Collins
SPANISH
DICTIONARY
& GRAMMAR

HarperCollins Publishers
Westerhill Road
Bishopbriggs
Glasgow
G64 2QT

Eighth Edition 2018

10 9 8 7 6 5 4 3 2 1

© HarperCollins Publishers 1997, 2000,
2004, 2006, 2008, 2010, 2014, 2018

ISBN 978-0-00-824139-1

Collins® is a registered trademark of
HarperCollins Publishers Limited

www.collinsdictionary.com
www.collins.co.uk

A catalogue record for this book is
available from the British Library

Typeset by Palimpsest Book Production
Limited and Davidson Publishing Solutions

Printed in Italy by Grafica Veneta S.p.A.

Acknowledgements
We would like to thank those authors
and publishers who kindly gave
permission for copyright material to be
used in the Collins Corpus. We would also
like to thank Times Newspapers Ltd for
providing valuable data.

EDITORS
Teresa Alvarez
Susie Beattie

CONTRIBUTORS
Tony Gálvez
Cordelia Lilly
Joyce Littlejohn
Persephone Lock
Sinda López

FOR THE PUBLISHER
Gerry Breslin
Janice McNeillie
Sheena Shanks

TECHNICAL SUPPORT
Claire Dimeo
Ross Taggart
Agnieszka Urbanowicz

MIX
Paper from
responsible sources
FSC™ C007454

This book is produced from independently certified FSC™ paper
to ensure responsible forest management.

For more information visit: www.harpercollins.co.uk/green

Índice de materias

Contents

Índice de materias   Contents

Introduction

You may be starting Spanish for the first time, or you may wish to extend your knowledge of the language. Perhaps you want to read and study Spanish books, newspapers and magazines, or perhaps simply have a conversation with Spanish speakers. Whatever the reason, whether you're a student, a tourist or want to use Spanish for business, this is the ideal book to help you understand and communicate. This modern, user-friendly dictionary gives priority to everyday vocabulary and the language of current affairs, business, computing and tourism, and, as in all Collins dictionaries, the emphasis is firmly placed on contemporary language and expressions.

How to use the dictionary

Below you will find an outline of how information is presented in your dictionary. Our aim is to give you the maximum amount of detail in the clearest and most helpful way.

Entries

A typical entry in your dictionary will be made up of the elements below.

Phonetic transcription

Phonetics appear in square brackets immediately after the headword. They are shown using the International Phonetic Alphabet (IPA), and a complete list of the symbols used in this system can be found on page x. The pronunciation given is for Castilian Spanish except where a word is solely used in Latin America, when we give the Latin American pronunciation. A further guide to the differences in types of Spanish pronunciation is given on page x.

Grammatical information

All words belong to one of the following parts of speech: noun, verb, adjective, adverb, pronoun, article, conjunction, preposition, exclamation, abbreviation. Nouns can be singular or plural and, in Spanish, masculine or feminine. Verbs can be transitive, intransitive, reflexive or impersonal, or else they can be auxiliaries. On the Spanish side, each verb is followed by a bold number, which corresponds to verb tables on pages xiii–xiv. Parts of speech appear in SMALL CAPS after the phonetic spelling of the headword. The gender of a noun translation also appears in *italics* after it, except where this is a regular masculine singular noun ending in "o", or a regular feminine singular noun ending in "a".

Often a word can have more than one part of speech. Just as the English word **chemical** can be an adjective or a noun, the Spanish word **conocido** can be an adjective ("(well-)known") or a noun ("acquaintance"). In the same way, the verb **to walk** is sometimes transitive, i.e. it takes an object ("to walk the dog") and sometimes intransitive, i.e. it doesn't take an object ("to walk to school"). To help you find the meaning you are looking for quickly and for clarity of presentation, the different part of speech categories are separated by a solid black triangle ▶.

Meaning divisions

Most words have more than one meaning. Take, for example, **punch**, which can be, amongst other things, a blow with the fist or an object used for making holes. Other words are translated differently depending on the context in which they are used. The transitive verb **to put on**, for example, can be translated by "ponerse", "encender" etc depending on *what* it is you are putting on. To help you select the most appropriate translation in every context, entries are divided according to meaning. Each different meaning is introduced by an "indicator" in *italics* and in brackets. Thus, the examples given above will be shown as follows:

> **punch** [pʌntʃ] N (*blow*) golpe *m*, puñetazo; (*tool*) punzón *m*

Likewise, some words can have a different meaning when used to talk about a specific subject area or field. For example **bishop**, which in a religious context means a high-ranking member of the clergy, is also the name of a chess piece. To show English speakers which translation to use, we have added "subject field labels" in brackets, in this case (*Chess*):

> **bishop** ['bɪʃəp] N obispo; (*Chess*) alfil *m*

Field labels are often shortened to save space. You will find a complete list of abbreviations used in the dictionary on pages viii and ix.

Translations

Most English words have a direct translation in Spanish and vice versa, as shown in the examples given above. Sometimes, however, no exact equivalent exists in the target language. In such cases we have given an approximate equivalent, indicated by the sign ≈. An example is **Open University**, the Spanish equivalent of which is the "Universidad Nacional de Educación a Distancia" or "UNED". There is no exact equivalent since the bodies in the two countries are quite different.

> **Open University** N (*Brit*) ≈ Universidad *f* Nacional de Educación a Distancia, ≈ UNED *f*

On occasion it is impossible to find even an approximate equivalent. This may be the case, for example, with the names of types of food:

> **fabada** [fa'βaða] NF *bean and sausage stew*

Here the translation (which doesn't exist) is replaced by an explanation. For increased clarity, the explanation, or "gloss", is shown in *italics*.

It is often the case that a word, or a particular meaning of a word, cannot be translated in isolation. The translation of **Dutch**, for example, is "holandés(-esa)". However, the phrase **to go Dutch** is rendered by "pagar a escote". Even an expression as simple as **washing powder** needs a separate translation since it translates as "detergente (en polvo)", not "polvo para lavar". This is where your dictionary will prove to be particularly informative and useful since it contains an abundance of compounds, phrases and idiomatic expressions.

Levels of formality and familiarity

In English you instinctively know when to say **I'm broke** or **I'm a bit short of cash** and when to say **I don't have any money**. When you are trying to understand someone who is speaking Spanish, however, or when you yourself try to speak Spanish, it is important to know what is polite and what is less so, and what you can say in a relaxed situation but not in a formal context. To help you with this, on the Spanish-English side we have added the label *(fam)* to show that a Spanish meaning or expression is colloquial, while those meanings or expressions which are vulgar are given an exclamation mark *(fam!)*, warning you they can cause serious offence. Note also that on the English-Spanish side, translations which are vulgar are followed by an exclamation mark in brackets. In addition to this, any word that we think may cause offence, whether vulgar or not, has also been identified using an exclamation mark in brackets.

Frequent words

The bold star symbol ★ that appears in front of words such as **ability** and **alegre** has been introduced to highlight core vocabulary. This symbol will help you quickly identify the key words you need to know.

Keywords

Words such as **have** and **do** or their Spanish equivalents **tener** and **hacer** have been given special treatment because they form the basic elements of the language. These entries are presented on a grey shaded background with the keyword itself at the top inside a white box with a black outline. This extra help will ensure that you know how to use these complex words with confidence.

Cultural information

Entries which appear inside a grey shaded box with rounded edges explain aspects of culture in Spanish- and English-speaking countries. Subject areas covered include politics, education, media and national festivals.

Language notes

Notes on the Spanish language have been added to supplement the information given in the entries themselves. These usage notes help users avoid common mistakes made by English speakers speaking Spanish, and also explain differences between the two languages in detail.

Abreviaturas

Abbreviations

abreviatura	AB(B)R	abbreviation
adjetivo, locución adjetiva	ADJ	adjective, adjectival phrase
administración, lenguaje administrativo	Admin	administration
adverbio, locución adverbial	ADV	adverb, adverbial phrase
agricultura	Agr	agriculture
alguien	algn	somebody
anatomía	Anat	anatomy
arquitectura	Arq, Arch	architecture
astronomía	Astro	astronomy
el automóvil	Aut(o)	automobiles
verbo auxiliar	AUX VB	auxiliary verb
aviación, viajes en avión	Aviat	flying, air travel
biología	Bio(l)	biology
botánica, flores	Bot	botany
inglés británico	BRIT	British English
química	Chem	chemistry
cine	Cine	cinema
comercio, finanzas, banca	Com(m)	commerce, finance, banking
informática	Comput	computing
conjunción	CONJ	conjunction
construcción	Constr	building, construction industry
sustantivo usado como adjetivo, que siempre va delante del sustantivo al que modifica	CPD, cpd	compound element (used before nouns)
cocina	Culin	cookery
economía	Econ	economics
electricidad, electrónica	Elec	electricity, electronics
enseñanza, sistema escolar	Escol	schooling, schools
España	Esp	Spain
especialmente	esp	especially
exclamación, interjección	EXCL	exclamation, interjection
femenino	f	feminine
lenguaje familiar	fam	colloquial usage
lenguaje vulgar	fam!	vulgar usage
ferrocarril	Ferro	railways
uso figurado	fig	figurative use
fotografía	Foto	photography
(verbo inglés) del cual la partícula es inseparable	FUS	(phrasal verb) where the particle is inseparable
generalmente	gen	generally
geografía, geología	Geo	geography, geology
geometría	Geom	geometry
lenguaje familiar	inf	informal usage
lenguaje vulgar	inf!	vulgar usage
informática	Inform	computing
invariable	inv	invariable
irregular	irreg	irregular
lo jurídico	Jur	law
América Latina	LAm	Latin America
gramática, lingüística	Ling	grammar, linguistics
literatura	Lit	literature
masculino	m	masculine
matemáticas	Mat(h)	mathematics
medicina	Med	medical term, medicine

masculino y femenino	*mf*	masculine and feminine
masculino/femenino	*m/f*	masculine/feminine
lo militar, el ejército	*Mil*	military matters
música	*Mus*	music
sustantivo	N	noun
navegación, náutica	*Naut*	sailing, navigation
sustantivo femenino	NF	feminine noun
sustantivo femenino plural	NFPL	feminine plural noun
sustantivo masculino	NM	masculine noun
sustantivo masculino y femenino	NMF	masculine and feminine noun
sustantivo masculino/femenino	NM/F	masculine/feminine noun
sustantivo masculino plural	NMPL	masculine plural noun
sustantivo no empleado en el plural	*no pl*	collective (uncountable) noun, not used in plural
numeral	NUM	number
complemento	*obj*	(grammatical) object
	o.s.	oneself
peyorativo	*pey, pej*	derogatory, pejorative
fotografía	*Phot*	photography
fisiología	*Physiol*	physiology
plural	*pl*	plural
política	*Pol*	politics
participio de pasado	*pp*	past participle
prefijo	PREF	prefix
preposición	PREP	preposition
pronombre	PRON	pronoun
psicología, psiquiatría	*Psico, Psych*	psychology, psychiatry
tiempo pasado	*pt*	past tense
ferrocarril	*Rail*	railways
religión, lo eclesiástico	*Rel*	religion, church service
Río de la Plata	RPL	River Plate
alguien	*sb*	somebody
enseñanza, sistema escolar	*Scol*	schooling, schools
singular	*sg*	singular
España	SP	Spain
algo	*sth*	something
subjuntivo	*subjun*	subjunctive
sujeto	*su(b)j*	(grammatical) subject
sufijo	*suff*	suffix
tauromaquia	*Taur*	bullfighting
también	*tb*	also
teatro	*Teat*	*theatre*
técnica, tecnología	*Tec(h)*	technical term, technology
telecomunicaciones	*Telec, Tel*	telecommunications
teatro	*Theat*	theatre
imprenta, tipografía	*Tip, Typ*	typography, printing
televisión	TV	television
sistema universitario	*Univ*	universities
inglés norteamericano	US	American English
verbo	VB	verb
verbo intransitivo	VI	intransitive verb
verbo pronominal	VR	reflexive verb
verbo transitivo	VT	transitive verb
zoología, animales	*Zool*	zoology
marca registrada	®	registered trademark
indica un equivalente cultural	≈	introduces a cultural equivalent
lenguaje ofensivo o vulgar	*!*	offensive or vulgar usage

Spanish pronunciation

Consonants

b	[b]	see notes on *v* below	*b*omba
	[β]		la*b*or
c	[k]	*c* before *a, o* or *u* is pronounced as in *c*at	*c*aja
ce, ci	[θe, θi]	*c* before *e* or *i* is pronounced as *th* in *th*in and as *s*	*ce*ro, *ci*elo
	[se, si¹]	in *s*in in Latin America and parts of Spain	vo*ce*ro, noti*ci*ero
ch	[tʃ]	*ch* is pronounced as *ch* in *ch*air	*ch*iste
d	[d]	at the beginning of a word or after *l* or *n*,	*d*anés
	[ð]	*d* is pronounced as in English. In any other position it is like *th* in *th*e	ciu*d*ad
g	[g]	*g* before *a, o* or *u* is pronounced as in *g*ap if	*g*afas, *g*uerra
	[ɤ]	at the beginning of a word or after *n*. In other positions the sound is softened	pa*g*a
ge, gi	[xe, xi]	*g* before *e* or *i* is pronounced much like *ch* in Scottish lo*ch*	*ge*nte, *gi*rar
h		*h* is always silent in Spanish	*h*aber
j	[x]	*j* is pronounced like *ch* in Scottish lo*ch*	*j*ugar
ll	[ʎ]	*ll* is pronounced like the *lli* in mi*lli*on	ta*ll*e
	[j]	or like *y* in *y*es. It can also be pronounced like	
	[ʒ]	*s* in mea*s*ure	
ñ	[ɲ]	*ñ* is pronounced like the *ni* in o*ni*on	ni*ñ*o
q	[k]	*q* is pronounced as *k* in *k*ing	*q*ue
r, rr	[r]	*r* is always pronounced in Spanish, unlike	quita*r*
	[rr]	the *r* in dance*r*. *rr* and *r* at the beginning of a word are trilled, like a Scottish *r*	ga*rr*a
s	[s]	*s* is usually pronounced as in pa*ss*, but before	quizá*s*
		b, d, g, l, m or *n* it is closer to the *s* in ro*s*e	i*s*la
v	[b]	*v* is pronounced something like *b*. At the	*v*ía
	[β]	beginning of a word or after *m* or *n* it is pronounced as *b* in *b*oy. In any other position it is pronounced with the lips in position to pronounce *b* of *b*oy, but not meeting	di*v*idir
w	[b]	pronounced occasionally like Spanish *b*,	*w*áter
	[w]	or else like English *w*	*w*hiskey
z	[θ]	*z* is pronounced as *th* in *th*in and as *s* in *s*in in	tena*z*
	[s¹]	Latin America and parts of Spain	i*z*ada

x

x	[ks]	*x* is pronounced as in to*x*in except in informal	tó*x*ico
	[s]	Spanish or at the beginning of a word,	*x*enofobia
		when it is pronounced like *s* in pa*ss*	

f, k, l, m, n, p and *t* are pronounced as in English
¹ only shown in Latin American entries

Vowels

a	[a]	not as long as *a* in f*a*r. When followed by a consonant in the same syllable (i.e. in a closed syllable), as in am*a*nte, the *a* is short as in b*a*t	p*a*ta
e	[e]	like *e* in th*ey*. In a closed syllable, as in g*e*nte, the *e* is short as in p*e*t	m*e*
i	[i]	as in m*ea*n or mach*i*ne	p*i*no
o	[o]	as in l*o*cal. In a closed syllable, as in c*o*ntrol, the *o* is short as in c*o*t	l*o*
u	[u]	as in r*u*le. It is silent after *q*, and in g*ue*, g*ui*, unless marked g*üe*, g*üi*, e.g. antig*üe*dad, when it is pronounced like *w* in *w*olf	l*u*nes

Semi-vowels

| i, y | [j] | pronounced like *y* in *y*es | b*i*en, h*i*elo, *y*unta |
| u | [w] | unstressed *u* between consonant and vowel is pronounced like *w* in *w*ell. See also notes on *u* above | h*u*evo, f*u*ente, antig*ü*edad |

Diphthongs

ai, ay	[ai]	as *i* in r*i*de	b*ai*le
au	[au]	as *ou* in sh*ou*t	*au*to
ei, ey	[ei]	as *ey* in gr*ey*	bu*ey*
eu	[eu]	both elements pronounced independently [e] + [u]	d*eu*da
oi, oy	[oi]	as *oy* in t*oy*	h*oy*

Stress

The rules of stress in Spanish are as follows:

(a)   when a word ends in a vowel or in *n* or *s*, the second last syllable is stressed: pa*ta*ta, pa*ta*tas, *co*me, *co*men

(b)   when a word ends in a consonant other than *n* or *s*, the stress falls on the last syllable: pa*red*, ha*blar*

(c)   when the rules set out in (a) and (b) are not applied, an acute accent appears over the stressed vowel: co*mún*, geogra*fía*, in*glés*

In the phonetic transcription, the symbol ['] precedes the syllable on which the stress falls.

In general, we give the pronunciation of each entry in square brackets after the word in question.

Spanish irregular verbs

1 Gerund **2** Imperative **3** Present **4** Preterite **5** Future **6** Present subjunctive
7 Imperfect subjunctive **8** Past participle **9** Imperfect

Etc indicates that the irregular root is used for all persons of the tense, e.g. **oír:**
6 oiga, oigas, oigamos, oigáis, oigan

/1a/ HABLAR 1 hablando **2** habla, hablad
3 hablo, hablas, habla, hablamos,
habláis, hablan **4** hablé, hablaste,
habló, hablamos, hablasteis, hablaron
5 hablaré, hablarás, hablará,
hablaremos, hablaréis, hablarán
6 hable, hables, hable, hablemos,
habléis, hablen **7** hablara, hablaras,
hablara, habláramos, hablarais,
hablaran **8** hablado **9** hablaba,
hablabas, hablaba, hablábamos,
hablabais, hablaban

/1b/ cambiar 2 cambia **3** cambio *etc*
6 cambie *etc*

/1c/ enviar 2 envía **3** envío, envías, envía,
envíen **6** envíe, envíes, envíe, envíen

/1d/ evacuar 2 evacua **3** evacuo *etc*
6 evacue *etc*

/1e/ situar 2 sitúa **3** sitúo, sitúas, sitúa,
sitúen **6** sitúe, sitúes, sitúe, sitúen

/1f/ cruzar 4 crucé **6** cruce *etc*

/1g/ picar 4 piqué **6** pique *etc*

/1h/ pagar 4 pagué **6** pague *etc*

/1i/ averiguar 4 averigüé **6** averigüe *etc*

/1j/ cerrar 2 cierra **3** cierro, cierras, cierra,
cierran **6** cierre, cierres, cierre, cierren

/1k/ errar 2 yerra **3** yerro, yerras, yerra,
yerran **6** yerre, yerres, yerre, yerren

/1l/ contar 2 cuenta **3** cuento, cuentas,
cuenta, cuentan **6** cuente, cuentes,
cuente, cuenten

/1m/ degollar 2 degüella **3** degüello,
degüellas, degüella, degüellan
6 degüelle, degüelles, degüelle,
degüellen

/1n/ jugar 2 juega **3** juego, juegas, juega,
jueguen **6** juegue, juegues, juegue,
jueguen

/1o/ ESTAR 2 está **3** estoy, estás, está,
están **4** estuve, estuviste, estuvo,
estuvimos, estuvisteis, estuvieron
6 esté, estés, esté, estén **7** estuviera *etc*

/1p/ andar 4 anduve *etc* **7** anduviera *etc*

/1q/ dar 3 doy **4** di, diste, dio, dimos,
disteis, dieron **7** diera *etc*

/2a/ COMER 1 comiendo **2** come, comed
3 como, comes, come, comemos,
coméis, comen **4** comí, comiste, comió,
comimos, comisteis, comieron
5 comeré, comerás, comerá,
comeremos, comeréis, comerán
6 coma, comas, coma, comamos,
comáis, coman **7** comiera, comieras,
comiera, comiéramos, comierais,
comieran **8** comido **9** comía, comías,
comía, comíamos, comíais, comían

/2b/ vencer 3 venzo **6** venza *etc*

/2c/ coger 3 cojo **6** coja *etc*

/2d/ parecer 3 parezco **6** parezca *etc*

/2e/ leer 1 leyendo **4** leyó, leyeron **7** leyera
etc **8** leído

/2f/ tañer 1 tañendo **4** tañó, tañeron

/2g/ perder 2 pierde **3** pierdo, pierdes,
pierde, pierden **6** pierda, pierdas,
pierda, pierdan

/2h/ mover 2 mueve **3** muevo, mueves,
mueve, mueven **6** mueva, muevas,
mueva, muevan

/2i/ oler 2 huele **3** huelo, hueles, huele,
huelen **6** huela, huelas, huela,
huelan

/2j/ HABER 3 he, has, ha, hemos, han
4 hube, hubiste, hubo, hubimos,
hubisteis, hubieron **5** habré *etc* **6** haya
etc **7** hubiera *etc*

/2k/ tener 2 ten **3** tengo, tienes, tiene,
tienen **4** tuve, tuviste, tuvo, tuvimos,
tuvisteis, tuvieron **5** tendré *etc* **6** tenga
etc **7** tuviera *etc*

/2l/ caber 3 quepo **4** cupe, cupiste, cupo,
cupimos, cupisteis, cupieron **5** cabré *etc*
6 quepa *etc* **7** cupiera *etc*

/2m/ **saber** **3** sé **4** supe, supiste, supo, supimos, supisteis, supieron **5** sabré *etc* **6** sepa *etc* **7** supiera *etc*

/2n/ **caer** **1** cayendo **3** caigo **4** cayó, cayeron **6** caiga *etc* **7** cayera *etc* **8** caído

/2o/ **traer** **1** trayendo **3** traigo **4** traje, trajiste, trajo, trajimos, trajisteis, trajeron **6** traiga *etc* **7** trajera *etc* **8** traído

/2p/ **valer** **2** vale **3** valgo **5** valdré *etc* **6** valga *etc*

/2q/ **poner** **2** pon **3** pongo **4** puse, pusiste, puso, pusimos, pusisteis, pusieron **5** pondré *etc* **6** ponga *etc* **7** pusiera *etc* **8** puesto

/2r/ **hacer** **2** haz **3** hago **4** hice, hiciste, hizo, hicimos, hicisteis, hicieron **5** haré *etc* **6** haga *etc* **7** hiciera *etc* **8** hecho

/2s/ **poder** **1** pudiendo **2** puede **3** puedo, puedes, puede, pueden **4** pude, pudiste, pudo, pudimos, pudisteis, pudieron **5** podré *etc* **6** pueda, puedas, pueda, puedan **7** pudiera *etc*

/2t/ **querer** **2** quiere **3** quiero, quieres, quiere, quieren **4** quise, quisiste, quiso, quisimos, quisisteis, quisieron **5** querré *etc* **6** quiera, quieras, quiera, quieran **7** quisiera *etc*

/2u/ **ver** **3** veo **6** vea *etc* **8** visto **9** veía *etc*

/2v/ **SER** **2** sé **3** soy, eres, es, somos, sois, son **4** fui, fuiste, fue, fuimos, fuisteis, fueron **6** sea *etc* **7** fuera *etc* **9** era, eras, era, éramos, erais, eran

/2w/ **placer** **3** plazco **6** plazca *etc*

/2x/ **yacer** **2** yace or yaz **3** yazco or yazgo **6** yazca or yazga *etc*

/2y/ **roer** **1** royendo **3** roo or roigo **7** royó, royeron, **6** roa or roiga *etc* **7** royera *etc* **8** roído

/3a/ **VIVIR** **1** viviendo **2** vive, vivid **3** vivo, vives, vive, vivimos, vivís, viven **4** viví, viviste, vivió, vivimos, vivisteis, vivieron **5** viviré, vivirás, vivirá, viviremos, viviréis, vivirán **6** viva, vivas, viva, vivamos, viváis, vivan **7** viviera, vivieras, viviera, viviéramos, vivierais, vivieran **8** vivido **9** vivía, vivías, vivía, vivíamos, vivías, vivían

/3b/ **esparcir** **3** esparzo **6** esparza *etc*

/3c/ **dirigir** **3** dirijo **6** dirija *etc*

/3d/ **distinguir** **3** distingo **6** distinga *etc*

/3e/ **delinquir** **3** delinco **6** delinca *etc*

/3f/ **lucir** **3** luzco **6** luzca *etc*

/3g/ **instruir** **1** instruyendo **2** instruye **3** instruyo, instruyes, instruye, instruyen **4** instruyó, instruyeron **6** instruya *etc* **7** instruyera *etc*

/3h/ **gruñir** **1** gruñendo **4** gruñó, gruñeron

/3i/ **sentir** **1** sintiendo **2** siente **3** siento, sientes, siente, sienten **4** sintió, sintieron **6** sienta, sientas, sienta, sintamos, sintáis, sientan **7** sintiera *etc*

/3j/ **dormir** **1** durmiendo **2** duerme **3** duermo, duermes, duerme, duermen **4** durmió, durmieron **6** duerma, duermas, duerma, durmamos, durmáis, duerman **7** durmiera *etc*

/3k/ **pedir** **1** pidiendo **2** pide **3** pido, pides, pide, piden **4** pidió, pidieron **6** pida *etc* **7** pidiera *etc*

/3l/ **reír** **2** ríe **3** río, ríes, ríe, ríen **4** reí, rio, rieron **6** ría, rías, ría, riamos, riáis, rían **7** riera *etc* **8** reído

/3m/ **erguir** **1** irguiendo **2** yergue **3** yergo, yergues, yergue, yerguen **6** irguió, irguieron **7** irguiera *etc*

/3n/ **reducir** **3** reduzco **5** reduje *etc* **6** reduzca *etc* **7** redujera *etc*

/3o/ **decir** **2** di **3** digo **4** dije, dijiste, dijo, dijimos, dijisteis, dijeron **5** diré *etc* **6** diga *etc* **7** dijera *etc* **8** dicho

/3p/ **oír** **1** oyendo **2** oye **3** oigo, oyes, oye, oyen **4** oyó, oyeron **6** oiga *etc* **7** oyera *etc* **8** oído

/3q/ **salir** **2** sal **3** salgo **5** saldré *etc* **6** salga *etc*

/3r/ **venir** **2** ven **3** vengo, vienes, viene, vienen **4** vine, viniste, vino, vinimos, vinisteis, vinieron **5** vendré *etc* **6** venga *etc* **7** viniera *etc*

/3s/ **ir** **1** yendo **2** ve **3** voy, vas, va, vamos, vais, van **4** fui, fuiste, fue, fuimos, fuisteis, fueron **6** vaya, vayas, vaya, vayamos, vayáis, vayan **7** fuera *etc* **9** iba, ibas, iba, íbamos, ibais, iban

Números

Numbers

Spanish	Number	English
uno (un, una)*	1	one
dos	2	two
tres	3	three
cuatro	4	four
cinco	5	five
seis	6	six
siete	7	seven
ocho	8	eight
nueve	9	nine
diez	10	ten
once	11	eleven
doce	12	twelve
trece	13	thirteen
catorce	14	fourteen
quince	15	fifteen
dieciséis	16	sixteen
diecisiete	17	seventeen
dieciocho	18	eighteen
diecinueve	19	nineteen
veinte	20	twenty
veintiuno(-ún, -una)*	21	twenty-one
veintidós	22	twenty-two
treinta	30	thirty
treinta y uno(un, una)*	31	thirty-one
treinta y dos	32	thirty-two
cuarenta	40	forty
cincuenta	50	fifty
sesenta	60	sixty
setenta	70	seventy
ochenta	80	eighty
noventa	90	ninety
cien(ciento)**	100	a hundred, one hundred
ciento uno(un, una)*	101	a hundred and one
ciento dos	102	a hundred and two
ciento cincuenta y seis	156	a hundred and fifty-six
doscientos(-as)	200	two hundred
trescientos(-as)	300	three hundred
quinientos(-as)	500	five hundred
mil	1,000	a thousand
mil tres	1,003	a thousand and three
dos mil	2,000	two thousand
un millón	1,000,000	a million

*'uno' (+'veintiuno' etc) agrees in gender (but not number) with its noun: **treinta y una personas**; the masculine form is shortened to 'un' unless it stands alone: **veintiún caballos, veintiuno**.

'ciento' is used in compound numbers, except when it multiplies: **ciento diez, but **cien mil**. 'Cien' is used before nouns: **cien hombres, cien casas**.

Números

primero (primer, primera) 1°, $1^{er}/1^a$, 1^{era}
segundo(-a) $2^o/2^a$
tercero (tercer, tercera) 3°, $3^{er}/3^a$, 3^{era}
cuarto(-a) $4^o/4^a$
quinto(-a)
sexto(-a)
séptimo(-a)
octavo(-a)
noveno(-a); nono(-a)
décimo(-a)
undécimo(-a)
duodécimo(-a)
decimotercero(-a)
decimocuarto(-a)
decimoquinto(-a)
decimosexto(-a)
decimoséptimo(-a)
decimoctavo(-a)
decimonoveno(-a)
vigésimo(-a)
vigésimo(-a) primero(-a)
vigésimo(-a) segundo(-a)
trigésimo(-a)
trigésimo(-a) primero(-a)
trigésimo(-a) segundo(-a)
cuadragésimo(-a)
quincuagésimo(-a)
sexagésimo(-a)
septuagésimo(-a)
octogésimo(-a)
nonagésimo(-a)
centésimo(-a)
centésimo(-a) primero(-a)
milésimo(-a)

Numbers

first, 1st, 1st
second, 2nd, 2nd
third, 3rd, 3rd
fourth, 4th, 4th
fifth, 5th, 5th
sixth, 6th, 6th
seventh
eighth
ninth
tenth
eleventh
twelfth
thirteenth
fourteenth
fifteenth
sixteenth
seventeenth
eighteenth
nineteenth
twentieth
twenty-first
twenty-second
thirtieth
thirty-first
thirty-second
fortieth
fiftieth
sixtieth
seventieth
eightieth
ninetieth
hundredth
hundred-and-first
thousandth

La hora

¿qué hora es?
es la una
son las cuatro
medianoche, las doce de la noche
la una (de la madrugada)
la una y cinco
la una y diez
la una y cuarto, la una quince
la una y veinticinco
la una y media, la una treinta
las dos menos veinticinco,
    la una treinta y cinco
las dos menos veinte, la una cuarenta
las dos menos cuarto,
    la una cuarenta y cinco
las dos menos diez, la una cincuenta
mediodía, las doce (de la mañana)
las dos (de la tarde)
las siete (de la tarde)

¿a qué hora?
a medianoche
a las siete
a la una
dentro de veinte minutos
hace diez minutos

La fecha

hoy
mañana
pasado mañana
ayer
antes de ayer, anteayer
la víspera
el día siguiente
la mañana
la tarde
esta mañana
esta tarde
ayer por la mañana
ayer por la tarde
mañana por la mañana
mañana por la tarde
en la noche del sábado al domingo

The time

what time is it?
it's one o'clock
it's four o'clock
midnight
one o'clock (in the morning), one (a.m.)
five past one
ten past one
a quarter past one, one fifteen
twenty-five past one, one twenty-five
half past one, one thirty
twenty-five to two, one thirty-five

twenty to two, one forty
a quarter to two, one forty-five

ten to two, one fifty
twelve o'clock, midday, noon
two o'clock (in the afternoon), two (p.m.)
seven o'clock (in the evening), seven (p.m.)

(at) what time?
at midnight
at seven o'clock
at one o'clock
in twenty minutes
ten minutes ago

The date

today
tomorrow
the day after tomorrow
yesterday
the day before yesterday
the day before, the previous day
the next or following day
morning
evening
this morning
this evening, this afternoon
yesterday morning
yesterday evening, yesterday afternoon
tomorrow morning
tomorrow evening, tomorrow afternoon
during Saturday night, during the night
    of Saturday to Sunday

vendrá el sábado	he's coming on Saturday
los sábados	on Saturdays
todos los sábados	every Saturday
el sábado pasado	last Saturday
el sábado que viene, el próximo sábado	next Saturday
del sábado en ocho días	a week on Saturday
del sábado en quince días	a fortnight *or* two weeks on Saturday
de lunes a sábado	from Monday to Saturday
todos las días	every day
una vez a la semana	once a week
una vez al mes	once a month
dos veces a la semana	twice a week
hace una semana *u* ocho días	a week ago
hace quince días	a fortnight *or* two weeks ago
el año pasado	last year
dentro de dos días	in two days
dentro de ocho días *o* una semana	in a week
dentro de quince días	in a fortnight *or* two weeks
el mes que viene, el próximo mes	next month
el año que viene, el próximo año	next year

¿a qué o a cuántos estamos?	*what's the date?*
el 1/22 octubre de 2018	the 1st/22nd of October 2018, October 1st/22nd 2018
en 2018	in 2018
mil novecientos noventa y cinco	nineteen ninety-five
dos mil dieciocho	two thousand and eighteen, twenty eighteen
44 a. de J.C.	44 BC
14 d. de J.C.	14 AD
en el (siglo) XIX	in the nineteenth century
en los años treinta	in the thirties
érase una vez ...	once upon a time ...

ESPAÑOL – INGLÉS

SPANISH – ENGLISH

Aa

A, a [a] NF (*letra*) A, a; **A de Antonio** A for Andrew (BRIT) o Able (US)

---

a [a]

PREP (**a + el = al**) **1** (*dirección*) to; **fueron a Madrid/Grecia** they went to Madrid/Greece; **me voy a casa** I'm going home

2 (*distancia*): **está a 15 km de aquí** it's 15 km from here

3 (*posición*): **estar a la mesa** to be at table; **al lado de** next to, beside; **a la derecha/izquierda** on the right/left; *ver tb* **puerta**

4 (*tiempo*): **a las 10/a medianoche** at 10/midnight; **¿a qué hora?** (at) what time?; **a la mañana siguiente** the following morning; **a los pocos días** after a few days; **estamos a 9 de julio** it's the 9th of July; **a los 24 años** at the age of 24; **ocho horas al día** eight hours a day; **al año/a la semana** (AM) a year/week later

5 (*manera*): **a la francesa** the French way; **a caballo** on horseback; **a oscuras** in the dark; **a rayas** striped; **le echaron a patadas** they kicked him out

6 (*medio, instrumento*): **a lápiz** in pencil; **a mano** by hand; **cocina a gas** gas stove

7 (*razón*): **a dos euros el kilo** at two euros a kilo; **a más de 50 km por hora** at more than 50 km per hour; **poco a poco** little by little

8 (*dativo*): **se lo di a él** I gave it to him; **se lo compré a él** I bought it from him

9 (*complemento directo*): **vi al policía** I saw the police officer

10 (*tras ciertos verbos*): **voy a verle** I'm going to see him; **empezó a trabajar** he started working o to work; **sabe a queso** it tastes of cheese

11 (+ *infin*): **al verle, le reconocí inmediatamente** when I saw him I recognized him at once; **el camino a recorrer** the distance we *etc* have to travel; **¡a callar!** keep quiet!; **¡a comer!** let's eat!

12: **a que**: **¡a que llueve!** I bet it's going to rain!; **¿a qué viene eso?** what's the meaning of this?; **¿a que sí va a venir?** he IS coming, isn't he?; **¿a que no lo haces? — ¡a que sí!** bet you don't do it! — yes, I WILL!

A. ABR (*Escol*: = *aprobado*) pass

AA NF PL ABR = **Aerolíneas Argentinas**

AA.EE. ABR (= *Asuntos Exteriores*): **Min. de ~** ≈ FO (BRIT)

ab. ABR (= *abril*) Apr.

abad, esa [a'βað, 'ðesa] NM/F abbot (abbess)

abadía [aβa'ðia] NF abbey

★**abajo** [a'βaxo] ADV (*situación*) (down) below, underneath; (*en edificio*) downstairs; (*dirección*) down, downwards; **~ de** (*prep*) below, under; **el piso de ~** the downstairs flat; **la parte de ~** the lower part; **¡~ el gobierno!** down with the government!; **cuesta/río ~** downhill/downstream; **de arriba ~** from top to bottom; **el ~ firmante** the undersigned; **más ~** lower o further down

abalance *etc* [aβa'lanθe] VB *ver* **abalanzarse**

abalanzarse [aβalan'θarse] /**1f**/ VR: **~ sobre** o **contra** to throw o.s. at

abalear [aβale'ar] /**1a**/ VT (AM *fam*) to shoot

abalorios [aβa'lorjos] NMPL (*chucherías*) trinkets

abanderado, -a [aβande'raðo, a] NM/F (*portaestandarte*) standard bearer; (*de un movimiento*) champion, leader; (AM: *linier*) linesman, assistant referee

abandonado, -a [aβando'naðo, a] ADJ derelict; (*desatendido*) abandoned; (*desierto*) deserted; (*descuidado*) neglected

abandonar [aβando'nar] /**1a**/ VT to leave; (*persona*) to abandon, desert; (*cosa*) to abandon, leave behind; (*descuidar*) to neglect; (*renunciar a*) to give up; (*Inform*) to quit ■ **abandonarse** VR: **abandonarse a** to abandon o.s. to; **abandonarse al alcohol** to take to drink

abandono [aβan'dono] NM (*acto*) desertion, abandonment; (*estado*) abandon, neglect;

a

(*renuncia*) withdrawal, retirement; **ganar por ~** to win by default

abanicar [aβani'kar] /**1g**/ VT to fan

★**abanico** [aβa'niko] NM fan; (*Naut*) derrick; **en ~** fan-shaped

abanique *etc* [aβa'nike] VB *ver* **abanicar**

abaratar [aβara'tar] /**1a**/ VT to lower the price of ▶ VI, **abaratarse** VR to go *o* come down in price

abarcar [aβar'kar] /**1g**/ VT to include, embrace; (*contener*) to comprise; (*Am*) to monopolize; **quien mucho abarca poco aprieta** don't bite off more than you can chew

abarque *etc* [a'βarke] VB *ver* **abarcar**

abarrotado, -a [aβarro'taðo, a] ADJ packed; **~ de** packed *o* bursting with

abarrotar [aβarro'tar] /**1a**/ VT (*local, estadio, teatro*) to fill, pack

abarrote [aβa'rrote] NM packing ▪ **abarrotes** NMPL (*Am*) groceries; **tienda de abarrotes** (*Am*) grocery store

abarrotería [aβarrote'ria] NF (*Am*) grocery store

abarrotero, -a [aβarro'tero, a] NM/F (*Am*) grocer

abastecedor, a [aβasteθe'ðor, a] ADJ supplying ▶ NM/F supplier

abastecer [aβaste'θer] /**2d**/ VT: **~ (de)** to supply (with)

abastecimiento [aβasteθi'mjento] NM supply

abastezca *etc* [aβas'teθka] VB *ver* **abastecer**

abasto [a'βasto] NM supply; (*abundancia*) abundance; **no dar ~ a algo** not to be able to cope with sth

abatible [aβa'tiβle] ADJ: **asiento ~** tip-up seat; (*Auto*) reclining seat

abatido, -a [aβa'tiðo, a] ADJ dejected, downcast; **estar muy ~** to be very depressed

abatimiento [aβati'mjento] NM (*depresión*) dejection, depression

abatir [aβa'tir] /**3a**/ VT (*muro*) to demolish; (*pájaro*) to shoot *o* bring down; (*fig*) to depress ▪ **abatirse** VR to get depressed; **abatirse sobre** to swoop *o* pounce on

abdicación [aβðika'θjon] NF abdication

abdicar [aβðı'kar] /**1g**/ VI to abdicate; **~ en algn** to abdicate in favour of sb

abdique *etc* [aβ'ðike] VB *ver* **abdicar**

abdomen [aβ'ðomen] NM abdomen

abdominal [aβðomi'nal] ADJ abdominal ▶ NM: **abdominales** abdominals, stomach muscles; (*Deporte: tb:* **ejercicios abdominales**) sit-ups

abecedario [aβeθe'ðarjo] NM alphabet

abedul [aβe'ðul] NM birch

★**abeja** [a'βexa] NF bee; (*fig: hormiguita*) hard worker

abejorro [aβe'xorro] NM bumblebee

aberración [aβerra'θjon] NF aberration

aberrante [aβe'rrante] ADJ (*disparatado*) ridiculous

abertura [aβer'tura] NF = **apertura**

abertzale [aβer'tʃale] ADJ, NMF Basque nationalist

abeto [a'βeto] NM fir

★**abierto, -a** [a'βjerto, a] PP *de* **abrir** ▶ ADJ open; (*fig: carácter*) frank

abigarrado, -a [aβiɣa'rraðo, a] ADJ multicoloured; (*fig*) motley

abismal [aβis'mal] ADJ (*fig*) vast, enormous

abismar [aβis'mar] /**1a**/ VT to humble, cast down ▪ **abismarse** VR to sink; (*Am*) to be amazed; **abismarse en** (*fig*) to be plunged into

abismo [a'βismo] NM abyss; **de sus ideas a las mías hay un ~** our views are worlds apart

abjurar [aβxu'rar] /**1a**/ VT to abjure, forswear ▶ VI: **~ de** to abjure, forswear

ablandar [aβlan'dar] /**1a**/ VT to soften; (*conmover*) to touch; (*Culin*) to tenderize ▶ VI, **ablandarse** VR to get softer

abnegación [aβneɣa'θjon] NF self-denial

abnegado, -a [aβne'ɣaðo, a] ADJ self-sacrificing

abobado, -a [aβo'βaðo, a] ADJ silly

abobamiento [aβoβa'mjento] NM (*asombro*) bewilderment

abocado, -a [aβo'kaðo, a] ADJ: **verse ~ al desastre** to be heading for disaster

abochornar [aβotʃor'nar] /**1a**/ VT to embarrass ▪ **abochornarse** VR to get flustered; (*Bot*) to wilt; **abochornarse de** to get embarrassed about

abofetear [aβofete'ar] /**1a**/ VT to slap (in the face)

abogacía [aβoɣa'θia] NF legal profession; (*ejercicio*) practice of the law

★**abogado, -a** [aβo'ɣaðo, a] NM/F lawyer; (*notario*) solicitor; (*asesor*) counsel; (*en tribunal*) barrister, advocate, attorney (*US*); **~ defensor** defence lawyer (*Brit*), defense attorney (*US*); **~ del diablo** devil's advocate

> **Lawyer** es el término general que se aplica a todo licenciado en derecho. *Abogado* también se puede traducir por **solicitor** o **barrister** en inglés británico. Un **solicitor** se encarga de preparar documentos legales, como testamentos y contratos, y casos que se llevan en los tribunales. Puede además representar a sus clientes ante algunos de ellos, pero no ante los tribunales superiores, ya que esto solo lo puede hacer un **barrister**. En inglés americano se usa **attorney** en ambos casos.

abogar [aβo'ɣar] /**1h**/ VI: **~ por** to plead for; (*fig*) to advocate

abogue *etc* [a'βoɣe] VB *ver* **abogar**

abolengo [aβo'lengo] NM ancestry, lineage

abolición [aβoli'θjon] NF abolition

abolir [aβo'lir] /**3a**/ VT to abolish

abolladura [aβoʎaˈðura] NF dent

abollar [aβoˈʎar] /1a/ VT to dent

abombarse [aβomˈbarse] /1a/ VR (AM) to go bad

abominable [aβomiˈnaβle] ADJ abominable

abominación [aβominaˈθjon] NF abomination

abonado, -a [aβoˈnaðo, a] ADJ (deuda) paid(-up) ▸ NM/F subscriber

★**abonar** [aβoˈnar] /1a/ VT to pay; (deuda) to settle; (terreno) to fertilize; (idea) to endorse; ~ dinero en una cuenta to pay money into an account, credit money to an account ▪ **abonarse** VR to subscribe

★**abono** [aˈβono] NM payment; fertilizer; subscription

abordable [aβorˈðaβle] ADJ (persona) approachable

abordar [aβorˈðar] /1a/ VT (barco) to board; (asunto) to broach; (individuo) to approach

aborigen [aβoˈrixen] NMF aborigine

aborrecer [aβorreˈθer] /2d/ VT to hate, loathe

aborrezca etc [aβoˈrreθka] VB ver **aborrecer**

abortar [aβorˈtar] /1a/ VI (malparir) to have a miscarriage; (deliberadamente) to have an abortion

aborto [aˈβorto] NM miscarriage; abortion

abotagado, -a [aβotaˈɣaðo, a] ADJ swollen

abotonar [aβotoˈnar] /1a/ VT to button (up), do up

abovedado, -a [aβoβeˈðaðo, a] ADJ vaulted, domed

abr. ABR (= abril) Apr

abrace etc [aˈβraθe] VB ver **abrazar**

abrasar [aβraˈsar] /1a/ VT to burn (up); (Agr) to dry up, parch

abrazadera [aβraθaˈðera] NF bracket

★**abrazar** [aβraˈθar] /1f/ VT to embrace, hug ▪ **abrazarse** VR to embrace, hug each other

★**abrazo** [aˈβraθo] NM embrace, hug; un ~ (en carta) with best wishes

abrebotellas [aβreβoˈteʎas] NM INV bottle opener

abrecartas [aβreˈkartas] NM INV letter opener

abrefácil [aβreˈfaθil] NM easy-open packaging ▸ ADJ (envase) easy-open

★**abrelatas** [aβreˈlatas] NM INV tin (BRIT) o can (US) opener

abrevadero [aβreβaˈðero] NM watering place

abreviar [aβreˈβjar] /1b/ VT to abbreviate; (texto) to abridge; (plazo) to reduce ▸ VI: bueno, para ~ well, to cut a long story short

abreviatura [aβreβjaˈtura] NF abbreviation

abridor [aβriˈðor] NM (de botellas) bottle opener; (de latas) tin (BRIT) o can (US) opener

abrigador, a [aβriɣaˈðor, a] ADJ (AM) warm

★**abrigar** [aβriˈɣar] /1h/ VT (proteger) to shelter; (suj: ropa) to keep warm; (fig) to cherish ▪ **abrigarse** VR (con ropa) to cover (o.s.) up; **abrigarse** (de) to take shelter (from), protect o.s. (from); ¡abrígate bien! wrap up well!

★**abrigo** [aˈβriɣo] NM (prenda) coat, overcoat; (lugar protegido) shelter; al ~ de in the shelter of

abrigue etc [aˈβriɣe] VB ver **abrigar**

★**abril** [aˈβril] NM April; ver tb **julio**

abrillantador [aβriʎantaˈðor] NM polish

abrillantar [aβriʎanˈtar] /1a/ VT (pulir) to polish; (fig) to enhance

★**abrir** [aˈβrir] /3a/ VT to open (up); (camino etc) to open up; (apetito) to whet; (lista) to head; ~ un negocio to start up a business ▸ VI to open ▪ **abrirse** VR to open (up); (extenderse) to open out; (cielo) to clear; **abrirse paso** to find o force a way through; **en un ~ y cerrar de ojos** in the twinkling of an eye

abrochar [aβroˈtʃar] /1a/ VT (con botones) to button (up); (zapato, con broche) to do up ▪ **abrocharse** VR: **abrocharse los zapatos** to tie one's shoelaces

abrogación [aβroɣaˈθjon] NF repeal

abrogar [aβroˈɣar] /1h/ VT to repeal

abrumador, a [aβrumaˈðor, a] ADJ (mayoría) overwhelming

abrumar [aβruˈmar] /1a/ VT to overwhelm; (sobrecargar) to weigh down

abrupto, -a [aˈβrupto, a] ADJ abrupt; (empinado) steep

absceso [aβsˈθeso] NM abscess

absentismo [aβsenˈtismo] NM (de obreros) absenteeism

absolución [aβsoluˈθjon] NF (Rel) absolution; (Jur) acquittal

absoluto, -a [aβsoˈluto, a] ADJ absolute; (total) utter, complete; **en ~** adv not at all

absolver [aβsolˈβer] /2h/ VT to absolve; (Jur) to pardon; (: acusado) to acquit

absorbente [aβsorˈβente] ADJ absorbent; (interesante) absorbing, interesting; (exigente) demanding

absorber [aβsorˈβer] /2a/ VT to absorb; (embeber) to soak up ▪ **absorberse** VR to become absorbed

absorción [aβsorˈθjon] NF absorption; (Com) takeover

absorto, -a [aβsˈorto, a] PP de **absorber** ▸ ADJ absorbed, engrossed

abstemio, -a [aβsˈtemjo, a] ADJ teetotal

abstención [aβstenˈθjon] NF abstention

abstendré etc [aβstenˈdre] VB ver **abstenerse**

abstenerse [aβsteˈnerse] /2k/ VR: ~ (de) to abstain o refrain (from)

abstenga etc [aβsˈtenga] VB ver **abstenerse**

abstinencia [aβstiˈnenθja] NF abstinence; (ayuno) fasting

abstracción [aβstrakˈθjon] NF abstraction

abstracto, -a [aβsˈtrakto, a] ADJ abstract; **en ~** in the abstract

abstraer [aβstra'er] /**2o**/ vt to abstract ■ **abstraerse** vr to be o become absorbed

abstraído, -a [aβstra'iðo, a] ADJ absent-minded

abstraiga etc [aβs'traiɣa], **abstraje** etc [aβs'traxe], **abstrayendo** etc [aβstra'jendo] vB ver **abstraer**

abstuve etc [aβs'tuβe] vB ver **abstenerse**

absuelto [aβ'swelto] PP de **absolver**

absurdo, -a [aβ'surðo, a] ADJ absurd ▶ NM absurdity; **lo ~ es que ...** the ridiculous thing is that ...

abuchear [aβutʃe'ar] /**1a**/ vt to boo

abucheo [aβu'tʃeo] NM booing; **ganarse un ~** (Teat) to be booed

★**abuela** [a'βwela] NF grandmother; **¡cuéntaselo a tu ~!** (fam) do you think I was born yesterday? (fam); **no tener/necesitar ~** (fam) to be full of o.s./blow one's own trumpet

abuelita [aβwe'lita] NF granny

★**abuelo** [a'βwelo] NM grandfather; (antepasado) ancestor ■ **abuelos** NMPL grandparents

abulense [aβu'lense] ADJ of Ávila ▶ NMF native o inhabitant of Ávila

abulia [a'βulja] NF lethargy

abúlico, -a [a'βuliko, a] ADJ lethargic

abultado, -a [aβul'taðo, a] ADJ bulky

abultar [aβul'tar] /**1a**/ vt to enlarge; (aumentar) to increase; (fig) to exaggerate ▶ vi to be bulky

abundancia [aβun'danθja] NF: **una ~ de** plenty of; **en ~** in abundance

abundante [aβun'dante] ADJ abundant, plentiful

abundar [aβun'dar] /**1a**/ vi to abound, be plentiful; **~ en una opinión** to share an opinion

aburguesarse [aβurɣe'sarse] /**1a**/ vr to become middle-class

★**aburrido, -a** [aβu'rriðo, a] ADJ (hastiado) bored; (que aburre) boring

---

Aburrido se traduce por **bored** *para referirse al hecho de estar aburrido: Si estás aburrida podrías ayudarme con esto.* **If you're bored you could help me with this**.
Se traduce por **boring** *para indicar que alguien o algo es aburrido: No me gusta salir con él; es muy aburrido.* **I don't like going out with him; he's really boring**.

★**aburrimiento** [aβurri'mjento] NM boredom, tedium

aburrir [aβu'rrir] /**3a**/ vt to bore ■ **aburrirse** vr to be bored, get bored; **aburrirse como una almeja** u **ostra** (fam) to be bored stiff

abusado, -a [aβu'saðo, a] ADJ (Am fam: astuto) sharp, cunning ▶ EXCL: **¡~!** (inv) look out!, careful!

abusar [aβu'sar] /**1a**/ vi to go too far; **~ de** to abuse

abusivo, -a [aβu'siβo, a] ADJ (precio) exorbitant

abuso [a'βuso] NM abuse; **~ de confianza** betrayal of trust

abyecto, -a [aβ'jekto, a] ADJ wretched, abject

a. C. ABR (= antes de Cristo) B.C.

a/c ABR (= al cuidado de) c/o; (= a cuenta) on account

acá [a'ka] ADV (lugar) here; **pasearse de ~ para allá** to walk up and down; **¡vente para ~!** come over here!; **¿de cuándo ~?** since when?

acabado, -a [aka'βaðo, a] ADJ finished, complete; (perfecto) perfect; (agotado) worn out; (fig) masterly ▶ NM finish

★**acabar** [aka'βar] /**1a**/ vt (llevar a su fin) to finish, complete; (consumir) to use up; (rematar) to finish off ▶ vi to finish, end; (morir) to die; **~ con** to put an end to; **esto acabará conmigo** this will be the end of me; **~ mal** to come to a sticky end; **~ de llegar** to have just arrived; **acababa de hacerlo** I had just done it; **~ haciendo** o **por hacer algo** to end up (by) doing sth ■ **acabarse** vr to finish, stop; (terminarse) to be over; (agotarse) to run out; **¡se acabó!** (¡basta!) that's enough!; (se terminó) it's all over!; **se me acabó el tabaco** I ran out of cigarettes

acabose [aka'βose] NM: **esto es el ~** this is the last straw

acacia [a'kaθja] NF acacia

★**academia** [aka'ðemja] NF academy; (Escol) private school; **~ de idiomas** language school; ver tb **colegio**

académico, -a [aka'ðemiko, a] ADJ academic

acaecer [akae'θer] /**2d**/ vi to happen, occur

acaezca etc [aka'eθka] vB ver **acaecer**

acallar [aka'ʎar] /**1a**/ vt (silenciar) to silence; (calmar) to pacify

acalorado, -a [akalo'raðo, a] ADJ (discusión) heated

acalorarse [akalo'rarse] /**1a**/ vr (fig) to get heated

acampada [akam'paða] NF: **ir de ~** to go camping

acampanado, -a [akampa'naðo, a] ADJ flared

★**acampar** [akam'par] /**1a**/ vi to camp

acanalado, -a [akana'laðo, a] ADJ (hierro) corrugated

acanalar [akana'lar] /**1a**/ vt to groove; (ondular) to corrugate

★**acantilado** [akanti'laðo] NM cliff

acaparador, a [akapara'ðor, a] NM/F monopolizer

acaparar [akapa'rar] /**1a**/ vt to monopolize; (acumular) to hoard

acápite [a'kapite] NM (Am) paragraph; **punto ~** full stop, new paragraph

acaramelado, -a [akarame'laðo, a] ADJ (Culin) toffee-coated; (fig) sugary

acariciar [akari'θjar] /**1b**/ vt to caress; (esperanza) to cherish

ácaro ['akaro] NM mite; **~ del polvo** dust mite

acarrear [akarre'ar] /1a/ VT to transport; (fig) to cause, result in; **le acarreó muchos disgustos** it brought him lots of problems

acaso [a'kaso] ADV perhaps, maybe; **¿~ es mi culpa?** (Am fam) what makes you think it's my fault?; **(por) si ~** (just) in case ▶ NM chance

acatamiento [akata'mjento] NM respect; (de la ley) observance

acatar [aka'tar] /1a/ VT to respect; (ley) to obey, observe

acatarrarse [akata'rrarse] /1a/ VR to catch a cold

acaudalado, -a [akauða'laðo, a] ADJ well-off

acaudillar [akauði'ʎar] /1a/ VT to lead, command

★**acceder** [akθe'ðer] /2a/ VI to accede, agree; **~ a** (petición etc) to agree to; (tener acceso a) to have access to; (Inform) to access

accesible [akθe'siβle] ADJ accessible; **~ a** open to

accésit [ak'θesit] (pl **accésits** [ak'θesits]) NM consolation prize

★**acceso** [ak'θeso] NM access, entry; (camino) access road; (Med) attack, fit; (de cólera) fit; (Pol) accession; (Inform) access; **~ aleatorio/directo/secuencial o en serie** (Inform) random/direct/sequential o serial access; **de ~ múltiple** multi-access

accesorio, -a [akθe'sorjo, a] ADJ accessory ▶ NM accessory ■ **accesorios** NMPL (Auto) accessories, extras; (Teat) props

accidentado, -a [akθiðen'taðo, a] ADJ uneven; (montañoso) hilly; (azaroso) eventful ▶ NM/F accident victim

accidental [akθiðen'tal] ADJ accidental; (empleo) temporary

accidentarse [akθiðen'tarse] /1a/ VR to have an accident

★**accidente** [akθi'ðente] NM accident; **por ~** by chance; **~ laboral o de trabajo/de tráfico** industrial/road o traffic accident ■ **accidentes** NMPL (de terreno) unevenness sg, roughness sg

acción [ak'θjon] NF action; (acto) action, act; (Teat) plot; (Com) share; (Jur) action, lawsuit; **capital en acciones** share capital; **~ liberada/ordinaria/preferente** fully-paid/ordinary/preference share

accionamiento [akθjona'mjento] NM (de máquina) operation

accionar [akθjo'nar] /1a/ VT to work, operate; (ejecutar) to activate

accionista [akθjo'nista] NMF shareholder

acebo [a'θeβo] NM holly; (árbol) holly tree

acechanza [aθe'tʃanθa] NF = **acecho**

acechar [aθe'tʃar] /1a/ VT to spy on; (aguardar) to lie in wait for

acecho [a'θetʃo] NM: **estar al ~ (de)** to lie in wait (for)

acedera [aθe'ðera] NF sorrel

aceitar [aθei'tar] /1a/ VT to oil, lubricate

★**aceite** [a'θeite] NM oil; **~ de girasol/oliva** sunflower/olive oil; **~ de hígado de bacalao** cod-liver oil

aceitera [aθei'tera] NF oilcan

aceitoso, -a [aθei'toso, a] ADJ oily

★**aceituna** [aθei'tuna] NF olive; **~ rellena** stuffed olive

aceitunado, -a [aθeitu'naðo, a] ADJ olive cpd; **de tez aceitunada** olive-skinned

acelerador [aθelera'ðor] NM accelerator

★**acelerar** [aθele'rar] /1a/ VT to accelerate ■ **acelerarse** VR to hurry

acelga [a'θelɣa] NF chard, beet

acendrado, -a [aθen'draðo, a] ADJ: **de ~ carácter español** typically Spanish

acendrar [aθen'drar] /1a/ VT to purify

★**acento** [a'θento] NM accent; (acentuación) stress; **~ cerrado** strong o thick accent

acentuar [aθen'twar] /1e/ VT to accent; to stress; (fig) to accentuate

acepción [aθep'θjon] NF meaning

★**aceptable** [aθep'taβle] ADJ acceptable

aceptación [aθepta'θjon] NF acceptance; (aprobación) approval

★**aceptar** [aθep'tar] /1a/ VT to accept; (aprobar) to approve; **~ hacer algo** to agree to do sth

acequia [a'θekja] NF irrigation ditch

★**acera** [a'θera] NF pavement (BRIT), sidewalk (US)

acerado, -a [aθe'raðo, a] ADJ steel; (afilado) sharp; (fig: duro) steely; (: mordaz) biting

acerbo, -a [a'θerβo, a] ADJ bitter; (fig) harsh

acerca [a'θerka]: **~ de** prep about, concerning

acercar [aθer'kar] /1g/ VT to bring o move nearer ■ **acercarse** VR to approach, come near

acerico [aθe'riko] NM pincushion

★**acero** [a'θero] NM steel; **~ inoxidable** stainless steel

acerque etc [a'θerke] VB ver **acercar**

acérrimo, -a [a'θerrimo, a] ADJ (partidario) staunch; (enemigo) bitter

acertado, -a [aθer'taðo, a] ADJ correct; (apropiado) apt; (sensato) sensible

★**acertar** [aθer'tar] /1j/ VT (blanco) to hit; (solución) to get right; (adivinar) to guess ▶ VI to get it right, be right; **~ a** to manage to; **~ con** to happen o hit on

acertijo [aθer'tixo] NM riddle, puzzle

acervo [a'θerβo] NM heap; **~ común** undivided estate

achacar [atʃa'kar] /1g/ VT to attribute

achacoso, -a [atʃa'koso, a] ADJ sickly

achantar [atʃan'tar] /1a/ VT (fam) to scare, frighten ■ **achantarse** VR to back down

achaque etc [a'tʃake] VB ver **achacar** ▶ NM ailment

achatar [atʃa'tar] /**1a**/ vᴛ to flatten

achicar [atʃi'kar] /**1g**/ vᴛ to reduce; (*humillar*) to humiliate; (*Naut*) to bale out ■ **achicarse** vʀ (*ropa*) to shrink; (*fig*) to humble o.s.

achicharrar [atʃitʃa'rrar] /**1a**/ vᴛ to scorch, burn

achichincle [atʃi'tʃinkle] ɴᴍF (*Am fam*) minion

achicoria [atʃi'korja] ɴF chicory

achinado, -a [atʃi'naðo, a] ᴀᴅJ (*ojos*) slanting; (*Am*) of mixed race

achique *etc* [a'tʃike] vʙ *ver* **achicar**

acholado, -a [atʃo'laðo, a] ᴀᴅJ (*Am*) of mixed race

achuchar [atʃu'tʃar] /**1a**/ vᴛ to crush

achuchón [atʃu'tʃon] ɴᴍ shove; **tener un ~** (*Med*) to be poorly

achuras [a'tʃuras] ɴFPL (*Am Culin*) offal

aciago, -a [a'θjaɣo, a] ᴀᴅJ ill-fated, fateful

acicalar [aθika'lar] /**1a**/ vᴛ to polish; (*adornar*) to bedeck ■ **acicalarse** vʀ to get dressed up

acicate [aθi'kate] ɴᴍ spur; (*fig*) incentive

acidez [aθi'ðeθ] ɴF acidity

ácido, -a ['aθiðo, a] ᴀᴅJ sour, acid ▸ ɴᴍ acid; (*fam: droga*) LSD

acierto *etc* [a'θjerto] vʙ *ver* **acertar** ▸ ɴᴍ success; (*buen paso*) wise move; (*solución*) solution; (*habilidad*) skill, ability; (*al adivinar*) good guess; **fue un ~ suyo** it was a sensible choice on his part

acitronar [aθitro'nar] /**1a**/ vᴛ (*Am fam*) to brown

aclamación [aklama'θjon] ɴF acclamation; (*aplausos*) applause

aclamar [akla'mar] /**1a**/ vᴛ to acclaim; (*aplaudir*) to applaud

aclaración [aklara'θjon] ɴF clarification, explanation

aclarar [akla'rar] /**1a**/ vᴛ to clarify, explain; (*ropa*) to rinse ▸ vɪ to clear up ■ **aclararse** vʀ (*suj: persona: explicarse*) to understand; (*fig: asunto*) to become clear; **aclararse la garganta** to clear one's throat

aclaratorio, -a [aklara'torjo, a] ᴀᴅJ explanatory

aclimatación [aklimata'θjon] ɴF acclimatization

aclimatar [aklima'tar] /**1a**/ vᴛ to acclimatize ■ **aclimatarse** vʀ to become *o* get acclimatized; **aclimatarse a algo** to get used to sth

acné [ak'ne] ɴᴍ acne

ACNUR [ak'nur] ɴᴍ ᴀʙʀ (= *Alto Comisionado de las Naciones Unidas para los Refugiados*) UNHCR

acobardar [akoβar'ðar] /**1a**/ vᴛ to daunt, intimidate ■ **acobardarse** vʀ (*atemorizarse*) to be intimidated; (*echarse atrás*): **acobardarse (ante)** to shrink back (from)

acodarse [ako'ðarse] /**1a**/ vʀ: **~ en** to lean on

★**acogedor, a** [akoxe'ðor, a] ᴀᴅJ welcoming; (*hospitalario*) hospitable

★**acoger** [ako'xer] /**2c**/ vᴛ to welcome; (*abrigar*) to shelter ■ **acogerse** vʀ to take refuge; **acogerse a** (*pretexto*) to take refuge in; (*ley*) to resort to

★**acogida** [ako'xiða] ɴF reception; refuge

acoja *etc* [a'koxa] vʙ *ver* **acoger**

acojonante [akoxo'nante] ᴀᴅJ (*Esp fam*) tremendous

acolchar [akol'tʃar] /**1a**/ vᴛ to pad; (*fig*) to cushion

acólito [a'kolito] ɴᴍ (*Rel*) acolyte; (*fig*) minion

acomedido, -a [akome'ðiðo, a] ᴀᴅJ (*Am*) helpful, obliging

acometer [akome'ter] /**2a**/ vᴛ to attack; (*emprender*) to undertake

acometida [akome'tiða] ɴF attack, assault

acomodado, -a [akomo'ðaðo, a] ᴀᴅJ (*persona*) well-to-do

acomodador, a [akomoða'ðor, a] ɴᴍ/F usher(ette)

acomodar [akomo'ðar] /**1a**/ vᴛ to adjust; (*alojar*) to accommodate ■ **acomodarse** vʀ to conform; (*instalarse*) to install o.s.; (*adaptarse*) to adapt o.s.; **acomodarse (a)** to adapt (to); **¡acomódese a su gusto!** make yourself comfortable!

acomodaticio, -a [akomoða'tiθjo, a] ᴀᴅJ (*complaciente*) accommodating, obliging; (*manejable*) pliable

acompañamiento [akompaɲa'mjento] ɴᴍ (*Mus*) accompaniment

acompañante, -a [akompa'ɲante, a] ɴᴍ/F companion

★**acompañar** [akompa'ɲar] /**1a**/ vᴛ to accompany, go with; (*documentos*) to enclose; **¿quieres que te acompañe?** do you want me to come with you?; **~ a algn a la puerta** to see sb to the door *o* out; **le acompaño en el sentimiento** please accept my condolences

acompasar [akompa'sar] /**1a**/ vᴛ (*Mus*) to mark the rhythm of

acomplejado, -a [akomple'xaðo, a] ᴀᴅJ neurotic

acomplejar [akomple'xar] /**1a**/ vᴛ to give a complex to ■ **acomplejarse** vʀ: **acomplejarse (con)** to get a complex (about)

acondicionado, -a [akondiθjo'naðo, a] ᴀᴅJ (*Tec*) in good condition

acondicionador [akondiθjona'ðor] ɴᴍ conditioner

acondicionar [akondiθjo'nar] /**1a**/ vᴛ to get ready, prepare; (*pelo*) to condition

acongojar [akongo'xar] /**1a**/ vᴛ to distress, grieve

aconsejable [akonse'xaβle] ᴀᴅJ advisable

★**aconsejar** [akonse'xar] /**1a**/ vᴛ to advise, counsel; **~ a algn hacer** *o* **que haga algo** to advise sb to do sth ■ **aconsejarse** vʀ: **aconsejarse con** *o* **de** to consult

acontecer [akonte'θer] /**2d**/ VI to happen, occur

acontecimiento [akonteθi'mjento] NM event

acontezca etc [akon'teθka] VB ver **acontecer**

acopiar [ako'pjar] /**1b**/ VT (recoger) to gather; (Com) to buy up

acopio [a'kopjo] NM store, stock

acoplador [akopla'ðor] NM: **~ acústico** (Inform) acoustic coupler

acoplamiento [akopla'mjento] NM coupling, joint

acoplar [ako'plar] /**1a**/ VT to fit; (Elec) to connect; (vagones) to couple

acoquinar [akoki'nar] /**1a**/ VT to scare ■ **acoquinarse** VR to get scared

acorazado, -a [akora'θaðo, a] ADJ armour-plated, armoured ▶ NM battleship

acordar [akor'ðar] /**1l**/ VT (resolver) to agree, resolve; (recordar) to remind; **~ hacer algo** to agree to do sth ■ **acordarse** VR to agree; **acordarse (de algo)** to remember (sth)

acorde [a'korðe] ADJ (Mus) harmonious ▶ NM chord; **~ con** (medidas etc) in keeping with

acordeón [akorðe'on] NM accordion

acordonado, -a [akorðo'naðo, a] ADJ (calle) cordoned-off

acorralar [akorra'lar] /**1a**/ VT to round up, corral; (fig) to intimidate

acortar [akor'tar] /**1a**/ VT to shorten; (duración) to cut short; (cantidad) to reduce ■ **acortarse** VR to become shorter

acosar [ako'sar] /**1a**/ VT to pursue relentlessly; (fig) to hound, pester; **~ a algn a preguntas** to pester sb with questions

★**acoso** [a'koso] NM relentless pursuit; (fig) harassment; **~ escolar** bullying; **~ sexual** sexual harassment

acostar [akos'tar] /**1l**/ VT (en cama) to put to bed; (en suelo) to lay down; (barco) to bring alongside ■ **acostarse** VR to go to bed; to lie down; **acostarse con algn** to sleep with sb

acostumbrado, -a [akostum'braðo, a] ADJ (habitual) usual; **estar ~ a (hacer) algo** to be used to (doing) sth

acostumbrar [akostum'brar] /**1a**/ VT: **~ a algn a algo** to get sb used to sth ▶ VI: **~ (a hacer algo)** to be in the habit of (doing sth) ■ **acostumbrarse** VR: **acostumbrarse a** to get used to

acotación [akota'θjon] NF (apunte) marginal note; (Geo) elevation mark; (de límite) boundary mark; (Teat) stage direction

acotamiento [akota'mjento] NM (Am) hard shoulder (Brit), berm (US)

acotar [ako'tar] /**1a**/ VT (terreno) to mark out; (fig) to limit; (caza) to protect

acotejar [akote'xar] /**1a**/ VT (Am) to put in order, arrange

ácrata ['akrata] ADJ, NMF anarchist

acre ['akre] ADJ (sabor) sharp, bitter; (olor) acrid; (fig) biting ▶ NM acre

acrecentar [akreθen'tar] /**1j**/ VT to increase, augment

acreciente etc [akre'θjente] VB ver **acrecentar**

acreditado, -a [akreði'taðo, a] ADJ (Pol) accredited; (Com): **una casa acreditada** a reputable firm

acreditar [akreði'tar] /**1a**/ VT (garantizar) to vouch for, guarantee; (autorizar) to authorize; (dar prueba de) to prove; (Com: abonar) to credit; (embajador) to accredit ■ **acreditarse** VR to become famous; (demostrar valía) to prove one's worth; **acreditarse de** to get a reputation for

acreedor, a [akree'ðor, a] ADJ: **~ a** worthy of ▶ NM/F creditor; **~ común/diferido/con garantía** (Com) unsecured/deferred/secured creditor

acribillar [akriβi'ʎar] /**1a**/ VT: **~ a balazos** to riddle with bullets

acrimonia [akri'monja], **acritud** [akri'tuð] NF acrimony

acrobacia [akro'βaθja] NF acrobatics; **~ aérea** aerobatics

acróbata [a'kroβata] NMF acrobat

acta ['akta] NF certificate; (de comisión) minutes pl, record; **~ de nacimiento/de matrimonio** birth/marriage certificate; **~ notarial** affidavit; **levantar ~** (Jur) to make a formal statement o deposition

★**actitud** [akti'tuð] NF attitude; (postura) posture; **adoptar una ~ firme** to take a firm stand

activar [akti'βar] /**1a**/ VT to activate; (acelerar) to speed up

★**actividad** [aktiβi'ðað] NF activity; **estar en plena ~** to be in full swing

★**activo, -a** [ak'tiβo, a] ADJ active; (vivo) lively ▶ NM (Com) assets pl; **~ y pasivo** assets and liabilities; **~ circulante/fijo/inmaterial/invisible** (Com) current/fixed/intangible/invisible assets; **~ realizable** liquid assets; **activos congelados** o **bloqueados** frozen assets; **~ tóxico** toxic asset; **estar en ~** (Mil) to be on active service

acto ['akto] NM act, action; (ceremonia) ceremony; (Teat) act; **en el ~** immediately; **hacer ~ de presencia** (asistir) to attend (formally)

★**actor** [ak'tor] NM actor; (Jur) plaintiff ▶ ADJ: **parte actora** prosecution

actora [ak'tora] ADJ: **parte ~** prosecution; (demandante) plaintiff

★**actriz** [ak'triθ] NF actress

★**actuación** [aktwa'θjon] NF action; (comportamiento) conduct, behaviour; (Jur) proceedings pl; (desempeño) performance

★**actual** [ak'twal] ADJ present(-day), current; **el 6 del ~** the 6th of this month

> Do not translate the Spanish word **actual** by actual.

actualice etc [aktwa'liθe] VB ver **actualizar**

actualidad [aktwali'ðað] NF present; **ser de gran ~** to be current; **en la ~** at present; (hoy día) nowadays, at present ■ **actualidades** NFPL (*noticias*) news *sg*

actualización [aktwaliθa'θjon] NF updating, modernization

actualizar [aktwali'θar] /**1f**/ VT to update, modernize

★**actualmente** [aktwal'mente] ADV at present; (*hoy día*) nowadays

★**actuar** [ak'twar] /**1e**/ VI (*obrar*) to work, operate; (*actor*) to act, perform; **~ de** to act as ▸ VT to work, operate

actuario, -a [ak'twarjo, a] NM/F clerk; (*Com*) actuary

acuarela [akwa'rela] NF watercolour

acuario [a'kwarjo] NM aquarium; **A~** (*Astro*) Aquarius

acuartelar [akwarte'lar] /**1a**/ VT (*Mil: alojar*) to quarter

acuático, -a [a'kwatiko, a] ADJ aquatic

acuchillar [akutʃi'ʎar] /**1a**/ VT (*Tec*) to plane (down), smooth

acuciar [aku'θjar] /**1b**/ VT to urge on

acuclillarse [akukli'ʎarse] /**1a**/ VR to crouch down

★**acudir** [aku'ðir] /**3a**/ VI to attend, turn up; (*ir*) to go; **~ a** to turn to; **~ en ayuda de** to go to the aid of; **~ a una cita** to keep an appointment; **~ a una llamada** to answer a call; **no tener a quién ~** to have nobody to turn to

★**acuerdo** [a'kwerðo] VB *ver* **acordar** ▸ NM agreement; (*Pol*) resolution; **~ de pago respectivo** (*Com*) knock-for-knock agreement; **A~ General sobre Aranceles Aduaneros y Comercio** (*Com*) General Agreement on Tariffs and Trade; **tomar un ~** to pass a resolution; **¡de ~!** agreed!; **de ~ con** (*persona*) in agreement with; (*acción, documento*) in accordance with; **de común ~** by common consent; **estar de ~** (*persona*) to agree; **llegar a un ~** to come to an understanding

acueste *etc* [a'kweste] VB *ver* **acostar**

acullá [aku'ʎa] ADV over there

acumular [akumu'lar] /**1a**/ VT to accumulate, collect

acunar [aku'nar] /**1a**/ VT to rock (to sleep)

acuñar [aku'ɲar] /**1a**/ VT (*moneda*) to mint; (*frase*) to coin

acuoso, -a [a'kwoso, a] ADJ watery

acupuntura [akupun'tura] NF acupuncture

acurrucarse [akurru'karse] /**1g**/ VR to crouch; (*ovillarse*) to curl up

acurruque *etc* [aku'rruke] VB *ver* **acurrucarse**

acusación [akusa'θjon] NF accusation

acusado, -a [aku'saðo, a] ADJ (*Jur*) accused; (*marcado*) marked; (*acento*) strong

★**acusar** [aku'sar] /**1a**/ VT to accuse; (*revelar*) to reveal; (*denunciar*) to denounce; (*emoción*) to show; **~ recibo** to acknowledge receipt; **su rostro acusó extrañeza** his face registered

surprise ■ **acusarse** VR: **acusarse (de)** to confess (to)

acuse [a'kuse] NM: **~ de recibo** acknowledgement of receipt

acústico, -a [a'kustiko, a] ADJ acoustic ▸ NF (*de una sala etc*) acoustics *pl*; (*ciencia*) acoustics *sg*

adagio [a'ðaxjo] NM adage; (*Mus*) adagio

adalid [aða'lið] NM leader, champion

adaptación [aðapta'θjon] NF adaptation

adaptador [aðapta'ðor] NM (*Elec*) adapter; **~ universal** universal adapter

adaptar [aðap'tar] /**1a**/ VT to adapt; (*acomodar*) to fit; (*convertir*): **~ (para)** to convert (to)

adecentar [aðeθen'tar] /**1a**/ VT to tidy up

adecuado, -a [aðe'kwaðo, a] ADJ (*apto*) suitable; (*oportuno*) appropriate; **el hombre ~ para el puesto** the right man for the job

adecuar [aðe'kwar] /**1d**/ VT (*adaptar*) to adapt; (*hacer apto*) to make suitable

adefesio [aðe'fesjo] NM (*fam*): **estaba hecha un ~** she looked a sight

a. de J.C. ABR (= *antes de Jesucristo*) B.C.

★**adelantado, -a** [aðelan'taðo, a] ADJ advanced; (*reloj*) fast; **pagar por ~** to pay in advance

adelantamiento [aðelanta'mjento] NM advance, advancement; (*Auto*) overtaking

★**adelantar** [aðelan'tar] /**1a**/ VT to move forward; (*avanzar*) to advance; (*acelerar*) to speed up; (*Auto*) to overtake ▸ VI (*ir delante*) to go ahead; (*progresar*) to improve ■ **adelantarse** VR (*tomar la delantera: corredor*) to move forward; **adelantarse a algn** to get ahead of sb; **adelantarse a los deseos de algn** to anticipate sb's wishes

★**adelante** [aðe'lante] ADV forward(s), onward(s), ahead; **de hoy en ~** from now on; **más ~** later on; (*más allá*) further on ▸ EXCL come in!

adelanto [aðe'lanto] NM advance; (*mejora*) improvement; (*progreso*) progress; (*dinero*) advance; **los adelantos de la ciencia** the advances of science

adelgace *etc* [aðel'ɣaθe] VB *ver* **adelgazar**

adelgazar [aðelɣa'θar] /**1f**/ VT to thin (down); (*afilar*) to taper ▸ VI to get thin; (*con régimen*) to slim down, lose weight

ademán [aðe'man] NM gesture; **en ~ de** as if to ■ **ademanes** NMPL manners

★**además** [aðe'mas] ADV besides; (*por otra parte*) moreover; (*también*) also; **~ de** besides, in addition to

ADENA [a'ðena] NF ABR (*Esp*: = *Asociación para la Defensa de la Naturaleza*) organization for nature conservation

adentrarse [aðen'trarse] /**1a**/ VR: **~ en** to go into, get inside; (*penetrar*) to penetrate (into)

★**adentro** [a'ðentro] ADV inside, in; **mar ~** out at sea; **tierra ~** inland ▸ NM: **dijo para sus adentros** he said to himself

adepto, -a [a'ðepto, a] NM/F supporter

aderece *etc* [aðe'reθe] VB *ver* **aderezar**

aderezar [aðere'θar] /**1f**/ VT (*ensalada*) to dress; (*comida*) to season

aderezo [aðe'reθo] NM dressing; seasoning

adeudar [aðeu'ðar] /**1a**/ VT to owe; ~ **una suma en una cuenta** to debit an account with a sum ◼ **adeudarse** VR to run into debt

adherirse [aðe'rirse] /**3i**/ VR: ~ **a** to adhere to; (*partido*) to join; (*fig*) to follow

adhesión [aðe'sjon] NF adhesion; (*fig*) adherence

adhesivo, -a [aðe'siβo, a] ADJ adhesive ▶ NM sticker

adhiera *etc* [a'ðjera], **adhiriendo** *etc* [aði'rjendo] VB *ver* **adherirse**

★**adicción** [aðik'θjon] NF addiction

adición [aði'θjon] NF addition

adicional [aðiθjo'nal] ADJ additional; (*Inform*) add-on

adicionar [aðiθjo'nar] /**1a**/ VT to add

★**adicto, -a** [a'ðikto, a] ADJ: ~ **a** (*droga etc*) addicted to; (*dedicado*) devoted to ▶ NM/F supporter, follower; (*toxicómano etc*) addict

adiestrar [aðjes'trar] /**1a**/ VT to train, teach; (*conducir*) to guide, lead ◼ **adiestrarse** VR to practise; (*aprender*) to train o.s.

adinerado, -a [aðine'raðo, a] ADJ wealthy

★**adiós** [a'ðjos] EXCL (*para despedirse*) goodbye!, cheerio!; (*al pasar*) hello!

aditivo [aði'tiβo] NM additive

adivinanza [aðiβi'nanθa] NF riddle

★**adivinar** [aðiβi'nar] /**1a**/ VT (*profetizar*) to prophesy; (*conjeturar*) to guess

adivino, -a [aði'βino, a] NM/F fortune-teller

adj. ABR (= *adjunto*) encl; (= *adjetivo*) adj

adjetivo [aðxe'tiβo] NM adjective

adjudicación [aðxuðika'θjon] NF award; (*Com*) adjudication

adjudicar [aðxuði'kar] /**1g**/ VT to award ◼ **adjudicarse** VR: **adjudicarse algo** to appropriate sth

adjudique *etc* [aðxu'ðike] VB *ver* **adjudicar**

adjuntar [aðxun'tar] /**1a**/ VT to attach, enclose

★**adjunto, -a** [að'xunto, a] ADJ attached, enclosed ▶ NM/F assistant

adminículo [aðmi'nikulo] NM gadget

administración [aðministra'θjon] NF administration; (*dirección*) management; ~ **pública** civil service; **A~ de Correos** General Post Office

administrador, a [aðministra'ðor, a] NM/F administrator; manager(ess)

administrar [aðminis'trar] /**1a**/ VT to administer

administrativo, -a [aðministra'tiβo, a] ADJ administrative

admirable [aðmi'raβle] ADJ admirable

admiración [aðmira'θjon] NF admiration; (*asombro*) wonder; (*Ling*) exclamation mark

★**admirar** [aðmi'rar] /**1a**/ VT to admire; (*extrañar*) to surprise; **no es de ~ que** ... it's not surprising that ... ◼ **admirarse** VR to be surprised; **se admiró de saberlo** he was amazed to hear it

admisible [aðmi'siβle] ADJ admissible

admisión [aðmi'sjon] NF admission; (*reconocimiento*) acceptance

admitir [aðmi'tir] /**3a**/ VT to admit; (*aceptar*) to accept; (*dudas*) to leave room for; **esto no admite demora** this must be dealt with immediately

admón. ABR (= *administración*) admin

admonición [aðmoni'θjon] NF warning

ADN NM ABR (= *ácido desoxirribonucleico*) DNA

adobar [aðo'βar] /**1a**/ VT (*preparar*) to prepare; (*cocinar*) to season

adobe [a'ðoβe] NM adobe, sun-dried brick

adocenado, -a [aðoθe'naðo, a] ADJ (*fam*) mediocre

adoctrinar [aðoktri'nar] /**1a**/ VT to indoctrinate

adolecer [aðole'θer] /**2d**/ VI: ~ **de** to suffer from

★**adolescente** [aðoles'θente] NMF adolescent, teenager ▶ ADJ adolescent, teenage

adolezca *etc* [aðo'leθka] VB *ver* **adolecer**

★**adonde** CONJ (to) where

★**adónde** [a'ðonde] ADV = **dónde**

adondequiera [aðonde'kjera] ADV wherever

adopción [aðop'θjon] NF adoption

★**adoptar** [aðop'tar] /**1a**/ VT to adopt

★**adoptivo, -a** [aðop'tiβo, a] ADJ (*padres*) adoptive; (*hijo*) adopted

adoquín [aðo'kin] NM paving stone

★**adorar** [aðo'rar] /**1a**/ VT to adore

adormecer [aðorme'θer] /**2d**/ VT to put to sleep ◼ **adormecerse** VR to become sleepy; (*dormirse*) to fall asleep

adormezca *etc* [aðor'meθka] VB *ver* **adormecer**

adormilarse [aðormi'larse] /**1a**/ VR to doze

adornar [aðor'nar] /**1a**/ VT to adorn

adorno [a'ðorno] NM (*objeto*) ornament; (*decoración*) decoration, adornment

adosado, -a [aðo'saðo, a] ADJ (*casa*) semidetached

adosar [aðo'sar] /**1a**/ VT (AM: *adjuntar*) to attach, enclose (*with a letter*)

adquiera *etc* [að'kjera] VB *ver* **adquirir**

adquirir [aðki'rir] /**3i**/ VT to acquire, obtain

adquisición [aðkisi'θjon] NF acquisition; (*compra*) purchase

★**adrede** [a'ðreðe] ADV on purpose

Adriático [að'rjatiko] NM: **el (mar)** ~ the Adriatic (Sea)

adscribir [aðskri'βir] /**3a**/ VT to appoint; **estuvo adscrito al servicio de** ... he was attached to ...

adscrito [aðˈskrito] PP *de* **adscribir**

ADSL NM ABR ADSL

★**aduana** [aˈðwana] NF customs *pl*; *(impuesto)* (customs) duty

★**aduanero, -a** [aðwaˈnero, a] ADJ customs *cpd* ▶ NM/F customs officer

aducir [aðuˈθir] /**3n**/ VT to adduce; *(dar como prueba)* to offer as proof

adueñarse [aðweˈɲarse] /**1a**/ VR: **~ de** to take possession of

adulación [aðulaˈθjon] NF flattery

adular [aðuˈlar] /**1a**/ VT to flatter

adulterar [aðulteˈrar] /**1a**/ VT to adulterate ▶ VI to commit adultery

adulterio [aðulˈterjo] NM adultery

adúltero, -a [aˈðultero, a] ADJ adulterous ▶ NM/F adulterer/adulteress

★**adulto, -a** [aˈðulto, a] ADJ, NM/F adult

adusto, -a [aˈðusto, a] ADJ stern; *(austero)* austere

aduzca *etc* [aˈðuθka] VB *ver* **aducir**

advenedizo, -a [aðβeneˈðiθo, a] NM/F upstart

advenimiento [aðβeniˈmjento] NM arrival; *(al trono)* accession

adverbio [aðˈβerβjo] NM adverb

adversario, -a [aðβerˈsarjo, a] NM/F adversary

adversidad [aðβersiˈðað] NF adversity; *(contratiempo)* setback

adverso, -a [aðˈβerso, a] ADJ adverse; *(suerte)* bad

advertencia [aðβerˈtenθja] NF warning; *(prefacio)* preface, foreword

★**advertir** [aðβerˈtir] /**3i**/ VT *(observar)* to notice; *(avisar)*: **~ a algn de** to warn sb about *o* of

Adviento [aðˈβjento] NM Advent

advierta *etc* [aðˈβjerta], **advirtiendo** *etc* [aðβirˈtjendo] VB *ver* **advertir**

adyacente [aðjaˈθente] ADJ adjacent

aéreo, -a [aˈereo, a] ADJ aerial; *(tráfico)* air *cpd*

aerobic [aeˈroβik] NM, *(AM)* **aerobics** [aeˈroβiks] NMPL aerobics *sg*

aerodeslizador [aeroðesliθaˈðor] NM hovercraft

aerodinámico, -a [aeroðiˈnamiko, a] ADJ aerodynamic

aeródromo [aeˈroðromo] NM aerodrome

aerogenerador [aeroxeneraˈðor] NM wind turbine

aerograma [aeroˈɣrama] NM airmail letter

aeromodelismo [aeromoðeˈlismo] NM model aircraft making, aeromodelling

aeromozo, -a [aeroˈmoθo, a] NM/F *(AM)* flight attendant, air steward(ess)

aeronáutica [aeroˈnautika] NF aeronautics *sg*

aeronáutico, -a [aeroˈnautiko, a] ADJ aeronautical

aeronave [aeroˈnaβe] NM spaceship

aeroplano [aeroˈplano] NM aeroplane

★**aeropuerto** [aeroˈpwerto] NM airport

aerosol [aeroˈsol] NM aerosol, spray

a/f ABR (= *a favor*) in favour

afabilidad [afaβiliˈðað] NF affability, pleasantness

afable [aˈfaβle] ADJ affable, pleasant

afamado, -a [afaˈmaðo, a] ADJ famous

afán [aˈfan] NM hard work; *(deseo)* desire; **con ~** keenly

afanador, a [afanaˈðor, a] NM/F *(AM: de limpieza)* cleaner

afanar [afaˈnar] /**1a**/ VT to harass; *(fam)* to pinch ■ **afanarse** VR: **afanarse por** to strive to

afanoso, -a [afaˈnoso, a] ADJ *(trabajo)* hard; *(trabajador)* industrious

AFE [ˈafe] NF ABR (= *Asociación de Futbolistas Españoles*) ≈ FA

afear [afeˈar] /**1a**/ VT to disfigure

afección [afekˈθjon] NF affection; *(Med)* disease

afectación [afektaˈθjon] NF affectation

afectado, -a [afekˈtaðo, a] ADJ affected

★**afectar** [afekˈtar] /**1a**/ VT to affect, have an effect on; *(AM: dañar)* to hurt; **por lo que afecta a esto** as far as this is concerned

afectísimo, -a [afekˈtisimo, a] ADJ affectionate; **suyo ~** yours truly

afectivo, -a [afekˈtiβo, a] ADJ *(problema etc)* emotional

afecto, -a [aˈfekto, a] ADJ: **~ a** fond of; *(Jur)* subject to ▶ NM affection; **tenerle ~ a algn** to be fond of sb

afectuoso, -a [afekˈtwoso, a] ADJ affectionate

afeitar [afeiˈtar] /**1a**/ VT to shave ■ **afeitarse** VR to shave

afeminado, -a [afemiˈnaðo, a] ADJ effeminate

aferrar [afeˈrrar] /**1j**/ VT to moor; *(fig)* to grasp ▶ VI to moor ■ **aferrarse** VR *(agarrarse)* to cling on; **aferrarse a un principio** to stick to a principle; **aferrarse a una esperanza** to cling to a hope

Afganistán [afɣanisˈtan] NM Afghanistan

afgano, -a [afˈɣano, a] ADJ, NM/F Afghan

afiance *etc* [aˈfjanθe] VB *ver* **afianzar**

afianzamiento [afjanθaˈmjento] NM strengthening; security

afianzar [afjanˈθar] /**1f**/ VT to strengthen, secure ■ **afianzarse** VR to steady o.s.; *(establecerse)* to become established

afiche [aˈfitʃe] NM *(AM)* poster

★**afición** [afiˈθjon] NF: **~ a** fondness *o* liking for; **la ~** the fans *pl*; **pinto por ~** I paint as a hobby

★**aficionado, -a** [afiθjoˈnaðo, a] ADJ keen, enthusiastic; *(no profesional)* amateur; **ser ~ a algo** to be very keen on *o* fond of sth ▶ NM/F enthusiast, fan; amateur

aficionar [afiθjo'nar] /**1a**/ VT: ~ **a algn a algo** to make sb like sth ■ **aficionarse** VR: **aficionarse a algo** to grow fond of sth

afilado, -a [afi'laðo, a] ADJ sharp

afilador [afila'ðor] NM knife grinder

afilalápices [afila'lapiθes] NM INV pencil sharpener

afilar [afi'lar] /**1a**/ VT to sharpen ■ **afilarse** VR (cara) to grow thin

afiliación [afilja'θjon] NF (de sindicatos) membership

afiliado, -a [afi'ljaðo, a] ADJ subsidiary ▶ NM/F affiliate

afiliarse [afi'ljarse] /**1b**/ VR to affiliate

afín [a'fin] ADJ (parecido) similar; (conexo) related

afinar [afi'nar] /**1a**/ VT (Tec) to refine; (Mus) to tune ▶ VI (tocar) to play in tune; (cantar) to sing in tune

afincarse [afin'karse] /**1g**/ VR to settle

afinidad [afini'ðað] NF affinity; (parentesco) relationship; **por** ~ by marriage

afirmación [afirma'θjon] NF affirmation

afirmar [afir'mar] /**1a**/ VT to affirm, state; (sostener) to strengthen ■ **afirmarse** VR (recuperar el equilibrio) to steady o.s.; **afirmarse en lo dicho** to stand by what one has said

afirmativo, -a [afirma'tiβo, a] ADJ affirmative

aflicción [aflik'θjon] NF affliction; (dolor) grief

afligir [afli'xir] /**3c**/ VT to afflict; (apenar) to distress ■ **afligirse** VR: **afligirse (por** o **con** o **de)** to grieve (about o at); **no te aflijas tanto** you must not let it affect you like this

aflija etc [a'flixa] VB ver **afligir**

aflojar [aflo'xar] /**1a**/ VT to slacken; (desatar) to loosen, undo; (relajar) to relax ▶ VI (amainar) to drop; (bajar) to go down ■ **aflojarse** VR to relax

aflorar [aflo'rar] /**1a**/ VI (Geo, fig) to come to the surface, emerge

afluencia [aflu'enθja] NF flow

afluente [aflu'ente] ADJ flowing ▶ NM (Geo) tributary

afluir [aflu'ir] /**3g**/ VI to flow

afluya etc [a'fluja], **afluyendo** etc [aflu'jendo] VB ver **afluir**

afmo., -a. ABR (= afectísimo/a suyo/a) Yours

afónico, -a [a'foniko, a] ADJ: **estar** ~ to have a sore throat; to have lost one's voice

aforar [afo'rar] /**1a**/ VT (Tec) to gauge; (fig) to value

aforo [a'foro] NM (Tec) gauging; (de teatro etc) capacity; **el teatro tiene un ~ de 2,000** the theatre can seat 2,000

★**afortunadamente** [afortunaða'mente] ADV fortunately, luckily

★**afortunado, -a** [afortu'naðo, a] ADJ fortunate, lucky

afrancesado, -a [afranθe'saðo, a] ADJ francophile; (pey) Frenchified

afrenta [a'frenta] NF affront, insult; (deshonra) dishonour (BRIT), dishonor (US), shame

afrentoso, -a [afren'toso, a] ADJ insulting; shameful

★**África** ['afrika] NF Africa; ~ **del Sur** South Africa

★**africano, -a** [afri'kano, a] ADJ, NM/F African

afrontar [afron'tar] /**1a**/ VT to confront; (poner cara a cara) to bring face to face

afrutado, -a [afru'taðo, a] ADJ fruity

after ['after] (pl **afters** o ~) NM, **afterhours** ['afterauars] NM INV after-hours club

★**afuera** [a'fwera] ADV out, outside; **por** ~ on the outside ■ **afueras** NFPL outskirts

ag. ABR (= agosto) Aug.

agachar [aɣa'tʃar] /**1a**/ VT to bend, bow ■ **agacharse** VR to stoop, bend

agalla [a'ɣaʎa] NF (Zool) gill ■ **agallas** NFPL (fam) guts; **tener agallas** to have guts

agarradera [aɣarra'ðera] NF, (AM) **agarradero** [aɣarra'ðero] NM handle ■ **agarraderas** NFPL pull sg, influence sg

agarrado, -a [aɣa'rraðo, a] ADJ mean, stingy

★**agarrar** [aɣa'rrar] /**1a**/ VT to grasp; grab; (AM: tomar) to take, catch; (recoger) to pick up ▶ VI (planta) to take root; **agarró y se fue** (esp AM fam) he upped and went ■ **agarrarse** VR to hold on (tightly); (meterse uno con otro) to grapple (with each other); **agarrársela con algn** (AM) to pick on sb

agarrotar [aɣarro'tar] /**1a**/ VT (lío) to tie tightly; (persona) to squeeze tightly; (reo) to garrotte ■ **agarrotarse** VR (motor) to seize up; (Med) to stiffen

agasajar [aɣasa'xar] /**1a**/ VT to treat well, fête

agave [a'ɣaβe] NF agave

agazapar [aɣaθa'par] /**1a**/ VT (coger) to grab hold of ■ **agazaparse** VR (agacharse) to crouch down

agencia [a'xenθja] NF agency; ~ **de créditos/ publicidad/viajes** credit/advertising/travel agency; ~ **inmobiliaria** estate agent's (office) (BRIT), real estate office (US); ~ **matrimonial** marriage bureau

agenciar [axen'θjar] /**1b**/ VT to bring about ■ **agenciarse** VR to look after o.s.; **agenciarse algo** to get hold of sth

★**agenda** [a'xenda] NF diary; ~ **electrónica** PDA; ~ **telefónica** telephone directory

Do not translate the Spanish word **agenda** by agenda.

agente [a'xente] NMF agent; (tb: **agente de policía**) police officer; ~ **de bolsa** stockbroker; ~ **de negocios** (Com) business agent; ~ **de seguros** insurance broker; ~ **de tránsito** (AM) traffic cop; ~ **de viajes** travel agent; ~ **inmobiliario** estate agent (BRIT), realtor (US); **agentes sociales** social partners

ágil ['axil] ADJ agile, nimble

agilidad [axili'ðað] NF agility, nimbleness

agilizar [axili'θar] /**1f**/ vt (*trámites*) to speed up

agiotista [axjo'tista] NMF (*AM: usurero*) usurer

agitación [axita'θjon] NF (*de mano etc*) shaking, waving; (*de líquido etc*) stirring; agitation

agitado, -a [axi'aðo, a] ADJ hectic; (*viaje*) bumpy

★**agitar** [axi'tar] /**1a**/ vt to wave, shake; (*líquido*) to stir; (*fig*) to stir up, excite ■ **agitarse** VR to get excited; (*inquietarse*) to get worried o upset

aglomeración [aɣlomera'θjon] NF: ~ **de tráfico** traffic jam; ~ **de gente** mass of people

aglomerar [aɣlome'rar] /**1a**/ vt, **aglomerarse** VR to crowd together

agnóstico, -a [aɣ'nostiko, a] ADJ, NM/F agnostic

agobiante [aɣo'βjante] ADJ (*calor*) oppressive

agobiar [aɣo'βjar] /**1b**/ vt to weigh down; (*oprimir*) to oppress; (*cargar*) to burden; **sentirse agobiado por** to be overwhelmed by

agobio [a'ɣoβjo] NM (*peso*) burden; (*fig*) oppressiveness

agolpamiento [aɣolpa'mjento] NM crush

agolparse [aɣol'parse] /**1a**/ VR to crowd together

agonía [aɣo'nia] NF death throes *pl*; (*fig*) agony, anguish

agonice *etc* [aɣo'niθe] VB *ver* **agonizar**

agonizante [aɣoni'θante] ADJ dying

agonizar [aɣoni'θar] /**1f**/ vi to be dying

agorero, -a [aɣo'rero, a] ADJ ominous; **ave agorera** bird of ill omen ▶ NM/F soothsayer

agostar [aɣo'star] /**1a**/ vt (*quemar*) to parch; (*fig*) to wither

★**agosto** [a'ɣosto] NM August; (*fig*) harvest; **hacer su** ~ to make one's pile; *ver tb* **julio**

agotado, -a [aɣo'taðo, a] ADJ (*persona*) exhausted; (*acabado*) finished; (*Com*) sold out; (: *libros*) out of print; (*pila*) flat

agotador, a [aɣota'ðor, a] ADJ exhausting

agotamiento [aɣota'mjento] NM exhaustion

★**agotar** [aɣo'tar] /**1a**/ vt to exhaust; (*consumir*) to drain; (*recursos*) to use up, deplete ■ **agotarse** VR to be exhausted; (*acabarse*) to run out; (*libro*) to go out of print

agraciado, -a [aɣra'θjaðo, a] ADJ (*atractivo*) attractive; (*en sorteo etc*) lucky

agraciar [aɣra'θjar] /**1b**/ vt (*Jur*) to pardon; (*con premio*) to reward; (*hacer más atractivo*) to make more attractive

★**agradable** [aɣra'ðaβle] ADJ pleasant, nice

agradar [aɣra'ðar] /**1a**/ vt, vi to please; **él me agrada** I like him ■ **agradarse** VR to like each other

★**agradecer** [aɣraðe'θer] /**2d**/ vt to thank; (*favor etc*) to be grateful for; **le agradecería me enviara ...** I would be grateful if you would send me ... ■ **agradecerse** VR: **¡se agradece!** much obliged!

★**agradecido, -a** [aɣraðe'θiðo, a] ADJ grateful; **¡muy ~!** thanks a lot!

agradecimiento [aɣraðeθi'mjento] NM thanks *pl*; gratitude

agradezca *etc* [aɣra'ðeθka] VB *ver* **agradecer**

★**agrado** [a'ɣraðo] NM: **ser de tu** *etc* ~ to be to your *etc* liking

agrandar [aɣran'dar] /**1a**/ vt to enlarge; (*fig*) to exaggerate ■ **agrandarse** VR to get bigger

agrario, -a [a'ɣrarjo, a] ADJ agrarian, land *cpd*; (*política*) agricultural, farming *cpd*

agravante [aɣra'βante] ADJ aggravating ▶ NM o F complication; **con el** or **la** ~ **de que ...** with the further difficulty that ...

agravar [aɣra'βar] /**1a**/ vt (*pesar sobre*) to make heavier; (*irritar*) to aggravate ■ **agravarse** VR to worsen, get worse

agraviar [aɣra'βjar] /**1b**/ vt to offend; (*ser injusto con*) to wrong ■ **agraviarse** VR to take offence

agravio [a'ɣraβjo] NM offence; wrong; (*Jur*) grievance

agraz [a'ɣraθ] NM (*uva*) sour grape; **en** ~ (*fig*) immature

agredir [aɣre'ðir] /**3a**/ vt to attack

agregado [aɣre'ɣaðo] NM aggregate; (*persona*) attaché; (*profesor*) assistant professor; **A-** = teacher (*who is not head of department*)

agregar [aɣre'ɣar] /**1h**/ vt to gather; (*añadir*) to add; (*persona*) to appoint

agregue *etc* [a'ɣreɣe] VB *ver* **agregar**

agresión [aɣre'sjon] NF aggression; (*ataque*) attack

★**agresivo, -a** [aɣre'siβo, a] ADJ aggressive

agreste [a'ɣreste] ADJ (*rural*) rural; (*fig*) rough

agriar [a'ɣrjar] /**1c**/ vt (*fig*) to turn sour ■ **agriarse** VR to turn sour

agrícola [a'ɣrikola] ADJ farming *cpd*, agricultural

agricultor, a [aɣrikul'tor, a] NM/F farmer

★**agricultura** [aɣrikul'tura] NF agriculture, farming

agridulce [aɣri'ðulθe] ADJ bittersweet; (*Culin*) sweet and sour

agrietarse [aɣrje'tarse] /**1a**/ VR to crack; (*la piel*) to chap

agrimensor, a [aɣrimen'sor, a] NM/F surveyor

agringado, -a [aɣrin'gaðo, a] ADJ gringolike

agrio, -a ['aɣrjo, a] ADJ bitter

agronomía [aɣrono'mia] NF agronomy, agriculture

agrónomo, -a [a'ɣronomo, a] NM/F agronomist, agricultural expert

agropecuario, -a [aɣrope'kwarjo, a] ADJ farming *cpd*, agricultural

agrupación [aɣrupa'θjon] NF group; (*acto*) grouping

agrupar [aɣru'par] /**1a**/ vt to group; (*Inform*) to block ■ **agruparse** VR (*Pol*) to form a group; (*juntarse*) to gather

★**agua** ['aɣwa] NF water; (*Naut*) wake; (*Arq*) slope

of a roof; **~ bendita/destilada/potable** holy/distilled/drinking water; **~ caliente** hot water; **~ corriente** running water; **~ de colonia** eau de cologne; **~ mineral (con/sin gas)** (sparkling/still) mineral water; **~ oxigenada** hydrogen peroxide; **~ pasada no mueve molino** it's no use crying over spilt milk; **estar con el ~ al cuello** to be up to one's neck; **venir como ~ de mayo** to be a godsend ■ **aguas** NFPL (*de joya*) sparkle *sg*; (*Med*) water *sg*, urine *sg*; (*Naut*) waters; **aguas abajo/arriba** downstream/upstream; **aguas jurisdiccionales** territorial waters; **aguas mayores** excrement *sg*

aguacate [aɣwaˈkate] NM avocado (pear)

aguacero [aɣwaˈθero] NM (heavy) shower, downpour

aguachirle [aɣwaˈtʃirle] NM (*bebida*) slops *pl*

aguado, -a [aˈɣwaðo, a] ADJ watery, watered down ▶ NF (*Agr*) watering place; (*Naut*) water supply; (*Arte*) watercolour

aguafiestas [aɣwaˈfjestas] NMF INV spoilsport

aguafuerte [aɣwaˈfwerte] NF etching

aguaitar [aɣwaiˈtar] /1a/ VT (*Am*) to watch

aguamiel [aɣwaˈmjel] NF (*Am*) fermented maguey o agave juice

aguanieve [aɣwaˈnjeβe] NF sleet

aguantable [aɣwanˈtaβle] ADJ bearable, tolerable

★**aguantar** [aɣwanˈtar] /1a/ VT to bear, put up with; (*sostener*) to hold up ▶ VI to last; **no sé cómo aguanta** I don't know how he can take it ■ **aguantarse** VR to restrain o.s.

aguante [aˈɣwante] NM (*paciencia*) patience; (*resistencia*) endurance; (*Deporte*) stamina

aguar [aˈɣwar] /1i/ VT to water down; (*fig*): **~ la fiesta a algn** to spoil sb's fun

★**aguardar** [aɣwarˈðar] /1a/ VT to wait for

aguardentoso, -a [aɣwarðenˈtoso, a] ADJ (*pey: voz*) husky, gruff

aguardiente [aɣwarˈðjente] NM brandy, liquor

aguarrás [aɣwaˈrras] NM turpentine

aguaviva [aɣwaˈbiβa] NF (*RPL*) jellyfish

aguce etc [aˈɣuθe] VB ver **aguzar**

agudeza [aɣuˈðeθa] NF sharpness; (*ingenio*) wit

agudice etc [aɣuˈðiθe] VB ver **agudizar**

agudizar [aɣuðiˈθar] /1f/ VT to sharpen; (*crisis*) to make worse ■ **agudizarse** VR to worsen, deteriorate

★**agudo, -a** [aˈɣuðo, a] ADJ sharp; (*voz*) high-pitched, piercing; (*dolor, enfermedad*) acute

agüe etc [ˈaɣwe] VB ver **aguar**

agüero [aˈɣwero] NM: **buen/mal ~** good/bad omen; **ser de buen ~** to augur well; **pájaro de mal ~** bird of ill omen

aguerrido, -a [aɣeˈrriðo, a] ADJ hardened; (*fig*) experienced

aguijar [aɣiˈxar] /1a/ VT to goad; (*incitar*) to urge on ▶ VI to hurry along

aguijón [aɣiˈxon] NM sting; (*fig*) spur

aguijonear [aɣixoneˈar] /1a/ VT = **aguijar**

águila [ˈaɣila] NF eagle; (*fig*) genius

aguileño, -a [aɣiˈleɲo, a] ADJ (*nariz*) aquiline; (*rostro*) sharp-featured

aguinaldo [aɣiˈnaldo] NM Christmas box

★**aguja** [aˈɣuxa] NF needle; (*de reloj*) hand; (*Arq*) spire; (*Tec*) firing-pin ■ **agujas** NFPL (*Zool*) ribs; (*Ferro*) points

agujerear [aɣuxereˈar] /1a/ VT to make holes in; (*penetrar*) to pierce

★**agujero** [aɣuˈxero] NM hole; (*Com*) deficit

agujetas [aɣuˈxetas] NFPL stitch *sg*; (*rigidez*) stiffness *sg*

aguzar [aɣuˈθar] /1f/ VT to sharpen; (*fig*) to incite; **~ el oído** to prick up one's ears

aherrumbrarse [aerrumˈbrarse] /1a/ VR to get rusty

★**ahí** [aˈi] ADV there; (*allá*) over there; **de ~ que** so that, with the result that; **~ llega** here he comes; **por ~** (*dirección*) that way; **¡hasta ~ hemos llegado!** so it has come to this!; **¡~ va!** (*objeto*) here it comes!; (*individuo*) there he goes!; **~ donde le ve** as sure as he's standing there; **200 o por ~** 200 or so

ahijado, -a [aiˈxaðo, a] NM/F godson(-daughter)

ahijar [aiˈxar] /1a/ VT: **~ algo a algn** (*fig*) to attribute sth to sb

ahínco [aˈinko] NM earnestness; **con ~** eagerly

ahíto, -a [aˈito, a] ADJ: **estoy ~** I'm full up

ahogado, -a [aoˈɣaðo, a] ADJ (*en agua*) drowned; (*emoción*) pent-up; (*grito*) muffled

ahogar [aoˈɣar] /1h/ VT (*en agua*) to drown; (*asfixiar*) to suffocate, smother; (*fuego*) to put out ■ **ahogarse** VR (*en agua*) to drown; (*por asfixia*) to suffocate

ahogo [aˈoɣo] NM (*Med*) breathlessness; (*fig*) distress; (*económico*) financial difficulty

ahogue etc [aˈoɣe] VB ver **ahogar**

ahondar [aonˈdar] /1a/ VT to deepen, make deeper; (*fig*) to study thoroughly ▶ VI: **~ en** to study thoroughly

★**ahora** [aˈora] ADV now; (*hace poco*) a moment ago, just now; (*dentro de poco*) in a moment; **~ voy** I'm coming; **~ mismo** right now; **~ bien** now then; **por ~** for the present

ahorcado, -a [aorˈkaðo, a] NM/F hanged person

ahorcar [aorˈkar] /1g/ VT to hang ■ **ahorcarse** VR to hang o.s.

ahorita [aoˈrita], **ahoritita** [aoriˈtita] ADV (*esp Am fam: en este momento*) right now; (: *hace poco*) just now; (: *dentro de poco*) in a minute

ahorque etc [aˈorke] VB ver **ahorcar**

★**ahorrar** [aoˈrrar] /1a/ VT (*dinero*) to save; (*esfuerzos*) to save, avoid ■ **ahorrarse** VR: **ahorrarse molestias** to save o.s. trouble

ahorrativo, -a [aorraˈtiβo, a] ADJ thrifty

ahorro [a'orro] NM (*acto*) saving; (*frugalidad*) thrift ■ **ahorros** NMPL (*dinero*) savings

ahuecar [awe'kar] /**1g**/ VT to hollow (out); (*voz*) to deepen ▶ VI: **¡ahueca!** (*fam*) beat it! (*fam*) ■ **ahuecarse** VR to give o.s. airs

ahueque *etc* [a'weke] VB *ver* **ahuecar**

ahumar [au'mar] /**1a**/ VT to smoke, cure; (*llenar de humo*) to fill with smoke ▶ VI to smoke ■ **ahumarse** VR to fill with smoke

ahuyentar [aujen'tar] /**1a**/ VT to drive off, frighten off; (*fig*) to dispel

AI NF ABR (= *Amnistía Internacional*) AI

aimara [ai'mara], **aimará** [aima'ra] ADJ, NMF Aymara

aindiado, -a [aindi'aðo, a] ADJ (*Am*) Indian-like

airado, -a [ai'raðo, a] ADJ angry

airar [ai'rar] /**1a**/ VT to anger ■ **airarse** VR to get angry

★**aire** ['aire] NM air; (*viento*) wind; (*corriente*) draught; (*Mus*) tune; **al ~ libre** in the open air; **~ climatizado** *o* **acondicionado** air conditioning; **tener ~ de** to look like; **estar de buen/mal ~** to be in a good/bad mood; **estar en el ~** (*Radio*) to be on the air; (*fig*) to be up in the air ■ **aires** NMPL: **darse aires** to give o.s. airs

airear [aire'ar] /**1a**/ VT to ventilate; (*fig: asunto*) to air ■ **airearse** VR to get some fresh air

airoso, -a [ai'roso, a] ADJ windy; draughty; (*fig*) graceful

★**aislado, -a** [ais'laðo, a] ADJ (*remoto*) isolated; (*incomunicado*) cut off; (*Elec*) insulated

aislante [ais'lante] NM (*Elec*) insulator

aislar [ais'lar] /**1a**/ VT to isolate; (*Elec*) to insulate ■ **aislarse** VR to cut o.s. off

ajar [a'xar] /**1a**/ VT to spoil; (*fig*) to abuse ■ **ajarse** VR to get crumpled; (*fig: piel*) to get wrinkled

ajardinado, -a [axarði'naðo, a] ADJ landscaped

★**ajedrez** [axe'ðreθ] NM chess

ajenjo [a'xenxo] NM (*bebida*) absinth(e)

ajeno, -a [a'xeno, a] ADJ (*que pertenece a otro*) somebody else's; **~ a** foreign to; **~ de** free from, devoid of; **por razones ajenas a nuestra voluntad** for reasons beyond our control

ajetreado, -a [axetre'aðo, a] ADJ busy

ajetrearse [axetre'arse] /**1a**/ VR (*atarearse*) to bustle about; (*fatigarse*) to tire o.s. out

ajetreo [axe'treo] NM bustle

ají [a'xi] NM chil(l)i, red pepper; (*salsa*) chil(l)i sauce

ajiaco [axi'ako] NM (*Am*) potato and chil(l)i stew

ajilimoje [axili'moxe] NM (*Am*) *sauce of garlic and pepper* ■ **ajilimojes** NMPL (*fam*) odds and ends

ajillo [a'xiʎo] NM: **gambas al ~** garlic prawns

★**ajo** ['axo] NM garlic; **~ porro** *o* **puerro** leek; **(tieso) como un ~** (*fam*) snobbish; **estar en el ~** to be mixed up in it

ajorca [a'xorka] NF bracelet

ajuar [a'xwar] NM household furnishings *pl*; (*de novia*) trousseau; (*de niño*) layette

ajustado, -a [axus'taðo, a] ADJ (*tornillo*) tight; (*cálculo*) right; (*ropa*) tight(-fitting); (*Deporte: resultado*) close

ajustar [axus'tar] /**1a**/ VT (*adaptar*) to adjust; (*encajar*) to fit; (*Tec*) to engage; (*Tip*) to make up; (*apretar*) to tighten; (*concertar*) to agree (on); (*reconciliar*) to reconcile; (*cuenta, deudas*) to settle; **~ las cuentas a algn** to get even with sb ▶ VI to fit ■ **ajustarse** VR: **ajustarse a** (*precio etc*) to be in keeping with, fit in with

ajuste [a'xuste] NM adjustment; (*Costura*) fitting; (*acuerdo*) compromise; (*de cuenta*) settlement

al [al] (= *a + el*) *ver* **a**

ala ['ala] NF wing; (*de sombrero*) brim; (*futbolista*) winger; **~ delta** hang-glider; **andar con el ~ caída** to be downcast; **cortar las alas a algn** to clip sb's wings; **dar alas a algn** to encourage sb

alabanza [ala'βanθa] NF praise

alabar [ala'βar] /**1a**/ VT to praise

alacena [ala'θena] NF cupboard (*Brit*), closet (*US*)

alacrán [ala'kran] NM scorpion

ALADI [a'laði] NF ABR = **Asociación Latinoamericana de Integración**

alado, -a [a'laðo, a] ADJ winged

alambicado, -a [alambi'kaðo, a] ADJ distilled; (*fig*) affected

alambicar [alambi'kar] /**1g**/ VT to distil

alambique *etc* [alam'bike] VB *ver* **alambicar** ▶ NM still

alambrada [alam'braða] NF, **alambrado** [alam'braðo] NM wire fence; (*red*) wire netting

alambre [a'lambre] NM wire; **~ de púas** barbed wire

alambrista [alam'brista] NMF tightrope walker

alameda [ala'meða] NF (*plantío*) poplar grove; (*lugar de paseo*) avenue, boulevard

álamo ['alamo] NM poplar; **~ temblón** aspen

alano [a'lano] NM mastiff

alarde [a'larðe] NM show, display; **hacer ~ de** to boast of

alardear [alarðe'ar] /**1a**/ VI to boast

alargador [alarɣa'ðor] NM extension cable *o* lead

alargar [alar'ɣar] /**1h**/ VT to lengthen, extend; (*paso*) to hasten; (*brazo*) to stretch out; (*cuerda*) to pay out; (*conversación*) to spin out ■ **alargarse** VR to get longer

alargue *etc* [a'larɣe] VB *ver* **alargar**

alarido [ala'riðo] NM shriek

★**alarma** [a'larma] NF alarm; **voz de ~** warning note; **dar la ~** to raise the alarm; **~ de incendios** fire alarm

alarmante [alar'mante] ADJ alarming

alarmar [alar'mar] /**1a**/ VT to alarm ■ **alarmarse** VR to get alarmed

alavés, -esa [ala'βes, esa] ADJ of Álava ▸ NM/F native o inhabitant of Álava

alazán [ala'θan] NM sorrel

alba ['alβa] NF dawn

albacea [alβa'θea] NMF executor (executrix)

albaceteño, -a [alβaθe'teɲo, a] ADJ of Albacete ▸ NM/F native o inhabitant of Albacete

albahaca [al'βaka] NF (Bot) basil

Albania [al'βanja] NF Albania

albañal [alβa'ɲal] NM drain, sewer

★**albañil** [alβa'ɲil] NM bricklayer; (cantero) mason

albarán [alβa'ran] NM (Com) delivery note, invoice

albarda [al'βarða] NF packsaddle

★**albaricoque** [alβari'koke] NM apricot

albedrío [alβe'ðrio] NM: **libre ~** free will

alberca [al'βerka] NF reservoir; (Am) swimming pool

albergar [alβer'ɣar] /1h/ VT to shelter; (esperanza) to cherish ■ **albergarse** VR (refugiarse) to shelter; (alojarse) to lodge

★**albergue** [al'βerɣe] VB ver **albergar** ▸ NM shelter, refuge; **~ juvenil** youth hostel

albis ['alβis] ADV: **quedarse en ~** not to have a clue

albóndiga [al'βondiɣa] NF meatball

albor [al'βor] NM whiteness; (amanecer) dawn

alborada [alβo'raða] NF dawn; (diana) reveille

alborear [alβore'ar] /1a/ VI to dawn

albornoz [alβor'noθ] NM (de los árabes) burnous; (para el baño) bathrobe

alboroce etc [alβo'roθe] VB ver **alborozar**

alborotar [alβoro'tar] /1a/ VI to make a row ▸ VT to agitate, stir up ■ **alborotarse** VR to get excited; (mar) to get rough

alboroto [alβo'roto] NM row, uproar

alborozar [alβoro'θar] /1f/ VT to gladden ■ **alborozarse** VR to rejoice, be overjoyed

alborozo [alβo'roθo] NM joy

albricias [al'βriθjas] NFPL: **¡~!** good news!

álbum ['alβum] (pl **álbums** o **álbumes**) NM album; **~ de recortes** scrapbook

albumen [al'βumen] NM egg white, albumen

albur [al'βur] (Am) NM (juego de palabras) pun; (doble sentido) double entendre

alcabala [alka'βala] NF (Am) roadblock

alcachofa [alka'tʃofa] NF (globe) artichoke; (Tip) golf ball; (de ducha) shower head

alcahueta [alka'weta] NF procuress

alcahuete [alka'wete] NM pimp

★**alcalde, -esa** [al'kalde, alkal'desa] NM/F mayor(ess)

alcaldía [alkal'dia] NF mayoralty; (lugar) mayor's office

álcali ['alkali] NM (Química) alkali

★**alcance** [al'kanθe] VB ver **alcanzar** ▸ NM (Mil, Radio) range; (fig) scope; (Com) adverse balance,

deficit; **estar al/fuera del ~ de algn** to be within/beyond sb's reach; (fig) to be within sb's powers/over sb's head; **de gran ~** (Mil) long-range; (fig) far-reaching

alcancía [alkan'θia] (Am) NF (para ahorrar) money box; (para colectas) collection box

alcanfor [alkan'for] NM camphor

alcantarilla [alkanta'riʎa] NF (de aguas cloacales) sewer; (en la calle) gutter

★**alcanzar** [alkan'θar] /1f/ VT (algo: con la mano, el pie) to reach; (alguien: en el camino etc) to catch up (with); (autobús) to catch; (suj: bala) to hit, strike; **~ algo a algn** to hand sth to sb; **alcánzame la sal, por favor** pass the salt please ▸ VI (ser suficiente) to be enough; **~ a hacer** to manage to do

alcaparra [alka'parra] NF (Bot) caper

alcatraz [alka'traθ] NM gannet

alcayata [alka'jata] NF hook

alcázar [al'kaθar] NM fortress; (Naut) quarterdeck

alce etc ['alθe] VB ver **alzar**

alcista [al'θista] NM speculator ▸ ADJ (Com, Econ): **mercado ~** bull market; **la tendencia ~** the upward trend

alcoba [al'koβa] NF bedroom

★**alcohol** [al'kol] NM alcohol; **no bebe ~** he doesn't drink (alcohol); **~ metílico** methylated spirits (BRIT), wood alcohol (US)

alcoholemia [alkoo'lemia] NF blood alcohol level; **prueba de la ~** breath test

alcoholice etc [alko'liθe] VB ver **alcoholizarse**

★**alcohólico, -a** [al'koliko, a] ADJ, NM/F alcoholic

alcoholímetro [alko'limetro] NM Breathalyser®, drunkometer (US)

★**alcoholismo** [alko'lismo] NM alcoholism

alcoholizarse [alkoli'θarse] /1f/ VR to become an alcoholic

alcornoque [alkor'noke] NM cork tree; (fam) idiot

alcotana [alko'tana] NF pickaxe; (Deporte) ice axe

alcurnia [al'kurnja] NF lineage

alcuza [al'kuθa] NF (Am) cruet

aldaba [al'daβa] NF (door) knocker

★**aldea** [al'dea] NF village

aldeano, -a [alde'ano, a] ADJ village cpd ▸ NM/F villager

ale ['ale] EXCL come on!, let's go!

aleación [alea'θjon] NF alloy

aleatorio, -a [alea'torjo, a] ADJ random, contingent; **acceso ~** (Inform) random access

aleccionador, a [alekθjona'ðor, a] ADJ instructive

aleccionar [alekθjo'nar] /1a/ VT to instruct; (adiestrar) to train

aledaño, -a [ale'ðaɲo, a] ADJ: **~ a** bordering on ▸ NM: **aledaños** outskirts

alegación [aleɣa'θjon] NF allegation

alegar [ale'ɣar] /1h/ VT (dificultad etc) to plead; (Jur) to allege; ~ **que ...** to give as an excuse that ... ▶ VI (AM) to argue

alegato [ale'ɣato] NM (Jur) allegation; (escrito) indictment; (declaración) statement; (AM) argument

alegoría [aleɣo'ria] NF allegory

alegrar [ale'ɣrar] /1a/ VT (causar alegría) to cheer (up); (fuego) to poke; (fiesta) to liven up ■ **alegrarse** VR (fam) to get merry o tight; **alegrarse de** to be glad about

★**alegre** [a'leɣre] ADJ happy, cheerful; (fam) merry, tight; (chiste) risqué, blue

★**alegría** [ale'ɣria] NF happiness; merriment; ~ **vital** joie de vivre

alegrón [ale'ɣron] NM (fig) sudden joy

alegue etc [a'leɣe] VB ver **alegar**

alejamiento [alexa'mjento] NM removal; (distancia) remoteness

alejar [ale'xar] /1a/ VT to move away, remove; (fig) to estrange ■ **alejarse** VR to move away

alelado, -a [ale'laðo, a] ADJ (bobo) foolish

alelar [ale'lar] /1a/ VT to bewilder

aleluya [ale'luja] NM (canto) hallelujah

★**alemán, -ana** [ale'man, ana] ADJ, NM/F German ▶ NM (lengua) German

★**Alemania** [ale'manja] NF Germany

alentador, a [alenta'ðor, a] ADJ encouraging

alentar [alen'tar] /1j/ VT to encourage

alergia [a'lerxja] NF allergy

alero [a'lero] NM (de tejado) eaves pl; (Deporte) forward; (Auto) mudguard

alerta [a'lerta] ADJ INV, NM alert

aleta [a'leta] NF (de pez) fin; (de ave) wing; (de foca, Deporte) flipper; (de coche) mudguard

aletargar [aletar'ɣar] /1h/ VT to make drowsy; (entumecer) to make numb ■ **aletargarse** VR to grow drowsy; to become numb

aletargue etc [ale'tarɣe] VB ver **aletargar**

aletear [alete'ar] /1a/ VI to flutter; (ave) to flap its wings; (individuo) to wave one's arms

alevín [ale'βin] NM fry, young fish

alevosía [aleβo'sia] NF treachery

alfabetización [alfaβetiθa'θjon] NF: **campaña de** ~ literacy campaign

alfabeto [alfa'βeto] NM alphabet

alfajor [alfa'xor] NM (Esp: polvorón) cake eaten at Christmas time

alfalfa [al'falfa] NF alfalfa, lucerne

alfaque [al'fake] NM (Naut) bar, sandbank

alfar [al'far] NM (taller) potter's workshop; (arcilla) clay

alfarería [alfare'ria] NF pottery; (tienda) pottery shop

alfarero, -a [alfa'rero, a] NM/F potter

alféizar [al'feiθar] NM window-sill

alférez [al'fereθ] NM (Mil) second lieutenant; (Naut) ensign

alfil [al'fil] NM (Ajedrez) bishop

★**alfiler** [alfi'ler] NM pin; (broche) clip; (pinza) clothes peg (BRIT) o pin (US); ~ **de gancho** (AM) safety pin; **prendido con alfileres** shaky

alfiletero [alfile'tero] NM needle case

★**alfombra** [al'fombra] NF carpet; (más pequeña) rug

alfombrar [alfom'brar] /1a/ VT to carpet

alfombrilla [alfom'briʎa] NF rug, mat; (Inform) mouse mat o pad

alforja [al'forxa] NF saddlebag

alforza [al'forθa] NF pleat

algarabía [alɣara'βia] NF (fam) gibberish; (griterío) hullabaloo

algarada [alɣa'raða] NF outcry; **hacer** o **levantar una** ~ to kick up a tremendous fuss

Algarbe [al'ɣarβe] NM: **el** ~ the Algarve

algarroba [alɣa'rroβa] NF carob

algarrobo [alɣa'rroβo] NM carob tree

algas ['alɣas] NFPL seaweed sg

algazara [alɣa'θara] NF din, uproar

álgebra ['alxeβra] NF algebra

álgido, -a ['alxiðo, a] ADJ icy; (momento etc) crucial, decisive

★**algo** ['alɣo] PRON something; (en frases interrogativas) anything; **¿~ más?** anything else?; (en tienda) is that all?; **por ~ será** there must be some reason for it ▶ ADV somewhat, rather; **es ~ difícil** it's a bit awkward

---

Algo se traduce por **something** en oraciones afirmativas y en aquellas interrogativas para las que se espera una respuesta afirmativa:
Ha ocurrido algo. **Something has happened.**
¿Has tomado algo de beber? **Did you have something to drink?**
En el resto de las oraciones interrogativas se traduce por **anything**: *¿Algo más?* **Anything else?**
Delante de un sustantivo, *algo de* se traduce por **some** o **any**:
Aún queda algo de café. **There's still some coffee left.**
¿Te queda algo de comer? **Do you have any food left?**

★**algodón** [alɣo'ðon] NM cotton; (planta) cotton plant; ~ **de azúcar** candy floss (BRIT), cotton candy (US); ~ **hidrófilo** cotton wool (BRIT), absorbent cotton (US)

algodonero, -a [alɣoðo'nero, a] ADJ cotton cpd ▶ NM/F cotton grower ▶ NM cotton plant

algoritmo [alɣo'ritmo] NM algorithm

alguacil [alɣwa'θil] NM bailiff; (Taur) mounted official

★**alguien** ['alɣjen] PRON someone, somebody; (en frases interrogativas) anyone, anybody

Alguien se traduce por **someone** o **somebody** en oraciones afirmativas y en aquellas interrogativas para las que se espera una respuesta afirmativa:
Alguien llama a la puerta. **There's somebody knocking at the door.**
¿Necesitas que te ayude alguien? **Do you need somebody to help you?**
En el resto de las oraciones interrogativas se traduce por **anyone** o **anybody**: *¿Conoces a alguien aquí?* **Do you know anybody here?**
Tanto **somebody** como **anybody** llevan el verbo en singular: *Alguien ha escrito mi nombre en la pared.* **Somebody has written my name on the wall.**

★**alguno, -a** [al'ɣuno, a] ADJ (*antes de n msg*: **algún**) some; (*después de n*): **no tiene talento ~** he has no talent, he doesn't have any talent; **algún que otro libro** some book or other; **algún día iré** I'll go one o some day; **sin interés ~** without the slightest interest ▶ PRON (*alguien*) someone, somebody; **~ que otro** an occasional one; **algunos piensan** some (people) think; **~ de ellos** one of them

En oraciones afirmativas y en aquellas interrogativas para las que se espera una respuesta afirmativa, *algún* se traduce por **some**:
Algunas personas no están de acuerdo. **Some people disagree.**
¿Me dejas alguno? **Can I borrow some?**
En el resto de las oraciones interrogativas se utilizan **any** o sus derivados:
¿Se te ocurre alguna otra idea? **Do you have any other ideas?**
¿Hay algún sitio donde esconderse? **Is there anywhere to hide?**

alhaja [a'laxa] NF jewel; (*tesoro*) precious object, treasure
alhelí [ale'li] NM wallflower, stock
aliado, -a [a'ljaðo, a] ADJ allied
alianza [a'ljanθa] NF (*Pol etc*) alliance; (*anillo*) wedding ring
aliar [a'ljar] /1c/ VT to ally ∎ **aliarse** VR to form an alliance
alias ['aljas] ADV alias
alicaído, -a [alika'iðo, a] ADJ (*Med*) weak; (*fig*) depressed
alicantino, -a [alikan'tino, a] ADJ of Alicante ▶ NM/F native o inhabitant of Alicante
alicatado [alika'taðo] NM (*Esp*) tiling
alicatar [alika'tar] /1a/ VT to tile
alicate [ali'kate] NM, **alicates** [ali'kates] NMPL pliers *pl*; **~(s) de uñas** nail clippers
aliciente [ali'θjente] NM incentive; (*atracción*) attraction
alienación [aljena'θjon] NF alienation
★**aliento** [a'ljento] VB *ver* **alentar** ▶ NM breath; (*respiración*) breathing; **sin ~** breathless; **de un ~** in one breath; (*fig*) in one go

aligerar [alixe'rar] /1a/ VT to lighten; (*reducir*) to shorten; (*aliviar*) to alleviate; (*mitigar*) to ease; (*paso*) to quicken
alijo [a'lixo] NM (*Naut: descarga*) unloading; (: *contrabando*) consignment (of smuggled goods)
alimaña [ali'maɲa] NF pest
★**alimentación** [alimenta'θjon] NF (*comida*) food; (*acción*) feeding; (*tienda*) grocer's (shop); **~ continua** (*en fotocopiadora etc*) stream feed
alimentador [alimenta'ðor] NM: **~ de papel** sheet-feeder
alimentar [alimen'tar] /1a/ VT to feed; (*nutrir*) to nourish ∎ **alimentarse** VR: **alimentarse (de)** to feed (on)
alimenticio, -a [alimen'tiθjo, a] ADJ food *cpd*; (*nutritivo*) nourishing, nutritious
alimento [ali'mento] NM food; (*nutrición*) nourishment; **alimentos transgénicos** GM foods
alimón [ali'mon]: **al ~** *adv* jointly, together
alineación [alinea'θjon] NF alignment; (*Deporte*) line-up
alineado, -a [aline'aðo, a] ADJ (*Tip*): **(no) ~** (un) justified; **~ a la izquierda/derecha** ranged left/right
alinear [aline'ar] /1a/ VT to align; (*Tip*) to justify; (*Deporte*) to select, pick ∎ **alinearse** VR to line up; **alinearse en** to fall in with
aliñar [ali'ɲar] /1a/ VT (*Culin*) to season; (: *ensalada*) to dress
aliño [a'liɲo] NM (*Culin*) dressing
alioli [ali'oli] NM garlic mayonnaise
alisar [ali'sar] /1a/ VT to smooth
aliso [a'liso] NM alder
alistamiento [alista'mjento] NM recruitment
alistar [ali'star] /1a/ VT to recruit ∎ **alistarse** VR to enlist; (*inscribirse*) to enrol; (*Am: prepararse*) to get ready
★**aliviar** [ali'βjar] /1b/ VT (*carga*) to lighten; (*persona*) to relieve; (*dolor*) to relieve, alleviate
alivio [a'liβjo] NM alleviation, relief; **~ de luto** half-mourning
aljibe [al'xiβe] NM cistern
★**allá** [a'ʎa] ADV (*lugar*) there; (*por ahí*) over there; (*tiempo*) then; **~ abajo** down there; **más ~** further on; **más ~ de** beyond; **¡~ tú!** that's your problem!
allanamiento [aʎana'mjento] NM (*Am Policía*) raid, search; **~ de morada** breaking and entering
allanar [aʎa'nar] /1a/ VT to flatten, level (out); (*igualar*) to smooth (out); (*fig*) to subdue; (*Jur*) to burgle, break into; (*Am Policía*) to raid, search ∎ **allanarse** VR to fall down; **allanarse a** to submit to, accept
allegado, -a [aʎe'ɣaðo, a] ADJ near, close ▶ NM/F relation
allende [a'ʎende] ADV on the other side ▶ PREP: **~ los mares** beyond the seas

★**allí** [a'ʎi] ADV there; **~ mismo** right there; **por ~** over there; (*por ese camino*) that way

alma ['alma] NF soul; (*persona*) person; (*Tec*) core; **se le cayó el ~ a los pies** he became very disheartened; **entregar el ~** to pass away; **estar con el ~ en la boca** to be scared to death; **lo siento en el ~** I am truly sorry; **tener el ~ en un hilo** to have one's heart in one's mouth; **estar como ~ en pena** to suffer; **ir como ~ que lleva el diablo** to go at breakneck speed

★**almacén** [alma'θen] NM (*depósito*) warehouse, store; (*Mil*) magazine; (*Am*) grocer's shop, food store, grocery store (*US*); **~ depositario** (*Com*) depository ■ **(grandes) almacenes** NMPL department store *sg*

almacenaje [almaθe'naxe] NM storage; **~ secundario** backup storage

almacenamiento [almaθena'mjento] NM (*Inform*) storage; **~ temporal en disco** disk spooling

almacenar [almaθe'nar] /**1a**/ VT to store, put in storage; (*Inform*) to store; (*proveerse*) to stock up with

almacenero [almaθe'nero] NM warehouse-man; (*Am*) grocer, shopkeeper

almanaque [alma'nake] NM almanac

almeja [al'mexa] NF clam

almenas [al'menas] NFPL battlements

★**almendra** [al'mendra] NF almond

almendro [al'mendro] NM almond tree

almeriense [alme'rjense] ADJ of Almería ▶ NMF native o inhabitant of Almería

almiar [al'mjar] NM haystack

almíbar [al'miβar] NM syrup

almidón [almi'ðon] NM starch

almidonado, -a [almiðo'naðo, a] ADJ starched

almidonar [almiðo'nar] /**1a**/ VT to starch

almirantazgo [almiran'taθɣo] NM admiralty

almirante [almi'rante] NM admiral

almirez [almi'reθ] NM mortar

almizcle [al'miθkle] NM musk

almizclero [almiθ'klero] NM musk deer

★**almohada** [almo'aða] NF pillow; (*funda*) pillowcase

almohadilla [almoa'ðiʎa] NF cushion; (*Tec*) pad; (*Am*) pincushion; (*Inform*) hash key, hashtag

almohadillado, -a [almoaði'ʎaðo, a] ADJ (*acolchado*) padded

almohadón [almoa'ðon] NM large pillow

almorcé [almor'θe], **almorcemos** *etc* [almor'θemos] VB *ver* **almorzar**

almorranas [almo'rranas] NFPL piles, haemorrhoids (*BRIT*), hemorrhoids (*US*)

★**almorzar** [almor'θar] /**1f, 1l**/ VT: **~ una tortilla** to have an omelette for lunch ▶ VI to (have) lunch

almuerce *etc* [al'mwerθe] VB *ver* **almorzar**

★**almuerzo** [al'mwerθo] VB *ver* **almorzar** ▶ NM lunch

aló [a'lo] EXCL (*esp Am Telec*) hello!

alocado, -a [alo'kaðo, a] ADJ crazy

★**alojamiento** [aloxa'mjento] NM lodging(s) (*pl*); (*viviendas*) housing

alojar [alo'xar] /**1a**/ VT to lodge ■ **alojarse** VR: **alojarse en** to stay at; (*bala*) to lodge in

alondra [a'londra] NF lark, skylark

alpaca [al'paka] NF alpaca

alpargata [alpar'ɣata] NF rope-soled shoe, espadrille

Alpes ['alpes] NMPL: **los ~** the Alps

★**alpinismo** [alpi'nismo] NM mountaineering, climbing

★**alpinista** [alpi'nista] NMF mountaineer, climber

alpino, -a [al'pino, a] ADJ alpine

alpiste [al'piste] NM (*semillas*) birdseed; (*Am fam: dinero*) dough; (*fam: alcohol*) booze

alquería [alke'ria] NF farmhouse

★**alquilar** [alki'lar] /**1a**/ VT (*suj: propietario: inmuebles*) to let, rent (out); (*: coche*) to hire out; (*: TV*) to rent (out); (*suj: alquilador: inmuebles, TV*) to rent; (*: coche*) to hire; **"se alquila casa"** "house to let (*BRIT*) o for rent (*US*)"

★**alquiler** [alki'ler] NM renting; letting; hiring; (*arriendo*) rent; hire charge; **de ~** for hire; **~ de automóviles** car hire

alquimia [al'kimja] NF alchemy

alquitrán [alki'tran] NM tar

★**alrededor** [alreðe'ðor] ADV around, about; **~ de** *prep* around, about ▶ NM: **mirar a su ~** to look (round) about one ■ **alrededores** NMPL surroundings

Alsacia [al'saθja] NF Alsace

alta ['alta] NF (certificate of) discharge; **dar a algn de ~** to discharge sb; **darse de ~** (*Mil*) to join, enrol; (*Deporte*) to declare o.s. fit

altanería [altane'ria] NF haughtiness, arrogance

altanero, -a [alta'nero, a] ADJ haughty, arrogant

altar [al'tar] NM altar

altavoz [alta'βoθ] NM loudspeaker; (*amplificador*) amplifier

alteración [altera'θjon] NF alteration; (*alboroto*) disturbance; **~ del orden público** breach of the peace

alterar [alte'rar] /**1a**/ VT to alter; to disturb ■ **alterarse** VR (*persona*) to get upset

altercado [alter'kaðo] NM argument

alternar [alter'nar] /**1a**/ VT to alternate ▶ VI to alternate; (*turnar*) to take turns; **~ con** to mix with ■ **alternarse** VR to alternate; (*turnar*) to take turns

alternativo, -a [alterna'tiβo, a] ADJ alternative; (*alterno*) alternating ▶ NF alternative; (*elección*) choice; **tomar la alternativa** (*Taur*) to become a fully-qualified bullfighter ■ **alternativas** NFPL ups and downs

alterno, -a [al'terno, a] ADJ (*Bot, Mat*) alternate; (*Elec*) alternating

Alteza [al'teθa] NF (*tratamiento*) Highness

altibajos [alti'βaxos] NMPL ups and downs

altillo [al'tiʎo] NM (*Geo*) small hill; (*Am*) attic

altiplanicie [altipla'niθje] NF, **altiplano** [alti'plano] NM high plateau

altisonante [altiso'nante] ADJ high-flown, high-sounding

altitud [alti'tuð] NF height; (*Aviat, Geo*) altitude; **a una ~ de** at a height of

altivez [alti'βeθ] NF haughtiness, arrogance

altivo, -a [al'tiβo, a] ADJ haughty, arrogant

★**alto, -a** [ˈalto, a] ADJ high; (*persona*) tall; (*sonido*) high, sharp; (*noble*) high, lofty; (*Geo, clase*) upper; **en alta mar** on the high seas; **en voz alta** in a loud voice; **las altas horas de la noche** the small (*Brit*) o wee (*US*) hours; **en lo ~ de** at the top of ▶ NM halt; (*Mus*) alto; (*Geo*) hill; (*Am*) pile; **la pared tiene dos metros de ~** the wall is two metres high; **pasar por ~** to overlook; **altos y bajos** ups and downs ▶ ADV (*estar*) high; (*hablar*) loud, loudly; **poner la radio más ~** to turn the radio up; **¡más ~, por favor!** louder, please! ▶ EXCL halt!

altoparlante [altopar'lante] NM (*Am*) loudspeaker

altramuz [altra'muθ] NM lupin

altruismo [al'truismo] NM altruism

★**altura** [al'tura] NF height; (*Naut*) depth; (*Geo*) latitude; **la pared tiene 1.80 de ~** the wall is 1 metre 80 (cm) high; **a estas alturas** at this stage; **a esta ~ del año** at this time of the year; **estar a la ~ de las circunstancias** to rise to the occasion; **ha sido un partido de gran ~** it has been a terrific match

alubia [a'luβja] NF bean; (*judía verde*) French bean; (*judía blanca*) cannellini bean

alucinación [aluθina'θjon] NF hallucination

alucinante [aluθi'nante] ADJ (*fam: estupendo*) great, super

alucinar [aluθi'nar] /1a/ VI to hallucinate ▶ VT to deceive; (*fascinar*) to fascinate

alud [a'luð] NM avalanche; (*fig*) flood

aludir [alu'ðir] /3a/ VI: **~ a** to allude to; **darse por aludido** to take the hint; **no te des por aludido** don't take it personally

alumbrado [alum'braðo] NM lighting

alumbramiento [alumbra'mjento] NM lighting; (*Med*) childbirth, delivery

alumbrar [alum'brar] /1a/ VT to light (up) ▶ VI (*iluminar*) to give light; (*Med*) to give birth

aluminio [alu'minjo] NM aluminium (*Brit*), aluminum (*US*)

alumnado [alum'naðo] NM (*Univ*) student body; (*Escol*) pupils *pl*

★**alumno, -a** [a'lumno, a] NM/F pupil, student

alunice *etc* [alu'niθe] VB *ver* **alunizar**

alunizaje [aluni'θaxe] NM (*en la luna*) moon landing; (*robo*) smash-and-grab

alunizar [aluni'θar] /1f/ VI to land on the moon

alusión [alu'sjon] NF allusion

alusivo, -a [alu'siβo, a] ADJ allusive

aluvión [alu'βjon] NM (*Geo*) alluvium; (*fig*) flood; **~ de improperios** torrent of abuse

alvéolo [al'βeolo] NM (*Anat*) alveolus; (*fig*) network

alverja [al'βerxa] NF (*Am*) pea

alza [ˈalθa] NF rise; (*Mil*) sight; **alzas fijas/graduables** fixed/adjustable sights; **al** o **en ~** (*precio*) rising; **jugar al ~** to speculate on a rising o bull market; **cotizarse** o **estar en ~** to be rising

alzado, -a [al'θaðo, a] ADJ (*gen*) raised; (*Com: precio*) fixed; (: *quiebra*) fraudulent; **por un tanto ~** for a lump sum ▶ NF (*de caballos*) height; (*Jur*) appeal

alzamiento [alθa'mjento] NM (*aumento*) rise, increase; (*acción*) lifting, raising; (*mejor postura*) higher bid; (*rebelión*) rising; (*Com*) fraudulent bankruptcy

alzar [al'θar] /1f/ VT to lift (up); (*precio, muro*) to raise; (*cuello de abrigo*) to turn up; (*Agr*) to gather in; (*Tip*) to gather ■ **alzarse** VR to get up, rise; (*rebelarse*) to revolt; (*Com*) to go fraudulently bankrupt; (*Jur*) to appeal; **alzarse con el premio** to carry off the prize

a.m. ABR (= *ante meridiem*) a.m.

ama [ˈama] NF lady of the house; (*dueña*) owner; (*institutriz*) governess; (*madre adoptiva*) foster mother; **~ de casa** housewife; **~ de cría** o **de leche** wet-nurse; **~ de llaves** housekeeper

amabilidad [amaβili'ðað] NF kindness; (*simpatía*) niceness

amabilísimo, -a [amaβi'lisimo, a] ADJ SUPERLATIVO *de* **amable**

★**amable** [a'maβle] ADJ kind; nice; **es usted muy ~** that's very kind of you

amaestrado, -a [amaes'traðo, a] ADJ (*animal*) trained; (: *en circo etc*) performing

amaestrar [amaes'trar] /1a/ VT to train

amagar [ama'ɣar] /1h/ VT, VI to threaten

amago [a'maɣo] NM threat; (*gesto*) threatening gesture; (*Med*) symptom

amague *etc* [a'maɣe] VB *ver* **amagar**

amainar [amai'nar] /1a/ VT (*Naut*) to lower, take in; (*fig*) to calm ▶ VI (*viento*) to die down; **el viento amaina** the wind is dropping ■ **amainarse** VR to drop, die down

amalgama [amal'ɣama] NF amalgam

amalgamar [amalɣa'mar] /1a/ VT to amalgamate; (*combinar*) to combine, mix

amamantar [amaman'tar] /1a/ VT to suckle, nurse

amancebarse [amanθe'βarse] /1a/ VR (*pareja*) to live together

★**amanecer** [amane'θer] /2d/ VI (*día*) to dawn; (*fig*) to appear, begin to show; (*persona*) to wake up; **~ afiebrado** to wake up with a fever ▶ NM dawn

amanerado, -a [amane'raðo, a] ADJ affected

amanezca *etc* [amaˈneθka] VB *ver* **amanecer**

amansar [amanˈsar] /1a/ VT to tame; (*persona*) to subdue ■ **amansarse** VR (*persona*) to calm down

amante [aˈmante] ADJ: ~ **de** fond of ▸ NMF lover

amanuense [amaˈnwense] NM (*escribiente*) scribe; (*copista*) copyist; (*Pol*) secretary

amañar [amaˈɲar] /1a/ VT (*gen*) to do skilfully; (*pey: resultado*) to alter

amaño [aˈmaɲo] NM (*habilidad*) skill ■ **amaños** NMPL (*Tec*) tools; (*fig*) tricks

amapola [amaˈpola] NF poppy

★**amar** [aˈmar] /1a/ VT to love

amargado, -a [amarˈɣaðo, a] ADJ bitter; embittered

amargar [amarˈɣar] /1h/ VT to make bitter; (*fig*) to embitter ■ **amargarse** VR to become embittered

★**amargo, -a** [aˈmarɣo, a] ADJ bitter

amargor [amarˈɣor] NM (*sabor*) bitterness; (*fig*) grief

amargue *etc* [aˈmarɣe] VB *ver* **amargar**

amargura [amarˈɣura] NF grief

amarillento, -a [amariˈʎento, a] ADJ yellowish; (*tez*) sallow

amarillismo [amariˈʎismo] NM (*de prensa*) sensationalist journalism

★**amarillo, -a** [amaˈriʎo, a] ADJ, NM yellow

amarra [aˈmarra] NF (*Naut*) mooring line; **soltar amarras** to set sail ■ **amarras** NFPL (*fig*) protection *sg*; **tener buenas amarras** to have good connections

amarrado, -a [amaˈrraðo, a] ADJ (*Am fam*) mean, stingy

amarrar [amaˈrrar] /1a/ VT to moor; (*sujetar*) to tie up

amartillar [amartiˈʎar] /1a/ VT (*fusil*) to cock

amasar [amaˈsar] /1a/ VT (*masa*) to knead; (*mezclar*) to mix, prepare; (*confeccionar*) to concoct

amasijo [amaˈsixo] NM kneading; mixing; (*fig*) hotchpotch

amateur [ˈamatur] NMF amateur

amatista [amaˈtista] NF amethyst

amazacotado, -a [amaθakoˈtaðo, a] ADJ (*terreno, arroz etc*) lumpy

amazona [amaˈθona] NF horsewoman

Amazonas [amaˈθonas] NM: **el (río) ~** the Amazon

ambages [amˈbaxes] NMPL: **sin ~** in plain language

ámbar [ˈambar] NM amber

Amberes [amˈberes] NM Antwerp

★**ambición** [ambiˈθjon] NF ambition

ambicionar [ambiθjoˈnar] /1a/ VT to aspire to

★**ambicioso, -a** [ambiˈθjoso, a] ADJ ambitious

ambidextro, -a [ambiˈðekstro, a], **ambidiestro, -a** [ambiˈðjestro, a] ADJ ambidextrous

ambientación [ambjentaˈθjon] NF (*Cine, Lit etc*) setting; (*Radio etc*) sound effects *pl*

ambientador [ambjentaˈðor] NM air freshener

ambientar [ambjenˈtar] /1a/ VT (*gen*) to give an atmosphere to; (*Lit etc*) to set

★**ambiente** [amˈbjente] NM (*tb fig*) atmosphere; (*medio*) environment; (*Am*) room

ambigüedad [ambiɣweˈðað] NF ambiguity

ambiguo, -a [amˈbiɣwo, a] ADJ ambiguous

ámbito [ˈambito] NM (*campo*) field; (*fig*) scope

★**ambos, -as** [ˈambos, as] ADJ PL, PRON PL both

★**ambulancia** [ambuˈlanθja] NF ambulance

ambulante [ambuˈlante] ADJ travelling, itinerant; (*biblioteca*) mobile

ambulatorio [ambulaˈtorio] NM state health service clinic

ameba [aˈmeβa] NF amoeba

amedrentar [ameðrenˈtar] /1a/ VT to scare

amén [aˈmen] EXCL amen; ~ **de** *prep* besides, in addition to; **en un decir ~** in the twinkling of an eye; **decir ~ a todo** to have no mind of one's own

amenace *etc* [ameˈnaθe] VB *ver* **amenazar**

amenaza [ameˈnaθa] NF threat

★**amenazar** [amenaˈθar] /1f/ VT to threaten ▸ VI: ~ **con hacer** to threaten to do

amenidad [ameniˈðað] NF pleasantness

ameno, -a [aˈmeno, a] ADJ pleasant

★**América** [aˈmerika] NF (*continente*) America, the Americas; (*EEUU*) America; (*Hispanoamérica*) Latin *o* South America; ~ **del Norte/del Sur** North/South America; ~ **Central/Latina** Central/Latin America

americanismo [amerikaˈnismo] NM Americanism

★**americano, -a** [ameriˈkano, a] ADJ, NM/F (*del continente*) American; (*hispanoamericano*) Latin *o* South American ▸ NF (*abrigo*) coat; (*chaqueta*) jacket

americe *etc* [ameˈriθe] VB *ver* **amerizar**

amerindio, -a [ameˈrindjo, a] ADJ, NM/F Amerindian, American Indian

amerizaje [ameriˈθaxe] NM (*Aviat*) landing (on the sea)

amerizar [ameriˈθar] /1f/ VI (*Aviat*) to land (on the sea)

ametralladora [ametraʎaˈðora] NF machine gun

amianto [aˈmjanto] NM asbestos

amigable [amiˈɣaβle] ADJ friendly

amígdala [aˈmiɣðala] NF tonsil

amigdalitis [amiɣðaˈlitis] NF tonsillitis

★**amigo, -a** [aˈmiɣo, a] ADJ friendly; **ser muy amigos** to be close friends; **ser ~ de** to like, be fond of ▸ NM/F friend; (*amante*) lover; ~ **de lo ajeno** thief; ~ **corresponsal** penfriend; **hacerse amigos** to become friends

amigote [amiˈɣote] NM mate (BRIT), buddy

amilanar [amilaˈnar] /**1a**/ VT to scare ■ **amilanarse** VR to get scared

aminorar [aminoˈrar] /**1a**/ VT to diminish; (*reducir*) to reduce; **~ la marcha** to slow down

★**amistad** [amisˈtað] NF friendship ■ **amistades** NFPL (*amigos*) friends

★**amistoso, -a** [amisˈtoso, a] ADJ friendly

amnesia [amˈnesja] NF amnesia

amnistía [amnisˈtia] NF amnesty

amnistiar [amnisˈtjar] /**1c**/ VT to amnesty, grant an amnesty to

★**amo** [ˈamo] NM owner; (*jefe*) boss

amodorrarse [amoðoˈrrarse] /**1a**/ VR to get sleepy

amolar [amoˈlar] /**1l**/ VT to annoy; (MÉXICO *fam*) to ruin, damage

amoldar [amolˈdar] /**1a**/ VT to mould; (*adaptar*) to adapt

amonestación [amonestaˈθjon] NF warning ■ **amonestaciones** NFPL marriage banns

amonestar [amonesˈtar] /**1a**/ VT to warn; (*Rel*) to publish the banns of

amoniaco [amoˈnjako] NM ammonia

amontonar [amontoˈnar] /**1a**/ VT to collect, pile up ■ **amontonarse** VR (*gente*) to crowd together; (*acumularse*) to pile up; (*datos*) to accumulate; (*desastres*) to come one on top of another

★**amor** [aˈmor] NM love; (*amante*) lover; **hacer el ~** to make love; **~ interesado** cupboard love; **~ propio** self-respect; **por (el) ~ de Dios** for God's sake; **estar al ~ de la lumbre** to be close to the fire

amoratado, -a [amoraˈtaðo, a] ADJ purple, blue with cold; (*con cardenales*) bruised

amordace *etc* [amorˈðaθe] VB *ver* **amordazar**

amordazar [amorðaˈθar] /**1f**/ VT to muzzle; (*fig*) to gag

amorfo, -a [aˈmorfo, a] ADJ amorphous, shapeless

amorío [amoˈrio] NM (*fam*) love affair

amoroso, -a [amoˈroso, a] ADJ affectionate, loving

amortajar [amortaˈxar] /**1a**/ VT (*fig*) to shroud

amortice *etc* [amorˈtiθe] VB *ver* **amortizar**

amortiguador [amortiɣwaˈðor] NM shock absorber; (*parachoques*) bumper; (*silenciador*) silencer ■ **amortiguadores** NMPL (*Auto*) suspension *sg*

amortiguar [amortiˈɣwar] /**1i**/ VT to deaden; (*ruido*) to muffle; (*color*) to soften

amortigüe *etc* [amorˈtiɣwe] VB *ver* **amortiguar**

amortización [amortiθaˈθjon] NF redemption; repayment; (*Com*) capital allowance

amortizar [amortiˈθar] /**1f**/ VT (*Econ: bono*) to redeem; (: *capital*) to write off; (: *préstamo*) to pay off

amoscarse [amosˈkarse] /**1g**/ VR to get cross

amosque *etc* [aˈmoske] VB *ver* **amoscarse**

amotinar [amotiˈnar] /**1a**/ VT to stir up, incite (to riot) ■ **amotinarse** VR to mutiny

amparar [ampaˈrar] /**1a**/ VT to protect ■ **ampararse** VR to seek protection; (*de la lluvia etc*) to shelter

amparo [amˈparo] NM help, protection; **al ~ de** under the protection of

amperímetro [ampeˈrimetro] NM ammeter

amperio [amˈperjo] NM ampère, amp

ampliable [amˈpljaβle] ADJ (*Inform*) expandable

ampliación [ampljaˈθjon] NF enlargement; (*extensión*) extension

ampliar [amˈpljar] /**1c**/ VT to enlarge; to extend

amplificación [amplifikaˈθjon] NF enlargement

amplificador [amplifikaˈðor] NM amplifier

amplificar [amplifiˈkar] /**1g**/ VT to amplify

amplifique *etc* [ampliˈfike] VB *ver* **amplificar**

★**amplio, -a** [ˈampljo, a] ADJ spacious; (*falda etc*) full; (*extenso*) extensive; (*ancho*) wide

amplitud [ampliˈtuð] NF spaciousness; extent; (*fig*) amplitude; **~ de miras** broadmindedness; **de gran ~** far-reaching

ampolla [amˈpoʎa] NF blister; (*Med*) ampoule

ampolleta [ampoˈʎeta] NF (AM) (light) bulb

ampuloso, -a [ampuˈloso, a] ADJ bombastic, pompous

amputar [ampuˈtar] /**1a**/ VT to cut off, amputate

amueblar [amweˈβlar] /**1a**/ VT to furnish

amuleto [amuˈleto] NM (lucky) charm

amurallar [amuraˈʎar] /**1a**/ VT to wall up *o* in

anacarado, -a [anakaˈraðo, a] ADJ mother-of-pearl *cpd*

anacardo [anaˈkarðo] NM cashew (nut)

anaconda [anaˈkonda] NF anaconda

anacronismo [anakroˈnismo] NM anachronism

ánade [ˈanaðe] NM duck

anagrama [anaˈɣrama] NM anagram

anales [aˈnales] NMPL annals

analfabetismo [analfaβeˈtismo] NM illiteracy

analfabeto, -a [analfaˈβeto, a] ADJ, NM/F illiterate

analgésico [analˈxesiko] NM painkiller, analgesic

analice *etc* [anaˈliθe] VB *ver* **analizar**

análisis [aˈnalisis] NM INV analysis; **~ de costos-beneficios** cost-benefit analysis; **~ de mercados** market research; **~ de sangre** blood test

analista [anaˈlista] NMF (*gen*) analyst; (*Pol, Historia*) chronicler; **~ de sistemas** (*Inform*) systems analyst

analizar [analiˈθar] /**1f**/ VT to analyse

analogía [analoˈxia] NF analogy; **por ~ con** on the analogy of

analógico, -a [anaˈloxiko, a] ADJ (Inform) analog; (reloj) analogue (BRIT), analog (US)

análogo, -a [aˈnaloɣo, a] ADJ analogous, similar

ananá [anaˈna], **ananás** [anaˈnas] NM pineapple

anaquel [anaˈkel] NM shelf

anaranjado, -a [anaranˈxaðo, a] ADJ orange(-coloured)

anarquía [anarˈkia] NF anarchy

anarquismo [anarˈkismo] NM anarchism

anarquista [anarˈkista] NMF anarchist

anatematice etc [anatemaˈtiθe] VB ver **anatematizar**

anatematizar [anatematiˈθar] /1f/ VT (Rel) to anathematize; (fig) to curse

anatomía [anatoˈmia] NF anatomy

anca [ˈanka] NF rump, haunch ■ **ancas** NFPL (fam) behind sg; **llevar a algn en ancas** to carry sb behind one

ancestral [anθesˈtral] ADJ (costumbre) age-old

★**ancho, -a** [ˈantʃo, a] ADJ wide; (falda) full; (fig) liberal; **le viene muy ~ el cargo** (fig) the job is too much for him; **ponerse ~** to get conceited; **quedarse tan ~** to go on as if nothing had happened ▶ NM width; (Ferro) gauge; **estar a sus anchas** to be at one's ease

anchoa [anˈtʃoa] NF anchovy

anchura [anˈtʃura] NF width; (amplitud) wideness

anchuroso, -a [antʃuˈroso, a] ADJ wide

★**anciano, -a** [anˈθjano, a] ADJ old, aged ▶ NM/F old man/woman ▶ NM elder

ancla [ˈankla] NF anchor; **levar anclas** to weigh anchor

ancladero [anklaˈðero] NM anchorage

anclar [anˈklar] /1a/ VI to (drop) anchor

andadas [anˈdaðas] NFPL (aventuras) adventures; **volver a las ~** to backslide

andaderas [andaˈðeras] NFPL baby-walker sg

andadura [andaˈðura] NF gait; (de caballo) pace

★**Andalucía** [andaluˈθia] NF Andalusia

★**andaluz, a** [andaˈluθ, a] ADJ, NM/F Andalusian

andamiaje [andaˈmjaxe], **andamio** [anˈdamjo] NM scaffold(ing)

andanada [andaˈnaða] NF (fig) reprimand; **soltarle a algn una ~** to give sb a rocket

andante [anˈdante] ADJ: **caballero ~** knight errant

★**andar** [anˈdar] /1p/ VT to go, cover, travel ▶ VI to go, walk, travel; (funcionar) to go, work; (estar) to be; **~ a pie/a caballo/en bicicleta** to go on foot/on horseback/by bicycle; **¡anda!** (sorpresa) go on!; **anda en o por los 40** he's about 40; **¿en qué andas?** what are you up to?; **andamos mal de dinero/tiempo** we're badly off for money/

we're short of time; **anda por aquí** it's round here somewhere; **~ haciendo algo** to be doing sth ▶ NM walk, gait, pace ■ **andarse** VR (irse) to go away o off; **andarse por las ramas** to beat about the bush; **no andarse con rodeos** to call a spade a spade (fam); **todo se andará** all in good time

andariego, -a [andaˈrjeɣo, a] ADJ fond of travelling

andas [ˈandas] NFPL stretcher sg

★**andén** [anˈden] NM (Ferro) platform; (Naut) quayside; (AM: acera) pavement (BRIT), sidewalk (US)

★**Andes** [ˈandes] NMPL: **los ~** the Andes

andinismo [andiˈnismo] NM (AM) mountaineering, climbing

andino, -a [anˈdino, a] ADJ Andean, of the Andes

Andorra [anˈdorra] NF Andorra

andrajo [anˈdraxo] NM rag

andrajoso, -a [andraˈxoso, a] ADJ ragged

andurriales [anduˈrrjales] NMPL out-of-the-way place sg, the sticks; **en esos ~** in that godforsaken spot

anduve [anˈduβe], **anduviera** etc [anduˈβjera] VB ver **andar**

anécdota [aˈnekðota] NF anecdote, story

anegar [aneˈɣar] /1h/ VT to flood; (ahogar) to drown ■ **anegarse** VR to drown; (hundirse) to sink

anegue etc [aˈneɣe] VB ver **anegar**

anejo, -a [aˈnexo, a] ADJ attached ▶ NM (Arq) annexe

anemia [aˈnemja] NF anaemia

anestesia [anesˈtesja] NF anaesthetic; **~ general/local** general/local anaesthetic

anestesiar [anesteˈsjar] /1b/ VT to anaesthetize (BRIT), anesthetize (US)

anestésico [anesˈtesiko] NM anaesthetic

anexar [anekˈsar] /1a/ VT to annex; (documento) to attach; (Inform) to append

anexión [anekˈsjon] NF, **anexionamiento** [aneksjonaˈmjento] NM annexation

anexionar [aneksjoˈnar] /1a/ VT to annex ■ **anexionarse** VR: **anexionarse un país** to annex a country

anexo, -a [aˈnekso, a] ADJ attached ▶ NM annexe

anfetamina [anfetaˈmina] NF amphetamine

anfibio, -a [anˈfiβjo, a] ADJ amphibious ▶ NM amphibian

★**anfiteatro** [anfiteˈatro] NM amphitheatre; (Teat) dress circle

anfitrión, -ona [anfiˈtrjon, ona] NM/F host(ess)

ánfora [ˈanfora] NF (cántaro) amphora; (AM Pol) ballot box

ángel [ˈanxel] NM angel; **~ de la guarda** guardian angel; **tener ~** to have charm

Ángeles ['anxeles] NMPL: **los ~** Los Angeles

angélico, -a [an'xeliko, a], **angelical** [anxeli'kal] ADJ angelic(al)

angina [an'xina] NF (*Med*) inflammation of the throat; **~ de pecho** angina; **tener anginas** to have tonsillitis, have a sore throat

anglicano, -a [angli'kano, a] ADJ, NM/F Anglican

anglicismo [angli'θismo] NM anglicism

anglosajón, -ona [anglosa'xon, 'xona] ADJ, NM/F Anglo-Saxon

Angola [an'gola] NF Angola

angoleño, -a [ango'leɲo, a] ADJ, NM/F Angolan

angosto, -a [an'gosto, a] ADJ narrow

anguila [an'gila] NF eel ■ **anguilas** NFPL slipway *sg*

angula [an'gula] NF elver, baby eel

ángulo ['angulo] NM angle; (*esquina*) corner; (*curva*) bend

angustia [an'gustja] NF anguish

angustiar [angus'tjar] /**1b**/ VT to distress, grieve ■ **angustiarse** VR: **angustiarse (por)** to be distressed (at *o* on account of)

anhelante [ane'lante] ADJ eager; (*deseoso*) longing

anhelar [ane'lar] /**1a**/ VT to be eager for; (*desear*) to long for, desire ▶ VI to pant, gasp

anhelo [a'nelo] NM eagerness; desire

anhídrido [a'niðriðo] NM: **~ carbónico** carbon dioxide

anidar [ani'ðar] /**1a**/ VT (*acoger*) to take in, shelter ▶ VI to nest; (*fig*) to make one's home

anilina [ani'lina] NF aniline

anilla [a'niʎa] NF ring; **(las) anillas** (*Deporte*) the rings

★**anillo** [a'niʎo] NM ring; **~ de boda** wedding ring; **~ de compromiso** engagement ring; **venir como ~ al dedo** to suit to a tee

ánima ['anima] NF soul; **las ánimas** the Angelus (bell) *sg*

animación [anima'θjon] NF liveliness; (*vitalidad*) life; (*actividad*) bustle

★**animado, -a** [ani'maðo, a] ADJ (*vivo*) lively; (*vivaz*) animated; (*concurrido*) bustling; (*alegre*) in high spirits; **dibujos animados** cartoon *sg*

animador, a [anima'ðor, a] NM/F (*TV*) host(ess), compère ▶ NF (*Deporte*) cheerleader

animadversión [animaðβer'sjon] NF ill-will, antagonism

★**animal** [ani'mal] ADJ animal; (*fig*) stupid ▶ NM animal; (*fig*) fool; (*bestia*) brute

animalada [anima'laða] NF (*gen*) silly thing (to do *o* say); (*ultraje*) disgrace

animalista [anima'lista] ADJ pro-animal-rights, animalist ▶ NMF animal-rights campaigner, animalist

★**animar** [ani'mar] /**1a**/ VT (*Bio*) to animate, give life to; (*fig*) to liven up, brighten up, cheer up;

(*estimular*) to stimulate ■ **animarse** VR to cheer up, feel encouraged; (*decidirse*) to make up one's mind

anime [a'nime] NM (*japonés*) anime

★**ánimo** ['animo] NM (*alma*) soul; (*mente*) mind; (*valentía*) courage; **cobrar ~** to take heart; **dar ~(s) a** to encourage ▶ EXCL cheer up!

animoso, -a [ani'moso, a] ADJ brave; (*vivo*) lively

aniñado, -a [ani'ɲaðo, a] ADJ (*facción*) childlike; (*carácter*) childish

aniquilar [aniki'lar] /**1a**/ VT to annihilate, destroy

anís [a'nis] NM (*grano*) aniseed; (*licor*) anisette

★**aniversario** [aniβer'sarjo] NM anniversary

Ankara [an'kara] NF Ankara

ano ['ano] NM anus

★**anoche** [a'notʃe] ADV last night; **antes de ~** the night before last

★**anochecer** [anotʃe'θer] /**2d**/ VI to get dark ▶ NM nightfall, dark; **al ~** at nightfall

anochezca *etc* [ano'tʃeθka] VB *ver* **anochecer**

anodino, -a [ano'ðino, a] ADJ dull, anodyne

anomalía [anoma'lia] NF anomaly

anonadado, -a [anona'ðaðo, a] ADJ: **estar ~** to be stunned

anonimato [anoni'mato] NM anonymity

anónimo, -a [a'nonimo, a] ADJ anonymous; (*Com*) limited ▶ NM (*carta*) anonymous letter; (: *maliciosa*) poison-pen letter

anorak [ano'rak] (*pl* **anoraks**) NM anorak

anorexia [ano'reksja] NF anorexia

anormal [anor'mal] ADJ abnormal

anotación [anota'θjon] NF note; annotation

anotar [ano'tar] /**1a**/ VT to note down; (*comentar*) to annotate

anquilosado, -a [ankilo'saðo, a] ADJ (*fig*) stale, out of date

anquilosamiento [ankilosa'mjento] NM (*fig*) paralysis, stagnation

ansia ['ansja] NF anxiety; (*añoranza*) yearning

ansiar [an'sjar] /**1b**/ VT to long for

ansiedad [ansje'ðað] NF anxiety

★**ansioso, -a** [an'sjoso, a] ADJ anxious; (*anhelante*) eager; **~ de** *o* **por algo** greedy for sth

antagónico, -a [anta'ɣoniko, a] ADJ antagonistic; (*opuesto*) contrasting

antagonista [antaɣo'nista] NMF antagonist

antaño [an'taɲo] ADV in years gone by, long ago

Antártico [an'tartiko] NM: **el (océano) ~** the Antarctic (Ocean)

Antártida [an'tartiða] NF Antarctica

ante ['ante] PREP before, in the presence of; (*encarado con*) faced with; **~ todo** above all ▶ NM (*piel*) suede

anteanoche [antea'notʃe] ADV the night before last

★**anteayer** [antea'jer] ADV the day before yesterday

antebrazo [ante'βraθo] NM forearm

antecámara [ante'kamara] NF (*Arq*) anteroom; (*antesala*) waiting room; (*Pol*) lobby

antecedente [anteθe'ðente] ADJ previous ▶ NM antecedent ■ **antecedentes** NMPL (*profesionales*) background *sg*; **antecedentes penales** criminal record; **no tener antecedentes** to have a clean record; **estar en antecedentes** to be well-informed; **poner a algn en antecedentes** to put sb in the picture

anteceder [anteθe'ðer] /**2a**/ VT to precede, go before

antecesor, a [anteθe'sor, a] NM/F predecessor

antedicho, -a [ante'ðitʃo, a] ADJ aforementioned

antelación [antela'θjon] NF: **con ~** in advance

antemano [ante'mano]: **de ~** *adv* beforehand, in advance

★**antena** [an'tena] NF antenna; (*de televisión etc*) aerial; **~ de telefonía móvil** mobile phone mast (*BRIT*), cell tower (*US*); **~ parabólica** satellite dish

antenoche [ante'notʃe] ADV (*AM*) the night before last

anteojeras [anteo'xeras] NFPL blinkers (*BRIT*), blinders (*US*)

anteojo [ante'oxo] NM eyeglass ■ **anteojos** NMPL (*esp AM*) glasses, spectacles

antepasados [antepa'saðos] NMPL ancestors

antepecho [ante'petʃo] NM guardrail, parapet; (*repisa*) ledge, sill

antepondré *etc* [antepon'dre] VB *ver* **anteponer**

anteponer [antepo'ner] /**2q**/ VT to place in front; (*fig*) to prefer

anteponga *etc* [ante'ponɣa] VB *ver* **anteponer**

anteproyecto [antepro'jekto] NM preliminary sketch; (*fig*) blueprint; (*Pol*): **~ de ley** draft bill

antepuesto, -a [ante'pwesto, a] PP *de* **anteponer**

antepuse *etc* [ante'puse] VB *ver* **anteponer**

★**anterior** [ante'rjor] ADJ preceding, previous

anterioridad [anterjori'ðað] NF: **con ~ a** prior to, before

anteriormente [anterjor'mente] ADV previously, before

★**antes** ['antes] ADV sooner; (*primero*) first; (*con anterioridad*) before; (*hace tiempo*) previously, once; (*más bien*) rather; **dos días ~** two days before *o* previously; **mucho/poco ~** long/shortly before; **~ muerto que esclavo** better dead than enslaved; **no quiso venir ~** she didn't want to come any earlier; **cuanto ~, lo ~ posible** as soon as possible; **~ de** *o* **que nada** (*en el tiempo*) first of all; (*indicando preferencia*) above all; **~ que yo** before me; **cuanto ~ mejor** the sooner the better ▶ PREP: **~ de** before ▶ CONJ: **~ (de) que** before; **tomo el avión ~ que el barco** I take the plane rather than the boat; **~ bien** (but) rather

antesala [ante'sala] NF anteroom

antiadherente [antiaðe'rente] ADJ non-stick

antiaéreo, -a [antia'ereo, a] ADJ anti-aircraft

antialcohólico, -a [antial'koliko, a] ADJ: **centro ~** (*Med*) detoxification unit

antibalas [anti'βalas] ADJ INV: **chaleco ~** bulletproof jacket

antibiótico [anti'βjotiko] NM antibiotic

anticaspa [anti'kaspa] ADJ INV anti-dandruff *cpd*

anticiclón [antiθi'klon] NM (*Meteorología*) anticyclone

anticipación [antiθipa'θjon] NF anticipation; **con 10 minutos de ~** 10 minutes early

anticipado, -a [antiθi'paðo, a] ADJ (in) advance; **por ~** in advance

anticipar [antiθi'par] /**1a**/ VT to anticipate; (*adelantar*) to bring forward; (*Com*) to advance ■ **anticiparse** VR: **anticiparse a su época** to be ahead of one's time

anticipo [anti'θipo] NM (*Com*) advance; *ver tb* **anticipación**

anticonceptivo, -a [antikonθep'tiβo, a] ADJ, NM contraceptive; **métodos anticonceptivos** methods of birth control

anticongelante [antikonxe'lante] NM antifreeze

anticonstitucional [antikonstituθjo'nal] ADJ unconstitutional

★**anticuado, -a** [anti'kwaðo, a] ADJ out-of-date, old-fashioned; (*desusado*) obsolete

anticuario [anti'kwarjo] NM antique dealer

anticuerpo [anti'kwerpo] NM (*Med*) antibody

antidemocrático, -a [antiðemo'kratiko, a] ADJ undemocratic

antideportivo, -a [antiðepor'tiβo, a] ADJ unsporting

antidepresivo [antiðepre'siβo] NM antidepressant

antideslumbrante [antiðeslum'brante] ADJ (*Inform*) anti-dazzle

antidoping [anti'ðopin] ADJ INV anti-drug; **control ~** drugs test

antídoto [an'tiðoto] NM antidote

antidroga [anti'ðroɣa] ADJ INV anti-drug; **brigada ~** drug squad

antiestético, -a [anties'tetiko, a] ADJ unsightly

antifaz [anti'faθ] NM mask; (*velo*) veil

antigás [anti'gas] ADJ INV: **careta ~** gas mask

antiglobalización [antiɣlobaliθa'θjon] NF anti-globalization; **manifestantes ~** anti-globalization protesters

antiglobalizador, a [antiɣlobaliθa'ðor, a] ADJ anti-globalization *cpd*

antigualla [anti'ɣwaʎa] NF antique; (*reliquia*) relic ■ **antiguallas** NFPL old things

antiguamente [antiɣwa'mente] ADV formerly; (*hace mucho tiempo*) long ago

Antigua y Barbuda [an'tiɣwaibar'βuða] NF Antigua and Barbuda

antigüedad [antiɣwe'ðað] NF antiquity; (*artículo*) antique; (*rango*) seniority

★**antiguo, -a** [an'tiɣwo, a] ADJ old, ancient; (*que fue*) former; **a la antigua** in the old-fashioned way

antihigiénico, -a [anti'xjeniko, a] ADJ unhygienic

antihistamínico, -a [antista'miniko, a] ADJ, NM antihistamine

antiinflacionista [antinflaθjo'nista] ADJ anti-inflationary, counter-inflationary

antillano, -a [anti'ʎano, a] ADJ, NM/F West Indian

Antillas [an'tiʎas] NFPL: **las ~** the West Indies, the Antilles; **el mar de las ~** the Caribbean Sea

antílope [an'tilope] NM antelope

antimonopolios [antimono'poljos] ADJ INV: **ley ~** anti-trust law

antinatural [antinatu'ral] ADJ unnatural

antiparras [anti'parras] NFPL (*fam*) specs

antipatía [antipa'tia] NF antipathy, dislike

★**antipático, -a** [anti'patiko, a] ADJ disagreeable, unpleasant

Antípodas [an'tipoðas] NFPL: **las ~** the Antipodes

antiquísimo, -a [anti'kisimo, a] ADJ ancient

antirreglamentario, -a [antirreɣlamen'tarjo, a] ADJ (*gen*) unlawful; (*Pol etc*) unconstitutional

antirrobo [anti'rroβo] NM (*tb:* **dispositivo antirrobo**: *para casas etc*) burglar alarm; (*: para coches*) car alarm ▶ ADJ INV (*alarma etc*) anti-theft

antisemita [antise'mita] ADJ anti-Semitic ▶ NMF anti-Semite

antiséptico, -a [anti'septiko, a] ADJ antiseptic ▶ NM antiseptic

antisistema [antisis'tema] ADJ INV anticapitalist

antiterrorismo [antiterro'rismo] NM counterterrorism

antiterrorista [antiterro'rista] ADJ antiterrorist, counterterrorist; **la lucha ~** the fight against terrorism

antítesis [an'titesis] NF INV antithesis

antivírico, -a [anti'βiriko, a] ADJ (*Med*) antiviral

antivirus [anti'birus] NM INV (*Inform*) antivirus program

antojadizo, -a [antoxa'ðiθo, a] ADJ capricious

antojarse [anto'xarse] /1a/ VR (*desear*): **se me antoja comprarlo** I have a mind to buy it; (*pensar*): **se me antoja que ...** I have a feeling that ...

antojo [an'toxo] NM caprice, whim; (*rosa*) birthmark; (*lunar*) mole; **hacer a su ~** to do as one pleases

antología [antolo'xia] NF anthology

antonomasia [antono'masja] NF: **por ~** par excellence

antorcha [an'tortʃa] NF torch

antro ['antro] NM cavern; **~ de corrupción** (*fig*) den of iniquity

antropófago, -a [antro'pofaɣo, a] ADJ, NM/F cannibal

antropología [antropolo'xia] NF anthropology

antropólogo, -a [antro'poloɣo, a] NM/F anthropologist

★**anual** [a'nwal] ADJ annual

anualidad [anwali'ðað] NF annuity, annual payment; **~ vitalicia** life annuity

anuario [a'nwarjo] NM yearbook

anublado, -a [anu'βlaðo, a] ADJ overcast

anudar [anu'ðar] /1a/ VT to knot, tie; (*unir*) to join ▪ **anudarse** VR to get tied up; **se me anudó la voz** I got a lump in my throat

anulación [anula'θjon] NF (*de un matrimonio*) annulment; (*cancelación*) cancellation; (*de una ley*) repeal

anular [anu'lar] /1a/ VT (*contrato*) to annul, cancel; (*suscripción*) to cancel; (*ley*) to repeal ▶ NM ring finger

anunciación [anunθja'θjon] NF announcement; **A~** (*Rel*) Annunciation

anunciante [anun'θjante] NMF (*Com*) advertiser

★**anunciar** [anun'θjar] /1b/ VT to announce; (*proclamar*) to proclaim; (*Com*) to advertise

★**anuncio** [a'nunθjo] NM announcement; (*señal*) sign; (*Com*) advertisement; (*cartel*) poster; (*Teat*) bill; **anuncios por palabras** classified ads

anverso [am'berso] NM obverse

anzuelo [an'θwelo] NM hook; (*para pescar*) fish hook; **tragar el ~** to swallow the bait

añadido [aɲa'ðiðo] NM addition

añadidura [aɲaði'ðura] NF addition, extra; **por ~** besides, in addition

★**añadir** [aɲa'ðir] /3a/ VT to add

añejo, -a [a'ɲexo, a] ADJ old; (*vino*) mature; (*jamón*) well-cured

añicos [a'ɲikos] NMPL: **hacer ~** to smash, shatter; **hacerse ~** to smash, shatter

añil [a'ɲil] NM (*Bot, color*) indigo

★**año** ['aɲo] NM year; **¡Feliz A~ Nuevo!** Happy New Year!; **tener 15 años** to be 15 (years old); **los años 80** the eighties; **~ bisiesto/escolar/fiscal/sabático** leap/school/tax/sabbatical year; **~ fiscal** o **tax** year; **estar de buen ~** to be in good shape; **en el ~ de la nana** in the year dot; **el ~ que viene** next year

añoranza [aɲo'ranθa] NF nostalgia; (*anhelo*) longing

añorar [aɲo'rar] /1a/ VT to long for

añoso, -a [a'ɲoso, a] ADJ ancient, old

aovado, -a [ao'βaðo, a] ADJ oval

aovar [ao'βar] /1a/ VI to lay eggs

apa ['apa] EXCL (Am) goodness me!, good gracious!

apabullar [apaβu'ʎar] /1a/ VT (lit, fig) to crush

apacentar [apaθen'tar] /1j/ VT to pasture, graze

apacible [apa'θiβle] ADJ gentle, mild

apaciente etc [apa'θjente] VB ver **apacentar**

apaciguar [apaθi'ɣwar] /1i/ VT to pacify, calm (down)

apacigüe etc [apa'θiɣwe] VB ver **apaciguar**

apadrinar [apaðri'nar] /1a/ VT to sponsor, support; (Rel: niño) to be godfather to

apagado, -a [apa'ɣaðo, a] ADJ (volcán) extinct; (color) dull; (voz) quiet; (sonido) muffled; (persona: apático) listless; **estar ~** (fuego, luz) to be out; (radio, TV etc) to be off

★**apagar** [apa'ɣar] /1h/ VT to put out; (color) to tone down; (sonido) to silence, muffle; (sed) to quench; (Elec, Radio, TV) to turn off; (Inform) to toggle off; **~ el sistema** (Inform) to close o shut down ■ **apagarse** VR (luz, fuego) to go out; (sonido) to die away; (pasión) to wither

apagón [apa'ɣon] NM blackout, power cut

apague etc [a'paɣe] VB ver **apagar**

apaisado, -a [apai'saðo, a] ADJ (papel) landscape cpd

apalabrar [apala'βrar] /1a/ VT to agree to; (obrero) to engage

Apalaches [apa'latʃes] NMPL: **(Montes) ~** Appalachians

apalear [apale'ar] /1a/ VT to beat, thrash; (Agr) to winnow

apantallar [apanta'ʎar] /1a/ VT (Am) to impress

apañado, -a [apa'ɲaðo, a] ADJ (mañoso) resourceful; (arreglado) tidy; (útil) handy

apañar [apa'ɲar] /1a/ VT to pick up; (asir) to take hold of, grasp; (reparar) to mend, patch up ■ **apañarse** VR to manage, get along; **apañárselas por su cuenta** to look after number one (fam)

apaño [a'paɲo] NM (Costura) patch; (maña) skill; **esto no tiene ~** there's no answer to this one

apapachar [apapa'tʃar] /1a/ VT (Am fam) to cuddle, hug

aparador [apara'ðor] NM sideboard; (Am: escaparate) shop window

★**aparato** [apa'rato] NM apparatus; (máquina) machine; (doméstico) appliance; (boato) ostentation; (Inform) device; **al ~** (Telec) speaking; **~ de facsímil** facsimile (machine), fax; **~ respiratorio** respiratory system; **~ digestivo** digestive system; **aparatos de mando** (Aviat etc) controls

aparatoso, -a [apara'toso, a] ADJ showy, ostentatious

★**aparcamiento** [aparka'mjento] NM car park (BRIT), parking lot (US); **~ disuasorio** park and ride

★**aparcar** [apar'kar] /1g/ VT, VI to park

aparear [apare'ar] /1a/ VT (objetos) to pair, match; (animales) to mate ■ **aparearse** VR to form a pair; to mate

★**aparecer** [apare'θer] /2d/ VI to appear; **apareció borracho** he turned up drunk ■ **aparecerse** VR to appear

aparejado, -a [apare'xaðo, a] ADJ fit, suitable; **ir ~ con** to go hand in hand with; **llevar** o **traer ~** to involve

aparejador, a [aparexa'ðor, a] NM/F (Arq) quantity surveyor

aparejar [apare'xar] /1a/ VT to prepare; (caballo) to saddle, harness; (Naut) to fit out, rig out

aparejo [apa'rexo] NM preparation; (de caballo) harness; (Naut) rigging; (de poleas) block and tackle

aparentar [aparen'tar] /1a/ VT (edad) to look; (fingir): **~ tristeza** to pretend to be sad

aparente [apa'rente] ADJ apparent; (adecuado) suitable

aparezca etc [apa'reθka] VB ver **aparecer**

aparición [apari'θjon] NF appearance; (de libro) publication; (de fantasma) apparition

apariencia [apa'rjenθja] NF (outward) appearance; **en ~** outwardly, seemingly

aparque etc [a'parke] VB ver **aparcar**

apartado, -a [apar'taðo, a] ADJ separate; (lejano) remote ▸ NM (tipográfico) paragraph; **~ de correos** (ESP), **~ postal** (Am) post office box

★**apartamento** [aparta'mento] NM apartment, flat (BRIT)

apartamiento [aparta'mjento] NM separation; (aislamiento) remoteness; (Am) apartment, flat (BRIT)

apartar [apar'tar] /1a/ VT to separate; (quitar) to remove; (Minería) to extract ■ **apartarse** VR (separarse) to separate, part; (irse) to move away; (mantenerse aparte) to keep away

★**aparte** [a'parte] ADV (separadamente) separately; (además) besides; **"punto y ~"** "new paragraph" ▸ PREP: **~ de** apart from ▸ NM (Teat) aside; (tipográfico) new paragraph

aparthotel [aparto'tel] NM serviced apartments

apasionado, -a [apasjo'naðo, a] ADJ passionate; (pey) biassed, prejudiced ▸ NM/F admirer

apasionante [apasjo'nante] ADJ exciting

apasionar [apasjo'nar] /1a/ VT to excite; **le apasiona el fútbol** she's crazy about football ■ **apasionarse** VR to get excited

apatía [apa'tia] NF apathy

apático, -a [a'patiko, a] ADJ apathetic

apátrida [a'patriða] ADJ stateless

Apdo. NM ABR (= Apartado (de Correos)) P.O. Box

apeadero [apea'ðero] NM halt, stopping place

apearse [ape'arse] /1a/ VR (jinete) to dismount; (bajarse) to get down o out; (de coche) to get out, alight; **no ~ del burro** to refuse to climb down

apechugar [apetʃu'ɣar] /1h/ VI: **~ con algo** to face up to sth

apechugue etc [ape'tʃuɣe] VB ver **apechugar**

apedrear [apeðre'ar] /**1a**/ VT to stone

apegarse [ape'ɣarse] /**1h**/ VR: ~ **a** to become attached to

apego [a'peɣo] NM attachment, devotion

apegue etc [a'peɣe] VB ver **apegarse**

apelación [apela'θjon] NF appeal

apelar [ape'lar] /**1a**/ VI to appeal; ~ **a** (fig) to resort to

apelativo [apela'tiβo] NM (Ling) appellative; (AM) surname

apellidar [apeʎi'ðar] /**1a**/ VT to call, name ■ **apellidarse** VR: **se apellida Pérez** her (sur)name's Pérez

★**apellido** [ape'ʎiðo] NM surname

In the Spanish-speaking world most people use two **apellidos**, the first being their father's first surname, and the second their mother's first surname: eg the children of Juan García López, married to Carmen Pérez Rodríguez, would have as their surname García Pérez. Married women retain their own surname(s) and sometimes add their husband's first surname on to theirs: eg Carmen Pérez de García. She could also be referred to as (la) Señora de García. In Latin America it is usual for the second surname to be shortened to an initial in correspondence eg: Juan García L.

apelmazado, -a [apelma'θaðo, a] ADJ compact, solid

apelotonar [apeloto'nar] /**1a**/ VT to roll into a ball ■ **apelotonarse** VR (gente) to crowd together

apenar [ape'nar] /**1a**/ VT to grieve, trouble; (AM: avergonzar) to embarrass ■ **apenarse** VR to grieve; (AM: avergonzarse) to be embarrassed

★**apenas** [a'penas] ADV scarcely, hardly ▶ CONJ as soon as, no sooner

apéndice [a'pendiθe] NM appendix

apendicitis [apendi'θitis] NF appendicitis

Apeninos [ape'ninos] NMPL Apennines

apercibimiento [aperθiβi'mjento] NM (aviso) warning

apercibir [aperθi'βir] /**3a**/ VT to prepare; (avisar) to warn; (Jur) to summon; (AM) to notice, see ■ **apercibirse** VR to get ready; **apercibirse de** to notice

★**aperitivo** [aperi'tiβo] NM (bebida) aperitif; (comida) appetizer

apero [a'pero] NM (Agr) implement ■ **aperos** NMPL farm equipment sg

★**apertura** [aper'tura] NF (gen) opening; (Pol) openness, liberalization; (Teat etc) beginning; ~ **de un juicio hipotecario** (Com) foreclosure

aperturismo [apertu'rismo] NM (Pol) (policy of) liberalization

apesadumbrar [apesaðum'brar] /**1a**/ VT to grieve, sadden ■ **apesadumbrarse** VR to distress o.s.

apestar [apes'tar] /**1a**/ VT to infect ▶ VI: ~ **(a)** to stink (of)

apestoso, -a [apes'toso, a] ADJ (hediondo) stinking; (asqueroso) sickening

★**apetecer** [apete'θer] /**2d**/ VT: **¿te apetece una tortilla?** do you fancy an omelette?

apetecible [apete'θiβle] ADJ desirable; (comida) appetizing

apetezca etc [ape'teθka] VB ver **apetecer**

★**apetito** [ape'tito] NM appetite

★**apetitoso, -a** [apeti'toso, a] ADJ (gustoso) appetizing; (fig) tempting

apiadarse [apja'ðarse] /**1a**/ VR: ~ **de** to take pity on

ápice ['apiθe] NM apex; (fig) whit, iota; **ni un** ~ not a whit; **no ceder un** ~ not to budge an inch

apicultor, a [apikul'tor, a] NM/F beekeeper, apiarist

apicultura [apikul'tura] NF beekeeping

apiladora [apila'ðora] NF (para máquina impresora) stacker

apilar [api'lar] /**1a**/ VT to pile o heap up ■ **apilarse** VR to pile up

apiñado, -a [api'naðo, a] ADJ (apretado) packed

apiñar [api'nar] /**1a**/ VT to crowd ■ **apiñarse** VR to crowd o press together

apio ['apjo] NM celery

apisonadora [apisona'ðora] NF (máquina) steamroller

aplacar [apla'kar] /**1g**/ VT to placate ■ **aplacarse** VR to calm down

aplace etc [a'plaθe] VB ver **aplazar**

aplanamiento [aplana'mjento] NM smoothing, levelling

aplanar [apla'nar] /**1a**/ VT to smooth, level; (allanar) to roll flat, flatten ■ **aplanarse** VR (edificio) to collapse; (persona) to get discouraged

aplaque etc [a'plake] VB ver **aplacar**

aplastante [aplas'tante] ADJ overwhelming; (lógica) compelling

★**aplastar** [aplas'tar] /**1a**/ VT to squash (flat); (fig) to crush

aplatanarse [aplata'narse] /**1a**/ VR to get lethargic

aplaudir [aplau'ðir] /**3a**/ VT to applaud

aplauso [a'plauso] NM applause; (fig) approval, acclaim

aplazamiento [aplaθa'mjento] NM postponement

aplazar [apla'θar] /**1f**/ VT to postpone, defer

aplicación [aplika'θjon] NF application; (para móvil, internet) app; (esfuerzo) effort; **aplicaciones de gestión** business applications

★**aplicado, -a** [apli'kaðo, a] ADJ diligent, hardworking

aplicar [apli'kar] /**1g**/ VT (ejecutar) to apply; (poner en vigor) to put into effect; (esfuerzos) to devote ■ **aplicarse** VR to apply o.s.

aplique *etc* [a'plike] VB *ver* **aplicar** ▶ NM wall light *o* lamp

aplomo [a'plomo] NM aplomb, self-assurance

apocado, -a [apo'kaðo, a] ADJ timid

apocamiento [apoka'mjento] NM timidity; (*depresión*) depression

apocarse [apo'karse] /**1g**/ VR to feel small *o* humiliated

apocopar [apoko'par] /**1a**/ VT (*Ling*) to shorten

apócope [a'pokope] NF apocopation; **gran es ~ de grande** "gran" is the shortened form of "grande"

apócrifo, -a [a'pokrifo, a] ADJ apocryphal

apodar [apo'ðar] /**1a**/ VT to nickname

apoderado [apoðe'raðo] NM agent, representative

apoderar [apoðe'rar] /**1a**/ VT to authorize, empower; (*Jur*) to grant (a) power of attorney to ■ **apoderarse** VR: **apoderarse de** to take possession of

★**apodo** [a'poðo] NM nickname

apogeo [apo'xeo] NM peak, summit

apolillado, -a [apoli'ʎaðo, a] ADJ moth-eaten

apolillarse [apoli'ʎarse] /**1a**/ VR to get moth-eaten

apología [apolo'xia] NF eulogy; (*defensa*) defence

apoltronarse [apoltro'narse] /**1a**/ VR to get lazy

apoplejía [apople'xia] NF apoplexy, stroke

apoque *etc* [a'poke] VB *ver* **apocarse**

apoquinar [apoki'nar] /**1a**/ VT (*fam*) to cough up, fork out

aporrear [aporre'ar] /**1a**/ VT to beat (up)

aportación [aporta'θjon] NF contribution

aportar [apor'tar] /**1a**/ VT to contribute ▶ VI to reach port ■ **aportarse** VR (*Am*: *llegar*) to arrive, come

aporte [a'porte] NM (*aportación*) contribution; (*Am*: *a la seguridad social*) contribution; **~ calórico** calorie content; **~ jubilatorio** (*Am*) pension contribution

aposentar [aposen'tar] /**1a**/ VT to lodge, put up

aposento [apo'sento] NM lodging; (*habitación*) room

apósito [a'posito] NM (*Med*) dressing

aposta [a'posta] ADV deliberately, on purpose

apostar [apos'tar] /**1a**, **1l**/ VT to bet, stake; (*tropas etc*) to station, post ▶ VI to bet

apostatar [aposta'tar] /**1a**/ VI (*Rel*) to apostatize; (*fig*) to change sides

a posteriori [aposte'rjori] ADV at a later date *o* stage; (*Filosofía*) a posteriori

apostilla [apos'tiʎa] NF note, comment

apóstol [a'postol] NM apostle

apóstrofo [a'postrofo] NM apostrophe

apostura [apos'tura] NF neatness, elegance

apoteósico, -a [apote'osiko, a] ADJ tremendous

★**apoyar** [apo'jar] /**1a**/ VT to lean, rest; (*fig*) to support, back ■ **apoyarse** VR: **apoyarse en** to lean on

★**apoyo** [a'pojo] NM support, backing

app [ap] (*pl* **apps**) NF (*para móvil, Internet*) app

apreciable [apre'θjaβle] ADJ considerable; (*fig*) esteemed

apreciación [apreθja'θjon] NF appreciation; (*Com*) valuation

★**apreciar** [apre'θjar] /**1b**/ VT to evaluate, assess; (*Com*) to appreciate, value; (*persona*) to respect; (*tamaño*) to gauge, assess; (*detalles*) to notice ▶ VI (*Econ*) to appreciate

aprecio [a'preθjo] NM valuation, estimate; (*fig*) appreciation

aprehender [apreen'der] /**2a**/ VT to apprehend, detain; (*ver*) to see, observe

aprehensión [apreen'sjon] NF detention, capture

apremiante [apre'mjante] ADJ urgent, pressing

apremiar [apre'mjar] /**1b**/ VT to compel, force ▶ VI to be urgent, press

apremio [a'premjo] NM urgency; **~ de pago** demand note

★**aprender** [apren'der] /**2a**/ VT, VI to learn; **~ a conducir** to learn to drive ■ **aprenderse** VR: **aprenderse algo de memoria** to learn sth (off) by heart

★**aprendiz, a** [apren'diθ, a] NM/F apprentice; (*principiante*) learner, trainee; **~ de comercio** business trainee

★**aprendizaje** [aprendi'θaxe] NM apprenticeship

aprensión [apren'sjon] NM apprehension, fear

aprensivo, -a [apren'siβo, a] ADJ apprehensive

apresar [apre'sar] /**1a**/ VT to seize; (*capturar*) to capture

aprestar [apres'tar] /**1a**/ VT to prepare, get ready; (*Tec*) to prime, size ■ **aprestarse** VR to get ready

apresto [a'presto] NM (*gen*) preparation; (*sustancia*) size

apresurado, -a [apresu'raðo, a] ADJ hurried, hasty

apresuramiento [apresura'mjento] NM hurry, haste

apresurar [apresu'rar] /**1a**/ VT to hurry, accelerate ■ **apresurarse** VR to hurry, make haste; **me apresuré a sugerir que ...** I hastily suggested that ...

apretado, -a [apre'taðo, a] ADJ tight; (*escritura*) cramped

apretar [apre'tar] /**1j**/ VT to squeeze, press; (*mano*) to clasp; (*dientes*) to grit; (*Tec*) to tighten; (*presionar*) to press together, pack; **~ la mano a algn** to shake sb's hand; **~ el paso** to quicken one's step ▶ VI to be too tight ■ **apretarse** VR to crowd together

apretón [apre'ton] NM squeeze; **~ de manos** handshake

aprieto [a'prjeto] VB ver **apretar** ▶ NM squeeze; (*dificultad*) difficulty, predicament; **estar en un ~** to be in a fix; **ayudar a algn a salir de un ~** to help sb out of trouble

a priori [apri'ori] ADV beforehand; (*Filosofía*) a priori

aprisa [a'prisa] ADV quickly, hurriedly

aprisionar [aprisjo'nar] /**1a**/ VT to imprison

aprobación [aproβa'θjon] NF approval

aprobado [apro'βaðo] NM (*nota*) pass mark

★**aprobar** [apro'βar] /**1l**/ VT to approve (of); (*examen, materia*) to pass ▶ VI to pass

apropiación [apropja'θjon] NF appropriation

★**apropiado, -a** [apro'pjaðo, a] ADJ appropriate, suitable

apropiarse [apro'pjarse] /**1b**/ VR: **~ de** to appropriate

aprovechado, -a [aproβe't∫aðo, a] ADJ industrious, hardworking; (*económico*) thrifty; (*pey*) unscrupulous

aprovechamiento [aproβet∫a'mjento] NM use, exploitation

★**aprovechar** [aproβe't∫ar] /**1a**/ VT to use; (*explotar*) to exploit; (*experiencia*) to profit from; (*oferta, oportunidad*) to take advantage of ▶ VI to progress, improve; **¡que aproveche!** enjoy your meal! ■ **aprovecharse** VR: **aprovecharse de** to make use of; (*pey*) to take advantage of

aprovisionar [aproβisjo'nar] /**1a**/ VT to supply

aproximación [aproksima'θjon] NF approximation; (*de lotería*) consolation prize

★**aproximadamente** [aproksimaða'mente] ADV approximately

aproximado, -a [aproksi'maðo, a] ADJ approximate

aproximar [aproksi'mar] /**1a**/ VT to bring nearer ■ **aproximarse** VR to come near, approach

apruebe etc [a'prweβe] VB ver **aprobar**

★**aptitud** [apti'tuð] NF aptitude; (*capacidad*) ability; **~ para los negocios** business sense

apto, -a ['apto, a] ADJ (*hábil*) capable; (*apropiado*): **~ (para)** fit (for), suitable (for); **~/no ~ para menores** (*Cine*) suitable/unsuitable for children

apuesto, -a [a'pwesto, a] VB ver **apostar** ▶ ADJ neat, elegant ▶ NF bet, wager

apuntador [apunta'ðor] NM prompter

apuntalar [apunta'lar] /**1a**/ VT to prop up

★**apuntar** [apun'tar] /**1a**/ VT (*con arma*) to aim at; (*con dedo*) to point at o to; (*anotar*) to note (down); (*datos*) to record; (*Teat*) to prompt; **~ una cantidad en la cuenta de algn** to charge a sum to sb's account ■ **apuntarse** VR (*Deporte: tanto, victoria*) to score; (*Escol*) to enrol; **apuntarse en un curso** to enrol on a course; **¡yo me apunto!** count me in!

apunte [a'punte] NM note; (*Teat: voz*) prompt; (*: texto*) prompt book

apuñalar [apuɲa'lar] /**1a**/ VT to stab

apurado, -a [apu'raðo, a] ADJ needy; (*difícil*) difficult; (*peligroso*) dangerous; (*Am: con prisa*) hurried, rushed; **estar en una situación apurada** to be in a tight spot; **estar ~** to be in a hurry

apurar [apu'rar] /**1a**/ VT (*agotar*) to drain; (*recursos*) to use up; (*molestar*) to annoy ■ **apurarse** VR (*preocuparse*) to worry; (*esp Am: darse prisa*) to hurry

apuro [a'puro] NM (*aprieto*) fix, jam; (*escasez*) want, hardship; (*vergüenza*) embarrassment; (*Am: prisa*) haste, urgency

aquejado, -a [ake'xaðo, a] ADJ: **~ de** (*Med*) afflicted by

aquejar [ake'xar] /**1a**/ VT (*afligir*) to distress; **le aqueja una grave enfermedad** he suffers from a serious disease

aquel, aquella, aquellos, -as [a'kel, a'keʎa, a'keʎos, as] ADJ that, those pl ▶ PRON that (one), those (ones) pl

aquél, aquélla, aquéllos, -as [a'kel, a'keʎa, a'keʎos, as] PRON that (one), those (ones) pl

★**aquello** [a'keʎo] PRON that, that business

★**aquí** [a'ki] ADV (*lugar*) here; (*tiempo*) now; **~ arriba** up here; **~ mismo** right here; **~ yace** here lies; **de ~ a siete días** a week from now

aquietar [akje'tar] /**1a**/ VT to quieten (down), calm (down)

Aquisgrán [akis'ɣran] NM Aachen, Aix-la-Chapelle

A.R. ABR (= *Alteza Real*) R.H.

★**árabe** ['araβe] ADJ Arab, Arabian; (*Ling*) Arabic ▶ NMF Arab ▶ NM (*Ling*) Arabic

Arabia [a'raβja] NF Arabia; **~ Saudí** o **Saudita** Saudi Arabia

arábigo, -a [a'raβiɣo, a] ADJ Arab, Arabian, Arabic

arácnido [a'rakniðo] NM arachnid

arado [a'raðo] NM plough

Aragón [ara'ɣon] NM Aragon

aragonés, -esa [araɣo'nes, esa] ADJ, NM/F Aragonese ▶ NM (*Ling*) Aragonese

arancel [aran'θel] NM tariff, duty; **~ de aduanas** (customs) duty

arandela [aran'dela] NF (*Tec*) washer; (*chorrera*) frill

araña [a'raɲa] NF (*Zool*) spider; (*lámpara*) chandelier

arañar [ara'ɲar] /**1a**/ VT to scratch

arañazo [ara'ɲaθo] NM scratch

arar [a'rar] /**1a**/ VT to plough, till

aras ['aras] NFPL: **en ~ de** for the sake of

araucano, -a [arau'kano, a] ADJ, NM/F Araucanian

arbitraje [arβi'traxe] NM arbitration

arbitrar [arβi'trar] /**1a**/ VT to arbitrate in; (*recur-*

sos) to bring together; (*Deporte*) to referee ▶ vɪ to arbitrate

arbitrariedad [arβitrarje'ðað] NF arbitrariness; (*acto*) arbitrary act

arbitrario, -a [arβi'trarjo, a] ADJ arbitrary

arbitrio [ar'βitrjo] NM free will; (*Jur*) adjudication, decision; **dejar al ~ de algn** to leave to sb's discretion

★**árbitro, -a** ['arβitro, a] NM/F arbitrator; (*Deporte*) referee; (*Tenis*) umpire

★**árbol** ['arβol] NM (*Bot*) tree; (*Naut*) mast; (*Tec*) axle, shaft; **~ de Navidad** Christmas tree

arbolado, -a [arβo'laðo, a] ADJ wooded; (*camino*) tree-lined ▶ NM woodland

arboladura [arβola'ðura] NF rigging

arbolar [arβo'lar] /1a/ vт to hoist, raise

arboleda [arβo'leða] NF grove, plantation

★**arbusto** [ar'βusto] NM bush, shrub

arca ['arka] NF chest, box; **A~ de la Alianza** Ark of the Covenant; **A~ de Noé** Noah's Ark

arcada [ar'kaða] NF arcade; (*de puente*) arch, span ▪ **arcadas** NFPL (*náuseas*) retching *sg*

arcaico, -a [ar'kaiko, a] ADJ archaic

arce ['arθe] NM maple tree

arcén [ar'θen] NM (*de autopista*) hard shoulder; (*de carretera*) verge

archiconocido, -a [artʃikono'θiðo, a] ADJ extremely well-known

archipiélago [artʃi'pjelaɣo] NM archipelago

archisabido, -a [artʃisa'βiðo, a] ADJ extremely well-known

archivador [artʃiβa'ðor] NM filing cabinet; **~ colgante** suspension file

★**archivar** [artʃi'βar] /1a/ vт to file (away); (*Inform*) to archive

★**archivo** [ar'tʃiβo] NM archive(s) *pl*; (*Inform*) file; **A~ Nacional** Public Record Office; **archivos policíacos** police files; **nombre de ~** (*Inform*) filename; **~ adjunto** (*Inform*) attachment; **~ de seguridad** (*Inform*) backup file

arcilla [ar'θiʎa] NF clay

arco ['arko] NM arch; (*Mat*) arc; (*Mil, Mus*) bow; (*Am Deporte*) goal; **~ iris** rainbow

arcón [ar'kon] NM large chest

★**arder** [ar'ðer] /2a/ vт, vɪ to burn; **~ sin llama** to smoulder; **estar que arde** (*persona*) to fume

ardid [ar'ðið] NM ploy, trick

ardiente [ar'ðjente] ADJ ardent

ardilla [ar'ðiʎa] NF squirrel

ardor [ar'ðor] NM (*calor*) heat, warmth; (*fig*) ardour; **~ de estómago** heartburn

ardoroso, -a [arðo'roso, a] ADJ passionate

arduo, -a ['arðwo, a] ADJ arduous

área ['area] NF area; (*Deporte*) penalty area

★**arena** [a'rena] NF sand; (*de una lucha*) arena

arenal [are'nal] NM (*terreno arenoso*) sandy area; (*arena movediza*) quicksand

arenga [a'renga] NF (*fam*) sermon

arengar [aren'gar] /1h/ vт to harangue

arengue *etc* [a'renge] VB *ver* **arengar**

arenillas [are'niʎas] NFPL (*Med*) stones

arenisca [are'niska] NF sandstone; (*cascajo*) grit

arenoso, -a [are'noso, a] ADJ sandy

arenque [a'renke] NM herring

arepa [a'repa] NF (*Am*) corn pancake

arete [a'rete] NM (*Am*) earring

argamasa [arɣa'masa] NF mortar, plaster

Argel [ar'xel] NM Algiers

Argelia [ar'xelja] NF Algeria

argelino, -a [arxe'lino, a] ADJ, NM/F Algerian

★**Argentina** [arxen'tina] NF: **(la) ~** Argentina, the Argentine

★**argentino, -a** [arxen'tino, a] ADJ Argentinian; (*de plata*) silvery ▶ NM/F Argentinian

argolla [ar'ɣoʎa] NF (large) ring; (*Am: de matrimonio*) wedding ring

argot [ar'ɣo] (*pl* **argots** [ar'ɣo, ar'ɣos]) NM slang

argucia [ar'ɣuθja] NF subtlety, sophistry

argüir [ar'ɣwir] /3g/ vт to deduce; (*discutir*) to argue; (*indicar*) to indicate, imply; (*censurar*) to reproach ▶ vɪ to argue

argumentación [arɣumenta'θjon] NF (line of) argument

argumentar [arɣumen'tar] /1a/ vт, vɪ to argue

★**argumento** [arɣu'mento] NM argument; (*razonamiento*) reasoning; (*de novela etc*) plot; (*Cine, TV*) storyline

arguyendo *etc* [arɣu'jendo] VB *ver* **argüir**

aria ['arja] NF aria

aridez [ari'ðeθ] NF aridity, dryness

árido, -a ['ariðo, a] ADJ arid, dry ▪ **áridos** NMPL dry goods

Aries ['arjes] NM Aries

ariete [a'rjete] NM battering ram

ario, -a ['arjo, a] ADJ Aryan

arisco, -a [a'risko, a] ADJ surly; (*insociable*) unsociable

aristocracia [aristo'kraθja] NF aristocracy

aristócrata [aris'tokrata] NMF aristocrat

aristocrático, -a [aristo'kratiko, a] ADJ aristocratic

aritmética [arit'metika] NF arithmetic

aritmético, -a [arit'metiko, a] ADJ arithmetic(al) ▶ NM/F arithmetician

★**arma** ['arma] NF arm; **~ blanca** blade, knife; (*espada*) sword; **~ de doble filo** double-edged sword; **~ de fuego** firearm ▪ **armas** NFPL arms; **armas cortas** small arms; **armas de destrucción masiva** weapons of mass destruction; **rendir las armas** to lay down one's arms; **ser de armas tomar** to be somebody to be reckoned with

armada [ar'maða] NF armada; (*flota*) fleet; *ver tb* **armado**

armadillo [arma'ðiʎo] NM armadillo

armado, -a [ar'maðo, a] ADJ armed; (Tec) reinforced

armador [arma'ðor] NM (Naut) shipowner

armadura [arma'ðura] NF (Mil) armour; (Tec) framework; (Zool) skeleton; (Física) armature

armamentista [armamen'tista], **armamentístico, -a** [armamen'tistiko, a] ADJ arms cpd

armamento [arma'mento] NM armament; (Naut) fitting-out

armar [ar'mar] /**1a**/ VT (soldado) to arm; (máquina) to assemble; (navío) to fit out; **armarla, ~ un lío** to start a row, kick up a fuss ■ **armarse** VR: **armarse de valor** to summon up one's courage

★armario [ar'marjo] NM wardrobe; (de cocina, baño) cupboard; **~ empotrado** built-in cupboard; **salir del ~** to come out (of the closet)

armatoste [arma'toste] NM (mueble) monstrosity; (máquina) contraption

armazón [arma'θon] NM O F body, chassis; (de mueble etc) frame; (Arq) skeleton

Armenia [ar'menja] NF Armenia

armería [arme'ria] NF (museo) military museum; (tienda) gunsmith's

armiño [ar'miɲo] NM stoat; (piel) ermine

armisticio [armis'tiθjo] NM armistice

armonía [armo'nia] NF harmony

armónica [ar'monika] NF harmonica; ver tb **armónico**

armonice etc [armo'niθe] VB ver **armonizar**

armónico, -a [ar'moniko, a] ADJ harmonic

armonioso, -a [armo'njoso, a] ADJ harmonious

armonizar [armoni'θar] /**1f**/ VT to harmonize; (diferencias) to reconcile ► VI to harmonize; **~ con** (fig) to be in keeping with's; (colores) to tone in with

arnés [ar'nes] NM armour ■ **arneses** NMPL harness sg

aro ['aro] NM ring; (tejo) quoit; (Am: pendiente) earring; **entrar por el ~** to give in

aroma [a'roma] NM aroma

aromaterapia [aromate'rapja] NF aromatherapy

aromático, -a [aro'matiko, a] ADJ aromatic

arpa ['arpa] NF harp

arpegio [ar'pexjo] NM (Mus) arpeggio

arpía [ar'pia] NF (fig) shrew

arpillera [arpi'ʎera] NF sacking, sackcloth

arpón [ar'pon] NM harpoon

arquear [arke'ar] /**1a**/ VT to arch, bend ■ **arquearse** VR to arch, bend

arqueo [ar'keo] NM (gen) arching; (Naut) tonnage

arqueología [arkeolo'xia] NF archaeology

arqueológico, -a [arkeo'loxiko, a] ADJ archaeological

arqueólogo, -a [arke'oloɣo, a] NM/F archaeologist

arquero [ar'kero] NM archer, bowman; (Am Deporte) goalkeeper

arquetipo [arke'tipo] NM archetype

★arquitecto, -a [arki'tekto, a] NM/F architect; **~ paisajista** O **de jardines** landscape gardener

arquitectónico, -a [arkitek'toniko, a] ADJ architectural

arquitectura [arkitek'tura] NF architecture

arrabal [arra'βal] NM suburb; (Am) slum ■ **arrabales** NMPL (afueras) outskirts

arrabalero, -a [arraβa'lero, a] ADJ (fig) common, coarse

arracimarse [arraθi'marse] /**1a**/ VR to cluster together

arraigado, -a [arrai'ɣaðo, a] ADJ deep-rooted; (fig) established

arraigar [arrai'ɣar] /**1h**/ VI to take root ■ **arraigarse** VR (persona) to settle

arraigo [a'rraiɣo] NM (raíces) roots pl; (bienes) property; (influencia) hold; **hombre de ~** man of property

arraigue etc [a'rraiɣe] VB ver **arraigar**

arrancada [arran'kaða] NF (arranque) sudden start

★arrancar [arran'kar] /**1g**/ VT (sacar) to extract, pull out; (arrebatar) to snatch (away); (pedazo) to tear off; (página) to rip out; (suspiro) to heave; (Auto) to start; (Inform) to boot; (fig) to extract; **~ información a algn** to extract information from sb ► VI (Auto, máquina) to start; (ponerse en marcha) to get going; **~ de** to stem from

arranque etc [a'rranke] VB ver **arrancar** ► NM sudden start; (Auto) start; (fig) fit, outburst

arras ['arras] NFPL pledge sg, security sg

arrasar [arra'sar] /**1a**/ VT (aplanar) to level, flatten; (destruir) to demolish

arrastrado, -a [arras'traðo, a] ADJ poor, wretched

arrastrador [arrastra'ðor] NM (en máquina impresora) tractor

arrastrar [arras'trar] /**1a**/ VT to drag (along); (fig) to drag down, degrade; (suj: agua, viento) to carry away; **llevar algo arrastrado** to drag sth along ► VI to drag, trail on the ground ■ **arrastrarse** VR to crawl; (fig) to grovel

arrastre [a'rrastre] NM drag, dragging; (Deporte) crawl; **estar para el ~** (fig) to have had it

array [a'rrai] NM (Inform) array; **~ empaquetado** (Inform) packed array

arrayán [arra'jan] NM myrtle

arre ['arre] EXCL gee up!

arrear [arre'ar] /**1a**/ VT to drive on, urge on ► VI to hurry along

arrebañar [arreβa'ɲar] /**1a**/ VT (juntar) to scrape together

arrebatado, -a [arreβa'taðo, a] ADJ rash, impetuous; (repentino) sudden, hasty

arrebatar [arreβa'tar] /**1a**/ VT to snatch (away),

seize; (*fig*) to captivate ▪ **arrebatarse** VR to get carried away, get excited

arrebato [arre'βato] NM fit of rage, fury; (*éxtasis*) rapture; **en un ~ de cólera** in an outburst of anger

arrebolar [arreβo'lar] /**1a**/ VT to redden ▪ **arrebolarse** VR (*enrojecer*) to blush

arrebujar [arreβu'xar] /**1a**/ VT (*objetos*) to jumble together ▪ **arrebujarse** VR to wrap o.s. up

arrechar [arre'tʃar] /**1a**/ VT (*AM*) to arouse, excite ▪ **arrecharse** VR to become aroused

arrechucho [arre'tʃutʃo] NM (*Med*) turn

arreciar [arre'θjar] /**1b**/ VI to get worse; (*viento*) to get stronger

arrecife [arre'θife] NM reef

arredrar [arre'ðrar] /**1a**/ VT (*hacer retirarse*) to drive back ▪ **arredrarse** VR (*apartarse*) to draw back; **arredrarse ante algo** to shrink away from sth

arreglado, -a [arre'ɣlaðo, a] ADJ (*ordenado*) neat, orderly; (*moderado*) moderate, reasonable

★**arreglar** [arre'ɣlar] /**1a**/ VT (*poner orden*) to tidy up; (*algo roto*) to fix, repair; (*problema*) to solve ▪ **arreglarse** VR to reach an understanding; **arreglárselas** (*fam*) to get by, manage

arreglo [a'rreɣlo] NM settlement; (*orden*) order; (*acuerdo*) agreement; (*Mus*) arrangement, setting; (*Inform*) array; **con ~ a** in accordance with; **llegar a un ~** to reach a compromise

arrellanarse [arreʎa'narse] /**1a**/ VR to sprawl; **~ en el asiento** to lie back in one's chair

arremangar [arreman'gar] /**1h**/ VT to roll up, turn up ▪ **arremangarse** VR to roll up one's sleeves

arremangue *etc* [arre'mange] VB *ver* **arremangar**

arremeter [arreme'ter] /**2a**/ VT to attack, assault ▸ VI: **~ contra algn** to attack sb

arremetida [arreme'tiða] NF assault

arremolinarse [arremoli'narse] /**1a**/ VR to crowd around, mill around; (*corriente*) to swirl, eddy

arrendador, a [arrenda'ðor, a] NM/F landlord/lady

arrendamiento [arrenda'mjento] NM letting; (*el alquilar*) hiring; (*contrato*) lease; (*alquiler*) rent

arrendar [arren'dar] /**1j**/ VT to let; to hire; to lease; to rent

arrendatario, -a [arrenda'tarjo, a] NM/F tenant

arreos [a'rreos] NMPL (*de caballo*) harness *sg*, trappings

arrepentido, -a [arrepen'tiðo, a] NM/F (*Pol*) reformed terrorist

arrepentimiento [arrepenti'mjento] NM regret, repentance

★**arrepentirse** [arrepen'tirse] /**3i**/ VR to repent; **~ de (haber hecho) algo** to regret (doing) sth

arrepienta *etc* [arre'pjenta], **arrepintiendo** *etc* [arrepin'tjendo] VB *ver* **arrepentirse**

arrestar [arres'tar] /**1a**/ VT to arrest; (*encarcelar*) to imprison

arresto [a'rresto] NM arrest; (*Mil*) detention; (*audacia*) boldness, daring; **~ domiciliario** house arrest

arriar [a'rrjar] /**1c**/ VT (*velas*) to haul down; (*bandera*) to lower, strike; (*un cable*) to pay out

arriate [a'rrjate] NM (*Bot*) bed; (*camino*) road

---

arriba [a'rriβa]

ADV **1** (*posición*) above; **desde arriba** from above; **arriba del todo** at the very top, right on top; **Juan está arriba** Juan is upstairs; **lo arriba mencionado** the aforementioned; **aquí/allí arriba** up here/there; **está hasta arriba de trabajo** (*fam*) he's up to his eyes in work (*fam*)

2 (*dirección*) up, upwards; **más arriba** higher *o* further up; **calle arriba** up the street

3: **de arriba abajo** from top to bottom; **mirar a algn de arriba abajo** to look sb up and down

4: **para arriba**: **de 50 euros para arriba** from 50 euros up(wards); **de la cintura (para) arriba** from the waist up

▸ ADJ: **de arriba: el piso de arriba** the upstairs flat (*BRIT*) *o* apartment; **la parte de arriba** the top *o* upper part

▸ PREP: **arriba de** (*AM*: *por encima de*) above; **arriba de 200 dólares** more than 200 dollars

▸ EXCL: **¡arriba!** up!; **¡manos arriba!** hands up!; **¡arriba España!** long live Spain!

---

arribar [arri'βar] /**1a**/ VI to put into port; (*esp AM*: *llegar*) to arrive

arribista [arri'βista] NMF parvenu(e), upstart

arribo [a'rriβo] NM (*esp AM*) arrival

arriendo *etc* [a'rrjendo] VB *ver* **arrendar** ▸ NM = **arrendamiento**

arriero [a'rrjero] NM muleteer

arriesgado, -a [arrjes'ɣaðo, a] ADJ (*peligroso*) risky; (*audaz*) bold, daring

★**arriesgar** [arrjes'ɣar] /**1h**/ VT to risk; (*poner en peligro*) to endanger ▪ **arriesgarse** VR to take a risk

arriesgue *etc* [a'rrjesɣe] VB *ver* **arriesgar**

arrimar [arri'mar] /**1a**/ VT (*acercar*) to bring close; (*poner de lado*) to set aside ▪ **arrimarse** VR to come close *o* closer; **arrimarse a** to lean on; (*fig*) to keep company with; (*buscar ayuda*) to seek the protection of; **arrímate a mí** cuddle up to me

arrinconado, -a [arrinko'naðo, a] ADJ forgotten, neglected

arrinconar [arrinko'nar] /**1a**/ VT (*colocar*) to put in a corner; (*enemigo*) to corner; (*fig*) to put on one side; (*abandonar*) to push aside

arriscado, -a [arris'kaðo, a] ADJ (*Geo*) craggy; (*fig*) bold, resolute

★**arroba** [aˈrroβa] NF (peso) 25 pounds; (Inform: en dirección electrónica) at sign, @; **tiene talento por arrobas** he has loads o bags of talent

arrobado, -a [arroˈβaðo, a] ADJ entranced, enchanted

arrobamiento [arroβaˈmjento] NM ecstasy

arrobar [arroˈβar] /1a/ VT to enchant ■ **arrobarse** VR to be enraptured; (místico) to go into a trance

arrodillarse [arroðiˈʎarse] /1a/ VR to kneel (down)

arrogancia [arroˈɣanθja] NF arrogance

arrogante [arroˈɣante] ADJ arrogant

★**arrojar** [arroˈxar] /1a/ VT to throw, hurl; (humo) to emit, give out; (Com) to yield, produce ■ **arrojarse** VR to throw o hurl o.s.

arrojo [aˈrroxo] NM daring

arrollador, a [arroˈʎaðor, a] ADJ crushing, overwhelming

arrollar [arroˈʎar] /1a/ VT (enrollar) to roll up; (suj: inundación) to wash away; (Auto) to run over; (Deporte) to crush

arropar [arroˈpar] /1a/ VT to cover (up), wrap up ■ **arroparse** VR to wrap o.s. up

arrostrar [arrosˈtrar] /1a/ VT to face (up to) ■ **arrostrarse** VR: **arrostrarse con algn** to face up to sb

★**arroyo** [aˈrroʝo] NM stream; (de la calle) gutter; **poner a algn en el ~** to turn sb onto the streets

★**arroz** [aˈrroθ] NM rice; **~ con leche** rice pudding

arrozal [arroˈθal] NM paddy field

arruga [aˈrruɣa] NF fold; (de cara) wrinkle; (de vestido) crease

arrugar [arruˈɣar] /1h/ VT to fold; to wrinkle; to crease ■ **arrugarse** VR to get wrinkled; to get creased

arrugue etc [aˈrruɣe] VB ver **arrugar**

★**arruinar** [arrwiˈnar] /1a/ VT to ruin, wreck ■ **arruinarse** VR to be ruined

arrullar [arruˈʎar] /1a/ VI to coo ▶ VT to lull to sleep

arrumaco [arruˈmako] NM (caricia) caress; (halago) piece of flattery

arrumbar [arrumˈbar] /1a/ VT (objeto) to discard; (individuo) to silence

arrurruz [arruˈrruθ] NM arrowroot

arsenal [arseˈnal] NM naval dockyard; (Mil) arsenal

arsénico [arˈseniko] NM arsenic

★**arte** [ˈarte] NM (gen m en sg, f en pl) art; (maña) skill, guile; **por ~ de magia** (as if) by magic; **no tener ~ ni parte en algo** to have nothing whatsoever to do with sth ■ **artes** NFPL arts; **artes y oficios** arts and crafts; **Bellas Artes** Fine Art sg

artefacto [arteˈfakto] NM appliance; (Arqueología) artefact

arteria [arˈterja] NF artery

arterial [arteˈrjal] ADJ arterial; (presión) blood cpd

arterioesclerosis [arterjoeskleˈrosis], **arteriosclerosis** [arterjoskleˈrosis] NF INV hardening of the arteries, arteriosclerosis

artesa [arˈtesa] NF trough

artesanía [artesaˈnia] NF craftsmanship; (artículos) handicrafts pl

artesano, -a [arteˈsano, a] NM/F artisan, craftsman/woman

ártico, -a [ˈartiko, a] ADJ Arctic ▶ NM: **el (océano) Á~** the Arctic (Ocean)

articulación [artikulaˈθjon] NF articulation; (Med, Tec) joint

articulado, -a [artikuˈlaðo, a] ADJ articulated; jointed

articular [artikuˈlar] /1a/ VT to articulate; to join together

articulista [artikuˈlista] NMF columnist, contributor (to a newspaper)

★**artículo** [arˈtikulo] NM article; (cosa) thing, article; (TV) feature, report; **~ de fondo** leader, editorial ■ **artículos** NMPL goods; **artículos de escritorio** stationery; **artículos de marca** (Com) proprietary goods

artífice [arˈtifiθe] NMF artist, craftsman; (fig) architect

artificial [artifiˈθjal] ADJ artificial

artificio [artiˈfiθjo] NM art, skill; (artesanía) craftsmanship; (astucia) cunning

artillería [artiʎeˈria] NF artillery

artillero [artiˈʎero] NM artilleryman, gunner

artilugio [artiˈluxjo] NM gadget

artimaña [artiˈmaɲa] NF trap, snare; (astucia) cunning

★**artista** [arˈtista] NMF (pintor) artist, painter; (Teat) artist, artiste; **~ de cine** film actor/actress

artístico, -a [arˈtistiko, a] ADJ artistic

artritis [arˈtritis] NF arthritis

artrosis [arˈtrosis] NF osteoarthritis

arveja [arˈβexa] NF (AM) pea

Arz. ABR (= Arzobispo) Abp

arzobispo [arθoˈβispo] NM archbishop

as [as] NM ace; **as del fútbol** star player

asa [ˈasa] NF handle; (fig) lever

★**asado** [aˈsaðo] NM roast (meat); (AM: barbacoa) barbecue

asador [asaˈðor] NM (varilla) spit; (aparato) spit roaster

asadura, asaduras [asaˈðura(s)] NF, NFPL entrails pl, offal sg; (Culin) chitterlings pl

asaetear [asaeteˈar] /1a/ VT (fig) to bother

asalariado, -a [asalaˈrjaðo, a] ADJ paid, wage-earning, salaried ▶ NM/F wage earner

asaltador, a [asaltaˈðor, a], **asaltante** [asalˈtante] NM/F assailant

asaltar [asalˈtar] /1a/ VT to attack, assault; (fig) to assail

asalto [aˈsalto] NM attack, assault; (Deporte) round

★asamblea [asam'blea] NF assembly; (*reunión*) meeting

★asar [a'sar] /**1a**/ VT to roast; **~ al horno/a la parrilla** to bake/grill ■ **asarse** VR (*fig*): **me aso de calor** I'm roasting; **aquí se asa uno vivo** it's boiling hot here

asbesto [as'βesto] NM asbestos

ascendencia [asθen'denθja] NF ancestry; (*AM: influencia*) ascendancy; **de ~ francesa** of French origin

ascender [asθen'der] /**2g**/ VI (*subir*) to ascend, rise; (*ser promovido*) to gain promotion; **~ a** to amount to ▶ VT to promote

ascendiente [asθen'djente] NM influence ▶ NMF ancestor

ascensión [asθen'sjon] NF ascent; **la A~** the Ascension

ascenso [as'θenso] NM ascent; (*promoción*) promotion

★ascensor [asθen'sor] NM lift (BRIT), elevator (US)

ascético, -a [as'θetiko, a] ADJ ascetic

ascienda *etc* [as'θjenda] VB *ver* **ascender**

★asco ['asko] NM: **el ajo me da ~** I hate *o* loathe garlic; **hacer ascos de algo** to turn up one's nose at sth; **estar hecho un ~** to be filthy; **poner a algn de ~** to call sb all sorts of names *o* every name under the sun; **¡qué ~!** how revolting *o* disgusting!

ascua ['askwa] NF ember; **arrimar el ~ a su sardina** to look after number one; **estar en ascuas** to be on tenterhooks

aseado, -a [ase'aðo, a] ADJ clean; (*arreglado*) tidy; (*pulcro*) smart

asear [ase'ar] /**1a**/ VT (*lavar*) to wash; (*ordenar*) to tidy (up)

asechanza [ase't∫anθa] NF trap, snare

asediar [ase'ðjar] /**1b**/ VT (*Mil*) to besiege, lay siege to; (*fig*) to chase, pester

asedio [a'seðjo] NM siege; (*Com*) run

asegurado, a [aseɣu'raðo, a] ADJ insured

asegurador, -a [aseɣura'ðor, a] NM/F insurer

★asegurar [aseɣu'rar] /**1a**/ VT (*consolidar*) to secure, fasten; (*dar garantía de*) to guarantee; (*preservar*) to safeguard; (*afirmar, dar por cierto*) to assure, affirm; (*tranquilizar*) to reassure; (*hacer un seguro*) to insure ■ **asegurarse** VR to assure o.s., make sure

asemejarse [aseme'xarse] /**1a**/ VR to be alike; **~ a** to be like, resemble

asentado, -a [asen'taðo, a] ADJ established, settled

asentar [asen'tar] /**1j**/ VT (*sentar*) to seat, sit down; (*poner*) to place, establish; (*alisar*) to level, smooth down *o* out; (*anotar*) to note down ▶ VI to be suitable, suit

asentimiento [asenti'mjento] NM assent, agreement

asentir [asen'tir] /**3i**/ VI to assent, agree; **~ con la cabeza** to nod (one's head)

★aseo [a'seo] NM cleanliness ■ **aseos** NMPL toilet *sg* (BRIT), cloakroom *sg* (BRIT), restroom *sg* (US)

aséptico, -a [a'septiko, a] ADJ germ-free, free from infection

asequible [ase'kiβle] ADJ (*precio*) reasonable; (*meta*) attainable; (*persona*) approachable

aserradero [aserra'ðero] NM sawmill

aserrar [ase'rrar] /**1j**/ VT to saw

★asesinar [asesi'nar] /**1a**/ VT to murder; (*Pol*) to assassinate

> *Asesinar* suele traducirse por **to murder**, pero cuando se trata del asesinato de figuras políticas importantes, como presidentes del gobierno *o* primeros ministros, se utiliza **to assassinate**: *Robert Kennedy fue asesinado en 1968.* **Robert Kennedy was assassinated in 1968.**
> Del mismo modo, **murder** es el sustantivo que se usa normalmente como traducción de *asesinato*, mientras que en el contexto político se habla de **assassination**.

★asesinato [asesi'nato] NM murder; (*Pol*) assassination

asesino, -a [ase'sino, a] NM/F murderer, killer; (*Pol*) assassin

asesor, a [ase'sor, a] NM/F adviser, consultant; (*Com*) assessor, consultant; **~ administrativo** management consultant

asesorar [aseso'rar] /**1a**/ VT (*Jur*) to advise, give legal advice to; (*Com*) to act as consultant to ■ **asesorarse** VR: **asesorarse con** *o* **de** to take advice from, consult

asesoría [aseso'ria] NF (*cargo*) consultancy; (*oficina*) consultant's office

asestar [ases'tar] /**1a**/ VT (*golpe*) to deal; (*arma*) to aim; (*tiro*) to fire

aseverar [aseβe'rar] /**1a**/ VT to assert

asfaltado, -a [asfal'taðo, a] ADJ asphalted ▶ NM (*pavimento*) asphalt

asfalto [as'falto] NM asphalt

asfixia [as'fiksja] NF asphyxia, suffocation

asfixiar [asfik'sjar] /**1b**/ VT to asphyxiate, suffocate ■ **asfixiarse** VR to be asphyxiated, suffocate

asga *etc* ['asɣa] VB *ver* **asir**

★así [a'si] ADV (*de esta manera*) in this way, like this, thus; (*aunque*) although; (*tan pronto como*) as soon as; **~ que** so; **~ como** as well as; **~ y todo** even so; **¿no es ~?** isn't it?, didn't you? *etc*; **~ de grande** this big; **¡~ sea!** so be it!; **~ es la vida** such is life, that's life

★Asia ['asja] NF Asia

asiático, -a [a'sjatiko, a] ADJ, NM/F Asian, Asiatic

asidero [asi'ðero] NM handle

asiduidad [asiðwi'ðað] NF assiduousness

asiduo, -a [a'siðwo, a] ADJ assiduous; (*frecuente*) frequent ▶ NM/F regular (customer)

★asiento [a'sjento] vb ver **asentar**; **asentir** ▶ NM (*mueble*) seat, chair; (*de coche, en tribunal etc*) seat; (*localidad*) seat, place; (*fundamento*) site; **~ delantero/trasero** front/back seat

asierre etc [a'sjerre] vb ver **aserrar**

asignación [asiɣna'θjon] NF (*atribución*) assignment; (*reparto*) allocation; (*sueldo*) salary; (*Com*) allowance; **~ (semanal)** (weekly) pocket money; **~ de presupuesto** budget appropriation

asignar [asiɣ'nar] /1a/ vt to assign, allocate

★asignatura [asiɣna'tura] NF subject; (*curso*) course; **~ pendiente** (*fig*) matter pending

asilado, -a [asi'laðo, a] NM/F refugee

asilo [a'silo] NM (*refugio*) asylum, refuge; (*establecimiento*) home, institution; **~ político** political asylum

asimilación [asimila'θjon] NF assimilation

asimilar [asimi'lar] /1a/ vt to assimilate

asimismo [asi'mismo] ADV in the same way, likewise

asintiendo etc [asin'tjendo] vb ver **asentir**

asir [a'sir] /3a/ vt to seize, grasp ■ **asirse** vr to take hold; **asirse a** o **de** to seize

asistencia [asis'tenθja] NF presence; (*Teat*) audience; (*Med*) attendance; (*ayuda*) assistance; **~ social** social o welfare work; **~ en carretera** roadside assistance

asistente, -a [asis'tente, a] NM/F assistant; **los asistentes** those present; **~ social** social worker ▶ NM (*Mil*) orderly ▶ NF daily help

asistido, -a [asis'tiðo, a] ADJ (*Auto: dirección*) power-assisted; **~ por ordenador** computer-aided

★asistir [asis'tir] /3a/ vt to assist, help ▶ vi: **~ a** to attend, be present at

asma ['asma] NF asthma

asno ['asno] NM donkey; (*fig*) ass

asociación [asoθja'θjon] NF association; (*Com*) partnership

asociado, -a [aso'θjaðo, a] ADJ associate ▶ NM/F associate; (*Com*) partner

asociar [aso'θjar] /1b/ vt to associate ■ **asociarse** vr to become partners

asolar [aso'lar] /1a/ vt to destroy

asolear [asole'ar] /1a/ vt to put in the sun ■ **asolearse** vr to sunbathe

asomar [aso'mar] /1a/ vt to show, stick out; **~ la cabeza por la ventana** to put one's head out of the window ▶ vi to appear ■ **asomarse** vr to appear, show up

★asombrar [asom'brar] /1a/ vt to amaze, astonish ■ **asombrarse** vr: **asombrarse (de)** (*sorprenderse*) to be amazed (at); (*asustarse*) to be frightened (at)

asombro [a'sombro] NM amazement, astonishment; (*susto*) fright

★asombroso, -a [asom'broso, a] ADJ amazing, astonishing

asomo [a'somo] NM hint, sign; **ni por ~** by no means

asonancia [aso'nanθja] NF (*Lit*) assonance; (*fig*) connection; **no tener ~ con** to bear no relation to

asorocharse [asoro'tʃarse] /1a/ vr (*Am*) to get mountain sickness

aspa ['aspa] NF (*cruz*) cross; (*de molino*) sail; **en ~** X-shaped

aspaviento [aspa'βjento] NM exaggerated display of feeling; (*fam*) fuss

★aspecto [as'pekto] NM (*apariencia*) look, appearance; (*fig*) aspect; **bajo ese ~** from that point of view

aspereza [aspe'reθa] NF roughness; (*de fruta*) sharpness; (*de carácter*) surliness

áspero, -a ['aspero, a] ADJ (*al tacto*) rough; (*al gusto*) sharp, sour; (*voz*) harsh

aspersión [asper'sjon] NF sprinkling; (*Agr*) spraying

aspersor [asper'sor] NM sprinkler

aspiración [aspira'θjon] NF breath, inhalation; (*Mus*) short pause ■ **aspiraciones** NFPL (*ambiciones*) aspirations

aspirador [aspira'ðor] NM = **aspiradora**

★aspiradora [aspira'ðora] NF vacuum cleaner, Hoover®

aspirante [aspi'rante] NMF (*candidato*) candidate; (*Deporte*) contender

aspirar [aspi'rar] /1a/ vt to breathe in ▶ vi: **~ a** to aspire to

★aspirina [aspi'rina] NF aspirin

asquear [aske'ar] /1a/ vt to sicken ▶ vi to be sickening ■ **asquearse** vr to feel disgusted

asquerosidad [askerosi'ðað] NF (*suciedad*) filth; (*dicho*) obscenity; (*faena*) dirty trick

★asqueroso, -a [aske'roso, a] ADJ disgusting, sickening

asta ['asta] NF lance; (*arpón*) spear; (*mango*) shaft, handle; (*Zool*) horn; **a media ~** at half mast

astado, -a [as'taðo, a] ADJ horned ▶ NM bull

asterisco [aste'risko] NM asterisk

asteroide [aste'roiðe] NM asteroid

astigmatismo [astiɣma'tismo] NM astigmatism

astilla [as'tiʎa] NF splinter; (*pedacito*) chip ■ **astillas** NFPL (*leña*) firewood sg

astillarse [asti'ʎarse] /1a/ vr to splinter; (*fig*) to shatter

astillero [asti'ʎero] NM shipyard

astringente [astrin'xente] ADJ, NM astringent

astro ['astro] NM star

astrología [astrolo'xia] NF astrology

astrólogo, -a [as'troloɣo, a] NM/F astrologer

astronauta [astro'nauta] NMF astronaut

astronave [astro'naβe] NM spaceship

astronomía [astrono'mia] NF astronomy

astronómico, -a [astroˈnomiko, a] ADJ (tb fig) astronomical

astrónomo, -a [asˈtronomo, a] NM/F astronomer

astroso, -a [asˈtroso, a] ADJ (desaliñado) untidy; (vil) contemptible

astucia [asˈtuθja] NF astuteness; (destreza) clever trick

asturiano, -a [astuˈrjano, a] ADJ, NM/F Asturian

Asturias [asˈturjas] NFPL Asturias; **Príncipe de ~** crown prince

astuto, -a [asˈtuto, a] ADJ astute; (taimado) cunning

asueto [aˈsweto] NM holiday; (tiempo libre) time off; **día de ~** day off; **tarde de ~** (trabajo) afternoon off; (Escol) half-holiday

asumir [asuˈmir] /3a/ VT to assume

asunción [asunˈθjon] NF assumption; **la A~** the Assumption

★**asunto** [aˈsunto] NM (tema) matter, subject; (negocio) business; **¡eso es ~ mío!** that's my business!; **asuntos exteriores** foreign affairs; **asuntos a tratar** agenda sg

asustadizo, -a [asustaˈðiθo, a] ADJ easily frightened

asustar [asusˈtar] /1a/ VT to frighten ■ **asustarse** VR to be/become frightened

atacante [ataˈkante] NMF attacker

★**atacar** [ataˈkar] /1g/ VT to attack

atadura [ataˈðura] NF bond, tie

atajar [ataˈxar] /1a/ VT (enfermedad, mal) to stop; (ruta de fuga) to cut off; (discurso) to interrupt ▶ VI (persona) to take a short cut

atajo [aˈtaxo] NM short cut; (Deporte) tackle

atalaya [ataˈlaja] NF watchtower

atañer [ataˈɲer] /2f/ VI: **~ a** to concern; **en lo que atañe a eso** with regard to that

ataque etc [aˈtake] VB ver **atacar** ▶ NM attack; **~ cardíaco** heart attack

★**atar** [aˈtar] /1a/ VT to tie, tie up; **~ la lengua a algn** (fig) to silence sb

atarantado, -a [ataranˈtaðo, a] ADJ (Am: aturdido) dazed

atardecer [atarðeˈθer] /2d/ VI to get dark ▶ NM evening; (crepúsculo) dusk

atardezca etc [atarˈðeθka] VB ver **atardecer**

atareado, -a [atareˈaðo, a] ADJ busy

atascar [atasˈkar] /1g/ VT to clog up; (obstruir) to jam; (fig) to hinder ■ **atascarse** VR to stall; (cañería) to get blocked up; (fig) to get bogged down; (en discurso) to dry up

★**atasco** [aˈtasko] NM obstruction; (Auto) traffic jam

atasque etc [aˈtaske] VB ver **atascar**

ataúd [ataˈuð] NM coffin

ataviar [ataˈβjar] /1c/ VT to deck, array ■ **ataviarse** VR to dress up

atavío [ataˈβio] NM attire, dress ■ **atavíos** NMPL finery sg

ateísmo [ateˈismo] NM atheism

atemorice etc [atemoˈriθe] VB ver **atemorizar**

atemorizar [atemoriˈθar] /1f/ VT to frighten, scare ■ **atemorizarse** VR to get frightened o scared

Atenas [aˈtenas] NF Athens

★**atención** [atenˈθjon] NF attention; (bondad) kindness; **en ~ a esto** in view of this ▶ EXCL (be) careful!, look out!

atender [atenˈder] /2g/ VT to attend to, look after; (Tec) to service; (enfermo) to care for; (ruego) to comply with; (Telec) to answer; **~ a** to attend to; (detalles) to take care of ▶ VI to pay attention

atendré etc [atenˈdre] VB ver **atenerse**

atenerse [ateˈnerse] /2k/ VR: **~ a** to abide by, adhere to

atenga etc [aˈtenga] VB ver **atenerse**

ateniense [ateˈnjense] ADJ, NMF Athenian

atentado [atenˈtaðo] NM crime, illegal act; (asalto) assault; (tb: **atentado terrorista**) terrorist attack; **~ contra la vida de algn** attempt on sb's life; **~ golpista** attempted coup; **~ suicida** suicide bombing, suicide attack

★**atentamente** [atentaˈmente] ADV: **Le saluda ~** Yours faithfully

atentar [atenˈtar] /1a/ VI: **~ a** o **contra** to commit an outrage against

★**atento, -a** [aˈtento, a] ADJ attentive, observant; (cortés) polite, thoughtful; **estar ~ a** (explicación) to pay attention to; **su atenta (carta)** (Com) your letter

atenuante [ateˈnwante] ADJ: **circunstancias atenuantes** extenuating o mitigating circumstances ▶ NF: **atenuantes** extenuating o mitigating circumstances

atenuar [ateˈnwar] /1e/ VT to attenuate; (disminuir) to lessen, minimize

ateo, -a [aˈteo, a] ADJ atheistic ▶ NM/F atheist

aterciopelado, -a [aterθjopeˈlaðo, a] ADJ velvety

aterido, -a [ateˈriðo, a] ADJ: **~ de frío** frozen stiff

aterrador, a [aterraˈðor, a] ADJ frightening

aterrar [ateˈrrar] /1a/ VT to frighten; (aterrorizar) to terrify ■ **aterrarse** VR to be frightened; to be terrified

aterrice etc [ateˈrriθe] VB ver **aterrizar**

★**aterrizaje** [aterriˈθaxe] NM landing; **~ forzoso** emergency o forced landing

★**aterrizar** [aterriˈθar] /1f/ VI to land

aterrorice etc [aterroˈriθe] VB ver **aterrorizar**

aterrorizar [aterroriˈθar] /1f/ VT to terrify

atesorar [atesoˈrar] /1a/ VT to hoard, store up

atestado, -a [atesˈtaðo, a] ADJ packed ▶ NM (Jur) affidavit

atestar [atesˈtar] /1a, 1j/ VT to pack, stuff; (Jur) to attest, testify to

atestiguar [atesti'ɣwar] /**1i**/ VT to testify to, bear witness to

atestigüe etc [ates'tiɣwe] VB ver **atestiguar**

atiborrar [atiβo'rrar] /**1a**/ VT to fill, stuff ■ **atiborrarse** VR to stuff o.s.

atice etc [a'tiθe] VB ver **atizar**

★**ático** ['atiko] NM (desván) attic; ~ **de lujo** penthouse flat

atienda etc [a'tjenda] VB ver **atender**

atildar [atil'dar] /**1a**/ VT to criticize; (Tip) to put a tilde over ■ **atildarse** VR to spruce o.s. up

atinado, -a [ati'naðo, a] ADJ correct; (sensato) wise, sensible

atinar [ati'nar] /**1a**/ VI (acertar) to be right; ~ **con** o **en** (solución) to hit upon; ~ **al blanco** to hit the target; (fig) to be right; ~ **a hacer** to manage to do

atípico, -a [a'tipiko, a] ADJ atypical

atiplado, -a [ati'plaðo, a] ADJ (voz) high-pitched

atisbar [atis'βar] /**1a**/ VT to spy on; (echar ojeada) to peep at

atizar [ati'θar] /**1f**/ VT to poke; (horno etc) to stoke; (fig) to stir up, rouse

atlántico, -a [at'lantiko, a] ADJ Atlantic ▶ NM: **el (océano) A~** the Atlantic (Ocean)

atlas ['atlas] NM INV atlas

★**atleta** [at'leta] NMF athlete

atlético, -a [at'letiko, a] ADJ athletic

★**atletismo** [atle'tismo] NM athletics sg

★**atmósfera** [at'mosfera] NF atmosphere

atmosférico, -a [atmos'feriko, a] ADJ atmospheric

atol [a'tol], **atole** [a'tole] NM (AM) cornflour drink

atolladero [atoʎa'ðero] NM: **estar en un ~** to be in a jam

atollarse [ato'ʎarse] /**1a**/ VR to get stuck; (fig) to get into a jam

atolondrado, -a [atolon'draðo, a] ADJ scatterbrained

atolondramiento [atolondra'mjento] NM bewilderment; (insensatez) silliness

atómico, -a [a'tomiko, a] ADJ atomic

atomizador [atomiθa'ðor] NM atomizer

átomo ['atomo] NM atom

★**atónito, -a** [a'tonito, a] ADJ astonished, amazed

atontado, -a [aton'taðo, a] ADJ stunned; (bobo) silly, daft

atontar [aton'tar] /**1a**/ VT to stun ■ **atontarse** VR to become confused

atorar [ato'rar] /**1a**/ VT to obstruct ■ **atorarse** VR (atragantarse) to choke

atormentar [atormen'tar] /**1a**/ VT to torture; (molestar) to torment; (acosar) to plague, harass

atornillar [atorni'ʎar] /**1a**/ VT to screw on o down

atorón [ato'ron] NM (AM) traffic jam

atosigar [atosi'ɣar] /**1h**/ VT to harass, pester

atosigue etc [ato'siɣe] VB ver **atosigar**

atrabiliario, -a [atraβi'ljarjo, a] ADJ bad-tempered

atracadero [atraka'ðero] NM pier

atracador, a [atraka'ðor, a] NM/F robber

★**atracar** [atra'kar] /**1g**/ VT (Naut) to moor; (robar) to hold up, rob ▶ VI to moor ■ **atracarse** VR: **atracarse (de)** (fam) to stuff o.s. (with)

atracción [atrak'θjon] NF attraction

★**atraco** [a'trako] NM holdup, robbery

atracón [atra'kon] NM: **darse** o **pegarse un ~ (de)** (fam) to stuff o.s. (with)

★**atractivo, -a** [atrak'tiβo, a] ADJ attractive ▶ NM appeal; (belleza) attractiveness

★**atraer** [atra'er] /**2o**/ VT to attract; **dejarse ~ por** to be tempted by

atragantarse [atraɣan'tarse] /**1a**/ VR: ~ **(con algo)** to choke (on sth); **se me ha atragantado el chico ese/el inglés** I can't stand that boy/English

atraiga etc [a'traiɣa], **atraje** etc [a'traxe] VB ver **atraer**

atrancar [atran'kar] /**1g**/ VT (con tranca, barra) to bar, bolt

atranque etc [a'tranke] VB ver **atrancar**

atrapar [atra'par] /**1a**/ VT to trap; (resfriado etc) to catch

atraque etc [a'trake] VB ver **atracar**

★**atrás** [a'tras] ADV (movimiento) back(wards); (lugar) behind; (tiempo) previously; **ir hacia ~** to go back(wards); to go to the rear; **estar ~** to be behind o at the back

★**atrasado, -a** [atra'saðo, a] ADJ slow; (pago) overdue, late; (país) backward

★**atrasar** [atra'sar] /**1a**/ VI to be slow ■ **atrasarse** VR to stay behind; (tren) to be o run late; (llegar tarde) to be late

atraso [a'traso] NM slowness; lateness, delay; (de país) backwardness ■ **atrasos** NMPL (Com) arrears

atravesado, -a [atraβe'saðo, a] ADJ: **un tronco ~ en la carretera** a tree trunk lying across the road

★**atravesar** [atraβe'sar] /**1j**/ VT (cruzar) to cross (over); (traspasar) to pierce; (período) to go through; (poner al través) to lay o put across ■ **atravesarse** VR to come in between; (intervenir) to interfere

atraviese etc [atra'βjese] VB ver **atravesar**

atrayendo [atra'jendo] VB ver **atraer**

atrayente [atra'jente] ADJ attractive

★**atreverse** [atre'βerse] /**2a**/ VR to dare; (insolentarse) to be insolent

★**atrevido, -a** [atre'βiðo, a] ADJ daring; insolent

atrevimiento [atreβi'mjento] NM daring; insolence

atribución [atriβu'θjon] NF (Lit) attribution ■ **atribuciones** NFPL (Pol) powers, functions; (Admin) responsibilities

atribuir [atriβu'ir] /3g/ VT to attribute; (funciones) to confer

atribular [atriβu'lar] /1a/ VT to afflict, distress

atributo [atri'βuto] NM attribute

atribuya etc [atri'βuja], **atribuyendo** etc [atriβu'jendo] VB ver **atribuir**

atril [a'tril] NM (para libro) lectern; (Mus) music stand

atrincherarse [atrintʃe'rarse] /1a/ VR (Mil) to dig (o.s.) in; ~ **en** (fig) to hide behind

atrio ['atrjo] NM (Rel) porch

atrocidad [atroθi'ðað] NF atrocity, outrage

atrofiado, -a [atro'fjaðo, a] ADJ (extremidad) withered

atrofiarse [atro'fjarse] /1b/ VR (tb fig) to atrophy

atronador, a [atrona'ðor, a] ADJ deafening

★**atropellar** [atrope'ʎar] /1a/ VT (derribar) to knock over o down; (empujar) to push (aside); (Auto) to run over o down; (agraviar) to insult ■ **atropellarse** VR to act hastily

atropello [atro'peʎo] NM (Auto) accident; (empujón) push; (agravio) wrong; (atrocidad) outrage

atroz [a'troθ] ADJ atrocious, awful

ATS [ate'ese] NMF INV (= Ayudante Técnico Sanitario) nurse

attrezzo [a'treθo] NM props pl

atuendo [a'twendo] NM attire

atufar [atu'far] /1a/ VT (suj: olor) to overcome; (molestar) to irritate ■ **atufarse** VR (fig) to get cross

★**atún** [a'tun] NM tuna, tunny

aturdir [atur'ðir] /3a/ VT to stun; (suj: ruido) to deafen; (fig) to dumbfound, bewilder

aturrullar /1a/, **aturullar** /1a/ [atur(r)u'ʎar] VT to bewilder

atusar [atu'sar] /1a/ VT (cortar) to trim; (alisar) to smooth (down)

atuve etc [a'tuβe] VB ver **atenerse**

audacia [au'ðaθja] NF boldness, audacity

audaz [au'ðaθ] ADJ bold, audacious

audible [au'ðiβle] ADJ audible

audición [auði'θjon] NF hearing; (Teat) audition; ~ **radiofónica** radio concert

audiencia [au'ðjenθja] NF audience; (Jur) high court; (Pol): ~ **pública** public inquiry

audífono [au'ðifono] NM (para sordos) hearing aid

audioguía [auðjo'ɣia] NF audioguide

audiovisual [auðjoβi'swal] ADJ audio-visual

auditivo, -a [auði'tiβo, a] ADJ hearing cpd; (conducto, nervio) auditory

auditor [auði'tor] NM (Jur) judge advocate; (Com) auditor

auditoría [auðito'ria] NF audit; (profesión) auditing

auditorio [auði'torjo] NM audience; (sala) auditorium

auge ['auxe] NM boom; (clímax) climax; (Econ) expansion; **estar en ~** to thrive

augurar [auɣu'rar] /1a/ VT to predict; (presagiar) to portend

augurio [au'ɣurjo] NM omen

★**aula** ['aula] NF classroom; (en universidad etc) lecture room

aullar [au'ʎar] /1a/ VI to howl, yell

aullido [au'ʎiðo] NM howl, yell

★**aumentar** [aumen'tar] /1a/ VT to increase; (precios) to put up; (producción) to step up; (con microscopio, anteojos) to magnify ▶ VI to increase, be on the increase

★**aumento** [au'mento] NM increase; rise

★**aun** [a'un] ADV even; ~ **así** even so; ~ **más** even o yet more

★**aún** [a'un] ADV still, yet; ~ **está aquí** he's still here; ~ **no lo sabemos** we don't know yet; **¿no ha venido ~?** hasn't she come yet?

★**aunque** [a'unke] CONJ though, although, even though

aúpa [a'upa] EXCL up!, come on!; (fam): **una función de ~** a slap-up do; **una paliza de ~** a good hiding

aupar [au'par] /1a/ VT (levantar) to help up; (fig) to praise

aura ['aura] NF (atmósfera) aura

aureola [aure'ola] NF halo

auricular [auriku'lar] NM (Telec) earpiece, receiver ■ **auriculares** NMPL (cascos) headphones

aurora [au'rora] NF dawn; ~ **boreal** northern lights pl

auscultar [auskul'tar] /1a/ VT (Med: pecho) to listen to, sound

★**ausencia** [au'senθja] NF absence

ausentarse [ausen'tarse] /1a/ VR to go away; (por poco tiempo) to go out

★**ausente** [au'sente] ADJ absent ▶ NMF (Escol) absentee; (Jur) missing person

auspiciar [auspi'sjar] /1b/ VT (AM) to back, sponsor

auspicios [aus'piθjos] NMPL auspices; (protección) protection sg

austericidio [austeri'θiðjo] NM impact of austerity

austeridad [austeri'ðað] NF austerity

austero, -a [aus'tero, a] ADJ austere

austral [aus'tral] ADJ southern ▶ NM monetary unit of Argentina (1985-1991)

★**Australia** [aus'tralja] NF Australia

australiano, -a [austra'ljano, a] ADJ, NM/F Australian

★**Austria** ['austrja] NF Austria

★**austriaco, -a** [aus'trjako, a], **austríaco, -a** [aus'triako, a] ADJ Austrian ▶ NM/F Austrian

autenticar [autenti'kar] /**1g**/ VT to authenticate

auténtico, -a [au'tentiko, a] ADJ authentic

autentificar [autentifi'kar] /**1g**/ VT to authenticate

autentique *etc* [auten'tike] VB *ver* **autenticar**

auto ['auto] NM (*coche*) car; (*Jur*) edict, decree; (: *orden*) writ; **~ de comparecencia** summons, subpoena; **~ de ejecución** writ of execution ■ **autos** NMPL (*Jur*) proceedings; (: *acta*) court record *sg*

autoadhesivo, -a [autoaðe'siβo, a] ADJ self-adhesive; (*sobre*) self-sealing

autoalimentación [autoalimenta'θjon] NF (*Inform*): **~ de hojas** automatic paper feed

autobiografía [autoβjoɣra'fia] NF autobiography

autobomba [auto'bomba] NM (*RPL*) fire engine

autobronceador, a [autoβronθea'ðor, a] ADJ (self-)tanning

★**autobús** [auto'βus] NM bus; **~ de línea** long-distance coach

★**autocar** [auto'kar] NM coach (*BRIT*), (passenger) bus (*US*); **~ de línea** intercity coach *or* bus

autocomprobación [autokomproβa'θjon] NF (*Inform*) self-test

autóctono, -a [au'toktono, a] ADJ native, indigenous

autodefensa [autoðe'fensa] NF self-defence

autodeterminación [autoðetermina'θjon] NF self-determination

autodidacta [autoðiˈðakta] ADJ self-taught ▶ NMF: **ser un(a) ~** to be self-taught

autoescuela [autoes'kwela] NF (*ESP*) driving school

autofinanciado, -a [autofinan'θjaðo, a] ADJ self-financing

autofoto [auto'foto] NF selfie

autogestión [autoxes'tjon] NF self-management

autógrafo [au'toɣrafo] NM autograph

autolesionarse [auto'lesjonarsi] VT to self-harm

automación [automa'θjon] NF = **automatización**

autómata [au'tomata] NM automaton

automáticamente [auto'matikamente] ADV automatically

automatice *etc* [automa'tiθe] VB *ver* **automatizar**

automático, -a [auto'matiko, a] ADJ automatic ▶ NM press stud

automatización [automatiθa'θjon] NF: **~ de fábricas** factory automation; **~ de oficinas** office automation

automatizar [automati'θar] /**1f**/ VT to automate

automontable [automon'taβle] ADJ self-assembly

automotor, -triz [automo'tor, 'triθ] ADJ self-propelled ▶ NM diesel train

automóvil [auto'moβil] NM (motor) car (*BRIT*), automobile (*US*)

automovilismo [automoβi'lismo] NM (*actividad*) motoring; (*Deporte*) motor racing

automovilista [automoβi'lista] NMF motorist, driver

automovilístico, -a [automoβi'listiko, a] ADJ (*industria*) car *cpd*

autonomía [autono'mia] NF autonomy; (*ESP Pol*) autonomy, self-government; (: *comunidad*) autonomous region

autonómico, -a [auto'nomiko, a] ADJ (*ESP Pol*) relating to autonomy, autonomous; **gobierno ~** autonomous government

autónomo, -a [au'tonomo, a] ADJ autonomous; (*Inform*) stand-alone, offline

★**autopista** [auto'pista] NF motorway (*BRIT*), freeway (*US*); **~ de cuota** (*AM*), **~ de peaje** (*ESP*) toll (*BRIT*) *o* turnpike (*US*) road

autopsia [au'topsja] NF post-mortem, autopsy

★**autor, a** [au'tor, a] NM/F author; **los autores del atentado** those responsible for the attack

autorice *etc* [auto'riθe] VB *ver* **autorizar**

★**autoridad** [autori'ðað] NF authority; **~ local** local authority

autoritario, -a [autori'tarjo, a] ADJ authoritarian

autorización [autoriθa'θjon] NF authorization

autorizado, -a [autori'θaðo, a] ADJ authorized; (*aprobado*) approved

autorizar [autori'θar] /**1f**/ VT to authorize; to approve

autorretrato [autorre'trato] NM self-portrait

★**autoservicio** [autoser'βiðjo] NM (*tienda*) self-service shop *o* store; (*restaurante*) self-service restaurant

★**autostop** [auto'stop] NM hitch-hiking; **hacer ~** to hitch-hike

autostopista [autosto'pista] NMF hitch-hiker

autosuficiencia [autosufi'θjenθja] NF self-sufficiency

autosuficiente [autosufi'θjente] ADJ self-sufficient; (*pey*) smug

autosugestión [autosuxes'tjon] NF autosuggestion

autovía [auto'βia] NF ≈ dual carriageway (*BRIT*), ≈ divided highway (*US*)

auxiliar [auksi'ljar] /**1b**/ VT to help ▶ NMF assistant

auxilio [auk'siljo] NM assistance, help; **primeros auxilios** first aid *sg*

Av ABR (= *Avenida*) Av(e)

a/v ABR (*Com*: = *a vista*) at sight

aval [a'βal] NM guarantee; (*persona*) guarantor

avalancha [aβa'lantʃa] NF avalanche

avalar [aβa'lar] /**1a**/ VT (*Com etc*) to underwrite; (*fig*) to endorse

avalista [aβa'lista] NM (*Com*) endorser

avance [a'βanθe] VB *ver* **avanzar** ▶ NM advance; (*pago*) advance payment; (*Cine*) trailer

avanzado, -a [aβan'θaðo, a] ADJ advanced; **de edad avanzada, ~ de edad** elderly

avanzar [aβan'θar] /**1f**/ VT, VI to advance

avaricia [aβa'riθja] NF avarice, greed

★**avaricioso, -a** [aβari'θjoso, a] ADJ avaricious, greedy

★**avaro, -a** [a'βaro, a] ADJ miserly, mean ▶ NM/F miser

avasallar [aβasa'ʎar] /**1a**/ VT to subdue, subjugate

avatar [aβa'tar] NM change; **avatares** ups and downs

Avda. ABR (= *Avenida*) Av(e)

AVE ['aβe] NM ABR (= *Alta Velocidad Española*) ≈ bullet train

★**ave** ['aβe] NF bird; **~ de rapiña** bird of prey

avecinarse [aβeθi'narse] /**1a**/ VR (*tormenta, fig*) to approach, be on the way

avejentar [aβexen'tar] /**1a**/ VT, VI, **avejentarse** VR to age

avellana [aβe'ʎana] NF hazelnut

avellano [aβe'ʎano] NM hazel tree

avemaría [aβema'ria] NM Hail Mary, Ave Maria

avena [a'βena] NF oats *pl*

avendré *etc* [aβen'dre], **avenga** *etc* [a'βenga] VB *ver* **avenir**

★**avenida** [aβe'niða] NF (*calle*) avenue

avenir [aβe'nir] /**3a**/ VT to reconcile ■ **avenirse** VR to come to an agreement, reach a compromise

aventado, -a [aβen'taðo, a] ADJ (*AM*) daring

aventajado, -a [aβenta'xaðo, a] ADJ outstanding

aventajar [aβenta'xar] /**1a**/ VT (*sobrepasar*) to surpass, outstrip

aventar [aβen'tar] /**1j**/ VT to fan, blow; (*grano*) to winnow; (*AM fam: echar*) to chuck out

aventón [aβen'ton] NM (*AM*) push; **pedir ~** to hitch a lift, hitch a ride (*US*)

★**aventura** [aβen'tura] NF adventure; **~ sentimental** love affair

aventurado, -a [aβentu'raðo, a] ADJ risky

aventurar [aβentu'rar] /**1a**/ VT to risk ■ **aventurarse** VR to dare; **aventurarse a hacer algo** to venture to do sth

aventurero, -a [aβentu'rero, a] ADJ adventurous

avergoncé [aβeryon'θe], **avergoncemos** *etc* [aβeryon'θemos] VB *ver* **avergonzar**

avergonzar [aβeryon'θar] /**1f, 1l**/ VT to shame; (*desconcertar*) to embarrass ■ **avergonzarse** VR to be ashamed; to be embarrassed

avergüence *etc* [aβer'ɣwenθe] VB *ver* **avergonzar**

★**avería** [aβe'ria] NF (*Tec*) breakdown, fault

averiado, -a [aβe'rjaðo, a] ADJ broken-down; **"~"** "out of order"

averiar [aβe'rjar] /**1c**/ VT to break ■ **averiarse** VR to break down

averiguación [aβeriɣwa'θjon] NF investigation

★**averiguar** [aβeri'ɣwar] /**1i**/ VT to investigate; (*descubrir*) to find out, ascertain

averigüe *etc* [aβe'riɣwe] VB *ver* **averiguar**

aversión [aβer'sjon] NF aversion, dislike; **cobrar ~ a** to take a strong dislike to

avestruz [aβes'truθ] NM ostrich

aviación [aβja'θjon] NF aviation; (*fuerzas aéreas*) air force

aviado, -a [a'βjaðo, a] ADJ: **estar ~** to be in a mess

aviador, a [aβja'ðor, a] NM/F aviator, airman/ woman

aviar [a'βjar] /**1c**/ VT to prepare, get ready

avícola [a'βikola] ADJ poultry *cpd*

avicultura [aβikul'tura] NF poultry farming

avidez [aβi'ðeθ] NF avidity, eagerness

ávido, -a ['aβiðo, a] ADJ avid, eager

aviente *etc* [a'βjente] VB *ver* **aventar**

avieso, -a [a'βjeso, a] ADJ (*torcido*) distorted; (*perverso*) wicked

avinagrado, -a [aβina'ɣraðo, a] ADJ sour, acid

avinagrarse [aβina'ɣrarse] /**1a**/ VR to go o turn sour

avine *etc* [a'βine] VB *ver* **avenir**

Aviñón [aβi'ɲon] NM Avignon

avío [a'βio] NM preparation ■ **avíos** NMPL gear *sg*, kit *sg*

★**avión** [a'βjon] NM aeroplane; (*ave*) martin; **~ de reacción** jet (plane); **por ~** (*Correos*) by air mail

avioneta [aβjo'neta] NF light aircraft

★**avisar** [aβi'sar] /**1a**/ VT (*advertir*) to warn, notify; (*informar*) to tell; (*aconsejar*) to advise, counsel

★**aviso** [a'βiso] NM warning; (*noticia*) notice; (*Com*) demand note; (*Inform*) prompt; **~ escrito** notice in writing; **sin previo ~** without warning; **estar sobre ~** to be on the look-out

★**avispa** [a'βispa] NF wasp

avispado, -a [aβis'paðo, a] ADJ sharp, clever

avispero [aβis'pero] NM wasp's nest

avispón [aβis'pon] NM hornet

avistar [aβis'tar] /**1a**/ VT to sight, spot

avitaminosis [aβitami'nosis] NF INV vitamin deficiency

avituallar [aβitwa'ʎar] /**1a**/ VT to supply with food

avivar [aβi'βar] /**1a**/ VT to strengthen, intensify

■ **avivarse** VR to revive, acquire new life

avizor [aβiˈθor] ADJ: **estar ojo ~** to be on the alert

avizorar [aβiθoˈrar] /**1a**/ VT to spy on

axila [akˈsila] NF armpit

axioma [akˈsjoma] NM axiom

★**ay** [ai] EXCL (dolor) ow!, ouch!; (aflicción) oh!, oh dear!; **¡ay de mí!** poor me!

aya [ˈaja] NF governess; (niñera) nanny

★**ayer** [aˈjer] ADV, NM yesterday; **antes de ~** the day before yesterday; **~ por la tarde** yesterday afternoon/evening; **~ mismo** only yesterday

aymara, aymará [aiˈmara, aimaˈra] ADJ, NMF Aymara

ayo [ˈajo] NM tutor

ayote [aˈjote] NM (Am) pumpkin

Ayto. ABR = **ayuntamiento**

★**ayuda** [aˈjuða] NF help, assistance; (Med) enema; **~ humanitaria** humanitarian aid ▶ NM page

ayudante, -a [ajuˈðante, a] NM/F assistant, helper; (Escol) assistant; (Mil) adjutant

★**ayudar** [ajuˈðar] /**1a**/ VT to help, assist

ayunar [ajuˈnar] /**1a**/ VI to fast

ayunas [aˈjunas] NFPL: **estar en ~** (no haber comido) to be fasting; (ignorar) to be in the dark

ayuno [aˈjuno] NM fast; fasting

★**ayuntamiento** [ajuntaˈmjento] NM (consejo) town/city council; (edificio) town/city hall; (cópula) sexual intercourse

azabache [aθaˈβatʃe] NM jet

azada [aˈθaða] NF hoe

★**azafata** [aθaˈfata] NF air hostess (BRIT) o stewardess

azafate [asaˈfate] NM (Am) tray

azafrán [aθaˈfran] NM saffron

azahar [aθaˈar] NM orange/lemon blossom

azalea [aθaˈlea] NF azalea

★**azar** [aˈθar] NM (casualidad) chance, fate; (desgracia) misfortune, accident; **por ~** by chance; **al ~** at random

azaroso, -a [aθaˈroso, a] ADJ (arriesgado) risky; (vida) eventful

Azerbaiyán [aθerbaˈjan] NM Azerbaijan

azerbaiyano, -a [aθerbaˈjano, a], **azerí** [aθeˈri] ADJ, NM/F Azerbaijani, Azeri

azogue [aˈθoɣe] NM mercury

azor [aˈθor] NM goshawk

azoramiento [aθoraˈmjento] NM alarm; (confusión) confusion

azorar [aθoˈrar] /**1a**/ VT to alarm ■ **azorarse** VR to get alarmed

Azores [aˈθores] NFPL: **las (Islas) ~** the Azores

azotaina [aθoˈtaina] NF beating

azotar [aθoˈtar] /**1a**/ VT to whip, beat; (pegar) to spank

azote [aˈθote] NM (látigo) whip; (latigazo) lash, stroke; (en las nalgas) spank; (calamidad) calamity

azotea [aθoˈtea] NF (flat) roof

azteca [aθˈteka] ADJ, NMF Aztec

★**azúcar** [aˈθukar] NM sugar

azucarado, -a [aθukaˈraðo, a] ADJ sugary, sweet

azucarero, -a [aθukaˈrero, a] ADJ sugar cpd ▶ NM sugar bowl

azuce etc [aˈθuθe] VB ver **azuzar**

azucena [aθuˈθena] NF white lily

azufre [aˈθufre] NM sulphur

★**azul** [aˈθul] ADJ, NM blue; **~ celeste/marino** sky/navy blue

azulejo [aθuˈlexo] NM tile

azulgrana [aθulˈɣrana] ADJ INV of Barcelona Football Club ▶ NM: **los A~** the Barcelona Football Club players o team

azuzar [aθuˈθar] /**1f**/ VT to incite, egg on

Bb

B, b [(Esp) be, (Am) be'larɣa] NF (letra) B, b; **B de Barcelona** B for Benjamin (BRIT) o Baker (US)

B.A. ABR (= Buenos Aires) B.A.

baba ['baβa] NF spittle, saliva; **se le caía la ~** (fig) he was thrilled to bits

babear [baβe'ar] /1a/ VI (echar saliva) to slobber; (niño) to dribble; (fig) to drool, slaver

babel [ba'βel] NM o F bedlam

babero [ba'βero] NM bib

Babia ['baβja] NF: **estar en ~** to be daydreaming

bable ['baβle] NM Asturian (dialect)

babor [ba'βor] NM port (side); **a ~** to port

babosada [baβo'saða] NF: **decir babosadas** (Am fam) to talk rubbish

baboso, -a [ba'βoso, a] ADJ slobbering; (Zool) slimy; (Am fam) silly ▶ NM/F (Am fam) fool

babucha [ba'βutʃa] NF slipper

baca ['baka] NF (Auto) luggage o roof rack

★**bacalao** [baka'lao] NM cod(fish)

bacanal [baka'nal] NF orgy

bache ['batʃe] NM pothole, rut; (fig) bad patch

bachillerato [batʃiʎe'rato] NM two-year advanced secondary school course; ver tb **sistema educativo**

bacilo [ba'θilo] NM bacillus, germ

bacinica [baθi'nika], **bacinilla** [baθi'niʎa] NF potty

★**bacteria** [bak'terja] NF bacterium, germ

bacteriológico, -a [bakterjo'loxiko, a] ADJ bacteriological; **guerra bacteriológica** germ warfare

báculo ['bakulo] NM stick, staff; (fig) support

badajo [ba'ðaxo] NM clapper (of a bell)

bádminton ['baðminton] NM badminton

bafle ['bafle] **baffle** ['bafle] NM (Elec) speaker

bagaje [ba'ɣaxe] NM baggage; (fig) background

bagatela [baɣa'tela] NF trinket, trifle

Bagdad [baɣ'ðað] NM Baghdad

Bahama [ba'ama]: **las Islas ~(s), las Bahamas** nfpl the Bahamas

★**bahía** [ba'ia] NF bay

★**bailar** [bai'lar] /1a/ VT, VI to dance

★**bailarín, -ina** [baila'rin, ina] NM/F dancer; (de ballet) ballet dancer

★**baile** ['baile] NM dance; (formal) ball

baja ['baxa] NF drop, fall; (Econ) slump; (Mil) casualty; (paro) redundancy; **dar de ~** (soldado) to discharge; (empleado) to dismiss, sack; **darse de ~** (retirarse) to drop out; (Med) to go sick; (dimitir) to resign; **estar de ~** (enfermo) to be off sick; (Bolsa) to be dropping o falling; **jugar a la ~** (Econ) to speculate on a fall in prices; ver tb **bajo**

bajada [ba'xaða] NF descent; (camino) slope; (de aguas) ebb

bajamar [baxa'mar] NF low tide

★**bajar** [ba'xar] /1a/ VI to go o come down; (temperatura, precios) to drop, fall; **~ de** (coche) to get out of; (autobús) to get off ▶ VT (cabeza) to bow; (escalera) to go o come down; (radio etc) to turn down; (precio, voz) to lower; (llevar abajo) to take down; **bajarle los humos a algn** (fig) to cut sb down to size ■ **bajarse** VR (de vehículo) to get out; (de autobús) to get off; **bajarse algo de Internet** to download sth from the internet

bajeza [ba'xeθa] NF baseness; (una bajeza) vile deed

bajío [ba'xio] NM shoal, sandbank; (Am) lowlands pl

bajista [ba'xista] NMF (Mus) bassist ▶ ADJ (Bolsa) bear cpd

★**bajo, -a** ['baxo, a] ADJ (terreno) low(-lying); (mueble, número, precio) low; (piso) ground cpd; (de estatura) small, short; (color) pale; (sonido) faint, soft, low; (voz, tono) deep; (metal) base; (humilde) low, humble; **hablar en voz baja** to whisper ▶ ADV (hablar) softly, quietly; (volar) low ▶ PREP under, below, underneath; **~ la lluvia** in the rain ▶ NM (Mus) bass

bajón [ba'xon] NM fall, drop

bajura [baˈxura] NF: **pesca de ~** coastal fishing
bakalao [bakaˈlao] NM (*Mus*) rave music
bala [ˈbala] NF bullet; **~ de goma** plastic bullet
balacear [balaθeˈar] /**1a**/ VT (*Am*) to shoot
balacera [balaˈsera] NF (*Am*) shoot-out
balada [baˈlaða] NF ballad
baladí [balaˈði] ADJ trivial
baladronada [balaðroˈnaða] NF (*dicho*) boast, brag; (*hecho*) piece of bravado
balance [baˈlanθe] NM (*Com*) balance; (: *libro*) balance sheet; (: *cuenta general*) stocktaking; **~ de comprobación** trial balance; **~ consolidado** consolidated balance sheet; **hacer ~** to take stock
balancear [balanθeˈar] /**1a**/ VT to balance ▶ VI to swing (to and fro); (*vacilar*) to hesitate ■ **balancearse** VR to swing (to and fro); (*vacilar*) to hesitate
balanceo [balanˈθeo] NM swinging
balandro [baˈlandro] NM yacht
balanza [baˈlanθa] NF scales pl, balance; **~ comercial** balance of trade; **~ de pagos/de poder(es)** balance of payments/of power; **B~** (*Astro*) Libra
balar [baˈlar] /**1a**/ VI to bleat
balaustrada [balausˈtraða] NF balustrade; (*pasamanos*) banister
balazo [baˈlaθo] NM (*tiro*) shot; (*herida*) bullet wound
balboa [balˈβoa] NM Panamanian currency unit
balbucear [balβuθeˈar] /**1a**/ VI, VT to stammer, stutter
balbuceo [balβuˈθeo] NM stammering, stuttering
balbucir [balβuˈθir] /**3f**/ VI, VT to stammer, stutter
Balcanes [balˈkanes] NMPL: **los (Montes) ~** the Balkans, the Balkan Mountains; **la Península de los ~** the Balkan Peninsula
balcánico, -a [balˈkaniko, a] ADJ Balkan
★**balcón** [balˈkon] NM balcony
balda [ˈbalda] NF (*estante*) shelf
baldar [balˈdar] /**1a**/ VT to cripple; (*agotar*) to exhaust
balde [ˈbalde] NM (*esp Am*) bucket, pail; **de ~** adv (for) free, for nothing; **en ~** adv in vain
baldío, -a [balˈdio, a] ADJ uncultivated; (*terreno*) waste; (*inútil*) vain ▶ NM wasteland
baldosa [balˈdosa] NF (*azulejo*) floor tile; (*grande*) flagstone
baldosín [baldoˈsin] NM tile
balear [baleˈar] /**1a**/ ADJ Balearic, of the Balearic Islands ▶ NMF native o inhabitant of the Balearic Islands ▶ VT (*Am*) to shoot (at)
Baleares [baleˈares] NFPL: **las (Islas) ~** the Balearics, the Balearic Islands
balero [baˈlero] NM (*Am*: *juguete*) cup-and-ball toy
balido [baˈliðo] NM bleat, bleating

balín [baˈlin] NM pellet ■ **balines** NMPL buckshot sg
balística [baˈlistika] NF ballistics pl
baliza [baˈliθa] NF (*Aviat*) beacon; (*Naut*) buoy
ballena [baˈʎena] NF whale
ballenero, -a [baʎeˈnero, a] ADJ: **industria ballenera** whaling industry ▶ NM (*pescador*) whaler; (*barco*) whaling ship
ballesta [baˈʎesta] NF crossbow; (*Auto*) spring
ballet [baˈle] (pl **ballets** [baˈles]) NM ballet
★**balneario, -a** [balneˈarjo, a] ADJ: **estación balnearia** (bathing) resort ▶ NM spa, health resort; (*Am*: *en la costa*) seaside resort
balompié [balomˈpje] NM football
balón [baˈlon] NM ball
★**baloncesto** [balonˈθesto] NM basketball
balonmano [balonˈmano] NM handball
balonred [balonˈreð] NM netball
balonvolea [balomboˈlea] NM volleyball
balsa [ˈbalsa] NF raft; (*Bot*) balsa wood
bálsamo [ˈbalsamo] NM balsam, balm
balsón [balˈson] NM (*Am*) swamp, bog
báltico, -a [ˈbaltiko, a] ADJ Baltic; **el (mar) B~** the Baltic (Sea)
baluarte [baˈlwarte] NM bastion, bulwark
bambolearse [bamboleˈarse] /**1a**/ VR to swing, sway; (*silla*) to wobble
bamboleo [bamboˈleo] NM swinging, swaying; wobbling
bambú [bamˈbu] NM bamboo
banal [baˈnal] ADJ banal, trivial
banana [baˈnana] NF (*Am*) banana
bananal [banaˈnal] NM (*Am*) banana plantation
banano [baˈnano] NM (*Am*) (*árbol*) banana tree; (*fruta*) banana
banasta [baˈnasta] NF large basket, hamper
banca [ˈbanka] NF (*asiento*) bench; (*Com*) banking
★**bancario, -a** [banˈkarjo, a] ADJ banking cpd, bank cpd; **giro ~** bank draft
bancarrota [bankaˈrrota] NF bankruptcy; **declararse en o hacer ~** to go bankrupt
★**banco** [ˈbanko] NM bench; (*Escol*) desk; (*Com*) bank; (*Geo*) stratum; **~ comercial o mercantil** commercial bank; **~ por acciones** joint-stock bank; **~ de crédito/de ahorros** credit/savings bank; **~ de arena** sandbank; **~ de datos** (*Inform*) data bank; **~ de hielo** iceberg
★**banda** [ˈbanda] NF band; (*cinta*) ribbon; (*pandilla*) gang; (*Mus*) brass band; (*Naut*) side, edge; **~ ancha** broadband; **~ gástrica** gastric band; **la B~ Oriental** Uruguay; **~ sonora** soundtrack; **~ transportadora** conveyor belt
bandada [banˈdaða] NF (*de pájaros*) flock; (*de peces*) shoal
bandazo [banˈdaθo] NM: **dar bandazos** (*coche*) to veer from side to side
★**bandeja** [banˈdexa] NF tray; **~ de entrada/salida** in-tray/out-tray

b

bandera [ban'dera] NF (*de tela*) flag; (*estandarte*) banner; **izar la ~** to hoist the flag

banderilla [bande'riʎa] NF banderilla; (*tapa*) *savoury appetizer* (*served on a cocktail stick*)

banderín [bande'rin] NM pennant, small flag

banderola [bande'rola] NF (*Mil*) pennant

bandido [ban'diðo] NM bandit

bando ['bando] NM (*edicto*) edict, proclamation; (*facción*) faction; **pasar al otro ~** to change sides; **los bandos** (*Rel*) the banns

bandolera [bando'lera] NF: **llevar en ~** to wear across one's chest; **bolsa de ~** shoulder bag

bandolero [bando'lero] NM bandit, brigand

bandoneón [bandone'on] NM (*Am*) large accordion

banquero [ban'kero] NM banker

banqueta [ban'keta] NF stool; (*Am: acera*) pavement (*Brit*), sidewalk (*US*)

banquete [ban'kete] NM banquet; (*para convidados*) formal dinner; **~ de boda** wedding reception

banquillo [ban'kiʎo] NM (*Jur*) dock, prisoner's bench; (*banco*) bench; (*para los pies*) footstool

banquina [ban'kina] NF (*RPL*) hard shoulder (*Brit*), berm (*US*)

bañadera [baɲa'ðera] NF (*Am*) bath(tub)

bañado [ba'ɲaðo] NM (*Am*) swamp

bañador [baɲa'ðor] NM swimming costume (*Brit*), bathing suit (*US*)

bañar [ba'ɲar] /1a/ VT (*niño*) to bath, bathe; (*objeto*) to dip; (*de barniz*) to coat ■ **bañarse** VR (*en el mar*) to bathe, swim; (*en la bañera*) to have a bath

bañera [ba'ɲera] NF (*Esp*) bath(tub)

bañero, -a [ba'ɲero, a] NM/F lifeguard ▶ NF bath(tub)

bañista [ba'ɲista] NMF bather

baño ['baɲo] NM (*en bañera*) bath; (*en río, mar*) dip, swim; (*cuarto*) bathroom; (*bañera*) bath(tub); (*capa*) coating; **darse** o **tomar un ~** (*en bañera*) to have o take a bath; (*en mar, piscina*) to have a swim; **~ María** bain-marie

baptista [bap'tista] NMF Baptist

baqueano, -a [bake'ano, a, baki'ano, a], **baquiano, -a** NM/F (*Am*) guide

baqueta [ba'keta] NF (*Mus*) drumstick

bar [bar] NM bar

barahúnda [bara'unda] NF uproar, hubbub

baraja [ba'raxa] NF pack (of cards)

The **baraja española** is the traditional Spanish deck of cards and differs from a standard poker deck. The four *palos* (suits) are *oros* (golden coins), *copas* (goblets), *espadas* (swords), and *bastos* ("clubs", but not like the clubs in a poker pack). Every suit has 9 numbered cards, although for certain games only 7 are used, and 3 face cards: *sota* (Jack), *caballo* (queen) and *rey* (king).

barajar [bara'xar] /1a/ VT (*naipes*) to shuffle; (*fig*) to jumble up

baranda [ba'randa], **barandilla** [baran'diʎa] NF rail, railing

barata [ba'rata] NF (*Am*) (bargain) sale

baratija [bara'tixa] NF trinket; (*fig*) trifle ■ **baratijas** NFPL (*Com*) cheap goods

baratillo [bara'tiʎo] NM (*tienda*) junk shop; (*subasta*) bargain sale; (*conjunto de cosas*) second-hand goods pl

barato, -a [ba'rato, a] ADJ cheap ▶ ADV cheap, cheaply

baratura [bara'tura] NF cheapness

baraúnda [bara'unda] NF = **barahúnda**

barba ['barβa] NF (*mentón*) chin; (*pelo*) beard; **tener ~** to be unshaven; **hacer algo en las barbas de algn** to do sth under sb's very nose; **reírse en las barbas de algn** to laugh in sb's face

barbacoa [barβa'koa] NF (*parrilla*) barbecue; (*carne*) barbecued meat

barbaridad [barβari'ðað] NF barbarity; (*acto*) barbarism; (*atrocidad*) outrage; **una ~ de** (*fam*) loads of; **¡qué ~!** (*fam*) how awful!; **cuesta una ~** (*fam*) it costs a fortune

barbarie [bar'βarje] NF, **barbarismo** [barβa'rismo] NM barbarism; (*crueldad*) barbarity

bárbaro, -a ['barβaro, a] ADJ barbarous, cruel; (*grosero*) rough, uncouth; **un éxito ~** (*fam*) a terrific success; **es un tipo ~** (*fam*) he's a great bloke; **¡qué ~!** (*fam*) how marvellous! ▶ NM/F barbarian ▶ ADV: **lo pasamos ~** (*fam*) we had a great time

barbecho [bar'βetʃo] NM fallow land

barbero [bar'βero] NM barber, hairdresser

barbilampiño, -a [barβilam'piɲo, a] ADJ smooth-faced; (*fig*) inexperienced

barbilla [bar'βiʎa] NF chin, tip of the chin

barbitúrico [barβi'turiko] NM barbiturate

barbo ['barβo] NM: **~ de mar** red mullet

barbotar [barβo'tar] /1a/, **barbotear** [barβo-te'ar] /1a/ VT, VI to mutter, mumble

barbudo, -a [bar'βuðo, a] ADJ bearded

barbullar [barβu'ʎar] /1a/ VI to jabber away

barca ['barka] NF (small) boat; **~ pesquera** fishing boat; **~ de pasaje** ferry

barcaza [bar'kaθa] NF barge; **~ de desembarco** landing craft

Barcelona [barθe'lona] NF Barcelona

barcelonés, -esa [barθelo'nes, esa] ADJ of o from Barcelona ▶ NM/F native o inhabitant of Barcelona

barco ['barko] NM boat; (*buque*) ship; (*Com etc*) vessel; **~ de carga** cargo boat; **~ de guerra** warship; **~ de vela** sailing ship; **ir en ~** to go by boat

barda ['barða] NF (*Am: de madera*) fence

baremo [ba'remo] NM scale; (*tabla de cuentas*) ready reckoner

barítono [ba'ritono] NM baritone

barman ['barman] NM barman

Barna ABR = **Barcelona**

barnice etc [bar'niθe] VB ver **barnizar**

barniz [bar'niθ] NM varnish; (en la loza) glaze; (fig) veneer

barnizar [barni'θar] /1f/ VT to varnish; (loza) to glaze

barómetro [ba'rometro] NM barometer

barón [ba'ron] NM baron

baronesa [baro'nesa] NF baroness

barquero [bar'kero] NM boatman

barquilla [bar'kiʎa] NF (Naut) log

barquillo [bar'kiʎo] NM cone, cornet

★**barra** ['barra] NF bar, rod; (Jur) rail; (: banquillo) dock; (de un bar, café) bar; (de pan) French loaf; (palanca) lever; ~ **de carmín** o **de labios** lipstick; ~ **de herramientas** (Inform) toolbar; ~ **de espaciado** (Inform) space bar; ~ **inversa** backslash; ~ **libre** free bar; **no pararse en barras** to stick o stop at nothing

barrabasada [barraβa'saða] NF (piece of) mischief

barraca [ba'rraka] NF hut, cabin; (en Valencia) thatched farmhouse; (en feria) booth

barracón [barra'kon] NM (caseta) big hut

barragana [barra'yana] NF concubine

barranca [ba'rranka] NF ravine, gully

barranco [ba'rranko] NM ravine; (fig) difficulty

barrena [ba'rrena] NF drill

barrenar [barre'nar] /1a/ VT to drill (through), bore

barrendero, -a [barren'dero, a] NM/F street sweeper

barreno [ba'rreno] NM large drill

barreño [ba'rreɲo] NM washing-up bowl

★**barrer** [ba'rrer] /2a/ VT to sweep; (quitar) to sweep away; (Mil, Naut) to sweep, rake (with gunfire) ▸ VI to sweep up

★**barrera** [ba'rrera] NF barrier; (Mil) barricade; (Ferro) crossing gate; **poner barreras a** to hinder; ~ **arancelaria** (Com) tariff barrier; ~ **comercial** (Com) trade barrier

barriada [ba'rrjaða] NF quarter, district

barricada [barri'kaða] NF barricade

barrida [ba'rriða] NF, **barrido** [ba'rriðo] NM sweep, sweeping

barriga [ba'rriya] NF belly; (panza) paunch; (vientre) guts pl; **echar** ~ to get middle-age spread

barrigón, -ona [barri'ɣon, ona], **barrigudo, -a** [barri'ɣuðo, a] ADJ potbellied

barril [ba'rril] NM barrel, cask; **cerveza de** ~ draught beer

★**barrio** ['barrjo] NM (vecindad) area, neighborhood (US); (en las afueras) suburb; **barrios bajos** poor quarter sg; ~ **chino** red-light district

barriobajero, -a [barrjobβa'xero, a] ADJ (vulgar) common

barro ['barro] NM (lodo) mud; (objetos) earthenware; (Med) pimple

barroco, -a [ba'rroko, a] ADJ Baroque; (fig) elaborate ▸ NM Baroque

barrote [ba'rrote] NM (de ventana etc) bar

barruntar [barrun'tar] /1a/ VT (conjeturar) to guess; (presentir) to suspect

barrunto [ba'rrunto] NM guess; suspicion

bartola [bar'tola] NF: **tirarse a la** ~ to take it easy, be lazy

bártulos ['bartulos] NMPL things, belongings

barullo [ba'ruʎo] NM row, uproar

basa ['basa] NF (Arq) base

basamento [basa'mento] NM base, plinth

basar [ba'sar] /1a/ VT to base ■ **basarse** VR: **basarse en** to be based on

basca ['baska] NF nausea

báscula ['baskula] NF (platform) scales pl

base ['base] NF base; **a** ~ **de** on the basis of, based on; (mediante) by means of; **a** ~ **de bien** in abundance; ~ **de conocimiento** knowledge base; ~ **de datos** database

básico, -a ['basiko, a] ADJ basic

Basilea [basi'lea] NF Basle

basílica [ba'silika] NF basilica

basilisco [basi'lisko] NM (Am) iguana; **estar hecho un** ~ to be hopping mad

basket, básquet ['basket] NM basketball

básquetbol ['basketbol] NM (Am) basketball

---

bastante [bas'tante]

ADJ **1** (suficiente) enough; **bastante dinero** enough o sufficient money; **bastantes libros** enough books

2 (valor intensivo): **bastante gente** quite a lot of people; **tener bastante calor** to be rather hot; **hace bastante tiempo que ocurrió** it happened quite o rather a long time ago

▸ ADV: **bastante bueno/malo** quite good/rather bad; **bastante rico** pretty rich; **(lo) bastante inteligente (como) para hacer algo** clever enough o sufficiently clever to do sth; **voy a tardar bastante** I'm going to be a while o quite some time

---

★**bastar** [bas'tar] /1a/ VI to be enough o sufficient; ~ **para** to be enough to; **¡basta!** (that's) enough! ■ **bastarse** VR to be self-sufficient

bastardilla [bastar'ðiʎa] NF italics pl

bastardo, -a [bas'tarðo, a] ADJ, NM/F bastard

bastidor [basti'ðor] NM frame; (de coche) chassis; (Arte) stretcher; (Teat) wing; **entre bastidores** behind the scenes

basto, -a ['basto, a] ADJ coarse, rough ▸ NM: **bastos** (Naipes) one of the suits in the Spanish card deck; ver tb **baraja española**

bastón [bas'ton] NM stick, staff; (para pasear) walking stick; ~ **de mando** baton

bastonazo [basto'naθo] NM blow with a stick

bastoncillo [baston'θiʎo] NM (tb: **bastoncillo de algodón**) cotton bud

★**basura** [ba'sura] NF rubbish, refuse (BRIT), garbage (US) ▶ ADJ: **comida/televisión ~** junk food/TV

★**basurero** [basu'rero] NM (hombre) dustman (BRIT), garbage collector o man (US); (lugar) rubbish dump; (cubo) (rubbish) bin (BRIT), trash can (US)

★**bata** ['bata] NF (gen) dressing gown; (cubretodo) smock, overall; (Med, Tec etc) lab(oratory) coat

batacazo [bata'kaθo] NM bump

★**batalla** [ba'taʎa] NF battle; **de ~** for everyday use; **~ campal** pitched battle

batallar [bata'ʎar] /1a/ VI to fight

batallón [bata'ʎon] NM battalion

batata [ba'tata] NF (AM Culin) sweet potato

bate ['bate] NM (Deporte) bat

batea [ba'tea] NF (AM) washing trough

bateador [batea'ðor] NM (Deporte) batter, batsman

★**batería** [bate'ria] NF battery; (Mus) drums pl; (Teat) footlights pl; **~ de cocina** kitchen utensils pl

batiburrillo [batiβu'rriʎo] NM hotchpotch

★**batido, -a** [ba'tiðo, a] ADJ (camino) beaten, well-trodden ▶ NM (Culin) batter; **~ (de leche)** milk shake ▶ NF (AM) (police) raid

batidora [bati'ðora] NF beater, mixer; **~ eléctrica** food mixer, blender

★**batir** [ba'tir] /3a/ VT to beat, strike; (vencer) to beat, defeat; (revolver) to beat, mix; (pelo) to back-comb; **~ palmas** to clap, applaud ▪ **batirse** VR to fight

baturro, -a [ba'turro, a] NM/F Aragonese peasant

batuta [ba'tuta] NF baton; **llevar la ~** (fig) to be the boss

baudio ['bauðjo] NM (Inform) baud

baúl [ba'ul] NM trunk; (AM Auto) boot (BRIT), trunk (US)

bautice etc [bau'tiθe] VB ver **bautizar**

bautismo [bau'tismo] NM baptism, christening

bautista [bau'tista] ADJ, NMF Baptist

bautizar [bauti'θar] /1f/ VT to baptize, christen; (fam: diluir) to water down; (dar apodo) to dub

bautizo [bau'tiθo] NM baptism, christening

bávaro, -a ['baβaro, a] ADJ, NM/F Bavarian

Baviera [ba'βjera] NF Bavaria

baya ['baja] NF berry; ver tb **bayo**

bayeta [ba'jeta] NF (trapo) floor cloth; (AM: pañal) nappy (BRIT), diaper (US)

bayo, -a ['bajo, a] ADJ bay

bayoneta [bajo'neta] NF bayonet

baza ['baθa] NF trick; **meter ~** to butt in

bazar [ba'θar] NM bazaar

bazo ['baθo] NM spleen

bazofia [ba'θofja] NF pigswill (BRIT), hogwash (US); (libro etc) trash

BCE NM ABR (= Banco Central Europeo) ECB

be [be] NF name of the letter B; **be chica/grande** (AM) V/B; **be larga** (AM) B

beatificar [beatifi'kar] /1g/ VT to beatify

beato, -a [be'ato, a] ADJ blessed; (piadoso) pious

★**bebé** [be'βe] (pl **bebés** [be'βes]), (AM) **bebe** ['beβe] (pl **bebes** ['beβes]) NM baby; **~ de diseño** designer baby

bebedero [beβe'ðero] NM (para animales) drinking trough; (AM: para personas) drinking fountain

bebedizo, -a [beβe'ðiθo, a] ADJ drinkable ▶ NM potion

bebedor, a [beβe'ðor, a] ADJ hard-drinking

bebé-probeta [be'βepro'βeta] (pl **bebés-probeta**) NM test-tube baby

★**beber** [be'βer] /2a/ VT, VI to drink; **~ a sorbos/tragos** to sip/gulp; **se lo bebió todo** he drank it all up

bebido, -a [be'βiðo, a] ADJ drunk ▶ NF drink; **bebida energética** energy drink

beca ['beka] NF grant, scholarship

becado, -a [be'kaðo, a] NM/F = **becario**

becario, -a [be'karjo, a] NM/F scholarship holder, grant holder; (en prácticas laborales) intern

becerro [be'θerro] NM yearling calf

bechamel [betʃa'mel] NF = **besamel**

becuadro [be'kwaðro] NM (Mus) natural sign

bedel [be'ðel] NM porter, janitor; (Univ) porter

beduino, -a [be'ðwino, a] ADJ, NM/F Bedouin

befarse [be'farse] /1a/ VR: **~ de algo** to scoff at sth

beige ['beix], **beis** ['beis] ADJ, NM beige

béisbol ['beisβol] NM baseball

bejuco [be'xuko] NM (AM) reed, liana

beldad [bel'dað] NF beauty

Belén [be'len] NM Bethlehem; **belén** (de Navidad) nativity scene, crib

★**belga** ['belɣa] ADJ, NMF Belgian

★**Bélgica** ['belxika] NF Belgium

Belgrado [bel'ɣraðo] NM Belgrade

Belice [be'liθe] NM Belize

bélico, -a ['beliko, a] ADJ (actitud) warlike

belicoso, -a [beli'koso, a] ADJ (guerrero) warlike; (agresivo) aggressive, bellicose

beligerante [belixe'rante] ADJ belligerent

bellaco, -a [be'ʎako, a] ADJ sly, cunning ▶ NM villain, rogue

belladona [beʎa'ðona] NF deadly nightshade

bellaquería [beʎake'ria] NF (acción) dirty trick; (calidad) wickedness

belleza [be'ʎeθa] NF beauty

★**bello, -a** ['beʎo, a] ADJ beautiful, lovely; **Bellas Artes** Fine Art sg

bellota [beˈʎota] NF acorn

bemol [beˈmol] NM (*Mus*) flat; **esto tiene bemoles** (*fam*) this is a tough one

bencina [benˈsina] NF (*Am*: *gasolina*) petrol (*Brit*), gas (*US*)

bendecir [bendeˈθir] /3o/ VT to bless; **~ la mesa** to say grace

bendición [bendiˈθjon] NF blessing

bendiga *etc* [benˈdiɣa], **bendije** *etc* [benˈdixe] VB *ver* **bendecir**

bendito, -a [benˈdito, a] PP *de* **bendecir** ▶ ADJ (*santo*) blessed; (*agua*) holy; (*afortunado*) lucky; (*feliz*) happy; (*sencillo*) simple; **¡~ sea Dios!** thank goodness! ▶ NM/F simple soul; **es un ~** he's sweet; **dormir como un ~** to sleep like a log

benedictino, -a [beneðikˈtino, a] ADJ, NM Benedictine

benefactor, a [benefakˈtor, a] NM/F benefactor/benefactress

beneficencia [benefiˈθenθja] NF charity

beneficiar [benefiˈθjar] /1b/ VT to benefit, be of benefit to ■ **beneficiarse** VR to benefit, profit

beneficiario, -a [benefiˈθjarjo, a] NM/F beneficiary; (*de cheque*) payee

★**beneficio** [beneˈfiθjo] NM (*bien*) benefit, advantage; (*Com*) profit, gain; **a ~ de** for the benefit of; **en ~ propio** to one's own advantage; **~ bruto/neto** gross/net profit; **~ por acción** earnings *pl* per share

beneficioso, -a [benefiˈθjoso, a] ADJ beneficial

benéfico, -a [beˈnefiko, a] ADJ charitable; **sociedad benéfica** charity (organization)

benemérito, -a [beneˈmerito, a] ADJ meritorious ▶ NF: **la Benemérita** (*Esp*) the Civil Guard; *ver tb* **Guardia Civil**

beneplácito [beneˈplaθito] NM approval, consent

benevolencia [beneβoˈlenθja] NF benevolence, kindness

benévolo, -a [beˈneβolo, a] ADJ benevolent, kind

Bengala [benˈgala] NF Bengal; **el Golfo de ~** the Bay of Bengal

bengala [benˈgala] NF (*Mil*) flare; (*fuego*) Bengal light; (*materia*) rattan

bengalí [bengaˈli] ADJ, NMF Bengali

benignidad [beniɣniˈðað] NF (*afabilidad*) kindness; (*suavidad*) mildness

benigno, -a [beˈniɣno, a] ADJ kind; (*suave*) mild; (*Med*: *tumor*) benign, non-malignant

Benín [beˈnin] NM Benin

benjamín [benxaˈmin] NM youngest child

beodo, -a [beˈoðo, a] ADJ drunk ▶ NM/F drunkard

berberecho [berβeˈretʃo] NM cockle

berenjena [berenˈxena] NF aubergine (*Brit*), eggplant (*US*)

berenjenal [berenxeˈnal] NM (*Agr*) aubergine bed; (*fig*) mess; **en buen ~ nos hemos metido** we've got ourselves into a fine mess

bergantín [berɣanˈtin] NM brig(antine)

Berlín [berˈlin] NM Berlin

berlinés, -esa [berliˈnes, esa] ADJ of o from Berlin ▶ NM/F Berliner

berlinesa [berliˈnesa] NF (*Am*) doughnut, donut (*US*)

bermejo, -a [berˈmexo, a] ADJ red

bermellón [bermeˈʎon] NM vermilion

bermudas [berˈmuðas] NFPL Bermuda shorts

berrear [berreˈar] /1a/ VI to bellow, low

berrido [beˈrriðo] NM bellow(ing)

berrinche [beˈrrintʃe] NM (*fam*) temper, tantrum

berro [ˈberro] NM watercress

berza [ˈberθa] NF cabbage; **~ lombarda** red cabbage

besamel [besaˈmel], **besamela** [besaˈmela] NF (*Culin*) white sauce, bechamel sauce

★**besar** [beˈsar] /1a/ VT to kiss; (*fig*: *tocar*) to graze ■ **besarse** VR to kiss (one another)

★**beso** [ˈbeso] NM kiss

bestia [ˈbestja] NF beast, animal; (*fig*) idiot; **~ de carga** beast of burden; **¡~!** you idiot!; **¡no seas ~!** (*bruto*) don't be such a brute!; (*idiota*) don't be such an idiot!

bestial [besˈtjal] ADJ bestial; (*fam*) terrific

bestialidad [bestjaliˈðað] NF bestiality; (*fam*) stupidity

besugo [beˈsuɣo] NM sea bream; (*fam*) idiot

besuguera [besuˈɣera] NF (*Culin*) fish pan

besuquear [besukeˈar] /1a/ VT to cover with kisses ■ **besuquearse** VR to kiss and cuddle

betabel [betaˈbel] NM (*Am*) beetroot (*Brit*), beet (*US*)

bético, -a [ˈbetiko, a] ADJ Andalusian

betún [beˈtun] NM shoe polish; (*Química*) bitumen, asphalt

Bib. ABR = **biblioteca**

biberón [biβeˈron] NM feeding bottle

Biblia [ˈbiβlja] NF Bible

bíblico, -a [ˈbiβliko, a] ADJ biblical

bibliografía [biβljoɣraˈfia] NF bibliography

★**biblioteca** [biβljoˈteka] NF library; (*estantes*) bookcase, bookshelves *pl*; **~ de consulta** reference library

bibliotecario, -a [biβljoteˈkarjo, a] NM/F librarian

BIC [bik] NF ABR (= *Brigada de Investigación Criminal*) ≈ CID (*Brit*), FBI (*US*)

bicarbonato [bikarβoˈnato] NM bicarbonate

bíceps [ˈbiθeps] NM INV biceps

bicho [ˈbitʃo] NM (*animal*) small animal; (*sabandija*) bug, insect; (*Taur*) bull; **~ raro** (*fam*) queer fish

★**bici** [ˈbiθi] NF (*fam*) bike

★**bicicleta** [biθiˈkleta] NF bicycle, cycle; **ir en ~** to cycle; **~ estática/de montaña** exercise/mountain bike

bicoca [bi'koka] NF (*Esp fam*) cushy job

bidé [bi'ðe] NM bidet

bidireccional [biðirekθjo'nal] ADJ bidirectional

bidón [bi'ðon] NM (*grande*) drum; (*pequeño*) can

Bielorrusia [bjelo'rrusja] NF Belarus, Byelorussia

bielorruso, -a [bjelo'rruso, a] ADJ, NM/F Belarussian, Belorussian ▶ NM (*Ling*) Belarussian, Belorussian

---

bien [bjen]

NM **1** (*bienestar*) good; **te lo digo por tu bien** I'm telling you for your own good; **el bien y el mal** good and evil

2 (*posesión*): **bienes** goods; **bienes de consumo/equipo** consumer/capital goods; **bienes inmuebles** o **raíces** real estate *sg*; **bienes muebles** personal property *sg*

▶ ADV **1** (*de manera satisfactoria, correcta etc*) well; **trabaja/come bien** she works/eats well; **contestó bien** he answered correctly; **oler bien** to smell nice o good; **me siento bien** I feel fine; **no me siento bien** I don't feel very well

2: **hiciste bien en llamarme** you were right to call me

3 (*valor intensivo*) very; **un cuarto bien caliente** a nice warm room; **bien de veces** lots of times; **bien se ve que ...** it's quite clear that ...

4: **estar bien**: **estoy muy bien aquí** I feel very happy here; **te está bien la falda** (*ser la talla*) the skirt fits you; (*sentar*) the skirt suits you; **el libro está muy bien** the book is really good; **está bien que vengan** it's all right for them to come; **¡está bien! lo haré** oh all right, I'll do it; **ya está bien de quejas** that's quite enough complaining; **¿te encuentras bien?** are you all right?; **se está bien aquí** it's nice here

5 (*de buena gana*): **yo bien que iría pero ...** I'd gladly go but ...

▶ EXCL: **¡bien!** (*aprobación*) OK!; **¡muy bien!** well done!; **¡qué bien!** great!; **bien, gracias, ¿y usted?** fine thanks, and you?

▶ ADJ INV: **niño bien** rich kid; **gente bien** posh people

▶ CONJ **1**: **bien ... bien**: **bien en coche bien en tren** either by car or by train

2: **no bien** (*esp AM*): **no bien llegue te llamaré** as soon as I arrive I'll call you

3: **si bien** even though; *ver tb* **más**

---

bienal [bje'nal] ADJ biennial

bienaventurado, -a [bjenaβentu'raðo, a] ADJ (*feliz*) happy; (*afortunado*) fortunate; (*Rel*) blessed

bienestar [bjenes'tar] NM well-being; **estado de ~** welfare state

bienhechor, a [bjene'tʃor, a] ADJ beneficent ▶ NM/F benefactor/benefactress

bienio ['bjenjo] NM two-year period

★**bienvenido, -a** [bjembe'niðo, a] ADJ welcome ▶ EXCL welcome! ▶ NF welcome; **dar la bienvenida a algn** to welcome sb

bies ['bjes] NM: **falda al ~** bias-cut skirt; **cortar al ~** to cut on the bias

bifásico, -a [bi'fasiko, a] ADJ (*Elec*) two-phase

bife ['bife] NM (*AM*) steak

bifocal [bifo'kal] ADJ bifocal

bifurcación [bifurka'θjon] NF fork; (*Ferro, Inform*) branch

bifurcarse [bifur'karse] /**1g**/ VR to fork

bigamia [bi'ɣamja] NF bigamy

bígamo, -a ['biɣamo, a] ADJ bigamous ▶ NM/F bigamist

bígaro ['biɣaro] NM winkle

★**bigote** [bi'ɣote] NM (*tb*: **bigotes**) moustache

bigotudo, -a [biɣo'tuðo, a] ADJ with a big moustache

bigudí [biɣu'ði] NM (hair-)curler

bikini [bi'kini] NM bikini; (*Culin*) toasted cheese and ham sandwich

bilateral [bilate'ral] ADJ bilateral

bilbaíno, -a [bilβa'ino, a] ADJ of o from Bilbao ▶ NM/F native o inhabitant of Bilbao

bilingüe [bi'lingwe] ADJ bilingual

bilis ['bilis] NF INV bile

★**billar** [bi'ʎar] NM billiards *sg*; **~ americano** pool ■ **billares** NMPL (*lugar*) billiard hall; (*galería de atracciones*) amusement arcade

★**billete** [bi'ʎete] NM ticket; (*de banco*) banknote (BRIT), bill (US); (*carta*) note; **~ de ida y sencillo** single (BRIT) o one-way (US) ticket; **~ de ida y vuelta** return (BRIT) o round-trip (US) ticket; **~ electrónico** e-ticket; **sacar (un) ~** to get a ticket; **un ~ de cinco libras** a five-pound note

billetera [biʎe'tera] NF, **billetero** [biʎe'tero] NM wallet

billón [bi'ʎon] NM billion

bimensual [bimen'swal] ADJ twice monthly

bimestral [bimes'tral] ADJ bimonthly

bimestre [bi'mestre] NM two-month period

bimotor, a [bimo'tor, a] ADJ twin-engined ▶ NM twin-engined plane

binario, -a [bi'narjo, a] ADJ (*Inform*) binary

bingo ['bingo] NM (*juego*) bingo; (*sala*) bingo hall

binóculo [bi'nokulo] NM pince-nez

binomio [bi'nomjo] NM (*Mat*) binomial

biocarburante [biokarβu'rante], **biocombustible** [biokombus'tiβle] NM biofuel

biodegradable [bioðeɣra'ðaβle] ADJ biodegradable

biodiésel [bio'disel] NM biodiesel

biodiversidad [bioðiβersi'ðað] NF biodiversity

biografía [bjoɣra'fia] NF biography

biográfico, -a [bio'ɣrafiko, a] ADJ biographical

biógrafo, -a [bi'oɣrafo, a] NM/F biographer

★biología [bioloˈxia] NF biology

biológico, -a [bioˈloxiko, a] ADJ biological; (*cultivo, producto*) organic; **guerra biológica** biological warfare

biólogo, -a [biˈoloɣo, a] NM/F biologist

biombo [ˈbjombo] NM (folding) screen

biométrico, -a [bioˈmetriko, a] ADJ biometric

biopsia [biˈopsja] NF biopsy

bioquímico, -a [bioˈkimiko, a] ADJ biochemical ▶ NM/F biochemist ▶ NF biochemistry

biosfera [biosˈfera] NF biosphere

bioterrorismo [bioterroˈrismo] NM bioterrorism

bióxido [biˈoksiðo] NM dioxide

bipartidismo [bipartiˈðismo] NM (*Pol*) two-party system

bipolar [biˈpolar] ADJ (*Med*) bipolar

biquini [biˈkini] NM = **bikini**

birlar [birˈlar] /1a/ VT (*fam*) to pinch

birlibirloque [birliβirˈloke] NM: **por arte de ~** (as if) by magic

Birmania [birˈmanja] NF Burma

birmano, -a [birˈmano, a] ADJ, NM/F Burmese

birome [biˈrome] NF (*Am*) ballpoint (pen)

birrete [biˈrrete] NM (*Jur*) judge's cap

birria [ˈbirrja] NF (*fam*): **ser una ~** (*película, libro*) to be rubbish; **ir hecho una ~** to be o look a sight

bis [bis] EXCL encore! ▶ NM encore ▶ ADV (*dos veces*) twice; **viven en el 27 ~** they live at 27a

bisabuelo, -a [bisaˈβwelo, a] NM/F great-grandfather/mother ■ **bisabuelos** NMPL great-grandparents

bisagra [biˈsaɣra] NF hinge

bisbisar [bisβiˈsar] /1a/, **bisbisear** [bisβiseˈar] /1a/ VT to mutter, mumble

bisbiseo [bisβiˈseo] NM muttering

biselar [biseˈlar] /1a/ VT to bevel

bisexual [bisekˈswal] ADJ, NMF bisexual

bisiesto [biˈsjesto] ADJ: **año ~** leap year

bisnieto, -a [bisˈnjeto, a] NM/F great-grandson/daughter ■ **bisnietos** NMPL great-grandchildren

bisonte [biˈsonte] NM bison

bisoñé [bisoˈɲe] NM toupée

bisoño, -a [biˈsoɲo, a] ADJ green, inexperienced

★bistec [bisˈtek], **bisté** [bisˈte] NM steak

bisturí [bistuˈri] NM scalpel

bisutería [bisuteˈria] NF imitation o costume jewellery

bit [bit] NM (*Inform*) bit; **~ de parada** stop bit; **~ de paridad** parity bit

bitácora [biˈtakora] NF: **cuaderno de ~** logbook, ship's log

bizantino, -a [biθanˈtino, a] ADJ Byzantine; (*fig*) pointless

bizarría [biθaˈrria] NF (*valor*) bravery; (*generosidad*) generosity

bizarro, -a [biˈθarro, a] ADJ brave; generous

bizco, -a [ˈbiθko, a] ADJ cross-eyed

bizcocho [biθˈkotʃo] NM (*Culin*) sponge cake

biznieto, -a [biθˈnjeto, a] NM/F = **bisnieto**

bizquear [biθkeˈar] /1a/ VI to squint

★blanco, -a [ˈblanko, a] ADJ white ▶ NM/F white man/woman, white ▶ NM (*color*) white; (*en texto*) blank; (*Mil, fig*) target; **en ~** blank; **cheque en ~** blank cheque; **noche en ~** sleepless night; **me quedé en ~** my mind went blank; **votar en ~** to spoil one's vote; **ser el ~ de las burlas** to be the butt of jokes ▶ NF (*Mus*) minim (*BRIT*), half note (*US*); **estar sin blanca** to be broke

blancura [blanˈkura] NF whiteness

blandengue [blanˈdenge] ADJ (*fam*) soft, weak

blandir [blanˈdir] /3a/ VT to brandish

blando, -a [ˈblando, a] ADJ soft; (*tierno*) tender, gentle; (*carácter*) mild; (*fam*) cowardly ▶ NM/F (*Pol etc*) soft-liner

blandura [blanˈdura] NF softness; tenderness; mildness

blanqueador [blankeaˈðor] NM (*Am*) bleach

blanquear [blankeˈar] /1a/ VT to whiten; (*fachada*) to whitewash; (*paño*) to bleach; (*dinero*) to launder ▶ VI to turn white

blanquecino, -a [blankeˈθino, a] ADJ whitish

blanqueo [blanˈkeo] NM (*de pared*) whitewashing; (*de dinero*) laundering

blanquillo [blanˈkiʎo] NM (*CAm*) egg

blasfemar [blasfeˈmar] /1a/ VI to blaspheme; (*fig*) to curse

blasfemia [blasˈfemja] NF blasphemy

blasfemo, -a [blasˈfemo, a] ADJ blasphemous ▶ NM/F blasphemer

blasón [blaˈson] NM coat of arms; (*fig*) honour

blasonar [blasoˈnar] /1a/ VT to emblazon ▶ VI to boast, brag

bledo [ˈbleðo] NM: **(no) me importa un ~** I couldn't care less

blindado, -a [blinˈdaðo, a] ADJ (*Mil*) armour-plated; (*antibalas*) bulletproof; **coche** o (*Am*) **carro ~** armoured car; **puertas blindadas** security doors

blindaje [blinˈdaxe] NM armour, armour-plating

bloc [blok] (*pl* **blocs**) NM writing pad; (*Escol*) jotter; **~ de dibujos** sketch pad

blof [blof] NM (*Am*) bluff

blofear [blofeˈar] /1a/ VI (*Am*) to bluff

blog [bloɣ] (*pl* **blogs**) NM blog

blogging [ˈbloɣin] NM blogging

blogosfera [bloɣosˈfera] NF blogosphere

bloguear [bloɣeˈar] /1a/ VI to blog

bloguero, -a [bloˈɣero, a] NM/F blogger

★bloque [ˈbloke] NM (*tb Inform*) block; (*Pol*) bloc; **~ de cilindros** cylinder block

bloquear [blokeˈar] /1a/ VT (*Naut etc*) to blockade; (*aislar*) to cut off; (*Com, Econ*) to freeze; **fondos bloqueados** frozen assets

bloqueo [blo'keo] NM blockade; (*Com*) freezing, blocking; **~ mental** mental block

bluejean [blu'jin] NM (*Am*) jeans *pl*, denims *pl*

★**blusa** ['blusa] NF blouse

B.° ABR (*Finanzas*: = *banco*) bank; (*Com*: = *beneficiario*) beneficiary

boa ['boa] NF boa

boato [bo'ato] NM show, ostentation

bobada [bo'βaða] NF foolish action (*o* statement); **decir bobadas** to talk nonsense

bobalicón, -ona [boβali'kon, ona] ADJ utterly stupid

bobería [boβe'ria] NF = **bobada**

bobina [bo'βina] NF (*Tec*) bobbin; (*Foto*) spool; (*Elec*) coil, winding

bobo, -a ['boβo, a] ADJ (*tonto*) daft, silly; (*cándido*) naïve ▶ NM/F fool, idiot ▶ NM (*Teat*) clown, funny man

★**boca** ['boka] NF mouth; (*de crustáceo*) pincer; (*de cañón*) muzzle; (*entrada*) mouth, entrance; **~ abajo/arriba** face down/up; **a ~ jarro** point-blank; **se me hace la ~ agua** my mouth is watering; **todo salió a pedir de ~** it all turned out perfectly; **en ~ de** (*esp Am*) according to; **la cosa anda de ~ en ~** the story is going the rounds; **¡cállate la ~!** (*fam*) shut up!; **quedarse con la ~ abierta** to be dumbfounded; **no abrir la ~** to keep quiet; **~ de incendios** hydrant; **~ del estómago** pit of the stomach; **~ de metro** tube (*Brit*) *o* subway (*US*) entrance ∎ **bocas** NFPL (*de río*) mouth *sg*

★**bocacalle** [boka'kaʎe] NF side street; **la primera ~** the first turning *o* street

★**bocadillo** [boka'ðiʎo] NM sandwich

bocado [bo'kaðo] NM mouthful, bite; (*de caballo*) bridle; **~ de Adán** Adam's apple

bocajarro [boka'xarro]: **a ~** *adv* (*Mil*) at point-blank range; **decir algo a ~** to say sth bluntly

bocanada [boka'naða] NF (*de vino*) mouthful, swallow; (*de aire*) gust, puff

bocata [bo'kata] NM (*fam*) sandwich

bocazas [bo'kaθas] NMF INV (*fam*) bigmouth

boceto [bo'θeto] NM sketch, outline

bocha ['botʃa] NF bowl ∎ **bochas** NFPL bowls *sg*

bochinche [bo'tʃintʃe] NM (*fam*) uproar

bochorno [bo'tʃorno] NM (*vergüenza*) embarrassment; (*calor*): **hace ~** it's very muggy

bochornoso, -a [botʃor'noso, a] ADJ muggy; embarrassing

bocina [bo'θina] NF (*Mus*) trumpet; (*Auto*) horn; (*para hablar*) megaphone; **tocar la ~** (*Auto*) to sound *o* blow one's horn

bocinazo [boθi'naθo] NM (*Auto*) toot

bocio [bo'θjo] NM (*Med*) goitre

★**boda** ['boða] NF (*tb*: **bodas**) wedding, marriage; (*fiesta*) wedding reception; **bodas de plata/de oro** silver/golden wedding *sg*

★**bodega** [bo'ðeɣa] NF (*de vino*) (wine) cellar; (*bar*) bar; (*restaurante*) restaurant; (*depósito*) storeroom; (*de barco*) hold

bodegón [boðe'ɣon] NM (*Arte*) still life

bodrio [bo'ðrio] NM: **el libro es un ~** the book is awful *o* rubbish

body ['boði] (*pl* **bodies**) NM body stocking; **~ milk** body milk

BOE ['boe] NM ABR = **Boletín Oficial del Estado**

> The *Boletín Oficial del Estado*, or **B.O.E.** is the official bulletin which records all the laws and resolutions passed by the *Cortes* (the Spanish Parliament). The work is available in print and online and is widely consulted, especially because it contains details of *oposiciones* (Civil Service examinations).

bofe ['bofe] NM (*tb*: **bofes**: *de res*) lights *pl*; **echar los bofes** to slave (away)

★**bofetada** [bofe'taða] NF slap (in the face); **dar de bofetadas a algn** to punch sb

bofetón [bofe'ton] NM = **bofetada**

boga ['boɣa] NF: **en ~** in vogue

bogar [bo'ɣar] /**1h**/ VI (*remar*) to row; (*navegar*) to sail

bogavante [boɣa'βante] NM (*Naut*) stroke, first rower; (*Zool*) lobster

Bogotá [boɣo'ta] NF Bogota

bogotano, -a [boɣo'tano, a] ADJ *o*f *o* from Bogota ▶ NM/F native *o* inhabitant of Bogota

bogue *etc* ['boɣe] VB *ver* **bogar**

bohemio, -a [bo'emjo, a] ADJ, NM/F Bohemian

bohío [bo'io] NM (*Am*) shack, hut

boicot [boi'ko(t)] (*pl* **boicots**) NM boycott

boicotear [boikote'ar] /**1a**/ VT to boycott

boicoteo [boiko'teo] NM boycott

bóiler ['boiler] NM (*Am*) boiler

boina ['boina] NF beret

★**bola** ['bola] NF ball; (*canica*) marble; (*Naipes*) (grand) slam; (*betún*) shoe polish; (*mentira*) tale, story; **~ de billar** billiard ball; **~ de nieve** snowball ∎ **bolas** NFPL (*Am*) bolas

bolchevique [boltʃe'βike] ADJ, NMF Bolshevik

boleadoras [bolea'ðoras] NFPL (*Am*) bolas *sg*

bolear [bole'ar] /**1a**/ VT (*Am*: *zapatos*) to polish, shine

★**bolera** [bo'lera] NF skittle *o* bowling alley

bolero, -a [bo'lero, a] NM bolero ▶ NM/F (*Am*: *limpiabotas*) shoeshine boy/girl

boleta [bo'leta] NF (*Am*: *permiso*) pass, permit; (: *de rifa*) ticket; (: *recibo*) receipt; (: *para votar*) ballot; **~ de calificaciones** report card

boletería [bolete'ria] NF (*Am*) ticket office

boletero, -a [bole'tero, a] NM/F (*Am*) ticket seller

★**boletín** [bole'tin] NM bulletin; (*periódico*) journal, review; **~ escolar** (*Esp*) school report; **~ de noticias** news bulletin; **~ de pedido** application form; **~ de precios** price list; **~ de prensa** press release

boleto [bo'leto] NM (*esp Am*) ticket; **~ de apuestas** betting slip; **~ de ida y vuelta** (*Am*) return (*Brit*) o round-trip (*US*) ticket; **~ electrónico** (*Am*) e-ticket; **~ redondo** (*Am*) return (*Brit*) o round-trip (*US*) ticket

★**boli** ['boli] NM Biro®

boliche [bo'litʃe] NM (*bola*) jack; (*juego*) bowls *sg*; (*lugar*) bowling alley; (*Am: tienda*) small grocery store

bólido ['boliðo] NM meteorite; (*Auto*) racing car

★**bolígrafo** [bo'liɣrafo] NM ball-point pen, Biro®

bolilla [bo'liʎa] NF (*Am*) topic

bolillo [bo'liʎo] NM (*Costura*) bobbin (for lace-making); (*Am*) (bread) roll

bolita [bo'lita] NF (*Am*) marble

bolívar [bo'liβar] NM *monetary unit of Venezuela*

★**Bolivia** [bo'liβja] NF Bolivia

boliviano, -a [boli'βjano, a] ADJ, NM/F Bolivian

bollería [boʎe'ria] NF cakes *pl* and pastries *pl*

bollo ['boʎo] NM (*de pan*) roll; (*dulce*) scone; (*chichón*) bump, lump; (*abolladura*) dent ■ **bollos** NMPL (*Am*) troubles

bolo ['bolo] NM skittle; (*píldora*) (large) pill; **(juego de) bolos** skittles *sg*

Bolonia [bo'lonja] NF Bologna

★**bolsa** ['bolsa] NF (*cartera*) purse; (*saco*) bag; (*Am*) pocket; (*de mujer*) handbag; (*Anat*) cavity, sac; (*Com*) stock exchange; (*Minería*) pocket; **~ de agua caliente** hot water bottle; **~ de aire** air pocket; **~ de (la) basura** bin-liner; **~ de dormir** (*Am*) sleeping bag; **~ de papel** paper bag; **~ de plástico** plastic (o carrier) bag; **~ de la compra** shopping bag; **"B~ de la propiedad"** "Property Mart"; **~ de trabajo** employment bureau; **jugar a la ~** to play the market

★**bolsillo** [bol'siʎo] NM pocket; (*cartera*) purse; **de ~** pocket *cpd*; **meterse a algn en el ~** to get sb eating out of one's hand

bolsista [bol'sista] NMF stockbroker

★**bolso** ['bolso] NM (*bolsa*) bag; (*de mujer*) handbag

boludo, -a [bo'luðo, a] ADJ (*Am fam!*) stupid ▶ NM/F prat (*fam!*)

★**bomba** ['bomba] NF (*Mil*) bomb; (*Tec*) pump; (*Am: borrachera*) drunkenness; **~ atómica/de humo/de retardo** atomic/smoke/time bomb; **~ de gasolina** petrol pump; **~ de incendios** fire engine ▶ ADJ (*fam!*): **noticia ~** bombshell ▶ ADV (*fam*): **pasarlo ~** to have a great time

bombacha [bom'batʃa] NF (*Am*) panties *pl*

bombacho, -a [bom'batʃo, a] ADJ baggy

bombardear [bombarðe'ar] /1a/ VT to bombard; (*Mil*) to bomb

bombardeo [bombar'ðeo] NM bombardment; bombing

bombardero [bombar'ðero] NM bomber

bombazo [bom'baθo] NM (*Am: explosión*) explo-

sion; (*fam: notición*) bombshell; (: *éxito*) smash hit

bombear [bombe'ar] /1a/ VT (*agua*) to pump (out o up); (*Mil*) to bomb; (*Fútbol*) to lob ■ **bombearse** VR to warp

bombero [bom'bero] NM firefighter; **(cuerpo de) bomberos** fire brigade

★**bombilla** [bom'biʎa] NF (*Esp*), **bombillo** [bom'biʎo] NM (*Am*) (light) bulb

bombín [bom'bin] NM bowler hat

bombita [bom'bita] NF (*Am*) (light) bulb

bombo ['bombo] NM (*Mus*) bass drum; (*Tec*) drum; (*fam*) exaggerated praise; **hacer algo a ~ y platillo** to make a great song and dance about sth; **tengo la cabeza hecha un ~** I've got a splitting headache

★**bombón** [bom'bon] NM chocolate; (*Am: de caramelo*) marshmallow; (*belleza*) gem

bombona [bom'bona] NF: **~ de butano** gas cylinder

bombonería [bombone'ria] NF sweetshop

bonachón, -ona [bona'tʃon, ona] ADJ good-natured

bonaerense [bonae'rense] ADJ of o from Buenos Aires ▶ NMF native o inhabitant of Buenos Aires

bonancible [bonan'θiβle] ADJ (*tiempo*) fair, calm

bonanza [bo'nanθa] NF (*Naut*) fair weather; (*fig*) bonanza; (*Minería*) rich pocket o vein

bondad [bon'dað] NF goodness, kindness; **tenga la ~ de** (please) be good enough to

bondadoso, -a [bonda'ðoso, a] ADJ good, kind

bongo ['bonɣo] NM large canoe

boniato [bo'njato] NM sweet potato, yam

bonificación [bonifika'θjon] NF (*Com*) allowance, discount; (*pago*) bonus; (*Deporte*) extra points *pl*

★**bonito, -a** [bo'nito, a] ADJ (*lindo*) pretty; (*agradable*) nice ▶ ADV (*Am fam*) well ▶ NM (*atún*) tuna (fish)

bono ['bono] NM voucher; (*Finanzas*) bond; **~ de billetes de metro** booklet of metro tickets; **~ del Tesoro** treasury bill

bonobús [bono'βus] NM (*Esp*) bus pass

Bono Loto, bonoloto [bono'loto] NM o F (*Esp*) state-run weekly lottery; *ver tb* **lotería**

boom [bum] (*pl* **booms** [bums]) NM boom

boquear [boke'ar] /1a/ VI to gasp

boquerón [boke'ron] NM (*pez*) (kind of) anchovy; (*agujero*) large hole

boquete [bo'kete] NM gap, hole

boquiabierto, -a [bokia'βjerto, a] ADJ open-mouthed (in astonishment); **quedarse ~** to be amazed o flabbergasted

boquilla [bo'kiʎa] NF (*de riego*) nozzle; (*de cigarro*) cigarette holder; (*Mus*) mouthpiece

borbollar [borβo'ʎar] /1a/, **borbollear** [borβoʎe'ar] /1a/ VI to bubble

51

borbollón [borβo'ʎon] NM bubbling; **hablar a borbollones** to gabble; **salir a borbollones** (*agua*) to gush out

borbotar [borβo'tar] /**1a**/ VI = **borbollar**

borbotón [borβo'ton] NM: **salir a borbotones** to gush out

borda ['borða] NF (*Naut*) gunwale, rail; **echar** *o* **tirar algo por la ~** to throw sth overboard

bordado [bor'ðaðo] NM embroidery

bordar [bor'ðar] /**1a**/ VT to embroider

★**borde** ['borðe] NM edge, border; (*de camino etc*) side; (*en la costura*) hem; **al ~ de** (*fig*) on the verge *o* brink of ▸ ADJ: **ser ~** (*Esp fam*) to be rude

bordear [borðe'ar] /**1a**/ VT to border

bordillo [bor'ðiʎo] NM kerb (*Brit*), curb (*US*)

★**bordo** ['borðo] NM (*Naut*) side; **a ~ on** board

Borgoña [bor'ɣoɲa] NF Burgundy

borgoña [bor'ɣoɲa] NM burgundy

boricua [bo'rikwa], **borinqueño, -a** [borin'keɲo, a] ADJ, NM/F Puerto Rican

borla ['borla] NF (*gen*) tassel; (*de gorro*) pompon

borlote [bor'lote] NM (*Am*) row, uproar

borra ['borra] NF (*pelusa*) fluff; (*sedimento*) sediment

borrachera [borra'tʃera] NF (*ebriedad*) drunkenness; (*orgía*) spree, binge

★**borracho, -a** [bo'rratʃo, a] ADJ drunk ▸ NM/F (*que bebe mucho*) drunkard, drunk; (*temporalmente*) drunk, drunk man/woman ▸ NM (*Culin*) cake soaked in liqueur or spirit

borrador [borra'ðor] NM (*escritura*) first draft, rough sketch; (*cuaderno*) scribbling pad; (*goma*) rubber (*Brit*), eraser; (*Com*) daybook; (*para pizarra*) duster; **hacer un nuevo ~ de** (*Com*) to redraft

★**borrar** [bo'rrar] /**1a**/ VT to erase, rub out; (*tachar*) to delete; (*cinta*) to wipe out; (*Inform: archivo*) to delete, erase; (*Pol etc: eliminar*) to deal with

★**borrasca** [bo'rraska] NF (*Meteorología*) storm

borrascoso, -a [borras'koso, a] ADJ stormy

borrego, -a [bo'rreɣo, a] NM/F (*oveja*) sheep; (*fig*) simpleton ▸ NM (*Am fam*) false rumour

borricada [borri'kaða] NF foolish action/statement

borrico, -a [bo'rriko, a] NM donkey; (*fig*) stupid man ▸ NF she-donkey; (*fig*) stupid woman

borrón [bo'rron] NM (*mancha*) stain; **~ y cuenta nueva** let bygones be bygones

borroso, -a [bo'rroso, a] ADJ vague, unclear; (*escritura*) illegible; (*escrito*) smudgy; (*Foto*) blurred

Bósforo ['bosforo] NM: **el (Estrecho del) ~** the Bosp(h)orus

Bosnia ['bosnja] NF Bosnia

Bosnia-Herzegovina ['bosnjaerθeɣo'βina] NF Bosnia and Herzegovina

bosnio, -a ['bosnjo, a] ADJ, NM/F Bosnian

★**bosque** ['boske] NM wood; (*grande*) forest

bosquejar [boske'xar] /**1a**/ VT to sketch

bosquejo [bos'kexo] NM sketch

bosta ['bosta] NF dung, manure

bostece *etc* [bos'teθe] VB *ver* **bostezar**

bostezar [boste'θar] /**1f**/ VI to yawn

bostezo [bos'teθo] NM yawn

★**bota** ['bota] NF (*calzado*) boot; (*de vino*) leather wine bottle; **botas de agua** *o* **goma** Wellingtons; **ponerse las botas** (*fam*) to strike it rich

botadura [bota'ðura] NF launching

botanas [bo'tanas] NFPL (*Am*) hors d'œuvres

botánico, -a [bo'taniko, a] ADJ botanical ▸ NM/F botanist ▸ NF botany

botar [bo'tar] /**1a**/ VT to throw, hurl; (*Naut*) to launch; (*esp Am fam*) to throw out ▸ VI to bounce

botarate [bota'rate] NM (*imbécil*) idiot

★**bote** ['bote] NM (*salto*) bounce; (*golpe*) thrust; (*vasija*) tin, can; (*embarcación*) boat; (*Am pey: cárcel*) jail; **de ~ en ~** packed, jammed full; **~ salvavidas** lifeboat; **dar un ~** to jump; **dar botes** (*Auto etc*) to bump; **~ de la basura** (*Am*) dustbin (*Brit*), trash can (*US*)

★**botella** [bo'teʎa] NF bottle; **~ de vino** (*contenido*) bottle of wine; (*recipiente*) wine bottle

botellero [bote'ʎero] NM wine rack

botellín [bote'ʎin] NM small bottle

botellón [bote'ʎon] NM (*Esp fam*) outdoor drinking session (*involving groups of young people*)

botica [bo'tika] NF chemist's (shop) (*Brit*), pharmacy

boticario, -a [boti'karjo, a] NM/F chemist (*Brit*), pharmacist

botijo [bo'tixo] NM (earthenware) jug; (*tren*) excursion train

botín [bo'tin] NM (*calzado*) half boot; (*polaina*) spat; (*Mil*) booty; (*de ladrón*) loot

botiquín [boti'kin] NM (*armario*) medicine chest; (*portátil*) first-aid kit

★**botón** [bo'ton] NM button; (*Bot*) bud; (*de florete*) tip; **~ de arranque** (*Auto etc*) starter; **~ de oro** buttercup; **pulsar el ~** to press the button

botones [bo'tones] NM INV bellboy, bellhop (*US*)

Botox® ['botoks] NM Botox®

botulismo [botu'lismo] NM botulism, food poisoning

bóveda ['boβeða] NF (*Arq*) vault

bovino, -a [bo'βino, a] ADJ bovine; (*Agr*): **ganado ~** cattle

box [boks] NM (*Am*) boxing

boxeador [boksea'ðor] NM boxer

boxear [bokse'ar] /**1a**/ VI to box

★**boxeo** [bok'seo] NM boxing

boya ['boja] NF (*Naut*) buoy; (*flotador*) float

boyante [bo'jante] ADJ (*Naut*) buoyant; (*feliz*) buoyant; (*próspero*) prosperous

bozal [bo'θal] NM (*de caballo*) halter; (*de perro*) muzzle

bozo ['boθo] NM (*pelusa*) fuzz; (*boca*) mouth

bracear [braθe'ar] /**1a**/ VI (*agitar los brazos*) to wave one's arms

bracero [bra'θero] NM labourer; (*en el campo*) farmhand

braga ['braɣa] NF, **bragas** ['braɣas] NFPL (*de mujer*) panties

braguero [bra'ɣero] NM (*Med*) truss

bragueta [bra'ɣeta] NF fly (*BRIT*), flies pl (*BRIT*), zipper (*US*)

braguetazo [braɣe'taθo] NM marriage of convenience

braille [breil] NM braille

bramante [bra'mante] NM twine, string

bramar [bra'mar] /**1a**/ VI to bellow, roar

bramido [bra'miðo] NM bellow, roar

branquias ['brankjas] NFPL gills

brasa ['brasa] NF live o hot coal; **carne a la ~** grilled meat; **dar la ~** (*fam: dar la lata, molestar*) to be a pain (*fam*); **dar la ~ a algn** to go on at sb (*fam*); **¡deja de darme la ~!** stop going on at me! (*fam*)

brasero [bra'sero] NM brazier; (*Am: chimenea*) fireplace

brasier [bra'sjer] NM (*AM*) bra

Brasil [bra'sil] NM: **(el) ~** Brazil

brasileño, -a [brasi'leɲo, a] ADJ, NM/F Brazilian

brassier [bra'sjer] NM (*AM*) *ver* **brasier**

bravata [bra'βata] NF boast

braveza [bra'βeθa] NF (*valor*) bravery; (*ferocidad*) ferocity

bravío, -a [bra'βio, a] ADJ wild; (*feroz*) fierce

★**bravo, -a** ['braβo, a] ADJ (*valiente*) brave; (*bueno*) fine, splendid; (*feroz*) ferocious; (*salvaje*) wild; (*mar etc*) rough, stormy; (*Culin*) hot, spicy ▶ EXCL bravo!

bravucón, -ona [braβu'kon, ona] ADJ swaggering ▶ NM/F braggart

bravura [bra'βura] NF bravery; ferocity; (*pey*) boast

braza ['braθa] NF fathom; **nadar a ~** to swim (the) breast-stroke

brazada [bra'θaða] NF stroke

brazalete [braθa'lete] NM (*pulsera*) bracelet; (*banda*) armband

★**brazo** ['braθo] NM arm; (*Zool*) foreleg; (*Bot*) limb, branch; **~ derecho** (*fig*) right-hand man; **a ~ partido** hand-to-hand; **cogidos** *etc* **del ~** arm in arm; **no dar su ~ a torcer** not to give way easily ■ **brazos** NMPL (*braceros*) hands, workers; **huelga de brazos caídos** sit-down strike

brea ['brea] NF pitch, tar

brebaje [bre'βaxe] NM potion

brecha ['bretʃa] NF (*hoyo, vacío*) gap, opening; (*Mil, fig*) breach

brécol ['brekol] NM broccoli

brega ['breɣa] NF (*lucha*) struggle; (*trabajo*) hard work

bregar [bre'ɣar] /**1h**/ VI (*luchar*) to struggle; (*trabajar mucho*) to slog away

bregue *etc* ['breɣe] VB *ver* **bregar**

breña ['breɲa] NF rough ground

Bretaña [bre'taɲa] NF Brittany

brete ['brete] NM (*cepo*) shackles pl; (*fig*) predicament; **estar en un ~** to be in a jam

breteles [bre'teles] NMPL (*AM*) straps

bretón, -ona [bre'ton, ona] ADJ, NM/F Breton

breva ['breβa] NF (*Bot*) early fig; (*puro*) flat cigar; **¡no caerá esa ~!** no such luck!

★**breve** ['breβe] ADJ short, brief; **en ~** (*pronto*) shortly; (*en pocas palabras*) in short ▶ NF (*Mus*) breve

brevedad [breβe'ðað] NF brevity, shortness; **con o a la mayor ~** as soon as possible

breviario [bre'βjarjo] NM (*Rel*) breviary

brezal [bre'θal] NM moor(land), heath

brezo ['breθo] NM heather

bribón, -ona [bri'βon, ona] ADJ idle, lazy ▶ NM/F (*vagabundo*) vagabond; (*pícaro*) rascal, rogue

★**bricolaje** [briko'laxe] NM do-it-yourself, DIY

brida ['briða] NF bridle, rein; (*Tec*) clamp; **a toda ~** at top speed

bridge [britʃ] NM (*Naipes*) bridge

brigada [bri'ɣaða] NF (*unidad*) brigade; (*trabajadores*) squad, gang ▶ NM ≈ sergeant major

brigadier [briɣa'ðjer] NM brigadier(-general)

brillante [bri'ʎante] ADJ brilliant; (*color*) bright; (*joya*) sparkling ▶ NM diamond

brillantez [briʎan'teθ] NF (*de color etc*) brightness; (*fig*) brilliance

★**brillar** [bri'ʎar] /**1a**/ VI (*tb fig*) to shine; (*joyas*) to sparkle; **~ por su ausencia** to be conspicuous by one's absence

brillo ['briʎo] NM shine; (*brillantez*) brilliance; (*fig*) splendour; **sacar ~ a** to polish

brilloso, -a [bri'ʎoso, a] ADJ (*AM*) = **brillante**

brincar [brin'kar] /**1g**/ VI to skip about, hop about, jump about; **está que brinca** he's hopping mad

brinco ['brinko] NM jump, leap; **a brincos** by fits and starts; **de un ~** at one bound

brindar [brin'dar] /**1a**/ VI: **~ a o por** to drink (a toast) to ▶ VT to offer, present; **le brinda la ocasión de** it offers o affords him the opportunity to ■ **brindarse** VR: **brindarse a hacer algo** to offer to do sth

brindis ['brindis] NM INV toast; (*Taur*) (ceremony of) dedication

brinque *etc* ['brinke] VB *ver* **brincar**

brío ['brio] NM spirit, dash

brioso, -a [bri'oso, a] ADJ spirited, dashing

brisa ['brisa] NF breeze

★**británico, -a** [bri'taniko, a] ADJ British ▶ NM/F Briton, British person; **los británicos** the British

53

brizna [ˈbriθna] NF (*hebra*) strand, thread; (*de hierba*) blade; (*de tabaco*) leaf; (*trozo*) piece

broca [ˈbroka] NF (*Costura*) bobbin; (*Tec*) drill bit; (*clavo*) tack

brocado [broˈkaðo] NM brocade

brocal [broˈkal] NM rim

brocha [ˈbrotʃa] NF (large) paintbrush; **~ de afeitar** shaving brush; **pintor de ~ gorda** painter and decorator; (*fig*) poor painter

brochazo [broˈtʃaθo] NM brush-stroke; **a grandes brochazos** (*fig*) in general terms

broche [ˈbrotʃe] NM brooch

★**broma** [ˈbroma] NF joke; (*inocentada*) practical joke; **en ~** in fun, as a joke; **gastar una ~ a algn** to play a joke on sb; **tomar algo a ~** to take sth as a joke; **~ pesada** practical joke

bromear [bromeˈar] /1a/ VI to joke

bromista [broˈmista] ADJ fond of joking ▶ NMF joker, wag

bromuro [broˈmuro] NM bromide

bronca [ˈbronka] NF row; (*regañada*) ticking-off; **armar una ~** to kick up a fuss; **echar una ~ a algn** to tell sb off

bronce [ˈbronθe] NM bronze; (*latón*) brass

bronceado, -a [bronθeˈaðo, a] ADJ bronze *cpd*; (*por el sol*) tanned ▶ NM (sun)tan; (*Tec*) bronzing

bronceador [bronθeaˈðor] NM suntan lotion

broncearse [bronθeˈarse] /1a/ VR to get a suntan

bronco, -a [ˈbronko, a] ADJ (*manera*) rude, surly; (*voz*) harsh

bronquios [ˈbronkjos] NMPL bronchial tubes

bronquitis [bronˈkitis] NF INV bronchitis

brotar [broˈtar] /1a/ VT (*tierra*) to produce ▶ VI (*Bot*) to sprout; (*aguas*) to gush (forth); (*lágrimas*) to well up; (*Med*) to break out

brote [ˈbrote] NM (*Bot*) shoot; (*Med, fig*) outbreak

broza [ˈbroθa] NF (*Bot*) dead leaves *pl*; (*fig*) rubbish

bruces [ˈbruθes]: **de ~** (*adv*): **caer** o **dar de ~** to fall headlong, fall flat

bruja [ˈbruxa] NF witch

Brujas [ˈbruxas] NF Bruges

brujería [bruxeˈria] NF witchcraft

brujo [ˈbruxo] NM wizard, magician

brújula [ˈbruxula] NF compass

★**bruma** [ˈbruma] NF mist

brumoso, -a [bruˈmoso, a] ADJ misty

Brunéi [bruˈnei] NM Brunei

bruñendo *etc* [bruˈɲendo] VB *ver* **bruñir**

bruñido [bruˈɲiðo] NM polish

bruñir [bruˈɲir] /3h/ VT to polish

★**brusco, -a** [ˈbrusko, a] ADJ (*súbito*) sudden; (*áspero*) brusque

Bruselas [bruˈselas] NF Brussels

brusquedad [bruskeˈðað] NF suddenness; brusqueness

brutal [bruˈtal] ADJ brutal

brutalidad [brutaliˈðað] NF brutality

bruto, -a [ˈbruto, a] ADJ (*idiota*) stupid; (*bestial*) brutish; (*peso*) gross; **a la bruta, a lo ~** roughly; **en ~** raw, unworked ▶ NM brute

Bs. ABR = **bolívares**

Bs.As. ABR (= *Buenos Aires*) B.A.

bucal [buˈkal] ADJ oral; **por vía ~** orally

bucanero [bukaˈnero] NM buccaneer

Bucarest [bukaˈrest] NM Bucharest

★**bucear** [buθeˈar] /1a/ VI to dive ▶ VT to explore

buceo [buˈθeo] NM diving; (*fig*) investigation

buche [ˈbutʃe] NM (*de ave*) crop; (*Zool*) maw; (*fam*) belly

bucle [ˈbukle] NM curl; (*Inform*) loop

budín [buˈðin] NM pudding

budismo [buˈðismo] NM Buddhism

budista [buˈðista] ADJ, NMF Buddhist

buen [bwen] ADJ *ver* **bueno**

buenamente [bwenaˈmente] ADV (*fácilmente*) easily; (*voluntariamente*) willingly

buenaventura [bwenaβenˈtura] NF (*suerte*) good luck; (*adivinación*) fortune; **decir** o **echar la ~ a algn** to tell sb's fortune

buenmozo [bwenˈmoθo] ADJ (*Am*) handsome

---

bueno, -a [ˈbweno, a]

(*antes de nmsg:* **buen**) ADJ **1** (*excelente etc*) good; **es un libro bueno, es un buen libro** it's a good book; **hace bueno, hace buen tiempo** the weather is fine, it is fine; **es buena persona** he's a good sort; **el bueno de Paco** good old Paco; **fue muy bueno conmigo** he was very nice o kind to me; **ya está bueno** he's fine now

2 (*apropiado*): **ser bueno para** to be good for; **creo que vamos por buen camino** I think we're on the right track

3 (*irónico*): **le di un buen rapapolvo** I gave him a good o real ticking off; **¡buen conductor estás hecho!** some driver o a fine driver you are!; **¡estaría bueno que …!** a fine thing it would be if …!

4 (*atractivo, sabroso*): **está bueno este bizcocho** this sponge is delicious; **Julio está muy bueno** (*fam*) Julio's gorgeous

5 (*saludos*): **¡buen día!** (*Am*), **¡buenos días!** (good) morning!; **¡buenas tardes!** good afternoon!; (*más tarde*) good evening!; **¡buenas noches!** good night!

6 (*Med*) well

7 (*otras locuciones*): **estar de buenas** to be in a good mood; **por las buenas o por las malas** by hook or by crook; **de buenas a primeras** all of a sudden

8 (*grande*) good, big; **un buen número de …** a good number of …; **un buen trozo de …** a nice big piece of …

▶ EXCL: **¡bueno!** all right!; **bueno, ¿y qué?** well, so what?; **bueno, lo que pasa es que …** well, the thing is …; **pero ¡bueno!** well, I like that!; **bueno, pues …** right, (then) …

Buenos Aires [bweno'saires] NM Buenos Aires

buey [bwei] NM ox

búfalo ['bufalo] NM buffalo

★**bufanda** [bu'fanda] NF scarf

bufar [bu'far] /1a/ VI to snort

bufete [bu'fete] NM (*despacho de abogado*) lawyer's office; **establecer su ~** to set up in legal practice

buffer ['bufer] NM (*Inform*) buffer

bufón [bu'fon] NM clown

bufonada [bufo'naða] NF (*dicho*) jest; (*hecho*) piece of buffoonery; (*Teat*) farce

buhardilla [buar'ðiʎa] NF attic

★**búho** ['buo] NM owl; (*fig*) hermit, recluse

buhonero [buo'nero] NM pedlar

buitre ['bwitre] NM vulture

bujía [bu'xia] NF (*vela*) candle; (*Elec*) candle (power); (*Auto*) spark plug

bula ['bula] NF (*papal*) bull

bulbo ['bulβo] NM (*Bot*) bulb

bulevar [bule'βar] NM boulevard

Bulgaria [bul'ɣarja] NF Bulgaria

búlgaro, -a ['bulɣaro, a] ADJ, NM/F Bulgarian

bulimia [bu'limja] NF bulimia

bulla ['buʎa] NF (*ruido*) uproar; (*de gente*) crowd; **armar** o **meter ~** to kick up a row

bullendo *etc* [bu'ʎendo] VB *ver* **bullir**

bullicio [bu'ʎiθjo] NM (*ruido*) uproar; (*movimiento*) bustle

bullicioso, -a [buʎi'θjoso, a] ADJ (*ruidoso*) noisy; (*calle*) busy; (*situación*) turbulent

bullir [bu'ʎir] /3h/ VI (*hervir*) to boil; (*burbujear*) to bubble; (*moverse*) to move, stir; (*insectos*) to swarm; **~ de** (*fig*) to teem o seethe with

bulo ['bulo] NM false rumour

bulto ['bulto] NM (*paquete*) package; (*fardo*) bundle; (*tamaño*) size, bulkiness; (*Med*) swelling, lump; (*silueta*) vague shape; (*estatua*) bust, statue; **hacer ~** to take up space; **escurrir el ~** to make o.s. scarce; (*fig*) to dodge the issue

buñuelo [bu'ɲwelo] NM ≈ doughnut, ≈ donut (US); (*fruta de sartén*) fritter

★**buque** ['buke] NM ship, vessel; **~ de guerra** warship; **~ mercante** merchant ship; **~ de vela** sailing ship

burbuja [bur'βuxa] NF bubble; **hacer burbujas** to bubble; (*gaseosa*) to fizz

burbujear [burβuxe'ar] /1a/ VI to bubble

burdel [bur'ðel] NM brothel

Burdeos [bur'ðeos] NM Bordeaux

burdo, -a ['burðo, a] ADJ coarse, rough

burgalés, -esa [burɣa'les, esa] ADJ of o from Burgos ▶ NM/F native o inhabitant of Burgos

burgués, -esa [bur'ɣes, esa] ADJ middle-class, bourgeois; **pequeño ~** lower middle-class; (*Pol, pey*) petty bourgeois

burguesía [burɣe'sia] NF middle class, bourgeoisie

Burkina Faso [bur'kina'faso] NF Burkina Faso

burla ['burla] NF (*mofa*) gibe; (*broma*) joke; (*engaño*) trick; **hacer ~ de** to make fun of

burladero [burla'ðero] NM (bullfighter's) refuge

burlador, a [burla'ðor, a] ADJ mocking ▶ NM/F mocker; (*bromista*) joker ▶ NM (*libertino*) seducer

burlar [bur'lar] /1a/ VT (*engañar*) to deceive; (*seducir*) to seduce ▶ VI to joke ■ **burlarse** VR to joke; **burlarse de** to make fun of

burlesco, -a [bur'lesko, a] ADJ burlesque

burlón, -ona [bur'lon, ona] ADJ mocking

buró [bu'ro] NM bureau

burocracia [buro'kraθja] NF bureaucracy

burócrata [bu'rokrata] NMF bureaucrat

buromática [buro'matika] NF office automation

burrada [bu'rraða] NF stupid act; **decir burradas** to talk nonsense; **hacer burradas** to act stupid; **una ~** (*Esp: mucho*) a (hell of a) lot

★**burro, -a** ['burro, a] NM/F (*Zool*) donkey; (*fig*) ass, idiot; **caerse del ~** to realise one's mistake; **no ver tres en un ~** to be as blind as a bat ▶ ADJ stupid

bursátil [bur'satil] ADJ stock-exchange *cpd*

Burundi [bu'rundi] NM Burundi

bus [bus] NM bus

★**busca** ['buska] NF search, hunt; **en ~ de** in search of ▶ NM bleeper, pager

buscador, a [buska'ðor, a] NM/F searcher ▶ NM (*Internet*) search engine

buscapiés [buska'pjes] NM INV jumping jack (BRIT), firecracker (US)

buscapleitos [buska'pleitos] NMF INV troublemaker

★**buscar** [bus'kar] /1g/ VT to look for; (*objeto perdido*) to have a look for; (*beneficio*) to seek; (*enemigo*) to seek out; (*traer*) to bring, fetch; (*provocar*) to provoke; (*Inform*) to search; **ven a buscarme a la oficina** come and pick me up at the office; **buscarle 3** o **4 pies al gato** to split hairs; **se busca secretaria** secretary wanted; **se la buscó** he asked for it ▶ VI to look, search, seek; **"~ y reemplazar"** (*Inform*) "search and replace"

buscavidas [buska'βiðas] NMF INV snooper; (*persona ambiciosa*) go-getter

buscona [bus'kona] NF whore

busilis [bu'silis] NM INV (*fam*) snag

busque *etc* ['buske] VB *ver* **buscar**

búsqueda ['buskeða] NF = **busca**

busto ['busto] NM (*Anat, Arte*) bust

★**butaca** [bu'taka] NF armchair; (*de cine, teatro*) stall, seat

Bután [bu'tan] NM Bhutan

butano [bu'tano] NM butane (gas); **bombona de ~** gas cylinder

butifarra [buti'farra] NF Catalan sausage

buzo ['buθo] NM diver; (*Am*: *chandal*) tracksuit

★**buzón** [bu'θon] NM (*gen*) letter box; (*en la calle*) pillar box (*Brit*); (*Telec*) mailbox; **echar al ~** to post; **~ de entrada** (*Inform*) inbox; **~ de salida** (*Inform*) outbox

buzonear [buθone'ar] /**1a**/ VT to leaflet

buzoneo [buθo'neo] NM direct mail, mailshot (*Brit*)

byte [bait] NM (*Inform*) byte

Cc

C, c [θe, (*esp* Am) se] NF (*letra*) C, c; **C de Carmen** C for Charlie

C. ABR (= *centígrado*) C.; (= *compañía*) Co

c. ABR (= *capítulo*) ch

C/ ABR (= *calle*) St, Rd

c/ ABR (*Com*: = *cuenta*) a/c

ca [ka] EXCL not a bit of it!

c.a. ABR (= *corriente alterna*) A.C.

cabal [ka'βal] ADJ (*exacto*) exact; (*correcto*) right, proper; (*acabado*) finished, complete ■ **cabales** NMPL: **estar en sus cabales** to be in one's right mind

cábala ['kaβala] NF (*Rel*) cab(b)ala; (*fig*) cabal, intrigue ■ **cábalas** NFPL guess *sg*, supposition *sg*; **hacer cábalas** to guess

cabalgadura [kaβalɣa'ðura] NF mount, horse

cabalgar [kaβal'ɣar] /**1h**/ VT, VI to ride

cabalgata [kaβal'ɣata] NF procession; *ver tb* **Reyes Magos**

cabalgue *etc* [ka'βalɣe] VB *ver* **cabalgar**

cabalístico, -a [kaβa'listiko, a] ADJ (*fig*) mysterious

caballa [ka'βaʎa] NF mackerel

caballeresco, -a [kaβaʎe'resko, a] ADJ noble, chivalrous

caballería [kaβaʎe'ria] NF mount; (*Mil*) cavalry

caballeriza [kaβaʎe'riθa] NF stable

caballerizo [kaβaʎe'riθo] NM groom, stableman

★**caballero** [kaβa'ʎero] NM gentleman; (*de la orden de caballería*) knight; (*trato directo*) sir; **"Caballeros"** "Gents"

caballerosidad [kaβaʎerosi'ðað] NF chivalry

caballete [kaβa'ʎete] NM (*Agr*) ridge; (*Arte*) easel; (*Tec*) trestle

caballito [kaβa'ʎito] NM (*caballo pequeño*) small horse, pony; (*juguete*) rocking horse; **~ de mar** seahorse; **~ del diablo** dragonfly ■ **caballitos** NMPL merry-go-round *sg*

★**caballo** [ka'βaʎo] NM horse; (*Ajedrez*) knight; (*Naipes*) ≈ queen; **ir en ~** to ride; **~ de carreras** racehorse; **~ de vapor** o **de fuerza** horsepower; **es su ~ de batalla** it's his hobby-horse; **~ blanco** (*Com*) backer; *ver tb* **baraja española**

cabaña [ka'βaɲa] NF (*casita*) hut, cabin

cabaré, cabaret [kaβa're] (*pl* **cabarés** o **cabarets** [kaβa'res]) NM cabaret

cabecear [kaβeθe'ar] /**1a**/ VT, VI to nod

cabecera [kaβe'θera] NF (*gen*) head; (*de distrito*) chief town; (*de cama*) headboard; (*Imprenta*) headline

cabecilla [kaβe'θiʎa] NM ringleader

cabellera [kaβe'ʎera] NF (head of) hair; (*de cometa*) tail

★**cabello** [ka'βeʎo] NM (*tb*: **cabellos**) hair *sg*; **~ de ángel** confectionery and pastry filling made of pumpkin and syrup

cabelludo [kaβe'ʎuðo] ADJ *ver* **cuero**

★**caber** [ka'βer] /**2l**/ VI (*entrar*) to fit, go; **caben tres más** there's room for three more; **cabe preguntar si...** one might ask whether...; **cabe que venga más tarde** he may come later

cabestrillo [kaβes'triʎo] NM sling

cabestro [ka'βestro] NM halter

★**cabeza** [ka'βeθa] NF head; (*Pol*) chief, leader; **~ de ajo** bulb of garlic; **~ de familia** head of the household; **~ rapada** skinhead; **caer de ~** to fall head first; **sentar la ~** to settle down; **~ de lectura/escritura** read/write head; **~ impresora** o **de impresión** printhead

cabezada [kaβe'θaða] NF (*golpe*) butt; **dar una ~** to nod off

cabezal [kaβe'θal] NM: **~ impresor** print head

cabezazo [kaβe'θaθo] NM (*golpe*) headbutt; (*Fútbol*) header

cabezón, -ona [kaβe'θon, ona] ADJ with a big head; (*vino*) heady; (*obstinado*) pig-headed

cabezota [kaβe'θota] ADJ obstinate, stubborn

cabezudo, -a [kaβe'θuðo, a] ADJ with a big head; (*obstinado*) obstinate, stubborn

cabida [ka'βiða] NF space; **dar ~ a** to make room for; **tener ~ para** to have room for

cabildo [ka'βildo] NM (*de iglesia*) chapter; (*Pol*) town council

★**cabina** [ka'βina] NF cabin; (*de avión*) cockpit; (*de camión*) cab; **~ telefónica** (tele)phone box (*BRIT*) o booth

cabizbajo, -a [kaβiθ'βaxo, a] ADJ crestfallen, dejected

★**cable** ['kaβle] NM cable; (*de aparato*) lead; **~ aéreo** (*Elec*) overhead cable; **conectar con ~** (*Inform*) to hardwire

★**cabo** ['kaβo] NM (*de objeto*) end, extremity; (*Naut*) rope, cable; (*Geo*) cape; (*Tec*) thread; **al ~ de tres días** after three days; **de ~ a rabo** o **~ from beginning to end**; (*libro: leer*) from cover to cover; **llevar a ~** to carry out; **atar cabos** to tie up the loose ends; **C~ de Buena Esperanza** Cape of Good Hope; **C~ de Hornos** Cape Horn; **C~ Verde** Cape Verde ▶ NMF (*Mil*) corporal

★**cabra** ['kaβra] NF goat; **estar como una ~** (*fam*) to be nuts

cabré *etc* [ka'βre] VB *ver* **caber**

cabrear [kaβre'ar] /**1a**/ VT to annoy ■ **cabrearse** VR (*enfadarse*) to fly off the handle

cabrío, -a [ka'βrio, a] ADJ goatish; **macho ~** (he-)goat, billy goat

cabriola [ka'βrjola] NF caper

cabritilla [kaβri'tiʎa] NF kid, kidskin

cabrito [ka'βrito] NM kid

cabrón [ka'βron] NM cuckold; (*fam!*) bastard (*fam!*)

cabronada [kaβro'naða] NF (*fam!*): **hacer una ~ a algn** to be a bastard to sb

caca ['kaka] NF (*palabra de niños*) pooh ▶ EXCL: **no toques, ¡~!** don't touch, it's dirty!

cacahuete [kaka'wete] NM (*Esp*) peanut

cacao [ka'kao] NM cocoa; (*Bot*) cacao

cacarear [kakare'ar] /**1a**/ VI (*persona*) to boast; (*gallo*) to cluck; (*gallo*) to crow

cacarizo, -a [kaka'riθo, a] ADJ (*Am*) pockmarked

cacatúa [kaka'tua] NF cockatoo

cacereño, -a [kaθe'reɲo, a] ADJ of o from Cáceres ▶ NM/F native o inhabitant of Cáceres

cacería [kaθe'ria] NF hunt

★**cacerola** [kaθe'rola] NF pan, saucepan

cacha ['katʃa] NF (*mango*) handle; (*nalga*) buttock

cachalote [katʃa'lote] NM sperm whale

cacharro [ka'tʃarro] NM (*cazo*) pot; (*cerámica*) piece of pottery; (*fam*) useless object ■ **cacharros** NMPL pots and pans

cachear [katʃe'ar] /**1a**/ VT to search, frisk

cachemir [katʃe'mir] NM cashmere

cacheo [ka'tʃeo] NM searching, frisking

cachetada [katʃe'taða] NF (*Am fam*: *bofetada*) slap (in the face)

cachete [ka'tʃete] NM (*Anat*) cheek; (*bofetada*) slap (in the face)

cachimba [ka'tʃimba] NF, **cachimbo** [ka'tʃimbo] NM (*Am*) pipe

cachiporra [katʃi'porra] NF truncheon

cachivache [katʃi'βatʃe] NM piece of junk ■ **cachivaches** NMPL trash *sg*, junk *sg*

cacho ['katʃo] NM (small) bit; (*Am*: *cuerno*) horn

cachondearse [katʃonde'arse] /**1a**/ VR: **~ de algn** to tease sb

cachondeo [katʃon'deo] NM (*Esp fam*) farce, joke; (*guasa*) laugh

cachondo, -a [ka'tʃondo, a] ADJ (*Zool*) on heat; (*caliente*) randy, sexy; (*gracioso*) funny

cachorro, -a [ka'tʃorro, a] NM/F (*de perro*) pup, puppy; (*de león*) cub

cachucha [ka'tʃutʃa] NF (*México fam*) cap

cacique [ka'θike] NM chief, local ruler; (*Pol*) local party boss; (*fig*) despot

caco ['kako] NM pickpocket

cacofonía [kakofo'nia] NF cacophony

cacto ['kakto] NM, **cactus** ['kaktus] NM INV cactus

CAD NM ABR (= *computer-aided design*) CAD

★**cada** ['kaða] ADJ INV each; (*antes de número*) every; **~ día** each day, every day; **~ dos días** every other day; **~ uno/a** each one, every one; **~ vez más/menos** more and more/less and less; **~ vez que ...** whenever, every time (that) ...; **uno de ~ diez** one out of every ten; **¿~ cuánto?** how often?

Cada se traduce por **each** cuando se quieren resaltar los elementos individuales dentro del grupo al que se hace referencia: *A cada miembro del personal se le asignó una tarea específica.* **Each member of staff was allocated a specific task.**

Cuando se desconoce o no se da importancia al número de miembros del grupo, o para generalizar, se traduce por **every**: *Cada empresa funciona de manera distinta.* **Every company works differently.**

También se utiliza **every** delante de una cantidad: *cada dos meses* **every two months**.

cadalso [ka'ðalso] NM scaffold

cadáver [ka'ðaβer] NM (dead) body, corpse

cadavérico, -a [kaða'βeriko, a] ADJ cadaverous; (*pálido*) deathly pale

★**cadena** [ka'ðena] NF chain; (*TV*) channel; **reacción en ~** chain reaction; **trabajo en ~** assembly line work; **~ midi/mini** (*Mus*) midi/mini system; **~ montañosa** mountain range; **~ perpetua** (*Jur*) life imprisonment; **~ de caracteres** (*Inform*) character string

cadencia [ka'ðenθja] NF cadence, rhythm

cadera [ka'ðera] NF hip

cadete [ka'ðete] NM cadet

Cádiz ['kaðiθ] NM Cadiz

caducar [kaðu'kar] /**1g**/ VI to expire

caducidad [kaðuθi'ðað] NF: **fecha de ~** expiry date; (*de comida*) sell-by date

caduco, -a [ka'ðuko, a] ADJ (*idea etc*) outdated, outmoded; **de hoja caduca** deciduous

caduque *etc* [ka'ðuke] VB *ver* **caducar**

★**caer** [ka'er] /**2n**/ VI to fall; (*premio*) to go; (*sitio*) to be, lie; (*pago*) to fall due; **dejar ~** to drop; **estar al ~** to be due to happen; (*persona*) to be about to arrive; **me cae bien/mal** I like/don't like him; **~ en la cuenta** to catch on; **su cumpleaños cae en viernes** her birthday falls on a Friday ■ **caerse** VR to fall (down); **se me ha caído el guante** I've dropped my glove

★**café** [ka'fe] (*pl* **cafés** [ka'fes]) NM (*bebida, planta*) coffee; (*lugar*) café; **~ con leche** white coffee; **~ solo, ~ negro** (*AM*) (small) black coffee ▸ ADJ (*color*) brown

cafeína [kafe'ina] NF caffein(e)

cafetal [kafe'tal] NM coffee plantation

★**cafetera** [kafe'tera] NF *ver* **cafetero**

★**cafetería** [kafete'ria] NF cafe

cafetero, -a [kafe'tero, a] ADJ coffee *cpd*; **ser muy ~** to be a coffee addict ▸ NF coffee pot

cafishio [ka'fiʃjo] NM (*AM*) pimp

cafre ['kafre] NMF: **como cafres** (*fig*) like savages

cagalera [kaɣa'lera] NF (*fam!*): **tener ~** to have the runs

cagar [ka'ɣar] /**1h**/ (*fam!*) VT to shit (*fam!*); (*fig*) to bungle, mess up ▸ VI to have a shit (*fam!*) ■ **cagarse** VR: **¡me cago en diez!** Christ! (*fam!*)

cague *etc* ['kaɣe] VB *ver* **cagar**

caído, -a [ka'iðo, a] ADJ fallen; (*Inform*) down; **~ del cielo** out of the blue ▸ NF fall; (*declive*) slope; (*disminución*) fall, drop; **a la caída del sol** at sunset; **sufrir una caída** to have a fall

caiga *etc* ['kaiɣa] VB *ver* **caer**

caimán [kai'man] NM alligator

caipiriña [kaipi'riɲa] NF caipirinha

Cairo ['kairo] NM: **el ~** Cairo

★**caja** ['kaxa] NF box; (*ataúd*) coffin, casket (*US*); (*para reloj*) case; (*de ascensor*) shaft; (*Com*) cash box; (*Econ*) fund; (*donde se hacen los pagos*) cash desk; (*en supermercado*) checkout, till; (*Tip*) case; (*de parking*) pay station; **~ de ahorros** savings bank; **~ de cambios** gearbox; **~ de fusibles** fuse box; **~ fuerte** *o* **de caudales** safe, strongbox; **ingresar en ~** to be paid in

★**cajero, -a** [ka'xero, a] NM/F cashier; (*en banco*) (bank) teller ▸ NM: **~ automático** cash dispenser, automatic telling machine, ATM

cajetilla [kaxe'tiʎa] NF (*de cigarrillos*) packet

cajista [ka'xista] NMF typesetter

★**cajón** [ka'xon] NM big box; (*de mueble*) drawer

cajuela [kax'wela] NF (*MÉXICO Auto*) boot (*BRIT*), trunk (*US*)

cal [kal] NF lime; **cerrar algo a ~ y canto** to shut sth firmly

cal. ABR (= *caloría(s)*) cal. (= *calorie(s)*)

cala ['kala] NF (*Geo*) cove, inlet; (*de barco*) hold

calabacín [kalaβa'θin] NM (*Bot*) baby marrow; (: *más pequeño*) courgette (*BRIT*), zucchini (*US*)

calabacita [kalaβa'θita] NF (*AM*) courgette (*BRIT*), zucchini (*US*)

calabaza [kala'βaθa] NF (*Bot*) pumpkin; **dar calabazas a** (*candidato*) to fail

calabozo [kala'βoθo] NM (*cárcel*) prison; (*celda*) cell

calado, -a [ka'laðo, a] ADJ (*prenda*) lace *cpd*; **estar ~ (hasta los huesos)** to be soaked (to the skin) ▸ NM (*Tec*) fretwork; (*Naut*) draught ▸ NF (*de cigarrillo*) puff

★**calamar** [kala'mar] NM squid

calambre [ka'lambre] NM (*Elec*) shock; (*tb*: **calambres**) cramp

calamidad [kalami'ðað] NF calamity, disaster; (*persona*): **es una ~** he's a dead loss

calamina [kala'mina] NF calamine

cálamo ['kalamo] NM (*Bot*) stem; (*Mus*) reed

calaña [ka'laɲa] NF model, pattern; (*fig*) nature, stamp

calar [ka'lar] /**1a**/ VT to soak, drench; (*penetrar*) to pierce, penetrate; (*comprender*) to see through; (*vela, red*) to lower ■ **calarse** VR (*Auto*) to stall; **calarse las gafas** to stick one's glasses on

calavera [kala'βera] NF skull

calcañal [kalka'ɲal], **calcañar** [kalka'ɲar] NM heel

calcar [kal'kar] /**1g**/ VT (*reproducir*) to trace; (*imitar*) to copy

calce *etc* ['kalθe] VB *ver* **calzar**

cal. cen. ABR = **calefacción central**

calceta [kal'θeta] NF (knee-length) stocking; **hacer ~** to knit

★**calcetín** [kalθe'tin] NM sock

calcinar [kalθi'nar] /**1a**/ VT to burn, blacken

calcio ['kalθjo] NM calcium

calco ['kalko] NM tracing

calcomanía [kalkoma'nia] NF transfer

calculador, a [kalkula'ðor, a] ADJ calculating ▸ NF calculator

★**calcular** [kalku'lar] /**1a**/ VT (*Mat*) to calculate, compute; **~ que ...** to reckon that ...

★**cálculo** ['kalkulo] NM calculation; (*Med*) (gall) stone; (*Mat*) calculus; **~ de costo** costing; **~ diferencial** differential calculus; **obrar con mucho ~** to act cautiously

caldear [kalde'ar] /**1a**/ VT to warm (up), heat (up); (*metales*) to weld

caldera [kal'dera] NF boiler

calderero [kalde'rero] NM boilermaker

calderilla [kalde'riʎa] NF (*moneda*) small change

caldero [kal'dero] NM small boiler

★**caldo** ['kaldo] NM stock; (*consomé*) consommé;

~ de cultivo (*Bio*) culture medium; **poner a ~ a algn** to tear sb off a strip; **los caldos jerezanos** sherries

caldoso, -a [kal'doso, a] ADJ (*guisado*) juicy; (*sopa*) thin

calé [ka'le] ADJ gipsy *cpd*

★**calefacción** [kalefak'θjon] NF heating; **~ central** central heating

calefón [kale'fon] NM (*RPL*) boiler

caleidoscopio [kaleiðos'kopjo] NM kaleidoscope

calendario [kalen'darjo] NM calendar

calentador [kalenta'ðor] NM heater

★**calentamiento** [kalenta'mjento] NM (*Deporte*) warm-up; **~ global** global warming

★**calentar** [kalen'tar] /**1j**/ VT to heat (up); (*fam: excitar*) to turn on; (*Am: enfurecer*) to anger ▪ **calentarse** VR to heat up, warm up; (*fig: discusión etc*) to get heated

calentón, -ona [kalen'ton, ona] ADJ (*fam: sexualmente*) horny, randy (*BRIT*)

calentura [kalen'tura] NF (*Med*) fever, (high) temperature; (*de boca*) mouth sore

calenturiento, -a [kalentu'rjento, a] ADJ (*mente*) overactive

calesita [kale'sita] NF (*AM*) merry-go-round, carousel

calibrar [kali'βrar] /**1a**/ VT to gauge, measure

calibre [ka'liβre] NM (*de cañón*) calibre, bore; (*diámetro*) diameter; (*fig*) calibre

★**calidad** [kali'ðað] NF quality; **de ~** quality *cpd*; **~ de borrador** (*Inform*) draft quality; **~ de carta** *o* **de correspondencia** (*Inform*) letter quality; **~ texto** (*Inform*) text quality; **~ de vida** quality of life; **en ~ de** in the capacity of

cálido, -a ['kaliðo, a] ADJ hot; (*fig*) warm

★**caliente** [ka'ljente] VB *ver* **calentar** ▶ ADJ hot; (*fig*) fiery; (*disputa*) heated; (*fam: cachondo*) randy

Caliente se traduce por **warm** cuando se refiere a algo que está templado, que no quema o que no está lo suficientemente frío: *¡Esta cerveza está caliente!* **This beer is warm!** Se utiliza **hot** para algo que está muy caliente, a veces tanto que quema: *No toques la sartén, está muy caliente.* **Don't touch the frying pan; it's very hot**.

califa [ka'lifa] NM caliph

★**calificación** [kalifika'θjon] NF qualification; (*de alumno*) grade, mark (*BRIT*); **~ de sobresaliente** first-class mark

calificado, -a [kalifi'kaðo, a] ADJ (*AM: competente*) qualified; (*: obrero*) skilled

calificar [kalifi'kar] /**1g**/ VT to qualify; (*alumno*) to grade, mark; **~ de** to describe as

calificativo, -a [kalifika'tiβo, a] ADJ qualifying ▶ NM qualifier, epithet

califique *etc* [kali'fike] VB *ver* **calificar**

californiano, -a [kalifor'njano, a] ADJ, NM/F Californian

caligrafía [kaliɣra'fia] NF calligraphy

calima [ka'lima] NF (*cerca del mar*) mist

calina [ka'lina] NF haze

cáliz ['kaliθ] NM (*Bot*) calyx; (*Rel*) chalice

caliza [ka'liθa] NF limestone

★**callado, -a** [ka'ʎaðo, a] ADJ quiet, silent

★**callar** [ka'ʎar] /**1a**/ VT (*asunto delicado*) to keep quiet about, say nothing about; (*persona, oposición*) to silence ▶ VI to keep quiet, be silent; (*dejar de hablar*) to stop talking; **¡calla!** be quiet! ▪ **callarse** VR to keep quiet, be silent; (*dejar de hablar*) to stop talking; **¡cállate!, ¡cállese!** shut up!; **¡cállate la boca!** shut your mouth!

★**calle** ['kaʎe] NF street; (*Deporte*) lane; **~ arriba/abajo** up/down the street; **~ de sentido único** one-way street; **~ mayor** (*ESP*) high (*BRIT*) *o* main (*US*) street; **~ peatonal** pedestrianized *o* pedestrian street; **~ principal** (*AM*) high (*BRIT*) *o* main (*US*) street; **poner a algn (de patitas) en la ~** to kick sb out

calleja [ka'ʎexa] NF alley, narrow street

callejear [kaʎexe'ar] /**1a**/ VI to wander (about) the streets

callejero, -a [kaʎe'xero, a] ADJ street *cpd* ▶ NM street map

callejón [kaʎe'xon] NM alley, passage; (*Geo*) narrow pass; **~ sin salida** cul-de-sac; (*fig*) blind alley

callejuela [kaʎe'xwela] NF side-street, alley

callista [ka'ʎista] NMF chiropodist

callo ['kaʎo] NM callus; (*en el pie*) corn ▪ **callos** NMPL (*Culin*) tripe *sg*

callosidad [kaʎosi'ðað] NF (*de pie*) corn; (*de mano*) callus

calloso, -a [ka'ʎoso, a] ADJ horny, rough

calma ['kalma] NF calm; (*pachorra*) slowness; (*Com, Econ*) calm, lull; **~ chicha** dead calm; **¡~!, ¡con ~!** take it easy!

calmante [kal'mante] ADJ soothing ▶ NM sedative, tranquillizer

calmar [kal'mar] /**1a**/ VT to calm, calm down; (*dolor*) to relieve ▪ **calmarse** VR (*tempestad*) to abate; (*mente etc*) to become calm

calmoso, -a [kal'moso, a] ADJ calm, quiet

caló [ka'lo] NM (*de gitanos*) gipsy language, Romany; (*argot*) slang

★**calor** [ka'lor] NM heat; (*calor agradable*) warmth; **entrar en ~** to get warm; **tener ~** to be *o* feel hot

caloría [kalo'ria] NF calorie

calorífero, -a [kalo'rifero, a] ADJ heat-producing, heat-giving ▶ NM heating system

calque *etc* ['kalke] VB *ver* **calcar**

calumnia [ka'lumnja] NF slander; (*por escrito*) libel

calumniar [kalum'njar] /**1b**/ VT to slander; to libel

calumnioso, -a [kalum'njoso, a] ADJ slanderous; libellous

★**caluroso, -a** [kalu'roso, a] ADJ hot; (sin exceso) warm; (fig) enthusiastic

calva ['kalβa] NF bald patch; (en bosque) clearing

calvario [kal'βarjo] NM stations pl of the cross; (fig) cross, heavy burden

calvicie [kal'βiθje] NF baldness

★**calvo, -a** ['kalβo, a] ADJ bald; (terreno) bare, barren; (tejido) threadbare ▶ NM bald man

calza ['kalθa] NF wedge, chock

★**calzado, -a** [kal'θaðo, a] ADJ shod ▶ NM footwear ▶ NF roadway, highway

calzador [kalθa'ðor] NM shoehorn

calzar [kal'θar] /1f/ VT (zapatos etc) to wear; (un mueble) to put a wedge under; (Tec: rueda etc) to scotch; ¿qué (número) calza? what size do you take? ■ **calzarse** VR: **calzarse los zapatos** to put on one's shoes

calzón [kal'θon] NM (tb: **calzones**) shorts pl; (AM: de hombre) pants pl; (: de mujer) panties pl

calzoncillos [kalθon'θiʎos] NMPL underpants

★**cama** ['kama] NF bed; (Geo) stratum; **~ individual/de matrimonio** single/double bed; **hacer la ~** to make the bed; **guardar ~** to be ill in bed

camada [ka'maða] NF litter; (de personas) gang, band

camafeo [kama'feo] NM cameo

camaleón [kamale'on] NM chameleon

★**cámara** ['kamara] NF (Pol etc) chamber; (habitación) room; (sala) hall; (Cine) cine camera; (fotográfica) camera; **~ de aire** inner tube; **~ alta/baja** upper/lower house; **~ de circuito cerrado de televisión** CCTV camera; **~ de comercio** chamber of commerce; **~ de control de velocidad** speed camera; **~ digital** digital camera; **~ de gas** gas chamber; **~ de vídeo** video camera; **a ~ lenta** in slow motion; **~ frigorífica** cold-storage room

camarada [kama'raða] NM comrade, companion

camaradería [kamaraðe'ria] NF comradeship

★**camarero, -a** [kama'rero, a] NM waiter ▶ NF (en restaurante) waitress; (en casa, hotel) maid

camarilla [kama'riʎa] NF (clan) clique; (Pol) lobby

camarín [kama'rin] NM (Teat) dressing room

camarógrafo, -a [kama'rografo, a] NM/F (AM) cameraman/camerawoman

camarón [kama'ron] NM shrimp

★**camarote** [kama'rote] NM (Naut) cabin

cambiable [kam'bjaβle] ADJ (variable) changeable, variable; (intercambiable) interchangeable

cambiante [kam'bjante] ADJ variable

★**cambiar** [kam'bjar] /1b/ VT to change; (trocar) to exchange ▶ VI to change; **~ de idea** u **opinión** to change one's mind ■ **cambiarse** VR (mudarse) to move; (de ropa) to change; **cambiarse de ropa** to change (one's clothes)

cambiazo [kam'bjaθo] NM: **dar el ~ a algn** to swindle sb

★**cambio** ['kambjo] NM change; (trueque) exchange; (Com) rate of exchange; (oficina) bureau de change; (dinero menudo) small change; **a ~ de** in return o exchange for; **en ~** on the other hand; (en lugar de eso) instead; **~ climático** climate change; **~ de divisas** (Com) foreign exchange; **~ de línea** (Inform) line feed; **~ de página** (Inform) form feed; **~ a término** (Com) forward exchange; **~ de velocidades** gear lever; **~ de vía** points pl

cambista [kam'bista] NM (Com) exchange broker

Camboya [kam'boja] NF Cambodia, Kampuchea

camboyano, -a [kambo'jano, a] ADJ, NM/F Cambodian, Kampuchean

camelar [kame'lar] /1a/ VT (con mujer) to flirt with; (persuadir) to sweet-talk

camelia [ka'melia] NF camellia

camello [ka'meʎo] NM camel; (fam: traficante) pusher

camelo [ka'melo] NM: **me huele a ~** it smells fishy

cameo [ka'meo] NM cameo appearance

camerino [kame'rino] NM (Teat) dressing room

camilla [ka'miʎa] NF (Med) stretcher

caminante [kami'nante] NMF traveller

★**caminar** [kami'nar] /1a/ VI (marchar) to walk, go; (viajar) to travel, journey ▶ VT (recorrer) to cover, travel

★**caminata** [kami'nata] NF long walk; (por el campo) hike

★**camino** [ka'mino] NM way, road; (sendero) track; **a medio ~** halfway (there); **en el ~** on the way, en route; **~ de** on the way to; **~ particular** private road; **~ vecinal** country road; **Caminos, Canales y Puertos** (Univ) Civil Engineering; **ir por buen ~** (fig) to be on the right track; **C~ de Santiago** Way of St James

The **Camino de Santiago** is a medieval pilgrim route stretching from the Pyrenees to Santiago de Compostela in north-west Spain, where tradition has it the body of the Apostle James is buried. Nowadays, it is a popular tourist route as well as a religious one. The **concha** (cockleshell) is a symbol of the **Camino de Santiago**, because it is said that when St James's body was found, it was covered in shells.

★**camión** [ka'mjon] NM lorry, truck (US); (AM: autobús) bus; **~ cisterna** tanker; **~ de la basura** dustcart, refuse lorry; **~ de mudanzas** removal (BRIT) o moving (US) van; **~ de bomberos** fire engine

★**camionero** [kamjo'nero] NM lorry (BRIT) o truck (US) driver, trucker (esp US)

★**camioneta** [kamjo'neta] NF van, small truck

camionista [kamjo'nista] NMF (AM) lorry (BRIT) o truck (US) driver, trucker (esp US)

★**camisa** [kaˈmisa] NF shirt; (*Bot*) skin; ~ **de dormir** nightdress; ~ **de fuerza** straitjacket

camisería [kamiseˈria] NF outfitter's (shop)

★**camiseta** [kamiˈseta] NF tee-shirt; (*ropa interior*) vest; (*de deportista*) top

★**camisón** [kamiˈson] NM nightdress, nightgown

camomila [kamoˈmila] NF camomile

camorra [kaˈmorra] NF: **armar** ~ to kick up a row; **buscar** ~ to look for trouble

camorrista [kamoˈrrista] NMF thug

camote [kaˈmote] NM (*Am*) sweet potato; (*bulbo*) tuber, bulb; (*fam: enamoramiento*) crush

campal [kamˈpal] ADJ: **batalla** ~ pitched battle

campamento [kampaˈmento] NM camp

campana [kamˈpana] NF bell

campanada [kampaˈnaða] NF peal

campanario [kampaˈnarjo] NM belfry

campanilla [kampaˈniʎa] NF (*campana*) small bell

campante [kamˈpante] ADJ: **siguió tan** ~ he went on as if nothing had happened

★**campaña** [kamˈpaɲa] NF (*Mil, Pol*) campaign; **hacer** ~ **(en pro de/contra)** to campaign (for/against); ~ **de venta** sales campaign; ~ **electoral** election campaign

campechano, -a [kampeˈtʃano, a] ADJ (*franco*) open

★**campeón, -ona** [kampeˈon, ona] NM/F champion

★**campeonato** [kampeoˈnato] NM championship

cámper [ˈkamper] NM O F (*Am*) caravan (*Brit*), trailer (*US*)

campera [kamˈpera] NF (*RPL*) anorak

★**campesino, -a** [kampeˈsino, a] ADJ country cpd, rural; (*gente*) peasant cpd ▶ NM/F countryman/woman; (*agricultor*) farmer

campestre [kamˈpestre] ADJ country cpd, rural

★**camping** [ˈkampin] NM camping; (*lugar*) campsite; **ir de** O **hacer** ~ to go camping

campiña [kamˈpiɲa] NF countryside

campista [kamˈpista] NMF camper

★**campo** [ˈkampo] NM (*fuera de la ciudad*) country, countryside; (*Agr, Elec, Inform*) field; (*de fútbol*) pitch; (*de golf*) course; (*Mil*) camp; ~ **de batalla** battlefield; ~ **de minas** minefield; ~ **petrolífero** oilfield; ~ **visual** field of vision; ~ **de concentración/de internación/de trabajo** concentration/internment/labour camp; ~ **de deportes** sports ground, playing field

camposanto [kamposˈanto] NM cemetery

campus [ˈkampus] NM INV (*Univ*) campus

camuflaje [kamuˈflaxe] NM camouflage

camuflar [kamuˈflar] /**1a**/ VT to camouflage

can [kan] NM dog, mutt (*fam*)

cana [ˈkana] NF *ver* **cano**

Canadá [kanaˈða] NM Canada

★**canadiense** [kanaˈðjense] ADJ, NMF Canadian ▶ NF fur-lined jacket

★**canal** [kaˈnal] NM canal; (*Geo*) channel, strait; (*de televisión*) channel; (*de tejado*) gutter; **C~ de la Mancha** English Channel; **C~ de Panamá** Panama Canal

canaleta [kanaˈleta] NF (*Am: de tejado*) gutter

canalice *etc* [kanaˈliθe] VB *ver* **canalizar**

canalizar [kanaliˈθar] /**1f**/ VT to channel

canalla [kaˈnaʎa] NF rabble, mob ▶ NM swine

canallada [kanaˈʎaða] NF (*hecho*) dirty trick

canalón [kanaˈlon] NM (*conducto vertical*) drainpipe; (*del tejado*) gutter ■ **canalones** NMPL (*Culin*) cannelloni

canapé [kanaˈpe] (*pl* **canapés** [kanaˈpes]) NM sofa, settee; (*Culin*) canapé

Canarias [kaˈnarjas] NFPL: **las (Islas)** ~ the Canaries, the Canary Isles

★**canario, -a** [kaˈnarjo, a] ADJ of O from the Canary Isles ▶ NM/F native O inhabitant of the Canary Isles ▶ NM (*Zool*) canary

canasta [kaˈnasta] NF (*round*) basket

canastilla [kanasˈtiʎa] NF small basket; (*de niño*) layette

canasto [kaˈnasto] NM large basket

cancela [kanˈθela] NF (*wrought-iron*) gate

cancelación [kanθelaˈθjon] NF cancellation

★**cancelar** [kanθeˈlar] /**1a**/ VT to cancel; (*una deuda*) to write off

cáncer [ˈkanθer] NM (*Med*) cancer; **C~** (*Astro*) Cancer

cancerígeno, -a [kanθeˈrixeno, a] ADJ carcinogenic

★**cancha** [ˈkantʃa] NF (*de baloncesto, tenis etc*) court; (*Am: de fútbol etc*) pitch; ~ **de tenis** tennis court

canciller [kanθiˈʎer] NM chancellor; **C~** (*Am*) Foreign Minister, ≈ Foreign Secretary (*Brit*)

Cancillería [kansiʎeˈria] NF (*Am*) Foreign Ministry, ≈ Foreign Office (*Brit*)

★**canción** [kanˈθjon] NF song; ~ **de cuna** lullaby

cancionero [kanθjoˈnero] NM song book

candado [kanˈdaðo] NM padlock

candela [kanˈdela] NF candle

candelabro [kandeˈlaβro] NM candelabra

candelero [kandeˈlero] NM (*para vela*) candlestick; (*de aceite*) oil lamp

candente [kanˈdente] ADJ red-hot; (*tema*) burning

★**candidato, -a** [kandiˈðato, a] NM/F candidate; (*para puesto*) applicant

candidatura [kandiðaˈtura] NF candidature

candidez [kandiˈðeθ] NF (*sencillez*) simplicity; (*simpleza*) naiveté

cándido, -a [ˈkandiðo, a] ADJ simple; naive

candil [kanˈdil] NM oil lamp

candilejas [kandiˈlexas] NFPL (*Teat*) footlights

candor [kanˈdor] NM (*sinceridad*) frankness; (*inocencia*) innocence

canela [ka'nela] NF cinnamon

canelo [ka'nelo] NM: **hacer el ~** to act the fool

canelones [kane'lones] NMPL cannelloni

★**cangrejo** [kan'grexo] NM crab

★**canguro** [kan'guro] NM (Zool) kangaroo; (de niños) baby-sitter; **hacer de ~** to baby-sit

caníbal [ka'niβal] ADJ, NMF cannibal

canica [ka'nika] NF marble

caniche [ka'nitʃe] NM poodle

canícula [ka'nikula] NF midsummer heat

canijo, -a [ka'nixo, a] ADJ frail, sickly

canilla [ka'niʎa] NF (Tec) bobbin; (AM) tap (BRIT), faucet (US)

canino, -a [ka'nino, a] ADJ canine ▶ NM canine (tooth)

canje [kan'xe] NM exchange; (trueque) swap

canjear [kanxe'ar] /**1a**/ VT to exchange; (trocar) to swap

cano, -a ['kano, a] ADJ grey-haired, white-haired ▶ NF (tb: **canas**) white o grey hair; **tener canas** to be going grey

canoa [ka'noa] NF canoe

canon ['kanon] NM canon; (pensión) rent; (Com) tax

canonice etc [kano'niθe] VB ver **canonizar**

canónico, -a [ka'noniko, a] ADJ: **derecho ~** canon law

canónigo [ka'noniɣo] NM canon

canonizar [kanoni'θar] /**1f**/ VT to canonize

canoro, -a [ka'noro, a] ADJ melodious

canoso, -a [ka'noso, a] ADJ (pelo) grey (BRIT), gray (US); (persona) grey-haired

★**cansado, -a** [kan'saðo, a] ADJ tired, weary; (tedioso) tedious, boring; **estoy ~ de hacerlo** I'm sick of doing it

★**cansancio** [kan'sanθjo] NM tiredness, fatigue

cansar [kan'sar] /**1a**/ VT (fatigar) to tire, tire out; (aburrir) to bore; (fastidiar) to bother ■ **cansarse** VR to tire, get tired; (aburrirse) to get bored

cantábrico, -a [kan'taβriko, a] ADJ Cantabrian; **montes cantábricos, cordillera cantábrica** Cantabrian Mountains; **el (mar) C~** Cantabrian Sea

cántabro, -a ['kantaβro, a] ADJ, NM/F Cantabrian

★**cantante** [kan'tante] ADJ singing ▶ NMF singer

cantaor, a [kanta'or, a] NM/F Flamenco singer

★**cantar** [kan'tar] /**1a**/ VT to sing; **~ a algn las cuarenta** to tell sb a few home truths ▶ VI to sing; (insecto) to chirp; (rechinar) to squeak; (fam: criminal) to squeal; **~ a dos voces** to sing a duet ▶ NM (acción) singing; (canción) song; (poema) poem

cántara ['kantara] NF large pitcher

cántaro ['kantaro] NM pitcher, jug; **llover a cántaros** to rain cats and dogs

cantautor, a [kantau'tor, a] NM/F singer-songwriter

cante ['kante] NM Andalusian folk song; **~ jondo** flamenco singing

cantera [kan'tera] NF quarry

cantero [kan'tero] NM (AM: arriate) border

cántico [kan'tiko] NM (Rel) canticle; (fig) song

★**cantidad** [kanti'ðað] NF quantity, amount; (Econ) sum; **~ alzada** lump sum; **~ de** lots of ▶ ADV (fam) a lot

cantilena [kanti'lena] NF = **cantinela**

cantimplora [kantim'plora] NF water bottle, canteen

cantina [kan'tina] NF canteen; (de estación) buffet; (esp AM) bar

cantinela [kanti'nela] NF ballad, song

cantinero, -a [kanti'nero, a] NM/F (AM) barman/barmaid, bartender (US)

canto ['kanto] NM singing; (canción) song; (borde) edge, rim; (de un cuchillo) back; **~ rodado** boulder

cantón [kan'ton] NM canton

cantor, a [kan'tor, a] NM/F singer

canturrear [kanturre'ar] /**1a**/ VI to sing softly

canutas [ka'nutas] NFPL: **pasarlas ~** (fam) to have a rough time (of it)

canuto [ka'nuto] NM (tubo) small tube; (fam: porro) joint

caña ['kaɲa] NF (Bot: tallo) stem, stalk; (: carrizo) reed; (de cerveza) glass of beer; (Anat) shinbone; (AM: aguardiente) cane liquor; **~ de azúcar** sugar cane; **~ de pescar** fishing rod

cañada [ka'ɲaða] NF (entre dos montañas) gully, ravine; (camino) cattle track

cáñamo ['kaɲamo] NM (Bot) hemp

cañaveral [kaɲaβe'ral] NM (Bot) reedbed; (Agr) sugar-cane field

cañería [kaɲe'ria] NF piping; (tubo) pipe

caño ['kaɲo] NM (tubo) tube, pipe; (de aguas servidas) sewer; (Mus) pipe; (Naut) navigation channel; (de fuente) jet

cañón [ka'ɲon] NM (Mil) cannon; (de fusil) barrel; (Geo) canyon, gorge

cañonazo [kaɲo'naθo] NM (Mil) gunshot

cañonera [kaɲo'nera] NF (tb: **lancha cañonera**) gunboat

caoba [ka'oβa] NF mahogany

caos ['kaos] NM chaos

caótico, -a [ka'otiko, a] ADJ chaotic

CAP [kap] NM ABR (= Certificado de Aptitud Pedagógica) teaching certificate

cap. ABR (= capítulo) ch.

★**capa** ['kapa] NF cloak, cape; (Culin) coating; (Geo) layer, stratum; (de pintura) coat; **de ~ y espada** cloak-and-dagger; **so ~ de** under the pretext of; **~ de ozono** ozone layer; **capas sociales** social groups

capacho [ka'patʃo] NM wicker basket

capacidad [kapaθi'ðað] NF (medida) capacity; (aptitud) capacity, ability; **una sala con ~ para**

900 a hall seating 900; **~ adquisitiva** purchasing power

capacitación [kapaθita'θjon] NF training

capacitar [kapaθi'tar] /1a/ VT: **~ a algn para algo** to qualify sb for sth; (*Tec*) to train sb for sth ■ **capacitarse** VR: **capacitarse para algo** to qualify for sth

capar [ka'par] /1a/ VT to castrate, geld

caparazón [kapara'θon] NM (*Zool*) shell

capataz [kapa'taθ] NM foreman, charge hand

★capaz [ka'paθ] ADJ able, capable; (*amplio*) capacious, roomy; **es ~ que venga mañana** (*Am*) he'll probably come tomorrow

capcioso, -a [kap'θjoso, a] ADJ wily, deceitful; **pregunta capciosa** trick question

capea [ka'pea] NF (*Taur*) bullfight with young bulls

capear [kape'ar] /1a/ VT (*dificultades*) to dodge; **~ el temporal** to weather the storm

capellán [kape'ʎan] NM chaplain; (*sacerdote*) priest

caperuza [kape'ruθa] NF hood; (*de bolígrafo*) cap

capi ['kapi] NF (*esp Am fam*) capital (city)

capicúa [kapi'kua] ADJ INV (*número, fecha*) reversible ▶ NM *reversible number, e.g.* 1441, *palindromic number*

capilar [kapi'lar] ADJ hair cpd

capilla [ka'piʎa] NF chapel

★capital [kapi'tal] ADJ capital ▶ NM (*Com*) capital ▶ NF (*de nación*) capital (city); (*tb:* **capital de provincia**) provincial capital, = county town; **~ activo/en acciones** working/share *o* equity capital; **~ arriesgado** venture capital; **~ autorizado** *o* **social** authorised capital; **~ emitido** issued capital; **~ improductivo** idle money; **~ invertido** *o* **utilizado** capital employed; **~ pagado** paid-up capital; **~ de riesgo** risk capital; **~ social** equity *o* share capital; **inversión de capitales** capital investment; *ver tb* **provincia**

capitalice etc [kapita'liθe] VB *ver* **capitalizar**

capitalino, -a [kapita'lino, a] ADJ (*Am*) of *o* from the capital ▶ NM/F native *o* inhabitant of the capital

capitalismo [kapita'lismo] NM capitalism

capitalista [kapita'lista] ADJ, NMF capitalist

capitalizar [kapitali'θar] /1f/ VT to capitalize

capitán, -ana [kapi'tan, ana] NM/F captain; (*fig*) leader

capitana [kapi'tana] NF flagship

capitanear [kapitane'ar] /1a/ VT to captain

capitanía [kapita'nia] NF captaincy

capitel [kapi'tel] NM (*Arq*) capital

capitolio [kapi'toljo] NM capitol

capitulación [kapitula'θjon] NF (*rendición*) capitulation, surrender; (*acuerdo*) agreement, pact; **capitulaciones matrimoniales** marriage contract sg

capitular [kapitu'lar] /1a/ VI to come to terms, make an agreement; (*Mil*) to surrender

capítulo [ka'pitulo] NM chapter

capo ['kapo] NM drugs baron

capó [ka'po] NM (*Auto*) bonnet (BRIT), hood (US)

capón [ka'pon] NM (*gallo*) capon

caporal [kapo'ral] NM chief, leader

capota [ka'pota] NF (*de mujer*) bonnet; (*Auto*) hood (BRIT), top (US)

capote [ka'pote] NM (*abrigo: de militar*) greatcoat; (*: de torero*) cloak

capricho [ka'pritʃo] NM whim, caprice

caprichoso, -a [kapri'tʃoso, a] ADJ capricious

Capricornio [kapri'kornjo] NM Capricorn

cápsula ['kapsula] NF capsule; **~ espacial** space capsule

captar [kap'tar] /1a/ VT (*comprender*) to understand; (*Radio*) to pick up; (*atención, apoyo*) to attract

captura [kap'tura] NF capture; (*Jur*) arrest; **~ de pantalla** (*Inform*) screenshot

capturar [kaptu'rar] /1a/ VT to capture; (*Jur*) to arrest; (*datos*) to input

capucha [ka'putʃa] NF hood, cowl

capuchón [kapu'tʃon] NM (*Esp: de bolígrafo*) cap

capullo¹ [ka'puʎo] NM (*Zool*) cocoon; (*Bot*) bud

capullo², -a [ka'puʎo, a] NM/F (*fam!*) berk (BRIT fam), jerk (*esp US fam*)

caqui ['kaki] NM khaki

★cara ['kara] NF (*Anat, de moneda*) face; (*aspecto*) appearance; (*de disco*) side; (*fig*) boldness; (*descaro*) cheek, nerve; **de ~ a** opposite, facing; **dar la ~ a** to face the consequences; **echar algo en ~ a algn** to reproach sb for sth; **¿~ o cruz?** heads or tails?; **¡qué ~ más dura!** what a nerve!; **de una ~** (*disquete*) single-sided ▶ PREP: **~ a** facing

carabina [kara'βina] NF carbine, rifle; (*persona*) chaperone

carabinero [karaβi'nero] NM (*de aduana*) customs officer; (*Am*) gendarme

Caracas [ka'rakas] NF Caracas

★caracol [kara'kol] NM (*Zool*) snail; (*concha*) (sea) shell; **escalera de ~** spiral staircase

caracolear [karakole'ar] /1a/ VI (*caballo*) to prance about

★carácter [ka'rakter] (pl **caracteres** [karak'teres]) NM character; **caracteres de imprenta** (*Tip*) type(face) sg; **~ libre** (*Inform*) wildcard character; **tener buen/mal ~** to be good-natured/bad-tempered

caracterice etc [karakte'riθe] VB *ver* **caracterizar**

característico, -a [karakte'ristiko, a] ADJ characteristic ▶ NF characteristic

caracterizar [karakteri'θar] /1f/ VT (*distinguir*) to characterize, typify; (*honrar*) to confer a distinction on

caradura [kara'ðura] NMF cheeky person; **es un ~** he's got a nerve

carajillo [kara'xiʎo] NM *black coffee with brandy*

carajo [ka'raxo] NM (*esp Am fam!*): ¡~! shit! (*fam!*); ¡qué ~! what the hell!; **me importa un** ~ I don't give a damn

★**caramba** [ka'ramba] EXCL well!, good gracious!

carámbano [ka'rambano] NM icicle

carambola [karam'bola] NF: **por ~** by a fluke

★**caramelo** [kara'melo] NM (*dulce*) sweet; (*azúcar fundido*) caramel

carantoñas [karan'toɲas] NFPL: **hacer ~ a algn** to (try to) butter sb up

caraqueño, -a [kara'keɲo, a] ADJ *o* from Caracas ▶ NM/F native *o* inhabitant of Caracas

carátula [ka'ratula] NF (*máscara*) mask; (*Teat*): **la ~** the stage

★**caravana** [kara'βana] NF caravan; (*fig*) group; (*de autos*) tailback

carbo ['karβo] NM (*fam: = carbohidrato*) carb

carbón [kar'βon] NM coal; ~ **de leña** charcoal; **papel** ~ carbon paper

carbonatado, -a [karβona'taðo, a] ADJ carbonated

carbonato [karβo'nato] NM carbonate; ~ **sódico** sodium carbonate

carboncillo [karβon'θiʎo] NM (*Arte*) charcoal

carbonice *etc* [karβo'niθe] VB *ver* **carbonizar**

carbonilla [karβo'niʎa] NF coal dust

carbonizar [karβoni'θar] /1f/ VT to carbonize; (*quemar*) to char; **quedar carbonizado** (*Elec*) to be electrocuted

carbono [kar'βono] NM carbon; ~ **neutral** carbon-neutral

carburador [karβura'ðor] NM carburettor

carburante [karβu'rante] NM fuel

carca ['karka] ADJ, NMF reactionary

carcajada [karka'xaða] NF (loud) laugh, guffaw

carcajearse [karkaxe'arse] /1a/ VR to roar with laughter

★**cárcel** ['karθel] NF prison, jail; (*Tec*) clamp

carcelero, -a [karθe'lero, a] ADJ prison *cpd* ▶ NM/F warder

carcoma [kar'koma] NF woodworm

carcomer [karko'mer] /2a/ VT to bore into, eat into; (*fig*) to undermine ■ **carcomerse** VR to become worm-eaten; (*fig*) to decay

carcomido, -a [karko'miðo, a] ADJ worm-eaten; (*fig*) rotten

cardar [kar'ðar] /1a/ VT (*Tec*) to card, comb; (*pelo*) to backcomb

cardenal [karðe'nal] NM (*Rel*) cardinal; (*Med*) bruise

cárdeno, -a ['karðeno, a] ADJ purple; (*lívido*) livid

cardiaco, -a [kar'ðjako, a], **cardíaco, -a** [kar'ðiako, a] ADJ cardiac; (*ataque*) heart *cpd*

cardinal [karði'nal] ADJ cardinal

cardiólogo, -a [karðj'oloɣo, a] NM/F cardiologist

cardo ['karðo] NM thistle

carear [kare'ar] /1a/ VT to bring face to face; (*comparar*) to compare ■ **carearse** VR to come face to face, meet

carecer [kare'θer] /2d/ VI: ~ **de** to lack, be in need of

carencia [ka'renθja] NF lack; (*escasez*) shortage; (*Med*) deficiency

carente [ka'rente] ADJ: ~ **de** lacking in, devoid of

carestía [kares'tia] NF (*escasez*) scarcity, shortage; (*Com*) high cost; **época de** ~ period of shortage

careta [ka'reta] NF mask

carey [ka'rei] NM (*tortuga*) turtle; (*concha*) tortoiseshell

carezca *etc* [ka'reθka] VB *ver* **carecer**

carga ['karɣa] NF (*peso, Elec*) load; (*de barco*) cargo, freight; (*Finanzas*) tax, duty; (*Mil*) charge; (*Inform*) loading; (*obligación, responsabilidad*) duty, obligation; ~ **aérea** (*Com*) air cargo; ~ **útil** (*Com*) payload; **la ~ fiscal** the tax burden

cargadero [karɣa'ðero] NM goods platform, loading bay

cargado, -a [kar'ɣaðo, a] ADJ loaded; (*Elec*) live; (*café, té*) strong; (*cielo*) overcast

cargador, a [karɣa'ðor, a] NM/F loader; (*Naut*) docker ▶ NM (*Inform*): ~ **de discos** disk pack; (*Telec: del móvil*) charger

cargamento [karɣa'mento] NM (*acción*) loading; (*mercancías*) load, cargo

cargante [kar'ɣante] ADJ (*persona*) trying

★**cargar** [kar'ɣar] /1h/ VT (*barco, arma*) to load; (*Elec*) to charge; (*impuesto*) to impose; (*Com: algo en cuenta*) to charge, debit; (*Mil: enemigo*) to charge; (*Inform*) to load ▶ VI (*Auto*) to load (up); (*inclinarse*) to lean; ~ **con** to pick up, carry away; (*peso, tb fig*) to shoulder, bear ■ **cargarse** VR (*fam: estropear*) to break; (: *matar*) to bump off; (*Elec*) to become charged

cargo ['karɣo] NM (*Com etc*) charge, debit; (*puesto*) post, office; (*responsabilidad*) duty, obligation; (*fig*) weight, burden; (*Jur*) charge; **altos cargos** high-ranking officials; **una cantidad en ~ a algn** a sum chargeable to sb; **hacerse ~ de** to take charge of *o* responsibility for

cargue *etc* ['karɣe] VB *ver* **cargar**

carguero [kar'ɣero] NM freighter, cargo boat; (*avión*) freight plane

Caribe [ka'riβe] NM: **el ~** the Caribbean; **del ~** Caribbean

caribeño, -a [kari'βeɲo, a] ADJ Caribbean

caricatura [karika'tura] NF caricature

caricia [ka'riθja] NF caress; (*a animal*) pat, stroke

caridad [kari'ðað] NF charity

caries ['karjes] NF INV (*Med*) tooth decay

★**cariño** [ka'riɲo] NM affection, love; (*caricia*) caress; (*en carta*) love ...; **tener ~ a** to be fond of

★**cariñoso, -a** [kari'ɲoso, a] ADJ affectionate

carioca [ka'rjoka] ADJ (*Am*) of *o* from Rio de Janeiro ▸ NMF native *o* inhabitant of Rio de Janeiro

carisma [ka'risma] NM charisma

carismático, -a [karis'matiko, a] ADJ charismatic

caritativo, -a [karita'tiβo, a] ADJ charitable

cariz [ka'riθ] NM: **tener** *o* **tomar buen/mal ~** to look good/bad

carmesí [karme'si] ADJ, NM crimson

carmín [kar'min] NM (*color*) carmine; (*tb: carmín de labios*) lipstick

carnal [kar'nal] ADJ carnal; **primo ~** first cousin

carnaval [karna'βal] NM carnival

The 3 days before *miércoles de ceniza* (Ash Wednesday), when fasting traditionally starts, are the time for **carnaval**, an exuberant celebration which dates back to pre-Christian times. Although in decline during the Franco years, the *carnaval* has grown in popularity recently in Spain, with Cádiz and Tenerife being particularly well-known for their celebrations. *El martes de carnaval* (Shrove Tuesday) is the biggest day, with colourful street parades, fancy dress, fireworks and a general party atmosphere.

★**carne** ['karne] NF flesh; (*Culin*) meat; **se me pone la ~ de gallina solo verlo** I get the creeps just seeing it; **~ de cerdo/de cordero/de ternera/de vaca** pork/lamb/veal/beef; **~ molida** (*Am*), **~ picada** (*Esp*) mince (*Brit*), ground meat (*US*); **~ de gallina** (*fig*) gooseflesh

★**carné** [kar'ne] (*pl* **carnés**) NM: **~ de conducir** driving licence (*Brit*), driver's license (*US*); **~ de identidad** identity card; **~ de socio** membership card; *ver tb* **Documento Nacional de Identidad**

carnero [kar'nero] NM sheep, ram; (*carne*) mutton

★**carnet** [kar'ne] (*pl* **carnets** [kar'nes]) NM (*Esp*) = **carné**

★**carnicería** [karniθe'ria] NF butcher's (shop); (*fig: matanza*) carnage, slaughter

★**carnicero, -a** [karni'θero, a] ADJ carnivorous ▸ NM/F (*tb fig*) butcher ▸ NM carnivore

carnívoro, -a [kar'niβoro, a] ADJ carnivorous ▸ NM carnivore

carnoso, -a [kar'noso, a] ADJ beefy, fat

★**caro, -a** ['karo, a] ADJ dear; (*Com*) dear, expensive ▸ ADV dear, dearly; **vender ~** to sell at a high price

carpa ['karpa] NF (*pez*) carp; (*de circo*) big top; (*Am: de camping*) tent

★**carpeta** [kar'peta] NF folder, file

carpintería [karpinte'ria] NF carpentry, joinery

★**carpintero** [karpin'tero] NM carpenter; **pájaro ~** woodpecker

carraca [ka'rraka] NF (*Deporte*) rattle

carraspear [karraspe'ar] /**1a**/ VI (*aclararse la garganta*) to clear one's throat

carraspera [karras'pera] NF hoarseness

★**carrera** [ka'rrera] NF (*acción*) run(ning); (*espacio recorrido*) run; (*certamen*) race; (*trayecto*) course; (*profesión*) career; (*Escol, Univ*) course; (*de taxi*) ride; (*en medias*) ladder; **a la ~** at (full) speed; **caballo de ~(s)** racehorse; **~ de obstáculos** (*Deporte*) steeplechase; **~ de armamentos** arms race

carrerilla [karre'riʎa] NF: **decir algo de ~** to reel sth off; **tomar ~** to get up speed

carreta [ka'rreta] NF wagon, cart

carrete [ka'rrete] NM reel, spool; (*Tec*) coil

★**carretera** [karre'tera] NF (*main*) road, highway; **~ nacional** ≈ A road (*Brit*), ≈ state highway (*US*); **~ de circunvalación** ring road

carretilla [karre'tiʎa] NF trolley; (*Agr*) (wheel)barrow

carril [ka'rril] NM furrow; (*de autopista*) lane; (*Ferro*) rail

carril-bici [karil'βiθi] (*pl* **carriles-bici** [kariles'βiθi]) NM cycle lane, bikeway (*US*)

carrillo [ka'rriʎo] NM (*Anat*) cheek; (*Tec*) pulley

carrito [ka'rrito] NM trolley, cart (*US*); **~ de la compra** (*tb Inform*) shopping trolley, shopping cart (*US*)

★**carro** ['karro] NM cart, wagon; (*Mil*) tank; (*Am: coche*) car; (*Tip*) carriage; **~ blindado** armoured car; **~ patrulla** (*Am*) patrol *o* (*Brit*) panda car

carrocería [karroθe'ria] NF body, bodywork *no pl* (*Brit*)

carroña [ka'rroɲa] NF carrion *no pl*

carroza [ka'rroθa] NF (*vehículo*) coach ▸ NMF (*fam*) old fogey

carruaje [ka'rrwaxe] NM carriage

carrusel [karru'sel] NM merry-go-round, roundabout (*Brit*)

★**carta** ['karta] NF letter; (*Culin*) menu; (*naipe*) card; (*mapa*) map; (*Jur*) document; **~ de crédito** credit card; **~ de crédito documentaria** (*Com*) documentary letter of credit; **~ de crédito irrevocable** (*Com*) irrevocable letter of credit; **~ certificada/urgente** registered/special delivery letter; **~ marítima** chart; **~ de pedido** (*Com*) order; **~ verde** (*Auto*) green card; **~ de vinos** wine list; **echar una ~ al correo** to post a letter; **echar las cartas a algn** to tell sb's fortune

cartabón [karta'βon] NM set square

cartearse [karte'arse] /**1a**/ VR to correspond

★**cartel** [kar'tel] NM (*anuncio*) poster, placard; (*Escol*) wall chart; (*Com*) cartel

★**cartelera** [karte'lera] NF hoarding, billboard; (*en periódico etc*) listings *pl*, entertainments guide; **"en ~"** "showing"

★**cartera** [kar'tera] NF (*de bolsillo*) wallet; (*de colegial, cobrador*) satchel; (*Am: de señora*) handbag (*Brit*), purse (*US*); (*para documentos*) briefcase; (*Com*) portfolio; **ministro sin ~** (*Pol*) minister without portfolio; **ocupa la ~ de Agricultura** he is Minister of Agriculture; **~ de pedidos** (*Com*) order book; **efectos en ~** (*Econ*) holdings

carterista [karte'rista] NMF pickpocket

★**cartero** [kar'tero] NM postman

cartílago [kar'tilaɣo] NM cartilage

cartilla [kar'tiʎa] NF (*Escol*) primer, first reading book; **~ de ahorros** savings book

cartografía [kartoɣra'fia] NF cartography

★**cartón** [kar'ton] NM cardboard; **~ piedra** papier-mâché

cartucho [kar'tutʃo] NM (*Mil*) cartridge; (*bolsita*) paper cone; **~ de datos** (*Inform*) data cartridge; **~ de tinta** ink cartridge

cartulina [kartu'lina] NF fine cardboard, card

CASA ['kasa] NF ABR (*Esp Aviat*) = **Construcciones Aeronáuticas S.A.**

★**casa** ['kasa] NF (*vivienda*) house; (*hogar*) home; (*Com*) firm, company; **~ consistorial** town hall; **~ de huéspedes** boarding house; **~ de socorro** first aid post; **~ de citas** (*fam*) brothel; **~ independiente** detached house; **~ rural** (*de alquiler*) holiday cottage; (*pensión*) rural B&B; **~ rodante** (*RPL*) caravan (*Brit*), trailer (*US*); **en ~** at home; **ir a ~** to go home; **salir de ~** to go out; (*para siempre*) to leave home; **echar la ~ por la ventana** (*gastar*) to spare no expense; *ver tb* **hotel**

> En el sentido de edificio, *casa* se traduce por **house**: *Queremos comprar una casa*. **We want to buy a house**.
> En cambio, en el sentido de hogar se traduce por **home**: *Quiero irme a casa*. **I want to go home**.
> **Home** nunca va detrás de **to**, excepto cuando le precede un adjetivo: *Quiere volver a su antigua casa*. **She wants to return to her former home**.

casadero, -a [kasa'ðero, a] ADJ marriageable

★**casado, -a** [ka'saðo, a] ADJ married ▶ NM/F married man/woman

★**casamiento** [kasa'mjento] NM marriage, wedding

casar [ka'sar] /1a/ VT to marry; (*Jur*) to quash, annul ■ **casarse** VR to marry, get married; **casarse por lo civil** to have a civil wedding, get married in a registry office (*Brit*)

cascabel [kaska'βel] NM (small) bell; (*Zool*) rattlesnake

cascada [kas'kaða] NF waterfall

cascajo [kas'kaxo] NM gravel, stone chippings *pl*

cascanueces [kaska'nweθes] NM INV nutcracker *sg*; **un ~** a pair of nutcrackers

cascar [kas'kar] /1g/ VT to split; (*nuez*) to crack ▶ VI to chatter ■ **cascarse** VR to crack, split, break (open)

cáscara ['kaskara] NF (*de huevo, fruta seca*) shell; (*de fruta*) skin; (*de limón*) peel

cascarón [kaska'ron] NM (broken) eggshell

cascarrabias [kaska'rraβjas] NMF INV (*fam*) hothead

★**casco** ['kasko] NM (*de bombero, soldado*) helmet; (*cráneo*) skull; (*Naut: de barco*) hull; (*Zool: de caballo*) hoof; (*botella*) empty bottle; (*de ciudad*): **el ~ antiguo** the old part; **el ~ urbano** the town centre; **los cascos azules** the UN peacekeeping force, the blue helmets

cascote [kas'kote] NM piece of rubble ■ **cascotes** NMPL rubble *sg*

caserío [kase'rio] NM hamlet, group of houses; (*casa*) farmhouse

casero, -a [ka'sero, a] ADJ (*pan etc*) home-made; (*persona*): **ser muy ~** to be home-loving; **"comida casera"** "home cooking" ▶ NM/F (*propietario*) landlord/lady; (*Com*) house agent

caserón [kase'ron] NM large (ramshackle) house

caseta [ka'seta] NF hut; (*para bañista*) cubicle; (*de feria*) stall

casete [ka'sete] NM O F cassette; **~ digital** digital audio tape, DAT

★**casi** ['kasi] ADV almost; **~ nunca** hardly ever, almost never; **~ nada** next to nothing; **~ te caes** you almost o nearly fell

★**casilla** [ka'siʎa] NF (*de formulario*) box; (*en juegos*) square; (*para cartas*) pigeonhole; **C~ postal** o **de Correo(s)** (*Am*) P.O. Box; **sacar a algn de sus casillas** to drive sb round the bend (*fam*), make sb lose his temper

casillero [kasi'ʎero] NM (*para cartas*) pigeonholes *pl*

casino [ka'sino] NM club; (*de juego*) casino

★**caso** ['kaso] NM case; (*suceso*) event; **en ~ de ...** in case of ...; **el ~ es que** the fact is that; **en el mejor de los casos** at best; **en ese ~** in that case; **en todo ~** in any case; **en último ~** as a last resort; **hacer ~ a** to pay attention to; **hacer ~ omiso de** to fail to mention, pass over; **hacer** o **venir al ~** to be relevant

caspa ['kaspa] NF dandruff

Caspio ['kaspjo] NM: **el (mar) ~** Caspian Sea

casque *etc* ['kaske] VB *ver* **cascar**

casquillo [kas'kiʎo] NM (*de bombilla*) fitting; (*de bala*) cartridge case

cassette [ka'set] NM O F = **casete**

casta ['kasta] NF caste; (*raza*) breed

castaña [kas'taɲa] NF *ver* **castaño**

castañetear [kastaɲete'ar] /1a/ VI (*dientes*) to chatter

★**castaño, -a** [kas'taɲo, a] ADJ chestnut, chestnut-coloured, brown ▶ NM chestnut tree; **~ de Indias** horse chestnut tree ▶ NF chestnut; (*fam: golpe*) punch

★**castañuelas** [kasta'ɲwelas] NFPL castanets

★**castellano, -a** [kaste'ʎano, a] ADJ Castilian; (*fam*) Spanish ▶ NM/F Castilian; (*fam*) Spaniard ▶ NM (*Ling*) Castilian, Spanish

The term **castellano** is sometimes used in Spain and Spanish America to refer to the Spanish language, since *español* is too closely associated with Spain as a nation. In Spain, *castellano* is generally used to refer to the language spoken throughout the country in contrast to the other regional co-official languages: Catalan, Basque, and Galician.

castellonense [kasteʎo'nense] ADJ of o from Castellón de la Plana ▸ NMF native o inhabitant of Castellón de la Plana

castidad [kasti'ðað] NF chastity, purity

★**castigar** [kasti'ɣar] /1h/ VT to punish; (Deporte) to penalize; (afligir) to afflict

★**castigo** [kas'tiɣo] NM punishment; (Deporte) penalty

castigue etc [kas'tiɣe] VB ver **castigar**

Castilla [kas'tiʎa] NF Castile

★**castillo** [kas'tiʎo] NM castle

castizo, -a [kas'tiθo, a] ADJ (Ling) pure; (de buena casta) purebred, pedigree; (auténtico) genuine

casto, -a ['kasto, a] ADJ chaste, pure

castor [kas'tor] NM beaver

castrar [kas'trar] /1a/ VT to castrate; (gato) to doctor; (Bot) to prune

castrense [kas'trense] ADJ army cpd, military

casual [ka'swal] ADJ chance, accidental

Do not translate the Spanish word **casual** by *casual*.

---

casualidad [kaswali'ðað] NF chance, accident; (combinación de circunstancias) coincidence; **da la ~ de que ...** it (just) so happens that ...; **¡qué ~!** what a coincidence!

casualmente [kaswal'mente] ADV by chance

cataclismo [kata'klismo] NM cataclysm

catador [kata'ðor] NM taster

catadura [kata'ðura] NF (aspecto) looks pl

★**catalán, -ana** [kata'lan, ana] ADJ, NM/F Catalan ▸ NM (Ling) Catalan; ver tb **lenguas cooficiales**

catalejo [kata'lexo] NM telescope

catalizador [kataliθa'ðor] NM catalyst; (Auto) catalytic converter

catalogar [katalo'ɣar] /1h/ VT to catalogue; **~ (de)** (fig) to classify as

catálogo [ka'taloɣo] NM catalogue

catalogue etc [kata'loɣe] VB ver **catalogar**

★**Cataluña** [kata'luɲa] NF Catalonia

cataplasma [kata'plasma] NF (Med) poultice

catapulta [kata'pulta] NF catapult

catar [ka'tar] /1a/ VT to taste, sample

catarata [kata'rata] NF (Geo) (water)fall; (Med) cataract

★**catarro** [ka'tarro] NM catarrh; (constipado) cold

catarsis [ka'tarsis] NF catharsis

catastro [ka'tastro] NM property register

★**catástrofe** [ka'tastrofe] NF catastrophe

catear [kate'ar] /1a/ VT (fam: examen, alumno) to fail

catecismo [kate'θismo] NM catechism

cátedra ['kateðra] NF (Univ) chair, professorship; (Escol) principal teacher's post; **sentar ~ sobre un argumento** to take one's stand on an argument

★**catedral** [kate'ðral] NF cathedral

catedrático, -a [kate'ðratiko, a] NM/F professor; (Escol) principal teacher

categoría [kateɣo'ria] NF category; (rango) rank, standing; (calidad) quality; **de ~** (hotel) top-class; **de baja ~** (oficial) low-ranking; **de segunda ~** second-rate; **no tiene ~** he has no standing

categórico, -a [kate'ɣoriko, a] ADJ categorical

catequesis [kate'kesis] NF catechism lessons

caterva [ka'terβa] NF throng, crowd

cateto, -a [ka'teto, a] NM/F yokel

cátodo ['katoðo] NM cathode

catolicismo [katoli'θismo] NM Catholicism

★**católico, -a** [ka'toliko, a] ADJ, NM/F Catholic

★**catorce** [ka'torθe] NUM fourteen

catre ['katre] NM camp bed (BRIT), cot (US); (fam) pit

Cáucaso ['kaukaso] NM Caucasus

cauce ['kauθe] NM (de río) riverbed; (fig) channel

caucho ['kautʃo] NM rubber; (AM: llanta) tyre

caución [kau'θjon] NF bail

caucionar [kauθjo'nar] /1a/ VT (Jur) to bail (out), go bail for

caudal [kau'ðal] NM (de río) volume, flow; (fortuna) wealth; (abundancia) abundance

caudaloso, -a [kauða'loso, a] ADJ (río) large; (persona) wealthy, rich

caudillaje [kauði'ʎaxe] NM leadership

caudillo [kau'ðiʎo] NM leader, chief

★**causa** ['kausa] NF cause; (razón) reason; (Jur) lawsuit, case; **a o por ~ de** because of, on account of

★**causar** [kau'sar] /1a/ VT to cause

cáustico, -a ['kaustiko, a] ADJ caustic

cautela [kau'tela] NF caution, cautiousness

cauteloso, -a [kaute'loso, a] ADJ cautious, wary

cautivar [kauti'βar] /1a/ VT to capture; (fig) to captivate

cautiverio [kauti'βerjo] NM, **cautividad** [kautiβi'ðað] NF captivity

cautivo, -a [kau'tiβo, a] ADJ, NM/F captive

cauto, -a ['kauto, a] ADJ cautious, careful

cava ['kaβa] NF (bodega) (wine) cellar ▸ NM (vino) champagne-type wine

★**cavar** [ka'βar] /1a/ VT to dig; (Agr) to dig over

caverna [ka'βerna] NF cave, cavern

cavernoso, -a [kaβer'noso, a] ADJ cavernous; (voz) resounding

caviar [ka'βjar] NM caviar(e)

cavidad [kaβi'ðað] NF cavity

cavilación [kaβila'θjon] NF deep thought

cavilar [kaβi'lar] /**1a**/ VT to ponder

cayado [ka'jaðo] NM (de pastor) crook; (de obispo) crozier

cayendo etc [ka'jendo] VB ver **caer**

★**caza** ['kaθa] NF (acción: gen) hunting; (: con fusil) shooting; (una caza) hunt, chase; (animales) game; **coto de ~** hunting estate; **ir de ~** to go hunting; **~ mayor** game hunting ▶ NM (Aviat) fighter

cazabe [ka'saβe] NM (AM) cassava bread o flour

cazador, a [kaθa'ðor, a] NM/F hunter/huntress ▶ NF jacket

cazaejecutivos [kaθaexeku'tiβos] NMF INV (Com) headhunter

★**cazar** [ka'θar] /**1f**/ VT to hunt; (perseguir) to chase; (prender) to catch; **cazarlas al vuelo** to be pretty sharp

cazasubmarinos [kaθasuβma'rinos] NM INV (Naut) destroyer; (Aviat) anti-submarine craft

cazo ['kaθo] NM saucepan

cazuela [ka'θwela] NF (vasija) pan; (guisado) casserole

cazurro, -a [ka'θurro, a] ADJ surly

CC ABR (= compensación de carbono) carbon offsetting ▶ NM ABR (Pol: = Comité Central) Central Committee

c/c. ABR (Com: = cuenta corriente) current account

CC AA ABR (ESP) = **Comunidades Autónomas**

CCI NF ABR (Com: = Cámara de Comercio Internacional) ICC

CC OO ABR = **Comisiones Obreras**

★**CD** [θe'ðe] NM ABR (= compact disc) CD; (Pol: = Cuerpo Diplomático) CD (= Diplomatic Corps)

c/d ABR (= en casa de) c/o, care of

CDN NM ABR (= Centro Dramático Nacional) ≈ RADA (BRIT)

CD-ROM [θeðe'rom] NM ABR CD-ROM

CE NM ABR (= Consejo de Europa) Council of Europe ▶ NF ABR (= Comunidad Europea) EC

cebada [θe'βaða] NF barley

cebar [θe'βar] /**1a**/ VT (animal) to fatten (up); (anzuelo) to bait; (Mil, Tec) to prime ■ **cebarse** VR: **cebarse en** to vent one's fury on, take it out on

cebo ['θeβo] NM (gen: para animales) feed, food; (para peces, fig) bait; (de arma) charge

★**cebolla** [θe'βoʎa] NF onion

cebolleta [θeβo'ʎeta] NF spring onion

cebollino [θeβo'ʎino] NM spring onion

cebón, -ona [θe'βon, ona] ADJ fat, fattened

cebra ['θeβra] NF zebra; **paso de ~** zebra crossing

CECA ['θeka] NF ABR (= Comunidad Europea del Carbón y del Acero) ECSC

ceca ['θeka] NF: **andar** o **ir de la ~ a la Meca** to chase about all over the place

cecear [θeθe'ar] /**1a**/ VI to lisp

ceceo [θe'θeo] NM lisp

cecina [θe'θina] NF cured o smoked meat

cedazo [θe'ðaθo] NM sieve

ceder [θe'ðer] /**2a**/ VT (entregar) to hand over; (renunciar a) to give up, part with; **"ceda el paso"** (Auto) "give way" ▶ VI (renunciar) to give in, yield; (disminuir) to diminish, decline; (romperse) to give way; (viento) to drop; (fiebre etc) to abate

cederom [θeðe'rom] NM CD-ROM

cedro ['θeðro] NM cedar

cédula ['θeðula] NF certificate, document; **~ de identidad** (AM) identity card; **~ electoral** (AM) ballot; **~ en blanco** blank cheque; ver tb **Documento Nacional de Identidad**

cegar [θe'ɣar] /**1h, 1j**/ VT to blind; (tubería etc) to block up, stop up ▶ VI to go blind ■ **cegarse** VR: **cegarse (de)** to be blinded (by)

cegué etc [θe'ɣe] VB ver **cegar**

ceguemos etc [θe'ɣemos] VB ver **cegar**

ceguera [θe'ɣera] NF blindness

CEI ['θei] NF ABR (= Comunidad de Estados Independientes) CIS

Ceilán [θei'lan] NM Ceylon, Sri Lanka

ceja ['θexa] NF eyebrow; **cejas pobladas** bushy eyebrows; **arquear las cejas** to raise one's eyebrows; **fruncir las cejas** to frown

cejar [θe'xar] /**1a**/ VI (fig) to back down; **no ~** to keep it up, stick at it

cejijunto, -a [θexi'xunto, a] ADJ with bushy eyebrows; (fig) scowling

celada [θe'laða] NF ambush, trap

celador, a [θela'ðor, a] NM/F (de edificio) watchman; (de museo etc) attendant; (de cárcel) warder

celda ['θelda] NF cell

celebérrimo, -a [θele'βerrimo, a] ADJ SUPERLATIVO de **célebre**

celebración [θeleβra'θjon] NF celebration

★**celebrar** [θele'βrar] /**1a**/ VT to celebrate; (alabar) to praise ▶ VI to be glad ■ **celebrarse** VR to occur, take place

★**célebre** ['θeleβre] ADJ famous

celebridad [θeleβri'ðað] NF fame; (persona) celebrity

celeridad [θeleri'ðað] NF: **con ~** promptly

celeste [θe'leste] ADJ sky-blue; (cuerpo etc) heavenly ▶ NM sky blue

celestial [θeles'tjal] ADJ celestial, heavenly

celibato [θeli'βato] NM celibacy

célibe ['θeliβe] ADJ, NMF celibate

celo[1] ['θelo] NM zeal; (Rel) fervour; (pey) envy; **en ~** (animales) on heat ■ **celos** NMPL jealousy sg; **tener celos de algn** to be jealous of sb; **dar celos a algn** to make sb jealous

celo[2] ® ['θelo] NM Sellotape®

celofán [θelo'fan] NM Cellophane®

celosía [θelo'sia] NF lattice (window)

★celoso, -a [θeˈloso, a] ADJ (*envidioso*) jealous; (*trabajador*) zealous; (*desconfiado*) suspicious

celta [ˈθelta] ADJ Celtic ▶ NMF Celt

célula [ˈθelula] NF cell

celular [θeluˈlar] NM (AM) mobile (phone) (BRIT), cellphone (US) ▶ ADJ: **tejido ~ cell** tissue

celulitis [θeluˈlitis] NF (*enfermedad*) cellulitis; (*grasa*) cellulite

celuloide [θeluˈloiðe] NM celluloid

celulosa [θeluˈlosa] NF cellulose

cementerio [θemenˈterjo] NM cemetery, graveyard; **~ de coches** scrap yard

cemento [θeˈmento] NM cement; (*hormigón*) concrete; (AM: *cola*) glue

★cena [ˈθena] NF evening meal, dinner

cenagal [θenaˈɣal] NM bog, quagmire

★cenar [θeˈnar] /1a/ VT to have for dinner, dine on ▶ VI to have dinner, dine

cencerro [θenˈθerro] NM cowbell; **estar como un ~** (*fam*) to be round the bend

★cenicero [θeniˈθero] NM ashtray

ceniciento, -a [θeniˈθjento, a] ADJ ashen, ash-coloured

cenit [θeˈnit] NM zenith

ceniza [θeˈniθa] NF ash, ashes *pl*

censar [θenˈsar] /1a/ VT to take a census of

censo [ˈθenso] NM census; **~ electoral** electoral roll

censor [θenˈsor] NM censor; **~ de cuentas** (Com) auditor; **~ jurado de cuentas** chartered (BRIT) o certified public (US) accountant

censura [θenˈsura] NF (Pol) censorship; (*moral*) censure, criticism

censurable [θensuˈraβle] ADJ reprehensible

censurar [θensuˈrar] /1a/ VT (*idea*) to censure; (*cortar: película*) to censor

centavo [θenˈtaβo] NM hundredth (part); (AM) cent

centella [θenˈteʎa] NF spark

centellear [θenteʎeˈar] /1a/ VI (*metal*) to gleam; (*estrella*) to twinkle; (*fig*) to sparkle

centelleo [θenteˈʎeo] NM gleam(ing); twinkling; sparkling

centena [θenˈtena] NF hundred

centenar [θenteˈnar] NM hundred

centenario, -a [θenteˈnarjo, a] ADJ hundred-year-old; **ser ~** to be one hundred years old ▶ NM centenary

centeno [θenˈteno] NM rye

centésimo, -a [θenˈtesimo, a] ADJ, NM hundredth

centígrado [θenˈtiɣraðo] ADJ centigrade

centigramo [θentiˈɣramo] NM centigramme

centilitro [θentiˈlitro] NM centilitre (BRIT), centiliter (US)

★centímetro [θenˈtimetro] NM centimetre (BRIT), centimeter (US)

★céntimo [ˈθentimo] NM cent

centinela [θentiˈnela] NM sentry, guard

centollo, -a [θenˈtoʎo, a] NM/F large (*o* spider) crab

central [θenˈtral] ADJ central ▶ NF head office; (*Tec*) plant; (*Telec*) exchange; **~ eléctrica** power station; **~ nuclear** nuclear power station; **~ telefónica** telephone exchange

centralice *etc* [θentraˈliθe] VB *ver* **centralizar**

centralita [θentraˈlita] NF switchboard

centralización [θentraliθaˈθjon] NF centralization

centralizar [θentraliˈθar] /1f/ VT to centralize

centrar [θenˈtrar] /1a/ VT to centre

★céntrico, -a [ˈθentriko, a] ADJ central

centrifugar [θentrifuˈɣar] /1h/ VT (*ropa*) to spin-dry

centrífugo, -a [θenˈtrifuɣo, a] ADJ centrifugal

centrifugue *etc* [θentriˈfuɣe] VB *ver* **centrifugar**

centrista [θenˈtrista] ADJ centre *cpd*

★centro [ˈθentro] NM centre; **ser de ~** (*Pol*) to be a moderate; **~ de acogida (para niños)** children's home; **~ de beneficios** (Com) profit centre; **~ cívico** community centre; **~ comercial** shopping centre; **~ de informática** computer centre; **~ (de determinación) de costos** (Com) cost centre; **~ delantero** (*Deporte*) centre forward; **~ de atención al cliente** call centre; **~ de salud** health centre; **~ docente** teaching institution; **~ escolar** school; **~ juvenil** youth club; **~ social** community centre; **~ turístico** (*lugar muy visitado*) tourist centre; **~ urbano** urban area, city

centroafricano, -a [θentroafriˈkano, a] ADJ: **la República Centroafricana** the Central African Republic

centroamericano, -a [θentroameriˈkano, a] ADJ, NM/F Central American

centrocampista [θentrokamˈpista] NMF (*Deporte*) midfielder

ceñido, -a [θeˈɲiðo, a] ADJ tight

ceñir [θeˈɲir] /3h, 3k/ VT (*rodear*) to encircle, surround; (*ajustar*) to fit (tightly); (*apretar*) to tighten ■ **ceñirse** VR: **ceñirse algo** to put sth on; **ceñirse al asunto** to stick to the matter in hand

ceño [ˈθeɲo] NM frown, scowl; **fruncir el ~** to frown, knit one's brow

CEOE [ˈθeoe] NF ABR (= *Confederación Española de Organizaciones Empresariales*) ≈ CBI (BRIT)

cepa [ˈθepa] NF (*de vid, fig*) stock; (Bio) strain

CEPAL [θeˈpal] NF ABR (= *Comisión Económica de las Naciones Unidas para la América Latina*) ECLA

★cepillar [θepiˈʎar] /1a/ VT to brush; (*madera*) to plane (down)

★cepillo [θeˈpiʎo] NM brush; (*para madera*) plane; (*Rel*) poor box, alms box; **~ de dientes** toothbrush

cepo [ˈθepo] NM (*de caza*) trap

CEPSA ['θepsa] NF ABR (*Com*) = **Compañía Española de Petróleos, S.A.**

CEPYME [θe'pime] NF ABR = **Confederación Española de la Pequeña y Mediana Empresa**

cera ['θera] NF wax; **~ de abejas** beeswax

cerámica [θe'ramika] NF pottery; (*arte*) ceramics *sg*

ceramista [θera'mista] NMF potter

cerbatana [θerβa'tana] NF blowpipe

★**cerca** ['θerka] NF fence ▶ ADV near, nearby, close; **por aquí ~** nearby ▶ PREP: **~ de** (*cantidad*) nearly, about; (*distancia*) near, close to

cercado [θer'kaðo] NM enclosure

cercanía [θerka'nia] NF nearness, closeness ▪ **cercanías** NFPL outskirts, suburbs; **tren de cercanías** commuter o local train

★**cercano, -a** [θer'kano, a] ADJ close, near; (*pueblo etc*) nearby; **C~ Oriente** Near East

cercar [θer'kar] /**1g**/ VT to fence in; (*rodear*) to surround

cerciorar [θerθjo'rar] /**1a**/ VT (*asegurar*) to assure ▪ **cerciorarse** VR: **cerciorarse (de)** (*descubrir*) to find out (about); (*asegurarse*) to make sure (of)

cerco ['θerko] NM (*Agr*) enclosure; (*Am*) fence; (*Mil*) siege

cerda ['θerða] NF (*de cepillo*) bristle; (*Zool*) sow

cerdada [θer'ðaða] NF (*fam*): **hacer una ~ a algn** to play a dirty trick on sb

Cerdeña [θer'ðeɲa] NF Sardinia

★**cerdo** ['θerðo] NM pig; **carne de ~** pork

★**cereal** [θere'al] NM cereal ▪ **cereales** NMPL cereals, grain *sg*

cerebral [θere'βral] ADJ (*tb fig*) cerebral; (*tumor*) brain *cpd*

★**cerebro** [θe'reβro] NM brain; (*fig*) brains *pl*; **ser un ~** (*fig*) to be brilliant

ceremonia [θere'monja] NF ceremony; **reunión de ~** formal meeting; **hablar sin ~** to speak plainly

ceremonial [θeremo'njal] ADJ, NM ceremonial

ceremonioso, -a [θeremo'njoso, a] ADJ ceremonious; (*cumplido*) formal

★**cereza** [θe'reθa] NF cherry

cerezo [θe'reθo] NM cherry tree

cerilla [θe'riʎa] NF, **cerillo** [se'riʎo] NM (*Am*) match

cerner [θer'ner] /**2g**/ VT to sift, sieve ▪ **cernerse** VR to hover

cero ['θero] NM nothing, zero; (*Deporte*) nil; **8 grados bajo ~** 8 degrees below zero; **a partir de ~** from scratch

cerque *etc* ['θerke] VB *ver* **cercar**

cerquillo [θer'kiʎo] NM (*Am*) fringe (*Brit*), bangs *pl* (*US*)

★**cerrado, -a** [θe'rraðo, a] ADJ closed, shut; (*con llave*) locked; (*tiempo*) cloudy, overcast; (*curva*) sharp; (*acento*) thick, broad; **a puerta cerrada** (*Jur*) in camera

★**cerradura** [θerra'ðura] NF (*acción*) closing; (*mecanismo*) lock

cerrajería [θerraxe'ria] NF locksmith's craft; (*tienda*) locksmith's (shop)

cerrajero, -a [θerra'xero, a] NM/F locksmith

★**cerrar** [θe'rrar] /**1j**/ VT to close, shut; (*paso, carretera*) to close; (*grifo*) to turn off; (*trato, cuenta, negocio*) to close; **~ con llave** to lock; **~ el sistema** (*Inform*) to close o shut down the system; **~ un trato** to strike a bargain ▶ VI to close, shut; (*la noche*) to come down ▪ **cerrarse** VR to close, shut; (*herida*) to heal

cerro ['θerro] NM hill; **andar por los cerros de Úbeda** to wander from the point, digress

cerrojo [θe'rroxo] NM (*herramienta*) bolt; (*de puerta*) latch

certamen [θer'tamen] NM competition, contest

certero, -a [θer'tero, a] ADJ accurate

certeza [θer'teθa], **certidumbre** [θerti'ðumbre] NF certainty

certidumbre [θerti'ðumβre] NF = **certeza**

certificación [θertifika'θjon] NF certification; (*Jur*) affidavit

★**certificado, -a** [θertifi'kaðo, a] ADJ certified; (*Correos*) registered ▶ NM certificate; **~ médico** medical certificate

certificar [θertifi'kar] /**1g**/ VT (*asegurar, atestar*) to certify

certifique *etc* [θerti'fike] VB *ver* **certificar**

cervatillo [θerβa'tiʎo] NM fawn

cervecería [θerβeθe'ria] NF (*fábrica*) brewery; (*taberna*) public house, pub

★**cerveza** [θer'βeθa] NF beer; **~ de barril** draught beer

cervical [θerβi'kal] ADJ cervical

cerviz [θer'βiθ] NF nape of the neck

cesación [θesa'θjon] NF cessation, suspension

cesante [θe'sante] ADJ redundant; (*Am*) unemployed; (*ministro*) outgoing; (*diplomático*) recalled ▶ NMF redundant worker

cesantía [θesan'tia] NF (*Am*) unemployment

★**cesar** [θe'sar] /**1a**/ VI to cease, stop; (*de un trabajo*) to leave ▶ VT (*en el trabajo*) to dismiss; (*alto cargo*) to remove from office

cesárea [θe'sarea] NF Caesarean (section)

cese ['θese] NM (*de trabajo*) dismissal; (*de pago*) suspension

CESID [θe'sið] NM ABR (*Esp*: = *Centro Superior de Investigación de la Defensa Nacional*) military intelligence service

cesión [θe'sjon] NF: **~ de bienes** surrender of property

★**césped** ['θespeð] NM grass, lawn

★**cesta** ['θesta] NF basket

★**cesto** ['θesto] NM (large) basket, hamper

cetrería [θetre'ria] NF falconry

cetrino, -a [θe'trino, a] ADJ (*tez*) sallow

cetro [ˈθetro] NM sceptre

Ceuta [ˈθeˈuta] NF Ceuta

ceutí [θeuˈti] ADJ of o from Ceuta ▶ NMF native o inhabitant of Ceuta

C.F. ABR (= *Club de Fútbol*) F.C.

CFC [θeefeˈθe] NM ABR (= *clorofluorocarbono*) CFC

cfr. ABR (= *confróntese, compárese*) cf

cg ABR (= *centígramo*) cg

CGPJ NM ABR (= *Consejo General del Poder Judicial*) *governing body of Spanish legal system*

CGT [θexeˈte] NF ABR (COLOMBIA, MÉXICO, NICARA-GUA, ESP) = **Confederación General de Trabaja-dores**; (ARGENTINA) = **Confederación General del Trabajo**

Ch, ch [tʃe] NF *former letter in the Spanish alphabet*

chabacano, -a [tʃaβaˈkano, a] ADJ vulgar, coarse

chabola [tʃaˈβola] NF shack; **barriada** *or* **barrio de chabolas** shanty town

chabolismo [tʃaβoˈlismo] NM: **el problema del ~** the problem of substandard housing, the shanty town problem

chacal [tʃaˈkal] NM jackal

chacarero [tʃakaˈrero] NM (AM) small farmer

chacha [ˈtʃatʃa] NF (*fam*) maid

cháchara [ˈtʃatʃara] NF chatter; **estar de ~** to chatter away

chacra [ˈtʃakra] NF (AM) smallholding

chafa [ˈtʃafa] ADJ (AM *fam*) useless, dud

chafar [tʃaˈfar] /1a/ VT (*aplastar*) to crush, flatten; (*arruinar*) to ruin

chaflán [tʃaˈflan] NM (*Tec*) bevel

chal [tʃal] NM shawl

chalado, -a [tʃaˈlaðo, a] ADJ (*fam*) crazy

chalé [tʃaˈle] (*pl* **chalés** [tʃaˈles]) NM = **chalet**

★**chaleco** [tʃaˈleko] NM waistcoat, vest (US); **~ anti-balas** bulletproof vest; **~ salvavidas** life jacket; **~ de seguridad**, **~ reflectante** high-visibility vest

★**chalet** [tʃaˈle] (*pl* **chalets** [tʃaˈles]) NM villa, ≈ detached house; **~ adosado** semi-detached house

chalupa [tʃaˈlupa] NF launch, boat

chamaco, -a [tʃaˈmako, a] NM/F (AM) kid

chamarra [tʃaˈmarra] NF sheepskin jacket; (AM: *poncho*) blanket

★**champán** [tʃamˈpan] NM, **champaña** [tʃamˈpaɲa] NM champagne

★**champiñón** [tʃampiˈɲon] NM mushroom

★**champú** [tʃamˈpu] (*pl* **champús** *o* **champúes**) NM shampoo

chamuscar [tʃamusˈkar] /1g/ VT to scorch, singe

chamusque *etc* [tʃaˈmuske] VB *ver* **chamuscar**

chamusquina [tʃamusˈkina] NF singeing

chance [ˈtʃanθe] NM o F (AM) chance, opportunity

chanchada [tʃanˈtʃaða] NF (AM *fam*) dirty trick

chancho, -a [ˈtʃantʃo, a] NM/F (AM) pig

chanchullo [tʃanˈtʃuʎo] NM (*fam*) fiddle, wangle

chancla [ˈtʃankla], **chancleta** [tʃanˈkleta] NF flip-flop; (*zapato viejo*) old shoe

★**chandal** [tʃanˈdal] NM tracksuit; **~ (de Tactel®)** shellsuit

chantaje [tʃanˈtaxe] NM blackmail; **hacer ~ a uno** to blackmail sb

chanza [ˈtʃanθa] NF joke

chao [ˈtʃao] EXCL (*fam*) cheerio

chapa [ˈtʃapa] NF (*de metal*) plate, sheet; (*de madera*) board, panel; (*de botella*) bottle top; (*insignia*) (lapel) badge; (AM *Auto*: *tb*: **chapa de matrícula**) number (BRIT) o license (US) plate; (AM: *cerradura*) lock; **de 3 chapas** (*madera*) 3-ply

chapado, -a [tʃaˈpaðo, a] ADJ (*metal*) plated; (*muebles etc*) finished; **~ en oro** gold-plated

chaparro, -a [tʃaˈparro, a] ADJ squat; (AM: *bajito*) short

★**chaparrón** [tʃapaˈrron] NM downpour, cloud-burst

chapata [tʃaˈpata] NF ciabatta

chaperón, -ona [tʃapeˈron, ona] NM/F (AM): **hacer de ~** to play gooseberry

chapotear [tʃapoteˈar] /1a/ VT to sponge down ▶ VI (*fam*) to splash about

chapucero, -a [tʃapuˈθero, a] ADJ rough, crude ▶ NM/F bungler

chapulín [tʃapuˈlin] NM (AM) grasshopper

chapurrar [tʃapurˈrar] /1a/, **chapurrear** [tʃapurreˈar] /1a/ VT (*idioma*) to speak badly

chapuza [tʃaˈpuθa] NF botched job

chapuzón [tʃapuˈθon] NM: **darse un ~** to go for a dip

chaqué [tʃaˈke] NM morning coat

★**chaqueta** [tʃaˈketa] NF jacket; **cambiar la ~** (*fig*) to change sides

chaquetón [tʃakeˈton] NM (three-quarter-length) coat

charca [ˈtʃarka] NF pond, pool

charco [ˈtʃarko] NM pool, puddle

charcutería [tʃarkuteˈria] NF (*tienda*) *shop sell-ing chiefly pork meat products*; (*productos*) cooked pork meats *pl*

charla [ˈtʃarla] NF talk, chat; (*conferencia*) lecture

★**charlar** [tʃarˈlar] /1a/ VI to talk, chat

charlatán, -ana [tʃarlaˈtan, ana] NM/F chatterbox; (*estafador*) trickster

charol[1] [tʃaˈrol] NM varnish; (*cuero*) patent leather

charol[2] [tʃaˈrol] NM, **charola** [tʃaˈrola] NF (AM) tray

charqui [ˈtʃarki] NM (AM) dried beef, jerky (US)

charro, -a [ˈtʃarro, a] ADJ Salamancan; (AM) Mexican; (*ropa*) loud, gaudy; (*costumbres*) traditional ▶ NM/F Salamancan ▶ NM (*vaquero*) typical Mexican

chárter ['tʃarter] ADJ INV: **vuelo ~** charter flight

chascarrillo [tʃaska'rriʎo] NM (fam) funny story

chasco ['tʃasko] NM (broma) trick, joke; (desengaño) disappointment

chasis ['tʃasis] NM INV (Auto) chassis; (Foto) plate holder

chasquear [tʃaske'ar] /1a/ VT (látigo) to crack; (lengua) to click

chasquido [tʃas'kiðo] NM (de lengua) click; (de látigo) crack

chat [tʃat] NM (Internet) chat room

chatarra [tʃa'tarra] NF scrap (metal)

★**chatear** [tʃate'ar] /1a/ VI (Internet) to chat

chatero, -a [tʃa'tero, a] ADJ chat cpd ▶ NM/F chat-room user

chato, -a ['tʃato, a] ADJ flat; (nariz) snub ▶ NM wine tumbler; **beber unos chatos** to have a few drinks

chau [tʃau], **chaucito** [tʃau'sito] EXCL (fam) cheerio

chaucha ['tʃautʃa] NF (Am) runner (Brit) o pole (US) bean

chauvinismo [tʃoβi'nismo] NM chauvinism

chauvinista [tʃoβi'nista] ADJ, NMF chauvinist

chaval, a [tʃa'βal, a] NM/F kid (fam), lad/lass

chavo, -a ['tʃaβo, a] NM/F (Am fam) guy/girl

checar [tʃe'kar] /1g/ VT (Am): **~ tarjeta** (al entrar) to clock in o on; (al salir) to clock off o out

checo, -a ['tʃeko, a] ADJ, NM/F Czech; **la República Checa** the Czech Republic ▶ NM (Ling) Czech

checo(e)slovaco, -a [tʃeko(e)slo'βako, a] ADJ, NM/F (Historia) Czech, Czechoslovak

Checo(e)slovaquia [tʃeko(e)slo'βakja] NF (Historia) Czechoslovakia

chepa ['tʃepa] NF hump

★**cheque** ['tʃeke] NM cheque (Brit), check (US); **cobrar un ~** to cash a cheque; **~ abierto/en blanco/cruzado** open/blank/crossed cheque; **~ al portador** cheque payable to bearer; **~ de viajero** traveller's cheque

chequeo [tʃe'keo] NM (Med) check-up; (Auto) service

chequera [tʃe'kera] NF (Am) chequebook (Brit), checkbook (US)

Chequia ['tʃekja] NF Czechia

chévere ['tʃeβere] ADJ (Am) great, fabulous (fam)

chicano, -a [tʃi'kano, a] ADJ, NM/F chicano, Mexican-American

chicha ['tʃitʃa] NF (Am) maize liquor

chícharo ['tʃitʃaro] NM (Am) pea

chicharra [tʃi'tʃarra] NF harvest bug, cicada

chicharrón [tʃitʃa'rron] NM (pork) crackling

chichón [tʃi'tʃon] NM bump, lump

chicle ['tʃikle] NM chewing gum

★**chico, -a** ['tʃiko, a] ADJ small, little ▶ NM/F child; (muchacho) boy; (muchacha) girl

chicote [tʃi'kote] NM (Am) whip

chiflado, -a [tʃi'flaðo, a] ADJ (fam) crazy, round the bend ▶ NM/F nutcase

chiflar [tʃi'flar] /1a/ VT to hiss, boo ▶ VI (esp Am) to whistle

chilango, -a [tʃi'lango, a] ADJ (Am) of o from Mexico City

★**Chile** ['tʃile] NM Chile

chile ['tʃile] NM chilli pepper

★**chileno, -a** [tʃi'leno, a] ADJ, NM/F Chilean

★**chillar** [tʃi'ʎar] /1a/ VI (persona) to yell, scream; (animal salvaje) to howl; (cerdo) to squeal; (puerta) to creak

chillido [tʃi'ʎiðo] NM (de persona) yell, scream; (de animal) howl; (de frenos) screech(ing)

chillón, -ona [tʃi'ʎon, ona] ADJ (niño) noisy; (color) loud, gaudy

★**chimenea** [tʃime'nea] NF chimney; (hogar) fireplace

chimpancé [tʃimpan'θe] (pl **chimpancés** [tʃimpan'θes]) NM chimpanzee

★**China** ['tʃina] NF: **(la) ~** China

china ['tʃina] NF pebble

chinchar [tʃin'tʃar] /1a/ (fam) VT to pester, annoy ■ **chincharse** VR to get cross; **¡chínchate!** tough!

chinche ['tʃintʃe] NF bug; (Tec) drawing pin (Brit), thumbtack (US) ▶ NMF nuisance, pest

chincheta [tʃin'tʃeta] NF drawing pin (Brit), thumbtack (US)

chinchorro [tʃin'tʃorro] NM (Am) hammock

chingado, -a [tʃin'gaðo, a] ADJ (esp Am fam!) lousy, bloody (fam!); **hijo de la chingada** bastard (fam!), son of a bitch (US fam!)

chingar [tʃin'gar] /1h/ VT (Am fam!) to fuck (up) (fam!), screw (up) (fam!) ■ **chingarse** VR (Am: emborracharse) to get pissed (Brit), get plastered; (: fracasar) to fail

chingue etc ['tʃinge] VB ver **chingar**

★**chino, -a** ['tʃino, a] ADJ, NM/F Chinese ▶ NM (Ling) Chinese; (Culin) chinois, conical strainer

chip [tʃip] NM (Inform) chip

chipirón [tʃipi'ron] NM squid

Chipre ['tʃipre] NF Cyprus

chipriota [tʃi'prjota] ADJ Cypriot, Cyprian ▶ NMF Cypriot

chiquillada [tʃiki'ʎaða] NF childish prank; (Am: chiquillos) kids pl

chiquillo, -a [tʃi'kiʎo, a] NM/F kid (fam), youngster, child

chiquito, -a [tʃi'kito, a] ADJ very small, tiny ▶ NM/F kid (fam)

chirigota [tʃiri'ɣota] NF joke

chirimbolo [tʃirim'bolo] NM thingummyjig (fam)

chirimoya [tʃiri'moja] NF custard apple

chiringuito [tʃirin'gito] NM small open-air bar

chiripa [tʃi'ripa] NF fluke; **por ~** by chance

chirona [tʃi'rona], (AM) **chirola** [tʃi'rola] NF (*fam*) clink, jail

chirriar [tʃi'rrjar] /**1b**/ VI (*goznes*) to creak, squeak; (*pájaros*) to chirp, sing

chirrido [tʃi'rriðo] NM creak(ing), squeak(ing); (*de pájaro*) chirp(ing)

chis [tʃis] EXCL sh!

★**chisme** ['tʃisme] NM (*habladurías*) piece of gossip; (*fam: objeto*) thingummyjig

chismoso, -a [tʃis'moso, a] ADJ gossiping ▶ NM/F gossip

chispa ['tʃispa] NF spark; (*fig*) sparkle; (*ingenio*) wit; (*fam*) drunkenness

chispeante [tʃispe'ante] ADJ (*tb fig*) sparkling

chispear [tʃispe'ar] /**1a**/ VI to spark; (*lloviznar*) to drizzle

chisporrotear [tʃisporrote'ar] /**1a**/ VI (*fuego*) to throw out sparks; (*leña*) to crackle; (*aceite*) to hiss, splutter

chistar [tʃis'tar] /**1a**/ VI: **no ~** not to say a word

★**chiste** ['tʃiste] NM joke, funny story; **~ verde** blue joke

chistera [tʃis'tera] NF top hat

chistoso, -a [tʃis'toso, a] ADJ (*gracioso*) funny, amusing; (*bromista*) witty

chivarse [tʃi'βarse] /**1a**/ VR (*fam*) to grass

chivatazo [tʃiβa'taθo] NM (*fam*) tip-off; **dar ~** to inform

chivo, -a ['tʃiβo, a] NM/F (billy/nanny-)goat; **~ expiatorio** scapegoat

chocante [tʃo'kante] ADJ startling; (*extraño*) odd; (*ofensivo*) shocking

★**chocar** [tʃo'kar] /**1g**/ VI (*coches etc*) to collide, crash; (*Mil, fig*) to clash; **~ con** to collide with; (*fig*) to run into, run up against ▶ VT to shock; (*sorprender*) to startle; **¡chócala!** (*fam*) put it there!

chochear [tʃotʃe'ar] /**1a**/ VI to dodder, be senile

chocho, -a ['tʃotʃo, a] ADJ doddering, senile; (*fig*) soft, doting

choclo ['tʃoklo] NM (*Am: grano*) sweetcorn; (*mazorca*) corn on the cob

★**chocolate** [tʃoko'late] ADJ chocolate ▶ NM chocolate; (*fam*) dope, marijuana

chocolatería [tʃokolate'ria] NF chocolate factory (o shop)

chocolatina [tʃokola'tina] NF chocolate

★**chófer** ['tʃofer], (*esp* AM) **chofer** [tʃo'fer] NMF driver

chollo ['tʃoʎo] NM (*fam*) bargain, snip

chomba ['tʃomba], **chompa** ['tʃompa] NF (AM) jumper, sweater

chopo ['tʃopo] NM black poplar

★**choque** ['tʃoke] VB ver **chocar** ▶ NM (*impacto*) impact; (*golpe*) jolt; (*Auto*) crash; (*fig*) conflict; **~ frontal** head-on collision

★**chorizo** [tʃo'riθo] NM hard pork sausage (*type of salami*); (*ladrón*) crook

chorra ['tʃorra] NF luck

chorrada [tʃo'rraða] NF (*fam*): **¡es una ~!** that's crap! (*fam!*); **decir chorradas** to talk crap (*fam!*)

chorrear [tʃorre'ar] /**1a**/ VT to pour ▶ VI to gush (out), spout (out); (*gotear*) to drip, trickle

chorreras [tʃo'rreras] NFPL (*adorno*) frill sg

chorro ['tʃorro] NM jet; (*caudalito*) dribble, trickle; (*fig*) stream; **salir a chorros** to gush forth; **con propulsión a ~** jet-propelled

chotearse [tʃote'arse] /**1a**/ VR to joke

choto ['tʃoto] NM (*cabrito*) kid

chovinismo [tʃoβi'nismo] NM = **chauvinismo**

chovinista [tʃoβi'nista] ADJ, NMF = **chauvinista**

choza ['tʃoθa] NF hut, shack

★**chubasco** [tʃu'βasko] NM squall

chubasquero [tʃuβas'kero] NM cagoule, raincoat

chuche ['tʃutʃe] NF (*fam*) sweetie (BRIT *fam*), candy (US)

chuchería [tʃutʃe'ria] NF trinket

chucho ['tʃutʃo] NM (*Zool*) mongrel

chufa ['tʃufa] NF chufa, earth almond, tiger nut; **horchata de chufas** *drink made from chufas*

★**chuleta** [tʃu'leta] NF chop, cutlet; (*Escol: fam*) crib

chulo, -a ['tʃulo, a] ADJ (*encantador*) charming; (*aire*) proud; (*pey*) fresh; (*fam: estupendo*) great, fantastic ▶ NM (*pícaro*) rascal; (*madrileño*) working-class person from Madrid; (*rufián: tb*: **chulo de putas**) pimp

chumbera [tʃum'bera] NF prickly pear

chungo, -a ['tʃungo, a] (*fam*) ADJ lousy ▶ NF: **estar de chunga** to be in a merry mood

chupa ['tʃupa] NF (*fam*) jacket

chupado, -a [tʃu'paðo, a] ADJ (*delgado*) skinny, gaunt; **está ~** (*fam*) it's simple, it's dead easy

chupaleta [tʃupa'leta] NF (AM) lollipop

chupar [tʃu'par] /**1a**/ VT to suck; (*absorber*) to absorb ■ **chuparse** VR to grow thin; **para chuparse los dedos** mouthwatering

chupatintas [tʃupa'tintas] NM INV penpusher

chupe ['tʃupe] NM (AM) stew

chupete [tʃu'pete] NM dummy (BRIT), pacifier (US)

chupetín [tʃupe'tin] NF (AM) lollipop

chupetón [tʃupe'ton] NM suck

chupito [tʃu'pito] NM (*fam*) shot

chupón [tʃu'pon] NM (*piruleta*) lollipop; (*Am: chupete*) dummy (BRIT), pacifier (US)

churrasco [tʃu'rrasko] NM (AM) barbecue, barbecued meat

churrería [tʃurre'ria] NF *stall or shop which sells "churros"*

churrete [tʃu'rrete] NM grease spot

churretón [tʃurre'ton] NM stain

churrigueresco, -a [tʃurrige'resko, a] ADJ (*Arq*) baroque; (*fig*) excessively ornate

churro, -a ['tʃurro, a] ADJ coarse ▶ NM (*Culin*) (type of) fritter; *see note*; (*fam*: *chapuza*) botch, mess

Churros, long fritters made with flour and water, are very popular in much of Spain and are often eaten with thick hot chocolate, either for breakfast or as a snack. In Madrid, they eat a thicker variety of *churro* called *porra*.

churruscar [tʃurrus'kar] /1g/ VT to fry crisp

churrusque *etc* [tʃu'rruske] VB *ver* **churruscar**

churumbel [tʃurum'bel] NM (*fam*) kid

chus [tʃus] EXCL: **no decir ni ~ ni mus** not to say a word

chusco, -a ['tʃusko, a] ADJ funny

chusma ['tʃusma] NF rabble, mob

chutar [tʃu'tar] /1a/ VI (*Deporte*) to shoot (at goal); **esto va que chuta** it's going fine

chuzo ['tʃuθo] NM: **llueve a chuzos, llueven chuzos de punta** it's raining cats and dogs

C.I. ABR (= *coeficiente intelectual*; *coeficiente de inteligencia*) I.Q.

Cía. ABR (= *compañía*) Co.

cianuro [θja'nuro] NM cyanide

ciática ['θjatika] NF sciatica

ciberacoso [θiβera'koso] NM cyberbullying

ciberataque [θiβera'take] NM cyber attack

cibercafé [θiβerka'fe] NM cybercafé

ciberdelito [θiβerðe'lito] NM cybercrime

ciberespacio [θiβeres'paθjo] NM cyberspace

ciberespionaje [θiβerespio'naxe] NM cyberspying, cyberespionage

ciberfraude [θiβer'frauðe] NM cybercrime

cibernauta [θiβer'nauta] NMF cybernaut

cibernética [θiβer'netika] NF cybernetics *sg*

ciberseguridad [θiβerseyuri'ðað] NF cybersecurity

ciberterrorista [θiβerterro'rista] NMF cyberterrorist

cibertienda [θiβer'tjenda] NF online shop, online store

cicatrice *etc* [θika'triθe] VB *ver* **cicatrizar**

cicatriz [θika'triθ] NF scar

cicatrizar [θikatri'θar] /1f/ VT to heal ■ **cicatrizarse** VR to heal (up), form a scar

cíclico, -a ['θikliko, a] ADJ cyclical

ciclismo [θi'klismo] NM cycling

ciclista [θi'klista] ADJ cycle *cpd* ▶ NMF cyclist

ciclo ['θiklo] NM cycle

ciclomotor [θiklomo'tor] NM moped

ciclón [θi'klon] NM cyclone

cicloturismo [θiklotu'rismo] NM touring by bicycle

cicuta [θi'kuta] NF hemlock

ciego, -a ['θjeyo, a] VB *ver* **cegar** ▶ ADJ blind; **a ciegas** blindly; **me puse ciega de mariscos** (*fam*) I stuffed myself with seafood ▶ NM/F blind man/woman

ciegue *etc* ['θjeye] VB *ver* **cegar**

★**cielo** ['θjelo] NM sky; (*Rel*) heaven; (*Arq*: *tb*: **cielo raso**) ceiling; **¡cielos!** good heavens!; **ver el ~ abierto** to see one's chance

ciempiés [θjem'pjes] NM INV centipede

★**cien** [θjen] NUM *ver* **ciento**

ciénaga ['θjenaya] NF marsh, swamp

★**ciencia** ['θjenθja] NF science; **saber algo a ~ cierta** to know sth for certain ■ **ciencias** NFPL science *sg*

★**ciencia-ficción** ['θjenθjafik'θjon] NF science fiction

cieno ['θjeno] NM mud, mire

★**científico, -a** [θjen'tifiko, a] ADJ scientific ▶ NM/F scientist

★**ciento** ['θjento], **cien** NUM hundred; **pagar al 10 por ~** to pay at 10 per cent

cierne *etc* ['θjerne] VB *ver* **cerner** ▶ NM: **en ~** in blossom; **en ~(s)** (*fig*) in its infancy

cierre ['θjerre] VB *ver* **cerrar** ▶ NM closing, shutting; (*con llave*) locking; (*Radio, TV*) close-down; **~ de cremallera** zip (fastener); **precios de ~** (*Bolsa*) closing prices; **~ del sistema** (*Inform*) system shutdown

cierro *etc* VB *ver* **cerrar**

★**cierto, -a** ['θjerto, a] ADJ sure, certain; (*un tal*) a certain; (*correcto*) right, correct; **~ hombre** a certain man; **ciertas personas** certain *o* some people; **sí, es ~** yes, that's correct; **por ~** by the way; **lo ~ es que ...** the fact is that ...; **estar en lo ~** to be right

ciervo ['θjerβo] NM (*Zool*) deer; (*: macho*) stag

cierzo ['θjerθo] NM north wind

★**cifra** ['θifra] NF number, figure; (*cantidad*) number, quantity; (*secreta*) code; **~ global** lump sum; **~ de negocios** (*Com*) turnover; **en cifras redondas** in round figures; **~ de referencia** (*Com*) bench mark; **~ de ventas** (*Com*) sales figures

cifrado, -a [θi'fraðo, a] ADJ in code

cifrar [θi'frar] /1a/ VT to code, write in code; (*resumir*) to abridge; (*calcular*) to reckon

cigala [θi'yala] NF Norway lobster

cigarra [θi'yarra] NF cicada

cigarrera [θiya'rrera] NF cigar case

★**cigarrillo** [θiya'rriʎo] NM cigarette; **~ electrónico** e-cigarette

★**cigarro** [θi'yarro] NM cigarette; (*puro*) cigar

cigüeña [θi'ɣweɲa] NF stork

CIJ [θix] NF ABR (= *Corte Internacional de Justicia*) ICJ

cilíndrico, -a [θi'lindriko, a] ADJ cylindrical

cilindro [θi'lindro] NM cylinder

★**cima** ['θima] NF (*de montaña*) top, peak; (*de árbol*) top; (*fig*) height

címbalo ['θimbalo] NM cymbal

cimbrear [θimbre'ar] /1a/ VT to brandish ■ **cimbrearse** VR to sway

cimentar [θimenˈtar] /**1j**/ vT to lay the foundations of; (*fig: reforzar*) to strengthen; (: *fundar*) to found

cimiento [θiˈmjento] vB *ver* **cimentar** ▶ NM foundation

cinc [θink] NM zinc

cincel [θinˈθel] NM chisel

cincelar [θinθeˈlar] /**1a**/ vT to chisel

cincha [ˈθintʃa] NF girth, saddle strap

cincho [ˈθintʃo] NM sash, belt

★**cinco** [ˈθinko] NUM five; (*fecha*) fifth; **las ~ five** o'clock; **no estar en sus ~** (*fam*) to be off one's rocker

cincuenta [θinˈkwenta] NUM fifty

cincuentón, -ona [θinkwenˈton, ona] ADJ, NM/F fifty-year-old

★**cine** [ˈθine] NM cinema; **el ~ mudo** silent films *pl*; **hacer ~** to make films

cineasta [θineˈasta] NMF (*director*) film-maker *o* director

cine-club [ˈθineˈklub] NM film club

cinéfilo, -a [θiˈnefilo, a] NM/F film buff

cinematográfico, -a [θinematoˈɣrafiko, a] ADJ cine-, film *cpd*

cínico, -a [ˈθiniko, a] ADJ cynical; (*descarado*) shameless ▶ NM/F cynic

cinismo [θiˈnismo] NM cynicism

★**cinta** [ˈθinta] NF band, strip; (*de tela*) ribbon; (*película*) reel; (*de máquina de escribir*) ribbon; (*métrica*) tape measure; (*magnetofónica*) tape; **~ adhesiva** sticky tape; **~ aislante** insulating tape; **~ de vídeo** videotape; **~ de carbón** carbon ribbon; **~ magnética** (*Inform*) magnetic tape; **~ métrica** tape measure; **~ de múltiples impactos** (*en impresora*) multistrike ribbon; **~ de tela** (*para máquina de escribir*) fabric ribbon; **~ transportadora** conveyor belt

cinto [ˈθinto] NM belt, girdle

★**cintura** [θinˈtura] NF waist; (*medida*) waistline

★**cinturón** [θintuˈron] NM belt; (*fig*) belt, zone; **~ salvavidas** lifebelt; **~ de seguridad** safety belt

ciña *etc* [ˈθiɲa], **ciñendo** *etc* [θiˈɲendo] vB *ver* ceñir

ciprés [θiˈpres] NM cypress (tree)

★**circo** [ˈθirko] NM circus

circuito [θirˈkwito] NM circuit; (*Deporte*) lap; **TV por ~ cerrado** closed-circuit TV; **~ experimental** (*Inform*) breadboard; **~ impreso** printed circuit; **~ lógico** (*Inform*) logical circuit

★**circulación** [θirkulaˈθjon] NF circulation; (*Auto*) traffic; **"cerrado a la ~ rodada"** "closed to vehicles"

★**circular** [θirkuˈlar] /**1a**/ ADJ, NF circular ▶ vT to circulate ▶ vI to circulate; (*dinero*) to be in circulation; (*Auto*) to run; (*autobús*) to run; **"circule por la derecha"** "keep (to the) right"

★**círculo** [ˈθirkulo] NM circle; (*centro*) clubhouse; (*Pol*) political group; **~ vicioso** vicious circle

circuncidar [θirkunθiˈdar] /**1a**/ vT to circumcise

circunciso, -a [θirkunˈθiso, a] PP *de* **circuncidar**

circundante [θirkunˈdante] ADJ surrounding

circundar [θirkunˈdar] /**1a**/ vT to surround

circunferencia [θirkunfeˈrenθja] NF circumference

circunloquio [θirkunˈlokjo] NM circumlocution

circunscribir [θirkunskriˈβir] /**3a**/ vT to circumscribe ■ **circunscribirse** vR to be limited

circunscripción [θirkunskripˈθjon] NF division; (*Pol*) constituency

circunscrito [θirkunsˈkrito] PP *de* **circunscribir**

circunspección [θirkunspekˈθjon] NF circumspection, caution

circunspecto, -a [θirkunsˈpekto, a] ADJ circumspect, cautious

circunstancia [θirkunsˈtanθja] NF circumstance; **circunstancias agravantes/extenuantes** aggravating/extenuating circumstances; **estar a la altura de las circunstancias** to rise to the occasion

circunvalación [θirkumbalaˈθjon] NF: **carretera de ~** ring road

cirio [ˈθirjo] NM (wax) candle

cirrosis [θiˈrrosis] NF cirrhosis (of the liver)

★**ciruela** [θiˈrwela] NF plum; **~ pasa** prune

ciruelo [θiˈrwelo] NM plum tree

cirugía [θiruˈxia] NF surgery; **~ estética** *o* **plástica** plastic surgery

★**cirujano** [θiruˈxano] NM surgeon

cisco [ˈθisko] NM: **armar un ~** to kick up a row; **estar hecho ~** to be a wreck

cisma [ˈθisma] NM schism; (*Pol etc*) split

cisne [ˈθisne] NM swan; **canto de ~** swan song

cisterna [θisˈterna] NF cistern, tank

cistitis [θisˈtitis] NF cystitis

★**cita** [ˈθita] NF appointment, meeting; (*de novios*) date; (*referencia*) quotation; **acudir/faltar a una ~** to turn up for/miss an appointment

citación [θitaˈθjon] NF (*Jur*) summons *sg*

citadino, -a [sitaˈðino, a] (*Am*) ADJ urban ▶ NM/F urban *o* city dweller

citar [θiˈtar] /**1a**/ vT to make an appointment with, arrange to meet; (*Jur*) to summons; (*un autor, texto*) to quote ■ **citarse** vR: **citarse con algn** to arrange to meet sb; **se citaron en el cine** they arranged to meet at the cinema

cítara [ˈθitara] NF zither

citología [θitoloˈxia] NF smear test

cítrico, -a [ˈθitriko, a] ADJ citric ▶ NM: **cítricos** citrus fruits

CiU [ˈθiu] NM ABR (*Pol*) = **Convergència i Unió**

★**ciudad** [θjuˈðað] NF town; (*capital de país etc*) city; **~ universitaria** university campus; **C~ del Cabo** Cape Town; **la C~ Condal** Barcelona

ciudadanía [θjuðaðaˈnia] NF citizenship

★**ciudadano, -a** [θjuðaˈðano, a] ADJ civic ▸ NM/F citizen

ciudadrealeño, -a [θjuðaðreaˈleɲo, a] ADJ of o from Ciudad Real ▸ NM/F native o inhabitant of Ciudad Real

cívico, -a [ˈθiβiko, a] ADJ civic; (fig) public-spirited

civil [θiˈβil] ADJ civil ▸ NM (guardia) police officer

civilice etc [θiβiˈliθe] VB ver **civilizar**

civilización [θiβiliθaˈθjon] NF civilization

civilizar [θiβiliˈθar] /1f/ VT to civilize

civismo [θiˈβismo] NM public spirit

cizaña [θiˈθaɲa] NF (fig) discord; **sembrar ~** to sow discord

cl ABR (= centilitro) cl

clamar [klaˈmar] /1a/ VT to clamour for, cry out for ▸ VI to cry out, clamour

clamor [klaˈmor] NM (grito) cry, shout; (fig) clamour, protest

clamoroso, -a [klamoˈroso, a] ADJ (éxito etc) resounding

clan [klan] NM clan; (de gángsters) gang

clandestinidad [klandestiniˈðað] NF secrecy

clandestino, -a [klandesˈtino, a] ADJ clandestine; (Pol) underground

clara [ˈklara] NF (de huevo) egg white

claraboya [klaraˈβoja] NF skylight

clarear [klareˈar] /1a/ VI (el día) to dawn; (el cielo) to clear up, brighten up ■ **clarearse** VR to be transparent

clarete [klaˈrete] NM rosé (wine)

claridad [klariˈðað] NF (del día) brightness; (de estilo) clarity

clarificar [klarifiˈkar] /1g/ VT to clarify

clarifique etc [klariˈfike] VB ver **clarificar**

clarín [klaˈrin] NM bugle

clarinete [klariˈnete] NM clarinet

clarividencia [klariβiˈðenθja] NF clairvoyance; (fig) far-sightedness

★**claro, -a** [ˈklaro, a] ADJ clear; (luminoso) bright; (color) light; (evidente) clear, evident; (poco espeso) thin ▸ NM (en bosque) clearing; **a las claras** openly; **no sacamos nada en ~** we couldn't get anything definite ▸ ADV clearly; **hablar ~** (fig) to speak plainly ▸ EXCL: **¡~ que sí!** of course!; **¡~ que no!** of course not!

clase [ˈklase] NF class; (tipo) kind, sort; (Escol etc) class; (: aula) classroom; **~ alta/media/obrera** upper/middle/working class; **dar clases** to teach; **clases particulares** private lessons o tuition sg

clásico, -a [ˈklasiko, a] ADJ classical; (fig) classic

clasificable [klasifiˈkaβle] ADJ classifiable

clasificación [klasifikaˈθjon] NF classification; (Deporte) league (table); (Com) ratings pl

clasificador [klasifikaˈðor] NM filing cabinet

★**clasificar** [klasifiˈkar] /1g/ VT to classify; (Inform)

to sort ■ **clasificarse** VR (Deporte: en torneo) to qualify

clasifique etc [klasiˈfike] VB ver **clasificar**

clasista [klaˈsista] ADJ (fam: actitud) snobbish

claudicar [klauðiˈkar] /1g/ VI (fig) to back down

claudique etc [klauˈðike] VB ver **claudicar**

claustro [ˈklaustro] NM cloister; (Univ) staff; (junta) senate

claustrofobia [klaustroˈfoβja] NF claustrophobia

cláusula [ˈklausula] NF clause; **~ de exclusión** (Com) exclusion clause

clausura [klauˈsura] NF closing, closure

clausurar [klausuˈrar] /1a/ VT (congreso etc) to close, bring to a close; (Pol etc) to adjourn; (cerrar) to close (down)

clavado, -a [klaˈβaðo, a] ADJ nailed ▸ EXCL exactly!, precisely!

clavar [klaˈβar] /1a/ VT (tablas etc) to nail (together); (con alfiler) to pin; (clavo) to hammer in; (cuchillo) to stick, thrust; (mirada) to fix; (fam: estafar) to cheat

clave [ˈklaβe] NF key; (Mus) clef; **~ de acceso** password; **~ lada** (AM) dialling (BRIT) o area (US) code ▸ ADJ INV key cpd

clavel [klaˈβel] NM carnation

clavicémbalo [klaβiˈθembalo] NM harpsichord

clavicordio [klaβiˈkorðjo] NM clavichord

clavícula [klaˈβikula] NF collar bone

clavija [klaˈβixa] NF peg, pin; (Mus) peg; (Elec) plug

★**clavo** [ˈklaβo] NM (de metal) nail; (Bot) clove; **dar en el ~** (fig) to hit the nail on the head

claxon [ˈklakson] NM (pl **claxons**) NM horn; **tocar el ~** to sound one's horn

clemencia [kleˈmenθja] NF mercy, clemency

clemente [kleˈmente] ADJ merciful, clement

cleptómano, -a [klepˈtomano, a] NM/F kleptomaniac

clerical [kleriˈkal] ADJ clerical

clérigo [ˈkleriɣo] NM priest, clergyman

clero [ˈklero] NM clergy

clic [klik] NM click; **hacer ~/doble ~ en algo** to click/double-click on sth

clicar [kliˈkar] /1a/ VI (Inform) to click; **clica en el icono** click on the icon; **~ dos veces** to double-click

cliché [kliˈtʃe] NM cliché; (Tip) stencil; (Foto) negative

★**cliente, -a** [ˈkljente, a] NM/F client, customer

clientela [kljenˈtela] NF clientele, customers pl; (Com) goodwill; (Med) patients pl

★**clima** [ˈklima] NM climate

climatizado, -a [klimatiˈθaðo, a] ADJ air-conditioned

clímax [ˈklimaks] NM INV climax

clínico, -a ['kliniko, a] ADJ clinical ▸ NF clinic; (*particular*) private hospital

clip [klip] (*pl* **clips** [klips]) NM paper clip

cliquear [klike'ar] /**1a**/ VI (*Inform*) to click; **cliquea en el icono** click on the icon

clítoris ['klitoris] NM INV clitoris

cloaca [klo'aka] NF sewer, drain

clonación [klona'θjon] NF cloning

clonar [klo'nar] /**1a**/ VT to clone

clorhídrico, -a [klo'ridriko, a] ADJ hydrochloric

cloro ['kloro] NM chlorine

clorofila [kloro'fila] NF chlorophyl(l)

cloroformo [kloro'formo] NM chloroform

cloruro [klo'ruro] NM chloride; **~ sódico** sodium chloride

★**club** [klub] (*pl* **clubs** [kluβs] *o* **clubes** ['kluβes]) NM club; **~ de jóvenes** youth club; **~ nocturno** night club

cm ABR (= *centímetro*) cm

CNT [θeene'te] NF ABR (*Esp*: = *Confederación Nacional de Trabajo*) *Anarchist Union Confederation*; (*Am*) = **Confederación Nacional de Trabajadores**

coacción [koak'θjon] NF coercion, compulsion

coaccionar [koakθjo'nar] /**1a**/ VT to coerce, compel

coagular [koaɣu'lar] /**1a**/ VT, **coagularse** VR (*sangre*) to clot; (*leche*) to curdle

coágulo [ko'aɣulo] NM clot

coalición [koali'θjon] NF coalition

coartada [koar'taða] NF alibi

coartar [koar'tar] /**1a**/ VT to limit, restrict

coba ['koβa] NF: **dar ~ a algn** (*adular*) to suck up to sb

★**cobarde** [ko'βarðe] ADJ cowardly ▸ NMF coward

cobardía [koβar'ðia] NF cowardice

★**cobaya** [ko'βaja] NF guinea pig

cobertizo [koβer'tiθo] NM shelter

cobertor [koβer'tor] NM bedspread

cobertura [koβer'tura] NF cover; (*Com*) coverage; **~ de dividendo** (*Com*) dividend cover; **no tengo ~** (*Telec*) I can't get a signal

cobija [ko'βixa] NF (*Am*) blanket

cobijar [koβi'xar] /**1a**/ VT (*cubrir*) to cover; (*abrigar*) to shelter ■ **cobijarse** VR to take shelter

cobijo [ko'βixo] NM shelter

cobra ['koβra] NF cobra

cobrador, a [koβra'ðor, a] NM/F (*de autobús*) conductor/conductress; (*de impuestos, gas*) collector

★**cobrar** [ko'βrar] /**1a**/ VT (*sueldo*) to earn; (*precio*) to charge; (*deuda*) to collect; (*cheque*) to cash; **¿me cobra, por favor?** (*en tienda*) how much do I owe you?; (*en restaurante*) can I have the bill, please?; **cóbrese al entregar** cash on delivery (COD) (*Brit*), collect on delivery (COD) (*US*) ▸ VI (*como sueldo*) to be paid; (*por servicio*) to charge; **a ~** (*Com*) receivable; **cantidades por ~** sums due

■ **cobrarse** VR (*muertos, víctimas*) to claim; (*recibir dinero*): **¡cóbrese, por favor!** can I pay, please?

cobre ['koβre] NM copper; (*Am fam*) cent ■ **cobres** NMPL (*Mus*) brass instruments

cobrizo, -a [ko'βriθo, a] ADJ coppery

cobro [ko'βro] NM (*de cheque*) cashing; (*pago*) payment; **presentar al ~** to cash; *ver tb* **llamada**

coca ['koka] NF coca; (*droga*) coke

★**cocaína** [koka'ina] NF cocaine

cocainómano, -a [kokai'nomano, a] NM/F cocaine addict

cocción [kok'θjon] NF (*Culin*) cooking; (*el hervir*) boiling

cocear [koθe'ar] /**1a**/ VI to kick

cocer [ko'θer] /**2b, 2h**/ VT, VI to cook; (*en agua*) to boil; (*en horno*) to bake

★**coche** ['kotʃe] NM (*Auto*) car, automobile (*US*); (*de tren, de caballos*) coach, carriage; (*para niños*) pram (*Brit*), baby carriage (*US*); **ir en ~** to drive; **~ de bomberos** fire engine; **~ celular** police van, patrol wagon (*US*); **~ (comedor)** (*Ferro*) (dining) car; **~ de carreras** racing car; **coche-escuela** learner car; **~ fúnebre** hearse

coche-bomba ['kotʃe'βomba] (*pl* **coches-bomba**) NM car bomb

coche-cama ['kotʃe'kama] (*pl* **coches-cama**) NM (*Ferro*) sleeping car, sleeper

coche-escuela ['kotʃees'kwela] NM INV learner car

cochera [ko'tʃera] NF garage; (*de autobuses, trenes*) depot

coche-restaurante ['kotʃerestau'rante] (*pl* **coches-restaurante**) NM (*Ferro*) dining-car, diner

cochinada [kotʃi'naða] NF dirty trick

cochinillo [kotʃi'niʎo] NM piglet, suckling pig

cochino, -a [ko'tʃino, a] ADJ filthy, dirty ▸ NM/F pig

★**cocido, -a** [ko'θiðo, a] ADJ boiled; (*fam*) plastered ▸ NM stew

cociente [ko'θjente] NM quotient

★**cocina** [ko'θina] NF kitchen; (*aparato*) cooker, stove; (*actividad*) cookery; **~ casera** home cooking; **~ eléctrica** electric cooker; **~ francesa** French cuisine; **~ de gas** gas cooker

★**cocinar** [koθi'nar] /**1a**/ VT, VI to cook

★**cocinero, -a** [koθi'nero, a] NM/F cook

coco ['koko] NM coconut; (*fantasma*) bogeyman; (*fam: cabeza*) nut; **comer el ~ a algn** (*fam*) to brainwash sb

cocodrilo [koko'ðrilo] NM crocodile

cocotero [koko'tero] NM coconut palm

cóctel ['koktel] NM (*bebida*) cocktail; (*reunión*) cocktail party; **~ Molotov** Molotov cocktail, petrol bomb

coctelera [kokte'lera] NF cocktail shaker

cod. ABR (= *código*) code

codazo [ko'ðaθo] NM: **dar un ~ a algn** to nudge sb

codear [koðe'ar] **/1a/** VI to elbow, jostle ■ **codearse** VR: **codearse con** to rub shoulders with

códice ['koðiθe] NM manuscript, codex

codicia [ko'ðiθja] NF greed; (*fig*) lust

codiciar [koði'θjar] **/1b/** VT to covet

codicioso, -a [koði'θjoso, a] ADJ covetous

codificador [koðifika'ðor] NM (*Inform*) encoder; **~ digital** digitizer

codificar [koðifi'kar] **/1g/** VT (*mensaje*) to (en)code; (*leyes*) to codify

★**código** ['koðiɣo] NM code; **~ de barras** (*Com*) bar code; **~ binario** binary code; **~ de caracteres** (*Inform*) character code; **~ de (la) circulación** highway code; **~ de la zona** (*Am*) dialling (*Brit*) o area (*US*) code; **~ postal** postcode; **~ civil** common law; **~ de control** (*Inform*) control code; **~ máquina** (*Inform*) machine code; **~ militar** military law; **~ de operación** (*Inform*) operational o machine code; **~ penal** penal code; **~ de práctica** code of practice

codillo [ko'ðiʎo] NM (*Zool*) knee; (*Tec*) elbow (joint)

★**codo** ['koðo] NM (*Anat, de tubo*) elbow; (*Zool*) knee; **hablar por los codos** to talk nineteen to the dozen

codorniz [koðor'niθ] NF quail

COE ['koe] NM ABR (= *Comité Olímpico Español*) Spanish Olympic® Committee

coeficiente [koefi'θjente] NM (*Mat*) coefficient; (*Econ etc*) rate; **~ intelectual** o **de inteligencia** I.Q.

coerción [koer'θjon] NF coercion

coercitivo, -a [koerθi'tiβo, a] ADJ coercive

coetáneo, -a [koe'taneo, a] NM/F: **coetáneos** contemporaries

coexistencia [koeksis'tenθja] NF coexistence

coexistir [koeksis'tir] **/3a/** VI to coexist

cofia ['kofja] NF (*de enfermera*) (white) cap

cofradía [kofra'ðia] NF brotherhood, fraternity; *ver tb* **semana**

cofre ['kofre] NM (*baúl*) trunk; (*de joyas*) box; (*de dinero*) chest; (*Am Auto*) bonnet (*Brit*), hood (*US*)

cogedor [koxe'ðor] NM dustpan

★**coger** [ko'xer] **/2c/** VT (*Esp*) to take (hold of); (: *objeto caído*) to pick up; (: *frutas*) to pick, harvest; (: *resfriado, ladrón, pelota*) to catch; (*Am fam!*) to lay (*fam!*); **~ a algn desprevenido** to take sb unawares ▶ VI: **~ por el buen camino** to take the right road ■ **cogerse** VR (*el dedo*) to catch; **cogerse a algo** to get hold of sth

cogida [ko'xiða] NF gathering, harvesting; (*de peces*) catch; (*Taur*) goring

cognitivo, -a [koɣni'tiβo, a] ADJ cognitive

cogollo [ko'ɣoʎo] NM (*de lechuga*) heart; (*fig*) core, nucleus

cogorza [ko'ɣorθa] NF (*fam*): **agarrar una ~** to get smashed

cogote [ko'ɣote] NM back o nape of the neck

cohabitar [koaβi'tar] **/1a/** VI to live together, cohabit

cohecho [ko'etʃo] NM (*acción*) bribery; (*soborno*) bribe

coherencia [koe'renθja] NF coherence

coherente [koe'rente] ADJ coherent

cohesión [koe'sjon] NM cohesion

cohete [ko'ete] NM rocket

cohibido, -a [koi'βiðo, a] ADJ (*Psico*) inhibited; (*tímido*) shy; **sentirse ~** to feel embarrassed

cohibir [koi'βir] **/3a/** VT to restrain, restrict ■ **cohibirse** VR to feel inhibited

COI ['koi] NM ABR (= *Comité Olímpico Internacional*) IOC

coima ['koima] NF (*Am fam*) bribe

coincidencia [koinθi'ðenθja] NF coincidence

coincidir [koinθi'ðir] **/3a/** VI (*en idea*) to coincide, agree; (*en lugar*) to coincide

coito ['koito] NM intercourse, coitus

coja *etc* VB *ver* **coger**

cojear [koxe'ar] **/1a/** VI (*persona*) to limp, hobble; (*mueble*) to wobble, rock

cojera [ko'xera] NF lameness; (*andar cojo*) limp

★**cojín** [ko'xin] NM cushion

cojinete [koxi'nete] NM small cushion, pad; (*Tec*) (ball) bearing

★**cojo, -a** ['koxo, a] VB *ver* **coger** ▶ ADJ (*que no puede andar*) lame, crippled; (*mueble*) wobbly ▶ NM/F lame person

cojón [ko'xon] NM (*fam!*) ball (*fam!*), testicle; **¡cojones!** shit! (*fam!*)

cojonudo, -a [koxo'nuðo, a] ADJ (*Esp fam*) great, fantastic

★**col** [kol] NF cabbage; **coles de Bruselas** Brussels sprouts

★**cola** ['kola] NF tail; (*de gente*) queue; (*lugar*) end, last place; (*para pegar*) glue, gum; (*de vestido*) train; **hacer ~** to queue (up)

colaboración [kolaβora'θjon] NF (*gen*) collaboration; (*en periódico*) contribution

colaborador, a [kolaβora'ðor, a] NM/F collaborator; (*en periódico*) contributor

colaborar [kolaβo'rar] **/1a/** VI to collaborate

colación [kola'θjon] NF: **sacar a ~** to bring up

colado, -a [ko'laðo, a] ADJ (*metal*) cast ▶ NF: **hacer la colada** to do the washing

colador [kola'ðor] NM (*de té*) strainer; (*para verduras etc*) colander

colapsar [kolap'sar] **/1a/** VT (*tráfico etc*) to bring to a standstill

colapso [ko'lapso] NM collapse; **~ nervioso** nervous breakdown

colar [ko'lar] **/1l/** VT (*líquido*) to strain off; (*metal*) to cast ▶ VI to ooze, seep (through) ■ **colarse** VR to jump the queue; (*en mitin*) to sneak in; (*equi-*

vocarse) to slip up; **colarse en** to get into without paying; (*en una fiesta*) to gatecrash

colateral [kolate'ral] NM collateral

colcha ['koltʃa] NF bedspread

★**colchón** [kol'tʃon] NM mattress; **~ inflable** air bed, inflatable mattress

colchoneta [koltʃo'neta] NF (*en gimnasio*) mat; **~ hinchable** air bed, inflatable mattress

colear [kole'ar] /**1a**/ VI (*perro*) to wag its tail

★**colección** [kolek'θjon] NF collection

★**coleccionar** [kolekθjo'nar] /**1a**/ VT to collect

coleccionista [kolekθjo'nista] NMF collector

colecta [ko'lekta] NF collection

colectivo, -a [kolek'tiβo, a] ADJ collective, joint ▶ NM (AM: *autobús*) (small) bus; (: *taxi*) collective taxi

colector [kolek'tor] NM collector; (*sumidero*) sewer

★**colega** [ko'leɣa] NMF colleague; (ESP: *amigo*) mate

colegiado, -a [kole'xjaðo, a] ADJ (*profesional*) registered ▶ NM/F referee

colegial, a [kole'xjal, a] ADJ (*Escol etc*) school *cpd*, college *cpd* ▶ NM/F schoolboy/girl

★**colegio** [ko'lexjo] NM college; (*escuela*) school; (*de abogados etc*) association; **~ de internos** boarding school; **ir al ~** to go to school; **~ electoral** polling station; **~ mayor** (ESP) hall of residence

A **colegio** is often a private primary or secondary school. In the state system it means a primary school although these are also called *escuela*. State secondary schools are called *institutos*. Extracurricular subjects, such as computing or foreign languages, are offered in private schools called *academias*.

colegir [kole'xir] /**3c, 3k**/ VT (*juntar*) to collect, gather; (*deducir*) to infer, conclude

cólera ['kolera] NF (*ira*) anger; **montar en ~** to get angry ▶ NM (*Med*) cholera

colérico, -a [ko'leriko, a] ADJ angry, furious

colesterol [koleste'rol] NM cholesterol

coleta [ko'leta] NF pigtail

coletazo [kole'taθo] NM: **dar un ~** (*animal*) to flap its tail; **los últimos coletazos** death throes

coletilla [kole'tiʎa] NF (*en carta*) postscript; (*en conversación*) filler phrase

colgado, -a [kol'ɣaðo, a] PP *de* **colgar** ▶ ADJ hanging; (*ahorcado*) hanged; **dejar ~ a algn** to let sb down

colgajo [kol'ɣaxo] NM tatter

colgante [kol'ɣante] ADJ hanging; *ver* **puente** ▶ NM (*joya*) pendant

★**colgar** [kol'ɣar] /**1h, 1l**/ VT to hang (up); (*tender: ropa*) to hang out ▶ VI to hang; (*teléfono*) to hang up; **no cuelgue** please hold

colgué [kol'ɣe], **colguemos** *etc* [kol'ɣemos] VB *ver* **colgar**

colibrí [koli'βri] NM hummingbird

cólico ['koliko] NM colic

★**coliflor** [koli'flor] NF cauliflower

coligiendo *etc* [koli'xjenðo] VB *ver* **colegir**

colija *etc* [ko'lixa] VB *ver* **colegir**

colilla [ko'liʎa] NF cigarette end, butt

★**colina** [ko'lina] NF hill

colindante [kolin'dante] ADJ adjacent, neighbouring

colindar [kolin'dar] /**1a**/ VI to adjoin, be adjacent

★**colisión** [koli'sjon] NF collision; **~ frontal** head-on crash

colitis [ko'litis] NF INV: **tener ~** to have diarrhoea

★**collar** [ko'ʎar] NM necklace; (*de perro*) collar

colmado, -a [kol'maðo, a] ADJ full ▶ NM grocer's (shop) (BRIT), grocery store (US)

colmar [kol'mar] /**1a**/ VT to fill to the brim; (*fig*) to fulfil, realize

colmena [kol'mena] NF beehive

colmillo [kol'miʎo] NM (*diente*) eye tooth; (*de elefante*) tusk; (*de perro*) fang

colmo ['kolmo] NM height, summit; **para ~ de desgracias** to cap it all; **¡eso es ya el ~!** that's beyond a joke!

colocación [koloka'θjon] NF (*acto*) placing; (*empleo*) job, position; (*situación*) place, position; (*Com*) placement

★**colocar** [kolo'kar] /**1g**/ VT to place, put, position; (*poner en empleo*) to find a job for; **~ dinero** to invest money ■ **colocarse** VR to place o.s.; (*conseguir trabajo*) to find a job

colofón [kolo'fon] NM: **como ~ de las conversaciones** as a sequel to o following the talks

★**Colombia** [ko'lombja] NF Colombia

★**colombiano, -a** [kolom'bjano, a] ADJ, NM/F Colombian

colon ['kolon] NM colon

colón [ko'lon] NM *monetary unit of Costa Rica and El Salvador*

Colonia [ko'lonja] NF Cologne

colonia [ko'lonja] NF colony; (*de casas*) housing estate; (*agua de colonia*) cologne; **~ escolar** summer camp (for schoolchildren); **~ proletaria** (AM) shantytown

colonice *etc* [kolo'niθe] VB *ver* **colonizar**

colonización [koloniθa'θjon] NF colonization

colonizador, a [koloniθa'ðor, a] ADJ colonizing ▶ NM/F colonist, settler

colonizar [koloni'θar] /**1f**/ VT to colonize

colono [ko'lono] NM (*Pol*) colonist, settler; (*Agr*) tenant farmer

coloque *etc* [ko'loke] VB *ver* **colocar**

coloquial [kolo'kjal] ADJ colloquial

coloquio [ko'lokjo] NM conversation; (*congreso*) conference

★color [ko'lor] NM colour; **a todo ~** in full colour; **verlo todo ~ de rosa** to see everything through rose-coloured spectacles; **le salieron los colores** she blushed

colorado, -a [kolo'raðo, a] ADJ (*rojo*) red; (*AM: chiste*) rude, blue; **ponerse ~** to blush

colorante [kolo'rante] NM colouring (matter)

colorar [kolo'rar] /1a/ VT to colour; (*teñir*) to dye

colorear [kolore'ar] /1a/ VT to colour

colorete [kolo'rete] NM blusher

colorido [kolo'riðo] NM colour(ing)

coloso [ko'loso] NM colossus

columbrar [kolum'brar] /1a/ VT to glimpse, spy

columna [ko'lumna] NF column; (*pilar*) pillar; (*apoyo*) support; **~ blindada** (*Mil*) armoured column; **~ vertebral** spine, spinal column; (*fig*) backbone

columpiar [kolum'pjar] /1b/ VT to swing ■ **columpiarse** VR to swing

★columpio [ko'lumpjo] NM swing

colza ['kolθa] NF rape; **aceite de ~** rapeseed oil

coma ['koma] NF comma ▶ NM (*Med*) coma

comadre [ko'maðre] NF (*madrina*) godmother; (*vecina*) neighbour; (*chismosa*) gossip

comadrear [komaðre'ar] /1a/ VI (*esp AM*) to gossip

comadreja [koma'ðrexa] NF weasel

comadrona [koma'ðrona] NF midwife

comal [ko'mal] NM (*AM*) griddle

comandancia [koman'danθja] NF command

comandante [koman'dante] NM commandant; (*grado*) major

comandar [koman'dar] /1a/ VT to command

comando [ko'mando] NM (*Mil: mando*) command; (: *grupo*) commando unit; (*Inform*) command; **~ de búsqueda** search command

comarca [ko'marka] NF region; *ver tb* **provincia**

comarcal [komar'kal] ADJ local

comba ['komba] NF (*curva*) curve; (*en viga*) warp; (*cuerda*) skipping rope; **saltar a la ~** to skip

combar [kom'bar] /1a/ VT to bend, curve

combate [kom'bate] NM fight; (*fig*) battle; **fuera de ~** out of action

combatiente [komba'tjente] NM combatant

combatir [komba'tir] /3a/ VT to fight, combat

combatividad [kombatiβi'ðað] NF (*actitud*) fighting spirit; (*agresividad*) aggressiveness

combativo, -a [komba'tiβo, a] ADJ full of fight

combi ['kombi] NM fridge-freezer

combinación [kombina'θjon] NF combination; (*Química*) compound; (*bebida*) cocktail; (*plan*) scheme, setup; (*prenda*) slip

combinado, -a [kombi'naðo, a] ADJ: **plato ~** main course served with vegetables

combinar [kombi'nar] /1a/ VT to combine; (*colores*) to match

combustible [kombus'tiβle] NM fuel

combustión [kombus'tjon] NF combustion

★comedia [ko'meðja] NF comedy; (*Teat*) play, drama; (*fig*) farce

comediante [kome'ðjante] NMF (*comic*) actor/actress

comedido, -a [kome'ðiðo, a] ADJ moderate

comedirse [kome'ðirse] /3k/ VR to behave moderately; (*ser cortés*) to be courteous

★comedor, a [kome'ðor, a] NM/F (*persona*) glutton ▶ NM (*habitación*) dining room; (*restaurante*) restaurant; (*cantina*) canteen

comencé [komen'θe], **comencemos** *etc* [komen'θemos] VB *ver* **comenzar**

comensal [komen'sal] NMF fellow guest/diner

★comentar [komen'tar] /1a/ VT to comment on; (*fam*) to discuss; **comentó que ...** he made the comment that ...

comentario [komen'tarjo] NM comment, remark; (*Lit*) commentary ■ **comentarios** NMPL gossip *sg*; **dar lugar a comentarios** to cause gossip

comentarista [komenta'rista] NMF commentator

★comenzar [komen'θar] /1f, 1j/ VT, VI to begin, start, commence; **~ a hacer algo** to begin *o* start doing *o* to do sth

★comer [ko'mer] /2a/ VT to eat; (*Damas, Ajedrez*) to take, capture; **~ el coco a** (*fam*) to brainwash ▶ VI to eat; (*almorzar*) to have lunch; **¡a ~!** food's ready! ■ **comerse** VR to eat up; (*párrafo etc*) to skip

comercial [komer'θjal] ADJ commercial; (*relativo al negocio*) business *cpd*

comercializar [komerθjali'θar] /1f/ VT (*producto*) to market; (*pey*) to commercialize

★comerciante [komer'θjante] NMF trader, merchant; (*tendero*) shopkeeper; **~ exclusivo** (*Com*) sole trader

comerciar [komer'θjar] /1b/ VI to trade, do business

★comercio [ko'merθjo] NM commerce, trade; (*tienda*) shop, store; (*negocio*) business; (*grandes empresas*) big business; (*fig*) dealings *pl*; **~ autorizado** (*Com*) licensed trade; **~ electrónico** e-commerce; **~ exterior** foreign trade

comestible [komes'tiβle] ADJ eatable, edible ▶ NM: **comestibles** food *sg*, foodstuffs; (*Com*) groceries

cometa [ko'meta] NM comet ▶ NF kite

★cometer [kome'ter] /2a/ VT to commit

cometido [kome'tiðo] NM (*misión*) task, assignment; (*deber*) commitment

comezón [kome'θon] NF itch, itching

cómic ['komik] (*pl* **cómics** ['komiks]) NM comic

comicios [ko'miθjos] NMPL elections; (*voto*) voting *sg*

★cómico, -a ['komiko, a] ADJ comic(al) ▶ NM/F comedian; (*de teatro*) (*comic*) actor/actress

★comida [ko'miða] VB *ver* **comedirse** ▶ NF (*ali-*

mento) food; (*almuerzo, cena*) meal; (*de mediodía*) lunch; (*AM*) dinner; **~ basura** junk food; **~ chatarra** (*AM*) junk food

comidilla [komiˈðiʎa] NF: **ser la ~ del barrio** o **pueblo** to be the talk of the town

comience *etc* [koˈmjenθe] VB *ver* **comenzar**

★**comienzo** [koˈmjenθo] VB *ver* **comenzar** ▶ NM beginning, start; **dar ~ a un acto** to begin a ceremony; **~ del archivo** (*Inform*) top-of-file

comillas [koˈmiʎas] NFPL quotation marks

comilón, -ona [komiˈlon, ona] ADJ greedy ▶ NF (*fam*) blow-out

comino [koˈmino] NM cumin (seed); **no me importa un ~** I don't give a damn!

★**comisaría** [komisaˈria] NF police station, precinct (*US*); (*Mil*) commissariat

comisario [komiˈsarjo] NM (*Mil etc*) commissary; (*Pol*) commissar

★**comisión** [komiˈsjon] NF (*Com: pago*) commission, rake-off (*fam*); (: *junta*) board; (*encargo*) assignment; **~ mixta/permanente** joint/ standing committee; **Comisiones Obreras** (*Esp*) Communist Union Confederation

comisura [komiˈsura] NF: **~ de los labios** corner of the mouth

★**comité** [komiˈte] (*pl* **comités** [komiˈtes]) NM committee; **~ de empresa** works council

comitiva [komiˈtiβa] NF suite, retinue

★**como** [ˈkomo] ADV as; (*tal como*) like; (*aproximadamente*) about, approximately; **es tan alto ~ ancho** it is as high as it is wide ▶ CONJ (*ya que, puesto que*) as, since; (*en seguida que*) as soon as; (*si: +subjun*) if; **~ no lo haga hoy** unless he does it today; **~ si** as if

> **How** no se utiliza para preguntar cómo es alguien sino para preguntar cómo está: *¿Cómo está Ana?* **How is Ana?**
> Para saber qué aspecto tiene una persona se usa **what**: *¿Cómo es Ana físicamente?* **What does Ana look like?**
> Si lo que interesa es saber qué carácter tiene, se pregunta: *¿Cómo es Ana (de carácter)?* **What is Ana like?**

★**cómo** [ˈkomo] ADV how?, why?; **¿~ está usted?** how are you?; **¿~ son?** what are they like?; **¿~ no?** why not?; **¡~ no!** (*esp AM*) of course! ▶ EXCL what?, I beg your pardon? ▶ NM: **el ~ y el porqué** the whys and wherefores

★**cómoda** [ˈkomoða] NF chest of drawers

★**comodidad** [komoðiˈðað] NF comfort; **venga a su ~** come at your convenience

comodín [komoˈðin] NM joker; (*Inform*) wild card; **símbolo ~** wild-card character

★**cómodo, -a** [ˈkomoðo, a] ADJ comfortable; (*práctico, de fácil uso*) convenient

comodón, -ona [komoˈðon, -ona] ADJ comfort-loving ▶ NM/F: **ser un(a) ~(-ona)** to like one's home comforts

comoquiera [komoˈkjera] CONJ: **~ que** (*+subjun*) in whatever way; **~ que sea eso** however that may be

Comoras [koˈmoras] NFPL Comoros

comp. ABR (= *compárese*) cp

compact [komˈpakt] (*pl* **compacts**) NM (*tb*: **compact disc**) compact disk

compacto, -a [komˈpakto, a] ADJ compact

compadecer [kompaðeˈθer] /2d/ VT to pity, be sorry for ■ **compadecerse** VR: **compadecerse de** to pity, be sorry for

compadezca *etc* [kompaˈðeθka] VB *ver* **compadecer**

compadre [komˈpaðre] NM (*padrino*) godfather; (*esp AM: amigo*) friend, pal

compaginar [kompaxiˈnar] /1a/ VT: **~ A con B** to bring A into line with B ■ **compaginarse** VR: **compaginarse con** to tally with, square with

compañerismo [kompaɲeˈrismo] NM comradeship

★**compañero, -a** [kompaˈɲero, a] NM/F companion; (*novio*) boyfriend/girlfriend; **~ de clase** classmate

★**compañía** [kompaˈɲia] NF company; **~ afiliada** associated company; **~ concesionaria** franchiser; **~ (no) cotizable** (un)listed company; **~ inversionista** investment trust; **hacer ~ a algn** to keep sb company

★**comparación** [komparaˈθjon] NF comparison; **en ~ con** in comparison with

★**comparar** [kompaˈrar] /1a/ VT to compare

comparativo, -a [komparaˈtiβo, a] ADJ comparative

comparecencia [kompareˈθenθja] NF (*Jur*) appearance (in court); **orden de ~** summons *sg*

comparecer [kompareˈθer] /2d/ VI to appear (in court)

comparezca *etc* [kompaˈreθka] VB *ver* **comparecer**

comparsa [komˈparsa] NMF extra

compartim(i)ento [kompartiˈm(j)ento] NM (*Ferro*) compartment; (*de mueble, cajón*) section; **~ estanco** (*fig*) watertight compartment

★**compartir** [komparˈtir] /3a/ VT to share; (*dinero, comida etc*) to divide (up), share (out)

compás [komˈpas] NM (*Mus*) beat, rhythm; (*Mat*) compasses *pl*; (*Naut etc*) compass; **al ~** in time

compasión [kompaˈsjon] NF compassion, pity

compasivo, -a [kompaˈsiβo, a] ADJ compassionate

compatibilidad [kompatiβiliˈðað] NF (*tb Inform*) compatibility

compatible [kompaˈtiβle] ADJ compatible

compatriota [kompaˈtrjota] NMF compatriot, fellow countryman/woman

compendiar [kompenˈdjar] /1b/ VT to summarize; (*libro*) to abridge

compendio [kom'pendjo] NM summary; abridgement

compenetración [kompenetra'θjon] NF (fig) mutual understanding

compenetrarse [kompene'trarse] /1a/ VR to be in tune; (fig): **~ (muy) bien** to get on (very) well together

compensación [kompensa'θjon] NF compensation; (Jur) damages pl; (Com) clearing; **~ (de emisiones) de carbono** (crédito) carbon offset; (sistema) carbon offsetting

compensar [kompen'sar] /1a/ VT to compensate; (pérdida) to make up for

competencia [kompe'tenθja] NF (incumbencia) domain, field; (Com) receipt; (Jur, habilidad) competence; (rivalidad) competition

★**competente** [kompe'tente] ADJ (Jur, persona) competent; (conveniente) suitable

competer [kompe'ter] /2a/ VI: **~ a** to be the responsibility of, fall to

★**competición** [kompeti'θjon] NF competition

competidor, a [kompeti'ðor, a] NM/F competitor

competir [kompe'tir] /3k/ VI to compete

competitivo, -a [kompeti'tiβo, a] ADJ competitive

compilación [kompila'θjon] NF compilation; **tiempo de ~** (Inform) compile time

compilador [kompila'ðor] NM compiler

compilar [kompi'lar] /1a/ VT to compile

compinche [kom'pintʃe] NMF (AM fam) mate, buddy (US)

compita etc [kom'pita] VB ver **competir**

complacencia [kompla'θenθja] NF (placer) pleasure; (satisfacción) satisfaction; (buena voluntad) willingness

complacer [kompla'θer] /2w/ VT to please ■ **complacerse** VR to be pleased

complaciente [kompla'θjente] ADJ kind, obliging, helpful

complazca etc [kom'plaθka] VB ver **complacer**

complejo, -a [kom'plexo, a] ADJ, NM complex

complementario, -a [komplemen'tarjo, a] ADJ complementary

complemento [komple'mento] NM (de moda, diseño) accessory; (Ling) complement

★**completar** [komple'tar] /1a/ VT to complete

★**completo, -a** [kom'pleto, a] ADJ complete; (perfecto) perfect; (lleno) full ▸ NM full complement

complexión [komple'ksjon] NF constitution

complicación [komplika'θjon] NF complication

★**complicado, -a** [kompli'kaðo, a] ADJ complicated; **estar ~ en** to be mixed up in

complicar [kompli'kar] /1g/ VT to complicate

cómplice ['kompliθe] NMF accomplice

complique etc [kom'plike] VB ver **complicar**

complot [kom'plo(t)] (pl **complots** [kom'plo(t)s]) NM plot; (conspiración) conspiracy

compondré etc [kompon'dre] VB ver **componer**

componenda [kompo'nenda] NF compromise; (pey) shady deal

componente [kompo'nente] ADJ, NM component

★**componer** [kompo'ner] /2q/ VT to make up, put together; (Mus, Lit, Imprenta) to compose; (algo roto) to mend, repair; (adornar) to adorn; (arreglar) to arrange; (reconciliar) to reconcile ■ **componerse** VR: **componerse de** to consist of; **componérselas para hacer algo** to manage to do sth

componga etc [kom'ponga] VB ver **componer**

★**comportamiento** [komporta'mjento] NM behaviour, conduct

★**comportarse** [kompor'tarse] /1a/ VR to behave

composición [komposi'θjon] NF composition

compositor, a [komposi'tor, a] NM/F composer

compostelano, -a [komposte'lano, a] ADJ of o from Santiago de Compostela ▸ NM/F native o inhabitant of Santiago de Compostela

compostura [kompos'tura] NF (reparación) mending, repair; (composición) composition; (acuerdo) agreement; (actitud) composure

compota [kom'pota] NF compote, preserve

★**compra** ['kompra] NF purchase; **hacer la ~/ir de compras** to do the/go shopping; **~ a granel** (Com) bulk buying; **~ proteccionista** (Com) support buying ■ **compras** NFPL purchases, shopping sg

comprador, a [kompra'ðor, a] NM/F buyer, purchaser

★**comprar** [kom'prar] /1a/ VT to buy, purchase; **~ deudas** (Com) to factor

compraventa [kompra'βenta] NF (Jur) contract of sale

★**comprender** [kompren'der] /2a/ VT to understand; (incluir) to comprise, include

comprensible [kompren'siβle] ADJ understandable

comprensión [kompren'sjon] NF understanding; (totalidad) comprehensiveness

★**comprensivo, -a** [kompren'siβo, a] ADJ comprehensive; (actitud) understanding

compresa [kom'presa] NF compress; (higiénica) sanitary towel (BRIT) o napkin (US)

compresión [kompre'sjon] NF compression

comprimido, -a [kompri'miðo, a] ADJ compressed ▸ NM (Med) pill, tablet; **en caracteres comprimidos** (Tip) condensed

comprimir [kompri'mir] /3a/ VT to compress; (fig) to control; (Inform) to compress, zip

comprobación [komproβa'θjon] NF: **~ general de cuentas** (Com) general audit

comprobante [kompro'βante] NM proof; (Com) voucher; **~ (de pago)** receipt; **~ de compra** proof of purchase

★**comprobar** [kompro'βar] /**1l**/ VT to check; (*probar*) to prove; (*Tec*) to check, test

comprometedor, a [kompromete'ðor, a] ADJ compromising

comprometer [komprome'ter] /**2a**/ VT to compromise; (*exponer*) to endanger ∎ **comprometerse** VR to compromise o.s.; (*involucrarse*) to get involved

comprometido, -a [komprome'tiðo, a] ADJ (*situación*) awkward; (*escritor etc*) committed

★**compromiso** [kompro'miso] NM (*obligación*) obligation; (*cita*) engagement, date; (*cometido*) commitment; (*convenio*) agreement; (*dificultad*) awkward situation; **libre de ~** (*Com*) without obligation

comprueba *etc* [kom'prweβa] VB *ver* **comprobar**

compuerta [kom'pwerta] NF (*en canal*) sluice, floodgate; (*Inform*) gate

compuesto, -a [kom'pwesto, a] PP *de* **componer** ▶ ADJ: **~ de** composed of, made up of ▶ NM compound; (*Med*) preparation

compulsar [kompul'sar] /**1a**/ VT (*cotejar*) to collate, compare; (*Jur*) to make an attested copy of

compulsivo, -a [kompul'siβo, a] ADJ compulsive

compungido, -a [kompun'xiðo, a] ADJ remorseful

compuse *etc* [kom'puse] VB *ver* **componer**

computación [komputa'θjon] NF computing; **~ en (la) nube** cloud computing

★**computador** [komputa'ðor] NM, **computadora** [komputa'ðora] NF computer; **~ central** mainframe computer; **~ de escritorio** desktop; **~ especializado** dedicated computer; **~ personal** personal computer

computar [kompu'tar] /**1a**/ VT to calculate, compute

cómputo ['komputo] NM calculation

comulgar [komul'ɣar] /**1h**/ VI to receive communion

comulgue *etc* [ko'mulɣe] VB *ver* **comulgar**

común [ko'mun] ADJ (*gen*) common; (*corriente*) ordinary; **por lo ~** generally ▶ NM: **el ~** the community

comuna [ko'muna] NF commune; (*Am*) district

comunicación [komunika'θjon] NF communication; (*informe*) report

comunicado [komuni'kaðo] NM announcement; **~ de prensa** press release

★**comunicar** [komuni'kar] /**1g**/ VT to communicate; (*Arq*) to connect ▶ VI to communicate; to send a report; **está comunicando** (*Telec*) the line's engaged (*Brit*) o busy (*US*) ∎ **comunicarse** VR to communicate

comunicativo, -a [komunika'tiβo, a] ADJ communicative

comunidad [komuni'ðað] NF community; **~ autónoma** (*Esp*) autonomous region; **~ de vecinos** residents' association

The 1978 Constitution provides for a degree of self-government for the 17 regions and two cities, called *comunidades autónomas* or *autonomías*. Some, such as Catalonia and the Basque Country, with their own language, history and culture, have long felt separate from the rest of Spain. The regions are: Andalusia, Aragon, Asturias, the Balearics, the Canaries, Cantabria, Castile and Leon, Castile-La Mancha, Catalonia, Extremadura, Galicia, Madrid, Murcia, Navarre, the Basque Country, La Rioja, the Community of Valencia, and the cities of Ceuta and Melilla.

comunión [komu'njon] NF communion

comunique *etc* [komu'nike] VB *ver* **comunicar**

comunismo [komu'nismo] NM communism

comunista [komu'nista] ADJ, NMF communist

comunitario, -a [komuni'tarjo, a] ADJ (*de la* UE) Community *cpd*, EU *cpd*

---

con [kon]

PREP **1** (*medio, compañía, modo*) with; **comer con cuchara** to eat with a spoon; **café con leche** white coffee; **estoy con un catarro** I've got a cold; **pasear con algn** to go for a walk with sb; **con habilidad** skilfully

2 (*a pesar de*): **con todo, merece nuestros respetos** all the same o even so, he deserves our respect

3 (*para con*): **es muy bueno para con los niños** he's very good with (the) children

4 (+ *infin*): **con llegar tan tarde se quedó sin comer** by arriving o because he arrived so late he missed out on eating; **con estudiar un poco apruebas** with a bit of studying you should pass

5 (*queja*): **¡con las ganas que tenía de ir!** and I really wanted to go (too)!

▶ CONJ: **con que: será suficiente con que le escribas** it will be enough if you write to her

---

conato [ko'nato] NM attempt; **~ de robo** attempted robbery

cóncavo, -a ['konkaβo, a] ADJ concave

concebir [konθe'βir] /**3k**/ VT to conceive; (*imaginar*) to imagine ▶ VI to conceive

conceder [konθe'ðer] /**2a**/ VT to concede

concejal, a [konθe'xal, a] NM/F town councillor

concejo [kon'θexo] NM council

concentración [konθentra'θjon] NF concentration

concentrar [konθen'trar] /**1a**/ VT to concentrate ∎ **concentrarse** VR to concentrate

concéntrico, -a [kon'θentriko, a] ADJ concentric

concepción [konθep'θjon] NF conception

concepto [kon'θepto] NM concept; **por ~ de** as, by way of; **tener buen ~ de algn** to think highly of sb; **bajo ningún ~** under no circumstances

conceptuar [konθep'twar] /**1e**/ VT to judge

concernir [konθer'nir] /3i/ VI to concern; **en lo que concierne a ...** with regard to ...; **en lo que a mí concierne** as far as I'm concerned

concertar [konθer'tar] /1j/ VT (entrevista) to arrange; (precio) to agree; (esfuerzos) to coordinate; (Mus) to harmonize ▶ VI to harmonize, be in tune

concesión [konθe'sjon] NF concession; (Com: fabricación) licence

concesionario, -a [konθesjo'narjo, a] NM/F (Com) (licensed) dealer, agent, concessionaire; (: de venta) franchisee; (: de transportes etc) contractor

concha ['kontʃa] NF shell; (Am fam!) cunt (fam!)

conchabarse [kontʃa'βarse] /1a/ VR: **~ contra** to gang up on

conciencia [kon'θjenθja] NF (moral) conscience; (conocimiento) awareness; **libertad de ~** freedom of worship; **tener/tomar ~ de** to be/become aware of; **tener la ~ limpia** o **tranquila** to have a clear conscience; **tener plena ~ de** to be fully aware of

concienciar [konθjen'θjar] /1b/ VT to make aware ■ **concienciarse** VR to become aware

concienzudo, -a [konθjen'θuðo, a] ADJ conscientious

concierne etc [kon'θjerne] VB ver **concernir**

★**concierto** [kon'θjerto] VB ver **concertar** ▶ NM concert; (obra) concerto

conciliación [konθilja'θjon] NF conciliation

conciliar [konθi'ljar] /1b/ VT to reconcile; **~ el sueño** to get to sleep ▶ ADJ (Rel) council cpd

concilio [kon'θiljo] NM council

concisión [konθi'sjon] NF conciseness

conciso, -a [kon'θiso, a] ADJ concise

conciudadano, -a [konθjuða'ðano, a] NM/F fellow citizen

concluir [konklu'ir] /3g/ VT (acabar) to conclude; (inferir) to infer, deduce ▶ VI to conclude; **todo ha concluido** it's all over ■ **concluirse** VR to conclude

conclusión [konklu'sjon] NF conclusion; **llegar a la ~ de que ...** to come to the conclusion that ...

concluya etc [kon'kluja] VB ver **concluir**

concluyente [konklu'jente] ADJ (prueba, información) conclusive

concordancia [konkor'ðanθja] NF agreement

concordar [konkor'ðar] /1l/ VT to reconcile ▶ VI to agree, tally

concordia [kon'korðja] NF harmony

concretamente [konkreta'mente] ADV specifically, to be exact

concretar [konkre'tar] /1a/ VT to make concrete, make more specific; (problema) to pinpoint ■ **concretarse** VR to become more definite

concreto, -a [kon'kreto, a] ADJ, NM (Am) concrete; **en ~** (en resumen) to sum up; (específica-

mente) specifically; **no hay nada en ~** there's nothing definite

concubina [konku'βina] NF concubine

concuerde etc [kon'kwerðe] VB ver **concordar**

concupiscencia [konkupis'θenθja] NF (avaricia) greed; (lujuria) lustfulness

concurrencia [konku'rrenθja] NF turnout

★**concurrido, -a** [konku'rriðo, a] ADJ (calle) busy; (local, reunión) crowded

concurrir [konku'rrir] /3a/ VI (juntarse: ríos) to meet, come together; (: personas) to gather, meet

concursante [konkur'sante] NM competitor

concursar [konkur'sar] /1a/ VI to compete

★**concurso** [kon'kurso] NM (de público) crowd; (Escol, Deporte, competición) competition; (Com) invitation to tender; (examen) open competition; (TV etc) quiz; (ayuda) help, cooperation

condado [kon'daðo] NM county

condal [kon'dal] ADJ: **la ciudad ~** Barcelona

conde ['konde] NM count

condecoración [kondekora'θjon] NF (Mil) medal, decoration

condecorar [kondeko'rar] /1a/ VT to decorate

condena [kon'dena] NF sentence; **cumplir una ~** to serve a sentence

condenación [kondena'θjon] NF condemnation; (Rel) damnation

condenado, -a [konde'naðo, a] ADJ (Jur) condemned; (fam: maldito) damned ▶ NM/F (Jur) convicted person

condenar [konde'nar] /1a/ VT to condemn; (Jur) to convict ■ **condenarse** VR (Jur) to confess (one's guilt); (Rel) to be damned

condensar [konden'sar] /1a/ VT to condense

condesa [kon'desa] NF countess

condescendencia [kondesθen'denθja] NF condescension; **aceptar algo por ~** to accept sth so as not to hurt feelings

condescender [kondesθen'der] /2g/ VI to acquiesce, comply

condescienda etc [kondes'θjenda] VB ver **condescender**

★**condición** [kondi'θjon] NF (gen) condition; (rango) social class; **a ~ de que ...** on condition that ... ■ **condiciones** NFPL (cualidades) qualities; (estado) condition; **las condiciones del contrato** the terms of the contract; **condiciones de trabajo** working conditions; **condiciones de venta** conditions of sale

condicional [kondiθjo'nal] ADJ conditional

condicionamiento [kondiθjona'mjento] NM conditioning

condicionar [kondiθjo'nar] /1a/ VT (acondicionar) to condition; **~ algo a algo** to make sth conditional o dependent on sth

condimento [kondi'mento] NM seasoning

condiscípulo, -a [kondis'θipulo, a] NM/F fellow student

condolerse [kondoˈlerse] /**2h**/ VR to sympathize

condominio [kondoˈminjo] NM (*Com*) joint ownership; (*Am*) condominium, apartment

condón [konˈdon] NM condom

condonar [kondoˈnar] /**1a**/ VT (*Jur: reo*) to reprieve; (*Com: deuda*) to cancel

cóndor [ˈkondor] NM condor

conducente [konduˈθente] ADJ: ~ **a** conducive to, leading to

★**conducir** [konduˈθir] /**3n**/ VT to take, convey; (*Elec etc*) to carry; (*Auto*) to drive; (*negocio*) to manage ▶ VI to drive; (*fig*) to lead ■ **conducirse** VR to behave

★**conducta** [konˈdukta] NF conduct, behaviour

conducto [konˈdukto] NM pipe, tube; (*fig*) channel; (*Elec*) lead; **por ~ de** through

★**conductor, a** [kondukˈtor, a] ADJ leading, guiding ▶ NM (*Física*) conductor; (*de vehículo*) driver

conduela *etc* [konˈdwela] VB *ver* **condolerse**

conduje *etc* [konˈduxe] VB *ver* **conducir**

conduzco *etc* [konˈduθko] VB *ver* **conducir**

conectado, -a [konekˈtaðo, a] ADJ (*Elec*) connected, plugged in; (*Inform*) on-line

★**conectar** [konekˈtar] /**1a**/ VT to connect (up); (*enchufar*) to plug in; (*Inform*) to toggle on ■ **conectarse** VR (*Inform*) to log in *or* on

conectividad [konektiβiˈðað] NF connectivity

conejillo [koneˈxiʎo] NM: ~ **de Indias** guinea pig

★**conejo** [koˈnexo] NM rabbit

conexión [konekˈsjon] NF connection; (*Inform*) logging in *or* on

confabularse [konfaβuˈlarse] /**1a**/ VR: ~ **(para hacer algo)** to plot *o* conspire (to do sth)

confección [konfekˈθjon] NF (*preparación*) preparation, making-up; (*industria*) clothing industry; (*producto*) article; **de ~** (*ropa*) off-the-peg

confeccionar [konfekθjoˈnar] /**1a**/ VT to make (up)

confederación [konfeðeraˈθjon] NF confederation

★**conferencia** [konfeˈrenθja] NF conference; (*lección*) lecture; (*Telec*) call; ~ **de cobro revertido** (*Telec*) reversed-charge (*Brit*) *o* collect (*US*) call; ~ **cumbre** summit (conference); ~ **de prensa** press conference

conferenciante [konferenˈθjante] NMF lecturer

conferir [konfeˈrir] /**3i**/ VT to award

confesar [konfeˈsar] /**1j**/ VT (*admitir*) to confess, admit; (*error*) to acknowledge; (*crimen*) to own up to

confesión [konfeˈsjon] NF confession

confesionario [konfesjoˈnarjo] NM confessional

confeso, -a [konˈfeso, a] ADJ (*Jur etc*) self-confessed

confeti [konˈfeti] NM confetti

confiado, -a [konˈfjaðo, a] ADJ (*crédulo*) trusting; (*seguro*) confident; (*presumido*) conceited, vain

★**confianza** [konˈfjanθa] NF trust; (*aliento, confidencia*) confidence; (*familiaridad*) intimacy, familiarity; (*pey*) vanity, conceit; **margen de ~** credibility gap; **tener ~ con algn** to be on close terms with sb

★**confiar** [konˈfjar] /**1c**/ VT to entrust ▶ VI (*fiarse*) to trust; (*contar con*) to rely; ~ **en algn** to trust sb; ~ **en que ...** to hope that ... ■ **confiarse** VR to put one's trust in

confidencia [konfiˈðenθja] NF confidence

confidencial [konfiðenˈθjal] ADJ confidential

confidente [konfiˈðente] NMF confidant/confidante; (*policial*) informer

confiera *etc* [konˈfjera] VB *ver* **conferir**

confiese *etc* [konˈfjese] VB *ver* **confesar**

configuración [konfiɣuraˈθjon] NF (*tb Inform*) configuration; **la ~ del terreno** the lie of the land; ~ **de bits** (*Inform*) bit pattern

configurar [konfiɣuˈrar] /**1a**/ VT to shape, form

confín [konˈfin] NM limit ■ **confines** NMPL confines, limits

confinar [konfiˈnar] /**1a**/ VI to confine; (*desterrar*) to banish

confiriendo *etc* [konfiˈrjendo] VB *ver* **conferir**

confirmación [konfirmaˈθjon] NF confirmation; (*Rel*) Confirmation

★**confirmar** [konfirˈmar] /**1a**/ VT to confirm; (*Jur etc*) to corroborate; **la excepción confirma la regla** the exception proves the rule

confiscar [konfisˈkar] /**1g**/ VT to confiscate

confisque *etc* [konˈfiske] VB *ver* **confiscar**

confitado, -a [konfiˈtaðo, a] ADJ: **fruta confitada** crystallized fruit

confite [konˈfite] NM sweet (*Brit*), candy (*US*)

★**confitería** [konfiteˈria] NF confectionery; (*tienda*) confectioner's (shop)

confitura [konfiˈtura] NF jam

conflagración [konflaɣraˈθjon] NF conflagration

conflictivo, -a [konflikˈtiβo, a] ADJ (*asunto, propuesta*) controversial; (*país, situación*) troubled

★**conflicto** [konˈflikto] NM conflict; (*fig*) clash; (: *dificultad*): **estar en un ~** to be in a jam; ~ **laboral** labour dispute

confluir [konfluˈir] /**3g**/ VI (*ríos etc*) to meet; (*gente*) to gather

confluya *etc* [konˈfluja] VB *ver* **confluir**

conformar [konforˈmar] /**1a**/ VT to shape, fashion ▶ VI to agree ■ **conformarse** VR to conform; (*resignarse*) to resign o.s.; **conformarse con algo** to be happy with sth

★**conforme** [konˈforme] ADJ alike, similar; (*correspondiente*): ~ **con** in line with; (*de acuerdo*) agreed, in agreement; (*satisfecho*) satisfied; **estar conformes (con algo)** to be in agreement (with sth); **quedarse ~ (con algo)** to be satisfied (with sth) ▶ ADV as ▶ EXCL agreed! ▶ NM agreement ▶ PREP: ~ **a** in accordance with

conformidad [komformiˈðað] NF (*semejanza*) similarity; (*acuerdo*) agreement; (*resignación*) resignation; **de/en ~ con** in accordance with; **dar su ~** to consent

conformismo [komforˈmismo] NM conformism

conformista [komforˈmista] NMF conformist

confort [konˈfor] (*pl* **conforts** [konˈfor(t)s]) NM comfort

★**confortable** [komforˈtaβle] ADJ comfortable

confortar [komforˈtar] /1a/ VT to comfort

confraternidad [komfraterniˈðað] NF brotherhood; **espíritu de ~** feeling of unity

confraternizar [komfraterniˈθar] /1f/ VI to fraternize

confrontación [komfrontaˈθjon] NF confrontation

confrontar [komfronˈtar] /1a/ VT to confront; (*dos personas*) to bring face to face; (*cotejar*) to compare ▶ VI to border

confundir [komfunˈdir] /3a/ VT (*borrar*) to blur; (*equivocar*) to mistake, confuse; (*mezclar*) to mix; (*turbar*) to confuse ■ **confundirse** VR (*hacerse borroso*) to become blurred; (*turbarse*) to get confused; (*equivocarse*) to make a mistake; (*mezclarse*) to mix

confusión [komfuˈsjon] NF confusion

confusionismo [komfusjoˈnismo] NM confusion, uncertainty

confuso, -a [komˈfuso, a] ADJ (*gen*) confused; (*recuerdo*) hazy; (*estilo*) obscure

congelación [konxelaˈθjon] NF freezing; **~ de créditos** credit freeze

congelado, -a [konxeˈlaðo, a] ADJ frozen ▶ NM: **congelados** frozen food *sg o* foods

★**congelador** [konxelaˈðor] NM freezer, deep freeze

★**congelar** [konxeˈlar] /1a/ VT to freeze ■ **congelarse** VR (*sangre, grasa*) to congeal

congénere [konˈxenere] NMF: **sus congéneres** his peers

congeniar [konxeˈnjar] /1b/ VI to get on (BRIT) *o* along (US) (well)

congénito, -a [konˈxenito, a] ADJ congenital

congestión [konxesˈtjon] NF congestion

congestionado, -a [konxestjoˈnaðo, a] ADJ congested

congestionar [konxestjoˈnar] /1a/ VT to congest ■ **congestionarse** VR to become congested; **se le congestionó la cara** his face became flushed

conglomerado [konglomeˈraðo] NM conglomerate

Congo [ˈkongo] NM: **el ~** the Congo

congoja [konˈgoxa] NF distress, grief

congraciarse [kongraˈθjarse] /1b/ VR to ingratiate o.s.

congratular [kongratuˈlar] /1a/ VT to congratulate

congregación [kongreɣaˈθjon] NF congregation

congregar [kongreˈɣar] /1h/ VT to gather together ■ **congregarse** VR to gather together

congregue *etc* [konˈgreɣe] VB *ver* **congregar**

congresista [kongreˈsista] NMF delegate, congressman/woman

congreso [konˈgreso] NM congress; **C~ de los Diputados** (*ESP Pol*) ≈ House of Commons (*BRIT*), House of Representatives (*US*); *ver tb* **corte**

congrio [ˈkongrjo] NM conger (eel)

congruente [konˈgrwente] ADJ congruent, congruous

conífera [koˈnifera] NF conifer

conjetura [konxeˈtura] NF guess; (*Com*) guesstimate

conjeturar [konxetuˈrar] /1a/ VT to guess

conjugación [konxuɣaˈθjon] NF conjugation

conjugar [konxuˈɣar] /1h/ VT to combine, fit together; (*Ling*) to conjugate

conjugue *etc* [konˈxuɣe] VB *ver* **conjugar**

conjunción [konxunˈθjon] NF conjunction

conjuntivitis [konxuntiˈβitis] NF conjunctivitis

★**conjunto, -a** [konˈxunto, a] ADJ joint, united ▶ NM whole; (*Mus*) band; (*de ropa*) ensemble; (*Inform*) set; **en ~** as a whole; **~ integrado de programas** (*Inform*) integrated software suite

conjura [konˈxura] NF plot, conspiracy

conjurar [konxuˈrar] /1a/ VT (*Rel*) to exorcise; (*peligro*) to ward off ▶ VI to plot

conjuro [konˈxuro] NM spell

conllevar [konʎeˈβar] /1a/ VT to bear; (*implicar*) to imply, involve

conmemoración [konmemoraˈθjon] NF commemoration

conmemorar [konmemoˈrar] /1a/ VT to commemorate

★**conmigo** [konˈmiɣo] PRON with me

conminar [konmiˈnar] /1a/ VT to threaten

conmiseración [konmiseraˈθjon] NF pity, commiseration

conmoción [konmoˈθjon] NF shock; (*Pol*) disturbance; (*fig*) upheaval; **~ cerebral** (*Med*) concussion

conmovedor, a [konmoβeˈðor, a] ADJ touching, moving; (*emocionante*) exciting

conmover [konmoˈβer] /2h/ VT to shake, disturb; (*fig*) to move ■ **conmoverse** VR (*fig*) to be moved

conmueva *etc* [konˈmweβa] VB *ver* **conmover**

conmutación [konmutaˈθjon] NF (*Inform*) switching; **~ de mensajes** message switching; **~ por paquetes** packet switching

conmutador [konmutaˈðor] NM switch; (*AM*

Telec) switchboard; (: *central)* telephone exchange

conmutar [konmuˈtar] /**1a**/ vт *(Jur)* to commute

connivencia [konniˈβenθja] NF: **estar en ~ con** to be in collusion with

connotación [konnotaˈθjon] NF connotation

cono [ˈkono] NM cone; **C~ Sur** Southern Cone

conocedor, a [konoθeˈðor, a] ADJ expert, knowledgeable ▶ NM/F expert, connoisseur

★**conocer** [konoˈθer] /**2d**/ vт to know; *(por primera vez)* to meet, get to know; *(entender)* to know about; *(reconocer)* to recognize; **~ a algn de vista** to know sb by sight; **darse a ~** *(presentarse)* to make o.s. known; **se conoce que ...** *(parece)* apparently ... ▪ **conocerse** VR *(una persona)* to know o.s.; *(dos personas)* to (get to) know each other

conocido, -a [konoˈθiðo, a] ADJ (well-)known ▶ NM/F acquaintance

★**conocimiento** [konoθiˈmjento] NM knowledge; *(Med)* consciousness; *(Naut: tb:* **conocimiento de embarque***)* bill of lading; **hablar con ~ de causa** to speak from experience; **~ (de embarque) aéreo** *(Com)* air waybill ▪ **conocimientos** NMPL *(personas)* acquaintances; *(saber)* knowledge *sg*

conozco *etc* [koˈnoθko] vв *ver* **conocer**

conque [ˈkonke] conj and so, so then

conquense [konˈkense] ADJ of o from Cuenca ▶ NMF native o inhabitant of Cuenca

conquista [konˈkista] NF conquest

conquistador, a [konkistaˈðor, a] ADJ conquering ▶ NM conqueror

conquistar [konkisˈtar] /**1a**/ vт *(Mil)* to conquer; *(puesto, simpatía)* to win; *(enamorar)* to win the heart of

consabido, -a [konsaˈβiðo, a] ADJ *(frase etc)* old; *(pey)*: **las consabidas excusas** the same old excuses

consagrado, -a [konsaˈɣraðo, a] ADJ *(Rel)* consecrated; *(actor)* established

consagrar [konsaˈɣrar] /**1a**/ vт *(Rel)* to consecrate; *(fig)* to devote

consciente [konsˈθjente] ADJ conscious; **ser** o **estar ~ de** to be aware of

consecución [konsekuˈθjon] NF acquisition; *(de fin)* attainment

★**consecuencia** [konseˈkwenθja] NF consequence, outcome; *(firmeza)* consistency; **de ~ of** importance

consecuente [konseˈkwente] ADJ consistent

consecutivo, -a [konsekuˈtiβo, a] ADJ consecutive

★**conseguir** [konseˈɣir] /**3d, 3k**/ vт to get, obtain; *(sus fines)* to attain

consejería [konsexeˈria] NF *(Pol)* ministry *(in a regional government)*

consejero, -a [konseˈxero, a] NM/F adviser, consultant; *(Pol)* minister *(in a regional government)*; *(Com)* director; *(en comisión)* member

★**consejo** [konˈsexo] NM advice; *(Pol)* council; *(Com)* board; **un ~** a piece of advice; **~ de administración** board of directors; **~ de guerra** court-martial; **~ de ministros** cabinet meeting; **C~ de Europa** Council of Europe

consenso [konˈsenso] NM consensus

consentido, -a [konsenˈtiðo, a] ADJ *(mimado)* spoiled

consentimiento [konsentiˈmjento] NM consent

consentir [konsenˈtir] /**3i**/ vт *(permitir, tolerar)* to consent to; *(mimar)* to pamper, spoil; *(aguantar)* to put up with; **~ que algn haga algo** to allow sb to do sth ▶ vi to agree, consent

★**conserje** [konˈserxe] NM caretaker; *(portero)* porter

conserva [konˈserβa] NF: **en ~** *(alimentos)* tinned (BRIT), canned ▪ **conservas** NFPL *(tb:* **conservas alimenticias***)* tinned (BRIT) o canned foods

conservación [konserβaˈθjon] NF conservation; *(de alimentos, vida)* preservation

conservador, a [konserβaˈðor, a] ADJ *(Pol)* conservative ▶ NM/F conservative

conservadurismo [konserβaðuˈrismo] NM *(Pol etc)* conservatism

conservante [konserˈβante] NM preservative

conservar [konserˈβar] /**1a**/ vт *(gen)* to preserve; *(recursos)* to conserve, keep; *(alimentos, vida)* to preserve ▪ **conservarse** VR to survive

conservatorio [konserβaˈtorjo] NM *(Mus)* conservatoire, conservatory; *(AM)* greenhouse

considerable [konsiðeˈraβle] ADJ considerable

consideración [konsiðeraˈθjon] NF consideration; *(estimación)* respect; **de ~** important; **De mi** o **nuestra (mayor) ~** *(AM)* Dear Sir(s) o Madam; **tomar en ~** to take into account

considerado, -a [konsiðeˈraðo, a] ADJ *(atento)* considerate; *(respetado)* respected

considerar [konsiðeˈrar] /**1a**/ vт *(gen)* to consider; *(meditar)* to think about; *(tener en cuenta)* to take into account

consienta *etc* [konˈsjenta] vв *ver* **consentir**

★**consigna** [konˈsiɣna] NF *(orden)* order, instruction; *(para equipajes)* left-luggage office (BRIT), checkroom (US)

consignación [konsiɣnaˈθjon] NF consignment; **~ de créditos** allocation of credits

consignador [konsiɣnaˈðor] NM *(Com)* consignor

consignar [konsiɣˈnar] /**1a**/ vт *(Com)* to send; *(créditos)* to allocate

consignatario, -a [konsiɣnaˈtarjo, a] NM/F *(Com)* consignee

★**consigo** [konˈsiɣo] vв *ver* **conseguir** ▶ PRON *(m)* with him; *(f)* with her; *(usted)* with you; *(reflexivo)* with o.s.

consiguiendo *etc* [konsiˈɣjendo] vв *ver* **conseguir**

consiguiente [konsi'ɣjente] ADJ consequent; **por ~** and so, therefore, consequently

consintiendo etc [konsin'tjendo] VB ver **consentir**

consistente [konsis'tente] ADJ consistent; (sólido) solid, firm; (válido) sound; **~ en** consisting of

consistir [konsis'tir] /3a/ VI: **~ en** (componerse de) to consist of; (ser resultado de) to be due to

consola [kon'sola] NF console, control panel; (mueble) console table; **~ de juegos** games console; **~ de mandos** (Inform) control console; **~ de visualización** visual display console

consolación [konsola'θjon] NF consolation

consolar [konso'lar] /1l/ VT to console

consolidar [konsoli'ðar] /1a/ VT to consolidate

consomé [konso'me] (pl **consomés** [konso'mes]) NM consommé, clear soup

consonancia [konso'nanθja] NF harmony; **en ~ con** in accordance with

consonante [konso'nante] ADJ consonant, harmonious ▸ NF consonant

consorcio [kon'sorθjo] NM (Com) consortium, syndicate

consorte [kon'sorte] NMF consort

conspicuo, -a [kons'pikwo, a] ADJ conspicuous

conspiración [konspira'θjon] NF conspiracy

conspirador, a [konspira'ðor, a] NM/F conspirator

conspirar [konspi'rar] /1a/ VI to conspire

constancia [kons'tanθja] NF (gen) constancy; (certeza) certainly; **dejar ~ de algo** to put sth on record

★**constante** [kons'tante] ADJ, NF constant

constar [kons'tar] /1a/ VI (evidenciarse) to be clear o evident; **~ (en)** to appear (in); **~ de** to consist of; **hacer ~** to put on record; **me consta que ...** I have evidence that ...; **que conste que lo hice por ti** believe me, I did it for your own good

constatar [konsta'tar] /1a/ VT (controlar) to check; (observar) to note

constelación [konstela'θjon] NF constellation

consternación [konsterna'θjon] NF consternation

★**constipado, -a** [konsti'paðo, a] ADJ: **estar ~** to have a cold ▸ NM cold

> Do not translate the Spanish word **constipado** by constipated.

constiparse [konsti'parse] /1a/ VR to catch a cold

constitución [konstitu'θjon] NF constitution; **Día de la C~** (ESP) Constitution Day (6th December)

constitucional [konstituθjo'nal] ADJ constitutional

constituir [konstitu'ir] /3g/ VT (formar, componer) to constitute, make up; (fundar, erigir, ordenar) to constitute, establish; (ser) to be ■ **constituirse**

VR (Pol etc: cuerpo) to be composed; (: fundarse) to be established

constitutivo, -a [konstitu'tiβo, a] ADJ constitutive, constituent

constituya etc [konsti'tuja] VB ver **constituir**

constituyente [konstitu'jente] ADJ constituent

constreñir [konstre'nir] /3h, 3k/ VT (obligar) to compel, oblige; (restringir) to restrict

constriño etc [kons'trino], **constriñendo** etc [konstri'nendo] VB ver **constreñir**

★**construcción** [konstruk'θjon] NF construction, building

constructivo, -a [konstruk'tiβo, a] ADJ constructive

★**constructor, a** [konstruk'tor, a] NM/F builder

★**construir** [konstru'ir] /3g/ VT to build, construct

construyendo etc [konstru'jendo] VB ver **construir**

consuelo [kon'swelo] VB ver **consolar** ▸ NM consolation, solace

consuetudinario, -a [konswetuði'narjo, a] ADJ customary; **derecho ~** common law

cónsul ['konsul] NM consul

★**consulado** [konsu'laðo] NM (sede) consulate; (cargo) consulship

★**consulta** [kon'sulta] NF consultation; (Med: consultorio) consulting room; (Inform) enquiry; **horas de ~** (Med) surgery hours; **obra de ~** reference book

★**consultar** [konsul'tar] /1a/ VT to consult; **~ un archivo** (Inform) to interrogate a file; **~ algo con algn** to discuss sth with sb

consultor, a [konsul'tor, a] NM: **~ en dirección de empresas** management consultant

★**consultorio** [konsul'torjo] NM (Med) surgery

consumado, -a [konsu'maðo, a] ADJ perfect; (bribón) out-and-out

consumar [konsu'mar] /1a/ VT to complete, carry out; (crimen) to commit; (sentencia) to carry out

consumición [konsumi'θjon] NF consumption; (bebida) drink; (comida) food; **~ mínima** cover charge

consumido, -a [konsu'miðo, a] ADJ (flaco) skinny

★**consumidor, a** [konsumi'ðor, a] NM/F consumer

★**consumir** [konsu'mir] /3a/ VT to consume ■ **consumirse** VR to be consumed; (persona) to waste away

consumismo [konsu'mismo] NM (Com) consumerism

consumo [kon'sumo] NM consumption; **bienes de ~** consumer goods

contabilice etc [kontaβi'liθe] VB ver **contabilizar**

contabilidad [kontaβili'ðað] NF accounting, book-keeping; (profesión) accountancy; (Com): **~ analítica** variable costing; **~ de costos** cost accounting; **~ de doble partida** double-entry book-keeping; **~ de gestión** management accounting; **~ por partida simple** single-entry book-keeping

contabilizar [kontaβi'liθar] /**1f**/ VT to enter in the accounts

★**contable** [kon'taβle] NMF bookkeeper; (licenciado) accountant; **~ de costos** (Com) cost accountant

★**contactar** [kontak'tar] /**1a**/ VI: **~ con algn** to contact sb

contacto [kon'takto] NM contact; (Auto) ignition; **lentes de ~** contact lenses; **estar en ~ con** to be in touch with

contado, -a [kon'taðo, a] ADJ: **contados** (escasos) numbered, scarce, few ▶ NM: **al ~** for cash; **pagar al ~** to pay (in) cash; **precio al ~** cash price

contador [konta'ðor] NM (aparato) meter; (Am: contable) accountant

contaduría [kontaðu'ria] NF accountant's office

contagiar [konta'xjar] /**1b**/ VT (enfermedad) to pass on, transmit; (persona) to infect ■ **contagiarse** VR to become infected

contagio [kon'taxjo] NM infection

contagioso, -a [konta'xjoso, a] ADJ infectious; (fig) catching

★**contaminación** [kontamina'θjon] NF (gen) contamination; (del ambiente etc) pollution

★**contaminar** [kontami'nar] /**1a**/ VT (gen) to contaminate; (aire, agua) to pollute; (fig) to taint

contante [kon'tante] ADJ: **dinero ~ (y sonante)** hard cash

★**contar** [kon'tar] /**1l**/ VT (páginas, dinero) to count; (anécdota etc) to tell; **le cuento entre mis amigos** I reckon him among my friends ▶ VI to count; **~ con** to rely on, count on; **sin ~** not to mention ■ **contarse** VR to be counted, figure

contemplación [kontempla'θjon] NF contemplation; **no andarse con contemplaciones** not to stand on ceremony

contemplar [kontem'plar] /**1a**/ VT to contemplate; (mirar) to look at

contemporáneo, -a [kontempo'raneo, a] ADJ, NM/F contemporary

contemporizar [kontempori'θar] /**1f**/ VI: **~ con** to keep in with

contención [konten'θjon] NF (Jur) suit; **muro de ~** retaining wall

contencioso, -a [konten'θjoso, a] ADJ (Jur etc) contentious ▶ NM (Pol) conflict, dispute

contender [konten'der] /**2g**/ VI to contend; (en un concurso) to compete

contendiente [konten'djente] NMF contestant

contendrá etc [konten'dra] VB ver **contener**

★**contenedor** [kontene'ðor] NM container; (de escombros) skip; **~ de (la) basura** wheelie-bin

(BRIT); **~ de vidrio** bottle bank

★**contener** [konte'ner] /**2k**/ VT to contain, hold; (risa etc) to hold back, contain ■ **contenerse** VR to control o restrain o.s.

contenga etc [kon'tenga] VB ver **contener**

★**contenido, -a** [konte'niðo, a] ADJ (moderado) restrained; (risa etc) suppressed ▶ NM contents pl, content

contentar [konten'tar] /**1a**/ VT (satisfacer) to satisfy; (complacer) to please; (Com) to endorse ■ **contentarse** VR to be satisfied

★**contento, -a** [kon'tento, a] ADJ contented, content; (alegre) pleased; (feliz) happy

★**contestación** [kontesta'θjon] NF answer, reply; **~ a la demanda** (Jur) defence plea

★**contestador** [kontesta'ðor] NM: **~ automático** answering machine

★**contestar** [kontes'tar] /**1a**/ VT to answer (back), reply; (Jur) to corroborate, confirm

contestatario, -a [kontesta'tarjo, a] ADJ anti-establishment, nonconformist

contexto [kon'teksto] NM context

contienda [kon'tjenda] NF contest, struggle

contiene etc [kon'tjene] VB ver **contener**

★**contigo** [kon'tiɣo] PRON with you

contiguo, -a [kon'tiɣwo, a] ADJ (de al lado) next; (vecino) adjacent, adjoining

continental [kontinen'tal] ADJ continental

continente [konti'nente] ADJ, NM continent

contingencia [kontin'xenθja] NF contingency; (riesgo) risk; (posibilidad) eventuality

contingente [kontin'xente] ADJ contingent ▶ NM contingent; (Com) quota

continuación [kontinwa'θjon] NF continuation; **a ~** then, next

★**continuamente** [kon'tinwamente] ADV (sin interrupción) continuously; (a todas horas) constantly

★**continuar** [konti'nwar] /**1e**/ VT to continue, go on with; (reanudar) to resume ▶ VI to continue, go on; **~ hablando** to continue talking o to talk

continuidad [kontinwi'ðað] NF continuity

continuo, -a [kon'tinwo, a] ADJ (sin interrupción) continuous; (acción perseverante) continual

contonearse [kontone'arse] /**1a**/ VR (hombre) to swagger; (mujer) to swing one's hips

contorno [kon'torno] NM outline; (Geo) contour ■ **contornos** NMPL neighbourhood sg, surrounding area sg

contorsión [kontor'sjon] NF contortion

★**contra** ['kontra] PREP against; (Com: giro) on ▶ ADV against ▶ ADJ, NMF (Pol: fam) counter-revolutionary ▶ NM con ▶ NF: **la C~ (nicaragüense)** the Contras pl

contraalmirante [kontraalmi'rante] NM rear admiral

contraanálisis [kontraa'nalisis] NM follow-up test, countertest

contraataque [kontraa'take] NM counterattack

contrabajo [kontra'βaxo] NM double bass

contrabandista [kontraβan'dista] NMF smuggler

contrabando [kontra'βando] NM (acción) smuggling; (mercancías) contraband; **~ de armas** gun-running

contracción [kontrak'θjon] NF contraction

contrachapado [kontratʃa'paðo] NM plywood

contracorriente [kontrako'rrjente] NF crosscurrent

contradecir [kontraðe'θir] /3o/ VT to contradict

contradicción [kontraðik'θjon] NF contradiction; **espíritu de ~** contrariness

contradicho [kontra'ðitʃo] PP de **contradecir**

contradiciendo etc [kontraði'θjendo] VB ver **contradecir**

contradictorio, -a [kontraðik'torjo, a] ADJ contradictory

contradiga etc [kontra'ðiɣa], **contradije** etc [kontra'ðixe], **contradirá** etc [kontraði'ra] VB ver **contradecir**

contraer [kontra'er] /2o/ VT to contract; (hábito) to acquire; (limitar) to restrict ▪ **contraerse** VR to contract; (limitarse) to limit o.s.

contraespionaje [kontraespjo'naxe] NM counter-espionage

contrafuerte [kontra'fwerte] NM (Arq) buttress

contragolpe [kontra'ɣolpe] NM backlash

contrahacer [kontraa'θer] /2r/ VB (copiar) to copy, imitate; (moneda) to counterfeit; (documento) to forge, fake; (libro) to pirate

contrahaga etc [kontra'aɣa], **contraharé** etc [kontraa're] VB ver **contrahacer**

contrahecho, -a [kontra'etʃo, a] PP de **contrahacer** ▸ ADJ fake; (Anat) hunchbacked

contrahice etc [kontra'iθe] VB ver **contrahacer**

contraiga etc [kon'traiɣa] VB ver **contraer**

contraindicaciones [kontraindika'θjones] NFPL (Med) contraindications

contraje etc [kon'traxe] VB ver **contraer**

contralor [kontra'lor] NM (Am) government accounting inspector

contraluz [kontra'luθ] NM o F view against the light; (Foto etc) back lighting; **a ~** against the light

contramaestre [kontrama'estre] NM foreman

contraofensiva [kontraofen'siβa] NF counteroffensive

contraorden [kontra'orðen] NF counterorder, countermand

contrapartida [kontrapar'tiða] NF (Com) balancing entry; **como ~ (de)** in return (for), as o in compensation (for)

contrapelo [kontra'pelo]: **a ~** adv the wrong way

contrapesar [kontrape'sar] /1a/ VT to counterbalance; (fig) to offset

contrapeso [kontra'peso] NM counterweight; (fig) counterbalance; (Com) makeweight

contrapondré etc [kontrapon'dre] VB ver **contraponer**

contraponer [kontrapo'ner] /2q/ VT (cotejar) to compare; (oponer) to oppose

contraponga etc [kontra'ponga] VB ver **contraponer**

contraportada [kontrapor'taða] NF (de revista) back cover

contraproducente [kontraproðu'θente] ADJ counterproductive

contrapuesto [kontra'pwesto] PP de **contraponer**

contrapunto [kontra'punto] NM counterpoint

contrapuse etc [kontra'puse] VB ver **contraponer**

contrariar [kontra'rjar] /1c/ VT (oponerse) to oppose; (poner obstáculo) to impede; (enfadar) to vex

contrariedad [kontrarje'ðað] NF (oposición) opposition; (obstáculo) obstacle, setback; (disgusto) vexation, annoyance

★**contrario, -a** [kon'trarjo, a] ADJ contrary; (persona) opposed; (sentido, lado) opposite ▸ NM/F enemy, adversary; (Deporte) opponent; **al ~, por el ~** on the contrary; **de lo ~** otherwise

Contrarreforma [kontrarre'forma] NF Counter-Reformation

contrarreloj [kontrarre'lo(x)] NF (tb: **prueba contrarreloj**) time trial

contrarrestar [kontrarres'tar] /1a/ VT to counteract

contrarrevolución [kontrarreβolu'θjon] NF counter-revolution

contrasentido [kontrasen'tiðo] NM contradiction; **es un ~ que él ...** it doesn't make sense for him to ...

★**contraseña** [kontra'seɲa] NF countersign; (frase) password

contrastar [kontras'tar] /1a/ VT to verify ▸ VI to contrast

contraste [kon'traste] NM contrast

contrata [kon'trata] NF (Jur) written contract; (empleo) hiring

contratar [kontra'tar] /1a/ VT (firmar un acuerdo para) to contract for; (empleados, obreros) to hire, engage; (Deporte) to sign up ▪ **contratarse** VR to sign on

contratiempo [kontra'tjempo] NM (revés) setback; (accidente) mishap; **a ~** (Mus) off-beat

contratista [kontra'tista] NMF contractor

★**contrato** [kon'trato] NM contract; **~ de compraventa** contract of sale; **~ a precio fijo** fixed-price contract; **~ a término** forward contract; **~ de trabajo** contract of employment *o* service

contravalor [kontraβa'lor] NM exchange value

contravención [kontraβen'θjon] NF contravention, violation

contravendré *etc* [kontraβen'dre], **contravenga** *etc* [kontra'βenga] VB *ver* **contravenir**

contravenir [kontraβe'nir] **/3r/** VI: **~ a** to contravene, violate

contraventana [kontraβen'tana] NF shutter

contraviene *etc* [kontra'βjene], **contraviniendo** *etc* [kontraβi'njendo] VB *ver* **contravenir**

contrayendo [kontra'jendo] VB *ver* **contraer**

contribución [kontriβu'θjon] NF (*municipal etc*) tax; (*ayuda*) contribution; **exento de contribuciones** tax-free

★**contribuir** [kontriβu'ir] **/3g/** VT, VI to contribute; (*Com*) to pay (in taxes)

contribuyendo *etc* [kontriβu'jendo] VB *ver* **contribuir**

contribuyente [kontriβu'jente] NMF (*Com*) taxpayer; (*que ayuda*) contributor

contrincante [kontrin'kante] NM opponent, rival

control [kon'trol] NM control; (*inspección*) inspection, check; (*Com*): **~ de calidad** quality control; **~ de cambios** exchange control; **~ de costos** cost control; **~ de créditos** credit control; **~ de existencias** stock control; **~ de precios** price control; **~ de pasaportes** passport inspection

controlador, a [kontrola'ðor, a] NM/F controller; **~ aéreo** air-traffic controller

★**controlar** [kontro'lar] **/1a/** VT to control; to inspect, check; (*Com*) to audit

controversia [kontro'βersja] NF controversy

contubernio [kontu'βernjo] NM ring, conspiracy

contumaz [kontu'maθ] ADJ obstinate, stubbornly disobedient

contundente [kontun'dente] ADJ (*prueba*) conclusive; (*fig: argumento*) convincing; **instrumento ~** blunt instrument

contusión [kontu'sjon] NF bruise

contuve *etc* [kon'tuβe] VB *ver* **contener**

convalecencia [kombale'θenθja] NF convalescence

convalecer [kombale'θer] **/2d/** VI to convalesce, get better

convaleciente [kombale'θjente] ADJ, NMF convalescent

convalezca *etc* [komba'leθka] VB *ver* **convalecer**

convalidar [kombali'ðar] **/1a/** VT (*título*) to recognize

★**convencer** [komben'θer] **/2b/** VT to convince; (*persuadir*) to persuade

convencimiento [kombenθi'mjento] NM (*acción*) convincing; (*persuasión*) persuasion; (*certidumbre*) conviction; **tener el ~ de que ...** to be convinced that ...

convención [komben'θjon] NF convention

convencional [kombenθjo'nal] ADJ conventional

convendré *etc* [komben'dre], **convenga** *etc* [kom'benga] VB *ver* **convenir**

conveniencia [kombe'njenθja] NF suitability; (*conformidad*) agreement; (*utilidad, provecho*) usefulness; **ser de la ~ de algn** to suit sb ■ **conveniencias** NFPL conventions; (*Com*) property *sg*

conveniente [kombe'njente] ADJ suitable; (*útil*) useful; (*correcto*) fit, proper; (*aconsejable*) advisable

convenio [kom'benjo] NM agreement, treaty; **~ de nivel crítico** threshold agreement

convenir [kombe'nir] **/3r/** VI (*estar de acuerdo*) to agree; (*ser conveniente*) to suit, be suitable; **"sueldo a ~"** "salary to be agreed"; **conviene recordar que ...** it should be remembered that ...

convento [kom'bento] NM monastery; (*de monjas*) convent

convenza *etc* [kom'benθa] VB *ver* **convencer**

convergencia [komber'xenθja] NF convergence

converger [komber'xer] **/2c/**, **convergir** [komber'xir] **/3c/** VI to converge; **sus esfuerzos convergen a un fin común** their efforts are directed towards the same objective

converja *etc* [kom'berxa] VB *ver* **converger**

★**conversación** [kombersa'θjon] NF conversation

★**conversar** [komber'sar] **/1a/** VI to talk, converse

conversión [komber'sjon] NF conversion

converso, -a [kom'berso, a] NM/F convert

★**convertir** [komber'tir] **/3i/** VT to convert; (*transformar*) to transform, turn; (*Com*) to (ex)change ■ **convertirse** VR (*Rel*) to convert

convexo, -a [kom'bekso, a] ADJ convex

convicción [kombik'θjon] NF conviction

convicto, -a [kom'bikto, a] ADJ convicted; (*condenado*) condemned

convidado, -a [kombi'ðaðo, a] NM/F guest

convidar [kombi'ðar] **/1a/** VT to invite; **~ a algn a una cerveza** to buy sb a beer

conviene *etc* [kom'bjene] VB *ver* **convenir**

convierta *etc* [kom'bjerta] VB *ver* **convertir**

convincente [kombin'θente] ADJ convincing

conviniendo *etc* [kombi'njendo] VB *ver* **convenir**

convirtiendo *etc* [kombir'tjendo] VB *ver* **convertir**

convite [kom'bite] NM invitation; (*banquete*) banquet

convivencia [kombi'βenθja] NF coexistence, living together

convivir [kombi'βir] /**3a**/ vi to live together; (*Pol*) to coexist

convocar [kombo'kar] /**1g**/ vt to summon, call (together)

convocatoria [komboka'torja] nf summons *sg*; (*anuncio*) notice of meeting; (*Escol*) examination session

convoque *etc* [kom'boke] vb *ver* **convocar**

convoy [kom'boj] nm (*Ferro*) train

convulsión [kombul'sjon] nf convulsion; (*Pol etc*) upheaval

conyugal [konju'ɣal] adj conjugal; **vida ~** married life

cónyuge ['konjuxe] nmf spouse, partner

coña ['koɲa] nf (*fam!*): **tomar algo a ~** to take sth as a joke

coñac ['koɲa(k)] (*pl* **coñacs** ['koɲa(k)s]) nm cognac, brandy

coñazo [ko'ɲaθo] nm (*fam!*) pain; **dar el ~** to be a real pain

coño ['koɲo] (*fam!*) nm cunt (*fam!*); (*Am pey*) Spaniard ▶ excl (*enfado*) shit (*fam!*); (*sorpresa*) bloody hell (*fam!*); **¡qué ~!** what a pain in the arse! (*fam!*)

cookie ['kuki] nf (*Inform*) cookie

cool [kul] adj (*fam*) cool

cooperación [koopera'θjon] nf cooperation

cooperar [koope'rar] /**1a**/ vi to cooperate

cooperativo, -a [koopera'tiβo, a] adj cooperative ▶ nf cooperative

coordenada [koorðe'naða] nf (*Mat*) coordinate ■ **coordenadas** nfpl (*fig*) guidelines, framework *sg*

coordinación [koorðina'θjon] nf coordination

coordinador, a [koorðina'ðor, a] nm/f coordinator ▶ nf coordinating committee

coordinar [koorði'nar] /**1a**/ vt to coordinate

★**copa** ['kopa] nf (*tb Deporte*) cup; (*vaso*) glass; (*de árbol*) top; (*de sombrero*) crown; **(tomar una) ~** (to have a) drink ■ **copas** nfpl (*Naipes*) one of the suits in the Spanish card deck; **ir de copas** to go out for a drink; *ver tb* **baraja española**

copago [ko'paɣo] nm (*Med: sistema, cuota*) copayment, copay

copar [ko'par] /**1a**/ vt (*puestos*) to monopolize

coparticipación [kopartiθipa'θjon] nf (*Com*) co-ownership

COPE ['kope] nf abr (= *Cadena de Ondas Populares Españolas*) *Spanish radio network*

Copenhague [kope'naɣe] nm Copenhagen

copete [ko'pete] nm tuft (of hair); **de alto ~** aristocratic, upper-crust (*fam*)

★**copia** ['kopja] nf copy; (*Arte*) replica; (*Com etc*) duplicate; (*Inform*): **~ impresa** hard copy; **~ de respaldo** *o* **de seguridad** backup copy; **hacer ~ de seguridad** to back up; **~ de trabajo** working copy

copiadora [kopja'ðora] nf photocopier; **~ al alcohol** spirit duplicator

★**copiar** [ko'pjar] /**1b**/ vt to copy; **~ al pie de la letra** to copy word for word

copiloto [kopi'loto] nm (*Aviat*) co-pilot; (*Auto*) co-driver

copioso, -a [ko'pjoso, a] adj copious, plentiful

copipega [kopi'peɣa] nm copy and paste

copipegar [kopipe'ɣar] /**1h**/ vt to copy and paste

copita [ko'pita] nf (small) glass; (*Golf*) tee

copla ['kopla] nf verse; (*canción*) (popular) song

copo ['kopo] nm: **copos de maíz** cornflakes; **~ de nieve** snowflake

coprocesador [koproθesa'ðor] nm (*Inform*) co-processor

coproducción [koproðuk'θjon] nf (*Cine etc*) joint production

copropietarios [kopropje'tarjos] nmpl (*Com*) joint owners

cópula ['kopula] nf copulation

copular [kopu'lar] /**1a**/ vi to copulate

coqueta [ko'keta] adj flirtatious, coquettish ▶ nf (*mujer*) flirt

coquetear [kokete'ar] /**1a**/ vi to flirt

coraje [ko'raxe] nm courage; (*ánimo*) spirit; (*ira*) anger

coral [ko'ral] adj choral ▶ nf choir ▶ nm (*Zool*) coral

Corán [ko'ran] nm: **el ~** the Koran

coraza [ko'raθa] nf (*armadura*) armour; (*blindaje*) armour-plating

★**corazón** [kora'θon] nm heart; (*Bot*) core; **de buen ~** kind-hearted; **de todo ~** wholeheartedly; **estar mal del ~** to have heart trouble ■ **corazones** nmpl (*Naipes*) hearts

corazonada [koraθo'naða] nf impulse; (*presentimiento*) presentiment, hunch

★**corbata** [kor'βata] nf tie

corbeta [kor'βeta] nf corvette

Córcega ['korθeɣa] nf Corsica

corcel [kor'θel] nm steed

corchea [kor'tʃea] nf quaver

corchete [kor'tʃete] nm catch, clasp ■ **corchetes** nmpl (*Tip*) square brackets

★**corcho** ['kortʃo] nm cork; (*Pesca*) float

corcovado, -a [korko'βaðo, a] adj hunchbacked ▶ nm/f hunchback

cordel [kor'ðel] nm cord, line

★**cordero** [kor'ðero] nm lamb; (*piel*) lambskin

cordial [kor'ðjal] adj cordial ▶ nm cordial, tonic

cordialidad [korðjali'ðað] nf warmth, cordiality

cordillera [korði'ʎera] nf range (of mountains)

Córdoba ['korðoβa] nf Cordova

cordobés, -esa [korðo'βes, esa] adj, nm/f Cordovan

★**cordón** [kor'ðon] nm (*cuerda*) cord, string; (*de*

zapatos) lace; (*Elec*) flex, wire (*US*); (*Mil etc*) cordon; **~ umbilical** umbilical cord

cordura [kor'ðura] NF (*Med*) sanity; (*fig*) good sense; **con ~** (*obrar, hablar*) sensibly

Corea [ko'rea] NF Korea; **~ del Norte/Sur** North/South Korea

coreano, -a [kore'ano, a] ADJ, NM/F Korean

corear [kore'ar] /**1a**/ VT to chorus

coreografía [koreoɣra'fia] NF choreography

corista [ko'rista] NF (*Teat etc*) chorus girl

cornada [kor'naða] NF (*Taur etc*) butt, goring

córner ['korner] (*pl* **córners** ['korners]) NM corner (kick)

corneta [kor'neta] NF bugle

cornisa [kor'nisa] NF cornice

Cornualles [kor'nwaʎes] NM Cornwall

cornudo, -a [kor'nuðo, a] ADJ (*Zool*) horned; (*marido*) cuckolded

★**coro** ['koro] NM chorus; (*conjunto de cantores*) choir

corolario [koro'larjo] NM corollary

★**corona** [ko'rona] NF crown; (*de flores*) garland

coronación [korona'θjon] NF coronation

coronar [koro'nar] /**1a**/ VT to crown

coronel [koro'nel] NM colonel

coronilla [koro'niʎa] NF (*Anat*) crown (of the head); **estar hasta la ~ (de)** to be utterly fed up (with)

corpiño [kor'piɲo] NM bodice; (*AM: sostén*) bra

corporación [korpora'θjon] NF corporation

corporal [korpo'ral] ADJ corporal, bodily

corporativo, -a [korpora'tiβo, a] ADJ corporate

corpulento, -a [korpu'lento, a] ADJ (*persona*) heavily-built

corral [ko'rral] NM (*patio*) farmyard; (*Agr: de aves*) poultry yard; (*redil*) pen

correa [ko'rrea] NF strap; (*cinturón*) belt; (*de perro*) lead, leash; **~ transportadora** conveyor belt; **~ del ventilador** (*Auto*) fan belt

correaje [korre'axe] NM (*Agr*) harness

corrección [korrek'θjon] NF correction; (*reprensión*) rebuke; (*cortesía*) good manners; (*Inform*): **~ por líneas** line editing; **~ en pantalla** screen editing; **~ (de pruebas)** (*Tip*) proof-reading

correccional [korrekθjo'nal] NM reformatory

★**correcto, -a** [ko'rrekto, a] ADJ correct; (*persona*) well-mannered

corrector, a [korrek'tor, a] NM/F: **~ de pruebas** proofreader

corredera [korre'ðera] NF: **puerta de ~** sliding door

corredizo, -a [korre'ðiθo, a] ADJ (*puerta etc*) sliding; (*nudo*) running

corredor, a [korre'ðor, a] ADJ running; (*rápido*) fast ▶ NM/F (*Deporte*) runner; **~ de bienes raíces** real-estate broker; **~ de bolsa** stockbroker; **~ de seguros** insurance broker ▶ NM (*pasillo*)

corridor; (*balcón corrido*) gallery; (*Com*) agent, broker

★**corregir** [korre'xir] /**3c, 3k**/ VT (*error*) to correct; (*amonestar, reprender*) to rebuke, reprimand ■ **corregirse** VR to reform

★**correo** [ko'rreo] NM post, mail; (*persona*) courier; **~ aéreo** airmail; **~ basura** (*por carta*) junk mail; (*por Internet*) spam; **~ certificado** registered mail; **~ electrónico** email, electronic mail; **~ urgente** special delivery; **~ web** webmail; **a vuelta de ~** by return (of post) ■ **Correos** NMPL Post Office *sg*

★**correr** [ko'rrer] /**2a**/ VT to run; (*viajar*) to cover, travel; (*riesgo*) to run; (*aventura*) to have; (*cortinas*) to draw; (*cerrojo*) to shoot ▶ VI to run; (*líquido*) to run, flow; (*rumor*) to go round; **echar a ~** to break into a run; **~ con los gastos** to pay the expenses; **eso corre de mi cuenta** I'll take care of that ■ **correrse** VR to slide, move; (*colores*) to run; (*fam: tener orgasmo*) to come

★**correspondencia** [korrespon'denθja] NF correspondence; (*Ferro*) connection; (*reciprocidad*) return; **~ directa** (*Com*) direct mail

★**corresponder** [korrespon'der] /**2a**/ VI to correspond; (*convenir*) to be suitable; (*pertenecer*) to belong; (*tocar*) to concern; (*favor*) to repay; **"a quien corresponda"** "to whom it may concern" ■ **corresponderse** VR (*por escrito*) to correspond; (*amarse*) to love one another

★**correspondiente** [korrespon'djente] ADJ corresponding; (*respectivo*) respective

★**corresponsal** [korrespon'sal] NMF (newspaper) correspondent; (*Com*) agent

corretaje [korre'taxe] NM (*Com*) brokerage

corretear [korrete'ar] /**1a**/ VI to loiter

corrido, -a [ko'rriðo, a] ADJ (*avergonzado*) abashed; (*fluido*) fluent; **un kilo ~** a good kilo; **tres noches corridas** three nights running; **de ~** fluently ▶ NF run, dash; (*de toros*) bullfight

corriente [ko'rrjente] ADJ (*agua*) running; (*fig*) flowing; (*dinero, cuenta etc*) current; (*común*) ordinary, normal ▶ NF current; (*fig: tendencia*) course; **~ de aire** draught; **~ eléctrica** electric current; **las corrientes modernas del arte** modern trends in art; **estar al ~ de** to be informed about ▶ NM current month

corrigiendo *etc* [korri'xjendo] VB *ver* **corregir**

corrija *etc* [ko'rrixa] VB *ver* **corregir**

corrillo [ko'rriʎo] NM ring, circle (of people); (*fig*) clique

corro ['korro] NM ring, circle (of people); (*baile*) ring-a-ring-a-roses; **la gente hizo ~** the people formed a ring

corroborar [korroβo'rar] /**1a**/ VT to corroborate

corroer [korro'er] /**2a**/ VT (*tb fig*) to corrode, eat away; (*Geo*) to erode

corromper [korrom'per] /**2a**/ VT (*madera*) to rot; (*fig*) to corrupt

corrompido, -a [korrom'piðo, a] ADJ corrupt

corrosivo, -a [korro'siβo, a] ADJ corrosive

corroyendo *etc* [korro'jendo] VB *ver* **corroer**

corrupción [korrup'θjon] NF rot, decay; (*fig*) corruption

corrupto, -a [ko'rrupto, a] ADJ corrupt

corsario [kor'sarjo] NM privateer, corsair

corsé [kor'se] NM corset

corso, -a ['korso, a] ADJ, NM/F Corsican

cortacésped [korta'θespeð] NM lawn mower

cortado, -a [kor'taðo, a] ADJ (*con cuchillo*) cut; (*leche*) sour; (*confuso*) confused; (*desconcertado*) embarrassed; (*tímido*) shy ▶ NM *coffee with a little milk*

cortadora [korta'ðora] NF cutter, slicer

cortadura [korta'ðura] NF cut

cortafuegos [korta'fweɣos] NM INV (*en el bosque*) firebreak, fire lane (*US*); (*Internet*) firewall

cortalápices [korta'lapiθes] NM INV (pencil) sharpener

cortante [kor'tante] ADJ (*viento*) biting; (*frío*) bitter

cortapega [korta'peɣa] NM cut and paste

cortapegar [kortape'ɣar] /1h/ VT to cut and paste

cortapisa [korta'pisa] NF (*restricción*) restriction; (*traba*) snag

★**cortar** [kor'tar] /1a/ VT to cut; (*suministro*) to cut off; (*un pasaje*) to cut out; (*comunicación, teléfono*) to cut off ▶ VI to cut; (*AM Telec*) to hang up; **~ por lo sano** to settle things once and for all ■ **cortarse** VR (*turbarse*) to become embarrassed; (*leche*) to turn, curdle; **cortarse el pelo** to have one's hair cut; **se cortó la línea** *o* **el teléfono** I got cut off

cortasetos [korta'setos] NM INV hedge trimmer

cortauñas [korta'uɲas] NM INV nail clippers *pl*

corte ['korte] NM cut, cutting; (*filo*) edge; (*de tela*) piece, length; (*Costura*) tailoring; **~ y confección** dressmaking; **~ de corriente** *o* **luz** power cut; **~ de pelo** haircut; **me da ~ pedírselo** I'm embarrassed to ask him for it; **¡qué ~ le di!** I left him with no comeback! ▶ NF (*real*) (royal) court; **C~ Internacional de Justicia** International Court of Justice; **las Cortes** the Spanish Parliament *sg*; **hacer la ~ a** to woo, court

---

The Spanish Parliament, *Las Cortes (Españolas)*, has a Lower and an Upper Chamber, the *Congreso de los Diputados* and the *Senado* respectively. Members of Parliament are called *diputados* and are elected in national elections by proportional representation. Some Senate members, *senadores*, are chosen by being voted in during national elections and others are appointed by the regional parliaments.

---

cortejar [korte'xar] /1a/ VT to court

cortejo [kor'texo] NM entourage; **~ fúnebre** funeral procession, cortège

★**cortés** [kor'tes] ADJ courteous, polite

cortesano, -a [korte'sano, a] ADJ courtly

★**cortesía** [korte'sia] NF courtesy

corteza [kor'teθa] NF (*de árbol*) bark; (*de pan*) crust; (*de fruta*) peel, skin; (*de queso*) rind

cortijo [kor'tixo] NM (*ESP*) farm, farmhouse

★**cortina** [kor'tina] NF curtain; **~ de humo** smoke screen

★**corto, -a** ['korto, a] ADJ (*breve*) short; (*tímido*) bashful; **~ de luces** not very bright; **~ de oído** hard of hearing; **~ de vista** short-sighted; **estar ~ de fondos** to be short of funds

cortocircuito [kortoθir'kwito] NM short-circuit

cortometraje [kortome'traxe] NM (*Cine*) short

Coruña [ko'ruɲa] NF: **La ~** Corunna

coruñés, -esa [koru'ɲes, esa] ADJ of *o* from Corunna ▶ NM/F native *o* inhabitant of Corunna

corvo, -a ['korβo, a] ADJ curved; (*nariz*) hooked ▶ NF back of knee

★**cosa** ['kosa] NF thing; (*asunto*) affair; **~ de** about; **eso es ~ mía** that's my business; **es poca ~** it's not important; **¡qué ~ más rara!** how strange!

cosaco, -a [ko'sako, a] ADJ, NM/F Cossack

coscorrón [kosko'rron] NM bump on the head

★**cosecha** [ko'setʃa] NF (*Agr*) harvest; (*acto*) harvesting; (*de vino*) vintage; (*producción*) yield

cosechadora [kosetʃa'ðora] NF combine harvester

★**cosechar** [kose'tʃar] /1a/ VT to harvest, gather (in)

★**coser** [ko'ser] /2a/ VT to sew; (*Med*) to stitch (up)

cosido [ko'siðo] NM sewing

cosmético, -a [kos'metiko, a] ADJ, NM cosmetic ▶ NF cosmetics *pl*

cosmopolita [kosmopo'lita] ADJ cosmopolitan

cosmos ['kosmos] NM INV cosmos

coso ['koso] NM bullring

cosquillas [kos'kiʎas] NFPL: **hacer ~** to tickle; **tener ~** to be ticklish

cosquilleo [koski'ʎeo] NM tickling (sensation)

★**costa** ['kosta] NF (*Geo*) coast; **C~ Brava** Costa Brava; **C~ Cantábrica** Cantabrian Coast; **C~ de Marfil** Ivory Coast; **C~ del Sol** Costa del Sol; **a ~** (*Com*) at cost; **a ~ de** at the expense of; **a toda ~** at any price

costado [kos'taðo] NM side; **de ~** (*dormir*) on one's side; **español por los 4 costados** Spanish through and through

costal [kos'tal] NM sack

costalada [kosta'laða] NF bad fall

costanera [kosta'nera] NF (*AM*) promenade, sea front

★**costar** [kos'tar] /1l/ VT (*valer*) to cost; **me cuesta hablarle** I find it hard to talk to him; **¿cuánto cuesta?** how much does it cost?

Costa Rica [kostaˈrika] NF Costa Rica

costarricense [kostarriˈθense], **costarri-queño, -a** [kostarriˈkeɲo, a] ADJ, NM/F Costa Rican

★**coste** [ˈkoste] NM cost; (Com): **~ promedio** average cost; **costes fijos** fixed costs

costear [kosteˈar] /1a/ VT to pay for; (Com etc) to finance; (Naut) to sail along the coast of ■ **costearse** VR (negocio) to pay for itself, cover its costs

costeño, -a [kosˈteɲo, a] ADJ coastal

costero [kosˈtero, a] ADJ coastal, coast cpd

costilla [kosˈtiʎa] NF rib; (Culin) cutlet

costo [ˈkosto] NM cost, price; **~ directo** direct cost; **~ de expedición** shipping charges; **~ de sustitución** replacement cost; **~ unitario** unit cost; **~ de la vida** cost of living

★**costoso, -a** [kosˈtoso, a] ADJ costly, expensive

costra [ˈkostra] NF (corteza) crust; (Med) scab

★**costumbre** [kosˈtumbre] NF custom, habit; **como de ~** as usual

costumbrismo [kostumˈbrismo] NM see note

Costumbrismo is a literary genre which emerged in the 19th century in Spain and aims to give a faithful portrait of the traditions and regional and social customs, in some cases contrasting them with the changes brought about by industrial development. Among the key writers belonging to this artistic movement are: Fernán Caballero, Pedro Antonio de Alarcón, Juan Valera and José María de Pereda.

★**costura** [kosˈtura] NF sewing, needlework; (confección) dressmaking; (zurcido) seam

costurera [kostuˈrera] NF dressmaker

costurero [kostuˈrero] NM sewing box o case

cota [ˈkota] NF (Geo) height above sea level; (fig) height

cotarro [koˈtarro] NM: **dirigir el ~** (fam) to rule the roost

cotejar [koteˈxar] /1a/ VT to compare

cotejo [koˈtexo] NM comparison

cotice etc [koˈtiθe] VB ver **cotizar**

★**cotidiano, -a** [kotiˈðjano, a] ADJ daily, day to day

cotilla [koˈtiʎa] NF busybody, gossip

cotillear [kotiʎeˈar] /1a/ VI to gossip

cotilleo [kotiˈʎeo] NM gossip(ing)

cotización [kotiθaˈθjon] NF (Com) quotation, price; (de club) dues pl

cotizado, -a [kotiˈθaðo, a] ADJ (fig) highly-prized

cotizar [kotiˈθar] /1f/ VT (Com) to quote, price ■ **cotizarse** VR (fig) to be highly prized; **cotizarse a** to sell at, fetch; (Bolsa) to stand at, be quoted at

coto [ˈkoto] NM (terreno cercado) enclosure; (de caza) reserve; (Com) price-fixing agreement; **poner ~ a** to put a stop to

cotorra [koˈtorra] NF (Zool: loro) parrot; (fam: persona) windbag

coyote [koˈjote] NM coyote, prairie wolf

coyuntura [kojunˈtura] NF (Anat) joint; (fig) juncture, occasion; **esperar una ~ favorable** to await a favourable moment

coz [koθ] NF kick

CP NM ABR (= código postal) post code

CPN NM ABR (Esp) = **Cuerpo de la Policía Nacional**

cps ABR (= caracteres por segundo) c.p.s.

crac [krak] NM (Econ) crash

crack [krak] NM (droga) crack

cráneo [ˈkraneo] NM skull, cranium

crápula [ˈkrapula] NF drunkenness

cráter [ˈkrater] NM crater

crayón [kraˈjon] NM (Am: lápiz) (coloured) pencil; (cera) crayon

creación [kreaˈθjon] NF creation

creador, a [kreaˈðor, a] ADJ creative ▶ NM/F creator

★**crear** [kreˈar] /1a/ VT to create, make; (originar) to originate; (Inform: archivo) to create ■ **crearse** VR (comité etc) to be set up

★**creativo, -a** [kreaˈtiβo, a] ADJ creative

★**crecer** [kreˈθer] /2d/ VI to grow; (precio) to rise ■ **crecerse** VR (engreírse) to get cocky

creces [ˈkreθes] **: con ~** adv amply, fully

crecido, -a [kreˈθiðo, a] ADJ (persona, planta) full-grown; (cantidad) large ▶ NF (de río) spate, flood

creciente [kreˈθjente] ADJ growing; (cantidad) increasing; (luna) crescent ▶ NM crescent

crecimiento [kreθiˈmjento] NM growth; (aumento) increase; (Com) rise

credencial [kreðenˈθjal] NF (Am: tarjeta) card; **~ de socio** (Am) membership card ■ **credenciales** NFPL credentials

crédito [ˈkreðito] NM credit; **a ~** on credit; **dar ~ a** to believe (in); **~ al consumidor** consumer credit; **~ rotativo** o **renovable** revolving credit

credo [ˈkreðo] NM creed

crédulo, -a [ˈkreðulo, a] ADJ credulous

creencia [kreˈenθja] NF belief

★**creer** [kreˈer] /2e/ VT, VI to think, believe; (considerar) to think, consider; **~ en** to believe in; **creo que sí/no** I think/don't think so; **¡ya lo creo!** I should think so! ■ **creerse** VR to believe o.s. (to be)

creíble [kreˈiβle] ADJ credible, believable

creído, -a [kreˈiðo, a] ADJ (engreído) conceited

★**crema** [ˈkrema] ADJ INV cream (coloured) ▶ NF cream; (natillas) custard; **~ batida** (Am) whipped cream; **~ pastelera** (confectioner's) custard; **la ~ de la sociedad** the cream of society

★**cremallera** [kremaˈʎera] NF zip (fastener) (Brit), zipper (US)

crematorio [krema'torjo] NM crematorium (BRIT), crematory (US)

cremoso, -a [kre'moso, a] ADJ creamy

crepe ['krepe] NF (ESP) pancake

crepitar [krepi'tar] /1a/ VI (fuego) to crackle

crepúsculo [kre'puskulo] NM twilight, dusk

crespo, -a ['krespo, a] ADJ (pelo) curly

crespón [kres'pon] NM crêpe

cresta ['kresta] NF (Geo, Zool) crest

Creta ['kreta] NF Crete

cretino, -a [kre'tino, a] ADJ cretinous ▶ NM/F cretin

creyendo etc [kre'jendo] VB ver **creer**

creyente [kre'jente] NMF believer

creyó etc [kre'jo] VB ver **creer**

crezca etc ['kreθka] VB ver **crecer**

cría ['kria] VB ver **criar** ▶ NF (de animales) rearing, breeding; (animal) young; ver tb **crío**

★**criada** [kri'aða] NF ver **criado**

criadero [kria'ðero] NM nursery; (Zool) breeding place

criadillas [kria'ðiʎas] NFPL (Culin) bull's (o sheep's) testicles

criado, -a [kri'aðo, a] NM servant ▶ NF servant, maid

criador [kria'ðor] NM breeder

crianza [kri'anθa] NF rearing, breeding; (fig) breeding; (Med) lactation

★**criar** [kri'ar] /1c/ VT (amamantar) to suckle, feed; (educar) to bring up; (producir) to grow, produce; (animales) to breed; ~ **cuervos** to nourish a viper in one's bosom; **Dios los cría y ellos se juntan** birds of a feather flock together ▪ **criarse** VR to grow (up)

criatura [kria'tura] NF creature; (niño) baby, (small) child

criba ['kriβa] NF sieve

cribar [kri'βar] /1a/ VT to sieve

★**crimen** ['krimen] NM crime; ~ **pasional** crime of passion

★**criminal** [krimi'nal] ADJ, NMF criminal

crin [krin] NF (tb: **crines**) mane

★**crío, -a** ['krio, a] NM/F (fam: chico) kid ▶ NF (de animales) rearing, breeding; (animal) young

criollo, -a [kri'oʎo, a] ADJ (gen) Creole (AM) native (to America), national ▶ NM/F (gen) Creole; (AM) native American

cripta ['kripta] NF crypt

★**crisis** ['krisis] NF INV crisis; ~ **nerviosa** nervous breakdown

crisma ['krisma] NF: **romperle la ~ a algn** (fam) to knock sb's block off

crismas ['krismas] NM INV (ESP) Christmas card

crisol [kri'sol] NM (Tec) crucible; (fig) melting pot

crispación [krispa'θjon] NF tension

crispar [kris'par] /1a/ VT (músculo) to cause to contract; (nervios) to set on edge

★**cristal** [kris'tal] NM crystal; (de ventana) glass, pane; (lente) lens; **de ~** glass cpd; ~ **ahumado/tallado** smoked/cut glass

cristalería [kristale'ria] NF (tienda) glassware shop; (objetos) glassware

cristalice etc [krista'liθe] VB ver **cristalizar**

cristalino, -a [krista'lino, a] ADJ crystalline; (fig) clear ▶ NM lens of the eye

cristalizar [kristali'θar] /1f/ VT, VI to crystallize

cristiandad [kristjan'dað] NF Christianity

cristianismo [kristja'nismo] NM Christianity

★**cristiano, -a** [kris'tjano, a] ADJ, NM/F Christian; **hablar en ~** to speak proper Spanish; (fig) to speak clearly

Cristo ['kristo] NM (dios) Christ; (crucifijo) crucifix

Cristóbal [kris'toβal] NM: ~ **Colón** Christopher Columbus

criterio [kri'terjo] NM criterion; (juicio) judgement; (enfoque) attitude, approach; (punto de vista) view, opinion; ~ **de clasificación** (Inform) sort criterion

★**criticar** [kriti'kar] /1g/ VT to criticize

crítico, -a ['kritiko, a] ADJ critical ▶ NM critic ▶ NF criticism; (Teat etc) review, notice; **la crítica** the critics pl

critique etc [kri'tike] VB ver **criticar**

Croacia [kro'aθja] NF Croatia

croar [kro'ar] /1a/ VI to croak

croata [kro'ata] ADJ, NMF Croat(ian) ▶ NM (Ling) Croat(ian)

croissan, croissant [krwa'san] NM croissant

crol [krol] NM crawl

cromado [kro'maðo] NM chromium plating, chrome

cromo ['kromo] NM chrome; (Tip) coloured print

cromosoma [kromo'soma] NM chromosome

crónico, -a ['kroniko, a] ADJ chronic ▶ NF chronicle, account; (de periódico) feature, article

cronoescalada [kronoeska'laða] NF (Deporte: cycling) mountain time trial

cronología [kronolo'xia] NF chronology

cronológico, -a [krono'loxiko, a] ADJ chronological

cronometraje [kronome'traxe] NM timing

cronometrar [kronome'trar] /1a/ VT to time

cronómetro [kro'nometro] NM (Deporte) stopwatch; (Tec etc) chronometer

croqueta [kro'keta] NF croquette, rissole

croquis ['krokis] NM INV sketch

★**cruce** ['kruθe] VB ver **cruzar** ▶ NM (para peatones) crossing; (de carreteras) crossroads; (Auto etc) junction, intersection; (Bio: proceso) crossbreeding; **luces de ~** dipped headlights

crucero [kru'θero] NM (*Naut: barco*) cruise ship; (: *viaje*) cruise

crucial [kru'θjal] ADJ crucial

crucificar [kruθifi'kar] /**1g**/ VT to crucify; (*fig*) to torment

crucifijo [kruθi'fixo] NM crucifix

crucifique *etc* [kruθi'fike] VB *ver* **crucificar**

★**crucigrama** [kruθi'ɣrama] NM crossword (puzzle)

cruda ['kruða] NF (*Am fam*) hangover

crudeza [kru'ðeθa] NF (*rigor*) harshness; (*aspereza*) crudeness

crudo, -a ['kruðo, a] ADJ raw; (*no maduro*) unripe; (*petróleo*) crude; (*rudo, cruel*) cruel; (*agua*) hard; (*clima etc*) harsh ▶ NM crude (oil)

★**cruel** [krwel] ADJ cruel

crueldad [krwel'ðað] NF cruelty

cruento, -a ['krwento, a] ADJ bloody

crujido [kru'xiðo] NM (*de madera etc*) creak

crujiente [kru'xjente] ADJ (*galleta etc*) crunchy

crujir [kru'xir] /**3a**/ VI (*madera etc*) to creak; (*dedos*) to crack; (*dientes*) to grind; (*nieve, arena*) to crunch

★**cruz** [kruθ] NF cross; (*de moneda*) tails *sg*; (*fig*) burden; **~ gamada** swastika; **C~ Roja** Red Cross

cruzado, -a [kru'θaðo, a] ADJ crossed ▶ NM crusader ▶ NF crusade

★**cruzar** [kru'θar] /**1f**/ VT to cross; (*palabras*) to exchange ■ **cruzarse** VR (*líneas etc*) to cross, intersect; (*personas*) to pass each other; **cruzarse de brazos** to fold one's arms; (*fig*) not to lift a finger to help; **cruzarse con algn en la calle** to pass sb in the street

CSIC [θe'sik] NM ABR (*Esp Escol*) = **Consejo Superior de Investigaciones Científicas**

cta., c.ᵗᵃ NF ABR (= *cuenta*) a/c

cta. cto. ABR (= *carta de crédito*) L.C.

cte. ABR = **corriente**; (= *de los corrientes*) inst.

CTNE NF ABR (*Telec*) = **Compañía Telefónica Nacional de España**

c/u ABR (= *cada uno*) ea

cuaco ['kwako] NM (*Am*) nag

★**cuaderno** [kwa'ðerno] NM notebook; (*de escuela*) exercise book; (*Naut*) logbook

cuadra ['kwaðra] NF (*caballeriza*) stable; (*Am*) (city) block

★**cuadrado, -a** [kwa'ðraðo, a] ADJ square ▶ NM (*Mat*) square

cuadragésimo, -a [kwaðra'xesimo, a] NUM fortieth

cuadrángulo [kwa'ðrangulo] NM quadrangle

cuadrante [kwa'ðrante] NM quadrant

cuadrar [kwa'ðrar] /**1a**/ VT to square; (*Tip*) to justify ▶ VI: **~ con** (*cuenta*) to square with, tally with; **~ por la derecha/izquierda** to right-/left-justify ■ **cuadrarse** VR (*soldado*) to stand to attention

cuadrícula [kwa'ðrikula] NF (*Tip etc*) grid, ruled squares

cuadriculado, -a [kwaðriku'laðo, a] ADJ: **papel ~** squared *o* graph paper

cuadrilátero [kwaðri'latero] NM (*Deporte*) boxing ring; (*Mat*) quadrilateral

cuadrilla [kwa'ðriʎa] NF (*de amigos*) party, group; (*de delincuentes*) gang; (*de obreros*) team

★**cuadro** ['kwaðro] NM square; (*Arte*) painting; (*Teat*) scene; (*diagrama*: *tb*: **cuadro sinóptico**) chart, table, diagram; (*Deporte, Med*) team; (*Pol*) executive; **~ de mandos** control panel; **a cuadros** check *cpd*; **tela a cuadros** checked (*Brit*) *o* chequered (*US*) material

cuadruplicarse [kwaðrupli'karse] /**1g**/ VR to quadruple

cuádruplo, -a ['kwaðruplo, a], **cuádruple** ['kwaðruple] ADJ quadruple

cuajado, -a [kwa'xaðo, a] ADJ: **~ de** (*fig*) full of ▶ NF (*de leche*) curd

cuajar [kwa'xar] /**1a**/ VT to thicken; (*leche*) to curdle; (*sangre*) to congeal; (*adornar*) to adorn; (*Culin*) to set ▶ VI (*nieve*) to lie; (*fig*) to become set, become established; (*idea*) to be received, be acceptable ■ **cuajarse** VR to curdle; to congeal; (*llenarse*) to fill up

cuajo ['kwaxo] NM: **de ~** (*arrancar*) by the roots; (*cortar*) completely; **arrancar algo de ~** to tear sth out by its roots

★**cual** [kwal] ADV like, as ▶ PRON: **el ~** *etc* which; (*persona*: *sujeto*) who; (*persona*: *objeto*) whom; **lo ~** (*relativo*) which; **cada ~** each one; **allá cada ~** every man to his own taste; **son a ~ más gandul** each is as idle as the other ▶ ADJ such as; **tal ~** just as it is

★**cuál** [kwal] PRON INTERROGATIVO which (one), what

cualesquier [kwales'kjer], **cualesquiera** [kwales'kjera] ADJ PL, PRON PL *de* **cualquier**

★**cualidad** [kwali'ðað] NF quality

cualificado, -a [kwalifi'kaðo, a] ADJ (*obrero*) skilled, qualified

★**cualquier** [kwal'kjer], **cualquiera** [kwal'kjera] (*pl* **cualesquier(a)**) ADJ any; **en ~ momento** any time; **~ día/libro** any day/book; **en ~ parte** anywhere; **un coche cualquiera servirá** any car will do; **no es un hombre cualquiera** he isn't just anybody ▶ PRON anybody, anyone; (*quienquiera*) whoever; **cualquiera que sea** whichever it is; (*persona*) whoever it is; **eso cualquiera lo sabe hacer** anybody can do that; **es un cualquiera** he's a nobody

cuán [kwan] ADV how

★**cuando** ['kwando] ADV when; (*aún si*) if, even if; **~ más** at (the) most; **~ menos** at least; **~ no** if not, otherwise; **de ~ en ~** from time to time ▶ CONJ (*puesto que*) since; **ven ~ quieras** come when(ever) you like; **~ no sea así** even if it is not so ▶ PREP: **yo, ~ niño ...** when I was a child *o* as a child I ...

★cuándo [ˈkwando] ADV when; **¿desde ~?, ¿de ~ acá?** since when?

cuantía [kwanˈtia] NF (*importe: de pérdidas, deuda, daños*) extent; (*importancia*) importance

cuantioso, -a [kwanˈtjoso, a] ADJ substantial

---

cuanto, -a [ˈkwanto, a]

ADJ **1** (*todo*): **tiene todo cuanto desea** he's got everything he wants; **le daremos cuantos ejemplares necesite** we'll give him as many copies as *o* all the copies he needs; **cuantos hombres la ven** all the men who see her

2: **unos cuantos: había unos cuantos periodistas** there were (quite) a few journalists

3 (+ *más*): **cuanto más vino bebas peor te sentirás** the more wine you drink the worse you'll feel; **cuantos más, mejor** the more the merrier

▶ PRON: **tiene cuanto desea** he has everything he wants; **tome cuanto/cuantos quiera** take as much/many as you want

▶ ADV: **en cuanto**: **en cuanto profesor** as a teacher; **en cuanto a mí** as for me; *ver tb* **antes**

▶ CONJ **1**: **cuanto más gana menos gasta** the more he earns the less he spends; **cuanto más joven se es más se es confiado** the younger you are the more trusting you are

2: **en cuanto**: **en cuanto llegue/llegué** as soon as I arrive/arrived

---

★cuánto, -a [ˈkwanto, a] ADJ (*exclamación*) what a lot of; (*interrogativo: sg*) how much?; (: *pl*) how many?; **¡cuánta gente!** what a lot of people!; **¿~ tiempo?** how long? ▶ PRON, ADV how; (*interrogativo: sg*) how much?; (: *pl*) how many?; **¿~ cuesta?** how much does it cost?; **¿a cuántos estamos?** what's the date?; **¿~ hay de aquí a Bilbao?** how far is it from here to Bilbao?; **Señor no sé cuántos** Mr. So-and-So ▶ EXCL: **¡~ me alegro!** I'm so glad!

★cuarenta [kwaˈrenta] NUM forty

cuarentena [kwarenˈtena] NF (*Med etc*) quarantine; (*conjunto*) forty-(odd)

cuarentón, -ona [kwarenˈton, ona] ADJ forty-year-old, fortyish ▶ NM/F person of about forty

cuaresma [kwaˈresma] NF Lent

cuarta [ˈkwarta] NF *ver* **cuarto**

cuartear [kwarteˈar] /**1a**/ VT to quarter; (*dividir*) to divide up ■ **cuartearse** VR to crack, split

cuartel [kwarˈtel] NM (*de ciudad*) quarter, district; (*Mil*) barracks pl; **~ de bomberos** (*Am*) fire station; **~ general** headquarters pl

cuartelazo [kwarteˈlaθo] NM coup, military uprising

cuarteto [kwarˈteto] NM quartet

cuartilla [kwarˈtiʎa] NF (*hoja*) sheet (of paper) ■ **cuartillas** NFPL (*Tip*) copy sg

★cuarto, -a [ˈkwarto, a] ADJ fourth ▶ NM (*Mat*) quarter, fourth; (*habitación*) room ▶ NF (*Mat*) quar-

ter, fourth; (*palmo*) span; **~ de baño** bathroom; **~ de estar** living room; **~ de hora** quarter (of an) hour; **~ de kilo** quarter kilo; **cuartos de final** quarter finals; **no tener un ~** to be broke (*fam*)

cuarzo [ˈkwarθo] NM quartz

cuatrero [kwaˈtrero] NM (*Am*) rustler, stock thief

cuatrimestre [kwatriˈmestre] NM four-month period

★cuatro [ˈkwatro] NUM four; **las ~** four o'clock; **el ~ de octubre** (on) the fourth of October; *ver tb* **seis**

cuatrocientos, -as [kwatroˈθjentos, as] NUM four hundred; *ver tb* **seiscientos**

Cuba [ˈkuβa] NF Cuba

cuba [ˈkuβa] NF cask, barrel; **estar como una ~** (*fam*) to be sloshed

cubalibre [kuβaˈliβre] NM (white) rum and coke®

cubano, -a [kuˈβano, a] ADJ, NM/F Cuban

cubata [kuˈβata] NM = **cubalibre**

cubertería [kuβerteˈria] NF cutlery

cubeta [kuˈβeta] NF (*balde*) bucket, tub

cúbico, -a [ˈkuβiko, a] ADJ cubic

★cubierto, -a [kuˈβjerto, a] PP *de* **cubrir** ▶ ADJ covered; (*cielo*) overcast ▶ NM cover; (*en la mesa*) place; **a ~** under cover; **a ~ de** covered with *o* in; **precio del ~** cover charge ▶ NF cover, covering; (*neumático*) tyre; (*Naut*) deck ■ **cubiertos** NMPL cutlery sg

cubil [kuˈβil] NM den

cubilete [kuβiˈlete] NM (*en juegos*) cup

cubito [kuˈβito] NM: **~ de hielo** ice cube

★cubo [ˈkuβo] NM cube; (*balde*) bucket, tub; (*Tec*) drum; **~ de (la) basura** dustbin (*Brit*), trash can (*US*)

cubrecama [kuβreˈkama] NM bedspread

★cubrir [kuˈβrir] /**3a**/ VT to cover; (*vacante*) to fill; (*Bio*) to mate with; (*gastos*) to meet; **~ las formas** to keep up appearances; **lo cubrieron las aguas** the waters closed over it; **el agua casi me cubría** I was almost out of my depth ■ **cubrirse** VR (*cielo*) to become overcast; (*Com: gastos*) to be met *o* paid; (: *deuda*) to be covered

★cucaracha [kukaˈratʃa] NF cockroach

★cuchara [kuˈtʃara] NF spoon; (*Tec*) scoop

★cucharada [kutʃaˈraða] NF spoonful; **~ colmada** heaped spoonful

cucharadita [kutʃaraˈðita] NF teaspoonful

★cucharilla [kutʃaˈriʎa] NF teaspoon

cucharita [kutʃaˈrita] NF teaspoon

cucharón [kutʃaˈron] NM ladle

cuchichear [kutʃitʃeˈar] /**1a**/ VI to whisper

cuchicheo [kutʃiˈtʃeo] NM whispering

cuchilla [kuˈtʃiʎa] NF (large) knife; (*de arma blanca*) blade; **~ de afeitar** razor blade; **pasar a ~** to put to the sword

99

cuchillada [kutʃi'ʎaða] NF (golpe) stab; (herida) knife o stab wound

⋆**cuchillo** [ku'tʃiʎo] NM knife

cuchitril [kutʃi'tril] NM hovel; (habitación etc) pigsty

cuclillas [ku'kliʎas] NFPL: **en ~** squatting

cuco, -a ['kuko, a] ADJ pretty; (astuto) sharp ▶ NM cuckoo

cucurucho [kuku'rutʃo] NM paper cone, cornet

cueca ['kweka] NF Chilean national dance

cuece etc ['kweθe] VB ver **cocer**

cuele etc ['kwele] VB ver **colar**

cuelgue etc ['kwelɣe] VB ver **colgar**

⋆**cuello** ['kweʎo] NM (Anat) neck; (de vestido, camisa) collar

cuenca ['kwenka] NF (Anat) eye socket; (Geo: valle) bowl, deep valley; (: fluvial) basin

cuenco ['kwenko] NM (earthenware) bowl

⋆**cuenta** ['kwenta] VB ver **contar** ▶ NF (cálculo) count, counting; (en café, restaurante) bill (BRIT), check (US); (Com) account; (de collar) bead; (fig) account; **a fin de cuentas** in the end; **en resumidas cuentas** in short; **caer en la ~** to catch on; **dar ~ a algn de sus actos** to account to sb for one's actions; **darse ~ de** to realize; **tener en ~** to bear in mind; **echar cuentas** to take stock; **~ atrás** countdown; **~ corriente/de ahorros/a plazo (fijo)** current/savings/deposit account; **~ de caja** cash account; **~ de capital** capital account; **~ por cobrar** account receivable; **~ de correo** (Internet) email account; **~ de crédito** credit o loan account; **~ de gastos e ingresos** income and expenditure account; **~ por pagar** account payable; **abonar una cantidad en ~ a algn** to credit a sum to sb's account; **ajustar o liquidar una ~** to settle an account; **pasar la ~** to send the bill

cuentagotas [kwenta'ɣotas] NM INV (Med) dropper; **a o con ~** (fam: fig) drop by drop, bit by bit

cuentakilómetros [kwentaki'lometros] NM INV (de distancias) ≈ milometer, clock; (velocímetro) speedometer

cuentista [kwen'tista] NMF gossip; (Lit) short story writer

⋆**cuento** ['kwento] VB ver **contar** ▶ NM story; (Lit) short story; **~ chino** tall story; **~ de hadas** fairy tale o story; **es el ~ de nunca acabar** it's an endless business; **eso no viene a ~** that's irrelevant

cuerda ['kwerða] NF rope; (hilo) string; (de reloj) spring; (Mus: de violín etc) string; (Mat) chord; (Anat) cord; **~ floja** tightrope; **cuerdas vocales** vocal cords; **dar ~ a un reloj** to wind up a clock

cuerdo, -a ['kwerðo, a] ADJ sane; (prudente) wise, sensible

cuerear [kwere'ar] /1a/ VT (AM) to skin

cuerno ['kwerno] NM (Zool: gen) horn; (: de ciervo) antler; **poner los cuernos a** (fam) to cuckold; **saber a ~ quemado** to leave a nasty taste

⋆**cuero** ['kwero] NM (Zool) skin, hide; (Tec) leather; **en cueros** stark naked; **~ cabelludo** scalp

⋆**cuerpo** ['kwerpo] NM body; (cadáver) corpse; (fig) main part; **~ de bomberos** fire brigade; **~ diplomático** diplomatic corps; **luchar ~ a ~** to fight hand-to-hand; **tomar ~** (plan etc) to take shape

cuervo ['kwerβo] NM (Zool) raven, crow; ver **criar**

⋆**cuesta** ['kwesta] VB ver **costar** ▶ NF slope; (en camino etc) hill; **~ arriba/abajo** uphill/downhill; **a cuestas** on one's back

cueste etc VB ver **costar**

cuestión [kwes'tjon] NF matter, question, issue; (riña) quarrel, dispute; **eso es otra ~** that's another matter

cuestionar [kwestjo'nar] /1a/ VT to question

cuestionario [kwestjo'narjo] NM questionnaire

cuete ['kwete] ADJ (AM fam) drunk ▶ NM (cohete) rocket; (AM fam: embriaguez) drunkenness; (Culin) steak

⋆**cueva** ['kweβa] NF cave

cueza etc ['kweθa] VB ver **cocer**

⋆**cuidado** [kwi'ðaðo] NM care, carefulness; (preocupación) care, worry; **eso me tiene sin ~** I'm not worried about that ▶ EXCL careful!, look out!

⋆**cuidadoso, -a** [kwiða'ðoso, a] ADJ careful; (preocupado) anxious

⋆**cuidar** [kwi'ðar] /1a/ VT (Med) to care for; (ocuparse de) to take care of, look after; (detalles) to pay attention to ▶ VI: **~ de** to take care of, look after ■ **cuidarse** VR to look after o.s.; **cuidarse de hacer algo** to take care to do sth

cuita ['kwita] NF (preocupación) worry, trouble; (pena) grief

culata [ku'lata] NF (de fusil) butt

culatazo [kula'taθo] NM kick, recoil

⋆**culebra** [ku'leβra] NF snake; **~ de cascabel** rattlesnake

culebrear [kuleβre'ar] /1a/ VI to wriggle along; (río) to meander

⋆**culebrón** [kule'βron] NM (fam) soap (opera)

culinario, -a [kuli'narjo, a] ADJ culinary, cooking cpd

culminación [kulmina'θjon] NF culmination

culminante [kulmi'nante] ADJ: **momento ~** climax, highlight, highspot

culminar [kulmi'nar] /1a/ VI to culminate

culo ['kulo] NM (fam: trasero) bottom, backside, bum (BRIT); (: ano) arse(hole) (BRIT fam!), ass(hole) (US fam!); (de vaso) bottom

⋆**culpa** ['kulpa] NF fault; (Jur) guilt; **por ~ de** through, because of; **echar la ~ de algo a algn** to blame sb for sth; **tener la ~ (de)** to be to blame (for) ■ **culpas** NFPL sins

culpabilidad [kulpaβili'ðað] NF guilt

⋆**culpable** [kul'paβle] ADJ guilty; **confesarse ~** to

plead guilty; **declarar ~ a algn** to find sb guilty
▶ NMF culprit

culpar [kul'par] /**1a**/ VT to blame; (acusar) to accuse

cultivadora [kultiβa'ðora] NF cultivator

★**cultivar** [kulti'βar] /**1a**/ VT to cultivate; (cosecha) to raise; (talento) to develop

cultivo [kul'tiβo] NM (acto) cultivation; (plantas) crop; (Bio) culture; **~ transgénico** GM crop

culto, -a ['kulto, a] ADJ (cultivado) cultivated; (que tiene cultura) cultured, educated ▶ NM (homenaje) worship; (religión) cult; (Pol etc) cult

★**cultura** [kul'tura] NF culture

cultural [kultu'ral] ADJ cultural

culturismo [kultu'rismo] NM body-building

cumbia ['kumbja] NF popular Colombian dance

★**cumbre** ['kumbre] NF summit, top; (fig) top, height; **conferencia (en la) ~** summit (conference)

★**cumpleaños** [kumple'aɲos] NM INV birthday

cumplido, -a [kum'pliðo, a] ADJ complete, perfect; (abundante) plentiful; (cortés) courteous ▶ NM compliment; **visita de ~** courtesy call

cumplidor, a [kumpli'ðor, a] ADJ reliable

cumplimentar [kumplimen'tar] /**1a**/ VT to congratulate; (órdenes) to carry out

cumplimiento [kumpli'mjento] NM (de un deber) fulfilment, execution, performance; (acabamiento) completion; (Com) expiry, end

★**cumplir** [kum'plir] /**3a**/ VT (orden) to carry out, obey; (promesa) to carry out, fulfil; (condena) to serve; (años) to reach, attain; **hoy cumple dieciocho años** he is eighteen today ▶ VI (pago) to fall due; (plazo) to expire; **~ con** (deber) to carry out, fulfil ■ **cumplirse** VR (plazo) to expire; (plan etc) to be fulfilled; (vaticinio) to come true

cúmulo ['kumulo] NM (montón) heap; (nube) cumulus

cuna ['kuna] NF cradle, cot; **canción de ~** lullaby

cundir [kun'dir] /**3a**/ VI (noticia, rumor, pánico) to spread; (rendir) to go a long way

cuneta [ku'neta] NF ditch

cuña ['kuɲa] NF (Tec) wedge; (Com) advertising spot; (Med) bedpan; **tener cuñas** to have influence

★**cuñado, -a** [ku'ɲaðo, a] NM/F brother-/sister-in-law

cuño ['kuɲo] NM (Tec) die-stamp; (fig) stamp

cuota ['kwota] NF (parte proporcional) share; (cotización) fee, dues pl; **~ inicial** (Com) down payment

cupe etc ['kupe] VB ver **caber**

cupiera etc [ku'pjera] VB ver **caber**

cupo etc ['kupo] VB ver **caber** ▶ NM quota, share; (Com): **~ de importación** import quota; **~ de ventas** sales quota

cupón [ku'pon] NM coupon; **~ de la ONCE** o **de los ciegos** ONCE lottery ticket; ver tb **lotería**

cúpula ['kupula] NF (Arq) dome

★**cura** ['kura] NF (curación) cure; (método curativo) treatment; **~ de emergencia** emergency treatment ▶ NM priest

curación [kura'θjon] NF cure; (acción) curing

curado, -a [ku'raðo, a] ADJ (Culin) cured; (pieles) tanned

curandero, -a [kuran'dero, a] NM/F healer; (pey) quack

★**curar** [ku'rar] /**1a**/ VT (Med: herida) to treat, dress; (: enfermo) to cure; (Culin) to cure, salt; (cuero) to tan ▶ VI, **curarse** VR to get well, recover

curda ['kurða] (fam) NM drunk ▶ NF: **agarrar una/estar ~** to get/be sloshed

curiosear [kurjose'ar] /**1a**/ VT to glance at, look over ▶ VI to look round, wander round; (explorar) to poke about

★**curiosidad** [kurjosi'ðað] NF curiosity

★**curioso, -a** [ku'rjoso, a] ADJ curious; (aseado) neat; **¡qué ~!** how odd! ▶ NM/F bystander, onlooker

curita [ku'rita] NF (Am) sticking plaster

currante [ku'rrante] NMF (fam) worker

currar [ku'rrar] /**1a**/, **currelar** [kurre'lar] /**1a**/ VI (fam) to work

currículo [ku'rrikulo], **currículum** [ku'rrikulum] NM curriculum vitae

curro ['kurro] NM (fam) work, job

cursar [kur'sar] /**1a**/ VT (Escol) to study

cursi ['kursi] ADJ (fam) pretentious; (: amanerado) affected

cursilada [kursi'laða] NF: **¡qué ~!** how tacky!

cursilería [kursile'ria] NF (vulgaridad) bad taste; (amaneramiento) affectation

cursillo [kur'siʎo] NM short course

cursiva [kur'siβa] NF italics pl

★**curso** ['kurso] NM (dirección) course; (fig) progress; (Escol) school year; (Univ) academic year; **en ~** (año) current; (proceso) going on, under way; **moneda de ~ legal** legal tender

cursor [kur'sor] NM (Inform) cursor; (Tec) slide

curtido, -a [kur'tiðo, a] ADJ (cara etc) weather-beaten; (fig: persona) experienced

curtir [kur'tir] /**3a**/ VT (piel) to tan; (fig) to harden

curul [ku'rul] NM (Am: escaño) seat

curvo, -a ['kurβo, a] ADJ (gen) curved; (torcido) bent ▶ NF (gen) curve, bend; **curva de rentabilidad** (Com) break-even chart

cúspide ['kuspiðe] NF (Geo) summit, peak; (fig) top, pinnacle

custodia [kus'toðja] NF (cuidado) safekeeping; (Jur) custody

custodiar [kusto'ðjar] /**1b**/ VT (conservar) to keep, take care of; (vigilar) to guard

custodio [kus'toðjo] NM guardian, keeper

cutáneo, -a [ku'taneo, a] ADJ skin cpd

cutícula [ku'tikula] NF cuticle

cutis ['kutis] NM INV skin, complexion

cutre ['kutre] ADJ (*fam: lugar*) grotty; (: *persona*) naff

★**cuyo, -a** ['kujo, a] PRON (*de quien*) whose; (*de que*) whose, of which; **la señora en cuya casa me hospedé** the lady in whose house I stayed; **el** asunto cuyos detalles conoces the affair the details of which you know; **por ~ motivo** for which reason; **en ~ caso** in which case

C.V. ABR (= *Curriculum Vitae*) CV; (= *caballos de vapor*) H.P.

Dd

D, d [de] NF (*letra*) D, d; **D de Dolores** D for David (BRIT), D for Dog (US)

D. ABR (= *Don*) Esq

D.ª ABR = **doña**

dación [daˈθjon] NF: **~ en pago** (*Jur*) surrender in lieu of foreclosure

dactilar [daktiˈlar] ADJ: **huellas dactilares** fingerprints

dactilógrafo, -a [daktiˈloɣrafo, a] NM/F typist

dadaísta [daðaˈista] ADJ, NMF (*Arte*) Dadaist

dádiva [ˈdaðiβa] NF (*donación*) donation; (*regalo*) gift

dadivoso, -a [daðiˈβoso, a] ADJ generous

dado, -a [ˈdaðo, a] PP *de* **dar** ▶ NM die ■ **dados** NMPL dice ▶ ADJ: **en un momento ~** at a certain point; **ser ~ a (hacer algo)** to be very fond of (doing sth); **~ que** *conj* given that

daga [ˈdaɣa] NF dagger

daltónico, -a [dalˈtoniko, a] ADJ colour-blind

daltonismo [daltoˈnismo] NM colour blindness

dama [ˈdama] NF (*gen*) lady; (*Ajedrez*) queen; **primera ~** (*Teat*) leading lady; (*Pol*) president's wife, first lady (US); **~ de honor** (*de reina*) lady-in-waiting; (*de novia*) bridesmaid ■ **damas** NFPL draughts

damasco [daˈmasko] NM (*tela*) damask; (*AM: árbol*) apricot tree; (: *fruta*) apricot

damnificado, -a [damnifiˈkaðo, a] NM/F: **los damnificados** the victims

damnificar [damnifiˈkar] /1g/ VT to harm; (*persona*) to injure

damnifique *etc* [damniˈfike] VB *ver* **damnificar**

dance *etc* [ˈdanθe] VB *ver* **danzar**

★**danés, -esa** [daˈnes, esa] ADJ Danish ▶ NM/F Dane ▶ NM (*Ling*) Danish

Danubio [daˈnuβjo] NM Danube

danza [ˈdanθa] NF (*gen*) dancing; (*una danza*) dance

danzar [danˈθar] /1f/ VT, VI to dance

danzarín, -ina [danθaˈrin, ina] NM/F dancer

★**dañar** [daˈɲar] /1a/ VT (*objeto*) to damage; (*persona*) to hurt; (*estropear*) to spoil ■ **dañarse** VR (*objeto*) to get damaged

dañino, -a [daˈɲino, a] ADJ harmful

★**daño** [ˈdaɲo] NM (*a un objeto*) damage; (*a una persona*) harm, injury; **daños y perjuicios** (*Jur*) damages; **hacer ~ a** to damage; (*persona*) to hurt, injure; **hacerse ~** to hurt o.s.

dañoso, -a [daˈɲoso, a] ADJ harmful

---

dar [dar]

/1q/ VT **1** (*gen*) to give; (*obra de teatro*) to put on; (*film*) to show; (*fiesta*) to have; **dar algo a algn** to give sb *o* sth to sb; **dar una patada a algn/algo** to kick sb/sth, give sb/sth a kick; **dar un susto a algn** to give sb a fright; **dar de beber a algn** to give sb a drink; **dar de comer** to feed

2 (*producir: intereses*) to yield; (: *fruta*) to produce

3 (*locuciones* + *n*): **da gusto escucharlo** it's a pleasure to listen to him; **me da pena** it frightens me; *ver tb* **paseo**

4 (+ *n*: = *perífrasis de verbo*): **me da asco** it sickens me

5 (*considerar*): **dar algo por descontado/ entendido** to take sth for granted/as read; **dar algo por concluido** to consider sth finished; **lo dieron por desaparecido** they gave him up as lost

6 (*hora*): **el reloj dio las seis** the clock struck six (o'clock)

7: **me da lo mismo** it's all the same to me; *ver tb* **igual; más**

8: **¡y dale!** (*¡otra vez!*) not again!; **estar/seguir dale que dale** *o* **dale que te pego** *o* (AM) **dale y dale** to go/keep on and on

▶ VI **1**: **dar a** (*habitación*) to overlook, look on to; (*accionar: botón etc*) to press, hit

2: **dar con**: **dimos con él dos horas más tarde** we came across him two hours later; **al final**

di con la solución I eventually came up with the answer
3: dar en (*blanco, suelo*) to hit; **el sol me da en la cara** the sun is shining (right) in my face
4: dar de sí (*zapatos etc*) to stretch, give
5: dar para to be enough for; **nuestro presupuesto no da para más** our budget's really tight
6: dar por: le ha dado por estudiar música now he's into studying music
7: dar que hablar to set people talking; **una película que da que pensar** a thought-provoking film
■ **darse** VR **1: darse un baño** to have a bath; **darse un golpe** to hit o.s.
2: darse por vencido to give up; **con eso me doy por satisfecho** I'd settle for that
3 (*ocurrir*): **se han dado muchos casos** there have been a lot of cases
4: darse a: se ha dado a la bebida he's taken to drinking
5: se me dan bien/mal las ciencias I'm good/bad at science
6: dárselas de: se las da de experto he fancies himself o poses as an expert

dardo ['darðo] NM dart
dársena ['darsena] NF (*Naut*) dock
datar [da'tar] /**1a**/ VI: **~ de** to date from
dátil ['datil] NM date
dativo [da'tiβo] NM (*Ling*) dative
dato ['dato] NM fact, piece of information; (*Mat*) datum ■ **datos** NMPL (*Inform*) data; **datos de entrada/salida** input/output data; **datos personales** personal details
dcha. ABR (= *derecha*) r (= *right*)
d. de C. ABR (= *después de Cristo*) A.D. (= *Anno Domini*)

---

de [de]

PREP (**de + el = del**) **1** (*posesión, pertenencia*) of; **la casa de Isabel/mis padres** Isabel's/my parents' house; **es de ellos/ella** it's theirs/hers; **un libro de Unamuno** a book by Unamuno
2 (*origen, distancia, con números*) from; **soy de Gijón** I'm from Gijón; **de 8 a 20** from 8 to 20; **5 metros de largo** 5 metres long; **salir del cine** to go out of o leave the cinema; **de ... en ...** from ... to ...; **de 2 en 2** 2 by 2, 2 at a time; **9 de cada 10** 9 out of every 10
3 (*valor descriptivo*): **un vaso de agua** a glass of water; **una silla de madera** a wooden chair; **la mesa de la cocina** the kitchen table; **un viaje de dos días** a two-day journey; **un billete de 50 euros** a 50-euro note; **un niño de tres años** a three-year-old (child); **una máquina de coser** a sewing machine; **la ciudad de Madrid** the city of Madrid; **el tonto de Juan** that idiot Juan; **ir vestido de gris** to be dressed in grey; **la niña del vestido azul** the girl in the blue dress; **la chica del pelo largo** the girl with

long hair; **trabaja de profesora** she works as a teacher; **de lado** sideways; **de atrás/delante** rear/front
4 (*hora, tiempo*): **a las 8 de la mañana** at 8 o'clock in the morning; **de día/noche** by day/night; **de hoy en ocho días** a week from now; **de niño era gordo** as a child he was fat
5 (*comparaciones*): **más/menos de cien personas** more/fewer than a hundred people; **el más caro de la tienda** the most expensive in the shop; **menos/más de lo esperado** less/more than expected
6 (*causa*): **del calor** from the heat; **de puro tonto** out of sheer stupidity
7 (*tema*) about; **clases de inglés** English classes; **¿sabes algo de él?** do you know anything about him?; **un libro de física** a physics book
8 (*adj + de + infin*): **fácil de entender** easy to understand
9 (*oraciones pasivas*): **fue respetado de todos** he was loved by all
10 (*condicional + infin*) if; **de ser posible** if possible; **de no terminarlo hoy** if I *etc* don't finish it today

---

dé [de] VB *ver* **dar**
deambular [deambu'lar] /**1a**/ VI to stroll, wander
★**debajo** [de'βaxo] ADV underneath; **~ de** below, under; **por ~ de** beneath
debate [de'βate] NM debate
debatir [deβa'tir] /**3a**/ VT to debate ■ **debatirse** VR to struggle
debe ['deβe] NM (*en cuenta*) debit side; **~ y haber** debit and credit
★**deber** [de'βer] /**2a**/ NM duty ▶ VT to owe; **¿qué o cuánto le debo?** how much is it? ▶ VI: **debe (de)** it must, it should; **debe de ir** he should go; **debo hacerlo** I must do it ■ **deberse** VR: **deberse a** to be owing o due to ■ **deberes** NMPL (*Escol*) homework *sg*
debidamente [deβiða'mente] ADV properly; (*rellenar*) duly
debido, -a [de'βiðo, a] ADJ proper, due; **~ a** due to, because of; **en debida forma** duly
★**débil** ['deβil] ADJ weak; (*persona: físicamente*) feeble; (*salud*) poor; (*voz, ruido*) faint; (*luz*) dim
debilidad [deβili'ðað] NF weakness; feebleness; dimness; **tener ~ por algn** to have a soft spot for sb
debilitar [deβili'tar] /**1a**/ VT to weaken ■ **debilitarse** VR to grow weak
débito ['deβito] NM debit; (*deuda*) debt; **~ bancario** (*Am*) direct debit (*Brit*) o billing (*US*)
debutante [deβu'tante] NMF beginner
debutar [deβu'tar] /**1a**/ VI to make one's debut
década ['dekaða] NF decade
decadencia [deka'ðenθja] NF (*estado*) decadence; (*proceso*) decline, decay
decadente [deka'ðente] ADJ decadent

decaer [deka'er] /2n/ VI (declinar) to decline; (debilitarse) to weaken; (salud) to fail; (negocio) to fall off

decaído, -a [deka'iðo, a] ADJ: **estar ~** (persona) to be down

decaiga etc [de'kaiɣa] VB ver **decaer**

decaimiento [dekai'mjento] NM (declinación) decline; (desaliento) discouragement; (Med: depresión) depression

decanato [deka'nato] NM (cargo) deanship; (despacho) dean's office

decano, -a [de'kano, a] NM/F (Univ etc) dean; (de grupo) senior member

decantar [dekan'tar] /1a/ VT (vino) to decant

decapitar [dekapi'tar] /1a/ VT to behead

decayendo etc [deka'jendo] VB ver **decaer**

★**decena** [de'θena] NF: **una ~** ten (or so)

decencia [de'θenθja] NF (modestia) modesty; (honestidad) respectability

decenio [de'θenjo] NM decade

decente [de'θente] ADJ decent

decepción [deθep'θjon] NF disappointment

> Do not translate the Spanish word **decepción** by deception.

decepcionante [deθepθjo'nante] ADJ disappointing

★**decepcionar** [deθepθjo'nar] /1a/ VT to disappoint

decibelio [deθi'βeljo] NM decibel

decidido, -a [deθi'ðiðo, a] ADJ decided; (resuelto) resolute

★**decidir** [deθi'ðir] /3a/ VT (persuadir) to convince, persuade; (resolver) to decide ▶ VI to decide ■ **decidirse** VR: **decidirse a** to make up one's mind to; **decidirse por** to decide o settle on, choose

decimal [deθi'mal] ADJ, NM decimal

★**décimo, -a** ['deθimo, a] NUM tenth ▶ NF (Mat) tenth; **tiene unas décimas de fiebre** he has a slight temperature

decimoctavo, -a [deθimok'taβo, a] NUM eighteenth; ver tb **sexto**

decimocuarto, -a [deθimo'kwarto, a] NUM fourteenth; ver tb **sexto**

decimonoveno, -a [deθimono'βeno, a] NUM nineteenth; ver tb **sexto**

decimoquinto, -a [deθimo'kinto, a] NUM fifteenth; ver tb **sexto**

decimoséptimo, -a [deθimo'septimo, a] NUM seventeenth; ver tb **sexto**

decimosexto, -a [deθimo'seksto, a] NUM sixteenth; ver tb **sexto**

decimotercero, -a [deθimoter'θero, a] NUM thirteenth; ver tb **sexto**

★**decir** [de'θir] /3o/ VT (expresar) to say; (contar) to tell; (hablar) to speak; (indicar) to show; (revelar) to reveal; (fam: nombrar) to call; **~ para** o **entre sí** to say to o.s.; **dar que ~ (a la gente)** to make people talk; **querer ~** to mean; **es ~** that is to say, namely; **ni que ~ tiene que ...** it goes without saying that ...; **como quien dice** so to speak; **¡quién lo diría!** would you believe it!; **el qué dirán** gossip; **le dije que fuera más tarde** I told her to go later ▶ VI: **¡diga!, ¡dígame!** (en tienda etc) can I help you?; (Telec) hello?; **~ por ~** to talk for talking's sake ▶ NM saying; **es un ~** it's just a phrase ■ **decirse** VR: **se dice** it is said, they say; (se cuenta) the story goes; **¿cómo se dice en inglés "cursi"?** what's the English for "cursi"?

★**decisión** [deθi'sjon] NF decision; (firmeza) decisiveness; (voluntad) determination

decisivo, -a [deθi'siβo, a] ADJ decisive

declamar [dekla'mar] /1a/ VT, VI to declaim; (versos etc) to recite

★**declaración** [deklara'θjon] NF (manifestación) statement; (de amor) declaration; (explicación) explanation; (Jur: testimonio) evidence; **~ de derechos** (Pol) bill of rights; **~ de impuestos** (Com) tax return; **~ de ingresos** o **de la renta** income tax return; **~ jurada** affidavit; **falsa ~** (Jur) misrepresentation

★**declarar** [dekla'rar] /1a/ VT to declare; **~ culpable/no culpable a algn** to find sb guilty/not guilty ▶ VI to declare; (Jur) to testify ■ **declararse** VR (a una chica) to propose; (guerra, incendio) to break out; **declararse culpable/inocente** to plead guilty/not guilty

declinación [deklina'θjon] NF (decaimiento) decline; (Ling) declension

declinar [dekli'nar] /1a/ VT (gen, Ling) to decline; (Jur) to reject ▶ VI (el día) to draw to a close

declive [de'kliβe] NM (cuesta) slope; (inclinación) incline; (fig) decline; (Com: tb: **declive económico**) slump

decodificador [dekoðifika'ðor] NM (Inform) decoder

decolorarse [dekolo'rarse] /1a/ VR to become discoloured

decomisar [dekomi'sar] /1a/ VT to seize, confiscate

decomiso [deko'miso] NM seizure

decoración [dekora'θjon] NF decoration; (Teat) scenery, set; **~ de escaparates** window dressing

decorado [deko'raðo] NM (Cine, Teat) scenery, set

★**decorador, a** [dekora'ðor, a] NM/F (de interiores) (interior) decorator; (Teat) stage o set designer

★**decorar** [deko'rar] /1a/ VT to decorate

decorativo, -a [dekora'tiβo, a] ADJ ornamental, decorative

decoro [de'koro] NM (respeto) respect; (dignidad) decency; (recato) propriety

decoroso, -a [deko'roso, a] ADJ (decente) decent; (modesto) modest; (digno) proper

decrecer [dekre'θer] /2d/ VI to decrease, diminish; (nivel de agua) to go down; (días) to draw in

decrépito, -a [de'krepito, a] ADJ decrepit

decretar [dekre'tar] /1a/ VT to decree

decreto [de'kreto] NM decree; (Pol) act

decreto-ley [dekreto'lei] (pl **decretos-leyes**) NM decree

decrezca etc [de'kreθka] VB ver **decrecer**

decúbito [de'kuβito] NM (Med): ~ **prono/ supino** prone/supine position

dedal [de'ðal] NM thimble

dedalera [deða'lera] NF foxglove

dédalo ['deðalo] NM (laberinto) labyrinth; (fig) tangle, mess

dedicación [deðika'θjon] NF dedication; **con ~ exclusiva** o **plena** full-time

dedicar [deði'kar] /1g/ VT (libro) to dedicate; (tiempo, dinero) to devote; (palabras: decir, consagrar) to dedicate, devote ■ **dedicarse** VR: **dedicarse a (hacer algo)** to devote o.s. to (doing sth); (carrera, estudio) to go in for (doing sth), take up (doing sth); **¿a qué se dedica usted?** what do you do (for a living)?

dedicatoria [deðika'torja] NF (de libro) dedication

dedillo [de'ðiʎo] NM: **saber algo al ~** to have sth at one's fingertips

dedique etc [de'ðike] VB ver **dedicar**

★**dedo** ['deðo] NM finger; (de vino etc) drop; ~ **(del pie)** toe; ~ **anular** ring finger; ~ **índice** index finger; ~ **mayor** o **cordial** middle finger; ~ **meñique** little finger; ~ **pulgar** thumb; **contar con los dedos** to count on one's fingers; **comerse los dedos** to get very impatient; **entrar a ~** to get a job by pulling strings; **hacer ~** (fam) to hitch (a lift); **poner el ~ en la llaga** to put one's finger on it; **no tiene dos dedos de frente** he's pretty dim

deducción [deðuk'θjon] NF deduction

deducir [deðu'θir] /3n/ VT (concluir) to deduce, infer; (Com) to deduct

deduje etc [de'ðuxe], **dedujera** etc [deðu'xera], **deduzca** etc [de'ðuθka] VB ver **deducir**

defección [defek'θjon] NF defection, desertion

★**defecto** [de'fekto] NM defect, flaw; (de cara) imperfection; ~ **de pronunciación** speech defect; **por ~** (Inform) default; ~ **latente** (Com) latent defect

defectuoso, -a [defek'twoso, a] ADJ defective, faulty

★**defender** [defen'der] /2g/ VT to defend; (ideas) to uphold; (causa) to champion; (amigos) to stand up for ■ **defenderse** VR to defend o.s.; **defenderse bien** to give a good account of o.s.; **me defiendo en inglés** (fig) I can get by in English

defendible [defen'diβle] ADJ defensible

defensa [de'fensa] NF defence; (Naut) fender; **en ~ propia** in self-defence ► NM (Deporte) defender, back

defensivo, -a [defen'siβo, a] ADJ defensive ► NF: **a la defensiva** on the defensive

defensor, -a [defen'sor, a] ADJ defending ► NM/F (abogado defensor) defending counsel; (protector) protector; ~ **del pueblo** (ESP) ≈ ombudsman

deferente [defe'rente] ADJ deferential

deferir [defe'rir] /3k/ VT (Jur) to refer, delegate ► VI: ~ **a** to defer to

deficiencia [defi'θjenθja] NF deficiency

deficiente [defi'θjente] ADJ (defectuoso) defective; ~ **en** lacking o deficient in ► NMF: **ser un ~ mental** to have learning difficulties

déficit ['defiθit] (pl **déficits**) NM (Com) deficit; (fig) lack, shortage; ~ **presupuestario** budget deficit

deficitario, -a [defiθi'tarjo, a] ADJ (Com) in deficit; (: empresa) loss-making

defienda etc [de'fjenda] VB ver **defender**

defiera etc [de'fjera] VB ver **deferir**

definición [defini'θjon] NF definition; (Inform: de pantalla) resolution

definido, -a [defi'niðo, a] ADJ (tb Ling) definite; **bien ~** well o clearly defined; ~ **por el usuario** (Inform) user-defined

definir [defi'nir] /3a/ VT (determinar) to determine, establish; (decidir, Inform) to define; (aclarar) to clarify

definitivo, -a [defini'tiβo, a] ADJ (edición, texto) definitive; (fecha) definite; **en definitiva** definitively; (en conclusión) finally; (en resumen) in short

defiriendo etc [defi'rjendo] VB ver **deferir**

deflacionario, -a [deflaθjo'narjo, a], **deflacionista** [deflaθjo'nista] ADJ deflationary

deflector [deflek'tor] NM (Tec) baffle

deforestación [deforesta'θjon] NF deforestation

deformación [deforma'θjon] NF (alteración) deformation; (Radio etc) distortion

deformar [defor'mar] /1a/ VT (gen) to deform ■ **deformarse** VR to become deformed

deforme [de'forme] ADJ (informe) deformed; (feo) ugly; (mal hecho) misshapen

deformidad [deformi'ðað] NF (forma anormal) deformity; (fig: defecto) (moral) shortcoming

defraudar [defrau'ðar] /1a/ VT (decepcionar) to disappoint; (estafar) to defraud, cheat; ~ **impuestos** to evade tax

defunción [defun'θjon] NF death, demise

degeneración [dexenera'θjon] NF (de las células) degeneration; (moral) degeneracy

degenerar [dexene'rar] /1a/ VI to degenerate; (empeorar) to get worse

deglutir [deɣlu'tir] /3a/ VT, VI to swallow

degolladero [deɣoʎa'ðero] NM (Anat) throat; (cadalso) scaffold; (matadero) slaughterhouse

degollar [deɣo'ʎar] /1m/ VT to slaughter

degradar [deɣra'ðar] /1a/ VT to debase, degrade; (Inform: datos) to corrupt ■ **degradarse** VR to demean o.s.

degüelle etc [de'ɣweʎe] vʙ ver **degollar**

degustación [deɣusta'θjon] ɴꜰ sampling, tasting

deificar [deifi'kar] /**1g**/ vᴛ (persona) to deify

deifique etc [dei'fike] vʙ ver **deificar**

dejadez [dexa'ðeθ] ɴꜰ (negligencia) neglect; (descuido) untidiness, carelessness

dejado, -a [de'xaðo, a] ADJ (desaliñado) slovenly; (negligente) careless; (indolente) lazy

★**dejar** [de'xar] /**1a**/ vᴛ (gen) to leave; (permitir) to allow, let; (abandonar) to abandon, forsake; (actividad, empleo) to give up; (beneficios) to produce, yield; **~ entrar/salir** to let in/out; **~ pasar** to let through; **~ a un lado** to leave o set aside; **~ caer** to drop; **¡déjalo!** (no te preocupes) don't worry about it; **te dejo en tu casa** I'll drop you off at your place; **deja mucho que desear** it leaves a lot to be desired ▸ vɪ: **~ de** (parar) to stop; (no hacer) to fail to; **no puedo ~ de fumar** I can't give up smoking; **no dejes de visitarlos** don't fail to visit them; **no dejes de comprar un billete** make sure you buy a ticket ∎ **dejarse** vʀ (abandonarse) to let o.s. go; **dejarse persuadir** to allow o.s. to o let o.s. be persuaded; **¡déjate de tonterías!** stop messing about!

deje ['dexe] ɴᴍ (trace of) accent

dejo ['dexo] ɴᴍ (Ling) accent

del [del] (= de + el) ver **de**

del. ABR (Admin: = Delegación) district office

★**delantal** [delan'tal] ɴᴍ apron

★**delante** [de'lante] ADV in front; (enfrente) opposite; (adelante) ahead; **la parte de ~** the front part; **estando otros ~** with others present ▸ PREP: **~ de** in front of, before

delantero, -a [delan'tero, a] ADJ front; (patas de animal) fore ▸ ɴᴍ (Deporte) forward, striker ▸ ɴꜰ (de vestido, casa etc) front part; (Teat) front row; (Deporte) forward line; **llevar la delantera (a algn)** to be ahead (of sb)

delatar [dela'tar] /**1a**/ vᴛ to inform on o against, betray; **los delató a la policía** he reported them to the police

delator, -a [dela'tor, a] ɴᴍ/ꜰ informer

delegación [deleɣa'θjon] ɴꜰ (acción: delegados) delegation; (Com: oficina) district office, branch; **~ de poderes** (Pol) devolution; **~ de policía** (Aᴍ) police station, precinct (US)

delegado, -a [dele'ɣaðo, a] ɴᴍ/ꜰ delegate; (Com) agent

delegar [dele'ɣar] /**1h**/ vᴛ to delegate

delegue etc [de'leɣe] vʙ ver **delegar**

deleitar [delei'tar] /**1a**/ vᴛ to delight ∎ **deleitarse** vʀ: **deleitarse con o en** to delight in, take pleasure in

deleite [de'leite] ɴᴍ delight, pleasure

★**deletrear** [deletre'ar] /**1a**/ vᴛ (tb fig) to spell (out)

deletreo [dele'treo] ɴᴍ spelling; (fig) interpretation, decipherment

deleznable [deleθ'naβle] ADJ (frágil) fragile; (fig: malo) poor; (: excusa) feeble

delfín [del'fin] ɴᴍ dolphin

delgadez [delɣa'ðeθ] ɴꜰ thinness, slimness

★**delgado, -a** [del'ɣaðo, a] ADJ thin; (persona) slim, thin; (tierra) poor; (tela etc) light, delicate ▸ ADV: **hilar (muy) ~** (fig) to split hairs

deliberación [deliβera'θjon] ɴꜰ deliberation

deliberar [deliβe'rar] /**1a**/ vᴛ to debate, discuss ▸ vɪ to deliberate

delicadeza [delika'ðeθa] ɴꜰ delicacy; (refinamiento, sutileza) refinement

delicado, -a [deli'kaðo, a] ADJ delicate; (sensible) sensitive; (rasgos) dainty; (gusto) refined; (situación: difícil) tricky; (: violento) embarrassing; (punto, tema) sore; (persona: difícil de contentar) hard to please; (: sensible) touchy, hypersensitive; (: atento) considerate

delicia [de'liθja] ɴꜰ delight

★**delicioso, -a** [deli'θjoso, a] ADJ (gracioso) delightful; (exquisito) delicious

delictivo, -a [delik'tiβo, a] ADJ criminal cpd

delimitar [delimi'tar] /**1a**/ vᴛ to delimit; (función, responsabilidades) to define

delincuencia [delin'kwenθja] ɴꜰ: **~ juvenil** juvenile delinquency; **cifras de la ~** crime rate

delincuente [delin'kwente] ɴᴍꜰ delinquent; (criminal) criminal; **~ sin antecedentes** first offender; **~ habitual** hardened criminal

delineante [deline'ante] ɴᴍꜰ draughtsman (draughtswoman); (US) draftsman (draftswoman)

delinear [deline'ar] /**1a**/ vᴛ to delineate; (dibujo) to draw; (contornos, fig) to outline; **~ un proyecto** to outline a project

delinquir [delin'kir] /**3e**/ vɪ to commit an offence

delirante [deli'rante] ADJ delirious

delirar [deli'rar] /**1a**/ vɪ to be delirious, rave; (fig: desatinar) to talk nonsense

delirio [de'lirjo] ɴᴍ (Med) delirium; (palabras insensatas) ravings pl; **~ de grandeza** megalomania; **~ de persecución** persecution mania; **con ~** (fam) madly; **¡fue el ~!** (fam) it was great!

★**delito** [de'lito] ɴᴍ (gen) crime; (infracción) offence

delta ['delta] ɴᴍ delta

demacrado, -a [dema'kraðo, a] ADJ emaciated; **estar ~** to look pale and drawn, be wasted away

demagogia [dema'ɣoxja] ɴꜰ demagogy, demagoguery

demagogo, -a [dema'ɣoɣo, a] ɴᴍ/ꜰ demagogue

demanda [de'manda] ɴꜰ (pedido, Com) demand; (petición) request; (pregunta) inquiry; (reivindicación) claim; (Jur) action, lawsuit; (Teat) call; (Elec) load; **~ de pago** demand for payment; **escribir en ~ de ayuda** to write asking for help;

entablar ~ (*Jur*) to sue; **presentar ~ de divorcio** to sue for divorce; **~ final** final demand; **~ indirecta** derived demand; **~ de mercado** market demand

demandado, -a [deman'daðo, a] NM/F defendant; (*en divorcio*) respondent

demandante [deman'dante] NMF claimant; (*Jur*) plaintiff

demandar [deman'dar] /**1a**/ VT (*gen*) to demand; (*Jur*) to sue, file a lawsuit against, start proceedings against; **~ a algn por calumnia/daños y perjuicios** to sue sb for libel/damages

demarcación [demarka'θjon] NF (*de terreno*) demarcation

★**demás** [de'mas] ADJ: **los ~ niños** the other children, the remaining children ▶ PRON: **los/las ~** the others, the rest (of them); **lo ~** the rest (of it); **por ~** moreover; (*en vano*) in vain; **y ~** et cetera

demasía [dema'sia] NF (*exceso*) excess, surplus; **comer en ~** to eat to excess

★**demasiado, -a** [dema'sjaðo, a] ADJ: **~ vino** too much wine; **demasiados libros** too many books; **hace ~ calor** it's too hot; **¡es ~!** it's too much! ▶ ADV (*antes de adj, adv*) too; **es ~ pesado para levantarlo** it is too heavy to lift; **~ despacio** too slowly; **~ lo sé** I know it only too well ▶ PRON: **demasiados** too many

> *Demasiado* se traduce por **too** delante de adjetivos y adverbios:
> *Hace demasiado calor.* **It's too hot.**
> *Hablas demasiado deprisa.* **You talk too quickly.**
> Se traduce por **too much** delante de sustantivos incontables o cuando modifica al verbo:
> *Le he echado demasiada sal al agua.* **I've put too much salt in the water.**
> *Habla demasiado.* **He talks too much.**
> En plural la traducción es **too many**: *Tiene demasiadas preocupaciones.* **He has too many worries.**
> Si acompaña a un verbo de tiempo, suele traducirse por **too long**: *He tardado demasiado en acabarlo.* **I've taken too long to finish it.**

demencia [de'menθja] NF (*Med*) dementia; (*locura*) madness

demencial [demen'θjal] ADJ crazy

demente [de'mente] ADJ mad, insane ▶ NMF lunatic (!)

democracia [demo'kraθja] NF democracy

demócrata [de'mokrata] NMF democrat

democratacristiano, -a [demokratakris'tjano, a], **democristiano, -a** [demokris'tjano, a] ADJ, NM/F Christian Democrat

democrático, -a [demo'kratiko, a] ADJ democratic

demográfico, -a [demo'ɣrafiko, a] ADJ demographic, population *cpd*; **la explosión demográfica** the population explosion

demoledor, a [demole'ðor, a] ADJ (*fig: argumento*) overwhelming; (: *ataque*) shattering

demoler [demo'ler] /**2h**/ VT to demolish; (*edificio*) to pull down

demolición [demoli'θjon] NF demolition

demonio [de'monjo] NM devil, demon; **¡demonios!** hell!, damn!; **¿cómo demonios?** how the hell?; **¿qué demonios será?** what the devil can it be?; **¿dónde ~ lo habré dejado?** where the devil can I have left it?; **tener el ~ en el cuerpo** (*no parar*) to be always on the go

demora [de'mora] NF delay

demorar [demo'rar] /**1a**/ VT (*retardar*) to delay, hold back; (*dilatar*) to hold up ▶ VI to linger, stay on ■ **demorarse** VR to linger, stay on; (*retrasarse*) to take a long time; **demorarse en hacer algo** (*esp Am*) to take time doing sth

demos ['demos] VB *ver* **dar**

demostración [demostra'θjon] NF (*gen*) demonstration; (*de cariño, fuerza*) show; (*de teorema*) proof; (*de amistad*) gesture; (*de cólera, gimnasia*) display; **~ comercial** commercial exhibition

demostrar [demos'trar] /**1l**/ VT (*probar*) to prove; (*mostrar*) to show; (*manifestar*) to demonstrate

demostrativo, -a [demostra'tiβo, a] ADJ demonstrative

demudado, -a [demu'ðaðo, a] ADJ (*rostro*) pale; (*fig*) upset; **tener el rostro ~** to look pale

demudar [demu'ðar] /**1a**/ VT to change, alter ■ **demudarse** VR (*expresión*) to alter; (*perder color*) to change colour

demuela *etc* [de'mwela] VB *ver* **demoler**

demuestre *etc* [de'mwestre] VB *ver* **demostrar**

den [den] VB *ver* **dar**

denegación [deneɣa'θjon] NF refusal

denegar [dene'ɣar] /**1h, 1j**/ VT (*rechazar*) to refuse; (*negar*) to deny; (*Jur*) to reject

denegué [dene'ɣe], **deneguemos** *etc* [dene'ɣemos], **deniego** *etc* [de'njeɣo], **deniegue** *etc* [de'njeɣe] VB *ver* **denegar**

dengue ['denɣe] NM dengue *o* breakbone fever

denigrante [deni'ɣrante] ADJ (*injurioso*) insulting; (*deshonroso*) degrading

denigrar [deni'ɣrar] /**1a**/ VT (*desacreditar*) to denigrate; (*injuriar*) to insult

denodado, -a [deno'ðaðo, a] ADJ bold, brave

denominación [denomina'θjon] NF (*acto*) naming; (*clase*) denomination

> The *denominación de origen*, often abbreviated to *D.O.*, is a prestigious product classification given to designated regions by the awarding body, the *Consejo Regulador de la Denominación de Origen*, when their produce meets the required quality and production standards. It is often associated with fine delicatessen products and many of the wines from the various wine-producing regions in the country such as Rioja and Jerez.

denominador [denominaˈðor] NM: **~ común** common denominator

denostar [denosˈtar] /1l/ VT to insult

denotar [denoˈtar] /1a/ VT (indicar) to indicate, denote

densidad [densiˈðað] NF (Física) density; (fig) thickness

denso, -a [ˈdenso, a] ADJ (apretado) solid; (espeso, pastoso) thick, dense; (fig) heavy

dentado, -a [denˈtaðo, a] ADJ (rueda) cogged; (filo) jagged; (sello) perforated; (Bot) dentate

dentadura [dentaˈðura] NF (set of) teeth pl; **~ postiza** false teeth pl

dental [denˈtal] ADJ dental

dentellada [denteˈʎaða] NF (mordisco) bite, nip; (señal) tooth mark; **partir algo a dentelladas** to sever sth with one's teeth

dentera [denˈtera] NF (sensación desagradable) the shivers pl; (grima) **dar ~ a algn** to set sb's teeth on edge

dentición [dentiˈθjon] NF (acto) teething; (Anat) dentition; **estar con la ~** to be teething

dentífrico, -a [denˈtifriko, a] ADJ dental, tooth cpd; **pasta dentífrica** toothpaste ▶ NM toothpaste

★**dentista** [denˈtista] NMF dentist

★**dentro** [ˈdentro] ADV inside; **por ~** (on the) inside; **allí ~** in there; **mirar por ~** to look inside ▶ PREP: **~ de** in, inside, within; **~ de lo posible** as far as possible; **~ de todo** all in all; **~ de tres meses** within three months

denuedo [deˈnweðo] NM boldness, daring

denuesto [deˈnwesto] NM insult

denuncia [deˈnunθja] NF (delación) denunciation; (acusación) accusation; (de accidente) report; **hacer o poner una ~** to report an incident to the police

denunciable [denunˈθjaβle] ADJ indictable, punishable

denunciante [denunˈθjante] NMF accuser; (delator) informer

★**denunciar** [denunˈθjar] /1b/ VT to report; (delatar) to inform on o against

Dep. ABR (= Departamento) Dept.; (= Depósito) dep.

deparar [depaˈrar] /1a/ VT (brindar) to provide o furnish with; (futuro, destino) to have in store for; **los placeres que el viaje nos deparó** the pleasures which the trip afforded us

★**departamento** [departaˈmento] NM (sección) department, section; (Am: piso) flat (BRIT), apartment (US); (distrito) department, province; **~ de envíos** (Com) dispatch department; **~ de máquinas** (Naut) engine room

departir [deparˈtir] /3a/ VI to talk, converse

dependencia [depenˈdenθja] NF dependence; (Pol) dependency; (Com) office, section; (sucursal) branch office; (Arq: cuarto) room ■ **dependencias** NFPL outbuildings

★**depender** [depenˈder] /2a/ VI: **~ de** to depend on; (contar con) to rely on; (autoridad) to be under, be answerable to; **depende** it (all) depends; **no depende de mí** it's not up to me

dependienta [depenˈdjenta] NF saleswoman, shop assistant

★**dependiente** [depenˈdjente] ADJ dependent ▶ NM salesman, shop assistant

depilación [depilaˈθjon] NF hair removal

depilar [depiˈlar] /1a/ VT (con cera: piernas) to wax; (cejas) to pluck

depilatorio, -a [depilaˈtorjo, a] ADJ depilatory ▶ NM hair remover

deplorable [deploˈraβle] ADJ deplorable

deplorar [deploˈrar] /1a/ VT to deplore

depondré etc [deponˈdre] VB ver **deponer**

deponer [depoˈner] /2q/ VT (armas) to lay down; (rey) to depose; (gobernante) to oust; (ministro) to remove from office ▶ VI (Jur) to give evidence; (declarar) to make a statement

deponga etc [deˈponga] VB ver **deponer**

deportación [deportaˈθjon] NF deportation

deportar [deporˈtar] /1a/ VT to deport

★**deporte** [deˈporte] NM sport; **hacer ~** to play sports

★**deportista** [deporˈtista] ADJ sports cpd ▶ NMF sportsman(-woman)

★**deportivo, -a** [deporˈtiβo, a] ADJ (club, periódico) sports cpd ▶ NM sports car

deposición [deposiˈθjon] NF (de funcionario etc) removal from office; (Jur: testimonio) evidence

depositante [deposiˈtante] NMF depositor

depositar [deposiˈtar] /1a/ VT (dinero) to deposit; (mercaderías) to put away, store; **~ la confianza en algn** to place one's trust in sb ■ **depositarse** VR to settle

depositario, -a [deposiˈtarjo, a] NM/F trustee; **~ judicial** official receiver

★**depósito** [deˈposito] NM (gen) deposit; (de mercaderías) warehouse, store; (de animales, coches) pound; (de agua, gasolina etc) tank; (en retrete) cistern; **~ afianzado** bonded warehouse; **~ bancario** bank deposit; **~ de cadáveres** mortuary; **~ de maderas** timber yard; **~ de suministro** feeder bin

depravar [depraˈβar] /1a/ VT to deprave, corrupt ■ **depravarse** VR to become depraved

depreciación [depreθjaˈθjon] NF depreciation

depreciar [depreˈθjar] /1b/ VT to depreciate, reduce the value of ■ **depreciarse** VR to depreciate, lose value

depredador, a [depreðaˈðor, a] (Zool) ADJ predatory ▶ NM predator

depredar [depreˈðar] /1a/ VT to pillage

★**depresión** [depreˈsjon] NF (gen, Med) depression; (hueco) hollow; (en horizonte, camino) dip; (merma) drop; (Econ) slump, recession; **~ nerviosa** nervous breakdown

deprimente [depriˈmente] ADJ depressing

★**deprimido, -a** [depriˈmiðo, a] ADJ depressed

deprimir [depri'mir] /**3a**/ VT to depress ■ **deprimirse** VR (*persona*) to become depressed

★**deprisa** [de'prisa] ADV quickly, hurriedly

depuesto [de'pwesto] PP *de* **deponer**

depuración [depura'θjon] NF purification; (*Pol*) purge

depurador [depura'ðor] NM purifier

depuradora [depura'ðora] NF (*de agua*) water treatment plant; (*tb*: **depuradora de aguas residuales**) sewage farm

depurar [depu'rar] /**1a**/ VT to purify; (*purgar*) to purge

depuse *etc* [de'puse] VB *ver* **deponer**

der.¹, der.° ABR (= *derecho*) r

der.², der.ª ABR (= *derecha*) r

★**derecha** [de'retʃa] NF *ver* **derecho**

derechazo [dere'tʃaθo] NM (*Boxeo*) right; (*Tenis*) forehand drive; (*Taur*) *a pass with the cape*

derechista [dere'tʃista] (*Pol*) ADJ right-wing ▶ NMF right-winger

★**derecho, -a** [de'retʃo, a] ADJ right, right-hand ▶ NM (*privilegio*) right; (*título*) claim, title; (*lado*) right(-hand) side; (*leyes*) law; **~ de propiedad literaria** copyright; **~ de timbre** (*Com*) stamp duty; **~ de votar** right to vote; **~ a voto** voting right; **Facultad de D~** Faculty of Law; **tener ~ a** to have a right to; **¡no hay ~!** it's not fair! ▶ NF right(-hand) side; (*Pol*) right; **la(s) derecha(s)** (*Pol*) the Right; **a derechas** rightly, correctly; **de derechas** (*Pol*) right-wing; **a la derecha** on the right; (*dirección*) to the right ▶ ADV straight, directly; **siga todo ~** carry o (*Brit*) go straight on ■ **derechos** NMPL dues; (*profesionales*) fees; (*impuestos*) taxes; (*de autor*) royalties; **derechos civiles** civil rights; **derechos de patente** patent rights; **derechos portuarios** (*Com*) harbour dues; **"reservados todos los derechos"** "all rights reserved"

deriva [de'riβa] NF: **ir** o **estar a la ~** to drift, be adrift

derivación [deriβa'θjon] NF derivation

derivado, -a [deri'βaðo, a] ADJ derived ▶ NM (*Ling*) derivative; (*Industria, Química*) by-product

derivar [deri'βar] /**1a**/ VT to derive; (*desviar*) to direct ▶ VI to derive, be derived; (*Naut*) to drift ■ **derivarse** VR to derive, be derived; **~(se) de** (*consecuencia*) to spring from

dermatólogo, -a [derma'toloɣo, a] NM/F dermatologist

dérmico, -a ['dermiko, a] ADJ skin *cpd*

dermoprotector, a [dermoprotek'tor, a] ADJ protective

derogación [deroɣa'θjon] NF repeal

derogar [dero'ɣar] /**1h**/ VT (*ley*) to repeal; (*contrato*) to revoke

derogue *etc* [de'roɣe] VB *ver* **derogar**

derramamiento [derrama'mjento] NM (*dispersión*) spilling; (*fig*) squandering; **~ de sangre** bloodshed

derramar [derra'mar] /**1a**/ VT to spill; (*verter*) to pour out; (*esparcir*) to scatter; **~ lágrimas** to weep ■ **derramarse** VR to pour out

derrame [de'rrame] NM (*de líquido*) spilling; (*de sangre*) shedding; (*de tubo etc*) overflow; (*pérdida*) leakage; (*Med*) discharge; (*declive*) slope; **~ cerebral** brain haemorrhage; **~ sinovial** water on the knee

derrapar [derra'par] /**1a**/ VI to skid

derredor [derre'ðor] ADV: **al** o **en ~ de** around, about

derrengado, -a [derren'gaðo, a] ADJ (*torcido*) bent; (*cojo*) crippled; **estar ~** (*fig*) to ache all over; **dejar ~ a algn** (*fig*) to wear sb out

derretido, -a [derre'tiðo, a] ADJ melted; (*metal*) molten; **estar ~ por algn** (*fig*) to be crazy about sb

derretir [derre'tir] /**3k**/ VT (*gen*) to melt; (*nieve*) to thaw; (*fig*) to squander ■ **derretirse** VR to melt

derribar [derri'βar] /**1a**/ VT to knock down; (*construcción*) to demolish; (*persona, gobierno, político*) to bring down

derribo [de'rriβo] NM (*de edificio*) demolition; (*Lucha*) throw; (*Aviat*) shooting down; (*Pol*) overthrow ■ **derribos** NMPL rubble *sg*, debris *sg*

derrita *etc* [de'rrita] VB *ver* **derretir**

derrocar [derro'kar] /**1g**/ VT (*gobierno*) to bring down, overthrow; (*ministro*) to oust

derrochador, a [derrotʃa'ðor, a] ADJ, NM/F spendthrift

derrochar [derro'tʃar] /**1a**/ VT (*dinero, recursos*) to squander; (*energía, salud*) to be bursting with o full of

derroche [de'rrotʃe] NM (*despilfarro*) waste, squandering; (*exceso*) extravagance; **con un ~ de buen gusto** with a fine display of good taste

derroque *etc* [de'rroke] VB *ver* **derrocar**

derrota [de'rrota] NF (*Naut*) course; (*Mil*) defeat, rout; **sufrir una grave ~** (*fig*) to suffer a grave setback

derrotar [derro'tar] /**1a**/ VT (*gen*) to defeat

derrotero [derro'tero] NM (*rumbo*) course; **tomar otro ~** (*fig*) to adopt a different course

derrotista [derro'tista] ADJ, NMF defeatist

derruir [derru'ir] /**3g**/ VT to demolish, tear down

derrumbamiento [derrumba'mjento] NM (*caída*) plunge; (*demolición*) demolition; (*desplome*) collapse; **~ de tierra** landslide

derrumbar [derrum'bar] /**1a**/ VT to throw down; (*despeñar*) to fling o hurl down; (*edificio*) to knock down; (*volcar*) to upset ■ **derrumbarse** VR (*hundirse*) to collapse; (: *techo*) to fall in, cave in; (*fig: esperanzas*) to collapse

derrumbe [de'rrumbe] NM = **derrumbamiento**

derruyendo *etc* [derru'jendo] VB *ver* **derruir**

des [des] VB *ver* **dar**

desabastecido, -a [desaβaste'θiðo, a] ADJ: **estar ~ de algo** to be short of o out of sth

desabotonar [desaβoto'nar] /**1a**/ VT to unbutton, undo ▶ VI (flores) to blossom ▪ **desabotonarse** VR to come undone

desabrido, -a [desa'βriðo, a] ADJ (comida) insipid, tasteless; (persona: soso) dull; (: antipático) rude, surly; (respuesta) sharp; (tiempo) unpleasant

desabrigado, -a [desaβri'ɣaðo, a] ADJ (sin abrigo) not sufficiently protected; (fig) exposed

desabrigar [desaβri'ɣar] /**1h**/ VT (quitar ropa a) to remove the clothing of; (descubrir) to uncover; (fig) to deprive of protection ▪ **desabrigarse** VR: **me desabrigué en la cama** the bedclothes came off

desabrigue etc [desa'βriɣe] VB ver **desabrigar**

desabrochar [desaβro'tʃar] /**1a**/ VT (botones, broches) to undo, unfasten ▪ **desabrocharse** VR (ropa etc) to come undone

desacatar [desaka'tar] /**1a**/ VT (ley) to disobey

desacato [desa'kato] NM (falta de respeto) disrespect; (Jur) contempt

desacertado, -a [desaθer'taðo, a] ADJ (equivocado) mistaken; (inoportuno) unwise

desacierto [desa'θjerto] NM (error) mistake, error; (dicho) unfortunate remark

desaconsejable [desakonse'xaβle] ADJ inadvisable

desaconsejado, -a [desakonse'xaðo, a] ADJ ill-advised

desaconsejar [desakonse'xar] /**1a**/ VT: **~ algo a algn** to advise sb against sth

desacoplar [desako'plar] /**1a**/ VT (Elec) to disconnect; (Tec) to take apart

desacorde [desa'korðe] ADJ (Mus) discordant; (fig: opiniones) conflicting; **estar ~ con algo** to disagree with sth

desacreditar [desakreði'tar] /**1a**/ VT (desprestigiar) to discredit, bring into disrepute; (denigrar) to run down

desactivar [desakti'βar] /**1a**/ VT to deactivate; (bomba) to defuse

desacuerdo [desa'kwerðo] NM (conflicto) disagreement, discord; (error) error, blunder; **en ~** out of keeping

desafiante [desa'fjante] ADJ (insolente) defiant; (retador) challenging ▶ NMF challenger

desafiar [desa'fjar] /**1c**/ VT (retar) to challenge; (enfrentarse a) to defy

desafilado, -a [desafi'laðo, a] ADJ blunt

desafinado, -a [desafi'naðo, a] ADJ: **estar ~** to be out of tune

desafinar [desafi'nar] /**1a**/ VI to be out of tune ▪ **desafinarse** VR to go out of tune

desafío [desa'fio] NM (reto) challenge; (combate) duel; (resistencia) defiance

desaforadamente [desaforaða'mente] ADV: **gritar ~** to shout one's head off

desaforado, -a [desafo'raðo, a] ADJ (grito) ear-splitting; (comportamiento) outrageous

desafortunadamente [desafortunaða'mente] ADV unfortunately

★**desafortunado, -a** [desafortu'naðo, a] ADJ (desgraciado) unfortunate, unlucky

★**desagradable** [desaɣra'ðaβle] ADJ (fastidioso, enojoso) unpleasant; (irritante) disagreeable; **ser ~ con algn** to be rude to sb

desagradar [desaɣra'ðar] /**1a**/ VI (disgustar) to displease; (molestar) to bother

desagradecido, -a [desaɣraðe'θiðo, a] ADJ ungrateful

desagrado [desa'ɣraðo] NM (disgusto) displeasure; (contrariedad) dissatisfaction; **con ~** unwillingly

desagraviar [desaɣra'βjar] /**1b**/ VT to make amends to

desagravio [desa'ɣraβjo] NM (satisfacción) amends; (compensación) compensation

desaguadero [desaɣwa'ðero] NM drain

desagüe [de'saɣwe] NM (de un líquido) drainage; (cañería: tb: **tubo de desagüe**) drainpipe; (salida) outlet, drain

desaguisado, -a [desaɣi'saðo, a] ADJ illegal ▶ NM outrage

desahogado, -a [desao'ɣaðo, a] ADJ (holgado) comfortable; (espacioso) roomy

desahogar [desao'ɣar] /**1h**/ VT (aliviar) to ease, relieve; (ira) to vent ▪ **desahogarse** VR (distenderse) to relax; (desfogarse) to let off steam (fam); (confesarse) to confess, get sth off one's chest (fam)

desahogo [desa'oɣo] NM (alivio) relief; (comodidad) comfort, ease; **vivir con ~** to be comfortably off

desahogue etc [desa'oɣe] VB ver **desahogar**

desahuciado, -a [desau'θjaðo, a] ADJ hopeless

desahuciar [desau'θjar] /**1b**/ VT (enfermo) to give up hope for; (inquilino) to evict

desahucio [de'sauθjo] NM eviction

desairado, -a [desai'raðo, a] ADJ (menospreciado) disregarded; (desgarbado) shabby; (sin éxito) unsuccessful; **quedar ~** to come off badly

desairar [desai'rar] /**1a**/ VT (menospreciar) to slight, snub; (cosa) to disregard; (Com) to default on

desaire [des'aire] NM (menosprecio) slight; (falta de garbo) unattractiveness; **dar** o **hacer un ~ a algn** to offend sb; **¿me va usted a hacer ese ~?** I won't take no for an answer!

desajustar [desaxus'tar] /**1a**/ VT (desarreglar) to disarrange; (desconcertar) to throw off balance; (fig: planes) to upset ▪ **desajustarse** VR to get out of order; (aflojarse) to loosen

desajuste [desa'xuste] NM (de máquina) disorder; (avería) breakdown; (situación) imbalance; (desacuerdo) disagreement

desalentador, -a [desalenta'ðor, a] ADJ discouraging

desalentar [desalen'tar] /**1j**/ VT (*desanimar*) to discourage ■ **desalentarse** VR to get discouraged

desaliento *etc* [desa'ljento] VB *ver* **desalentar** ▶ NM discouragement; (*abatimiento*) depression

desaliñado, -a [desali'naðo, a] ADJ (*descuidado*) slovenly; (*raído*) shabby; (*desordenado*) untidy; (*negligente*) careless

desaliño [desa'lino] NM (*descuido*) slovenliness; (*negligencia*) carelessness

desalmado, -a [desal'maðo, a] ADJ (*cruel*) cruel, heartless

desalojar [desalo'xar] /**1a**/ VT (*gen*) to remove, expel; (*expulsar, echar*) to eject; (*abandonar*) to move out of; **la policía desalojó el local** the police cleared people out of the place ▶ VI to move out

desalquilar [desalki'lar] /**1a**/ VT to vacate, move out ■ **desalquilarse** VR to become vacant

desamarrar [desama'rrar] /**1a**/ VT to untie; (*Naut*) to cast off

desamor [desa'mor] NM (*frialdad*) indifference; (*odio*) dislike

desamparado, -a [desampa'raðo, a] ADJ (*persona*) helpless; (*lugar: expuesto*) exposed; (: *desierto*) deserted

desamparar [desampa'rar] /**1a**/ VT (*abandonar*) to desert, abandon; (*Jur*) to leave defenceless; (*barco*) to abandon

desamparo [desam'paro] NM (*acto*) desertion; (*estado*) helplessness

desamueblado, -a [desamwe'βlaðo, a] ADJ unfurnished

desandar [desan'dar] /**1p**/ VT: ~ **lo andado** *o* **el camino** to retrace one's steps

desanduve *etc* [desan'duβe], **desanduviera** *etc* [desandu'βjera] VB *ver* **desandar**

desangelado, -a [desanxe'laðo, a] ADJ (*habitación, edificio*) lifeless

desangrar [desan'grar] /**1a**/ VT to bleed; (*fig: persona*) to bleed dry; (*lago*) to drain ■ **desangrarse** VR to lose a lot of blood; (*morir*) to bleed to death

desanimado, -a [desani'maðo, a] ADJ (*persona*) downhearted; (*espectáculo, fiesta*) dull

desanimar [desani'mar] /**1a**/ VT (*desalentar*) to discourage; (*deprimir*) to depress ■ **desanimarse** VR to lose heart

desánimo [de'sanimo] NM despondency; (*abatimiento*) dejection; (*falta de animación*) dullness

desanudar [desanu'ðar] /**1a**/ VT to untie; (*fig*) to clear up

desapacible [desapa'θiβle] ADJ unpleasant

★**desaparecer** [desapare'θer] /**2d**/ VI to disappear; (*el sol, la luz*) to vanish; (*desaparecer de vista*) to drop out of sight; (*efectos, señales*) to wear off ▶ VT (*esp AM Pol*) to cause to disappear; (: *eufemismo*) to murder

desaparecido, -a [desapare'θiðo, a] ADJ missing; (*especie*) extinct ▶ NM/F (*Pol*) kidnapped *o* missing person

★**desaparición** [desapari'θjon] NF disappearance; (*de especie etc*) extinction

desapasionado, -a [desapasjo'naðo, a] ADJ dispassionate, impartial

desapego [desa'peγo] NM (*frialdad*) coolness; (*distancia*) detachment

desapercibido, -a [desaperθi'βiðo, a] ADJ unnoticed; (*desprevenido*) unprepared; **pasar ~** to go unnoticed

desaplicado, -a [desapli'kaðo, a] ADJ slack, lazy

desaprensivo, -a [desapren'siβo, a] ADJ unscrupulous

desaprobar [desapro'βar] /**1l**/ VT (*reprobar*) to disapprove of; (*condenar*) to condemn; (*no consentir*) to reject

desaprovechado, -a [desaproβe'tʃaðo, a] ADJ (*oportunidad, tiempo*) wasted; (*estudiante*) slack

desaprovechar [desaproβe'tʃar] /**1a**/ VT to waste; (*talento*) not to use to the full ▶ VI (*perder terreno*) to lose ground

desapruebe *etc* [desa'prweβe] VB *ver* **desaprobar**

desarmador [desarma'ðor] NM (*Am*) screwdriver

desarmar [desar'mar] /**1a**/ VT to disarm; (*Tec*) to take apart, dismantle

desarme [de'sarme] NM disarmament

desarraigado, -a [desarrai'γaðo, a] ADJ (*persona*) without roots, rootless

desarraigar [desarrai'γar] /**1h**/ VT to uproot; (*fig: costumbre*) to root out; (: *persona*) to banish

desarraigo [desa'rraiγo] NM uprooting

desarraigue *etc* [desa'rraiγe] VB *ver* **desarraigar**

desarrapado, -a [desarra'paðo, a] ADJ ragged; **(de aspecto) ~** shabby

desarreglado, -a [desarre'γlaðo, a] ADJ (*desordenado*) disorderly, untidy; (*hábitos*) irregular

desarreglar [desarre'γlar] /**1a**/ VT to mess up; (*desordenar*) to disarrange; (*trastocar*) to upset, disturb

desarreglo [desa'rreγlo] NM (*de casa, persona*) untidiness; (*desorden*) disorder; (*Tec*) trouble; (*Med*) upset; **viven en el mayor ~** they live in complete chaos

desarrollado, -a [desarro'ʎaðo, a] ADJ developed

desarrollar [desarro'ʎar] /**1a**/ VT (*gen*) to develop; (*extender*) to unfold; (*teoría*) to explain; **aquí desarrollan un trabajo muy importante** they carry on *o* out very important work here ■ **desarrollarse** VR to develop; (*ocurrir*) to take place; (*extenderse*) to open (out); (*film*) to develop; (*fig*) to grow; (*tener lugar*) to take place; **la acción se desarrolla en Roma** (*Cine etc*) the scene is set in Roma

desarrollo [desa'rroʎo] NM development; (*de*

acontecimientos) unfolding; (*de industria, mercado*) expansion, growth; **país en vías de ~** developing country; **la industria está en pleno ~** industry is expanding steadily; **~ sostenible** sustainable development

desarrugar [desarruˈɣar] /**1h**/ VT (*alisar*) to smooth (out); (*ropa*) to remove the creases from

desarrugue *etc* [desaˈrruɣe] VB *ver* **desarrugar**

desarticulado, -a [desartikuˈlaðo, a] ADJ disjointed

desarticular [desartikuˈlar] /**1a**/ VT (*huesos*) to dislocate, put out of joint; (*objeto*) to take apart; (*grupo terrorista etc*) to break up

desaseado, -a [desaseˈaðo, a] ADJ (*sucio*) dirty; (*desaliñado*) untidy

desaseo [desaˈseo] NM (*suciedad*) dirtiness; (*desarreglo*) untidiness

desasga *etc* [deˈsasɣa] VB *ver* **desasir**

desasir [desaˈsir] /**3a**/ VT to loosen ■ **desasirse** VR to extricate o.s.; **desasirse de** to let go, give up

desasosegar [desasoseˈɣar] /**1h, 1j**/ VT (*inquietar*) to disturb, make uneasy ■ **desasosegarse** VR to become uneasy

desasosegué [desasoseˈɣe], **desasoseguemos** *etc* [desasoseˈɣemos] VB *ver* **desasosegar**

desasosiego *etc* [desaˈsjeɣo] VB *ver* **desasosegar** ▶ NM (*intranquilidad*) uneasiness, restlessness; (*ansiedad*) anxiety; (*Pol etc*) unrest

desasosiegue *etc* [desaˈsjeɣe] VB *ver* **desasosegar**

desastrado, -a [desasˈtraðo, a] ADJ (*desaliñado*) shabby; (*sucio*) dirty

★**desastre** [deˈsastre] NM disaster; **¡un ~!** how awful!; **la función fue un ~** the show was a shambles

★**desastroso, -a** [desasˈtroso, a] ADJ disastrous

desatado, -a [desaˈtaðo, a] ADJ (*desligado*) untied; (*violento*) violent, wild

desatar [desaˈtar] /**1a**/ VT (*nudo*) to untie; (*paquete*) to undo; (*perro, odio*) to unleash; (*misterio*) to solve; (*separar*) to detach ■ **desatarse** VR (*zapatos*) to come untied; (*tormenta*) to break; (*perder control de sí mismo*) to lose self-control; **desatarse en injurias** to pour out a stream of insults

desatascar [desatasˈkar] /**1g**/ VT (*cañería*) to unblock, clear

desatasque *etc* [desaˈtaske] VB *ver* **desatascar**

desatención [desatenˈθjon] NF (*descuido*) inattention; (*distracción*) absent-mindedness

desatender [desatenˈder] /**2g**/ VT (*no prestar atención a*) to disregard; (*abandonar*) to neglect

desatento, -a [desaˈtento, a] ADJ (*distraído*) inattentive; (*descortés*) discourteous

desatienda *etc* [desaˈtjenda] VB *ver* **desatender**

desatinado, -a [desatiˈnaðo, a] ADJ foolish, silly

desatino [desaˈtino] NM (*idiotez*) foolishness, folly; (*error*) blunder; **¡qué ~!** how silly!, what rubbish! ■ **desatinos** NMPL nonsense *sg*

desatornillar [desatorniˈʎar] /**1a**/ VT to unscrew

desatrancar [desatranˈkar] /**1g**/ VT (*puerta*) to unbolt; (*cañería*) to unblock

desatranque *etc* [desaˈtranke] VB *ver* **desatrancar**

desautorice *etc* [desautoˈriθe] VB *ver* **desautorizar**

desautorizado, -a [desautoriˈθaðo, a] ADJ unauthorized

desautorizar [desautoriˈθar] /**1f**/ VT (*oficial*) to deprive of authority; (*informe*) to deny

desavendré *etc* [desaβenˈdre] VB *ver* **desavenir**

desavenencia [desaβeˈnenθja] NF (*desacuerdo*) disagreement; (*discrepancia*) quarrel

desavenga *etc* [desaˈβenga] VB *ver* **desavenir**

desavenido, -a [desaβeˈniðo, a] ADJ (*opuesto*) contrary; (*reñido*) in disagreement; **ellos están desavenidos** they are at odds

desavenir [desaβeˈnir] /**3r**/ VT (*enemistar*) to make trouble between ■ **desavenirse** VR to fall out

desaventajado, -a [desaβentaˈxaðo, a] ADJ (*inferior*) inferior; (*poco ventajoso*) disadvantageous

desaviene *etc* [desaˈβjene], **desaviniendo** *etc* [desaβiˈnjendo] VB *ver* **desavenir**

★**desayunar** [desajuˈnar] /**1a**/ VI to have breakfast; **~ con algo** (*fig*) to get the first news of sth ▶ VT to have for breakfast; **~ café** to have coffee for breakfast

★**desayuno** [desaˈjuno] NM breakfast

desazón [desaˈθon] NF (*angustia*) anxiety; (*Med*) discomfort; (*fig*) annoyance

desazonar [desaθoˈnar] /**1a**/ VT (*fig*) to annoy, upset ■ **desazonarse** VR (*enojarse*) to be annoyed; (*preocuparse*) to worry, be anxious

desbancar [desβanˈkar] /**1g**/ VT (*quitar el puesto a*) to oust; (*suplantar*) to supplant (in sb's affections)

desbandada [desβanˈdaða] NF rush; **~ general** mass exodus; **a la ~** in disorder

desbandarse [desβanˈdarse] /**1a**/ VR (*Mil*) to disband; (*fig*) to flee in disorder

desbanque *etc* [desˈβanke] VB *ver* **desbancar**

desbarajuste [desβaraˈxuste] NM confusion, disorder; **¡qué ~!** what a mess!

desbaratar [desβaraˈtar] /**1a**/ VT (*gen*) to mess up; (*plan*) to spoil; (*deshacer, destruir*) to ruin ▶ VI to talk nonsense ■ **desbaratarse** VR (*máquina*) to break down; (*persona: irritarse*) to fly off the handle (*fam*)

desbarrar [desβaˈrrar] /**1a**/ VI to talk nonsense

desbloquear [desβlokeˈar] /**1a**/ VT (*negociaciones, tráfico*) to get going again; (*Com: cuenta*) to unfreeze

desbocado – descendencia

desbocado, -a [desβo'kaðo, a] ADJ (*caballo*) runaway; (*herramienta*) worn

desbocar [desβo'kar] /**1g**/ VT (*vasija*) to break the rim of ■ **desbocarse** VR (*caballo*) to bolt; (*persona: soltar injurias*) to let out a stream of insults

desboque *etc* [des'βoke] VB *ver* **desbocar**

desbordamiento [desβorða'mjento] NM (*de río*) overflowing; (*Inform*) overflow; (*de cólera*) outburst; (*de entusiasmo*) upsurge

desbordar [desβor'ðar] /**1a**/ VT (*sobrepasar*) to go beyond; (*exceder*) to exceed ▶ VI, **desbordarse** VR (*líquido, río*) to overflow; (*entusiasmo*) to erupt; (*persona: exaltarse*) to get carried away

desbravar [desβra'βar] /**1a**/ VT (*caballo*) to break in; (*animal*) to tame

descabalgar [deskaβal'γar] /**1h**/ VI to dismount

descabalgue *etc* [deska'βalγe] VB *ver* **descabalgar**

descabellado, -a [deskaβe'ʎaðo, a] ADJ (*disparatado*) wild, crazy; (*insensato*) preposterous

descabellar [deskaβe'ʎar] /**1a**/ VT to ruffle; (*Taur: toro*) to give the coup de grace to

descabezado, -a [deskaβe'θaðo, a] ADJ (*sin cabeza*) headless; (*insensato*) wild

descafeinado, -a [deskafei'naðo, a] ADJ decaffeinated ▶ NM decaffeinated coffee, de-caff

descalabrar [deskala'βrar] /**1a**/ VT to smash; (*persona*) to hit; (: *en la cabeza*) to hit on the head; (*Naut*) to cripple; (*dañar*) to harm, damage ■ **descalabrarse** VR to hurt one's head

descalabro [deska'laβro] NM blow; (*desgracia*) misfortune

descalce *etc* [des'kalθe] VB *ver* **descalzar**

descalificación [deskalifika'θjon] NF disqualification ■ **descalificaciones** NFPL discrediting *sg*

descalificar [deskalifi'kar] /**1g**/ VT to disqualify; (*desacreditar*) to discredit

descalifique *etc* [deskali'fike] VB *ver* **descalificar**

descalzar [deskal'θar] /**1f**/ VT (*zapato*) to take off; (*persona*) to take the shoes off

descalzo, -a [des'kalθo, a] ADJ barefoot(ed); (*fig*) destitute; **estar (con los pies) ~(s)** to be barefooted

descambiar [deskam'bjar] /**1b**/ VT to exchange

descaminado, -a [deskami'naðo, a] ADJ (*equivocado*) on the wrong road; (*fig*) misguided; **en eso no anda usted muy ~** you're not far wrong there

descamisado, -a [deskami'saðo, a] ADJ barechested

descampado [deskam'paðo] NM open space, piece of empty ground; **comer al ~** to eat in the open air

descansado, -a [deskan'saðo, a] ADJ (*gen*) rested; (*que tranquiliza*) restful

★**descansar** [deskan'sar] /**1a**/ VT (*gen*) to rest; (*apoyar*): **~ (sobre)** to lean (on) ▶ VI to rest, have a rest; (*echarse*) to lie down; (*cadáver, restos*) to lie; **¡que usted descanse!** sleep well!; **~ en** (*argumento*) to be based on

descansillo [deskan'siʎo] NM (*de escalera*) landing

★**descanso** [des'kanso] NM (*reposo*) rest; (*alivio*) relief; (*pausa*) break; (*Deporte*) interval, half time; **día de ~** day off; **~ de enfermedad/maternidad** sick/maternity leave; **tomarse unos días de ~** to take a few days' leave *o* rest

descapitalizado, -a [deskapitali'θaðo, a] ADJ undercapitalized

descapotable [deskapo'taβle] NM (*tb:* **coche descapotable**) convertible

descarado, -a [deska'raðo, a] ADJ (*sin vergüenza*) shameless; (*insolente*) cheeky

descarga [des'karγa] NF (*Arq, Elec, Mil*) discharge; (*Naut*) unloading; (*Inform*) download

descargable [deskar'γaβle] ADJ downloadable

descargador [deskarγa'ðor] NM (*de barcos*) docker

★**descargar** [deskar'γar] /**1h**/ VT to unload; (*golpe*) to let fly; (*arma*) to fire; (*Elec*) to discharge; (*Inform*) to download; (*pila*) to run down; (*conciencia*) to relieve; (*Com*) to take up; (*persona: de una obligación*) to release; (: *de una deuda*) to free; (*Jur*) to clear; **~ algo de Internet** to download sth from the internet ▶ VI (*río*): **~ (en)** to flow (into) ■ **descargarse** VR to unburden o.s.; **descargarse de algo** to get rid of sth

descargo [des'karγo] NM (*de obligación*) release; (*Com: recibo*) receipt; (: *de deuda*) discharge; (*Jur*) evidence; **~ de una acusación** acquittal on a charge

descargue *etc* [des'karγe] VB *ver* **descargar**

descarnado, -a [deskar'naðo, a] ADJ scrawny; (*fig*) bare; (*estilo*) straightforward

descaro [des'karo] NM nerve

descarriar [deska'rrjar] /**1c**/ VT (*descaminar*) to misdirect; (*fig*) to lead astray ■ **descarriarse** VR (*perderse*) to lose one's way; (*separarse*) to stray; (*pervertirse*) to err, go astray

descarrilamiento [deskarrila'mjento] NM (*de tren*) derailment

descarrilar [deskarri'lar] /**1a**/ VI to be derailed

descartable [deskar'taβle] ADJ (*Inform*) temporary

descartar [deskar'tar] /**1a**/ VT (*rechazar*) to reject; (*eliminar*) to rule out ■ **descartarse** VR (*Naipes*) to discard; **descartarse de** to shirk

descascarar [deskaska'rar] /**1a**/ VT (*naranja, limón*) to peel; (*nueces, huevo duro*) to shell ■ **descascararse** VR to peel (off)

descascarillado, -a [deskaskari'ʎaðo, a] ADJ (*paredes*) peeling

descendencia [desθen'denθja] NF (*origen*)

origin, descent; (*hijos*) offspring; **morir sin dejar ~** to die without issue

descendente [desθen'dente] ADJ (*cantidad*) diminishing; (*Inform*) top-down

descender [desθen'der] /**2g**/ VT (*bajar: escalera*) to go down ▸ VI to descend; (*temperatura, nivel*) to fall, drop; (*líquido*) to run; (*cortina etc*) to hang; (*fuerzas, persona*) to fail, get weak; **~ de** to be descended from

descendiente [desθen'djente] NMF descendant

descenso [des'θenso] NM descent; (*de temperatura*) drop; (*de producción*) downturn; (*de calidad*) decline; (*Minería*) collapse; (*bajada*) slope; (*fig: decadencia*) decline; (*de empleado etc*) demotion

descentrado, -a [desθen'traðo, a] ADJ (*pieza de una máquina*) off-centre; (*rueda*) out of true; (*persona*) bewildered; (*desequilibrado*) unbalanced; (*problema*) out of focus; **todavía está algo ~** he is still somewhat out of touch

descentralice *etc* [desθentra'liθe] VB *ver* **descentralizar**

descentralizar [desθentrali'θar] /**1f**/ VT to decentralize

descerrajar [desθerra'xar] /**1a**/ VT (*puerta*) to break open

descienda *etc* [des'θjenda] VB *ver* **descender**

descifrable [desθi'fraβle] ADJ (*gen*) decipherable; (*letra*) legible

descifrar [desθi'frar] /**1a**/ VT (*escritura*) to decipher; (*mensaje*) to decode; (*problema*) to puzzle out; (*misterio*) to solve

descocado, -a [desko'kaðo, a] ADJ (*descarado*) cheeky; (*desvergonzado*) brazen

descoco [des'koko] NM (*descaro*) cheek; (*atrevimiento*) brazenness

descodificador [deskoðifika'ðor] NM decoder

descodificar [deskoðifi'kar] /**1g**/ VT to decode

★**descolgar** [deskol'ɣar] /**1h, 1l**/ VT (*bajar*) to take down; (*desde una posición alta*) to lower; (*de una pared etc*) to unhook; (*teléfono*) to pick up; **dejó el teléfono descolgado** he left the phone off the hook ◾ **descolgarse** VR to let o.s. down; **descolgarse por** (*bajar escurriéndose*) to slip down; (*pared*) to climb down

descolgué [deskol'ɣe], **descolguemos** *etc* [deskol'ɣemos] VB *ver* **descolgar**

descollar [desko'ʎar] /**1l**/ VI (*sobresalir*) to stand out; (*montaña etc*) to rise; **la obra que más descuella de las suyas** his most outstanding work

descolocado, -a [deskolo'kaðo, a] ADJ: **estar ~** (*cosa*) to be out of place; (*criada*) to be unemployed

descolorido, -a [deskolo'riðo, a] ADJ (*color, tela*) faded; (*pálido*) pale; (*fig: estilo*) colourless

descompaginar [deskompaxi'nar] /**1a**/ VT (*desordenar*) to disarrange, mess up

descompasado, -a [deskompa'saðo, a] ADJ (*sin proporción*) out of all proportion; (*excesivo*) excessive; (*hora*) unearthly

descompensar [deskompen'sar] /**1a**/ VT to unbalance

descompondré *etc* [deskompon'dre] VB *ver* **descomponer**

descomponer [deskompo'ner] /**2q**/ VT (*gen, Ling, Mat*) to break down; (*desordenar*) to disarrange, disturb; (*materia orgánica*) to rot, decompose; (*Tec*) to put out of order; (*facciones*) to distort; (*estómago etc*) to upset; (*planes*) to mess up; (*persona: molestar*) to upset; (: *irritar*) to annoy ◾ **descomponerse** VR (*corromperse*) to rot, decompose; (*estómago*) to get upset; (*el tiempo*) to change (for the worse); (*Tec*) to break down

descomponga *etc* [deskom'ponga] VB *ver* **descomponer**

descomposición [deskomposi'θjon] NF (*de un objeto*) breakdown; (*de fruta etc*) decomposition; (*putrefacción*) rotting; (*de cara*) distortion; **~ de vientre** (*Med*) stomach upset, diarrhoea, diarrhea (*US*)

descompostura [deskompos'tura] NF (*Tec*) breakdown, fault; (*desorganización*) disorganization; (*desorden*) untidiness; (*AM: diarrea*) diarrhoea, diarrhea (*US*)

descompuesto, -a [deskom'pwesto, a] PP *de* **descomponer** ▸ ADJ (*corrompido*) decomposed; (*roto*) broken (down)

descompuse *etc* [deskom'puse] VB *ver* **descomponer**

descomunal [deskomu'nal] ADJ (*enorme*) huge; (*fam: excelente*) fantastic

desconcertado, -a [deskonθer'taðo, a] ADJ disconcerted, bewildered

desconcertar [deskonθer'tar] /**1j**/ VT (*confundir*) to baffle; (*incomodar*) to upset, put out; (*orden*) to disturb ◾ **desconcertarse** VR (*turbarse*) to be upset; (*confundirse*) to be bewildered

desconchado, -a [deskon'tʃaðo, a] ADJ (*pintura*) peeling

desconchar [deskon'tʃar] /**1a**/ VT (*pared*) to strip off; (*loza*) to chip off

desconcierto *etc* [deskon'θjerto] VB *ver* **desconcertar** ▸ NM (*gen*) disorder; (*desorientación*) uncertainty; (*inquietud*) uneasiness; (*confusión*) bewilderment

desconectado, -a [deskonek'taðo, a] ADJ (*Elec*) disconnected, switched off; (*Inform*) offline; **estar ~ de** (*fig*) to have no contact with

★**desconectar** [deskonek'tar] /**1a**/ VT to disconnect; (*desenchufar*) to unplug; (*radio, televisión*) to switch off; (*Inform*) to toggle off

desconfiado, -a [deskon'fjaðo, a] ADJ suspicious

desconfianza [deskon'fjanθa] NF distrust

★**desconfiar** [deskon'fjar] /**1c**/ VI to be distrustful; **~ de** (*sospechar*) to mistrust, suspect; (*no tener confianza en*) to have no faith o confidence in; **desconfío de ello** I doubt it; **desconfíe de las imitaciones** (*Com*) beware of imitations

desconforme [deskon'forme] ADJ = **disconforme**

descongelar [deskonxe'lar] /**1a**/ VT (*nevera*) to defrost; (*comida*) to thaw; (*Auto*) to de-ice; (*Com, Pol*) to unfreeze

descongestionar [deskonxestjo'nar] /**1a**/ VT (*cabeza, tráfico*) to clear; (*calle, ciudad*) to relieve congestion in; (*fig: despejar*) to clear

desconocer [deskono'θer] /**2d**/ VT (*ignorar*) not to know, to be ignorant of; (*no aceptar*) to deny; (*repudiar*) to disown

★**desconocido, -a** [deskono'θiðo, a] ADJ unknown; (*que no se conoce*) unfamiliar; (*no reconocido*) unrecognized; **está ~** he is hardly recognizable ▸ NM/F stranger; (*recién llegado*) newcomer

desconocimiento [deskonoθi'mjento] NM (*falta de conocimientos*) ignorance; (*repudio*) disregard

desconozca *etc* [desko'noθka] VB *ver* **desconocer**

desconsiderado, -a [deskonsiðe'raðo, a] ADJ inconsiderate; (*insensible*) thoughtless

desconsolado, -a [deskonso'laðo, a] ADJ (*afligido*) disconsolate; (*cara*) sad; (*desanimado*) dejected

desconsolar [deskonso'lar] /**1l**/ VT to distress ■ **desconsolarse** VR to despair

desconsuelo [deskon'swelo] VB *ver* **desconsolar** ▸ NM (*tristeza*) distress; (*desesperación*) despair

descontado, -a [deskon'taðo, a] ADJ: **por ~** of course; **dar por ~ (que)** to take it for granted (that)

descontar [deskon'tar] /**1l**/ VT (*deducir*) to take away, deduct; (*rebajar*) to discount

descontento, -a [deskon'tento, a] ADJ dissatisfied ▸ NM dissatisfaction, discontent

descontrol [deskon'trol] NM lack of control

descontrolado, -a [deskontro'laðo, a] ADJ uncontrolled

descontrolarse [deskontro'larse] /**1a**/ VR (*persona*) to lose control

desconvenir [deskombe'nir] /**3s**/ VI (*personas*) to disagree; (*no corresponder*) not to fit; (*no convenir*) to be inconvenient

desconvocar [deskombo'kar] /**1g**/ VT to call off

descorazonar [deskoraθo'nar] /**1a**/ VT to discourage, dishearten ■ **descorazonarse** VR to get discouraged, lose heart

descorchador [deskortʃa'ðor] NM corkscrew

descorchar [deskor'tʃar] /**1a**/ VT to uncork, open

descorrer [desko'rrer] /**2a**/ VT (*cortina, cerrojo*) to draw back; (*velo*) to remove

descortés [deskor'tes] ADJ (*mal educado*) discourteous; (*grosero*) rude

descortesía [deskorte'sia] NF discourtesy; (*grosería*) rudeness

descoser [desko'ser] /**2a**/ VT to unstitch ■ **des-coserse** VR to come apart (at the seams); (*fam: descubrir un secreto*) to blurt out a secret; **descoserse de risa** to split one's sides laughing

descosido, -a [desko'siðo, a] ADJ (*costura*) unstitched; (*desordenado*) disjointed ▸ NM: **como un ~** (*obrar*) wildly; (*beber, comer*) to excess; (*estudiar*) like mad

descoyuntar [deskojun'tar] /**1a**/ VT (*Anat*) to dislocate; (*hechos*) to twist; **estar descoyuntado** (*persona*) to be double-jointed ■ **descoyuntarse** VR: **descoyuntarse un hueso** (*Anat*) to put a bone out of joint; **descoyuntarse de risa** (*fam*) to split one's sides laughing

descrédito [des'kreðito] NM discredit; **caer en ~** to fall into disrepute; **ir en ~ de** to be to the discredit of

descreído, -a [deskre'iðo, a] ADJ (*incrédulo*) incredulous; (*falto de fe*) unbelieving

descremado, -a [deskre'maðo, a] ADJ skimmed

descremar [deskre'mar] /**1a**/ VT (*leche*) to skim

★**describir** [deskri'βir] /**3a**/ VT to describe

★**descripción** [deskrip'θjon] NF description

descrito [des'krito] PP *de* **describir**

descuajar [deskwa'xar] /**1a**/ VT (*disolver*) to melt; (*planta*) to pull out by the roots; (*extirpar*) to eradicate, wipe out; (*desanimar*) to dishearten

descuajaringarse [deskwaxarin'garse] /**1h**/ VR to fall to bits

descuajaringue *etc* [deskwaxa'ringe] VB *ver* **descuajaringarse**

descuartice *etc* [deskwar'tiθe] VB *ver* **descuartizar**

descuartizar [deskwarti'θar] /**1f**/ VT (*animal*) to carve up, cut up; (*fig: hacer pedazos*) to tear apart

descubierto, -a [desku'βjerto, a] PP *de* **descubrir** ▸ ADJ uncovered, bare; (*persona*) bare-headed; (*cielo*) clear; (*coche*) open; (*campo*) treeless ▸ NM (*lugar*) open space; (*Com: en el presupuesto*) shortage; (*: bancario*) overdraft; **al ~** in the open; **poner al ~** to lay bare; **quedar al ~** to be exposed; **estar en ~** to be overdrawn

descubridor, a [deskuβri'ðor, a] NM/F discoverer

★**descubrimiento** [deskuβri'mjento] NM (*hallazgo*) discovery; (*de criminal, fraude*) detection; (*revelación*) revelation; (*de secreto etc*) disclosure; (*de estatua etc*) unveiling

★**descubrir** [desku'βrir] /**3a**/ VT to discover, find out; (*petróleo*) to strike; (*inaugurar*) to unveil; (*vislumbrar*) to detect; (*sacar a la luz: crimen*) to bring to light; (*revelar*) to reveal, show; (*poner al descubierto*) to expose to view; (*naipes*) to lay down; (*quitar la tapa de*) to uncover; (*cacerola*) to take the lid off; (*enterarse de: causa, solución*) to find out; (*divisar*) to see, make out; (*delatar*) to give away, betray ■ **descubrirse** VR to reveal o.s.; (*quitarse sombrero*) to take off one's hat; (*confesar*) to confess; (*fig: salir a la luz*) to come out *o* to light

descuelga *etc* [des'kwelɣa], **descuelgue** *etc* [des'kwelɣe] VB *ver* **descolgar**

descuelle etc [des'kweʎe] VB ver **descollar**

★**descuento** [des'kwento] VB ver **descontar**
▶ NM discount; **~ del 3%** 3% off; **con ~** at a discount; **~ por pago al contado** (Com) cash discount; **~ por volumen de compras** (Com) volume discount

★**descuidado, -a** [deskwi'ðaðo, a] ADJ (sin cuidado) careless; (desordenado) untidy; (olvidadizo) forgetful; (dejado) neglected; (desprevenido) unprepared

descuidar [deskwi'ðar] /1a/ VT (dejar) to neglect; (olvidar) to overlook ▶ VI: **¡descuida!** don't worry! ■ **descuidarse** VR (distraerse) to be careless; (estar desaliñado) to let o.s. go; (desprevenirse) to drop one's guard

descuido [des'kwiðo] NM (dejadez) carelessness; (olvido) negligence; (un error) oversight; **al ~** casually; (sin cuidado) carelessly; **al menor ~** if my etc attention wanders for a minute; **con ~** thoughtlessly; **por ~** by an oversight

---

desde ['desðe]

PREP **1** (lugar) from; **desde Burgos hasta mi casa hay 30 km** it's 30 km from Burgos to my house; **desde lejos** from a distance

2 (posición): **hablaba desde el balcón** she was speaking from the balcony

3 (tiempo: + adv, n): **desde ahora** from now on; **desde entonces/la boda** since then/the wedding; **desde niño** since I etc was a child; **desde tres años atrás** since three years ago

4 (tiempo: + vb) since; for; **nos conocemos desde 1988/desde hace 20 años** we've known each other since 1988/for 20 years; **no lo veo desde 2005/desde hace 5 años** I haven't seen him since 2005/for 5 years; **¿desde cuándo vives aquí?** how long have you lived here?

5 (gama): **desde los más lujosos hasta los más económicos** from the most luxurious to the most reasonably priced

6: desde luego (que no) of course (not)

▶ CONJ: **desde que: desde que recuerdo** for as long as I can remember; **desde que llegó no ha salido** he hasn't been out since he arrived

---

En expresiones de tiempo, desde se traduce por **since** para indicar cuándo comenzó una situación o una acción que continúa en el momento presente: Llevo aquí desde el viernes. **I have been here since Friday**.

Si la situación o la acción se da por terminada, se usa **from**: Desde aquel día no volvió a hablar del asunto. **From that day on, he never spoke about the subject again**.

La construcción desde ... hasta se traduce por **from ... until** o por **from .... to**: desde julio hasta octubre **from July until** o to **October**.

Desde hace expresa duración, por lo que su traducción es **for**: Estoy esperando desde hace una hora. **I have been waiting for an hour**.

---

desdecir [desðe'θir] /3o/ VI: **~ de** (no merecer) to be unworthy of; (no corresponder) to clash with ■ **desdecirse** VR: **desdecirse de** to go back on

desdén [des'ðen] NM scorn

desdentado, -a [desðen'taðo, a] ADJ toothless

desdeñable [desðe'naβle] ADJ contemptible; **nada ~** far from negligible, considerable

desdeñar [desðe'nar] /1a/ VT (despreciar) to scorn

desdeñoso, -a [desðe'noso, a] ADJ scornful

desdibujar [desðiβu'xar] /1a/ VT to blur (the outlines of) ■ **desdibujarse** VR to get blurred, fade (away); **el recuerdo se ha desdibujado** the memory has become blurred

desdicha [des'ðitʃa] NF (desgracia) misfortune; (infelicidad) unhappiness

desdichado, -a [desði'tʃaðo, a] ADJ (sin suerte) unlucky; (infeliz) unhappy; (día) ill-fated ▶ NM/F (pobre desgraciado) poor devil

desdicho, -a [des'ðitʃo, a] PP de **desdecir** ▶ NF (desgracia) misfortune; (infelicidad) unhappiness

desdiciendo etc [desði'θjendo] VB ver **desdecir**

desdiga etc [des'ðiɣa], **desdije** etc [des'ðixe] VB ver **desdecir**

desdoblado, -a [desðo'βlaðo, a] ADJ (personalidad) split

desdoblar [desðo'βlar] /1a/ VT (extender) to spread out; (desplegar) to unfold

deseable [dese'aβle] ADJ desirable

★**desear** [dese'ar] /1a/ VT to want, desire, wish for; **¿qué desea la señora?** (tienda etc) what can I do for you, madam?; **estoy deseando que esto termine** I'm longing for this to finish

desecar [dese'kar] /1g/ VT, **desecarse** VR to dry up

desechable [dese'tʃaβle] ADJ (envase etc) disposable

desechar [dese'tʃar] /1a/ VT (basura) to throw out o away; (ideas) to reject, discard; (miedo) to cast aside; (plan) to drop

desecho [de'setʃo] NM (desprecio) contempt; (lo peor) dregs pl; **de ~** (hierro) scrap; (producto) waste; (ropa) cast-off ■ **desechos** NMPL rubbish sg, waste sg

desembalar [desemba'lar] /1a/ VT to unpack

desembarace etc [desemba'raθe] VB ver **desembarazar**

desembarazado, -a [desembara'θaðo, a] ADJ (libre) clear, free; (desenvuelto) free and easy

desembarazar [desembara'θar] /1f/ VT (desocupar) to clear; (desenredar) to free ■ **desembarazarse** VR: **desembarazarse de** to free o.s. of, get rid of

desembarazo [desemba'raθo] NM (acto) clearing; (Am: parto) birth; (desenfado) ease

desembarcadero [desembarka'ðero] NM quay

★**desembarcar** [desembar'kar] /**1g**/ vT (*personas*) to land; (*mercancías etc*) to unload ▶ vI (*de barco, avión*) to disembark

desembarco [desem'barko] NM landing

desembargar [desembar'ɣar] /**1h**/ vT (*gen*) to free; (*Jur*) to remove the embargo on

desembargue *etc* [desem'βarɣe] VB *ver* **desembargar**

desembarque *etc* [desem'barke] VB *ver* **desembarcar** ▶ NM disembarkation; (*de pasajeros*) landing; (*de mercancías*) unloading

desembocadura [desemboka'ðura] NF (*de río*) mouth; (*de calle*) opening

desembocar [desembo'kar] /**1g**/ vI: **~ en** to flow into; (*fig*) to result in

desemboce *etc* [desem'boθe] VB *ver* **desembozar**

desembolsar [desembol'sar] /**1a**/ vT (*pagar*) to pay out; (*gastar*) to lay out

desembolso [desem'bolso] NM payment

desemboque *etc* [desem'boke] VB *ver* **desembocar**

desembozar [desembo'θar] /**1f**/ vT to unmask

desembragar [desembra'ɣar] /**1h**/ vT (*Tec*) to disengage, release ▶ vI (*Auto*) to declutch

desembrague *etc* [desem'βraɣe] VB *ver* **desembragar**

desembrollar [desembro'ʎar] /**1a**/ vT (*madeja*) to unravel; (*asunto, malentendido*) to sort out

desembuchar [desembu'tʃar] /**1a**/ vT to disgorge; (*fig*) to come out with ▶ vI (*confesar*) to spill the beans (*fam*); **¡desembucha!** out with it!

desemejante [deseme'xante] ADJ dissimilar; **~ de** different from, unlike

desemejanza [deseme'xanθa] NF dissimilarity

desempacar [desempa'kar] /**1g**/ vT (*esp Am*) to unpack

desempañar [desempa'ɲar] /**1a**/ vT (*cristal*) to clean, demist

desempaque *etc* [desem'pake] VB *ver* **desempacar**

desempaquetar [desempake'tar] /**1a**/ vT (*regalo*) to unwrap; (*mercancía*) to unpack

desempatar [desempa'tar] /**1a**/ vI to break a tie; **volvieron a jugar para ~** they held a play-off

desempate [desem'pate] NM (*Fútbol*) replay, play-off; (*Tenis*) tie-break(er)

desempeñar [desempe'ɲar] /**1a**/ vT (*cargo*) to hold; (*papel*) to play; (*deber, función*) to perform, carry out; (*lo empeñado*) to redeem; **~ un papel** (*fig*) to play a role ■ **desempeñarse** VR to get out of debt

desempeño [desem'peɲo] NM occupation; (*de lo empeñado*) redeeming; **de mucho ~** very capable

★**desempleado, -a** [desemple'aðo, a] ADJ unemployed, out of work ▶ NM/F unemployed person

★**desempleo** [desem'pleo] NM unemployment

desempolvar [desempol'βar] /**1a**/ vT (*muebles etc*) to dust; (*lo olvidado*) to revive

desencadenar [desenkaðe'nar] /**1a**/ vT to unchain; (*ira*) to unleash; (*provocar*) to cause, set off ■ **desencadenarse** VR to break loose; (*tormenta*) to burst; (*guerra*) to break out; **se desencadenó una lucha violenta** a violent struggle ensued

desencajar [desenka'xar] /**1a**/ vT (*hueso*) to put out of joint; (*mandíbula*) to dislocate; (*mecanismo, pieza*) to disconnect, disengage

desencantar [desenkan'tar] /**1a**/ vT to disillusion, disenchant

desencanto [desen'kanto] NM disillusionment, disenchantment

desenchufar [desentʃu'far] /**1a**/ vT to unplug, disconnect

desenfadado, -a [desenfa'ðaðo, a] ADJ (*desenvuelto*) uninhibited; (*descarado*) forward; (*en el vestir*) casual

desenfado [desen'faðo] NM (*libertad*) freedom; (*comportamiento*) free and easy manner; (*descaro*) forwardness; (*desenvoltura*) self-confidence

desenfocado, -a [desenfo'kaðo, a] ADJ (*Foto*) out of focus

desenfrenado, -a [desenfre'naðo, a] ADJ (*descontrolado*) uncontrolled; (*inmoderado*) unbridled

desenfrenarse [desenfre'narse] /**1a**/ VR (*persona: desmandarse*) to lose all self-control; (*multitud*) to run riot; (*tempestad*) to burst; (*viento*) to rage

desenfreno [desen'freno] NM (*vicio*) wildness; (*falta de control*) lack of self-control; (*de pasiones*) unleashing

desenganchar [desengan'tʃar] /**1a**/ vT (*gen*) to unhook; (*Ferro*) to uncouple; (*Tec*) to disengage

desengañar [desenga'ɲar] /**1a**/ vT to disillusion; (*abrir los ojos a*) to open the eyes of ■ **desengañarse** VR to become disillusioned; **¡desengáñate!** don't you believe it!

desengaño [desen'gaɲo] NM disillusionment; (*decepción*) disappointment; **sufrir un ~ amoroso** to be disappointed in love

desengrasar [desengra'sar] /**1a**/ vT to degrease

desenlace *etc* [desen'laθe] VB *ver* **desenlazar** ▶ NM outcome; (*Lit*) ending

desenlazar [desenla'θar] /**1f**/ vT (*desatar*) to untie; (*problema*) to solve; (*aclarar: asunto*) to unravel ■ **desenlazarse** VR (*desatarse*) to come undone; (*Lit*) to end

desenmarañar [desenmara'ɲar] /**1a**/ vT (*fig*) to unravel

desenmascarar [desenmaska'rar] /**1a**/ vT to unmask, expose

desenredar [desenre'ðar] /**1a**/ vT (*pelo*) to untangle; (*problema*) to sort out

desenrollar [desenroˈʎar] /1a/ VT to unroll, unwind

desenroscar [desenrosˈkar] /1g/ VT (*tornillo etc*) to unscrew

desenrosque *etc* [desenˈroske] VB *ver* **desenroscar**

desentenderse [desentenˈderse] /2g/ VR: ~ **de** to pretend not to know about; (*apartarse*) to have nothing to do with

desentendido, -a [desentenˈdiðo, a] ADJ: **hacerse el** ~ to pretend not to notice; **se hizo el** ~ he didn't take the hint

desenterrar [desenteˈrrar] /1j/ VT to exhume; (*tesoro, fig*) to unearth, dig up

desentierre *etc* [desenˈtjerre] VB *ver* **desenterrar**

desentonar [desentoˈnar] /1a/ VI (*Mus*) to sing (*o play*) out of tune; (*no encajar*) to be out of place; (*color*) to clash

desentorpecer [desentorpeˈθer] /2d/ VT (*miembro*) to stretch; (*fam: persona*) to polish up

desentorpezca *etc* [desentorˈpeθka] VB *ver* **desentorpecer**

desentrañar [desentraˈɲar] /1a/ VT (*misterio*) to unravel

desentrenado, -a [desentreˈnaðo, a] ADJ out of training

desentumecer [desentumeˈθer] /2d/ VT (*pierna etc*) to stretch; (*Deporte*) to loosen up

desentumezca *etc* [desentuˈmeθka] VB *ver* **desentumecer**

desenvainar [desembaiˈnar] /1a/ VT (*espada*) to draw, unsheathe

desenvoltura [desembolˈtura] NF (*libertad, gracia*) ease; (*descaro*) free and easy manner; (*al hablar*) fluency

desenvolver [desembolˈβer] /2h/ VT (*paquete*) to unwrap; (*fig*) to develop ■ **desenvolverse** VR (*desarrollarse*) to unfold, develop; (*suceder*) to go off; (*prosperar*) to prosper; (*arreglárselas*) to cope

desenvolvimiento [desembolβiˈmjento] NM (*desarrollo*) development; (*de idea*) exposition

desenvuelto, -a [desemˈbwelto, a] PP *de* **desenvolver** ▸ ADJ (*suelto*) easy; (*desenfadado*) confident; (*al hablar*) fluent; (*pey*) forward

desenvuelva *etc* [desemˈbwelβa] VB *ver* **desenvolver**

deseo [deˈseo] NM desire, wish; ~ **de saber** thirst for knowledge; **buen** ~ good intentions *pl*; **arder en deseos de algo** to yearn for sth

deseoso, -a [deseˈoso, a] ADJ: **estar** ~ **de hacer** to be anxious to do

deseque *etc* [deˈseke] VB *ver* **desecar**

desequilibrado, -a [desekiliˈβraðo, a] ADJ unbalanced ▸ NM/F unbalanced person; ~ **mental** mentally disturbed person

desequilibrar [desekiliˈβrar] /1a/ VT (*mente*) to unbalance; (*objeto*) to throw out of balance; (*persona*) to throw off balance

desequilibrio [desekiˈliβrio] NM (*mental*) unbalance; (*entre cantidades*) imbalance; (*Med*) unbalanced mental condition

desertar [deserˈtar] /1a/ VT (*Jur: derecho de apelación*) to forfeit ▸ VI to desert; ~ **de sus deberes** to neglect one's duties

desértico, -a [deˈsertiko, a] ADJ desert *cpd*; (*vacío*) deserted

desertor, a [deserˈtor, a] NM/F deserter

desesperación [desesperaˈθjon] NF desperation, despair; (*irritación*) fury; **es una** ~ it's maddening; **es una** ~ **tener que ...** it's infuriating to have to ...

desesperado, -a [desespeˈraðo, a] ADJ (*persona: sin esperanza*) desperate; (*caso, situación*) hopeless; (*esfuerzo*) furious ▸ NM: **como un** ~ like mad ▸ NF: **hacer algo a la desesperada** to do sth as a last resort *o* in desperation

desesperance *etc* [desespeˈranθe] VB *ver* **desesperanzar**

desesperante [desespeˈrante] ADJ (*exasperante*) infuriating; (*persona*) hopeless

desesperanzar [desesperanˈθar] /1f/ VT to drive to despair ■ **desesperanzarse** VR to lose hope, despair

desesperar [desespeˈrar] /1a/ VT to drive to despair; (*exasperar*) to drive to distraction ▸ VI: ~ **de** to despair of ■ **desesperarse** VR to despair, lose hope

desespero [desesˈpero] NM (*AM*) despair

desestabilice *etc* [desestaβiˈliθe] VB *ver* **desestabilizar**

desestabilizar [desestaβiliˈθar] /1f/ VT to destabilize

desestimar [desestiˈmar] /1a/ VT (*menospreciar*) to have a low opinion of; (*rechazar*) to reject

desfachatez [desfatʃaˈteθ] NF (*insolencia*) impudence; (*descaro*) rudeness

desfalco [desˈfalko] NM embezzlement

desfallecer [desfaʎeˈθer] /2d/ VI (*perder las fuerzas*) to become weak; (*desvanecerse*) to faint

desfallecido, -a [desfaʎeˈθiðo, a] ADJ (*débil*) weak

desfallezca *etc* [desfaˈʎeθka] VB *ver* **desfallecer**

desfasado, -a [desfaˈsaðo, a] ADJ (*anticuado*) old-fashioned; (*Tec*) out of phase

desfasar [desfaˈsar] /1a/ VT to phase out

desfase [desˈfase] NM (*diferencia*) gap

desfavorable [desfaβoˈraβle] ADJ unfavourable

desfavorecer [desfaβoreˈθer] /2d/ VT (*sentar mal*) not to suit

desfavorezca *etc* [desfaβoˈreθka] VB *ver* **desfavorecer**

desfiguración [desfiɣuraˈθjon] NF, **desfiguramiento** [desfiɣuraˈmjento] NM (*de persona*) disfigurement; (*de monumento*) defacement; (*Foto*) blurring

desfigurar [desfiɣuˈrar] /1a/ VT (*cara*) to disfigure; (*cuerpo*) to deform; (*cuadro, monumento*) to deface; (*Foto*) to blur; (*sentido*) to twist; (*suceso*) to misrepresent

desfiladero [desfila'ðero] NM gorge, defile

desfilar [desfi'lar] /1a/ VI to parade; **desfilaron ante el general** they marched past the general

desfile [des'file] NM procession; (*Mil*) parade; **~ de modelos** fashion show

desflorar [desflo'rar] /1a/ VT (*mujer*) to deflower; (*arruinar*) to tarnish; (*asunto*) to touch on

desfogar [desfo'ɣar] /1h/ VT (*fig*) to vent ▸ VI (*Naut: tormenta*) to burst ■ **desfogarse** VR (*fig*) to let off steam

desfogue *etc* [des'foɣe] VB *ver* **desfogar**

desgajar [desɣa'xar] /1a/ VT (*arrancar*) to tear off; (*romper*) to break off; (*naranja*) to split into segments ■ **desgajarse** VR to come off

desgana [des'ɣana] NF (*falta de apetito*) loss of appetite; (*renuencia*) unwillingness; **hacer algo a ~** to do sth unwillingly

desganado, -a [desɣa'naðo, a] ADJ: **estar ~** (*sin apetito*) to have no appetite; (*sin entusiasmo*) to have lost interest

desgañitarse [desɣaɲi'tarse] /1a/ VR to shout o.s. hoarse

desgarbado, -a [desɣar'βaðo, a] ADJ (*sin gracia*) clumsy, ungainly

desgarrador, a [desɣarra'ðor, a] ADJ heartrending

desgarrar [desɣa'rrar] /1a/ VT to tear (up); (*fig*) to shatter

desgarro [des'ɣarro] NM (*en tela*) tear; (*aflicción*) grief; (*descaro*) impudence

desgastar [desɣas'tar] /1a/ VT (*deteriorar*) to wear away o down; (*estropear*) to spoil ■ **desgastarse** VR to get worn out

desgaste [des'ɣaste] NM wear (and tear); (*de roca*) erosion; (*de cuerda*) fraying; (*de metal*) corrosion; **~ económico** drain on one's resources

desglosar [desɣlo'sar] /1a/ VT to detach; (*factura*) to break down

desgobernar [desɣoβer'nar] /1j/ VB (*Pol*) to misgovern, misrule; (*asunto*) to handle badly; (*Anat*) to dislocate

desgobierno *etc* [desɣo'βjerno] VB *ver* **desgobernar** ▸ NM (*Pol*) misgovernment, misrule

★**desgracia** [des'ɣraθja] NF misfortune; (*accidente*) accident; (*vergüenza*) disgrace; (*contratiempo*) setback; **por ~** unfortunately; **en el accidente no hay que lamentar desgracias personales** there were no casualties in the accident; **caer en ~** to fall from grace; **tener la ~ de** to be unlucky enough to

desgraciadamente [desɣraθjaða'mente] ADV unfortunately

desgraciado, -a [desɣra'θjaðo, a] ADJ (*sin suerte*) unlucky, unfortunate; (*miserable*) wretched; (*infeliz*) miserable ▸ NM/F (*malvado*) swine; (*infeliz*) poor creature; **¡esa radio desgraciada!** (*esp Am*) that lousy radio!

desgraciar [desɣra'θjar] /1b/ VT (*estropear*) to spoil; (*ofender*) to displease

desgranar [desɣra'nar] /1a/ VT (*trigo*) to thresh; (*guisantes*) to shell; **~ un racimo** to pick the grapes from a bunch; **~ mentiras** to come out with a string of lies

desgravación [desɣraβa'θjon] NF (*Com*): **~ de impuestos** tax relief; **~ personal** personal allowance

desgravar [desɣra'βar] /1a/ VT (*producto*) to reduce the tax o duty on

desgreñado, -a [desɣre'naðo, a] ADJ dishevelled

desguace [des'ɣwaθe] NM (*de coches*) scrapping; (*lugar*) scrapyard

desguazar [desɣwa'θar] /1f/ VT (*coche*) to scrap

deshabitado, -a [desaβi'taðo, a] ADJ uninhabited

deshabitar [desaβi'tar] /1a/ VT (*casa*) to leave empty; (*despoblar*) to depopulate

deshacer [desa'θer] /2r/ VT (*lo hecho*) to undo, unmake; (*proyectos: arruinar*) to spoil; (*casa*) to break up; (*Tec*) to take apart; (*enemigo*) to defeat; (*diluir*) to melt; (*contrato*) to break; (*intriga*) to solve; (*cama*) to strip; (*maleta*) to unpack; (*paquete*) to unwrap; (*nudo*) to untie; (*costura*) to unpick ■ **deshacerse** VR (*desatarse*) to come undone; (*estropearse*) to be spoiled; (*descomponerse*) to fall to pieces; (*disolverse*) to melt; (*despedazarse*) to come apart o undone; **deshacerse de** to get rid of; (*Com*) to dump, unload; **deshacerse en** (*cumplidos, elogios*) to be lavish with; **deshacerse en lágrimas** to burst into tears; **deshacerse por algo** to be crazy about sth

deshaga *etc* [de'saɣa], **desharé** *etc* [desa're] VB *ver* **deshacer**

desharrapado, -a [desarra'paðo, a] ADJ = **desarrapado**

deshecho, -a [de'setʃo, a] PP *de* **deshacer** ▸ ADJ (*lazo, nudo*) undone; (*roto*) smashed; (*despedazado*) in pieces; (*cama*) unmade; (*Med: persona*) weak, emaciated; (: *salud*) broken; **estoy ~** I'm shattered

deshelar [dese'lar] /1j/ VT (*cañería*) to thaw; (*heladera*) to defrost

desheredar [desere'ðar] /1a/ VT to disinherit

deshice *etc* [de'siθe] VB *ver* **deshacer**

deshidratación [desiðrata'θjon] NF dehydration

deshidratar [desiðra'tar] /1a/ VT to dehydrate

deshielo [des'jelo] VB *ver* **deshelar** ▸ NM thaw

deshilachar [desila'tʃar] /1a/ VT, **deshilacharse** VR to fray

deshilar [desi'lar] /1a/ VT (*tela*) to unravel

deshilvanado, -a [desilβa'naðo, a] ADJ (*fig*) disjointed, incoherent

deshinchar [desin'tʃar] /1a/ VT (*neumático*) to let down; (*herida etc*) to reduce (the swelling of) ■ **deshincharse** VR (*neumático*) to go flat; (*hinchazón*) to go down

deshojar [deso'xar] /**1a**/ VT (*árbol*) to strip the leaves off; (*flor*) to pull the petals off ■ **deshojarse** VR to lose its leaves *etc*

deshollinar [desoʎi'nar] /**1a**/ VT (*chimenea*) to sweep

deshonesto, -a [deso'nesto, a] ADJ (*no honrado*) dishonest; (*indecente*) indecent

deshonor [deso'nor] NM dishonour, disgrace; (*un deshonor*) insult, affront

deshonra [de'sonra] NF (*deshonor*) dishonour; (*vergüenza*) shame

deshonrar [deson'rar] /**1a**/ VT to dishonour

deshonroso, -a [deson'roso, a] ADJ dishonourable, disgraceful

deshora [de'sora]: **a ~** *adv* at the wrong time; (*llegar*) unexpectedly; (*acostarse*) at some unearthly hour

deshuesadero [deswesa'ðero] NM (*AM*) junkyard

deshuesar [deswe'sar] /**1a**/ VT (*carne*) to bone; (*fruta*) to stone

desidia [de'siðja] NF (*pereza*) idleness

★**desierto, -a** [de'sjerto, a] ADJ (*casa, calle, negocio*) deserted; (*paisaje*) bleak ▶ NM desert

designación [desiɣna'θjon] NF (*para un cargo*) appointment; (*nombre*) designation

designar [desiɣ'nar] /**1a**/ VT (*nombrar*) to designate; (*indicar*) to fix

designio [de'siɣnjo] NM plan; **con el ~ de** with the intention of

desigual [desi'ɣwal] ADJ (*lucha*) unequal; (*diferente*) different; (*terreno*) uneven; (*tratamiento*) unfair; (*cambiadizo: tiempo*) changeable; (: *carácter*) unpredictable

desigualdad [desiɣwal'ðað] NF (*Econ, Pol*) inequality; (*de carácter, tiempo*) unpredictability; (*de escritura*) unevenness; (*de terreno*) roughness

desilusión [desilu'sjon] NF disillusionment; (*decepción*) disappointment

desilusionar [desilusjo'nar] /**1a**/ VT to disillusion; (*decepcionar*) to disappoint ■ **desilusionarse** VR to become disillusioned

desinencia [desi'nenθja] NF (*Ling*) ending

desinfectar [desinfek'tar] /**1a**/ VT to disinfect

desinfestar [desinfes'tar] /**1a**/ VT to decontaminate

desinflación [desinfla'θjon] NF (*Com*) disinflation

desinflar [desin'flar] /**1a**/ VT to deflate ■ **desinflarse** VR (*neumático*) to go down *o* flat

desinstalar [desinsta'lar] /**1a**/ VT uninstall

desintegración [desinteɣra'θjon] NF disintegration; **~ nuclear** nuclear fission

desintegrar [desinte'ɣrar] /**1a**/ VT (*gen*) to disintegrate; (*átomo*) to split; (*grupo*) to break up ■ **desintegrarse** VR to disintegrate; to split; to break up

desinterés [desinte'res] NM (*desgana*) lack of interest; (*altruismo*) unselfishness

desinteresado, -a [desintere'saðo, a] ADJ (*imparcial*) disinterested; (*altruista*) unselfish

desintoxicación [desintoksika'θjon] NF detox

desintoxicar [desintoksi'kar] /**1g**/ VT to detoxify ■ **desintoxicarse** VR (*drogadicto*) to undergo detoxification; **desintoxicarse de** (*rutina, trabajo*) to get away from

desintoxique *etc* [desintok'sike] VB *ver* **desintoxicar**

desistir [desis'tir] /**3a**/ VI (*renunciar*) to stop, desist; **~ de** (*empresa*) to give up; (*derecho*) to waive

deslavazado, -a [deslaβa'θaðo, a] ADJ (*lacio*) limp; (*desteñido*) faded; (*insípido*) colourless; (*incoherente*) disjointed

desleal [desle'al] ADJ (*infiel*) disloyal; (*Com: competencia*) unfair

deslealtad [desleal'tað] NF disloyalty

desleído, -a [desle'iðo, a] ADJ weak, woolly

desleír [desle'ir] /**3l**/ VT (*líquido*) to dilute; (*sólido*) to dissolve

deslenguado, -a [deslen'gwaðo, a] ADJ (*grosero*) foul-mouthed

deslía *etc* [des'lia] VB *ver* **desleír**

desliar [des'ljar] /**1c**/ VT (*desatar*) to untie; (*paquete*) to open ■ **desliarse** VR to come undone

deslice *etc* [des'liθe] VB *ver* **deslizar**

desliendo *etc* [desli'endo] VB *ver* **desleír**

desligar [desli'ɣar] /**1h**/ VT (*desatar*) to untie, undo; (*separar*) to separate ■ **desligarse** VR (*de un compromiso*) to extricate o.s.

desligue *etc* [des'liɣe] VB *ver* **desligar**

deslindar [deslin'dar] /**1a**/ VT (*señalar las lindes de*) to mark out, fix the boundaries of; (*fig*) to define

desliz [des'liθ] NM (*fig*) lapse; **~ de lengua** slip of the tongue; **cometer un ~** to slip up

deslizar [desli'θar] /**1f**/ VT to slip, slide ■ **deslizarse** VR (*escurrirse: persona*) to slip, slide; (: *coche*) to skid; (*aguas mansas*) to flow gently; (*error*) to creep in; (*tiempo*) to pass; (*persona: irse*) to slip away; **deslizarse en un cuarto** to slip into a room

deslomar [deslo'mar] /**1a**/ VT (*romper el lomo de*) to break the back of; (*fig*) to wear out ■ **deslomarse** VR (*fig: fam*) to work one's guts out

deslucido, -a [deslu'θiðo, a] ADJ dull; (*torpe*) awkward, graceless; (*deslustrado*) tarnished; (*fracasado*) unsuccessful; **quedar ~** to make a poor impression

deslucir [deslu'θir] /**3f**/ VT (*deslustrar*) to tarnish; (*estropear*) to spoil, ruin; (*persona*) to discredit; **la lluvia deslució el acto** the rain ruined the ceremony

deslumbrar [deslum'brar] /**1a**/ VT (*con la luz*) to dazzle; (*cegar*) to blind; (*impresionar*) to dazzle; (*dejar perplejo a*) to puzzle, confuse

deslustrar [deslus'trar] /**1a**/ VT (*vidrio*) to frost; (*quitar lustre a*) to dull; (*reputación*) to sully

desluzca *etc* [des'luθka] VB *ver* **deslucir**

desmadrarse [desma'ðrarse] /**1a**/ VR (*fam: descontrolarse*) to run wild; (: *divertirse*) to let one's hair down

desmadre [des'maðre] NM (*fam: desorganización*) chaos; (: *jaleo*) commotion

desmán [des'man] NM (*exceso*) outrage; (*abuso de poder*) abuse

desmandarse [desman'darse] /**1a**/ VR (*portarse mal*) to behave badly; (*excederse*) to get out of hand; (*caballo*) to bolt

desmano [des'mano]: **a ~** *adv*: **me coge** *o* **pilla a ~** it's out of my way

desmantelar [desmante'lar] /**1a**/ VT (*deshacer*) to dismantle; (*casa*) to strip; (*organización*) to disband; (*Mil*) to raze; (*andamio*) to take down; (*Naut*) to unrig

desmaquillador [desmakiλa'ðor] NM make-up remover

desmaquillarse [desmaki'λarse] /**1a**/ VR to take off one's make-up

desmarcarse [desmar'karse] /**1g**/ VR: **~ de** (*Deporte*) to get clear of; (*fig*) to distance o.s. from

desmayado, -a [desma'jaðo, a] ADJ (*sin sentido*) unconscious; (*carácter*) dull; (*débil*) faint, weak; (*color*) pale

desmayar [desma'jar] /**1a**/ VI to lose heart ■ **desmayarse** VR (*Med*) to faint

desmayo [des'majo] NM (*Med: acto*) faint; (: *estado*) unconsciousness; (: *depresión*) dejection; (*de voz*) faltering; **sufrir un ~** to have a fainting fit

desmedido, -a [desme'ðiðo, a] ADJ excessive; (*ambición*) boundless

desmejorado, -a [desmexo'raðo, a] ADJ: **está muy desmejorada** (*Med*) she's not looking too well

desmejorar [desmexo'rar] /**1a**/ VT (*dañar*) to impair, spoil; (*Med*) to weaken

desmembración [desmembra'θjon] NF dismemberment; (*fig*) break-up

desmembrar [desmem'brar] /**1j**/ VT (*Med*) to dismember; (*fig*) to separate

desmemoriado, -a [desmemo'rjaðo, a] ADJ forgetful, absent-minded

desmentir [desmen'tir] /**3i**/ VT (*contradecir*) to contradict; (*refutar*) to deny; (*rumor*) to scotch ► VI: **~ de** to refute ■ **desmentirse** VR to contradict o.s.

desmenuce *etc* [desme'nuθe] VB *ver* **desmenuzar**

desmenuzar [desmenu'θar] /**1f**/ VT (*deshacer*) to crumble; (*carne*) to chop; (*examinar*) to examine closely

desmerecer [desmere'θer] /**2d**/ VT to be unworthy of ► VI (*deteriorarse*) to deteriorate

desmerezca *etc* [desme're θka] VB *ver* **desmerecer**

desmesurado, -a [desmesu'raðo, a] ADJ (*desmedido*) disproportionate; (*enorme*) enormous; (*ambición*) boundless; (*descarado*) insolent

desmiembre *etc* [des'mjembre] VB *ver* **desmembrar**

desmienta *etc* [des'mjenta] VB *ver* **desmentir**

desmigajar [desmiɣa'xar] /**1a**/, **desmigar** [desmi'ɣar] /**1h**/ VT to crumble

desmigue *etc* [des'miɣe] VB *ver* **desmigajar**

desmilitarice *etc* [desmilita'riθe] VB *ver* **desmilitarizar**

desmilitarizar [desmilitari'θar] /**1f**/ VT to demilitarize

desmintiendo *etc* [desmin'tjendo] VB *ver* **desmentir**

desmochar [desmo'tʃar] /**1a**/ VT (*árbol*) to lop; (*texto*) to cut, hack about

desmontable [desmon'taβle] ADJ (*que se quita*) detachable; (*en compartimientos*) sectional; (*que se puede plegar etc*) collapsible, folding

desmontar [desmon'tar] /**1a**/ VT (*deshacer*) to dismantle; (*motor*) to strip down; (*máquina*) to take apart; (*escopeta*) to uncock; (*tienda de campaña*) to take down; (*tierra*) to level; (*quitar los árboles a*) to clear; (*jinete*) to throw ► VI to dismount

desmonte [des'monte] NM (*de tierra*) levelling; (*de árboles*) clearing; (*terreno*) levelled ground; (*Ferro*) cutting

desmoralice *etc* [desmora'liθe] VB *ver* **desmoralizar**

desmoralizador, a [desmoraliθa'ðor, a] ADJ demoralizing

desmoralizar [desmorali'θar] /**1f**/ VT to demoralize

desmoronado, -a [desmoro'naðo, a] ADJ (*casa, edificio*) dilapidated

desmoronamiento [desmorona'mjento] NM (*tb fig*) crumbling

desmoronar [desmoro'nar] /**1a**/ VI to wear away, erode ■ **desmoronarse** VR (*edificio, dique*) to collapse; (*economía*) to decline

desmovilice *etc* [desmoβi'liθe] VB *ver* **desmovilizar**

desmovilizar [desmoβili'θar] /**1f**/ VT to demobilize

desnacionalización [desnaθjonaliθa'θjon] NF denationalization

desnacionalizado, -a [desnaθjonali'θaðo, a] ADJ (*industria*) denationalized; (*persona*) stateless

desnatado, -a [desna'taðo, a] ADJ (*leche*) skimmed; (*yogur, queso*) low-fat

desnatar [desna'tar] /**1a**/ VT (*leche*) to skim; **leche sin ~** whole milk

desnaturalice *etc* [desnatura'liθe] VB *ver* **desnaturalizar**

desnaturalizado, -a [desnaturali'θaðo, a] ADJ (*persona*) unnatural; **alcohol ~** methylated spirits

desnaturalizar [desnaturali'θar] /**1f**/ VT (*Quí-*

mica) to denature; (*corromper*) to pervert; (*sentido de algo*) to distort ■ **desnaturalizarse** VR (*perder la nacionalidad*) to give up one's nationality

desnivel [desni'βel] NM (*de terreno*) unevenness; (Pol) inequality; (*diferencia*) difference

desnivelar [desniβe'lar] /**1a**/ VT (*terreno*) to make uneven; (*fig: desequilibrar*) to unbalance; (*balanza*) to tip

desnuclearizado, -a [desnukleari'θaðo, a] ADJ: **región desnuclearizada** nuclear-free zone

desnudar [desnu'ðar] /**1a**/ VT (*desvestir*) to undress; (*despojar*) to strip ■ **desnudarse** VR (*desvestirse*) to get undressed

desnudez [desnu'ðeθ] NF (*de persona*) nudity; (*fig*) bareness

desnudo, -a [des'nuðo, a] ADJ (*cuerpo*) naked; (*árbol, brazo*) bare; (*paisaje*) flat; (*estilo*) unadorned; (*verdad*) plain; ~ **de** devoid o bereft of ▶ NM nude; **la retrató al** ~ he painted her in the nude; **poner al** ~ to lay bare

desnutrición [desnutri'θjon] NF malnutrition

desnutrido, -a [desnu'triðo, a] ADJ undernourished

★**desobedecer** [desoβeðe'θer] /**2d**/ VT, VI to disobey

desobedezca etc [desoβe'ðeθka] VB ver **desobedecer**

desobediencia [desoβe'ðjenθja] NF disobedience

★**desobediente** [desoβe'ðjente] ADJ disobedient

desocupación [desokupa'θjon] NF (AM) unemployment

desocupado, -a [desoku'paðo, a] ADJ at leisure; (AM: *desempleado*) unemployed; (*deshabitado*) empty, vacant

desocupar [desoku'par] /**1a**/ VT to vacate ■ **desocuparse** VR (*quedar libre*) to be free; **se ha desocupado aquella mesa** that table's free now

★**desodorante** [desoðo'rante] NM deodorant

desoiga etc [de'soiγa] VB ver **desoír**

desoír [deso'ir] /**3p**/ VT to ignore, disregard

desolación [desola'θjon] NF (*de lugar*) desolation; (*fig*) grief

desolar [deso'lar] /**1a**/ VT to ruin, lay waste

desollar [deso'ʎar] /**1l**/ VT (*quitar la piel a*) to skin; (*criticar*): ~ **vivo a** to criticize unmercifully

desorbitado, -a [desorβi'taðo, a] ADJ (*excesivo: ambición*) boundless; (: *deseos*) excessive; (: *precio*) exorbitant; **con los ojos desorbitados** pop-eyed

desorbitar [desorβi'tar] /**1a**/ VT (*exagerar*) to exaggerate; (*interpretar mal*) to misinterpret ■ **desorbitarse** VR (*persona*) to lose one's sense of proportion; (*asunto*) to get out of hand

desorden [de'sorðen] NM confusion; (*de casa, cuarto*) mess; (*político*) disorder; **en** ~ (*gente*) in confusion ■ **desórdenes** NMPL (*alborotos*) disturbances; (*excesos*) excesses

desordenado, -a [desorðe'naðo, a] ADJ (*habitación, persona*) untidy; (*objetos revueltos*) in a mess, jumbled; (*conducta*) disorderly

desordenar [desorðe'nar] /**1a**/ VT (*gen*) to disarrange; (*pelo*) to mess up; (*cuarto*) to make a mess in; (*causar confusión a*) to throw into confusion

desorganice etc [desorγa'niθe] VB ver **desorganizar**

desorganización [desorγaniθa'θjon] NF (*de persona*) disorganization; (*en empresa, oficina*) disorder, chaos

desorganizar [desorγani'θar] /**1f**/ VT to disorganize

desorientar [desorjen'tar] /**1a**/ VT (*extraviar*) to mislead; (*confundir, desconcertar*) to confuse ■ **desorientarse** VR (*perderse*) to lose one's way

desovar [deso'βar] /**1l**/ VI (*peces*) to spawn; (*insectos*) to lay eggs

desoyendo etc [deso'jendo] VB ver **desoír**

despabilado, -a [despaβi'laðo, a] ADJ (*despierto*) wide-awake; (*fig*) alert, sharp

despabilar [despaβi'lar] /**1a**/ VT (*despertar*) to wake up; (*fig: persona*) to liven up; (*trabajo*) to get through quickly ▶ VI, **despabilarse** VR to wake up; (*fig*) to get a move on

despachar [despa'tʃar] /**1a**/ VT (*negocio*) to do, complete; (*resolver: problema*) to settle; (: *correspondencia*) to deal with; (*fam: comida*) to polish off; (: *bebida*) to knock back; (*enviar*) to send, dispatch; (*vender*) to sell, deal in; (Com: *cliente*) to attend to; (: *billete*) to issue; (*mandar ir*) to send away ▶ VI (*decidirse*) to get things settled; (*apresurarse*) to hurry up; **¿quién despacha?** is anybody serving? ■ **despacharse** VR to finish off; (*apresurarse*) to hurry up; **despacharse de algo** to get rid of sth; **despacharse a su gusto con algn** to give sb a piece of one's mind

★**despacho** [des'patʃo] NM (*oficina*) office; (: *en una casa*) study; (*de paquetes*) dispatch; (Com: *venta*) sale (of goods); (: *comunicación*) message; ~ **de billetes** o (AM) **boletos** booking office; ~ **de localidades** box office; **géneros sin** ~ unsaleable goods; **tener buen** ~ to find a ready sale

despachurrar [despatʃu'rrar] /**1a**/ VT (*aplastar*) to crush; (*persona*) to flatten

★**despacio** [des'paθjo] ADV (*lentamente*) slowly; (*esp AM: en voz baja*) softly; **¡~!** take it easy!

despacito [despa'θito] ADV (*fam*) slowly; (*suavemente*) softly

despampanante [despampa'nante] ADJ (*fam: chica*) stunning

desparejado, -a [despare'xaðo, a] ADJ odd

desparpajo [despar'paxo] NM (*desenvoltura*) self-confidence; (*pey*) nerve

desparramar [desparra'mar] /**1a**/ VT (*esparcir*) to scatter; (*líquido*) to spill

despatarrarse [despata'rrarse] /**1a**/ VR (*abrir las piernas*) to open one's legs wide; (*caerse*) to tumble; (*fig*) to be flabbergasted

d

despavorido, -a [despaβo'riðo,a] ADJ terrified

despecho [des'petʃo] NM spite; **a ~ de** in spite of; **por ~** out of (sheer) spite

despectivo, -a [despek'tiβo, a] ADJ (*despreciativo*) derogatory; (*Ling*) pejorative

despedace *etc* [despe'ðaθe] VB *ver* **despedazar**

despedazar [despeða'θar] /1f/ VT to tear to pieces

despedida [despe'ðiða] NF (*adiós*) goodbye, farewell; (*antes de viaje*) send-off; (*en carta*) closing formula; (*de obrero*) sacking; (*Inform*) logout; **cena/función de ~** farewell dinner/performance; **regalo de ~** parting gift; **~ de soltero/soltera** stag/hen party

★**despedir** [despe'ðir] /3k/ VT (*visita*) to see off, show out; (*empleado*) to dismiss; (*inquilino*) to evict; (*objeto*) to hurl; (*olor etc*) to give out *o* off ■ **despedirse** VR (*dejar un empleo*) to give up one's job; (*Inform*) to log out *o* off; **despedirse de** to say goodbye to; **se despidieron** they said goodbye to each other

despegado, -a [despe'ɣaðo, a] ADJ (*separado*) detached; (*persona: poco afectuoso*) cold, indifferent ▶ NM/F: **es un ~** he has cut himself off from his family

★**despegar** [despe'ɣar] /1h/ VT to unstick; (*sobre*) to open; **sin ~ los labios** without uttering a word ▶ VI (*avión*) to take off; (*cohete*) to blast off ■ **despegarse** VR to come loose, come unstuck

despego [des'peɣo] NM detachment

despegue *etc* [des'peɣe] VB *ver* **despegar** ▶ NM takeoff; (*de cohete*) blast-off

despeinado, -a [despei'naðo, a] ADJ dishevelled, unkempt

despeinar [despei'nar] /1a/ VT (*pelo*) to ruffle; **¡me has despeinado todo!** you've completely ruined my hairdo!

★**despejado, -a** [despe'xaðo, a] ADJ (*lugar*) clear, free; (*cielo*) clear; (*persona*) wide-awake, bright

★**despejar** [despe'xar] /1a/ VT (*gen*) to clear; (*misterio*) to clarify, clear up; (*Mat: incógnita*) to find ▶ VI (*el tiempo*) to clear; **¡despejen!** (*moverse*) move along!; (*salirse*) everybody out! ■ **despejarse** VR (*tiempo, cielo*) to clear (up); (*misterio*) to become clearer; (*cabeza*) to clear

despeje [des'pexe] NM (*Deporte*) clearance

despellejar [despeʎe'xar] /1a/ VT (*animal*) to skin; (*criticar*) to criticize unmercifully; (*fam: arruinar*) to fleece

despelotarse [despelo'tarse] /1a/ VR (*fam*) to strip off; (*fig*) to let one's hair down

despelote [despe'lote] NM (*Am fam*: *lío*) mess; **¡qué *o* vaya ~!** what a riot *o* laugh!

despenalizar [despenali'θar] /1f/ VT to decriminalize

despensa [des'pensa] NF (*armario*) larder; (*Naut*) storeroom; (*provisión de comestibles*) stock of food

despeñadero [despeɲa'ðero] NM (*Geo*) cliff, precipice

despeñar [despe'ɲar] /1a/ VT (*arrojar*) to fling

down ■ **despeñarse** VR to fling o.s. down; (*caer*) to fall headlong; (*coche*) to tumble over

desperdiciar [desperði'θjar] /1b/ VT (*comida, tiempo*) to waste; (*oportunidad*) to throw away

★**desperdicio** [desper'ðiθjo] NM (*despilfarro*) squandering; (*residuo*) waste; **el libro no tiene ~** the book is excellent from beginning to end ■ **desperdicios** NMPL (*basura*) rubbish *sg*, refuse *sg*, garbage *sg* (US); (*residuos*) waste *sg*; **desperdicios de cocina** kitchen scraps

desperdigar [desperði'ɣar] /1h/ VT (*esparcir*) to scatter; (*energía*) to dissipate ■ **desperdigarse** VR to scatter

desperdigue *etc* [desper'ðiɣe] VB *ver* **desperdigar**

desperece *etc* [despe'reθe] VB *ver* **desperezarse**

desperezarse [despere'θarse] /1f/ VR to stretch

desperfecto [desper'fekto] NM (*deterioro*) slight damage; (*defecto*) flaw, imperfection

★**despertador** [desperta'ðor] NM alarm clock; **~ de viaje** travelling clock

★**despertar** [desper'tar] /1j/ VT (*persona*) to wake up; (*recuerdos*) to revive; (*esperanzas*) to raise; (*sentimiento*) to arouse ▶ VI to awaken, wake up ■ **despertarse** VR to awaken, wake up; **despertarse a la realidad** to wake up to reality ▶ NM awakening

despiadado, -a [despja'ðaðo, a] ADJ (*ataque*) merciless; (*persona*) heartless

despido *etc* [des'piðo] VB *ver* **despedir** ▶ NM dismissal, sacking; **~ improcedente** *o* **injustificado** wrongful dismissal; **~ injusto** unfair dismissal; **~ libre** right to hire and fire; **~ voluntario** voluntary redundancy

despierto, -a [des'pjerto, a] PP *de* **despertar** ▶ ADJ awake; (*fig*) sharp, alert

despilfarrar [despilfa'rrar] /1a/ VT (*gen*) to waste; (*dinero*) to squander

despilfarro [despil'farro] NM (*derroche*) squandering; (*lujo desmedido*) extravagance

despintar [despin'tar] /1a/ VT (*quitar pintura a*) to take the paint off; (*hechos*) to distort ▶ VI: **A no despinta a B** A is in no way inferior to B ■ **despintarse** VR (*desteñir*) to fade

despiojar [despjo'xar] /1a/ VT to delouse

despistado, -a [despis'taðo, a] ADJ (*distraído*) vague, absent-minded; (*poco práctico*) unpractical; (*confuso*) confused; (*desorientado*) off the track ▶ NM/F (*persona distraída*) scatterbrain, absent-minded person

despistar [despis'tar] /1a/ VT to throw off the track *o* scent; (*fig*) to mislead, confuse ■ **despistarse** VR to take the wrong road; (*fig*) to become confused

despiste [des'piste] NM (*Auto etc*) swerve; (*error*) slip; (*distracción*) absent-mindedness; **un ~** a mistake *o* slip; **tiene un terrible ~** he's terribly absent-minded

desplace *etc* [des'plaθe] VB *ver* **desplazar**

desplante [des'plante] NM: **hacer un ~ a algn** to be rude to sb

desplazado, -a [despla'θaðo, a] ADJ (*pieza*) wrongly placed; **sentirse un poco ~** to feel rather out of place ▸ NM/F (*inadaptado*) misfit

desplazamiento [desplaθa'mjento] NM displacement; (*viaje*) journey; (*de opinión, votos*) shift, swing; (*Inform*) scrolling; **~ hacia arriba/abajo** (*Inform*) scroll up/down

★**desplazar** [despla'θar] /1f/ VT (*gen*) to move; (*Física, Naut, Tec*) to displace; (*tropas*) to transfer; (*suplantar*) to take the place of; (*fig*) to oust; (*Inform*) to scroll ■ **desplazarse** VR (*persona, vehículo*) to travel, go; (*objeto*) to move, shift; (*votos, opinión*) to shift, swing

desplegable [desple'ɣaβle] ADJ (*libro, tb Inform*) pop-up

desplegar [desple'ɣar] /1h, 1j/ VT (*tela, papel*) to unfold, open out; (*bandera*) to unfurl; (*alas*) to spread; (*Mil*) to deploy; (*manifestar*) to display

desplegué [desple'ɣe], **despleguemos** etc [desple'ɣemos] VB ver **desplegar**

despliegue etc [des'pljeɣe] VB ver **desplegar** ▸ NM unfolding, opening; deployment, display

desplomarse [desplo'marse] /1a/ VR (*edificio, gobierno, persona*) to collapse; (*derrumbarse*) to topple over; (*precios*) to slump; **se ha desplomado el techo** the ceiling has fallen in

desplumar [desplu'mar] /1a/ VT (*ave*) to pluck; (*fam: estafar*) to fleece

despoblado, -a [despo'βlaðo, a] ADJ (*sin habitantes*) uninhabited; (*con pocos habitantes*) depopulated; (*con insuficientes habitantes*) underpopulated ▸ NM deserted spot

despojar [despo'xar] /1a/ VT (*a alguien: de sus bienes*) to divest of, deprive of; (*casa*) to strip, leave bare; (*de su cargo*) to strip of ■ **despojarse** VR (*desnudarse*) to undress; **despojarse de** (*ropa, hojas*) to shed; (*poderes*) to relinquish

despojo [des'poxo] NM (*acto*) plundering; (*objetos*) plunder, loot ■ **despojos** NMPL (*de ave, res*) offal *sg*

desposado, -a [despo'saðo, a] ADJ, NM/F newly-wed

desposar [despo'sar] /1a/ VT (*sacerdote, pareja*) to marry ■ **desposarse** VR (*casarse*) to marry, get married

desposeer [despose'er] /2e/ VT (*despojar*) to dispossess; **~ a algn de su autoridad** to strip sb of his authority

desposeído, -a [despose'iðo, a] NM/F: **los desposeídos** the have-nots

desposeyendo etc [despose'jendo] VB ver **desposeer**

desposorios [despo'sorjos] NMPL (*esponsales*) betrothal *sg*; (*boda*) marriage ceremony *sg*

déspota ['despota] NMF despot

despotismo [despo'tismo] NM despotism

despotricar [despotri'kar] /1g/ VI: **~ contra** to moan o complain about

despotrique etc [despo'trike] VB ver **despotricar**

despreciable [despre'θjaβle] ADJ (*moralmente*) despicable; (*objeto*) worthless; (*cantidad*) negligible

despreciar [despre'θjar] /1b/ VT (*desdeñar*) to despise, scorn; (*afrentar*) to slight

despreciativo, -a [despre'θja'tiβo, a] ADJ (*observación, tono*) scornful, contemptuous; (*comentario*) derogatory

desprecio [des'preθjo] NM scorn, contempt; slight

desprender [despren'der] /2a/ VT (*soltar*) to loosen; (*separar*) to separate; (*desatar*) to unfasten; (*olor*) to give off ■ **desprenderse** VR (*botón: caerse*) to fall off; (*broche*) to come unfastened; (*olor, perfume*) to be given off; **desprenderse de** to follow from; **desprenderse de algo** (*ceder*) to give sth up; (*desembarazarse*) to get rid of sth; **desprenderse de algo que ...** to draw from sth that ...; **se desprende que ...** it transpires that ...

desprendido, -a [despren'dido, a] ADJ (*pieza*) loose; (*sin abrochar*) unfastened; (*desinteresado*) disinterested; (*generoso*) generous

desprendimiento [desprendi'mjento] NM (*gen*) loosening; (*generosidad*) disinterestedness; (*indiferencia*) detachment; (*de gas*) leak; (*de tierra, rocas*) landslide; **~ de retina** detachment of the retina

despreocupado, -a [despreoku'paðo, a] ADJ (*sin preocupación*) unworried, unconcerned; (*tranquilo*) nonchalant; (*en el vestir*) casual; (*negligente*) careless

despreocuparse [despreoku'parse] /1a/ VR to be carefree, not to worry; (*dejar de inquietarse*) to stop worrying; (*ser indiferente*) to be unconcerned; **~ de** to have no interest in

desprestigiar [despresti'xjar] /1b/ VT (*criticar*) to run down, disparage; (*desacreditar*) to discredit

desprestigio [despres'tixjo] NM (*denigración*) disparagement; (*impopularidad*) unpopularity

desprevenido, -a [despreβe'niðo, a] ADJ (*no preparado*) unprepared, unready; **coger** (*ESP*) o **agarrar** (*AM*) **a algn ~** to catch sb unawares

desproporción [despropor'θjon] NF disproportion, lack of proportion

desproporcionado, -a [desproporθjo'naðo, a] ADJ disproportionate, out of proportion

despropósito [despro'posito] NM (*salida de tono*) irrelevant remark; (*disparate*) piece of nonsense

desprovisto, -a [despro'βisto, a] ADJ: **~ de** devoid of; **estar ~ de** to lack

★**después** [des'pwes] ADV afterwards, later; (*desde entonces*) since (then); (*próximo paso*) next; **poco ~** soon after; **un año ~** a year later; **~ se debatió el tema** next the matter was discussed; **~ de** (*tiempo*) after, since; (*orden*) next (to); **mi nombre está ~ del tuyo** my name comes next to yours; **~ de esa fecha** (*pasado*) since that date; (*futuro*) from *o* after that date; **~ de comer** after lunch; **~ de verlo** after seeing it, after I *etc* saw it; **~ de todo** after all; **~ de corregido el texto** after the text had been corrected; **~ de que** after; **~ de que lo escribí** after *o* since I wrote it, after writing it

despuntar [despun'tar] /**1a**/ vt (*lápiz*) to blunt ▶ vi (*Bot: plantas*) to sprout; (: *flores*) to bud; (*alba*) to break; (*día*) to dawn; (*persona: descollar*) to stand out

desquiciado, -a [deski'θjaðo, a] ADJ deranged

desquiciar [deski'θjar] /**1b**/ vt (*puerta*) to take off its hinges; (*descomponer*) to upset; (*persona: turbar*) to disturb; (: *volver loco a*) to unhinge

desquitarse [deski'tarse] /**1a**/ vr to obtain satisfaction; (*Com*) to recover a debt; (*fig: vengarse de*) to get one's own back; **~ de una pérdida** to make up for a loss

desquite [des'kite] NM (*satisfacción*) satisfaction; (*venganza*) revenge

Dest. ABR = **destinatario**

destacado, -a [desta'kaðo, a] ADJ outstanding

destacamento [destaka'mento] NM (*Mil*) detachment

destacar [desta'kar] /**1g**/ vt (*Arte: hacer resaltar*) to make stand out; (: *subrayar*) to emphasize, point up; (*Mil*) to detach, detail; (*Inform*) to highlight; **quiero ~ que...** I wish to emphasize that... ▶ vi (*resaltarse*) to stand out; (*persona*) to be outstanding *o* exceptional ■ **destacarse** vr (*resaltarse*) to stand out; (*persona*) to be outstanding *o* exceptional; **~(se) contra *o* en *o* sobre** to stand out *o* be outlined against

destajo [des'taxo] NM: **a ~** (*por pieza*) by the job; (*con afán*) eagerly; **trabajar a ~** to do piecework; (*fig*) to work one's fingers to the bone

destapar [desta'par] /**1a**/ vt (*botella*) to open; (*cacerola*) to take the lid off; (*descubrir*) to uncover ■ **destaparse** vr (*descubrirse*) to get uncovered; (*revelarse*) to reveal one's true character

destape [des'tape] NM nudity; (*fig*) permissiveness; **el ~ español** *the process of liberalization in Spain after Franco's death*

destaque *etc* [des'take] vb *ver* **destacar**

destartalado, -a [destarta'laðo, a] ADJ (*desordenado*) untidy; (*casa etc: grande*) rambling; (: *ruinoso*) tumbledown

destellar [deste'ʎar] /**1a**/ vi (*diamante*) to sparkle; (*metal*) to glint; (*estrella*) to twinkle

destello [des'teʎo] NM (*de diamante*) sparkle; (*de metal*) glint; (*de estrella*) twinkle; (*de faro*) signal light; **no tiene un ~ de verdad** there's not a grain of truth in it

destemplado, -a [destem'plaðo, a] ADJ (*Mus*) out of tune; (*voz*) harsh; (*Med*) out of sorts; (*Meteorología*) unpleasant, nasty

destemplar [destem'plar] /**1a**/ vt (*Mus*) to put out of tune; (*alterar*) to upset ■ **destemplarse** vr (*Mus*) to lose its pitch; (*descomponerse*) to get

out of order; (*persona: irritarse*) to get upset; (*Med*) to get out of sorts

desteñir [deste'ɲir] /**3h, 3k**/ vt, vi to fade; **esta tela no destiñe** this fabric will not run ■ **desteñirse** vr to fade

desternillarse [desterni'ʎarse] /**1a**/ vr: **~ de risa** to split one's sides laughing

desterrado, -a [deste'rraðo, a] NM/F (*exiliado*) exile

desterrar [deste'rrar] /**1j**/ vt (*exiliar*) to exile; (*fig*) to banish, dismiss

destetar [deste'tar] /**1a**/ vt to wean

destiempo [des'tjempo]: **a ~** adv at the wrong time

destierro *etc* [des'tjerro] vb *ver* **desterrar** ▶ NM exile; **vivir en el ~** to live in exile

destilar [desti'lar] /**1a**/ vt to distil; (*pus, sangre*) to ooze; (*fig: rebosar*) to exude; (: *revelar*) to reveal ▶ vi (*gotear*) to drip

destilería [destile'ria] NF distillery; **~ de petróleo** oil refinery

destinar [desti'nar] /**1a**/ vt (*funcionario*) to appoint, assign; (*fondos*) to set aside; **es un libro destinado a los niños** it is a book (intended *o* meant) for children; **una carta que viene destinada a usted** a letter for you, a letter addressed to you

destinatario, -a [destina'tarjo, a] NM/F addressee; (*Com*) payee

★**destino** [des'tino] NM (*suerte*) destiny; (*de viajero*) destination; (*función*) use; (*puesto*) post, placement; **~ público** public appointment; **salir con ~ a** to leave for; **con ~ a Londres** (*avión, barco*) (bound) for London; (*carta*) to London

destiña *etc* [des'tiɲa], **destiñendo** *etc* [desti'ɲendo] vb *ver* **desteñir**

destitución [destitu'θjon] NF dismissal, removal

destituir [desti'tuir] /**3g**/ vt (*despedir*) to dismiss; (: *ministro, funcionario*) to remove from office

destituyendo *etc* [destitu'jendo] vb *ver* **destituir**

destornillador [destorniʎa'ðor] NM screwdriver

destornillar [destorni'ʎar] /**1a**/ vt (*tornillo*) to unscrew ■ **destornillarse** vr to unscrew

destreza [des'treθa] NF (*habilidad*) skill; (*maña*) dexterity

destripar [destri'par] /**1a**/ vt (*animal*) to gut; (*reventar*) to mangle

destroce *etc* [des'troθe] vb *ver* **destrozar**

destronar [destro'nar] /**1a**/ vt (*rey*) to dethrone; (*fig*) to overthrow

destroncar [destron'kar] /**1h**/ vt (*árbol*) to chop off, lop; (*proyectos*) to ruin; (*discurso*) to interrupt

destronque *etc* [des'tronke] vb *ver* **destroncar**

destrozar [destro'θar] /**1f**/ vt (*romper*) to smash, break (up); (*estropear*) to ruin; (*nervios*) to shatter; **~ a algn en una discusión** to crush sb in an argument

destrozo [des'troθo] NM *(acción)* destruction; *(desastre)* smashing ▪ **destrozos** NMPL *(pedazos)* pieces; *(daños)* havoc *sg*

★**destrucción** [destruk'θjon] NF destruction

destructor, a [destruk'tor, a] ADJ destructive ▶ NM *(Naut)* destroyer

★**destruir** [destru'ir] /3g/ VT to destroy; *(casa)* to demolish; *(equilibrio)* to upset; *(proyecto)* to spoil; *(esperanzas)* to dash; *(argumento)* to demolish

destruyendo *etc* [destru'jendo] VB *ver* **destruir**

desuelle *etc* [de'sweʎe] VB *ver* **desollar**

desunión [desu'njon] NF *(separación)* separation; *(discordia)* disunity

desunir [desu'nir] /3a/ VT to separate; *(Tec)* to disconnect; *(fig)* to cause a quarrel *o* rift between

desuso [de'suso] NM disuse; **caer en ~** to fall into disuse, become obsolete; **una expresión caída en ~** an obsolete expression

desvaído, -a [desβa'iðo, a] ADJ *(color)* pale; *(contorno)* blurred

desvalido, -a [desβa'liðo, a] ADJ *(desprotegido)* destitute; *(sin fuerzas)* helpless; **niños desvalidos** waifs and strays

desvalijar [desβali'xar] /1a/ VT *(persona)* to rob; *(casa, tienda)* to burgle; *(coche)* to break into

desvalorice *etc* [desβalo'riθe] VB *ver* **desvalorizar**

desvalorizar [desβalori'θar] /1f/ VT to devalue

★**desván** [des'βan] NM attic

desvanecer [desβane'θer] /2d/ VT *(disipar)* to dispel; *(recuerdo, temor)* to banish; *(borrar)* to erase ▪ **desvanecerse** VR *(humo etc)* to vanish, disappear; *(duda)* to be dispelled; *(color)* to fade; *(recuerdo, sonido)* to fade away; *(Med)* to pass out

desvanecido, -a [desβane'θiðo, a] ADJ *(Med)* faint; **caer ~** to fall in a faint

desvanecimiento [desβaneθi'mjento] NM *(desaparición)* disappearance; *(de dudas)* dispelling; *(de colores)* fading; *(evaporación)* evaporation; *(Med)* fainting fit

desvanezca *etc* [desβa'neθka] VB *ver* **desvanecer**

desvariar [desβa'rjar] /1c/ VI *(enfermo)* to be delirious; *(delirar)* to talk nonsense

desvarío [desβa'rio] NM delirium; *(desatino)* absurdity ▪ **desvaríos** NMPL ravings

desvelar [desβe'lar] /1a/ VT to keep awake ▪ **desvelarse** VR *(no poder dormir)* to stay awake; *(vigilar)* to be vigilant o watchful; **desvelarse por algo** *(inquietarse)* to be anxious about sth; *(poner gran cuidado)* to take great care over sth

desvelo [des'βelo] NM lack of sleep; *(insomnio)* sleeplessness; *(fig)* vigilance ▪ **desvelos** NMPL *(preocupación)* anxiety *sg*, effort *sg*

desvencijado, -a [desβenθi'xaðo, a] ADJ *(silla)* rickety; *(máquina)* broken-down

desvencijar [desβenθi'xar] /1a/ VT *(romper)* to break; *(soltar)* to loosen; *(persona: agotar)* to exhaust ▪ **desvencijarse** VR to come apart

★**desventaja** [desβen'taxa] NF disadvantage; *(inconveniente)* drawback

desventajoso, -a [desβenta'xoso, a] ADJ disadvantageous, unfavourable

desventura [desβen'tura] NF misfortune

desventurado, -a [desβentu'raðo, a] ADJ *(desgraciado)* unfortunate; *(de poca suerte)* ill-fated

desvergonzado, -a [desβerɣon'θaðo, a] ADJ *(sin vergüenza)* shameless; *(descarado)* insolent ▶ NM/F shameless person

desvergüenza [desβer'ɣwenθa] NF *(descaro)* shamelessness; *(insolencia)* impudence; *(mala conducta)* effrontery; **esto es una ~** this is disgraceful; **¡qué ~!** what a nerve!

desvestir [desβes'tir] /3k/ VT to undress ▪ **desvestirse** VR to undress

desviación [desβja'θjon] NF deviation; *(Auto: rodeo)* diversion, detour; *(: carretera de circunvalación)* ring road *(Brit)*, circular route *(US)*; **~ de la circulación** traffic diversion; **es una ~ de sus principios** it is a departure from his usual principles

★**desviar** [des'βjar] /1c/ VT to turn aside; *(balón, flecha, golpe)* to deflect; *(pregunta)* to parry; *(ojos)* to avert, turn away; *(río)* to alter the course of; *(navío)* to divert, re-route; *(conversación)* to sidetrack ▪ **desviarse** VR *(apartarse del camino)* to turn aside; *(: barco)* to go off course; *(Auto: dar un rodeo)* to make a detour; **desviarse de un tema** to get away from the point

desvincular [desβinku'lar] /1a/ VT to free, release ▪ **desvincularse** VR *(aislarse)* to be cut off; *(alejarse)* to cut o.s. off

★**desvío** [des'βio] VB *ver* **desviar** ▶ NM *(desviación)* detour, diversion; *(fig)* indifference

desvirgar [desβir'ɣar] /1h/ VT to deflower

desvirtuar [desβir'twar] /1e/ VT *(estropear)* to spoil; *(argumento, razonamiento)* to detract from; *(efecto)* to counteract; *(sentido)* to distort ▪ **desvirtuarse** VR to spoil

desvistiendo *etc* [desβis'tjendo] VB *ver* **desvestir**

desvitalizar [desβitali'θar] /1f/ VT *(nervio)* to numb

desvivirse [desβi'βirse] /3a/ VR: **~ por** to long for, crave for; **~ por los amigos** to do anything for one's friends

detalladamente [detaʎaða'mente] ADV *(en detalle)* in detail; *(extensamente)* at great length

detallar [deta'ʎar] /1a/ VT to detail; *(asunto por asunto)* to itemize

★**detalle** [de'taʎe] NM detail; *(fig)* gesture, token; **al ~** in detail; *(Com)* retail *cpd*; **comercio al ~** retail trade; **vender al ~** to sell retail; **no pierde ~** he doesn't miss a trick; **me observaba sin perder ~** he watched my every move; **tiene muchos detalles** she is very considerate

detallista [deta'ʎista] NMF retailer ▸ ADJ (*meticuloso*) meticulous; **comercio ~** retail trade

detectar [detek'tar] /1a/ VT to detect

detective [detek'tiβe] NMF detective; **~ privado** private detective

detector [detek'tor] NM (*Naut, Tec etc*) detector; **~ de mentiras/de minas** lie/mine detector

detención [deten'θjon] NF (*acción*) stopping; (*estancamiento*) stoppage; (*retraso*) holdup, delay; (Jur: *arresto*) arrest; (: *prisión*) detention; (: *cuidado*) care; **~ de juego** (*Deporte*) stoppage of play; **~ ilegal** unlawful detention

detendré *etc* [deten'dre] VB *ver* **detener**

★**detener** [dete'ner] /2k/ VT (*gen*) to stop; (Jur: *arrestar*) to arrest; (: *encarcelar*) to detain; (*objeto*) to keep; (*retrasar*) to hold up, delay; (*aliento*) to hold ■ **detenerse** VR to stop; **detenerse en** (*demorarse*) to delay over, linger over

detenga *etc* [de'tenga] VB *ver* **detener**

detenidamente [deteniða'mente] ADV (*minuciosamente*) carefully; (*extensamente*) at great length

detenido, -a [dete'niðo, a] ADJ (*arrestado*) under arrest; (*minucioso*) detailed; (*examen*) thorough; (*tímido*) timid ▸ NM/F person under arrest, prisoner

detenimiento [deteni'mjento] NM care; **con ~** thoroughly; (*observar, considerar*) carefully

detentar [deten'tar] /1a/ VT to hold; (*sin derecho: título*) to hold unlawfully; (: *puesto*) to occupy unlawfully

★**detergente** [deter'xente] ADJ, NM detergent

deteriorado, -a [deterjo'raðo, a] ADJ (*estropeado*) damaged; (*desgastado*) worn

deteriorar [deterjo'rar] /1a/ VT to spoil, damage ■ **deteriorarse** VR to deteriorate

deterioro [dete'rjoro] NM deterioration

determinación [determina'θjon] NF (*empeño*) determination; (*decisión*) decision; (*de fecha, precio*) settling, fixing

determinado, -a [determi'naðo, a] ADJ (*preciso*) certain; (Ling: *artículo*) definite; (*persona: resuelto*) determined; **un día ~** on a certain day; **no hay ningún tema ~** there is no particular theme

determinar [determi'nar] /1a/ VT (*plazo*) to fix; (*precio*) to settle; (*daños, impuestos*) to assess; (*pleito*) to decide; (*causar*) to cause; **el reglamento determina que ...** the rules lay it down or state that ...; **aquello determinó la caída del gobierno** that brought about the fall of the government; **esto le determinó** this decided him ■ **determinarse** VR to decide

detestable [detes'taβle] ADJ (*persona*) hateful; (*acto*) detestable

★**detestar** [detes'tar] /1a/ VT to detest

detonación [detona'θjon] NF detonation; (*sonido*) explosion

detonante [deto'nante] NM (*fig*) trigger

detonar [deto'nar] /1a/ VI to detonate

detractor, a [detrak'tor, a] ADJ disparaging ▸ NM/F detractor

★**detrás** [de'tras] ADV behind; (*atrás*) at the back; **salir de ~** to come out from behind; **por ~** behind ▸ PREP: **~ de** behind; **por ~ de algn** (*fig*) behind sb's back

detrasito [detra'sito] ADV (*AM fam*) behind

detrimento [detri'mento] NM: **en ~ de** to the detriment of

detuve *etc* [de'tuβe] VB *ver* **detener**

deuda [de'uða] NF (*condición*) indebtedness, debt; (*cantidad*) debt; **~ a largo plazo** long-term debt; **~ exterior/pública** foreign/national debt; **~ incobrable** o **morosa** bad debt; **deudas activas/pasivas** assets/liabilities; **contraer deudas** to get into debt

deudor, a [deu'ðor, a] NM/F debtor; **~ hipotecario** mortgager; **~ moroso** slow payer

devaluación [deβalwa'θjon] NF devaluation

devaluar [deβalu'ar] /1e/ VT to devalue

devanar [deβa'nar] /1a/ VT (*hilo*) to wind ■ **devanarse** VR: **devanarse los sesos** to rack one's brains

devaneo [deβa'neo] NM (*Med*) delirium; (*desatino*) nonsense; (*fruslería*) idle pursuit; (*amorío*) flirtation

devastar [deβas'tar] /1a/ VT (*destruir*) to devastate

devendré *etc* [deβen'dre], **devenga** *etc* [de'βenga] VB *ver* **devenir**

devengar [deβen'gar] /1h/ VT (*salario: ganar*) to earn; (: *tener que cobrar*) to be due; (*intereses*) to bring in, accrue, earn

devengue *etc* [de'βenge] VB *ver* **devengar**

devenir [deβe'nir] /3r/ VI: **~ en** to become, turn into ▸ NM (*movimiento progresivo*) process of development; (*transformación*) transformation

deveras [de'βeras] NF INV (*AM*): **un amigo de (a) ~** a true o real friend

deviene *etc* [de'βjene], **deviniendo** *etc* [deβi'njendo] VB *ver* **devenir**

devoción [deβo'θjon] NF devotion; (*afición*) strong attachment

devolución [deβolu'θjon] NF (*reenvío*) return, sending back; (*reembolso*) repayment; (Jur) devolution

★**devolver** [deβol'βer] /2h/ VT to return; (*lo extraviado, prestado*) to give back; (*a su sitio*) to put back; (*carta al correo*) to send back; (*Com*) to repay, refund; (*visita, la palabra*) to return; (*salud, vista*) to restore; (*fam: vomitar*) to throw up; **~ mal por bien** to return ill for good; **~ la pelota a algn** to give sb tit for tat ▸ VI (*fam*) to be sick ■ **devolverse** VR (*AM*) to return

devorar [deβo'rar] /1a/ VT to devour; (*comer ávidamente*) to gobble up; (*fig: fortuna*) to run through; **todo lo devoró el fuego** the fire consumed everything; **le devoran los celos** he is consumed with jealousy

devoto, -a [de'βoto, a] ADJ (Rel: *persona*) devout;

d

(: *obra*) devotional; (*amigo*): **~ (de algn)** devoted (to sb); **su muy ~ servidor** your devoted servant ▶ NM/F admirer ▦ **los devotos** NMPL (*Rel*) the faithful

devuelto [de'βwelto], **devuelva** *etc* [de'βwelβa] VB *ver* **devolver**

D.F. [de'efe] NM ABR (*MÉXICO*) = **Distrito Federal**

dg ABR (= *decigramo*) dg

D.G. ABR = **Dirección General**; (= *Director General*) DG

DGT [dexe'te] NF ABR = **Dirección General de Tráfico**

di [di] VB *ver* **dar; decir**

★**día** ['dia] NM day; **~ de asueto** day off; **~ feriado** (*Am*) *o* **festivo** (public) holiday; **~ hábil/inhábil** working/non-working day; **~ lunes** (*Am*) Monday; **~ lectivo** teaching day; **~ libre** day off; **D~ de Reyes** Epiphany (*6 January*); **D~ de la Independencia** Independence Day; **¿qué ~ es?** what's the date?; **estar/poner al ~** to be/keep up to date; **el ~ de hoy/de mañana** today/tomorrow; **el ~ menos pensado** when you least expect it; **al ~ siguiente** on the following day; **todos los días** every day; **un ~ sí y otro no** every other day; **vivir al ~** to live from hand to mouth; **de ~** during the day, by day; **es de ~** it's daylight; **del ~** (*estilos*) fashionable; (*menú*) today's; **de un ~ para otro** any day now; **en pleno ~** in full daylight; **en su ~** in due time; **¡hasta otro ~!** so long!

diabetes [dja'betes] NF diabetes *sg*

diabético, -a [dja'betiko, a] ADJ, NM/F diabetic

diablo ['djaβlo] NM (*tb fig*) devil; **pobre ~** poor devil; **hace un frío de todos los diablos** it's hellishly cold

diablura [dja'βlura] NF prank; (*travesura*) mischief

diabólico, -a [dja'βoliko, a] ADJ diabolical

Diada ['djaða] NF *Catalonia's national holiday (September 11th)*

The **Diada**, Catalonia's national holiday, is celebrated on September 11th commemorating the fall of Barcelona into the hands of Philip V of Spain (Philippe de Bourbon) at the end of the War of the Spanish Succession in 1714. Before this event, Catalonia enjoyed great autonomy with its own government, the *Generalitat*, which it lost at the time but which has existed again continuously since 1977. For the *Diada*, the roads and balconies are draped in the official Catalan flag, the *Senyera*, with its four red stripes on a yellow background and the *Estelada*, which is the flag preferred by supporters of Catalan independence.

diadema [dja'ðema] NF (*para el pelo*) Alice band, headband; (*joya*) tiara

diáfano, -a ['djafano, a] ADJ (*tela*) diaphanous; (*agua*) crystal-clear; (*espacio*) open-plan

diafragma [dja'fraɣma] NM diaphragm

diagnosis [djaɣ'nosis] NF INV, **diagnóstico** [diaɣ'nostiko] NM diagnosis

diagnosticar [djaɣnosti'kar] /**1g**/ VT to diagnose

diagnóstico [diaɣ'nostiko] NM = **diagnosis**

diagonal [djaɣo'nal] ADJ diagonal ▶ NF (*Mat*) diagonal; **en ~** diagonally

diagrama [dja'ɣrama] NM diagram; **~ de barras** (*Com*) bar chart; **~ de dispersión** (*Com*) scatter diagram; **~ de flujo** (*Inform*) flowchart

dial [di'al] NM dial

dialecto [dja'lekto] NM dialect

dialogar [djalo'ɣar] /**1h**/ VT to write in dialogue form ▶ VI (*conversar*) to have a conversation; **~ con** (*Pol*) to hold talks with

★**diálogo** ['djaloɣo] NM dialogue

dialogue *etc* [dja'loɣe] VB *ver* **dialogar**

★**diamante** [dja'mante] NM diamond

diametralmente [djametral'mente] ADV diametrically; **~ opuesto a** diametrically opposed to

diámetro [di'ametro] NM diameter; **~ de giro** (*Auto*) turning circle; **faros de gran ~** wide-angle headlights

diana ['djana] NF (*Mil*) reveille; (*de blanco*) centre, bull's-eye

diantre ['djantre] NM: **¡~!** (*fam*) oh hell!

diapasón [djapa'son] NM (*instrumento*) tuning fork; (*de violín etc*) fingerboard; (*de voz*) tone

★**diapositiva** [djaposi'tiβa] NF (*Foto*) slide, transparency

★**diario, -a** ['djarjo, a] ADJ daily ▶ NM newspaper; (*libro diario*) diary; (*Com*) daybook; (: *gastos*) daily expenses; **~ de navegación** (*Naut*) logbook; **~ hablado** (*Radio*) news (bulletin); **~ de sesiones** parliamentary report; **a ~** daily; **de** *o* **para ~** everyday

diarrea [dja'rrea] NF diarrhoea

diatriba [dja'triβa] NF diatribe, tirade

dibujante [diβu'xante] NMF (*de bosquejos*) sketcher; (*de dibujos animados*) cartoonist; (*de moda*) designer; **~ de publicidad** commercial artist

★**dibujar** [diβu'xar] /**1a**/ VT to draw, sketch ▦ **dibujarse** VR (*emoción*) to show; **dibujarse contra** to be outlined against

★**dibujo** [di'βuxo] NM drawing; (*Tec*) design; (*en papel, tela*) pattern; (*en periódico*) cartoon; (*fig*) description; **dibujos animados** cartoons; **~ del natural** drawing from life

dic., dic.ᵉ ABR (= *diciembre*) Dec.; *ver tb* **julio**

★**diccionario** [dikθjo'narjo] NM dictionary

dice *etc* VB *ver* **decir**

dicharachero, -a [ditʃara'tʃero, a] ADJ talkative ▶ NM/F (*con ingenio*) wit; (*parlanchín*) chatterbox

dicho, -a ['ditʃo, a] PP *de* **decir** ▶ ADJ (*susodicho*) aforementioned; **mejor ~** rather; **~ y hecho** no sooner said than done ▶ NM saying; (*proverbio*) proverb; *(ocurrencia)* bright remark ▸ NF *(buena suerte)* good luck

dichoso, -a [di'tʃoso, a] ADJ *(feliz)* happy; *(afortunado)* lucky; **¡aquel ~ coche!** *(fam)* that blessed car!

★**diciembre** [di'θjembre] NM December; *ver tb* **julio**

diciendo *etc* [di'θjendo] VB *ver* **decir**

dictado [dik'taðo] NM dictation; **escribir al ~** to take dictation; **los dictados de la conciencia** *(fig)* the dictates of conscience

★**dictador** [dikta'ðor] NM dictator

dictadura [dikta'ðura] NF dictatorship

dictáfono® [dik'tafono] NM Dictaphone®

dictamen [dik'tamen] NM *(opinión)* opinion; *(informe)* report; **~ contable** auditor's report; **~ facultativo** *(Med)* medical report

dictar [dik'tar] /1a/ VT *(carta)* to dictate; *(Jur: sentencia)* to pass; *(decreto)* to issue; *(Am: clase)* to give; *(: conferencia)* to deliver

didáctico, -a [di'ðaktiko, a] ADJ didactic; *(material)* teaching *cpd*; *(juguete)* educational

★**diecinueve** [djeθinu'eβe] NUM nineteen; *(fecha)* nineteenth; *ver tb* **seis**

dieciochesco, -a [djeθio'tʃesko, a] ADJ eighteenth-century

★**dieciocho** [djeθi'otʃo] NUM eighteen; *(fecha)* eighteenth; *ver tb* **seis**

★**dieciséis** [djeθi'seis] NUM sixteen; *(fecha)* sixteenth; *ver tb* **seis**

★**diecisiete** [djeθi'sjete] NUM seventeen; *(fecha)* seventeenth; *ver tb* **seis**

★**diente** ['djente] NM *(Anat, Tec)* tooth; *(Zool)* fang; *(: de elefante)* tusk; *(de ajo)* clove; **~ de león** dandelion; **dientes postizos** false teeth; **enseñar los dientes** *(fig)* to show one's claws; **hablar entre dientes** to mutter, mumble; **hincar el ~ en** *(comida)* to bite into

diera *etc* ['djera] VB *ver* **dar**

diéresis [di'eresis] NF diaeresis

dieron ['djeron] VB *ver* **dar**

diesel ['disel] ADJ: **motor ~** diesel engine

diestro, -a ['djestro, a] ADJ *(derecho)* right; *(hábil)* skilful; *(: con las manos)* handy ▸ NM *(Taur)* matador ▸ NF right hand; **a ~ y siniestro** *(sin método)* wildly

★**dieta** ['djeta] NF diet; **estar a ~** to be on a diet ■ **dietas** NFPL expenses

dietético, -a [dje'tetiko, a] ADJ dietetic ▸ NM/F dietician ▸ NF dietetics *sg*

dietista [dje'tista] NMF dietician

★**diez** [djeθ] NUM ten; *(fecha)* tenth; **hacer las ~ de últimas** *(Naipes)* to sweep the board; *ver tb* **seis**

diezmar [djeθ'mar] /1a/ VT to decimate

difamación [difama'θjon] NF slander; libel

difamar [difa'mar] /1a/ VT *(Jur: hablando)* to slander; *(: por escrito)* to libel

difamatorio, -a [difama'torjo, a] ADJ slanderous; libellous

★**diferencia** [dife'renθja] NF difference; **a ~ de** unlike; **hacer ~ entre** to make a distinction between; **~ salarial** *(Com)* wage differential

diferencial [diferen'θjal] NM *(Auto)* differential

diferenciar [diferen'θjar] /1b/ VT to differentiate between ▸ VI to differ ■ **diferenciarse** VR to differ, be different; *(distinguirse)* to distinguish o.s.

★**diferente** [dife'rente] ADJ different

diferido [dife'riðo] NM: **en ~** *(TV etc)* recorded

diferir [dife'rir] /3i/ VT to defer

★**difícil** [di'fiθil] ADJ difficult; *(tiempos, vida)* hard; *(situación)* delicate; **es un hombre ~** he's a difficult man to get on with

difícilmente [di'fiθilmente] ADV *(con dificultad)* with difficulty; *(apenas)* hardly

★**dificultad** [difikul'taδ] NF difficulty; *(problema)* trouble; *(objeción)* objection

dificultar [difikul'tar] /1a/ VT *(complicar)* to complicate, make difficult; *(estorbar)* to obstruct; **las restricciones dificultan el comercio** the restrictions hinder trade

dificultoso, -a [difikul'toso, a] ADJ *(difícil)* difficult, hard; *(fam: cara)* odd, ugly; *(persona: exigente)* fussy

difiera *etc* [di'fjera], **difiriendo** *etc* [difi'rjendo] VB *ver* **diferir**

difuminar [difumi'nar] /1a/ VT to blur

difundir [difun'dir] /3a/ VT *(calor, luz)* to diffuse; *(Radio)* to broadcast; **~ una noticia** to spread a piece of news ■ **difundirse** VR to spread (out)

difunto, -a [di'funto, a] ADJ dead, deceased ▸ NM/F deceased (person); **el ~** the deceased

difusión [difu'sjon] NF *(de calor, luz)* diffusion; *(de noticia, teoría)* dissemination; *(de programa)* broadcasting; *(programa)* broadcast

difuso, -a [di'fuso, a] ADJ *(luz)* diffused; *(conocimientos)* widespread; *(estilo, explicación)* wordy

diga *etc* ['diɣa] VB *ver* **decir**

digerir [dixe'rir] /3i/ VT to digest; *(fig)* to absorb; *(reflexionar sobre)* to think over

digestión [dixes'tjon] NF digestion; **corte de ~** indigestion

digestivo, -a [dixes'tiβo, a] ADJ digestive ▸ NM *(bebida)* liqueur, digestif

digiera *etc* [di'xjera], **digiriendo** *etc* [dixi'rjendo] VB *ver* **digerir**

digital [dixi'tal] ADJ *(Inform)* digital; *(dactilar)* finger *cpd* ▸ NF *(Bot)* foxglove; *(droga)* digitalis

digitalizador [dixitaliθa'ðor] NM *(Inform)* digitizer

dignarse [diɣ'narse] /1a/ VR to deign to

dignidad [diɣni'ðaδ] NF dignity; *(honra)* honour; *(rango)* rank; *(persona)* dignitary; **herir la ~ de algn** to hurt sb's pride

dignificar [diɣnifiˈkar] /**1g**/ vt to dignify

dignifique *etc* [diɣniˈfike] vb *ver* **dignificar**

digno, -a [ˈdiɣno, a] ADJ worthy; (*persona: honesto*) honourable; ~ **de elogio** praiseworthy; ~ **de mención** worth mentioning; **es ~ de verse** it is worth seeing; **poco ~** unworthy

digo *etc* vb *ver* **decir**

digresión [diɣreˈsjon] NF digression

dije *etc* [ˈdixe], **dijera** *etc* [diˈxera] vb *ver* **decir**

dilación [dilaˈθjon] NF delay; **sin ~** without delay, immediately

dilapidar [dilapiˈðar] /**1a**/ vt to squander, waste

dilatación [dilataˈθjon] NF (*expansión*) dilation

dilatado, -a [dilaˈtaðo, a] ADJ dilated; (*período*) long drawn-out; (*extenso*) extensive

dilatar [dilaˈtar] /**1a**/ vt (*gen*) to dilate; (*prolongar*) to prolong; (*aplazar*) to delay ■ **dilatarse** VR (*pupila etc*) to dilate; (*agua*) to expand

dilema [diˈlema] NM dilemma

diligencia [diliˈxenθja] NF diligence; (*rapidez*) speed; (*ocupación*) errand, job; (*carruaje*) stagecoach ■ **diligencias** NFPL (*Jur*) formalities; **diligencias judiciales** judicial proceedings; **diligencias previas** inquest *sg*

diligente [diliˈxente] ADJ diligent; **poco ~** slack

dilucidar [diluθiˈðar] /**1a**/ vt (*aclarar*) to elucidate, clarify; (*misterio*) to clear up

diluir [diluˈir] /**3g**/ vt to dilute; (*aguar, tb fig*) to water down

diluviar [diluˈβjar] /**1b**/ vi to pour with rain

diluvio [diˈluβjo] NM deluge, flood; **un ~ de cartas** (*fig*) a flood of letters

diluyendo *etc* [diluˈjendo] vb *ver* **diluir**

dimanar [dimaˈnar] /**1a**/ vi: ~ **de** to arise o spring from

dimensión [dimenˈsjon] NF dimension ■ **dimensiones** NFPL size *sg*; **tomar las dimensiones de** to take the measurements of

dimes [ˈdimes] NMPL: **andar en ~ y diretes con algn** to bicker o squabble with sb

diminutivo [diminuˈtiβo] NM diminutive

diminuto, -a [dimiˈnuto, a] ADJ tiny, diminutive

dimisión [dimiˈsjon] NF resignation

dimitir [dimiˈtir] /**3a**/ vt (*cargo*) to give up; (*despedir*) to sack ▶ vi to resign

dimos [ˈdimos] vb *ver* **dar**

Dinamarca [dinaˈmarka] NF Denmark

dinamarqués, -esa [dinamarˈkes, esa] ADJ Danish ▶ NM/F Dane ▶ NM (*Ling*) Danish

dinámico, -a [diˈnamiko, a] ADJ dynamic ▶ NF dynamics *sg*

dinamita [dinaˈmita] NF dynamite

dinamitar [dinamiˈtar] /**1a**/ vt to dynamite

dinamo [diˈnamo], (*Am*) **dínamo** [ˈdinamo] NF dynamo

dinastía [dinasˈtia] NF dynasty

dineral [dineˈral] NM fortune

★**dinero** [diˈnero] NM money; (*dinero en circulación*) currency; ~ **caro** (*Com*) dear money; ~ **contante (y sonante)** hard cash; ~ **de curso legal** legal tender; ~ **efectivo** o **metálico** cash, ready cash; ~ **suelto** (loose) change; **es hombre de ~** he is a man of means; **andar mal de ~** to be short of money; **ganar ~ a espuertas** to make money hand over fist

dinosaurio [dinoˈsaurjo] NM dinosaur

dintel [dinˈtel] NM lintel; (*umbral*) threshold

diñar [diˈnar] /**1a**/ vt (*fam*) to give; **diñarla** to kick the bucket

dio [djo] vb *ver* **dar**

diócesis [ˈdjoθesis] NF INV diocese

★**dios** [djos] NM god; **D~** God; **D~ mediante** God willing; **a D~ gracias** thank heaven; **a la buena de D~** any old how; **una de D~ es Cristo** an almighty row; **D~ los cría y ellos se juntan** birds of a feather flock together; **como D~ manda** as is proper; **¡D~ mío!** (oh) my God!; **¡por D~!** for God's sake!; **¡válgame D~!** bless my soul!

diosa [ˈdjosa] NF goddess

Dip. ABR (= *Diputación*) ≈ CC

diploma [diˈploma] NM diploma

diplomacia [diploˈmaθja] NF diplomacy; (*fig*) tact

diplomado, -a [diploˈmaðo, a] ADJ qualified ▶ NM/F holder of a diploma; (*Univ*) graduate; *ver tb* **licenciado**

diplomático, -a [diploˈmatiko, a] ADJ (*cuerpo*) diplomatic; (*que tiene tacto*) tactful ▶ NM/F diplomat

diptongo [dipˈtongo] NM diphthong

diputación [diputaˈθjon] NF deputation; (*tb*: **diputación provincial**) ≈ county council; ~ **permanente** (*Pol*) standing committee

diputado, -a [dipuˈtaðo, a] NM/F delegate; (*Pol*) ≈ member of parliament (*Brit*), ≈ representative (*US*); *ver tb* **cortes**

dique [ˈdike] NM dyke; (*rompeolas*) breakwater; ~ **de contención** dam

Dir. ABR = **dirección**; (= *director*) Mgr

diré *etc* [diˈre] vb *ver* **decir**

dirección [direkˈθjon] NF direction; (*fig: tendencia*) trend; (*señas, tb Inform*) address; (*Auto*) steering; (*gerencia*) management; (*de periódico*) editorship; (*en escuela*) headship; (*Pol*) leadership; (*junta*) board of directors; (*despacho*) director's/manager's/head teacher's/editor's office; ~ **administrativa** office management; ~ **asistida** power-assisted steering; **D~ General de Seguridad/Turismo** State Security/Tourist Office; "~ **única**" "one-way street"; "~ **prohibida**" "no entry"; **tomar la ~ de una empresa** to take over the running of a company

direccional [direkθjo'nal] NF (*Am Auto*) indicator

direccionamiento [direkθjona'mjento] NM (*Inform*) addressing

directa [di'rekta] NF (*Auto*) top gear

directivo, -a [direk'tiβo, a] ADJ (*junta*) managing; (*función*) administrative ▶ NM/F (*Com*) manager ▶ NF (*norma*) directive; (*tb:* **junta directiva**) board of directors

★**directo, -a** [di'rekto, a] ADJ direct; (*línea*) straight; (*inmediato*) immediate; (*tren*) through; (*TV*) live; **programa en ~** live programme; **transmitir en ~** to broadcast live

★**director, a** [direk'tor, a] ADJ leading ▶ NM/F director; (*Escol*) head (teacher) (*BRIT*), principal (*US*); (*gerente*) manager/manageress; (*de compañía*) president; (*jefe*) head; (*Prensa*) editor; (*de prisión*) governor (*BRIT*), warden (*US*); (*Mus*) conductor; **~ adjunto** assistant manager; **~ de cine** film director; **~ comercial** marketing manager; **~ ejecutivo** executive director; **~ de empresa** company director; **~ general** general manager; **~ gerente** managing director; **~ de sucursal** branch manager

directorio [direk'torjo] NM (*Inform*) directory; (*Am: telefónico*) phone book

directrices [direk'triθes] NFPL guidelines

dirigente [diri'xente] ADJ leading ▶ NMF (*Pol*) leader; **los dirigentes del partido** the party leaders

dirigible [diri'xiβle] ADJ (*Aviat, Naut*) steerable ▶ NM airship

★**dirigir** [diri'xir] /3c/ VT to direct; (*acusación*) to level; (*carta*) to address; (*obra de teatro, película*) to direct; (*Mus*) to conduct; (*comercio*) to manage; (*expedición*) to lead; (*sublevación*) to head; (*periódico*) to edit; (*guiar*) to guide ▪ **dirigirse** VR: **dirigirse a** to go towards, make one's way towards; (*hablar con*) to speak to; **dirigirse a algn solicitando algo** to apply to sb for sth; **"diríjase a ..."** "apply to ..."

dirigismo [diri'xismo] NM management, control; **~ estatal** state control

dirija *etc* [di'rixa] VB *ver* **dirigir**

dirimir [diri'mir] /3a/ VT (*contrato, matrimonio*) to dissolve

discado [dis'kaðo] NM: **~ automático** autodial

discapacidad [diskapaθi'ðað] NF disability

discapacitado, -a [diskapaθi'taðo, a] ADJ disabled ▶ NM/F disabled person

discernir [disθer'nir] /3k/ VT to discern ▶ VI to distinguish

discierna *etc* [dis'θjerna] VB *ver* **discernir**

★**disciplina** [disθi'plina] NF discipline

disciplinar [disθipli'nar] /1a/ VT to discipline; (*enseñar*) to school; (*Mil*) to drill; (*azotar*) to whip

discípulo, -a [dis'θipulo, a] NM/F disciple; (*seguidor*) follower; (*Escol*) pupil

Discman® ['diskman] NM Discman®, personal CD player

★**disco** ['disko] NM disc (*BRIT*), disk (*US*); (*Deporte*) discus; (*Telec*) dial; (*Auto: semáforo*) light; (*Mus*) record; (*Inform*) disk; **~ de arranque** boot disk; **~ compacto** compact disc; **~ de densidad sencilla/doble** single/double density disk; **~ de larga duración** long-playing record (LP); **~ flexible** o **floppy** floppy disk; **~ de freno** brake disc; **~ maestro** master disk; **~ de reserva** backup disk; **~ rígido** hard disk; **~ de una cara/dos caras** single-/double-sided disk; **~ virtual** RAM disk

discóbolo [dis'koβolo] NM discus thrower

discográfico, -a [disko'ɣrafiko, a] ADJ record *cpd*; **casa discográfica** record company; **sello ~** label

díscolo, -a ['diskolo, a] ADJ (*rebelde*) unruly

disconforme [diskon'forme] ADJ differing; **estar ~ (con)** to be in disagreement (with)

discontinuo, -a [diskon'tinwo, a] ADJ discontinuous; (*Auto: línea*) broken

discordar [diskor'ðar] /1l/ VI (*Mus*) to be out of tune; (*estar en desacuerdo*) to disagree; (*colores, opiniones*) to clash

discorde [dis'korðe] ADJ (*sonido*) discordant; (*opiniones*) clashing

discordia [dis'korðja] NF discord

★**discoteca** [disko'teka] NF disco(theque)

discreción [diskre'θjon] NF discretion; (*reserva*) prudence; **¡a ~!** (*Mil*) stand easy!; **añadir azúcar a ~** (*Culin*) add sugar to taste; **comer a ~** to eat as much as one wishes

discrecional [diskreθjo'nal] ADJ (*facultativo*) discretionary; **parada ~** request stop

discrepancia [diskre'panθja] NF (*diferencia*) discrepancy; (*desacuerdo*) disagreement

discrepante [diskre'pante] ADJ divergent; **hubo varias voces discrepantes** there were some dissenting voices

discrepar [diskre'par] /1a/ VI to disagree

discreto, -a [dis'kreto, a] ADJ (*diplomático*) discreet; (*sensato*) sensible; (*reservado*) quiet; (*sobrio*) sober; (*mediano*) fair, fairly good; **le daremos un plazo ~** we'll allow him a reasonable time

★**discriminación** [diskrimina'θjon] NF discrimination

discriminar [diskrimi'nar] /1a/ VT to discriminate against; (*diferenciar*) to discriminate between

discuerde *etc* [dis'kwerðe] VB *ver* **discordar**

★**disculpa** [dis'kulpa] NF excuse; (*para pedir perdón*) apology; **pedir disculpas a/por** to apologize to/for

★**disculpar** [diskul'par] /1a/ VT to excuse, pardon ▪ **disculparse** VR to excuse o.s.; to apologize

discurrir [disku'rrir] /3a/ VT to contrive, think up ▶ VI (*pensar, reflexionar*) to think, meditate;

(*recorrer*) to roam, wander; (*río*) to flow; (*el tiempo*) to pass, flow by

★**discurso** [dis'kurso] NM speech; **~ de clausura** closing speech; **pronunciar un ~** to make a speech; **en el ~ del tiempo** with the passage of time

★**discusión** [disku'sjon] NF (*diálogo*) discussion; (*riña*) argument; **tener una ~** to have an argument

discutible [disku'tiβle] ADJ debatable; **de mérito ~** of dubious worth

discutido, -a [disku'tiðo, a] ADJ controversial

★**discutir** [disku'tir] /**3a**/ VT (*debatir*) to discuss; (*pelear*) to argue about; (*contradecir*) to argue against ► VI to discuss; (*disputar*) to argue; **~ de política** to argue about politics; **¡no discutas!** don't argue!

disecar [dise'kar] /**1g**/ VT (*para conservar: animal*) to stuff; (: *planta*) to dry

diseminar [disemi'nar] /**1a**/ VT to disseminate, spread

disentir [disen'tir] /**3i**/ VI to dissent, disagree

diseñador, a [diseɲa'dor, a] NM/F designer

★**diseñar** [dise'ɲar] /**1a**/ VT, VI to design

★**diseño** [di'seɲo] NM (*Tec*) design; (*Arte*) drawing; (*Costura*) pattern; **de ~ italiano** Italian-designed; **~ asistido por ordenador** computer-aided design, CAD

diseque *etc* [di'seke] VB *ver* **disecar**

disertar [diser'tar] /**1a**/ VI to speak

disfrace *etc* [dis'fraθe] VB *ver* **disfrazar**

disfraz [dis'fraθ] NM (*máscara*) disguise; (*traje*) fancy dress; (*excusa*) pretext; **bajo el ~ de** under the cloak of

disfrazado, -a [disfra'θaðo, a] ADJ disguised; **ir ~ de** to masquerade as

disfrazar [disfra'θar] /**1f**/ VT to disguise ■ **disfrazarse** VR to dress (o.s.) up; **disfrazarse de** to disguise o.s. as

★**disfrutar** [disfru'tar] /**1a**/ VT to enjoy ► VI to enjoy o.s.; **¡que disfrutes!** have a good time!; **~ de** to enjoy, possess; **~ de buena salud** to enjoy good health

disfrute [dis'frute] NM (*goce*) enjoyment; (*aprovechamiento*) use

disgregar [disɣre'ɣar] /**1h**/ VT (*desintegrar*) to disintegrate; (*manifestantes*) to disperse ■ **disgregarse** VR to disintegrate, break up

disgregue *etc* [dis'ɣreɣe] VB *ver* **disgregar**

disgustar [disɣus'tar] /**1a**/ VT (*no gustar*) to displease; (*contrariar, enojar*) to annoy, upset; **estaba muy disgustado con el asunto** he was very upset about the affair ■ **disgustarse** VR to get upset; (*dos personas*) to fall out

disgusto [dis'ɣusto] NM (*repugnancia*) disgust; (*contrariedad*) annoyance; (*desagrado*) displeasure; (*tristeza*) grief; (*riña*) quarrel; (*desgracia*) misfortune; **hacer algo a ~** to do sth unwillingly; **matar a algn a disgustos** to drive sb to distraction

disidente [disi'ðente] NM dissident

disienta *etc* [di'sjenta] VB *ver* **disentir**

disimulado, -a [disimu'laðo, a] ADJ (*solapado*) furtive, underhand; (*oculto*) covert; **hacerse el ~** to pretend not to notice

disimular [disimu'lar] /**1a**/ VT (*ocultar*) to hide, conceal ► VI to dissemble

disimulo [disi'mulo] NM (*fingimiento*) dissimulation; **con ~** cunningly

disipar [disi'par] /**1a**/ VT (*duda, temor*) to dispel; (*esperanza*) to destroy; (*fortuna*) to squander ■ **disiparse** VR (*nubes*) to vanish; (*dudas*) to be dispelled; (*indisciplinarse*) to dissipate

diskette [dis'ket] NM (*Inform*) diskette, floppy disk

dislate [dis'late] NM (*absurdo*) absurdity ■ **dislates** NMPL nonsense *sg*

dislexia [dis'leksja] NF dyslexia

dislocar [dislo'kar] /**1g**/ VT (*gen*) to dislocate; (*tobillo*) to sprain ■ **dislocarse** VR (*articulación*) to sprain, dislocate

disloque *etc* [dis'loke] VB *ver* **dislocar** ► NM: **es el ~** (*fam*) it's the last straw

disminución [disminu'θjon] NF decrease, reduction

disminuido, -a [disminu'iðo, a] NM/F: **~ mental/físico** person with a mental/physical disability

★**disminuir** [disminu'ir] /**3g**/ VT to decrease, diminish; (*estrechar*) to lessen; (*temperatura*) to lower; (*gastos, raciones*) to cut down; (*dolor*) to relieve; (*autoridad, prestigio*) to weaken; (*entusiasmo*) to dampen ► VI (*días*) to grow shorter; (*precios, temperatura*) to drop, fall; (*velocidad*) to slacken; (*población*) to decrease; (*beneficios, número*) to fall off; (*memoria, vista*) to fail

disminuyendo *etc* [disminu'jendo] VB *ver* **disminuir**

disociar [diso'θjar] /**1b**/ VT to disassociate ■ **disociarse** VR to disassociate o.s.

disoluble [diso'luβle] ADJ soluble

disolución [disolu'θjon] NF (*acto*) dissolution; (*Química*) solution; (*Com*) liquidation; (*moral*) dissoluteness

disoluto, -a [diso'luto, a] ADJ dissolute

disolvente [disol'βente] NM solvent, thinner

disolver [disol'βer] /**2h**/ VT (*gen*) to dissolve; (*manifestación*) to break up ■ **disolverse** VR to dissolve; (*Com*) to go into liquidation

disonar [diso'nar] /**1l**/ VI (*Mus*) to be out of tune; (*no armonizar*) to lack harmony; **~ con** to be out of keeping with, clash with

dispar [dis'par] ADJ (*distinto*) different; (*irregular*) uneven

disparado, -a [dispa'raðo, a] ADJ: **entrar ~** to shoot in; **salir ~** to shoot out; **ir ~** to go like mad

disparador [dispara'ðor] NM (*de arma*) trigger; (*Foto, Tec*) release; **~ atómico** aerosol; **~ de bombas** bomb release

disparar [dispa'rar] /**1a**/ VT, VI to shoot, fire ■ **dispararse** VR (*arma de fuego*) to go off; (*persona: marcharse*) to rush off; (: *enojarse*) to lose control; (*caballo*) to bolt

disparatado, -a [dispara'taðo, a] ADJ crazy

disparate [dispa'rate] NM (*tontería*) foolish remark; (*error*) blunder; **decir disparates** to talk nonsense; **¡qué ~!** how absurd!; **costar un ~** to cost a hell of a lot

disparo [dis'paro] NM shot; (*acto*) firing; **~ inicial** (*de cohete*) blast-off ■ **disparos** NMPL shooting *sg*, exchange *sg* of shots, shots

dispendio [dis'pendjo] NM waste

dispensar [dispen'sar] /**1a**/ VT to dispense; (*ayuda*) to give; (*honores*) to grant; (*disculpar*) to excuse; **¡usted dispense!** I beg your pardon!; **~ a algn de hacer algo** to excuse sb from doing sth

dispensario [dispen'sarjo] NM (*clínica*) community clinic; (*de hospital*) outpatients' department

dispersar [disper'sar] /**1a**/ VT to disperse; (*manifestación*) to break up ■ **dispersarse** VR to scatter

disperso, -a [dis'perso, a] ADJ scattered

displicencia [displi'θenθja] NF (*mal humor*) peevishness; (*desgana*) lack of enthusiasm

displicente [displi'θente] ADJ (*malhumorado*) peevish; (*poco entusiasta*) unenthusiastic

dispondré *etc* [dispon'dre] VB *ver* **disponer**

disponer [dispo'ner] /**2q**/ VT (*arreglar*) to arrange; (*ordenar*) to put in order; (*preparar*) to prepare, get ready; **la ley dispone que ...** the law provides that ... ▶ VI: **~ de** to have, own; **no puede ~ de esos bienes** she cannot dispose of those properties ■ **disponerse** VR: **disponerse para** to prepare to, prepare for

disponga *etc* [dis'ponga] VB *ver* **disponer**

disponibilidad [disponiβili'ðað] NF availability ■ **disponibilidades** NFPL (*Com*) resources, financial assets

★**disponible** [dispo'niβle] ADJ available; (*tiempo*) spare; (*dinero*) on hand

disposición [disposi'θjon] NF arrangement, disposition; (*voluntad*) willingness; (*de casa, Inform*) layout; (*ley*) order; (*cláusula*) provision; (*aptitud*) aptitude; **~ de ánimo** attitude of mind; **última ~** last will and testament; **a la ~ de** at the disposal of; **a su ~** at your service

dispositivo [disposi'tiβo] NM device, mechanism; **~ de alimentación** hopper; **~ de almacenaje** storage device; **~ periférico** peripheral (device); **~ de seguridad** safety catch; (*fig*) security measure

★**dispuesto, -a** [dis'pwesto, a] PP *de* **disponer** ▶ ADJ (*arreglado*) arranged; (*preparado*) disposed; (*persona: dinámico*) bright; **estar ~/poco ~ a hacer algo** to be inclined/reluctant to do sth

dispuse *etc* [dis'puse] VB *ver* **disponer**

★**disputa** [dis'puta] NF (*discusión*) dispute, argument; (*controversia*) controversy

disputar [dispu'tar] /**1a**/ VT (*discutir*) to dispute, question; (*contender*) to contend for; (*carrera*) to compete in ▶ VI to argue

disquete [dis'kete] NM (*Inform*) diskette, floppy disk

disquetera [diske'tera] NF disk drive

Dist. ABR (= *Distrito*) dist.

★**distancia** [dis'tanθja] NF distance; (*de tiempo*) interval; **~ de parada** braking distance; **~ del suelo** (*Auto etc*) height off the ground; **a gran** o **a larga ~** long-distance; **mantenerse a ~** to keep one's distance; (*fig*) to remain aloof; **guardar las distancias** to keep one's distance

distanciado, -a [distan'θjaðo, a] ADJ (*remoto*) remote; (*fig: alejado*) far apart; **estamos distanciados en ideas** our ideas are poles apart

distanciamiento [distanθja'mjento] NM (*acto*) spacing out; (*estado*) remoteness; (*fig*) distance

distanciar [distan'θjar] /**1b**/ VT to space out ■ **distanciarse** VR to become estranged

distante [dis'tante] ADJ distant

distar [dis'tar] /**1a**/ VI: **dista 5 km de aquí** it is 5 km from here; **¿dista mucho?** is it far?; **dista mucho de la verdad** it's very far from the truth

diste ['diste], **disteis** ['disteis] VB *ver* **dar**

distensión [disten'sjon] NF distension; (*Pol*) détente; **~ muscular** (*Med*) muscular strain

distinción [distin'θjon] NF distinction; (*elegancia*) elegance; (*honor*) honour; **a ~ de** unlike; **sin ~** indiscriminately; **sin ~ de edades** irrespective of age

distinga *etc* [dis'tinga] VB *ver* **distinguir**

distinguido, -a [distin'giðo, a] ADJ distinguished; (*famoso*) prominent, well-known; (*elegante*) elegant

★**distinguir** [distin'gir] /**3d**/ VT to distinguish; (*divisar*) to make out; (*escoger*) to single out; (*caracterizar*) to mark out ■ **distinguirse** VR to be distinguished; (*destacarse*) to distinguish o.s.; **a lo lejos no se distingue** it's not visible from a distance

distintivo, -a [distin'tiβo, a] ADJ distinctive; (*signo*) distinguishing ▶ NM (*de policía etc*) badge; (*fig*) characteristic

★**distinto, -a** [dis'tinto, a] ADJ different; (*claro*) clear; **distintos** several, various

distorsión [distor'sjon] NF (*Anat*) twisting; (*Radio etc*) distortion

distorsionar [distorsjo'nar] /**1a**/ VT, VI to distort

★**distracción** [distrak'θjon] NF distraction; (*pasatiempo*) hobby, pastime; (*olvido*) absent-mindedness, distraction

distraer [distra'er] /**2o**/ VT (*atención*) to distract; (*divertir*) to amuse; (*fondos*) to embezzle;

~ a algn de su pensamiento to divert sb from his train of thought ▶ VI to be relaxing; **el pescar distrae** fishing is a relaxation ■ **distraerse** VR (*entretenerse*) to amuse o.s.; (*perder la concentración*) to allow one's attention to wander

distraído, -a [distra'iðo, a] ADJ (*gen*) absent-minded; (*desatento*) inattentive; (*entretenido*) amusing; **con aire ~** idly; **me miró distraída** she gave me a casual glance ▶ NM: **hacerse el ~** to pretend not to notice

distraiga etc [dis'traiɣa], **distraje** etc [dis'traxe], **distrajera** etc [distra'xera], **distrayendo** [distra'jendo] VB ver **distraer**

distribución [distriβu'θjon] NF distribution; (*entrega*) delivery; (*en estadística*) distribution, incidence; (*Arq*) layout; **~ de premios** prize-giving; **la ~ de los impuestos** the incidence of taxes

distribuidor, a [distriβui'ðor, a] NM/F (*persona: gen*) distributor; (: *Correos*) sorter; (: *Com*) dealer, agent; **su ~ habitual** your regular dealer

★**distribuir** [distriβu'ir] /3g/ VT to distribute; (*prospectos*) to hand out; (*cartas*) to deliver; (*trabajo*) to allocate; (*premios*) to award; (*dividendos*) to pay; (*peso*) to distribute; (*Arq*) to plan

distribuyendo etc [distriβu'jendo] VB ver **distribuir**

distrito [dis'trito] NM (*sector, territorio*) region; (*barrio*) district; **~ electoral** constituency; **~ postal** postal district; **D~ Federal** (*AM*) Federal District

disturbio [dis'turβjo] NM disturbance; (*desorden*) riot ■ **los disturbios** NMPL the troubles

disuadir [diswa'ðir] /3a/ VT to dissuade

disuasión [diswa'sjon] NF dissuasion; (*Mil*) deterrent; **~ nuclear** nuclear deterrent

disuasivo, -a [diswa'siβo, a] ADJ dissuasive; **arma disuasiva** deterrent

disuasorio, -a [diswa'sorjo, a] ADJ = **disuasivo**

disuelto [di'swelto] PP de **disolver**

disuelva etc [di'swelβa] VB ver **disolver**

disuene etc [di'swene] VB ver **disonar**

disyuntiva [disjun'tiβa] NF (*dilema*) dilemma

DIU ['diu] NM ABR (= *dispositivo intrauterino*) IUD

diurno, -a ['djurno, a] ADJ day cpd, diurnal

diva ['diβa] NF prima donna

divagar [diβa'ɣar] /1h/ VI (*desviarse*) to digress

divague etc [di'βaɣe] VB ver **divagar**

diván [di'βan] NM divan

divergencia [diβer'xenθja] NF divergence

divergir [diβer'xir] /3c/ VI (*líneas*) to diverge; (*opiniones*) to differ; (*personas*) to disagree

diverja etc [di'βerxa] VB ver **divergir**

diversidad [diβersi'ðað] NF diversity, variety

diversificación [diβersifika'θjon] NF (*Com*) diversification

diversificar [diβersifi'kar] /1g/ VT to diversify

diversifique etc [diβersi'fike] VB ver **diversificar**

★**diversión** [diβer'sjon] NF (*gen*) entertainment; (*actividad*) hobby, pastime

diverso, -a [di'βerso, a] ADJ diverse; (*diferente*) different; **diversos libros** several books ▶ NM: **diversos** (*Com*) sundries

★**divertido, -a** [diβer'tiðo, a] ADJ (*chiste*) amusing, funny; (*fiesta etc*) enjoyable; (*película, libro*) entertaining; **está ~** (*irónico*) this is going to be fun

★**divertir** [diβer'tir] /3i/ VT (*entretener, recrear*) to amuse, entertain ■ **divertirse** VR (*pasarlo bien*) to have a good time; (*distraerse*) to amuse o.s.

dividendo [diβi'ðendo] NM (*Com*) dividend, dividends; **~ definitivo** final dividend; **dividendos por acción** earnings per share

★**dividir** [diβi'ðir] /3a/ VT (*gen*) to divide; (*separar*) to separate; (*distribuir*) to distribute, share out

divierta etc [di'βjerta] VB ver **divertir**

divinidad [diβini'ðað] NF (*esencia divina*) divinity; **la D~** God

divino, -a [di'βino, a] ADJ divine; (*fig*) lovely

divirtiendo etc [diβir'tjendo] VB ver **divertir**

divisa [di'βisa] NF (*emblema*) emblem, badge; **~ de reserva** reserve currency ■ **divisas** NFPL currency sg; (*Com*) foreign exchange sg; **control de divisas** exchange control

divisar [diβi'sar] /1a/ VT to make out, distinguish

división [diβi'sjon] NF division; (*de partido*) split; (*de país*) partition

divisorio, -a [diβi'sorjo, a] ADJ (*línea*) dividing; **línea divisoria de las aguas** watershed

divorciado, -a [diβor'θjaðo, a] ADJ divorced; (*opinión*) split ▶ NM/F divorcé(e)

divorciar [diβor'θjar] /1b/ VT to divorce ■ **divorciarse** VR to get divorced

★**divorcio** [di'βorθjo] NM divorce; (*fig*) split

divulgación [diβulɣa'θjon] NF (*difusión*) spreading; (*popularización*) popularization

divulgar [diβul'ɣar] /1h/ VT (*desparramar*) to spread; (*popularizar*) to popularize; (*hacer circular*) to divulge, circulate ■ **divulgarse** VR (*secreto*) to leak out; (*rumor*) to get about

divulgue etc [di'βulɣe] VB ver **divulgar**

dizque ['diske] ADV (*AM fam*) apparently

Dls, dls ABR (*AM*) = **dólares**

dm ABR (= *decímetro*) dm

★**DNI** NM ABR (*ESP*) = **Documento Nacional de Identidad**

The *Documento Nacional de Identidad* is a Spanish ID card which must be carried at all times and produced on request for the police. It contains the holder's photo, fingerprints and personal details. It is also known as the **DNI** or *carnet de identidad*.

Dña. ABR (= *Doña*) Mrs

do [do] NM (*Mus*) C

D.O. ABR = **Denominación de Origen**; *ver* **denominación**

dobladillo [doβla'ðiʎo] NM (*de vestido*) hem; (*de pantalón: vuelta*) turn-up (BRIT), cuff (US)

doblaje [do'βlaxe] NM (*Cine*) dubbing

★**doblar** [do'βlar] /**1a**/ VT to double; (*papel*) to fold; (*caño*) to bend; (*la esquina*) to turn, go round; (*film*) to dub ▶ VI to turn; (*campana*) to toll; **~ a la derecha/izquierda** to turn right/left ■ **doblarse** VR (*plegarse*) to fold (up), crease; (*encorvarse*) to bend

★**doble** ['doβle] ADJ (*gen*) double; (*de dos aspectos*) dual; (*cuerda*) thick; (*fig*) two-faced; **~ o nada** double or quits; **~ página** double-page spread; **con ~ sentido** with a double meaning; (*Inform*) **de ~ cara** double-sided; **~ densidad** double density; **~ espacio** double spacing ▶ NM double; **el ~** twice the quantity *o* as much; **su sueldo es el ~ del mío** his salary is twice (as much as) mine ▶ NMF (*Teat*) double, stand-in ■ **dobles** NMPL (*Deporte*) doubles *sg*

doblegar [doβle'ɣar] /**1h**/ VT to fold, crease ■ **doblegarse** VR to yield

doblegue *etc* [do'βleɣe] VB *ver* **doblegar**

doblez [do'βleθ] NM (*pliegue*) fold, hem ▶ NF (*falsedad*) duplicity

doc. ABR (= *docena*) doz.; (= *documento*) doc.

★**doce** ['doθe] NUM twelve; (*fecha*) twelfth; **las ~** twelve o'clock; *ver tb* **seis**

★**docena** [do'θena] NF dozen; **por docenas** by the dozen

docente [do'θente] ADJ: **personal ~** teaching staff; **centro ~** educational institution

dócil ['doθil] ADJ (*pasivo*) docile; (*manso*) gentle; (*obediente*) obedient

docto, -a ['dokto, a] ADJ learned, erudite ▶ NM/F scholar

★**doctor, a** [dok'tor, a] NM/F doctor; **~ en filosofía** Doctor of Philosophy

doctorado [dokto'raðo] NM doctorate

> In Spain, the **doctorado** (PhD) is divided into two stages: the first stage which can begin at a Master's level and must accrue a minimum of 60 credits; and a second stage which focuses on research and concludes with a viva. In theory, the PhD should be completed within a maximum period of three years if done on a full-time basis, although it is possible to do it in five years on a part-time basis.

doctorarse [dokto'rarse] /**1a**/ VR to get a doctorate

doctrina [dok'trina] NF doctrine, teaching

★**documentación** [dokumenta'θjon] NF documentation; (*de identidad etc*) papers *pl*

★**documental** [dokumen'tal] ADJ, NM documentary

documentar [dokumen'tar] /**1a**/ VT to document ■ **documentarse** VR to gather information

★**documento** [doku'mento] NM (*certificado*) document; (*Jur*) exhibit; **~ adjunto** (*Inform*) attachment; **~ justificativo** voucher; **D~ Nacional de Identidad** national identity card ■ **documentos** NMPL papers; *ver tb* **DNI**

dogma ['doɣma] NM dogma

dogmático, -a [doɣ'matiko, a] ADJ dogmatic

dogo ['doɣo] NM bulldog

dólar ['dolar] NM dollar

dolencia [do'lenθja] NF (*achaque*) ailment; (*dolor*) ache

★**doler** [do'ler] /**2h**/ VI to hurt; (*fig*) to grieve; **me duele el brazo** my arm hurts; **no me duele el dinero** I don't mind about the money; **¡ahí le duele!** you've put your finger on it! ■ **dolerse** VR (*de su situación*) to grieve, feel sorry; (*de las desgracias ajenas*) to sympathize; (*quejarse*) to complain

doliente [do'ljente] ADJ (*enfermo*) sick; (*dolorido*) aching; (*triste*) sorrowful; **la familia ~** the bereaved family

★**dolor** [do'lor] NM pain; (*fig*) grief, sorrow; **~ de cabeza** headache; **~ de estómago** stomach ache; **~ de oídos** earache; **~ sordo** dull ache

dolorido, -a [dolo'riðo, a] ADJ (*Med*) sore; **la parte dolorida** the part which hurts

doloroso, -a [dolo'roso, a] ADJ (*Med*) painful; (*fig*) distressing

dom. ABR (= *domingo*) Sun.

domar [do'mar] /**1a**/ VT to tame

domesticado, -a [domesti'kaðo, a] ADJ (*amansado*) tame

domesticar [domesti'kar] /**1g**/ VT to tame

doméstico, -a [do'mestiko, a] ADJ domestic; (*vida, servicio*) home; (*tareas*) household; (*animal*) tame, pet; **economía doméstica** home economy; **gastos domésticos** household expenses ▶ NM/F servant

domestique *etc* [domes'tike] VB *ver* **domesticar**

domiciliación [domiθilja'θjon] NF: **~ de pagos** (*Com*) direct debit

domiciliar [domiθi'ljar] /**1b**/ VT to domicile ■ **domiciliarse** VR to take up (one's) residence

domiciliario, -a [domiθi'ljarjo, a] ADJ: **arresto ~** house arrest

★**domicilio** [domi'θiljo] NM home; **~ particular** private residence; **~ social** (*Com*) head office, registered office; **servicio a ~** delivery service; **sin ~ fijo** of no fixed abode

dominante [domi'nante] ADJ dominant; (*persona*) domineering

dominar [domi'nar] /**1a**/ VT (*gen*) to dominate; (*países*) to rule over; (*adversario*) to overpower; (*caballo, nervios, emoción*) to control; (*incendio, epidemia*) to bring under control; (*idiomas*) to be fluent in ▶ VI to dominate, prevail ■ **dominarse** VR to control o.s.

*domingo [do'mingo] NM Sunday; **D~ de Ramos** Palm Sunday; **D~ de Resurrección** Easter Sunday; *ver tb* **sábado**; **Semana Santa**

dominguero, -a [domin'gero, a] ADJ Sunday *cpd*

Dominica [domi'nika] NF Dominica

dominical [domini'kal] ADJ Sunday *cpd*; **periódico ~** Sunday newspaper

dominicano, -a [domini'kano, a] ADJ, NM/F Dominican

dominio [do'minjo] NM (*tierras*) domain; (*Pol*) dominion; (*autoridad*) power, authority; (*supremacía*) supremacy; (*de las pasiones*) grip, hold; (*de idioma*) command; **ser del ~ público** to be widely known

dominó [domi'no] NM (*pieza*) domino; (*juego*) dominoes

*don [don] NM (*talento*) gift; **D~ Juan Gómez** Mr Juan Gómez, Juan Gómez Esq. (BRIT); **tener ~ de gentes** to know how to handle people; **~ de lenguas** gift for languages; **~ de mando** (qualities of) leadership; **~ de palabra** gift of the gab; *see note*

> **Don** or *doña* is a term used before someone's first name – eg Don Diego, Doña Inés – when showing respect or being polite to a superior or an older person. It is becoming somewhat rare, but it does however continue to be used with names and surnames in official documents and in correspondence: eg Sr. D. Pedro Rodríguez Hernández, Sra. Dña. Inés Rodríguez Hernández.

dona ['dona] NF (*Am*) doughnut, donut (*US*)

donación [dona'θjon] NF donation

donaire [do'naire] NM charm

donante [do'nante] NMF donor; **~ de sangre** blood donor

donar [do'nar] /1a/ VT to donate

donativo [dona'tiβo] NM donation

doncella [don'θeʎa] NF (*criada*) maid

*donde ['donde] ADV where; **por ~** through which; **a ~** to where, to which; **en ~** where, in which; **es a ~ vamos nosotros** that's where we're going ▶ PREP: **el coche está allí ~ el farol** the car is over there by the lamppost *o* where the lamppost is

*dónde ['donde] ADV INTERROGATIVO where?; **¿a ~ vas?** where are you going (to)?; **¿de ~ vienes?** where have you been?; **¿en ~?** where?; **¿por ~?** where?, whereabouts?; **¿por ~ se va al estadio?** how do you get to the stadium?

dondequiera [donde'kjera] ADV anywhere; **por ~** everywhere, all over the place ▶ CONJ: **~ que** wherever

donostiarra [donos'tjarra] ADJ of *o* from San Sebastián ▶ NMF native *o* inhabitant of San Sebastián

donut® [do'nut] NM (*Esp*) doughnut, donut (*US*)

*doña ['doɲa] NF: **~ Alicia** Alicia; **D~ Carmen Gómez** Mrs Carmen Gómez; *ver tb* **don**

dopar [do'par] /1a/ VT to dope, drug

doping ['dopin] NM doping, drugging

doquier [do'kjer] ADV: **por ~** all over, everywhere

dorado, -a [do'raðo, a] ADJ (*color*) golden; (*Tec*) gilt

dorar [do'rar] /1a/ VT (*Tec*) to gild; (*Culin*) to brown, cook lightly; **~ la píldora** to sweeten the pill

dormilón, -ona [dormi'lon, ona] ADJ fond of sleeping ▶ NM/F sleepyhead

*dormir [dor'mir] /3j/ VT: **~ la siesta** to have an afternoon nap; **dormirla** (*fam*) to sleep it off; **~ la mona** (*fam*) to sleep off a hangover ▶ VI to sleep; **~ como un lirón** *o* **tronco** to sleep like a log; **~ a pierna suelta** to sleep soundly ■ **dormirse** VR (*persona*) to fall asleep; (*brazo, pierna*) to go to sleep

dormitar [dormi'tar] /1a/ VI to doze

*dormitorio [dormi'torjo] NM bedroom; **~ común** dormitory

dorsal [dor'sal] ADJ dorsal ▶ NM (*Deporte*) number

dorso ['dorso] NM (*de mano*) back; (*de hoja*) other side; **escribir algo al ~** to write sth on the back; **"véase al ~"** "see other side", "please turn over"

*dos [dos] NUM two; (*fecha*) second; **los ~** the two of them, both of them; **cada ~ por tres** every five minutes; **de ~ en ~** in twos; **estamos a ~** (*Tenis*) the score is deuce; *ver tb* **seis**

doscientos, -as [dos'θjentos, as] NUM two hundred

dosel [do'sel] NM canopy

dosificar [dosifi'kar] /1g/ VT (*Culin, Med, Química*) to measure out; (*no derrochar*) to be sparing with

dosifique *etc* [dosi'fike] VB *ver* **dosificar**

dosis ['dosis] NF INV dose, dosage

dossier [do'sjer] NM dossier, file

dotación [dota'θjon] NF (*acto, dinero*) endowment; (*plantilla*) staff; (*Naut*) crew; **la ~ es insuficiente** we are understaffed

dotado, -a [do'taðo, a] ADJ gifted; **~ de** (*persona*) endowed with; (*máquina*) equipped with

dotar [do'tar] /1a/ VT to endow; (*Tec*) to fit; (*barco*) to man; (*oficina*) to staff

dote ['dote] NF (*de novia*) dowry ■ **dotes** NFPL (*talentos*) gifts

doy [doi] VB *ver* **dar**

Dpto. ABR (= *Departamento*) dept.

Dr., Dra. ABR (= *Doctor; Doctora*) Dr

draga ['draɣa] NF dredge

dragado [dra'ɣaðo] NM dredging

dragar [dra'ɣar] /1h/ VT to dredge; (*minas*) to sweep

dragón [dra'ɣon] NM dragon

drague *etc* ['draɣe] VB *ver* **dragar**

drama ['drama] NM drama; (*obra*) play

dramático, -a [dra'matiko, a] ADJ dramatic; **obra dramática** play ▸ NM/F dramatist; (*actor*) actor

dramaturgo, -a [drama'turɣo, a] NM/F dramatist, playwright

dramón [dra'mon] NM (*Teat*) melodrama; **¡qué ~!** what a scene!

drástico, -a ['drastiko, a] ADJ drastic

drenaje [dre'naxe] NM drainage

drenar [dre'nar] /**1a**/ VT to drain

★**droga** ['droɣa] NF drug; (*Deporte*) dope; **el problema de la ~** the drug problem

★**drogadicto, -a** [droɣa'ðikto, a] NM/F drug addict

drogar [dro'ɣar] /**1h**/ VT to drug; (*Deporte*) to dope ∎ **drogarse** VR to take drugs

drogodependencia [droɣoðepen'denθja] NF drug addiction

drogue *etc* ['droɣe] VB *ver* **drogar**

★**droguería** [droɣe'ria] NF ≈ hardware shop (*BRIT*) o store (*US*)

dromedario [drome'ðarjo] NM dromedary

dron [dron] NM drone

Dto. ABR = **descuento**

Dtor., Dtora. ABR (= *Director; Directora*) Dir.

ducado [du'kaðo] NM duchy, dukedom

★**ducha** ['dutʃa] NF (*baño*) shower; (*Med*) douche

★**ducharse** [du'tʃarse] /**1a**/ VR to have a shower, take a shower

ducho, -a ['dutʃo, a] ADJ: **~ en** (*experimentado*) experienced in; (*hábil*) skilled at

dúctil ['duktil] ADJ (*metal*) ductile; (*persona*) easily influenced

duda ['duða] NF doubt; **sin ~** no doubt, doubtless; **¡sin ~!** of course!; **no cabe ~** there is no doubt about it; **no le quepa ~** make no mistake about it; **no quiero poner en ~ su conducta** I don't want to call his behaviour into question; **sacar a algn de la ~** to settle sb's doubts; **tengo una ~** I have a query

★**dudar** [du'ðar] /**1a**/ VT to doubt; **dudan que sea verdad** they doubt whether o if it's true ▸ VI to doubt, have doubts; **~ acerca de algo** to be uncertain about sth; **dudó en comprarlo** he hesitated to buy it

dudoso, -a [du'ðoso, a] ADJ (*incierto*) hesitant; (*sospechoso*) doubtful; (*conducta*) dubious

duela *etc* VB *ver* **doler**

duelo ['dwelo] VB *ver* **doler** ▸ NM (*combate*) duel; (*luto*) mourning; **batirse en ~** to fight a duel

duende ['dwende] NM imp, goblin; **tiene ~** he's got real soul

★**dueño, -a** ['dweɲo, a] NM/F (*propietario*) owner; (*de pensión, taberna*) landlord(-lady); (*de casa, perro*) master (mistress); (*empresario*) employer; **ser ~ de sí mismo** to have self-control; (*libre*) to be one's own boss; **eres ~ de hacer como te**

parezca you're free to do as you think fit; **hacerse ~ de una situación** to take command of a situation

duerma *etc* ['dwerma] VB *ver* **dormir**

duermevela [dwerme'βela] NF (*fam*) nap, snooze

Duero ['dwero] NM Douro

★**dulce** ['dulθe] ADJ sweet; (*carácter, clima*) gentle, mild ▸ ADV gently, softly ▸ NM sweet

dulcería [dulθe'ria] NF (*Am*) confectioner's (shop)

dulcificar [dulθifi'kar] /**1g**/ VT (*fig*) to soften

dulcifique *etc* [dulθi'fike] VB *ver* **dulcificar**

dulzón, -ona [dul'θon, ona] ADJ (*alimento*) sickly-sweet, too sweet; (*canción etc*) gooey

dulzura [dul'θura] NF sweetness; (*ternura*) gentleness

duna ['duna] NF dune

Dunquerque [dun'kerke] NM Dunkirk

dúo ['duo] NM duet, duo

duodécimo, -a [duo'deθimo, a] ADJ twelfth; *ver tb* **sexto**

dup., dup.^{do} ABR (= *duplicado*) duplicated

dúplex ['dupleks] NM INV (*piso*) duplex (apartment); (*Telec*) link-up; (*Inform*): **~ integral** full duplex

duplicar [dupli'kar] /**1g**/ VT (*hacer el doble de*) to duplicate; (*cantidad*) to double ∎ **duplicarse** VR to double

duplique *etc* [du'plike] VB *ver* **duplicar**

duque ['duke] NM duke

duquesa [du'kesa] NF duchess

durable [du'raβle] ADJ durable

★**duración** [dura'θjon] NF (*de película, disco etc*) length; (*de pila etc*) life; (*curso: de acontecimientos etc*) duration; **~ media de la vida** average life expectancy; **de larga ~** (*enfermedad*) lengthy; (*pila*) long-life; (*disco*) long-playing; **de poca ~** short

duradero, -a [dura'ðero, a] ADJ (*material*) hard-wearing; (*fe, paz*) lasting

★**durante** [du'rante] ADV during; **~ toda la noche** all night long; **habló ~ una hora** he spoke for an hour

★**durar** [du'rar] /**1a**/ VI (*permanecer*) to last; (*recuerdo*) to remain; (*ropa*) to wear (well)

durazno [du'rasno] NM (*Am: fruta*) peach; (: *árbol*) peach tree

durex ['dureks] NM (*Am: tira adhesiva*) Sellotape® (*BRIT*), Scotch tape® (*US*)

dureza [du'reθa] NF (*cualidad*) hardness; (*de carácter*) toughness

durmiendo *etc* [dur'mjendo] VB *ver* **dormir**

durmiente [dur'mjente] ADJ sleeping ▸ NMF sleeper

★**duro, -a** ['duro, a] ADJ hard; (*carácter*) tough; (*pan*) stale; (*cuello, puerta*) stiff; (*clima, luz*) harsh; **el sector ~ del partido** the hardliners pl in the party; **ser ~ con algn** to be tough with o hard on sb; **~ de mollera** (torpe) dense; **~ de oído** hard of hearing ▶ ADV hard; **trabajar ~** to work hard ▶ NM (moneda) five peseta coin; **estar sin un ~** to be broke

DVD NM ABR (= disco de vídeo digital) DVD

Ee

E, e [e] NF (letra) E, e; **E de Enrique** E for Edward (BRIT) o Easy (US)

E ABR (= este) E

★**e** [e] CONJ (delante de i- e hi- pero no hie-) and; ver tb **y**

e/ ABR (Com: = envío) shpt.

EA ABR = **Ejército del Aire**

EAU NMPL ABR (= Emiratos Árabes Unidos) UAE

ebanista [eβa'nista] NMF cabinetmaker

ébano ['eβano] NM ebony

e-book ['ibuk] NM e-book

ebrio, -a ['eβrjo, a] ADJ drunk

Ebro ['eβro] NM Ebro

ebullición [eβuʎi'θjon] NF boiling; **punto de ~** boiling point

e-card ['ikard] NF e-card

eccema [ek'θema] NM (Med) eczema

★**echar** [e'tʃar] /1a/ VT to throw; (agua, vino) to pour (out); (Culin) to put in, add; (dientes) to cut; (discurso) to give; (empleado: despedir) to fire, sack; (hojas) to sprout; (cartas) to post; (humo) to emit, give out; (reprimenda) to deal out; (cuenta) to make up; (freno) to put on; **~ llave a** to lock (up); **~ abajo** (gobierno) to overthrow; (edificio) to demolish; **~ la buenaventura a algn** to tell sb's fortune; **~ mano a** to lay hands on; **~ una mano a algn** (ayudar) to give sb a hand; **~ la culpa a** to lay the blame on; **~ de menos** to miss; **~ una mirada** to give a look; **~ sangre** to bleed ▶ VI: **~ a correr** to start running o to run, break into a run; **~ a llorar** to burst into tears; **~ a reír** to burst out laughing ∎ **echarse** VR to lie down; **echarse atrás** to throw o.s. back(wards); (fig) to back out; **echarse una novia** to get o.s. a girlfriend; **echarse una siestecita** to have a nap

echarpe [e'tʃarpe] NM (woman's) stole

eclesiástico, -a [ekle'sjastiko, a] ADJ ecclesiastical; (autoridades etc) church cpd ▶ NM clergyman

eclipsar [eklip'sar] /1a/ VT to eclipse; (fig) to outshine, overshadow

eclipse [e'klipse] NM eclipse

eco ['eko] NM echo; **encontrar un ~ en** to produce a response from; **hacerse ~ de una opinión** to echo an opinion; **tener ~** to catch on

ecografía [ekoɣra'fia] NF ultrasound

★**ecología** [ekolo'xia] NF ecology

★**ecológico, -a** [eko'loxiko, a] ADJ ecological; (producto, método) environmentally friendly; (agricultura) organic

ecologista [ekolo'xista] ADJ environmental, conservation cpd ▶ NMF environmentalist

economato [ekono'mato] NM cooperative store

★**economía** [ekono'mia] NF (sistema) economy; (carrera) economics; (cualidad) thrift; **~ dirigida** planned economy; **~ doméstica** housekeeping; **~ de mercado** market economy; **~ mixta** mixed economy; **~ sumergida** black economy; **hacer economías** to economize; **economías de escala** economies of scale

economice etc [ekono'miθe] VB ver **economizar**

★**económico, -a** [eko'nomiko, a] ADJ (barato) cheap, economical; (persona) thrifty; (Com: año etc) financial; (: situación) economic

economista [ekono'mista] NMF economist

economizar [ekonomi'θar] /1f/ VT to economize on ▶ VI (ahorrar) to save up; (pey) to be miserly

ecosistema [ekosis'tema] NM ecosystem

ecotasa [eko'tasa] NF green tax

ecoturismo [ekotu'rismo] NM ecotourism

ecuación [ekwa'θjon] NF equation

Ecuador [ekwa'ðor] NM Ecuador

ecuador [ekwa'ðor] NM equator

ecuánime [e'kwanime] ADJ (carácter) level-headed; (estado) calm

ecuatorial [ekwato'rjal] ADJ equatorial

ecuatoriano, -a [ekwato'rjano, a] ADJ, NM/F Ecuador(i)an

ecuestre [e'kwestre] ADJ equestrian

eczema [ek'θema] NM = **eccema**

ed. ABR (= *edición*) ed.

★**edad** [e'ðað] NF age; **¿qué ~ tienes?** how old are you?; **tiene ocho años de ~** he is eight (years old); **de corta ~** young; **ser de ~ mediana/ avanzada** to be middle-aged/getting on; **ser mayor de ~** to be of age; **llegar a mayor ~** to come of age; **ser menor de ~** to be under age; **la E~ Media** the Middle Ages; **la E~ de Oro** the Golden Age

Edén [e'ðen] NM Eden

edición [eði'θjon] NF (*acto*) publication; (*ejemplar*) edition; **"al cerrar la ~"** (*Tip*) "stop press"

edicto [e'ðikto] NM edict, proclamation

edificante [eðifi'kante] ADJ edifying

edificar [eðifi'kar] /1g/ VT, VI (*Arq*) to build

★**edificio** [eði'fiθjo] NM building; (*fig*) edifice, structure

edifique *etc* [eði'fike] VB *ver* **edificar**

Edimburgo [eðim'burɣo] NM Edinburgh

editar [eði'tar] /1a/ VT (*publicar*) to publish; (*preparar textos, tb Inform*) to edit

editor, a [eði'tor, a] NM/F (*que publica*) publisher; (*redactor*) editor ▶ ADJ: **casa editora** publishing company

editorial [eðito'rjal] ADJ editorial ▶ NM leading article, editorial; (*tb*: **casa editorial**) publisher

editorialista [eðitorja'lista] NMF leader writer

edredón [eðre'ðon] NM eiderdown, quilt; **~ nórdico** duvet, continental quilt

★**educación** [eðuka'θjon] NF education; (*crianza*) upbringing; (*modales*) (good) manners *pl*; (*formación*) training; **sin ~** ill-mannered; **¡qué falta de ~!** how rude!

educado, -a [eðu'kaðo, a] ADJ well-mannered; **mal ~** ill-mannered

★**educar** [eðu'kar] /1g/ VT to educate; (*criar*) to bring up; (*voz*) to train

★**educativo, -a** [eðuka'tiβo, a] ADJ educational; (*política*) education *cpd*

eduque *etc* [e'ðuke] VB *ver* **educar**

EE UU NMPL ABR (= *Estados Unidos*) USA

efectista [efek'tista] ADJ sensationalist

efectivamente [efektiβa'mente] ADV (*como respuesta*) exactly, precisely; (*verdaderamente*) really; (*de hecho*) in fact

★**efectivo, -a** [efek'tiβo, a] ADJ effective; (*real*) actual, real; **hacer ~ un cheque** to cash a cheque ▶ NM: **pagar en ~** to pay (in) cash

★**efecto** [e'fekto] NM effect, result; (*objetivo*) purpose, end; **~ invernadero** greenhouse effect; **efectos de consumo** consumer goods; **efectos a cobrar** bills receivable; **efectos especiales** special effects; **efectos personales** personal effects; **efectos secundarios** side effects; **efectos sonoros** sound effects; **hacer ~** to have the desired effect; **hacer ~** (*impresionar*) to make an impression; **llevar algo a ~** to carry

sth out; **en ~** in fact; (*respuesta*) exactly, indeed ■ **efectos** NMPL (*personales*) effects; (*bienes*) goods; (*Com*) assets; (*Econ*) bills, securities

★**efectuar** [efek'twar] /1e/ VT to carry out; (*viaje*) to make

efervescente [eferβes'θente] ADJ (*bebida*) fizzy, bubbly

eficacia [efi'kaθja] NF (*de persona*) efficiency; (*de medicamento etc*) effectiveness

★**eficaz** [efi'kaθ] ADJ (*persona*) efficient; (*acción*) effective

eficiencia [efi'θjenθja] NF efficiency

eficiente [efi'θjente] ADJ efficient

efigie [e'fixje] NF effigy

efímero, -a [e'fimero, a] ADJ ephemeral

EFTA SIGLA F = **Asociación Europea de Libre Comercio**

efusión [efu'sjon] NF outpouring; (*en el trato*) warmth; **con ~** effusively

efusivo, -a [efu'siβo, a] ADJ effusive; **mis más efusivas gracias** my warmest thanks

EGB NF ABR (*Esp Escol*: = *Educación General Básica*) *former primary education for six- to fourteen-year olds*

Egeo [e'xeo] NM: **el (mar) ~** Aegean (Sea)

egipcio, -a [e'xipθjo, a] ADJ, NM/F Egyptian

Egipto [e'xipto] NM Egypt

egocéntrico, -a [eɣo'θentriko, a] ADJ self-centred

egoísmo [eɣo'ismo] NM egoism

★**egoísta** [eɣo'ista] ADJ egoistical, selfish ▶ NMF egoist

ególatra [e'ɣolatra] ADJ big-headed

egregio, -a [e'ɣrexjo, a] ADJ eminent, distinguished

egresado, -a [eɣre'saðo, a] NM/F (*Am*) graduate

egresar [eɣre'sar] /1a/ VI (*Am*) to graduate

eh [e] EXCL hey!, hi!

Eire ['eire] NM Eire

ej. ABR (= *ejemplo*) ex.

eje ['exe] NM (*Geo, Mat*) axis; (*Pol, fig*) axis, main line; (*de rueda*) axle; (*de máquina*) shaft, spindle

ejecución [exeku'θjon] NF execution; (*cumplimiento*) fulfilment; (*actuación*) performance; (*Jur: embargo de deudor*) attachment

ejecutar [exeku'tar] /1a/ VT to execute, carry out; (*matar*) to execute; (*cumplir*) to fulfil; (*Mus*) to perform; (*Jur: embargar*) to attach, distrain; (*deseos*) to fulfil; (*Inform*) to run

★**ejecutivo, -a** [exeku'tiβo, a] ADJ, NM/F executive; **el (poder) ~** the executive (power)

ejecutor [exeku'tor] NM (*tb*: **ejecutor testamentario**) executor

ejecutoria [exeku'torja] NF (*Jur*) final judgment

ejemplar [exem'plar] ADJ exemplary ▶ NM example; (*Zool*) specimen; (*de libro*) copy; (*de periódico*) number, issue; **~ de regalo** complimentary copy; **sin ~** unprecedented

ejemplificar [exemplifi'kar] /**1g**/ VT to exemplify, illustrate

ejemplifique *etc* [exempli'fike] VB *ver* **ejemplificar**

★**ejemplo** [e'xemplo] NM example; (*caso*) instance; **por ~** for example; **dar ~** to set an example

ejercer [exer'θer] /**2b**/ VT to exercise; (*funciones*) to perform; (*negocio*) to manage; (*influencia*) to exert; (*un oficio*) to practise; (*poder*) to wield ▶ VI: **~ de** to practise as

★**ejercicio** [exer'θiθjo] NM exercise; (*Mil*) drill; (*Com*) fiscal o financial year; (*período*) tenure; **~ acrobático** (*Aviat*) stunt; **~ comercial** business year; **ejercicios espirituales** (*Rel*) retreat *sg*; **hacer ~** to take exercise

ejercitar [exerθi'tar] /**1a**/ VT to exercise; (*Mil*) to drill

★**ejército** [e'xerθito] NM army; **E~ del Aire/de Tierra** Air Force/Army; **~ de ocupación** army of occupation; **~ permanente** standing army; **entrar en el ~** to join the army, join up

ejerza *etc* [e'xerθa] VB *ver* **ejercer**

ejote [e'xote] NM (*Am*) green bean

---

el [el]

(*fem* **la**, *neutro* **lo**, *pl* **los**, *pl* **las**) ARTÍCULO DEFINIDO **1** the; **el libro/la mesa/los estudiantes/las flores** the book/table/students/flowers; **me gusta el fútbol** I like football; **está en la cama** she's in bed

2 (*con nombre abstracto o propio: no se traduce*): **el amor/la juventud** love/youth; **el Conde Drácula** Count Dracula

3 (*posesión: se traduce a menudo por adj posesivo*): **romperse el brazo** to break one's arm; **levantó la mano** he put his hand up; **se puso el sombrero** she put her hat on

4 (*valor descriptivo*): **tener la boca grande/los ojos azules** to have a big mouth/blue eyes

5 (*con días*) on; **me iré el viernes** I'll leave on Friday; **los domingos suelo ir a nadar** on Sundays I generally go swimming

6 (*lo + adj*): **lo difícil/caro** what is difficult/expensive; (*cuán*): **no se da cuenta de lo pesado que es** he doesn't realize how boring he is

▶ PRON DEMOSTRATIVO **1**: **mi libro y el de usted** my book and yours; **las de Pepe son mejores** Pepe's are better; **no la(s) blanca(s) sino la(s) gris(es)** not the white one(s) but the grey one(s)

2: **lo de: lo de ayer** what happened yesterday; **lo de las facturas** that business about the invoices

▶ PRON RELATIVO **1**: **el que** *etc* (*indef*): **el (los) que quiera(n) que se vaya(n)** anyone who wants to can leave; **llévese el/la que más le guste** take the one you like best; (*def*): **el que compré ayer** the one I bought yesterday; **los que se van** those who leave

2: **lo que: lo que pienso yo/más me gusta** what I think/like most

▶ CONJ: **el que: el que lo diga** the fact that he says so; **el que sea tan vago me molesta** his being so lazy bothers me

▶ EXCL: **¡el susto que me diste!** what a fright you gave me!

▶ PRON PERSONAL **1** (*persona: m*) him; (: *f*) her; (: *pl*) them; **lo/las veo** I can see him/them

2 (*animal, cosa: sg*) it; (: *pl*) them; **lo** (*o* **la**) **veo** I can see it; **los** (*o* **las**) **veo** I can see them

3: **lo** (*como sustituto de frase*): **no lo sabía** I didn't know; **ya lo entiendo** I understand now

---

★**él** [el] PRON (*persona*) he; (*cosa*) it; (*después de prep: persona*) him; (: *cosa*) it; **mis libros y los de él** my books and his

elaboración [elaβora'θjon] NF (*producción*) manufacture; **~ de presupuestos** (*Com*) budgeting

elaborar [elaβo'rar] /**1a**/ VT (*producto*) to make, manufacture; (*preparar*) to prepare; (*madera, metal etc*) to work; (*proyecto etc*) to work on o out

elasticidad [elastiθi'ðað] NF elasticity

elástico, -a [e'lastiko, a] ADJ elastic; (*flexible*) flexible ▶ NM elastic; (*gomita*) elastic band

ELE ['ele] SIGLA M (= *español como lengua extranjera*) Spanish as a Foreign Language

★**elección** [elek'θjon] NF election; (*selección*) choice, selection; **elecciones parciales** by-election *sg*; **elecciones generales** general election *sg*

electo, -a [e'lekto, a] ADJ elect; **el presidente ~** the president-elect

electorado [elekto'raðo] NM electorate, voters *pl*

electoral [elekto'ral] ADJ electoral

electrice *etc* [elek'triθe] VB *ver* **electrizar**

★**electricidad** [elektriθi'ðað] NF electricity

★**electricista** [elektri'θista] NMF electrician

★**eléctrico, -a** [e'lektriko, a] ADJ electric

electrificar [elektrifi'kar] /**1g**/ VT to electrify

electrizar [elektri'θar] /**1f**/ VT (*Ferro, fig*) to electrify

electro... [elektro] PREF electro...

electrocardiograma [elektrokarðjo'ɣrama] NM electrocardiogram

electrocución [elektroku'θjon] NF electrocution

electrocutar [elektroku'tar] /**1a**/ VT to electrocute

electrodo [elek'troðo] NM electrode

electrodomésticos [elektroðo'mestikos] NMPL (*electrical*) household appliances; (*Com*) white goods

electroimán [elektroi'man] NM electromagnet

electromagnético, -a [elektromaɣ'netiko, a] ADJ electromagnetic

electrón [elek'tron] NM electron

★**electrónico, -a** [elek'troniko, a] ADJ electronic
▶ NF electronics *sg*

electrotecnia [elektro'teknja] NF electrical engineering

electrotécnico, -a [elektro'tekniko, a] NM/F electrical engineer

electrotren [elektro'tren] NM express electric train

★**elefante** [ele'fante] NM elephant

elegancia [ele'ɣanθja] NF elegance, grace; (*estilo*) stylishness

★**elegante** [ele'ɣante] ADJ elegant, graceful; (*estiloso*) stylish, fashionable; (*traje etc*) smart; (*decoración*) tasteful

elegía [ele'xia] NF elegy

★**elegir** [ele'xir] /3c, 3k/ VT (*escoger*) to choose, select; (*optar*) to opt for; (*presidente*) to elect

elemental [elemen'tal] ADJ (*claro, obvio*) elementary; (*fundamental*) elemental, fundamental

elemento [ele'mento] NM element; (*fig*) ingredient; (*AM*) person, individual; (*tipo raro*) odd person; (*de pila*) cell; **estar en su ~** to be in one's element; **vino a verle un ~** someone came to see you ■ **elementos** NMPL (*nociones*) elements, rudiments

elenco [e'lenko] NM catalogue, list; (*Teat*) cast; (*AM: equipo*) team

elepé [ele'pe] NM LP

elevación [eleβa'θjon] NF elevation; (*acto*) raising, lifting; (*de precios*) rise; (*Geo etc*) height, altitude

★**elevado, -a** [ele'βaðo, a] PP *de* **elevar** ▶ ADJ high

elevador [eleβa'ðor] NM (*AM*) lift (*BRIT*), elevator (*US*)

elevar [ele'βar] /1a/ VT to raise, lift (up); (*precio*) to put up; (*producción*) to step up; (*informe etc*) to present ■ **elevarse** VR (*edificio*) to rise; (*precios*) to go up; (*transportarse, enajenarse*) to get carried away; **la cantidad se eleva a ...** the total amounts to ...

eligiendo *etc* [eli'xjenðo], **elija** *etc* [e'lixa] VB *ver* **elegir**

eliminar [elimi'nar] /1a/ VT to eliminate, remove; (*olor, persona*) to get rid of; (*Deporte*) to eliminate, knock out

eliminatoria [elimina'torja] NF heat, preliminary (round)

elite [e'lite], **élite** ['elite] NF elite, élite

elitista [eli'tista] ADJ elitist

elixir [elik'sir] NM elixir; (*tb:* **elixir bucal**) mouthwash

ella ['eʎa] PRON (*persona*) she; (*cosa*) it; (*después de prep: persona*) her; (: *cosa*) it; **de ~** hers

ellas ['eʎas] PRON *ver* **ellos**

ello ['eʎo] PRON NEUTRO it; **es por ~ que ...** that's why ...

ellos, -as ['eʎos, as] PRON PERSONAL PL they; (*después de prep*) them; **de ~** theirs

elocuencia [elo'kwenθja] NF eloquence

elocuente [elo'kwente] ADJ eloquent; (*fig*) significant; **un dato ~** a fact which speaks for itself

elogiar [elo'xjar] /1b/ VT to praise, eulogize

elogio [e'loxjo] NM praise; **queda por encima de todo ~** it's beyond praise; **hacer ~ de** to sing the praises of

elote [e'lote] NM (*AM*) corn on the cob

El Salvador NM El Salvador

eludir [elu'ðir] /3a/ VT (*evitar*) to avoid, evade; (*escapar*) to escape, elude

E.M. ABR (*Mil*) = **Estado Mayor**

Em.ª ABR (= *Eminencia*) Mgr

email ['imeil] NM (*gen*) email *m*; (*dirección*) email address; **mandar un ~ a algn** to email sb, send sb an email

emanar [ema'nar] /1a/ VI: **~ de** to emanate from, come from; (*derivar de*) to originate in

emancipar [emanθi'par] /1a/ VT to emancipate ■ **emanciparse** VR to become emancipated, free o.s.

embadurnar [embaður'nar] /1a/ VT to smear

embajada [emba'xaða] NF embassy

embajador, a [embaxa'ðor, a] NM/F ambassador (ambassadress)

embaladura [embala'ðura] NF, (*AM*) **embalaje** [emba'laxe] NM packing

embalar [emba'lar] /1a/ VT (*envolver*) to parcel, wrap (up); (*envasar*) to package ▶ VI to sprint ■ **embalarse** VR to go fast

embalsamar [embalsa'mar] /1a/ VT to embalm

embalsar [embal'sar] /1a/ VT (*río*) to dam (up); (*agua*) to retain

★**embalse** [em'balse] NM (*presa*) dam; (*lago*) reservoir

embarace *etc* [emba'raθe] VB *ver* **embarazar**

★**embarazada** [embara'θaða] ADJ F pregnant ▶ NF pregnant woman

embarazar [embara'θar] /1f/ VT to obstruct, hamper ■ **embarazarse** VR (*aturdirse*) to become embarrassed; (*confundirse*) to get into a mess

embarazo [emba'raθo] NM (*de mujer*) pregnancy; (*impedimento*) obstacle, obstruction; (*timidez*) embarrassment

embarazoso, -a [embara'θoso, a] ADJ (*molesto*) awkward; (*violento*) embarrassing

embarcación [embarka'θjon] NF (*barco*) boat, craft; (*acto*) embarkation; **~ de arrastre** trawler; **~ de cabotaje** coasting vessel

embarcadero [embarka'ðero] NM pier, landing stage

★**embarcar** [embar'kar] /1g/ VT (*cargamento*) to ship, stow; (*persona*) to embark, put on board; (*fig*): **~ a algn en una empresa** to involve sb in an undertaking ■ **embarcarse** VR to embark, go on board; (*marinero*) to sign on; (*AM: en tren etc*) to get on, get in

embargar [embar'ɣar] /**1h**/ VT (*frenar*) to restrain; (*sentidos*) to overpower; (*Jur*) to seize, impound

embargo [em'barɣo] NM (*Jur*) seizure; (*Com etc*) embargo; **sin ~** still, however, nonetheless

embargue *etc* [em'barɣe] VB *ver* **embargar**

embarque *etc* [em'barke] VB *ver* **embarcar** ▶ NM shipment, loading

embarrancar [embarran'kar] /**1g**/ VT, VI (*Naut*) to run aground; (*Auto etc*) to run into a ditch

embarranque *etc* [emba'rranke] VB *ver* **embarrancar**

embarullar [embaru'ʎar] /**1a**/ VT to make a mess of

embate [em'bate] NM (*de mar, viento*) beating, violence

embaucador, a [embauka'ðor, a] NM/F (*estafador*) trickster; (*impostor*) impostor

embaucar [embau'kar] /**1g**/ VT to trick, fool

embauque *etc* [em'bauke] VB *ver* **embaucar**

embeber [embe'βer] /**2a**/ VT (*absorber*) to absorb, soak up; (*empapar*) to saturate ▶ VI to shrink ∎ **embeberse** VR: **embeberse en un libro** to be engrossed o absorbed in a book

embelesado, -a [embele'saðo, a] ADJ spell-bound

embelesar [embele'sar] /**1a**/ VT to enchant ∎ **embelesarse** VR: **embelesarse (con)** to be enchanted (by)

embellecer [embeʎe'θer] /**2d**/ VT to embellish, beautify

embellezca *etc* [embe'ʎeθka] VB *ver* **embellecer**

embestida [embes'tiða] NF attack, onslaught; (*carga*) charge

embestir [embes'tir] /**3k**/ VT to attack, assault; to charge, attack ▶ VI to attack

embistiendo *etc* [embis'tjendo] VB *ver* **embestir**

emblanquecer [emblanke'θer] /**2d**/ VT to whiten, bleach ∎ **emblanquecerse** VR to turn white

emblanquezca *etc* [emblan'keθka] VB *ver* **emblanquecer**

emblema [em'blema] NM emblem

embobado, -a [embo'βaðo, a] ADJ (*atontado*) stunned, bewildered

embobar [embo'βar] /**1a**/ VT (*asombrar*) to amaze; (*fascinar*) to fascinate ∎ **embobarse** VR: **embobarse con** o **de** o **en** to be amazed at; to be fascinated by

embocadura [emboka'ðura] NF narrow entrance; (*de río*) mouth; (*Mus*) mouthpiece

embolado [embo'laðo] NM (*Teat*) bit part, minor role; (*fam*) trick

embolia [em'bolja] NF (*Med*) clot, embolism; **~ cerebral** clot on the brain

émbolo ['embolo] NM (*Auto*) piston

embolsar [embol'sar] /**1a**/ VT to pocket

emboquillado, -a [emboki'ʎaðo, a] ADJ (*cigarrillo*) tipped, filter *cpd*

emborrachar [emborra'tʃar] /**1a**/ VT to make drunk, intoxicate ∎ **emborracharse** VR to get drunk

emboscada [embos'kaða] NF (*celada*) ambush

embotar [embo'tar] /**1a**/ VT to blunt, dull ∎ **embotarse** VR (*adormecerse*) to go numb

★**embotellamiento** [emboteʎa'mjento] NM (*Auto*) traffic jam

embotellar [embote'ʎar] /**1a**/ VT to bottle ∎ **embotellarse** VR (*circulación*) to get into a jam

embozo [em'boθo] NM muffler, mask; (*de sábana*) turnover

embragar [embra'ɣar] /**1h**/ VT (*Auto, Tec*) to engage; (*partes*) to connect ▶ VI to let in the clutch

embrague [em'braɣe] VB *ver* **embragar** ▶ (*tb:* **pedal de embrague**) clutch

embravecer [embraβe'θer] /**2d**/ VT to enrage, infuriate ∎ **embravecerse** VR to become furious; (*mar*) to get rough; (*tormenta*) to rage

embravecido, -a [embraβe'θiðo, a] ADJ (*mar*) rough; (*persona*) furious

embriagador, a [embrjaɣa'ðor, a] ADJ intoxicating

embriagar [embrja'ɣar] /**1h**/ VT (*emborrachar*) to make drunk; (*alegrar*) to delight ∎ **embriagarse** VR (*emborracharse*) to get drunk

embriague *etc* [em'brjaɣe] VB *ver* **embriagar**

embriaguez [embrja'ɣeθ] NF (*borrachera*) drunkenness

embrión [em'brjon] NM embryo

embrionario, -a [embrjo'narjo, a] ADJ embryonic

embrollar [embro'ʎar] /**1a**/ VT (*asunto*) to confuse, complicate; (*persona*) to involve, embroil ∎ **embrollarse** VR (*confundirse*) to get into a muddle o mess

embrollo [em'broʎo] NM (*enredo*) muddle, confusion; (*aprieto*) fix, jam

embromado, -a [embro'maðo, a] ADJ (*Am fam*) tricky, difficult

embromar [embro'mar] /**1a**/ VT (*burlarse de*) to tease, make fun of; (*Am fam: molestar*) to annoy

embrujado, -a [embru'xaðo, a] ADJ (*persona*) bewitched; **casa embrujada** haunted house

embrujo [em'bruxo] NM (*de mirada etc*) charm, magic

embrutecer [embrute'θer] /**2d**/ VT (*atontar*) to stupefy ∎ **embrutecerse** VR to be stupefied

embrutezca *etc* [embru'teθka] VB *ver* **embrutecer**

embudo [em'buðo] NM funnel

embuste [em'buste] NM trick; (*mentira*) lie; (*humorístico*) fib

embustero, -a [embus'tero, a] ADJ lying, deceitful ▶ NM/F (*tramposo*) cheat; (*mentiroso*) liar; (*humorístico*) fibber

embutido [embu'tiðo] NM (*Culin*) sausage; (*Tec*) inlay

embutir [embu'tir] /3a/ VT to insert; (*Tec*) to inlay; (*llenar*) to pack tight, cram

emergencia [emer'xenθja] NF emergency; (*surgimiento*) emergence

emergente [emer'xente] ADJ resultant, consequent; (*nación*) emergent; (*Inform*) pop-up *cpd*; **menú/ventana** ~ pop-up menu/window

emerger [emer'xer] /2c/ VI to emerge, appear

emeritense [emeri'tense] ADJ of *o* from Mérida ▶ NMF native *o* inhabitant of Mérida

emerja *etc* [e'merxa] VB *ver* **emerger**

emigración [emiɣra'θjon] NF emigration; (*de pájaros*) migration

emigrado, -a [emi'ɣraðo, a] NM/F emigrant; (*Pol etc*) émigré(e)

emigrante [emi'ɣrante] ADJ, NMF emigrant

★**emigrar** [emi'ɣrar] /1a/ VI (*personas*) to emigrate; (*pájaros*) to migrate

eminencia [emi'nenθja] NF eminence; (*en títulos*): **Su E~** His Eminence; **Vuestra E~** Your Eminence

eminente [emi'nente] ADJ eminent, distinguished; (*elevado*) high

emisario [emi'sarjo] NM emissary

emisión [emi'sjon] NF (*acto*) emission; (*Com etc*) issue; (*Radio, TV: acto*) broadcasting; (: *programa*) broadcast, programme, program (*US*); ~ **de acciones** (*Com*) share issue; ~ **gratuita de acciones** (*Com*) rights issue; ~ **de valores** (*Com*) flotation

emisor, a [emi'sor, a] NM transmitter ▶ NF radio *o* broadcasting station

emitir [emi'tir] /3a/ VT (*olor etc*) to emit, give off; (*moneda etc*) to issue; (*opinión*) to express; (*voto*) to cast; (*señal*) to send out; (*Radio*) to broadcast; ~ **una señal sonora** to beep

emoción [emo'θjon] NF emotion; (*excitación*) excitement; (*sentimiento*) feeling; **¡qué ~!** how exciting!; (*irónico*) what a thrill!

emocionado, -a [emoθjo'naðo, a] ADJ deeply moved, stirred

★**emocionante** [emoθjo'nante] ADJ (*excitante*) exciting, thrilling

emocionar [emoθjo'nar] /1a/ VT (*excitar*) to excite, thrill; (*conmover*) to move, touch; (*impresionar*) to impress ■ **emocionarse** VR to get excited

emoticón [emoti'kon], **emoticono** [emoti'kono] NM smiley, emoticon

★**emotivo, -a** [emo'tiβo, a] ADJ emotional

empacar [empa'kar] /1g/ VT (*gen*) to pack; (*en caja*) to bale, crate

empacharse [empa'tʃarse] /1a/ VR (*Med*) to get indigestion

empacho [em'patʃo] NM (*Med*) indigestion; (*fig*) embarrassment

empadronamiento [empaðrona'mjento] NM census; (*de electores*) electoral register

empadronarse [empaðro'narse] /1a/ VR (*Pol: como elector*) to register

empalagar [empala'ɣar] /1h/ VT (*comida*) to cloy; (*hartar*) to pall on ▶ VI to pall

empalagoso, -a [empala'ɣoso, a] ADJ cloying; (*fig*) tiresome

empalague *etc* [empa'laɣe] VB *ver* **empalagar**

empalizada [empali'θaða] NF fence; (*Mil*) palisade

empalmar [empal'mar] /1a/ VT to join, connect ▶ VI (*dos caminos*) to meet, join

empalme [em'palme] NM joint, connection; (*de vías*) junction; (*de trenes*) connection

empanada [empa'naða] NF pie, pasty

empanar [empa'nar] /1a/ VT (*Culin*) to cook *o* roll in breadcrumbs *o* pastry

empantanarse [empanta'narse] /1a/ VR to get swamped; (*fig*) to get bogged down

empañarse [empa'ɲarse] /1a/ VR (*nublarse*) to get misty, steam up

empapar [empa'par] /1a/ VT (*mojar*) to soak, saturate; (*absorber*) to soak up, absorb ■ **empaparse** VR: **empaparse de** to soak up

empapelar [empape'lar] /1a/ VT (*paredes*) to paper

empaque *etc* [em'pake] VB *ver* **empacar**

empaquetar [empake'tar] /1a/ VT to pack, parcel up; (*Com*) to package

emparedado [empare'ðaðo] NM sandwich

★**emparejar** [empare'xar] /1a/ VT to pair, match

emparentar [emparen'tar] /1j/ VI: ~ **con** to marry into

empariente *etc* [empa'rjente] VB *ver* **emparentar**

empastar [empas'tar] /1a/ VT (*embadurnar*) to paste; (*diente*) to fill

★**empaste** [em'paste] NM (*de diente*) filling

empatar [empa'tar] /1a/ VI to draw, tie; **empataron a dos** they drew two-all

★**empate** [em'pate] NM draw, tie; **un ~ a cero** a no-score draw

empecé [empe'θe], **empecemos** *etc* [empe'θemos] VB *ver* **empezar**

empecinado, -a [empeθi'naðo, a] ADJ stubborn

empedernido, -a [empeðer'niðo, a] ADJ hard, heartless; (*fijado*) hardened, inveterate; **un fumador** ~ a heavy smoker

empedrado, -a [empe'ðraðo, a] ADJ paved ▶ NM paving

empedrar [empe'ðrar] /1j/ VT to pave

empeine [em'peine] NM (*de pie, zapato*) instep

empellón [empe'ʎon] NM push, shove; **abrirse paso a empellones** to push *o* shove one's way past *o* through

empeñado, -a [empe'ɲaðo, a] ADJ (*persona*) determined; (*objeto*) pawned

empeñar [empe'ɲar] /1a/ VT (*objeto*) to pawn, pledge; (*persona*) to compel ■ **empeñarse** VR (*obligarse*) to bind o.s., pledge o.s.; (*endeudarse*) to get into debt; **empeñarse en hacer** to be set on doing, be determined to do

empeño [em'peɲo] NM (*determinación*) determination; (*cosa prendada*) pledge; **casa de empeños** pawnshop; **con ~** insistently; (*con celo*) eagerly; **tener ~ en hacer algo** to be bent on doing sth

empeoramiento [empeora'mjento] NM worsening

empeorar [empeo'rar] /1a/ VT to make worse, worsen ▶ VI to get worse, deteriorate

empequeñecer [empekeɲe'θer] /2d/ VT to dwarf; (*fig*) to belittle

empequeñezca etc [empeke'ɲeθka] VB ver **empequeñecer**

emperador [empera'ðor] NM emperor

emperatriz [empera'triθ] NF empress

emperrarse [empe'rrarse] /1a/ VR to get stubborn; **~ en algo** to persist in sth

★**empezar** [empe'θar] /1f, 1j/ VT, VI to begin, start; **empezó a llover** it started to rain; **bueno, para ~** well, to start with

empiece etc [em'pjeθe] VB ver **empezar**

empiedre etc [em'pjeðre] VB ver **empedrar**

empiezo etc [em'pjeθo] VB ver **empezar**

empinado, -a [empi'naðo, a] ADJ steep

empinar [empi'nar] /1a/ VT to raise; (*botella*) to tip up; **~ el codo** to booze (*fam*) ■ **empinarse** VR (*persona*) to stand on tiptoe; (*animal*) to rear up; (*camino*) to climb steeply

empingorotado, -a [empingoro'taðo, a] ADJ (*fam*) stuck-up

empírico, -a [em'piriko, a] ADJ empirical

emplace etc [em'plaθe] VB ver **emplazar**

emplaste [em'plaste], **emplasto** [em'plasto] NM (*Med*) plaster

emplasto [em'plasto] NM (*Med*) plaster

emplazamiento [emplaθa'mjento] NM site, location; (*Jur*) summons sg

emplazar [empla'θar] /1f/ VT (*ubicar*) to site, place, locate; (*Jur*) to summons; (*convocar*) to summon

★**empleado, -a** [emple'aðo, a] NM/F (*gen*) employee; (*de banco etc*) clerk; **~ público** civil servant

★**emplear** [emple'ar] /1a/ VT (*usar*) to use, employ; (*dar trabajo a*) to employ; **~ mal el tiempo** to waste time; **¡te está bien empleado!** it serves you right! ■ **emplearse** VR (*conseguir trabajo*) to be employed; (*ocuparse*) to occupy o.s.

★**empleo** [em'pleo] NM (*puesto*) job; (*puestos: colectivamente*) employment; (*uso*) use, employment; **"modo de ~"** "instructions for use"

emplumar [emplu'mar] /1a/ VT (*estafar*) to swindle

empobrecer [empoβre'θer] /2d/ VT to impoverish ■ **empobrecerse** VR to become poor o impoverished

empobrecimiento [empoβreθi'mjento] NM impoverishment

empobrezca etc [empo'βreθka] VB ver **empobrecer**

empoderar [empoðe'rar] /1a/ VT to empower

empollar [empo'ʎar] /1a/ VT to incubate; (*Escol: fam*) to swot (up) ▶ VI (*gallina*) to brood; (*Escol: fam*) to swot

empollón, -ona [empo'ʎon, ona] NM/F (*Escol: fam*) swot

empolvar [empol'βar] /1a/ VT (*cara*) to powder ■ **empolvarse** VR to powder one's face; (*superficie*) to get dusty

emponzoñar [emponθo'ɲar] /1a/ VT (*esp fig*) to poison

emporio [em'porjo] NM emporium, trading centre; (*Am: gran almacén*) department store

empotrado, -a [empo'traðo, a] ADJ (*armario etc*) built-in

empotrar [empo'trar] /1a/ VT to embed; (*armario etc*) to build in

emprendedor, a [emprende'ðor, a] ADJ enterprising

emprender [empren'der] /2a/ VT to undertake; (*empezar*) to begin, embark on; (*acometer*) to tackle, take on; **~ marcha a** to set out for

★**empresa** [em'presa] NF enterprise; (*Com: sociedad*) firm, company; (: *negocio*) business; (*esp Teat*) management; **~ filial** (*Com*) affiliated company; **~ matriz** (*Com*) parent company

empresarial [empresa'rjal] ADJ (*función, clase*) managerial; **sector ~** business sector

empresariales [empresa'rjales] NFPL business studies

★**empresario, -a** [empre'sarjo, a] NM/F (*Com*) businessman(-woman), entrepreneur; (*Tec*) manager; (*Mus: de ópera etc*) impresario; **~ de pompas fúnebres** undertaker (*BRIT*), mortician (*US*)

empréstito [em'prestito] NM (public) loan; (*Com*) loan capital

★**empujar** [empu'xar] /1a/ VT to push, shove

empuje [em'puxe] NM thrust; (*presión*) pressure; (*fig*) vigour, drive

empujón [empu'xon] NM push, shove; **abrirse paso a empujones** to shove one's way through

empuñadura [empuɲa'ðura] NF (*de espada*) hilt; (*de herramienta etc*) handle

empuñar [empu'ɲar] /1a/ VT (*asir*) to grasp, take (firm) hold of; **~ las armas** (*fig*) to take up arms

emulación [emula'θjon] NF emulation

emular [emu'lar] /1a/ VT to emulate; (*rivalizar*) to rival

émulo, -a ['emulo, a] NM/F rival, competitor

emulsión [emul'sjon] NF emulsion

---

en [en]

PREP **1** (*posición*) in; (: *sobre*) on; **está en el cajón** it's in the drawer; **en Argentina/La Paz** in Argentina/La Paz; **en el colegio/la oficina** at school/the office; **en casa** at home; **está en el suelo/quinto piso** it's on the floor/the fifth floor; **en el periódico** in the paper

2 (*dirección*) into; **entró en el aula** she went into the classroom; **meter algo en el bolso** to put sth into one's bag; **ir de puerta en puerta** to go from door to door

3 (*tiempo*) in; on; **en 1605/3 semanas/ invierno** in 1605/3 weeks/winter; **en (el mes de) enero** in (the month of) January; **en aquella ocasión/época** on that occasion/at that time

4 (*precio*) for; **lo vendió en 20 dólares** he sold it for 20 dollars

5 (*diferencia*) by; **reducir/aumentar en una tercera parte/un 20 por ciento** to reduce/ increase by a third/20 per cent

6 (*manera: forma*): **en avión/autobús** by plane/ bus; **escrito en inglés** written in English; **en serio** seriously; **en espiral/círculo** in a spiral/circle

7 (*después de vb que indica gastar etc*) on; **han cobrado demasiado en dietas** they've charged too much to expenses; **se le va la mitad del sueldo en comida** half his salary goes on food

8 (*tema, ocupación*): **experto en la materia** expert on the subject; **trabaja en la construcción** he works in the building industry

9 (*adj + en + infin*): **lento en reaccionar** slow to react

---

enagua(s) [eˈnaɣwa(s)] NF(PL) (*esp Am*) petticoat *sg*, underskirt *sg*

enajenación [enaxenaˈθjon] NF, **enajenamiento** [enaxenaˈmjento] NM alienation; (*tb*: **enajenación mental**) mental derangement; (*fig: distracción*) absent-mindedness; (: *embelesamiento*) rapture, trance

enajenar [enaxeˈnar] /1a/ VT to alienate; (*fig*) to carry away

★**enamorado, -a** [enamoˈraðo, a] ADJ in love; **estar ~ (de)** to be in love (with) ▶ NM/F lover

enamorar [enamoˈrar] /1a/ VT to win the love of ■ **enamorarse** VR: **enamorarse (de)** to fall in love (with)

enano, -a [eˈnano, a] ADJ tiny, dwarf ▶ NM/F (*persona*) person of small stature; (*en cuentos*) dwarf; (*pey*) runt

enarbolar [enarβoˈlar] /1a/ VT (*bandera etc*) to hoist; (*espada etc*) to brandish

enardecer [enarðeˈθer] /2d/ VT (*pasiones*) to fire, inflame; (*persona*) to fill with enthusiasm ■ **enardecerse** VR to get excited; **enardecerse por** to get enthusiastic about

enardezca *etc* [enarˈdeθka] VB *ver* **enardecer**

encabece *etc* [enkaˈβeθe] VB *ver* **encabezar**

encabezado [enkaβeˈθaðo] NM (*Com*) header

encabezamiento [enkaβeθaˈmjento] NM (*de carta*) heading; (*Com*) billhead, letterhead; (*de periódico*) headline; (*preámbulo*) foreword, preface; **~ normal** (*Tip etc*) running head

encabezar [enkaβeˈθar] /1f/ VT (*movimiento, revolución*) to lead, head; (*lista*) to head; (*carta*) to put a heading to; (*libro*) to entitle

encadenar [enkaðeˈnar] /1a/ VT to chain (together); (*poner grilletes a*) to shackle

encajar [enkaˈxar] /1a/ VT (*meter a la fuerza*) to push in; (*máquina etc*) to house; (*partes*) to join; (*fam: golpe*) to give, deal; (*entremeter*) to insert; (*ajustar*): **~ en** to fit (into) ▶ VI to fit (well); (*fig: corresponder a*) to match ■ **encajarse** VR: **encajarse en un sillón** to squeeze into a chair

encaje [enˈkaxe] NM (*labor*) lace

encajonar [enkaxoˈnar] /1a/ VT to box (up), put in a box

encalar [enkaˈlar] /1a/ VT (*pared*) to whitewash

encallar [enkaˈʎar] /1a/ VI (*Naut*) to run aground

encaminado, -a [enkamiˈnaðo, a] ADJ: **medidas encaminadas a …** measures designed to *o* aimed at …

encaminar [enkamiˈnar] /1a/ VT to direct, send; **~ por** (*expedición etc*) to route via ■ **encaminarse** VR: **encaminarse a** to set out for

encandilar [enkandiˈlar] /1a/ VT to dazzle; (*persona*) to daze, bewilder

encanecer [enkaneˈθer] /2d/ VI, **encanecerse** VR (*pelo*) to go grey

encanezca *etc* [enkaˈneθka] VB *ver* **encanecer**

★**encantado, -a** [enkanˈtaðo, a] ADJ (*hechizado*) bewitched; (*muy contento*) delighted; **¡~!** how do you do!, pleased to meet you

★**encantador, a** [enkantaˈðor, a] ADJ charming, lovely ▶ NM/F magician, enchanter (enchantress)

★**encantar** [enkanˈtar] /1a/ VT to charm, delight; (*cautivar*) to fascinate; (*hechizar*) to bewitch, cast a spell on; **me encanta eso** I love that

encanto [enˈkanto] NM (*magia*) spell, charm; (*fig*) charm, delight; (*expresión de ternura*) sweetheart; **como por ~** as if by magic

encapotado, -a [enkapoˈtaðo, a] ADJ (*cielo*) overcast

encapricharse [enkapriˈtʃarse] /1a/ VR: **se ha encaprichado con ir** he's taken it into his head to go; **se ha encaprichado** he's digging his heels in

encaramar [enkaraˈmar] /1a/ VT (*subir*) to raise, lift up ■ **encaramarse** VR (*subir*) to perch; **encaramarse a** (*árbol etc*) to climb

encararse [enkaˈrarse] /1a/ VR: **~ a** *o* **con** to confront, come face to face with

encarcelar [enkarθeˈlar] /1a/ VT to imprison, jail

147

encarecer [enkareˈθer] /**2d**/ VT to put up the price of ▸ VI, **encarecerse** VR to get dearer

encarecidamente [enkareθiðaˈmente] ADV earnestly

encarecimiento [enkareθiˈmjento] NM price increase

encarezca etc [enkaˈreθka] VB ver **encarecer**

★**encargado, -a** [enkarˈɣaðo, a] ADJ in charge ▸ NM/F agent, representative; (responsable) person in charge

encargar [enkarˈɣar] /**1h**/ VT to entrust; (Com) to order; (recomendar) to urge, recommend; ~ **algo a algn** to put sb in charge of sth ∎ **encargarse** VR: **encargarse de** to look after, take charge of

encargo [enˈkarɣo] NM (pedido) assignment, job; (responsabilidad) responsibility; (recomendación) recommendation; (Com) order

encargue etc [enˈkarɣe] VB ver **encargar**

encariñarse [enkariˈɲarse] /**1a**/ VR: ~ **con** to grow fond of, get attached to

encarnación [enkarnaˈθjon] NF incarnation, embodiment

encarnado, -a [enkarˈnaðo, a] ADJ (color) red; **ponerse** ~ to blush

encarnar [enkarˈnar] /**1a**/ VT to personify; (Teat: papel) to play ▸ VI (Rel etc) to become incarnate

encarnizado, -a [enkarniˈθaðo, a] ADJ (lucha) bloody, fierce

encarrilar [enkarriˈlar] /**1a**/ VT (tren) to put back on the rails; (fig) to correct, put on the right track

encasillar [enkasiˈʎar] /**1a**/ VT (Teat) to typecast; (clasificar: pey) to pigeonhole

encasquetar [enkaskeˈtar] /**1a**/ VT (sombrero) to pull down o on; ~ **algo a algn** to offload sth onto sb ∎ **encasquetarse** VR: **encasquetarse el sombrero** to pull one's hat down o on

encauce etc [enˈkauθe] VB ver **encauzar**

encausar [enkauˈsar] /**1a**/ VT to prosecute, sue

encauzar [enkauˈθar] /**1f**/ VT to channel; (fig) to direct

★**encendedor** [enθendeˈðor] NM lighter

★**encender** [enθenˈder] /**2g**/ VT (con fuego) to light; (incendiar) to set fire to; (luz, radio) to put on, switch on; (Inform) to toggle on, switch on; (avivar: pasiones etc) to inflame; (despertar: entusiasmo) to arouse; (: odio) to awaken ∎ **encenderse** VR to catch fire; (excitarse) to get excited; (de cólera) to flare up; (el rostro) to blush

encendidamente [enθendiðaˈmente] ADV passionately

encendido, -a [enθenˈdiðo, a] ADJ alight; (aparato) (switched) on; (mejillas) glowing; (cara: por el vino etc) flushed; (mirada) passionate ▸ NM (Auto) ignition; (de faroles) lighting

encerado, -a [enθeˈraðo, a] ADJ (suelo) waxed, polished ▸ NM (Escol) blackboard; (hule) oilcloth

encerar [enθeˈrar] /**1a**/ VT (suelo) to wax, polish

★**encerrar** [enθeˈrrar] /**1j**/ VT (confinar) to shut in o up; (con llave) to lock in o up; (comprender, incluir) to include, contain ∎ **encerrarse** VR to shut o lock o.s. up o in

encerrona [enθeˈrrona] NF trap

encestar [enθesˈtar] /**1a**/ VI to score a basket

encharcado, -a [entʃarˈkaðo, a] ADJ (terreno) flooded

encharcar [entʃarˈkar] /**1g**/ VT to swamp, flood ∎ **encharcarse** VR to become flooded

encharque etc [enˈtʃarke] VB ver **encharcar**

enchufado, -a [entʃuˈfaðo, a] NM/F (fam) well-connected person

★**enchufar** [entʃuˈfar] /**1a**/ VT (Elec) to plug in; (Tec) to connect, fit together; (Com) to merge

★**enchufe** [enˈtʃufe] NM (Elec: clavija) plug; (: toma) socket; (de dos tubos) joint, connection; (fam: influencia) contact, connection; (: puesto) cushy job; ~ **de clavija** jack plug; **tiene un ~ en el ministerio** he can pull strings at the ministry

encía [enˈθia] NF (Anat) gum

enciclopedia [enθikloˈpeðja] NF encyclopaedia

encienda etc [enˈθjenda] VB ver **encender**

encierro etc [enˈθjerro] VB ver **encerrar** ▸ NM shutting in o up; (calabozo) prison; (Agr) pen; (Taur) penning

★**encima** [enˈθima] ADV (sobre) above, over; (además) besides; ~ **de** (en) on, on top of; (sobre) above, over; (además de) besides, on top of; **por** ~ **de** over; **¿llevas dinero ~?** have you (got) any money on you?; **se me vino** ~ it took me by surprise

encina [enˈθina] NF (holm) oak

encinta [enˈθinta] ADJ F pregnant

enclave [enˈklaβe] NM enclave

enclenque [enˈklenke] ADJ weak, sickly

★**encoger** [enkoˈxer] /**2c**/ VT (gen) to shrink, contract; (fig: asustar) to scare; (: desanimar) to discourage ∎ **encogerse** VR to shrink, contract; (fig) to cringe; **encogerse de hombros** to shrug one's shoulders

encoja etc [enˈkoxa] VB ver **encoger**

encolar [enkoˈlar] /**1a**/ VT (engomar) to glue, paste; (pegar) to stick down

encolerice etc [enkoleˈriθe] VB ver **encolerizar**

encolerizar [enkoleriˈθar] /**1f**/ VT to anger, provoke ∎ **encolerizarse** VR to get angry

encomendar [enkomenˈdar] /**1j**/ VT to entrust, commend ∎ **encomendarse** VR: **encomendarse a** to put one's trust in

encomiar [enkoˈmjar] /**1b**/ VT to praise, pay tribute to

encomienda etc [enkoˈmjenda] VB ver **encomendar** ▸ NF (encargo) charge, commission; (elogio) tribute; (Am) parcel, package; ~ **postal** (Am: servicio) parcel post

encomio [enˈkomjo] NM praise, tribute

encono [enˈkono] NM (rencor) rancour, spite

encontrado, -a [enkon'traðo, a] ADJ (*contrario*) contrary, conflicting; (*hostil*) hostile

★**encontrar** [enkon'trar] /**1l**/ VT (*hallar*) to find; (*inesperadamente*) to meet, run into ■ **encontrarse** VR to meet (each other); (*situarse*) to be (situated); (*persona*) to find o.s., be; (*entrar en conflicto*) to crash, collide; **encontrarse con** to meet; **encontrarse bien (de salud)** to feel well; **no se encuentra aquí en este momento** he's not in at the moment

encontronazo [enkontro'naθo] NM collision, crash

encorvar [enkor'βar] /**1a**/ VT to curve; (*inclinar*) to bend (down) ■ **encorvarse** VR to bend down, bend over

encrespado, -a [enkres'paðo, a] ADJ (*pelo*) curly; (*mar*) rough

encrespar [enkres'par] /**1a**/ VT (*cabellos*) to curl; (*fig*) to anger, irritate ■ **encresparse** VR (*el mar*) to get rough; (*fig*) to get cross o irritated

encriptar [enkrip'tar] /**1a**/ VT encrypt

encrucijada [enkruθi'xaða] NF crossroads *sg*; (*empalme*) junction

encuadernación [enkwaðerna'θjon] NF binding; (*taller*) binder's

encuadernador, a [enkwaðerna'ðor, a] NM/F bookbinder

encuadrar [enkwa'ðrar] /**1a**/ VT (*retrato*) to frame; (*ajustar*) to fit, insert; (*encerrar*) to contain

encubierto [enku'βjerto] PP *de* **encubrir**

encubrir [enku'βrir] /**3a**/ VT (*ocultar*) to hide, conceal; (*criminal*) to harbour, shelter; (*ayudar*) to be an accomplice in

★**encuentro** [en'kwentro] VB *ver* **encontrar** ▶ NM (*de personas*) meeting; (*Auto etc*) collision, crash; (*Deporte*) match, game; (*Mil*) encounter

encuerado, -a [enkwe'raðo, a] ADJ (*AM*) nude, naked

★**encuesta** [en'kwesta] NF inquiry, investigation; (*sondeo*) public opinion poll; **~ judicial** post-mortem

encumbrado, -a [enkum'braðo, a] ADJ eminent, distinguished

encumbrar [enkum'brar] /**1a**/ VT (*persona*) to exalt ■ **encumbrarse** VR (*fig*) to become conceited

endeble [en'deβle] ADJ (*argumento, excusa, persona*) weak

endémico, -a [en'demiko, a] ADJ endemic

endemoniado, -a [endemo'njaðo, a] ADJ possessed (of the devil); (*travieso*) devilish

enderece *etc* [ende're θe] VB *ver* **enderezar**

enderezar [endere'θar] /**1f**/ VT (*poner derecho*) to straighten (out); (: *verticalmente*) to set upright; (*fig*) to straighten o sort out; (*dirigir*) to direct ■ **enderezarse** VR (*persona sentada*) to sit up straight

endeudarse [endeu'ðarse] /**1a**/ VR to get into debt

endiablado, -a [endja'βlaðo, a] ADJ devilish, diabolical; (*humorístico*) mischievous

endibia [en'diβja] NF endive

endilgar [endil'ɣar] /**1h**/ VT (*fam*): **~ algo a algn** to lumber sb with sth; **~ un sermón a algn** to give sb a lecture

endilgue *etc* [en'dilɣe] VB *ver* **endilgar**

endiñar [endi'nar] /**1a**/ VT: **~ algo a algn** to land sth on sb

endomingarse [endomin'garse] /**1h**/ VR to dress up, put on one's best clothes

endomingue *etc* [endo'minge] VB *ver* **endomingarse**

endosar [endo'sar] /**1a**/ VT (*cheque etc*) to endorse

endulce *etc* [en'dulθe] VB *ver* **endulzar**

endulzar [endul'θar] /**1f**/ VT to sweeten; (*suavizar*) to soften

endurecer [endure'θer] /**2d**/ VT to harden ■ **endurecerse** VR to harden, grow hard

endurecido, -a [endure'θiðo, a] ADJ (*duro*) hard; (*fig*) hardy, tough; **estar ~ a algo** to be hardened o used to sth

endurezca *etc* [endu're θka] VB *ver* **endurecer**

ene. ABR (= *enero*) Jan.; *ver tb* **julio**

enema [e'nema] NM (*Med*) enema

★**enemigo, -a** [ene'miɣo, a] ADJ enemy, hostile ▶ NM/F enemy; **ser ~ de** (*persona*) to dislike; (*tendencia*) to be inimical to ▶ NF enmity, hostility

enemistad [enemis'tað] NF enmity

enemistar [enemis'tar] /**1a**/ VT to make enemies of, cause a rift between ■ **enemistarse** VR to become enemies; (*amigos*) to fall out

energético, -a [ener'xetiko, a] ADJ: **política energética** energy policy

★**energía** [ener'xia] NF (*vigor*) energy, drive; (*empuje*) push; (*Tec, Elec*) energy, power; **~ atómica/eléctrica/eólica** atomic/electric/wind power; **~ solar** solar energy o power; **energías renovables** renewable energy sources

★**enérgico, -a** [e'nerxiko, a] ADJ (*gen*) energetic; (*ataque*) vigorous; (*ejercicio*) strenuous; (*medida*) bold; (*voz, modales*) forceful

energúmeno, -a [ener'ɣumeno, a] NM/F madman(-woman); **ponerse como un ~ con algn** to get furious with sb

★**enero** [e'nero] NM January; *ver tb* **julio**

enervar [ener'βar] /**1a**/ VT (*poner nervioso a*) to get on sb's nerves

enésimo, -a [e'nesimo, a] ADJ (*Mat*) nth; **por enésima vez** (*fig*) for the umpteenth time

★**enfadado, -a** [enfa'ðaðo, a] ADJ angry, annoyed

enfadar [enfa'ðar] /**1a**/ VT to anger, annoy ■ **enfadarse** VR to get angry o annoyed

enfado [en'faðo] NM (*enojo*) anger, annoyance; (*disgusto*) trouble, bother

énfasis ['enfasis] NM emphasis, stress; **poner ~ en** to stress

enfático, -a [en'fatiko, a] ADJ emphatic

enfatizado, -a [enfati'θaðo, a] ADJ: **en caracteres enfatizados** (*Inform*) emphasized

enfermar [enfer'mar] /**1a**/ VT to make ill; **su actitud me enferma** his attitude makes me sick ▶ VI to fall ill, be taken ill; **~ del corazón** to develop heart trouble

★**enfermedad** [enferme'ðað] NF illness; **~ venérea** venereal disease

> *Enfermedad* se traduce por **illness** cuando no se especifica la enfermedad de que se trata, o cuando se refiere al tiempo que una persona está enferma: *Adelgazó mucho durante su enfermedad*. **He lost a lot of weight during his illness**.
> Se traduce por **disease** cuando se especifica el tipo de enfermedad: *mineros que sufren una enfermedad pulmonar* **miners suffering from lung disease**; *enfermedad de Alzheimer* **Alzheimer's disease**.

enfermera [enfer'mera] NF ver **enfermero**

enfermería [enferme'ria] NF infirmary; (*de colegio etc*) sick bay

★**enfermero, -a** [enfer'mero, a] NM (male) nurse ▶ NF nurse; **enfermera jefa** matron

enfermizo, -a [enfer'miθo, a] ADJ (*persona*) sickly, unhealthy; (*fig*) unhealthy

★**enfermo, -a** [en'fermo, a] ADJ ill, sick; **caer o ponerse ~** to fall ill ▶ NM/F invalid, sick person; (*en hospital*) patient

enfilar [enfi'lar] /**1a**/ VT (*aguja*) to thread; (*calle*) to go down

enflaquecer [enflake'θer] /**2d**/ VT (*adelgazar*) to make thin; (*debilitar*) to weaken

enflaquezca etc [enfla'keθka] VB ver **enflaquecer**

enfocar [enfo'kar] /**1g**/ VT (*foto etc*) to focus; (*problema etc*) to consider, look at

enfoque etc [en'foke] VB ver **enfocar** ▶ NM focus; (*acto*) focusing; (*óptica*) approach

enfrascado, -a [enfras'kaðo, a] ADJ: **estar ~ en algo** (*fig*) to be wrapped up in sth

enfrascarse [enfras'karse] /**1g**/ VR: **~ en un libro** to bury o.s. in a book

enfrasque etc [en'fraske] VB ver **enfrascarse**

enfrentamiento [enfrenta'mjento] NM confrontation

enfrentar [enfren'tar] /**1a**/ VT (*peligro*) to face (up to), confront; (*oponer*) to bring face to face ■ **enfrentarse** VR (*dos personas*) to face o confront each other; (*Deporte: dos equipos*) to meet; **enfrentarse a** o **con** to face up to, confront

★**enfrente** [en'frente] ADV opposite; **~ de** opposite, facing; **la casa de ~** the house opposite, the house across the street

enfriamiento [enfria'mjento] NM chilling, refrigeration; (*Med*) cold, chill

enfriar [enfri'ar] /**1c**/ VT (*alimentos*) to cool, chill; (*algo caliente*) to cool down; (*habitación*) to air, freshen; (*entusiasmo*) to dampen ■ **enfriarse** VR to cool down; (*Med*) to catch a chill; (*amistad*) to cool

enfurecer [enfure'θer] /**2d**/ VT to enrage, madden ■ **enfurecerse** VR to become furious, fly into a rage; (*mar*) to get rough

enfurezca etc [enfu'reθka] VB ver **enfurecer**

engalanar [engala'nar] /**1a**/ VT (*adornar*) to adorn; (*ciudad*) to decorate ■ **engalanarse** VR to get dressed up

★**enganchar** [engan'tʃar] /**1a**/ VT to hook; (*ropa*) to hang up; (*dos vagones*) to hitch up; (*Tec*) to couple, connect; (*Mil*) to recruit; (*fam: atraer: persona*) to rope into ■ **engancharse** VR (*Mil*) to enlist, join up; **engancharse (a)** (*drogas*) to get hooked (on)

enganche [en'gantʃe] NM hook; (*Tec*) coupling, connection; (*acto*) hooking (up); (*Mil*) recruitment, enlistment; (*Am: depósito*) deposit

★**engañar** [enga'ɲar] /**1a**/ VT to deceive; (*estafar*) to cheat, swindle; **engaña a su mujer** he's unfaithful to o cheats on his wife ▶ VI: **las apariencias engañan** appearances can be deceptive ■ **engañarse** VR (*equivocarse*) to be wrong; (*a sí mismo*) to deceive o kid o.s.

engaño [en'gaɲo] NM deceit; (*estafa*) trick, swindle; (*error*) mistake, misunderstanding; (*ilusión*) delusion

engañoso, -a [enga'ɲoso, a] ADJ (*tramposo*) crooked; (*mentiroso*) dishonest, deceitful; (*aspecto*) deceptive; (*consejo*) misleading

engarce etc [en'garθe] VB ver **engarzar**

engarzar [engar'θar] /**1f**/ VT (*joya*) to set, mount; (*fig*) to link, connect

engatusar [engatu'sar] /**1a**/ VT (*fam*) to coax

engendrar [enxen'drar] /**1a**/ VT to breed; (*procrear*) to beget; (*fig*) to cause, produce

engendro [en'xendro] NM (*Bio*) foetus; (*fig*) monstrosity; (*: idea*) brainchild

englobar [englo'βar] /**1a**/ VT (*comprender*) to include, comprise; (*incluir*) to lump together

engomar [engo'mar] /**1a**/ VT to glue, stick

engordar [engor'ðar] /**1a**/ VT to fatten ▶ VI to get fat, put on weight

engorro [en'gorro] NM bother, nuisance

engorroso, -a [engo'rroso, a] ADJ bothersome, trying

engranaje [engra'naxe] NM (*Auto*) gear; (*juego*) gears pl

engrandecer [engrande'θer] /**2d**/ VT to enlarge, magnify; (*alabar*) to praise, speak highly of; (*exagerar*) to exaggerate

engrandezca etc [engran'deθka] VB ver **engrandecer**

engrasar [engra'sar] /**1a**/ VT (*Tec: poner grasa*) to grease; (*: lubricar*) to lubricate, oil; (*manchar*) to make greasy

engrase [en'grase] NM greasing, lubrication

engreído, -a [engre'iðo, a] ADJ vain, conceited

engrosar [engro'sar] /**1l**/ vT (*ensanchar*) to enlarge; (*aumentar*) to increase; (*hinchar*) to swell

engrudo [en'gruðo] NM paste

engruese *etc* [en'grwese] vB *ver* **engrosar**

engullir [engu'ʎir] /**3a, 3h**/ vT to gobble, gulp (down)

enhebrar [ene'βrar] /**1a**/ vT to thread

enhiesto, -a [e'njesto, a] ADJ (*derecho*) erect; (*bandera*) raised; (*edificio*) lofty

★**enhorabuena** [enora'βwena] EXCL: **¡~!** congratulations! ▶ NF: **dar la ~ a** to congratulate

enigma [e'niɣma] NM enigma; (*problema*) puzzle; (*misterio*) mystery

enigmático, -a [eniɣ'matiko, a] ADJ enigmatic

enjabonar [enxaβo'nar] /**1a**/ vT to soap; (*barba*) to lather; (*fam: adular*) to soft-soap; (*: regañar*) to tick off

enjalbegar [enxalβe'ɣar] /**1h**/ vT (*pared*) to whitewash

enjalbegue *etc* [enxal'βeɣe] vB *ver* **enjalbegar**

enjambre [en'xamβre] NM swarm

enjaular [enxau'lar] /**1a**/ vT to (put in a) cage; (*fam*) to jail, lock up

enjuagar [enxwa'ɣar] /**1h**/ vT (*ropa*) to rinse (out)

enjuague *etc* [en'xwaɣe] vB *ver* **enjuagar** ▶ NM (*Med*) mouthwash; (*de ropa*) rinse, rinsing

enjugar [enxu'ɣar] /**1h**/ vT to wipe (off); (*lágrimas*) to dry; (*déficit*) to wipe out

enjugue *etc* [en'xuɣe] vB *ver* **enjugar**

enjuiciar [enxwi'θjar] /**1b**/ vT (*Jur: procesar*) to prosecute, try; (*fig*) to judge

enjuto, -a [en'xuto, a] ADJ dry, dried up; (*fig*) lean, skinny

enlace [en'laθe] vB *ver* **enlazar** ▶ NM link, connection; (*relación*) relationship; (*tb:* **enlace matrimonial**) marriage; (*de trenes*) connection; **~ de datos** data link; **~ sindical** shop steward; **~ telefónico** telephone link-up

enlatado, -a [enla'taðo, a] ADJ (*alimentos, productos*) tinned, canned

enlazar [enla'θar] /**1f**/ vT (*unir con lazos*) to bind together; (*atar*) to tie; (*conectar*) to link, connect; (*Am*) to lasso

enlodar [enlo'ðar] /**1a**/ vT to cover in mud; (*fig: manchar*) to stain; (*: rebajar*) to debase

enloquecer [enloke'θer] /**2d**/ vT to drive mad ▶ vi to go mad

enloquezca *etc* [enlo'keθka] vB *ver* **enloquecer**

enlutado, -a [enlu'taðo, a] ADJ (*persona*) in mourning

enlutar [enlu'tar] /**1a**/ vT to dress in mourning ■ **enlutarse** vR to go into mourning

enmarañar [enmara'ɲar] /**1a**/ vT (*enredar*) to tangle up, entangle; (*complicar*) to complicate; (*confundir*) to confuse ■ **enmarañarse** vR (*enredarse*) to become entangled; (*confundirse*) to get confused

enmarcar [enmar'kar] /**1g**/ vT (*cuadro*) to frame; (*fig*) to provide a setting for

enmarque *etc* [en'marke] vB *ver* **enmarcar**

enmascarar [enmaska'rar] /**1a**/ vT to mask; (*intenciones*) to disguise ■ **enmascararse** vR to put on a mask

enmendar [enmen'dar] /**1j**/ vT to emend, correct; (*constitución etc*) to amend; (*comportamiento*) to reform ■ **enmendarse** vR to reform, mend one's ways

enmienda [en'mjenda] vB *ver* **enmendar** ▶ NF correction; amendment; reform

enmohecerse [enmoe'θerse] /**2d**/ vR (*metal*) to rust, go rusty; (*muro, plantas*) to go mouldy

enmohezca *etc* [enmo'eθka] vB *ver* **enmohecerse**

enmudecer [enmuðe'θer] /**2d**/ vT to silence ▶ vi (*perder el habla*) to fall silent; (*guardar silencio*) to remain silent; (*por miedo*) to be struck dumb

enmudezca *etc* [enmu'ðeθka] vB *ver* **enmudecer**

ennegrecer [enneɣre'θer] /**2d**/ vT (*poner negro*) to blacken; (*oscurecer*) to darken ■ **ennegrecerse** vR to turn black; (*oscurecerse*) to get dark, darken

ennegrezca *etc* [enne'ɣreθka] vB *ver* **ennegrecer**

ennoblecer [ennoβle'θer] /**2d**/ vT to ennoble

ennoblezca *etc* [enno'βleθka] vB *ver* **ennoblecer**

en.° ABR (= *enero*) Jan.

enojadizo, -a [enoxa'ðiθo, a] ADJ irritable, short-tempered

enojado, -a [eno'xaðo, a] ADJ (*Am*) angry

enojar [eno'xar] /**1a**/ vT (*encolerizar*) to anger; (*disgustar*) to annoy, upset ■ **enojarse** vR to get angry; to get annoyed

enojo [e'noxo] NM (*esp Am: cólera*) anger; (*irritación*) annoyance

enojoso, -a [eno'xoso, a] ADJ annoying

enorgullecerse [enorɣuʎe'θerse] /**2d**/ vR to be proud; **~ de** to pride o.s. on, be proud of

enorgullezca *etc* [enorɣu'ʎeθka] vB *ver* **enorgullecerse**

★**enorme** [e'norme] ADJ enormous, huge; (*fig*) monstrous

enormidad [enormi'ðað] NF hugeness, immensity

enraice *etc* [en'raiθe] vB *ver* **enraizar**

enraizar [enrai'θar] /**1f**/ vi to take root

enrarecido, -a [enrare'θiðo, a] ADJ rarefied

enredadera [enreða'ðera] NF (*Bot*) creeper, climbing plant

enredar [enre'ðar] /**1a**/ vT (*cables, hilos etc*) to tangle (up), entangle; (*situación*) to complicate, confuse; (*meter cizaña*) to sow discord among o between; (*implicar*) to embroil, implicate ■ **enredarse** vR to get entangled, get tangled (up); (*situación*) to get complicated; (*persona*) to get embroiled; (*Am fam*) to meddle

enredo [enˈreðo] NM (*maraña*) tangle; (*confusión*) mix-up, confusion; (*intriga*) intrigue; (*apuro*) jam; (*amorío*) love affair

enrejado [enreˈxaðo] NM grating; (*de ventana*) lattice; (*en jardín*) trellis

enrevesado, -a [enreβeˈsaðo, a] ADJ (*asunto*) complicated, involved

enriquecer [enrikeˈθer] /2d/ VT to make rich; (*fig*) to enrich ■ **enriquecerse** VR to get rich

enriquezca *etc* [enriˈkeθka] VB *ver* **enriquecer**

enrojecer [enroxeˈθer] /2d/ VT to redden ▸ VI (*persona*) to blush ■ **enrojecerse** VR to blush

enrojezca *etc* [enroˈxeθka] VB *ver* **enrojecer**

enrolar [enroˈlar] /1a/ VT (*Mil*) to enlist; (*reclutar*) to recruit ■ **enrolarse** VR (*Mil*) to join up; (*afiliarse*) to enrol, sign on

enrollar [enroˈʎar] /1a/ VT to roll (up), wind (up) ■ **enrollarse** VR: **enrollarse con algn** to get involved with sb

enroque [enˈroke] NM (*Ajedrez*) castling

enroscar [enrosˈkar] /1g/ VT (*torcer, doblar*) to twist; (*arrollar*) to coil (round), wind; (*tornillo, rosca*) to screw in ■ **enroscarse** VR to coil, wind

enrosque *etc* [enˈroske] VB *ver* **enroscar**

★**ensalada** [ensaˈlaða] NF salad; (*lío*) mix-up

ensaladilla [ensalaˈðiʎa] NF (*tb*: **ensaladilla rusa**) ≈ Russian salad

ensalce *etc* [enˈsalθe] VB *ver* **ensalzar**

ensalzar [ensalˈθar] /1f/ VT (*alabar*) to praise, extol; (*exaltar*) to exalt

ensamblador [ensamblaˈðor] NM (*Inform*) assembler

ensambladura [ensamblaˈðura] NF, **ensamblaje** [ensamˈblaxe] NM assembly; (*Tec*) joint

ensamblar [ensamˈblar] /1a/ VT (*montar*) to assemble; (*madera etc*) to join

ensanchar [ensanˈtʃar] /1a/ VT (*hacer más ancho*) to widen; (*agrandar*) to enlarge, expand; (*Costura*) to let out ■ **ensancharse** VR to get wider, expand; (*pey*) to give o.s. airs

ensanche [enˈsantʃe] NM (*de calle*) widening; (*de negocio*) expansion

ensangrentado, -a [ensangrenˈtaðo, a] ADJ bloodstained, covered with blood

ensangrentar [ensangrenˈtar] /1j/ VT to stain with blood

ensangriente *etc* [ensanˈgrjente] VB *ver* **ensangrentar**

ensañarse [ensaˈɲarse] /1a/ VR: ~ **con** to treat brutally

ensartar [ensarˈtar] /1a/ VT (*gen*) to string (together); (*carne*) to spit, skewer

ensayar [ensaˈjar] /1a/ VT to test, try (out); (*Teat*) to rehearse

ensayista [ensaˈjista] NMF essayist

★**ensayo** [enˈsajo] NM test, trial; (*Química*) experiment; (*Teat*) rehearsal; (*Deporte*) try; (*Escol, Lit*)

essay; **pedido de** ~ (*Com*) trial order; ~ **general** (*Teat*) dress rehearsal; (*Mus*) full rehearsal

★**enseguida** [enseˈɣwiða] ADV at once, right away; ~ **termino** I've nearly finished, I shan't be long now

ensenada [enseˈnaða] NF inlet, cove

enseña [enˈseɲa] NF ensign, standard

enseñante [enseˈɲante] NMF teacher

★**enseñanza** [enseˈɲanθa] NF (*educación*) education; (*acción*) teaching; (*doctrina*) teaching, doctrine; ~ **primaria/secundaria/superior** primary/secondary/higher education

★**enseñar** [enseˈɲar] /1a/ VT (*educar*) to teach; (*instruir*) to teach, instruct; (*mostrar, señalar*) to show

enseres [enˈseres] NMPL belongings

ensillar [ensiˈʎar] /1a/ VT to saddle (up)

ensimismarse [ensimisˈmarse] /1a/ VR (*abstraerse*) to become lost in thought; (*estar absorto*) to be lost in thought; (*Am*) to become conceited

ensopar [ensoˈpar] /1a/ VT (*Am*) to soak

ensordecer [ensorðeˈθer] /2d/ VT to deafen ▸ VI to go deaf

ensordezca *etc* [ensorˈðeθka] VB *ver* **ensordecer**

ensortijado, -a [ensortiˈxaðo, a] ADJ (*pelo*) curly

★**ensuciar** [ensuˈθjar] /1b/ VT (*manchar*) to dirty, soil; (*fig*) to defile ■ **ensuciarse** VR (*mancharse*) to get dirty; (*bebé*) to dirty one's nappy

ensueño [enˈsweɲo] NM (*sueño*) dream, fantasy; (*ilusión*) illusion; (*soñando despierto*) daydream; **de** ~ dream-like

entablado [entaˈβlaðo] NM (*piso*) floorboards *pl*; (*armazón*) boarding

entablar [entaˈβlar] /1a/ VT (*recubrir*) to board (up); (*Ajedrez, Damas*) to set up; (*conversación*) to strike up; (*Jur*) to file ▸ VI to draw

entablillar [entaβliˈʎar] /1a/ VT (*Med*) to (put in a) splint

entallado, -a [entaˈʎaðo, a] ADJ waisted

entallar [entaˈʎar] /1a/ VT (*traje*) to tailor ▸ VI: **el traje entalla bien** the suit fits well

ente [ˈente] NM (*organización*) body, organization; (*compañía*) company; (*fam: persona*) odd character; (*ser*) being; ~ **público** (*Esp*) state(-owned) body

★**entender** [entenˈder] /2g/ VT (*comprender*) to understand; (*darse cuenta*) to realize; (*querer decir*) to mean; ~ **algo de** to know a little about; **dar a** ~ **que ...** to lead to believe that ... ▸ VI to understand; (*creer*) to think, believe; ~ **de** to know all about; ~ **en** to deal with, have to do with; ¿**entiendes?** (do you) understand? ▸ NM: **a mi** ~ in my opinion ■ **entenderse** VR (*comprenderse*) to be understood; (*2 personas*) to get on together; (*ponerse de acuerdo*) to agree, reach an agreement; **entenderse mal** to get on badly

★**entendido, -a** [entenˈdiðo, a] ADJ (*comprendido*) understood; (*hábil*) skilled; (*inteligente*) knowledgeable ▸ NM/F (*experto*) expert ▸ EXCL agreed!

entendimiento [entendi'mjento] NM (*comprensión*) understanding; (*inteligencia*) mind, intellect; (*juicio*) judgement

enterado, -a [ente'raðo, a] ADJ well-informed; **estar ~ de** to know about, be aware of; **no darse por ~** to pretend not to understand

enteramente [entera'mente] ADV entirely, completely

enterar [ente'rar] /**1a**/ VT (*informar*) to inform, tell ∎ **enterarse** VR to find out, get to know; **para que te enteres ...** (*fam*) for your information ...

entereza [ente'reθa] NF (*totalidad*) entirety; (*fig: de carácter*) strength of mind; (*honradez*) integrity

enterito [ente'rito] NM (*Am*) boiler suit (*Brit*), overalls (*US*)

enternecedor, a [enterneθe'ðor, a] ADJ touching

enternecer [enterne'θer] /**2d**/ VT (*ablandar*) to soften; (*apiadar*) to touch, move ∎ **enternecerse** VR to be touched, be moved

enternezca *etc* [enter'neθka] VB *ver* **enternecer**

★**entero, -a** [en'tero, a] ADJ (*total*) whole, entire; (*fig: recto*) honest; (: *firme*) firm, resolute ▶ NM (*Mat*) integer; (*Com: punto*) point; (*Am: pago*) payment; **las acciones han subido dos enteros** the shares have gone up two points

enterrador [enterra'ðor] NM gravedigger

enterrar [ente'rrar] /**1j**/ VT to bury; (*fig*) to forget

entibiar [enti'βjar] /**1b**/ VT (*enfriar*) to cool; (*calentar*) to warm ∎ **entibiarse** VR (*fig*) to cool

entidad [enti'ðað] NF (*empresa*) firm, company; (*organismo*) body; (*sociedad*) society; (*Filosofía*) entity

entienda *etc* [en'tjenda] VB *ver* **entender**

entierro [en'tjerro] NM *ver* **enterrar** ▶ NM (*acción*) burial; (*funeral*) funeral

entomología [entomolo'xia] NF entomology

entomólogo, -a [ento'moloɣo, a] NM/F entomologist

entonación [entona'θjon] NF (*Ling*) intonation; (*fig*) conceit

entonar [ento'nar] /**1a**/ VT (*canción*) to intone; (*colores*) to tone; (*Med*) to tone up ▶ VI to be in tune ∎ **entonarse** VR (*engreírse*) to give o.s. airs

entonces [en'tonθes] ADV then, at that time; **desde ~** since then; **en aquel ~** at that time; **(pues) ~** and so; **el ~ embajador de España** the then Spanish ambassador

entornar [entor'nar] /**1a**/ VT (*puerta, ventana*) to half close, leave ajar; (*los ojos*) to screw up

★**entorno** [en'torno] NM setting, environment; **~ de redes** (*Inform*) network environment

entorpecer [entorpe'θer] /**2d**/ VT (*entendimiento*) to dull; (*impedir*) to obstruct, hinder; (: *tránsito*) to slow down, delay

entorpezca *etc* [entor'peθka] VB *ver* **entorpecer**

entrado, -a [en'traðo, a] ADJ: **~ en años** elderly;

(una vez) ~ el verano in the summer(time), when summer comes ▶ NF (*sitio*) entrance, way in; (*acción*) entry, access; (*principio*) beginning; (*para espectáculo*) ticket; (*Culin*) entrée; (*Deporte*) innings *sg*; (*Teat: público*) house, audience; (*Teat: recaudación*) receipts *pl*, takings *pl*; (*Inform*) input; **entrada de aire** (*Tec*) air intake *o* inlet; **de entrada** from the outset; **"entrada gratis"** "admission free" ∎ **entradas** NFPL (*Com*) income *sg*; **entradas brutas** gross receipts; **entradas y salidas** income and expenditure; **tiene entradas** he's losing his hair

entramparse [entram'parse] /**1a**/ VR to get into debt

entrante [en'trante] ADJ next, coming; (*Pol*) incoming; **mes/año ~** next month/year ▶ NM (*Geo*) inlet; (*Culin*) starter

entraña [en'trapa] NF (*fig: centro*) heart, core; (*raíz*) root ∎ **entrañas** NFPL (*Anat*) entrails; (*fig*) heart *sg*

entrañable [entra'paβle] ADJ (*amigo*) dear; (*recuerdo*) fond; (*acto*) intimate

entrañar [entra'par] /**1a**/ VT to entail

★**entrar** [en'trar] /**1a**/ VT (*introducir*) to bring in; (*persona*) to show in; (*Inform*) to input; **le entraron ganas de reír** he felt a sudden urge to laugh; **me entró sed/sueño** I started to feel thirsty/sleepy; **no me entra** I can't get the hang of it ▶ VI (*meterse*) to go *o* come in, enter; (*comenzar*): **~ diciendo** to begin by saying; **entré en** *o* **a la casa** (*Am*) I went into the house

★**entre** ['entre] PREP (*dos*) between; (*en medio de*) among(st); (*por*): **se abrieron paso ~ la multitud** they forced their way through the crowd; **~ una cosa y otra** what with one thing and another; **~ más estudia más aprende** (*Am*) the more he studies the more he learns

entreabierto [entrea'βjerto] PP *de* **entreabrir**

entreabrir [entrea'βrir] /**3a**/ VT to half-open, open halfway

entreacto [entre'akto] NM interval

entrecano, -a [entre'kano, a] ADJ greying; **ser ~** (*persona*) to be going grey

entrecejo [entre'θexo] NM: **fruncir el ~** to frown

entrechocar [entretʃo'kar] /**1g**/ VI (*dientes*) to chatter

entrechoque *etc* [entre'tʃoke] VB *ver* **entrechocar**

entrecomillado, -a [entrekomi'ʎaðo, a] ADJ in inverted commas

entrecortado, -a [entrekor'taðo, a] ADJ (*respiración*) laboured, difficult; (*habla*) faltering

entrecot [entre'ko(t)] NM (*Culin*) sirloin steak

entrecruce *etc* [entre'kruθe] VB *ver* **entrecruzarse**

entrecruzarse [entrekru'θarse] /**1f**/ VR (*Bio*) to interbreed

entredicho [entre'ðitʃo] NM (*Jur*) injunction;

poner en ~ to cast doubt on; **estar en ~** to be in doubt

entrega [en'treɣa] NF (*de mercancías*) delivery; (*de premios*) presentation; (*de novela etc*) instalment; **"~ a domicilio"** "door-to-door delivery service"

★**entregar** [entre'ɣar] /**1h**/ VT (*dar*) to hand (over), deliver; (*ejercicios*) to hand in ■ **entregarse** VR (*rendirse*) to surrender, give in, submit; **entregarse a** (*dedicarse*) to devote o.s. to; **a ~** (*Com*) to be supplied

entregue *etc* [en'treɣe] VB *ver* **entregar**

entrelace *etc* [entre'laθe] VB *ver* **entrelazar**

entrelazar [entrela'θar] /**1f**/ VT to entwine

entremedias [entre'meðjas] ADV (*en medio*) in between, halfway

★**entremeses** [entre'meses] NMPL hors d'œuvres

entremeter [entreme'ter] /**2a**/ VT to insert, put in ■ **entremeterse** VR to meddle, interfere

entremetido, -a [entreme'tiðo, a] ADJ meddling, interfering

entremezclar [entremeθ'klar] /**1a**/ VT to intermingle ■ **entremezclarse** VR to intermingle

entrenador, a [entrena'ðor, a] NM/F trainer, coach

★**entrenamiento** [entrena'mjento] NM training

entrenar [entre'nar] /**1a**/ VT (*Deporte*) to train; (*caballo*) to exercise ▶ VI, **entrenarse** VR to train

entrepierna [entre'pjerna] NF (*tb:* **entrepiernas**) crotch, crutch

entresacar [entresa'kar] /**1g**/ VT to pick out, select

entresaque *etc* [entre'sake] VB *ver* **entresacar**

entresuelo [entre'swelo] NM mezzanine, entresol; (*Teat*) dress o first circle

★**entretanto** [entre'tanto] ADV meanwhile, meantime

entretecho [entre'tetʃo] NM (*Am*) attic

entretejer [entrete'xer] /**2a**/ VT to interweave

entretela [entre'tela] NF (*de ropa*) interlining ■ **entretelas** NFPL heartstrings

entretención [entreten'sjon] NF (*Am*) entertainment

entretendré *etc* [entreten'dre] VB *ver* **entretener**

entretener [entrete'ner] /**2k**/ VT (*divertir*) to entertain, amuse; (*detener*) to hold up, delay; (*mantener*) to maintain; **no le entretengo más** I won't keep you any longer ■ **entretenerse** VR (*divertirse*) to amuse o.s.; (*retrasarse*) to delay, linger

entretenga *etc* [entre'tenga] VB *ver* **entretener**

★**entretenido, -a** [entrete'niðo, a] ADJ entertaining, amusing

entretenimiento [entreteni'mjento] NM entertainment, amusement; (*mantenimiento*) upkeep, maintenance

entretiempo [entre'tjempo] NM: **ropa de ~** clothes for spring and autumn

entretiene *etc* [entre'tjene], **entretuve** *etc* [entre'tuβe] VB *ver* **entretener**

entreveía *etc* [entreβe'ia] VB *ver* **entrever**

entrever [entre'βer] /**2u**/ VT to glimpse, catch a glimpse of

★**entrevista** [entre'βista] NF interview

entrevistador, a [entreβista'ðor, a] NM/F interviewer

★**entrevistar** [entreβis'tar] /**1a**/ VT to interview ■ **entrevistarse** VR: **entrevistarse con** to have an interview with, see; **el ministro se entrevistó con el Rey ayer** the minister had an audience with the King yesterday

entrevisto [entre'βisto] PP *de* **entrever**

entristecer [entriste'θer] /**2d**/ VT to sadden, grieve ■ **entristecerse** VR to grow sad

entristezca *etc* [entris'teθka] VB *ver* **entristecer**

entrometerse [entrome'terse] /**2a**/ VR: **~ (en)** to interfere (in o with)

entrometido, -a [entrome'tiðo, a] ADJ interfering, meddlesome

entroncar [entron'kar] /**1g**/ VI to be connected o related

entronque *etc* [en'tronke] VB *ver* **entroncar**

entuerto [en'twerto] NM wrong, injustice ■ **entuertos** NMPL (*Med*) afterpains

entumecer [entume'θer] /**2d**/ VT to numb, benumb ■ **entumecerse** VR (*por el frío*) to go o become numb

entumecido, -a [entume'θiðo, a] ADJ numb, stiff

entumezca *etc* [entu'meθka] VB *ver* **entumecer**

enturbiar [entur'βjar] /**1b**/ VT (*el agua*) to make cloudy; (*fig*) to confuse ■ **enturbiarse** VR (*oscurecerse*) to become cloudy; (*fig*) to get confused, become obscure

entusiasmar [entusjas'mar] /**1a**/ VT to excite, fill with enthusiasm; (*gustar mucho*) to delight ■ **entusiasmarse** VR: **entusiasmarse con** o **por** to get enthusiastic o excited about

★**entusiasmo** [entu'sjasmo] NM enthusiasm; (*excitación*) excitement

★**entusiasta** [entu'sjasta] ADJ enthusiastic ▶ NMF enthusiast

enumerar [enume'rar] /**1a**/ VT to enumerate

enunciación [enunθja'θjon] NF, **enunciado** [enun'θjaðo] NM enunciation; (*declaración*) declaration, statement

enunciar [enun'θjar] /**1b**/ VT to enunciate; to declare, state

envainar [embai'nar] /**1a**/ VT to sheathe

envalentonar [embalento'nar] /**1a**/ VT to give courage to ■ **envalentonarse** VR (*pey: jactarse*) to boast, brag

envanecer [embane'θer] /**2d**/ VT to make conceited ■ **envanecerse** VR to grow conceited

envanezca etc [embaˈneθka] VB ver **envanecer**

envasar [embaˈsar] /**1a**/ VT (empaquetar) to pack, wrap; (enfrascar) to bottle; (enlatar) to can; (embolsar) to pocket

★**envase** [emˈbase] NM packing, wrapping; bottling; canning; pocketing; (recipiente) container; (paquete) package; (botella) bottle; (lata) tin (BRIT), can

envejecer [embexeˈθer] /**2d**/ VT to make old, age ▶ VI (volverse viejo) to grow old; (parecer viejo) to age

envejecido, -a [embexeˈθiðo, a] ADJ old, aged; (de aspecto) old-looking

envejezca etc [embeˈxeθka] VB ver **envejecer**

envenenar [embeneˈnar] /**1a**/ VT to poison; (fig) to embitter

envergadura [emberɣaˈðura] NF (expansión) expanse; (Naut) breadth; (fig) scope; **un programa de gran ~** a wide-ranging programme

envés [emˈbes] NM (de tela) back, wrong side

enviado, -a [emˈbjaðo, a] NM/F (Pol) envoy; **~ especial** (de periódico, TV) special correspondent

★**enviar** [emˈbjar] /**1c**/ VT to send; **~ un mensaje a algn** (por móvil) to text sb, send sb a text message

enviciar [embiˈθjar] /**1b**/ VT to corrupt ▶ VI (trabajo etc) to be addictive ■ **enviciarse** VR: **enviciarse (con o en)** to get addicted (to)

envidia [emˈbiðja] NF envy; **tener ~ a** to envy, be jealous of

envidiar [embiˈðjar] /**1b**/ VT (desear) to envy; (tener celos de) to be jealous of

envidioso, -a [embiˈðjoso, a] ADJ envious, jealous

envío [emˈbio] NM (acción) sending; (de mercancías) consignment; (de dinero) remittance; (en barco) shipment; **gastos de ~** postage and packing; **~ contra reembolso** COD shipment

enviudar [embjuˈðar] /**1d**/ VI to be widowed

envoltorio [embolˈtorjo] NM package

envoltura [embolˈtura] NF (cobertura) cover; (embalaje) wrapper, wrapping

★**envolver** [embolˈβer] /**2h**/ VT to wrap (up); (cubrir) to cover; (enemigo) to surround; (implicar) to involve, implicate

envuelto [emˈbwelto], **envuelva** etc [emˈbwelβa] VB ver **envolver**

enyesar [enjeˈsar] /**1a**/ VT (pared) to plaster; (Med) to put in plaster

enzarzarse [enθarˈθarse] /**1f**/ VR: **~ en algo** to get mixed up in sth; (disputa) to get involved in sth

epa [ˈepa], (AM) **épale** [ˈepale] EXCL hey!, wow!

E.P.D. ABR (= en paz descanse) RIP

epicentro [epiˈθentro] NM epicentre

épico, -a [ˈepiko, a] ADJ epic ▶ NF epic (poetry)

epidemia [epiˈðemja] NF epidemic

epidémico, -a [epiˈðemiko, a] ADJ epidemic

epidermis [epiˈðermis] NF epidermis

epidural [epiðuˈral] ADJ, NF (Med) epidural

epifanía [epifaˈnia] NF Epiphany

epilepsia [epiˈlepsja] NF epilepsy

epiléptico, -a [epiˈleptiko, a] ADJ epileptic

epílogo [eˈpiloɣo] NM epilogue

episcopado [episkoˈpaðo] NM (cargo) bishopric; (obispos) bishops pl (collectively)

episodio [epiˈsoðjo] NM episode; (suceso) incident

epístola [eˈpistola] NF epistle

epitafio [epiˈtafjo] NM epitaph

epíteto [eˈpiteto] NM epithet

★**época** [ˈepoka] NF period, time; (temporada) season; (Historia) age, epoch; **hacer ~** to be epoch-making

equidad [ekiˈðað] NF equity, fairness

equilibrar [ekiliˈβrar] /**1a**/ VT to balance

equilibrio [ekiˈliβrjo] NM balance, equilibrium; **mantener/perder el ~** to keep/lose one's balance; **~ político** balance of power

equilibrista [ekiliˈβrista] NMF (funámbulo) tightrope walker; (acróbata) acrobat

equinoccio [ekiˈnokθjo] NM equinox

★**equipaje** [ekiˈpaxe] NM luggage (BRIT), baggage (US); (avíos) equipment, kit; **~ de mano** hand luggage; **hacer el ~** to pack

equipamiento [ekipaˈmjento] NM equipment; **~ de serie** standard equipment

equipar [ekiˈpar] /**1a**/ VT (proveer) to equip

equiparar [ekipaˈrar] /**1a**/ VT (igualar) to put on the same level; (comparar): **~ con** to compare with ■ **equipararse** VR: **equipararse con** to be on a level with

★**equipo** [eˈkipo] NM (conjunto de cosas) equipment; (Deporte, grupo) team; (de obreros) shift; (de máquinas) plant; (turbinas etc) set; **~ de caza** hunting gear; **~ de música** music centre; **~ físico** (Inform) hardware; **~ médico** medical team

equis [ˈekis] NF (the letter) X

★**equitación** [ekitaˈθjon] NF (acto) riding; (arte) horsemanship

equitativo, -a [ekitaˈtiβo, a] ADJ equitable, fair

equivaldré etc [ekiβalˈdre] VB ver **equivaler**

equivalencia [ekiβaˈlenθja] NF equivalence

equivalente [ekiβaˈlente] ADJ, NM equivalent

equivaler [ekiβaˈler] /**2p**/ VI: **~ a** to be equivalent o equal to; (en rango) to rank as

equivalga etc [ekiˈβalɣa] VB ver **equivaler**

equivocación [ekiβokaˈθjon] NF mistake, error; (malentendido) misunderstanding

★**equivocado, -a** [ekiβoˈkaðo, a] ADJ wrong, mistaken

★**equivocarse** [ekiβoˈkarse] /**1g**/ VR to be wrong, make a mistake; **~ de camino** to take the wrong road

equívoco, -a [eˈkiβoko, a] ADJ (dudoso) suspect;

(*ambiguo*) ambiguous ▶ NM ambiguity; (*malen-tendido*) misunderstanding

equivoque *etc* [ekiˈβoke] VB *ver* **equivocarse**

era [ˈera] VB *ver* **ser** ▶ NF era, age; (*Agr*) threshing floor

erais [ˈerais], **éramos** [ˈeramos], **eran** [ˈeran] VB *ver* **ser**

erario [eˈrarjo] NM exchequer, treasury

eras [ˈeras], **eres** [ˈeres] VB *ver* **ser**

e-reader [ˈirider] NM e-reader

erección [erekˈθjon] NF erection

erecto, -a [eˈrekto, a] ADJ erect

ergonomía [erɣonoˈmia] NF ergonomics *sg*, human engineering

erguir [erˈɣir] /**3m**/ VT to raise, lift; (*poner derecho*) to straighten ■ **erguirse** VR to straighten up

erice *etc* [eˈriθe] VB *ver* **erizarse**

erigir [eriˈxir] /**3c**/ VT to erect, build ■ **erigirse** VR: **erigirse en** to set o.s. up as

erija *etc* [eˈrixa] VB *ver* **erigir**

erizado, -a [eriˈθaðo, a] ADJ bristly

erizarse [eriˈθarse] /**1f**/ VR (*pelo: de perro*) to bris-tle; (: *de persona*) to stand on end

erizo [eˈriθo] NM hedgehog; **~ de mar** sea urchin

ermita [erˈmita] NF hermitage

ermitaño, -a [ermiˈtaɲo, a] NM/F hermit

erosión [eroˈsjon] NF erosion

erosionar [erosjoˈnar] /**1a**/ VT to erode

erótico, -a [eˈrotiko, a] ADJ erotic

erotismo [eroˈtismo] NM eroticism

erradicar [erraðiˈkar] /**1g**/ VT to eradicate

erradique *etc* [erraˈðike] VB *ver* **erradicar**

errado, -a [eˈrraðo, a] ADJ mistaken, wrong

errante [eˈrrante] ADJ wandering, errant

errar [eˈrrar] /**1k**/ VT: **~ el tiro** to miss; **~ el camino** to take the wrong road ▶ VI (*vagar*) to wander, roam; (*equivocarse*) to be mistaken

errata [eˈrrata] NF misprint

erre [ˈerre] NF (the letter) R; **~ que ~** stubbornly

erróneo, -a [eˈrroneo, a] ADJ (*equivocado*) wrong, mistaken; (*falso*) false, untrue

★**error** [eˈrror] NM error, mistake; (*Inform*) bug; **~ de imprenta** misprint; **~ de lectura/escri-tura** (*Inform*) read/write error; **~ sintáctico** syntax error; **~ judicial** miscarriage of justice

---

Los sustantivos **mistake** y **error** tienen el mismo significado, pero **mistake** es una palabra de uso corriente, mientras que **error** suele utilizarse en un contexto formal o en lenguaje técnico:
No hay duda de que fue un error dejar el trabajo. **Leaving the job was definitely a mistake**.
La NASA ha descubierto un error matemático en sus cálculos. **NASA has discovered a mathe-matical error in its calculations**.
Ambos se utilizan con el verbo **make**, no con **do**.

Ertzaintza [erˈtʃantʃa] NF Basque police; *ver tb* **policía**

eructar [erukˈtar] /**1a**/ VT to belch, burp

eructo [eˈrukto] NM belch

erudición [eruðiˈθjon] NF erudition, learning

erudito, -a [eruˈðito, a] ADJ erudite, learned ▶ NM/F scholar; **los eruditos en esta materia** the experts in this field

erupción [erupˈθjon] NF eruption; (*Med*) rash; (*de violencia*) outbreak; (*de ira*) outburst

es [es] VB *ver* **ser**

E/S ABR (*Inform*: = *entrada/salida*) I/O

★**esa** [ˈesa], **esas** [ˈesas] ADJ DEMOSTRATIVO, PRON *ver* **ese²**

★**ésa** [ˈesa], **ésas** [ˈesas] PRON *ver* **ése**

esbelto, -a [esˈβelto, a] ADJ slim, slender

esbirro [esˈβirro] NM henchman

esbozar [esβoˈθar] /**1f**/ VT to sketch, outline

esbozo [esˈβoθo] NM sketch, outline

escabeche [eskaˈβetʃe] NM brine; (*de aceitunas etc*) pickle; **en ~** pickled

escabechina [eskaβeˈtʃina] NF (*batalla*) mas-sacre; **hacer una ~** (*Escol*) to fail a lot of stu-dents

escabroso, -a [eskaˈβroso, a] ADJ (*accidentado*) rough, uneven; (*fig*) tough, difficult; (: *atrevido*) risqué

escabullirse [eskaβuˈʎirse] /**3a**/ VR to slip away; (*largarse*) to clear out

escacharrar [eskatʃaˈrrar] /**1a**/ VT (*fam*) to break ■ **escacharrarse** VR to get broken

escafandra [eskaˈfandra] NF (*buzo*) diving suit; (*escafandra espacial*) spacesuit

★**escala** [esˈkala] NF (*proporción, Mus*) scale; (*de mano*) ladder; (*Aviat*) stopover; (*de colores etc*) range; **~ de tiempo** time scale; **~ de sueldos** salary scale; **una investigación a ~ nacional** a nationwide inquiry; **reproducir a ~** to repro-duce to scale; **hacer ~ en** (*gen*) to stop off at *o* call in at; (*Aviat*) to stop over in

escalada [eskaˈlaða] NF (*de montaña*) climb; (*de pared*) scaling

escalafón [eskalaˈfon] NM (*escala de salarios*) salary scale, wage scale

★**escalar** [eskaˈlar] /**1a**/ VT to climb, scale ▶ VI (*Mil, Pol*) to escalate

escaldar [eskalˈdar] /**1a**/ VT (*quemar*) to scald; (*escarmentar*) to teach a lesson

★**escalera** [eskaˈlera] NF stairs *pl*, staircase; (*escala*) ladder; (*Naipes*) run; (*de camión*) tail-board; **~ mecánica** escalator; **~ de caracol** spiral staircase; **~ de incendios** fire escape

escalerilla [eskaleˈriʎa] NF (*de avión*) steps *pl*

escalfar [eskalˈfar] /**1a**/ VT (*huevos*) to poach

escalinata [eskaliˈnata] NF staircase

escalofriante [eskaloˈfrjante] ADJ chilling

escalofrío [eskaloˈfrio] NM (*Med*) chill ■ **esca-lofríos** NMPL (*fig*) shivers

escalón [eskaˈlon] NM step, stair; (*de escalera*) rung; (*fig: paso*) step; (*al éxito*) ladder

escalonar [eskaloˈnar] /1a/ VT to spread out; (*tierra*) to terrace; (*horas de trabajo*) to stagger

escalope [eskaˈlope] NM (*Culin*) escalope

escama [esˈkama] NF (*de pez, serpiente*) scale; (*de jabón*) flake; (*fig*) resentment

escamar [eskaˈmar] /1a/ VT (*pez*) to scale; (*producir recelo*) to make wary

escamotear [eskamoteˈar] /1a/ VT (*fam: robar*) to lift, swipe; (*hacer desaparecer*) to make disappear

escampar [eskamˈpar] /1a/ VB IMPERSONAL to stop raining

escanciar [eskanˈθjar] /1b/ VT (*vino*) to pour (out)

escandalice *etc* [eskandaˈliθe] VB *ver* **escandalizar**

escandalizar [eskandaliˈθar] /1f/ VT to scandalize, shock ■ **escandalizarse** VR to be shocked; (*ofenderse*) to be offended

escándalo [esˈkandalo] NM scandal; (*alboroto, tumulto*) row, uproar; **armar un ~** to make a scene; **¡es un ~!** it's outrageous!

escandaloso, -a [eskandaˈloso, a] ADJ scandalous, shocking; (*risa*) hearty; (*niño*) noisy

Escandinavia [eskandiˈnaβja] NF Scandinavia

escandinavo, -a [eskandiˈnaβo, a] ADJ, NM/F Scandinavian

escanear [eskaneˈar] /1a/ VT to scan

escaneo [esˈkaneo] NM scanning

escáner [esˈkaner] NM scanner

escaño [esˈkaɲo] NM bench; (*Pol*) seat

escapada [eskaˈpaða] NF (*huida*) escape, flight; (*Deporte*) breakaway; (*viaje*) quick trip

★**escapar** [eskaˈpar] /1a/ VI (*gen*) to escape, run away; (*Deporte*) to break away ■ **escaparse** VR to escape, get away; (*agua, gas, noticias*) to leak (out); **se me escapa su nombre** his name escapes me

★**escaparate** [eskapaˈrate] NM shop window; (*Com*) showcase; **ir de escaparates** to go window shopping

escapatoria [eskapaˈtorja] NF: **no tener ~** (*fig*) to have no way out

escape [esˈkape] NM (*huida*) escape; (*de agua, gas*) leak; (*de motor*) exhaust; **salir a ~** to rush out

escapismo [eskaˈpismo] NM escapism

escaquearse [eskakeˈarse] /1a/ VR (*fam*) to duck out

escarabajo [eskaraˈβaxo] NM beetle

escaramuza [eskaraˈmuθa] NF skirmish; (*fig*) brush

escarbar [eskarˈβar] /1a/ VT (*gallina*) to scratch; (*fig*) to inquire into, investigate

escarceos [eskarˈθeos] NMPL: **en sus ~ con la política** in his occasional forays into politics; **~ amorosos** love affairs

★**escarcha** [esˈkartʃa] NF frost

escarchado, -a [eskarˈtʃaðo, a] ADJ (*Culin: fruta*) crystallized

escarlata [eskarˈlata] ADJ INV scarlet

escarlatina [eskarlaˈtina] NF scarlet fever

escarmentar [eskarmenˈtar] /1j/ VT to punish severely ▸ VI to learn one's lesson; **¡para que escarmientes!** that'll teach you!

escarmiento *etc* [eskarˈmjento] VB *ver* **escarmentar** ▸ NM (*ejemplo*) lesson; (*castigo*) punishment

escarnio [esˈkarnjo] NM mockery; (*injuria*) insult

escarola [eskaˈrola] NF (*Bot*) endive

escarpado, -a [eskarˈpaðo, a] ADJ (*pendiente*) sheer, steep; (*rocas*) craggy

escasamente [eskasaˈmente] ADV (*insuficientemente*) scantily; (*apenas*) scarcely

escasear [eskaseˈar] /1a/ VI to be scarce

★**escasez** [eskaˈseθ] NF (*falta*) shortage, scarcity; (*pobreza*) poverty; **vivir con ~** to live on the breadline

escaso, -a [esˈkaso, a] ADJ (*poco*) scarce; (*raro*) rare; (*ralo*) thin, sparse; (*limitado*) limited; (*recursos*) scanty; (*público*) sparse; (*posibilidad*) slim; (*visibilidad*) poor

escatimar [eskatiˈmar] /1a/ VT (*limitar*) to skimp (on), be sparing with; **no ~ esfuerzos (para)** to spare no effort (to)

escayola [eskaˈjola] NF plaster

escayolar [eskajoˈlar] /1a/ VT to put in plaster

★**escena** [esˈθena] NF scene; (*decorado*) scenery; (*escenario*) stage; **poner en ~** to put on

escenario [esθeˈnarjo] NM (*Teat*) stage; (*Cine*) set; (*fig*) scene; **el ~ del crimen** the scene of the crime; **el ~ político** the political scene

escenografía [esθenoɣraˈfia] NF set o stage design

escepticismo [esθeptiˈθismo] NM scepticism

escéptico, -a [esˈθeptiko, a] ADJ sceptical ▸ NM/F sceptic

escindir [esθinˈdir] /3a/ VT to split ■ **escindirse** VR (*facción*) to split off; **escindirse en** to split into

escisión [esθiˈsjon] NF (*Med*) excision; (*fig, Pol*) split; **~ nuclear** nuclear fission

esclarecer [esklareˈθer] /2d/ VT (*iluminar*) to light up, illuminate; (*misterio, problema*) to shed light on

esclarezca *etc* [esklaˈreθka] VB *ver* **esclarecer**

esclavice *etc* [esklaˈβiθe] VB *ver* **esclavizar**

esclavitud [esklaβiˈtuð] NF slavery

esclavizar [esklaβiˈθar] /1f/ VT to enslave

esclavo, -a [esˈklaβo, a] NM/F slave

esclusa [esˈklusa] NF (*de canal*) lock; (*compuerta*) floodgate

escoba [esˈkoβa] NF broom; **pasar la ~** to sweep up

escobazo [eskoˈβaθo] NM (*golpe*) blow with a

broom; **echar a algn a escobazos** to kick sb out

escobilla [esko'βiʎa] NF brush

escocer [esko'θer] /**2b, 2h**/ VI to burn, sting ▪ **escocerse** VR to chafe, get chafed

★**escocés, -esa** [esko'θes, esa] ADJ Scottish; (*whisky*) Scotch; **tela escocesa** tartan ▸ NM/F Scotsman(-woman), Scot ▸ NM (*Ling*) Scots *sg*

★**Escocia** [es'koθja] NF Scotland

★**escoger** [esko'xer] /**2c**/ VT to choose, pick, select

escogido, -a [esko'xiðo, a] ADJ chosen, selected; (*calidad*) choice, select; (*persona*): **ser muy ~** to be very fussy

escoja *etc* [es'koxa] VB *ver* **escoger**

★**escolar** [esko'lar] ADJ school *cpd* ▸ NMF schoolboy(-girl), pupil

escolaridad [eskolari'ðað] NF schooling; **libro de ~** school record

escolarización [eskolariθa'θjon] NF: **~ obligatoria** compulsory education

escolarizado, -a [eskolari'θaðo, a] ADJ, NM/F: **los escolarizados** those in *o* attending school

escollo [es'koʎo] NM (*arrecife*) reef, rock; (*fig*) pitfall

escolta [es'kolta] NF escort

escoltar [eskol'tar] /**1a**/ VT to escort; (*proteger*) to guard

escombros [es'kombros] NMPL (*basura*) rubbish *sg*; (*restos*) debris *sg*

★**esconder** [eskon'der] /**2a**/ VT to hide, conceal ▪ **esconderse** VR to hide

escondidas [eskon'diðas] NFPL (*Am*) hide-and-seek *sg*; **a ~** secretly; **hacer algo a ~ de algn** to do sth behind sb's back

escondite [eskon'dite] NM hiding place; (*juego*) hide-and-seek

escondrijo [eskon'drixo] NM hiding place, hideout

escopeta [esko'peta] NF shotgun; **~ de aire comprimido** air gun

escoria [es'korja] NF (*desecho mineral*) slag; (*fig*) scum, dregs *pl*

Escorpio [es'korpjo] NM (*Astro*) Scorpio

escorpión [eskor'pjon] NM scorpion

escotado, -a [esko'taðo, a] ADJ low-cut

escotar [esko'tar] /**1a**/ VT (*vestido: ajustar*) to cut to fit; (*cuello*) to cut low

escote [es'kote] NM (*de vestido*) low neck; **pagar a ~** to share the expenses

escotilla [esko'tiʎa] NF (*Naut*) hatchway

escotillón [eskoti'ʎon] NM trapdoor

escozor [esko'θor] NM (*dolor*) sting(ing)

escrache [es'kratʃe] NM public protest

escribano, -a [eskri'βano, a], **escribiente** [eskri'βjente] NM/F clerk; (*secretario judicial*) court *o* lawyer's clerk

escribible [eskri'βiβle] ADJ writable

★**escribir** [eskri'βir] /**3a**/ VT, VI to write; **~ a máquina** to type; **¿cómo se escribe?** how do you spell it?

escrito, -a [es'krito, a] PP *de* **escribir** ▸ ADJ written, in writing; (*examen*) written ▸ NM (*documento*) document; (*manuscrito*) text, manuscript; **por ~** in writing

★**escritor, a** [eskri'tor, a] NM/F writer

★**escritorio** [eskri'torjo] NM desk; (*oficina*) office; (*Inform*) desktop

escritura [eskri'tura] NF (*acción*) writing; (*caligrafía*) (hand)writing; (*Jur: documento*) deed; (*Com*) indenture; **~ de propiedad** title deed; **Sagrada E~** (Holy) Scripture; **~ social** articles *pl* of association

escroto [es'kroto] NM scrotum

escrúpulo [es'krupulo] NM scruple; (*minuciosidad*) scrupulousness

escrupuloso, -a [eskrupu'loso, a] ADJ scrupulous

escrutar [eskru'tar] /**1a**/ VT to scrutinize, examine; (*votos*) to count

escrutinio [eskru'tinjo] NM (*examen atento*) scrutiny; (*Pol: recuento de votos*) count(ing)

escuadra [es'kwaðra] NF (*Tec*) square; (*Mil etc*) squad; (*Naut*) squadron; (*de coches etc*) fleet

escuadrilla [eskwa'ðriʎa] NF (*de aviones*) squadron; (*Am: de obreros*) gang

escuadrón [eskwa'ðron] NM squadron

escuálido, -a [es'kwaliðo, a] ADJ skinny, scraggy; (*sucio*) squalid

escucha [es'kutʃa] NF (*acción*) listening; **estar a la ~** to listen in; **estar de ~** to spy; **escuchas telefónicas** (phone-)tapping *sg* ▸ NM (*Telec: sistema*) monitor; (: *oyente*) listener

★**escuchar** [esku'tʃar] /**1a**/ VT to listen to; (*consejo*) to heed; (*esp Am: oír*) to hear ▸ VI to listen ▪ **escucharse** VR: **se escucha muy mal** (*Telec*) it's a very bad line

escudarse [esku'ðarse] /**1a**/ VR: **~ en** (*fig*) to hide behind

escudería [eskuðe'ria] NF: **la ~ Ferrari** the Ferrari team

escudero [esku'ðero] NM squire

escudilla [esku'ðiʎa] NF bowl, basin

escudo [es'kuðo] NM shield; **~ de armas** coat of arms

escudriñar [eskuðri'ɲar] /**1a**/ VT (*examinar*) to investigate, scrutinize; (*mirar de lejos*) to scan

escuece *etc* [es'kweθe] VB *ver* **escocer**

★**escuela** [es'kwela] NF (*tb fig*) school; **~ normal** teacher training college; **~ técnica superior** *university offering five-year courses in engineering and technical subjects*; **~ universitaria** *university offering three-year diploma courses*; **~ de párvulos** kindergarten; **~ de artes y oficios** (*Esp*) ≈ technical college; **~ de choferes** (*Am*) driving school; **~ de manejo** (*Am*) driving school; *ver tb* **colegio**

escueto, -a [es'kweto, a] ADJ plain; (*estilo*) simple; (*explicación*) concise

escueza *etc* [es'kweθa] VB *ver* **escocer**

escuincle [es'kwinkle] NM (*Am fam*) kid

esculpir [eskul'pir] /3a/ VT to sculpt; (*grabar*) to engrave; (*tallar*) to carve

escultor, a [eskul'tor, a] NM/F sculptor

★**escultura** [eskul'tura] NF sculpture

escupidera [eskupi'ðera] NF spittoon

★**escupir** [esku'pir] /3a/ VT to spit (out) ▶ VI to spit

escupitajo [eskupi'taxo] NM (*fam*) gob of spit

escurreplatos [eskurre'platos] NM INV plate rack

escurridero [eskurri'ðero] NM (*Am*) draining board (*Brit*), drainboard (*US*)

escurridizo, -a [eskurri'ðiθo, a] ADJ slippery

escurridor [eskurri'ðor] NM colander

escurrir [esku'rrir] /3a/ VT (*ropa*) to wring out; (*verduras, platos*) to drain ▶ VI (*los líquidos*) to drip ■ **escurrirse** VR (*secarse*) to drain; (*resbalarse*) to slip, slide; (*escaparse*) to slip away

ese[1] ['ese] NF (the letter) S; **hacer eses** (*carretera*) to zigzag; (*borracho*) to reel about

★**ese**[2] ['ese], **esa** ['esa], **esos** ['esos], **esas** ['esas] ADJ DEMOSTRATIVO that *sg*, those *pl* ▶ PRON that (one) *sg*, those (ones) *pl*; **~ ... este ...** the former ... the latter ...; **¡no me vengas con esas!** don't give me any more of that nonsense!

★**ése** ['ese], **ésa** ['esa], **ésos** ['esos], **ésas** ['esas] PRON that (one) *sg*, those (ones) *pl*

esencia [e'senθja] NF essence

★**esencial** [esen'θjal] ADJ essential; (*principal*) chief; **lo ~** the main thing

esfera [es'fera] NF sphere; (*de reloj*) face; **~ de acción** scope; **~ terrestre** globe

esférico, -a [es'feriko, a] ADJ spherical

esfinge [es'finxe] NF sphinx

esforcé [esfor'θe], **esforcemos** *etc* [esfor'θemos] VB *ver* **esforzarse**

esforzado, -a [esfor'θaðo, a] ADJ (*enérgico*) energetic, vigorous

esforzarse [esfor'θarse] /1f, 1l/ VR to exert o.s., make an effort

esfuerce *etc* [es'fwerθe] VB *ver* **esforzarse**

★**esfuerzo** [es'fwerθo] VB *ver* **esforzarse** ▶ NM effort; **sin ~** effortlessly

esfumarse [esfu'marse] /1a/ VR (*apoyo, esperanzas*) to fade away; (*persona*) to vanish

★**esgrima** [es'ɣrima] NF fencing

esgrimidor [esɣrimi'ðor] NM fencer

esgrimir [esɣri'mir] /3a/ VT (*arma*) to brandish; (*argumento*) to use ▶ VI to fence

esguince [es'ɣinθe] NM (*Med*) sprain

eslabón [esla'βon] NM link; **~ perdido** (*Bio, fig*) missing link

eslabonar [eslaβo'nar] /1a/ VT to link, connect

eslálom [es'lalom] NM slalom

eslavo, -a [es'laβo, a] ADJ Slav, Slavonic ▶ NM/F Slav ▶ NM (*Ling*) Slavonic

eslip [es'lip] NM pants *pl* (*Brit*), briefs *pl*

eslogan [es'loɣan] (*pl* **eslogans**) NM slogan

eslora [es'lora] NF (*Naut*) length

eslovaco, -a [eslo'βako, a] ADJ, NM/F Slovak, Slovakian ▶ NM (*Ling*) Slovak, Slovakian

Eslovaquia [eslo'βakja] NF Slovakia

Eslovenia [eslo'βenja] NF Slovenia

esloveno, -a [eslo'βeno, a] ADJ, NM/F Slovene, Slovenian ▶ NM (*Ling*) Slovene, Slovenian

esmaltar [esmal'tar] /1a/ VT to enamel

esmalte [es'malte] NM enamel; **~ de uñas** nail varnish *o* polish

esmerado, -a [esme'raðo, a] ADJ careful, neat

esmeralda [esme'ralda] NF emerald

esmerarse [esme'rarse] /1a/ VR (*aplicarse*) to take great pains, exercise great care; (*afanarse*) to work hard; (*hacer lo mejor*) to do one's best

esmero [es'mero] NM (great) care

esmirriado, -a [esmi'rrjaðo, a] ADJ puny

esmoquin [es'mokin] NM dinner jacket (*Brit*), tuxedo (*US*)

esnob [es'nob] ADJ INV (*persona*) snobbish; (*coche etc*) posh ▶ NMF snob

esnobismo [esno'βismo] NM snobbery

ESO ['eso] NF ABR (*Esp*: = *Educación Secundaria Obligatoria*) compulsory secondary education for 12 to 16 year-olds

La **ESO**, or *Educación Secundaria Obligatoria* (Secondary education), is aimed at young people aged between 12 and 16. It is free and compulsory and offers both academic and vocational subjects. If they pass their exams, students receive the diploma called *Título de Graduado en Educación Secundaria* when they are 16, which coincides with the end of compulsory education. If they wish to continue their studies, they can choose to do the *Bachillerato* (equivalent A-Level course) if they want to go to university or the *Formación Profesional Específica* (vocational course) if they decide to pursue a vocational path.

★**eso** ['eso] PRON that, that thing *o* matter; **~ de su coche** that business about his car; **~ de ir al cine** all that about going to the cinema; **a ~ de las cinco** at about five o'clock; **en ~** thereupon, at that point; **por ~** therefore; **~ es** that's it; **nada de ~** far from it; **¡~ sí que es vida!** now this is really living!; **por ~ te lo dije** that's why I told you; **y ~ que llovía** in spite of the fact it was raining

esófago [e'sofaɣo] NM (*Anat*) oesophagus

esos ['esos] ADJ DEMOSTRATIVO *ver* **ese**[2]

ésos ['esos] PRON *ver* **ése**

esotérico, -a [eso'teriko, a] ADJ esoteric

esp. ABR (= *español*) Sp., Span.; = **especialmente**

espabilado, -a [espaβi'laðo, a] ADJ quick-witted

espabilar [espaβi'lar] /**1a**/ VT, **espabilarse** VR = **despabilar**

espachurrar [espatʃu'rrar] /**1a**/ VT to squash ■ **espachurrarse** VR to get squashed

espaciado [espa'θjaðo] NM (*Inform*) spacing

espacial [espa'θjal] ADJ (*del espacio*) space *cpd*

espaciar [espa'θjar] /**1b**/ VT to space (out)

★espacio [es'paθjo] NM space; (*Mus*) interval; (*Radio, TV*) programme, program (*US*); **el ~** space; **ocupar mucho ~** to take up a lot of room; **a dos espacios, a doble ~** (*Tip*) double-spaced; **por ~ de** during, for; **~ aéreo/ exterior** air/outer space

espacioso, -a [espa'θjoso, a] ADJ spacious, roomy

espada [es'paða] NF sword; **estar entre la ~ y la pared** to be between the devil and the deep blue sea ▶ NM swordsman; (*Taur*) matador ■ **espadas** NFPL (*Naipes*) one of the suits in the Spanish card deck; *ver tb* **baraja española**

espadachín [espaða'tʃin] NM (*esgrimidor*) skilled swordsman

★espaguetis [espa'ɣetis] NMPL spaghetti *sg*

★espalda [es'palda] NF (*gen*) back; (*Natación*) backstroke ■ **espaldas** NFPL (*hombros*) shoulders; **a espaldas de algn** behind sb's back; **estar de espaldas** to have one's back turned; **tenderse de espaldas** to lie (down) on one's back; **volver la ~ a algn** to cold-shoulder sb

espaldarazo [espalda'raθo] NM (*tb fig*) slap on the back

espaldilla [espal'ðiʎa] NF shoulder blade

espantadizo, -a [espanta'ðiθo, a] ADJ timid, easily frightened

espantajo [espan'taxo] NM, **espantapájaros** [espanta'paxaros] NM INV scarecrow

★espantar [espan'tar] /**1a**/ VT (*asustar*) to frighten, scare; (*ahuyentar*) to frighten off; (*asombrar*) to horrify, appal ■ **espantarse** VR to get frightened *o* scared; to be appalled

espanto [es'panto] NM (*susto*) fright; (*terror*) terror; (*asombro*) astonishment; **¡qué ~!** how awful!

★espantoso, -a [espan'toso, a] ADJ frightening, terrifying; (*ruido*) dreadful

★España [es'paɲa] NF Spain; **la ~ de pandereta** touristy Spain

★español, a [espa'ɲol, a] ADJ Spanish ▶ NM/F Spaniard ▶ NM (*Ling*) Spanish; *ver tb* **castellano**

españolice *etc* [espaɲo'liθe] VB *ver* **españolizar**

españolizar [espaɲoli'θar] /**1f**/ VT to make Spanish, Hispanicize ■ **españolizarse** VR to adopt Spanish ways

★esparadrapo [espara'ðrapo] NM surgical tape

esparcido, -a [espar'θiðo, a] ADJ scattered

esparcimiento [esparθi'mjento] NM (*disper-sión*) spreading; (*derramamiento*) scattering; (*fig*) cheerfulness

esparcir [espar'θir] /**3b**/ VT to spread; (*derramar*) to scatter ■ **esparcirse** VR to spread (out); to scatter; (*divertirse*) to enjoy o.s.

★espárrago [es'parraɣo] NM (*tb*: **espárragos**) asparagus; **estar hecho un ~** to be as thin as a rake; **¡vete a freír espárragos!** (*fam*) go to hell!

esparto [es'parto] NM esparto (grass)

esparza *etc* [es'parθa] VB *ver* **esparcir**

espasmo [es'pasmo] NM spasm

espátula [es'patula] NF (*Med*) spatula; (*Arte*) palette knife; (*Culin*) fish slice

especia [es'peθja] NF spice

★especial [espe'θjal] ADJ special

★especialidad [espeθjali'ðað] NF speciality, specialty (*US*); (*Escol: ramo*) specialism

especialista [espeθja'lista] NMF specialist; (*Cine*) stuntman(-woman)

especializado, -a [espeθjali'θaðo, a] ADJ specialized; (*obrero*) skilled

especialmente [espeθjal'mente] ADV particularly, especially

En inglés son posibles tanto **especially** como **specially**. En el sentido de *sobre todo* se utiliza más **especially**: *Vuelva a aplicar la crema con filtro solar cada dos horas, especialmente si ha estado en el agua.* **Reapply sunscreen every two hours, especially if you have been swimming**.
Specially se utiliza hablando de una finalidad concreta: *un jabón pensado especialmente para pieles sensibles* **a soap that has been specially formulated for sensitive skins**.

★especie [es'peθje] NF (*Bio*) species; (*clase*) kind, sort; **pagar en ~** to pay in kind

especificar [espeθifi'kar] /**1g**/ VT to specify

específico, -a [espe'θifiko, a] ADJ specific

especifique *etc* [espeθi'fike] VB *ver* **especificar**

espécimen [es'peθimen] (*pl* **especímenes**) NM specimen

★espectáculo [espek'takulo] NM (*gen*) spectacle; (*Teat etc*) show; (*función*) performance; **dar un ~** to make a scene

★espectador, a [espekta'ðor, a] NM/F spectator; (*de incidente*) onlooker ■ **los espectadores** NMPL (*Teat*) the audience *sg*

espectro [es'pektro] NM ghost; (*fig*) spectre

especulación [espekula'θjon] NF speculation; **~ bursátil** speculation on the Stock Market

especular [espeku'lar] /**1a**/ VT, VI to speculate

especulativo, -a [espekula'tiβo, a] ADJ speculative

espejismo [espe'xismo] NM mirage

★espejo [es'pexo] NM mirror; (*fig*) model; **~ retrovisor** rear-view mirror; **mirarse al ~** to look (at o.s.) in the mirror

espeleología [espeleolo'xia] NF potholing

espeluznante [espeluθ'nante] ADJ horrifying, hair-raising

espera [es'pera] NF (*pausa, intervalo*) wait; (*Jur: plazo*) respite; **en ~ de** waiting for; (*con expectativa*) expecting; **en ~ de su contestación** awaiting your reply

esperance *etc* [espe'ranθe] VB *ver* **esperanzar**

★**esperanza** [espe'ranθa] NF (*confianza*) hope; (*expectativa*) expectation; **hay pocas esperanzas de que venga** there is little prospect of his coming; **~ de vida** life expectancy

esperanzador, a [esperanθa'ðor, a] ADJ hopeful, encouraging

esperanzar [esperan'θar] /**1f**/ VT to give hope to

★**esperar** [espe'rar] /**1a**/ VT (*aguardar*) to wait for; (*tener expectativa de*) to expect; (*desear*) to hope for; **hacer ~ a algn** to keep sb waiting; **ir a ~ a algn** to go and meet sb; **~ un bebé** to be expecting (a baby) ► VI to wait; to expect; to hope ■ **esperarse** VR: **como podía esperarse** as was to be expected

esperma [es'perma] NF sperm

espermatozoide [espermato'θoiðe] NM spermatozoid

esperpento [esper'pento] NM (*persona*) sight (*fam*); (*disparate*) (piece of) nonsense

espesar [espe'sar] /**1a**/ VT to thicken ■ **espesarse** VR to thicken, get thicker

★**espeso, -a** [es'peso, a] ADJ thick; (*bosque*) dense; (*nieve*) deep; (*sucio*) dirty

espesor [espe'sor] NM thickness; (*de nieve*) depth

espesura [espe'sura] NF (*de bosque*) thicket

espetar [espe'tar] /**1a**/ VT (*reto, sermón*) to give

★**espía** [es'pia] NMF spy

espiar [espi'ar] /**1c**/ VT (*observar*) to spy on ► VI: **~ para** to spy for

espiga [es'piɣa] NF (*Bot: de trigo etc*) ear; (: *de flores*) spike

espigado, -a [espi'ɣaðo, a] ADJ (*Bot*) ripe; (*fig*) tall, slender

espigón [espi'ɣon] NM (*Bot*) ear; (*Naut*) breakwater

espina [es'pina] NF thorn; (*de pez*) bone; **~ dorsal** (*Anat*) spine; **me da mala ~** I don't like the look of it

espinaca [espi'naka] NF (*tb*: **espinacas**) spinach

espinar [espi'nar] NM (*matorral*) thicket

espinazo [espi'naθo] NM spine, backbone

espinilla [espi'niʎa] NF (*Anat: tibia*) shin(bone); (: *en la piel*) blackhead

espino [es'pino] NM hawthorn

espinoso, -a [espi'noso, a] ADJ (*planta*) thorny, prickly; (*fig*) bony; (*asunto*) difficult; (*problema*) knotty

espionaje [espjo'naxe] NM spying, espionage

espiral [espi'ral] ADJ, NF spiral; **la ~ inflacionista** the inflationary spiral

espirar [espi'rar] /**1a**/ VT, VI to breathe out, exhale

espiritista [espiri'tista] ADJ, NMF spiritualist

★**espíritu** [es'piritu] NM spirit; (*mente*) mind; (*inteligencia*) intelligence; (*Rel*) spirit, soul; **con ~ amplio** with an open mind; **E~ Santo** Holy Ghost, Holy Spirit

espiritual [espiri'twal] ADJ spiritual

espita [es'pita] NF tap (BRIT), faucet (US)

esplendidez [esplendi'ðeθ] NF (*abundancia*) lavishness; (*magnificencia*) splendour

★**espléndido, -a** [es'plendiðo, a] ADJ (*magnífico*) magnificent, splendid; (*generoso*) generous, lavish

esplendor [esplen'dor] NM splendour

espliego [es'pljeɣo] NM lavender

espolear [espole'ar] /**1a**/ VT to spur on

espoleta [espo'leta] NF (*de bomba*) fuse

espolvorear [espolβore'ar] /**1a**/ VT to dust, sprinkle

esponja [es'ponxa] NF sponge; (*fig*) sponger

esponjoso, -a [espon'xoso, a] ADJ spongy

esponsales [espon'sales] NMPL betrothal *sg*

espontaneidad [espontanei'ðað] NF spontaneity

espontáneo, -a [espon'taneo, a] ADJ spontaneous; (*improvisado*) impromptu; (*persona*) natural

espora [es'pora] NF spore

esporádico, -a [espo'raðiko, a] ADJ sporadic

★**esposa** [es'posa] NF *ver* **esposo**

esposar [espo'sar] /**1a**/ VT to handcuff

★**esposo, -a** [es'poso, a] NM husband ► NF wife ■ **esposas** NFPL handcuffs

espray [es'prai] NM spray

espuela [es'pwela] NF spur; (*fam: trago*) one for the road

espuerta [es'pwerta] NF basket, pannier

espuma [es'puma] NF foam; (*de cerveza*) froth, head; (*de jabón*) lather; (*de olas*) surf; **~ de afeitar** shaving foam

espumadera [espuma'ðera] NF skimmer

espumarajo [espuma'raxo] NM froth, foam; **echar espumarajos (de rabia)** to splutter with rage

espumoso, -a [espu'moso, a] ADJ frothy, foamy; (*vino*) sparkling

esputo [es'puto] NM (*de saliva*) spit; (*Med*) sputum

esqueje [es'kexe] NM (*Bot*) cutting

esquela [es'kela] NF: **~ mortuoria** announcement of death

esquelético, -a [eske'letiko, a] ADJ (*fam*) skinny

esqueleto [eske'leto] NM skeleton; (*lo esencial*) bare bones (of a matter); **en ~** unfinished

esquema [es'kema] NM (*diagrama*) diagram; (*dibujo*) plan; (*plan*) scheme; (*Filosofía*) schema

esquemático, -a [eske'matiko, a] ADJ schematic; **un resumen ~** a brief outline

★**esquí** [es'ki] (*pl* **esquís**) NM (*objeto*) ski; (*deporte*) skiing; **~ acuático** water-skiing; **hacer ~** to go skiing

esquiador, a [eskja'ðor, a] NM/F skier

★**esquiar** [es'kjar] /1c/ VI to ski

esquila [es'kila] NF (*campanilla*) small bell; (*cencerro*) cowbell

esquilar [eski'lar] /1a/ VT to shear

esquimal [eski'mal] ADJ, NMF Eskimo (!)

★**esquina** [es'kina] NF corner; **doblar la ~** to turn the corner

esquinazo [eski'naθo] NM: **dar ~ a algn** to give sb the slip

esquirla [es'kirla] NF splinter

esquirol [eski'rol] NM (*ESP*) strikebreaker, blackleg

esquivar [eski'βar] /1a/ VT to avoid; (*evadir*) to dodge, elude

esquivo, -a [es'kiβo, a] ADJ (*altanero*) aloof; (*desdeñoso*) scornful, disdainful

esquizofrenia [eskiθo'frenja] NF schizophrenia

★**esta** ['esta] ADJ DEMOSTRATIVO, PRON *ver* **este²**

está [es'ta] VB *ver* **estar**

★**ésta** ['esta] PRON *ver* **éste**

estabilice *etc* [estaβi'liθe] VB *ver* **estabilizar**

estabilidad [estaβili'ðað] NF stability

estabilización [estaβiliθa'θjon] NF (*Com*) stabilization

estabilizador, a [estabiliθa'ðor, a] ADJ (*Foto*) antishake

estabilizar [estaβili'θar] /1f/ VT to stabilize; (*fijar*) to make steady; (*precios*) to peg ■ **estabilizarse** VR to become stable

★**estable** [es'taβle] ADJ stable

establecer [estaβle'θer] /2d/ VT to establish; (*fundar*) to set up; (*colonos*) to settle; (*récord*) to set (up) ■ **establecerse** VR to establish o.s.; (*echar raíces*) to settle (down); (*Com*) to start up

★**establecimiento** [estaβleθi'mjento] NM establishment; (*fundación*) institution; (*de negocio*) start-up; (*de colonias*) settlement; (*local*) establishment; **~ comercial** business house

establezca *etc* [esta'βleθka] VB *ver* **establecer**

establo [es'taβlo] NM (*Agr*) stall; (*para vacas*) cowshed; (*para caballos*) stable; (*esp AM*) barn

estaca [es'taka] NF stake, post; (*de tienda de campaña*) peg

estacada [esta'kaða] NF (*cerca*) fence, fencing; (*palenque*) stockade; **dejar a algn en la ~** to leave sb in the lurch

★**estación** [esta'θjon] NF station; (*del año*) season; **~ de autobuses/ferrocarril** bus/railway station; **~ de esquí** ski resort; **~ de servicio** service

station; **~ terminal** terminus; **~ de trabajo** (*Com*) work station; **~ transmisora** transmitter; **~ de visualización** display unit

estacionamiento [estaθjona'mjento] NM (*Auto*) parking; (*Mil*) stationing

★**estacionar** [estaθjo'nar] /1a/ VT (*Auto*) to park; (*Mil*) to station

estacionario, -a [estaθjo'narjo, a] ADJ stationary; (*Com: mercado*) slack

estada [es'taða], **estadía** [esta'ðia] NF (*AM*) stay

★**estadio** [es'taðjo] NM (*fase*) stage, phase; (*Deporte*) stadium

estadista [esta'ðista] NM (*Pol*) statesman; (*Estadística*) statistician

estadística [esta'ðistika] NF (*una estadística*) figure, statistic; (*ciencia*) statistics *sg*

★**estado** [es'taðo] NM (*Pol: condición*) state; **~ civil** marital status; **~ de ánimo** state of mind; **~ de cuenta(s)** bank statement, statement of accounts; **~ de excepción** (*Pol*) state of emergency; **~ financiero** (*Com*) financial statement; **~ mayor** (*Mil*) staff; **~ de pérdidas y ganancias** (*Com*) profit and loss statement, operating statement; **Estados Unidos (EE UU)** United States (of America) (USA); **estar en ~ (de buena esperanza)** to be pregnant

★**estadounidense** [estaðouni'ðense] ADJ United States *cpd*, American ▶ NMF United States citizen, American

estafa [es'tafa] NF swindle, trick; (*Com etc*) racket

estafar [esta'far] /1a/ VT to swindle, defraud

estafeta [esta'feta] NF (*oficina de correos*) post office; **~ diplomática** diplomatic bag

estáis VB *ver* **estar**

estalactita [estalak'tita] NF stalactite

estalagmita [estalaɣ'mita] NF stalagmite

★**estallar** [esta'ʎar] /1a/ VI to burst; (*bomba*) to explode, go off; (*volcán*) to erupt; (*vidrio*) to shatter; (*látigo*) to crack; (*epidemia, guerra, rebelión*) to break out; **~ en llanto** to burst into tears

estallido [esta'ʎiðo] NM explosion; (*de látigo, trueno*) crack; (*fig*) outbreak

estambre [es'tambre] NM (*tela*) worsted; (*Bot*) stamen

Estambul [estam'bul] NM Istanbul

estamento [esta'mento] NM (*social*) class

estampa [es'tampa] NF (*impresión, imprenta*) print, engraving; (*imagen, figura: de persona*) appearance

estampado, -a [estam'paðo, a] ADJ printed ▶ NM (*dibujo*) print; (*impresión*) printing

estampar [estam'par] /1a/ VT (*imprimir*) to print; (*marcar*) to stamp; (*metal*) to engrave; (*poner sello en*) to stamp; (*fig*) to stamp, imprint

estampida [estam'piða] NF stampede

estampido [estam'piðo] NM bang, report

estampilla [estamˈpiʎa] NF (*sello de goma*) (rubber) stamp; (AM) (postage) stamp

están [esˈtan] VB *ver* **estar**

estancado, -a [estanˈkaðo, a] ADJ (*agua*) stagnant

estancamiento [estankaˈmjento] NM stagnation

estancar [estanˈkar] /**1g**/ VT (*aguas*) to hold up, hold back; (*Com*) to monopolize; (*fig*) to block, hold up ■ **estancarse** VR to stagnate

★**estancia** [esˈtanθja] NF (*permanencia*) stay; (*sala*) room; (AM) farm, ranch

estanciero [estanˈsjero] NM (AM) farmer, rancher

★**estanco, -a** [esˈtanko, a] ADJ watertight ▶ NM tobacconist's (shop)

In the past, cigarettes, tobacco, postage stamps and official forms were all sold under state monopoly and usually through a shop called an **estanco**. Tobacco products are now also sold in *quioscos*, bars and convenience stores but are generally more expensive. The number of *estanco* licences is regulated by the state.

estándar [esˈtandar] ADJ, NM standard

estandarice *etc* [estandaˈriθe] VB *ver* **estandarizar**

estandarizar [estandariˈθar] /**1f**/ VT to standardize

estandarte [estanˈdarte] NM banner, standard

estanque [esˈtanke] VB *ver* **estancar** ▶ NM (*lago*) pool, pond; (*Agr*) reservoir

estanquero, -a [estanˈkero, a] NM/F tobacconist

estante [esˈtante] NM (*armario*) rack, stand; (*biblioteca*) bookcase; (*anaquel*) shelf; (AM) prop

estantería [estanteˈria] NF shelving, shelves *pl*

estaño [esˈtaɲo] NM tin

---

estar [esˈtar]

/**1o**/ VI **1** (*posición*) to be; **está en la plaza** it's in the square; **¿está Juan?** is Juan in?; **estamos a 30 km de Junín** we're 30 km from Junín

2 (+ *adj o adv: estado*) to be; **estar enfermo** to be ill; **está muy elegante** he's looking very smart; **estar lejos** to be far (away); **¿cómo estás?** how are you keeping?

3 (+ *gerundio*) to be; **estoy leyendo** I'm reading

4 (*uso pasivo*): **está condenado a muerte** he's been condemned to death; **está envasado en ...** it's packed in ...

5: **estar a**: **¿a cuántos estamos?** what's the date today?; **estamos a 9 de mayo** it's the 9th of May; **las manzanas están a 1,50 euros** apples are (selling at) 1.5 euros; **estamos a 25 grados** it's 25 degrees today

6 (*locuciones*): **¿estamos?** (*¿de acuerdo?*) okay?; (*¿listo?*) ready?; **¡ya está bien!** that's enough!; **¿está la comida?** is dinner ready?; **¡ya está!**, **¡ya estuvo!** (AM) that's it!

7: **estar con**: **está con gripe** he's got (the) flu

8: **estar de**: **estar de vacaciones/viaje** to be on holiday/away *o* on a trip; **está de camarero** he's working as a waiter

9: **estar para**: **está para salir** he's about to leave; **no estoy para bromas** I'm not in the mood for jokes

10: **estar por** (*propuesta etc*) to be in favour of; (*persona etc*) to support, side with; **está por limpiar** it still has to be cleaned; **¡estoy por dejarlo!** I think I'm going to leave this!

11: **estar sin**: **estar sin dinero** to have no money; **está sin terminar** it isn't finished yet

12 (+ *que*): **está que rabia** (*fam*) he's hopping mad (*fam*); **estoy que me caigo de sueño** I'm terribly sleepy, I can't keep my eyes open

■ **estarse** VR: **se estuvo en la cama toda la tarde** he stayed in bed all afternoon; **¡estate quieto!** stop fidgeting!

---

estárter [esˈtarter] NM (*Auto*) choke

estas [ˈestas] ADJ DEMOSTRATIVO, PRON *ver* **este¹**

estás [esˈtas] VB *ver* **estar**

éstas [ˈestas] PRON *ver* **éste**

estatal [estaˈtal] ADJ state *cpd*

estático, -a [esˈtatiko, a] ADJ static

★**estatua** [esˈtatwa] NF statue

estatura [estaˈtura] NF stature, height

estatus [esˈtatus] NM INV status

estatutario, -a [estatuˈtarjo, a] ADJ statutory

estatuto [estaˈtuto] NM (*Jur*) statute; (*de ciudad*) bye-law; (*de comité*) rule; **estatutos sociales** (*Com*) articles of association

★**este¹** [ˈeste] ADJ (*lado*) east; (*dirección*) easterly ▶ NM east; **en la parte del ~** in the eastern part

★**este²** [ˈeste], **esta** [ˈesta], **estos** [ˈestos], **estas** [ˈestas] ADJ DEMOSTRATIVO this *sg*, these *pl*; (AM: *como muletilla*) er, um ▶ PRON this (one) *sg*, these (ones) *pl*; **ese ... ~ ...** the former ... the latter ...

esté [esˈte] VB *ver* **estar**

★**éste** [ˈeste], **ésta** [ˈesta], **éstos** [ˈestos], **éstas** [ˈestas] PRON this (one) *sg*, these (ones) *pl*; **ése ... ~ ...** the former ... the latter ...

estela [esˈtela] NF wake, wash; (*fig*) trail

estelar [esteˈlar] ADJ (*Astro*) stellar; (*Teat*) star *cpd*

estén [esˈten] VB *ver* **estar**

estenografía [estenoɣraˈfia] NF shorthand

estentóreo, -a [estenˈtoreo, a] ADJ (*sonido*) strident; (*voz*) booming

estepa [esˈtepa] NF (*Geo*) steppe

estera [esˈtera] NF (*alfombra*) mat; (*tejido*) matting

estercolero [esterkoˈlero] NM manure heap, dunghill

★**estéreo** [esˈtereo] ADJ INV, NM stereo

estereofónico, -a [estereoˈfoniko, a] ADJ stereophonic

estereotipar [estereoti'par] /**1a**/ VT to stereo-type

estereotipo [estereo'tipo] NM stereotype

estéril [es'teril] ADJ sterile, barren; (fig) vain, futile

esterilice etc [esteri'liθe] VB ver **esterilizar**

esterilizar [esterili'θar] /**1f**/ VT to sterilize

esterilla [este'riʎa] NF (alfombrilla) small mat

esterlina [ester'lina] ADJ: **libra ~** pound sterling

esternón [ester'non] NM breastbone

estero [es'tero] NM (Am) swamp

estertor [ester'tor] NM death rattle

estés [es'tes] VB ver **estar**

esteta [es'teta] NMF aesthete

esteticienne [esteti'θjen] NF beautician

estético, -a [es'tetiko, a] ADJ aesthetic ▶ NF aesthetics sg

estetoscopio [estetos'kopjo] NM stethoscope

estibador [estiβa'ðor] NM stevedore

estibar [esti'βar] /**1a**/ VT (Naut) to stow

estiércol [es'tjerkol] NM dung, manure

estigma [es'tiɣma] NM stigma

estigmatice etc [estiɣma'tiθe] VB ver **estigmatizar**

estigmatizar [estiɣmati'θar] /**1f**/ VT to stigmatize

estilarse [esti'larse] /**1a**/ VR (estar de moda) to be in fashion; (usarse) to be used

estilice etc [esti'liθe] VB ver **estilizar**

estilizar [estili'θar] /**1f**/ VT to stylize; (Tec) to design

★**estilo** [es'tilo] NM style; (Tec) stylus; (Natación) stroke; **~ de vida** lifestyle; **al ~ de** in the style of; **algo por el ~** something along those lines

estilográfica [estilo'ɣrafika] NF fountain pen

estima [es'tima] NF esteem, respect

estimación [estima'θjon] NF (evaluación) estimation; (aprecio, afecto) esteem, regard

★**estimado, -a** [esti'maðo, a] ADJ esteemed; **"E~ Señor"** "Dear Sir"

estimar [esti'mar] /**1a**/ VT (evaluar) to estimate; (valorar) to value; (apreciar) to esteem, respect; (pensar, considerar) to think, reckon

estimulante [estimu'lante] ADJ stimulating ▶ NM stimulant

estimular [estimu'lar] /**1a**/ VT to stimulate; (excitar) to excite; (animar) to encourage

estímulo [es'timulo] NM stimulus; (ánimo) encouragement

estío [es'tio] NM summer

estipendio [esti'pendjo] NM salary; (Com) stipend

estipulación [estipula'θjon] NF stipulation, condition

estipular [estipu'lar] /**1a**/ VT to stipulate

estirado, -a [esti'raðo, a] ADJ (tenso) (stretched

o drawn) tight; (fig: persona) stiff, pompous; (engreído) stuck-up

estirar [esti'rar] /**1a**/ VT to stretch; (dinero, suma etc) to stretch out; (cuello) to crane; (discurso) to spin out; **~ la pata** (fam) to kick the bucket ■ **estirarse** VR to stretch

estirón [esti'ron] NM pull, tug; (crecimiento) spurt, sudden growth; **dar un ~** (niño) to shoot up

estirpe [es'tirpe] NF stock, lineage

estival [esti'βal] ADJ summer cpd

★**esto** ['esto] PRON this, this thing o matter; (como muletilla) er, um; **~ de la boda** this business about the wedding; **en ~** at this o that point; **por ~** for this reason

estocada [esto'kaða] NF (acción) stab; (Taur) death blow

Estocolmo [esto'kolmo] NM Stockholm

estofa [es'tofa] NF: **de baja ~** poor-quality

estofado [esto'faðo] NM stew

estofar [esto'far] /**1a**/ VT (bordar) to quilt; (Culin) to stew

estoico, -a [es'toiko, a] ADJ (Filosofía) stoic(al); (fig) cold, indifferent

estomacal [estoma'kal] ADJ stomach cpd; **trastorno ~** stomach upset

★**estómago** [es'tomaɣo] NM stomach; **tener ~** to be thick-skinned

Estonia [es'tonja] NF Estonia

estonio, -a [es'tonjo, a] ADJ, NM/F Estonian ▶ NM (Ling) Estonian

estoque [es'toke] NM rapier, sword

estor [es'tor] NM roller blind

estorbar [estor'βar] /**1a**/ VT to hinder, obstruct; (fig) to bother, disturb ▶ VI to be in the way

estorbo [es'torβo] NM (molestia) bother, nuisance; (obstáculo) hindrance, obstacle

estornino [estor'nino] NM starling

estornudar [estornu'ðar] /**1a**/ VI to sneeze

estornudo [estor'nuðo] NM sneeze

estos ['estos] ADJ DEMOSTRATIVO ver **este²**

éstos ['estos] PRON ver **éste**

estoy [es'toi] VB ver **estar**

estrabismo [estra'βismo] NM squint

estrado [es'traðo] NM (tarima) platform; (Mus) bandstand

estrafalario, -a [estrafa'larjo, a] ADJ odd, eccentric; (desarreglado) slovenly, sloppy

estrago [es'traɣo] NM ruin, destruction; **hacer estragos en** to wreak havoc among

estragón [estra'ɣon] NM (Culin) tarragon

estrambótico, -a [estram'botiko, a] ADJ odd, eccentric; (peinado, ropa) outlandish

estrangulación [estrangula'θjon] NF strangulation

estrangulador, -a [estrangula'ðor, a] NM/F strangler ▶ NM (Tec) throttle; (Auto) choke

estrangulamiento [estrangula'mjento] NM (Auto) bottleneck

estrangular [estrangu'lar] /**1a**/ VT (*persona*) to strangle; (*Med*) to strangulate

estraperlista [estraper'lista] NMF black marketeer

estraperlo [estra'perlo] NM black market

estratagema [estrata'xema] NF (*Mil*) stratagem; (*astucia*) cunning

estratega [estra'teɣa] NMF strategist

estrategia [estra'texja] NF strategy

estratégico, -a [estra'texiko, a] ADJ strategic

estratificar [estratifi'kar] /**1g**/ VT to stratify

estratifique *etc* [estrati'fike] VB *ver* **estratificar**

estrato [es'trato] NM stratum, layer

estratosfera [estratos'fera] NF stratosphere

estrechar [estre'tʃar] /**1a**/ VT (*reducir*) to narrow; (*vestido*) to take in; (*persona*) to hug, embrace; **~ la mano** to shake hands ■ **estrecharse** VR (*reducirse*) to narrow, grow narrow; (*2 personas*) to embrace

estrechez [estre'tʃeθ] NF narrowness; (*de ropa*) tightness; (*intimidad*) intimacy; (*Com*) want o shortage of money ■ **estrecheces** NFPL (*dificultades*) financial difficulties

★**estrecho, -a** [es'tretʃo, a] ADJ narrow; (*apretado*) tight; (*íntimo*) close, intimate; (*miserable*) mean ▶ NM strait; **~ de miras** narrow-minded; **E~ de Gibraltar** Straits of Gibraltar

★**estrella** [es'treʎa] NF star; **~ fugaz** shooting star; **~ de mar** starfish; **tener (buena) ~/mala ~** to be lucky/unlucky

estrellado, -a [estre'ʎaðo, a] ADJ (*forma*) star-shaped; (*cielo*) starry; (*huevos*) fried

estrellar [estre'ʎar] /**1a**/ VT (*hacer añicos*) to smash (to pieces); (*huevos*) to fry ■ **estrellarse** VR to smash; (*chocarse*) to crash; (*fracasar*) to fail

estrellato [estre'ʎato] NM stardom

estremecer [estreme'θer] /**2d**/ VT to shake ▶ VI: **~ de** (*horror*) to shudder with; (*frío*) to shiver with ■ **estremecerse** VR to shake, tremble

estremecimiento [estremeθi'mjento] NM (*temblor*) trembling, shaking

estremezca *etc* [estre'meθka] VB *ver* **estremecer**

★**estrenar** [estre'nar] /**1a**/ VT (*vestido*) to wear for the first time; (*casa*) to move into; (*película, obra de teatro*) to première ■ **estrenarse** VR (*persona*) to make one's début; (*película*) to have its première; (*Teat*) to open

★**estreno** [es'treno] NM (*primer uso*) first use; (*Cine etc*) première

estreñido, -a [estre'niðo, a] ADJ constipated

estreñimiento [estreni'mjento] NM constipation

estreñir [estre'nir] /**3h, 3k**/ VT to constipate

estrépito [es'trepito] NM noise, racket; (*fig*) fuss

estrepitoso, -a [estrepi'toso, a] ADJ noisy; (*fiesta*) rowdy

★**estrés** [es'tres] NM stress

estresante [estre'sante] ADJ stressful

estría [es'tria] NF groove; **estrías (en el cutis)** stretch marks

estribaciones [estriβa'θjones] NFPL foothills

estribar [estri'βar] /**1a**/ VI (*Arq*): **~ en** to rest on, be supported by; **la dificultad estriba en el texto** the difficulty lies in the text

estribillo [estri'βiʎo] NM (*Lit*) refrain; (*Mus*) chorus

estribo [es'triβo] NM (*de jinete*) stirrup; (*de coche, tren*) step; (*de puente*) support; (*Geo*) spur; **perder los estribos** to fly off the handle

estribor [estri'βor] NM (*Naut*) starboard

estricnina [estrik'nina] NF strychnine

★**estricto, -a** [es'trikto, a] ADJ (*riguroso*) strict; (*severo*) severe

estridente [estri'ðente] ADJ (*color*) loud; (*voz*) raucous

estro ['estro] NM inspiration

estrofa [es'trofa] NF verse

estropajo [estro'paxo] NM scourer

estropeado, -a [estrope'aðo, a] ADJ: **está ~** it's not working

★**estropear** [estrope'ar] /**1a**/ VT (*arruinar*) to spoil; (*dañar*) to damage; (: *máquina*) to break ■ **estropearse** VR (*objeto*) to get damaged; (*coche*) to break down; (*la piel etc*) to be ruined

estropicio [estro'piθjo] NM (*rotura*) breakage; (*efectos*) harmful effects *pl*

estructura [estruk'tura] NF structure

estruendo [es'trwendo] NM (*ruido*) racket, din; (*fig: alboroto*) uproar, turmoil

estrujar [estru'xar] /**1a**/ VT (*apretar*) to squeeze; (*aplastar*) to crush; (*fig*) to drain, bleed

estuario [es'twarjo] NM estuary

★**estuche** [es'tutʃe] NM box, case

★**estudiante** [estu'ðjante] NMF student

estudiantil [estuðjan'til] ADJ INV student *cpd*

estudiantina [estuðjan'tina] NF student music group

★**estudiar** [estu'ðjar] /**1b**/ VT to study; (*propuesta*) to think about o over; **~ para abogado** to study to become a lawyer

★**estudio** [es'tuðjo] NM study; (*encuesta*) research; (*proyecto*) plan; (*piso*) studio flat; (*Cine, Arte, Radio*) studio; **~ de casos prácticos** case study; **~ de desplazamientos y tiempos** (*Com*) time and motion study; **~ del trabajo** (*Com*) work study; **~ de viabilidad** (*Com*) feasibility study ■ **estudios** NMPL (*educación*) studies; (*erudición*) learning *sg*; **cursar** o **hacer estudios** to study; **estudios de motivación** motivational research *sg*

estudioso, -a [estu'ðjoso, a] ADJ studious

estufa [es'tufa] NF heater, fire

estulticia [estul'tiθja] NF foolishness

estupefaciente [estupefa'θjente] ADJ, NM narcotic

165

estupefacto, -a [estupeˈfakto, a] ADJ speechless, thunderstruck

estupendamente [estupendaˈmente] ADV (*fam*): **estoy ~** I feel great; **le salió ~** he did it very well

★**estupendo, -a** [estuˈpendo, a] ADJ wonderful, terrific; (*fam*) great; **¡~!** that's great!, fantastic!

estupidez [estupiˈðeθ] NF (*torpeza*) stupidity; (*acto*) stupid thing (to do); **fue una ~ mía** that was a silly thing for me to do *o* say

★**estúpido, -a** [esˈtupiðo, a] ADJ stupid, silly

estupor [estuˈpor] NM stupor; (*fig*) astonishment, amazement

estupro [esˈtupro] NM rape

estuve *etc* [esˈtuβe], **estuviera** *etc* [estuˈβjera] VB *ver* **estar**

esvástica [esˈβastika] NF swastika

ET ABR = **Ejército de Tierra**

ETA [ˈeta] NF ABR (*Pol*: = *Euskadi Ta Askatasuna*) ETA

★**etapa** [eˈtapa] NF (*de viaje*) stage; (*Deporte*) leg; (*parada*) stopping place; (*fig*) stage, phase; **por etapas** gradually, in stages

etarra [eˈtarra] ADJ ETA *cpd* ▶ NMF member of ETA

etc. ABR (= *etcétera*) etc

etcétera [etˈθetera] ADV etcetera

etéreo, -a [eˈtereo, a] ADJ ethereal

eternice *etc* [eterˈniθe] VB *ver* **eternizarse**

eternidad [eterniˈðað] NF eternity

eternizarse [eterniˈθarse] /**1f**/ VR: **~ en hacer algo** to take ages to do sth

eterno, -a [eˈterno, a] ADJ eternal, everlasting; (*despectivo*) never-ending

ético, -a [ˈetiko, a] ADJ ethical ▶ NF ethics

etimología [etimoloˈxia] NF etymology

etiqueta [etiˈketa] NF (*modales*) etiquette; (*rótulo*) label, tag; **de ~** formal

etnia [ˈetnja] NF ethnic group

étnico, -a [ˈetniko, a] ADJ ethnic

ETS SIGLA F (= *Enfermedad de Transmisión Sexual*) STD

eucalipto [eukaˈlipto] NM eucalyptus

Eucaristía [eukarisˈtia] NF Eucharist

eufemismo [eufeˈmismo] NM euphemism

euforia [euˈforja] NF euphoria

eufórico, -a [euˈforiko, a] ADJ euphoric

eunuco [euˈnuko] NM eunuch

★**euro** [ˈeuro] NM (*moneda*) euro

eurodiputado, -a [euroðipuˈtaðo, a] NM/F Euro MP, MEP

Eurolandia [euroˈlandja] NF Euroland

★**Europa** [euˈropa] NF Europe

europeice *etc* [euroˈpeiθe] VB *ver* **europeizar**

europeizar [europeiˈθar] /**1f**/ VT to Europeanize ■ **europeizarse** VR to become Europeanized

★**europeo, -a** [euroˈpeo, a] ADJ, NM/F European

Eurotúnel [euroˈtunel] NM (*estructura*) Channel Tunnel

eurozona [euroˈθona] NF Eurozone

Euskadi [eusˈkaði] NM the Basque Provinces *pl*

euskera, eusquera [eusˈkera] NM (*Ling*) Basque; *ver tb* **lengua**

eutanasia [eutaˈnasja] NF euthanasia

evacuación [eβakwaˈθjon] NF evacuation

evacuar [eβaˈkwar] /**1d**/ VT to evacuate

evadir [eβaˈðir] /**3a**/ VT to evade, avoid ■ **evadirse** VR to escape

evaluación [eβalwaˈθjon] NF evaluation, assessment

evaluar [eβaˈlwar] /**1e**/ VT to evaluate, assess

evangélico, -a [eβanˈxeliko, a] ADJ evangelical

evangelio [eβanˈxeljo] NM gospel

evaporación [eβaporaˈθjon] NF evaporation

evaporar [eβapoˈrar] /**1a**/ VT to evaporate ■ **evaporarse** VR to vanish

evasión [eβaˈsjon] NF escape, flight; (*fig*) evasion; **~ fiscal** *o* **tributaria** tax evasion; **~ de capitales** flight of capital

evasivo, -a [eβaˈsiβo, a] ADJ evasive, non-committal ▶ NF (*pretexto*) excuse; **contestar con evasivas** to avoid giving a straight answer

evento [eˈβento] NM event; (*eventualidad*) eventuality

eventual [eβenˈtwal] ADJ possible, conditional (upon circumstances); (*trabajador*) casual, temporary

Everest [eβeˈrest] NM: **el (Monte) ~** (Mount) Everest

evidencia [eβiˈðenθja] NF evidence, proof; **poner en ~** to make clear; **ponerse en ~** (*persona*) to show o.s. up

evidenciar [eβiðenˈθjar] /**1b**/ VT (*hacer patente*) to make evident; (*probar*) to prove, show ■ **evidenciarse** VR to be evident

★**evidente** [eβiˈðente] ADJ obvious, clear, evident

★**evitar** [eβiˈtar] /**1a**/ VT (*evadir*) to avoid; (*impedir*) to prevent; (*peligro*) to escape; (*molestia*) to save; (*tentación*) to shun; **~ hacer algo** to avoid doing sth; **si puedo evitarlo** if I can help it

evocador, a [eβokaˈðor, a] ADJ (*sugestivo*) evocative

evocar [eβoˈkar] /**1g**/ VT to evoke, call forth

evolución [eβoluˈθjon] NF (*desarrollo*) evolution, development; (*cambio*) change; (*Mil*) manoeuvre

evolucionar [eβoluθjoˈnar] /**1a**/ VI to evolve; (*Mil, Aviat*) to manoeuvre

evoque *etc* [eˈβoke] VB *ver* **evocar**

ex [eks] ADJ ex-; **el ex ministro** the former minister, the ex-minister

exabrupto [eksaˈβrupto] NM interjection

exacción [eksakˈθjon] NF (*acto*) exaction; (*de impuestos*) demand

exacerbar [eksaθer'βar] /**1a**/ VT to irritate, annoy

★**exactamente** [eksakta'mente] ADV exactly

exactitud [eksakti'tuð] NF exactness; (*precisión*) accuracy; (*puntualidad*) punctuality

★**exacto, -a** [ek'sakto, a] ADJ exact; accurate; punctual; ¡~! exactly!; **eso no es del todo ~** that's not quite right; **para ser ~** to be precise

exageración [eksaxera'θjon] NF exaggeration

exagerado, -a [eksaxe'raðo, a] ADJ (*relato*) exaggerated; (*precio*) excessive; (*persona*) over-demonstrative; (*gesto*) theatrical

★**exagerar** [eksaxe'rar] /**1a**/ VT to exaggerate; (*exceder*) to overdo

exaltado, -a [eksal'taðo, a] ADJ (*apasionado*) over-excited, worked up; (*exagerado*) extreme; (*fanático*) hot-headed; (*discurso*) impassioned ▶ NM/F (*fanático*) hothead; (*Pol*) extremist

exaltar [eksal'tar] /**1a**/ VT to exalt, glorify ■ **exaltarse** VR (*excitarse*) to get excited o worked up

★**examen** [ek'samen] NM examination; (*de problema*) consideration; ~ **de** (*encuesta*) inquiry into; ~ **de conducir** driving test; ~ **de ingreso** entrance examination; ~ **eliminatorio** qualifying examination

★**examinar** [eksami'nar] /**1a**/ VT to examine; (*poner a prueba*) to test; (*inspeccionar*) to inspect ■ **examinarse** VR to be examined, take an examination

exánime [ek'sanime] ADJ lifeless; (*fig*) exhausted

exasperar [eksaspe'rar] /**1a**/ VT to exasperate ■ **exasperarse** VR to get exasperated, lose patience

Exc.ª ABR = **Excelencia**

excarcelar [ekskarθe'lar] /**1a**/ VT to release (from prison)

excavador, a [ekskaβa'ðor, a] NM/F (*persona*) excavator ▶ NF (*Tec*) digger

excavar [ekska'βar] /**1a**/ VT to excavate, dig (out)

excedencia [eksθe'ðenθja] NF (*Mil*) leave; (*Escol*) sabbatical; **estar en ~** to be on leave; **pedir** o **solicitar la ~** to ask for leave

excedente [eksθe'ðente] ADJ, NM excess, surplus

exceder [eksθe'ðer] /**2a**/ VT to exceed, surpass ■ **excederse** VR (*extralimitarse*) to go too far; (*sobrepasarse*) to excel o.s.

excelencia [eksθe'lenθja] NF excellence; **E~** Excellency; **por ~** par excellence

★**excelente** [eksθe'lente] ADJ excellent

excelso, -a [eks'θelso, a] ADJ lofty, sublime

excentricidad [eksθentriθi'ðað] NF eccentricity

excéntrico, -a [eks'θentriko, a] ADJ, NM/F eccentric

excepción [eksθep'θjon] NF exception; **a ~ de** with the exception of, except for; **la ~ confirma la regla** the exception proves the rule

★**excepcional** [eksθepθjo'nal] ADJ exceptional

★**excepto** [eks'θepto] ADV excepting, except (for)

exceptuar [eksθep'twar] /**1e**/ VT to except, exclude

excesivo, -a [eksθe'siβo, a] ADJ excessive

exceso [eks'θeso] NM excess; (*Com*) surplus; ~ **de equipaje/peso** excess luggage/weight; ~ **de velocidad** speeding; **en** o **por ~** excessively

excitación [eksθita'θjon] NF (*sensación*) excitement; (*acción*) excitation

excitado, -a [eksθi'taðo, a] ADJ excited; (*emociones*) aroused

excitante [eksθi'tante] ADJ exciting; (*Med*) stimulating ▶ NM stimulant

excitar [eksθi'tar] /**1a**/ VT to excite; (*incitar*) to urge; (*emoción*) to stir up; (*esperanzas*) to raise; (*pasión*) to arouse ■ **excitarse** VR to get excited

exclamación [eksklama'θjon] NF exclamation

exclamar [ekskla'mar] /**1a**/ VI to exclaim ■ **exclamarse** VR: **exclamarse (contra)** to complain (about)

excluir [eksklu'ir] /**3g**/ VT to exclude; (*dejar fuera*) to shut out; (*solución*) to reject; (*posibilidad*) to rule out

exclusión [eksklu'sjon] NF exclusion

exclusiva [eksklu'siβa] NF *ver* **exclusivo**

exclusive [eksklu'siβe] PREP exclusive of, not counting

exclusivo, -a [eksklu'siβo, a] ADJ exclusive; **derecho ~** sole o exclusive right ▶ NF (*Prensa*) exclusive, scoop; (*Com*) sole right o agency

excluyendo *etc* [eksklu'jendo] VB *ver* **excluir**

Excma. ABR (= *Excelentísima*) *courtesy title*

Excmo. ABR (= *Excelentísimo*) *courtesy title*

excombatiente [ekskomba'tjente] NM ex-serviceman, war veteran (*US*)

excomulgar [ekskomul'ɣar] /**1h**/ VT (*Rel*) to excommunicate

excomulgue *etc* [eksko'mulɣe] VB *ver* **excomulgar**

excomunión [ekskomu'njon] NF excommunication

excoriar [eksko'rjar] /**1b**/ VT to flay, skin

excremento [ekskre'mento] NM excrement

exculpar [ekskul'par] /**1a**/ VT to exonerate; (*Jur*) to acquit ■ **exculparse** VR to exonerate o.s.

★**excursión** [ekskur'sjon] NF excursion, outing; **ir de ~** to go (off) on a trip

excursionista [ekskursjo'nista] NMF (*turista*) sightseer

★**excusa** [eks'kusa] NF excuse; (*disculpa*) apology; **presentar sus excusas** to excuse o.s.

excusado, -a [eksku'saðo, a] ADJ unnecessary; (*disculpado*) excused, forgiven

excusar [eksku'sar] /**1a**/ VT to excuse; (*evitar*) to avoid, prevent ∎ **excusarse** VR (*disculparse*) to apologize

execrable [ekse'kraβle] ADJ appalling

exención [eksen'θjon] NF exemption

exento, -a [ek'sento, a] PP *de* **eximir** ▶ ADJ exempt

exequias [ek'sekjas] NFPL funeral rites

exfoliar [eksfo'ljar] /**1b**/ VT to exfoliate

exhalación [eksala'θjon] NF (*del aire*) exhalation; (*de vapor*) fumes *pl*, vapour; (*rayo*) shooting star; **salir como una ~** to shoot out

exhalar [eksa'lar] /**1a**/ VT to exhale, breathe out; (*olor etc*) to give off; (*suspiro*) to breathe, heave

exhaustivo, -a [eksaus'tiβo, a] ADJ (*análisis*) thorough; (*estudio*) exhaustive

exhausto, -a [ek'sausto, a] ADJ exhausted, worn-out

exhibición [eksiβi'θjon] NF exhibition; (*demostración*) display, show; (*de película*) showing; (*de equipo*) performance

exhibicionista [eksiβiθjo'nista] ADJ, NMF exhibitionist

exhibir [eksi'βir] /**3a**/ VT (*cuadros*) to exhibit; (*colección*) to display, show; (*artículos*) to display; (*pasaporte*) to show; (*película*) to screen; (*mostrar con orgullo*) to show off ∎ **exhibirse** VR (*mostrarse en público*) to show o.s. off; (*fam: indecentemente*) to expose o.s.

exhortación [eksorta'θjon] NF exhortation

exhortar [eksor'tar] /**1a**/ VT: **~ a** to exhort to

exhumar [eksu'mar] /**1a**/ VT to exhume

exigencia [eksi'xenθja] NF demand, requirement

★**exigente** [eksi'xente] ADJ demanding; (*profesor*) strict; **ser ~ con algn** to be hard on sb

★**exigir** [eksi'xir] /**3c**/ VT (*gen*) to demand, require; (*impuestos*) to exact, levy; **~ el pago** to demand payment

exiguo, -a [ek'siɣwo, a] ADJ (*cantidad*) meagre; (*objeto*) tiny

exija *etc* [e'ksixa] VB *ver* **exigir**

exiliado, -a [eksi'ljaðo, a] ADJ exiled, in exile ▶ NM/F exile

exiliar [eksi'ljar] /**1b**/ VT to exile ∎ **exiliarse** VR to go into exile

exilio [ek'siljo] NM exile

eximio, -a [ek'simjo, a] ADJ (*eminente*) distinguished, eminent

eximir [eksi'mir] /**3a**/ VT to exempt

existencia [eksis'tenθja] NF existence; **~ de mercancías** (*Com*) stock-in-trade; **tener en ~** to have in stock; **amargar la ~ a algn** to make sb's life a misery ∎ **existencias** NFPL (*productos*) stock *sg*

★**existir** [eksis'tir] /**3a**/ VI to exist, be

★**éxito** ['eksito] NM (*resultado*) result, outcome; (*triunfo*) success; (*Mus, Teat*) hit; **~ editorial** best-

seller; **~ rotundo** smash hit; **tener ~** to be successful

---

Do not translate the Spanish word **éxito** by *exit*.

---

exitoso, -a [eksi'toso, a] ADJ (*esp Am*) successful

éxodo ['eksoðo] NM exodus; **el ~ rural** the drift from the land

ex oficio [ekso'fiθjo] ADJ, ADV ex officio

exonerar [eksone'rar] /**1a**/ VT to exonerate; **~ de una obligación** to free from an obligation

exoplaneta [ekspla'neta] NM exoplanet

exorbitante [eksorβi'tante] ADJ (*precio*) exorbitant; (*cantidad*) excessive

exorcice *etc* [eksor'θiθe] VB *ver* **exorcizar**

exorcismo [eksor'θismo] NM exorcism

exorcizar [eksorθi'θar] /**1f**/ VT to exorcize

exótico, -a [ek'sotiko, a] ADJ exotic

expandido, -a [ekspan'diðo, a] ADJ: **en caracteres expandidos** (*Inform*) double width

expandir [ekspan'dir] /**3a**/ VT to expand; (*Com*) to expand, enlarge ∎ **expandirse** VR to expand, spread

expansión [ekspan'sjon] NF expansion; (*recreo*) relaxation; **la ~ económica** economic growth; **economía en ~** expanding economy

expansionarse [ekspansjo'narse] /**1a**/ VR (*dilatarse*) to expand; (*recrearse*) to relax

expansivo, -a [ekspan'siβo, a] ADJ expansive; (*efusivo*) communicative; **onda expansiva** shock wave

expatriado, -a [ekspa'trjaðo, a] NM/F (*emigrado*) expatriate; (*exiliado*) exile

expatriarse [ekspa'trjarse] /**1b**/ VR to emigrate; (*Pol*) to go into exile

expectación [ekspekta'θjon] NF (*esperanza*) expectation; (*ilusión*) excitement

★**expectativa** [ekspekta'tiβa] NF (*espera*) expectation; (*perspectiva*) prospect; **~ de vida** life expectancy; **estar a la ~** to wait and see (what will happen)

expedición [ekspeði'θjon] NF (*excursión*) expedition; **gastos de ~** shipping charges

expedientar [ekspeðjen'tar] /**1a**/ VT to open a file on; (*funcionario*) to discipline, start disciplinary proceedings against

expediente [ekspe'ðjente] NM expedient; (*Jur: procedimiento*) action, proceedings *pl*; (*: papeles*) dossier, file, record; **~ judicial** court proceedings *pl*; **~ académico** (student's) record

expedir [ekspe'ðir] /**3k**/ VT (*despachar*) to send, forward; (*pasaporte*) to issue; (*cheque*) to make out

expedito, -a [ekspe'ðito, a] ADJ (*libre*) clear, free

expeler [ekspe'ler] /**2a**/ VT to expel, eject

expendedor, -a [ekspende'ðor, a] NM/F (*vendedor*) dealer; (*Teat*) ticket agent ▶ NM (*aparato*) (vending) machine; **~ de cigarrillos** cigarette machine

expendeduría [ekspendedu'ria] NF (*estanco*) tobacconist's (shop) (*BRIT*), cigar store (*US*)

expendio [eks'pendjo] NM (*AM*) small shop (*BRIT*) o store (*US*)

expensas [eks'pensas] NFPL (*Jur*) costs; **a ~ de** at the expense of

★**experiencia** [ekspe'rjenθja] NF experience

experimentado, -a [eksperimen'taðo, a] ADJ experienced

★**experimentar** [eksperimen'tar] /**1a**/ VT (*en laboratorio*) to experiment with; (*probar*) to test, try out; (*notar, observar*) to experience; (*deterioro, pérdida*) to suffer; (*aumento*) to show; (*sensación*) to feel

★**experimento** [eksperi'mento] NM experiment

experto, -a [eks'perto, a] ADJ expert ▶ NM/F expert

expiar [ekspi'ar] /**1c**/ VT to atone for

expida *etc* [eks'piða] VB *ver* **expedir**

expirar [ekspi'rar] /**1a**/ VI to expire

explanada [ekspla'naða] NF (*paseo*) esplanade; (*a orillas del mar*) promenade

explayarse [ekspla'jarse] /**1a**/ VR (*en discurso*) to speak at length; **~ con algn** to confide in sb

★**explicación** [eksplika'θjon] NF explanation

★**explicar** [ekspli'kar] /**1g**/ VT to explain; (*teoría*) to expound; (*Univ*) to lecture in ■ **explicarse** VR to explain (o.s.); **no me lo explico** I can't understand it

explícito, -a [eks'pliθito, a] ADJ explicit

explique *etc* [eks'plike] VB *ver* **explicar**

exploración [eksplora'θjon] NF exploration; (*Mil*) reconnaissance

explorador, a [eksplora'ðor, a] NM/F (*pionero*) explorer; (*Mil*) scout ▶ NM (*Med*) probe; (*radar*) (radar) scanner

explorar [eksplo'rar] /**1a**/ VT to explore; (*Med*) to probe; (*radar*) to scan

explosión [eksplo'sjon] NF explosion

explosivo, -a [eksplo'siβo, a] ADJ explosive

explotación [eksplota'θjon] NF exploitation; (*de planta etc*) running; (*de mina*) working; (*de recurso*) development; **~ minera** mine; **gastos de ~** operating costs

explotar [eksplo'tar] /**1a**/ VT to exploit; (*planta*) to run, operate; (*mina*) to work ▶ VI (*bomba etc*) to explode, go off

expondré *etc* [ekspon'dre] VB *ver* **exponer**

exponer [ekspo'ner] /**2q**/ VT to expose; (*cuadro*) to display; (*vida*) to risk; (*idea*) to explain; (*teoría*) to expound; (*hechos*) to set out; **según lo expuesto arriba** according to what has been stated above ■ **exponerse** VR: **exponerse a (hacer) algo** to run the risk of (doing) sth

exponga *etc* [eks'ponga] VB *ver* **exponer**

exportación [eksporta'θjon] NF (*acción*) export; (*mercancías*) exports pl

exportador, a [eksporta'ðor, a] ADJ (*país*) exporting ▶ NM/F exporter

exportar [ekspor'tar] /**1a**/ VT to export

★**exposición** [eksposi'θjon] NF (*gen*) exposure; (*de arte*) show, exhibition; (*Com*) display; (*feria*) show, fair; (*explicación*) explanation; (*de teoría*) exposition; (*narración*) account, statement

exprés [eks'pres] ADJ INV (*café*) espresso ▶ NM (*Ferro*) express (train)

expresamente [ekspresa'mente] ADV (*decir*) clearly; (*concretamente*) expressly; (*a propósito*) on purpose

expresar [ekspre'sar] /**1a**/ VT to express; (*redactar*) to phrase, put; (*emoción*) to show ■ **expresarse** VR to express o.s.; (*dato*) to be stated; **como abajo se expresa** as stated below

★**expresión** [ekspre'sjon] NF expression; **~ familiar** colloquialism

expresivo, -a [ekspre'siβo, a] ADJ expressive; (*cariñoso*) affectionate

★**expreso, -a** [eks'preso, a] ADJ (*explícito*) express; (*claro*) specific, clear; (*tren*) fast ▶ NM (*Ferro*) fast train

express [eks'pres] ADV (*AM*): **enviar algo ~** to send sth special delivery

exprimidor [eksprimi'ðor] NM (lemon) squeezer

exprimir [ekspri'mir] /**3a**/ VT (*fruta*) to squeeze; (*zumo*) to squeeze out

ex profeso [ekspro'feso] ADV expressly

expropiar [ekspro'pjar] /**1b**/ VT to expropriate

expuesto, -a [eks'pwesto, a] PP *de* **exponer** ▶ ADJ exposed; (*cuadro etc*) on show, on display

expulsar [ekspul'sar] /**1a**/ VT (*echar*) to eject, throw out; (*alumno*) to expel; (*despedir*) to sack, fire; (*Deporte*) to send off

expulsión [ekspul'sjon] NF expulsion; sending-off

expurgar [ekspur'ɣar] /**1h**/ VT to expurgate

expuse *etc* [eks'puse] VB *ver* **exponer**

exquisito, -a [ekski'sito, a] ADJ exquisite; (*comida*) delicious; (*afectado*) affected

Ext. ABR (= *Exterior*) ext.; (= *Extensión*) ext.

éxtasis ['ekstasis] NM (*tb droga*) ecstasy

extemporáneo, -a [ekstempo'raneo, a] ADJ unseasonal

extender [eksten'der] /**2g**/ VT to extend; (*los brazos*) to stretch out, hold out; (*mapa, tela*) to spread (out), open (out); (*mantequilla*) to spread; (*certificado*) to issue; (*cheque, recibo*) to make out; (*documento*) to draw up ■ **extenderse** VR to extend; (*terreno*) to stretch o spread (out); (*persona: en el suelo*) to stretch out; (: *en el tiempo*) to extend, last; (*costumbre, epidemia*) to spread; (*guerra*) to escalate; **extenderse sobre un tema** to enlarge on a subject

extendido, -a [eksten'diðo, a] ADJ (*abierto*) spread out, open; (*brazos*) outstretched; (*costumbre etc*) widespread

extensible [eksten'siβle] ADJ extending

extensión [eksten'sjon] NF (*de terreno, mar*)

expanse, stretch; (*Mus*) range; (*de conocimientos*) extent; (*de programa*) scope; (*de tiempo*) length, duration; (*Telec*) extension; **~ de plazo** (*Com*) extension; **en toda la ~ de la palabra** in every sense of the word; **de ~** (*Inform*) add-on

extenso, -a [eks'tenso, a] ADJ extensive

extenuar [ekste'nwar] /**1e**/ VT (*debilitar*) to weaken

★**exterior** [ekste'rjor] ADJ (*de fuera*) external; (*afuera*) outside, exterior; (*apariencia*) outward; (*deuda, relaciones*) foreign; **asuntos exteriores** foreign affairs ▶ NM exterior, outside; (*aspecto*) outward appearance; (*Deporte*) wing(er); (*países extranjeros*) abroad; **al ~** outwardly, on the outside; **en el ~** abroad; **noticias del ~** foreign o overseas news

exteriorice *etc* [eksterjo'riθe] VB *ver* **exteriorizar**

exteriorizar [eksterjori'θar] /**1f**/ VT (*emociones*) to show, reveal

exteriormente [eksterjor'mente] ADV outwardly

exterminar [ekstermi'nar] /**1a**/ VT to exterminate

exterminio [ekster'minjo] NM extermination

externo, -a [eks'terno, a] ADJ (*exterior*) external, outside; (*superficial*) outward ▶ NM/F day pupil

extienda *etc* [eks'tjenda] VB *ver* **extender**

extinción [ekstin'θjon] NF extinction

extinga *etc* [eks'tinga] VB *ver* **extinguir**

extinguido, -a [ekstin'giðo, a] ADJ (*animal, volcán*) extinct; (*fuego*) out, extinguished

extinguir [ekstin'gir] /**3d**/ VT (*fuego*) to extinguish, put out; (*raza, población*) to wipe out ■ **extinguirse** VR (*fuego*) to go out; (*Bio*) to die out, become extinct

extinto, -a [eks'tinto, a] ADJ extinct

extintor [ekstin'tor] NM (fire) extinguisher

extirpar [ekstir'par] /**1a**/ VT (*vicios*) to eradicate, stamp out; (*Med*) to remove (surgically)

extorsión [ekstor'sjon] NF blackmail

extra ['ekstra] ADJ INV (*tiempo*) extra; (*vino*) vintage; (*chocolate*) good-quality; (*gasolina*) high-octane ▶ NMF extra ▶ NM extra; (*bono*) bonus; (*periódico*) special edition

extracción [ekstrak'θjon] NF extraction; (*en lotería*) draw; (*de carbón*) mining

extracto [eks'trakto] NM extract

extractor [ekstrak'tor] NM (*tb:* **extractor de humos**) extractor fan

extradición [ekstraði'θjon] NF extradition

extraditar [ekstraði'tar] /**1a**/ VT to extradite

extraer [ekstra'er] /**2o**/ VT to extract, take out

extraescolar [ekstraesko'lar] ADJ: **actividad ~** extracurricular activity

extrafino, -a [ekstra'fino, a] ADJ extra-fine; **azúcar ~** caster sugar

extraiga *etc* [eks'traiɣa], **extraje** *etc* [eks'traxe], **extrajera** *etc* [ekstra'xera] VB *ver* **extraer**

extralimitarse [ekstralimi'tarse] /**1a**/ VR to go too far

extranjerismo [ekstranxe'rismo] NM foreign word o phrase *etc*

★**extranjero, -a** [ekstran'xero, a] ADJ foreign ▶ NM/F foreigner ▶ NM foreign countries *pl*; **en el ~** abroad

extrañamiento [ekstraɲa'mjento] NM estrangement

extrañar [ekstra'ɲar] /**1a**/ VT (*sorprender*) to find strange o odd; (*echar de menos*) to miss; **me extraña** I'm surprised ■ **extrañarse** VR (*sorprenderse*) to be amazed, be surprised; (*distanciarse*) to become estranged, grow apart

extrañeza [ekstra'ɲeθa] NF (*rareza*) strangeness, oddness; (*asombro*) amazement, surprise

★**extraño, -a** [eks'traɲo, a] ADJ (*extranjero*) foreign; (*raro, sorprendente*) strange, odd

extraoficial [ekstraofi'θjal] ADJ unofficial, informal

★**extraordinario, -a** [ekstraorði'narjo, a] ADJ extraordinary; (*edición, número*) special; **horas extraordinarias** overtime *sg* ▶ NM (*de periódico*) special edition

extrarradio [ekstra'rraðjo] NM suburbs *pl*

extrasensorial [ekstrasenso'rjal] ADJ: **percepción ~** extrasensory perception

extraterrestre [ekstrate'rrestre] ADJ of o from outer space ▶ NMF creature from outer space

extravagancia [ekstraβa'ɣanθja] NF oddness; outlandishness; (*rareza*) peculiarity ■ **extravagancias** NFPL (*tonterías*) nonsense *sg*

extravagante [ekstraβa'ɣante] ADJ (*excéntrico*) eccentric; (*estrafalario*) outlandish

extraviado, -a [ekstra'βjaðo, a] ADJ lost, missing

extraviar [ekstra'βjar] /**1c**/ VT to mislead, misdirect; (*perder*) to lose, misplace ■ **extraviarse** VR to lose one's way, get lost; (*objeto*) to go missing, be mislaid

extravío [ekstra'βio] NM loss; (*fig*) misconduct

extrayendo [ekstra'jendo] VB *ver* **extraer**

extremado, -a [ekstre'maðo, a] ADJ extreme, excessive

Extremadura [ekstrema'ðura] NF Estremadura

extremar [ekstre'mar] /**1a**/ VT to carry to extremes ■ **extremarse** VR to do one's utmost, make every effort

extremaunción [ekstremaun'θjon] NF extreme unction, last rites *pl*

extremidad [ekstremi'ðað] NF (*punta*) extremity; (*fila*) edge ■ **extremidades** NFPL (*Anat*) extremities

extremista [ekstre'mista] ADJ, NMF extremist

★**extremo, -a** [eks'tremo, a] ADJ extreme; (*más alejado*) furthest; (*último*) last; **E~ Oriente** Far East; **la extrema derecha** (*Pol*) the far right; **~ derecho/izquierdo** (*Deporte*) outside right/left ▶ NM end; (*situación*) extreme; **en último ~** as a last resort; **pasar de un ~ a otro** (*fig*) to go from one

extreme to the other; **con ~** in the extreme
extrínseco, -a [eks'trinseko, a] ADJ extrinsic
★**extrovertido, -a** [ekstroβer'tiðo, a] ADJ extrovert, outgoing ▶ NM/F extrovert
exuberancia [eksuβe'ranθja] NF exuberance
exuberante [eksuβe'rante] ADJ exuberant; (fig) luxuriant, lush

exudar [eksu'ðar] /1a/ VT, VI to exude
exultar [eksul'tar] /1a/ VI: **~ (en)** to exult (in); (pey) to gloat (over)
exvoto [eks'βoto] NM votive offering
eyaculación [ejakula'θjon] NF ejaculation
eyacular [ejaku'lar] /1a/ VT, VI to ejaculate

e

Ff

F, f ['efe] NF (*letra*) F, f; **F de Francia** F for Frederick (BRIT), F for Fox (US)

fa [fa] NM (*Mus*) F

f.ª ABR (*Com:* = *factura*) Inv.

fabada [fa'βaða] NF *bean and sausage stew*

★fábrica ['faβrika] NF factory; **~ de moneda** mint; **marca de ~** trademark; **precio de ~** factory price

> Do not translate the Spanish word **fábrica** by *fabric*.

fabricación [faβrika'θjon] NF (*manufactura*) manufacture; (*producción*) production; **de ~ casera** home-made; **de ~ nacional** home produced; **~ en serie** mass production

fabricante [faβri'kante] NMF manufacturer

★fabricar [faβri'kar] /**1g**/ VT (*manufacturar*) to manufacture, make; (*construir*) to build; (*cuento*) to fabricate, devise; **~ en serie** to mass-produce

fabril [fa'βril] ADJ: **industria ~** manufacturing industry

fabrique *etc* [fa'βrike] VB *ver* **fabricar**

fábula ['faβula] NF (*cuento*) fable; (*chisme*) rumour; (*mentira*) fib

fabuloso, -a [faβu'loso, a] ADJ fabulous, fantastic

facción [fak'θjon] NF (*Pol*) faction ■ **facciones** NFPL (*del rostro*) features

Facebook® ['feisβuk] M Facebook®

faceta [fa'θeta] NF facet

facha ['fatʃa] (*fam*) NMF fascist, right-wing extremist ▶ NF (*aspecto*) look; (*cara*) face; **¡qué ~ tienes!** you look a sight!

fachada [fa'tʃaða] NF (*Arq*) façade, front; (*Tip*) title page; (*fig*) façade, outward show

facial [fa'θjal] ADJ facial

★fácil ['faθil] ADJ (*simple*) easy; (*sencillo*) simple, straightforward; (*probable*) likely; (*respuesta*) facile; **~ de usar** (*Inform*) user-friendly

facilidad [faθili'ðað] NF (*capacidad*) ease; (*senci-*

llez) simplicity; (*de palabra*) fluency ■ **facilidades** NFPL facilities; **"facilidades de pago"** (*Com*) "credit facilities", "payment terms"

facilitar [faθili'tar] /**1a**/ VT (*hacer fácil*) to make easy; (*proporcionar*) to provide; (*documento*) to issue; **le agradecería me facilitara ...** I would be grateful if you could let me have ...

fácilmente ['faθilmente] ADV easily

facsímil [fak'simil] NM (*documento*) facsimile; **enviar por ~** to fax

factible [fak'tiβle] ADJ feasible

factor [fak'tor] NM factor; (*Com*) agent; (*Ferro*) freight clerk

factoría [fakto'ria] NF (*Com: fábrica*) factory

factura [fak'tura] NF (*cuenta*) bill; (*nota de pago*) invoice; (*hechura*) manufacture; **presentar ~ a** to invoice

facturación [faktura'θjon] NF (*Com*) invoicing; (*: ventas*) turnover; **~ de equipajes** luggage check-in; **~ online** online check-in

facturar [faktu'rar] /**1a**/ VT (*Com*) to invoice, charge for; (*Aviat*) to check in; (*equipaje*) to register, check (US)

facultad [fakul'tað] NF (*aptitud, Escol etc*) faculty; (*poder*) power

facultativo, -a [fakulta'tiβo, a] ADJ optional; (*de un oficio*) professional; **prescripción facultativa** medical prescription

FAD [fað] NM ABR (*Esp*) = **Fondo de Ayuda al Desarrollo**

★faena [fa'ena] NF (*trabajo*) work; (*quehacer*) task, job; **faenas domésticas** housework *sg*

faenar [fae'nar] /**1a**/ VI to fish

fagot [fa'ɣot] NM (*Mus*) bassoon

faisán [fai'san] NM pheasant

faja ['faxa] NF (*para la cintura*) sash; (*de mujer*) corset; (*de tierra*) strip

fajo ['faxo] NM (*de papeles*) bundle; (*de billetes*) role, wad

falange [fa'lanxe] NF: **la F~** (*Pol*) the Falange

f

★**falda** [ˈfalda] NF (*prenda de vestir*) skirt; (*Geo*) foothill; **~ pantalón** culottes *pl*, split skirt; **~ escocesa** kilt

fálico, -a [ˈfaliko, a] ADJ phallic

falla [ˈfaʎa] NF (*defecto*) fault, flaw; **~ humana** (AM) human error

fallar [faˈʎar] /**1a**/ VT (*Jur*) to pronounce sentence on; (*Naipes*) to trump ▶ VI (*memoria*) to fail; (*plan*) to go wrong; (*motor*) to miss; **~ a algn** to let sb down

Fallas [ˈfaʎas] NFPL *see note*

In the week of the 19th March (the feast of St Joseph, San José), Valencia honours its patron saint with a spectacular *fiesta* called *las Fallas*. The **Fallas** are huge sculptures, made of wood, cardboard, paper and cloth, depicting famous politicians and other targets for ridicule, which are judged before being set alight and burned by the *falleros*, members of the competing local groups who have just spent months preparing them. Only the winner escapes the flames.

fallecer [faʎeˈθer] /**2d**/ VI to pass away, die

fallecido, -a [faʎeˈθiðo, a] ADJ late ▶ NM/F deceased

fallecimiento [faʎeθiˈmjento] NM decease, demise

fallero, -a [faˈʎero, a] NM/F maker of "Fallas"

fallezca *etc* [faˈʎeθka] VB *ver* **fallecer**

fallido, -a [faˈʎiðo, a] ADJ vain; (*intento*) frustrated, unsuccessful

fallo [ˈfaʎo] NM (*Jur*) verdict, ruling; (*decisión*) decision; (*de jurado*) findings; (*fracaso*) failure; (*Deporte*) miss; (*Inform*) bug; **~ cardíaco** heart failure; **~ humano** (ESP) human error

falo [ˈfalo] NM phallus

falsear [falseˈar] /**1a**/ VT to falsify; (*firma etc*) to forge ▶ VI (*Mus*) to be out of tune

falsedad [falseˈðað] NF falseness; (*hipocresía*) hypocrisy; (*mentira*) falsehood

falsificación [falsifikaˈθjon] NF (*acto*) falsification; (*objeto*) forgery

falsificar [falsifiˈkar] /**1g**/ VT (*firma etc*) to forge; (*voto etc*) to rig; (*moneda*) to counterfeit

falsifique *etc* [falsiˈfike] VB *ver* **falsificar**

★**falso, -a** [ˈfalso, a] ADJ false; (*erróneo*) wrong, mistaken; (*firma, documento*) forged; (*moneda etc*) fake; **en ~** falsely; **dar un paso en ~** to trip; (*fig*) to take a false step

★**falta** [ˈfalta] NF (*defecto*) fault, flaw; (*privación*) lack, want; (*ausencia*) absence; (*carencia*) shortage; (*equivocación*) mistake; (*Jur*) default; (*Deporte*) foul; (*Tenis*) fault; **~ de educación** bad manners *pl*; **~ de ortografía** spelling mistake; **~ de respeto** disrespect; **echar en ~** to miss; **hacer ~ hacer algo** to be necessary to do sth; **me hace ~ una pluma** I need a pen; **sin ~** without fail; **por ~ de** through *o* for lack of

★**faltar** [falˈtar] /**1a**/ VI (*escasear*) to be lacking, be

wanting; (*ausentarse*) to be absent, be missing; **¿falta algo?** is anything missing?; **falta mucho todavía** there's plenty of time yet; **¿falta mucho?** is there long to go?; **faltan dos horas para llegar** we should arrive in two hours; **~ (al respeto) a algn** to be disrespectful to sb; **~ a una cita** to miss an appointment; **~ a la verdad** to lie; **¡no faltaba más!** (*no hay de qué*) don't mention it!

falto, -a [ˈfalto, a] ADJ (*desposeído*) deficient, lacking; (*necesitado*) poor, wretched; **estar ~ de** to be short of

fama [ˈfama] NF (*renombre*) fame; (*reputación*) reputation

famélico, -a [faˈmeliko, a] ADJ starving

★**familia** [faˈmilja] NF family; **~ numerosa** large family; **~ política** in-laws *pl*

★**familiar** [famiˈljar] ADJ (*relativo a la familia*) family *cpd*; (*conocido, informal*) familiar; (*estilo*) informal; (*Ling*) colloquial ▶ NMF relative, relation

familiarice *etc* [familjaˈriθe] VB *ver* **familiarizarse**

familiaridad [familjariˈðað] NF familiarity; (*informalidad*) homeliness

familiarizarse [familjariˈθarse] /**1f**/ VR: **~ con** to familiarize o.s. with

★**famoso, -a** [faˈmoso, a] ADJ famous ▶ NM/F celebrity

fan [fan] (*pl* **fans** [fans]) NM fan

fanático, -a [faˈnatiko, a] ADJ fanatical ▶ NM/F fanatic; (*Cine, Deporte etc*) fan

fanatismo [fanaˈtismo] NM fanaticism

fanfarrón, -ona [fanfaˈrron, ona] ADJ boastful; (*pey*) showy

fanfarronear [fanfarroneˈar] /**1a**/ VI to boast

fango [ˈfango] NM mud

fangoso, -a [fanˈgoso, a] ADJ muddy

fantasear [fantaseˈar] /**1a**/ VI to fantasize; **~ con una idea** to toy with an idea

fantasía [fantaˈsia] NF fantasy, imagination; (*Mus*) fantasia; (*capricho*) whim; **joyas de ~** imitation jewellery *sg*

fantasma [fanˈtasma] NM (*espectro*) ghost, apparition; (*presumido*) show-off

★**fantástico, -a** [fanˈtastiko, a] ADJ (*irreal, fam*) fantastic

fanzine [fanˈθine] NM fanzine

FAO [ˈfao] NF ABR (= *Organización de las Naciones Unidas para la Agricultura y la Alimentación*) FAO

faquir [faˈkir] NM fakir

faraón [faraˈon] NM Pharaoh

faraónico, -a [faraˈoniko, a] ADJ Pharaonic; (*fig*) grandiose

FARC [fark] NFPL ABR = **Fuerzas Armadas Revolucionarias de Colombia;** = **Fuerza Alternativa Revolucionaria Común**

fardar [farˈðar] /**1a**/ VI to show off; **~ de** to boast about

173

fardo ['farðo] NM bundle; (fig) burden

faringe [fa'rinxe] NF pharynx

faringitis [farin'xitis] NF pharyngitis

★**farmacéutico, -a** [farma'θeutiko, a] ADJ pharmaceutical ▶ NM/F chemist (BRIT), pharmacist

★**farmacia** [far'maθja] NF (ciencia) pharmacy; (tienda) chemist's (shop) (BRIT), pharmacy, drugstore (US); ~ **de turno** duty chemist; ~ **de guardia** all-night chemist

fármaco ['farmako] NM medicine, drug

★**faro** ['faro] NM (Naut: torre) lighthouse; (: señal) beacon; (Auto) headlamp; **faros antiniebla** fog lamps; **faros delanteros/traseros** headlights/rear lights

farol [fa'rol] NM (luz) lantern, lamp; (Ferro) headlamp; (poste) lamppost; **echarse un ~** (fam) to show off

farola [fa'rola] NF street lamp (BRIT) o light (US), lamppost

farra ['farra] NF (AM fam) party; **ir de ~** to go on a binge

farruco, -a [fa'rruko, a] ADJ (fam): **estar** o **ponerse ~** to get aggressive

farsa ['farsa] NF farce

farsante [far'sante] NMF fraud, fake

fascículo [fas'θikulo] NM part, instalment (BRIT), installment (US)

★**fascinante** [fasθi'nante] ADJ fascinating

fascinar [fasθi'nar] /1a/ VT to fascinate; (encantar) to captivate

fascismo [fas'θismo] NM fascism

fascista [fas'θista] ADJ, NMF fascist

fase ['fase] NF phase

fashion ['faʃon] ADJ (fam) trendy

★**fastidiar** [fasti'ðjar] /1b/ VT (disgustar) to annoy, bother; (estropear) to spoil ▶ VI: **¡no fastidies!** you're joking! ■ **fastidiarse** VR (disgustarse) to get annoyed o cross; **¡que se fastidie!** (fam) he'll just have to put up with it!

fastidio [fas'tiðjo] NM (disgusto) annoyance

fastidioso, -a [fasti'ðjoso, a] ADJ (molesto) annoying

fastuoso, -a [fas'twoso, a] ADJ (espléndido) magnificent; (banquete etc) lavish

★**fatal** [fa'tal] ADJ (gen) fatal; (desgraciado) ill-fated; (fam: malo, pésimo) awful ▶ ADV terribly; **lo pasó ~** he had a terrible time (of it)

fatalidad [fatali'ðað] NF (destino) fate; (mala suerte) misfortune

fatídico, -a [fa'tiðiko, a] ADJ fateful

fatiga [fa'tiɣa] NF (cansancio) fatigue, weariness ■ **fatigas** NFPL hardships

fatigar [fati'ɣar] /1h/ VT to tire, weary ■ **fatigarse** VR to get tired

fatigoso, -a [fati'ɣoso, a] ADJ (que cansa) tiring

fatigue etc [fa'tiɣe] VB ver **fatigar**

fatuo, -a ['fatwo, a] ADJ (vano) fatuous; (presuntuoso) conceited

fauces ['fauθes] NFPL (Anat) gullet sg; (fam) jaws

fauna ['fauna] NF fauna

★**favor** [fa'βor] NM favour (BRIT), favor (US); **haga el ~ de ...** would you be so good as to ..., kindly ...; **por ~** please; **a ~** in favo(u)r; **a ~ de** in favo(u)r of; (Com) to the order of

favorable [faβo'raβle] ADJ favourable (BRIT), favorable (US); (condiciones etc) advantageous

favorecer [faβore'θer] /2d/ VT to favour (BRIT), favor (US); (amparar) to help; (vestido etc) to become, flatter; **este peinado le favorece** this hairstyle suits him

favorezca etc [faβo'reθka] VB ver **favorecer**

★**favorito, -a** [faβo'rito, a] ADJ, NM/F favourite (BRIT), favorite (US)

fax [faks] NM INV fax; **mandar por ~** to fax

faz [faθ] NF face; **la ~ de la tierra** the face of the earth

FBI NM ABR FBI

F.C., f.c. ABR = **ferrocarril**; (= Fútbol Club) FC

fe [fe] NF (Rel) faith; (confianza) belief; (documento) certificate; **de buena fe** (Jur) bona fide; **prestar fe a** to believe, credit; **actuar con buena/mala fe** to act in good/bad faith; **dar fe de** to bear witness to; **fe de erratas** errata

fealdad [feal'dað] NF ugliness

feb., feb.º ABR (= febrero) Feb.

★**febrero** [fe'βrero] NM February; ver tb **julio**

febril [fe'βril] ADJ feverish; (movido) hectic

★**fecha** ['fetʃa] NF date; ~ **límite** o **tope** closing o last date; ~ **límite de venta** (de alimentos) sell-by date; ~ **de caducidad** (de alimentos) sell-by date; (de contrato) expiry date; **con ~ adelantada** postdated; **en ~ próxima** soon; **hasta la ~** to date, so far; ~ **de vencimiento** (Com) due date; ~ **de vigencia** (Com) effective date

fechar [fe'tʃar] /1a/ VT to date

fechoría [fetʃo'ria] NF misdeed

fécula ['fekula] NF starch

fecundación [fekunda'θjon] NF fertilization; ~ **in vitro** in vitro fertilization, I.V.F.

fecundar [fekun'dar] /1a/ VT (generar) to fertilize, make fertile

fecundidad [fekundi'ðað] NF fertility; (fig) productiveness

fecundo, -a [fe'kundo, a] ADJ (fértil) fertile; (fig) prolific; (productivo) productive

FED [feð] NM ABR (= Fondo Europeo de Desarrollo) EDF

FEDER ['feðer] NM ABR (= Fondo Europeo de Desarrollo Regional) ERDF

federación [feðera'θjon] NF federation

federal [feðe'ral] ADJ federal

federalismo [feðera'lismo] NM federalism

FEF NF ABR (= Federación Española de Fútbol) Spanish Football Federation

★**felicidad** [feliθi'ðað] NF (satisfacción, contento) happiness ■ **felicidades** NFPL best wishes, congratulations; (*en cumpleaños*) happy birthday

felicitación [feliθita'θjon] NF (*tarjeta*) greetings card; **~ navideña** o **de Navidad** Christmas Greetings ■ **felicitaciones** NFPL (*enhorabuena*) congratulations

★**felicitar** [feliθi'tar] /**1a**/ VT to congratulate

feligrés, -esa [feli'ɣres, esa] NM/F parishioner

felino, -a [fe'lino, a] ADJ cat-like; (*Zool*) feline ▶ NM feline

★**feliz** [fe'liθ] ADJ (*contento*) happy; (*afortunado*) lucky

felonía [felo'nia] NF felony, crime

felpa ['felpa] NF (*terciopelo*) plush; (*toalla*) towelling

felpudo [fel'puðo] NM doormat

★**femenino, -a** [feme'nino, a] ADJ feminine; (*Zool etc*) female ▶ NM (*Ling*) feminine

Al traducir *femenino*, el adjetivo **female** señala que se está haciendo referencia a algo relativo al sexo femenino por oposición al masculino: *las protagonistas femeninas* **the female protagonists**.
El adjetivo **feminine** se utiliza en relación a cualidades que se consideran típicas de la mujer y no del hombre: *Tiene un encanto muy femenino*. **She has lots of feminine charm**. Se utiliza además para indicar el género gramatical: *un nombre femenino* **a feminine noun**.

feminicidio [femini'θiðjo] NM femicide

feminismo [femi'nismo] NM feminism

feminista [femi'nista] ADJ, NMF feminist

★**fenomenal** [fenome'nal] ADJ phenomenal; (*fam*) great, terrific

fenómeno [fe'nomeno] NM phenomenon; (*fig*) freak, accident ▶ ADV: **lo pasamos ~** we had a great time ▶ EXCL great!, marvellous!

★**feo, -a** ['feo, a] ADJ (*gen*) ugly; (*desagradable*) bad, nasty; **más ~ que Picio** as ugly as sin ▶ NM insult; **hacer un ~ a algn** to offend sb

féretro ['feretro] NM (*ataúd*) coffin; (*sarcófago*) bier

★**feria** ['ferja] NF (*gen*) fair; (*Am: mercado*) market; (*descanso*) holiday, rest day; (*Am: cambio*) small change; **~ comercial** trade fair; **~ de muestras** trade show

feriado, -a [fe'rjaðo, a] (*Am*) ADJ: **día ~** (public) holiday ▶ NM (public) holiday

fermentar [fermen'tar] /**1a**/ VI to ferment

fermento [fer'mento] NM leaven, leavening

ferocidad [feroθi'ðað] NF fierceness, ferocity

ferocísimo, -a [fero'θisimo, a] ADJ SUPERLATIVO *de* **feroz**

feroz [fe'roθ] ADJ (*cruel*) cruel; (*salvaje*) fierce

férreo, -a ['ferreo, a] ADJ iron *cpd*; (*Tec*) ferrous; (*fig*) (of) iron

★**ferretería** [ferrete'ria] NF (*tienda*) ironmonger's (shop) (BRIT), hardware store

ferretero [ferre'tero] NM ironmonger

★**ferrocarril** [ferroka'rril] NM railway, railroad (US); **~ de vía estrecha/única** narrow-gauge/single-track railway o line

ferroviario, -a [ferroβja'rjo, a] ADJ rail *cpd*, railway *cpd* (BRIT), railroad *cpd* (US) ▶ NM: **ferroviarios** railway (BRIT) o railroad (US) workers

ferry ['ferri] (*pl* **ferrys** o **ferries**) NM ferry

fértil ['fertil] ADJ (*productivo*) fertile; (*rico*) rich

fertilice *etc* [ferti'liθe] VB *ver* **fertilizar**

fertilidad [fertili'ðað] NF (*gen*) fertility; (*productividad*) fruitfulness

fertilizante [fertili'θante] NM fertilizer

fertilizar [fertili'θar] /**1f**/ VT to fertilize

ferviente [fer'βjente] ADJ fervent

fervor [fer'βor] NM fervour (BRIT), fervor (US)

fervoroso, -a [ferβo'roso, a] ADJ fervent

festejar [feste'xar] /**1a**/ VT (*agasajar*) to wine and dine, fête; (*galantear*) to court; (*celebrar*) to celebrate

festejo [fes'texo] NM (*diversión*) entertainment; (*galanteo*) courtship; (*fiesta*) celebration ■ **festejos** NMPL (*fiestas*) festivals

festín [fes'tin] NM feast, banquet

★**festival** [festi'βal] NM festival

festividad [festiβi'ðað] NF festivity

festivo, -a [fes'tiβo, a] ADJ (*de fiesta*) festive; (*fig*) witty; (*Cine, Lit*) humorous; **día ~** holiday

fetiche [fe'titʃe] NM fetish

fetichista [feti'tʃista] ADJ fetishistic ▶ NMF fetishist

fétido, -a ['fetiðo, a] ADJ foul-smelling

feto ['feto] NM foetus; (*fam*) monster

FEVE ['feβe] NF ABR (= *Ferrocarriles Españoles de Vía Estrecha*) *Spanish narrow-gauge railways*

FF.AA. NFPL ABR (*Mil*) = **Fuerzas Armadas**

FF.CC. NMPL ABR (= *Ferrocarriles*) *ver* **ferrocarril**

fiable [fi'aβle] ADJ (*persona*) trustworthy; (*máquina*) reliable

fiado [fi'aðo] NM: **comprar al ~** to buy on credit; **en ~** on bail

fiador, a [fia'ðor, a] NM/F (*Jur*) surety, guarantor; (*Com*) backer; **salir ~ por algn** to stand bail for sb

fiambre ['fjambre] ADJ (*Culin*) served cold ▶ NM (*Culin*) cold meat (BRIT), cold cut (US); (*fam*) corpse, stiff

fiambrera [fjam'brera] NF ≈ lunch box, ≈ dinner pail (US)

★**fianza** ['fjanθa] NF surety; (*Jur*): **libertad bajo ~** release on bail

★**fiar** [fi'ar] /**1c**/ VT (*salir garante de*) to guarantee; (*Jur*) to stand bail o (US) bond for; (*vender a crédito*) to sell on credit; (*secreto*) to confide ▶ VI: **~ (de)** to trust (in); **ser de ~** to be trustworthy ■ **fiarse**

VR: **fiarse de** to trust (in), rely on; **fiarse de algn** to rely on sb

fiasco ['fjasko] NM fiasco

fibra ['fiβra] NF fibre (BRIT), fiber (US); (fig) vigour (BRIT), vigor (US); **~ óptica** (Inform) optical fibre (BRIT) o fiber (US)

ficción [fik'θjon] NF fiction

★**ficha** ['fitʃa] NF (Telec) token; (en juegos) counter, marker; (en casino) chip; (Com, Econ) tally, check (US); (Inform) file; (tarjeta) (index) card; (Elec) plug; (en hotel) registration form; **~ policíaca** police dossier

fichaje [fi'tʃaxe] NM signing(-up)

fichar [fi'tʃar] /**1a**/ VT (archivar) to file, index; (Deporte) to sign (up); **estar fichado** to have a record ▶ VI (deportista) to sign (up); (obrero) to clock in o on

★**fichero** [fi'tʃero] NM card index; (archivo) filing cabinet; (Com) box file; (Inform) file, archive; (de policía) criminal records; **~ activo** (Inform) active file; **~ archivado** (Inform) archived file; **~ indexado** (Inform) index file; **~ de reserva** (Inform) backup file; **~ de tarjetas** card index; **nombre de ~** filename

ficticio, -a [fik'tiθjo, a] ADJ (imaginario) fictitious; (falso) fabricated

ficus ['fikus] NM INV (Bot) rubber plant

fidedigno, -a [fiðe'ðiɣno, a] ADJ reliable

fideicomiso [fiðeiko'miso] NM (Com) trust

fidelidad [fiðeli'ðað] NF (lealtad) fidelity, loyalty; (exactitud: de dato etc) accuracy; **alta ~** high fidelity, hi-fi

fidelísimo, -a [fiðe'lisimo, a] ADJ SUPERLATIVO de **fiel**

fidelizar [fiðeli'θar] /**1f**/ VT (Com) to develop customer loyalty

fideos [fi'ðeos] NMPL noodles

fiduciario, -a [fiðu'θjarjo, a] NM/F fiduciary

★**fiebre** ['fjeβre] NF (Med) fever; (fig) fever, excitement; **~ amarilla/del heno** yellow/hay fever; **~ palúdica** malaria; **tener ~** to have a temperature; **~ aftosa** foot-and-mouth disease

fiel [fjel] ADJ (leal) faithful, loyal; (fiable) reliable; (exacto) accurate ▶ NM (aguja) needle, pointer ■ **los fieles** NMPL the faithful

fieltro ['fjeltro] NM felt

fiera ['fjera] NF ver **fiero**

fiereza [fje'reθa] NF (Zool) wildness; (bravura) fierceness

fiero, -a ['fjero, a] ADJ (cruel) cruel; (feroz) fierce; (duro) harsh ▶ NM/F (fig) fiend ▶ NF (animal feroz) wild animal o beast; (fig) dragon

fierro ['fjerro] NM (AM) iron

★**fiesta** ['fjesta] NF party; (de pueblo) festival; **la ~ nacional** bullfighting; **(día de) ~** (public) holiday; **mañana es ~** it's a holiday tomorrow; **~ mayor** annual festival; **~ patria** (AM) independence day; **~ de guardar** (Rel) day of obligation; see note

Fiestas can be official public holidays (such as the Día de la Constitución), or special holidays for each comunidad autónoma, many of which are religious feast days. All over Spain, there are also special local fiestas for a patron saint or the Virgin Mary. These often last several days and can include religious processions, carnival parades, bullfights, dancing and feasts of typical local produce.

FIFA ['fifa] NF ABR (= Federación Internacional de Fútbol Asociación) FIFA

★**figura** [fi'ɣura] NF (gen) figure; (forma, imagen) shape, form; (Naipes) face card

figurado, -a [fiɣu'raðo, a] ADJ figurative

figurante [fiɣu'rante] NMF (Teat) walk-on part; (Cine) extra

figurar [fiɣu'rar] /**1a**/ VT (representar) to represent; (fingir) to feign ▶ VI to figure ■ **figurarse** VR (imaginarse) to imagine; (suponer) to suppose; **ya me lo figuraba** I thought as much

fijador [fixa'ðor] NM (Foto etc) fixative; (de pelo) gel

★**fijar** [fi'xar] /**1a**/ VT (gen) to fix; (cartel) to post, put up; (estampilla) to affix, stick (on); (pelo) to set; (fig) to settle (on), decide ■ **fijarse** VR: **fijarse en** to notice; **¡fíjate!** just imagine!; **¿te fijas?** see what I mean?

★**fijo, -a** ['fixo, a] ADJ (gen) fixed; (firme) firm; (permanente) permanent; (trabajo) steady; (colorfast) fast; **teléfono ~** landline ▶ ADV: **mirar ~** to stare

★**fila** ['fila] NF row; (Mil) rank; (cadena) line; (en marcha) file; **~ india** single file; **ponerse en ~** to line up, get into line; **primera ~** front row

filántropo, -a [fi'lantropo, a] NM/F philanthropist

filarmónico, a [filar'moniko, a] ADJ, NF philharmonic

filatelia [fila'telja] NF philately, stamp collecting

filatelista [filate'lista] NMF philatelist, stamp collector

★**filete** [fi'lete] NM (de carne) fillet steak; (de cerdo) tenderloin; (pescado) fillet; (Mecánica: rosca) thread

filiación [filja'θjon] NF (Pol etc) affiliation; (señas) particulars pl; (Mil, Policía) records pl

filial [fi'ljal] ADJ filial ▶ NF subsidiary; (sucursal) branch

Filipinas [fili'pinas] NFPL: **las (Islas) ~** the Philippines

filipino, -a [fili'pino, a] ADJ, NM/F Philippine

film [film] (pl **films**) NM = **filme**

filmación [filma'θjon] NF filming, shooting

filmar [fil'mar] /**1a**/ VT to film, shoot

filme ['filme] NM film, movie (US)

filmoteca [filmo'teka] NF film library

filo ['filo] NM (gen) edge; **sacar ~ a** to sharpen; **al ~ del mediodía** at about midday; **de doble ~** double-edged

filología [filoloˈxia] NF philology; **~ inglesa** (Univ) English Studies

filólogo, -a [fiˈloloɣo, a] NM/F philologist

filón [fiˈlon] NM (Minería) vein, lode; (fig) gold mine

filoso, -a [fiˈloso, a] ADJ (Am) sharp

filosofía [filosoˈfia] NF philosophy

filosófico, -a [filoˈsofiko, a] ADJ philosophic(al)

filósofo, -a [fiˈlosofo, a] NM/F philosopher

filtración [filtraˈθjon] NF (Tec) filtration; (Inform) sorting; (fig: de fondos) misappropriation; (de datos) leak

filtrar [filˈtrar] /1a/ VT, VI to filter, strain; (información) to leak ■ **filtrarse** VR to filter; (fig: dinero) to dwindle

filtro [ˈfiltro] NM (Tec, utensilio) filter

filudo, -a [fiˈluðo, a] ADJ (Am) sharp

⭑**fin** [fin] NM end; (objetivo) aim, purpose; **al ~ y al cabo** when all's said and done; **a ~ de** in order to; **a ~ de cuentas** at the end of the day; **por ~** finally; **en ~** (resumiendo) in short; **¡en ~!** (resignación) oh, well!; **~ de archivo** (Inform) end-of-file; **~ de semana** weekend; **sin ~** endless(ly)

⭑**final** [fiˈnal] ADJ final ▶ NM end, conclusion ▶ NF (Deporte) final; **al ~** in the end; **a finales de** at the end of

finalice etc [finaˈliθe] VB ver **finalizar**

finalidad [finaliˈðað] NF finality; (propósito) purpose, aim

finalista [finaˈlista] NMF finalist

finalizar [finaliˈθar] /1f/ VT to end, finish; **~ la sesión** (Inform) to log out o off ▶ VI to end, come to an end

financiación [finanθjaˈθjon] NF financing

financiar [finanˈθjar] /1b/ VT to finance

financiero, -a [finanˈθjero, a] ADJ financial ▶ NM/F financier

financista [finanˈsista] NMF (Am) financier

finanzas [fiˈnanθas] NFPL finances

⭑**finca** [ˈfinka] NF (casa de recreo) house in the country; (Esp: bien inmueble) property, land; (Am: granja) farm

finde [ˈfinde] NM (fam) (= fin de semana) weekend

fineza [fiˈneθa] NF (cualidad) fineness; (de modales) refinement

fingir [finˈxir] /3c/ VT (simular) to simulate, feign; (pretextar) to sham, fake ▶ VI (aparentar) to pretend ■ **fingirse** VR: **fingirse dormido** to pretend to be asleep

finiquitar [finikiˈtar] /1a/ VT (Econ: cuenta) to settle and close

Finisterre [finisˈterre] NM: **el cabo de ~** Cape Finisterre

finja etc [ˈfinxa] VB ver **fingir**

⭑**finlandés, -esa** [finlanˈdes, esa] ADJ Finnish ▶ NM/F Finn ▶ NM (Ling) Finnish

⭑**Finlandia** [finˈlandja] NF Finland

fino, -a [ˈfino, a] ADJ fine; (delgado) slender; (de buenas maneras) polite, refined; (inteligente) shrewd; (punta) sharp; (gusto) discriminating; (oído) sharp; (jerez) fino, dry ▶ NM (jerez) dry sherry

finura [fiˈnura] NF (calidad) fineness; (cortesía) politeness; (elegancia) elegance; (agudeza) shrewdness

⭑**firma** [ˈfirma] NF signature; (Com) firm, company

firmamento [firmaˈmento] NM firmament

firmante [firˈmante] ADJ, NMF signatory; **los abajo firmantes** the undersigned

⭑**firmar** [firˈmar] /1a/ VT to sign; **~ un contrato** (Com: colocarse) to sign on; **firmado y sellado** signed and sealed

firme [ˈfirme] ADJ firm; (estable) stable; (sólido) solid; (constante) steady; (decidido) resolute; (duro) hard; **¡firmes!** (Mil) attention! ▶ NM road (surface); **oferta en ~** (Com) firm offer

firmemente [firmeˈmente] ADV firmly

firmeza [firˈmeθa] NF firmness; (constancia) steadiness; (solidez) solidity

fiscal [fisˈkal] ADJ fiscal; **año ~** tax o fiscal year ▶ NM (Jur) public prosecutor, ≈ district attorney (US)

fiscalice etc [fiskaˈliθe] VB ver **fiscalizar**

fiscalizar [fiskaliˈθar] /1f/ VT (controlar) to control; (registrar) to inspect (officially); (fig) to criticize

fisco [ˈfisko] NM (hacienda) treasury, exchequer; **declarar algo al ~** to declare sth for tax purposes

fisgar [fisˈɣar] /1h/ VT to pry into

fisgón, -ona [fisˈɣon, ona] ADJ nosey

fisgonear [fisɣoneˈar] /1a/ VT to poke one's nose into ▶ VI to pry, spy

fisgue etc [ˈfisɣe] VB ver **fisgar**

⭑**físico, -a** [ˈfisiko, a] ADJ physical ▶ NM physique; (aspecto) appearance, looks pl ▶ NM/F physicist ▶ NF physics sg

fisioterapeuta [fisjoteraˈpeuta] NMF physiotherapist

fisioterapia [fisjoteˈrapja] NF physiotherapy

fisioterapista [fisjoteraˈpista] NMF (Am) physiotherapist

fisonomía [fisonoˈmia] NF physiognomy, features pl

fisonomista [fisonoˈmista] NMF: **ser buen ~** to have a good memory for faces

fisura [fiˈsura] NF crack; (Med) fracture

flaccidez [flakθiˈðeθ], **flacidez** [flaθiˈðeθ] NF softness, flabbiness

fláccido [ˈflakθiðo, a], **flácido** [ˈflaθiðo, a] ADJ flabby

⭑**flaco, -a** [ˈflako, a] ADJ (muy delgado) skinny, thin; (débil) weak, feeble

flagrante [flaˈɣrante] ADJ flagrant

flama [ˈflama] NF (Am) flame

flamable [flaˈmaβle] ADJ (Am) flammable

flamante [fla'mante] ADJ (*fam*) brilliant; (: *nuevo*) brand-new

flamear [flame'ar] /**1a**/ VT (*Culin*) to flambé

★**flamenco, -a** [fla'menko, a] ADJ (*de Flandes*) Flemish; (*baile, música*) flamenco ▶ NM/F Fleming; **los flamencos** the Flemish ▶ NM (*Ling*) Flemish; (*baile, música*) flamenco; (*Zool*) flamingo

flamingo [fla'mingo] NM (*Am*) flamingo

★**flan** [flan] NM creme caramel

flanco ['flanko] NM side; (*Mil*) flank

Flandes ['flandes] NM Flanders

flanquear [flanke'ar] /**1a**/ VT to flank; (*Mil*) to outflank

flaquear [flake'ar] /**1a**/ VI (*debilitarse*) to weaken; (*persona*) to slack

flaqueza [fla'keθa] NF (*delgadez*) thinness, leanness; (*fig*) weakness

flaquísimo, -a [fla'kisimo, a] ADJ SUPERLATIVO *de* **flaco**

flash [flaʃ, flas] (*pl* **flashes**) NM (*Foto*) flash; (*Inform*): **~ drive** flash drive

flato ['flato] NM: **el** (*o* **un**) **~** the (*o* a) stitch

★**flauta** ['flauta] (*Mus*) NF flute; **¡la gran ~!** (*Am*) my God!; **hijo de la gran ~** (*Am fam!*) bastard (*fam!*), son of a bitch (*US fam!*) ▶ NMF flautist, flute player

★**flecha** ['fletʃa] NF arrow

flechazo [fle'tʃaθo] NM (*acción*) bowshot; (*fam*): **fue un ~** it was love at first sight

fleco ['fleko] NM fringe

flema ['flema] NM phlegm

flemático, -a [fle'matiko, a] ADJ phlegmatic; (*tono etc*) matter-of-fact

flemón [fle'mon] NM (*Med*) gumboil

flequillo [fle'kiʎo] NM (*de pelo*) fringe, bangs (*US*)

fletar [fle'tar] /**1a**/ VT (*Com*) to charter; (*embarcar*) to load; (*Auto*) to lease(-purchase)

flete ['flete] NM (*carga*) freight; (*alquiler*) charter; (*precio*) freightage; **~ debido** (*Com*) freight forward; **~ sobre compras** (*Com*) freight inward

★**flexible** [flek'siβle] ADJ flexible; (*individuo*) compliant

flexión [flek'sjon] NF (*Deporte*) bend; (: *en el suelo*) press-up

flexo ['flekso] NM adjustable table lamp

flipper ['fliper] NM pinball machine

flirtear [flirte'ar] /**1a**/ VI to flirt

FLN NM ABR (*Pol: ESP, PERÚ, VENEZUELA*: = *Frente de Liberación Nacional*) *political party*

flojear [floxe'ar] /**1a**/ VI (*piernas: al andar*) to give way; (*alumno*) to do badly; (*cosecha, mercado*) to be poor

flojera [flo'xera] NF (*Am*) laziness; **me da ~** I can't be bothered

★**flojo, -a** ['floxo, a] ADJ (*gen*) loose; (*sin fuerzas*) limp; (*débil*) weak; (*viento*) light; (*bebida*) weak;

(*trabajo*) poor; (*actitud*) slack; (*precio*) low; (*Com: mercado*) dull, slack; (*Am*) lazy

★**flor** [flor] NF flower; (*piropo*) compliment; **la ~ y nata de la sociedad** (*fig*) the cream of society; **en la ~ de la vida** in the prime of life; **a ~ de** on the surface of

flora ['flora] NF flora

florecer [flore'θer] /**2d**/ VI (*Bot*) to flower, bloom; (*fig*) to flourish

floreciente [flore'θjente] ADJ (*Bot*) in flower, flowering; (*fig*) thriving

Florencia [flo'renθja] NF Florence

florería [flore'ria] NF (*Am*) florist's (shop)

★**florero** [flo'rero] NM vase

florezca *etc* [flo'reθka] VB *ver* **florecer**

florista [flo'rista] NMF florist

floristería [floriste'ria] NF florist's (shop)

flota ['flota] NF fleet

flotación [flota'θjon] NF (*Com*) flotation

flotador [flota'ðor] NM (*gen*) float; (*para nadar*) rubber ring; (*de cisterna*) ballcock

flotante [flo'tante] ADJ floating; (*Inform*): **de coma ~** floating-point

★**flotar** [flo'tar] /**1a**/ VI to float

flote ['flote] NM: **a ~** afloat; **salir a ~** (*fig*) to get back on one's feet

FLS NM ABR (*Pol: NICARAGUA*) = **Frente de Liberación Sandinista**

fluctuación [fluktwa'θjon] NF fluctuation

fluctuante [fluk'twante] ADJ fluctuating

fluctuar [fluk'twar] /**1e**/ VI (*oscilar*) to fluctuate

fluidez [flui'ðeθ] NF fluidity; (*fig*) fluency

fluido, -a ['flwiðo, a] ADJ fluid; (*lenguaje*) fluent; (*estilo*) smooth ▶ NM (*líquido*) fluid

fluir [flu'ir] /**3g**/ VI to flow

flujo ['fluxo] NM flow; (*Pol*) swing; (*Naut*) rising tide; **~ y reflujo** ebb and flow; **~ de sangre** (*Med*) haemorrhage (*BRIT*), hemorrhage (*US*); **~ positivo/negativo de efectivo** (*Com*) positive/negative cash flow

flúor ['fluor] NM fluorine; (*en dentífrico*) fluoride

fluorescente [flwores'θente] ADJ fluorescent ▶ NM (*tb*: **tubo fluorescente**) fluorescent tube

fluoruro [flwo'ruro] NM fluoride

fluvial [fluβi'al] ADJ (*navegación, cuenca*) fluvial, river *cpd*

fluyendo *etc* [flu'jendo] VB *ver* **fluir**

FM NF ABR (= *Frecuencia Modulada*) FM

FMI NM ABR (= *Fondo Monetario Internacional*) IMF

FN NM ABR = **Frente Nacional**

f.° ABR (= *folio*) fo., fol.

fobia ['fobja] NF phobia; **~ a las alturas** fear of heights

foca ['foka] NF seal

foco ['foko] NM focus; (*centro*) focal point; (*fuente*) source; (*de incendio*) seat; (*Elec*) floodlight; (*Teat*) spotlight; (*Am*) (light) bulb, light

fofo, -a ['fofo, a] ADJ (*esponjoso*) soft, spongy; (*músculo*) flabby

fogata [fo'ɣata] NF (*hoguera*) bonfire

fogón [fo'ɣon] NM (*de cocina*) ring, burner

fogoso, -a [fo'ɣoso, a] ADJ spirited

foja ['foxa] NF (*Am*) sheet (of paper); **~ de servicios** record (file)

fol. ABR (= *folio*) fo., fol.

folder, fólder ['folder] NM (*Am*) folder

folio ['foljo] NM folio; (*hoja*) sheet (of paper), page

folklore [fol'klore] NM folklore

folklórico, -a [fol'kloriko, a] ADJ traditional

follaje [fo'ʎaxe] NM foliage

follar [fo'ʎar] /1l/ VT, VI (*fam!*) to fuck (*fam!*)

folletinesco, -a [foʎetin'esko, a] ADJ melodramatic

★**folleto** [fo'ʎeto] NM pamphlet; (*Com*) brochure; (*prospecto*) leaflet; (*Escol etc*) handout

follón [fo'ʎon] NM (*fam*: *lío*) mess; (: *conmoción*) fuss, rumpus, shindy; **armar un ~** to kick up a fuss; **se armó un ~** there was a hell of a row

fomentar [fomen'tar] /1a/ VT (*Med*) to foment; (*fig: promover*) to promote, foster; (*odio etc*) to stir up

fomento [fo'mento] NM (*fig: ayuda*) fostering; (*promoción*) promotion

fonda ['fonda] NF ≈ boarding house; *ver tb* **hotel**

fondear [fonde'ar] /1a/ VT (*Naut: sondear*) to sound; (*barco*) to search

★**fondo** ['fondo] NM (*de caja etc*) bottom; (*medida*) depth; (*de coche, sala*) back; (*Arte etc*) background; (*reserva*) fund; (*fig: carácter*) nature; **~ de escritorio** (*Inform*) wallpaper; **F~ Monetario Internacional** International Monetary Fund; **~ del mar** sea bed *o* floor; **una investigación a ~** a thorough investigation; **en el ~** at bottom, deep down; **tener buen ~** to be good-natured ■ **fondos** NMPL (*Com*) funds, resources

fonética [fo'netika] NF phonetics *sg*

fono ['fono] NM (*Am*) telephone (number)

fonobuzón [fonoβu'θon] NM voice mail

fonógrafo [fo'noɣrafo] NM (*esp Am*) gramophone, phonograph (*US*)

fonología [fonolo'xia] NF phonology

fontanería [fontane'ria] NF plumbing

★**fontanero** [fonta'nero] NM plumber

★**footing** ['futin] NM jogging; **hacer ~** to jog

F.O.P. [fop] NFPL ABR (*Esp*) = **Fuerza del Orden Público**

forajido [fora'xiðo] NM outlaw

foráneo, -a [fo'raneo, a] ADJ foreign ▶ NM/F outsider

forastero, -a [foras'tero, a] NM/F stranger

forcé [for'θe] VB *ver* **forzar**

forcejear [forθexe'ar] /1a/ VI (*luchar*) to struggle

forcemos *etc* [for'θemos] VB *ver* **forzar**

fórceps ['forθeps] NM INV forceps *pl*

forense [fo'rense] ADJ forensic ▶ NMF pathologist

forestal [fores'tal] ADJ forest *cpd*

forjar [for'xar] /1a/ VT to forge; (*formar*) to form

★**forma** ['forma] NF (*figura*) form, shape; (*molde*) mould, pattern; (*Med*) fitness; (*método*) way, means; **estar en ~** to be fit; **~ de pago** (*Com*) method of payment; **las formas** the conventions; **de ~ que ...** so that ...; **de todas formas** in any case

★**formación** [forma'θjon] NF (*gen*) formation; (*enseñanza*) training; **~ profesional** vocational training; **~ fuera del trabajo** off-the-job training; **~ en el trabajo** *o* **sobre la práctica** on-the-job training

> In Spain, there are two levels of **formación profesional** (vocational training): an intermediate level which is open to those who have an *ESO* (Secondary education) diploma or anyone over 17 who passes the entrance exam; and the advanced vocational training level, which people with the *Bachillerato* (equivalent to an A-Level course) qualification can do, as well as anyone over 19 (or over 18 if they have an intermediate-level qualification in the chosen subject). The first level leads to a technical diploma, and the second to an advanced technical diploma which is accepted as an entrance qualification by universities.

★**formal** [for'mal] ADJ (*gen*) formal; (*fig: persona*) serious; (: *de fiar*) reliable; (: *conducta*) steady

formalice *etc* [forma'liθe] VB *ver* **formalizar**

formalidad [formali'ðað] NF (*requisito*) formality; (*seriedad*) seriousness; (*fiabilidad*) reliability, steadiness

formalizar [formali'θar] /1f/ VT (*Jur*) to formalize; (*plan*) to draw up; (*situación*) to put in order, regularize ■ **formalizarse** VR (*situación*) to be put in order, be regularized

formar [for'mar] /1a/ VT (*componer*) to form, shape; (*constituir*) to make up, constitute; (*Escol*) to train, educate ▶ VI (*Mil*) to fall in; (*Deporte*) to line up ■ **formarse** VR (*Escol*) to be trained (*o* educated); (*cobrar forma*) to form, take form; (*desarrollarse*) to develop

formatear [formate'ar] /1a/ VT (*Inform*) to format

formateo [forma'teo] NM (*Inform*) formatting

formato [for'mato] NM (*Inform*) format; **sin ~** (*disco, texto*) unformatted; **~ de registro** record format

formidable [formi'ðaβle] ADJ (*temible*) formidable; (*asombroso*) tremendous

fórmula ['formula] NF formula

formular [formu'lar] /1a/ VT (*queja*) to lodge; (*petición*) to draw up; (*pregunta*) to pose, formulate; (*idea*) to formulate

★**formulario** [formu'larjo] NM form; **~ de solicitud/de pedido** (*Com*) application/order form;

llenar un ~ to fill in a form; **~ continuo desplegable** (*Inform*) fanfold paper

fornicar [forni'kar] /**1g**/ vɪ to fornicate

fornido, -a [for'niðo, a] ADJ well-built

fornique *etc* [for'nike] vв *ver* **fornicar**

foro ['foro] NM (*gen*) forum; (*Jur*) court; **~ de debate/discusión** (*Internet*) discussion forum, message board

forofo, -a [fo'rofo, a] NM/F fan

FORPRONU [for'pronu] NF ABR (= *Fuerza de Protección de las Naciones Unidas*) UNPROFOR

forrado, -a [fo'rraðo, a] ADJ (*ropa*) lined; (*fam*) well-heeled

forrar [fo'rrar] /**1a**/ vт (*abrigo*) to line; (*libro*) to cover; (*coche*) to upholster ■ **forrarse** vʀ (*fam*) to line one's pockets

forro ['forro] NM (*de cuaderno*) cover; (*costura*) lining; (*de sillón*) upholstery; **~ polar** fleece

fortalecer [fortale'θer] /**2d**/ vт to strengthen ■ **fortalecerse** vʀ to fortify o.s.; (*opinión etc*) to become stronger

fortaleza [forta'leθa] NF (*Mil*) fortress, stronghold; (*fuerza*) strength; (*determinación*) resolution

fortalezca *etc* [forta'leθka] vв *ver* **fortalecer**

fortificar [fortifi'kar] /**1g**/ vт to fortify; (*fig*) to strengthen

fortifique *etc* [forti'fike] vв *ver* **fortificar**

fortísimo, -a [for'tisimo, a] ADJ SUPERLATIVO *de* **fuerte**

fortuito, -a [for'twito, a] ADJ accidental, chance *cpd*

fortuna [for'tuna] NF (*suerte*) fortune, (good) luck; (*riqueza*) fortune, wealth

★**forzar** [for'θar] /**1f**, **1l**/ vт (*puerta*) to force (open); (*compeler*) to compel; (*violar*) to rape; (*ojos etc*) to strain

forzoso, -a [for'θoso, a] ADJ necessary; (*inevitable*) inescapable; (*obligatorio*) compulsory

forzudo, -a [for'θuðo, a] ADJ burly

fosa ['fosa] NF (*sepultura*) grave; (*en tierra*) pit; (*Med*) cavity; **fosas nasales** nostrils

fosfato [fos'fato] NM phosphate

fosforescente [fosfores'θente] ADJ phosphorescent

★**fósforo** ['fosforo] NM (*Química*) phosphorus; (*esp Am*: *cerilla*) match

fósil ['fosil] ADJ fossil, fossilized ▶ NM fossil

foso ['foso] NM ditch; (*Teat*) pit; (*Auto*): **~ de reconocimiento** inspection pit

★**foto** ['foto] NF photo, snap(shot); **sacar una ~** to take a photo *o* picture; **~ (de) carné** passport(-size) photo

fotocopia [foto'kopja] NF photocopy

fotocopiadora [fotokopja'ðora] NF photocopier

fotocopiar [fotoko'pjar] /**1b**/ vт to photocopy

fotogénico, -a [foto'xeniko, a] ADJ photogenic

★**fotografía** [fotoɣra'fia] NF (*arte*) photography; (*una fotografía*) photograph

fotografiar [fotoɣra'fjar] /**1c**/ vт to photograph

★**fotógrafo, -a** [fo'toɣrafo, a] NM/F photographer

fotomatón [fotoma'ton] NM (*cabina*) photo booth

fotómetro [fo'tometro] NM (*Foto*) light meter

fotonovela [fotono'βela] NF photo-story

foulard [fu'lar] NM (head)scarf

FP NF ABR (*Esp Escol*, *Com*) = **Formación Profesional** ▶ NM ABR (*Pol*) = **Frente Popular**

FPLP NM ABR (*Pol*: = *Frente Popular para la Liberación de Palestina*) PFLP

Fr. ABR (= *Fray*) Fr.

fra. ABR = **factura**

frac [frak] (*pl* **fracs** *o* **fraques** ['frakes]) NM dress coat, tails

★**fracasar** [fraka'sar] /**1a**/ vɪ (*gen*) to fail; (*plan etc*) to fall through

★**fracaso** [fra'kaso] NM (*desgracia*, *revés*) failure; (*de negociaciones etc*) collapse, breakdown

fracción [frak'θjon] NF fraction; (*Pol*) faction, splinter group

fraccionamiento [fraksjona'mjento] NM (*Am*) housing estate

fracking ['frakin] NM fracking

fractura [frak'tura] NF fracture, break; **~ hidráulica** fracking

fragancia [fra'ɣanθja] NF (*olor*) fragrance, perfume

fragante [fra'ɣante] ADJ fragrant, scented

fraganti [fra'ɣanti]: **in ~** *adv*: **coger a algn en ~** to catch sb red-handed

fragata [fra'ɣata] NF frigate

frágil ['fraxil] ADJ (*débil*) fragile; (*Com*) breakable; (*fig*) frail, delicate

fragilidad [fraxili'ðað] NF fragility; (*de persona*) frailty

fragmento [fraɣ'mento] NM fragment; (*pedazo*) piece; (*de discurso*) excerpt; (*de canción*) snatch

fragor [fra'ɣor] NM (*ruido intenso*) din

fragua ['fraɣwa] NF forge

fraguar [fra'ɣwar] /**1i**/ vт to forge; (*fig*) to concoct ▶ vɪ to harden

fragüe *etc* ['fraɣwe] vв *ver* **fraguar**

fraile ['fraile] NM (*Rel*) friar; (: *monje*) monk

★**frambuesa** [fram'bwesa] NF raspberry

★**francés, -esa** [fran'θes, esa] ADJ French ▶ NM/F Frenchman(-woman) ▶ NM (*Ling*) French

★**Francia** ['franθja] NF France

★**franco, -a** ['franko, a] ADJ (*cándido*) frank, open; (*Com*: *exento*) free; **~ de derechos** duty-free; **~ al costado del buque** (*Com*) free alongside ship; **~ puesto sobre vagón** (*Com*) free on rail; **~ a bordo** free on board ▶ NM (*moneda*) franc

francotirador, a [frankotira'ðor, a] NM/F sniper

franela [fra'nela] NF flannel

franja ['franxa] NF fringe; (de uniforme) stripe; (de tierra etc) strip

franquear [franke'ar] /1a/ VT (camino) to clear; (carta, paquete) to frank, stamp; (obstáculo) to overcome; (Com etc) to free, exempt

franqueo [fran'keo] NM postage

franqueza [fran'keθa] NF frankness

franquicia [fran'kiθja] NF exemption; ~ adua-nera exemption from customs duties

franquismo [fran'kismo] NM: **el ~** (sistema) the Franco system; (período) the Franco years; see note

The political reign and style of government of Francisco Franco, from the end of the Spanish Civil War in 1939 until his death in 1975, are commonly referred to as **franquismo**. Franco was a powerful, authoritarian, right-wing dictator, who promoted a traditional, Catholic and self-sufficient country. From the 1960s, Spain gradually opened its doors to the international community, coinciding with a rise in economic growth and internal political opposition. On his death, Spain became a democratic constitutional monarchy.

franquista [fran'kista] ADJ pro-Franco ▶ NMF supporter of Franco

frasco ['frasko] NM bottle, flask; **~ al vacío** (vacuum) flask

★**frase** ['frase] NF sentence; (locución) phrase, expression; **~ hecha** set phrase; (pey) stock phrase

fraternal [frater'nal] ADJ brotherly, fraternal

fraterno, -a [fra'terno, a] ADJ brotherly, fraternal

fraude ['frauðe] NM (cualidad) dishonesty; (acto) fraud, swindle

fraudulento, -a [frauðu'lento, a] ADJ fraudulent

frazada [fra'saða] NF (AM) blanket

frecuencia [fre'kwenθja] NF frequency; **con ~** frequently, often; **~ de red** (Inform) mains frequency; **~ del reloj** (Inform) clock speed; **~ tele-fónica** voice frequency

frecuentar [frekwen'tar] /1a/ VT (lugar) to frequent; (persona) to see frequently o often; **~ la buena sociedad** to mix in high society

frecuente [fre'kwente] ADJ frequent; (costumbre) common; (vicio) rife

★**fregadero** [freɣa'ðero] NM (kitchen) sink

fregado, -a [fre'ɣaðo, a] ADJ (AM fam!) damn, bloody (fam!)

★**fregar** [fre'ɣar] /1h, 1j/ VT (frotar) to scrub; (platos) to wash (up); (AM fam: fastidiar) to annoy; (: malo-grar) to screw up

fregón, -ona [fre'ɣon, ona] ADJ = **fregado** ▶ NF (utensilio) mop; (pey: sirvienta) skivvy

fregué [fre'ɣe], **freguemos** etc [fre'ɣemos] VB ver **fregar**

freidora [frei'ðora] NF deep-fat fryer

★**freír** [fre'ir] /3l/ VT to fry

fréjol ['frexol] NM = **frijol**

★**frenar** [fre'nar] /1a/ VT to brake; (fig) to check

frenazo [fre'naθo] NM: **dar un ~** to brake sharply

frenesí [frene'si] NM frenzy

frenético, -a [fre'netiko, a] ADJ frantic; **ponerse ~** to lose one's head

★**freno** ['freno] NM (Tec, Auto) brake; (de cabalga-dura) bit; (fig) check; **~ de mano** handbrake

★**frente** ['frente] NM (Arq, Mil, Pol) front; (de objeto) front part; **~ de batalla** battle front; **hacer ~ común con algn** to make common cause with sb; **chocar de ~** to crash head-on; **hacer ~ a** to face up to; **~ a** in front of; (en situación opuesta a) opposite ▶ NF forehead, brow

★**fresa** ['fresa] NF (ESP: fruta) strawberry; (de den-tista) drill

★**fresco, -a** ['fresko, a] ADJ (nuevo) fresh; (huevo) newly-laid; (frío) cool; (fam: descarado) cheeky, bad-mannered; **¡qué ~!** what a cheek! ▶ NM (aire) fresh air; (Arte) fresco; (AM: bebida) fruit juice o drink; **tomar el ~** to get some fresh air ▶ NM/F (fam) shameless person; (: persona inso-lente) impudent person; **ser un(a) ~(-a)** to have a nerve

frescor [fres'kor] NM freshness

frescura [fres'kura] NF freshness; (descaro) cheek, nerve; (calma) calmness

fresno ['fresno] NM ash (tree)

fresón [fre'son] NM strawberry

frialdad [frjal'daθ] NF (gen) coldness; (indiferen-cia) indifference

fricción [frik'θjon] NF (gen) friction; (acto) rub(bing); (Med) massage; (Pol, fig etc) friction, trouble

friega etc ['frjeɣa], **friegue** etc ['frjeɣe] VB ver **fregar**

friendo etc [fri'endo] VB ver **freír**

frigidez [frixi'ðeθ] NF frigidity

frígido, -a ['frixiðo, a] ADJ frigid

frigo ['friɣo] NM fridge

★**frigorífico, -a** [friɣo'rifiko, a] ADJ refrigerat-ing; **instalación frigorífica** cold-storage plant ▶ NM refrigerator; (camión) freezer lorry o (US) truck

frijol [fri'xol], **fríjol** ['frixol] NM kidney bean

friki ['friki] (fam) ADJ weird (fam); **me pasó una cosa muy ~** something really weird (fam) hap-pened to me; **¡qué tío más ~!** what a weirdo! (fam) ▶ NMF weirdo (fam)

frio [fri'o] VB ver **freír**

★**frío, -a** ['frio, a] VB ver **freír** ▶ ADJ cold; (fig: indife-rente) unmoved, indifferent; (poco entusiasta) chilly; **¡qué ~!** how cold it is! ▶ NM cold(ness); indifference; **hace ~** it's cold; **tener ~** to be cold

friolento, -a [frjo'lento, a] (AM), **friolero, -a** [frjo'lero, a] ADJ sensitive to cold

friqui ['friki] NMF (*fam*) = **friki**

★**frito, -a** ['frito, a] PP *de* **freír** ▶ ADJ fried; **me trae ~ ese hombre** I'm sick and tired of that man ▶ NM fry ∎ **fritos** NMPL fried food; **fritos variados** mixed grill

frívolo, -a ['friβolo, a] ADJ frivolous

frondoso, -a [fron'doso, a] ADJ leafy

frontal [fron'tal] ADJ frontal ▶ NM: **choque ~** head-on collision

★**frontera** [fron'tera] NF frontier; (*línea divisoria*) border; (*zona*) frontier area

fronterizo, -a [fronte'riθo, a] ADJ frontier *cpd*; (*contiguo*) bordering

frontón [fron'ton] NM (*Deporte: cancha*) pelota court; (*juego*) pelota

frotar [fro'tar] /**1a**/ VT to rub; (*fósforo*) to strike ∎ **frotarse** VR: **frotarse las manos** to rub one's hands

fructífero, -a [fruk'tifero, a] ADJ productive, fruitful

frugal [fru'ɣal] ADJ frugal

fruncir [frun'θir] /**3b**/ VT to pucker; (*Costura*) to gather; (*ceño*) to frown; (*labios*) to purse; **~ el ceño** to knit one's brow

frunza *etc* ['frunθa] VB *ver* **fruncir**

frustración [frustra'θjon] NF frustration

frustrar [frus'trar] /**1a**/ VT to frustrate ∎ **frustrarse** VR to be frustrated; (*plan etc*) to fail

★**fruta** ['fruta] NF fruit

frutal [fru'tal] ADJ fruit-bearing, fruit *cpd* ▶ NM: (**árbol**) **~** fruit tree

★**frutería** [frute'ria] NF fruit shop

frutero, -a [fru'tero, a] ADJ fruit *cpd* ▶ NM/F fruiterer ▶ NM fruit dish *o* bowl

frutilla [fru'tiʎa] NF (*Am*) strawberry

fruto ['fruto] NM (*Bot*) fruit; (*fig: resultado*) result, outcome; (*: beneficio*) benefit; **frutos secos** nuts and dried fruit

FSLN NM ABR (*Pol: NICARAGUA*) = **Frente Sandinista de Liberación Nacional**

fucsia ['fuksja] NF fuchsia

fue [fwe] VB *ver* **ser; ir**

★**fuego** ['fweɣo] NM (*gen*) fire; (*Culin: gas*) burner, ring; (*Mil*) fire; (*fig: pasión*) fire, passion; **~ amigo** friendly fire; **fuegos artificiales** *o* **de artificio** fireworks; **prender ~ a** to set fire to; **a ~ lento** on a low flame *o* gas; **¡alto el ~!** cease fire!; **estar entre dos fuegos** to be in the crossfire; **¿tienes ~?** have you (got) a light?

fuelle ['fweʎe] NM bellows *pl*

fueloil [fuel'oil] NM paraffin (*BRIT*), kerosene (*US*)

★**fuente** ['fwente] NF fountain; (*manantial*, *fig*) spring; (*origen*) source; (*plato*) large dish; **~ de alimentación** (*Inform*) power supply; **de ~ desconocida/fidedigna** from an unknown/reliable source

★**fuera** ['fwera] VB *ver* **ser; ir** ▶ ADV out(side); (*en otra parte*) away; (*excepto, salvo*) except, save; **por**

~ (on the) outside; **los de ~** strangers, newcomers; **estar ~** (*en el extranjero*) to be abroad ▶ PREP: **~ de** outside; (*fig*) besides; **~ de alcance** out of reach; **~ de combate** out of action; (*boxeo*) knocked out; **~ de sí** beside o.s.

fuera-borda [fwera'βorða] NM INV (*barca*) speedboat; (*motor*) outboard engine *o* motor

fuerce *etc* ['fwerθe] VB *ver* **forzar**

fuereño, -a [fwe'reɲo, a] NM/F (*Am*) outsider

fuero ['fwero] NM (*carta municipal*) municipal charter; (*leyes locales*) local *o* regional law code; (*privilegio*) privilege; (*autoridad*) jurisdiction; (*fig*): **en mi** *etc* **~ interno ...** in my *etc* heart of hearts ..., deep down ...

★**fuerte** ['fwerte] ADJ strong; (*golpe*) hard; (*ruido*) loud; (*comida*) rich; (*lluvia*) heavy; (*dolor*) intense; **ser ~ en** (*fig*) to be good at ▶ ADV strongly; hard; loud(ly) ▶ NM (*Mil*) fort, strongpoint; **el canto no es mi ~** singing is not my strong point

★**fuerza** ['fwerθa] VB *ver* **forzar** ▶ NF (*fortaleza*) strength; (*Tec, Elec*) power; (*coacción*) force; (*violencia*) violence; (*Mil: tb:* **fuerzas**) forces *pl*; **~ de arrastre** (*Tec*) pulling power; **~ de brazos** manpower; **~ mayor** force majeure; **~ bruta** brute force; **fuerzas armadas (FF.AA.)** armed forces; **~ del orden público (F.O.P.)** police (forces); **fuerzas aéreas** air force *sg*; **~ vital** vitality; **a ~ de** by (dint of); **cobrar fuerzas** to recover one's strength; **tener fuerzas para** to have the strength to; **hacer algo a la ~** to be forced to do sth; **con ~ legal** (*Com*) legally binding; **a la ~** forcibly, by force; **por ~** of necessity; **~ de voluntad** willpower

fuete ['fwete] NM (*Am*) whip

fuga ['fuɣa] NF (*huida*) flight, escape; (*de enamorados*) elopement; (*de gas etc*) leak; **~ de cerebros** (*fig*) brain drain

fugarse [fu'ɣarse] /**1h**/ VR to flee, escape

fugaz [fu'ɣaθ] ADJ fleeting

fugitivo, -a [fuxi'tiβo, a] ADJ fugitive, fleeing ▶ NM/F fugitive

fugue *etc* ['fuɣe] VB *ver* **fugarse**

fui *etc* [fwi] VB *ver* **ser; ir**

fulano, -a [fu'lano, a] NM/F so-and-so, what's-his-name

fulgor [ful'ɣor] NM brilliance

fulminante [fulmi'nante] ADJ (*pólvora*) fulminating; (*fig: mirada*) withering; (*Med*) sudden, serious; (*fam*) terrific, tremendous; (*éxito, golpe*) sudden; **ataque ~** stroke

fulminar [fulmi'nar] /**1a**/ VT: **caer fulminado por un rayo** to be struck down by lightning; **~ a algn con la mirada** to look daggers at sb

★**fumador, a** [fuma'ðor, a] NM/F smoker; **no ~** non-smoker

★**fumar** [fu'mar] /**1a**/ VT, VI to smoke; **~ en pipa** to smoke a pipe ∎ **fumarse** VR (*disipar*) to squander

fumigar [fumi'ɣar] /**1h**/ VT to fumigate

funámbulo, -a [fuˈnambulo, a], **funambu-lista** [funambuˈlista] NMF/F tightrope walker

★**función** [funˈθjon] NF function; (de puesto) duties pl; (Teat etc) show; **entrar en funciones** to take up one's duties; **~ de tarde/de noche** matinée/evening performance

funcional [funθjoˈnal] ADJ functional

funcionamiento [funθjonaˈmjento] NM functioning; (Tec) working; **en ~** (Com) on stream; **entrar en ~** to come into operation

★**funcionar** [funθjoˈnar] /1a/ VI (gen) to function; (máquina) to work; **"no funciona"** "out of order"

★**funcionario, -a** [funθjoˈnarjo, a] NM/F official; (público) civil servant

funda [ˈfunda] NF (gen) cover; (de almohada) pillowcase; **~ protectora del disco** (Inform) disk jacket

fundación [fundaˈθjon] NF foundation

fundado, -a [funˈdaðo, a] ADJ (justificado) well-founded

fundamental [fundamenˈtal] ADJ fundamental, basic

fundamentalismo [fundamentaˈlismo] NM fundamentalism

fundamentalista [fundamentaˈlista] ADJ, NMF fundamentalist

fundamentar [fundamenˈtar] /1a/ VT (poner base) to lay the foundations of; (establecer) to found; (fig) to base

fundamento [fundaˈmento] NM (base) foundation; (razón) grounds pl; **eso carece de ~** that is groundless

fundar [funˈdar] /1a/ VT to found; (crear) to set up; (fig: basar): **~ (en)** to base o found (on) ▪ **fundarse** VR: **fundarse en** to be founded on

fundición [fundiˈθjon] NF (acción) smelting; (fábrica) foundry; (Tip) font

fundir [funˈdir] /3a/ VT (gen) to fuse; (metal) to smelt, melt down; (nieve etc) to melt; (Com) to merge; (estatua) to cast ▪ **fundirse** VR (colores etc) to merge, blend; (unirse) to fuse together; (Elec: fusible, lámpara etc) to blow; (nieve etc) to melt

fúnebre [ˈfuneβre] ADJ funeral cpd, funereal

funeral [funeˈral] NM funeral

funeraria [funeˈrarja] NF undertaker's (Brit), mortician's (US)

funesto, -a [fuˈnesto, a] ADJ ill-fated; (desastroso) fatal

fungir [funˈxir] /3c/ VI: **~ de** (Am) to act as

funicular [funikuˈlar] NM (tren) funicular; (teleférico) cable car

furgón [furˈɣon] NM wagon

furgoneta [furɣoˈneta] NF (Auto, Com) (transit) van (Brit), pickup (truck) (US)

furia [ˈfurja] NF (ira) fury; (violencia) violence

furibundo, -a [furiˈβundo, a] ADJ furious

★**furioso, -a** [fuˈrjoso, a] ADJ (iracundo) furious; (violento) violent

furor [fuˈror] NM (cólera) rage; (pasión) frenzy, passion; **hacer ~** to be a sensation

furtivo, -a [furˈtiβo, a] ADJ furtive ▶ NM poacher

furúnculo [fuˈrunkulo] NM (Med) boil

fuselaje [fuseˈlaxe] NM fuselage

fusible [fuˈsiβle] NM fuse

★**fusil** [fuˈsil] NM rifle

fusilamiento [fusilaˈmjento] NM (Jur) execution by firing squad

fusilar [fusiˈlar] /1a/ VT to shoot

fusión [fuˈsjon] NF (gen) melting; (unión) fusion; (Com) merger, amalgamation

fusionar [fusjoˈnar] /1a/ VT to fuse (together); (Com) to merge ▪ **fusionarse** VR (Com) to merge, amalgamate

fusta [ˈfusta] NF (látigo) riding crop

★**fútbol** [ˈfutβol] NM football (Brit), soccer (US); **~ americano** American football (Brit), football (US); **~ sala** indoor football (Brit) o soccer (US)

futbolín [futβoˈlin] NM table football

★**futbolista** [futβoˈlista] NMF footballer

fútil [ˈfutil] ADJ trifling

futilidad [futiliˈðað], **futileza** [futiˈleθa] NF triviality

futón [fuˈton] NM futon

★**futuro, -a** [fuˈturo, a] ADJ future ▶ NM future; (Ling) future tense ▪ **futuros** NMPL (Com) futures

Gg

G, g [xe] NF (*letra*) G, g; **G de Gerona** G for George

gabacho, -a [gaˈβatʃo, a] ADJ Pyrenean; (*fam*) Frenchified ▶ NM/F Pyrenean villager; (*fam*) Frenchy

gabán [gaˈβan] NM overcoat

gabardina [gaβarˈðina] NF (*tela*) gabardine; (*prenda*) raincoat

gabinete [gaβiˈnete] NM (*Pol*) cabinet; (*estudio*) study; (*de abogados etc*) office; **~ de consulta/de lectura** consulting/reading room

gacela [gaˈθela] NF gazelle

gaceta [gaˈθeta] NF gazette

gacetilla [gaθeˈtiʎa] NF (*en periódico*) news in brief; (*de personalidades*) gossip column

gachas [ˈgatʃas] NFPL porridge *sg*

gacho, -a [ˈgatʃo, a] ADJ (*encorvado*) bent down; (*orejas*) drooping

gaditano, -a [gaðiˈtano, a] ADJ of o from Cadiz ▶ NM/F native o inhabitant of Cadiz

gaélico, -a [gaˈeliko, a] ADJ Gaelic ▶ NM/F Gael ▶ NM (*Ling*) Gaelic

gafar [gaˈfar] /1a/ VT (*fam: traer mala suerte*) to put a jinx on

★**gafas** [ˈgafas] NFPL glasses; **~ oscuras** dark glasses; **~ de sol** sunglasses

gafe [ˈgafe] ADJ: **ser ~** to be jinxed ▶ NM (*fam*) jinx

gaita [ˈgaita] NF flute; (*tb*: **gaita gallega**) bagpipes *pl*; (*dificultad*) bother; (*cosa engorrosa*) tough job

gajes [ˈgaxes] NMPL (*salario*) pay *sg*; **los ~ del oficio** occupational hazards; **~ y emolumentos** perquisites

gajo [ˈgaxo] NM (*gen*) bunch; (*de árbol*) bough; (*de naranja*) segment

gala [ˈgala] NF full dress; (*fig: lo mejor*) cream, flower; **estar de ~** to be in one's best clothes; **hacer ~ de** to display, show off; **tener algo a ~** to be proud of sth ∎ **galas** NFPL finery *sg*

galaico, -a [gaˈlaiko, a] ADJ Galician

galán [gaˈlan] NM lover, gallant; (*hombre atractivo*) ladies' man; (*Teat*): **primer ~** leading man

galante [gaˈlante] ADJ gallant; (*atento*) charming; (*cortés*) polite

galantear [galanteˈar] /1a/ VT (*hacer la corte a*) to court, woo

galanteo [galanˈteo] NM (*coqueteo*) flirting; (*de pretendiente*) wooing

galantería [galanteˈria] NF (*caballerosidad*) gallantry; (*cumplido*) politeness; (*piropo*) compliment

galápago [gaˈlapaɣo] NM (*Zool*) turtle, sea/freshwater turtle (*US*)

galardón [galarˈðon] NM award, prize

galardonar [galarðoˈnar] /1a/ VT (*premiar*) to reward; (*una obra*) to award a prize for

galaxia [gaˈlaksja] NF galaxy

galbana [galˈβana] NF (*pereza*) sloth, laziness

galeote [galeˈote] NM galley slave

galera [gaˈlera] NF (*nave*) galley; (*carro*) wagon; (*Med*) hospital ward; (*Tip*) galley

★**galería** [galeˈria] NF (*gen*) gallery; (*balcón*) veranda(h); (*de casa*) corridor; (*fam: público*) audience; **~ secreta** secret passage; **~ comercial** shopping mall

★**Gales** [ˈgales] NM: **(el País de) ~** Wales

★**galés, -esa** [gaˈles, esa] ADJ Welsh ▶ NM/F Welshman(-woman) ▶ NM (*Ling*) Welsh

galgo, -a [ˈgalɣo, a] NM/F greyhound

Galia [ˈgalja] NF Gaul

★**Galicia** [gaˈliθja] NF Galicia

galicismo [galiˈθismo] NM gallicism

Galilea [galiˈlea] NF Galilee

galimatías [galimaˈtias] NM INV (*asunto*) rigmarole; (*lenguaje*) gibberish, nonsense

gallardía [gaʎarˈðia] NF (*galantería*) dash; (*gracia*) gracefulness; (*valor*) bravery; (*elegancia*) elegance; (*nobleza*) nobleness

★**gallego, -a** [gaˈʎeɣo, a] ADJ Galician; (*Am pey*)

Spanish ▸ NM/F Galician; (AM pey) Spaniard ▸ NM (Ling) Galician; ver tb **lengua**

★**galleta** [ga'ʎeta] NF biscuit (BRIT), cookie (US); (fam: bofetada) whack, slap

★**gallina** [ga'ʎina] NF hen; **~ ciega** blind man's buff; **~ llueca** broody hen ▸ NM (fam) chicken

gallinazo [gaʎi'naso] NM (AM) turkey buzzard

gallinero [gaʎi'nero] NM (criadero) henhouse; (Teat) gods sg, top gallery; (voces) hubbub

★**gallo** ['gaʎo] NM cock, rooster; (Mus) false o wrong note; (cambio de voz) break in the voice; **en menos que canta un ~** in an instant

galo, -a ['galo, a] ADJ Gallic; (= francés) French ▸ NM/F Gaul

galón [ga'lon] NM (Costura) braid; (Mil) stripe; (medida) gallon

galopante [galo'pante] ADJ galloping

galopar [galo'par] /1a/ VI to gallop

galope [ga'lope] NM gallop; **al ~** (fig) in great haste; **a ~ tendido** at full gallop

galvanice etc [galβa'niθe] VB ver **galvanizar**

galvanizar [galβani'θar] /1f/ VT to galvanize

gama ['gama] NF (Mus) scale; (fig) range; (Zool) doe

★**gamba** ['gamba] NF prawn (BRIT), shrimp (US)

gamberrada [gambe'rraða] NF act of hooliganism

★**gamberro, -a** [gam'berro, a] NM/F hooligan, lout

gamo ['gamo] NM (Zool) buck

gamuza [ga'muθa] NF chamois; (bayeta) duster; (AM: piel) suede

★**gana** ['gana] NF (deseo) desire, wish; (apetito) appetite; (voluntad) will; (añoranza) longing; **de buena ~** willingly; **de mala ~** reluctantly; **me da ganas de** I feel like, I want to; **tener ganas de** to feel like; **no me da la (real) ~** I (really) don't feel like it; **son ganas de molestar** they're just trying to be awkward

ganadería [ganaðe'ria] NF (ganado) livestock; (ganado vacuno) cattle pl; (cría, comercio) cattle raising

ganadero, -a [gana'ðero, a] ADJ stock cpd ▸ NM/F (hacendado) rancher

ganado [ga'naðo] NM livestock; **~ caballar/cabrío** horses pl/goats pl; **~ lanar** u **ovejuno** sheep pl; **~ porcino/vacuno** pigs pl/cattle pl

★**ganador, -a** [gana'ðor, a] ADJ winning ▸ NM/F winner; (Econ) earner

★**ganancia** [ga'nanθja] NF (lo ganado) gain; (aumento) increase; (beneficio) profit; **~ bruta/líquida** gross/net profit; **sacar ~ de** to draw profit from ■ **ganancias** NFPL (ingresos) earnings; (beneficios) profit sg, winnings; **ganancias y pérdidas** profit and loss; **ganancias de capital** capital gains

ganapán [gana'pan] NM (obrero casual) odd-job man; (individuo tosco) lout

★**ganar** [ga'nar] /1a/ VT (obtener) to get, obtain;

(sacar ventaja) to gain; (Com) to earn; (Deporte, premio) to win; (derrotar) to beat; (alcanzar) to reach; (Mil: objetivo) to take; (: apoyo) to gain, win; **~ tiempo** to gain time ▸ VI (Deporte) to win ■ **ganarse** VR: **ganarse la vida** to earn one's living; **se lo ha ganado** he deserves it

ganchillo [gan'tʃiʎo] NM (para croché) crochet hook; (arte) crochet

gancho ['gantʃo] NM (gen) hook; (colgador) hanger; (pey: revendedor) tout; (fam: atractivo) sex appeal; (Boxeo: golpe) hook

gandul, -a [gan'dul, a] ADJ, NM/F good-for-nothing, layabout

★**ganga** ['ganga] NF (cosa) bargain; (chollo) cushy job

Ganges ['ganxes] NM: **el (río) ~** the Ganges

ganglio ['gangljo] NM (Anat) ganglion; (Med) swelling

gangrena [gan'grena] NF gangrene

gansada [gan'saða] NF (fam) stupid thing (to do)

★**ganso, -a** ['ganso, a] NM/F (Zool) goose (: macho) gander; (fam) idiot

Gante ['gante] NM Ghent

ganzúa [gan'θua] NF skeleton key ▸ NMF burglar

gañán [ga'ɲan] NM farmhand, farm labourer

garabatear [garaβate'ar] /1a/ VT to scribble, scrawl

garabato [gara'βato] NM (gancho) hook; (garfio) grappling iron; (escritura) scrawl, scribble; (fam) sex appeal

★**garaje** [ga'raxe] NM garage

garajista [gara'xista] NMF mechanic

garante [ga'rante] ADJ responsible ▸ NMF guarantor

garantía [garan'tia] NF guarantee; (seguridad) pledge; (compromiso) undertaking; (Jur: caución) warranty; **de máxima ~** absolutely guaranteed; **~ de trabajo** job security

garantice etc [garan'tiθe] VB ver **garantizar**

garantizar [garanti'θar] /1f/ VT (hacerse responsable de) to vouch for; (asegurar) to guarantee

garbanzo [gar'βanθo] NM chickpea

garbeo [gar'βeo] NM: **darse un ~** to go for a walk

garbo ['garβo] NM grace, elegance; (desenvoltura) jauntiness; (de mujer) glamour; **andar con ~** to walk gracefully

garboso, -a [gar'βoso, a] ADJ graceful, elegant

garete [ga'rete] NM: **irse al ~** to go to the dogs

garfio ['garfjo] NM grappling iron; (gancho) hook; (Alpinismo) climbing iron

gargajo [gar'ɣaxo] NM phlegm, sputum

★**garganta** [gar'ɣanta] NF (interna) throat; (externa, de botella) neck; (Geo: barranco) ravine; (: desfiladero) narrow pass

gargantilla [garɣan'tiʎa] NF necklace

gárgara ['garɣara] NF gargle, gargling; **hacer gárgaras** to gargle; **¡vete a hacer gárgaras!** (*fam*) go to blazes!

gargarear [garɣare'ar] /**1a**/ VI (*Am*) to gargle

gárgola ['garɣola] NF gargoyle

garita [ga'rita] NF cabin, hut; (*Mil*) sentry box; (*puesto de vigilancia*) lookout post

garito [ga'rito] NM (*lugar*) gaming house *o* den

garra ['garra] NF (*de gato, Tec*) claw; (*de ave*) talon; (*fam*) hand, paw; (*fig: de canción etc*) bite; **caer en las garras de algn** to fall into sb's clutches

garrafa [ga'rrafa] NF carafe, decanter

garrafal [garra'fal] ADJ enormous, terrific; (*error*) terrible

garrapata [garra'pata] NF (*Zool*) tick

garrotazo [garro'taθo] NM blow with a stick *o* club

garrote [ga'rrote] NM (*palo*) stick; (*porra*) club, cudgel; (*suplicio*) garrotte

garza ['garθa] NF heron

★**gas** [gas] NM gas; (*vapores*) fumes *pl*; **gases de escape** exhaust (fumes); **gases lacrimógenos** tear gas *sg*

gasa ['gasa] NF gauze; (*de pañal*) nappy liner

gaseoso, -a [gase'oso, a] ADJ gassy, fizzy ▶ NF lemonade, pop (*fam*)

gasoducto [gaso'ðukto] NM gas pipeline

gasoil [ga'soil], **gasóleo** [ga'soleo] NM diesel (oil)

★**gasolina** [gaso'lina] NF petrol, gas(oline) (*US*); **~ sin plomo** unleaded petrol

★**gasolinera** [gasoli'nera] NF petrol (*BRIT*) *o* gas (*US*) station

★**gastado, -a** [gas'taðo, a] ADJ (*dinero*) spent; (*ropa*) worn out; (*usado: frase etc*) trite

★**gastar** [gas'tar] /**1a**/ VT (*dinero, tiempo*) to spend; (*consumir*) to use (up), consume; (*desperdiciar*) to waste; (*llevar*) to wear; **~ en** to spend on; **~ bromas** to crack jokes; **¿qué número gastas?** what size (shoe) do you take? ■ **gastarse** VR to wear out; (*terminarse*) to run out; (*estropearse*) to waste

★**gasto** ['gasto] NM (*desembolso*) expenditure, spending; (*cantidad gastada*) outlay, expense; (*consumo, uso*) use; (*desgaste*) waste ■ **gastos** NMPL (*desembolsos*) expenses; (*cargos*) charges, costs; **gastos bancarios** bank charges; **gastos corrientes** (*Com*) running expenses; (*Admin*) revenue expenditure; **gastos de distribución** (*Com*) distribution costs; **gastos de mantenimiento** maintenance expenses; **gastos de tramitación** (*Com*) handling charge *sg*; **gastos fijos** (*Com*) fixed charges; **gastos generales** overheads; **gastos operacionales** operating costs; **gastos vencidos** (*Com*) accrued charges; **cubrir gastos** to cover expenses; **meterse en gastos** to incur expense

gastronomía [gastrono'mia] NF gastronomy

gata ['gata] NF (*Zool*) she-cat; **andar a gatas** to go on all fours

gatear [gate'ar] /**1a**/ VI (*andar a gatas*) to go on all fours

gatillo [ga'tiʎo] NM (*de arma de fuego*) trigger; (*de dentista*) forceps

★**gato** ['gato] NM (*Zool*) cat; (*Tec*) jack; **~ de Angora** Angora cat; **~ montés** wildcat; **dar a algn ~ por liebre** to take sb in; **aquí hay ~ encerrado** there's something fishy here

GATT [gat] SIGLA M (= *Acuerdo General sobre Aranceles Aduaneros y Comercio*) GATT

gatuno, -a [ga'tuno, a] ADJ feline

gaucho, -a ['gautʃo, a] ADJ, NM/F gaucho

gaveta [ga'βeta] NF drawer

gavilán [gaβi'lan] NM sparrowhawk

gavilla [ga'βiʎa] NF sheaf

gaviota [ga'βjota] NF seagull

gay [ge] ADJ gay, homosexual

gazapo [ga'θapo] NM young rabbit

gaznate [gaθ'nate] NM (*pescuezo*) gullet; (*garganta*) windpipe

★**gazpacho** [gaθ'patʃo] NM gazpacho

GB ABR (= *gigabyte*) GB

gel [xel] NM gel; **~ de baño/ducha** bath/shower gel

gelatina [xela'tina] NF jelly; (*polvos etc*) gelatine

gema ['xema] NF gem

★**gemelo, -a** [xe'melo, a] ADJ, NM/F twin ■ **gemelos** NMPL (*de camisa*) cufflinks; **gemelos de campo** field glasses, binoculars; **gemelos de teatro** opera glasses

gemido [xe'miðo] NM (*quejido*) moan, groan; (*lamento*) wail, howl

Géminis ['xeminis] NM (*Astro*) Gemini

gemir [xe'mir] /**3k**/ VI (*quejarse*) to moan, groan; (*animal*) to whine; (*viento*) to howl

gen [xen] NM gene

gen. ABR (*Ling*) = **género**; **genitivo**

gendarme [xen'darme] NM (*Am*) policeman

genealogía [xenealo'xia] NF genealogy

★**generación** [xenera'θjon] NF generation; **primera/segunda/tercera/cuarta ~** (*Inform*) first/second/third/fourth generation

generado, -a [xene'raðo, a] ADJ (*Inform*): **~ por ordenador** computer generated

generador [xenera'ðor] NM generator; **~ de programas** (*Inform*) program generator

★**general** [xene'ral] ADJ general; (*común*) common; (*pey: corriente*) rife; (*frecuente*) usual ▶ NM general; **~ de brigada/de división** brigadier-/major-general; **por lo o en ~** in general

generalice *etc* [xenera'liθe] VB *ver* **generalizar**

generalidad [xenerali'ðað] NF generality

Generalitat [jenerali'tat] NF regional government of Catalonia; **~ Valenciana** regional government of Valencia

generalización [xeneraliθa'θjon] NF generalization

generalizar [xenerali'θar] /**1f**/ VT to generalize

■ **generalizarse** VR to become generalized, spread; (*difundirse*) to become widely known

★**generalmente** [xeneral'mente] ADV generally

generar [xene'rar] /**1a**/ VT to generate

genérico, -a [xe'neriko, a] ADJ generic

★**género** ['xenero] NM (*clase*) kind, sort; (*tipo*) type; (*Bio*) genus; (*Ling*) gender; (*Com*) material; **~ humano** human race; **~ chico** (*zarzuela*) Spanish operetta ■ **géneros** NMPL (*productos*) goods; **géneros de punto** knitwear *sg*

generosidad [xenerosi'ðað] NF generosity

★**generoso, -a** [xene'roso, a] ADJ generous

genético, -a [xe'netiko, a] ADJ genetic ▶ NF genetics *sg*

★**genial** [xe'njal] ADJ inspired; (*idea*) brilliant; (*estupendo*) wonderful; (*afable*) genial

genialidad [xenjali'ðað] NF (*singularidad*) genius; (*acto genial*) stroke of genius; **es una ~ suya** it's one of his brilliant ideas

genio ['xenjo] NM (*carácter*) nature, disposition; (*humor*) temper; (*facultad creadora*) genius; **mal ~** bad temper; **~ vivo** quick o hot temper; **de mal ~** bad-tempered

genital [xeni'tal] ADJ genital ▶ NM: **genitales** genitals, genital organs

genitivo [xeni'tiβo] NM (*Ling*) genitive

genocidio [xeno'θiðjo] NM genocide

genoma [xe'noma] NM genome

Génova ['xenoβa] NF Genoa

genovés, -esa [xeno'βes, esa] ADJ, NM/F Genoese

★**gente** ['xente] NF (*personas*) people *pl*; (*raza*) race; (*nación*) nation; (*parientes*) relatives *pl*; **~ bien/baja** posh/lower-class people *pl*; **~ menuda** (*niños*) children *pl*; **es buena ~** (*esp AM fam*) he's a good sort; **una ~ como usted** (*AM*) a person like you

gentil [xen'til] ADJ (*elegante*) graceful; (*encantador*) charming; (*Rel*) gentile

> Do not translate the Spanish word **gentil** by *gentle*.

gentileza [xenti'leθa] NF grace; charm; (*cortesía*) courtesy; **por ~ de** by courtesy of

gentilicio, -a [xenti'liθjo, a] ADJ (*familiar*) family *cpd*

gentío [xen'tio] NM crowd, throng

gentuza [xen'tuθa] NF (*pey: plebe*) rabble; (: *chusma*) riffraff

genuflexión [xenuflek'sjon] NF genuflexion

genuino, -a [xe'nwino, a] ADJ genuine

GEO ['xeo] NMPL ABR (*ESP*: = *Grupos Especiales de Operaciones*) *Special Police Units used in anti-terrorist operations etc*

★**geografía** [xeoɣra'fia] NF geography

geográfico, -a [xeo'ɣrafiko, a] ADJ geographic(al)

geolocalización [xeolokaliθa'θjon] NF geolocation

geolocalizar [xeolokali'θar] /**1f**/ VT to geolocate

geología [xeolo'xia] NF geology

geólogo, -a [xe'oloɣo, a] NM/F geologist

geometría [xeome'tria] NF geometry

geométrico, -a [xeo'metriko, a] ADJ geometric(al)

Georgia [xe'orxja] NF Georgia

georgiano, -a [xeor'xjano, a] ADJ, NM/F Georgian ▶ NM (*Ling*) Georgian

geranio [xe'ranjo] NM (*Bot*) geranium

gerencia [xe'renθja] NF management; (*cargo*) post of manager; (*oficina*) manager's office

★**gerente** [xe'rente] NMF (*supervisor*) manager; (*jefe*) director

geriatría [xerja'tria] NF (*Med*) geriatrics *sg*

geriátrico, -a [xer'jatriko, a] ADJ geriatric

germano, -a [xer'mano, a] ADJ German, Germanic ▶ NM/F German

germen ['xermen] NM germ

germinar [xermi'nar] /**1a**/ VI to germinate; (*brotar*) to sprout

gerundense [xerun'dense] ADJ of o from Gerona ▶ NMF native o inhabitant of Gerona

gerundio [xe'rundjo] NM (*Ling*) gerund

gestación [xesta'θjon] NF gestation

gesticulación [xestikula'θjon] NF (*ademán*) gesticulation; (*mueca*) grimace

gesticular [xestiku'lar] /**1a**/ VI (*con ademanes*) to gesticulate; (*con muecas*) to make faces

gestión [xes'tjon] NF management; (*diligencia, acción*) negotiation; **hacer las gestiones preliminares** to do the groundwork; **~ de cartera** (*Com*) portfolio management; **~ financiera** (*Com*) financial management; **~ interna** (*Inform*) housekeeping; **~ de personal** personnel management; **~ de riesgos** (*Com*) risk management

gestionar [xestjo'nar] /**1a**/ VT (*tratar de arreglar*) to try to arrange; (*llevar*) to manage

gesto ['xesto] NM (*mueca*) grimace; (*ademán*) gesture; **hacer gestos** to make faces

gestor, a [xes'tor, a] ADJ managing ▶ NM/F manager; (*promotor*) promoter; (*agente*) business agent

gestoría [xesto'ria] NF *agency undertaking business with government departments, insurance companies etc*

Gibraltar [xiβral'tar] NM Gibraltar

gibraltareño, -a [xiβralta'reɲo, a] ADJ of o from Gibraltar, Gibraltarian ▶ NM/F Gibraltarian

giga ['xiɣa] N gig (= *gigabyte*)

gigabyte ['xiɣaβait] NM gigabyte

gigante [xi'ɣante] ADJ, NMF giant

gigantesco, -a [xiɣan'tesko, a] ADJ gigantic

gijonés, -esa [xixo'nes, esa] ADJ of o from Gijón ▶ NM/F native o inhabitant of Gijón

gilipollas [xili'poʎas] (*fam!*) ADJ INV daft ▶ NMF INV berk (*BRIT fam*), jerk (*esp US fam*)

gilipollez [xilipoˈʎeθ] NF (*fam*): **es una ~** that's a load of crap (*fam*!); **decir gilipolleces** to talk crap (*fam*!)

gima *etc* [ˈxima] VB *ver* **gemir**

★**gimnasia** [ximˈnasja] NF gymnastics *pl*; **confundir la ~ con la magnesia** to get things mixed up

★**gimnasio** [ximˈnasjo] NM gym(nasium)

★**gimnasta** [ximˈnasta] NMF gymnast

gimnástica [ximˈnastika] NF gymnastics *sg*

gimotear [ximoteˈar] /1a/ VI to whine, whimper; (*lloriquear*) to snivel

gincana [jinˈkana] NF gymkhana

Ginebra [xiˈneβra] NF Geneva

ginebra [xiˈneβra] NF gin

ginecología [xinekoloˈxia] NF gyn(a)ecology

ginecológico, -a [xinekoˈloxiko, a] ADJ gyn(a)ecological

ginecólogo, -a [xineˈkoloɣo, a] NM/F gyn(a)ecologist

gira [ˈxira] NF tour, trip

★**girar** [xiˈrar] /1a/ VT (*dar la vuelta*) to turn (around); (: *rápidamente*) to spin; (*Com: giro postal*) to draw; (*comerciar: letra de cambio*) to issue ▶ VI to turn (round); (*dar vueltas*) to rotate; (*rápido*) to spin; **la conversación giraba en torno a las elecciones** the conversation centred on the election; **~ en descubierto** to overdraw

girasol [xiraˈsol] NM sunflower

giratorio, -a [xiraˈtorjo, a] ADJ (*gen*) revolving; (*puente*) swing *cpd*; (*silla*) swivel *cpd*

giro [ˈxiro] NM (*movimiento*) turn, revolution; (*Ling*) expression; (*Com*) draft; (*de sucesos*) trend, course; **~ bancario** bank draft, bank giro; **~ de existencias** (*Com*) stock turnover; **~ postal** money order

gis [xis] NM (*Am*) chalk

gitano, -a [xiˈtano, a] ADJ, NM/F gypsy

glacial [glaˈθjal] ADJ icy, freezing

glaciar [glaˈθjar] NM glacier

glándula [ˈglandula] NF (*Anat*, *Bot*) gland

glicerina [gliθeˈrina] NF (*Tec*) glycerin(e)

global [gloˈβal] ADJ (*en conjunto*) global; (*completo*) total; (*investigación*) full; (*suma*) lump *cpd*

globalización [gloβaliθaˈθjon] NF globalization

globo [ˈgloβo] NM (*esfera*) globe, sphere; (*aeróstato, juguete*) balloon

glóbulo [ˈgloβulo] NM globule; (*Anat*) corpuscle; **~ blanco/rojo** white/red corpuscle

gloria [ˈglorja] NF glory; (*fig*) delight; (*delicia*) bliss

★**glorieta** [gloˈrjeta] NF (*de jardín*) bower, arbour, arbor (*US*); (*Auto*) roundabout (*BRIT*), traffic circle (*US*); (*plaza redonda*) circus; (*cruce*) junction

glorificar [glorifiˈkar] /1g/ VT (*enaltecer*) to glorify, praise

glorifique *etc* [gloriˈfike] VB *ver* **glorificar**

glorioso, -a [gloˈrjoso, a] ADJ glorious

glosa [ˈglosa] NF comment; (*explicación*) gloss

glosar [gloˈsar] /1a/ VT (*comentar*) to comment on

glosario [gloˈsarjo] NM glossary

★**glotón, -ona** [gloˈton, ona] ADJ gluttonous, greedy ▶ NM/F glutton

glotonería [glotoneˈria] NF gluttony, greed

glucosa [gluˈkosa] NF glucose

glúteo [ˈgluteo] NM (*fam: nalga*) buttock

G.N. ABR (*NICARAGUA*, *PANAMA*: = Guardia Nacional) police

gnomo [ˈnomo] NM gnome

gobernación [goβernaˈθjon] NF government, governing; (*Pol*) Provincial Governor's office; **Ministro de la G~** Minister of the Interior, Home Secretary (*BRIT*)

gobernador, -a [goβernaˈðor, a] ADJ governing ▶ NM/F governor

gobernanta [goβerˈnanta] NF (*esp Am: niñera*) governess

gobernante [goβerˈnante] ADJ governing ▶ NM ruler, governor ▶ NF (*en hotel etc*) housekeeper

gobernar [goβerˈnar] /1j/ VT (*dirigir*) to guide, direct; (*Pol*) to rule, govern ▶ VI to govern; (*Naut*) to steer; **~ mal** to misgovern

★**gobierno** [goˈβjerno] VB *ver* **gobernar** ▶ NM (*Pol*) government; (*gestión*) management; (*dirección*) guidance, direction; (*Naut*) steering; (*puesto*) governorship

goce *etc* [ˈgoθe] VB *ver* **gozar** ▶ NM enjoyment

godo, -a [ˈgoðo, a] NM/F Goth; (*Am pey*) Spaniard

★**gol** [gol] NM goal

golear [goleˈar] /1a/ VT (*marcar*) to score a goal against

golf [golf] NM golf

golfo, -a [ˈgolfo, a] NM/F (*pilluelo*) street urchin; (*vagabundo*) tramp; (*gorrón*) loafer; (*gamberro*) lout ▶ NM (*Geo*) gulf ▶ NF (!: *insulto*) slut (!)

golondrina [golonˈdrina] NF swallow

golosina [goloˈsina] NF titbit; (*dulce*) sweet

★**goloso, -a** [goˈloso, a] ADJ sweet-toothed; (*fam: glotón*) greedy

★**golpe** [ˈgolpe] NM blow; (*de puño*) punch; (*de mano*) smack; (*de remo*) stroke; (*Fútbol*) kick; (*Tenis etc*) hit, shot; (*mala suerte*) misfortune; (*fam: atraco*) job, heist (*US*); (*fig: choque*) clash; **no dar ~** to be bone idle; **de un ~** with one blow; **de ~** suddenly; **~ (de estado)** coup (d'état); **~ de gracia** coup de grâce (*tb fig*); **~ de fortuna/maestro** stroke of luck/genius; **cerrar una puerta de ~** to slam a door

★**golpear** [golpeˈar] /1a/ VT, VI to strike, knock; (*asestar*) to beat; (*de puño*) to punch; (*golpetear*) to tap; (*mesa*) to bang

golpista [golˈpista] ADJ: **intentona ~** coup attempt ▶ NMF participant in a coup (d'état)

golpiza [gol'pisa] NF: **dar una ~ a algn** (AM) to beat sb up

★**goma** ['goma] NF (*caucho*) rubber; (*elástico*) elastic; (*tira*) rubber o (BRIT) elastic band; (*fam: preservativo*) condom; (*droga*) hashish; (*explosivo*) plastic explosive; **~ (de borrar)** eraser, rubber (BRIT); **~ de mascar** chewing gum; **~ de pegar** gum, glue

goma-espuma [gomaes'puma] NF foam rubber

gomina [go'mina] NF hair gel

gomita [go'mita] NF rubber o (BRIT) elastic band

góndola ['gondola] NF (*barco*) gondola; (*de tren*) goods wagon

Google® ['gugel] NM Google®

googlear [guɣle'ar] /**1a**/ VT to google

★**gordo, -a** ['gorðo, a] ADJ (*gen*) fat; (*persona*) plump; (*agua*) hard; (*fam*) enormous; **el (premio) ~** (*en lotería*) first prize ▶ NM/F fat man o woman; **¡~!** (*fam*) fatty!; *see note*

The **Gordo** refers to the jackpot associated with the *Lotería Nacional* (Spanish national lottery), especially at Christmas. Winnings from the *Sorteo Extraordinario de Navidad* (special Christmas draw) on December 22nd amount to several million euros and many communities throughout the country tune in to the draw in the hope of winning a life-changing amount of money.

gordura [gor'ðura] NF fat; (*corpulencia*) fatness, stoutness

gorgojo [gor'ɣoxo] NM (*insecto*) grub

gorgorito [gorɣo'rito] NM (*gorjeo*) trill, warble

gorila [go'rila] NM gorilla; (*fam*) tough, thug; (*guardaespaldas*) bodyguard

gorjear [gorxe'ar] /**1a**/ VI to twitter, chirp

gorjeo [gor'xeo] NM twittering, chirping

★**gorra** ['gorra] NF (*gen*) cap; (*de niño*) bonnet; (*militar*) bearskin; **~ de montar/de paño/de punto/de visera** riding/cloth/knitted/peaked cap; **andar** o **ir** o **vivir de ~** to sponge, scrounge; **entrar de ~** (*fam*) to gatecrash

gorrión [go'rrjon] NM sparrow

gorro ['gorro] NM cap; (*de niño, mujer*) bonnet; **estoy hasta el ~** I am fed up

gorrón, -ona [go'rron, ona] NM pebble; (*Tec*) pivot ▶ NM/F scrounger

gorronear [gorrone'ar] /**1a**/ VI (*fam*) to sponge, scrounge

★**gota** ['gota] NF (*gen*) drop; (*de pintura*) blob; (*de sudor*) bead; (*Med*) gout; **~ a ~** drop by drop; **caer a gotas** to drip

gotear [gote'ar] /**1a**/ VI to drip; (*escurrir*) to trickle; (*salirse*) to leak; (*cirio*) to gutter; (*lloviznar*) to drizzle

gotera [go'tera] NF leak

gótico, -a ['gotiko, a] ADJ Gothic

★**gozar** [go'θar] /**1f**/ VI to enjoy o.s.; **~ de** (*disfrutar*) to enjoy; (*poseer*) to possess; **~ de buena salud** to enjoy good health

gozne ['goθne] NM hinge

gozo ['goθo] NM (*alegría*) joy; (*placer*) pleasure; **¡mi ~ en el pozo!** that's torn it!, just my luck!

g.p. NM ABR (= *giro postal*) m.o.

GPS NM ABR (= *global positioning system*) GPS

gr. ABR (= *gramo(s)*) g

grabación [graβa'θjon] NF recording

grabado, -a [gra'βaðo, a] ADJ (*Mus*) recorded; (*en cinta*) taped, on tape ▶ NM print, engraving; **~ al agua fuerte** etching; **~ al aguatinta** aquatint; **~ en cobre** copperplate; **~ en madera** woodcut; **~ rupestre** rock carving

grabador, -a [graβa'ðor, a] NM/F engraver ▶ NF tape-recorder; **grabadora de CD/DVD** CD/DVD writer

★**grabar** [gra'βar] /**1a**/ VT to engrave; (*discos, cintas*) to record; (*impresionar*) to impress

gracejo [gra'θexo] NM (*ingenio*) wit, humour; (*elegancia*) grace

gracia ['graθja] NF (*encanto*) grace, gracefulness; (*Rel*) grace; (*chiste*) joke; (*humor*) humour, wit; **¡muchas gracias!** thanks very much!; **gracias a** thanks to; **tener ~** (*chiste etc*) to be funny; **¡qué ~!** how funny!; (*irónico*) what a nerve!; **no me hace ~** (*broma*) it's not funny; (*plan*) I am not too keen; **con gracias anticipadas/repetidas** thanking you in advance/again; **dar las gracias a algn por algo** to thank sb for sth

grácil ['graθil] ADJ (*sutil*) graceful; (*delgado*) slender; (*delicado*) delicate

★**gracioso, -a** [gra'θjoso, a] ADJ (*garboso*) graceful; (*chistoso*) funny; (*cómico*) comical; (*agudo*) witty; (*título*) gracious; **su graciosa Majestad** His/Her Gracious Majesty ▶ NM/F (*Teat*) comic character, fool

grada ['graða] NF (*de escalera*) step; (*de anfiteatro*) tier, row ■ **gradas** NFPL (*de estadio*) terraces

gradación [graða'θjon] NF gradation; (*serie*) graded series

gradería [graðe'ria] NF (*gradas*) (flight of) steps pl; (*de anfiteatro*) tiers pl, rows pl; **~ cubierta** covered stand

★**grado** ['graðo] NM degree; (*etapa*) stage, step; (*nivel*) rate; (*de parentesco*) order of lineage; (*de aceite, vino*) grade; (*grada*) step; (*Escol*) class, year, grade (US); (*Univ*) degree; (*Ling*) degree of comparison; (*Mil*) rank; **de buen ~** willingly; **en sumo ~, en ~ superlativo** in the highest degree; **~ centígrado/Fahrenheit** degree centigrade/Fahrenheit; *see note*

The **Grado** is the degree awarded at the end of an undergraduate course which replaces the former *Diplomado* and *Licenciado* qualifications. Lasting four years, the course consists of a basic training element, compulsory subjects, optional subjects, a work experience placement, a dissertation, and cultural activities.

graduación [graðwa'θjon] NF (*acto*) gradation; (*clasificación*) rating; (*del alcohol*) proof, strength; (*Escol*) graduation; (*Mil*) rank; **de alta ~** high-ranking

gradual [gra'ðwal] ADJ gradual

graduar [gra'ðwar] /**1e**/ VT (*gen*) to graduate; (*medir*) to gauge; (*Tec*) to calibrate; (*Univ*) to confer a degree on; (*Mil*) to commission ■ **graduarse** VR to graduate; **graduarse la vista** to have one's eyes tested

grafía [gra'fia] NF (*escritura*) writing; (*ortografía*) spelling

gráfico, -a ['grafiko, a] ADJ graphic; (*fig: vívido*) vivid, lively ▶ NM diagram ▶ NF graph; **~ de barras** (*Com*) bar chart; **~ de sectores** o **de tarta** (*Com*) pie chart ■ **gráficos** NMPL (*tb Inform*) graphics; **gráficos empresariales** (*Com*) business graphics

grafitero, -a [grafi'tero, a] NM/F graffiti artist

grafito [gra'fito] NM (*Tec*) graphite, black lead

grafología [grafolo'xia] NF graphology

gragea [gra'xea] NF (*Med*) pill; (*caramelo*) dragée

grajo ['graxo] NM rook

Gral. ABR (*Mil*: = *General*) Gen.

gramático, -a [gra'matiko, a] NM/F (*persona*) grammarian ▶ NF grammar

★**gramo** ['gramo] NM gramme (BRIT), gram (US)

gran [gran] ADJ (*antes de nmsg*) ver **grande**

grana ['grana] NF (*Bot*) seedling; (*color*) scarlet; **ponerse como la ~** to go as red as a beetroot

Granada [gra'naða] NF (*ciudad*) Granada; (*país*) Grenada

granada [gra'naða] NF pomegranate; (*Mil*) grenade; **~ de mano** hand grenade; **~ de metralla** shrapnel shell

granadilla [grana'ðiʎa] NF (*Am*) passion fruit

granadino, -a [grana'ðino, a] ADJ of o from Granada ▶ NM/F native o inhabitant of Granada ▶ NF grenadine

granar [gra'nar] /**1a**/ VI to seed

granate [gra'nate] ADJ INV maroon ▶ NM garnet; (*color*) maroon

★**Gran Bretaña** [grambre'taɲa] NF Great Britain

Gran Canaria [granka'narja] NF Grand Canary

grancanario, -a [granka'narjo, a] ADJ of o from Grand Canary ▶ NM/F native o inhabitant of Grand Canary

★**grande** ['grande] ADJ (*antes de nmsg* o *nfsg*: **gran**) (*de tamaño*) big, large; (*alto*) tall; (*distinguido*) great; (*impresionante*) grand; **¿cómo es de ~?** how big is it?, what size is it?; **pasarlo en ~** to have a tremendous time ▶ NM grandee

---

Big se usa con más frecuencia que **large** para referirse a algo grande: *¡Qué jardín tan grande!* **What a big garden!**
Ambos se utilizan en relación a objetos, pero para cantidades se usa más **large**: *grandes cantidades de dinero* **large sums of money**.

---

grandeza [gran'deθa] NF greatness; (*tamaño*) bigness; (*esplendor*) grandness; (*nobleza*) nobility

grandioso, -a [gran'djoso, a] ADJ magnificent, grand

grandullón, -ona [granðu'ʎon, ona] ADJ oversized

granel [gra'nel] NM (*montón*) heap; **a ~** (*Com*) in bulk

granero [gra'nero] NM granary, barn

granice *etc* [gra'niθe] VB ver **granizar**

granito [gra'nito] NM (*Agr*) small grain; (*roca*) granite

granizada [grani'θaða] NF hailstorm; (*fig*) hail; **una ~ de balas** a hail of bullets

granizado [grani'θaðo] NM iced drink; **~ de café** iced coffee

granizar [grani'θar] /**1f**/ VI to hail

★**granizo** [gra'niθo] NM hail

★**granja** ['granxa] NF (*gen*) farm; **~ avícola** chicken o poultry farm

granjear [granxe'ar] /**1a**/ VT (*cobrar*) to earn; (*ganar*) to win; (*avanzar*) to gain ■ **granjearse** VR (*amistad etc*) to gain for o.s.

★**granjero, -a** [gran'xero, a] NM/F farmer

grano ['grano] NM grain; (*semilla*) seed; (*baya*) berry; (*Med*) pimple, spot; (*partícula*) particle; (*punto*) speck; **~ de café** coffee bean; **ir al ~** to get to the point ■ **granos** NMPL cereals

granuja [gra'nuxa] NM rogue; (*golfillo*) urchin

grapa ['grapa] NF staple; (*Tec*) clamp; (*sujetador*) clip, fastener; (*Arq*) cramp

grapadora [grapa'ðora] NF stapler

GRAPO ['grapo] NM ABR (*Esp Pol*) = **Grupo de Resistencia Antifascista Primero de Octubre**

★**grasa** ['grasa] NF ver **graso**

grasiento, -a [gra'sjento, a] ADJ greasy; (*de aceite*) oily; (*mugriento*) filthy

graso, -a ['graso, a] ADJ fatty; (*aceitoso*) greasy, oily ▶ NF (*gen*) grease; (*de cocina*) fat, lard; (*sebo*) suet; (*mugre*) filth; (*Auto*) oil; (*lubricante*) grease; **grasa de ballena** blubber; **grasa de pescado** fish oil

grasoso, -a [gra'soso, a] ADJ (*Am*) greasy, sticky

gratificación [gratifika'θjon] NF (*propina*) tip; (*aguinaldo*) gratuity; (*bono*) bonus; (*recompensa*) reward

gratificar [gratifi'kar] /**1g**/ VT (*dar propina*) to tip; (*premiar*) to reward; **"se gratificará"** "a reward is offered"

gratifique *etc* [grati'fike] VB ver **gratificar**

gratinar [grati'nar] /**1a**/ VT to cook au gratin

★**gratis** ['gratis] ADV free, for nothing

gratitud [grati'tuð] NF gratitude

grato, -a ['grato, a] ADJ (*agradable*) pleasant, agreeable; (*bienvenido*) welcome; **nos es ~ informarle que ...** we are pleased to inform you that ...

★gratuito, -a [gra'twito, a] ADJ (*gratis*) free; (*sin razón*) gratuitous; (*acusación*) unfounded

grava ['graβa] NF (*guijos*) gravel; (*piedra molida*) crushed stone; (*en carreteras*) road metal

gravamen [gra'βamen] NM (*carga*) burden; (*impuesto*) tax; **libre de ~** (*Econ*) free from encumbrances

gravar [gra'βar] /1a/ VT to burden; (*Com*) to tax; (*Econ*) to assess for tax; **~ con impuestos** to burden with taxes

★grave ['graβe] ADJ heavy; (*fig, Med*) grave, serious; (*importante*) important; (*herida*) severe; (*Mus*) low, deep; (*Ling: acento*) grave; **estar ~** to be seriously ill

gravedad [graβe'ðað] NF gravity; (*fig*) seriousness; (*grandeza*) importance; (*dignidad*) dignity; (*Mus*) depth

grávido, -a ['graβiðo, a] ADJ (*preñada*) pregnant

gravilla [gra'βiʎa] NF gravel

gravitación [graβita'θjon] NF gravitation

gravitar [graβi'tar] /1a/ VI to gravitate; **~ sobre** to rest on

gravoso, -a [gra'βoso, a] ADJ (*pesado*) burdensome; (*costoso*) costly

graznar [graθ'nar] /1a/ VI (*cuervo*) to squawk; (*pato*) to quack; (*hablar ronco*) to croak

graznido [graθ'niðo] NM squawk; croak

Grecia ['greθja] NF Greece

gregario, -a [gre'ɣarjo, a] ADJ gregarious; **instinto ~** herd instinct

gremio ['gremjo] NM trade, industry; (*asociación*) professional association, guild

greña ['greɲa] NF (*cabellos*) shock of hair; (*maraña*) tangle; **andar a la ~** to bicker, squabble

greñudo, -a [gre'ɲuðo, a] ADJ (*persona*) dishevelled; (*pelo*) tangled

gresca ['greska] NF uproar; (*trifulca*) row

griego, -a ['grjeɣo, a] ADJ Greek, Grecian ▶ NM/F Greek ▶ NM (*Ling*) Greek

grieta ['grjeta] NF crack; (*hendidura*) chink; (*quiebra*) crevice; (*Med*) chap; (*Pol*) rift

grifa ['grifa] NF (*fam: droga*) marijuana

grifo ['grifo] NM tap (*BRIT*), faucet (*US*); (*AM*) petrol (*BRIT*) o gas (*US*) station

grilletes [gri'ʎetes] NMPL fetters, shackles

grillo ['griʎo] NM (*Zool*) cricket; (*Bot*) shoot ■ **grillos** NMPL shackles, irons

grima ['grima] NF (*horror*) loathing; (*desagrado*) reluctance; (*desazón*) uneasiness; **me da ~** it makes me sick

gringo, -a ['gringo, a] (*AM fam, pey*) ADJ (*norteamericano*) Yankee; (*idioma*) foreign; (*extranjero*) foreign ▶ NM/F (*extranjero*) foreigner; (*norteamericano*) Yank

gripa ['gripa] NF (*AM*) flu, influenza

gripe ['gripe] NF flu, influenza; **~ A** swine flu; **~ porcina** swine flu; **~ aviar** bird flu

gris [gris] ADJ grey

grisáceo, -a [gri'saθeo, a] ADJ greyish

grisoso, -a [gri'soso, a] ADJ (*AM*) greyish

★gritar [gri'tar] /1a/ VT, VI to shout, yell; **¡no grites!** stop shouting!

★grito ['grito] NM shout, yell; (*de horror*) scream; **a ~ pelado** at the top of one's voice; **poner el ~ en el cielo** to scream blue murder; **es el último ~** (*de moda*) it's all the rage

groenlandés, -esa [groenlan'des, esa] ADJ Greenland *cpd* ▶ NM/F Greenlander

Groenlandia [groen'landja] NF Greenland

grosella [gro'seʎa] NF (red)currant; **~ negra** blackcurrant

grosería [grose'ria] NF (*actitud*) rudeness; (*comentario*) vulgar comment; (*palabrota*) swearword

★grosero, -a [gro'sero, a] ADJ (*poco cortés*) rude, bad-mannered; (*ordinario*) vulgar, crude

grosor [gro'sor] NM thickness

grotesco, -a [gro'tesko, a] ADJ grotesque; (*absurdo*) bizarre

grúa ['grua] NF (*Tec*) crane; (*de petróleo*) derrick; **~ corrediza** o **móvil/de pescante/puente/de torre** travelling/jib/overhead/tower crane

★grueso, -a ['grweso, a] ADJ thick; (*persona*) stout; (*calidad*) coarse ▶ NM bulk; (*espesor*) thickness; (*densidad*) density; (*de gente*) main body, mass; **el ~ de** the bulk of

grulla ['gruʎa] NF (*Zool*) crane

grumete [gru'mete] NM (*Naut*) cabin o ship's boy

grumo ['grumo] NM (*coágulo*) clot, lump; (*masa*) dollop

gruñido [gru'niðo] NM grunt, growl; (*fig*) grumble

gruñir [gru'nir] /3h/ VI (*animal*) to grunt, growl; (*fam*) to grumble

gruñón, -ona [gru'non, ona] ADJ grumpy ▶ NM/F grumbler

grupa ['grupa] NF (*Zool*) rump

★grupo ['grupo] NM group; (*Tec*) unit, set; (*de árboles*) cluster; **~ sanguíneo** blood group; **~ de presión** pressure group

gruta ['gruta] NF grotto

Gta. ABR (*Auto*) = **glorieta**

guaca ['gwaka] NF Indian tomb

guacamole [gwaka'mole] NM (*AM*) avocado salad

guachimán [gwatʃi'man] NM (*AM*) night watchman

guacho, -a ['gwatʃo, a] NM/F (*AM*) homeless child

guadalajareño, -a [gwaðalaxa'reɲo, a] ADJ of o from Guadalajara ▶ NM/F native o inhabitant of Guadalajara

Guadalquivir [gwaðalki'βir] NM: **el (río) ~** the Guadalquivir

guadaña [gwa'ðaɲa] NF scythe

guadañar [gwaða'ɲar] /**1a**/ VT to scythe, mow
Guadiana [gwa'ðjana] NM: **el (río) ~** the Guadiana
guagua ['gwaɣwa] NF (AM, CANARIAS) bus; (AM: *criatura*) baby
guajolote [gwaxo'lote] NM (AM) turkey
guano ['gwano] NM guano
guantada [gwan'taða] NF, **guantazo** [gwan'taθo] NM slap
★**guante** ['gwante] NM glove; **guantes de goma** rubber gloves; **se ajusta como un ~** it fits like a glove; **echar el ~ a algn** to catch hold of sb; (*fig: policía*) to catch sb
guantera [gwan'tera] NF glove compartment
★**guapo, -a** ['gwapo, a] ADJ good-looking; (*mujer*) pretty, attractive; (*hombre*) handsome; (*elegante*) smart ▶ NM lover, gallant; (AM *fam*) tough guy, bully
guaraní [gwara'ni] ADJ, NMF Guarani ▶ NM (*moneda*) monetary unit of Paraguay
guarapo [gwa'rapo] NM (AM) fermented cane juice
guarda ['gwarða] NMF (*persona*) warden, keeper; **~ forestal** game warden; **~ jurado** (armed) security guard ▶ NF (*acto*) guarding; (*custodia*) custody; (*Tip*) flyleaf, endpaper
guardaagujas [gwarða'ɣuxas] NM INV (*Ferro*) switchman
guardabarros [gwarða'βarros] NM INV mudguard (BRIT), fender (US)
guardabosques [gwarða'βoskes] NMF INV gamekeeper
guardacoches [gwarða'kotʃes] NMF INV parking attendant
guardacostas [gwarða'kostas] NMF INV coastguard ▶ NM INV coastguard vessel
guardador, a [gwarða'ðor, a] ADJ protective; (*tacaño*) mean, stingy ▶ NM/F guardian, protector
guardaespaldas [gwardaes'paldas] NMF INV bodyguard
guardagujas [gwarda'ɣuxas] NM INV = **guardaagujas**
guardameta [gwarða'meta] NM goalkeeper
guardapolvo [gwarða'polβo] NM dust cover; (*prenda de vestir*) overalls *pl*
★**guardar** [gwar'ðar] /**1a**/ VT (*gen*) to keep; (*vigilar*) to guard, watch over; (*conservar*) to put away; (*dinero: ahorrar*) to save; (*promesa etc*) to keep; (*ley*) to observe; (*rencor*) to bear, harbour; (*Inform: archivo*) to save; **~ cama** to stay in bed ■ **guardarse** VR (*preservarse*) to protect o.s.; **guardarse de algo** (*evitar*) to avoid sth; (*abstenerse*) to refrain from sth; **guardarse de hacer algo** to be careful not to do sth; **guardársela a algn** to have it in for sb
★**guardarropa** [gwarða'rropa] NM (*armario*) wardrobe; (*en establecimiento público*) cloakroom
★**guardería** [gwarðe'ria] NF nursery

★**guardia** ['gwarðja] NF (*Mil*) guard; (*cuidado*) care, custody; **estar de ~** to be on guard; **montar ~** to mount guard; **la G~ Civil** the Civil Guard; **~ municipal** o **urbana** municipal police ▶ NMF guard; (*policía*) police officer; **un ~ civil** a civil guard(sman); **un(a) ~ nacional** a police officer; **~ urbano** traffic police officer; *see note*

guardián, -ana [gwar'ðjan, ana] NM/F (*gen*) guardian, keeper
guarecer [gware'θer] /**2d**/ VT (*proteger*) to protect; (*abrigar*) to shelter ■ **guarecerse** VR to take refuge
guarezca *etc* [gwa're θka] VB *ver* **guarecer**
guarida [gwa'riða] NF (*de animal*) den, lair; (*de persona*) haunt, hideout; (*refugio*) refuge
guarnecer [gwarne'θer] /**2d**/ VT (*equipar*) to provide; (*adornar*) to adorn; (*Tec*) to reinforce
guarnezca *etc* [gwar'neθka] VB *ver* **guarnecer**
guarnición [gwarni'θjon] NF (*de vestimenta*) trimming; (*de piedra*) mount; (*Culin*) garnish; (*arneses*) harness; (*Mil*) garrison
guarrada [gwa'rraða] NF (*fam: cosa sucia*) dirty mess; (: *acto o dicho obsceno*) obscenity; **hacer una ~ a algn** to do the dirty on sb
guarrería [gwarre'ria] NF = **guarrada**
guarro, -a ['gwarro, a] NM/F (*fam*) pig; (*fig*) dirty o slovenly person
guasa ['gwasa] NF joke; **con** o **de ~** jokingly, in fun
guasón, -ona [gwa'son, ona] ADJ witty; (*bromista*) joking ▶ NM/F wit; (*bromista*) joker
Guatemala [gwate'mala] NF Guatemala
guatemalteco, -a [gwatemal'teko, a] ADJ, NM/F Guatemalan
guateque [gwa'teke] NM (*fiesta*) party
★**guay** [gwai] ADJ (*fam*) super, great
guayaba [gwa'jaβa] NF (*Bot*) guava
Guayana [gwa'jana] NF Guyana, Guiana
gubernamental [guβernamen'tal], **gubernativo, -a** [guβerna'tiβo, a] ADJ governmental
guedeja [ge'ðexa] NF long hair
güero, -a ['gwero, a] ADJ (AM) blond(e)
★**guerra** ['gerra] NF war; (*arte*) warfare; (*pelea*) struggle; **~ atómica/bacteriológica/nuclear/de guerrillas** atomic/germ/nuclear/guerrilla warfare; **Primera/Segunda G~ Mundial** First/Second World War; **~ de precios** (*Com*) price war; **~ civil/fría** civil/cold war; **~ a muerte**

fight to the death; **de ~** military, war *cpd*; **estar en ~** to be at war; **dar ~** to be a nuisance; **dar ~ a algn** to give s.o. a lot of bother

guerrear [gerre'ar] /**1a**/ vi to wage war

guerrero, -a [ge'rrero, a] ADJ fighting; (*carácter*) warlike ▶ NM/F warrior

guerrilla [ge'rriʎa] NF guerrilla warfare; (*tropas*) guerrilla band o group

guerrillero, -a [gerri'ʎero, a] NM/F guerrilla (fighter); (*contra invasor*) partisan

gueto ['geto] NM ghetto

★**guía** ['gia] VB ver **guiar** ▶ NMF (*persona*) guide ▶ NF (*libro*) guidebook; (*manual*) handbook; **~ de ferrocarriles** railway timetable; **~ telefónica** telephone directory; **~ del turista/del viajero** tourist/traveller's guide

★**guiar** [gi'ar] /**1c**/ VT to guide, direct; (*dirigir*) to lead; (*orientar*) to advise; (*Auto*) to steer ■ **guiarse** VR: **guiarse por** to be guided by

guijarro [gi'xarro] NM pebble

guillotina [giʎo'tina] NF guillotine

guinda ['ginda] NF morello cherry; (*licor*) cherry liqueur

guindar [gin'dar] /**1a**/ VT to hoist; (*fam: robar*) to nick

guindilla [gin'diʎa] NF chil(l)i pepper

Guinea [gi'nea] NF Guinea

Guinea-Bissau [gi'neaβi'sau] NF Guinea-Bissau

guineo, -a [gi'neo, a] ADJ Guinea *cpd*, Guinean ▶ NM/F Guinean

guiñapo [gi'ɲapo] NM (*harapo*) rag; (*persona*) rogue

guiñar [gi'ɲar] /**1a**/ VI to wink

guiño ['giɲo] NM (*parpadeo*) wink; (*muecas*) grimace; **hacer guiños a** (*enamorados*) to make eyes at

guiñol [gi'ɲol] NM (*Teat*) puppet theatre

guión [gi'on] NM (*Ling*) hyphen, dash; (*esquema*) summary, outline; (*Cine*) script

guionista [gjo'nista] NMF scriptwriter

guipuzcoano, -a [gipuθko'ano, a] ADJ of o from Guipúzcoa ▶ NM/F native o inhabitant of Guipúzcoa

guiri ['giri] NMF (*fam, pey*) foreigner

guirigay [giri'gai] NM (*griterío*) uproar; (*confusión*) chaos

guirnalda [gir'nalda] NF garland

guisa ['gisa] NF: **a ~ de** as, like

guisado [gi'saðo] NM stew

★**guisante** [gi'sante] NM pea

guisar [gi'sar] /**1a**/ VT, VI to cook; (*fig*) to arrange

guiso ['giso] NM cooked dish

guita ['gita] NF twine; (*fam: dinero*) dough

★**guitarra** [gi'tarra] NF guitar

guitarrista [gita'rrista] NMF guitarist

gula ['gula] NF gluttony, greed

gusano [gu'sano] NM maggot, worm; (*de mariposa, polilla*) caterpillar; (*lombriz*) earthworm; (*fig*) worm; (*ser despreciable*) creep; **~ de seda** silkworm

★**gustar** [gus'tar] /**1a**/ VT to taste, sample ▶ VI to please, be pleasing; **~ de algo** to like o enjoy sth; **me gustan las uvas** I like grapes; **le gusta nadar** she likes o enjoys swimming; **¿gusta usted?** would you like some?; **como usted guste** as you wish

★**gusto** ['gusto] NM (*sentido, sabor*) taste; (*agrado*) liking; (*placer*) pleasure; **tiene un ~ amargo** it has a bitter taste; **tener buen ~** to have good taste; **sobre gustos no hay nada escrito** there's no accounting for tastes; **de buen/mal ~** in good/bad taste; **sentirse a ~** to feel at ease; **¡mucho o tanto ~ (en conocerle)!** how do you do?, pleased to meet you; **el ~ es mío** the pleasure is mine; **tomar ~ a** to take a liking to; **con ~** willingly, gladly

gustoso, -a [gus'toso, a] ADJ (*sabroso*) tasty; (*agradable*) pleasant; (*con voluntad*) willing, glad; **lo hizo ~** he did it gladly

gutural [gutu'ral] ADJ guttural

guyanés, -esa [gwaja'nes, esa] ADJ, NM/F Guyanese

g

Hh

H, h ['atʃe] NF (*letra*) H, h; **H de Historia** H for Harry (BRIT) o How (US)

H. ABR (*Química*: = *Hidrógeno*) H; (= *Hectárea(s)*) ha.

h. ABR (= *hora(s)*) h., hr(s). ▶ NMPL ABR (= *habitantes*) pop.

ha¹ [a] VB *ver* **haber**

ha² ABR (= *Hectárea(s)*) ha

★**haba** ['aβa] NF bean; **son habas contadas** it goes without saying; **en todas partes cuecen habas** it's the same (story) the whole world over

Habana [a'βana] NF: **la ~** Havana

habanero, -a [aβa'nero, a] ADJ of o from Havana ▶ NM/F native o inhabitant of Havana ▶ NF (*Mus*) habanera

habano [a'βano] NM Havana cigar

habeas corpus [a'βeas'korpus] NM (*Jur*) habeas corpus

habéis VB *ver* **haber**

---

haber [a'βer]

/**2j**/ VB AUXILIAR **1** (*tiempos compuestos*) to have; **he/había comido** I have/had eaten; **antes/después de haberlo visto** before seeing o having seen it; **si lo hubiera sabido habría ido** if I had known I would have gone **2**: **¡haberlo dicho antes!** you should have said so before!; **¿habrase visto (cosa igual)?** have you ever seen anything like it?

3: **haber de: he de hacerlo** I must do it; **ha de llegar mañana** it should arrive tomorrow

▶ VB IMPERSONAL **1** (*existencia*: *sg*) there is; (: *pl*) there are; **hay un hermano/dos hermanos** there is one brother/there are two brothers; **¿cuánto hay de aquí a Sucre?** how far is it from here to Sucre?; **habrá unos 4 grados** it must be about 4 degrees; **no hay quien te entienda** there's no understanding you **2** (*obligación*): **hay que hacer algo** something must be done; **hay que apuntarlo para acordarse** you have to write it down or you'll forget

3: **¡hay que ver!** well I never!

4: **¡no hay de qué!**, (AM) **¡no hay por qué!** don't mention it!, not at all!

5: **¿qué hay?** (*¿qué pasa?*) what's up?, what's the matter?; (*¿qué tal?*) how's it going?

■ **haberse** VB IMPERSONAL: **habérselas con algn** to have it out with sb

▶ VT: **he aquí unas sugerencias** here are some suggestions; **todos los inventos habidos y por haber** all inventions present and future; **en el encuentro habido ayer** in yesterday's game

▶ NM (*en cuenta*) credit side; **¿cuánto tengo en el haber?** how much do I have in my account?; **tiene varias novelas en su haber** he has several novels to his credit

■ **haberes** NMPL assets

Cuando *hay* va seguido de un complemento singular, se traduce por **there is**: *Hay una iglesia en la esquina*. **There is a church on the corner**.
En cambio, cuando le sigue uno plural se traduce por **there are**: *¿Hay entradas?* **Are there any tickets?**

---

habichuela [aβi'tʃwela] NF kidney bean

★**hábil** ['aβil] ADJ (*listo*) clever, smart; (*capaz*) fit, capable; (*experto*) expert; **día ~** working day

★**habilidad** [aβili'ðað] NF (*gen*) skill, ability; (*inteligencia*) cleverness; (*destreza*) expertness, expertise; (*Jur*) competence; **~ (para)** fitness (for); **tener ~ manual** to be clever with one's hands

habilitación [aβilita'θjon] NF qualification; (*colocación de muebles*) fitting out; (*financiamiento*) financing; (*oficina*) paymaster's office

habilitado [aβili'taðo] NM paymaster

habilitar [aβili'tar] /**1a**/ VT to qualify; (*autorizar*) to authorize; (*capacitar*) to enable; (*dar instrumentos*) to equip; (*financiar*) to finance

hábilmente [aβil'mente] ADV skilfully, expertly

habitable [aβi'taβle] ADJ inhabitable

habitación [aβita'θjon] NF (*cuarto*) room; (*casa*) dwelling, abode; (*Bio: morada*) habitat; ~ **sencilla** o **individual** single room; ~ **doble** o **de matrimonio** double room

habitante [aβi'tante] NMF inhabitant

habitar [aβi'tar] /1a/ VT (*residir en*) to inhabit; (*ocupar*) to occupy ▶ VI to live

hábitat ['aβitat] (*pl* **hábitats** ['aβitats]) NM habitat

hábito ['aβito] NM habit; **tener el ~ de hacer algo** to be in the habit of doing sth

habitual [aβi'twal] ADJ habitual

habituar [aβi'twar] /1e/ VT to accustom ■ **habituarse** VR: **habituarse a** to get used to

habla ['aβla] NF (*capacidad de hablar*) speech; (*idioma*) language; (*dialecto*) dialect; **perder el ~** to become speechless; **de ~ francesa** French-speaking; **estar al ~** to be in contact; (*Telec*) to be on the line; **¡González al ~!** (*Telec*) Gonzalez speaking!

hablador, a [aβla'ðor, a] ADJ talkative ▶ NM/F chatterbox

habladuría [aβlaðu'ria] NF rumour ■ **habladurías** NFPL gossip *sg*

hablante [a'βlante] ADJ speaking ▶ NMF speaker

hablar [a'βlar] /1a/ VT to speak, talk; "**se habla inglés**" "English spoken here" ▶ VI to speak; ~ **con** to speak to; **¡hable!, ¡puede ~!** (*Telec*) you're through!; **de eso ni ~** no way, that's out of the question; ~ **alto/bajo/claro** to speak loudly/quietly/plainly o bluntly; ~ **de** to speak of o about ■ **hablarse** VR to speak to each other; **no se hablan** they are not on speaking terms

---

Al traducir *hablar*, se utiliza **speak** en los casos en que una persona se dirige a otra u otras que se limitan a escuchar, por lo que no hay una conversación propiamente dicha. En cambio, se utiliza **talk** cuando hay dos o más personas conversando. **Speak** se usa además en relación con la habilidad de alguien para hablar una lengua: ¿Hablas francés? **Do you speak French?**
Para indicar en qué lengua se está hablando, se puede utilizar tanto **speak** como **talk**: *Hablaban en español.* **They were talking** o **speaking Spanish**.

---

habré *etc* [a'βre] VB *ver* **haber**

hacedor, a [aθe'ðor, a] NM/F maker

hacendado, -a [aθen'daðo, a] ADJ property-owning ▶ NM/F (*AM*) rancher, farmer; (*terrateniente*) large landowner

hacendoso, -a [aθen'doso, a] ADJ industrious, hard-working

---

hacer [a'θer]

/2r/ VT **1** (*fabricar, producir, conseguir*) to make; **hacer una película/un ruido** to make a film/noise; **el guisado lo hice yo** I made o cooked the stew; **hacer amigos** to make friends

2 (*ejecutar: trabajo etc*) to do; **hacer la colada** to do the washing; **hacer la comida** to do the cooking; **¿qué haces?** what are you doing?; **¡eso está hecho!** you've got it!; **hacer el tonto/indio** to act the fool/clown; **hacer el malo** o **el papel del malo** (*Teat*) to play the villain

3 (*estudios, algunos deportes*) to do; **hacer español/económicas** to do o study Spanish/economics; **hacer yoga/gimnasia** to do yoga/go to the gym

4 (*transformar, incidir en*): **esto lo hará más difícil** this will make it more difficult; **salir te hará sentir mejor** going out will make you feel better; **te hace más joven** it makes you look younger

5 (*cálculo*): **2 y 2 hacen 4** 2 and 2 make 4; **este hace 100** this one makes 100

6 (+ *sub*): **esto hará que ganemos** this will make us win; **harás que no quiera venir** you'll stop him wanting to come

7 (*como sustituto de vb*) to do; **él bebió y yo hice lo mismo** he drank and I did likewise

8: **no hace más que criticar** all he does is criticize

▶ VB SEMI-AUXILIAR (+ *infin*) **1** (*directo*): **les hice venir** I made o had them come; **hacer trabajar a los demás** to get others to work

2 (*por intermedio de otros*): **hacer reparar algo** to get sth repaired

▶ VI **1**: **haz como que no lo sabes** act as if you don't know; **hiciste bien en decírmelo** you were right to tell me

2 (*ser apropiado*): **si os hace** if it's alright with you

3: **hacer de: hacer de madre para uno** to be like a mother to sb; (*Teat*): **hacer de Otelo** to play Othello; **la tabla hace de mesa** the board does as a table

▶ VB IMPERSONAL **1**: **hace calor/frío** it's hot/cold; *ver tb* **bueno; sol; tiempo**

2 (*tiempo*): **hace tres años** three years ago; **hace un mes que voy/no voy** I've been going/I haven't been for a month; **no le veo desde hace mucho** I haven't seen him for a long time

3: **¿cómo has hecho para llegar tan rápido?** how did you manage to get here so quickly?

■ **hacerse** VR **1** (*volverse*) to become; **se hicieron amigos** they became friends; **hacerse viejo** to get o grow old; **se hace tarde** it's getting late

2: **hacerse algo: me hice un traje** I got a suit made

3 (*acostumbrarse*): **hacerse a** to get used to; **hacerse a la idea** to get used to the idea

4: **se hace con huevos y leche** it's made out of eggs and milk; **eso no se hace** that's not done

5 (*obtener*): **hacerse de** o **con algo** to get hold of sth

6 (*fingirse*): **hacerse el sordo/sueco** to turn a deaf ear/pretend not to notice

En la traducción de *hacer* se utiliza **make** cuando se habla de crear o construir algo, o de preparar comidas o bebidas. Cuando se utiliza en este sentido, **make** puede llevar objeto indirecto:
Carmen se hace ella misma toda la ropa. **Carmen makes all her own clothes.**
Acabo de hacer café. **I've just made some coffee.**
Se utiliza **do** sobre todo cuando se habla en general: *Has hecho mucho por nosotros.* **You've done a lot to help us.**

hacha [ˈatʃa] NF axe; (*antorcha*) torch
hachazo [aˈtʃaθo] NM axe blow
hache [ˈatʃe] NF (the letter) H; **llámele usted ~** call it what you will
hachís [aˈtʃis] NM hashish
★**hacia** [ˈaθja] PREP (*en dirección de*) towards; (*cerca de*) near; (*actitud*) towards; **~ adelante/atrás** forwards/backwards; **~ arriba/abajo** up(wards)/down(wards); **~ mediodía** about noon
hacienda [aˈθjenda] NF (*propiedad*) property; (*finca*) farm; (*AM*) ranch; **~ pública** public finance; **(Ministerio de) H~** Exchequer (*BRIT*), Treasury Department (*US*)
hacinar [aθiˈnar] /1a/ VT to pile (up); (*Agr*) to stack; (*fig*) to overcrowd
hada [ˈaða] NF fairy; **~ madrina** fairy godmother
hado [ˈaðo] NM fate, destiny
haga *etc* [ˈaɣa] VB *ver* **hacer**
Haití [aiˈti] NM Haiti
haitiano, -a [aiˈtjano, a] ADJ, NM/F Haitian
hala [ˈala] EXCL (*vamos*) come on!; (*anda*) get on with it!
halagar [alaˈɣar] /1h/ VT (*lisonjear*) to flatter
halago [aˈlaɣo] NM (*adulación*) flattery
halague *etc* [aˈlaɣe] VB *ver* **halagar**
halagüeño, -a [alaˈɣweɲo, a] ADJ flattering
halcón [alˈkon] NM falcon, hawk
hálito [ˈalito] NM breath
halitosis [aliˈtosis] NF halitosis, bad breath
★**hallar** [aˈʎar] /1a/ VT (*gen*) to find; (*descubrir*) to discover; (*toparse con*) to run into ■ **hallarse** VR to be (situated); (*encontrarse*) to find o.s.; **se halla fuera** he is away; **no se halla** he feels out of place
hallazgo [aˈʎaθɣo] NM discovery; (*cosa*) find
halo [ˈalo] NM halo
halógeno, -a [aˈloxeno, a] ADJ: **faro ~** halogen lamp
halterofilia [alteroˈfilja] NF weightlifting
hamaca [aˈmaka] NF hammock
★**hambre** [ˈambre] NF hunger; (*carencia*) famine; (*inanición*) starvation; (*fig*) longing; **tener ~** to be hungry; **¡me muero de ~!** I'm starving!
hambriento, -a [amˈbrjento, a] ADJ hungry,

starving; **~ de** hungry *o* longing for ▶ NM/F starving person; **los hambrientos** the hungry
hambruna [amˈbruna] NF famine
Hamburgo [amˈburɣo] NM Hamburg
★**hamburguesa** [amburˈɣesa] NF hamburger, burger
hamburguesería [amburɣeseˈria] NF burger bar
hampa [ˈampa] NF underworld
hampón [amˈpon] NM thug
★**hámster** [ˈxamster] NM hamster
han [an] VB *ver* **haber**
haragán, -ana [araˈɣan, ana] ADJ, NM/F good-for-nothing
haraganear [araɣaneˈar] /1a/ VI to idle, loaf about
harapiento, -a [araˈpjento, a] ADJ tattered, in rags
harapo [aˈrapo] NM rag
hardware [ˈxardwer] NM (*Inform*) hardware
haré *etc* [aˈre] VB *ver* **hacer**
harén [aˈren] NM harem
★**harina** [aˈrina] NF flour; **~ de maíz** cornflour (*BRIT*), cornstarch (*US*); **~ de trigo** wheat flour; **eso es ~ de otro costal** that's another kettle of fish
harinero, -a [ariˈnero, a] NM/F flour merchant
harinoso, -a [ariˈnoso, a] ADJ floury
hartar [arˈtar] /1a/ VT to satiate, glut; (*fig*) to tire, sicken ■ **hartarse** VR (*de comida*) to fill o.s., gorge o.s.; (*cansarse*): **hartarse de** to get fed up with
hartazgo [arˈtaθɣo] NM surfeit, glut
★**harto, -a** [ˈarto, a] ADJ (*lleno*) full; (*cansado*) fed up; **estar ~ de** to be fed up with; **¡estoy ~ de decírtelo!** I'm sick and tired of telling you (so)! ▶ ADV (*bastante*) enough; (*muy*) very
hartura [arˈtura] NF (*exceso*) surfeit; (*abundancia*) abundance; (*satisfacción*) satisfaction
has¹ [as] VB *ver* **haber**
has² ABR (= *Hectáreas*) ha
hashtag [xasˈtaɣ] NM (*en Twitter*) hashtag
★**hasta** [ˈasta] ADV even; **~ en Valencia hiela a veces** even in Valencia it freezes sometimes ▶ PREP (*alcanzando a*) as far as, up/down to; (*de tiempo: a tal hora*) till, until; (: *antes de*) before; **~ luego** *o* **ahora/el sábado** see you soon/on Saturday; **~ la fecha** (up) to date; **~ nueva orden** until further notice; **~ pronto** see you soon ▶ CONJ: **~ que** until

En expresiones de tiempo, *hasta* suele traducirse por **till** o **until**. **Till** tiene un registro más coloquial que **until** y no suele ir al principio de la frase:
Hasta entonces las cosas nos habían ido bien. **Until then, things had been going well for us.**
¿Por qué no esperas hasta el lunes para llamar? **Why don't you wait till Monday to call?**

hastiar [as'tjar] /**1c**/ VT (*gen*) to weary; (*aburrir*) to bore ■ **hastiarse** VR: **hastiarse de** to get fed up with

hastío [as'tio] NM weariness; (*aburrimiento*) boredom

hatajo [a'taxo] NM: **un ~ de gamberros** a bunch of hooligans

hatillo [a'tiʎo] NM belongings *pl*, kit; (*montón*) bundle, heap

Hawai [a'wai] NM (*tb*: **las Islas Hawai**) Hawaii

hawaianas [awa'janas] NFPL (*esp* AM) flip-flops (BRIT), thongs

hawaiano, -a [awa'jano, a] ADJ, NM/F Hawaian

★**hay** [ai] VB *ver* **haber**

Haya ['aja] NF: **la ~** The Hague

haya *etc* ['aja] VB *ver* **haber** ▸ NF beech tree

hayal [a'jal] NM beech grove

haz [aθ] VB *ver* **hacer** ▸ NM bundle, bunch; (*rayo: de luz*) beam ▸ NF: **~ de la tierra** face of the earth

hazaña [a'θaɲa] NF feat, exploit; **sería una ~** it would be a great achievement

hazmerreír [aθmerre'ir] NM INV laughing stock

he [e] VB *ver* **haber** ▸ ADV: **he aquí** here is, here are; **he aquí por qué ...** that is why ...

hebilla [e'βiʎa] NF buckle, clasp

hebra ['eβra] NF thread; (*Bot: fibra*) fibre, grain

hebreo, -a [e'βreo, a] ADJ, NM/F Hebrew ▸ NM (*Ling*) Hebrew

Hébridas ['eβriðas] NFPL: **las ~** the Hebrides

hechice *etc* [e'tʃiθe] VB *ver* **hechizar**

hechicero, -a [etʃi'θero, a] NM/F sorcerer (sorceress)

hechizar [etʃi'θar] /**1f**/ VT to cast a spell on, bewitch

hechizo [e'tʃiθo] NM witchcraft, magic; (*acto de magia*) spell, charm

★**hecho, -a** ['etʃo, a] PP *de* **hacer** ▸ ADJ complete; (*maduro*) mature; (*carne*) done; (*Costura*) ready-to-wear; **¡bien ~!** well done!; **~ a la medida** made-to-measure; **a lo ~, pecho** it's no use crying over spilt milk ▸ NM deed, act; (*dato*) fact; (*cuestión*) matter; (*suceso*) event; **de ~** in fact, as a matter of fact; (*Pol etc: adj, adv*) de facto; **de ~ y de derecho** de facto and de jure; **el ~ es que ...** the fact is that ... ▸ EXCL agreed!, done!

hechura [e'tʃura] NF making, creation; (*producto*) product; (*forma*) form, shape; (*de persona*) build; (*Tec*) craftsmanship

hectárea [ek'tarea] NF hectare

heder [e'ðer] /**2g**/ VI to stink, smell; (*fig*) to be unbearable

hediondez [eðjon'deθ] NF stench, stink; (*cosa*) stinking thing

hediondo, -a [e'ðjondo, a] ADJ stinking

hedor [e'ðor] NM stench

hegemonía [exemo'nia] NF hegemony

helada [e'laða] NF frost

heladera [ela'ðera] NF (AM: *refrigerador*) refrigerator

★**heladería** [elaðe'ria] NF ice-cream stall (*o* parlour)

★**helado, -a** [e'laðo, a] ADJ frozen; (*glacial*) icy; (*fig*) chilly, cold; **dejar ~ a algn** to dumbfound sb ▸ NM ice-cream

helador, a [ela'ðor, a] ADJ (*viento etc*) icy, freezing

★**helar** [e'lar] /**1j**/ VT to freeze, ice (up); (*dejar atónito*) to amaze ▸ VI to freeze ■ **helarse** VR to freeze; (*Aviat, Ferro etc*) to ice (up), freeze up

helecho [e'letʃo] NM bracken, fern

helénico, -a [e'leniko, a] ADJ Hellenic, Greek

heleno, -a [e'leno, a] NM/F Hellene, Greek

hélice ['eliθe] NF spiral; (*Tec*) propeller; (*Mat*) helix

helicóptero [eli'koptero] NM helicopter

helio ['eljo] NM helium

helmántico, -a [el'mantiko, a] ADJ of *o* from Salamanca

Helsinki [xel'sinki] NM Helsinki

helvético, -a [el'βetiko, a] ADJ, NM/F Swiss

hematoma [ema'toma] NM bruise

hembra ['embra] NF (*Bot, Zool*) female; (*mujer*) woman; (*Tec*) nut; **un elefante ~** a she-elephant

hemeroteca [emero'teka] NF newspaper library

hemiciclo [emi'θiklo] NM: **el ~** (*Pol*) the floor

hemisferio [emis'ferjo] NM hemisphere

hemofilia [emo'filja] NF haemophilia (BRIT), hemophilia (US)

hemorragia [emo'rraxja] NF haemorrhage (BRIT), hemorrhage (US)

hemorroides [emo'rroiðes] NFPL haemorrhoids (BRIT), hemorrhoids (US)

hemos ['emos] VB *ver* **haber**

henar [e'nar] NM meadow, hayfield

henchir [en'tʃir] /**3h**/ VT to fill, stuff ■ **henchirse** VR (*llenarse de comida*) to stuff o.s. (with food); (*inflarse*) to swell (up)

Hendaya [en'daja] NF Hendaye

hender [en'der] /**2g**/ VT to cleave, split

hendidura [endi'ðura] NF crack, split; (*Geo*) fissure

henequén [ene'ken] NM (AM) henequen

heno ['eno] NM hay

hepatitis [epa'titis] NF INV hepatitis

herbario, -a [er'βarjo, a] ADJ herbal ▸ NM (*colección*) herbarium; (*especialista*) herbalist; (*botánico*) botanist

herbicida [erβi'θiða] NM weedkiller

herbívoro, -a [er'βiβoro, a] ADJ herbivorous

herboristería [erβoriste'ria] NF herbalist's shop

heredad [ere'ðað] NF landed property; (*granja*) farm

heredar [ere'ðar] /**1a**/ VT to inherit

heredero, -a [ere'ðero, a] NM/F heir(ess); **~ del trono** heir to the throne

hereditario, -a [ereði'tarjo, a] ADJ hereditary

hereje [e'rexe] NMF heretic

herejía [ere'xia] NF heresy

herencia [e'renθja] NF inheritance; (*fig*) heritage; (*Bio*) heredity

herético, -a [e'retiko, a] ADJ heretical

★**herido, -a** [e'riðo, a] ADJ injured, wounded; (*fig*) offended ▶ NM/F casualty ▶ NF wound, injury

★**herir** [e'rir] /**3i**/ VT to wound, injure; (*fig*) to offend; (*conmover*) to touch, move

★**hermana** [er'mana] NF ver **hermano**

hermanación [ermana'θjon] NF (*de ciudades*) twinning

hermanado, -a [erma'naðo, a] PP de **hermanar** ▶ ADJ (*ciudad*) twinned

hermanar [erma'nar] /**1a**/ VT to match; (*unir*) to join; (*ciudades*) to twin

★**hermanastro, -a** [erma'nastro, a] NM/F stepbrother(-sister)

hermandad [erman'dað] NF brotherhood; (*de mujeres*) sisterhood; (*sindicato etc*) association

★**hermano, -a** [er'mano, a] ADJ similar ▶ NM brother; **~ gemelo** twin brother; **~ político** brother-in-law; **mis hermanos** my brothers, my brothers and sisters ▶ NF sister; **hermana política** sister-in-law

hermético, -a [er'metiko, a] ADJ hermetic; (*fig*) watertight

★**hermoso, -a** [er'moso, a] ADJ beautiful, lovely; (*estupendo*) splendid; (*guapo*) handsome

hermosura [ermo'sura] NF beauty; (*de hombre*) handsomeness

hernia ['ernja] NF hernia, rupture; **~ discal** slipped disc

herniarse [er'njarse] /**1b**/ VR to rupture o.s.; (*fig*) to break one's back

héroe ['eroe] NM hero

heroicidad [eroiθi'ðað] NF heroism; (*una heroicidad*) heroic deed

heroico, -a [e'roiko, a] ADJ heroic

heroína [ero'ina] NF (*mujer*) heroine; (*droga*) heroin

heroinómano, -a [eroi'nomano, a] NM/F heroin addict

heroísmo [ero'ismo] NM heroism

herpes ['erpes] NMPL O NFPL (*Med*: *gen*) herpes *sg*; (: *de la piel*) shingles *sg*

herradura [erra'ðura] NF horseshoe

herraje [e'rraxe] NM (*trabajos*) ironwork

★**herramienta** [erra'mjenta] NF tool

herrería [erre'ria] NF smithy; (*Tec*) forge

herrero [e'rrero] NM blacksmith

herrumbre [e'rrumbre] NF rust

herrumbroso, -a [errum'broso, a] ADJ rusty

hervidero [erβi'ðero] NM (*fig*) swarm; (*Pol etc*) hotbed

★**hervir** [er'βir] /**3i**/ VI to boil; (*burbujear*) to bubble; (*fig*): **~ de** to teem with; **~ a fuego lento** to simmer

hervor [er'βor] NM boiling; (*fig*) ardour, fervour

heterogéneo, -a [etero'xeneo, a] ADJ heterogeneous

heterosexual [eterosek'swal] ADJ, NMF heterosexual

hez [eθ] NF (*tb*: **heces**) dregs *pl*

hibernar [iβer'nar] /**1a**/ VI to hibernate

híbrido, -a ['iβriðo, a] ADJ hybrid

hice *etc* ['iθe] VB ver **hacer**

hidalgo, -a [i'ðalɣo, a] ADJ noble; (*honrado*) honourable (*BRIT*), honorable (*US*) ▶ NM/F noble(man(-woman))

hidratante [iðra'tante] ADJ: **crema ~** moisturizing cream, moisturizer

hidratar [iðra'tar] /**1a**/ VT to moisturize

hidrato [i'ðrato] NM hydrate; **~ de carbono** carbohydrate

hidráulico, -a [i'ðrauliko, a] ADJ hydraulic ▶ NF hydraulics *sg*

hidro... [iðro] PREF hydro..., water-...

hidroavión [iðroa'βjon] NM seaplane

hidrodeslizador [iðrodesliθa'ðor] NM hovercraft

hidroeléctrico, -a [iðroe'lektriko, a] ADJ hydroelectric

hidrófilo, -a [i'ðrofilo, a] ADJ absorbent; **algodón ~** cotton wool (*BRIT*), absorbent cotton (*US*)

hidrofobia [iðro'foβja] NF hydrophobia, rabies

hidrófugo, -a [i'ðrofuɣo, a] ADJ damp-proof

hidrógeno [i'ðroxeno] NM hydrogen

hieda *etc* ['jeða] VB ver **heder**

hiedra ['jeðra] NF ivy

hiel [jel] NF gall, bile; (*fig*) bitterness

★**hielo** ['jelo] VB ver **helar** ▶ NM (*gen*) ice; (*escarcha*) frost; (*fig*) coldness, reserve; **romper el ~** (*fig*) to break the ice

hiena ['jena] NF (*Zool*) hyena

hiera *etc* ['jera] VB ver **herir**

★**hierba** ['jerβa] NF (*pasto*) grass; (*Culin*, *Med*: *planta*) herb; **mala ~** weed; (*fig*) evil influence

hierbabuena [jerβa'βwena] NF mint

★**hierro** ['jerro] NM (*metal*) iron; (*objeto*) iron object; **~ acanalado** corrugated iron; **~ colado** o **fundido** cast iron; **de ~** iron *cpd*

hierva *etc* ['jerβa] VB ver **hervir**

★**hígado** ['iɣaðo] NM liver ■ **hígados** NMPL (*fig*) guts; **echar los hígados** to wear o.s. out

higiene [i'xjene] NF hygiene

higiénico, -a [i'xjeniko, a] ADJ hygienic

★**higo** ['iɣo] NM fig; **~ seco** dried fig; **~ chumbo**

prickly pear; **de higos a brevas** once in a blue moon

higuera [i'gera] NF fig tree

hijastro, -a [i'xastro, a] NM/F stepson(-daughter)

hijo, -a ['ixo, a] NM/F son (daughter), child; (*uso vocativo*) dear; **~ adoptivo** adopted child; **~ de papá/mamá** daddy's/mummy's boy; **~ de puta** (*fam!*) bastard (*fam!*), son of a bitch (*fam!*); **~/hija político/a** son-/daughter-in-law; **~ pródigo** prodigal son; **~ único** only child; **cada ~ de vecino** any Tom, Dick or Harry ∎ **hijos** NMPL children, sons and daughters; **sin hijos** childless

hilacha [i'latʃa] NF ravelled thread; **~ de acero** steel wool

hilado, -a [i'laðo, a] ADJ spun

hilandero, -a [ilan'dero, a] NM/F spinner

hilar [i'lar] /1a/ VT to spin; (*fig*) to reason, infer; **~ delgado** to split hairs

hilera [i'lera] NF row, file

hilo ['ilo] NM thread; (*Bot*) fibre; (*tela*) linen; (*de metal*) wire; (*de agua*) trickle, thin stream; (*de luz*) beam, ray; (*de conversación*) thread, theme; (*de pensamientos*) train; **~ dental** dental floss; **colgar de un ~** (*fig*) to hang by a thread; **traje de ~** linen suit

hilvanar [ilβa'nar] /1a/ VT (*Costura*) to tack (BRIT), baste (US); (*fig*) to do hurriedly

Himalaya [ima'laja] NM: **el ~, los Montes ~** the Himalayas

himno ['imno] NM hymn; **~ nacional** national anthem

hincapié [inka'pje] NM: **hacer ~ en** to emphasize, stress

hincar [in'kar] /1g/ VT to drive (in), thrust (in); (*diente*) to sink ∎ **hincarse** VR: **hincarse de rodillas** (*esp Am*) to kneel down

hincha ['intʃa] NMF (*fam: Deporte*) fan

hinchado, -a [in'tʃaðo, a] ADJ (*gen*) swollen; (*persona*) pompous ▸ NF (group of) supporters *o* fans

hinchar [in'tʃar] /1a/ VT (*gen*) to swell; (*inflar*) to blow up, inflate; (*fig*) to exaggerate ∎ **hincharse** VR (*inflarse*) to swell up; (*fam: llenarse*) to stuff o.s.; (*fig*) to get conceited; **hincharse de reír** to have a good laugh

hinchazón [intʃa'θon] NF (*Med*) swelling; (*protuberancia*) bump, lump; (*altivez*) arrogance

hindú [in'du] ADJ, NMF Hindu

hinojo [i'noxo] NM fennel

hinque *etc* ['inke] VB *ver* **hincar**

hipar [i'par] /1a/ VI to hiccup

hiper... [iper] PREF hyper...

hiperactivo, -a [iperak'tiβo, a] ADJ hyperactive

hiperenlace [iperen'laθe] NM (*Inform*) hyperlink

hipermercado [ipermer'kaðo] NM hypermarket, superstore

hipersensible [ipersen'siβle] ADJ hypersensitive

hipertensión [iperten'sjon] NF high blood pressure, hypertension

hípico, -a ['ipiko, a] ADJ horse *cpd*, equine; **club ~** riding club

hipnosis [ip'nosis] NF INV hypnosis

hipnotice *etc* [ipno'tiθe] VB *ver* **hipnotizar**

hipnotismo [ipno'tismo] NM hypnotism

hipnotizar [ipnoti'θar] /1f/ VT to hypnotize

hipo ['ipo] NM hiccups *pl*; **quitar el ~ a algn** to cure sb's hiccups

hipocondría [ipokon'dria] NF hypochondria

hipocondríaco, -a [ipokon'driako, a] ADJ, NM/F hypochondriac

hipocresía [ipokre'sia] NF hypocrisy

hipócrita [i'pokrita] ADJ hypocritical ▸ NMF hypocrite

hipodérmico, -a [ipo'ðermiko, a] ADJ: **aguja hipodérmica** hypodermic needle

hipódromo [i'poðromo] NM racetrack

hipopótamo [ipo'potamo] NM hippopotamus

hipoteca [ipo'teka] NF mortgage; **redimir una ~** to pay off a mortgage

hipotecar [ipote'kar] /1g/ VT to mortgage; (*fig*) to jeopardize

hipotecario, -a [ipote'karjo, a] ADJ mortgage *cpd*

hipótesis [i'potesis] NF INV hypothesis; **es una ~ (nada más)** that's just a theory

hipotético, -a [ipo'tetiko, a] ADJ hypothetic(al)

hiriendo *etc* [i'rjendo] VB *ver* **herir**

hiriente [i'rjente] ADJ offensive, wounding

hirsuto, -a [ir'suto, a] ADJ hairy

hirviendo *etc* [ir'βjendo] VB *ver* **hervir**

hisopo [i'sopo] NM (*Rel*) sprinkler; (*Bot*) hyssop; (*de algodón*) swab

hispánico, -a [is'paniko, a] ADJ Hispanic, Spanish

hispanidad [ispani'ðað] NF (*cualidad*) Spanishness; (*Pol*) Spanish *o* Hispanic world

hispanista [ispa'nista] NMF (*Univ etc*) Hispan(ic)ist

hispano, -a [is'pano, a] ADJ Hispanic, Spanish, Hispano- ▸ NM/F Spaniard

Hispanoamérica [ispanoa'merika] NF Spanish *o* Latin America

hispanoamericano, -a [ispanoameri'kano, a] ADJ, NM/F Spanish *o* Latin American

hispanohablante [ispanoa'βlante], **hispanoparlante** [ispanopar'lante] ADJ Spanish-speaking

histeria [is'terja] NF hysteria

histérico, -a [is'teriko, a] ADJ hysterical

histerismo [iste'rismo] NM (*Med*) hysteria; (*fig*) hysterics

histograma [isto'ɣrama] NM histogram

★**historia** [is'torja] NF history; (*cuento*) story, tale; **pasar a la ~** to go down in history ▪ **historias** NFPL (*chismes*) gossip *sg*; **dejarse de historias** to come to the point

historiador, a [istorja'ðor, a] NM/F historian

historial [isto'rjal] NM record; (*profesional*) curriculum vitae, C.V., résumé (US); (*Med*) case history

★**histórico, -a** [is'toriko, a] ADJ historical; (*fig*) historic

historieta [isto'rjeta] NF tale, anecdote; (*de dibujos*) comic strip

histrionismo [istrjo'nismo] NM (*Teat*) acting; (*fig*) histrionics *pl*

hito ['ito] NM (*fig*) landmark; (*objetivo*) goal, target; (*fig*) milestone

hizo ['iθo] VB *ver* hacer

Hna., Hnas. ABR (= *Hermana(s)*) Sr(s).

Hno., Hnos. ABR (= *Hermano(s)*) Bro(s).

hocico [o'θiko] NM snout; (*fig*) grimace

hockey ['xoki] NM hockey; **~ sobre hielo** ice hockey

★**hogar** [o'ɣar] NM fireplace, hearth; (*casa*) home; (*vida familiar*) home life

hogareño, -a [oɣa'reɲo, a] ADJ home *cpd*; (*persona*) home-loving

hogaza [o'ɣaθa] NF (*de pan*) large loaf

hoguera [o'ɣera] NF (*gen*) bonfire; (*para herejes*) stake

★**hoja** ['oxa] NF (*gen*) leaf; (*de flor*) petal; (*de hierba*) blade; (*de papel*) sheet; (*página*) page; (*formulario*) form; (*de puerta*) leaf; **~ de afeitar** razor blade; **~ de cálculo electrónica** spreadsheet; **~ informativa** leaflet, handout; **~ de ruta** road map; **~ de solicitud** application form; **~ de trabajo** (*Inform*) worksheet; **de ~ ancha** broad-leaved; **de ~ caduca/perenne** deciduous/evergreen

hojalata [oxa'lata] NF tin(plate)

hojaldre [o'xaldre] NM (*Culin*) puff pastry

hojarasca [oxa'raska] NF (*hojas*) dead o fallen leaves *pl*; (*fig*) rubbish

hojear [oxe'ar] /1a/ VT to leaf through, turn the pages of

hojuela [o'xwela] NF (AM) flake

★**hola** ['ola] EXCL hello!

★**Holanda** [o'landa] NF Holland

★**holandés, -esa** [olan'des, esa] ADJ Dutch ▶ NM/F Dutchman(-woman); **los holandeses** the Dutch ▶ NM (*Ling*) Dutch

holgado, -a [ol'ɣaðo, a] ADJ loose, baggy; (*rico*) well-to-do

holgar [ol'ɣar] /1h, 1l/ VI (*descansar*) to rest; (*sobrar*) to be superfluous; **huelga decir que** it goes without saying that

holgazán, -ana [olɣa'θan, ana] ADJ idle, lazy ▶ NM/F loafer

holgazanear [olɣaθane'ar] /1a/ VI to laze o loaf around

holgura [ol'ɣura] NF looseness, bagginess;

(*Tec*) play, free movement; (*vida*) comfortable living, luxury

hollar [o'ʎar] /1l/ VT to tread (on), trample

hollín [o'ʎin] NM soot

★**hombre** ['ombre] NM man; (*raza humana*): **el ~** man(kind); **~ de bien** o **pro** honest man; **~ de confianza** right-hand man; **~ de estado** statesman; **~ de negocios** businessman; **el ~ medio** the average man; **hombre-rana** frogman ▶ EXCL (*para énfasis*) man, old chap; **¡sí ~!** (*claro*) of course!

hombrera [om'brera] NF shoulder strap

★**hombro** ['ombro] NM shoulder; **arrimar el ~** to lend a hand; **encogerse de hombros** to shrug one's shoulders

hombruno, -a [om'bruno, a] ADJ mannish

homenaje [ome'naxe] NM (*gen*) homage; (*tributo*) tribute; **un partido ~** a benefit match

homeopatía [omeopa'tia] NF hom(o)eopathy

homeopático, -a [omeo'patiko, a] ADJ hom(o)eopathic

homicida [omi'θiða] ADJ homicidal ▶ NMF murderer

homicidio [omi'θiðjo] NM murder, homicide; (*involuntario*) manslaughter

homologación [omoloɣa'θjon] NF (*de sueldo, condiciones*) parity

homologar [omolo'ɣar] /1h/ VT (*Com*) to standardize; (*Escol*) to officially approve; (*Deporte*) to officially recognize; (*sueldos*) to equalize

homólogo, -a [o'moloɣo, a] NM/F counterpart, opposite number

homónimo [o'monimo] NM (*tocayo*) namesake

homoparental [omoparen'tal] ADJ same-sex; **adopción ~** adoption by a same-sex couple

homosexual [omosek'swal] ADJ, NMF homosexual

honda ['onda] NF (*RPL*) catapult

hondo, -a ['ondo, a] ADJ deep; **lo ~** the depth(s) (*pl*), the bottom; **con ~ pesar** with deep regret

hondonada [ondo'naða] NF hollow, depression; (*cañón*) ravine; (*Geo*) lowland

hondura [on'dura] NF depth, profundity

★**Honduras** [on'duras] NF Honduras

hondureño, -a [ondu'reɲo, a] ADJ, NM/F Honduran

honestidad [onesti'ðað] NF purity, chastity; (*decencia*) decency

★**honesto, -a** [o'nesto, a] ADJ chaste; decent, honest; (*justo*) just

hongo ['ongo] NM (*Bot: gen*) fungus; (: *comestible*) mushroom; (: *venenoso*) toadstool; (*sombrero*) bowler (hat), derby (US); **hongos del pie** foot rot *sg*, athlete's foot *sg*

honor [o'nor] NM (*gen*) honour (BRIT), honor (US); (*gloria*) glory; **~ profesional** professional etiquette; **en ~ a la verdad** to be fair

honorable [ono'raβle] ADJ honourable (BRIT), honorable (US)

honorario, -a [ono'rarjo, a] ADJ honorary
▶ NM: **honorarios** fees

honorífico, -a [ono'rifiko, a] ADJ honourable (BRIT), honorable (US); **mención honorífica** hono(u)rable mention

honra ['onra] NF (gen) honour (BRIT), honor (US); (renombre) good name; **honras fúnebres** funeral rites; **tener algo a mucha ~** to be proud of sth

honradez [onra'ðeθ] NF honesty; (de persona) integrity

★**honrado, -a** [on'raðo, a] ADJ honest, upright

honrar [on'rar] /1a/ VT to honour (BRIT) o honor (US) ■ **honrarse** VR: **honrarse con algo/de hacer algo** to be honoured (BRIT) o honored (US) by sth/to do sth

honroso, -a [on'roso, a] ADJ (honrado) honourable (BRIT) o honorable (US); (respetado) respectable

★**hora** ['ora] NF hour; (tiempo) time; **¿qué ~ es?** what time is it?; **¿a qué ~?** (at) what time?; **media ~** half an hour; **a la ~ de comer/del recreo** at lunchtime/at playtime; **a primera ~** first thing (in the morning); **a última ~** at the last moment; **"última ~"** "breaking news"; **noticias de última ~** last-minute news; **a altas horas** in the small hours; **a la ~ en punto** on the dot; **¡a buena ~!** about time, too!; **en mala ~** unluckily; **pedir ~** to make an appointment; **dar la ~** to strike the hour; **poner el reloj en ~** to set one's watch; **~ punta** rush hour; **horas de oficina/de trabajo** office/working hours; **horas de visita** visiting times; **horas extras** o **extraordinarias** overtime sg; **horas pico** (AM) rush o peak hours; **no ver la ~ de** to look forward to; **¡ya era ~!** and about time too!

horadar [ora'ðar] /1a/ VT to drill, bore

★**horario, -a** [o'rarjo, a] ADJ hourly, hour cpd
▶ NM timetable; **~ comercial** business hours

horca ['orka] NF gallows sg; (Agr) pitchfork

horcajadas [orka'xaðas]: **a ~** adv astride

★**horchata** [or'tʃata] NF tiger nut milk

horda ['orða] NF horde

horizontal [oriθon'tal] ADJ horizontal

horizonte [ori'θonte] NM horizon

horma ['orma] NF mould; **~ (de calzado)** last; **~ de sombrero** hat block

hormiga [or'miɣa] NF ant ■ **hormigas** NFPL (Med) pins and needles

hormigón [ormi'ɣon] NM concrete; **~ armado/ pretensado** reinforced/prestressed concrete

hormigonera [ormiɣon'era] NF cement mixer

hormigueo [ormi'ɣeo] NM (comezón) itch; (fig) uneasiness

hormiguero [ormi'ɣero] NM (Zool) ants' nest; **era un ~** it was swarming with people

hormona [or'mona] NF hormone

hornada [or'naða] NF batch of loaves (etc)

hornillo [or'niʎo] NM (cocina) portable stove; **~ de gas** gas ring

★**horno** ['orno] NM (Culin) oven; (Tec) furnace; (para cerámica) kiln; **~ microondas** microwave (oven); **alto ~** blast furnace; **~ crematorio** crematorium

horóscopo [o'roskopo] NM horoscope

horquilla [or'kiʎa] NF hairpin; (Agr) pitchfork

horrendo, -a [o'rrendo, a] ADJ horrendous, frightful

★**horrible** [o'rriβle] ADJ horrible, dreadful

horripilante [orripi'lante] ADJ hair-raising, horrifying

horripilar [orripi'lar] /1a/ VT: **~ a algn** to horrify sb ■ **horripilarse** VR to be horrified

horror [o'rror] NM horror, dread; (atrocidad) atrocity; **¡qué ~!** (fam) how awful!; **estudia horrores** he studies a hell of a lot

horrorice etc [orro'riθe] VB ver **horrorizar**

horrorizar [orrori'θar] /1f/ VT to horrify, frighten ■ **horrorizarse** VR to be horrified

★**horroroso, -a** [orro'roso, a] ADJ horrifying, ghastly

★**hortaliza** [orta'liθa] NF vegetable

hortelano, -a [orte'lano, a] NM/F (market) gardener

hortera [or'tera] ADJ (fam) tacky

horterada [orte'raða] NF (fam): **es una ~** it's really naff

hortícola [or'tikola] ADJ horticultural

horticultura [ortikul'tura] NF horticulture

hortofrutícola [ortofru'tikola] ADJ fruit and vegetable cpd

hosco, -a ['osko, a] ADJ dark; (persona) sullen, gloomy

hospedaje [ospe'ðaxe] NM (cost of) board and lodging

hospedar [ospe'ðar] /1a/ VT to put up ■ **hospedarse** VR: **hospedarse (con/en)** to stay o lodge (with/at)

hospedería [ospeðe'ria] NF (edificio) inn; (habitación) guest room

hospicio [os'piθjo] NM (para niños) orphanage

★**hospital** [ospi'tal] NM hospital

hospitalario, -a [ospita'larjo, a] ADJ (acogedor) hospitable

hospitalice etc [ospita'liθe] VB ver **hospitalizar**

★**hospitalidad** [ospitali'ðað] NF hospitality

hospitalizar [ospitali'θar] /1f/ VT to send o take to hospital, hospitalize

hosquedad [oske'ðað] NF sullenness

★**hostal** [os'tal] NM small hotel; ver tb **hotel**

hostelería [ostele'ria] NF hotel business o trade

hostia ['ostja] NF (Rel) host, consecrated wafer; (fam: golpe) whack, punch ▶ EXCL: **¡~(s)!** (fam!) damn!

hostigar [osti'ɣar] /1h/ VT to whip; (fig) to harass, pester

hostigue etc [os'tiɣe] VB ver **hostigar**

h

hostil [os'til] ADJ hostile

hostilidad [ostili'ðað] NF hostility

hotdog [ot'doɣ] NM (AM) hot dog

★**hotel** [o'tel] NM hotel

> In Spain, you can choose from the following categories of accommodation in descending order of quality and price: **hotel** (from 5 stars to 1 star), *hostal*, *pensión*. Quality can vary widely even within these categories. The State also runs luxury hotels called *paradores*, which are usually sited in places of particular historical interest and are often historic buildings themselves.

hotelero, -a [ote'lero, a] ADJ hotel *cpd* ▶ NM/F hotelier

★**hoy** ['oi] ADV (*este día*) today; (*en la actualidad*) now(adays) ▶ NM present time; **~ (en) día** now(adays); **el día de ~, ~ día** (AM) this very day; **~ por ~** right now; **de ~ en ocho días** a week today; **de ~ en adelante** from now on

hoya ['oja] NF pit; (*sepulcro*) grave; (*Geo*) valley

hoyo ['ojo] NM hole, pit; (*tumba*) grave; (*Golf*) hole; (*Med*) pockmark

hoyuelo [oj'welo] NM dimple

hoz [oθ] NF sickle

hube *etc* ['uβe] VB *ver* **haber**

hucha ['utʃa] NF money box

hueco, -a ['weko, a] ADJ (*vacío*) hollow, empty; (*resonante*) booming; (*sonido*) resonant; (*persona*) conceited; (*estilo*) pompous ▶ NM hollow, cavity; (*agujero*) hole; (*de escalera*) well; (*de ascensor*) shaft; (*vacante*) vacancy; **~ de la mano** hollow of the hand

huela *etc* ['wela] VB *ver* **oler**

★**huelga** ['welɣa] VB *ver* **holgar** ▶ NF strike; **declararse en ~** to go on strike, come out on strike; **~ general** general strike; **~ de hambre** hunger strike; **~ oficial** official strike

huelgue *etc* ['welɣe] VB *ver* **holgar**

huelguista [wel'ɣista] NMF striker

huella ['weʎa] NF (*acto de pisar, pisada*) tread(ing); (*marca del paso*) footprint, footstep; (: *de animal, máquina*) track; **~ de carbono** carbon footprint; **~ dactilar** o **digital** fingerprint; **sin dejar ~** without leaving a trace

huelo *etc* VB *ver* **oler**

★**huérfano, -a** ['werfano, a] ADJ orphan(ed); (*fig*) unprotected ▶ NM/F orphan

huerta ['werta] NF market garden (BRIT), truck farm (US); (*de Murcia, Valencia*) irrigated region

★**huerto** ['werto] NM kitchen garden; (*de árboles frutales*) orchard

★**hueso** ['weso] NM (*Anat*) bone; (*de fruta*) stone, pit (US); **sin ~** (*carne*) boned; **estar en los huesos** to be nothing but skin and bone; **ser un ~** (*profesor*) to be terribly strict; **un ~ duro de roer** a hard nut to crack

huesoso, -a [we'soso, a] ADJ (*esp* AM) bony

★**huésped, a** ['wespeð, a] NM/F (*invitado*) guest; (*habitante*) resident; (*anfitrión*) host(ess)

huesudo, -a [we'suðo, a] ADJ bony, big-boned

huevas ['weβas] NFPL eggs, roe *sg*; (AM *fam!*) balls (*fam!*)

huevera [we'βera] NF eggcup

★**huevo** ['weβo] NM egg; (*fam!*) ball (*fam!*), testicle; **~ duro/escalfado/estrellado** o **frito/pasado por agua** hard-boiled/poached/fried/soft-boiled egg; **huevos revueltos** scrambled eggs; **~ tibio** (AM) soft-boiled egg; **me costó un ~** (*fam!*) it was hard work; **tener huevos** (*fam!*) to have guts

huevón, -ona [we'βon, ona] NM/F (AM *fam!*) stupid bastard (*fam!*), stupid idiot

★**huida** [u'iða] NF escape, flight; **~ de capitales** (*Com*) flight of capital

huidizo, -a [ui'ðiθo, a] ADJ (*tímido*) shy; (*pasajero*) fleeting

★**huir** [u'ir] /**3g**/ VT (*escapar*) to flee, escape; (*evadir*) to avoid ▶ VI to flee, run away

hule ['ule] NM (*encerado*) oilskin; (*esp* AM) rubber

hulera [u'lera] NF (AM) catapult

hulla ['uʎa] NF bituminous coal

humanice *etc* [uma'niθe] VB *ver* **humanizar**

humanidad [umani'ðað] NF (*género humano*) man(kind); (*cualidad*) humanity; (*fam: gordura*) corpulence

humanitario, -a [umani'tarjo, a] ADJ humanitarian; (*benévolo*) humane

humanizar [umani'θar] /**1f**/ VT to humanize ■ **humanizarse** VR to become more human

humano, -a [u'mano, a] ADJ (*gen*) human; (*humanitario*) humane; **ser ~** human being ▶ NM human

humareda [uma'reða] NF cloud of smoke

humeante [ume'ante] ADJ smoking, smoky

humedad [ume'ðað] NF (*del clima*) humidity; (*de pared etc*) dampness; **a prueba de ~** damp-proof

humedecer [umeðe'θer] /**2d**/ VT to moisten, wet ■ **humedecerse** VR to get wet

humedezca *etc* [ume'ðeθka] VB *ver* **humedecer**

★**húmedo, -a** [u'meðo, a] ADJ (*mojado*) damp, wet; (*tiempo etc*) humid

humidificador [umiðifika'ðor] NM humidifier

humildad [umil'dað] NF humility, humbleness

humilde [u'milde] ADJ humble, modest; (*clase etc*) low, modest

humillación [umiʎa'θjon] NF humiliation

humillante [umi'ʎante] ADJ humiliating

humillar [umi'ʎar] /**1a**/ VT to humiliate ■ **humillarse** VR to humble o.s., grovel

★**humo** ['umo] NM (*de fuego*) smoke; (*gas nocivo*) fumes *pl*; (*vapor*) steam, vapour; **irse todo en ~** (*fig*) to vanish without trace ■ **humos** NMPL (*fig*) conceit *sg*; **bajar los humos a algn** to take sb down a peg or two

★**humor** [u'mor] NM (*disposición*) mood, temper; (*lo que divierte*) humour; **de buen/mal ~** in a good/bad mood

humorismo [umo'rismo] NM humour

humorista [umo'rista] NMF comic

humorístico, -a [umo'ristiko, a] ADJ funny, humorous

hundimiento [undi'mjento] NM (*gen*) sinking; (*colapso*) collapse

hundir [un'dir] /3a/ VT to sink; (*edificio, plan*) to ruin, destroy ■ **hundirse** VR to sink, collapse; (*fig: arruinarse*) to be ruined; (*desaparecer*) to disappear; **se hundió la economía** the economy collapsed; **se hundieron los precios** prices slumped

húngaro, -a ['ungaro, a] ADJ, NM/F Hungarian ▶ NM (*Ling*) Hungarian, Magyar

Hungría [un'gria] NF Hungary

huracán [ura'kan] NM hurricane

huraño, -a [u'raɲo, a] ADJ shy; (*antisocial*) unsociable

hurgar [ur'ɣar] /1h/ VT to poke, jab; (*remover*) to stir (up) ■ **hurgarse** VR: **hurgarse (las narices)** to pick one's nose

hurgonear [urɣone'ar] /1a/ VT to poke

hurgue *etc* ['urɣe] VB *ver* **hurgar**

hurón [u'ron] NM (*Zool*) ferret

hurra ['urra] EXCL hurray!, hurrah!

hurtadillas [urta'ðiʎas]: **a ~** *adv* stealthily, on the sly

hurtar [ur'tar] /1a/ VT to steal ■ **hurtarse** VR to hide, keep out of the way

hurto ['urto] NM theft, stealing; (*lo robado*) (piece of) stolen property, loot

husmear [usme'ar] /1a/ VT (*oler*) to sniff out, scent; (*fam*) to pry into ▶ VI to smell bad

huso ['uso] NM (*Tec*) spindle; (*de torno*) drum

huy ['ui] EXCL (*dolor*) ow!, ouch!; (*sorpresa*) well!; (*alivio*) phew!; **¡~, perdona!** oops, sorry!

huyendo *etc* [u'jendo] VB *ver* **huir**

huyo *etc* VB *ver* **huir**

h

I i

I, i [i] NF (*letra*) I, i; **I de Inés** I for Isaac (*BRIT*) *o* Item (*US*)

IA ABR = **inteligencia artificial**

iba *etc* [ˈiβa] VB *ver* **ir**

Iberia [iˈβerja] NF Iberia

ibérico, -a [iˈβeriko, a] ADJ Iberian; **la Península ibérica** the Iberian Peninsula

ibero, -a [iˈβero, a], **íbero, -a** [ˈiβero, a] ADJ, NM/F Iberian

iberoamericano, -a [iβeroameriˈkano, a] ADJ, NM/F Latin American

íbice [ˈiβiθe] NM ibex

ibicenco, -a [iβiˈθenko, a] ADJ of *o* from Ibiza ▶ NM/F native *o* inhabitant of Ibiza

Ibiza [iˈβiθa] NF Ibiza

ice *etc* [ˈiθe] VB *ver* **izar**

iceberg [iθeˈber] NM iceberg

ICONA [iˈkona] NM ABR (*ESP*) = **Instituto Nacional para la Conservación de la Naturaleza**

icono [iˈkono] NM (*tb Inform*) icon

iconoclasta [ikonoˈklasta] ADJ iconoclastic ▶ NMF iconoclast

ictericia [ikteˈriθja] NF jaundice

I+D NF ABR (= *Investigación y Desarrollo*) R&D

íd. ABR = **ídem**

★**ida** [ˈiða] NF going, departure; **~ y vuelta** round trip, return; **idas y venidas** comings and goings

IDE [ˈiðe] NF ABR (= *Iniciativa de Defensa Estratégica*) SDI

★**idea** [iˈðea] NF idea; (*impresión*) opinion; (*propósito*) intention; **~ genial** brilliant idea; **a mala ~** out of spite; **no tengo la menor ~** I haven't a clue

★**ideal** [iðeˈal] ADJ, NM ideal

idealice *etc* [iðeaˈliθe] VB *ver* **idealizar**

idealista [iðeaˈlista] ADJ idealistic ▶ NMF idealist

idealizar [iðealiˈθar] /**1f**/ VT to idealize

idear [iðeˈar] /**1a**/ VT to think up; (*aparato*) to invent; (*viaje*) to plan

ídem [ˈiðem] PRON ditto

idéntico, -a [iˈðentiko, a] ADJ identical

identidad [iðentiˈðað] NF identity; **~ corporativa** corporate identity *o* image

identificación [iðentifikaˈθjon] NF identification

identificador de llamadas [iðentifikaˈðor-] NM caller ID

identificar [iðentifiˈkar] /**1g**/ VT to identify ■ **identificarse** VR: **identificarse con** to identify with

identifique *etc* [iðentiˈfike] VB *ver* **identificar**

ideología [iðeoloˈxia] NF ideology

ideológico, -a [iðeoˈloxiko, a] ADJ ideological

idílico, -a [iˈðiliko, a] ADJ idyllic

idilio [iˈðiljo] NM love affair

★**idioma** [iˈðjoma] NM language

idiomático, -a [iðjoˈmatiko, a] ADJ idiomatic

★**idiota** [iˈðjota] ADJ idiotic ▶ NMF idiot

idiotez [iðjoˈteθ] NF idiocy

idolatrar [iðolaˈtrar] /**1a**/ VT (*fig*) to idolize

ídolo [ˈiðolo] NM (*tb fig*) idol

idoneidad [iðoneiˈðað] NF suitability; (*capacidad*) aptitude

idóneo, -a [iˈðoneo, a] ADJ suitable

IES NM ABR = **Instituto de Enseñanza Secundaria**

★**iglesia** [iˈɣlesja] NF church; **~ parroquial** parish church; **¡con la ~ hemos topado!** now we're really up against it!

iglú [iˈɣlu] NM igloo; (*contenedor*) bottle bank

IGME NM ABR = **Instituto Geográfico y Minero**

ignición [iɣniˈθjon] NF ignition

ignominia [iɣnoˈminja] NF ignominy

ignominioso, -a [iɣnomiˈnjoso, a] ADJ ignominious

ignorado, -a [iɣnoˈraðo, a] ADJ unknown; (*dato*) obscure

ignorancia [iɣnoˈranθja] NF ignorance; **por ~** through ignorance

ignorante [iɣnoˈrante] ADJ ignorant, uninformed ▶ NMF ignoramus

ignorar [iɣnoˈrar] /**1a**/ VT not to know, be ignorant of; (*no hacer caso a*) to ignore; **ignoramos su paradero** we don't know his whereabouts

ignoto, -a [iɣˈnoto, a] ADJ unknown

igual [iˈɣwal] ADJ equal; (*similar*) like, similar; (*mismo*) (the) same; (*constante*) constant; (*temperatura*) even; **~ que** the same as; **son iguales** they're the same ▶ ADV: **me da ο es ~** I don't care, it makes no difference; **al ~ que** prep like, just like ▶ NMF equal; **sin ~** peerless; **no tener ~** to be unrivalled

iguala [iˈɣwala] NF equalization; (*Com*) agreement

igualada [iɣwaˈlaða] NF equalizer

igualar [iɣwaˈlar] /**1a**/ VT (*gen*) to equalize, make equal; (*terreno*) to make even; (*allanar, nivelar*) to level (off); (*Com*) to agree upon ▪ **igualarse** VR (*platos de balanza*) to balance out; **igualarse (a)** (*equivaler*) to be equal (to)

igualdad [iɣwalˈdað] NF equality; (*similaridad*) sameness; (*uniformidad*) uniformity; **en ~ de condiciones** on an equal basis

igualmente [iɣwalˈmente] ADV equally; (*también*) also, likewise ▶ EXCL the same to you!

iguana [iˈɣwana] NF iguana

ikurriña [ikuˈrrina] NF Basque flag

ilegal [ileˈɣal] ADJ illegal

ilegitimidad [ilexitimiˈðað] NF illegitimacy

ilegítimo, -a [ileˈxitimo, a] ADJ illegitimate

ileso, -a [iˈleso, a] ADJ unhurt, unharmed

ilícito, -a [iˈliθito, a] ADJ illicit

ilimitado, -a [ilimiˈtaðo, a] ADJ unlimited

Ilma., Ilmo. ABR (= *Ilustrísima, Ilustrísimo*) *courtesy title*

ilógico, -a [iˈloxiko, a] ADJ illogical

iluminación [iluminaˈθjon] NF illumination; (*alumbrado*) lighting; (*fig*) enlightenment

iluminar [ilumiˈnar] /**1a**/ VT to illuminate, light (up); (*fig*) to enlighten

ilusión [iluˈsjon] NF illusion; (*quimera*) delusion; (*esperanza*) hope; (*emoción*) excitement, thrill; **hacerse ilusiones** to build up one's hopes; **no te hagas ilusiones** don't build up your hopes ο get too excited

◂**ilusionado, -a** [ilusjoˈnaðo, a] ADJ excited

ilusionar [ilusjoˈnar] /**1a**/ VT: **~ a algn** (*falsamente*) to build up sb's hopes ▶ VI: **le ilusiona ir de vacaciones** he's looking forward to going on holiday ▪ **ilusionarse** VR (*falsamente*) to build up one's hopes; (*entusiasmarse*) to get excited; **me ilusiona mucho el viaje** I'm really excited about the trip

ilusionista [ilusjoˈnista] NMF conjurer

iluso, -a [iˈluso, a] ADJ gullible, easily deceived ▶ NM/F dreamer, visionary

ilusorio, -a [iluˈsorjo, a] ADJ (*de ilusión*) illusory, deceptive; (*esperanza*) vain

ilustración [ilustraˈθjon] NF illustration; (*saber*) learning, erudition; **la I~** the Enlightenment

ilustrado, -a [ilusˈtraðo, a] ADJ illustrated; learned

ilustrar [ilusˈtrar] /**1a**/ VT to illustrate; (*instruir*) to instruct; (*explicar*) to explain, make clear ▪ **ilustrarse** VR to acquire knowledge

ilustre [iˈlustre] ADJ famous, illustrious

★**imagen** [iˈmaxen] NF (*gen*) image; (*dibujo, TV*) picture; (*Rel*) statue; **ser la viva ~ de** to be the spitting ο living image of; **a su ~** in one's own image

imaginación [imaxinaˈθjon] NF imagination; (*fig*) fancy; **ni por ~** on no account; **no se me pasó por la ~ que ...** it never even occurred to me that ...

imaginar [imaxiˈnar] /**1a**/ VT (*gen*) to imagine; (*idear*) to think up; (*suponer*) to suppose ▪ **imaginarse** VR to imagine; **¡imagínate!** just imagine!, just fancy!; **imagínese que ...** suppose that ...; **me imagino que sí** I should think so

imaginario, -a [imaxiˈnarjo, a] ADJ imaginary

imaginativo, -a [imaxinaˈtiβo, a] ADJ imaginative ▶ NF imagination

imán [iˈman] NM magnet; (*Rel*) imam

imanar [imaˈnar] /**1a**/, **imantar** [imaˈntar] /**1a**/ VT to magnetize

★**imbécil** [imˈbeθil] NMF imbecile, idiot

imbecilidad [imbeθiliˈðað] NF imbecility, stupidity

imberbe [imˈberβe] ADJ beardless

imborrable [imboˈrraβle] ADJ indelible; (*inolvidable*) unforgettable

imbuir [imbuˈir] /**3g**/ VI to imbue

imbuyendo *etc* [imbuˈjendo] VB *ver* **imbuir**

imitación [imitaˈθjon] NF imitation; (*parodia*) mimicry; **a ~ de** in imitation of; **desconfíe de las imitaciones** (*Com*) beware of copies ο imitations

imitador, a [imitaˈðor, a] ADJ imitative ▶ NM/F imitator; (*Teat*) mimic

imitar [imiˈtar] /**1a**/ VT to imitate; (*parodiar, remedar*) to mimic, ape; (*copiar*) to follow

impaciencia [impaˈθjenθja] NF impatience

impacientar [impaθjenˈtar] /**1a**/ VT to make impatient; (*enfadar*) to irritate ▪ **impacientarse** VR to get impatient; (*inquietarse*) to fret

★**impaciente** [impaˈθjente] ADJ impatient; (*nervioso*) anxious

impacto [imˈpakto] NM impact; (*esp Am fig*) shock

impagado, -a [impaˈɣaðo, a] ADJ unpaid, still to be paid

impar [imˈpar] ADJ odd ▶ NM odd number

imparable [impaˈraβle] ADJ unstoppable

imparcial [imparˈθjal] ADJ impartial, fair

imparcialidad [imparθjaliˈðað] NF impartiality, fairness

impartir [impar'tir] /**3a**/ VT to impart, give

impasible [impa'siβle] ADJ impassive

impávido, -a [im'paβiðo, a] ADJ fearless, intrepid

impecable [impe'kaβle] ADJ impeccable

impedido, -a [impe'ðiðo, a] ADJ: **estar ~** to be an invalid ▶ NM/F: **ser un ~ físico** to be an invalid

impedimento [impeði'mento] NM impediment, obstacle

★**impedir** [impe'ðir] /**3k**/ VT (obstruir) to impede, obstruct; (estorbar) to prevent; **~ a algn hacer o que algn haga algo** to prevent sb (from) doing sth; **~ el tráfico** to block the traffic

impeler [impe'ler] /**2a**/ VT to drive, propel; (fig) to impel

impenetrabilidad [impenetraβili'ðað] NF impenetrability

impenetrable [impene'traβle] ADJ impenetrable; (fig) incomprehensible

impensable [impen'saβle] ADJ unthinkable

impepinable [impepi'naβle] ADJ (fam) certain, inevitable

imperante [impe'rante] ADJ prevailing

imperar [impe'rar] /**1a**/ VI (reinar) to rule, reign; (fig) to prevail, reign; (precio) to be current

imperativo, -a [impera'tiβo, a] ADJ (persona) imperious; (urgente, Ling) imperative

imperceptible [imperθep'tiβle] ADJ imperceptible

imperdible [imper'ðiβle] NM safety pin

imperdonable [imperðo'naβle] ADJ unforgivable, inexcusable

imperecedero, -a [impereθe'ðero, a] ADJ undying

imperfección [imperfek'θjon] NF imperfection; (falla) flaw, fault

imperfecto, -a [imper'fekto, a] ADJ faulty, imperfect ▶ NM (Ling) imperfect tense

imperial [impe'rjal] ADJ imperial

imperialismo [imperja'lismo] NM imperialism

imperialista [imperja'lista] ADJ imperialist(ic) ▶ NMF imperialist

impericia [impe'riθja] NF (torpeza) unskilfulness; (inexperiencia) inexperience

imperio [im'perjo] NM empire; (autoridad) rule, authority; (fig) pride, haughtiness; **vale un ~** (fig) it's worth a fortune

imperioso, -a [impe'rjoso, a] ADJ imperious; (urgente) urgent; (imperativo) imperative

★**impermeable** [imperme'aβle] ADJ (a prueba de agua) waterproof ▶ NM raincoat, mac (BRIT)

impersonal [imperso'nal] ADJ impersonal

impertérrito, -a [imper'territo, a] ADJ undaunted

impertinencia [imperti'nenθja] NF impertinence

impertinente [imperti'nente] ADJ impertinent

imperturbable [impertur'βaβle] ADJ imperturbable; (sereno) unruffled; (impasible) impassive

ímpetu ['impetu] NM (impulso) impetus, impulse; (impetuosidad) impetuosity; (violencia) violence

impetuosidad [impetwosi'ðað] NF impetuousness; (violencia) violence

impetuoso, -a [impe'twoso, a] ADJ impetuous; (río) rushing; (acto) hasty

impida etc [im'piða] VB ver **impedir**

impío, -a [im'pio, a] ADJ impious, ungodly; (cruel) cruel, pitiless

implacable [impla'kaβle] ADJ implacable, relentless

implantación [implanta'θjon] NF introduction; (Bio) implantation

implantar [implan'tar] /**1a**/ VT (costumbre) to introduce; (Bio) to implant ■ **implantarse** VR to be introduced

implemento [imple'mento] NM (AM) tool, implement

implicar [impli'kar] /**1g**/ VT to involve; (entrañar) to imply; **esto no implica que ...** this does not mean that ...

implícito, -a [im'pliθito, a] ADJ (tácito) implicit; (sobreentendido) implied

implique etc [im'plike] VB ver **implicar**

implorar [implo'rar] /**1a**/ VT to beg, implore

impondré etc [impon'dre] VB ver **imponer**

imponente [impo'nente] ADJ (impresionante) impressive, imposing; (solemne) grand ▶ NMF (Com) depositor

imponer [impo'ner] /**2q**/ VT (gen) to impose; (tarea) to set; (exigir) to exact; (miedo) to inspire; (Com) to deposit ■ **imponerse** VR to assert o.s.; (prevalecer) to prevail; (costumbre) to grow up; **imponerse un deber** to assume a duty

imponga etc [im'ponga] VB ver **imponer**

imponible [impo'niβle] ADJ (Com) taxable, subject to tax; (importación) dutiable, subject to duty; **no ~** tax-free, tax-exempt (US)

impopular [impopu'lar] ADJ unpopular

importación [importa'θjon] NF (acto) importing; (mercancías) imports pl

importancia [impor'tanθja] NF importance; (valor) value, significance; (extensión) size, magnitude; **no dar ~ a** to consider unimportant; (fig) to make light of; **no tiene ~** it's nothing

★**importante** [impor'tante] ADJ important; (considerable) valuable, significant

★**importar** [impor'tar] /**1a**/ VT (del extranjero) to import; (costar) to amount to; (implicar) to involve ▶ VI to be important, matter; **me importa un rábano** or **un bledo** I couldn't care less, I don't give a damn; **¿le importa que fume?** do you mind if I smoke?; **¿te importa prestármelo?** would you mind lending it to me?; **¿qué importa?** what difference does it make?; **no importa** it doesn't matter; **no le importa** he doesn't care, it doesn't bother him; **"no importa precio"** "cost no object"

importe [im'porte] NM (*cantidad*) amount; (*valor*) value

importunar [importu'nar] /1a/ VT to bother, pester

importuno, -a [impor'tuno, a] ADJ (*inoportuno, molesto*) inopportune; (*indiscreto*) troublesome

imposibilidad [imposiβili'ðað] NF impossibility; **mi ~ para hacerlo** my inability to do it

imposibilitado, -a [imposiβili'taðo, a] ADJ: **verse ~ para hacer algo** to be unable to do sth

imposibilitar [imposiβili'tar] /1a/ VT to make impossible, prevent

★**imposible** [impo'siβle] ADJ impossible; (*insoportable*) unbearable, intolerable; **es ~** it's out of the question; **es ~ de predecir** it's impossible to forecast o predict

imposición [imposi'θjon] NF imposition; (*Com*) tax; (*inversión*) deposit; **efectuar una ~** to make a deposit

impostor, a [impos'tor, a] NM/F impostor

impostura [impos'tura] NF fraud, imposture

impotencia [impo'tenθja] NF impotence

impotente [impo'tente] ADJ impotent

impracticable [imprakti'kaβle] ADJ (*irrealizable*) impracticable; (*intransitable*) impassable

imprecar [impre'kar] /1g/ VI to curse

imprecisión [impreθi'sjon] NF lack of precision, vagueness

impreciso, -a [impre'θiso, a] ADJ imprecise, vague

impredecible [impreðe'θiβle], **impredictible** [impreðik'tiβle] ADJ unpredictable

impregnar [impreɣ'nar] /1a/ VT to impregnate; (*fig*) to pervade ■ **impregnarse** VR to become impregnated

imprenta [im'prenta] NF (*acto*) printing; (*aparato*) press; (*casa*) printer's; (*letra*) print

impreque *etc* [im'preke] VB *ver* **imprecar**

★**imprescindible** [impresθin'diβle] ADJ essential, vital

impresión [impre'sjon] NF impression; (*Imprenta*) printing; (*edición*) edition; (*Foto*) print; (*marca*) imprint; **~ digital** fingerprint

impresionable [impresjo'naβle] ADJ (*sensible*) impressionable

impresionado, -a [impresjo'naðo, a] ADJ impressed; (*Foto*) exposed

★**impresionante** [impresjo'nante] ADJ impressive; (*tremendo*) tremendous; (*maravilloso*) great, marvellous

impresionar [impresjo'nar] /1a/ VT (*conmover*) to move; (*afectar*) to impress, strike; (*película fotográfica*) to expose ■ **impresionarse** VR to be impressed; (*conmoverse*) to be moved

impresionista [impresjo'nista] ADJ impressionist(ic); (*Arte*) impressionist ▶ NMF impressionist

impreso, -a [im'preso, a] PP *de* **imprimir** ▶ ADJ printed ▶ NM printed paper/book *etc*; **~ de solicitud** application form ■ **impresos** NMPL printed matter *sg*

★**impresora** [impre'sora] NF (*Inform*) printer; **~ de chorro de tinta** ink-jet printer; **~ (por) láser** laser printer; **~ de línea** line printer; **~ de matriz (de agujas)** dot-matrix printer; **~ de rueda** o **de margarita** daisy-wheel printer

imprevisible [impreβi'siβle] ADJ unforeseeable; (*individuo*) unpredictable

imprevisión [impreβi'sjon] NF shortsightedness; (*irreflexión*) thoughtlessness

imprevisto, -a [impre'βisto, a] ADJ unforeseen; (*inesperado*) unexpected ▶ NM: **imprevistos** (*dinero*) incidentals, unforeseen expenses

★**imprimir** [impri'mir] /3a/ VT to stamp; (*textos*) to print; (*Inform*) to output, print out

improbabilidad [improβaβili'ðað] NF improbability, unlikelihood

improbable [impro'βaβle] ADJ improbable; (*inverosímil*) unlikely

improcedente [improθe'ðente] ADJ inappropriate; (*Jur*) inadmissible

improductivo, -a [improðuk'tiβo, a] ADJ unproductive

impronunciable [impronun'θjaβle] ADJ unpronounceable

improperio [impro'perjo] NM insult ■ **improperios** NMPL abuse *sg*

impropiedad [impropje'ðað] NF impropriety (of language)

impropio, -a [im'propjo, a] ADJ improper; (*inadecuado*) inappropriate

improvisación [improβisa'θjon] NF improvisation

improvisado, -a [improβi'saðo, a] ADJ improvised, impromptu

improvisar [improβi'sar] /1a/ VT to improvise; (*comida*) to rustle up ▶ VI to improvise; (*Mus*) to extemporize; (*Teat etc*) to ad-lib

improviso [impro'βiso] ADV: **de ~** unexpectedly, suddenly; (*Mus etc*) impromptu

imprudencia [impru'ðenθja] NF imprudence; (*indiscreción*) indiscretion; (*descuido*) carelessness

imprudente [impru'ðente] ADJ unwise, imprudent; (*indiscreto*) indiscreet

Impte. ABR (= *Importe*) amt.

impúdico, -a [im'puðiko, a] ADJ shameless; (*lujurioso*) lecherous

impudor [impu'ðor] NM shamelessness; (*lujuria*) lechery

★**impuesto, -a** [im'pwesto, a] PP *de* **imponer** ▶ ADJ imposed ▶ NM tax; **anterior al ~** pre-tax; **sujeto a ~** taxable; **~ ambiental** green tax, environmental tax; **~ ecológico** green tax; **~ de lujo** luxury tax; **~ de plusvalía** capital gains tax; **~ sobre la propiedad** property tax; **~ sobre la renta** income tax; **~ sobre la renta**

de las personas físicas (IRPF) personal income tax; **~ sobre la riqueza** wealth tax; **~ de transferencia de capital** capital transfer tax; **~ de venta** sales tax; **~ sobre el valor añadido (IVA)** value added tax (VAT)

impugnar [impuɣˈnar] /**1a**/ ᴠᴛ to oppose, contest; (*refutar*) to refute, impugn

impulsar [impulˈsar] /**1a**/ ᴠᴛ to drive; (*promover*) to promote, stimulate

impulsivo, -a [impulˈsiβo, a] ᴀᴅᴊ impulsive

impulso [imˈpulso] ɴᴍ impulse; (*fuerza, empuje*) thrust, drive; (*fig: sentimiento*) urge, impulse; **a impulsos del miedo** driven on by fear

impune [imˈpune] ᴀᴅᴊ unpunished

impunemente [impuneˈmente] ᴀᴅᴠ with impunity

impureza [impuˈreθa] ɴꜰ impurity; (*fig*) lewdness

impuro, -a [imˈpuro, a] ᴀᴅᴊ impure; lewd

impuse *etc* [imˈpuse] ᴠʙ *ver* **imponer**

imputación [imputaˈθjon] ɴꜰ imputation

imputar [impuˈtar] /**1a**/ ᴠᴛ: **~ a** to attribute to, impute to

IMSERSO [inˈserso] ɴᴍ ᴀʙʀ (= *Instituto de Mayores y Servicios Sociales*) branch of social services

inabordable [inaβorˈðaβle] ᴀᴅᴊ unapproachable

inacabable [inakaˈβaβle] ᴀᴅᴊ (*infinito*) endless; (*interminable*) interminable

inaccesible [inakθeˈsiβle] ᴀᴅᴊ inaccessible; (*fig: precio*) beyond one's reach, prohibitive; (*individuo*) aloof

inacción [inakˈθjon] ɴꜰ inactivity

inaceptable [inaθepˈtaβle] ᴀᴅᴊ unacceptable

inactividad [inaktiβiˈðað] ɴꜰ inactivity; (*Com*) dullness

inactivo, -a [inakˈtiβo, a] ᴀᴅᴊ inactive; (*Com*) dull; (*población*) non-working

inadaptación [inaðaptaˈθjon] ɴꜰ maladjustment

inadaptado, -a [inaðapˈtaðo, a] ᴀᴅᴊ maladjusted ▶ ɴᴍ/ꜰ misfit

inadecuado, -a [inaðeˈkwaðo, a] ᴀᴅᴊ (*insuficiente*) inadequate; (*inapto*) unsuitable

inadmisible [inaðmiˈsiβle] ᴀᴅᴊ inadmissible

inadvertido, -a [inaðβerˈtiðo, a] ᴀᴅᴊ (*no visto*) unnoticed

inagotable [inaɣoˈtaβle] ᴀᴅᴊ inexhaustible

inaguantable [inaɣwanˈtaβle] ᴀᴅᴊ unbearable

inalámbrico, -a [inaˈlambriko, a] ᴀᴅᴊ cordless, wireless

inalcanzable [inalkanˈθaβle] ᴀᴅᴊ unattainable

inalterable [inalteˈraβle] ᴀᴅᴊ immutable, unchangeable

inamovible [inamoˈβiβle] ᴀᴅᴊ fixed, immovable; (*Tec*) undetachable

inanición [inaniˈθjon] ɴꜰ starvation

inanimado, -a [inaniˈmaðo, a] ᴀᴅᴊ inanimate

inapelable [inapeˈlaβle] ᴀᴅᴊ (*Jur*) unappealable; (*fig*) irremediable

inapetencia [inapeˈtenθja] ɴꜰ lack of appetite

inaplicable [inapliˈkaβle] ᴀᴅᴊ not applicable

inapreciable [inapreˈθjaβle] ᴀᴅᴊ invaluable

inarrugable [inarruˈɣaβle] ᴀᴅᴊ crease-resistant

inasequible [inaseˈkiβle] ᴀᴅᴊ unattainable

inaudito, -a [inauˈðito, a] ᴀᴅᴊ unheard-of

inauguración [inauɣuraˈθjon] ɴꜰ inauguration; (*de exposición*) opening

inaugurar [inauɣuˈrar] /**1a**/ ᴠᴛ to inaugurate; (*exposición*) to open

INBA ᴀʙʀ (*Aᴍ*) = **Instituto Nacional de Bellas Artes**

inca [ˈinka] ɴᴍꜰ Inca

INCAE [inˈkae] ɴᴍ ᴀʙʀ = **Instituto Centroamericano de Administración de Empresas**

incaico, -a [inˈkaiko, a] ᴀᴅᴊ Inca

incalculable [inkalkuˈlaβle] ᴀᴅᴊ incalculable

incandescente [inkandesˈθente] ᴀᴅᴊ incandescent

incansable [inkanˈsaβle] ᴀᴅᴊ tireless, untiring

incapacidad [inkapaθiˈðað] ɴꜰ incapacity; (*incompetencia*) incompetence; **~ física/mental** physical/mental disability

incapacitar [inkapaθiˈtar] /**1a**/ ᴠᴛ (*inhabilitar*) to incapacitate, handicap; (*descalificar*) to disqualify

incapaz [inkaˈpaθ] ᴀᴅᴊ incapable; **~ de hacer algo** unable to do sth

incautación [inkautaˈθjon] ɴꜰ seizure, confiscation

incautarse [inkauˈtarse] /**1a**/ ᴠʀ: **~ de** to seize, confiscate

incauto, -a [inˈkauto, a] ᴀᴅᴊ (*imprudente*) incautious, unwary

incendiar [inθenˈdjar] /**1b**/ ᴠᴛ to set fire to; (*fig*) to inflame ■ **incendiarse** ᴠʀ to catch fire

incendiario, -a [inθenˈdjarjo, a] ᴀᴅᴊ incendiary ▶ ɴᴍ/ꜰ fire-raiser, arsonist

★incendio [inˈθendjo] ɴᴍ fire; **~ intencionado** arson

incentivo [inθenˈtiβo] ɴᴍ incentive

incertidumbre [inθertiˈðumbre] ɴꜰ (*inseguridad*) uncertainty; (*duda*) doubt

incesante [inθeˈsante] ᴀᴅᴊ incessant

incesto [inˈθesto] ɴᴍ incest

incidencia [inθiˈðenθja] ɴꜰ (*Mat*) incidence; (*fig*) effect

★incidente [inθiˈðente] ɴᴍ incident

incidir [inθiˈðir] /**3a**/ ᴠɪ: **~ en** (*influir*) to influence; (*afectar*) to affect; **~ en un error** to be mistaken

incienso [inˈθjenso] ɴᴍ incense

incierto, -a [inˈθjerto, a] ᴀᴅᴊ uncertain

incineración [inθine'raθjon] NF incineration; (*de cadáveres*) cremation

incinerar [inθine'rar] /**1a**/ VT to burn; (*cadáveres*) to cremate

incipiente [inθi'pjente] ADJ incipient

incisión [inθi'sjon] NF incision

incisivo, -a [inθi'siβo, a] ADJ sharp, cutting; (*fig*) incisive

inciso [in'θiso] NM (*Ling*) clause, sentence; (*coma*) comma; (*Jur*) subsection

incitante [inθi'tante] ADJ (*estimulante*) exciting; (*provocativo*) provocative

incitar [inθi'tar] /**1a**/ VT to incite, rouse

incivil [inθi'βil] ADJ rude, uncivil

inclemencia [inkle'menθja] NF (*severidad*) harshness, severity; (*del tiempo*) inclemency

inclemente [inkle'mente] ADJ harsh, severe; inclement

inclinación [inklina'θjon] NF (*gen*) inclination; (*de tierras*) slope, incline; (*de cabeza*) nod, bow; (*fig*) leaning, bent

inclinado, -a [inkli'naðo, a] ADJ (*objeto*) leaning; (*superficie*) sloping

★**inclinar** [inkli'nar] /**1a**/ VT to incline; (*cabeza*) to nod, bow ■ **inclinarse** VR to lean, slope; (*en reverencia*) to bow; (*encorvarse*) to stoop; **inclinarse a** (*parecerse*) to take after, resemble; **inclinarse ante** to bow down to; **me inclino a pensar que ...** I'm inclined to think that ...

★**incluir** [inklu'ir] /**3g**/ VT to include; (*incorporar*) to incorporate; (*meter*) to enclose; **todo incluido** (*Com*) inclusive, all-in

inclusive [inklu'siβe] ADV inclusive ▶ PREP including

★**incluso, -a** [in'kluso, a] ADJ included ▶ ADV inclusively; (*hasta*) even

incluyendo *etc* [inklu'jendo] VB *ver* **incluir**

incobrable [inko'βraβle] ADJ irrecoverable; (*deuda*) bad

incógnita [in'koɣnita] NF (*Mat*) unknown quantity; (*fig*) mystery

incógnito [in'koɣnito] NM: **de ~** incognito

incoherencia [inkoe'renθja] NF incoherence; (*falta de conexión*) disconnectedness

incoherente [inkoe'rente] ADJ incoherent

incoloro, -a [inko'loro, a] ADJ colourless

incólume [in'kolume] ADJ safe; (*indemne*) unhurt, unharmed

incombustible [inkombus'tiβle] ADJ (*gen*) fire-resistant; (*telas*) fireproof

incomodar [inkomo'ðar] /**1a**/ VT to inconvenience; (*molestar*) to bother, trouble; (*fastidiar*) to annoy ■ **incomodarse** VR to put o.s. out; (*fastidiarse*) to get annoyed; **no se incomode** don't bother

incomodidad [inkomoði'ðað] NF inconvenience; (*fastidio, enojo*) annoyance; (*de vivienda*) discomfort

★**incómodo, -a** [in'komoðo, a] ADJ (*inconfortable*) uncomfortable; (*molesto*) annoying; (*inconveniente*) inconvenient; **sentirse ~** to feel ill at ease

incomparable [inkompa'raβle] ADJ incomparable

incomparecencia [inkompare'θenθja] NF (*Jur etc*) failure to appear

incompatible [inkompa'tiβle] ADJ incompatible

incompetencia [inkompe'tenθja] NF incompetence

incompetente [inkompe'tente] ADJ incompetent

incompleto, -a [inkom'pleto, a] ADJ incomplete, unfinished

incomprendido, -a [inkompren'diðo, a] ADJ misunderstood

incomprensible [inkompren'siβle] ADJ incomprehensible

incomunicado, -a [inkomuni'kaðo, a] ADJ (*aislado*) cut off, isolated; (*confinado*) in solitary confinement

incomunicar [inkomuni'kar] /**1g**/ VT (*gen*) to cut off; (*preso*) to put into solitary confinement ■ **incomunicarse** VR (*fam*) to go into one's shell

incomunique *etc* [inkomu'nike] VB *ver* **incomunicar**

inconcebible [inkonθe'βiβle] ADJ inconceivable

inconcluso, -a [inkon'kluso, a] ADJ (*inacabado*) unfinished

incondicional [inkondiθjo'nal] ADJ unconditional; (*apoyo*) wholehearted; (*partidario*) staunch

inconexo, -a [inko'nekso, a] ADJ unconnected; (*desunido*) disconnected; (*incoherente*) incoherent

inconfeso, -a [inkon'feso, a] ADJ unconfessed; **un homosexual ~** a closet homosexual

inconformista [inkonfor'mista] ADJ, NMF non-conformist

inconfundible [inkonfun'diβle] ADJ unmistakable

incongruente [inkon'grwente] ADJ incongruous

inconmensurable [inkonmensu'raβle] ADJ immeasurable, vast

inconsciencia [inkons'θjenθja] NF unconsciousness; (*fig*) thoughtlessness

inconsciente [inkons'θjente] ADJ unconscious; thoughtless; (*ignorante*) unaware; (*involuntario*) unwitting

inconsecuencia [inkonse'kwenθja] NF inconsistency

inconsecuente [inkonse'kwente] ADJ inconsistent

inconsiderado, -a [inkonsiðe'raðo, a] ADJ inconsiderate

inconsistente [inkonsis'tente] ADJ inconsistent; (*Culin*) lumpy; (*endeble*) weak; (*tela*) flimsy

inconstancia [inkons'tanθja] NF inconstancy; (*de tiempo*) changeability; (*capricho*) fickleness

inconstante [inkons'tante] ADJ inconstant; (*tiempo*) changeable; (*persona*) fickle

incontable [inkon'taβle] ADJ countless, innumerable

incontestable [inkontes'taβle] ADJ unanswerable; (*innegable*) undeniable

incontinencia [inkonti'nenθja] NF incontinence

incontrolado, -a [inkontro'laðo, a] ADJ uncontrolled

incontrovertible [inkontroβer'tiβle] ADJ undeniable, incontrovertible

inconveniencia [inkombe'njenθja] NF unsuitability, inappropriateness; (*falta de cortesía*) impoliteness

★**inconveniente** [inkombe'njente] ADJ unsuitable; impolite ▶ NM obstacle; (*desventaja*) disadvantage; **el ~ es que ...** the trouble is that ...; **no hay ~ en** o **para hacer eso** there is no objection to doing that; **no tengo ~** I don't mind

incordiar [inkor'ðjar] /**1b**/ VT (*fam*) to hassle

incorporación [inkorpora'θjon] NF incorporation; (*fig*) inclusion

incorporado, -a [inkorpo'raðo, a] ADJ (*Tec*) built-in

incorporar [inkorpo'rar] /**1a**/ VT to incorporate; (*abarcar*) to embody; (*Culin*) to mix ■ **incorporarse** VR to sit up; **incorporarse a** to join

incorrección [inkorrek'θjon] NF incorrectness, inaccuracy; (*descortesía*) bad-mannered behaviour

★**incorrecto, -a** [inko'rrekto, a] ADJ incorrect, wrong; (*comportamiento*) bad-mannered

incorregible [inkorre'xiβle] ADJ incorrigible

incorruptible [inkorrup'tiβle] ADJ incorruptible

incorrupto, -a [inko'rrupto, a] ADJ uncorrupted; (*fig*) pure

incredulidad [inkreðuli'ðað] NF incredulity; (*escepticismo*) scepticism

incrédulo, -a [in'kreðulo, a] ADJ incredulous, unbelieving; (*escéptico*) sceptical

★**increíble** [inkre'iβle] ADJ incredible

incrementar [inkremen'tar] /**1a**/ VT (*aumentar*) to increase; (*alzar*) to raise ■ **incrementarse** VR to increase

incremento [inkre'mento] NM increment; (*aumento*) rise, increase; **~ de precio** rise in price

increpar [inkre'par] /**1a**/ VT to reprimand

incriminar [inkrimi'nar] /**1a**/ VT (*Jur*) to incriminate

incruento, -a [in'krwento, a] ADJ bloodless

incrustar [inkrus'tar] /**1a**/ VT to incrust; (*piedras: en joya*) to inlay; (*fig*) to graft; (*Tec*) to set

incubar [inku'βar] /**1a**/ VT to incubate; (*fig*) to hatch

incuestionable [inkwestjo'naβle] ADJ unchallengeable

inculcar [inkul'kar] /**1g**/ VT to inculcate

inculpar [inkul'par] /**1a**/ VT: **~ de** (*acusar*) to accuse of; (*achacar, atribuir*) to charge with, blame for

inculque *etc* [in'kulke] VB *ver* **inculcar**

inculto, -a [in'kulto, a] ADJ (*persona*) uneducated, uncultured; (*fig: grosero*) uncouth ▶ NM/F ignoramus

incumbencia [inkum'benθja] NF obligation; **no es de mi ~** it is not my field

incumbir [inkum'bir] /**3a**/ VI: **~ a** to be incumbent upon; **no me incumbe a mí** it is no concern of mine

incumplimiento [inkumpli'mjento] NM non-fulfilment; (*Com*) repudiation; **~ de contrato** breach of contract; **por ~** by default

incurable [inku'raβle] ADJ (*enfermedad*) incurable; (*paciente*) incurably ill

incurrir [inku'rrir] /**3a**/ VI: **~ en** to incur; (*crimen*) to commit; **~ en un error** to make a mistake

indagación [indaɣa'θjon] NF investigation; (*búsqueda*) search; (*Jur*) inquest

indagar [inda'ɣar] /**1h**/ VT to investigate; to search; (*averiguar*) to ascertain

indague *etc* [in'daɣe] VB *ver* **indagar**

indebido, -a [inde'βiðo, a] ADJ undue; (*dicho*) improper

indecencia [inde'θenθja] NF indecency; (*dicho*) obscenity

indecente [inde'θente] ADJ indecent, improper; (*lascivo*) obscene

indecible [inde'θiβle] ADJ unspeakable; (*indescriptible*) indescribable

indeciso, -a [inde'θiso, a] ADJ (*por decidir*) undecided; (*vacilante*) hesitant

indefenso, -a [inde'fenso, a] ADJ defenceless

indefinido, -a [indefi'niðo, a] ADJ indefinite; (*vago*) vague, undefined

indeleble [inde'leβle] ADJ indelible

indemne [in'demne] ADJ (*objeto*) undamaged; (*persona*) unharmed, unhurt

indemnice *etc* [indem'niθe] VB *ver* **indemnizar**

indemnización [indemniθa'θjon] NF (*acto*) indemnification; (*suma*) indemnity; **~ por cese** redundancy payment; **~ por despido** severance pay; **doble ~** double indemnity

indemnizar [indemni'θar] /**1f**/ VT to indemnify; (*compensar*) to compensate

★**independencia** [indepen'denθja] NF independence

independice *etc* [indepen'diθe] VB *ver* **independizar**

★**independiente** [indepen'djente] ADJ (*libre*) independent; (*autónomo*) self-sufficient; (*Inform*) stand-alone

independizar [independi'θar] /**1f**/ VT to make independent ■ **independizarse** VR to become independent

indescifrable [indesθiˈfraβle] ADJ (Mil: código) indecipherable; (fig: misterio) impenetrable

indeseable [indeseˈaβle] ADJ, NMF undesirable

indeterminado, -a [indetermiˈnaðo, a] ADJ (tb Ling) indefinite; (desconocido) indeterminate

★**India** [ˈindja] NF: **la ~** India

indiano, -a [inˈdjano, a] ADJ (Spanish-)American ▶ NM Spaniard who has made good in America

indicación [indikaˈθjon] NF indication; (dato) piece of information; (señal) sign; (sugerencia) suggestion, hint ■ **indicaciones** NFPL (Com) instructions

indicado, -a [indiˈkaðo, a] ADJ (momento, método) right; (tratamiento) appropriate; (solución) likely

indicador [indikaˈðor] NM indicator; (Tec) gauge, meter; (aguja) hand, pointer; (de carretera) road sign; **~ de encendido** (Inform) power-on indicator

★**indicar** [indiˈkar] /**1g**/ VT (mostrar) to indicate, show; (suj: termómetro etc) to read, register; (señalar) to point to

indicativo, -a [indikaˈtiβo, a] ADJ indicative ▶ NM (Radio) call sign; **~ de nacionalidad** (Auto) national identification plate

índice [ˈindiθe] NM index; (catálogo) catalogue; (Anat) index finger, forefinger; **~ del coste de (la) vida** cost-of-living index; **~ de crédito** credit rating; **~ de materias** table of contents; **~ de natalidad** birth rate; **~ de precios al por menor (IPM)** (Com) retail price index (RPI)

indicio [inˈdiθjo] NM indication, sign; (en pesquisa etc) clue

indiferencia [indifeˈrenθja] NF indifference; (apatía) apathy

indiferente [indifeˈrente] ADJ indifferent; **me es ~** it makes no difference to me

indígena [inˈdixena] ADJ indigenous, native ▶ NMF native

indigencia [indiˈxenθja] NF poverty, need

indigenista [indixeˈnista] (Am) ADJ pro-Indian ▶ NMF (estudiante) student of Indian cultures; (Pol etc) promoter of Indian cultures

indigestar [indixesˈtar] /**1a**/ VT to cause indigestion to ■ **indigestarse** VR to get indigestion

indigestión [indixesˈtjon] NF indigestion

indigesto, -a [indiˈxesto, a] ADJ undigested; (indigerible) indigestible; (fig) turgid

indignación [indiɣnaˈθjon] NF indignation

indignante [indiɣˈnante] ADJ outrageous, infuriating

indignar [indiɣˈnar] /**1a**/ VT to anger, make indignant ■ **indignarse** VR: **indignarse por** to get indignant about

indigno, -a [inˈdiɣno, a] ADJ (despreciable) low, contemptible; (inmerecido) unworthy

★**indio, -a** [ˈindjo, a] ADJ, NM/F Indian

indique etc [inˈdike] VB ver **indicar**

indirecto, -a [indiˈrekto, a] ADJ indirect ▶ NF insinuation, innuendo; (sugerencia) hint

indisciplina [indisθiˈplina] NF (gen) lack of discipline; (Mil) insubordination

indiscreción [indiskreˈθjon] NF (imprudencia) indiscretion; (irreflexión) tactlessness; (acto) gaffe, faux pas; **si no es ~** ..., if I may say so

indiscreto, -a [indisˈkreto, a] ADJ indiscreet

indiscriminado, -a [indiskrimiˈnaðo, a] ADJ indiscriminate

indiscutible [indiskuˈtiβle] ADJ indisputable, unquestionable

indispensable [indispenˈsaβle] ADJ indispensable, essential

indispondré etc [indisponˈdre] VB ver **indisponer**

indisponer [indispoˈner] /**2q**/ VT to spoil, upset; (salud) to make ill ■ **indisponerse** VR to fall ill; **indisponerse con algn** to fall out with sb

indisponga etc [indisˈpoŋga] VB ver **indisponer**

indisposición [indisposiˈθjon] NF indisposition; (desgana) unwillingness

indispuesto, -a [indisˈpwesto, a] PP de **indisponer** ▶ ADJ (enfermo) unwell, indisposed; **sentirse ~** to feel unwell o indisposed

indispuse etc [indisˈpuse] VB ver **indisponer**

indistinto, -a [indisˈtinto, a] ADJ indistinct; (vago) vague

★**individual** [indiβiˈðwal] ADJ individual; (habitación) single ▶ NM (Deporte) singles sg

★**individuo** [indiˈβiðwo] NM individual

Indochina [indoˈtʃina] NF Indochina

indocumentado, -a [indokumenˈtaðo, a] ADJ without identity papers

indoeuropeo, -a [indoeuroˈpeo, a] ADJ, NM/F Indo-European

índole [ˈindole] NF (naturaleza) nature; (clase) sort, kind

indolencia [indoˈlenθja] NF indolence, laziness

indoloro, -a [inˈdoloro, a] ADJ painless

indomable [indoˈmaβle] ADJ (animal) untameable; (espíritu) indomitable

indómito, -a [inˈdomito, a] ADJ indomitable

Indonesia [indoˈnesja] NF Indonesia

indonesio, -a [indoˈnesjo, a] ADJ, NM/F Indonesian

inducción [indukˈθjon] NF (Filosofía, Elec) induction; **por ~** by induction

inducir [induˈθir] /**3n**/ VT to induce; (inferir) to infer; (persuadir) to persuade; **~ a algn en el error** to mislead sb

indudable [induˈðaβle] ADJ undoubted; (incuestionable) unquestionable; **es ~ que ...** there is no doubt that ...

indulgencia [indulˈxenθja] NF indulgence; (Jur etc) leniency; **proceder sin ~ contra** to proceed ruthlessly against

indultar [indulˈtar] /**1a**/ VT (perdonar) to pardon, reprieve; (librar de pago) to exempt

indulto [in'dulto] NM pardon; (*exención*) exemption

indumentaria [indumen'tarja] NF (*ropa*) clothing, dress

★**industria** [in'dustrja] NF industry; (*habilidad*) skill; **~ agropecuaria** farming and fishing; **~ pesada** heavy industry; **~ petrolífera** oil industry

★**industrial** [indus'trjal] ADJ industrial ▶ NMF industrialist

industrializar [industrjali'θar] /**1f**/ VT to industrialize ■ **industrializarse** VR to become industrialized

INE ['ine] NM ABR (*Esp*) = **Instituto Nacional de Estadística**

inédito, -a [i'neðito, a] ADJ (*libro*) unpublished; (*nuevo*) new

inefable [ine'faβle] ADJ ineffable, indescribable

ineficacia [inefi'kaθja] NF (*de medida*) ineffectiveness; (*de proceso*) inefficiency

ineficaz [inefi'kaθ] ADJ (*inútil*) ineffective; (*ineficiente*) inefficient

ineludible [inelu'ðiβle] ADJ inescapable, unavoidable

INEM [i'nem] NM ABR (*Esp*: = *Instituto Nacional de Empleo*) ≈ Department of Employment (*Brit*)

INEN ['inen] NM ABR (*México*) = **Instituto Nacional de Energía Nuclear**

inenarrable [inena'rraβle] ADJ inexpressible

ineptitud [inepti'tuð] NF ineptitude, incompetence

inepto, -a [i'nepto, a] ADJ inept, incompetent

inequívoco, -a [ine'kiβoko, a] ADJ unequivocal; (*inconfundible*) unmistakable

inercia [i'nerθja] NF inertia; (*pasividad*) passivity

inerme [i'nerme] ADJ (*sin armas*) unarmed; (*indefenso*) defenceless

inerte [i'nerte] ADJ inert; (*inmóvil*) motionless

inescrutable [ineskru'taβle] ADJ inscrutable

inesperado, -a [inespe'raðo, a] ADJ unexpected, unforeseen

inestable [ines'taβle] ADJ unstable

inestimable [inesti'maβle] ADJ inestimable; **de valor ~** invaluable

inevitable [ineβi'taβle] ADJ inevitable

inexactitud [ineksakti'tuð] NF inaccuracy

inexacto, -a [inek'sakto, a] ADJ inaccurate; (*falso*) untrue

inexistente [ineksis'tente] ADJ non-existent

inexorable [inekso'raβle] ADJ inexorable

inexperiencia [inekspe'rjenθja] NF inexperience, lack of experience

inexperto, -a [ineks'perto, a] ADJ (*novato*) inexperienced

inexplicable [inekspli'kaβle] ADJ inexplicable

inexpresable [inekspre'saβle] ADJ inexpressible

inexpresivo, -a [inekspre'siβo, a] ADJ inexpressive; (*ojos*) dull; (*cara*) wooden

inexpugnable [inekspuɣ'naβle] ADJ (*Mil*) impregnable; (*fig*) firm

infalible [infa'liβle] ADJ infallible; (*indefectible*) certain, sure; (*plan*) foolproof

infame [in'fame] ADJ infamous

infamia [in'famja] NF infamy; (*deshonra*) disgrace

infancia [in'fanθja] NF infancy, childhood; **jardín de ~** nursery school

infanta [in'fanta] NF (*hija del rey*) infanta, princess

infante [in'fante] NM (*hijo del rey*) infante, prince

infantería [infante'ria] NF infantry

★**infantil** [infan'til] ADJ child's, children's; (*pueril, aniñado*) infantile; (*cándido*) childlike

infarto [in'farto] NM (*tb*: **infarto de miocardio**) heart attack; **~ cerebral** stroke

infatigable [infati'ɣaβle] ADJ tireless, untiring

infección [infek'θjon] NF infection

infeccioso, -a [infek'θjoso, a] ADJ infectious

infectar [infek'tar] /**1a**/ VT to infect ■ **infectarse** VR: **infectarse (de)** (*tb fig*) to become infected (with)

infecundidad [infekundi'ðað] NF (*de tierra*) infertility, barrenness; (*de mujer*) sterility

infecundo, -a [infe'kundo, a] ADJ (*tierra*) infertile, barren; (*mujer*) sterile

infeliz [infe'liθ] ADJ (*desgraciado*) unhappy, wretched; (*inocente*) gullible ▶ NMF (*desgraciado*) wretch; (*inocentón*) simpleton

inferior [infe'rjor] ADJ inferior; (*situación, Mat*) lower; **una cantidad ~** a lesser quantity; **cualquier número ~ a nueve** any number less than o under o below nine ▶ NMF inferior, subordinate

inferioridad [inferjori'ðað] NF inferiority; **estar en ~ de condiciones** to be at a disadvantage

inferir [infe'rir] /**3i**/ VT (*deducir*) to infer, deduce; (*causar*) to cause

infernal [infer'nal] ADJ infernal

infértil [in'fertil] ADJ infertile

infestar [infes'tar] /**1a**/ VT to infest

infidelidad [infiðeli'ðað] NF infidelity, unfaithfulness

infiel [in'fjel] ADJ unfaithful, disloyal; (*falso*) inaccurate ▶ NMF infidel, unbeliever

infiera *etc* [in'fjera] VB *ver* **inferir**

infierno [in'fjerno] NM hell; **¡vete al ~!** go to hell; **está en el quinto ~** it's in the back of beyond

infiltrar [infil'trar] /**1a**/ VT to infiltrate ■ **infiltrarse** VR to infiltrate; **infiltrarse en** to infiltrate in(to); (*persona*) to work one's way in(to)

ínfimo, -a ['infimo, a] ADJ (*vil*) vile, mean; (*más bajo*) lowest; (*peor*) worst; (*miserable*) wretched

infinidad [infini'ðað] NF infinity; (*abundancia*) great quantity; ~ **de** vast numbers of; ~ **de veces** countless times

infinitivo [infini'tiβo] NM infinitive

infinito, -a [infi'nito, a] ADJ infinite; (*fig*) boundless ▶ ADV infinitely ▶ NM infinite; (*Mat*) infinity; **hasta lo** ~ ad infinitum

infiriendo *etc* [infi'rjendo] VB *ver* **inferir**

inflación [infla'θjon] NF (*hinchazón*) swelling; (*monetaria*) inflation; (*fig*) conceit

inflacionario, -a [inflaθjo'narjo, a] ADJ inflationary

inflacionismo [inflaθjo'nismo] NM (*Econ*) inflation

inflacionista [inflaθjo'nista] ADJ inflationary

inflamable [infla'maβle] ADJ flammable

inflamar [infla'mar] /**1a**/ VT to set on fire; (*Med, fig*) to inflame ▪ **inflamarse** VR to catch fire; to become inflamed

inflar [in'flar] /**1a**/ VT (*hinchar*) to inflate, blow up; (*fig*) to exaggerate ▪ **inflarse** VR to swell (up); (*fig*) to get conceited

inflexible [inflek'siβle] ADJ inflexible; (*fig*) unbending

infligir [infli'xir] /**3c**/ VT to inflict

inflija *etc* [in'flixa] VB *ver* **infligir**

★**influencia** [in'flwenθja] NF influence

influenciador, a [inflwenθja'ðor, a] NM/F influencer

influenciar [inflwen'θjar] /**1b**/ VT to influence

influir [influ'ir] /**3g**/ VT to influence ▶ VI to have influence, carry weight; ~ **en** *o* **sobre** to influence, affect; (*contribuir a*) to have a hand in

influjo [in'fluxo] NM influence; ~ **de capitales** (*Econ etc*) capital influx

influya *etc* VB *ver* **influir**

influyente [influ'jente] ADJ influential

★**información** [informa'θjon] NF information; (*noticias*) news *sg*; (*informe*) report; (*Inform: datos*) data; (*Jur*) inquiry; **I~** (*oficina, mostrador*) Information Desk; (*Telec*) Directory Enquiries (*BRIT*), Directory Assistance (*US*); **una** ~ a piece of information; **abrir una** ~ (*Jur*) to begin proceedings; ~ **deportiva** (*en periódico*) sports section

informal [infor'mal] ADJ informal

informante [infor'mante] NMF informant

★**informar** [infor'mar] /**1a**/ VT (*gen*) to inform; (*revelar*) to reveal, make known ▶ VI (*Jur*) to plead; (*denunciar*) to inform; (*dar cuenta de*) to report on ▪ **informarse** VR to find out; **informarse de** to inquire into

★**informática** [infor'matika] NF *ver* **informático**

informatice *etc* [informa'tiθe] VB *ver* **informatizar**

★**informático, -a** [infor'matiko, a] ADJ computer *cpd* ▶ NF (*Tec*) information technology; computing; (*Escol*) computer science *o* studies; **informática de gestión** commercial computing

informativo, -a [informa'tiβo, a] ADJ (*libro*) informative; (*folleto*) information *cpd*; (*Radio, TV*) news *cpd* ▶ NM (*Radio, TV*) news programme

informatización [informatiθa'θjon] NF computerization

informatizar [informati'θar] /**1f**/ VT to computerize

★**informe** [in'forme] ADJ shapeless ▶ NM report; (*dictamen*) statement; (*Mil*) briefing; (*Jur*) plea; ~ **anual** annual report; ~ **del juez** summing-up ▪ **informes** NMPL information *sg*; (*datos*) data

infortunio [infor'tunjo] NM misfortune

infracción [infrak'θjon] NF infraction, infringement; (*Auto*) offence

infraestructura [infraestruk'tura] NF infrastructure

in fraganti [infra'ɣanti] ADV: **pillar a algn** ~ to catch sb red-handed

infranqueable [infranke'aβle] ADJ impassable; (*fig*) insurmountable

infrarrojo, -a [infra'rroxo, a] ADJ infrared

infravalorar [infraβalo'rar] /**1a**/ VT to undervalue; (*Finanzas*) to underestimate

infringir [infrin'xir] /**3c**/ VT to infringe, contravene

infrinja *etc* [in'frinxa] VB *ver* **infringir**

infructuoso, -a [infruk'twoso, a] ADJ fruitless, unsuccessful

infundado, -a [infun'daðo, a] ADJ groundless, unfounded

infundir [infun'dir] /**3a**/ VT to infuse, instil; ~ **ánimo a algn** to encourage sb; ~ **miedo a algn** to intimidate sb

infusión [infu'sjon] NF infusion; ~ **de manzanilla** camomile tea

Ing. ABR (*AM*) = **ingeniero**

ingeniar [inxe'njar] /**1a**/ VT to think up, devise ▪ **ingeniarse** VR to manage; **ingeniarse para** to manage to

★**ingeniería** [inxenje'ria] NF engineering; ~ **genética** genetic engineering; ~ **de sistemas** (*Inform*) systems engineering

★**ingeniero, -a** [inxe'njero, a] NM/F engineer; (*AM*) courtesy title; ~ **de sonido** sound engineer; ~ **de caminos** civil engineer

ingenio [in'xenjo] NM (*talento*) talent; (*agudeza*) wit; (*habilidad*) ingenuity, inventiveness; (*Tec*): ~ **azucarero** sugar refinery

ingenioso, -a [inxe'njoso, a] ADJ ingenious, clever; (*divertido*) witty

ingente [in'xente] ADJ huge, enormous

ingenuidad [inxenwi'ðað] NF ingenuousness; (*sencillez*) simplicity

ingenuo, -a [in'xenwo, a] ADJ ingenuous

ingerir [inxe'rir] /**3i**/ VT to ingest; (*tragar*) to swallow; (*consumir*) to consume

ingiera *etc* [in'xjera], **ingiriendo** *etc* [inxi-'rjendo] VB *ver* **ingerir**

★**Inglaterra** [ingla'terra] NF England

ingle ['ingle] NF groin

★**inglés, -esa** [in'gles, esa] ADJ English ▶ NM/F Englishman(-woman); **los ingleses** the English ▶ NM (*Ling*) English

ingratitud [ingrati'tuð] NF ingratitude

ingrato, -a [in'grato, a] ADJ ungrateful; (*tarea*) thankless

ingravidez [ingraβi'ðeθ] NF weightlessness

ingrediente [ingre'ðjente] NM ingredient ■ **ingredientes** NMPL (*Am*) (*tapas*) titbits

ingresar [ingre'sar] /**1a**/ VT (*dinero*) to deposit ▶ VI to come o go in; **~ a** (*esp Am*) to enter; **~ en** (*club*) to join; (*Mil, Escol*) to enrol in; **~ en el hospital** to go into hospital

★**ingreso** [in'greso] NM (*entrada*) entry; (: *en hospital etc*) admission; (*Mil, Escol*) enrolment ■ **ingresos** NMPL (*dinero*) income *sg*; (: *Com*) takings *pl*; **ingresos accesorios** fringe benefits; **ingresos brutos** gross receipts; **ingresos devengados** earned income *sg*; **ingresos exentos de impuestos** non-taxable income *sg*; **ingresos gravables** taxable income *sg*; **ingresos personales disponibles** disposable personal income *sg*

íngrimo, -a ['ingrimo, a] ADJ (*Am*: *tb*: **íngrimo y solo**) all alone

inhábil [i'naβil] ADJ unskilful, clumsy

inhabilitar [inaβili'tar] /**1a**/ VT (*Pol, Med*): **~ a algn (para hacer algo)** to disqualify sb (from doing sth)

inhabitable [inaβi'taβle] ADJ uninhabitable

inhabituado, -a [inaβi'twaðo, a] ADJ unaccustomed

inhalador [inala'ðor] NM (*Med*) inhaler

inhalar [ina'lar] /**1a**/ VT to inhale

inherente [ine'rente] ADJ inherent

inhibición [iniβi'θjon] NF inhibition

inhibir [ini'βir] /**3a**/ VT to inhibit; (*Rel*) to restrain ■ **inhibirse** VR to keep out

inhospitalario, -a [inospita'larjo, a], **inhóspito, -a** [i'nospito, a] ADJ inhospitable

inhóspito, -a [i'nospito, a] ADJ (*región, paisaje*) inhospitable

inhumación [inuma'θjon] NF burial, interment

inhumano, -a [inu'mano, a] ADJ inhuman

inicial [ini'θjal] ADJ, NF initial

inicialice *etc* [iniθja'liθe] VB *ver* **inicializar**

inicializar [iniθjali'θar] /**1f**/ VT (*Inform*) to initialize

iniciar [ini'θjar] /**1b**/ VT (*persona*) to initiate; (*empezar*) to begin, commence; (*conversación*) to start up; **~ a algn en un secreto** to let sb into a secret; **~ la sesión** (*Inform*) to log in o on

iniciativa [iniθja'tiβa] NF initiative; (*liderazgo*) leadership; **~ privada** private enterprise

inicio [i'niθjo] NM start, beginning

inicuo, -a [i'nikwo, a] ADJ iniquitous

inigualado, -a [iniɣwa'laðo, a] ADJ unequalled

ininteligible [ininteli'xiβle] ADJ unintelligible

ininterrumpido, -a [ininterrum'piðo, a] ADJ uninterrupted; (*proceso*) continuous; (*progreso*) steady

injerencia [inxe'renθja] NF interference

injertar [inxer'tar] /**1a**/ VT to graft

injerto [in'xerto] NM graft; **~ de piel** skin graft

injuria [in'xurja] NF (*agravio, ofensa*) offence; (*insulto*) insult ■ **injurias** NFPL abuse *sg*

injuriar [inxu'rjar] /**1b**/ VT to insult

injurioso, -a [inxu'rjoso, a] ADJ offensive, insulting

injusticia [inxus'tiθja] NF injustice, unfairness; **con ~** unjustly

★**injusto, -a** [in'xusto, a] ADJ unjust, unfair

inmaculado, -a [inmaku'laðo, a] ADJ immaculate, spotless

inmadurez [inmaðu'reθ] NF immaturity

inmaduro, -a [inma'ðuro, a] ADJ immature; (*fruta*) unripe

inmediaciones [inmeðja'θjones] NFPL neighbourhood *sg*, environs

★**inmediatamente** [inmeðjata'mente] ADV immediately

inmediatez [inmeðja'teθ] NF immediacy

★**inmediato, -a** [inme'ðjato, a] ADJ immediate; (*contiguo*) adjoining; (*rápido*) prompt; (*próximo*) neighbouring, next; **de ~** (*esp Am*) immediately

inmejorable [inmexo'raβle] ADJ unsurpassable; (*precio*) unbeatable

inmemorable [inmemo'raβle], **inmemorial** [inmemo'rjal] ADJ immemorial

★**inmenso, -a** [in'menso, a] ADJ immense, huge

inmerecido, -a [inmere'θiðo, a] ADJ undeserved

inmersión [inmer'sjon] NF immersion; (*buzo*) dive

inmigración [inmiɣra'θjon] NF immigration

★**inmigrante** [inmi'ɣrante] ADJ, NMF immigrant

inminente [inmi'nente] ADJ imminent, impending

inmiscuirse [inmisku'irse] /**3g**/ VR to interfere, meddle

inmiscuyendo *etc* [inmisku'jendo] VB *ver* **inmiscuirse**

inmobiliario, -a [inmoβi'ljarjo, a] ADJ real estate *cpd*, property *cpd* ▶ NF estate agency

inmolar [inmo'lar] /**1a**/ VT to immolate, sacrifice

inmoral [inmo'ral] ADJ immoral

inmortal [inmor'tal] ADJ immortal

inmortalice *etc* [inmorta'liθe] VB *ver* **inmortalizar**

inmortalizar [inmortali'θar] /**1f**/ VT to immortalize

inmotivado, -a [inmoti'βaðo, a] ADJ motiveless; (*sospecha*) groundless

★**inmóvil** [in'moβil] ADJ immobile

inmovilizar [inmoβili'θar] /**1f**/ vt to immobilize; (*paralizar*) to paralyse ∎ **inmovilizarse** vr: **se le inmovilizó la pierna** her leg was paralysed

inmueble [in'mweβle] ADJ: **bienes inmuebles** real estate *sg*, landed property *sg* ▶ NM property

inmundicia [inmun'diθja] NF filth

inmundo, -a [in'mundo, a] ADJ filthy

inmune [in'mune] ADJ: **~ (a)** (*Med*) immune (to)

inmunidad [inmuni'ðað] NF immunity; (*fisco*) exemption; **~ diplomática/parlamentaria** diplomatic/parliamentary immunity

inmunitario, -a [inmuni'tarjo, a] ADJ: **sistema ~** immune system

inmunización [inmuniθa'θjon] NF immunization

inmunizar [inmuni'θar] /**1f**/ vt to immunize

inmutable [inmu'taβle] ADJ immutable; **permaneció ~** he didn't flinch

inmutarse [inmu'tarse] /**1a**/ vr to turn pale; **no se inmutó** he didn't turn a hair; **siguió sin ~** he carried on unperturbed

innato, -a [in'nato, a] ADJ innate

innecesario, -a [inneθe'sarjo, a] ADJ unnecessary

innegable [inne'ɣaβle] ADJ undeniable

innoble [in'noβle] ADJ ignoble

innovación [innoβa'θjon] NF innovation

innovador, a [innoβa'ðor, a] ADJ innovatory, innovative ▶ NM/F innovator

innovar [inno'βar] /**1a**/ vt to introduce

innumerable [innume'raβle] ADJ countless

inocencia [ino'θenθja] NF innocence

inocentada [inoθen'taða] NF practical joke

inocente [ino'θente] ADJ (*ingenuo*) naive, innocent; (*no culpable*) innocent; (*sin malicia*) harmless ▶ NMF simpleton; **día de los (Santos) Inocentes** ≈ April Fools' Day; *see note*

The 28th December, **el día de los (Santos) Inocentes**, is when the Church commemorates the story of Herod's slaughter of the innocent children of Judea in the time of Christ. On this day, people in Spanish-speaking countries play *inocentadas* (practical jokes) on each other, much like our April Fools' Day pranks, such as sticking a *monigote* (cut-out paper figure) on someone's back, or broadcasting unlikely news stories.

inocuidad [inokwi'ðað] NF harmlessness

inocular [inoku'lar] /**1a**/ vt to inoculate

inocuo, -a [i'nokwo, a] ADJ (*sustancia*) harmless

inodoro, -a [ino'ðoro, a] ADJ odourless ▶ NM toilet (*Brit*), lavatory (*Brit*), washroom (*US*)

inofensivo, -a [inofen'siβo, a] ADJ inoffensive

inolvidable [inolβi'ðaβle] ADJ unforgettable

inoperante [inope'rante] ADJ ineffective

inopinado, -a [inopi'naðo, a] ADJ unexpected

inoportuno, -a [inopor'tuno, a] ADJ untimely; (*molesto*) inconvenient; (*inapropiado*) inappropriate

inoxidable [inoksi'ðaβle] ADJ stainless; **acero ~** stainless steel

inquebrantable [inkeβran'taβle] ADJ unbreakable; (*fig*) unshakeable

inquiera *etc* [in'kjera] VB *ver* **inquirir**

inquietante [inkje'tante] ADJ worrying

★**inquietar** [inkje'tar] /**1a**/ vt to worry, trouble ∎ **inquietarse** vr to worry, get upset

★**inquieto, -a** [in'kjeto, a] ADJ anxious, worried; **estar ~ por** to be worried about

inquietud [inkje'tuð] NF anxiety, worry

★**inquilino, -a** [inki'lino, a] NM/F tenant; (*Com*) lessee

inquiriendo *etc* [inki'rjendo] VB *ver* **inquirir**

inquirir [inki'rir] /**3i**/ vt to enquire into, investigate

insaciable [insa'θjaβle] ADJ insatiable

insalubre [insa'luβre] ADJ unhealthy; (*condiciones*) insanitary

INSALUD [insa'luð] NM ABR (*Esp*) = **Instituto Nacional de la Salud**

insano, -a [in'sano, a] ADJ (*loco*) insane; (*malsano*) unhealthy

insatisfacción [insatisfak'θjon] NF dissatisfaction

insatisfecho, -a [insatis'fetʃo, a] ADJ (*condición*) unsatisfied; (*estado de ánimo*) dissatisfied

inscribir [inskri'βir] /**3a**/ vt to inscribe; (*en lista*) to put; (*en censo*) to register ∎ **inscribirse** vr to register; (*Escol etc*) to enrol

inscripción [inskrip'θjon] NF inscription; (*Escol etc*) enrolment; (*en censo*) registration

inscrito [ins'krito] PP *de* **inscribir**

insecticida [insekti'θiða] NM insecticide

★**insecto** [in'sekto] NM insect

inseguridad [inseɣuri'ðað] NF insecurity; **~ ciudadana** lack of safety in the streets

★**inseguro, -a** [inse'ɣuro, a] ADJ insecure; (*inconstante*) unsteady; (*incierto*) uncertain

inseminación [insemina'θjon] NF: **~ artificial** artificial insemination (A.I.)

inseminar [insemi'nar] /**1a**/ vt to inseminate, fertilize

insensato, -a [insen'sato, a] ADJ foolish, stupid

insensibilice *etc* [insensiβi'liθe] VB *ver* **insensibilizar**

insensibilidad [insensiβili'ðað] NF (*gen*) insensitivity; (*dureza de corazón*) callousness

insensibilizar [insensiβili'θar] /**1f**/ vt to desensitize; (*Med*) to anaesthetize (*Brit*), anesthetize (*US*); (*eufemismo*) to knock out *o* unconscious

insensible [insen'siβle] ADJ (*gen*) insensitive; (*movimiento*) imperceptible; (*sin sensación*) numb

inseparable [insepa'raβle] ADJ inseparable

insertar [inser'tar] /**1a**/ vt to insert

inservible [inser'βiβle] ADJ useless

insidioso, -a [insi'ðjoso, a] ADJ insidious

insigne [in'siɣne] ADJ distinguished; (*famoso*) notable

★**insignia** [in'siɣnja] NF (*señal distintiva*) badge; (*estandarte*) flag

insignificante [insiɣnifi'kante] ADJ insignificant

insinuar [insi'nwar] /**1e**/ VT to insinuate, imply ■ **insinuarse** VR: **insinuarse con algn** to ingratiate o.s. with sb

insípido, -a [in'sipiðo, a] ADJ insipid

insistencia [insis'tenθja] NF insistence

insistir [insis'tir] /**3a**/ VI to insist; **~ en algo** to insist on sth; (*enfatizar*) to stress sth

in situ [in'situ] ADV on the spot, in situ

insobornable [insoβor'naβle] ADJ incorruptible

insociable [inso'θjaβle] ADJ unsociable

★**insolación** [insola'θjon] NF (*Med*) sunstroke

insolencia [inso'lenθja] NF insolence

★**insolente** [inso'lente] ADJ insolent

insólito, -a [in'solito, a] ADJ unusual

insoluble [inso'luβle] ADJ insoluble

insolvencia [insol'βenθja] NF insolvency

insomne [in'somne] ADJ sleepless ▶ NMF insomniac

insomnio [in'somnjo] NM insomnia

insondable [inson'daβle] ADJ bottomless

insonorización [insonoriθa'θjon] NF soundproofing

insonorizado, -a [insonori'θaðo, a] ADJ (*cuarto etc*) soundproof

★**insoportable** [insopor'taβle] ADJ unbearable

insoslayable [insosla'jaβle] ADJ unavoidable

insospechado, -a [insospe'tʃaðo, a] ADJ (*inesperado*) unexpected

insostenible [insoste'niβle] ADJ untenable

inspección [inspek'θjon] NF inspection, check; **I~** inspectorate; **~ técnica (de vehículos)** ≈ MOT (test) (*BRIT*)

inspeccionar [inspekθjo'nar] /**1a**/ VT (*examinar*) to inspect, examine; (*controlar*) to check

★**inspector, a** [inspek'tor, a] NM/F inspector

inspectorado [inspekto'raðo] NM inspectorate

inspiración [inspira'θjon] NF inspiration

inspirador, a [inspira'ðor, a] ADJ inspiring

inspirar [inspi'rar] /**1a**/ VT to inspire; (*Med*) to inhale ■ **inspirarse** VR: **inspirarse en** to be inspired by

instalación [instala'θjon] NF (*equipo*) fittings *pl*, equipment; **~ eléctrica** wiring

instalador, a [instala'ðor, a] NM/F installer

★**instalar** [insta'lar] /**1a**/ VT (*establecer*) to instal; (*erguir*) to set up, erect ■ **instalarse** VR to establish o.s.; (*en una vivienda*) to move into

instancia [ins'tanθja] NF (*solicitud*) application; (*ruego*) request; (*Jur*) petition; **a ~ de** at the request of; **en última ~** as a last resort

instantáneo, -a [instan'taneo, a] ADJ instantaneous; **café ~** instant coffee ▶ NF snap(shot)

★**instante** [ins'tante] NM instant, moment; **al ~** right now; **en un ~** in a flash

instar [ins'tar] /**1a**/ VT to press, urge

instaurar [instau'rar] /**1a**/ VT (*costumbre*) to establish; (*normas, sistema*) to bring in, introduce; (*gobierno*) to install

insti ['insti] NM (*Esp fam: instituto*) ≈ secondary school (*BRIT*), ≈ high school

instigador, a [instiɣa'ðor, a] NM/F instigator; **~ de un delito** (*Jur*) accessory before the fact

instigar [insti'ɣar] /**1h**/ VT to instigate

instigue *etc* [ins'tiɣe] VB *ver* **instigar**

instintivo, -a [instin'tiβo, a] ADJ instinctive

instinto [ins'tinto] NM instinct; **por ~** instinctively

institución [institu'θjon] NF institution, establishment; **~ benéfica** charitable foundation

instituir [institu'ir] /**3g**/ VT to establish; (*fundar*) to found

★**instituto** [insti'tuto] NM (*gen*) institute; **I~ Nacional de Enseñanza** (*Esp*) ≈ comprehensive (*BRIT*) *o* high school; **I~ Nacional de Industria (INI)** (*Esp Com*) ≈ National Enterprise Board (*BRIT*)

institutriz [institu'triθ] NF governess

instituyendo *etc* [institu'jendo] VB *ver* **instituir**

instrucción [instruk'θjon] NF instruction; (*enseñanza*) education, teaching; (*Jur*) proceedings *pl*; (*Mil*) training; (*Deporte*) coaching; (*conocimientos*) knowledge; (*Inform*) statement; **instrucciones para el uso** directions for use; **instrucciones de funcionamiento** operating instructions

instructivo, -a [instruk'tiβo, a] ADJ instructive

★**instructor** [instruk'tor] NM instructor; **~ de fitness** fitness instructor

instruir [instru'ir] /**3g**/ VT (*gen*) to instruct; (*enseñar*) to teach, educate; (*Jur: proceso*) to prepare, draw up ■ **instruirse** VR to learn, teach o.s.

★**instrumento** [instru'mento] NM (*gen, Mus*) instrument; (*herramienta*) tool, implement; (*Com*) indenture; (*Jur*) legal document; **~ de percusión/cuerda/viento** percussion/string(ed)/wind instrument

instruyendo *etc* [instru'jendo] VB *ver* **instruir**

insubordinarse [insuβorði'narse] /**1a**/ VR to rebel

insuficiencia [insufi'θjenθja] NF (*carencia*) lack; (*inadecuación*) inadequacy; **~ cardíaca/renal** heart/kidney failure

insuficiente [insufi'θjente] ADJ (*gen*) insufficient; (*Escol: nota*) D, fail

insufrible [insu'friβle] ADJ insufferable

insular [insuˈlar] ADJ insular

insulina [insuˈlina] NF insulin

insulso, -a [inˈsulso, a] ADJ insipid; (fig) dull

★**insultar** [insulˈtar] /1a/ VT to insult

insulto [inˈsulto] NM insult

insumisión [insumiˈsjon] NF refusal to do military service or community service

insumiso, -a [insuˈmiso, a] ADJ (rebelde) rebellious ▶ NM/F (Pol) person who refuses to do military service or community service

insuperable [insupeˈraβle] ADJ (excelente) unsurpassable; (problema etc) insurmountable

insurgente [insurˈxente] ADJ, NMF insurgent

insurrección [insurrekˈθjon] NF insurrection, rebellion

insustituible [insustiˈtwiβle] ADJ irreplaceable

intachable [intaˈtʃaβle] ADJ irreproachable

intacto, -a [inˈtakto, a] ADJ (sin tocar) untouched; (entero) intact

integrado, -a [inteˈɣraðo, a] ADJ (Inform): **circuito ~** integrated circuit

integral [inteˈɣral] ADJ integral; (completo) complete; (Tec) built-in; **pan ~** wholemeal bread

integrante [inteˈɣrante] ADJ integral ▶ NMF member

integrar [inteˈɣrar] /1a/ VT to make up, compose; (Mat, fig) to integrate

integridad [inteɣriˈðað] NF wholeness; (carácter, tb Inform) integrity; **en su ~** completely

integrismo [inteˈɣrismo] NM fundamentalism

integrista [inteˈɣrista] ADJ, NMF fundamentalist

íntegro, -a [ˈinteɣro, a] ADJ whole, entire; (texto) uncut, unabridged; (honrado) honest

intelectual [intelekˈtwal] ADJ, NMF intellectual

intelectualidad [intelektwaliˈðað] NF intelligentsia, intellectuals pl

inteligencia [inteliˈxenθja] NF intelligence; (ingenio) ability; **~ artificial** artificial intelligence

★**inteligente** [inteliˈxente] ADJ intelligent

inteligible [inteliˈxiβle] ADJ intelligible

intemperancia [intempeˈranθja] NF excess, intemperance

intemperie [intemˈperje] NF: **a la ~** outdoors, out in the open, exposed to the elements

intempestivo, -a [intempesˈtiβo, a] ADJ untimely

★**intención** [intenˈθjon] NF intention, purpose; **con segundas intenciones** maliciously; **con ~** deliberately

intencionado, -a [intenθjoˈnaðo, a] ADJ deliberate; **bien ~** well-meaning; **mal ~** ill-disposed, hostile

intendencia [intenˈdenθja] NF management, administration; (Mil: tb: **cuerpo de intendencia**) ≈ service corps

intensidad [intensiˈðað] NF (gen) intensity; (Elec, Tec) strength; (de recuerdo) vividness; **llover con ~** to rain hard

intensificar [intensifiˈkar] /1g/ VT, **intensificarse** VR to intensify

intensifique etc [intensiˈfike] VB ver **intensificar**

intensivo, -a [intenˈsiβo, a] ADJ intensive; **curso ~** crash course

intenso, -a [inˈtenso, a] ADJ intense; (impresión) vivid; (sentimiento) profound, deep

★**intentar** [intenˈtar] /1a/ VT (tratar) to try, attempt

intento [inˈtento] NM (intención) intention, purpose; (tentativa) attempt

intentona [intenˈtona] NF (Pol) attempted coup

interaccionar [interakθjoˈnar] /1a/ VI (Inform) to interact

interactividad [interaktiβiˈðað] NF interactivity

interactivo, -a [interakˈtiβo, a] ADJ interactive; (Inform): **computación interactiva** interactive computing

intercalación [interkalaˈθjon] NF (Inform) merging

intercalar [interkaˈlar] /1a/ VT to insert; (Inform: archivos, texto) to merge

intercambiable [interkamˈbjaβle] ADJ interchangeable

★**intercambio** [interˈkambjo] NM (canje) exchange; (trueque) swap

interceder [interθeˈðer] /2a/ VI to intercede

interceptar [interθepˈtar] /1a/ VT to intercept, cut off; (Auto) to hold up

interceptor [interθepˈtor] NM interceptor; (Tec) trap

intercesión [interθeˈsjon] NF intercession

★**interés** [inteˈres] NM (gen, Com) interest; (importancia) concern; (parte) share, part; (pey) self-interest; **~ compuesto** compound interest; **~ simple** simple interest; **con un ~ del 9 por ciento** at an interest of 9%; **dar a ~** to lend at interest; **tener ~ en** (Com) to hold a share in; **intereses acumulados** accrued interest sg; **intereses por cobrar** interest receivable sg; **intereses creados** vested interests; **intereses por pagar** interest payable sg

interesado, -a [intereˈsaðo, a] ADJ interested; (prejuiciado) prejudiced; (pey) mercenary, self-seeking ▶ NM/F person concerned; (firmante) the undersigned

★**interesante** [intereˈsante] ADJ interesting

★**interesar** [intereˈsar] /1a/ VT to interest, be of interest to ▶ VI to interest, be of interest; (importar) to be important; **no me interesan los toros** bullfighting does not appeal to me ■ **interesarse** VR: **interesarse en** o **por** to take an interest in

interestatal [interestaˈtal] ADJ inter-state

interface [interˈfaθe], **interfase** [interˈfase] NM (Inform) interface; **~ hombre/máquina/por menús** man/machine/menu interface

interfaz [inter'faθ] NM = **interface**

interferencia [interfe'renθja] NF interference

interferir [interfe'rir] /**3i**/ VT to interfere with; (*Telec*) to jam ▶ VI to interfere

interfiera *etc* [inter'fjera], **interfiriendo** *etc* [interfi'rjendo] VB *ver* **interferir**

interfón [inter'fon] NM (*Am*) = **interfono**

interfono [inter'fono] NM intercom, entry phone

ínterin ['interin] ADV meanwhile ▶ NM interim; **en el ~** in the meantime

interino, -a [inte'rino, a] ADJ temporary; (*empleado etc*) provisional ▶ NM/F temporary holder of a post; (*Med*) locum; (*Escol*) supply teacher; (*Teat*) stand-in

★**interior** [inte'rjor] ADJ inner, inside; (*Com*) domestic, internal ▶ NM interior, inside; (*fig*) soul, mind; (*Deporte*) inside forward; **Ministerio del I-** ≈ Home Office (*BRIT*), ≈ Department of the Interior (*US*); **dije para mi ~** I said to myself

interjección [interxek'θjon] NF interjection

interlínea [inter'linea] NF (*Inform*) line feed

interlocutor, a [interloku'tor, a] NM/F speaker; (*al teléfono*) person at the other end (of the line); **mi ~** the person I was speaking to

intermediario, -a [interme'ðjarjo, a] ADJ (*mediador*) mediating ▶ NM/F intermediary, go-between; (*mediador*) mediator

intermedio, -a [inter'meðjo, a] ADJ intermediate; (*tiempo*) intervening ▶ NM interval; (*Pol*) recess

interminable [intermi'naβle] ADJ endless, interminable

intermitente [intermi'tente] ADJ intermittent ▶ NM (*Auto*) indicator

internacional [internaθjo'nal] ADJ international

internado [inter'naðo] NM boarding school

internamiento [interna'mjento] NM internment

internar [inter'nar] /**1a**/ VT to intern; (*en un manicomio*) to commit ■ **internarse** VR (*penetrar*) to penetrate; **internarse en** to go into o right inside; **internarse en un estudio** to study a subject in depth

★**internauta** [inter'nauta] NMF web surfer, internet user

★**Internet** [inter'net] NM O F internet, Internet

★**interno, -a** [in'terno, a] ADJ internal, interior; (*Pol etc*) domestic ▶ NM/F (*alumno*) boarder

interpelación [interpela'θjon] NF appeal, plea

interpelar [interpe'lar] /**1a**/ VT (*rogar*) to implore; (*hablar*) to speak to; (*Pol*) to ask for explanations, question formally

interpondré *etc* [interpon'dre] VB *ver* **interponer**

interponer [interpo'ner] /**2q**/ VT to interpose, put in ■ **interponerse** VR to intervene

interponga *etc* [inter'ponga] VB *ver* **interponer**

interposición [interposi'θjon] NF insertion

interpretación [interpreta'θjon] NF interpretation; (*Mus, Teat*) performance; **mala ~** misinterpretation

interpretar [interpre'tar] /**1a**/ VT to interpret; (*Teat, Mus*) to perform, play

★**intérprete** [in'terprete] NMF (*Ling*) interpreter, translator; (*Mus, Teat*) performer, artist(e)

interpuesto [inter'pwesto], **interpuse** *etc* [inter'puse] VB *ver* **interponer**

interrogación [interroγa'θjon] NF interrogation; (*Ling: tb:* **signo de interrogación**) question mark; (*Telec*) polling

interrogante [interro'γante] ADJ questioning ▶ NM question mark; (*fig*) question mark, query

interrogar [interro'γar] /**1h**/ VT to interrogate, question

interrogatorio [interroγa'torjo] NM interrogation; (*Mil*) debriefing; (*Jur*) examination

interrogue *etc* [inte'rroγe] VB *ver* **interrogar**

interrumpir [interrum'pir] /**3a**/ VT to interrupt; (*vacaciones*) to cut short; (*servicio*) to cut off; (*tráfico*) to block

interrupción [interrup'θjon] NF interruption

interruptor [interrup'tor] NM (*Elec*) switch

intersección [intersek'θjon] NF intersection; (*Auto*) junction

interurbano, -a [interur'βano, a] ADJ inter city; (*Telec*) long-distance

intervalo [inter'βalo] NM interval; (*descanso*) break; **a intervalos** at intervals, every now and then

intervención [interβen'θjon] NF supervision; (*Com*) audit(ing); (*Med*) operation; (*Telec*) tapping; (*participación*) intervention; **~ quirúrgica** surgical operation; **la política de no ~** the policy of non-intervention

intervencionista [interβenθjo'nista] ADJ: **no ~** (*Com*) laissez-faire

intervendré *etc* [interβen'dre], **intervenga** *etc* [inter'βenga] VB *ver* **intervenir**

★**intervenir** [interβe'nir] /**3r**/ VT (*controlar*) to control, supervise; (*Com*) to audit; (*Med*) to operate on; (*Telec*) to tap ▶ VI (*participar*) to take part, participate; (*mediar*) to intervene

interventor, a [interβen'tor, a] NM/F inspector; (*Com*) auditor

interviniendo *etc* [interβi'njendo] VB *ver* **intervenir**

interviú [inter'βju] NF interview

intestino [intes'tino] NM intestine

inti ['inti] NM *former monetary unit of Peru*

intimar [inti'mar] /**1a**/ VT to intimate, announce; (*mandar*) to order ▶ VI to become friendly

intimidad [intimi'ðað] NF intimacy; (*familiaridad*) familiarity; (*vida privada*) private life; (*Jur*) privacy

intimidar [intimi'ðar] /**1a**/ VT to intimidate, scare

íntimo, -a ['intimo, a] ADJ intimate; (*pensamientos*) innermost; (*vida*) personal, private; **una boda íntima** a quiet wedding

intolerable [intole'raβle] ADJ intolerable, unbearable

intolerancia [intole'ranθja] NF intolerance

intoxicación [intoksika'θjon] NF poisoning; **~ alimenticia** food poisoning

intraducible [intraðu'θiβle] ADJ untranslatable

intranet [intra'net] NF intranet

intranquilice *etc* [intranki'liθe] VB *ver* **intranquilizarse**

intranquilizarse [intrankili'θarse] /**1f**/ VR to get worried *o* anxious

intranquilo, -a [intran'kilo, a] ADJ worried

intranscendente [intransθen'dente] ADJ unimportant

intransferible [intransfe'riβle] ADJ not transferable

intransigente [intransi'xente] ADJ intransigent

intransitable [intransi'taβle] ADJ impassable

intransitivo, -a [intransi'tiβo, a] ADJ intransitive

intratable [intra'taβle] ADJ (*problema*) intractable; (*dificultad*) awkward; (*individuo*) unsociable

intrepidez [intrepi'ðeθ] NF courage, bravery

intrépido, -a [in'trepiðo, a] ADJ intrepid, fearless

intriga [in'triɣa] NF intrigue; (*plan*) plot

intrigar [intri'ɣar] /**1h**/ VT, VI to intrigue

intrigue *etc* [in'triɣe] VB *ver* **intrigar**

intrincado, -a [intrin'kaðo, a] ADJ intricate

intrínseco, -a [in'trinseko, a] ADJ intrinsic

introducción [introðuk'θjon] NF introduction; (*de libro*) foreword; (*Inform*) input

★**introducir** [introðu'θir] /**3n**/ VT (*gen*) to introduce; (*moneda*) to insert; (*Inform*) to input, enter

introduje *etc* [intro'ðuxe], **introduzca** *etc* [intro'ðuθka] VB *ver* **introducir**

intromisión [intromi'sjon] NF interference, meddling

★**introvertido, -a** [introβer'tiðo, a] ADJ introverted ▶ NM/F introvert

intruso, -a [in'truso, a] ADJ intrusive ▶ NM/F intruder

intuición [intwi'θjon] NF intuition

intuir [intu'ir] /**3g**/ VT to know by intuition, intuit

intuyendo *etc* [intu'jendo] VB *ver* **intuir**

★**inundación** [inunda'θjon] NF flood(ing)

inundar [inun'dar] /**1a**/ VT to flood; (*fig*) to swamp, inundate

inusitado, -a [inusi'taðo, a] ADJ unusual

★**inútil** [i'nutil] ADJ useless; (*esfuerzo*) vain, fruitless

inutilice *etc* [inuti'liθe] VB *ver* **inutilizar**

inutilidad [inutili'ðað] NF uselessness

inutilizar [inutili'θar] /**1f**/ VT to make unusable, put out of action; (*incapacitar*) to disable ■ **inutilizarse** VR to become useless

invadir [imba'ðir] /**3a**/ VT to invade

invalidar [imbali'ðar] /**1a**/ VT to invalidate

invalidez [imbali'ðeθ] NF (*Med*) disablement; (*Jur*) invalidity

inválido, -a [im'baliðo, a] ADJ invalid; (*Jur*) null and void ▶ NM/F invalid

invariable [imba'rjable] ADJ invariable

invasión [imba'sjon] NF invasion

invasor, a [imba'sor, a] ADJ invading ▶ NM/F invader

invencible [imben'θiβle] ADJ invincible; (*timidez, miedo*) unsurmountable

invención [imben'θjon] NF invention

★**inventar** [imben'tar] /**1a**/ VT to invent

inventario [imben'tarjo] NM inventory; (*Com*) stocktaking

inventiva [imben'tiβa] NF inventiveness

invento [im'bento] NM invention; (*fig*) brainchild; (*pey*) silly idea

inventor, a [imben'tor, a] NM/F inventor

invernadero [imberna'ðero] NM greenhouse

invernal [imber'nal] ADJ wintry, winter *cpd*

invernar [imber'nar] /**1j**/ VI (*Zool*) to hibernate

inverosímil [imbero'simil] ADJ implausible

inversión [imber'sjon] NF (*Com*) investment; **~ de capitales** capital investment; **inversiones extranjeras** foreign investment *sg*

inverso, -a [im'berso, a] ADJ inverse, opposite; **en el orden ~** in reverse order; **a la inversa** inversely, the other way round

inversor, -a [imber'sor, a] NM/F (*Com*) investor

invertebrado, -a [imberte'βraðo, a] ADJ, NM invertebrate

invertido, -a [imber'tiðo, a] ADJ inverted; (*al revés*) reversed

invertir [imber'tir] /**3i**/ VT (*Com*) to invest; (*volcar*) to turn upside down; (*tiempo etc*) to spend

investigación [imbestiɣa'θjon] NF investigation; (*indagación*) inquiry; (*Univ*) research; **~ y desarrollo** (*Com*) research and development (R & D); **~ de los medios de publicidad** media research; **~ del mercado** market research

investigador, a [imbestiɣa'ðor, a] NM/F investigator; (*Univ*) research fellow

investigar [imbesti'ɣar] /**1h**/ VT to investigate; (*estudiar*) to do research into

investigue *etc* [imbes'tiɣe] VB *ver* **investigar**

investir [imbes'tir] /**3k**/ VT: **~ a algn con algo** to confer sth on sb; **fue investido Doctor Honoris Causa** he was awarded an honorary doctorate

invicto, -a [im'bikto, a] ADJ unconquered

invidente [imbi'ðente] ADJ sightless ▶ NMF blind person; **los invidentes** the sightless

219

★**invierno** [imˈbjerno] NM winter

invierta etc [imˈbjerta] VB ver **invertir**

inviolabilidad [imbjolaβiliˈðað] NF inviolability; **~ parlamentaria** parliamentary immunity

invirtiendo etc [imbirˈtjendo] VB ver **invertir**

invisible [imbiˈsiβle] ADJ invisible; **exportaciones/importaciones invisibles** invisible exports/imports

★**invitación** [imbitaˈθjon] NF invitation

★**invitado, -a** [imbiˈtaðo, a] NM/F guest

★**invitar** [imbiˈtar] /**1a**/ VT to invite; (incitar) to entice; **~ a algn a hacer algo** to invite sb to do sth; **~ a algo** to pay for sth; **nos invitó a cenar fuera** she took us out for dinner; **invito yo** it's on me

in vitro [imˈbitro] ADV in vitro

invocar [imboˈkar] /**1g**/ VT to invoke, call on

involucrar [imboluˈkrar] /**1a**/ VT: **~ algo en un discurso** to bring something irrelevant into a discussion; **~ a algn en algo** to involve sb in sth ■ **involucrarse** VR (interesarse) to get involved

involuntario, -a [imbolunˈtarjo, a] ADJ involuntary; (ofensa etc) unintentional

invoque etc [imˈboke] VB ver **invocar**

★**inyección** [injekˈθjon] NF injection

inyectar [injekˈtar] /**1a**/ VT to inject

ión [iˈon] NM ion

IPC NM ABR (Esp: = índice de precios al consumo) CPI

IPM NM ABR (= índice de precios al por menor) RPI

iPod® [ˈipoð] (pl **iPods**) NM iPod®

---

ir [ir]

/**3s**/ VI **1** to go; (a pie) to walk; (viajar) to travel; **ir caminando** to walk; **fui en tren** I went o travelled by train; **voy a la calle** I'm going out; **ir en coche/en bicicleta** to drive/cycle; **ir a pie** to walk, go on foot; **ir de pesca** to go fishing; **¡(ahora) voy!** (I'm just) coming!

2: **ir (a) por**: **ir (a) por el médico** to fetch the doctor

3 (progresar: persona, cosa) to go; **el trabajo va muy bien** work is going very well; **¿cómo te va?** how are things going?; **me va muy bien** I'm getting on very well; **le fue fatal** it went awfully badly for him

4 (funcionar): **el coche no va muy bien** the car isn't running very well

5 (sentar): **me va estupendamente** (ropa, color) it suits me really well; (medicamento) it works really well for me; **ir bien con algo** to go well with sth; **te va estupendamente ese color** that colour really suits you o looks fantastic on you

6 (aspecto): **iba muy bien vestido** he was very well dressed; **ir con zapatos negros** to wear black shoes

7 (locuciones): **¿vino? — ¡que va!** did he come? — of course not!; **vamos, no llores** come on, don't cry; **¡vaya coche!** (admiración) what a car!, that's some car!; (desprecio) that's a terrible car!; **¡vaya!** (regular) so so; (desagrado) come on!; **¡vamos!** come on!; **¡que le vaya bien!** (adiós) take care!

8: **no vaya a ser: tienes que correr, no vaya a ser que pierdas el tren** you'll have to run so as not to miss the train

9: **no me** etc **va ni me viene** I etc don't care

▶ VB AUXILIAR **1**: **ir a: voy/iba a hacerlo hoy** I am/was going to do it today

2 (+gerundio): **iba anocheciendo** it was getting dark; **todo se me iba aclarando** everything was gradually becoming clearer to me

3 (+ pp = pasivo): **van vendidos 300 ejemplares** 300 copies have been sold so far

■ **irse** VR **1**: **¿por dónde se va al zoológico?** which is the way to the zoo?

2 (marcharse) to leave; **ya se habrán ido** they must already have left o gone; **¡vámonos!**, **¡nos fuimos!** (AM) let's go!; **¡vete!** go away!; **¡vete a saber!** your guess is as good as mine!, who knows!

IRA [ˈira] NM ABR (= Irish Republican Army) IRA

ira [ˈira] NF anger, rage

iracundo, -a [iraˈkundo, a] ADJ irascible

Irak [iˈrak] NM = **Iraq**

irakí ADJ, NMF Iraqui

Irán [iˈran] NM Iran

iraní [iraˈni] ADJ, NMF Iranian

Iraq [iˈrak] NM Iraq

iraquí [iraˈki] ADJ, NMF Iraqi

irascible [irasˈθiβle] ADJ irascible

irguiendo etc [irˈɣjendo] VB ver **erguir**

iris [ˈiris] NM INV (arco iris) rainbow; (Anat) iris

★**Irlanda** [irˈlanda] NF Ireland; **~ del Norte** Northern Ireland, Ulster

★**irlandés, -esa** [irlanˈdes, esa] ADJ Irish ▶ NM/F Irishman(-woman) ▶ NM (Ling) Gaelic, Irish ■ **los irlandeses** NMPL the Irish

ironía [iroˈnia] NF irony

irónico, -a [iˈroniko, a] ADJ ironic(al)

IRPF NM ABR (Esp) = **impuesto sobre la renta de las personas físicas**

irracional [iraθjoˈnal] ADJ irrational

irrazonable [iraθoˈnaβle] ADJ unreasonable

irreal [irreˈal] ADJ unreal

irrealizable [irrealiˈθaβle] ADJ (gen) unrealizable; (meta) unrealistic

irrebatible [irreβaˈtiβle] ADJ irrefutable

irreconocible [irrekonoˈθiβle] ADJ unrecognizable

irrecuperable [irrekupeˈraβle] ADJ irrecoverable, irretrievable

irreembolsable [irreembolˈsaβle] ADJ (Com) non-returnable

irreflexión [irreflekˈsjon] NF thoughtlessness; (ímpetu) rashness

irregular [irreɣuˈlar] ADJ irregular; (situación)

abnormal, anomalous; **margen izquierdo/ derecho ~** (*texto*) ragged left/right (margin)

irregularidad [irreɣulariˈðað] NF irregularity

irremediable [irremeˈðjaβle] ADJ irremediable; (*vicio*) incurable

irreparable [irrepaˈraβle] ADJ (*daños*) irreparable; (*pérdida*) irrecoverable

irreprochable [irreproˈtʃaβle] ADJ irreproachable

irresistible [irresisˈtiβle] ADJ irresistible

irresoluto, -a [irresoˈluto, a] ADJ irresolute, hesitant; (*sin resolver*) unresolved

irrespetuoso, -a [irrespeˈtwoso, a] ADJ disrespectful

irresponsable [irresponˈsaβle] ADJ irresponsible

irreverente [irreβeˈrente] ADJ disrespectful

irreversible [irreβerˈsiβle] ADJ irreversible

irrevocable [irreβoˈkaβle] ADJ irrevocable

irrigar [irriˈɣar] /**1h**/ VT to irrigate

irrigue *etc* [iˈrriɣe] VB *ver* **irrigar**

irrisorio, -a [irriˈsorjo, a] ADJ derisory, ridiculous; (*precio*) bargain *cpd*

irritación [irritaˈθjon] NF irritation

irritar [irriˈtar] /**1a**/ VT to irritate, annoy ■ **irritarse** VR to get angry, lose one's temper

irrompible [irromˈpiβle] ADJ unbreakable

irrumpir [irrumˈpir] /**3a**/ VI: **~ en** to burst o rush into

irrupción [irrupˈθjon] NF irruption; (*invasión*) invasion

ISBN NM ABR (= *International Standard Book Number*) ISBN

isla [ˈisla] NF (*Geo*) island; **Islas Británicas** British Isles; **Islas Filipinas/Malvinas/Canarias** Philippines/Falklands/Canaries; **Islas Marshall** Marshall Islands

Islam [isˈlam] NM Islam

islámico, -a [isˈlamiko, a] ADJ Islamic

islamofobia [islamoˈfoβja] NF Islamophobia

islandés, -esa [islanˈdes, esa] ADJ Icelandic ▶ NM/F Icelander ▶ NM (*Ling*) Icelandic

Islandia [isˈlandja] NF Iceland

isleño, -a [isˈleɲo, a] ADJ island *cpd* ▶ NM/F islander

islote [isˈlote] NM small island

isotónico, -a [isoˈtoniko, a] ADJ isotonic

isótopo [iˈsotopo] NM isotope

Israel [israˈel] NM Israel

israelí [israeˈli] ADJ, NMF Israeli

istmo [ˈistmo] NM isthmus; **el I~ de Panamá** the Isthmus of Panama

★**Italia** [iˈtalja] NF Italy

★**italiano, -a** [itaˈljano, a] ADJ, NM/F Italian ▶ NM (*Ling*) Italian

itinerancia [itineˈranθja] NF (*de teléfono móvil*) roaming

itinerante [itineˈrante] ADJ travelling; (*embajador*) roving

itinerario [itineˈrarjo] NM itinerary, route

ITV NF ABR (= *Inspección Técnica de Vehículos*) ≈ MOT (test)

★**IVA** [ˈiβa] NM ABR (*Esp Com*: = *Impuesto sobre el Valor Añadido*) VAT

IVP NM ABR = **Instituto Venezolano de Petroquímica**

izada [iˈsaða] NF (*Am*) lifting, raising

izar [iˈθar] /**1f**/ VT to hoist

izda., izq.ª ABR (= *izquierda*) L, l

izdo., izq.º ABR (= *izquierdo*) L, l

★**izquierda** [iθˈkjerða] NF *ver* **izquierdo**

izquierdista [iθkjerˈðista] ADJ leftist, left-wing ▶ NMF left-winger, leftist

izquierdo, -a [iθˈkjerðo, a] ADJ left ▶ NF left; (*Pol*) left (wing); **a la izquierda** on the left; (*torcer etc*) (to the) left; **es un cero a la izquierda** (*fam*) he is a nonentity; **conducción por la izquierda** left-hand drive

J, j [ˈxota] NF (*letra*) J, j; **J de José** J for Jack (BRIT) o Jig (US)

J ABR (= *julio(s)*) J

jabalí [xaβaˈli] NM wild boar

jabalina [xaβaˈlina] NF javelin

jabato, -a [xaˈβato, a] ADJ brave, bold ▸ NM young wild boar

★**jabón** [xaˈβon] NM soap; (*fam: adulación*) flattery; **~ de afeitar** shaving soap; **~ de tocador** toilet soap; **dar ~ a algn** to soft-soap sb

jabonar [xaβoˈnar] /**1a**/ VT to soap

jaca [ˈxaka] NF pony

jacal [xaˈkal] NM (*AM*) shack

jacinto [xaˈθinto] NM hyacinth

jactancia [xakˈtanθja] NF boasting, boastfulness

jactarse [xakˈtarse] /**1a**/ VR: **~ (de)** to boast o brag (about o of)

jadear [xaðeˈar] /**1a**/ VI to pant, gasp for breath

jadeo [xaˈðeo] NM panting, gasping

jaguar [xaˈɣwar] NM jaguar

jaiba [ˈxaiβa] NF (*AM*) crab

jalar [xaˈlar] /**1a**/ VT (*AM*) to pull

jalbegue [xalˈβeɣe] NM whitewash

jalea [xaˈlea] NF jelly

jaleo [xaˈleo] NM racket, uproar; **armar un ~** to kick up a racket

jalón [xaˈlon] NM (*AM*) tug

jalonar [xaloˈnar] /**1a**/ VT to stake out; (*fig*) to mark

Jamaica [xaˈmaika] NF Jamaica

jamaicano, -a [xamaiˈkano, a] ADJ, NM/F Jamaican

★**jamás** [xaˈmas] ADV never, not ... ever; (*interrogativo*) ever; **¿~ se vio tal cosa?** did you ever see such a thing?

★**jamón** [xaˈmon] NM ham; **~ (de) York** boiled ham; **~ dulce/serrano** boiled/cured ham

★**Japón** [xaˈpon] NM Japan

★**japonés, -esa** [xapoˈnes, esa] ADJ, NM/F Japanese ▸ NM (*Ling*) Japanese

jaque [ˈxake] NM: **~ mate** checkmate

jaqueca [xaˈkeka] NF (very bad) headache, migraine

★**jarabe** [xaˈraβe] NM syrup; **~ para la tos** cough syrup o mixture

jarana [xaˈrana] NF (*juerga*) spree (*fam*); **andar/ir de ~** to be/go on a spree

jarcia [ˈxarθja] NF (*Naut*) ropes *pl*, rigging

★**jardín** [xarˈðin] NM garden; **~ botánico** botanical garden; **~ de (la) infancia** (*ESP*) o **de niños** (*AM*) o **infantil** kindergarten, nursery school

jardinaje [xarðiˈnaxe] NM gardening

jardinería [xarðineˈria] NF gardening

★**jardinero, -a** [xarðiˈnero, a] NM/F gardener

★**jarra** [ˈxarra] NF jar; (*jarro*) jug; (*de leche*) churn; (*de cerveza*) mug; **de** o **en jarras** with arms akimbo

★**jarro** [ˈxarro] NM jug

jarrón [xaˈrron] NM vase; (*Arqueología*) urn

jaspeado, -a [xaspeˈaðo, a] ADJ mottled, speckled

★**jaula** [ˈxaula] NF cage; (*embalaje*) crate

jauría [xauˈria] NF pack of hounds

jazmín [xaθˈmin] NM jasmine

J. C. ABR = **Jesucristo**

jeans [jins] NMPL (*AM*) jeans, denims; **unos ~** a pair of jeans

jeep® [jip] (*pl* **jeeps** [jips]) NM jeep®

jefa [ˈxefa] NF *ver* **jefe**

jefatura [xefaˈtura] NF (*liderazgo*) leadership; (*sede*) central office; **J~ de la aviación civil** ≈ Civil Aviation Authority; **~ de policía** police headquarters *sg*

jefazo [xeˈfaθo] NM bigwig

★**jefe, -a** [ˈxefe, a] NM/F (*gen*) chief, head; (*patrón*) boss; (*Pol*) leader; (*Com*) manager(ess); **~ de camareros** head waiter; **~ de cocina** chef;

~ ejecutivo (*Com*) chief executive; **~ de estación** stationmaster; **~ de estado** head of state; **~ de oficina** (*Com*) office manager; **~ de producción** (*Com*) production manager; **~ supremo** commander-in-chief; **~ de estudios** (*Escol*) director of studies; **~ de gobierno** head of government; **ser el ~** (*fig*) to be the boss

JEN [xen] NF ABR (*ESP*) = **Junta de Energía Nuclear**

jengibre [xen'xiβre] NM ginger

jeque ['xeke] NM sheik(h)

jerarquía [xerar'kia] NF (*orden*) hierarchy; (*rango*) rank

jerárquico, -a [xe'rarkiko, a] ADJ hierarchic(al)

✱jerez [xe'reθ] NM sherry; **J~ de la Frontera** Jerez

jerezano, -a [xere'θano, a] ADJ of *o* from Jerez ▶ NM/F native *o* inhabitant of Jerez

jerga ['xerɣa] NF (*tela*) coarse cloth; (*lenguaje*) jargon; **~ informática** computer jargon

jerigonza [xeri'ɣonθa] NF (*jerga*) jargon, slang; (*galimatías*) nonsense, gibberish

jeringa [xe'ringa] NF syringe; (*AM*) annoyance, bother; **~ de engrase** grease gun

jeringar [xerin'gar] /**1h**/ VT to annoy, bother

jeringue *etc* [xe'ringe] VB *ver* **jeringar**

jeringuilla [xerin'guiʎa] NF syringe

jeroglífico [xero'ɣlifiko] NM hieroglyphic

✱jersey [xer'sei] (*pl* **jerseys**) NM jersey, pullover, jumper

Jerusalén [xerusa'len] NF Jerusalem

Jesucristo [xesu'kristo] NM Jesus Christ

jesuita [xe'swita] ADJ, NM Jesuit

Jesús [xe'sus] NM Jesus; **¡~!** good heavens!; (*al estornudar*) bless you!

jet [jet] (*pl* **jets** [jet]) NM jet (plane) ▶ NF: **la ~** the jet set

jeta ['xeta] NF (*Zool*) snout; (*fam: cara*) mug; **¡que ~ tienes!** (*fam*) (*insolencia*) you've got a nerve!

jíbaro, -a ['xiβaro, a] ADJ, NM/F Jíbaro (Indian)

jícara ['xikara] NF small cup

jiennense [xjen'nense] ADJ of *o* from Jaén ▶ NMF native *o* inhabitant of Jaén

jilguero [xil'ɣero] NM goldfinch

jinete, -a [xi'nete, a] NM/F horseman(-woman)

jipijapa [xipi'xapa] NM (*AM*) straw hat

jira ['xira] NF (*de tela*) strip; (*excursión*) picnic

jirafa [xi'rafa] NF giraffe

jirón [xi'ron] NM rag, shred

jitomate [xito'mate] NM (*AM*) tomato

JJ. OO. NMPL ABR = **Juegos Olímpicos**

jocosidad [xokosi'ðað] NF humour; (*chiste*) joke

jocoso, -a [xo'koso, a] ADJ humorous, jocular

joder [xo'ðer] /**2a**/ (*fam!*) VT to fuck (*fam!*), screw (*fam!*); (*fig: fastidiar*) to piss off (*fam!*), bug ▶ EXCL: **¡~!** bloody hell! (*fam!*), damn it! ▪ **joderse** VR (*fracasar*) to fail; **se jodió todo** everything was ruined

jodido, -a [xo'ðiðo, a] ADJ (*fam!: difícil*) awkward; **estoy ~** I'm knackered

jofaina [xo'faina] NF washbasin

jogging ['joɣin] NM (*AM*) tracksuit (*BRIT*), sweat suit (*US*)

jojoba [xo'xoβa] NF jojoba

jolgorio [xol'ɣorjo] NM (*juerga*) fun, revelry

jonrón [xon'ron] NM home run

Jordania [xor'ðanja] NF Jordan

jornada [xor'naða] NF (*viaje de un día*) day's journey; (*camino o viaje entero*) journey; (*día de trabajo*) working day; **~ de 8 horas** 8-hour day; (**trabajar a**) **~ partida** (to work a) split shift

jornal [xor'nal] NM (day's) wage

jornalero, -a [xorna'lero, a] NM/F (day) labourer

joroba [xo'roβa] NF hump

jorobado, -a [xoro'βaðo, a] ADJ hunchbacked ▶ NM/F hunchback

jorobar [xoro'βar] /**1a**/ VT to annoy, pester, bother; **¡esto me joroba!** I'm fed up with this! ▪ **jorobarse** VR to get cross; **¡hay que jorobarse!** to hell with it!

jota ['xota] NF letter J; (*danza*) Aragonese dance; (*fam*) jot, iota; **no saber ni ~** to have no idea

✱joven ['xoβen] ADJ young ▶ NM young man, youth ▶ NF young woman, girl

jovencito, -a [xoβen'θito, a] NM/F youngster

jovial [xo'βjal] ADJ cheerful, jolly

jovialidad [xoβjali'ðað] NF cheerfulness

✱joya ['xoja] NF jewel, gem; (*fig: persona*) gem; **joyas de fantasía** imitation jewellery *sg*

✱joyería [xoje'ria] NF (*joyas*) jewellery; (*tienda*) jeweller's (shop)

joyero [xo'jero] NM (*persona*) jeweller; (*caja*) jewel case

juanete [xwa'nete] NM (*del pie*) bunion

jubilación [xuβila'θjon] NF (*retiro*) retirement

✱jubilado, -a [xuβi'laðo, a] ADJ retired ▶ NM/F retired person, pensioner (*BRIT*), senior citizen

jubilar [xuβi'lar] /**1a**/ VT to pension off, retire; (*fam*) to discard ▪ **jubilarse** VR to retire

jubileo [xuβi'leo] NM jubilee

júbilo ['xuβilo] NM joy, rejoicing

jubiloso, -a [xuβi'loso, a] ADJ jubilant

judaísmo [xuða'ismo] NM Judaism

✱judía [xu'ðia] NF *ver* **judío**

judicatura [xuðika'tura] NF (*cargo de juez*) office of judge; (*cuerpo de jueces*) judiciary

judicial [xuði'θjal] ADJ judicial

✱judío, -a [xu'ðio, a] ADJ Jewish ▶ NM Jew ▶ NF Jewish woman; (*Culin*) bean; **judía blanca** haricot bean; **judía verde** French *o* string bean

judo ['xuðo] NM judo

✱juego ['xweɣo] VB *ver* **jugar** ▶ NM (*gen*) play; (*pasatiempo, partido*) game; (*en casino*) gambling; (*deporte*) sport; (*conjunto*) set; (*herramientas*) kit; **~ de azar** game of chance; **~ de café** coffee set;

~ **de caracteres** (*Inform*) font; ~ **limpio/sucio** fair/foul *o* dirty play; ~ **de mesa** board game; ~ **de palabras** pun, play on words; **Juegos Olímpicos** Olympic Games®; ~ **de programas** (*Inform*) suite of programs; **fuera de** ~ (*Deporte: persona*) offside; (: *pelota*) out of play; **por** ~ in fun, for fun

juegue *etc* [ˈxweɣe] VB *ver* **jugar**

juerga [ˈxwerɣa] NF binge; (*fiesta*) party; **ir de** ~ to go out on a binge

juerguista [xwerˈɣista] NMF reveller

★**jueves** [ˈxweβes] NM INV Thursday; *ver tb* **sábado**

★**juez, a** [ˈxweθ, a] NM/F judge; (*Tenis*) umpire; ~ **de instrucción** examining magistrate; ~ **de línea** linesman(-woman); ~ **de paz** justice of the peace; ~ **de salida** starter

jugada [xuˈɣaða] NF play; **buena** ~ good move (*o* shot *o* stroke) *etc*

★**jugador, a** [xuɣaˈðor, a] NM/F player; (*en casino*) gambler

★**jugar** [xuˈɣar] /**1h, 1n**/ VI to play; (*por dinero*) to gamble; ~ **al fútbol** to play football; ~ **a la bolsa** to play the stock market; **¿quién juega?** whose move is it? ▶ VT to play; (*en casino*) to gamble; (*apostar*) to bet; **¡me la han jugado!** (*fam*) I've been had! ■ **jugarse** VR to gamble (away); **jugarse el todo por el todo** to stake one's all, go for bust

jugarreta [xuɣaˈrreta] NF (*mala jugada*) bad move; (*trampa*) dirty trick; **hacer una** ~ **a algn** to play a dirty trick on sb

juglar [xuˈɣlar] NM minstrel

★**jugo** [ˈxuɣo] NM (*Bot, de fruta*) juice; (*fig*) essence, substance; ~ **de naranja** (*esp Am*) orange juice

jugoso, -a [xuˈɣoso, a] ADJ juicy; (*fig*) substantial, important

jugué [xuˈɣe], **juguemos** *etc* [xuˈɣemos] VB *ver* **jugar**

★**juguete** [xuˈɣete] NM toy

juguetear [xuɣeteˈar] /**1a**/ VI to play

★**juguetería** [xuɣeteˈria] NF toyshop

juguetón, -ona [xuɣeˈton, ona] ADJ playful

juicio [ˈxwiθjo] NM judgement; (*sana razón*) sanity, reason; (*opinión*) opinion; (*Jur: proceso*) trial; **estar fuera de** ~ to be out of one's mind; **a mi** ~ in my opinion

juicioso, -a [xwiˈθjoso, a] ADJ wise, sensible

JUJEM [xuˈxem] NF ABR (*Esp Mil*) = **Junta de Jefes del Estado Mayor**

jul. ABR (= *julio*) Jul.

★**julio** [ˈxuljo] NM July; **el uno** *o* **el primero de** ~ the first of July; **en el mes de** ~ during July; **en** ~ **del año que viene** in July of next year

jumento, -a [xuˈmento, a] NM/F donkey

jumper [ˈjumper] NM (*Am*) pinafore dress (*Brit*), jumper (*US*)

jun. ABR (= *junio*) Jun.

junco [ˈxunko] NM rush, reed

jungla [ˈxungla] NF jungle

★**junio** [ˈxunjo] NM June; *ver tb* **julio**

junta [ˈxunta] NF *ver* **junto**

juntar [xunˈtar] /**1a**/ VT to join, unite; (*maquinaria*) to assemble, put together; (*dinero*) to collect ■ **juntarse** VR to join, meet; (*reunirse: personas*) to meet, assemble; (*arrimarse*) to approach, draw closer; **juntarse con algn** to join sb

★**junto, -a** [ˈxunto, a] ADJ joined; (*unido*) united; (*anexo*) near, close; (*contiguo, próximo*) next, adjacent; **juntos** together ▶ NF (*asamblea*) meeting, assembly; (*comité, consejo*) board, council, committee; (*Mil, Pol*) junta; (*articulación*) joint; **junta constitutiva** (*Com*) statutory meeting; **junta directiva** (*Com*) board of management; **junta general extraordinaria** (*Com*) extraordinary general meeting ▶ ADV: **todo** ~ all at once; ~ **con** (together) with ▶ PREP: ~ **a** near (to), next to

juntura [xunˈtura] NF (*punto de unión*) join, junction; (*articulación*) joint

jura [ˈxura] NF oath, pledge; ~ **de bandera** (ceremony of taking the) oath of allegiance

jurado [xuˈraðo] NM (*Jur: individuo*) juror; (: *grupo*) jury; (*de concurso: grupo*) panel (of judges); (: *individuo*) member of a panel

juramentar [xuramenˈtar] /**1a**/ VT to swear in, administer the oath to ■ **juramentarse** VR to be sworn in, take the oath

juramento [xuraˈmento] NM oath; (*maldición*) oath, curse; **bajo** ~ on oath; **prestar** ~ to take the oath; **tomar** ~ **a** to swear in, administer the oath to

jurar [xuˈrar] /**1a**/ VT, VI to swear; ~ **en falso** to commit perjury; **jurárselas a algn** to have it in for sb

jurídico, -a [xuˈriðiko, a] ADJ legal, juridical

jurisdicción [xurisðikˈθjon] NF (*poder, autoridad*) jurisdiction; (*territorio*) district

jurisprudencia [xurispruˈðenθja] NF jurisprudence

jurista [xuˈrista] NMF jurist

justamente [xustaˈmente] ADV justly, fairly; (*precisamente*) just, exactly

justicia [xusˈtiθja] NF justice; (*equidad*) fairness, justice; **de** ~ deservedly

justiciero, -a [xustiˈθjero, a] ADJ just, righteous

justificable [xustifiˈkaβle] ADJ justifiable

justificación [xustifikaˈθjon] NF justification; ~ **automática** (*Inform*) automatic justification

justificado, -a [xustifiˈkaðo, a] ADJ (*Tip*): **(no)** ~ (un)justified

justificante [xustifiˈkante] NM voucher; ~ **médico** sick note

★**justificar** [xustifiˈkar] /**1g**/ VT (*tb Tip*) to justify; (*probar*) to verify

justifique *etc* [xustiˈfike] VB *ver* **justificar**

★**justo, -a** [ˈxusto, a] ADJ (*equitativo*) just, fair, right; (*preciso*) exact, correct; (*ajustado*) tight ▶ ADV (*precisamente*) exactly, precisely; (*apenas a tiempo*) just in time; **¡~!** that's it!, correct!; **lle-**

gaste muy ~ you just made it; **vivir muy ~** to be hard up

juvenil [xuβeˈnil] ADJ youthful

★**juventud** [xuβenˈtuð] NF (*adolescencia*) youth; (*jóvenes*) young people *pl*

juzgado [xuθˈɣaðo] NM tribunal; (*Jur*) court

★**juzgar** [xuθˈɣar] /1h/ VT to judge; **a ~ por ...** to judge by ..., judging by ...; **~ mal** to misjudge; **júzguelo usted mismo** see for yourself

Kk

K, k [ka] NF (*letra*) K, k; **K de Kilo** K for King

K ABR (= *1.000*) K; (*Inform*: = *1.024*) K

Kampuchea [kampuˈtʃea] NF Kampuchea

karaoke [karaˈoke] NM karaoke

kárate [ˈkarate], **karate** [kaˈrate] NM karate

Kazajstán [kaθaxsˈtan] NM Kazakhstan

k/c. ABR (= *kilociclos*) kc.

Kenia [ˈkenja] NF Kenya

keniata [keˈnjata] ADJ, NMF Kenyan

kepí, kepis [keˈpi, ˈkepis] NM (*esp AM*) kepi, military hat

kerosene [keroˈsene] NM kerosene

Kg, kg ABR (= *kilogramo(s)*) K, kg

KGB SIGLA M KGB

kilate [kiˈlate] NM = **quilate**

★**kilo** [ˈkilo] NM kilo

kilobyte [ˈkiloβait] NM (*Inform*) kilobyte

kilogramo [kiloˈɣramo] NM kilogramme (*BRIT*), kilogram (*US*)

kilolitro [kiloˈlitro] NM kilolitre (*BRIT*), kiloliter (*US*)

kilometraje [kilomeˈtraxe] NM distance in kilometres (*BRIT*) o kilometers (*US*), ≈ mileage

kilométrico, -a [kiloˈmetriko, a] ADJ kilometric; (*fam*) very long; **(billete)** ~ (*Ferro*) mileage ticket

★**kilómetro** [kiˈlometro] NM kilometre (*BRIT*), kilometer (*US*)

kiloocteto [kilookˈteto] NM (*Inform*) kilobyte

kilovatio [kiloˈβatjo] NM kilowatt

★**kiosco** [ˈkjosko] NM = **quiosco**

Kirguistán [kirɣisˈtan], **Kirguizistán** [kirɣiθisˈtan] NM Kyrgyzstan

Kiribati [kiriˈβati] NM Kiribati

kiwi [ˈkiwi] NM kiwi (fruit)

kleenex® [kliˈneks] NM paper handkerchief, tissue

km ABR (= *kilómetro(s)*) km

km/h ABR (= *kilómetros por hora*) km/h

knock-out [ˈnokau], **K.O.** [ˈkao] NM knockout; (*golpe*) knockout blow; **dejar** o **poner a algn** ~ to knock sb out

kosovar, a [kosoˈβar, a] ADJ Kosovan

Kosovo [kosoˈβo] NM Kosovo

k.p.h. ABR (= *kilómetros por hora*) km/h

kurdo, -a [ˈkurðo, a] ADJ Kurdish ▶ NM/F Kurd ▶ NM (*Ling*) Kurdish

kuwaití [kuβaiˈti] ADJ, NMF Kuwaiti

kv ABR (= *kilovatio*) kw

kv/h ABR (= *kilovatios-hora*) kw-h

Ll

L, l ['ele] NF (*letra*) L, l; **L de Lorenzo** L for Lucy (*BRIT*) o Love (*US*)

l ABR (= *litro(s)*) l; (= *libro*) bk

L/ ABR (*Com*) = **letra**

★la [la] ARTÍCULO DEFINIDO FSG the; **está en la cárcel** he's in jail ▶ PRON her; (*en relación a usted*) you; (*en relación a una cosa*) it; **la del sombrero rojo** the woman/girl/one in the red hat ▶ NM (*Mus*) A

laberinto [laβe'rinto] NM labyrinth

labia ['laβja] NF fluency; (*pey*) glibness; **tener mucha ~** to have the gift of the gab

labial [la'βjal] ADJ labial

★labio ['laβjo] NM lip; (*de vasija etc*) edge, rim; **~ inferior/superior** lower/upper lip

labor [la'βor] NF labour; (*Agr*) farm work; (*tarea*) job, task; (*Costura*) needlework, sewing; (*punto*) knitting; **~ de equipo** teamwork; **~ de ganchillo** crochet; **labores domésticas** o **del hogar** household chores

laborable [laβo'raβle] ADJ (*Agr*) workable; **día ~** working day

★laboral [laβo'ral] ADJ (*accidente, conflictividad*) industrial; (*jornada*) working; (*derecho, relaciones*) labour *cpd*

laboralista [laβora'lista] ADJ: **abogado ~** labour lawyer

laborar [laβo'rar] /1a/ VI to work

★laboratorio [laβora'torjo] NM laboratory

laborioso, -a [laβo'rjoso, a] ADJ (*persona*) hard-working; (*trabajo*) tough

laborista [laβo'rista] (*Pol*) ADJ: **Partido L~** Labour Party (*BRIT*) ▶ NMF Labour Party member o supporter (*BRIT*)

labrado, -a [la'βraðo, a] ADJ worked; (*madera*) carved; (*metal*) wrought ▶ NM (*Agr*) cultivated field

Labrador [laβra'ðor] NM Labrador

labrador, a [laβra'ðor, a] ADJ farming *cpd* ▶ NM/F farmer

labranza [la'βranθa] NF (*Agr*) cultivation

labrar [la'βrar] /1a/ VT (*gen*) to work; (*madera etc*) to carve; (*fig*) to cause, bring about

labriego, -a [la'βrjeɣo, a] NM/F peasant

laca ['laka] NF lacquer; (*de pelo*) hairspray; **~ de uñas** nail varnish

lacayo [la'kajo] NM lackey

lacerar [laθe'rar] /1a/ VT to lacerate

lacio, -a ['laθjo, a] ADJ (*pelo*) lank, straight

lacón [la'kon] NM shoulder of pork

lacónico, -a [la'koniko, a] ADJ laconic

lacra ['lakra] NF (*defecto*) blemish; **~ social** social disgrace

lacrar [la'krar] /1a/ VT (*cerrar*) to seal (with sealing wax)

lacre ['lakre] NM sealing wax

lacrimógeno, -a [lakri'moxeno, a] ADJ (*fig*) sentimental; **gas ~** tear gas

lacrimoso, -a [lakri'moso, a] ADJ tearful

lactancia [lak'tanθja] NF lactation, breast-feeding

lactar [lak'tar] /1a/ VT, VI to suckle, breast-feed

lácteo, -a ['lakteo, a] ADJ: **productos lácteos** dairy products

ladear [laðe'ar] /1a/ VT to tip, tilt ▶ VI to tilt **■ladearse** VR to lean; (*Deporte*) to swerve; (*Aviat*) to bank, turn

ladera [la'ðera] NF slope

ladino, -a [la'ðino, a] ADJ cunning

★lado ['laðo] NM (*gen*) side; (*fig*) protection; (*Mil*) flank; **~ izquierdo** left(-hand) side; **~ a ~** side by side; **al ~ de** next to, beside; **hacerse a un ~** to stand aside; **poner de ~** to put on its side; **poner a un ~** to put aside; **me da de ~** I don't care; **por un ~ ..., por otro ~ ...** on the one hand ..., on the other (hand) ...; **por todos lados** on all sides, all round (*BRIT*)

ladrar [la'ðrar] /1a/ VI to bark

ladrido [la'ðriðo] NM bark, barking

★**ladrillo** [la'ðriʎo] NM (gen) brick; (azulejo) tile; (fam: negocio) real estate (business)

★**ladrón, -ona** [la'ðron, ona] NM/F thief

lagar [la'ɣar] NM (wine/oil) press

lagartija [laɣar'tixa] NF (small) lizard, wall lizard

lagarto [la'ɣarto] NM (Zool) lizard; (AM) alligator

★**lago** ['laɣo] NM lake

Lagos ['laɣos] NM Lagos

★**lágrima** ['laɣrima] NF tear

lagrimal [laɣri'mal] NM (inner) corner of the eye

lagrimear [laɣrime'ar] /1a/ VI to weep; (ojos) to water

laguna [la'ɣuna] NF (lago) lagoon; (en escrito, conocimientos) gap

laico, -a ['laiko, a] ADJ lay ▶ NM/F layman(-woman)

laja ['laxa] NF rock

lamber [lam'ber] /2a/ VT (AM) to lick

lambiscón, -ona [lambis'kon, ona] ADJ flattering ▶ NM/F flatterer

lameculos [lame'kulos] NMF (fam!) arse licker (fam!), crawler (fam)

lamentable [lamen'taβle] ADJ lamentable, regrettable; (miserable) pitiful

lamentación [lamenta'θjon] NF lamentation; **ahora no sirven lamentaciones** it's no good crying over spilt milk

★**lamentar** [lamen'tar] /1a/ VT (sentir) to regret; (deplorar) to lament; **lo lamento mucho** I'm very sorry ■ **lamentarse** VR to lament

lamento [la'mento] NM lament

lamer [la'mer] /2a/ VT to lick

lámina ['lamina] NF (plancha delgada) sheet; (para estampar, estampa) plate; (grabado) engraving

laminar [lami'nar] /1a/ VT (en libro) to laminate; (Tec) to roll

★**lámpara** ['lampara] NF lamp; **~ de alcohol/gas** spirit/gas lamp; **~ de pie** standard lamp

lamparilla [lampa'riʎa] NF night-light

lamparón [lampa'ron] NM (Med) scrofula; (mancha) (large) grease spot

lampiño, -a [lam'piɲo, a] ADJ (sin pelo) hairless

★**lana** ['lana] NF wool; (tela) woollen (BRIT) o woolen (US) cloth; (AM fam: dinero) dough; **(hecho) de ~** wool cpd

lance etc ['lanθe] VB ver **lanzar** ▶ NM (golpe) stroke; (suceso) event, incident

lanceta [lan'seta] NF (AM) sting

lancha ['lantʃa] NF launch; **~ motora** motorboat; **~ neumática** rubber dinghy; **~ de pesca** fishing boat; **~ salvavidas/torpedera** lifeboat/torpedo boat

lanero, -a [la'nero, a] ADJ wool cpd

★**langosta** [lan'gosta] NF (insecto) locust; (crustáceo) lobster; (: de río) crayfish

langostino [langos'tino] NM prawn; (de agua dulce) crayfish

languidecer [langiðe'θer] /2d/ VI to languish

languidez [langi'ðeθ] NF languor

languidezca etc [langi'ðeθka] VB ver **languidecer**

lánguido, -a ['langiðo, a] ADJ (gen) languid; (sin energía) listless

lanilla [la'niʎa] NF nap; (tela) thin flannel cloth

lanolina [lano'lina] NF lanolin(e)

lanudo, -a [la'nuðo, a] ADJ woolly, fleecy

lanza ['lanθa] NF (arma) lance, spear; **medir lanzas** to cross swords

lanzacohetes [lanθako'etes] NM INV rocket launcher

lanzadera [lanθa'ðera] NF shuttle

lanzado, -a [lan'θaðo, a] ADJ (atrevido) forward; (decidido) determined; **ir ~** (rápido) to fly along

lanzallamas [lanθa'ʎamas] NM INV flamethrower

lanzamiento [lanθa'mjento] NM (gen) throwing; (Naut, Com) launch, launching; **~ de pesos** putting the shot

★**lanzar** [lan'θar] /1f/ VT (gen) to throw; (con violencia) to fling; (Deporte: pelota) to bowl, pitch (US); (Naut, Com) to launch; (Jur) to evict; (grito) to give, utter ■ **lanzarse** VR to throw o.s.; (fig) to take the plunge; **lanzarse a** (fig) to embark upon

Lanzarote [lanθa'rote] NM Lanzarote

lanzatorpedos [lanθator'peðos] NM INV torpedo tube

lapa ['lapa] NF limpet

La Paz NF La Paz

lapicero [lapi'θero] NM (lápiz) pencil; (AM: portaminas) propelling (BRIT) o mechanical (US) pencil; (: bolígrafo) ballpoint pen, Biro®

lápida ['lapiða] NF stone; **~ conmemorativa** memorial stone; **~ mortuoria** headstone

lapidar [lapi'ðar] /1a/ VT to stone; (Tec) to polish, lap

lapidario, -a [lapi'ðarjo, a] ADJ, NM lapidary

★**lápiz** ['lapiθ] NM pencil; **~ de color** coloured pencil; **~ de labios** lipstick; **~ de ojos** eyebrow pencil; **~ óptico** o **luminoso** light pen

lapón, -ona [la'pon, ona] ADJ Lapp ▶ NM/F Laplander, Lapp ▶ NM (Ling) Lapp

Laponia [la'ponja] NF Lapland

lapso ['lapso] NM lapse; (error) error; **~ de tiempo** interval of time

lapsus ['lapsus] NM INV error, mistake

largamente [larɣa'mente] ADV for a long time; (relatar) at length

largar [lar'ɣar] /1h/ VT (soltar) to release; (aflojar) to loosen; (lanzar) to launch; (fam) to let

fly; (*velas*) to unfurl; (*Am*) to throw ■ **largarse**
VR (*fam*) to beat it; **largarse a** (*Am*) to start
to

★**largo, -a** ['larɣo, a] ADJ (*longitud*) long; (*tiempo*)
lengthy; (*persona: alta*) tall; (: *fig*) generous; **dos
años largos** two long years; **a ~ plazo** in the
long term; **a lo ~** (*posición*) lengthways ▶ NM
length; (*Mus*) largo; **tiene nueve metros de ~** it
is nine metres long ▶ NF: **a la larga** in the long
run; **me dio largas con una promesa** she put
me off with a promise ▶ EXCL: **¡~ de aquí!** (*fam*)
clear off!; **a lo ~ de** along; (*tiempo*) all through,
throughout

> Do not translate the Spanish word **largo** by
> *large*.

largometraje [larɣome'traxe] NM full-length
o feature film

largue *etc* ['larɣe] VB *ver* **largar**

larguero [lar'ɣero] NM (*Arq*) main beam, chief
support; (*de puerta*) jamb; (*Deporte*) crossbar; (*de
cama*) bolster

largueza [lar'ɣeθa] NF generosity

larguirucho, -a [larɣi'rutʃo, a] ADJ lanky, gangling

larguísimo, -a [lar'ɣisimo, a] ADJ SUPERLATIVO
de **largo**

largura [lar'ɣura] NF length

laringe [la'rinxe] NF larynx

laringitis [larin'xitis] NF laryngitis

larva ['larβa] NF larva

~**las** [las] ARTÍCULO DEFINIDO FPL the ▶ PRON
them; **~ que cantan** the ones/women/girls
who sing

lasaña [la'saɲa] NF lasagne, lasagna

lasca ['laska] NF chip of stone

lascivia [las'θiβja] NF lewdness; (*lujuria*) lust;
(*fig*) playfulness

lascivo, -a [las'θiβo, a] ADJ lewd

láser ['laser] NM laser

Las Palmas NF Las Palmas

~**lástima** ['lastima] NF (*pena*) pity; **dar ~** to be
pitiful; **es una ~ que** it's a pity that; **¡qué ~!**
what a pity!; **estar hecho una ~** to be a sorry
sight

lastimar [lasti'mar] /1a/ VT (*herir*) to wound;
(*ofender*) to offend ■ **lastimarse** VR to hurt o.s.

lastimero, -a [lasti'mero, a] ADJ pitiful,
pathetic

lastre ['lastre] NM (*Tec, Naut*) ballast; (*fig*) dead
weight

lata ['lata] NF (*metal*) tin; (*envase*) tin, can; (*fam*)
nuisance; **en ~** tinned; **dar (la) ~** to be a nuisance

latente [la'tente] ADJ latent

lateral [late'ral] ADJ side, lateral ▶ NM (*Teat*)
wings *pl*

latido [la'tiðo] NM (*del corazón*) beat; (*de herida*)
throb(bing)

latifundio [lati'fundjo] NM large estate

latifundista [latifun'dista] NMF owner of a
large estate

latigazo [lati'ɣaθo] NM (*golpe*) lash; (*sonido*)
crack; (*fig: regaño*) dressing-down

látigo ['latiɣo] NM whip

latiguillo [lati'ɣiʎo] NM (*Teat*) hamming

★**latín** [la'tin] NM Latin; **saber (mucho) ~** (*fam*) to
be pretty sharp

latinajo [lati'naxo] NM dog Latin; **echar latina-
jos** to come out with Latin words

latino, -a [la'tino, a] ADJ Latin

★**Latinoamérica** [latinoa'merika] NF Latin
America

★**latinoamericano, -a** [latinoameri'kano, a]
ADJ, NM/F Latin American

latir [la'tir] /3a/ VI (*corazón, pulso*) to beat

latitud [lati'tuð] NF (*Geo*) latitude; (*fig*) breadth,
extent

lato, -a ['lato, a] ADJ broad

latón [la'ton] NM brass

latoso, -a [la'toso, a] ADJ (*molesto*) annoying;
(*aburrido*) boring

latrocinio [latro'θinjo] NM robbery

LAU ['lau] NF ABR (*Esp Jur*) = **Ley de Arrenda-
mientos Urbanos**

laúd [la'uð] NM lute

laudatorio, -a [lauða'torjo, a] ADJ laudatory

laudo ['lauðo] NM (*Jur*) decision, finding

laurear [laure'ar] /1a/ VT to honour, reward

laurel [lau'rel] NM (*Bot*) laurel; (*Culin*) bay

Lausana [lau'sana] NF Lausanne

lava ['laβa] NF lava

lavable [la'βaβle] ADJ washable

★**lavabo** [la'βaβo] NM (*jofaina*) washbasin;
(*retrete*) lavatory (*Brit*), toilet (*Brit*), washroom
(*US*)

lavadero [laβa'ðero] NM laundry

★**lavado** [la'βaðo] NM washing; (*de ropa*) wash,
laundry; (*Arte*) wash; **~ de cerebro** brainwash-
ing; **~ en seco** dry-cleaning

★**lavadora** [laβa'ðora] NF washing machine

lavanda [la'βanda] NF lavender

★**lavandería** [laβande'ria] NF laundry; **~ automática** launderette

lavaparabrisas [laβapara'βrisas] NM INV
windscreen washer

★**lavaplatos** [laβa'platos] NM INV dishwasher

★**lavar** [la'βar] /1a/ VT to wash; (*borrar*) to wipe
away; **~ y marcar** (*pelo*) to shampoo and set;
~ en seco to dry-clean; **~ los platos** to wash the
dishes ■ **lavarse** VR to wash o.s.; **lavarse las
manos** to wash one's hands; (*fig*) to wash one's
hands of it; **lavarse los dientes** to brush one's
teeth

lavarropas [laβa'rropas] NM INV (*RPL*) washing
machine

lavativa [laβa'tiβa] NF (*Med*) enema

★lavavajillas [laβaβa'xiʎas] NM INV dish-washer

laxante [lak'sante] NM laxative

laxitud [laksi'tuð] NF laxity, slackness

lazada [la'θaða] NF bow

lazarillo [laθa'riʎo] NM: **perro de ~** guide dog

lazo ['laθo] NM knot; (*lazada*) bow; (*para animales*) lasso; (*trampa*) snare; (*vínculo*) tie; **~ corredizo** slipknot

lb ABR = **libra**

lbs ABR = **libras**

L/C ABR (= *Letra de Crédito*) B/E

LCD NF ABR (= *liquid crystal display*) LCD

Lda., Ldo. ABR = **Licenciada, o**

le [le] PRON (*directo*) him (*o* her); (: *en relación a usted*) you; (*indirecto*) to him (*o* her *o* it); (: *a usted*) to you

leal [le'al] ADJ loyal

lealtad [leal'tað] NF loyalty

lebrel [le'βrel] NM greyhound

★lección [lek'θjon] NF lesson; **~ práctica** object lesson; **dar lecciones** to teach, give lessons; **dar una ~ a algn** (*fig*) to teach sb a lesson

★leche ['letʃe] NF milk; (*fam!*) semen, spunk (*fam!*); **dar una ~ a algn** (*fam*) to belt sb; **estar de mala ~** (*fam*) to be in a foul mood; **tener mala ~** (*fam*) to be a nasty piece of work; **~ condensada/en polvo** condensed/powdered milk; **~ desnatada** skimmed milk; **~ de magnesia** milk of magnesia; **¡~!** hell!

lechera [le'tʃera] NF ver **lechero**

lechería [letʃe'ria] NF dairy

lechero, -a [le'tʃero, a] ADJ milk cpd ▶ NM milk-man ▶ NF (*vendedora*) milkwoman; (*recipiente*) milk pan; (*para servir*) milk churn

lecho ['letʃo] NM (*cama, de río*) bed; (*Geo*) layer; **~ mortuorio** deathbed

lechón [le'tʃon] NM sucking (BRIT) *o* suckling (US) pig

lechoso, -a [le'tʃoso, a] ADJ milky

★lechuga [le'tʃuɣa] NF lettuce

lechuza [le'tʃuθa] NF (barn) owl

lectivo, -a [lek'tiβo, a] ADJ (*horas*) teaching cpd; **año** *o* **curso ~** (*Escol*) school year; (*Univ*) academic year

lector, a [lek'tor, a] NM/F reader; (*Escol, Univ*) (conversation) assistant ▶ NM: **~ de discos compactos** CD player; **~ óptico de caracteres** (*Inform*) optical character reader; **~ de libros electrónicos** e-reader, eReader ▶ NF: **lectora de fichas** (*Inform*) card reader

★lectura [lek'tura] NF reading; **~ de marcas sensibles** (*Inform*) mark sensing

★leer [le'er] /2e/ VT to read; **~ entre líneas** to read between the lines

legación [leɣa'θjon] NF legation

legado [le'ɣaðo] NM (*don*) bequest; (*herencia*) legacy; (*enviado*) legate

legajo [le'ɣaxo] NM file, bundle (of papers)

legal [le'ɣal] ADJ legal, lawful; (*persona*) trustworthy

legalice *etc* [leɣa'liθe] VB ver **legalizar**

legalidad [leɣali'ðað] NF legality

legalizar [leɣali'θar] /1f/ VT to legalize; (*documento*) to authenticate

legaña [le'ɣaɲa] NF sleep (*in eyes*)

legar [le'ɣar] /1h/ VT to bequeath, leave

legatario, -a [leɣa'tarjo, a] NM/F legatee

legendario, -a [lexen'darjo, a] ADJ legendary

legible [le'xiβle] ADJ legible; **~ por máquina** (*Inform*) machine-readable

legión [le'xjon] NF legion

legionario, -a [lexjo'narjo, a] ADJ legionary ▶ NM legionnaire

legislación [lexisla'θjon] NF legislation; (*leyes*) laws pl; **~ antimonopolio** (*Com*) anti-trust legislation

legislar [lexis'lar] /1a/ VT to legislate

legislativo, -a [lexisla'tiβo, a] ADJ: **(elecciones) legislativas** = general election

legislatura [lexisla'tura] NF (*Pol*) period of office

legitimar [lexiti'mar] /1a/ VT to legitimize

legítimo, -a [le'xitimo, a] ADJ (*genuino*) authentic; (*legal*) legitimate, rightful

lego, -a ['leɣo, a] ADJ (*Rel*) secular; (*ignorante*) ignorant ▶ NM layman

legua ['leɣwa] NF league; **se ve** (*o* **nota**) **a la ~** you can tell (it) a mile off

legue *etc* ['leɣe] VB ver **legar**

leguleyo [leɣu'lejo] NM (*pey*) petty *o* (US) shyster lawyer

legumbres [le'ɣumbres] NFPL pulses

leído, -a [le'iðo, a] ADJ well-read

lejanía [lexa'nia] NF distance

★lejano, -a [le'xano, a] ADJ far-off; (*en el tiempo*) distant; (*fig*) remote; **L~ Oriente** Far East

lejía [le'xia] NF bleach

lejísimos [le'xisimos] ADV a long, long way

★lejos ['lexos] ADV far, far away; **a lo ~** in the distance; **de** *o* **desde ~** from a distance; **está muy ~** it's a long way (away); **¿está ~?** is it far?; **~ de** prep far from

lelo, -a ['lelo, a] ADJ silly ▶ NM/F idiot

lema ['lema] NM motto; (*Pol*) slogan

lencería [lenθe'ria] NF (*telas*) linen, drapery; (*ropa interior*) lingerie

lendakari [lenda'kari] NM *head of the Basque Autonomous Government*

★lengua ['lengwa] NF tongue; (*Ling*) language; **~ materna** mother tongue; **~ de tierra** (*Geo*) spit *o* tongue of land; **dar a la ~** to chatter; **morderse la ~** to hold one's tongue; **sacar la ~ a algn** (*fig*) to cock a snook at sb; *see note*

Under the Spanish constitution, **lenguas co-oficiales** or *oficiales* enjoy the same status as *castellano* in those regions which have retained their own distinct language, such as *gallego* in Galicia, *euskera* in the Basque Country, and *catalán* in Catalonia, the Community of Valencia, and the Balearics. The regional governments actively promote their own language through the media and the education system. Of the three regions with their own language, Catalonia has the highest number of people who speak the *lengua cooficial*.

lenguado [len'gwaðo] NM sole

lenguaje [len'gwaxe] NM language; (*forma de hablar*) (mode of) speech; **~ comercial** business language; **~ ensamblador** o **de alto nivel** (*Inform*) high-level language; **~ máquina** (*Inform*) machine language; **~ original** source language; **~ periodístico** journalese; **~ de programación** (*Inform*) programming language; **en ~ llano** ≈ in plain English

lenguaraz [lengwa'raθ] ADJ talkative; (*pey*) foul-mouthed

lengüeta [len'gweta] NF (*Anat*) epiglottis; (*de zapatos*) tongue; (*Mus*) reed

lenidad [leni'ðað] NF lenience

Leningrado [lenin'graðo] NM Leningrad

lente ['lente] NM o F lens; (*lupa*) magnifying glass ■ **lentes** NMPL glasses; **lentes bifocales/de sol** (*Am*) bifocals/sunglasses; **lentes de contacto** contact lenses; **lentes progresivas** varifocal lenses

lenteja [len'texa] NF lentil

lentejuela [lente'xwela] NF sequin

lentilla [len'tiʎa] NF contact lens

lentitud [lenti'tuð] NF slowness; **con ~** slowly

★**lento, -a** ['lento, a] ADJ slow

★**leña** ['leɲa] NF firewood; **dar ~ a** to thrash; **echar ~ al fuego** to add fuel to the flames

leñador, a [leɲa'ðor, a] NM/F woodcutter

leño ['leɲo] NM (*trozo de árbol*) log; (*madera*) timber; (*fig*) blockhead

Leo ['leo] NM (*Astro*) Leo

★**león** [le'on] NM lion; **~ marino** sea lion

★**leona** [le'ona] NF lioness

leonera [leo'nera] NF (*jaula*) lion's cage; **parece una ~** it's shockingly dirty

leonés, -esa [leo'nes, esa] ADJ, NM/F Leonese ► NM (*Ling*) Leonese

leonino, -a [leo'nino, a] ADJ leonine

leopardo [leo'parðo] NM leopard

leotardos [leo'tarðos] NMPL tights

lepra ['lepra] NF leprosy

leprosería [leprose'ria] NF leper colony

leproso, -a [le'proso, a] NM/F leper

lerdo, -a ['lerðo, a] ADJ (*lento*) slow; (*patoso*) clumsy

leridano, -a [leri'ðano, a] ADJ of o from Lérida ► NM/F native o inhabitant of Lérida

les [les] PRON (*directo*) them; (: *en relación a ustedes*) you; (*indirecto*) to them; (: *a ustedes*) to you

lesbiana [les'βjana] ADJ, NF lesbian

lesión [le'sjon] NF wound, lesion; (*Deporte*) injury

lesionado, -a [lesjo'naðo, a] ADJ injured ► NM/F injured person

lesionar [lesjo'nar] /1a/ VT (*dañar*) to hurt; (*herir*) to wound ■ **lesionarse** VR to get hurt

letal [le'tal] ADJ lethal

letanía [leta'nia] NF litany; (*retahíla*) long list

letárgico, -a [le'tarxiko, a] ADJ lethargic

letargo [le'taryo] NM lethargy

letón, -ona [le'ton, ona] ADJ, NM/F Latvian ► NM (*Ling*) Latvian

Letonia [le'tonja] NF Latvia

★**letra** ['letra] NF letter; (*escritura*) handwriting; (*Com*) letter, bill, draft; (*Mus*) lyrics pl; **~ bancaria** (*Com*) bank draft; **~ bastardilla/negrilla** italics pl/bold type; **~ de cambio** bill of exchange; **~ de imprenta** print; **~ inicial/mayúscula/minúscula** initial/capital/small letter; **lo tomó al pie de la ~** he took it literally; **~ de patente** (*Com*) letters patent pl ■ **letras** NFPL (*Univ*) arts; **escribir cuatro letras a algn** to drop a line to sb

letrado, -a [le'traðo, a] ADJ learned; (*fam*) pedantic ► NM/F lawyer

★**letrero** [le'trero] NM (*cartel*) sign; (*etiqueta*) label

letrina [le'trina] NF latrine

leucemia [leu'θemja] NF leukaemia

leucocito [leuko'θito] NM white blood cell, leucocyte

leva ['leβa] NF (*Naut*) weighing anchor; (*Mil*) levy; (*Tec*) lever

levadizo, -a [leβa'ðiθo, a] ADJ: **puente ~** drawbridge

levadura [leβa'ðura] NF yeast, leaven; **~ de cerveza** brewer's yeast

levantamiento [leβanta'mjento] NM raising, lifting; (*rebelión*) revolt, rising; (*Geo*) survey; **~ de pesos** weightlifting

★**levantar** [leβan'tar] /1a/ VT (*gen*) to raise; (*del suelo*) to pick up; (*hacia arriba*) to lift (up); (*plan*) to make, draw up; (*mesa*) to clear; (*campamento*) to strike; (*fig*) to cheer up, hearten; **~ el ánimo** to cheer up ■ **levantarse** VR to get up; (*enderezarse*) to straighten up; (*rebelarse*) to rebel; (*sesión*) to be adjourned; (*niebla*) to lift; (*viento*) to rise; **levantarse (de la cama)** to get up, get out of bed

levante [le'βante] NM east; (*viento*) east wind; **el L~** region of Spain extending along the coast from Castellón to Murcia

levantino, -a [leβan'tino, a] ADJ of o from the Levante ► NM/F: **los levantinos** the people of the Levante

levar [le'βar] /1a/ VT, VI: **~ (anclas)** to weigh anchor

leve ['leβe] ADJ light; (*fig*) trivial; (*mínimo*) slight

levedad [leβe'ðað] NF lightness; (fig) levity

levita [le'βita] NF frock coat

léxico, -a ['leksiko, a] ADJ lexical ▶ NM (vocabulario) vocabulary; (Ling) lexicon

★**ley** [lei] NF (gen) law; (metal) standard; **decreto-ley** decree law; **de buena ~** (fig) genuine; **según la ~** in accordance with the law, by law, in law

leyenda [le'jenda] NF legend; (Tip) inscription

leyendo etc [le'jendo] VB ver **leer**

leyó etc VB ver **leer**

LGBT ABR (= lesbianas, gays, bisexuales y transexuales) LGBT

liar [li'ar] /1c/ VT to tie (up); (unir) to bind; (envolver) to wrap (up); (enredar) to confuse; (cigarrillo) to roll ■ **liarse** VR (fam) to get involved; (confundirse) to get mixed up; **liarse a palos** to get involved in a fight

lib. ABR (= libro) bk.

libanés, -esa [liβa'nes, esa] ADJ, NM/F Lebanese

Líbano ['liβano] NM: **el ~** the Lebanon

libar [li'βar] /1a/ VT to suck

libelo [li'βelo] NM satire, lampoon; (Jur) petition

libélula [li'βelula] NF dragonfly

liberación [liβera'θjon] NF liberation; (de la cárcel) release

liberado, -a [liβe'raðo, a] ADJ liberated; (Com) paid-up, paid-in (US)

liberal [liβe'ral] ADJ, NMF liberal

★**liberar** [liβe'rar] /1a/ VT to liberate

★**libertad** [liβer'tað] NF liberty, freedom; **~ de asociación/de culto/de prensa/de comercio/de palabra** freedom of association/of worship/ of the press/of trade/of speech; **~ condicional** probation; **~ bajo palabra** parole; **~ bajo fianza** bail; **estar en ~** to be free; **poner a algn en ~** to set sb free

libertador, a [liβerta'ðor, a] ADJ liberating ▶ NM/F liberator; **El L~** (Am) The Liberator

libertar [liβer'tar] /1a/ VT (preso) to set free; (de una obligación) to release; (eximir) to exempt

libertinaje [liβerti'naxe] NM licentiousness

libertino, -a [liβer'tino, a] ADJ permissive ▶ NM/F permissive person

Libia ['liβja] NF Libya

libidinoso, -a [liβiði'noso, a] ADJ lustful; (viejo) lecherous

libido [li'βiðo] NF libido

libio, -a ['liβjo, a] ADJ, NM/F Libyan

★**libra** ['liβra] NF pound; **L~** (Astro) Libra; **~ esterlina** pound sterling

librador, a [liβra'ðor, a] NM/F drawer

libramiento [liβra'mjento] NM (Am) ring road (Brit), beltway (US)

libranza [li'βranθa] NF (Com) draft; (letra de cambio) bill of exchange

librar [li'βrar] /1a/ VT (de peligro) to save; (batalla) to wage, fight; (de impuestos) to exempt; (cheque)

to make out; (Jur) to exempt ■ **librarse** VR: **librarse de** to escape from, free o.s. from; **de buena nos hemos librado** we're well out of that

★**libre** ['liβre] ADJ (gen) free; (lugar) unoccupied; (tiempo) spare; (asiento) vacant; (de deudas) free of debts; (Com): **~ a bordo** free on board; **~ de franqueo** post-free; **~ de impuestos** free of tax; **tiro ~** free kick; **los 100 metros ~** the 100 metres freestyle (race); **al aire ~** in the open air; **¿estás ~?** are you free?

librecambio [liβre'kambjo] NM free trade

librecambista [liβrekam'bista] ADJ free-trade cpd ▶ NM free-trader

★**librería** [liβre'ria] NF (tienda) bookshop, bookstore (esp US); (estante) bookcase; **~ de ocasión** secondhand bookshop

> Do not translate the Spanish word **librería** by library.

librero, -a [li'βrero, a] NM/F bookseller

libreta [li'βreta] NF notebook; (pan) one-pound loaf; **~ de ahorros** savings book

★**libro** ['liβro] NM book; **~ de actas** minute book; **~ de bolsillo** paperback; **~ de cabecera** bedside book; **~ de caja** (Com) cashbook; **~ de cocina** cookery book (Brit), cookbook (US); **~ de consulta** reference book; **~ de cuentas** account book; **~ de cuentos** storybook; **~ de cheques** chequebook (Brit), checkbook (US); **~ de entradas y salidas** (Com) daybook; **~ de honor** visitors' book; **~ diario** journal; **~ electrónico** e-book; (aparato) e-reader; **~ mayor** (Com) general ledger; **~ de reclamaciones** complaints book; **~ de texto** textbook

Lic. ABR = **Licenciado, a**

★**licencia** [li'θenθja] NF (gen) licence; (permiso) permission; **~ por enfermedad** sick leave; **~ con goce de sueldo** (Am) paid leave; **~ de armas/de caza** gun/game licence; **~ de exportación** (Com) export licence; **~ poética** poetic licence

★**licenciado, -a** [liθen'θjaðo, a] ADJ licensed ▶ NM/F graduate; **L~ en Filosofía y Letras** ≈ Bachelor of Arts; see note

> Prior to 2010, when students finished university after an average of five years, they used to receive the degree of **licenciado**. If the course was only three years, they were awarded the degree of diplomado. Now the average length of a university degree or grado is four years, in line with the rest of Europe. Cursos de posgrado, postgraduate courses, are becoming increasingly popular, especially one-year specialist courses called masters.

licenciar [liθen'θjar] /1b/ VT (empleado) to dismiss; (permitir) to permit, allow; (soldado) to discharge; (estudiante) to confer a degree upon ■ **licenciarse** VR: **licenciarse en derecho** to graduate in law; **licenciarse en letras** to get an arts degree

★**licenciatura** [liθenθja'tura] NF (*título*) degree; (*estudios*) degree course

licencioso, -a [liθen'θjoso, a] ADJ licentious

liceo [li'θeo] NM (*esp Am*) (high) school

licitación [liθita'θjon] NF bidding; (*oferta*) tender, offer

licitador [liθita'ðor] NM bidder

licitar [liθi'tar] /1a/ VT to bid for ▶ VI to bid

lícito, -a ['liθito, a] ADJ (*legal*) lawful; (*justo*) fair, just; (*permisible*) permissible

licor [li'kor] NM spirits *pl* (BRIT), liquor (US); (*con hierbas etc*) liqueur

licra® ['likra] NF Lycra®

licuadora [likwa'ðora] NF blender

licuar [li'kwar] /1d/ VT to liquidize

lid [lið] NF combat; (*fig*) controversy

líder ['liðer] NMF leader

liderazgo [liðe'raθγo], **liderato** [liðe'rato] NM leadership

lidia ['liðja] NF bullfighting; (*una lidia*) bullfight; **toros de ~** fighting bulls

lidiar [li'ðjar] /1b/ VT, VI to fight

liebre ['ljeβre] NF hare; **dar gato por ~** to con

Liechtenstein ['lixtenstain] NM Liechtenstein

Lieja ['ljexa] NF Liège

lienzo ['ljenθo] NM linen; (*Arte*) canvas; (*Arq*) wall

lifting ['liftin] NM facelift

★**liga** ['liγa] NF (*de medias*) garter, suspender; (*confederación*) league; (*Am: gomita*) rubber band

ligadura [liγa'ðura] NF bond, tie; (*Med, Mus*) ligature

ligamento [liγa'mento] NM (*Anat*) ligament; (*atadura*) tie; (*unión*) bond

ligar [li'γar] /1h/ VT (*atar*) to tie; (*unir*) to join; (*Med*) to bind up; (*Mus*) to slur; (*fam*) to get off with, pick up ▶ VI to mix, blend; (*fam*) to get off with sb; (: *dos personas*) to get off with one another; **(él) liga mucho** (*fam*) he pulls a lot of women; **~ con** (*fam*) to get off with, pick up ∎ **ligarse** VR (*fig*) to commit o.s.; **ligarse a algn** to get off with *o* pick up sb

ligereza [lixe'reθa] NF lightness; (*rapidez*) swiftness; (*agilidad*) agility; (*superficialidad*) flippancy

★**ligero, -a** [li'xero, a] ADJ (*de peso*) light; (*tela*) thin; (*rápido*) swift, quick; (*ágil*) agile, nimble; (*de importancia*) slight; (*de carácter*) flippant, superficial; **a la ligera** superficially; **juzgar a la ligera** to jump to conclusions ▶ ADV quickly, swiftly

light ['lait] ADJ INV (*cigarrillo*) low-tar; (*comida*) diet *cpd*

ligón [li'γon] NM (*fam*) Romeo

ligue *etc* [li'γe] VB *ver* **ligar** ▶ NMF boyfriend (girlfriend) ▶ NM (*persona*) pick-up

liguero [li'γero] NM suspender (BRIT) *o* garter (US) belt

lija ['lixa] NF (*Zool*) dogfish; **(papel de) ~** sandpaper

lijar [li'xar] /1a/ VT to sand

lila ['lila] ADJ INV, NF lilac ▶ NM (*fam*) twit

lima ['lima] NF file; (*Bot*) lime; **~ de uñas** nail file; **comer como una ~** to eat like a horse

limar [li'mar] /1a/ VT to file; (*alisar*) to smooth over; (*fig*) to polish up

limbo ['limbo] NM (*Rel*) limbo; **estar en el ~** to be on another planet

limitación [limita'θjon] NF limitation, limit; **~ de velocidad** speed limit

limitado, -a [limi'taðo, a] ADJ limited; **sociedad limitada** (*Com*) limited company

limitar [limi'tar] /1a/ VT to limit; (*reducir*) to reduce, cut down ▶ VI: **~ con** to border on ∎ **limitarse** VR: **limitarse a** to limit *o* confine o.s. to

límite ['limite] NM (*gen*) limit; (*fin*) end; (*frontera*) border; **como ~** at (the) most; (*fecha*) at the latest; **no tener límites** to know no bounds; **~ de crédito** (*Com*) credit limit; **~ de página** (*Inform*) page break; **~ de velocidad** speed limit

limítrofe [li'mitrofe] ADJ bordering, neighbouring

★**limón** [li'mon] NM lemon ▶ ADJ: **amarillo ~** lemon-yellow

★**limonada** [limo'naða] NF lemonade

★**limonero** [limo'nero] NM lemon tree

limosna [li'mosna] NF alms *pl*; **pedir ~** to beg; **vivir de ~** to live on charity

limpiabotas [limpja'βotas] NMF INV bootblack (BRIT), shoeshine boy/girl

limpiacristales [limpjakris'tales] NM INV (*detergente*) window cleaner

limpiador, a [limpja'ðor, a] ADJ cleaning, cleansing ▶ NM/F cleaner ▶ NM (*Am*) = **limpiaparabrisas**

limpiaparabrisas [limpjapara'βrisas] NM INV windscreen (BRIT) *o* windshield (US) wiper

★**limpiar** [lim'pjar] /1b/ VT to clean; (*con trapo*) to wipe; (*quitar*) to wipe away; (*zapatos*) to shine, polish; (*casa*) to tidy up; (*Inform*) to debug; (*fig*) to clean up; (: *purificar*) to cleanse, purify; (*Mil*) to mop up; **~ en seco** to dry-clean

limpieza [lim'pjeθa] NF (*estado*) cleanliness; (*acto*) cleaning; (: *de las calles*) cleansing; (: *de zapatos*) polishing; (*habilidad*) skill; (*fig: Policía*) clean-up; (*pureza*) purity; (*Mil*): **operación de ~** mopping-up operation; **~ étnica** ethnic cleansing; **~ en seco** dry cleaning

★**limpio, -a** ['limpjo, a] ADJ clean; (*moralmente*) pure; (*ordenado*) tidy; (*despejado*) clear; (*Com*) clear, net; (*fam*) honest; **~ de** free from ▶ ADV: **jugar ~** to play fair ▶ NM: **pasar a ~** to make a fair copy; **sacar algo en ~** to get benefit from sth

linaje [li'naxe] NM lineage, family

linaza [li'naθa] NF linseed; **aceite de ~** linseed oil

233

lince ['linθe] NM lynx; **ser un ~** (*fig: observador*) to be very observant; (: *astuto*) to be shrewd

linchar [lin'tʃar] /**1a**/ VT to lynch

lindante [lin'dante] ADJ adjoining; **~ con** bordering on

lindar [lin'dar] /**1a**/ VI to adjoin; **~ con** to border on; (*Arq*) to abut on

linde ['linde] NM O F boundary

lindero, -a [lin'dero, a] ADJ adjoining ▶ NM boundary

lindo, -a ['lindo, a] ADJ pretty, lovely; **se divertían de lo ~** they enjoyed themselves enormously ▶ ADV (*esp Am fam*) nicely, very well; **canta muy ~** (*Am*) he sings beautifully

★**línea** ['linea] NF (*gen, moral, Pol etc*) line; (*talle*) figure; (*Inform*): **en ~** on line; **fuera de ~** off line; **~ de estado** status line; **~ de formato** format line; **~ aérea** airline; **~ de alto el fuego** ceasefire line; **~ de fuego** firing line; **~ de meta** goal line; (*de carrera*) finishing line; **~ de montaje** assembly line; **~ discontinua** (*Auto*) broken line; **~ dura** (*Pol*) hard line; **~ recta** straight line; **la ~ de 2018** (*moda*) the 2018 look

lineal [line'al] ADJ linear

lingote [lin'gote] NM ingot

lingüista [lin'gwista] NMF linguist

lingüística [lin'gwistika] NF linguistics *sg*

linimento [lini'mento] NM liniment

lino ['lino] NM linen; (*Bot*) flax

linóleo [li'noleo] NM lino, linoleum

★**linterna** [lin'terna] NF (*eléctrica*) torch (BRIT), flashlight (US); (*farolillo*) lantern, lamp

lío ['lio] NM bundle; (*desorden*) muddle, mess; (*fam: follón*) fuss; (: *relación amorosa*) affair; **armar un ~** to make a fuss; **meterse en un ~** to get into a jam; **tener un ~ con algn** to be having an affair with sb

lipotimia [lipo'timja] NF blackout

liquen ['liken] NM lichen

★**liquidación** [likiða'θjon] NF liquidation; (*de cuenta*) settlement; **venta de ~** clearance sale

liquidar [liki'ðar] /**1a**/ VT (*Química*) to liquefy; (*Com*) to liquidate; (*deudas*) to pay off; (*empresa*) to wind up; **~ a algn** to bump sb off, rub sb out (*fam*)

liquidez [liki'ðeθ] NF liquidity

líquido, -a ['likiðo, a] ADJ liquid; (*ganancia*) net ▶ NM liquid; (*Com: efectivo*) ready cash O money; (: *ganancia*) net amount O profit; **~ imponible** net taxable income

lira ['lira] NF (*Mus*) lyre; (*moneda*) lira

lírico, -a ['liriko, a] ADJ lyrical

lirio ['lirjo] NM (*Bot*) iris

lirismo [li'rismo] NM lyricism; (*sentimentalismo*) sentimentality

lirón [li'ron] NM (*Zool*) dormouse; (*fig*) sleepyhead

Lisboa [lis'βoa] NF Lisbon

lisboeta [lisβo'eta] ADJ of O from Lisbon ▶ NMF native O inhabitant of Lisbon

lisiado, -a [li'sjaðo, a] ADJ injured ▶ NM/F cripple (!)

lisiar [li'sjar] /**1b**/ VT to maim ■ **lisiarse** VR to injure o.s.

★**liso, -a** ['liso, a] ADJ (*terreno*) flat; (*cabello*) straight; (*superficie*) even; (*tela*) plain; **lisa y llanamente** in plain language, plainly

lisonja [li'sonxa] NF flattery

lisonjear [lisonxe'ar] /**1a**/ VT to flatter; (*fig*) to please

lisonjero, -a [lison'xero, a] ADJ flattering; (*agradable*) gratifying, pleasing ▶ NM/F flatterer

★**lista** ['lista] NF list; (*en escuela*) school register; (*de libros*) catalogue; (*tb*: **lista de correos**) poste restante, general delivery (US); (*tb*: **lista de platos**) menu; (*tb*: **lista de precios**) price list; **pasar ~** to call the roll; (*Escol*) to call the register; **~ de direcciones** mailing list; **~ electoral** electoral roll; **~ de espera** waiting list; **tela a listas** striped material

listado, -a [lis'taðo, a] ADJ striped ▶ NM (*Com, Inform*) listing; **~ paginado** (*Inform*) paged listing

listar [lis'tar] /**1a**/ VT (*Inform*) to list

★**listo, -a** ['listo, a] ADJ (*perspicaz*) smart, clever; (*preparado*) ready; **~ para usar** ready-to-use; **¿estás ~?** are you ready?; **pasarse de ~** to be too clever by half

listón [lis'ton] NM (*de tela*) ribbon; (*de madera, metal*) strip

litera [li'tera] NF (*en barco, tren*) berth; (*en dormitorio*) bunk, bunk bed

literal [lite'ral] ADJ literal

literario, -a [lite'rarjo, a] ADJ literary

literato, -a [lite'rato, a] ADJ literary ▶ NM/F writer

★**literatura** [litera'tura] NF literature

litigante [liti'ɣante] NMF litigant, claimant

litigar [liti'ɣar] /**1h**/ VT to fight ▶ VI (*Jur*) to go to law; (*fig*) to dispute, argue

litigio [li'tixjo] NM (*Jur*) lawsuit; (*fig*): **en ~ con** in dispute with

litigue *etc* [li'tiɣe] VB *ver* **litigar**

litografía [litoɣra'fia] NF lithography; (*una litografía*) lithograph

litoral [lito'ral] ADJ coastal ▶ NM coast, seaboard

★**litro** ['litro] NM litre, liter (US)

Lituania [li'twanja] NF Lithuania

lituano, -a [li'twano, a] ADJ, NM/F Lithuanian ▶ NM (*Ling*) Lithuanian

liturgia [li'turxja] NF liturgy

liviano, -a [li'βjano, a] ADJ (*persona*) fickle; (*cosa, objeto*) trivial; (*Am*) light

lívido, -a ['liβiðo, a] ADJ livid

living ['liβin] (*pl* **livings**) NM (*esp Am*) sitting room

Ll, ll [ˈeʎe] NF *former letter in the Spanish alphabet*

llaga [ˈʎaɣa] NF wound

llagar [ʎaˈɣar] /1h/ VT to make sore; (*herir*) to wound

llague *etc* [ˈʎaɣe] VB *ver* **llagar**

llama [ˈʎama] NF flame; (*fig*) passion; (*Zool*) llama; **en llamas** burning, ablaze

★**llamada** [ʎaˈmaða] NF call; (*a la puerta*) knock; (: *al timbre*) ring; **~ a cobro revertido** reverse-charge call; **~ al orden** call to order; **~ de atención** warning; **~ a pie de página** reference note; **~ a procedimiento** (*Inform*) procedure call; **~ interurbana** trunk call; **~ metropolitana**, **~ local** local call; **~ por cobrar** (*Am*) reverse-charge call

llamado [ʎaˈmaðo] NM (*Am*) (telephone) call; (*llamamiento*) appeal, call

llamamiento [ʎamaˈmjento] NM call; **hacer un ~ a algn para que haga algo** to appeal to sb to do sth

★**llamar** [ʎaˈmar] /1a/ VT to call; (*convocar*) to summon; (*invocar*) to invoke; (*atraer con gesto*) to beckon; (*atención*) to attract; (*Telec*: tb: **llamar por teléfono**) to call, ring up, telephone; (*Mil*) to call up; **no me llama la atención** (*fam*) I don't fancy it ▶ VI (*por teléfono*) to phone; (*a la puerta*) to knock (o ring); (*por señas*) to beckon; **¿quién llama?** (*Telec*) who's calling?, who's that? ■ **llamarse** VR to be called, be named; **¿cómo se llama usted?** what's your name?

llamarada [ʎamaˈraða] NF (*llamas*) blaze; (*rubor*) flush; (*fig*) flare-up

llamativo, -a [ʎamaˈtiβo, a] ADJ showy; (*color*) loud

llamear [ʎameˈar] /1a/ VI to blaze

llanamente [ʎanaˈmente] ADV (*lisamente*) smoothly; (*sin ostentaciones*) plainly; (*sinceramente*) frankly; *ver tb* **liso**

llaneza [ʎaˈneθa] NF (*gen*) simplicity; (*honestidad*) straightforwardness, frankness

llano, -a [ˈʎano, a] ADJ (*superficie*) flat; (*persona*) straightforward; (*estilo*) clear ▶ NM plain, flat ground

llanta [ˈʎanta] NF (*wheel*) rim; (*Am*: *neumático*) tyre; (: *cámara*) (inner) tube; **~ de repuesto** (*Am*) spare tyre

llanto [ˈʎanto] NM weeping; (*fig*) lamentation; (*canción*) dirge, lament

llanura [ʎaˈnura] NF (*lisura*) flatness, smoothness; (*Geo*) plain

★**llave** [ˈʎaβe] NF key; (*de gas, agua*) tap (BRIT), faucet (US); (*Mecánica*) spanner; (*de la luz*) switch; (*Mus*) key; **~ inglesa** monkey wrench; **~ maestra** master key; **~ de contacto**, **~ de encendido** (*Am Auto*) ignition key; **~ de paso** stopcock; **echar ~ a** to lock up

llavero [ʎaˈβero] NM keyring

llavín [ʎaˈβin] NM latchkey

★**llegada** [ʎeˈɣaða] NF arrival

★**llegar** [ʎeˈɣar] /1h/ VT to bring up, bring over ▶ VI to arrive; (*bastar*) to be enough; **~ a** (*alcanzar*) to reach; (*lograr*) to manage to, succeed in; **~ a saber** to find out; **~ a ser famoso/el jefe** to become famous/the boss; **~ a las manos** to come to blows; **~ a las manos de** to come into the hands of; **no llegues tarde** don't be late; **esta cuerda no llega** this rope isn't long enough ■ **llegarse** VR: **llegarse a** to approach

llegue *etc* [ˈʎeɣe] VB *ver* **llegar**

★**llenar** [ʎeˈnar] /1a/ VT to fill; (*superficie*) to cover; (*espacio, tiempo*) to fill, take up; (*formulario*) to fill in o out; (*fig*) to heap ■ **llenarse** VR to fill (up); **llenarse de** (*fam*) to stuff o.s. with

★**lleno, -a** [ˈʎeno, a] ADJ full, filled; (*repleto*) full up; **dar de ~ contra un muro** to hit a wall head-on ▶ NM (*abundancia*) abundance; (*Teat*) full house

llevadero, -a [ʎeβaˈðero, a] ADJ bearable, tolerable

★**llevar** [ʎeˈβar] /1a/ VT to take; (*ropa*) to wear; (*cargar*) to carry; (*quitar*) to take away; (*en coche*) to drive; (*transportar*) to transport; (*dinero*) to carry; (*conducir*) to lead; (*ruta*) to follow, keep to; (*Mat*) to carry; (*aguantar*) to bear; (*negocio*) to conduct, direct; (*dirigir*) to manage; **llevamos dos días aquí** we have been here for two days; **él me lleva dos años** he's two years older than me; **~ adelante** (*fig*) to carry forward; **~ por delante a algn** (*en coche etc*) to run sb over; (*fig*) to ride roughshod over sb; **~ ventaja** to be winning o in the lead; **~ los libros** (*Com*) to keep the books; **llevo las de perder** I'm likely to lose; **no las lleva todas consigo** he's not all there; **nos llevó a cenar fuera** she took us out for a meal ▶ VI (*suj: camino etc*): **~ a** to lead to ■ **llevarse** VR to carry off, take away; **llevarse a algn por delante** (*atropellar*) to run sb over; **llevarse bien** to get on well (together)

★**llorar** [ʎoˈrar] /1a/ VT to cry, weep ▶ VI to cry, weep; (*ojos*) to water; **~ a moco tendido** to sob one's heart out; **~ de risa** to cry with laughter

lloriquear [ʎorikeˈar] /1a/ VI to snivel, whimper

lloro [ˈʎoro] NM crying, weeping

llorón, -ona [ʎoˈron, ona] ADJ tearful ▶ NM/F cry-baby

lloroso, -a [ʎoˈroso, a] ADJ (*gen*) weeping, tearful; (*triste*) sad, sorrowful

★**llover** [ʎoˈβer] /2h/ VI to rain; **~ a cántaros** o **a cubos** o **a mares** to rain cats and dogs, pour (down); **ser una cosa llovida del cielo** to be a godsend; **llueve sobre mojado** it never rains but it pours

llovizna [ʎoˈβiθna] NF drizzle

lloviznar [ʎoβiθˈnar] /1a/ VI to drizzle

llueve *etc* [ˈʎweβe] VB *ver* **llover**

★**lluvia** [ˈʎuβja] NF rain; (*cantidad*) rainfall; (*fig*: *de balas etc*) hail, shower; **~ radioactiva** radioactive fallout; **día de ~** rainy day; **una ~ de regalos** a shower of gifts

★**lluvioso, -a** [ʎu'βjoso, a] ADJ rainy

★**lo** [lo] ARTÍCULO DEFINIDO NEUTRO: **lo bueno** the good (thing); **lo mío** what is mine; **lo difícil es que ...** the difficult thing about it is that ...; **no saben lo aburrido que es** they don't know how boring it is; **viste a lo americano** he dresses in the American style; **lo de** that matter of; **toma lo que quieras** take what(ever) you want; **lo que** what, that which; **lo que sea** whatever; **¡toma lo que he dicho!** I stand by what I said! ▶ PRON (*en relación a una persona*) him; (*en relación a una cosa*) it; *ver tb* **el**

loa ['loa] NF praise

loable [lo'aβle] ADJ praiseworthy

loar [lo'ar] /**1a**/ VT to praise

lobato [lo'βato] NM (*Zool*) wolf cub

lobo ['loβo] NM wolf; **~ de mar** (*fig*) sea dog; **~ marino** seal

lóbrego, -a ['loβreɣo, a] ADJ dark; (*fig*) gloomy

lóbulo ['loβulo] NM lobe

LOC NM ABR (= *lector óptico de caracteres*) OCR

local [lo'kal] ADJ local ▶ NM place, site; (*oficinas*) premises *pl*

localice *etc* [loka'liθe] VB *ver* **localizar**

★**localidad** [lokali'ðað] NF (*barrio*) locality; (*lugar*) location; (*Teat*) seat, ticket

localizador NM (*de un vuelo*) booking reference, reservation code

localizar [lokali'θar] /**1f**/ VT (*ubicar*) to locate, find; (*encontrar*) to find, track down; (*restringir*) to localize; (*situar*) to place

loción [lo'θjon] NF lotion, wash

★**loco, -a** ['loko, a] ADJ mad; (*fig*) wild, mad; **~ de atar, ~ de remate, ~ rematado** raving mad; **a lo ~** without rhyme or reason; **ando ~ con el examen** the exam is driving me crazy; **estar ~ con** *o* **por algo/por algn** to be mad about sth/sb; **estar ~ de alegría** to be overjoyed *o* over the moon ▶ NM/F madman(-woman)

locomoción [lokomo'θjon] NF locomotion

locomotora [lokomo'tora] NF engine, locomotive

locuaz [lo'kwaθ] ADJ loquacious, talkative

locución [loku'θjon] NF expression

locura [lo'kura] NF madness; (*acto*) crazy act

locutor, a [loku'tor, a] NM/F (*Radio*) announcer; (*comentarista*) commentator; (*TV*) newscaster, newsreader

locutorio [loku'torjo] NM (*Telec*) telephone box *o* booth; (*negocio*) shop or internet café providing telephone services

lodo ['lodo] NM mud

logia ['loxja] NF (*Mil, de masones*) lodge; (*Arq*) loggia

★**lógico, -a** ['loxiko, a] ADJ logical; (*correcto*) nat-ural; (*razonable*) reasonable; **es ~ que ...** it stands to reason that ... ▶ NM/F logician ▶ NF logic; **ser de una lógica aplastante** to be as clear as day

login ['loxin] NM login

logístico, -a [lo'xistiko, a] ADJ logistical ▶ NF logistics *pl*

logotipo [loɣo'tipo] NM logo

logrado, -a [lo'ɣraðo, a] PP *de* **lograr** ▶ ADJ (*interpretación, reproducción*) polished, excellent

★**lograr** [lo'ɣrar] /**1a**/ VT (*obtener*) to get, obtain; (*conseguir*) to achieve, attain; **~ hacer** to manage to do; **~ que algn venga** to manage to get sb to come; **~ acceso a** (*Inform*) to access

logro ['loɣro] NM achievement, success; (*Com*) profit

logroñés, -esa [loɣro'ɲes, esa] ADJ of *o* from Logroño ▶ NM/F native *o* inhabitant of Logroño

Loira ['loira] NM Loire

lóker ['loker] NM (*Am*) locker

loma ['loma] NF hillock, low ridge

Lombardía [lombar'ðia] NF Lombardy

lombriz [lom'briθ] NF (earth)worm

lomo ['lomo] NM (*de animal*) back; (*Culin: de cerdo*) pork loin; (*: de vaca*) rib steak; (*de libro*) spine

lona ['lona] NF canvas

★**loncha** ['lontʃa] NF = **lonja**

lonche ['lontʃe] NM (*Am*) lunch

lonchería [lontʃe'ria] NF (*Am*) snack bar, diner (*US*)

londinense [londi'nense] ADJ London *cpd*, of *o* from London ▶ NMF Londoner

★**Londres** ['londres] NM London

longaniza [longa'niθa] NF pork sausage

longevidad [lonxeβi'ðað] NF longevity

longitud [lonxi'tuð] NF length; (*Geo*) longitude; **tener tres metros de ~** to be three metres long; **~ de onda** wavelength; **salto de ~** long jump

longitudinal [lonxituði'nal] ADJ longitudinal

lonja ['lonxa] NF slice; (*de tocino*) rasher; (*Com*) market, exchange; **~ de pescado** fish market

lontananza [lonta'nanθa] NF background; **en ~** far away, in the distance

Lorena [lo'rena] NF Lorraine

★**loro** ['loro] NM parrot

★**los** [los] ARTÍCULO DEFINIDO MPL the; **~ libros** the books; **mis libros y ~ tuyos** my books and yours ▶ PRON them; (*en relación a ustedes*) you

losa ['losa] NF stone; **~ sepulcral** gravestone

lote ['lote] NM portion, share; (*Com*) lot; (*Inform*) batch

★**lotería** [lote'ria] NF lottery; (*juego*) lotto; **le tocó la ~** he won the lottery; (*fig*) he struck lucky; **~ nacional** national lottery; **~ primitiva** (*Esp*) *type of state-run lottery; see note*

Millions of euros are spent every year on **loterías** (lotteries). There are two state-run lotteries: the *lotería nacional*, which is particularly popular at Christmas because of the size of the jackpot known as *el gordo*, and the *(lotería) primitiva*. One of the most famous lotteries is run by the wealthy and influential society for the blind, *la ONCE*, and the ticket is called *el cupón de la ONCE* or *el cupón de los ciegos*.

lotero, -a [lo'tero, a] NM/F seller of lottery tickets

Lovaina [lo'βaina] NF Louvain

loza ['loθa] NF crockery; **~ fina** china

lozanía [loθa'nia] NF (*lujo*) luxuriance

lozano, -a [lo'θano, a] ADJ luxuriant; (*animado*) lively

LSD SIGLA M (= *Dietilamida del Ácido Lisérgico*) LSD

lubina [lu'βina] NF (Zool) sea bass

lubricante [luβri'kante] ADJ, NM lubricant

lubricar [luβri'kar] /1g/, **lubrificar** [luβrifi'kar] /1a/ VT to lubricate

lubrique *etc* [lu'βrike] VB *ver* **lubricar**

lucense [lu'θense] ADJ of *o* from Lugo ▶ NMF native *o* inhabitant of Lugo

Lucerna [lu'θerna] NF Lucerne

lucero [lu'θero] NM (*Astro*) bright star; (*fig*) brilliance; **~ del alba/de la tarde** morning/evening star

luces ['luθes] NFPL *de* **luz**

★**lucha** ['lutʃa] NF fight, struggle; **~ de clases** class struggle; **~ libre** wrestling

★**luchar** [lu'tʃar] /1a/ VI to fight

lucidez [luθi'ðeθ] NF lucidity

lucido, -a [lu'θiðo, a] ADJ (*espléndido*) splendid, brilliant; (*elegante*) elegant; (*exitoso*) successful

lúcido, -a ['luθiðo, a] ADJ (*persona*) lucid; (*mente*) logical; (*idea*) crystal-clear

luciérnaga [lu'θjernaɣa] NF glow-worm

lucimiento [luθi'mjento] NM (*brillo*) brilliance; (*éxito*) success

lucio ['luθjo] NM (Zool) pike

lucir [lu'θir] /3f/ VT to illuminate, light (up); (*ostentar*) to show off ▶ VI (*brillar*) to shine; (*Am: parecer*) to look, seem; **la casa luce limpia** the house looks clean ■ **lucirse** VR (*irónico*) to make a fool of o.s.; (*presumir*) to show off

lucrativo, -a [lukra'tiβo, a] ADJ lucrative, profitable; **institución no lucrativa** non profit-making institution

lucro ['lukro] NM profit, gain; **lucros y daños** (Com) profit and loss *sg*

luctuoso, -a [luk'twoso, a] ADJ mournful

lúdico, -a ['luðiko, a] ADJ playful; (*actividad*) recreational

ludopatía [luðopa'tia] NF addiction to gambling (*o* videogames)

★**luego** ['lweɣo] ADV (*después*) next; (*más tarde*) later, afterwards; (*Am fam: en seguida*) at once, immediately; **desde ~** of course; **¡hasta ~!** see you later!, so long!; **¿y ~?** what next?

★**lugar** [lu'ɣar] NM place; (*sitio*) spot; (*pueblo*) village, town; **en ~ de** instead of; **en primer ~** in the first place, firstly; **dar ~ a** to give rise to; **hacer ~** to make room; **fuera de ~** out of place; **sin ~ a dudas** without doubt, undoubtedly; **tener ~** to take place; **~ común** commonplace; **yo en su ~** if I were him; **no hay ~ para preocupaciones** there is no cause for concern

lugareño, -a [luɣa'reɲo, a] ADJ village *cpd* ▶ NM/F villager

lugarteniente [luɣarte'njente] NM deputy

lúgubre ['luɣuβre] ADJ mournful

★**lujo** ['luxo] NM luxury; (*fig*) profusion, abundance; **de ~** luxury *cpd*, de luxe

★**lujoso, -a** [lu'xoso, a] ADJ luxurious

lujuria [lu'xurja] NF lust

lumbago [lum'baɣo] NM lumbago

lumbre ['lumbre] NF (*luz*) light; (*fuego*) fire; **cerca de la ~** near the fire, at the fireside; **¿tienes ~?** (*para cigarro*) have you got a light?

lumbrera [lum'brera] NF luminary; (*fig*) leading light

luminoso, -a [lumi'noso, a] ADJ luminous, shining; (*idea*) bright, brilliant

★**luna** ['luna] NF moon; (*vidrio: escaparate*) plate glass; (: *de un espejo*) glass; (: *de gafas*) lens; (*fig*) crescent; **~ creciente/llena/menguante/nueva** crescent/full/waning/new moon; **~ de miel** honeymoon; **estar en la ~** to have one's head in the clouds

lunar [lu'nar] ADJ lunar ▶ NM (*Anat*) mole; **tela a lunares** polka-dot material

★**lunes** ['lunes] NM INV Monday; *ver tb* **sábado**

luneta [lu'neta] NF lens

lupa ['lupa] NF magnifying glass

lusitano, -a [lusi'tano, a], **luso, -a** ['luso, a] ADJ, NM/F Portuguese

lustrador [lustra'ðor] NM (*Am*) bootblack

lustrar [lus'trar] /1a/ VT (*esp Am: mueble*) to polish; (: *zapatos*) to shine

lustre ['lustre] NM polish; (*fig*) lustre; **dar ~ a** to polish

lustro ['lustro] NM period of five years

lustroso, -a [lus'troso, a] ADJ shining

luterano, -a [lute'rano, a] ADJ Lutheran

luto ['luto] NM mourning; (*congoja*) grief, sorrow; **llevar el *o* vestirse de ~** to be in mourning

luxación [luksa'θjon] NF (*Med*) dislocation; **tener una ~ de tobillo** to have a dislocated ankle

★**Luxemburgo** [luksem'burɣo] NM Luxembourg

★**luz** [luθ] (*pl* **luces**) NF (*tb fig*) light; (*fam*) electricity; **dar a ~ un niño** to give birth to a child; **sacar** a la ~ to bring to light; **dar la ~** to switch on the light; **encender** (Esp) o **prender** (Am)/**apagar la ~** to switch the light on/off; **les cortaron la ~** their (electricity) supply was cut off; **a la ~ de** in the light of; **a todas luces** by any reckoning; **hacer la ~ sobre** to shed light on; **tener pocas luces** to be dim o stupid; **~ de la luna/del sol** o **solar** moonlight/sunlight; **~ eléctrica** electric light; **~ roja/verde** red/green light; **~ de cruce** (Auto) dipped headlight; **~ de freno** brake light; **~ intermitente/trasera** flashing/rear light; **luces de tráfico** traffic lights; **el Siglo de las Luces** the Age of Enlightenment; **traje de luces** bullfighter's costume

Mm

M, m ['eme] NF (*letra*) M, m; **M de Madrid** M for Mike

m ABR (= *metro(s)*) m; (= *minuto(s)*) min., m; (= *masculino*) m., masc

M. ABR (*Ferro*) = **metro**; (= *mujer*) F

M.ª ABR = **María**

macabro, -a [ma'kaβro, a] ADJ macabre

macaco [ma'kako] NM (*Zool*) rhesus monkey; (*fam*) runt, squirt

macana [ma'kana] NF (*Am: porra*) club; (: *mentira*) lie, fib; (: *tontería*) piece of nonsense

macanudo, -a [maka'nuðo, a] ADJ (*Am fam*) great

macarra [ma'karra] NM (*fam*) thug

macarrones [maka'rrones] NMPL macaroni *sg*

Macedonia [maθe'ðonja] NF Macedonia

macedonia [maθe'ðonja] NF: **~ de frutas** fruit salad

macedonio, -a [maθe'ðonjo, a] ADJ, NM/F Macedonian ▶ NM (*Ling*) Macedonian

macerar [maθe'rar] /1a/ VT (*Culin*) to soak, macerate ▪ **macerarse** VR to soak, soften

maceta [ma'θeta] NF (*de flores*) pot of flowers; (*para plantas*) flowerpot

macetero [maθe'tero] NM flowerpot stand *o* holder

machacar [matʃa'kar] /1g/ VT to crush, pound; (*moler*) to grind (up); (*aplastar*) to mash ▶ VI (*insistir*) to go on, keep on

machacón, -ona [matʃa'kon, ona] ADJ (*pesado*) tiresome; (*insistente*) insistent; (*monótono*) monotonous

machamartillo [matʃamar'tiʎo]: **a ~** *adv*: **creer a ~** (*firmemente*) to firmly believe

machaque *etc* [ma'tʃake] VB *ver* **machacar**

machete [ma'tʃete] NM machete, (large) knife

machetear [matʃete'ar] /1a/ VT (*Am*) to swot (*BRIT*), grind away (*US*)

machismo [ma'tʃismo] NM sexism, male chauvinism

machista [ma'tʃista] ADJ, NM male chauvinist

macho ['matʃo] ADJ male; (*fig*) virile ▶ NM male; (*fig*) he-man, tough guy (*US*); (*Tec: perno*) pin, peg; (*Elec*) pin, plug; (*Costura*) hook

macilento, -a [maθi'lento, a] ADJ (*pálido*) pale; (*ojeroso*) haggard

macizo, -a [ma'θiθo, a] ADJ (*grande*) massive; (*fuerte, sólido*) solid ▶ NM mass, chunk; (*Geo*) massif

macramé [makra'me] NM macramé

macrobiótico, -a [makro'βjotiko, a] ADJ macrobiotic

macrocomando [makroko'mando] NM (*Inform*) macro (command)

macroeconomía [makroekono'mia] NF (*Com*) macroeconomics *sg*

mácula ['makula] NF stain, blemish

macuto [ma'kuto] NM (*Mil*) knapsack

Madagascar [maðaɣas'kar] NM Madagascar

madeja [ma'ðexa] NF (*de lana*) skein, hank; (*de pelo*) mass, mop

★**madera** [ma'ðera] NF wood; (*fig*) nature, character; (: *aptitud*) aptitude; **una ~** a piece of wood; **~ contrachapada** *o* **laminada** plywood; **tiene buena ~** he's made of solid stuff; **tiene ~ de futbolista** he's got the makings of a footballer

maderaje [maðe'raxe], **maderamen** [maðe'ramen] NM timber; (*trabajo*) woodwork, timbering

maderero [maðe'rero] NM timber merchant

madero [ma'ðero] NM beam; (*fig*) ship

★**madrastra** [ma'ðrastra] NF stepmother

★**madre** ['maðre] ADJ mother *cpd*; (*Am*) tremendous ▶ NF mother; (*de vino etc*) dregs *pl*; **~ adoptiva/política/soltera** foster mother/mother-in-law/unmarried mother; **la M~ Patria** the Mother Country; **sin ~** motherless; **¡~ mía!** oh dear!; **¡tu ~!** (*fam!*) fuck off! (*fam!*); **salirse de ~** (*río*) to burst its banks; (*persona*) to lose all self-control

madreperla [maðreˈperla] NF mother-of-pearl

madreselva [maðreˈselβa] NF honeysuckle

★**Madrid** [maˈðrið] NM Madrid

madriguera [maðriˈɣera] NF burrow

★**madrileño, -a** [maðriˈleɲo, a] ADJ of o from Madrid ▶ NM/F native o inhabitant of Madrid

Madriles [maˈðriles] NMPL: **Los ~** (*fam*) Madrid *sg*

madrina [maˈðrina] NF godmother; (*Arq*) prop, shore; (*Tec*) brace; **~ de boda** bridesmaid

madroño [maˈðroɲo] NM (*Bot*) strawberry tree, arbutus

★**madrugada** [maðruˈɣaða] NF early morning, small hours; (*alba*) dawn, daybreak; **a las cuatro de la ~** at four o'clock in the morning

madrugador, a [maðruɣaˈðor, a] ADJ early-rising

★**madrugar** [maðruˈɣar] /**1h**/ VI to get up early; (*fig*) to get ahead

madrugue *etc* [maˈðruɣe] VB *ver* **madrugar**

madurar [maðuˈrar] /**1a**/ VT, VI (*fruta*) to ripen; (*fig*) to mature

madurez [maðuˈreθ] NF ripeness; (*fig*) maturity

★**maduro, -a** [maˈðuro, a] ADJ ripe; (*fig*) mature; **poco ~** unripe

MAE NM ABR (*Esp Pol*) = **Ministerio de Asuntos Exteriores**

maestra [maˈestra] NF *ver* **maestro**

maestría [maesˈtria] NF mastery; (*habilidad*) skill, expertise; (*Am*) Master's Degree

★**maestro, -a** [maˈestro, a] ADJ masterly; (*perito*) skilled, expert; (*principal*) main; (*educado*) trained ▶ NM/F master/mistress; (*profesor*) teacher; **~ albañil** master mason; **~ de obras** foreman ▶ NM (*autoridad*) authority; (*Mus*) maestro; (*experto*) master; (*obrero*) skilled workman

mafia [ˈmafja] NF mafia; **la M~** the Mafia

mafioso [maˈfjoso] NM gangster

Magallanes [maɣaˈʎanes] NM: **Estrecho de ~** Strait of Magellan

magdalena [maɣðaˈlena] NF fairy cake

magia [ˈmaxja] NF magic

★**mágico, -a** [ˈmaxiko, a] ADJ magic(al) ▶ NM/F magician

magisterio [maxisˈterjo] NM (*enseñanza*) teaching; (*profesión*) teaching profession; (*maestros*) teachers *pl*

magistrado [maxisˈtraðo] NM magistrate; **Primer M~** (*Am*) President, Prime Minister

magistral [maxisˈtral] ADJ magisterial; (*fig*) masterly

magistratura [maxistraˈtura] NF magistracy; **M~ del Trabajo** (*Esp*) ≈ Industrial Tribunal

magnánimo, -a [maɣˈnanimo, a] ADJ magnanimous

magnate [maɣˈnate] NM magnate, tycoon; **~ de la prensa** press baron

magnesio [maɣˈnesjo] NM (*Química*) magnesium

magnetice *etc* [maɣneˈtiθe] VB *ver* **magnetizar**

magnético, -a [maɣˈnetiko, a] ADJ magnetic

magnetismo [maɣneˈtismo] NM magnetism

magnetizar [maɣnetiˈθar] /**1f**/ VT to magnetize

magnetofón [maɣnetoˈfon], **magnetófono** [maɣneˈtofono] NM tape recorder

magnetofónico, -a [maɣnetoˈfoniko, a] ADJ: **cinta magnetofónica** recording tape

magnicidio [maɣniˈθiðjo] NM assassination (*of an important person*)

★**magnífico, -a** [maɣˈnifiko, a] ADJ splendid, magnificent

magnitud [maɣniˈtuð] NF magnitude

mago, -a [ˈmaɣo, a] NM/F magician, wizard; **los Reyes Magos** the Magi, the Three Wise Men; *ver tb* **rey**

magrear [maɣreˈar] /**1a**/ VT (*fam*) to touch up

magro, -a [ˈmaɣro, a] ADJ (*persona*) thin, lean; (*carne*) lean

maguey [maˈɣei] NM (*Bot*) agave

magulladura [maɣuʎaˈðura] NF bruise

magullar [maɣuˈʎar] /**1a**/ VT (*amoratar*) to bruise; (*dañar*) to damage; (*fam: golpear*) to bash, beat

Maguncia [maˈɣunθja] NF Mainz

mahometano, -a [maomeˈtano, a] ADJ Mohammedan

mahonesa [maoˈnesa] NF mayonnaise

maicena [maiˈθena] NF cornflour, corn starch (*US*)

mail [meil] NM (*fam*) email

maillot [maˈjot] NM swimming costume; (*Deporte*) vest

maître [ˈmetre] NM head waiter

maíz [maˈiθ] NM maize (*Brit*), corn (*US*); (*dulce*) sweetcorn

maizal [maiˈθal] NM maize field, cornfield

majadero, -a [maxaˈðero, a] ADJ silly, stupid

majar [maˈxar] /**1a**/ VT to crush, grind

majareta [maxaˈreta] ADJ (*fam*) cracked, potty

majestad [maxesˈtað] NF majesty; **Su M~** His/Her Majesty; **(Vuestra) M~** Your Majesty

majestuoso, -a [maxesˈtwoso, a] ADJ majestic

majo, -a [ˈmaxo, a] ADJ nice; (*guapo*) attractive, good-looking; (*elegante*) smart

★**mal** [mal] ADV badly; (*equivocadamente*) wrongly; (*con dificultad*) with difficulty; **me entendió ~** he misunderstood me; **hablar ~ de algn** to speak ill of sb; **oigo/veo ~** I can't hear/see very well; **si ~ no recuerdo** if my memory serves me right; **huele ~** it smells bad; **~ que bien** rightly or wrongly; **¡menos ~!** just as well!; **ir de ~ en peor** to go from bad to worse ▶ ADJ = **malo** ▶ NM evil; (*desgracia*) misfortune; (*daño*) harm, damage; (*Med*) illness; **no hay ~ que por bien**

no venga every cloud has a silver lining; **~ de ojo** evil eye ► CONJ: **~ que le pese** whether he likes it or not

malabarismo [malaβa'rismo] NM juggling

malabarista [malaβa'rista] NMF juggler

malaconsejado, -a [malakonse'xaðo, a] ADJ ill-advised

malacostumbrado, -a [malakostum'braðo, a] ADJ (consentido) spoiled

malacostumbrar [malakostum'brar] /1a/ VT: **~ a algn** to get sb into bad habits

malagueño, -a [mala'ɣeɲo, a] ADJ of o from Málaga ► NM/F native o inhabitant of Málaga

Malaisia [ma'laisja] NF Malaysia

malaria [ma'larja] NF malaria

Malasia [ma'lasja] NF Malaysia

malavenido, -a [malaβe'niðo, a] ADJ incompatible

malayo, -a [ma'lajo, a] ADJ Malay(an) ► NM/F Malay ► NM (Ling) Malay

Malaysia [ma'laisja] NF Malaysia

malcarado, -a [malka'raðo, a] ADJ ugly, grim-faced

malcriado, -a [mal'krjaðo, a] ADJ (consentido) spoiled

malcriar [mal'krjar] /1c/ VT to spoil, pamper

maldad [mal'dað] NF evil, wickedness

maldecir [malde'θir] /3o/ VT to curse ► VI: **~ de** to speak ill of

maldiciendo etc [maldi'θjendo] VB ver **maldecir**

maldición [maldi'θjon] NF curse; **¡~!** curse it!, damn!

maldiga etc [mal'diɣa], **maldije** etc [mal'dixe] VB ver **maldecir**

maldito, -a [mal'dito, a] ADJ (condenado) damned; (perverso) wicked; **¡~ sea!** damn it!; **no le hace ~ (el) caso** he doesn't take a blind bit of notice ► NM: **el ~** the devil

maleable [male'aβle] ADJ malleable

maleante [male'ante] ADJ wicked ► NMF criminal, crook

malecón [male'kon] NM pier, jetty; (rompeolas) breakwater; (Am: paseo) sea front, promenade

maledicencia [maleði'θenθja] NF slander, scandal

★**maleducado, -a** [maleðu'kaðo, a] ADJ bad-mannered, rude

maleficio [male'fiθjo] NM curse, spell

malentendido [malenten'diðo] NM misunderstanding

malestar [males'tar] NM (gen) discomfort; (enfermedad) indisposition; (fig: inquietud) uneasiness; (Pol) unrest; **siento un ~ en el estómago** my stomach is upset

★**maleta** [ma'leta] NF case, suitcase; (Auto) boot (BRIT), trunk (US); **hacer la ~** to pack

maletera [male'tera] NF (Am Auto) boot (BRIT), trunk (US)

★**maletero** [male'tero] NM (Auto) boot (BRIT), trunk (US); (persona) porter

maletín [male'tin] NM small case, bag; (portafolio) briefcase

malevolencia [maleβo'lenθja] NF malice, spite

malévolo, -a [ma'leβolo, a] ADJ malicious, spiteful

maleza [ma'leθa] NF (malas hierbas) weeds pl; (arbustos) thicket

malgache [mal'ɣatʃe] ADJ of o from Madagascar ► NMF native o inhabitant of Madagascar

★**malgastar** [malɣas'tar] /1a/ VT (tiempo, dinero) to waste; (recursos) to squander; (salud) to ruin

malhaya [ma'laja] EXCL (esp Am fam!) damn (it)! (fam!); **¡~ sea/sean!** damn it/them! (fam!)

malhechor, a [male'tʃor, a] NM/F delinquent; (criminal) criminal

malherido, -a [male'riðo, a] ADJ badly injured

★**malhumorado, -a** [malumo'raðo, a] ADJ bad-tempered

Mali ['mali], **Malí** [ma'li] NM Mali

malicia [ma'liθja] NF (maldad) wickedness; (astucia) slyness, guile; (mala intención) malice, spite; (carácter travieso) mischievousness

malicioso, -a [mali'θjoso, a] ADJ (malintencionado) malicious, spiteful; (pícaro) mischievous; (astuto) sly, crafty; (malo) wicked, evil

malignidad [maliɣni'ðað] NF (Med) malignancy; (malicia) malice

maligno, -a [ma'liɣno, a] ADJ evil; (dañino) pernicious, harmful; (malévolo) malicious; (Med) malignant ► NM: **el ~** the devil

malintencionado, -a [malintenθjo'naðo, a] ADJ (comentario) hostile; (persona) malicious

malla ['maʎa] NF (de una red) mesh; (red) network; (Am: de baño) swimsuit; (de ballet, gimnasia) leotard; **~ de alambre** wire mesh ■ **mallas** NFPL tights

Mallorca [ma'ʎorka] NF Majorca

mallorquín, -ina [maʎor'kin, ina] ADJ, NM/F Majorcan ► NM (Ling) Majorcan

malnutrido, -a [malnu'triðo, a] ADJ undernourished

★**malo, -a** ['malo, a] ADJ (mal antes de nmsg) bad; (calidad) poor; (falso) false; (espantoso) dreadful; (niño) naughty; **estar ~** to be ill; **lo ~ es que ...** the trouble is that ... ► NM/F villain; **andar a malas con algn** to be on bad terms with sb; **estar de malas** (mal humor) to be in a bad mood ► NM (Cine: fam) bad guy ► NF spell of bad luck

malograr [malo'ɣrar] /1a/ VT to spoil; (plan) to upset; (ocasión) to waste ■ **malograrse** VR (plan etc) to fail, come to grief; (persona) to die before one's time

maloliente [malo'ljente] ADJ stinking, smelly

malparado, -a [malpa'raðo, a] ADJ: **salir ~** to come off badly

malpensado, -a [malpen'saðo, a] ADJ nasty

malquerencia [malkeˈrenθja] NF dislike

malquistar [malkisˈtar] /1a/ VT: **~ a dos personas** to cause a rift between two people ■ **malquistarse** VR to fall out

malsano, -a [malˈsano, a] ADJ unhealthy

malsonante [malsoˈnante] ADJ (*palabra*) nasty, rude

Malta [ˈmalta] NF Malta

malta [ˈmalta] NF malt

malteada [malteˈaða] NF (AM) milk shake

maltés, -esa [malˈtes, esa] ADJ, NM/F Maltese

maltraer [maltraˈer] /2o/ VT (*abusar*) to insult, abuse; (*maltratar*) to ill-treat

maltratador, a [maltrataˈðor, a] NM/F abuser

★**maltratar** [maltraˈtar] /1a/ VT (*tratar mal*) to ill-treat, mistreat; (*pegar*) to abuse

maltrato [malˈtrato] NM (*gen*) mistreatment, ill-treatment; (*infantil, psicológico*) abuse

maltrecho, -a [malˈtretʃo, a] ADJ battered, damaged

malva [ˈmalβa] NF mallow; **~ loca** hollyhock; (**de color de**) **~** mauve

malvado, -a [malˈβaðo, a] ADJ evil, villainous

malvavisco [malβaˈβisko] NM marshmallow

malvender [malβenˈder] /2a/ VT to sell off cheap *o* at a loss

malversación [malβersaˈθjon] NF embezzlement, misappropriation

malversar [malβerˈsar] /1a/ VT to embezzle, misappropriate

Malvinas [malˈβinas] NFPL: **Islas ~** Falkland Islands

malware [ˈmalwer] NM malware

mama [ˈmama] (*pl* **mamás**) NF (*de animal*) teat; (*de mujer*) breast

★**mamá** [maˈma] NF (*fam*) mum, mummy

mamacita [mamaˈsita] NF (AM *fam*) mum, mummy

mamadera [mamaˈdera] NF (AM) baby's bottle

mamagrande [mamaˈgrande] NF (AM) grandmother

mamar [maˈmar] /1a/ VT (*pecho*) to suck; (*fig*) to absorb, assimilate; **dar de ~** to (breast-)feed; (*animal*) to suckle ▶ VI to suck

mamarracho [mamaˈrratʃo] NM sight, mess

mambo [ˈmambo] NF (*Mus*) mambo

mameluco [mameˈluko] NM (AM) dungarees *pl* (BRIT), overalls *pl* (US)

mamífero, -a [maˈmifero, a] ADJ mammalian, mammal *cpd* ▶ NM mammal

mamón, -ona [maˈmon, ona] ADJ small, baby *cpd* ▶ NM/F small baby; (*fam!*) wanker (*fam!*)

mamotreto [mamoˈtreto] NM hefty volume; (*fam*) whacking great thing

mampara [mamˈpara] NF (*entre habitaciones*) partition; (*biombo*) screen

mamporro [mamˈporro] NM (*fam*): **dar un ~ a** to clout

mampostería [mampposteˈria] NF masonry

mamut [maˈmut] NM mammoth

maná [maˈna] NM manna

manada [maˈnaða] NF (*Zool*) herd; (*: de leones*) pride; (*: de lobos*) pack; **llegaron en manadas** (*fam*) they came in droves

Managua [maˈnaɣwa] NF Managua

manantial [mananˈtjal] NM spring; (*fuente*) fountain; (*fig*) source

manar [maˈnar] /1a/ VT to run with, flow with ▶ VI to run, flow; (*abundar*) to abound

manaza [maˈnaθa] NF big hand ▶ ADJ, NMF: **manazas, ser un manazas** to be clumsy

mancebo [manˈθeβo] NM (*joven*) young man

★**mancha** [ˈmantʃa] NF stain, mark; (*de tinta*) blot; (*de vegetación*) patch; (*imperfección*) stain, blemish, blot; (*boceto*) sketch, outline; **la M~** La Mancha

manchado, -a [manˈtʃaðo, a] ADJ (*sucio*) dirty; (*animal*) spotted; (*ave*) speckled; (*de tinta*) smudged

★**manchar** [manˈtʃar] /1a/ VT to stain, mark; (*Zool*) to patch; (*ensuciar*) to soil, dirty ■ **mancharse** VR to get dirty; (*fig*) to dirty one's hands

manchego, -a [manˈtʃeɣo, a] ADJ of *o* from La Mancha ▶ NM/F native *o* inhabitant of La Mancha

mancilla [manˈθiʎa] NF stain, blemish

mancillar [manθiˈʎar] /1a/ VT to stain, sully

manco, -a [ˈmanko, a] ADJ (*de un brazo*) one-armed; (*de una mano*) one-handed; (*fig*) defective, faulty; **no ser ~** to be useful *o* active

mancomunar [mankomuˈnar] /1a/ VT to unite, bring together; (*recursos*) to pool; (*Jur*) to make jointly responsible

mancomunidad [mankomuniˈðað] NF union, association; (*comunidad*) community; (*Jur*) joint responsibility

mandado [manˈdaðo] NM (*orden*) order; (*recado*) commission, errand

mandamás [mandaˈmas] ADJ, NMF boss; **ser un ~** to be very bossy

mandamiento [mandaˈmjento] NM (*orden*) order, command; (*Rel*) commandment; **~ judicial** warrant

★**mandar** [manˈdar] /1a/ VT (*ordenar*) to order; (*dirigir*) to lead, command; (*país*) to rule over; (*enviar*) to send; (*pedir*) to order, ask for; **¿manda usted algo más?** is there anything else?; **~ a algn a paseo** *o* **a la porra** to tell sb to go to hell; **se lo mandaremos por correo** we'll post it to you; **~ hacer un traje** to have a suit made ▶ VI to be in charge; (*pey*) to be bossy; **¿mande?** pardon?, excuse me? (US) ■ **mandarse** VR: **mandarse mudar** (AM *fam*) to go away, clear off

mandarín [mandaˈrin] NM petty bureaucrat

mandarina [mandaˈrina] NF (*fruta*) tangerine, mandarin (orange)

mandatario, -a [mandaˈtarjo, a] NM/F (*representante*) agent; **primer ~** (*esp* AM) head of state

mandato [man'dato] NM (*orden*) order; (*Pol: período*) term of office; (: *territorio*) mandate; **~ judicial** (search) warrant

mandíbula [man'diβula] NF jaw

mandil [man'dil] NM (*delantal*) apron

Mandinga [man'dinɣa] NM (*Am*) Devil

mandioca [man'djoka] NF cassava

mando ['mando] NM (*Mil*) command; (*de país*) rule; (*el primer lugar*) lead; (*Pol*) term of office; (*Tec*) control; **~ a la izquierda** left-hand drive; **los altos mandos** the high command *sg*; **~ por botón** push-button control; **~ a distancia** remote control; **al ~ de** in charge of; **tomar el ~** to take the lead

mandolina [mando'lina] NF mandolin(e)

mandón, -ona [man'don, ona] ADJ bossy, domineering

manecilla [mane'θiʎa] NF (*Tec*) pointer; (*de reloj*) hand

manejable [mane'xaβle] ADJ manageable; (*fácil de usar*) handy

★**manejar** [mane'xar] /**1a**/ VT to manage; (*máquina*) to work, operate; (*caballo etc*) to handle; (*casa*) to run, manage; (*Am Auto*) to drive ▶ VI (*Am Auto*) to drive; **"~ con cuidado"** "handle with care" ■ **manejarse** VR (*comportarse*) to act, behave; (*arreglárselas*) to manage

manejo [ma'nexo] NM (*de bicicleta*) handling; (*de negocio*) management, running; (*Auto*) driving; (*facilidad de trato*) ease, confidence; (*de idioma*) command; **tengo ~ del francés** I have a good command of French ■ **manejos** NMPL intrigues

★**manera** [ma'nera] NF way, manner, fashion; (*Arte, Lit etc: estilo*) manner, style; **su ~ de ser** the way he is; (*aire*) his manner; **de mala ~** (*fam*) badly, unwillingly; **de ninguna ~** no way, by no means; **de otra ~** otherwise; **en gran ~** to a large extent; **a mi ~ de ver** in my view; **no hay ~ de persuadirle** there's no way of convincing him ■ **maneras** NFPL (*modales*) manners; **de todas maneras** at any rate

manga ['manga] NF (*de camisa*) sleeve; (*de riego*) hose; **de ~ corta/larga** short-/long-sleeved; **andar ~ por hombro** (*desorden*) to be topsy-turvy; **tener ~ ancha** to be easy-going

mangante [man'gante] ADJ (*descarado*) brazen ▶ NM (*mendigo*) beggar

mangar [man'gar] /**1h**/ VT (*unir*) to plug in; (*fam: birlar*) to pinch, nick, swipe; (*mendigar*) to beg

mango ['mango] NM handle; (*Bot*) mango; **~ de escoba** broomstick

mangonear [mangone'ar] /**1a**/ VT to boss about ▶ VI to be bossy

mangue *etc* ['mange] VB *ver* **mangar**

manguera [man'gera] NF (*de riego*) hose; (*tubo*) pipe; **~ de incendios** fire hose

maní [ma'ni] (*pl* **maníes** *o* **manises**) NM (*Am: cacahuete*) peanut; (: *planta*) groundnut plant

manía [ma'nia] NF (*Med*) mania; (*fig: moda*) rage, craze; (*disgusto*) dislike; (*malicia*) spite; **tiene manías** she's a bit fussy; **coger ~ a algn** to take a dislike to sb; **tener ~ a algn** to dislike sb

maníaco, -a [ma'niako, a] ADJ maniac(al) ▶ NM/F maniac

maniatar [manja'tar] /**1a**/ VT to tie the hands of

maniático, -a [ma'njatiko, a] ADJ maniac(al); (*loco*) crazy; (*tiquismiquis*) fussy ▶ NM/F maniac

manicomio [mani'komjo] NM psychiatric hospital

manicuro, -a [mani'kuro, a] NM/F manicurist ▶ NF manicure

manido, -a [ma'niðo, a] ADJ (*tema etc*) trite, stale

★**manifestación** [manifesta'θjon] NF (*declaración*) statement, declaration; (*demostración*) show, display; (*Pol*) demonstration; (*concentración*) mass meeting

manifestante [manifes'tante] NMF demonstrator

manifestar [manifes'tar] /**1j**/ VT to show, manifest; (*declarar*) to state, declare ■ **manifestarse** VR to show, become apparent; (*Pol: desfilar*) to demonstrate; (: *reunirse*) to hold a mass meeting

manifiesto, -a [mani'fjesto, a] VB *ver* **manifestar** ▶ ADJ clear, manifest; **quedar ~** to be plain *o* clear; **poner algo de ~** (*aclarar*) to make sth clear; (*revelar*) to reveal sth ▶ NM manifesto; (*Anat, Naut*) manifest

manija [ma'nixa] NF handle

manilla [ma'niʎa] NF (*de reloj*) hand; (*Am*) handle, lever; **manillas (de hierro)** *nfpl* handcuffs

manillar [mani'ʎar] NM handlebars *pl*

maniobra [ma'njoβra] NF manœuvring; (*manejo*) handling; (*fig: movimiento*) manœuvre, move; (: *estratagema*) trick, stratagem ■ **maniobras** NFPL manœuvres

maniobrar [manio'βrar] /**1a**/ VT to manœuvre; (*manejar*) to handle ▶ VI to manœuvre

manipulación [manipula'θjon] NF manipulation; (*Com*) handling

manipular [manipu'lar] /**1a**/ VT to manipulate; (*manejar*) to handle

maniquí [mani'ki] NMF model ▶ NM dummy

manirroto, -a [mani'rroto, a] ADJ lavish, extravagant ▶ NM/F spendthrift

manita [ma'nita] NF little hand; **manitas de plata** artistic hands

manitas [ma'nitas] (*fam*) ADJ INV good with one's hands ▶ NMF INV: **ser un ~** to be very good with one's hands

manito [ma'nito] NM (*Am: en conversación*) mate (*fam*), chum

manivela [mani'βela] NF crank

manjar [man'xar] NM (tasty) dish

★**mano¹** ['mano] NF hand; (*Zool*) foot, paw; (*de pintura*) coat; (*serie*) lot, series; **a ~** by hand; **a**

~ derecha/izquierda on (o to) the right(-hand side)/left(-hand side); **a manos llenas** lavishly, generously; **hecho a ~** handmade; **robo a ~ armada** armed robbery; **darse la(s) ~(s)** to shake hands; **de primera ~** (at) first hand; **de segunda ~** (at) second hand; **echar ~ de** to make use of; **echar una ~** to lend a hand; **echar una ~ a** to lay hands on; **está en tus manos** it's up to you; **estrechar la ~ a algn** to shake sb's hand; **~ de obra** labour, manpower; **~ de santo** sure remedy; **¡manos a la obra!** (let's) get on with it!; **manos libres** hands-free; **Pedro es mi ~ derecha** Pedro is my right-hand man; **se le fue la ~** his hand slipped; (*fig*) he went too far; **traer** o **llevar algo entre manos** to deal o be busy with sth

mano² [ˈmano] NM (AM *fam*) friend, mate

manojo [maˈnoxo] NM handful, bunch; **~ de llaves** bunch of keys

manómetro [maˈnometro] NM (pressure) gauge

manopla [maˈnopla] NF (*paño*) flannel ■ **manoplas** NFPL mittens

manoseado, -a [manoseˈaðo, a] ADJ well-worn

manosear [manoseˈar] /**1a**/ VT (*tocar*) to handle, touch; (*desordenar*) to mess up, rumple; (*insistir en*) to overwork; (*acariciar*) to caress, fondle; (*pey: persona*) to feel o touch up

manos libres ADJ INV (*dispositivo*) hands-free ▶ NM INV hands-free kit

manotazo [manoˈtaθo] NM slap, smack

mansalva [manˈsalβa]: **a ~** *adv* indiscriminately

mansedumbre [manseˈðumbre] NF gentleness, meekness; (*de animal*) tameness

mansión [manˈsjon] NF mansion

manso, -a [ˈmanso, a] ADJ gentle, mild; (*animal*) tame

★**manta** [ˈmanta] NF blanket; (AM) poncho

manteca [manˈteka] NF fat; (AM) butter; **~ de cacahuete/cacao** peanut/cocoa butter; **~ de cerdo** lard

mantecado [manteˈkaðo] NM (ESP: *dulce navideño*) Christmas sweet made from flour, almonds and lard; (: *helado*) ice cream

mantecoso, -a [manteˈkoso, a] ADJ fat, greasy; **queso ~** soft cheese

★**mantel** [manˈtel] NM tablecloth

mantelería [manteleˈria] NF table linen

mantendré *etc* [mantenˈdre] VB *ver* **mantener**

★**mantener** [manteˈner] /**2k**/ VT to support, maintain; (*alimentar*) to sustain; (*conservar*) to keep; (*Tec*) to maintain, service; **~ algo en equilibrio** to keep sth balanced ■ **mantenerse** VR (*seguir de pie*) to be still standing; (*no ceder*) to hold one's ground; (*subsistir*) to sustain o.s., keep going; **mantenerse a distancia** to keep one's distance; **mantenerse firme** to hold one's ground

mantenga *etc* [manˈtenga] VB *ver* **mantener**

mantenimiento [manteniˈmjento] NM main-

tenance; (*alimento*) sustenance; (*sustento*) support

mantequería [mantekeˈria] NF (*ultramarinos*) grocer's (shop)

★**mantequilla** [manteˈkiʎa] NF butter

mantilla [manˈtiʎa] NF mantilla ■ **mantillas** NFPL baby clothes; **estar en mantillas** (*persona*) to be terribly innocent; (*proyecto*) to be in its infancy

manto [ˈmanto] NM (*capa*) cloak; (*de ceremonia*) robe, gown

mantón [manˈton] NM shawl

mantuve *etc* [manˈtuβe] VB *ver* **mantener**

manual [maˈnwal] ADJ manual; **habilidad ~** manual skill ▶ NM manual, handbook

manubrio [maˈnuβrio] NM (AM *Auto*) steering wheel

manufactura [manufakˈtura] NF manufacture; (*fábrica*) factory

manufacturado, -a [manufaktuˈraðo, a] ADJ manufactured

manuscrito, -a [manusˈkrito, a] ADJ handwritten ▶ NM manuscript

manutención [manutenˈθjon] NF maintenance; (*sustento*) support

★**manzana** [manˈθana] NF apple; (*Arq*) block; **~ de la discordia** (*fig*) bone of contention

manzanal [manθaˈnal] NM apple orchard

manzanilla [manθaˈniʎa] NF (*planta*) camomile; (*infusión*) camomile tea; (*vino*) manzanilla

manzano [manˈθano] NM apple tree

maña [ˈmaɲa] NF (*destreza*) skill; (*pey*) guile; (*ardid*) trick; **con ~** craftily

★**mañana** [maˈɲana] ADV tomorrow; **¡hasta ~!** see you tomorrow!; **pasado ~** the day after tomorrow ▶ NM future ▶ NF morning; **de** o **por la ~** in the morning; **~ por la ~** tomorrow morning

mañanero, -a [maɲaˈnero, a] ADJ early-rising

maño, -a [ˈmaɲo, a] ADJ Aragonese ▶ NM/F native o inhabitant of Aragon

mañoso, -a [maˈɲoso, a] ADJ (*hábil*) skilful; (*astuto*) smart, clever

★**mapa** [ˈmapa] NM map

maple [ˈmaple] NM (AM) maple

mapuche [maˈputʃe] ADJ, NMF Mapuche, Araucanian

maqueta [maˈketa] NF (scale) model

maquiavélico, -a [makjaˈβeliko, a] ADJ Machiavellian

maquillador, a [makiʎaˈðor, a] NM/F (*Teat etc*) make-up artist ▶ NF (AM *Com*) bonded assembly plant

★**maquillaje** [makiˈʎaxe] NM make-up; (*acto*) making up

maquillar [makiˈʎar] /**1a**/ VT to make up ■ **maquillarse** VR to put on (some) make-up

★**máquina** [ˈmakina] NF machine; (*de tren*) locomotive, engine; (*Foto*) camera; (AM: *coche*) car;

(*fig*) machinery; (: *proyecto*) plan, project; **a toda ~** at full speed; **escrito a ~** typewritten; **~ de afeitar** electric razor; **~ de coser** sewing machine; **~ de escribir** typewriter; **~ fotográfica** camera; **~ de lavar** washing machine; **~ de facsímil** facsimile (machine), fax; **~ de franqueo** franking machine; **~ tragaperras** fruit machine; (*Com*) slot machine

maquinación [makina'θjon] NF machination, plot

maquinal [maki'nal] ADJ (*fig*) mechanical, automatic

maquinar [maki'nar] /1a/ VT, VI to plot

maquinaria [maki'narja] NF (*máquinas*) machinery; (*mecanismo*) mechanism, works *pl*

maquinilla [maki'niʎa] NF small machine; (*torno*) winch; **~ de afeitar** razor; **~ eléctrica** electric razor

maquinista [maki'nista] NMF (*Ferro*) engine driver (BRIT), engineer (US); (*Tec*) operator; (*Naut*) engineer

★mar [mar] NM O F sea; **~ adentro** (*ir*) out to sea; (*estar*) out at sea; **~ de fondo** groundswell; **en alta ~** on the high seas; **por ~** by sea O boat; **hacerse a la ~** to put to sea; **a mares** in abundance; **un ~ de** lots of; **es la ~ de guapa** she is ever so pretty; **el M~ Negro/Báltico** the Black/Baltic Sea; **el M~ Muerto/Rojo** the Dead/Red Sea; **el M~ del Norte** the North Sea

mar. ABR (= *marzo*) Mar.

maraca [ma'raka] NF maraca

maraña [ma'raɲa] NF (*maleza*) thicket; (*confusión*) tangle

maravilla [mara'βiʎa] NF marvel, wonder; (*Bot*) marigold; **hacer maravillas** to work wonders; **a (las mil) maravillas** wonderfully well

maravillar [maraβi'ʎar] /1a/ VT to astonish, amaze ■ **maravillarse** VR to be amazed, be amazed

★maravilloso, -a [maraβi'ʎoso, a] ADJ wonderful, marvellous

marbellí [marβe'ʎi] ADJ of O from Marbella ▶ NMF native O inhabitant of Marbella

★marca ['marka] NF mark; (*sello*) stamp; (*Com*) make, brand; (*de ganado*) brand; (: *acto*) branding; (*Naut*) seamark; (: *boya*) marker; (*Deporte*) record; **de ~** excellent, outstanding; **~ de fábrica** trademark; **~ propia** own brand; **~ registrada** registered trademark

marcación [marka'θjon] NF (*Telec*): **~ automática** autodial

marcado, -a [mar'kaðo, a] ADJ marked, strong

marcador [marka'ðor] NM marker; (*rotulador*) marker (pen); (*de libro*) bookmark; (*Deporte*) scoreboard; (: *persona*) scorer

marcapasos [marka'pasos] NM INV pacemaker

★marcar [mar'kar] /1g/ VT to mark; (*número de teléfono*) to dial; (*gol*) to score; (*números*) to record, keep a tally of; (*el pelo*) to set; (*ganado*) to brand; (*suj: termómetro*) to register, read; (: *reloj*) to say;

(*tarea*) to assign; (*Com*) to put a price on; **mi reloj marca las dos** it's two o'clock by my watch; **~ el compás** (*Mus*) to keep time; **~ el paso** (*Mil*) to mark time ▶ VI (*Deporte*) to score; (*Telec*) to dial

marcha ['martʃa] NF march; (*Deporte*) walk; (*Tec*) running, working; (*Auto*) gear; (*velocidad*) speed; (*fig*) progress; (*curso*) course; **dar ~ atrás** to reverse, put into reverse; **estar en ~** to be under way, be in motion; **hacer algo sobre la ~** to do sth as you *etc* go along; **poner en ~** to put into gear; **ponerse en ~** to start, get going; **a marchas forzadas** (*fig*) with all speed; **¡en ~!** (*Mil*) forward march!; (*fig*) let's go!; **"~ moderada"** (*Auto*) "drive slowly"; **que tiene** O **de mucha ~** (*fam*) very lively

marchante, -a [mar'tʃante, a] NM/F dealer, merchant

marchar [mar'tʃar] /1a/ VI (*ir*) to go; (*funcionar*) to work, go; (*fig*) to go, proceed; **todo marcha bien** everything is going well ■ **marcharse** VR to go (away), leave

marchitar [martʃi'tar] /1a/ VT to wither, dry up ■ **marchitarse** VR (*Bot*) to wither; (*fig*) to fade away

marchito, -a [mar'tʃito, a] ADJ withered, faded; (*fig*) in decline

marchoso, -a [mar'tʃoso, a] ADJ (*fam: animado*) lively; (: *moderno*) modern

marcial [mar'θjal] ADJ martial, military

marciano, -a [mar'θjano, a] ADJ Martian, of O from Mars

marco ['marko] NM frame; (*Deporte*) goalposts *pl*; (*moneda*) mark; (*fig*) setting; (: *contexto*) framework; **~ de chimenea** mantelpiece

★marea [ma'rea] NF tide; (*llovizna*) drizzle; **~ alta/baja** high/low tide; **~ negra** oil slick

★mareado, -a [mare'aðo, a] ADJ: **estar ~** (*con náuseas*) to feel sick; (*aturdido*) to feel dizzy

marear [mare'ar] /1a/ VT (*fig: irritar*) to annoy, upset; (*Med*): **~ a algn** to make sb feel sick ■ **marearse** VR (*tener náuseas*) to feel sick; (*desvanecerse*) to feel faint; (*aturdirse*) to feel dizzy; (*fam: emborracharse*) to get tipsy

marejada [mare'xaða] NF (*Naut*) swell, heavy sea

maremágnum [mare'maɣnum] NM (*fig*) ocean, abundance

maremoto [mare'moto] NM tidal wave

★mareo [ma'reo] NM (*náusea*) sick feeling; (*en viaje*) travel sickness; (*aturdimiento*) dizziness; (*fam: lata*) nuisance

marfil [mar'fil] NM ivory

margarina [marɣa'rina] NF margarine

margarita [marɣa'rita] NF (*Bot*) daisy; **(rueda) ~** (*en máquina impresora*) daisy wheel

margen ['marxen] NM (*borde*) edge, border; (*fig*) margin, space ▶ NF (*de río etc*) bank; **~ de beneficio** O **de ganancia** profit margin; **~ comercial** mark-up; **~ de confianza** credibility gap; **dar**

m

~ para to give an opportunity for; **dejar a algn al ~** to leave sb out (in the cold); **mantenerse al ~** to keep out (of things); **al ~ de lo que digas** despite what you say

marginado, -a [marxi'naðo, a] NM/F outcast

marginal [marxi'nal] ADJ (tema, error) minor; (grupo) fringe cpd; (anotación) marginal

marginar [marxi'nar] /1a/ VT to exclude; (socialmente) to marginalize, ostracize

maría [ma'ria] NF (fam: mujer) housewife

mariachi [ma'rjatʃi] NM (música) mariachi music; (grupo) mariachi band; (persona) mariachi musician

marica [ma'rika] NM (!: insulto) sissy (!); (: homosexual) queer (!)

Maricastaña [marikas'taɲa] NF: **en los días** o **en tiempos de ~** way back, in the good old days

maricón [mari'kon] NM (!) queer (!)

★**marido** [ma'riðo] NM husband

marihuana [mari'wana] NF marijuana, cannabis

marimacho [mari'matʃo] NF (fam) mannish woman

marimorena [marimo'rena] NF fuss, row; **armar una ~** to kick up a row

marina [ma'rina] NF navy; **~ mercante** merchant navy

★**marinero, -a** [mari'nero, a] ADJ sea cpd; (barco) seaworthy ▶ NM sailor, seaman

marino, -a [ma'rino, a] ADJ sea cpd, marine ▶ NM sailor; **~ de agua dulce/de cubierta/de primera** landlubber/deckhand/able seaman

marioneta [marjo'neta] NF puppet

mariposa [mari'posa] NF butterfly

mariposear [maripose'ar] /1a/ VI (revolotear) to flutter about; (ser inconstante) to be fickle; (coquetear) to flirt

mariquita [mari'kita] NM (!: insulto) sissy (!); (: homosexual) queer (!) ▶ NF (Zool) ladybird (BRIT), ladybug (US)

marisco [ma'risko] NM (tb: **mariscos**) shellfish, seafood

marisma [ma'risma] NF marsh, swamp

marisquería [mariske'ria] NF shellfish bar, seafood restaurant

marítimo, -a [ma'ritimo, a] ADJ sea cpd, maritime

marmita [mar'mita] NF pot

mármol ['marmol] NM marble

marmóreo, -a [mar'moreo, a] ADJ marble

marmota [mar'mota] NF (Zool) marmot; (fig) sleepyhead

maroma [ma'roma] NF rope

marque etc ['marke] VB ver **marcar**

marqués, -esa [mar'kes, esa] NM/F marquis/marchioness

marquesina [marke'sina] NF (de parada) bus shelter

marquetería [markete'ria] NF marquetry, inlaid work

marranada [marra'naða] NF (fam): **es una ~** that's disgusting; **hacer una ~ a algn** to do the dirty on sb

marrano, -a [ma'rrano, a] ADJ filthy, dirty ▶ NM (Zool) pig; (malo) swine; (sucio) dirty pig

marras ['marras]: **de ~** adv: **es el problema de ~** it's the same old problem

★**marrón** [ma'rron] ADJ brown

marroquí [marro'ki] ADJ, NMF Moroccan ▶ NM Morocco (leather)

★**Marruecos** [ma'rrwekos] NM Morocco

marta ['marta] NF (animal) (pine) marten; (piel) sable

Marte ['marte] NM Mars

★**martes** ['martes] NM INV Tuesday; **~ de carnaval** Shrove Tuesday; **~ y trece** ≈ Friday 13th; ver tb **carnaval**; **sábado**

According to Spanish superstition, it's Tuesday rather than Friday that is an unlucky day when it falls on the 13th of the month.

martillar [marti'ʎar] /1a/, **martillear** [martiʎe'ar] /1a/ VT to hammer

martilleo [marti'ʎeo] NM hammering

martillo [mar'tiʎo] NM hammer; (de presidente de asamblea, comité) gavel; **~ neumático** pneumatic drill (BRIT), jackhammer (US)

Martinica [marti'nika] NF Martinique

mártir ['martir] NMF martyr

martirice etc [marti'riθe] VB ver **martirizar**

martirio [mar'tirjo] NM martyrdom; (fig) torture, torment

martirizar [martiri'θar] /1f/ VT (Rel) to martyr; (fig) to torture, torment

maruja [ma'ruxa] NF (fam) = **maría**

marxismo [mark'sismo] NM Marxism

marxista [mark'sista] ADJ, NMF Marxist

★**marzo** ['marθo] NM March; **11 de ~** the Madrid train bombings of 11 March 2004 (also 11-M); ver tb **julio**

★**mas** [mas] CONJ but

más [mas]

ADJ, ADV **1**: **más (que/de)** (compar) more (than), ...+ -er (than); **más inteligente** more intelligent; **más grande** bigger; **trabaja más (que yo)** he works more (than me); **más de seis** more than six; **es más de medianoche** it's after midnight; **durar más** to last longer; ver tb **cada**

2 (superl): **el más** the most, the ...+ -est; **el más alto/inteligente (de)** the tallest/most intelligent (in)

3 (negativo): **no tengo más dinero** I haven't got any more money; **no viene más por aquí** he doesn't come round here any more; **no sé más** I don't know any more, that's all I know

4 (*adicional*): **un kilómetro más** one more kilometre; **no le veo más solución que …** I see no other solution than to …; **¿algo más?** anything else?; (*en tienda*) will that be all?; **¿quién más?** anybody else?

5 (+ *adj*: *valor intensivo*): **¡qué perro más sucio!** what a filthy dog!; **¡es más tonto!** he's so stupid!

6 (*locuciones*): **más o menos** more or less; **los más** most people; **es más** in fact, furthermore; **más bien** rather; **¡qué más da!** what does it matter!; *ver tb* **no**

7: **por más**: **por más que lo intento** no matter how much o hard I try; **por más que quisiera ayudar** much as I should like to help

8: **de más**: **veo que aquí estoy de más** I can see I'm not needed here; **tenemos uno de más** we've got one extra

9 (*AM*): **no más** only, just; **ayer no más** just yesterday

▶ PREP: **2 más 2 son 4** 2 and o plus 2 are 4

▶ NM INV: **este trabajo tiene sus más y sus menos** this job's got its good points and its bad points

Para formar el comparativo, la mayoría de los adjetivos y adverbios ingleses de una sílaba, o los de dos que terminan en *-y*, añaden el sufijo **–er**: *barato, más barato* **cheap, cheaper**.
A veces se produce algún cambio ortográfico: *grande, más grande* **big, bigger**; *contento, más contento* **happy, happier**.
El resto de los adjetivos forma el comparativo con **more**: *inteligente, más inteligente* **intelligent, more intelligent**.
Los adverbios de modo terminados en **-ly** siempre forman así el comparativo, independientemente del número de sílabas que tengan: *deprisa, más deprisa* **quickly, more quickly**.
Siguiendo las mismas normas del comparativo, el superlativo se forma añadiendo **the …-est** o **the most …**: *el bolígrafo más barato* **the cheapest pen**; *el más inteligente de todos* **the most intelligent of all of them**.

masa ['masa] NF (*mezcla*) dough; (*volumen*) volume, mass; (*Física*) mass; **en ~** en masse; **las masas** (*Pol*) the masses

masacrar [masa'krar] /1a/ VT to massacre

masacre [ma'sakre] NF massacre

masaje [ma'saxe] NM massage; **dar ~ a** to massage

masajista [masa'xista] NMF masseur/masseuse

mascar [mas'kar] /1g/ VT, VI to chew; (*fig*) to mumble, mutter

máscara ['maskara] NF (*tb Inform*) mask; **~ antigás** gas mask ▶ NMF masked person

mascarada [maska'raða] NF masquerade

mascarilla [maska'riʎa] NF mask; (*vaciado*) deathmask; (*de maquillaje*) face pack

mascarón [maska'ron] NM large mask; **~ de proa** figurehead

★**mascota** [mas'kota] NF (*animal doméstico*) pet; (*de un club*) mascot

★**masculino, -a** [masku'lino, a] ADJ masculine; (*Bio*) male ▶ NM (*Ling*) masculine

mascullar [masku'ʎar] /1a/ VT to mumble, mutter

masía [ma'sia] NF farmhouse

masificación [masifika'θjon] NF overcrowding

masilla [ma'siʎa] NF putty

masivo, -a [ma'siβo, a] ADJ (*en masa*) mass

masón [ma'son] NM (free)mason

masonería [masone'ria] NF (free)masonry

masoquista [maso'kista] ADJ masochistic ▶ NMF masochist

masque *etc* ['maske] VB *ver* **mascar**

mastectomía [mastekto'mia] NF mastectomy

máster ['master] (*pl* **masters** ['masters]) NM master's degree; *ver tb* **licenciado**

The **máster** is the degree awarded to graduates at the end of a university course following on from an undergraduate degree. In Spain, a master's course lasts one or two years and combines university, vocational, and research studies.

masticar [masti'kar] /1g/ VT to chew; (*fig*) to ponder over

mástil ['mastil] NM (*de navío*) mast; (*de guitarra*) neck

mastín [mas'tin] NM mastiff

mastique *etc* [mas'tike] VB *ver* **masticar**

masturbación [masturβa'θjon] NF masturbation

masturbarse [mastur'βarse] /1a/ VR to masturbate

Mat. ABR = **matemáticas**

mata ['mata] NF (*arbusto*) bush, shrub; (*de hierbas*) tuft; (*campo*) field; (*manojo*) tuft, blade; **~ de pelo** mop of hair; **a salto de ~** (*día a día*) from day to day; (*al azar*) haphazardly ■ **matas** NFPL scrub *sg*

matadero [mata'ðero] NM slaughterhouse, abattoir

matador, a [mata'ðor, a] ADJ killing ▶ NM/F killer ▶ NM (*Taur*) matador, bullfighter

matamoscas [mata'moskas] NM INV (*palo*) fly swat

matanza [ma'tanθa] NF slaughter

★**matar** [ma'tar] /1a/ VT to kill; (*tiempo, pelota*) to kill; **~ el hambre** to stave off hunger; **~ a algn a disgustos** to make sb's life a misery; **matarlas callando** to go about things slyly ▶ VI to kill ■ **matarse** VR (*suicidarse*) to kill o.s., commit suicide; (*morir*) to be o get killed; (*gastarse*) to wear o.s. out; **matarse trabajando** to kill o.s. with work; **matarse por hacer algo** to struggle to do sth

m

matarife [mata'rife] NM slaughterman

matasanos [mata'sanos] NM INV quack

matasellos [mata'seʎos] NM INV postmark

mate ['mate] ADJ (sin brillo: color) dull, matt ▶ NM (en ajedrez) (check)mate; (Am: hierba) maté; (: vasija) gourd

★**matemáticas** [mate'matikas] NFPL mathematics

matemático, -a [mate'matiko, a] ADJ mathematical ▶ NM/F mathematician

materia [ma'terja] NF (gen) matter; (Tec) material; (Escol) subject; **en ~ de** on the subject of; (en cuanto a) as regards; **~ prima** raw material; **entrar en ~** to get down to business

★**material** [mate'rjal] ADJ material; (dolor) physical; (real) real; (literal) literal; **máximo jefe** o **líder** (Am) President, leader ▶ NM material; (Tec) equipment; **~ de construcción** building material; **materiales de derribo** rubble sg

materialismo [materja'lismo] NM materialism

materialista [materja'lista] ADJ materialist(ic)

materialmente [materjal'mente] ADV materially; (fig) absolutely

maternal [mater'nal] ADJ motherly, maternal

maternidad [materni'ðað] NF motherhood, maternity

materno, -a [ma'terno, a] ADJ maternal; (lengua) mother cpd

matice etc [ma'tiθe] VB ver **matizar**

matinal [mati'nal] ADJ morning cpd

matiz [ma'tiθ] NM shade; (de sentido) shade, nuance; (de ironía etc) touch

matizar [mati'θar] /1f/ VT (variar) to vary; (Arte) to blend; **~ de** to tinge with

matón [ma'ton] NM bully

matorral [mato'rral] NM thicket

matraca [ma'traka] NF rattle; (fam) nuisance

matraz [ma'traθ] NM (Química) flask

matriarcado [matrjar'kaðo] NM matriarchy

★**matrícula** [ma'trikula] NF (registro) register; (Escol: inscripción) registration; (Auto) registration number; (: placa) number plate; **~ de honor** (Univ) top marks in a subject at university

matricular [matriku'lar] /1a/ VT to register, enrol

matrimonial [matrimo'njal] ADJ matrimonial

★**matrimonio** [matri'monjo] NM (pareja) (married) couple; (acto) marriage; **~ civil/clandestino** civil/secret marriage; **contraer ~ (con)** to marry

matriz [ma'triθ] NF (Anat) womb; (Tec) mould; (Mat) matrix; **casa ~** (Com) head office

matrona [ma'trona] NF (mujer de edad) matron; (comadrona) midwife

matufia [ma'tufja] NF (Am fam) put-up job

matutino, -a [matu'tino, a] ADJ morning cpd

maula ['maula] ADJ (persona) good-for-nothing ▶ NMF (vago) idler, slacker ▶ NF (persona) dead loss (fam)

maullar [mau'ʎar] /1a/ VI to mew, miaow

maullido [mau'ʎiðo] NM mew(ing), miaow(ing)

Mauricio [mau'riθjo] NM Mauritius

Mauritania [mauri'tanja] NF Mauritania

mausoleo [mauso'leo] NM mausoleum

max. ABR (= máximo) max.

maxilar [maksi'lar] NM jaw(bone)

máxima ['maksima] NF ver **máximo**

máxime ['maksime] ADV especially

★**máximo, -a** ['maksimo, a] ADJ maximum; (más alto) highest; (más grande) greatest; **~ jefe** o **líder** (Am) President, leader ▶ NM maximum; **como ~** at most; **al ~** to the utmost ▶ NF (frase) maxim

maya ['maja] ADJ Mayan ▶ NMF Maya(n)

★**mayo** ['majo] NM May; ver tb **julio**

mayonesa [majo'nesa] NF mayonnaise

★**mayor** [ma'jor] ADJ main, chief; (adulto) adult, grown-up; (Jur) of age; (de edad avanzada) elderly, old; (Mus) major; (: de tamaño) bigger; (: de edad) older; (superlativo: de tamaño) biggest; (: fig) greatest; (: de edad) oldest; **al por ~** wholesale; ▶ NMF (adulto) adult, grown-up; **~ de edad** adult ■ **mayores** NMPL (adultos) adults, grown-ups; (antepasados) ancestors; **llegar a mayores** to get out of hand

mayoral [majo'ral] NM foreman

mayordomo [major'ðomo] NM butler

mayoreo [majo'reo] NM (Am) wholesale (trade)

★**mayoría** [majo'ria] NF majority, greater part; **en la ~ de los casos** in most cases; **en su ~** on the whole

mayorista [majo'rista] NMF wholesaler

mayoritario, -a [majori'tarjo, a] ADJ majority cpd; **gobierno ~** majority government

mayúsculo, -a [ma'juskulo, a] ADJ (fig) big, tremendous ▶ NF capital (letter) ■ **mayúsculas** NFPL capitals; (Tip) upper case sg

maza ['maθa] NF (arma) mace; (Deporte) bat; (Polo) stick

mazacote [maθa'kote] NM hard mass; (Culin) dry doughy food; (Arte, Lit etc) mess, hotchpotch

mazapán [maθa'pan] NM marzipan

mazmorra [maθ'morra] NF dungeon

mazo ['maθo] NM (martillo) mallet; (de mortero) pestle; (de flores) bunch; (Deporte) bat

mazorca [ma'θorka] NF (Bot) spike; (de maíz) cob, ear

MB ABR (= megabyte) MB

MCCA NM ABR = **Mercado Común Centroamericano**

m.c.d. ABR (= mínimo común denominador) lcd

m.c.m. ABR = **mínimo común múltiplo**

me [me] PRON (directo) me; (indirecto) (to) me; (reflexivo) (to) myself; **¡dámelo!** give it to me!; **me lo compró** (de mí) he bought it from me; (para mí) he bought it for me

meandro [me'andro] NM meander

mear [me'ar] /**1a**/ (fam) VT to piss on (fam!) ▸ VI to pee, piss (fam!), have a piss (fam!) ■ **mearse** VR to wet o.s.

Meca ['meka] NF: **La ~** Mecca

mecánica [me'kanika] NF ver **mecánico**

mecanice etc [meka'niθe] VB ver **mecanizar**

★**mecánico, -a** [me'kaniko, a] ADJ mechanical; (repetitivo) repetitive ▸ NM/F mechanic ▸ NF (estudio) mechanics sg; (mecanismo) mechanism

mecanismo [meka'nismo] NM mechanism; (engranaje) gear

mecanizar [mekani'θar] /**1f**/ VT to mechanize

mecanografía [mekanoɣra'fia] NF typewriting

mecanografiado, -a [mekanoɣra'fjaðo, a] ADJ typewritten ▸ NM typescript

mecanógrafo, -a [meka'noɣrafo, a] NM/F (copy) typist

mecate [me'kate] NM (Am) rope

mecedor [mese'ðor] NM (Am), **mecedora** [meθe'ðora] NF rocking chair

mecenas [me'θenas] NMF INV patron

mecenazgo [meθe'naθɣo] NM patronage

mecer [me'θer] /**2b**/ VT (cuna) to rock ■ **mecerse** VR to rock; (rama) to sway

mecha ['metʃa] NF (de vela) wick; (de bomba) fuse; **a toda ~** at full speed; **ponerse mechas** to streak one's hair

mechero [me'tʃero] NM (cigarette) lighter

mechón [me'tʃon] NM (gen) tuft; (manojo) bundle; (de pelo) lock

★**medalla** [me'ðaʎa] NF medal

★**media** ['meðja] NF ver **medio**

★**mediación** [meða'θjon] NF mediation; **por ~ de** through

mediado, -a [me'ðjaðo, a] ADJ half-full; (trabajo) half-completed; **a mediados de** in the middle of, halfway through

medianamente [meðjana'mente] ADV (moderadamente) moderately, fairly; (regularmente) moderately well

★**mediano, -a** [me'ðjano, a] ADJ (regular) medium, average; (mediocre) mediocre; **(de tamaño) ~** medium-sized ▸ NF (Auto) central reservation, median (US)

★**medianoche** [meðja'notʃe] NF midnight

mediante [me'ðjante] ADV by (means of), through

mediar [me'ðjar] /**1b**/ VI (tiempo) to elapse; (interceder) to mediate, intervene; (existir) to exist; **media el hecho de que ...** there is the fact that ...

medicación [meðika'θjon] NF medication, treatment

★**medicamento** [meðika'mento] NM medicine, drug

★**medicina** [meði'θina] NF medicine

medicinal [meðiθi'nal] ADJ medicinal

medición [meði'θjon] NF measurement

★**médico, -a** ['meðiko, a] ADJ medical ▸ NM/F doctor; **~ de cabecera** family doctor; **~ pediatra** paediatrician; **~ residente** house physician, intern (US)

★**medida** [me'ðiða] NF measure; (medición) measurement; (de camisa, zapato etc) size, fitting; (moderación) moderation, prudence; **en cierta/gran ~** up to a point/to a great extent; **un traje a la ~** a made-to-measure suit; **~ de cuello** collar size; **a ~ de** in proportion to; (de acuerdo con) in keeping with; **con ~** with restraint; **sin ~** immoderately; **a ~ que ...** (at the same time) as ...; **tomar medidas** to take steps

medidor [meði'ðor] NM (Am) meter

medieval [meðje'βal] ADJ medieval

★**medio, -a** ['meðjo, a] ADJ half (a); (punto) mid, middle; (promedio) average; **media hora** half an hour; **~ litro** half a litre; **las tres y media** half past three; **M~ Oriente** Middle East; **a ~ camino** halfway (there) ▸ ADV half-; (esp Am: un tanto) rather, quite; **~ dormido** half asleep; **~ enojado** (esp Am) rather annoyed; **a ~ terminar** half finished ▸ NM (centro) middle, centre; (método) means, way; (ambiente) environment; **en ~** in the middle; (entre) in between; **por ~ de** by (means of), through; **encontrarse en su ~** to be in one's element; **~ ambiente** environment; **~ circulante** (Com) money supply; **~ de transporte** means of transport; **en los medios financieros** in financial circles ▸ NF (prenda de vestir) stocking; (Am) sock; (promedio) average ■ **medias** NFPL tights; **a medias**: **ir a medias** to go fifty-fifty; **lo dejó a medias** he left it half-done; ver tb **medios**

medioambiental [meðjoambjen'tal] ADJ environmental

mediocre [me'ðjokre] ADJ middling, average; (pey) mediocre

mediocridad [meðjokri'ðað] NF middling quality; (pey) mediocrity

★**mediodía** [meðjo'ðia] NM midday, noon

mediopensionista [meðjopensjo'nista] NMF day boy (girl)

★**medios** ['meðjos] NMPL means, resources; **los ~ de comunicación** the media; **los ~ sociales** social media

★**medir** [me'ðir] /**3k**/ VT (gen) to measure; **¿cuánto mides?** — **mido 1.50 m** how tall are you? — I am 1.50 m tall ▸ VI to measure ■ **medirse** VR (moderarse) to be moderate, act with restraint

meditabundo, -a [meðita'βundo, a] ADJ pensive

meditar [meði'tar] /**1a**/ VT to ponder, think over, meditate on; (planear) to think out ▸ VI to ponder, think, meditate

★**mediterráneo, -a** [meðite'rraneo, a] ADJ Mediterranean ▸ NM: **el (mar) M~** the Mediterranean (Sea)

medrar [me'ðrar] /**1a**/ VI to increase, grow; (mejorar) to improve; (prosperar) to prosper, thrive; (animal, planta etc) to grow

medroso, -a [me'ðroso, a] ADJ fearful, timid

médula ['meðula] NF (*Anat*) marrow; (*Bot*) pith; **~ espinal** spinal cord; **hasta la ~** (*fig*) to the core

medusa [me'ðusa] NF (*Esp*) jellyfish

megabyte ['meɣaβait] NM (*Inform*) megabyte

megafonía [meɣafo'nia] NF PA *o* public address system

megáfono [me'ɣafono] NM megaphone

megalomanía [meɣaloma'nia] NF megalomania

megalómano, -a [meɣa'lomano, a] NM/F megalomaniac

megaocteto [meɣaok'teto] NM (*Inform*) megabyte

megapíxel [meɣa'piksel] (*pl* **megapixels** *o* **megapíxeles**) NM megapixel

mejicano, -a [mexi'kano, a] ADJ, NM/F Mexican

Méjico ['mexiko] NM Mexico

★**mejilla** [me'xiʎa] NF cheek

★**mejillón** [mexi'ʎon] NM mussel

★**mejor** [me'xor] ADJ, ADV (*comparativo*) better; (*superlativo*) best; **lo ~** the best thing; **lo ~ de la vida** the prime of life; **a lo ~** probably; (*quizá*) maybe; **~ dicho** rather; **tanto ~** so much the better; **es el ~ de todos** he's the best of all

★**mejora** [me'xora] NF, **mejoramiento** [mexora'mjento] NM improvement

★**mejorar** [mexo'rar] /**1a**/ VT to improve, make better ▶ VI to improve, get better; (*Com*) to do well, prosper; **~ a** to be better than; **los negocios mejoran** business is picking up ■ **mejorarse** VR to improve, get better

mejoría [mexo'ria] NF improvement; (*restablecimiento*) recovery

mejunje [me'xunxe] NM (*pey*) concoction

melancolía [melanko'lia] NF melancholy

melancólico, -a [melan'koliko, a] ADJ (*triste*) sad, melancholy; (*soñador*) dreamy

melena [me'lena] NF (*de persona*) long hair; (*Zool*) mane

melillense [meli'ʎense] ADJ of *o* from Melilla ▶ NMF native *o* inhabitant of Melilla

mella ['meʎa] NF (*rotura*) notch, nick; **hacer ~** (*fig*) to make an impression

mellizo, -a [me'ʎiθo, a] ADJ, NM/F twin

★**melocotón** [meloko'ton] NM (*Esp*) peach

melodía [melo'ðia] NF melody; (*tonada*) tune; (*de móvil*) ringtone

melodrama [melo'ðrama] NM melodrama

melodramático, -a [meloðra'matiko, a] ADJ melodramatic

★**melón** [me'lon] NM melon

melopea [melo'pea] NF (*fam*): **tener una ~** to be sloshed

meloso, -a [me'loso, a] ADJ honeyed, sweet; (*empalagoso*) sickly, cloying; (*voz*) sweet; (*zalamero*) smooth

membrana [mem'brana] NF membrane

membrete [mem'brete] NM letterhead; **papel con ~** headed notepaper

membrillo [mem'briʎo] NM quince; **carne de ~** quince jelly

meme ['meme] NM (*Internet: fam*) meme

memo, -a ['memo, a] ADJ silly, stupid ▶ NM/F idiot

memorable [memo'raβle] ADJ memorable

memorándum [memo'randum] NM (*libro*) notebook; (*comunicación*) memorandum

memoria [me'morja] NF (*gen*) memory; (*artículo*) (learned) paper; **~ anual** annual report; **aprender algo de ~** to learn sth by heart; **si tengo buena ~** if my memory serves me right; **venir a la ~** to come to mind; (*Inform*) **~ auxiliar** backing storage; **~ de acceso aleatorio** random access memory, RAM; **~ del teclado** keyboard memory; **~ fija** read-only memory, ROM; **~ flash** flash drive ■ **memorias** NFPL (*de autor*) memoirs

memorice *etc* [memo'riθe] VB *ver* **memorizar**

memorizar [memori'θar] /**1f**/ VT to memorize

menaje [me'naxe] NM (*muebles*) furniture; (*tb*: **artículos de menaje**) household items *pl*; **~ de cocina** kitchenware

mención [men'θjon] NF mention; **digno de ~** noteworthy; **hacer ~ de** to mention

★**mencionar** [menθjo'nar] /**1a**/ VT to mention; (*nombrar*) to name; **sin ~ ...** let alone ...

mendicidad [mendiθi'ðað] NF begging

mendigar [mendi'ɣar] /**1h**/ VT to beg (for)

mendigo, -a [men'diɣo, a] NM/F beggar

mendigue *etc* [men'diɣe] VB *ver* **mendigar**

mendrugo [men'druɣo] NM crust

menear [mene'ar] /**1a**/ VT to move; (*cola*) to wag; (*cadera*) to swing; (*fig*) to handle ■ **menearse** VR to shake; (*balancearse*) to sway; (*moverse*) to move; (*fig*) to get a move on

menester [menes'ter] NM (*necesidad*) necessity; **es ~ hacer algo** it is necessary to do sth, sth must be done ■ **menesteres** NMPL (*deberes*) duties

menestra [me'nestra] NF: **~ de verduras** vegetable stew

mengano, -a [men'gano, a] NM/F Mr (*o* Mrs *o* Miss) So-and-so

mengua ['mengwa] NF (*disminución*) decrease; (*falta*) lack; (*pobreza*) poverty; (*fig*) discredit; **en ~ de** to the detriment of

menguante [men'gwante] ADJ decreasing, diminishing; (*luna*) waning; (*marea*) ebb *cpd*

menguar [men'gwar] /**1i**/ VT to lessen, diminish; (*fig*) to discredit ▶ VI to diminish, decrease; (*fig*) to decline

mengüe *etc* [men'gwe] VB *ver* **menguar**

menhir [me'nir] NM menhir

menopausia [meno'pausja] NF menopause

★**menor** [me'nor] ADJ (*más pequeño: comparativo*) smaller; (: *número*) less, lesser; (: *superlativo*) smallest; (: *número*) least; (*más joven: comparativo*) younger; (: *superlativo*) youngest; (*Mus*) minor; **Juanito es ~ que Pepe** Juanito is younger than Pepe; **no tengo la ~ idea** I haven't the faintest idea; **al por ~** retail ▶ NMF (*joven*) child, minor; **ella es la ~ de todas** she is the youngest of all; **~ de edad** minor

Menorca [me'norka] NF Minorca

menorquín, -ina [menor'kin, ina] ADJ, NM/F Minorcan

---

menos ['menos]

ADJ **1** (*compar*): **menos (que/de)** (*cantidad*) less (than); (*número*) fewer (than); **con menos entusiasmo** with less enthusiasm; **menos gente** fewer people; *ver tb* **cada**
2 (*superl*): **es el que menos culpa tiene** he is the least to blame; **donde menos problemas hay** where there are fewest problems
▶ ADV **1** (*compar*): **menos (que/de)** less (than); **me gusta menos que el otro** I like it less than the other one; **menos de cinco** fewer than five; **menos de lo que piensas** less than you think
2 (*superl*): **es el menos listo (de su clase)** he's the least bright (in his class); **de todas ellas es la que menos me agrada** out of all of them she's the one I like least; **(por) lo menos** at (the very) least; **es lo menos que puedo hacer** it's the least I can do; **lo menos posible** as little as possible
3 (*locuciones*): **no quiero verlo y menos visitarlo** I don't want to see him let alone visit him; **tenemos siete (de) menos** we're seven short; **eso es lo de menos** that's the least of it; **¡todo menos eso!** anything but that!; **al/por lo menos** at (the very) least; **si al menos** if only; **¡menos mal!** thank goodness!
▶ PREP except; (*cifras*) minus; **todos menos él** everyone except (for) him; **5 menos 2** 5 minus 2; **las 7 menos 20** (*hora*) 20 to 7
▶ CONJ: **a menos que**: **a menos que venga mañana** unless he comes tomorrow

---

Para formar el comparativo de *menos* en inglés, se usa **less** delante de un sustantivo incontable y **fewer** delante de uno contable: *menos harina* **less flour**; *menos gatos* **fewer cats**.
Para el superlativo se usan **least** delante de los sustantivos incontables y **fewest** delante de los contables: *el método que lleva menos tiempo* **the method which takes the least time**; *el examen con menos errores* **the exam paper with the fewest mistakes**.
Sin embargo, en inglés coloquial muchos hablantes utilizan **less** y **least** también en el caso de sustantivos contables, aunque se considera un uso incorrecto.

---

menoscabar [menoska'βar] /**1a**/ VT (*estropear*) to damage, harm; (*fig*) to discredit

menospreciar [menospre'θjar] /**1b**/ VT to

underrate, undervalue; (*despreciar*) to scorn, despise

menosprecio [menos'preθjo] NM (*subestimación*) underrating, undervaluation; (*desdén*) scorn, contempt

★**mensaje** [men'saxe] NM message; **enviar un ~ a algn** (*por móvil*) to text sb, send sb a text message; **~ de error** (*Inform*) error message; **~ de texto** text message; **~ electrónico** email

★**mensajero, -a** [mensa'xero, a] NM/F messenger

menso, -a ['menso, a] ADJ (*Am fam*) stupid

menstruación [menstrwa'θjon] NF menstruation

menstruar [mens'trwar] /**1e**/ VI to menstruate

★**mensual** [men'swal] ADJ monthly; **10 euros mensuales** 10 euros a month

mensualidad [menswali'ðað] NF (*salario*) monthly salary; (*Com*) monthly payment *o* instalment

menta ['menta] NF mint

mentado, -a [men'taðo, a] ADJ (*mencionado*) aforementioned; (*famoso*) well-known ▶ NF: **hacerle una mentada a algn** (*Am fam*) to (seriously) insult sb

mental [men'tal] ADJ mental

mentalidad [mentali'ðað] NF mentality

mentalizar [mentali'θar] /**1f**/ VT (*sensibilizar*) to make aware; (*convencer*) to convince; (*preparar mentalmente*) to prepare mentally ▪ **mentalizarse** VR (*concienciarse*) to become aware; (*prepararse mentalmente*) to prepare o.s. mentally; **mentalizarse (de)** to get used to the idea (of); **mentalizarse de que ...** (*convencerse*) to get it into one's head that ...

mentar [men'tar] /**1j**/ VT to mention, name; **~ la madre a algn** to swear at sb

mente ['mente] NF mind; (*inteligencia*) intelligence; **no tengo en ~ hacer eso** it is not my intention to do that

mentecato, -a [mente'kato, a] ADJ silly, stupid ▶ NM/F fool, idiot

★**mentir** [men'tir] /**3i**/ VI to lie; **¡miento!** sorry, I'm wrong!

★**mentira** [men'tira] NF (*una mentira*) lie; (*acto*) lying; (*invención*) fiction; **~ piadosa** white lie; **una ~ como una casa** a whopping great lie (*fam*); **parece ~ que ...** it seems incredible that ..., I can't believe that ...

★**mentiroso, -a** [menti'roso, a] ADJ lying; (*falso*) deceptive ▶ NM/F liar

mentís [men'tis] NM INV denial; (*tb*: **dar el mentís a**) to deny

mentón [men'ton] NM chin

★**menú** [me'nu] NM (*tb Inform*) menu; (*tb*: **menú del día**) set meal; **~ turístico** tourist menu; **guiado por ~** (*Inform*) menu-driven

menudear [menuðe'ar] /**1a**/ VT (*repetir*) to repeat frequently ▶ VI (*ser frecuente*) to be frequent; (*detallar*) to go into great detail

m

menudencia [menu'ðenθja] NF (*bagatela*) trifle ■ **menudencias** NFPL odds and ends; (*Culin*) giblets

menudeo [menu'ðeo] NM retail sales *pl*

menudillos [menu'ðiʎos] NMPL giblets

★**menudo, -a** [me'nuðo, a] ADJ (*pequeño*) small, tiny; (*sin importancia*) petty, insignificant; **¡~ negocio!** (*fam*) some deal!; **a ~** often, frequently

meñique [me'ɲike] NM little finger

meollo [me'oʎo] NM (*fig*) essence, core

mequetrefe [meke'trefe] NM good-for-nothing, whippersnapper

mercader [merka'ðer] NM merchant

mercadería [merkaðe'ria] NF commodity ■ **mercaderías** NFPL goods, merchandise *sg*

mercadillo [merka'ðiʎo] NM (*ESP*) flea market

★**mercado** [mer'kaðo] NM market; **~ en baja** falling market; **M~ Común** Common Market; **~ de demanda/de oferta** seller's/buyer's market; **~ laboral** labour market; **~ objetivo** target market; **~ de productos básicos** commodity market; **~ de pulgas** (*AM*) flea market; **~ de valores** stock market; **~ exterior/interior** o **nacional/libre** overseas/home/free market

mercancía [merkan'θia] NF commodity ■ **mercancías** NFPL goods, merchandise *sg*; goods train, freight train (*US*); **mercancías en depósito** bonded goods; **mercancías perecederas** perishable goods

mercantil [merkan'til] ADJ mercantile, commercial

mercenario, -a [merθe'narjo, a] ADJ, NM mercenary

mercería [merθe'ria] NF (*artículos*) haberdashery (*BRIT*), notions *pl* (*US*); (*tienda*) haberdasher's shop (*BRIT*), drapery (*BRIT*), notions store (*US*)

Mercosur [merko'sur] NM ABR (= *Mercado Común del Sur*) Argentina, Brazil, Paraguay and Uruguay

mercurio [mer'kurjo] NM mercury

merecedor, a [mereθe'ðor, a] ADJ deserving; **~ de confianza** trustworthy

★**merecer** [mere'θer] /2d/ VT to deserve, merit; **merece la pena** it's worthwhile ▸ VI to be deserving, be worthy

merecido, -a [mere'θiðo, a] ADJ (well) deserved; **llevarse su ~** to get one's deserts

★**merendar** [meren'dar] /1j/ VT to have for tea ▸ VI to have tea; (*en el campo*) to have a picnic

merendero [meren'dero] NM (open-air) café; (*en el campo*) picnic spot

merengue [me'reŋge] NM meringue

merezca *etc* [me'reθka] VB *ver* **merecer**

meridiano [meri'ðjano] NM (*Astro, Geo*) meridian; **la explicación es de una claridad meridiana** the explanation is as clear as day

meridional [meriðjo'nal] ADJ Southern ▸ NMF Southerner

★**merienda** [me'rjenda] VB *ver* **merendar** ▸ NF (light) tea, afternoon snack; (*de campo*) picnic; **~ de negros** (!) free-for-all

mérito ['merito] NM merit; (*valor*) worth, value; **hacer méritos** to make a good impression; **restar ~ a** to detract from

meritorio, -a [meri'torjo, a] ADJ deserving

★**merluza** [mer'luθa] NF hake; **coger una ~** (*fam*) to get sozzled

merma ['merma] NF decrease; (*pérdida*) wastage

mermar [mer'mar] /1a/ VT to reduce, lessen ▸ VI to decrease, dwindle

★**mermelada** [merme'laða] NF jam; **~ de naranja** marmalade

mero, -a ['mero, a] ADJ mere, simple; (*AM fam*) very ▸ ADV just, right ▸ NM (*Zool*) grouper; **el ~** (*AM fam*) the boss

merodear [meroðe'ar] /1a/ VI (*Mil*) to maraud; (*de noche*) to prowl (about); (*curiosear*) to snoop around

★**mes** [mes] NM month; (*salario*) month's pay; **el ~ corriente** this o the current month

★**mesa** ['mesa] NF table; (*de trabajo*) desk; (*Com*) counter; (*en mitin*) platform; (*Geo*) plateau; (*Arq*) landing; **~ de noche/de tijera/de operaciones** u **operatoria** bedside/folding/operating table; **~ electoral** officials in charge of a polling station; **~ redonda** (*reunión*) round table; **~ digitalizadora** (*Inform*) graph pad; **~ directiva** board; **~ y cama** bed and board; **poner/quitar la ~** to lay/clear the table

mesarse [me'sarse] /1a/ VR: **~ el pelo** o **los cabellos** to tear one's hair out

mesero, -a [me'sero, a] NM/F (*AM*) waiter (waitress)

meseta [me'seta] NF (*Geo*) tableland; (*Arq*) landing

mesilla [me'siʎa], **mesita** [me'sita] NF: **~ de noche** bedside table

mesón [me'son] NM inn

mestizo, -a [mes'tiθo, a] ADJ mixed-race; (*Zool*) crossbred ▸ NM/F person of mixed race

mesura [me'sura] NF (*calma*) calm; (*moderación*) moderation, restraint; (*cortesía*) courtesy

mesurar [mesu'rar] /1a/ VT (*contener*) to restrain ■ **mesurarse** VR to restrain o.s.

meta ['meta] NF goal; (*de carrera*) finish; (*fig*) goal, aim, objective

metabolismo [metaβo'lismo] NM metabolism

metafísico, -a [meta'fisiko, a] ADJ metaphysical ▸ NF metaphysics *sg*

metáfora [me'tafora] NF metaphor

metafórico, -a [meta'foriko, a] ADJ metaphorical

★**metal** [me'tal] NM (*materia*) metal; (*Mus*) brass

★**metálico, -a** [me'taliko, a] ADJ metallic; (*de metal*) metal ▸ NM (*dinero contante*) cash

metalurgia [meta'lurxja] NF metallurgy

metalúrgico, -a [meta'lurxiko, a] ADJ metallurgic(al); **industria metalúrgica** engineering industry

metamorfosear [metamorfose'ar] /**1a**/ VT: ~ **(en)** to metamorphose o transform (into)

metamorfosis [metamor'fosis] NF INV metamorphosis, transformation

metedura [mete'ðura] NF: ~ **de pata** (fam) blunder

meteorito [meteo'rito] NM meteorite

meteoro [mete'oro] NM meteor

meteorología [meteorolo'xia] NF meteorology

meteorólogo, -a [meteo'roloɣo, a] NM/F meteorologist; (Radio, TV) weather reporter

★**meter** [me'ter] /**2a**/ VT (colocar) to put, place; (introducir) to put in, insert; (involucrar) to involve; (causar) to make, cause; ~ **prisa a algn** to hurry sb up ■ **meterse** VR: **meterse en** to go into, enter; (fig) to interfere in, meddle in; **meterse a** to start; **meterse a escritor** to become a writer; **meterse con algn** to provoke sb, pick a quarrel with sb

meticuloso, -a [metiku'loso, a] ADJ meticulous, thorough

metido, -a [me'tiðo, a] ADJ: **estar muy ~ en un asunto** to be deeply involved in a matter; ~ **en años** elderly; ~ **en carnes** plump

metódico, -a [me'toðiko, a] ADJ methodical

metodismo [meto'ðismo] NM Methodism

★**método** ['metoðo] NM method

metodología [metoðolo'xia] NF methodology

metomentodo [metomen'toðo] NM INV meddler, busybody

metraje [me'traxe] NM (Cine) length; **cinta de largo/corto ~** full-length film/short

metralla [me'traʎa] NF shrapnel

metralleta [metra'ʎeta] NF sub-machine gun

métrico, -a ['metriko, a] ADJ metric; **cinta métrica** tape measure ▶ NF metrics pl

★**metro** ['metro] NM metre; (tren: tb: **metropolitano**) underground (BRIT), subway (US); (instrumento) rule; ~ **cuadrado/cúbico** square/cubic metre

metrópoli [me'tropoli], **metrópolis** [me'tropolis] NF (ciudad) metropolis; (colonial) mother country

metrosexual [metrosexu'al] ADJ, NM metrosexual

★**mexicano, -a** [mexi'kano, a] ADJ, NM/F (AM) Mexican

★**México** ['mexiko] NM (AM) Mexico; **Ciudad de ~** Mexico City

mezcla ['meθkla] NF mixture; (fig) blend

mezclar [meθ'klar] /**1a**/ VT to mix (up); (armonizar) to blend; (combinar) to merge; ~ **en** to get mixed up in, get involved in ■ **mezclarse** VR to mix, mingle

mezcolanza [meθko'lanθa] NF hotchpotch, jumble

mezquindad [meθkin'dað] NF (cicatería) meanness; (miras estrechas) pettiness; (acto) mean action

★**mezquino, -a** [meθ'kino, a] ADJ (cicatero) mean ▶ NM/F (avaro) mean person; (miserable) petty individual

★**mezquita** [meθ'kita] NF mosque

mg ABR (= miligramo(s)) mg

★**mi** [mi] ADJ POSESIVO my ▶ NM (Mus) E

★**mí** [mi] PRON me, myself; **¿y a mí qué?** so what?

mía ['mia] PRON ver **mío**

miaja ['mjaxa] NF crumb; **ni una ~** (fig) not the least little bit

miau [mjau] NM miaow

michelín [mitʃe'lin] NM (fam) spare tyre

mico ['miko] NM monkey

micro ['mikro] NM (Radio) mike, microphone; (AM: pequeño) minibus; (: grande) coach, bus

microbio [mi'kroβjo] NM microbe

microblog [mikro'βloɣ] NM microblog

microbús [mikro'βus] NM minibus

microchip [mikro'tʃip] NM microchip

microcomputador [mikrokomputa'ðor] NM, **microcomputadora** [mikrokomputa'ðora] NF micro(computer)

microeconomía [mikroekono'mia] NF microeconomics sg

microficha [mikro'fitʃa] NF microfiche

microfilm [mikro'film] (pl **microfilms** [mikro'films]) NM microfilm

micrófono [mi'krofono] NM microphone

microinformática [mikroinfor'matika] NF microcomputing

micromecenazgo [mikromeθe'naθɣo] NM crowdfunding

micrómetro [mi'krometro] NM micrometer

microonda [mikro'onda] NF, **microondas** [mikro'ondas] NM INV microwave; **(horno) microondas** microwave (oven)

microordenador [mikroordena'ðor] NM microcomputer

micropastilla [mikropas'tiʎa], **microplaqueta** [mikropla'keta] NF (Inform) chip, wafer

microplaquita [mikropla'kita] NF: ~ **de silicio** silicon chip

microprocesador [mikroproθesa'ðor] NM microprocessor

microscópico, -a [mikros'kopiko, a] ADJ microscopic

microscopio [mikros'kopjo] NM microscope

midiendo etc [mi'ðjendo] VB ver **medir**

★**miedo** ['mjeðo] NM fear; (nerviosismo) apprehension, nervousness; **meter ~ a** to scare, frighten; **tener ~ a** to be afraid; **de ~** wonderful, marvellous; **¡qué ~!** (fam) how awful!; **me da ~** it scares me; **hace un frío de ~** (fam) it's terribly cold

miedoso, -a [mje'ðoso, a] ADJ fearful, timid

★miel [mjel] NF honey; **no hay ~ sin hiel** there's no rose without a thorn

★miembro ['mjembro] NM limb; (*socio*) member; (*de institución*) fellow; **~ viril** penis

mientes *etc* ['mjentes] VB *ver* **mentar; mentir** ▶ NFPL: **no parar ~ en** to pay no attention to; **traer a las ~** to recall

★mientras ['mjentras] CONJ while; (*duración*) as long as; **~ más tiene, más quiere** the more he has, the more he wants; **~ (que)** whereas ▶ ADV meanwhile; **~ tanto** meanwhile

★miércoles ['mjerkoles] NM INV Wednesday; **~ de ceniza** Ash Wednesday; *ver tb* **carnaval; sábado**

mierda ['mjerða] NF (*fam!*) shit (*fam!*), crap (*fam!*); (*fig*) filth, dirt; **¡vete a la ~!** go to hell!

mies [mjes] NF (*ripe*) corn, wheat, grain

miga ['miɣa] NF crumb; (*fig: meollo*) essence; **hacer buenas migas** (*fam*) to get on well; **esto tiene su ~** there's more to this than meets the eye

migaja [mi'ɣaxa] NF: **una ~ de** (*un poquito*) a little ■ **migajas** NFPL (*pey*) crumbs; (*sobras*) leftovers

migración [miɣra'θjon] NF migration

migratorio, -a [miɣra'torjo, a] ADJ migratory

mil [mil] NUM thousand; **dos ~ libras** two thousand pounds

milagro [mi'laɣro] NM miracle; **hacer milagros** (*fig*) to work wonders

milagroso, -a [mila'ɣroso, a] ADJ miraculous

Milán [mi'lan] NM Milan

milenario, -a [mile'narjo, a] ADJ millennial; (*fig*) very ancient

milenio [mi'lenjo] NM millennium

milésima [mi'lesima] NF (*de segundo*) thousandth

milésimo, -a [mi'lesimo, a] NUM thousandth

mileurista NMF *person earning around a thousand euros or less;* **un ~ no puede comprar ese piso** no one on a salary of a thousand euros could afford that flat ▶ ADJ of (around) a thousand euros; **un sueldo ~** a salary of (around) a thousand euros

mili ['mili] NF: **hacer la ~** (*fam*) to do one's military service

milicia [mi'liθja] NF (*Mil*) militia; (*servicio militar*) military service

miligramo [mili'ɣramo] NM milligram

milímetro [mi'limetro] NM millimetre (*Brit*), millimeter (*US*)

militante [mili'tante] ADJ militant

★militar [mili'tar] **/1a/** ADJ military ▶ NM/F soldier ▶ VI to serve in the army; (*fig*) to militate, fight

militarismo [milita'rismo] NM militarism

mill. ABR = **millón;** (= *millones*) M

★milla ['miʎa] NF mile; **~ marina** nautical mile

millar [mi'ʎar] NUM thousand; **a millares** in thousands

★millón [mi'ʎon] NUM million

★millonario, -a [miʎo'narjo, a] NM/F millionaire

millonésimo, -a [miʎo'nesimo, a] NUM millionth

milusos [mi'lusos] NM INV (*AM*) odd-job man

mimado, -a [mi'maðo, a] ADJ spoiled

mimar [mi'mar] **/1a/** VT to spoil, pamper

mimbre ['mimbre] NM wicker; **de ~** wicker *cpd*, wickerwork

mimetismo [mime'tismo] NM mimicry

mímica ['mimika] NF (*para comunicarse*) sign language; (*imitación*) mimicry

mimo ['mimo] NM (*caricia*) caress; (*de niño*) spoiling; (*Teat*) mime; (: *actor*) mime artist

mina ['mina] NF mine; (*pozo*) shaft; (*de lápiz*) lead refill; **hullera** *o* **~ de carbón** coal mine

minar [mi'nar] **/1a/** VT to mine; (*fig*) to undermine

mineral [mine'ral] ADJ mineral ▶ NM (*Geo*) mineral; (*mena*) ore

minería [mine'ria] NF mining

★minero, -a [mi'nero, a] ADJ mining *cpd* ▶ NM/F miner

miniatura [minja'tura] ADJ INV, NF miniature

minicadena [minika'ðena] NF (*Mus*) mini hi-fi

minicomputador [minikomputa'ðor] NM minicomputer

MiniDisc® [mini'disk] NM MiniDisc®

minidisco [mini'ðisko] NM diskette

minifalda [mini'falda] NF miniskirt

minifundio [mini'fundjo] NM smallholding, small farm

minimizar [minimi'θar] **/1f/** VT to minimize

★mínimo, -a ['minimo, a] ADJ minimum; (*insignificante*) minimal; **precio/salario ~** minimum price/wage; **lo ~ que pueden hacer** the least they can do ▶ NM minimum

minino, -a [mi'nino, a] NM/F (*fam*) puss, pussy

ministerio [minis'terjo] NM ministry (*Brit*), department (*US*); **M~ de Asuntos Exteriores** Foreign Office (*Brit*), State Department (*US*); **M~ de Comercio e Industria** Department of Trade and Industry; **M~ de (la) Gobernación** *o* **del Interior** ≈ Home Office (*Brit*), Ministry of the Interior; **M~ de Hacienda** Treasury (*Brit*), Treasury Department (*US*)

★ministro, -a [mi'nistro, a] NM/F minister, secretary (*esp US*); **M~ de Hacienda** Chancellor of the Exchequer, Secretary of the Treasury (*US*); **M~ de (la) Gobernación** *o* **del Interior** ≈ Home Secretary (*Brit*), Secretary of the Interior (*US*)

minoría [mino'ria] NF minority

minorista [mino'rista] NM retailer

mintiendo *etc* [min'tjendo] VB *ver* **mentir**

minucia [mi'nuθja] NF (*detalle insignificante*) trifle; (*bagatela*) mere nothing

minuciosidad [minuθjosi'ðað] NF (*meticulosidad*) thoroughness, meticulousness

minucioso, -a [minu'θjoso, a] ADJ thorough, meticulous; (*prolijo*) very detailed

minúsculo, -a [mi'nuskulo, a] ADJ tiny, minute ▶ NF small letter ▪ **minúsculas** NFPL (*Tip*) lower case *sg*

minusvalía [minusβa'lia] NF physical disability; (*Com*) depreciation, capital loss

minusválido, -a [minus'βaliðo, a] ADJ (physically) disabled ▶ NM/F person with a disability

minuta [mi'nuta] NF (*de comida*) menu; (*de abogado etc*) fee

minutero [minu'tero] NM minute hand

★**minuto** [mi'nuto] NM minute

Miño ['miɲo] NM: **el (río) ~** the Miño

★**mío, -a** ['mio, a] ADJ, PRON: **el ~** mine; **un amigo ~** a friend of mine; **lo ~** what is mine; **los míos** my people, my relations

miope ['mjope] ADJ short-sighted

miopía [mjo'pia] NF near-*o* short-sightedness

MIR [mir] NM ABR (*Pol*) = **Movimiento de Izquierda Revolucionaria**; (*Esp Med*) = **Médico Interno y Residente**

mira ['mira] NF (*de arma*) sight(s) *pl*; (*fig*) aim, intention; **de amplias/estrechas miras** broad-/narrow-minded

mirada [mi'raða] NF look, glance; (*expresión*) look, expression; **~ de soslayo** sidelong glance; **~ fija** stare, gaze; **~ perdida** distant look; **clavar la ~ en** to stare at; **echar una ~ a** to glance at; **levantar/bajar la ~** to look up/down; **resistir la ~ de algn** to stare sb out

mirado, -a [mi'raðo, a] ADJ (*sensato*) sensible; (*considerado*) considerate; **bien/mal ~** well/not well thought of; **bien ~ ...** all things considered ...

mirador [mira'ðor] NM viewpoint, vantage point

miramiento [mira'mjento] NM (*consideración*) considerateness; **tratar sin miramientos a algn** to ride roughshod over sb

mirar [mi'rar] /**1a**/ VT to look at; (*observar*) to watch; (*considerar*) to consider, think over; (*vigilar, cuidar*) to watch, look after; **~ algo/a algn de reojo** o **de través** to look askance at sth/sb; **~ algo/a algn por encima del hombro** to look down on sth/sb; **~ bien/mal algo** to think highly of/have a poor opinion of sth; **~ fijamente algo/a algn** to stare o gaze at sth/sb ▶ VI to look; (*Arq*) to face; **~ por** (*fig*) to look after; **~ por la ventana** to look out of the window ▪ **mirarse** VR (*dos personas*) to look at each other; **mirarse al espejo** to look at o.s. in the mirror; **mirarse a los ojos** to look into each other's eyes

---

Cuando la acción de *mirar* se dirige a algo que no se está moviendo, se traduce por **look at**: *Le pedí que mirara la foto*. **I asked him to look at the photo**.
Cuando se mira algo que se está moviendo, o que está cambiando, se traduce por **watch**: *Miraba a los niños que jugaban en el jardín*. **He watched the children playing in the garden**.

---

mirilla [mi'riʎa] NF (*agujero*) spyhole, peephole

mirlo ['mirlo] NM blackbird

★**misa** ['misa] NF mass; **~ del gallo** midnight mass (*on Christmas Eve*); **~ de difuntos** requiem mass; **como en ~** in dead silence; **estos datos van a ~** (*fig*) these facts are utterly trustworthy

misántropo [mi'santropo] NM misanthrope, misanthropist

miscelánea [misθe'lanea] NF miscellany

miserable [mise'raβle] ADJ (*avaro*) mean, stingy; (*nimio*) miserable, paltry; (*fam*) vile, despicable ▶ NMF (*malvado*) rogue

miseria [mi'serja] NF misery; (*pobreza*) poverty; (*tacañería*) meanness, stinginess; (*condiciones*) squalor; **una ~** a pittance

misericordia [miseri'korðja] NF (*compasión*) compassion, pity; (*perdón*) forgiveness, mercy

misil [mi'sil] NM missile

misión [mi'sjon] NF mission; (*tarea*) job, duty; (*Pol*) assignment ▪ **misiones** NFPL (*Rel*) overseas missions

misionero, -a [misjo'nero, a] NM/F missionary

mismamente [misma'mente] ADV (*fam: solo*) only, just

mismísimo, -a [mis'misimo, a] ADJ SUPERLATIVO selfsame, very (same)

★**mismo, -a** ['mismo, a] ADJ (*semejante*) same; (*después de pronombre*) -self; (*para énfasis*) very; **por lo ~** for the same reason; **el ~ traje** the same suit; **en ese ~ momento** at that very moment; **yo ~ lo vi** I saw it myself; **lo hizo por sí ~** he did it by himself; **vino el ~ Ministro** the Minister himself came; **lo ~** the same (thing); **quedamos en las mismas** we're no further forward ▶ ADV: **aquí/ayer/hoy ~** right here/only yesterday/this very day; **ahora ~** right now; **da lo ~** it's all the same ▶ CONJ: **lo ~ que** just like, just as

misógino, -a [mi'soxino, a] NM/F misogynist ▶ ADJ misogynistic, misogynist

miss [mis] NF beauty queen

misterio [mis'terjo] NM mystery; (*lo secreto*) secrecy

★**misterioso, -a** [miste'rjoso, a] ADJ mysterious; (*inexplicable*) puzzling

misticismo [misti'θismo] NM mysticism

místico, -a ['mistiko, a] ADJ mystic(al) ▶ NM/F mystic ▶ NF mysticism

★**mitad** [mi'tað] NF (*medio*) half; (*centro*) middle; **~ (y) ~** half-and-half; (*fig*) yes and no; **a ~ de precio** (at) half-price; **en** o **a ~ del camino** halfway along the road; **cortar por la ~** to cut through the middle

mítico, -a ['mitiko, a] ADJ mythical

mitigar [miti'ɣar] /**1h**/ VT to mitigate; (*dolor*) to relieve; (*sed*) to quench; (*ira*) to appease; (*preocupación*) to allay; (*soledad*) to alleviate

mitigue *etc* [mi'tiɣe] VB *ver* **mitigar**

mitin ['mitin] NM (*esp Pol*) meeting

mito ['mito] NM myth

mitología [mitolo'xia] NF mythology

mitológico, -a [mito'loxiko, a] ADJ mythological

★**mixto, -a** ['miksto, a] ADJ mixed; (*comité*) joint

ml ABR (= *mililitro(s)*) ml

mm ABR (= *milímetro(s)*) mm

M.N., m/n ABR (*AM Econ*) = **moneda nacional**

M.° ABR (*Pol*: = *Ministerio*) Min

m/o ABR (*Com*) = **mi orden**

mobiliario [moβi'ljarjo] NM furniture

mocasín [moka'sin] NM moccasin

mocedad [moθe'ðað] NF youth

★**mochila** [mo't∫ila] NF rucksack (*BRIT*), backpack

moción [mo'θjon] NF motion; **~ compuesta** (*Pol*) composite motion

moco ['moko] NM mucus; **no es ~ de pavo** it's no trifle ■ **mocos** NMPL (*fam*) snot; **limpiarse los mocos** to blow one's nose

mocoso, -a [mo'koso, a] ADJ snivelling; (*fig*) ill-bred ▶ NM/F (*fam*) brat

★**moda** ['moða] NF fashion; (*estilo*) style; **de** *o* **a la ~** in fashion, fashionable; **pasado de ~** out of fashion; **vestido a la última ~** trendily dressed

modal [mo'ðal] ADJ modal ■ **modales** NMPL manners

modalidad [moðali'ðað] NF (*clase*) kind, variety; (*manera*) way; (*Inform*) mode; **~ de texto** (*Inform*) text mode

modelar [moðe'lar] /1a/ VT to model

★**modelo** [mo'ðelo] ADJ INV model ▶ NMF model ▶ NM (*patrón*) pattern; (*norma*) standard

módem ['moðem] NM (*Inform*) modem

moderado, -a [moðe'raðo, a] ADJ moderate

moderar [moðe'rar] /1a/ VT to moderate; (*violencia*) to restrain, control; (*velocidad*) to reduce ■ **moderarse** VR to restrain o.s., control o.s.

modernice *etc* [moðer'niθe] VB *ver* **modernizar**

modernizar [moðerni'θar] /1f/ VT to modernize; (*Inform*) to upgrade

★**moderno, -a** [mo'ðerno, a] ADJ modern; (*actual*) present-day; (*equipo etc*) up-to-date

modestia [mo'ðestja] NF modesty

modesto, -a [mo'ðesto, a] ADJ modest

módico, -a ['moðiko, a] ADJ moderate, reasonable

modificar [moðifi'kar] /1g/ VT to modify

modifique *etc* [moði'fike] VB *ver* **modificar**

modismo [mo'ðismo] NM idiom

modisto, -a [mo'ðisto, a] NM/F (*diseñador*) couturier, designer; (*que confecciona*) dressmaker

★**modo** ['moðo] NM (*manera, forma*) way, manner; (*Inform, Mus*) mode; (*Ling*) mood; **"~ de empleo"** "instructions for use"; **~ de gobierno** form of government; **a ~ de** like; **de este ~** in this way; **de ningún ~** in no way; **de un ~ u otro** (in) one way or another ■ **modos** NMPL manners; **de todos modos** at any rate

modorra [mo'ðorra] NF drowsiness

modoso, -a [mo'ðoso, a] ADJ (*educado*) quiet, well-mannered

modulación [moðula'θjon] NF modulation; **~ de frecuencia** (*Radio*) frequency modulation, FM

módulo ['moðulo] NM module; (*de mueble*) unit

mofarse [mo'farse] /1a/ VR: **~ de** to mock, scoff at

mofle ['mofle] NM (*AM*) silencer (*BRIT*), muffler (*US*)

moflete [mo'flete] NM fat cheek, chubby cheek

mogollón [moɣo'ʎon] (*fam*) NM: **~ de discos** *etc* loads of records *etc* ▶ ADV: **un ~** a hell of a lot

mohín [mo'in] NM (*mueca*) (wry) face; (*pucheros*) pout

mohíno, -a [mo'ino, a] ADJ (*triste*) gloomy, depressed; (*enojado*) sulky

moho ['moo] NM (*Bot*) mould, mildew; (*en metal*) rust

mohoso, -a [mo'oso, a] ADJ mouldy; (*metal*) rusty

★**mojado, -a** [mo'xaðo, a] ADJ wet; (*húmedo*) damp; (*empapado*) drenched

★**mojar** [mo'xar] /1a/ VT to wet; (*humedecer*) to damp(en), moisten; (*calar*) to soak; **~ el pan en el café** to dip *o* dunk one's bread in one's coffee ■ **mojarse** VR to get wet

mojigato, -a [moxi'ɣato, a] ADJ (*hipócrita*) hypocritical; (*santurrón*) sanctimonious; (*gazmoño*) prudish ▶ NM/F hypocrite; sanctimonious person; prude

mojón [mo'xon] NM (*hito*) landmark; (*en un camino*) signpost; (*tb:* **mojón kilométrico**) milestone

mol. ABR (= *molécula*) mol

molar [mo'lar] /1a/ NM molar ▶ VT (*fam*): **lo que más me mola es …** what I'm really into is …; **¿te mola un cigarrillo?** do you fancy a smoke?

molcajete [molka'xete] NM (*AM*) mortar

Moldavia [mol'ðaβja], **Moldova** [mol'ðoβa] NF Moldavia, Moldova

moldavo, -a [mol'ðaβo, a] ADJ, NM/F Moldavian, Moldovan

molde ['molde] NM mould; (*vaciado*) cast; (*de costura*) pattern; (*fig*) model

moldeado [molde'aðo] PP *de* **moldear** ▶ NM soft perm

moldear [molde'ar] /1a/ VT to mould; (*en yeso etc*) to cast

mole ['mole] NF mass, bulk; (*edificio*) pile

molécula [mo'lekula] NF molecule

moler [mo'ler] VT to grind, crush; (*pulverizar*) to pound; (*trigo etc*) to mill; (*cansar*) to tire out, exhaust; **~ a algn a palos** to give sb a beating

★**molestar** [moles'tar] /1a/ VT to bother; (*fastidiar*) to annoy; (*incomodar*) to inconvenience, put out; (*perturbar*) to trouble, upset; **¿le molesta el**

ruido? do you mind the noise?; **siento molestarle** I'm sorry to trouble you ▶ vi to be a nuisance ■ **molestarse** vr to bother; (*incomodarse*) to go to a lot of trouble; (*ofenderse*) to take offence

> Do not translate the Spanish word **molestar** by *molest*.

★**molestia** [mo'lestja] NF bother, trouble; (*incomodidad*) inconvenience; (*Med*) discomfort; **es una ~** it's a nuisance; **no es ninguna ~** it's no trouble at all

molesto, -a [mo'lesto, a] ADJ (*que fastidia*) annoying; (*incómodo*) inconvenient; (*inquieto*) uncomfortable, ill at ease; (*enfadado*) annoyed; **estar ~** (*Med*) to be in some discomfort; **estar ~ con algn** (*fig*) to be cross with sb; **me sentí ~** I felt embarrassed

molido, -a [mo'liðo, a] ADJ (*machacado*) ground; (*pulverizado*) powdered; **estar ~** (*fig*) to be exhausted o dead beat

molinero [moli'nero] NM miller

molinillo [moli'niʎo] NM hand mill; **~ de carne/ café** mincer/coffee grinder

molino [mo'lino] NM (*edificio*) mill; (*máquina*) grinder

mollera [mo'ʎera] NF (*Anat*) crown of the head; (*fam: seso*) brains pl; **duro de ~** (*estúpido*) thick

Molucas [mo'lukas] NFPL: **las (Islas) ~** the Moluccas, the Molucca Islands

molusco [mo'lusko] NM mollusc

momentáneo, -a [momen'taneo, a] ADJ momentary

★**momento** [mo'mento] NM (*gen*) moment; (*Tec*) momentum; **de ~** at the moment, for the moment; **en ese ~** at that moment, just then; **por el ~** for the time being

momia ['momja] NF mummy

mona ['mona] NF *ver* **mono**

Mónaco ['monako] NM Monaco

monada [mo'naða] NF (*gracia*) charming habit; (*cosa primorosa*) lovely thing; (*chica*) pretty girl; **¡qué ~!** isn't it cute?

monaguillo [mona'ɣiʎo] NM altar boy

monarca [mo'narka] NMF monarch, ruler

monarquía [monar'kia] NF monarchy

monárquico, -a [mo'narkiko, a] NM/F royalist, monarchist

monasterio [monas'terjo] NM monastery

Moncloa [mon'kloa] NF: **la ~** *official residence of the Spanish Prime Minister*

> The Moncloa Palace in Madrid is the official residence of the Spanish prime minister. By extension, the **Moncloa** is often used to mean the prime minister and the government.

monda ['monda] NF (*poda*) pruning; (*: de árbol*) lopping; (*: de fruta*) peeling; (*cáscara*) skin; **¡es la ~!** (*fam*) (*fantástico*) it's great!; (*el colmo*) it's the limit!; (*es gracioso*) he's a knockout!

mondadientes [monda'ðjentes] NM INV toothpick

mondar [mon'dar] /1a/ VT (*limpiar*) to clean; (*pelar*) to peel ■ **mondarse** VR: **mondarse de risa** (*fam*) to split one's sides laughing

mondongo [mon'dongo] NM (*Am*) tripe

★**moneda** [mo'neða] NF (*tipo de dinero*) currency, money; (*pieza*) coin; **una ~ de 50 céntimos** a 50-cent coin; **~ de curso** legal tender; **~ extranjera** foreign exchange; **~ única** single currency; **es ~ corriente** (*fig*) it's common knowledge

★**monedero** [mone'ðero] NM purse

monegasco, -a [mone'ɣasko, a] ADJ of o from Monaco, Monegasque ▶ NM/F Monegasque

monetario, -a [mone'tarjo, a] ADJ monetary, financial

monetarista [moneta'rista] ADJ, NMF monetarist

mongol, -a [mon'gol, a] ADJ, NM/F Mongol ▶ NM (*Ling*) Mongol

monigote [moni'ɣote] NM (*dibujo*) doodle; (*de papel*) cut-out figure; (*pey*) wimp; *ver tb* **inocente**

★**monitor, a** [moni'tor, a] NM/F instructor, coach; **~ en color** colour monitor ▶ NM (*TV*) set; (*Inform*) monitor

monja ['monxa] NF nun

monje ['monxe] NM monk

★**mono, -a** ['mono, a] ADJ (*bonito*) lovely, pretty; (*gracioso*) nice, charming; **una chica muy mona** a very pretty girl ▶ NM/F monkey, ape ▶ NM dungarees pl; (*traje de faena*) overalls pl; (*fam: de drogadicto*) cold turkey ▶ NF: **dormir la mona** to sleep it off

monóculo [mo'nokulo] NM monocle

monografía [monoɣra'fia] NF monograph

monolingüe [mono'lingwe] ADJ monolingual

monólogo [mo'noloɣo] NM monologue

monomando [mono'mando] NM (*tb*: **grifo monomando**) mixer tap

monoparental [monoparen'tal] ADJ: **familia ~** single-parent family

★**monopatín** [monopa'tin] NM skateboard

monopolice etc [monopo'liθe] VB *ver* **monopolizar**

monopolio [mono'poljo] NM monopoly; **~ total** absolute monopoly

monopolista [monopo'lista] ADJ, NMF monopolist

monopolizar [monopoli'θar] /1f/ VT to monopolize

monosílabo, -a [mono'silaβo, a] ADJ monosyllabic ▶ NM monosyllable

monotonía [monoto'nia] NF (*sonido*) monotone; (*fig*) monotony

monótono, -a [mo'notono, a] ADJ monotonous

mono-usuario, -a [monou'swarjo, a] ADJ (*Inform*) single-user

m

monóxido [mo'noksiðo] NM monoxide; **~ de carbono** carbon monoxide

Mons. ABR (*Rel*) = **monseñor**

monseñor [monse'ɲor] NM monsignor

monserga [mon'serɣa] NF (*lenguaje confuso*) gibberish; (*tonterías*) drivel

monstruo ['monstrwo] NM monster ▶ ADJ INV fantastic

monstruoso, -a [mons'trwoso, a] ADJ monstrous

monta ['monta] NF total, sum; **de poca ~** unimportant, of little account

montacargas [monta'karɣas] NM INV service lift (*BRIT*), freight elevator (*US*)

montador [monta'ðor] NM (*para montar*) mounting block; (*profesión*) fitter; (*Cine*) film editor

montaje [mon'taxe] NM assembly; (*organización*) fitting up; (*Teat*) décor; (*Cine*) montage

montante [mon'tante] NM (*poste*) upright; (*soporte*) stanchion; (*Arq: de puerta*) transom; (: *de ventana*) mullion; (*suma*) amount, total

★**montaña** [mon'taɲa] NF (*monte*) mountain; (*sierra*) mountains *pl*, mountainous area; (*AM: selva*) forest; **~ rusa** roller coaster

montañero, -a [monta'ɲero, a] ADJ mountain *cpd* ▶ NM/F mountaineer, climber

montañés, -esa [monta'ɲes, esa] ADJ mountain *cpd*; (*de Santander*) of o from the Santander region ▶ NM/F highlander; native o inhabitant of the Santander region

montañismo [monta'ɲismo] NM mountaineering, climbing

★**montañoso, -a** [monta'ɲoso, a] ADJ mountainous

★**montar** [mon'tar] /**1a**/ VT to mount, get on; (*caballo etc*) to ride; (*Tec*) to assemble, put together; (*negocio*) to set up; (*colocar*) to lift on to; (*Cine: película*) to edit; (*Teat: obra*) to stage, put on; (*Culin: batir*) to whip, beat; **~ un número o numerito** to make a scene ▶ VI to mount, get on; (*sobresalir*) to overlap; **~ en bicicleta** to ride a bicycle; **~ en cólera** to get angry; **~ a caballo** to ride, go horseriding; **tanto monta** it makes no odds

montaraz [monta'raθ] ADJ mountain *cpd*, highland *cpd*; (*pey*) uncivilized

★**monte** ['monte] NM (*montaña*) mountain; (*bosque*) woodland; (*área sin cultivar*) wild area, wild country; **~ de piedad** pawnshop; **~ alto** forest; **~ bajo** scrub(land)

Montenegro [monte'neɣro] NM Montenegro

montera [mon'tera] NF (*sombrero*) cloth cap; (*de torero*) bullfighter's hat

Montevideo [monteβi'ðeo] NM Montevideo

monto ['monto] NM total, amount

★**montón** [mon'ton] NM heap, pile; **un ~ de** (*fig*) heaps of, lots of; **a montones** by the score, galore

montura [mon'tura] NF (*cabalgadura*) mount; (*silla*) saddle; (*arreos*) harness; (*de joya*) mounting; (*de gafas*) frame

monumental [monumen'tal] ADJ (*tb fig*) monumental; **zona ~** area of historical interest

★**monumento** [monu'mento] NM monument; (*de conmemoración*) memorial

monzón [mon'θon] NM monsoon

moña ['moɲa] NF hair ribbon

moño ['moɲo] NM (*de pelo*) bun; **estar hasta el ~** (*fam*) to be fed up to the back teeth

★**moqueta** [mo'keta] NF fitted carpet

moquillo [mo'kiʎo] NM (*enfermedad*) distemper

mora ['mora] NF (*Bot*) mulberry; (: *zarzamora*) blackberry; (*Com*): **en ~** in arrears

★**morado, -a** [mo'raðo, a] ADJ purple, violet; **pasarlas moradas** to have a tough time of it ▶ NM bruise ▶ NF (*casa*) dwelling, abode

moral [mo'ral] ADJ moral ▶ NF (*ética*) ethics *pl*; (*moralidad*) morals *pl*, morality; (*ánimo*) morale; **tener baja la ~** to be in low spirits

moraleja [mora'lexa] NF moral

moralice *etc* [mora'liθe] VB *ver* **moralizar**

moralidad [morali'ðað] NF morals *pl*, morality

moralizar [morali'θar] /**1f**/ VT to moralize

morar [mo'rar] /**1a**/ VI to live, dwell

moratón [mora'ton] NM bruise

moratoria [mora'torja] NF moratorium

morbo ['morβo] NM (*fam*) morbid pleasure

morbosidad [morβosi'ðað] NF morbidity

morboso, -a [mor'βoso, a] ADJ morbid

morcilla [mor'θiʎa] NF blood sausage, ≈ black pudding (*BRIT*)

mordaz [mor'ðaθ] ADJ (*crítica*) biting, scathing

mordaza [mor'ðaθa] NF (*para la boca*) gag; (*Tec*) clamp

★**morder** [mor'ðer] /**2h**/ VT to bite; (*mordisquear*) to nibble; (*fig: consumir*) to eat away, eat into ▶ VI to bite; **está que muerde** he's hopping mad ■ **morderse** VR to bite; **morderse la lengua** to hold one's tongue

mordida [mor'ðiða] NF (*AM fam*) bribe

mordisco [mor'ðisko] NM bite

mordisquear [morðiske'ar] /**1a**/ VT to nibble at

★**moreno, -a** [mo'reno, a] ADJ (*color*) (dark) brown; (*de tez*) dark; (*de pelo moreno*) dark-haired; (*negro*) black ▶ NM/F (*de tez*) dark-skinned man/woman; (*de pelo*) dark-haired man/woman

morfina [mor'fina] NF morphine

morfinómano, -a [morfi'nomano, a] ADJ addicted to hard drugs ▶ NM/F drug addict

morgue ['morgue] NF (*AM*) mortuary (*BRIT*), morgue (*US*)

moribundo, -a [mori'βundo, a] ADJ dying ▶ NM/F dying person

★**morir** [mo'rir] /**3j**/ VI to die; (*fuego*) to die down; (*luz*) to go out; **~ de frío/hambre** to die of cold/starve to death ■ **morirse** VR to die; (*fig*) to be dying; (*Ferro etc: vías*) to end; (: *calle*) to come out;

¡me muero de hambre! (*fig*) I'm starving!; **morirse por algo** to be dying for sth; **morirse por algn** to be crazy about sb

mormón, -ona [mor'mon, ona] NM/F Mormon

moro, -a ['moro, a] ADJ Moorish ▶ NM/F Moor; **¡hay moros en la costa!** watch out!

moroso, -a [mo'roso, a] ADJ (*lento*) slow; **deudor ~** (*Com*) slow payer ▶ NM/F (*Com*) bad debtor, defaulter

morral [mo'rral] NM haversack

morriña [mo'rriɲa] NF homesickness; **tener ~** to be homesick

morro ['morro] NM (*Zool*) snout, nose; (*Auto, Aviat*) nose; (*fam: labio*) (thick) lip; **beber a ~** to drink from the bottle; **caer de ~** to nosedive; **estar de morros (con algn)** to be in a bad mood (with sb); **tener ~** to have a nerve

morrocotudo, -a [morroko'tuðo, a] ADJ (*fam: fantástico*) smashing; (: *riña, golpe*) tremendous; (: *fuerte*) strong; (: *pesado*) heavy; (: *difícil*) awkward

morsa ['morsa] NF walrus

morse ['morse] NM Morse (code)

mortadela [morta'ðela] NF mortadella, bologna sausage

mortaja [mor'taxa] NF shroud; (*Tec*) mortise; (*Am*) cigarette paper

mortal [mor'tal] ADJ mortal; (*golpe*) deadly

mortalidad [mortali'ðað], **mortandad** [mortan'dað] NF mortality

mortecino, -a [morte'θino, a] ADJ (*débil*) weak; (*luz*) dim; (*color*) dull

mortero [mor'tero] NM mortar

mortífero, -a [mor'tifero, a] ADJ deadly, lethal

mortificar [mortifi'kar] /**1g**/ VT to mortify; (*atormentar*) to torment

mortifique *etc* [morti'fike] VB *ver* **mortificar**

mortuorio, -a [mor'tworjo, a] ADJ mortuary, death *cpd*

Mosa ['mosa] NM: **el (río) ~** the Meuse

mosaico [mo'saiko] NM mosaic

mosca ['moska] NF fly; **por si las moscas** just in case; **estar ~** (*desconfiar*) to smell a rat; **tener la ~ en** o **detrás de la oreja** to be wary

moscovita [mosko'βita] ADJ Muscovite, Moscow *cpd* ▶ NMF Muscovite

Moscú [mos'ku] NM Moscow

mosquear [moske'ar] /**1a**/ (*fam*) VT (*hacer sospechar*) to make suspicious; (*fastidiar*) to annoy ■ **mosquearse** VR (*enfadarse*) to get annoyed; (*ofenderse*) to take offence

mosquita [mos'kita] NF: **parece una ~ muerta** he looks as though butter wouldn't melt in his mouth

mosquitero [moski'tero] NM mosquito net

★**mosquito** [mos'kito] NM mosquito

Mossos ['mosos] NMPL: **~ d'Esquadra** Catalan police; *ver tb* **policía**

★**mostaza** [mos'taθa] NF mustard

mosto ['mosto] NM unfermented grape juice

★**mostrador** [mostra'ðor] NM (*de tienda*) counter; (*de café*) bar

★**mostrar** [mos'trar] /**1l**/ VT to show; (*exhibir*) to display, exhibit; (*explicar*) to explain; **~ en pantalla** (*Inform*) to display ■ **mostrarse** VR: **mostrarse amable** to be kind, prove to be kind; **no se muestra muy inteligente** he doesn't seem (to be) very intelligent

mota ['mota] NF speck, tiny piece; (*en diseño*) dot

mote ['mote] NM (*apodo*) nickname

motín [mo'tin] NM (*del pueblo*) revolt, rising; (*del ejército*) mutiny

motivación [motiβa'θjon] NF motivation

motivar [moti'βar] /**1a**/ VT (*causar*) to cause, motivate; (*explicar*) to explain, justify

★**motivo** [mo'tiβo] NM motive, reason; (*Arte, Mus*) motif; **con ~ de** (*debido a*) because of; (*en ocasión de*) on the occasion of; (*con el fin de*) in order to; **sin ~** for no reason at all

★**moto** ['moto], **motocicleta** [motoθi'kleta] NF motorbike (BRIT), motorcycle

motociclista [motoθi'klista] NMF motorcyclist, biker

motoneta [moto'neta] NF (*Am*) (*motor*) scooter

★**motor, a** [mo'tor, a] ADJ (*Tec*) motive; (*Anat*) motor ▶ NM motor, engine ▶ NF motorboat; **~ a chorro** o **de reacción/de explosión** jet engine/ internal combustion engine; **~ de búsqueda** (*Internet*) search engine

motorismo [moto'rismo] NM motorcycling

motorista [moto'rista] NMF (*esp Am: automovilista*) motorist; (: *motociclista*) motorcyclist

motorizado, -a [motori'θaðo, a] ADJ motorized

motosierra [moto'sjerra] NF mechanical saw

motriz [mo'triθ] ADJ: **fuerza ~** motive power; (*fig*) driving force

movedizo, -a [moβe'ðiθo, a] ADJ (*inseguro*) unsteady; (*fig*) unsettled, changeable; (*persona*) fickle

★**mover** [mo'βer] /**2h**/ VT to move; (*cambiar de lugar*) to shift; (*cabeza: para negar*) to shake; (: *para asentir*) to nod; (*accionar*) to drive; (*fig*) to cause, provoke ■ **moverse** VR to move; (*mar*) to get rough; (*viento*) to rise; (*fig: apurarse*) to get a move on; (: *transformarse*) to be on the move

movible [mo'βiβle] ADJ (*no fijo*) movable; (*móvil*) mobile; (*cambiadizo*) changeable

movido, -a [mo'βiðo, a] ADJ (*Foto*) blurred; (*persona: activo*) active; (*mar*) rough; (*día*) hectic ▶ NF move; **la movida madrileña** the Madrid scene

★**móvil** ['moβil] ADJ mobile; (*pieza de máquina*) moving; (*mueble*) movable ▶ NM (*motivo*) motive; (*teléfono*) mobile (BRIT), cellphone (US)

movilice *etc* [moβi'liθe] VB *ver* **movilizar**

movilidad [moβili'ðað] NF mobility

movilizar [moβili'θar] /**1f**/ VT to mobilize

m

★**movimiento** [moβi'mjento] NM (gen, Lit, Pol) movement; (Tec) motion; (actividad) activity; (Mus) tempo; **el M~** the Falangist Movement; **~ de bloques** (Inform) block move; **~ de mercancías** (Com) turnover, volume of business; **~ obrero/sindical** workers'/trade union movement; **~ sísmico** earth tremor

Mozambique [moθam'bike] NM Mozambique

mozambiqueño, -a [moθambi'keɲo, a] ADJ, NM/F Mozambican

★**mozo, -a** ['moθo, a] ADJ (joven) young; (soltero) single, unmarried ▶ NM/F (joven) youth, young man (girl); (camarero) waiter; (camarera) waitress; **~ de estación** porter

MP3 NM MP3; **reproductor (de) ~** MP3 player

mucama [mu'kama] NF (Am) maid

★**muchacho, -a** [mu'tʃatʃo, a] NM/F (niño) boy/girl; (criado) servant/servant o maid

muchedumbre [mutʃe'ðumbre] NF crowd

muchísimo, -a [mu'tʃisimo, a] ADJ SUPERLATIVO de **mucho** lots and lots of, ever so much ▶ ADV ever so much

---

mucho, -a ['mutʃo, a]

ADJ **1** (cantidad) a lot of, much; (número) lots of, a lot of, many; **mucho dinero** a lot of money; **hace mucho calor** it's very hot; **muchas amigas** lots of o a lot of o many friends

2 (sg: fam): **esta es mucha casa para él** this house is much too big for him; **había mucho borracho** there were a lot o lots of drunks

▶ PRON: **tengo mucho que hacer** I've got a lot to do; **muchos dicen que ...** a lot of people say that ...; ver tb **tener**

▶ ADV **1**: **me gusta mucho** I like it a lot o very much; **lo siento mucho** I'm very sorry; **come mucho** he eats a lot; **trabaja mucho** he works hard; **¿te vas a quedar mucho?** are you going to be staying long?; **mucho más/menos** much o a lot more/less

2 (respuesta) very; **¿estás cansado? — ¡mucho!** are you tired? — very!

3 (locuciones): **como mucho** at (the) most; **el mejor con mucho** by far the best; **¡ni mucho menos!** far from it!; **no es rico ni mucho menos** he's far from rich

4: **por mucho que**: **por mucho que le creas** however much o no matter how much you believe him

---

Como traducción de mucho, tanto **many** como **a lot of** preceden a sustantivos en plural: Hay mucha gente que no está de acuerdo. **A lot of people** o **many people disagree**.
En el caso de sustantivos incontables se utilizan **much** o **a lot of**: No tenía mucho dinero. **He didn't have much money** o **a lot of money**.
En inglés hablado tiende a utilizarse **a lot of** en vez de **many** y **much**, especialmente en oraciones afirmativas.

---

muda ['muða] NF (de ropa) change of clothing; (Zool) moult; (de serpiente) slough

★**mudanza** [mu'ðanθa] NF (cambio) change; (de casa) move; **estar de ~** to be moving

mudar [mu'ðar] /1a/ VT to change; (Zool) to shed ▶ VI to change ■ **mudarse** VR (la ropa) to change; **mudarse de casa** to move house

mudo, -a ['muðo, a] ADJ with a speech impairment; (callado: película) silent; (Ling: letra) mute; (: consonante) voiceless; **quedarse ~ (de)** (fig) to be dumb with; **quedarse ~ de asombro** to be speechless

★**mueble** ['mweβle] NM piece of furniture ■ **muebles** NMPL furniture sg

mueble-bar [mweβle'βar] NM cocktail cabinet

mueca ['mweka] NF face, grimace; **hacer muecas a** to make faces at

★**muela** ['mwela] VB ver **moler** ▶ NF (diente) tooth; (: de atrás) back tooth; (de molino) millstone; (de afilar) grindstone; **~ del juicio** wisdom tooth

muelle ['mweʎe] ADJ (blando) soft; (fig) soft, easy ▶ NM spring; (Naut) wharf; (malecón) pier

muera etc ['mwera] VB ver **morir**

muerda etc ['mwerða] VB ver **morder**

muermo ['mwermo] NM (fam) wimp

★**muerte** ['mwerte] NF (death); (homicidio) murder; **dar ~ a** to kill; **de mala ~** (fam) lousy, rotten; **es la ~** (fam) it's deadly boring

★**muerto, -a** ['mwerto, a] PP de **morir** ▶ ADJ dead; (color) dull; **estar ~ de cansancio** to be dead tired; **fue ~ a tiros/en un accidente** he was shot (dead)/was killed in an accident ▶ NM/F dead man(-woman); (difunto) deceased; (cadáver) corpse; **cargar con el ~** (fam) to carry the can; **echar el ~ a algn** to pass the buck; **hacer el ~** (nadando) to float; **Día de los Muertos** (Am) Day of the Dead

---

The **Día de los Muertos** (Day of the Dead) in Mexico coincides with All Souls' Day, which is celebrated in the Catholic countries of Latin America on November 2nd. The Day of the Dead is actually a celebration which often now begins on the evening of October 31st and continues until November 2nd. It is a combination of the Catholic tradition of honouring the Christian saints and martyrs, and the ancient Mexican or Aztec traditions, in which death was not something sinister. For this reason, all the dead are honoured by bringing offerings of food, flowers, and candles to the cemetery.

---

muesca ['mweska] NF nick

muestra ['mwestra] VB ver **mostrar** ▶ NF (señal) indication, sign; (demostración) demonstration; (prueba) proof; (estadística) sample; (modelo) model, pattern; (testimonio) token; **~ al azar** (Com) random sample; **dar muestras de** to show signs of

muestrario [mwes'trarjo] NM collection of samples; (exposición) showcase

muestreo [mwes'treo] NM sample, sampling

muestro etc VB ver **mostrar**

muevo etc ['mweβo] VB ver **mover**

mugir [mu'xir] /3c/ VI (vaca) to moo

mugre ['muɣre] NF dirt, filth, muck

mugriento, -a [mu'ɣrjento, a] ADJ dirty, filthy, grubby

mugroso, -a [muɣ'roso, a] ADJ (Am) dirty, filthy, grubby

muja etc ['muxa] VB ver **mugir**

★**mujer** [mu'xer] NF woman; (esposa) wife

mujeriego [muxe'rjeɣo] NM womaniser

mula ['mula] NF mule

mulato, -a [mu'lato, a] ADJ, NM/F mulatto (!)

muleta [mu'leta] NF (para andar) crutch; (Taur) stick with red cape attached

muletilla [mule'tiʎa] NF (palabra) pet word, tag; (de cómico) catch phrase

mullido, -a [mu'ʎiðo, a] ADJ (cama) soft; (hierba) soft, springy

★**multa** ['multa] NF fine; **echar** o **poner una ~ a** to fine

multar [mul'tar] /1a/ VT to fine; (Deporte) to penalize

multiacceso [multjak'θeso] ADJ (Inform) multi-access

multicines [multi'θine] NMPL multiscreen cinema

multicolor [multiko'lor] ADJ multicoloured

multimillonario, -a [multimiʎo'narjo, a] ADJ (contrato) multimillion pound o dollar cpd ▶ NM/F multimillionaire/-millionairess

multinacional [multinaθjo'nal] ADJ, NF multinational

múltiple ['multiple] ADJ multiple, many pl, numerous; **de tarea ~** (Inform) multi-tasking; **de usuario ~** (Inform) multi-user

multiplicar [multipli'kar] /1g/ VT (Mat) to multiply; (fig) to increase ▪ **multiplicarse** VR (Bio) to multiply; (fig) to be everywhere at once

multiplique etc [multi'plike] VB ver **multiplicar**

múltiplo ['multiplo] ADJ, NM multiple

multitud [multi'tuð] NF (muchedumbre) crowd; **~ de** lots of

multitudinario, -a [multituði'narjo, a] ADJ (numeroso) multitudinous; (de masas) mass cpd

mundanal [munda'nal] ADJ worldly; **alejarse del ~ ruido** to get away from it all

mundano, -a [mun'dano, a] ADJ worldly; (de moda) fashionable

★**mundial** [mun'djal] ADJ world-wide, universal; (guerra, récord) world cpd

mundialización [mundjaliθa'θjon] NF globalization

mundialmente [mundjal'mente] ADV world-wide; **~ famoso** world-famous

★**mundo** ['mundo] NM world; (ámbito) world, circle; **el otro ~** the next world; **el ~ del espec-**

táculo show business; **todo el ~** everybody; **tener ~** to be experienced, know one's way around; **el ~ es un pañuelo** it's a small world; **no es nada del otro ~** it's nothing special; **se le cayó el ~ (encima)** his world fell apart

Munich ['munitʃ] NM Munich

munición [muni'θjon] NF (Mil: provisiones) stores pl, supplies pl; (: de armas) ammunition

★**municipal** [muniθi'pal] ADJ (elección) municipal; (concejo) town cpd, local; (piscina etc) public ▶ NM (guardia) policeman

municipio [muni'θipjo] NM (ayuntamiento) town council, corporation; (territorio administrativo) town, municipality

★**muñeca** [mu'ɲeka] NF (Anat) wrist; (juguete) doll

muñeco [mu'ɲeko] NM (figura) figure; (marioneta) puppet; (fig) puppet, pawn; (niño) pretty little boy; **~ de nieve** snowman

muñequera [muɲe'kera] NF wristband

muñón [mu'ɲon] NM (Anat) stump

mural [mu'ral] ADJ mural, wall cpd ▶ NM mural

muralla [mu'raʎa] NF (city) walls pl

murciano, -a [mur'θjano, a] ADJ of o from Murcia ▶ NM/F native o inhabitant of Murcia

murciélago [mur'θjelaɣo] NM bat

murga ['murɣa] NF (banda) band of street musicians; **dar la ~** to be a nuisance

murmullo [mur'muʎo] NM murmur(ing); (cuchicheo) whispering; (de arroyo) murmur, rippling; (de hojas, viento) rustle, rustling; (ruido confuso) hum(ming)

murmuración [murmura'θjon] NF gossip; (críticas) backbiting

murmurador, a [murmura'ðor, a] ADJ gossiping; (criticón) backbiting ▶ NM/F gossip; (criticón) backbiter

murmurar [murmu'rar] /1a/ VI to murmur, whisper; (criticar) to criticize; (cotillear) to gossip

★**muro** ['muro] NM wall; **~ de contención** retaining wall

mus [mus] NM card game

musaraña [musa'raɲa] NF (Zool) shrew; (insecto) creepy-crawly; **pensar en las musarañas** to daydream

muscular [musku'lar] ADJ muscular

músculo ['muskulo] NM muscle

musculoso, -a [musku'loso, a] ADJ muscular

★**museo** [mu'seo] NM museum; **~ de arte** o **de pintura** art gallery; **~ de cera** waxworks

En inglés, la palabra **museum** se refiere al lugar donde se exponen objetos de interés general o valor histórico o científico. Cuando lo que se exponen son cuadros, esculturas y, en general, objetos de valor artístico, se usa **gallery**.

musgo ['musɣo] NM moss

musical [musi'kal] ADJ, NM musical

m

★**músico, -a** ['musiko, a] ADJ musical ▶ NM/F musician ▶ NF music; **irse con la música a otra parte** to clear off

musitar [musi'tar] /1a/ VT, VI to mutter, mumble

muslo ['muslo] NM thigh; (*de pollo*) leg, drumstick

mustio, -a ['mustjo, a] ADJ (*persona*) depressed, gloomy; (*planta*) faded, withered

musulmán, -ana [musul'man, ana] NM/F Moslem, Muslim

mutación [muta'θjon] NF (*Bio*) mutation; (*cambio*) (sudden) change

mutilar [muti'lar] /1a/ VT to mutilate; (*a una persona*) to maim

mutis ['mutis] NM INV (*Teat*) exit; **hacer ~** (*Teat: retirarse*) to exit, go off; (*fig*) to say nothing

mutismo [mu'tismo] NM silence

mutualidad [mutwali'ðað] NF (*reciprocidad*) mutual character; (*asociación*) friendly o (*US*) benefit society

mutuamente [mutwa'mente] ADV mutually

mutuo, -a ['mutwo, a] ADJ mutual

★**muy** [mwi] ADV very; (*demasiado*) too; **M~ Señor mío** Dear Sir; **~ bien** (*de acuerdo*) all right; **~ de noche** very late at night; **eso es ~ de él** that's just like him; **eso es ~ español** that's typically Spanish

Nn

N, n ['ene] NF (letra) N, n; **N de Navarra** N for Nellie (BRIT) o Nan (US)

N ABR (= norte) N

N. ABR (= noviembre) Nov; = **carretera nacional**; (AM: = moneda nacional) local currency; **le entregaron solo N.\$2.000** they only gave him \$2000 pesos

N.º ABR (= número) No.

n. ABR (Ling: = nombre) n; = **nacido, a**

n/ ABR = **nuestro, a**

N.ª ABR = **Nuestra Señora**

nabo ['naβo] NM turnip

nácar ['nakar] NM mother-of-pearl

★**nacer** [na'θer] **/2d/** VI to be born; (huevo) to hatch; (vegetal) to sprout; (río) to rise; (fig) to begin, originate, have its origins; **nací en Barcelona** I was born in Barcelona; **nació para poeta** he was born to be a poet; **nadie nace enseñado** we all have to learn; **nació una sospecha en su mente** a suspicion formed in her mind

nacido, -a [na'θiðo, a] ADJ born; **recién ~** newborn

naciente [na'θjente] ADJ new, emerging; (sol) rising

★**nacimiento** [naθi'mjento] NM birth; (fig) birth, origin; (de Navidad) Nativity; (linaje) descent, family; (de río) source; **ciego de ~** blind from birth

★**nación** [na'θjon] NF nation; (pueblo) people; **Naciones Unidas** United Nations

nacional [naθjo'nal] ADJ national; (Com, Econ) domestic, home cpd

nacionalice etc [naθjona'liθe] VB ver **nacionalizar**

★**nacionalidad** [naθjonali'ðað] NF nationality; (Esp Pol) autonomous region

nacionalismo [naθjona'lismo] NM nationalism

nacionalista [naθjona'lista] ADJ, NMF nationalist

nacionalizar [naθjonali'θar] **/1f/** VT to nationalize ■ **nacionalizarse** VR (persona) to become naturalized

★**nada** ['naða] PRON nothing; **no decir ~ (más)** to say nothing (else), not to say anything (else); **¡~ más!** that's all; **de ~** don't mention it; **~ de eso** nothing of the kind; **antes de ~** right away ▶ ADV not at all, in no way; **como si ~** as if it didn't matter; **no ha sido ~** it's nothing ▶ NF nothingness; **la ~** the void

> Como traducción de nada, **nothing** se usa con el verbo en forma afirmativa: No podemos hacer nada. **There's nothing we can do**.
> **Anything**, en cambio, se usa con el verbo en forma negativa: **There isn't anything we can do**.
> Esto es debido a que en inglés se considera incorrecta la doble negación, de modo que **nothing** no debería aparecer junto a **not**, **never**, **none**, **hardly**, **without**, etc: Nunca dice nada. **He never says anything**.
> No hay que olvidar que **nothing** lleva el verbo en singular: No hay nada seguro. **Nothing is certain**.

nadador, a [naða'ðor, a] NM/F swimmer

★**nadar** [na'ðar] **/1a/** VI to swim; **~ en la abundancia** (fig) to be rolling in money

★**nadie** ['naðje] PRON nobody, no-one; **~ habló** nobody spoke; **no había ~** there was nobody there, there wasn't anybody there; **es un don ~** he's a nobody o nonentity

> Como traducción de nadie, **nobody** y **no-one** se usan con el verbo en forma afirmativa: No había nadie. **There was nobody there**.
> **Anybody** y **anyone** se usan, en cambio, con el verbo en forma negativa: No había nadie en el parque. **There wasn't anybody in the park**.
> Esto es debido a que en inglés se considera incorrecta la doble negación, de modo que **nobody** no debería aparecer junto a **not**,

n

never, **none**, **hardly**, **without**, etc: *Nunca viene nadie.* **Nobody ever comes**.
No hay que olvidar que **nobody** y **no-one** llevan el verbo en singular.

nadita [na'ðita] (*esp Am fam*) = **nada**

nado ['naðo]: **a ~** *adv*: **pasar a ~** to swim across

nafta ['nafta] NF (*Am*) petrol (*Brit*), gas(oline) (*US*)

naftalina [nafta'lina] NF: **bolas de ~** mothballs

náhuatl ['nawatl] ADJ, NM Nahuatl

★**naipe** ['naipe] NM (playing) card ■ **naipes** NMPL cards

nal. ABR (= *nacional*) nat

nalgas ['nalɣas] NFPL buttocks

nalguear [nalɣe'ar] /**1a**/ VT (*Am*, *Cam*) to spank

Namibia [na'miβja] NF Namibia

nana ['nana] NF lullaby

nanopartícula [nanopar'tikula] NF nanoparticle

napias ['napjas] NFPL (*fam*) conk *sg*

Nápoles ['napoles] NF Naples

napolitano, -a [napoli'tano, a] ADJ of *o* from Naples, Neapolitan ▶ NM/F Neapolitan

★**naranja** [na'ranxa] ADJ INV, NF orange; **media ~** (*fam*) better half; **¡naranjas de la China!** nonsense!

naranjada [naran'xaða] NF orangeade

naranjo [na'ranxo] NM orange tree

Narbona [nar'βona] NF Narbonne

narcisista [narθi'sista] ADJ narcissistic

narciso [nar'θiso] NM narcissus

narcotice *etc* [narko'tiθe] VB *ver* **narcotizar**

narcótico, -a [nar'kotiko, a] ADJ, NM narcotic

narcotizar [narkoti'θar] /**1f**/ VT to drug

narcotraficante [narkotrafi'kante] NMF narcotics *o* drug trafficker

narcotráfico [narko'trafiko] NM narcotics *o* drug trafficking

nardo ['narðo] NM lily

narices [na'riθes] NFPL *ver* **nariz**

narigón, -ona [nari'ɣon, ona], **narigudo, -a** [nari'ɣuðo, a] ADJ big-nosed

★**nariz** [na'riθ] NF nose; **~ chata/respingona** snub/turned-up nose ■ **narices** NFPL nostrils; **¡narices!** (*fam*) rubbish!; **delante de las narices de algn** under one's (very) nose; **estar hasta las narices** to be completely fed up; **meter las narices en algo** to poke one's nose into sth

narración [narra'θjon] NF narration

narrador, a [narra'ðor, a] NM/F narrator

narrar [na'rrar] /**1a**/ VT to narrate, recount

narrativo, -a [narra'tiβo, a] ADJ narrative ▶ NF narrative, story

nasal [na'sal] ADJ nasal

★**nata** ['nata] NF cream (*tb fig*); (*en leche cocida etc*) skin; **~ batida** whipped cream

★**natación** [nata'θjon] NF swimming

natal [na'tal] ADJ natal; (*país*) native; **ciudad ~** home town

natalicio [nata'liθjo] NM birthday

natalidad [natali'ðað] NF birth rate

natillas [na'tiʎas] NFPL (egg) custard *sg*

natividad [natiβi'ðað] NF nativity

nativo, -a [na'tiβo, a] ADJ, NM/F native

nato, -a ['nato, a] ADJ born; **un músico ~** a born musician

★**natural** [natu'ral] ADJ natural; (*fruta etc*) fresh ▶ NMF native ▶ NM disposition, temperament; **buen ~** good nature; **fruta al ~** fruit in its own juice

★**naturaleza** [natura'leθa] NF nature; (*género*) nature, kind; **~ muerta** still life

naturalice *etc* [natura'liθe] VB *ver* **naturalizarse**

naturalidad [naturali'ðað] NF naturalness

naturalización [naturaliθa'θjon] NF naturalization

naturalizarse [naturali'θarse] /**1f**/ VR to become naturalized; (*aclimatarse*) to become acclimatized

naturalmente [natural'mente] ADV naturally; (*de modo natural*) in a natural way; **¡~!** of course!

naturista [natu'rista] ADJ (*Med*) naturopathic ▶ NMF naturopath

naufragar [naufra'ɣar] /**1h**/ VI (*barco*) to sink; (*gente*) to be shipwrecked; (*fig*) to fail

naufragio [nau'fraxjo] NM shipwreck

náufrago, -a ['naufraɣo, a] NM/F castaway, shipwrecked person

naufrague *etc* [nau'fraɣe] VB *ver* **naufragar**

Nauru [na'uru] NM Nauru

náusea ['nausea] NF nausea; **me da náuseas** it makes me feel sick

nauseabundo, -a [nausea'βundo, a] ADJ nauseating, sickening

náutico, -a ['nautiko, a] ADJ nautical; **club ~** sailing *o* yacht club ▶ NF navigation, seamanship

navaja [na'βaxa] NF (*cortaplumas*) clasp knife (*Brit*), penknife; **~ (de afeitar)** razor

navajazo [naβa'xaθo] NM (*herida*) gash; (*acto*) slash

naval [na'βal] ADJ (*Mil*) naval; **construcción ~** shipbuilding; **sector ~** shipbuilding industry

Navarra [na'βarra] NF Navarre

navarro, -a [na'βarro, a] ADJ of *o* from Navarre, Navarrese ▶ NM/F Navarrese ▶ NM (*Ling*) Navarrese

nave ['naβe] NF (*barco*) ship, vessel; (*Arq*) nave; **~ espacial** spaceship; **quemar las naves** to burn one's boats; **~ industrial** factory premises *pl*

navegación [naβeɣa'θjon] NF navigation; (*viaje*) sea journey; **~ aérea** air traffic; **~ cos-**

tera coastal shipping; **~ fluvial** river navigation

navegador [naβeɣa'ðor] NM (*Inform*) browser; (*de coche*) sat nav

navegante [naβe'ɣante] NMF navigator

★**navegar** [naβe'ɣar] /**1h**/ VI (*barco*) to sail; (*avión*) to fly; **~ por Internet** to surf the Net ▶ VT to sail; to fly; (*dirigir el rumbo de*) to navigate

navegue *etc* [na'βeɣe] VB *ver* **navegar**

★**Navidad** [naβi'ðað] NF Christmas; **día de ~** Christmas Day; **¡Feliz ~!** Merry Christmas! ■ **Navidades** NFPL Christmas time *sg*; **por Navidades** at Christmas (time)

navideño, -a [naβi'ðeɲo, a] ADJ Christmas *cpd*

navío [na'βio] NM ship

nazca *etc* VB *ver* **nacer**

nazi ['naθi] ADJ, NMF Nazi

nazismo [na'θismo] NM Nazism

N. de la R. ABR (= *nota de la redacción*) editor's note

N. de la T./del T. ABR (= *nota de la traductora/del traductor*) translator's note

NE ABR (= *nor(d)este*) NE

★**neblina** [ne'βlina] NF mist

nebuloso, -a [neβu'loso, a] ADJ foggy; (*calinoso*) misty; (*indefinido*) nebulous, vague ▶ NF nebula

necedad [neθe'ðað] NF foolishness; (*una necedad*) foolish act

★**necesario, -a** [neθe'sarjo, a] ADJ necessary; **si fuera** *o* **fuese ~** if need(s) be

neceser [neθe'ser] NM toilet bag; (*bolsa grande*) holdall

★**necesidad** [neθesi'ðað] NF need; (*lo inevitable*) necessity; (*miseria*) poverty, need; **en caso de ~** in case of need *o* emergency; **hacer sus necesidades** to relieve o.s.

necesitado, -a [neθesi'taðo, a] ADJ needy, poor; **~ de** in need of

★**necesitar** [neθesi'tar] /**1a**/ VT to need, require ▶ VI: **~ de** to have need of ■ **necesitarse** VR to be needed; (*en anuncios*): **"se necesita coche"** "car wanted"

necio, -a ['neθjo, a] ADJ foolish ▶ NM/F fool

necrología [nekrolo'xia] NF obituary

necrópolis [ne'kropolis] NF INV cemetery

néctar ['nektar] NM nectar

nectarina [nekta'rina] NF nectarine

neerlandés, -esa [neerlan'des, esa] ADJ Dutch ▶ NM/F Dutchman(-woman); **los neerlandeses** the Dutch ▶ NM (*Ling*) Dutch

nefando, -a [ne'fando, a] ADJ unspeakable

nefasto, -a [ne'fasto, a] ADJ ill-fated, unlucky

negación [neɣa'θjon] NF negation; (*Ling*) negative; (*rechazo*) refusal, denial

negado, -a [ne'ɣaðo, a] ADJ: **~ para** inept at, unfitted for

★**negar** [ne'ɣar] /**1h, 1j**/ VT (*renegar, rechazar*) to refuse; (*prohibir*) to refuse, deny; (*desmentir*) to deny ■ **negarse** VR: **negarse a hacer algo** to refuse to do sth

★**negativo, -a** [neɣa'tiβo, a] ADJ negative ▶ NM (*Foto*) negative; (*Mat*) minus ▶ NF (*gen*) negative; (*rechazo*) refusal, denial; **negativa rotunda** flat refusal

negligencia [neɣli'xenθja] NF negligence

negligente [neɣli'xente] ADJ negligent

negociable [neɣo'θjaβle] ADJ negotiable

★**negociación** [neɣoθja'θjon] NF negotiation

negociado [neɣo'θjaðo] NM department, section

negociante [neɣo'θjante] NMF businessman(-woman)

negociar [neɣo'θjar] /**1b**/ VT, VI to negotiate; **~ en** to deal in, trade in

★**negocio** [ne'ɣoθjo] NM (*Com*) business; (*asunto*) affair, business; (*operación comercial*) deal, transaction; (*Am*) shop, store; (*lugar*) place of business; **los negocios** business *sg*; **hacer ~** to do business; **el ~ del libro** the book trade; **~ autorizado** licensed trade; **hombre de negocios** businessman; **~ sucio** shady deal; **hacer un buen ~** to pull off a profitable deal; **¡mal ~!** it looks bad!

negra ['neɣra] NF (*Mus*) crotchet; *ver tb* **negro**

negrita [ne'ɣrita] NF (*Tip*) bold face; **en ~** in bold (type)

★**negro, -a** ['neɣro, a] ADJ black; (*suerte*) awful, atrocious; (*humor etc*) sad; (*lúgubre*) gloomy; **~ como la boca del lobo** pitch-black; **estoy ~ con esto** I'm getting desperate about it; **ponerse ~** (*fam*) to get cross ▶ NM (*color*) black ▶ NM/F black person ▶ NF (*Mus*) crotchet

negrura [ne'ɣrura] NF blackness

negué [ne'ɣe], **neguemos** *etc* [ne'ɣemos] VB *ver* **negar**

nene, -a ['nene, a] NM/F baby, small child

nenúfar [ne'nufar] NM water lily

neologismo [neolo'xismo] NM neologism

neón [ne'on] NM neon; **luces/lámpara de ~** neon lights/lamp

neopreno [neo'preno] NM neoprene

neoyorquino, -a [neojor'kino, a] ADJ New York *cpd* ▶ NM/F New Yorker

neozelandés, -esa [neoθelan'des, esa] ADJ New Zealand *cpd* ▶ NM/F New Zealander

nepotismo [nepo'tismo] NM nepotism

nervio ['nerβjo] NM (*Anat*) nerve; (: *tendón*) tendon; (*fig*) vigour; (*Tec*) rib; **crispar los nervios a algn, poner los nervios de punta a algn** to get on sb's nerves

nerviosismo [nerβjo'sismo] NM nervousness, nerves *pl*

★**nervioso, -a** [ner'βjoso, a] ADJ nervous; (*sensible*) nervy, highly-strung; (*impaciente*) restless; **¡no te pongas ~!** take it easy!

nervudo, -a [ner'βuðo, a] ADJ tough; (*mano*) sinewy

netiqueta [neti'keta] NF netiquette

neto, -a ['neto, a] ADJ clear; (*limpio*) clean; (*Com*) net

★**neumático, -a** [neu'matiko, a] ADJ pneumatic ▶ NM (*ESP*) tyre (*BRIT*), tire (*US*); **~ de recambio** spare tyre

neumonía [neumo'nia] NF pneumonia; **~ asiática** SARS

neura ['neura] NF (*fam: obsesión*) obsession

neuralgia [neu'ralxja] NF neuralgia

neurálgico, -a [neu'ralxiko, a] ADJ neuralgic; (*fig: centro*) nerve *cpd*

neurastenia [neuras'tenja] NF neurasthenia; (*fig*) excitability

neurasténico, -a [neuras'teniko, a] ADJ neurasthenic; (*fig*) excitable

neurólogo, -a [neu'roloɣo, a] NM/F neurologist

neurona [neu'rona] NF neuron

neurosis [neu'rosis] NF INV neurosis

neurótico, -a [neu'rotiko, a] ADJ, NM/F neurotic

neutral [neu'tral] ADJ neutral

neutralice *etc* [neutra'liθe] VB *ver* **neutralizar**

neutralizar [neutrali'θar] /**1f**/ VT to neutralize; (*contrarrestar*) to counteract

neutro, -a ['neutro, a] ADJ (*Bio*, *Ling*) neuter; **~ en carbono** carbon-neutral

neutrón [neu'tron] NM neutron

nevado, -a [ne'βaðo, a] ADJ snow-covered; (*montaña*) snow-capped; (*fig*) snowy, snow-white ▶ NF (*tormenta*) snowstorm; (*caída de nieve*) snowfall

★**nevar** [ne'βar] /**1j**/ VI to snow ▶ VT (*fig*) to whiten

★**nevera** [ne'βera] NF (*ESP*) refrigerator (*BRIT*), icebox (*US*)

nevería [neβe'ria] NF (*AM*) ice-cream parlour

nevisca [ne'βiska] NF flurry of snow

nexo ['nekso] NM link, connection

n/f ABR (*Com*) = **nuestro favor**

★**ni** [ni] CONJ nor, neither; (*tb*: **ni siquiera**) not even; **ni que** not even if; **ni blanco ni negro** neither white nor black; **ni el uno ni el otro** neither one nor the other

Nicaragua [nika'raɣwa] NF Nicaragua

nicaragüense [nikara'ɣwense] ADJ, NMF Nicaraguan

nicho ['nitʃo] NM niche

nick [nik] NM (*Internet*) nickname, user name, nick

nicotina [niko'tina] NF nicotine

nido ['niðo] NM nest; (*fig*) hiding place; **~ de ladrones** den of thieves

★**niebla** ['njeβla] NF fog; (*neblina*) mist; **hay ~** it is foggy

niego *etc* ['njeɣo], **niegue** *etc* ['njeɣe] VB *ver* **negar**

★**nieto, -a** ['njeto, a] NM/F grandson/grand-daughter ∎ **nietos** NMPL grandchildren

★**nieve** ['njeβe] VB *ver* **nevar** ▶ NF snow; (*AM*) ice cream; **copo de ~** snowflake

N.I.F. [nif] NM ABR (= *Número de Identificación Fiscal*) ID number used for tax purposes

Nigeria [ni'xerja] NF Nigeria

nigeriano, -a [nixe'rjano, a] ADJ, NM/F Nigerian

nigromancia [niɣro'manθja] NF necromancy, black magic

nihilista [nii'lista] ADJ nihilistic ▶ NMF nihilist

Nilo ['nilo] NM: **el (río) ~** the Nile

nimbo ['nimbo] NM (*aureola*) halo; (*nube*) nimbus

nimiedad [nimje'ðað] NF small-mindedness; (*trivialidad*) triviality; (*una nimiedad*) trifle, tiny detail

nimio, -a ['nimjo, a] ADJ trivial, insignificant

ninfa ['ninfa] NF nymph

ninfómana [nin'fomana] NF nymphomaniac

ningún [nin'ɣun] ADJ *ver* **ninguno**

★**ninguno, -a** [nin'ɣuno, a] ADJ (*antes de nmsg*: **ningún**) no; **de ninguna manera** by no means, not at all; **no voy a ninguna parte** I'm not going anywhere ▶ PRON (*nadie*) nobody; (*ni uno*) none, not one; (*ni uno ni otro*) neither

---

El adjetivo *ninguno* se traduce por **no** si el verbo está en forma afirmativa: *No tengo ningún interés en ir.* **I have no interest in going.**
Si está en forma negativa se traduce por **any**: *No practico ningún deporte.* **I don't play any sports.**
El pronombre *ninguno* se traduce por **none**: *No me queda ninguno.* **I have none left.**
Ninguno de nosotros va a ir a la fiesta. **None of us is going to the party.**
A no ser que se refiera a solo dos personas o cosas, en cuyo caso se traduce por **neither** si el verbo está en forma afirmativa: *No vino ninguno de los dos.* **Neither of them came.**
Si el verbo está en forma negativa se traduce por **either**: *No vi a ninguno de los dos.* **I didn't see either of them.**

---

nini ['nini] ADJ (*fam*) NEET; **la generación ~** the NEET generation ▶ NMF ≈ NEET

★**niña** ['niɲa] NF *ver* **niño**

niñera [ni'ɲera] NF nursemaid, nanny

niñería [niɲe'ria] NF childish act

★**niñez** [ni'ɲeθ] NF childhood; (*infancia*) infancy

★**niño, -a** ['niɲo, a] ADJ (*joven*) young; (*inmaduro*) immature ▶ NM/F (*chico*) boy, child; (*chica*) girl, child; **los niños** the children; **~ bien** rich kid; **~ expósito** foundling; **~ de pecho** babe-in-arms; **~ prodigio** child prodigy; **ser el ~ mimado de algn** to be sb's pet; **de ~** as a child ▶ NF (*Anat*) pupil; **ser la niña de los ojos de algn** to be the apple of sb's eye

nipón, -ona [ni'pon, ona] ADJ, NM/F Japanese; **los nipones** the Japanese

níquel ['nikel] NM nickel

niquelar [nike'lar] /**1a**/ VT (Tec) to nickel-plate

níspero ['nispero] NM loquat

nitidez [niti'ðeθ] NF (claridad) clarity; (: de atmósfera) brightness; (: de imagen) sharpness

nítido, -a ['nitiðo, a] ADJ bright; (fig) pure; (imagen) clear, sharp

nitrato [ni'trato] NM nitrate

nitrógeno [ni'troxeno] NM nitrogen

nitroglicerina [nitroɣliθe'rina] NF nitroglycerine

★**nivel** [ni'βel] NM (Geo) level; (norma) level, standard; (altura) height; **~ de aceite** oil level; **~ de aire** spirit level; **~ de vida** standard of living; **al ~ de** on a level with, at the same height as; (fig) on a par with; **a 900 m sobre el ~ del mar** at 900 m above sea level

nivelado, -a [niβe'laðo, a] ADJ level, flat; (Tec) flush

nivelar [niβe'lar] /**1a**/ VT to level out; (fig) to even up; (Com) to balance

Niza ['niθa] NF Nice

n/l. ABR (Com) = **nuestra letra**

NNE ABR (= nornordeste) NNE

NNO ABR (= nornoroeste) NNW

NO ABR (= noroeste) NW

★**no** [no] ADV no; (con verbo) not; **no tengo nada** I don't have anything, I have nothing; **no es el mío** it's not mine; **ahora no** not now; **¿no lo sabes?** don't you know?; **no mucho** not much; **no bien termine, lo entregaré** as soon as I finish, I'll hand it over; **ayer no más** just yesterday; **¡pase no más!** come in!; **¡a que no lo sabes!** I bet you don't know!; **¡cómo no!** of course!; **pacto de no agresión** non-aggression pact; **los países no alineados** the non-aligned countries; **el no va más** the ultimate; **la no intervención** non-intervention ▶ EXCL no!

n/o ABR (Com) = **nuestra orden**

noble ['noβle] ADJ, NMF noble; **los nobles** the nobility sg

nobleza [noβ'leθa] NF nobility

★**noche** ['notʃe] NF night, night-time; (la tarde) evening; (fig) darkness; **de ~, por la ~** at night; **ayer por la ~** last night; **esta ~** tonight; **(en) toda la ~** all night; **hacer ~ en un sitio** to spend the night in a place; **se hace de ~** it's getting dark; **es de ~** it's dark; **ver tb San Juan**

★**Nochebuena** [notʃe'βwena] NF Christmas Eve

In Spanish-speaking countries, families come together for **Nochebuena** (Christmas Eve) to share a special meal. The more religiously inclined attend la misa del gallo (midnight mass). Although, traditionally, presents are given on el Día de Reyes (the feast of the Three Kings) on the 6th of January, children also now tend to receive presents from Santa Claus on Christmas Day.

★**Nochevieja** [notʃe'βjexa] NF New Year's Eve; ver tb **uva**

In Spain, the campanadas, the 12 chimes that ring out from the clock at the Puerta del Sol in Madrid, which are broadcast live to mark the start of the New Year, and are the peak point of the **Nochevieja** (New Year's Eve) celebrations. When the clock strikes midnight, the tradition known as las uvas de la suerte or las doce uvas, involves eating 12 grapes, one per each stroke.

noción [no'θjon] NF notion ■ **nociones** NFPL elements, rudiments

nocivo, -a [no'θiβo, a] ADJ harmful

noctambulismo [noktambu'lismo] NM sleepwalking

noctámbulo, -a [nok'tambulo, a] NM/F sleepwalker

nocturno, -a [nok'turno, a] ADJ (de la noche) nocturnal, night cpd; (de la tarde) evening cpd ▶ NM nocturne

Noé [no'e] NM Noah

nogal [no'ɣal] NM walnut tree; (madera) walnut

nómada ['nomaða] ADJ nomadic ▶ NMF nomad

nomás [no'mas] (AM) ADV (gen) just; (tan solo) only; **así ~** (fam) just like that; **ayer ~** only yesterday ▶ CONJ (en cuanto): **~ se fue se acordó** she remembered as soon as she left

nombramiento [nombra'mjento] NM naming; (para un empleo) appointment; (Pol etc) nomination; (Mil) commission

nombrar [nom'brar] /**1a**/ VT (gen) to name; (mencionar) to mention; (designar) to appoint, nominate; (Mil) to commission

★**nombre** ['nombre] NM name; (sustantivo) noun; (fama) renown; **~ y apellidos** name in full; **poner ~ a** to call, name; **~ común/propio** common/proper noun; **~ de pila/de soltera** Christian/maiden name; **~ de usuario** (Inform) username; **~ de fichero** (Inform) file name; **en ~ de** in the name of, on behalf of; **sin ~** nameless; **su conducta no tiene ~** his behaviour is utterly despicable

nomenclatura [nomenkla'tura] NF nomenclature

nomeolvides [nomeol'βiðes] NM INV forget-me-not

nómina ['nomina] NF (lista) list; (Com: tb: **nóminas**) payroll; (hoja) payslip

nominal [nomi'nal] ADJ nominal; (valor) face cpd; (Ling) noun cpd, substantival

nominar [nomi'nar] /**1a**/ VT to nominate

nominativo, -a [nomina'tiβo, a] ADJ (Ling) nominative; (Com): **un cheque ~ a X** a cheque made out to X

non [non] ADJ odd, uneven ▶ NM odd number; **pares y nones** odds and evens

nonagésimo, -a [nona'xesimo, a] NUM ninetieth

nono, -a ['nono, a] NUM ninth

nordeste [nor'ðeste] ADJ north-east, north-eastern, north-easterly ▶ NM north-east; (viento) north-east wind, north-easterly

nórdico, -a ['norðiko, a] ADJ (*del norte*) northern, northerly; (*escandinavo*) Nordic, Norse ▶ NM/F northerner; (*escandinavo*) Norseman/-woman ▶ NM (*Ling*) Norse

★**noreste** [no'reste] ADJ, NM = **nordeste**

noria ['norja] NF (*Agr*) waterwheel; (*de feria*) big (BRIT) o Ferris (US) wheel

★**norma** ['norma] NF standard, norm, rule; (*patrón*) pattern; (*método*) method

★**normal** [nor'mal] ADJ (*corriente*) normal; (*habitual*) usual, natural; (*Tec*) standard; **Escuela N~** teacher training college; **(gasolina) ~** two-star petrol

normalice *etc* [norma'liθe] VB *ver* **normalizar**

normalidad [normali'ðað] NF normality

normalización [normaliθa'θjon] NF (*Com*) standardization

normalizar [normali'θar] /**1f**/ VT (*reglamentar*) to normalize; (*Com, Tec*) to standardize ■ **normalizarse** VR to return to normal

★**normalmente** [normal'mente] ADV (*con normalidad*) normally; (*habitualmente*) usually

Normandía [norman'dia] NF Normandy

normando, -a [nor'mando, a] ADJ, NM/F Norman

normativo, -a [norma'tiβo, a] ADJ: **es ~ en todos los coches nuevos** it is standard in all new cars ▶ NF rules *pl*, regulations *pl*

★**noroeste** [noro'este] ADJ north-west, north-western, north-westerly ▶ NM north-west; (*viento*) north-west wind, north-westerly

★**norte** ['norte] ADJ north, northern, northerly ▶ NM north; (*fig*) guide

Norteamérica [nortea'merika] NF North America

★**norteamericano, -a** [norteameri'kano, a] ADJ, NM/F (North) American

norteño, -a [nor'teɲo, a] ADJ northern ▶ NM/F northerner

Noruega [no'rweɣa] NF Norway

noruego, -a [no'rweɣo, a] ADJ, NM/F Norwegian ▶ NM (*Ling*) Norwegian

nos [nos] PRON (*directo*) us; (*indirecto*) (to) us; (*reflexivo*) (to) ourselves; (*recíproco*) (to) each other; **ayer ~ levantamos a las siete** we got up at seven yesterday

nosocomio [noso'komjo] NM (*Am*) hospital

nosotros, -as [no'sotros, as] PRON (*sujeto*) we; (*después de prep*) us; **~ (mismos)** ourselves

nostalgia [nos'talxja] NF nostalgia, homesickness

nostálgico, -a [nos'talxiko, a] ADJ nostalgic, homesick

★**nota** ['nota] NF note; (*Escol*) mark; (*de fin de año*) report; (*Univ etc*) footnote; (*Com*) account; **~ de aviso** advice note; **~ de crédito/débito** credit/debit note; **~ de gastos** expenses claim; **~ de sociedad** gossip column; **tomar notas** to take notes

notable [no'taβle] ADJ noteworthy, notable; (*Escol etc*) outstanding ▶ NMF notable

★**notar** [no'tar] /**1a**/ VT to notice, note; (*percibir*) to feel; (*ver*) to see ■ **notarse** VR to be obvious; **se nota que ...** you can tell that ...

notaría [nota'ria] NF (*profesión*) profession of notary; (*despacho*) notary's office

notarial [nota'rjal] ADJ (*estilo*) legal; **acta ~** affidavit

notario [no'tarjo] NM notary; (*abogado*) solicitor

★**noticia** [no'tiθja] NF (*información*) piece of news; (*TV etc*) news item; **las noticias** the news *sg*; **según nuestras noticias** according to our information; **tener noticias de algn** to hear from sb

---

Aunque a veces se confunde *noticia* con **notice**, esta palabra inglesa significa *letrero*: *El letrero dice 'prohibida la entrada'.* **The notice says 'keep out'.**
Frases como ¿*Hay alguna noticia?* se traducen utilizando el sustantivo **news**: **Any news?**

---

noticiario [noti'θjarjo] NM (*Cine*) newsreel; (*TV*) news bulletin

noticiero [noti'θjero] NM newspaper, gazette; (*Am: tb:* **noticiero telediario**) news bulletin

notificación [notifika'θjon] NF notification

notificar [notifi'kar] /**1g**/ VT to notify, inform

notifique *etc* [noti'fike] VB *ver* **notificar**

notoriedad [notorje'ðað] NF fame, renown

notorio, -a [no'torjo, a] ADJ (*público*) well-known; (*evidente*) obvious

nov. ABR (= *noviembre*) Nov.

novatada [noβa'taða] NF (*burla*) teasing, hazing (US); **pagar la ~** to learn the hard way

★**novato, -a** [no'βato, a] ADJ inexperienced ▶ NM/F beginner, novice

novecientos, -as [noβe'θjentos, as] NUM nine hundred

novedad [noβe'ðað] NF (*calidad de nuevo*) newness, novelty; (*noticia*) piece of news; (*cambio*) change, (new) development; (*sorpresa*) surprise ■ **novedades** NFPL (*noticia*) latest (news) *sg*

novedoso, -a [noβe'ðoso, a] ADJ novel

novel [no'βel] ADJ new; (*inexperto*) inexperienced ▶ NMF beginner

★**novela** [no'βela] NF novel; **~ policíaca** detective story

novelero, -a [noβe'lero, a] ADJ highly imaginative

novelesco, -a [noβe'lesko, a] ADJ fictional; (*romántico*) romantic; (*fantástico*) fantastic

novelista [noβe'lista] NMF novelist

novelística [noβe'listika] NF: **la ~** fiction, the novel

★**noveno, -a** [no'βeno, a] NUM ninth

★**noventa** [no'βenta] NUM ninety

★**novia** ['noβja] NF *ver* **novio**

★**noviazgo** [no'βjaθɣo] NM engagement

novicio, -a [no'βiθjo, a] NM/F novice

★**noviembre** [no'βjembre] NM November; *ver tb* **julio**

novilla [no'βiʎa] NF heifer

novillada [noβi'ʎaða] NF (*Taur*) bullfight with young bulls

novillero [noβi'ʎero] NM novice bullfighter

novillo [no'βiʎo] NM young bull, bullock; **hacer novillos** (*fam*) to play truant (*BRIT*) o hooky (*US*)

★**novio, -a** ['noβjo, a] NM/F boyfriend (girlfriend); (*prometido*) fiancé (fiancée); (*recién casado*) bridegroom (bride); **los novios** the newly-weds

novísimo, -a [no'βisimo, a] ADJ SUPERLATIVO *de* **nuevo**

N. S. ABR = **Nuestro Señor**

ns/nc ABR = **no sabe(n)/no contesta(n)**

ntra., ntro. ABR = **nuestra, nuestro**

Ntro. Sr. ABR = **Nuestro Señor**

nubarrón [nuβa'rron] NM storm cloud

★**nube** ['nuβe] NF cloud; (*Med: ocular*) cloud, film; (*fig*) mass; **una ~ de críticas** a storm of criticism; **los precios están por las nubes** prices are sky-high; **estar en las nubes** to be away with the fairies

★**nublado, -a** [nu'βlaðo, a] ADJ cloudy ▶ NM storm cloud

nublar [nu'βlar] /1a/ VT (*oscurecer*) to darken; (*confundir*) to cloud ■ **nublarse** VR to cloud over

★**nuboso, -a** [nu'βoso, a] ADJ cloudy

nuca ['nuka] NF nape of the neck

★**nuclear** [nukle'ar] ADJ nuclear

nuclearizado, -a [nukleari'θaðo, a] ADJ: **países nuclearizados** countries possessing nuclear weapons

núcleo ['nukleo] NM (*centro*) core; (*Física*) nucleus; **~ urbano** city centre

nudillo [nu'ðiʎo] NM knuckle

nudista [nu'dista] ADJ, NMF nudist

nudo ['nuðo] NM knot; (*unión*) bond; (*de problema*) crux; (*Ferro*) junction; (*fig*) lump; **~ corredizo** slipknot; **con un ~ en la garganta** with a lump in one's throat

nudoso, -a [nu'ðoso, a] ADJ knotty; (*tronco*) gnarled; (*bastón*) knobbly

nueces ['nweθes] NFPL *de* **nuez**

nuera ['nwera] NF daughter-in-law

★**nuestro, -a** ['nwestro, a] ADJ POSESIVO our; **~ padre** our father; **un amigo ~** a friend of ours ▶ PRON ours; **es el ~** it's ours; **los nuestros** our people; (*Deporte*) our o the local team o side

nueva ['nweβa] NF *ver* **nuevo**

Nueva Escocia NF Nova Scotia

nuevamente [nweβa'mente] ADV (*otra vez*) again; (*de nuevo*) anew

Nueva York [-'jork] NF New York

Nueva Zelanda [-θe'landa], **Nueva Zelandia** [-θe'landja] NF New Zealand

★**nueve** ['nweβe] NUM nine

★**nuevo, -a** ['nweβo, a] ADJ (*gen*) new; **de ~** again; **¿qué hay de ~?** (*fam*) what's new? ▶ NF piece of news

Nuevo México NM New Mexico

★**nuez** [nweθ] (*pl* **nueces**) NF nut; (*del nogal*) walnut; **~ de Adán** Adam's apple; **~ moscada** nutmeg

nulidad [nuli'ðað] NF (*incapacidad*) incompetence; (*abolición*) nullity; (*individuo*) nonentity; **es una ~** he's a dead loss

nulo, -a ['nulo, a] ADJ (*inepto, torpe*) useless; (*inválido*) (null and) void; (*Deporte*) drawn, tied

núm. ABR (= *número*) no.

numen ['numen] NM inspiration

numeración [numera'θjon] NF (*cifras*) numbers pl; (*arábiga, romana etc*) numerals pl; **~ de línea** (*Inform*) line numbering

numerador [numera'ðor] NM (*Mat*) numerator

numeral [nume'ral] NM numeral

numerar [nume'rar] /1a/ VT to number ■ **numerarse** VR (*Mil etc*) to number off

numerario, -a [nume'rarjo, a] ADJ numerary; **profesor** o **permanent** o tenured member of teaching staff ▶ NM hard cash

numérico, -a [nu'meriko, a] ADJ numerical

★**número** ['numero] NM (*gen*) number; (*tamaño: de zapato*) size; (*ejemplar: de diario*) number, issue; (*Teat etc*) turn, act, number; **sin ~** numberless, unnumbered; **~ binario** (*Inform*) binary number; **~ de matrícula/de teléfono** registration/telephone number; **~ personal de identificación** (*Inform etc*) personal identification number; **~ impar/par** odd/even number; **~ romano** Roman numeral; **~ de serie** (*Com*) serial number; **~ atrasado** back number

numeroso, -a [nume'roso, a] ADJ numerous; **familia numerosa** large family

numerus ['numerus] NM: **~ clausus** (*Univ*) restricted o selective entry

★**nunca** ['nunka] ADV (*jamás*) never; (*con verbo negativo*) ever; **~ lo pensé** I never thought it; **no viene ~** he never comes; **~ más** never again; **más que ~** more than ever

> Como traducción de *nunca*, **never** se usa con el verbo en forma afirmativa: *Últimamente nunca voy al cine*. **I never go to the cinema these days.**
> En cambio, **ever** se usa con el verbo en forma negativa: *Nunca ha estado en París*. **He hasn't ever been to Paris.**
> Esto es debido a que la doble negación se considera incorrecta en inglés, de modo que **never** no puede aparecer junto a **not**, **nothing**, **none**, **hardly**, **without**, etc: *Nunca dice nada*. **He never says anything.**
> **Ever** se utiliza también en frases enfáticas: *¡No vuelvas nunca jamás!* **Don't ever come here again!**

nuncio ['nunθjo] NM (*Rel*) nuncio

nupcial [nup'θjal] ADJ wedding *cpd*

nupcias ['nupθjas] NFPL wedding *sg*, nuptials

nutria ['nutrja] NF otter

nutrición [nutri'θjon] NF nutrition

nutrido, -a [nu'triðo, a] ADJ (*alimentado*) nourished; (*fig: grande*) large; (*abundante*) abundant; **mal ~** undernourished; **~ de** full of

nutrir [nu'trir] /3a/ VT (*alimentar*) to nourish; (*dar de comer*) to feed; (*fig*) to strengthen

nutritivo, -a [nutri'tiβo, a] ADJ nourishing, nutritious

nylon [ni'lon] NM nylon

Ñ ñ

Ñ, ñ [ˈeɲe] NF (*letra*) Ñ ñ

ñango, -a [ˈɲaŋɡo, a] ADJ (*Am*) puny

ñapa [ˈɲapa] NF (*Am*) extra

ñata [ˈɲata] NF (*Am fam*) nose; *ver tb* **ñato**

ñato, -a [ˈɲato, a] ADJ (*Am*) snub-nosed

ñoñería [ɲoɲeˈria], **ñoñez** [ɲoˈɲeθ] NF insipidness

ñoño, -a [ˈɲoɲo, a] ADJ (*tonto*) silly, stupid; (*soso*) insipid; (*débil: persona*) spineless; (*Esp: película, novela*) sentimental

ñoquis [ˈɲokis] NMPL (*Culin*) gnocchi

Oo

O, o [o] NF (letra) O, o; **O de Oviedo** O for Oliver (BRIT) o Oboe (US)

O ABR (= oeste) W

★**o** [o] CONJ or; **o … o** either … or; **o sea** that is

ó [o] CONJ (en números para evitar confusión) or; **cinco ó seis** five or six

o/ NM (Com: = orden) o

OACI NF ABR (= Organización de la Aviación Civil Internacional) ICAO

oasis [oˈasis] NM INV oasis

obcecado, -a [oβθeˈkaðo, a] ADJ blind; (terco) stubborn

obcecarse [oβθeˈkarse] /1g/ VR to become obsessed; **~ en hacer** to insist on doing

obceque etc [oβˈθeke] VB ver **obcecarse**

★**obedecer** [oβeðeˈθer] /2d/ VT to obey; **~ a** (Med etc) to yield to; **~ al hecho de que …** (fig) to be due to …, arise from …

obedezca etc [oβeˈðeθka] VB ver **obedecer**

obediencia [oβeˈðjenθja] NF obedience

★**obediente** [oβeˈðjente] ADJ obedient

obertura [oβerˈtura] NF overture

obesidad [oβesiˈðað] NF obesity

obeso, -a [oˈβeso, a] ADJ obese

óbice [ˈoβiθe] NM obstacle, impediment

obispado [oβisˈpaðo] NM bishopric

obispo [oˈβispo] NM bishop

óbito [ˈoβito] NM demise

obituario [oβiˈtwarjo] NM (AM) obituary

objeción [oβxeˈθjon] NF objection; **hacer una ~, poner objeciones** to raise objections, object

objetar [oβxeˈtar] /1a/ VT, VI to object

★**objetivo, -a** [oβxeˈtiβo, a] ADJ objective ▶ NM objective; (fig) aim; (Foto) lens

★**objeto** [oβˈxeto] NM (cosa) object; (fin) aim

objetor, a [oβxeˈtor, a] NM/F objector; **~ de conciencia** conscientious objector

oblea [oˈβlea] NF (Rel, fig) wafer

oblicuo, -a [oˈβlikwo, a] ADJ oblique; (mirada) sidelong

obligación [oβliɣaˈθjon] NF obligation; (Com) bond, debenture

★**obligar** [oβliˈɣar] /1h/ VT to force ▪ **obligarse** VR: **obligarse a** to commit o.s. to

★**obligatorio, -a** [oβliɣaˈtorjo, a] ADJ compulsory, obligatory

obligue etc [oˈβliɣe] VB ver **obligar**

Ob.° ABR (= Obispo) Bp

oboe [oˈβoe] NM oboe; (músico) oboist

Ob.ᵖᵒ ABR = **obispo**

★**obra** [ˈoβra] NF work; (producción) piece of work; (Arq) construction, building; (libro) book; (Mus) opus; (Teat) play; **~ de arte** work of art; **~ maestra** masterpiece; **~ de consulta** reference book; **obras completas** complete works; **~ benéfica** charity; **"obras"** (en carretera) "men at work"; **obras públicas** public works; **por ~ de** thanks to (the efforts of); **obras son amores y no buenas razones** actions speak louder than words

obrar [oˈβrar] /1a/ VT to work; (tener efecto) to have an effect on ▶ VI to act, behave; (tener efecto) to have an effect; **la carta obra en su poder** the letter is in his/her possession

obr. cit. ABR (= obra citada) op. cit.

★**obrero, -a** [oˈβrero, a] ADJ working; (movimiento) labour cpd; **clase obrera** working class ▶ NM/F (gen) worker; (sin oficio) labourer

obscenidad [oβsθeniˈðað] NF obscenity

obsceno, -a [oβsˈθeno, a] ADJ obscene

obscu… PREF = **oscu…**

obsequiar [oβseˈkjar] /1b/ VT (ofrecer) to present; (agasajar) to make a fuss of, lavish attention on

obsequio [oβˈsekjo] NM (regalo) gift; (cortesía) courtesy, attention

obsequioso, -a [oβseˈkjoso, a] ADJ attentive

observación [oβserβaˈθjon] NF observation; (reflexión) remark; (objeción) objection

observador, a [oβserβa'ðor, a] ADJ observant
  ▶ NM/F observer

observancia [oβser'βanθja] NF observance

observar [oβser'βar] /**1a**/ VT to observe; (*notar*)
  to notice; (*leyes*) to observe, respect; (*reglas*) to
  abide by ▪ **observarse** VR to keep to, observe

observatorio [oβserβa'torjo] NM observatory;
  ~ del tiempo weather station

obsesión [oβse'sjon] NF obsession

obsesionar [oβsesjo'nar] /**1a**/ VT to obsess

obsesivo, -a [obse'siβo, a] ADJ obsessive

obseso, -a [oβ'seso, a] NM/F (*sexual*) sex maniac

obsolescencia [oβsoles'θenθja] NF: **~ incorpo-
rada** (*Com*) built-in obsolescence

obsoleto, -a [oβso'leto, a] ADJ obsolete

obstaculice *etc* [oβstaku'liθe] VB *ver* **obstaculizar**

obstaculizar [oβstaku'liθar] /**1f**/ VT (*dificultar*)
  to hinder, hamper

obstáculo [oβs'takulo] NM (*gen*) obstacle;
  (*impedimento*) hindrance, drawback

obstante [oβs'tante]: **no ~** *adv* nevertheless; (*de
todos modos*) all the same ▶ PREP in spite of

obstetra [oβs'tetra] NMF obstetrician

obstetricia [oβste'triθja] NF obstetrics *sg*

obstinado, -a [oβsti'naðo, a] ADJ (*gen*) obstinate; (*terco*) stubborn

obstinarse [oβsti'narse] /**1a**/ VR to be obstinate; **~ en** to persist in

obstrucción [oβstruk'θjon] NF obstruction

obstruir [oβstru'ir] /**3g**/ VT to obstruct; (*bloquear*) to block; (*estorbar*) to hinder

obstruyendo *etc* [oβstru'jendo] VB *ver* **obstruir**

obtención [oβten'θjon] NF (*Com*) procurement

obtendré *etc* [oβten'dre] VB *ver* **obtener**

★**obtener** [oβte'ner] /**2k**/ VT (*conseguir*) to obtain;
  (*ganar*) to gain; (*premio*) to win

obtenga *etc* [oβ'tenga] VB *ver* **obtener**

obturación [oβtura'θjon] NF plugging, stopping; (*Foto*): **velocidad de ~** shutter speed

obturador [oβtura'ðor] NM (*Foto*) shutter

obtuso, -a [oβ'tuso, a] ADJ (*filo*) blunt; (*Mat, fig*)
  obtuse

obtuve *etc* [oβ'tuβe] VB *ver* **obtener**

obús [o'βus] NM (*Mil*) shell

obviar [oβ'βjar] /**1c**/ VT to obviate, remove

obvio, -a [o'βββjo, a] ADJ obvious

oca ['oka] NF goose; (*tb:* **juego de la oca**)
  ≈ snakes and ladders

★**ocasión** [oka'sjon] NF (*oportunidad*) opportunity,
  chance; (*momento*) occasion, time; (*causa*) cause;
  de ~ secondhand; **con ~ de** on the occasion of;
  en algunas ocasiones sometimes; **aprovechar la ~** to seize on one's opportunity

ocasionar [okasjo'nar] /**1a**/ VT to cause

ocaso [o'kaso] NM sunset; (*fig*) decline

occidental [okθiðen'tal] ADJ western ▶ NMF
  westerner ▶ NM west

occidente [okθi'ðente] NM west; **el O~** the
  West

occiso, -a [ok'θiso, a] NM/F: **el ~** the deceased;
  (*de asesinato*) the victim

OCDE NF ABR (= *Organización de Cooperación y Desarrollo Económicos*) OECD

océano [o'θeano] NM ocean; **el ~ Índico** the
  Indian Ocean

★**ochenta** [o'tʃenta] NUM eighty

★**ocho** ['otʃo] NUM eight; (*fecha*) eighth; **~ días** a
  week; **dentro de ~ días** within a week

ochocientos, -as [otʃo'θjentos, as] NUM eight
  hundred

OCI ['oθi] NF ABR (*Pol: VENEZUELA, PERÚ*) = **Oficina
Central de Información**

★**ocio** ['oθjo] NM (*tiempo*) leisure; (*pey*) idleness;
  "guía del ~" "what's on"

ociosidad [oθjosi'ðað] NF idleness

ocioso, -a [o'θjoso, a] ADJ (*inactivo*) idle; (*inútil*)
  useless

OCR ABR (*Inform*: = *reconocimiento óptico de caracteres*) OCR

oct. ABR (= *octubre*) Oct.

octanaje [okta'naxe] NM: **de alto ~** high octane

octano [ok'tano] NM octane

octavilla [okta'βiʎa] NF leaflet, pamphlet

★**octavo, -a** [ok'taβo, a] NUM eighth

octeto [ok'teto] NM (*Inform*) byte

octogenario, -a [oktoxe'narjo, a] ADJ, NM/F
  octogenarian

★**octubre** [ok'tuβre] NM October; *ver tb* **julio**

OCU ['oku] NF ABR (*ESP*: = *Organización de Consumidores y Usuarios*) ≈ Consumers' Association

ocular [oku'lar] ADJ ocular, eye *cpd*; **testigo ~**
  eyewitness

oculista [oku'lista] NMF oculist

ocultar [okul'tar] /**1a**/ VT (*esconder*) to hide;
  (*callar*) to conceal; (*disfrazar*) to screen ▪ **ocultarse** VR to hide (o.s.); **ocultarse a la vista** to
  keep out of sight

oculto, -a [o'kulto, a] ADJ hidden; (*fig*) secret

ocupación [okupa'θjon] NF occupation; (*tenencia*) occupancy

★**ocupado, -a** [oku'paðo, a] ADJ (*persona*) busy;
  (*plaza*) occupied, taken; (*teléfono*) engaged;
  ¿está ocupada la silla? is this seat taken?

★**ocupar** [oku'par] /**1a**/ VT (*gen*) to occupy; (*puesto*)
  to hold, fill; (*individuo*) to engage; (*obreros*) to
  employ; (*confiscar*) to seize ▪ **ocuparse** VR: **ocuparse de** *o* **en** to concern o.s. with; (*cuidar*) to
  look after; **ocuparse de lo suyo** to mind one's
  own business

ocurrencia [oku'rrenθja] NF (*ocasión*) occurrence; (*agudeza*) witticism; (*idea*) bright idea

★**ocurrir** [oku'rrir] /**3a**/ VI to happen; **¿qué
ocurre?** what's going on? ▪ **ocurrirse** VR: **se
me ocurrió que ...** it occurred to me that ...; **¿se
te ocurre algo?** can you think of *o* come up
  with anything?

oda [ˈoða] NF ode

ODECA [oˈðeka] NF ABR = **Organización de Estados Centroamericanos**

★**odiar** [oˈðjar] /**1b**/ VT to hate

odio [ˈoðjo] NM (gen) hate, hatred; (disgusto) dislike

odioso, -a [oˈðjoso, a] ADJ (gen) hateful; (malo) nasty

odisea [oðiˈsea] NF odyssey

odontología [oðontoloˈxia] NF dentistry, dental surgery

odontólogo, -a [oðonˈtoloɣo, a] NM/F dentist, dental surgeon

odre [ˈoðre] NM wineskin

OEA NF ABR (= Organización de Estados Americanos) O.A.S.

OECE NF ABR (= Organización Europea de Cooperación Económica) OEEC

OELA [oˈela] NF ABR = **Organización de Estados Latinoamericanos**

★**oeste** [oˈeste] NM west; **una película del ~** a western

★**ofender** [ofenˈder] /**2a**/ VT (agraviar) to offend; (insultar) to insult ▪ **ofenderse** VR to take offence

ofensa [oˈfensa] NF offence; (insulto) slight

ofensivo, -a [ofenˈsiβo, a] ADJ (insultante) insulting; (Mil) offensive ▸ NF offensive

★**oferta** [oˈferta] NF offer; (propuesta) proposal; (para contrato) bid, tender; **la ~ y la demanda** supply and demand; **artículos en ~** goods on offer; **~ excedentaria** (Com) excess supply; **~ monetaria** money supply; **~ pública de adquisición (OPA)** (Com) takeover bid; **ofertas de trabajo** (en periódicos) situations vacant column

offset [ˈofset] NM offset

oficial [ofiˈθjal] ADJ official ▸ NM official; (Mil) officer

oficialista [ofisjaˈlista] ADJ (AM) (pro-) government; **el candidato ~** the governing party's candidate

oficiar [ofiˈθjar] /**1b**/ VT to inform officially ▸ VI (Rel) to officiate

★**oficina** [ofiˈθina] NF office; **~ de correos** post office; **~ de empleo** employment agency; **~ de información** information bureau; **~ de objetos perdidos** lost property office (BRIT), lost-and-found department (US); **~ de turismo** tourist office; **~ principal** (Com) head office, main branch

oficinista [ofiθiˈnista] NMF clerk; **los oficinistas** white-collar workers

★**oficio** [oˈfiθjo] NM (profesión) profession; (puesto) post; (Rel) service; (función) function; (comunicado) official letter; **ser del ~** to be an old hand; **tener mucho ~** to have a lot of experience; **~ de difuntos** funeral service; **de ~** officially

oficioso, -a [ofiˈθjoso, a] ADJ (pey) officious; (no oficial) unofficial, informal

ofimática [ofiˈmatika] NF office automation

★**ofrecer** [ofreˈθer] /**2d**/ VT (dar) to offer; (proponer) to propose ▪ **ofrecerse** VR (persona) to offer o.s., volunteer; (situación) to present itself; **¿qué se le ofrece?, ¿se le ofrece algo?** what can I do for you?, can I get you anything?

ofrecimiento [ofreθiˈmjento] NM offer, offering

ofrendar [ofrenˈdar] /**1a**/ VT to offer, contribute

ofrezca etc [oˈfreθka] VB ver **ofrecer**

oftalmología [oftalmoloˈxia] NF ophthalmology

oftalmólogo, -a [oftalˈmoloɣo, a] NM/F ophthalmologist

ofuscación [ofuskaˈθjon] NF, **ofuscamiento** [ofuskaˈmjento] NM (fig) bewilderment

ofuscar [ofusˈkar] /**1g**/ VT (confundir) to bewilder; (enceguecer) to dazzle, blind

ofusque etc [oˈfuske] VB ver **ofuscar**

ogro [ˈoɣro] NM ogre

OIC NF ABR (Com) = **Organización Interamericana del Café**; **Organización Internacional del Comercio**

oída [oˈiða] NF: **de oídas** by hearsay

★**oído** [oˈiðo] NM (Anat, Mus) ear; (sentido) hearing; **~ interno** inner ear; **de ~** by ear; **apenas pude dar crédito a mis oídos** I could scarcely believe my ears; **hacer oídos sordos a** to turn a deaf ear to

OIEA NM ABR (= Organismo Internacional de Energía Atómica) IAEA

oigo etc VB ver **oír**

★**oír** [oˈir] /**3p**/ VT (gen) to hear; (esp AM: escuchar) to listen to; **¡oye!** (sorpresa) I say!, say! (US); **¡oiga!** excuse me!; (Telec) hello?; **~ misa** to attend mass; **como quien oye llover** without paying (the slightest) attention

OIT NF ABR (= Organización Internacional del Trabajo) ILO

ojal [oˈxal] NM buttonhole

★**ojalá** [oxaˈla] EXCL if only (it were so)!, some hope!; **~ que venga hoy** I hope he comes today; **¡~ pudiera!** I wish I could! ▸ CONJ if only ...!, would that ...!

ojeada [oxeˈaða] NF glance; **echar una ~ a** to take a quick look at

ojera [oˈxera] NF: **tener ojeras** to have bags under one's eyes

ojeriza [oxeˈriθa] NF ill-will; **tener ~ a** to have a grudge against, have it in for

ojeroso, -a [oxeˈroso, a] ADJ haggard

ojete [oˈxete] NM eye(let)

★**ojo** [ˈoxo] NM eye; (de puente) span; (de cerradura) keyhole; **tener ~ para** to have an eye for; **ojos saltones** bulging o goggle eyes; **~ de buey** porthole; **~ por ~** an eye for an eye; **en un abrir y cerrar de ojos** in the twinkling of an eye; **a ojos vistas** openly; (crecer etc) before one's (very) eyes; **a ~ (de buen cubero)** roughly; **ojos que no ven, corazón que no siente** out of sight, out of mind; **ser el ~ derecho de algn** (*fig*) to be the apple of sb's eye ▶ EXCL careful!

okey ['okei] EXCL (*AM*) O.K.

okupa [o'kupa] NMF (*fam*) squatter

OL ABR (= *onda larga*) LW, long wave

★**ola** ['ola] NF wave; **~ de calor/frío** heatwave/cold spell; **la nueva ~** the latest fashion; (*Cine, Mus*) (the) new wave

OLADE [o'laðe] NF ABR = **Organización Latinoamericana de Energía**

olé [o'le] EXCL bravo!, olé!

oleada [ole'aða] NF big wave, swell; (*fig*) wave

oleaje [ole'axe] NM swell

óleo ['oleo] NM oil

oleoducto [oleo'ðukto] NM (oil) pipeline

★**oler** [o'ler] /2i/ VT (*gen*) to smell; (*inquirir*) to pry into; (*fig: sospechar*) to sniff out ▶ VI to smell; **~ a** to smell of; **huele mal** it smells bad, it stinks

olfatear [olfate'ar] /1a/ VT to smell; (*fig: sospechar*) to sniff out; (*inquirir*) to pry into

olfato [ol'fato] NM sense of smell

oligarquía [oliɣar'kia] NF oligarchy

olimpiada [olim'piaða] NF: **la ~** *o* **las olimpiadas** the Olympics®

olímpicamente [o'limpikamente] ADV: **pasar ~ de algo** to totally ignore sth

olímpico, -a [o'limpiko, a] ADJ Olympian; (*deportes*) Olympic®

oliva [o'liβa] NF (*aceituna*) olive; **aceite de ~** olive oil

olivar [oli'βar] NM olive grove *o* plantation

olivo [o'liβo] NM olive tree

olla ['oʎa] NF pan; (*para hervir agua*) kettle; (*comida*) stew; **~ a presión** pressure cooker; **~ podrida** *type of Spanish stew*

olmo ['olmo] NM elm (tree)

★**olor** [o'lor] NM smell

oloroso, -a [olo'roso, a] ADJ scented

OLP NF ABR (= *Organización para la Liberación de Palestina*) PLO

olvidadizo, -a [olβiða'ðiθo, a] ADJ (*desmemoriado*) forgetful; (*distraído*) absent-minded

★**olvidar** [olβi'ðar] /1a/ VT to forget; (*omitir*) to omit; (*abandonar*) to leave behind ▪ **olvidarse** VR (*fig*) to forget o.s.; **se me olvidó** I forgot

olvido [ol'βiðo] NM oblivion; (*acto*) oversight; (*descuido*) slip; (*despiste*) forgetfulness; **caer en el ~** to fall into oblivion

OM ABR (= *onda media*) MW, medium wave; (*Pol*) = **Orden Ministerial**; (= *Oriente Medio*) Middle East

ombligo [om'bliɣo] NM navel

omelette [ome'lete] NF (*AM*) omelet(te)

OMI NF ABR (= *Organización Marítima Internacional*) IMO

ominoso, -a [omi'noso, a] ADJ ominous

omisión [omi'sjon] NF (*abstención*) omission; (*descuido*) neglect

omiso, -a [o'miso, a] ADJ: **hacer caso ~ de** to ignore, pass over

omitir [omi'tir] /3a/ VT to leave *o* miss out, omit

ómnibus ['omniβus] NM (*AM*) bus

omnipotente [omnipo'tente] ADJ omnipotent

omnipresente [omnipre'sente] ADJ omnipresent

omnívoro, -a [om'niβoro, a] ADJ omnivorous

omoplato [omo'plato], **omóplato** [o'moplato] NM shoulder-blade

OMS NF ABR (= *Organización Mundial de la Salud*) WHO

ONCE ['onθe] NF ABR (= *Organización Nacional de Ciegos Españoles*) *charity for the blind*

★**once** ['onθe] NUM eleven ▪ **onces** NFPL tea break *sg*

onda ['onda] NF wave; **~ corta/larga/media** short/long/medium wave; **ondas acústicas/hertzianas** acoustic/Hertzian waves; **~ sonora** sound wave

ondear [onde'ar] /1a/ VI to wave; (*tener ondas*) to be wavy; (*agua*) to ripple ▪ **ondearse** VR to swing, sway

ondulación [ondula'θjon] NF undulation

ondulado, -a [ondu'laðo, a] ADJ wavy ▶ NM wave

ondulante [ondu'lante] ADJ undulating

ondular [ondu'lar] /1a/ VT (*el pelo*) to wave ▶ VI, **ondularse** VR to undulate

oneroso, -a [one'roso, a] ADJ onerous

ONG NF ABR (= *organización no gubernamental*) NGO

onomástico, -a [ono'mastiko, a] ADJ: **fiesta onomástica** saint's day ▶ NM saint's day

★**ONU** ['onu] NF ABR (= *Organización de las Naciones Unidas*) UN

onubense [onu'βense] ADJ of *o* from Huelva ▶ NMF native *o* inhabitant of Huelva

ONUDI [o'nuði] NF ABR (= *Organización de las Naciones Unidas para el Desarrollo Industrial*) UNIDO (= *United Nations Industrial Development Organization*)

onza ['onθa] NF ounce

OPA ['opa] NF ABR (= *Oferta Pública de Adquisición*) takeover bid

opaco, -a [o'pako, a] ADJ opaque; (*fig*) dull

ópalo ['opalo] NM opal

★**opción** [op'θjon] NF (*gen*) option; (*derecho*) right, option; **no hay ~** there is no alternative

opcional [opθjo'nal] ADJ optional

OPEP [o'pep] NF ABR (= *Organización de Países Exportadores de Petróleo*) OPEC

★**ópera** ['opera] NF opera; **~ bufa** *o* **cómica** comic opera

★**operación** [opera'θjon] NF (*gen*) operation; (*Com*) transaction, deal; **~ a plazo** (*Com*) forward transaction; **operaciones accesorias** (*Inform*) housekeeping; **operaciones a término** (*Com*) futures

operador, a [opera'ðor, a] NM/F operator; (*Cine: proyección*) projectionist; (: *rodaje*) cameraman

operar [ope'rar] /**1a**/ VT (*producir*) to produce, bring about; (*Med*) to operate on ▶ VI (*Com*) to operate, deal ■ **operarse** VR to occur; (*Med*) to have an operation; **se han operado grandes cambios** great changes have been made *o* have taken place

operario, -a [ope'rarjo, a] NM/F worker

opereta [ope'reta] NF operetta

★**opinar** [opi'nar] /**1a**/ VT (*estimar*) to think ▶ VI (*enjuiciar*) to give one's opinion; **~ bien de** to think well of

★**opinión** [opi'njon] NF (*creencia*) belief; (*criterio*) opinion; **la ~ pública** public opinion

opio ['opjo] NM opium

opíparo, -a [o'piparo, a] ADJ sumptuous

opondré etc [opon'dre] VB ver **oponer**

oponente [opo'nente] NMF opponent

oponer [opo'ner] /**2q**/ VT (*resistencia*) to put up, offer; (*negativa*) to raise; **~ A a B** to set A against B ■ **oponerse** VR (*objetar*) to object; (*estar frente a frente*) to be opposed; (*dos personas*) to oppose each other; **me opongo a pensar que ...** I refuse to believe *o* think that ...

oponga etc [o'ponga] VB ver **oponer**

Oporto [o'porto] NM Oporto

oporto [o'porto] NM port

★**oportunidad** [oportuni'ðað] NF (*ocasión*) opportunity; (*posibilidad*) chance

oportunismo [oportu'nismo] NM opportunism

oportunista [oportu'nista] NMF opportunist; (*infección*) opportunistic

oportuno, -a [opor'tuno, a] ADJ (*en su tiempo*) opportune, timely; (*respuesta*) suitable; **en el momento ~** at the right moment

oposición [oposi'θjon] NF opposition ■ **oposiciones** NFPL (*examen*) public examinations; **hacer oposiciones a, presentarse a unas oposiciones a** to sit a competitive examination for; **ganar un puesto por oposiciones** to win a post by public competitive examination; *see note*

The **oposiciones** are exams that are held nationally and locally for posts in the public sector, state education, the judiciary etc. These posts are permanent and the number of candidates is high so the exams are tough. The candidates, *opositores*, have to study a great number of subjects relating to their field and also the Constitution. People can spend years studying and resitting exams.

opositar [oposi'tar] /**1a**/ VI to sit a public entrance examination

opositor, -a [oposi'tor, a] NM/F (*Admin*) candidate to a public examination; (*adversario*) opponent; **~ (a)** candidate (for)

opresión [opre'sjon] NF oppression

opresivo, -a [opre'siβo, a] ADJ oppressive

opresor, a [opre'sor, a] NM/F oppressor

oprimir [opri'mir] /**3a**/ VT to squeeze; (*asir*) to grasp; (*pulsar*) to press; (*fig*) to oppress

★**optar** [op'tar] /**1a**/ VI (*elegir*) to choose; **~ a** *o* **por** to opt for

★**optativo, -a** [opta'tiβo, a] ADJ optional

óptico, -a ['optiko, a] ADJ optic(al) ▶ NM/F optician ▶ NF (*ciencia*) optics sg; (*tienda*) optician's; (*fig*) viewpoint; **desde esta óptica** from this point of view

optimismo [opti'mismo] NM optimism

★**optimista** [opti'mista] NMF optimist

óptimo, -a ['optimo, a] ADJ (*el mejor*) very best

opuesto, -a [o'pwesto, a] PP de **oponer** ▶ ADJ (*contrario*) opposite; (*antagónico*) opposing

opulencia [opu'lenθja] NF opulence

opulento, -a [opu'lento, a] ADJ opulent

opuse etc [o'puse] VB ver **oponer**

ora ['ora] ADV: **~ tú ~ yo** now you, now me

oración [ora'θjon] NF (*Rel*) prayer; (*Ling*) sentence

oráculo [o'rakulo] NM oracle

orador, a [ora'ðor, a] NM/F orator; (*conferenciante*) speaker

oral [o'ral] ADJ oral; **por vía ~** (*Med*) orally

orangután [orangu'tan] NM orang-utan

orar [o'rar] /**1a**/ VI (*Rel*) to pray

oratoria [ora'torja] NF oratory

orbe ['orβe] NM orb, sphere; (*fig*) world; **en todo el ~** all over the globe

órbita ['orβita] NF orbit; (*Anat: ocular*) (eye-)socket

★**orden** ['orðen] NM (*colocación*) order ▶ NF (*mandato*) order; (*Inform*) command; **~ público** public order, law and order; **del ~ de** (*números*) about; **de primer ~** first-rate; **en ~ de prioridad** in order of priority; **~ bancaria** banker's order; **una ~ de compra** (*Com*) a purchase order; **el ~ del día** the agenda; **eso ahora está a la ~ del día** that is now the order of the day; **a la ~ de usted** at your service; **dar la ~ de hacer algo** to give the order to do sth

ordenación [orðena'θjon] NF (*estado*) order; (*acto*) ordering; (*Rel*) ordination

ordenado, -a [orðe'naðo, a] ADJ (*metódico*) methodical; (*arreglado*) orderly

★**ordenador** [orðena'ðor] NM computer; **~ central** mainframe computer; **~ de gestión** business computer; **~ portátil** laptop (computer); **~ de sobremesa** desktop

ordenamiento [orðena'mjento] NM legislation

ordenanza [orðe'nanθa] NF ordinance; **ordenanzas municipales** by-laws ▶ NM (*Com etc*) messenger; (*Mil*) orderly; (*bedel*) porter

★**ordenar** [orðe'nar] /**1a**/ VT (*mandar*) to order;

(*poner orden*) to put in order, arrange ■ **ordenarse** VR (*Rel*) to be ordained

ordeñadora [orðeɲaˈðora] NF milking machine

ordeñar [orðeˈnar] /**1a**/ VT to milk

ordinariez [orðinaˈrjeθ] NF (*cualidad*) coarseness, vulgarity; (*una ordinariez*) coarse remark *o* joke *etc*

★**ordinario, -a** [orðiˈnarjo, a] ADJ (*común*) ordinary, usual; (*vulgar*) vulgar, common

ordinograma [orðinoˈɣrama] NM flowchart

orear [oreˈar] /**1a**/ VT to air ■ **orearse** VR (*ropa*) to air

orégano [oˈreɣano] NM oregano

★**oreja** [oˈrexa] NF ear; (*Mecánica*) lug, flange

orensano, -a [orenˈsano, a] ADJ of *o* from Orense ▸ NM/F native *o* inhabitant of Orense

orfanato [orfaˈnato], **orfanatorio** [orfanaˈtorjo] NM orphanage

orfandad [orfanˈdað] NF orphanhood

orfebre [orˈfeβre] NM gold-/silversmith

orfebrería [orfeβreˈria] NF gold/silver work

orfelinato [orfeliˈnato] NM orphanage

orfeón [orfeˈon] NM (*Mus*) choral society

organice *etc* [orɣaˈniθe] VB *ver* **organizar**

orgánico, -a [orˈɣaniko, a] ADJ organic

organigrama [orɣaniˈɣrama] NM flow chart; (*de organización*) organization chart

organillo [orɣaˈniʎo] NM barrel organ

organismo [orɣaˈnismo] NM (*Bio*) organism; (*Pol*) organization; **O~ Internacional de Energía Atómica** International Atomic Energy Agency

organista [orɣaˈnista] NMF organist

organización [orɣaniθaˈθjon] NF organization; **O~ de las Naciones Unidas (ONU)** United Nations Organization; **O~ del Tratado del Atlántico Norte (OTAN)** North Atlantic Treaty Organization (NATO)

organizador, a [orɣaniθaˈðor, a] ADJ organizing; **el comité ~** the organizing committee ▸ NM/F organizer

★**organizar** [orɣaniˈθar] /**1f**/ VT to organize

órgano [ˈorɣano] NM organ

orgasmo [orˈɣasmo] NM orgasm

orgía [orˈxia] NF orgy

★**orgullo** [orˈɣuʎo] NM (*altanería*) pride; (*autorrespeto*) self-respect

★**orgulloso, -a** [orɣuˈʎoso, a] ADJ (*gen*) proud; (*altanero*) haughty

orientación [orjentaˈθjon] NF (*posición*) position; (*dirección*) direction; **~ profesional** occupational guidance

oriental [orjenˈtal] ADJ oriental; (*región etc*) eastern ▸ NMF oriental

orientar [orjenˈtar] /**1a**/ VT (*situar*) to orientate; (*señalar*) to point; (*dirigir*) to direct; (*guiar*) to guide ■ **orientarse** VR to get one's bearings; (*decidirse*) to decide on a course of action

oriente [oˈrjente] NM east; **el O~** the East, the Orient; **Cercano/Medio/Lejano O~** Near/Middle/Far East

orificio [oriˈfiθjo] NM hole; (*Anat*) orifice

★**origen** [oˈrixen] NM origin; (*nacimiento*) lineage, birth; **dar ~ a** to cause, give rise to

original [orixiˈnal] ADJ (*nuevo*) original; (*extraño*) odd, strange ▸ NM original; (*Tip*) manuscript; (*Tec*) master (copy)

originalidad [orixinaliˈðað] NF originality

originar [orixiˈnar] /**1a**/ VT to start, cause ■ **originarse** VR to originate

originario, -a [orixiˈnarjo, a] ADJ (*nativo*) native; (*primordial*) original; **ser ~ de** to originate from; **país ~** country of origin

★**orilla** [oˈriʎa] NF (*borde*) border; (*de río*) bank; (*de bosque, tela*) edge; (*de mar*) shore; **a orillas de** on the banks of

orillar [oriˈʎar] /**1a**/ VT (*bordear*) to skirt, go round; (*Costura*) to edge; (*resolver*) to wind up; (*tocar: asunto*) to touch briefly on; (: *dificultad*) to avoid

orín [oˈrin] NM rust

orina [oˈrina] NF urine

orinal [oriˈnal] NM (chamber) pot

orinar [oriˈnar] /**1a**/ VI to urinate ■ **orinarse** VR to wet o.s.

orines [oˈrines] NMPL urine *sg*

oriundo, -a [oˈrjundo, a] ADJ: **~ de** native of

orla [ˈorla] NF edge, border; (*Escol*) graduation photograph

ornamentar [ornamenˈtar] /**1a**/ VT (*adornar, ataviar*) to adorn; (*revestir*) to bedeck

ornar [orˈnar] /**1a**/ VT to adorn

ornitología [ornitoloˈxia] NF ornithology, bird watching

ornitólogo, -a [orniˈtoloɣo, a] NM/F ornithologist

★**oro** [ˈoro] NM gold; **~ en barras** gold ingots; **de ~** gold, golden; **no es ~ todo lo que reluce** all that glitters is not gold; **hacerse de ~** to make a fortune; *ver tb* **oros**

orondo, -a [oˈrondo, a] ADJ (*vasija*) rounded; (*individuo*) smug, self-satisfied

oropel [oroˈpel] NM tinsel

oros [ˈoros] NMPL (*Naipes*) one of the suits in the Spanish card deck; *ver tb* **baraja española**

★**orquesta** [orˈkesta] NF orchestra; **~ de cámara/sinfónica** chamber/symphony orchestra; **~ de jazz** jazz band

orquestar [orkesˈtar] /**1a**/ VT to orchestrate

orquídea [orˈkiðea] NF orchid

ortiga [orˈtiɣa] NF nettle

ortodoncia [ortoˈðonθja] NF orthodontics *sg*

ortodoxo, -a [ortoˈðokso, a] ADJ orthodox

ortografía [ortoɣraˈfia] NF spelling

ortopedia [ortoˈpeðja] NF orthop(a)edics *sg*

ortopédico, -a [ortoˈpeðiko, a] ADJ orthop(a)edic

o

oruga [o'ruɣa] NF caterpillar

orujo [o'ruxo] NM *type of strong grape liqueur made from grape pressings*

orzuelo [or'θwelo] NM (*Med*) stye

os [os] PRON (*gen*) you; (*a vosotros*) (to) you; (*reflexivo*) (to) yourselves; (*mutuo*) (to) each other; **vosotros os laváis** you wash yourselves; **¡callaos!** (*fam*) shut up!

osa ['osa] NF (she-)bear; **O~ Mayor/Menor** Great/Little Bear, Ursa Major/Minor

osadía [osa'ðia] NF daring; (*descaro*) impudence

osamenta [osa'menta] NF skeleton

osar [o'sar] /1a/ VI to dare

oscense [os'θense] ADJ of *o* from Huesca ▶ NMF native *o* inhabitant of Huesca

oscilación [osθila'θjon] NF (*movimiento*) oscillation; (*fluctuación*) fluctuation; (*vacilación*) hesitation; (*de columpio*) swinging, movement to and fro

oscilar [osθi'lar] /1a/ VI to oscillate; (*precio, peso, temperatura*) to fluctuate; (*dudar*) to hesitate

ósculo ['oskulo] NM kiss

oscurecer [oskure'θer] /2d/ VT to darken ▶ VI to grow dark ■ **oscurecerse** VR to grow *o* get dark

oscurezca etc [osku're θka] VB ver **oscurecer**

★**oscuridad** [oskuri'ðað] NF obscurity; (*tinieblas*) darkness

★**oscuro, -a** [os'kuro, a] ADJ dark; (*fig*) obscure; (*indefinido*) confused; (*cielo*) overcast, cloudy; (*futuro etc*) uncertain; **a oscuras** in the dark

óseo, -a ['oseo, a] ADJ bony; (*Med etc*) bone *cpd*

Oslo ['oslo] NM Oslo

★**oso** ['oso] NM bear; **~ blanco/gris/pardo** polar/grizzly/brown bear; **~ de peluche** teddy bear; **~ hormiguero** anteater; **hacer el ~** to play the fool

Ostende [os'tende] NM Ostend

ostensible [osten'siβle] ADJ obvious

ostensiblemente [ostensiβle'mente] ADV perceptibly, visibly

ostentación [ostenta'θjon] NF (*gen*) ostentation; (*acto*) display

ostentar [osten'tar] /1a/ VT (*gen*) to show; (*pey*) to flaunt, show off; (*poseer*) to have, possess

ostentoso, -a [osten'toso, a] ADJ ostentatious, showy

osteópata [oste'opata] NMF osteopath

ostión [os'tjon] NM (*Am*) = **ostra**

★**ostra** ['ostra] NF oyster ▶ EXCL: **¡ostras!** (*fam*) sugar!

ostracismo [ostra'θismo] NM ostracism

OTAN ['otan] NF ABR (= *Organización del Tratado del Atlántico Norte*) NATO

otear [ote'ar] /1a/ VT to observe; (*fig*) to look into

otero [o'tero] NM low hill, hillock

otitis [o'titis] NF earache

otoñal [oto'ɲal] ADJ autumnal

★**otoño** [o'toɲo] NM autumn, fall (*US*)

otorgamiento [otorɣa'mjento] NM conferring, granting; (*Jur*) execution

otorgar [otor'ɣar] /1h/ VT (*conceder*) to concede; (*dar*) to grant; (*poderes*) to confer; (*premio*) to award

otorgue etc [o'torɣe] VB ver **otorgar**

otorrinolaringólogo, -a [otorrinolarin'goloɣo, a] NM/F (*Med: tb:* **otorrino**) ear, nose and throat specialist

---

otro, -a ['otro, a]

ADJ **1** (*distinto: sg*) another; (*: pl*) other; **otra cosa/persona** something/someone else; **con otros amigos** with other *o* different friends; **a/en otra parte** elsewhere, somewhere else

2 (*adicional*): **tráigame otro café (más), por favor** can I have another coffee, please?; **otros 10 días más** another 10 days

▶ PRON **1** (*sg*) another one; **el otro** the other one; **¡otra!** (*Mus*) more!; **de otro** somebody *o* someone else's; **que lo haga otro** let somebody *o* someone else do it; **ni uno ni otro** neither one nor the other

2 (*pl*): **(los) otros** (the) others

3 (*recíproco*): **se odian (la) una a (la) otra** they hate one another *o* each other

4: **otro tanto**: **comer otro tanto** to eat the same *o* as much again; **recibió una decena de telegramas y otras tantas llamadas** he got about ten telegrams and as many calls

---

Por regla general, al traducir *otro*, se utiliza **another** con sustantivos en singular y **other** con sustantivos en plural:
Me das otra manzana, por favor? **Can I have another apple, please?**
Tengo otros planes. **I have other plans.**
Sin embargo, se utiliza **another** con un sustantivo en plural precedido de un número:
Tenemos que esperar todavía otros 10 minutos. **We've still got another 10 minutes to wait.**
Se utiliza **other** con un sustantivo en singular acompañado de un determinante, como **some**, **any**, **the** o un adjetivo posesivo:
Hay alguna otra manera de hacerlo? **Is there any other way of doing it?**
No quiero este, quiero el otro. **I don't want this one, I want the other one.**
mi otro coche **my other car**.

---

otrora [o'trora] ADV formerly; **el ~ señor del país** the one-time ruler of the country

OUA NF ABR (= *Organización de la Unidad Africana*) OAU

outlet ['autlet] (*pl* **outlets**) NM (*tienda*) outlet

ovación [oβa'θjon] NF ovation

ovacionar [oβaθjo'nar] /1a/ VT to cheer

oval [o'βal] , **ovalado, -a** [oβa'laðo, a] ADJ oval

óvalo [ˈoβalo] NM oval

ovario [oˈβarjo] NM ovary

★**oveja** [oˈβexa] NF sheep; **~ negra** (*fig*) black sheep (of the family)

overol [oβeˈrol] NM (*AM*) overalls *pl*

ovetense [oβeˈtense] ADJ of *o* from Oviedo ▶ NMF native *o* inhabitant of Oviedo

ovillo [oˈβiʎo] NM (*de lana*) ball; (*fig*) tangle; **hacerse un ~** to curl up (into a ball)

OVNI [ˈoβni] NM ABR (= *objeto volante* (*o volador*) *no identificado*) UFO

ovulación [oβulaˈθjon] NF ovulation

óvulo [ˈoβulo] NM ovum

oxidación [oksiðaˈθjon] NF rusting

oxidar [oksiˈðar] /**1a**/ VT to rust ■ **oxidarse** VR to go rusty; (*Tec*) to oxidize

óxido [ˈoksiðo] NM oxide

oxigenado, -a [oksixeˈnaðo, a] ADJ (*Química*) oxygenated; (*pelo*) bleached

oxigenar [oksixeˈnar] /**1a**/ VT to oxygenate ■ **oxigenarse** VR to become oxygenated; (*fam*) to get some fresh air

★**oxígeno** [okˈsixeno] NM oxygen

oyendo *etc* [oˈjendo] VB *ver* **oír**

oyente [oˈjente] NMF listener, hearer; (*Escol*) unregistered *o* occasional student

oyes *etc* VB *ver* **oír**

ozono [oˈθono] NM ozone

P p

P, p [pe] NF (*letra*) P, p; **P de Pamplona** P for Peter

P ABR (*Rel*: = *padre*) Fr.; (= *pregunta*) Q; = **papa**

p. ABR (= *página*) p; (*Costura*) = **punto**

p.a. ABR = **por autorización; por ausencia**

pabellón [paβeˈʎon] NM bell tent; (*Arq*) pavilion; (*de hospital etc*) block, section; (*bandera*) flag; **~ de conveniencia** (*Com*) flag of convenience; **~ de la oreja** outer ear

pábilo [ˈpaβilo] NM wick

pábulo [ˈpaβulo] NM food; **dar ~ a** to feed, encourage

PAC NF ABR (= *Política Agrícola Común*) CAP

pacense [paˈθense] ADJ of o from Badajoz ▶ NMF native o inhabitant of Badajoz

paceño, -a [paˈθeɲo, a] ADJ of o from La Paz ▶ NM/F native o inhabitant of La Paz

pacer [paˈθer] /2d/ VI to graze ▶ VT to graze on

pachá [paˈtʃa] NM: **vivir como un ~** to live like a king

pachanga [paˈtʃanga] (*CAm, México*) NF (*Mus*) pachanga, Cuban dance; (*fam: en fútbol, baloncesto*) friendly game, friendly (*Brit*)

pachanguero, -a [patʃanˈgero, a] ADJ (*fam, pey: música*) catchy

pachorra [paˈtʃorra] NF (*indolencia*) slowness; (*tranquilidad*) calmness

pachucho, -a [paˈtʃutʃo, a] ADJ (*fruta*) overripe; (*persona*) off-colour, poorly

paciencia [paˈθjenθja] NF patience; **¡~!** be patient!; **¡~ y barajar!** don't give up!; **perder la ~** to lose one's temper

★**paciente** [paˈθjente] ADJ, NMF patient

pacificación [paθifikaˈθjon] NF pacification

pacificar [paθifiˈkar] /1g/ VT to pacify; (*tranquilizar*) to calm

★**pacífico, -a** [paˈθifiko, a] ADJ peaceful; (*persona*) peaceable; (*existencia*) peaceful; **el (océano) P~** the Pacific (Ocean)

pacifique *etc* [paθiˈfike] VB *ver* **pacificar**

pacifismo [paθiˈfismo] NM pacifism

pacifista [paθiˈfista] NMF pacifist

pack [pak] NM (*de yogures, latas*) pack; (*de vacaciones*) package

pacotilla [pakoˈtiʎa] NF trash; **de ~** shoddy

pactar [pakˈtar] /1a/ VT to agree to, agree on ▶ VI to come to an agreement

pacto [ˈpakto] NM (*tratado*) pact; (*acuerdo*) agreement

padecer [paðeˈθer] /2d/ VT (*sufrir*) to suffer; (*soportar*) to endure, put up with; (*ser víctima de*) to be a victim of ▶ VI: **~ de** to suffer from

padecimiento [paðeθiˈmjento] NM suffering

pádel [ˈpaðel] NM paddle tennis

padezca *etc* [paˈðeθka] VB *ver* **padecer**

★**padrastro** [paˈðrastro] NM stepfather

★**padre** [ˈpaðre] NM father; **~ espiritual** confessor; **P~ Nuestro** Lord's Prayer; **~ político** father-in-law; **García ~** García senior; **¡tu ~!** (*fam!*) up yours! (*fam!*) ▶ ADJ (*fam*): **un éxito ~** a tremendous success ■ **padres** NMPL parents

padrino [paˈðrino] NM godfather; (*fig*) sponsor, patron; **~ de boda** best man ■ **padrinos** NMPL godparents

padrón [paˈðron] NM (*censo*) census, roll; (*de socios*) register

padrote [paˈðrote] NM (*Am fam*) pimp

★**paella** [paˈeʎa] NF paella, *dish of rice with meat, shellfish etc*

pág(s). ABR (= *página(s)*) p(p)

★**paga** [ˈpaɣa] NF (*dinero pagado*) payment; (*sueldo*) pay, wages *pl*

pagadero, -a [paɣaˈðero, a] ADJ payable; **~ a la entrega/a plazos** payable on delivery/in instalments

pagano, -a [paˈɣano, a] ADJ, NM/F pagan, heathen

★**pagar** [paˈɣar] /1h/ VT (*gen*) to pay; (*las compras, crimen*) to pay for; (*deuda*) to pay (off); (*fig: favor*) to repay; **¡me las pagarás!** I'll get you for this!

▶ VI to pay; **~ al contado/a plazos** to pay (in) cash/in instalments ■ **pagarse** VR: **pagarse con algo** to be pleased with sth

pagaré [paɣaˈre] NM IOU

★**página** [ˈpaxina] NF page; **~ de inicio** (*Inform*) home page; **~ personal** (*Internet*) personal web page; **~ web** (*Internet*) web page; **páginas amarillas** Yellow Pages®

paginación [paxinaˈθjon] NF (*Inform, Tip*) pagination

paginar [paxiˈnar] /**1a**/ VT (*Inform, Tip*) to paginate

★**pago** [ˈpaɣo] NM (*dinero*) payment; (*fig*) return; **~ anticipado/a cuenta/a la entrega/en especie/inicial** advance payment/payment on account/cash on delivery/payment in kind/down payment; **~ a título gracioso** ex gratia payment; **en ~ de** in return for

pague *etc* [ˈpaɣe] VB *ver* **pagar**

paila [ˈpaila] NF (*Am*) frying pan

★**país** [paˈis] NM (*gen*) country; (*región*) land; **los Países Bajos** the Low Countries; **el P~ Vasco** the Basque Country

★**paisaje** [paiˈsaxe] NM countryside, landscape; (*vista*) scenery

paisano, -a [paiˈsano, a] ADJ of the same country ▶ NM/F (*compatriota*) fellow countryman(-woman); **vestir de ~** (*soldado*) to be in civilian clothes; (*guardia*) to be in plain clothes

paja [ˈpaxa] NF straw; (*fig*) trash, rubbish; (*en libro, ensayo*) padding, waffle; **riñeron por un quítame allá esas pajas** they quarrelled over a trifle

pajar [paˈxar] NM hay loft

pajarita [paxaˈrita] NF bow tie

★**pájaro** [ˈpaxaro] NM bird; (*fam: astuto*) clever fellow; **tener la cabeza a pájaros** to be featherbrained; **~ carpintero** woodpecker

pajita [paˈxita] NF (drinking) straw

pajizo, -a [paˈxiθo, a] ADJ (*de paja*) straw *cpd*; (*techo*) thatched; (*color*) straw-coloured

pakistaní [pakistaˈni] ADJ, NM/F Pakistani

pala [ˈpala] NF (*de mango largo*) spade; (*de mango corto*) shovel; (*raqueta etc*) bat; (: *de tenis*) racquet; (*Culin*) slice; **~ matamoscas** fly swat; **~ mecánica** power shovel

★**palabra** [paˈlaβra] NF (*gen, promesa*) word; (*facultad*) (power of) speech; (*derecho de hablar*) right to speak; **faltar a su ~** to go back on one's word; **quedarse con la ~ en la boca** to stop short; **tomar la ~** (*en reunión, comité etc*) to speak, take the floor; **pedir la ~** to ask to be allowed to speak; **tener la ~** to have the floor; **no encuentro palabras para expresarme** words fail me

palabrería [palaβreˈria] NF hot air

palabrota [palaˈβrota] NF swearword

★**palacio** [paˈlaθjo] NM palace; (*mansión*) mansion, large house; **~ de justicia** courthouse; **~ municipal** town/city hall

palada [paˈlaða] NF shovelful, spadeful; (*de remo*) stroke

paladar [palaˈðar] NM palate

paladear [palaðeˈar] /**1a**/ VT to taste

palanca [paˈlanka] NF lever; (*fig*) pull, influence; **~ de cambio** (*Auto*) gear lever, gearshift (*US*); **~ de freno** (*Auto*) brake lever; **~ de gobierno** *o* **de control** (*Inform*) joystick

palangana [palanˈgana] NF washbasin

palco [ˈpalko] NM box

palenque [paˈlenke] NM (*cerca*) stockade, fence; (*área*) arena, enclosure; (*de gallos*) pit

palentino, -a [palenˈtino, a] ADJ of *o* from Palencia ▶ NM/F native *o* inhabitant of Palencia

paleolítico, -a [paleoˈlitiko, a] ADJ palaeolithic (*Brit*), paleolithic (*US*)

paleontología [paleontoloˈxia] NF palaeontology (*Brit*), paleontology (*US*)

Palestina [palesˈtina] NF Palestine

palestino, -a [palesˈtino, a] ADJ, NM/F Palestinian

palestra [paˈlestra] NF: **salir** *o* **saltar a la ~** to come into the spotlight

paleto, -a [paˈleto, a] NM/F yokel, hick (*US*) ▶ NF (*pala*) small shovel; (*Arte*) palette; (*Anat*) shoulder blade; (*Deporte: de ping-pong*) bat; (*Am: helado*) ice lolly (*Brit*), Popsicle® (*US*)

paliar [paˈljar] /**1b**/ VT (*mitigar*) to mitigate; (*disfrazar*) to conceal

paliativo [paljaˈtiβo] NM palliative

palidecer [paliðeˈθer] /**2d**/ VI to turn pale

palidez [paliˈðeθ] NF paleness

palidezca *etc* [paliˈðeθka] VB *ver* **palidecer**

★**pálido, -a** [ˈpaliðo, a] ADJ pale

palillo [paˈliʎo] NM small stick; (*para dientes*) toothpick; **palillos (chinos)** chopsticks; **estar hecho un ~** to be as thin as a rake

palio [ˈpaljo] NM canopy

palique [paˈlike] NM: **estar de ~** (*fam*) to have a chat

paliza [paˈliθa] NF beating, thrashing; **dar** *o* **propinar** (*fam*) **una ~ a algn** to give sb a thrashing

palma [ˈpalma] NF (*Anat*) palm; (*árbol*) palm tree; **batir** *o* **dar palmas** to clap, applaud; **llevarse la ~** to triumph, win

palmada [palˈmaða] NF slap ■ **palmadas** NFPL clapping *sg*, applause *sg*

Palma de Mallorca NF Palma

palmar [palˈmar] /**1a**/ VI (*tb*: **palmarla**) to die, kick the bucket (*fam*)

palmarés [palmaˈres] NM (*lista*) list of winners; (*historial*) track record

palmear [palmeˈar] /**1a**/ VI to clap

palmera [palˈmera] NF (*Bot*) palm tree

palmero, -a [palˈmero, a] ADJ of the island of Palma ▶ NM/F native *o* inhabitant of the island of Palma

palmo [ˈpalmo] NM (*medida*) span; (*fig*) small amount; **~ a ~** inch by inch

P

palmotear [palmote'ar] /**1a**/ vi to clap, applaud
palmoteo [palmo'teo] NM clapping, applause
palo ['palo] NM stick; (*poste*) post, pole; (*mango*) handle, shaft; (*golpe*) blow, hit; (*de golf*) club; (*de béisbol*) bat; (*Naut*) mast; (*Naipes*) suit; **vermut a ~ seco** straight vermouth; **de tal ~ tal astilla** like father like son
paloma [pa'loma] NF dove, pigeon; **~ mensajera** carrier o homing pigeon
palomilla [palo'miʎa] NF moth; (*Tec: tuerca*) wing nut; (:*soporte*) bracket
palomitas [palo'mitas] NFPL popcorn *sg*
paloselfi [palo'selfi] NM selfie stick
palpable [pal'paβle] ADJ palpable; (*fig*) tangible
palpar [pal'par] /**1a**/ vt to touch, feel
palpitación [palpita'θjon] NF palpitation
palpitante [palpi'tante] ADJ palpitating; (*fig*) burning
palpitar [palpi'tar] /**1a**/ vi to palpitate; (*latir*) to beat
palta ['palta] NF (*AM*) avocado
palúdico, -a [pa'luðiko, a] ADJ marshy
paludismo [palu'ðismo] NM malaria
palurdo, -a [pa'lurðo, a] ADJ coarse, uncouth ▶ NM/F yokel, hick (*US*)
pamela [pa'mela] NF sun hat
pampa ['pampa] NF (*AM*) pampa(s), prairie
pamplinas [pam'plinas] NFPL nonsense *sg*
pamplonés, -esa [pamplo'nes, esa], **pamplonica** [pamplo'nika] ADJ of o from Pamplona ▶ NM/F native o inhabitant of Pamplona
★**pan** [pan] NM bread; (*una barra*) loaf; **~ de molde** sliced loaf; **~ integral** wholemeal bread; **~ rallado** breadcrumbs *pl*; **~ tostado** toast; **eso es ~ comido** it's a cinch; **llamar al ~ ~ y al vino vino** to call a spade a spade
pana ['pana] NF corduroy
★**panadería** [panaðe'ria] NF baker's (shop)
★**panadero, -a** [pana'ðero, a] NM/F baker
panal [pa'nal] NM honeycomb
Panamá [pana'ma] NM Panama
panameño, -a [pana'meɲo, a] ADJ Panamanian
pancarta [pan'karta] NF placard, banner
panceta [pan'θeta] NF bacon
pancho, -a ['pantʃo, a] ADJ: **estar tan ~** to remain perfectly calm ▶ NM (*AM*) hot dog
pancito [pan'sito] NM (*AM*) (bread) roll
páncreas ['pankreas] NM pancreas
panda ['panda] NM panda ▶ NF gang
pandemia [pan'demja] NF pandemic
pandereta [pande'reta] NF tambourine
pandilla [pan'diʎa] NF set, group; (*de criminales*) gang; (*pey*) clique
pando, -a ['pando, a] ADJ sagging
panecillo [pane'θiʎo] NM (bread) roll
panel [pa'nel] NM panel; **~ acústico** acoustic screen; **~ solar** solar panel

panera [pa'nera] NF bread basket
panfleto [pan'fleto] NM (*Pol etc*) pamphlet; lampoon
pánico ['paniko] NM panic
panificadora [panifika'ðora] NF bakery
panorama [pano'rama] NM panorama; (*vista*) view
panqué [pan'ke], **panqueque** [pan'keke] NM (*AM*) pancake
pantaletas [panta'letas] NFPL (*AM*) panties
★**pantalla** [pan'taʎa] NF (*de cine*) screen; (*de lámpara*) lampshade; (*Inform*) screen, display; **servir de ~ a** to be a blind for; **~ de ayuda** help screen; **~ de cristal líquido** liquid crystal display; **~ de plasma** plasma screen; **~ plana** flatscreen; **~ táctil** touchscreen
pantallazo [panta'ʎaθo] NM (*Inform*) screenshot
pantalón, pantalones [panta'lon(es)] NM(PL) trousers *pl*, pants *pl* (*US*); **pantalones cortos** shorts *pl*; **pantalones vaqueros** jeans *pl*
pantano [pan'tano] NM (*ciénaga*) marsh, swamp; (*depósito: de agua*) reservoir; (*fig*) jam, fix, difficulty
panteón [pante'on] NM (*monumento*) pantheon
pantera [pan'tera] NF panther
pantimedias [panti'meðjas] NFPL (*AM*) = **pantis**
pantis ['pantis] NMPL tights (*BRIT*), pantyhose (*US*)
pantomima [panto'mima] NF pantomime
pantorrilla [panto'rriʎa] NF calf (of the leg)
pants [pants] NMPL (*AM*) tracksuit (*BRIT*), sweat suit (*US*)
pantufla [pan'tufla] NF slipper
panty(s) ['panti(s)] NM(PL) tights (*BRIT*), pantyhose (*US*)
panza ['panθa] NF belly, paunch
panzón, -ona [pan'θon, ona], **panzudo, -a** [pan'θuðo, a] ADJ fat, potbellied
pañal [pa'ɲal] NM nappy, diaper (*US*); (*fig*) early stages, infancy *sg*; **estar todavía en pañales** to be still wet behind the ears
pañería [paɲe'ria] NF (*artículos*) drapery; (*tienda*) draper's (shop), dry-goods store (*US*)
paño ['paɲo] NM (*tela*) cloth; (*pedazo de tela*) (piece of) cloth; (*trapo*) duster, rag; **~ de cocina** dishcloth; **~ higiénico** sanitary towel; **paños menores** underclothes; **paños calientes** (*fig*) half-measures; **no andarse con paños calientes** to pull no punches
★**pañuelo** [pa'ɲwelo] NM handkerchief, hanky (*fam*); (*para la cabeza*) (head)scarf
★**papa** ['papa] NF (*AM: patata*) potato; **papas fritas** (*AM*) French fries, chips (*BRIT*); (*de bolsa*) crisps (*BRIT*), potato chips (*US*) ▶ NM: **el P~** the Pope
★**papá** [pa'pa] NM (*pl* **papás**) (*fam*) dad, daddy, pop (*US*); **hijo de ~** Hooray Henry (*fam*) ■ **papás** NMPL parents
papada [pa'paða] NF double chin

papagayo [papaˈɣajo] NM parrot

papalote [papaˈlote] NM (AM) kite

papanatas [papaˈnatas] NM INV (fam) sucker, simpleton

paparrucha [papaˈrrutʃa] NF (tontería) piece of nonsense

papaya [paˈpaja] NF papaya

papear [papeˈar] /1a/ VT, VI (fam) to eat

★**papel** [paˈpel] NM (gen) paper; (hoja de papel) sheet of paper; (Teat) part, role; ~ **de calco/carbón/de cartas** tracing paper/carbon paper/stationery; ~ **continuo** (Inform) continuous stationery; ~ **de arroz/envolver/fumar** rice/wrapping/cigarette paper; ~ **de aluminio/lija** tinfoil/sandpaper; ~ **del** o **de pagos al Estado** government bonds pl; ~ **higiénico** toilet paper; ~ **moneda** paper money; ~ **plegado (en abanico** o **en acordeón)** fanfold paper; ~ **pintado** wallpaper; ~ **secante** blotting paper; ~ **térmico** thermal paper ■ **papeles** NMPL identification papers

papeleo [papeˈleo] NM red tape

★**papelera** [papeˈlera] NF (cesto) wastepaper basket; (escritorio) desk; ~ **de reciclaje** (Inform) wastebasket

★**papelería** [papeleˈria] NF (tienda) stationer's (shop)

papeleta [papeˈleta] NF (pedazo de papel) slip o bit of paper; (Pol) ballot paper; (Escol) report; ¡**vaya ~!** this is a tough one!

paperas [paˈperas] NFPL mumps sg

papilla [paˈpiʎa] NF (de bebé) baby food; (pey) mush; **estar hecho ~** to be dog-tired

Papúa Nueva Guinea [papˈuanweβagiˈnea] NF Papua New Guinea

paquete [paˈkete] NM (caja) packet; (bulto) parcel; (AM fam) nuisance, bore; (Inform) package (of software); (de vacaciones) package tour; ~ **de aplicaciones** (Inform) applications package; ~ **integrado** (Inform) integrated package; ~ **de gestión integrado** combined management suite; **paquetes postales** parcel post sg

paquistaní [pakistaˈni] = **pakistaní**

★**par** [par] ADJ (igual) like, equal; (Mat) even ▶ NM equal; (de guantes) pair; (de veces) couple; (título) peer; (Golf, Com) par; **pares o nones** odds or evens; **abrir de ~ en ~** to open wide ▶ NF par; **a la ~** par; **sobre/bajo la ~** above/below par

★**para** [ˈpara] PREP for; **no es ~ comer** it's not for eating; **decir ~ sí** to say to o.s.; ¿~ **qué lo quieres?** what do you want it for?; **se casaron ~ separarse otra vez** they married only to separate again; ~ **entonces** by then o that time; **lo tendré ~ mañana** I'll have it for tomorrow; **ir ~ casa** to go home, head for home; ~ **profesor es muy estúpido** he's very stupid for a teacher; ¿**quién es usted ~ gritar así?** who are you to shout like that?; **tengo bastante ~ vivir** I have enough to live on

parabellum [paraβeˈlum] NM (automatic) pistol

parabién [paraˈβjen] NM congratulations pl

parábola [paˈraβola] NF parable; (Mat) parabola

parabólica [paraˈβolika] NF (tb: **antena parabólica**) satellite dish

★**parabrisas** [paraˈβrisas] NM INV windscreen, windshield (US)

paracaídas [parakaˈiðas] NM INV parachute

paracaidista [parakaiˈðista] NMF parachutist; (Mil) paratrooper

parachoques [paraˈtʃokes] NM INV bumper, fender (US); (Mecánica) shock absorber

★**parada** [paˈraða] NF ver **parado**

paradero [paraˈðero] NM stopping-place; (situación) whereabouts

★**parado, -a** [paˈraðo, a] ADJ (persona) motionless, standing still; (fábrica) closed, at a standstill; (coche) stopped; (AM: de pie) standing (up); (sin empleo) unemployed, idle; (confuso) confused; **salir bien ~** to come off well ▶ NF (gen) stop; (acto) stopping; (de industria) shutdown, stoppage; (lugar) stopping-place; **parada de autobús** bus stop; **parada discrecional** request stop; **parada en seco** sudden stop; **parada de taxis** taxi rank

paradoja [paraˈðoxa] NF paradox

paradójico, -a [paraˈðoxiko, a] ADJ paradoxical

★**parador** [paraˈðor] NM (ESP) (luxury) hotel (owned by the state)

The network of **paradores** was established by the government in the 1950s, when tourism was beginning to take off in Spain. They are first-class hotels, in unique locations or places of historical interest, often set up in old castles or monasteries. Currently, there are just under a hundred, all 3-star or above, offering top-quality service as well as a large range of local specialities.

parafrasear [parafraseˈar] /1a/ VT to paraphrase

paráfrasis [paˈrafrasis] NF INV paraphrase

paragolpes [paraˈɡolpes] NM INV (AM Auto) bumper, fender (US)

★**paraguas** [paˈraɣwas] NM INV umbrella

★**Paraguay** [paraˈɣwai] NM Paraguay

paraguayo, -a [paraˈɣwajo, a] ADJ, NM/F Paraguayan

paraíso [paraˈiso] NM paradise, heaven; ~ **fiscal** (Com) tax haven

paraje [paˈraxe] NM place, spot

paralelo, -a [paraˈlelo, a] ADJ, NM parallel; **en ~** (Elec, Inform) (in) parallel

paralice etc [paraˈliθe] VB ver **paralizar**

parálisis [paˈralisis] NF INV paralysis; ~ **cerebral** cerebral palsy; ~ **progresiva** creeping paralysis

paralítico, -a [paraˈlitiko, a] ADJ, NM/F paralytic

paralizar [parali'θar] /**1f**/ vт to paralyse ■ **paralizarse** vʀ to become paralysed; (*fig*) to come to a standstill

parámetro [pa'rametro] ɴм parameter

paramilitar [paramili'tar] ᴀᴅᴊ paramilitary

páramo ['paramo] ɴм bleak plateau

parangón [paran'gon] ɴм: **sin ~** incomparable

paraninfo [para'ninfo] ɴм (*Escol*) assembly hall

paranoia [para'noia] ɴ ꜰ paranoia

paranoico, -a [para'noiko, a] ᴀᴅᴊ, ɴм/ꜰ paranoid

paranormal [paranor'mal] ᴀᴅᴊ paranormal

parapente [para'pente] ɴм (*deporte*) paragliding; (*aparato*) paraglider

parapetarse [parape'tarse] /**1a**/ vʀ to shelter

parapléjico, -a [para'plexiko, a] ᴀᴅᴊ, ɴм/ꜰ paraplegic

★**parar** [pa'rar] /**1a**/ vт to stop; (*progreso etc*) to check, halt; (*golpe*) to ward off ▸ vɪ to stop; (*hospedarse*) to stay, put up; **no ~ de hacer algo** to keep on doing sth; **ha parado de llover** it has stopped raining; **van a ~ en la comisaría** they're going to end up in the police station; **no sabemos en qué va a ~ todo esto** we don't know where all this is going to end ■ **pararse** vʀ to stop; (*Am*) to stand up; **pararse a hacer algo** to stop to do sth; **pararse en** to pay attention to

pararrayos [para'rrajos] ɴм ɪɴᴠ lightning conductor

parásito, -a [pa'rasito, a] ɴм/ꜰ parasite

parasol [para'sol] ɴм parasol, sunshade

parcela [par'θela] ɴ ꜰ plot, piece of ground, smallholding

parche ['partʃe] ɴм patch

parchís [par'tʃis] ɴм ludo

parcial [par'θjal] ᴀᴅᴊ (*pago*) part-; (*eclipse*) partial; (*juez*) prejudiced, biased; (*Pol*) partisan

parcialidad [parθjali'ðað] ɴ ꜰ (*prejuicio*) prejudice, bias

parco, -a ['parko, a] ᴀᴅᴊ (*frugal*) sparing; (*moderado*) moderate

pardillo, -a [par'ðiʎo, a] ᴀᴅᴊ (*pey*) provincial ▸ ɴм/ꜰ (*pey*) country bumpkin ▸ ɴм (*Zool*) linnet

pardo, -a ['parðo, a] ᴀᴅᴊ (*color*) brown; (*cielo*) overcast; (*voz*) flat, dull

parear [pare'ar] /**1a**/ vт (*juntar, hacer par*) to match, put together; (*calcetines*) to put into pairs; (*Bio*) to mate, pair

★**parecer** [pare'θer] /**2d**/ ɴм (*opinión*) opinion, view; (*aspecto*) looks *pl* ▸ vɪ (*tener apariencia*) to seem, look; (*asemejarse*) to look like, seem like; (*aparecer, llegar*) to appear; **según parece** evidently, apparently; **al ~** apparently; **me parece que** I think (that), it seems to me that ■ **parecerse** vʀ to look alike, resemble each other; **parecerse a** to look like, resemble

Cuando *parecer* se refiere a la apariencia física de alguien o algo, se traduce por **look** cuando va con adjetivos o **look like** cuando va con sustantivos:
Parece mayor. **He looks older**.
Ese cuadro parece una pintura del Renacimiento. **That picture looks like a Renaissance painting**.

★**parecido, -a** [pare'θiðo, a] ᴀᴅᴊ similar; **~ a** like, similar to; **bien ~** good-looking, nice-looking ▸ ɴм similarity, likeness, resemblance

★**pared** [pa'reð] ɴ ꜰ wall; **~ divisoria/medianera** dividing/party wall; **subirse por las paredes** (*fam*) to go up the wall

paredón [pare'ðon] ɴм: **llevar a algn al ~** to put sb up against a wall, shoot sb

parejo, -a [pa'rexo, a] ᴀᴅᴊ (*igual*) equal; (*liso*) smooth, even ▸ ɴ ꜰ (*dos*) pair; (: *de personas*) couple; (*el otro: de un par*) other one (of a pair); (: *persona*) partner; (*de Guardias*) Civil Guard patrol

parentela [paren'tela] ɴ ꜰ relations *pl*

parentesco [paren'tesko] ɴм relationship

paréntesis [pa'rentesis] ɴм ɪɴᴠ parenthesis; (*digresión*) digression; (*en escrito*) bracket

parezco *etc* vʙ *ver* **parecer**

parida [pa'riða] ɴ ꜰ: **~ mental** (*fam*) dumb idea

paridad [pari'ðað] ɴ ꜰ (*Econ*) parity

★**pariente, -a** [pa'rjente, a] ɴм/ꜰ relative, relation

Do not translate the Spanish word **pariente** by *parent*.

parihuela [pari'wela] ɴ ꜰ stretcher

paripé [pari'pe] ɴм: **hacer el ~** to put on an act

parir [pa'rir] /**3a**/ vт to give birth to ▸ vɪ (*mujer*) to give birth, have a baby; (*yegua*) to foal; (*vaca*) to calve

París [pa'ris] ɴм Paris

parisiense [pari'sjense] ᴀᴅᴊ, ɴм ꜰ Parisian

paritario, -a [pari'tarjo, a] ᴀᴅᴊ equal

parka ['parka] ɴ ꜰ (*Am*) anorak

★**parking** ['parkin] ɴм car park, parking lot (*US*)

parlamentar [parlamen'tar] /**1a**/ vɪ (*negociar*) to parley

parlamentario, -a [parlamen'tarjo, a] ᴀᴅᴊ parliamentary ▸ ɴм/ꜰ member of parliament

parlamento [parla'mento] ɴм (*Pol*) parliament; (*Jur*) speech

parlanchín, -ina [parlan'tʃin, ina] ᴀᴅᴊ loose-tongued, indiscreet ▸ ɴм/ꜰ chatterbox

parlante [par'lante] ɴм (*Am*) loudspeaker

parlar [par'lar] /**1a**/ vɪ to chatter (away)

parlotear [parlote'ar] /**1a**/ vɪ to chatter, prattle

parloteo [parlo'teo] ɴм chatter, prattle

★**paro** ['paro] ɴм (*huelga*) stoppage (of work), strike; (*desempleo*) unemployment; **~ cardiaco** cardiac arrest; **estar en ~** (*Esp*) to be unemployed; **subsidio de ~** unemployment benefit; **hay ~ en la industria** work in the industry is at a standstill; **~ del sistema** (*Inform*) system shutdown

parodia [pa'roðja] NF parody

parodiar [paro'ðjar] /**1b**/ VT to parody

parpadear [parpaðe'ar] /**1a**/ VI (*los ojos*) to blink; (*luz*) to flicker

parpadeo [parpa'ðeo] NM (*de ojos*) blinking, winking; (*de luz*) flickering

párpado ['parpaðo] NM eyelid

★**parque** ['parke] NM (*lugar verde*) park; (*AM: munición*) ammunition; **~ de atracciones/de bomberos** fairground/fire station; **~ infantil/temático/zoológico** playground/theme park/zoo

parqué, parquet [par'ke] NM parquet

parqueadero [parkea'ðero] NM (*AM*) car park, parking lot (*US*)

parquímetro [par'kimetro] NM parking meter

parra ['parra] NF grapevine

párrafo ['parrafo] NM paragraph; **echar un ~** (*fam*) to have a chat

parranda [pa'rranda] NF (*fam*) spree, binge

parrilla [pa'rriʎa] NF (*Culin*) grill; (*AM Auto*) roof-rack; **~ (de salida)** (*Auto*) starting grid; **(carne a la) ~** grilled meat, barbecue

parrillada [parri'ʎaða] NF barbecue

párroco ['parroko] NM parish priest

parroquia [pa'rrokja] NF parish; (*iglesia*) parish church; (*Com*) clientele, customers *pl*

parroquiano, -a [parro'kjano, a] NM/F parishioner; client, customer

parsimonia [parsi'monja] NF (*frugalidad*) sparingness; (*calma*) deliberateness; **con ~** calmly

★**parte** ['parte] NM message; (*informe*) report; **dar ~ a algn** to report to sb; **~ meteorológico** weather forecast *o* report ▶ NF part; (*lado, cara*) side; (*de reparto*) share; (*Jur*) party; **en alguna ~ de Europa** somewhere in Europe; **en cualquier ~** anywhere; **por ahí no se va a ninguna ~** that leads nowhere; (*fig*) this is getting us nowhere; **en** *o* **por todas partes** everywhere; **en gran ~** to a large extent; **la mayor ~ de los españoles** most Spaniards; **de algún tiempo a esta ~** for some time past; **de ~ de algn** on sb's behalf; **¿de ~ de quién?** (*Telec*) who is speaking?; **por ~ de** on the part of; **yo por mi ~** I for my part; **por una ~ ... por otra ~** on the one hand, ... on the other (hand); **tomar ~** to take part

partera [par'tera] NF midwife

parterre [par'terre] NM (flower)bed

partición [parti'θjon] NF division, sharing-out; (*Pol*) partition

participación [partiθipa'θjon] NF (*acto*) participation, taking part; (*parte*) share; (*Com*) share, stock (*US*); (*de lotería*) (share in a) lottery ticket; (*aviso*) notice, notification; **~ en los beneficios** profit-sharing; **~ minoritaria** minority interest

participante [partiθi'pante] NMF participant

★**participar** [partiθi'par] /**1a**/ VT to notify, inform; **le participo que ...** I have to tell you that ... ▶ VI to take part, participate; **~ en una empresa** (*Com*) to invest in an enterprise

partícipe [par'tiθipe] NMF participant; **hacer ~ a algn de algo** to inform sb of sth

participio [parti'θipjo] NM participle; **~ de pasado/presente** past/present participle

partícula [par'tikula] NF particle

★**particular** [partiku'lar] ADJ (*especial*) particular, special; (*individual, personal*) private, personal; **tiene coche ~** he has a car of his own ▶ NM (*punto, asunto*) particular, point; (*individuo*) individual; **no dijo mucho sobre el ~** he didn't say much about the matter

particularice *etc* [partikula'riθe] VB *ver* **particularizar**

particularidad [partikulari'ðað] NF peculiarity; **tiene la ~ de que ...** one of its special features is (that) ...

particularizar [partikulari'θar] /**1f**/ VT to distinguish; (*especificar*) to specify; (*detallar*) to give details about

partida [par'tiða] NF (*salida*) departure; (*Com*) entry, item; (*juego*) game; (*grupo, bando*) band, group; **mala ~** dirty trick; **~ de nacimiento/matrimonio/defunción** birth/marriage/death certificate; **echar una ~** to have a game

partidario, -a [parti'ðarjo, a] ADJ partisan ▶ NM/F (*Deporte*) supporter; (*Pol*) partisan

partidismo [parti'ðismo] NM (*Jur*) partisanship, bias; (*Pol*) party politics

★**partido** [par'tiðo] NM (*Pol*) party; (*encuentro*) game, match; (*apoyo*) support; (*equipo*) team; **~ amistoso** (*Deporte*) friendly (game); **~ de fútbol** football match; **sacar ~ de** to profit from, benefit from; **tomar ~** to take sides

★**partir** [par'tir] /**3a**/ VT (*dividir*) to split, divide; (*compartir, distribuir*) to share (out), distribute; (*romper*) to break open, split open; (*rebanada*) to cut (off) ▶ VI (*ponerse en camino*) to set off, set out; **a ~ de** (starting) from ■ **partirse** VR to crack *o* split *o* break (in two *etc*); **partirse de risa** to split one's sides (laughing)

partitura [parti'tura] NF score

parto ['parto] NM birth, delivery; (*fig*) product, creation; **estar de ~** to be in labour

parvulario [parβu'larjo] NM nursery school, kindergarten

párvulo, -a ['parβulo, a] NM/F infant

pasa ['pasa] NF *ver* **paso**

pasable [pa'saβle] ADJ passable

pasacintas [pasa'θintas] NM (*AM*) cassette player

pasada [pa'saða] NF *ver* **pasado**

pasadizo [pasa'ðiθo] NM (*pasillo*) passage, corridor; (*callejuela*) alley

★**pasado, -a** [pa'saðo, a] ADJ past; (*malo: comida, fruta*) bad; (*muy cocido*) overdone; (*anticuado*) out of date; **~ mañana** the day after tomorrow; **el mes ~** last month; **pasados dos días** after two days; **~ de moda** old-fashioned; **lo ~**, **~** let bygones be bygones; **~ por agua** (*huevo*) boiled; **estar ~ de vueltas** o **de rosca** (*grifo, tuerca*) to be worn ▶ NM past; (*Ling*) past (tense) ▶ NF (*con un trapo*) wipe; **de pasada** in passing, incidentally; **una mala pasada** a dirty trick

pasador [pasa'ðor] NM (*gen*) bolt; (*de pelo*) slide; (*horquilla*) grip ∎ **pasadores** NMPL (*Am: cordones*) shoelaces

pasaje [pa'saxe] NM (*gen*) passage; (*pago de viaje*) fare; (*los pasajeros*) passengers pl; (*pasillo*) passageway

★**pasajero, -a** [pasa'xero, a] ADJ passing; (*situación, estado*) temporary; (*amor, enfermedad*) brief; (*ave*) migratory ▶ NM/F passenger; (*viajero*) traveller

pasamanos [pasa'manos] NM INV rail, handrail; (*de escalera*) banister

pasamontañas [pasamon'taɲas] NM INV balaclava (helmet)

★**pasaporte** [pasa'porte] NM passport

★**pasar** [pa'sar] /1a/ VT (*gen*) to pass; (*tiempo*) to spend; (*durezas*) to suffer, endure; (*noticia*) to give, pass on; (*película*) to show; (*persona*) to take, conduct; (*río*) to cross; (*barrera*) to pass through; (*falta*) to overlook, tolerate; (*contrincante*) to surpass, do better than; (*coche*) to overtake; (*contrabando*) to smuggle (in/out); (*enfermedad*) to give, infect with; **~ la aspiradora** to do the vacuuming or hoovering, hoover; **~ por alto** to skip; **pasarlo bien/bomba** o **de maravilla** to have a good/great time; **¡que lo pases bien!** have a good time!; **¿qué pasa?** what's happening?, what's going on?, what's up?; **¿qué te pasa?** what's wrong?; **¡cómo pasa el tiempo!** time just flies! ▶ VI (*gen*) to pass, go; (*terminarse*) to be over; (*ocurrir*) to happen; **~ de** to go beyond, exceed; **¡pase!** come in!; **nos hicieron ~** they showed us in; **~ por** to fetch; **~ por una crisis** to go through a crisis; **se hace ~ por médico** he passes himself off as a doctor; **el autobús pasa por nuestra casa** the bus goes past our house; **pase lo que pase** come what may ∎ **pasarse** VR (*efectos*) to pass, be over; (*flores*) to fade; (*comida*) to go bad, go off; (*fig*) to overdo it, go too far o over the top; **pasarse al enemigo** to go over to the enemy; **pasarse de la raya** to go too far; **¡no te pases!** watch it!; **se me pasó** I forgot; **se me pasó el turno** I missed my turn; **no se le pasa nada** nothing escapes him, he misses nothing; **ya se te pasará** you'll get over it

pasarela [pasa'rela] NF footbridge; (*en barco*) gangway

★**pasatiempo** [pasa'tjempo] NM pastime, hobby; (*distracción*) amusement

★**Pascua, pascua** ['paskwa] NF: **~ (de Resurrección)** Easter; **~ de Navidad** Christmas; **hacer la ~ a** (*fam*) to annoy, bug ∎ **Pascuas** NFPL Christmas time sg; **¡felices Pascuas!** Merry Christmas!; **de Pascuas a Ramos** once in a blue moon

pase ['pase] NM pass; (*Cine*) performance, showing; (*Com*) permit; (*Jur*) licence; **~ de diapositivas** slide show

★**pasear** [pase'ar] /1a/ VT to take for a walk; (*exhibir*) to parade, show off ▶ VI to walk, go for a walk; **~ en coche** to go for a drive ∎ **pasearse** VR to walk, go for a walk

★**paseo** [pa'seo] NM (*distancia corta*) (short) walk, stroll; (*avenida*) avenue; **~ marítimo** promenade; **dar un ~** to go for a walk; **~ en bicicleta** (bike) ride; **~ en barco** boat trip; **mandar a algn a ~** to tell sb to go to blazes; **¡vete a ~!** get lost!

★**pasillo** [pa'siʎo] NM passage, corridor

pasión [pa'sjon] NF passion

pasional [pasjo'nal] ADJ passionate; **crimen ~** crime of passion

pasivo, -a [pa'siβo, a] ADJ passive; (*inactivo*) inactive ▶ NM (*Com*) liabilities pl, debts pl; (*de cuenta*) debit side; **~ circulante** current liabilities

pasma ['pasma] NM (*fam*) cop

pasmado, -a [pas'maðo, a] ADJ (*asombrado*) astonished; (*atontado*) bewildered

pasmar [pas'mar] /1a/ VT (*asombrar*) to amaze, astonish ∎ **pasmarse** VR to be amazed o astonished

pasmo ['pasmo] NM amazement, astonishment; (*fig*) wonder, marvel

pasmoso, -a [pas'moso, a] ADJ amazing, astonishing

★**paso, -a** ['paso, a] ADJ dried ▶ NM (*gen, de baile*) step; (*modo de andar*) walk; (*huella*) footprint; (*rapidez*) speed, pace, rate; (*camino accesible*) way through, passage; (*cruce*) crossing; (*pasaje*) passing, passage; (*Rel*) religious float or sculpture; (*Geo*) pass; (*estrecho*) strait; (*fig*) step, measure; (*apuro*) difficulty; **~ a ~** step by step; **a ese ~** (*fig*) at that rate; **salir al ~ de** o **a** to waylay; **salir del ~** to get out of trouble; **dar un ~ en falso** to trip; (*fig*) to take a false step; **estar de ~** to be passing through; **~ atrás** step backwards; (*fig*) backward step; **~ elevado** flyover; **~ subterráneo** subway, underpass (US); **prohibido el ~** no entry; **ceda el ~** give way; **~ a nivel** (*Ferro*) level crossing; **~ (de) cebra** (*Esp*) zebra crossing; **~ de peatones** pedestrian crossing ▶ NF raisin; **pasa de Corinto/de Esmirna** currant/sultana; ver tb **Semana Santa**

pasota [pa'sota] ADJ, NMF (*fam*) ≈ dropout; **ser un (tipo) ~** to be a bit of a dropout; (*ser indiferente*) not to care about anything

pasotismo [paso'tismo] NM underground o alternative culture

★**pasta** ['pasta] NF (*gen*) paste; (*Culin: masa*) dough; (: *de bizcochos etc*) pastry; (*fam*) money, dough; (*encuadernación*) hardback; **~ de dientes** o **dentífrica** toothpaste; **~ de madera** wood pulp ∎ **pastas** NFPL (*bizcochos*) pastries, small cakes; (*espaguetis etc*) pasta sg

pastar [pas'tar] /1a/ VT, VI to graze

★**pastel** [pas'tel] NM (*dulce*) cake; (*Arte*) pastel; (*fig*) plot; **~ de carne** meat pie ■ **pasteles** NMPL pastry *sg*, confectionery *sg*

★**pastelería** [pastele'ria] NF cake shop, pastry shop

pasteurizado, -a [pasteuri'θaðo, a] ADJ pasteurized

★**pastilla** [pas'tiʎa] NF (*de jabón, chocolate*) cake, bar; (*píldora*) tablet, pill

pastizal [pasti'θal] NM pasture

pasto ['pasto] NM (*hierba*) grass; (*lugar*) pasture, field; (*fig*) food, nourishment

pastón [pas'ton] NM (*fam*): **cuesta un ~** it costs a fortune, it costs a packet (BRIT *fam*)

pastor, a [pas'tor, a] NM/F shepherd(ess) ▶ NM clergyman, pastor; (*Zool*) sheepdog; **~ alemán** Alsatian

pastoso, -a [pas'toso, a] ADJ (*material*) doughy, pasty; (*lengua*) furry; (*voz*) mellow

pat. ABR (= *patente*) pat

★**pata** ['pata] NF (*pierna*) leg; (*pie*) foot; (*de muebles*) leg; **patas arriba** upside down; **a cuatro patas** on all fours; **meter la ~** to put one's foot in it; **~ de cabra** (*Tec*) crowbar; **patas de gallo** crow's feet; **metedura de ~** (*fam*) gaffe; **tener buena/mala ~** to be lucky/unlucky

★**patada** [pa'taða] NF stamp; (*puntapié*) kick; **a patadas** (*muchos*) in abundance; (*trato*) roughly; **echar a algn a patadas** to kick sb out

patagón, -ona [pata'ɣon, ona] ADJ, NM/F Patagonian

Patagonia [pata'ɣonja] NF: **la ~** Patagonia

patalear [patale'ar] /1a/ VI to stamp one's feet

pataleo [pata'leo] NM stamping

patán [pa'tan] NM rustic, yokel

★**patata** [pa'tata] NF potato; **patatas fritas** o **a la española** chips (BRIT), French fries; (*de bolsa*) crisps (BRIT), potato chips (US); **ni ~** (*fam*) nothing at all; **no entendió ni ~** he didn't understand a single word

★**paté** [pa'te] NM pâté

patear [pate'ar] /1a/ VT (*pisar*) to stamp on, trample (on); (*pegar con el pie*) to kick ▶ VI to stamp (with rage), stamp one's foot

patentar [paten'tar] /1a/ VT to patent

patente [pa'tente] ADJ obvious, evident; (*Com*) patent ▶ NF patent

patera [pa'tera] NF boat

paternal [pater'nal] ADJ fatherly, paternal

paternalista [paterna'lista] ADJ (*tono, actitud etc*) patronizing

paternidad [paterni'ðað] NF fatherhood, parenthood; (*Jur*) paternity

paterno, -a [pa'terno, a] ADJ paternal

patético, -a [pa'tetiko, a] ADJ pathetic, moving

patíbulo [pa'tiβulo] NM scaffold, gallows *sg*

patilla [pa'tiʎa] NF (*de gafas*) sidepiece ■ **patillas** NFPL sideburns

★**patín** [pa'tin] NM skate; (*de tobogán*) runner; **patines de hielo** ice skates; **patines de ruedas** rollerskates

★**patinaje** [pati'naxe] NM skating

★**patinar** [pati'nar] /1a/ VI to skate; (*resbalarse*) to skid, slip; (*fam*) to slip up, blunder

patinazo [pati'naθo] NM (*Auto*) skid; **dar un ~** (*fam*) to blunder

patineta [pati'neta] NF (*patinete*) scooter; (*Am: monopatín*) skateboard

patinete [pati'nete] NM scooter

★**patio** ['patjo] NM (*de casa*) patio, courtyard; **~ de recreo** playground

★**pato** ['pato] NM duck; **pagar el ~** (*fam*) to take the blame, carry the can

patológico, -a [pato'loxiko, a] ADJ pathological

patoso, -a [pa'toso, a] ADJ awkward, clumsy

patotero [pato'tero] NM (*Am*) hooligan, lout

patraña [pa'traɲa] NF story, fib

patria ['patrja] NF native land, mother country; **~ chica** home town

patrimonio [patri'monjo] NM inheritance; (*fig*) heritage; (*Com*) net worth

patriota [pa'trjota] NMF patriot

patriotero, -a [patrjo'tero, a] ADJ chauvinistic

patriótico, -a [pa'trjotiko, a] ADJ patriotic

patriotismo [patrjo'tismo] NM patriotism

patrocinador, a [patroθina'ðor, a] NM/F sponsor

patrocinar [patroθi'nar] /1a/ VT to sponsor; (*apoyar*) to back, support

patrocinio [patro'θinjo] NM sponsorship; backing, support

★**patrón, -ona** [pa'tron, ona] NM/F (*jefe*) boss, chief, master (mistress); (*propietario*) landlord(-lady); (*Rel*) patron saint ▶ NM (*Costura*) pattern; (*Tec*) standard; **~ oro** gold standard

patronal [patro'nal] ADJ: **la clase ~** management; **cierre ~** lockout

patronato [patro'nato] NM sponsorship; (*acto*) patronage; (*Com*) employers' association; (*fundación*) trust; **el ~ de turismo** the tourist board

patrulla [pa'truʎa] NF patrol

patrullar [patru'ʎar] /1a/ VI to patrol

paulatino, -a [paula'tino, a] ADJ gradual, slow

paupérrimo, -a [pau'perrimo, a] ADJ very poor, poverty-stricken

★**pausa** ['pausa] NF pause; (*intervalo*) break; (*interrupción*) interruption; (*Tec: en videograbadora*) hold; **con ~** slowly

pausado, -a [pau'saðo, a] ADJ slow, deliberate

pauta ['pauta] NF line, guide line

pava ['paβa] NF (*Am*) kettle

pavimento [paβi'mento] NM (*Arq*) flooring; (*de losa*) pavement, paving

★**pavo** ['paβo] NM turkey; (*necio*) silly thing, idiot; **~ real** peacock; **¡no seas ~!** don't be silly!

P

pavonearse [paβone'arse] /**1a**/ VR to swagger, show off

pavor [pa'βor] NM dread, terror

payasada [paja'saða] NF ridiculous thing (to do) ▪ **payasadas** NFPL clowning sg

★**payaso, -a** [pa'jaso, a] NM/F clown

payo, -a ['pajo, a] ADJ, NM/F non-gipsy

★**paz** [paθ] NF peace; (tranquilidad) peacefulness, tranquillity; **dejar a algn en ~** to leave sb alone o in peace; **hacer las paces** to make peace; (fig) to make up; **¡déjame en ~!** leave me alone!; **¡haya ~!** stop it!

pazca etc ['paθka] VB ver **pacer**

PC NM ABR (Pol: = Partido Comunista) CP ▶ NM PC, personal computer

PCE [pe'θe] NM ABR = **Partido Comunista de España**

P.D. ABR (= posdata) P.S.

pdo. ABR (= pasado) ult.

★**peaje** [pe'axe] NM toll; **autopista de ~** toll motorway (BRIT), turnpike (US)

★**peatón** [pea'ton] NM pedestrian; **paso de peatones** pedestrian crossing, crosswalk (US)

peatonal [peato'nal] ADJ pedestrian

peca ['peka] NF freckle

pecado [pe'kaðo] NM sin

pecador, a [peka'ðor, a] ADJ sinful ▶ NM/F sinner

pecaminoso, -a [pekami'noso, a] ADJ sinful

pecar [pe'kar] /**1g**/ VI (Rel) to sin; (fig): **~ de generoso** to be too generous

pecera [pe'θera] NF fish tank; (redonda) goldfish bowl

★**pecho** ['petʃo] NM (Anat) chest; (de mujer) breast(s pl), bosom; (corazón) heart, breast; (valor) courage, spirit; **dar el ~ a** to breast-feed; **tomar algo a ~** to take sth to heart; **no le cabía en el ~** he was bursting with happiness

pechuga [pe'tʃuɣa] NF breast

pecoso, -a [pe'koso, a] ADJ freckled

peculiar [peku'ljar] ADJ special, peculiar; (característico) typical, characteristic

peculiaridad [pekuljari'ðað] NF peculiarity; (característica) special feature, characteristic

pedagogía [peðaɣo'ɣia] NF education

pedagogo [peða'ɣoɣo] NM pedagogue, teacher

pedal [pe'ðal] NM pedal; **~ de embrague** clutch (pedal); **~ de freno** brake pedal

pedalear [peðale'ar] /**1a**/ VI to pedal

pédalo ['peðalo] NM pedalo, pedal boat

pedante [pe'ðante] ADJ pedantic ▶ NMF pedant

pedantería [peðante'ria] NF pedantry

★**pedazo** [pe'ðaθo] NM piece, bit; **hacerse pedazos** to fall to pieces; (romperse) to smash, shatter; **un ~ de pan** a scrap of bread; (fig) a terribly nice person

pedernal [peðer'nal] NM flint

pedestal [peðes'tal] NM base; **tener/poner a algn en un ~** to put sb on a pedestal

pedestre [pe'ðestre] ADJ pedestrian; **carrera ~** foot race

pediatra [pe'ðjatra] NMF paediatrician (BRIT), pediatrician (US)

pediatría [peðja'tria] NF paediatrics sg (BRIT), pediatrics sg (US)

pedicuro, -a [peði'kuro, a] NM/F chiropodist (BRIT), podiatrist (US)

★**pedido** [pe'ðiðo] NM (Com) order; (petición) request; **pedidos en cartera** (Com) backlog sg

pedigrí [peði'ɣri] NM pedigree

★**pedir** [pe'ðir] /**3k**/ VT to ask for, request; (comida, Com: mandar) to order; (exigir: precio) to ask; (necesitar) to need, demand, require; **~ prestado** to borrow; **~ disculpas** to apologize; **me pidió que cerrara la puerta** he asked me to shut the door; **¿cuánto piden por el coche?** how much are they asking for the car? ▶ VI to ask

pedo ['peðo] (fam) ADJ INV: **estar ~** to be plastered o (BRIT fam!) pissed ▶ NM fart (fam!)

pedrada [pe'ðraða] NF throw of a stone; (golpe) blow from a stone; **herir a algn de una ~** to hit sb with a stone

pedrea [pe'ðrea] NF (granizada) hailstorm; (de lotería) minor prizes

pedrisco [pe'ðrisko] NM (granizo) hail; (granizada) hailstorm

Pedro ['peðro] NM Peter; **entrar como ~ por su casa** to come in as if one owned the place

pega ['peɣa] NF (dificultad) snag; **de ~** false, dud; **poner pegas** to raise objections

pegadizo, -a [peɣa'ðiθo, a] ADJ (canción etc) catchy

pegajoso, -a [peɣa'xoso, a] ADJ sticky, adhesive

pegamento [peɣa'mento] NM gum, glue

★**pegar** [pe'ɣar] /**1h**/ VT (papel, sellos) to stick (on); (con cola) to glue; (cartel) to post, stick up; (coser) to sew (on); (unir: partes) to join, fix together; (Inform) to paste; (Med) to give, infect with; (dar: golpe) to give, deal; **~ un grito** to let out a yell; **~ un salto** to jump (with fright); **~ fuego** to catch fire; **pegarle a algo** to be a great one for sth ▶ VI (adherirse) to stick, adhere; (Inform) to paste; (ir juntos: colores) to match, go together; (golpear) to hit; (quemar: el sol) to strike hot, burn; **~ en** to touch; **no pega** that doesn't seem right; **ese sombrero no pega con el abrigo** that hat doesn't go with the coat ▪ **pegarse** VR (gen) to stick; (dos personas) to hit each other, fight; **pegarse un tiro** to shoot o.s.

pegatina [peɣa'tina] NF (Pol etc) sticker

pego ['peɣo] NM: **dar el ~** (pasar por verdadero) to look like the real thing

pegote [pe'ɣote] NM (fam) eyesore, sight; (fig) patch, ugly mend; **tirarse pegotes** (fam) to come on strong

pegue etc ['peɣe] VB ver **pegar**

★**peinado** [pei'naðo] NM (*en peluquería*) hairdo; (*estilo*) hairstyle

peinar [pei'nar] /**1a**/ VT to comb sb's hair; (*con un cierto estilo*) to style ▪ **peinarse** VR to comb one's hair

★**peine** ['peine] NM comb

peineta [pei'neta] NF ornamental comb

p.ej. ABR (= *por ejemplo*) e.g.

Pekín [pe'kin] NM Beijing, Peking

pela ['pela] NF (ESP *fam*) peseta; *ver tb* **pelas**

pelado, -a [pe'laðo, a] ADJ (*cabeza*) shorn; (*fruta*) peeled; (*campo, fig*) bare; (*fam: sin dinero*) broke

pelaje [pe'laxe] NM (*Zool*) fur, coat; (*fig*) appearance

pelambre [pe'lambre] NM long hair, mop

★**pelar** [pe'lar] /**1a**/ VT (*fruta, patatas*) to peel; (*cortar el pelo a*) to cut the hair of; (*quitar la piel: animal*) to skin; (: *ave*) to pluck; (: *habas etc*) to shell ▪ **pelarse** VR (*la piel*) to peel off; **voy a pelarme** I'm going to get my hair cut; **corre que se las pela** (*fam*) he runs like nobody's business

pelas ['pelas] NFPL (ESP *fam*) dough

peldaño [pel'daɲo] NM step; (*de escalera portátil*) rung

★**pelea** [pe'lea] NF (*lucha*) fight; (*discusión*) quarrel, row

peleado, -a [pele'aðo, a] ADJ: **estar ~ (con algn)** to have fallen out (with sb)

★**pelear** [pele'ar] /**1a**/ VI to fight ▪ **pelearse** VR to fight; (*reñir*) to fall out, quarrel

pelela [pe'lela] NF (AM) potty

pelele [pe'lele] NM (*figura*) guy, dummy; (*fig*) puppet

peletería [pelete'ria] NF furrier's, fur shop

peliagudo, -a [pelja'ɣuðo, a] ADJ tricky

pelícano [pe'likano] NM pelican

★**película** [pe'likula] NF (*Cine*) film, movie (US); (*cobertura ligera*) film, thin covering; (*Foto: rollo*) roll *o* reel of film; **~ de dibujos (animados)** cartoon film; **~ muda** silent film; **de ~** (*fam*) astonishing, out of this world

peligrar [peli'ɣrar] /**1a**/ VI to be in danger

★**peligro** [pe'liɣro] NM danger; (*riesgo*) risk; **"~ de muerte"** "danger"; **correr ~ de** to be in danger of, run the risk of; **con ~ de la vida** at the risk of one's life

peligrosidad [peliɣrosi'ðað] NF danger, riskiness

peligroso, -a [peli'ɣroso, a] ADJ dangerous; risky

★**pelirrojo, -a** [peli'rroxo, a] ADJ red-haired, red-headed ▸ NM/F redhead

pellejo [pe'ʎexo] NM (*de animal*) skin, hide; **salvar el ~** to save one's skin

pellizcar [peʎiθ'kar] /**1g**/ VT to pinch, nip

pellizco [pe'ʎiθko] NM pinch

pellizque *etc* [pe'ʎiθke] VB *ver* **pellizcar**

pelma ['pelma] NMF, **pelmazo, -a** [pel'maθo, a] NM/F (*fam*) pain (in the neck)

★**pelo** ['pelo] NM (*cabellos*) hair; (*de barba, bigote*) whisker; (*de animal: piel*) fur, coat; (*de perro etc*) hair, coat; (*de ave*) down; (*de tejido*) nap; (*Tec*) fibre; **a ~** bareheaded; (*desnudo*) naked; **al ~** just right; **venir al ~** to be exactly what one needs; **un hombre de ~ en pecho** a brave man; **por los pelos** by the skin of one's teeth; **escaparse por un ~** to have a close shave; **se me pusieron los pelos de punta** my hair stood on end; **no tener pelos en la lengua** to be outspoken, not mince words; **con pelos y señales** in minute detail; **tomar el ~ a algn** to pull sb's leg

pelón, -ona [pe'lon, ona] ADJ hairless, bald

★**pelota** [pe'lota] NF ball; (*fam: cabeza*) nut (*fam*); **en ~(s)** stark naked; **~ vasca** pelota; **devolver la ~ a algn** (*fig*) to turn the tables on sb; **hacer la ~ (a algn)** to creep (to sb)

pelotera [pelo'tera] NF (*fam*) barney

pelotón [pelo'ton] NM (*Mil*) squad, detachment

peluca [pe'luka] NF wig

peluche [pe'lutʃe] NM: **muñeco de ~** soft toy

peludo, -a [pe'luðo, a] ADJ hairy, shaggy

★**peluquería** [peluke'ria] NF hairdresser's; (*para hombres*) barber's (shop)

★**peluquero, -a** [pelu'kero, a] NM/F hairdresser; barber

peluquín [pelu'kin] NM toupée

pelusa [pe'lusa] NF (*Bot*) down; (*Costura*) fluff

pelvis ['pelβis] NF pelvis

PEMEX [pe'meks] NM ABR = **Petróleos Mexicanos**

PEN [pen] NM ABR (ESP) = **Plan Energético Nacional**; (ARGENTINA) = **Poder Ejecutivo Nacional**

★**pena** ['pena] NF (*congoja*) grief, sadness; (*remordimiento*) regret; (*dificultad*) trouble; (*dolor*) pain; (AM: *vergüenza*) shame; (*Jur*) sentence; (*Deporte*) penalty; **~ capital** capital punishment; **~ de muerte** death penalty; **~ pecuniaria** fine; **merecer** *o* **valer la ~** to be worthwhile; **a duras penas** with great difficulty; **so ~ de** on pain of; **me dan ~** I feel sorry for them; **¡no te da ~ hacerlo?** (AM) aren't you embarrassed doing that?; **¡qué ~!** what a shame *o* pity!

penal [pe'nal] ADJ penal ▸ NM (*cárcel*) prison

penalidad [penali'ðað] NF (*problema, dificultad*) trouble, hardship; (*Jur*) penalty, punishment ▪ **penalidades** NFPL trouble *sg*, hardship *sg*

penalizar [penali'θar] /**1f**/ VT to penalize

penalti, penalty [pe'nalti] (*pl* **penalties** *o* **penaltys**) NM (*Deporte*) penalty (kick)

penar [pe'nar] /**1a**/ VT to penalize; (*castigar*) to punish ▸ VI to suffer

pendejo, -a [pen'dexo, a] NM/F (AM *fam!*) wanker (BRIT *fam!*), jerk (*esp* US *fam*)

pender [pen'der] /**2a**/ VI (*colgar*) to hang; (*Jur*) to be pending

★**pendiente** [pen'djente] ADJ pending, unsettled; **tener una asignatura ~** to have to resit a subject ▸ NM earring ▸ NF hill, slope

pendón [pen'don] NM banner, standard

péndulo ['pendulo] NM pendulum

pene ['pene] NM penis

penene [pe'nene] NMF = **PNN**

penetración [penetra'θjon] NF (acto) penetration; (agudeza) sharpness, insight

penetrante [pene'trante] ADJ (herida) deep; (persona, arma) sharp; (sonido) penetrating, piercing; (mirada) searching; (viento, ironía) biting

penetrar [pene'trar] /**1a**/ VT to penetrate, pierce; (entender) to grasp ▶ VI to penetrate, go in; (entrar) to enter; (líquido) to soak in; (emoción) to pierce

penicilina [peniθi'lina] NF penicillin

★**península** [pe'ninsula] NF peninsula; **P~ Ibérica** Iberian Peninsula

peninsular [peninsu'lar] ADJ peninsular

★**penique** [pe'nike] NM penny ■ **peniques** NMPL pence

penitencia [peni'tenθja] NF (remordimiento) penitence; (castigo) penance; **en ~** as a penance

penitencial [peniten'θjal] ADJ penitential

penitenciaría [penitenθja'ria] NF prison, penitentiary

penitenciario, -a [peniten'θjarjo, a] ADJ prison cpd

penoso, -a [pe'noso, a] ADJ laborious, difficult; (lamentable) distressing

pensado, -a [pen'saðo, a] ADJ: **bien/mal ~** well intentioned/cynical; **en el momento menos ~** when least expected

pensador, a [pensa'ðor, a] NM/F thinker

pensamiento [pensa'mjento] NM (gen) thought; (mente) mind; (idea) idea; (Bot) pansy; **no se la pasó por el ~** it never occurred to him

★**pensar** [pen'sar] /**1j**/ VT to think; (considerar) to think over, think out; (proponerse) to intend, plan, propose; (imaginarse) to think up, invent ▶ VI to think; **~ en** to think of o about; (anhelar) to aim at, aspire to; **dar que ~ a algn** to give sb food for thought

pensativo, -a [pensa'tiβo, a] ADJ thoughtful, pensive

★**pensión** [pen'sjon] NF (casa) ≈ guest house; (dinero) pension; (cama y comida) board and lodging; **~ de jubilación** retirement pension; **~ escalada** graduated pension; **~ completa** full board; **media ~** half board

pensionista [pensjo'nista] NMF (jubilado) (old-age) pensioner; (el que vive en una pensión) lodger; (Escol) boarder

pentágono [pen'taɣono] NM pentagon; **el P~** the Pentagon

pentagrama [penta'ɣrama] NM (Mus) stave, staff

penúltimo, -a [pe'nultimo, a] ADJ penultimate, second last

penumbra [pe'numbra] NF half-light, semi-darkness

penuria [pe'nurja] NF shortage, want

peña ['peɲa] NF (roca) rock; (acantilado) cliff, crag; (grupo) group, circle; (Am: club) folk club; (Deporte) supporters' club

peñasco [pe'ɲasko] NM large rock, boulder

peñón [pe'ɲon] NM crag; **el P~** the Rock (of Gibraltar)

peón [pe'on] NM labourer; (Am) farm labourer, farmhand; (Tec) spindle, shaft; (Ajedrez) pawn

peonza [pe'onθa] NF spinning top

★**peor** [pe'or] ADJ (comparativo) worse; (superlativo) worst; **A es ~ que B** A is worse than B; **Z es el ~ de todos** Z is the worst of all ▶ ADV (comparativo) worse; (superlativo) worst; **de mal en ~** from bad to worse; **tanto ~** so much the worse

pepenar [pepe'nar] /**1a**/ VI (Am) to sift through rubbish o garbage

pepinillo [pepi'niʎo] NM gherkin

★**pepino** [pe'pino] NM cucumber; **(no) me importa un ~** I don't care one bit

pepita [pe'pita] NF (Bot) pip; (Minería) nugget

pepito [pe'pito] NM (Esp: tb: **pepito de ternera**) steak sandwich

peque etc ['peke] VB ver **pecar**

pequeñez [peke'ɲeθ] NF smallness, littleness; (trivialidad) trifle, triviality

★**pequeño, -a** [pe'keɲo, a] ADJ small, little; (cifra) small, low; (bajo) short; **~ burgués** lower middle-class

pequinés, -esa [peki'nes, esa] ADJ, NM/F Pekinese

★**pera** ['pera] ADJ INV classy; **niño ~** spoiled upper-class brat ▶ NF pear; **eso es pedir peras al olmo** that's asking the impossible

peral [pe'ral] NM pear tree

percance [per'kanθe] NM setback, misfortune

per cápita [per'kapita] ADJ: **renta ~** per capita income

percatarse [perka'tarse] /**1a**/ VR: **~ de** to notice, take note of

percebe [per'θeβe] NM (Zool) barnacle; (fam) idiot

percepción [perθep'θjon] NF (vista) perception; (idea) notion, idea; (Com) collection

perceptible [perθep'tiβle] ADJ perceptible, noticeable; (Com) payable, receivable

percha ['pertʃa] NF (poste) pole, support; (gancho) peg; (de abrigos) coat stand; (colgador) coat hanger; (ganchos) coat hooks pl; (de ave) perch

perchero [per'tʃero] NM clothes rack

★**percibir** [perθi'βir] /**3a**/ VT to perceive, notice; (ver) to see; (peligro etc) to sense; (Com) to earn, receive, get

percusión [perku'sjon] NF percussion

percusor [perku'sor], **percutor** [perku'tor] NM (Tec) hammer; (de arma) firing pin

perdedor, a [perðe'ðor, a] ADJ losing ▶ NM/F loser

★perder [per'ðer] /**2g**/ vт to lose; *(tiempo, palabras)* to waste; *(oportunidad)* to lose, miss; *(tren)* to miss; **he perdido la costumbre** I have got out of the habit ▶ vı to lose; **echar a ~** *(comida)* to spoil, ruin; *(oportunidad)* to waste; **tener buen ~** to be a good loser ■ **perderse** vʀ *(extraviarse)* to get lost; *(desaparecer)* to disappear, be lost to view; *(arruinarse)* to be ruined; **¡no te lo pierdas!** don't miss it!

perdición [perði'θjon] ɴF perdition; *(fig)* ruin

★pérdida ['perðiða] ɴF loss; *(de tiempo)* waste; *(Com)* net loss; **¡no tiene ~!** you can't go wrong!; **~ contable** *(Com)* book loss ■ **pérdidas** ɴFPL *(Com)* losses

perdido, -a [per'ðiðo, a] ADJ lost; **estar ~ por** to be crazy about; **es un caso ~** he is a hopeless case

perdigón [perði'ɣon] ɴM pellet

perdiz [per'ðiθ] ɴF partridge

★perdón [per'ðon] ɴM *(disculpa)* pardon, forgiveness; *(clemencia)* mercy; **¡~!** sorry!, I beg your pardon!; **con ~** if I may, if you don't mind

★perdonar [perðo'nar] /**1a**/ vт to pardon, forgive; *(la vida)* to spare; *(excusar)* to exempt, excuse ▶ vı to pardon, forgive; **¡perdone (usted)!** sorry!, I beg your pardon!; **perdone, pero me parece que ...** excuse me, but I think ...

perdurable [perðu'raβle] ADJ lasting; *(eterno)* everlasting

perdurar [perðu'rar] /**1a**/ vı *(resistir)* to last, endure; *(seguir existiendo)* to stand, still exist

perecedero, -a [pereθe'ðero, a] ADJ perishable

perecer [pere'θer] /**2d**/ vı to perish, die

peregrinación [pereɣrina'θjon] ɴF *(Rel)* pilgrimage

peregrino, -a [pere'ɣrino, a] ADJ *(extraño)* strange; *(singular)* rare ▶ ɴM/F pilgrim

perejil [pere'xil] ɴM parsley

perenne [pe'renne] ADJ perennial

perentorio, -a [peren'torjo, a] ADJ *(urgente)* urgent; *(terminante)* peremptory; *(fijo)* set, fixed

pereza [pe'reθa] ɴF *(flojera)* laziness; *(lentitud)* sloth, slowness

perezca *etc* [pe'reθka] vʙ *ver* **perecer**

★perezoso, -a [pere'θoso, a] ADJ *(flojo)* lazy; *(lento)* slow, sluggish

perfección [perfek'θjon] ɴF perfection; **a la ~** to perfection

perfeccionar [perfekθjo'nar] /**1a**/ vт to perfect; *(mejorar)* to improve; *(acabar)* to complete, finish

★perfectamente [perfekta'mente] ADV perfectly

★perfecto, -a [per'fekto, a] ADJ perfect ▶ ɴM *(Ling)* perfect (tense)

perfidia [per'fiðja] ɴF perfidy, treachery

pérfido, -a ['perfiðo, a] ADJ perfidious, treacherous

perfil [per'fil] ɴM *(parte lateral)* profile; *(silueta)* silhouette, outline; *(Tec)* (cross) section; **~ del cliente** *(Com)* customer profile; **en ~** from the side, in profile ■ **perfiles** ɴMPL *(fig)* features; *(cortesías)* social graces

perfilado, -a [perfi'laðo, a] ADJ *(bien formado)* well-shaped; *(largo: cara)* long

perfilar [perfi'lar] /**1a**/ vт *(trazar)* to outline; *(dar carácter a)* to shape, give character to ■ **perfilarse** vʀ: **perfilarse (en)** to be silhouetted (against); **el proyecto se va perfilando** the project is taking shape

perforación [perfora'θjon] ɴF perforation; *(con taladro)* drilling

perforadora [perfora'ðora] ɴF drill; *(tb: perforadora de fichas)* card-punch

perforar [perfo'rar] /**1a**/ vт to perforate; *(agujero)* to drill, bore; *(papel)* to punch a hole in ▶ vı to drill, bore

perfumar [perfu'mar] /**1a**/ vт to scent, perfume

★perfume [per'fume] ɴM perfume, scent

★perfumería [perfume'ria] ɴF perfume shop

pergamino [perɣa'mino] ɴM parchment

pericia [pe'riθja] ɴF skill, expertise

periferia [peri'ferja] ɴF periphery; *(de ciudad)* outskirts *pl*

periférico, -a [peri'feriko, a] ADJ peripheral; **barrio ~** outlying district ▶ ɴM *(Inform)* peripheral; *(Am Auto)* ring road (Brit), beltway (US)

perilla [pe'riʎa] ɴF *(barba)* goatee; *(Am: de puerta)* doorknob, door handle

perímetro [pe'rimetro] ɴM perimeter

★periódico, -a [pe'rjoðiko, a] ADJ periodic(al) ▶ ɴM (news)paper; **~ dominical** Sunday (news)paper

★periodismo [perjo'ðismo] ɴM journalism

★periodista [perjo'ðista] ɴMF journalist

periodístico, -a [perjo'ðistiko, a] ADJ journalistic

periodo [pe'rjoðo], **período** [pe'rioðo] ɴM period; **~ contable** *(Com)* accounting period

peripecias [peri'peθjas] ɴFPL adventures

peripuesto, -a [peri'pwesto, a] ADJ dressed up; **tan ~** all dressed up (to the nines)

★periquito [peri'kito] ɴM budgerigar, budgie *(fam)*

perito, -a [pe'rito, a] ADJ *(experto)* expert; *(diestro)* skilled, skilful ▶ ɴM/F *(experto)* expert; *(especialista)* skilled worker; *(técnico)* technician

perjudicar [perxuði'kar] /**1g**/ vт *(gen)* to damage, harm; *(fig)* to prejudice

perjudicial [perxuði'θjal] ADJ damaging, harmful; *(en detrimento)* detrimental

perjudique *etc* [perxu'ðike] vʙ *ver* **perjudicar**

perjuicio [per'xwiθjo] ɴM damage, harm; **en/sin ~ de** to the detriment of/without prejudice to

perjurar [perxu'rar] /**1a**/ vı to commit perjury

perla ['perla] ɴF pearl; **me viene de perlas** it suits me fine

★**permanecer** [permane'θer] /**2d**/ vi (*quedarse*) to stay, remain; (*seguir*) to continue to be

permanencia [perma'nenθja] NF (*duración*) permanence; (*estancia*) stay

★**permanente** [perma'nente] ADJ (*que queda*) permanent; (*constante*) constant; (*comisión etc*) standing ▶ NF perm; **hacerse una ~** to have one's hair permed

permanezca *etc* [perma'neθka] VB *ver* **permanecer**

permisible [permi'siβle] ADJ permissible, allowable

★**permiso** [per'miso] NM permission; (*licencia*) permit, licence (BRIT), license (US); **con ~** excuse me; **estar de ~** (*Mil*) to be on leave; **~ de conducir** o **conductor** driving licence (BRIT), driver's license (US); **~ de exportación/importación** export/import licence; **~ por asuntos familiares** compassionate leave; **~ por enfermedad** (*AM*) sick leave

★**permitir** [permi'tir] /**3a**/ VT to permit, allow; **¿me permite?** may I?; **si lo permite el tiempo** weather permitting ■ **permitirse** VR: **permitirse algo** to allow o.s. sth; **no me puedo ~ ese lujo** I can't afford that

permuta [per'muta] NF exchange

permutar [permu'tar] /**1a**/ VT to switch, exchange; **~ destinos con algn** to swap o exchange jobs with sb

pernera [per'nera] NF trouser leg

pernicioso, -a [perni'θjoso, a] ADJ (*maligno, Med*) pernicious; (*persona*) wicked

perno ['perno] NM bolt

pernoctar [pernok'tar] /**1a**/ vi to stay the night

★**pero** ['pero] CONJ but; (*aún*) yet ▶ NM (*defecto*) flaw, defect; (*reparo*) objection; **¡no hay ~ que valga!** there are no buts about it

perogrullada [peroɣru'ʎaða] NF platitude, truism

perol [pe'rol] NM, **perola** [pe'rola] NF pan

peronista [pero'nista] ADJ, NMF Peronist

perorata [pero'rata] NF long-winded speech

perpendicular [perpendiku'lar] ADJ perpendicular; **el camino es ~ al río** the road is at right angles to the river

perpetrar [perpe'trar] /**1a**/ VT to perpetrate

perpetuamente [perpetwa'mente] ADV perpetually

perpetuar [perpe'twar] /**1e**/ VT to perpetuate

perpetuo, -a [per'petwo, a] ADJ perpetual; (*Jur etc*: *condena*) life *cpd*

Perpiñán [perpi'ɲan] NM Perpignan

perplejo, -a [per'plexo, a] ADJ perplexed, bewildered

perra ['perra] NF (*Zool*) bitch; (*fam*: *dinero*) money; (: *manía*) mania, crazy idea; (: *rabieta*) tantrum; **estar sin una ~** to be flat broke

perrera [pe'rrera] NF kennel

perrito [pe'rrito] NM (*tb*: **perrito caliente**) hot dog

★**perro** ['perro] NM dog; **~ caliente** hot dog; **"~ peligroso"** "beware of the dog"; **ser ~ viejo** to be an old hand; **tiempo de perros** filthy weather; **~ que ladra no muerde** his bark is worse than his bite

perroflauta [perro'flauta] NMF (*fam*) down-and-out (*fam*), bum (*esp US fam*)

persa ['persa] ADJ, NMF Persian ▶ NM (*Ling*) Persian

persecución [perseku'θjon] NF pursuit, hunt, chase; (*Rel, Pol*) persecution

perseguir [perse'ɣir] /**3d, 3k**/ VT to pursue, hunt; (*cortejar*) to chase after; (*molestar*) to pester, annoy; (*Rel, Pol*) to persecute; (*Jur*) to prosecute

perseverante [perseβe'rante] ADJ persevering, persistent

perseverar [perseβe'rar] /**1a**/ vi to persevere, persist; **~ en** to persevere in, persist with

★**persiana** [per'sjana] NF (Venetian) blind

persiga *etc* [per'siɣa] VB *ver* **perseguir**

persignarse [persiɣ'narse] /**1a**/ VR to cross o.s.

persiguiendo *etc* [persi'ɣjenðo] VB *ver* **perseguir**

persistente [persis'tente] ADJ persistent

persistir [persis'tir] /**3a**/ vi to persist

★**persona** [per'sona] NF person; **10 personas** 10 people; **~ mayor** elderly person; **tercera ~** third person; (*Ling*) third person; **en ~** in person o the flesh; **por ~** a head; **es buena ~** he's a good sort

★**personaje** [perso'naxe] NM important person, celebrity; (*Teat*) character

★**personal** [perso'nal] ADJ (*particular*) personal; (*para una persona*) single, for one person ▶ NM (*plantilla*) personnel, staff; (*Naut*) crew; (*fam*: *gente*) people

★**personalidad** [personali'ðað] NF personality; (*Jur*) status

personalizar [personali'θar] /**1f**/ VT to personalize ▶ VI (*al hablar*) to name names

personarse [perso'narse] /**1a**/ VR to appear in person; **~ en** to present o.s. at, report to

personero, -a [perso'nero, a] NM/F (*AM*) (government) official

personificar [personifi'kar] /**1g**/ VT to personify

personifique *etc* [personi'fike] VB *ver* **personificar**

★**perspectiva** [perspek'tiβa] NF perspective; (*vista, panorama*) view, panorama; (*posibilidad futura*) outlook, prospect; **tener algo en ~** to have sth in view

perspicacia [perspi'kaθja] NF discernment, perspicacity

perspicaz [perspi'kaθ] ADJ shrewd

★**persuadir** [perswa'ðir] /**3a**/ VT (*gen*) to persuade; (*convencer*) to convince ■ **persuadirse** VR to become convinced

persuasión [perswaˈsjon] NF (*acto*) persuasion; (*convicción*) conviction

persuasivo, -a [perwaˈsiβo, a] ADJ persuasive; convincing

★**pertenecer** [perteneˈθer] /**2d**/ VI: ~ **a** to belong to; (*fig*) to concern

perteneciente [perteneˈθjente] ADJ: ~ **a** belonging to

pertenencia [perteˈnenθja] NF ownership ■ **pertenencias** NFPL possessions, property *sg*

pertenezca *etc* [perteˈneθka] VB *ver* **pertenecer**

pértiga [ˈpertiɣa] NF pole; **salto de ~** pole vault

pertinaz [pertiˈnaθ] ADJ (*persistente*) persistent; (*terco*) obstinate

pertinente [pertiˈnente] ADJ relevant, pertinent; (*apropiado*) appropriate; ~ **a** concerning, relevant to

pertrechar [pertreˈtʃar] /**1a**/ VT (*gen*) to supply; (*Mil*) to supply with ammunition and stores ■ **pertrecharse** VR: **pertrecharse de algo** to provide o.s. with sth

pertrechos [perˈtretʃos] NMPL (*gen*) implements; (*Mil*) supplies and stores

perturbación [perturβaˈθjon] NF (*Pol*) disturbance; (*Med*) upset, disturbance; ~ **del orden público** breach of the peace

perturbador, a [perturβaˈðor, a] ADJ (*que perturba*) perturbing, disturbing; (*subversivo*) subversive

perturbar [perturˈβar] /**1a**/ VT (*el orden*) to disturb; (*Med*) to upset, disturb; (*mentalmente*) to perturb

★**Perú** [peˈru] NM Peru

★**peruano, -a** [peˈrwano, a] ADJ, NM/F Peruvian

perversión [perβerˈsjon] NF perversion

perverso, -a [perˈβerso, a] ADJ perverse; (*depravado*) depraved

pervertido, -a [perβerˈtiðo, a] ADJ perverted ▶ NM/F pervert

pervertir [perβerˈtir] /**3i**/ VT to pervert, corrupt

pervierta *etc* [perˈβjerta], **pervirtiendo** *etc* [perβirˈtjendo] VB *ver* **pervertir**

pesa [ˈpesa] NF weight; (*Deporte*) shot

pesadez [pesaˈðeθ] NF (*calidad de pesado*) heaviness; (*lentitud*) slowness; (*aburrimiento*) tediousness; **es una ~ tener que ...** it's a bind having to ...

★**pesadilla** [pesaˈðiʎa] NF nightmare, bad dream; (*fig*) worry, obsession

★**pesado, -a** [peˈsaðo, a] ADJ (*gen*) heavy; (*lento*) slow; (*difícil, duro*) tough, hard; (*aburrido*) tedious, boring; (*bochornoso*) sultry; **tener el estómago ~** to feel bloated; **¡no seas ~!** come off it! ▶ NM/F bore

pesadumbre [pesaˈðumbre] NF grief, sorrow

pésame [ˈpesame] NM expression of condolence, message of sympathy; **dar el ~** to express one's condolences

★**pesar** [peˈsar] /**1a**/ VT to weigh; (*fig*) to weigh heavily on; (*afligir*) to grieve; **no me pesa haberlo hecho** I'm not sorry I did it ▶ VI to weigh; (*ser pesado*) to weigh a lot, be heavy; (*fig: opinión*) to carry weight; **no pesa mucho** it's not very heavy ▶ NM (*sentimiento*) regret; (*pena*) grief, sorrow; **a ~ de (que)** in spite of, despite

★**pesca** [ˈpeska] NF (*acto*) fishing; (*cantidad de pescado*) catch; ~ **de altura/en bajura** deep sea/coastal fishing; **ir de ~** to go fishing

★**pescadería** [peskaðeˈria] NF fish shop, fishmonger's

pescadilla [peskaˈðiʎa] NF whiting

★**pescado** [pesˈkaðo] NM fish

★**pescador, a** [peskaˈðor, a] NM/F fisherman(-woman)

★**pescar** [pesˈkar] /**1g**/ VT (*coger*) to catch; (*tratar de coger*) to fish for; (*fam: lograr*) to get hold of, land; (*conseguir: trabajo*) to manage to get; (*sorprender*) to catch unawares ▶ VI to fish, go fishing

pescuezo [pesˈkweθo] NM neck

pese [ˈpese] PREP: ~ **a** despite, in spite of

pesebre [peˈseβre] NM manger

★**peseta** [peˈseta] NF (*Historia*) peseta

pesetero, -a [peseˈtero, a] ADJ money-grubbing

pesimismo [pesiˈmismo] NM pessimism

★**pesimista** [pesiˈmista] ADJ pessimistic ▶ NMF pessimist

pésimo, -a [ˈpesimo, a] ADJ awful, dreadful

★**peso** [ˈpeso] NM weight; (*balanza*) scales *pl*; (*Am Com*) monetary unit; (*moneda*) peso; (*Deporte*) shot; ~ **bruto/neto** gross/net weight; ~ **mosca/pesado** fly-/heavyweight; **de poco ~** light(-weight); **levantamiento de pesos** weightlifting; **vender a ~** to sell by weight; **argumento de ~** weighty argument; **eso cae por su propio ~** that goes without saying

pesque *etc* [ˈpeske] VB *ver* **pescar**

pesquero, -a [pesˈkero, a] ADJ fishing *cpd*

pesquisa [pesˈkisa] NF inquiry, investigation

pestaña [pesˈtaɲa] NF (*Anat*) eyelash; (*borde*) rim

pestañear [pestaɲeˈar] /**1a**/ VI to blink

peste [ˈpeste] NF plague; (*fig*) nuisance; (*mal olor*) stink, stench; ~ **negra** Black Death; **echar pestes de algn** to slag sb off (*fam*)

★**pesticida** [pestiˈθiða] NM pesticide

pestilencia [pestiˈlenθja] NF (*mal olor*) stink, stench

pestillo [pesˈtiʎo] NM bolt, latch; (*cerrojo*) catch; (*picaporte*) (door) handle

petaca [peˈtaka] NF (*de cigarrillos*) cigarette case; (*de pipa*) tobacco pouch; (*Am: maleta*) suitcase

petado, -a [peˈtaðo, a] (*fam*) ADJ: **estar ~ de gente** to be packed (with people); **ir ~ de trabajo** to be drowning in work

pétalo [ˈpetalo] NM petal

petanca [peˈtanka] NF *a game in which metal bowls are thrown at a target bowl*

P

petar [pe'tar] /**1a**/ VT: **petarlo** (*fam: arrasar*) to be all the rage

petardo [pe'tarðo] NM firework, firecracker

petición [peti'θjon] NF (*pedido*) request, plea; (*memorial*) petition; (*Jur*) plea; **a ~ de** at the request of; **~ de aumento de salarios** wage demand *o* claim

petirrojo [peti'rroxo] NM robin

peto ['peto] NM dungarees *pl*, overalls *pl* (US); (*corpiño*) bodice; (*Taur*) horse's padding

pétreo, -a ['petreo, a] ADJ stony, rocky

petrificar [petrifi'kar] /**1g**/ VT to petrify

petrifique *etc* [petri'fike] VB *ver* **petrificar**

petrodólar [petro'ðolar] NM petrodollar

petróleo [pe'troleo] NM oil, petroleum

★**petrolero, -a** [petro'lero, a] ADJ petroleum *cpd* ▶ NM (*Com*) oil man; (*buque*) (oil) tanker

PETROVEN [petro'ben] NM ABR = **Petróleos de Venezuela**

petulancia [petu'lanθja] NF (*insolencia*) vanity, opinionated nature

peyorativo, -a [pejora'tiβo, a] ADJ pejorative

★**pez** [peθ] NM fish; **~ de colores** goldfish; **~ espada** swordfish; **estar como el ~ en el agua** to feel completely at home

pezón [pe'θon] NM teat, nipple

pezuña [pe'θuɲa] NF hoof

Photoshop® [foto'sop] NM Photoshop®

piadoso, -a [pja'ðoso, a] ADJ (*devoto*) pious, devout; (*misericordioso*) kind, merciful

Piamonte [pja'monte] NM Piedmont

pianista [pja'nista] NMF pianist

★**piano** ['pjano] NM piano; **~ de cola** grand piano

piar [pjar] /**1c**/ VI to cheep

piara ['pjara] NF (*manada*) herd, drove

PIB NM ABR (*Esp Com*: = *Producto Interior Bruto*) GDP

★**pibe, -a** ['piβe, a] NM/F (*Am*) boy (girl), kid, child

pica ['pika] NF (*Mil*) pike; (*Taur*) goad; **poner una ~ en Flandes** to bring off something difficult

picadero [pika'ðero] NM riding school

picadillo [pika'ðiʎo] NM mince, minced meat

picado, -a [pi'kaðo, a] ADJ pricked, punctured; (*Culin*) minced, chopped; (*mar*) choppy; (*diente*) bad; (*tabaco*) cut; (*enfadado*) cross

picador [pika'ðor] NM (*Taur*) picador; (*minero*) faceworker

picadora [pika'ðora] NF mincer

★**picadura** [pika'ðura] NF (*pinchazo*) puncture; (*de abeja*) sting; (*de mosquito*) bite; (*tabaco picado*) cut tobacco

picana [pi'kana] (*Am*) NF (*Agr*) cattle prod; (*Pol: para tortura*) electric prod

★**picante** [pi'kante] ADJ (*comida, sabor*) hot; (*comentario*) racy, spicy

picaporte [pika'porte] NM (*tirador*) handle; (*pestillo*) latch

★**picar** [pi'kar] /**1g**/ VT (*agujerear, perforar*) to prick,

puncture; (*billete*) to punch, clip; (*abeja*) to sting; (*mosquito, serpiente*) to bite; (*Culin*) to mince, chop; (*persona*) to nibble (at); (*incitar*) to incite, goad; (*dañar, irritar*) to annoy, bother; (*quemar: lengua*) to burn, sting; **me pican los ojos** my eyes sting; **me pica el brazo** my arm itches ▶ VI (*pez*) to bite, take the bait; (*el sol*) to burn, scorch; (*abeja, Med*) to sting; (*mosquito*) to bite ▪ **picarse** VR (*agriarse*) to turn sour, go off; (*mar*) to get choppy; (*ofenderse*) to take offence

picardía [pikar'ðia] NF villainy; (*astucia*) slyness, craftiness; (*una picardía*) dirty trick; (*palabra*) rude/bad word *o* expression

picaresco, -a [pika'resko, a] ADJ (*travieso*) roguish, rascally; (*Lit*) picaresque

pícaro, -a ['pikaro, a] ADJ (*malicioso*) villainous; (*travieso*) mischievous ▶ NM (*astuto*) sly sort; (*sinvergüenza*) rascal, scoundrel

picazón [pika'θon] NF (*comezón*) itch; (*ardor*) sting(ing feeling); (*remordimiento*) pang of conscience

pichi ['pitʃi] NM (*Esp*) pinafore dress (BRIT), jumper (US)

pichón, -ona [pi'tʃon, ona] NM (*de paloma*) young pigeon ▶ NM/F (*apelativo*) darling, dearest

★**pico** ['piko] NM (*de ave*) beak; (*punta aguda*) peak, sharp point; (*Tec*) pick, pickaxe; (*Geo*) peak, summit; (*labia*) talkativeness; **no abrir el ~** to keep quiet; **~ parásito** (*Elec*) spike; **y ~** and a bit; **las seis y ~** six and a bit; **son las tres y ~** it's just after three; **tiene 50 libros y ~** he has 50-odd books; **me costó un ~** it cost me quite a bit

picor [pi'kor] NM itch; (*ardor*) sting(ing feeling)

picoso, -a [pi'koso, a] ADJ (*Am: comida*) hot

picota [pi'kota] NF pillory; **poner a algn en la ~** (*fig*) to ridicule sb

picotada [piko'taða] NF, **picotazo** [piko'taθo] NM (*de pájaro*) peck; (*de insecto*) sting, bite

picotear [pikote'ar] /**1a**/ VT to peck ▶ VI to nibble, pick

pictórico, -a [pik'toriko, a] ADJ pictorial; **tiene dotes pictóricas** she has a talent for painting

picudo, -a [pi'kuðo, a] ADJ pointed, with a point

pidiendo *etc* [pi'ðjendo] VB *ver* **pedir**

pidió *etc* VB *ver* **pedir**

pido *etc* VB *ver* **pedir**

★**pie** [pje] (*pl* **pies**) NM (*gen, Mat*) foot; (*de cama, página, escalera*) foot, bottom; (*Teat*) cue; (*fig: motivo*) motive, basis; (: *fundamento*) foothold; **pies planos** flat feet; **ir a ~** to go on foot, walk; **estar de ~** to be standing (up); **ponerse de ~** to stand up; **al ~ de la letra** (*citar*) literally, verbatim; (*copiar*) exactly, word for word; **de pies a cabeza** from head to foot; **en ~ de guerra** on a war footing; **sin pies ni cabeza** pointless, absurd; **dar ~ a** to give cause for; **hacer ~** (*en el agua*) to touch (the) bottom; **no dar ~ con bola** to be no good at anything; **saber de qué ~ cojea algn** to know sb's weak spots

★**piedad** [pjeˈðað] NF (*lástima*) pity, compassion; (*clemencia*) mercy; (*devoción*) piety, devotion; **tener ~ de** to take pity on

★**piedra** [ˈpjeðra] NF stone; (*roca*) rock; (*de mechero*) flint; (*Meteorología*) hailstone; **primera ~** foundation stone; **~ de afilar** grindstone; **~ arenisca/caliza** sand-/limestone; **~ preciosa** precious stone

★**piel** [pjel] NF (*Anat*) skin; (*Zool*) skin, hide; (*de oso*) fur; (*cuero*) leather; (*Bot*) skin, peel ▶ NMF: **~ roja** redskin (!)

pienso *etc* [ˈpjenso] VB *ver* **pensar** ▶ NM (*Agr*) feed

piercing [ˈpjersin] NM piercing

pierdo *etc* [ˈpjerðo] VB *ver* **perder**

★**pierna** [ˈpjerna] NF leg; **en piernas** bare-legged

★**pieza** [ˈpjeθa] NF piece; (*esp Am: habitación*) room; (*Mus*) piece, composition; (*Teat*) work, play; **~ de recambio** *o* **repuesto** spare (part), extra (*US*); **~ de ropa** article of clothing; **quedarse de una ~** to be dumbfounded

pigmento [piɣˈmento] NM pigment

pigmeo, -a [piɣˈmeo, a] ADJ, NM/F pigmy

★**pijama** [piˈxama] NM pyjamas *pl*

pijo, -a [ˈpixo, a] NM/F (*fam*) upper-class twit

pijoprogre [pixoˈproɣre] NMF (*fam, pey*) middle-class lefty

pijotada [pixoˈtaða] NF nuisance

★**pila** [ˈpila] NF (*Elec*) battery; (*montón*) heap, pile; (*de fuente*) sink; (*Rel: tb:* **pila bautismal**) font; **nombre de ~** Christian *o* first name; **tengo una ~ de cosas que hacer** (*fam*) I have heaps *o* stacks of things to do

pilar [piˈlar] NM pillar; (*de puente*) pier; (*fig*) prop, mainstay

Pilates [piˈlates] NM Pilates

★**píldora** [ˈpildora] NF pill; **la ~ (anticonceptiva)** the pill; **tragarse la ~** to be taken in

pileta [piˈleta] NF basin, bowl; (*Am: de cocina*) sink; (*: piscina*) swimming pool

pillaje [piˈʎaxe] NM pillage, plunder

pillar [piˈʎar] /**1a**/ VT (*saquear*) to pillage, plunder; (*fam: coger*) to catch; (*: agarrar*) to grasp, seize; (*: entender*) to grasp, catch on to; (*suj: coche etc*) to run over; **~ un resfriado** (*fam*) to catch a cold ◼ **pillarse** VR: **pillarse un dedo con la puerta** to catch one's finger in the door

pillo, -a [ˈpiʎo, a] ADJ villainous; (*astuto*) sly, crafty ▶ NM/F rascal, rogue, scoundrel

pilón [piˈlon] NM pillar, post; (*Elec*) pylon; (*bebedero*) drinking trough; (*de fuente*) basin

pilotar [piloˈtar] /**1a**/ VT (*avión*) to pilot; (*barco*) to steer

★**piloto** [piˈloto] NMF (*de avión*) pilot; (*de coche*) driver ▶ NM (*de aparato*) (pilot) light; (*Auto*) rear light, tail light; **~ automático** automatic pilot ▶ ADJ INV: **planta ~** pilot plant

piltrafa [pilˈtrafa] NF (*carne*) poor quality meat; (*fig*) worthless object; (*: individuo*) wretch

pimentón [pimenˈton] NM (*polvo*) paprika

★**pimienta** [piˈmjenta] NF pepper

★**pimiento** [piˈmjento] NM pepper, pimiento

PIN NM ABR (*Esp Com*: = *Producto Interior Neto*) net domestic product; (*Inform*: = *número personal de identificación*) PIN

pin [pin] (*pl* **pins** [pins]) NM badge

pinacoteca [pinakoˈteka] NF art gallery

pinar [piˈnar] NM pinewood

pincel [pinˈθel] NM paintbrush

pincelada [pinθeˈlaða] NF brushstroke; **última ~** (*fig*) finishing touch

pinchadiscos [pintʃaˈdiskos] NMF INV disc jockey, DJ

pinchar [pinˈtʃar] /**1a**/ VT (*perforar*) to prick, pierce; (*neumático*) to puncture; (*incitar*) to prod; (*Inform*) to click; **tener un neumático pinchado** to have a puncture *o* a flat tyre ▶ VI (*Mus: fam*) to be DJ; **no ~ ni cortar** (*fam*) to cut no ice ◼ **pincharse** VR (*con droga*) to inject o.s.; (*neumático*) to burst, puncture

★**pinchazo** [pinˈtʃaθo] NM (*perforación*) prick; (*de llanta*) puncture, flat (*US*); (*fig*) prod

pinche [ˈpintʃe] NM (*de cocina*) kitchen boy, scullion

pinchito [pinˈtʃito] NM shish kebab

pincho [ˈpintʃo] NM point; (*aguijón*) spike; (*Culin*) savoury (snack); (*Inform*) dongle; **~ moruno** shish kebab; **~ de tortilla** small slice of omelette

★**ping-pong** [ˈpimpon] NM table tennis

pingüe [ˈpingwe] ADJ (*cosecha*) bumper *cpd*; (*negocio*) lucrative

pingüino [pinˈgwino] NM penguin

pinitos [piˈnitos] NMPL: **hacer sus primeros ~** to take one's first steps

pino [ˈpino] NM pine (tree); **vivir en el quinto ~** to live in the back of beyond

pinta [ˈpinta] NF spot; (*gota*) spot, drop; (*aspecto*) appearance, look(s) *pl*; (*medida*) pint; **tener buena ~** to look good, look well; **por la ~** by the look of it

pintado, -a [pinˈtaðo, a] ADJ spotted; (*de muchos colores*) colourful; **me sienta que ni ~**, **me viene que ni ~** it suits me a treat ▶ NF piece of political graffiti ◼ **pintadas** NFPL political graffiti *sg*

pintalabios [pintaˈlaβjos] NM INV (*Esp*) lipstick

★**pintar** [pinˈtar] /**1a**/ VT to paint ▶ VI to paint; (*fam*) to count, be important; **no pinta nada** (*fam*) he has no say ◼ **pintarse** VR to put on make-up; **pintárselas solo para hacer algo** to manage to do sth by o.s.

★**pintor, a** [pinˈtor, a] NM/F painter; **~ de brocha gorda** house painter; (*fig*) bad painter

★**pintoresco, -a** [pintoˈresko, a] ADJ picturesque

★**pintura** [pinˈtura] NF painting; **~ a la acuarela** watercolour; **~ al óleo** oil painting; **~ rupestre** cave painting

pinza ['pinθa] NF (*Zool*) claw; (*para colgar ropa*) clothes peg, clothespin (*US*); (*Tec*) pincers *pl* ■ **pinzas** NFPL (*para depilar*) tweezers

★**piña** ['piɲa] NF (*fruto del pino*) pine cone; (*fruta*) pineapple; (*fig*) group

piñata [pi'ɲata] NF piñata (*cardboard figure hung up at parties that is beaten with sticks until sweets or presents fall out*)

piñón [pi'ɲon] NM (*Bot*) pine nut; (*Tec*) pinion

pío, -a ['pio, a] ADJ (*devoto*) pious, devout; (*misericordioso*) merciful ▶ NM: **no decir ni ~** not to breathe a word

piojo ['pjoxo] NM louse

piojoso, -a [pjo'xoso, a] ADJ lousy; (*sucio*) dirty

piolet [pjo'le] (*pl* **piolets**) NM ice axe

pionero, -a [pjo'nero, a] ADJ pioneering ▶ NM/F pioneer

★**pipa** ['pipa] NF pipe; (*Bot*) seed, pip; (*de girasol*) sunflower seed

pipí [pi'pi] NM (*fam*): **hacer ~** to have a wee(-wee)

pipiolo [pi'pjolo] NM youngster; (*novato*) novice, greenhorn

pique ['pike] VB *ver* **picar** ▶ NM (*resentimiento*) pique, resentment; (*rivalidad*) rivalry, competition; **irse a ~** to sink; (*familia*) to be ruined; **tener un ~ con algn** to have a grudge against sb

piqueta [pi'keta] NF pick(axe)

piquete [pi'kete] NM (*agujerito*) small hole; (*Mil*) squad, party; (*de obreros*) picket; (*Am*: *de insecto*) bite; **~ secundario** secondary picket

pirado, -a [pi'raðo, a] ADJ (*fam*) round the bend ▶ NM/F nutter

piragua [pi'raɣwa] NF canoe

★**piragüismo** [pira'ɣwismo] NM (*Deporte*) canoeing

pirámide [pi'ramiðe] NF pyramid

piraña [pi'raɲa] NF piranha

pirarse [pi'rarse] /1a/ VR (*tb*: **pirárselas**: *largarse*) to beat it (*fam*); (: *Escol*) to cut class

pirata [pi'rata] ADJ: **edición/disco ~** pirate edition/bootleg record ▶ NM pirate; (*tb*: **pirata informático**) hacker

pirenaico, -a [pire'naiko, a] ADJ Pyrenean

Pirineo(s) [piri'neo(s)] NM(PL) Pyrenees *pl*

pirómano, -a [pi'romano, a] NM/F (*Psico*) pyromaniac; (*Jur*) arsonist

piropo [pi'ropo] NM compliment, (piece of) flattery; **echar piropos a** to make flirtatious remarks to

pirueta [pi'rweta] NF pirouette

piruleta [piru'leta] NF lollipop

pirulí [piru'li] NM lollipop

pis [pis] NM (*fam*) pee; **hacer ~** to have a pee; (*para niños*) to wee-wee

pisada [pi'saða] NF (*paso*) footstep; (*huella*) footprint

★**pisar** [pi'sar] /1a/ VT (*caminar sobre*) to walk on, tread on; (*apretar con el pie*) to press; (*fig*) to tram-

ple on, walk all over; **~ el acelerador** to step on the accelerator ▶ VI to tread, step, walk; **~ fuerte** (*fig*) to act determinedly

piscifactoría [pisθifakto'ria] NF fish farm

★**piscina** [pis'θina] NF swimming pool; **~ de bolas** ball pool, ball pit

Piscis ['pisθis] NM (*Astro*) Pisces

★**piso** ['piso] NM (*suelo*: *de edificio*) floor; (*Am*) ground; (*apartamento*) flat, apartment; **primer ~** (*Esp*) first o second (*US*) floor; (*Am*) ground o first (*US*) floor

pisotear [pisote'ar] /1a/ VT to trample (on o underfoot); (*fig*: *humillar*) to trample on

pisotón [piso'ton] NM (*con el pie*) stamp

★**pista** ['pista] NF track, trail; (*indicio*) clue; (*Inform*) track; **~ de auditoría** (*Com*) audit trail; **~ de aterrizaje** runway; **~ de baile** dance floor; **~ de tenis** tennis court; **~ de hielo** ice rink; **estar sobre la ~ de algn** to be on sb's trail

pisto ['pisto] NM (*Culin*) ratatouille; **darse ~** (*fam*) to show off

★**pistola** [pis'tola] NF pistol; (*Tec*) spray-gun

pistolero, -a [pisto'lero, a] NM/F gunman, gangster ▶ NF holster

pistón [pis'ton] NM (*Tec*) piston; (*Mus*) key

pitar [pi'tar] /1a/ VT (*hacer sonar*) to blow; (*partido*) to referee; (*rechiflar*) to whistle at, boo; (*actor, obra*) to hiss ▶ VI to whistle; (*Auto*) to sound o toot one's horn; (*Am*) to smoke; **salir pitando** to beat it

pitido [pi'tiðo] NM whistle; (*sonido agudo*) beep; (*sonido corto*) pip

pitillera [piti'ʎera] NF cigarette case

pitillo [pi'tiʎo] NM cigarette

pito ['pito] NM whistle; (*de coche*) horn; (*cigarrillo*) cigarette; (*fam*: *de marihuana*) joint; (*fam!*) prick (*fam!*); **me importa un ~** I don't care two hoots

pitón [pi'ton] NM (*Zool*) python

pitonisa [pito'nisa] NF fortune-teller

pitorrearse [pitorre'arse] /1a/ VR: **~ de** to scoff at, make fun of

pitorreo [pito'rreo] NM joke, laugh; **estar de ~** to be in a joking mood

píxel ['piksel] NM (*Inform*) pixel

pixelar [pikse'lar] /1a/ VT (*Inform*) to pixelate

piyama [pi'jama] NM (*Am*) pyjamas *pl*, pajamas *pl* (*US*)

★**pizarra** [pi'θarra] NF (*piedra*) slate; (*encerado*) blackboard; **~ blanca** whiteboard; **~ interactiva** interactive whiteboard

pizarrón [piθa'rron] NM (*Am*) blackboard

pizca ['piθka] NF pinch, spot; (*fig*) spot, speck, trace; **ni ~** not a bit

pizza ['pitsa] NF pizza

placa ['plaka] NF plate; (*Med*) dental plate; (*distintivo*) badge; **~ de matrícula** number plate; **~ madre** (*Inform*) mother board

placaje [pla'kaxe] NM tackle

placard [plaˈkar] NM (Am) built-in cupboard, (clothes) closet (US)

placenta [plaˈθenta] NF placenta; (tras el parto) afterbirth

placentero, -a [plaθenˈtero, a] ADJ pleasant, agreeable

★**placer** [plaˈθer] /2w/ NM pleasure; **a ~** at one's pleasure ▸ VT to please

plácido, -a [ˈplaθiðo, a] ADJ placid

plafón [plaˈfon] NM (Am) ceiling

plaga [ˈplaɣa] NF (Zool) pest; (Med) plague; (fig) swarm; (: abundancia) abundance

plagar [plaˈɣar] /1h/ VT to infest, plague; (llenar) to fill; **plagado de** riddled with; **han plagado la ciudad de carteles** they have plastered the town with posters

plagiar [plaˈɣjar] /1b/ VT to plagiarize; (Am) to kidnap

plagiario, -a [plaˈɣjario, a] NM/F plagiarist; (Am) kidnapper

plagio [ˈplaxjo] NM plagiarism; (Am) kidnap

plague etc [ˈplaɣe] VB ver **plagar**

★**plan** [plan] NM (esquema, proyecto) plan; (idea, intento) idea, intention; (de curso) programme; **~ cotizable de jubilación** contributory pension scheme; **~ de estudios** curriculum, syllabus; **~ de incentivos** (Com) incentive scheme; **tener ~** (fam) to have a date; **tener un ~** (fam) to have an affair; **en ~ de cachondeo** for a laugh; **en ~ económico** (fam) on the cheap; **vamos en ~ de turismo** we're going as tourists; **si te pones en ese ~ ...** if that's your attitude ...

plana [ˈplana] NF ver **plano**

★**plancha** [ˈplantʃa] NF (para planchar) iron; (rótulo) plate, sheet; (Naut) gangway; (Culin) grill; **pescado a la ~** grilled fish; **~ de pelo** straighteners; **a la ~** (Culin) grilled

planchado, -a [planˈtʃaðo, a] ADJ (ropa) ironed; (traje) pressed ▸ NM ironing

planchar [planˈtʃar] /1a/ VT to iron ▸ VI to do the ironing

planeador [planeaˈðor] NM glider

planear [planeˈar] /1a/ VT to plan ▸ VI to glide

★**planeta** [plaˈneta] NM planet

planetario, -a [planeˈtarjo, a] ADJ planetary ▸ NM planetarium

planicie [plaˈniθje] NF plain

planificación [planifikaˈθjon] NF planning; **~ corporativa** (Com) corporate planning; **~ familiar** family planning; **diagrama de ~** (Com) planner

planilla [plaˈniʎa] NF (Am) form

★**plano, -a** [ˈplano, a] ADJ flat, level, even; (liso) smooth ▸ NM (Mat, Tec, Aviat) plane; (Foto) shot; (Arq) plan; (Geo) map; (de ciudad) map, street plan; **primer ~** close-up; **caer de ~** to fall flat; **rechazar algo de ~** to turn sth down flat; **le daba el sol de ~** (fig) the sun shone directly on it ▸ NF sheet of paper, page; (Tec) trowel; **en primera plana** on the front page; **plana mayor** staff

★**planta** [ˈplanta] NF (Bot, Tec) plant; (Anat) sole of the foot, foot; (piso) floor; (Am: personal) staff; **~ baja** ground floor

plantación [plantaˈθjon] NF (Agr) plantation; (acto) planting

plantar [planˈtar] /1a/ VT (Bot) to plant; (puesto) to put in; (levantar) to erect, set up; **~ a algn en la calle** to chuck sb out; **dejar plantado a algn** (fam) to stand sb up ■ **plantarse** VR to stand firm; **plantarse en** to reach, get to

plantear [planteˈar] /1a/ VT (problema) to pose; (dificultad) to raise; **se lo plantearé** I'll put it to him

plantel [planˈtel] NM (fig) group, set

plantilla [planˈtiʎa] NF (de zapato) insole; (personal) personnel; **ser de ~** to be on the staff

plantío [planˈtio] NM (acto) planting; (lugar) plot, bed, patch

plantón [planˈton] NM (Mil) guard, sentry; (fam) long wait; **dar (un) ~ a algn** to stand sb up

plañir [plaˈɲir] /3h/ VI to mourn

plasma [ˈplasma] NM plasma

plasmar [plasˈmar] /1a/ VT (dar forma) to mould, shape; (representar) to represent ▸ VI: **~ en** to take the form of

plasta [ˈplasta] NF soft mass, lump; (desastre) botch, mess ▸ NMF (Esp fam) bore ▸ ADJ (Esp fam) boring

plasticidad [plastiθiˈðað] NF (fig) expressiveness

★**plástico, -a** [ˈplastiko, a] ADJ plastic ▸ NF (art of) sculpture, modelling ▸ NM plastic

plastificar [plastifiˈkar] /1g/ VT (documento) to laminate

plastifique etc [plastiˈfike] VB ver **plastificar**

Plastilina® [plastiˈlina] NF Plasticine®

★**plata** [ˈplata] NF (metal) silver; (cosas hechas de plata) silverware; (Am) cash, dough (fam); **hablar en ~** to speak bluntly o frankly

plataforma [plataˈforma] NF platform; **~ de lanzamiento/perforación** launch(ing) pad/drilling rig

★**plátano** [ˈplatano] NM (fruta) banana; (árbol) plane tree; banana tree

platea [plaˈtea] NF (Teat) pit

plateado, -a [plateˈaðo, a] ADJ silver; (Tec) silver-plated

platense [plaˈtense] (fam) = **rioplatense**

plática [ˈplatika] NF (Am) talk, chat; (Rel) sermon

platicar [platiˈkar] /1g/ VI (Am) to talk, chat

★**platillo** [plaˈtiʎo] NM saucer; (de limosnas) collecting bowl; **~ volador o volante** flying saucer; **pasar el ~** to pass the hat round ■ **platillos** NMPL cymbals

platina [plaˈtina] NF (Mus) tape deck

platino [plaˈtino] NM platinum ■ **platinos** NMPL (Auto) (contact) points

platique etc [plaˈtike] VB ver **platicar**

p

★**plato** [ˈplato] NM plate, dish; (*parte de comida*) course; (*guiso*) dish; ~ **frutero/sopero** fruit/soup dish; **primer** ~ first course; ~ **combinado** set main course (*served on one plate*); ~ **fuerte** main course; **pagar los platos rotos** (*fam*) to carry the can (*fam*)

plató [plaˈto] NM set

platónico, -a [plaˈtoniko, a] ADJ platonic

★**playa** [ˈplaja] NF beach; (*costa*) seaside; ~ **de estacionamiento** (AM) car park

playero, -a [plaˈjero, a] ADJ beach *cpd* ▸ NF (AM: *camiseta*) T-shirt ▪ **playeras** NFPL canvas shoes; (*Tenis*) tennis shoes

★**plaza** [ˈplaθa] NF square; (*mercado*) market(place); (*sitio*) room, space; (*en vehículo*) seat, place; (*colocación*) post, job; ~ **de abastos** food market; ~ **mayor** main square; ~ **de toros** bullring; **hacer la** ~ to do the daily shopping; **reservar una** ~ to reserve a seat; **el hotel tiene 100 plazas** the hotel has 100 beds

plazca *etc* [ˈplaθka] VB *ver* **placer**

plazo [ˈplaθo] NM (*lapso de tiempo*) time, period, term; (*fecha de vencimiento*) expiry date; (*pago parcial*) instalment; **a corto/largo** ~ short-/long-term; **comprar a plazos** to buy on hire purchase, pay for in instalments; **nos dan un** ~ **de ocho días** they allow us a week

plazoleta [plaθoˈleta], **plazuela** [plaˈθwela] NF small square

pleamar [pleaˈmar] NF high tide

plebe [ˈpleβe] NF: **la** ~ the common people *pl*, the masses *pl*; (*pey*) the plebs *pl*

plebeyo, -a [pleˈβejo, a] ADJ plebeian; (*pey*) coarse, common

plebiscito [pleβisˈθito] NM plebiscite

pleca [ˈpleka] NF (*Inform*) backslash

plegable [pleˈɣaβle] ADJ pliable; (*silla*) folding

plegar [pleˈɣar] /**1h, 1j**/ VT (*doblar*) to fold, bend; (*Costura*) to pleat ▪ **plegarse** VR to yield, submit

plegaria [pleˈɣarja] NF (*oración*) prayer

plegué [pleˈɣe], **pleguemos** *etc* [pleˈɣemos] VB *ver* **plegar**

pleitear [pleiteˈar] /**1a**/ VI (*Jur*) to plead, conduct a lawsuit; (*litigar*) to go to law

pleito [ˈpleito] NM (*Jur*) lawsuit, case; (*fig*) dispute, feud; **entablar** ~ to bring an action o a lawsuit; **poner** ~ to sue ▪ **pleitos** NMPL litigation *sg*

plenario, -a [pleˈnarjo, a] ADJ plenary, full

plenilunio [pleniˈlunjo] NM full moon

plenitud [pleniˈtuð] NF plenitude, fullness; (*abundancia*) abundance

pleno, -a [ˈpleno, a] ADJ full; (*completo*) complete; **en** ~ **día** in broad daylight; **en** ~ **verano** at the height of summer; **en plena cara** full in the face ▸ NM plenum; **en** ~ as a whole; (*por unanimidad*) unanimously

pletina NF (*Mus*) tape deck

pleuresía [pleureˈsia] NF pleurisy

plexiglás [pleksiˈɣlas] NM acrylic

pliego [ˈpljeɣo] VB *ver* **plegar** ▸ NM (*hoja*) sheet (of paper); (*carta*) sealed letter/document; ~ **de condiciones** details *pl*, specifications *pl*

pliegue [ˈpljeɣe] VB *ver* **plegar** ▸ NM fold, crease; (*de vestido*) pleat

plisado [pliˈsaðo] NM pleating

plomería [plomeˈria] NF (AM) plumbing

plomero, -a [ploˈmero, a] NM/F (AM) plumber

plomizo, -a [ploˈmiθo, a] ADJ leaden, lead-coloured

★**plomo** [ˈplomo] NM (*metal*) lead; (*Elec*) fuse; **sin** ~ unleaded; **caer a** ~ to fall heavily o flat

★**pluma** [ˈpluma] NF (*Zool*) feather; (*para escribir*): ~ **(estilográfica)** ink pen; ~ **fuente** (AM) fountain pen

plumazo [pluˈmaθo] NM (*lit, fig*) stroke of the pen

plumero [pluˈmero] NM (*quitapolvos*) feather duster; **ya te veo el** ~ I know what you're up to

plumón [pluˈmon] NM (*de ave*) down; (AM) felt-tip pen

plural [pluˈral] ADJ plural ▸ NM: **en** ~ in the plural

pluralidad [pluraliˈðað] NF plurality; **una ~ de votos** a majority of votes

pluriempleo [pluriemˈpleo] NM having more than one job

plus [plus] NM bonus

plusmarquista [plusmarˈkista] NMF (*Deporte*) record holder

plusvalía [plusβaˈlia] NF (*mayor valor*) appreciation, added value; (*Com*) goodwill

plutocracia [plutoˈkraθja] NF plutocracy

PM NF ABR (*Mil*: = *Policía Militar*) MP

p.m. ABR (= *post meridiem*) p.m.; (= *por minuto*) per minute

PMA NM ABR (= *Programa Mundial de Alimentos*) World Food Programme

P.M.A. NM ABR (= **peso máximo autorizado**)

pmo. ABR (= *próximo*) prox.

PN NF ABR (*Mil*: = *Policía Naval*) Naval Police

PNB NM ABR (*Esp Com*: = *Producto Nacional Bruto*) GNP

PNN [peˈnene] NMF (= *profesor(a) no numerario(-a)*) untenured teacher ▸ NM ABR (*Esp Com*: = *Producto Nacional Neto*) net national product

PNUD NM ABR (= *Programa de las Naciones Unidas para el Desarrollo*) United Nations Development Programme

PNV NM ABR (*Esp Pol*) = **Partido Nacionalista Vasco**

P.° ABR (= *Paseo*) Av(e).

p.o. ABR = **por orden**

★**población** [poβlaˈθjon] NF population; (*pueblo, ciudad*) town, city; ~ **activa** working population

poblado, -a [poˈβlaðo, a] ADJ inhabited; (*barba*)

thick; (*cejas*) bushy; **~ de** (*lleno de*) filled with; **densamente ~** densely populated ▶ NM (*aldea*) village; (*pueblo*) (small) town

poblador, a [poβla'ðor, a] NM/F settler, colonist

poblar [po'βlar] /**1l**/ VT (*colonizar*) to colonize; (*fundar*) to found; (*habitar*) to inhabit ∎ **poblarse** VR: **poblarse de** to fill up with; (*irse cubriendo*) to become covered with

★**pobre** ['poβre] ADJ poor; **~ diablo** (*fig*) poor wretch *o* devil ▶ NMF poor person; (*mendigo*) beggar; **los pobres** the poor; **¡~!** poor thing!

★**pobreza** [po'βreθa] NF poverty; **~ energética** fuel poverty

pocho, -a ['potʃo, a] ADJ (*flor, color*) faded, discoloured; (*persona*) pale; (*fruta*) overripe; (*deprimido*) depressed

pocilga [po'θilɣa] NF pigsty

pocillo [po'siʎo] NM (*AM*) coffee cup

pócima ['poθima], **poción** [po'θjon] NF potion; (*brebaje*) concoction, nasty drink

---

poco, -a ['poko, a]

ADJ **1** (*sg*) little, not much; **poco tiempo** little *o* not much time; **de poco interés** of little interest, not very interesting; **poca cosa** not much

2 (*pl*) few, not many; **unos pocos** a few, some; **pocos niños comen lo que les conviene** few children eat what they should

▶ ADV **1** little, not much; **cuesta poco** it doesn't cost much; **poco más o menos** more or less

2 (+ *adj: negativo, antónimo*): **poco amable/inteligente** not very nice/intelligent

3: **por poco me caigo** I almost fell

4 (*tiempo*): **poco después** soon after that; **dentro de poco** shortly; **hace poco** a short time ago, not long ago; **a poco de haberse casado** shortly after getting married

5: **poco a poco** little by little

6 (*AM*): **¿a poco no está divino?** isn't it just divine?; **de a poco** gradually

▶ NM a little, a bit; **un poco triste/de dinero** a little sad/money

---

poda ['poða] NF (*acto*) pruning; (*temporada*) pruning season

podar [po'ðar] /**1a**/ VT to prune

podcast ['poðkast] NM podcast

podcastear [poðkaste'ar] /**1a**/ VI to podcast

podenco [po'ðenko] NM hound

---

poder [po'ðer]

/**2s**/ VI **1** (*capacidad*) can, be able to; **no puedo hacerlo** I can't do it, I'm unable to do it

2 (*permiso*) can, may, be allowed to; **¿se puede?** may I (*o* we)?; **puedes irte ahora** you may go now; **no se puede fumar en este hospital** smoking is not allowed in this hospital

3 (*posibilidad*) may, might, could; **puede llegar**

---

mañana he may *o* might arrive tomorrow; **pudiste haberte hecho daño** you might *o* could have hurt yourself; **¡podías habérmelo dicho antes!** you might have told me before!

4: **puede (ser)** perhaps; **puede que lo sepa Tomás** Tomás may *o* might know

5: **¡no puedo más!** I've had enough!; **no pude menos que dejarlo** I couldn't help but leave it; **es tonto a más no poder** he's as stupid as they come

6: **poder con**: **no puedo con este crío** this kid's too much for me; **¿puedes con eso?** can you manage that?

7: **él me puede** (*fam*) he's stronger than me

▶ NM power; **el poder** the Government; **poder adquisitivo** purchasing power; **detentar** *u* **ocupar** *o* **estar en el poder** to be in power *o* office; **estar** *u* **obrar en poder de** to be in the hands *o* possession of; **por poder(es)** by proxy; **poder judicial** judiciary

---

> El verbo **can** no tiene forma de infinitivo ni futuro. La forma del pasado es **could**. Para formar el futuro se utiliza **be able to**.
> **May**, **might** y **could** expresan distintos grados de probabilidad. **Might** indica un grado menor de probabilidad que **may**, mientras que **could** indica la probabilidad más remota.

---

poderío [poðe'rio] NM power; (*autoridad*) authority

poderoso, -a [poðe'roso, a] ADJ powerful

podio ['poðjo] NM podium

pódium ['poðjum] = **podio**

podólogo, -a [po'ðoloɣo, a] NM/F chiropodist (BRIT), podiatrist (US)

podré *etc* [po'ðre] VB *ver* **poder**

podrido, -a [po'ðriðo, a] ADJ rotten, bad; (*fig*) rotten, corrupt

podrir [po'ðrir] = **pudrir**

poema [po'ema] NM poem

poesía [poe'sia] NF poetry

poeta [po'eta] NM poet

poético, -a [po'etiko, a] ADJ poetic(al)

poetisa [poe'tisa] NF (woman) poet

póker ['poker] NM poker

polaco, -a [po'lako, a] ADJ Polish ▶ NM/F Pole ▶ NM (*Ling*) Polish

polar [po'lar] ADJ polar

polarice *etc* [pola'riθe] VB *ver* **polarizar**

polaridad [polari'ðað] NF polarity

polarizar [polari'θar] /**1f**/ VT to polarize

polea [po'lea] NF pulley

polémica [po'lemika] NF polemics *sg*; (*una polémica*) controversy

polemice *etc* [pole'miθe] VB *ver* **polemizar**

polémico, -a [po'lemiko, a] ADJ polemic(al)

polemizar [polemi'θar] /**1f**/ VI argue

polen ['polen] NM pollen

poleo [po'leo] NM pennyroyal

poli ['poli] NM (fam) cop (fam) ▶ NF: **la ~** the cops pl (fam)

★**policía** [poli'θia] NMF policeman(-woman) ▶ NF police

> There are two branches of the police in Spain, both armed: the *policía nacional*, in charge of national security and public order in general, and the *policía municipal*, with duties of regulating traffic and policing the local community. Catalonia and the Basque Country have their own police forces, the *Mossos d'Esquadra* and the *Ertzaintza* respectively.

★**policíaco, -a** [poli'θiako, a] ADJ police cpd; **novela policíaca** detective story

policial [poli'θjal] ADJ police cpd

★**polideportivo** [poliðepor'tiβo] NM sports centre

poliéster [poli'ester] NM polyester

polietileno [polieti'leno] NM polythene (BRIT), polyethylene (US)

polifacético, -a [polifa'θetiko, a] ADJ (persona, talento) many-sided, versatile

poligamia [poli'ɣamja] NF polygamy

polígamo, -a [po'liɣamo, a] ADJ polygamous ▶ NM polygamist

polígono [po'liɣono] NM (Mat) polygon; (solar) building lot; (zona) area; (residencial) housing estate; **~ industrial** industrial estate

polígrafo [po'liɣrafo] NM polygraph

polilla [po'liʎa] NF moth

Polinesia [poli'nesja] NF Polynesia

polinesio, -a [poli'nesjo, a] ADJ, NM/F Polynesian

polio ['poljo] NF polio

Polisario [poli'sarjo] NM ABR (Pol: tb: **Frente Polisario**) = **Frente Político de Liberación del Sáhara y Río de Oro**

politécnico [poli'tekniko] NM polytechnic

★**político, -a** [po'litiko, a] ADJ political; (discreto) tactful; (pariente) in-law; **padre ~** father-in-law ▶ NM/F politician ▶ NF politics sg; (económica, agraria) policy; **política exterior/de ingresos y precios** foreign/prices and incomes policy

póliza ['poliθa] NF certificate, voucher; (impuesto) tax o fiscal stamp; **~ de seguro(s)** insurance policy

polizón [poli'θon] NM (Aviat, Naut) stowaway

pollera [po'ʎera] NF (criadero) hencoop; (AM) skirt, overskirt

pollería [poʎe'ria] NF poulterer's (shop)

★**pollo** ['poʎo] NM chicken; (joven) young man; (señorito) playboy; **~ asado** roast chicken

polo ['polo] NM (Geo, Elec) pole; (helado) ice lolly (BRIT), Popsicle® (US); (Deporte) polo; (suéter) polo-neck; **P~ Norte/Sur** North/South Pole;

esto es el ~ opuesto de lo que dijo antes this is the exact opposite of what he said before

Polonia [po'lonja] NF Poland

poltrona [pol'trona] NF reclining chair, easy chair

polución [polu'θjon] NF pollution; **~ ambiental** environmental pollution

polvera [pol'βera] NF powder compact

★**polvo** ['polβo] NM dust; (Química, Culin, Med) powder; (fam!) screw (fam!); **en ~** powdered; **~ de talco** talcum powder; **estar hecho ~** to be worn out o exhausted; **hacer algo ~** to smash sth; **hacer ~ a algn** to shatter sb ■ **polvos** NMPL (maquillaje) powder sg

pólvora ['polβora] NF gunpowder; (fuegos artificiales) fireworks pl; **propagarse como la ~** (noticia) to spread like wildfire

polvoriento, -a [polβo'rjento, a] ADJ (superficie) dusty; (sustancia) powdery

polvorín [polβo'rin] NM (fig) powder keg

polvorosa [polβo'rosa] ADJ (fam): **poner pies en ~** to beat it

polvoso, -a [pol'βoso, a] ADJ (AM) dusty

★**pomada** [po'maða] NF cream

★**pomelo** [po'melo] NM grapefruit

pómez ['pomeθ] NF: **piedra ~** pumice stone

pomo ['pomo] NM knob, handle

pompa ['pompa] NF (burbuja) bubble; (bomba) pump; (esplendor) pomp, splendour; **pompas fúnebres** funeral sg

pomposo, -a [pom'poso, a] ADJ splendid, magnificent; (pey) pompous

pómulo ['pomulo] NM cheekbone

pon [pon] VB ver **poner**

ponchadura [pontʃa'dura] NF (AM) puncture (BRIT), flat (US)

ponchar [pon'tʃar] /1a/ VT (AM: llanta) to puncture

ponche ['pontʃe] NM punch

poncho ['pontʃo] NM (AM) poncho, cape

ponderar [ponde'rar] /1a/ VT (considerar) to weigh up, consider; (elogiar) to praise highly, speak in praise of

pondré etc [pon'dre] VB ver **poner**

ponencia [po'nenθja] NF (exposición) (learned) paper, communication; (informe) report

---

poner [po'ner]

/2q/ VT **1** to put; (colocar) to place, set; (ropa) to put on; (problema, la mesa) to set; (interés) to show; (telegrama) to send; (obra de teatro) to put on; (película) to show; **ponlo más alto** turn it up; **¿qué ponen en el Excelsior?** what's on at the Excelsior?; **poner algo a secar** to put sth (out) to dry; **¡no pongas esa cara!** don't look at me like that!

2 (tienda) to open; (instalar: gas etc) to put in; (radio, TV) to switch o turn on

3 (suponer): **pongamos que ...** let's suppose that ...

4 (*contribuir*): **el gobierno ha puesto otro millón** the government has contributed another million

5 (*Telec*): **póngame con el Sr. López** can you put me through to Mr. López?

6: poner de: le han puesto de director general they've appointed him general manager

7 (+ *adj*) to make; **me estás poniendo nerviosa** you're making me nervous

8 (*dar nombre*): **al hijo le pusieron Diego** they called their son Diego

9 (*estar escrito*) to say; **¿qué pone aquí?** what does it say here?

▶ VI (*gallina*) to lay

■ **ponerse** VR **1** (*colocarse*): **se puso a mi lado** he came and stood beside me; **tú ponte en esa silla** you go and sit on that chair; **ponerse en camino** to set off

2 (*vestido, cosméticos*) to put on; **¿por qué no te pones el vestido nuevo?** why don't you put on *o* wear your new dress?

3 (*sol*) to set

4 (+ *adj*) to get, become; **ponerse enfermo/gordo/triste** to get ill/fat/sad; **se puso muy serio** he got very serious; **después de lavarla la tela se puso azul** after washing it the material turned blue; **¡no te pongas así!** don't be like that!; **ponerse cómodo** to make o.s. comfortable

5: ponerse a: se puso a llorar he started to cry; **tienes que ponerte a estudiar** you must get down to studying; **ponerse a bien con algn** to make it up with sb; **ponerse a mal con algn** to get on the wrong side of sb

6 (*AM*): **se me pone que ...** it seems to me that ..., I think that ...

pongo etc ['pongo] VB ver **poner**

poniente [po'njente] NM west; (*viento*) west wind

pontevedrés, -esa [ponteβe'ðres, esa] ADJ of *o* from Pontevedra ▶ NM/F native *o* inhabitant of Pontevedra

pontificado [pontifi'kaðo] NM papacy, pontificate

pontífice [pon'tifiθe] NM pope, pontiff; **el Sumo P~** His Holiness the Pope

pontón [pon'ton] NM pontoon

ponzoña [pon'θoɲa] NF poison, venom

ponzoñoso, -a [ponθo'ɲoso, a] ADJ poisonous, venomous

pop [pop] ADJ INV, NM (*Mus*) pop

popa ['popa] NF stern; **a ~** astern, abaft; **de ~ a proa** fore and aft

popote [po'pote] NM (*AM*) straw

★**popular** [popu'lar] ADJ popular; (*del pueblo*) of the people

popularice etc [popula'riθe] VB ver **popularizarse**

popularidad [populari'ðað] NF popularity

popularizarse [populari'θarse] /1f/ VR to become popular

poquísimo, -a [po'kisimo, a] ADJ SUPERLATIVO de **poco** very little, very few pl; (*casi nada*) hardly any

poquito [po'kito] NM: **un ~** a little bit; **a poquitos** bit by bit ▶ ADV a little, a bit

---

por [por]

PREP **1** (*objetivo*) for; **luchar por la patria** to fight for one's country; **hazlo por mí** do it for my sake

2 (+ *infin*): **por no llegar tarde** so as not to arrive late; **por citar unos ejemplos** to give a few examples

3 (*causa*) out of, because of; **no es por eso** that's not the reason; **por escasez de fondos** through *o* for lack of funds

4 (*tiempo*): **por la mañana/noche** in the morning/at night; **se queda por una semana** she's staying (for) a week

5 (*lugar*): **pasar por Madrid** to pass through Madrid; **ir a Guayaquil por Quito** to go to Guayaquil via Quito; **caminar por la calle** to walk along the street; **por allí** over there; **se va por ahí** we have to go that way; **¿hay un banco por aquí?** is there a bank near here?; **¿por dónde?** which way?; **está por el norte** it's somewhere in the north; **por todo el país** throughout the country

6 (*cambio; precio*): **te doy uno nuevo por el que tienes** I'll give you a new one (in return) for the one you've got; **lo vendí por 15 dólares** I sold it for 15 dollars

7 (*valor distributivo*): **30 euros por hora/cabeza** 30 euros an *o* per hour/a *o* per head; **10 por ciento** 10 per cent; **80 (km) por hora** 80 (km) an *o* per hour

8 (*modo, medio*) by; **por correo/avión** by post/air; **día por día** day by day; **por orden** in order; **entrar por la entrada principal** to go in through the main entrance

9 (*agente*) by; **hecho por él** done by him; **"dirigido por"** "directed by"

10: 10 por 10 son 100 10 times 10 is 100

11 (*en lugar de*): **vino él por su jefe** he came instead of his boss

12: por mí que revienten as far as I'm concerned they can drop dead

13 (*evidencia*): **por lo que dicen** judging by *o* from what they say

14: estar/quedar por hacer to be still *o* remain to be done

15: por (muy) difícil que sea however hard it is *o* may be; **por más que lo intente** no matter how *o* however hard I try

16: por qué why; **¿por qué?** why?; **¿por qué no?** why not?; **¿por?** (*fam*) why (do you ask)?

porcelana [porθe'lana] NF porcelain; (*china*) china

★**porcentaje** [porθen'taxe] NM percentage; **~ de actividad** (*Inform*) hit rate

porche ['portʃe] NM (*de una plaza*) arcade; (*de casa*) porch

porción [por'θjon] NF (*parte*) portion, share; (*cantidad*) quantity, amount

pordiosero, -a [porðjo'sero, a] NM/F beggar

porfía [por'fia] NF persistence; (*terquedad*) obstinacy

porfiado, -a [por'fjaðo, a] ADJ persistent; (*terco*) obstinate

porfiar [por'fjar] /1c/ VI to persist, insist; (*disputar*) to argue stubbornly

pormenor [porme'nor] NM detail, particular

pormenorice *etc* [pormeno'riθe] VB *ver* **pormenorizar**

pormenorizar [pormenori'θar] /1f/ VT to (set out in) detail ▶ VI to go into detail

porno ['porno] ADJ INV porno ▶ NM porn

pornografía [pornoɣra'fia] NF pornography

poro ['poro] NM pore

pororó [poro'ro] NM (*Am*) popcorn

poroso, -a [po'roso, a] ADJ porous

poroto [po'roto] NM (*Am*) kidney bean

★**porque** ['porke] CONJ (*a causa de*) because; (*ya que*) since; (*con el fin de*) so that, in order that; ~ **sí** because I feel like it

★**porqué** [por'ke] NM reason, cause

porquería [porke'ria] NF (*suciedad*) filth, muck, dirt; (*acción*) dirty trick; (*objeto*) small thing, trifle; (*fig*) rubbish

porqueriza [porke'riθa] NF pigsty

porra ['porra] NF (*arma*) stick, club; (*cachiporra*) truncheon; **¡porras!** (*fam*) oh heck!; **¡vete a la ~!** (*fam*) go to hell!

porrazo [po'rraθo] NM (*golpe*) blow; (*caída*) bump; **de un ~** in one go

porro ['porro] NM (*fam: droga*) joint

porrón [po'rron] NM *glass wine jar with a long spout*

portaaviones [port(a)a'βjones] NM INV aircraft carrier

portada [por'taða] NF (*Tip*) title page; (: *de revista*) cover

portador, a [porta'ðor, a] NM/F carrier, bearer; (*Com*) bearer, payee; (*Med*) carrier; **ser ~ del virus del sida** to be HIV-positive

portaequipajes [portaeki'paxes] NM INV boot (*Brit*), trunk (*US*); (*baca*) luggage rack

portafolio [porta'foljo], **portafolios** [porta'foljos] NM (*Am*) briefcase; **~(s) de inversiones** (*Com*) investment portfolio

portal [por'tal] NM (*entrada*) vestibule, hall; (*pórtico*) porch, doorway; (*puerta de entrada*) main door; (*Deporte*) goal; (*Internet*) portal ■ **portales** NMPL arcade *sg*

portaligas [porta'liɣas] NM INV (*Am*) suspender belt

portamaletas [portama'letas] NM INV (*Auto: maletero*) boot; (: *baca*) roof rack

portamonedas [portamo'neðas] NM INV (*Am*) purse

portar [por'tar] /1a/ VT to carry, bear ■ **portarse** VR to behave, conduct o.s.; **portarse mal** to misbehave; **se portó muy bien conmigo** he treated me very well

★**portátil** [por'tatil] ADJ portable; **(ordenador) ~** laptop (computer)

portaviones [porta'βjones] NM INV aircraft carrier

portavoz [porta'βoθ] NMF spokesman(-woman)

portazo [por'taθo] NM: **dar un ~** to slam the door

porte ['porte] NM (*Com*) transport; (*precio*) transport charges *pl*; (*Correos*) postage; **~ debido** (*Com*) carriage forward; **~ pagado** (*Com*) carriage paid, post-paid

portento [por'tento] NM marvel, wonder

portentoso, -a [porten'toso, a] ADJ marvellous, extraordinary

porteño, -a [por'teɲo, a] ADJ of o from Buenos Aires ▶ NM/F native o inhabitant of Buenos Aires

portería [porte'ria] NF (*oficina*) porter's office; (*gol*) goal

★**portero, -a** [por'tero, a] NM/F porter; (*conserje*) caretaker; (*ujier*) doorman; (*Deporte*) goalkeeper; **~ automático** (*Esp*) entry phone

pórtico ['portiko] NM (*porche*) portico, porch; (*fig*) gateway; (*arcada*) arcade

portilla [por'tiʎa] NF, **portillo** [por'tiʎo] NM gate

portorriqueño, -a [portorri'keɲo, a] ADJ, NM/F Puerto Rican

portuario, -a [por'twarjo, a] ADJ (*del puerto*) port *cpd*, harbour *cpd*; (*del muelle*) dock *cpd*; **trabajador ~** docker

★**Portugal** [portu'ɣal] NM Portugal

★**portugués, -esa** [portu'ɣes, esa] ADJ, NM/F Portuguese ▶ NM (*Ling*) Portuguese

★**porvenir** [porβe'nir] NM future

pos [pos]: **en ~ de** *prep* after, in pursuit of

posada [po'saða] NF (*refugio*) shelter, lodging; (*mesón*) guest house; **dar ~ a** to give shelter to, take in

posaderas [posa'ðeras] NFPL backside *sg*, buttocks

posar [po'sar] /1a/ VT (*en el suelo*) to lay down, put down; (*la mano*) to place, put gently ▶ VI to sit, pose ■ **posarse** VR to settle; (*pájaro*) to perch; (*avión*) to land, come down

posavasos [posa'basos] NM INV coaster; (*para cerveza*) beermat

posdata [pos'ðata] NF postscript

pose ['pose] NF (*Arte, afectación*) pose

poseedor, a [posee'ðor, a] NM/F owner, possessor; (*de récord, puesto*) holder

poseer [pose'er] /2e/ VT to have, possess, own; (*ventaja*) to enjoy; (*récord, puesto*) to hold

poseído, -a [pose'iðo, a] ADJ possessed; **estar muy ~ de** to be very vain about

posesión [pose'sjon] NF possession; **tomar ~ (de)** to take over

posesionarse [posesjo'narse] /**1a**/ VR: **~ de** to take possession of, take over

posesivo, -a [pose'siβo, a] ADJ possessive

poseyendo etc [pose'jendo] VB ver **poseer**

posgrado [pos'ɣraðo] NM = **postgrado**

posgraduado, -a [posɣra'ðwaðo, a] ADJ, NM/F = **postgraduado**

posguerra [pos'ɣerra] NF = **postguerra**

★**posibilidad** [posiβili'ðað] NF possibility; (oportunidad) chance

posibilitar [posiβili'tar] /**1a**/ VT to make possible, permit; (hacer factible) to make feasible

★**posible** [po'siβle] ADJ possible; (factible) feasible; **de ser ~** if possible; **en** o **dentro de lo ~** as far as possible; **lo antes ~** as quickly as possible ▶ NM: **posibles** means; (bienes) funds, assets

posición [posi'θjon] NF (gen) position; (rango social) status

★**positivo, -a** [posi'tiβo, a] ADJ positive ▶ NF (Foto) print

poso ['poso] NM sediment; (heces) dregs pl

posoperatorio, -a [posopera'torjo, a] ADJ, NM = **postoperatorio**

posponer [pospo'ner] /**2q**/ VT (relegar) to put behind o below; (aplazar) to postpone

posponga etc [pos'ponga], **pospuesto** [pos'pwesto], **pospuse** etc [pos'puse] VB ver **posponer**

post [post] (pl **posts**) NM (en sitio web) post

posta ['posta] NF (de caballos) relay, team; **a ~** on purpose, deliberately

★**postal** [pos'tal] ADJ postal ▶ NF postcard

poste ['poste] NM (de telégrafos) post, pole; (columna) pillar

postear [poste'ar] /**1a**/ VT (en blog, redes sociales) to post

★**póster** ['poster] (pl **posters** ['posters]) NM poster

postergar [poster'ɣar] /**1h**/ VT (esp AM) to put off, postpone, delay

postergue etc [pos'terɣe] VB ver **postergar**

posteridad [posteri'ðað] NF posterity

posterior [poste'rjor] ADJ back, rear; (siguiente) following, subsequent; (más tarde) later; **ser ~ a** to be later than

posterioridad [posterjori'ðað] NF: **con ~** later, subsequently

postgrado [post'ɣraðo] NM: **curso de ~** postgraduate course

postgraduado, -a [postɣra'ðwaðo, a] ADJ, NM/F postgraduate

postguerra [post'ɣerra] NF postwar period; **en la ~** after the war

postigo [pos'tiɣo] NM (portillo) postern; (contraventana) shutter

postín [pos'tin] NM (fam) elegance; **de ~** posh; **darse ~** to show off

postizo, -a [pos'tiθo, a] ADJ false, artificial; (sonrisa) false, phoney ▶ NM hairpiece

postoperatorio, -a [postopera'torjo, a] ADJ postoperative ▶ NM postoperative period

postor, a [pos'tor, a] NM/F bidder; **mejor ~** highest bidder

postrado, -a [pos'traðo, a] ADJ prostrate

postrar [pos'trar] /**1a**/ VT (derribar) to cast down, overthrow; (humillar) to humble; (Med) to weaken, exhaust ■ **postrarse** VR to prostrate o.s.

★**postre** ['postre] NM sweet, dessert; **para ~** (fam) to crown it all; **llegar a los postres** (fig) to come too late ▶ NF: **a la ~** in the end, when all is said and done

postrero, -a [pos'trero, a] ADJ (antes de nmsg: **postrer**) (último) last; (que viene detrás) rear

postrimerías [postrime'rias] NFPL final stages

postulado [postu'laðo] NM postulate

postulante [postu'lante] NMF petitioner; (Rel) postulant

póstumo, -a ['postumo, a] ADJ posthumous

postura [pos'tura] NF (del cuerpo) posture, position; (fig) attitude, position

postureo [postu'reo] NM (fam) posing

post-venta [pos'βenta] ADJ (Com) after-sales

★**potable** [po'taβle] ADJ drinkable; **agua ~** drinking water

potaje [po'taxe] NM thick vegetable soup

pote ['pote] NM pot, jar

potencia [po'tenθja] NF power; (capacidad) capacity; **~ (en caballos)** horsepower; **en ~** potential, in the making; **las grandes potencias** the great powers

potencial [poten'θjal] ADJ, NM potential

potenciar [poten'θjar] /**1b**/ VT (promover) to promote; (fortalecer) to boost

potente [po'tente] ADJ powerful

potestad [potes'tað] NF authority; **patria ~** paternal authority

potosí [poto'si] NM fortune; **cuesta un ~** it costs the earth

potra ['potra] NF (Zool) filly; **tener ~** to be lucky

potro ['potro] NM (Zool) colt; (Deporte) vaulting horse

pozo ['poθo] NM well; (de río) deep pool; (de mina) shaft; **~ negro** cesspool; **ser un ~ de ciencia** (fig) to be deeply learned

PP ABR (= por poderes) pp; (= porte pagado) carriage paid ▶ NM ABR = **Partido Popular**

p.p. ABR = **por poderes**

p.p.m. ABR (= palabras por minuto) wpm

★**práctica** ['praktika] NF ver **práctico**

practicable [prakti'kaβle] ADJ practicable; (camino) passable, usable

prácticamente ['praktikamente] ADV practically

practicante [prakti'kante] NMF (Med: ayudante

de doctor) medical assistant; (: *enfermero*) nurse; (*el que practica algo*) practitioner ▶ ADJ practising

★**practicar** [prakti'kar] /**1g**/ VT to practise; (*deporte*) to go in for, play; (*ejecutar*) to carry out, perform

★**práctico, -a** ['praktiko, a] ADJ (*gen*) practical; (*conveniente*) handy; (*instruido: persona*) skilled, expert ▶ NF practice; (*método*) method; (*arte, capacidad*) skill; **en la práctica** in practice

practique *etc* [prak'tike] VB *ver* **practicar**

pradera [pra'ðera] NF meadow; (*de Canadá*) prairie

★**prado** ['praðo] NM (*campo*) meadow, field; (*pastizal*) pasture; (*AM*) lawn

Praga ['praɣa] NF Prague

pragmático, -a [praɣ'matiko, a] ADJ pragmatic

preámbulo [pre'ambulo] NM preamble, introduction; **decir algo sin preámbulos** to say sth without beating about the bush

precalentamiento [prekalenta'mjento] NM (*Deporte*) warm-up

precalentar [prekalen'tar] /**1j**/ VT to preheat

precaliente *etc* [preka'ljente] VB *ver* **precalentar**

precario, -a [pre'karjo, a] ADJ precarious

precaución [prekau'θjon] NF (*medida preventiva*) preventive measure, precaution; (*prudencia*) caution, wariness

precaver [preka'βer] /**2a**/ VT to guard against; (*impedir*) to forestall ■ **precaverse** VR: **precaverse de** *o* **contra algo** to (be on one's) guard against sth

precavido, -a [preka'βiðo, a] ADJ cautious, wary

precedencia [preθe'ðenθja] NF precedence; (*prioridad*) priority; (*superioridad*) greater importance, superiority

precedente [preθe'ðente] ADJ preceding; (*anterior*) former ▶ NM precedent; **sin ~(s)** unprecedented; **establecer** *o* **sentar un ~** to establish *o* set a precedent

preceder [preθe'ðer] /**2a**/ VT, VI to precede, go/come before

precepto [pre'θepto] NM precept

preceptor [preθep'tor] NM (*maestro*) teacher; (: *particular*) tutor

preciado, -a [pre'θjaðo, a] ADJ (*estimado*) esteemed, valuable

preciar [pre'θjar] /**1b**/ VT to esteem, value ■ **preciarse** VR to boast; **preciarse de** to pride o.s. on

precintar [preθin'tar] /**1a**/ VT (*local*) to seal off; (*producto*) to seal

precinto [pre'θinto] NM (*Com: tb:* **precinto de garantía**) seal

★**precio** ['preθjo] NM (*de mercado*) price; (*costo*) cost; (*valor*) value, worth; (*de viaje*) fare; **~ de coste** *o* **de cobertura** cost price; **~ al contado** cash price; **~ al detalle** *o* **al por menor** retail price; **~ al detallista** trade price; **~ de entrega inmediata** spot price; **~ de oferta** offer price, bargain price; **~ de salida** upset price; **~ tope** top price; **~ unitario** unit price; **no tener ~** (*fig*) to be priceless; **"no importa ~"** "cost no object"

preciosidad [preθjosi'ðað] NF (*valor*) (high) value, (great) worth; (*encanto*) charm; (*cosa bonita*) beautiful thing; **es una ~** it's lovely, it's really beautiful

★**precioso, -a** [pre'θjoso, a] ADJ precious; (*de mucho valor*) valuable; (*fam*) lovely, beautiful

precipicio [preθi'piθjo] NM cliff, precipice; (*fig*) abyss

precipitación [preθipita'θjon] NF (*prisa*) haste; (*lluvia*) rainfall; (*Química*) precipitation

precipitado, -a [preθipi'taðo, a] ADJ hasty, rash; (*salida*) hasty, sudden ▶ NM (*Química*) precipitate

precipitar [preθipi'tar] /**1a**/ VT (*arrojar*) to hurl, throw; (*apresurar*) to hasten; (*acelerar*) to speed up, accelerate; (*Química*) to precipitate ■ **precipitarse** VR to throw o.s.; (*apresurarse*) to rush; (*actuar sin pensar*) to act rashly; **precipitarse hacia** to rush towards

precisado, -a [preθi'saðo, a] ADJ: **verse ~ a hacer algo** to be obliged to do sth

precisamente [preθisa'mente] ADV precisely; (*justo*) precisely, exactly, just; **~ por eso** for that very reason; **~ fue él quien lo dijo** as a matter of fact he said it; **no es eso ~** it's not really that

precisar [preθi'sar] /**1a**/ VT (*necesitar*) to need, require; (*fijar*) to determine exactly, fix; (*especificar*) to specify; (*señalar*) to pinpoint

precisión [preθi'sjon] NF (*exactitud*) precision

★**preciso, -a** [pre'θiso, a] ADJ (*exacto*) precise; (*necesario*) necessary, essential; (*estilo, lenguaje*) concise; **es ~ que lo hagas** you must do it

precocidad [prekoθi'ðað] NF precociousness, precocity

preconcebido, -a [prekonθe'βiðo, a] ADJ preconceived

preconice *etc* [preko'niθe] VB *ver* **preconizar**

preconizar [prekoni'θar] /**1f**/ VT (*aconsejar*) to advise; (*prever*) to foresee

precoz [pre'koθ] ADJ (*persona*) precocious; (*calvicie*) premature

precuela [pre'kwela] NF prequel

precursor, a [prekur'sor, a] NM/F precursor

predecesor, a [preðeθe'sor, a] NM/F predecessor

predecir [preðe'θir] /**3o**/ VT to predict, foretell, forecast

predestinado, -a [preðesti'naðo, a] ADJ predestined

predeterminar [preðetermi'nar] /**1a**/ VT to predetermine

predicado [preði'kaðo] NM predicate

predicador, a [preðika'ðor, a] NM/F preacher

predicar [preði'kar] /**1g**/ VT, VI to preach

predicción [preðik'θjon] NF prediction; (*pronóstico*) forecast; **~ del tiempo** weather forecast(ing)

predicho [pre'ðitʃo], **prediga** *etc* [pre'ðiɣa], **predije** *etc* [pre'ðixe] VB *ver* **predecir**

predictivo, -a [preðik'tiβo, a] ADJ (*texto*) predictive

predilecto, -a [preði'lekto, a] ADJ favourite (BRIT), favorite (US)

predique *etc* [pre'ðike] VB *ver* **predicar**

prediré *etc* [preði're] VB *ver* **predecir**

predispondré *etc* [preðispon'dre] VB *ver* **predisponer**

predisponer [preðispo'ner] /2q/ VT to predispose; (*pey*) to prejudice

predisponga *etc* [preðis'ponga] VB *ver* **predisponer**

predisposición [preðisposi'θjon] NF predisposition, inclination; (*prejuicio*) prejudice, bias; (*Med*) tendency

predispuesto [preðis'pwesto], **predispuse** *etc* [preðis'puse] VB *ver* **predisponer**

predominante [preðomi'nante] ADJ predominant; (*preponderante*) prevailing; (*interés*) controlling

predominar [preðomi'nar] /1a/ VT to dominate ▶ VI to predominate; (*prevalecer*) to prevail

predominio [preðo'minjo] NM predominance

preescolar [preesko'lar] ADJ preschool

preestreno [prees'treno] NM preview, press view

prefabricado, -a [prefaβri'kaðo, a] ADJ prefabricated

prefacio [pre'faθjo] NM preface

★**preferencia** [prefe'renθja] NF preference; **de ~** preferably, for preference; **localidad de ~** reserved seat

preferible [prefe'riβle] ADJ preferable

★**preferido, -a** [prefe'riðo, a] ADJ, NM/F favourite (BRIT), favorite (US)

★**preferir** [prefe'rir] /3i/ VT to prefer

prefiero *etc* [pre'fjero] VB *ver* **preferir**

★**prefijo** [pre'fixo] NM prefix; (*Telec*) (dialling) code

prefiriendo *etc* [prefi'rjendo] VB *ver* **preferir**

pregón [pre'ɣon] NM proclamation, announcement

pregonar [preɣo'nar] /1a/ VT to proclaim, announce; (*mercancía*) to hawk

pregonero [preɣo'nero] NM town crier

★**pregunta** [pre'ɣunta] NF question; **~ capciosa** catch question; **hacer una ~** to ask a question; **preguntas frecuentes** FAQs, frequently asked questions

★**preguntar** [preɣun'tar] /1a/ VT to ask; (*cuestionar*) to question ▶ VI to ask; **~ por algn** to ask for sb; **~ por la salud de algn** to ask after sb's health ■ **preguntarse** VR to wonder

preguntón, -ona [preɣun'ton, ona] ADJ inquisitive

prehistórico, -a [preis'toriko, a] ADJ prehistoric

★**prejuicio** [pre'xwiθjo] NM prejudgement; (*preconcepción*) preconception; (*pey*) prejudice, bias

prejuzgar [prexuθ'ɣar] /1h/ VT (*predisponerse*) to prejudge

prejuzgue *etc* [pre'xuθɣe] VB *ver* **prejuzgar**

preliminar [prelimi'nar] ADJ, NM preliminary

preludio [pre'luðjo] NM (*Mus, fig*) prelude

premamá [prema'ma] ADJ: **vestido ~** maternity dress

prematrimonial [prematrimo'njal] ADJ: **relaciones prematrimoniales** premarital sex

prematuro, -a [prema'turo, a] ADJ premature

premeditación [premeðita'θjon] NF premeditation

premeditado, -a [premeði'taðo, a] ADJ premeditated, deliberate; (*intencionado*) wilful

premeditar [premeði'tar] /1a/ VT to premeditate

premiar [pre'mjar] /1b/ VT to reward; (*en un concurso*) to give a prize to

★**premio** ['premjo] NM reward; (*en un concurso*) prize; (*Com*) premium; **~ gordo** first prize

premisa [pre'misa] NF premise

premonición [premoni'θjon] NF premonition

premura [pre'mura] NF (*prisa*) haste, urgency

prenatal [prena'tal] ADJ antenatal, prenatal

prenda ['prenda] NF (*de ropa*) garment, article of clothing; (*garantía*) pledge; (*fam*) darling!; **dejar algo en ~** to pawn sth; **no soltar ~** to give nothing away; (*fig*) not to say a word ■ **prendas** NFPL talents, gifts

prendar [pren'dar] /1a/ VT to captivate, enchant; **prendarse de algo** to fall in love with sth

prendedor [prende'ðor] NM brooch

prender [pren'der] /2a/ VT (*captar*) to catch, capture; (*detener*) to arrest; (*coser*) to pin, attach; (*sujetar*) to fasten; (*AM*) to switch on ▶ VI to catch; (*arraigar*) to take root ■ **prenderse** VR (*encenderse*) to catch fire

prendido, -a [pren'diðo, a] ADJ (*AM: luz*) on

★**prensa** ['prensa] NF press; **la P~** the press; **tener mala ~** to have *o* get a bad press; **la ~ nacional** the national press

prensar [pren'sar] /1a/ VT to press

preñado, -a [pre'naðo, a] ADJ (*mujer*) pregnant; **~ de** pregnant with, full of

★**preocupación** [preokupa'θjon] NF worry, concern; (*ansiedad*) anxiety

★**preocupado, -a** [preoku'paðo, a] ADJ worried, concerned

★**preocupar** [preoku'par] /1a/ VT to worry ■ **preocuparse** VR to worry; **preocuparse de algo** (*hacerse cargo de algo*) to take care of sth; **preocuparse por algo** to worry about sth

P

preparación [prepara'θjon] NF (*acto*) preparation; (*estado*) preparedness, readiness; (*entrenamiento*) training

preparado, -a [prepa'raðo, a] ADJ (*dispuesto*) prepared; (*Culin*) ready (to serve); **¡preparados, listos, ya!** ready, steady, go! ▶ NM (*Med*) preparation

★**preparar** [prepa'rar] /1a/ VT (*disponer*) to prepare, get ready; (*Tec: tratar*) to prepare, process, treat; (*entrenar*) to teach, train ■ **prepararse** VR: **prepararse a** o **para hacer algo** to prepare o get ready to do sth

preparativo, -a [prepara'tiβo, a] ADJ preparatory, preliminary ■ **preparativos** NMPL preparations

preparatoria [prepara'torja] NF (*Am*) sixth form college (BRIT); senior high school (US)

preposición [preposi'θjon] NF preposition

prepotencia [prepo'tenθja] NF abuse of power; (*Pol*) high-handedness; (*soberbia*) arrogance

prepotente [prepo'tente] ADJ (*autoritario*) high-handed; (*soberbio*) arrogant

prerrogativa [prerroɣa'tiβa] NF prerogative, privilege

presa ['presa] NF (*cosa apresada*) catch; (*víctima*) victim; (*de animal*) prey; (*de agua*) dam; **hacer ~ en** to clutch (on to), seize; **ser ~ de** (*fig*) to be a prey to

presagiar [presa'xjar] /1b/ VT to presage

presagio [pre'saxjo] NM omen

presbítero [pres'βitero] NM priest

★**prescindir** [presθin'dir] /3a/ VI: **~ de** (*privarse de*) to do without, go without; (*descartar*) to dispense with; **no podemos ~ de él** we can't manage without him

prescribir [preskri'βir] /3a/ VT to prescribe

prescripción [preskrip'θjon] NF prescription; **~ facultativa** medical prescription

prescrito [pres'krito] PP *de* **prescribir**

preseleccionar [preselekθjo'nar] /1a/ VT (*Deporte*) to seed

presencia [pre'senθja] NF presence; **en ~ de** in the presence of

presencial [presen'θjal] ADJ: **testigo ~** eyewitness

presenciar [presen'θjar] /1b/ VT to be present at; (*asistir a*) to attend; (*ver*) to see, witness

presentación [presenta'θjon] NF presentation; (*introducción*) introduction

presentador, a [presenta'ðor, a] NM/F compère

★**presentar** [presen'tar] /1a/ VT to present; (*ofrecer*) to offer; (*mostrar*) to show, display; (*renuncia*) to tender; (*moción*) to propose; (*a una persona*) to introduce; **~ al cobro** (*Com*) to present for payment ■ **presentarse** VR (*llegar inesperadamente*) to appear, turn up; (*ofrecerse: como candidato*) to run, stand; (*aparecer*) to show, appear; (*solicitar empleo*) to apply; **presentarse a la policía** to report to the police

★**presente** [pre'sente] ADJ present; **hacer ~** to state, declare; **tener ~** to remember, bear in mind; **la carta ~** this letter ▶ NM present; (*Ling*) present (tense); (*regalo*) gift; **los presentes** those present; **la ~** this letter

presentimiento [presenti'mjento] NM premonition, presentiment

presentir [presen'tir] /3i/ VT to have a premonition of

preservación [preserβa'θjon] NF protection, preservation

preservar [preser'βar] /1a/ VT to protect, preserve

preservativo [preserβa'tiβo] NM sheath, condom

presidencia [presi'ðenθja] NF presidency; (*de comité*) chairmanship; **ocupar la ~** to preside, be in o take the chair

★**presidente, -a** [presi'ðente, a] NM/F president; (*de comité*) chairman(-woman); (*en parlamento*) speaker; (*Jur*) presiding magistrate

presidiario [presi'ðjarjo] NM convict

presidio [pre'siðjo] NM prison, penitentiary

presidir [presi'ðir] /3a/ VT (*dirigir*) to preside at, preside over; (: *comité*) to take the chair at; (*dominar*) to dominate, rule ▶ VI (*en ceremonia*) to preside; (*en reunión*) to take the chair

presienta *etc* [pre'sjenta], **presintiendo** *etc* [presin'tjendo] VB *ver* **presentir**

★**presión** [pre'sjon] NF pressure; **~ atmosférica** atmospheric o air pressure; **~ arterial** o **sanguínea** blood pressure; **a ~** under pressure

presionar [presjo'nar] /1a/ VT to press; (*botón*) to push, press; (*fig*) to press, put pressure on ▶ VI: **~ para** o **por** to press for

preso, -a ['preso, a] ADJ: **tomar** o **llevar ~ a algn** to arrest sb, take sb prisoner; **estar ~ de terror** o **pánico** to be panic-stricken ▶ NM/F prisoner

prestación [presta'θjon] NF (*aportación*) lending; (*Inform*) capability; (*servicio*) service; (*subsidio*) benefit; **~ de juramento** oath-taking; **~ personal** obligatory service; **P~ Social Sustitutoria** community service for conscientious objectors ■ **prestaciones** NFPL (*Auto*) performance features

prestado, -a [pres'taðo, a] ADJ on loan; **dar algo ~** to lend sth; **pedir ~** to borrow

prestamista [presta'mista] NMF moneylender

préstamo ['prestamo] NM loan; **~ con garantía** loan against collateral; **~ hipotecario** mortgage

★**prestar** [pres'tar] /1a/ VT to lend, loan; (*atención*) to pay; (*ayuda*) to give; (*servicio*) to do, render; (*juramento*) to take, swear ■ **prestarse** VR (*ofrecerse*) to offer o volunteer

prestatario, -a [presta'tarjo, a] NM/F borrower

presteza [pres'teθa] NF speed, promptness

prestidigitador [prestiðixita'ðor] NM conjurer

prestigio [pres'tixjo] NM prestige; (*reputación*) face; (*renombre*) good name

prestigioso, -a [presti'xjoso, a] ADJ (*honorable*) prestigious; (*famoso, renombrado*) renowned, famous

presto, -a ['presto, a] ADJ (*rápido*) quick, prompt; (*dispuesto*) ready ▶ ADV at once, right away

presumido, -a [presu'miðo, a] ADJ conceited

presumir [presu'mir] /3a/ VT to presume ▶ VI (*darse aires*) to be conceited; **según cabe ~** as may be presumed, presumably; **~ de listo** to think o.s. very smart

presunción [presun'θjon] NF presumption; (*sospecha*) suspicion; (*vanidad*) conceit

presunto, -a [pre'sunto, a] ADJ (*supuesto*) supposed, presumed; (*así llamado*) so-called

presuntuoso, -a [presun'twoso, a] ADJ conceited, presumptuous

presupondré etc [presupon'dre] VB ver **presuponer**

presuponer [presupo'ner] /2q/ VT to presuppose

presuponga etc [presu'ponga] VB ver **presuponer**

presupuestar [presupwes'tar] /1a/ VI to budget ▶ VT: **~ algo** to budget for sth

presupuestario, -a [presupwes'tarjo, a] ADJ (*Finanzas*) budgetary, budget *cpd*

presupuesto [presu'pwesto] PP *de* **presuponer** ▶ NM (*Finanzas*) budget; (*estimación: de costo*) estimate; **asignación de ~** (*Com*) budget appropriation

presupuse etc [presu'puse] VB ver **presuponer**

presuroso, -a [presu'roso, a] ADJ (*rápido*) quick, speedy; (*que tiene prisa*) hasty

pretencioso, -a [preten'θjoso, a] ADJ pretentious

pretender [preten'der] /2a/ VT (*intentar*) to try to, seek to; (*reivindicar*) to claim; (*buscar*) to seek, try for; (*cortejar*) to woo, court; **~ que** to expect that; **¿qué pretende usted?** what are you after?

pretendiente [preten'djente] NMF (*candidato*) candidate, applicant; (*amante*) suitor; (*al trono*) pretender

pretensión [preten'sjon] NF (*aspiración*) aspiration; (*reivindicación*) claim; (*orgullo*) pretension

pretérito, -a [pre'terito, a] ADJ (*Ling*) past; (*fig*) past, former

pretextar [preteks'tar] /1a/ VT to plead, use as an excuse

pretexto [pre'teksto] NM pretext; (*excusa*) excuse; **so ~ de** under pretext of

pretil [pre'til] NM (*valla*) parapet; (*baranda*) handrail

prevalecer [preβale'θer] /2d/ VI to prevail

prevaleciente [preβale'θjente] ADJ prevailing, prevalent

prevalezca etc [preβa'leθka] VB ver **prevalecer**

prevención [preβen'θjon] NF (*preparación*) preparation; (*estado*) preparedness, readiness;

(*medida*) prevention; (*previsión*) foresight, forethought; (*precaución*) precaution

prevendré etc [preβen'dre], **prevenga** etc [pre'βenga] VB ver **prevenir**

prevenido, -a [preβe'niðo, a] ADJ prepared, ready; (*cauteloso*) cautious; **estar ~** (*preparado*) to be ready; **ser ~** (*cuidadoso*) to be cautious; **hombre ~ vale por dos** forewarned is forearmed

prevenir [preβe'nir] /3r/ VT (*impedir*) to prevent; (*prever*) to foresee, anticipate; (*predisponer*) to prejudice, bias; (*avisar*) to warn; (*preparar*) to prepare, get ready ■ **prevenirse** VR to get ready, prepare; **prevenirse contra** to take precautions against

preventivo, -a [preβen'tiβo, a] ADJ preventive, precautionary

★**prever** [pre'βer] /2u/ VT to foresee; (*anticipar*) to anticipate

previniendo etc [preβi'njendo] VB ver **prevenir**

previo, -a ['preβjo, a] ADJ (*anterior*) previous, prior; (*preliminar*) preliminary ▶ PREP: **~ acuerdo de los otros** subject to the agreement of the others; **~ pago de los derechos** on payment of the fees

previsible [preβi'siβle] ADJ foreseeable

previsión [preβi'sjon] NF (*perspicacia*) foresight; (*predicción*) forecast; (*prudencia*) caution; **~ de ventas** (*Com*) sales forecast

previsor, a [preβi'sor, a] ADJ (*precavido*) far-sighted; (*prudente*) thoughtful

★**previsto, -a** [pre'βisto, a] PP *de* **prever** ▶ ADJ anticipated, forecast

PRI [pri] NM ABR (*Am*: = *Partido Revolucionario Institucional*) Mexican political party

prieto, -a ['prjeto, a] ADJ (*oscuro*) dark; (*Am*) dark(-skinned); (*fig*) mean; (*comprimido*) tight, compressed

prima ['prima] NF ver **primo**

primacía [prima'θia] NF primacy

primar [pri'mar] /1a/ VI (*tener primacía*) to occupy first place; **~ sobre** to have priority over

★**primario, -a** [pri'marjo, a] ADJ primary ▶ NF primary education

★**primavera** [prima'βera] NF (*temporada*) spring; (*período*) springtime; **P~ árabe** Arab Spring, Arab Awakening

primaveral [primaβe'ral] ADJ spring *cpd*, springlike

Primer Ministro [pri'mer-] NM Prime Minister

★**primero, -a** [pri'mero, a] ADJ (*antes de nmsg*: **primer**) first; (*fig*) prime; (*anterior*) former; (*básico*) fundamental; **primera dama** (*Teat*) leading lady; **primera plana** front page ▶ ADV first; (*más bien*) sooner, rather ▶ NF (*Auto*) first gear; (*Ferro*) first class; **de primera** (*fam*) first-class, first-rate; **de buenas a primeras** suddenly

primicia [pri'miθja] NF (*Prensa*) scoop ■ **primicias** NFPL (*tb fig*) first fruits

primitivo, -a [primiˈtiβo, a] ADJ primitive; (*original*) original; (*Com: acción*) ordinary ▶ NF: **(Lotería) Primitiva** weekly state-run lottery; ver tb **lotería**

★**primo, -a** [ˈprimo, a] ADJ (*Mat*) prime; **materias primas** raw materials ▶ NM/F cousin; (*fam*) fool, idiot; **~ hermano** first cousin; **hacer el ~** to be taken for a ride ▶ NF (*Com*) bonus; (*de seguro*) premium; (*a la exportación*) subsidy

primogénito, -a [primoˈxenito, a] ADJ first-born

primor [priˈmor] NM (*cuidado*) care; **es un ~** it's lovely

primordial [primorˈðjal] ADJ basic, fundamental

primoroso, -a [primoˈroso, a] ADJ exquisite, fine

★**princesa** [prinˈθesa] NF princess

principado [prinθiˈpaðo] NM principality

★**principal** [prinθiˈpal] ADJ principal, main; (*más destacado*) foremost; (*piso*) first, second (*US*); (*Inform*) foreground ▶ NM (*jefe*) chief, principal

★**príncipe** [ˈprinθipe] NM prince; **~ heredero** crown prince; **P~ de Asturias** King's son and heir to the Spanish throne; **~ de Gales** (*tela*) check

principiante [prinθiˈpjante] NMF beginner; (*novato*) novice

★**principio** [prinˈθipjo] NM (*comienzo*) beginning, start; (*origen*) origin; (*base*) rudiment, basic idea; (*moral*) principle; **a principios de** at the beginning of; **desde el ~** from the first; **en un ~** at first

pringado, a [prinˈɣaðo, a] NM/F (*fam*) loser (*fam*)

pringar [prinˈgar] /**1h**/ VT (*Culin: pan*) to dip; (*ensuciar*) to dirty; **~ a algn en un asunto** (*fam*) to involve sb in a matter ■ **pringarse** VR to get splashed o soiled

pringoso, -a [prinˈgoso, a] ADJ greasy; (*pegajoso*) sticky

pringue [ˈpringe] VB ver **pringar** ▶ NM (*grasa*) grease, fat, dripping

★**prioridad** [prioriˈðað] NF priority; (*Auto*) right of way

prioritario, -a [prioriˈtarjo, a] ADJ (*Inform*) foreground

★**prisa** [ˈprisa] NF (*apresuramiento*) hurry, haste; (*rapidez*) speed; (*urgencia*) (sense of) urgency; **a** o **de ~** quickly; **correr ~** to be urgent; **darse ~** to hurry up; **estar de** o **tener ~** to be in a hurry

prisión [priˈsjon] NF (*cárcel*) prison; (*período de cárcel*) imprisonment

★**prisionero, -a** [prisjoˈnero, a] NM/F prisoner

prismáticos [prisˈmatikos] NMPL binoculars

privación [priβaˈθjon] NF deprivation; (*falta*) want, privation ■ **privaciones** NFPL hardships, privations

★**privado, -a** [priˈβaðo, a] ADJ (*particular*) private; (*Pol: favorito*) favourite (*BRIT*), favorite (*US*); **en ~** privately, in private; **"~ y confidencial"** "private and confidential"

privar [priˈβar] /**1a**/ VT to deprive ■ **privarse** VR: **privarse de** (*abstenerse de*) to deprive o.s. of; (*renunciar a*) to give up

privativo, -a [priβaˈtiβo, a] ADJ exclusive

privatizar [priβatiˈθar] /**1f**/ VT to privatize

privilegiado, -a [priβileˈxjaðo, a] ADJ privileged; (*memoria*) very good ▶ NM/F (*afortunado*) privileged person

privilegiar [priβileˈxjar] /**1b**/ VT to grant a privilege to; (*favorecer*) to favour (*BRIT*), to favor (*US*)

privilegio [priβiˈlexjo] NM privilege; (*concesión*) concession

pro [pro] NM o F profit, advantage; **en ~ de** on behalf of, for; **los pros y los contras** the pros and cons ▶ PREP: **asociación ~ ciegos** association for the blind ▶ PREF: **~ soviético/americano** pro-Soviet/-American

proa [ˈproa] NF (*Naut*) bow, prow; **de ~** bow cpd, fore; ver tb **popa**

probabilidad [proβaβiliˈðað] NF probability, likelihood; (*oportunidad, posibilidad*) chance, prospect

★**probable** [proˈβaβle] ADJ probable, likely; **es ~ que** (+ subjun) it is probable o likely that; **es ~ que no venga** he probably won't come

★**probador** [proβaˈðor] NM (*persona*) taster (*of wine etc*); (*en una tienda*) fitting room

★**probar** [proˈβar] /**1l**/ VT (*demostrar*) to prove; (*someter a prueba*) to test, try out; (*ropa*) to try on; (*comida*) to taste ▶ VI to try ■ **probarse** VR: **probarse un traje** to try on a suit

probeta [proˈβeta] NF test tube

★**problema** [proˈβlema] NM problem

procaz [proˈkaθ] ADJ insolent, impudent

procedencia [proθeˈðenθja] NF (*principio*) source, origin; (*lugar de salida*) point of departure

★**procedente** [proθeˈðente] ADJ (*razonable*) reasonable; (*conforme a derecho*) proper, fitting; **~ de** coming from, originating in

proceder [proθeˈðer] /**2a**/ VI (*avanzar*) to proceed; (*actuar*) to act; (*ser correcto*) to be right (and proper), be fitting; **no procede obrar así** it is not right to act like that; **~ de** to come from, originate in ▶ NM (*comportamiento*) behaviour, conduct

procedimiento [proθeðiˈmjento] NM procedure; (*proceso*) process; (*método*) means, method; (*trámite*) proceedings pl

prócer [ˈproθer] NM (*persona eminente*) worthy; (*líder*) great man, leader; (*esp AM*) national hero

procesado, -a [proθeˈsaðo, a] NM/F accused (person)

procesador [proθesaˈðor] NM: **~ de textos** (*Inform*) word processor

procesamiento [proθesaˈmjento] NM (*Inform*) processing; **~ de datos** data processing; **~ por lotes** batch processing; **~ solapado** multiprogramming; **~ de textos** word processing

procesar [proθeˈsar] /**1a**/ VT to try, put on trial; (*Inform*) to process

procesión [proθe'sjon] NF procession; **la ~ va por dentro** he keeps his troubles to himself

proceso [pro'θeso] NM process; (*Jur*) trial; (*lapso*) course (of time); (*Inform*): **~ (automático) de datos** (automatic) data processing; **~ no prioritario** background process; **~ por pasadas** batch processing; **~ en tiempo real** real-time programming

proclama [pro'klama] NF (*acto*) proclamation; (*cartel*) poster

proclamar [prokla'mar] /1a/ VT to proclaim

proclive [pro'kliβe] ADJ: **~ (a)** inclined *o* prone (to)

procreación [prokrea'θjon] NF procreation

procrear [prokre'ar] /1a/ VT, VI to procreate

procurador, a [prokura'ðor, a] NM/F attorney, solicitor

procurar [proku'rar] /1a/ VT (*intentar*) to try, endeavour; (*conseguir*) to get, obtain; (*asegurar*) to secure; (*producir*) to produce

prodigar [proði'ɣar] /1h/ VT to lavish ▪ **prodigarse** VR: **prodigarse en** to be lavish with

prodigio [pro'ðixjo] NM prodigy; (*milagro*) wonder, marvel; **niño ~** child prodigy

prodigioso, -a [proði'xjoso, a] ADJ prodigious, marvellous

pródigo, -a ['proðiɣo, a] ADJ (*rico*) rich, productive; **hijo ~** prodigal son

producción [proðuk'θjon] NF production; (*suma de productos*) output; (*producto*) product; **~ en serie** mass production

★**producir** [proðu'θir] /3n/ VT to produce; (*generar*) to cause, bring about; (*impresión*) to give; (*Com: interés*) to bear ▪ **producirse** VR (*cambio*) to come about, happen; (*hacerse*) to be produced, be made; (*estallar*) to break out; (*accidente*) to take place; (*problema etc*) to arise

productividad [proðuktiβi'ðað] NF productivity

productivo, -a [proðuk'tiβo, a] ADJ productive; (*provechoso*) profitable

producto [pro'ðukto] NM (*resultado*) product; (*producción*) production; **~ alimenticio** foodstuff; **~ (nacional) bruto** gross (national) product; **~ interior bruto** gross domestic product

productor, a [proðuk'tor, a] ADJ productive, producing ▶ NM/F producer

produje [pro'ðuxe], **produjera** [proðu'xera], **produzca** *etc* [pro'ðuθka] VB *ver* **producir**

proeza [pro'eθa] NF exploit, feat

profanar [profa'nar] /1a/ VT to desecrate, profane

profano, -a [pro'fano, a] ADJ profane; **soy ~ en música** I don't know anything about music ▶ NM/F (*inexperto*) layman(-woman)

profecía [profe'θia] NF prophecy

proferir [profe'rir] /3i/ VT (*palabra, sonido*) to utter; (*injuria*) to hurl, let fly

profesar [profe'sar] /1a/ VT (*declarar*) to profess; (*practicar*) to practise

★**profesión** [profe'sjon] NF profession; (*en formulario*) occupation; (*confesión*) avowal; **abogado de ~, de ~ abogado** a lawyer by profession

★**profesional** [profesjo'nal] ADJ professional

★**profesor, a** [profe'sor, a] NM/F teacher; (*instructor*) instructor; **~ de universidad** lecturer; **~ adjunto** assistant lecturer, associate professor (*US*)

profesorado [profeso'raðo] NM (*profesión*) teaching profession; (*cuerpo*) teaching staff, faculty (*US*); (*cargo*) professorship

profeta [pro'feta] NMF prophet

profetice *etc* [profe'tiθe] VB *ver* **profetizar**

profetizar [profeti'θar] /1f/ VT, VI to prophesy

profiera *etc* [pro'fjera], **profiriendo** *etc* [profi'rjendo] VB *ver* **proferir**

profilaxis [profi'laksis] NF INV prevention

prófugo, -a ['profuɣo, a] NM/F fugitive; (*desertor*) deserter

profundice *etc* [profun'diθe] VB *ver* **profundizar**

★**profundidad** [profundi'ðað] NF depth; **tener una ~ de 30 cm** to be 30 cm deep

profundizar [profundi'θar] /1f/ (*fig*) VT to go into deeply, study in depth ▶ VI: **~ en** to go into deeply

profundo, -a [pro'fundo, a] ADJ deep; (*misterio, pensador*) profound; **poco ~** shallow

profusión [profu'sjon] NF (*abundancia*) profusion; (*prodigalidad*) wealth

progenie [pro'xenje] NF offspring

progenitor [proxeni'tor] NM ancestor ▪ **progenitores** NMPL (*fam*) parents

★**programa** [pro'ɣrama] NM programme; (*Inform*) program; **~ de estudios** curriculum, syllabus; **~ verificador de ortografía** (*Inform*) spelling checker

programación [proɣrama'θjon] NF (*Inform*) programming; **~ estructurada** structured programming

★**programador, a** [proɣrama'ðor, a] NM/F (computer) programmer; **~ de aplicaciones** applications programmer

programar [proɣra'mar] /1a/ VT (*Inform*) to program

progre ['proɣre] ADJ (*fam*) liberal

progresar [proɣre'sar] /1a/ VI to progress, make progress

progresión [proɣre'sjon] NF: **~ geométrica/aritmética** geometric/arithmetic progression

progresista [proɣre'sista] ADJ, NMF progressive

progresivo, -a [proɣre'siβo, a] ADJ progressive; (*gradual*) gradual; (*continuo*) continuous

★**progreso** [pro'ɣreso] NM (*tb*: **progresos**) progress; **hacer progresos** to progress, advance

prohibición [proiβi'θjon] NF prohibition, ban; **levantar la ~ de** to remove the ban on

★**prohibir** [proi'βir] /3a/ VT to prohibit, ban, forbid; **se prohíbe fumar** no smoking; **"prohibido el paso"** "no entry"

prohibitivo, -a [proiβi'tiβo, a] ADJ prohibitive

prójimo, -a ['proximo, a] NM fellow man ▶ NM/F (*vecino*) neighbour

prole ['prole] NF (*descendencia*) offspring

proletariado [proleta'rjaðo] NM proletariat

proletario, -a [prole'tarjo, a] ADJ, NM/F proletarian

proliferación [prolifera'θjon] NF proliferation; **~ de armas nucleares** spread of nuclear arms

proliferar [prolife'rar] /1a/ VI to proliferate

prolífico, -a [pro'lifiko, a] ADJ prolific

prolijo, -a [pro'lixo, a] ADJ long-winded, tedious; (*AM*) neat

prólogo ['proloɣo] NM prologue; (*preámbulo*) preface, introduction

prolongación [prolonga'θjon] NF extension

prolongado, -a [prolon'gaðo, a] ADJ (*largo*) long; (*alargado*) lengthy

prolongar [prolon'gar] /1h/ VT (*gen*) to extend; (*en el tiempo*) to prolong; (*calle, tubo*) to make longer, extend ■ **prolongarse** VR (*alargarse*) to extend, go on

prolongue *etc* [pro'longe] VB *ver* **prolongar**

prom. ABR (= *promedio*) av.

promedio [pro'meðjo] NM average; (*de distancia*) middle, mid-point

promesa [pro'mesa] NF promise; **faltar a una ~** to break a promise ▶ ADJ: **jugador ~** promising player

★**prometer** [prome'ter] /2a/ VT to promise ▶ VI to show promise ■ **prometerse** VR (*dos personas*) to get engaged

prometido, -a [prome'tiðo, a] ADJ promised; engaged ▶ NM/F fiancé (fiancée)

prominente [promi'nente] ADJ prominent

promiscuidad [promiskwi'ðað] NF promiscuity

promiscuo, -a [pro'miskwo, a] ADJ promiscuous

★**promoción** [promo'θjon] NF promotion; (*año*) class, year; **~ por correspondencia directa** (*Com*) direct mailshot; **~ de ventas** sales promotion *o* drive

promocionar [promoθjo'nar] /1a/ VT (*Com: dar publicidad*) to promote

promontorio [promon'torjo] NM promontory

promotor [promo'tor] NM promoter; (*instigador*) instigator

promover [promo'βer] /2h/ VT to promote; (*causar*) to cause; (*juicio*) to bring; (*motín*) to instigate, stir up

promueva *etc* [pro'mweβa] VB *ver* **promover**

promulgar [promul'ɣar] /1h/ VT to promulgate; (*fig*) to proclaim

promulgue *etc* [pro'mulɣe] VB *ver* **promulgar**

pronombre [pro'nombre] NM pronoun

pronosticar [pronosti'kar] /1g/ VT to predict, foretell, forecast

★**pronóstico** [pro'nostiko] NM prediction, forecast; (*profecía*) omen; (*Med: diagnóstico*) prognosis; **de ~ leve** slight, not serious; **~ del tiempo** weather forecast

pronostique *etc* [pronos'tike] VB *ver* **pronosticar**

prontitud [pronti'tuð] NF speed, quickness

★**pronto, -a** ['pronto, a] ADJ (*rápido*) prompt, quick; (*preparado*) ready ▶ ADV quickly, promptly; (*en seguida*) at once, right away; (*dentro de poco*) soon; (*temprano*) early; **¡hasta ~!** see you soon!; **lo más ~ posible** as soon as possible; **por lo ~** meanwhile, for the present; **al ~** at first; **tan ~ como** as soon as; **de ~** suddenly ▶ NM urge, sudden feeling; **tener prontos de enojo** to be quick-tempered; **tiene unos prontos muy malos** he gets ratty all of a sudden (*fam*)

pronunciación [pronunθja'θjon] NF pronunciation

pronunciado, -a [pronun'θjaðo, a] ADJ (*marcado*) pronounced; (*curva etc*) sharp; (*facciones*) marked

pronunciamiento [pronunθja'mjento] NM (*rebelión*) insurrection

★**pronunciar** [pronun'θjar] /1b/ VT to pronounce; (*discurso*) to make, deliver; (*Jur: sentencia*) to pass, pronounce ■ **pronunciarse** VR to revolt, rise, rebel; (*declararse*) to declare o.s.; **pronunciarse sobre** to pronounce on

propagación [propaɣa'θjon] NF propagation; (*difusión*) spread(ing)

propaganda [propa'ɣanda] NF (*política*) propaganda; (*comercial*) advertising; **hacer ~ de** (*Com*) to advertise

propagar [propa'ɣar] /1h/ VT to propagate; (*difundir*) to spread, disseminate ■ **propagarse** VR (*Bio*) to propagate; (*fig*) to spread

propague *etc* [pro'paɣe] VB *ver* **propagar**

propalar [propa'lar] /1a/ VT (*divulgar*) to divulge; (*publicar*) to publish an account of

propano [pro'pano] NM propane

propasarse [propa'sarse] /1a/ VR (*excederse*) to go too far; (*sexualmente*) to take liberties

propensión [propen'sjon] NF inclination, propensity

propenso, -a [pro'penso, a] ADJ: **~ a** prone *o* inclined to; **ser ~ a hacer algo** to be inclined *o* have a tendency to do sth

propiamente [propja'mente] ADV properly; (*realmente*) really, exactly; **~ dicho** real, true

propicio, -a [pro'piθjo, a] ADJ favourable (*BRIT*), favorable (*US*), propitious

propiedad [propje'ðað] NF property; (*posesión*) possession, ownership; (*conveniencia*) suitability; (*exactitud*) accuracy; **~ particular** private property; **~ pública** (*Com*) public ownership; **ceder algo a algn en ~** to transfer to sb the full rights over sth

★**propietario, -a** [propje'tarjo, a] NM/F owner, proprietor

propina [pro'pina] NF tip; **dar algo de ~** to give something extra; **darle una ~ a algn** to give sb a tip

propinar [propi'nar] /1a/ VT (*golpe*) to strike; (*azotes*) to give

propio, -a ['propjo, a] ADJ own, of one's own; (*característico*) characteristic, typical; (*conveniente*) proper; (*mismo*) selfsame, very; **el ~ ministro** the minister himself; **¿tienes casa propia?** do you have a house of your own?; **eso es muy ~ de él** that's just like him; **tiene un olor muy ~** it has a smell of its own

propondré *etc* [propon'dre] VB *ver* **proponer**

proponente [propo'nente] NM proposer, mover

proponer [propo'ner] /2q/ VT to propose, put forward; (*candidato*) to propose, nominate; (*problema*) to pose ∎ **proponerse** VR to propose, plan, intend

proponga *etc* [pro'ponga] VB *ver* **proponer**

proporción [propor'θjon] NF proportion; (*Mat*) ratio; (*razón, porcentaje*) rate; **en ~ con** in proportion to ∎ **proporciones** NFPL dimensions (*fig*); size *sg*

proporcionado, -a [proporθjo'naðo, a] ADJ proportionate; (*regular*) medium, middling; (*justo*) just right; **bien ~** well-proportioned

proporcional [proporθjo'nal] ADJ proportional; **~ a** proportional to

proporcionar [proporθjo'nar] /1a/ VT (*dar*) to give, supply, provide; **esto le proporciona una renta anual de ...** this brings him in a yearly income of ...

proposición [proposi'θjon] NF proposition; (*propuesta*) proposal

propósito [pro'posito] NM (*intención*) purpose; (*intento*) aim, intention; **a ~ de** about, with regard to ▶ ADV: **a ~** by the way, incidentally; (*a posta*) on purpose, deliberately

propuesto, -a [pro'pwesto, a] PP *de* **proponer** ▶ NF proposal

propugnar [propuɣ'nar] /1a/ VT to uphold

propulsar [propul'sar] /1a/ VT to drive, propel; (*fig*) to promote, encourage

propulsión [propul'sjon] NF propulsion; **~ a chorro** o **por reacción** jet propulsion

propuse *etc* [pro'puse] VB *ver* **proponer**

prorrata [pro'rrata] NF (*porción*) share, quota, prorate (US) ▶ ADV (*Com*) pro rata

prorratear [prorrate'ar] /1a/ VT (*dividir*) to share out, prorate (US)

prórroga ['prorroɣa] NF (*gen*) extension; (*Jur*) stay; (*Com*) deferment; (*Deporte*) extra time

prorrogable [prorro'ɣaβle] ADJ which can be extended

prorrogar [prorro'ɣar] /1h/ VT (*período*) to extend; (*decisión*) to defer, postpone

prorrogue *etc* [pro'rroɣe] VB *ver* **prorrogar**

prorrumpir [prorrum'pir] /3a/ VI to burst forth, break out; **~ en gritos** to start shouting; **~ en lágrimas** to burst into tears

prosa ['prosa] NF prose

prosaico, -a [pro'saiko, a] ADJ prosaic, dull

proscribir [proskri'βir] /3a/ VT to prohibit, ban; (*desterrar*) to exile, banish; (*partido*) to proscribe

proscripción [proskrip'θjon] NF (*prohibition*) prohibition (*frm*), ban; (*de partido*) proscription; (*destierro*) banishment

proscrito, -a [pros'krito, a] PP *de* **proscribir** ▶ ADJ (*prohibido*) banned; (*desterrado*) outlawed ▶ NM/F (*exilado*) exile; (*bandido*) outlaw

prosecución [proseku'θjon] NF continuation; (*persecución*) pursuit

proseguir [prose'ɣir] /3d, 3k/ VT to continue, carry on, proceed with; (*investigación, estudio*) to pursue ▶ VI to continue, go on

prosiga *etc* [pro'siɣa], **prosiguiendo** *etc* [pro-si'ɣjenðo] VB *ver* **proseguir**

prosista [pro'sista] NMF (*escritor*) prose writer

prospección [prospek'θjon] NF exploration; (*del petróleo, del oro*) prospecting

prospecto [pros'pekto] NM prospectus; (*folleto*) leaflet, sheet of instructions

prosperar [prospe'rar] /1a/ VI to prosper, thrive, flourish

prosperidad [prosperi'ðað] NF prosperity; (*éxito*) success

próspero, -a ['prospero, a] ADJ prosperous, thriving; (*que tiene éxito*) successful

prostíbulo [pros'tiβulo] NM brothel

prostitución [prostitu'θjon] NF prostitution

prostituir [prosti'twir] /3g/ VT to prostitute ∎ **prostituirse** VR to prostitute o.s., become a prostitute

prostituta [prosti'tuta] NF prostitute

prostituyendo *etc* [prostitu'jenðo] VB *ver* **prostituir**

protagonice *etc* [protaɣo'niθe] VB *ver* **protagonizar**

protagonista [protaɣo'nista] NMF protagonist; (*Lit: personaje*) main character, hero/heroine

protagonizar [protaɣoni'θar] /1f/ VT to head, take the chief role in

★**protección** [protek'θjon] NF protection

proteccionismo [protekθjo'nismo] NM (*Com*) protectionism

protector, a [protek'tor, a] ADJ protective, protecting; (*tono*) patronizing ▶ NM/F protector; (*bienhechor*) patron; (*de la tradición*) guardian

★**proteger** [prote'xer] /2c/ VT to protect; **~ contra grabación** o **contra escritura** (*Inform*) to write-protect

protegido, -a [prote'xiðo, a] NM/F protégé (protégée)

proteína [prote'ina] NF protein

proteja *etc* [pro'texa] VB *ver* **proteger**

prótesis ['protesis] NF (*Med*) prosthesis

protesta [pro'testa] NF protest; (*declaración*) protestation

P

★protestante [protes'tante] ADJ Protestant

★protestar [protes'tar] /**1a**/ VT to protest, declare; (*fe*) to protest; **cheque protestado por falta de fondos** cheque referred to drawer ▶ VI to protest; (*objetar*) to object

protocolo [proto'kolo] NM protocol; **sin protocolos** (*formalismo*) informal(ly)

protón [pro'ton] NM proton

prototipo [proto'tipo] NM prototype; (*ideal*) model

protuberancia [protuβe'ranθja] NF protuberance

prov. ABR (= *provincia*) prov.

provecho [pro'βetʃo] NM advantage, benefit; (*Finanzas*) profit; **¡buen ~!** bon appétit!; **en ~ de** to the benefit of; **sacar ~ de** to benefit from, profit by

provechoso, -a [proβe'tʃoso, a] ADJ (*ventajoso*) advantageous; (*beneficioso*) beneficial, useful; (*Finanzas*: *lucrativo*) profitable

proveedor, a [proβee'ðor, a] NM/F (*abastecedor*) supplier; (*distribuidor*) dealer; **~ de (acceso a) Internet** internet service provider

proveer [proβe'er] /**2e**/ VT to provide, supply; (*preparar*) to provide, get ready; (*vacante*) to fill; (*negocio*) to transact, dispatch ▶ VI: **~ a** to provide for ■ **proveerse** VR: **proveerse de** to provide o.s. with

provendré *etc* [proβen'dre], **provenga** *etc* [pro'βenga] VB *ver* **provenir**

provenir [proβe'nir] /**3r**/ VI: **~ de** to come from

Provenza [pro'βenθa] NF Provence

proverbial [proβer'βjal] ADJ proverbial; (*fig*) notorious

proverbio [pro'βerβjo] NM proverb

proveyendo *etc* [proβe'jendo] VB *ver* **proveer**

providencia [proβi'ðenθja] NF providence; (*previsión*) foresight ■ **providencias** NFPL measures, steps

★provincia [pro'βinθja] NF province; (*ESP Admin*) ≈ county, ≈ region (*SCOT*); **un pueblo de ~(s)** a country town; *see note*

Spain is divided up into 50 administrative **provincias**, including the islands, and territories in North Africa. Each one has a *capital de provincia*, which generally bears the same name. *Provincias* are grouped by geography, history and culture into *comunidades autónomas*. It should be noted that the term *comarca* normally has a purely geographical function in Spanish, but in Catalonia it designates administrative boundaries.

provinciano, -a [proβin'θjano, a] ADJ provincial; (*del campo*) country *cpd*

proviniendo *etc* [proβi'njendo] VB *ver* **provenir**

provisión [proβi'sjon] NF provision; (*abastecimiento*) provision, supply; (*medida*) measure, step

★provisional [proβisjo'nal] ADJ provisional

provisorio, -a [proβi'sorjo, a] ADJ (*esp AM*) provisional

provisto, -a [pro'βisto, a] ADJ: **~ de** provided o supplied with; (*que tiene*) having, possessing

provocación [proβoka'θjon] NF provocation

provocador, a [proβoka'ðor, a] ADJ provocative, provoking

★provocar [proβo'kar] /**1g**/ VT to provoke; (*alentar*) to tempt, invite; (*causar*) to bring about, lead to; (*promover*) to promote; (*estimular*) to rouse, stir, stimulate; (*protesta, explosión*) to cause, spark off; (*AM*): **¿te provoca un café?** would you like a coffee?

provocativo, -a [proβoka'tiβo, a] ADJ provocative

provoque *etc* [pro'βoke] VB *ver* **provocar**

proxeneta [prokse'neta] NMF go-between; (*de prostitutas*) pimp (procuress)

próximamente [proksima'mente] ADV shortly, soon

proximidad [proksimi'ðað] NF closeness, proximity

★próximo, -a ['proksimo, a] ADJ near, close; (*vecino*) neighbouring; (*el que viene*) next; **en fecha próxima** at an early date; **el mes ~** next month

proyección [projek'θjon] NF projection; (*Cine*) showing; (*diapositiva*) slide, transparency; (*influencia*) influence; **el tiempo de ~ es de 35 minutos** the film runs for 35 minutes

proyectar [projek'tar] /**1a**/ VT (*objeto*) to hurl, throw; (*luz*) to cast, shed; (*Cine*) to screen, show; (*planear*) to plan

proyectil [projek'til] NM projectile, missile; **~ (tele)dirigido** guided missile

★proyecto [pro'jekto] NM plan; (*idea*) project; (*estimación de coste*) detailed estimate; **tener algo en ~** to be planning sth; **~ de ley** (*Pol*) bill

★proyector [projek'tor] NM (*Cine*) projector

prudencia [pru'ðenθja] NF (*sabiduría*) wisdom, prudence; (*cautela*) care

★prudente [pru'ðente] ADJ sensible, wise, prudent; (*cauteloso*) careful

★prueba ['prweβa] VB *ver* **probar** ▶ NF proof; (*ensayo*) test, trial; (*cantidad*) taste, sample; (*saboreo*) testing, sampling; (*de ropa*) fitting; (*Deporte*) event; **a ~** on trial; (*Com*) on approval; **a ~ de** proof against; **a ~ de agua/fuego** waterproof/fireproof; **~ de capacitación** (*Com*) proficiency test; **~ de fuego** (*fig*) acid test; **~ de vallas** hurdles; **someter a ~** to put to the test; **¿tiene usted ~ de ello?** can you prove it?, do you have proof?

prurito [pru'rito] NM itch; (*de bebé*) nappy rash; (*anhelo*) urge

psico... [siko] PREF psycho...

psicoanálisis [sikoa'nalisis] NM psychoanalysis

psicoanalista [sikoana'lista] NMF psychoanalyst

psicología [sikoloˈxia] NF psychology
psicológico, -a [sikoˈloxiko, a] ADJ psychological
psicólogo, -a [siˈkoloɣo, a] NM/F psychologist
psicópata [siˈkopata] NMF psychopath
psicosis [siˈkosis] NF INV psychosis
psicosomático, -a [sikosoˈmatiko, a] ADJ psychosomatic
psicoterapia [sikoteˈrapja] NF psychotherapy
psiquiatra [siˈkjatra] NMF psychiatrist
psiquiátrico, -a [siˈkjatriko, a] ADJ psychiatric
▶ NM mental hospital
psíquico, -a [ˈsikiko, a] ADJ psychic(al)
PSOE [peˈsoe] NM ABR = **Partido Socialista Obrero Español**
pta(s) ABR (*Historia*) = **peseta**
Pta. ABR (*Geo*: = *Punta*) Pt.
pts ABR (*Historia*) = **pesetas**
púa [ˈpua] NF sharp point; (*Bot, Zool*) prickle, spine; (*para guitarra*) plectrum; **alambre de púas** barbed wire
pub [paβ] NM bar
púber, a [ˈpuβer, a] ADJ, NM/F adolescent
pubertad [puβerˈtað] NF puberty
publicación [puβlikaˈθjon] NF publication
★**publicar** [puβliˈkar] /1g/ VT (*editar*) to publish; (*hacer público*) to publicize; (*divulgar*) to make public, divulge
★**publicidad** [puβliθiˈðað] NF publicity; (*Com*) advertising; **dar ~ a** to publicize, give publicity to; **~ gráfica** display advertising; **~ en el punto de venta** point-of-sale advertising
publicitar [puβliθiˈtar] /1a/ VT to publicize
publicitario, -a [puβliθiˈtarjo, a] ADJ publicity *cpd*; advertising *cpd*
★**público, -a** [ˈpuβliko, a] ADJ public; **hacer ~** to publish; (*difundir*) to disclose ▶ NM public; (*Teat etc*) audience; (*Deporte*) spectators *pl*, crowd; (*en restaurantes etc*) clients *pl*; **el gran ~** the general public; **~ objetivo** (*Com*) target audience
publique *etc* [puˈβlike] VB *ver* **publicar**
pucherazo [putʃeˈraθo] NM (*fraude*) electoral fiddle; **dar ~** to rig an election
puchero [puˈtʃero] NM (*Culin*: *olla*) cooking pot; (: *guiso*) stew; **hacer pucheros** to pout
pucho [ˈputʃo] NM (*Am fam*) cigarette, fag (*Brit*)
pude *etc* VB *ver* **poder**
pudibundo, -a [puðiˈβundo, a] ADJ bashful
púdico, -a [ˈpuðiko, a] ADJ modest; (*pudibundo*) bashful
pudiendo *etc* [puˈðjendo] VB *ver* **poder**
pudiente [puˈðjente] ADJ (*opulento*) wealthy; (*poderoso*) powerful
pudiera *etc* VB *ver* **poder**
pudín [puˈðin] NM pudding
pudor [puˈðor] NM modesty; (*vergüenza*) (sense of) shame

pudoroso, -a [puðoˈroso, a] ADJ (*modesto*) modest; (*casto*) chaste
pudrir [puˈðrir] /3a/ VT to rot; (*fam*) to upset, annoy ▪ **pudrirse** VR to rot, decay; (*fig*) to rot, languish
pueblerino, -a [pweβleˈrino, a] ADJ (*lugareño*) small-town *cpd*; (*persona*) rustic, provincial ▶ NM/F (*aldeano*) country person
★**pueblo** [ˈpweβlo] VB *ver* **poblar** ▶ NM people; (*nación*) nation; (*aldea*) village; (*plebe*) common people; (*población pequeña*) small town, country town
puedo *etc* [ˈpweðo] VB *ver* **poder**
★**puente** [ˈpwente] NM (*gen*) bridge; (*Naut*: *tb*: **puente de mando**) bridge; (: *cubierta*) deck; **~ aéreo** shuttle service; **~ colgante** suspension bridge; **~ levadizo** drawbridge; **hacer ~** (*fam*) to take a long weekend

> When a public holiday in Spain falls on a Tuesday or Thursday it is common practice for employers to make the Monday or Friday a holiday as well and to give everyone a four-day weekend. This is known as **hacer puente**. When a named public holiday such as, for example, the *Día de la Constitución* falls on a Tuesday or Thursday, people refer to the whole holiday period as *el puente de la Constitución*.

puenting [ˈpwentin] NM bungee jumping
★**puerco, -a** [ˈpwerko, a] ADJ (*sucio*) dirty, filthy; (*obsceno*) disgusting ▶ NM/F pig (sow); **~ espín** porcupine
pueril [pweˈril] ADJ childish
★**puerro** [ˈpwerro] NM leek
★**puerta** [ˈpwerta] NF door; (*de jardín*) gate; (*portal*) doorway; (*fig*) gateway; (*gol*) goal; (*Inform*) port; **a la ~** at the door; **a ~ cerrada** behind closed doors; **~ corredera/giratoria** sliding/swing *o* revolving door; **~ principal/trasera** *o* **de servicio** front/back door; **~ (de transmisión en) paralelo/serie** (*Inform*) parallel/serial port; **tomar la ~** (*fam*) to leave
★**puerto** [ˈpwerto] NM (*tb Inform*) port; (*de mar*) seaport; (*paso*) pass; (*fig*) haven, refuge; **llegar a ~** (*fig*) to get over a difficulty
★**Puerto Rico** [pwertoˈriko] NM Puerto Rico
puertorriqueño, -a [pwertorriˈkeɲo, a] ADJ, NM/F Puerto Rican
★**pues** [pwes] ADV (*entonces*) then; (*¡entonces!*) well, well then; (*así que*) so ▶ CONJ (*porque*) since; **¡~ sí!** yes!, certainly!; **~, no sé** well, I don't know
★**puesto, -a** [ˈpwesto, a] PP *de* **poner** ▶ ADJ dressed; **tener algo ~** to have sth on, be wearing sth ▶ NM (*lugar, posición*) place; (*trabajo*) post, job; (*Mil*) post; (*Com*) stall; (*quiosco*) kiosk; **~ de mercado** market stall; **~ de policía** police station; **~ de socorro** first aid post ▶ CONJ: **~ que** since, as ▶ NF (*apuesta*) bet, stake; **puesta en escena** staging; **puesta al día** updating; **puesta en marcha** starting; **puesta a punto**

P

fine tuning; **puesta del sol** sunset; **puesta a cero** (*Inform*) reset

púgil ['puxil] NM boxer

pugna ['puɣna] NF battle, conflict

pugnar [puɣ'nar] /**1a**/ VI (*luchar*) to struggle, fight; (*pelear*) to fight

puja ['puxa] NF (*esfuerzo*) attempt; (*en una subasta*) bid

pujante [pu'xante] ADJ strong, vigorous

pujar [pu'xar] /**1a**/ VT (*precio*) to raise, push up ▶ VI (*en licitación*) to bid, bid up; (*fig: esforzarse*) to struggle, strain

pulcro, -a ['pulkro, a] ADJ neat, tidy

pulga ['pulɣa] NF flea; **tener malas pulgas** to be short-tempered

pulgada [pul'ɣaða] NF inch

pulgar [pul'ɣar] NM thumb

pulgón [pul'ɣon] NM plant louse, greenfly

pulir [pu'lir] /**3a**/ VT to polish; (*alisar*) to smooth; (*fig*) to polish up, touch up

pulla ['puʎa] NF cutting remark

pulmón [pul'mon] NM lung; **a pleno ~** (*respirar*) deeply; (*gritar*) at the top of one's voice; **~ de acero** iron lung

pulmonía [pulmo'nia] NF pneumonia

pulpa ['pulpa] NF pulp; (*de fruta*) flesh, soft part

pulpería [pulpe'ria] NF (*AM*) small grocery store

púlpito ['pulpito] NM pulpit

★**pulpo** ['pulpo] NM octopus

pulque ['pulke] NM pulque

pulsación [pulsa'θjon] NF beat, pulsation; (*Anat*) throb(bing); (*en máquina de escribir*) tap; (*de pianista, mecanógrafo*) touch; **~ (de una tecla)** (*Inform*) keystroke; **~ doble** (*Inform*) strikeover; **pulsaciones** pulse rate

pulsador [pulsa'ðor] NM button, push button

pulsar [pul'sar] /**1a**/ VT (*tecla*) to touch, tap; (*Mus*) to play; (*botón*) to press, push ▶ VI to pulsate; (*latir*) to beat, throb

★**pulsera** [pul'sera] NF bracelet; **reloj de ~** wristwatch

pulso ['pulso] NM (*Med*) pulse; (*fuerza*) strength; (*firmeza*) steadiness, steady hand; **hacer algo a ~** to do sth unaided o by one's own efforts

pulular [pulu'lar] /**1a**/ VI (*estar plagado*) **~ (de)** to swarm (with)

pulverice *etc* [pulβe'riθe] VB *ver* **pulverizar**

pulverizador [pulβeriθa'ðor] NM spray, spray gun

pulverizar [pulβeri'θar] /**1f**/ VT to pulverize; (*líquido*) to spray

puna ['puna] NF (*AM Med*) mountain sickness

punce *etc* ['punθe] VB *ver* **punzar**

punción [pun'θjon] NF (*Med*) puncture

pundonor [pundo'nor] NM (*dignidad*) self-respect

punición [puni'θjon] NF punishment

punitivo, -a [puni'tiβo, a] ADJ punitive

punki ['punki] ADJ, NMF punk

punta ['punta] NF point, tip; (*extremidad*) end; (*promontorio*) headland; (*Costura*) corner; (*Tec*) small nail; (*fig*) touch, trace; **horas puntas** peak hours, rush hours; **sacar ~ a** to sharpen; **de ~** on end; **de ~ a ~** from one end to the other; **estar de ~** to be edgy; **ir de ~ en blanco** to be all dressed up to the nines; **tener algo en la ~ de la lengua** to have sth on the tip of one's tongue; **se le pusieron los pelos de ~** her hair stood on end

puntada [pun'taða] NF (*Costura*) stitch

puntal [pun'tal] NM prop, support

puntapié [punta'pje] (*pl* **puntapiés**) NM kick; **echar a algn a puntapiés** to kick sb out

punteado, -a [punte'aðo, a] ADJ (*moteado*) dotted; (*diseño*) of dots ▶ NM (*Mus*) twang

puntear [punte'ar] /**1a**/ VT to tick, mark; (*Mus*) to pluck

puntería [punte'ria] NF (*de arma*) aim, aiming; (*destreza*) marksmanship

puntero, -a [pun'tero, a] ADJ leading ▶ NM (*señal, Inform*) pointer; (*dirigente*) leader

puntiagudo, -a [puntja'ɣuðo, a] ADJ sharp, pointed

puntilla [pun'tiʎa] NF (*Tec*) tack, braid; (*Costura*) lace edging; **(andar) de puntillas** (to walk) on tiptoe

puntilloso, -a [punti'ʎoso, a] ADJ (*pundonoroso*) punctilious; (*susceptible*) touchy

★**punto** ['punto] NM (*gen*) point; (*señal diminuta*) spot, dot; (*lugar*) spot, place; (*momento*) point, moment; (*en un examen*) mark; (*tema*) item; (*Costura*) stitch; (*Inform: impresora*) pitch; (: *pantalla*) pixel; **a ~** ready; **estar a ~ de** to be on the point of o about to; **llegar a ~** to come just at the right moment; **al ~** at once; **en ~** on the dot; **estar en su ~** (*Culin*) to be done to a turn; **hasta cierto ~** to some extent; **hacer ~** to knit; **poner un motor en ~** to tune an engine; **~ de partida/de congelación/de fusión** starting/freezing/ melting point; **~ de vista** point of view, viewpoint; **~ muerto** dead centre; (*Auto*) neutral (gear); **puntos a tratar** matters to be discussed, agenda *sg*; **~ final** full stop; **dos puntos** colon; **~ y coma** semicolon; **~ acápite** (*AM*) full stop, new paragraph; **~ de interrogación** question mark; **puntos suspensivos** suspension points; **~ de equilibrio/de pedido** (*Com*) breakeven/reorder point; **~ inicial** o **de partida** (*Inform*) home; **~ de referencia/de venta** (*Com*) benchmark point/point-of-sale

puntocom [punto'kom] NF INV, ADJ INV dotcom, dot.com

puntuación [puntwa'θjon] NF punctuation; (*puntos: en examen*) mark(s) *pl*; (: *Deporte*) score

puntual [pun'twal] ADJ (*a tiempo*) punctual; (*cálculo*) exact, accurate; (*informe*) reliable

puntualice *etc* [puntwa'liθe] VB *ver* **puntualizar**

puntualidad [puntwali'ðað] NF (*de llegada*)

punctuality; (*exactitud*) exactness, accuracy; (*fiabilidad*) reliability

puntualizar [puntwali'θar] /**1f**/ vt to fix, specify

puntuar [pun'twar] /**1e**/ vt (*Ling, Tip*) to punctuate; (*examen*) to mark ▶ vi (*Deporte*) to score, count

punzada [pun'θaða] nf (*puntura*) prick; (*Med*) stitch; (*dolor*) twinge (of pain)

punzante [pun'θante] adj (*dolor*) shooting, sharp; (*herramienta*) sharp; (*comentario*) biting

punzar [pun'θar] /**1f**/ vt to prick, pierce ▶ vi to shoot, stab

punzón [pun'θon] nm (*Tec*) punch

puñado [pu'ɲaðo] nm handful (*tb fig*); **a puñados** by handfuls

puñal [pu'ɲal] nm dagger

puñalada [puɲa'laða] nf stab

puñeta [pu'ɲeta] nf: **¡~!, ¡qué ~(s)!** (*fam!*) hell!; **mandar a algn a hacer puñetas** (*fam*) to tell sb to go to hell

puñetazo [puɲe'taθo] nm punch

puño ['puɲo] nm (*Anat*) fist; (*cantidad*) fistful, handful; (*Costura*) cuff; (*de herramienta*) handle; **como un ~** (*verdad*) obvious; (*palpable*) tangible, visible; **de ~ y letra del poeta** in the poet's own handwriting

pupila [pu'pila] nf (*Anat*) pupil

pupitre [pu'pitre] nm desk

puré [pu're] (*pl* **purés**) nm purée; (*sopa*) (thick) soup; **~ de patatas** (*Esp*), **~ de papas** (*Am*) mashed potatoes; **estar hecho ~** (*fig*) to be knackered

pureza [pu'reθa] nf purity

purga ['purɣa] nf purge

purgante [pur'ɣante] adj, nm purgative

purgar [pur'ɣar] /**1h**/ vt to purge; (*Pol: depurar*) to purge, liquidate ▪ **purgarse** vr (*Med*) to take a purge

purgatorio [purɣa'torjo] nm purgatory

purgue *etc* ['purɣe] vb ver **purgar**

purificar [purifi'kar] /**1g**/ vt to purify; (*refinar*) to refine

purifique *etc* [puri'fike] vb ver **purificar**

puritano, -a [puri'tano, a] adj (*actitud*) puritanical; (*iglesia, tradición*) puritan ▶ nm/f puritan

★**puro, -a** ['puro, a] adj pure; (*depurado*) unadulterated; (*oro*) solid; (*cielo*) clear; (*verdad*) simple, plain; **por pura casualidad** by sheer chance ▶ adv: **de ~ cansado** out of sheer tiredness ▶ nm cigar

púrpura ['purpura] nf purple

purpúreo, -a [pur'pureo, a] adj purple

pus [pus] nm pus

puse *etc* ['puse] vb ver **poner**

pusiera *etc* vb ver **poder**

pústula ['pustula] nf pimple, sore

puta ['puta] nf (*fam!*) whore (*fam!*), prostitute

putada [pu'taða] nf (*fam!*): **hacer una ~ a algn** to play a dirty trick on sb; **¡qué ~!** what a pain in the arse! (*fam!*)

putería [pute'ria] nf (*prostitución*) prostitution; (*prostíbulo*) brothel

putrefacción [putrefak'θjon] nf rotting, putrefaction

pútrido, -a ['putriðo, a] adj rotten

puzzle ['puθle] nm puzzle

PVP abr (*Esp*: = *Precio Venta al Público*) ≈ RRP

PYME ['pime] nf abr (= *Pequeña y Mediana Empresa*) SME

Pza abr = **plaza**

Qq

Q, q [ku] NF (*letra*) Q, q; **Q de Querido** Q for Queen

q.e.p.d. ABR (= *que en paz descanse*) R.I.P

qm ABR = **quintal métrico; quintales métricos**

qts. ABR = **quilates**

quad [kwað] NM quad, quad bike

---

que [ke]

CONJ **1** (*con oración subordinada: muchas veces no se traduce*) that; **dijo que vendría** he said (that) he would come; **espero que lo encuentres** I hope (that) you find it; **dile que me llame** ask him to call me; *ver tb* **el**

2 (*en oración independiente*): **¡que entre!** send him in!; **¡que aproveche!** enjoy your meal!; **¡que se mejore tu padre!** I hope your father gets better; **¡que lo haga él!** he can do it!; (*orden*) get him to do it!

3 (*enfático*): **¿me quieres? — ¡que sí!** do you love me? — of course!; **te digo que sí** I'm telling you

4 (*consecutivo: muchas veces no se traduce*) that; **es tan grande que no lo puedo levantar** it's so big (that) I can't lift it

5 (*comparaciones*) than; **yo que tú/él** if I were you/him; *ver tb* **más; menos**

6 (*valor disyuntivo*): **que le guste o no** whether he likes it or not; **que venga o que no venga** whether he comes or not

7 (*porque*): **no puedo, que tengo que quedarme en casa** I can't, I've got to stay in

8: **siguió toca que toca** he kept on playing

▶ PRON **1** (*cosa*) that, which; (: + *prep*) which; **el sombrero que te compraste** the hat (that *o* which) you bought; **la cama en que dormí** the bed (that *o* which) I slept in; **el día (en) que ella nació** the day (when) she was born

2 (*persona: suj*) that, who; (: *objeto*) that, whom; **el amigo que me acompañó al museo** the friend that *o* who went to the museum with me; **la chica que invité** the girl (that *o* whom) I invited

---

★**qué** [ke] ADJ what?, which?; **¡~ día más espléndido!** what a glorious day!; **¿~ edad tienes?** how old are you? ▶ ADV how; **¡~ divertido/asco!** how funny/revolting! ▶ PRON what?; **¿de ~ me hablas?** what are you talking about?; **¿~ tal?** how are you?, how are things?; **¿~ hay (de nuevo)?** what's new?; **¿~ más?** anything else?

quebrada [ke'βraða] NF *ver* **quebrado**

quebradero [keβra'ðero] NM: **~ de cabeza** headache, worry

quebradizo, -a [keβra'ðiθo, a] ADJ fragile; (*persona*) frail

quebrado, -a [ke'βraðo, a] ADJ (*roto*) broken; (*terreno*) rough, uneven ▶ NM/F bankrupt; **~ rehabilitado** discharged bankrupt ▶ NM (*Mat*) fraction ▶ NF ravine

quebradura [keβra'ðura] NF (*fisura*) fissure; (*Med*) rupture

quebrantamiento [keβranta'mjento] NM (*acto*) breaking; (*de ley*) violation; (*estado*) exhaustion

quebrantar [keβran'tar] /**1a**/ VT (*infringir*) to violate, transgress ■ **quebrantarse** VR (*persona, salud*) to decline

quebranto [ke'βranto] NM damage, harm; (*decaimiento*) exhaustion; (*dolor*) grief, pain

★**quebrar** [ke'βrar] /**1j**/ VT to break, smash ▶ VI to go bankrupt ■ **quebrarse** VR to break, get broken; (*Med*) to be ruptured

quechua ['ketʃua] ADJ, NMF Quechua

queda ['keða] NF: **(toque de) ~** curfew

★**quedar** [ke'ðar] /**1a**/ VI to stay, remain; (*encontrarse*) to be; (*restar*) to remain, be left; **~ en** (*acordar*) to agree on/to; (*acabar siendo*) to end up as; **~ ciego/mudo** to be left blind/with a speech impairment; **~ por hacer** to be still to be done; **no te queda bien ese vestido** that dress doesn't suit you; **quedamos a las seis** we agreed to meet at six; **eso queda muy lejos** that's a long way (away); **nos quedan 12 kiló-**

metros para llegar al pueblo there are still 12 km before we get to the village; **no queda otra** there's no alternative ▪**quedarse** VR to remain, stay (behind); **quedarse (con) algo** to keep sth; **quedarse con algn** (*fam*) to swindle sb; **quedarse en nada** to come to nothing o nought; **quedarse frito** (*fam*) to fall asleep, crash out; **quedarse sin** to run out of

quedo, -a [ˈkeðo, a] ADJ still ▶ ADV softly, gently

quehacer [keaˈθer] NM task, job; **quehaceres (domésticos)** household chores

★**queja** [ˈkexa] NF complaint

★**quejarse** [keˈxarse] /1a/ VR (*enfermo*) to moan, groan; (*protestar*) to complain; **~ de que ...** to complain (about the fact) that ...

quejica [keˈxika] ADJ grumpy, complaining ▶ NMF grumbler, whinger

quejido [keˈxiðo] NM moan

quejoso, -a [keˈxoso, a] ADJ complaining

quema [ˈkema] NF fire; (*combustión*) burning

quemado, -a [keˈmaðo, a] ADJ burnt; (*irritado*) annoyed

★**quemadura** [kemaˈðura] NF burn, scald; (*de sol*) sunburn; (*de fusible*) blow-out

★**quemar** [keˈmar] /1a/ VT to burn; (*fig: malgastar*) to burn up, squander; (*Com: precios*) to slash, cut; (*fastidiar*) to annoy, bug ▶ VI to be burning hot ▪**quemarse** VR (*consumirse*) to burn (up); (*del sol*) to get sunburnt

quemarropa [kemaˈrropa] : **a ~** adv point-blank

quemazón [kemaˈθon] NF burn; (*calor*) intense heat; (*sensación*) itch

quena [ˈkena] NF (*Am*) Indian flute

quepo *etc* [ˈkepo] VB *ver* **caber**

querella [keˈreʎa] NF (*Jur*) charge; (*disputa*) dispute

querellarse [kereˈʎarse] /1a/ VR to file a complaint

querencia [keˈrenθja] NF (*Zool*) homing instinct; (*fig*) homesickness

---

querer [keˈrer]

/2t/ VT **1** (*desear*) to want; **quiero más dinero** I want more money; **quisiera** o **querría un té** I'd like a tea; **sin querer** unintentionally; **quiero ayudar/que vayas** I want to help/you to go; **como usted quiera** as you wish, as you please; **ven cuando quieras** come when you like; **lo hizo sin querer** he didn't mean to do it; **no quiero** I don't want to; **le pedí que me dejara ir pero no quiso** I asked him to let me go but he refused

2 (*preguntas: para pedir u ofrecer algo*): **¿quiere abrir la ventana?** could you open the window?; **¿quieres echarme una mano?** can you give me a hand?; **¿quiere un café?** would you like some coffee?

3 (*amar*) to love; **te quiero** I love you; **no estoy enamorado, pero la quiero mucho** I'm not in

---

love, but I'm very fond of her

4 (*requerir*): **esta planta quiere más luz** this plant needs more light

5: **querer decir** to mean; **¿qué quieres decir?** what do you mean?

★**querido, -a** [keˈriðo, a] ADJ dear; **nuestra querida patria** our beloved country ▶ NM/F darling; (*amante*) lover

querosén [keroˈsen], **querosene** [keroˈsene] NM (*Am*) kerosene, paraffin

querré *etc* [keˈrre] VB *ver* **querer**

quesería [keseˈria] NF dairy; (*fábrica*) cheese factory

quesero, -a [keˈsero, a] ADJ: **la industria quesera** the cheese industry ▶ NM/F cheesemaker ▶ NF cheese dish

quesito [keˈsito] NM soft-cheese triangle

★**queso** [ˈkeso] NM cheese; **~ rallado** grated cheese; **~ crema** (*Am*), **~ de untar** (*Esp*) cream cheese; **~ manchego** *sheep's milk cheese made in La Mancha*; **dárselas con ~ a algn** (*fam*) to take sb in

quetzal [ketˈsal] NM *monetary unit of Guatemala*

quicio [ˈkiθjo] NM hinge; **estar fuera de ~** to be beside o.s.; **sacar a algn de ~** to drive sb up the wall

quid [kið] NM gist, crux; **dar en el ~** to hit the nail on the head

quiebra [ˈkjeβra] NF break, split; (*Com*) bankruptcy; (*Econ*) slump

quiebro *etc* [ˈkjeβro] VB *ver* **quebrar** ▶ NM (*del cuerpo*) swerve

★**quien** [kjen] PRON RELATIVO (*suj*) who; (*complemento*) whom; (*indefinido*): **~ dice eso es tonto** whoever says that is a fool; **hay ~ piensa que** there are those who think that; **no hay ~ lo haga** no-one will do it; **~ más, ~ menos tiene sus problemas** everybody has problems

★**quién** [kjen] PRON INTERROGATIVO who; (*complemento*) whom; **¿~ es?** who is it?, who's there?; (*Telec*) who's calling?

quienquiera [kjenˈkjera] (*pl* **quienesquiera**) PRON whoever

quiero *etc* [ˈkjero] VB *ver* **querer**

★**quieto, -a** [ˈkjeto, a] ADJ still; (*carácter*) placid; **¡estate ~!** keep still!

Do not translate the Spanish word **quieto** by *quiet*.

quietud [kjeˈtuð] NF stillness

quijada [kiˈxaða] NF jaw, jawbone

quijote [kiˈxote] NM dreamer; **Don Q~** Don Quixote

quil. ABR = **quilates**

quilate [kiˈlate] NM carat

quilla [ˈkiʎa] NF keel

quilo ... [ˈkilo] = **kilo...**

quimera [kiˈmera] NF (*sueño*) pipe dream

quimérico, -a [kiˈmeriko, a] ADJ fantastic

q

★químico, -a ['kimiko, a] ADJ chemical ▸ NM/F chemist ▸ NF chemistry

quimioterapia [kimiote'rapia] NF chemotherapy

quina ['kina] NF quinine

quincalla [kin'kaʎa] NF hardware, ironmongery (BRIT)

quincallería [kinkaʎe'ria] NF ironmonger's (shop), hardware store (US)

★quince ['kinθe] NUM fifteen; **~ días** a fortnight

★quinceañero, -a [kinθea'ɲero, a] ADJ fifteen-year-old; (adolescente) teenage ▸ NM/F fifteen-year-old; (adolescente) teenager

★quincena [kin'θena] NF fortnight; (pago) fortnightly pay

quincenal [kinθe'nal] ADJ fortnightly

quincuagésimo, -a [kinkwa'xesimo, a] NUM fiftieth

quiniela [ki'njela] NF football pools pl ■ **quinielas** NFPL pools coupon sg

quinientos, -as [ki'njentos, as] NUM five hundred

quinina [ki'nina] NF quinine

quinqué [kin'ke] NM oil lamp

quinquenal [kinke'nal] ADJ five-year cpd

quinqui ['kinki] NM delinquent

quinta ['kinta] NF ver **quinto**

quintaesencia [kintae'senθja] NF quintessence

quintal [kin'tal] NM (CASTILLA: peso) = 46kg; **~ métrico** = 100kg

quinteto [kin'teto] NM quintet

★quinto, -a ['kinto, a] ADJ fifth ▸ NM (Mil) conscript, draftee ▸ NF country house; (Mil) call-up, draft

quíntuplo, -a [kin'tuplo, a] ADJ quintuple, five-fold

★quiosco ['kjosko] NM (de música) bandstand; (de periódicos) news stand (also selling sweets, cigarettes etc)

quirófano [ki'rofano] NM operating theatre

quiromancia [kiro'manθja] NF palmistry

quirúrgico, -a [ki'rurxiko, a] ADJ surgical

quise etc ['kise] VB ver **querer**

quisiera etc VB ver **querer**

quisque ['kiske] PRON (fam): **cada** o **todo ~** (absolutely) everyone

quisquilloso, -a [kiski'ʎoso, a] ADJ (susceptible) touchy; (meticuloso) pernickety

quiste ['kiste] NM cyst

quitaesmalte [kitaes'malte] NM nail polish remover

quitamanchas [kita'mantʃas] NM INV stain remover

quitanieves [kita'njeβes] NM INV snowplough (BRIT), snowplow (US)

★quitar [ki'tar] **/1a/** VT to remove, take away; (ropa) to take off; (dolor) to relieve; (vida) to take; (valor) to reduce; (hurtar) to remove, steal; **me quita mucho tiempo** it takes up a lot of my time; **el café me quita el sueño** coffee stops me sleeping; **~ de en medio a algn** to get rid of sb ▸ VI: **¡quita de ahí!** get out of the way! ■ **quitarse** VR to withdraw; (mancha) to come off o out; (ropa) to take off; **quitarse algo de encima** to get rid of sth; **quitarse del tabaco** to give up smoking; **se quitó el sombrero** he took off his hat

quitasol [kita'sol] NM sunshade (BRIT), parasol

quite ['kite] NM (en esgrima) parry; (evasión) dodge; **estar al ~** to be ready to go to sb's aid

Quito ['kito] NM Quito

★quizá(s) [ki'θa(s)] ADV perhaps, maybe

quórum ['kworum] (pl **quórums** ['kworum]) NM quorum

Rr

R, r ['erre] NF (*letra*) R, r; **R de Ramón** R for Robert (BRIT) o Roger (US)

R. ABR (*Rel*) = **real; reverendo; remite; remitente; río**

rabadilla [raβa'ðiʎa] NF base of the spine

rábano ['raβano] NM radish; **me importa un ~** I don't give a damn

rabia ['raβja] NF (*Med*) rabies *sg*; (*fig: ira*) fury, rage; **¡qué ~!** isn't it infuriating!; **me da ~** it maddens me; **tener ~ a algn** to have a grudge against sb

rabiar [ra'βjar] /**1b**/ VI to have rabies; (*encolerizarse*) to rage, be furious; **~ por algo** to long for sth

rabieta [ra'βjeta] NF tantrum, fit of temper

rabino [ra'βino] NM rabbi

rabioso, -a [ra'βjoso, a] ADJ rabid; (*fig*) furious

rabo ['raβo] NM tail

racanear [rakane'ar] /**1a**/ VI (*fam*) to skive

rácano ['rakano] NM (*fam*) slacker, skiver

RACE ['raθe] NM ABR (= *Real Automóvil Club de España*) ≈ RAC

racha ['ratʃa] NF gust of wind; (*serie*) string, series; **buena/mala ~** spell of good/bad luck

racial [ra'θjal] ADJ racial, race *cpd*

racimo [ra'θimo] NM bunch

raciocinio [raθjo'θinjo] NM reason; (*razonamiento*) reasoning

★ración [ra'θjon] NF portion ■ **raciones** NFPL rations

racional [raθjo'nal] ADJ (*razonable*) reasonable; (*lógico*) rational

racionalice *etc* [raθjona'liθe] VB *ver* **racionalizar**

racionalizar [raθjonali'θar] /**1f**/ VT to rationalize; (*Com*) to streamline

racionamiento [raθjona'mjento] NM (*Com*) rationing

racionar [raθjo'nar] /**1a**/ VT to ration (out)

★racismo [ra'θismo] NM racialism, racism

★racista [ra'θista] ADJ, NMF racist

radar [ra'ðar] NM radar

radiación [raðja'θjon] NF radiation; (*Telec*) broadcasting

radiactividad [raðjaktiβi'ðað] NF radioactivity

radiactivo, -a [raðjak'tiβo, a] ADJ radioactive

radiado, -a [ra'ðjaðo, a] ADJ radio *cpd*, broadcast

★radiador [raðja'ðor] NM radiator

radial [ra'ðjal] ADJ (*Am*) radio *cpd*

radiante [ra'ðjante] ADJ radiant

radiar [ra'ðjar] /**1b**/ VT to radiate; (*Telec*) to broadcast; (*Med*) to give radiotherapy to

radical [raði'kal] ADJ, NMF radical ▶ NM (*Ling*) root; (*Mat*) square-root sign

radicar [raði'kar] /**1g**/ VI to take root; **~ en** (*dificultad, problema*) to lie in; (*solución*) to consist in ■ **radicarse** VR to establish o.s., put down (one's) roots

★radio ['raðjo] NF radio; (*aparato*) radio (set); **~ de acción** extent of one's authority, sphere of influence ▶ NM (*Mat*) radius; (*Am*) radio; (*Química*) radium

radioactividad [raðjoaktiβi'ðað] NF radioactivity

radioactivo, -a [raðjoak'tiβo, a] ADJ radioactive

radioaficionado, -a [raðjoafiθjo'naðo, a] NM/F radio ham

radiocasete [raðjoka'sete] NM radiocassette (player)

radiodifusión [raðjodifu'sjon] NF broadcasting

radioemisora [raðjoemi'sora] NF transmitter, radio station

radiofónico, -a [raðjo'foniko, a] ADJ radio *cpd*

radiografía [raðjoɣra'fia] NF X-ray

r

radiólogo, -a [ra'ðjoloɣo, a] NM/F radiologist
radionovela [raðjono'βela] NF radio series
radiotaxi [raðjo'taksi] NM radio taxi
radioterapia [raðjote'rapja] NF radiotherapy
radioyente [raðjo'jente] NMF listener
radique *etc* [ra'ðike] VB *ver* **radicar**
RAE ['rae] NF ABR (= *Real Academia Española*) *ver* **real**
ráfaga ['rafaɣa] NF gust; (*de luz*) flash; (*de tiros*) burst
raído, -a [ra'iðo, a] ADJ (*ropa*) threadbare; (*persona*) shabby
raigambre [rai'ɣambre] NF (*Bot*) roots *pl*; (*fig*) tradition
raíz [ra'iθ] (*pl* **raíces**) NF root; **~ cuadrada** square root; **a ~ de** as a result of; (*después de*) immediately after
raja ['raxa] NF (*de melón etc*) slice; (*hendidura*) slit, split; (*grieta*) crack
rajar [ra'xar] /1a/ VT to split; (*fam*) to slash ■ **rajarse** VR to split, crack; **rajarse de** to back out of
rajatabla [raxa'taβla]: **a ~** *adv* (*estrictamente*) strictly, to the letter
ralea [ra'lea] NF (*pey*) kind, sort
ralentí [ra'lenti] NM (*TV etc*) slow motion; (*Auto*) neutral; **al ~** in slow motion; (*Auto*) ticking over
rallador [raʎa'ðor] NM grater
rallar [ra'ʎar] /1a/ VT to grate
ralo, -a ['ralo, a] ADJ thin, sparse
RAM [ram] NF ABR (= *random access memory*) RAM
rama ['rama] NF bough, branch; **andarse por las ramas** (*fig: fam*) to beat about the bush
ramaje [ra'maxe] NM branches *pl*, foliage
ramal [ra'mal] NM (*de cuerda*) strand; (*Ferro*) branch line; (*Auto*) branch (road)
rambla ['rambla] NF (*avenida*) avenue
ramera [ra'mera] NF whore, hooker (US)
ramificación [ramifika'θjon] NF ramification
ramificarse [ramifi'karse] /1g/ VR to branch out
ramifique *etc* [rami'fike] VB *ver* **ramificarse**
ramillete [rami'ʎete] NM bouquet; (*fig*) select group
★**ramo** ['ramo] NM branch, twig; (*sección*) department, section; (*sector*) field, sector
rampa ['rampa] NF ramp; **~ de acceso** entrance ramp
ramplón, -ona [ram'plon, ona] ADJ uncouth, coarse
★**rana** ['rana] NF frog; **salto de ~** leapfrog; **cuando las ranas críen pelos** when pigs fly
ranchero [ran'tʃero] NM (*AM*) rancher; (*pequeño propietario*) smallholder
rancho ['rantʃo] NM (*Mil*) food; (*AM: grande*) ranch; (*: pequeño*) small farm

rancio, -a ['ranθjo, a] ADJ (*comestibles*) stale, rancid; (*vino*) aged, mellow; (*fig*) ancient
★**rango** ['rango] NM rank; (*prestigio*) standing
★**ranura** [ra'nura] NF groove; (*de teléfono etc*) slot; **~ de expansión** (*Inform*) expansion slot
rap [rap] NM (*Mus*) rap
rapacidad [rapaθi'ðað] NF rapacity
rapapolvo [rapa'polβo] NM: **echar un ~ a algn** to give sb a ticking off
rapar [ra'par] /1a/ VT to shave; (*los cabellos*) to crop
rapaz [ra'paθ] ADJ (*Zool*) predatory ▶ NM young boy
rape ['rape] NM quick shave; (*pez*) monkfish; **al ~ cropped**
rapé [ra'pe] NM snuff
rapel [ra'pel] NM = **rappel**
★**rápidamente** ['rapiðamente] ADV quickly
rapidez [rapi'ðeθ] NF speed, rapidity
★**rápido, -a** ['rapiðo, a] ADJ fast, quick ▶ ADV quickly ▶ NM (*Ferro*) express ■ **rápidos** NMPL rapids
rapiña [ra'piɲa] NF robbery; **ave de ~** bird of prey
rappel [ra'pel] NM (*Deporte*) abseiling
raptar [rap'tar] /1a/ VT to kidnap
rapto ['rapto] NM kidnapping; (*impulso*) sudden impulse; (*éxtasis*) ecstasy, rapture
raqueta [ra'keta] NF racket
raquítico, -a [ra'kitiko, a] ADJ stunted; (*fig*) poor, inadequate
raquitismo [raki'tismo] NM rickets *sg*
★**raramente** [rara'mente] ADV rarely
rareza [ra'reθa] NF rarity; (*fig*) eccentricity
★**raro, -a** ['raro, a] ADJ (*poco común*) rare; (*extraño*) odd, strange; (*excepcional*) remarkable; **¡qué ~!** how (very) odd!; **¡(qué) cosa más rara!** how strange!
ras [ras] NM: **a ~ de** level with; **a ~ de tierra** at ground level
rasar [ra'sar] /1a/ VT to level
★**rascacielos** [raska'θjelos] NM INV skyscraper
rascar [ras'kar] /1g/ VT (*con las uñas etc*) to scratch; (*raspar*) to scrape ■ **rascarse** VR to scratch (o.s.)
★**rasgar** [ras'ɣar] /1h/ VT to tear, rip (up)
rasgo ['rasɣo] NM (*con pluma*) stroke ■ **rasgos** NMPL features, characteristics; **a grandes rasgos** in outline, broadly
rasgue *etc* ['rasɣe] VB *ver* **rasgar**
rasguear [rasɣe'ar] /1a/ VT (*Mus*) to strum
rasguñar [rasɣu'ɲar] /1a/ VT to scratch; (*bosquejar*) to sketch
rasguño [ras'ɣuɲo] NM scratch
raso, -a ['raso, a] ADJ (*liso*) flat, level; (*a baja altura*) very low; **cielo ~** clear sky ▶ NM satin; (*campo llano*) flat country; **al ~** in the open
raspado [ras'paðo] NM (*Med*) scrape

raspador [raspaˈðor] NM scraper

raspadura [raspaˈðura] NF (acto) scrape, scraping; (marca) scratch ■ **raspaduras** NFPL (de papel etc) scrapings

raspar [rasˈpar] /1a/ VT to scrape; (arañar) to scratch; (limar) to file ▶ VI (manos) to be rough; (vino) to be sharp, have a rough taste

rasque etc [ˈraske] VB ver **rascar**

rastra [ˈrastra] NF (Agr) rake; **a rastras** by dragging; (fig) unwillingly

rastreador [rastreaˈðor] NM tracker; **~ de minas** minesweeper

rastrear [rastreˈar] /1a/ VT (seguir) to track; (minas) to sweep

rastrero, -a [rasˈtrero, a] ADJ (Bot, Zool) creeping; (fig) despicable, mean

rastrillar [rastriˈʎar] /1a/ VT to rake

rastrillo [rasˈtriʎo] NM rake; (AM) safety razor

rastro [ˈrastro] NM (Agr) rake; (pista) track, trail; (vestigio) trace; (mercado) flea market; **el R~** the Madrid flea market; **perder el ~** to lose the scent; **desaparecer sin ~** to vanish without trace

rastrojo [rasˈtroxo] NM stubble

rasurado [rasuˈraðo] NM (AM) shaving

rasuradora [rasuraˈðora] NF, (AM) **rasuradora** [rasuraˈðora] NF electric shaver o razor

rasurar [rasuˈrar] /1a/ VT (AM) to shave ■ **rasurarse** VR to shave

★**rata** [ˈrata] NF rat

ratear [rateˈar] /1a/ VT (robar) to steal

ratero, -a [raˈtero, a] ADJ light-fingered ▶ NM/F (carterista) pickpocket; (ladrón) petty thief; (AM: de casas) burglar

ratificar [ratifiˈkar] /1g/ VT to ratify

ratifique etc [ratiˈfike] VB ver **ratificar**

★**rato** [ˈrato] NM while, short time; **a ratos** from time to time; **al poco ~** shortly after, soon afterwards; **ratos libres** o **de ocio** free o leisure time sg; **hay para ~** there's still a long way to go; **pasar el ~** to kill time; **pasar un buen/mal ~** to have a good/rough time

★**ratón** [raˈton] NM (tb Inform) mouse

ratonera [ratoˈnera] NF mousetrap

raudal [rauˈðal] NM torrent; **a raudales** in abundance; **entrar a raudales** to pour in

raya [ˈraja] NF line; (marca) scratch; (en tela) stripe; (puntuación) dash; (de pelo) parting; (límite) boundary; (pez) ray; **a rayas** striped; **pasarse de la ~** to overstep the mark; **tener a ~** to keep in check

rayado, -a [raˈjaðo, a] ADJ (papel) ruled; (tela, diseño) striped

rayar [raˈjar] /1a/ VT to line; (marcar) to scratch; (subrayar) to underline; **~ a algn** (fam) to do sb's head in (fam); **está siempre rayándome con esa historia** he's doing my head in with that business (fam) ▶ VI: **~ en** o **con** to border on; **al ~ el alba** at first light

★**rayo** [ˈrajo] NM (del sol) ray, beam; (de luz) shaft;

(en una tormenta) (flash of) lightning; **~ solar** o **de sol** sunbeam; **rayos infrarrojos** infrared rays; **rayos X** X-rays; **como un ~** like a shot; **la noticia cayó como un ~** the news was a bombshell; **pasar como un ~** to flash past

raza [ˈraθa] NF race; (de animal) breed; **~ humana** human race; **de pura ~** (caballo) thoroughbred; (perro etc) pedigree

★**razón** [raˈθon] NF reason; (justicia) right, justice; (razonamiento) reasoning; (motivo) reason, motive; (proporción) rate; (Mat) ratio; **a ~ de 10 cada día** at the rate of 10 a day; **"razón: …"** "inquiries to …"; **en ~ de** with regard to; **perder la ~** to go out of one's mind; **dar ~ a algn** to agree that sb is right; **dar ~ de** to give an account of, report on; **tener/no tener ~** to be right/wrong; **~ directa/inversa** direct/inverse proportion; **~ de ser** raison d'être

razonable [raθoˈnaβle] ADJ reasonable; (justo, moderado) fair

razonado, -a [raθoˈnaðo, a] ADJ (Com: cuenta etc) itemized

razonamiento [raθonaˈmjento] NM (juicio) judgement; (argumento) reasoning

razonar [raθoˈnar] /1a/ VT, VI to reason, argue

RDA NF ABR (Historia: = República Democrática Alemana) ver **república**

RDC NF (= República Democrática del Congo) DRC

Rdo. ABR (Rel: = Reverendo) Rev

RDSI NF ABR (= Red Digital de Servicios Integrados) ISDN

re [re] NM (Mus) D

reabierto [reaˈβjerto] PP de **reabrir**

reabrir [reaˈβrir] /3a/ VT, **reabrirse** VR to reopen

★**reacción** [reakˈθjon] NF reaction; **avión a ~** jet plane; **~ en cadena** chain reaction

reaccionar [reakθjoˈnar] /1a/ VI to react

reaccionario, -a [reakθjoˈnarjo, a] ADJ reactionary

reacio, -a [reˈaθjo, a] ADJ stubborn; **ser** o **estar ~ a** to be opposed to

reactivar [reaktiˈβar] /1a/ VT to reactivate; (economía) revitalize ■ **reactivarse** VR (economía) to be on the upturn

reactor [reakˈtor] NM reactor; (avión) jet plane; **~ nuclear** nuclear reactor

readaptación [reaðaptaˈθjon] NF: **~ profesional** industrial retraining

readmitir [reaðmiˈtir] /3a/ VT to readmit

reafirmar [reafirˈmar] /1a/ VT to reaffirm

reagrupar [reaɣruˈpar] /1a/ VT to regroup

reajustar [reaxusˈtar] /1a/ VT (Inform) to reset

reajuste [reaˈxuste] NM readjustment; **~ salarial** wage increase; **~ de plantilla** rationalization

★**real** [reˈal] ADJ real; (del rey, fig) royal; (espléndido) grand; **la R~ Academia Española** see note ▶ NM (de feria) fairground

The **Real Academia Española** (*RAE*) is the regulatory body for the Spanish language in Spain and was founded in 1713. It was given royal approval by Philip V of Spain under the motto *Limpia, fija y da esplendor* (It purifies, fixes and gives splendour) with the aim of preserving the purity of the Spanish language. The 46 lifetime members of this institution are among the greatest writers and linguists in Spain. The first dictionary, *el Diccionario de Autoridades* in six volumes, was published between 1726 and 1739. There have been over 21 editions since the publication of the original single-volume abridged version in 1780. It produces dictionaries and grammars bearing its own name, and is considered the authority on the language, although it has been criticized for being too conservative. In 1994, along with the Spanish American *academias*, it approved a change to the Spanish alphabet, no longer treating "ch" and "ll" as separate letters though "ñ" continues to be treated separately.

realce *etc* [reˈalθe] VB *ver* **realzar** ▶ NM (*Tec*) embossing; **poner de ~** to emphasize

real-decreto [reˈaldeˈkreto] (*pl* **reales-decretos**) NM royal decree

realeza [reaˈleθa] NF royalty

realice *etc* [reaˈliθe] VB *ver* **realizar**

realidad [realiˈðað] NF reality; (*verdad*) truth; **~ virtual** virtual reality; **en ~** in fact

realismo [reaˈlismo] NM realism

realista [reaˈlista] NMF realist

realización [realiθaˈθjon] NF fulfilment, realization; (*Com*) selling up (*BRIT*), conversion into money (*US*); **~ de plusvalías** profit-taking

realizador, a [realiθaˈðor, a] NM/F film-maker; (*TV etc*) producer

★**realizar** [realiˈθar] /1f/ VT (*objetivo*) to achieve; (*plan*) to carry out; (*viaje*) to make, undertake; (*Com*) to realize ■ **realizarse** VR to come about, come true; **realizarse como persona** to fulfil one's aims in life

realmente [realˈmente] ADV really, actually

realojar [realoˈxar] /1a/ VT to rehouse

realquilar [realkiˈlar] /1a/ VT (*subarrendar*) to sublet; (*alquilar de nuevo*) to relet

realzar [realˈθar] /1f/ VT (*Tec*) to raise; (*embellecer*) to enhance; (*acentuar*) to highlight

reanimar [reaniˈmar] /1a/ VT to revive; (*alentar*) to encourage ■ **reanimarse** VR to revive

reanudar [reanuˈðar] /1a/ VT (*renovar*) to renew; (*historia, viaje*) to resume

reaparición [reapariˈθjon] NF reappearance; (*vuelta*) return

reapertura [reaperˈtura] NF reopening

rearme [reˈarme] NM rearmament

reata [reˈata] NF (*AM*) lasso

reavivar [reaβiˈβar] /1a/ VT (*persona*) to revive; (*fig*) to rekindle

★**rebaja** [reˈβaxa] NF reduction, lowering; (*Com*) discount ■ **rebajas** NFPL (*Com*) sale; **"grandes rebajas"** "big reductions", "sale"

rebajar [reβaˈxar] /1a/ VT (*bajar*) to lower; (*reducir*) to reduce; (*precio*) to cut; (*disminuir*) to lessen; (*humillar*) to humble ■ **rebajarse** VR: **rebajarse a hacer algo** to stoop to doing sth

★**rebanada** [reβaˈnaða] NF slice

rebañar [reβaˈɲar] /1a/ VT (*comida*) to scrape up; (*plato*) to scrape clean

rebaño [reˈβaɲo] NM herd; (*de ovejas*) flock

rebasar [reβaˈsar] /1a/ VT (*tb*: **rebasar de**) to exceed; (*Auto*) to overtake

rebatir [reβaˈtir] /3a/ VT to refute; (*rebajar*) to reduce; (*ataque*) to repel

rebato [reˈβato] NM alarm; (*ataque*) surprise attack; **llamar** o **tocar a ~** (*fig*) to sound the alarm

★**rebeca** [reˈβeka] NF cardigan

rebelarse [reβeˈlarse] VR to rebel, revolt

rebelde [reˈβelde] ADJ rebellious; (*niño*) unruly; **ser ~ a** to be in revolt against, rebel against ▶ NMF rebel

rebeldía [reβelˈdia] NF rebelliousness; (*desobediencia*) disobedience; (*Jur*) default

rebelión [reβeˈljon] NF rebellion

rebenque [reˈβenke] NM (*AM*) whip

reblandecer [reβlandeˈθer] /2d/ VT to soften

reblandezca *etc* [reβlanˈdeθka] VB *ver* **reblandecer**

rebobinar [reβoβiˈnar] /1a/ VT to rewind

reboce *etc* [reˈβoθe] VB *ver* **rebozar**

rebosante [reβoˈsante] ADJ: **~ de** (*fig*) brimming o overflowing with

rebosar [reβoˈsar] /1a/ VI to overflow; (*abundar*) to abound, be plentiful; **~ de salud** to be bursting o brimming with health

rebotar [reβoˈtar] /1a/ VT to bounce; (*rechazar*) to repel ▶ VI (*pelota*) to bounce; (*bala*) to ricochet

rebote [reˈβote] NM rebound; **de ~** on the rebound

rebozado, -a [reβoˈθaðo, a] ADJ (*Culin*) fried in batter o breadcrumbs o flour

rebozar [reβoˈθar] /1f/ VT to wrap up; (*Culin*) to fry in batter *etc*

rebozo [reˈβoθo] NM: **sin ~** openly

rebuscado, -a [reβusˈkaðo, a] ADJ (*amanerado*) affected; (*palabra*) recherché; (*idea*) far-fetched

rebuscar [reβusˈkar] /1g/ VI (*en bolsillo, cajón*) to fish; (*en habitación*) to search high and low

rebuznar [reβuθˈnar] /1a/ VI to bray

recabar [rekaˈβar] /1a/ VT (*obtener*) to manage to get; **~ fondos** to collect money

recadero [rekaˈðero] NM messenger

★**recado** [reˈkaðo] NM message; (*encargo*) errand; **dejar/tomar un ~** (*Telec*) to leave/take a message

recaer [rekaˈer] /2n/ VI to relapse; **~ en** to fall to *o* on; (*criminal etc*) to fall back into, relapse into; (*premio*) to go to

recaída [reka'iða] NF relapse

recaiga *etc* [re'kaiɣa] VB *ver* **recaer**

recalcar [rekal'kar] /**1g**/ VT (*fig*) to stress, emphasize

recalcitrante [rekalθi'trante] ADJ recalcitrant

recalentamiento [rekalenta'mjento] NM: **~ global** global warming

recalentar [rekalen'tar] /**1j**/ VT (*comida*) to warm up, reheat; (*demasiado*) to overheat ■ **recalentarse** VR to overheat, get too hot

recaliente *etc* [reka'ljente] VB *ver* **recalentar**

recalque *etc* [re'kalke] VB *ver* **recalcar**

recámara [re'kamara] NF side room; (*AM*) bedroom

recamarera [rekama'rera] NF (*AM*) maid

recambio [re'kambjo] NM spare; (*de pluma*) refill; **piezas de ~** spares

recapacitar [rekapaθi'tar] /**1a**/ VI to reflect

recapitular [rekapitu'lar] /**1a**/ VT to recap

recargable [rekar'ɣaβle] ADJ (*batería, pila*) rechargeable; (*mechero, pluma*) refillable

recargado, -a [rekar'ɣaðo, a] ADJ overloaded; (*exagerado*) over-elaborate

recargar [rekar'ɣar] /**1h**/ VT to overload; (*batería*) to recharge; (*mechero, pluma*) to refill; (*tarjeta de teléfono*) to top up

recargo [re'karɣo] NM surcharge; (*aumento*) increase

recargue *etc* [re'karɣe] VB *ver* **recargar**

recatado, -a [reka'taðo, a] ADJ (*modesto*) modest, demure; (*prudente*) cautious

recato [re'kato] NM (*modestia*) modesty, demureness; (*cautela*) caution

recauchutado, -a [rekautʃu'taðo, a] ADJ remould *cpd*

recaudación [rekauða'θjon] NF (*acción*) collection; (*cantidad*) takings *pl*; (*en deporte*) gate; (*oficina*) tax office

recaudador, a [rekauða'ðor, a] NM/F tax collector

recaudar [rekau'ðar] /**1a**/ VT to collect

recaudo [re'kauðo] NM: **estar a buen ~** to be in safekeeping; **poner algo a buen ~** to put sth in a safe place

recayendo *etc* [reka'jendo] VB *ver* **recaer**

rece *etc* ['reθe] VB *ver* **rezar**

recelar [reθe'lar] /**1a**/ VT: **~ que** (*sospechar*) to suspect that; (*temer*) to fear that ▶ VI: **~(se) de** to distrust

recelo [re'θelo] NM distrust, suspicion

receloso, -a [reθe'loso, a] ADJ distrustful, suspicious

★recepción [reθep'θjon] NF reception; (*acto de recibir*) receipt

★recepcionista [reθepθjo'nista] NMF receptionist

receptáculo [reθep'takulo] NM receptacle

receptivo, -a [reθep'tiβo, a] ADJ receptive

receptor, a [reθep'tor, a] NM/F recipient ▶ NM (*Telec*) receiver; **descolgar el ~** to pick up the receiver

recesión [reθe'sjon] NF (*Com*) recession

★receta [re'θeta] NF (*Culin*) recipe; (*Med*) prescription

recetar [reθe'tar] /**1a**/ VT to prescribe

rechace *etc* [re'tʃaθe] VB *ver* **rechazar**

rechazar [retʃa'θar] /**1f**/ VT to repel, drive back; (*idea*) to reject; (*oferta*) to turn down

rechazo [re'tʃaθo] NM (*de propuesta, tb Med: de un órgano*) rejection; (*rebote*) rebound; (*de fusil*) recoil

rechifla [re'tʃifla] NF hissing, booing; (*fig*) derision

rechinar [retʃi'nar] /**1a**/ VI to creak; (*dientes*) to grind; (*máquina*) to clank, clatter; (*metal seco*) to grate; (*motor*) to hum

rechistar [retʃis'tar] /**1a**/ VI: **sin ~** without complaint

rechoncho, -a [re'tʃontʃo, a] ADJ (*fam*) stocky, thickset (*BRIT*), heavy-set (*US*)

rechupete [retʃu'pete]: **de ~** *adv* (*comida*) delicious

recibidor [reθiβi'ðor] NM entrance hall

recibimiento [reθiβi'mjento] NM reception, welcome

★recibir [reθi'βir] /**3a**/ VT to receive; (*dar la bienvenida*) to welcome; (*salir al encuentro de*) to go and meet ▶ VI to entertain ■ **recibirse** VR: **recibirse de** to qualify as

★recibo [re'θiβo] NM receipt; **acusar ~ de** to acknowledge receipt of

reciclable [reθi'klaβle] ADJ recyclable

★reciclaje [reθi'klaxe] NM recycling; (*de trabajadores*) retraining; **cursos de ~** refresher courses

★reciclar [reθi'klar] /**1a**/ VT to recycle; (*trabajador*) to retrain

recién [re'θjen] ADV recently, newly; (*AM*) just, recently; **~ casado** newly-wed; **el ~ llegado** the newcomer; **el ~ nacido** the newborn child; **~ a las seis** only at six o'clock

★reciente [re'θjente] ADJ recent; (*fresco*) fresh

★recientemente [reθjente'mente] ADV recently

recinto [re'θinto] NM enclosure; (*área*) area, place

recio, -a ['reθjo, a] ADJ strong, tough; (*voz*) loud ▶ ADV hard; loud(ly)

recipiente [reθi'pjente] NM (*objeto*) container, receptacle; (*persona*) recipient

reciprocidad [reθiproθi'ðað] NF reciprocity

recíproco, -a [re'θiproko, a] ADJ reciprocal

recital [reθi'tal] NM (*Mus*) recital; (*Lit*) reading

recitar [reθi'tar] /**1a**/ VT to recite

reclamación [reklama'θjon] NF claim, demand; (*queja*) complaint; **libro de reclamaciones** complaints book; **~ salarial** pay claim

r

reclamar [rekla'mar] /**1a**/ VT to claim, demand; **~ a algn en justicia** to take sb to court ▶ VI: **~ contra** to complain about

reclamo [re'klamo] NM (*anuncio*) advertisement; (*tentación*) attraction

reclinar [rekli'nar] /**1a**/ VT to recline, lean ◼ **reclinarse** VR to lean back

recluir [reklu'ir] /**3g**/ VT to intern, confine

reclusión [reklu'sjon] NF (*prisión*) prison; (*refugio*) seclusion; **~ perpetua** life imprisonment

recluso, -a [re'kluso, a] ADJ imprisoned; **población reclusa** prison population ▶ NM/F (*solitario*) recluse; (*Jur*) prisoner

recluta [re'kluta] NMF recruit ▶ NF recruitment

reclutamiento [rekluta'mjento] NM recruitment

reclutar [reklu'tar] /**1a**/ VT (*datos*) to collect; (*dinero*) to collect up

recluyendo *etc* [reklu'jendo] VB *ver* **recluir**

recobrar [reko'βrar] /**1a**/ VT (*recuperar*) to recover; (*rescatar*) to get back; (*ciudad*) to recapture; (*tiempo*) to make up (for) ◼ **recobrarse** VR to recover

recochineo [rekotʃi'neo] NM (*fam*) mickeytaking

recodo [re'koðo] NM (*de río, camino*) bend

recogedor, a [rekoxe'ðor, a] NM dustpan ▶ NM/F picker, harvester

★recoger [reko'xer] /**2c**/ VT to collect; (*Agr*) to harvest; (*fruta*) to pick; (*levantar*) to pick up; (*juntar*) to gather; (*pasar a buscar*) to come for, get; (*dar asilo*) to give shelter to; (*faldas*) to gather up; (*mangas*) to roll up; (*pelo*) to put up ◼ **recogerse** VR (*retirarse*) to retire; **me recogieron en la estación** they picked me up at the station

recogido, -a [reko'xiðo, a] ADJ (*lugar*) quiet, secluded; (*pequeño*) small ▶ NF (*Correos*) collection; (*Agr*) harvest; **recogida de datos** (*Inform*) data capture

recogimiento [rekoxi'mjento] NM collection; (*Agr*) harvesting

recoja *etc* [re'koxa] VB *ver* **recoger**

recolección [rekolek'θjon] NF (*Agr*) harvesting; (*colecta*) collection

recomencé [rekomen'θe], **recomencemos** *etc* [rekomen'θemos] VB *ver* **recomenzar**

recomendable [rekomen'daβle] ADJ recommendable; **poco ~** inadvisable

recomendación [rekomenda'θjon] NF (*sugerencia*) suggestion, recommendation; (*referencia*) reference; **carta de ~ para** letter of introduction to

★recomendar [rekomen'dar] /**1j**/ VT to suggest, recommend; (*confiar*) to entrust

recomenzar [rekomen'θar] /**1f, 1j**/ VT, VI to begin again, recommence

recomience *etc* [reko'mjenθe] VB *ver* **recomenzar**

recomiende *etc* [reko'mjende] VB *ver* **recomendar**

recomienzo *etc* [reko'mjenθo] VB *ver* **recomenzar**

★recompensa [rekom'pensa] NF reward, recompense; (*compensación*): **~ (de una pérdida)** compensation (for a loss); **como o en ~ por** in return for

recompensar [rekompen'sar] /**1a**/ VT to reward, recompense

recompondré *etc* [rekompon'dre] VB *ver* **recomponer**

recomponer [rekompo'ner] /**2q**/ VT to mend; (*Inform*: *texto*) to reformat

recomponga *etc* [rekom'ponga], **recompuesto** [rekom'pwesto], **recompuse** *etc* [rekom'puse] VB *ver* **recomponer**

reconciliación [rekonθilja'θjon] NF reconciliation

reconciliar [rekonθi'ljar] /**1b**/ VT to reconcile ◼ **reconciliarse** VR to become reconciled

recóndito, -a [re'kondito, a] ADJ (*lugar*) hidden, secret

reconfortar [rekonfor'tar] /**1a**/ VT to comfort

★reconocer [rekono'θer] /**2d**/ VT to recognize; (*registrar*) to search; (*Med*) to examine; **~ los hechos** to face the facts

reconocido, -a [rekono'θiðo, a] ADJ recognized; (*agradecido*) grateful

reconocimiento [rekonoθi'mjento] NM recognition; (*registro*) search; (*inspección*) examination; (*gratitud*) gratitude; (*confesión*) admission; **~ óptico de caracteres** (*Inform*) optical character recognition; **~ de la voz** (*Inform*) speech recognition

reconozca *etc* [reko'noθka] VB *ver* **reconocer**

reconquista [rekon'kista] NF reconquest; **la R~** the Reconquest (of Spain)

reconquistar [rekonkis'tar] /**1a**/ VT (*Mil*) to reconquer; (*fig*) to recover, win back

reconstituyente [rekonstitu'jente] NM tonic

reconstruir [rekonstru'ir] /**3g**/ VT to reconstruct

reconstruyendo *etc* [rekonstru'jendo] VB *ver* **reconstruir**

reconversión [rekomber'sjon] NF restructuring, reorganization; (*tb*: **reconversión industrial**) rationalization

recopilación [rekopila'θjon] NF (*resumen*) summary; (*compilación*) compilation

recopilar [rekopi'lar] /**1a**/ VT to compile

récord ['rekorð] ADJ INV record; **cifras ~** record figures ▶ NM (*pl* **récords** o **records**) record; **batir el ~** to break the record

★recordar [rekor'ðar] /**1l**/ VT (*acordarse de*) to remember; (*traer a la memoria*) to recall; (*recordar a otro*) to remind; **recuérdale que me debe cinco dólares** remind him that he owes me five dollars ▶ VI to remember; **que yo recuerde** as far as I can remember; **creo ~, si mal no recuerdo** if my memory serves me right

recordatorio [rekorða'torjo] NM (*de falleci-miento*) in memoriam card; (*de bautizo, comunión*) commemorative card

recorrer [reko'rrer] /2a/ VT (*país*) to cross, travel through; (*distancia*) to cover; (*registrar*) to search; (*repasar*) to look over

recorrido [reko'rriðo] NM run, journey; **tren de largo ~** main-line *o* (*BRIT*) inter-city train

recortado, -a [rekor'taðo, a] ADJ uneven, irregular

recortar [rekor'tar] /1a/ VT (*papel*) to cut out; (*el pelo*) to trim; (*dibujar*) to draw in outline ■ **recortarse** VR to stand out, be silhouetted

recorte [re'korte] NM (*acción, de prensa*) cutting; (*de telas, chapas*) trimming; **~ presupuestario** budget cut; **~ salarial** wage cut

recostado, -a [rekos'taðo, a] ADJ leaning; **estar ~** to be lying down

recostar [rekos'tar] /1l/ VT to lean ■ **recostarse** VR to lie down

recoveco [reko'βeko] NM (*de camino, río etc*) bend; (*en casa*) cubbyhole

recreación [rekrea'θjon] NF recreation

recrear [rekre'ar] /1a/ VT (*entretener*) to enter-tain; (*volver a crear*) to recreate

recreativo, -a [rekrea'tiβo, a] ADJ recreational

★**recreo** [re'kreo] NM recreation; (*Escol*) break, playtime

recriminar [rekrimi'nar] /1a/ VT to reproach ▶ VI to recriminate ■ **recriminarse** VR to reproach each other

recrudecer [rekruðe'θer] /2d/ VT, VI to worsen ■ **recrudecerse** VR to worsen

recrudecimiento [rekruðeθi'mjento] NM upsurge

recrudezca *etc* [rekru'ðeθka] VB *ver* **recrudecer**

recta ['rekta] NF *ver* **recto**

rectangular [rektangu'lar] ADJ rectangular

rectángulo, -a [rek'tangulo, a] ADJ rectangu-lar ▶ NM rectangle

rectificable [rektifi'kaβle] ADJ rectifiable; **fácilmente ~** easily rectified

rectificación [rektifika'θjon] NF correction

rectificar [rektifi'kar] /1g/ VT to rectify; (*volverse recto*) to straighten ▶ VI to correct o.s.

rectifique *etc* [rekti'fike] VB *ver* **rectificar**

rectitud [rekti'tuð] NF straightness; (*fig*) recti-tude

★**recto, -a** ['rekto, a] ADJ straight; (*persona*) honest, upright; (*estricto*) strict; (*juez*) fair; (*juicio*) sound; **siga todo ~** go straight on; **en el sentido ~ de la palabra** in the proper sense of the word ▶ NM rectum; (*Atletismo*) straight ▶ NF straight line; **recta final** *o* **de llegada** home straight

rector, a [rek'tor, a] ADJ governing ▶ NM/F head, chief; (*Escol*) rector, president (*US*)

rectorado [rekto'raðo] NM (*cargo*) rectorship, presidency (*US*); (*oficina*) rector's office

recuadro [re'kwaðro] NM box; (*Tip*) inset

recubrir [reku'βir] /3a/ VT: **~ (con)** (*pintura, crema*) to cover (with)

recuento [re'kwento] NM inventory; **hacer el ~ de** to count *o* reckon up

★**recuerdo** [re'kwerðo] VB *ver* **recordar** ▶ NM sou-venir; **"R~ de Mallorca"** "a present from Majorca" ■ **recuerdos** NMPL memories; **¡recuerdos a tu madre!** give my regards to your mother!; **contar los recuerdos** to reminisce

recueste *etc* [re'kweste] VB *ver* **recostar**

recular [reku'lar] /1a/ VI to back down

recuperable [rekupe'raβle] ADJ recoverable

recuperación [rekupera'θjon] NF recovery; **~ de datos** (*Inform*) data retrieval

★**recuperar** [rekupe'rar] /1a/ VT to recover; (*tiempo*) to make up; (*Inform*) to retrieve ■ **recu-perarse** VR to recuperate

recurrir [reku'rrir] /3a/ VI (*Jur*) to appeal; **~ a** to resort to; (*persona*) to turn to

★**recurso** [re'kurso] NM resort; (*medio*) means *pl*, resource; (*Jur*) appeal; **como último ~** as a last resort; **recursos económicos** economic resources; **recursos naturales** natural resources

recusar [reku'sar] /1a/ VT to reject, refuse

★**red** [reð] NF net, mesh; (*Ferro, Inform*) network; (*Elec, de agua*) mains, supply system; (*de tiendas*) chain; (*trampa*) trap; **la R~** (*Internet*) the Net; **estar conectado con la ~** to be connected to the mains; **~ de transmisión** (*Inform*) data net-work; **~ local** (*Inform*) local area network; **redes sociales** social networks; (*páginas web*) social networking sites

redacción [reðak'θjon] NF (*acción*) writing; (*Escol*) essay, composition; (*limpieza de texto*) editing; (*personal*) editorial staff

redactar [reðak'tar] /1a/ VT to draw up, draft; (*periódico, Inform*) to edit

redactor, a [reðak'tor, a] NM/F writer; (*en perió-dico*) editor

redada [re'ðaða] NF (*Pesca*) cast, throw; (*fig*) catch; **~ policial** police raid, round-up

rededor [reðe'ðor] NM: **al** *o* **en ~** around, round about

redención [reðen'θjon] NF redemption

redentor, a [reðen'tor, a] ADJ redeeming ▶ NM/F (*Com*) redeemer

redescubierto [reðesku'βjerto] PP *de* **redescu-brir**

redescubrir [reðesku'βrir] /3a/ VT to rediscover

redesignar [reðesiɣ'nar] /1a/ VT (*Inform*) to rename

redicho, -a [re'ðitʃo, a] ADJ affected

redil [re'ðil] NM sheepfold

redimir [reði'mir] /3a/ VT to redeem; (*rehén*) to ransom

redistribución [reðistriβu'θjon] NF (*Com*) re-deployment

r

rédito [ˈreðito] NM interest, yield

redoblar [reðoˈβlar] /1a/ VT to redouble ▶ VI (*tambor*) to roll

redoble [reˈðoβle] NM (*Mus*) drumroll, drumbeat; (*de trueno*) roll

redomado, -a [reðoˈmaðo, a] ADJ (*astuto*) sly, crafty; (*perfecto*) utter

redonda [reˈðonda] NF *ver* **redondo**

redondear [reðondeˈar] /1a/ VT to round, round off; (*cifra*) to round up

redondel [reðonˈdel] NM (*círculo*) circle; (*Taur*) bullring, arena; (*Auto*) roundabout

★**redondo, -a** [reˈðondo, a] ADJ (*circular*) round; (*completo*) complete; **rehusar en ~** to give a flat refusal ▶ NF: **a la redonda** around, round about; **en muchas millas a la redonda** for many miles around

★**reducción** [reðukˈθjon] NF reduction; **~ del activo** (*Com*) divestment; **~ de precios** (*Com*) price-cutting

reducido, -a [reðuˈθiðo, a] ADJ reduced; (*limitado*) limited; (*pequeño*) small; **quedar ~ a** to be reduced to

★**reducir** [reðuˈθir] /3n/ VT to reduce, limit; (*someter*) to bring under control; (*Mat*) **~ (a)** to reduce (to), convert (into); **~ las millas a kilómetros** to convert miles into kilometres ■ **reducirse** VR to diminish; **reducirse a** (*fig*) to come *o* boil down to

reducto [reˈðukto] NM redoubt

reduje *etc* [reˈðuxe] VB *ver* **reducir**

redundancia [reðunˈdanθja] NF redundancy

reduzca *etc* [reˈðuθka] VB *ver* **reducir**

reedición [re(e)ðiˈθjon] NF reissue

reeditar [re(e)ðiˈtar] /1a/ VT to reissue

reelección [re(e)lekˈθjon] NF re-election

reelegir [re(e)leˈxir] /3c, 3k/ VT to re-elect

reembolsable [re(e)mbolˈsaβle] ADJ (*Com*) redeemable, refundable

★**reembolsar** [re(e)mbolˈsar] /1a/ VT (*persona*) to reimburse; (*dinero*) to repay, pay back; (*depósito*) to refund

★**reembolso** [re(e)mˈbolso] NM (*de gastos*) reimbursement; (*de depósito*) refund; **enviar algo contra ~** to send sth cash on delivery; **contra ~ del flete** freight forward; **~ fiscal** tax rebate

reemplace *etc* [re(e)mˈplaθe] VB *ver* **reemplazar**

reemplazar [re(e)mplaˈθar] /1f/ VT to replace

reemplazo [re(e)mˈplaθo] NM replacement; **de ~** (*Mil*) reserve

reencuentro [re(e)nˈkwentro] NM reunion

reengancharse [re(e)nganˈtʃarse] /1a/ VR (*Mil*) to re-enlist

reescribible [reeskriˈβiβle] ADJ rewritable

reestreno [re(e)sˈtreno] NM rerun

reestructurar [re(e)struktuˈrar] /1a/ VT to restructure

reexportación [re(e)ksportaˈθjon] NF (*Com*) re-export

reexportar [re(e)ksporˈtar] /1a/ VT (*Com*) to re-export

Ref.ª ABR (= *referencia*) ref

refacción [refakˈθjon] NF (*Am*) repair(s) ■ **refacciones** NFPL (*piezas de repuesto*) spare parts

referencia [refeˈrenθja] NF reference; **con ~ a** with reference to; **hacer ~ a** to refer *o* allude to; **~ comercial** (*Com*) trade reference

referéndum [refeˈrendum] (*pl* **referéndums**) NM referendum

referente [refeˈrente] ADJ: **~ a** concerning, relating to

réferi [ˈreferi] NMF (*Am*) referee

referir [refeˈrir] /3i/ VT (*contar*) to tell, recount; (*relacionar*) to refer, relate; **~ al lector a un apéndice** to refer the reader to an appendix; **~ a** (*Com*) to convert into ■ **referirse** VR: **referirse a** to refer to; **por lo que se refiere a eso** as for that, as regards that

refiera *etc* [reˈfjera] VB *ver* **referir**

refilón [refiˈlon]: **de ~** *adv* obliquely; **mirar a algn de ~** to look out of the corner of one's eye at sb

refinado, -a [refiˈnaðo, a] ADJ refined

refinamiento [refinaˈmjento] NM refinement; **~ por pasos** (*Inform*) stepwise refinement

refinar [refiˈnar] /1a/ VT to refine

refinería [refineˈria] NF refinery

refiriendo *etc* [refiˈrjendo] VB *ver* **referir**

reflector [reflekˈtor] NM reflector; (*Elec*) spotlight; (*Aviat, Mil*) searchlight

reflejar [refleˈxar] /1a/ VT to reflect ■ **reflejarse** VR to be reflected

reflejo, -a [reˈflexo, a] ADJ reflected; (*movimiento*) reflex ▶ NM reflection; (*Anat*) reflex; **reflejos** *nmpl* (*en el pelo*) highlights; **tiene el pelo castaño con reflejos rubios** she has chestnut hair with blond highlights

reflexión [reflekˈsjon] NF reflection

★**reflexionar** [refleksjoˈnar] /1a/ VT to reflect on ▶ VI to reflect; (*detenerse*) to pause (to think); **¡reflexione!** you think it over!

reflexivo, -a [reflekˈsiβo, a] ADJ thoughtful; (*Ling*) reflexive

refluir [refluˈir] /3g/ VI to flow back

reflujo [reˈfluxo] NM ebb

refluyendo *etc* [refluˈjendo] VB *ver* **refluir**

reforcé [reforˈθe], **reforcemos** *etc* [reforˈθemos] VB *ver* **reforzar**

reforma [reˈforma] NF reform; (*Arq etc*) repair; **~ agraria** agrarian reform

reformar [reforˈmar] /1a/ VT to reform; (*modificar*) to change, alter; (*texto*) to revise; (*Arq*) to repair ■ **reformarse** VR to mend one's ways

reformatear [reformateˈar] /1a/ VT (*Inform: disco*) to reformat

reformatorio [reforma'torjo] NM reformatory; **~ de menores** remand home

reformista [refor'mista] ADJ, NMF reformist

reforzamiento [reforθa'mjento] NM reinforcement

reforzar [refor'θar] /**1f, 1l**/ VT to strengthen; (*Arq*) to reinforce; (*fig*) to encourage

refractario, -a [refrak'tarjo, a] ADJ (*Tec*) heat-resistant; **ser ~ a una reforma** to resist *o* be opposed to a reform

refrán [re'fran] NM proverb, saying

refregar [refre'ɣar] /**1h, 1j**/ VT to scrub

refrenar [refre'nar] /**1a**/ VT to check, restrain

refrendar [refren'dar] /**1a**/ VT (*firma*) to endorse, countersign; (*ley*) to approve

refrescante [refres'kante] ADJ refreshing, cooling

refrescar [refres'kar] /**1g**/ VT to refresh ▶ VI to cool down ■ **refrescarse** VR to get cooler; (*tomar aire fresco*) to go out for a breath of fresh air; (*beber*) to have a drink

★**refresco** [re'fresko] NM soft drink, cool drink; **"refrescos"** "refreshments"

refresque etc [re'freske] VB ver **refrescar**

refriega etc [re'frjeɣa] VB ver **refregar** ▶ NF scuffle, brawl

refriegue etc [re'frjeɣe] VB ver **refregar**

refrigeración [refrixera'θjon] NF refrigeration; (*de casa*) air-conditioning

refrigerado, -a [refrixe'raðo, a] ADJ cooled; (*sala*) air-conditioned

refrigerador [refrixera'ðor] NM, (*Am*) **refrigeradora** [refrixera'ðora] NF refrigerator, icebox (*US*)

refrigerar [refrixe'rar] /**1a**/ VT to refrigerate; (*sala*) to air-condition

refrito [re'frito] NM (*Culin*): **un ~ de cebolla y tomate** sautéed onions and tomatoes; **un ~** (*fig*) a rehash

refuerce etc [re'fwerθe] VB ver **reforzar**

refuerzo etc [re'fwerθo] VB ver **reforzar** ▶ NM reinforcement; (*Tec*) support

refugiado, -a [refu'xjaðo, a] NM/F refugee

★**refugiarse** [refu'xjarse] /**1b**/ VR to take refuge, shelter

★**refugio** [re'fuxjo] NM refuge; (*protección*) shelter; (*Auto*) street *o* traffic island; **~ alpino** *o* **de montaña** mountain hut; **~ subterráneo** (*Mil*) underground shelter

refulgencia [reful'xenθja] NF brilliance

refulgir [reful'xir] /**3c**/ VI to shine, be dazzling

refulja etc [re'fulxa] VB ver **refulgir**

refundir [refun'dir] /**3a**/ VT to recast; (*escrito etc*) to adapt, rewrite

refunfuñar [refunfu'ɲar] /**1a**/ VI to grunt, growl; (*quejarse*) to grumble

refunfuñón, -ona [refunfu'ɲon, ona] (*fam*) ADJ grumpy ▶ NM/F grouch

refutación [refuta'θjon] NF refutation

refutar [refu'tar] /**1a**/ VT to refute

regadera [reɣa'ðera] NF watering can; (*Am*) shower; **estar como una ~** (*fam*) to be as mad as a hatter

regadío [reɣa'ðio] NM irrigated land

regalado, -a [reɣa'laðo, a] ADJ comfortable, luxurious; (*gratis*) free, for nothing; **lo tuvo ~** it was handed to him on a plate

★**regalar** [reɣa'lar] /**1a**/ VT (*dar*) to give (as a present); (*entregar*) to give away; (*mimar*) to pamper, make a fuss of ■ **regalarse** VR to treat o.s. to

regalía [reɣa'lia] NF privilege, prerogative; (*Com*) bonus; (*de autor*) royalty

regaliz [reɣa'liθ] NM liquorice

★**regalo** [re'ɣalo] NM (*obsequio*) gift, present; (*gusto*) pleasure; (*comodidad*) comfort

regañadientes [reɣaɲa'ðjentes]: **a ~** adv reluctantly

regañar [reɣa'ɲar] /**1a**/ VT to scold ▶ VI to grumble; (*dos personas*) to fall out, quarrel

regañón, -ona [reɣa'ɲon, ona] ADJ nagging

★**regar** [re'ɣar] /**1h, 1j**/ VT to water, irrigate; (*fig*) to scatter, sprinkle

regata [re'ɣata] NF (*Naut*) race

regatear [reɣate'ar] /**1a**/ VT (*Com*) to bargain over; (*escatimar*) to be mean with; **no ~ esfuerzos** to spare no effort ▶ VI to bargain, haggle; (*Deporte*) to dribble

regateo [reɣa'teo] NM bargaining; (*Deporte*) dribbling; (*con el cuerpo*) swerve, dodge

regazo [re'ɣaθo] NM lap

regencia [re'xenθja] NF regency

regeneración [rexenera'θjon] NF regeneration

regenerar [rexene'rar] /**1a**/ VT to regenerate

regentar [rexen'tar] /**1a**/ VT to direct, manage; (*puesto*) to hold in an acting capacity; (*negocio*) to be in charge of

regente, -a [re'xente, a] ADJ (*príncipe*) regent; (*director*) managing ▶ NM (*Com*) manager; (*Pol*) regent

★**régimen** ['reximen] (*pl* **regímenes** [re'ximenes]) NM regime; (*reinado*) rule; (*Med*) diet; (*reglas*) (set of) rules *pl*; (*manera de vivir*) lifestyle; **estar a ~** to be on a diet

regimiento [rexi'mjento] NM regiment

regio, -a ['rexjo, a] ADJ royal, regal; (*fig: suntuoso*) splendid; (*Am fam*) great, terrific

★**región** [re'xjon] NF region; (*área*) area

regional [rexjo'nal] ADJ regional

regir [re'xir] /**3c, 3k**/ VT to govern, rule; (*dirigir*) to manage, run; (*Econ, Jur, Ling*) to govern ▶ VI to apply, be in force

registrador [rexistra'ðor] NM registrar, recorder

★**registrar** [rexis'trar] /**1a**/ VT (*buscar*) to search; (*en cajón*) to look through; (*inspeccionar*) to inspect; (*anotar*) to register, record; (*Inform*) to log; (*Mus*) to record ■ **registrarse** VR to register; (*ocurrir*) to happen

registro [re'xistro] NM (*acto*) registration; (*Mus, libro*) register; (*lista*) list, record; (*Inform*) record; (*inspección*) inspection, search; **~ civil** registry office; **~ electoral** voting register; **~ de la propiedad** land registry (office)

★**regla** ['reɣla] NF (*ley*) rule, regulation; (*de medir*) ruler, rule; (*Med: período*) period; **en ~** in order; (*regla científica*) law, principle; **no hay ~ sin excepción** there's an exception to every rule

reglamentación [reɣlamenta'θjon] NF (*acto*) regulation; (*lista*) rules *pl*

reglamentar [reɣlamen'tar] /**1a**/ VT to regulate

reglamentario, -a [reɣlamen'tarjo, a] ADJ statutory; **en la forma reglamentaria** in the properly established way

reglamento [reɣla'mento] NM rules *pl*, regulations *pl*; **~ del tráfico** highway code

reglar [re'ɣlar] /**1a**/ VT (*acciones*) to regulate ■ **reglarse** VR: **reglarse por** to be guided by

regocijarse [reɣoθi'xarse] /**1a**/ VR: **~ de** o **por** to rejoice at, be glad about

regocijo [reɣo'θixo] NM joy, happiness

regodearse [reɣoðe'arse] /**1a**/ VR to be glad, be delighted; (*pey*): **~ con** o **en** to gloat over

regodeo [reɣo'ðeo] NM delight; (*pey*) perverse pleasure

regrabadora [regraβa'ðora] NF rewriter; **~ de DVD** DVD rewriter

★**regresar** [reɣre'sar] /**1a**/ VI to come/go back, return ■ **regresarse** VR (*Am*) to return

regresivo, -a [reɣre'siβo, a] ADJ backward; (*fig*) regressive

★**regreso** [re'ɣreso] NM return; **estar de ~** to be back, be home

regué [re'ɣe], **reguemos** *etc* [re'ɣemos] VB *ver* **regar**

reguero [re'ɣero] NM (*de sangre*) trickle; (*de humo*) trail

reguetón [reɣe'ton] NM (*Mus*) reggaeton

regulación [reɣula'θjon] NF regulation; (*Tec*) adjustment; (*control*) control; **~ de empleo** redundancies *pl*; **~ del tráfico** traffic control

regulador [reɣula'ðor] NM (*Tec*) regulator; (*de radio etc*) knob, control

★**regular** [reɣu'lar] /**1a**/ ADJ regular; (*normal*) normal, usual; (*común*) ordinary; (*organizado*) regular, orderly; (*mediano*) average; (*fam*) not bad, so-so; **por lo ~** as a rule ▶ ADV: **estar ~** to be so-so o all right ▶ VT (*controlar*) to control, regulate; (*Tec*) to adjust

regularice *etc* [reɣula'riθe] VB *ver* **regularizar**

regularidad [reɣulari'ðað] NF regularity; **con ~** regularly

regularizar [reɣulari'θar] /**1f**/ VT to regularize

regusto [re'ɣusto] NM aftertaste

rehabilitación [reaβilita'θjon] NF rehabilitation; (*Arq*) restoration

rehabilitar [reaβili'tar] /**1a**/ VT to rehabilitate; (*Arq*) to restore; (*reintegrar*) to reinstate

rehacer [rea'θer] /**2r**/ VT (*reparar*) to mend, repair; (*volver a hacer*) to redo, repeat ■ **rehacerse** VR (*Med*) to recover

rehaga *etc* [re'aɣa], **reharé** *etc* [rea're], **rehaz** [re'aθ], **rehecho** [re'etʃo] VB *ver* **rehacer**

rehén [re'en] NMF hostage

rehice *etc* [re'iθe], **rehizo** [re'iθo] VB *ver* **rehacer**

rehogar [reo'ɣar] /**1h**/ VT to sauté, toss in oil

rehuir [reu'ir] /**3g**/ VT to avoid, shun

rehusar [reu'sar] /**1a**/ VT, VI to refuse

rehuyendo *etc* [reu'jendo] VB *ver* **rehuir**

★**reina** ['reina] NF queen

reinado [rei'naðo] NM reign

reinante [rei'nante] ADJ (*fig*) prevailing

reinar [rei'nar] /**1a**/ VI to reign; (*fig: prevalecer*) to prevail, be general

reincidir [reinθi'ðir] /**3a**/ VI to relapse; (*criminal*) to repeat an offence

reincorporarse [reinkorpo'rarse] /**1a**/ VR: **~ a** to rejoin

reinicializar [reiniθjali'θar] /**1f**/ VT (*Inform*) to reset

reino ['reino] NM kingdom; **~ animal/vegetal** animal/plant kingdom; **el R~ Unido** the United Kingdom

reinserción [reinser'θjon] NF rehabilitation

reinsertar [reinser'tar] /**1a**/ VT to rehabilitate

reintegración [reinteɣra'θjon] NF (*Com*) reinstatement

reintegrar [reinte'ɣrar] /**1a**/ VT (*reconstituir*) to reconstruct; (*persona*) to reinstate; (*dinero*) to refund, pay back ■ **reintegrarse** VR: **reintegrarse a** to return to

reintegro [rein'teɣro] NM refund, reimbursement; (*en banco*) withdrawal

★**reír** [re'ir] /**3l**/ VI to laugh ■ **reírse** VR to laugh; **reírse de** to laugh at

reiterado, -a [reite'raðo, a] ADJ repeated

reiterar [reite'rar] /**1a**/ VT to reiterate; (*repetir*) to repeat

reivindicación [reiβindika'θjon] NF (*demanda*) claim, demand; (*justificación*) vindication

reivindicar [reiβindi'kar] /**1g**/ VT to claim

reivindique *etc* [reiβin'dike] VB *ver* **reivindicar**

reja ['rexa] NF (*de ventana*) grille, bars *pl*; (*en la calle*) grating

rejilla [re'xiʎa] NF grating, grille; (*muebles*) wickerwork; (*de ventilación*) vent; (*de coche etc*) luggage rack

rejoneador [rexonea'ðor] NM mounted bullfighter

rejuvenecer [rexuβene'θer] /**2d**/ VT, VI to rejuvenate

rejuvenezca *etc* [rexuβe'neθka] VB *ver* **rejuvenecer**

relación [rela'θjon] NF relation, relationship; (*Mat*) ratio; (*lista*) list; (*narración*) report; **costo-efectivo** o **costo-rendimiento** (*Com*) cost-effectiveness; **con ~ a**, **en ~ con** in relation to; **relaciones carnales** sexual relations; **relaciones empresariales/humanas** industrial/human relations; **relaciones laborales/públicas** labour/public relations; **estar en** *o* **tener buenas relaciones con** to be on good terms with ■ **relaciones** NFPL (*enchufes*) connections, influential friends; **relaciones comerciales** business connections

relacionar [relaθjo'nar] /**1a**/ VT to relate, connect ■ **relacionarse** VR to be connected *o* linked

relajación [relaxa'θjon] NF relaxation

relajado, -a [rela'xaðo, a] ADJ (*disoluto*) loose; (*cómodo*) relaxed; (*Med*) ruptured

relajante [rela'xante] ADJ relaxing; (*Med*) sedative

★**relajar** [rela'xar] /**1a**/ VT to relax ■ **relajarse** VR to relax

relamerse [rela'merse] /**2a**/ VR to lick one's lips

relamido, -a [rela'miðo, a] ADJ (*pulcro*) overdressed; (*afectado*) affected

★**relámpago** [re'lampaɣo] NM flash of lightning; **como un ~** as quick as lightning, in a flash ▶ ADJ lightning *cpd*; **visita/huelga ~** lightning visit/strike

relampaguear [relampaɣe'ar] /**1a**/ VI to flash

relanzar [relan'θar] /**1f**/ VT to relaunch

relatar [rela'tar] /**1a**/ VT to tell, relate

relatividad [relatiβi'ðað] NF relativity

relativo, -a [rela'tiβo, a] ADJ relative; **en lo ~ a** concerning

★**relato** [re'lato] NM (*narración*) story, tale

relax [re'las] NM rest; "**R~**" (*en anuncio*) "Personal services"

relegar [rele'ɣar] /**1h**/ VT to relegate; **~ algo al olvido** to banish sth from one's mind

relegue *etc* [re'leɣe] VB *ver* **relegar**

relevante [rele'βante] ADJ eminent, outstanding

relevar [rele'βar] /**1a**/ VT (*sustituir*) to relieve; **~ a algn de un cargo** to relieve sb of his post ■ **relevarse** VR to relay

relevo [re'leβo] NM relief; **carrera de relevos** relay race; **coger** *o* **tomar el ~** to take over, stand in

relieve [re'ljeβe] NM (*Arte, Tec*) relief; (*fig*) prominence, importance; **bajo ~** bas-relief; **un personaje de ~** an important man; **dar ~ a** to highlight

★**religión** [reli'xjon] NF religion

religioso, -a [reli'xjoso, a] ADJ religious ▶ NM/F monk/nun

relinchar [relin'tʃar] /**1a**/ VI to neigh

relincho [re'lintʃo] NM neigh; (*acto*) neighing

reliquia [re'likja] NF relic; **~ de familia** heirloom

rellano [re'ʎano] NM (*Arq*) landing

★**rellenar** [reʎe'nar] /**1a**/ VT (*llenar*) to fill up; (*Culin*) to stuff; (*Costura*) to pad; (*formulario etc*) to fill in *o* out

relleno, -a [re'ʎeno, a] ADJ full up; (*Culin*) stuffed ▶ NM stuffing; (*de tapicería*) padding

★**reloj** [re'lo(x)] NM clock; **poner el ~ (en hora)** to set one's watch *o* the clock; **~ de pie** grandfather clock; **~ (de pulsera)** (wrist)watch; **~ de sol** sundial; **~ despertador** alarm (clock); **~ digital** digital watch; **como un ~** like clockwork; **contra (el) ~** against the clock

★**relojería** [reloxe'ria] NF (*tienda*) watchmaker's (shop); **aparato de ~** clockwork; **bomba de ~** time bomb

relojero, -a [relo'xero, a] NM/F clockmaker, watchmaker

reluciente [relu'θjente] ADJ brilliant, shining

relucir [relu'θir] /**3f**/ VI to shine; (*fig*) to excel; **sacar algo a ~** to show sth off

relumbrante [relum'brante] ADJ dazzling

relumbrar [relum'brar] /**1a**/ VI to dazzle, shine brightly

reluzca *etc* [re'luθka] VB *ver* **relucir**

remachar [rema'tʃar] /**1a**/ VT to rivet; (*fig*) to hammer home, drive home

remache [re'matʃe] NM rivet

remanente [rema'nente] NM remainder; (*Com*) balance; (*de producto*) surplus

remangar [reman'gar] /**1h**/ VT to roll up ■ **remangarse** VR to roll one's sleeves up

remanso [re'manso] NM pool

★**remar** [re'mar] /**1a**/ VI to row

rematado, -a [rema'taðo, a] ADJ complete, utter; **es un loco ~** he's a raving lunatic (!)

rematar [rema'tar] /**1a**/ VT to finish off; (*animal*) to put out of its misery; (*Com*) to sell off cheap ▶ VI to end, finish off; (*Deporte*) to shoot

remate [re'mate] NM end, finish; (*punta*) tip; (*Deporte*) shot; (*Arq*) top; (*Com*) auction sale; **de** *o* **para ~** to crown it all (*BRIT*), to top it off

remedar [reme'ðar] /**1a**/ VT to imitate

remediable [reme'ðjaβle] ADJ: **fácilmente ~** easily remedied

remediar [reme'ðjar] /**1b**/ VT (*gen*) to remedy; (*subsanar*) to make good, repair; (*evitar*) to avoid; **sin poder remediarlo** without being able to prevent it

★**remedio** [re'meðjo] NM remedy; (*alivio*) relief, help; (*Jur*) recourse, remedy; **poner ~ a** to correct, stop; **no tener más ~** to have no alternative; **¡qué ~!** there's no choice!; **como último ~** as a last resort; **sin ~** inevitable; (*Med*) hopeless

remedo [re'meðo] NM imitation; (*pey*) parody

remendar [remen'dar] /**1j**/ VT to repair; (*con parche*) to patch; (*fig*) to correct

remesa [re'mesa] NF remittance; (*Com*) shipment

remiendo *etc* [re'mjendo] VB *ver* **remendar** ▶ NM mend; (*con parche*) patch; (*cosido*) darn; (*fig*) correction

r

remilgado, -a [remil'ɣaðo, a] ADJ prim; (*afectado*) affected

remilgo [re'milɣo] NM primness; (*afectación*) affectation

reminiscencia [reminis'θenθja] NF reminiscence

remirar [remi'rar] /1a/ VT (*volver a mirar*) to look at again; (*examinar*) to look hard at

remisión [remi'sjon] NF (*acto*) sending, shipment; (*Rel*) forgiveness, remission; **sin ~** hopelessly

remiso, -a [re'miso, a] ADJ slack, slow

★**remite** [re'mite] NM (*en sobre*) name and address of sender

★**remitente** [remi'tente] NMF (*Correos*) sender

remitir [remi'tir] /3a/ VT to remit, send ▶ VI to slacken; (*en carta*): **remite: X** sender: X

remo ['remo] NM (*de barco*) oar; (*Deporte*) rowing; **cruzar un río a ~** to row across a river

remoce etc [re'moθe] VB ver **remozar**

remodelación [remodela'θjon] NF **~ del gobierno** cabinet reshuffle

remojar [remo'xar] /1a/ VT to steep, soak; (*galleta etc*) to dip, dunk; (*fam*) to celebrate with a drink

remojo [re'moxo] NM steeping, soaking; (*por la lluvia*) drenching, soaking; **dejar la ropa en ~** to leave clothes to soak

remojón [remo'xon] NM soaking; **darse un ~** (*fam*) to go (in) for a dip

remolacha [remo'latʃa] NF beet, beetroot (BRIT)

remolcador [remolka'ðor] NM (*Naut*) tug; (*Auto*) breakdown lorry

remolcar [remol'kar] /1g/ VT to tow

remolino [remo'lino] NM eddy; (*de agua*) whirlpool; (*de viento*) whirlwind; (*de gente*) crowd

remolón, -ona [remo'lon, ona] ADJ lazy ▶ NM/F slacker, shirker

remolque [re'molke] VB ver **remolcar** ▶ NM tow, towing; (*cuerda*) towrope; **llevar a ~** to tow

remontar [remon'tar] /1a/ VT to mend; (*obstáculo*) to negotiate, get over; **~ el vuelo** to soar ■ **remontarse** VR to soar; **remontarse a** (*Com*) to amount to; (*en tiempo*) to go back to, date from

rémora ['remora] NF hindrance

remorder [remor'ðer] /2h/ VT to distress, disturb; **remorderle la conciencia a algn** to have a guilty conscience

remordimiento [remorði'mjento] NM remorse

remotamente [remota'mente] ADV vaguely

remoto, -a [re'moto, a] ADJ remote

remover [remo'βer] /2h/ VT to stir; (*tierra*) to turn over; (*objetos*) to move round

remozar [remo'θar] /1f/ VT (*Arq*) to refurbish; (*fig*) to brighten o polish up

remuerda etc [re'mwerða] VB ver **remorder**

remueva etc [re'mweβa] VB ver **remover**

remuneración [remunera'θjon] NF remuneration

remunerado, -a [remune'raðo, a] ADJ: **trabajo bien/mal ~** well-/badly-paid job

remunerar [remune'rar] /1a/ VT to remunerate; (*premiar*) to reward

renacer [rena'θer] /2d/ VI to be reborn; (*fig*) to revive

renacimiento [renaθi'mjento] NM rebirth; **el R~** the Renaissance

renacuajo [rena'kwaxo] NM (*Zool*) tadpole

renal [re'nal] ADJ renal, kidney *cpd*

Renania [re'nanja] NF Rhineland

renazca etc [re'naθka] VB ver **renacer**

rencilla [ren'θiʎa] NF quarrel ■ **rencillas** NFPL bickering *sg*

rencor [ren'kor] NM rancour, bitterness; (*resentimiento*) ill feeling, resentment; **guardar ~ a** to have a grudge against

rencoroso, -a [renko'roso, a] ADJ spiteful

rendición [rendi'θjon] NF surrender

★**rendido, -a** [ren'diðo, a] ADJ (*sumiso*) submissive; (*agotado*) worn-out, exhausted; (*enamorado*) devoted

rendija [ren'dixa] NF (*hendidura*) crack; (*abertura*) aperture; (*fig*) rift, split; (*Jur*) loophole

rendimiento [rendi'mjento] NM (*producción*) output; (*Com*) yield, profit(s) *nf*; (*Tec, Com*) efficiency; **~ de capital** (*Com*) return on capital

rendir [ren'dir] /3k/ VT (*vencer*) to defeat; (*producir*) to produce; (*dar beneficio*) to yield; (*agotar*) to exhaust; **~ homenaje** o **culto a** to pay homage to ▶ VI to pay; (*Com*) to yield, produce; **el negocio no rinde** the business doesn't pay ■ **rendirse** VR (*someterse*) to surrender; (*ceder*) to yield; (*cansarse*) to wear o.s. out

renegado, -a [rene'ɣaðo, a] ADJ, NM/F renegade

renegar [rene'ɣar] /1h, 1j/ VT (*negar*) to deny vigorously ▶ VI (*blasfemar*) to blaspheme; **~** (*renunciar*) to renounce; (*quejarse*) to complain about

renegué [rene'ɣe], **reneguemos** etc [rene'ɣemos] VB ver **renegar**

RENFE ['renfe] NF ABR (*Esp Ferro*) = **Red Nacional de Ferrocarriles Españoles**

renglón [ren'glon] NM (*línea*) line; (*Com*) item, article; **a ~ seguido** immediately after

rengo, -a ['rengo, a] ADJ (*AM*) lame

reniego etc [re'njeɣo], **reniegue** etc [re'njeɣe] VB ver **renegar**

reno ['reno] NM reindeer

renombrado, -a [renom'braðo, a] ADJ renowned

renombre [re'nombre] NM renown

renovable [reno'βaβle] ADJ renewable

renovación [renoβa'θjon] NF (*de contrato*) renewal; (*Arq*) renovation

renovar [reno'βar] /**1l**/ vt to renew; (Arq) to renovate; (sala) to redecorate

renquear [renke'ar] /**1a**/ vi to limp; (fam) to get along, scrape by

renta ['renta] NF (ingresos) income; (beneficio) profit; (alquiler) rent; ~ **gravable** o **imponible** taxable income; ~ **nacional (bruta)** (gross) national income; ~ **no salarial** unearned income; ~ **sobre el terreno** (Com) ground rent; ~ **vitalicia** annuity; **política de rentas** incomes policy; **vivir de sus rentas** to live on one's private income

rentabilizar [rentaβili'θar] /**1f**/ vt to make profitable

rentable [ren'taβle] ADJ profitable; **no ~** unprofitable

rentar [ren'tar] /**1a**/ vt to produce, yield; (AM) to rent

rentista [ren'tista] NMF (accionista) shareholder (BRIT), stockholder (US)

renuencia [re'nwenθja] NF reluctance

renuente [re'nwente] ADJ reluctant

renueve etc [re'nweβe] VB ver **renovar**

renuncia [re'nunθja] NF resignation

renunciar [renun'θjar] /**1b**/ vt to renounce, give up ▶ vi to resign; ~ **a** (tabaco, alcohol etc) to give up; (oferta, oportunidad) to turn down; (puesto) to resign; ~ **a hacer algo** to give up doing sth

reñido, -a [re'niðo, a] ADJ (batalla) bitter, hard-fought; **estar ~ con algn** to be on bad terms with sb; **está ~ con su familia** he has fallen out with his family

reñir [re'nir] /**3h, 3k**/ vt (regañar) to scold ▶ vi (estar peleado) to quarrel, fall out; (combatir) to fight

reo ['reo] NMF culprit, offender; (Jur) accused

reojo [re'oxo]: **de ~** adv out of the corner of one's eye

reorganice etc [reorγa'niθe] VB ver **reorganizar**

reorganizar [reorγani'θar] /**1f**/ vt to reorganize

Rep. ABR = **república**

★**reparación** [repara'θjon] NF (acto) mending, repairing; (Tec) repair; (fig) amends, reparation; **"reparaciones en el acto"** "repairs while you wait"

reparador, -a [repara'ðor, a] ADJ refreshing; (comida) fortifying ▶ NM repairer

★**reparar** [repa'rar] /**1a**/ vt to repair; (fig) to make amends for; (suerte) to retrieve; (observar) to observe ▶ vi: ~ **en** (darse cuenta de) to notice; (poner atención en) to pay attention to; **sin ~ en los gastos** regardless of the cost

reparo [re'paro] NM (advertencia) observation; (duda) doubt; (dificultad) difficulty; (escrúpulo) scruple, qualm; **poner reparos (a)** to raise objections (to); (criticar) to criticize; **no tuvo ~ en hacerlo** he did not hesitate to do it

repartición [reparti'θjon] NF distribution; (división) division

repartidor, a [reparti'ðor, a] NM/F distributor; ~ **de leche** milkman

★**repartir** [repar'tir] /**3a**/ vt to distribute, share out; (Com, Correos) to deliver; (Mil) to partition; (libros) to give out; (comida) to serve out; (Naipes) to deal

reparto [re'parto] NM distribution; (Com, Correos) delivery; (Teat, Cine) cast; (AM: urbanización) housing estate (BRIT), real estate development (US); **"~ a domicilio"** "home delivery service"

★**repasar** [repa'sar] /**1a**/ vt (Escol) to revise; (Mecánica) to check, overhaul; (Costura) to mend

repaso [re'paso] NM revision; (Mecánica) overhaul, checkup; (Costura) mending; ~ **general** servicing, general overhaul; **curso de ~** refresher course

repatriar [repa'trjar] /**1b**/ vt to repatriate ■ **repatriarse** VR to return home

repecho [re'petʃo] NM steep incline

repelente [repe'lente] ADJ repellent, repulsive

repeler [repe'ler] /**2a**/ vt to repel; (idea, oferta) to reject

repensar [repen'sar] /**1j**/ vt to reconsider

repente [re'pente] NM sudden movement; (fig) impulse; **de ~** suddenly; ~ **de ira** fit of anger

repentice etc [repen'tiθe] VB ver **repentizar**

repentino, -a [repen'tino, a] ADJ sudden; (imprevisto) unexpected

repentizar [repenti'θar] /**1f**/ vi (Mus) to sight-read

repercusión [reperku'sjon] NF repercussion; **de amplia** o **ancha ~** far-reaching

repercutir [reperku'tir] /**3a**/ vi (objeto) to rebound; (sonido) to echo; ~ **en** (fig) to have repercussions o effects on

repertorio [reper'torjo] NM list; (Teat) repertoire

repesca [re'peska] NF (Escol: fam) resit

repetición [repeti'θjon] NF repetition

repetido, -a [repe'tiðo, a] ADJ repeated; **repetidas veces** repeatedly

★**repetir** [repe'tir] /**3k**/ vt to repeat; (plato) to have a second helping of; (Teat) to give as an encore, sing etc again ▶ vi to repeat; (sabor) to come back ■ **repetirse** VR to repeat o.s.; (suceso) to recur

repetitivo, -a [repeti'tiβo, a] ADJ repetitive, repetitious

repicar [repi'kar] /**1g**/ vi (campanas) to ring (out)

repiense etc [re'pjense] VB ver **repensar**

repipi [re'pipi] ADJ la-di-da ▶ NF: **es una ~** she's a little madam

repique [re'pike] VB ver **repicar** ▶ NM pealing, ringing

repiqueteo [repike'teo] NM pealing; (de tambor) drumming

repisa [re'pisa] NF ledge, shelf; ~ **de chimenea** mantelpiece; ~ **de ventana** windowsill

r

repito etc VB ver **repetir**

replantear [replante'ar] /**1a**/ VT (cuestión pública) to readdress; (problema personal) to reconsider; (en reunión) to raise again ■ **replantearse** VR: **replantearse algo** to reconsider sth

replegarse [reple'ɣarse] /**1h, 1j**/ VR to fall back, retreat

replegué [reple'ɣe], **repleguemos** etc [reple'ɣemos] VB ver **replegarse**

repleto, -a [re'pleto, a] ADJ replete, full up; ~ **de** filled o crammed with

réplica ['replika] NF answer; (Arte) replica; **derecho de** ~ right of o to reply

replicar [repli'kar] /**1g**/ VI to answer; (objetar) to argue, answer back

repliego etc [re'pljeɣo] VB ver **replegarse**

repliegue [re'pljeɣe] VB ver **replegarse** ▶ NM (Mil) withdrawal

replique etc [re'plike] VB ver **replicar**

repoblación [repoβla'θjon] NF repopulation; (de río) restocking; ~ **forestal** reafforestation

repoblar [repo'βlar] /**1l**/ VT to repopulate; to restock; (con árboles) to reafforest

repollito [repo'ʎito] NM (AM): **repollitos de Bruselas** (Brussels) sprouts

★**repollo** [re'poʎo] NM cabbage

repondré etc [repon'dre] VB ver **reponer**

reponer [repo'ner] /**2q**/ VT to replace, put back; (máquina) to re-set; (Teat) to revive; ~ **que** to reply that ■ **reponerse** VR to recover

reponga etc [re'ponga] VB ver **reponer**

★**reportaje** [repor'taxe] NM report, article; ~ **gráfico** illustrated report

reportar [repor'tar] /**1a**/ VT (traer) to bring, carry; (conseguir) to obtain; (fig) to check; **la cosa no le reportó sino disgustos** the affair brought him nothing but trouble ■ **reportarse** VR (contenerse) to control o.s.; (calmarse) to calm down

reportero, -a [repor'tero, a] NM/F reporter; ~ **gráfico/a** news photographer

reposacabezas [reposaka'βeθas] NM INV headrest

reposado, -a [repo'saðo, a] ADJ (descansado) restful; (tranquilo) calm

reposar [repo'sar] /**1a**/ VI to rest, repose; (muerto) to lie, rest

reposición [reposi'θjon] NF replacement; (Cine) second showing; (Teat) revival

reposo [re'poso] NM rest

repostar [repos'tar] /**1a**/ VT to replenish; (Auto) to fill up (with petrol o gasoline)

repostería [reposte'ria] NF (arte) confectionery, pastry-making; (tienda) confectioner's (shop)

repostero, -a [repos'tero, a] NM/F confectioner

reprender [repren'der] /**2a**/ VT to reprimand; (niño) to scold

reprensión [repren'sjon] NF rebuke, reprimand; (de niño) telling-off, scolding

represa [re'presa] NF dam; (lago artificial) lake, pool

represalia [repre'salja] NF reprisal; **tomar represalias** to take reprisals, retaliate

representación [representa'θjon] NF representation; (Teat) performance; **en ~ de** representing; **por ~** by proxy

representante [represen'tante] NMF (Pol, Com) representative; (Teat) performer

representar [represen'tar] /**1a**/ VT to represent; (significar) to mean; (Teat) to perform; (edad) to look; **tal acto representaría la guerra** such an act would mean war ■ **representarse** VR to imagine

representativo, -a [representa'tiβo, a] ADJ representative

represión [repre'sjon] NF repression

represivo, -a [repre'siβo, a] ADJ repressive

reprimenda [repri'menda] NF reprimand, rebuke

reprimir [repri'mir] /**3a**/ VT to repress ■ **reprimirse** VR: **reprimirse de hacer algo** to stop o.s. from doing sth

reprobación [reproβa'θjon] NF reproval; (culpa) blame

reprobar [repro'βar] /**1l**/ VT to censure, reprove

réprobo, -a ['reproβo, a] NM/F reprobate

reprochar [repro'tʃar] /**1a**/ VT to reproach; (censurar) to condemn, censure

reproche [re'protʃe] NM reproach

reproducción [reproðuk'θjon] NF reproduction

reproducir [reproðu'θir] /**3n**/ VT to reproduce ■ **reproducirse** VR to breed; (situación) to recur

reproductor, a [reproðuk'tor, a] ADJ reproductive ▶ NM: ~ **de CD** CD player; ~ **MP3/MP4** MP3/MP4 player

reproduje [repro'ðuxe], **reprodujera** etc [reproðu'xera], **reproduzca** etc [repro'ðuθka] VB ver **reproducir**

repruebe etc [re'prweβe] VB ver **reprobar**

reptar [rep'tar] /**1a**/ VI to creep, crawl

reptil [rep'til] NM reptile

★**república** [re'puβlika] NF republic; **R~ Dominicana** Dominican Republic; **R~ Federal Alemana (RFA)** Federal Republic of Germany

republicano, -a [repuβli'kano, a] ADJ, NM/F republican

repudiar [repu'ðjar] /**1b**/ VT to repudiate; (fe) to renounce

repudio [re'puðjo] NM repudiation

repueble etc [re'pweβle] VB ver **repoblar**

repuesto [re'pwesto] PP de **reponer** ▶ NM (pieza de recambio) spare (part); (abastecimiento) supply; **rueda de** ~ spare wheel; **y llevamos otro de** ~ and we have another as a spare o in reserve

repugnancia [repuɣ'nanθja] NF repugnance

repugnante [repuɣ'nante] ADJ repugnant, repulsive

repugnar [repuɣ'nar] /**1a**/ vт to disgust ▶ vi, **repugnarse** vr (*contradecirse*) to contradict each other

repujar [repu'xar] /**1a**/ vт to emboss

repulsa [re'pulsa] nf rebuff

repulsión [repul'sjon] nf repulsion, aversion

repulsivo, -a [repul'siβo, a] adj repulsive

repuse *etc* [re'puse] vв ver **reponer**

reputación [reputa'θjon] nf reputation

reputar [repu'tar] /**1a**/ vт to consider, deem

requemado, -a [reke'maðo, a] adj (*quemado*) scorched; (*bronceado*) tanned

requemar [reke'mar] /**1a**/ vт (*quemar*) to scorch; (*secar*) to parch; (*Culin*) to overdo, burn; (*la lengua*) to burn, sting

requerimiento [rekeri'mjento] nm request; (*demanda*) demand; (*Jur*) summons

requerir [reke'rir] /**3i**/ vт (*pedir*) to ask, request; (*exigir*) to require; (*ordenar*) to call for; (*llamar*) to send for, summon

requesón [reke'son] nm whey cheese (*similar to ricotta*)

requete... [rekete] pref extremely

requiebro [re'kjeβro] nm (*piropo*) compliment, flirtatious remark

réquiem ['rekjem] nm requiem

requiera *etc* [re'kjera], **requiriendo** *etc* [reki'rjendo] vв ver **requerir**

requisa [re'kisa] nf (*inspección*) survey, inspection; (*Mil*) requisition

requisar [reki'sar] /**1a**/ vт (*Mil*) to requisition; (*confiscar*) to seize, confiscate

requisito [reki'sito] nm requirement, requisite; **~ previo** prerequisite; **tener los requisitos para un cargo** to have the essential qualifications for a post

res [res] nf beast, animal

resabio [re'saβjo] nm (*maña*) vice, bad habit; (*dejo*) (unpleasant) aftertaste

resaca [re'saka] nf (*en el mar*) undertow, undercurrent; (*fig*) backlash; (*fam*) hangover

resaltar [resal'tar] /**1a**/ vi to project, stick out; (*fig*) to stand out

resarcir [resar'θir] /**3b**/ vт to compensate; (*pagar*) to repay; **~ a algn de una pérdida** to compensate sb for a loss; **~ a algn de una cantidad** to repay sb a sum ■ **resarcirse** vr to make up for

resarza *etc* [re'sarθa] vв ver **resarcir**

resbalada [resβa'laða] nf (*AM*) slip

resbaladero [resβala'ðero] nm (*AM*) slide

resbaladizo, -a [resβala'ðiθo, a] adj slippery

★**resbalar** [resβa'lar] /**1a**/ vi to slip, slide; (*fig*) to slip (up); **le resbalaban las lágrimas por las mejillas** tears were trickling down his cheeks ■ **resbalarse** vr to slip, slide; (*fig*) to slip (up)

resbalón [resβa'lon] nm (*acción*) slip; (*deslizamiento*) slide; (*fig*) slip

★**rescatar** [reska'tar] /**1a**/ vт (*salvar*) to save, rescue; (*objeto*) to get back, recover; (*cautivos*) to ransom

★**rescate** [res'kate] nm rescue; (*de objeto*) recovery; (*Com*) bailout; **pagar un ~** to pay a ransom

rescindir [resθin'dir] /**3a**/ vт (*contrato*) to annul, rescind

rescisión [resθi'sjon] nf cancellation

rescoldo [res'koldo] nm embers pl

resecar [rese'kar] /**1g**/ vт to dry off, dry thoroughly; (*Med*) to cut out, remove ■ **resecarse** vr to dry up

reseco, -a [re'seko, a] adj very dry; (*fig*) skinny

resentido, -a [resen'tiðo, a] adj resentful; **es un ~** he's bitter

resentimiento [resenti'mjento] nm resentment, bitterness

resentirse [resen'tirse] /**3i**/ vr (*debilitarse: persona*) to suffer; **~ con** to resent; **~ de** (*sufrir las consecuencias de*) to feel the effects of; **~ de o por algo** to resent sth, be bitter about sth

reseña [re'seɲa] nf (*cuenta*) account; (*informe*) report; (*Lit*) review

reseñar [rese'ɲar] /**1a**/ vт to describe; (*Lit*) to review

reseque *etc* [re'seke] vв ver **resecar**

★**reserva** [re'serβa] nf reserve; (*reservación*) reservation; **a ~ de que ...** unless ...; **con toda ~** in strictest confidence; **de ~** spare; **tener algo de ~** to have sth in reserve; **~ de indios** Indian reservation; (*Com*) **~ para amortización** depreciation allowance; **~ de caja o en efectivo** cash reserves; **reservas del Estado** government stock; **reservas en oro** gold reserves

reservación [reserβa'θjon] nf (*AM*) reservation

★**reservado, -a** [reser'βaðo, a] adj reserved; (*retraído*) cold, distant ▶ nm private room; (*Ferro*) reserved compartment

★**reservar** [reser'βar] /**1a**/ vт (*guardar*) to keep; (*Ferro, Teat etc*) to reserve, book; **~ con exceso** to overbook ■ **reservarse** vr to save o.s.; (*callar*) to keep to o.s.

★**resfriado** [res'friaðo] nm cold

resfriarse [res'friarse] /**1c**/ vr to cool off; (*Med*) to catch (a) cold

resfrío [res'frio] nm (*esp AM*) cold

resguardar [resɣwar'ðar] /**1a**/ vт to protect, shield ■ **resguardarse** vr: **resguardarse de** to guard against

resguardo [res'ɣwarðo] nm defence; (*vale*) voucher; (*recibo*) receipt, slip

★**residencia** [resi'ðenθja] nf residence; (*Univ*) hall of residence; **~ para ancianos** o **jubilados** residential home, old people's home

★**residencial** [resiðen'θjal] adj residential ▶ nf (*urbanización*) housing estate (*BRIT*), real estate development (*US*)

residente [resi'ðente] adj, nmf resident

r

residir [resiˈðir] /3a/ vi to reside, live; **~ en** to reside o lie in; (*consistir en*) to consist of

residual [resiˈðwal] ADJ residual; **aguas residuales** sewage

residuo [reˈsiðwo] NM residue; **residuos atmosféricos** o **radiactivos** fallout *sg*

resienta *etc* [reˈsjenta] VB *ver* **resentirse**

resignación [resiɣnaˈθjon] NF resignation

resignarse [resiɣˈnarse] /1a/ VR: **~ a** o **con** to resign o.s. to, be resigned to

resina [reˈsina] NF resin

resintiendo *etc* [resinˈtjendo] VB *ver* **resentirse**

resistencia [resisˈtenθja] NF (*dureza*) endurance, strength; (*oposición, Elec*) resistance; **la R~** (*Mil*) the Resistance

resistente [resisˈtente] ADJ strong, hardy; (*Tec*) resistant; **~ al calor** heat-resistant

resistir [resisˈtir] /3a/ VT (*soportar*) to bear; (*oponerse a*) to resist, oppose; (*aguantar*) to put up with; **no puedo ~ este frío** I can't bear o stand this cold ▶ vi to resist; (*aguantar*) to last, endure ■ **resistirse** VR: **resistirse a** to refuse to, resist; **me resisto a creerlo** I refuse to believe it; **se le resiste la química** chemistry escapes her

resol [reˈsol] NM glare of the sun

resollar [resoˈʎar] /1l/ vi to breathe noisily, wheeze

resolución [resoluˈθjon] NF resolution; (*decisión*) decision; (*moción*) motion; **~ judicial** legal ruling; **tomar una ~** to take a decision

resoluto, -a [resoˈluto, a] ADJ resolute

★**resolver** [resolˈβer] /2h/ VT to resolve; (*solucionar*) to solve, resolve; (*decidir*) to decide, settle ■ **resolverse** VR to make up one's mind

resonancia [resoˈnanθja] NF (*del sonido*) resonance; (*repercusión*) repercussion; (*fig*) wide effect, impact

resonante [resoˈnante] ADJ resonant, resounding; (*fig*) tremendous

resonar [resoˈnar] /1l/ vi to ring, echo

resoplar [resoˈplar] /1a/ vi to snort; (*por cansancio*) to puff

resoplido [resoˈpliðo] NM heavy breathing

resorte [reˈsorte] NM spring; (*fig*) lever

resortera [resorˈtera] NF (*Am*) catapult

respaldar [respalˈdar] /1a/ VT to back (up), support; (*Inform*) to back up ■ **respaldarse** VR to lean back; **respaldarse con** o **en** (*fig*) to take one's stand on

respaldo [resˈpaldo] NM (*de sillón*) back; (*fig*) support, backing

respectivo, -a [respekˈtiβo, a] ADJ respective; **en lo ~ a** with regard to

respecto [resˈpekto] NM: **al ~** on this matter; **con ~ a, ~ de** with regard to, in relation to

respetable [respeˈtaβle] ADJ respectable

★**respetar** [respeˈtar] /1a/ VT to respect

★**respeto** [resˈpeto] NM respect; (*acatamiento*) deference; **por ~ a** out of consideration for

■ **respetos** NMPL respects; **presentar sus respetos a** to pay one's respects to

respetuoso, -a [respeˈtwoso, a] ADJ respectful

respingo [resˈpingo] NM start, jump

respiración [respiraˈθjon] NF breathing; (*Med*) respiration; (*ventilación*) ventilation; **~ asistida** artificial respiration (*by machine*)

★**respirar** [respiˈrar] /1a/ VT, vi to breathe; **no dejar ~ a algn** to keep on at sb; **estuvo escuchándole sin ~** he listened to him in complete silence

respiratorio, -a [respiraˈtorjo, a] ADJ respiratory

respiro [resˈpiro] NM breathing; (*fig: descanso*) respite, rest; (*Com*) period of grace

resplandecer [resplandeˈθer] /2d/ vi to shine

resplandeciente [resplandeˈθjente] ADJ resplendent, shining

resplandezca *etc* [resplanˈdeθka] VB *ver* **resplandecer**

resplandor [resplanˈdor] NM brilliance, brightness; (*del fuego*) blaze

★**responder** [responˈder] /2a/ VT to answer ▶ vi to answer; (*fig*) to respond; (*pey*) to answer back; (*corresponder*) to correspond; **~ a** (*situación etc*) to respond to; **~ a una pregunta** to answer a question; **~ a una descripción** to fit a description; **~ de** o **por** to answer for

respondón, -ona [responˈdon, ona] ADJ cheeky

responsabilice *etc* [responsaβiˈliθe] VB *ver* **responsabilizarse**

★**responsabilidad** [responsaβiliˈðað] NF responsibility; **bajo mi ~** on my authority; **~ ilimitada** (*Com*) unlimited liability

responsabilizarse [responsaβiliˈθarse] /1f/ VR to make o.s. responsible, take charge

★**responsable** [responˈsable] ADJ responsible; **la persona ~** the person in charge; **hacerse ~ de algo** to assume responsibility for sth

★**respuesta** [resˈpwesta] NF answer, reply; (*reacción*) response

resquebrajar [reskeβraˈxar] /1a/ VT to crack, split ■ **resquebrajarse** VR to crack, split

resquemor [reskeˈmor] NM resentment

resquicio [resˈkiθjo] NM chink; (*hendidura*) crack

resta [ˈresta] NF (*Mat*) remainder

restablecer [restaβleˈθer] /2d/ VT to re-establish, restore ■ **restablecerse** VR to recover

restablecimiento [restaβleθiˈmjento] NM re-establishment; (*restauración*) restoration; (*Med*) recovery

restablezca *etc* [restaˈβleθka] VB *ver* **restablecer**

restallar [restaˈʎar] /1a/ vi to crack

restante [resˈtante] ADJ remaining; **lo ~** the remainder; **los restantes** the rest, those left (over)

restar [resˈtar] /1a/ VT (*Mat*) to subtract; (*descon-*

tar) to deduct; (*fig*) to take away ▶ VI to remain, be left

restauración [restaura'θjon] NF restoration

restaurador, a [restaura'ðor, a] NM/F (*persona*) restorer

★**restaurante** [restau'rante] NM restaurant

restaurar [restau'rar] /**1a**/ VT to restore

restitución [restitu'θjon] NF return, restitution

restituir [restitu'ir] /**3g**/ VT (*devolver*) to return, give back; (*rehabilitar*) to restore

restituyendo *etc* [restitu'jendo] VB *ver* **restituir**

★**resto** ['resto] NM (*residuo*) rest, remainder; (*apuesta*) stake ▥ **restos** NMPL remains; (*Culin*) leftovers, scraps; **restos mortales** mortal remains

restorán [resto'ran] NM (*Am*) restaurant

restregar [restre'ɣar] /**1h, 1j**/ VT to scrub, rub

restregué [restre'ɣe], **restreguemos** *etc* [restre'ɣemos] VB *ver* **restregar**

restricción [restrik'θjon] NF restriction; **sin ~ de** without restrictions on *o* as to; **hablar sin restricciones** to talk freely

restrictivo, -a [restrik'tiβo, a] ADJ restrictive

restriego *etc* [res'trjeɣo], **restriegue** *etc* [res-'trjeɣe] VB *ver* **restregar**

restringir [restrin'xir] /**3c**/ VT to restrict, limit

restrinja *etc* [res'trinxa] VB *ver* **restringir**

resucitar [resuθi'tar] /**1a**/ VT, VI to resuscitate, revive

resuello *etc* [re'sweʎo] VB *ver* **resollar** ▶ NM (*aliento*) breath

resuelto, -a [re'swelto, a] PP *de* **resolver** ▶ ADJ resolute, determined; **estar ~ a algo** to be set on sth; **estar ~ a hacer algo** to be determined to do sth

resuelva *etc* [re'swelβa] VB *ver* **resolver**

resuene *etc* [re'swene] VB *ver* **resonar**

resulta [re'sulta] NF result; **de resultas de** as a result of

★**resultado** [resul'taðo] NM result; (*conclusión*) outcome; **dar ~** to produce results ▥ **resultados** NMPL (*Inform*) output *sg*

resultante [resul'tante] ADJ resulting, resultant

★**resultar** [resul'tar] /**1a**/ VI (*ser*) to be; (*llegar a ser*) to turn out to be; (*salir bien*) to turn out well; (*seguir*) to ensue; **~ de** to stem from; **~ en** to result in, produce; **resulta que ...** it turns out that ...; **el conductor resultó muerto** the driver was killed; **no resultó** it didn't work *o* come off; **me resulta difícil hacerlo** it's difficult for me to do it

★**resumen** [re'sumen] NM summary, résumé; **en ~ in** short

resumir [resu'mir] /**3a**/ VT to sum up; (*condensar*) to summarize; (*cortar*) to abridge, cut down ▥ **resumirse** VR: **la situación se resume en pocas palabras** the situation can be summed up in a few words

resurgir [resur'xir] /**3c**/ VI (*reaparecer*) to reappear

resurrección [resurrek'θjon] NF resurrection

retablo [re'taβlo] NM altarpiece

retaguardia [reta'ɣwarðja] NF rearguard

retahíla [reta'ila] NF series, string; (*de injurias*) volley, stream

retal [re'tal] NM remnant

retar [re'tar] /**1a**/ VT (*gen*) to challenge; (*desafiar*) to defy, dare

retardar [retar'ðar] /**1a**/ VT (*demorar*) to delay; (*hacer más lento*) to slow down; (*retener*) to hold back

retardo [re'tarðo] NM delay

retazo [re'taθo] NM snippet (*Brit*), fragment

rete ... ['rete] PREF very, extremely

retén [re'ten] NM (*Am*) roadblock, checkpoint

retención [reten'θjon] NF retention; (*de pago*) deduction; (*tráfico*) hold-up; **~ fiscal** deduction for tax purposes; **~ de llamadas** (*Telec*) hold facility

retendré *etc* [reten'dre] VB *ver* **retener**

retener [rete'ner] /**2k**/ VT (*guardar*) to retain, keep; (*intereses*) to withhold

retenga *etc* [re'tenga] VB *ver* **retener**

reticencia [reti'θenθja] NF (*insinuación*) insinuation, (*malevolent*) suggestion; (*verdad a medias*) half-truth

reticente [reti'θente] ADJ (*insinuador*) insinuating; (*engañoso*) deceptive; (*postura*) reluctant; **ser ~ a hacer algo** to be reluctant *o* unwilling to do sth

retiene *etc* [re'tjene] VB *ver* **retener**

retina [re'tina] NF retina

retintín [retin'tin] NM jangle, jingle; **decir algo con ~** to say sth sarcastically

retirado, -a [reti'raðo, a] ADJ (*lugar*) remote; (*vida*) quiet; (*jubilado*) retired ▶ NF (*Mil*) retreat; (*de dinero*) withdrawal; (*de embajador*) recall; **batirse en retirada** to retreat

retirar [reti'rar] /**1a**/ VT to withdraw; (*la mano*) to draw back; (*quitar*) to remove; (*dinero*) to take out, withdraw; (*jubilar*) to retire, pension off ▥ **retirarse** VR to retreat, withdraw; (*jubilarse*) to retire; (*acostarse*) to retire, go to bed

retiro [re'tiro] NM retreat; (*jubilación, tb Deporte*) retirement; (*pago*) pension; (*lugar*) quiet place

reto ['reto] NM dare, challenge

retocar [reto'kar] /**1g**/ VT (*fotografía*) to touch up, retouch

retoce *etc* [re'toθe] VB *ver* **retozar**

retoño [re'toɲo] NM sprout, shoot; (*fig*) offspring, child

retoque [re'toke] VB *ver* **retocar** ▶ NM retouching

retorcer [retor'θer] /**2b, 2h**/ VT to twist; (*argumento*) to turn, twist; (*manos, lavado*) to wring ▥ **retorcerse** VR to become twisted; (*persona*) to writhe; **retorcerse de dolor** to writhe in *o* squirm with pain

r

retorcido, -a [retorˈθiðo, a] ADJ (tb fig) twisted

retorcijón [retorθiˈxon] NM (Am: tb: **retorcijón de tripas**) stomach cramp

retorcimiento [retorθiˈmjento] NM twist, twisting; (fig) deviousness

retórico, -a [reˈtoriko, a] ADJ rhetorical; (pey) affected, windy ▶ NF rhetoric; (pey) affectedness

retornable [retorˈnaβle] ADJ returnable

retornar [retorˈnar] /1a/ VT to return, give back ▶ VI to return, go/come back

retorno [reˈtorno] NM return; **~ del carro** (Inform, Tip) carriage return

retortero [retorˈtero] NM: **andar al ~** to bustle about, have heaps of things to do; **andar al ~ por algn** to be madly in love with sb

retortijón [retortiˈxon] NM twist, twisting; **~ de tripas** stomach cramp

retorzamos etc [retorˈθamos] VB ver **retorcer**

retozar [retoˈθar] /1f/ VI (juguetear) to frolic, romp; (saltar) to gambol

retozón, -ona [retoˈθon, ona] ADJ playful

retracción [retrakˈθjon] NF retraction

retractarse [retrakˈtarse] /1a/ VR to retract; **me retracto** I take that back

retraerse [retraˈerse] /2o/ VR to retreat, withdraw

retraído, -a [retraˈiðo, a] ADJ shy, retiring

retraiga etc [reˈtraiɣa] VB ver **retraerse**

retraimiento [retraiˈmjento] NM retirement; (timidez) shyness

retraje etc [reˈtraxe], **retrajera** etc [retraˈxera] VB ver **retraerse**

retransmisión [retransmiˈsjon] NF repeat (broadcast)

retransmitir [retransmiˈtir] /3a/ VT (mensaje) to relay; (TV etc) to repeat, retransmit; (: en vivo) to broadcast live

retrasado, -a [retraˈsaðo, a] ADJ late; (mentalmente) backward (!); (país etc) backward (pey), underdeveloped; **estar ~** (reloj) to be slow; (persona, industria) to be o lag behind

retrasar [retraˈsar] /1a/ VT (demorar) to postpone, put off; (retardar) to slow down ▶ VI (atrasarse) to be late; (reloj) to be slow; (producción) to fall (off); (quedarse atrás) to lag behind ■ **retrasarse** VR (atrasarse) to be late; (suj: reloj) to be slow; (producción) to fall (off); (quedarse atrás) to lag behind

★**retraso** [reˈtraso] NM (demora) delay; (lentitud) slowness; (tardanza) lateness; (pey: atraso) backwardness; **llegar con ~** to arrive late; **llegar con 25 minutos de ~** to be 25 minutes late; **llevo un ~ de seis semanas** I'm six weeks behind (with my work etc); **~ mental** learning disability ■ **retrasos** NMPL (Com) arrears; (deudas) deficit sg, debts

retratar [retraˈtar] /1a/ VT (Arte) to paint the portrait of; (fotografiar) to photograph; (fig) to depict, describe ■ **retratarse** VR (en cuadro) to have one's portrait painted; (en fotografía) to have one's photograph taken

retratista [retraˈtista] NMF (Arte) (portrait) painter; (Foto) photographer

retrato [reˈtrato] NM portrait; (Foto) photograph; (descripción) portrayal, depiction; (fig) likeness; **ser el vivo ~ de** to be the spitting image of

retrato-robot [reˈtratoroˈβo(t)] (pl **retratos-robot**) NM Identikit® picture

retrayendo etc [retraˈjendo] VB ver **retraerse**

retreta [reˈtreta] NF retreat

★**retrete** [reˈtrete] NM toilet

retribución [retriβuˈθjon] NF (recompensa) reward; (pago) pay, payment

retribuir [retriβuˈir] /3g/ VT (recompensar) to reward; (pagar) to pay

retribuyendo etc [retriβuˈjendo] VB ver **retribuir**

retro... [retro] PREF retro...

retroactivo, -a [retroakˈtiβo, a] ADJ retroactive, retrospective; **dar efecto ~ a un pago** to backdate a payment

retroalimentación [retroalimentaˈθjon] NF (Inform) feedback

retroceder [retroθeˈðer] /2a/ VI (echarse atrás) to move back(wards); (fig) to back down; **no ~** to stand firm; **la policía hizo ~ a la multitud** the police forced the crowd back

retroceso [retroˈθeso] NM backward movement; (Med) relapse; (Com) recession, depression; (fig) backing down

retrógrado, -a [reˈtroɣraðo, a] ADJ retrograde, retrogressive; (Pol) reactionary

retroiluminado, -a [retroilumiˈnaðo, a] ADJ (teclado) backlit

retropropulsión [retropropulˈsjon] NF jet propulsion

retrospectivo, -a [retrospekˈtiβo, a] ADJ retrospective; **mirada retrospectiva** backward glance

★**retrovisor** [retroβiˈsor] NM rear-view mirror

retuerce etc [reˈtwerθe], **retuerza** etc [reˈtwerθa] VB ver **retorcer**

retuit [reˈtwit] NM (en Twitter) retweet

retuitear [retwiteˈar] /1a/ VT (en Twitter) to retweet

retumbante [retumˈbante] ADJ resounding

retumbar [retumˈbar] /1a/ VI to echo, resound; (continuamente) to reverberate

retuve etc [reˈtuβe] VB ver **retener**

reuma [ˈreuma] NM rheumatism

reumático, -a [reuˈmatiko, a] ADJ rheumatic

reumatismo [reumaˈtismo] NM rheumatism

reunificar [reunifiˈkar] /1g/ VT to reunify

reunifique etc [reuniˈfike] VB ver **reunificar**

★**reunión** [reuˈnjon] NF (asamblea) meeting; (fiesta) party; **~ en la cumbre** summit meeting; **~ de ventas** (Com) sales meeting

reunir [reu'nir] /**3a**/ vt (*juntar*) to reunite, join (together); (*recoger*) to gather (together); (*personas*) to bring o get together; (*cualidades*) to combine; **reunió a sus amigos para discutirlo** he got his friends together to talk it over ■ **reunirse** vr (*personas: en asamblea*) to meet, gather

reválida [re'βaliða] nf (*Escol*) final examination

revalidar [reβali'ðar] /**1a**/ vt (*ratificar*) to confirm, ratify

revalorar [reβalo'rar] /**1a**/ vt to revalue, reassess

revalorización [reβaloriθa'θjon], **revaloración** [reβalora'θjon] nf revaluation; (*Econ*) reassessment

revalorizar [reβalori'θar] /**1f**/ vt to revalue, reassess

revancha [re'βantʃa] nf revenge; (*Deporte*) return match; (*Boxeo*) return fight

revelación [reβela'θjon] nf revelation

revelado [reβe'laðo] nm developing

revelador, a [reβela'ðor, a] adj revealing

revelar [reβe'lar] /**1a**/ vt to reveal; (*secreto*) to disclose; (*mostrar*) to show; (*Foto*) to develop

revendedor, a [reβende'ðor, a] nm/f retailer; (*pey*) ticket tout

revendré *etc* [reβen'dre], **revenga** *etc* [re'βenga] vb *ver* **revenir**

revenirse [reβe'nirse] /**3r**/ vr to shrink; (*comida*) to go bad o off; (*vino*) to sour; (*Culin*) to get tough

reventa [re'βenta] nf resale; (*de entradas*) touting

reventar [reβen'tar] /**1j**/ vt to burst, explode; (*molestar*) to annoy, rile; **me revienta tener que ponérmelo** I hate having to wear it ▶ vi (*estallar*) to burst, explode; **~ de** (*fig*) to be bursting with; **~ por** to be bursting to ■ **reventarse** vr (*estallar*) to burst, explode

reventón [reβen'ton] nm (*Auto*) blow-out (*Brit*), flat (*US*)

reverberación [reβerβera'θjon] nf reverberation

reverberar [reβerβe'rar] /**1a**/ vi (*luz*) to play, be reflected; (*superficie*) to shimmer; (*nieve*) to glare; (*sonido*) to reverberate

reverbero [reβer'βero] nm (*de luz*) play; (*de superficie*) shimmer, shine; (*de nieve*) glare; (*de sonido*) reverberation

reverencia [reβe'renθja] nf reverence; (*inclinación*) bow

reverenciar [reβeren'θjar] /**1b**/ vt to revere

reverendo, -a [reβe'rendo, a] adj reverend; (*fam*) big, awful; **un ~ imbécil** an awful idiot

reverente [reβe'rente] adj reverent

reversa [re'βersa] nf (*Am*) (reverse) gear

reversible [reβer'siβle] adj reversible

reverso [re'βerso] nm back, other side; (*de moneda*) reverse

revertir [reβer'tir] /**3i**/ vi to revert; **~ en benefi-** cio de to be to the advantage of; **~ en perjuicio de** to be to the detriment of

★**revés** [re'βes] nm back, wrong side; (*fig*) reverse, setback; (*Deporte*) backhand; **al ~** the wrong way round; (*de arriba abajo*) upside down; (*ropa*) inside out; **y al ~** and vice versa; **volver algo del ~** to turn sth round; (*ropa*) to turn sth inside out; **los reveses de la fortuna** the blows of fate

revestir [reβes'tir] /**3k**/ vt (*poner*) to put on; (*cubrir*) to cover, coat; (*cualidad*) to have, possess; **el acto revestía gran solemnidad** the ceremony had great dignity ■ **revestirse** vr (*Rel*) to put on one's vestments; (*ponerse*) to put on; **revestirse con** o **de** to arm o.s. with

reviejo, -a [re'βjexo, a] adj very old, ancient

reviene *etc* [re'βjene] vb *ver* **revenirse**

reviente *etc* [re'βjente] vb *ver* **reventar**

revierta *etc* [re'βjerta] vb *ver* **revertir**

reviniendo *etc* [reβi'njendo] vb *ver* **revenirse**

revirtiendo *etc* [reβir'tjendo] vb *ver* **revertir**

revisar [reβi'sar] /**1a**/ vt (*examinar*) to check; (*texto etc*) to revise; (*Jur*) to review

revisión [reβi'sjon] nf revision; **~ aduanera** customs inspection; **~ de cuentas** audit; **~ salarial** wage review

★**revisor, a** [reβi'sor, a] nm/f inspector; (*Ferro*) ticket collector; **~ de cuentas** auditor

★**revista** [re'βista] vb *ver* **revestir** ▶ nf magazine, review; (*Teat*) revue; (*inspección*) inspection; **~ literaria** literary review; **~ de libros** book reviews (page); **~ del corazón** *magazine featuring celebrity gossip and real-life romance stories*; **pasar ~ a** to review, inspect

revivir [reβi'βir] /**3a**/ vt (*recordar*) to revive memories of ▶ vi to revive

revocación [reβoka'θjon] nf repeal

revocar [reβo'kar] /**1g**/ vt (*decisión*) to revoke; (*Arq*) to plaster

revolcar [reβol'kar] /**1g, 1l**/ vt to knock down, send flying ■ **revolcarse** vr to roll about

revolcón [reβol'kon] nm tumble

revolotear [reβolote'ar] /**1a**/ vi to flutter

revoloteo [reβolo'teo] nm fluttering

revolqué [reβol'ke], **revolquemos** *etc* [reβol'kemos] vb *ver* **revolcar**

revoltijo [reβol'tixo] nm mess, jumble

★**revoltoso, -a** [reβol'toso, a] adj (*travieso*) naughty, unruly

revolución [reβolu'θjon] nf revolution

revolucionar [reβoluθjo'nar] /**1a**/ vt to revolutionize

revolucionario, -a [reβoluθjo'narjo, a] adj, nm/f revolutionary

★**revolver** [reβol'βer] /**2h**/ vt (*desordenar*) to disturb, mess up; (*agitar*) to shake; (*líquido*) to stir; (*mover*) to move about; (*Pol*) to stir up; **han revuelto toda la casa** they've turned the whole house upside down ▶ vi: **~ en** to go through, rummage (about) in ■ **revolverse** vr

r

(*en cama*) to toss and turn; (*Meteorología*) to break, turn stormy; **revolverse contra** to turn on *o* against

revólver [re'βolβer] NM revolver

revoque *etc* [re'βoke] VB *ver* **revocar**

revuelco *etc* [re'βwelko] VB *ver* **revolcar**

revuelo [re'βwelo] NM fluttering; (*fig*) commotion; **armar** *o* **levantar un gran ~** to cause a great stir

revuelque *etc* [re'βwelke] VB *ver* **revolcar**

★**revuelto, -a** [re'βwelto, a] PP *de* **revolver** ▶ ADJ (*mezclado*) mixed-up, in disorder; (*mar*) rough; (*tiempo*) unsettled; **todo estaba ~** everything was in disorder *o* was topsy-turvy ▶ NF (*motín*) revolt; (*agitación*) commotion

revuelva *etc* [re'βwelβa] VB *ver* **revolver**

revulsivo [reβul'siβo] NM: **servir de ~** to have a salutary effect

★**rey** [rei] NM king; **Día de Reyes** Epiphany; **los Reyes Magos** the Three Wise Men, the Magi; **los Reyes** the King and Queen; *ver tb* **baraja española**; *see note*

> The night before *Reyes* (Epiphany), which is celebrated on the 6th of January and is a holiday in Spain, children go to bed expecting **los Reyes Magos**, the Three Wise Men who visited the baby Jesus, to bring them presents. Twelfth night processions, known as *cabalgatas*, take place that evening, when three people dressed as *los Reyes Magos* arrive in the town by land or sea to the delight of the children.

reyerta [re'jerta] NF quarrel, brawl

rezagado, -a [reθa'γaðo, a] ADJ: **quedar ~** to be left behind; (*estar retrasado*) to be late, be behind ▶ NM/F straggler

rezagar [reθa'γar] /**1h**/ VT (*dejar atrás*) to leave behind; (*retrasar*) to delay, postpone ▪ **rezagarse** VR (*atrasarse*) to fall behind

rezague *etc* [re'βaγe] VB *ver* **rezagar**

★**rezar** [re'θar] /**1f**/ VI to pray; **~ con** (*fam*) to concern, have to do with

rezo ['reθo] NM prayer

rezongar [reθon'gar] /**1h**/ VI to grumble; (*murmurar*) to mutter; (*refunfuñar*) to growl

rezongue *etc* [re'θonge] VB *ver* **rezongar**

rezumar [reθu'mar] /**1a**/ VT to ooze ▶ VI to leak ▪ **rezumarse** VR to leak out

RFA NF ABR (*Historia*) = **República Federal Alemana**

RFEF NF ABR (= *Real Federación Española de Fútbol*) Spanish Football Federation

ría ['ria] NF estuary

riachuelo [rja'tʃwelo] NM stream

riada [ri'aða] NF flood

ribera [ri'βera] NF (*de río*) bank; (: *área*) riverside

ribete [ri'βete] NM (*de vestido*) border; (*fig*) addition

ribetear [riβete'ar] /**1a**/ VT to edge, border

rice *etc* ['riθe] VB *ver* **rizar**

ricino [ri'θino] NM: **aceite de ~** castor oil

★**rico, -a** ['riko, a] ADJ (*adinerado*) rich, wealthy; (*lujoso*) luxurious; (*comida*) delicious; (*niño*) lovely, cute ▶ NM/F rich person; **nuevo ~** nouveau riche

rictus ['riktus] NM (*mueca*) sneer, grin; **~ de amargura** bitter smile

ridiculez [riðiku'leθ] NF absurdity

ridiculice *etc* [riðiku'liθe] VB *ver* **ridiculizar**

ridiculizar [riðikuli'θar] /**1f**/ VT to ridicule

★**ridículo, -a** [ri'ðikulo, a] ADJ ridiculous; **hacer el ~** to make a fool of o.s.; **poner a algn en ~** to make a fool of sb; **ponerse en ~** to make a fool of o.s.

riego ['rjeγo] VB *ver* **regar** ▶ NM (*aspersión*) watering; (*irrigación*) irrigation; **~ sanguíneo** blood flow *o* circulation

riegue *etc* ['rjeγe] VB *ver* **regar**

riel [rjel] NM rail

rienda ['rjenda] NF rein; (*fig*) restraint, moderating influence; **dar ~ suelta a** to give free rein to; **llevar las riendas** to be in charge

riendo ['rjendo] VB *ver* **reír**

★**riesgo** ['rjesγo] NM risk; **seguro a** *o* **contra todo ~** comprehensive insurance; **~ para la salud** health hazard; **correr el ~ de** to run the risk of

Rif [rif] NM Rif(f)

rifa ['rifa] NF (*lotería*) raffle

rifar [ri'far] /**1a**/ VT to raffle

rifeño, -a [ri'feɲo, a] ADJ of the Rif(f), Rif(f)ian ▶ NM/F Rif(f)ian, Rif(f)

rifle ['rifle] NM rifle

rigidez [rixi'ðeθ] NF rigidity, stiffness; (*fig*) strictness

rígido, -a ['rixiðo, a] ADJ rigid, stiff; (*moralmente*) strict, inflexible; (*cara*) wooden, expressionless

rigiendo *etc* [ri'xjendo] VB *ver* **regir**

rigor [ri'γor] NM strictness, rigour; (*dureza*) toughness; (*inclemencia*) harshness; (*meticulosidad*) accuracy; **el ~ del verano** the hottest part of the summer; **con todo ~ científico** with scientific precision; **de ~** de rigueur, essential; **después de los saludos de ~** after the inevitable greetings

★**riguroso, -a** [riγu'roso, a] ADJ rigorous; (*Meteorología*) harsh; (*severo*) severe

rija *etc* ['rixa] VB *ver* **regir** ▶ NF quarrel

rima ['rima] NF rhyme; **~ imperfecta** assonance; **~ rimando** (*fam*) merrily ▪ **rimas** NFPL verse *sg*

rimar [ri'mar] /**1a**/ VI to rhyme

rimbombante [rimbom'bante] ADJ (*fig*) pompous

rímel, rimmel ['rimel] NM mascara

rimero [ri'mero] NM stack, pile

rímmel ['rimel] NM = **rímel**

Rin [rin] NM Rhine

rin [rin] NM (*Am*) (wheel) rim

★**rincón** [rin'kon] NM corner (*inside*)

rindiendo *etc* [rin'djendo] VB *ver* **rendir**

ring [rin] NM (*Boxeo*) ring

rinoceronte [rinoθe'ronte] NM rhinoceros

riña ['riɲa] NF (*disputa*) argument; (*pelea*) brawl

riñendo *etc* [ri'ɲendo] VB *ver* **reñir**

★**riñón** [ri'ɲon] NM kidney; **me costó un ~** (*fam*) it cost me an arm and a leg; **tener riñones** to have guts

rio [ri'o] VB *ver* **reír**

★**río** ['rio] VB *ver* **reír** ▸ NM river; (*fig*) torrent, stream; **~ abajo/arriba** downstream/upstream; **cuando el ~ suena, agua lleva** there's no smoke without fire

Río de Janeiro ['rioðexa'neiro] NM Rio de Janeiro

Río de la Plata ['rioðela'plata] NM Rio de la Plata, River Plate

rioja [ri'oxa] NM rioja wine ▸ NF: **La R~** La Rioja

riojano, -a [rjo'xano,a] ADJ, NM/F Riojan

rioplatense [riopla'tense] ADJ of *o* from the River Plate region ▸ NMF native *o* inhabitant of the River Plate region

★**riqueza** [ri'keθa] NF wealth, riches *pl*; (*cualidad*) richness

★**risa** ['risa] NF laughter; (*una risa*) laugh; **¡qué ~!** what a laugh!; **caerse *o* morirse de ~** to split one's sides laughing, die laughing; **tomar algo a ~** to laugh sth off

risco ['risko] NM crag, cliff

risible [ri'siβle] ADJ ludicrous, laughable

risotada [riso'taða] NF guffaw, loud laugh

ristra ['ristra] NF string

ristre ['ristre] NM: **en ~** at the ready

risueño, -a [ri'sweɲo,a] ADJ (*sonriente*) smiling; (*contento*) cheerful

★**ritmo** ['ritmo] NM rhythm; **a ~ lento** slowly; **trabajar a ~ lento** to go slow; **~ cardíaco** heart rate

rito ['rito] NM rite

ritual [ri'twal] ADJ, NM ritual

rival [ri'βal] ADJ, NMF rival

rivalice *etc* [riβa'liθe] VB *ver* **rivalizar**

rivalidad [riβali'ðað] NF rivalry, competition

rivalizar [riβali'θar] /1f/ VI: **~ con** to rival, vie with

★**rizado, -a** [ri'θaðo,a] ADJ (*pelo*) curly; (*superficie*) ridged; (*terreno*) undulating; (*mar*) choppy ▸ NM curls *pl*

rizar [ri'θar] /1f/ VT to curl ■ **rizarse** VR (*el pelo*) to curl; (*agua*) to ripple; (*el mar*) to become choppy

rizo ['riθo] NM curl; (*en agua*) ripple

Rma. ABR (= *Reverendísima*) *courtesy title*

Rmo. ABR (= *Reverendísimo*) Rt. Rev.

RNE NF ABR = **Radio Nacional de España**

R.O. ABR (= *Real Orden*) royal order

★**robar** [ro'βar] /1a/ VT to rob; (*objeto*) to steal; (*casa etc*) to break into; (*Naipes*) to draw; (*atención*) to steal, capture; (*paciencia*) to exhaust

roble ['roβle] NM oak

robledal [roβle'ðal], **robledo** [ro'βleðo] NM oakwood

★**robo** ['roβo] NM robbery, theft; (*objeto robado*) stolen article *o* goods *pl*; **¡esto es un ~!** this is daylight robbery!

robot [ro'βo(t)] (*pl* **robots**) ADJ, NM robot ▸ NM (*tb*: **robot de cocina**) food processor

robótica [ro'βotika] NF robotics *sg*

robustecer [roβuste'θer] /2d/ VT to strengthen

robustezca *etc* [roβus'teθka] VB *ver* **robustecer**

★**robusto, -a** [ro'βusto,a] ADJ robust, strong

★**roca** ['roka] NF rock; **la R~** the Rock (of Gibraltar)

★**roce** ['roθe] VB *ver* **rozar** ▸ NM rub, rubbing; (*caricia*) brush; (*Tec*) friction; (*en la piel*) graze; **tener ~ con** to have a brush with

rociar [ro'θjar] /1c/ VT to sprinkle, spray

rocín [ro'θin] NM nag, hack

rocío [ro'θio] NM dew

rock [rok] ADJ INV, NM (*Mus*) rock *cpd*

rockero, -a [ro'kero,a] ADJ rock *cpd* ▸ NM/F rocker

rocódromo [ro'koðromo] NM climbing centre, climbing wall

rocola [ro'kola] NF (*Am*) jukebox

rocoso, -a [ro'koso,a] ADJ rocky

rodaballo [roða'baʎo] NM turbot

rodado, -a [ro'ðaðo,a] ADJ (*con ruedas*) wheeled ▸ NF rut

rodaja [ro'ðaxa] NF (*raja*) slice

rodaje [ro'ðaxe] NM (*Cine*) shooting, filming; (*Auto*): **en ~** running in

rodamiento [roða'mjento] NM (*Auto*) tread

Ródano ['roðano] NM Rhône

rodar [ro'ðar] /1l/ VT (*vehículo*) to wheel (along); (*escalera*) to roll down; (*viajar por*) to travel (over) ▸ VI to roll; (*coche*) to go, run; (*Cine*) to shoot, film; (*persona*) to move about (from place to place), drift; **echarlo todo a ~** (*fig*) to mess it all up

Rodas ['roðas] NF Rhodes

★**rodear** [roðe'ar] /1a/ VT to surround ▸ VI to go round ■ **rodearse** VR: **rodearse de amigos** to surround o.s. with friends

rodeo [ro'ðeo] NM (*ruta indirecta*) long way round, roundabout way; (*desvío*) detour; (*evasión*) evasion; (*Am*) rodeo; **dejarse de rodeos** to talk straight; **hablar sin rodeos** to come to the point, speak plainly

★**rodilla** [ro'ðiʎa] NF knee; **de rodillas** kneeling; **ponerse de rodillas** to kneel (down)

rodillo [ro'ðiʎo] NM roller; (*Culin*) rolling-pin; (*en máquina de escribir, impresora*) platen

rododendro [roðo'ðendro] NM rhododendron

roedor, a [roe'ðor, a] ADJ gnawing ▶ NM rodent

roer [ro'er] /2y/ VT (*masticar*) to gnaw; (*corroer, fig*) to corrode

★**rogar** [ro'ɣar] /1h, 1l/ VT (*pedir*) to beg, ask for; **~ que** (+*subjun*) to ask to ...; **ruegue a este señor que nos deje en paz** please ask this gentleman to leave us alone ▶ VI (*suplicar*) to beg, plead; **no se hace de ~** he doesn't have to be asked twice ▪ **rogarse** VR: **se ruega no fumar** please do not smoke

rogué [ro'ɣe], **roguemos** *etc* [ro'ɣemos] VB *ver* **rogar**

rojizo, -a [ro'xiθo, a] ADJ reddish

★**rojo, -a** ['roxo, a] ADJ red; **ponerse ~** to turn red, blush ▶ NM red (colour); (*Pol*) red; **al ~ vivo** red-hot

rol [rol] NM list, roll; (*esp Am: papel*) role

rollito [ro'ʎito] NM (*tb:* **rollito de primavera**) spring roll

rollizo, -a [ro'ʎiθo, a] ADJ (*objeto*) cylindrical; (*persona*) plump

rollo, -a ['roʎo, a] ADJ (*fam*) boring, tedious ▶ NM roll; (*de cuerda*) coil; (*de madera*) log; (*fam*) bore; (*discurso*) boring speech; **¡qué ~!** what a carry-on!; **la conferencia fue un ~** the lecture was a big drag

ROM [rom] NF ABR (= *memoria de solo lectura*) ROM

Roma ['roma] NF Rome; **por todas partes se va a ~** all roads lead to Rome

romance [ro'manθe] NM (*amoroso*) romance; (*Ling*) Romance language; (*Lit*) ballad; **hablar en ~** to speak plainly

románico, -a [ro'maniko, a] ADJ, NM Romanesque

romano, -a [ro'mano, a] ADJ Roman, of Rome ▶ NM/F Roman; **a la romana** in batter

romanticismo [romanti'θismo] NM romanticism

★**romántico, -a** [ro'mantiko, a] ADJ romantic

rombo ['rombo] NM (*Mat*) rhombus; (*diseño*) diamond; (*Tip*) lozenge

romería [rome'ria] NF (*Rel*) pilgrimage; (*excursión*) trip, outing

Originally a pilgrimage to a shrine or church to express devotion to Our Lady or a local Saint, the **romería** has also become a rural *fiesta* which accompanies the pilgrimage. People come from all over to attend, bringing their own food and drink, and spend the day in celebration.

romero, -a [ro'mero, a] NM/F pilgrim ▶ NM (*Bot*) rosemary

romo, -a ['romo, a] ADJ blunt; (*fig*) dull

rompecabezas [rompeka'βeθas] NM INV riddle, puzzle; (*juego*) jigsaw (puzzle)

rompehielos [rompe'jelos] NM INV icebreaker

rompehuelgas [rompe'welɣas] NM INV (*Am*) strikebreaker, scab

rompeolas [rompe'olas] NM INV breakwater

★**romper** [rom'per] /2a/ VT to break; (*hacer pedazos*) to smash; (*papel, tela etc*) to tear, rip; (*relaciones*) to break off; **~ un contrato** to break a contract ▶ VI (*olas*) to break; (*sol, diente*) to break through; **~ a** to start (suddenly) to; **~ a llorar** to burst into tears; **~ con algn** to fall out with sb; **ha roto con su novio** she has broken up with her fiancé

rompimiento [rompi'mjento] NM (*acto*) breaking; (*fig*) break; (*quiebra*) crack; **~ de relaciones** breaking off of relations

ron [ron] NM rum

★**roncar** [ron'kar] /1g/ VI (*al dormir*) to snore; (*animal*) to roar

roncha ['rontʃa] NF (*cardenal*) bruise; (*hinchazón*) swelling

★**ronco, -a** ['ronko, a] ADJ (*afónico*) hoarse; (*áspero*) raucous

★**ronda** ['ronda] NF (*de bebidas etc*) round; (*patrulla*) patrol; (*de naipes*) hand, game; **ir de ~** to do one's rounds

rondar [ron'dar] /1a/ VT to patrol; (*a una persona*) to hang round; (*molestar*) to harass; (*a una chica*) to court ▶ VI to patrol; (*fig*) to prowl round; (*Mus*) to go serenading

rondeño, -a [ron'deɲo, a] ADJ of o from Ronda ▶ NM/F native o inhabitant of Ronda

ronque *etc* [ronke] VB *ver* **roncar**

ronquido [ron'kiðo] NM snore, snoring

ronronear [ronrone'ar] /1a/ VI to purr

ronroneo [ronro'neo] NM purr

roña ['roɲa] NF (*en veterinaria*) mange; (*mugre*) dirt, grime; (*óxido*) rust

roñica [ro'ɲika] NMF (*fam*) skinflint

roñoso, -a [ro'ɲoso, a] ADJ (*mugriento*) filthy; (*tacaño*) mean

★**ropa** ['ropa] NF clothes *pl*, clothing; **~ blanca** linen; **~ de cama** bed linen; **~ de color** coloureds *pl*; **~ interior** underwear; **~ lavada** o **para lavar** washing; **~ planchada** ironing; **~ sucia** dirty clothes *pl*, dirty washing; **~ usada** secondhand clothes

ropaje [ro'paxe] NM gown, robes *pl*

ropero [ro'pero] NM linen cupboard; (*guardarropa*) wardrobe

★**rosa** ['rosa] ADJ INV pink ▶ NF rose; (*Anat*) red birthmark; **~ de los vientos** the compass; **estar como una ~** to feel as fresh as a daisy; **(color) de ~** pink

★**rosado, -a** [ro'saðo, a] ADJ pink ▶ NM rosé

rosal [ro'sal] NM rosebush

rosaleda [rosa'leða] NF rose bed o garden

rosario [ro'sarjo] NM (*Rel*) rosary; (*fig: serie*) string; **rezar el ~** to say the rosary

rosbif [ros'βif] NM roast beef

rosca ['roska] NF (*de tornillo*) thread; (*de humo*) coil, spiral; (*pan, postre*) ring-shaped roll/pastry; **hacerla ~ a algn** (*fam*) to suck up to sb; **pasarse de ~** (*fig*) to go too far

Rosellón [rose'ʎon] NM Roussillon

rosetón [rose'ton] NM rosette; (*Arq*) rose window

rosquilla [ros'kiʎa] NF *ring-shaped cake*; (*de humo*) ring

rosticería [rostise'ria] NF (*Am*) rotisserie

★**rostro** ['rostro] NM (*cara*) face; (*fig*) cheek

rotación [rota'θjon] NF rotation; **~ de cultivos** crop rotation

rotativo, -a [rota'tiβo, a] ADJ rotary ▶ NM newspaper

★**roto, -a** ['roto, a] PP *de* **romper** ▶ ADJ broken; (*en pedazos*) smashed; (*tela, papel*) torn; (*vida*) shattered ▶ NM (*en vestido*) hole, tear

rotonda [ro'tonda] NF roundabout

rótula ['rotula] NF kneecap; (*Tec*) ball-and-socket joint

★**rotulador** [rotula'ðor] NM felt-tip pen

rotular [rotu'lar] /**1a**/ VT (*carta, documento*) to head, entitle; (*objeto*) to label

rótulo ['rotulo] NM (*título*) heading, title; (*etiqueta*) label; (*letrero*) sign

rotundamente [rotunda'mente] ADV (*negar*) flatly; (*responder, afirmar*) emphatically

rotundo, -a [ro'tundo, a] ADJ round; (*enfático*) emphatic

rotura [ro'tura] NF (*rompimiento*) breaking; (*Med*) fracture

roturar [rotu'rar] /**1a**/ VT to plough

roulotte [ru'lote] NF caravan (*Brit*), trailer (*US*)

rozado, -a [ro'θaðo, a] ADJ worn

rozadura [roθa'ðura] NF abrasion, graze

rozar [ro'θar] /**1f**/ VT (*frotar*) to rub; (*arañar*) to scratch; (*ensuciar*) to dirty; (*Med*) to graze; (*tocar ligeramente*) to shave, skim; (*fig*) to touch o border on ▶ VI: **~ con** (*fam*) to rub shoulders with ■ **rozarse** VR to rub (together)

Rte. ABR = **remite; remitente**

RTVE NF ABR (*TV*) = **Radiotelevisión Española**

Ruán [ru'an] NM Rouen

Ruanda [ru'anda] NF Rwanda

rubéola [ru'βeola] NF German measles, rubella

rubí [ru'βi] NM ruby; (*de reloj*) jewel

★**rubio, -a** ['ruβjo, a] ADJ fair-haired, blond(e); **tabaco ~** Virginia tobacco; **(cerveza) rubia** lager ▶ NM/F blond/blonde

rubor [ru'βor] NM (*sonrojo*) blush; (*timidez*) bashfulness

ruborice *etc* [ruβo'riθe] VB *ver* **ruborizarse**

ruborizarse [ruβori'θarse] /**1f**/ VR to blush

ruboroso, -a [ruβo'roso, a] ADJ blushing

rúbrica ['ruβrika] NF (*título*) title, heading; (*de la firma*) flourish; **bajo la ~ de** under the heading of

rubricar [ruβri'kar] /**1g**/ VT (*firmar*) to sign with a flourish; (*concluir*) to sign and seal

rubrique *etc* [ru'βrike] VB *ver* **rubricar**

rudeza [ru'ðeθa] NF (*tosquedad*) coarseness; (*sencillez*) simplicity

rudimentario, -a [ruðimen'tarjo, a] ADJ rudimentary, basic

rudo, -a ['ruðo, a] ADJ (*sin pulir*) unpolished; (*grosero*) coarse; (*violento*) violent; (*sencillo*) simple

★**rueda** ['rweða] NF wheel; (*círculo*) ring, circle; (*rodaja*) slice, round; (*en impresora etc*) sprocket; **~ de auxilio** (*Am*) spare tyre; **~ delantera/trasera/de repuesto** front/back/spare wheel; **~ impresora** (*Inform*) print wheel; **~ de prensa** press conference; **~ gigante** (*Am*) big (*Brit*) o Ferris (*US*) wheel

ruedo ['rweðo] VB *ver* **rodar** ▶ NM (*contorno*) edge, border; (*de vestido*) hem; (*círculo*) circle; (*Taur*) arena, bullring; (*esterilla*) (round) mat

ruego *etc* ['rweɣo] VB *ver* **rogar** ▶ NM request; **a ~ de** at the request of; **"ruegos y preguntas"** "question and answer session"

ruegue *etc* ['rweɣe] VB *ver* **rogar**

rufián [ru'fjan] NM scoundrel

rugby ['ruɣβi] NM rugby

rugido [ru'xiðo] NM roar

rugir [ru'xir] /**3c**/ VI to roar; (*toro*) to bellow; (*estómago*) to rumble

rugoso, -a [ru'ɣoso, a] ADJ (*arrugado*) wrinkled; (*áspero*) rough; (*desigual*) ridged

ruibarbo [rwi'βarβo] NM rhubarb

★**ruido** ['rwiðo] NM noise; (*sonido*) sound; (*alboroto*) racket, row; (*escándalo*) commotion, rumpus; **~ de fondo** background noise; **hacer** o **meter ~** to cause a stir

★**ruidoso, -a** [rwi'ðoso, a] ADJ noisy, loud; (*fig*) sensational

ruin [rwin] ADJ contemptible, mean

ruina ['rwina] NF ruin; (*hundimiento*) collapse; (*de persona*) ruin, downfall; **estar hecho una ~** to be a wreck; **la empresa lo llevó a la ~** the venture ruined him (financially)

ruindad [rwin'dað] NF lowness, meanness; (*acto*) low o mean act

ruinoso, -a [rwi'noso, a] ADJ ruinous; (*destartalado*) dilapidated, tumbledown; (*Com*) disastrous

ruiseñor [rwise'ɲor] NM nightingale

ruja *etc* ['ruxa] VB *ver* **rugir**

rulero [ru'lero] NM (*Am*) roller

ruleta [ru'leta] NF roulette

rulo ['rulo] NM (*para el pelo*) curler

rulot [ru'lot], **rulote** [ru'lote] NF caravan (*Brit*), trailer (*US*)

Rumania [ru'manja] NF Rumania

rumano, -a [ru'mano, a] ADJ, NM/F Rumanian

rumba ['rumba] NF rumba

rumbo ['rumbo] NM (*ruta*) route, direction; (*ángulo de dirección*) course, bearing; (*fig*) course of events; **con ~ a** in the direction of; **ir con ~ a** to be heading for; (*Naut*) to be bound for

rumboso, -a [rum'boso, a] ADJ (*generoso*) generous

rumiante [ru'mjante] NM ruminant

rumiar [ruˈmjar] /**1b**/ VT to chew; (*fig*) to chew over ▸ VI to chew the cud

rumor [ruˈmor] NM (*ruido sordo*) low sound; (*murmuración*) murmur, buzz

rumorearse [rumoreˈarse] /**1a**/ VR: **se rumorea que** it is rumoured that

rumoroso, -a [rumoˈroso, a] ADJ full of sounds; (*arroyo*) murmuring

runrún [runˈrun] NM (*de voces*) murmur, sound of voices; (*fig*) rumour; (*de una máquina*) whirr

rupestre [ruˈpestre] ADJ rock *cpd*; **pintura ~** cave painting

ruptura [rupˈtura] NF (*gen*) rupture; (*disputa*) split; (*de contrato*) breach; (*de relaciones*) breaking-off

rural [ruˈral] ADJ rural

★**Rusia** [ˈrusja] NF Russia

★**ruso, -a** [ˈruso, a] ADJ, NM/F Russian ▸ NM (*Ling*) Russian

rústico, -a [ˈrustiko, a] ADJ rustic; (*ordinario*) coarse, uncouth ▸ NM/F yokel ▸ NF: **libro en rústica** paperback (book)

★**ruta** [ˈruta] NF route

rutina [ruˈtina] NF routine; **~ diaria** daily routine; **por ~** as a matter of course

rutinario, -a [rutiˈnarjo, a] ADJ routine

Ss

S, s ['ese] NF (*letra*) S, s; **S de Santander** S for Sugar

S ABR (= *san; santo, a*) St.; (= *sur*) S

s. ABR (= *siglo*) C.; (= *siguiente*) foll.

S/ ABR (*Com*) = **su; sus**

S.ª ABR (= *Sierra*) Mts

S.A. ABR (= *Sociedad Anónima*) Ltd., Inc. (*US*); (= *Su Alteza*) H.H.

sáb. ABR (= *sábado*) Sat.

★**sábado** ['saβaðo] NM Saturday; (*de los judíos*) Sabbath; **del ~ en ocho días** a week on Saturday; **un ~ sí y otro no, cada dos sábados** every other Saturday; **S~ Santo** Easter Saturday; *ver tb* **Semana Santa**

sabana [sa'βana] NF savannah

★**sábana** ['saβana] NF sheet; **se le pegan las sábanas** he can't get up in the morning

sabandija [saβan'dixa] NF (*bicho*) bug; (*fig*) louse

sabañón [saβa'ɲon] NM chilblain

sabático, -a [sa'βatiko, a] ADJ (*Rel, Univ*) sabbatical

sabelotodo [saβelo'toðo] NMF know-all

★**saber** [sa'βer] /2m/ VT to know; (*llegar a conocer*) to find out, learn; (*tener capacidad de*) to know how to; **¿sabes conducir/nadar?** can you drive/swim?; **¿sabes francés?** do you *o* can you speak French?; **~ de memoria** to know by heart; **lo sé** I know; **hacer ~** to inform, let know; **que yo sepa** as far as I know ▶ VI: **~ a** to taste of, taste like; **a ~** namely; **vete** *o* **anda a ~** your guess is as good as mine, who knows!; **¿sabe?** (*fam*) you know (what I mean)?; **me supo muy mal lo que hicieron** I didn't like what they did ▶ NM knowledge, learning ■**saberse** VR: **se sabe que ...** it is known that ...; **no se sabe** nobody knows

En general, cuando *saber* va seguido de un infinitivo, se traduce por **can** cuando indica una habilidad permanente y por **know how** cuando se trata de la capacidad de resolver un problema concreto. La construcción correspondiente será el verbo **can** seguido por un infinitivo sin **to**, o el verbo **know how** seguido por un infinitivo con **to**:
Jaime sabe tocar el piano. **Jaime can play the piano**.
¿Sabes cambiar una rueda? **Do you know how to change a wheel?**

sabido, -a [sa'βiðo, a] ADJ well-known; **como es ~** as we all know

sabiduría [saβiðu'ria] NF (*conocimientos*) wisdom; (*instrucción*) learning; **~ popular** folklore

sabiendas [sa'βjendas]: **a ~** *adv* knowingly; **a ~ de que ...** knowing full well that ...

sabihondo, -a [sa'βjondo, a] ADJ, NM/F know-all, know-it-all (*US*)

★**sabio, -a** ['saβjo, a] ADJ (*docto*) learned; (*prudente*) wise, sensible

sablazo [sa'βlaθo] NM (*herida*) sword wound; (*fam*) sponging; **dar un ~ a algn** to tap sb for money

sable [sa'βle] NM sabre

★**sabor** [sa'βor] NM taste, flavour; (*fig*) flavour; **sin ~** flavourless

saborear [saβore'ar] /1a/ VT to taste, savour; (*fig*) to relish

sabotaje [saβo'taxe] NM sabotage

saboteador, a [saβotea'ðor, a] NM/F saboteur

sabotear [saβote'ar] /1a/ VT to sabotage

Saboya [sa'βoja] NF Savoy

sabré *etc* [sa'βre] VB *ver* **saber**

★**sabroso, -a** [sa'βroso, a] ADJ tasty; (*fig: fam*) racy, salty

saca ['saka] NF big sack; **~ de correo(s)** mailbag; (*Com*) withdrawal

sacacorchos [saka'kortʃos] NM INV corkscrew

★**sacapuntas** [saka'puntas] NM INV pencil sharpener

S

★**sacar** [sa'kar] /**1g**/ VT to take out; (*fig: extraer*) to get (out); (*quitar*) to remove, get out; (*hacer salir*) to bring out; (*fondos: de cuenta*) to draw out, withdraw; (*obtener: legado etc*) to get; (*demostrar*) to show; (*conclusión*) to draw; (*novela etc*) to publish, bring out; (*ropa*) to take off; (*obra*) to make; (*premio*) to receive; (*entradas*) to get; (*Tenis*) to serve; (*Fútbol*) to put into play; ~ **adelante** (*niño*) to bring up; (*negocio*) to carry on, go on with; ~ **a algn a bailar** to get sb up to dance; ~ **a algn de sí** to infuriate sb; ~ **una foto** to take a photo; ~ **la lengua** to stick out one's tongue; ~ **buenas/malas notas** to get good/bad marks

sacarina [saka'rina] NF saccharin(e)

★**sacerdote** [saθer'ðote] NM priest

saciar [sa'θjar] /**1b**/ VT (*hartar*) to satiate; (*fig*) to satisfy ◼ **saciarse** VR (*de comida*) to get full up; (*fig*) to be satisfied

saciedad [saθje'ðað] NF satiety; **hasta la ~** (*comer*) one's fill; (*repetir*) ad nauseam

★**saco** ['sako] NM bag; (*grande*) sack; (*contenido*) bagful; (*AM: chaqueta*) jacket; ~ **de dormir** sleeping bag

sacramento [sakra'mento] NM sacrament

sacrificar [sakrifi'kar] /**1g**/ VT to sacrifice; (*animal*) to slaughter; (*perro etc*) to put to sleep ◼ **sacrificarse** VR to sacrifice o.s.

sacrificio [sakri'fiθjo] NM sacrifice

sacrifique *etc* [sakri'fike] VB *ver* **sacrificar**

sacrilegio [sakri'lexjo] NM sacrilege

sacrílego, -a [sa'krileɣo, a] ADJ sacrilegious

sacristán [sakris'tan] NM verger

sacristía [sakris'tia] NF sacristy

sacro, -a ['sakro, a] ADJ sacred

sacudida [saku'ðiða] NF (*agitación*) shake, shaking; (*sacudimiento*) jolt, bump; (*fig*) violent change; (*Pol etc*) upheaval; ~ **eléctrica** electric shock

★**sacudir** [saku'ðir] /**3a**/ VT to shake; (*golpear*) to hit; (*ala*) to flap; (*alfombra*) to beat; ~ **a algn** (*fam*) to belt sb

sádico, -a ['saðiko, a] ADJ sadistic ► NM/F sadist

sadismo [sa'ðismo] NM sadism

sadomasoquismo [saðomaso'kismo] NM sadomasochism, S & M

sadomasoquista [saðomaso'kista] ADJ sadomasochistic ► NMF sadomasochist

saeta [sa'eta] NF (*flecha*) arrow; (*Mus*) *sacred song in flamenco style*

safari [sa'fari] NM safari

sagacidad [saɣaθi'ðað] NF shrewdness, cleverness

sagaz [sa'ɣaθ] ADJ shrewd, clever

Sagitario [saxi'tarjo] NM (*Astro*) Sagittarius

sagrado, -a [sa'ɣraðo, a] ADJ sacred, holy

Sáhara ['saara] NM: **el ~** the Sahara (desert)

saharaui [saxa'rawi] ADJ Saharan ► NMF native o inhabitant of the Sahara

sajón, -ona [sa'xon, 'xona] ADJ, NM/F Saxon

Sajonia [sa'xonja] NF Saxony

★**sal** [sal] VB *ver* **salir** ► NF salt; (*gracia*) wit; (*encanto*) charm; ~ **gorda** o **de cocina** kitchen o cooking salt; **sales de baño** bath salts

★**sala** ['sala] NF (*cuarto grande*) large room; (*tb*: **sala de estar**) living room; (*Teat*) house, auditorium; (*de hospital*) ward; ~ **de apelación** court; ~ **de conferencias** lecture hall; ~ **de espera** waiting room; ~ **de embarque** departure lounge; ~ **de estar** living room; ~ **de juntas** (*Com*) boardroom; ~ **VIP** (*en aeropuerto, discoteca*) VIP lounge

★**salado, -a** [sa'laðo, a] ADJ salty; (*fig*) witty, amusing; **agua salada** salt water

salar [sa'lar] /**1a**/ VT to salt, add salt to

salariado, -a [sala'rjaðo, a] ADJ (*empleado*) salaried

salarial [sala'rjal] ADJ (*aumento, revisión*) wage cpd, salary cpd, pay cpd

★**salario** [sa'larjo] NM wage, pay

★**salchicha** [sal'tʃitʃa] NF (pork) sausage

★**salchichón** [saltʃi'tʃon] NM (salami-type) sausage

saldar [sal'dar] /**1a**/ VT to pay; (*vender*) to sell off; (*fig*) to settle, resolve

saldo ['saldo] NM (*pago*) settlement; (*de una cuenta*) balance; (*lo restante*) remnant(s) (*pl*), remainder; (*de móvil*) credit; (*Com*) ~ **anterior** balance brought forward; ~ **acreedor/deudor** o **pasivo** credit/debit balance; ~ **final** final balance ◼ **saldos** NMPL (*en tienda*) sale

saldré *etc* [sal'dre] VB *ver* **salir**

salero [sa'lero] NM salt cellar; (*ingenio*) wit; (*encanto*) charm

salgo *etc* ['salɣo] VB *ver* **salir**

★**salida** [sa'liða] NF (*puerta etc*) exit, way out; (*acto*) leaving, going out; (*de tren, Aviat*) departure; (*Com, Tec*) output, production; (*fig*) way out; (*resultado*) outcome; (*Com: oportunidad*) opening; (*Geo, válvula*) outlet; (*de gas*) leak; (*ocurrencia*) joke; **calle sin ~** cul-de-sac; ~ **de baño** (*AM*) bathrobe; **a la ~ del teatro** after the theatre; **dar la ~** (*Deporte*) to give the starting signal; ~ **de incendios** fire escape; ~ **impresa** (*Inform*) hard copy; **no hay ~** there's no way out of it; **no tenemos otra ~** we have no option; **tener salidas** to be witty

salido, -a [sa'liðo, a] ADJ (*fam*) randy

saliente [sa'ljente] ADJ (*Arq*) projecting; (*sol*) rising; (*fig*) outstanding

salina [sa'lina] NF salt mine ◼ **salinas** NFPL saltworks *sg*

---

salir [sa'lir]

/**3q**/ VI **1** (*persona*) to come o go out; (*tren, avión*) to leave; **Juan ha salido** Juan has gone out; **salió de la cocina** he came out of the kitchen; **salimos de Madrid a las ocho** we left Madrid at eight (o'clock); **salió corriendo (del**

cuarto) he ran out (of the room); **salir de un apuro** to get out of a jam

2 (*pelo*) to grow; (*diente*) to come through; (*disco, libro*) to come out; (*planta, número de lotería*) to come up; **salir a la superficie** to come to the surface; **anoche salió en la tele** she appeared *o* was on TV last night; **salió en todos los periódicos** it was in all the papers; **le salió un trabajo** he got a job

3 (*resultar*): **la muchacha nos salió muy trabajadora** the girl turned out to be a very hard worker; **la comida te ha salido exquisita** the food was delicious; **sale muy caro** it's very expensive; **la entrevista que hice me salió bien/mal** the interview I did turned out *o* went well/badly; **nos salió a 50 euros cada uno** it worked out at 50 euros each; **no salen las cuentas** it doesn't work out *o* add up; **salir ganando** to come out on top; **salir perdiendo** to lose out

4 (*Deporte*) to start; (*Naipes*) to lead

5: **salir con algn** to go out with sb

6: **salir adelante: no sé como haré para salir adelante** I don't know how I'll get by

■ **salirse** VR **1** (*líquido*) to spill; (*animal*) to escape

2 (*desviarse*): **salirse de la carretera** to leave *o* go off the road; **salirse de lo normal** to be unusual; **salirse del tema** to get off the point

3: **salirse con la suya** to get one's own way

saliva [sa'liβa] NF saliva

salivadera [saliβa'ðera] NF (*AM*) spittoon

salmantino, -a [salman'tino, a] ADJ of *o* from Salamanca ▶ NM/F native *o* inhabitant of Salamanca

salmo ['salmo] NM psalm

★**salmón** [sal'mon] NM salmon

salmonete [salmo'nete] NM red mullet

salmuera [sal'mwera] NF pickle, brine

★**salón** [sa'lon] NM (*de casa*) living-room, lounge; (*muebles*) lounge suite; **~ de belleza** beauty parlour; **~ de baile** dance hall; **~ de actos/sesiones** assembly hall

salpicadera [salpika'ðera] NF (*AM*) mudguard (*BRIT*), fender (*US*)

salpicadero [salpika'ðero] NM (*Auto*) dashboard

salpicar [salpi'kar] /1g/ VT (*de barro, pintura*) to splash; (*rociar*) to sprinkle, spatter; (*esparcir*) to scatter

salpicón [salpi'kon] NM (*acto*) splashing; (*Culin*) meat *o* fish salad; (*tb*: **salpicón de marisco**) seafood salad

salpimentar [salpimen'tar] /1a/ VT (*Culin*) to season

salpique *etc* [sal'pike] VB *ver* **salpicar**

★**salsa** ['salsa] NF sauce; (*con carne asada*) gravy; (*fig*) spice; **~ mayonesa** mayonnaise; **estar en su ~** (*fam*) to be in one's element

saltamontes [salta'montes] NM INV grasshopper

★**saltar** [sal'tar] /1a/ VT to jump (over), leap (over); (*dejar de lado*) to skip, miss out ▶ VI to jump, leap; (*pelota*) to bounce; (*al aire*) to fly up; (*quebrarse*) to break; (*al agua*) to dive; (*fig*) to explode, blow up; (*botón*) to come off; (*corcho*) to pop out; **salta a la vista** it's obvious ■ **saltarse** VR (*omitir*) to skip, miss; **saltarse todas las reglas** to break all the rules

salteado, -a [salte'aðo, a] ADJ (*Culin*) sauté(ed)

salteador [saltea'ðor] NM (*tb*: **salteador de caminos**) highwayman

saltear [salte'ar] /1a/ VT (*robar*) to rob (in a holdup); (*asaltar*) to assault, attack; (*Culin*) to sauté

saltimbanqui [saltim'banki] NMF acrobat

salto ['salto] NM jump, leap; (*al agua*) dive; **a saltos** by jumping; **~ de agua** waterfall; **~ de altura** high jump; **~ de cama** negligee; **~ mortal** somersault; (*Inform*) **~ de línea** line feed; **~ de línea automático** wordwrap; **~ de página** formfeed

saltón, -ona [sal'ton, ona] ADJ (*ojos*) bulging, popping; (*dientes*) protruding

salubre [sa'luβre] ADJ healthy, salubrious

★**salud** [sa'luð] NF health; **estar bien/mal de ~** to be in good/poor health; **¡(a su) ~!** cheers!, good health!; **beber a la ~** to drink (to) the health of

★**saludable** [salu'ðaβle] ADJ (*de buena salud*) healthy; (*provechoso*) good, beneficial

★**saludar** [salu'ðar] /1a/ VT to greet; (*Mil*) to salute; **ir a ~ algn** to drop in to see sb; **salude de mi parte a X** give my regards to X; **le saluda atentamente** (*en carta*) yours faithfully

★**saludo** [sa'luðo] NM greeting; **saludos** (*en carta*) best wishes, regards; **un ~ afectuoso** *o* **cordial** yours sincerely

salva ['salβa] NF (*Mil*) salvo; **una ~ de aplausos** thunderous applause

salvación [salβa'θjon] NF salvation; (*rescate*) rescue

salvado [sal'βaðo] NM bran

salvador [salβa'ðor] NM rescuer, saviour; **el S~** (*Rel*) the Saviour; **El S~** (*Geo*) El Salvador; **San S~** (*Geo*) San Salvador

salvadoreño, -a [salβaðo'reɲo, a] ADJ, NM/F Salvadoran, Salvadorian

salvaeslip [salβaes'lip] (*pl* **salvaeslips**) [ru'anða] NM panty liner

salvaguardar [salβaɣwar'ðar] /1a/ VT to safeguard; (*Inform*) to back up, make a backup copy of

salvajada [salβa'xaða] NF savage deed, atrocity

★**salvaje** [sal'βaxe] ADJ wild; (*tribu*) savage

salvajismo [salβa'xismo] NM savagery

salvamanteles [salβaman'teles] NM INV table mat

salvamento [salβa'mento] NM (*acción*) rescue; (*de naufragio*) salvage; **~ y socorrismo** life-saving

salvapantallas [salβapan'taʎas] NM INV screensaver

★**salvar** [sal'βar] /1a/ VT (*rescatar*) to save, rescue; (*resolver*) to overcome, resolve; (*cubrir distancias*) to cover, travel; (*hacer excepción*) to except, exclude; (*un barco*) to salvage ■ **salvarse** VR to save o.s., escape; **¡sálvese el que pueda!** every man for himself!

★**salvavidas** [salβa'βiðas] ADJ INV: **bote/chaleco/cinturón ~** lifeboat/lifejacket/lifebelt

salvedad [salβe'ðað] NF reservation, qualification; **con la ~ de que ...** with the proviso that ...

salvia ['salβja] NF sage

★**salvo, -a** ['salβo, a] ADJ safe; **a ~** out of danger ▶ PREP except (for), save; **~ error u omisión** (*Com*) errors and omissions excepted ▶ CONJ: **~ que** unless

salvoconducto [salβokon'dukto] NM safe-conduct

samba ['samba] NF samba

Samoa [sa'moa] NF Samoa

san [san] N (*apócope de* **santo**) saint; **S~ Juan** St. John

San Juan is a celebration that takes place on June 24th, around the time of the summer solstice, and has its roots in ancient pagan festivals. In many areas, especially in coastal regions, people traditionally light huge bonfires on the night of the 23rd, known as *la Noche de San Juan* (the eve of *San Juan*). These *San Juan* bonfires, made of piled-up furniture and other wood with an effigy at the top, are often accompanied by fireworks, music, and dancing, with many people enjoying this summer's evening until the flames go out in the early morning.

sanar [sa'nar] /1a/ VT (*herida*) to heal; (*persona*) to cure ▶ VI (*persona*) to get well, recover; (*herida*) to heal

sanatorio [sana'torjo] NM sanatorium

sanción [san'θjon] NF sanction

sancionar [sanθjo'nar] /1a/ VT to sanction

sancochado, -a [sanko'tʃaðo, a] ADJ (*Am Culin*) underdone, rare

sancocho [san'kotʃo] NM (*Am Culin*) stew

San Cristóbal y Nieves NM St Kitts and Nevis

★**sandalia** [san'dalja] NF sandal

sándalo ['sandalo] NM sandal(wood)

sandez [san'deθ] NF (*cualidad*) foolishness; (*acción*) stupid thing; **decir sandeces** to talk nonsense

★**sandía** [san'dia] NF watermelon

sandinista [sandi'nista] ADJ, NMF Sandinist(a)

sándwich ['sandwitʃ] (*pl* **sándwichs** *o* **sandwiches**) NM sandwich

saneamiento [sanea'mjento] NM sanitation

sanear [sane'ar] /1a/ VT to drain; (*indemnizar*) to compensate; (*Econ*) to reorganize

Sanfermines [sanfer'mines] NMPL festivities in celebration of San Fermín

The **Sanfermines** are a week of *fiestas* in Pamplona, the capital of Navarre, made famous by Ernest Hemingway. From the 7th of July, the feast of San Fermín, crowds of mainly young people take to the streets drinking, singing and dancing. Early in the morning, bulls are released along the narrow streets leading to the bullring, and people risk serious injury by running out in front of them.

sangrar [san'grar] /1a/ VT, VI to bleed; (*texto*) to indent

★**sangre** ['sangre] NF blood; **~ fría** sangfroid; **a ~ fría** in cold blood

★**sangría** [san'gria] NF (*Med*) bleeding; (*Culin*) sangria (*sweetened drink of red wine with fruit*), ≈ fruit cup

sangriento, -a [san'grjento, a] ADJ bloody

sanguijuela [sangi'xwela] NF (*Zool, fig*) leech

sanguinario, -a [sangi'narjo, a] ADJ bloodthirsty

sanguíneo, -a [san'gineo, a] ADJ blood *cpd*

sanidad [sani'ðað] NF sanitation; (*calidad de sano*) health, healthiness; **~ pública** public health (department)

San Isidro [sani'sidro] NM *patron saint of Madrid*

San Isidro is the patron saint of Madrid, and gives his name to the week-long festivities which take place around the 15th May. Originally an 18th-century trade fair, the *San Isidro* celebrations now include music, dance, a famous *romería*, theatre and bullfighting.

sanitario, -a [sani'tarjo, a] ADJ sanitary; (*de la salud*) health *cpd* ■ **sanitarios** NMPL toilets (*BRIT*), restroom *sg* (*US*)

San Marino [sanma'rino] NM: **(La República de) ~** San Marino

★**sano, -a** ['sano, a] ADJ healthy; (*sin daños*) sound; (*comida*) wholesome; (*entero*) whole, intact; **~ y salvo** safe and sound

Santa Lucía ['santalu'θia] NF St Lucia

santanderino, -a [santande'rino, a] ADJ of *o* from Santander ▶ NM/F native *o* inhabitant of Santander

Santiago [san'tjaɣo] NM: **~ (de Chile)** Santiago

santiamén [santja'men] NM: **en un ~** in no time at all

santidad [santi'ðað] NF holiness, sanctity

santificar [santifi'kar] /1g/ VT to sanctify

santifique *etc* [santi'fike] VB *ver* **santificar**

santiguarse [santi'ɣwarse] /1i/ VR to make the sign of the cross

santigüe *etc* [san'tiɣwe] VB *ver* **santiguarse**

★**santo, -a** ['santo, a] ADJ holy; (*fig*) wonderful, miraculous; **hacer su santa voluntad** to do as one jolly well pleases ▶ NM/F saint ▶ NM saint's day; **¿a ~ de qué ...?** why on earth ...?; **se le fue el ~ al cielo** he forgot what he was about to say; **~ y seña** password; *see note*

People in Spanish-speaking countries traditionally celebrate **el santo** (their Saint's day), when the Saint they are named after, eg San Pedro or Santa Teresa, is honoured in the Christian calendar. For some people, their Saint's day is just as important or even more so than their birthday.

santuario [san'twarjo] NM sanctuary, shrine

San Vicente y las Granadinas [sanβi'θenteilasɣrana'ðinas] NM St Vincent and the Grenadines

saña ['saɲa] NF rage, fury

sapo ['sapo] NM toad

saque ['sake] VB ver **sacar** ▶ NM (*Tenis*) service, serve; (*Fútbol*) throw-in; **~ inicial** kick-off; **~ de esquina** corner (kick); **tener buen ~** to eat heartily

saquear [sake'ar] /1a/ VT (*Mil*) to sack; (*robar*) to loot, plunder; (*fig*) to ransack

saqueo [sa'keo] NM sacking; (*robbery*) looting, plundering; (*fig*) ransacking

S.A.R. ABR (= *Su Alteza Real*) HRH

★**sarampión** [saram'pjon] NM measles *sg*

sarape [sa'rape] NM (*Am*) blanket

sarcasmo [sar'kasmo] NM sarcasm

sarcástico, -a [sar'kastiko, a] ADJ sarcastic

sarcófago [sar'kofaɣo] NM sarcophagus

★**sardina** [sar'ðina] NF sardine

sardo, -a ['sarðo, a] ADJ, NM/F Sardinian

sardónico, -a [sar'ðoniko, a] ADJ sardonic; (*irónico*) ironical, sarcastic

sargento [sar'xento] NM sergeant

sarmiento [sar'mjento] NM vine shoot

sarna ['sarna] NF itch; (*Med*) scabies

sarpullido [sarpu'ʎiðo] NM (*Med*) rash

sarro ['sarro] NM deposit; (*en dientes*) tartar, plaque

sarta ['sarta] NF (*fig*): **una ~ de mentiras** a pack of lies

★**sartén** [sar'ten] NF frying pan; **tener la ~ por el mango** to rule the roost

sastre ['sastre] NM tailor

sastrería [sastre'ria] NF (*arte*) tailoring; (*tienda*) tailor's (shop)

Satanás [sata'nas] NM Satan

★**satélite** [sa'telite] NM satellite

satinado, -a [sati'naðo, a] ADJ glossy ▶ NM gloss, shine

sátira ['satira] NF satire

satírico, -a [sa'tiriko, a] ADJ satiric(al)

sátiro ['satiro] NM (*Mitología*) satyr; (*fig*) sex maniac

satisfacción [satisfak'θjon] NF satisfaction

satisfacer [satisfa'θer] /2r/ VT to satisfy; (*gastos*) to meet; (*deuda*) to pay; (*Com*: *letra de cambio*) to honour (BRIT), honor (US); (: *pérdida*) to make good ■ **satisfacerse** VR to satisfy o.s., be satisfied; (*vengarse*) to take revenge

satisfaga *etc* [satis'faɣa], **satisfaré** *etc* [satisfa're] VB ver **satisfacer**

★**satisfecho, -a** [satis'fetʃo, a] PP *de* **satisfacer** ▶ ADJ satisfied; (*contento*) content(ed), happy; (*tb*: **satisfecho de sí mismo**) self-satisfied, smug

satisfice *etc* [satis'fiθe] VB ver **satisfacer**

saturación [satura'θjon] NF saturation; **llegar a la ~** to reach saturation point

saturar [satu'rar] /1a/ VT to saturate; **¡estoy saturado de tanta televisión!** I can't take any more television! ■ **saturarse** VR (*mercado, aeropuerto*) to reach saturation point

sauce ['sauθe] NM willow; **~ llorón** weeping willow

saúco [sa'uko] NM (*Bot*) elder

saudí [sau'ði] ADJ, NMF Saudi

sauna ['sauna] NF sauna

savia ['saβja] NF sap

saxo ['sakso] NM sax

saxofón [sakso'fon] NM saxophone

saya ['saja] NF (*falda*) skirt; (*enagua*) petticoat

sayo ['sajo] NM smock

sazón [sa'θon] NF (*de fruta*) ripeness; **a la ~** then, at that time

sazonado, -a [saθo'naðo, a] ADJ (*fruta*) ripe; (*Culin*) flavoured, seasoned

sazonar [saθo'nar] /1a/ VT to ripen; (*Culin*) to flavour, season

s/c ABR (*Com*: = *su casa*) your firm; (= *su cuenta*) your account

scooter [e'skuter] NF (*Esp*) scooter

Scotch® [skotʃ] NM (*Am*) Sellotape® (BRIT), Scotch tape® (US)

SE ABR (= *sudeste*) SE

---

se [se]

PRON **1** (*reflexivo*: *sg*: *m*) himself; (: *f*) herself; (: *pl*) themselves; (: *cosa*) itself; (: *de usted*) yourself; (: *de ustedes*) yourselves; (: *indefinido*) oneself; **se mira en el espejo** he looks at himself in the mirror; **¡siéntese!** sit down!; **se durmió** he fell asleep; **se está preparando** she's getting (herself) ready (*para usos léxicos del pron ver el vb en cuestión, p. ej.* **arrepentirse**)

2 (*como complemento indirecto*: *sg*: *m*) to him; (: *f*) to her; (: *pl*) to them; (: *cosa*) to it; (: *a usted, pl*) to you; **se lo dije ayer** (*a usted*) I told you yesterday; **se compró un sombrero** he bought himself a hat; **se rompió la pierna** he broke his leg; **cortarse el pelo** to get one's hair cut; (*uno mismo*) to cut one's hair; **se comió un pastel** he ate a cake

3 (*uso recíproco*) each other, one another; **se miraron (el uno al otro)** they looked at each other *o* one another

4 (*en oraciones pasivas*): **se han vendido muchos libros** a lot of books have been sold; **"se vende coche"** "car for sale"

5 (*impers*): **se dice que** people say that, it is said that; **allí se come muy bien** the food there is very good, you can eat very well there

347

sé [se] VB ver **saber**; **ser**

sea etc ['sea] VB ver **ser**

SEAT ['seat] NF ABR = **Sociedad Española de Automóviles de Turismo**

sebo ['seβo] NM fat, grease

Sec. ABR (= Secretario) Sec

seca ['seka] NF ver **seco**

secado [se'kaðo] NM drying; **~ a mano** blow-dry

secador [seka'ðor] NM: **~ para el pelo** hairdryer

★**secadora** [seka'ðora] NF tumble dryer; **~ centrífuga** spin-dryer

secano [se'kano] NM (Agr: tb: **tierra de secano**) dry land o region; **cultivo de ~** dry farming

secante [se'kante] ADJ (viento) drying ▶ NM blotting paper

★**secar** [se'kar] /1g/ VT to dry; (superficie) to wipe dry; (frente, suelo) to mop; (líquido) to mop up; (tinta) to blot ■ **secarse** VR to dry (off); (río, planta) to dry up

★**sección** [sek'θjon] NF section; (Com) department; **~ deportiva** (en periódico) sports page(s)

★**seco, -a** ['seko, a] ADJ dry; (fruta) dried; (persona: magro) thin, skinny; (carácter) cold; (antipático) disagreeable; (respuesta) sharp, curt; **parar en ~** to stop dead ▶ NF dry season; **habrá pan a secas** there will be just bread; **decir algo a secas** to say sth curtly

secreción [sekre'θjon] NF secretion

secretaría [sekreta'ria] NF secretariat; (oficina) secretary's office

secretariado [sekreta'rjaðo] NM (oficina) secretariat; (cargo) secretaryship; (curso) secretarial course

★**secretario, -a** [sekre'tarjo, a] NM/F secretary; **~ adjunto** (Com) assistant secretary

secreto, -a [se'kreto, a] ADJ secret; (información) confidential; (persona) secretive ▶ NM secret; (calidad) secrecy

secta ['sekta] NF sect

sectario, -a [sek'tarjo, a] ADJ sectarian

sector [sek'tor] NM (tb Inform) sector; (de opinión) section; (fig: campo) area, field; **~ privado/público** (Com, Econ) private/public sector

secuela [se'kwela] NF consequence

secuencia [se'kwenθja] NF sequence

★**secuestrar** [sekwes'trar] /1a/ VT to kidnap; (avión) to hijack; (bienes) to seize, confiscate

★**secuestro** [se'kwestro] NM (de persona) kidnapping; (de avión) hijack; (Jur: de cargamento, propiedad) seizure, confiscation

secular [seku'lar] ADJ secular

secundar [sekun'dar] /1a/ VT to second, support

★**secundario, -a** [sekun'darjo, a] ADJ secondary; (carretera) side cpd; (Inform) background cpd ▶ NF secondary education

★**sed** [seð] NF thirst; (fig) thirst, craving; **tener ~** to be thirsty

★**seda** ['seða] NF silk; **~ dental** dental floss

sedal [se'ðal] NM fishing line

sedán [se'ðan] NM (Am) saloon (Brit), sedan (US)

sedante [se'ðante] NM sedative

sede ['seðe] NF (de gobierno) seat; (de compañía) headquarters pl, head office; **Santa S~** Holy See

sedentario, -a [seðen'tarjo, a] ADJ sedentary

sedición [seði'θjon] NF sedition

sediento, -a [se'ðjento, a] ADJ thirsty

sedimentar [seðimen'tar] /1a/ VT to deposit ■ **sedimentarse** VR to settle

sedimento [seði'mento] NM sediment

sedoso, -a [se'ðoso, a] ADJ silky, silken

seducción [seðuk'θjon] NF seduction

seducir [seðu'θir] /3n/ VT to seduce; (sobornar) to bribe; (cautivar) to charm, fascinate; (atraer) to attract

seductor, a [seðuk'tor, a] ADJ (sexualmente) seductive; (cautivador: persona) charming; (: idea) tempting; (engañoso) deceptive, misleading ▶ NM/F seducer

seduje etc [se'ðuxe], **seduzca** etc [se'ðuθka] VB ver **seducir**

sefardí [sefar'ði], **sefardita** [sefar'ðita] ADJ Sephardi(c) ▶ NM/F Sephardi

segador, a [seɣa'ðor, a] NM/F (persona) harvester ▶ NF (Tec) mower, reaper

segadora-trilladora [seɣaˈðoratriʎaˈðora] NF combine harvester

segar [se'ɣar] /1h, 1j/ VT (mies) to reap, cut; (hierba) to mow, cut; (esperanzas) to ruin

seglar [se'ɣlar] ADJ secular, lay

segoviano, -a [seɣo'βjano, a] ADJ of o from Segovia ▶ NM/F native o inhabitant of Segovia

segregación [seɣreɣa'θjon] NF segregation; **~ racial** racial segregation

segregar [seɣre'ɣar] /1h/ VT to segregate, separate

segregue etc [se'ɣreɣe] VB ver **segregar**

segué [se'ɣe], **seguemos** etc [se'ɣemos] VB ver **segar**

seguidamente [seɣiða'mente] ADV (sin parar) without a break; (inmediatamente después) immediately after

seguido, -a [se'ɣiðo, a] ADJ (continuo) continuous, unbroken; (recto) straight; **cinco días seguidos** five days running, five days in a row ▶ ADV (directo) straight (on); (después) after; (Am: a menudo) often ▶ NF: **en seguida** at once, right away; **en seguida termino** I've nearly finished, I shan't be long now

seguidor, a [seɣi'ðor, a] NM/F follower

seguimiento [seɣi'mjento] NM chase, pursuit; (continuación) continuation

★**seguir** [se'ɣir] /3d, 3k/ VT to follow; (venir después) to follow on, come after; (proseguir) to continue; (perseguir) to chase, pursue; (indicio) to follow up; (mujer) to court ▶ VI (gen) to follow; (continuar) to

continue, carry *o* go on; **a ~** to be continued; **sigo sin comprender** I still don't understand; **sigue lloviendo** it's still raining; **sigue** (*en carta*) P.T.O.; (*en libro, TV*) continued; **"hágase ~"** "please forward"; **¡siga!** (*Am: pase*) come in!
■ **seguirse** VR to follow

★**según** [se'ɣun] PREP according to ▶ ADV: **~ (y conforme)** it all depends ▶ CONJ as; **~ esté el tiempo** depending on the weather; **~ me consta** as far as I know; **está ~ lo dejaste** it is just as you left it

★**segundo, -a** [se'ɣundo, a] ADJ second; (*en discurso*) secondly; **de segunda mano** second hand; **segunda clase** (*Ferro*) second class; **segunda marcha** (*Auto*) second gear ▶ NM (*gen, medida de tiempo*) second; (*piso*) second floor; **~ (de a bordo)** (*Naut*) first mate ▶ NF (*sentido*) double meaning; (*Ferro*) second (class); (*Auto*) second (gear)

seguramente [seɣura'mente] ADV surely; (*con certeza*) for sure, with certainty; (*probablemente*) probably; **¿lo va a comprar? — ~** is he going to buy it? — I should think so

★**seguridad** [seɣuri'ðað] NF safety; (*del estado, de casa etc*) security; (*certidumbre*) certainty; (*confianza*) confidence; (*estabilidad*) stability; **~ social** social security (BRIT), welfare (US); **~ contra incendios** fire precautions *pl*; **~ en sí mismo** (self-)confidence; **~ cibernética** cybersecurity

★**seguro, -a** [se'ɣuro, a] ADJ (*cierto*) sure, certain; (*fiel*) trustworthy; (*libre de peligro*) safe; (*bien defendido, firme*) secure; (*datos etc*) reliable; (*fecha*) firm ▶ ADV for sure, certainly ▶ NM (*dispositivo*) safety device; (*de cerradura*) tumbler; (*de arma*) safety catch; (*Com*) insurance; **~ contra accidentes/incendios** accident/fire insurance; **~ contra terceros/a todo riesgo** third-party/comprehensive insurance; **~ dotal con beneficios** with-profits endowment assurance; **S~ de Enfermedad** health insurance; **~ marítimo** marine insurance; **~ mixto** endowment assurance; **~ temporal** term insurance; **~ de vida** life insurance; **~ social** (*Am*) social security (BRIT), welfare (US)

★**seis** [seis] NUM six; **~ mil** six thousand; **tiene ~ años** she is six (years old); **unos ~** about six; **hoy es el ~** today is the sixth

seiscientos, -as [seis'θjentos, as] NUM six hundred

seísmo [se'ismo] NM tremor, earthquake

SELA SIGLA M = **Sistema Económico Latinoamericano**

★**selección** [selek'θjon] NF selection; **~ múltiple** multiple choice; **~ nacional** (*Deporte*) national team

seleccionador, a [selekθjona'ðor, a] NM/F (*Deporte*) selector

★**seleccionar** [selekθjo'nar] /**1a**/ VT to pick, choose, select

selectividad [selektiβi'ðað] NF (*Univ*) entrance examination

selecto, -a [se'lekto, a] ADJ select, choice; (*escogido*) selected

selfi, selfie ['selfi] NM O F selfie

sellado, -a [se'ʎaðo, a] ADJ (*documento oficial*) sealed; (*pasaporte*) stamped

sellar [se'ʎar] /**1a**/ VT (*documento oficial*) to seal; (*pasaporte, visado*) to stamp; (*marcar*) to brand; (*pacto, labios*) to seal

★**sello** ['seʎo] NM stamp; (*precinto*) seal; (*fig: tb:* **sello distintivo**) hallmark; **~ fiscal** revenue stamp; **sellos de prima** (*Com*) trading stamps

★**selva** ['selβa] NF (*bosque*) forest, woods *pl*; (*jungla*) jungle; **la S~ Negra** the Black Forest

S.Em. ABR = **Su Eminencia**

★**semáforo** [se'maforo] NM (*Auto*) traffic lights *pl*; (*Ferro*) signal

★**semana** [se'mana] NF week; **~ inglesa** five-day (working) week; **~ laboral** working week; **S~ Santa** Holy Week; **entre ~** during the week; *see note*

Semana Santa is a holiday in Spain. *Viernes Santo* (Good Friday), *Sábado Santo* (Holy Saturday), and *Domingo de Resurrección* (Easter Sunday) are celebrated throughout the whole of the country and various regions have their own additional holidays around this time. There are spectacular *procesiones* all over the country, with members of *cofradías* (brotherhoods) dressing in hooded robes and parading their *pasos* (religious floats or sculptures) through the streets. Seville has the most renowned celebrations, on account of the religious fervour shown by the locals.

★**semanal** [sema'nal] ADJ weekly

semanario [sema'narjo] NM weekly (magazine)

semántica [se'mantika] NF semantics *sg*

semblante [sem'blante] NM face; (*fig*) look

sembrar [sem'brar] /**1j**/ VT to sow; (*objetos*) to sprinkle, scatter about; (*noticias etc*) to spread

semejante [seme'xante] ADJ (*parecido*) similar; (*tal*) such; **ser semejantes** to be alike *o* similar; **son muy semejantes** they are very much alike; **nunca hizo cosa ~** he never did such a thing ▶ NM fellow man, fellow creature

semejanza [seme'xanθa] NF similarity, resemblance; **a ~ de** like, as

semejar [seme'xar] /**1a**/ VI to seem like, resemble ■ **semejarse** VR to look alike, be similar

semen ['semen] NM semen

semental [semen'tal] NM (*macho*) stud

sementera [semen'tera] NF (*acto*) sowing; (*temporada*) seedtime; (*tierra*) sown land

semestral [semes'tral] ADJ half-yearly, bi-annual

semestre [se'mestre] NM period of six months; (*Univ*) semester; (*Com*) half-yearly payment

semicírculo [semi'θirkulo] NM semicircle

S

semiconductor [semikonduk'tor] NM semi-conductor

semiconsciente [semikons'θjente] ADJ semiconscious

semidesnatado, -a [semiðesna'taðo, a] ADJ semi-skimmed

semifinal [semifi'nal] NF semifinal

semiinconsciente [semi(i)nkons'θjente] ADJ semiconscious

semilla [se'miʎa] NF seed

semillero [semi'ʎero] NM (Agr etc) seedbed; (fig) hotbed

seminario [semi'narjo] NM (Rel) seminary; (Escol) seminar; ~ **web** (Inform) webinar

semiseco [semi'seko] NM medium-dry

semita [se'mita] ADJ Semitic ▶ NMF Semite

sémola ['semola] NF semolina

sempiterno, -a [sempi'terno, a] ADJ everlasting

Sena ['sena] NM: **el ~** the (river) Seine

senado [se'naðo] NM senate; ver tb **las Cortes**

senador, a [sena'ðor, a] NM/F senator

sencillez [senθi'ʎeθ] NF simplicity; (de persona) naturalness

★**sencillo, -a** [sen'θiʎo, a] ADJ simple; (carácter) natural, unaffected; (billete) single ▶ NM (disco) single; (Am) small change

senda ['senda] NF, **sendero** [sen'dero] NM path, track; **Sendero Luminoso** (Am Pol) the Shining Path (guerrilla movement)

senderismo [sende'rismo] NM hiking

★**sendero** [sen'dero] NM path, track

sendos, -as ['sendos, as] ADJ PL: **les dio ~ golpes** he hit both of them

senil [se'nil] ADJ senile

seno ['seno] NM (Anat) bosom, bust; (fig) bosom; ~ **materno** womb ■ **senos** NMPL breasts

★**sensación** [sensa'θjon] NF sensation; (sentido) sense; (sentimiento) feeling; **causar** o **hacer ~** to cause a sensation

★**sensacional** [sensaθjo'nal] ADJ sensational

sensatez [sensa'teθ] NF common sense

sensato, -a [sen'sato, a] ADJ sensible

sensibilidad [sensiβili'ðað] NF sensitivity; (para el arte) feel

sensibilizar [sensiβili'θar] /1f/ VT: ~ **a la población/opinión pública** to raise public awareness

★**sensible** [sen'sible] ADJ sensitive; (apreciable) perceptible, appreciable; (pérdida) considerable

---

Do not translate the Spanish word **sensible** by sensible.

---

sensiblero, -a [sensi'βlero, a] ADJ sentimental, slushy

sensitivo, -a [sensi'tiβo, a] ADJ sense cpd

sensor [sen'sor] NM: ~ **de fin de papel** paper out sensor

sensorial [senso'rjal] ADJ sensory

sensual [sen'swal] ADJ sensual

★**sentado, -a** [sen'taðo, a] ADJ (establecido) settled; (carácter) sensible; **dar por ~** to take for granted, assume; **dejar algo ~** to establish sth firmly; **estar ~** to sit, be sitting (down) ▶ NF sitting; (Pol) sit-in, sit-down protest; **de una sentada** at one sitting

sentar [sen'tar] /1j/ VT to sit, seat; (fig) to establish ▶ VI (vestido) to suit; (alimento): ~ **bien/mal a** to agree/disagree with ■ **sentarse** VR (persona) to sit, sit down; (el tiempo) to settle (down); (los depósitos) to settle; **¡siéntese!** (do) sit down, take a seat

sentencia [sen'tenθja] NF (máxima) maxim, saying; (Jur) sentence; ~ **de muerte** death sentence

sentenciar [senten'θjar] /1b/ VT to sentence

★**sentido, -a** [sen'tiðo, a] ADJ (pérdida) regrettable; (carácter) sensitive; **mi más ~ pésame** my deepest sympathy ▶ NM sense; (sentimiento) feeling; (significado) sense, meaning; (dirección) direction; ~ **del humor** sense of humour; ~ **común** common sense; **en el buen ~ de la palabra** in the best sense of the word; **sin ~** meaningless; **tener ~** to make sense; ~ **único** one-way (street)

sentimental [sentimen'tal] ADJ sentimental; **vida ~** love life

★**sentimiento** [senti'mjento] NM (emoción) feeling, emotion; (sentido) sense; (pesar) regret, sorrow

★**sentir** [sen'tir] /3i/ VT to feel; (percibir) to perceive, sense; (esp Am: oír) to hear; (lamentar) to regret, be sorry for; (música etc) to have a feeling for; **lo siento** I'm sorry ▶ VI to feel; (lamentarse) to feel sorry ▶ NM opinion, judgement ■ **sentirse** VR to feel; **sentirse mejor/mal** to feel better/ill; **sentirse como en su casa** to feel at home

seña ['seɲa] NF sign; (Mil) password ■ **señas** NFPL address sg; **señas personales** personal description sg; **por más señas** moreover; **dar señas de** to show signs of

★**señal** [se'ɲal] NF sign; (síntoma) symptom; (indicio) indication; (Ferro, Telec) signal; (marca) mark; (Com) deposit; (Inform) marker, mark; **en ~ de** as a token of, as a sign of; **dar señales de** to show signs of; ~ **de auxilio/de peligro** distress/danger signal; ~ **de llamada** ringing tone; ~ **para marcar** dialling (Brit) o dial (US) tone

señalado, -a [seɲa'laðo, a] ADJ (persona) distinguished; (pey) notorious

señalar [seɲa'lar] /1a/ VT to mark; (indicar) to point out, indicate; (significar) to denote; (referirse a) to allude to; (fijar) to fix, settle; (pey) to criticize

señalice etc [seɲa'liθe] VB ver **señalizar**

señalización [seɲaliθa'θjon] NF (Auto) signposting; (Ferro) signals pl

señalizar [seɲali'θar] /1f/ VT (Auto) to put up

road signs on; (*Ferro*) to put signals on; (*Auto: ruta*): **está bien señalizada** it's well sign-posted

señas ['seɲas] NFPL *ver* **seña**

★**señor, a** [se'ɲor, a] ADJ (*fam*) lordly ▶ NM (*hombre*) man; (*caballero*) gentleman; (*dueño*) owner, master; (*trato: antes de nombre propio*) Mr; (: *hablando directamente*) sir; **los señores González** Mr and Mrs González; **S~ Don Jacinto Benavente** (*en sobre*) Mr J. Benavente, J. Benavente Esq.; **S~ Director ...** (*de periódico*) Dear Sir ...; **~ juez** my lord, your worship (*US*); **~ Presidente** Mr Chairman o President; **Muy ~ mío** Dear Sir; **Muy señores nuestros** Dear Sirs; **Nuestro S~** (*Rel*) Our Lord ▶ NF (*dama*) lady; (*trato: antes de nombre propio*) Mrs; (: *hablando directamente*) madam; (*esposa*) wife; **¿está la señora?** is the lady of the house in?; **la señora de Smith** Mrs Smith; **Nuestra Señora** (*Rel*) Our Lady

señoría [seɲo'ria] NF rule; **su** o **vuestra S~** your o his/her lordship/ladyship

señorío [seɲo'rio] NM manor; (*fig*) rule

★**señorita** [seɲo'rita] NF (*gen*) Miss; (*mujer joven*) young lady; (*maestra*) schoolteacher

señorito [seɲo'rito] NM young gentleman; (*lenguaje de criados*) master; (*pey*) toff

señuelo [se'ɲwelo] NM decoy

Sep. ABR (= *septiembre*) Sept

sepa *etc* ['sepa] VB *ver* **saber**

separable [sepa'raβle] ADJ separable; (*Tec*) detachable

separación [separa'θjon] NF separation; (*división*) division; (*distancia*) gap, distance; **~ de bienes** division of property

★**separado, -a** [sepa'raðo, a] ADJ separate; (*Tec*) detached; **vive ~ de su mujer** he is separated from his wife; **por ~** separately

separador [separa'ðor] NM (*Inform*) delimiter

separadora [separa'ðora] NF: **~ de hojas** burster

★**separar** [sepa'rar] /**1a**/ VT to separate; (*silla (de la mesa)*) to move away; (*Tec: pieza*) to detach; (: *persona: de un cargo*) to remove, dismiss; (*dividir*) to divide ▪ **separarse** VR (*parte*) to come away; (*partes*) to come apart; (*persona*) to leave, go away; (*matrimonio*) to separate

separata [sepa'rata] NF offprint

separatismo [separa'tismo] NM (*Pol*) separatism

sepelio [se'peljo] NM burial, interment

sepia ['sepja] NF cuttlefish

Sept. ABR (= *septiembre*) Sept.

septentrional [septentrjo'nal] ADJ north *cpd*, northern

★**septiembre** [sep'tjembre] NM September; *ver tb* julio

★**séptimo, -a** ['septimo, a] ADJ, NM seventh

septuagésimo, -a [septwa'xesimo, a] ADJ seventieth

sepulcral [sepul'kral] ADJ sepulchral; (*fig*) gloomy, dismal; (*silencio, atmósfera*) deadly

sepulcro [se'pulkro] NM tomb, grave, sepulchre

sepultar [sepul'tar] /**1a**/ VT to bury; (*en accidente*) to trap; **quedaron sepultados en la caverna** they were trapped in the cave

sepultura [sepul'tura] NF (*acto*) burial; (*tumba*) grave, tomb; **dar ~ a** to bury; **recibir ~** to be buried

sepulturero, -a [sepultu'rero, a] NM/F grave-digger

seque *etc* ['seke] VB *ver* **secar**

sequedad [seke'ðað] NF dryness; (*fig*) brusqueness, curtness

★**sequía** [se'kia] NF drought

séquito ['sekito] NM (*de rey etc*) retinue; (*Pol*) followers *pl*

SER [ser] NF ABR (*Radio*: = *Sociedad Española de Radiodifusión*) Spanish radio network

---

ser [ser]

/2v/ VI **1** (*descripción, identidad*) to be; **es médica/muy alta** she's a doctor/very tall; **su familia es de Cuzco** his family is from Cuzco; **ser de madera** to be made of wood; **soy Ana** I'm Ana; (*por teléfono*) it's Ana

2 (*propiedad*): **es de Joaquín** it's Joaquín's, it belongs to Joaquín

3 (*horas, fechas, números*): **es la una** it's one o'clock; **son las seis y media** it's half-past six; **es el 1 de junio** it's the first of June; **somos/son seis** there are six of us/them; **2 y 2 son 4** 2 and 2 are o make 4

4 (*suceso*): **¿qué ha sido eso?** what was that?; **la fiesta es en mi casa** the party's at my house; **¿qué será de mí?** what will become of me?; **"érase una vez ..."** "once upon a time ..."

5 (*en oraciones pasivas*): **ha sido descubierto ya** it's already been discovered

6: **es de esperar que ...** it is to be hoped o I etc hope that ...

7 (*locuciones con subjun*): **o sea** that is to say; **sea él sea su hermana** either him or his sister; **tengo que irme, no sea que mis hijos estén esperándome** I have to go in case my children are waiting for me

8: **a** o **de no ser por él ...** but for him ...

9: **a no ser que**: **a no ser que tenga uno ya** unless he's got one already

▶ NM being; **ser humano** human being; **ser vivo** living creature

---

Serbia ['serβja] NF Serbia

serbio, -a ['serβjo, a] ADJ Serbian ▶ NM/F Serb

serenarse [sere'narse] /**1a**/ VR to calm down; (*mar*) to grow calm; (*tiempo*) to clear up

serenidad [sereni'ðað] NF calmness

sereno, -a [se'reno, a] ADJ (*persona*) calm, unruffled; (*tiempo*) fine, settled; (*ambiente*) calm, peaceful ▶ NM night watchman

serial [se'rjal] NM serial

★**serie** ['serje] NF series; (*cadena*) sequence, succession; (*TV etc*) serial; (*de inyecciones*) course; **fuera de ~** out of order; (*fig*) special, out of the ordinary; **fabricación en ~** mass production; (*Inform*) **interface/impresora en ~** serial interface/printer

seriedad [serje'ðað] NF seriousness; (*formalidad*) reliability; (*de crisis*) gravity, seriousness

serigrafía [seriɣra'fia] NF silk screen printing

★**serio, -a** ['serjo, a] ADJ serious; (*fiable: persona*) reliable, dependable; **poco ~** (*actitud*) undignified; (*carácter*) unreliable; **en ~** seriously

sermón [ser'mon] NM (*Rel*) sermon

sermonear [sermone'ar] /1a/ VT (*fam*) to lecture ▶ VI to sermonize

seropositivo, -a [seroposi'tiβo, a] ADJ HIV-positive

serpentear [serpente'ar] /1a/ VI to wriggle; (*camino, río*) to wind, snake

serpentina [serpen'tina] NF streamer

★**serpiente** [ser'pjente] NF snake; **~ boa** boa constrictor; **~ de cascabel** rattlesnake

serranía [serra'nia] NF mountainous area

serrano, -a [se'rrano, a] ADJ highland *cpd*, hill *cpd* ▶ NM/F highlander

serrar [se'rrar] /1j/ VT to saw

serrín [se'rrin] NM sawdust

serrucho [se'rrutʃo] NM handsaw

service ['serβis] NM (*Am Auto*) service

servicial [serβi'θjal] ADJ helpful, obliging

★**servicio** [ser'βiθjo] NM service; (*Am Auto*) service; (*Culin etc*) set; **estar de ~** to be on duty; **~ aduanero** o **de aduana** customs service; **~ a domicilio** home delivery service; **~ incluido** (*en hotel etc*) service charge included; **~ militar** military service; **~ público** (*Com*) public utility ■ **servicios** NMPL toilet(s)

servidor, a [serβi'ðor, a] NM/F servant ▶ NM (*Inform*) server; **su seguro ~ (s.s.s.)** yours faithfully; **un ~** (*el que habla o escribe*) your humble servant

servidumbre [serβi'ðumbre] NF (*sujeción*) servitude; (*criados*) servants *pl*, staff

servil [ser'βil] ADJ servile

★**servilleta** [serβi'ʎeta] NF serviette, napkin

servilletero [serβiʎe'tero] NM (*aro*) napkin ring

★**servir** [ser'βir] /3k/ VT to serve; (*comida*) to serve out o up; (*Tenis etc*) to serve; **¿en qué puedo servirle?** how can I help you?; **~ vino a algn** to pour sb some wine ▶ VI to serve; (*camarero*) to serve, wait; (*tener utilidad*) to be of use, be useful; **~ de guía** to act o serve as a guide; **no sirve para nada** it's no use at all ■ **servirse** VR to serve o help o.s.; **servirse de algo** to make use of sth, use sth; **sírvase pasar** please come in

★**sesenta** [se'senta] NUM sixty

sesentón, -ona [sesen'ton, ona] ADJ, NM/F sixty-year-old

sesgado, -a [ses'ɣaðo, a] ADJ slanted, slanting

sesgo ['sesɣo] NM slant; (*fig*) slant, twist

★**sesión** [se'sjon] NF (*Pol*) session, sitting; (*Cine*) showing; (*Teat*) performance; **abrir/levantar la ~** to open/close o adjourn the meeting; **la segunda ~** the second showing

seso ['seso] NM brain; (*fig*) intelligence ■ **sesos** NMPL (*Culin*) brains; **devanarse los sesos** to rack one's brains

sesudo, -a [se'suðo, a] ADJ sensible, wise

set [set] (*pl* **sets** [sets]) NM (*Tenis*) set

Set. ABR (= *setiembre*) Sept.

★**seta** ['seta] NF mushroom; **~ venenosa** toadstool

setecientos, -as [sete'θjentos, as] NUM seven hundred

★**setenta** [se'tenta] NUM seventy

setiembre [se'tjembre] NM = **septiembre**; *ver tb* **julio**

seto ['seto] NM fence; **~ vivo** hedge

seudo... [seuðo] PREF pseudo...

seudónimo [seu'ðonimo] NM pseudonym

Seúl [se'ul] NM Seoul

s.e.u.o. ABR (= *salvo error u omisión*) E&OE

severidad [seβeri'ðað] NF severity

★**severo, -a** [se'βero, a] ADJ severe; (*disciplina*) strict; (*frío*) bitter

Sevilla [se'βiʎa] NF Seville

sevillano, -a [seβi'ʎano, a] ADJ of o from Seville ▶ NM/F native o inhabitant of Seville

sexagenario, -a [seksaxe'narjo, a] ADJ sixty-year-old ▶ NM/F person in his/her sixties

sexagésimo, -a [seksa'xesimo, a] NUM sixtieth

S.Exc. ABR = **Su Excelencia**

★**sexo** ['sekso] NM sex; **el ~ femenino/masculino** the female/male sex

★**sexto, -a** ['seksto, a] NUM sixth; **Juan S~** John the Sixth

sexual [sek'swal] ADJ sexual; **vida ~** sex life

sexualidad [sekswali'ðað] NF sexuality

s.f. ABR (= *sin fecha*) no date

s/f ABR (*Com*: = *su favor*) your favour (BRIT), your favor (US)

sgte(s). ABR (= *siguiente*) foll.

★**si** [si] CONJ if; (*en pregunta indirecta*) if, whether; **si ... si ...** whether ... or ...; **me pregunto si ...** I wonder if o whether ...; **si no** if not, otherwise; **¡si fuera verdad!** if only it were true!; **por si viene** in case he comes ▶ NM (*Mus*) B

En las oraciones dubitativas y en las interrogativas en estilo indirecto *si* se puede traducir por **whether** o **if**:
No sé si me dejará quedarme. **I don't know whether** o **if he'll let me stay**.
Les pregunté si podían ayudarme. **I asked them if** o **whether they could help me**.

Si se traduce solo por **whether** cuando se hacen explícitas las opciones a elegir, cuando va detrás de una preposición o delante de un infinitivo:

Hablamos de si deberíamos comprar una casa. **We talked about whether we should buy a house**.

No sé si ir a Canadá o a Estados Unidos. **I can't decide whether to go to Canada or the United States**.

★**sí** [si] ADV yes; **él no quiere pero yo sí** he doesn't want to but I do; **ella sí vendrá** she will certainly come, she is sure to come; **claro que sí** of course; **creo que sí** I think so; **porque sí** because that's the way it is; (*porque lo digo yo*) because I say so; **¡sí que lo es!** I'll say it is!; **¡eso sí que no!** never! ▶ PRON (*uso impersonal*) oneself; (*sg: m*) himself; (: *f*) herself; (: *de cosa*) itself; (: *de usted*) yourself; (*pl*) themselves; (: *de ustedes*) yourselves; (: *recíproco*) each other; **se ríe de sí misma** she laughs at herself; **de por sí** in itself; **cambiaron una mirada entre sí** they gave each other a look ▶ NM consent

siamés, -esa [sja'mes, esa] ADJ, NM/F Siamese

sibarita [siβa'rita] ADJ sybaritic ▶ NMF sybarite

sicario [si'karjo] NM hired killer

SICAV [si'kaß] NF ABR (= *sociedad de inversión de capital variable*) SICAV

Sicilia [si'θilja] NF Sicily

siciliano, -a [siθi'ljano, a] ADJ, NM/F Sicilian ▶ NM (*Ling*) Sicilian

★**sida, SIDA** ['siða] NM ABR (= *síndrome de inmunodeficiencia adquirida*) AIDS

siderurgia [siðe'rurxja] NF iron and steel industry

siderúrgico, -a [siðe'rurxiko, a] ADJ iron and steel *cpd*

★**sidra** ['siðra] NF cider

siega *etc* ['sjeɣa] VB *ver* **segar** ▶ NF (*el cosechar*) reaping; (*el segar*) mowing; (*época*) harvest (time)

siegue *etc* ['sjeɣe] VB *ver* **segar**

siembra ['sjembra] VB *ver* **sembrar** ▶ NF sowing

★**siempre** ['sjempre] ADV always; (*todo el tiempo*) all the time; (*Am: así y todo*) still; **es lo de** ~ it's the same old story; **como** ~ as usual; **para** ~ forever; ~ **me voy mañana** (*Am*) I'm still leaving tomorrow ▶ CONJ: ~ **que ...** (+ *indic*) whenever ...; (+ *subjun*) provided that ...

sien [sjen] NF (*Anat*) temple

siento *etc* ['sjento] VB *ver* **sentar; sentir**

★**sierra** ['sjerra] VB *ver* **serrar** ▶ NF (*Tec*) saw; (*Geo*) mountain range; **S~ Leona** Sierra Leone

siervo, -a ['sjerβo, a] NM/F slave

★**siesta** ['sjesta] NF siesta, nap; **dormir la** o **echarse una** o **tomar una** ~ to have an afternoon nap o a doze

★**siete** ['sjete] NUM seven ▶ EXCL (*Am fam*): **¡la gran** ~! wow!, hell!; **hijo de la gran** ~ (*fam!*) bastard (*fam!*), son of a bitch (*US fam!*)

sífilis ['sifilis] NF syphilis

sifón [si'fon] NM syphon; **whisky con** ~ whisky and soda

siga *etc* ['siɣa] VB *ver* **seguir**

sigilo [si'xilo] NM secrecy; (*discreción*) discretion

sigla ['siɣla] NF initial, abbreviation

★**siglo** ['siɣlo] NM century; (*fig*) age; **S~ de las Luces** Age of Enlightenment; **S~ de Oro** Golden Age

significación [siɣnifika'θjon] NF significance

significado [siɣnifi'kaðo] NM significance; (*de palabra etc*) meaning

★**significar** [siɣnifi'kar] /1g/ VT to mean, signify; (*notificar*) to make known, express

significativo, -a [siɣnifika'tiβo, a] ADJ significant

signifique *etc* [siɣni'fike] VB *ver* **significar**

★**signo** ['siɣno] NM sign; ~ **de admiración** o **exclamación** exclamation mark; ~ **igual** equals sign; ~ **de interrogación** question mark; ~ **de más/de menos** plus/minus sign; **signos de puntuación** punctuation marks

sigo *etc* VB *ver* **seguir**

siguiendo *etc* [si'ɣjendo] VB *ver* **seguir**

★**siguiente** [si'ɣjente] ADJ following; (*próximo*) next

siguió *etc* VB *ver* **seguir**

sílaba ['silaβa] NF syllable

★**silbar** [sil'βar] /1a/ VT, VI to whistle; (*silbato*) to blow; (*Teat etc*) to hiss

silbato [sil'βato] NM (*instrumento*) whistle

silbido [sil'βiðo] NM whistle, whistling; (*abucheo*) hiss

silenciador [silenθja'ðor] NM silencer

silenciar [silen'θjar] /1b/ VT (*persona*) to silence; (*escándalo*) to hush up

★**silencio** [si'lenθjo] NM silence, quiet; **en el** ~ **más absoluto** in dead silence; **guardar** ~ to keep silent

★**silencioso, -a** [silen'θjoso, a] ADJ silent, quiet

sílfide ['silfiðe] NF sylph

silicio [si'liθjo] NM silicon

★**silla** ['siʎa] NF (*asiento*) chair; (*tb:* **silla de montar**) saddle; ~ **de ruedas** wheelchair

sillería [siʎe'ria] NF (*asientos*) chairs *pl*, set of chairs; (*Rel*) choir stalls *pl*; (*taller*) chairmaker's workshop

sillín [si'ʎin] NM saddle, seat

★**sillón** [si'ʎon] NM armchair, easy chair

★**silueta** [si'lweta] NF silhouette; (*de edificio*) outline; (*figura*) figure

silvestre [sil'βestre] ADJ (*Bot*) wild; (*fig*) rustic, rural

sima ['sima] NF abyss, chasm

simbolice *etc* [simbo'liθe] VB *ver* **simbolizar**

simbólico, -a [sim'boliko, a] ADJ symbolic(al)

simbolizar [simboli'θar] /1f/ VT to symbolize

S

353

símbolo ['simbolo] NM symbol; **~ gráfico** (*Inform*) icon

simetría [sime'tria] NF symmetry

simétrico, -a [si'metriko, a] ADJ symmetrical

simiente [si'mjente] NF seed

similar [simi'lar] ADJ similar

similitud [simili'tuð] NF similarity, resemblance

simio ['simjo] NM ape

★**simpatía** [simpa'tia] NF liking; (*afecto*) affection; (*amabilidad*) kindness; (*de ambiente*) friendliness; (*de persona, lugar*) charm, attractiveness; (*solidaridad*) mutual support, solidarity; **tener ~ a** to like; **la famosa ~ andaluza** that well-known Andalusian charm

simpatice *etc* [simpa'tiθe] VB *ver* **simpatizar**

★**simpático, -a** [sim'patiko, a] ADJ nice, pleasant; (*bondadoso*) kind; **no le hemos caído muy simpáticos** she didn't really take to us

---

Do not translate the Spanish word **simpático** by *sympathetic*.

---

simpatiquísimo, -a [simpati'kisimo, a] ADJ SUPERLATIVO *de* **simpático** ever so nice; ever so kind

simpatizante [simpati'θante] NMF sympathizer

simpatizar [simpati'θar] /1f/ VI: **~ con** to get on well with

simple ['simple] ADJ simple; (*elemental*) simple, easy; (*mero*) mere; (*puro*) pure, sheer; **un ~ soldado** an ordinary soldier ▶ NMF simpleton

simpleza [sim'pleθa] NF simpleness; (*necedad*) silly thing

simplicidad [simpliθi'ðað] NF simplicity

simplificar [simplifi'kar] /1g/ VT to simplify

simplifique *etc* [simpli'fike] VB *ver* **simplificar**

simplón, -ona [sim'plon, ona] ADJ simple, gullible ▶ NM/F simple soul

simposio [sim'posjo] NM symposium

simulacro [simu'lakro] NM (*apariencia*) semblance; (*fingimiento*) sham

simular [simu'lar] /1a/ VT to simulate; (*fingir*) to feign, sham

simultanear [simultane'ar] /1a/ VT: **~ dos cosas** to do two things simultaneously

simultáneo, -a [simul'taneo, a] ADJ simultaneous

★**sin** [sin] PREP without; (*a no ser por*) but for; **~ decir nada** without a word; **~ verlo yo** without my seeing it; **platos ~ lavar** unwashed *o* dirty dishes; **la ropa está ~ lavar** the washing hasn't been done; **~ embargo** however ▶ CONJ: **~ que** (+ *subjun*) without; **~ que lo sepa él** without his knowing

sinagoga [sina'ɣoɣa] NF synagogue

Sinaí [sina'i] NM: **El ~** Sinai, the Sinai Peninsula; **el Monte ~** Mount Sinai

sinceridad [sinθeri'ðað] NF sincerity

★**sincero, -a** [sin'θero, a] ADJ sincere; (*persona*) genuine; (*opinión*) frank; (*felicitaciones*) heartfelt

síncope ['sinkope] NM (*desmayo*) blackout; **~ cardíaco** (*Med*) heart failure

sincronice *etc* [sinkro'niθe] VB *ver* **sincronizar**

sincronizar [sinkroni'θar] /1f/ VT to synchronize

sindical [sindi'kal] ADJ union *cpd*, trade-union *cpd*

sindicalista [sindika'lista] ADJ trade-union *cpd* ▶ NMF trade unionist

sindicar [sindi'kar] /1g/ VT (*obreros*) to organize, unionize ■ **sindicarse** VR (*obrero*) to join a union

★**sindicato** [sindi'kato] NM (*de trabajadores*) trade(s) *o* (*US*) labor union; (*de negociantes*) syndicate

sindique *etc* [sin'dike] VB *ver* **sindicar**

síndrome ['sindrome] NM syndrome; **~ de abstinencia** withdrawal symptoms; **~ de la clase turista** economy-class syndrome

sine qua non [sine'kwanon] ADJ: **condición ~** sine qua non

sinfín [sin'fin] NM: **un ~ de** a great many, no end of

sinfonía [sinfo'nia] NF symphony

sinfónico, -a [sin'foniko, a] ADJ (*música*) symphonic; **orquesta sinfónica** symphony orchestra

Singapur [singa'pur] NM Singapore

singular [singu'lar] ADJ singular; (*fig*) outstanding, exceptional; (*pey*) peculiar, odd ▶ NM (*Ling*) singular; **en ~** in the singular

singularice *etc* [singula'riθe] VB *ver* **singularizar**

singularidad [singulari'ðað] NF singularity, peculiarity

singularizar [singulari'θar] /1f/ VT to single out ■ **singularizarse** VR to distinguish o.s., stand out

siniestro, -a [si'njestro, a] ADJ left; (*fig*) sinister ▶ NM (*accidente*) accident; (*desastre*) natural disaster

sinnúmero [sin'numero] NM = **sinfín**

★**sino** ['sino] NM fate, destiny ▶ CONJ (*pero*) but; (*salvo*) except, save; **no son 8 ~ 9** there are not 8 but 9; **todos ~ él** all except him

sinónimo, -a [si'nonimo, a] ADJ synonymous ▶ NM synonym

sinrazón [sinra'θon] NF wrong, injustice

sinsabor [sinsa'βor] NM (*molestia*) trouble; (*dolor*) sorrow; (*preocupación*) uneasiness

sintaxis [sin'taksis] NF syntax

síntesis ['sintesis] NF INV synthesis

sintetice *etc* [sinte'tiθe] VB *ver* **sintetizar**

sintético, -a [sin'tetiko, a] ADJ synthetic

sintetizador [sintetiθa'ðor] NM synthesizer

sintetizar [sinteti'θar] /1f/ VT to synthesize

sintiendo etc [sin'tjendo] VB ver **sentir**

sintió VB ver **sentir**

★**síntoma** ['sintoma] NM symptom

sintomático, -a [sinto'matiko, a] ADJ symptomatic

sintonía [sinto'nia] NF (Radio) tuning; (melodía) signature tune

sintonice etc [sinto'niθe] VB ver **sintonizar**

sintonizador [sintoniθa'ðor] NM (Radio) tuner

sintonizar [sintoni'θar] /1f/ VT (Radio) to tune (in) to, pick up

sinuoso, -a [si'nwoso, a] ADJ (camino) winding; (rumbo) devious

sinvergüenza [simber'ɣwenθa] NMF rogue, scoundrel; **¡es un ~!** he's got a nerve!

sionismo [sjo'nismo] NM Zionism

siquiera [si'kjera] CONJ even if, even though ▶ ADV (esp Am) at least; **ni ~** not even; **~ bebe algo** at least drink something

sirena [si'rena] NF siren, mermaid; (bocina) siren, hooter

Siria ['sirja] NF Syria

sirio, -a ['sirjo, a] ADJ, NM/F Syrian

sirviendo etc [sir'βjendo] VB ver **servir**

★**sirviente, -a** [sir'βjente, a] NM/F servant

sirvo etc VB ver **servir**

sisa ['sisa] NF petty theft; (Costura) dart; (sobaquera) armhole

sisar [si'sar] /1a/ VT (robar) to thieve; (Costura) to take in

sisear [sise'ar] /1a/ VT, VI to hiss

sísmico, -a ['sismiko, a] ADJ: **movimiento ~** earthquake

sismógrafo [sis'moɣrafo] NM seismograph

sistema [sis'tema] NM system; (método) method; **~ binario** (Inform) binary system; **~ de alerta inmediata** early-warning system; **~ de facturación** (Com) invoicing system; **~ de fondo fijo** (Com) imprest system; **~ de lógica compartida** (Inform) shared logic system; **~ educativo** educational system; **~ experto** expert system; **~ impositivo** o **tributario** taxation, tax system; **~ métrico** metric system; **~ operativo (en disco)** (Inform) (disk-based) operating system

The reform of the **Sistema educativo** (Spanish education system) dates from the 1990s. The former EGB, BUP, and COU cycles have been replaced respectively by Primaria (Primary), a compulsory six-year stage, Secundaria (Secondary), a compulsory four-year stage, and the Bachillerato (equivalent to A Levels), an optional two-year secondary-education course.

sistemático, -a [siste'matiko, a] ADJ systematic

sitiar [si'tjar] /1b/ VT to besiege, lay siege to

★**sitio** ['sitjo] NM (lugar) place; (espacio) room, space; (Mil) siege; **~ de taxis** (Am: parada) taxi stand o (Brit) rank ; **~ web** website; **¿hay ~?** is there any room?; **hay ~ de sobra** there's plenty of room

★**situación** [sitwa'θjon] NF situation, position; (estatus) position, standing

★**situado, -a** [si'twaðo, a] ADJ situated, placed; **estar ~** to be financially secure

situar [si'twar] /1e/ VT to place, put; (edificio) to locate, situate

S.L. ABR (Com: = Sociedad Limitada) Ltd

slip [es'lip] (pl **slips**) NM pants pl, briefs pl

slot [es'lot] (pl **slots**) NM: **~ de expansión** expansion slot

S.M. ABR (= Su Majestad) HM

smartphone [(e)'smarfon] NM smartphone

SME NM ABR (= Sistema Monetario Europeo) EMS; **(mecanismo de cambios del) ~** ERM

smoking [(e)'smokin] (pl **smokings**) NM dinner jacket (Brit), tuxedo (US)

SMS NM ABR (= short message service) SMS; (: mensaje) text (message)

s/n ABR (= sin número) no number

snob [es'nob] = **esnob**

snowboard [es'nouβor] NM snowboarding; **tabla de ~** snowboard

SO ABR (= suroeste) SW

so [so] EXCL whoa!; **¡so burro!** you idiot! ▶ PREP under

s/o ABR (Com: = su orden) your order

sobaco [so'βako] NM armpit

sobado, -a [so'βaðo, a] ADJ (ropa) worn; (arrugado) crumpled; (libro) well-thumbed; (Culin: bizcocho) short

sobar [so'βar] /1a/ VT (tela) to finger; (ropa) to rumple, mess up; (músculos) to rub, massage; (comida) to play around with

soberanía [soβera'nia] NF sovereignty

soberano, -a [soβe'rano, a] ADJ sovereign; (fig) supreme ▶ NM/F sovereign; **los soberanos** the king and queen

soberbio, -a [so'βerβjo, a] ADJ (orgulloso) proud; (altanero) haughty, arrogant; (magnífico) magnificent, superb ▶ NF (orgullo) pride; (altanería) haughtiness, arrogance; (magnificencia) magnificence

sobornar [soβor'nar] /1a/ VT to bribe

soborno [so'βorno] NM (un soborno) bribe; (el soborno) bribery

sobra ['soβra] NF excess, surplus; **de ~** surplus, extra; **lo sé de ~** I'm only too aware of it; **tengo de ~** I've more than enough ◼ **sobras** NFPL leftovers, scraps

sobradamente [soβraða'mente] ADV amply; (saber) only too well

sobrado, -a [so'βraðo, a] ADJ (más que suficiente) more than enough; (superfluo) excessive; **sobradas veces** repeatedly ▶ ADV too, exceedingly

sobrante [so'βrante] ADJ remaining, extra ▶ NM surplus, remainder

S

★**sobrar** [soˈβrar] /**1a**/ vi (*tener de más*) to be more than enough; (*quedar*) to remain, be left (over); **con este dinero sobrará** this money will be more than enough; **ha sobrado mucha comida** there's a lot of food left (over)

sobrasada [soβraˈsaða] NF cured Majorcan sausage

★**sobre** [ˈsoβre] PREP (*gen*) on; (*encima*) on (top of); (*por encima de, arriba de*) over, above; (*más que*) more than; (*además*) in addition to, besides; (*alrededor de*) about; (*porcentaje*) in, out of; (*tema*) about, on; ~ **todo** above all; **3 ~ 100** 3 in a 100, 3 out of every 100; **un libro ~ Tirso** a book about Tirso ▶ NM envelope; ~ **de ventanilla** window envelope

sobrecama [soβreˈkama] NF bedspread

sobrecapitalice *etc* [soβrekapitaˈliθe] VB *ver* **sobrecapitalizar**

sobrecapitalizar [soβrekapitaliˈθar] /**1f**/ vi to overcapitalize

sobrecargar [soβrekarˈɣar] /**1h**/ VT (*camión*) to overload; (*Com*) to surcharge

sobrecargue *etc* [soβreˈkarɣe] VB *ver* **sobrecargar**

sobrecoger [soβrekoˈxer] /**2c**/ VT (*sobresaltar*) to startle; (*asustar*) to scare ■ **sobrecogerse** VR (*sobresaltarse*) to be startled; (*asustarse*) to get scared; (*quedar impresionado*) **sobrecogerse (de)** to be overawed (by)

sobrecoja *etc* [soβreˈkoxa] VB *ver* **sobrecoger**

sobredosis [soβreˈðosis] NF INV overdose

sobreentender [soβreenˈender] /**2g**/ VT to understand; (*adivinar*) to deduce, infer ■ **sobreentenderse** VR: **se sobreentiende que ...** it is implied that ...

sobreescribir [soβreeskriˈβir] /**3a**/ VT (*Inform*) to overwrite

sobreestimar [soβreestiˈmar] /**1a**/ VT to overestimate

sobregiro [soβreˈxiro] NM (*Com*) overdraft

sobrehumano, -a [soβreuˈmano, a] ADJ superhuman

sobreimprimir [soβreimpriˈmir] /**3a**/ VT (*Com*) to merge

sobrellevar [soβreʎeˈβar] /**1a**/ VT (*fig*) to bear, endure

sobremanera [soβremaˈnera] ADV exceedingly

sobremesa [soβreˈmesa] NF (*después de comer*) sitting on after a meal; (*Inform*) desktop; **durante la ~** after dinner; **conversación de ~** table talk

sobremodo [soβreˈmoðo] ADV very much, enormously

sobrenatural [soβrenatuˈral] ADJ supernatural

sobrenombre [soβreˈnombre] NM nickname

sobrentender [soβrenˈender] /**2g**/ VT = **sobreentender**

sobrepasar [soβrepaˈsar] /**1a**/ VT to exceed, surpass

sobrepondré *etc* [soβreponˈdre] VB *ver* **sobreponer**

sobreponer [soβrepoˈner] /**2q**/ VT (*poner encima*) to put on top; (*añadir*) to add ■ **sobreponerse** VR: **sobreponerse a** to overcome

sobreponga *etc* [soβreˈponga] VB *ver* **sobreponer**

sobreprima [soβreˈprima] NF (*Com*) loading

sobreproducción [soβreproðukˈθjon] NF overproduction

sobrepuesto [soβreˈpwesto], **sobrepuse** *etc* [soβreˈpuse] VB *ver* **sobreponer**

sobresaldré *etc* [soβresalˈdre], **sobresalga** *etc* [soβreˈsalɣa] VB *ver* **sobresalir**

★**sobresaliente** [soβresaˈljente] ADJ projecting; (*excelente*) outstanding, excellent ▶ NM (*Escol*) ≈ A; **sacar un ~** to get an A o a 9

sobresalir [soβresaˈlir] /**3q**/ vi to project, jut out; (*fig*) to stand out, excel

sobresaltar [soβresalˈtar] /**1a**/ VT (*asustar*) to scare, frighten; (*sobrecoger*) to startle

sobresalto [soβreˈsalto] NM (*movimiento*) start; (*susto*) scare; (*turbación*) sudden shock

sobrescribir [soβreskriˈβir] /**3a**/ VT = **sobreescribir**

sobreseer [soβreseˈer] /**2e**/ VT: ~ **una causa** (*Jur*) to dismiss a case

sobrestadía [soβrestaˈðia] NF (*Com*) demurrage

sobrestimar [soβrestiˈmar] /**1a**/ VT = **sobreestimar**

sobretensión [soβretenˈsjon] NF (*Elec*): ~ **transitoria** surge

sobretiempo [soβreˈtjempo] NM (*Am*) overtime

sobretodo [soβreˈtoðo] NM overcoat

sobrevendré *etc* [soβreβenˈdre], **sobrevenga** *etc* [soβreˈβenga] VB *ver* **sobrevenir**

sobrevenir [soβreβeˈnir] /**3r**/ vi (*ocurrir*) to happen (unexpectedly); (*resultar*) to follow, ensue

sobreviene *etc* [soβreˈβjene], **sobrevine** *etc* [soβreˈβine] VB *ver* **sobrevenir**

sobreviviente [soβreβiˈβjente] ADJ surviving ▶ NMF survivor

sobrevivir [soβreβiˈβir] /**3a**/ vi to survive; (*persona*) to outlive; (*objeto etc*) to outlast

sobrevolar [soβreβoˈlar] /**1l**/ VT to fly over

sobrevuele *etc* [soβreˈβwele] VB *ver* **sobrevolar**

sobriedad [soβrjeˈðað] NF sobriety, soberness; (*moderación*) moderation, restraint

★**sobrino, -a** [soˈβrino, a] NM/F nephew/niece

sobrio, -a [ˈsoβrjo, a] ADJ sober; (*moderado*) moderate, restrained

socarrón, -ona [sokaˈrron, ona] ADJ (*sarcástico*) sarcastic, ironic(al)

socavar [sokaˈβar] /**1a**/ VT to undermine; (*excavar*) to dig underneath o below

socavón [sokaˈβon] NM (*en mina*) gallery; (*hueco*) hollow; (*en la calle*) hole

sociable [so'θjaβle] ADJ (persona) sociable, friendly; (animal) social

social [so'θjal] ADJ social; (Com) company cpd

socialdemócrata [soθjalde'mokrata] ADJ social-democratic ▶ NMF social democrat

socialice etc [soθja'liθe] VB ver **socializar**

socialista [soθja'lista] ADJ, NMF socialist

socializar [soθjali'θar] /1f/ VT to socialize

★**sociedad** [soθje'ðað] NF society; (Com) company; ~ **de ahorro y préstamo** savings and loan society; ~ **anónima (S.A.)** limited company (Ltd) (BRIT), incorporated company (Inc) (US); ~ **de beneficiencia** friendly society (BRIT), benefit association (US); ~ **de cartera** investment trust; ~ **comanditaria** (Com) co-ownership; ~ **conjunta** (Com) joint venture; ~ **de consumo** consumer society; ~ **inmobiliaria** building society (BRIT), savings and loan (society) (US); ~ **de responsabilidad limitada** (Com) private limited company

★**socio, -a** ['soθjo, a] NM/F (miembro) member; (Com) partner; ~ **activo** active partner; ~ **capitalista** o **comanditario** sleeping o (US) silent partner

socioeconómico, -a [soθjoekono'miko, a] ADJ socio-economic

sociología [soθjolo'xia] NF sociology

sociólogo, -a [so'θjoloɣo, a] NM/F sociologist

socorrer [soko'rrer] /2a/ VT to help

socorrido, -a [soko'rriðo, a] ADJ (tienda) well-stocked; (útil) handy; (persona) helpful

socorrismo [soko'rrismo] NM life-saving

★**socorrista** [soko'rrista] NMF first aider; (en piscina, playa) lifeguard

★**socorro** [so'korro] NM (ayuda) help, aid; (Mil) relief; ¡~! help!

soda ['soða] NF (sosa) soda; (bebida) soda (water)

sódico, -a ['soðiko, a] ADJ sodium cpd

soez [so'eθ] ADJ dirty, obscene

★**sofá** [so'fa] NM sofa, settee

sofá-cama [so'fakama] NM studio couch, sofa bed

Sofía ['sofja] NF Sofia

sofisticación [sofistika'θjon] NF sophistication

sofisticado, -a [sofisti'kaðo, a] ADJ sophisticated

sofocado, -a [sofo'kaðo, a] ADJ: **estar ~** (fig) to be out of breath; (ahogarse) to feel stifled

sofocar [sofo'kar] /1g/ VT to suffocate; (apagar) to smother, put out ■ **sofocarse** VR to suffocate; (fig) to blush, feel embarrassed

sofoco [so'foko] NM suffocation; (azoro) embarrassment

sofocón [sofo'kon] NM: **llevarse** o **pasar un ~** to have a sudden shock

sofreír [sofre'ir] /3l/ VT to fry lightly

sofría etc [so'fria], **sofriendo** etc [so'frjendo], **sofrito** [so'frito] VB ver **sofreír**

soft [sof], **software** ['sofwer] NM (Inform) software

soga ['soɣa] NF rope

sois [sois] VB ver **ser**

soja ['soxa] NF soya

sojuzgar [soxuθ'ɣar] /1h/ VT to subdue, rule despotically

sojuzgue etc [so'xuθɣe] VB ver **sojuzgar**

★**sol** [sol] NM sun; (luz) sunshine, sunlight; (Mus) G; (PERÚ: moneda) Peruvian Sol; ~ **naciente/ poniente** rising/setting sun; **tomar el ~** to sunbathe; **hace ~** it is sunny

solace etc [so'laθe] VB ver **solazar**

★**solamente** [sola'mente] ADV only, just

solapa [so'lapa] NF (de chaqueta) lapel; (de libro) jacket

solapado, -a [sola'paðo, a] ADJ (intenciones) underhand; (gestos, movimiento) sly

solar [so'lar] ADJ solar, sun cpd ▶ NM (terreno) plot (of ground); (local) undeveloped site

solaz [so'laθ] NM recreation, relaxation

solazar [sola'θar] /1f/ VT (divertir) to amuse ■ **solazarse** VR to enjoy o.s., relax

soldada [sol'daða] NF pay

★**soldado** [sol'daðo] NM soldier; ~ **raso** private

soldador [solda'ðor] NM soldering iron; (persona) welder

soldar [sol'dar] /1l/ VT to solder, weld; (unir) to join, unite

★**soleado, -a** [sole'aðo, a] ADJ sunny

soledad [sole'ðað] NF solitude; (estado infeliz) loneliness

solemne [so'lemne] ADJ solemn; (tontería) utter; (error) complete

solemnidad [solemni'ðað] NF solemnity

★**soler** [so'ler] /2h/ VI to be in the habit of, be accustomed to; **suele salir a las ocho** she usually goes out at 8 o'clock; **solíamos ir todos los años** we used to go every year

solera [so'lera] NF (tradición) tradition; **vino de ~** vintage wine

solfeo [sol'feo] NM sol-fa, singing of scales; **ir a clases de ~** to take singing lessons

★**solicitar** [soliθi'tar] /1a/ VT (permiso) to ask for, seek; (puesto) to apply for; (votos) to canvass for; (atención) to attract; (persona) to pursue, chase after

solícito, -a [so'liθito, a] ADJ (diligente) diligent; (cuidadoso) careful

★**solicitud** [soliθi'tuð] NF (calidad) great care; (petición) request; (a un puesto) application

solidaridad [soliðari'ðað] NF solidarity; **por ~ con** (Pol etc) out of o in solidarity with

solidario, -a [soli'ðarjo, a] ADJ (participación) joint, common; (compromiso) mutually binding; **hacerse ~ de** to declare one's solidarity with

solidarizarse [soliðari'θarse] /1f/ VR: ~ **con algn** to support sb, sympathize with sb

solidez [soliˈðeθ] NF solidity

★**sólido, -a** [ˈsoliðo, a] ADJ solid; (Tec) solidly made; (bien construido) well built

soliloquio [soliˈlokjo] NM soliloquy

solista [soˈlista] NMF soloist

solitario, -a [soliˈtarjo, a] ADJ (persona) lonely, solitary; (lugar) lonely, desolate ▶ NM/F (recluso) recluse; (en la sociedad) loner ▶ NM solitaire ▶ NF tapeworm

soliviantar [soliβjanˈtar] /1a/ VT to stir up, rouse (to revolt); (enojar) to anger; (sacar de quicio) to exasperate

solloce etc [soˈʎoθe] VB ver **sollozar**

sollozar [soʎoˈθar] /1f/ VI to sob

sollozo [soˈʎoθo] NM sob

★**solo¹, -a** [ˈsolo, a] ADJ (único) single, sole; (sin compañía) alone; (Mus) solo; (solitario) lonely; **hay una sola dificultad** there is just one difficulty; **a solas** alone, by o.s.

★**solo², sólo** [ˈsolo] ADV only, just; (exclusivamente) solely; **tan ~** only just

★**solomillo** [soloˈmiʎo] NM sirloin

solsticio [solsˈtiθjo] NM solstice

soltar [solˈtar] /1l/ VT (dejar ir) to let go of; (desprender) to unfasten, loosen; (librar) to release, set free; (amarras) to cast off; (Auto: freno etc) to release; (: suspiro) to heave; (: risa etc) to let out ■ **soltarse** VR (desanudarse) to come undone; (desprenderse) to come off; (adquirir destreza) to become expert; (en idioma) to become fluent

★**soltero, -a** [solˈtero, a] ADJ single, unmarried ▶ NM bachelor ▶ NF single woman, spinster

solterón [solteˈron] NM confirmed bachelor

solterona [solteˈrona] NF spinster, maiden lady; (pey) old maid

soltura [solˈtura] NF looseness, slackness; (de los miembros) agility, ease of movement; (en el hablar) fluency, ease

soluble [soˈluβle] ADJ (Química) soluble; (problema) solvable; **~ en agua** soluble in water

solución [soluˈθjon] NF solution; **~ de continuidad** break in continuity

solucionar [soluθjoˈnar] /1a/ VT (problema) to solve; (asunto) to settle, resolve

solvencia [solˈβenθja] NF (Com: estado) solvency; (: acción) settlement, payment

solventar [solβenˈtar] /1a/ VT (pagar) to settle, pay; (resolver) to resolve

solvente [solˈβente] ADJ solvent, free of debt

Somalia [soˈmalja] NF Somalia

★**sombra** [ˈsombra] NF shadow; (como protección) shade; **sin ~ de duda** without a shadow of doubt; **tener buena/mala ~** (suerte) to be lucky/unlucky; (carácter) to be likeable/disagreeable ■ **sombras** NFPL darkness sg, shadows

★**sombrero** [somˈbrero] NM hat; **~ hongo** bowler (hat), derby (US); **~ de copa** o **de pelo** (AM) top hat

★**sombrilla** [somˈbriʎa] NF parasol, sunshade

sombrío, -a [somˈbrio, a] ADJ (oscuro) dark; (fig) sombre, sad; (persona) gloomy

somero, -a [soˈmero, a] ADJ superficial

someter [someˈter] /2a/ VT (país) to conquer; (persona) to subject to one's will; (informe) to present, submit; **~ a** to subject to ■ **someterse** VR to give in, yield, submit; **someterse a** to submit to; **someterse a una operación** to undergo an operation

sometimiento [sometiˈmjento] NM (estado) submission; (acción) presentation

somier [soˈmjer] (pl **somiers**) NM spring mattress

somnífero [somˈnifero] NM sleeping pill o tablet

somnolencia [somnoˈlenθja] NF sleepiness, drowsiness

somos [ˈsomos] VB ver **ser**

son [son] VB ver **ser** ▶ NM sound; **en ~ de broma** as a joke

sonado, -a [soˈnaðo, a] ADJ (comentado) talked-of; (famoso) famous; (Com: pey) hyped(-up)

sonaja [soˈnaxa] NF (AM) = **sonajero**

sonajero [sonaˈxero] NM (baby's) rattle

sonambulismo [sonambuˈlismo] NM sleepwalking

sonámbulo, -a [soˈnambulo, a] NM/F sleepwalker

★**sonar** [soˈnar] /1l/ VT (campana) to ring; (trompeta, sirena) to blow; **me suena ese nombre** that name rings a bell ▶ VI to sound; (hacer ruido) to make a noise; (Ling) to be sounded, be pronounced; (ser conocido) to sound familiar; (campana) to ring; (reloj) to strike, chime; **es un nombre que suena** people know the name ■ **sonarse** VR: **sonarse (la nariz)** to blow one's nose

sonda [ˈsonda] NF (Naut) sounding; (Tec) bore, drill; (Med) probe

sondear [sondeˈar] /1a/ VT (Med) to probe, sound; (Naut) to sound; (Tec) to bore (into), drill; (fig: persona, intenciones) to sound out

★**sondeo** [sonˈdeo] NM (Med, Naut) sounding; (Tec) boring, drilling; (encuesta) poll, enquiry; **~ de la opinión pública** public opinion poll

sónico, -a [ˈsoniko, a] ADJ sonic, sound cpd

★**sonido** [soˈniðo] NM sound

sonoro, -a [soˈnoro, a] ADJ sonorous; (resonante) loud, resonant; (Ling) voiced; **efectos sonoros** sound effects

★**sonreír** [sonreˈir] /3l/ VI to smile ■ **sonreírse** VR to smile

sonría etc [sonˈria], **sonriendo** etc [sonˈrjendo] VB ver **sonreír**

sonriente [sonˈrjente] ADJ smiling

★**sonrisa** [sonˈrisa] NF smile

sonrojar [sonroˈxar] /1a/ VT: **~ a algn** to make sb blush ■ **sonrojarse** VR: **sonrojarse (de)** to blush (at)

sonrojo [son'roxo] NM blush

sonsacar [sonsa'kar] /1g/ VT to wheedle, coax; **~ a algn** to pump sb for information

sonsaque etc [son'sake] VB ver **sonsacar**

sonsonete [sonso'nete] NM (golpecitos) tap(ping); (voz monótona) monotonous delivery, singsong (voice)

soñador, a [soɲa'ðor, a] NM/F dreamer

★**soñar** [so'ɲar] /1l/ VT, VI to dream; **~ con** to dream about o of; **soñé contigo anoche** I dreamed about you last night

soñoliento, -a [soɲo'ljento, a] ADJ sleepy, drowsy

★**sopa** ['sopa] NF soup; **~ de fideos** noodle soup

sopero, -a [so'pero, a] ADJ (plato, cuchara) soup cpd ▸ NM soup plate ▸ NF soup tureen

sopesar [sope'sar] /1a/ VT to try the weight of; (fig) to weigh up

sopetón [sope'ton] NM: **de ~** suddenly, unexpectedly

★**soplar** [so'plar] /1a/ VT (polvo) to blow away, blow off; (inflar) to blow up; (vela) to blow out; (ayudar a recordar) to prompt; (birlar) to nick; (delatar) to split on ▸ VI to blow; (delatar) to squeal; (beber) to booze, bend the elbow

soplete [so'plete] NM blowlamp; **~ soldador** welding torch

soplo ['soplo] NM blow, puff; (de viento) puff, gust

soplón, -ona [so'plon, ona] NM/F (fam: chismoso) telltale; (: de policía) informer, grass

soponcio [so'ponθjo] NM dizzy spell

sopor [so'por] NM drowsiness

soporífero, -a [sopo'rifero, a] ADJ sleep-inducing; (fig) soporific ▸ NM sleeping pill

soportable [sopor'taβle] ADJ bearable

soportal [sopor'tal] NM porch ■ **soportales** NMPL arcade sg

soportar [sopor'tar] /1a/ VT to bear, carry; (fig) to bear, put up with

soporte [so'porte] NM support; (fig) pillar, support; (Inform) medium; **~ de entrada/salida** input/output medium

soprano [so'prano] NF soprano

sor [sor] NF: **S~ María** Sister Mary

sorber [sor'βer] /2a/ VT (chupar) to sip; (inhalar) to sniff, inhale; (absorber) to soak up, absorb

sorbete [sor'βete] NM iced fruit drink

sorbo ['sorβo] NM (trago) gulp, swallow; (chupada) sip; **beber a sorbos** to sip

sordera [sor'ðera] NF deafness

sórdido, -a ['sorðiðo, a] ADJ dirty, squalid

★**sordo, -a** ['sorðo, a] ADJ (persona) deaf; (ruido) dull; (Ling) voiceless; **quedarse ~** to go deaf ▸ NM/F deaf person

sordomudo, -a [sorðo'muðo, a] ADJ speech-and-hearing impaired ▸ NM/F person with a speech and hearing impairment

soriano, -a [so'rjano, a] ADJ of o from Soria ▸ NM/F native o inhabitant of Soria

sorna ['sorna] NF (malicia) slyness; (tono burlón) sarcastic tone

soroche [so'rotʃe] NM (Am Med) mountain sickness

★**sorprendente** [sorpren'dente] ADJ surprising

★**sorprender** [sorpren'der] /2a/ VT to surprise; (asombrar) to amaze; (sobresaltar) to startle; (coger desprevenido) to catch unawares ■ **sorprenderse** VR: **sorprenderse (de)** to be surprised o amazed (at)

★**sorpresa** [sor'presa] NF surprise

sorpresivo, -a [sorpre'siβo, a] ADJ (Am) surprising; (imprevisto) sudden

sortear [sorte'ar] /1a/ VT to draw lots for; (rifar) to raffle; (dificultad) to dodge, avoid

★**sorteo** [sor'teo] NM (en lotería) draw; (rifa) raffle

★**sortija** [sor'tixa] NF ring; (rizo) ringlet, curl

sortilegio [sorti'lexjo] NM (hechicería) sorcery; (hechizo) spell

SOS SIGLA M SOS

sosegado, -a [sose'γaðo, a] ADJ quiet, calm

sosegar [sose'γar] /1h, 1j/ VT to quieten, calm; (el ánimo) to reassure ▸ VI to rest

sosegué [sose'γe], **soseguemos** etc [sose'γemos] VB ver **sosegar**

sosiego [so'sjeγo] VB ver **sosegar** ▸ NM quiet(-ness), calm(ness)

sosiegue etc [so'sjeγe] VB ver **sosegar**

soslayar [sosla'jar] /1a/ VT (preguntas) to get round

soslayo [sos'lajo]: **de ~** adv obliquely, sideways; **mirar de ~** to look out of the corner of one's eye (at)

soso, -a ['soso, a] ADJ (Culin) tasteless; (fig) dull, uninteresting

★**sospecha** [sos'petʃa] NF suspicion

★**sospechar** [sospe'tʃar] /1a/ VT to suspect ▸ VI: **~ de** to be suspicious of

sospechoso, -a [sospe'tʃoso, a] ADJ suspicious; (testimonio, opinión) suspect ▸ NM/F suspect

★**sostén** [sos'ten] NM (apoyo) support; (sujetador) bra; (alimentación) sustenance, food

sostendré etc [sosten'dre] VB ver **sostener**

★**sostener** [soste'ner] /2k/ VT to support; (mantener) to keep up, maintain; (alimentar) to sustain, keep going ■ **sostenerse** VR to support o.s.; (seguir) to continue, remain

sostenga etc [sos'tenga] VB ver **sostener**

sostenibilidad [sosteniβili'ðað] NF sustainability

sostenido, -a [soste'niðo, a] ADJ continuous, sustained; (prolongado) prolonged; (Mus) sharp ▸ NM (Mus) sharp

sostuve etc [sos'tuβe] VB ver **sostener**

sota ['sota] NF (Naipes) ≈ jack; ver tb **baraja española**

sotana [so'tana] NF (Rel) cassock

★**sótano** ['sotano] NM basement

sotavento [sota'βento] NM (Naut) lee, leeward

soterrar [sote'rrar] /1j/ VT to bury; (esconder) to hide away

sotierre etc [so'tjerre] VB ver **soterrar**

soviético, -a [so'βjetiko, a] ADJ, NM/F Soviet; **los soviéticos** the Soviets, the Russians

soy [soi] VB ver **ser**

soya ['soja] NF (AM) soya (bean)

SP ABR (Auto) = **servicio público**

SPM NM ABR (= síndrome premenstrual) PMS

spooling [es'pulin] NM (Inform) spooling

sport [es'por(t)] NM sport

spot [es'pot] (pl **spots**) NM (publicitario) ad

spyware [es'paiwer] NM spyware

squash [es'kwas] NM (Deporte) squash

Sr. ABR (= Señor) Mr

Sra. ABR (= Señora) Mrs

Sras. ABR (= Señoras) Mrs

S.R.C. ABR (= se ruega contestación) R.S.V.P.

Sres., Srs. ABR (= Señores) Messrs

Sri Lanka [sri'lanka] NM Sri Lanka

Srta. ABR = **señorita**

SS ABR = **Santos**; (= Santas) SS

ss. ABR (= siguientes) foll

S.S. ABR (Rel: = Su Santidad) H.H.; = **Seguridad Social**

SSE ABR (= sursudeste) SSE

SS MM ABR (= Sus Majestades) Their Royal Highnesses

SSO ABR (= sursudoeste) SSW

Sta. ABR (= Santa) St; (= Señorita) Miss

stand [es'tan] (pl **stands** [es'tan(s)]) NM (Com) stand

stárter [es'tarter] NM (Auto) self-starter, starting motor

statu quo [es'tatu'kuo], **status quo** [es'ta-tus'kuo] NM status quo

status ['status, es'tatus] NM INV status

Sto. ABR (= Santo) St

stop [es'top] (pl **stops** [es'top(s)]) NM (Auto) stop sign

★**su** [su] PRON (de él) his; (de ella) her; (de una cosa) its; (de ellos, ellas) their; (de usted, ustedes) your

★**suave** ['swaβe] ADJ gentle; (superficie) smooth; (trabajo) easy; (música, voz) soft, sweet; (clima, sabor) mild

suavice etc [swa'βiθe] VB ver **suavizar**

suavidad [swaβi'ðað] NF gentleness; (de superficie) smoothness; (de música) softness, sweetness

suavizante [swaβi'θante] NM (de ropa) softener; (del pelo) conditioner

suavizar [swaβi'θar] /1f/ VT to soften; (quitar la aspereza) to smooth (out); (pendiente) to ease; (colores) to tone down; (carácter) to mellow; (dureza) to temper

subalimentado, -a [suβalimen'taðo, a] ADJ undernourished

subalterno, -a [suβal'terno, a] ADJ (importancia) secondary; (personal) minor, auxiliary ▸ NM subordinate

subarrendar [suβarren'dar] /1j/ VT (Com) to lease back

subarriendo [suβa'rrjendo] NM (Com) leaseback

subasta [su'βasta] NF auction; **poner en o sacar a pública ~** to put up for public auction; **~ a la rebaja** Dutch auction

subastador, a [suβasta'ðor, a] NM/F auctioneer

subastar [suβas'tar] /1a/ VT to auction (off)

subcampeón, -ona [suβkampe'on, ona] NM/F runner-up

subconsciente [suβkons'θjente] ADJ subconscious

subcontratar [suβkontra'tar] /1a/ VT (Com) to subcontract

subcontrato [suβkon'trato] NM (Com) subcontract

subdesarrollado, -a [suβðesarro'ʎaðo, a] ADJ underdeveloped

subdesarrollo [suβðesa'rroʎo] NM underdevelopment

subdirector, a [suβðirek'tor, a] NM/F assistant o deputy manager

subdirectorio [suβðirek'torjo] NM (Inform) subdirectory

súbdito, -a ['suβðito, a] NM/F subject

subdividir [suβðiβi'ðir] /3a/ VT to subdivide

subempleo [suβem'pleo] NM underemployment

subestimar [suβesti'mar] /1a/ VT to underestimate, underrate

subido, -a [su'βiðo, a] ADJ (color) bright, strong; (precio) high ▸ NF (de montaña etc) ascent, climb; (de precio) rise, increase; (pendiente) slope, hill

subíndice [su'βindiθe] NM (Inform, Tip) subscript

★**subir** [su'βir] /3a/ VT (objeto) to raise, lift up; (cuesta, calle) to go up; (colina, montaña) to climb; (precio) to raise, put up; (empleado etc) to promote ▸ VI to go/come up; (a un coche) to get in; (a un autobús, tren) to get on; (precio) to rise, go up; (en el empleo) to be promoted; (río, marea) to rise ▪ **subirse** VR to get up, climb; **subirse a un coche** to get in(to) a car

súbito, -a ['suβito, a] ADJ (repentino) sudden; (imprevisto) unexpected

subjetivo, -a [suβxe'tiβo, a] ADJ subjective

subjuntivo [suβxun'tiβo] NM subjunctive (mood)

sublevación [suβleβa'θjon] NF revolt, rising

sublevar [suβle'βar] /1a/ VT to rouse to revolt ▪ **sublevarse** VR to revolt, rise

sublimar [suβli'mar] /1a/ VT (persona) to exalt; (deseos etc) to sublimate

sublime [su'βlime] ADJ sublime

subliminal [suβlimi'nal] ADJ subliminal

submarinismo [suβmari'nismo] NM scuba diving

submarinista [suβmari'nista] NMF scuba diver

submarino, -a [suβma'rino, a] ADJ underwater ▶ NM submarine

subnormal [suβnor'mal] ADJ subnormal ▶ NMF subnormal person

suboficial [suβofi'θjal] NM non-commissioned officer

subordinado, -a [suβorði'naðo, a] ADJ, NM/F subordinate

subproducto [suβpro'ðukto] NM by-product

subrayado [suβra'jaðo] NM underlining

★**subrayar** [suβra'jar] /**1a**/ VT to underline; (*recalcar*) to underline, emphasize

subrepticio, -a [suβrep'tiθjo, a] ADJ surreptitious

subrutina [suβru'tina] NF (*Inform*) subroutine

subsanar [suβsa'nar] /**1a**/ VT (*reparar*) to rectify; (*perdonar*) to excuse; (*sobreponerse a*) to overcome

subscribir [suβskri'βir] /**3a**/ VT = **suscribir**

subscrito [suβs'krito] PP de **subscribir**

subsecretario, -a [suβsekre'tarjo, a] NM/F undersecretary, assistant secretary

subsidiariedad [suβsiðjarie'ðað] NF (*Pol*) subsidiarity

subsidiario, -a [suβsi'ðjarjo, a] ADJ subsidiary

subsidio [suβ'siðjo] NM (*ayuda*) aid, financial help; (*subvención*) subsidy, grant; (*de enfermedad, paro etc*) benefit, allowance

subsistencia [suβsis'tenθja] NF subsistence

subsistir [suβsis'tir] /**3a**/ VI to subsist; (*vivir*) to live; (*sobrevivir*) to survive, endure

subsuelo [suβ'swelo] NM subsoil

subte ['suβte] NM (*RPL*) underground (*BRIT*), subway (*US*)

subterfugio [suβter'fuxjo] NM subterfuge

★**subterráneo, -a** [suβte'rraneo, a] ADJ underground, subterranean ▶ NM underpass, underground passage; (*AM*) underground, subway (*US*)

★**subtitulado, -a** [suβtitu'laðo, a] ADJ subtitled

subtítulo [suβ'titulo] NM subtitle, subheading

suburbano, -a [suβur'βano, a] ADJ suburban

suburbio [su'βurβjo] NM (*barrio*) slum quarter; (*afueras*) suburbs *pl*

subvención [suββen'θjon] NF subsidy, subvention, grant; ~ **estatal** state subsidy *o* support; ~ **para la inversión** (*Com*) investment grant

subvencionar [suββenθjo'nar] /**1a**/ VT to subsidize

subversión [suββer'sjon] NF subversion

subversivo, -a [suββer'siβo, a] ADJ subversive

subyacente [suβja'θente] ADJ underlying

subyugar [suβju'ɣar] /**1h**/ VT (*país*) to subjugate, subdue; (*enemigo*) to overpower; (*voluntad*) to dominate

subyugue *etc* [sub'juɣe] VB *ver* **subyugar**

succión [suk'θjon] NF suction

succionar [sukθjo'nar] /**1a**/ VT (*sorber*) to suck; (*Tec*) to absorb, soak up

sucedáneo, -a [suθe'ðaneo, a] ADJ substitute ▶ NM substitute (food)

★**suceder** [suθe'ðer] /**2a**/ VI to happen; ~ **a** (*seguir*) to succeed, follow; **lo que sucede es que ...** the fact is that ...; ~ **al trono** to succeed to the throne

sucesión [suθe'sjon] NF succession; (*serie*) sequence, series; (*hijos*) issue, offspring

sucesivamente [suθesiβa'mente] ADV: **y así ~** and so on

sucesivo, -a [suθe'siβo, a] ADJ successive, following; **en lo ~** in future, from now on

★**suceso** [su'θeso] NM (*hecho*) event, happening; (*incidente*) incident

sucesor, a [suθe'sor, a] NM/F successor; (*heredero*) heir/heiress

suciedad [suθje'ðað] NF (*estado*) dirtiness; (*mugre*) dirt, filth

sucinto, -a [su'θinto, a] ADJ (*conciso*) succinct, concise

★**sucio, -a** ['suθjo, a] ADJ dirty; (*mugriento*) grimy; (*manchado*) grubby; (*borroso*) smudged; (*conciencia*) bad; (*conducta*) vile; (*táctica*) dirty, unfair

Sucre ['sukre] NF Sucre

sucre ['sukre] NM (*Historia*) *former Ecuadorean monetary unit*

suculento, -a [suku'lento, a] ADJ (*sabroso*) tasty; (*jugoso*) succulent

sucumbir [sukum'bir] /**3a**/ VI to succumb

★**sucursal** [sukur'sal] NF branch (office); (*filial*) subsidiary

★**sudadera** [suða'ðera] NF sweatshirt

Sudáfrica [su'ðafrika] NF South Africa

sudafricano, -a [suðafri'kano, a] ADJ, NM/F South African

★**Sudamérica** [suða'merika] NF South America

★**sudamericano, -a** [suðameri'kano, a] ADJ, NM/F South American

Sudán [su'ðan] NM Sudan; ~ **del Sur** South Sudan

sudanés, -esa [suða'nes, esa] ADJ, NM/F Sudanese

★**sudar** [su'ðar] /**1a**/ VT, VI to sweat; (*Bot*) to ooze, give out *o* off

★**sudeste** [su'ðeste] ADJ south-east(ern); (*rumbo, viento*) south-easterly ▶ NM south-east; (*viento*) south-east wind

★**sudoeste** [suðo'este] ADJ south-west(ern); (*rumbo, viento*) south-westerly ▶ NM south-west; (*viento*) south-west wind

sudoku [su'ðoku] NM sudoku

sudor [su'ðor] NM sweat

sudoroso, -a [suðo'roso, a] ADJ sweaty, sweating

★**Suecia** ['sweθja] NF Sweden

★**sueco, -a** ['sweko, a] ADJ Swedish ▶ NM/F Swede; **hacerse el ~** to pretend not to hear o understand ▶ NM (*Ling*) Swedish

★**suegro, -a** ['sweɣro, a] NM/F father-/mother-in-law; **los suegros** one's in-laws

suela ['swela] NF (*de zapato, tb pescado*) sole

★**sueldo** ['sweldo] VB *ver* **soldar** ▶ NM pay, wage(s) (*pl*)

★**suelo** ['swelo] VB *ver* **soler** ▶ NM (*tierra*) ground; (*de casa*) floor

★**suelto, -a** ['swelto, a] VB *ver* **soltar** ▶ ADJ loose; (*libre*) free; (*separado*) detached; (*ágil*) quick, agile; (*fue corre*) fluent, flowing; **está muy ~ en inglés** he is very good at o fluent in English ▶ NM (*loose*) change, small change

suene *etc* ['swene] VB *ver* **sonar**

sueñito [swe'ɲito] NM (*Am*) nap

★**sueño** ['sweɲo] VB *ver* **soñar** ▶ NM sleep; (*somnolencia*) sleepiness, drowsiness; (*lo soñado, fig*) dream; **~ pesado** o **profundo** deep o heavy sleep; **tener ~** to be sleepy

suero ['swero] NM (*Med*) serum; (*de leche*) whey

★**suerte** ['swerte] NF (*fortuna*) luck; (*azar*) chance; (*destino*) fate, destiny; (*condición*) lot; (*género*) sort, kind; **le echaron a suertes** they drew lots o tossed for it; **tener ~** to be lucky; **de otra ~** otherwise, if not; **de ~ que** so that, in such a way that

★**suéter** ['sweter] (*pl* **suéters**) NM sweater

suficiencia [sufi'θjenθja] NF (*cabida*) sufficiency; (*idoneidad*) suitability; (*aptitud*) adequacy

★**suficiente** [sufi'θjente] ADJ enough, sufficient ▶ NM (*Escol*) pass

sufijo [su'fixo] NM suffix

sufragar [sufra'ɣar] /1h/ VT (*ayudar*) to help; (*gastos*) to meet; (*proyecto*) to pay for

sufragio [su'fraxjo] NM (*voto*) vote; (*derecho de voto*) suffrage

sufrague *etc* [su'fraɣe] VB *ver* **sufragar**

sufrido, -a [su'friðo, a] ADJ (*de carácter fuerte*) tough; (*paciente*) long-suffering, patient; (*tela*) hard-wearing; (*color*) that does not show the dirt; (*marido*) complaisant

sufrimiento [sufri'mjento] NM suffering

★**sufrir** [su'frir] /3a/ VT (*padecer*) to suffer; (*soportar*) to bear, stand, put up with; (*apoyar*) to hold up, support ▶ VI to suffer

sugerencia [suxe'renθja] NF suggestion

★**sugerir** [suxe'rir] /3i/ VT to suggest; (*sutilmente*) to hint; (*idea: incitar*) to prompt

sugestión [suxes'tjon] NF suggestion; (*sutil*) hint; (*poder*) hypnotic power

sugestionar [suxestjo'nar] /1a/ VT to influence

sugestivo, -a [suxes'tiβo, a] ADJ stimulating; (*atractivo*) attractive; (*fascinante*) fascinating

sugiera *etc* [su'xjera], **sugiriendo** *etc* [suxi'rjendo] VB *ver* **sugerir**

suicida [sui'θiða] ADJ suicidal ▶ NMF suicidal person; (*muerto*) suicide, person who has committed suicide

suicidarse [suiθi'ðarse] /1a/ VR to commit suicide, kill o.s.

suicidio [sui'θiðjo] NM suicide

★**Suiza** ['swiθa] NF Switzerland

★**suizo, -a** ['swiθo, a] ADJ, NM/F Swiss ▶ NM sugared bun

sujeción [suxe'θjon] NF subjection

sujetador [suxeta'ðor] NM fastener, clip; (*prenda femenina*) bra, brassiere

sujetapapeles [suxetapa'peles] NM INV paper clip

★**sujetar** [suxe'tar] /1a/ VT (*fijar*) to fasten; (*detener*) to hold down; (*fig*) to subject, subjugate; (*pelo etc*) to keep o hold in place; (*papeles*) to fasten together ■ **sujetarse** VR to subject o.s.

sujeto, -a [su'xeto, a] ADJ fastened, secure; **~ a** subject to ▶ NM subject; (*individuo*) individual; (*fam: tipo*) fellow, character, type, guy (US)

sulfurar [sulfu'rar] /1a/ VT (*Tec*) to sulphurate; (*sacar de quicio*) to annoy ■ **sulfurarse** VR (*enojarse*) to get riled, see red, blow up

sulfuro [sul'furo] NM sulphide

★**suma** ['suma] NF (*cantidad*) total, sum; (*de dinero*) sum; (*acto*) adding (up), addition; **en ~** in short

sumador [suma'ðor] NM (*Inform*) adder

sumamente [suma'mente] ADV extremely, exceedingly

sumar [su'mar] /1a/ VT to add (up); (*reunir*) to collect, gather ▶ VI to add up; **suma y sigue** (*Com*) carry forward

sumario, -a [su'marjo, a] ADJ brief, concise ▶ NM summary

sumergir [sumer'xir] /3c/ VT to submerge; (*hundir*) to sink; (*bañar*) to immerse, dip ■ **sumergirse** VR (*hundirse*) to sink beneath the surface

sumerja *etc* [su'merxa] VB *ver* **sumergir**

sumidero [sumi'ðero] NM drain, sewer; (*Tec*) sump

suministrador, a [suministra'ðor, a] NM/F supplier

suministrar [suminis'trar] /1a/ VT to supply, provide

suministro [sumi'nistro] NM supply; (*acto*) supplying, providing

sumir [su'mir] /3a/ VT to sink, submerge; (*fig*) to plunge ■ **sumirse** VR (*objeto*) to sink; **sumirse en el estudio** to become absorbed in one's studies

sumisión [sumi'sjon] NF (*acto*) submission; (*calidad*) submissiveness, docility

sumiso, -a [su'miso, a] ADJ submissive, docile

súmmum ['sumum] NM INV (*fig*) height

sumo, -a ['sumo, a] ADJ great, extreme; (*mayor*)

highest, supreme ▸ NM sumo (wrestling); **a lo
~** at most

suntuoso, -a [sun'twoso, a] ADJ sumptuous,
magnificent; (*lujoso*) lavish

sup. ABR (= *superior*) sup

supe *etc* ['supe] VB *ver* **saber**

supeditar [supeði'tar] /**1a**/ VT to subordinate;
(*sojuzgar*) to subdue; (*oprimir*) to oppress ◾ **supeditarse** VR: **supeditarse a** to subject o.s. to

súper ['super] ADJ (*fam*) super, great ▸ NF (*gasolina*) four-star (petrol)

★**super...** [super] PREF super..., over...

superable [supe'raβle] ADJ (*dificultad*) sur-
mountable; (*tarea*) that can be performed

superación [supera'θjon] NF (*tb*: **superación
personal**) self-improvement

★**superar** [supe'rar] /**1a**/ VT (*sobreponerse a*) to overcome; (*rebasar*) to surpass, do better than;
(*pasar*) to go beyond; (*marca, récord*) to break;
(*etapa: dejar atrás*) to get past ◾ **superarse** VR to
excel o.s.

superávit [supe'raβit] (*pl* **superávits**) NM surplus

superbueno, a [super'bweno, a] ADJ great,
fantastic

superchería [supertʃe'ria] NF fraud, trick,
swindle

superficial [superfi'θjal] ADJ superficial;
(*medida*) surface *cpd*

superficie [super'fiθje] NF surface; (*área*) area;
grandes superficies (*Com*) superstores

superfluo, -a [su'perflwo, a] ADJ superfluous

superíndice [supe'rindiθe] NM (*Inform, Tip*)
superscript

superintendente [superinten'dente] NMF
supervisor, superintendent

★**superior** [supe'rjor] ADJ (*piso, clase*) upper; (*temperatura, número, nivel*) higher; (*mejor: calidad, producto*) superior, better ▸ NMF superior

superiora [supe'rjora] NF (*Rel*) mother superior

superioridad [superjori'ðað] NF superiority

superlativo, -a [superla'tiβo, a] ADJ, NM superlative

★**supermercado** [supermer'kaðo] NM supermarket

superpoblación [superpoβla'θjon] NF over-
population; (*congestionamiento*) overcrowding

superponer [superpo'ner] /**2q**/ VT to superimpose; (*Inform*) to overstrike

superposición [superposi'θjon] NF (*en impresora*) overstrike

superpotencia [superpo'tenθja] NF superpower, great power

superproducción [superproðuk'θjon] NF
overproduction

supersónico, -a [super'soniko, a] ADJ supersonic

superstición [supersti'θjon] NF superstition

supersticioso, -a [supersti'θjoso, a] ADJ superstitious

supervisar [superβi'sar] /**1a**/ VT to supervise;
(*Com*) to superintend

supervisor, a [superβi'sor, a] NM/F supervisor

supervivencia [superβi'βenθja] NF survival

superviviente [superβi'βjente] ADJ surviving
▸ NMF survivor

supiera *etc* VB *ver* **saber**

suplantar [suplan'tar] /**1a**/ VT (*persona*) to supplant; (*hacerse pasar por otro*) to take the place of

suplementario, -a [suplemen'tarjo, a] ADJ
supplementary

★**suplemento** [suple'mento] NM supplement

suplencia [su'plenθja] NF substitution,
replacement; (*etapa*) period during which one
deputizes *etc*

suplente [su'plente] ADJ substitute; (*disponible*)
reserve ▸ NMF substitute

supletorio, -a [suple'torjo, a] ADJ supplementary; (*adicional*) extra; **mesa supletoria** spare
table; **teléfono ~** extension ▸ NM supplement

súplica ['suplika] NF request; (*Rel*) supplica-
tion; (*Jur: instancia*) petition ◾ **súplicas** NFPL
entreaties

suplicar [supli'kar] /**1g**/ VT (*cosa*) to beg (for),
plead for; (*persona*) to beg, plead with; (*Jur*) to
appeal to, petition

suplicio [su'pliθjo] NM torture; (*tormento*) torment; (*emoción*) anguish; (*experiencia penosa*)
ordeal

suplique *etc* [su'plike] VB *ver* **suplicar**

suplir [su'plir] /**3a**/ VT (*compensar*) to make good,
make up for; (*reemplazar*) to replace, substitute
▸ VI: **~ a** to take the place of, substitute for

supo *etc* ['supo] VB *ver* **saber**

supondré *etc* [supon'dre] VB *ver* **suponer**

★**suponer** [supo'ner] /**2q**/ VT to suppose; (*significar*) to mean; (*acarrear*) to involve; **era de
~ que ...** it was to be expected that ... ▸ VI to
count, have authority

suponga *etc* [su'ponga] VB *ver* **suponer**

suposición [suposi'θjon] NF supposition

supositorio [suposi'torjo] NM suppository

supremacía [suprema'θia] NF supremacy

supremo, -a [su'premo, a] ADJ supreme

supresión [supre'sjon] NF suppression; (*de derecho*) abolition; (*de dificultad*) removal; (*de palabra
etc*) deletion; (*de restricción*) cancellation, lifting

suprimir [supri'mir] /**3a**/ VT to suppress; (*derecho, costumbre*) to abolish; (*dificultad*) to remove;
(*palabra etc, Inform*) to delete; (*restricción*) to
cancel, lift

supuestamente [supwesta'mente] ADV supposedly

supuesto, -a [su'pwesto, a] PP *de* **suponer** ▸ ADJ
(*hipotético*) supposed; (*falso*) false; **dar por ~ algo**
to take sth for granted; **por ~** of course ▸ NM
assumption, hypothesis ▸ CONJ: **~ que** since

S

supurar [supu'rar] /**1a**/ vi to fester, suppurate

supuse etc [su'puse] vb ver **suponer**

★**sur** [sur] ADJ southern; (rumbo) southerly ▶ NM south; (viento) south wind

Suráfrica etc [su'rafrika] = **Sudáfrica** etc

Suramérica etc [sura'merika] = **Sudamérica** etc

suramericano, -a [surameri'kano, a] ADJ South American ▶ NM/F South American

surcar [sur'kar] /**1g**/ vt to plough; (superficie) to cut, score

surco ['surko] NM (en metal, disco) groove; (Agr) furrow

surcoreano, -a [surkore'ano, a] ADJ, NM/F South Korean

sureño, -a [su'reɲo, a] ADJ southern ▶ NM/F southerner

★**sureste** [su'reste] = **sudeste**

surf [surf] NM surfing

surfear [surfe'ar] /**1a**/ vт: ~ **por Internet** to surf the internet

surgir [sur'xir] /**3c**/ vi to arise, emerge; (dificultad) to come up, crop up

Surinam [suri'nam] NM Suriname

surja etc ['surxa] vb ver **surgir**

★**suroeste** [suro'este] NM south-west

surque etc ['surke] vb ver **surcar**

surrealismo [surrea'lismo] NM surrealism

surrealista [surrea'lista] ADJ, NMF surrealist

★**surtido, -a** [sur'tiðo, a] ADJ mixed, assorted ▶ NM (selección) selection, assortment; (abastecimiento) supply, stock

surtidor [surti'ðor] NM (chorro) jet, spout; (fuente) fountain; ~ **de gasolina** petrol (BRIT) o gas (US) pump

surtir [sur'tir] /**3a**/ vт to supply, provide; (efecto) to have, produce ▶ vi to spout, spurt ■ **surtirse** vR: **surtirse de** to provide o.s. with

susceptible [susθep'tiβle] ADJ susceptible; (sensible) sensitive; ~ **de** capable of

suscitar [susθi'tar] /**1a**/ vт to cause, provoke; (discusión) to start; (duda, problema) to raise; (interés, sospechas) to arouse

suscribir [suskri'βir] /**3a**/ vт (firmar) to sign; (respaldar) to subscribe to, endorse; (Com: acciones) to take out an option on; ~ **a algn a una revista** to take out a subscription to a journal for sb ■ **suscribirse** vR to subscribe

suscripción [suskrip'θjon] NF subscription

suscrito, -a [sus'krito, a] PP de **suscribir** ▶ ADJ: ~ **en exceso** oversubscribed

sushi ['suʃi] NM sushi

susodicho, -a [suso'ditʃo, a] ADJ above-mentioned

★**suspender** [suspen'der] /**2a**/ vт (objeto) to hang (up), suspend; (trabajo) to stop, suspend; (Escol) to fail; (interrumpir) to adjourn; (atrasar) to postpone

suspense [sus'pense] NM suspense; **película/ novela de ~** thriller

suspensión [suspen'sjon] NF suspension; (fig) stoppage, suspension; (Jur) stay; ~ **de fuego** o **de hostilidades** ceasefire, cessation of hostilities; ~ **de pagos** suspension of payments

suspensivo, -a [suspen'siβo, a] ADJ: **puntos suspensivos** dots, suspension points

suspenso, -a [sus'penso, a] ADJ hanging, suspended; (Escol) failed ▶ NM (Escol) fail(ure); **quedar** o **estar en ~** to be pending; **película** o **novela de ~** (AM) thriller

suspicacia [suspi'kaθja] NF suspicion, mistrust

suspicaz [suspi'kaθ] ADJ suspicious, distrustful

suspirar [suspi'rar] /**1a**/ vi to sigh

suspiro [sus'piro] NM sigh

sustancia [sus'tanθja] NF substance; ~ **gris** (Anat) grey matter; **sin ~** lacking in substance, shallow

sustancial [sustan'θjal] ADJ substantial

sustancioso, -a [sustan'θjoso, a] ADJ substantial; (discurso) solid

sustantivo, -a [sustan'tiβo, a] ADJ substantive; (Ling) substantival, noun cpd ▶ NM noun, substantive

sustentar [susten'tar] /**1a**/ vт (alimentar) to sustain, nourish; (objeto) to hold up, support; (idea, teoría) to maintain, uphold; (fig) to sustain, keep going

sustento [sus'tento] NM support; (alimento) sustenance, food

★**sustituir** [sustitu'ir] /**3g**/ vт to substitute, replace

sustituto, -a [susti'tuto, a] NM/F substitute, replacement

sustituyendo etc [sustitu'jendo] vb ver **sustituir**

★**susto** ['susto] NM fright, scare; **dar un ~ a algn** to give sb a fright; **darse** o **pegarse un ~** (fam) to get a fright

sustraer [sustra'er] /**2p**/ vт to remove, take away; (Mat) to subtract

sustraiga etc [sus'traiɣa], **sustraje** etc [sus-'traxe] vb ver **sustraer**

sustrato [sus'trato] NM substratum

sustrayendo etc [sustra'jendo] vb ver **sustraer**

susurrar [susu'rrar] /**1a**/ vi to whisper

susurro [su'surro] NM whisper

sutil [su'til] ADJ (aroma) subtle; (tenue) thin; (hilo, hebra) fine; (olor) delicate; (brisa) gentle; (diferencia) fine, subtle; (inteligencia) sharp, keen

sutileza [suti'leθa] NF subtlety; (delgadez) thinness; (delicadeza) delicacy; (agudeza) keenness

sutura [su'tura] NF suture

suturar [sutu'rar] /**1a**/ vт to suture; (juntar con puntos) to stitch

★**suyo, -a** ['sujo, a] ADJ (con artículo o después del verbo ser: de él) his; (: de ella) hers; (: de ellos, ellas) theirs; (: de usted, ustedes) yours; (: después de un *nombre: de él*) of his; (: *de ella*) of hers; (: *de ellos, ellas*) of theirs; (: *de usted, ustedes*) of yours; **lo ~** (what is) his; (*su parte*) his share, what he deserves; **los suyos** (*su familia*) one's family *o* relations; (*sus partidarios*) one's own people *o* supporters; **~ afectísimo** (*en carta*) yours faithfully *o* sincerely; **de ~** in itself; **eso es muy ~** that's just like him; **hacer de las suyas** to get up to one's old tricks; **ir a la suya, ir a lo ~** to go one's own way; **salirse con la suya** to get one's way; **un amigo ~** a friend of his (*o* hers *o* theirs *o* yours)

Tt

T, t [te] NF (*letra*) T, t; **T de Tarragona** T for Tommy

t ABR = **tonelada**

T. ABR (= *Teléfon*; *Telégrafo*) tel.; (*Com*) = **tarifa**; **tasa**

t. ABR (= *tomo(s)*) vol(s)

Tabacalera [taβaka'lera] NF *former Spanish state tobacco monopoly*

★**tabaco** [ta'βako] NM tobacco; (*fam*) cigarettes *pl*

tábano ['taβano] NM horsefly

tabaquería [tabake'ria] NF tobacconist's (*BRIT*), cigar store (*US*)

tabarra [ta'βarra] NF (*fam*) nuisance; **dar la ~** to be a pain in the neck

★**taberna** [ta'βerna] NF bar

tabernero, -a [taβer'nero, a] NM/F (*encargado*) publican; (*camarero*) barman/barmaid

tabique [ta'βike] NM (*pared*) thin wall; (*para dividir*) partition

★**tabla** ['taβla] NF (*de madera*) plank; (*estante*) shelf; (*de anuncios*) board; (*lista, catálogo*) list; (*de vestido*) pleat; (*Arte*) panel; **~ de consulta** (*Inform*) lookup table ▪ **tablas** NFPL (*Taur, Teat*) boards; **estar** *o* **quedar en tablas** to draw

tablado [ta'βlaðo] NM (*plataforma*) platform; (*suelo*) plank floor; (*Teat*) stage

tablao [ta'βlao] NM (*tb*: **tablao flamenco**) flamenco show

tablero [ta'βlero] NM (*de madera*) plank, board; (*pizarra*) blackboard; (*de ajedrez, damas*) board; (*Auto*) dashboard; **~ de gráficos** (*Inform*) graph pad; **~ de mandos** (*Am Auto*) dashboard

tablet ['taβlet] NF (*Inform*) tablet

tableta [ta'βleta] NF (*Med*) tablet; (*de chocolate*) bar; (*Inform*) tablet

tablilla [ta'βliʎa] NF small board; (*Med*) splint

tablón [ta'βlon] NM (*de suelo*) plank; (*de techo*) beam; (*de anuncios*) notice board

tabú [ta'βu] NM taboo

tabulación [taβula'θjon] NF (*Inform*) tab(bing)

tabulador [taβula'ðor] NM (*Inform, Tip*) tab

tabuladora [taβula'ðora] NF: **~ eléctrica** electric accounting machine

tabular [taβu'lar] /**1a**/ VT to tabulate; (*Inform*) to tab

taburete [taβu'rete] NM stool

tacaño, -a [ta'kaɲo, a] ADJ (*avaro*) mean; (*astuto*) crafty

tacha ['tatʃa] NF (*defecto*) flaw, defect; (*Tec*) stud; **poner ~ a** to find fault with; **sin ~** flawless

tachar [ta'tʃar] /**1a**/ VT (*borrar*) to cross out; (*corregir*) to correct; (*criticar*) to criticize; **~ de** to accuse of

tacho ['tatʃo] NM (*Am*) bucket, pail; **~ de la basura** rubbish bin (*BRIT*), trash can (*US*)

tachón [ta'tʃon] NM erasure; (*tachadura*) crossing-out; (*Tec*) ornamental stud; (*Costura*) trimming

tachuela [ta'tʃwela] NF (*clavo*) tack

tácito, -a ['taθito, a] ADJ tacit; (*acuerdo*) unspoken; (*Ling*) understood; (*ley*) unwritten

taciturno, -a [taθi'turno, a] ADJ (*callado*) silent; (*malhumorado*) sullen

taco ['tako] NM (*Billar*) cue; (*libro de billetes*) book; (*manojo de billetes*) wad; (*Am*) heel; (*tarugo*) peg; (*fam: bocado*) snack; (: *palabrota*) swear word; (: *trago de vino*) swig; (*MÉXICO*) filled tortilla; **armarse** *o* **hacerse un ~** to get into a mess

tacógrafo [ta'koɣrafo] NM (*Com*) tachograph

tacón [ta'kon] NM heel; **de ~ alto** high-heeled

taconear [takone'ar] /**1a**/ VI (*dar golpecitos*) to tap with one's heels; (*Mil etc*) to click one's heels

taconeo [tako'neo] NM (heel) tapping *o* clicking

táctico, -a ['taktiko, a] ADJ tactical ▶ NF tactics *pl*

táctil [ˈtaktil] ADJ (sensibilidad) tactile; (Telec: aparato) touchscreen, touch-sensitive

tacto [ˈtakto] NM touch; (acción) touching; (fig) tact

TAE NF ABR (= tasa anual equivalente) APR

tafetán [tafeˈtan] NM taffeta; **~ adhesivo** o **inglés** sticking plaster ■**tafetanes** NMPL (fam) frills

tafilete [tafiˈlete] NM morocco leather

tahona [taˈona] NF (panadería) bakery; (molino) flour mill

tahúr [taˈur] NM gambler; (pey) cheat

tailandés, -esa [tailanˈdes, esa] ADJ, NM/F Thai ▶ NM (Ling) Thai

Tailandia [tailanˈdja] NF Thailand

taimado, -a [taiˈmaðo, a] ADJ (astuto) sly; (resentido) sullen

taita [ˈtaita] NM dad, daddy

tajada [taˈxaða] NF slice; (fam) rake-off; **sacar ~** to get one's share

tajante [taˈxante] ADJ (afirmación) categorical; (crítica) sharp; (negativa) emphatic

tajar [taˈxar] /1a/ VT to cut, slice

Tajo [ˈtaxo] NM Tagus

tajo [ˈtaxo] NM (corte) cut; (filo) cutting edge; (Geo) cleft

★**tal** [tal] ADJ such; **un ~ García** a man called García; **~ vez** perhaps ▶ PRON (persona) someone, such a one; (cosa) something, such a thing; **~ como** such as; **~ para cual** tit for tat; (dos iguales) two of a kind; **hablábamos de que si ~ si cual** we were talking about this, that and the other ▶ ADV: **~ como** (igual) just as; **~ cual** (como es) just as it is; **~ el padre, cual el hijo** like father, like son; **¿qué ~?** how are things?; **¿qué ~ te gusta?** how do you like it? ▶ CONJ: **con ~ (de) que** provided that

tala [ˈtala] NF (de árboles) tree felling

taladradora [talaðraˈðora] NF drill; **~ neumática** pneumatic drill

taladrar [talaˈðrar] /1a/ VT to drill; (fig: ruido) to pierce

taladro [taˈlaðro] NM (gen) drill; (hoyo) drill hole; **~ neumático** pneumatic drill

talante [taˈlante] NM (humor) mood; (voluntad) will, willingness

talar [taˈlar] /1a/ VT to fell, cut down; (fig) to devastate

talco [ˈtalko] NM (polvos) talcum powder; (Minería) talc

talega [taˈleɣa] NF sack

talego [taˈleɣo] NM sack; **tener ~** (fam) to have money

talento [taˈlento] NM talent; (capacidad) ability; (don) gift

Talgo [ˈtalɣo] NM ABR (= tren articulado ligero Goicoechea Oriol) high-speed train

talidomida [taliðoˈmiða] NM thalidomide

talismán [talisˈman] NM talisman

★**talla** [ˈtaʎa] NF (estatura, Med) height; (fig) stature; (de ropa) size, fitting; (palo) measuring rod; (Arte: de madera) carving; (: de piedra) sculpture

tallado, -a [taˈʎaðo, a] ADJ carved ▶ NM (de madera) carving; (de piedra) sculpture

tallar [taˈʎar] /1a/ VT (trabajar) to work, carve; (grabar) to engrave; (medir) to measure; (repartir) to deal ▶ VI to deal

tallarín [taʎaˈrin] NM noodle

talle [ˈtaʎe] NM (Anat) waist; (medida) size; (física) build; (: de mujer) figure; (fig) appearance; **de ~ esbelto** with a slim figure

★**taller** [taˈʎer] NM (Tec) workshop; (fábrica) factory; (Auto) garage; (de artista) studio

tallo [ˈtaʎo] NM (de planta) stem; (de hierba) blade; (brote) shoot; (col) cabbage; (Culin) candied peel

talmente [talˈmente] ADV (de esta forma) in such a way; (hasta tal punto) to such an extent; (exactamente) exactly

talón [taˈlon] NM (gen) heel; (Com) counterfoil; (cheque) cheque (BRIT), check (US); (Tec) rim; **~ de Aquiles** Achilles heel

talonario [taloˈnarjo] NM (de cheques) chequebook (BRIT), checkbook (US); (de billetes) book of tickets; (de recibos) receipt book

★**tamaño, -a** [taˈmaɲo, a] ADJ (tan grande) such a big; (tan pequeño) such a small ▶ NM size; **de ~ natural** full-size; **¿de qué ~ es?** what size is it?

tamarindo [tamaˈrindo] NM tamarind

tambaleante [tambaleˈante] ADJ (persona) staggering; (mueble) wobbly; (vehículo) swaying

tambalearse [tambaleˈarse] /1a/ VR (persona) to stagger; (mueble) to wobble; (vehículo) to sway

★**también** [tamˈbjen] ADV (igualmente) also, too, as well; (además) besides; **estoy cansado — yo ~** I'm tired — me too o so am I

> *También* puede traducirse por **also**, **too** o **as well**. **Also** es el menos coloquial de los tres y normalmente va delante del verbo principal y detrás de los verbos auxiliares si los hay; además suele ir delante de aquello a lo que se refiere: *También he estado en Moscú.* **I've also been to Moscow.**
> **Too** y **as well** suelen ir al final de la frase: **I've been to Moscow too** o **as well**.
> **Too** se puede cambiar de posición para mayor énfasis: *Tú también puedes aprender ruso.* **You too can learn Russian.**

tambor [tamˈbor] NM drum; (Anat) eardrum; **~ del freno** brake drum; **~ magnético** (Inform) magnetic drum

tamboril [tamboˈril] NM small drum

tamborilear [tamborileˈar] /1a/ VI (Mus) to drum; (con los dedos) to drum with one's fingers

tamborilero, -a [tamboriˈlero, a] NM/F drummer

Támesis [ˈtamesis] NM Thames

tamice etc [taˈmiθe] VB ver **tamizar**

tamiz [taˈmiθ] NM sieve

tamizar [tamiˈθar] /1f/ VT to sieve

★**tampoco** [tamˈpoko] ADV nor, neither; **yo ~ lo compré** I didn't buy it either

tampón [tamˈpon] NM plug; (Med) tampon

★**tan** [tan] ADV so; **~ es así que** so much so that; **¡qué cosa ~ rara!** how strange!; **no es una idea ~ buena** it is not such a good idea

tanatorio [tanaˈtorjo] NM (privado) funeral home o parlour; (público) mortuary

tanda [ˈtanda] NF (gen) series; (de inyecciones) course; (juego) set; (turno) shift; (grupo) gang

tándem [ˈtandem] NM tandem; (Pol) duo

tanga [ˈtanga] NM (bikini) tanga; (ropa interior) tanga briefs

tangente [tanˈxente] NF tangent; **salirse por la ~** to go off at a tangent

Tánger [ˈtanxer] NM Tangier

tangerina [tanxeˈrina] NF (Am) tangerine

tangerino, -a [tanxeˈrino, a] ADJ of o from Tangier ▶ NM/F native o inhabitant of Tangier

tangible [tanˈxiβle] ADJ tangible

tango [ˈtango] NM tango

tanino [taˈnino] NM tannin

tankini [tanˈkini] NM tankini

tanque [ˈtanke] NM (gen) tank; (Auto, Naut) tanker

tanqueta [tanˈketa] NF (Mil) small tank, armoured vehicle

tantear [tanteˈar] /1a/ VT (calcular) to reckon (up); (medir) to take the measure of; (probar) to test, try out; (tomar la medida: persona) to take the measurements of; (considerar) to weigh up; (persona, opinión) to sound out ▶ VI (Deporte) to score

tanteo [tanˈteo] NM (cálculo aproximado) (rough) calculation; (prueba) test, trial; (Deporte) scoring; (adivinanzas) guesswork; **al ~** by trial and error

tantísimo, -a [tanˈtisimo, a] ADJ so much; **tantísimos** so many

---

tanto, -a [ˈtanto, a]

ADJ (cantidad) so much, as much; **tantos** so many, as many; **20 y tantos** 20-odd
▶ ADV (cantidad) so much, as much; (tiempo) so long, as long; **tanto tú como yo** both you and I; **tanto como eso** as much as that; **tanto más ... cuanto que** it's all the more ... because; **tanto mejor/peor** so much the better/the worse; **tanto si viene como si va** whether he comes or whether he goes; **tanto es así que** so much so that; **por tanto, por lo tanto** therefore; **me he vuelto ronco de** o **con tanto hablar** I have become hoarse with so much talking
▶ CONJ: **con tanto que** provided (that); **en tanto que** while; **hasta tanto (que)** until such time as
▶ NM **1** (punto) point
2 (gol) goal
3 (locuciones): **tanto alzado** agreed price; **tanto por ciento** percentage; **al tanto** up to date; **estar al tanto de los acontecimientos** to be fully abreast of events; **al tanto de que** because of the fact that
▶ PRON: **cada uno paga tanto** each one pays so much; **uno de tantos** one of many; **a tantos de agosto** on such and such a day in August; **entre tanto** meanwhile

---

tañer [taˈɲer] /2f/ VT (Mus) to play; (campana) to ring

T/año ABR = **toneladas por año**

TAO NF ABR (= traducción asistida por ordenador) MAT

★**tapa** [ˈtapa] NF (de caja, olla) lid; (de botella) top; (de libro) cover; (de comida) snack

tapacubos [tapaˈkuβos] NM INV hub cap

tapadera [tapaˈðera] NF lid, cover

tapado [taˈpaðo] NM (Am: abrigo) coat

tapar [taˈpar] /1a/ VT (cubrir) to cover; (envolver) to wrap o cover up; (la vista) to obstruct; (persona, falta) to conceal; (Am) to fill ■ **taparse** VR to wrap o.s. up

taparrabo [tapaˈrraβo] NM loincloth

tapete [taˈpete] NM table cover; **estar sobre el ~** (fig) to be under discussion

tapia [ˈtapja] NF (garden) wall

tapiar [taˈpjar] /1b/ VT to wall in

tapice etc [taˈpiθe] VB ver **tapizar**

tapicería [tapiθeˈria] NF tapestry; (para muebles) upholstery; (tienda) upholsterer's (shop)

tapicero, -a [tapiˈθero, a] NM/F (de muebles) upholsterer

tapiz [taˈpiθ] NM (alfombra) carpet; (tela tejida) tapestry

tapizar [tapiˈθar] /1f/ VT (pared) to wallpaper; (suelo) to carpet; (muebles) to upholster

tapón [taˈpon] NM (de botella) top; (corcho) stopper; (Tec) plug; (Med) tampon; **~ de rosca** o **de tuerca** screw-top

taponar [tapoˈnar] /1a/ VT (botella) to cork; (tubería) to block

taponazo [tapoˈnaθo] NM (de tapón) pop

tapujo [taˈpuxo] NM (embozo) muffler; (engaño) deceit; **sin tapujos** honestly

taquigrafía [takiɣraˈfia] NF shorthand

taquígrafo, -a [taˈkiɣrafo, a] NM/F shorthand writer, stenographer (US)

★**taquilla** [taˈkiʎa] NF (de estación etc) booking office; (de teatro) box office; (suma recogida) takings pl; (archivador) filing cabinet

taquillero, -a [takiˈʎero, a] ADJ: **función**

taquillera box office success ▸ NM/F ticket clerk

taquimecanografía [takimekanoɣraˈfia] NF shorthand and typing

taquímetro [taˈkimetro] NM speedometer; (de control) tachymeter

tara [ˈtara] NF (defecto) defect; (Com) tare

tarado, -a [taˈraðo, a] ADJ (Com) defective, imperfect; (fam: insulto: idiota) stupid; (: loco) crazy, nuts ▸ NM/F (fam: insulto) idiot, cretin

tarántula [taˈrantula] NF tarantula

tararear [tarareˈar] /1a/ VI to hum

tardanza [tarˈðanθa] NF (demora) delay; (lentitud) slowness

★**tardar** [tarˈðar] /1a/ VI (tomar tiempo) to take a long time; (llegar tarde) to be late; (demorar) to delay; **¿tarda mucho el tren?** does the train take long?; **a más ~** at the (very) latest; **~ en hacer algo** to be slow o take a long time to do sth; **no tardes en venir** come soon, come before long

★**tarde** [ˈtarðe] ADV (hora) late; (fuera de tiempo) too late; **~ o temprano** sooner or later ▸ NF (de día) afternoon; (de noche) evening; **de ~ en ~** from time to time; **¡buenas tardes!** (de día) good afternoon!; (de noche) good evening!; **a o por la ~** in the afternoon; in the evening

tardío, -a [tarˈðio, a] ADJ (retrasado) late; (lento) slow (to arrive)

tardo, -a [ˈtarðo, a] ADJ (lento) slow; (torpe) dull; **~ de oído** hard of hearing

★**tarea** [taˈrea] NF task; **~ de ocasión** chore ▪ **tareas** NFPL (Escol) homework sg

★**tarifa** [taˈrifa] NF (lista de precios) price list; (Com) tariff; **~ básica** basic rate; **~ completa** all-in cost; **~ a destajo** piece rate; **~ doble** double time

tarima [taˈrima] NF (plataforma) platform

★**tarjeta** [tarˈxeta] NF card; **~ postal/de crédito/de Navidad** postcard/credit card/Christmas card; **~ de circuitos** (Inform) circuit board; **~ cliente** loyalty card; **~ comercial** (Com) calling card; **~ dinero** cash card; **~ gráficos** (Inform) graphics card; **~ monedero** electronic purse o wallet; **~ de embarque** boarding pass; **~ de memoria** memory card; **~ prepago** top-up card; **~ SIM** SIM card

tarot [taˈrot] NM tarot

tarraconense [tarrakoˈnense] ADJ of o from Tarragona ▸ NMF native o inhabitant of Tarragona

★**tarro** [ˈtarro] NM jar, pot

★**tarta** [ˈtarta] NF (pastel) cake; (torta) tart

tartajear [tartaxeˈar] /1a/ VI to stammer

tartamudear [tartamuðeˈar] /1a/ VI to stutter, stammer

tartamudo, -a [tartaˈmuðo, a] ADJ stuttering, stammering ▸ NM/F stutterer, stammerer

tartárico, -a [tarˈtariko, a] ADJ: **ácido ~** tartaric acid

tártaro, -a [ˈtartaro, a] ADJ: **salsa tártara** tartar(e) sauce ▸ NM Tartar; (Química) tartar

tarugo, -a [taˈruɣo, a] ADJ stupid ▸ NM (de madera) lump

tarumba [taˈrumba] ADJ (confuso) confused

★**tasa** [ˈtasa] NF (precio) (fixed) price, rate; (valoración) valuation; (medida, norma) measure, standard; **~ básica** (Com) basic rate; **~ de cambio** exchange rate; **de ~ cero** (Com) zero-rated; **tasas de aeropuerto** airport tax; **~ de crecimiento** growth rate; **~ de interés/de nacimiento** rate of interest/birth rate; **~ de rendimiento** (Com) rate of return; **tasas universitarias** university fees

tasación [tasaˈθjon] NF assessment, valuation; (fig) appraisal

tasador, a [tasaˈðor, a] NM/F valuer; (Com: de impuestos) assessor

tasar [taˈsar] /1a/ VT (arreglar el precio) to fix a price for; (valorar) to value, assess; (limitar) to limit

tasca [ˈtaska] NF (fam) pub

tata [ˈtata] NM (fam) dad(dy) ▸ NF (niñera) nanny, maid

tatarabuelo, -a [tataraˈβwelo, a] NM/F great-great-grandfather/mother; **los tatarabuelos** one's great-great-grandparents

tatuaje [taˈtwaxe] NM (dibujo) tattoo; (acto) tattooing

tatuar [taˈtwar] /1d/ VT to tattoo

taumaturgo [taumaˈturɣo] NM miracle worker

taurino, -a [tauˈrino, a] ADJ bullfighting cpd

Tauro [ˈtauro] NM Taurus

tauromaquia [tauroˈmakja] NF (art of) bullfighting

tautología [tautoloˈxia] NF tautology

taxativo, -a [taksaˈtiβo, a] ADJ (restringido) limited; (sentido) specific

★**taxi** [ˈtaksi] NM taxi

taxidermia [taksiˈðermja] NF taxidermy

taxímetro [takˈsimetro] NM taximeter

★**taxista** [takˈsista] NMF taxi driver

Tayikistán [tajikisˈtan] NM Tajikistan

★**taza** [ˈtaθa] NF cup; (de retrete) bowl; **~ para café** coffee cup; **~ de café** cup of coffee

★**tazón** [taˈθon] NM mug, large cup; (escudilla) basin

TB ABR (= terabyte) TB

TDT NF ABR (= televisión digital terrestre) DTT, DTTV

★**te** [te] PRON (complemento de objeto) you; (complemento indirecto) (to) you; (reflexivo) (to) yourself; **¿te duele mucho el brazo?** does your arm hurt a lot?; **te equivocas** you're wrong; **¡cálmate!** calm yourself!

★**té** [te] (pl **tés**) NM tea; (reunión) tea party

tea [ˈtea] NF (antorcha) torch

t

teatral [tea'tral] ADJ theatre *cpd* (BRIT), theater *cpd* (US); (*fig*) theatrical

★**teatro** [te'atro] NM theatre (BRIT), theater (US); (*Lit*) plays *pl*, drama; **el ~** (*carrera*) the theatre, acting; **~ de aficionados/de variedades** amateur/variety theatre, vaudeville theater (US); **hacer ~** (*fig*) to make a fuss

★**tebeo** [te'βeo] NM children's comic

techado [te'tʃaðo] NM (*techo*) roof; **bajo ~** under cover

★**techo** ['tetʃo] NM (*externo*) roof; (*interno*) ceiling

techumbre [te'tʃumbre] NF roof

tecla ['tekla] NF (*Inform, Mus, Tip*) key; (*Inform*): **~ de anulación/de borrar** cancel/delete key; **~ de control/de edición** control/edit key; **~ con flecha** arrow key; **~ programable** user-defined key; **~ de retorno/de tabulación** return/tab key; **~ del cursor** cursor key; **teclas de control direccional del cursor** cursor control keys

★**teclado** [te'klaðo] NM (*tb Inform*) keyboard; **~ numérico** (*Inform*) numeric keypad

teclear [tekle'ar] /1a/ VI to strum; (*fam*) to drum ▸ VT (*Inform*) to key (in), type in

tecleo [te'kleo] NM (*Mus: sonido*) strumming; (: *forma de tocar*) fingering; (*fam*) drumming

tecnicismo [tekni'θismo] NM (*carácter técnico*) technical nature; (*Ling*) technical term

★**técnico, -a** ['tekniko, a] ADJ technical ▸ NM/F technician; (*experto*) expert ▸ NF (*procedimientos*) technique; (*tecnología*) technology; (*arte, oficio*) craft

tecnicolor [tekniko'lor] NM Technicolor®

tecnócrata [tek'nokrata] NMF technocrat

★**tecnología** [teknolo'xia] NF technology; **~ de estado sólido** (*Inform*) solid-state technology; **~ de la información** information technology; **~ limpia** clean technology

★**tecnológico, -a** [tekno'loxiko, a] ADJ technological

tecnólogo, -a [tek'noloɣo, a] NM/F technologist

tecolote [teko'lote] NM (*AM*) owl

tedio ['teðjo] NM (*aburrimiento*) boredom; (*apatía*) apathy; (*fastidio*) depression

tedioso, -a [te'ðjoso, a] ADJ boring; (*cansado*) wearisome, tedious

Teherán [tee'ran] NM Teheran

teja ['texa] NF (*azulejo*) tile; (*Bot*) lime (tree)

★**tejado** [te'xaðo] NM (tiled) roof

tejano, -a [te'xano, a] ADJ, NM/F Texan ▸ NMPL: **tejanos** (*vaqueros*) jeans

Tejas ['texas] NM Texas

tejemaneje [texema'nexe] NM (*actividad*) bustle; (*lío*) fuss, to-do; (*intriga*) intrigue

tejer [te'xer] /2a/ VT to weave; (*tela de araña*) to spin; (*AM*) to knit; (*fig*) to fabricate ▸ VI: **~ y destejer** to chop and change

tejido [te'xiðo] NM fabric; (*estofa, tela*) (knitted) material; (*telaraña*) web; (*Anat*) tissue; (*textura*) texture

tejo ['texo] NM (*Bot*) yew (tree)

tel. ABR (= *teléfono*) tel.

★**tela** ['tela] NF (*material*) material; (*de fruta, en líquido*) skin; (*del ojo*) film; **hay ~ para rato** there's lots to talk about; **poner en ~ de juicio** to (call in) question; **~ de araña** cobweb, spider's web

telar [te'lar] NM (*máquina*) loom; (*de teatro*) gridiron ■ **telares** NMPL textile mill *sg*

telaraña [tela'raɲa] NF cobweb, spider's web

tele ['tele] NF (*fam*) TV

tele... [tele] PREF tele...

telebasura [teleβa'sura] NF trash TV

telecargar [telekar'ɣar] /1h/ VT (*Inform*) to download

telecomunicación [telekomunika'θjon] NF telecommunication

teleconferencia [telekonfe'renθja] NF (*reunión*) teleconference; (*sistema*) teleconferencing

telecontrol [telekon'trol] NM remote control

telecopiadora [telekopja'ðora] NF: **~ facsímil** fax copier

★**telediario** [tele'ðjarjo] NM television news

teledifusión [teleðifu'sjon] NF (television) broadcast

teledirigido, -a [teleðiri'xiðo, a] ADJ remote-controlled

teléf. ABR (= *teléfono*) tel.

★**teleférico** [tele'feriko] NM (*tren*) cable-railway; (*de esquí*) ski-lift

telefilm [tele'film], **telefilme** [tele'filme] NM TV film

telefonazo [telefo'naθo] NM (*fam*) telephone call; **te daré un ~** I'll give you a ring

★**telefonear** [telefone'ar] /1a/ VI to telephone

telefonía [telefo'nia] NF telephony; **~ móvil** *o* **celular** mobile telephony; **~ fija** fixed telephony, landline phones *pl*; **red de ~ móvil** mobile phone (BRIT) *o* cellphone (US) network; **servicios de ~ móvil** mobile phone (BRIT) *o* cellphone (US) services

telefónicamente [tele'fonikamente] ADV by (tele)phone

telefónico, -a [tele'foniko, a] ADJ telephone *cpd* ▸ NF: **Telefónica** (*ESP*) *former Spanish national telephone company*

telefonillo [telefo'niʎo] NM (*de puerta*) intercom

telefonista [telefo'nista] NMF telephonist

★**teléfono** [te'lefono] NM (tele)phone; **~ móvil** mobile phone (BRIT), cellphone (US); **está hablando por ~** he's on the phone; **llamar a algn por ~** to ring sb (up) *o* phone sb (up); **~ celular** (*AM*) mobile phone (BRIT), cellphone (US); **~ con cámara** camera phone; **~ inalámbrico** cordless phone

telefoto [tele'foto] NF telephoto
telegrafía [teleɣra'fia] NF telegraphy
telégrafo [te'leɣrafo] NM telegraph; (*fam: persona*) telegraph boy
telegrama [tele'ɣrama] NM telegram
teleimpresor [teleimpre'sor] NM teleprinter
telemática [tele'matika] NF telematics *sg*
telémetro [te'lemetro] NM rangefinder
★**telenovela** [teleno'βela] NF soap (opera)
teleobjetivo [teleobxe'tiβo] NM telephoto lens
telepatía [telepa'tia] NF telepathy
telepático, -a [tele'patiko, a] ADJ telepathic
telepredicador, a [telepreðika'ðor, a] NM/F televangelist
teleproceso [telepro'θeso] NM teleprocessing
telerrealidad [telerreali'ðað] NF reality TV
telescópico, -a [tele'skopiko, a] ADJ telescopic
telescopio [tele'skopjo] NM telescope
telesilla [tele'siʎa] NM chairlift
★**telespectador, a** [telespekta'ðor, a] NM/F viewer
telesquí [teles'ki] NM ski-lift
teletarjeta [teletar'xeta] NF phonecard
teletex [tele'teks], **teletexto** [tele'teksto] NM teletext
teletipo [tele'tipo] NM teletype(writer)
teletrabajador, a [teletraβaxa'ðor, a] NM/F teleworker
★**teletrabajo** [teletra'βaxo] NM teleworking
televentas [tele'βentas] NFPL telesales
televidente [teleβi'ðente] NMF viewer
televisar [teleβi'sar] /1a/ VT to televise
★**televisión** [teleβi'sjon] NF television; **~ en color/por satélite** colour/satellite television; **~ digital** digital television
televisivo, -a [teleβi'siβo, a] ADJ television *cpd*
★**televisor** [teleβi'sor] NM television set
télex ['teleks] NM telex; **máquina ~** telex (machine); **enviar por ~** to telex
telón [te'lon] NM curtain; **~ de boca/seguridad** front/safety curtain; **~ de acero** (*Historia*) Iron Curtain; **~ de fondo** backcloth, background
telonero, -a [telo'nero, a] NM/F support act; **los teloneros** (*Mus*) the support band
★**tema** ['tema] NM (*asunto*) subject, topic; (*Mus*) theme; **temas de actualidad** current affairs ▶ NF (*obsesión*) obsession; (*manía*) ill-will; **tener ~ a algn** to have a grudge against sb
temario [te'marjo] NM (*Escol*) set of topics; (*de una conferencia*) agenda
temático, -a [te'matiko, a] ADJ thematic ▶ NF subject matter

tembladera [tembla'ðera] NF shaking; (*Am*) quagmire
★**temblar** [tem'blar] /1j/ VI to shake, tremble; (*de frío*) to shiver
tembleque [tem'bleke] ADJ shaking ▶ NM shaking
temblón, -ona [tem'blon, ona] ADJ shaking
temblor [tem'blor] NM trembling; (*de tierra*) earthquake
tembloroso, -a [temblo'roso, a] ADJ trembling
temer [te'mer] /2a/ VT to fear; **temo que Juan llegue tarde** I am afraid Juan may be late ▶ VI to be afraid
temerario, -a [teme'rarjo, a] ADJ (*imprudente*) rash; (*descuidado*) reckless; (*arbitrario*) hasty
temeridad [temeri'ðað] NF (*imprudencia*) rashness; (*audacia*) boldness
temeroso, -a [teme'roso, a] ADJ (*miedoso*) fearful; (*que inspira temor*) frightful
temible [te'miβle] ADJ fearsome
temor [te'mor] NM (*miedo*) fear; (*duda*) suspicion
témpano ['tempano] NM (*Mus*) kettledrum; **~ de hielo** ice floe
★**temperamento** [tempera'mento] NM temperament; **tener ~** to be temperamental
temperar [tempe'rar] /1a/ VT to temper, moderate
★**temperatura** [tempera'tura] NF temperature
★**tempestad** [tempes'tað] NF storm; **~ en un vaso de agua** (*fig*) storm in a teacup, tempest in a teapot (*US*)
tempestuoso, -a [tempes'twoso, a] ADJ stormy
★**templado, -a** [tem'plaðo, a] ADJ (*agua*) lukewarm; (*clima*) mild; (*Mus*) in tune, well-tuned; (*moderado*) moderate
templanza [tem'planθa] NF moderation; (*en el beber*) abstemiousness; (*del clima*) mildness
templar [tem'plar] /1a/ VT (*moderar*) to moderate; (*furia*) to restrain; (*calor*) to reduce; (*solución*) to dilute; (*afinar*) to tune (up); (*acero*) to temper; (*tuerca*) to tighten up ▶ VI to moderate ■ **templarse** VR to be restrained
temple ['temple] NM (*humor*) mood; (*coraje*) courage; (*ajuste*) tempering; (*afinación*) tuning; (*pintura*) tempera
templo ['templo] NM (*iglesia*) church; (*pagano etc*) temple; **~ metodista** Methodist chapel
★**temporada** [tempo'raða] NF time, period; (*estación, social, Deporte*) season; **en plena ~** at the height of the season
★**temporal** [tempo'ral] ADJ (*no permanente*) temporary; (*Rel*) temporal ▶ NM storm
temporario, -a [tempo'rarjo, a] ADJ (*Am*) temporary
tempranero, -a [tempra'nero, a] ADJ (*Bot*) early; (*persona*) early-rising

t

★**temprano, -a** [tem'prano, a] ADJ early ▸ ADV early; (*demasiado pronto*) too soon, too early; **lo más ~ posible** as soon as possible

ten [ten] VB ver **tener**

tenaces [te'naθes] ADJ PL ver **tenaz**

tenacidad [tenaθi'ðað] NF (*gen*) tenacity; (*dureza*) toughness; (*terquedad*) stubbornness

tenacillas [tena'θiʎas] NFPL (*gen*) tongs; (*para el pelo*) curling tongs; (*Med*) forceps

tenaz [te'naθ] ADJ (*material*) tough; (*persona*) tenacious; (*pegajoso*) sticky; (*terco*) stubborn

tenaza(s) [te'naθ(as)] NF(PL) (*Med*) forceps; (*Tec*) pliers; (*Zool*) pincers

tendal [ten'dal] NM awning

tendedero [tende'ðero] NM (*para ropa*) drying-place; (*cuerda*) clothes line

tendencia [ten'denθja] NF tendency; (*proceso*) trend; **~ imperante** prevailing tendency; **~ del mercado** run of the market; **tener ~ a** to tend o have a tendency to

tendenciosidad [tendenθjosi'ðað] NF tendentiousness

tendencioso, -a [tenden'θjoso, a] ADJ tendentious

tender [ten'der] /2g/ VT (*extender*) to spread out; (*ropa*) to hang out; (*vía férrea, cable*) to lay; (*cuerda*) to stretch; (*trampa*) to set; **~ la cama/la mesa** (AM) to make the bed/lay the table ▸ VI to tend ■ **tenderse** VR to lie down; (*fig: dejarse llevar*) to let o.s. go; (: *dejar ir*) to let things go

ténder ['tender] NM (*Ferro*) tender

tenderete [tende'rete] NM (*puesto*) stall; (*carretilla*) barrow; (*exposición*) display of goods

★**tendero, -a** [ten'dero, a] NM/F shopkeeper, storekeeper (*US*)

tendido, -a [ten'diðo, a] ADJ (*acostado*) lying down, flat; (*colgado*) hanging; **a galope ~** flat out ▸ NM (*ropa*) washing; (*Taur*) front rows pl of seats; (*colocación*) laying; (*Arq: enyesado*) coat of plaster

tendón [ten'don] NM tendon

tendré etc [ten'dre] VB ver **tener**

tenducho [ten'dutʃo] NM small dirty shop

tenebroso, -a [tene'βroso, a] ADJ (*oscuro*) dark; (*fig*) gloomy; (*siniestro*) sinister

★**tenedor** [tene'ðor] NM (*Culin*) fork; (*poseedor*) holder; **~ de libros** book-keeper; **~ de acciones** shareholder; **~ de póliza** policyholder

teneduría [teneðu'ria] NF keeping; **~ de libros** book-keeping

tenencia [te'nenθja] NF (*de casa*) tenancy; (*de oficio*) tenure; (*de propiedad*) possession; **~ asegurada** security of tenure; **~ ilícita de armas** illegal possession of weapons

---
tener [te'ner]

/2k/ VT **1** (*poseer: gen*) to have; (: *en la mano*) to hold; **¿tienes un boli?** have you got a pen?; **va a tener un niño** she's going to have a baby; **tiene los ojos azules** he's got blue eyes; **¡ten o tenga!, ¡aquí tienes o tiene!** here you are!

2 (*edad, medidas*) to be; **tiene siete años** she's seven (years old); **tiene 15 cm de largo** it's 15 cm long

3 (*sentimientos, sensaciones*): **tener sed/hambre/frío/calor** to be thirsty/hungry/cold/hot; **tener celos** to be jealous; **tener cuidado** to be careful; **tener razón** to be right; **tener suerte** to be lucky

4 (*considerar*): **lo tengo por brillante** I consider him to be brilliant; **tener en mucho a algn** to think very highly of sb

5 (+ *pp*, + *adj*, + *gerundio*): **tengo terminada ya la mitad del trabajo** I've done half the work already; **tenía el sombrero puesto** he had his hat on; **tenía pensado llamarte** I had been thinking of phoning you; **nos tiene hartos** we're fed up with him; **me ha tenido tres horas esperando** he kept me waiting three hours

6: **tener que hacer algo** to have to do sth; **tengo que acabar este trabajo hoy** I have to finish this job today

7: **¿qué tienes, estás enfermo?** what's the matter with you, are you ill?

8 (*locuciones*): **¿conque esas tenemos?** so it's like that, then?; **no las tengo todas conmigo** I'm a bit unsure (about it); **lo tiene difícil** he'll have a hard job

■ **tenerse** VR **1**: **tenerse en pie** to stand up

2: **tenerse por** to think o.s.; **se tiene por un gran cantante** he thinks himself a great singer

---

Tener suele traducirse por **to have**:
Tengo dos hermanas. **I have two sisters**.
¿Tienes hora? **Do you have the time?**
En inglés coloquial británico suele añadirse **got** cuando se habla del tiempo presente, en cuyo caso se utilizan las correspondientes contracciones:
Tengo dos hermanas. **I've got two sisters**.
¿Tienes hora? **Have you got the time?**
Sin embargo, en muchas ocasiones se traduce por **to be** cuando se refiere al estado en que se encuentra una parte del cuerpo o cuando *tener* va seguido de un sustantivo:
Tenía el pelo mojado. **His hair was wet**.
tener miedo **to be frightened**.

---

tengo etc ['tengo] VB ver **tener**

tenia ['tenja] NF tapeworm

teniente [te'njente] NMF lieutenant; (*ayudante*) deputy; **~ coronel** lieutenant colonel

★**tenis** ['tenis] NM tennis; **~ de mesa** table tennis

★**tenista** [te'nista] NMF tennis player

tenor [te'nor] NM (*tono*) tone; (*sentido*) meaning; (*Mus*) tenor; **a ~ de** on the lines of

tenorio [te'norjo] NM (*fam*) ladykiller, Don Juan

tensar [ten'sar] /**1a**/ VT to tauten; (*arco*) to draw

tensión [ten'sjon] NF tension; (*Tec*) stress; (*Med*): **~ arterial** blood pressure; **~ nerviosa** nervous strain; **tener la ~ alta** to have high blood pressure

tenso, -a ['tenso, a] ADJ tense; (*relaciones*) strained

★**tentación** [tenta'θjon] NF temptation

tentáculo [ten'takulo] NM tentacle

tentador, a [tenta'ðor, a] ADJ tempting ▶ NM/F tempter/temptress

tentar [ten'tar] /**1j**/ VT (*tocar*) to touch, feel; (*seducir*) to tempt; (*atraer*) to attract; (*probar*) to try (out); (*Med*) to probe; **~ hacer algo** to try to do sth

tentativa [tenta'tiβa] NF attempt; **~ de asesinato** attempted murder

tentempié [tentem'pje] NM (*fam*) snack

tenue ['tenwe] ADJ (*delgado*) thin, slender; (*alambre*) fine; (*insustancial*) tenuous; (*sonido*) faint; (*neblina*) light; (*lazo, vínculo*) slight

teñir [te'ɲir] /**3h, 3k**/ VT to dye; (*fig*) to tinge ■ **teñirse** VR to dye; **teñirse el pelo** to dye one's hair

teología [teolo'xia] NF theology

teólogo, -a [te'oloɣo, a] NM/F theologist, theologian

teorema [teo'rema] NM theorem

teoría [teo'ria] NF theory; **en ~** in theory

teóricamente [te'orikamente] ADV theoretically

teorice *etc* [teo'riθe] VB *ver* **teorizar**

teórico, -a [te'oriko, a] ADJ theoretic(al) ▶ NM/F theoretician, theorist

teorizar [teori'θar] /**1f**/ VI to theorize

tequila [te'kila] NM O F tequila

terapeuta [tera'peuta] NMF therapist

terapéutico, -a [tera'peutiko, a] ADJ therapeutic(al) ▶ NF therapeutics *sg*

terapia [te'rapja] NF therapy; **~ laboral** occupational therapy

tercer [ter'θer] ADJ *ver* **tercero**

tercermundista [terθermun'dista] ADJ Third World *cpd*

★**tercero, -a** [ter'θero, a] ADJ (*antes de nmsg:* **tercer**) third ▶ NM (*árbitro*) mediator; (*Jur*) third party

terceto [ter'θeto] NM trio

terciado, -a [ter'θjaðo, a] ADJ slanting; **azúcar ~** brown sugar

terciar [ter'θjar] /**1b**/ VT (*Mat*) to divide into three; (*inclinarse*) to slope; (*llevar*) to wear across one's chest ▶ VI (*participar*) to take part; (*hacer de árbitro*) to mediate ■ **terciarse** VR to arise

terciario, -a [ter'θjarjo, a] ADJ tertiary

tercio ['terθjo] NM third

terciopelo [terθjo'pelo] NM velvet

★**terco, -a** ['terko, a] ADJ obstinate, stubborn; (*material*) tough

tergal® [ter'ɣal] NM Terylene®, Dacron® (*US*)

tergiversación [terxiβersa'θjon] NF (*deformación*) distortion; (*evasivas*) prevarication

tergiversar [terxiβer'sar] /**1a**/ VT to distort ▶ VI to prevaricate

termal [ter'mal] ADJ thermal

termas ['termas] NFPL hot springs

térmico, -a ['termiko, a] ADJ thermic, thermal, heat *cpd*

terminación [termina'θjon] NF (*final*) end; (*conclusión*) conclusion, ending

terminal [termi'nal] ADJ terminal ▶ NM (*Elec, Inform*) terminal; **un ~ interactivo** an interactive terminal; **un ~ de pantalla** a visual display unit ▶ NF (*en aeropuerto, estación*) terminal

terminante [termi'nante] ADJ (*final*) final, definitive; (*tajante*) categorical

terminantemente [terminante'mente] ADV: **~ prohibido** strictly forbidden

★**terminar** [termi'nar] /**1a**/ VT (*completar*) to complete, finish; (*concluir*) to end ▶ VI (*llegar a su fin*) to end; (*parar*) to stop; (*acabar*) to finish; **~ por hacer algo** to end up (by) doing sth ■ **terminarse** VR to come to an end

término ['termino] NM end, conclusion; (*parada*) terminus; (*límite*) boundary; (*en discusión*) point; (*Ling, Com*) term; **~ medio** average; (*fig*) middle way; **en otros términos** in other words; **en último ~** (*a fin de cuentas*) in the last analysis; (*como último recurso*) as a last resort; **~ medio** average; (*fig*) middle way; **en términos de** in terms of; **según los términos del contrato** according to the terms of the contract

terminología [terminolo'xia] NF terminology

termita [ter'mita] NF termite

termo® ['termo] NM Thermos® (flask)

termodinámico, -a [termoði'namiko, a] ADJ thermodynamic ▶ NF thermodynamics *sg*

termoimpresora [termoimpre'sora] NF thermal printer

termómetro [ter'mometro] NM thermometer

termonuclear [termonukle'ar] ADJ thermonuclear

termostato [termos'tato] NM thermostat

ternero, -a [ter'nero, a] NM/F (*animal*) calf ▶ NF (*carne*) veal, beef

terneza [ter'neθa] NF tenderness

ternilla [ter'niʎa] NF gristle; (*cartílago*) cartilage

terno ['terno] NM (*traje*) three-piece suit; (*conjunto*) set of three

ternura [ter'nura] NF (*trato*) tenderness; (*palabra*) endearment; (*cariño*) fondness

terquedad [terkeˈðað] NF obstinacy; (*dureza*) harshness

terrado [teˈrraðo] NM terrace

Terranova [terraˈnoβa] NF Newfoundland

terraplén [terraˈplen] NM (*Agr*) terrace; (*Ferro*) embankment; (*Mil*) rampart; (*cuesta*) slope

terráqueo, -a [teˈrrakeo, a] ADJ: **globo ~** globe

terrateniente [terrateˈnjente] NMF landowner

★**terraza** [teˈrraθa] NF (*balcón*) balcony; (*techo*) flat roof; (*Agr*) terrace

★**terremoto** [terreˈmoto] NM earthquake

terrenal [terreˈnal] ADJ earthly

★**terreno, -a** [teˈrreno, a] ADJ (*de la tierra*) earthly, worldly ▶ NM (*tierra*) land; (*parcela*) plot; (*suelo*) soil; (*fig*) field; **un ~** a piece of land; **sobre el ~** on the spot; **ceder/perder ~** to give/lose ground; **preparar el ~ (a)** (*fig*) to pave the way (for)

terrestre [teˈrrestre] ADJ terrestrial; (*ruta*) land *cpd*

★**terrible** [teˈrriβle] ADJ (*espantoso*) terrible; (*aterrador*) dreadful; (*tremendo*) awful

territorial [territoˈrjal] ADJ territorial

territorio [territoˈrjo] NM territory; **~ bajo mandato** mandated territory

terrón [teˈrron] NM (*de azúcar*) lump; (*de tierra*) clod, lump ■ **terrones** NMPL land *sg*

terror [teˈrror] NM terror

terrorífico, -a [terroˈrifiko, a] ADJ terrifying

terrorismo [terroˈrismo] NM terrorism

★**terrorista** [terroˈrista] ADJ, NMF terrorist; **~ suicida** suicide bomber

terroso, -a [teˈrroso, a] ADJ earthy

terruño [teˈrruɲo] NM (*pedazo*) clod; (*parcela*) plot; (*fig*) native soil; **apego al ~** attachment to one's native soil

terso, -a [ˈterso, a] ADJ (*liso*) smooth; (*pulido*) polished; (*fig: estilo*) flowing

tersura [terˈsura] NF smoothness; (*brillo*) shine

tertulia [terˈtulja] NF (*reunión informal*) social gathering; (*grupo*) group, circle; (*sala*) clubroom; **~ literaria** literary circle

tesina [teˈsina] NF dissertation

tesis [ˈtesis] NF INV thesis

tesón [teˈson] NM (*firmeza*) firmness; (*tenacidad*) tenacity

tesorería [tesoreˈria] NF treasurership

tesorero, -a [tesoˈrero, a] NM/F treasurer

★**tesoro** [teˈsoro] NM treasure; (*Com, Pol*) treasury; **T~ público** (*Pol*) Exchequer

test [tes(t)] (*pl* **tests** [tes(t)]) NM test

testaferro [testaˈferro] NM figurehead

testamentaría [testamentaˈria] NF execution of a will

testamentario, -a [testamenˈtarjo, a] ADJ testamentary ▶ NM/F executor/executrix

testamento [testaˈmento] NM will; **~ vital** living will

testar [tesˈtar] /1a/ VI to make a will

testarada [testaˈraða] NF, **testarazo** [testaˈraθo] NM: **darse una ~ o un testarazo** (*fam*) to bump one's head

testarudo, -a [testaˈruðo, a] ADJ stubborn

testículo [tesˈtikulo] NM testicle

testificar [testifiˈkar] /1g/ VT to testify; (*fig*) to attest ▶ VI to give evidence

testifique *etc* [testiˈfike] VB *ver* **testificar**

★**testigo** [tesˈtiɣo] NMF witness; **~ de cargo/descargo** witness for the prosecution/defence; **~ ocular** eye witness; **poner a algn por ~** to cite sb as a witness

testimonial [testimoˈnjal] ADJ (*prueba*) testimonial; (*gesto*) token

testimoniar [testimoˈnjar] /1b/ VT to testify to; (*fig*) to show

★**testimonio** [testiˈmonjo] NM testimony; **en ~ de** as a token *o* mark of; **falso ~** perjured evidence, false witness

teta [ˈteta] NF (*de biberón*) teat; (*Anat*) nipple; (:*fam*) breast; (*fam!*) tit (*fam!*)

tétanos [ˈtetanos] NM tetanus

★**tetera** [teˈtera] NF teapot; **~ eléctrica** (electric) kettle

tetilla [teˈtiʎa] NF (*Anat*) nipple; (*de biberón*) teat

tetrapléjico, -a [tetraˈplexiko, a] ADJ, NM/F quadriplegic

tétrico, -a [ˈtetriko, a] ADJ gloomy, dismal

textear [teksteˈar] /1a/ VT (*Am*) to text

textil [teksˈtil] ADJ textile

★**texto** [ˈteksto] NM text

textual [teksˈtwal] ADJ textual; **palabras textuales** exact words

textura [teksˈtura] NF (*de tejido*) texture; (*de mineral*) structure

tez [teθ] NF (*cutis*) complexion; (*color*) colouring

tfno. ABR (= *teléfono*) tel.

ti [ti] PRON you; (*reflexivo*) yourself

★**tía** [ˈtia] NF (*pariente*) aunt; (*fam: mujer*) girl

Tibet [tiˈβet] NM: **El ~** Tibet

tibetano, -a [tiβeˈtano, a] ADJ, NM/F Tibetan ▶ NM (*Ling*) Tibetan

tibia [ˈtiβja] NF tibia

tibieza [tiˈβjeθa] NF (*temperatura*) tepidness; (*fig*) coolness

★**tibio, -a** [ˈtiβjo, a] ADJ lukewarm, tepid

tiburón [tiβuˈron] NM shark

tic [tik] NM (*ruido*) click; (*de reloj*) tick; **~ nervioso** (*Med*) nervous tic

tico, -a [ˈtiko, a] ADJ, NM/F (*Am fam*) Costa Rican

tictac [tikˈtak] NM (*de reloj*) tick tock

tiemble *etc* [ˈtjemble] VB *ver* **temblar**

★**tiempo** [ˈtjempo] NM (*gen*) time; (*época, período*) age, period; (*Meteorología*) weather; (*Ling*) tense;

(*edad*) age; (*de juego*) half; **a** ~ in time; **a un** *o* **al mismo** ~ at the same time; **al poco** ~ very soon (after); **andando el** ~ in due course; **cada cierto** ~ every so often; **con** ~ in time; **con el** ~ eventually; **se quedó poco** ~ he didn't stay very long; **hace poco** ~ not long ago; **mucho** ~ a long time; **de** ~ **en** ~ from time to time; **en mis tiempos** in my time; **en los buenos tiempos** in the good old days; **hace buen/mal** ~ the weather is fine/bad; **estar a** ~ to be in time; **hace** ~ some time ago; **hacer** ~ to while away the time; **¿qué** ~ **tiene?** how old is he?; **motor de 2 tiempos** two-stroke engine; ~ **compartido** (*Inform*) time sharing; ~ **de ejecución** (*Inform*) run time; ~ **inactivo** (*Com*) downtime; ~ **libre** spare time; ~ **de paro** (*Com*) idle time; **a** ~ **partido** (*trabajar*) part-time; ~ **preferencial** (*Com*) prime time; **en** ~ **real** (*Inform*) real time; **primer** ~ first half

★**tienda** ['tjenda] VB *ver* **tender** ▶ NF shop; (*más grande*) store; (*Naut*) awning; ~ **de campaña** tent; ~ **de comestibles** grocer's (shop) (*BRIT*), grocery (store) (*US*)

tiene *etc* ['tjene] VB *ver* **tener**

tienta ['tjenta] VB *ver* **tentar** ▶ NF (*Med*) probe; (*fig*) tact; **andar a tientas** to grope one's way along

tiento *etc* ['tjento] VB *ver* **tentar** ▶ NM (*tacto*) touch; (*precaución*) wariness; (*pulso*) steady hand; (*Zool*) feeler, tentacle

tierno, -a ['tjerno, a] ADJ (*blando, dulce*) tender; (*fresco*) fresh

★**tierra** ['tjerra] NF earth; (*suelo*) soil; (*mundo*) world; (*país*) country, land; (*Elec*) earth, ground (*US*); ~ **adentro** inland; ~ **natal** native land; **echar** ~ **a un asunto** to hush an affair up; **no es de estas tierras** he's not from these parts; **la T~ Santa** the Holy Land

★**tieso, -a** ['tjeso, a] ADJ (*rígido*) rigid; (*duro*) stiff; (*fig: testarudo*) stubborn; (*fam: orgulloso*) conceited ▶ ADV strongly

tiesto ['tjesto] NM flowerpot; (*pedazo*) piece of pottery

tifoidea [tifoi'ðea] NF typhoid

tifón [ti'fon] NM (*huracán*) typhoon; (*de mar*) tidal wave

tifus ['tifus] NM typhus; ~ **icteroides** yellow fever

★**tigre** ['tiɣre] NM tiger; (*AM*) jaguar

TIJ SIGLA M (= *Tribunal Internacional de Justicia*) ICJ

tijera [ti'xera] NF (*utensilio*) (pair of) scissors *pl*; (*Zool*) claw; (*persona*) gossip; **de** ~ folding ■ **tijeras** NFPL scissors; (*para plantas*) shears; **unas tijeras** a pair of scissors

tijeretear [tixerete'ar] /1a/ VT to snip ▶ VI (*fig*) to meddle

tila ['tila] NF (*Bot*) lime tree; (*Culin*) lime flower tea

tildar [til'dar] /1a/ VT: ~ **de** to brand as

tilde ['tilde] NF (*defecto*) defect; (*trivialidad*) triviality; (*Tip*) tilde

tilín [ti'lin] NM tinkle

tilo ['tilo] NM lime tree

timador, a [tima'ðor, a] NM/F swindler

timar [ti'mar] /1a/ VT (*robar*) to steal; (*estafar*) to swindle; (*persona*) to con ■ **timarse** VR (*fam*): **timarse con algn** to make eyes at sb

timbal [tim'bal] NM small drum

timbrar [tim'brar] /1a/ VT to stamp; (*sellar*) to seal; (*carta*) to postmark

timbrazo [tim'braθo] NM ring; **dar un** ~ to ring the bell

★**timbre** ['timbre] NM (*sello*) stamp; (*campanilla*) bell; (*tono*) timbre; (*Com*) stamp duty

timidez [timi'ðeθ] NF shyness

★**tímido, -a** ['timiðo, a] ADJ shy, timid

timo ['timo] NM swindle; **dar un** ~ **a algn** to swindle sb

timón [ti'mon] NM helm, rudder; (*AM*) steering wheel; **coger el** ~ (*fig*) to take charge

timonel [timo'nel] NMF helmsman/helmswoman

timorato, -a [timo'rato, a] ADJ God-fearing; (*mojigato*) sanctimonious

Timor Este [tim'or'este] NM East Timor

tímpano ['timpano] NM (*Anat*) eardrum; (*Mus*) small drum

tina ['tina] NF tub; (*AM: baño*) bath(tub)

tinaja [ti'naxa] NF large earthen jar

tinerfeño, -a [tiner'feɲo, a] ADJ of *o* from Tenerife ▶ NM/F native *o* inhabitant of Tenerife

tinglado [tin'glaðo] NM (*cobertizo*) shed; (*fig: truco*) trick; (*intriga*) intrigue; **armar un** ~ to lay a plot

tinieblas [ti'njeβlas] NFPL darkness *sg*; (*sombras*) shadows; **estamos en** ~ **sobre sus proyectos** (*fig*) we are in the dark about his plans

tino ['tino] NM (*habilidad*) skill; (*Mil*) marksmanship; (*juicio*) insight; (*moderación*) moderation; **sin** ~ immoderately; **coger el** ~ to get the feel *o* hang of it

tinta ['tinta] NF ink; (*Tec*) dye; (*Arte*) colour; ~ **china** Indian ink; **saber algo de buena** ~ to have sth on good authority ■ **tintas** NFPL (*fig*) shades; **medias tintas** (*fig*) half measures

tinte ['tinte] NM dye; (*acto*) dyeing; (*fig*) tinge; (*barniz*) veneer

tintero [tin'tero] NM inkwell; **se le quedó en el** ~ he clean forgot about it

tintinear [tintine'ar] /1a/ VT to tinkle

★**tinto, -a** ['tinto, a] ADJ (*teñido*) dyed; (*manchado*) stained ▶ NM red wine

tintorera [tinto'rera] NF shark

tintorería [tintore'ria] NF dry cleaner's

tintorero [tinto'rero] NM dry cleaner('s)

tintura [tin'tura] NF (*acto*) dyeing; (*Química*) dye; (*farmacéutico*) tincture

tiña *etc* ['tiɲa] VB *ver* **teñir** ▶ NF (*Med*) ringworm

★tío ['tio] NM (*pariente*) uncle; (*fam: hombre*) bloke, guy

tiovivo [tio'βiβo] NM merry-go-round

★típico, -a ['tipiko, a] ADJ typical; (*pintoresco*) picturesque

tiple ['tiple] NM soprano (voice) ▸ NF soprano

★tipo ['tipo] NM (*clase*) type, kind; (*norma*) norm; (*patrón*) pattern; (*fam: hombre*) fellow, bloke, guy; (*Anat*) build; (: *de mujer*) figure; (*Imprenta*) type; **~ bancario/de descuento** bank/discount rate; **~ de interés** interest rate; **~ de interés vigente** (*Com*) standard rate; **~ de cambio** exchange rate; **~ base** (*Com*) base rate; **~ a término** (*Com*) forward rate; **dos tipos sospechosos** two suspicious characters; **~ de letra** (*Inform, Tip*) typeface; **~ de datos** (*Inform*) data type

tipografía [tipoɣra'fia] NF (*tipo*) printing; (*lugar*) printing press

tipográfico, -a [tipo'ɣrafiko, a] ADJ typographic, printing *cpd*

tipógrafo, -a [ti'poɣrafo, a] NM/F printer

tique, tíquet ['tike] (*pl* ~**(t)s** ['tikes]) NM ticket; (*en tienda*) cash slip

tiquismiquis [tikis'mikis] NM fussy person ▸ NMPL (*querellas*) squabbling *sg*; (*escrúpulos*) silly scruples

TIR SIGLA MPL = **Transportes internacionales por carretera**

tira ['tira] NF strip; (*fig*) abundance; **la ~ de ...** (*fam*) lots of ... ▸ NM: **~ y afloja** give and take

tirabuzón [tiraβu'θon] NM corkscrew; (*rizo*) curl

tirachinas [tira'tʃinas] NM INV catapult

tiradero [tira'ðero] NM (*AM*) rubbish dump (*BRIT*), garbage dump (*US*)

tirado, -a [ti'raðo, a] ADJ (*barato*) dirt-cheap; (*fam: fácil*) very easy; **está ~** (*fam*) it's a cinch ▸ NF (*acto*) cast, throw; (*distancia*) distance; (*serie*) series; (*Tip*) printing, edition; **de una tirada** at one go

tirador, a [tira'ðor, a] NM/F (*persona*) shooter; **~ certero** sniper ▸ NM (*mango*) handle; (*Elec*) flex

tiralíneas [tira'lineas] NM INV ruling-pen

tiranía [tira'nia] NF tyranny

tiránico, -a [ti'raniko, a] ADJ tyrannical

tiranizar [tirani'θar] /1f/ VT (*pueblo, empleado*) to tyrannize

tirano, -a [ti'rano, a] ADJ tyrannical ▸ NM/F tyrant

tirante [ti'rante] ADJ (*cuerda*) tight, taut; (*relaciones*) strained ▸ NM (*Arq*) brace; (*Tec*) stay; (*correa*) shoulder strap ▪ **tirantes** NMPL braces, suspenders (*US*)

tirantez [tiran'teθ] NF tightness; (*fig*) tension

★tirar [ti'rar] /1a/ VT to throw; (*volcar*) to upset; (*derribar*) to knock down *o* over; (*tiro*) to fire; (*cohete*) to launch; (*bomba*) to drop; (*edificio*) to pull down; (*desechar*) to throw out *o* away; (*disipar*) to squander; (*imprimir*) to print; (*dar: golpe*) to

deal; **~ abajo** to bring down, destroy ▸ VI (*disparar*) to shoot; (*dar un tirón*) to pull; (*fig*) to draw; (*interesar*) to appeal; (*fam: andar*) to go; (*tender a*) to tend to; (*Deporte*) to shoot; **tira más a su padre** he takes more after his father; **~ de algo** to pull *o* tug (on) sth; **ir tirando** to manage; **~ a la derecha** to turn *o* go right; **a todo ~** at the most ▪ **tirarse** VR to throw o.s.; (*fig*) to demean o.s.; (*fam!*) to screw (*fam!*)

★tirita [ti'rita] NF (sticking) plaster, Band-Aid® (*US*)

tiritar [tiri'tar] /1a/ VI to shiver

tiritona [tiri'tona] NF shivering (fit)

tiro ['tiro] NM (*lanzamiento*) throw; (*disparo*) shot; (*tiroteo*) shooting; (*Deporte*) shot; (*Tenis, Golf*) drive; (*alcance*) range; (*de escalera*) flight (of stairs); (*golpe*) blow; (*engaño*) hoax; **~ al blanco** target practice; **caballo de ~** carthorse; **andar a tiros largos** to be all dressed up; **al ~** (*AM*) at once; **de a ~** (*AM fam*) completely; **se pegó un ~** he shot himself; **le salió el ~ por la culata** it backfired on him

tiroides [ti'roiðes] NM INV thyroid

Tirol [ti'rol] NM: **El ~** the Tyrol

tirolés, -esa [tiro'les, esa] ADJ, NM/F Tyrolean

tirolina [tiro'lina] NF zip line

tirón [ti'ron] NM (*sacudida*) pull, tug; **de un ~** in one go; **dar un ~ a** to pull at, tug at

tirotear [tirote'ar] /1a/ VT to shoot at ▪ **tirotearse** VR to exchange shots

tiroteo [tiro'teo] NM exchange of shots, shooting; (*escaramuza*) skirmish

tirria ['tirrja] NF: **tener ~ a algn** to have a grudge against sb

tísico, -a ['tisiko, a] ADJ, NM/F consumptive

tisis ['tisis] NF consumption, tuberculosis

tít. ABR = **título**

titánico, -a [ti'taniko, a] ADJ titanic

títere ['titere] NM puppet; **no dejar ~ con cabeza** to turn everything upside-down

titilar [titi'lar] /1a/ VI (*luz, estrella*) to twinkle; (*párpado*) to flutter

titiritero, -a [titiri'tero, a] NM/F (*acróbata*) acrobat; (*malabarista*) juggler

titubeante [tituβe'ante] ADJ (*inestable*) shaky, tottering; (*farfullante*) stammering; (*dudoso*) hesitant

titubear [tituβe'ar] /1a/ VI to stagger; (*balbucear*) to stammer; (*vacilar*) to hesitate

titubeo [titu'βeo] NM staggering; (*balbuceo*) stammering; (*vacilación*) hesitation

titulado, -a [titu'laðo, a] ADJ (*libro*) entitled; (*persona*) titled

titular [titu'lar] /1a/ ADJ titular ▸ NM/F (*de oficina*) occupant; (*de pasaporte*) holder ▸ NM headline ▸ VT to title ▪ **titularse** VR to be entitled

★título ['titulo] NM (*gen*) title; (*de diario*) headline; (*certificado*) professional qualification; (*universi-*

tario) university degree; (*Com*) bond; (*fig*) right; **a ~ de** by way of; (*en calidad de*) in the capacity of; **a ~ de curiosidad** as a matter of interest; **~ de propiedad** title deed ∎ **títulos** NMPL qualifications; **títulos convertibles de interés fijo** (*Com*) convertible loan stock *sg*

⭐**tiza** [ˈtiθa] NF chalk; **una ~** a piece of chalk

tizna [ˈtiθna] NF grime

tiznar [tiθˈnar] /**1a**/ VT to blacken; (*manchar*) to smudge, stain; (*fig*) to tarnish

tizón [tiˈθon], **tizo** [ˈtiθo] NM brand; (*fig*) stain

TLC NM ABR (= *Tratado de Libre Comercio*) NAFTA

Tm. ABR = **tonelada(s) métrica(s)**

TNT SIGLA M (= *trinitrotolueno*) TNT

⭐**toalla** [toˈaʎa] NF towel

toallita [toaˈʎita] NF (*tb*: **toallita húmeda**) wet wipe

⭐**tobillo** [toˈβiʎo] NM ankle

tobogán [toβoˈɣan] NM toboggan; (*resbaladilla*) slide, chute; (*montaña rusa*) roller-coaster

toca [ˈtoka] NF headdress

tocadiscos [tokaˈðiskos] NM INV record player

tocado, -a [toˈkaðo, a] ADJ (*fruta etc*) rotten; (*fam*) touched; **estar ~ de la cabeza** (*fam*) to be weak in the head ▶ NM headdress

tocador [tokaˈðor] NM (*mueble*) dressing table; (*cuarto*) boudoir; (*neceser*) toilet case; (*fam*) ladies' room

tocante [toˈkante]: **~ a** prep with regard to; **en lo ~ a** as for, so far as concerns

⭐**tocar** [toˈkar] /**1g**/ VT to touch; (*sentir*) to feel; (*con la mano*) to handle; (*Mus*) to play; (*campana*) to ring; (*tambor*) to beat; (*trompeta*) to blow; (*topar con*) to run into, strike; (*referirse a*) to allude to; (*estar emparentado con*) to be related to; **tocarle a algn** to fall to sb's lot; **por lo que a mí me toca** as far as I am concerned; **te toca a ti** it's your turn ▶ VI (*a la puerta*) to knock (on o at the door); (*ser el turno*) to fall to, be the turn of; (*ser hora*) to be due; (*atañer*) to concern; **~ en** (*Naut*) to call at; **esto toca en la locura** this verges on madness ∎ **tocarse** VR (*cubrirse la cabeza*) to cover one's head; (*tener contacto*) to touch (each other)

tocateja [tokaˈtexa]: **a ~** adv (*fam*) in readies

tocayo, -a [toˈkajo, a] NM/F namesake

tocino [toˈθino] NM (bacon) fat; **~ de panceta** bacon

⭐**todavía** [toðaˈβia] ADV (*aun*) even; (*aún*) still, yet; **~ más** yet o still more; **~ no** not yet; **~ en 1970** as late as 1970; **está lloviendo ~** it's still raining

toditito, -a [toðiˈtito, a], **todito, -a** [toˈðito, a] ADJ (*Am fam*) (absolutely) all

---

todo, -a [ˈtoðo, a]

ADJ **1** (*sg*) all; **toda la carne** all the meat; **toda la noche** all night, the whole night; **todo el libro** the whole book; **toda una botella** a whole bottle; **todo lo contrario** quite the opposite; **está toda sucia** she's all dirty; **a toda velocidad** at full speed; **por todo el país** throughout the whole country; **es todo un hombre** he's every inch a man; **soy todo oídos** I'm all ears

2 (*pl*) all; every; **todos los libros** all the books; **todas las noches** every night; **todos los que quieran salir** all those who want to leave; **todos vosotros** all of you

▶ PRON **1** everything, all; **todos** everyone, everybody; **lo sabemos todo** we know everything; **todos querían más tiempo** everybody o everyone wanted more time; **nos marchamos todos** all of us left; **corriendo y todo, no llegaron a tiempo** even though they ran, they still didn't arrive in time

2 (*con preposición*): **a pesar de todo** even so, in spite of everything; **con todo él me sigue gustando** even so I still like him; **le llamaron de todo** they called him all the names under the sun; **no me agrada del todo** I don't entirely like it

▶ ADV all; **vaya todo seguido** keep straight on o ahead

▶ NM: **como un todo** as a whole; **arriba del todo** at the very top; **todo a cien** = pound store (*BRIT*), ≈ dollar store (*US*)

---

todopoderoso, -a [toðopoðeˈroso, a] ADJ all-powerful; (*Rel*) almighty

todoterreno [toðoteˈrreno] NM (*tb*: **vehículo todoterreno**) four-wheel drive, SUV (*esp US*)

toga [ˈtoɣa] NF toga; (*Escol*) gown

Tokio [ˈtokjo] NM Tokyo

toldo [ˈtoldo] NM (*para el sol*) sunshade; (*en tienda*) marquee; (*fig*) pride

tole [ˈtole] NM (*fam*) commotion

toledano, -a [toleˈðano, a] ADJ of o from Toledo ▶ NM/F native o inhabitant of Toledo

tolerable [toleˈraβle] ADJ tolerable

tolerancia [toleˈranθja] NF tolerance

⭐**tolerante** [toleˈrante] ADJ tolerant; (*sociedad*) liberal; (*fig*) open-minded

tolerar [toleˈrar] /**1a**/ VT to tolerate; (*resistir*) to endure

Tolón [toˈlon] NM Toulon

toma [ˈtoma] NF (*gen*) taking; (*Med*) dose; (*Elec*: *tb*: **toma de corriente**) socket; (*Mecánica*) inlet; **~ de posesión** (*por presidente*) taking up office; **~ de tierra** (*Elec*) earth (wire), ground (wire) (*US*); (*Aviat*) landing ▶ NM: **~ y daca** give and take

tomacorriente [tomakoˈrrjente] NM (*Am*) socket

tomadura [tomaˈðura] NF: **~ de pelo** hoax

⭐**tomar** [toˈmar] /**1a**/ VT (*gen, Cine, Foto, TV*) to take; (*actitud*) to adopt; (*aspecto*) to take on; (*notas*) to take down; (*beber*) to drink; **~ asiento** to sit down; **~ a algn por loco** to think sb mad; **~ algo a bien/a mal** to take sth well/badly; **~ algo en serio** to take sth seriously; **~ el pelo a algn** to pull sb's leg; **tomarla con algn** to pick a quarrel with sb; **~ el sol** to sunbathe; **~ por escrito** to write down ▶ vi to take; (*Am*) to drink; **¡toma!** here you are! ■ **tomarse** vr to take; **tomarse por** to consider o.s. to be

★**tomate** [to'mate] nm tomato

tomatera [toma'tera] nf tomato plant

tomavistas [toma'βistas] nm inv movie camera

tomillo [to'miʎo] nm thyme

tomo ['tomo] nm (*libro*) volume; (*fig*) importance

ton [ton] abr = **tonelada** ▶ nm: **sin ~ ni son** without rhyme or reason

tonada [to'naða] nf tune

tonalidad [tonali'ðað] nf tone

tonel [to'nel] nm barrel

tonelada [tone'laða] nf ton; **~(s) métrica(s)** metric ton(s)

tonelaje [tone'laxe] nm tonnage

tonelero [tone'lero] nm cooper

tongo ['tongo] nm (*Deporte*) fix

tónico, -a ['toniko, a] adj tonic ▶ nm (*Med*) tonic ▶ nf (*Mus*) tonic; (*fig*) keynote

tonificador, a [tonifika'ðor, a], **tonificante** [tonifi'kante] adj invigorating, stimulating

tonificar [tonifi'kar] /1g/ vt to tone up

tonifique etc [toni'fike] vb ver **tonificar**

tonillo [to'niʎo] nm monotonous voice

★**tono** ['tono] nm (*Mus*) tone; (*altura*) pitch; (*color*) shade; **fuera de ~** inappropriate; **~ de llamada** ringtone; **~ de marcar** dialling tone (*Brit*), dial tone (*US*); **darse ~** to put on airs

tontear [tonte'ar] /1a/ vi (*fam*) to fool about; (*enamorados*) to flirt

★**tontería** [tonte'ria] nf (*estupidez*) foolishness; (*una tontería*) silly thing ■ **tonterías** nfpl rubbish *sg*, nonsense *sg*

★**tonto, -a** ['tonto, a] adj stupid; (*ridículo*) silly ▶ nm/f fool; (*payaso*) clown; **a tontas y a locas** anyhow; **hacer(se) el ~** to act the fool

topacio [to'paθjo] nm topaz

topar [to'par] /1a/ vt (*tropezar*) to bump into; (*encontrar*) to find, come across; (*cabra etc*) to butt ▶ vi: **~ contra** o **en** to run into; **~ con** to run up against; **el problema topa en eso** that's where the problem lies

tope ['tope] adj maximum; **fecha ~** closing date; **precio ~** top price; **sueldo ~** maximum salary ▶ nm (*fin*) end; (*límite*) limit; (*Ferro*) buffer; (*Auto*) bumper; **al ~** end to end; **~ de tabulación** tab stop

★**tópico, -a** ['topiko, a] adj topical; (*Med*) local; **de uso ~** for external application ▶ nm platitude, cliché

topo ['topo] nm (*Zool*) mole; (*fig*) blunderer

topografía [topoɣra'fia] nf topography

topógrafo, -a [to'poɣrafo, a] nm/f topographer; (*agrimensor*) surveyor

toponimia [topo'nimja] nf place names *pl*; (*estudio*) study of place names

toque etc ['toke] vb ver **tocar** ▶ nm touch; (*Mus*) beat; (*de campana*) chime, ring; (*Mil*) bugle call; (*fig*) crux; **dar un ~ a** to test; **dar el último ~ a** to put the final touch to; **~ de queda** curfew

toqué etc vb ver **tocar**

toquetear [tokete'ar] /1a/ vt to finger; (*fam!*) to touch up

toquilla [to'kiʎa] nf (*pañuelo*) headscarf; (*chal*) shawl

tórax ['toraks] nm inv thorax

torbellino [torbe'ʎino] nm whirlwind; (*fig*) whirl

torcedura [torθe'ðura] nf twist; (*Med*) sprain

★**torcer** [tor'θer] /2b, 2h/ vt to twist; (*la esquina*) to turn; (*Med*) to sprain; (*cuerda*) to plait; (*ropa, manos*) to wring; (*persona*) to corrupt; (*sentido*) to distort; **~ el gesto** to scowl ▶ vi (*cambiar de dirección*) to turn; (*desviar*) to turn off; **el coche torció a la derecha** the car turned right ■ **torcerse** vr to twist; (*doblar*) to bend; (*desviarse*) to go astray; (*fracasar*) to go wrong; **torcerse un pie** to twist one's foot

torcido, -a [tor'θiðo, a] adj twisted; (*fig*) crooked ▶ nm curl

tordo, -a ['torðo, a] adj dappled ▶ nm thrush

★**torear** [tore'ar] /1a/ vt (*fig: evadir*) to dodge; (*jugar con*) to tease; (*toro*) to fight ▶ vi to fight bulls

toreo [to'reo] nm bullfighting

★**torero, -a** [to'rero, a] nm/f bullfighter

toril [to'ril] nm bullpen

★**tormenta** [tor'menta] nf storm; (*fig: confusión*) turmoil

tormento [tor'mento] nm torture; (*fig*) anguish

tormentoso, -a [tormen'toso, a] adj stormy

tornar [tor'nar] /1a/ vt (*devolver*) to return, give back; (*transformar*) to transform ▶ vi to go back ■ **tornarse** vr (*ponerse*) to become; (*volver*) to return

tornasol [torna'sol] nm (*Bot*) sunflower; **papel de ~** litmus paper

tornasolado, -a [tornaso'laðo, a] adj (*brillante*) iridescent; (*reluciente*) shimmering

★**torneo** [tor'neo] nm tournament

tornero, -a [tor'nero, a] nm/f machinist

★**tornillo** [tor'niʎo] nm screw; **apretar los tornillos a algn** to apply pressure on sb; **le falta un ~** (*fam*) he's got a screw loose

torniquete [torni'kete] nm (*puerta*) turnstile; (*Med*) tourniquet

torno ['torno] nm (*Tec: grúa*) winch; (: *de carpintero*) lathe; (*tambor*) drum; **~ de banco** vice, vise (*US*); **en ~ (a)** round, about

★**toro** ['toro] nm bull; (*fam*) he-man; **los toros** bullfighting *sg*

toronja [to'ronxa] NF grapefruit

★**torpe** ['torpe] ADJ (*poco hábil*) clumsy, awkward; (*movimiento*) sluggish; (*necio*) dim; (*lento*) slow; (*indecente*) crude; (*no honrado*) dishonest

torpedo [tor'peðo] NM torpedo

torpemente [torpe'mente] ADV (*sin destreza*) clumsily; (*lentamente*) slowly

torpeza [tor'peθa] NF (*falta de agilidad*) clumsiness; (*lentitud*) slowness; (*rigidez*) stiffness; (*error*) mistake; (*crudeza*) obscenity

★**torre** ['torre] NF tower; (*de petróleo*) derrick; (*de electricidad*) pylon; (*Ajedrez*) rook; (*Aviat, Mil, Naut*) turret; **~ de telefonía móvil** mobile phone mast (BRIT), cell tower (US)

torrefacto, -a [torre'fakto, a] ADJ roasted; **café ~** high roast coffee

torrencial [torren'θjal] ADJ torrential

torrente [to'rrente] NM torrent

tórrido, -a ['torriðo, a] ADJ torrid

torrija [to'rrixa] NF fried bread; **torrijas** French toast *sg*

torsión [tor'sjon] NF twisting

torso ['torso] NM torso

★**torta** ['torta] NF cake; (*fam*) slap; **~ de huevos** (AM) omelette; **no entendió ni ~** he didn't understand a word of it

tortazo [tor'taθo] NM (*bofetada*) slap; (*de coche*) crash

tortícolis [tor'tikolis] NF stiff neck

★**tortilla** [tor'tiʎa] NF omelette; (AM) maize pancake; **~ francesa/española** plain/potato omelette; **cambiar** *o* **volver la ~ a algn** to turn the tables on sb

tortillera [torti'ʎera] NF (*fam!*) lesbian

tórtola ['tortola] NF turtledove

★**tortuga** [tor'tuɣa] NF tortoise; **~ marina** turtle

tortuoso, -a [tor'twoso, a] ADJ winding

tortura [tor'tura] NF torture

torturar [tortu'rar] /1a/ VT to torture

torvo, -a ['torβo, a] ADJ grim, fierce

torzamos *etc* [tor'θamos] VB *ver* **torcer**

★**tos** [tos] NF INV cough; **~ ferina** whooping cough

Toscana [tos'kana] NF: **La ~** Tuscany

tosco, -a ['tosko, a] ADJ coarse

★**toser** [to'ser] /2a/ VI to cough; **no hay quien le tosa** he's in a class by himself

tostado, -a [tos'taðo, a] ADJ toasted; (*por el sol*) dark brown; (*piel*) tanned ▶ NF (*pan*) piece of toast ∎ **tostadas** NFPL toast *sg*

tostador [tosta'ðor] NM, **tostadora** [tosta'ðora] NF toaster

tostar [tos'tar] /1l/ VT to toast; (*café*) to roast; (*al sol*) to tan ∎ **tostarse** VR to get brown

tostón [tos'ton] NM: **ser un ~** to be a drag

★**total** [to'tal] ADJ total ▶ ADV in short; (*al fin y al cabo*) when all is said and done; **~ que** to cut a long story short ▶ NM total; **en ~** in all; **~ de**

comprobación (*Inform*) hash total; **~ debe/ haber** (*Com*) debit/assets total

totalidad [totali'ðað] NF whole

totalitario, -a [totali'tarjo, a] ADJ totalitarian

totalmente [to'talmente] ADV totally

★**tóxico, -a** ['toksiko, a] ADJ toxic ▶ NM poison

★**toxicómano, -a** [toksi'komano, a] ADJ addicted to drugs ▶ NM/F drug addict

toxina [to'ksina] NF toxin

tozudo, -a [to'θuðo, a] ADJ obstinate

traba ['traβa] NF bond, tie; (*cadena*) fetter; **poner trabas a** to restrain

★**trabajador, a** [traβaxa'ðor, a] NM/F worker; **~ autónomo** *o* **por cuenta propia** self-employed person ▶ ADJ hard-working

★**trabajar** [traβa'xar] /1a/ VT to work; (*arar*) to till; (*empeñarse en*) to work at; (*empujar: persona*) to push; (*convencer*) to persuade ▶ VI to work; (*esforzarse*) to strive; **¡a ~!** let's get to work!; **~ por hacer algo** to strive to do sth

★**trabajo** [tra'βaxo] NM work; (*tarea*) task; (*Pol*) labour; (*fig*) effort; **tomarse el ~ de** to take the trouble to; **~ por turnos/a destajo** shift work/ piecework; **~ en equipo** teamwork; **~ en proceso** (*Com*) work-in-progress; **trabajos forzados** hard labour *sg*

trabajoso, -a [traβa'xoso, a] ADJ hard; (*Med*) pale

trabalenguas [traβa'lengwas] NM INV tongue twister

trabar [tra'βar] /1a/ VT (*juntar*) to join, unite; (*atar*) to tie down, fetter; (*agarrar*) to seize; (*amistad*) to strike up ∎ **trabarse** VR to become entangled; (*reñir*) to squabble; **se le traba la lengua** he gets tongue-tied

trabazón [traβa'θon] NF (*Tec*) joining, assembly; (*fig*) bond, link

trabucar [traβu'kar] /1g/ VT (*confundir*) to confuse, mix up; (*palabras*) to misplace

trabuque *etc* [tra'βuke] VB *ver* **trabucar**

tracción [trak'θjon] NF traction; **~ delantera/ trasera** front-wheel/rear-wheel drive

trace *etc* ['traθe] VB *ver* **trazar**

★**tractor** [trak'tor] NM tractor

trad. ABR (= *traducido*) trans

★**tradición** [traði'θjon] NF tradition

★**tradicional** [traðiθjo'nal] ADJ traditional

traducción [traðuk'θjon] NF translation; **~ asistida por ordenador** computer-assisted translation

traducible [traðu'θiβle] ADJ translatable

★**traducir** [traðu'θir] /3n/ VT to translate ∎ **traducirse** VR: **traducirse en** (*fig*) to entail, result in

★**traductor, a** [traðuk'tor, a] NM/F translator

traduzca *etc* [tra'ðuθka] VB *ver* **traducir**

★**traer** [tra'er] /2o/ VT to bring; (*llevar*) to carry; (*ropa*) to wear; (*incluir*) to carry; (*fig*) to cause; **~ consigo** to involve, entail ∎ **traerse** VR:

traerse algo to be up to sth; **traerse bien/mal** to dress well/badly; **traérselas** to be annoying; **es un problema que se las trae** it's a difficult problem

traficante [trafiˈkante] NMF trader, dealer

traficar [trafiˈkar] /**1g**/ VI to trade; **~ con** (pey) to deal illegally in

★**tráfico** [ˈtrafiko] NM (Com) trade; (Auto) traffic

trafique etc [traˈfike] VB ver **traficar**

tragaderas [traɣaˈðeras] NFPL (garganta) throat sg, gullet sg; (credulidad) gullibility sg

tragaluz [traɣaˈluθ] NM skylight

tragamonedas [traɣamoˈneðas] NM INV, **tragaperras** [traɣaˈperras] NM INV slot machine

★**tragar** [traˈɣar] /**1h**/ VT to swallow; (devorar) to devour, bolt down; **no lo puedo ~** (persona) I can't stand him ■ **tragarse** VR to swallow; (tierra) to absorb, soak up

★**tragedia** [traˈxeðja] NF tragedy

trágico, -a [ˈtraxiko, a] ADJ tragic

trago [ˈtraɣo] NM (de líquido) drink; (comido de golpe) gulp; (fam: de bebida) swig; (desgracia) blow; **echar un ~** to have a drink; **~ amargo** (fig) hard time

trague etc [ˈtraɣe] VB ver **tragar**

traición [traiˈθjon] NF treachery; (Jur) treason; (una traición) act of treachery

traicionar [traiθjoˈnar] /**1a**/ VT to betray

traicionero, -a [traiθjoˈnero, a] = **traidor**

traída [traˈiða] NF carrying; **~ de aguas** water supply

traidor, a [traiˈðor, a] ADJ treacherous ▸ NM/F traitor

traigo etc [ˈtraiɣo] VB ver **traer**

trailer [ˈtrailer] (pl **trailers** [ˈtrailer(s)]) NM trailer

★**traje** [ˈtraxe] VB ver **traer** ▸ NM (gen) dress; (de hombre) suit; (traje típico) costume; (fig) garb; **~ de baño** swimsuit; **~ de luces** bullfighter's costume; **~ a la medida** made-to-measure suit

trajera etc [traˈxera] VB ver **traer**

trajín [traˈxin] NM haulage; (fam: movimiento) bustle ■ **trajines** NMPL goings-on

trajinar [traxiˈnar] /**1a**/ VT (llevar) to carry, transport ▸ VI (moverse) to bustle about; (viajar) to travel around

trama [ˈtrama] NF (fig) link; (: intriga) plot; (de tejido) weft

tramar [traˈmar] /**1a**/ VT to plot; (Tec) to weave ■ **tramarse** VR (fig): **algo se está tramando** there's something going on

tramitar [tramiˈtar] /**1a**/ VT (asunto) to transact; (negociar) to negotiate; (manejar) to handle

trámite [ˈtramite] NM (paso) step; (Jur) transaction ■ **trámites** NMPL (burocracia) paperwork sg, procedures; (Jur) proceedings

tramo [ˈtramo] NM (de tierra) plot; (de escalera) flight; (de vía) section

tramoya [traˈmoja] NF (Teat) piece of stage machinery; (fig) trick

tramoyista [tramoˈjista] NMF scene shifter; (fig) trickster

trampa [ˈtrampa] NF trap; (en el suelo) trapdoor; (prestidigitación) conjuring trick; (engaño) trick; (fam) fiddle; **caer en la ~** to fall into the trap; **hacer trampas** (trampear) to cheat

trampear [trampeˈar] /**1a**/ VT, VI to cheat

trampilla [tramˈpiʎa] NF trap, hatchway

trampolín [trampoˈlin] NM trampoline; (de piscina etc) diving board

tramposo, -a [tramˈposo, a] ADJ crooked, cheating ▸ NM/F crook, cheat

tranca [ˈtranka] NF (palo) stick; (viga) beam; (de puerta, ventana) bar; (borrachera) binge; **a trancas y barrancas** with great difficulty

trancar [tranˈkar] /**1g**/ VT to bar ▸ VI to stride along

trancazo [tranˈkaθo] NM (golpe) blow

trance [ˈtranθe] NM (momento difícil) difficult moment; (situación crítica) critical situation; (estado de hipnosis) trance; **estar en ~ de muerte** to be at death's door

tranco [ˈtranko] NM stride

tranque etc [ˈtranke] VB ver **trancar**

tranquilamente [tranˈkilamente] ADV (sin preocupaciones: leer, trabajar) peacefully; (sin enfadarse: hablar, discutir) calmly

tranquilice etc [trankiˈliθe] VB ver **tranquilizar**

tranquilidad [trankiliˈðað] NF (calma) calmness, stillness; (paz) peacefulness

tranquilizador, a [trankiliθaˈðor, a] ADJ (música) soothing; (hecho) reassuring

tranquilizante [trankiliˈθante] NM tranquillizer

tranquilizar [trankiliˈθar] /**1f**/ VT (calmar) to calm (down); (asegurar) to reassure ■ **tranquilizarse** VR to calm down

★**tranquilo, -a** [tranˈkilo, a] ADJ (calmado) calm; (apacible) peaceful; (mar) calm; (mente) untroubled

Trans. ABR (Com) = **transferencia**

transacción [transakˈθjon] NF transaction

transar [tranˈsar] /**1a**/ VI (Am) = **transigir**

transatlántico, -a [transatˈlantiko, a] ADJ transatlantic ▸ NM (ocean) liner

transbordador [transβorðaˈðor] NM ferry

transbordar [transβorˈðar] /**1a**/ VT to transfer ■ **transbordarse** VR to change

★**transbordo** [transˈβorðo] NM transfer; **hacer ~** to change (trains)

transcender [transθenˈder] /**2g**/ VT = **trascender**

transcribir [transkriˈβir] /**3a**/ VT to transcribe

transcurrir [transkuˈrrir] /**3a**/ VI (tiempo) to pass; (hecho) to turn out

transcurso [transˈkurso] NM passing, lapse;

~ del tiempo passing of time; **en el ~ de ocho días** in the course of a week

★**transeúnte** [transeˈunte] ADJ transient ▶ NMF passer-by

transexual [transeˈkswal] ADJ, NMF transsexual

transferencia [transfeˈrenθja] NF transference; (Com) transfer; **~ bancaria** banker's order; **~ de crédito** (Com) credit transfer; **~ electrónica de fondos** (Com) electronic funds transfer

transferir [transfeˈrir] /3i/ VT to transfer; (aplazar) to postpone

transfiera etc [transˈfjera] VB ver **transferir**

transfigurar [transfiɣuˈrar] /1a/ VT to transfigure

transfiriendo etc [transfiˈrjendo] VB ver **transferir**

★**transformación** [transformaˈθjon] NF transformation

★**transformador** [transformaˈðor] NM transformer

★**transformar** [transforˈmar] /1a/ VT to transform; (convertir) to convert

tránsfuga [ˈtransfuɣa] NMF (Mil) deserter; (Pol) turncoat

transfusión [transfuˈsjon] NF (tb: **transfusión de sangre**) (blood) transfusion

transgénico, -a [transˈxeniko, a] ADJ genetically modified

transgredir [transɣreˈdir] /3a/ VT to transgress

transgresión [transɣreˈsjon] NF transgression

transición [transiˈθjon] NF transition; **período de ~** transitional period

transido, -a [tranˈsiðo, a] ADJ overcome; **~ de angustia** beset with anxiety; **~ de dolor** racked with pain

transigir [transiˈxir] /3c/ VI to compromise; (ceder) to make concessions

transija etc [tranˈsixa] VB ver **transigir**

Transilvania [transilˈβanja] NF Transylvania

transistor [transisˈtor] NM transistor

transitable [transiˈtaβle] ADJ (camino) passable

transitar [transiˈtar] /1a/ VI to go (from place to place)

transitivo, -a [transiˈtiβo, a] ADJ transitive

★**tránsito** [ˈtransito] NM transit; (Auto) traffic; (parada) stop; **horas de máximo ~** rush hours; **"se prohíbe el ~"** "no thoroughfare"

transitorio, -a [transiˈtorjo, a] ADJ transitory

transmisión [transmiˈsjon] NF (Radio, TV) transmission, broadcast(ing); (transferencia) transfer; **~ en circuito** hookup; **~ en directo/exterior** live/outside broadcast; **~ de datos (en paralelo/en serie)** (Inform) (parallel/serial) data transfer o transmission; **plena/media ~ bidireccional** (Inform) full/half duplex

transmitir [transmiˈtir] /3a/ VT to transmit; (Radio, TV) to broadcast; (enfermedad) to give, pass on

transparencia [transpaˈrenθja] NF transparency; (claridad) clearness, clarity; (diapositiva) slide

transparentar [transparenˈtar] /1a/ VT to reveal ▶ VI to be transparent

transparente [transpaˈrente] ADJ transparent; (aire) clear; (ligero) diaphanous ▶ NM curtain

transpirar [transpiˈrar] /1a/ VI to perspire; (fig) to transpire

transpondré etc [transponˈdre] VB ver **transponer**

transponer [transpoˈner] /2q/ VT to transpose; (cambiar de sitio) to move about ▶ VI (desaparecer) to disappear; (ir más allá) to go beyond ■ **transponerse** VR to change places; (ocultarse) to hide; (sol) to go down

transponga etc [transˈponga] VB ver **transponer**

transportador [transportaˈðor] NM (Mecánica): **~ de correa** conveyor belt

★**transportar** [transporˈtar] /1a/ VT to transport; (llevar) to carry

★**transporte** [transˈporte] NM transport; (Com) haulage; **Ministerio de Transportes** Ministry of Transport

transpuesto [transˈpwesto], **transpuse** etc [transˈpuse] VB ver **transponer**

transversal [transβerˈsal] ADJ transverse, cross ▶ NF (tb: **calle transversal**) cross street

transversalmente [transβersalˈmente] ADV obliquely

★**tranvía** [tramˈbia] NM tram, streetcar (US)

trapeador [trapeaˈðor] NM (Am) mop

trapear [trapeˈar] /1a/ VT (Am) to mop

trapecio [traˈpeθjo] NM trapeze

trapecista [trapeˈθista] NMF trapeze artist

trapero, -a [traˈpero, a] NM/F ragman

trapicheos [trapiˈtʃeos] NMPL (fam) schemes, fiddles

trapisonda [trapiˈsonda] NF (jaleo) row; (estafa) swindle

★**trapo** [ˈtrapo] NM (tela) rag; (de cocina) cloth; **a todo ~** under full sail; **soltar el ~** (llorar) to burst into tears ■ **trapos** NMPL (fam: de mujer) clothes, dresses

tráquea [ˈtrakea] NF trachea, windpipe

traqueteo [trakeˈteo] NM (crujido) crack; (golpeteo) rattling

tras [tras] PREP (detrás) behind; (después) after; **~ de** besides; **día ~ día** day after day; **uno ~ otro** one after the other

trasatlántico [trasatˈlantiko] NM (barco) (ocean) liner

trascendencia [trasθen'denθja] NF (*importancia*) importance; (*en filosofía*) transcendence

trascendental [trasθenden'tal] ADJ important; transcendental

trascender [trasθen'der] /2g/ VI (*oler*) to smell; (*noticias*) to come out, leak out; (*sucesos, sentimientos*) to spread, have a wide effect; **~ a** (*afectar*) to reach, have an effect on; (*oler a*) to smack of; **en su novela todo trasciende a romanticismo** everything in his novel smacks of romanticism

trascienda *etc* [tras'θjenda] VB *ver* **trascender**

trasegar [trase'ɣar] /1h, 1j/ VT (*mover*) to move about; (*vino*) to decant

trasegué [trase'ɣe], **traseguemos** *etc* [trase'ɣemos] VB *ver* **trasegar**

trasero, -a [tra'sero, a] ADJ back, rear ▶ NM (*Anat*) bottom ▪ **traseros** NMPL ancestors

trasfondo [tras'fondo] NM background

trasgo ['trasɣo] NM (*duende*) goblin

trasgredir [trasɣre'ðir] /3a/ VT to contravene

trashumante [trasu'mante] ADJ migrating

trasiego *etc* [tra'sjeɣo] VB *ver* **trasegar** ▶ NM (*cambiar de sitio*) move, switch; (*de vino*) decanting; (*trastorno*) upset

trasiegue *etc* [tra'sjeɣe] VB *ver* **trasegar**

trasladar [trasla'ðar] /1a/ VT to move; (*persona*) to transfer; (*postergar*) to postpone; (*copiar*) to copy; (*interpretar*) to interpret ▪ **trasladarse** VR (*irse*) to go; (*mudarse*) to move; **trasladarse a otro puesto** to move to a new job

traslado [tras'laðo] NM move; (*mudanza*) move, removal; (*de persona*) transfer; (*copia*) copy; **~ de bloque** (*Inform*) block move, cut-and-paste

traslucir [traslu'θir] /3f/ VT to show ▪ **traslucirse** VR to be translucent; (*fig*) to be revealed

trasluz [tras'luθ] NM reflected light; **al ~** against *o* up to the light

trasluzca *etc* [tras'luθka] VB *ver* **traslucir**

trasmano [tras'mano] **a ~** *adv* (*fuera de alcance*) out of reach; (*apartado*) out of the way

trasnochado, -a [trasno'tʃaðo, a] ADJ dated

trasnochador, a [trasnotʃa'ðor, a] ADJ given to staying up late ▶ NM/F (*fig*) night owl

trasnochar [trasno'tʃar] /1a/ VI (*acostarse tarde*) to stay up late; (*no dormir*) to have a sleepless night; (*pasar la noche*) to stay the night

traspapelar [traspape'lar] /1a/ VT (*documento, carta*) to mislay, misplace

traspasar [traspa'sar] /1a/ VT (*bala*) to pierce, go through; (*propiedad*) to sell, transfer; (*calle*) to cross over; (*límites*) to go beyond; (*ley*) to break; **"traspaso negocio"** "business for sale"

traspaso [tras'paso] NM (*venta*) transfer, sale; (*fig*) anguish

traspié [tras'pje] (*pl* **traspiés**) NM (*caída*) stumble; (*tropezón*) trip; (*fig*) blunder

trasplantar [trasplan'tar] /1a/ VT to transplant

trasplante [tras'plante] NM transplant

traspuesto, -a [tras'pwesto, a] ADJ: **quedarse ~** to doze off

trastada [tras'taða] NF (*fam*) prank

trastazo [tras'taθo] NM (*fam*) bump; **darse un ~** (*persona*) to bump o.s.; (*en coche*) to have a bump

traste ['traste] NM (*Mus*) fret; **dar al ~ con algo** to ruin sth; **ir al ~** to fall through

trastero [tras'tero] NM lumber room

trastienda [tras'tjenda] NF back room (*of shop*); **obtener algo por la ~** to get sth by underhand means

trasto ['trasto] NM (*mueble*) piece of furniture; (*tarro viejo*) old pot; (*pey: cosa*) piece of junk; (: *persona*) dead loss ▪ **trastos** NMPL (*Teat*) scenery *sg*; **tirar los trastos a la cabeza** to have a blazing row

trastocar [trasto'kar] /1g, 1l/ VT (*papeles*) to mix up

trastornado, -a [trastor'naðo, a] ADJ (*loco*) mad; (*agitado*) crazy

trastornar [trastor'nar] /1a/ VT to overturn, upset; (*fig: ideas*) to confuse; (: *nervios*) to shatter; (: *persona*) to drive crazy ▪ **trastornarse** VR (*plan*) to fall through; (*volverse loco*) to go mad *o* crazy

trastorno [tras'torno] NM (*acto*) overturning; (*confusión*) confusion; (*Pol*) disturbance, upheaval; (*Med*) upset; **~ estomacal** stomach upset; **~ mental** mental disorder, breakdown

trasunto [tra'sunto] NM copy

trasvase [tras'βase] NM (*de río*) diversion

tratable [tra'taβle] ADJ friendly

tratado [tra'taðo] NM (*Pol*) treaty; (*Com*) agreement; (*Lit*) treatise

tratamiento [trata'mjento] NM treatment; (*Tec*) processing; (*de problema*) handling; **~ de datos** (*Inform*) data processing; **~ de gráficos** (*Inform*) graphics; **~ de márgenes** margin settings; **~ de textos** (*Inform*) word processing; **~ por lotes** (*Inform*) batch processing; **~ de tú** familiar address

tratante [tra'tante] NMF dealer, merchandiser

★tratar [tra'tar] /1a/ VT (*ocuparse de*) to treat; (*manejar, Tec*) to handle; (*Inform*) to process; (*Med*) to treat; (*dirigirse a: persona*) to address ▶ VI: **~ de** (*hablar sobre*) to deal with, be about; (*intentar*) to try to; **~ con** (*Com*) to trade in; (*negociar con*) to negotiate with; (*tener tratos con*) to have dealings with ▪ **tratarse** VR to treat each other; **se trata de la nueva piscina** it's about the new pool; **¿de qué se trata?** what's it about?

trato ['trato] NM dealings *pl*; (*relaciones*) relationship; (*comportamiento*) manner; (*Com, Jur*) agreement, contract; (*título*) (form of) address; **de ~ agradable** pleasant; **de fácil ~** easy to get on with; **~ equitativo** fair deal; **¡~ hecho!** it's a deal!; **malos tratos** ill-treatment *sg*

trauma ['trauma] NM trauma

traumático, -a [trau'matiko, a] ADJ traumatic

través [tra'βes] NM (*contratiempo*) reverse; **al ~** across, crossways; **a ~ de** across; (*sobre*) over; (*por*) through; **de ~** across; (*de lado*) sideways

travesaño [traβe'saɲo] NM (*Arq*) crossbeam; (*Deporte*) crossbar

★**travesía** [traβe'sia] NF (*calle*) cross-street; (*Naut*) crossing

travesti [tra'βesti] NMF transvestite

travesura [traβe'sura] NF (*broma*) prank; (*ingenio*) wit

★**travieso, -a** [tra'βjeso, a] ADJ (*niño*) naughty; (*adulto*) restless; (*ingenioso*) witty ▶ NF crossing; (*Arq*) crossbeam; (*Ferro*) sleeper

★**trayecto** [tra'jekto] NM (*ruta*) road, way; (*viaje*) journey; (*tramo*) stretch; (*curso*) course; **final del ~** end of the line

trayectoria [trajek'torja] NF trajectory; (*desarrollo*) development; (*fig*) path; **la ~ actual del partido** the party's present line

trayendo *etc* [tra'jendo] VB *ver* **traer**

traza ['traθa] NF (*Arq*) plan, design; (*aspecto*) looks *pl*; (*señal*) sign; (*engaño*) trick; (*habilidad*) skill; (*Inform*) trace

trazado, -a [tra'θaðo, a] ADJ: **bien ~** shapely, well-formed ▶ NM (*Arq*) plan, design; (*fig*) outline; (*de carretera etc*) line, route

trazador [traθa'ðor] NM plotter; **~ plano** flat-bed plotter

trazar [tra'θar] /1f/ VT (*Arq*) to plan; (*Arte*) to sketch; (*fig*) to trace; (*hacer: itinerario*) to plot; (*plan*) to draw up

trazo ['traθo] NM (*línea*) line; (*bosquejo*) sketch ▪ **trazos** NMPL (*de cara*) lines, features

TRB ABR = **toneladas de registro bruto**

trébol ['treβol] NM (*Bot*) clover ▪ **tréboles** NMPL (*Naipes*) clubs

★**trece** ['treθe] NUM thirteen; **estar en sus ~** to stand firm

trecho ['tretʃo] NM (*distancia*) distance; (*de tiempo*) while; (*fam*) piece; **de ~ en ~** at intervals

tregua ['treɣwa] NF (*Mil*) truce; (*fig*) lull, respite; **sin ~** without respite

★**treinta** ['treinta] NUM thirty

treintena [trein'tena] NF (about) thirty

tremendo, -a [tre'mendo, a] ADJ (*terrible*) terrible; (*imponente: cosa*) imposing; (*fam: fabuloso*) tremendous; (*divertido*) entertaining

trémulo, -a ['tremulo, a] ADJ quivering; (*luz*) flickering

★**tren** [tren] NM (*Ferro*) train; **~ de aterrizaje** undercarriage; **~ directo/expreso/(de) mer-**

cancías/de pasajeros/suplementario through/fast/goods *o* freight/passenger/relief train; **~ de cercanías** suburban train; **~ de vida** way of life

trenca ['trenka] NF duffel coat

trence *etc* ['trenθe] VB *ver* **trenzar**

trenza ['trenθa] NF (*de pelo*) plait

trenzar [tren'θar] /1f/ VT (*el pelo*) to plait ▶ VI (*en baile*) to weave in and out ▪ **trenzarse** VR (*Am*) to become involved

trepa ['trepa] NF (*subida*) climb; (*ardid*) trick

trepador, a [trepa'ðor, a] NM/F (*fam*): **ser un(a) ~(a)** to be on the make ▶ NF (*Bot*) climber

trepar [tre'par] /1a/ VT, VI to climb; (*Tec*) to drill

trepidación [trepiða'θjon] NF shaking, vibration

trepidar [trepi'ðar] /1a/ VI to shake, vibrate

★**tres** [tres] NUM three; (*fecha*) third; **las ~** three o'clock

trescientos, -as [tres'θjentos, as] NUM three hundred

tresillo [tre'siʎo] NM three-piece suite; (*Mus*) triplet

treta ['treta] NF (*Com etc*) gimmick; (*fig*) trick

tri ... [tri] PREF tri..., three-...

tríada ['triaða] NF triad

triangular [trjangu'lar] ADJ triangular

triángulo [tri'angulo] NM triangle

triatleta [trjat'leta] NMF triathlete

tribal [tri'βal] ADJ tribal

tribu ['triβu] NF tribe

tribuna [tri'βuna] NF (*plataforma*) platform; (*Deporte*) stand; (*fig*) public speaking; **~ de la prensa** press box; **~ del acusado** (*Jur*) dock; **~ del jurado** jury box

tribunal [triβu'nal] NM (*en juicio*) court; (*comisión, fig*) tribunal; (*Escol: examinadores*) board of examiners; **T~ Supremo** High Court, Supreme Court (US); **T~ de Justicia de las Comunidades Europeas** European Court of Justice; **~ popular** jury

tributar [triβu'tar] /1a/ VT to pay; (*las gracias*) to give; (*cariño*) to show

tributario, -a [triβu'tarjo, a] ADJ (*Geo, Pol*) tributary *cpd*; (*Econ*) tax *cpd*, taxation *cpd*; **sistema ~** tax system ▶ NM (*Geo*) tributary ▶ NM/F (*Com*) taxpayer

tributo [tri'βuto] NM (*Com*) tax

tríceps ['triθeps] NM INV triceps

triciclo [tri'θiklo] NM tricycle

tricornio [tri'kornjo] NM three-cornered hat

tricota [tri'kota] NF (*Am*) knitted sweater

tricotar [triko'tar] /1a/ VI to knit

tridimensional [triðimensjo'nal] ADJ three-dimensional

trienal [trje'nal] ADJ triennial, three-yearly

trifulca [tri'fulka] NF (*fam*) row, shindy

trigal [tri'ɣal] NM wheat field

383

trigésimo, -a [tri'xesimo, a] NUM thirtieth

trigo ['triɣo] NM wheat ■ **trigos** NMPL wheat field(s)

trigueño, -a [tri'ɣeɲo, a] ADJ (pelo) corn-coloured; (piel) olive-skinned

trillado, -a [tri'ʎaðo, a] ADJ threshed; (fig) trite, hackneyed

trilladora [triʎa'ðora] NF threshing machine

trillar [tri'ʎar] /1a/ VT (Agr) to thresh; (fig) to frequent

trillizos, -as [tri'ʎiθos, as] NMPL/NFPL triplets

trilogía [trilo'xia] NF trilogy

trimestral [trimes'tral] ADJ quarterly; (Escol) termly

★**trimestre** [tri'mestre] NM (Escol) term; (Com) quarter, financial period; (: pago) quarterly payment

trinar [tri'nar] /1a/ VI (Mus) to trill; (ave) to sing, warble; (rabiar) to fume, be angry; **está que trina** he's hopping mad

trincar [trin'kar] /1g/ VT (atar) to tie up; (Naut) to lash; (agarrar) to pinion

trinchante [trin'tʃante] NM (para cortar carne) carving knife; (tenedor) meat fork

trinchar [trin'tʃar] /1a/ VT to carve

trinchera [trin'tʃera] NF (fosa) trench; (para vía) cutting; (impermeable) trench-coat

trineo [tri'neo] NM sledge

Trinidad [trini'ðað] NF (Geografía) Trinidad; (Rel): **la (Santísima)** ~ the (Holy) Trinity; ~ **y Tobago** Trinidad and Tobago

trinidad [trini'ðað] NF trio

trino ['trino] NM trill

trinque etc ['trinke] VB ver **trincar**

trinquete [trin'kete] NM (Tec) pawl; (Naut) foremast

trío ['trio] NM trio

tripa ['tripa] NF (Anat) intestine; (fam) belly; **tener mucha** ~ to be fat; **me duele la** ~ I have a stomach ache ■ **tripas** NFPL (Anat) insides; (Culin) tripe sg

tripartito, -a [tripar'tito, a] ADJ tripartite

triple ['triple] ADJ triple; (tres veces) threefold

triplicado, -a [tripli'kaðo, a] ADJ: **por** ~ in triplicate

triplicar [tripli'kar] /1g/ VT to treble

triplo, -a ['triplo, a] ADJ = **triple**

trípode ['tripoðe] NM tripod

Trípoli ['tripoli] NM Tripoli

tríptico ['triptiko] NM (Arte) triptych; (documento) three-part document

tripulación [tripula'θjon] NF crew

tripulante [tripu'lante] NMF crew member; **los tripulantes** the crew

tripular [tripu'lar] /1a/ VT (barco) to man; (Auto) to drive

triquiñuela [triki'ɲwela] NF trick

tris [tris] NM crack; **en un** ~ in an instant;

estar en un ~ **de hacer algo** to be within an inch of doing sth

★**triste** ['triste] ADJ (afligido) sad; (sombrío) melancholy, gloomy; (desolado) desolate; (lamentable) sorry, miserable; (viejo) old; (único) single; **no queda sino un** ~ **penique** there's just one miserable penny left

tristeza [tris'teθa] NF (aflicción) sadness; (melancolía) melancholy; (de lugar) desolation; (pena) misery

tristón, -ona [tris'ton, ona] ADJ sad, downhearted

trituradora [tritura'ðora] NF shredder

triturar [tritu'rar] /1a/ VT (moler) to grind; (mascar) to chew; (documentos) to shred

triunfador, a [triunfa'ðor, a] ADJ triumphant; (ganador) winning ▶ NM/F winner

triunfal [triun'fal] ADJ triumphant; (arco) triumphal

triunfante [triun'fante] ADJ triumphant; (ganador) winning

triunfar [triun'far] /1a/ VI (tener éxito) to triumph; (ganar) to win; (Naipes) to be trumps; **triunfan corazones** hearts are trumps; ~ **en la vida** to succeed in life

triunfo [tri'unfo] NM triumph; (Naipes) trump

trivial [tri'βjal] ADJ trivial

trivialice etc [triβja'liθe] VB ver **trivializar**

trivializar [triβjali'θar] /1f/ VT to minimize, play down

triza ['triθa] NF bit, piece; **hacer algo trizas** to smash sth to bits; (papel) to tear sth to shreds

trocar [tro'kar] /1g, 1l/ VT (Com) to exchange; (dinero, de lugar) to change; (palabras) to exchange; (confundir) to confuse ■ **trocarse** VR (confundirse) to get mixed up; (transformarse) **trocarse (en)** to change (into)

trocear [troθe'ar] /1a/ VT to cut up

trocha ['trotʃa] NF (sendero) bypath; (atajo) shortcut

troche ['trotʃe]: **a** ~ **y moche** (adv) helter-skelter, pell-mell

trofeo [tro'feo] NM (premio) trophy

trol [trol] NMF (Internet) troll ▶ NM (duende) troll

trola ['trola] NF (fam) fib

trolear [trole'ar] /1a/ VT (Internet) to troll

troll [trol] NMF (Internet) troll

tromba ['tromba] NF whirlwind; ~ **de agua** downpour

trombón [trom'bon] NM trombone

trombosis [trom'bosis] NF INV thrombosis

tromba ['trompa] NF (Mus) horn; (de elefante) trunk; (trompo) humming top; (hocico) snout; (Anat) tube, duct; ~ **de Falopio** Fallopian tube; **cogerse una** ~ (fam) to get tight ▶ NM (Mus) horn player

trompada [trom'paða] NF, **trompazo**

[trom'paθo] NM (choque) bump, bang; (puñetazo) punch

★**trompeta** [trom'peta] NF trumpet; (clarín) bugle ▶ NMF trumpeter

trompetilla [trompe'tiʎa] NF ear trumpet

trompicón [trompi'kon]: **a trompicones** (adv) in fits and starts

trompo ['trompo] NM spinning top

trompón [trom'pon] NM bump

tronado, -a [tro'naðo, a] ADJ broken-down

tronar [tro'nar] /1l/ VT (AM) to shoot, execute; (: examen) to flunk ▶ VI to thunder; (fig) to rage; (fam) to go broke

tronchar [tron'tʃar] /1a/ VT (árbol) to chop down; (fig: vida) to cut short; (esperanza) to shatter; (persona) to tire out ■ **troncharse** VR to fall down; **troncharse de risa** to split one's sides with laughter

tronco ['tronko] NM (de árbol, Anat) trunk; (de planta) stem; **estar hecho un ~** to be sound asleep

tronera [tro'nera] NF (Mil) loophole; (Arq) small window

trono ['trono] NM throne

tropa ['tropa] NF (Mil) troop; (soldados) soldiers pl; (soldados rasos) ranks pl; (gentío) mob

tropecé [trope'θe], **tropecemos** etc [trope'θemos] VB ver **tropezar**

tropel [tro'pel] NM (muchedumbre) crowd; (prisa) rush; (montón) throng; **acudir (etc) en ~** to come (etc) in a mad rush

tropelía [trope'lia] NF outrage

tropezar [trope'θar] /1f, 1j/ VI to trip, stumble; (fig) to slip up; **~ con** (encontrar) to run into; (topar con) to bump into ■ **tropezarse** VR (dos personas) to run into each other

tropezón [trope'θon] NM trip; (fig) blunder; (traspié): **dar un ~** to trip

tropical [tropi'kal] ADJ tropical

trópico ['tropiko] NM tropic

tropiece etc [tro'pjeθe] VB ver **tropezar**

tropiezo etc [tro'pjeθo] VB ver **tropezar** ▶ NM (error) slip, blunder; (desgracia) misfortune; (revés) setback; (obstáculo) snag; (discusión) quarrel

troqué [tro'ke], **troquemos** etc [tro'kemos] VB ver **trocar**

trotamundos [trota'mundos] NMF INV globetrotter

trotar [tro'tar] /1a/ VI to trot; (viajar) to travel about

trote ['trote] NM trot; (fam) travelling; **de mucho ~** hard-wearing

Troya ['troja] NF Troy; **aquí fue ~** now there's nothing but ruins

trozar [tro'θar] /1f/ VT (AM) to cut up, cut into pieces

★**trozo** ['troθo] NM bit, piece; (Lit, Mus) passage; **a trozos** in bits

★**trucha** ['trutʃa] NF (pez) trout; (Tec) crane

truco ['truko] NM (habilidad) knack; (engaño) trick; (Cine) trick effect o photography; **~ publicitario** advertising gimmick ■ **trucos** NMPL billiards sg

trueco etc ['trweko] VB ver **trocar**

★**trueno** ['trweno] VB ver **tronar** ▶ NM (gen) thunder; (estampido) boom; (: de arma) bang

trueque ['trweke] VB ver **trocar** ▶ NM exchange; (Com) barter

trufa ['trufa] NF (Bot) truffle; (fig: fam) fib

truhán, -ana [tru'an, ana] NM/F rogue

truncado, -a [trun'kaðo, a] ADJ truncated

truncar [trun'kar] /1g/ VT (cortar) to truncate; (la vida etc) to cut short; (el desarrollo) to stunt

trunque etc ['trunke] VB ver **truncar**

Tte. ABR (= Teniente) Lt.

★**tu** [tu] ADJ your

★**tú** [tu] PRON you

tubérculo [tu'βerkulo] NM (Bot) tuber

tuberculosis [tuβerku'losis] NF INV tuberculosis

tubería [tuβe'ria] NF pipes pl, piping; (conducto) pipeline

★**tubo** ['tuβo] NM tube, pipe; **~ de desagüe** drainpipe; **~ de ensayo** test tube; **~ de escape** exhaust (pipe); **~ digestivo** alimentary canal

tuerca ['twerka] NF (Tec) nut

tuerce etc ['twerθe] VB ver **torcer**

tuerto, -a ['twerto, a] ADJ (sin un ojo) one-eyed; (ciego de un ojo) blind in one eye ▶ NM/F (sin un ojo) one-eyed person; (ciego de un ojo) person who is blind in one eye ▶ NM (ofensa) wrong

tuerza etc ['twerθa] VB ver **torcer**

tueste etc ['tweste] VB ver **tostar**

tuétano [t'twetano] NM (Anat: médula) marrow; (Bot) pith; **hasta los tuétanos** through and through, utterly

tufo ['tufo] NM vapour; (fig: pey) stench

tugurio [tu'ɣurjo] NM slum

tuit [twit] (pl **tuits**) NM (en Twitter) tweet; Twitter® post

tuitear [twite'ar] /1a/ VT, VI (Inform) to tweet

tuitero, -a [twi'tero, a] NM/F Twitter® user

tul [tul] NM tulle

tulipán [tuli'pan] NM tulip

tullido, -a [tu'ʎiðo, a] ADJ crippled; (cansado) exhausted

tumba ['tumba] NF (sepultura) tomb; (sacudida) shake; (voltereta) somersault; **ser (como) una ~** to keep one's mouth shut

tumbar [tum'bar] /1a/ VT to knock down; (doblar) to knock over; (fam: suj: olor) to overpower ▶ VI to fall down ■ **tumbarse** VR (echarse) to lie down; (extenderse) to stretch out

tumbo ['tumbo] NM (caída) fall; (de vehículo) jolt; (momento crítico) critical moment; **dar tumbos** to stagger

tumbona [tum'bona] NF (*butaca*) easy chair; (*de playa: para acostarse*) lounger; (*: para sentarse*) deckchair (BRIT), beach chair (US)

tumor [tu'mor] NM tumour

tumulto [tu'multo] NM turmoil; (*Pol: motín*) riot

tuna ['tuna] NF (*Mus*) student music group; *ver tb* **tuno**

A **tuna** is made up of university students, or quite often former students, who dress up in costumes from the *Edad de Oro*, the Spanish Golden Age. These musical troupes go through the town playing their guitars, lutes and tambourines and serenade the young ladies in the halls of residence, or make impromptu appearances at weddings or parties singing traditional Spanish songs for a few coins.

tunante [tu'nante] ADJ rascally ▶ NM rogue, villain; ¡~! you villain!

tunda ['tunda] NF (*de tela*) shearing; (*de golpes*) beating

tundir [tun'dir] /3a/ VT (*tela*) to shear; (*hierba*) to mow; (*fig*) to exhaust; (*fam: golpear*) to beat

tunear [tune'ar] /1a/ VT (*fam: vehículo*) to tune

tunecino, -a [tune'θino, a] ADJ, NM/F Tunisian

★**túnel** ['tunel] NM tunnel

Túnez ['tuneθ] NM Tunis

túnica ['tunika] NF tunic; (*vestido largo*) long dress; (*Anat, Bot*) tunic

Tunicia [tu'niθja] NF Tunisia

tuning ['tunin] NM (*Auto*) tuning

tuno, -a ['tuno, a] NM/F (*fam*) rogue ▶ NM (*Mus*) member of a "tuna"; *ver* **tuna**

tuntún [tun'tun] ADV: **al ~** thoughtlessly

tupamaro, -a [tupa'maro, a] ADJ, NM/F (AM) urban guerrilla

tupé [tu'pe] NM quiff

tupí [tu'pi], **tupí-guaraní** [tupigwara'ni] ADJ, NMF Tupi-Guarani

tupido, -a [tu'piðo, a] ADJ (*denso*) dense; (*fig: torpe*) dim; (*tela*) close-woven

turba ['turβa] NF (*combustible*) turf; (*muchedumbre*) crowd

turbación [turβa'θjon] NF (*molestia*) disturbance; (*preocupación*) worry

turbado, -a [tur'βaðo, a] ADJ (*molesto*) disturbed; (*preocupado*) worried

turbante [tur'βante] NM turban

turbar [tur'βar] /1a/ VT (*molestar*) to disturb; (*incomodar*) to upset ■ **turbarse** VR to be disturbed

turbina [tur'βina] NF turbine

turbio, -a ['turβjo, a] ADJ (*agua etc*) cloudy; (*vista*) dim, blurred; (*tema*) unclear, confused; (*negocio*) shady ▶ ADV indistinctly

turbión [tur'βjon] NF downpour; (*fig*) shower, hail

turbo ['turβo] ADJ INV turbo(-charged) ▶ NM (*tb coche*) turbo

turbulencia [turβu'lenθja] NF turbulence; (*fig*) restlessness

turbulento, -a [turβu'lento, a] ADJ turbulent; (*fig: intranquilo*) restless; (*ruidoso*) noisy

turco, -a ['turko, a] ADJ Turkish ▶ NM/F Turk ▶ NM (*Ling*) Turkish

Turena [tu'rena] NF Touraine

turgente [tur'xente], **túrgido, a** ['turxiðo, a] ADJ (*tirante*) turgid, swollen

Turín [tu'rin] NM Turin

★**turismo** [tu'rismo] NM tourism; (*coche*) saloon car; **hacer ~** to go travelling (abroad)

★**turista** [tu'rista] NMF tourist; (*visitante*) sightseer

★**turístico, -a** [tu'ristiko, a] ADJ tourist *cpd*

Turkmenistán [turkmenis'tan] NM Turkmenistan

turnarse [tur'narse] /1a/ VR to take (it in) turns

turno ['turno] NM (*de trabajo*) shift; (*oportunidad, orden de prioridad*) opportunity; (*Deporte etc*) turn; **es su ~** it's his turn (next); **~ de día/de noche** day/night shift

turolense [turo'lense] ADJ of o from Teruel ▶ NMF native o inhabitant of Teruel

turquesa [tur'kesa] NF turquoise

Turquía [tur'kia] NF Turkey

★**turrón** [tu'rron] NM (*dulce*) nougat; (*fam*) sinecure, cushy job o number

Turrón is a type of nougat of oriental origin made with honey, egg whites, and almonds which is eaten at Christmas. There are two types of traditional *turrón*: hard with whole almonds known as *Alicante*; or soft, made with ground almonds, known as *Jijona*. There is also a wide variety of other *turrones* like coconut, crystallized fruits, or chocolate.

tute ['tute] NM (*Naipes*) card game; **darse un ~** to break one's back

★**tutear** [tute'ar] /1a/ VT to address as familiar "tú" ■ **tutearse** VR to be on familiar terms

tutela [tu'tela] NF (*legal*) guardianship; (*instrucción*) guidance; **estar bajo la ~ de** (*fig*) to be under the protection of

tutelar [tute'lar] /1a/ ADJ tutelary ▶ VT to protect

★**tutor, a** [tu'tor, a] NM/F (*legal*) guardian; (*Escol*) tutor; **~ de curso** form master/mistress

tutorial [tuto'rial] NM tutorial

Tuvalu [tuβa'lu] NM Tuvalu

tuve *etc* ['tuβe] VB *ver* **tener**

tuviera *etc* VB *ver* **tener**

★**tuyo, -a** ['tujo, a] ADJ yours, of yours; **un amigo**

~ a friend of yours ▶ PRON yours; **los tuyos**
(*fam*) your relations, your family

TV NF ABR (= *televisión*) TV

TVE NF ABR = **Televisión Española**

tweet [twit] (*pl* **tweets**) NM (*en Twitter*) tweet,
Twitter® post

Uu

U, u [u] NF (*letra*) U, u; **viraje en U** U-turn; **U de Ulises** U for Uncle

★**u** [u] CONJ or

u. ABR = **unidad**

ubérrimo, -a [u'βerrimo, a] ADJ very rich, fertile

ubicación [uβika'θjon] NF (*esp AM*) place, position, location

★**ubicado, -a** [uβi'kaðo, a] ADJ (*esp AM*) situated

ubicar [uβi'kar] /**1g**/ VT (*esp AM*) to place, situate; (: *encontrar*) to find ■ **ubicarse** VR to be situated, be located

ubicuo, -a [u'βikwo, a] ADJ ubiquitous

ubique *etc* [u'βike] VB *ver* **ubicar**

ubre ['uβre] NF udder

UCI ['uθi] SIGLA F (= *Unidad de Cuidados Intensivos*) ICU

Ucrania [u'kranja] NF Ukraine

ucraniano, -a [ukra'njano, a] ADJ, NM/F Ukrainian ▶ NM (*Ling*) Ukrainian

ucranio [u'kranjo] NM (*Ling*) Ukrainian

Ud(s). ABR = **usted**

★**UE** NF ABR (= *Unión Europea*) EU

UEFA [w'efa] NF ABR (= *Unión de Asociaciones de Fútbol Europeo*) UEFA

UEM NF ABR (= *Unión Económica y Monetaria*) EMU

UEO NF ABR (= *Unión Europea Occidental*) WEU

UER SIGLA F = **Unión Europea de Radiodifusión**

uf [uf] EXCL (*cansancio*) phew!; (*repugnancia*) ugh!

ufanarse [ufa'narse] /**1a**/ VR to boast; **~ de** to pride o.s. on

ufano, -a [u'fano, a] ADJ (*arrogante*) arrogant; (*presumido*) conceited

UGT NF ABR *ver* **Unión General de Trabajadores**

UIT SIGLA F = **Unión Internacional de Telecomunicaciones**

ujier [u'xjer] NM usher; (*portero*) doorkeeper

úlcera ['ulθera] NF ulcer

ulcerar [ulθe'rar] /**1a**/ VT to make sore ■ **ulcerarse** VR to ulcerate

ulterior [ulte'rjor] ADJ (*más allá*) farther, further; (*subsecuente, siguiente*) subsequent

ulteriormente [ulterjor'mente] ADV later, subsequently

★**últimamente** ['ultimamente] ADV (*recientemente*) lately, recently; (*finalmente*) finally; (*como último recurso*) as a last resort

ultimar [ulti'mar] /**1a**/ VT to finish; (*finalizar*) to finalize; (*AM: matar*) to kill

ultimátum [ulti'matum] NM (*pl* **ultimátums**) ultimatum

★**último, -a** ['ultimo, a] ADJ last; (*más reciente*) latest, most recent; (*más bajo*) bottom; (*más alto*) top; (*fig*) final, extreme; **en las últimas** on one's last legs; **por ~** finally

ultra ['ultra] ADJ ultra ▶ NMF extreme right-winger

ultracongelar [ultrakonxe'lar] /**1a**/ VT to deep-freeze

ultraderecha [ultraðe'retʃa] NF extreme right (wing)

ultrajar [ultra'xar] /**1a**/ VT (*escandalizar*) to outrage; (*insultar*) to insult, abuse

ultraje [ul'traxe] NM outrage; insult

ultraligero [ultrali'xero] NM microlight (*BRIT*), microlite (*US*)

ultramar [ultra'mar] NM: **de** *o* **en ~** abroad, overseas; **los países de ~** the overseas countries

ultramarino, -a [ultrama'rino, a] ADJ overseas, foreign ▶ NM: **ultramarinos** groceries; **tienda de ultramarinos** grocer's (shop)

ultranza [ul'tranθa]: **a ~** *adv* to the death; (*a toda costa*) at all costs; (*completo*) outright; (*Pol etc*) out-and-out, extreme; **un nacionalista a ~** a rabid nationalist

ultrarrojo, -a [ultra'rroxo, a] ADJ = **infra-rrojo**

ultrasónico, -a [ultra'soniko, a] ADJ ultrasonic

ultratumba [ultra'tumba] NF: **la vida de ~** the next life; **una voz de ~** a ghostly voice

ultravioleta [ultraβjo'leta] ADJ INV ultraviolet

ulular [ulu'lar] /1a/ VI to howl; (búho) to hoot

umbilical [umbili'kal] ADJ: **cordón ~** umbilical cord

umbral [um'bral] NM (gen) threshold; **~ de rentabilidad** (Com) break-even point

umbrío, -a [um'brio, a] ADJ shady

---

un, una [un, 'una]

ARTÍCULO INDEFINIDO **1** a; (antes de vocal) an; **una mujer/naranja** a woman/an orange
2: **unos/unas**: **hay unos regalos para ti** there are some presents for you; **hay unas cervezas en la nevera** there are some beers in the fridge; ver tb **uno**
3 (enfático): **¡hace un frío!** it's so cold!; **¡tiene una casa!** he's got some house!

UNAM ['unam] NF ABR = **Universidad Nacional Autónoma de México**

unánime [u'nanime] ADJ unanimous

unanimidad [unanimi'ðað] NF unanimity; **por ~** unanimously

unción [un'θjon] NF anointing

uncir [un'θir] /3b/ VT to yoke

undécimo, -a [un'deθimo, a] ADJ, NM/F eleventh

UNED [u'ned] NF ABR (Esp Univ: = Universidad Nacional de Educación a Distancia) ≈ Open University (BRIT)

UNESCO, Unesco [u'nesko] SIGLA F (= United Nations Educación, Scientific and Cultural Organization) UNESCO

ungir [un'xir] /3c/ VT to rub with ointment; (Rel) to anoint

ungüento [un'gwento] NM ointment; (fig) salve, balm

únicamente ['unikamente] ADV solely; (solamente) only

UNICEF, Unicef [uni'θef] SIGLA F (= United Nations International Children's Emergency Fund) ≈ UNICEF

unicidad [uniθi'ðað] NF uniqueness

⋆**único, -a** ['uniko, a] ADJ only; (solo) sole, single; (sin par) unique; **hijo ~** only child

⋆**unidad** [uni'ðað] NF unity; (Tec) unit; **~ móvil** (TV) mobile unit; (Inform) **~ central** system unit, central processing unit; **~ de control** control unit; **~ de disco** disk drive; **~ de disco duro** hard drive; **~ de entrada/salida** input/output device; **~ de información** data item; **~ de presentación visual** o **de visualización** visual display unit; **~ periférica** peripheral

device; ~ procesadora central central processing unit

⋆**unido, -a** [u'niðo, a] ADJ joined, linked; (fig) united

unifamiliar [unifamil'jar] ADJ: **vivienda ~** single-family home

unificar [unifi'kar] /1g/ VT to unite, unify

unifique etc [uni'fike] VB ver **unificar**

uniformado, -a [unifor'maðo, a] ADJ uniformed, in uniform

uniformar [unifor'mar] /1a/ VT to make uniform; (persona) to put into uniform; (Tec) to standardize

⋆**uniforme** [uni'forme] ADJ uniform, equal; (superficie) even ▸ NM uniform

uniformidad [uniformi'ðað] NF uniformity; (llaneza) levelness, evenness

unilateral [unilate'ral] ADJ unilateral

unión [u'njon] NF (gen) union; (acto) uniting, joining; (calidad) unity; (Tec) joint; (fig) closeness, togetherness; **en ~ con** (together) with, accompanied by; **~ aduanera** customs union; **U~ General de Trabajadores** (Esp) Socialist Union Confederation; **U~ Europea** European Union; **la U~ Soviética** (Historia) the Soviet Union; **punto de ~** (Tec) junction

unir [u'nir] /3a/ VT (juntar) to join, unite; (atar) to tie, fasten; (combinar) to combine; **les une una fuerte simpatía** they are bound by (a) strong affection ▸ VI (ingredientes) to mix well ▪ **unirse** VR to join together, unite; (empresas) to merge; **unirse en matrimonio** to marry

unisex [uni'seks] ADJ INV unisex

unísono [u'nisono] NM: **al ~** in unison

unitario, -a [uni'tarjo, a] ADJ unitary; (Rel) Unitarian ▸ NM/F (Rel) Unitarian

universal [uniβer'sal] ADJ universal; (mundial) world cpd; **historia ~** world history

⋆**universidad** [uniβersi'ðað] NF university; **~ laboral** polytechnic, poly

universitario, -a [uniβersi'tarjo, a] ADJ university cpd ▸ NM/F (profesor) lecturer; (estudiante) (university) student; (graduado) graduate

universo [uni'βerso] NM universe

unja etc ['unxa] VB ver **ungir**

---

uno, -a ['uno, a]

ADJ one; **es todo uno** it's all one and the same; **unos pocos** a few; **unos cien** about a hundred
▸ PRON **1** one; **quiero uno solo** I only want one; **uno de ellos** one of them; **una de dos** either one or the other; **no doy una hoy** I can't do anything right today
2 (alguien) somebody, someone; **conozco a uno que se te parece** I know somebody o someone who looks like you; **unos querían quedarse** some (people) wanted to stay

3 (*impersonal*) one; **uno mismo** oneself; **uno nunca sabe qué hacer** one never knows what to do

4: **unos ... otros ...** some ... others; **una y otra son muy agradables** they're both very nice; **(los) uno(s) a (los) otro(s)** each other, one another

▶ NF one; **es la una** it's one o'clock

▶ NUM (number) one; **el día uno** the first; *ver* tb **un**

untar [un'tar] /**1a**/ VT (*gen*) to rub; (*mantequilla*) to spread; (*engrasar*) to grease, oil; (*Med*) to rub (with ointment); (*fig*) to bribe; **~ el pan con mantequilla** to spread butter on one's bread ■ **untarse** VR (*fig*) to be crooked

unto ['unto] NM animal fat; (*Med*) ointment

unza *etc* ['unθa] VB *ver* **uncir**

★**uña** ['uɲa] NF (*Anat*) nail; (*del pie*) toenail; (*garra*) claw; (*casco*) hoof; (*arrancaclavos*) claw; **ser ~ y carne** to be as thick as thieves; **enseñar** *o* **mostrar** *o* **sacar las uñas** to show one's claws

UPC NF ABR (= *unidad procesadora central*) CPU

uperizado, -a [uperi'θaðo, a] ADJ: **leche uperizada** UHT milk

Urales [u'rales] NMPL (*tb*: **Montes Urales**) Urals

uralita® [ura'lita] NF corrugated asbestos cement

uranio [u'ranjo] NM uranium

urbanidad [urβani'ðað] NF courtesy, politeness

urbanismo [urβa'nismo] NM town planning

urbanista [urβa'nista] NMF town planner

★**urbanización** [urβaniθa'θjon] NF (*colonia*, *barrio*) estate, housing scheme

urbanizar [urβani'θar] /**1f**/ VT (*zona*) to develop, urbanize

urbano, -a [ur'βano, a] ADJ (*de ciudad*) urban, town *cpd*; (*cortés*) courteous, polite

urbe ['urβe] NF large city, metropolis

urdimbre [ur'ðimbre] NF (*de tejido*) warp; (*intriga*) intrigue

urdir [ur'ðir] /**3a**/ VT to warp; (*fig*) to plot, contrive

★**urgencia** [ur'xenθja] NF urgency; (*prisa*) haste, rush; (*emergencia*) emergency; **salida de ~** emergency exit; **servicios de ~** emergency services; **"Urgencias"** "Accident & Emergency", "Casualty"

★**urgente** [ur'xente] ADJ urgent; (*insistente*) insistent; **carta ~** registered (BRIT) *o* special delivery (US) letter

urgir [ur'xir] /**3c**/ VI to be urgent; **me urge** I'm in a hurry for it; **me urge terminarlo** I must finish it as soon as I can

urinario, -a [uri'narjo, a] ADJ urinary ▶ NM urinal, public lavatory, comfort station (US)

urja *etc* ['urxa] VB *ver* **urgir**

urna ['urna] NF urn; (*Pol*) ballot box; **acudir a las urnas** (*fig*: *persona*) to (go and) vote; (*gobierno*) to go to the country

urología [urolo'xia] NF urology

urólogo, -a [u'roloɣo, a] NM/F urologist

urraca [u'rraka] NF magpie

URSS [urs] NF ABR (*Historia*: = *Unión de Repúblicas Socialistas Soviéticas*) USSR

★**Uruguay** [uru'ɣwai] NM Uruguay

uruguayo, -a [uru'ɣwajo, a] ADJ, NM/F Uruguayan

usado, -a [u'saðo, a] ADJ (*gen*) used; (*ropa etc*) worn; (*de segunda mano*) secondhand; **muy ~** worn out

usanza [u'sanθa] NF custom, usage

★**usar** [u'sar] /**1a**/ VT to use; (*ropa*) to wear; (*tener costumbre*) to be in the habit of ▶ VI: **~ de** to make use of ■ **usarse** VR to be used; (*ropa*) to be worn in fashion

USB NM ABR (*Inform*: = *universal serial bus*) USB

USO ['uso] NF ABR (ESP: = *Unión Sindical Obrera*) *workers' union*

★**uso** ['uso] NM use; (*Mecánica etc*) wear; (*costumbre*) usage, custom; (*moda*) fashion; **al ~** in keeping with custom; **al ~ de** in the style of; **de ~ externo** (*Med*) for external use; **estar en el ~ de la palabra** to be speaking, have the floor; **~ y desgaste** (*Com*) wear and tear; **~ compartido de archivos** (*Inform*) file sharing

★**usted** [us'teð] PRON (*sg formal*: *abr* **Ud.** *o* **Vd.**) you *sg*; **ustedes** (*pl formal*: *abr* **Uds.** *o* **Vds.**) you *pl*; (AM *frm*, *tb fam*) you *pl*

usual [u'swal] ADJ usual

★**usuario, -a** [usw'arjo, a] NM/F user; **~ final** (*Com*) end user

usufructo [usu'frukto] NM use; **~ vitalicio (de)** life interest (in)

usura [u'sura] NF usury

usurero, -a [usu'rero, a] NM/F usurer

usurpar [usur'par] /**1a**/ VT to usurp

utensilio [uten'siljo] NM tool; (*Culin*) utensil

útero ['utero] NM uterus, womb

★**útil** ['util] ADJ useful; (*servible*) usable, serviceable; **día ~** working day, weekday; **es muy ~ tenerlo aquí cerca** it's very handy having it here close by ▶ NM tool

utilice *etc* [uti'liθe] VB *ver* **utilizar**

utilidad [utili'ðað] NF usefulness, utility; (*Com*) profit; **utilidades líquidas** net profit *sg*

utilitario [utili'tarjo] NM (*Inform*) utility

★**utilizar** [utili'θar] /**1f**/ VT to use, utilize; (*explotar*) to harness

utopía [uto'pia] NF Utopia

utópico, -a [u'topiko, a] ADJ Utopian

UVA SIGLA MPL (= *ultravioleta A*) UVA

★**uva** ['uβa] NF grape; **~ pasa** raisin; **~ de Corinto** currant; **estar de mala ~** to be in a bad mood; *see note*

In Spain **las uvas** play a big part on New Year's Eve (*Nochevieja*), when on the stroke of midnight people from every part of Spain, at home, in restaurants, in open spaces and in public squares, eat a grape for each stroke of the clock – especially the one at Puerta del Sol in Madrid. It is said to bring luck for the following year.

uve ['uβe] NF *name of the letter V*; **en forma de ~** V-shaped; **~ doble** *name of the letter W*

UVI ['uβi] NF ABR (*ESP Med*: = *unidad de vigilancia intensiva*) ICU

Vv

V, v [(Esp) ˈuβe, (Am) beˈkorta, beˈtʃika] NF (letra) V, v; **V de Valencia** V for Victor

V. ABR = **usted**; (= visto) approved, passed

v. ABR (= voltio) v; (Lit: = verso) v; (= ver, véase) v.

va [ba] VB ver **ir**

★**vaca** [ˈbaka] NF (animal) cow; (carne) beef; (cuero) cowhide; **vacas flacas/gordas** (fig) bad/good times

★**vacaciones** [bakaˈθjones] NFPL holiday(s); **estar/irse o marcharse de ~** to be/go (away) on holiday

vacante [baˈkante] ADJ vacant, empty ▸ NF vacancy

vaciado, -a [baˈθjaðo, a] ADJ (hecho en molde) cast in a mould; (hueco) hollow ▸ NM cast, mould(ing)

★**vaciar** [baˈθjar] /1c/ VT to empty (out); (ahuecar) to hollow out; (moldear) to cast; (Inform) to dump ▸ VI (río): **~ en** to flow into ▪ **vaciarse** VR to empty; (fig) to blab, spill the beans

vaciedad [baθjeˈðað] NF emptiness

vacilación [baθilaˈθjon] NF hesitation

vacilante [baθiˈlante] ADJ unsteady; (habla) faltering; (luz) flickering; (fig) hesitant

vacilar [baθiˈlar] /1a/ VI (dudar) to hesitate, waver; (mueble) to be unsteady; (persona: al andar) to stagger, stumble; (: al hablar) to falter; (luz) to flicker; (memoria) to fail; (esp Am: divertirse) to have a great time

vacilón [baθiˈlon] NM (esp Am): **estar o ir de ~** to have a great time

★**vacío, -a** [baˈθio, a] ADJ empty; (puesto) vacant; (desocupado) idle; (vano) vain; (charla etc) light, superficial ▸ NM emptiness; (Física) vacuum; (un vacío) (empty) space; **hacer el ~ a algn** to send sb to Coventry

vacuna [baˈkuna] NF vaccine

vacunar [bakuˈnar] /1a/ VT to vaccinate ▪ **vacunarse** VR to get vaccinated

vacuno, -a [baˈkuno, a] ADJ bovine; **ganado ~** cattle

vacuo, -a [ˈbakwo, a] ADJ empty

vadear [baðeˈar] /1a/ VT (río) to ford; (problema) to overcome; (persona) to sound out

vado [ˈbaðo] NM ford; (solución) solution; (descanso) respite; **"~ permanente"** "keep clear"

★**vagabundo, -a** [baɣaˈβundo, a] ADJ wandering; (pey) vagrant ▸ NM/F (errante) wanderer; (vago) tramp, bum (US)

vagamente [baɣaˈmente] ADV vaguely

vagancia [baˈɣanθja] NF (pereza) idleness, laziness; (vagabundeo) vagrancy

vagar [baˈɣar] /1h/ VI to wander; (pasear) to saunter up and down; (no hacer nada) to idle ▸ NM leisure

vagido [baˈxiðo] NM wail

vagina [baˈxina] NF vagina

★**vago, -a** [ˈbaɣo, a] ADJ vague; (perezoso) lazy; (ambulante) wandering ▸ NM/F (vagabundo) tramp, bum (US); (perezoso) lazybones sg, idler

★**vagón** [baˈɣon] NM (de pasajeros) carriage; (de mercancías) wagon; **~ cama/restaurante** sleeping/dining car

vague etc [ˈbaɣe] VB ver **vagar**

vaguear [baɣeˈar] /1a/ VI to laze around

vaguedad [baɣeˈðað] NF vagueness

vahído [baˈiðo] NM dizzy spell

vaho [ˈbao] NM (vapor) vapour, steam; (olor) smell; (respiración) breath ▪ **vahos** NMPL (Med) inhalation sg

vaina [ˈbaina] NF sheath ▸ NM (Am) nuisance

★**vainilla** [baiˈniʎa] NF vanilla

vainita [baiˈnita] NF (Am) green o French bean

vais [bais] VB ver **ir**

vaivén [baiˈβen] NM to-and-fro movement; (de tránsito) coming and going ▪ **vaivenes** NMPL (fig) ups and downs

★**vajilla** [baˈxiʎa] NF crockery, dishes pl; (una vajilla) service; **~ de porcelana** chinaware

val [bal], **valdré** etc [balˈdre] VB ver **valer**

★**vale** ['bale] NM voucher; (*recibo*) receipt; (*pagaré*) IOU; **~ de regalo** gift voucher *o* token

valedero, -a [bale'ðero, a] ADJ valid

valenciano, -a [balen'θjano, a] ADJ, NM/F Valencian ▶ NM (*Ling*) Valencian

valentía [balen'tia] NF courage, bravery; (*pey*) boastfulness; (*acción*) heroic deed

valentísimo, -a [balen'tisimo, a] ADJ SUPERLATIVO *de* **valiente** very brave, courageous

valentón, -ona [balen'ton, ona] ADJ blustering

★**valer** [ba'ler] /2p/ VT to be worth; (*Mat*) to equal; (*costar*) to cost; (*amparar*) to aid, protect; **~ la pena** to be worthwhile ▶ VI (*ser útil*) to be useful; (*ser válido*) to be valid; **¿vale?** O.K.?; **¡vale!** (*¡basta!*) that'll do!; **¡eso no vale!** that doesn't count!; **¡eso a mí no me vale!** (*AM fam: no importa*) I couldn't care less about that; **no vale nada** it's no good; (*mercancía*) it's worthless; (*argumento*) it's no use; **no vale para nada** he's no good at all; **más vale tarde que nunca** better late than never; **más vale que nos vayamos** we'd better go ■ **valerse** VR to take care of o.s.; **valerse de** to make use of, take advantage of; **valerse por sí mismo** to help *o* manage by o.s.

valeroso, -a [bale'roso, a] ADJ brave, valiant

valgo etc ['balɣo] VB ver **valer**

valía [ba'lia] NF worth; **de gran ~** (*objeto*) very valuable

validar [bali'ðar] /1a/ VT to validate; (*Pol*) to ratify

validez [bali'ðeθ] NF validity; **dar ~ a** to validate

★**válido, -a** ['baliðo, a] ADJ valid

★**valiente** [ba'ljente] ADJ brave, valiant; (*audaz*) bold; (*pey*) boastful; (*con ironía*) fine, wonderful ▶ NMF brave man/woman

valija [ba'lixa] NF (*AM*) case, suitcase; (*mochila*) satchel; (*Correos*) mailbag; **~ diplomática** diplomatic bag

valioso, -a [ba'ljoso, a] ADJ valuable; (*rico*) wealthy

valla ['baʎa] NF fence; (*Deporte*) hurdle; (*fig*) barrier; **~ publicitaria** hoarding (*esp BRIT*), billboard (*esp US*)

vallar [ba'ʎar] /1a/ VT to fence in

★**valle** ['baʎe] NM valley, vale

vallisoletano, -a [baʎisole'tano, a] ADJ of *o* from Valladolid ▶ NM/F native *o* inhabitant of Valladolid

★**valor** [ba'lor] NM value, worth; (*precio*) price; (*valentía*) valour, courage; (*importancia*) importance; (*cara*) nerve, cheek (*fam*); **sin ~** worthless; **~ adquisitivo** *o* **de compra** purchasing power; **dar ~ a** to attach importance to; **quitar ~ a** to minimize the importance of; (*Com*) **~ según balance** book value; **~ comercial** *o* **de mercado** market value; **~ contable/desglosado** asset/break-up value; **~ de escasez** scarcity value; **~ intrínseco** intrinsic value; **~ a la**

par par value; **~ neto** net worth; **~ de rescate/de sustitución** surrender/replacement value; *ver tb* **valores**

valoración [balora'θjon] NF valuation

valorar [balo'rar] /1a/ VT to value; (*tasar*) to price; (*fig*) to assess

valores [ba'lores] NMPL (*Com*) securities; **~ en cartera** *o* **habidos** investments

vals [bals] NM waltz

válvula ['balβula] NF valve

vamos ['bamos] VB ver **ir**

vampiro, -iresa [bam'piro, i'resa] NM/F vampire ▶ NF (*Cine*) vamp, femme fatale

van [ban] VB ver **ir**

vanagloriarse [banaɣlo'rjarse] /1b/ VR to boast

★**vandalismo** [banda'lismo] NM vandalism

vándalo, -a ['bandalo, a] NM/F vandal

vanguardia [ban'gwardja] NF vanguard; **de ~** (*Arte*) avant-garde; **estar en** *o* **ir a la ~ de** (*fig*) to be in the forefront of

vanguardista [bangwar'ðista] ADJ avant-garde

vanidad [bani'ðað] NF vanity; (*inutilidad*) futility; (*irrealidad*) unreality

vanidoso, -a [bani'ðoso, a] ADJ vain, conceited

vano, -a ['bano, a] ADJ (*irreal*) unreal; (*irracional*) unreasonable; (*inútil*) vain, useless; (*persona*) vain, conceited; (*frívolo*) frivolous

Vanuatu [βa'nwatu] NM Vanuatu

★**vapor** [ba'por] NM vapour; (*vaho*) steam; (*de gas*) fumes *pl*; (*neblina*) mist; **al ~** (*Culin*) steamed; **~ de agua** water vapour ■ **vapores** NMPL (*Med*) hysterics

vaporice etc [bapo'riθe] VB ver **vaporizar**

vaporizador [baporiθa'ðor] NM (*de perfume etc*) spray

vaporizar [bapori'θar] /1f/ VT to vaporize; (*perfume*) to spray

vaporoso, -a [bapo'roso, a] ADJ vaporous; (*vahoso*) steamy; (*tela*) light, airy

vapulear [bapule'ar] /1a/ VT to thrash; (*fig*) to slate

vaquería [bake'ria] NF dairy

vaquero, -a [ba'kero, a] ADJ cattle *cpd* ▶ NM cowboy ■ **vaqueros** NMPL jeans

vaquilla [ba'kiʎa] NF heifer

vara ['bara] NF stick, pole; (*Tec*) rod; **~ mágica** magic wand

varado, -a [ba'raðo, a] ADJ (*Naut*) stranded; **estar ~** to be aground

varar [ba'rar] /1a/ VT to beach ▶ VI, **vararse** VR to be beached

varear [bare'ar] /1a/ VT to hit, beat; (*frutas*) to knock down (with poles)

★**variable** [ba'rjaβle] ADJ, NF (*tb Inform*) variable

variación [barja'θjon] NF variation; **sin ~** unchanged

variado, -a [ba'rjaðo, a] ADJ varied; (*dulces, galle-*

V

tas) assorted; **entremeses variados** a selection of starters

variante [baˈrjante] ADJ variant ▶ NF (*alternativa*) alternative; (*Auto*) bypass

★**variar** [baˈrjar] /**1c**/ VT (*cambiar*) to change; (*poner variedad*) to vary; (*modificar*) to modify; (*cambiar de posición*) to switch around ▶ VI to vary; **~ de** to differ from; **~ de opinión** to change one's mind; **para ~** just for a change

varicela [bariˈθela] NF chicken pox

varices [baˈriθes] NFPL varicose veins

variedad [barjeˈðað] NF variety

varilla [baˈriʎa] NF stick; (*Bot*) twig; (*Tec*) rod; (*de rueda*) spoke; **~ mágica** magic wand

vario, -a [ˈbarjo, a] ADJ (*variado*) varied; (*multicolor*) motley; (*cambiable*) changeable; **varios** various, several

variopinto, -a [barjoˈpinto, a] ADJ diverse; **un público ~** a mixed audience

varita [baˈrita] NF: **~ mágica** magic wand

varón [baˈron] NM male, man

varonil [baroˈnil] ADJ manly

Varsovia [barˈsoβja] NF Warsaw

vas [bas] VB *ver* **ir**

vasco, -a [ˈbasko, a], **vascongado, -a** [baskonˈgaðo, a] ADJ, NM/F Basque ▶ NM (*Ling*) Basque ▶ NFPL: **las Vascongadas** the Basque Country *sg*

vascuence [basˈkwenθe] NM (*Ling*) Basque

vasectomía [basektoˈmia] NF vasectomy

vaselina [baseˈlina] NF Vaseline®

vasija [baˈsixa] NF (earthenware) vessel

★**vaso** [ˈbaso] NM glass, tumbler; (*Anat*) vessel; (*cantidad*) glass(ful); **~ de vino** glass of wine; **~ para vino** wineglass

vástago [ˈbastaɣo] NM (*Bot*) shoot; (*Tec*) rod; (*fig*) offspring

vasto, -a [ˈbasto, a] ADJ vast, huge

váter [ˈbater] NM lavatory, W.C.

Vaticano [batiˈkano] NM: **el ~** the Vatican; **la Ciudad del ~** (the) Vatican City

vaticinar [batiθiˈnar] /**1a**/ VT to prophesy, predict

vaticinio [batiˈθinjo] NM prophecy

vatio [ˈbatjo] NM (*Elec*) watt

vaya *etc* [ˈbaja] VB *ver* **ir**

Vd. ABR = **usted**

Vda. ABR (= *viuda*) *ver* **viudo**

Vds. ABR = **ustedes**; *ver* **usted**

ve [be] VB *ver* **ir**; **ver**

vea *etc* [ˈbea] VB *ver* **ver**

vecinal [beθiˈnal] ADJ (*camino, impuesto etc*) local

vecindad [beθinˈdað] NF, **vecindario** [beθinˈdarjo] NM neighbourhood; (*habitantes*) residents *pl*

★**vecino, -a** [beˈθino, a] ADJ neighbouring ▶ NM/F neighbour; (*residente*) resident; **somos vecinos** we live next door to one another

vector [bekˈtor] NM vector

veda [ˈbeða] NF prohibition; (*temporada*) close season

vedado [beˈðaðo] NM preserve

vedar [beˈðar] /**1a**/ VT (*prohibir*) to ban, prohibit; (*idea, plan*) to veto; (*impedir*) to stop, prevent

vedette [beˈðet] NF (*Teat, Cine*) star(let)

vega [ˈbeɣa] NF fertile plain *o* valley

vegano, -a [beˈɣano, a] ADJ, NM/F vegan

vegetación [bexetaˈθjon] NF vegetation

vegetal [bexeˈtal] ADJ, NM vegetable

vegetar [bexeˈtar] /**1a**/ VI to vegetate

★**vegetariano, -a** [bexetaˈrjano, a] ADJ, NM/F vegetarian

vegetativo, -a [bexetaˈtiβo, a] ADJ vegetative

vehemencia [beeˈmenθja] NF (*insistencia*) vehemence; (*pasión*) passion; (*fervor*) fervour; (*violencia*) violence

vehemente [beeˈmente] ADJ vehement; passionate; fervent; violent

★**vehículo** [beˈikulo] NM vehicle; (*Med*) carrier; **~ de servicio público** public service vehicle; **~ espacial** spacecraft

veía *etc* VB *ver* **ver**

★**veinte** [ˈbeinte] NUM twenty; (*orden, fecha*) twentieth; **el siglo ~** the twentieth century

veintena [beinˈtena] NF: **una ~** (about) twenty, a score

vejación [bexaˈθjon] NF vexation; (*humillación*) humiliation

vejamen [beˈxamen] NM satire

vejar [beˈxar] /**1a**/ VT (*irritar*) to annoy, vex; (*humillar*) to humiliate

vejatorio, -a [bexaˈtorjo, a] ADJ humiliating, degrading

vejez [beˈxeθ] NF old age

vejiga [beˈxiɣa] NF (*Anat*) bladder

★**vela** [ˈbela] NF (*de cera*) candle; (*Naut*) sail; (*insomnio*) sleeplessness; (*vigilia*) vigil; (*Mil*) sentry duty; (*fam*) snot; **a toda ~** (*Naut*) under full sail; **estar a dos velas** (*fam*) to be skint; **pasar la noche en ~** to have a sleepless night

velado, -a [beˈlaðo, a] ADJ veiled; (*sonido*) muffled; (*Foto*) blurred ▶ NF soirée

velador [belaˈðor] NM watchman; (*candelero*) candlestick; (*AM*) bedside table

velar [beˈlar] /**1a**/ VT (*vigilar*) to keep watch over; (*cubrir*) to veil ▶ VI to stay awake; **~ por** to watch over, look after

velatorio [belaˈtorjo] NM (*funeral*) wake

veleidad [beleiˈðað] NF (*ligereza*) fickleness; (*capricho*) whim

velero [beˈlero] NM (*Naut*) sailing ship; (*Aviat*) glider

veleta [beˈleta] NMF fickle person ▶ NF weather vane

veliz [beˈlis] NM (*AM*) suitcase

vello [ˈbeʎo] NM down, fuzz

vellón [beˈʎon] NM fleece

velloso, -a [beˈʎoso, a] ADJ fuzzy

velludo, -a [beˈʎuðo, a] ADJ shaggy ▶ NM plush, velvet

velo [ˈbelo] NM veil; **~ de paladar** (*Anat*) soft palate

★**velocidad** [beloθiˈðað] NF speed; (*Tec*) rate, pace, velocity; (*Mecánica, Auto*) gear; **¿a qué ~?** how fast?; **de alta ~** high-speed; **cobrar ~** to pick up *o* gather speed; **meter la segunda ~** to change into second gear; **~ máxima de impresión** (*Inform*) maximum print speed

velocímetro [beloˈθimetro] NM speedometer

velódromo [beˈloðromo] NM cycle track

velorio [beˈlorjo] NM (*Am*) (*funeral*) wake

veloz [beˈloθ] ADJ fast, swift

ven [ben] VB *ver* **venir**

★**vena** [ˈbena] NF vein; (*fig*) vein, disposition; (*Geo*) seam, vein

venablo [beˈnaβlo] NM javelin

venado [beˈnaðo] NM deer; (*Culin*) venison

venal [beˈnal] ADJ (*Anat*) venous; (*pey*) venal

venalidad [benaliˈðað] NF venality

vencedor, a [benθeˈðor, a] ADJ victorious ▶ NM/F victor, winner

★**vencer** [benˈθer] /**2b**/ VT (*dominar*) to defeat, beat; (*derrotar*) to vanquish; (*superar, controlar*) to overcome, master ▶ VI (*triunfar*) to win (through), triumph; (*pago*) to fall due; (*plazo*) to expire; **dejarse ~** to yield, give in

vencido, -a [benˈθiðo, a] ADJ (*derrotado*) defeated, beaten; (*Com*) payable, due; **darse por ~** to give up; **le pagan por meses vencidos** he is paid at the end of the month ▶ ADV: **pagar ~** to pay in arrears

vencimiento [benθiˈmjento] NM collapse; (*Com: de plazo*) expiration; **a su ~** when it falls due

★**venda** [ˈbenda] NF bandage

vendaje [benˈdaxe] NM bandage, dressing

★**vendar** [benˈdar] /**1a**/ VT to bandage; **~ los ojos** to blindfold

vendaval [bendaˈβal] NM (*viento*) gale; (*huracán*) hurricane

★**vendedor, a** [bendeˈðor, a] NM/F seller; **~ ambulante** hawker, pedlar (*Brit*), peddler (*US*)

★**vender** [benˈder] /**2a**/ VT to sell; (*comerciar*) to market; (*traicionar*) to sell out, betray; **~ al contado/al por mayor/al por menor/a plazos** to sell for cash/wholesale/retail/on credit; **~ al descubierto** to sell short ■ **venderse** VR (*estar a la venta*) to be on sale; **"se vende"** "for sale"; **"véndese coche"** "car for sale"

★**vendimia** [benˈdimja] NF grape harvest; **la ~ de 1993** the 1993 vintage

vendimiar [bendiˈmjar] /**1b**/ VI to pick grapes

vendré *etc* [benˈdre] VB *ver* **venir**

Venecia [beˈneθja] NF Venice

veneciano, -a [beneˈθjano, a] ADJ, NM/F Venetian

veneno [beˈneno] NM poison; (*de serpiente*) venom

venenoso, -a [beneˈnoso, a] ADJ poisonous; venomous

venerable [beneˈraβle] ADJ venerable

veneración [beneraˈθjon] NF veneration

venerar [beneˈrar] /**1a**/ VT (*respetar*) to revere; (*reconocer*) to venerate; (*adorar*) to worship

venéreo, -a [beˈnereo, a] ADJ venereal; **enfermedad venérea** venereal disease

venezolano, -a [beneθoˈlano, a] ADJ, NM/F Venezuelan

★**Venezuela** [beneˈθwela] NF Venezuela

venga *etc* [ˈbenga] VB *ver* **venir**

vengador, a [bengaˈðor, a] ADJ avenging ▶ NM/F avenger

venganza [benˈganθa] NF vengeance, revenge

vengar [benˈgar] /**1h**/ VT to avenge ■ **vengarse** VR to take revenge

vengativo, -a [bengaˈtiβo, a] ADJ (*persona*) vindictive

vengo *etc* VB *ver* **venir**

vengue *etc* [ˈbenge] VB *ver* **vengar**

venia [ˈbenja] NF (*perdón*) pardon; (*permiso*) consent; **con su ~** by your leave

venial [beˈnjal] ADJ venial

venida [beˈniða] NF (*llegada*) arrival; (*regreso*) return; (*fig*) rashness

venidero, -a [beniˈðero, a] ADJ coming, future; **en lo ~ in** (the) future

★**venir** [beˈnir] /**3r**/ VI to come; (*llegar*) to arrive; (*ocurrir*) to happen; **~ a menos** (*persona*) to lose status; (*empresa*) to go downhill; **~ bien** to be suitable, come just right; (*ropa, gusto*) to suit; **~ mal** to be unsuitable *o* inconvenient, come awkwardly; **el año que viene** next year; **¡ven acá!** come (over) here!; **¡venga!** (*fam*) come on! ■ **venirse** VR: **venirse abajo** to collapse

★**venta** [ˈbenta] NF (*Com*) sale; (*posada*) inn; **~ a plazos** hire purchase; **"en ~"** "for sale"; **~ al contado/al por mayor/al por menor** *o* **al detalle** cash sale/wholesale/retail; **~ a domicilio** door-to-door selling; **~ y arrendamiento al vendedor** sale and lease back; **~ de liquidación** clearance sale; **estar de** *o* **en ~** to be (up) for sale *o* on the market; **ventas brutas** gross sales; **ventas a término** forward sales

★**ventaja** [benˈtaxa] NF advantage; **llevar la ~** (*en carrera*) to be leading *o* ahead

ventajoso, -a [benˈtaxoso, a] ADJ advantageous

★**ventana** [benˈtana] NF window; **~ de guillotina/galería** sash/bay window; **~ de la nariz** nostril

★**ventanilla** [bentaˈniʎa] NF (*de taquilla, tb Inform*) window

V

ventearse [bente'arse] /**1a**/ VR (*romperse*) to crack; (*Anat*) to break wind

ventilación [bentila'θjon] NF ventilation; (*corriente*) draught; (*fig*) airing

ventilador [bentila'ðor] NM ventilator; (*eléctrico*) fan

ventilar [benti'lar] /**1a**/ VT to ventilate; (*poner a secar*) to put out to dry; (*fig*) to air, discuss

ventisca [ben'tiska] NF blizzard

ventisquero [bentis'kero] NM snowdrift

ventolera [bento'lera] NF (*ráfaga*) gust of wind; (*idea*) whim, wild idea; **le dio la ~ de comprarlo** he had a sudden notion to buy it

ventosear [bentose'ar] /**1a**/ VI to break wind

ventosidad [bentosi'ðað] NF flatulence

ventoso, -a [ben'toso, a] ADJ windy ▶ NF (*Zool*) sucker; (*instrumento*) suction pad

ventrículo [ben'trikulo] NM ventricle

ventrílocuo, -a [ben'trilokwo, a] NM/F ventriloquist

ventriloquia [bentri'lokja] NF ventriloquism

ventura [ben'tura] NF (*felicidad*) happiness; (*buena suerte*) luck; (*destino*) fortune; **a la (buena) ~** at random

venturoso, -a [bentu'roso, a] ADJ happy; (*afortunado*) lucky, fortunate

venza *etc* ['benθa] VB *ver* **vencer**

veo *etc* VB *ver* **ver**

★**ver** [ber] /**2u**/ VT to see; (*mirar*) to look at, watch; (*investigar*) to look into; **a ~ let's see**; **a ~ si …** I wonder if …; **por lo que veo** apparently; **dejarse ~** to become apparent; **no tener nada que ~ con** to have nothing to do with; **no lo veo** I can't see it; **si te vi no me acuerdo** they *etc* just don't want to know; **¡viera(n) o hubiera(n) visto qué casa!** (*AM fam*) if only you'd seen the house!, what a house! ▶ VI to see; (*entender*) to see, understand; **a mi modo de ~** as I see it; **¡habrase visto!** did you ever! (*fam*); **ya veremos** we'll see ▶ NM looks *pl*, appearance ■ **verse** VR (*encontrarse*) to meet; (*dejarse ver*) to be seen; (*hallarse: en un apuro*) to find o.s., be; **merece verse** it's worth seeing; **¡nos vemos!** see you (later)!; **ya se ve que …** it is obvious that …

vera ['bera] NF edge, verge; (*de río*) bank; **a la ~ de** near, next to

veracidad [beraθi'ðað] NF truthfulness

veraneante [berane'ante] NMF holidaymaker, (summer) vacationer (*US*)

★**veranear** [berane'ar] /**1a**/ VI to spend the summer

veraneo [bera'neo] NM summer holiday; **estar de ~** to be away on (one's summer) holiday; **lugar de ~** holiday resort

veraniego, -a [bera'njeɣo, a] ADJ summer *cpd*

★**verano** [be'rano] NM summer

veras ['beras] NFPL truth *sg*; **de ~** really, truly; **esto va de ~** this is serious

veraz [be'raθ] ADJ truthful

verbal [ber'βal] ADJ verbal; (*mensaje etc*) oral

★**verbena** [ber'βena] NF street party; (*baile*) open-air dance

verbigracia [berβi'ɣraθja] ADV for example

verbo ['berβo] NM verb

verborrea [berβo'rrea] NF verbosity, verbal diarrhoea

verboso, -a [ber'βoso, a] ADJ verbose

★**verdad** [ber'ðað] NF (*lo verídico*) truth; (*fiabilidad*) reliability; **de ~** *adj* real, proper; **a decir ~, no quiero** to tell (you) the truth, I don't want to; **la pura ~** the plain truth ▶ ADV really; **¿~?, ¿no es ~?** isn't it?, aren't you?, don't you? *etc*

verdaderamente [berðaðera'mente] ADV really, indeed, truly

★**verdadero, -a** [berða'ðero, a] ADJ (*veraz*) true, truthful; (*fiable*) reliable; (*fig*) real

★**verde** ['berðe] ADJ green; (*fruta etc*) green, unripe; (*chiste etc*) blue, smutty, dirty; **viejo ~** dirty old man; **poner ~ a algn** to give sb a dressing-down ▶ NM green

verdear [berðe'ar] /**1a**/, **verdecer** [berðe'θer] /**2d**/ VI to turn green

verdezca *etc* [ber'ðeθka] VB *ver* **verdear**

verdor [ber'ðor] NM (*lo verde*) greenness; (*Bot*) verdure; (*fig*) youthful vigour

verdugo [ber'ðuɣo] NM executioner; (*Bot*) shoot; (*cardenal*) weal

verdulería [berðule'ria] NF greengrocer's (shop)

verdulero, -a [berðu'lero, a] NM/F greengrocer

★**verdura** [ber'ðura] NF greenness ■ **verduras** NFPL (*Culin*) greens

vereda [be'reða] NF path; (*AM*) pavement, sidewalk (*US*); **meter a algn en ~** to bring sb into line

veredicto [bere'ðikto] NM verdict

vergel [ber'xel] NM lush garden

vergonzoso, -a [berɣon'θoso, a] ADJ shameful; (*tímido*) timid, bashful

vergüenza [ber'ɣwenθa] NF shame, sense of shame; (*timidez*) bashfulness; (*pudor*) modesty; **tener ~** to be ashamed; **me da ~ decírselo** I feel too shy o it embarrasses me to tell him; **¡qué ~!** (*de situación*) what a disgrace!; (*a persona*) shame on you!

vericueto [beri'kweto] NM rough track

verídico, -a [be'riðiko, a] ADJ true, truthful

verificar [berifi'kar] /**1a**/ VT to check; (*corroborar, tb Inform*) to verify; (*testamento*) to prove; (*llevar a cabo*) to carry out ■ **verificarse** VR to occur, happen; (*mitin etc*) to be held; (*profecía etc*) to come o prove true

verifique *etc* [beri'fike] VB *ver* **verificar**

verja ['berxa] NF (*cancela*) iron gate; (*cerca*) railing(s); (*rejado*) grating

vermut [ber'mu] (*pl* **vermuts**) NM vermouth ▶ NF (*esp AM*) matinée

verosímil [bero'simil] ADJ likely, probable; (*relato*) credible

verosimilitud [berosimili'tuð] NF likeliness, probability

verruga [be'rruɣa] NF wart

versado, -a [ber'saðo, a] ADJ: ~ **en** versed in

Versalles [ber'saʎes] NM Versailles

versar [ber'sar] /1a/ VI to go round, turn; ~ **sobre** to deal with, be about

versátil [ber'satil] ADJ versatile

versículo [ber'sikulo] NM (Rel) verse

versión [ber'sjon] NF version; (traducción) translation

verso ['berso] NM verse; **un ~** a line of poetry; ~ **libre/suelto** free/blank verse

vértebra ['berteβra] NF vertebra

vertebrado, -a [berte'βraðo, a] ADJ, NM/F vertebrate

vertebral [berte'βral] ADJ vertebral; **columna ~** spine

vertedero [berte'ðero] NM rubbish dump, tip

★**verter** [ber'ter] /2g/ VT (vaciar) to empty, pour (out); (sin querer) to spill; (basura) to dump ▶ VI to flow

vertical [berti'kal] ADJ vertical; (postura, piano etc) upright ▶ NF vertical

vértice ['bertiθe] NM vertex, apex

vertidos [ber'tiðos] NMPL waste sg

vertiente [ber'tjente] NF slope; (fig) aspect

vertiginoso, -a [bertixi'noso, a] ADJ giddy, dizzy

vértigo ['bertiɣo] NM vertigo; (mareo) dizziness; (actividad) intense activity; **de ~** (fam: velocidad) giddy; (: ruido) tremendous; (: talento) fantastic

vesícula [be'sikula] NF blister; ~ **biliar** gall bladder

vespa® ['bespa] NF (motor) scooter

vespertino, -a [besper'tino, a] ADJ evening cpd

vespino® [bes'pino] NM O F ≈ moped

★**vestíbulo** [bes'tiβulo] NM hall; (de teatro) foyer

★**vestido** [bes'tiðo] NM (ropa) clothes pl, clothing; (de mujer) dress, frock

vestidor [besti'ðor] NM (Am Deporte) changing (Brit) o locker (US) room

vestigio [bes'tixjo] NM (trazo) trace; (señal) sign ■ **vestigios** NMPL remains

vestimenta [besti'menta] NF clothing

vestir [bes'tir] /3k/ VT (ropa: poner) to put on; (: llevar) to wear; (cubrir) to clothe, cover; (pagar la ropa a) to clothe, pay for the clothing of; (sastre) to make clothes for; **estar vestido de** to be dressed o clad in; (como disfraz) to be dressed as ▶ VI (ponerse: ropa) to dress; (verse bien) to look good; **traje de ~** (formal) formal suit ■ **vestirse** VR to get dressed, dress o.s.

★**vestuario** [bes'twarjo] NM clothes pl, wardrobe; (Teat: para actores) dressing room; (: para público) cloakroom; (Deporte) changing room

Vesubio [be'suβjo] NM Vesuvius

veta ['beta] NF (vena) vein, seam; (raya) streak; (de madera) grain

vetar [be'tar] /1a/ VT to veto

veterano, -a [bete'rano, a] ADJ, NM/F veteran

★**veterinario, -a** [beteri'narjo, a] NM/F vet(erinary surgeon) ▶ NF veterinary science

veto ['beto] NM veto

vetusto, -a [be'tusto, a] ADJ ancient

★**vez** [beθ] NF time; (turno) turn; **a la ~ que** at the same time as; **a su ~** in its turn; **cada ~ más/menos** more and more/less and less; **una ~** once; **dos veces** twice; **de una ~** in one go; **de una ~ para siempre** once and for all; **en ~ de** instead of; **a veces** sometimes; **otra ~** again; **una y otra ~** repeatedly; **muchas veces** (con frecuencia) often; **pocas veces** seldom; **de ~ en cuando** from time to time; **7 veces 9** 7 times 9; **hacer las veces de** to stand in for; **tal ~** perhaps; **¿lo viste alguna ~?** did you ever see it?; **¿cuántas veces?** how often?; **érase una ~** once upon a time (there was)

v. g., v. gr. ABR (= verbigracia) viz

VHF SIGLA F (= Very High Frequency) VHF

★**vía** ['bia] NF (calle) road; (ruta) track, route; (Ferro) line; (fig) way; (Anat) passage, tube; **por ~ bucal** orally; **por ~ judicial** by legal means; **por ~ oficial** through official channels; **por ~ de** by way of; **en vías de** in the process of; **un país en vías de desarrollo** a developing country; ~ **aérea** airway; **V~ Láctea** Milky Way; ~ **pública** public highway o thoroughfare; ~ **única** one-way street; **el tren está en la ~ 8** the train is (standing) at platform 8 ▶ PREP via, by way of

viable ['bjaβle] ADJ (Com) viable; (plan etc) feasible

viaducto [bja'ðukto] NM viaduct

viajante [bja'xante] NMF travelling (Brit) o traveling (US) salesman/saleswoman

★**viajar** [bja'xar] /1a/ VI to travel, journey

★**viaje** ['bjaxe] NM journey; (gira) tour; (Naut) voyage; (Com: carga) load; **los viajes** travel sg; **estar de ~** to be away; ~ **de ida y vuelta** round trip; ~ **de novios** honeymoon

> Cuando viaje se refiere a la acción de viajar, en general, se utiliza **travel**, que es siempre plural o incontable: En sus viajes por el extranjero. **On his travels abroad.**
>
> No se puede decir **a travel**; en su lugar se usan **trip**, **journey** o **voyage**. **Trip** es un viaje de ida y vuelta a algún lugar que normalmente conlleva una estancia en el mismo: un viaje de negocios **a business trip**.
>
> **Journey** puede ser por tierra, mar o aire.
>
> **Voyage** es un viaje muy largo por mar o en una nave espacial.

★**viajero, -a** [bja'xero, a] ADJ travelling (Brit), traveling (US); (Zool) migratory ▶ NM/F (quien viaja) traveller; (pasajero) passenger

vial [bjal] ADJ road cpd, traffic cpd

vianda [ˈbjanda] NF (tb: **viandas**) food

viáticos [ˈbjatikos] NMPL (Com) travelling (BRIT) o traveling (US) expenses

víbora [ˈbiβora] NF viper; (AM: venenoso) poisonous snake

vibración [biβraˈθjon] NF vibration

vibrador [biβraˈðor] NM vibrator

vibrante [biˈβrante] ADJ vibrant, vibrating

vibrar [biˈβrar] /**1a**/ VT to vibrate ▶ VI to vibrate; (pulsar) to throb, beat, pulsate

vicario [biˈkarjo] NM curate

vicecónsul [biθeˈkonsul] NMF vice-consul

vicegerente [biθexeˈrente] NMF assistant manager

vicepresidente, -a [biθepresiˈðente, a] NM/F vice-president; (de comité etc) vice-chair

viceversa [biθeˈβersa] ADV vice versa

viciado, -a [biˈθjaðo, a] ADJ (corrompido) corrupt; (contaminado) foul, contaminated

viciar [biˈθjar] /**1b**/ VT (pervertir) to pervert; (adulterar) to adulterate; (falsificar) to falsify; (Jur) to nullify; (estropear) to spoil; (sentido) to twist ■ **viciarse** VR to become corrupted; (aire, agua) to be(come) polluted

vicio [ˈbiθjo] NM (libertinaje) vice; (mala costumbre) bad habit; (mimo) spoiling; (alabeo) warp, warping; **de** o **por** ~ out of sheer habit

vicioso, -a [biˈθjoso, a] ADJ (muy malo) vicious; (corrompido) depraved; (mimado) spoiled ▶ NM/F depraved person; (adicto) addict

vicisitud [biθisiˈtuð] NF vicissitude

★**víctima** [ˈbiktima] NF victim; (de accidente etc) casualty

victimario [biktiˈmarjo] NM (AM) killer, murderer

victoria [bikˈtorja] NF victory

victorioso, -a [biktoˈrjoso, a] ADJ victorious

vicuña [biˈkuɲa] NF vicuna

vid [bið] NF vine

★**vida** [ˈbiða] NF life; (duración) lifetime; (modo de vivir) way of life; **¡~!, ¡~ mía!** (saludo cariñoso) my love!; **de por** ~ for life; **de ~ airada** o **libre** loose-living; **en la/mi** ~ never; **estar con** ~ to be still alive; **ganarse la** ~ to earn one's living; **¡esto es ~!** this is the life!; **le va la ~ en esto** his life depends on it

vidente [biˈðente] NMF (adivino) clairvoyant; (no ciego) sighted person

★**vídeo** [ˈbiðeo] NM video; (aparato) video (recorder); **cinta de** ~ videotape; **película de** ~ videofilm; **grabar en** ~ to record, (video)tape; **~ compuesto/inverso** (Inform) composite/reverse video

videoblog [biðeoˈbloɣ] NM (pl **videoblogs**) NM vlog, video blog

videocámara [biðeoˈkamara] NF video camera; (pequeña) camcorder

videocasete, videocassette [biðeokaˈset] NM video cassette

videoclip [biðeoˈklip] NM (music) video

videoclub [biðeoˈklub] NM video club; (tienda) video shop

videodatos [biðeoˈðatos] NMPL (Com) viewdata

★**videojuego** [biðeoˈxweɣo] NM video game

videojugador, -a [biðeoxuɣaˈðor, a] NM/F gamer

videollamada [biðeoʎaˈmada] NF video call

videoproyector [biðeoprojekˈtor] NM video projector

videoteléfono [biðeoteˈlefono] NF videophone

videotex [biðeoˈteks], **videotexto** [biðeoˈteksto] NM Videotex®

vidriero, -a [biˈðrjero, a] NM/F glazier ▶ NF (ventana) stained-glass window; (AM: de tienda) shop window; (puerta) glass door

★**vidrio** [ˈbiðrjo] NM glass; (AM) window; **~ cilindrado/inastillable** plate/splinter-proof glass

vidrioso, -a [biˈðrjoso, a] ADJ glassy; (frágil) fragile, brittle; (resbaladizo) slippery

vieira [ˈbjeira] NF scallop

★**viejo, -a** [ˈbjexo, a] ADJ old; **hacerse** o **ponerse** ~ to grow o get old ▶ NM/F old man/woman; **mi ~/vieja** (fam) my old man/woman

Viena [ˈbjena] NF Vienna

viene etc [ˈbjene] VB ver **venir**

vienés, -esa [bjeˈnes, esa] ADJ, NM/F Viennese

★**viento** [ˈbjento] NM wind; **hacer** ~ to be windy; **contra** ~ **y marea** at all costs; **ir** ~ **en popa** to go splendidly; (negocio) to prosper

★**vientre** [ˈbjentre] NM belly; (matriz) womb; **hacer de** ~ to have a bowel movement ■ **vientres** NMPL bowels

vier. ABR (= viernes) Fri.

★**viernes** [ˈbjernes] NM INV Friday; **V~ Santo** Good Friday; ver tb **Semana Santa**; **sábado**

vierta etc [ˈbjerta] VB ver **verter**

Vietnam [bjetˈnam] NM Vietnam

vietnamita [bjetnaˈmita] ADJ, NMF Vietnamese

viga [ˈbiɣa] NF beam, rafter; (de metal) girder

vigencia [biˈxenθja] NF validity; (de contrato etc) term, life; **estar/entrar en** ~ to be in/come into effect o force

vigente [biˈxente] ADJ valid, in force; (imperante) prevailing

vigésimo, -a [biˈxesimo, a] NUM twentieth

vigía [biˈxia] NM look-out ▶ NF (atalaya) watchtower; (acción) watching

vigilancia [bixiˈlanθja] NF vigilance; **tener a algn bajo** ~ to keep watch on sb

vigilante [bixiˈlante] ADJ vigilant ▶ NMF caretaker; (en cárcel) warder; (en almacén) shopwalker (BRIT), floor-walker (US); **~ jurado** security guard (licensed to carry a gun); **~ nocturno** night watchman

★**vigilar** [bixi'lar] /**1a**/ vt to watch over; (*cuidar*) to look after, keep an eye on ▶ vi to be vigilant; (*hacer guardia*) to keep watch; ~ **por** to take care of

vigilia [bi'xilja] nf wakefulness; (*Rel*) vigil; (: *ayuno*) fast; **comer de ~** to fast

vigor [bi'γor] nm vigour, vitality; **en ~** in force; **entrar/poner en ~** to come/put into effect

vigoroso, -a [biγo'roso, a] adj vigorous

VIH nm abr (= *virus de inmunodeficiencia humana*) HIV; ~ **negativo/positivo** HIV-negative/-positive

vil [bil] adj vile, low

vileza [bi'leθa] nf vileness; (*acto*) base deed

vilipendiar [bilipen'djar] /**1b**/ vt to vilify, revile

villa ['biʎa] nf (*casa*) villa; (*pueblo*) small town; (*municipalidad*) municipality; **la V~** (*Esp*) Madrid; ~ **miseria** shanty town

villancico [biʎan'θiko] nm (Christmas) carol

villorrio [bi'ʎorrjo] nm one-horse town, dump; (*Am: barrio pobre*) shanty town

vilo ['bilo] adv: **en ~** in the air, suspended; (*fig*) on tenterhooks, in suspense; **estar** o **quedar en ~** to be left in suspense

★**vinagre** [bi'naγre] nm vinegar

vinagrera [bina'γrera] nf vinegar bottle ■ **vinagreras** nfpl cruet stand *sg*

vinagreta [bina'γreta] nf vinaigrette, French dressing

vinatería [binate'ria] nf wine shop

vinatero, -a [bina'tero, a] adj wine *cpd* ▶ nm wine merchant

vinculación [binkula'θjon] nf (*lazo*) link, bond; (*acción*) linking

vincular [binku'lar] /**1a**/ vt to link, bind

vínculo ['binkulo] nm link, bond

vindicar [bindi'kar] /**1g**/ vt to vindicate; (*vengar*) to avenge; (*Jur*) to claim

vine *etc* vb ver **venir**

vinícola [bi'nikola] adj (*industria*) wine *cpd*; (*región*) wine-growing *cpd*

vinicultor, -a [binikul'tor, a] nm/f wine grower

vinicultura [binikul'tura] nf wine growing

viniera *etc* vb ver **venir**

★**vino** ['bino] vb ver **venir** ▶ nm wine; ~ **de solera/seco/tinto** vintage/dry/red wine; ~ **de Jerez** sherry; ~ **de Oporto** port (wine)

★**viña** ['biɲa] nf, **viñedo** [bi'ɲeðo] nm vineyard

viñeta [bi'ɲeta] nf (*en historieta*) cartoon

viola ['bjola] nf viola

violación [bjola'θjon] nf violation; (*Jur*) offence, infringement; (*estupro*): ~ **(sexual)** rape; ~ **de contrato** (*Com*) breach of contract

violar [bjo'lar] /**1a**/ vt to violate; (*Jur*) to infringe; (*cometer estupro*) to rape

★**violencia** [bjo'lenθja] nf (*fuerza*) violence, force; (*embarazo*) embarrassment; (*acto injusto*) unjust act

violentar [bjolen'tar] /**1a**/ vt to force; (*casa*) to break into; (*agredir*) to assault; (*violar*) to violate

★**violento, -a** [bjo'lento, a] adj violent; (*furioso*) furious; (*situación*) embarrassing; (*acto*) forced, unnatural; (*difícil*) awkward; **me es muy ~** it goes against the grain with me

★**violeta** [bjo'leta] nf violet

★**violín** [bjo'lin] nm violin

violón [bjo'lon] nm double bass

violoncelo [bjolon'θelo] nm cello

VIP [bip] sigla mf (= *Very Important Person*) VIP

virador [bira'ðor] nm (*para fotocopiadora*) toner

viraje [bi'raxe] nm turn; (*de vehículo*) swerve; (*de carretera*) bend; (*fig*) change of direction

viral [bi'ral] adj (*tb Inform*) viral

virar [bi'rar] /**1a**/ vi (*vehículo*) to turn; (: *con violencia*) to swerve; (*fig*) to change direction

virgen ['birxen] adj virgin; (*cinta*) blank ▶ nmf virgin; **la Santísima V~** (*Rel*) the Blessed Virgin

virginidad [birxini'ðað] nf virginity

Virgo ['birγo] nm Virgo

viril [bi'ril] adj virile

virilidad [birili'ðað] nf virility

virrey [bi'rrei] nm viceroy

virtual [bir'twal] adj (*real*) virtual; (*en potencia*) potential

virtud [bir'tuð] nf virtue; **en ~ de** by virtue of

virtuoso, -a [bir'twoso, a] adj virtuous ▶ nm/f virtuoso

viruela [bi'rwela] nf smallpox ■ **viruelas** nfpl pockmarks; **viruelas locas** chickenpox *sg*

virulento, -a [biru'lento, a] adj virulent

virus ['birus] nm inv virus

viruta [bi'ruta] nf wood o metal shaving

vis [bis] nf: ~ **cómica** sense of humour

visa ['bisa] nf (*Am*), **visado** [bi'saðo] nm (*Esp*) visa; ~ **de permanencia** residence permit

visar [bi'sar] /**1a**/ vt (*pasaporte*) to visa; (*documento*) to endorse

víscera ['bisθera] nf internal organ ■ **vísceras** nfpl entrails

visceral [bisθe'ral] adj (*odio*) deep-rooted; **reacción ~** gut reaction

viscoso, -a [bis'koso, a] adj viscous

visera [bi'sera] nf visor

★**visibilidad** [bisiβili'ðað] nf visibility

visible [bi'siβle] adj visible; (*fig*) obvious; **exportaciones/importaciones visibles** (*Com*) visible exports/imports

visillo [bi'siʎo] nm lace curtain

visión [bi'sjon] nf (*Anat*) vision, (eye)sight; (*fantasía*) vision, fantasy; (*panorama*) view; **ver visiones** to see o be seeing things

visionario, -a [bisjo'narjo, a] adj (*que prevé*) visionary; (*loco*) deluded ▶ nm/f visionary; (*loco*) deluded peson

★**visita** [bi'sita] nf call, visit; (*persona*) visitor;

horas/tarjeta de ~ visiting hours/card; **~ de cortesía/de cumplido/de despedida** courtesy/formal/farewell visit; **hacer una ~** to pay a visit; **ir de ~** to go visiting

★**visitante** [bisiˈtante] ADJ visiting ▶ NMF visitor

★**visitar** [bisiˈtar] /1a/ VT to visit, call on; (*inspeccionar*) to inspect

vislumbrar [bislumˈbrar] /1a/ VT to glimpse, catch a glimpse of

vislumbre [bisˈlumbre] NF glimpse; (*centelleo*) gleam; (*idea vaga*) glimmer

viso [ˈbiso] NM (*de metal*) glint, gleam; (*de tela*) sheen; (*aspecto*) appearance; **hay un ~ de verdad en esto** there is an element of truth in this

visón [biˈson] NM mink

visor [biˈsor] NM (*Foto*) viewfinder

★**víspera** [ˈbispera] NF day before; **la ~ o en vísperas de** on the eve of

★**vista** [ˈbista] NF sight, vision; (*capacidad de ver*) (eye)sight; (*mirada*) look(s); (*Foto etc*) view; (*Jur*) hearing; **a primera ~** at first glance; **~ general** overview; **fijar o clavar la ~ en** to stare at; **hacer la ~ gorda** to turn a blind eye; **volver la ~** to look back; **está a la ~ que** it's obvious that; **a la ~** (*Com*) at sight; **en ~ de** in view of; **en ~ de que** in view of the fact that; **¡hasta la ~!** so long!, see you!; **con vistas a** with a view to; *ver tb* **visto**

vistazo [bisˈtaθo] NM glance; **dar o echar un ~ a** to glance at

★**visto, -a** [ˈbisto, a] VB *ver* **vestir** ▶ PP *de ver* ▶ ADJ seen; (*considerado*) considered; **por lo ~** apparently; **está ~ que** it's clear that; **está bien/mal ~** it's acceptable/unacceptable; **está muy ~** it is very common; **estaba ~** it had to be; **~ que** *conj* since, considering that ▶ NM: **~ bueno** approval; **"~ bueno"** "approved"; **dar el ~ bueno a algo** to give sth the go-ahead

vistoso, -a [bisˈtoso, a] ADJ colourful; (*alegre*) gay; (*pey*) gaudy

visual [biˈswal] ADJ visual

visualice *etc* [biswaˈliθe] VB *ver* **visualizar**

visualizador [biswaliθaˈðor] NM (*Inform*) display screen, VDU

visualizar [biswaliˈθar] /1f/ VT (*imaginarse*) to visualize; (*Inform*) to display

vital [biˈtal] ADJ life *cpd*, living *cpd*; (*fig*) vital; (*persona*) lively, vivacious

vitalicio, -a [bitaˈliθjo, a] ADJ for life

vitalidad [bitaliˈðað] NF vitality; (*de persona, negocio*) energy; (*de ciudad*) liveliness

vitamina [bitaˈmina] NF vitamin

vitaminado, -a [bitamiˈnaðo, a] ADJ with added vitamins

vitamínico, -a [bitaˈminiko, a] ADJ vitamin *cpd*; **complejos vitamínicos** vitamin compounds

viticultor, a [bitikulˈtor, a] NM/F vine grower

viticultura [bitikulˈtura] NF vine growing

vitorear [bitoreˈar] /1a/ VT to cheer, acclaim

vítores [ˈbitores] NMPL cheers

vitoriano, -a [bitoˈrjano, a] ADJ of *o* from Vitoria ▶ NM/F native *o* inhabitant of Vitoria

vítreo, -a [ˈbitreo, a] ADJ vitreous

vitrina [biˈtrina] NF glass case; (*en casa*) display cabinet; (*AM*) shop window

vituperar [bitupeˈrar] /1a/ VT to condemn

vituperio [bituˈperjo] NM (*condena*) condemnation; (*censura*) censure; (*insulto*) insult

viudez [bjuˈðeθ] NF widowhood

★**viudo, -a** [ˈbjuðo, a] ADJ widowed ▶ NM widower ▶ NF widow

viva [ˈbiβa] EXCL hurrah!; **¡~ el rey!** long live the King! ▶ NM cheer

vivacidad [biβaθiˈðað] NF (*vigor*) vigour; (*vida*) vivacity

vivamente [biβaˈmente] ADV in lively fashion; (*describir*) vividly; (*protestar*) sharply; (*emocionarse*) acutely

vivaracho, -a [biβaˈratʃo, a] ADJ jaunty, lively; (*ojos*) bright, twinkling

vivaz [biˈβaθ] ADJ (*que dura*) enduring; (*vigoroso*) vigorous; (*vivo*) lively

vivencia [biˈβenθja] NF experience

víveres [ˈbiβeres] NMPL provisions

vivero [biˈβero] NM (*Horticultura*) nursery; (*para peces*) fishpond; (: *Com*) fish farm; (*fig*) hotbed

viveza [biˈβeθa] NF liveliness; (*agudeza: mental*) sharpness

vividor, a [biβiˈðor, a] ADJ (*pey*) opportunistic ▶ NM (*aprovechado*) hustler

★**vivienda** [biˈβjenda] NF (*alojamiento*) housing; (*morada*) dwelling; (*casa*) house; (*piso*) flat (BRIT), apartment (US); **viviendas protegidas** *o* **sociales** council housing *sg* (BRIT), public housing *sg* (US)

viviente [biˈβjente] ADJ living

vivificar [biβifiˈkar] /1g/ VT to give life to

vivifique *etc* [biβiˈfike] VB *ver* **vivificar**

★**vivir** [biˈβir] /3a/ VT (*experimentar*) to live *o* go through ▶ VI (*gen, Com*): **~ (de)** to live (by, off, on); **¡viva!** hurray!; **¡viva el rey!** long live the king! ▶ NM life, living

★**vivo, -a** [ˈbiβo, a] ADJ living, live, alive; (*fig*) vivid; (*movimiento*) quick; (*color*) bright; (*protesta*) strong; (*persona: astuto*) smart, clever; **en ~** (*TV etc*) live; **llegar a lo ~** to cut to the quick

vizcaíno, -a [biθkaˈino, a] ADJ, NM/F Biscayan

Vizcaya [biθˈkaja] NF Biscay; **el Golfo de ~** the Bay of Biscay

VO ABR = **versión original**

V.°B.° ABR = **visto bueno**

vocablo [boˈkaβlo] NM (*palabra*) word; (*término*) term

★**vocabulario** [bokaβuˈlarjo] NM vocabulary, word list

vocación [bokaˈθjon] NF vocation

vocacional [bokasjo'nal] NF (Am) ≈ technical college

vocal [bo'kal] ADJ vocal ▸ NMF member (of a committee etc) ▸ NM non-executive director ▸ NF vowel

vocalice etc [boka'liθe] VB ver **vocalizar**

vocalizar [bokali'θar] /**1f**/ VT to vocalize

voceador [bosea'ðor] NM (Am): **~ de periódicos** newspaper vendor o seller

vocear [boθe'ar] /**1a**/ VT (para vender) to cry; (aclamar) to acclaim; (fig) to proclaim ▸ VI to yell

vocerío [boθe'rio] NM shouting; (escándalo) hullabaloo

vocero, -a [bo'θero, a] NM/F (Am) spokesman/ spokeswoman

voces ['boθes] NFPL de **voz**

vociferar [boθife'rar] /**1a**/ VT to shout; (jactarse) to proclaim boastfully ▸ VI to yell

vocinglero, -a [boθin'glero, a] ADJ vociferous; (gárrulo) garrulous; (fig) blatant

vodevil [boðe'βil] NM music hall, variety, vaudeville (US)

vodka ['boðka] NM vodka

vodú [bo'ðu] NM voodoo

vol. ABR = **volumen**

volado, -a [bo'laðo, a] ADJ: **estar ~** (fam: inquieto) to be worried; (: loco) to be crazy ▸ ADV (Am) in a rush, hastily

volador, a [bola'ðor, a] ADJ flying

voladura [bola'ðura] NF blowing up, demolition; (Minería) blasting

volandas [bo'landas] ADV: **en ~** in o through the air; (fig) swiftly

★**volante** [bo'lante] ADJ flying ▸ NM (de máquina, coche) steering wheel; (de reloj) balance; (nota) note; **ir al ~** to be at the wheel, be driving

★**volar** [bo'lar] /**1l**/ VT (demoler) to blow up, demolish ▸ VI to fly; (fig: correr) to rush, hurry; (fam: desaparecer) to disappear; **voy volando** I must dash; **¡cómo vuela el tiempo!** how time flies!

volátil [bo'latil] ADJ volatile; (fig) changeable

volcán [bol'kan] NM volcano

volcánico, -a [bol'kaniko, a] ADJ volcanic

★**volcar** [bol'kar] /**1g, 1l**/ VT to upset, overturn; (tumbar, derribar) to knock over; (vaciar) to empty out ▸ VI to overturn ◼ **volcarse** VR to tip over; (barco) to capsize

★**voleibol** [bolei'βol] NM volleyball

voleo [bo'leo] NM volley; **a(l) ~** haphazardly; **de un ~** quickly

Volga ['bolɣa] NM Volga

volición [boli'θjon] NF volition

volqué [bol'ke], **volquemos** etc [bol'kemos] VB ver **volcar**

volquete [bol'kete] NM dumper, dump truck (US)

voltaje [bol'taxe] NM voltage

voltear [bolte'ar] /**1a**/ VT to turn over; (volcar) to knock over; (doblar) to peal ▸ VI to roll over; **~ a hacer algo** (Am) to do sth again ◼ **voltearse** VR (Am) to turn round

voltereta [bolte'reta] NF somersault; **~ sobre las manos** handspring; **~ lateral** cartwheel

voltio ['boltjo] NM volt

voluble [bo'luβle] ADJ fickle

volumen [bo'lumen] NM volume; **~ monetario** money supply; **~ de negocios** turnover; **bajar el ~** to turn down the volume; **poner la radio a todo ~** to turn the radio up full

voluminoso, -a [bolumi'noso, a] ADJ voluminous; (enorme) massive

voluntad [bolun'tað] NF will, willpower; (deseo) desire, wish; (afecto) fondness; **a ~** at will; (cantidad) as much as one likes; **buena ~** goodwill; **mala ~** ill will, malice; **por causas ajenas a mi ~** for reasons beyond my control

★**voluntario, -a** [bolun'tarjo, a] ADJ voluntary ▸ NM/F volunteer

voluntarioso, -a [bolunta'rjoso, a] ADJ headstrong

voluptuoso, -a [bolup'twoso, a] ADJ voluptuous

★**volver** [bol'βer] /**2h**/ VT to turn; (boca abajo) to turn (over); (voltear) to turn round, turn upside down; (poner del revés) to turn inside out; (devolver) to return; (transformar) to change, transform; (manga) to roll up; **~ la espalda** to turn one's back; **~ bien por mal** to return good for evil; **~ la vista atrás** to look back; **~ triste** etc **a algn** to make sb sad etc; **~ loco a algn** to drive sb mad ▸ VI to return, go/come back; **~ a hacer** to do again; **~ en sí** to come to o round, regain consciousness ◼ **volverse** VR to turn round; (llegar a ser) to become; **volverse loco** to go mad

★**vomitar** [bomi'tar] /**1a**/ VT, VI to vomit

vómito ['bomito] NM (acto) vomiting; (resultado) vomit

voracidad [boraθi'ðað] NF voracity

vorágine [bo'raxine] NF whirlpool; (fig) maelstrom

voraz [bo'raθ] ADJ voracious; (fig) fierce

vórtice ['bortiθe] NM whirlpool; (de aire) whirlwind

VOS ABR = **versión original subtitulada**

vos [bos] PRON (Am) you

In Argentina, Uruguay, Paraguay, and in most of Central America, the second person singular personal pronoun tú is replaced by **vos**, which was originally the formal form of address up to the 16th Century. Vos is used with the verb conjugation relating to the second person singular tú (¿Vos lo sabías?) and with the direct object te (Vos te lo mereces.). In other Spanish-speaking countries, tuteo (use of the standard tú form) is used as in Spain.

VOSE ABR = **versión original con subtítulos en español**

voseo [bo'seo] NM (AM) addressing a person as "vos" (familiar usage)

Vosgos ['bosɣos] NMPL Vosges

★**vosotros, -as** [bo'sotros, as] PRON you pl; (reflexivo) yourselves; **entre ~** among yourselves

votación [bota'θjon] NF (acto) voting; (voto) vote; **~ a mano alzada** show of hands; **someter algo a ~** to put sth to the vote

votar [bo'tar] /**1a**/ VT (Pol: partido etc) to vote for; (: proyecto: aprobar) to pass; (Rel) to vow ▶ VI to vote

voto ['boto] NM vote; (promesa) vow; (maldición) oath, curse; **~ de bloque/de grupo** block/card vote; **~ de censura/de (des)confianza/de gracias** vote of censure/(no) confidence/thanks; **dar su ~** to cast one's vote ▥ **votos** NMPL (good) wishes

voy [boi] VB ver **ir**

★**voz** [boθ] NF voice; (grito) shout; (chisme) rumour; (Ling: palabra) word; (: forma) voice; **dar voces** to shout, yell; **llamar a algn a voces** to shout to sb; **llevar la ~ cantante** (fig) to be the boss; **tener la ~ tomada** to be hoarse; **tener ~ y voto** to have the right to speak; **en ~ baja** in a low voice; **a ~ en cuello** o **en grito** at the top of one's voice; **de viva ~** verbally; **en ~ alta** aloud; **~ de mando** command

vozarrón [boθa'rron] NM booming voice

vro. ABR = **vuestro**

Vto. ABR (Com) = **vencimiento**

vudú [bu'ðu] NM voodoo

vuelco etc ['bwelko] VB ver **volcar** ▶ NM spill, overturning; (fig) collapse; **mi corazón dio un ~** my heart missed a beat

★**vuelo** ['bwelo] VB ver **volar** ▶ NM flight; (encaje) lace, frill; (de falda etc) loose part; (fig) importance; **de altos vuelos** (fig: plan) grandiose; (: persona) ambitious; **alzar el ~** to take flight; (fig) to dash off; **coger al ~** to catch in flight; **~ de bajo coste** low-cost flight; **~ en picado** dive; **~ libre** hang-gliding; **~ regular** scheduled flight; **falda de mucho ~** full o wide skirt

vuelque etc ['bwelke] VB ver **volcar**

★**vuelta** ['bwelta] NF turn; (curva) bend, curve; (regreso) return; (revolución) revolution; (paseo) stroll; (circuito) lap; (de papel, tela) reverse; (de pantalón) turn-up (BRIT), cuff (US); (cambio) change; **~ a empezar** back to square one; **~ al mundo** world trip; **~ ciclista** (Deporte) (cycle) tour; **V~ de Francia** Tour de France; **~ cerrada** hairpin bend; **a la ~** (ESP) on one's return; **a la ~ de la esquina, a la ~** (AM) round the corner; **a ~ de correo** by return of post; **dar vueltas** to turn, revolve; (cabeza) to spin; **dar(se) la ~** (volverse) to turn round; **dar vueltas a una idea** to turn over an idea (in one's mind); **dar una ~** to go for a walk; (en coche) to go for a drive; **dar media ~** (Auto) to do a U-turn; (fam) to beat it; **estar de ~** (fam) to be back; **poner a algn de ~ y media** to heap abuse on sb; **no tiene ~ de hoja** there's no alternative

vueltita [bwel'tita] NF (esp AM fam) (little) walk; (: en coche) (little) drive

vuelto ['bwelto] PP de **volver** ▶ NM (AM: moneda) change

vuelvo etc ['bwelβo] VB ver **volver**

★**vuestro, -a** ['bwestro, a] ADJ your; (después de n) of yours; **un amigo ~** a friend of yours; **una idea vuestra** an idea of yours ▶ PRON: **el ~/la vuestra/los vuestros/las vuestras** yours; **lo ~** (what is) yours

vulgar [bul'ɣar] ADJ (ordinario) vulgar; (común) common

vulgarice etc [bulɣa'riθe] VB ver **vulgarizar**

vulgaridad [bulɣari'ðað] NF commonness; (acto) vulgarity; (expresión) coarse expression ▥ **vulgaridades** NFPL banalities

vulgarismo [bulɣa'rismo] NM popular form of a word

vulgarizar [bulɣari'θar] /**1f**/ VT to popularize

vulgo ['bulɣo] NM common people

vulnerable [bulne'raβle] ADJ vulnerable

vulnerar [bulne'rar] /**1a**/ VT (Jur, Com) to violate; (derechos) to violate, interfere with; (reputación) to harm, damage

vulva ['bulβa] NF vulva

Ww

W ABR (= *vatio(s)*) w

W, w ['uβe'doβle, (*Am*) 'doβleβe] NF (*letra*) W, w; **W de Washington** W for William

walkie-talkie [walki'talki] NM walkie-talkie

walkman® ['wal(k)man] NM Walkman®

WAP [wap] ADJ, NM WAP; **teléfono ~ WAP** phone

wasap ['wasap] (*pl* **wasaps**) NM (*fam*) WhatsApp®; **mándame un ~** WhatsApp® me, send me a message on WhatsApp®

wasapear [wasape'ar] /1a/ VT, VI (*fam*) to WhatsApp®

★**wáter** ['bater] NM (*taza*) toilet; (*Am: lugar*) toilet (*Brit*), rest room (*US*)

waterpolo [water'polo] NM waterpolo

web [web] NF (*sitio*) website; **la W~** the Web ▶ ADJ INV (*página, sitio*) web *cpd*

webcam ['webkam] NF webcam

webinario [webi'narjo] NM webinar

webmaster ['webmaster] NMF webmaster

★**western** ['western] (*pl* **westerns**) NM western

whisky ['wiski] NM whisky

widget [wi'tʃet] (*pl* **widgets** [wi'tʃets]) NM (*Inform*) widget

wifi ['waifai] NM Wi-Fi

wiki ['wiki] NF wiki

Winchester ['wintʃester] NM (*Inform*): **disco ~** Winchester disk

★**windsurf** ['winsurf] NM windsurfing; **hacer ~** to go windsurfing

WWW NM O NF ABR (*Inform: = World Wide Web*) WWW

Xx

X, x [ˈekis] NF (*letra*) X, x; **X de xilófono** X for Xmas

xenofobia [senoˈfoβja] NF xenophobia

xenófobo, -a [seˈnofoβo, a] ADJ xenophobic ▸ NM/F xenophobe

xerografía [seroɣraˈfia] NF xerography

xilófono [siˈlofono] NM xylophone

xocoyote, -a [ksokoˈjote, a] NM/F (*AM*) baby of the family, youngest child

Xunta [ˈʃunta] NF (*tb:* **Xunta de Galicia**) *regional government of Galicia*

Yy

Y, y [i'ɣrjeɣa] NF (*letra*) Y, y; **Y de Yegua** Y for Yellow (BRIT) o Yoke (US)

★**y** [i] CONJ and; (*Am fam: pues*) well; (*hora*): **la una y cinco** five past one; **¿y eso?** why?, how so?; **¿y los demás?** what about the others?; **y bueno ...** (*Am*) well ...

★**ya** [ja] ADV (*gen*) already; (*ahora*) now; (*en seguida*) at once; (*pronto*) soon; **ya no** not any more, no longer; **ya lo sé** I know; **¡ya, ya!** yes, yes!; (*con impaciencia*) all right!, O.K.!; **¡ya está bien!** that's (quite) enough!; **¡ya voy!** (*enfático: no se suele traducir*) coming! ► EXCL all right!; (*por supuesto*) of course! ► CONJ (*ahora que*) now that; **ya dice que sí, ya dice que no** first he says yes, then he says no; **ya que** since

yacer [ja'θer] /2x/ VI to lie

yacimiento [jaθi'mjento] NM bed, deposit; (*arqueológico*) site; **~ petrolífero** oilfield

Yakarta [ja'karta] NF Jakarta

yanqui ['janki] ADJ Yankee ► NMF Yank, Yankee

yate ['jate] NM yacht

yayo, -a ['jajo, a] NM/F (*fam*) grandpa/grandma (*fam*)

yazco etc ['jaθko] VB ver **yacer**

yedra ['jeðra] NF ivy

yegua ['jeɣwa] NF mare

yema ['jema] NF (*del huevo*) yolk; (*Bot*) leaf bud; (*fig*) best part; **~ del dedo** fingertip

Yemen ['jemen] NM Yemen

yemení [jeme'ni] ADJ, NMF Yemeni

yendo ['jendo] VB ver **ir**

yerba ['jerβa] NF = **hierba**

yerbatero, -a [jerβa'tero, a] ADJ (*Am*) maté ► NM/F (*Am*) herbal healer

yerga etc ['jerɣa], **yergue** etc ['jerɣe] VB ver **erguir**

yermo, -a ['jermo, a] ADJ barren; (*de gente*) uninhabited ► NM waste land

★**yerno** ['jerno] NM son-in-law

yerre etc ['jerre] VB ver **errar**

yerto, -a ['jerto, a] ADJ stiff

yesca ['jeska] NF tinder

yeso ['jeso] NM (*Geo*) gypsum; (*Arq*) plaster

Yibuti [ji'βuti] NM Djibouti

yihadismo [jixa'ðismo] NM jihadism

yihadista [jixa'ðista] ADJ, NMF jihadist

★**yo** [jo] PRON PERSONAL I; **soy yo** it's me, it is I; **yo que tú/usted** if I were you

yodo ['joðo] NM iodine

yoga ['joɣa] NM yoga

★**yogur(t)** [jo'ɣur(t)] NM yogurt

yogurtera [joɣur'tera] NF yogurt maker

yuca ['juka] NF (*Bot*) yucca; (*alimento*) cassava, manioc root

yudo ['juðo] NM judo

yugo ['juɣo] NM yoke

Yugoslavia [juɣos'laβja] NF (*Historia*) Yugoslavia

yugoslavo, -a [juɣos'laβo, a] (*Historia*) ADJ Yugoslavian ► NM/F Yugoslav

yugular [juɣu'lar] ADJ jugular

yunque ['junke] NM anvil

yunta ['junta] NF yoke

yuntero [jun'tero] NM ploughman, plowman (US)

yute ['jute] NM jute

yuxtapondré etc [jukstapond're] VB ver **yuxtaponer**

yuxtaponer [jukstapo'ner] /2q/ VT to juxtapose

yuxtaponga etc [juksta'ponga] VB ver **yuxtaponer**

yuxtaposición [jukstaposi'θjon] NF juxtaposition

yuxtapuesto [juksta'pwesto], **yuxtapuse** etc [juksta'puse] VB ver **yuxtaponer**

yuyo ['jujo] NM (*Am: mala hierba*) weed

y

Zz

Z, z [ˈθeta, (esp Am) ˈseta] NF (letra) Z, z; **Z de Zaragoza** Z for Zebra

zafar [θaˈfar] /1a/ VT (soltar) to untie; (superficie) to clear ■ **zafarse** VR (escaparse) to escape; (ocultarse) to hide o.s. away; (Tec) to slip off; **zafarse de** (persona) to get away from

zafio, -a [ˈθafjo, a] ADJ coarse

zafiro [θaˈfiro] NM sapphire

zaga [ˈθaɣa] NF rear; **a la ~** behind, in the rear

zagal [θaˈɣal] NM boy, lad

zagala [θaˈɣala] NF girl, lass

zaguán [θaˈɣwan] NM hallway

zaherir [θaeˈrir] /3i/ VT (criticar) to criticize; (fig: herir) to wound

zahiera etc [θaˈjera], **zahiriendo** etc [θaiˈrjendo] VB ver **zaherir**

zahorí [θaoˈri] NMF clairvoyant

zaino, -a [ˈθaino, a] ADJ (color de caballo) chestnut; (pérfido) treacherous; (animal) vicious

zalamería [θalameˈria] NF flattery

zalamero, -a [θalaˈmero, a] ADJ flattering; (relamido) suave

zamarra [θaˈmarra] NF (piel) sheepskin; (chaqueta) sheepskin jacket

Zambeze [θamˈbeθe] NM Zambezi

zambo, -a [ˈθambo, a] ADJ knock-kneed ▶ NM/F (Am) person of Black and Native American parentage ▶ NF samba

zambullida [θambuˈʎiða] NF dive, plunge

zambullirse [θambuˈʎirse] /3h/ VR to dive; (ocultarse) to hide o.s.

zamorano, -a [θamoˈrano, a] ADJ of o from Zamora ▶ NM/F native o inhabitant of Zamora

zampar [θamˈpar] /1a/ VT (esconder) to hide o put away (hurriedly); (comer) to gobble; (arrojar) to hurl ▶ VI to eat voraciously ■ **zamparse** VR (chocar) to bump; (fig) to gatecrash

★**zanahoria** [θanaˈorja] NF carrot

zancada [θanˈkaða] NF stride

zancadilla [θankaˈðiʎa] NF trip; (fig) stratagem; **echar la ~ a algn** to trip sb up

zancajo [θanˈkaxo] NM (Anat) heel

zanco [ˈθanko] NM stilt

zancudo, -a [θanˈkuðo, a] ADJ long-legged ▶ NM (Am) mosquito

zángano [ˈθangano] NM drone; (holgazán) idler, slacker

zanja [ˈθanxa] NF (fosa) ditch; (tumba) grave

zanjar [θanˈxar] /1a/ VT (fosa) to ditch, trench; (problema) to surmount; (conflicto) to resolve

zapapico [θapaˈpiko] NM pick, pickaxe

zapata [θaˈpata] NF half-boot; (Mecánica) shoe

zapateado [θapateˈaðo] NM (flamenco) tap dance

zapatear [θapateˈar] /1a/ VT (tocar) to tap with one's foot; (patear) to kick; (fam) to ill-treat ▶ VI to tap with one's feet

★**zapatería** [θapateˈria] NF (oficio) shoemaking; (tienda) shoe-shop; (fábrica) shoe factory

★**zapatero, -a** [θapaˈtero, a] NM/F shoemaker; **~ remendón** cobbler

★**zapatilla** [θapaˈtiʎa] NF slipper; (Tec) washer; (de deporte) training shoe

★**zapato** [θaˈpato] NM shoe

zapear [θapeˈar] /1a/ VI to flick through the channels

zapping [ˈθapin] NM channel-hopping; **hacer ~** to channel-hop, flick through the channels

zar [θar] NM tsar, czar

zarabanda [θaraˈβanda] NF saraband; (fig) whirl

Zaragoza [θaraˈɣoθa] NF Saragossa

zaragozano, -a [θaraɣoˈθano, a] ADJ of o from Saragossa ▶ NM/F native o inhabitant of Saragossa

zaranda [θaˈranda] NF sieve

zarandear [θarandeˈar] /1a/ VT to sieve; (fam) to shake vigorously

zarpa ['θarpa] NF (*garra*) claw, paw; **echar la ~ a** to claw at; (*fam*) to grab

zarpar [θar'par] /**1a**/ VI to weigh anchor

zarpazo [θar'paθo] NM: **dar un ~** to claw

zarza ['θarθa] NF (*Bot*) bramble

zarzal [θar'θal] NM (*matorral*) bramble patch

zarzamora [θarθa'mora] NF blackberry

zarzuela [θar'θwela] NF Spanish light opera; **la Z~** *home of the Spanish Royal Family*

zasca ['θaska] NM (*ESP fam: comentario*) jibe; **se llevó un ~** he was jibed at

zigzag [θiɣ'θaɣ] NM zigzag

zigzaguear [θiɣθaɣe'ar] /**1a**/ VI to zigzag

zinc [θink] NM zinc

zíper ['siper] NM (*AM*) zip, zipper (*US*)

zócalo ['θokalo] NM (*Arq*) plinth, base; (*de pared*) skirting board (*BRIT*), baseboard (*US*)

zoclo ['θoklo] NM (*AM*) skirting board (*BRIT*), baseboard (*US*)

zoco ['θoko] NM (*Arab*) market, souk

zodíaco [θo'ðiako] NM zodiac; **signo del ~** star sign

★**zona** ['θona] NF area, zone; **~ cero** ground zero; **~ euro** eurozone; **los países de la ~ euro** the eurozone countries; **~ fronteriza** border area; **~ del dólar** (*Com*) dollar area; **~ de fomento** *o* **de desarrollo** development area; **~ roja** (*AM*) red-light district

zonzo, -a ['θonθo, a] (*AM*) ADJ silly ► NM/F fool

★**zoo** ['θoo] NM zoo

zoología [θoolo'xia] NF zoology

zoológico, -a [θoo'loxiko, a] ADJ zoological ► NM (*tb:* **parque zoológico**) zoo

zoólogo, -a [θo'oloɣo, a] NM/F zoologist

zoom [θum] NM zoom lens

zopenco, -a [θo'penko, a] (*fam*) ADJ dull, stupid ► NM/F clot, nitwit

zopilote [θopi'lote] NM (*AM*) buzzard

zoquete [θo'kete] NM (*de madera*) block; (*de pan*) crust; (*fam*) blockhead

★**zorro, -a** ['θorro, a] ADJ crafty ► NM/F fox/vixen ► NF (*fam*) whore, tart, hooker (*US*)

zote ['θote] (*fam*) ADJ dim, stupid ► NMF dimwit

zozobra [θo'θoβra] NF (*fig*) anxiety

zozobrar [θoθo'βrar] /**1a**/ VI (*hundirse*) to capsize; (*fig*) to fail

zueco ['θweko] NM clog

zulo ['θulo] NM (*de armas*) cache

zumba ['θumba] NM o F (*Mus*) Zumba®

zumbar [θum'bar] /**1a**/ VT (*burlar*) to tease; (*golpear*) to hit ► VI to buzz; (*fam*) to be very close; **me zumban los oídos** I have a buzzing *o* ringing in my ears ■ **zumbarse** VR: **zumbarse de** to tease

zumbido [θum'biðo] NM buzzing; (*fam*) punch; **~ de oídos** buzzing *o* ringing in one's ears

★**zumo** ['θumo] NM juice; (*ganancia*) profit; **~ de naranja** (fresh) orange juice

zurcir [θur'θir] /**3b**/ VT (*coser*) to darn; (*fig*) to put together; **¡que las zurzan!** to blazes with them!

zurdo, -a ['θurðo, a] ADJ (*mano*) left; (*persona*) left-handed

zurrar [θu'rrar] /**1a**/ VT (*Tec*) to dress; (*fam: pegar duro*) to wallop; (*: aplastar*) to flatten; (*: criticar*) to criticize harshly

zurriagazo [θurrja'ɣaθo] NM lash, stroke; (*desgracia*) stroke of bad luck

zurrón [θu'rron] NM pouch

zurza *etc* ['θurθa] VB *ver* **zurcir**

zutano, -a [θu'tano, a] NM/F so-and-so

z

ENGLISH – SPANISH

INGLÉS – ESPAÑOL

Aa

A, a [eɪ] N (*letter*) A, a; (*Scol: mark*) ≈ sobresaliente *m*; (*Mus*): **A** la *m*; **A for Andrew**, (US) **A for Able** A de Antonio; **A road** *n* (BRIT *Aut*) ≈ carretera nacional

---

a [ə]

INDEF ART (*before vowel and silent h* **an**) **1** un(a); **a book** un libro; **an apple** una manzana; **she's a nurse** (ella) es enfermera; **I haven't got a car** no tengo coche
2 (*instead of the number "one"*) un(a); **a year ago** hace un año; **a hundred/thousand pounds** cien/mil libras
3 (*in expressing ratios, prices etc*): **three a day/week** tres al día/a la semana; **10 km an hour** 10 km por hora; **£5 a person** £5 por persona; **30p a kilo** 30p el kilo; **three times a month** tres veces al mes

---

a. ABBR = **acre**

A2 N (BRIT *Scol*) segunda parte de los "A levels" (*módulos 4-6*)

AA N ABBR (BRIT: = *Automobile Association*) ≈ RACE *m* (SP); (= *Alcoholics Anonymous*) A.A.; (US: = *Associate in/of Arts*) título universitario; = **anti-aircraft**

AAA¹ [ˈtrɪplˈeɪ] N ABBR (= *American Automobile Association*) ≈ RACE *m* (SP)

AAA² [ˈθriːˈeɪz] N ABBR (BRIT: = *Amateur Athletics Association*) *asociación de atletismo amateur*

A & R N ABBR (*Mus*: = *artists and repertoire*) *nuevos artistas y canciones*; **~ man** *descubridor de jóvenes talentos*

AASCU N ABBR (US) = **American Association of State Colleges and Universities**

AAUP N ABBR (= *American Association of University Professors*) *asociación de profesores universitarios*

AB ABBR (BRIT) = **able-bodied seaman**; (CANADA) = **Alberta**

aback [əˈbæk] ADV: **to be taken ~** quedar(se) desconcertado

★**abandon** [əˈbændən] VT abandonar; (*renounce*) renunciar a; **to ~ ship** abandonar el barco ▸ N abandono; (*wild behaviour*): **with ~** con desenfreno

abandoned [əˈbændənd] ADJ (*child, house etc*) abandonado; (*unrestrained: manner*) desinhibido

abase [əˈbeɪs] VT: **to ~ o.s. (so far as to do ...)** rebajarse (hasta el punto de hacer ...)

abashed [əˈbæʃt] ADJ avergonzado

abate [əˈbeɪt] VI moderarse; (*lessen*) disminuir; (*calm down*) calmarse

abatement [əˈbeɪtmənt] N (*of pollution, noise*) disminución *f*

abattoir [ˈæbətwɑːʳ] N (BRIT) matadero

abbey [ˈæbɪ] N abadía

abbot [ˈæbət] N abad *m*

abbreviate [əˈbriːvɪeɪt] VT abreviar

abbreviation [əbriːvɪˈeɪʃən] N (*short form*) abreviatura; (*act*) abreviación *f*

ABC N ABBR (= *American Broadcasting Company*) *cadena de televisión*

abdicate [ˈæbdɪkeɪt] VT, VI abdicar

abdication [æbdɪˈkeɪʃən] N abdicación *f*

abdomen [ˈæbdəmən] N abdomen *m*

abdominal [æbˈdɒmɪnl] ADJ abdominal

abduct [æbˈdʌkt] VT raptar, secuestrar

abduction [æbˈdʌkʃən] N rapto, secuestro

abductor [æbˈdʌktəʳ] N raptor(a) *m/f*, secuestrador(a) *m/f*

Aberdonian [æbəˈdəunɪən] ADJ de Aberdeen ▸ N nativo(-a) *or* habitante *mf* de Aberdeen

aberration [æbəˈreɪʃən] N aberración *f*; **in a moment of mental ~** en un momento de enajenación mental

abet [əˈbɛt] VT *see* **aid**

abeyance [əˈbeɪəns] N: **in ~** (*law*) en desuso; (*matter*) en suspenso

abhor [əbˈhɔːʳ] VT aborrecer, abominar (de)

abhorrent [əbˈhɒrənt] ADJ aborrecible, detestable

abide [ə'baɪd] VT: **I can't ~ it/him** no lo/le puedo ver or aguantar
▸ **abide by** VT FUS atenerse a

abiding [ə'baɪdɪŋ] ADJ (*memory etc*) perdurable

★**ability** [ə'bɪlɪtɪ] N habilidad f, capacidad f; (*talent*) talento; **to the best of my ~** lo mejor que pueda *etc*

abject ['æbdʒɛkt] ADJ (*poverty*) sórdido; (*apology*) rastrero; (*coward*) vil

ablaze [ə'bleɪz] ADJ en llamas, ardiendo

★**able** ['eɪbl] ADJ capaz; (*skilled*) hábil; **to be ~ to do sth** poder hacer algo

> *to be able to*, *can*, and *could* can be translated by **poder** or **saber**. Use **saber** to talk about skills: *Can you swim?* **¿Sabes nadar?**
> Use **poder** for more general contexts: *He can stay here.* **Puede quedarse aquí.**
> If you want to emphasize the capability, you can also use **ser capaz de** as an alternative to **poder**: *I don't think he'll be able to resist it.* **No creo que sea capaz de or pueda resistirlo.**

able-bodied ['eɪbl'bɔdɪd] ADJ sano; **~ seaman** marinero de primera

ably ['eɪblɪ] ADV hábilmente

ABM N ABBR = **anti-ballistic missile**

abnormal [æb'nɔːməl] ADJ anormal

abnormality [æbnɔː'mælɪtɪ] N (*condition*) anormalidad f; (*instance*) anomalía

aboard [ə'bɔːd] ADV a bordo ▸ PREP a bordo de; **~ the train** en el tren

abode [ə'bəʊd] N (*old*) morada; (*Law*) domicilio; **of no fixed ~** sin domicilio fijo

abolish [ə'bɔlɪʃ] VT suprimir, abolir

abolition [æbə'lɪʃən] N supresión f, abolición f

abominable [ə'bɔmɪnəbl] ADJ abominable

aborigine [æbə'rɪdʒɪnɪ] N aborigen mf

abort [ə'bɔːt] VT abortar; (*Comput*) interrumpir ▸ VI (*Comput*) interrumpir el programa

★**abortion** [ə'bɔːʃən] N aborto; **to have an ~** abortar

abortionist [ə'bɔːʃənɪst] N persona que practica abortos

abortive [ə'bɔːtɪv] ADJ fracasado

abound [ə'baʊnd] VI: **to ~ (in** or **with)** abundar (de or en)

---

about [ə'baʊt]

ADV **1** (*approximately*) más o menos, aproximadamente; **about a hundred/thousand** *etc* unos(-as) or como cien/mil *etc*; **it takes about 10 hours** se tarda unas or más o menos 10 horas; **at about two o'clock** sobre las dos; **I've just about finished** casi he terminado
2 (*referring to place*) por todas partes; **to leave things lying about** dejar las cosas (tiradas) por ahí; **to run about** correr por todas partes; **to walk about** pasearse, ir y venir; **is Paul**

---

about? ¿está por aquí Paul?; **it's the other way about** es al revés
3: **to be about to do sth** estar a punto de hacer algo; **I'm not about to do all that for nothing** no pienso hacer todo eso para nada
▸ PREP **1** (*relating to*) de, sobre, acerca de; **a book about London** un libro sobre or acerca de Londres; **what is it about?** (*book, film*) ¿de qué se trata?; **we talked about it** hablamos de eso or ello; **what** or **how about doing this?** ¿qué tal si hacemos esto?
2 (*referring to place*) por; **to walk about the town** caminar por la ciudad

---

about face, about turn N (*Mil*) media vuelta; (*fig*) cambio radical

★**above** [ə'bʌv] ADV encima, por encima, arriba; **mentioned ~** susodicho ▸ PREP encima de; (*greater than: in number*) más de; (*: in rank*) superior a; **~ all** sobre todo; **he's not ~ a bit of blackmail** es capaz hasta de hacer chantaje

above board ADJ legítimo

above-mentioned [əbʌv'menʃnd] ADJ susodicho

abrasion [ə'breɪʒən] N (*on skin*) abrasión f

abrasive [ə'breɪzɪv] ADJ abrasivo

abreast [ə'brest] ADV uno al lado de otro; **to keep ~ of** mantenerse al corriente de

abridge [ə'brɪdʒ] VT abreviar

★**abroad** [ə'brɔːd] ADV (*be*) en el extranjero; (*go*) al extranjero; **there is a rumour ~ that ...** corre el rumor de que ...

abrupt [ə'brʌpt] ADJ (*sudden: departure*) repentino; (*manner*) brusco

abruptly [ə'brʌptlɪ] ADV (*leave*) repentinamente; (*speak*) bruscamente

abscess ['æbsɪs] N absceso

abscond [əb'skɔnd] VI fugarse

★**absence** ['æbsəns] N ausencia; **in the ~ of** (*person*) en ausencia de; (*thing*) a falta de

★**absent** ['æbsənt] ADJ ausente; **~ without leave (AWOL)** ausente sin permiso

absentee [æbsən'tiː] N ausente mf

absenteeism [æbsən'tiːɪzəm] N absentismo

absent-minded [æbsənt'maɪndɪd] ADJ distraído

absolute ['æbsəluːt] ADJ absoluto; **~ monopoly** monopolio total

★**absolutely** [æbsə'luːtlɪ] ADV totalmente; **oh yes, ~!** ¡claro or por supuesto que sí!

absolution [æbsə'luːʃən] N (*Rel*) absolución f

absolve [əb'zɔlv] VT: **to ~ sb (from)** absolver a algn (de)

absorb [əb'zɔːb] VT absorber; **to be absorbed in a book** estar absorto en un libro

absorbent [əb'zɔːbənt] ADJ absorbente

absorbent cotton N (*US*) algodón m hidrófilo

absorbing [əb'zɔːbɪŋ] ADJ absorbente; (*book etc*) interesantísimo

absorption [əbˈzɔ:pʃən] N absorción f
abstain [əbˈsteɪn] VI: **to ~ (from)** abstenerse (de)
abstemious [əbˈsti:mɪəs] ADJ abstemio
abstention [əbˈstɛnʃən] N abstención f
abstinence [ˈæbstɪnəns] N abstinencia
abstract [ˈæbstrækt] ADJ abstracto
abstruse [æbˈstru:s] ADJ abstruso, oscuro
absurd [əbˈsə:d] ADJ absurdo
absurdity [əbˈsə:dɪtɪ] N absurdo
ABTA [ˈæbtə] N ABBR = **Association of British Travel Agents**
abundance [əˈbʌndəns] N abundancia
abundant [əˈbʌndənt] ADJ abundante
★abuse N [əˈbju:s] (insults) insultos mpl, improperios mpl; (misuse) abuso; **open to ~** sujeto al abuso ▸ VT [əˈbju:z] (ill-treat) maltratar; (take advantage of) abusar de
abusive [əˈbju:sɪv] ADJ ofensivo
abysmal [əˈbɪzməl] ADJ pésimo; (failure) garrafal; (ignorance) supino
abyss [əˈbɪs] N abismo
AC ABBR (= alternating current) corriente f alterna ▸ N ABBR (US) = **athletic club**
a/c ABBR (Banking etc: = account) c/; (: = account current) c/c
★academic [ækəˈdɛmɪk] ADJ académico, universitario; (pej: issue) puramente teórico ▸ N estudioso(-a); (lecturer) profesor(a) m/f universitario(-a)
academic year N (Univ) año académico
academy [əˈkædəmɪ] N (learned body) academia; (school) instituto, colegio
academy of music N conservatorio
ACAS [ˈeɪkæs] N ABBR (Brit: = Advisory, Conciliation and Arbitration Service) ≈ Instituto de Mediación, Arbitraje y Conciliación
accede [ækˈsi:d] VI: **to ~ to** acceder a
accelerate [ækˈsɛləreɪt] VI acelerar
acceleration [æksɛləˈreɪʃən] N aceleración f
accelerator [ækˈsɛləreɪtəʳ] N (Brit) acelerador m
★accent [ˈæksɛnt] N acento; (fig) énfasis m
accentuate [ækˈsɛntjueɪt] VT (syllable) acentuar; (need, difference etc) recalcar, subrayar
★accept [əkˈsɛpt] VT aceptar; (approve) aprobar; (concede) admitir
★acceptable [əkˈsɛptəbl] ADJ aceptable, admisible
acceptance [əkˈsɛptəns] N aceptación f; aprobación f; **to meet with general ~** recibir la aprobación general
★access [ˈæksɛs] N acceso; **the burglars gained ~ through a window** los ladrones lograron entrar por una ventana; **to have ~ to** tener acceso a ▸ VT (Comput) acceder a
accessible [ækˈsɛsəbl] ADJ (place, person) accesible; (knowledge etc) asequible
accession [ækˈsɛʃən] N (of monarch) subida, ascenso; (addition) adquisición f

accessory [ækˈsɛsərɪ] N accesorio; (Law): **~ to** cómplice mf de; **toilet accessories** artículos mpl de tocador
access road N carretera de acceso; (to motorway) carril m de acceso
access time N (Comput) tiempo de acceso
★accident [ˈæksɪdənt] N accidente m; (chance) casualidad f; **by ~** (unintentionally) sin querer; (by coincidence) por casualidad; **accidents at work** accidentes mpl de trabajo; **to meet with or to have an ~** tener or sufrir un accidente
accidental [æksɪˈdɛntl] ADJ accidental, fortuito
accidentally [æksɪˈdɛntəlɪ] ADV sin querer; por casualidad
Accident and Emergency Department N (Brit) Urgencias fpl
accident insurance N seguro contra accidentes
accident-prone [ˈæksɪdəntˈprəun] ADJ propenso a los accidentes
acclaim [əˈkleɪm] VT aclamar, aplaudir ▸ N aclamación f, aplausos mpl
acclamation [ækləˈmeɪʃən] N (approval) aclamación f; (applause) aplausos mpl; **by ~** por aclamación
acclimatize [əˈklaɪmətaɪz], (US) **acclimate** [əˈklaɪmət] VT: **to become acclimatized** aclimatarse
accolade [ˈækəuleɪd] N (prize) premio; (praise) alabanzas fpl, homenaje m
accommodate [əˈkɔmədeɪt] VT alojar, hospedar; (car, hotel etc) tener cabida para; (oblige, help) complacer; **this car accommodates four people comfortably** en este coche caben cuatro personas cómodamente
accommodating [əˈkɔmədeɪtɪŋ] ADJ servicial, complaciente
★accommodation N [əkɔməˈdeɪʃən], (US) **accommodations** NPL [əkɔməˈdeɪʃənz] alojamiento; **"~ to let"** "se alquilan habitaciones"; **seating ~** asientos mpl
accompaniment [əˈkʌmpənɪmənt] N acompañamiento
accompanist [əˈkʌmpənɪst] N (Mus) acompañante mf
★accompany [əˈkʌmpənɪ] VT acompañar
accomplice [əˈkʌmplɪs] N cómplice mf
accomplish [əˈkʌmplɪʃ] VT (finish) concluir; (aim) realizar; (task) llevar a cabo
accomplished [əˈkʌmplɪʃt] ADJ experto, hábil
accomplishment [əˈkʌmplɪʃmənt] N (ending) conclusión f; (bringing about) realización f; (skill) talento
accord [əˈkɔ:d] N acuerdo; **of his own ~** espontáneamente; **with one ~** de or por común acuerdo ▸ VT conceder
accordance [əˈkɔ:dəns] N: **in ~ with** de acuerdo con

according [əˈkɔːdɪŋ]: **~ to** prep según; (in accordance with) conforme a; **it went ~ to plan** salió según lo previsto

accordingly [əˈkɔːdɪŋlɪ] ADV (thus) por consiguiente, en consecuencia; (appropriately) de acuerdo con esto

accordion [əˈkɔːdɪən] N acordeón m

accordionist [əˈkɔːdɪənɪst] N acordeonista mf

accost [əˈkɔst] VT abordar, dirigirse a

★**account** [əˈkaunt] N (Comm) cuenta, factura; (report) informe m; **"~ payee only"** "únicamente en cuenta del beneficiario"; **your ~ is still outstanding** su cuenta está todavía pendiente; **of little ~** de poca importancia; **on ~** a crédito; **to buy sth on ~** comprar algo a crédito; **on no ~** bajo ningún concepto; **on ~ of** a causa de, por motivo de; **to take into ~, take ~ of** tener en cuenta; **to keep an ~ of** llevar la cuenta de; **to bring sb to ~ for sth/for having done sth** pedirle cuentas a algn por algo/por haber hecho algo ■**accounts** NPL (Comm) cuentas fpl
▶ **account for** VT FUS (explain) explicar; **all the children were accounted for** no faltaba ningún niño

accountability [əkauntəˈbɪlɪtɪ] N responsabilidad f

accountable [əˈkauntəbl] ADJ: **~ (for)** responsable (de)

accountancy [əˈkauntənsɪ] N contabilidad f

accountant [əˈkauntənt] N contable mf, contador(a) m/f (LAM)

accounting [əˈkauntɪŋ] N contabilidad f

accounting period N período contable, ejercicio financiero

account number N (at bank etc) número de cuenta

account payable N cuenta por pagar

account receivable N cuenta por cobrar

accoutrements [əˈkuːtrəmənts] NPL equipo, pertrechos mpl

accredited [əˈkredɪtɪd] ADJ (agent etc) autorizado, acreditado

accretion [əˈkriːʃən] N acumulación f

accrue [əˈkruː] VI (mount up) aumentar, incrementarse; (interest) acumularse; **to ~ to** corresponder a; **accrued charges** gastos mpl vencidos; **accrued interest** interés m acumulado

accumulate [əˈkjuːmjuleɪt] VT acumular ▶ VI acumularse

accumulation [əkjuːmjuˈleɪʃən] N acumulación f

accuracy [ˈækjurəsɪ] N (of total) exactitud f; (of description etc) precisión f

★**accurate** [ˈækjurɪt] ADJ (number) exacto; (answer) acertado; (shot) certero

accurately [ˈækjurɪtlɪ] ADV (count, shoot, answer) con precisión

accursed [əˈkɔːst] ADJ maldito

accusation [ækjuˈzeɪʃən] N acusación f

accusative [əˈkjuːzətɪv] N acusativo

★**accuse** [əˈkjuːz] VT acusar; (blame) echar la culpa a; **to ~ sb (of sth)** acusar a algn (de algo)

accused [əˈkjuːzd] N acusado(-a)

accuser [əˈkjuːzər] N acusador(a) m/f

accustom [əˈkʌstəm] VT acostumbrar; **to ~ o.s. to sth** acostumbrarse a algo

accustomed [əˈkʌstəmd] ADJ: **~ to** acostumbrado a

AC/DC ABBR (= alternating current/direct current) CA/CC

ACE [eɪs] N ABBR = **American Council on Education**

ace [eɪs] N as m

acerbic [əˈsɜːbɪk] ADJ acerbo; (fig) mordaz

acetate [ˈæsɪteɪt] N acetato

★**ache** [eɪk] N dolor m; **I've got stomach ~** or (US) **a stomach ~** tengo dolor de estómago, me duele el estómago ▶ VI doler; **my head aches** me duele la cabeza; (yearn): **to ~ to do sth** ansiar hacer algo

★**achieve** [əˈtʃiːv] VT (reach) alcanzar; (realize) realizar; (victory, success) lograr, conseguir

★**achievement** [əˈtʃiːvmənt] N (completion) realización f; (success) éxito

Achilles heel [əˈkɪliːz-] N talón m de Aquiles

★**acid** [ˈæsɪd] ADJ ácido; (bitter) agrio ▶ N (Chem, inf: LSD) ácido

acidity [əˈsɪdɪtɪ] N acidez f; (Med) acedía

acid rain N lluvia ácida

acid test N (fig) prueba de fuego

acknowledge [əkˈnɔlɪdʒ] VT (letter: also: **acknowledge receipt of**) acusar recibo de; (fact) reconocer

acknowledgement [əkˈnɔlɪdʒmənt] N acuse m de recibo; reconocimiento; **acknowledgements** (in book) agradecimientos mpl

ACLU N ABBR (= American Civil Liberties Union) unión americana por libertades civiles

acme [ˈækmɪ] N súmmum m

acne [ˈæknɪ] N acné m

acorn [ˈeɪkɔːn] N bellota

acoustic [əˈkuːstɪk] ADJ acústico

acoustics [əˈkuːstɪks] N, NPL acústica sg

acquaint [əˈkweɪnt] VT: **to ~ sb with sth** (inform) poner a algn al corriente de algo; **to be acquainted with** (person) conocer; (fact) estar al corriente de

acquaintance [əˈkweɪntəns] N conocimiento; (person) conocido(-a); **to make sb's ~** conocer a algn

acquiesce [ækwɪˈɛs] VI (agree): **to ~ (in)** consentir (en), conformarse (con)

acquire [əˈkwaɪər] VT adquirir

acquired [əˈkwaɪəd] ADJ adquirido; **it's an ~ taste** es algo a lo que uno se aficiona poco a poco

acquisition [ækwɪˈzɪʃən] N adquisición f

acquisitive [əˈkwɪzɪtɪv] ADJ codicioso

acquit [əˈkwɪt] VT absolver, exculpar; **to ~ o.s. well** salir con éxito

acquittal [əˈkwɪtl] N absolución f, exculpación f

★**acre** [ˈeɪkəʳ] N acre m

acreage [ˈeɪkərɪdʒ] N extensión f

acrid [ˈækrɪd] ADJ (smell) acre; (fig) mordaz, sarcástico

acrimonious [ækrɪˈməʊnɪəs] ADJ (remark) mordaz; (argument) reñido

acrobat [ˈækrəbæt] N acróbata mf

acrobatic [ækrəˈbætɪk] ADJ acrobático

acrobatics [ækrəˈbætɪks] NPL acrobacia sg

acronym [ˈækrənɪm] N siglas fpl

★**across** [əˈkrɒs] PREP (on the other side of) al otro lado de; (crosswise) a través de ▶ ADV a través, al través, de un lado a otro; **to run/swim ~** atravesar corriendo/nadando; **~ from** enfrente de; **the lake is 12 km ~** el lago tiene 12 km de ancho; **to get sth ~ to sb** (fig) hacer comprender algo a algn

acrylic [əˈkrɪlɪk] ADJ acrílico

ACT N ABBR (= American College Test) prueba de aptitud estándar que por lo general hacen los estudiantes que quieren entrar a la universidad por primera vez

★**act** [ækt] N acto, acción f; (Theat) acto; (in music hall etc) número; (Law) decreto, ley f; **~ of God** fuerza mayor; **it's only an ~** es cuento; **to catch sb in the ~** coger a algn in fraganti or con las manos en la masa ▶ VI (behave) comportarse; (Theat) actuar; (pretend) fingir; (take action) tomar medidas; **to ~ as** actuar or hacer de; **acting in my capacity as chairman, I …** en mi calidad de presidente, yo …; **it acts as a deterrent** sirve para disuadir; **he's only acting** está fingiendo nada más ▶ VT (part) hacer, representar; **to ~ Hamlet** hacer el papel de Hamlet ▶ **act on** VT: **to ~ on sth** actuar or obrar sobre algo

▶ **act out** VT (event) representar; (fantasies) realizar

▶ **act up** VI (inf: person) portarse mal

acting [ˈæktɪŋ] ADJ suplente; **he is the ~ manager** es el gerente en funciones ▶ N: **to do some ~** hacer algo de teatro

★**action** [ˈækʃən] N acción f, acto; (Mil) acción f; (Law) proceso, demanda; **to put a plan into ~** poner un plan en acción or en marcha; **killed in ~** (Mil) muerto en acto de servicio or en combate; **out of ~** (person) fuera de combate; (thing) averiado, estropeado; **to take ~** tomar medidas; **to bring an ~ against sb** entablar or presentar demanda contra algn ▶ VT (Comm) llevar a cabo

action replay N (TV) repetición f

activate [ˈæktɪveɪt] VT activar

★**active** [ˈæktɪv] ADJ activo, enérgico; (volcano) en actividad; **to play an ~ part in** colaborar activamente en

active duty N (US Mil) servicio activo

actively [ˈæktɪvlɪ] ADV (participate) activamente; (discourage, dislike) enérgicamente

active partner N (Comm) socio activo

activist [ˈæktɪvɪst] N activista mf

★**activity** [ækˈtɪvɪtɪ] N actividad f

activity holiday N vacaciones con actividades organizadas

★**actor** [ˈæktəʳ] N actor m

★**actress** [ˈæktrɪs] N actriz f

★**actual** [ˈæktjuəl] ADJ verdadero, real

★**actually** [ˈæktjuəlɪ] ADV realmente, en realidad

actually no debe traducirse por actualmente.

actuary [ˈæktjuərɪ] N (Comm) actuario(-a) (de seguros)

actuate [ˈæktjueɪt] VT mover, impulsar

acumen [ˈækjumən] N perspicacia; **business ~** talento para los negocios

acupuncture [ˈækjupʌŋktʃəʳ] N acupuntura

acute [əˈkjuːt] ADJ agudo

acutely [əˈkjuːtlɪ] ADV profundamente, extremadamente

AD ADV ABBR (= Anno Domini) d.C. ▶ N ABBR (US Mil) = **active duty**

★**ad** [æd] N ABBR = **advertisement**

adage [ˈædɪdʒ] N refrán m, adagio

Adam [ˈædəm] N Adán m; **~'s apple** n nuez f (de la garganta)

adamant [ˈædəmənt] ADJ firme, inflexible

adapt [əˈdæpt] VT adaptar; (reconcile) acomodar ▶ VI: **to ~ (to)** adaptarse (a), ajustarse (a)

adaptability [ədæptəˈbɪlɪti] N (of person, device etc) adaptabilidad f

adaptable [əˈdæptəbl] ADJ (device) adaptable; (person) acomodadizo, que se adapta

adaptation [ædæpˈteɪʃən] N adaptación f

adapter, adaptor [əˈdæptəʳ] N (Elec) adaptador m; (for several plugs) ladrón m

ADC N ABBR (Mil) = **aide-de-camp**; (US: = Aid to Dependent Children) ayuda para niños dependientes

★**add** [æd] VT añadir, agregar (esp LAm); (figures: also: **add up**) sumar ▶ VI: **to ~ to** (increase) aumentar, acrecentar ▶ N (Internet): **thanks for the ~** gracias por agregarme

▶ **add on** VT añadir

▶ **add up** VT (figures) sumar ▶ VI (fig): **it doesn't ~ up** no tiene sentido; **it doesn't ~ up to much** es poca cosa, no tiene gran or mucha importancia

addendum [əˈdɛndəm] N adenda m or f

adder [ˈædəʳ] N víbora

addict [ˈædɪkt] N (to drugs etc) adicto(-a); (enthusiast) aficionado(-a), entusiasta mf; **heroin ~** heroinómano(-a)

addicted [əˈdɪktɪd] ADJ: **to be ~ to** ser adicto a; ser aficionado a

addiction [əˈdɪkʃən] N (to drugs etc) adicción f; (enthusiasm) afición f

addictive [əˈdɪktɪv] ADJ que causa adicción

adding machine [ˈædɪŋ-] N calculadora

Addis Ababa [ˈædɪsˈæbəbə] N Addis Abeba m

★**addition** [əˈdɪʃən] N (adding up) adición f; (thing added) añadidura, añadido; **in ~** además, por añadidura; **in ~ to** además de

additional [əˈdɪʃənl] ADJ adicional

additive [ˈædɪtɪv] N aditivo

addled [ˈædld] ADJ (BRIT: old: rotten) podrido; (: fig) confuso

★**address** [əˈdrɛs] N dirección f, señas fpl; (speech) discurso; (Comput) dirección f; **form of ~** tratamiento; **absolute/relative ~** (Comput) dirección f absoluta/relativa ▶ VT (letter) dirigir; (speak to) dirigirse a, dirigir la palabra a; **to ~ o.s. to sth** (issue, problem) abordar

address book N agenda (de direcciones)

addressee [ædrɛˈsiː] N destinatario(-a)

Aden [ˈeɪdn] N Adén m

adenoids [ˈædɪnɔɪdz] NPL vegetaciones fpl (adenoideas)

adept [ˈædɛpt] ADJ: **~ at** experto or ducho en

adequacy [ˈædɪkwəsɪ] N idoneidad f

adequate [ˈædɪkwɪt] ADJ (satisfactory) adecuado; (enough) suficiente; **to feel ~ to a task** sentirse con fuerzas para una tarea

adequately [ˈædɪkwɪtlɪ] ADV adecuadamente

adhere [ədˈhɪəʳ] VI: **to ~ to** adherirse a; (fig: abide by) observar

adherent [ədˈhɪərənt] N partidario(-a)

adhesion [ədˈhiːʒən] N adherencia

adhesive [ədˈhiːzɪv] ADJ, N adhesivo

adhesive tape N (BRIT) cinta adhesiva; (US Med) esparadrapo

ad hoc [ædˈhɔk] ADJ (decision) ad hoc; (committee) formado con fines específicos ▶ ADV ad hoc

adieu [əˈdjuː] EXCL ¡vaya con Dios!

ad inf [ˈædˈɪnf] ADV hasta el infinito

adjacent [əˈdʒeɪsənt] ADJ: **~ to** contiguo a, inmediato a

★**adjective** [ˈædʒɛktɪv] N adjetivo

adjoin [əˈdʒɔɪn] VT estar contiguo a; (land) lindar con

adjoining [əˈdʒɔɪnɪŋ] ADJ contiguo, vecino

adjourn [əˈdʒəːn] VT aplazar; (session) suspender, levantar; (US: end) terminar; **the meeting has been adjourned till next week** se ha levantado la sesión hasta la semana que viene ▶ VI suspenderse; **they adjourned to the pub** (inf) se trasladaron al bar

adjournment [əˈdʒəːnmənt] N (period) suspensión f; (postponement) aplazamiento

Adjt. ABBR (Mil) = **adjutant**

adjudicate [əˈdʒuːdɪkeɪt] VI sentenciar ▶ VT (contest) hacer de árbitro en, juzgar; (claim) decidir

adjudication [ədʒuːdɪˈkeɪʃən] N fallo

adjudicator [əˈdʒuːdɪkeɪtəʳ] N juez(a) m/f, árbitro(-a)

★**adjust** [əˈdʒʌst] VT (change) modificar; (arrange) arreglar; (machine) ajustar ▶ VI: **to ~ (to)** adaptarse (a)

adjustable [əˈdʒʌstəbl] ADJ ajustable

adjuster [əˈdʒʌstəʳ] N see **loss adjuster**

adjustment [əˈdʒʌstmənt] N adaptación f; arreglo; (of prices, wages) ajuste m

adjutant [ˈædʒətənt] N ayudante m

ad-lib [ædˈlɪb] VT, VI improvisar ▶ ADV: **ad lib** a voluntad, a discreción

adman [ˈædmæn] N (irreg) (inf) publicista m

admin [ˈædmɪn] N ABBR (inf) = **administration**

administer [ədˈmɪnɪstəʳ] VT proporcionar; (justice) administrar

★**administration** [ædmɪnɪˈstreɪʃən] N administración f; (government) gobierno; **the A~** (US) la Administración

administrative [ədˈmɪnɪstrətɪv] ADJ administrativo

administrator [ədˈmɪnɪstreɪtəʳ] N administrador(a) m/f

admirable [ˈædmərəbl] ADJ admirable

admiral [ˈædmərəl] N almirante m

Admiralty [ˈædmərəltɪ] N (BRIT) Ministerio de Marina, Almirantazgo

admiration [ædməˈreɪʃən] N admiración f

★**admire** [ədˈmaɪəʳ] VT admirar

admirer [ədˈmaɪərəʳ] N admirador(a) m/f; (suitor) pretendiente m

admiring [ədˈmaɪərɪŋ] ADJ (expression) de admiración

admissible [ədˈmɪsəbl] ADJ admisible

admission [ədˈmɪʃən] N (to exhibition, nightclub) entrada; (enrolment) ingreso; (confession) confesión f; **"~ free"** "entrada gratis or libre"; **by his own ~** él mismo reconoce que

★**admit** [ədˈmɪt] VT dejar entrar, dar entrada a; (permit) admitir; (acknowledge) reconocer; **"this ticket admits two"** "entrada para dos personas"; **children not admitted** se prohíbe la entrada a (los) menores de edad; **to be admitted to hospital** ingresar en el hospital; **I must ~ that ...** debo reconocer que ...
▶ **admit of** VT FUS admitir, permitir
▶ **admit to** VT FUS confesarse culpable de

admittance [ədˈmɪtəns] N entrada; **"no ~"** "se prohíbe la entrada", "prohibida la entrada"

admittedly [ədˈmɪtədlɪ] ADV es cierto que

admonish [ədˈmɔnɪʃ] VT amonestar; (advise) aconsejar

ad nauseam [ædˈnɔːsɪæm] ADV hasta la saciedad

ado [əˈduː] N: **without (any) more ~** sin más (ni más)

adolescence [ædəuˈlɛsns] N adolescencia

adolescent [ædəuˈlɛsnt] ADJ, N adolescente mf

★**adopt** [əˈdɔpt] VT adoptar

★**adopted** [əˈdɔptɪd] ADJ adoptivo

adoption [ə'dɔpʃən] N adopción f
adoptive [ə'dɔptɪv] ADJ adoptivo
adorable [ə'dɔ:rəbl] ADJ adorable
adoration [ædə'reɪʃən] N adoración f
adore [ə'dɔ:ʳ] VT adorar
adoring [ə'dɔ:rɪŋ] ADJ: **to his ~ public** a un público que le adora or le adoraba *etc*
adorn [ə'dɔ:n] VT adornar
adornment [ə'dɔ:nmənt] N adorno
ADP N ABBR = **automatic data processing**
adrenalin [ə'drenəlɪn] N adrenalina
Adriatic [eɪdrɪ'ætɪk] N: **the ~ (Sea)** el (mar) Adriático
adrift [ə'drɪft] ADV a la deriva; **to come ~** (*boat*) ir a la deriva, soltarse; (*wire, rope etc*) soltarse
adroit [ə'drɔɪt] ADJ diestro, hábil
ADSL N ABBR (= *asymmetric digital subscriber line*) ADSL *m*
ADT ABBR (US: = *Atlantic Daylight Time*) *hora de verano de Nueva York*
adulation [ædju'leɪʃən] N adulación f
★**adult** ['ædʌlt] N adulto(-a) ▶ ADJ: **~ education** educación f para adultos
adulterate [ə'dʌltəreɪt] VT adulterar
adulterer [ə'dʌltərəʳ] N adúltero
adulteress [ə'dʌltrɪs] N adúltera
adultery [ə'dʌltərɪ] N adulterio
adulthood ['ædʌlthud] N edad f adulta
★**advance** [əd'vɑ:ns] N adelanto, progreso; (*money*) anticipo; (*Mil*) avance *m*; **in ~** por adelantado; (*book*) con antelación; **to make advances to sb** (*gen*) hacer una proposición a algn; (*amorously*) insinuarse a algn ▶ VT avanzar, adelantar; (*money*) anticipar ▶ VI avanzar, adelantarse
★**advanced** ADJ avanzado; (*Scol: studies*) adelantado; **~ in years** entrado en años
Advanced Higher N (*SCOTTISH Scol*) titulación *que sigue al "Higher"*, ≈ Bachillerato
advancement [əd'vɑ:nsmənt] N progreso; (*in rank*) ascenso
advance notice N previo aviso
advance payment N (*part sum*) anticipo
★**advantage** [əd'vɑ:ntɪdʒ] N (*also Tennis*) ventaja; **to take ~ of** aprovecharse de; **it's to our ~** es ventajoso para nosotros
advantageous [ædvən'teɪdʒəs] ADJ ventajoso, provechoso
advent ['ædvənt] N advenimiento; **A~** Adviento
★**adventure** [əd'ventʃəʳ] N aventura
adventure playground N parque *m* infantil
adventurous [əd'ventʃərəs] ADJ aventurero; (*bold*) arriesgado
adverb ['ædvə:b] N adverbio
adversary ['ædvəsərɪ] N adversario(-a), contrario(-a)
adverse ['ædvə:s] ADJ adverso, contrario; **~ to** adverso a

adversity [əd'və:sɪtɪ] N infortunio
advert ['ædvə:t] N ABBR (*BRIT*) = **advertisement**
★**advertise** ['ædvətaɪz] VI hacer propaganda; (*in newspaper etc*) poner un anuncio, anunciarse; **to ~ for** (*staff*) buscar por medio de anuncios ▶ VT anunciar
advertisement [əd'və:tɪsmənt] N anuncio
advertiser ['ædvətaɪzəʳ] N anunciante *mf*
advertising ['ædvətaɪzɪŋ] N publicidad f, propaganda; anuncios *mpl*; (*industry*) industria publicitaria
advertising agency N agencia de publicidad
advertising campaign N campaña de publicidad
★**advice** [əd'vaɪs] N consejo, consejos *mpl*; (*notification*) aviso; **a piece of ~** un consejo; **to take legal ~** consultar a un abogado; **to ask (sb) for ~** pedir consejo (a algn)
advice note N (*BRIT*) nota de aviso
advisable [əd'vaɪzəbl] ADJ aconsejable, conveniente
★**advise** [əd'vaɪz] VT aconsejar; **to ~ sb of sth** (*inform*) informar a algn de algo; **to ~ sb against sth/doing sth** desaconsejar algo a algn/aconsejar a algn que no haga algo; **you will be well/ill advised to go** deberías/no deberías ir
advisedly [əd'vaɪzɪdlɪ] ADV deliberadamente
adviser [əd'vaɪzəʳ] N consejero(-a); (*business adviser*) asesor(a) *m/f*
advisory [əd'vaɪzərɪ] ADJ consultivo; **in an ~ capacity** como asesor
advocate VT ['ædvəkeɪt] (*argue for*) abogar por; (*give support to*) ser partidario de ▶ N ['ædvəkɪt] abogado(-a); (*supporter*): **~ of** defensor(a) *m/f* de
advt. ABBR = **advertisement**
AEA N ABBR (*BRIT*: = *Atomic Energy Authority*) *consejo de energía nuclear*; (*BRIT Scol*: = *Advanced Extension Award*) *titulación opcional para los alumnos mejor preparados de los "A levels"*
AEC N ABBR (*US*: = *Atomic Energy Commission*) AEC f
Aegean [iː'dʒiːən] N: **the ~ (Sea)** el (mar) Egeo
aegis ['iːdʒɪs] N: **under the ~ of** bajo la tutela de
aeon ['iːən] N eón *m*
aerial ['ɛərɪəl] N antena ▶ ADJ aéreo
aerie ['ɛərɪ] N (*US*) aguilera
aero- ['ɛərəu] PREF aero-
aerobatics [ɛərəu'bætɪks] NPL acrobacia aérea
★**aerobics** [ɛə'rəubɪks] NSG aerobic *m*, aerobismo (*LAM*)
aerodrome ['ɛərədrəum] N (*BRIT*) aeródromo
aerodynamic [ɛərəudaɪ'næmɪk] ADJ aerodinámico
aeronautics [ɛərəu'nɔ:tɪks] NSG aeronáutica
★**aeroplane** ['ɛərəpleɪn] N (*BRIT*) avión *m*
aerosol ['ɛərəsɔl] N aerosol *m*
aerospace industry ['ɛərəuspeɪs-] N industria aeroespacial
aesthetic [iːs'θetɪk] ADJ estético

aesthetics [iːsˈθɛtɪks] NPL estética

afar [əˈfɑːʳ] ADV lejos; **from ~** desde lejos

AFB N ABBR (US) = **Air Force Base**

AFDC N ABBR (US: = Aid to Families with Dependent Children) ayuda a familias con hijos menores

affable [ˈæfəbl] ADJ afable

★**affair** [əˈfɛəʳ] N asunto; (also: **love affair**) aventura f amorosa; **affairs** (business) asuntos mpl; **the Watergate ~** el asunto (de) Watergate

★**affect** [əˈfɛkt] VT afectar, influir en; (move) conmover

affectation [æfɛkˈteɪʃən] N afectación f

affected [əˈfɛktɪd] ADJ afectado

affection [əˈfɛkʃən] N afecto, cariño

affectionate [əˈfɛkʃənɪt] ADJ afectuoso, cariñoso

affectionately [əˈfɛkʃənɪtlɪ] ADV afectuosamente

affidavit [æfɪˈdeɪvɪt] N (Law) declaración f jurada

affiliated [əˈfɪlɪeɪtɪd] ADJ afiliado; **~ company** empresa or compañía filial or subsidiaria

affinity [əˈfɪnɪtɪ] N afinidad f

affirm [əˈfəːm] VT afirmar

affirmation [æfəˈmeɪʃən] N afirmación f

affirmative [əˈfəːmətɪv] ADJ afirmativo

affix [əˈfɪks] VT (signature) estampar; (stamp) pegar

afflict [əˈflɪkt] VT afligir

affliction [əˈflɪkʃən] N enfermedad f, aflicción f

affluence [ˈæfluəns] N opulencia, riqueza

affluent [ˈæfluənt] ADJ acomodado; **the ~ society** la sociedad opulenta

★**afford** [əˈfɔːd] VT poder permitirse; (provide) proporcionar; **can we ~ a car?** ¿podemos permitirnos el gasto de comprar un coche?

affordability [əfɔːdəˈbɪlɪtɪ] N asequibilidad f

affordable [əˈfɔːdəbl] ADJ asequible

affray [əˈfreɪ] N refriega, reyerta

affront [əˈfrʌnt] N afrenta, ofensa

affronted [əˈfrʌntɪd] ADJ ofendido

Afghan [ˈæfgæn] ADJ, N afgano(-a) m/f

Afghanistan [æfˈgænɪstæn] N Afganistán m

afield [əˈfiːld] ADV: **far ~** muy lejos

AFL-CIO N ABBR (US: = American Federation of Labor and Congress of Industrial Organizations) confederación sindicalista

afloat [əˈfləut] ADV (floating) a flote; (at sea) en el mar

afoot [əˈfut] ADV: **there is something ~** algo se está tramando

aforesaid [əˈfɔːsɛd] ADJ susodicho; (Comm) mencionado anteriormente

★**afraid** [əˈfreɪd] ADJ: **to be ~ of** (person) tener miedo a; (thing) tener miedo de; **to be ~ to** tener miedo de, temer; **I am ~ that** me temo que; **I'm ~ so** lo siento, pero es así, me temo que sí; **I'm ~ not** lo siento, pero no

afresh [əˈfrɛʃ] ADV de nuevo, otra vez

★**Africa** [ˈæfrɪkə] N África

African [ˈæfrɪkən] ADJ, N africano(-a) m/f

African-American ADJ, N afroamericano(-a) m/f

Afrikaans [æfrɪˈkɑːns] N africaans m

Afrikaner [æfrɪˈkɑːnəʳ] N afrikáner mf

Afro-American [ˈæfrəuəˈmerɪkən] ADJ, N afroamericano(-a) m/f

AFT N ABBR (= American Federation of Teachers) sindicato de profesores

aft [ɑːft] ADV (be) en popa; (go) a popa

★**after** [ˈɑːftəʳ] PREP (time) después de; (place, order) detrás de, tras; **the police are ~ him** la policía le está buscando; **~ dinner** después de cenar or comer; **the day ~ tomorrow** pasado mañana; **to ask ~ sb** preguntar por algn; **~ all** después de todo, al fin y al cabo; **~ you!** ¡pase usted!; **quarter ~ two** (US) las dos y cuarto; **what/who are you ~?** ¿qué/a quién buscas? ▸ ADV después ▸ CONJ después (de) que; **~ having done/he left** después de haber hecho/después de que se marchó

afterbirth [ˈɑːftəbəːθ] N placenta

aftercare [ˈɑːftəkɛəʳ] N (Med) asistencia postoperatoria

after-effects [ˈɑːftərɪfɛkts] NPL secuelas fpl, efectos mpl

afterlife [ˈɑːftəlaɪf] N vida después de la muerte

aftermath [ˈɑːftəmɑːθ] N consecuencias fpl, resultados mpl

★**afternoon** [ɑːftəˈnuːn] N tarde f; **good ~!** ¡buenas tardes!

afternoon tea N té m de la tarde

La hora del té es una tradición inglesa que se remonta al siglo XIX, cuando la alta sociedad se reunía para tomar el té a las 5 de la tarde. Hoy en día la tradición sigue viva, aunque lo más habitual es que la familia o los amigos se citen en el restaurante de un hotel o en una casa de té para celebrar alguna ocasión especial. El menú clásico del **afternoon tea** incluye varios sandwiches pequeños, con rellenos como huevo, pepino o salmón ahumado; bollitos dulces servidos con nata y mermelada; bollería variada servida en una fuente con varios pisos y, claro está, té o, para el que lo prefiera, café.

afterparty [ˈɑːftəpɑːtɪ] N fiesta f posterior

afters [ˈɑːftəz] N (inf: dessert) postre m

after-sales service [ɑːftəˈseɪlz-] N (BRIT Comm: for car, washing machine etc) servicio de asistencia pos-venta

after-shave [ˈɑːftəʃeɪv], **after-shave lotion** N loción f para después del afeitado, aftershave m

aftershock [ˈɑːftəʃɔk] N (of earthquake) pequeño temblor m posterior

aftersun [ˈɑːftəsʌn], **aftersun lotion** N aftersun m inv

aftertaste [ˈɑːftəteɪst] N regusto

afterthought [ˈɑːftəθɔːt] N ocurrencia (tardía)

★**afterwards** [ˈɑːftəwədz] ADV después, más tarde

★**again** [əˈgɛn] ADV otra vez, de nuevo; **to do sth ~** volver a hacer algo; **~ and ~** una y otra vez; **now and ~** de vez en cuando

★**against** [əˈgɛnst] PREP (*opposed*) en contra de; (*close to*) contra, junto a; **I was leaning ~ the desk** estaba apoyado en el escritorio; **(as) ~** frente a

★**age** [eɪdʒ] N edad *f*; (*old age*) vejez *f*; (*period*) época; **what ~ is he?** ¿qué edad *or* cuántos años tiene?; **he is 20 years of ~** tiene 20 años; **under ~** menor de edad; **to come of ~** llegar a la mayoría de edad; **it's been ages since I saw you** hace siglos que no te veo ▶ VI envejecer(se) ▶ VT envejecer

★**aged** ADJ [eɪdʒd]: **~ 10** de 10 años de edad ▶ NPL [ˈeɪdʒɪd]: **the ~** los ancianos

age group N: **to be in the same ~** tener la misma edad; **the 40 to 50 ~** las personas de 40 a 50 años

ageing [ˈeɪdʒɪŋ] ADJ que envejece; (*pej*) en declive ▶ N envejecimiento

ageless [ˈeɪdʒlɪs] ADJ (*eternal*) eterno; (*ever young*) siempre joven

age limit N límite *m* de edad, edad *f* tope

agency [ˈeɪdʒənsɪ] N agencia; **through** *or* **by the ~ of** por medio de

★**agenda** [əˈdʒɛndə] N orden *m* del día; **on the ~** (*Comm*) en el orden del día

> La palabra inglesa **agenda** no debe traducirse por *agenda*.

★**agent** [ˈeɪdʒənt] N (*gen*) agente *mf*; (*representative*) representante *mf* delegado(-a)

aggravate [ˈægrəveɪt] VT agravar; (*annoy*) irritar, exasperar

aggravating [ˈægrəveɪtɪŋ] ADJ irritante, molesto

aggravation [ægrəˈveɪʃən] N agravamiento

aggregate [ˈægrɪgɪt] N conjunto

aggression [əˈgrɛʃən] N agresión *f*

★**aggressive** [əˈgrɛsɪv] ADJ agresivo; (*vigorous*) enérgico

aggressiveness [əˈgrɛsɪvnɪs] N agresividad *f*

aggressor [əˈgrɛsəʳ] N agresor(a) *m/f*

aggrieved [əˈgriːvd] ADJ ofendido, agraviado

aggro [ˈægrəu] N (BRIT *inf*: *physical violence*) bronca; (: *bad feeling*) mal rollo; (: *hassle*) rollo, movida

aghast [əˈgɑːst] ADJ horrorizado

agile [ˈædʒaɪl] ADJ ágil

agility [əˈdʒɪlɪtɪ] N agilidad *f*

agitate [ˈædʒɪteɪt] VT (*shake*) agitar; (*trouble*) inquietar; **to ~ for** hacer campaña en pro de *or* en favor de

agitated [ˈædʒɪteɪtɪd] ADJ agitado

agitator [ˈædʒɪteɪtəʳ] N agitador(a) *m/f*

AGM N ABBR (= *annual general meeting*) junta *f* general

agnostic [ægˈnɔstɪk] ADJ, N agnóstico(-a) *m/f*

★**ago** [əˈgəu] ADV: **two days ~** hace dos días; **not long ~** hace poco; **how long ~?** ¿hace cuánto tiempo?; **as long ~ as 1980** ya en 1980

agog [əˈgɔg] ADJ (*anxious*) ansioso; (*excited*): **(all) ~ (for)** (todo) emocionado (por)

agonize [ˈægənaɪz] VI: **to ~ (over)** atormentarse (por)

agonized [ˈægənaɪzd] ADJ angustioso

agonizing [ˈægənaɪzɪŋ] ADJ (*pain*) atroz; (*suspense*) angustioso

agony [ˈægənɪ] N (*pain*) dolor *m* atroz; (*distress*) angustia; **to be in ~** retorcerse de dolor

agony aunt N (BRIT *inf*) consejera sentimental

agony column N consultorio sentimental

★**agree** [əˈgriː] VT (*price*) acordar, quedar en; **to ~ that** (*admit*) estar de acuerdo en que; **it was agreed that ...** se acordó que ... ▶ VI (*statements etc*) coincidir, concordar; **to ~ (with)** (*person*) estar de acuerdo (con), ponerse de acuerdo (con); **to ~ to do** aceptar hacer; **to ~ to sth** consentir en algo; **garlic doesn't ~ with me** el ajo no me sienta bien

agreeable [əˈgriːəbl] ADJ agradable; (*person*) simpático; (*willing*) de acuerdo, conforme

agreeably [əˈgriːəblɪ] ADV agradablemente

agreed [əˈgriːd] ADJ (*time, place*) convenido

★**agreement** [əˈgriːmənt] N acuerdo; (*Comm*) contrato; **in ~** de acuerdo, conforme; **by mutual ~** de común acuerdo

★**agricultural** [ægrɪˈkʌltʃərəl] ADJ agrícola

★**agriculture** [ˈægrɪkʌltʃəʳ] N agricultura

aground [əˈgraund] ADV: **to run ~** encallar, embarrancar

★**ahead** [əˈhɛd] ADV delante; **~ of** delante de; (*fig: schedule etc*) antes de; **~ of time** antes de la hora; **to be ~ of sb** (*fig*) llevar ventaja *or* la delantera a algn; **go right** *or* **straight ~** siga adelante; **they were (right) ~ of us** iban (justo) delante de nosotros

ahoy [əˈhɔɪ] EXCL ¡oiga!

AI N ABBR = **Amnesty International**; (*Comput*) = **artificial intelligence**

AID N ABBR (= *artificial insemination by donor*) inseminación artificial por donante; (US: = *Agency for International Development*) Agencia Internacional para el Desarrollo

★**aid** [eɪd] N ayuda, auxilio; **in ~ of** a beneficio de; **with the ~ of** con la ayuda de ▶ VT ayudar, auxiliar; **to ~ and abet** (*Law*) ser cómplice

aide [eɪd] N (*Pol*) ayudante *mf*

★**AIDS** [eɪdz] N ABBR (= *acquired immune (or immuno-) deficiency syndrome*) sida m, SIDA m

AIH N ABBR (= *artificial insemination by husband*) inseminación artificial por esposo

ailing [ˈeɪlɪŋ] ADJ (*person, economy*) enfermizo

ailment ['eɪlmənt] N enfermedad f, achaque m

★**aim** [eɪm] VT (gun) apuntar; (missile, remark) dirigir; (blow) asestar ▸ VI (also: **take aim**) apuntar; **to ~ at** (objective) aspirar a, pretender; **to ~ to do** tener la intención de hacer, aspirar a hacer ▸ N puntería; (objective) propósito, meta

aimless ['eɪmlɪs] ADJ sin propósito, sin objeto

aimlessly ['eɪmlɪslɪ] ADV sin rumbo fijo

ain't [eɪnt] (inf) = **are not; aren't; isn't**

★**air** [ɛəʳ] N aire m; (appearance) aspecto; **to throw sth into the ~** (ball etc) lanzar algo al aire; **by ~** (travel) en avión; **to be on the ~** (Radio, TV: programme) estarse emitiendo; (: station) estar en antena ▸ VT (room) ventilar; (clothes, bed, grievances, ideas) airear; (views) hacer público ▸ CPD aéreo

airbag ['ɛəbæg] N airbag m inv

air base N (Mil) base f aérea

air bed N (BRIT) colchoneta inflable or neumática

airborne ['ɛəbɔːn] ADJ (in the air) en el aire; (Mil) aerotransportado; **as soon as the plane was ~** tan pronto como el avión estuvo en el aire

air cargo N carga aérea

★**air-conditioned** ['ɛəkən'dɪʃənd] ADJ climatizado

air conditioning [-kən'dɪʃənɪŋ] N aire m acondicionado

air-cooled ['ɛəkuːld] ADJ refrigerado por aire

aircraft ['ɛəkrɑːft] N pl inv avión m

aircraft carrier N porta(a)viones m inv

air cushion N cojín m de aire; (Aviat) colchón m de aire

airdrome ['ɛədrəum] N (US) aeródromo

airfield ['ɛəfiːld] N campo de aviación

Air Force N fuerzas aéreas fpl, aviación f

air freight N flete m por avión

air freshener N ambientador m

air gun N escopeta de aire comprimido

air hostess N (BRIT) azafata, aeromoza (LAM)

airily ['ɛərɪlɪ] ADV muy a la ligera

airing ['ɛərɪŋ] N: **to give an ~ to** (linen) airear; (room) ventilar; (fig: ideas etc) airear, someter a discusión

airing cupboard N (BRIT) armario m para oreo

air letter N (BRIT) carta aérea

airlift ['ɛəlɪft] N puente m aéreo

★**airline** ['ɛəlaɪn] N línea aérea

airliner ['ɛəlaɪnəʳ] N avión m de pasajeros

airlock ['ɛəlɔk] N (in pipe) esclusa de aire

★**airmail** ['ɛəmeɪl] N: **by ~** por avión

air mattress N colchón m inflable or neumático

airplane ['ɛəpleɪn] N (US) avión m

air pocket N bolsa de aire

★**airport** ['ɛəpɔːt] N aeropuerto

air rage N conducta agresiva de pasajeros a bordo de un avión

air raid N ataque m aéreo

air rifle N escopeta de aire comprimido

airsick ['ɛəsɪk] ADJ: **to be ~** marearse (en avión)

airspace N espacio aéreo

airspeed ['ɛəspiːd] N velocidad f de vuelo

airstrip ['ɛəstrɪp] N pista de aterrizaje

air terminal N terminal f

airtight ['ɛətaɪt] ADJ hermético

air time N (Radio, TV) tiempo en antena

air traffic control N control m de tráfico aéreo

air traffic controller N controlador(a) m/f aéreo(-a)

airway ['ɛəweɪ] N (Aviat) vía aérea; (Anat) vía respiratoria

airy ['ɛərɪ] ADJ (room) bien ventilado; (manners) desenfadado

aisle [aɪl] N (of church) nave f lateral; (of theatre, plane) pasillo

aisle seat N (on plane) asiento de pasillo

ajar [ə'dʒɑːʳ] ADJ entreabierto

AK ABBR (US) = **Alaska**

aka ABBR (= also known as) alias

akin [ə'kɪn] ADJ: **~ to** semejante a

AL ABBR (US) = **Alabama**

ALA N ABBR = **American Library Association**

alabaster ['æləbɑːstəʳ] N alabastro

à la carte [ælæ'kɑːt] ADV a la carta

alacrity [ə'lækrɪtɪ] N: **with ~** con la mayor prontitud

★**alarm** [ə'lɑːm] N alarma; (anxiety) inquietud f ▸ VT asustar, alarmar

alarm call N (in hotel etc) alarma

alarm clock N despertador m

alarmed [ə'lɑːmd] ADJ (person) alarmado, asustado; (house, car etc) con alarma

alarming [ə'lɑːmɪŋ] ADJ alarmante

alarmingly [ə'lɑːmɪŋlɪ] ADV de forma alarmante; **~ quickly** a una velocidad alarmante

alarmist [ə'lɑːmɪst] N alarmista mf

alas [ə'læs] ADV desgraciadamente ▸ EXCL ¡ay!

Alaska [ə'læskə] N Alaska

Albania [æl'beɪnɪə] N Albania

Albanian [æl'beɪnɪən] ADJ albanés(-esa) ▸ N albanés(-esa) m/f; (Ling) albanés m

albatross ['ælbətrɔs] N albatros m

albeit [ɔːl'biːɪt] CONJ (although) aunque

★**album** ['ælbəm] N álbum m; (L.P.) elepé m

albumen ['ælbjumɪn] N albúmina

alchemy ['ælkɪmɪ] N alquimia

★**alcohol** ['ælkəhɔl] N alcohol m

alcohol-free ['ælkəhɔlfriː] ADJ sin alcohol

alcoholic [ælkə'hɔlɪk] ADJ, N alcohólico(-a) m/f

alcoholism ['ælkəhɔlɪzəm] N alcoholismo

alcopop ['ælkəupɔp] N combinado de refresco y alcohol que se vende ya embotellado

alcove ['ælkəuv] N nicho, hueco

Ald. ABBR = **alderman**

alderman ['ɔːldəmən] N (irreg) concejal m

ale [eɪl] N cerveza

alert [ə'ləːt] ADJ alerta inv; (sharp) despierto, atento ▶ N alerta m, alarma; **to be on the ~** estar alerta or sobre aviso ▶ VT poner sobre aviso; **to ~ sb (to sth)** poner sobre aviso or alertar a algn (de algo); **to ~ sb to the dangers of sth** poner sobre aviso or alertar a algn de los peligros de algo

alertness [ə'ləːtnɪs] N vigilancia

Aleutian Islands [ə'luːʃən-] NPL Islas fpl Aleutianas

A level N ABBR (BRIT Scol: = Advanced level) ≈ Bachillerato

> Los **A Levels** son exámenes optativos que se llevan a cabo en Inglaterra, Gales e Irlanda del Norte. Los dos años que se tarda en prepararlos equivaldrían a un bachillerato muy especializado. Los estudiantes pueden elegir entre tres y cinco A Levels, que se dividen en dos grupos de exámenes: los AS Levels al final del primer año, y los A Levels al final del segundo. Aunque los resultados de los AS Levels ya no cuenten para la nota final del A Level, siguen siendo importantes, puesto que las universidades ofrecen plazas a los candidatos en función de estos resultados. El objetivo es que los estudiantes trabajen para conseguir al final del curso unos resultados determinados en los A Levels.

Alexandria [ælɪg'zɑːndrɪə] N Alejandría

alfresco [æl'freskəu] ADJ, ADV al aire libre

algebra ['ældʒɪbrə] N álgebra

Algeria [æl'dʒɪərɪə] N Argelia

Algerian [æl'dʒɪərɪən] ADJ, N argelino(-a) m/f

Algiers [æl'dʒɪəz] N Argel m

algorithm ['ælgərɪðəm] N algoritmo

alias ['eɪlɪəs] ADV alias, conocido por ▶ N alias m; (of criminal) apodo; (of writer) seudónimo

alibi ['ælɪbaɪ] N coartada

alien ['eɪlɪən] N (foreigner) extranjero(-a); (extraterrestrial) extraterrestre mf ▶ ADJ: ~ **to** ajeno a

alienate ['eɪlɪəneɪt] VT enajenar, alejar

alienation [eɪlɪə'neɪʃən] N alejamiento m

alight [ə'laɪt] ADJ ardiendo ▶ VI apearse, bajar

align [ə'laɪn] VT alinear

alignment [ə'laɪnmənt] N alineación f; **the desks are out of ~** los pupitres no están bien alineados

alike [ə'laɪk] ADJ semejantes, iguales; **to look ~** parecerse ▶ ADV igualmente, del mismo modo

alimony ['ælɪmənɪ] N (Law) pensión f alimenticia

★**alive** [ə'laɪv] ADJ (gen) vivo; (lively) alegre

alkali ['ælkəlaɪ] N álcali m

---

all [ɔːl]

ADJ todo(-a) sg, todos(-as) pl; **all day** todo el día; **all night** toda la noche; **all men** todos los hombres; **all five came** vinieron los cinco; **all the books** todos los libros; **all the time/his life** todo el tiempo/toda su vida; **for all their efforts** a pesar de todos sus esfuerzos

▶ PRON **1** todo; **I ate it all, I ate all of it** me lo comí todo; **all of them** todos (ellos); **all of us went** fuimos todos; **all the boys went** fueron todos los chicos; **is that all?** ¿eso es todo?, ¿algo más?; (in shop) ¿algo más?, ¿alguna cosa más?

2 (in phrases): **above all** sobre todo; por encima de todo; **after all** después de todo; **at all:** **anything at all** lo que sea; **not at all** (in answer to question) en absoluto; (in answer to thanks) ¡de nada!, ¡no hay de qué!; **I'm not at all tired** no estoy nada cansado(-a); **anything at all will do** cualquier cosa viene bien; **all in all** a fin de cuentas

▶ ADV: **all alone** completamente solo(-a); **to be/feel all in** estar rendido; **it's not as hard as all that** no es tan difícil como lo pintas; **all the more/the better** tanto más/mejor; **all but** casi; **the score is two all** están empatados a dos

---

Allah ['ælə] N Alá m

all-around ['ɔːlə'raund] ADJ (US) = **all-round**

allay [ə'leɪ] VT (fears) aquietar; (pain) aliviar

all clear N (after attack etc) fin m de la alerta; (fig) luz f verde

allegation [ælɪ'geɪʃən] N alegato

allege [ə'ledʒ] VT pretender; **he is alleged to have said ...** se afirma que él dijo ...

alleged [ə'ledʒd] ADJ supuesto, presunto

allegedly [ə'ledʒɪdlɪ] ADV supuestamente, según se afirma

allegiance [ə'liːdʒəns] N lealtad f

allegory ['ælɪgərɪ] N alegoría

all-embracing ['ɔːləm'breɪsɪŋ] ADJ universal

★**allergic** [ə'ləːdʒɪk] ADJ: ~ **to** alérgico a

allergy ['ælədʒɪ] N alergia

alleviate [ə'liːvɪeɪt] VT aliviar

alleviation [əliːvɪ'eɪʃən] N alivio

alley ['ælɪ] N (street) callejuela; (in garden) paseo

alleyway ['ælɪweɪ] N callejón m

alliance [ə'laɪəns] N alianza

allied ['ælaɪd] ADJ aliado; (related) relacionado

alligator ['ælɪgeɪtə'] N caimán m

all-important ['ɔːlɪm'pɔːtənt] ADJ de suma importancia

all-in ['ɔːlɪn] ADJ, ADV (BRIT: charge) todo incluido

all-in wrestling N lucha libre

alliteration [əlɪtə'reɪʃən] N aliteración f

all-night ['ɔːl'naɪt] ADJ (café) abierto toda la noche; (party) que dura toda la noche

419

allocate ['æləkeɪt] VT (*share out*) repartir; (*devote*) asignar

allocation [ælə'keɪʃən] N (*of money*) ración f, cuota; (*distribution*) reparto

allot [ə'lɔt] VT asignar; **in the allotted time** en el tiempo asignado

allotment [ə'lɔtmənt] N porción f; (*garden*) parcela

all-out ['ɔ:laut] ADJ (*effort etc*) supremo ▶ ADV: **all out** con todas las fuerzas, a fondo

★**allow** [ə'lau] VT (*permit*) permitir, dejar; (*a claim*) admitir; (*sum to spend, time estimated*) dar, conceder; (*concede*): **to ~ that** reconocer que; **to ~ sb to do** permitir a algn hacer; **smoking is not allowed** prohibido or se prohíbe fumar; **he is allowed to ...** se le permite ...; **we must ~ three days for the journey** debemos dejar tres días para el viaje
▶ **allow for** VT FUS tener en cuenta

allowance [ə'lauəns] N concesión f; (*payment*) subvención f, pensión f; (*discount*) descuento, rebaja; (*tax allowance*) desgravación f; **to make allowances for** (*person*) disculpar a; (*thing: take into account*) tener en cuenta

alloy ['ælɔɪ] N aleación f

★**all right** ADV (*feel, work*) bien; (*as answer*) ¡de acuerdo!, ¡está bien!; **I'm/I feel ~ now** ya estoy bien ▶ EXCL ¡vale!, ¡está bien!

all-round ['ɔ:l'raund] ADJ completo; (*view*) amplio

all-rounder ['ɔ:l'raundə'] N: **to be a good ~** ser una persona que hace de todo

allspice ['ɔ:lspaɪs] N pimienta inglesa or de Jamaica

all-time ['ɔ:l'taɪm] ADJ (*record*) de todos los tiempos

allude [ə'lu:d] VI: **to ~ to** aludir a

alluring [ə'ljuərɪŋ] ADJ seductor(a), atractivo

allusion [ə'lu:ʒən] N referencia, alusión f

ally N ['ælaɪ] aliado(-a) ▶ VT [ə'laɪ]: **to ~ o.s. with** aliarse con

almanac ['ɔ:lmənæk] N almanaque m

almighty [ɔ:l'maɪtɪ] ADJ todopoderoso; (*row etc*) imponente

almond ['ɑ:mənd] N (*fruit*) almendra; (*tree*) almendro

★**almost** ['ɔ:lməust] ADV casi; **he ~ fell** casi or por poco se cae

alms [ɑ:mz] NPL limosna *sg*

aloft [ə'lɔft] ADV arriba

★**alone** [ə'ləun] ADJ solo; **to leave sb ~** dejar a algn en paz; **to leave sth ~** no tocar algo ▶ ADV solo, solamente; **let ~ ...** y mucho menos ..., y no digamos ...

★**along** [ə'lɔŋ] PREP a lo largo de, por ▶ ADV: **is he coming ~ with us?** ¿viene con nosotros?; **~ with** junto con; **he was limping ~** iba cojeando; **all ~** (*all the time*) desde el principio

alongside [ə'lɔŋ'saɪd] PREP al lado de ▶ ADV

(*Naut*) de costado; **we brought our boat ~** atracamos nuestro barco

aloof [ə'lu:f] ADJ distante ▶ ADV: **to stand ~** mantenerse a distancia

★**aloud** [ə'laud] ADV en voz alta

★**alphabet** ['ælfəbet] N alfabeto

alphabetical [ælfə'betɪkəl] ADJ alfabético; **in ~ order** por orden alfabético

alphanumeric [ælfənju:'mɛrɪk] ADJ alfanumérico

alpine ['ælpaɪn] ADJ alpino, alpestre

★**Alps** [ælps] NPL: **the ~** los Alpes

★**already** [ɔ:l'redɪ] ADV ya

alright ['ɔ:l'raɪt] ADV = **all right**

Alsatian [æl'seɪʃən] N (*dog*) pastor m alemán

★**also** ['ɔ:lsəu] ADV también, además

altar ['ɔltə'] N altar m

alter ['ɔltə'] VT cambiar, modificar ▶ VI cambiar, modificarse

alteration [ɔltə'reɪʃən] N cambio, modificación f; **timetable subject to ~** el horario puede cambiar ■ **alterations** NPL (*Arch*) reformas *fpl*; (*Sewing*) arreglos *mpl*

altercation [ɔltə'keɪʃən] N altercado

★**alternate** ADJ [ɔl'tə:nɪt] alterno; (*US*) = **alternative; on ~ days** en días alternos ▶ VI ['ɔltəneɪt]: **to ~ (with)** alternar (con)

alternately [ɔl'tə:nɪtlɪ] ADV alternativamente, por turno

alternating ['ɔltəneɪtɪŋ] ADJ (*current*) alterno

★**alternative** [ɔl'tə:nətɪv] ADJ alternativo ▶ N alternativa

alternatively [ɔl'tə:nətɪvlɪ] ADV: **~ one could ...** por otra parte se podría ...

alternative medicine N medicina alternativa

alternator ['ɔltəneɪtə'] N (*Aut*) alternador m

★**although** [ɔ:l'ðəu] CONJ aunque, si bien

altitude ['æltɪtju:d] N altitud f, altura

altitude sickness N mal m de altura, soroche m (*LAm*)

alto ['æltəu] N (*female*) contralto f; (*male*) alto

★**altogether** [ɔ:ltə'gɛðə'] ADV completamente, del todo; (*on the whole, in all*) en total, en conjunto; **how much is that ~?** ¿cuánto es todo or en total?

altruism ['æltruɪzəm] N altruismo

altruistic [æltru'ɪstɪk] ADJ altruista

aluminium [ælju'mɪnɪəm], (*US*) **aluminum** [ə'lu:mɪnəm] N aluminio

★**always** ['ɔ:lweɪz] ADV siempre

Alzheimer's ['æltshaɪməz] N (*also*: **Alzheimer's disease**) (enfermedad f de) Alzheimer m

AM ABBR (= *amplitude modulation*) A.M. f ▶ N ABBR (*Pol: in Wales*) = **Assembly Member**

am [æm] VB *see* **be**

a.m. ADV ABBR (= *ante meridiem*) de la mañana

AMA N ABBR = **American Medical Association**

amalgam [əˈmælgəm] N amalgama

amalgamate [əˈmælgəmeɪt] VI amalgamarse ▶ VT amalgamar

amalgamation [əmælgəˈmeɪʃən] N (Comm) fusión f

amass [əˈmæs] VT amontonar, acumular

amateur [ˈæmətəʳ] N aficionado(-a), amateur mf; ~ **dramatics** dramas mpl presentados por aficionados, representación f de aficionados

amateurish [ˈæmətərɪʃ] ADJ (pej) torpe, inexperto

amaze [əˈmeɪz] VT asombrar, pasmar

amazed [əˈmeɪzd] ADJ asombrado; **to be ~ (at)** asombrarse (de)

amazement [əˈmeɪzmənt] N asombro, sorpresa; **to my ~** para mi sorpresa

★**amazing** [əˈmeɪzɪŋ] ADJ extraordinario, asombroso; (bargain, offer) increíble

amazingly [əˈmeɪzɪŋlɪ] ADV extraordinariamente

Amazon [ˈæməzən] N (Geo) Amazonas m; (Mythology) amazona ▶ CPD: **the ~ basin/jungle** la cuenca/selva del Amazonas

Amazonian [æməˈzəunɪən] ADJ amazónico

ambassador [æmˈbæsədəʳ] N embajador(a) m/f

amber [ˈæmbəʳ] N ámbar m; **at ~** (BRIT Aut) en amarillo

ambidextrous [æmbɪˈdɛkstrəs] ADJ ambidextro

ambience [ˈæmbɪəns] N ambiente m

ambiguity [æmbɪˈgjuɪtɪ] N ambigüedad f; (of meaning) doble sentido

ambiguous [æmˈbɪgjuəs] ADJ ambiguo

★**ambition** [æmˈbɪʃən] N ambición f; **to achieve one's ~** realizar su ambición

ambitious [æmˈbɪʃəs] ADJ ambicioso; (plan) grandioso

ambivalent [æmˈbɪvələnt] ADJ ambivalente; (pej) equívoco

amble [ˈæmbl] VI (gen: also: **amble along**) deambular, andar sin prisa

★**ambulance** [ˈæmbjuləns] N ambulancia

ambulanceman [ˈæmbjulənsmən], **ambulancewoman** [-wumən] N (irreg) ambulanciero(-a)

ambush [ˈæmbuʃ] N emboscada ▶ VT tender una emboscada a; (fig) coger (SP) or agarrar (LAm) por sorpresa

ameba [əˈmiːbə] N (US) = **amoeba**

ameliorate [əˈmiːlɪəreɪt] VT mejorar

amelioration [əmiːlɪəˈreɪʃən] N mejora

amen [ɑːˈmɛn] EXCL amén

amenable [əˈmiːnəbl] ADJ: ~ **to** (advice etc) sensible a

amend [əˈmɛnd] VT (law, text) enmendar; **to make amends** (apologize) enmendarlo, dar cumplida satisfacción

amendment [əˈmɛndmənt] N enmienda

amenity [əˈmiːnɪtɪ] N servicio ■ **amenities** NPL (facilities) servicios, instalaciones fpl

★**America** [əˈmɛrɪkə] N América (del Norte); (USA) Estados mpl Unidos

American [əˈmɛrɪkən] ADJ, N (norte)americano(-a), estadounidense mf

American football N (BRIT) fútbol m americano

Americanism [əˈmɛrɪkənɪzəm] N americanismo

americanize [əˈmɛrɪkənaɪz] VT americanizar

Amerindian [æmərˈɪndɪən] ADJ, N amerindio(-a) m/f

amethyst [ˈæmɪθɪst] N amatista

Amex [ˈæmɛks] N ABBR = **American Stock Exchange**

amiable [ˈeɪmɪəbl] ADJ (kind) amable, simpático

amicable [ˈæmɪkəbl] ADJ amistoso, amigable

amicably [ˈæmɪkəblɪ] ADV amigablemente, amistosamente; **to part ~** separarse amistosamente

amid [əˈmɪd], **amidst** [əˈmɪdst] PREP entre, en medio de

amiss [əˈmɪs] ADV: **to take sth ~** tomar algo a mal; **there's something ~** pasa algo

ammo [ˈæməu] N ABBR (inf) = **ammunition**

ammonia [əˈməunɪə] N amoníaco

ammunition [æmjuˈnɪʃən] N municiones fpl; (fig) argumentos mpl

ammunition dump N depósito de municiones

amnesia [æmˈniːzɪə] N amnesia

amnesty [ˈæmnɪstɪ] N amnistía; **to grant an ~ to** amnistiar (a); **A~ International** Amnistía Internacional

amoeba, (US) **ameba** [əˈmiːbə] N amiba

amok [əˈmɔk] ADV: **to run ~** enloquecerse, desbocarse

★**among** [əˈmʌŋ], **amongst** [əˈmʌŋst] PREP entre, en medio de

amoral [æˈmɔrəl] ADJ amoral

amorous [ˈæmərəs] ADJ cariñoso

amorphous [əˈmɔːfəs] ADJ amorfo

amortization [əmɔːtaɪˈzeɪʃən] N amortización f

★**amount** [əˈmaunt] N (gen) cantidad f; (of bill etc) suma, importe m; **the total ~** (of money) la suma total ▶ VI: **to ~ to** (total) sumar; (be same as) equivaler a, significar; **this amounts to a refusal** esto equivale a una negativa

amp [æmp], **ampère** [ˈæmpɛəʳ] N amperio; **a 13 ~ plug** un enchufe de 13 amperios

ampersand [ˈæmpəsænd] N signo &, "y" comercial

amphetamine [æmˈfɛtəmiːn] N anfetamina

amphibian [æmˈfɪbɪən] N anfibio

amphibious [æmˈfɪbɪəs] ADJ anfibio

amphitheatre, (US) **amphitheater** ['æmfιθιətə'] N anfiteatro

ample ['æmpl] ADJ (spacious) amplio; (abundant) abundante; **to have ~ time** tener tiempo de sobra

amplifier ['æmplιfaιə'] N amplificador m

amplify ['æmplιfaι] VT amplificar, aumentar; (explain) explicar

amply ['æmplι] ADV ampliamente

ampoule, (US) **ampule** ['æmpu:l] N (Med) ampolla

amputate ['æmpjuteιt] VT amputar

amputee [æmpju'ti:] N persona que ha sufrido una amputación

Amsterdam ['æmstədæm] N Amsterdam m

amt ABBR = **amount**

Amtrak ['æmtræk] N (US) empresa nacional de ferrocarriles de los EE.UU.

amuck [ə'mʌk] ADV = **amok**

amuse [ə'mju:z] VT divertir; (distract) distraer, entretener; **to ~ o.s. with sth/by doing sth** distraerse con algo/haciendo algo; **he was amused at the joke** le divirtió el chiste

amusement [ə'mju:zmənt] N diversión f; (pastime) pasatiempo; (laughter) risa; **much to my ~** con gran regocijo mío

amusement arcade N salón m de juegos

amusement park N parque m de atracciones

amusing [ə'mju:zιŋ] ADJ divertido

an [æn, ən, n] INDEF ART see **a**

ANA N ABBR = **American Newspaper Association; American Nurses Association**

anachronism [ə'nækrənιzəm] N anacronismo

anaemia [ə'ni:mιə] N anemia

anaemic [ə'ni:mιk] ADJ anémico; (fig) flojo

anaesthetic [ænιs'θetιk] N anestesia; **local/ general ~** anestesia local/general

anaesthetist [æ'ni:sθιtιst] N anestesista mf

anagram ['ænəgræm] N anagrama m

anal ['eιnl] ADJ anal

analgesic [ænæl'dʒi:sιk] ADJ, N analgésico

analogous [ə'næləgəs] ADJ: **~ to or with** análogo a

analogue, analog ['ænəlɔg] ADJ analógico

analogy [ə'nælədʒι] N analogía; **to draw an ~ between** señalar la analogía entre

analyse ['ænəlaιz] VT (BRIT) analizar

analysis [ə'næləsιs] (pl **analyses** [-si:z]) N análisis m inv

analyst ['ænəlιst] N (political analyst, psychoanalyst) analista mf

analytic [ænə'lιtιk], **analytical** [ænə'lιtιkəl] ADJ analítico

analyze ['ænəlaιz] VT (US) = **analyse**

anarchic [æ'nɑ:kιk] ADJ anárquico

anarchist ['ænəkιst] ADJ, N anarquista mf

anarchy ['ænəkι] N anarquía, desorden m

anathema [ə'næθιmə] N: **that is ~ to him** eso es pecado para él

anatomical [ænə'tɔmιkəl] ADJ anatómico

anatomy [ə'nætəmι] N anatomía

ANC N ABBR = **African National Congress**

ancestor ['ænsιstə'] N antepasado(-a)

ancestral [æn'sɛstrəl] ADJ ancestral

ancestry ['ænsιstrι] N ascendencia, abolengo

anchor ['æŋkə'] N ancla, áncora; **to weigh ~** levar anclas ▶ VI (also: **to drop anchor**) anclar, echar el ancla ▶ VT (fig) sujetar, afianzar

anchorage ['æŋkərιdʒ] N ancladero

anchor man, anchor woman N (irreg) (Radio, TV) presentador(a) m/f

anchovy ['æntʃəvι] N anchoa

ancient ['eιnʃənt] ADJ antiguo; **~ monument** monumento histórico

ancillary [æn'sιlərι] ADJ (worker, staff) auxiliar

★**and** [ænd] CONJ y; (before i, hi) e; **~ so on** etcétera; **try ~ come** procura venir; **better ~ better** cada vez mejor

---

While *and* is usually translated by **y**, use **e** before words beginning with **i** or **hi** to avoid two 'i' sounds coming together: *Spain and England* **España e Inglaterra**; *grapes and figs* **uvas e higos**.
Words beginning with **hie** are preceded by **y**, since **hie** is not pronounced 'i': *flowers and grass* **flores y hierba**.

Andalusia [ændə'lu:zιə] N Andalucía

Andean ['ændιən] ADJ andino(-a); **~ high plateau** altiplanicie f, altiplano (LAM)

Andes ['ændi:z] NPL: **the ~** los Andes

Andorra [æn'dɔ:rə] N Andorra

anecdote ['ænιkdəut] N anécdota

anemia [ə'ni:mιə] N (US) = **anaemia**

anemic [ə'ni:mιk] ADJ (US) = **anaemic**

anemone [ə'nɛmənι] N (Bot) anémone f; **sea ~** anémona

anesthetic [ænιs'θetιk] ADJ, N (US) = **anaesthetic**

anesthetist [æ'ni:sθιtιst] N (US) = **anaesthetist**

anew [ə'nju:] ADV de nuevo, otra vez

★**angel** ['eιndʒəl] N ángel m

angel dust N polvo de ángel

angelic [æn'dʒelιk] ADJ angélico

★**anger** ['æŋgə'] N ira, cólera, enojo (LAM) ▶ VT enojar, enfurecer

angina [æn'dʒaιnə] N angina (de pecho)

★**angle** ['æŋgl] N ángulo; **from their ~** desde su punto de vista

angler ['æŋglə'] N pescador(a) m/f (de caña)

Anglican ['æŋglιkən] ADJ, N anglicano(-a) m/f

anglicize ['æŋglιsaιz] VT anglicanizar

angling ['æŋglιŋ] N pesca con caña

Anglo- [ˈæŋgləu] PREF anglo...
Angola [æŋˈgəulə] N Angola
Angolan [æŋˈgəulən] ADJ, N angoleño(-a) m/f
angrily [ˈæŋgrɪlɪ] ADV enfadado, enojado (esp LAM)
★**angry** [ˈæŋgrɪ] ADJ enfadado, enojado (esp LAM); **to be ~ with sb/at sth** estar enfadado con algn/por algo; **to get ~** enfadarse, enojarse (esp LAM)
anguish [ˈæŋgwɪʃ] N (physical) tormentos mpl; (mental) angustia
anguished [ˈæŋgwɪʃt] ADJ angustioso
angular [ˈæŋgjuləʳ] ADJ (shape) angular; (features) anguloso
★**animal** [ˈænɪməl] ADJ, N animal m; (pej: person) bestia
animal rights [-raɪts] NPL derechos mpl de los animales
animate VT [ˈænɪmeɪt] (enliven) animar; (encourage) estimular, alentar ▶ ADJ [ˈænɪmɪt] vivo, animado
animated [ˈænɪmeɪtɪd] ADJ vivo, animado
animation [ænɪˈmeɪʃən] N animación f
animosity [ænɪˈmɔsɪtɪ] N animosidad f, rencor m
aniseed [ˈænɪsiːd] N anís m
Ankara [ˈæŋkərə] N Ankara
ankle [ˈæŋkl] N tobillo m
ankle sock N calcetín m
annex N [ˈænɛks] (BRIT: also: **annexe**: building) edificio anexo ▶ VT [æˈnɛks] (territory) anexionar
annihilate [əˈnaɪəleɪt] VT aniquilar
annihilation [ənaɪəˈleɪʃən] N aniquilación f
★**anniversary** [ænɪˈvəːsərɪ] N aniversario
annotate [ˈænəuteɪt] VT anotar
★**announce** [əˈnauns] VT (gen) anunciar; (inform) comunicar; **he announced that he wasn't going** declaró que no iba
announcement [əˈnaunsmənt] N (gen) anuncio; (declaration) declaración f; **I'd like to make an ~** quisiera anunciar algo
announcer [əˈnaunsəʳ] N (Radio) locutor(a) m/f; (TV) presentador(a) m/f
annoy [əˈnɔɪ] VT molestar, fastidiar, fregar (LAM), embromar (LAM); **to be annoyed (at sth/with sb)** estar enfadado or molesto (por algo/con algn); **don't get annoyed!** ¡no se enfade!
annoyance [əˈnɔɪəns] N enojo; (thing) molestia
★**annoying** [əˈnɔɪɪŋ] ADJ molesto, fastidioso, fregado (LAM), embromado (LAM); (person) pesado
★**annual** [ˈænjuəl] ADJ anual ▶ N (Bot) anual m; (book) anuario
annual general meeting N junta general anual
annually [ˈænjuəlɪ] ADV anualmente, cada año
annual report N informe m or memoria anual
annuity [əˈnjuːɪtɪ] N renta or pensión f vitalicia

annul [əˈnʌl] VT anular; (law) revocar
annulment [əˈnʌlmənt] N anulación f
annum [ˈænəm] N see **per annum**
Annunciation [ənʌnsɪˈeɪʃən] N Anunciación f
anode [ˈænəud] N ánodo
anoint [əˈnɔɪnt] VT untar
anomalous [əˈnɔmələs] ADJ anómalo
anomaly [əˈnɔməlɪ] N anomalía
anon. [əˈnɔn] ABBR = **anonymous**
anonymity [ænəˈnɪmɪtɪ] N anonimato
anonymous [əˈnɔnɪməs] ADJ anónimo; **to remain ~** quedar en el anonimato
anorak [ˈænəræk] N anorak m
anorexia [ænəˈrɛksɪə] N (Med) anorexia
anorexic [ænəˈrɛksɪk] ADJ, N anoréxico(-a) m/f
★**another** [əˈnʌðəʳ] ADJ: **~ book** otro libro; **~ beer?** ¿(quieres) otra cerveza?; **in ~ five years** en cinco años más ▶ PRON otro; see also **one**
ANSI N ABBR (= American National Standards Institution) oficina de normalización de EE.UU.
★**answer** [ˈɑːnsəʳ] N respuesta, contestación f; (to problem) solución f; **in ~ to your letter** contestando or en contestación a su carta ▶ VI contestar, responder ▶ VT (reply to) contestar a, responder a; (problem) resolver; **to ~ the phone** contestar el teléfono; **to ~ the bell** or **the door** abrir la puerta
  ▶ **answer back** VI replicar, ser respondón(-ona)
  ▶ **answer for** VT FUS responder de or por
  ▶ **answer to** VT FUS (description) corresponder a
answerable [ˈɑːnsərəbl] ADJ: **~ to sb for sth** responsable ante algn de algo
answering machine [ˈɑːnsərɪŋ-] N contestador m automático
answerphone [ˈɑːnsəfəun] N (esp BRIT) contestador m (automático)
ant [ænt] N hormiga
ANTA N ABBR = **American National Theater and Academy**
antagonism [ænˈtægənɪzəm] N antagonismo m
antagonist [ænˈtægənɪst] N antagonista mf, adversario(-a)
antagonistic [æntægəˈnɪstɪk] ADJ antagónico; (opposed) contrario, opuesto
antagonize [ænˈtægənaɪz] VT provocar la enemistad de
Antarctic [æntˈɑːktɪk] ADJ antártico ▶ N: **the ~** el Antártico
Antarctica [ænˈtɑːktɪkə] N Antártida
Antarctic Circle N Círculo Polar Antártico
Antarctic Ocean N océano Antártico
ante [ˈæntɪ] N: **to up the ~** subir la apuesta
ante... [æntɪ] PREF ante...
anteater [ˈæntiːtəʳ] N oso hormiguero
antecedent [æntɪˈsiːdənt] N antecedente m
antechamber [ˈæntɪtʃeɪmbəʳ] N antecámara
antelope [ˈæntɪləup] N antílope m

antenatal [æntɪˈneɪtl] ADJ prenatal

antenatal clinic N clínica prenatal

antenna [ænˈtɛnə] (pl **antennae** [-niː]) N antena

anteroom [ˈæntɪrum] N antesala

anthem [ˈænθəm] N: **national ~** himno nacional

anthology [ænˈθɒlədʒɪ] N antología

anthrax [ˈænθræks] N ántrax m

anthropologist [ænθrəˈpɒlədʒɪst] N antropólogo(-a)

anthropology [ænθrəˈpɒlədʒɪ] N antropología

anti... [æntɪ] PREF anti...

anti-aircraft [ˈæntɪˈɛəkrɑːft] ADJ antiaéreo

antiballistic [æntɪbəˈlɪstɪk] ADJ antibalístico

antibiotic [æntɪbaɪˈɒtɪk] ADJ, N antibiótico

antibody [ˈæntɪbɒdɪ] N anticuerpo

anticipate [ænˈtɪsɪpeɪt] VT (foresee) prever; (expect) esperar, contar con; (forestall) anticiparse a, adelantarse a; **this is worse than I anticipated** esto es peor de lo que esperaba; **as anticipated** según se esperaba

anticipation [æntɪsɪˈpeɪʃən] N previsión f; esperanza; anticipación f

anticlimax [æntɪˈklaɪmæks] N decepción f

anticlockwise [æntɪˈklɒkwaɪz] ADV en dirección contraria a la de las agujas del reloj

antics [ˈæntɪks] NPL gracias fpl

anticyclone [æntɪˈsaɪkləun] N anticiclón m

antidepressant [ˈæntɪdɪˈpresnt] N antidepresivo

antidote [ˈæntɪdəut] N antídoto

antifreeze [ˈæntɪfriːz] N anticongelante m

anti-globalization [ˈæntɪgləubəlaɪˈzeɪʃən] N antiglobalización f; **~ protesters** manifestantes mf pl antiglobalización

Antigua and Barbuda [ænˈtiːgəændbɑːˈbuːdə] N Antigua y Barbuda f

antihistamine [æntɪˈhɪstəmiːn] N antihistamínico

Antilles [ænˈtɪliːz] NPL: **the ~** las Antillas

antipathy [ænˈtɪpəθɪ] N (between people) antipatía; (to person, thing) aversión f

antiperspirant [ˈæntɪpəˈspɪrənt] N antitranspirante m

Antipodean [æntɪpəˈdiːən] ADJ antípoda

Antipodes [ænˈtɪpədiːz] NPL: **the ~** las Antípodas

antiquarian [æntɪˈkwɛərɪən] N anticuario(-a)

antiquated [ˈæntɪkweɪtɪd] ADJ anticuado

★antique [ænˈtiːk] N antigüedad f ▸ ADJ antiguo

antique dealer N anticuario(-a)

antique shop N tienda de antigüedades

antiquity [ænˈtɪkwɪtɪ] N antigüedad f

anti-Semitic [ˈæntɪsɪˈmɪtɪk] ADJ antisemita

anti-Semitism [æntɪˈsɛmɪtɪzəm] N antisemitismo

antiseptic [æntɪˈsɛptɪk] ADJ, N antiséptico

antishake [ˈæntɪʃeɪk] ADJ estabilizador

antisocial [æntɪˈsəuʃəl] ADJ antisocial

antitank [æntɪˈtæŋk] ADJ antitanque

antithesis [ænˈtɪθɪsɪs] (pl **antitheses** [-siːz]) N antítesis f inv

antitrust [æntɪˈtrʌst] ADJ: **~ legislation** legislación f antimonopolio

antiviral [æntɪˈvaɪərəl] ADJ (Med) antivírico

antivirus [æntɪˈvaɪərəs] ADJ antivirus; **~ software** antivirus m

antlers [ˈæntləz] NPL cornamenta

anus [ˈeɪnəs] N ano

anvil [ˈænvɪl] N yunque m

anxiety [æŋˈzaɪətɪ] N (worry) inquietud f; (eagerness) ansia, anhelo

anxious [ˈæŋkʃəs] ADJ (worried) inquieto; (keen) deseoso; **to be ~ to do** tener muchas ganas de hacer; **I'm very ~ about you** me tienes muy preocupado

anxiously [ˈæŋkʃəslɪ] ADV con inquietud, de manera angustiada

any [ˈɛnɪ]

ADJ **1** (in questions etc) algún/alguna; **have you any butter/children?** ¿tienes mantequilla/hijos?; **if there are any tickets left** si quedan billetes, si queda algún billete

2 (with negative): **I haven't any money/books** no tengo dinero/libros

3 (no matter which) cualquier; **any excuse will do** valdrá or servirá cualquier excusa; **choose any book you like** escoge el libro que quieras; **any teacher you ask will tell you** cualquier profesor al que preguntes te lo dirá

4 (in phrases): **in any case** de todas formas, en cualquier caso; **any day now** cualquier día (de estos); **at any moment** en cualquier momento, de un momento a otro; **at any rate** en todo caso; **any time: come (at) any time** ven cuando quieras; **he might come (at) any time** podría llegar de un momento a otro

▸ PRON **1** (in questions etc): **have you got any?** ¿tienes alguno/a?; **can any of you sing?** ¿sabe cantar alguno de vosotros/ustedes?

2 (with negative): **I haven't any (of them)** no tengo ninguno

3 (no matter which one(s)): **take any of those books (you like)** toma el libro que quieras de esos

▸ ADV **1** (in questions etc): **do you want any more soup/sandwiches?** ¿quieres más sopa/bocadillos?; **are you feeling any better?** ¿te sientes algo mejor?

2 (with negative): **I can't hear him any more** ya no le oigo; **don't wait any longer** no esperes más

In questions and negative sentences, *any* is usually not translated:
Have you got any change? **¿Tienes cambio?**
He hasn't got any friends. **No tiene amigos**.
Use **algún/alguna** followed by a singular noun in questions where *any* is used with plural nouns: *Do you speak any foreign languages?* **¿Hablas algún idioma extranjero?**
Use **cualquier** in affirmative sentences: *Any teacher will tell you that.* **Cualquier profesor te lo dirá**.

★**anybody** [ˈɛnɪbɔdɪ] PRON cualquiera, cualquier persona; (*in interrogative sentences*) alguien; (*in negative sentences*) **I don't see ~** no veo a nadie

anyhow [ˈɛnɪhau] ADV de todos modos, de todas maneras; (*carelessly*) de cualquier manera; (*haphazardly*) de cualquier modo; **I shall go ~** iré de todas maneras

★**anyone** [ˈɛnɪwʌn] PRON = **anybody**

anyplace [ˈɛnɪpleɪs] ADV (*US*) = **anywhere**

★**anything** [ˈɛnɪθɪŋ] PRON cualquier cosa; (*in interrogative sentences*) algo; (*in negative sentences*) nada; (*everything*) todo; **~ else?** ¿algo más?; **can you see ~?** ¿ves algo?; **he'll eat ~** come de todo or lo que sea; **it can cost ~ between £15 and £20** puede costar entre 15 y 20 libras

anytime [ˈɛnɪtaɪm] ADV (*at any moment*) en cualquier momento, de un momento a otro; (*whenever*) no importa cuándo, cuando quiera

★**anyway** [ˈɛnɪweɪ] ADV (*at any rate*) de todos modos, de todas formas; (*besides*) además; **~, I couldn't come even if I wanted to** además, no podría venir aunque quisiera; **I shall go ~** iré de todos modos; **why are you phoning, ~?** ¿entonces, por qué llamas?, ¿por qué llamas, pues?

★**anywhere** [ˈɛnɪwɛəʳ] ADV dondequiera; (*interrogative*) en algún sitio; (*negative sense*) en ningún sitio; (*everywhere*) en or por todas partes; **I don't see him ~** no le veo en ningún sitio; **are you going ~?** ¿vas a algún sitio?; **~ in the world** en cualquier parte del mundo

Anzac [ˈænzæk] N ABBR = **Australia-New Zealand Army Corps**

Anzac Day N *ver nota*

El 25 de abril es uno de los festivos más importantes en Australia y Nueva Zelanda, durante el cual se rinde homenaje a los caídos en la batalla de Galípoli, en 1915, durante la Primera Guerra Mundial. **ANZAC** (acrónimo de *Australia-New Zealand Army Corps*) era el nombre que recibían las tropas conjuntas de Australia y Nueva Zelanda.

apace [əˈpeɪs] ADV aprisa

★**apart** [əˈpɑːt] ADV aparte, separadamente; **10 miles ~** separados por 10 millas; **to take ~** desmontar; **~ from** *prep* aparte de

apartheid [əˈpɑːteɪt] N apartheid *m*

★**apartment** [əˈpɑːtmənt] N (*US*) piso, departamento (*LAM*), apartamento; (*room*) cuarto

apartment block, apartment building N (*US*) bloque *m* de apartamentos

apathetic [æpəˈθɛtɪk] ADJ apático, indiferente

apathy [ˈæpəθɪ] N apatía, indiferencia

APB N ABBR (*US: police expression*: = *all points bulletin*) expresión usada por la policía que significa "descubrir y aprehender al sospechoso"

ape [eɪp] N mono ▸ VT imitar, remedar

Apennines [ˈæpənaɪnz] NPL: **the ~** los Apeninos *mpl*

aperitif [əˈpɛrɪtiːf] N aperitivo

aperture [ˈæpətʃuəʳ] N rendija, resquicio; (*Phot*) abertura

apex [ˈeɪpɛks] N ápice *m*; (*fig*) cumbre *f*

aphid [ˈeɪfɪd] N pulgón *m*

aphorism [ˈæfərɪzəm] N aforismo

aphrodisiac [æfrəuˈdɪzɪæk] ADJ, N afrodisíaco

API N ABBR = **American Press Institute**

apiece [əˈpiːs] ADV cada uno

aplomb [əˈplɔm] N aplomo, confianza

Apocalypse [əˈpɔkəlɪps] N Apocalipsis *m*

apocryphal [əˈpɔkrɪfəl] ADJ apócrifo

apolitical [eɪpəˈlɪtɪkl] ADJ apolítico

apologetic [əpɔləˈdʒɛtɪk] ADJ (*look, remark*) de disculpa

apologetically [əpɔləˈdʒɛtɪkəlɪ] ADV con aire de disculpa, excusándose, disculpándose

★**apologize** [əˈpɔlədʒaɪz] VI: **to ~ (for sth to sb)** disculparse (con algn por algo)

apology [əˈpɔlədʒɪ] N disculpa, excusa; **please accept my apologies** le ruego me disculpe

apoplectic [æpəˈplɛktɪk] ADJ (*Med*) apoplético; (*inf*): **~ with rage** furioso

apoplexy [ˈæpəplɛksɪ] N apoplejía

apostle [əˈpɔsl] N apóstol *mf*

★**apostrophe** [əˈpɔstrəfɪ] N apóstrofo *m*

app N ABBR (*inf: Comput*: = *application*) aplicación *f*

appal [əˈpɔːl] VT horrorizar, espantar

Appalachian Mountains [æpəˈleɪʃən-] NPL: **the ~** los (Montes) Apalaches

appalling [əˈpɔːlɪŋ] ADJ espantoso; (*awful*) pésimo; **she's an ~ cook** es una cocinera malísima

apparatus [æpəˈreɪtəs] N (*equipment*) equipo; (*organization*) aparato; (*in gymnasium*) aparatos *mpl*

apparel [əˈpærl] N (*US*) indumentaria

apparent [əˈpærənt] ADJ aparente; (*obvious*) manifiesto, evidente; **it is ~ that** está claro que

★**apparently** [əˈpærəntlɪ] ADV por lo visto, al parecer, dizque (*LAM*)

apparition [æpəˈrɪʃən] N aparición *f*

★**appeal** [əˈpiːl] VI (*Law*) apelar; **to ~ for** solicitar; **to ~ to** (*person*) rogar a, suplicar a; (*thing*) atraer, interesar; **to ~ to sb for mercy** rogar misericordia a algn; **it doesn't ~ to me** no me atrae, no me llama la atención ▸ N (*Law*) apelación *f*; (*request*) llamamiento, llamado (*LAM*); (*plea*) petición f; (charm) atractivo, encanto; **right of ~** derecho de apelación

appealing [əˈpiːlɪŋ] ADJ (nice) atractivo; (touching) conmovedor(a), emocionante

★**appear** [əˈpɪəʳ] VI aparecer, presentarse; (Law) comparecer; (publication) salir (a luz), publicarse; (seem) parecer; **to ~ on TV/in "Hamlet"** salir por la tele/hacer un papel en "Hamlet"; **it would ~ that** parecería que

★**appearance** [əˈpɪərəns] N aparición f; (look, aspect) apariencia, aspecto; **to keep up appearances** salvar las apariencias; **to all appearances** al parecer

appease [əˈpiːz] VT (pacify) apaciguar; (satisfy) satisfacer

appeasement [əˈpiːzmənt] N (Pol) apaciguamiento

append [əˈpend] VT (Comput) añadir (al final)

appendage [əˈpendɪdʒ] N añadidura

appendices [əˈpendɪsiːz] NPL of **appendix**

appendicitis [əpendɪˈsaɪtɪs] N apendicitis f

appendix [əˈpendɪks] (pl **appendices** [-dɪsiːz]) N apéndice m; **to have one's ~ out** operarse de apendicitis

appetite [ˈæpɪtaɪt] N apetito; (fig) deseo, anhelo; **that walk has given me an ~** ese paseo me ha abierto el apetito

appetizer [ˈæpɪtaɪzəʳ] N (drink) aperitivo; (food) tapas fpl (SP)

appetizing [ˈæpɪtaɪzɪŋ] ADJ apetitoso

applaud [əˈplɔːd] VT, VI aplaudir

applause [əˈplɔːz] N aplausos mpl

★**apple** [ˈæpl] N manzana

> Don't confuse **la manzana**, the fruit, with **el manzano**, which is the tree.

apple pie N pastel m de manzana, pay m de manzana (LAM)

apple tree N manzano

appliance [əˈplaɪəns] N aparato; **electrical appliances** electrodomésticos mpl

applicable [əˈplɪkəbl] ADJ aplicable, pertinente; **the law is ~ from January** la ley es aplicable or se pone en vigor a partir de enero; **to be ~ to** referirse a

applicant [ˈæplɪkənt] N candidato(-a); solicitante mf

★**application** [æplɪˈkeɪʃən] N (also Comput) aplicación f; (for a job, a grant etc) solicitud f

application form N solicitud f

application program N (Comput) (programa m de) aplicación f

applications package N (Comput) paquete m de programas de aplicación

applied [əˈplaɪd] ADJ (science, art) aplicado

★**apply** [əˈplaɪ] VT: **to ~ (to)** aplicar (a); (fig) emplear (para); **to ~ the brakes** echar el freno; **to ~ o.s. to** aplicarse a, dedicarse a ▶ VI: **to ~ to** (ask) dirigirse a; (be suitable for) ser aplicable a; (be relevant to) tener que ver con; **to ~ for** (permit, grant, job) solicitar

appoint [əˈpɔɪnt] VT (to post) nombrar; (date, place) fijar, señalar

appointee [əpɔɪnˈtiː] N persona nombrada

★**appointment** [əˈpɔɪntmənt] N (engagement) cita; (date) compromiso; (act) nombramiento; (post) puesto; **to make an ~ (with)** (doctor) pedir hora (con); (friend) citarse (con); **"appointments"** "ofertas de trabajo"; **by ~** mediante cita

apportion [əˈpɔːʃən] VT repartir

appraisal [əˈpreɪzl] N evaluación f

appraise [əˈpreɪz] VT (value) tasar, valorar; (situation etc) evaluar

appreciable [əˈpriːʃəbl] ADJ sensible

appreciably [əˈpriːʃəblɪ] ADV sensiblemente, de manera apreciable

★**appreciate** [əˈpriːʃɪeɪt] VT (like) apreciar, tener en mucho; (be grateful for) agradecer; (be aware of) comprender; **I appreciated your help** agradecí tu ayuda ▶ VI (Comm) aumentar en valor

appreciation [əpriːʃɪˈeɪʃən] N apreciación f; (gratitude) reconocimiento, agradecimiento; (Comm) aumento en valor

appreciative [əˈpriːʃɪətɪv] ADJ agradecido

apprehend [æprɪˈhend] VT percibir; (arrest) detener

apprehension [æprɪˈhenʃən] N (fear) aprensión f

apprehensive [æprɪˈhensɪv] ADJ aprensivo

apprentice [əˈprentɪs] N aprendiz(a) m/f ▶ VT: **to be apprenticed to** estar de aprendiz con

apprenticeship [əˈprentɪsʃɪp] N aprendizaje m; **to serve one's ~** hacer el aprendizaje

appro. [ˈæprəu] ABBR (BRIT Comm: inf) see **approval**

★**approach** [əˈprəutʃ] VI acercarse ▶ VT acercarse a; (be approximate) aproximarse a; (ask, apply to) dirigirse a; (problem) abordar; **to ~ sb about sth** hablar con algn sobre algo ▶ N acercamiento; aproximación f; (access) acceso; (proposal) proposición f; (to problem etc) enfoque m

approachable [əˈprəutʃəbl] ADJ (person) abordable; (place) accesible

approach road N vía de acceso

approbation [æprəˈbeɪʃən] N aprobación f

★**appropriate** ADJ [əˈprəuprɪɪt] apropiado, conveniente; **~ for or to** apropiado para; **it would not be ~ for me to comment** no estaría bien or sería pertinente que yo diera mi opinión ▶ VT [əˈprəuprɪeɪt] (take) apropiarse de; (allot): **to ~ sth for** destinar algo a

appropriation [əprəuprɪˈeɪʃən] N asignación f

★**approval** [əˈpruːvəl] N aprobación f, visto bueno; **on ~** (Comm) a prueba; **to meet with sb's ~** obtener la aprobación de algn

★**approve** [əˈpruːv] VT aprobar

▶ **approve of** VT FUS aprobar; **they don't ~ of her** (ella) no les parece bien

approved school [ə'pru:vd-] N (BRIT) correccional m

approx. ABBR (= approximately) aprox.

approximate [ə'prɔksɪmɪt] ADJ aproximado

approximately [ə'prɔksɪmɪtlɪ] ADV aproximadamente, más o menos

approximation [əprɔksɪ'meɪʃən] N aproximación f

apr N ABBR (= annual percentage rate) tasa de interés anual

apricot ['eɪprɪkɔt] N albaricoque m (SP), damasco (LAM)

★**April** ['eɪprəl] N abril m; see also **July**

April Fools' Day N ≈ día m de los (Santos) Inocentes

El 1 de abril es **April Fools' Day** en la tradición anglosajona. Tal día se les gastan bromas a los más desprevenidos, quienes reciben la denominación de April Fool (= inocente), y tanto la prensa escrita como la televisión difunden alguna historia falsa con la que sumarse al espíritu del día.

apron ['eɪprən] N delantal m; (Aviat) pista

apse [æps] N (Arch) ábside m

apt [æpt] ADJ (to the point) acertado, oportuno; (appropriate) apropiado; **~ to do** (likely) propenso a hacer

apt. ABBR = **apartment**

aptitude ['æptɪtju:d] N aptitud f, capacidad f

aptitude test N prueba de aptitud

aptly ['æptlɪ] ADJ acertadamente

aqualung ['ækwəlʌŋ] N escafandra autónoma

aquarium [ə'kwɛərɪəm] N acuario

Aquarius [ə'kwɛərɪəs] N Acuario

aquatic [ə'kwætɪk] ADJ acuático

aqueduct ['ækwɪdʌkt] N acueducto

AR ABBR (US) = **Arkansas**

ARA N ABBR (BRIT) = **Associate of the Royal Academy**

Arab ['ærəb] ADJ, N árabe mf

Arabia [ə'reɪbɪə] N Arabia

Arabian [ə'reɪbɪən] ADJ árabe, arábigo

Arabian Desert N Desierto de Arabia

Arabian Sea N mar m de Omán

Arabic ['ærəbɪk] ADJ (language, manuscripts) árabe, arábigo; **~ numerals** numeración f arábiga ▶ N árabe m

arable ['ærəbl] ADJ cultivable

Aragon ['ærəgən] N Aragón m

ARAM N ABBR (BRIT) = **Associate of the Royal Academy of Music**

arbiter ['ɑ:bɪtəʳ] N árbitro(-a)

arbitrary ['ɑ:bɪtrərɪ] ADJ arbitrario

arbitrate ['ɑ:bɪtreɪt] VI arbitrar

arbitration [ɑ:bɪ'treɪʃən] N arbitraje m; **the dispute went to ~** el conflicto laboral fue sometido al arbitraje

arbitrator ['ɑ:bɪtreɪtəʳ] N árbitro(-a)

ARC N ABBR = **American Red Cross**

arc [ɑːk] N arco

arcade [ɑː'keɪd] N (Arch) arcada; (round a square) soportales mpl; (shopping arcade) galería comercial

arch [ɑːtʃ] N arco; (vault) bóveda; (of foot) puente m ▶ VT arquear

archaeological [ɑːkɪə'lɔdʒɪkl] ADJ arqueológico

archaeologist [ɑːkɪ'ɔlədʒɪst] N arqueólogo(-a)

archaeology [ɑːkɪ'ɔlədʒɪ] N arqueología

archaic [ɑː'keɪɪk] ADJ arcaico

archangel ['ɑːkeɪndʒəl] N arcángel m

archbishop [ɑːtʃ'bɪʃəp] N arzobispo

arched [ɑːtʃt] ADJ abovedado

archenemy ['ɑːtʃ'enəmɪ] N enemigo jurado

archeology etc [ɑːkɪ'ɔlədʒɪ] (US) N see **archaeology** etc

archer ['ɑːtʃəʳ] N arquero(-a)

archery ['ɑːtʃərɪ] N tiro al arco

archetypal ['ɑːkɪtaɪpəl] ADJ arquetípico

archetype ['ɑːkɪtaɪp] N arquetipo

archipelago [ɑːkɪ'pelɪgəu] N archipiélago

architect ['ɑːkɪtekt] N arquitecto(-a)

architectural [ɑːkɪ'tektʃərəl] ADJ arquitectónico

architecture ['ɑːkɪtektʃəʳ] N arquitectura

archive ['ɑːkaɪv] N (gen pl) archivo

archive file N (Comput) fichero archivado

archivist ['ɑːkɪvɪst] N archivero(-a)

archway ['ɑːtʃweɪ] N arco, arcada

ARCM N ABBR (BRIT) = **Associate of the Royal College of Music**

Arctic ['ɑːktɪk] ADJ ártico ▶ N: **the ~** el Ártico

Arctic Circle N Círculo Polar Ártico

Arctic Ocean N océano (Glacial) Ártico

ardent ['ɑːdənt] ADJ (desire) ardiente; (supporter, lover) apasionado

ardour, (US) **ardor** ['ɑːdəʳ] N ardor m, pasión f

arduous ['ɑːdjuəs] ADJ (gen) arduo; (journey) penoso

are [ɑːʳ] VB see **be**

★**area** ['ɛərɪə] N área; (Math etc) superficie f, extensión f; (zone) región f, zona; (of knowledge, experience) campo; **the London ~** la zona de Londres

area code N (US Tel) prefijo

arena [ə'riːnə] N arena; (of circus) pista; (for bullfight) plaza, ruedo

aren't [ɑːnt] = **are not**

★**Argentina** [ɑːdʒən'tiːnə] N Argentina

Argentinian [ɑːdʒən'tɪnɪən] ADJ, N argentino(-a) m/f

arguable [ˈɑːgjuəbl] ADJ: **it is ~ whether ...** es dudoso que+*subjun*

arguably [ˈɑːgjuəblɪ] ADV: **it is ~ ...** es discutiblemente ...

★**argue** [ˈɑːgjuː] VT (*debate: case, matter*) mantener, argüir; **to ~ that** sostener que ▶ VI (*quarrel*) discutir; (*reason*) razonar, argumentar; **to ~ about sth (with sb)** pelearse (con algn) por algo

★**argument** [ˈɑːgjumənt] N (*reasons*) argumento; (*quarrel*) discusión *f*; (*debate*) debate *m*; **~ for/ against** argumento en pro/contra de

argumentative [ɑːgjuˈmɛntətɪv] ADJ discutidor(a)

aria [ˈɑːrɪə] N (*Mus*) aria

ARIBA N ABBR (*BRIT*) = **Associate of the Royal Institute of British Architects**

arid [ˈærɪd] ADJ árido

aridity [əˈrɪdɪtɪ] N aridez *f*

Aries [ˈɛərɪz] N Aries *m*

arise [əˈraɪz] (*pt* **arose**, *pp* **arisen** [əˈrɪzn]) VI (*rise up*) levantarse, alzarse; (*emerge*) surgir, presentarse; **to ~ from** derivar de; **should the need ~** si fuera necesario

aristocracy [ærɪsˈtɒkrəsɪ] N aristocracia

aristocrat [ˈærɪstəkræt] N aristócrata *mf*

aristocratic [ərɪstəˈkrætɪk] ADJ aristocrático

arithmetic [əˈrɪθmətɪk] N aritmética

arithmetical [ærɪθˈmɛtɪkl] ADJ aritmético

Ark [ɑːk] N: **Noah's ~** el Arca *f* de Noé

★**arm** [ɑːm] N (*Anat*) brazo; **~ in ~** cogidos del brazo ▶ VT armar; *see also* **arms**

armaments [ˈɑːməmənts] NPL (*weapons*) armamentos *mpl*

armchair [ˈɑːmtʃɛəʳ] N sillón *m*, butaca

armed [ɑːmd] ADJ armado; **the ~ forces** las fuerzas armadas

armed robbery N robo a mano armada

Armenia [ɑːˈmiːnɪə] N Armenia

Armenian [ɑːˈmiːnɪən] ADJ armenio ▶ N armenio(-a); (*Ling*) armenio

armful [ˈɑːmful] N brazada

armistice [ˈɑːmɪstɪs] N armisticio

armour, (*US*) **armor** [ˈɑːməʳ] N armadura

armoured car, (*US*) **armored car** N coche *m* or (*LAm*) carro blindado

armoury, (*US*) **armory** [ˈɑːmərɪ] N arsenal *m*

armpit [ˈɑːmpɪt] N sobaco, axila

armrest [ˈɑːmrɛst] N reposabrazos *m inv*, brazo

arms [ɑːmz] NPL (*weapons*) armas *fpl*; (*Heraldry*) escudo *sg*

arms control N control *m* de armamentos

arms race N carrera de armamentos

★**army** [ˈɑːmɪ] N ejército; (*fig*) multitud *f*

A road N (*BRIT*) ≈ carretera *f* nacional

aroma [əˈrəumə] N aroma *m*, fragancia

aromatherapy [ərəuməˈθɛrəpɪ] N aromaterapia

aromatic [ærəˈmætɪk] ADJ aromático, fragante

arose [əˈrəuz] PT *of* **arise**

★**around** [əˈraund] ADV alrededor; (*in the area*) a la redonda ▶ PREP alrededor de

arousal [əˈrauzəl] N (*sexual*) excitación *f*; (*of feelings, interest*) despertar *m*

arouse [əˈrauz] VT despertar; (*anger*) provocar

★**arrange** [əˈreɪndʒ] VT arreglar, ordenar; (*programme*) organizar; (*appointment*) concertar; **it was arranged that ...** se quedó en que ... ▶ VI: **we have arranged for a taxi to pick you up** hemos organizado todo para que le recoja un taxi; **to ~ to do sth** quedar en hacer algo

arrangement [əˈreɪndʒmənt] N arreglo; (*agreement*) acuerdo; **to come to an ~ (with sb)** llegar a un acuerdo (con algn); **by ~** a convenir ◼ **arrangements** NPL (*plans*) planes *mpl*, medidas *fpl*; (*preparations*) preparativos *mpl*; **I'll make arrangements for you to be met** haré los preparativos para que le estén esperando

arrant [ˈærənt] ADJ: **~ nonsense** una verdadera tontería

array [əˈreɪ] N (*Comput*) matriz *f*; **~ of** (*things*) serie *f* or colección *f* de; (*people*) conjunto de

arrears [əˈrɪəz] NPL atrasos *mpl*; **in ~** (*Comm*) en mora; **to be in ~ with one's rent** estar retrasado en el pago del alquiler

★**arrest** [əˈrɛst] VT detener; (*sb's attention*) llamar ▶ N detención *f*; **under ~** detenido

arresting [əˈrɛstɪŋ] ADJ (*fig*) llamativo

arrival [əˈraɪvəl] N llegada, arribo (*LAm*); **new ~** recién llegado(-a)

★**arrive** [əˈraɪv] VI llegar, arribar (*LAm*) ▶ **arrive at** VT FUS (*decision, solution*) llegar a

arrogance [ˈærəgəns] N arrogancia, prepotencia (*LAm*)

arrogant [ˈærəgənt] ADJ arrogante, prepotente (*LAm*)

arrow [ˈærəu] N flecha

arse [ɑːs] N (*BRIT inf!*) culo, trasero

arsenal [ˈɑːsɪnl] N arsenal *m*

arsenic [ˈɑːsnɪk] N arsénico

arson [ˈɑːsn] N incendio provocado

★**art** [ɑːt] N arte *m*; (*skill*) destreza; (*technique*) técnica; **work of ~** obra de arte ◼ **Arts** NPL (*Scol*) Letras *fpl*

art and design N (*BRIT Scol*) arte *m* y diseño, dibujo

art college N escuela *f* de Bellas Artes

artefact [ˈɑːtɪfækt] N artefacto

arterial [ɑːˈtɪərɪəl] ADJ (*Anat*) arterial; (*road etc*) principal

artery [ˈɑːtərɪ] N (*Med: road etc*) arteria

artful [ˈɑːtful] ADJ (*cunning: person, trick*) mañoso

art gallery N pinacoteca, museo de pintura; (*Comm*) galería de arte

arthritis [ɑːˈθraɪtɪs] N artritis *f*

artichoke [ˈɑːtɪtʃəuk] N alcachofa; **Jerusalem ~** aguaturma

a

★**article** ['ɑːtɪkl] N artículo, objeto, cosa; (in news-paper) artículo; **articles of clothing** prendas fpl de vestir ■ **articles** NPL (BRIT Law: training) contrato sg de aprendizaje

articles of association NPL (Comm) estatutos mpl sociales, escritura social

articulate ADJ [ɑːˈtɪkjulɪt] (speech) claro; (person) que se expresa bien ▶ VI [ɑːˈtɪkjuleɪt] articular ▶ VT [ɑːˈtɪkjuleɪt] expresar

articulated lorry N (BRIT) trailer m

artifice ['ɑːtɪfɪs] N artificio, truco

artificial [ɑːtɪˈfɪʃəl] ADJ artificial; (teeth etc) postizo

artificial insemination N inseminación f artificial

artificial intelligence N inteligencia artificial

artificial respiration N respiración f artificial

artillery [ɑːˈtɪlərɪ] N artillería

artisan ['ɑːtɪzæn] N artesano(-a)

★**artist** ['ɑːtɪst] N artista mf; (Mus) intérprete mf

artistic [ɑːˈtɪstɪk] ADJ artístico

artistry ['ɑːtɪstrɪ] N arte m, habilidad f (artística)

artless ['ɑːtlɪs] ADJ (innocent) natural, sencillo; (clumsy) torpe

art school N escuela de bellas artes

artwork ['ɑːtwəːk] N material m gráfico

arty ['ɑːtɪ] ADJ artistoide

ARV N ABBR (= American Revised Version) traducción americana de la Biblia

AS N ABBR (US Scol) = **Associate in** or **of Science**

---

as [æz]

CONJ **1** (referring to time: while) mientras; (: when) cuando; **she wept as she told her story** lloraba mientras contaba lo que le ocurrió; **as the years go by** con el paso de los años, a medida que pasan los años; **he came in as I was leaving** entró cuando me marchaba; **as from tomorrow** a partir de or desde mañana
2 (in comparisons): **as big as** tan grande como; **twice as big as** el doble de grande que; **as much money/many books as** tanto dinero/tantos libros como; **as soon as** en cuanto, no bien (LAM)
3 (since, because) como, ya que; **as I don't speak German I can't understand him** como no hablo alemán no le entiendo, no le entiendo ya que no hablo alemán
4 (although): **much as I like them, ...** aunque me gustan, ...
5 (referring to manner, way): **do as you wish** haz lo que quieras; **as she said** como dijo; **it's on the left as you go in** según se entra, a la izquierda
6 (concerning): **as for** or **to that** por or en lo que respecta a eso
7: **as if** or **though** como si; **he looked as if he was ill** parecía como si estuviera enfermo,

tenía aspecto de enfermo; see also **long**; **such**; **well**

▶ PREP (in the capacity of): **he works as a barman** trabaja de barman; **as chairman of the company, he ...** como presidente de la compañía, ...; **he gave it to me as a present** me lo dio de regalo

---

ASA N ABBR (= American Standards Association) instituto de normalización; (BRIT: = Advertising Standards Authority) departamento de control de la publicidad; (= Amateur Swimming Association) federación amateur de natación

a.s.a.p. ABBR (= as soon as possible) cuanto antes, lo más pronto posible

asbestos [æzˈbɛstəs] N asbesto, amianto

ascend [əˈsɛnd] VT subir, ascender

ascendancy [əˈsɛndənsɪ] N ascendiente m, dominio

ascendant [əˈsɛndənt] N: **to be in the ~** estar en auge, ir ganando predominio

Ascension [əˈsɛnʃən] N: **the ~** la Ascensión

Ascension Island N Isla Ascensión

ascent [əˈsɛnt] N subida; (slope) cuesta, pendiente f; (of plane) ascenso

ascertain [æsəˈteɪn] VT averiguar

ascetic [əˈsɛtɪk] ADJ ascético

asceticism [əˈsɛtɪsɪzəm] N ascetismo

ASCII ['æskiː] N ABBR (= American Standard Code for Information Interchange) ASCII

ascribe [əˈskraɪb] VT: **to ~ sth to** atribuir algo a

ASE N ABBR = **American Stock Exchange**

ASH [æʃ] N ABBR (BRIT: = Action on Smoking and Health) organización anti-tabaco

ash [æʃ] N ceniza; (tree) fresno

ashamed [əˈʃeɪmd] ADJ avergonzado; **to be ~ of** avergonzarse de

ashcan ['æʃkæn] N (US) cubo or (LAM) bote m de la basura

ashen ['æʃn] ADJ pálido

ashore [əˈʃɔːʳ] ADV en tierra; (swim etc) a tierra

ashtray ['æʃtreɪ] N cenicero

Ash Wednesday N miércoles m de Ceniza

★**Asia** ['eɪʃə] N Asia

Asian ['eɪʃən], **Asiatic** [eɪsɪˈætɪk] ADJ, N asiático(-a) m/f

aside [əˈsaɪd] ADV a un lado; **~ from** prep (as well as) aparte or además de ▶ N aparte m

★**ask** [ɑːsk] VT (question) preguntar; (demand) pedir; (invite) invitar; **to ~ sb sth/to do sth** preguntar algo a algn/pedir a algn que haga algo; **to ~ sb about sth** preguntar algo a algn; **to ~ (sb) a question** hacer una pregunta (a algn); **to ~ sb the time** preguntar la hora a algn; **to ~ sb out to dinner** invitar a cenar a algn ▶ VI: **to ~ about sth** preguntar acerca de algo
▶ **ask after** VT FUS preguntar por
▶ **ask for** VT FUS pedir; **it's just asking for trouble** or **for it** es buscarse problemas

ask can be translated by **preguntar** or **pedir**. Use **preguntar** for contexts in which someone wants to find out information: *Ask her what she thinks*. **Pregúntale qué le parece.** Use **pedir** when *ask* means *request* or *demand*: *I wasn't asked for any ID*. **No me pidieron identificación.**

askance [əˈskɑːns] ADV: **to look ~ at sb** mirar con recelo a algn

askew [əˈskjuː] ADV sesgado, ladeado

asking price N (*Comm*) precio inicial

★**asleep** [əˈsliːp] ADJ dormido; **to fall ~** dormirse, quedarse dormido

AS level N ABBR (*Brit Scol*: = *Advanced Subsidiary level*) título intermedio entre los "GCSEs" y los "A levels"

asp [æsp] N áspid m

asparagus [əsˈpærəgəs] N espárragos mpl

ASPCA N ABBR = **American Society for the Prevention of Cruelty to Animals**

★**aspect** [ˈæspɛkt] N aspecto, apariencia; (*direction in which a building etc faces*) orientación f

aspersions [əsˈpɜːʃənz] NPL: **to cast ~ on** difamar a, calumniar a

asphalt [ˈæsfælt] N asfalto

asphyxiate [æsˈfɪksɪeɪt] VT asfixiar

asphyxiation [aesfɪksɪˈeɪʃən] N asfixia

aspirate VT [ˈæspəreɪt] aspirar ▶ ADJ [ˈæspərɪt] aspirado

aspirations [æspəˈreɪʃənz] NPL aspiraciones fpl; (*ambition*) ambición f

aspire [əsˈpaɪəˀ] VI: **to ~ to** aspirar a, ambicionar

aspirin [ˈæsprɪn] N aspirina

aspiring [əsˈpaɪərɪŋ] ADJ: **an ~ actor** un aspirante a actor

ass [æs] N asno, burro; (*inf*) imbécil mf; (*US inf!*) culo, trasero

assailant [əˈseɪlənt] N agresor(a) m/f

assassin [əˈsæsɪn] N asesino(-a)

assassinate [əˈsæsɪneɪt] VT asesinar

assassination [əsæsɪˈneɪʃən] N asesinato

assault [əˈsɔːlt] N (*gen: attack*) asalto; (*Law*) agresión f ▶ VT asaltar, agredir; (*sexually*) violar

assemble [əˈsɛmbl] VT reunir, juntar; (*Tech*) montar ▶ VI reunirse, juntarse

assembly [əˈsɛmblɪ] N (*meeting*) reunión f, asamblea; (*parliament*) parlamento; (*construction*) montaje m

assembly language N (*Comput*) lenguaje m ensamblador

assembly line N cadena de montaje

Assembly Member N (*in Wales*) miembro mf de la Asamblea Nacional (de Gales)

assent [əˈsɛnt] N asentimiento, aprobación f ▶ VI consentir, asentir; **to ~ (to sth)** consentir (en algo)

assert [əˈsɜːt] VT afirmar; (*insist on*) hacer valer; **to ~ o.s.** imponerse

assertion [əˈsɜːʃən] N afirmación f

assertive [əˈsɜːtɪv] ADJ enérgico, agresivo, perentorio

assess [əˈsɛs] VT valorar, calcular; (*tax, damages*) fijar; (*property etc: for tax*) gravar

assessment [əˈsɛsmənt] N valoración f; gravamen m; (*judgment*): **~ (of)** juicio (sobre)

assessor [əˈsɛsəˀ] N asesor(a) m/f; (*of tax*) tasador(a) m/f

asset [ˈæsɛt] N posesión f; (*quality*) ventaja ■ **assets** NPL (*funds*) activo sg, fondos mpl

asset-stripping [ˈæsɛtˈstrɪpɪŋ] N (*Comm*) acaparamiento de activos

assiduous [əˈsɪdjuəs] ADJ asiduo

assign [əˈsaɪn] VT (*date*) fijar; (*task*) asignar; (*resources*) destinar; (*property*) traspasar

assignment [əˈsaɪnmənt] N asignación f; (*task*) tarea

assimilate [əˈsɪmɪleɪt] VT asimilar

assimilation [əsɪmɪˈleɪʃən] N asimilación f

assist [əˈsɪst] VT ayudar

assistance [əˈsɪstəns] N ayuda, auxilio

★**assistant** [əˈsɪstənt] N ayudante mf; (*Brit: also:* **shop assistant**) dependiente(-a) m/f

assistant manager N subdirector(a) m/f

assizes [əˈsaɪzɪz] NPL sesión f de un tribunal

associate ADJ, N [əˈsəuʃɪɪt] asociado(-a); socio(-a), colega mf; (*in crime*) cómplice mf; (*member*) miembro(-a); **~ director** subdirector(a) m/f ▶ VT [əˈsəuʃɪeɪt] asociar; (*ideas*) relacionar; **associated company** compañía afiliada ▶ VI [əˈsəuʃɪeɪt]: **to ~ with sb** tratar con algn

association [əsəuʃɪˈeɪʃən] N asociación f; (*Comm*) sociedad f; **in ~ with** en asociación con

association football N (*Brit*) fútbol m

assorted [əˈsɔːtɪd] ADJ surtido, variado; **in ~ sizes** en distintos tamaños

assortment [əˈsɔːtmənt] N (*of shapes, colours*) surtido; (*of books*) colección f; (*of people*) mezcla

Asst. ABBR = **assistant**

assuage [əˈsweɪdʒ] VT mitigar

assume [əˈsjuːm] VT (*suppose*) suponer; (*responsibilities etc*) asumir; (*attitude, name*) adoptar, tomar

assumed name [əˈsjuːmd-] N nombre m falso

assumption [əˈsʌmpʃən] N (*supposition*) suposición f, presunción f; (*act*) asunción f; **on the ~ that** suponiendo que

assurance [əˈʃuərəns] N garantía, promesa; (*confidence*) confianza, aplomo; (*Brit: insurance*) seguro; **I can give you no assurances** no puedo hacerle ninguna promesa

assure [əˈʃuəˀ] VT asegurar

assured [əˈʃuəd] ADJ seguro

assuredly [əˈʃuərɪdlɪ] ADV indudablemente

AST ABBR (= *Atlantic Standard Time*) hora oficial del este del Canadá

asterisk [ˈæstərɪsk] N asterisco

astern [əˈstɜːn] ADV a popa

asteroid [ˈæstərɔɪd] N asteroide *m*

★**asthma** [ˈæsmə] N asma

asthmatic [æsˈmætɪk] ADJ, N asmático(-a) *m/f*

astigmatism [əˈstɪɡmətɪzəm] N astigmatismo

astir [əˈstɜːʳ] ADV en acción

astonish [əˈstɒnɪʃ] VT asombrar, pasmar

astonished [əˈstɒnɪʃt] ADJ estupefacto, pasmado; **to be ~ (at)** asombrarse (de)

astonishing [əˈstɒnɪʃɪŋ] ADJ asombroso, pasmoso; **I find it ~ that ...** me asombra *or* pasma que ...

astonishingly [əˈstɒnɪʃɪŋlɪ] ADV increíblemente, asombrosamente

astonishment [əˈstɒnɪʃmənt] N asombro, sorpresa; **to my ~** con gran sorpresa mía

astound [əˈstaʊnd] VT asombrar, pasmar

astounding [əˈstaʊndɪŋ] ADJ asombroso

astray [əˈstreɪ] ADV: **to go ~** extraviarse; **to lead ~** llevar por mal camino; **to go ~ in one's calculations** equivocarse en sus cálculos

astride [əˈstraɪd] PREP a caballo *or* horcajadas sobre

astringent [əsˈtrɪndʒənt] ADJ, N astringente *m*

astrologer [əsˈtrɒlədʒəʳ] N astrólogo(-a)

astrology [əsˈtrɒlədʒɪ] N astrología

astronaut [ˈæstrənɔːt] N astronauta *mf*

astronomer [əsˈtrɒnəməʳ] N astrónomo(-a)

astronomical [æstrəˈnɒmɪkəl] ADJ astronómico

astronomy [æesˈtrɒnəmɪ] N astronomía

astrophysics [ˈæstrəʊˈfɪzɪks] N astrofísica

astute [əsˈtjuːt] ADJ astuto

asunder [əˈsʌndəʳ] ADV: **to tear ~** hacer pedazos

ASV N ABBR (= *American Standard Version*) traducción de la Biblia

asylum [əˈsaɪləm] N (*refuge*) asilo; (*hospital*) manicomio; **to seek political ~** pedir asilo político

asymmetric [eɪsɪˈmɛtrɪk], **asymmetrical** [eɪsɪˈmɛtrɪkl] ADJ asimétrico

---

at [æt]

PREP 1 (*referring to position*) en; (*direction*) a; **at the top** en lo alto; **at home/school** en casa/la escuela; **to look at sth/sb** mirar algo/a algn 2 (*referring to time*): **at four o'clock** a las cuatro; **at night** por la noche; **at Christmas** en Navidad; **at times** a veces

3 (*referring to rates, speed etc*): **at £1 a kilo** a una libra el kilo; **two at a time** de dos en dos; **at 50 km/h** a 50 km/h

4 (*referring to manner*): **at a stroke** de un golpe; **at peace** en paz

5 (*referring to activity*): **to be at work** estar trabajando; (*in office*) estar en el trabajo; **to play at cowboys** jugar a los vaqueros; **to be good at sth** ser bueno en algo

6 (*referring to cause*): **shocked/surprised/annoyed at sth** asombrado/sorprendido/fastidiado por algo; **I went at his suggestion** fui a instancias suyas

▶ N (*symbol @*) arroba

ate [ɛt, eɪt] PT *of* **eat**

atheism [ˈeɪθɪɪzəm] N ateísmo

atheist [ˈeɪθɪɪst] N ateo(-a)

Athenian [əˈθiːnɪən] ADJ, N ateniense *mf*

Athens [ˈæθɪnz] N Atenas *f*

★**athlete** [ˈæθliːt] N atleta *mf*

athletic [æθˈlɛtɪk] ADJ atlético

athletics [æθˈlɛtɪks] N atletismo

★**Atlantic** [ətˈlæntɪk] ADJ atlántico ▶ N: **the ~ (Ocean)** el (océano) Atlántico

★**atlas** [ˈætləs] N atlas *m inv*

Atlas Mountains NPL: **the ~** el Atlas

ATM N ABBR (= *Automated Telling Machine*) cajero automático

atmosphere [ˈætməsfɪəʳ] N (*air*) atmósfera; (*fig*) ambiente *m*

atom [ˈætəm] N átomo

atom bomb N bomba atómica

atomic [əˈtɒmɪk] ADJ atómico

atomic bomb N bomba atómica

atomic power N energía atómica

atomizer [ˈætəmaɪzəʳ] N atomizador *m*

atone [əˈtəʊn] VI: **to ~ for** expiar

atonement [əˈtəʊnmənt] N expiación *f*

A to Z® N guía alfabética; (*map*) callejero

ATP N ABBR (= *Association of Tennis Professionals*) sindicato de jugadores de tenis profesionales

atrocious [əˈtrəʊʃəs] ADJ atroz; (*fig*) horrible, infame

atrocity [əˈtrɒsɪtɪ] N atrocidad *f*

atrophy [ˈætrəfɪ] N atrofia ▶ VI atrofiarse

★**attach** [əˈtætʃ] VT sujetar; (*stick*) pegar; (*document, email, letter*) adjuntar; **to be attached to sb/sth** (*like*) tener cariño a algn/algo; **the attached letter** la carta adjunta

attaché [əˈtæʃeɪ] N agregado(-a)

attaché case N (*BRIT*) maletín *m*

attachment [əˈtætʃmənt] N (*tool*) accesorio; (*Comput*) archivo *o* documento adjunto; (*love*): **~ (to)** apego (a), cariño (a)

attack [əˈtæk] VT (*Mil*) atacar; (*criminal*) agredir, asaltar; (*criticize*) criticar; (*task etc*) emprender ▶ N ataque *m*, asalto; (*on sb's life*) atentado; (*fig: criticism*) crítica; **heart ~** infarto (de miocardio)

attacker [əˈtækəʳ] N agresor(a) *m/f*, asaltante *mf*

attain [əˈteɪn] VT (*also:* **attain to**) alcanzar; (*achieve*) lograr, conseguir

attainments [əˈteɪnmənts] NPL (*skill*) talento *sg*

★**attempt** [əˈtɛmpt] N tentativa, intento; (*attack*) atentado; **he made no ~ to help** ni siquiera intentó ayudar ▶ VT intentar, tratar de

attempted [ə'tɛmptɪd] ADJ: **~ murder/burglary/suicide** tentativa or intento de asesinato/robo/suicidio

attend [ə'tɛnd] VT asistir a; (patient) atender ▸ **attend to** VT FUS (needs, affairs etc) ocuparse de; (speech etc) prestar atención a; (customer) atender a

attendance [ə'tɛndəns] N asistencia, presencia; (people present) concurrencia

attendant [ə'tɛndənt] N sirviente(-a) m/f, ayudante mf; (Theat) acomodador(a) m/f ▸ ADJ concomitante

★**attention** [ə'tɛnʃən] N atención f; **for the ~ of ...** (Admin) a la atención de ...; **it has come to my ~ that ...** me he enterado de que ... ▸ EXCL (Mil) ¡firme(s)!

attentive [ə'tɛntɪv] ADJ atento; (polite) cortés

attenuate [ə'tɛnjueɪt] VT atenuar

attest [ə'tɛst] VI: **to ~ to** dar fe de

attic ['ætɪk] N desván m, altillo (LAM), entretecho (LAM)

attitude ['ætɪtju:d] N (gen) actitud f; (disposition) disposición f

attorney [ə'tɜ:nɪ] N (US: lawyer) abogado(-a); (having proxy) apoderado

Attorney General N (BRIT) ≈ fiscal mf general del Estado; (US) ≈ ministro(-a) de Justicia

attract [ə'trækt] VT atraer; (attention) llamar

attraction [ə'trækʃən] N (gen) encanto, atractivo; (Physics) atracción f; (towards sth) atracción f

★**attractive** [ə'træktɪv] ADJ atractivo

attribute N ['ætrɪbju:t] atributo ▸ VT [ə'trɪbju:t]: **to ~ sth to** atribuir algo a; (accuse) achacar algo a

attrition [ə'trɪʃən] N: **war of ~** guerra de agotamiento or desgaste

Atty. Gen. ABBR = **Attorney General**

ATV N ABBR (= all terrain vehicle) vehículo todo terreno

atypical [eɪ'tɪpɪkl] ADJ atípico

AU N ABBR (= African Union) UA f (= Unión Africana)

aubergine ['əubəʒi:n] N (BRIT) berenjena; (colour) morado

auburn ['ɔ:bən] ADJ color castaño rojizo

auction ['ɔ:kʃən] N (also: **sale by auction**) subasta ▸ VT subastar

auctioneer [ɔ:kʃə'nɪəʳ] N subastador(a) m/f

auction room N sala de subastas

audacious [ɔ:'deɪʃəs] ADJ (bold) audaz, osado; (impudent) atrevido, descarado

audacity [ɔ:'dæsɪtɪ] N audacia, atrevimiento; (pej) descaro

audible ['ɔ:dɪbl] ADJ audible, que se puede oír

★**audience** ['ɔ:dɪəns] N auditorio; (gathering) público; (Radio) radioescuchas mpl; (TV) telespectadores mpl; (interview) audiencia

audio-typist ['ɔ:dɪəu'taɪpɪst] N mecanógrafo(-a) de dictáfono

audiovisual [ɔ:dɪəu'vɪzjuəl] ADJ audiovisual

audiovisual aid N ayuda or medio audiovisual

audit ['ɔ:dɪt] VT revisar, intervenir

audition [ɔ:'dɪʃən] N audición f ▸ VI: **to ~ for the part of** hacer una audición para el papel de

auditor ['ɔ:dɪtəʳ] N interventor(a) m/f, censor(a) m/f de cuentas

auditorium [ɔ:dɪ'tɔ:rɪəm] N auditorio

Aug. ABBR (= August) ag.

augment [ɔ:g'mɛnt] VT, VI aumentar

augur ['ɔ:gəʳ] VI: **it augurs well** es de buen agüero

★**August** ['ɔ:gəst] N agosto; see also **July**

august [ɔ:'gʌst] ADJ augusto

★**aunt** [ɑ:nt] N tía

auntie, aunty ['ɑ:ntɪ] N DIMINUTIVE of **aunt**

★**au pair** ['əu'pɛəʳ] N (also: **au pair girl**) chica f au pair

aura ['ɔ:rə] N aura; (atmosphere) ambiente m

auspices ['ɔ:spɪsɪz] NPL: **under the ~ of** bajo los auspicios de

auspicious [ɔ:s'pɪʃəs] ADJ propicio, de buen augurio

austere [ɔs'tɪəʳ] ADJ austero; (manner) adusto

austerity [ɔ'stɛrɪtɪ] N austeridad f

Australasia [ɔ:strə'leɪzɪə] N Australasia

★**Australia** [ɔs'treɪlɪə] N Australia

Australian [ɔs'treɪlɪən] ADJ, N australiano(-a) m/f

★**Austria** ['ɔstrɪə] N Austria

Austrian ['ɔstrɪən] ADJ, N austríaco(-a) m/f

authentic [ɔ:'θɛntɪk] ADJ auténtico

authenticate [ɔ:'θɛntɪkeɪt] VT autentificar

authenticity [ɔ:θɛn'tɪsɪtɪ] N autenticidad f

★**author** ['ɔ:θəʳ] N autor(a) m/f

authoritarian [ɔ:θɔrɪ'tɛərɪən] ADJ autoritario

authoritative [ɔ:'θɔrɪtətɪv] ADJ autorizado; (manner) autoritario

authority [ɔ:'θɔrɪtɪ] N autoridad f; **to have ~ to do sth** tener autoridad para hacer algo ■ **the authorities** NPL las autoridades

authorization [ɔ:θəraɪ'zeɪʃən] N autorización f

authorize ['ɔ:θəraɪz] VT autorizar

authorized capital N (Comm) capital m autorizado or social

autistic [ɔ:'tɪstɪk] ADJ autista

auto ['ɔ:təu] N (US) coche m, carro (LAM), auto (LAM), automóvil m

autobiographical [ɔ:təbaɪə'græfɪkəl] ADJ autobiográfico

autobiography [ɔ:təbaɪ'ɔgrəfɪ] N autobiografía

autocratic [ɔ:tə'krætɪk] ADJ autocrático

Autocue® ['ɔ:təukju:] N autocue m, teleapuntador m

autograph ['ɔ:təgrɑ:f] N autógrafo ▸ VT firmar; (photo etc) dedicar

autoimmune [ɔ:təu'mju:n] ADJ autoinmune

automat [ˈɔːtəmæt] N (*US*) restaurante *m* de autoservicio

automate [ˈɔːtəmeɪt] VT automatizar

automated [ˈɔːtəmeɪtɪd] ADJ automatizado

★**automatic** [ɔːtəˈmætɪk] ADJ automático ▶ N (*gun*) pistola automática; (*washing machine*) lavadora

automatically [ɔːtəˈmætɪklɪ] ADV automáticamente

automatic data processing N proceso automático de datos

automation [ɔːtəˈmeɪʃən] N automatización *f*

automaton [ɔːˈtɔmətən] (*pl* **automata** [-tə]) N autómata

automobile [ˈɔːtəməbiːl] N (*US*) coche *m*, carro (*LAm*), auto (*LAm*), automóvil *m*

autonomous [ɔːˈtɔnəməs] ADJ autónomo

autonomy [ɔːˈtɔnəmɪ] N autonomía

autopsy [ˈɔːtɔpsɪ] N autopsia

★**autumn** [ˈɔːtəm] N otoño

auxiliary [ɔːɡˈzɪlɪərɪ] ADJ auxiliar

AV N ABBR (= *Authorized Version*) traducción inglesa de la Biblia ▶ ABBR = **audiovisual**

Av. ABBR (= *avenue*) Av., Avda

avail [əˈveɪl] VT: **to ~ o.s. of** aprovechar(se) de, valerse de ▶ N: **to no ~** en vano, sin resultado

availability [əveɪləˈbɪlɪtɪ] N disponibilidad *f*

★**available** [əˈveɪləbl] ADJ disponible; (*obtainable*) asequible; **to make sth ~ to sb** poner algo a la disposición de algn; **is the manager ~?** ¿está libre el gerente?

avalanche [ˈævəlɑːnʃ] N alud *m*, avalancha

avant-garde [ˈævɑ̃ˈɡɑːd] ADJ de vanguardia

avarice [ˈævərɪs] N avaricia

avaricious [ævəˈrɪʃəs] ADJ avaricioso

avatar [ˈævətɑːʳ] N (*Comput*) avatar *m*

avdp. ABBR = **avoirdupois**

Ave. ABBR (= *avenue*) Av., Avda

avenge [əˈvendʒ] VT vengar

avenue [ˈævənjuː] N avenida; (*fig*) camino, vía

★**average** [ˈævərɪdʒ] N promedio, media; **on ~** por término medio ▶ ADJ (*mean*) medio; (*ordinary*) regular, corriente ▶ VT alcanzar un promedio de
▶ **average out** VI: **to ~ out at** salir a un promedio de

averse [əˈvəːs] ADJ: **to be ~ to sth/doing** sentir aversión *or* antipatía por algo/por hacer

aversion [əˈvəːʃən] N aversión *f*, repugnancia

avert [əˈvəːt] VT prevenir; (*blow*) desviar; (*one's eyes*) apartar

aviary [ˈeɪvɪərɪ] N pajarera

aviation [eɪvɪˈeɪʃən] N aviación *f*

aviator [ˈeɪvɪeɪtəʳ] N aviador(a) *m/f*

avid [ˈævɪd] ADJ ávido, ansioso

avidly [ˈævɪdlɪ] ADV ávidamente, con avidez

avocado [ævəˈkɑːdəu] N (*BRIT: also:* **avocado pear**) aguacate *m*, palta (*LAm*)

★**avoid** [əˈvɔɪd] VT evitar, eludir

avoidable [əˈvɔɪdəbl] ADJ evitable, eludible

avoidance [əˈvɔɪdəns] N evasión *f*

avow [əˈvau] VT prometer

avowal [əˈvauəl] N promesa, voto

avowed [əˈvaud] ADJ declarado

AVP N ABBR (*US*) = **assistant vice-president**

avuncular [əˈvʌŋkjuləʳ] ADJ paternal

AWACS [ˈeɪwæks] N ABBR (= *airborne warning and control system*) AWACS *m*

await [əˈweɪt] VT esperar, aguardar; **long awaited** largamente esperado

awake [əˈweɪk] (*pt* **awoke** [əˈwəuk] *or* **awaked**, *pp* **awoken** [əˈwəukən] *or* **awaked**) ADJ despierto; **to be ~** estar despierto ▶ VT despertar ▶ VI despertarse

awakening [əˈweɪknɪŋ] N despertar *m*

award [əˈwɔːd] N (*prize*) premio; (*medal*) condecoración *f*; (*Law*) fallo, sentencia; (*act*) concesión *f* ▶ VT (*prize*) otorgar, conceder; (*Law: damages*) adjudicar

★**aware** [əˈwɛəʳ] ADJ consciente; (*awake*) despierto; (*informed*) enterado; **to become ~ of** darse cuenta de, enterarse de; **I am fully ~ that** sé muy bien que

awareness [əˈwɛənɪs] N conciencia, conocimiento

awash [əˈwɔʃ] ADJ inundado

★**away** [əˈweɪ] ADV (*gen*) fuera; (*far away*) lejos; **two kilometres ~** a dos kilómetros (de distancia); **two hours ~ by car** a dos horas en coche; **the holiday was two weeks ~** faltaban dos semanas para las vacaciones; **~ from** lejos de, fuera de; **he's ~ for a week** estará ausente una semana; **he's ~ in Barcelona** está en Barcelona; **to take ~** llevar(se); **to work/pedal ~** seguir trabajando/pedaleando; **to fade ~** desvanecerse; (*sound*) apagarse

away game N (*Sport*) partido de fuera

awe [ɔː] N respeto, admiración *f* respetuosa

awe-inspiring [ˈɔːɪnspaɪərɪŋ] ADJ imponente, pasmoso

awesome [ˈɔːsəm] ADJ (*esp US: excellent*) formidable; *see also* **awe-inspiring**

awestruck [ˈɔːstrʌk] ADJ pasmado

★**awful** [ˈɔːfəl] ADJ terrible; **an ~ lot of** (*people, cars, dogs*) la mar de, muchísimos

awfully [ˈɔːfəlɪ] ADV (*very*) terriblemente

awhile [əˈwaɪl] ADV (durante) un rato, algún tiempo

awkward [ˈɔːkwəd] ADJ (*clumsy*) desmañado, torpe; (*shape, situation*) incómodo; (*difficult: question*) difícil; (: *problem*) complicado

awkwardness [ˈɔːkwədnɪs] N (*clumsiness*) torpeza; (*of situation*) incomodidad *f*

awl [ɔːl] N lezna, subilla

awning [ˈɔːnɪŋ] N (*of shop*) toldo; (*of window etc*) marquesina

awoke [əˈwəuk] PT *of* **awake**

awoken [əˈwəukən] PP *of* **awake**

AWOL [ˈeɪwɔl] ABBR (*Mil etc*) = **absent without leave**

awry [əˈraɪ] ADV: **to be ~** estar descolocado *or* atravesado; **to go ~** salir mal, fracasar

axe, (*US*) **ax** [æks] N hacha; **to have an ~ to grind** (*fig*) tener un interés creado *or* algún fin interesado ▶ VT (*employee*) despedir; (*project etc*) cortar; (*jobs*) reducir

axes [ˈæksiːz] NPL *of* **axis**

axiom [ˈæksɪəm] N axioma *m*

axiomatic [æksɪəˈmætɪk] ADJ axiomático

axis [ˈæksɪs] (*pl* **axes** [ˈæksiːz]) N eje *m*

axle [ˈæksl] N eje *m*, árbol *m*

ay, aye [aɪ] EXCL (*yes*) sí; **the ayes** los que votan a favor

AYH N ABBR = **American Youth Hostels**

AZ ABBR (*US*) = **Arizona**

azalea [əˈzeɪlɪə] N azalea

Azerbaijan [æzəbaɪˈdʒɑːn] N Azerbaiyán *m*

Azerbaijani [æzəbaɪˈdʒɑːnɪ], **Azeri** [əˈzɛərɪ] ADJ, N azerbaiyano(-a), azerí *mf*

Azores [əˈzɔːz] NPL: **the ~** las (Islas) Azores

AZT N ABBR (= *azidothymidine*) AZT *m*

Aztec [ˈæztɛk] ADJ, N azteca *mf*

azure [ˈeɪʒəʳ] ADJ celeste

Bb

B, b [biː] N (*letter*) B, b f; (*Scol: mark*) N; (*Mus*): **B** si m; **B for Benjamin**, (*US*) **B for Baker** B de Barcelona; **B road** (*Brit Aut*) ≈ carretera secundaria

b. ABBR = **born**

BA N ABBR = **British Academy**; (*Scol*) = **Bachelor of Arts**; *see also* **bachelor's degree**

babble [ˈbæbl] VI farfullar

babe [beɪb] N criatura

baboon [bəˈbuːn] N mandril m

★**baby** [ˈbeɪbɪ] N bebé mf; (*US inf: darling*) mi amor

baby carriage N (*US*) cochecito

babyish [ˈbeɪbɪʃ] ADJ infantil

baby-minder [ˈbeɪbɪˈmaɪndəʳ] N niñera f (cualificada)

baby-sit [ˈbeɪbɪsɪt] VI hacer de canguro

baby-sitter [ˈbeɪbɪsɪtəʳ] N canguro mf

baby wipe N toallita húmeda (*para bebés*)

bachelor [ˈbætʃələʳ] N soltero; **B~ of Arts/Science (BA/BSc)** licenciado(-a) en Filosofía y Letras/Ciencias

bachelor's degree N licenciatura

Se denomina **Bachelor's degree** a la titulación que se recibe al finalizar el primer ciclo universitario, normalmente después de un período de estudio de tres o cuatro años. Las titulaciones más frecuentes son las de Letras, *BA* (*Bachelor of Arts*), Ciencias, *BSc* (*Bachelor of Science*) o simplemente BS en los Estados Unidos, Educación, *BEd* (*Bachelor of Education*) y Derecho, *LLB* (*Bachelor of Laws*).

★**back** [bæk] N (*of person*) espalda; (*of animal*) lomo; (*of hand, page*) dorso; (*as opposed to front*) parte f de atrás; (*of room*) fondo; (*of chair*) respaldo; (*of page*) reverso; (*Football*) defensa m; **to have one's ~ to the wall** (*fig*) estar entre la espada y la pared; **to break the ~ of a job** hacer lo más difícil de un trabajo; **at the ~ of my mind was the thought that ...** en el fondo tenía la idea de que ... ► VT (*candidate: also:* **back up**) respaldar, apoyar;

(*horse: at races*) apostar a; (*car*) dar marcha atrás a *or* con ► VI (*car etc*) dar marcha atrás ► ADJ (*in compounds: garden, room*) de atrás; **~ seats/wheels** (*Aut*) asientos mpl traseros, ruedas fpl traseras; **~ garden/room** jardín m/habitación f de atrás; **~ payments** pagos mpl con efecto retroactivo; **~ rent** renta atrasada; **to take a ~ seat** (*fig*) pasar a segundo plano ► ADV (*not forward*) (hacia) atrás; **he's ~** (*returned*) ha vuelto; **he ran ~** volvió corriendo; **he called ~** (*again*) volvió a llamar; **throw the ball ~** (*restitution*) devuelve la pelota; **when will you be ~?** ¿cuándo volverá?; **can I have it ~?** ¿me lo devuelve?; **as far ~ as the 13th century** ya en el siglo XIII; **~ to front** al revés; **~ and forth** de acá para allá

► **back down** VI echarse atrás

► **back on to** VT FUS: **the house backs on to the golf course** por atrás la casa da al campo de golf

► **back out** VI (*of promise*) volverse atrás

► **back up** VT (*support: person*) apoyar, respaldar; (: *theory*) defender; (: *car*) dar marcha atrás a; (*Comput*) hacer una copia de reserva de

backache [ˈbækeɪk] N dolor m de espalda

backbencher [ˈbækˈbentʃəʳ] N (*Brit*) *diputado sin cargo oficial en el gobierno o la oposición*

back benches NPL (*Brit*) *ver nota*

Reciben el nombre genérico de **back benches** los escaños más alejados del pasillo central en la Cámara de los Comunes del Parlamento británico, que son ocupados por los *backbenchers*, los miembros de la cámara que no tienen cargo en el gobierno o en la oposición.

backbiting [ˈbækbaɪtɪŋ] N murmuración f

backbone [ˈbækbəʊn] N columna vertebral; **the ~ of the organization** el pilar de la organización

backchat [ˈbæktʃæt] (*Brit inf*) N réplicas fpl

backcloth [ˈbækklɒθ] N telón m de fondo

backcomb [ˈbækkəʊm] VT cardar

backdate [bæk'deɪt] VT (*letter*) poner fecha atrasada a; **backdated pay rise** aumento de sueldo con efecto retroactivo

back door N puerta *f* trasera

backdrop ['bækdrɔp] N = **backcloth**

backer ['bækər] N partidario(-a); (*Comm*) promotor(a) *m/f*

backfire [bæk'faɪər] VI (*Aut*) petardear; (*plans*) fallar, salir mal

backgammon ['bækgæmən] N backgammon *m*

★**background** ['bækgraund] N fondo; (*of events*) antecedentes *mpl*; (*basic knowledge*) bases *fpl*; (*experience*) conocimientos *mpl*, educación *f*; **family ~** origen *m*, antecedentes *mpl* familiares ▶ CPD (*noise, music*) de fondo; (*Comput*) secundario; **~ reading** lectura de preparación

backhand ['bækhænd] N (*Tennis: also:* **backhand stroke**) revés *m*

backhanded [bæk'hændɪd] ADJ (*fig*) ambiguo, equívoco

backhander [bæk'hændər] N (*Brit: bribe*) soborno

★**backing** ['bækɪŋ] N (*fig*) apoyo, respaldo; (*Comm*) respaldo financiero; (*Mus*) acompañamiento

backlash ['bæklæʃ] N reacción *f* (en contra)

backlog ['bæklɔg] N: **~ of work** trabajo atrasado

back number N (*of magazine etc*) número atrasado

backpack ['bækpæk] N mochila

backpacker ['bækpækər] N mochilero(-a)

back pay N atrasos *mpl*

backpedal ['bækpɛdl] VI (*fig*) volverse/echarse atrás

backseat driver ['bæksi:t-] N *pasajero que se empeña en aconsejar al conductor*

backside ['bæksaɪd] N (*inf*) trasero

backslash ['bækslæʃ] N pleca, barra inversa

backslide ['bækslaɪd] VI reincidir, recaer

backspace ['bækspeɪs] VI (*in typing*) retroceder

backstage [bæk'steɪdʒ] ADV entre bastidores

back-street ['bækstri:t] ADJ de barrio; **~ abortionist** persona que practica abortos clandestinos

backstroke ['bækstrəuk] N espalda

backtrack ['bæktræk] VI (*fig*) = **backpedal**

backup ['bækʌp] ADJ (*train, plane*) suplementario; (*Comput: disk, file*) de reserva ▶ N (*support*) apoyo; (*also:* **backup file**) copia de reserva; (*US: congestion*) embotellamiento, retención *f*

back-up lights NPL (*US*) luces *fpl* de marcha atrás

backward ['bækwəd] ADJ (*movement*) hacia atrás; (*person, country*) atrasado; (*shy*) tímido

backwardness ['bækwədnɪs] N atraso

★**backwards** ['bækwədz] ADV (*move, go*) hacia atrás; (*read a list*) al revés; (*fall*) de espaldas; **to know sth ~ or** (*US*) **~ and forwards** (*inf*) saberse algo al dedillo

backwater ['bækwɔːtər] N (*fig*) lugar *m* atrasado *or* apartado

backyard [bæk'jɑːd] N patio trasero

★**bacon** ['beɪkən] N tocino, bacón *m*, beicon *m*

bacteria [bæk'tɪərɪə] NPL bacterias *fpl*

bacteriology [bæktɪərɪ'ɔlədʒɪ] N bacteriología

★**bad** [bæd] ADJ malo; (*serious*) grave; (*meat, food*) podrido, pasado; **to go ~** pasarse; **to have a ~ time of it** pasarlo mal; **I feel ~ about it** (*guilty*) me siento culpable; **~ debt** (*Comm*) cuenta incobrable; **in ~ faith** de mala fe

baddie, baddy ['bædɪ] N (*inf: Cine etc*) malo(-a)

bade [bæd, beɪd] PT *of* **bid**

badge [bædʒ] N insignia; (*metal badge*) chapa; (*of police officer*) placa; (*stick-on*) pegatina

badger ['bædʒər] N tejón *m*

★**badly** ['bædlɪ] ADV (*work, dress etc*) mal; **to reflect ~ on sb** influir negativamente en la reputación de algn; **~ wounded** gravemente herido; **he needs it ~** le hace mucha falta; **to be ~ off (for money)** andar mal de dinero; **things are going ~** las cosas van muy mal

bad-mannered ['bæd'mænəd] ADJ mal educado

badminton ['bædmɪntən] N bádminton *m*

bad-tempered ['bæd'tɛmpəd] ADJ de mal genio *or* carácter; (*temporarily*) de mal humor

baffle ['bæfl] VT desconcertar, confundir

baffling ['bæflɪŋ] ADJ incomprensible

★**bag** [bæg] N bolsa; (*handbag*) bolso; (*satchel*) mochila; (*case*) maleta; (*of hunter*) caza; **bags of** (*inf: lots of*) un montón de; **to pack one's bags** hacer las maletas ▶ VT (*inf: take*) coger (*Sp*), agarrar (*Lam*), pescar

bagful ['bægful] N saco (lleno)

baggage ['bægɪdʒ] N equipaje *m*

baggage allowance N límite *m* de equipaje

baggage claim, baggage reclaim N recogida de equipajes

baggy ['bægɪ] ADJ (*trousers*) ancho, holgado

Baghdad [bæg'dæd] N Bagdad *m*

bag lady N (*inf*) mujer *sin hogar cargada de bolsas*

bagpipes ['bægpaɪps] NPL gaita *sg*

bag-snatcher ['bægsnætʃər] N (*Brit*) ladrón(-ona) *m/f* de bolsos

bag-snatching ['bægsnætʃɪŋ] N (*Brit*) tirón *m* (de bolsos)

Bahamas [bə'hɑːməz] NPL: **the ~** las (Islas) Bahama

Bahrain [bɑː'reɪn] N Bahrein *m*

bail [beɪl] N fianza; **on ~** (*prisoner*) bajo fianza; **to be released on ~** ser puesto en libertad bajo fianza ▶ VT (*prisoner: also:* **grant bail to**) poner en libertad bajo fianza; (*boat: also:* **bail out**) achicar; **to ~ sb out** pagar la fianza de algn; *see also* **bale**

bailiff ['beɪlɪf] N alguacil *m*

bailout ['beɪlaut] N rescate *m* (financiero)

bait [beɪt] N cebo ▶ VT poner el cebo en

★**bake** [beɪk] VT cocer (al horno) ▶ VI (cook) cocerse; (be hot) hacer un calor terrible

baked beans NPL judías fpl en salsa de tomate

baked potato N patata al horno

★**baker** ['beɪkəʳ] N panadero(-a)

baker's dozen N docena del fraile

bakery ['beɪkərɪ] N (for bread) panadería; (for cakes) pastelería

baking ['beɪkɪŋ] N (act) cocción f; (batch) hornada

baking powder N levadura (en polvo)

baking tin N molde m (para horno)

balaclava [bælə'klɑːvə] N (also: **balaclava helmet**) pasamontañas m inv

★**balance** ['bæləns] N equilibrio; (Comm: sum) balance m; (remainder) resto; (scales) balanza; **~ of trade/payments** balanza de comercio/pagos; **~ carried forward** balance m pasado a cuenta nueva; **~ brought forward** saldo de hoja anterior ▶ VT equilibrar; (budget) nivelar; (account) saldar; (compensate) compensar; **to ~ the books** hacer el balance

balanced ['bælənst] ADJ (personality, diet) equilibrado; (report) objetivo

balance sheet N balance m

★**balcony** ['bælkənɪ] N (open) balcón m; (closed) galería; (in theatre) anfiteatro

bald [bɔːld] ADJ calvo; (tyre) liso

baldness ['bɔːldnɪs] N calvicie f

bale [beɪl] N (Agr) paca, fardo ▶ **bale out** VI (of a plane) lanzarse en paracaídas ▶ VT (Naut) achicar; **to ~ sb out of a difficulty** sacar a algn de un apuro

Balearic Islands [bælɪ'ærɪk-] NPL: **the ~** las (Islas) Baleares

baleful ['beɪlful] ADJ (look) triste; (sinister) funesto, siniestro

balk [bɔːk] VI: **to ~ (at)** resistirse (a); (horse) plantarse (ante)

Balkan ['bɔːlkən] ADJ balcánico ▶ N: **the Balkans** los Balcanes

★**ball** [bɔːl] N (sphere) bola; (football) balón m; (for tennis, golf etc) pelota; (of wool, string) ovillo; (dance) baile m; **to be on the ~** (fig: competent) ser un enterado; (: alert) estar al tanto; **to play ~ (with sb)** jugar a la pelota (con algn); (fig) cooperar; **to start the ~ rolling** (fig) empezar; **the ~ is in your court** (fig) le toca a usted

ballad ['bæləd] N balada, romance m

ballast ['bæləst] N lastre m

ball bearing N cojinete m de bolas

ballcock ['bɔːlkɔk] N llave f de bola or de flotador

ballerina [bælə'riːnə] N bailarina

ballet ['bæleɪ] N ballet m

ballet dancer N bailarín(-ina) m/f (de ballet)

ballistic [bə'lɪstɪk] ADJ balístico; **intercontinental ~ missile** misil m balístico intercontinental

ballistics [bə'lɪstɪks] N balística

★**balloon** [bə'luːn] N globo; (in comic strip) bocadillo ▶ VI dispararse

balloonist [bə'luːnɪst] N aeróstata mf

ballot ['bælət] N votación f

ballot box N urna (electoral)

ballot paper N papeleta

ballpark ['bɔːlpɑːk] N (US) estadio de béisbol

ballpark figure N (inf) cifra aproximada

ballpoint pen ['bɔːlpɔɪnt-] N bolígrafo

ballroom ['bɔːlrum] N salón m de baile

balm [bɑːm] N (also fig) bálsamo

balmy ['bɑːmɪ] ADJ (breeze, air) suave; (inf) = **barmy**

BALPA ['bælpə] N ABBR (= British Airline Pilots' Association) sindicato de pilotos de líneas aéreas

balsa ['bɔːlsə], **balsa wood** N (madera de) balsa

Baltic ['bɔːltɪk] ADJ báltico ▶ N: **the ~ (Sea)** el (mar) Báltico

balustrade ['bæləstreɪd] N barandilla

bamboo [bæm'buː] N bambú m

bamboozle [bæm'buːzl] VT (inf) embaucar, engatusar

★**ban** [bæn] N prohibición f ▶ VT prohibir; (exclude) excluir; **he was banned from driving** le retiraron el carnet de conducir

banal [bə'nɑːl] ADJ banal, vulgar

★**banana** [bə'nɑːnə] N plátano, banana (LAm)

★**band** [bænd] N (group) banda; (gang) pandilla; (strip) faja, tira; (at a dance) orquesta; (Mil) banda; (rock band) grupo ▶ **band together** VI juntarse, asociarse

bandage ['bændɪdʒ] N venda, vendaje m ▶ VT vendar

Band-Aid® ['bændeɪd] N (US) tirita, curita (LAm)

B & B N ABBR = **bed and breakfast**

bandit ['bændɪt] N bandido; **one-armed ~** máquina tragaperras

bandstand ['bændstænd] N quiosco de música

bandwagon ['bændwægən] N: **to jump on the ~** (fig) subirse al carro

bandy ['bændɪ] VT (jokes, insults) intercambiar

bandy-legged ['bændɪ'legd] ADJ patizambo

bane [beɪn] N: **it/he** etc **is the ~ of my life** me amarga la vida

bang [bæŋ] N (of gun, exhaust) estallido; (of door) portazo; (blow) golpe m ▶ VT (door) cerrar de golpe; (one's head) golpear; **to ~ the door** dar un portazo ▶ VI estallar; **to ~ into sth** chocar con algo, golpearse contra algo ▶ ADV: **to be ~ on time** (inf) llegar en punto; see also **bangs**

banger ['bæŋəʳ] N (Brit inf: car: also: **old banger**) armatoste m, cacharro; (: sausage) salchicha; (firework) petardo

Bangkok [bæŋ'kɔk] N Bangkok m

Bangladesh [bæŋglə'dɛʃ] N Bangladesh f

bangle [ˈbæŋgl] N brazalete m, ajorca

bangs [bæŋz] NPL (US) flequillo sg

banish [ˈbænɪʃ] VT desterrar

banister [ˈbænɪstəʳ] N, **banisters** [ˈbænɪstəz] NPL barandilla f, pasamanos m inv

banjo [ˈbændʒəu] (pl **banjoes** or **banjos**) N banjo

★**bank** [bæŋk] N (Comm) banco; (of river, lake) ribera, orilla; (of earth) terraplén m ▸ VI (Aviat) ladearse; (Comm): **to ~ with** tener la cuenta en
▸ **bank on** VT FUS contar con

bank account N cuenta bancaria

bank balance N saldo

bank card N tarjeta bancaria

bank charges NPL comisión fsg

bank draft N letra de cambio

★**banker** [ˈbæŋkəʳ] N banquero(-a); **~'s card** (BRIT) tarjeta bancaria; **~'s order** orden f bancaria

bank giro N giro bancario

bank holiday N (BRIT) día m festivo or de fiesta

> El término **bank holiday** se aplica en el Reino Unido a todo día festivo oficial en el que cierran bancos y comercios. Los más destacados coinciden con Navidad, Semana Santa, finales de mayo y finales de agosto. Al contrario que en los países de tradición católica, no se celebran las festividades dedicadas a los santos.

banking [ˈbæŋkɪŋ] N banca

bank loan N préstamo bancario

bank manager N director(a) m/f (de sucursal) de banco

banknote [ˈbæŋknəut] N billete m de banco

bank rate N tipo de interés bancario

bankrupt [ˈbæŋkrʌpt] N quebrado(-a) ▸ ADJ quebrado, insolvente; **to go ~** quebrar, hacer bancarrota; **to be ~** estar en quiebra

bankruptcy [ˈbæŋkrʌptsɪ] N quiebra, bancarrota

bank statement N extracto de cuenta

banned substance [ˈbænd-] N (Sport) sustancia prohibida

banner [ˈbænəʳ] N bandera; (in demonstration) pancarta

bannister [ˈbænɪstəʳ] N, **bannisters** [ˈbænɪstəz] NPL = **banister**

banns [bænz] NPL amonestaciones fpl

banquet [ˈbæŋkwɪt] N banquete m

banter [ˈbæntəʳ] N guasa, bromas fpl

baptism [ˈbæptɪzəm] N bautismo; (act) bautizo

baptize [bæpˈtaɪz] VT bautizar

★**bar** [bɑːʳ] N barra; (on door) tranca; (of window, cage) reja; (of soap) pastilla; (of chocolate) tableta; (fig: hindrance) obstáculo; (prohibition) prohibición f; (pub) bar m, cantina (esp LAM); (counter: in pub) barra, mostrador m; (Mus) barra; **behind bars** entre rejas; **the B~** (Law: profession) la abogacía; (: people) el cuerpo de abogados ▸ VT (road) obstruir; (window, door) atrancar; (person)

excluir; (activity) prohibir ▸ PREP: **~ none** sin excepción

Barbados [bɑːˈbeɪdɔs] N Barbados m

barbarian [bɑːˈbɛərɪən] N bárbaro(-a)

barbaric [bɑːˈbærɪk] ADJ bárbaro

barbarity [bɑːˈbærɪtɪ] N barbaridad f

barbarous [ˈbɑːbərəs] ADJ bárbaro

★**barbecue** [ˈbɑːbɪkjuː] N barbacoa, asado (LAM)

barbed wire [ˈbɑːbd-] N alambre m de espino

barber [ˈbɑːbəʳ] N peluquero, barbero

barber's (shop), (US) **barber (shop)** N peluquería

barbiturate [bɑːˈbɪtjurɪt] N barbitúrico

Barcelona [bɑːsɪˈləunə] N Barcelona

bar chart N gráfico de barras

bar code N código de barras

★**bare** [bɛəʳ] ADJ desnudo; (trees) sin hojas; (head) descubierto ▸ VT desnudar; **to ~ one's teeth** enseñar los dientes

bareback [ˈbɛəbæk] ADV a pelo

barefaced [ˈbɛəfeɪst] ADJ descarado

barefoot [ˈbɛəfut] ADJ, ADV descalzo

bareheaded [bɛəˈhɛdɪd] ADJ descubierto, sin sombrero

barely [ˈbɛəlɪ] ADV apenas

bareness [ˈbɛənɪs] N desnudez f

Barents Sea [ˈbærənts-] N: **the ~** el mar de Barents

★**bargain** [ˈbɑːgɪn] N pacto; (transaction) negocio; (good buy) ganga; **into the ~** además, por añadidura ▸ VI negociar; (haggle) regatear
▸ **bargain for** VT FUS: **he got more than he bargained for** le resultó peor de lo que esperaba

bargaining [ˈbɑːgənɪŋ] N negociación f, regateo; **~ table** mesa de negociaciones

bargaining position N: **to be in a strong/weak ~** estar/no estar en una posición de fuerza para negociar

barge [bɑːdʒ] N barcaza
▸ **barge in** VI irrumpir; (in conversation) entrometerse
▸ **barge into** VT FUS dar contra

baritone [ˈbærɪtəun] N barítono

barium meal [ˈbɛərɪəm-] N (Med) sulfato de bario

bark [bɑːk] N (of tree) corteza; (of dog) ladrido ▸ VI ladrar

barley [ˈbɑːlɪ] N cebada

barley sugar N azúcar m cande

barmaid [ˈbɑːmeɪd] N camarera

barman [ˈbɑːmən] N (irreg) camarero, barman m

barmy [ˈbɑːmɪ] ADJ (BRIT inf) chiflado, chalado

barn [bɑːn] N granero; (for animals) cuadra

barnacle [ˈbɑːnəkl] N percebe m

barn owl N lechuza

barometer [bəˈrɔmɪtəʳ] N barómetro

baron [ˈbærən] N barón m; (fig) magnate m; **the press barons** los magnates de la prensa

baroness ['bærənɪs] N baronesa

baroque [bə'rɔk] ADJ barroco

barrack ['bærək] VT (BRIT) abuchear

barracking ['bærəkɪŋ] N: **to give sb a ~** (BRIT) abuchear a algn

barracks ['bærəks] NPL cuartel *msg*

barrage ['bæra:ʒ] N (Mil) cortina de fuego; (dam) presa; (fig: of criticism etc) lluvia, aluvión *m*; **a ~ of questions** una lluvia de preguntas

barrel ['bærəl] N barril *m*; (of wine) tonel *m*, cuba; (of gun) cañón *m*

barren ['bærən] ADJ estéril

barrette [bə'rɛt] N (US) pasador *m*, broche *m* (MEX)

barricade [bærɪ'keɪd] N barricada ▶ VT cerrar con barricadas

barrier ['bærɪəʳ] N barrera; (crash barrier) barrera

barrier cream N crema protectora

barring ['ba:rɪŋ] PREP excepto, salvo

barrister ['bærɪstəʳ] N (BRIT) abogado(-a)

En el sistema legal inglés, **barrister** es el abogado que se ocupa de defender los casos de sus clientes en los tribunales superiores. El equivalente escocés es *advocate*. Normalmente actúan según instrucciones de un *solicitor*, abogado de despacho que no toma parte activa en los juicios de dichos tribunales. El título de *barrister* lo otorga el órgano colegiado correspondiente, *the Inns of Court*, y cada barrister debe pertenecer a una de estas asociaciones que les proporcionan servicios, apoyo y asesoramiento.

barrow ['bærəu] N (cart) carretilla

barstool ['ba:stu:l] N taburete *m* (de bar)

Bart. ABBR (BRIT) = **baronet**

bartender ['ba:tɛndəʳ] N (US) camarero(-a), barman *m*

barter ['ba:təʳ] VT: **to ~ sth for sth** trocar algo por algo

base [beɪs] N base *f* ▶ ADJ bajo, infame ▶ VT: **to ~ sth on** basar or fundar algo en; **I'm based in London** (work) trabajo en Londres ▶ VI: **to ~ at** (troops) estacionar en

★**baseball** ['beɪsbɔ:l] N béisbol *m*

baseball cap N gorra *f* de béisbol

base camp N campamento base

Basel ['ba:zəl] N Basilea

baseless ['beɪslɪs] ADJ infundado

baseline ['beɪslaɪn] N (Tennis) línea de fondo

★**basement** ['beɪsmənt] N sótano

base rate N tipo base

bases ['beɪsi:z] NPL of **basis**

bash [bæʃ] N: **I'll have a ~ (at it)** lo intentaré ▶ VT (inf) golpear
▶ **bash up** VT (inf: car) destrozar; (: person) aporrear, vapulear

bashful ['bæʃful] ADJ tímido, vergonzoso

bashing ['bæʃɪŋ] N (inf) paliza

BASIC ['beɪsɪk] N (Comput) BASIC *m*

basic ['beɪsɪk] ADJ (salary etc) básico; (elementary: principles) fundamental

★**basically** ['beɪsɪklɪ] ADV fundamentalmente, en el fondo

basic rate N (of tax) base *f* mínima imponible

basics NPL: **the ~** los fundamentos

basil ['bæzl] N albahaca

basin ['beɪsn] N (vessel) cuenco, tazón *m*; (Geo) cuenca; (also: **washbasin**) palangana, jofaina; (: in bathroom) lavabo

★**basis** ['beɪsɪs] (pl **bases** [-si:z]) N base *f*; **on a part-time/trial ~** a tiempo parcial/a prueba; **on the ~ of what you've said** en base a lo que has dicho

bask [ba:sk] VI: **to ~ in the sun** tomar el sol

★**basket** ['ba:skɪt] N cesta, cesto

★**basketball** ['ba:skɪtbɔ:l] N baloncesto

basketball player N jugador(a) *m/f* de baloncesto

basketwork ['ba:skɪtwə:k] N cestería

Basle [ba:l] N Basilea

basmati rice [bəz'mætɪ-] N arroz *m* basmati

Basque [bæsk] ADJ, N vasco(-a) *m/f*

Basque Country N Euskadi *m*, País *m* Vasco

bass [beɪs] N (Mus) bajo

bass clef N clave *f* de fa

bassoon [bə'su:n] N fagot *m*

bastard ['ba:stəd] N bastardo(-a); (inf!) cabrón *m* (inf!), hijo de puta (inf!)

baste [beɪst] VT (Culin) rociar (con su salsa)

bastion ['bæstɪən] N bastión *m*, baluarte *m*

★**bat** [bæt] N (Zool) murciélago; (for ball games) palo; (for cricket, baseball) bate *m*; (BRIT: for table tennis) pala ▶ VT: **he didn't ~ an eyelid** ni pestañeó, ni se inmutó

batch [bætʃ] N lote *m*, remesa; (of bread) hornada

bated ['beɪtɪd] ADJ: **with ~ breath** sin respirar

★**bath** [ba:θ] N (act) baño; (bathtub) bañera, tina (esp LAm); **to have a ~** bañarse, darse un baño ▶ VT bañar; see also **baths**

bath chair N silla de ruedas

bathe [beɪð] VI bañarse; (US) darse un baño, bañarse ▶ VT (wound etc) lavar; (US) bañar, dar un baño a

bather ['beɪðəʳ] N bañista *mf*

bathing ['beɪðɪŋ] N baño

bathing cap N gorro de baño

bathing costume, (US) **bathing suit** N bañador *m*, traje *m* de baño

bathing trunks NPL bañador *msg*

bathmat ['ba:θmæt] N alfombrilla de baño

bathrobe ['ba:θrəub] N albornoz *m*

★**bathroom** ['ba:θrum] N (cuarto de) baño

baths [ba:ðz] NPL piscina *sg*

bath towel N toalla de baño

bathtub ['ba:θtʌb] N bañera

batman ['bætmən] N (*irreg*) (BRIT) ordenanza *m*
baton ['bætən] N (*Mus*) batuta; (*weapon*) porra
battalion [bə'tælɪən] N batallón *m*
batten ['bætn] N (*Carpentry*) listón *m*; (*Naut*) junquillo, sable *m*
 ▶ **batten down** VT (*Naut*): **to ~ down the hatches** atrancar las escotillas
batter ['bætə*ʳ*] VT maltratar; (*wind, rain*) azotar
 ▶ N batido
battered ['bætəd] ADJ (*hat, pan*) estropeado
battery ['bætərɪ] N batería; (*of torch*) pila
battery charger N cargador *m* de baterías
battery farming N cría intensiva
★**battle** ['bætl] N batalla; (*fig*) lucha; **that's half the ~** (*inf*) ya hay medio camino andado; **to fight a losing ~** (*fig*) luchar por una causa perdida ▶ VI luchar
battlefield ['bætlfi:ld] N campo *m* de batalla
battlements ['bætlmənts] NPL almenas *fpl*
battleship ['bætlʃɪp] N acorazado
batty ['bætɪ] ADJ (*inf: person*) chiflado; (: *idea*) de chiflado
bauble ['bɔ:bl] N chuchería
baud rate N (*Comput*) velocidad *f* (de transmisión) en baudios
bauxite ['bɔ:ksaɪt] N bauxita
Bavaria [bə'vɛərɪə] N Baviera
Bavarian [bə'vɛərɪən] ADJ, N bávaro(-a) *m/f*
bawdy ['bɔ:dɪ] ADJ indecente; (*joke*) verde
bawl [bɔ:l] VI chillar, gritar
bay [beɪ] N (*Geo*) bahía; (*for parking*) parking *m*, estacionamiento; (*loading bay*) patio de carga; (*Bot*) laurel *m*; **to hold sb at ~** mantener a alguien a raya ▶ VI aullar
bay leaf N (hoja de) laurel *m*
bayonet ['beɪənɪt] N bayoneta
bay window N ventana salediza
bazaar [bə'zɑ:*ʳ*] N bazar *m*
bazooka [bə'zu:kə] N bazuca
BB N ABBR (*Brit*: = *Boys' Brigade*) organización juvenil para chicos
BBB N ABBR (*US*: = *Better Business Bureau*) organismo para la defensa del consumidor
BBC N ABBR (= *British Broadcasting Corporation*) BBC *f*

La **BBC** es el organismo público británico de radio y televisión, autónomo en cuanto a su política de programas pero regulado por un estatuto que ha de aprobar el Parlamento. Además de cadenas nacionales de televisión y de radio, transmite también un servicio informativo mundial (*BBC World Service*). La programación es accesible en línea mediante la app *BBC iPlayer*. Al no tener publicidad, se financia a través de operaciones comerciales paralelas y del cobro de una licencia anual obligatoria (*TV licence*).

BC ADV ABBR (= *before Christ*) a. de J.C. ▶ ABBR (CANADA) = **British Columbia**

BCG N ABBR (= *Bacillus Calmette-Guérin*) vacuna de la tuberculosis
BD N ABBR (= *Bachelor of Divinity*) Licenciado/a en Teología
B/D ABBR = **bank draft**
BDS N ABBR (= *Bachelor of Dental Surgery*) título universitario

be [bi:]

(*pt* **was** [wɔz], **were** [wə:*ʳ*], *pp* **been** [bi:n]) AUX VB **1** (*with present participle: forming continuous tenses*): **what are you doing?** ¿qué estás haciendo?, ¿qué haces?; **they're coming tomorrow** vienen mañana; **I've been waiting for you for hours** llevo horas esperándote **2** (*with pp: forming passives*) ser (*but often replaced by active or reflexive constructions*); **to be murdered** ser asesinado; **the box had been opened** habían abierto la caja; **the thief was nowhere to be seen** no se veía al ladrón por ninguna parte
3 (*in tag questions*): **it was fun, wasn't it?** fue divertido, ¿no? or ¿verdad?; **he's good-looking, isn't he?** es guapo, ¿no te parece?; **she's back again, is she?** entonces, ¿ha vuelto?
4 (+ *to* + *infin*): **the house is to be sold** (*necessity*) hay que vender la casa; (*future*) van a vender la casa; **he's not to open it** no tiene que abrirlo; **he was to have come yesterday** debía de haber venido ayer; **am I to understand that ...?** ¿debo entender que ...?
 ▶ VB + COMPLEMENT **1** (*with n or num complement*) ser; **he's a doctor** es médico; **2 and 2 are 4** 2 y 2 son 4
2 (*with adj complement: expressing permanent or inherent quality*) ser; (: *expressing state seen as temporary or reversible*) estar; **I'm English** soy inglés(-esa); **she's tall/pretty** es alta/bonita; **he's young** es joven; **be careful/good/quiet** ten cuidado/pórtate bien/cállate; **I'm tired** estoy cansado(-a); **I'm warm** tengo calor; **it's dirty** está sucio(-a)
3 (*of health*) estar; **how are you?** ¿cómo estás?; **he's very ill** está muy enfermo; **I'm better now** ya estoy mejor
4 (*of age*) tener; **how old are you?** ¿cuántos años tienes?; **I'm sixteen (years old)** tengo dieciséis años
5 (*cost*) costar; ser; **how much was the meal?** ¿cuánto fue or costó la comida?; **that'll be £5.75, please** son £5.75, por favor; **this shirt is £17** esta camisa cuesta £17
 ▶ VI **1** (*exist, occur etc*) existir, haber; **the best singer that ever was** el mejor cantante que existió jamás; **is there a God?** ¿hay un Dios?, ¿existe Dios?; **be that as it may** sea como sea; **so be it** así sea
2 (*referring to place*) estar; **I won't be here tomorrow** no estaré aquí mañana
3 (*referring to movement*): **where have you been?** ¿dónde has estado?
 ▶ IMPERS VB **1** (*referring to time*): **it's 5 o'clock**

son las 5; **it's the 28th of April** estamos a 28 de abril

2 (*referring to distance*): **it's 10 km to the village** el pueblo está a 10 km

3 (*referring to the weather*): **it's too hot/cold** hace demasiado calor/frío; **it's windy today** hace viento hoy

4 (*emphatic*): **it's me** soy yo; **it was Maria who paid the bill** fue Maria la que pagó la cuenta

There are two basic verbs to translate *be* into Spanish: **estar** and **ser**. **estar** is used with adjectives describing a temporary state: *I'm very happy*. **Estoy muy contento**.
ser is used with adjectives describing permanent states or characteristics: *She's English*. **Es inglesa**.
When referring to the weather, use **hacer**: *It's cold*. **Hace frío**.
With ages and certain adjectives, such as 'cold', 'hot', 'hungry', and 'thirsty', use **tener** and a noun or noun phrase in Spanish: *I'm twelve*. **Tengo doce años**. *I'm cold*. **Tengo frío**.

B/E ABBR = **bill of exchange**

★**beach** [biːtʃ] N playa ▶ VT varar

beach buggy [-bʌgɪ] N buggy *m*

beachcomber ['biːtʃkəʊmə^r] N raquero(-a)

beachwear ['biːtʃwɛə^r] N ropa de playa

beacon ['biːkən] N (*lighthouse*) faro; (*marker*) guía; (*radio beacon*) radiofaro

bead [biːd] N cuenta, abalorio; (*of dew, sweat*) gota ■ **beads** NPL (*necklace*) collar *m*

beady ['biːdɪ] ADJ (*eyes*) pequeño y brillante

beagle ['biːgl] N sabueso pequeño, beagle *m*

beak [biːk] N pico

beaker ['biːkə^r] N vaso

beam [biːm] N (*Arch*) viga; (*of light*) rayo, haz *m* de luz; (*Radio*) rayo; **to drive on full** or **main ~** conducir con las luces largas ▶ VI brillar; (*smile*) sonreír

beaming ['biːmɪŋ] ADJ (*sun, smile*) radiante

bean [biːn] N judía, fríjol/frijol *m* (*esp LAM*); **runner/broad ~** habichuela/haba; **coffee ~** grano de café

beanpole ['biːnpəʊl] N (*inf*) espárrago

bean sprouts ['biːnsprauts] NPL brotes *mpl* de soja

★**bear** [bɛə^r] (*pt* **bore** [bɔː^r], *pp* **borne** [bɔːn]) N oso; (*Stock Exchange*) bajista *m* ▶ VT (*weight etc*) llevar; (*cost*) pagar; (*responsibility*) tener; (*traces, signs*) mostrar; (*produce: fruit*) dar; (*Comm: interest*) devengar; (*endure*) soportar, aguantar; (*stand up to*) resistir a; (*children*) tener, dar a luz; (*fruit*) dar; **I can't ~ him** no le puedo ver, no lo soporto ▶ VI: **to ~ right/left** torcer a la derecha/izquierda; **to bring pressure to ~ on sb** ejercer presión sobre algn

▶ **bear on** VT FUS tener que ver con, referirse a

▶ **bear out** VT FUS (*suspicions*) corroborar, confirmar; (*person*) confirmar lo dicho por

▶ **bear up** VI (*cheer up*) animarse; **he bore up well under the strain** resistió bien la presión

▶ **bear with** VT FUS (*sb's moods, temper*) tener paciencia con

bearable ['bɛərəbl] ADJ soportable, aguantable

beard [bɪəd] N barba

bearded ['bɪədɪd] ADJ con barba

bearer ['bɛərə^r] N (*of news, cheque*) portador(a) *m/f*; (*of passport*) titular *mf*

bearing ['bɛərɪŋ] N porte *m*; (*connection*) relación *f*; **to take a ~** marcarse; **to find one's bearings** orientarse ■ **(ball) bearings** NPL cojinetes *mpl* a bolas

bearskin ['bɛəskɪn] N (*Mil*) gorro militar (*de piel de oso*)

beast [biːst] N bestia; (*inf*) bruto, salvaje *m*

beastly ['biːstlɪ] ADJ bestial; (*awful*) horrible

★**beat** [biːt] (*pt* ~, *pp* **beaten** ['biːtn]) N (*of heart*) latido; (*Mus*) ritmo, compás *m*; (*of police officer*) ronda ▶ VT (*hit*) golpear, pegar; (*eggs*) batir; (*defeat*) vencer, derrotar; (*better*) sobrepasar; (*drum*) redoblar; (*rhythm*) marcar; **that beats everything!** (*inf*) ¡eso es el colmo!; **off the beaten track** aislado; **to ~ it** largarse ▶ VI (*heart*) latir; **to ~ about the bush** andarse con rodeos; **to ~ on a door** dar golpes en una puerta

▶ **beat down** VT (*door*) derribar a golpes; (*price*) conseguir rebajar, regatear; (*seller*) hacer rebajar el precio ▶ VI (*rain*) llover a cántaros; (*sun*) caer de plomo

▶ **beat off** VT rechazar

▶ **beat up** VT (*inf: person*) dar una paliza a

beater ['biːtə^r] N (*for eggs, cream*) batidora

beating ['biːtɪŋ] N paliza, golpiza (*LAM*); **to take a ~** recibir una paliza

beat-up ['biːtʌp] ADJ (*inf*) destartalado

★**beautiful** ['bjuːtɪful] ADJ hermoso, bello, lindo (*esp LAM*)

beautifully ['bjuːtɪfəlɪ] ADV de maravilla

beautify ['bjuːtɪfaɪ] VT embellecer

★**beauty** ['bjuːtɪ] N belleza, hermosura; (*concept, person*) belleza; **the ~ of it is that ...** lo mejor de esto es que ...

beauty contest N concurso de belleza

beauty parlour, (*US*) **beauty parlor** N salón *m* de belleza

beauty queen N reina de la belleza

beauty salon N salón *m* de belleza

beauty sleep N: **to get one's ~** no perder horas de sueño

beauty spot N lunar *m* postizo; (*BRIT Tourism*) lugar *m* pintoresco

beaver ['biːvə^r] N castor *m*

becalmed [bɪ'kɑːmd] ADJ encalmado

became [bɪ'keɪm] PT *of* **become**

★**because** [bɪ'kɔz] CONJ porque; **~ of** PREP debido a, a causa de

beck [bɛk] N: **to be at the ~ and call of** estar a disposición de

beckon [ˈbɛkən] vт (*also:* **beckon to**) llamar con señas

★**become** [bɪˈkʌm] vɪ (*irreg: like* **come**) + *noun* hacerse, llegar a ser; + *adj* ponerse, volverse; **to ~ fat** engordar; **to ~ angry** enfadarse; **it became known that ...** se descubrió que ... ▶ vт (*suit*) favorecer, sentar bien a

becoming [bɪˈkʌmɪŋ] ADJ (*behaviour*) decoroso; (*clothes*) favorecedor(a)

becquerel [bɛkəˈrɛl] N becquerelio

BECTU [ˈbɛktuː] N ABBR (BRɪт) = **Broadcasting, Entertainment, Cinematograph and Theatre Union**

BEd N ABBR (= *Bachelor of Education*) título universitario; *see also* **bachelor's degree**

★**bed** [bɛd] N cama; (*of flowers*) macizo; (*of sea, lake*) fondo; (*of river*) lecho; (*of coal, clay*) capa; **to go to ~** acostarse
  ▶ **bed down** vɪ acostarse

bed and breakfast N ≈ pensión f

> Se llama **bed and breakfast** a la casa de hospedaje particular, o granja si es en el campo, que ofrece cama y desayuno a tarifas inferiores a las de un hotel. Aunque hoy en día se puedan encontrar en la web, el servicio se sigue anunciando con carteles colocados en las ventanas del establecimiento, en el jardín o en la carretera. En ellos aparece a menudo únicamente el símbolo B & B.

bedbug [ˈbɛdbʌg] N chinche f

bedclothes [ˈbɛdkləʊðz] NPL ropa de cama

bedding [ˈbɛdɪŋ] N ropa de cama

bedeck [bɪˈdɛk] vт engalanar, adornar

bedevil [bɪˈdɛvl] vт (*dog*) acosar; (*trouble*) fastidiar

bedfellow [ˈbɛdfɛləʊ] N: **they are strange bedfellows** (*fig*) hacen una pareja rara

bedlam [ˈbɛdləm] N confusión f

bed linen N (BRɪт) ropa f de cama

bedpan [ˈbɛdpæn] N cuña

bedraggled [bɪˈdrægld] ADJ desastrado

bedridden [ˈbɛdrɪdn] ADJ postrado (en cama)

bedrock [ˈbɛdrɔk] N (*Geo*) roca firme; (*fig*) pilar m

★**bedroom** [ˈbɛdrum] N dormitorio, alcoba

bed settee N sofá-cama m

bedside [ˈbɛdsaɪd] N: **at sb's ~** a la cabecera de alguien

bedside lamp N lámpara de noche

bedside table N mesilla de noche

bedsit [ˈbɛdsɪt], **bedsitter** [ˈbɛdsɪtəʳ] N (BRɪт) estudio

bedspread [ˈbɛdsprɛd] N cubrecama m, colcha

★**bedtime** [ˈbɛdtaɪm] N hora de acostarse; **it's ~** es hora de acostarse *or* de irse a la cama

bee [biː] N abeja; **to have a ~ in one's bonnet (about sth)** tener una idea fija (de algo)

beech [biːtʃ] N haya

★**beef** [biːf] N carne f de vaca; **roast ~** rosbif m
  ▶ **beef up** vт (*inf*) reforzar

★**beefburger** [ˈbiːfbəːgəʳ] N hamburguesa

beefeater [ˈbiːfiːtəʳ] N *alabardero de la Torre de Londres*

beehive [ˈbiːhaɪv] N colmena

bee-keeping [ˈbiːkiːpɪŋ] N apicultura

beeline [ˈbiːlaɪn] N: **to make a ~ for** ir derecho a

been [biːn] PP *of* **be**

beep [biːp] N pitido ▶ vɪ pitar

beeper [ˈbiːpəʳ] N (*of doctor etc*) busca m inv

★**beer** [bɪəʳ] N cerveza

beer belly N (*inf*) barriga (*de bebedor de cerveza*)

beer can N bote m *or* lata de cerveza

beer garden N (BRɪт) terraza f de verano, jardín m (de un bar)

beet [biːt] N (US) remolacha

beetle [ˈbiːtl] N escarabajo

beetroot [ˈbiːtruːt] N (BRɪт) remolacha

befall [bɪˈfɔːl] vɪ, vт (*irreg: like* **fall**) acontecer (a)

befit [bɪˈfɪt] vт convenir a, corresponder a

★**before** [bɪˈfɔːʳ] PREP (*of time*) antes de; (*of space*) delante de; **~ going** antes de marcharse ▶ CONJ antes (de) que; **~ she goes** antes de que se vaya ▶ ADV (*time*) antes; (*space*) delante, adelante; **the week ~** la semana anterior; **I've never seen it ~** no lo he visto nunca

beforehand [bɪˈfɔːhænd] ADV de antemano, con anticipación

befriend [bɪˈfrɛnd] vт ofrecer amistad a

befuddled [bɪˈfʌdld] ADJ aturdido, atontado

beg [bɛg] vɪ pedir limosna, mendigar ▶ vт pedir, rogar; (*entreat*) suplicar; **to ~ sb to do sth** rogar a algn que haga algo; *see also* **pardon**

began [bɪˈgæn] PT *of* **begin**

beggar [ˈbɛgəʳ] N mendigo(-a)

★**begin** [bɪˈgɪn] (*pt* **began** [bɪˈgæn], *pp* **begun** [bɪˈgʌn]) vт, vɪ empezar, comenzar; **to ~ doing** *or* **to do sth** empezar a hacer algo; **I can't ~ to thank you** no encuentro palabras para agradecerle; **to ~ with, I'd like to know ...** en primer lugar, quisiera saber ...; **beginning from Monday** a partir del lunes

beginner [bɪˈgɪnəʳ] N principiante mf

★**beginning** [bɪˈgɪnɪŋ] N principio, comienzo; **right from the ~** desde el principio

begrudge [bɪˈgrʌdʒ] vт: **to ~ sb sth** tenerle envidia a alguien por algo

beguile [bɪˈgaɪl] vт (*enchant*) seducir

beguiling [bɪˈgaɪlɪŋ] ADJ seductor(a), atractivo

begun [bɪˈgʌn] PP *of* **begin**

★**behalf** [bɪˈhɑːf] N: **on ~ of**, (US) **in ~ of** en nombre de, por; (*for benefit of*) en beneficio de; **on my/his ~** por mí/él

★**behave** [bɪˈheɪv] vɪ (*person*) portarse, comportarse; (*thing*) funcionar; (*well: also:* **behave o.s.**) portarse bien

behaviour, (US) **behavior** [bɪ'heɪvjər] N comportamiento, conducta

behead [bɪ'hɛd] VT decapitar

beheld [bɪ'hɛld] PT, PP of **behold**

★**behind** [bɪ'haɪnd] PREP detrás de; **to be ~ (schedule)** ir retrasado; **~ the scenes** (fig) entre bastidores; **we're ~ them in technology** (fig) nos dejan atrás en tecnología ▶ ADV detrás, por detrás, atrás; **to leave sth ~** olvidar or dejarse algo; **to be ~ with sth** estar atrasado en algo; **to be ~ with payments (on sth)** estar atrasado en el pago (de algo) ▶ N trasero

behold [bɪ'həʊld] VT (irreg: like **hold**) contemplar

beige [beɪʒ] ADJ (color) beige

Beijing [beɪ'dʒɪŋ] N Pekín m

being ['biːɪŋ] N ser m; **to come into ~** nacer, aparecer

Beirut [beɪ'ruːt] N Beirut m

Belarus [bɛlə'rus] N Bielorrusia

Belarussian [bɛlə'rʌʃən] ADJ, N bielorruso(-a) m/f ▶ N (Ling) bielorruso

belated [bɪ'leɪtɪd] ADJ atrasado, tardío

belch [bɛltʃ] VI eructar ▶ VT (also: **belch out**: smoke etc) vomitar, arrojar

beleaguered [bɪ'liːgəd] ADJ asediado

Belfast ['bɛlfɑːst] N Belfast m

belfry ['bɛlfrɪ] N campanario

★**Belgian** ['bɛldʒən] ADJ, N belga mf

★**Belgium** ['bɛldʒəm] N Bélgica

Belgrade [bɛl'greɪd] N Belgrado

belie [bɪ'laɪ] VT (give false impression of) desmentir, contradecir

belief [bɪ'liːf] N (opinion) opinión f; (trust, faith) fe f; (acceptance as true) creencia; **it's beyond ~** es increíble; **in the ~ that** creyendo que

believable [bɪ'liːvəbl] ADJ creíble

★**believe** [bɪ'liːv] VT, VI creer; **to ~ (that)** creer (que); **to ~ in** (God, ghosts) creer en; (method) ser partidario de; **he is believed to be abroad** se cree que está en el extranjero; **I don't ~ in corporal punishment** no soy partidario del castigo corporal

believer [bɪ'liːvər] N (in idea, activity) partidario(-a); (Rel) creyente mf, fiel mf

belittle [bɪ'lɪtl] VT despreciar

Belize [bɛ'liːz] N Belice f

★**bell** [bɛl] N campana; (small) campanilla; (on door) timbre m; (animal's) cencerro; (on toy etc) cascabel m; **that rings a ~** (fig) eso me suena

bellboy ['bɛlbɔɪ], (US) **bellhop** ['bɛlhɔp] N botones m inv

belligerent [bɪ'lɪdʒərənt] ADJ (at war) beligerante; (fig) agresivo

bellow ['bɛləʊ] VI bramar; (person) rugir ▶ VT (orders) gritar

bellows ['bɛləʊz] NPL fuelle msg

bell pepper N (esp US) pimiento, pimentón m (LAm)

bell push N pulsador m de timbre

belly ['bɛlɪ] N barriga, panza

bellyache ['bɛlɪeɪk] N dolor m de barriga or de tripa ▶ VI (inf) gruñir

belly button (inf) N ombligo

bellyful ['bɛlɪful] N: **to have had a ~ of ...** (inf) estar más que harto de ...

★**belong** [bɪ'lɔŋ] VI: **to ~ to** pertenecer a; (club etc) ser socio de; **this book belongs here** este libro va aquí

belongings [bɪ'lɔŋɪŋz] NPL (also: **personal belongings**) pertenencias fpl

Belorussia [bɛləʊ'rʌʃə] N Bielorrusia

Belorussian [bɛləʊ'rʌʃən] ADJ, N = **Belarussian**

beloved [bɪ'lʌvɪd] ADJ, N querido(-a) m/f, amado(-a) m/f

★**below** [bɪ'ləʊ] PREP bajo, debajo de; (less than) inferior a ▶ ADV abajo, (por) debajo; **see ~** véase más abajo

★**belt** [bɛlt] N cinturón m; (Tech) correa, cinta; **industrial ~** cinturón industrial ▶ VT (thrash) pegar con correa
▶ **belt out** VT (song) cantar a voz en grito or a grito pelado
▶ **belt up** VI (Aut) ponerse el cinturón de seguridad; (fig: inf) cerrar el pico

beltway ['bɛltweɪ] N (US Aut) carretera de circunvalación

bemoan [bɪ'məʊn] VT lamentar

bemused [bɪ'mjuːzd] ADJ perplejo

bench [bɛntʃ] N banco; (Brit Pol): **the Government/Opposition benches** (los asientos de) los miembros del Gobierno/de la Oposición; **the B~** (Law) la magistratura

benchmark ['bɛntʃmɑːk] N punto de referencia ▶ VT comparar; **to ~ sth against sth** comparar algo con algo

★**bend** [bɛnd] (pt, pp **bent** [bɛnt]) VT doblar; (body, head) inclinar ▶ VI inclinarse; (road) curvarse ▶ N (in road, river) recodo; (in pipe) codo; see also **bends**
▶ **bend down** VI inclinarse, doblarse
▶ **bend over** VI inclinarse

bends [bɛndz] NPL (Med) apoplejía por cambios bruscos de presión

★**beneath** [bɪ'niːθ] PREP bajo, debajo de; (unworthy of) indigno de ▶ ADV abajo, (por) debajo

benefactor ['bɛnɪfæktər] N bienhechor m

benefactress ['bɛnɪfæktrɪs] N bienhechora

beneficial [bɛnɪ'fɪʃəl] ADJ: **~ to** beneficioso para

beneficiary [bɛnɪ'fɪʃərɪ] N (Law) beneficiario(-a)

★**benefit** ['bɛnɪfɪt] N beneficio, provecho; (allowance of money) subsidio; **unemployment ~** subsidio de desempleo ▶ VT beneficiar ▶ VI: **he'll ~ from it** le sacará provecho

Benelux ['bɛnɪlʌks] N Benelux m

benevolence [bɪ'nɛvələns] N benevolencia

benevolent [bɪ'nɛvələnt] ADJ benévolo

BEng N ABBR (= *Bachelor of Engineering*) título universitario

benign [bɪˈnaɪn] ADJ (*person*) benigno; (*Med*) benigno; (*smile*) afable

Benin [bɛˈniːn] N Benín *m*

bent [bɛnt] PT, PP *of* **bend** ▶ N inclinación *f* ▶ ADJ (*wire, pipe*) doblado, torcido; (*inf: dishonest*) pringado, corrupto; **to be ~ on** estar empeñado en

bequeath [bɪˈkwiːð] VT legar

bequest [bɪˈkwɛst] N legado

bereaved [bɪˈriːvd] ADJ afligido ▶ N: **the ~** los allegados *mpl* del difunto

bereavement [bɪˈriːvmənt] N aflicción *f*

beret [ˈbɛreɪ] N boina

Bering Sea [ˈbɛərɪŋ-] N: **the ~** el Mar de Bering

berk [bəːk] N (BRIT *pej*) imbécil *mf*

Berlin [bəːˈlɪn] N Berlín *m*

berm [bəːm] N (US *Aut*) arcén *m*

Bermuda [bəːˈmjuːdə] N las (Islas) Bermudas

Bermuda shorts NPL bermudas *mf*

Bern [bəːn] N Berna

berry [ˈbɛrɪ] N baya

berserk [bəˈsəːk] ADJ: **to go ~** perder los estribos

berth [bəːθ] N (*bed*) litera; (*cabin*) camarote *m*; (*for ship*) amarradero; **to give sb a wide ~** (*fig*) evitar encontrarse con algn ▶ VI atracar, amarrar

beseech [bɪˈsiːtʃ] (*pt, pp* **besought** [-ˈsɔːt]) VT suplicar

beset [bɪˈsɛt] (*pt, pp ~*) VT (*person*) acosar ▶ ADJ: **a policy ~ with dangers** una política rodeada de peligros

besetting [bɪˈsɛtɪŋ] ADJ: **his ~ sin** su principal falta

★**beside** [bɪˈsaɪd] PREP junto a, al lado de; (*compared with*) comparado con; **to be ~ o.s. with anger** estar fuera de sí; **that's ~ the point** eso no tiene nada que ver

besides [bɪˈsaɪdz] ADV además ▶ PREP (*as well as*) además de; (*except*) excepto

besiege [bɪˈsiːdʒ] VT (*town*) sitiar; (*fig*) asediar

besmirch [bɪˈsməːtʃ] VT (*fig*) manchar, mancillar

besotted [bɪˈsɔtɪd] ADJ: **~ with** chiflado por

bespoke [bɪˈspəʊk] ADJ (*garment*) hecho a la medida; **~ tailor** sastre *m* que confecciona a la medida

★**best** [bɛst] ADJ (el/la) mejor; **the ~ part of** (*most*) la mayor parte de; **the ~ thing to do is ...** lo mejor (que se puede hacer) es ... ▶ ADV (lo) mejor ▶ N lo mejor; **to make the ~ of sth** sacar el mejor partido de algo; **to do one's ~** hacer todo lo posible; **to the ~ of my knowledge** que yo sepa; **to the ~ of my ability** como mejor puedo; **at ~** en el mejor de los casos; **he's not exactly patient at the ~ of times** no es que tenga mucha paciencia precisamente

best-before date N fecha de consumo preferente

bestial [ˈbɛstɪəl] ADJ bestial

best man N (*irreg*) padrino de boda

bestow [bɪˈstəʊ] VT otorgar; (*honour, praise*) dispensar; **to ~ sth on sb** conceder *or* dar algo a algn

bestseller [ˈbɛstˈsɛləʳ] N éxito de ventas, bestseller *m*

bet [bɛt] N apuesta; **it's a safe ~** (*fig*) es cosa segura ▶ VT, VI (*pt, pp ~ or* **betted**): **to ~ (on)** apostar (a)

Bethlehem [ˈbɛθlɪhɛm] N Belén *m*

betray [bɪˈtreɪ] VT traicionar; (*trust*) faltar a; (*inform on*) delatar

betrayal [bɪˈtreɪəl] N traición *f*

★**better** [ˈbɛtəʳ] ADJ mejor; **to get ~** mejorar(se); **that's ~!** ¡eso es!; **~ off** más acomodado ▶ ADV mejor; **you had ~ do it** más vale que lo hagas; **he thought ~ of it** cambió de parecer; **I had ~ go** tengo que irme ▶ VT mejorar; (*record etc*) superar ▶ N: **to get the ~ of sb** quedar por encima de algn; **a change for the ~** una mejora

betting [ˈbɛtɪŋ] N juego, apuestas *fpl*

betting shop N (BRIT) casa de apuestas

★**between** [bɪˈtwiːn] PREP entre; **the road ~ here and London** la carretera de aquí a Londres; **we only had 5 ~ us** teníamos solo 5 entre todos ▶ ADV (*also*: **in between**: *time*) mientras tanto; (: *place*) en medio

bevel [ˈbɛvəl] N (*also*: **bevel edge**) bisel *m*, chaflán *m*

beverage [ˈbɛvərɪdʒ] N bebida

bevy [ˈbɛvɪ] N: **a ~ of** una bandada de

bewail [bɪˈweɪl] VT lamentar

beware [bɪˈwɛəʳ] VI: **to ~ (of)** tener cuidado (con); **"~ of the dog"** "perro peligroso" ▶ EXCL ¡cuidado!

bewildered [bɪˈwɪldəd] ADJ aturdido, perplejo

bewildering [bɪˈwɪldərɪŋ] ADJ desconcertante

bewitching [bɪˈwɪtʃɪŋ] ADJ hechicero, encantador(a)

beyond [bɪˈjɔnd] PREP más allá de; (*past: understanding*) fuera de; (*after: date*) después de, más allá de; (*above*) superior a; **~ doubt** fuera de toda duda; **~ repair** irreparable ▶ ADV (*in space*) más allá; (*in time*) posteriormente

b/f ABBR (= *brought forward*) saldo previo

BFPO N ABBR (= *British Forces Post Office*) servicio postal del ejército

bhp N ABBR (*Aut*: = *brake horsepower*) potencia al freno

Bhutan [buːˈtɑːn] N Bután *m*

bi... [baɪ] PREF bi...

biannual [baɪˈænjuəl] ADJ semestral

bias [ˈbaɪəs] N (*prejudice*) prejuicio; (*preference*) predisposición *f*

biased, biassed [ˈbaɪəst] ADJ parcial; **to be ~ against** tener perjuicios contra

biathlon [baɪˈæθlən] N biatlón *m*

bib [bɪb] N babero

★**Bible** ['baɪbl] N Biblia

biblical ['bɪblɪkəl] ADJ bíblico

bibliography [bɪblɪ'ɔgrəfɪ] N bibliografía

bicarbonate of soda [baɪ'kɑːbənɪt-] N bicarbonato sódico

bicentenary [baɪsen'tiːnərɪ], (US) **bicentennial** [baɪsen'tenɪəl] N bicentenario

biceps ['baɪseps] N bíceps *m*

bicker ['bɪkəʳ] VI reñir

bickering ['bɪkərɪŋ] N riñas *fpl*, altercados *mpl*

★**bicycle** ['baɪsɪkl] N bicicleta

bicycle path N camino para ciclistas

bicycle pump N bomba de bicicleta

bid [bɪd] N (*at auction*) oferta, puja, postura; (*attempt*) tentativa, conato ▶ VI (*pt, pp* ~) hacer una oferta ▶ VT (*pt, pp* ~) (*offer*) ofrecer; (*pt* **bade** [bæd], *pp* **bidden** ['bɪdn]); **to ~ sb good day** dar a algn los buenos días

bidder ['bɪdəʳ] N: **the highest ~** el mejor postor

bidding ['bɪdɪŋ] N (*at auction*) ofertas *fpl*, puja; (*order*) orden *f*, mandato

bide [baɪd] VT: **to ~ one's time** esperar el momento adecuado

bidet ['biːdeɪ] N bidet *m*

bidirectional ['baɪdɪ'rekʃənl] ADJ bidireccional

biennial [baɪ'enɪəl] ADJ, N bienal *f*

bier [bɪəʳ] N féretro

bifocals [baɪ'fəuklz] NPL gafas *fpl* or (*LAM*) anteojos *mpl* bifocales

★**big** [bɪg] ADJ grande; (*brother, sister*) mayor; **~ business** gran negocio; **to do things in a ~ way** hacer las cosas en grande

bigamy ['bɪgəmɪ] N bigamia

Big Apple N *ver nota*

Muchos ya saben que **The Big Apple** (la Gran Manzana) es el término con el que se conoce a la ciudad de Nueva York (manzana es un término coloquial que significa gran ciudad). Pero los sobrenombres de otras ciudades estadounidenses son menos conocidos. A Chicago se le llama *Windy City* (la Ciudad del Viento), por las fuertes ráfagas que soplan desde el Lago Michigan; a Nueva Orleans se la conoce como *Big Easy* por su estilo de vida relajado; y la industria del automóvil da a Detroit el nombre de *Motown*.

big dipper [-'dɪpəʳ] N montaña rusa

big end N (*Aut*) cabeza de biela

biggish ['bɪgɪʃ] ADJ más bien grande; (*man*) más bien alto

bigheaded ['bɪg'hedɪd] ADJ engreído

bigot ['bɪgət] N fanático(-a), intolerante *mf*

bigoted ['bɪgətɪd] ADJ fanático, intolerante

bigotry ['bɪgətrɪ] N fanatismo, intolerancia

big toe N dedo gordo (del pie)

big top N (*circus*) circo; (*main tent*) carpa principal

big wheel N (*at fair*) noria

bigwig ['bɪgwɪg] N (*inf*) pez *m* gordo

★**bike** [baɪk] N bici *f*

bike lane N carril *m* de bicicleta, carril *m* bici

bikini [bɪ'kiːnɪ] N bikini *m*

bilateral [baɪ'lætərl] ADJ (*agreement*) bilateral

bile [baɪl] N bilis *f*

bilge [bɪldʒ] N (*water*) agua de sentina

bilingual [baɪ'lɪŋgwəl] ADJ bilingüe

bilious ['bɪlɪəs] ADJ bilioso (*also fig*)

★**bill** [bɪl] N (*gen*) cuenta; (*invoice*) factura; (*Pol*) proyecto de ley; (*US: banknote*) billete *m*; (*of bird*) pico; (*notice*) cartel *m*; (*Theat*) programa *m*; **may I have the ~ please?** ¿puede traerme la cuenta, por favor?; **~ of exchange** letra de cambio; **~ of lading** conocimiento de embarque; **~ of sale** escritura de venta; **"post no bills"** "prohibido fijar carteles"; **to fit** or **fill the ~** (*fig*) cumplir con los requisitos ▶ VT extender or pasar la factura a

billboard ['bɪlbɔːd] N valla publicitaria

billet ['bɪlɪt] N alojamiento ▶ VT: **to ~ sb (on sb)** alojar a algn (con algn)

billfold ['bɪlfəuld] N (US) cartera

billiards ['bɪljədz] N billar *m*

★**billion** ['bɪljən] N (*BRIT*) billón *m*; (*US*) mil millones *mpl*

billow ['bɪləu] N (*of smoke*) nube *f*; (*of sail*) ondulación *f* ▶ VI (*smoke*) salir en nubes; (*sail*) ondear, ondular

billy ['bɪlɪ] N (US) porra

billy goat N macho cabrío

bimbo ['bɪmbəu] N (*pej*) tía buena sin seso

bin [bɪn] N (*gen*) cubo or (*LAM*) bote *m* de la basura; (*litterbin*) papelera

binary ['baɪnərɪ] ADJ (*Math*) binario; **~ code** código binario

bind [baɪnd] (*pt, pp* **bound** [baund]) VT atar, liar; (*wound*) vendar; (*book*) encuadernar; (*oblige*) obligar ▶ N (*inf: nuisance*) lata
▶ **bind over** VT (*Law*) obligar por vía legal
▶ **bind up** VT (*wound*) vendar; **to be bound up in** (*work, research etc*) estar absorto en; **to be bound up with** (*person*) estar estrechamente ligado a

binder ['baɪndəʳ] N (*file*) archivador *m*

binding ['baɪndɪŋ] ADJ (*contract*) vinculante

binge [bɪndʒ] N borrachera, juerga; **to go on a ~** (*inf*) ir de juerga

bingo ['bɪŋgəu] N bingo *m*

bin-liner ['bɪnlaɪnəʳ] N bolsa de la basura

binoculars [bɪ'nɔkjuləz] NPL prismáticos *mpl*, gemelos *mpl*

biochemical [baɪəu'kemɪkl] ADJ bioquímico

biochemistry [baɪə'kemɪstrɪ] N bioquímica

biodegradable ['baɪəudɪ'greɪdəbl] ADJ biodegradable

biodiesel ['baɪəudiːzl] N biodiésel *m*

biodiversity [ˌbaɪəʊdaɪˈvɜːsɪtɪ] N biodiversidad f

biofuel [ˈbaɪəʊfjuəl] N biocombustible m, biocarburante m

biographer [baɪˈɒɡrəfəʳ] N biógrafo(-a)

biographical [baɪəˈɡræfɪkəl] ADJ biográfico

biography [baɪˈɒɡrəfɪ] N biografía

biological [baɪəˈlɒdʒɪkəl] ADJ biológico; (products, foodstuffs etc) orgánico(-a)

biological clock N reloj m biológico

biologist [baɪˈɒlədʒɪst] N biólogo(-a)

★**biology** [baɪˈɒlədʒɪ] N biología

biometric [baɪəˈmetrɪk] ADJ biométrico

biophysics [ˈbaɪəʊˈfɪzɪks] NSG biofísica

biopic [ˈbaɪəʊpɪk] N filme m biográfico

biopsy [ˈbaɪɒpsɪ] N biopsia

biosecurity [ˈbaɪəʊsɪˈkjʊərɪtɪ] N bioseguridad f

biosphere [ˈbaɪəsfɪəʳ] N biosfera

biotechnology [ˈbaɪəʊtɛkˈnɒlədʒɪ] N biotecnología

bioterrorism [ˈbaɪəʊˈtɛrərɪzəm] N bioterrorismo

biped [ˈbaɪpɛd] N bípedo

bipolar [baɪˈpəʊləʳ] ADJ bipolar

birch [bɜːtʃ] N abedul m; (cane) vara

★**bird** [bɜːd] N ave f, pájaro; (Brit pej: girl) chica

birdcage [ˈbɜːdkeɪdʒ] N jaula

bird flu N gripe aviar

bird of prey N ave f de presa

bird's-eye view [ˈbɜːdzaɪ-] N vista de pájaro

bird-watcher N ornitólogo(-a)

bird-watching N: **he likes to go ~ on Sundays** los domingos le gusta ir a ver pájaros

Biro® [ˈbaɪrəʊ] N bolígrafo

★**birth** [bɜːθ] N nacimiento; (Med) parto; **to give ~ to** parir, dar a luz a; (fig) dar origen a

birth certificate N partida de nacimiento

birth control N control m de natalidad; (methods) métodos mpl anticonceptivos

★**birthday** [ˈbɜːθdeɪ] N cumpleaños m inv

birthday card N tarjeta de cumpleaños

birthmark N [ˈbɜːθmɑːk] antojo, marca de nacimiento

birthplace [ˈbɜːθpleɪs] N lugar m de nacimiento

birth rate N (tasa de) natalidad f

Biscay [ˈbɪskeɪ] N: **the Bay of ~** el mar Cantábrico, el golfo de Vizcaya

★**biscuit** [ˈbɪskɪt] N (Brit) galleta

bisect [baɪˈsɛkt] VT (also Math) bisecar

bisexual [ˈbaɪˈsɛksjuəl] ADJ, N bisexual mf

bishop [ˈbɪʃəp] N obispo; (Chess) alfil m

bistro [ˈbiːstrəʊ] N café-bar m

★**bit** [bɪt] PT of **bite** ▶ N trozo, pedazo, pedacito; (Comput) bit m; (for horse) freno, bocado; **a ~ of** un poco de; **~ by ~** poco a poco; **to come to bits** (break) hacerse pedazos; **to do one's ~** aportar

su granito de arena; **bring all your bits and pieces** trae todas tus cosas ▶ ADV: **a ~ mad** un poco loco

bitch [bɪtʃ] N (dog) perra; (!: woman) zorra (!)

bitcoin [ˈbɪtkɔɪn] N (Comput) bitcoin m

★**bite** [baɪt] VT, VI (pt **bit** [bɪt], pp **bitten** [ˈbɪtn]) morder; (insect etc) picar; **to ~ one's nails** morderse las uñas ▶ N (wound: of dog, snake etc) mordedura; (: of insect) picadura; (mouthful) bocado; **let's have a ~ (to eat)** vamos a comer algo

biting [ˈbaɪtɪŋ] ADJ (wind) que traspasa los huesos; (criticism) mordaz

bit part N (Theat) papel m sin importancia, papelito

bitten [ˈbɪtn] PP of **bite**

★**bitter** [ˈbɪtəʳ] ADJ amargo; (wind, criticism) cortante, penetrante; (icy: weather) glacial; (: battle) encarnizado ▶ N (Brit: beer) cerveza típica británica a base de lúpulos

bitterly [ˈbɪtəlɪ] ADV (disappoint, complain, weep) desconsoladamente; (oppose, criticise) implacablemente; (jealous) agriamente; **it's ~ cold** hace un frío glacial

bitterness [ˈbɪtənɪs] N amargura; (anger) rencor m

bitty [ˈbɪtɪ] ADJ (inf) deshilvanado

bitumen [ˈbɪtjumɪn] N betún m

bivouac [ˈbɪvuæk] N vivac m, vivaque m

bizarre [bɪˈzɑːʳ] ADJ raro, extraño

BL N ABBR (= Bachelor of Law; Bachelor of Letters) títulos universitarios; (US: = Bachelor of Literature) título universitario; see also **bachelor's degree**

B/L ABBR = **bill of lading**

blab [blæb] VI cantar ▶ VT (also: **blab out**) soltar, contar

★**black** [blæk] ADJ (colour) negro; (dark) oscuro; **to give sb a ~ eye** ponerle a algn el ojo morado; **~ and blue** adj amoratado; **~ coffee** café m solo ▶ N (colour) color m negro; **there it is in ~ and white** (fig) ahí está bien claro; **to be in the ~** (in credit) tener saldo positivo ▶ VT (shoes) lustrar; (Brit Industry) boicotear ▶ **black out** VI (faint) desmayarse

black belt N (Sport) cinturón m negro; (US: area) zona negra

blackberry [ˈblækbərɪ] N zarzamora

blackbird [ˈblækbɜːd] N mirlo

blackboard [ˈblækbɔːd] N pizarra

black box N (Aviat) caja negra

Black Country N (Brit): **the ~** región industrial del centro de Inglaterra

blackcurrant [ˈblækˈkʌrənt] N grosella negra

black economy N economía sumergida

blacken [ˈblækən] VT ennegrecer; (fig) denigrar

Black Forest N: **the ~** la Selva Negra

blackguard [ˈblægɑːd] N canalla m, pillo

black hole N (Astro) agujero negro

black ice N hielo invisible en la carretera

blackjack [ˈblækdʒæk] N (US) veintiuna

blackleg [ˈblækleg] N (BRIT) esquirol mf

blacklist [ˈblæklɪst] N lista negra ▸ VT poner en la lista negra

blackmail [ˈblækmeɪl] N chantaje m ▸ VT chantajear

blackmailer [ˈblækmeɪləʳ] N chantajista mf

black market N mercado negro, estraperlo

blackness [ˈblæknɪs] N negrura

blackout [ˈblækaut] N (Elec) apagón m; (TV) bloqueo informativo; (fainting) desmayo, pérdida de conocimiento

black pepper N pimienta f negra

black pudding N morcilla

Black Sea N: the ~ el mar Negro

black sheep N oveja negra

blacksmith [ˈblæksmɪθ] N herrero

black spot N (Aut) punto negro

bladder [ˈblædəʳ] N vejiga

blade [bleɪd] N hoja; (cutting edge) filo; **a ~ of grass** una brizna de hierba

blame [bleɪm] N culpa ▸ VT: **to ~ sb for sth** echar a algn la culpa de algo; **to be to ~ (for)** tener la culpa (de); **and I don't ~ him** y lo comprendo perfectamente; **I'm not to ~** yo no tengo la culpa

blameless [ˈbleɪmlɪs] ADJ (person) inocente

blanch [blɑːntʃ] VI (person) palidecer; (Culin) escaldar

bland [blænd] ADJ suave; (taste) soso

blank [blæŋk] ADJ en blanco; (shot) de fogueo; (look) sin expresión ▸ N blanco, espacio en blanco; (cartridge) cartucho sin bala or de fogueo; **to draw a ~** (fig) no conseguir nada; **my mind is a ~** no puedo recordar nada

blank cheque, (US) **blank check** N cheque m en blanco

★**blanket** [ˈblæŋkɪt] N manta, frazada (LAM), cobija (LAM); (of snow) capa; (of fog) manto ▸ ADJ (statement, agreement) comprensivo, general; **to give ~ cover** (insurance policy) dar póliza a todo riesgo

blankly [ˈblæŋklɪ] ADV: **she looked at me ~** me miró sin comprender

blare [blɛəʳ] VI (brass band, horns, radio) resonar

blasé [ˈblɑːzeɪ] ADJ de vuelta de todo

blaspheme [blæsˈfiːm] VI blasfemar

blasphemous [ˈblæsfɪməs] ADJ blasfemo

blasphemy [ˈblæsfɪmɪ] N blasfemia

blast [blɑːst] N (of wind) ráfaga, soplo; (of whistle) toque m; (of explosive) explosión f; (force) choque m; **(at) full ~** (also fig) a toda marcha ▸ VT (blow up) volar; (blow open) abrir con carga explosiva ▸ EXCL (BRIT inf) ¡maldito sea! ▸ **blast off** VI (spacecraft etc) despegar

blast furnace N alto horno

blast-off [ˈblɑːstɔf] N (Space) lanzamiento

blatant [ˈbleɪtənt] ADJ descarado

blatantly [ˈbleɪtəntlɪ] ADV: **it's ~ obvious** está clarísimo

blather [ˈblæðəʳ] VI decir tonterías

blaze [bleɪz] N (fire) fuego; (flames) llamarada; (glow: of fire, sun etc) resplandor m; (fig) arranque m; **in a ~ of publicity** bajo los focos de la publicidad ▸ VI (fire) arder en llamas; (fig) brillar ▸ VT: **to ~ a trail** (fig) abrir (un) camino

blazer [ˈbleɪzəʳ] N chaqueta de uniforme de colegial o de socio de club

bleach [bliːtʃ] N (also: **household bleach**) lejía ▸ VT (linen) blanquear

bleached [bliːtʃt] ADJ (hair) decolorado; (clothes) blanqueado

bleachers [ˈbliːtʃəz] NPL (US Sport) gradas fpl

bleak [bliːk] ADJ (countryside) desierto; (landscape) desolado, desierto; (weather) desapacible; (smile) triste; (prospect, future) poco prometedor(a)

bleary-eyed [ˈblɪərɪˈaɪd] ADJ: **to be ~** tener ojos de cansado

bleat [bliːt] VI balar

bled [blɛd] PT, PP of **bleed**

bleed [bliːd] (pt, pp **bled** [blɛd]) VT sangrar; (brakes, radiator) desaguar ▸ VI sangrar; **my nose is bleeding** me está sangrando la nariz

bleeding [ˈbliːdɪŋ] ADJ sangrante

bleep [bliːp] N pitido ▸ VI pitar ▸ VT llamar por el busca

bleeper [ˈbliːpəʳ] N (of doctor etc) busca m

blemish [ˈblɛmɪʃ] N marca, mancha; (on reputation) tacha

blench [blɛntʃ] VI (shrink back) acobardarse; (grow pale) palidecer

blend [blɛnd] N mezcla ▸ VT mezclar ▸ VI (colours etc) combinarse, mezclarse

blender [ˈblɛndəʳ] N (Culin) batidora

bless [blɛs] (pt, pp **blessed** or **blest** [blɛst]) VT bendecir; **~ you!** (after sneeze) ¡Jesús!

blessed [ˈblɛsɪd] ADJ (Rel: holy) santo, bendito; (: happy) dichoso; **every ~ day** cada santo día

blessing [ˈblɛsɪŋ] N bendición f; (advantage) beneficio, ventaja; **to count one's blessings** agradecer lo que se tiene; **it was a ~ in disguise** no hay mal que por bien no venga

blew [bluː] PT of **blow**

blight [blaɪt] VT (hopes etc) frustrar, arruinar

blimey [ˈblaɪmɪ] EXCL (BRIT inf) ¡caray!

★**blind** [blaɪnd] ADJ ciego; **~ people** los ciegos ▸ N (for window) persiana ▸ VT cegar; (dazzle) deslumbrar; **to ~ sb to ...** (deceive) cegar a algn a ...

blind alley N callejón m sin salida

blind corner N (BRIT) esquina or curva sin visibilidad

blind date N cita a ciegas

blinders [ˈblaɪndəz] NPL (US) anteojeras fpl

blindfold [ˈblaɪndfəuld] N venda ▸ ADJ, ADV con los ojos vendados ▸ VT vendar los ojos a

blinding ['blaindiŋ] ADJ (*flash, light*) cegador; (*pain*) intenso

blindingly ['blaindiŋli] ADV: **it's ~ obvious** salta a la vista

blindly ['blaindli] ADV a ciegas, ciegamente

blindness ['blaindnis] N ceguera

blind spot N (*Aut*) ángulo muerto; **to have a ~ about sth** estar ciego para algo

blink [bliŋk] VI parpadear, pestañear; (*light*) oscilar; **to be on the ~** (*inf*) estar estropeado

blinkers ['bliŋkəz] NPL (*esp BRIT*) anteojeras *fpl*

blinking ['bliŋkiŋ] ADJ (*inf*): **this ~ ...** este condenado ...

blip [blip] N señal *f* luminosa; (*on graph*) pequeña desviación *f*; (*fig*) pequeña anomalía

bliss [blis] N felicidad *f*

blissful ['blisful] ADJ dichoso; **in ~ ignorance** feliz en la ignorancia

blissfully ['blisfuli] ADV (*sigh, smile*) con felicidad; **~ happy** sumamente feliz

blister ['blistə'] N (*on skin, paint*) ampolla ▶ VI ampollarse

blistering ['blistəriŋ] ADJ (*heat*) abrasador(a)

BLit, BLitt N ABBR (= *Bachelor of Literature*) título universitario

blithely ['blaiðli] ADV alegremente, despreocupadamente

blithering ['bliðəriŋ] ADJ (*inf*): **this ~ idiot** este tonto perdido

blitz [blits] N bombardeo aéreo; **to have a ~ on sth** (*fig*) emprenderla con algo

blizzard ['blizəd] N ventisca

BLM N ABBR (*US*) = **Bureau of Land Management**

bloated ['bləutid] ADJ hinchado

blob [blɔb] N (*drop*) gota; (*stain, spot*) mancha

bloc [blɔk] N (*Pol*) bloque *m*

★**block** [blɔk] N (*also Comput*) bloque *m*; (*in pipes*) obstáculo; (*of buildings*) manzana, cuadra (*LAM*); **~ of flats** (*BRIT*) bloque *m* de pisos; **mental ~** bloqueo mental; **~ and tackle** (*Tech*) aparejo de polea; **3 blocks from here** a 3 manzanas *or* (*LAM*) cuadras de aquí ▶ VT (*gen*) obstruir, cerrar; (*progress*) estorbar; (*Comput*) agrupar
  ▶ **block up** VT tapar, obstruir; (*pipe*) atascar

blockade [blɔ'keid] N bloqueo ▶ VT bloquear

blockage ['blɔkidʒ] N estorbo, obstrucción *f*

block booking N reserva en grupo

blockbuster ['blɔkbʌstə'] N (*book*) best-seller *m*; (*film*) éxito de público

block capitals NPL mayúsculas *fpl*

block letters NPL mayúsculas *fpl*

block release N (*BRIT*) exención *f* por estudios

block vote N (*BRIT*) voto por delegación

blog [blɔg] (*Comput*) N blog *m* ▶ VI bloguear; **he blogs about politics** tiene un blog sobre política

blogger ['blɔgə'] N (*person*) bloguero(-a)

blogging ['blɔgiŋ] N blogging *m*

blogosphere ['blɔgəsfiə'] N blogosfera

blogpost ['blɔgpəust] N entrada de un blog, post *m*

bloke [bləuk] N (*BRIT inf*) tipo, tío

blond, blonde [blɔnd] ADJ, N rubio(-a) *m/f*

★**blood** [blʌd] N sangre *f*; **new ~** (*fig*) gente *f* nueva

blood bank N banco de sangre

blood count N recuento de glóbulos rojos y blancos

blood donor N donante *mf* de sangre

blood group N grupo sanguíneo

bloodhound ['blʌdhaund] N sabueso

bloodless ['blʌdlis] ADJ (*pale*) exangüe; (*revolt etc*) sin derramamiento de sangre, incruento

bloodletting ['blʌdletiŋ] N (*Med*) sangría; (*fig*) sangría, carnicería

blood poisoning N septicemia, envenenamiento de la sangre

blood pressure N tensión *f*, presión *f* sanguínea; **to have high/low ~** tener la tensión alta/baja

bloodshed ['blʌdʃed] N baño de sangre

bloodshot ['blʌdʃɔt] ADJ inyectado en sangre

bloodstained ['blʌdsteind] ADJ manchado de sangre

bloodstream ['blʌdstri:m] N corriente *f* sanguínea

blood test N análisis *m* de sangre

bloodthirsty ['blʌdθə:sti] ADJ sanguinario

blood transfusion N transfusión *f* de sangre

blood type N grupo sanguíneo

blood vessel N vaso sanguíneo

bloody ['blʌdi] ADJ sangriento; (*BRIT infl*): **this ~ ...** este condenado *or* puñetero *or* (*LAM*) fregado ... (*infl*) ▶ ADV (*BRIT infl*): **~ strong/good** terriblemente fuerte/bueno

bloody-minded ['blʌdi'maindid] ADJ (*BRIT inf*) con malas pulgas

bloom [blu:m] N floración *f*; **in ~** en flor ▶ VI florecer

blooming ['blu:miŋ] ADJ (*inf*): **this ~ ...** este condenado ...

blossom ['blɔsəm] N flor *f* ▶ VI florecer; (*fig*) desarrollarse; **to ~ into** (*fig*) convertirse en

blot [blɔt] N borrón *m*; **to be a ~ on the landscape** estropear el paisaje ▶ VT (*dry*) secar; (*stain*) manchar; **to ~ out** (*view*) tapar; (*memories*) borrar; **to ~ one's copy book** (*fig*) manchar su reputación

blotchy ['blɔtʃi] ADJ (*complexion*) lleno de manchas

blotter ['blɔtə'] N secante *m*

blotting paper ['blɔtiŋ-] N papel *m* secante

blotto ['blɔtəu] ADJ (*inf*) mamado

★**blouse** [blauz] N blusa

★**blow** [bləu] (*pt* **blew** [blu:], *pp* **blown** [bləun]) N golpe *m*; **to come to blows** llegar a golpes ▶ vi soplar; (*fuse*) fundirse ▶ vt (*glass*) soplar; (*fuse*) quemar; (*instrument*) tocar; **to ~ one's nose** sonarse

▶ **blow away** vt llevarse, arrancar

▶ **blow down** vt derribar

▶ **blow off** vt arrebatar

▶ **blow out** vt apagar ▶ vi apagarse; (*tyre*) reventar

▶ **blow over** vi amainar

▶ **blow up** vi estallar ▶ vt volar; (*tyre*) inflar; (*Phot*) ampliar

blow-dry [ˈbləudraɪ] N secado con secador de mano ▶ vt secar con secador de mano

blowlamp [ˈbləulæmp] N (*BRIT*) soplete *m*, lámpara de soldar

blown [bləun] PP *of* **blow**

blowout [ˈbləuaut] N (*of tyre*) pinchazo; (*inf: big meal*) banquete *m*, festín *m*

blowtorch [ˈbləutɔːtʃ] N = **blowlamp**

blow-up [ˈbləuʌp] N (*Phot*) ampliación *f*

BLS N ABBR (*US*) = **Bureau of Labor Statistics**

blubber [ˈblʌbəʳ] N grasa de ballena ▶ vi (*pej*) lloriquear

bludgeon [ˈblʌdʒən] vt: **to ~ sb into doing sth** coaccionar a algn a hacer algo

★**blue** [bluː] ADJ azul; **~ film** película porno; **~ joke** chiste verde; **once in a ~ moon** de higos a brevas; **to come out of the ~** (*fig*) ser completamente inesperado; *see also* **blues**

blue baby N niño azul *or* cianótico

bluebell [ˈbluːbɛl] N campanilla, campánula azul

blueberry N [ˈbluːbərɪ] arándano

blue-blooded [bluːˈblʌdɪd] ADJ de sangre azul

bluebottle [ˈbluːbɒtl] N moscarda, mosca azul

blue cheese N queso azul

blue-chip [ˈbluːtʃɪp] N: **~ investment** inversión *f* asegurada

blue-collar worker [ˈbluːkɔləʳ-] N obrero(-a)

blue jeans NPL tejanos *mpl*, vaqueros *mpl*

blueprint [ˈbluːprɪnt] N proyecto; **~ (for)** (*fig*) anteproyecto (de)

blues [bluːz] NPL: **the ~** (*Mus*) el blues; **to have the ~** estar triste

bluetit [ˈbluːtɪt] N herrerillo *m* (común)

Bluetooth® [ˈbluːtuːθ] N Bluetooth® *f*; **~ technology** tecnología Bluetooth®

bluff [blʌf] vi tirarse un farol, farolear ▶ N bluff *m*, farol *m*; (*Geo*) precipicio, despeñadero; **to call sb's ~** coger a algn en un renuncio

bluish [ˈbluːɪʃ] ADJ azulado

blunder [ˈblʌndəʳ] N patinazo, metedura de pata ▶ vi cometer un error, meter la pata; **to ~ into sb/sth** tropezar con algn/algo

blunt [blʌnt] ADJ (*knife*) desafilado; (*person*) franco, directo; **this pencil is ~** este lápiz está despuntado; **~ instrument** (*Law*) instrumento contundente ▶ vt embotar, desafilar

bluntly [ˈblʌntlɪ] ADV (*speak*) francamente, de modo terminante

bluntness [ˈblʌntnɪs] N (*of person*) franqueza, brusquedad *f*

blur [bləːʳ] N aspecto borroso; **to become a ~** hacerse borroso ▶ vt (*vision*) enturbiar; (*memory*) empañar

blurb [bləːb] N propaganda

blurred [bləːd] ADJ borroso

blurt [bləːt]: **to ~ out** vt (*say*) descolgarse con, dejar escapar

blush [blʌʃ] vi ruborizarse, ponerse colorado ▶ N rubor *m*

blusher [ˈblʌʃəʳ] N colorete *m*

bluster [ˈblʌstəʳ] N fanfarronada, bravata ▶ vi fanfarronear, echar bravatas

blustering [ˈblʌstərɪŋ] ADJ (*person*) fanfarrón(-ona)

blustery [ˈblʌstərɪ] ADJ (*weather*) tempestuoso, tormentoso

Blvd ABBR = **boulevard**

BM N ABBR = **British Museum**; (*Univ*: = *Bachelor of Medicine*) título universitario

BMA N ABBR = **British Medical Association**

BMJ N ABBR = **British Medical Journal**

BMus N ABBR (= *Bachelor of Music*) título universitario

BMX N ABBR (= *bicycle motocross*) BMX *f*; **~ bike** bici(cleta) *f* BMX

bn ABBR = **billion**

BO N ABBR (*inf*: = *body odour*) olor *m* a sudor; (*US*) = **box office**

boa [ˈbəuə] N boa

boar [bɔːʳ] N verraco, cerdo

★**board** [bɔːd] N tabla, tablero; (*on wall*) tablón *m*; (*for chess etc*) tablero; (*committee*) junta, consejo; (*in firm*) mesa *or* junta directiva; (*Naut, Aviat*): **on ~** a bordo; **full ~** (*BRIT*) pensión *f* completa; **half ~** (*BRIT*) media pensión; **~ and lodging** alojamiento y comida; **to go by the ~** (*fig*) irse por la borda; **above ~** (*fig*) sin tapujos; **across the ~** (*fig: adv*) en todos los niveles; (: *adj*) general ▶ vt (*ship*) embarcarse en; (*train*) subir a

▶ **board up** vt (*door*) tapar, cegar

boarder [ˈbɔːdəʳ] N huésped(a) *m/f*; (*Scol*) interno(-a)

board game N juego de tablero

boarding card [ˈbɔːdɪŋ-] N (*BRIT Aviat, Naut*) tarjeta de embarque

boarding house [ˈbɔːdɪŋ-] N casa de huéspedes

boarding party [ˈbɔːdɪŋ-] N brigada de inspección

boarding pass [ˈbɔːdɪŋ-] N (*US*) = **boarding card**

boarding school [ˈbɔːdɪŋ-] N internado

board meeting N reunión *f* de la junta directiva

449

board room N sala de juntas

boardwalk ['bɔ:dwɔ:k] N (US) paseo entablado

boast [bəust] VI: **to ~ (about** or **of)** alardear (de) ▶ VT ostentar ▶ N alarde m, baladronada

boastful ['bəustfəl] ADJ presumido, jactancioso

boastfulness ['bəustfulnɪs] N fanfarronería, jactancia

★**boat** [bəut] N barco, buque m; (small) barca, bote m; **to go by ~** ir en barco

boater ['bəutər] N (hat) canotié m

boating ['bəutɪŋ] N canotaje m

boatman ['bəutmən] N (irreg) barquero

boat people N PL refugiados que huyen en barca

boatswain ['bəusn] N contramaestre m

bob [bɔb] VI (also: **bob up and down**: boat, cork on water) menearse, balancearse ▶ N (BRIT inf) = **shilling**
▶ **bob up** VI (re)aparecer de repente

bobbin ['bɔbɪn] N (of sewing machine) carrete m, bobina

bobby ['bɔbɪ] N (BRIT inf) poli mf

bobby pin N (US) horquilla

bobsleigh ['bɔbsleɪ] N bob m, trineo de competición f

bode [bəud] VI: **to ~ well/ill (for)** ser de buen/mal agüero (para)

bodice ['bɔdɪs] N corpiño

-bodied ['bɔdɪd] ADJ SUFF de cuerpo ...

bodily ['bɔdɪlɪ] ADJ (comfort, needs) corporal; (pain) corpóreo ▶ ADV (in person) en persona; (carry) corporalmente; (lift) en peso

★**body** ['bɔdɪ] N cuerpo; (corpse) cadáver m; (of car) caja, carrocería; (also: **body stocking**) body m; (fig: organization) organización f; (: public body) organismo; (quantity) masa; (of speech, document) parte f principal; **ruling ~** directiva; **in a ~** todos juntos, en masa

body blow N (fig) palo

body-building ['bɔdɪ'bɪldɪŋ] N culturismo

bodyguard ['bɔdɪgɑ:d] N guardaespaldas mf

body language N lenguaje m gestual

body search N cacheo; **to carry out a ~ on sb** registrar a algn; **to submit to** or **undergo a ~** ser registrado

bodywork ['bɔdɪwə:k] N carrocería

boffin ['bɔfɪn] N (BRIT) científico(-a)

bog [bɔg] N pantano, ciénaga ▶ VT: **to get bogged down** (fig) empantanarse, atascarse

boggle ['bɔgl] VI: **the mind boggles!** ¡no puedo creerlo!

Bogotá [bəugə'tɑ:] N Bogotá

bogus ['bəugəs] ADJ falso, fraudulento; (person) fingido

Bohemia [bə'hi:mɪə] N Bohemia

Bohemian [bə'hi:mɪən] ADJ, N bohemio(-a) m/f

★**boil** [bɔɪl] VT hervir; (eggs) pasar por agua; **boiled egg** huevo pasado por agua; **boiled potatoes** patatas f pl or (LAM) papas f pl cocidas ▶ VI hervir; (fig: with anger) estar furioso ▶ N (Med) furúnculo, divieso; **to bring to the ~** calentar hasta que hierva; **to come to the** (BRIT) or **a** (US) **~** comenzar a hervir
▶ **boil down** VI (fig): **to ~ down to** reducirse a
▶ **boil over** VI (liquid) salirse; (anger, resentment) llegar al colmo

boiler ['bɔɪlər] N caldera

boiler suit N (BRIT) mono, overol m (LAM)

boiling ['bɔɪlɪŋ] ADJ: **I'm ~ (hot)** (inf) estoy asado

boiling point N punto de ebullición f

boil-in-the-bag [bɔɪlɪnðə'bæg] ADJ: **~ meals** platos que se cuecen en su misma bolsa

boisterous ['bɔɪstərəs] ADJ (noisy) bullicioso; (excitable) exuberante; (crowd) tumultuoso

bold [bəuld] ADJ (brave) valiente, audaz; (pej) descarado; (outline) grueso; (colour) llamativo; **~ type** (Typ) negrita

boldly ['bəuldlɪ] ADV audazmente

boldness ['bəuldnɪs] N valor m, audacia; (cheek) descaro

Bolivia [bə'lɪvɪə] N Bolivia

Bolivian [bə'lɪvɪən] ADJ, N boliviano(-a) m/f

bollard ['bɔləd] N (BRIT Aut) poste m

Bollywood ['bɔlɪwud] N Bollywood m

bolshy ['bɔlʃɪ] ADJ (BRIT inf) protestón(-ona); **to be in a ~ mood** tener el día protestón

bolster ['bəulstər] N travesero, cabezal m
▶ **bolster up** VT reforzar; (fig) alentar

bolt [bəult] N (lock) cerrojo; (with nut) perno, tornillo ▶ ADV: **~ upright** rígido, erguido ▶ VT (door) echar el cerrojo a; (food) engullir ▶ VI fugarse; (horse) desbocarse

★**bomb** [bɔm] N bomba ▶ VT bombardear

bombard [bɔm'bɑ:d] VT bombardear; (fig) asediar

bombardment [bɔm'bɑ:dmənt] N bombardeo

bombastic [bɔm'bæstɪk] ADJ rimbombante; (person) pomposo

bomb disposal N desactivación f de explosivos

bomb disposal expert N artificiero(-a)

bomber ['bɔmər] N (Aviat) bombardero; (terrorist) persona que pone bombas

bombing ['bɔmɪŋ] N bombardeo

bomb scare N amenaza de bomba

bombshell ['bɔmʃel] N obús m, granada; (fig) bomba

bomb site N lugar m donde estalló una bomba

bona fide ['bəunə'faɪdɪ] ADJ genuino, auténtico

bonanza [bə'nænzə] N bonanza

bond [bɔnd] N (binding promise) fianza; (Finance) bono; (link) vínculo, lazo; **in ~** (Comm) en depósito bajo fianza

bondage ['bɔndɪdʒ] N esclavitud f

bonded goods ['bɔndɪd-] N PL mercancías f pl en depósito de aduanas

bonded warehouse ['bɔndɪd-] N depósito de aduanas

★**bone** [bəʊn] N hueso; (*of fish*) espina; **~ of contention** manzana de la discordia ▶ VT deshuesar; quitar las espinas a

bone china N porcelana fina

bone-dry ['bəʊn'draɪ] ADJ completamente seco

bone idle ADJ gandul

bone marrow N médula; **~ transplant** transplante *m* de médula

boner ['bəʊnə^r] N (*US inf*) plancha, patochada

bonfire ['bɒnfaɪə^r] N hoguera, fogata

bonk [bɒŋk] VT, VI (*hum, inf*) chingar (*inf!*)

bonkers ['bɒŋkəz] ADJ (*BRIT inf*) majareta

Bonn [bɒn] N Bonn *m*

bonnet ['bɒnɪt] N gorra; (*BRIT: of car*) capó *m*

bonny ['bɒnɪ] ADJ (*esp SCOTTISH*) bonito, hermoso, lindo

bonus ['bəʊnəs] N (*payment*) paga extraordinaria, plus *m*; (*fig*) bendición *f*

bony ['bəʊnɪ] ADJ (*arm, face*) huesudo; (*Med: tissue*) huesudo; (: *meat*) lleno de huesos; (: *fish*) lleno de espinas; (*thin: person*) flaco, delgado

boo [buː] EXCL ¡uh! ▶ VT abuchear

boob [buːb] N (*inf: mistake*) disparate *m*, sandez *f*; (: *breast*) teta

booby prize ['buːbɪ-] N premio de consolación (*al último*)

booby trap ['buːbɪ-] N (*Mil etc*) trampa explosiva

★**book** [bʊk] N libro; (*notebook*) libreta; (*of stamps etc*) librillo; **by the ~** según las reglas; **to throw the ~ at sb** echar un rapapolvo a algn ▶ VT (*ticket, seat, room*) reservar; (*driver*) fichar; (*Football*) amonestar ■ **books** NPL cuentas *fpl*, contabilidad *f*; **to keep the books** llevar las cuentas *or* los libros
▶ **book in** VI (*at hotel*) registrarse
▶ **book up** VT: **all seats are booked up** todas las plazas están reservadas; **the hotel is booked up** el hotel está completo

> Don't confuse **el libro**, which means *book*, with **la libra**, which means *pound*.

bookable ['bʊkəbl] ADJ: **seats are ~** los asientos se pueden reservar (de antemano)

bookcase ['bʊkkeɪs] N librería, estante *m* para libros

booking ['bʊkɪŋ] N reserva

booking office N (*BRIT: Rail*) despacho de billetes *or* (*LAM*) boletos; (: *Theat*) taquilla, boletería (*LAM*)

book-keeping ['bʊk'kiːpɪŋ] N contabilidad *f*

booklet ['bʊklɪt] N folleto

bookmaker ['bʊkmeɪkə^r] N corredor *m* de apuestas

bookmark ['bʊkmɑːk] N (*Comput*) favorito, marcador *m*

bookseller ['bʊksɛlə^r] N librero(-a)

bookshelf ['bʊkʃɛlf] N estante *m*

★**bookshop** ['bʊkʃɒp] N librería

bookstall ['bʊkstɔːl] N quiosco de libros

book store N = **bookshop**

book token N vale *m* para libros

book value N (*Comm*) valor *m* contable

bookworm ['bʊkwəːm] N (*fig*) ratón *m* de biblioteca

boom [buːm] N (*noise*) trueno, estampido; (*in prices etc*) alza rápida; (*Econ*) boom *m*, auge *m* ▶ VI (*cannon*) hacer gran estruendo, retumbar; (*Econ*) estar en alza

boomerang ['buːməræŋ] N bumerang *m* (*also fig*) ▶ VI: **to ~ on sb** (*fig*) ser contraproducente para algn

boom town N ciudad *f* de crecimiento rápido

boon [buːn] N favor *m*, beneficio

boorish ['bʊərɪʃ] ADJ grosero

boost [buːst] N estímulo, empuje *m*; **to give a ~ to** (*morale*) levantar; **it gave a ~ to his confidence** le dio confianza en sí mismo ▶ VT estimular, empujar; (*increase: sales, production*) aumentar

booster ['buːstə^r] N (*Med*) reinyección *f*; (*TV*) repetidor *m*; (*Elec*) elevador *m* de tensión; (*also:* **booster rocket**) cohete *m*

★**boot** [buːt] N bota; (*ankle boot*) botín *m*, borceguí *m*; (*BRIT: of car*) maleta, maletero, baúl *m* (*LAM*); **to give sb the ~** (*inf*) despedir a algn, poner a algn en la calle ▶ VT dar un puntapié a; (*Comput*) arrancar; **to ~** (*in addition*) además, por añadidura

booth [buːð] N (*at fair*) barraca; (*telephone booth, voting booth*) cabina

bootleg ['buːtlɛg] ADJ de contrabando; **~ record** disco pirata

booty ['buːtɪ] N botín *m*

booze [buːz] (*inf*) N bebida ▶ VI emborracharse

boozer ['buːzə^r] N (*inf: person*) bebedor(a) *m/f*; (: *BRIT: pub*) bar *m*

★**border** ['bɔːdə^r] N borde *m*, margen *m*; (*of a country*) frontera; (*for flowers*) arriate *m*; **the Borders** región fronteriza entre Escocia e Inglaterra ▶ ADJ fronterizo
▶ **border on** VT FUS lindar con; (*fig*) rayar en

borderline ['bɔːdəlaɪn] N (*fig*) frontera; **on the ~** en el límite

bore [bɔː^r] PT *of* **bear** ▶ VT (*hole*) hacer; (*person*) aburrir ▶ N (*person*) pelmazo(-a), pesado(-a); (*of gun*) calibre *m*

★**bored** [bɔːd] ADJ aburrido; **he's ~ to tears** *or* **to death** *or* **stiff** está aburrido como una ostra, está muerto de aburrimiento

boredom ['bɔːdəm] N aburrimiento

★**boring** ['bɔːrɪŋ] ADJ aburrido, pesado

★**born** [bɔːn] ADJ: **to be ~** nacer; **I was ~ in 2003** nací en 2003

born-again [bɔːnə'gɛn] ADJ: **~ Christian** evangelista *mf*

borne [bɔːn] PP *of* **bear**

Borneo ['bɔːnɪəʊ] N Borneo

b

borough ['bʌrə] N municipio

★**borrow** ['bɔrəu] VT: **to ~ sth (from sb)** tomar algo prestado (a alguien); **may I ~ your car?** ¿me prestas tu coche?

> The concepts of *borrowing* and *lending* are both expressed by the verbs **prestar** or **dejar** in Spanish. To ask to *borrow* something from somebody, you use the structure ¿**me prestas ...?** or ¿**me dejas ...?**: *Can I borrow your car?* ¿**Me prestas el coche?** or ¿**Me dejas el coche?**
> To say that someone is *lending* something to someone, you use the subject and object to clarify the action:
> *Josh lent David his bike.* **Josh le prestó la bicicleta a David.**
> *My dad always lends me his car.* **Mi padre siempre me deja el coche.**

borrower ['bɔrəuə'] N prestatario(-a)

borrowing ['bɔrəuɪŋ] N préstamos mpl

borstal ['bɔːstl] N (BRIT) reformatorio (de menores)

Bosnia ['bɔznɪə] N Bosnia

Bosnia and Herzegovina ['bɔznɪə-ændhɜːtsə'gəuvi:nə] N Bosnia-Herzegovina

Bosnian ['bɔznɪən] ADJ, N bosnio(-a) m/f

bosom ['buzəm] N pecho; (fig) seno

bosom friend N amigo(-a) íntimo(-a) or del alma

★**boss** [bɔs] N jefe(-a) m/f; (employer) patrón(-ona) m/f; (political etc) cacique m ▶ VT (also: **boss about** or **around**) mangonear; **stop bossing everyone about!** ¡deja de dar órdenes or de mangonear a todos!

bossy ['bɔsɪ] ADJ mandón(-ona)

bosun ['bəusn] N contramaestre m

botanical [bə'tænɪkl] ADJ botánico

botanist ['bɔtənɪst] N botanista mf

botany ['bɔtənɪ] N botánica

botch [bɔtʃ] VT (also: **botch up**) arruinar, estropear

★**both** [bəuθ] ADJ, PRON ambos(-as), los/las dos; **~ of us went, we ~ went** fuimos los dos, ambos fuimos ▶ ADV: **~ A and B** tanto A como B

★**bother** ['bɔðə'] VT (worry) preocupar; (disturb) molestar, fastidiar, fregar (LAM), embromar (LAM); **I'm sorry to ~ you** perdona que te moleste; **to ~ doing** tomarse la molestia de hacer ▶ VI (gen): **to ~ o.s.** molestarse; **please don't ~** no te molestes ▶ N (trouble) dificultad f; (nuisance) molestia, lata; **what a ~!** ¡qué lata! ▶ EXCL ¡maldita sea!, ¡caramba!

Botswana [bɔt'swɑːnə] N Botswana

★**bottle** ['bɔtl] N botella; (small) frasco; (baby's) biberón m; **~ of wine/milk** botella de vino/de leche; **wine/milk ~** botella de vino/de leche ▶ VT embotellar

▶ **bottle up** VT (fig) contener, reprimir

bottle bank N contenedor m de vidrio, iglú m

bottleneck ['bɔtlnɛk] N embotellamiento

bottle-opener ['bɔtləupnə'] N abrebotellas m inv

★**bottom** ['bɔtəm] N (of box, sea) fondo; (buttocks) trasero, culo; (of page, mountain, tree) pie m; (of list) final m; **to get to the ~ of sth** (fig) llegar al fondo de algo ▶ ADJ (lowest) más bajo; (last) último

bottomless ['bɔtəmlɪs] ADJ sin fondo, insondable

bottom line N: **the ~** lo fundamental; **the ~ is he has to go** el caso es que tenemos que despedirle

botulism ['bɔtjulɪzəm] N botulismo

bough [bau] N rama

bought [bɔːt] PT, PP of **buy**

bouillon cube ['buːjɔn-] N (US) cubito de caldo

boulder ['bəuldə'] N canto rodado

boulevard ['buːləvɑːd] N bulevar

bounce [bauns] VI (ball) (re)botar; (cheque) ser rechazado ▶ VT hacer (re)botar ▶ N (rebound) (re)bote m; **he's got plenty of ~** (fig) tiene mucha energía

bouncer ['baunsə'] N (inf) forzudo, gorila m

bouncy castle ['baunsɪ-] N castillo inflable

bound [baund] PT, PP of **bind** ▶ N (leap) salto; (gen pl: limit) límite m; **"out of bounds to the public"** "prohibido el paso" ▶ ADJ: **~ by** rodeado de; **to be ~ to do sth** (obliged) tener el deber de hacer algo; **he's ~ to come** es seguro que vendrá; **~ for** con destino a

boundary ['baundrɪ] N límite m, lindero

boundless ['baundlɪs] ADJ ilimitado

bountiful ['bauntɪful] ADJ (person) liberal, generoso; (God) bondadoso; (supply) abundante

bounty ['bauntɪ] N (generosity) generosidad f; (reward) prima

bounty hunter N cazarrecompensas mf

bouquet ['bukeɪ] N (of flowers) ramo, ramillete m; (of wine) aroma m

bourbon ['buəbən] N (US: also: **bourbon whiskey**) whisky m americano, bourbon m

bourgeois ['buəʒwɑː] ADJ, N burgués(-esa) m/f

bout [baut] N (of malaria etc) ataque m; (Boxing etc) combate m, encuentro

boutique [buː'tiːk] N boutique f, tienda de ropa

bow¹ [bəu] N (knot) lazo; (weapon, Mus) arco

bow² [bau] N (of the head) reverencia; (Naut: also: **bows**) proa ▶ VI inclinarse, hacer una reverencia; (yield): **to ~ to** or **before** ceder ante, someterse a; **to ~ to the inevitable** resignarse a lo inevitable

bowels ['bauəlz] NPL intestinos mpl, vientre m; (fig) entrañas fpl

★**bowl** [bəul] N tazón m, cuenco; (for washing) palangana, jofaina; (ball) bola; (US: stadium) estadio ▶ VI (Cricket) arrojar la pelota; see also **bowls**

bow-legged ['bəu'lɛgɪd] ADJ estevado
bowler ['bəulə'] N (Cricket) lanzador m (de la pelota); (BRIT: also: **bowler hat**) hongo, bombín m
bowling ['bəulɪŋ] N (game) bolos mpl, bochas fpl
bowling alley N bolera
bowling green N pista para bochas
bowls [bəulz] N juego de los bolos, bochas fpl
bow tie ['bəu-] N corbata de lazo, pajarita
★**box** [bɔks] N (also: **cardboard box**) caja, cajón m; (for jewels) estuche m; (for money) cofre m; (crate) cofre m, arca; (Theat) palco ▶ VT encajonar ▶ VI (Sport) boxear
boxer ['bɔksə'] N (person) boxeador m; (dog) bóxer m
boxer shorts ['bɔksəʃɔ:ts] NPL bóxers; **a pair of ~** unos bóxers
box file N fichero
boxing ['bɔksɪŋ] N (Sport) boxeo, box m (LAM)
Boxing Day N (BRIT) día m de San Esteban

El día después de Navidad es **Boxing Day**, fiesta en todo el Reino Unido, aunque si el 26 de diciembre cae en domingo el día de descanso se traslada al lunes. En dicho día solía ser tradición entregar *Christmas boxes* (aguinaldos) a empleados, repartidores, carteros, etc.

boxing gloves NPL guantes mpl de boxeo
boxing ring N ring m, cuadrilátero
box number N (for advertisements) apartado
box office N taquilla, boletería (LAM)
boxroom ['bɔksrum] N trastero
★**boy** [bɔɪ] N (young) niño; (older) muchacho, chico; (son) hijo
boy band N boy band m (grupo musical de chicos)
boycott ['bɔɪkɔt] N boicot m ▶ VT boicotear
★**boyfriend** ['bɔɪfrɛnd] N novio
boyish ['bɔɪɪʃ] ADJ de muchacho, inmaduro
boy scout N boy scout m
bp ABBR = **bishop**
Br. ABBR (Rel) = **brother**
bra [brɑ:] N sostén m, sujetador m, corpiño (LAM)
brace [breɪs] N refuerzo, abrazadera; (BRIT: on teeth) aparato m, bráket m; (tool) berbiquí m ▶ VT asegurar, reforzar; **to ~ o.s. (for)** (fig) prepararse (para); see also **braces**
bracelet ['breɪslɪt] N pulsera, brazalete m, pulso (LAM)
braces ['breɪsɪz] NPL (on teeth) aparato m, bráket m; (BRIT: for trousers) tirantes mpl, suspensores mpl (LAM)
bracing ['breɪsɪŋ] ADJ vigorizante, tónico
bracken ['brækən] N helecho
bracket ['brækɪt] N (Tech) soporte m, puntal m; (group) clase f, categoría; (also: **brace bracket**) soporte m, abrazadera; (also: **round bracket**) paréntesis m inv; **income ~** nivel m económico;

in brackets entre paréntesis ▶ VT (fig: also: **bracket together**) agrupar
brackish ['brækɪʃ] ADJ (water) salobre
brag [bræg] VI jactarse
braid [breɪd] N (trimming) galón m; (of hair) trenza
Braille [breɪl] N Braille m
★**brain** [breɪn] N cerebro; **she's got brains** es muy lista ■ **brains** NPL sesos mpl
brainchild ['breɪntʃaɪld] N invención f
braindead ['breɪndɛd] ADJ (Med) clínicamente muerto; (inf) subnormal, tarado
brainfood ['breɪnfu:d] N alimentos pl para el cerebro
brainless ['breɪnlɪs] ADJ estúpido, insensato
brainstorm ['breɪnstɔ:m] N (fig) ataque m de locura, frenesí m; (US: brainwave) idea luminosa or genial, inspiración f
brainstorming ['breɪnstɔ:mɪŋ] N discusión intensa para solucionar problemas
brainwash ['breɪnwɔʃ] VT lavar el cerebro a
brainwave ['breɪnweɪv] N idea luminosa or genial, inspiración f
brainy ['breɪnɪ] ADJ muy listo or inteligente
braise [breɪz] VT cocer a fuego lento
brake [breɪk] N (on vehicle) freno ▶ VT, VI frenar
brake drum N tambor m de freno
brake fluid N líquido de frenos
brake light N luz f de frenado
brake pedal N pedal m de freno
bramble ['bræmbl] N (fruit) zarza
bran [bræn] N salvado
★**branch** [brɑ:ntʃ] N rama; (fig) ramo; (Comm) sucursal f ▶ VI ramificarse; (fig) extenderse ▶ **branch off** VI: **a small road branches off to the right** hay una carretera pequeña que sale hacia la derecha ▶ **branch out** VI (fig) extenderse
branch line N (Rail) ramal m, línea secundaria
branch manager N director(a) m/f de sucursal
brand [brænd] N marca; (fig: type) tipo; (iron) hierro de marcar ▶ VT (cattle) marcar con hierro candente
brandish ['brændɪʃ] VT blandir
brand name N marca
brand-new ['brænd'nju:] ADJ flamante, completamente nuevo
brandy ['brændɪ] N coñac m, brandy m
brash [bræʃ] ADJ (rough) tosco; (cheeky) descarado
Brasilia [brə'zɪlɪə] N Brasilia
brass [brɑ:s] N latón m; **the ~** (Mus) los cobres
brass band N banda de metal
brassière ['bræsɪə'] N sostén m, sujetador m, corpiño (LAM)
brass tacks NPL: **to get down to ~** ir al grano
brat [bræt] N (pej) mocoso(-a)
bravado [brə'vɑ:dəu] N fanfarronería
★**brave** [breɪv] ADJ valiente, valeroso ▶ N gue-

453

rrero indio ▸ ᴠᴛ (*challenge*) desafiar; (*resist*) aguantar

bravely ['breɪvlɪ] ᴀᴅᴠ valientemente, con valor

bravery ['breɪvərɪ] ɴ valor *m*, valentía

bravo [brɑːˈvəu] ᴇxᴄʟ ¡bravo!, ¡olé!

brawl [brɔːl] ɴ pelea, reyerta ▸ ᴠɪ pelearse

brawn [brɔːn] ɴ fuerza muscular; (*meat*) carne *f* en gelatina

brawny ['brɔːnɪ] ᴀᴅᴊ fornido, musculoso

bray [breɪ] ɴ rebuzno ▸ ᴠɪ rebuznar

brazen ['breɪzn] ᴀᴅᴊ descarado, cínico ▸ ᴠᴛ: **to ~ it out** echarle cara al asunto

brazier ['breɪzɪər] ɴ brasero

Brazil [brəˈzɪl] ɴ (el) Brasil

Brazilian [brəˈzɪlɪən] ᴀᴅᴊ, ɴ brasileño(-a) *m/f*

breach [briːtʃ] ᴠᴛ abrir brecha en ▸ ɴ (*gap*) brecha; (*estrangement*) ruptura; (*breaking*): **~ of confidence** abuso de confianza; **~ of contract** infracción *f* de contrato; **in ~ of** por incumplimiento *or* infracción de; **~ of the peace** perturbación *f* del orden público

★**bread** [brɛd] ɴ pan *m*; (*inf: money*) pasta, lana (ʟᴀᴍ); **~ and butter** (*n*) pan con mantequilla; (*fig*) pan (de cada día); (*adj*) común y corriente; **to earn one's daily ~** ganarse el pan; **to know which side one's ~ is buttered (on)** saber dónde aprieta el zapato

breadbin ['brɛdbɪn] ɴ panera

breadboard ['brɛdbɔːd] ɴ (*Comput*) circuito experimental

breadbox ['brɛdbɔks] ɴ (*US*) panera

breadcrumbs ['brɛdkrʌmz] ɴᴘʟ migajas *fpl*; (*Culin*) pan *msg* rallado

breadline ['brɛdlaɪn] ɴ: **on the ~** en la miseria

breadth [brɛtθ] ɴ anchura; (*fig*) amplitud *f*

breadwinner ['brɛdwɪnər] ɴ sostén *m* de la familia

★**break** [breɪk] (*pt* **broke** [brəuk], *pp* **broken** ['brəukən]) ᴠᴛ (*gen*) romper; (*promise*) faltar a; (*fall*) amortiguar; (*journey*) interrumpir; (*law*) violar, infringir; (*record*) batir; (*news*) comunicar ▸ ᴠɪ romperse, quebrarse; (*storm*) estallar; (*weather*) cambiar; (*news etc*) darse a conocer; **to ~ with sb** (*fig*) romper con algn; **to ~ even** cubrir los gastos; **to ~ free** *or* **loose** escaparse ▸ ɴ (*gap*) abertura; (*crack*) grieta; (*fracture*) fractura; (*in relations*) ruptura; (*rest*) descanso; (*time*) intervalo; (: *at school*) (período de) recreo; (*holiday*) vacaciones *fpl*; (*chance*) oportunidad *f*; (*escape*) evasión *f*, fuga; **lucky ~** (*inf*) chiripa, racha de buena suerte; **to have** *or* **take a ~** (*few minutes*) descansar; **without a ~** sin descanso *or* descansar

▸ **break down** ᴠᴛ (*door etc*) echar abajo, derribar; (*resistance*) vencer, acabar con; (*figures, data*) analizar, descomponer; (*undermine*) acabar con ▸ ᴠɪ estropearse; (*Med*) sufrir un colapso; (*Aut*) averiarse, descomponerse (ʟᴀᴍ); (*person*) romper a llorar; (*talks*) fracasar

▸ **break in** ᴠᴛ (*horse etc*) domar ▸ ᴠɪ (*burglar*) forzar una entrada

▸ **break into** ᴠᴛ ꜰᴜs (*house*) forzar

▸ **break off** ᴠɪ (*speaker*) pararse, detenerse; (*branch*) partir ▸ ᴠᴛ (*talks*) suspender; (*engagement*) romper

▸ **break open** ᴠᴛ (*door etc*) abrir por la fuerza, forzar

▸ **break out** ᴠɪ estallar; (*prisoner*) escaparse; **to ~ out in spots** salir a algn granos

▸ **break through** ᴠɪ: **the sun broke through** asomó el sol ▸ ᴠᴛ ꜰᴜs (*defences, barrier, crowd*) abrirse paso por

▸ **break up** ᴠɪ (*marriage*) deshacerse; (*ship*) hacerse pedazos; (*crowd, meeting*) disolverse; (*Scol*) terminar (el curso); (*line*) cortarse; **the line's** *or* **you're breaking up** se corta ▸ ᴠᴛ (*rocks etc*) partir; (*journey*) partir; (*fight etc*) acabar con

breakable ['breɪkəbl] ᴀᴅᴊ quebradizo ▸ ɴ: **breakables** cosas *fpl* frágiles

breakage ['breɪkɪdʒ] ɴ rotura; **to pay for breakages** pagar por los objetos rotos

breakaway ['breɪkəweɪ] ᴀᴅᴊ (*group etc*) disidente

break-dancing ['breɪkdɑːnsɪŋ] ɴ break *m*

breakdown ['breɪkdaun] ɴ (*Aut*) avería; (*in communications*) interrupción *f*; (*Med: also*: **nervous breakdown**) colapso, crisis *f* nerviosa; (*of marriage, talks*) fracaso; (*of figures*) desglose *m*

breakdown truck, breakdown van ɴ (camión *m*) grúa

breaker ['breɪkər] ɴ rompiente *m*, ola grande

breakeven ['breɪkˈiːvn] ᴄᴘᴅ: **~ chart** gráfico del punto de equilibrio; **~ point** punto de breakeven *or* de equilibrio

★**breakfast** ['brɛkfəst] ɴ desayuno

breakfast cereal ɴ cereales *mpl* para el desayuno

break-in ['breɪkɪn] ɴ robo con allanamiento de morada

breaking and entering ['breɪkɪŋəndˈɛntərɪŋ] ɴ (*Law*) violación *f* de domicilio, allanamiento de morada

breaking point ['breɪkɪŋ-] ɴ punto de ruptura

breakthrough ['breɪkθruː] ɴ ruptura; (*fig*) avance *m*, adelanto

break-up ['breɪkʌp] ɴ (*of partnership, marriage*) disolución *f*

break-up value ɴ (*Comm*) valor *m* de liquidación

breakwater ['breɪkwɔːtər] ɴ rompeolas *m inv*

breast [brɛst] ɴ (*of woman*) pecho, seno; (*chest*) pecho; (*of bird*) pechuga

breast-feed ['brɛstfiːd] ᴠᴛ, ᴠɪ (*irreg: like* **feed**) amamantar, dar el pecho

breaststroke ['brɛststrəuk] ɴ braza de pecho

★**breath** [brɛθ] ɴ aliento, respiración *f*; **to take a deep ~** respirar hondo; **out of ~** sin aliento, sofocado; **to go out for a ~ of air** salir a tomar el fresco

Breathalyser® ['brɛθəlaɪzər] ɴ (*ʙʀɪᴛ*) alcoholímetro *m*; **~ test** *n* prueba de alcoholemia

★**breathe** [bri:ð] VT, VI respirar; (noisily) resollar; **I won't ~ a word about it** no diré ni una palabra de ello
▶ **breathe in** VT, VI aspirar
▶ **breathe out** VT, VI espirar

breather ['bri:ðə^r] N respiro, descanso

breathing ['bri:ðɪŋ] N respiración f

breathing space N (fig) respiro, pausa

breathless ['brɛθlɪs] ADJ sin aliento, jadeante; (with excitement) pasmado

breathtaking ['brɛθteɪkɪŋ] ADJ imponente, pasmoso

breath test N prueba de la alcoholemia

bred [brɛd] PT, PP of **breed**

-bred [brɛd] SUFF: **to be well/ill-bred** estar bien/mal criado

breed [bri:d] (pt, pp bred [brɛd]) VT criar; (fig: hate, suspicion) crear, engendrar ▶ VI reproducirse, procrear ▶ N raza, casta

breeder ['bri:də^r] N (person) criador(a) m/f; (Physics: also: **breeder reactor**) reactor m

breeding ['bri:dɪŋ] N (of person) educación f

breeze [bri:z] N brisa

breezeblock ['bri:zblɔk] N (BRIT) bovedilla

breezy ['bri:zɪ] ADJ de mucho viento, ventoso; (person) despreocupado

Breton ['brɛtən] ADJ bretón(-ona) ▶ N bretón(-ona) m/f; (Ling) bretón m

brevity ['brɛvɪtɪ] N brevedad f

brew [bru:] VT (tea) hacer; (beer) elaborar; (plot) tramar ▶ VI hacerse; elaborarse; tramarse; (fig: trouble) prepararse; (storm) amenazar

brewer ['bru:ə^r] N cervecero, fabricante m de cerveza

brewery ['bru:ərɪ] N fábrica de cerveza

briar ['braɪə^r] N (thorny bush) zarza; (wild rose) escaramujo, rosa silvestre

bribe [braɪb] N soborno ▶ VT sobornar, cohechar; **to ~ sb to do sth** sobornar a algn para que haga algo

bribery ['braɪbərɪ] N soborno, cohecho

bric-a-brac ['brɪkəbræk] N INV baratijas fpl

brick [brɪk] N ladrillo

bricklayer ['brɪkleɪə^r] N albañil m

brickwork ['brɪkwə:k] N enladrillado

brickworks ['brɪkwə:ks] N ladrillar m

bridal ['braɪdl] ADJ nupcial

bride [braɪd] N novia

bridegroom ['braɪdgru:m] N novio

bridesmaid ['braɪdzmeɪd] N dama de honor

★**bridge** [brɪdʒ] N puente m; (Naut) puente m de mando; (of nose) caballete m; (Cards) bridge m ▶ VT (river) tender un puente sobre; (fig): **to ~ a gap** llenar un vacío

bridgehead ['brɪdʒhɛd] N cabeza de puente

bridging loan ['brɪdʒɪŋ-] N crédito provisional

bridle ['braɪdl] N brida, freno ▶ VT poner la brida a; (fig) reprimir, refrenar ▶ VI (in anger etc) picarse

bridle path N camino de herradura

brief [bri:f] ADJ breve, corto ▶ N (Law) escrito; **in ~ ...** en resumen ... ▶ VT (inform) informar; (instruct) dar instrucciones a; **to ~ sb (about sth)** informar a algn (sobre algo)

briefcase ['bri:fkeɪs] N cartera, portafolio(s) m inv (LAm)

briefing ['bri:fɪŋ] N (Press) informe m

briefly ['bri:flɪ] ADV (smile, glance) brevemente; (explain, say) brevemente, en pocas palabras

briefs [bri:fs] NPL (for men) calzoncillos mpl; (for women) bragas fpl

Brig. ABBR = **brigadier**

brigade [brɪ'geɪd] N (Mil) brigada

brigadier [brɪgə'dɪə^r] N general m de brigada

★**bright** [braɪt] ADJ brillante; (room) luminoso; (day) de sol; (person: clever) listo, inteligente; (: lively) alegre, animado; (colour) vivo; (future) prometedor(a); **to look on the ~ side** mirar el lado bueno

brighten ['braɪtn], **brighten up** VT (room) hacer más alegre ▶ VI (weather) despejarse; (person) animarse, alegrarse

brill [brɪl] ADJ (BRIT inf) guay

brilliance ['brɪljəns] N brillo, brillantez f; (fig: of person) inteligencia

★**brilliant** ['brɪljənt] ADJ (light, idea, person, success) brillante; (clever) genial; (inf: great) genial

brilliantly ['brɪljəntlɪ] ADV brillantemente

brim [brɪm] N borde m; (of hat) ala

brimful ['brɪm'ful] ADJ lleno hasta el borde; (fig) rebosante

brine [braɪn] N (Culin) salmuera

★**bring** [brɪŋ] (pt, pp brought [brɔ:t]) VT (thing) traer; (person) conducir; **to ~ sth to an end** terminar con algo; **I can't ~ myself to sack him** no soy capaz de echarle
▶ **bring about** VT ocasionar, producir
▶ **bring back** VT volver a traer; (return) devolver
▶ **bring down** VT (government, plane) derribar; (price) rebajar
▶ **bring forward** VT adelantar; (Bookkeeping) sumar y seguir
▶ **bring in** VT (harvest) recoger; (person) hacer entrar or pasar; (object) traer; (Pol: bill, law) presentar; (Law: verdict) pronunciar; (produce: income) producir, rendir
▶ **bring off** VT (task, plan) lograr, conseguir; (deal) cerrar
▶ **bring on** VT (illness, attack) producir, causar; (player, substitute) sacar (de la reserva), hacer salir
▶ **bring out** VT (object) sacar; (new product) sacar; (book) publicar
▶ **bring round** VT (unconscious person) hacer volver en sí; (convince) convencer
▶ **bring up** VT (person) educar, criar; (carry up) subir; (question) sacar a colación; (food: vomit) devolver, vomitar

brink [brɪŋk] N borde m; **on the ~ of doing sth** a punto de hacer algo; **she was on the ~ of tears** estaba al borde de las lágrimas

brisk [brɪsk] ADJ (*walk*) enérgico, vigoroso; (*speedy*) rápido; (*wind*) fresco; (*trade*) activo, animado; (*abrupt*) brusco; **business is ~** el negocio va bien *or* a paso activo

brisket ['brɪskɪt] N falda de vaca

bristle ['brɪsl] N cerda ▸ VI (*fur*) erizarse; **to ~ in anger** temblar de rabia

bristly ['brɪslɪ] ADJ (*beard, hair*) erizado; **to have a ~ chin** tener la barba crecida

Brit [brɪt] N ABBR (*inf:* = *British person*) británico(-a)

★**Britain** ['brɪtən] N (*also:* **Great Britain**) Gran Bretaña

★**British** ['brɪtɪʃ] ADJ británico ■ **the British** NPL los británicos

British Isles NPL: **the ~** las Islas Británicas

British Rail N ≈ RENFE *f* (*SP*)

British Summer Time N *hora de verano británica*

Briton ['brɪtən] N británico(-a)

brittle ['brɪtl] ADJ quebradizo, frágil

Bro. ABBR (*Rel*) = **brother**

broach [brəutʃ] VT (*subject*) abordar

broad [brɔːd] ADJ ancho; (*range*) amplio; (*accent*) cerrado; **in ~ daylight** en pleno día; **the ~ outlines** las líneas generales ▸ N (*US pej*) tía

broadband ['brɔːdbænd] N banda ancha

broad bean N haba

broadcast ['brɔːdkɑːst] (*pt, pp* ~) N emisión *f* ▸ VT (*Radio*) emitir; (*TV*) transmitir ▸ VI emitir; transmitir

broadcaster ['brɔːdkɑːstər] N locutor(a) *m/f*

broadcasting ['brɔːdkɑːstɪŋ] N radiodifusión *f*, difusión *f*

broadcasting station N emisora

broaden ['brɔːdn] VT ampliar; **to ~ one's mind** hacer más tolerante a algn ▸ VI ensancharse

broadly ['brɔːdlɪ] ADV en general

broad-minded ['brɔːd'maɪndɪd] ADJ tolerante, liberal

broadsheet ['brɔːdʃiːt] N (*BRIT*) periódico de gran formato (*no sensacionalista*); *see also* **quality press**

brocade [brə'keɪd] N brocado

★**broccoli** ['brɔkəlɪ] N brécol *m*, brócoli *m*

brochure ['brəuʃuər] N folleto

brogue [brəug] N (*accent*) acento regional; (*shoe*) (*tipo de*) *zapato de cuero grueso*

broil [brɔɪl] VT (*US*) asar a la parrilla

broiler ['brɔɪlər] N (*grill*) parrilla; (*fowl*) pollo (para asar)

broke [brəuk] PT *of* **break** ▸ ADJ (*inf*) pelado, sin blanca; **to go ~** quebrar

broken ['brəukən] PP *of* **break** ▸ ADJ (*stick*) roto; (*fig: marriage*) deshecho; (: *promise, vow*) violado; **~ leg** pierna rota; **in ~ English** en un inglés chapurreado

broken-down ['brəukn'daun] ADJ (*car*) averiado; (*machine*) estropeado; (*house*) destartalado

broken-hearted ['brəukn'hɑːtɪd] ADJ con el corazón destrozado

broker ['brəukər] N corredor(a) *m/f* de bolsa

brokerage ['brəukərɪdʒ] N corretaje *m*

brolly ['brɔlɪ] N (*BRIT inf*) paraguas *m inv*

bromance ['brəumæns] N (*inf*) amistad *f* íntima entre hombres

bronchitis [brɔŋ'kaɪtɪs] N bronquitis *f*

bronze [brɔnz] N bronce *m*

bronzed [brɔnzd] ADJ bronceado

brooch [brəutʃ] N broche *m*

brood [bruːd] N camada, cría; (*children*) progenie *f* ▸ VI (*hen*) empollar; **to ~ over** dar vueltas a

broody ['bruːdɪ] ADJ (*fig*) triste, melancólico

brook [bruk] N arroyo

broom [brum] N escoba; (*Bot*) retama

broomstick ['brumstɪk] N palo de escoba

Bros. ABBR (*Comm:* = *Brothers*) Hnos

broth [brɔθ] N caldo

brothel ['brɔθl] N burdel *m*

★**brother** ['brʌðər] N hermano

brotherhood ['brʌðəhud] N hermandad *f*

brother-in-law ['brʌðərɪn'lɔː] N cuñado

brotherly ['brʌðəlɪ] ADJ fraternal

brought [brɔːt] PT, PP *of* **bring**

brow [brau] N (*forehead*) frente *f*; (*eyebrow*) ceja; (*of hill*) cumbre *f*

browbeat ['braubiːt] VT (*irreg: like* **beat**) intimidar

★**brown** [braun] ADJ marrón; (*hair*) castaño; (*tanned*) moreno ▸ N (*colour*) marrón *m*; **to go ~** (*person*) ponerse moreno; (*leaves*) dorarse ▸ VT (*tan*) poner moreno; (*Culin*) dorar

brown bread N pan *m* integral

Brownie ['braunɪ] N niña exploradora

brown paper N papel *m* de estraza

brown rice N arroz *m* integral

brown sugar N azúcar *m* moreno

browse [brauz] VI (*animal*) pacer; (*among books*) hojear libros; **to ~ through a book** hojear un libro

browser ['brauzər] N (*Comput*) navegador *m*

bruise [bruːz] N (*on person*) cardenal *m*, moretón *m* ▸ VT (*leg etc*) magullar; (*fig: feelings*) herir

Brum [brʌm] N ABBR, **Brummagem** ['brʌmədʒəm] N (*inf*) = **Birmingham**

Brummie ['brʌmɪ] N (*inf*) habitante *mf* de Birmingham

brunch [brʌntʃ] N desayuno-almuerzo

Brunei [bruːˈnaɪ, ˈbruːnaɪ] N Brunéi *m*

brunette [bruːˈnet] N morena, morocha (*LAM*)

brunt [brʌnt] N: **to bear the ~ of** llevar el peso de

★**brush** [brʌʃ] N cepillo, escobilla (*LAM*); (*large*) escoba; (*for painting, shaving etc*) brocha; (*artist's*) pincel *m*; (*Bot*) maleza; **to have a ~ with the police** tener un roce con la policía ▸ VT (*sweep*)

barrer; (*groom*) cepillar; (*gen*): **to ~ past,
~ against** rozar al pasar
▶ **brush aside** VT rechazar, no hacer caso a
▶ **brush up** VT (*knowledge*) repasar, refrescar

brushed [brʌʃt] ADJ (*nylon, denim etc*) afelpado;
(*Tech: steel, chrome etc*) cepillado

brushwood ['brʌʃwud] N (*bushes*) maleza;
(*sticks*) leña

brusque [bru:sk] ADJ (*person, manner*) brusco;
(*tone*) áspero

★**Brussels** ['brʌslz] N Bruselas

Brussels sprout N col f de Bruselas

brutal ['bru:tl] ADJ brutal

brutality [bru:'tælɪtɪ] N brutalidad f

brutalize ['bru:təlaɪz] VT (*harden*) embrutecer;
(*ill-treat*) tratar brutalmente a

brute [bru:t] N bruto; (*person*) bestia ▶ ADJ: **by
~ force** por la fuerza bruta

brutish ['bru:tɪʃ] ADJ brutal

BS N ABBR (*US: = Bachelor of Science*) título universitario

bs ABBR = **bill of sale**

BSA N ABBR (*US*) = **Boy Scouts of America**

BSc N ABBR (= *Bachelor of Science*) licenciado en Ciencias

BSE N ABBR (= *bovine spongiform encephalopathy*)
encefalopatía espongiforme bovina

BSI N ABBR (= *British Standards Institution*) institución
británica de normalización

BST N ABBR (= *British Summer Time*) hora de verano
británica

btu N ABBR (= *British thermal unit*) = 1054.2 *julios*

BTW ABBR (= *by the way*) por cierto

bubble ['bʌbl] N burbuja; (*in paint*) ampolla ▶ VI
burbujear, borbotar

bubble bath N espuma para el baño

bubble gum N chicle m (de globo)

bubbly ['bʌblɪ] ADJ (*person*) vivaracho; (*liquid*)
con burbujas ▶ N (*inf*) champán m

Bucharest [bu:kə'rest] N Bucarest m

buck [bʌk] N (*rabbit*) macho; (*deer*) gamo; (*US inf*)
dólar m; **to pass the ~ (to sb)** echar (a algn) el
muerto ▶ VI corcovear
▶ **buck up** VI (*cheer up*) animarse, cobrar ánimo
▶ VT: **to ~ one's ideas up** poner más empeño

bucket ['bʌkɪt] N cubo, balde m (*esp LAm*) ▶ VI:
the rain is bucketing (down) (*inf*) está lloviendo a cántaros

bucket list N lista de cosas que hacer antes de morir

Buckingham Palace ['bʌkɪŋəm-] N el Palacio
de Buckingham

buckle ['bʌkl] N hebilla ▶ VT abrochar con hebilla ▶ VI torcerse, combarse
▶ **buckle down** VI poner empeño

bud [bʌd] N (*of plant*) brote m, yema; (*of flower*)
capullo ▶ VI brotar, echar brotes

Budapest [bju:də'pest] N Budapest m

Buddhism ['budɪzm] N Budismo

Buddhist ['budɪst] ADJ, N budista mf

budding ['bʌdɪŋ] ADJ en ciernes, en embrión

buddy ['bʌdɪ] N (*US*) compañero(-a), compinche mf

budge [bʌdʒ] VT mover; (*fig*) hacer ceder ▶ VI
moverse

budgerigar ['bʌdʒərɪgɑ:ʳ] N periquito

★**budget** ['bʌdʒɪt] N presupuesto; **I'm on a tight
~** no puedo gastar mucho; **she works out her
~ every month** planea su presupuesto todos
los meses ▶ VI: **to ~ for sth** presupuestar algo

budget airline N compañía aérea de bajo coste

budgie ['bʌdʒɪ] N = **budgerigar**

Buenos Aires ['bweɪnɔs'aɪrɪz] N Buenos Aires
m ▶ ADJ bonaerense, porteño (*LAm*)

buff [bʌf] ADJ (*colour*) color de ante; (*inf: person: well-
muscled*) escultural ▶ N (*enthusiast*) entusiasta mf

buffalo ['bʌfələu] (*pl ~ or* **buffaloes**) N (*BRIT*)
búfalo; (*US: bison*) bisonte m

buffer ['bʌfəʳ] N amortiguador m; (*Rail*) tope m;
(*Comput*) memoria intermedia, buffer m ▶ VI
(*Comput*) almacenar temporalmente

buffering ['bʌfərɪŋ] N (*Comput*) almacenamiento en memoria intermedia

buffer zone N zona (que sirve de) colchón

buffet N ['bufeɪ] (*BRIT: bar*) bar m, cafetería;
(*food*) buffet m ▶ VT ['bʌfɪt] (*strike*) abofetear;
(*wind etc*) golpear

buffet car N (*BRIT Rail*) coche-restaurante m

buffet lunch N buffet m (almuerzo)

buffoon [bə'fu:n] N bufón m

bug [bʌg] N (*insect*) chinche m; (: *gen*) bicho,
sabandija; (*germ*) microbio, bacilo; (*spy device*)
micrófono oculto; (*Comput*) fallo, error m; **I've
got the travel ~** (*fig*) me encanta viajar ▶ VT
(*annoy*) fastidiar; (*room*) poner un micrófono
oculto en; (*phone*) pinchar; **it really bugs me**
me fastidia *or* molesta mucho

bugbear ['bʌgbɛəʳ] N pesadilla

bugger ['bʌgəʳ] (*inf!*) N hijo(-a) de puta (!) ▶ VI:
~ off! ¡vete a la mierda! (*inf!*) ▶ EXCL: **~!** (*also:*
bugger it!) ¡mierda! (*inf!*)

bugle ['bju:gl] N corneta, clarín m

★**build** [bɪld] N (*of person*) talle m, tipo ▶ VT (*pt, pp*
built [bɪlt]) construir, edificar
▶ **build on** VT FUS (*fig*) basar en
▶ **build up** VT (*morale, forces, production*) acrecentar; (*Med*) fortalecer; (*stocks*) acumular; (*establish: business*) fomentar, desarrollar; (: *reputation*)
crear(se); (*increase: production*) aumentar; **don't
~ your hopes up too soon** no te hagas demasiadas ilusiones

builder [ˈbɪldəʳ] N constructor(a) m/f; (contractor) contratista mf

★**building** [ˈbɪldɪŋ] N (act) construcción f; (habitation, offices) edificio

building contractor N contratista mf de obras

building industry N construcción f

building site N obra, solar m (SP)

building society N (BRIT) sociedad f de préstamo inmobiliario

> En el Reino Unido existe un tipo de entidad financiera llamada **building society** de la que sus clientes son también propietarios y cuyos servicios ahora son similares a los de los bancos, aunque en el pasado se centraban fundamentalmente en créditos hipotecarios y cuentas de ahorro.

building trade N = building industry

build-up [ˈbɪldʌp] N (publicity): **to give sb/sth a good ~** hacer mucha propaganda de algn/algo

built [bɪlt] PT, PP of build

built-in [ˈbɪltˈɪn] ADJ (cupboard) empotrado; (device) interior, incorporado; **~ obsolescence** caducidad f programada

built-up [ˈbɪltʌp] ADJ (area) urbanizado

bulb [bʌlb] N (Bot) bulbo; (Elec) bombilla, bombillo (LAM), foco (LAM)

bulbous [ˈbʌlbəs] ADJ bulboso

Bulgaria [bʌlˈɡɛərɪə] N Bulgaria

Bulgarian [bʌlˈɡɛərɪən] ADJ búlgaro ▸ N búlgaro(-a); (Ling) búlgaro

bulge [bʌldʒ] N bulto; (in birth rate, sales) alza, aumento ▸ VI bombearse, pandearse; (pocket etc) hacer bulto; **to ~ (with)** rebosar (de)

bulimia [bjuːˈlɪmɪə] N bulimia

bulimic [bjuːˈlɪmɪk] ADJ, N bulímico(-a) m/f

bulk [bʌlk] N (mass) bulto, volumen m; (major part) grueso; **in ~** (Comm) a granel; **the ~ of** la mayor parte de; **to buy in ~** comprar en grandes cantidades

bulk buying N compra a granel

bulk carrier N (buque m) granelero

bulkhead [ˈbʌlkhed] N mamparo

bulky [ˈbʌlkɪ] ADJ voluminoso, abultado

bull [bul] N toro; (Stock Exchange) alcista mf de bolsa; (Rel) bula

bulldog [ˈbuldɔɡ] N dogo

bulldoze [ˈbuldəuz] VT mover con excavadora; **I was bulldozed into doing it** (fig: inf) me obligaron a hacerlo

bulldozer [ˈbuldəuzəʳ] N bulldozer m, excavadora

bullet [ˈbulɪt] N bala; **~ wound** balazo

bulletin [ˈbulɪtɪn] N comunicado, parte m; (journal) boletín m

bulletin board N (US) tablón m de anuncios; (Comput) tablero de noticias

bulletproof [ˈbulɪtpruːf] ADJ a prueba de balas; **~ vest** chaleco antibalas

bullfight [ˈbulfaɪt] N corrida de toros

bullfighter [ˈbulfaɪtəʳ] N torero

bullfighting [ˈbulfaɪtɪŋ] N los toros mpl, el toreo; (art of bullfighting) tauromaquia

bullion [ˈbuljən] N oro or plata en barras

bullock [ˈbulək] N novillo

bullring [ˈbulrɪŋ] N plaza de toros

bull's-eye [ˈbulzaɪ] N blanco, diana

bullshit [ˈbulʃɪt] (inf!) EXCL chorradas ▸ N chorradas fpl ▸ VI decir chorradas ▸ VT: **to ~ sb** quedarse con algn

bully [ˈbulɪ] N valentón m, matón m ▸ VT intimidar, tiranizar

bullying [ˈbulɪŋ] N (at school) acoso escolar

bum [bʌm] N (inf: BRIT: backside) culo; (esp US: tramp) vagabundo; (: idler) holgazán(-ana) m/f, flojo(-a)

bumble [ˈbʌmbl] VI (walk unsteadily) andar de forma vacilante; (fig) farfullar, trastabillar

bumblebee [ˈbʌmblbiː] N abejorro

bumbling [ˈbʌmblɪŋ] N divagación f

bumf [bʌmf] N (inf: forms etc) papeleo

bump [bʌmp] N (blow) tope m, choque m; (jolt) sacudida; (noise) choque m, topetón m; (on road etc) bache m; (on head) chichón m ▸ VT (strike) chocar contra, topetar ▸ VI dar sacudidas
  ▸ **bump into** VT FUS chocar contra, tropezar con; (person) topar con; (inf: meet) tropezar con, toparse con

bumper [ˈbʌmpəʳ] N (BRIT) parachoques m inv ▸ ADJ: **~ crop/harvest** cosecha abundante

bumper cars NPL (US) autos or coches mpl de choque

bumph [bʌmf] N = bumf

bumptious [ˈbʌmpʃəs] ADJ engreído, presuntuoso

bumpy [ˈbʌmpɪ] ADJ (road) lleno de baches; (journey, flight) agitado

bun [bʌn] N (BRIT: cake) pastel m; (US: bread) bollo; (of hair) moño

★**bunch** [bʌntʃ] N (of flowers) ramo; (of keys) manojo; (of bananas) piña; (of people) grupo; (pej) pandilla ■ **bunches** NPL (in hair) coletas fpl

bundle [ˈbʌndl] N (gen) bulto, fardo; (of sticks) haz m; (of papers) legajo ▸ VT (also: **bundle up**) atar, envolver; **to ~ sth/sb into** meter algo/a algn precipitadamente en

bun fight N (BRIT inf: tea party) merienda; (: function) fiesta oficial

bung [bʌŋ] N tapón m, bitoque m ▸ VT (throw) arrojar; (also: **bung up**: pipe, hole) tapar; **my nose is bunged up** (inf) tengo la nariz atascada or taponada

bungalow [ˈbʌŋɡələu] N bungalow m, chalé m

bungee jumping [ˈbʌndʒiːˈdʒʌmpɪŋ] N puenting m, banyi m

bungle [ˈbʌŋɡl] VT chapucear

bunion [ˈbʌnjən] N juanete m

bunk [bʌŋk] N litera; **~ beds** npl literas fpl

bunker ['bʌŋkə^r] N (*coal store*) carbonera; (*Mil*) refugio; (*Golf*) búnker *m*

bunk off VI: **to ~ school** (*BRIT inf*) pirarse las clases; **I'll ~ at 3 this afternoon** me voy a pirar a las 3 esta tarde

bunny ['bʌnɪ] N (*also:* **bunny rabbit**) conejito

Bunsen burner ['bʌnsn-] N mechero Bunsen

bunting ['bʌntɪŋ] N empavesada, banderas *fpl*

buoy [bɔɪ] N boya
▶ **buoy up** VT mantener a flote; (*fig*) animar

buoyancy ['bɔɪənsɪ] N (*of ship*) flotabilidad *f*

buoyant ['bɔɪənt] ADJ (*ship*) capaz de flotar; (*carefree*) boyante, optimista; (*Comm: market, prices etc*) sostenido; (*: economy*) boyante

BUPA ['bu:pə] N ABBR (= *British United Provident Association*) *seguro médico privado*

burden ['bə:dn] N carga; **to be a ~ to sb** ser una carga para algn ▶ VT cargar

bureau ['bjuərəu] (*pl* **bureaux**) N (*BRIT: writing desk*) escritorio, buró *m*; (*US: chest of drawers*) cómoda; (*office*) oficina, agencia

bureaucracy [bjuə'rɔkrəsɪ] N burocracia

bureaucrat ['bjuərəkræt] N burócrata *mf*

bureaucratic [bjuərə'krætɪk] ADJ burocrático

bureau de change [-də'ʃɑ̃ʒ] (*pl* **bureaux de change**) N caja *f* de cambio

bureaux ['bjuərəuz] NPL *of* **bureau**

burgeon ['bə:dʒən] VI (*develop rapidly*) crecer, incrementarse; (*trade etc*) florecer

★**burger** ['bə:gə^r] N hamburguesa

burglar ['bə:glə^r] N ladrón(-ona) *m/f*

burglar alarm N alarma *f* contra robo

burglarize ['bə:gləraɪz] VT (*US*) robar (con allanamiento)

burglary ['bə:glərɪ] N robo con allanamiento *or* fractura, robo de una casa

burgle ['bə:gl] VT robar (con allanamiento)

Burgundy ['bə:gəndɪ] N Borgoña

burial ['berɪəl] N entierro

burial ground N cementerio

burkha ['bə:kə] N = **burqa**

Burkina Faso [bə:'ki:nə'fæsəu] N Burkina Faso *f*

burlap ['bə:læp] N arpillera

burlesque [bə:'lesk] N parodia

burly ['bə:lɪ] ADJ fornido, membrudo

Burma ['bə:mə] N Birmania

Burmese [bə:'mi:z] ADJ birmano ▶ N *pl inv* birmano(-a); (*Ling*) birmano

★**burn** [bə:n] (*pt, pp* **burned** *or* **burnt** [bə:nt]) VT quemar; (*house*) incendiar; **the cigarette burnt a hole in her dress** se ha quemado el vestido con el cigarrillo; **I've burnt myself!** ¡me he quemado! ▶ VI quemarse, arder; incendiarse; (*sting*) escocer ▶ N (*Med*) quemadura
▶ **burn down** VT incendiar
▶ **burn out** VT (*writer etc*): **to ~ o.s. out** agotarse

burner ['bə:nə^r] N (*gas*) quemador *m*

burning ['bə:nɪŋ] ADJ (*building, forest*) en llamas; (*hot: sand etc*) abrasador(a); (*ambition*) ardiente

Burns Night [bə:nz-] N *ver nota*

Cada veinticinco de enero los escoceses celebran la llamada **Burns Night** (noche de Burns), en honor al poeta escocés Robert Burns (1759-1796). Es tradición hacer una cena en la que, al son de la música de la gaita escocesa, se sirve *haggis*, plato tradicional de asadura de cordero cocida en el estómago del animal, acompañado de nabos y puré de patatas. Durante la misma se recitan poemas del autor y varios discursos conmemorativos de carácter festivo.

burnt [bə:nt] PT, PP *of* **burn**

burp [bə:p] (*inf*) N eructo ▶ VI eructar

burqa ['bə:kə] N burka *m*, burqa *m*

burrow ['bʌrəu] N madriguera ▶ VT hacer una madriguera

bursar ['bə:sə^r] N tesorero(-a); (*BRIT: student*) becario(-a)

bursary ['bə:sərɪ] N (*BRIT*) beca

★**burst** [bə:st] (*pt, pp* **~**) VT (*balloon, pipe*) reventar; (*banks etc*) romper; **the river has ~ its banks** el río se ha desbordado ▶ VI reventarse; romperse; (*tyre*) pincharse; **to ~ into flames** estallar en llamas; **to ~ out laughing** soltar la carcajada; **to ~ into tears** deshacerse en lágrimas; **to ~ open** abrirse de golpe; **to be bursting with** reventar de ▶ N (*explosion*) estallido; (*also:* **burst pipe**) reventón *m*; **a ~ of energy** una explosión de energía; **a ~ of applause** una salva de aplausos; **a ~ of speed** un acelerón
▶ **burst into** VT FUS (*room etc*) irrumpir en

Burundi [bə'rundi] N Burundi *m*

★**bury** ['berɪ] VT enterrar; (*body*) enterrar, sepultar; **to ~ the hatchet** enterrar el hacha (de guerra), echar pelillos a la mar

★**bus** [bʌs] N autobús *m*, camión *m* (*LAM*)

bus boy N (*US*) ayudante *mf* de camarero

bus conductor N cobrador(a) *m/f*

bush [buʃ] N arbusto; (*scrub land*) monte *m* bajo; **to beat about the ~** andar(se) con rodeos

bushed [buʃt] ADJ (*inf*) molido

bushel ['buʃl] N (*measure: BRIT*) = 36,36 *litros*; (*: US*) = 35,24 *litros*

bush fire N incendio en el monte

bushy ['buʃɪ] ADJ (*beard, eyebrows*) poblado; (*hair*) espeso; (*fur*) tupido

busily ['bɪzɪlɪ] ADV afanosamente

★**business** ['bɪznɪs] N (*matter, affair*) asunto; (*trading*) comercio, negocios *mpl*; (*firm*) empresa, casa; (*occupation*) oficio; **to be away on ~** estar en viaje de negocios; **it's my ~ to ...** me toca *or* corresponde ...; **it's none of my ~** no es asunto mío; **he means ~** habla en serio; **he's in the insurance ~** se dedica a los seguros; **I'm here on ~** estoy aquí por mi trabajo; **to do ~ with sb** hacer negocios con algn

business address N dirección *f* comercial

business card N tarjeta de visita

business class N (*Aviat*) clase *f* preferente

businesslike [ˈbɪznɪslaɪk] ADJ (*company*) serio; (*person*) eficiente

★**businessman** [ˈbɪznɪsmən] N (*irreg*) hombre *m* de negocios

business trip N viaje *m* de negocios

★**businesswoman** [ˈbɪznɪswumən] N (*irreg*) mujer *f* de negocios

busker [ˈbʌskəʳ] N (*BRIT*) músico(-a) ambulante

bus pass N bonobús

bus route N recorrido del autobús

bus shelter N parada cubierta

bus station N estación *f* or terminal *f* de autobuses

bus-stop [ˈbʌsstɔp] N parada de autobús, paradero (*LAM*)

bust [bʌst] N (*Anat*) pecho; (*sculpture*) busto ▸ ADJ (*inf: broken*) roto, estropeado; **to go ~** quebrar ▸ VT (*inf: Police: arrest*) detener

bustle [ˈbʌsl] N bullicio, movimiento ▸ VI menearse, apresurarse

bustling [ˈbʌslɪŋ] ADJ (*town*) animado, bullicioso

bust-up [ˈbʌstʌp] N (*inf*) riña

busty [ˈbʌstɪ] ADJ (*inf*) pechugona, con buena delantera

★**busy** [ˈbɪzɪ] ADJ ocupado, atareado; (*shop, street*) concurrido, animado; **he's a ~ man** (*normally*) es un hombre muy ocupado; (*temporarily*) está muy ocupado; **the line's ~** (*esp US*) está comunicando ▸ VT: **to ~ o.s. with** ocuparse en

busybody [ˈbɪzɪbɔdɪ] N entrometido(-a)

busy signal N (*US Tel*) señal *f* de comunicando

---

but [bʌt]

CONJ **1** pero; **he's not very bright, but he's hard-working** no es muy inteligente, pero es trabajador

2 (*in direct contradiction*) sino; **he's not English but French** no es inglés sino francés; **he didn't sing but he shouted** no cantó sino que gritó

3 (*showing disagreement, surprise etc*) **but that's far too expensive!** ¡pero eso es carísimo!; **but it does work!** ¡(pero) sí que funciona!

▸ PREP (*apart from, except*) menos, salvo; **we've had nothing but trouble** no hemos tenido más que problemas; **no-one but him can do it** nadie más que él puede hacerlo; **the last but one** el penúltimo; **who but a lunatic would do such a thing?** ¡sólo un loco haría una cosa así!; **but for you/your help** si no fuera por ti/tu ayuda; **anything but that** cualquier cosa menos eso

▸ ADV (*just, only*): **she's but a child** no es más que una niña; **had I but known** si lo hubiera sabido; **I can but try** al menos lo puedo intentar; **it's all but finished** está casi acabado

---

butane [ˈbjuːteɪn] N (*also:* **butane gas**) (gas *m*) butano

butch [butʃ] ADJ (*inf, pej: woman*) machirula, marimacho; (*inf: man*) muy macho

★**butcher** [ˈbutʃəʳ] N carnicero(-a); **~'s (shop)** carnicería ▸ VT hacer una carnicería con; (*cattle etc for meat*) matar

butler [ˈbʌtləʳ] N mayordomo

butt [bʌt] N (*cask*) tonel *m*; (*for rain*) tina; (*thick end*) cabo, extremo; (*of gun*) culata; (*of cigarette*) colilla; (*BRIT fig: target*) blanco ▸ VT dar cabezadas contra, topetar

▸ **butt in** VI (*interrupt*) interrumpir

★**butter** [ˈbʌtəʳ] N mantequilla, manteca (*LAM*) ▸ VT untar con mantequilla

butter bean N judía blanca

buttercup [ˈbʌtəkʌp] N ranúnculo

butterfingers [ˈbʌtəfɪŋgəz] N (*inf*) torpe *mf*

butterfly [ˈbʌtəflaɪ] N mariposa; (*Swimming: also:* **butterfly stroke**) (braza de) mariposa

buttocks [ˈbʌtəks] NPL nalgas *fpl*

★**button** [ˈbʌtn] N botón *m* ▸ VT (*also:* **button up**) abotonar, abrochar ▸ VI abrocharse

buttonhole [ˈbʌtnhəul] N ojal *m*; (*flower*) flor *f* que se lleva en el ojal ▸ VT obligar a escuchar

buttress [ˈbʌtrɪs] N contrafuerte *m*; (*fig*) apoyo, sostén *m*

buxom [ˈbʌksəm] ADJ (*woman*) frescachona, rolliza

★**buy** [baɪ] (*pt, pp* **bought** [bɔːt]) VT comprar; **to ~ sb sth/sth from sb** comprarle algo a algn; **to ~ sb a drink** invitar a algn a tomar algo ▸ N compra; **a good/bad ~** una buena/mala compra

▸ **buy back** VT volver a comprar

▸ **buy in** VT proveerse or abastecerse de

▸ **buy into** VT FUS comprar acciones en

▸ **buy off** VT (*inf: bribe*) sobornar

▸ **buy out** VT (*partner*) comprar la parte de

▸ **buy up** VT (*property*) acaparar; (*stock*) comprar todas las existencias de

buyer [ˈbaɪəʳ] N comprador(a) *m/f*; **~'s market** mercado favorable al comprador

buy-out [ˈbaɪaut] N (*Comm*) adquisición *f* de (la totalidad de) las acciones

buzz [bʌz] N zumbido; (*inf: phone call*) llamada (telefónica) ▸ VT (*call on intercom*) llamar; (*with buzzer*) hacer sonar; (*Aviat: plane, building*) pasar rozando ▸ VI zumbar; **my head is buzzing** me zumba la cabeza

▸ **buzz off** VI (*BRIT inf*) largarse

buzzard [ˈbʌzəd] N (*BRIT*) águila ratonera; (*US*) buitre *m*, gallinazo (*LAM*)

buzzer [ˈbʌzəʳ] N timbre *m*

buzz word N palabra que está de moda

---

by [baɪ]

PREP **1** (*referring to cause, agent*) por; de; **abandoned by his mother** abandonado por su

---

madre; **surrounded by enemies** rodeado de enemigos; **a painting by Picasso** un cuadro de Picasso

2 (*referring to method, manner, means*): **by bus/ car/train** en autobús/coche/tren; **to pay by cheque** pagar con cheque; **by moonlight/ candlelight** a la luz de la luna/una vela; **by saving hard, he ...** ahorrando, ...

3 (*via, through*) por; **we came by Dover** vinimos por Dover

4 (*close to, past*): **the house by the river** la casa junto al río; **she rushed by me** pasó a mi lado como una exhalación; **I go by the post office every day** paso por delante de Correos todos los días

5 (*time: not later than*) para; (: *during*): **by daylight** de día; **by 4 o'clock** para las cuatro; **by this time tomorrow** mañana a estas horas; **by the time I got here it was too late** cuando llegué ya era demasiado tarde

6 (*amount*): **by the metre/kilo** por metro/kilo; **paid by the hour** pagado por hora

7 (*in measurements, sums*): **to divide/multiply by 3** dividir/multiplicar por 3; **a room 3 metres by 4** una habitación de 3 metros por 4; **it's broader by a metre** es un metro más ancho; **the bus missed me by inches** no me pilló el autobús por un pelo

8 (*according to*) según, de acuerdo con; **it's 3 o'clock by my watch** según mi reloj, son las tres; **it's all right by me** por mí, está bien

9: **(all) by oneself** *etc* todo solo; **he did it (all) by himself** lo hizo él solo; **he was standing (all) by himself in a corner** estaba de pie solo en un rincón

10: **by the way** a propósito, por cierto; **this wasn't my idea, by the way** pues, no fue idea mía

▶ ADV **1** *see* **go**; **pass** *etc*

2: **by and by** finalmente; **they'll come back by and by** acabarán volviendo; **by and large** en líneas generales, en general

★**bye(-bye)** [ˈbaɪ(ˈbaɪ)] EXCL adiós, hasta luego, chao (*esp LAM*)

bye-law [ˈbaɪlɔː] N *see* **by-law**

by-election [ˈbaɪɪlɛkʃən] N (*BRIT*) elección *f* parcial

Byelorussia [bjɛləuˈrʌʃə] N Bielorrusia

Byelorussian [bjɛləuˈrʌʃən] ADJ, N = **Belarussian**

bygone [ˈbaɪgɔn] ADJ pasado, del pasado ▶ N: **let bygones be bygones** lo pasado, pasado está

by-law [ˈbaɪlɔː] N ordenanza municipal

bypass [ˈbaɪpɑːs] N carretera de circunvalación; (*Med*) (operación *f* de) bypass *m* ▶ VT evitar

by-product [ˈbaɪprɔdʌkt] N subproducto, derivado

bystander [ˈbaɪstændəʳ] N espectador(a) *m/f*

byte [baɪt] N (*Comput*) byte *m*, octeto

byway [ˈbaɪweɪ] N camino poco frecuentado

byword [ˈbaɪwəːd] N: **to be a ~ for** ser sinónimo de

by-your-leave [ˈbaɪjɔːˈliːv] N: **without so much as a ~** sin decir nada, sin dar ningún tipo de explicación

Cc

C, c [si:] N (*letter*) C, c f; (*Mus*): **C** do m; **C for Charlie** C de Carmen

C ABBR (= *Celsius, centigrade*) C

c ABBR (= *century*) S.; (*US etc*) = **cent**; (= *circa*) hacia

CA N ABBR = **Central America**; (*BRIT*) = **chartered accountant**; (*US Post*) = **California**

ca. ABBR (= *circa*) c

CAA N ABBR (*BRIT*: = *Civil Aviation Authority*) organismo de control y desarrollo de la aviación civil

CAB N ABBR (*BRIT*: = *Citizens' Advice Bureau*) ≈ Servicio de Información Ciudadana

cab [kæb] N taxi m; (*of truck*) cabina

cabaret [ˈkæbəreɪ] N cabaret m

★**cabbage** [ˈkæbɪdʒ] N col f, berza

cabbie, cabby [ˈkæbɪ] N (*inf*) taxista mf

cab driver N taxista mf

cabin [ˈkæbɪn] N cabaña; (*on ship*) camarote m

cabin crew N tripulación f de cabina

cabin cruiser N yate m de motor

cabinet [ˈkæbɪnɪt] N (*Pol*) consejo de ministros; (*furniture*) armario; (*also:* **display cabinet**) vitrina

cabinet-maker [ˈkæbɪnɪtˈmeɪkəʳ] N ebanista m

cabinet minister N ministro(-a) (del gabinete)

★**cable** [ˈkeɪbl] N cable m ▸ VT cablegrafiar

cable car N teleférico

cablegram [ˈkeɪblgræm] N cablegrama m

cable television N televisión f por cable

cache [kæʃ] N (*of drugs*) alijo; (*of arms*) zulo

cackle [ˈkækl] VI cacarear

cactus [ˈkæktəs] (*pl* **cacti** [-taɪ]) N cacto

CAD [kæd] N (= *computer-aided design*) DAO m

caddie, caddy [ˈkædɪ] N (*Golf*) cadi m

cadence [ˈkeɪdəns] N ritmo; (*Mus*) cadencia

cadet [kəˈdɛt] N (*Mil*) cadete m; **police ~** cadete m de policía

cadge [kædʒ] VT gorronear

cadger [ˈkædʒəʳ] N gorrón(-ona) m/f

cadre [ˈkædrɪ] N cuadro

Caesarean, (*US*) **Cesarean** [siːˈzɛərɪən] ADJ, N: **~ (section)** cesárea

CAF ABBR (*BRIT*: = *cost and freight*) C y F

café [ˈkæfeɪ] N café m

cafeteria [kæfɪˈtɪərɪə] N cafetería (*con autoservicio para comer*)

caffeine [ˈkæfiːn] N cafeína

cage [keɪdʒ] N jaula ▸ VT enjaular

cagey [ˈkeɪdʒɪ] ADJ (*inf*) cauteloso, reservado

cagoule [kəˈguːl] N chubasquero

cahoots [kəˈhuːts] N: **to be in ~ (with sb)** estar conchabado (con algn)

Cairo [ˈkaɪərəu] N El Cairo

cajole [kəˈdʒəul] VT engatusar

★**cake** [keɪk] N (*large*) tarta; (*small*) pastel m; (*of soap*) pastilla; **he wants to have his ~ and eat it** (*fig*) quiere estar en misa y repicando; **it's a piece of ~** (*inf*) es pan comido

caked [keɪkt] ADJ: **~ with** cubierto de

cake shop N pastelería

calamine [ˈkæləmaɪn] N calamina

calamitous [kəˈlæmɪtəs] ADJ calamitoso

calamity [kəˈlæmɪtɪ] N calamidad f

calcium [ˈkælsɪəm] N calcio

calculate [ˈkælkjuleɪt] VT (*estimate: chances, effect*) calcular
▸ **calculate on** VT FUS: **to ~ on sth/on doing sth** contar con algo/con hacer algo

calculated [ˈkælkjuleɪtɪd] ADJ: **we took a ~ risk** calculamos el riesgo

calculating [ˈkælkjuleɪtɪŋ] ADJ (*scheming*) calculador(a)

calculation [kælkjuˈleɪʃən] N cálculo, cómputo

★**calculator** [ˈkælkjuleɪtəʳ] N calculadora

calculus [ˈkælkjuləs] N cálculo

calendar [ˈkæləndəʳ] N calendario; **~ month/ year** n mes m/año civil

★**calf** [kɑːf] (pl **calves** [kɑːvz]) N (of cow) ternero, becerro; (of other animals) cría; (also: **calfskin**) piel f de becerro; (Anat) pantorrilla, canilla (LAM)

caliber [ˈkælɪbəʳ] N (US) = **calibre**

calibrate [ˈkælɪbreɪt] VT (gun etc) calibrar; (scale of measuring instrument) graduar

calibre, (US) **caliber** [ˈkælɪbəʳ] N calibre m

calico [ˈkælɪkəu] N calicó m

California [kælɪˈfɔːnɪə] N California

calipers [ˈkælɪpəz] NPL (US) = **callipers**

★**call** [kɔːl] VT (gen) llamar; (Tel) llamar; (announce: flight) anunciar; (: meeting, strike) convocar; **to be called** (person, object) llamarse; **to ~ sb names** poner verde a algn; **let's ~ it a day** (inf) ¡dejémoslo!, ¡ya está bien! ▶ VI (shout) llamar; (telephone) llamar (por teléfono), telefonear; (visit: also: **call in, call round**) hacer una visita; **who is calling?** ¿de parte de quién?; **London calling** (Radio) aquí Londres ▶ N (shout) llamada, llamado (LAM); (Tel) llamada, llamado (LAM); (of bird) canto; (appeal) llamamiento, llamado (LAM); (summons: for flight etc) llamada; (fig: lure) llamada; **on ~** (nurse, doctor etc) de guardia; **please give me a ~ at seven** despiérteme or llámeme a las siete, por favor; **long-distance ~** conferencia (interurbana); **to make a ~** llamar por teléfono; **port of ~** puerto de escala; **to pay a ~ on sb** pasarse a ver a algn; **there's not much ~ for these items** estos artículos no tienen mucha demanda
▶ **call at** VT FUS (ship) hacer escala en, tocar en; (train) parar en
▶ **call back** VI (return) volver; (Tel) volver a llamar
▶ **call for** VT FUS (demand) pedir, exigir; (fetch) pasar a recoger
▶ **call in** VT (doctor, expert, police) llamar
▶ **call off** VT (cancel: meeting, race) cancelar; (: deal) anular; (: strike) desconvocar
▶ **call on** VT FUS (visit) ir a ver; (turn to) acudir a
▶ **call out** VI gritar, dar voces ▶ VT (doctor) llamar; (police, troops) hacer intervenir
▶ **call up** VT (Mil) llamar a filas

Callanetics® [kæləˈnetɪks] NSG gimnasia de repetición de pequeños ejercicios musculares

callbox [ˈkɔːlbɔks] N (BRIT) cabina telefónica

call centre N (BRIT) centro de atención al cliente

caller [ˈkɔːləʳ] N visita f; (Tel) usuario(-a); **hold the line, ~!** ¡no cuelgue!

call girl N prostituta

call-in [ˈkɔːlɪn] N (US) programa de línea abierta al público

calling [ˈkɔːlɪŋ] N vocación f; (profession) profesión f

calling card N tarjeta de visita

callipers, (US) **calipers** [ˈkælɪpəz] NPL (Med) aparato ortopédico; (Math) calibrador m

callous [ˈkæləs] ADJ insensible, cruel

callousness [ˈkæləsnɪs] N insensibilidad, crueldad f

callow [ˈkæləu] ADJ inexperto, novato

★**calm** [kɑːm] ADJ tranquilo; (sea) tranquilo, en calma ▶ N calma, tranquilidad f ▶ VT calmar, tranquilizar
▶ **calm down** VI calmarse, tranquilizarse ▶ VT calmar, tranquilizar

calmly [ˈkɑːmlɪ] ADV tranquilamente, con calma

calmness [ˈkɑːmnɪs] N calma

Calor gas® [ˈkælə⁻-] N butano, camping gas® m inv

calorie [ˈkælərɪ] N caloría; **low-calorie product** producto bajo en calorías

calve [kɑːv] VI parir

calves [kɑːvz] NPL of **calf**

CAM N ABBR (= computer-aided manufacturing) producción f asistida por ordenador

camber [ˈkæmbəʳ] N (of road) combadura

Cambodia [kæmˈbəudjə] N Camboya

Cambodian [kæmˈbəudjən] ADJ, N camboyano(-a) m/f

camcorder [ˈkæmkɔːdəʳ] N videocámara

came [keɪm] PT of **come**

camel [ˈkæməl] N camello

cameo [ˈkæmɪəu] N camafeo

★**camera** [ˈkæmərə] N cámara (fotográfica), máquina fotográfica; (Cine, TV) cámara; (movie camera) cámara, tomavistas m inv; **in ~** (Law) a puerta cerrada

cameraman [ˈkæmərəmən] N (irreg) cámara m

camera phone N teléfono m con cámara

Cameroon, Cameroun [kæməˈruːn] N Camerún m

camomile tea [ˈkæməmaɪl-] N manzanilla

camouflage [ˈkæməflɑːʒ] N camuflaje m ▶ VT camuflar

★**camp** [kæmp] N campamento, camping m; (Mil) campamento; (for prisoners) campo; (fig: faction) bando; **to go camping** ir de or hacer camping ▶ VI acampar ▶ ADJ afectado, afeminado

★**campaign** [kæmˈpeɪn] N (Mil, Pol etc) campaña ▶ VI: **to ~ (for/against)** hacer campaña (a favor de/en contra de)

campaigner [kæmˈpeɪnəʳ] N: **~ for** defensor(a) m/f de; **~ against** persona que hace campaña contra

campbed [ˈkæmpbɛd] N (BRIT) cama plegable

camper [ˈkæmpəʳ] N campista mf; (vehicle) caravana

campground [ˈkæmpgraund] N (US) camping m, campamento

★**camping** [ˈkæmpɪŋ] N camping m

★**campsite** [ˈkæmpsaɪt] N camping m

campus [ˈkæmpəs] N campus m

camshaft [ˈkæmʃɑːft] N árbol m de levas

★**can¹** [kæn] N (of oil, water) bidón m; (tin) lata, bote m; **a ~ of beer** una lata or un bote de cerveza; **to**

carry the ~ (*inf*) pagar el pato ▶ VT enlatar; (*preserve*) conservar en lata

---

can² [kæn]

(*negative* **cannot** [ˈkænɔt] *or* **can't** [kɑːnt], *pt*, *conditional* **could** [kud]) AUX VB **1** (*be able to*) poder; **you can do it if you try** puedes hacerlo si lo intentas; **I can't see you** no te veo; **can you hear me?** (*not translated*) ¿me oyes?

2 (*know how to*) saber; **I can swim/play tennis/drive** sé nadar/jugar al tenis/conducir; **can you speak French?** ¿hablas *or* sabes hablar francés?

3 (*may*) poder; **can I use your phone?** ¿me dejas *or* puedo usar tu teléfono?; **could I have a word with you?** ¿podría hablar contigo un momento?

4 (*expressing disbelief, puzzlement etc*): **it can't be true!** ¡no puede ser (verdad)!; **what CAN he want?** ¿qué querrá?

5 (*expressing possibility, suggestion etc*): **he could be in the library** podría estar en la biblioteca; **she could have been delayed** puede que se haya retrasado

---

can is not explicitly translated with Spanish verbs such as **ver**, **entender**, and **oír**:
I can see her! **¡La veo!**
I can't understand him. **No lo entiendo**.
I can't hear you. **No te oigo**.

★**Canada** [ˈkænədə] N Canadá *m*
★**Canadian** [kəˈneɪdɪən] ADJ, N canadiense *mf*
canal [kəˈnæl] N canal *m*
canary [kəˈnɛərɪ] N canario
Canary Islands, Canaries [kəˈnɛərɪz] NPL las (Islas) Canarias
Canberra [ˈkænbərə] N Canberra, Camberra
★**cancel** [ˈkænsəl] VT cancelar; (*train*) suprimir; (*appointment, cheque*) anular; (*cross out*) tachar ▶ **cancel out** VT (*Math*) anular; (*fig*) contrarrestar; **they ~ each other out** se anulan mutuamente
cancellation [kænsəˈleɪʃən] N cancelación *f*; supresión *f*
★**cancer** [ˈkænsəʳ] N cáncer *m*; **C~** (*Astro*) Cáncer *m*
cancerous [ˈkænsərəs] ADJ canceroso
cancer patient N enfermo(-a) de cáncer
cancer research N investigación *f* del cáncer
C&F ABBR (= *cost and freight*) C y F
candid [ˈkændɪd] ADJ franco, abierto
candidacy [ˈkændɪdəsɪ] N candidatura
★**candidate** [ˈkændɪdeɪt] N candidato(-a)
candidature [ˈkændɪdətʃəʳ] N (*BRIT*) = **candidacy**
candidly [ˈkændɪdlɪ] ADV francamente, con franqueza

candle [ˈkændl] N vela; (*in church*) cirio
candle holder N *see* **candlestick**
candlelight [ˈkændllaɪt] N: **by ~** a la luz de una vela
candlestick [ˈkændlstɪk] N (*single*) candelero; (*low*) palmatoria; (*bigger, ornate*) candelabro
candour, (*US*) **candor** [ˈkændəʳ] N franqueza
C & W N ABBR = **country and western (music)**
candy [ˈkændɪ] N azúcar *m* cande; (*US*) caramelo ▶ VT (*fruit*) escarchar
candy bar (*US*) N barrita (*dulce*)
candyfloss [ˈkændɪflɔs] N (*BRIT*) algodón *m* (azucarado)
cane [keɪn] N (*Bot*) caña; (*for baskets, chairs etc*) mimbre *m*; (*stick*) vara, palmeta; (*for walking*) bastón *m*; **~ liquor** caña ▶ VT (*BRIT Scol*) castigar (con palmeta)
canine [ˈkænaɪn] ADJ canino
canister [ˈkænɪstəʳ] N bote *m*, lata
cannabis [ˈkænəbɪs] N canabis *m*
canned [kænd] ADJ en lata, de lata; (*inf: music*) grabado; (: *drunk*) mamado
cannibal [ˈkænɪbəl] N caníbal *mf*, antropófago(-a)
cannibalism [ˈkænɪbəlɪzəm] N canibalismo
cannon [ˈkænən] (*pl ~ or* **cannons**) N cañón *m*
cannonball [ˈkænənbɔːl] N bala (de cañón)
cannon fodder N carne *f* de cañón
cannot [ˈkænɔt] = **can not**
canny [ˈkænɪ] ADJ avispado
canoe [kəˈnuː] N canoa; (*Sport*) piragua
canoeing [kəˈnuːɪŋ] N (*Sport*) piragüismo
canoeist [kəˈnuːɪst] N piragüista *mf*
canon [ˈkænən] N (*clergyman*) canónigo; (*standard*) canon *m*
canonize [ˈkænənaɪz] VT canonizar
can opener N abrelatas *m inv*
canopy [ˈkænəpɪ] N dosel *m*, toldo
can't [kɑːnt] = **can not**
cantankerous [kænˈtæŋkərəs] ADJ arisco, malhumorado
canteen [kænˈtiːn] N (*eating place*) comedor *m*; (*BRIT: of cutlery*) juego
canter [ˈkæntəʳ] N medio galope ▶ VI ir a medio galope
cantilever [ˈkæntɪliːvəʳ] N viga voladiza
canvas [ˈkænvəs] N (*material*) lona; (*painting*) lienzo; (*Naut*) velamen *m*; **under ~** (*camping*) en tienda de campaña
canvass [ˈkænvəs] VI (*Pol*): **to ~ for** solicitar votos por ▶ VT (*Pol: district*) hacer campaña (puerta a puerta) en; (: *person*) solicitar el voto de; (*Comm: district*) sondear el mercado en; (: *citizens, opinions*) sondear
canvasser [ˈkænvəsəʳ] N (*Pol*) representante *mf* electoral; (*Comm*) corredor(a) *m/f*
canyon [ˈkænjən] N cañón *m*

CAP N ABBR (= *Common Agricultural Policy*) PAC f

★**cap** [kæp] N (*hat*) gorra; (*for swimming*) gorro; (*of pen*) capuchón *m*; (*of bottle*) tapón *m*, tapa; (: *metal*) chapa; (BRIT: *contraceptive*) diafragma *m* ▶ VT (*outdo*) superar; (*limit*) recortar; (BRIT *Sport*) seleccionar (para el equipo nacional); **and to ~ it all, he …** y para colmo, él …

capability [keɪpəˈbɪlɪtɪ] N capacidad f

★**capable** [ˈkeɪpəbl] ADJ capaz

capacious [kəˈpeɪʃəs] ADJ amplio

capacity [kəˈpæsɪtɪ] N capacidad f; (*position*) calidad f; **filled to ~** lleno a reventar; **this work is beyond my ~** este trabajo es superior a mí; **in an advisory ~** como asesor

cape [keɪp] N capa; (*Geo*) cabo

Cape of Good Hope N Cabo de Buena Esperanza

caper [ˈkeɪpəʳ] N (*Culin: gen pl*) alcaparra; (*prank*) travesura

Cape Town N Ciudad f del Cabo

Cape Verde [keɪpˈvɜːd] N Cabo Verde *m*

★**capital** [ˈkæpɪtl] N (*also:* **capital city**) capital f; (*money*) capital *m*; (*also:* **capital letter**) mayúscula

capital account N cuenta de capital

capital allowance N desgravación f sobre bienes del capital

capital assets N activo fijo

capital expenditure N inversión f de capital

capital gains tax N impuesto sobre la plusvalía

capital goods NPL bienes *mpl* de capital

capital-intensive [kæpɪtlɪnˈtɛnsɪv] ADJ de utilización intensiva de capital

capital investment N inversión f de capital

capitalism [ˈkæpɪtəlɪzəm] N capitalismo

capitalist [ˈkæpɪtəlɪst] ADJ, N capitalista *mf*

capitalize [ˈkæpɪtəlaɪz] VT (*Comm: provide with capital*) capitalizar
▶ **capitalize on** VT FUS (*fig*) sacar provecho de, aprovechar

capital punishment N pena de muerte

capital transfer tax N impuesto sobre plusvalía de cesión

Capitol [ˈkæpɪtl] N: **the ~** el Capitolio

El **Capitol** es el edificio en Washington DC que alberga a la Cámara de Representantes y al Senado de los Estados Unidos. Está situado en *Capitol Hill*, nombre que también se usa para referirse, por extensión, al poder legislativo.

capitulate [kəˈpɪtjuleɪt] VI capitular, rendirse

capitulation [kəpɪtjuˈleɪʃən] N capitulación f, rendición f

capricious [kəˈprɪʃəs] ADJ caprichoso

Capricorn [ˈkæprɪkɔːn] N Capricornio

caps [kæps] ABBR (= *capital letters*) may.

capsize [kæpˈsaɪz] VT volcar, hacer zozobrar ▶ VI volcarse, zozobrar

capstan [ˈkæpstən] N cabrestante *m*

capsule [ˈkæpsjuːl] N cápsula

Capt. ABBR = **captain**

★**captain** [ˈkæptɪn] N capitán(-ana) *m/f* ▶ VT capitanear

★**caption** [ˈkæpʃən] N (*heading*) título; (*to picture*) leyenda, pie *m*

captivate [ˈkæptɪveɪt] VT cautivar, encantar

captive [ˈkæptɪv] ADJ, N cautivo(-a) *m/f*

captivity [kæpˈtɪvɪtɪ] N cautiverio

captor [ˈkæptəʳ] N captor(a) *m/f*

capture [ˈkæptʃəʳ] VT capturar; (*place*) tomar; (*attention*) captar, llamar ▶ N captura; toma; (*Comput: also:* **data capture**) formulación f de datos

★**car** [kɑːʳ] N coche *m*, carro (LAM), automóvil *m*, auto (LAM); (*US Rail*) vagón *m*; **by ~** en coche

Caracas [kəˈrækəs] N Caracas *m*

carafe [kəˈræf] N jarra

caramel [ˈkærəməl] N caramelo

carat [ˈkærət] N quilate *m*; **18-carat gold** oro de 18 quilates

★**caravan** [ˈkærəvæn] N (BRIT) caravana, rulot *m*; (*of camels*) caravana

caravan site N (BRIT) camping *m* para caravanas

caraway [ˈkærəweɪ] N: **~ seed** carvi *m*

carb [kɑːb] N ABBR (*inf*: = *carbohydrate*) carbohidrato

carbohydrates [kɑːbəʊˈhaɪdreɪts] NPL (*foods*) hidratos *mpl* de carbono

carbolic [kɑːˈbɒlɪk] ADJ: **~ acid** ácido carbólico, fenol *m*

car bomb N coche-bomba *m*

carbon [ˈkɑːbən] N carbono

carbonated [ˈkɑːbəneɪtɪd] ADJ (*drink*) con gas

carbon copy N copia al carbón

carbon credit N crédito *m* de carbono

carbon dioxide N dióxido de carbono, anhídrido carbónico

carbon footprint N huella de carbono

carbon monoxide N monóxido de carbono

carbon-neutral [kɑːbnˈnjuːtrəl] ADJ neutro en carbono, carbono neutral

carbon offset N compensación f de emisiones de carbono

carbon offsetting [-ˈɒfsɛtɪŋ] N compensación f de carbono

carbon paper N papel *m* carbón

carbon ribbon N cinta de carbón

car boot sale N mercadillo (*de objetos usados expuestos en el maletero del coche*)

carburettor, (US) **carburetor** [kɑːbjuˈrɛtəʳ] N carburador *m*

carcass ['kɑːkəs] N (*of animal*) res *f* muerta; (*dead body*) cadáver *m*

carcinogenic [kɑːsɪnə'dʒɛnɪk] ADJ cancerígeno

★**card** [kɑːd] N (*thin cardboard*) cartulina; (*playing card*) carta, naipe *m*; (*visiting card, greetings card etc*) tarjeta; (*index card*) ficha; **membership ~** carnet *m*; **to play cards** jugar a las cartas *or* los naipes

cardamom ['kɑːdəməm] N cardamomo

★**cardboard** ['kɑːdbɔːd] N cartón *m*, cartulina

cardboard box N caja de cartón

cardboard city N zona de marginados sin hogar (*que se refugian entre cartones*)

card-carrying member ['kɑːdkærɪŋ-] N miembro con carnet

card game N juego de naipes *or* cartas

cardiac ['kɑːdɪæk] ADJ cardíaco

cardigan ['kɑːdɪgən] N chaqueta (de punto), rebeca

cardinal ['kɑːdɪnl] ADJ cardinal; (*importance, principle*) esencial ▸ N cardenal *m*

cardinal number N número cardinal

card index N fichero

cardphone ['kɑːdfəun] N cabina que funciona con tarjetas telefónicas

cardsharp ['kɑːdʃɑːp] N fullero(-a)

card vote N voto por delegación

CARE [kɛəʳ] N ABBR (= *Cooperative for American Relief Everywhere*) sociedad benéfica

★**care** [kɛəʳ] N cuidado; (*worry*) preocupación *f*; (*charge*) cargo, custodia; **~ of (c/o)** en casa de, al cuidado de; **in sb's ~** a cargo de algn; **the child has been taken into ~** pusieron al niño bajo custodia del gobierno; **"with ~"** "¡frágil!"; **to take ~ to** cuidarse de, tener cuidado de; **to take ~ of** *vt* cuidar; (*details, arrangements*) encargarse de ▸ VI: **to ~ about** preocuparse por; **I don't ~** no me importa; **I couldn't ~ less** me trae sin cuidado
  ▸ **care for** VT FUS cuidar; (*like*) querer

careen [kə'riːn] VI (*ship*) inclinarse, escorar ▸ VT carenar

★**career** [kə'rɪəʳ] N carrera (profesional); (*occupation*) profesión *f* ▸ VI (*also*: **career along**) correr a toda velocidad

career girl N mujer *f* dedicada a su profesión

careers officer N consejero(-a) de orientación profesional

carefree ['kɛəfriː] ADJ despreocupado

★**careful** ['kɛəful] ADJ cuidadoso; (*cautious*) cauteloso; **(be) ~!** ¡(ten) cuidado!; **he's very ~ with his money** mira mucho el dinero; (*pej*) es muy tacaño

carefully ['kɛəfəlɪ] ADV con cuidado, cuidadosamente

caregiver ['kɛəgɪvəʳ] N (*US: professional*) enfermero(-a); (: *unpaid*) persona que cuida a un pariente *o* vecino

careless ['kɛəlɪs] ADJ descuidado; (*heedless*) poco atento

carelessly ['kɛəlɪslɪ] ADV sin cuidado, a la ligera

carelessness ['kɛəlɪsnɪs] N descuido, falta de atención

carer ['kɛərəʳ] N (*professional*) enfermero(-a); (*unpaid*) persona que cuida a un pariente o vecino

caress [kə'rɛs] N caricia ▸ VT acariciar

★**caretaker** ['kɛəteɪkəʳ] N portero(-a), conserje *mf*

caretaker government N gobierno provisional

car ferry ['kɑːfɛrɪ] N transbordador *m* para coches

cargo ['kɑːgəu] (*pl* **cargoes**) N cargamento, carga

cargo boat N buque *m* de carga, carguero

cargo plane N avión *m* de carga

car hire N alquiler *m* de coches

Caribbean [kærɪ'biːən] ADJ caribe, caribeño; **the ~ (Sea)** el (mar) Caribe

caricature ['kærɪkətjuəʳ] N caricatura

caring ['kɛərɪŋ] ADJ humanitario

carnage ['kɑːnɪdʒ] N matanza, carnicería

carnal ['kɑːnl] ADJ carnal

carnation [kɑː'neɪʃən] N clavel *m*

carnival ['kɑːnɪvəl] N carnaval *m*; (*US*) parque *m* de atracciones

carnivore ['kɑːnɪvɔːʳ] N carnívoro(-a)

carnivorous [kɑː'nɪvərəs] ADJ carnívoro

carol ['kærəl] N: **(Christmas) ~** villancico

carouse [kə'rauz] VI estar de juerga

carousel [kærə'sɛl] N (*US*) tiovivo, caballitos *mpl*

carp [kɑːp] N (*fish*) carpa
  ▸ **carp at, carp about** VT FUS sacar faltas de

★**car park** N (*BRIT*) aparcamiento, parking *m*, playa de estacionamiento (*LAM*)

carpenter ['kɑːpɪntəʳ] N carpintero(-a)

carpentry ['kɑːpɪntrɪ] N carpintería

★**carpet** ['kɑːpɪt] N alfombra; **fitted ~** moqueta ▸ VT alfombrar

carpet bombing N bombardeo de arrasamiento

carpet slippers NPL zapatillas *fpl*

carpet sweeper [-'swiːpəʳ] N cepillo mecánico

car phone N teléfono de coche

carping ['kɑːpɪŋ] ADJ (*critical*) criticón(-ona)

car rental N (*US*) alquiler *m* de coches

carriage ['kærɪdʒ] N (*BRIT Rail*) vagón *m*; (*horse-drawn*) coche *m*; (*for goods*) transporte *m*; (*of typewriter*) carro; (*bearing*) porte *m*; **~ forward** porte *m* debido; **~ free** franco de porte; **~ paid** porte pagado; **~ inwards/outwards** gastos *mpl* de transporte a cargo del comprador/vendedor

carriage return N (*on typewriter etc*) tecla de regreso

carriageway ['kærɪdʒweɪ] N (BRIT: *part of road*) calzada; **dual ~** autovía

carrier ['kærɪər] N transportista *mf*; (*company*) empresa de transportes; (*Med*) portador(a) *m/f*

carrier bag N (BRIT) bolsa de papel *or* plástico

carrier pigeon N paloma mensajera

carrion ['kærɪən] N carroña

★**carrot** ['kærət] N zanahoria

★**carry** ['kærɪ] VT (*person*) llevar; (*transport*) transportar; (*a motion, bill*) aprobar; (*involve: responsibilities etc*) entrañar, conllevar; (*Comm: stock*) tener en existencia; (: *interest*) llevar; (*Math: figure*) llevarse; **this loan carries 10% interest** este empréstito devenga un interés del 10 por ciento; **to get carried away** (*fig*) entusiasmarse ▶ VI (*sound*) oírse

▶ **carry forward** VT (*Math, Comm*) pasar a la página/columna siguiente

▶ **carry on** VI (*continue*) seguir (adelante), continuar; (*inf: complain*) montar el número ▶ VT seguir, continuar

▶ **carry out** VT (*orders*) cumplir; (*investigation*) llevar a cabo, realizar

carrycot ['kærɪkɔt] N (BRIT) cuna portátil, capazo

carry-on ['kærɪˈɔn] N (*inf*) follón *m*

cart [kɑːt] N carro, carreta ▶ VT (*inf: transport*) cargar con

carte blanche ['kɑːt'blɒnʃ] N: **to give sb ~** dar carta blanca a algn

cartel [kɑːˈtel] N (*Comm*) cartel *m*

cartilage ['kɑːtɪlɪdʒ] N cartílago

cartographer [kɑːˈtɔgrəfər] N cartógrafo(-a)

carton ['kɑːtən] N caja (de cartón); (*of milk etc*) bote *m*; (*of cigarettes*) cartón *m*

★**cartoon** [kɑːˈtuːn] N (*Press*) chiste *m*; (*comic strip*) historieta, tira cómica; (*film*) dibujos *mpl* animados

cartoonist [kɑːˈtuːnɪst] N humorista *mf* gráfico

cartridge ['kɑːtrɪdʒ] N cartucho

cartwheel ['kɑːtwiːl] N: **to turn a ~** dar una voltereta lateral

carve [kɑːv] VT (*meat*) trinchar; (*wood*) tallar; (*stone*) cincelar, esculpir; (*on tree*) grabar

▶ **carve up** VT dividir, repartir; (*meat*) trinchar

carving ['kɑːvɪŋ] N (*in wood etc*) escultura; (*design*) talla

carving knife N trinchante *m*

car wash N túnel *m* de lavado

Casablanca [kæsəˈblæŋkə] N Casablanca

cascade [kæsˈkeɪd] N salto de agua, cascada; (*fig*) chorro ▶ VI caer a chorros

★**case** [keɪs] N (*container*) caja; (*Med*) caso; (*for jewels etc*) estuche *m*; (*Law*) causa, proceso; (BRIT: *also*: **suitcase**) maleta; **lower/upper ~** (*Typ*) caja baja/alta; **in ~ of** en caso de; **in any ~** en todo caso; **just in ~** por si acaso; **to have a good ~** tener buenas razones; **there's a strong ~ for reform** hay razones sólidas para exigir una reforma

case history N (*Med*) historial *m* médico, historia clínica

case study N estudio de casos prácticos

★**cash** [kæʃ] N (dinero en) efectivo; (*inf: money*) dinero; **to pay (in) ~** pagar al contado; **~ on delivery (COD)** entrega contra reembolso; **~ with order** paga al hacer el pedido; **to be short of ~** estar pelado, estar sin blanca ▶ VT cobrar, hacer efectivo

▶ **cash in** VT (*insurance policy etc*) cobrar ▶ VI: **to ~ in on sth** sacar partido *or* aprovecharse de algo

cash account N cuenta de caja

cash and carry N cash and carry *m*, autoservicio mayorista

cashback ['kæʃ'bæk] N (*discount*) devolución *f*; (*at supermarket etc*) retirada de dinero en efectivo de un establecimiento donde se ha pagado con tarjeta; *también dinero retirado*

cashbook ['kæʃbuk] N libro de caja

cash box N hucha

cash card N tarjeta *f* de(l) cajero (automático)

cash desk N (BRIT) caja

cash discount N descuento por pago al contado

cash dispenser N cajero automático

cashew [kæ'ʃuː] N (*also*: **cashew nut**) anacardo

cash flow N flujo de fondos, cash-flow *m*, movimiento de efectivo

cashier [kæ'ʃɪər] N cajero(-a) ▶ VT (*Mil*) destituir, expulsar

cashless ['kæʃlɪs] ADJ sin dinero

cashmere ['kæʃmɪər] N cachemir *m*, cachemira

cash payment N pago al contado

cash point N cajero automático

cash price N precio al contado

cash register N caja

cash reserves NPL reserva en efectivo

cash sale N venta al contado

casing ['keɪsɪŋ] N revestimiento

casino [kə'siːnəu] N casino

cask [kɑːsk] N tonel *m*, barril *m*

casket ['kɑːskɪt] N cofre *m*, estuche *m*; (US: *coffin*) ataúd *m*

Caspian Sea ['kæspɪən-] N: **the ~** el mar Caspio

cassava [kə'sɑːvə] N mandioca

casserole ['kæsərəul] N (*food, pot*) cazuela

cassette [kæ'set] N cas(s)et(t)e *m or f*

cassette deck N platina

cassette player, cassette recorder N cas(s)et(t)e *m*

cassock ['kæsək] N sotana

cast [kɑːst] (*pt, pp* ~) VT (*throw*) echar, arrojar, lanzar; (*skin*) mudar, perder; (*metal*) fundir; (*Theat*): **to ~ sb as Othello** dar a algn el papel de Otelo; **to ~ one's vote** votar; **to ~ loose**

soltar ▸ N (*Theat*) reparto; (*mould*) forma, molde *m*; (*also:* **plaster cast**) vaciado
▸ **cast aside** VT (*reject*) descartar, desechar
▸ **cast away** VT desechar
▸ **cast down** VT derribar
▸ **cast off** VI (*Naut*) soltar amarras; (*Knitting*) cerrar los puntos ▸ VT (*Knitting*) cerrar; **to ~ sb off** abandonar a algn, desentenderse de algn
▸ **cast on** VT (*Knitting*) montar

castanets [kæstəˈnets] NPL castañuelas *fpl*

castaway [ˈkɑːstəwəɪ] N náufrago(-a)

caste [kɑːst] N casta

caster sugar [ˈkɑːstər-] N (*Brit*) azúcar *m* extrafino

Castile [kæsˈtiːl] N Castilla

Castilian [kæsˈtɪlɪən] ADJ, N castellano(-a) *m/f*
▸ N (*Ling*) castellano

casting vote [ˈkɑːstɪŋ-] N (*Brit*) voto decisivo

cast iron N hierro fundido *or* colado

cast-iron [ˈkɑːstaɪən] ADJ (*lit*) (hecho) de hierro fundido *or* colado; (*fig: alibi*) irrebatible; (*will*) férreo

★**castle** [ˈkɑːsl] N castillo; (*Chess*) torre *f*

castor [ˈkɑːstər] N (*wheel*) ruedecilla

castor oil N aceite *m* de ricino

castrate [kæsˈtreɪt] VT castrar

casual [ˈkæʒjul] ADJ (*by chance*) fortuito; (*irregular: work etc*) eventual, temporero; (*unconcerned*) despreocupado; (*informal: clothes*) de sport

La palabra inglesa **casual** no debe traducirse por *casual*.

casually [ˈkæʒjulɪ] ADV por casualidad; de manera despreocupada

★**casualty** [ˈkæʒjultɪ] N víctima, herido; (*dead*) muerto; (*Mil*) baja; "**~**" (*Brit Med*) urgencias *fpl*; **heavy casualties** numerosas bajas *fpl*

casualty ward N urgencias *fpl*

★**cat** [kæt] N gato

catacombs [ˈkætəkuːmz] NPL catacumbas *fpl*

Catalan [ˈkætəlæn] ADJ, N catalán(-ana) *m/f*

catalogue, (*US*) **catalog** [ˈkætəlɒg] N catálogo ▸ VT catalogar

Catalonia [kætəˈləʊnɪə] N Cataluña

catalyst [ˈkætəlɪst] N catalizador *m*

catalytic converter [kætəˈlɪtɪkkənˈvəːtər] N catalizador *m*

catapult [ˈkætəpʌlt] N tirachinas *m inv*

cataract [ˈkætərækt] N (*Med*) cataratas *fpl*

catarrh [kəˈtɑːr] N catarro

catastrophe [kəˈtæstrəfɪ] N catástrofe *f*

catastrophic [kætəˈstrɒfɪk] ADJ catastrófico

catcall [ˈkætkɔːl] N (*at meeting etc*) rechifla, silbido

★**catch** [kætʃ] (*pt, pp* **caught** [kɔːt]) VT coger (*Sp*), agarrar (*LAm*); (*arrest*) atrapar, coger (*Sp*); (*grasp*) asir; (*breath*) recobrar; (*person: by surprise*) pillar; (*attract: attention*) captar; (*Med*) pillar, coger; (*also:* **catch up**) alcanzar; **to**

~ fire prenderse; (*house*) incendiarse; **to ~ sight of** divisar ▸ VI (*fire*) encenderse; (*in branches etc*) engancharse ▸ N (*fish etc*) captura; (*act of catching*) cogida; (*trick*) trampa; (*of lock*) pestillo, cerradura
▸ **catch on** VI (*understand*) caer en la cuenta; (*grow popular*) tener éxito, cuajar
▸ **catch out** VT (*fig: with trick question*) hundir
▸ **catch up** VI (*fig*) ponerse al día

catching [ˈkætʃɪŋ] ADJ (*Med*) contagioso

catchment area [ˈkætʃmənt-] N (*Brit*) zona de captación

catch phrase N frase *f* de moda

catch-22 [ˈkætʃtwentɪˈtuː] N: **it's a ~ situation** es un callejón sin salida, es un círculo vicioso

catchy [ˈkætʃɪ] ADJ (*tune*) pegadizo

catechism [ˈkætɪkɪzəm] N (*Rel*) catecismo

categoric [kætɪˈgɒrɪk], **categorical** [kætɪˈgɒrɪkəl] ADJ categórico, terminante

categorically [kætɪˈgɒrɪkəlɪ] ADV categóricamente, terminantemente

categorize [ˈkætɪgəraɪz] VT clasificar

category [ˈkætɪgərɪ] N categoría

cater [ˈkeɪtər] VI: **to ~ for** (*Brit*) abastecer a; (*needs*) atender a; (*consumers*) proveer a

caterer [ˈkeɪtərər] N abastecedor(a) *m/f*, proveedor(a) *m/f*

catering [ˈkeɪtərɪŋ] N (*trade*) hostelería

caterpillar [ˈkætəpɪlər] N oruga

caterpillar track N rodado de oruga

cat flap N gatera

cathedral [kəˈθiːdrəl] N catedral *f*

cathode-ray tube [ˈkæθəʊdreɪˈtjuːb] N tubo de rayos catódicos

catholic [ˈkæθəlɪk] ADJ católico; **C~** (*adj, n: Rel*) católico(-a) *m/f*

CAT scanner [kæt-] (*Med*) N ABBR (= *computerized axial tomography scanner*) escáner *m* TAC

Catseye® [ˈkætsaɪ] N (*Brit Aut*) catadióptrico

catsup [ˈkætsəp] N (*US*) ketchup, catsup *m*

cattle [ˈkætl] NPL ganado *sg*

catty [ˈkætɪ] ADJ malicioso

catwalk [ˈkætwɔːk] N pasarela

Caucasian [kɔːˈkeɪzɪən] ADJ, N caucásico(-a) *m/f*

Caucasus [ˈkɔːkəsəs] N Cáucaso

caucus [ˈkɔːkəs] N (*Pol: local committee*) comité *m* local; (: *US: to elect candidates*) comité *m* electoral; (: *group*) camarilla política

caught [kɔːt] PT, PP *of* **catch**

★**cauliflower** [ˈkɒlɪflauər] N coliflor *f*

★**cause** [kɔːz] N causa; (*reason*) motivo, razón *f* ▸ VT causar; (*provoke*) provocar; **to ~ sb to do sth** hacer que algn haga algo

causeway [ˈkɔːzweɪ] N (*road*) carretera elevada; (*embankment*) terraplén *m*

caustic [ˈkɔːstɪk] ADJ cáustico; (*fig*) mordaz

cauterize [ˈkɔːtəraɪz] VT cauterizar

caution [ˈkɔːʃən] N cautela, prudencia; (*warning*) advertencia, amonestación *f* ▶ VT amonestar

cautious [ˈkɔːʃəs] ADJ cauteloso, prudente, precavido

cautiously [ˈkɔːʃəslɪ] ADV con cautela

cautiousness [ˈkɔːʃəsnɪs] N cautela

cavalcade [kævəlˈkeɪd] N cabalgata

cavalier [kævəˈlɪəʳ] N (*knight*) caballero ▶ ADJ (*pej: offhand: person, attitude*) arrogante, desdeñoso

cavalry [ˈkævəlrɪ] N caballería

★**cave** [keɪv] N cueva, caverna ▶ VI: **to go caving** ir en una expedición espeleológica
   ▶ **cave in** VI (*roof etc*) derrumbarse, hundirse

caveman [ˈkeɪvmæn] N (*irreg*) cavernícola *m*

cavern [ˈkævən] N caverna

cavernous [ˈkævənəs] ADJ (*cheeks, eyes*) hundido

caviar, caviare [ˈkævɪɑːʳ] N caviar *m*

cavity [ˈkævɪtɪ] N hueco, cavidad *f*

cavity wall insulation N aislamiento térmico

cavort [kəˈvɔːt] VI hacer cabrioladas

cayenne [keɪˈɛn] N: **~ pepper** pimentón *m* picante

CBC N ABBR (= *Canadian Broadcasting Corporation*) cadena de radio y televisión

CBE N ABBR (*BRIT*: = *Companion of (the Order of) the British Empire*) título de nobleza

CBI N ABBR (= *Confederation of British Industry*) ≈ C.E.O.E. *f* (*SP*)

CC ABBR (*BRIT*) = **county council**

cc ABBR (= *cubic centimetres*) cc, cm³; (*on letter etc*) = **carbon copy**

CCA N ABBR (*US*: = *Circuit Court of Appeals*) tribunal de apelación itinerante

CCTV N ABBR = **closed-circuit television**

CCTV camera N cámara de vigilancia, cámara de circuito cerrado de televisión

CCU N ABBR (*esp US*: = *coronary care unit*) unidad *f* de cuidados cardiológicos

★**CD** N ABBR (= *compact disc*) CD *m*; (*Mil*: *BRIT*) = **Civil Defence (Corps)**; (: *US*: = *Civil Defense*) defensa civil ▶ ABBR (*BRIT*: = *Corps Diplomatique*) CD

CD burner N tostadora *or* grabadora de CDs

CDC N ABBR (*US*) = **center for disease control**

★**CD player** N reproductor *m* de CD

Cdr. ABBR = **commander**

★**CD-ROM** [ˈsiːˈdiːˈrɔm] N ABBR (= *compact disc read-only memory*) CD-ROM *m*

CDT N ABBR (*US*: = *Central Daylight Time*) hora de verano del centro; (*BRIT Scol*: = *Craft, Design and Technology*) artesanía, diseño y tecnología

CDW N ABBR = **collision damage waiver**

CD writer N grabadora *f* de CDs

cease [siːs] VT cesar

★**ceasefire** [ˈsiːsfaɪəʳ] N alto *m* el fuego

ceaseless [ˈsiːslɪs] ADJ incesante

ceaselessly [ˈsiːslɪslɪ] ADV sin cesar

CED N ABBR (*US*) = **Committee for Economic Development**

cedar [ˈsiːdəʳ] N cedro

cede [siːd] VT ceder

CEEB N ABBR (*US*: = *College Entrance Examination Board*) tribunal para las pruebas de acceso a la universidad

ceilidh [ˈkeɪlɪ] N baile con música y danzas tradicionales escocesas o irlandesas

★**ceiling** [ˈsiːlɪŋ] N techo; (*fig: upper limit*) límite *m*, tope *m*

★**celebrate** [ˈsɛlɪbreɪt] VT celebrar; (*have a party*) festejar ▶ VI: **let's ~!** ¡vamos a celebrarlo!

celebrated [ˈsɛlɪbreɪtɪd] ADJ célebre

celebration [sɛlɪˈbreɪʃən] N celebración *f*, festejo

celebrity [sɪˈlɛbrɪtɪ] N (*person*) famoso(-a)

celeriac [səˈlɛrɪæk] N apio-nabo

celery [ˈsɛlərɪ] N apio

celestial [sɪˈlɛstɪəl] ADJ (*of the sky*) celeste; (*divine*) celestial

celibacy [ˈsɛlɪbəsɪ] N celibato

★**cell** [sɛl] N (*in prison, monastery*) celda; (*Biol*) célula; (*Elec*) elemento

★**cellar** [ˈsɛləʳ] N sótano; (*for wine*) bodega

cellist [ˈtʃɛlɪst] N violoncelista *mf*

cello [ˈtʃɛləʊ] N violoncelo

Cellophane® [ˈsɛləfeɪn] N celofán *m*

cellphone [ˈsɛlfəʊn] N móvil

cell tower N (*US Tel*) torre *f* de telefonía móvil, antena de telefonía móvil

cellular [ˈsɛljʊləʳ] ADJ celular

celluloid [ˈsɛljʊlɔɪd] N celuloide *m*

cellulose [ˈsɛljʊləʊs] N celulosa

Celsius [ˈsɛlsɪəs] ADJ centígrado

Celt [kɛlt, sɛlt] N celta *mf*

Celtic [ˈkɛltɪk, ˈsɛltɪk] ADJ celta, céltico ▶ N (*Ling*) celta *m*

cement [səˈmɛnt] N cemento ▶ VT cementar; (*fig*) cimentar

cement mixer N hormigonera

cemetery [ˈsɛmɪtrɪ] N cementerio

cenotaph [ˈsɛnətɑːf] N cenotafio

censor [ˈsɛnsəʳ] N censor(a) *m/f* ▶ VT (*cut*) censurar

censorship [ˈsɛnsəʃɪp] N censura

censure [ˈsɛnʃəʳ] VT censurar

census [ˈsɛnsəs] N censo

★**cent** [sɛnt] N (*US: unit of dollar*) centavo; (*unit of euro*) céntimo; *see also* **per cent**

centenary [sɛnˈtiːnərɪ], (*US*) **centennial** [sɛnˈtɛnɪəl] N centenario

center [ˈsɛntəʳ] N (*US*) = **centre**

★**centigrade** [ˈsɛntɪɡreɪd] ADJ centígrado

centilitre, (US) **centiliter** [ˈsɛntɪliːtəʳ] N centilitro

centimetre, (US) **centimeter** [ˈsɛntɪmiːtəʳ] N centímetro

centipede [ˈsɛntɪpiːd] N ciempiés m inv

★**central** [ˈsɛntrəl] ADJ central; (house etc) céntrico

Central African Republic N República Centroafricana

Central America N Centroamérica

Central American ADJ, N centroamericano(-a) m/f

★**central heating** N calefacción f central

centralize [ˈsɛntrəlaɪz] VT centralizar

central processing unit N (Comput) unidad f procesadora central, unidad f central de proceso

central reservation N (Brit Aut) mediana

★**centre**, (US) **center** [ˈsɛntəʳ] N centro ▶ VT centrar ▶ VI: **to ~ (on)** (concentrate) concentrar (en)

centrefold, (US) **centerfold** [ˈsɛntəfəʊld] N página central plegable

centre-forward [ˈsɛntəˈfɔːwəd] N (Sport) delantero centro

centre-half [ˈsɛntəˈhɑːf] N (Sport) medio centro

centrepiece, (US) **centerpiece** [ˈsɛntəpiːs] N punto central

centre spread N (Brit) páginas fpl centrales

centre-stage [ˈsɛntəsteɪdʒ] N: **to take ~** pasar a primer plano

centrifuge [ˈsɛntrɪfjuːdʒ] N centrifugadora

★**century** [ˈsɛntjʊrɪ] N siglo; **20th ~** siglo veinte; **in the twentieth ~** en el siglo veinte

CEO N ABBR = **chief executive officer**

ceramic [sɪˈræmɪk] ADJ de cerámica

ceramics [sɪˈræmɪks] N cerámica

cereal [ˈsiːrɪəl] N cereal m

cerebral [ˈsɛrɪbrəl] ADJ cerebral

ceremonial [sɛrɪˈməʊnɪəl] N ceremonial

★**ceremony** [ˈsɛrɪmənɪ] N ceremonia; **to stand on ~** hacer ceremonias, andarse con cumplidos

cert [səːt] N (Brit inf): **it's a dead ~** ¡es cosa segura!

★**certain** [ˈsəːtən] ADJ seguro; (correct) cierto; (particular) cierto; **for ~** a ciencia cierta; **a ~ Mr Smith** un tal Sr. Smith

★**certainly** [ˈsəːtənlɪ] ADV desde luego, por supuesto

certainty [ˈsəːtəntɪ] N certeza, certidumbre f, seguridad f

★**certificate** [səˈtɪfɪkɪt] N certificado

certified [ˈsəːtɪfaɪd] ADJ: **~ mail** (US) correo certificado

certified public accountant N (US) contable mf diplomado(-a)

certify [ˈsəːtɪfaɪ] VT certificar; (declare insane) declarar loco

cervical [ˈsəːvɪkl] ADJ: **~ cancer** cáncer m cervical; **~ smear** citología

cervix [ˈsəːvɪks] N cerviz f, cuello del útero

Cesarean [sɪˈzɛərɪən] ADJ, N (US) = **Caesarean**

cessation [səˈseɪʃən] N cese m, suspensión f

cesspit [ˈsɛspɪt] N pozo negro

CET N ABBR (= Central European Time) hora de Europa central

Ceylon [sɪˈlɔn] N Ceilán m

cf. ABBR (= compare) cfr.

c/f ABBR (Comm) = **carried forward**

CFC N ABBR (= chlorofluorocarbon) CFC m

CG N ABBR (US) = **coastguard**

cg ABBR (= centigram) cg

CH N ABBR (Brit: = Companion of Honour) título de nobleza

ch. ABBR (= chapter) cap.

Chad [tʃæd] N Chad m

chafe [tʃeɪf] VT (rub) rozar; (irritate) irritar; **to ~ (against)** (fig) irritarse or enojarse (con)

chaffinch [ˈtʃæfɪntʃ] N pinzón m (vulgar)

chagrin [ˈʃægrɪn] N (annoyance) disgusto; (disappointment) desazón f

★**chain** [tʃeɪn] N cadena; (of mountains) cordillera; (of events) sucesión f ▶ VT (also: **chain up**) encadenar

chain reaction N reacción f en cadena

chain-smoke [ˈtʃeɪnsməʊk] VI fumar un cigarrillo tras otro

chain store N tienda de una cadena, ≈ grandes almacenes mpl

★**chair** [tʃɛəʳ] N silla; (armchair) sillón m; (of university) cátedra; (chairperson) presidente(-a) m/f; **the ~** (US: electric chair) la silla eléctrica; **please take a ~** siéntese or tome asiento, por favor ▶ VT (meeting) presidir

chairlift [ˈtʃɛəlɪft] N telesilla m

★**chairman** [ˈtʃɛəmən] N (irreg) presidente(-a) m/f

chairperson [ˈtʃɛəpəːsn] N presidente(-a) m/f

chairwoman [ˈtʃɛəwʊmən] N (irreg) presidenta

chalet [ˈʃæleɪ] N chalet m (de madera)

chalice [ˈtʃælɪs] N cáliz m

chalk [tʃɔːk] N (Geo) creta; (for writing) tiza, gis m (LAm)
▶ **chalk up** VT apuntar; (fig: success, victory) apuntarse

chalkboard [ˈtʃɔːkbɔːd] (US) N pizarrón (LAm), pizarra (Sp)

★**challenge** [ˈtʃælɪndʒ] N desafío, reto ▶ VT desafiar, retar; (statement, right) poner en duda; **to ~ sb to do sth** retar a algn a que haga algo

challenger [ˈtʃælɪndʒəʳ] N (Sport) contrincante mf

challenging [ˈtʃælɪndʒɪŋ] ADJ que supone un reto; (tone) de desafío

chamber [ˈtʃeɪmbəʳ] N cámara, sala

chambermaid [ˈtʃeɪmbəmeɪd] N camarera

chamber music N música de cámara
chamber of commerce N cámara de comercio
chamber pot [ˈtʃeɪmbəpɒt] N orinal *m*
chameleon [kəˈmiːlɪən] N camaleón *m*
chamois [ˈʃæmwɑː] N gamuza
champagne [ʃæmˈpeɪn] N champaña *m*, champán *m*
champers [ˈʃæmpəz] NSG (*inf*) champán *m*
★**champion** [ˈtʃæmpɪən] N campeón(-ona) *m/f*; (*of cause*) defensor(a) *m/f*, paladín *mf* ▶ VT defender, apoyar
★**championship** [ˈtʃæmpɪənʃɪp] N campeonato
★**chance** [tʃɑːns] N (*coincidence*) casualidad *f*; (*luck*) suerte *f*; (*fate*) azar *m*; (*opportunity*) ocasión *f*, oportunidad *f*, chance *m* or *f* (*LAм*); (*likelihood*) posibilidad *f*; (*risk*) riesgo; **to take a ~** arriesgarse; **by ~** por casualidad; **it's the ~ of a lifetime** es la oportunidad de su vida; **the chances are that ...** lo más probable es que ... ▶ VT arriesgar, probar; **to ~ it** arriesgarse, intentarlo; **to ~ to do sth** (*happen*) hacer algo por casualidad ▶ ADJ fortuito, casual
▶ **chance (up)on** VT FUS tropezar(se) con
chancel [ˈtʃɑːnsəl] N coro y presbiterio
chancellor [ˈtʃɑːnsələ^r] N canciller *m*; **C~ of the Exchequer** (*BRIT*) Ministro de Economía y Hacienda; *see also* **Downing Street**
chancy [ˈtʃɑːnsɪ] ADJ (*inf*) arriesgado
chandelier [ʃændəˈlɪə^r] N araña (de luces)
★**change** [tʃeɪndʒ] VT cambiar; (*clothes, house*) cambiarse de, mudarse de; (*transform*) transformar; **to ~ one's mind** cambiar de opinión o idea; **to ~ gear** (*Aut*) cambiar de marcha ▶ VI cambiar(se); (*change trains*) hacer transbordo; (*be transformed*): **to ~ into** transformarse en; **she changed into an old skirt** se puso una falda vieja ▶ N cambio; (*alteration*) modificación *f*, transformación *f*; (*coins*) suelto; (*money returned*) vuelta, vuelto (*LAм*); **for a ~** para variar; **can you give me ~ for £1?** ¿tiene cambio de una libra?; **keep the ~** quédese con la vuelta
▶ **change over** VI (*from sth to sth*) cambiar; (*players etc*) cambiar(se) ▶ VT cambiar
changeable [ˈtʃeɪndʒəbl] ADJ (*weather*) cambiable; (*person*) variable
changeless [ˈtʃeɪndʒlɪs] ADJ inmutable
change machine N máquina de cambio
changeover [ˈtʃeɪndʒəuvə^r] N (*to new system*) cambio
changing [ˈtʃeɪndʒɪŋ] ADJ cambiante
changing room N (*BRIT*) vestuario
★**channel** [ˈtʃænl] N (*TV*) canal *m*; (*of river*) cauce *m*; (*of sea*) estrecho; (*groove, fig: medium*) conducto, medio; **the (English) C~** el Canal (de la Mancha); **the C~ Islands** las Islas Anglonormandas; **channels of communication** canales *mpl* de comunicación; **green/red ~** (*Customs*) pasillo verde/rojo ▶ VT (*river etc*)

encauzar; **to ~ into** (*fig: interest, energies*) encauzar a, dirigir a
Channel Tunnel N: **the ~** el túnel del Canal de la Mancha, el Eurotúnel
chant [tʃɑːnt] N (*also Rel*) canto; (*of crowd*) gritos *mpl* ▶ VT cantar; (*slogan, word*) repetir a gritos; **the demonstrators chanted their disapproval** los manifestantes corearon su desaprobación
★**chaos** [ˈkeɪɒs] N caos *m*
chaos theory N teoría del caos
chaotic [keɪˈɒtɪk] ADJ caótico
chap [tʃæp] N (*BRIT inf: man*) tío, tipo; **old ~** amigo (mío)
chapel [ˈtʃæpəl] N capilla
chaperone [ˈʃæpərəun] N carabina
chaplain [ˈtʃæplɪn] N capellán *m*
chapped [tʃæpt] ADJ agrietado
★**chapter** [ˈtʃæptə^r] N capítulo
char [tʃɑː^r] VT (*burn*) carbonizar, chamuscar ▶ N (*BRIT*) = **charlady**
★**character** [ˈkærɪktə^r] N carácter *m*, naturaleza, índole *f*; (*in novel, film*) personaje *m*; (*role*) papel *m*; (*individuality*) carácter *m*; (*Comput*) carácter *m*; **a person of good ~** una persona de buena reputación
character code N código de caracteres
★**characteristic** [kærɪktəˈrɪstɪk] ADJ característico ▶ N característica
characterize [ˈkærɪktəraɪz] VT caracterizar
charade [ʃəˈrɑːd] N farsa, comedia; **charades** (*game*) charadas *fpl*
charcoal [ˈtʃɑːkəul] N carbón *m* vegetal; (*Art*) carboncillo
★**charge** [tʃɑːdʒ] N carga; (*Law*) cargo, acusación *f*; (*cost*) precio, coste *m*; (*responsibility*) cargo; (*task*) encargo; **extra ~** recargo, suplemento; **free of ~** gratis; **to reverse the charges** (*BRIT Tel*) llamar a cobro revertido; **to take ~ of** hacerse cargo de, encargarse de; **to be in ~ of** estar encargado de ▶ VT (*Law*): **to ~ (with)** acusar (de); (*gun, battery*) cargar; (*Mil: enemy*) cargar; (*price*) pedir; (*customer*) cobrar; (*person: with task*) encargar; **how much do you ~?** ¿cuánto cobra usted?; **to ~ an expense (up) to sb's account** cargar algo a cuenta de algn; **~ it to my account** póngalo *or* cárguelo a mi cuenta ▶ VI precipitarse; (*make pay*) cobrar ■ **charges** NPL: **bank charges** comisiones *fpl* bancarias
charge account N (*US*) cuenta abierta *or* a crédito
charge card N tarjeta de cuenta
chargé d'affaires [ˈʃɑːʒeɪdæˈfeə^r] N encargado de negocios
charge hand [ˈtʃɑːdʒhænd] N capataz *m*
charger [ˈtʃɑːdʒə^r] N (*also*: **battery charger**) cargador *m* (de baterías)
chariot [ˈtʃærɪət] N carro
charisma [kæˈrɪzmə] N carisma *m*

charismatic [kærɪz'mætɪk] ADJ carismático

charitable ['tʃærɪtəbl] ADJ caritativo

★**charity** ['tʃærɪtɪ] N (gen) caridad f; (organization) organización f benéfica; (money, gifts) limosnas fpl

charity shop N (BRIT) tienda de artículos de segunda mano que dedica su recaudación a causas benéficas

charlady ['tʃɑːleɪdɪ] N (BRIT) mujer f de la limpieza

charlatan ['ʃɑːlətən] N charlatán(-ana) m/f

charm [tʃɑːm] N encanto, atractivo; (spell) hechizo; (object) amuleto; (on bracelet) dije m ▶ VT encantar; hechizar

charm bracelet N pulsera amuleto

charming ['tʃɑːmɪŋ] ADJ encantador(a); (person) simpático

★**chart** [tʃɑːt] N (table) cuadro; (graph) gráfica; (map) carta de navegación; (weather chart) mapa m meteorológico; **to be in the charts** (record, pop group) estar en la lista de éxitos ▶ VT (course) trazar; (progress) seguir; (sales) hacer una gráfica de

charter ['tʃɑːtər] VT (bus) alquilar; (plane, ship) fletar ▶ N (document) estatuto, carta; **on ~** en alquiler, alquilado

chartered accountant ['tʃɑːtəd-] N (BRIT) contable mf diplomado(-a)

charter flight N vuelo chárter

charwoman ['tʃɑːwʊmən] N (irreg) = **charlady**

★**chase** [tʃeɪs] VT (pursue) perseguir; (hunt) cazar ▶ VI: **to ~ after** correr tras ▶ N persecución f; caza
▶ **chase up** VT (information) tratar de conseguir; **to ~ sb up about sth** recordar algo a algn

chasm ['kæzəm] N abismo

chassis ['ʃæsɪ] N chasis m

chaste [tʃeɪst] ADJ casto

chastened ['tʃeɪsənd] ADJ escarmentado

chastening ['tʃeɪsnɪŋ] ADJ aleccionador(a)

chastity ['tʃæstɪtɪ] N castidad f

★**chat** [tʃæt] VI (also: **have a chat**) charlar; (: Internet) chatear ▶ N charla; (Internet) chat m
▶ **chat up** VT (inf) ligar con, enrollarse con

chatline ['tʃætlaɪn] N servicio telefónico que permite a los que llaman conversar unos con otros

chat room N (Internet) chat m, canal m de charla

chat show N (BRIT) programa m de entrevistas

chattel ['tʃætl] N bien m mueble

chatter ['tʃætər] VI (person) charlar; (teeth) castañetear ▶ N (of birds) parloteo; (of people) charla, cháchara

chatterbox ['tʃætəbɔks] N parlanchín(-ina) m/f

chattering classes ['tʃætərɪŋ'klɑːsɪz] NPL (pej): **the ~** los intelectualillos

chatty ['tʃætɪ] ADJ (style) informal; (person) hablador(a)

chauffeur ['ʃəufər] N chófer mf

chauvinist ['ʃəuvɪnɪst] N (also: **male chauvinist**) machista m; (nationalist) chovinista mf, patriotero(-a)

ChE ABBR = **chemical engineer**

★**cheap** [tʃiːp] ADJ barato; (joke) de mal gusto, chabacano; (poor quality) de mala calidad; (reduced: ticket) económico; (: fare) barato ▶ ADV barato

cheap day return N billete de ida y vuelta el mismo día

cheapen ['tʃiːpn] VT rebajar el precio de, abaratar

cheaply ['tʃiːplɪ] ADV barato, a bajo precio

cheat [tʃiːt] VI hacer trampa; (in exam) copiar ▶ VT estafar, timar; **to ~ sb (out of sth)** estafar (algo) a algn ▶ N trampa; estafa; (person) tramposo(-a)
▶ **cheat on** VT FUS engañar; **he's been cheating on his wife** ha estado engañando a su esposa

cheating ['tʃiːtɪŋ] N trampa

cheat sheet N (US: in exam) chuleta

Chechnya ['tʃetʃniːə] N Chechenia

★**check** [tʃɛk] VT (examine) controlar; (facts) comprobar; (count) contar; (halt) frenar; (restrain) refrenar, restringir ▶ VI: **to ~ with sb** consultar con algn; (official etc) informarse por ▶ N (inspection) control m, inspección f; (curb) freno; (bill) nota, cuenta; (US) = **cheque**; (pattern: gen pl) cuadro; **to keep a ~ on sth/sb** controlar algo/a algn ▶ ADJ (pattern, cloth: also: **checked**) a cuadros
▶ **check in** VI (in hotel) registrarse; (at airport) facturar ▶ VT (luggage) facturar
▶ **check off** VT (esp US: check) comprobar; (: cross off) tachar
▶ **check out** VI (of hotel) desocupar la habitación ▶ VT (investigate: story) comprobar; (: person) informarse sobre
▶ **check up** VI: **to ~ up on sth** comprobar algo; **to ~ up on sb** investigar a algn

checkbook ['tʃɛkbuk] N (US) = **chequebook**

checked [tʃɛkt] ADJ a cuadros inv

checkered ['tʃɛkəd] ADJ (US) = **chequered**

checkers ['tʃɛkəz] N (US) damas fpl

check-in ['tʃɛkɪn] N (also: **check-in desk**: at airport) mostrador m de facturación

checking account ['tʃɛkɪŋ-] N (US) cuenta corriente

checklist ['tʃɛklɪst] N lista

checkmate ['tʃɛkmeɪt] N jaque m mate

checkout ['tʃɛkaut] N (in supermarket) caja

checkpoint ['tʃɛkpɔɪnt] N (punto de) control m, retén m (LAM)

checkroom ['tʃɛkrum] N (US) consigna

checkup ['tʃɛkʌp] N (Med) reconocimiento general; (of machine) revisión f

cheddar ['tʃedər] N (also: **cheddar cheese**) queso m cheddar

cheek [tʃiːk] N mejilla; (impudence) descaro; **what a ~!** ¡qué cara!

cheekbone ['tʃiːkbəun] N pómulo

⋆**cheeky** ['tʃiːkɪ] ADJ fresco, descarado

cheep [tʃiːp] N (of bird) pío ▶ VI piar

⋆**cheer** [tʃɪəʳ] VT vitorear, ovacionar; (gladden) alegrar, animar ▶ VI dar vivas ▶ N viva m ■ **cheers** NPL vítores mpl; **cheers!** (as toast) ¡salud!; (BRIT inf: thank you) ¡gracias!; (: goodbye) ¡hasta luego!
  ▶ **cheer on** VT (person etc) animar con aplausos or gritos
  ▶ **cheer up** VI animarse ▶ VT alegrar, animar

⋆**cheerful** ['tʃɪəful] ADJ alegre

cheerfulness ['tʃɪəfulnɪs] N alegría

cheering ['tʃɪərɪŋ] N ovaciones fpl, vítores mpl

cheerio [tʃɪərɪ'əu] EXCL (BRIT) ¡hasta luego!

cheerleader ['tʃɪəliːdəʳ] N animador(a) m/f

cheerless ['tʃɪələs] ADJ triste, sombrío

⋆**cheese** [tʃiːz] N queso

cheeseboard ['tʃiːzbɔːd] N tabla de quesos

cheeseburger ['tʃiːzbəːgəʳ] N hamburguesa con queso

cheesecake ['tʃiːzkeɪk] N pastel m de queso

cheetah ['tʃiːtə] N guepardo

⋆**chef** [ʃɛf] N jefe(-a) m/f de cocina

⋆**chemical** ['kɛmɪkəl] ADJ químico ▶ N producto químico

⋆**chemist** ['kɛmɪst] N (BRIT: pharmacist) farmacéutico(-a); (scientist) químico(-a); **~'s (shop)** n (BRIT) farmacia

⋆**chemistry** ['kɛmɪstrɪ] N química

chemotherapy [kiːməu'θɛrəpɪ] N quimioterapia

cheque, (US) **check** [tʃɛk] N cheque m; **to pay by ~** pagar con cheque

chequebook, (US) **checkbook** ['tʃɛkbuk] N talonario (de cheques), chequera (LAM)

cheque card N (BRIT) tarjeta de identificación bancaria

chequered, (US) **checkered** ['tʃɛkəd] ADJ (fig) accidentado; (pattern) de cuadros

cherish ['tʃɛrɪʃ] VT (love) querer, apreciar; (protect) cuidar; (hope etc) abrigar

cheroot [ʃə'ruːt] N puro (cortado en los dos extremos)

⋆**cherry** ['tʃɛrɪ] N (fruit) cereza; (also: **cherry tree**) cerezo

chess [tʃɛs] N ajedrez m

chessboard ['tʃɛsbɔːd] N tablero (de ajedrez)

chessman ['tʃɛsmən] N (irreg) pieza (de ajedrez)

⋆**chest** [tʃɛst] N (Anat) pecho; (box) cofre m; **to get sth off one's ~** (inf) desahogarse; **~ of drawers** n cómoda

chest measurement N talla (de chaqueta etc)

chestnut ['tʃɛsnʌt] N castaña; (also: **chestnut tree**) castaño; (colour) castaño ▶ ADJ (color) castaño inv

chesty ['tʃɛstɪ] ADJ (cough) de bronquios, de pecho

chew [tʃuː] VT mascar, masticar

chewing gum ['tʃuːɪŋ-] N chicle m

chic [ʃiːk] ADJ elegante

chicanery [ʃɪ'keɪnərɪ] N embustes mpl, sofismas mpl

Chicano [tʃɪ'kɑːnəu] ADJ, N chicano(-a) m/f

chick [tʃɪk] N pollito, polluelo; (US inf) chica

⋆**chicken** ['tʃɪkɪn] N gallina, pollo; (food) pollo; (inf: coward) gallina mf
  ▶ **chicken out** VI (inf) rajarse; **to ~ out of doing sth** rajarse y no hacer algo

chickenpox ['tʃɪkɪnpɔks] N varicela

chickpea ['tʃɪkpiː] N garbanzo

chicory ['tʃɪkərɪ] N (for coffee) achicoria; (salad) escarola

chide [tʃaɪd] VT: **to ~ sb for sth** reprender a algn por algo

⋆**chief** [tʃiːf] N jefe(-a) m/f; **C~ of Staff** (esp Mil) Jefe(-a) m/f del Estado Mayor ▶ ADJ principal, máximo (esp LAM)

chief executive, chief executive officer N (of company) presidente(-a) m/f general; (local government) director(-a) m/f general

chiefly ['tʃiːflɪ] ADV principalmente

chieftain ['tʃiːftən] N jefe m, cacique m

chiffon ['ʃɪfɔn] N gasa

chilblain ['tʃɪlbleɪn] N sabañón m

⋆**child** [tʃaɪld] (pl **children** ['tʃɪldrən]) N niño(-a); (offspring) hijo(-a)

child abuse N (with violence) malos tratos mpl a niños; (sexual) abuso m sexual de niños

child benefit N (BRIT) subsidio por cada hijo pequeño

childbirth ['tʃaɪldbəːθ] N parto

childcare ['tʃaɪldkɛəʳ] N cuidado de los niños

childhood ['tʃaɪldhud] N niñez f, infancia

childish ['tʃaɪldɪʃ] ADJ pueril, infantil

childless ['tʃaɪldlɪs] ADJ sin hijos

childlike ['tʃaɪldlaɪk] ADJ de niño, infantil

child minder N (BRIT) niñera, madre f de día

child prodigy N niño(-a) prodigio inv

⋆**children** ['tʃɪldrən] NPL of **child**

children's home N centro de acogida para niños

child's play N (fig): **this is ~** esto es coser y cantar

⋆**Chile** ['tʃɪlɪ] N Chile m

Chilean ['tʃɪlɪən] ADJ, N chileno(-a) m/f

chili ['tʃɪlɪ] N = **chilli**

chill [tʃɪl] N frío; (Med) resfriado ▶ ADJ frío ▶ VT enfriar; (Culin) refrigerar
  ▶ **chill out** VI (esp US inf) tranquilizarse

chilli, chili ['tʃɪlɪ] N (BRIT) chile m, ají m (LAM)

chilling ['tʃɪlɪŋ] ADJ escalofriante

chilly ['tʃɪlɪ] ADJ frío

chime [tʃaɪm] N repique m, campanada ▶ VI repicar, sonar

chimney ['tʃɪmnɪ] N chimenea
chimney sweep N deshollinador m
chimpanzee [tʃɪmpæn'ziː] N chimpancé m
chin [tʃɪn] N mentón m, barbilla
★**China** ['tʃaɪnə] N China
china ['tʃaɪnə] N porcelana; (crockery) loza
Chinese [tʃaɪ'niːz] ADJ chino ▶ N pl inv chino(-a); (Ling) chino
chink [tʃɪŋk] N (opening) rendija, hendedura; (noise) tintineo
chintz [tʃɪnts] N cretona
chinwag ['tʃɪnwæg] N (BRIT inf): **to have a ~** echar una parrafada
★**chip** [tʃɪp] N (gen pl: Culin: BRIT) patata or (LAM) papa frita; (: US: also: **potato chip**) patata or (LAM) papa frita; (of wood) astilla; (stone) lasca; (in gambling) ficha; (Comput) chip m; **when the chips are down** (fig) a la hora de la verdad ▶ VT (cup, plate) desconchar
▶ **chip in** VI (inf: interrupt) interrumpir, meterse; (: contribute) contribuir
chip and PIN N chip and PIN m (sistema de tarjetas chip con número PIN); **~ machine** lector m de tarjetas chip and PIN
chipboard ['tʃɪpbɔːd] N madera aglomerada
chipmunk ['tʃɪpmʌŋk] N ardilla listada
chip shop N ver nota

Se denomina **chip shop** o fish and chip shop a un tipo de tienda popular de comida rápida en la que se despachan platos tradicionales británicos, principalmente filetes de pescado rebozado frito y patatas fritas. La comida es más bien para llevar e incluso comer por la calle y muchas tiendas aún siguen la tradición de envolverla en periódico o papel.

chiropodist [kɪ'rɔpədɪst] N (BRIT) podólogo(-a)
chiropody [kɪ'rɔpədɪ] N (BRIT) podología
chirp [tʃəːp] VI gorjear; (cricket) cantar ▶ N (of cricket) canto
chirpy ['tʃəːpɪ] ADJ (inf) alegre, animado
chisel ['tʃɪzl] N (for wood) escoplo; (for stone) cincel m
chit [tʃɪt] N nota
chitchat ['tʃɪttʃæt] N chismes mpl, habladurías fpl
chivalrous ['ʃɪvəlrəs] ADJ caballeroso
chivalry ['ʃɪvəlrɪ] N caballerosidad f
chives [tʃaɪvz] NPL cebollinos mpl
chloride ['klɔːraɪd] N cloruro
chlorinate ['klɔːrɪneɪt] VT clorar
chlorine ['klɔːriːn] N cloro
choc-ice ['tʃɔkaɪs] N (BRIT) helado m cubierto de chocolate
chock-a-block ['tʃɔkə'blɔk], **chock-full** [tʃɔk'ful] ADJ atestado
★**chocolate** ['tʃɔklɪt] N chocolate m; (sweet) bombón m

★**choice** [tʃɔɪs] N elección f; (preference) preferencia; **I did it by** or **from ~** lo hice de buena gana; **a wide ~** un gran surtido, una gran variedad ▶ ADJ escogido
choir ['kwaɪər] N coro
choirboy ['kwaɪəbɔɪ] N niño de coro
choke [tʃəuk] VI ahogarse; (on food) atragantarse ▶ VT ahogar; (block) atascar ▶ N (Aut) estárter m
choker ['tʃəukər] N (necklace) gargantilla
cholera ['kɔlərə] N cólera m
cholesterol [kɔ'lɛstərəl] N colesterol m
chook [tʃuk] N (AUSTRALIA, NEW ZEALAND inf) N gallina; (as food) pollo
★**choose** [tʃuːz] (pt **chose** [tʃəuz], pp **chosen** ['tʃəuzn]) VT escoger, elegir; (team) seleccionar; **to ~ to do sth** optar por hacer algo ▶ VI: **to ~ between** elegir or escoger entre; **to ~ from** escoger entre
choosy ['tʃuːzɪ] ADJ remilgado
★**chop** [tʃɔp] VT (wood) cortar, talar; (Culin: also: **chop up**) picar ▶ N tajo, golpe m cortante; (Culin) chuleta; **to get the ~** (inf: project) ser suprimido; (: person: be sacked) ser despedido
▪ **chops** NPL (jaws) boca sg
▶ **chop down** VT (tree) talar
▶ **chop off** VT cortar (de un tajo)
chopper ['tʃɔpər] N (helicopter) helicóptero
choppy ['tʃɔpɪ] ADJ (sea) picado, agitado
chopsticks ['tʃɔpstɪks] NPL palillos mpl
choral ['kɔːrəl] ADJ coral
chord [kɔːd] N (Mus) acorde m
chore [tʃɔːr] N faena, tarea; (routine task) trabajo rutinario
choreographer [kɔrɪ'ɔgrəfər] N coreógrafo(-a)
choreography [kɔrɪ'ɔgrəfɪ] N coreografía
chorister ['kɔrɪstər] N corista mf; (US) director(a) m/f de un coro
chortle ['tʃɔːtl] VI reírse satisfecho
chorus ['kɔːrəs] N coro; (repeated part of song) estribillo
chose [tʃəuz] PT of **choose**
chosen ['tʃəuzn] PP of **choose**
chow [tʃau] N (dog) perro chino
chowder ['tʃaudər] N (esp US) sopa de pescado
Christ [kraɪst] N Cristo
christen ['krɪsn] VT bautizar
christening ['krɪsnɪŋ] N bautizo
Christian ['krɪstɪən] ADJ, N cristiano(-a) m/f
Christianity [krɪstɪ'ænɪtɪ] N cristianismo
Christian name N nombre m de pila
★**Christmas** ['krɪsməs] N Navidad f; **Merry ~!** ¡Felices Navidades!, ¡Felices Pascuas!
Christmas card N crismas m inv, tarjeta de Navidad
Christmas carol N villancico m
Christmas Day N día m de Navidad

Christmas Eve N Nochebuena

Christmas Island N Isla Christmas

Christmas pudding N (*esp BRIT*) pudín *m* de Navidad

Christmas tree N árbol *m* de Navidad

chrome [krəum] N = **chromium**

chromium ['krəumɪəm] N cromo; (*also:* **chromium plating**) cromado

chromosome ['krəuməsəum] N cromosoma *m*

chronic ['krɒnɪk] ADJ crónico; (*fig: liar, smoker*) empedernido

chronicle ['krɒnɪkl] N crónica

chronological [krɒnə'lɒdʒɪkəl] ADJ cronológico

chrysalis ['krɪsəlɪs] N (*Biol*) crisálida

chrysanthemum [krɪ'sænθəməm] N crisantemo

chubby ['tʃʌbɪ] ADJ rechoncho

chuck [tʃʌk] (*inf*) VT lanzar, arrojar; (*BRIT: also:* **chuck in, chuck up**) abandonar
  ▶ **chuck out** VT (*person*) echar (fuera); (*rubbish etc*) tirar

chuckle ['tʃʌkl] VI reírse entre dientes

chuffed [tʃʌft] ADJ (*inf*): **to be ~ (about sth)** estar encantado (con algo)

chug [tʃʌg] VI (*also:* **chug along**: *train*) ir despacio; (*: fig*) ir tirando

chugger ['tʃʌgər] N (*inf*) activista de ONG que aborda a las personas en la calle, a menudo de forma agresiva, para pedirles dinero

chum [tʃʌm] N amiguete(-a) *m/f*, coleguilla *mf*

chump [tʃʌmp] N (*inf*) tonto(-a), estúpido(-a)

chunk [tʃʌŋk] N pedazo, trozo

chunky ['tʃʌŋkɪ] ADJ (*furniture etc*) achaparrado; (*person*) fornido; (*knitwear*) de lana gorda, grueso

Chunnel ['tʃʌnl] N = **Channel Tunnel**

★**church** [tʃəːtʃ] N iglesia; **the C~ of England** la Iglesia Anglicana

churchyard ['tʃəːtʃjɑːd] N cementerio, camposanto

churlish ['tʃəːlɪʃ] ADJ grosero; (*mean*) arisco

churn [tʃəːn] N (*for butter*) mantequera; (*for milk*) lechera
  ▶ **churn out** VT producir en serie

chute [ʃuːt] N (*also:* **rubbish chute**) vertedero; (*BRIT: children's slide*) tobogán *m*

chutney ['tʃʌtnɪ] N *salsa picante de frutas y especias*

CIA N ABBR (*US:* = *Central Intelligence Agency*) CIA *f*, Agencia Central de Inteligencia

cicada [sɪ'kɑːdə] N cigarra

CID N ABBR (*BRIT:* = *Criminal Investigation Department*) ≈ B.I.C. *f* (*SP*)

cider ['saɪdər] N sidra

CIF ABBR (= *cost, insurance and freight*) c.s.f.

cigar [sɪ'gɑːr] N puro

★**cigarette** [sɪgə'ret] N cigarrillo, pitillo

cigarette case N pitillera

cigarette end N colilla

cigarette holder N boquilla

cigarette lighter N mechero

C-in-C ABBR (= *commander-in-chief*) comandante *mf* general

cinch [sɪntʃ] N (*inf*): **it's a ~** está tirado

Cinderella [sɪndə'relə] N Cenicienta

cinders ['sɪndəz] NPL cenizas *fpl*

cine-camera ['sɪnɪ'kæmərə] N (*BRIT*) cámara cinematográfica

cine-film ['sɪnɪfɪlm] N (*BRIT*) película de cine

★**cinema** ['sɪnəmə] N cine *m*

cinnamon ['sɪnəmən] N canela

cipher ['saɪfər] N clave *f*; (*fig*) cero; **in ~** en clave

★**circle** ['səːkl] N círculo; (*in theatre*) anfiteatro ▶ VI dar vueltas ▶ VT (*surround*) rodear, cercar; (*move round*) dar la vuelta a

circuit ['səːkɪt] N circuito; (*track*) pista; (*lap*) vuelta

circuit board N tarjeta de circuitos

circuitous [səː'kjuɪtəs] ADJ indirecto

circular ['səːkjulər] ADJ circular ▶ N circular *f*; (*as advertisement*) panfleto

circulate ['səːkjuleɪt] VI circular; (*person: socially*) alternar, circular ▶ VT poner en circulación

circulation [səːkju'leɪʃən] N circulación *f*; (*of newspaper etc*) tirada

circumcise ['səːkəmsaɪz] VT circuncidar

circumference [sə'kʌmfərəns] N circunferencia

circumscribe ['səːkəmskraɪb] VT circunscribir

circumspect ['səːkəmspekt] ADJ circunspecto, prudente

circumstances ['səːkəmstənsɪz] NPL circunstancias *fpl*; (*financial condition*) situación *f* económica; **in the ~** en *or* dadas las circunstancias; **under no ~** de ninguna manera, bajo ningún concepto

circumstantial [səːkəm'stænʃəl] ADJ detallado; **~ evidence** prueba indiciaria

circumvent ['səːkəmvent] VT (*rule etc*) burlar

circus ['səːkəs] N circo; (*also:* **Circus**: *in place names*) Plaza

cirrhosis [sɪ'rəusɪs] N (*also:* **cirrhosis of the liver**) cirrosis *f inv*

CIS N ABBR (= *Commonwealth of Independent States*) CEI *f*

cissy ['sɪsɪ] N = **sissy**

cistern ['sɪstən] N tanque *m*, depósito; (*in toilet*) cisterna

citation [saɪ'teɪʃən] N cita; (*Law*) citación *f*; (*Mil*) mención *f*

cite [saɪt] VT citar

★**citizen** ['sɪtɪzn] N (*Pol*) ciudadano(-a); (*of city*) habitante *mf*, vecino(-a)

Citizens' Advice Bureau N (BRIT) organización voluntaria británica que aconseja especialmente en temas legales o financieros

citizenship [ˈsɪtɪznʃɪp] N ciudadanía; (BRIT Scol) civismo

citric [ˈsɪtrɪk] ADJ: ~ **acid** ácido cítrico

citrus fruits [ˈsɪtrəs-] NPL cítricos mpl

★**city** [ˈsɪtɪ] N ciudad f; **the C~** centro financiero de Londres

city centre N centro de la ciudad

City Hall N (US) ayuntamiento

city technology college N (BRIT) ≈ centro de formación profesional

civic [ˈsɪvɪk] ADJ cívico; (authorities) municipal

civic centre N (BRIT) centro de administración municipal

civil [ˈsɪvɪl] ADJ civil; (polite) atento, cortés; (well-bred) educado

civil defence N protección f civil

civil engineer N ingeniero(-a) de caminos

civil engineering N ingeniería de caminos

civilian [sɪˈvɪlɪən] ADJ civil; (clothes) de paisano ▶ N civil mf

civilization [sɪvɪlaɪˈzeɪʃən] N civilización f

civilized [ˈsɪvɪlaɪzd] ADJ civilizado

civil law N derecho civil

civil liberties NPL libertades fpl civiles

civil partnership N ≈ unión f civil

civil rights NPL derechos mpl civiles

civil servant N funcionario(-a) (del Estado)

Civil Service N administración f pública

civil war N guerra civil

civvies [ˈsɪvɪz] NPL (inf): **in ~** de paisano

CJD N ABBR (= Creutzfeldt-Jakob disease) enfermedad de Creutzfeldt-Jakob

cl ABBR (= centilitre) cl

clad [klæd] ADJ: ~ **(in)** vestido (de)

★**claim** [kleɪm] VT exigir, reclamar; (rights etc) reivindicar; (assert) pretender ▶ VI (for insurance) reclamar ▶ N (for expenses) reclamación f; (Law) demanda; (pretension) pretensión f; **to put in a ~ for sth** presentar una demanda por algo

claimant [ˈkleɪmənt] N (Admin, Law) demandante mf

claim form N solicitud f

clairvoyant [klɛəˈvɔɪənt] N clarividente mf

clam [klæm] N almeja
  ▶ **clam up** VI (inf) cerrar el pico

clamber [ˈklæmbəʳ] VI trepar

clammy [ˈklæmɪ] ADJ (cold) frío y húmedo; (sticky) pegajoso

clamour, (US) **clamor** [ˈklæməʳ] N (noise) clamor m; (protest) protesta ▶ VI: **to ~ for sth** clamar por algo, pedir algo a voces

clamp [klæmp] N abrazadera; (laboratory clamp) grapa; (wheel clamp) cepo ▶ VT afianzar (con abrazadera)

  ▶ **clamp down on** VT FUS (government, police) poner coto a

clampdown [ˈklæmpdaun] N restricción f; **there has been a ~ on terrorism** se ha puesto coto al terrorismo

clan [klæn] N clan m

clandestine [klænˈdɛstɪn] ADJ clandestino

clang [klæŋ] N estruendo ▶ VI sonar con estruendo

clanger [ˈklæŋəʳ] N (BRIT inf): **to drop a ~** meter la pata

clansman [ˈklænzmən] N (irreg) miembro del clan

clap [klæp] VI aplaudir ▶ VT (hands) batir; **to ~ one's hands** dar palmadas, batir las palmas ▶ N (of hands) palmada; **a ~ of thunder** un trueno

clapping [ˈklæpɪŋ] N aplausos mpl

claptrap [ˈklæptræp] N (inf) gilipolleces fpl

claret [ˈklærət] N burdeos m inv

clarification [klærɪfɪˈkeɪʃən] N aclaración f

clarify [ˈklærɪfaɪ] VT aclarar

clarinet [klærɪˈnɛt] N clarinete m

clarity [ˈklærɪtɪ] N claridad f

clash [klæʃ] N estruendo; (fig) choque m ▶ VI enfrentarse; (beliefs) chocar; (disagree) estar en desacuerdo; (colours) desentonar; (two events) coincidir

clasp [klɑːsp] N (hold) apretón m; (of necklace, bag) cierre m ▶ VT abrochar; (hand) apretar; (embrace) abrazar

★**class** [klɑːs] N (gen) clase f; (group, category) clase f, categoría f ▶ CPD de clase ▶ VT clasificar

class-conscious [ˈklɑːsˈkɔnʃəs] ADJ clasista, con conciencia de clase

classic [ˈklæsɪk] ADJ clásico ▶ N (work) obra clásica, clásico ■ **classics** NPL (Univ) clásicas fpl

classical [ˈklæsɪkəl] ADJ clásico; ~ **music** música clásica

classification [klæsɪfɪˈkeɪʃən] N clasificación f

classified [ˈklæsɪfaɪd] ADJ (information) reservado

classified advertisement N anuncio por palabras

classify [ˈklæsɪfaɪ] VT clasificar

classless [ˈklɑːslɪs] ADJ: ~ **society** sociedad f sin clases

classmate [ˈklɑːsmeɪt] N compañero(-a) de clase

classroom [ˈklɑːsrum] N aula

classroom assistant N profesor(a) m/f de apoyo

classy [ˈklɑːsɪ] ADJ (inf) elegante, con estilo

clatter [ˈklætəʳ] N ruido, estruendo; (of hooves) trápala ▶ VI hacer ruido or estruendo

clause [klɔːz] N cláusula; (Ling) oración f

claustrophobia [klɔːstrəˈfəubɪə] N claustrofobia

claustrophobic [klɔːstrəˈfəubɪk] ADJ claustrofóbico; **I feel ~** me entra claustrofobia

claw [klɔː] N (*of cat*) uña; (*of bird of prey*) garra; (*of lobster*) pinza; (*Tech*) garfio ▸ VI: **to ~ at** arañar; (*tear*) desgarrar

clay [kleɪ] N arcilla

★**clean** [kliːn] ADJ limpio; (*record, reputation*) bueno, intachable; (*joke*) decente; (*copy*) en limpio; (*lines*) bien definido; **to have a ~ driving licence** tener el carnet de conducir sin sanciones ▸ VT limpiar; (*hands etc*) lavar; **to ~ one's teeth** lavarse los dientes ▸ ADV: **he ~ forgot** lo olvidó por completo; **to come ~** (*inf: admit guilt*) confesarlo todo
▸ **clean off** VT limpiar
▸ **clean out** VT limpiar (a fondo)
▸ **clean up** VT limpiar, asear ▸ VI (*fig: make profit*): **to ~ up on** sacar provecho de

clean-cut [ˈkliːnˈkʌt] ADJ bien definido; (*outline*) nítido; (*person*) de buen parecer

cleaner [ˈkliːnəʳ] N encargado(-a) de la limpieza; (*also:* **dry cleaner**) tintorero(-a); (*substance*) producto para la limpieza

cleaning [ˈkliːnɪŋ] N limpieza

cleaning lady N señora de la limpieza, asistenta

cleanliness [ˈklɛnlɪnɪs] N limpieza

cleanse [klɛnz] VT limpiar

cleanser [ˈklɛnzəʳ] N detergente *m*; (*cosmetic*) loción *f* or crema limpiadora

clean-shaven [ˈkliːnˈʃeɪvn] ADJ bien afeitado

cleansing department [ˈklɛnzɪŋ-] N (*Brit*) servicio municipal de limpieza

clean sweep N: **to make a ~** (*Sport*) arrasar, barrer

clean technology N tecnología limpia

★**clear** [klɪəʳ] ADJ claro; (*road, way*) libre; (*profit*) neto; (*majority*) absoluto; **to make o.s. ~** explicarse claramente; **to make it ~ to sb that ...** hacer entender a algn que ...; **I have a ~ day tomorrow** mañana tengo el día libre ▸ VT (*space*) despejar, limpiar; (*Law: suspect*) absolver; (*obstacle*) salvar, saltar por encima de; (*debt*) liquidar; (*cheque*) aceptar; (*site, woodland*) desmontar; **to ~ a profit of ...** sacar una ganancia de ...; **to ~ the table** recoger *or* quitar la mesa ▸ VI (*fog etc*) despejarse ▸ N: **to be in the ~** (*out of debt*) estar libre de deudas; (*out of suspicion*) estar fuera de toda sospecha; (*out of danger*) estar fuera de peligro ▸ ADV: **~ of** a distancia de; **to keep ~ of sth/sb** evitar algo/a algn
▸ **clear away** VT (*things, clothes etc*) quitar (de en medio); (*dishes*) retirar
▸ **clear off** VT (*inf: leave*) marcharse, mandarse mudar (*Lam*)
▸ **clear up** VT limpiar; (*mystery*) aclarar, resolver

clearance [ˈklɪərəns] N (*removal*) despeje *m*; (*permission*) acreditación *f*

clear-cut [ˈklɪəˈkʌt] ADJ bien definido, claro

clearing [ˈklɪərɪŋ] N (*in wood*) claro

clearing bank N (*Brit*) banco central

clearing house N (*Comm*) cámara de compensación

clearly [ˈklɪəlɪ] ADV claramente; (*evidently*) sin duda

clearway [ˈklɪəweɪ] N (*Brit*) carretera en la que no se puede estacionar

cleaver [ˈkliːvə] N cuchilla (de carnicero)

clef [klɛf] N (*Mus*) clave *f*

cleft [klɛft] N (*in rock*) grieta, hendedura

clemency [ˈklɛmənsɪ] N clemencia

clench [klɛntʃ] VT apretar, cerrar

clergy [ˈkləːdʒɪ] N clero

clergyman [ˈkləːdʒɪmən] N (*irreg*) clérigo

clerical [ˈklɛrɪkəl] ADJ de oficina; (*Rel*) clerical; (*error*) de copia

clerk [klɑːk, (*US*) kləːk] N oficinista *mf*; (*US*) dependiente(-a) *m/f*, vendedor(a) *m/f*; **C~ of the Court** secretario(-a) de juzgado

★**clever** [ˈklɛvəʳ] ADJ (*mentally*) inteligente, listo; (*skilful*) hábil; (*device, arrangement*) ingenioso

cleverly [ˈklɛvəlɪ] ADV ingeniosamente

clew [kluː] N (*US*) = **clue**

cliché [ˈkliːʃeɪ] N (*pej*) cliché *m*, frase *f* hecha

click [klɪk] VT (*tongue*) chasquear; **to ~ one's heels** taconear ▸ VI (*Comput*) hacer clic; **to ~ on an icon** hacer clic en un icono

clickable [ˈklɪkəbl] ADJ (*Comput*) cliqueable

★**client** [ˈklaɪənt] N cliente(-a) *m/f*

clientele [kliːɑːnˈtɛl] N clientela

cliff [klɪf] N acantilado

cliffhanger [ˈklɪfhæŋəʳ] N: **it was a ~** estuvimos *etc* en ascuas hasta el final

climactic [klaɪˈmæktɪk] ADJ culminante

★**climate** [ˈklaɪmɪt] N clima *m*; (*fig*) clima *m*, ambiente *m*

climate change N cambio climático

climax [ˈklaɪmæks] N (*of battle, career*) apogeo; (*of film, book*) punto culminante, clímax *m inv*; (*sexual*) orgasmo

★**climb** [klaɪm] VI subir, trepar; (*plane*) elevarse, remontar el vuelo; **to ~ over a wall** saltar una tapia ▸ VT (*stairs*) subir; (*tree*) trepar a; (*mountain*) escalar ▸ N subida, ascenso
▸ **climb down** VI (*fig*) volverse atrás

climbdown [ˈklaɪmdaun] N vuelta atrás

climber [ˈklaɪməʳ] N escalador(a) *m/f*

climbing [ˈklaɪmɪŋ] N escalada

clinch [klɪntʃ] VT (*deal*) cerrar; (*argument*) remachar

clincher [ˈklɪntʃəʳ] N (*inf*): **that was the ~ for me** eso me hizo decidir

cling [klɪŋ] (*pt, pp* **clung** [klʌŋ]) VI: **to ~ (to)** agarrarse (a); (*clothes*) pegarse (a)

clingfilm [ˈklɪŋfɪlm] N plástico adherente

clinic [ˈklɪnɪk] N clínica

clinical [ˈklɪnɪkl] ADJ clínico; (*fig*) frío, impasible

clink [klɪŋk] vɪ tintinear

clip [klɪp] N (for hair) horquilla; (also: **paper clip**) sujetapapeles m inv, clip m; (clamp) grapa ▶ VT (cut) cortar; (hedge) podar; (also: **clip together**) unir

clippers ['klɪpəz] NPL (for gardening) tijeras fpl de podar; (for hair) maquinilla sg; (for nails) cortauñas m inv

clipping ['klɪpɪŋ] N (from newspaper) recorte m

clique [kliːk] N (pej) camarilla

cloak [kləuk] N capa, manto ▶ VT (fig) encubrir, disimular

cloakroom ['kləukrum] N guardarropa m; (BRIT: WC) lavabo, aseos mpl, baño (esp LAM)

clobber ['klɔbəʳ] N (inf) bártulos mpl, trastos mpl ▶ VT dar una paliza a

★**clock** [klɔk] N reloj m; (in taxi) taxímetro; **to work against the ~** trabajar contra reloj; **around the ~** las veinticuatro horas; **to sleep round the ~** dormir un día entero; **30,000 on the ~** (Aut) treinta mil millas en el cuentakilómetros
  ▶ **clock in, clock on** vɪ fichar, picar
  ▶ **clock off, clock out** vɪ fichar or picar la salida
  ▶ **clock up** VT hacer

clockwise ['klɔkwaɪz] ADV en el sentido de las agujas del reloj

clockwork ['klɔkwəːk] N aparato de relojería ▶ ADJ (toy, train) de cuerda

clog [klɔg] N zueco, chanclo ▶ VT atascar ▶ VI (also: **clog up**) atascarse

cloister ['klɔɪstəʳ] N claustro

clone [kləun] N clon m ▶ VT clonar

★**close**[1] [kləus] ADJ cercano, próximo; (near): **~ (to)** cerca (de); (print, weave) tupido, compacto; (friend) íntimo; (connection) estrecho; (examination) detallado, minucioso; (weather) bochornoso; (atmosphere) sofocante; (room) mal ventilado; **to have a ~ shave** (fig) escaparse por un pelo; **how ~ is Edinburgh to Glasgow?** ¿qué distancia hay de Edimburgo a Glasgow?; **at ~ quarters** de cerca ▶ ADV cerca; **~ by, ~ at hand** muy cerca; **~ to** prep cerca de

★**close**[2] [kləuz] VT cerrar; (end) concluir, terminar ▶ VI (shop etc) cerrar; (end) concluir(se), terminar(se) ▶ N (end) fin m, final m, conclusión f; **to bring sth to a ~** terminar algo
  ▶ **close down** vɪ cerrar definitivamente
  ▶ **close in** vɪ (hunters) acercarse rodeando, rodear; (evening, night) caer; (fog) cerrarse; **to ~ in on sb** rodear or cercar a algn; **the days are closing in** los días son cada vez más cortos
  ▶ **close off** vT (area) cerrar al tráfico or al público

★**closed** [kləuzd] ADJ (shop etc) cerrado

closed-circuit ['kləuzd'səːkɪt] ADJ: **~ television** televisión f por circuito cerrado

closed shop N empresa en la que todo el personal está afiliado a un sindicato

close-knit ['kləus'nɪt] ADJ (fig) muy unido

closely ['kləuslɪ] ADV (study) con detalle; (listen) con atención; (watch) de cerca; **we are ~ related**

somos parientes cercanos; **a ~ guarded secret** un secreto rigurosamente guardado

close season [kləuz-] N (Football) temporada de descanso; (Hunting) veda

closet ['klɔzɪt] N (cupboard) armario, placar(d) m (LAM)

close-up ['kləusʌp] N primer plano

closing ['kləuzɪŋ] ADJ (stages, remarks) último, final; **~ price** (Stock Exchange) cotización f de cierre

closing time ['kləuzɪŋ-] N hora de cierre

closure ['kləuʒəʳ] N cierre m

clot [klɔt] N (also: **blood clot**) coágulo m; (inf: idiot) imbécil mf ▶ vɪ (blood) coagularse

cloth [klɔθ] N (material) tela, paño; (table cloth) mantel m; (rag) trapo

clothe [kləuð] VT vestir; (fig) revestir

★**clothes** [kləuðz] NPL ropa sg; **to put one's ~ on** vestirse, ponerse la ropa; **to take one's ~ off** desvestirse, desnudarse

clothes brush N cepillo (para la ropa)

clothes line N cuerda (para tender la ropa)

clothes peg, (US) **clothes pin** N pinza

clothing ['kləuðɪŋ] N = **clothes**

clotted cream ['klɔtɪd-] N nata muy espesa

★**cloud** [klaud] N nube f; (storm cloud) nubarrón m; **every ~ has a silver lining** no hay mal que por bien no venga ▶ VT (liquid) enturbiar; **to ~ the issue** empañar el problema
  ▶ **cloud over** vɪ (also fig) nublarse

cloudburst ['klaudbəːst] N chaparrón m

cloud computing N computación f en (la) nube

cloud-cuckoo-land ['klaud'kuku'lænd] N Babia

cloudy ['klaudɪ] ADJ nublado; (liquid) turbio

clout [klaut] N (fig) influencia, peso ▶ VT dar un tortazo a

clove [kləuv] N clavo; **~ of garlic** diente m de ajo

clover ['kləuvəʳ] N trébol m

clown [klaun] N payaso(-a) ▶ vɪ (also: **clown about, clown around**) hacer el payaso

cloying ['klɔɪɪŋ] ADJ (taste) empalagoso

★**club** [klʌb] N (society) club m; (weapon) porra, cachiporra; (also: **golf club**) palo ▶ VT aporrear ▶ vɪ: **to ~ together** (join forces) unir fuerzas
  ◼ **clubs** NPL (Cards) tréboles mpl

club car N (US Rail) coche m salón

club class N (Aviat) clase f preferente

clubhouse ['klʌbhaus] N local social, sobre todo en clubs deportivos

club soda N (US) soda

cluck [klʌk] vɪ cloquear

clue [kluː] N pista; (in crosswords) indicación f; **I haven't a ~** no tengo ni idea

clued up, (US) **clued in** [kluːd-] ADJ (inf) al tanto, al corriente

clueless ['klu:lɪs] ADJ (*inf*) desorientado

clump [klʌmp] N (*of trees*) grupo

clumsy ['klʌmzɪ] ADJ (*person*) torpe; (*tool*) difícil de manejar

clung [klʌŋ] PT, PP *of* **cling**

cluster ['klʌstə'] N grupo; (*Bot*) racimo ▶ VI agruparse, apiñarse

clutch [klʌtʃ] N (*Aut*) embrague *m*; (*pedal*) (pedal *m* de) embrague *m*; **to fall into sb's clutches** caer en las garras de algn ▶ VT agarrar

clutter ['klʌtə'] VT (*also:* **clutter up**) atestar, llenar desordenadamente ▶ N desorden *m*, confusión *f*

CM ABBR (US) = **North Mariana Islands**

cm ABBR (= *centimetre*) cm

CND N ABBR (BRIT: = *Campaign for Nuclear Disarmament*) plataforma pro desarme nuclear

CO N ABBR = **commanding officer**; (BRIT) = **Commonwealth Office** ▶ ABBR (US) = **Colorado**

Co. ABBR = **county**; **company**

c/o ABBR (= *care of*) c/a, a/c

★**coach** [kəutʃ] N (*bus*) autocar *m* (SP), autobús *m*; (*horse-drawn*) coche *m*; (*ceremonial*) carroza; (*of train*) vagón *m*, coche *m*; (*Sport*) entrenador(a) *m/f*, instructor(a) *m/f* ▶ VT (*Sport*) entrenar; (*student*) preparar, enseñar

coach station N (BRIT) estación *f* de autobuses *etc*

coach trip N excursión *f* en autocar

coagulate [kəu'ægjuleɪt] VI coagularse

★**coal** [kəul] N carbón *m*

coal face N frente *m* de carbón

coalfield ['kəulfi:ld] N yacimiento de carbón

coalition [kəuə'lɪʃən] N coalición *f*

coal man N (*irreg*) carbonero

coalmine ['kəulmaɪn] N mina de carbón

coalminer ['kəulmaɪnə'] N minero (de carbón)

coalmining ['keulmaɪnɪŋ] N minería (de carbón)

coarse [kɔ:s] ADJ basto, burdo; (*vulgar*) grosero, ordinario

★**coast** [kəust] N costa, litoral *m* ▶ VI (*Aut*) ir en punto muerto

coastal ['kəustl] ADJ costero

coaster ['kəustə'] N buque *m* costero, barco de cabotaje

coastguard ['kəustgɑ:d] N (*person*) guardacostas *mf inv*

coastline ['kəustlaɪn] N litoral *m*

★**coat** [kəut] N (*jacket*) chaqueta, saco (LAM); (*overcoat*) abrigo; (*of animal*) pelo, pelaje, lana; (*of paint*) mano *f*, capa ▶ VT cubrir, revestir

coat hanger N percha, gancho (LAM)

coating ['kəutɪŋ] N capa, baño

coat of arms N escudo de armas

co-author ['kəu'ɔ:θə'] N coautor(a) *m/f*

coax [kəuks] VT engatusar

cob [kɔb] N *see* **corn**

cobbled ['kɔbld] ADJ: **~ street** calle *f* empedrada, calle *f* adoquinada

cobbler ['kɔblə'] N zapatero (remendón)

cobbles ['kɔblz], **cobblestones** ['kɔblstəunz] NPL adoquines *mpl*

COBOL ['kəubɔl] N COBOL *m*

cobra ['kəubrə] N cobra

cobweb ['kɔbwɛb] N telaraña

cocaine [kə'keɪn] N cocaína

cock [kɔk] N (*rooster*) gallo; (*male bird*) macho ▶ VT (*gun*) amartillar

cock-a-hoop [kɔkə'hu:p] ADJ: **to be ~** estar más contento que unas pascuas

cockatoo [kɔkə'tu:] N cacatúa

cockerel ['kɔkərl] N gallito, gallo joven

cock-eyed ['kɔkaɪd] ADJ bizco; (*fig: crooked*) torcido; (: *idea*) disparatado

cockle ['kɔkl] N berberecho

cockney ['kɔknɪ] N habitante de ciertos barrios de Londres

cockpit ['kɔkpɪt] N (*in aircraft*) cabina

cockroach ['kɔkrəutʃ] N cucaracha

cocktail ['kɔkteɪl] N combinado, cóctel *m*; **prawn ~** cóctel *m* de gambas

cocktail cabinet N mueble-bar *m*

cocktail party N cóctel *m*

cocktail shaker [-ʃeɪkə'] N coctelera

cocky ['kɔkɪ] ADJ farruco, flamenco

cocoa ['kəukəu] N cacao; (*drink*) chocolate *m*

coconut ['kəukənʌt] N coco

cocoon [kə'ku:n] N capullo

COD ABBR (BRIT: = *cash on delivery*) C.A.E.; (US: = *collect on delivery*) C.A.E.

cod [kɔd] N bacalao

★**code** [kəud] N código; (*cipher*) clave *f*; (*Tel*) prefijo; **~ of behaviour** código de conducta; **~ of practice** código profesional ▶ VI (*Comput*) codificar, escribir código

codeine ['kəudi:n] N codeína

codger ['kɔdʒə'] N (BRIT *pej*): **an old ~** un abuelo

codicil ['kɔdɪsɪl] N codicilo

codify ['kəudɪfaɪ] VT codificar

cod-liver oil ['kɔdlɪvə'-] N aceite *m* de hígado de bacalao

co-driver ['kəu'draɪvə'] N (*in race*) copiloto *mf*; (*of lorry*) segundo conductor *m*

co-ed ['kəuɛd] ADJ ABBR = **coeducational** ▶ N ABBR (US: = *female student*) alumna de una universidad mixta; (BRIT: *school*) colegio mixto

coeducational [kəuɛdju'keɪʃənl] ADJ mixto

coerce [kəu'ə:s] VT forzar, coaccionar

coercion [kəu'ə:ʃən] N coacción *f*

coexistence ['kəuɪg'zɪstəns] N coexistencia

C. of C. N ABBR = **chamber of commerce**

C of E ABBR = **Church of England**

★**coffee** [ˈkɔfɪ] N café m; **white ~**, (US) **~ with cream** café con leche

coffee bar N (BRIT) cafetería

coffee bean N grano de café

coffee break N descanso (para tomar café)

coffee cup N taza de café, pocillo (LAM)

coffee maker N máquina de hacer café, cafetera

coffeepot [ˈkɔfɪpɔt] N cafetera

coffee shop N café m

coffee table N mesita baja

coffin [ˈkɔfɪn] N ataúd m

C of I ABBR = **Church of Ireland**

C of S ABBR = **Church of Scotland**

cog [kɔg] N diente m

cogent [ˈkəudʒənt] ADJ lógico, convincente

cognac [ˈkɔnjæk] N coñac m

cognitive [ˈkɔgnɪtɪv] ADJ cognitivo(-a), cognoscitivo(-a)

cogwheel [ˈkɔgwiːl] N rueda dentada

cohabit [kəuˈhæbɪt] VI (formal): **to ~ (with sb)** cohabitar (con algn)

coherent [kəuˈhɪərənt] ADJ coherente

cohesion [kəuˈhiːʒən] N cohesión f

cohesive [kəuˈhiːsɪv] ADJ (fig) cohesivo, unido

COI N ABBR (BRIT: = Central Office of Information) servicio de información gubernamental

coil [kɔɪl] N rollo; (of rope) vuelta; (of smoke) espiral f; (Aut, Elec) bobina, carrete m; (contraceptive) DIU m ▶ VT enrollar

coin [kɔɪn] N moneda ▶ VT acuñar; (word) inventar, acuñar

coinage [ˈkɔɪnɪdʒ] N moneda

coin-box [ˈkɔɪnbɔks] N (BRIT) caja recaudadora

coincide [kəuɪnˈsaɪd] VI coincidir

coincidence [kəuˈɪnsɪdəns] N casualidad f, coincidencia

coin-operated [ˈkɔɪnˈɔpəreɪtɪd] ADJ (machine) que funciona con monedas

Coke® [kəuk] N Coca Cola® f

coke [kəuk] N (coal) coque m

Col. ABBR (= colonel) Cnel., Cor.

COLA N ABBR (US: = cost-of-living adjustment) reajuste salarial de acuerdo con el coste de la vida

colander [ˈkɔləndəʳ] N escurridor m

★**cold** [kəuld] ADJ frío; **it's ~** hace frío; **to be ~** tener frío; **in ~ blood** a sangre fría; **the room's getting ~** está empezando a hacer frío en la habitación; **to give sb the ~ shoulder** tratar a algn con frialdad ▶ N frío; (Med) resfriado; **to catch a ~** resfriarse, acatarrarse, coger un catarro

cold-blooded [ˈkəuldˈblʌdɪd] ADJ (Zool) de sangre fría

cold cream N crema

coldly [ˈkəuldlɪ] ADJ fríamente

cold sore N calentura, herpes m labial

cold sweat N: **to be in a ~ (about sth)** tener sudores fríos (por algo)

cold turkey N (inf) mono

Cold War N: **the ~** la guerra fría

coleslaw [ˈkəulslɔː] N ensalada de col con zanahoria

colic [ˈkɔlɪk] N cólico

colicky [ˈkɔlɪkɪ] ADJ: **to be ~** tener un cólico

collaborate [kəˈlæbəreɪt] VI colaborar

collaboration [kəlæbəˈreɪʃən] N colaboración f; (Pol) colaboracionismo

collaborator [kəˈlæbəreɪtəʳ] N colaborador(a) m/f; (Pol) colaboracionista mf

collage [kɔˈlɑːʒ] N collage m

collagen [ˈkɔlədʒən] N colágeno

★**collapse** [kəˈlæps] VI (gen) hundirse, derrumbarse; (Med) sufrir un colapso ▶ N (gen) hundimiento, derrumbamiento; (Med) colapso; (of government) caída; (of plans, scheme) fracaso; (of business) ruina

collapsible [kəˈlæpsəbl] ADJ plegable

collar [ˈkɔləʳ] N (of coat, shirt) cuello; (for dog) collar m; (Tech) collar m ▶ VT (inf: person) agarrar; (: object) birlar

collarbone [ˈkɔləbəun] N clavícula

collate [kɔˈleɪt] VT cotejar

collateral [kɔˈlætərəl] N (Comm) garantía subsidiaria

collation [kəˈleɪʃən] N colación f

★**colleague** [ˈkɔliːg] N colega mf; (at work) compañero(-a)

★**collect** [kəˈlɛkt] VT reunir; (as a hobby) coleccionar; (BRIT: call and pick up) recoger; (wages) cobrar; (debts) recaudar; (donations, subscriptions) colectar; **to ~ one's thoughts** reponerse, recobrar el dominio de sí mismo ▶ VI (crowd) reunirse; **~ on delivery (COD)** (US) entrega contra reembolso ▶ ADV (US Tel): **to call ~** llamar a cobro revertido

★**collection** [kəˈlɛkʃən] N colección f; (of fares, wages) cobro; (of post) recogida

collective [kəˈlɛktɪv] ADJ colectivo

collective bargaining N negociación f del convenio colectivo

collector [kəˈlɛktəʳ] N coleccionista mf; (of taxes etc) recaudador(a) m/f; **~'s item** or **piece** pieza de coleccionista

★**college** [ˈkɔlɪdʒ] N colegio; (of technology, agriculture etc) escuela

collide [kəˈlaɪd] VI chocar

collie [ˈkɔlɪ] N (dog) collie m, perro pastor escocés

colliery [ˈkɔlɪərɪ] N (BRIT) mina de carbón

collision [kəˈlɪʒən] N choque m, colisión f; **to be on a ~ course** (also fig) ir rumbo al desastre

colloquial [kəˈləukwɪəl] ADJ coloquial

collusion [kəˈluːʒən] N confabulación f, connivencia; **in ~ with** en connivencia con

cologne [kəˈləun] N (also: **eau de cologne**) (agua de) colonia

Colombia [kəˈlɔmbɪə] N Colombia

Colombian [kəˈlɔmbɪən] ADJ, N colombiano(-a) *m/f*

colon [ˈkəulən] N (sign) dos puntos; (Med) colon *m*

colonel [ˈkɜːnl] N coronel *m*

colonial [kəˈləunɪəl] ADJ colonial

colonize [ˈkɔlənaɪz] VT colonizar

colonnade [kɔləˈneɪd] N columnata

colony [ˈkɔlənɪ] N colonia

color [ˈkʌləʳ] N (US) = **colour**

Colorado beetle [kɔləˈrɑːdəu-] N escarabajo de la patata

colossal [kəˈlɔsl] ADJ colosal

★**colour**, (US) **color** [ˈkʌləʳ] N color *m* ▶ VT colorear, pintar; (dye) teñir; (fig: account) adornar; (: judgement) distorsionar ▶ VI (blush) sonrojarse ■ **colours** NPL (of party, club) colores *mpl* ▶ **colour in** VT colorear

colour bar, (US) **color bar** N segregación *f* racial

colour-blind, (US) **color-blind** [ˈkʌləblaɪnd] ADJ daltónico

coloured, (US) **colored** [ˈkʌləd] ADJ de color; (photo) en color; (!: by race) de color

colour film, (US) **color film** N película en color

colourful, (US) **colorful** [ˈkʌləful] ADJ lleno de color; (person) pintoresco

colouring, (US) **coloring** [ˈkʌlərɪŋ] N colorido, color; (substance) colorante *m*

colourless, (US) **colorless** [ˈkʌləlɪs] ADJ incoloro, sin color

colour scheme, (US) **color scheme** N combinación *f* de colores

colour supplement N (Brit Press) suplemento semanal or dominical

colour television, (US) **color television** N televisión *f* en color

colt [kəult] N potro

column [ˈkɔləm] N columna; (fashion column, sports column etc) sección *f*, columna; **the editorial ~** el editorial

columnist [ˈkɔləmnɪst] N columnista *mf*

coma [ˈkəumə] N coma *m*

★**comb** [kəum] N peine *m*; (ornamental) peineta ▶ VT (hair) peinar; (area) registrar a fondo, peinar

combat [ˈkɔmbæt] N combate *m* ▶ VT combatir

★**combination** [kɔmbɪˈneɪʃən] N (gen) combinación *f*

combination lock N cerradura de combinación

★**combine** VT [kəmˈbaɪn] combinar; (qualities) reunir; **a combined effort** un esfuerzo conjunto ▶ VI combinarse ▶ N [ˈkɔmbaɪn] (Econ) cartel *m*; (also: **combine harvester**) cosechadora

combine harvester N cosechadora

combo [ˈkɔmbəu] N (jazz etc) conjunto

combustion [kəmˈbʌstʃən] N combustión *f*

come [kʌm]

(pt **came** [keɪm], pp **come**) VI **1** (movement towards) venir; **to come running** venir corriendo; **come with me** ven conmigo **2** (arrive) llegar; **he's come here to work** ha venido aquí para trabajar; **to come home** volver a casa; **we've just come from Seville** acabamos de llegar de Sevilla; **coming!** ¡voy! **3** (reach): **to come to** llegar a; **the bill came to £40** la cuenta ascendía a cuarenta libras **4** (occur): **an idea came to me** se me ocurrió una idea; **if it comes to it** llegado el caso **5** (be, become): **to come loose/undone** etc aflojarse/desabrocharse, desatarse etc; **I've come to like him** por fin ha llegado a gustarme

▶ **come about** VI suceder, ocurrir

▶ **come across** VT FUS (person) encontrarse con; (thing) encontrar ▶ VI: **to come across well/badly** causar buena/mala impresión

▶ **come along** VI (Brit: progress) ir

▶ **come away** VI (leave) marcharse; (become detached) desprenderse

▶ **come back** VI (return) volver; (reply): **can I come back to you on that one?** volvamos sobre ese punto

▶ **come by** VT FUS (acquire) conseguir

▶ **come down** VI (price) bajar; (building) derrumbarse; (: be demolished) ser derribado

▶ **come forward** VI presentarse

▶ **come from** VT FUS (place, source) ser de

▶ **come in** VI (visitor) entrar; (train, report) llegar; (fashion) ponerse de moda; (on deal etc) entrar

▶ **come in for** VT FUS (criticism etc) recibir

▶ **come into** VT FUS (money) heredar; (be involved) tener que ver con; **to come into fashion** ponerse de moda

▶ **come off** VI (button) soltarse, desprenderse; (attempt) salir bien

▶ **come on** VI (pupil, work, project) marchar; (lights) encenderse; (electricity) volver; **come on!** ¡vamos!

▶ **come out** VI (fact) salir a la luz; (book, sun) salir; (stain) quitarse; **to come out (on strike)** declararse en huelga; **to come out for/against** declararse a favor/en contra de

▶ **come over** VT FUS: **I don't know what's come over him!** ¡no sé lo que le pasa!

▶ **come round** VI (after faint, operation) volver en sí

▶ **come through** VI (survive) sobrevivir; (telephone call): **the call came through** recibimos la llamada

▶ **come to** VI (wake) volver en sí; (total) sumar; **how much does it come to?** ¿cuánto es en total?, ¿a cuánto asciende?

▶ **come under** VT FUS (heading) entrar dentro de; (influence) estar bajo

481

▶ **come up** VI (sun) salir; (problem) surgir; (event) aproximarse; (in conversation) mencionarse
▶ **come up against** VT FUS (resistance etc) tropezar con
▶ **come upon** VT FUS (find) dar con
▶ **come up to** VT FUS llegar hasta; **the film didn't come up to our expectations** la película no fue tan buena como esperábamos
▶ **come up with** VT FUS (idea) sugerir; (money) conseguir

comeback [ˈkʌmbæk] N (reaction) reacción f; (response) réplica; **to make a ~** (Theat) volver a las tablas

comedian [kəˈmiːdɪən] N humorista mf

comedienne [kəmiːdɪˈɛn] N humorista

comedown [ˈkʌmdaʊn] N revés m

★**comedy** [ˈkɔmɪdɪ] N comedia

comet [ˈkɔmɪt] N cometa m

comeuppance [kʌmˈʌpəns] N: **to get one's ~** llevar su merecido

comfort [ˈkʌmfət] N comodidad f, confort m; (well-being) bienestar m; (solace) consuelo; (relief) alivio ▶ VT consolar; see also **comforts**

★**comfortable** [ˈkʌmfətəbl] ADJ cómodo; (income) adecuado; (majority) suficiente; **I don't feel very ~ about it** la cosa me tiene algo preocupado

comfortably [ˈkʌmfətəblɪ] ADV (sit) cómodamente; (live) holgadamente

comforter [ˈkʌmfətəʳ] N (US: pacifier) chupete m; (: bed cover) colcha

comforts [ˈkʌmfəts] NPL comodidades fpl

comfort station N (US) servicios mpl

comic [ˈkɔmɪk] ADJ (also: **comical**) cómico, gracioso ▶ N (comedian) cómico(-a); (magazine) tebeo; (for adults) cómic m

comic book N (US) libro m de cómics

comic strip N tira cómica

coming [ˈkʌmɪŋ] N venida, llegada ▶ ADJ que viene; (next) próximo; (future) venidero; **in the ~ weeks** en las próximas semanas

comings and goings NPL, **coming and going** N ir y venir m, ajetreo

Comintern [ˈkɔmɪntəːn] N Comintern m

comma [ˈkɔmə] N coma

★**command** [kəˈmaːnd] N orden f, mandato; (Mil: authority) mando; (mastery) dominio; (Comput) orden f, comando; **to have at one's ~** (money, resources etc) disponer de; **to have/take ~ of** estar al/asumir el mando de ▶ VT (troops) mandar; (give orders to) mandar, ordenar; (be able to get) disponer de; (deserve) merecer

command economy N economía dirigida

commandeer [kɔmənˈdɪəʳ] VT requisar

commander [kəˈmaːndəʳ] N (Mil) comandante mf, jefe(-a) m/f

commanding [kəˈmaːndɪŋ] ADJ (appearance) imponente; (voice, tone) imperativo; (lead) abrumador(-a); (position) dominante

commanding officer N comandante mf

commandment [kəˈmaːndmənt] N (Rel) mandamiento

command module N módulo de mando

commando [kəˈmaːndəʊ] N comando

commemorate [kəˈmemərreɪt] VT conmemorar

commemoration [kəmeməˈreɪʃən] N conmemoración f

commemorative [kəˈmemərətɪv] ADJ conmemorativo

commence [kəˈmens] VT, VI comenzar

commencement [kəˈmensmənt] N (US Univ) (ceremonia de) graduación f

commend [kəˈmend] VT (praise) elogiar, alabar; (recommend) recomendar; (entrust) encomendar

commendable [kəˈmendəbl] ADJ encomiable

commendation [kɔmenˈdeɪʃən] N (for bravery etc) elogio, encomio

commensurate [kəˈmenʃərɪt] ADJ: **~ with** en proporción a

★**comment** [ˈkɔment] N comentario; **"no ~"** (written) "sin comentarios"; (spoken) "no tengo nada que decir" ▶ VT: **to ~ that** comentar or observar que ▶ VI: **to ~ (on)** comentar, hacer comentarios (sobre)

commentary [ˈkɔməntərɪ] N comentario

commentator [ˈkɔmənteɪtəʳ] N comentarista mf

commerce [ˈkɔməːs] N comercio

★**commercial** [kəˈməːʃəl] ADJ comercial ▶ N (TV) anuncio

commercial bank N banco comercial

commercial break N intermedio para publicidad

commercialism [kəˈməːʃəlɪzəm] N comercialismo

commercial television N televisión f comercial

commercial vehicle N vehículo comercial

commiserate [kəˈmɪzəreɪt] VI: **to ~ with** compadecerse de, condolerse de

★**commission** [kəˈmɪʃən] N (committee, fee, order for work of art etc) comisión f; (act) perpetración f; **out of ~** (machine) fuera de servicio; **~ of inquiry** comisión f investigadora; **I get 10% ~** me dan el diez por ciento de comisión ▶ VT (Mil) nombrar; (work of art) encargar; **to ~ sb to do sth** encargar a algn que haga algo; **to ~ sth from sb** (painting etc) encargar algo a algn

commissionaire [kəmɪʃəˈnɛəʳ] N (BRIT) portero, conserje m

commissioner [kəˈmɪʃənəʳ] N comisario(-a)

★**commit** [kəˈmɪt] VT (act) cometer; (resources) dedicar; (to sb's care) entregar; **to ~ o.s. (to do)** comprometerse (a hacer); **to ~ suicide** suicidarse; **to ~ sb for trial** remitir a algn al tribunal

commitment [kəˈmɪtmənt] N compromiso

committed [kə'mɪtɪd] ADJ (writer, politician etc) comprometido

★**committee** [kə'mɪtɪ] N comité m; **to be on a ~** ser miembro(-a) de un comité

committee meeting N reunión f del comité

commodious [kə'məudɪəs] ADJ grande, espacioso

commodity [kə'mɔdɪtɪ] N mercancía

commodity exchange N bolsa de productos or de mercancías

commodity market N mercado de productos básicos

commodore ['kɔmədɔːʳ] N comodoro

★**common** ['kɔmən] ADJ (gen) común; (pej) ordinario; **in ~ use** de uso corriente ▶ N campo común; **in ~** en común

common cold N: **the ~** el resfriado

common denominator N común denominador m

commoner ['kɔmənəʳ] N plebeyo(-a)

common land N campo comunal, ejido

common law N ley f consuetudinaria

common-law ['kɔmənlɔː] ADJ: **~ wife** esposa de hecho

commonly ['kɔmənlɪ] ADV comúnmente

Common Market N Mercado Común

commonplace ['kɔmənpleɪs] ADJ corriente

common room ['kɔmənrum] N sala de reunión

Commons ['kɔmənz] NPL (BRIT Pol): **the ~** (la Cámara de) los Comunes

common sense N sentido común

Commonwealth ['kɔmənwɛlθ] N: **the ~** la Comunidad (Británica) de Naciones, la Commonwealth

La **Commonwealth** es la asociación de estados soberanos independientes y territorios asociados que formaban parte del antiguo Imperio Británico. Este pasó a llamarse así después de la Segunda Guerra Mundial, aunque ya desde 1931 se le conocía como British Commonwealth of Nations. Organizan su propia competición deportiva cada cuatro años llamada the Commonwealth Games. Todos los estados miembros reconocen al monarca británico como Head of the Commonwealth.

commotion [kə'məuʃən] N tumulto, confusión f

communal ['kɔmjuːnl] ADJ comunal; (kitchen) común

commune N ['kɔmjuːn] (group) comuna ▶ VI [kə'mjuːn]: **to ~ with** comunicarse con

★**communicate** [kə'mjuːnɪkeɪt] VT comunicar ▶ VI: **to ~ (with)** comunicarse (con); (in writing) estar en contacto (con)

★**communication** [kəmjuːnɪ'keɪʃən] N comunicación f

communication cord N (BRIT) timbre m de alarma

communications network N red f de comunicaciones

communications satellite N satélite m de comunicaciones

communicative [kə'mjuːnɪkətɪv] ADJ comunicativo

communion [kə'mjuːnɪən] N (also: **Holy Communion**) comunión f

communiqué [kə'mjuːnɪkeɪ] N comunicado, parte m

communism ['kɔmjunɪzəm] N comunismo

communist ['kɔmjunɪst] ADJ, N comunista mf

★**community** [kə'mjuːnɪtɪ] N comunidad f; (large group) colectividad f; (local) vecindario

community centre N centro social

community chest N (US) fondo social

community health centre N centro médico, casa de salud

community service N trabajo m comunitario (prestado en lugar de cumplir una pena de prisión)

community spirit N civismo

commutation ticket [kɔmju'teɪʃən-] N (US) billete m de abono

commute [kə'mjuːt] VI viajar a diario de casa al trabajo ▶ VT conmutar

commuter [kə'mjuːtəʳ] N persona que viaja a diario de casa al trabajo

Comoros ['kɔmərəuz, kə'mɔːrəuz] NPL Comoras fpl

compact ADJ [kəm'pækt] compacto; (style) conciso; (dense) apretado ▶ N ['kɔmpækt] (pact) pacto; (also: **powder compact**) polvera

compact disc N compact disc m, disco compacto

compact disc player N lector m or reproductor m de discos compactos

companion [kəm'pænɪən] N compañero(-a)

companionship [kəm'pænjənʃɪp] N compañerismo

companionway [kəm'pænjənweɪ] N (Naut) escalerilla

★**company** ['kʌmpənɪ] N (gen) compañía; (Comm) empresa, compañía; **to keep sb ~** acompañar a algn; **Smith and C~** Smith y Compañía

company car N coche m de la empresa

company director N director(a) m/f de empresa

company secretary N (BRIT) administrador(a) m/f de empresa

comparable ['kɔmpərəbl] ADJ comparable

comparative [kəm'pærətɪv] ADJ (freedom, luxury, cost) relativo; (study, linguistics) comparado

comparatively [kəm'pærətɪvlɪ] ADV (relatively) relativamente

★**compare** [kəm'pɛəʳ] VT comparar; **compared with** or **to** comparado con or a ▶ VI: **to ~ (with)**

poder compararse (con); **how do the prices ~?** ¿cómo son los precios en comparación?

★**comparison** [kəmˈpærɪsn] N comparación f; **in ~ (with)** en comparación (con)

compartment [kəmˈpɑːtmənt] N compartim(i)ento; (*Rail*) departamento, compartimento

compass [ˈkʌmpəs] N brújula; **within the ~ of** al alcance de ■ **compasses** NPL compás m

compassion [kəmˈpæʃən] N compasión f

compassionate [kəmˈpæʃənɪt] ADJ compasivo; **on ~ grounds** por compasión

compassionate leave N permiso por asuntos familiares

compatibility [kəmpætɪˈbɪlɪtɪ] N compatibilidad f

compatible [kəmˈpætɪbl] ADJ compatible

compel [kəmˈpel] VT obligar

compelling [kəmˈpelɪŋ] ADJ (*fig: argument*) convincente

compendium [kəmˈpendɪəm] N compendio

compensate [ˈkɔmpənseɪt] VT compensar ▶ VI: **to ~ for** compensar

compensation [kɔmpənˈseɪʃən] N (*for loss*) indemnización f

compère [ˈkɔmpeəʳ] N presentador(a) m/f

★**compete** [kəmˈpiːt] VI (*take part*) competir; (*vie with*) competir, hacer la competencia

competence [ˈkɔmpɪtəns] N capacidad f, aptitud f

competent [ˈkɔmpɪtənt] ADJ competente, capaz

competing [kəmˈpiːtɪŋ] ADJ (*rival*) competidor(-a); (*ideas*) contrapuesto

★**competition** [kɔmpɪˈtɪʃən] N (*contest*) concurso; (*Sport*) competición f; (*Econ: rivalry*) competencia; **in ~ with** en competencia con

★**competitive** [kəmˈpetɪtɪv] ADJ (*Econ, Sport*) competitivo; (*spirit*) competidor(a), de competencia; (*selection*) por concurso

★**competitor** [kəmˈpetɪtəʳ] N (*rival*) competidor(a) m/f; (*participant*) concursante mf

compile [kəmˈpaɪl] VT recopilar

complacency [kəmˈpleɪsnsɪ] N autosatisfacción f

complacent [kəmˈpleɪsənt] ADJ autocomplaciente

★**complain** [kəmˈpleɪn] VI (*gen*) quejarse; (*Comm*) reclamar

★**complaint** [kəmˈpleɪnt] N (*gen*) queja; (*Comm*) reclamación f; (*Law*) demanda, querella; (*Med*) enfermedad f

complement N [ˈkɔmplɪmənt] complemento; (*esp ship's crew*) dotación f ▶ VT [ˈkɔmplɪment] (*enhance*) complementar

complementary [kɔmplɪˈmentərɪ] ADJ complementario

★**complete** [kəmˈpliːt] ADJ (*full*) completo; (*finished*) acabado; **it's a ~ disaster** es un desastre

total ▶ VT (*fulfil*) completar; (*finish*) acabar; (*a form*) rellenar

★**completely** [kəmˈpliːtlɪ] ADV completamente

completion [kəmˈpliːʃən] N (*gen*) conclusión f, terminación f; **to be nearing ~** estar a punto de terminarse; **on ~ of contract** cuando se realice el contrato

complex [ˈkɔmpleks] ADJ complejo ▶ N (*gen*) complejo

complexion [kəmˈplekʃən] N (*of face*) tez f, cutis m; (*fig*) aspecto

complexity [kəmˈpleksɪtɪ] N complejidad f

compliance [kəmˈplaɪəns] N (*submission*) sumisión f; (*agreement*) conformidad f; **in ~ with** de acuerdo con

compliant [kəmˈplaɪənt] ADJ sumiso; conforme

★**complicated** [ˈkɔmplɪkeɪtɪd] ADJ complicado

complication [kɔmplɪˈkeɪʃən] N complicación f

complicity [kəmˈplɪsɪtɪ] N complicidad f

compliment [ˈkɔmplɪmənt] N (*formal*) cumplido; (*flirtation*) piropo; **to pay sb a ~** (*formal*) hacer cumplidos a algn; (*flirt*) piropear, echar piropos a algn ▶ VT felicitar; **to ~ sb (on sth/on doing sth)** felicitar a algn (por algo/por haber hecho algo) ■ **compliments** NPL saludos mpl

complimentary [kɔmplɪˈmentərɪ] ADJ elogioso; (*copy*) de regalo; **~ ticket** invitación f

compliments slip N saluda m

comply [kəmˈplaɪ] VI: **to ~ with** acatar

component [kəmˈpəunənt] ADJ componente ▶ N (*Tech*) pieza, componente m

compose [kəmˈpəuz] VT componer; **to be composed of** componerse de, constar de; **to ~ o.s.** tranquilizarse

composed [kəmˈpəuzd] ADJ sosegado

composer [kəmˈpəuzəʳ] N (*Mus*) compositor(a) m/f

composite [ˈkɔmpəzɪt] ADJ compuesto; **~ motion** moción f compuesta

composition [kɔmpəˈzɪʃən] N composición f

compositor [kəmˈpɔzɪtəʳ] N (*Typ*) cajista mf

compos mentis [ˈkɔmpəsˈmentɪs] ADJ: **to be ~** estar en su sano juicio

compost [ˈkɔmpɔst] N abono

compost heap N montón de basura orgánica para abono

composure [kəmˈpəuʒəʳ] N serenidad f, calma

compound N [ˈkɔmpaund] (*Chem*) compuesto; (*Ling*) término compuesto; (*enclosure*) recinto ▶ ADJ (*gen*) compuesto; (*fracture*) complicado ▶ VT [kəmˈpaund] (*fig: problem, difficulty*) agravar

comprehend [kɔmprɪˈhend] VT comprender

comprehension [kɔmprɪˈhenʃən] N comprensión f

comprehensive [kɔmprɪˈhensɪv] ADJ (*broad*)

exhaustivo; (*general*) de conjunto; **~ (school)** *n* centro estatal de enseñanza secundaria, ≈ Instituto Nacional de Bachillerato (SP)

En los años 60 se creó un nuevo tipo de centro educativo de enseñanza secundaria (aproximadamente de los once años en adelante) denominado **comprehensive school**, abierto a todos los alumnos independientemente de sus capacidades, con el que se intentó poner fin a la división tradicional entre centros de enseñanzas teóricas para acceder a la educación superior (*grammar schools*) y otros de enseñanzas básicamente profesionales (*secondary modern schools*). Aunque estas últimas ya no existen, en algunas partes de Inglaterra aún hay alguna "grammar school", lo cual sigue siendo un asunto que genera debate político tanto en el gobierno como entre la población.

comprehensive insurance policy N seguro a todo riesgo

compress VT [kəm'pres] comprimir; (*Comput*) comprimir ▶ N ['kɒmpres] (*Med*) compresa

compression [kəm'preʃən] N compresión *f*

comprise [kəm'praɪz] VT (*also:* **be comprised of**) comprender, constar de

★**compromise** ['kɒmprəmaɪz] N solución *f* intermedia; (*agreement*) arreglo ▶ VT comprometer ▶ VI transigir, transar (LAM) ▶ CPD (*decision, solution*) de término medio

compulsion [kəm'pʌlʃən] N obligación *f*; **under ~** a la fuerza, por obligación

compulsive [kəm'pʌlsɪv] ADJ compulsivo; (*viewing, reading*) obligado

compulsory [kəm'pʌlsərɪ] ADJ obligatorio

compulsory purchase N expropiación *f*

compunction [kəm'pʌŋkʃən] N escrúpulo; **to have no ~ about doing sth** no tener escrúpulos en hacer algo

★**computer** [kəm'pjuːtəʳ] N ordenador *m*, computador *m*, computadora

★**computer game** N juego de ordenador

computerize [kəm'pjuːtəraɪz] VT (*data*) computerizar; (*system*) informatizar

computer language N lenguaje *m* de ordenador *or* computadora

computer literate ADJ: **to be ~** tener conocimientos de informática a nivel de usuario

computer peripheral N periférico

computer program N programa *m* informático *or* de ordenador

computer programmer N programador(a) *m/f*

computer programming N programación *f*

computer science N informática

computer studies NPL informática *fsg*, computación *fsg* (LAM)

computing [kəm'pjuːtɪŋ] N (*activity*) informática

comrade ['kɒmrɪd] N compañero(-a)

comradeship ['kɒmrɪdʃɪp] N camaradería, compañerismo

comsat® ['kɒmsæt] N ABBR = **communications satellite**

con [kɒn] VT timar, estafar; **to ~ sb into doing sth** (*inf*) engañar a algn para que haga algo ▶ N timo, estafa

concave ['kɒn'keɪv] ADJ cóncavo

conceal [kən'siːl] VT ocultar; (*thoughts etc*) disimular

concede [kən'siːd] VT (*point, argument*) reconocer; (*game*) darse por vencido en; (*territory*) ceder; **to ~ (defeat)** darse por vencido; **to ~ that** admitir que

conceit [kən'siːt] N orgullo, presunción *f*

conceited [kən'siːtɪd] ADJ orgulloso

conceivable [kən'siːvəbl] ADJ concebible; **it is ~ that ...** es posible que ...

conceivably [kən'siːvəblɪ] ADV: **he may ~ be right** es posible que tenga razón

conceive [kən'siːv] VT, VI concebir; **to ~ of sth/of doing sth** imaginar algo/imaginarse haciendo algo

★**concentrate** ['kɒnsəntreɪt] VI concentrarse ▶ VT concentrar

concentration [kɒnsən'treɪʃən] N concentración *f*

concentration camp N campo de concentración

concentric [kən'sentrɪk] ADJ concéntrico

concept ['kɒnsept] N concepto

conception [kən'sepʃən] N (*idea*) concepto, idea; (*Biol*) concepción *f*

concern [kən'sɜːn] N (*matter*) asunto; (*Comm*) empresa; (*anxiety*) preocupación *f* ▶ VT (*worry*) preocupar; (*involve*) afectar; (*relate to*) tener que ver con; **to be concerned (about)** interesarse (por), preocuparse (por); **to be concerned with** tratar de; **the department concerned** (*under discussion*) el departamento en cuestión; (*relevant*) el departamento competente; **as far as I am concerned** en cuanto a mí, por lo que a mí se refiere; **"to whom it may ~"** "a quien corresponda"

concerning [kən'sɜːnɪŋ] PREP sobre, acerca de

★**concert** ['kɒnsət] N concierto

concerted [kən'sɜːtɪd] ADJ (*efforts etc*) concertado

concert hall N sala de conciertos

concertina [kɒnsə'tiːnə] N concertina

concerto [kən'tʃɜːtəu] N concierto

concession [kən'seʃən] N concesión *f*; (*price concession*) descuento; **tax ~** privilegio fiscal

concessionaire [kənseʃə'neəʳ] N concesionario(-a)

concessionary [kən'seʃənərɪ] ADJ (*ticket, fare*) con descuento, a precio reducido

conciliation [kənsɪlɪ'eɪʃən] N conciliación *f*

conciliatory [kən'sɪlɪətrɪ] ADJ conciliador(a)

concise [kən'saıs] ADJ conciso

conclave ['kɒnkleıv] N cónclave m

conclude [kən'klu:d] VT (finish) concluir; (treaty etc) firmar; (agreement) llegar a; (decide): **to ~ that ...** llegar a la conclusión de que ... ▶ VI (events) concluir, terminar

concluding [kən'klu:dıŋ] ADJ (remarks etc) final

conclusion [kən'klu:ʒən] N conclusión f; **to come to the ~ that** llegar a la conclusión de que

conclusive [kən'klu:sıv] ADJ decisivo, concluyente

conclusively [kən'klu:sıvlı] ADV concluyentemente

concoct [kən'kɒkt] VT (food, drink) preparar; (story) inventar; (plot) tramar

concoction [kən'kɒkʃən] N (food) mezcla; (drink) brebaje m

concord ['kɒŋkɔ:d] N (harmony) concordia; (treaty) acuerdo

concourse ['kɒŋkɔ:s] N (hall) vestíbulo

concrete ['kɒnkri:t] N hormigón m ▶ ADJ de hormigón; (fig) concreto

concrete mixer N hormigonera

concur [kən'kə:ʳ] VI estar de acuerdo

concurrently [kən'kʌrntlı] ADV al mismo tiempo

concussion [kən'kʌʃən] N conmoción f cerebral

condemn [kən'dɛm] VT condenar; (building) declarar en ruina

condemnation [kɒndɛm'neıʃən] N (gen) condena; (blame) censura

condensation [kɒndɛn'seıʃən] N condensación f

condense [kən'dɛns] VI condensarse ▶ VT condensar; (text) abreviar

condensed milk [kən'dɛnst-] N leche f condensada

condescend [kɒndı'sɛnd] VI condescender; **to ~ to sb** tratar a algn con condescendencia; **to ~ to do sth** dignarse hacer algo

condescending [kɒndı'sɛndıŋ] ADJ superior

★**condition** [kən'dıʃən] N condición f; (of health) estado; (disease) enfermedad f; **on ~ that** a condición (de) que; **weather conditions** condiciones atmosféricas; **in good/poor ~** en buenas/malas condiciones, en buen/mal estado; **conditions of sale** condiciones de venta ▶ VT condicionar

conditional [kən'dıʃənl] ADJ condicional

conditioned reflex [kən'dıʃənd-] N reflejo condicionado

conditioner [kən'dıʃənəʳ] N (for hair) suavizante m, acondicionador m

condo ['kɒndəu] N ABBR (US inf) = **condominium**

condolences [kən'dəulənsız] NPL pésame msg

condom ['kɒndəm] N condón m

condominium [kɒndə'mınıəm] N (US: building) bloque m de pisos or apartamentos (propiedad de quienes lo habitan), condominio (LAM); (: apartment) piso or apartamento (en propiedad), condominio (LAM)

condone [kən'dəun] VT condonar

conducive [kən'dju:sıv] ADJ: **~ to** conducente a

conduct N ['kɒndʌkt] conducta, comportamiento ▶ VT [kən'dʌkt] (lead) conducir; (manage) llevar, dirigir; (Mus) dirigir; **to ~ o.s.** comportarse ▶ VI (Mus) llevar la batuta

conducted tour [kən'dʌktıd-] N (BRIT) visita con guía

conductor [kən'dʌktəʳ] N (of orchestra) director(a) m/f; (US: on train) revisor(a) m/f; (on bus) cobrador(a) m/f; (Elec) conductor m

cone [kəun] N cono; (pine cone) piña; (for ice cream) cucurucho

confectioner [kən'fɛkʃənəʳ] N (of cakes) pastelero(-a); (of sweets) confitero(-a); **~'s (shop)** n pastelería; confitería

confectionery [kən'fɛkʃənrı] N pasteles mpl; dulces mpl

confederate [kən'fɛdrıt] ADJ confederado ▶ N (pej) cómplice mf; (US History) confederado(-a)

confederation [kənfɛdə'reıʃən] N confederación f

confer [kən'fə:ʳ] VT: **to ~ (on)** otorgar (a) ▶ VI conferenciar; **to ~ (with sb about sth)** consultar (con algn sobre algo)

conference ['kɒnfərns] N (meeting) reunión f; (convention) congreso; **to be in ~** estar en una reunión

conference room N sala de conferencias

confess [kən'fɛs] VT confesar ▶ VI confesar; (Rel) confesarse

confession [kən'fɛʃən] N confesión f

confessional [kən'fɛʃənl] N confesionario

confessor [kən'fɛsəʳ] N confesor m

confetti [kən'fɛtı] N confeti m

confide [kən'faıd] VI: **to ~ in** confiar en

★**confidence** ['kɒnfıdns] N (also: **self-confidence**) confianza; (secret) confidencia; **in ~** (speak, write) en confianza; **to have (every) ~ that** estar seguro or confiado de que; **motion of no ~** moción f de censura; **to tell sb sth in strict ~** decir algo a algn de manera confidencial

confidence trick N timo

★**confident** ['kɒnfıdənt] ADJ seguro de sí mismo

confidential [kɒnfı'dɛnʃəl] ADJ confidencial; (secretary) de confianza

confidentiality [kɒnfıdɛnʃı'ælıtı] N confidencialidad f

configuration [kənfıgju'reıʃən] N (Comput) configuración f

confine [kən'faın] VT (limit) limitar; (shut up) encerrar; **to ~ o.s. to doing sth** limitarse a hacer algo

confined [kənˈfaɪnd] ADJ (*space*) reducido
confinement [kənˈfaɪnmənt] N (*prison*) reclusión f; (*Med*) parto; **in solitary ~** incomunicado
confines [ˈkɒnfaɪnz] NPL confines *mpl*
★**confirm** [kənˈfəːm] VT confirmar
confirmation [kɒnfəˈmeɪʃən] N confirmación f
confirmed [kənˈfəːmd] ADJ empedernido
confiscate [ˈkɒnfɪskeɪt] VT confiscar
confiscation [kɒnfɪsˈkeɪʃən] N incautación f
conflagration [kɒnfləˈgreɪʃən] N conflagración f
conflict N [ˈkɒnflɪkt] conflicto ▶ VI [kənˈflɪkt] (*opinions*) estar reñido; (*reports, evidence*) contradecirse
conflicting [kənˈflɪktɪŋ] ADJ (*reports, evidence, opinions*) contradictorio
conform [kənˈfɔːm] VI: **to ~ to** (*laws*) someterse a; (*usages, mores*) amoldarse a; (*standards*) ajustarse a
conformist [kənˈfɔːmɪst] N conformista *mf*
confound [kənˈfaund] VT confundir; (*amaze*) pasmar
confounded [kənˈfaundɪd] ADJ condenado
confront [kənˈfrʌnt] VT (*problems*) hacer frente a; (*enemy, danger*) enfrentarse con
confrontation [kɒnfrənˈteɪʃən] N enfrentamiento, confrontación f
confrontational [kɒnfrənˈteɪʃənəl] ADJ conflictivo
confuse [kənˈfjuːz] VT (*perplex*) desconcertar; (*mix up*) confundir; (*complicate*) complicar
confused [kənˈfjuːzd] ADJ confuso; (*person*) desconcertado; **to get ~** desconcertarse; (*muddled up*) hacerse un lío
confusing [kənˈfjuːzɪŋ] ADJ confuso
confusion [kənˈfjuːʒən] N confusión f
congeal [kənˈdʒiːl] VI coagularse
congenial [kənˈdʒiːnɪəl] ADJ agradable
congenital [kənˈdʒenɪtl] ADJ congénito
congested [kənˈdʒestɪd] ADJ (*gen*) atestado; (*telephone lines*) saturado
congestion [kənˈdʒestʃən] N congestión f
congestion charge N, **congestion charges** NPL tasa por congestión
conglomerate [kənˈglɒmərət] N (*Comm, Geo*) conglomerado
conglomeration [kənglɒməˈreɪʃən] N conglomeración f
Congo [ˈkɒŋgəu] N (*state*) Congo
congratulate [kənˈgrætjuleɪt] VT felicitar
★**congratulations** [kəngrætjuˈleɪʃənz] NPL: **~ (on)** felicitaciones *fpl* (por); **~!** ¡enhorabuena!, ¡felicidades!
congregate [ˈkɒŋgrɪgeɪt] VI congregarse
congregation [kɒŋgrɪˈgeɪʃən] N (*in church*) fieles *mpl*

congress [ˈkɒŋgres] N congreso; (*US Pol*): **C~** el Congreso (de los Estados Unidos)

En el Congreso de los Estados Unidos (**Congress**) se elaboran y aprueban las leyes federales. Consta de dos cámaras: la Cámara de Representantes (*House of Representatives*), cuyos 435 miembros son elegidos cada dos años por voto popular directo y en número proporcional a los habitantes de cada estado, y el Senado (*Senate*), con 100 senadores (*senators*), 2 por estado, elegidos por un período de seis años, aunque alrededor de un tercio de los escaños queda libre cada dos años debido al escalonamiento de las elecciones.

congressman [ˈkɒŋgresmən] N (*irreg*) (*US*) diputado, miembro del Congreso
congresswoman [ˈkɒŋgreswumən] N (*irreg*) (*US*) diputada, miembro f del Congreso
conical [ˈkɒnɪkl] ADJ cónico
conifer [ˈkɒnɪfər] N conífera
coniferous [kəˈnɪfərəs] ADJ (*forest*) conífero
conjecture [kənˈdʒektʃər] N conjetura
conjugal [ˈkɒndʒugl] ADJ conyugal
conjugate [ˈkɒndʒugeɪt] VT conjugar
conjugation [kɒndʒəˈgeɪʃən] N conjugación f
conjunction [kənˈdʒʌŋkʃən] N conjunción f; **in ~ with** junto con
conjunctivitis [kəndʒʌŋktɪˈvaɪtɪs] N conjuntivitis f
conjure [ˈkʌndʒər] VI hacer juegos de manos ▶ **conjure up** VT (*ghost, spirit*) hacer aparecer; (*memories*) evocar
conjurer [ˈkʌndʒərər] N ilusionista *mf*
conjuring trick [ˈkʌndʒərɪŋ-] N juego de manos
conker [ˈkɒŋkər] N (*BRIT*) castaño de Indias
conk out [kɒŋk-] VI (*inf*) estropearse, fastidiarse, descomponerse (*LAM*)
con man N (*irreg*) timador m
connect [kəˈnekt] VT juntar, unir; (*Elec*) conectar; (*pipes*) empalmar; (*fig*) relacionar, asociar; **to be connected with** (*associated*) estar relacionado con; (*related*) estar emparentado con; **I am trying to ~ you** (*Tel*) estoy intentando ponerle al habla ▶ VI: **to ~ with** (*train*) enlazar con
connecting flight [kəˈnektɪŋ-] N vuelo m de enlace
★**connection** [kəˈnekʃən] N juntura, unión f; (*Elec*) conexión f; (*Tech*) empalme m; (*Rail*) enlace m; (*Tel*) comunicación f; (*fig*) relación f; **what is the ~ between them?** ¿qué relación hay entre ellos?; **in ~ with** con respecto a, en relación a; **she has many business connections** tiene muchos contactos profesionales; **to miss/make a ~** perder/coger el enlace
connive [kəˈnaɪv] VI: **to ~ at** hacer la vista gorda a

connoisseur [kɒnɪˈsəːʳ] N experto(-a), entendido(-a)

connotation [kɒnəˈteɪʃən] N connotación f

conquer [ˈkɒŋkəʳ] VT (territory) conquistar; (enemy, feelings) vencer

conqueror [ˈkɒŋkərəʳ] N conquistador(a) m/f

conquest [ˈkɒŋkwɛst] N conquista

cons [kɒnz] NPL see mod cons; pro

conscience [ˈkɒnʃəns] N conciencia; in all ~ en conciencia

conscientious [kɒnʃɪˈɛnʃəs] ADJ concienzudo; (objection) de conciencia

conscientious objector N objetor m de conciencia

★**conscious** [ˈkɒnʃəs] ADJ consciente; (deliberate: insult, error) premeditado, intencionado; to become ~ of sth/that darse cuenta de algo/de que

consciousness [ˈkɒnʃəsnɪs] N conciencia; (Med) conocimiento

conscript [ˈkɒnskrɪpt] N recluta mf

conscription [kənˈskrɪpʃən] N servicio militar (obligatorio)

consecrate [ˈkɒnsɪkreɪt] VT consagrar

consecutive [kənˈsɛkjutɪv] ADJ consecutivo; on 3 ~ occasions en 3 ocasiones consecutivas

consensus [kənˈsɛnsəs] N consenso; the ~ of opinion el consenso general

consent [kənˈsɛnt] N consentimiento; by common ~ de común acuerdo ▶ VI: to ~ to consentir en

consenting adults [kənˈsɛntɪŋ-] NPL adultos con capacidad de consentir

★**consequence** [ˈkɒnsɪkwəns] N consecuencia; in ~ por consiguiente

consequently [ˈkɒnsɪkwəntlɪ] ADV por consiguiente

conservation [kɒnsəˈveɪʃən] N conservación f; (of nature) conservación, protección f

conservationist [kɒnsəˈveɪʃnɪst] N conservacionista mf

★**conservative** [kənˈsəːvətɪv] ADJ conservador(a); (cautious) moderado; C~ adj, n (BRIT Pol) conservador m/f; the C~ Party el partido conservador (británico)

conservatory [kənˈsəːvətrɪ] N (greenhouse) invernadero

conserve [kənˈsəːv] VT conservar ▶ N conserva

★**consider** [kənˈsɪdəʳ] VT considerar; (take into account) tener en cuenta; (study) estudiar, examinar; to ~ doing sth pensar en (la posibilidad de) hacer algo; all things considered pensándolo bien; ~ yourself lucky ¡date por satisfecho!

considerable [kənˈsɪdərəbl] ADJ considerable

considerably [kənˈsɪdərəblɪ] ADV bastante, considerablemente

considerate [kənˈsɪdərɪt] ADJ considerado

consideration [kənsɪdəˈreɪʃən] N consideración f; (reward) retribución f; to be under ~ estar estudiándose; my first ~ is my family mi primera consideración es mi familia

considered [kənˈsɪdəd] ADJ: it's my ~ opinion that ... después de haber reflexionado mucho, pienso que ...

considering [kənˈsɪdərɪŋ] PREP: ~ (that) teniendo en cuenta (que)

consign [kənˈsaɪn] VT consignar

consignee [kɒnsaɪˈniː] N consignatario(-a)

consignment [kənˈsaɪnmənt] N envío

consignment note N (Comm) talón m de expedición

consignor [kənˈsaɪnəʳ] N remitente mf

consist [kənˈsɪst] VI: to ~ of consistir en

consistency [kənˈsɪstənsɪ] N (of person etc) consecuencia, coherencia; (thickness) consistencia

consistent [kənˈsɪstənt] ADJ (person, argument) consecuente, coherente; (results) constante

consolation [kɒnsəˈleɪʃən] N consuelo

console VT [kənˈsəul] consolar ▶ N [ˈkɒnsəul] (control panel) consola

consolidate [kənˈsɒlɪdeɪt] VT consolidar

consols [ˈkɒnsɒlz] NPL (BRIT Stock Exchange) valores mpl consolidados

consommé [kənˈsɒmeɪ] N consomé m, caldo

consonant [ˈkɒnsənənt] N consonante f

consort N [ˈkɒnsɔːt] consorte mf; prince ~ príncipe m consorte ▶ VI [kənˈsɔːt]: to ~ with sb (often pej) asociarse con algn

consortium [kənˈsɔːtɪəm] N consorcio

conspicuous [kənˈspɪkjuəs] ADJ (visible) visible; (garish etc) llamativo; (outstanding) notable; to make o.s. ~ llamar la atención

conspiracy [kənˈspɪrəsɪ] N conjura, complot m

conspiratorial [kənspɪrəˈtɔːrɪəl] ADJ de conspirador

conspire [kənˈspaɪəʳ] VI conspirar

constable [ˈkʌnstəbl] N (BRIT) agente mf (de policía); chief ~ ≈ jefe(-a) m/f de policía

constabulary [kənˈstæbjulərɪ] N ≈ policía

constancy [ˈkɒnstənsɪ] N constancia; fidelidad f

★**constant** [ˈkɒnstənt] ADJ (gen) constante; (loyal) leal, fiel

constantly [ˈkɒnstəntlɪ] ADV constantemente

constellation [kɒnstəˈleɪʃən] N constelación f

consternation [kɒnstəˈneɪʃən] N consternación f

constipated [ˈkɒnstɪpeɪtəd] ADJ estreñido

> **constipated** no debe traducirse por constipado.

constipation [kɒnstɪˈpeɪʃən] N estreñimiento

constituency [kənˈstɪtjuənsɪ] N (Pol) distrito electoral; (people) electorado

constituency party N partido local

constituent [kənˈstɪtjuənt] N (*Pol*) elector(a) *m/f*; (*part*) componente *m*

constitute [ˈkɒnstɪtjuːt] VT constituir

constitution [kɒnstɪˈtjuːʃən] N constitución *f*

constitutional [kɒnstɪˈtjuːʃənl] ADJ constitucional; **~ monarchy** monarquía constitucional

constrain [kənˈstreɪn] VT obligar

constrained [kənˈstreɪnd] ADJ: **to feel ~ to ...** sentirse obligado a ...

constraint [kənˈstreɪnt] N (*force*) fuerza; (*limit*) restricción *f*; (*restraint*) reserva; (*embarrassment*) cohibición *f*

constrict [kənˈstrɪkt] VT oprimir

constriction [kənˈstrɪkʃən] N constricción *f*, opresión *f*

construct [kənˈstrʌkt] VT construir

construction [kənˈstrʌkʃən] N construcción *f*; (*fig: interpretation*) interpretación *f*; **under ~** en construcción

construction industry N industria de la construcción

constructive [kənˈstrʌktɪv] ADJ constructivo

construe [kənˈstruː] VT interpretar

consul [ˈkɒnsl] N cónsul *mf*

consulate [ˈkɒnsjulɪt] N consulado

★**consult** [kənˈsʌlt] VT, VI consultar; **to ~ sb (about sth)** consultar a algn (sobre algo)

consultancy [kənˈsʌltənsɪ] N (*Comm*) consultoría; (*Med*) puesto de especialista

consultant [kənˈsʌltənt] N (*BRIT Med*) especialista *mf*; (*other specialist*) asesor(a) *m/f*, consultor(a) *m/f*

consultation [kɒnsəlˈteɪʃən] N consulta; **in ~ with** en consulta con

consultative [kənˈsʌltətɪv] ADJ consultivo

consulting room [kənˈsʌltɪŋ-] N (*BRIT*) consulta, consultorio

consume [kənˈsjuːm] VT (*eat*) comerse; (*drink*) beberse; (*fire etc*) consumir; (*Comm*) consumir

★**consumer** [kənˈsjuːməʳ] N (*of electricity, gas etc*) consumidor(a) *m/f*

consumer association N asociación *f* de consumidores

consumer credit N crédito al consumidor

consumer durables NPL bienes *mpl* de consumo duraderos

consumer goods NPL bienes *mpl* de consumo

consumerism [kənˈsjuːmərɪzəm] N consumismo

consumer society N sociedad *f* de consumo

consumer watchdog N organización *f* protectora del consumidor

consummate [ˈkɒnsʌmeɪt] VT consumar

consumption [kənˈsʌmpʃən] N consumo; (*Med*) tisis *f*; **not fit for human ~** no apto para el consumo humano

cont. ABBR (= *continued*) sigue

★**contact** [ˈkɒntækt] N contacto; **to be in ~ with sb/sth** estar en contacto con algn/algo; **business contacts** relaciones *fpl* comerciales ▶ VT ponerse en contacto con

contact lens N lente *f* de contacto

contactless [ˈkɒntæktlɪs] ADJ sin contacto

contagious [kənˈteɪdʒəs] ADJ contagioso

★**contain** [kənˈteɪn] VT contener; **to ~ o.s.** contenerse

container [kənˈteɪnəʳ] N recipiente *m*; (*for shipping etc*) contenedor *m*

containerize [kənˈteɪnəraɪz] VT transportar en contenedores

container ship N buque *m* contenedor, portacontenedores *m inv*

contaminate [kənˈtæmɪneɪt] VT contaminar

contamination [kəntæmɪˈneɪʃən] N contaminación *f*

contemplate [ˈkɒntəmpleɪt] VT (*gen*) contemplar; (*reflect upon*) considerar; (*intend*) pensar

contemplation [kɒntəmˈpleɪʃən] N contemplación *f*

contemporary [kənˈtempərərɪ] ADJ, N (*of the same age*) contemporáneo(-a) *m/f*

contempt [kənˈtempt] N desprecio; **~ of court** (*Law*) desacato (a los tribunales *or* a la justicia)

contemptible [kənˈtemptɪbl] ADJ despreciable, desdeñable

contemptuous [kənˈtemptjuəs] ADJ desdeñoso

contend [kənˈtend] VT (*argue*) afirmar ▶ VI: **to ~ with/for** luchar contra/por; **he has a lot to ~ with** tiene que hacer frente a muchos problemas

contender [kənˈtendəʳ] N (*Sport*) contendiente *mf*

content ADJ [kənˈtent] (*happy*) contento; (*satisfied*) satisfecho; **to be ~ with** conformarse con ▶ VT [kənˈtent] contentar; satisfacer; **to ~ o.s. with sth/with doing sth** conformarse con algo/con hacer algo ▶ N [ˈkɒntent] contenido ■ **contents** NPL contenido *sg*; **(table of) contents** (*in book*) índice *m* de materias; (*in magazine*) sumario

contented [kənˈtentɪd] ADJ contento; satisfecho

contentedly [kənˈtentɪdlɪ] ADV con aire satisfecho

contention [kənˈtenʃən] N discusión *f*; (*belief*) argumento; **bone of ~** manzana de la discordia

contentious [kənˈtenʃəs] ADJ discutible

contentment [kənˈtentmənt] N satisfacción *f*

★**contest** N [ˈkɒntest] contienda; (*competition*) concurso ▶ VT [kənˈtest] (*dispute*) impugnar; (*Law*) disputar, litigar; (*Pol: election, seat*) presentarse como candidato(-a) a

contest no debe traducirse por *contestar*.

contestant [kənˈtestənt] N concursante *mf*; (*in fight*) contendiente *mf*

★**context** ['kɔntɛkst] N contexto; **in/out of ~** en/ fuera de contexto

★**continent** ['kɔntɪnənt] N continente *m*; **the C~** (Brit) el continente europeo, Europa; **on the C~** en el continente europeo, en Europa

continental [kɔntɪ'nɛntl] ADJ continental; (Brit: *European*) europeo

continental breakfast N desayuno estilo europeo

continental quilt N (Brit) edredón *m* (nórdico)

contingency [kən'tɪndʒənsɪ] N contingencia

contingent [kən'tɪndʒənt] N (*group*) representación *f*

continual [kən'tɪnjuəl] ADJ continuo

continually [kən'tɪnjuəlɪ] ADV continuamente

continuation [kəntɪnju'eɪʃən] N prolongación *f*; (*after interruption*) reanudación *f*; (*of story, episode*) continuación *f*

★**continue** [kən'tɪnjuː] VI, VT seguir, continuar; **continued on page 10** sigue en la página 10

continuing education [kən'tɪnjuɪŋ-] N educación *f* continua de adultos

continuity [kɔntɪ'njuɪtɪ] N (*also Cine*) continuidad *f*

continuity girl N (*Cine*) secretaria de continuidad

continuous [kən'tɪnjuəs] ADJ continuo; **~ performance** (*Cine*) sesión *f* continua

continuous assessment N (Brit) evaluación *f* continua

continuously [kən'tɪnjuəslɪ] ADV continuamente

contort [kən'tɔːt] VT retorcer

contortion [kən'tɔːʃən] N (*movement*) contorsión *f*

contortionist [kən'tɔːʃənɪst] N contorsionista *mf*

contour ['kɔntuə'] N contorno; (*also:* **contour line**) curva de nivel

contraband ['kɔntrəbænd] N contrabando ▸ ADJ de contrabando

contraception [kɔntrə'sɛpʃən] N contracepción *f*

contraceptive [kɔntrə'sɛptɪv] ADJ, N anticonceptivo

contract N ['kɔntrækt] contrato; **to be under ~ to do sth** estar bajo contrato para hacer algo; **~ of employment** *or* **of service** contrato de trabajo ▸ CPD ['kɔntrækt] (*price, date*) contratado, de contrato; (*work*) bajo contrato ▸ VI [kən'trækt] (*Comm*): **to ~ to do sth** comprometerse por contrato a hacer algo; (*become smaller*) contraerse, encogerse ▸ VT [kən'trækt] contraer

▸ **contract in** VI tomar parte

▸ **contract out** VI: **to ~ out (of)** optar por no tomar parte (en); **to ~ out of a pension scheme** dejar de cotizar en un plan de jubilación

contraction [kən'trækʃən] N contracción *f*

contractor [kən'træktə'] N contratista *mf*

contractual [kən'træktjuəl] ADJ contractual

contradict [kɔntrə'dɪkt] VT (*declare to be wrong*) desmentir; (*be contrary to*) contradecir

contradiction [kɔntrə'dɪkʃən] N contradicción *f*; **to be in ~ with** contradecir

contradictory [kɔntrə'dɪktərɪ] ADJ (*statements*) contradictorio; **to be ~ to** contradecir

contralto [kən'træltəu] N contralto *f*

contraption [kən'træpʃən] N (*pej*) artilugio

contrary¹ ['kɔntrərɪ] ADJ contrario; **~ to what we thought** al contrario de lo que pensábamos ▸ N lo contrario; **on the ~** al contrario; **unless you hear to the ~** a no ser que le digan lo contrario

contrary² [kən'trɛərɪ] ADJ (*perverse*) terco

★**contrast** N ['kɔntrɑːst] contraste *m*; **in ~ to** *or* **with** a diferencia de ▸ VT [kən'trɑːst] contrastar

contrasting [kən'trɑːstɪŋ] ADJ (*opinion*) opuesto; (*colour*) que hace contraste

contravene [kɔntrə'viːn] VT contravenir

contravention [kɔntrə'vɛnʃən] N: **~ (of)** contravención *f* (de)

★**contribute** [kən'trɪbjuːt] VI, VT contribuir; **to ~ to** (*gen*) contribuir a; (*newspaper*) colaborar en; (*discussion*) intervenir en

★**contribution** [kɔntrɪ'bjuːʃən] N (*money*) contribución *f*; (*to debate*) intervención *f*; (*to journal*) colaboración *f*

contributor [kən'trɪbjutə'] N (*to newspaper*) colaborador(a) *m/f*

contributory [kən'trɪbjutərɪ] ADJ (*cause*) contribuyente; **it was a ~ factor in …** fue un factor que contribuyó en …

contributory pension scheme N plan *m* cotizable de jubilación

contrivance [kən'traɪvəns] N (*machine, device*) aparato, dispositivo

contrive [kən'traɪv] VT (*invent*) idear ▸ VI: **to ~ to do** lograr hacer; (*try*) procurar hacer

★**control** [kən'trəul] VT controlar; (*traffic etc*) dirigir; (*machinery*) manejar; (*temper*) dominar; (*disease, fire*) dominar, controlar; **to ~ o.s.** controlarse, dominarse ▸ N (*command*) control *m*; (*of car*) conducción *f*; (*check*) freno; **everything is under ~** todo está bajo control; **to be in ~ of** estar al mando de; **the car went out of ~** perdió el control del coche ■ **controls** NPL (*of vehicle*) instrumentos *mpl* de mando; (*of radio*) controles *mpl*; (*governmental*) medidas *fpl* de control

control group N (*Med, Psych etc*) grupo de control

control key N (*Comput*) tecla de control

controlled economy N economía dirigida

controller [kən'trəulə'] N controlador(a) *m/f*

controlling interest [kən'trəulɪŋ-] N participación *f* mayoritaria

control panel N (*on aircraft, ship, TV etc*) tablero de instrumentos

control point N (puesto de) control *m*

control room N (*Naut, Mil*) sala de mandos; (*Radio, TV*) sala de control

control tower N (*Aviat*) torre *f* de control

control unit N (*Comput*) unidad *f* de control

★**controversial** [kɒntrə'vəːʃl] ADJ polémico

controversy ['kɒntrəvəːsɪ] N polémica

conurbation [kɒnə:'beɪʃən] N conurbación *f*

convalesce [kɒnvə'lɛs] VI convalecer

convalescence [kɒnvə'lɛsns] N convalecencia

convalescent [kɒnvə'lɛsnt] ADJ, N convaleciente *mf*

convector [kən'vɛktəʳ] N calentador *m* de convección

convene [kən'vi:n] VT (*meeting*) convocar ▶ VI reunirse

convenience [kən'vi:nɪəns] N (*comfort*) comodidad *f*; (*advantage*) ventaja; **at your earliest ~** (*Comm*) tan pronto como le sea posible; **all modern conveniences** (*BRIT*) todo confort

convenience foods NPL platos *mpl* preparados

convenient [kən'vi:nɪənt] ADJ (*useful*) útil; (*place*) conveniente; (*time*) oportuno; **if it is ~ for you** si le viene bien

conveniently [kən'vi:nɪəntlɪ] ADV (*happen*) oportunamente; (*situated*) convenientemente

convent ['kɒnvənt] N convento

convention [kən'vɛnʃən] N convención *f*; (*meeting*) asamblea

conventional [kən'vɛnʃənl] ADJ convencional

convent school N colegio de monjas

converge [kən'vəːdʒ] VI converger

conversant [kən'vəːsnt] ADJ: **to be ~ with** estar familiarizado con

★**conversation** [kɒnvə'seɪʃən] N conversación *f*

conversational [kɒnvə'seɪʃənl] ADJ (*familiar*) familiar; (*talkative*) locuaz; **~ mode** (*Comput*) modo de conversación

converse N ['kɒnvəːs] inversa ▶ VI [kən'vəːs] conversar; **to ~ (with sb about sth)** conversar or (*LAM*) platicar (con algn de algo)

conversely [kən'vəːslɪ] ADV a la inversa

conversion [kən'vəːʃən] N conversión *f*; (*house conversion*) reforma, remodelación *f*

conversion table N tabla de equivalencias

convert VT [kən'vəːt] (*Rel, Comm*) convertir; (*alter*) transformar ▶ N ['kɒnvəːt] converso(-a)

convertible [kən'vəːtəbl] ADJ convertible; **~ loan stock** obligaciones *fpl* convertibles ▶ N descapotable *m*

convex ['kɒn'vɛks] ADJ convexo

convey [kən'veɪ] VT transportar; (*thanks*) comunicar; (*idea*) expresar

conveyance [kən'veɪəns] N (*of goods*) transporte *m*; (*vehicle*) vehículo, medio de transporte

conveyancing [kən'veɪənsɪŋ] N (*Law*) preparación *f* de escrituras de traspaso

conveyor belt [kən'veɪəʳ-] N cinta transportadora

convict VT [kən'vɪkt] (*gen*) condenar; (*find guilty*) declarar culpable a ▶ N ['kɒnvɪkt] presidiario(-a)

conviction [kən'vɪkʃən] N condena; (*belief*) creencia, convicción *f*

★**convince** [kən'vɪns] VT convencer; **to ~ sb (of sth/that)** convencer a algn (de algo/de que)

convinced [kən'vɪnst] ADJ: **~ of/that** convencido de/de que

convincing [kən'vɪnsɪŋ] ADJ convincente

convincingly [kən'vɪnsɪŋlɪ] ADV de modo convincente, convincentemente

convivial [kən'vɪvɪəl] ADJ (*person*) sociable; (*atmosphere*) alegre

convoluted ['kɒnvəlu:tɪd] ADJ (*argument etc*) enrevesado; (*shape*) enrollado, enroscado

convoy ['kɒnvɔɪ] N convoy *m*

convulse [kən'vʌls] VT convulsionar; **to be convulsed with laughter** dislocarse de risa

convulsion [kən'vʌlʃən] N convulsión *f*

coo [ku:] VI arrullar

★**cook** [kuk] VT cocinar; (*stew etc*) guisar; (*meal*) preparar ▶ VI (*person*) cocinar; (*dish, food*) hacerse ▶ N cocinero(-a)
▶ **cook up** VT (*inf: excuse, story*) inventar

cookbook ['kukbuk] N libro de cocina

★**cooker** ['kukəʳ] N cocina

cookery ['kukərɪ] N cocina

cookery book N (*BRIT*) = **cookbook**

cookie ['kukɪ] N (*US*) galleta; (*Comput*) cookie *f*

★**cooking** ['kukɪŋ] N cocina ▶ CPD (*apples*) para cocinar; (*utensils, salt, foil*) de cocina

cooking chocolate N chocolate *m* fondant or de hacer

cookout ['kukaut] N (*US*) comida al aire libre

★**cool** [ku:l] ADJ fresco; (*not hot*) tibio; (*not afraid*) tranquilo; (*unfriendly*) frío; **it is ~** (*weather*) hace fresco; **to keep sth ~** or **in a ~ place** conservar algo fresco or en un sitio fresco ▶ VT enfriar ▶ VI enfriarse
▶ **cool down** VI enfriarse; (*fig: person, situation*) calmarse
▶ **cool off** VI (*become calmer*) calmarse, apaciguarse; (*lose enthusiasm*) perder (el) interés, enfriarse

coolant ['ku:lənt] N refrigerante *m*

cool box, (*US*) **cooler** ['ku:ləʳ] N nevera portátil

cooling ['ku:lɪŋ] ADJ refrescante

cooling-off period [ku:lɪŋ'ɔf-] N (*Industry*) plazo de negociaciones

cooling tower N torre *f* de refrigeración

coolly [ˈkuːlɪ] ADV (*calmly*) con tranquilidad; (*audaciously*) descaradamente; (*unenthusiastically*) fríamente, con frialdad

coolness [ˈkuːlnɪs] N frescura; tranquilidad *f*; (*hostility*) frialdad *f*; (*indifference*) falta de entusiasmo

coop [kuːp] N gallinero ▶ VT: **to ~ up** (*fig*) encerrar

co-op [ˈkəʊɒp] N ABBR (= *cooperative (society)*) cooperativa

cooperate [kəʊˈɒpəreɪt] VI cooperar, colaborar; **will he ~?** ¿querrá cooperar?

cooperation [kəʊɒpəˈreɪʃən] N cooperación *f*, colaboración *f*

cooperative [kəʊˈɒpərətɪv] ADJ cooperativo; (*person*) dispuesto a colaborar ▶ N cooperativa

co-opt [kəʊˈɒpt] VT: **to ~ sb into sth** nombrar a algn para algo

coordinate VT [kəʊˈɔːdɪneɪt] coordinar ▶ N [kəʊˈɔːdɪnət] (*Math*) coordenada ■ **coordinates** NPL (*clothes*) coordinados *mpl*

coordination [kəʊɔːdɪˈneɪʃən] N coordinación *f*

coot [kuːt] N focha (común)

co-ownership [kəʊˈəʊnəʃɪp] N copropiedad *f*

cop [kɒp] N (*inf*) poli *mf*

co-parent [ˈkəʊˈpɛərənt] VT compartir el cuidado de

co-parenting [kəʊˈpɛərəntɪŋ] N coparentalidad *f*

cope [kəʊp] VI: **to ~ with** poder con; (*problem*) hacer frente a

Copenhagen [kəʊpənˈheɪgən] N Copenhague *m*

copier [ˈkɒpɪəʳ] N (*photocopier*) (foto)copiadora

co-pilot [ˈkəʊˈpaɪlət] N copiloto *mf*

copious [ˈkəʊpɪəs] ADJ copioso, abundante

copper [ˈkɒpəʳ] N (*metal*) cobre *m*; (BRIT *inf: police officer*) poli *mf* ■ **coppers** NPL (BRIT *inf: money*) perras *fpl*; (: *small change*) calderilla

coppice [ˈkɒpɪs], **copse** [kɒps] N bosquecillo

copulate [ˈkɒpjuleɪt] VI copular

copulation [kɒpjuˈleɪʃən] N cópula

★**copy** [ˈkɒpɪ] N copia; (*of book*) ejemplar *m*; (*of magazine*) número; (*material: for printing*) original *m*; **to make good ~** (*fig*) ser una noticia de interés; **rough ~** borrador *m*; **fair ~** copia en limpio ▶ VT (*also Comput*) copiar; (*imitate*) copiar, imitar ▶ **copy out** VT copiar

copycat [ˈkɒpɪkæt] N (*pej*) imitador(a) *m/f*

copyright [ˈkɒpɪraɪt] N derechos *mpl* de autor

copy typist N mecanógrafo(-a)

coral [ˈkɒrəl] N coral *m*

coral reef N arrecife *m* (de coral)

Coral Sea N: **the ~** el mar del Coral

cord [kɔːd] N cuerda; (*Elec*) cable *m*; (*fabric*) pana ■ **cords** NPL (*trousers*) pantalones *mpl* de pana

cordial [ˈkɔːdɪəl] ADJ cordial ▶ N cordial *m*

cordless [ˈkɔːdlɪs] ADJ sin hilos; **~ telephone** teléfono inalámbrico

cordon [ˈkɔːdn] N cordón *m* ▶ **cordon off** VT acordonar

Cordova [ˈkɔːdəvə] N Córdoba

corduroy [ˈkɔːdərɔɪ] N pana

CORE [kɔːʳ] N ABBR (*US*) = **Congress of Racial Equality**

core [kɔːʳ] N (*of earth, nuclear reactor*) centro, núcleo; (*of fruit*) corazón *m*; (*of problem etc*) esencia, meollo ▶ VT quitar el corazón de

Corfu [kɔːˈfuː] N Corfú *m*

coriander [kɒrɪˈændəʳ] N culantro, cilantro

cork [kɔːk] N corcho; (*tree*) alcornoque *m*

corkage [ˈkɔːkɪdʒ] N precio que se cobra en un restaurante por una botella de vino traída de fuera

corked [kɔːkt] ADJ (*wine*) con sabor a corcho

corkscrew [ˈkɔːkskruː] N sacacorchos *m inv*

cormorant [ˈkɔːmərnt] N cormorán *m*

corn [kɔːn] N (BRIT: *wheat*) trigo; (*US: maize*) maíz *m*, choclo (LAM); (*on foot*) callo; **~ on the cob** (*Culin*) maíz en la mazorca

cornea [ˈkɔːnɪə] N córnea

corned beef [ˈkɔːnd-] N carne *f* de vaca acecinada

★**corner** [ˈkɔːnəʳ] N (*outside*) esquina; (*inside*) rincón *m*; (*in road*) curva; (*Football*) córner *m*, saque *m* de esquina; **to cut corners** atajar ▶ VT (*trap*) arrinconar; (*Comm*) acaparar ▶ VI (*in car*) tomar las curvas

corner flag N (*Football*) banderola de esquina

corner kick N (*Football*) córner *m*, saque *m* de esquina

corner shop N (BRIT) tienda de la esquina

cornerstone [ˈkɔːnəstəʊn] N piedra angular

cornet [ˈkɔːnɪt] N (*Mus*) corneta; (BRIT: *of ice cream*) cucurucho

cornflakes [ˈkɔːnfleɪks] NPL copos *mpl* de maíz, cornflakes *mpl*

cornflour [ˈkɔːnflaʊəʳ] N (BRIT) harina de maíz

cornice [ˈkɔːnɪs] N cornisa

Cornish [ˈkɔːnɪʃ] ADJ de Cornualles

corn oil N aceite *m* de maíz

cornstarch [ˈkɔːnstɑːtʃ] N (*US*) = **cornflour**

cornucopia [kɔːnjuˈkəʊpɪə] N cornucopia

Cornwall [ˈkɔːnwəl] N Cornualles *m*

corny [ˈkɔːnɪ] ADJ (*inf*) gastado

corollary [kəˈrɒlərɪ] N corolario

coronary [ˈkɒrənərɪ] N: **~ (thrombosis)** infarto

coronation [kɒrəˈneɪʃən] N coronación *f*

coroner [ˈkɒrənəʳ] N juez(a) *m/f* de instrucción

coronet [ˈkɒrənɪt] N corona

Corp. ABBR = **corporation**

corporal [ˈkɔːpərl] N cabo *mf* ▶ ADJ: **~ punishment** castigo corporal

corporate ['kɔːpərɪt] ADJ (action, ownership) colectivo; (finance, image) corporativo

corporate hospitality N obsequios a los clientes por cortesía de la empresa

corporate identity, corporate image N (of organization) identidad f corporativa

corporation [kɔːpə'reɪʃən] N (of town) ayuntamiento; (Comm) corporación f

corps [kɔːʳ] (pl ~ [kɔːz]) N cuerpo; **press ~** gabinete m de prensa

corpse [kɔːps] N cadáver m

corpulent ['kɔːpjulənt] ADJ corpulento(-a)

Corpus Christi ['kɔːpəs'krɪstɪ] N Corpus m (Christi)

corpuscle ['kɔːpʌsl] N corpúsculo

corral [kə'rɑːl] N corral m

★**correct** [kə'rɛkt] ADJ correcto; (accurate) exacto; **you are ~** tiene razón ▶ VT corregir

correction [kə'rɛkʃən] N (act) corrección f; (instance) rectificación f; (erasure) tachadura

correlate ['kɔrɪleɪt] VI: **to ~ with** tener correlación con

correlation [kɔrɪ'leɪʃən] N correlación f

correspond [kɔrɪs'pɔnd] VI: **to ~ (with)** (write) escribirse (con); (be in accordance) corresponder (con); **to ~ (to)** (be equivalent to) corresponder (a)

correspondence [kɔrɪs'pɔndəns] N correspondencia

correspondence course N curso por correspondencia

correspondent [kɔrɪs'pɔndənt] N corresponsal mf

corresponding [kɔrɪs'pɔndɪŋ] ADJ correspondiente

corridor ['kɔrɪdɔːʳ] N pasillo

corroborate [kə'rɔbəreɪt] VT corroborar

corroboration [kərɔbə'reɪʃən] N corroboración f, confirmación f

corrode [kə'rəud] VT corroer ▶ VI corroerse

corrosion [kə'rəuʒən] N corrosión f

corrosive [kə'rəusɪv] ADJ corrosivo

corrugated ['kɔrəgeɪtɪd] ADJ ondulado

corrugated cardboard N cartón m ondulado

corrugated iron N chapa ondulada

corrupt [kə'rʌpt] ADJ corrompido; (person) corrupto; **~ practices** (dishonesty, bribery) corrupción f ▶ VT corromper; (bribe) sobornar; (Comput: data) degradar

corruption [kə'rʌpʃən] N corrupción f; (Comput: of data) alteración f

corset ['kɔːsɪt] N faja; (old-style) corsé m

Corsica ['kɔːsɪkə] N Córcega

Corsican ['kɔːsɪkən] ADJ, N corso(-a) m/f

cortège [kɔː'teɪʒ] N cortejo, comitiva

cortisone ['kɔːtɪzəun] N cortisona

cosh [kɔʃ] N (BRIT) cachiporra

cosignatory ['kəu'sɪgnətərɪ] N cosignatario(-a)

cosine ['kəusaɪn] N coseno

cosiness ['kəuzɪnɪs] N comodidad f; (atmosphere) lo acogedor

cos lettuce [kɔs-] N lechuga romana

cosmetic [kɔz'mɛtɪk] N cosmético ▶ ADJ (also fig) cosmético

cosmetic surgery N cirugía f estética

cosmic ['kɔzmɪk] ADJ cósmico

cosmonaut ['kɔzmənɔːt] N cosmonauta mf

cosmopolitan [kɔzmə'pɔlɪtn] ADJ cosmopolita

cosmos ['kɔzmɔs] N cosmos m

cosset ['kɔsɪt] VT mimar

★**cost** [kɔst] (pt, pp ~) N (gen) coste m, costo; (price) precio; **the ~ of living** el coste or costo de la vida; **at all costs** cueste lo que cueste ▶ VT (gen) costar, valer; (Comm) preparar el presupuesto de; **how much does it ~?** ¿cuánto cuesta?, ¿cuánto vale?; **what will it ~ to have it repaired?** ¿cuánto costará repararlo?; **to ~ sb time/effort** costarle a algn tiempo/esfuerzo; **it ~ him his life** le costó la vida ◼ **costs** NPL (Law) costas fpl

cost accountant N contable mf de costos

co-star ['kəustɑːʳ] N coprotagonista mf

Costa Rica ['kɔstə'riːkə] N Costa Rica

Costa Rican ['kɔstə'riːkən] ADJ, N costarriqueño(-a) m/f, costarricense mf

cost centre N centro (de determinación) de coste

cost control N control m de costes

cost-effective [kɔstɪ'fɛktɪv] ADJ (Comm) rentable

cost-effectiveness ['kɔstɪ'fɛktɪvnɪs] N relación f coste-rendimiento

costing ['kɔstɪŋ] N cálculo del coste

costly ['kɔstlɪ] ADJ (expensive) costoso

cost-of-living [kɔstəv'lɪvɪŋ] ADJ: **~ allowance** plus m de carestía de vida; **~ index** índice m del coste de vida

cost price N (BRIT) precio de coste

costume ['kɔstjuːm] N traje m; (BRIT: also: **swimming costume**) traje de baño

costume jewellery N bisutería

cosy, (US) **cozy** ['kəuzɪ] ADJ cómodo, a gusto; (room, atmosphere) acogedor(a)

cot [kɔt] N (BRIT: child's) cuna; (US: folding bed) cama plegable

cot death N muerte f en la cuna

Cotswolds ['kɔtswəuldz] NPL región de colinas del suroeste inglés

★**cottage** ['kɔtɪdʒ] N casita de campo

cottage cheese N requesón m

cottage industry N industria artesanal

cottage pie N pastel de carne cubierta de puré de patatas

★**cotton** ['kɔtn] N algodón m; (thread) hilo ▶ **cotton on** VI (inf): **to ~ on (to sth)** caer en la cuenta (de algo)

cotton bud N (BRIT) bastoncillo de algodón

cotton candy N (US) algodón m (azucarado)

cotton wool N (BRIT) algodón m (hidrófilo)

couch [kautʃ] N sofá m; (in doctor's surgery) camilla; (psychiatrist's) diván m

couchette [ku:'ʃɛt] N litera

couch potato N (inf) persona comodona que no se mueve en todo el día

couchsurfing ['kautʃsə:fɪŋ] N alojamiento gratuito en casas de terceros

★**cough** [kɔf] VI toser ▶ N tos f
   ▶ **cough up** VT escupir

cough drop N pastilla para la tos

cough mixture N jarabe m para la tos

★**could** [kud] PT of **can²**

couldn't ['kudnt] = **could not**

★**council** ['kaunsl] N consejo; **city** or **town ~** ayuntamiento, consejo municipal; **C~ of Europe** Consejo de Europa

council estate N (BRIT) barriada de viviendas sociales de alquiler

council house N (BRIT) vivienda social de alquiler

councillor ['kaunslə'] N concejal mf

council tax N (BRIT) contribución f municipal (dependiente del valor de la vivienda)

counsel ['kaunsl] N (advice) consejo; (lawyer) abogado(-a); **~ for the defence/the prosecution** abogado(-a) defensor(a)/fiscal ▶ VT aconsejar; **to ~ sth/sb to do sth** aconsejar algo/a algn que haga algo

counselling, (US) **counseling** N (Psych) asistencia psicológica

counsellor, (US) **counselor** ['kaunslə'] N (Psych) consejero(-a); (US Law) abogado(-a)

★**count** [kaunt] VT (gen) contar; (include) incluir; **to ~ the cost of** calcular el coste de; **not counting the children** niños aparte; **10 counting him** diez incluyéndolo a él, diez con él; **~ yourself lucky** date por satisfecho ▶ VI contar; **that doesn't ~!** ¡eso no vale!; **to ~ (up) to 10** contar hasta diez; **it counts for very little** cuenta poco ▶ N cuenta; (of votes) escrutinio; (nobleman) conde m; (sum) total m, suma; **to keep ~ of sth** llevar la cuenta de algo
   ▶ **count in** (inf) VT: **to ~ sb in on sth** contar con algn para algo
   ▶ **count on** VT FUS contar con; **to ~ on doing sth** contar con hacer algo
   ▶ **count up** VT contar

countdown ['kauntdaun] N cuenta atrás

countenance ['kauntɪnəns] N semblante m, rostro ▶ VT (tolerate) aprobar, consentir

★**counter** ['kauntə'] N (in shop) mostrador m; (position: in post office, bank) ventanilla; (: in games) ficha; (Tech) contador m; **to buy under the ~** (fig) comprar de estraperlo or bajo mano ▶ VT contrarrestar; (blow) parar; (attack) contestar a; **to ~ sth with sth/by doing sth** contestar algo con algo/haciendo algo ▶ ADV: **~ to** contrario a

counteract ['kauntər'ækt] VT contrarrestar

counterattack ['kauntərə'tæk] N contraataque m ▶ VI contraatacar

counterbalance ['kauntə'bæləns] N contrapeso

counter-clockwise ['kauntə'klɔkwaız] ADV en sentido contrario al de las agujas del reloj

counter-espionage ['kauntər'ɛspɪənɑːʒ] N contraespionaje m

counterfeit ['kauntəfɪt] N falsificación f ▶ VT falsificar ▶ ADJ falso, falsificado

counterfoil ['kauntəfɔɪl] N (BRIT) matriz f, talón m

counterintelligence ['kauntərɪn'tɛlɪdʒəns] N contraespionaje m

countermand ['kauntəmɑːnd] VT revocar

counter-measure ['kauntəmɛʒə'] N contramedida

counteroffensive ['kauntərə'fɛnsɪv] N contraofensiva

counterpane ['kauntəpeɪn] N colcha

counterpart ['kauntəpɑːt] N (of person) homólogo(-a)

counter-productive [kauntəprə'dʌktɪv] ADJ contraproducente

counterproposal ['kauntəprə'pəuzl] N contrapropuesta

countersign ['kauntəsaın] VT ratificar, refrendar

counterterrorism [kauntə'tɛrərɪzəm] N antiterrorismo

countess ['kauntɪs] N condesa

countless ['kauntlıs] ADJ innumerable

countrified ['kʌntrɪfaɪd] ADJ rústico

★**country** ['kʌntrɪ] N país m; (native land) patria; (as opposed to town) campo; (region) región f, tierra; **in the ~** en el campo; **mountainous ~** región f montañosa

country and western, country and western music N música country

country dancing N (BRIT) baile m regional

country house N casa de campo

countryman ['kʌntrɪmən] N (irreg) (national) compatriota m; (rural) hombre m del campo

★**countryside** ['kʌntrɪsaɪd] N campo

countrywide ['kʌntrɪ'waɪd] ADJ nacional ▶ ADV por todo el país

county ['kauntɪ] N condado; see also **district council**

county council N (BRIT) ≈ diputación f provincial

county town N cabeza de partido

coup [ku:] (pl **coups** [ku:z]) N golpe m; (triumph) éxito; (also: **coup d'état**) golpe de estado

coupé ['ku:peɪ] N cupé m

★**couple** ['kʌpl] N (of things) par m; (of people) pareja; (married couple) matrimonio; **a ~ of** un par de ▶ VT (ideas, names) unir, juntar; (machinery) acoplar

couplet [ˈkʌplɪt] N pareado

coupling [ˈkʌplɪŋ] N (Rail) enganche m

coupon [ˈkuːpɔn] N cupón m; (voucher) valé m; (pools coupon) boleto (de quiniela)

★**courage** [ˈkʌrɪdʒ] N valor m, valentía

courageous [kəˈreɪdʒəs] ADJ valiente

courgette [kuəˈʒɛt] N (BRIT) calabacín m

courier [ˈkurɪəʳ] N mensajero(-a); (diplomatic) correo; (for tourists) guía mf (de turismo)

★**course** [kɔːs] N (direction) dirección f; (of river) curso; (Scol) curso; (of ship) rumbo; (fig) proceder m; (Golf) campo; (part of meal) plato; **of ~** adv desde luego, naturalmente; **of ~!** ¡claro!, ¡cómo no! (LAM); **(no) of ~ not!** ¡claro que no!, ¡por supuesto que no!; **in due ~** a su debido tiempo; **in the ~ the next few days** durante los próximos días; **we have no other ~ but to ...** no tenemos más remedio que ...; **there are two courses open to us** se nos ofrecen dos posibilidades; **the best ~ would be to ...** lo mejor sería ...; **~ of treatment** (Med) tratamiento

★**court** [kɔːt] N (royal) corte f; (Law) tribunal m, juzgado; (Tennis) pista, cancha (LAM); **to take to ~** demandar; **~ of appeal** tribunal m de apelación ▶ VT (woman) cortejar; (fig: favour, popularity) solicitar, buscar; (: death, disaster, danger etc) buscar

courteous [ˈkəːtɪəs] ADJ cortés

courtesan [kɔːtɪˈzæn] N cortesana

courtesy [ˈkəːtəsɪ] N cortesía; **by ~ of** (por) cortesía de

courtesy bus, courtesy coach N autobús m gratuito

courtesy light N (Aut) luz f interior

courthouse [ˈkɔːthaus] N (US) palacio de justicia

courtier [ˈkɔːtɪəʳ] N cortesano(-a)

court martial [ˈkɔːtˈmɑːʃəl] (pl **courts martial**) N consejo de guerra

court-martial [ˈkɔːtˈmɑːʃəl] VT someter a consejo de guerra

courtroom [ˈkɔːtrum] N sala de justicia

court shoe N zapato de mujer de estilo clásico

courtyard [ˈkɔːtjɑːd] N patio

★**cousin** [ˈkʌzn] N primo(-a); **first ~** primo(-a) carnal

cove [kəuv] N cala, ensenada

covenant [ˈkʌvənənt] N convenio ▶ VT: **to ~ £20 per year to a charity** concertar el pago de veinte libras anuales a una sociedad benéfica

Coventry [ˈkɔvəntrɪ] N: **to send sb to ~** (fig) hacer el vacío a algn

★**cover** [ˈkʌvəʳ] VT cubrir; (with lid) tapar; (chairs etc) revestir; (distance) cubrir, recorrer; (include) abarcar; (protect) abrigar; (journalist) investigar; (issues) tratar; **£10 will ~ everything** con diez libras cubriremos todos los gastos ▶ N cubierta; (lid) tapa; (for chair etc) funda; (for bed: blanket) manta; (: sheet) sábana; (envelope) sobre m; (of magazine) portada; (shelter) abrigo; (insurance) cobertura; **to**

take ~ (shelter) protegerse, resguardarse; **under ~** (indoors) bajo techo; **under ~ of darkness** al amparo de la oscuridad; **under separate ~** (Comm) por separado
  ▶ **cover up** VT (child, object) cubrir completamente, tapar; (fig: hide: truth, facts) ocultar ▶ VI: **to ~ up for sb** (fig) encubrir a algn

coverage [ˈkʌvərɪdʒ] N alcance m; (in media) cobertura informativa; (Insurance) cobertura

coveralls [ˈkʌvərɔːlz] NPL (US) mono sg

cover charge N precio del cubierto

covering [ˈkʌvərɪŋ] N cubierta, envoltura

covering letter, (US) **cover letter** N carta de explicación

cover note N (Insurance) póliza provisional

cover price N precio de cubierta

covert [ˈkəuvət] ADJ (secret) secreto, encubierto; (dissembled) furtivo

cover-up [ˈkʌvərʌp] N encubrimiento

covet [ˈkʌvɪt] VT codiciar

covetous [ˈkʌvɪtəs] ADJ codicioso

★**cow** [kau] N vaca ▶ VT intimidar

coward [ˈkauəd] N cobarde mf

cowardice [ˈkauədɪs] N cobardía

cowardly [ˈkauədlɪ] ADJ cobarde

cowboy [ˈkaubɔɪ] N vaquero

cower [ˈkauəʳ] VI encogerse (de miedo)

co-worker [ˈkəuwəːkəʳ] N colaborador(a) m/f

cowshed [ˈkauʃɛd] N establo

cowslip [ˈkauslɪp] N (Bot) primavera, prímula

cox [kɔks], **coxswain** [ˈkɔksn] N timonel mf

coy [kɔɪ] ADJ tímido

coyote [kɔɪˈəutɪ] N coyote m

cozy [ˈkəuzɪ] ADJ (US) = **cosy**

CP N ABBR (= Communist Party) PC m

cp. ABBR (= compare) cfr.

CPA N ABBR (US) = **certified public accountant**

CPI N ABBR (= Consumer Price Index) IPC m

Cpl. ABBR (Mil) = **corporal**

c.p.s. ABBR (= characters per second) c.p.s.

CPSA N ABBR (BRIT: = Civil and Public Services Association) sindicato de funcionarios

CPU N ABBR = **central processing unit**

cr. ABBR = **credit; creditor**

crab [kræb] N cangrejo

crab apple N manzana silvestre

★**crack** [kræk] N grieta; (noise) crujido; (: of whip) chasquido; (joke) chiste m; (inf: drug) crack m; (attempt): **to have a ~ at sth** intentar algo ▶ VT agrietar, romper; (nut) cascar; (safe) forzar; (whip etc) chasquear; (knuckles) crujir; (joke) contar; (case: solve) resolver; (code) descifrar; **to ~ jokes** (inf) bromear ▶ ADJ (athlete) de primera clase
  ▶ **crack down on** VT FUS reprimir fuertemente, adoptar medidas severas contra
  ▶ **crack up** VI sufrir una crisis nerviosa

crackdown [ˈkrækdaun] N: **~ (on)** (on crime) campaña (contra); (on spending) reducción f (en)

cracked [krækt] ADJ (cup, window) rajado; (wall) resquebrajado

cracker [ˈkrækəʳ] N (biscuit) galleta salada, cracker m; (Christmas cracker) tubito con decoración navideña que contiene un pequeño regalo sorpresa y que se abre al tirar dos personas de sus extremos

crackle [ˈkrækl] VI crepitar

crackling [ˈkræklɪŋ] N (on radio, telephone) interferencia; (of fire) chisporroteo, crepitación f; (of leaves etc) crujido; (of pork) chicharrón m

crackpot [ˈkrækpɔt] (inf) N pirado(-a) ▶ ADJ de pirado

cradle [ˈkreɪdl] N cuna ▶ VT (child) mecer, acunar; (object) abrazar

craft [krɑːft] N (skill) arte m; (trade) oficio; (cunning) astucia; (boat) embarcación f

craftsman [ˈkrɑːftsmən] N (irreg) artesano

craftsmanship [ˈkrɑːftsmənʃɪp] N destreza

crafty [ˈkrɑːftɪ] ADJ astuto

crag [kræg] N peñasco

craggy [ˈkrægɪ] ADJ escarpado

cram [kræm] VT (fill): **to ~ sth with** llenar algo (a reventar) de; (put): **to ~ sth into** meter algo a la fuerza en ▶ VI (for exams) empollar

crammed [kræmd] ADJ atestado

cramp [kræmp] N (Med) calambre m; (Tech) grapa ▶ VT (limit) poner trabas a

cramped [kræmpt] ADJ apretado; (room) minúsculo

crampon [ˈkræmpən] N crampón m

cranberry [ˈkrænbərɪ] N arándano agrio

crane [kreɪn] N (Tech) grúa; (bird) grulla ▶ VT, VI: **to ~ forward, to ~ one's neck** estirar el cuello

cranium [ˈkreɪnɪəm] N cráneo

crank [kræŋk] N manivela; (person) chiflado(-a)

crankshaft [ˈkræŋkʃɑːft] N cigüeñal m

cranky [ˈkræŋkɪ] ADJ (eccentric) maniático; (bad-tempered) de mal genio

cranny [ˈkrænɪ] N see **nook**

crap [kræp] N (inf!) mierda (inf!)

crappy [ˈkræpɪ] ADJ (inf) chungo

craps [kræps] N (US) dados mpl

★**crash** [kræʃ] N (noise) estrépito; (of cars, plane) accidente m; (of business) quiebra; (Stock Exchange) crac m ▶ VT (plane) estrellar; **he crashed the car into a wall** estrelló el coche contra una pared or tapia ▶ VI (plane) estrellarse; (two cars) chocar; (fall noisily) caer con estrépito
  ▶ **crash out** VI (inf: sleep) quedarse frito; (: of competition) quedar eliminado

crash barrier N (Aut) barrera de protección

crash course N curso acelerado

crash helmet N casco (protector)

crash landing N aterrizaje m forzoso

crass [kræs] ADJ grosero, maleducado

crate [kreɪt] N cajón m de embalaje; (for bottles) caja; (inf) armatoste m

crater [ˈkreɪtəʳ] N cráter m

cravat, cravate [krəˈvæt] N pañuelo

crave [kreɪv] VT, VI: **to ~ (for)** ansiar, anhelar

craving [ˈkreɪvɪŋ] N (for food, cigarettes etc) ansias fpl; (during pregnancy) antojo

crawl [krɔːl] VI (drag o.s.) arrastrarse; (child) andar a gatas, gatear; (vehicle) avanzar (lentamente); (inf): **to ~ to sb** dar coba a algn, hacerle la pelota a algn ▶ N (Swimming) crol m

crawler lane [krɔːlə-] N (BRIT Aut) carril m para tráfico lento

crayfish [ˈkreɪfɪʃ] (pl ~) N INV (freshwater) cangrejo (de río); (saltwater) cigala

crayon [ˈkreɪən] N lápiz m de color

craze [kreɪz] N manía; (fashion) moda

crazed [kreɪzd] ADJ (look, person) loco, demente; (pottery, glaze) agrietado, cuarteado

★**crazy** [ˈkreɪzɪ] ADJ (person) loco; (idea) disparatado; **to go ~** volverse loco; **to be ~ about sb/sth** (inf) estar loco por algn/algo

crazy paving N pavimento de baldosas irregulares

creak [kriːk] VI crujir; (hinge etc) chirriar, rechinar

★**cream** [kriːm] N (of milk) nata, crema; (lotion) crema; (fig) flor f y nata; **whipped ~** nata batida ▶ ADJ (colour) color m crema
  ▶ **cream off** VT (fig: best talents, part of profits) separar lo mejor de

cream cake N pastel m de nata

cream cheese N queso blanco cremoso

creamery [ˈkriːmərɪ] N (shop) quesería; (factory) central f lechera

creamy [ˈkriːmɪ] ADJ cremoso

crease [kriːs] N (fold) pliegue m; (in trousers) raya; (wrinkle) arruga ▶ VT (fold) doblar, plegar; (wrinkle) arrugar ▶ VI (wrinkle up) arrugarse

crease-resistant [ˈkriːsrɪzɪstənt] ADJ inarrugable

★**create** [kriːˈeɪt] VT (also Comput) crear; (impression) dar; (fuss, noise) hacer

creation [kriːˈeɪʃən] N creación f

★**creative** [kriːˈeɪtɪv] ADJ creativo

creativity [kriːeɪˈtɪvɪtɪ] N creatividad f

creator [kriːˈeɪtəʳ] N creador(a) m/f

creature [ˈkriːtʃəʳ] N (living thing) criatura; (animal) animal m; (insect) bicho; (person) criatura

creature comforts NPL comodidades fpl materiales

crèche, creche [kreʃ] N (BRIT) guardería (infantil)

credence [ˈkriːdəns] N: **to lend** or **give ~ to** creer en, dar crédito a

credentials [krɪˈdɛnʃlz] NPL credenciales *fpl*; (*letters of reference*) referencias *fpl*

credibility [krɛdɪˈbɪlɪtɪ] N credibilidad *f*

credible [ˈkrɛdɪbl] ADJ creíble; (*witness, source*) fidedigno

★**credit** [ˈkrɛdɪt] N (*gen*) crédito; (*merit*) honor *m*, mérito; **to be in ~** (*person, bank account*) tener saldo a favor; **on ~** a crédito; (*inf*) al fiado; **he's a ~ to his family** hace honor a su familia ▶ VT (*Comm*) abonar; (*believe*) creer, dar crédito a; **to ~ sb with** (*fig*) reconocer a algn el mérito de ▶ ADJ crediticio; *see also* **credits**

creditable [ˈkrɛdɪtəbl] ADJ estimable, digno de elogio

credit account N cuenta de crédito

credit agency N agencia de informes comerciales

credit balance N saldo acreedor

credit card N tarjeta de crédito

credit control N control *m* de créditos

credit crunch N crisis *f* crediticia

credit facilities NPL facilidades *fpl* de crédito

credit limit N límite *m* de crédito

credit note N nota de crédito

creditor [ˈkrɛdɪtər] N acreedor(a) *m/f*

credit rating N calificación *f* crediticia

credits [ˈkrɛdɪts] NPL títulos *mpl* or rótulos *mpl* de crédito, ficha técnica

credit transfer N transferencia de crédito

creditworthy [ˈkrɛdɪtwəːðɪ] ADJ solvente

credulity [krɪˈdjuːlɪtɪ] N credulidad *f*

creed [kriːd] N credo

creek [kriːk] N cala, ensenada; (*US*) riachuelo

creel [kriːl] N nasa

creep [kriːp] (*pt, pp* **crept** [krɛpt]) VI (*animal*) deslizarse; (*plant*) trepar; **to ~ up on sb** acercarse sigilosamente a algn; (*fig: old age etc*): **to ~ up (on sb)** acercarse a algn (*pej*): **he's a ~** ¡qué lameculos es!; **it gives me the creeps** me da escalofríos

creeper [ˈkriːpər] N enredadera

creepers [ˈkriːpəz] NPL (*US: for baby*) pelele *msg*

creepy [ˈkriːpɪ] ADJ (*frightening*) horripilante

creepy-crawly [ˈkriːpɪˈkrɔːlɪ] N (*inf*) bicho

cremate [krɪˈmeɪt] VT incinerar

cremation [krɪˈmeɪʃən] N incineración *f*, cremación *f*

crematorium [krɛməˈtɔːrɪəm] (*pl* **crematoria** [krɛməˈtɔːrɪə]) N crematorio

creosote [ˈkrɪəsəʊt] N creosota

crêpe [kreɪp] N (*fabric*) crespón *m*; (*also:* **crêpe rubber**) crep(é) *m*

crêpe bandage N (BRIT) venda elástica

crêpe paper N papel *m* crep(é)

crêpe sole N (*on shoes*) suela de crep(é)

crept [krɛpt] PT, PP *of* **creep**

crescent [ˈkrɛsnt] N media luna; (*street*) calle *f* (*en forma de semicírculo*)

cress [krɛs] N berro

crest [krɛst] N (*of bird*) cresta; (*of hill*) cima, cumbre *f*; (*of helmet*) cimera; (*of coat of arms*) blasón *m*

crestfallen [ˈkrɛstʃɔːlən] ADJ alicaído

Crete [kriːt] N Creta

cretin [ˈkrɛtɪn] N cretino(-a)

crevasse [krɪˈvæs] N grieta

crevice [ˈkrɛvɪs] N grieta, hendedura

crew [kruː] N (*of ship etc*) tripulación *f*; (*Cine etc*) equipo; (*gang*) pandilla, banda; (*Mil*) dotación *f*

crew-cut [ˈkruːkʌt] N corte *m* al rape

crew-neck [ˈkruːnɛk] N cuello a la caja

crib [krɪb] N cuna ▶ VT (*inf*) plagiar; (*Scol*) copiar

crib sheet N (BRIT: *in exam*) chuleta

crick [krɪk] N: **~ in the neck** tortícolis *f inv*

★**cricket** [ˈkrɪkɪt] N (*insect*) grillo; (*game*) críquet *m*

cricketer [ˈkrɪkɪtər] N jugador(a) *m/f* de críquet

★**crime** [kraɪm] N crimen *m*; (*less serious*) delito

crime wave N ola de crímenes *or* delitos

★**criminal** [ˈkrɪmɪnl] N criminal *mf*, delincuente *mf* ▶ ADJ criminal; (*law*) penal

Criminal Investigation Department N ≈ Brigada de Investigación Criminal *f* (SP)

crimp [krɪmp] VT (*hair*) rizar

crimson [ˈkrɪmzn] ADJ carmesí

cringe [krɪndʒ] VI encogerse

crinkle [ˈkrɪŋkl] VT arrugar

crinkly [ˈkrɪŋklɪ] ADJ (*hair*) rizado, crespo

cripple [ˈkrɪpl] N (!) lisiado(-a), cojo(-a) ▶ VT lisiar, mutilar; (*ship, plane*) inutilizar; (*production, exports*) paralizar; **crippled with arthritis** paralizado por la artritis

crippling [ˈkrɪplɪŋ] ADJ (*injury etc*) debilitador(a); (*prices, taxes*) devastador(a)

★**crisis** [ˈkraɪsɪs] (*pl* **crises** [ˈkraɪsiːz]) N crisis *f*

crisp [krɪsp] ADJ fresco; (*toast, snow*) crujiente; (*manner*) seco

★**crisps** [krɪsps] NPL (BRIT) patatas *fpl* fritas (chips)

crispy ADJ crujiente

crisscross [ˈkrɪskrɔs] ADJ entrelazado, entrecruzado ▶ VT entrecruzar(se)

criterion [kraɪˈtɪərɪən] (*pl* **criteria** [kraɪˈtɪərɪə]) N criterio

★**critic** [ˈkrɪtɪk] N crítico(-a)

critical [ˈkrɪtɪkl] ADJ (*gen*) crítico; (*illness*) grave; **to be ~ of sb/sth** criticar a algn/algo

critically [ˈkrɪtɪklɪ] ADV (*speak etc*) en tono crítico; (*ill*) gravemente

★**criticism** [ˈkrɪtɪsɪzm] N crítica

★**criticize** [ˈkrɪtɪsaɪz] VT criticar

critique [krɪˈtiːk] N crítica

croak [krəʊk] VI (*frog*) croar; (*raven*) graznar ▶ N (*of raven*) graznido

Croat [ˈkrəʊæt] ADJ, N = **Croatian**

C

497

Croatia [krəuˈeɪʃə] N Croacia

Croatian [krəuˈeɪʃən] ADJ, N croata *mf* ▶ N (*Ling*) croata *m*

crochet [ˈkrəuʃeɪ] N ganchillo

crock [krɔk] N cántaro; (*inf: person: also:* **old crock**) carcamal *mf*, vejestorio; (: *car etc*) cacharro

crockery [ˈkrɔkərɪ] N (*plates, cups etc*) loza, vajilla

crocodile [ˈkrɔkədaɪl] N cocodrilo

crocus [ˈkrəukəs] N crocus *m*, croco

croft [krɔft] N granja pequeña

crofter [ˈkrɔftər] N pequeño granjero

croissant [ˈkrwasã] N croissant *m*, medialuna (*esp* LAM)

crone [krəun] N arpía, bruja

crony [ˈkrəunɪ] N compinche *mf*

crook [kruk] N (*inf*) ladrón(-ona) *m/f*; (*of shepherd*) cayado; (*of arm*) pliegue *m*

crooked [ˈkrukɪd] ADJ torcido; (*path*) tortuoso; (*inf*) corrupto

★**crop** [krɔp] N (*produce*) cultivo; (*amount produced*) cosecha; (*riding crop*) látigo de montar; (*of bird*) buche *m* ▶ VT cortar, recortar; (*animals, grass*) pacer
  ▶ **crop up** VI surgir, presentarse

crop spraying [-ˈspreɪɪŋ] N fumigación *f* de los cultivos

croquet [ˈkrəukeɪ] N croquet *m*

croquette [krəˈkɛt] N croqueta (*de patata*)

★**cross** [krɔs] N cruz *f*; **it's a ~ between geography and sociology** es una mezcla de geografía y sociología ▶ VT (*street etc*) cruzar, atravesar; (*thwart: person*) contrariar, ir contra; **to ~ o.s.** santiguarse; **they've got their lines crossed** (*fig*) hay un malentendido entre ellos ▶ VI: **the boat crosses from Santander to Plymouth** el barco hace la travesía de Santander a Plymouth ▶ ADJ de mal humor, enojado; **to be/get ~ with sb (about sth)** estar enfadado/enfadarse con algn (por algo)
  ▶ **cross off** VT tachar
  ▶ **cross out** VT tachar
  ▶ **cross over** VI cruzar

crossbar [ˈkrɔsbɑːr] N travesaño; (*of bicycle*) barra

crossbow [ˈkrɔsbəu] N ballesta

cross-Channel ferry [ˈkrɔsˈtʃænl-] N transbordador *m* que cruza el Canal de la Mancha

cross-check [ˈkrɔstʃɛk] N verificación *f* ▶ VT verificar

cross-country [ˈkrɔsˈkʌntrɪ], **cross-country race** N carrera a campo traviesa, cross *m*

cross-dressing [krɔsˈdrɛsɪŋ] N travestismo

cross-examination [ˈkrɔsɪgzæmɪˈneɪʃən] N interrogatorio

cross-examine [ˈkrɔsɪgˈzæmɪn] VT interrogar

cross-eyed [ˈkrɔsaɪd] ADJ bizco

crossfire [ˈkrɔsfaɪər] N fuego cruzado

★**crossing** [ˈkrɔsɪŋ] N (*on road*) cruce *m*; (*Rail*) paso a nivel; (*sea passage*) travesía; (*also:* **pedestrian crossing**) paso de peatones

crossing guard N (*US*) persona encargada de ayudar a los niños a cruzar la calle

crossing point N paso; (*at border*) paso fronterizo

cross purposes NPL: **to be at ~ with sb** tener un malentendido con algn

cross-question [ˈkrɔsˈkwɛstʃən] VT interrogar

cross-reference [ˈkrɔsˈrɛfrəns] N remisión *f*

★**crossroads** [ˈkrɔsrəudz] NSG cruce *m*; (*fig*) encrucijada

cross section N corte *m* transversal; (*of population*) muestra (representativa)

crosswalk [ˈkrɔswɔːk] N (*US*) paso de peatones

crosswind [ˈkrɔswɪnd] N viento de costado

crossword [ˈkrɔswɜːd] N crucigrama *m*

crotch [krɔtʃ] N (*of garment*) entrepierna

crotchet [ˈkrɔtʃɪt] N (BRIT *Mus*) negra

crotchety [ˈkrɔtʃɪtɪ] ADJ (*person*) arisco

crouch [krautʃ] VI agacharse, acurrucarse

croup [kruːp] N (*Med*) crup *m*

croupier [ˈkruːpɪə] N crupier *mf*

crouton [ˈkruːtɔn] N cubito de pan frito

crow [krəu] N (*bird*) cuervo; (*of cock*) canto, cacareo ▶ VI (*cock*) cantar; (*fig*) jactarse

crowbar [ˈkrəubɑːr] N palanca

★**crowd** [kraud] N muchedumbre *f*; (*Sport*) público; (*common herd*) vulgo; **crowds of people** gran cantidad de gente ▶ VT (*gather*) amontonar; (*fill*) llenar ▶ VI (*gather*) reunirse; (*pile up*) amontonarse

crowded [ˈkraudɪd] ADJ (*full*) atestado; (*well-attended*) concurrido; (*densely populated*) superpoblado

crowd scene N (*Cine, Theat*) escena con muchos comparsas

crowdsource [ˈkraudsɔːs] VT aplicar el crowdsourcing en, aplicar la tercerización masiva en

crowdsourcing [ˈkraudsɔːsɪŋ] N crowdsourcing *m*, tercerización *f* masiva

★**crown** [kraun] N corona; (*of head*) coronilla; (*of hat*) copa; (*of hill*) cumbre *f*; (*for tooth*) funda ▶ VT (*also tooth*) coronar; **and to ~ it all ...** (*fig*) y para colmo *or* remate ...

crown court N (*Law*) tribunal *m* superior

En el sistema legal de Inglaterra y el País de Gales, los delitos graves como asesinato, violación o atraco son juzgados por un jurado en un tribunal superior llamado **crown court** con sede en unas noventa ciudades. Los jueces de paz (*Justices of the Peace*) juzgan delitos menores e infracciones de la ley en juzgados llamados *Magistrates' Courts*. Es el juez de paz quien decide remitir los casos pertinentes a la *crown court*, que en caso de recursos se remite al tribunal de apelación, *Court of Appeal*. Escocia e Irlanda del Norte tienen sus propios sistemas legales, aunque la *Supreme Court of the United Kingdom* es es la más alta instancia judicial de todo el Reino Unido.

crowning [ˈkraʊnɪŋ] ADJ (*achievement, glory*) máximo

crown jewels NPL joyas *fpl* reales

crown prince N príncipe *m* heredero

crow's feet [ˈkrəʊzfiːt] NPL patas *fpl* de gallo

crucial [ˈkruːʃl] ADJ crucial, decisivo; **his approval is ~ to the success of the project** su aprobación es crucial para el éxito del proyecto

crucifix [ˈkruːsɪfɪks] N crucifijo

crucifixion [kruːsɪˈfɪkʃən] N crucifixión *f*

crucify [ˈkruːsɪfaɪ] VT crucificar; (*fig*) martirizar

crude [kruːd] ADJ (*materials*) bruto; (*fig: basic*) tosco; (: *vulgar*) ordinario ▶ N (*also:* **crude oil**) (petróleo) crudo

crude oil N petróleo crudo

cruel [ˈkruːəl] ADJ cruel

cruelty [ˈkruːəltɪ] N crueldad *f*

cruet [ˈkruːɪt] N vinagreras *fpl*

cruise [kruːz] N crucero ▶ VI (*ship*) navegar; (*holidaymakers*) hacer un crucero; (*car*) ir a velocidad constante

cruise missile N misil *m* de crucero

cruiser [ˈkruːzər] N crucero

cruising speed [ˈkruːzɪŋ-] N velocidad *f* de crucero

crumb [krʌm] N miga, migaja

crumble [ˈkrʌmbl] VT desmenuzar ▶ VI (*gen*) desmenuzarse; (*building*) desmoronarse

crumbly [ˈkrʌmblɪ] ADJ desmenuzable

crummy [ˈkrʌmɪ] ADJ (*inf: poor quality*) pésimo, cutre (SP); (: *unwell*) fatal

crumpet [ˈkrʌmpɪt] N ≈ bollo para tostar

crumple [ˈkrʌmpl] VT (*paper*) estrujar; (*material*) arrugar

crunch [krʌntʃ] VT (*with teeth*) mascar; (*underfoot*) hacer crujir ▶ N (*fig*) hora de la verdad

crunchy [ˈkrʌntʃɪ] ADJ crujiente

crusade [kruːˈseɪd] N cruzada ▶ VI: **to ~ for/against** (*fig*) hacer una campaña en pro de/en contra de

crusader [kruːˈseɪdər] N (*fig*) paladín *mf*

crush [krʌʃ] N (*crowd*) aglomeración *f*; **to have a ~ on sb** estar enamorado de algn ▶ VT (*gen*) aplastar; (*paper*) estrujar; (*cloth*) arrugar; (*grind, break up: garlic, ice*) picar; (: *fruit*) exprimir; (: *grapes*) exprimir, prensar; (: *opposition*) aplastar; (: *hopes*) destruir

crush barrier N barrera de seguridad

crushing [ˈkrʌʃɪŋ] ADJ aplastante; (*burden*) agobiante

crust [krʌst] N corteza

crustacean [krʌsˈteɪʃən] N crustáceo

crusty [ˈkrʌstɪ] ADJ (*bread*) crujiente; (*person*) de mal carácter; (*remark*) brusco

crutch [krʌtʃ] N (*Med*) muleta; (*support*) apoyo

crux [krʌks] N: **the ~** lo esencial, el quid

★**cry** [kraɪ] VI llorar; **what are you crying about?** ¿por qué lloras?; **to ~ for help** pedir socorro a voces ▶ VT (*shout: also:* **cry out**) gritar ▶ N grito; (*of animal*) aullido; (*weep*): **she had a good ~** lloró a lágrima viva; **it's a far ~ from ...** (*fig*) dista mucho de ...

▶ **cry off** VI retirarse

▶ **cry out** VI (*call out, shout*) lanzar un grito, echar un grito ▶ VT gritar

crypt [krɪpt] N cripta

cryptic [ˈkrɪptɪk] ADJ enigmático

crystal [ˈkrɪstl] N cristal *m*

crystal-clear [ˈkrɪstlˈklɪər] ADJ claro como el agua; (*fig*) cristalino

crystallize [ˈkrɪstəlaɪz] VT (*fig*) cristalizar; **crystallized fruits** frutas *fpl* escarchadas ▶ VI cristalizarse

CSA N ABBR = **Confederate States of America**; (= *Child Support Agency*) organismo que supervisa el pago de la pensión a hijos de padres separados

CSC N ABBR (= *Civil Service Commission*) comisión para la contratación de funcionarios

CS gas N (BRIT) gas *m* lacrimógeno

CST N ABBR (US: = *Central Standard Time*) huso horario

CT, Ct. ABBR (US) = **Connecticut**

ct ABBR = **cent**; **court**; **carat**

CTC N ABBR (BRIT: = *city technology college*) ≈ centro de formación profesional

cu. ABBR = **cubic**

cub [kʌb] N cachorro; (*also:* **cub scout**) niño explorador

Cuba [ˈkjuːbə] N Cuba

Cuban [ˈkjuːbən] ADJ, N cubano(-a) *m/f*

cubbyhole [ˈkʌbɪhəʊl] N cuchitril *m*

cube [kjuːb] N cubo; (*of sugar*) terrón *m* ▶ VT (*Math*) elevar al cubo

cube root N raíz *f* cúbica

cubic [ˈkjuːbɪk] ADJ cúbico; **~ capacity** (*Aut*) capacidad *f* cúbica

cubicle [ˈkjuːbɪkl] N (*at pool*) caseta; (*for bed*) cubículo

cubism [ˈkjuːbɪzəm] N cubismo

cuckoo [ˈkuːkuː] N cuco

cuckoo clock N reloj *m* de cuco

★**cucumber** [ˈkjuːkʌmbər] N pepino

cuddle [ˈkʌdl] VT abrazar ▶ VI abrazarse

cuddly [ˈkʌdlɪ] ADJ mimoso; (*toy*) de peluche

cudgel [ˈkʌdʒəl] VT: **to ~ one's brains** devanarse los sesos

cue [kjuː] N (*snooker cue*) taco; (*Theat etc*) entrada

cuff [kʌf] N (BRIT: *of shirt, coat etc*) puño; (US: *of trousers*) vuelta; (*blow*) bofetada; **off the ~** adv improvisado ▶ VT bofetear

cufflinks [ˈkʌflɪŋks] NPL gemelos *mpl*

cu. ft. ABBR = **cubic feet**

cu. in. ABBR = **cubic inches**

cuisine [kwɪˈziːn] N cocina

cul-de-sac [ˈkʌldəsæk] N callejón m sin salida

culinary [ˈkʌlɪnərɪ] ADJ culinario

cull [kʌl] VT (select) entresacar; (kill selectively: animals) matar selectivamente ▶ N matanza selectiva; **seal ~** matanza selectiva de focas

culminate [ˈkʌlmɪneɪt] VI: **to ~ in** culminar en

culmination [kʌlmɪˈneɪʃən] N culminación f, colmo

culottes [kuːˈlɒts] NPL falda f pantalón

culpable [ˈkʌlpəbl] ADJ culpable

culprit [ˈkʌlprɪt] N culpable mf

cult [kʌlt] N culto; **a ~ figure** un ídolo

cultivate [ˈkʌltɪveɪt] VT (also fig) cultivar

cultivated [ˈkʌltɪveɪtɪd] ADJ culto

cultivation [kʌltɪˈveɪʃən] N cultivo; (fig) cultura

cultural [ˈkʌltʃərəl] ADJ cultural

★**culture** [ˈkʌltʃəʳ] N (also fig) cultura; (Biol) cultivo

cultured [ˈkʌltʃəd] ADJ culto

cumbersome [ˈkʌmbəsəm] ADJ voluminoso

cumin [ˈkʌmɪn] N (spice) comino

cummerbund [ˈkʌməbʌnd] N faja, fajín m

cumulative [ˈkjuːmjulətɪv] ADJ cumulativo

cunning [ˈkʌnɪŋ] N astucia ▶ ADJ astuto; (clever: device, idea) ingenioso

cunt [kʌnt] N (inf!) coño; (insult) mamonazo(-a) (!)

★**cup** [kʌp] N taza; (prize, event) copa; **a ~ of tea** una taza de té

★**cupboard** [ˈkʌbəd] N armario, placar(d) m (LAM); (in kitchen) alacena

cup final N (Football) final f de copa

cupful [ˈkʌpful] N taza

Cupid [ˈkjuːpɪd] N Cupido

cupola [ˈkjuːpələ] N cúpula

cuppa [ˈkʌpə] N (BRIT inf) (taza de) té m

cup-tie [ˈkʌptaɪ] N (BRIT) partido de copa

cur [kəːʳ] N perro de mala raza; (person) canalla m

curable [ˈkjuərəbl] ADJ curable

curate [ˈkjuərɪt] N coadjutor m

curator [kjuəˈreɪtəʳ] N director(a) m/f

curb [kəːb] VT refrenar; (powers, spending) limitar ▶ N freno; (US: kerb) bordillo

curd cheese [kəːd-] N requesón m

curdle [ˈkəːdl] VI cuajarse

curds [kəːdz] NPL requesón msg

cure [kjuəʳ] VT curar; **to be cured of sth** curarse de algo ▶ N cura, curación f; (fig: solution) remedio; **to take a ~** tomar un remedio

cure-all [ˈkjuərɔːl] N (also fig) panacea

curfew [ˈkəːfjuː] N toque m de queda

curio [ˈkjuərɪəu] N curiosidad f

curiosity [kjuərɪˈɒsɪtɪ] N curiosidad f

★**curious** [ˈkjuərɪəs] ADJ curioso; **I'm ~ about him** me intriga

curiously [ˈkjuərɪəslɪ] ADV curiosamente; **~ enough, ...** aunque parezca extraño ...

curl [kəːl] N rizo; (of smoke etc) espiral f, voluta ▶ VT (hair) rizar; (paper) arrollar; (lip) fruncir ▶ VI rizarse; arrollarse
▶ **curl up** VI arrollarse; (person) hacerse un ovillo; (inf) morirse de risa

curler [ˈkəːləʳ] N bigudí m, rulo

curlew [ˈkəːluː] N zarapito

curling tongs, (US) **curling irons** [ˈkəːlɪŋ-] NPL tenacillas fpl

curly [ˈkəːlɪ] ADJ rizado

currant [ˈkʌrnt] N pasa; (black, red) grosella

★**currency** [ˈkʌrnsɪ] N moneda; **to gain ~** (fig) difundirse

current [ˈkʌrnt] N corriente f; **direct/alternating ~** corriente directa/alterna; **in ~ use** de uso corriente ▶ ADJ actual; **the ~ issue of a magazine** el último número de una revista

current account N (BRIT) cuenta corriente

current affairs NPL (noticias fpl de) actualidad f

current assets NPL (Comm) activo disponible

current liabilities NPL (Comm) pasivo circulante

currently [ˈkʌrntlɪ] ADV actualmente

curriculum [kəˈrɪkjuləm] (pl **curriculums** or **curricula** [kəˈrɪkjulə]) N plan m de estudios

curriculum vitae [-ˈviːtaɪ] N currículum m (vitae)

curry [ˈkʌrɪ] N curry m ▶ VT: **to ~ favour with** buscar el favor de

curry powder N curry m en polvo

curse [kəːs] VI echar pestes, soltar palabrotas ▶ VT maldecir ▶ N maldición f; (swearword) palabrota, taco

cursor [ˈkəːsəʳ] N (Comput) cursor m

cursory [ˈkəːsərɪ] ADJ rápido, superficial

curt [kəːt] ADJ seco

curtail [kəːˈteɪl] VT (cut short) acortar; (restrict) restringir

★**curtain** [ˈkəːtn] N cortina; (Theat) telón m; **to draw the curtains** (together) cerrar las cortinas; (apart) abrir las cortinas

curtain call N (Theat) llamada a escena

curtain ring N anilla

curtsey, curtsy [ˈkəːtsɪ] N reverencia ▶ VI hacer una reverencia

curve [kəːv] N curva ▶ VI (road) hacer una curva; (line etc) curvarse

curved [kəːvd] ADJ curvo

cushion [ˈkuʃən] N cojín m; (Snooker) banda ▶ VT (seat) acolchar; (shock) amortiguar

cushy [ˈkuʃɪ] ADJ (inf): **a ~ job** un chollo; **to have a ~ time** tener la vida arreglada

custard [ˈkʌstəd] N (for pouring) natillas fpl

custard powder N polvos *mpl* para natillas

custodial sentence [kʌsˈtəudɪəl-] N pena de prisión

custodian [kʌsˈtəudɪən] N guardián(-ana) *m/f*; *(of museum etc)* conservador(a) *m/f*

custody [ˈkʌstədɪ] N custodia; **to take sb into ~** detener a algn; **in the ~ of** al cuidado *or* cargo de

custom [ˈkʌstəm] N costumbre *f*; *(Comm)* clientela; *see also* **customs**

customary [ˈkʌstəmərɪ] ADJ acostumbrado; **it is ~ to do …** es la costumbre hacer …

custom-built [ˈkʌstəmˈbɪlt] ADJ = **custom-made**

★**customer** [ˈkʌstəmər] N cliente(-a) *m/f*; **he's an awkward ~** *(inf)* es un tipo difícil

customer profile N perfil *m* del cliente

customize [ˈkʌstəmaɪz] VT personalizar

customized [ˈkʌstəmaɪzd] ADJ *(car etc)* hecho a encargo

custom-made [ˈkʌstəmˈmeɪd] ADJ hecho a la medida

customs [ˈkʌstəmz] NPL aduana *sg*; **to go through (the) ~** pasar la aduana

Customs and Excise N *(Brit)* Aduanas *fpl* y Arbitrios

customs officer N aduanero(-a), funcionario(-a) de aduanas

★**cut** [kʌt] *(pt, pp ~)* VT cortar; *(price)* rebajar; *(record)* grabar; *(reduce)* reducir; *(inf: avoid: class, lecture)* fumarse, faltar a; **to ~ one's finger** cortarse un dedo; **to get one's hair ~** cortarse el pelo; **to ~ and paste** *(Comput)* cortar y pegar; **to ~ a tooth** echar un diente; **to ~ sb dead** negarle el saludo *or* *(Lam)* cortarle a algn ▶ VI cortar; *(intersect)* cruzarse; **it cuts both ways** *(fig)* tiene doble filo ▶ N corte *m*; *(in skin)* corte, cortadura; *(with sword)* tajo; *(of knife)* cuchillada; *(in salary etc)* rebaja; *(in spending)* reducción *f*, recorte *m*; *(slice of meat)* tajada; **power ~** *(Brit)* apagón *m*
  ▶ **cut back** VT *(plants)* podar; *(production, expenditure)* reducir
  ▶ **cut down** VT *(tree)* cortar, derribar; *(consumption, expenses)* reducir; **to ~ sb down to size** *(fig)* bajarle los humos a algn
  ▶ **cut in** VI: **to ~ in (on)** *(interrupt: conversation)* interrumpir, intervenir (en); *(Aut)* cerrar el paso (a)
  ▶ **cut off** VT cortar; *(fig)* aislar; *(troops)* cercar; **we've been ~ off** *(Tel)* nos han cortado la comunicación
  ▶ **cut out** VT *(shape)* recortar; *(delete)* suprimir
  ▶ **cut up** VT cortar (en pedazos); *(chop: food)* trinchar, cortar

cut-and-dried [ˈkʌtənˈdraɪd], **cut-and-dry** [ˈkʌtənˈdraɪ] ADJ arreglado de antemano, seguro

cutback [ˈkʌtbæk] N reducción *f*

cute [kjuːt] ADJ lindo, mono; *(shrewd)* listo

cuticle [ˈkjuːtɪkl] N cutícula

cutlery [ˈkʌtlərɪ] N cubiertos *mpl*

cutlet [ˈkʌtlɪt] N chuleta

cutoff [ˈkʌtɔf] N *(also: **cutoff point**)* límite *m*

cutout [ˈkʌtaut] N *(cardboard cutout)* recortable *m*

cut-price [ˈkʌtˈpraɪs], *(US)* **cut-rate** [ˈkʌtˈreɪt] ADJ a precio reducido

cut-throat [ˈkʌtθrəut] N asesino(-a) ▶ ADJ feroz; **~ competition** competencia encarnizada *or* despiadada

cutting [ˈkʌtɪŋ] ADJ *(gen)* cortante; *(remark)* mordaz ▶ N *(Brit: from newspaper)* recorte *m*; *(from plant)* esqueje *m*; *(Brit Rail)* desmonte *m*; *(Cine)* montaje *m*

cutting edge N *(of knife)* filo; *(fig)* vanguardia; **a country on** *or* **at the ~ of space technology** un país puntero en tecnología del espacio

cutting-edge [kʌtɪŋˈɛdʒ] ADJ punta, de vanguardia

★**CV** N ABBR = **curriculum vitae**

CWO ABBR *(Comm)* = **cash with order**

cwt. ABBR = **hundredweight**

cyanide [ˈsaɪənaɪd] N cianuro

cyberattack [ˈsaɪbərətæk] N ciberataque *m*

cyberbully [ˈsaɪbəbulɪ] N ciberacosador(a) *m/f*

cyberbullying [ˈsaɪbəbulɪɪŋ] N ciberacoso

cybercafé [ˈsaɪbəkæfeɪ] N cibercafé *m*

cybernetics [saɪbəˈnɛtɪks] NSG cibernética

cybersecurity [saɪbəsɪˈkjuərɪtɪ] N ciberseguridad *f*, seguridad *f* cibernética

cyberspace [ˈsaɪbəspeɪs] N ciberespacio

cyberterrorism [ˈsaɪbətərərɪzəm] N ciberterrorismo *m*

cyclamen [ˈsɪkləmən] N ciclamen *m*

★**cycle** [ˈsaɪkl] N ciclo; *(bicycle)* bicicleta ▶ VI ir en bicicleta

cycle hire N alquiler *m* de bicicletas

cycle lane N carril *m* de bicicleta, carril *m* bici

cycle path N carril-bici *m*

cycle race N carrera ciclista

cycle rack N soporte *m* para bicicletas

cycling [ˈsaɪklɪŋ] N ciclismo

cycling holiday N vacaciones *fpl* en bicicleta

cyclist [ˈsaɪklɪst] N ciclista *mf*

cyclone [ˈsaɪkləun] N ciclón *m*

cygnet [ˈsɪgnɪt] N pollo de cisne

cylinder [ˈsɪlɪndər] N cilindro

cylinder block N bloque *m* de cilindros

cylinder head N culata de cilindro

cylinder-head gasket N junta de culata

cymbals [ˈsɪmblz] NPL platillos *mpl*, címbalos *mpl*

cynic [ˈsɪnɪk] N cínico(-a)

cynical [ˈsɪnɪkl] ADJ cínico

cynicism [ˈsɪnɪsɪzəm] N cinismo

cypress [ˈsaɪprɪs] N ciprés *m*
Cypriot [ˈsɪprɪət] ADJ, N chipriota *mf*
Cyprus [ˈsaɪprəs] N Chipre *f*
cyst [sɪst] N quiste *m*
cystitis [sɪsˈtaɪtɪs] N cistitis *f*
CZ N ABBR (*US*: = *Canal Zone*) *zona del Canal de Panamá*
czar [zɑːʳ] N zar *m*
czarina [zɑːˈriːnə] N zarina

Czech [tʃɛk] ADJ checo; **the ~ Republic** la República Checa ▶ N checo(-a); (*Ling*) checo
Czechia [ˈtʃɛkiə] N Chequia
Czechoslovak [tʃɛkəˈsləʊvæk] ADJ, N (*History*) = **Czechoslovakian**
Czechoslovakia [tʃɛkəsləˈvækiə] N (*History*) Checoslovaquia
Czechoslovakian [tʃɛkəsləˈvækiən] ADJ, N (*History*) checoslovaco(-a) *m/f*

Dd

d

D, d [di:] N (*letter*) D, d; (*Mus*): **D** re *m*; **D for David**, (*US*) **D for Dog** D de Dolores

D ABBR (*US Pol*) = **democrat; democratic**

d ABBR (*BRIT old*) = **penny**

d. ABBR = **died**

DA N ABBR (*US*) = **district attorney**

dab [dæb] VT: **to ~ ointment onto a wound** aplicar pomada sobre una herida; **to ~ with paint** dar unos toques de pintura a ▶ N (*light stroke*) toque *m*; (*small amount*) pizca

dabble ['dæbl] VI: **to ~ in** hacer por afición

Dacca ['dækə] N Dacca

dachshund ['dækshund] N perro tejonero

Dacron® ['deɪkrɔn] N (*US*) terylene *m*

★**dad** [dæd], **daddy** ['dædɪ] N papá *m*

daddy-long-legs [dædɪ'lɔŋlɛgz] N típula

daffodil ['dæfədɪl] N narciso

daft [dɑːft] ADJ tonto

dagger ['dægəʳ] N puñal *m*, daga; **to look daggers at sb** fulminar a algn con la mirada

dahlia ['deɪljə] N dalia

★**daily** ['deɪlɪ] ADJ diario, cotidiano ▶ N (*paper*) diario; (*domestic help*) asistenta ▶ ADV todos los días, cada día; **twice ~** dos veces al día

dainty ['deɪntɪ] ADJ delicado; (*tasteful*) elegante

dairy ['dɛərɪ] N (*shop*) lechería; (*on farm*) vaquería; (*products*) lácteos *mpl* ▶ ADJ (*cow etc*) lechero

dairy cow N vaca lechera

dairy farm N vaquería

dairy produce N productos *mpl* lácteos

dais ['deɪɪs] N estrado

daisy ['deɪzɪ] N margarita

dale [deɪl] N valle *m*

dally ['dælɪ] VI entretenerse

Dalmatian [dæl'meɪʃən] N (*dog*) (perro) dálmata *mf*

dam [dæm] N presa; (*reservoir*) embalse *m* ▶ VT embalsar

★**damage** ['dæmɪdʒ] N daño; (*fig*) perjuicio; (*to machine*) avería; **~ to property** daños materiales ▶ VT dañar; perjudicar; averiar ▓ **damages** NPL (*Law*) daños y perjuicios; **to pay £5000 in damages** pagar £5000 por daños y perjuicios

damaging ['dæmɪdʒɪŋ] ADJ: **~ (to)** perjudicial (a)

Damascus [də'mɑːskəs] N Damasco

dame [deɪm] N (*title*) dama; (*US inf*) tía; (*Theat*) vieja; *see also* **pantomime**

damn [dæm] VT condenar; (*curse*) maldecir; **~ (it)!** ¡maldito sea! ▶ N (*inf*): **I don't give a ~** me importa un pito ▶ ADJ (*inf: also:* **damned**) maldito, fregado (*LAM*)

damnable ['dæmnəbl] ADJ (*inf: behaviour*) detestable; (: *weather*) horrible

damnation [dæm'neɪʃən] N (*Rel*) condenación *f* ▶ EXCL (*inf*) ¡maldición!, ¡maldito sea!

damning ['dæmɪŋ] ADJ (*evidence*) irrecusable

damp [dæmp] ADJ húmedo, mojado ▶ N humedad *f* ▶ VT (*also:* **dampen**: *cloth, rag*) mojar; (: *enthusiasm*) enfriar

dampcourse ['dæmpkɔːs] N aislante *m* hidrófugo

damper ['dæmpəʳ] N (*Mus*) sordina; (*of fire*) regulador *m* de tiro; **to put a ~ on things** ser un jarro de agua fría

dampness ['dæmpnɪs] N humedad *f*

damson ['dæmzən] N ciruela damascena

★**dance** [dɑːns] N baile *m* ▶ VI bailar; **to ~ about** saltar

dance floor N pista *f* de baile

dance hall N salón *m* de baile

dancer ['dɑːnsəʳ] N bailador(a) *m/f*; (*professional*) bailarín(-ina) *m/f*

dancing ['dɑːnsɪŋ] N baile *m*

D and C N ABBR (*Med*: = *dilation and curettage*) raspado

dandelion ['dændɪlaɪən] N diente *m* de león

dandruff ['dændrəf] N caspa

D & T (Brit Scol) N ABBR (= *design and technology*) diseño y tecnología

dandy ['dændɪ] N dandi *m* ▶ ADJ (US *inf*) estupendo

Dane [deɪn] N danés(-esa) *m/f*

★**danger** ['deɪndʒəʳ] N peligro; (*risk*) riesgo; **~!** (*on sign*) ¡peligro!; **to be in ~ of** correr riesgo de; **out of ~** fuera de peligro

danger list N (Med): **to be on the ~** estar grave

★**dangerous** ['deɪndʒərəs] ADJ peligroso

dangerously ['deɪndʒərəslɪ] ADV peligrosamente; **~ ill** gravemente enfermo

danger zone N área or zona de peligro

dangle ['dæŋgl] VT colgar ▶ VI pender, estar colgado

★**Danish** ['deɪnɪʃ] ADJ danés(-esa) ▶ N (*Ling*) danés *m*

Danish pastry N *bollo de masa de hojaldre con pasas, manzana o crema*

dank [dæŋk] ADJ húmedo y malsano

dapper ['dæpəʳ] ADJ pulcro, apuesto

Dardanelles [dɑːdəˈnɛlz] NPL Dardanelos *mpl*

dare [dɛəʳ] VT: **to ~ sb to do** desafiar a algn a hacer ▶ VI: **to ~ (to) do sth** atreverse a hacer algo; **I ~ say** (I suppose) puede ser, a lo mejor; **I ~ say he'll turn up** puede ser que or quizás venga; **I daren't tell him** no me atrevo a decírselo

daredevil ['dɛədɛvl] N temerario(-a), atrevido(-a)

Dar-es-Salaam ['dɑːrɛssəˈlɑːm] N Dar es Salaam *m*

daring ['dɛərɪŋ] ADJ (*person*) osado; (*plan, escape*) atrevido ▶ N atrevimiento, osadía

★**dark** [dɑːk] ADJ oscuro; (*hair, complexion*) moreno; (*fig: cheerless*) triste, sombrío; **~ chocolate** chocolate *m* amargo; **it is/is getting ~** es de noche/ está oscureciendo ▶ N (*gen*) oscuridad *f*; (*night*) tinieblas *fpl*; **in the ~** a oscuras; **in the ~ about** (*fig*) ignorante de; **after ~** después del anochecer

darken ['dɑːkn] VT oscurecer; (*colour*) hacer más oscuro ▶ VI oscurecerse; (*cloud over*) nublarse

dark glasses NPL gafas *fpl* oscuras

dark horse N (*fig*) incógnita

darkly ['dɑːklɪ] ADV (*gloomily*) tristemente; (*sinisterly*) siniestramente

darkness ['dɑːknɪs] N (*in room*) oscuridad *f*; (*night*) tinieblas *fpl*

darkroom ['dɑːkrum] N cuarto oscuro

darling ['dɑːlɪŋ] ADJ, N querido(-a) *m/f*

darn [dɑːn] VT zurcir

dart [dɑːt] N dardo; (*in sewing*) pinza ▶ VI precipitarse; **to ~ away/along** salir/marchar disparado

dartboard ['dɑːtbɔːd] N diana

darts [dɑːts] N dardos *mpl*

dash [dæʃ] N (*small quantity: of liquid*) gota, chorrito; (: *of solid*) pizca; (*sign*) guión *m*; (: *long*) raya; **a ~ of soda** un poco or chorrito de sifón or soda ▶ VT (*break*) romper, estrellar; (*hopes*) defraudar ▶ VI precipitarse, ir de prisa

▶ **dash away, dash off** VI marcharse apresuradamente

dashboard ['dæʃbɔːd] N (Aut) salpicadero

dashing ['dæʃɪŋ] ADJ gallardo

dastardly ['dæstədlɪ] ADJ ruin, vil

DAT N ABBR (= *digital audio tape*) cas(s)et(t)e *m or f* digital

★**data** ['deɪtə] NPL datos *mpl*

database ['deɪtəbeɪs] N base *f* de datos

data capture N recogida de datos

data link N enlace *m* de datos

data processing N proceso or procesamiento de datos

data transmission N transmisión *f* de datos

★**date** [deɪt] N (*day*) fecha; (*with friend*) cita; (*fruit*) dátil *m*; **what's the ~ today?** ¿qué fecha es hoy?; **~ of birth** fecha de nacimiento; **closing ~** fecha tope; **to ~** adv hasta la fecha; **out of ~** pasado de moda; **up to ~** moderno; puesto al día; **to bring up to ~** (*correspondence, information*) poner al día; (*method*) actualizar; **to bring sb up to ~** poner a algn al corriente ▶ VT fechar; (*inf: girl etc*) salir con; **letter dated 5th July** or (US) **July 5th** carta fechada el 5 de julio

dated ['deɪtɪd] ADJ anticuado

date rape N *violación ocurrida durante una cita con un conocido*

date stamp N matasellos *m inv*; (*on fresh foods*) sello de fecha

dative ['deɪtɪv] N dativo

daub [dɔːb] VT embadurnar

★**daughter** ['dɔːtəʳ] N hija

daughter-in-law ['dɔːtərɪnlɔː] N nuera, hija política

daunting ['dɔːntɪŋ] ADJ desalentador(-a)

davenport ['dævnpɔːt] N escritorio; (US: *sofa*) sofá *m*

dawdle ['dɔːdl] VI (*waste time*) perder el tiempo; (*go slowly*) andar muy despacio; **to ~ over one's work** trabajar muy despacio

dawn [dɔːn] N alba, amanecer *m*; (*fig*) nacimiento; **at ~** al amanecer; **from ~ to dusk** de sol a sol ▶ VI amanecer; (*fig*): **it dawned on him that …** cayó en la cuenta de que …

dawn chorus N canto de los pájaros al amanecer

★**day** [deɪ] N día *m*; (*working day*) jornada; **the ~ before** el día anterior; **the ~ after tomorrow** pasado mañana; **the ~ before yesterday** anteayer, antes de ayer; **the ~ after, the following ~** el día siguiente; **by ~** de día; **~ by ~** día a día; **(on) the ~ that …** el día que …; **to work an eight-hour ~** trabajar ocho horas diarias or al día; **he works eight hours a ~** trabaja ocho horas al día; **paid by the ~** pagado por día; **these days, in the present ~** hoy en día

daybook ['deɪbuk] N (Brit) diario or libro de entradas y salidas

daybreak ['deɪbreɪk] N amanecer m

day-care centre ['deɪkɛə-] N centro de día; (for children) guardería infantil

daydream ['deɪdriːm] N ensueño ▶ VI soñar despierto

daylight ['deɪlaɪt] N luz f (del día)

daylight robbery N: **it's ~!** (fig: inf) ¡es un robo descarado!

Daylight Saving Time N (US) hora de verano

day-release course [deɪrɪ'liːs-] N curso de formación de un día a la semana

day return, day return ticket N (BRIT) billete m de ida y vuelta (en un día)

day shift N turno de día

daytime ['deɪtaɪm] N día m

day-to-day ['deɪtə'deɪ] ADJ cotidiano, diario; (expenses) diario; **on a ~ basis** día por día

day trip N excursión f (de un día)

day tripper N excursionista mf

daze [deɪz] VT (stun) aturdir ▶ N: **in a ~** aturdido

dazed [deɪzd] ADJ aturdido

dazzle ['dæzl] VT deslumbrar

dazzling ['dæzlɪŋ] ADJ (light, smile) deslumbrante; (colour) fuerte

dB ABBR = **decibel**

DBS N ABBR (= direct broadcasting by satellite) transmisión f vía satélite

DC ABBR (Elec) = **direct current**; (US) = **District of Columbia**

DD N ABBR (= Doctor of Divinity) título universitario ▶ ABBR = **direct debit**

dd. ABBR (Comm) = **delivered**

D-day ['diːdeɪ] N (fig) día m clave

DDS N ABBR (US: = Doctor of Dental Science; Doctor of Dental Surgery) títulos universitarios

DDT N ABBR (= dichlorodiphenyl trichloroethane) DDT m

DE ABBR (US) = **Delaware**

DEA N ABBR (US: = Drug Enforcement Administration) brigada especial dedicada a la lucha contra el tráfico de estupefacientes

deacon ['diːkən] N diácono

★**dead** [dɛd] ADJ muerto; (limb) dormido; (battery) agotado; **he was ~ on arrival** ingresó cadáver; **to shoot sb ~** matar a algn a tiros; **the ~** npl los muertos; **the line has gone ~** (Tel) se ha cortado la línea ▶ ADV (completely) totalmente; (exactly) justo; **~ tired** muerto (de cansancio); **to stop ~** parar en seco

dead beat ADJ: **to be ~** (inf) estar hecho polvo

deaden ['dɛdn] VT (blow, sound) amortiguar; (pain) calmar, aliviar

dead end N callejón m sin salida

dead-end ['dɛdɛnd] ADJ: **a ~ job** un trabajo sin porvenir

dead heat N (Sport) empate m

★**deadline** ['dɛdlaɪn] N fecha tope; **to work to a ~** trabajar con una fecha tope

deadlock ['dɛdlɔk] N punto muerto

dead loss N (inf): **to be a ~** (person) ser un inútil; (thing) ser una birria

deadly ['dɛdlɪ] ADJ mortal, fatal; **~ dull** aburridísimo

deadly nightshade [-'naɪtʃeɪd] N belladona

deadpan ['dɛdpæn] ADJ sin expresión

Dead Sea N: **the ~** el mar Muerto

dead season N (Tourism) temporada baja

★**deaf** [dɛf] ADJ sordo; **to turn a ~ ear to sth** hacer oídos sordos a algo

deaf-aid ['dɛfeɪd] N audífono

deaf-and-dumb ['dɛfən'dʌm] (!) ADJ (person) sordomudo; (alphabet) para sordomudos

deafen ['dɛfn] VT ensordecer

deafening ['dɛfnɪŋ] ADJ ensordecedor(a)

deaf-mute ['dɛfmjuːt] N (!) sordomudo(-a)

deafness ['dɛfnɪs] N sordera

★**deal** [diːl] N (agreement) pacto, convenio; (business) negocio, transacción f; (Cards) reparto; **a great ~ (of)** bastante, mucho; **it's a ~!** (inf) ¡trato hecho!, ¡de acuerdo!; **to do a ~ with sb** hacer un trato con algn; **he got a bad/fair ~ from them** le trataron mal/bien ▶ VT (pt, pp **dealt** [dɛlt]) (gen) dar; (card) repartir
▶ **deal in** VT FUS tratar en, comerciar en
▶ **deal with** VT FUS (people) tratar con; (problem) ocuparse de; (subject) tratar de

dealbreaker ['diːlbreɪkər] N: **it was a ~** fue un punto decisivo

dealer ['diːlər] N comerciante mf; (Cards) mano f

dealership ['diːləʃɪp] N concesionario

dealings ['diːlɪŋz] NPL (Comm) transacciones fpl; (relations) relaciones fpl

dealt [dɛlt] PT, PP of **deal**

dean [diːn] N (Rel) deán m; (Scol) decano(-a)

★**dear** [dɪər] ADJ querido; (expensive) caro; **~ me!** ¡Dios mío!; **D~ Sir/Madam** (in letter) Muy señor mío, Estimado señor/Estimada señora, De mí/nuestra (mayor) consideración (esp LAm); **D~ Mr/Mrs X** Estimado(-a) señor(a) X ▶ N: **my ~** querido(-a)

dearly ['dɪəlɪ] ADV (love) mucho; (pay) caro

dearth [dəːθ] N (of food, resources, money) escasez f

★**death** [dɛθ] N muerte f

deathbed ['dɛθbɛd] N lecho de muerte

death certificate N partida de defunción

death duties NPL (BRIT) derechos mpl de sucesión

deathly ['dɛθlɪ] ADJ mortal; (silence) profundo

death penalty N pena de muerte

death rate N tasa de mortalidad

death row N: **to be on ~** (US) estar condenado a muerte

death sentence N condena a muerte

death squad N escuadrón m de la muerte

death trap ['dɛθtræp] N lugar m (or vehículo etc) muy peligroso

deb [dɛb] N ABBR (inf) = **debutante**

debacle [deɪˈbɑːkl] N desastre m, catástrofe f

debar [dɪˈbɑːʳ] VT: **to ~ sb from doing** prohibir a algn hacer

debase [dɪˈbeɪs] VT degradar

debatable [dɪˈbeɪtəbl] ADJ discutible; **it is ~ whether ...** es discutible si ...

★**debate** [dɪˈbeɪt] N debate m ▶ VT discutir

debauched [dɪˈbɔːtʃt] ADJ vicioso

debauchery [dɪˈbɔːtʃərɪ] N libertinaje m

debenture [dɪˈbɛntʃəʳ] N (Comm) bono, obligación f

debenture capital N capital m hipotecario

debilitate [dɪˈbɪlɪteɪt] VT debilitar

debilitating [dɪˈbɪlɪteɪtɪŋ] ADJ (illness etc) debilitante

debit [ˈdɛbɪt] N debe m ▶ VT: **to ~ a sum to sb** or **to sb's account** cargar una suma en cuenta a algn

debit balance N saldo deudor or pasivo

debit card N tarjeta f de débito

debit note N nota de débito or cargo

debonair [dɛbəˈnɛəʳ] ADJ jovial, cortés(-esa)

debrief [diːˈbriːf] VT hacer dar parte

debriefing [diːˈbriːfɪŋ] N relación f (de un informe)

debris [ˈdɛbriː] N escombros mpl

debt [dɛt] N deuda; **to be in ~** tener deudas; **debts of £5000** deudas de cinco mil libras; **bad ~** deuda incobrable

debt collector N cobrador(a) m/f de deudas

debtor [ˈdɛtəʳ] N deudor(a) m/f

debug [ˈdiːˈbʌg] VT (Comput) depurar, limpiar

debunk [diːˈbʌŋk] VT (inf: theory) desprestigiar, desacreditar; (: claim) desacreditar; (: person, institution) desenmascarar

début [ˈdeɪbjuː] N presentación f

debutante [ˈdɛbjutænt] N debutante f

Dec. ABBR (= December) dic.

★**decade** [ˈdɛkeɪd] N década, decenio

decadence [ˈdɛkədəns] N decadencia

decadent [ˈdɛkədənt] ADJ decadente

de-caff [ˈdiːkæf] N (inf) descafeinado

decaffeinated [dɪˈkæfɪneɪtɪd] ADJ descafeinado

decamp [dɪˈkæmp] VI (inf) escaparse, largarse, rajarse (LAm)

decant [dɪˈkænt] VT decantar

decanter [dɪˈkæntəʳ] N jarra, decantador m

decathlon [dɪˈkæθlən] N decatlón m

decay [dɪˈkeɪ] N (fig) decadencia; (of building) desmoronamiento; (of tooth) caries f inv ▶ VI (rot) pudrirse; (fig) decaer

decease [dɪˈsiːs] N fallecimiento ▶ VI fallecer

deceased [dɪˈsiːst] N: **the ~** el (la) difunto(-a) ▶ ADJ difunto

deceit [dɪˈsiːt] N engaño

deceitful [dɪˈsiːtful] ADJ engañoso

deceive [dɪˈsiːv] VT engañar

decelerate [diːˈsɛləreɪt] VT moderar la marcha de ▶ VI decelerar

★**December** [dɪˈsɛmbəʳ] N diciembre m; see also **July**

decency [ˈdiːsənsɪ] N decencia

decent [ˈdiːsənt] ADJ (proper) decente; (person) amable, bueno

decently [ˈdiːsəntlɪ] ADV (respectably) decentemente; (kindly) amablemente

decentralization [diːsɛntrəlaɪˈzeɪʃən] N descentralización f

decentralize [diːˈsɛntrəlaɪz] VT descentralizar

deception [dɪˈsɛpʃən] N engaño

> **deception** no debe traducirse por decepción.

deceptive [dɪˈsɛptɪv] ADJ engañoso

decibel [ˈdɛsɪbɛl] N decibel(io) m

★**decide** [dɪˈsaɪd] VT (person) decidir; (question, argument) resolver; **to ~ to do/that** decidir hacer/que ▶ VI decidir; **to ~ on sth** tomar una decisión sobre algo; **to ~ against doing sth** decidir en contra de hacer algo

decided [dɪˈsaɪdɪd] ADJ (resolute) decidido; (clear, definite) indudable

decidedly [dɪˈsaɪdɪdlɪ] ADV decididamente

deciding [dɪˈsaɪdɪŋ] ADJ decisivo

deciduous [dɪˈsɪdjuəs] ADJ de hoja caduca

decimal [ˈdɛsɪməl] ADJ decimal; **to three ~ places** con tres cifras decimales ▶ N decimal f

decimalize [ˈdɛsɪməlaɪz] VT convertir al sistema decimal

decimal point N coma decimal

decimal system N sistema m métrico decimal

decimate [ˈdɛsɪmeɪt] VT diezmar

decipher [dɪˈsaɪfəʳ] VT descifrar

★**decision** [dɪˈsɪʒən] N decisión f; **to make a ~** tomar una decisión

decisive [dɪˈsaɪsɪv] ADJ (influence) decisivo; (manner, person) decidido; (reply) tajante

★**deck** [dɛk] N (Naut) cubierta; (of bus) piso; (of cards) baraja; **record ~** platina; **to go up on ~** subir a (la) cubierta; **below ~** en la bodega

deckchair [ˈdɛktʃɛəʳ] N tumbona

deckhand [ˈdɛkhænd] N marinero de cubierta

declaration [dɛkləˈreɪʃən] N declaración f

declare [dɪˈklɛəʳ] VT (gen) declarar

declassify [diːˈklæsɪfaɪ] VT permitir que salga a la luz

decline [dɪˈklaɪn] N decaimiento, decadencia; (lessening) disminución f; **~ in living standards** disminución f del nivel de vida ▶ VT rehusar; **to ~ to do sth** rehusar hacer algo ▶ VI (person, business) decaer; (strength) disminuir

declutch [ˈdiːˈklʌtʃ] VI desembragar

declutter [diːˈklʌtəʳ] VT deshacerse de lo que sobra en

decode [di:'kəud] VT descifrar; (Comput, TV) de(s)codificar

decoder [di:'kəudər] N (Comput, TV) de(s)codificador m

decompose [di:kəm'pəuz] VI descomponerse

decomposition [di:kɔmpə'zɪʃən] N descomposición f

decompression [di:kəm'preʃən] N descompresión f

decompression chamber N cámara de descompresión

decongestant [di:kən'dʒestənt] N descongestionante m

decontaminate [di:kən'tæmɪneɪt] VT descontaminar

decontrol [di:kən'trəul] VT (trade) quitar controles a; (prices) descongelar

décor ['deɪkɔːr] N decoración f; (Theat) decorado

★**decorate** ['dekəreɪt] VT (paint) pintar; (paper) empapelar; (adorn): **to ~ (with)** adornar (de), decorar (de)

decoration [dekə'reɪʃən] N adorno; (act) decoración f; (medal) condecoración f

decorative ['dekərətɪv] ADJ decorativo

decorator ['dekəreɪtər] N (also: **painter and decorator**) pintor(a) m/f decorador(a)

decorum [dɪ'kɔːrəm] N decoro

decoy ['di:kɔɪ] N señuelo; **police ~** trampa or señuelo policial

decrease N ['di:kri:s] disminución f; **to be on the ~** ir disminuyendo ▶ VT [dɪ'kri:s] disminuir, reducir ▶ VI reducirse

decreasing [dɪ'kri:sɪŋ] ADJ decreciente

decree [dɪ'kri:] N decreto; **~ absolute/nisi** sentencia absoluta/provisional de divorcio ▶ VT: **to ~ (that)** decretar (que)

decrepit [dɪ'krepɪt] ADJ (person) decrépito; (building) ruinoso

decry [dɪ'kraɪ] VT criticar, censurar

decrypt [di:'krɪpt] VT (Comput, Tel) descifrar

dedicate ['dedɪkeɪt] VT dedicar

dedicated ['dedɪkeɪtɪd] ADJ dedicado; (Comput) especializado; **~ word processor** procesador m de textos especializado or dedicado

dedication [dedɪ'keɪʃən] N (devotion) dedicación f; (in book) dedicatoria

deduce [dɪ'dju:s] VT deducir

deduct [dɪ'dʌkt] VT restar; (from wage etc) descontar, deducir

deduction [dɪ'dʌkʃən] N (amount deducted) descuento; (conclusion) deducción f, conclusión f

deed [di:d] N hecho, acto; (feat) hazaña; (Law) escritura; **~ of covenant** escritura de contrato

deem [di:m] VT (formal) juzgar, considerar; **to ~ it wise to do** considerar prudente hacer

★**deep** [di:p] ADJ profundo; (voice) bajo; (breath) profundo, a pleno pulmón; **to be four metres ~** tener cuatro metros de profundidad ▶ ADV: **the**

spectators stood 20 ~ los espectadores se formaron de 20 en fondo

deepen ['di:pn] VT ahondar, profundizar ▶ VI (darkness) intensificarse

deep-freeze ['di:p'fri:z] N arcón m congelador

deep-fry ['di:p'fraɪ] VT freír en aceite abundante

deeply ['di:plɪ] ADV (breathe) profundamente, a pleno pulmón; (interested, moved, grateful) profundamente, hondamente; **to regret sth ~** sentir algo profundamente

deep-rooted ['di:p'ru:tɪd] ADJ (prejudice, habit) profundamente arraigado; (affection) profundo

deep-sea ['di:p'si:] ADJ: **~ diver** buzo; **~ diving** buceo de altura

deep-seated ['di:p'si:tɪd] ADJ (beliefs) (profundamente) arraigado

deep-set ['di:p'set] ADJ (eyes) hundido

deep-vein thrombosis ['di:pveɪn-] N (Med) trombosis f venosa profunda

deer [dɪər] (pl **~**) N INV ciervo

deerstalker ['dɪəstɔːkər] N (hat) gorro de cazador

deface [dɪ'feɪs] VT desfigurar, mutilar

defamation [defə'meɪʃən] N difamación f

defamatory [dɪ'fæmətrɪ] ADJ difamatorio

default [dɪ'fɔːlt] VI faltar al pago; (Sport) no presentarse, no comparecer; **to ~ on a debt** dejar de pagar una deuda ▶ N (Comput) defecto; **by ~** (Law) en rebeldía; (Sport) por incomparecencia

defaulter [dɪ'fɔːltər] N (in debt) moroso(-a)

default option N (Comput) opción f por defecto

★**defeat** [dɪ'fi:t] N derrota ▶ VT derrotar, vencer; (fig: efforts) frustrar

defeatism [dɪ'fi:tɪzəm] N derrotismo

defeatist [dɪ'fi:tɪst] ADJ, N derrotista mf

defecate ['defəkeɪt] VI defecar

defect N ['di:fekt] defecto; **physical ~** defecto físico; **mental ~** (pej) deficiencia mental ▶ VI [dɪ'fekt]: **to ~ to the enemy** pasarse al enemigo

defective [dɪ'fektɪv] ADJ (gen) defectuoso; (pej: person) anormal

defector [dɪ'fektər] N tránsfuga mf

★**defence**, (US) **defense** [dɪ'fens] N defensa; **the Ministry of D~** el Ministerio de Defensa; **witness for the ~** testigo mf de descargo

defenceless [dɪ'fenslɪs] ADJ indefenso

defence spending N gasto militar

★**defend** [dɪ'fend] VT defender; (decision, action) defender; (opinion) mantener

defendant [dɪ'fendənt] N acusado(-a); (in civil case) demandado(-a)

defender [dɪ'fendər] N defensor(a) m/f; (Sport) defensa mf

defending champion [dɪ'fendɪŋ-] N (Sport) defensor(-a) m/f del título

defending counsel N (Law) abogado defensor

defense [dɪ'fens] N (US) = **defence**

defensive [dɪˈfɛnsɪv] ADJ defensivo ▸ N defensiva; **on the ~** a la defensiva

defer [dɪˈfəːʳ] VT (postpone) aplazar ▸ VI: **to ~ to** diferir a; (submit): **to ~ to sb/sb's opinion** someterse a algn/a la opinión de algn

deference [ˈdɛfərəns] N deferencia, respeto; **out of** or **in ~ to** por respeto a

deferential [dɛfəˈrɛnʃəl] ADJ respetuoso

deferred [dɪˈfəːd] ADJ: **~ creditor** acreedor(a) m/f diferido(-a)

defiance [dɪˈfaɪəns] N desafío; **in ~ of** en contra de

defiant [dɪˈfaɪənt] ADJ (insolent) insolente; (challenging) retador(a), desafiante

defiantly [dɪˈfaɪəntlɪ] ADV con aire de desafío

deficiency [dɪˈfɪʃənsɪ] N (lack) falta; (Comm) déficit m; (defect) defecto

deficient [dɪˈfɪʃənt] ADJ (lacking) insuficiente; (incomplete) incompleto; (defective) defectuoso; **~ in** deficiente en

deficit [ˈdɛfɪsɪt] N déficit m

defile [dɪˈfaɪl] VT manchar; (violate) violar

define [dɪˈfaɪn] VT (Comput) definir; (limits etc) determinar

definite [ˈdɛfɪnɪt] ADJ (fixed) determinado; (clear, obvious) claro; **he was ~ about it** no dejó lugar a dudas (sobre ello)

★**definitely** [ˈdɛfɪnɪtlɪ] ADV: **he's ~ mad** no cabe duda de que está loco

definition [dɛfɪˈnɪʃən] N definición f

definitive [dɪˈfɪnɪtɪv] ADJ definitivo

deflate [diːˈfleɪt] VT (gen) desinflar; (pompous person) quitar or rebajar los humos a; (Econ) deflacionar

deflation [diːˈfleɪʃən] N (Econ) deflación f

deflationary [diːˈfleɪʃənrɪ] ADJ (Econ) deflacionario

deflect [dɪˈflɛkt] VT desviar

defog [diːˈfɒg] VT desempañar

defogger [diːˈfɒgəʳ] N (US Aut) dispositivo antivaho

deform [dɪˈfɔːm] VT deformar

deformed [dɪˈfɔːmd] ADJ deformado

deformity [dɪˈfɔːmɪtɪ] N deformación f

Defra N ABBR (BRIT) = **Department for Environment, Food and Rural Affairs**

defraud [dɪˈfrɔːd] VT estafar; **to ~ sb of sth** estafar algo a algn

defray [dɪˈfreɪ] VT: **to ~ sb's expenses** reembolsar a algn los gastos

defriend [diːˈfrɛnd] VT (Internet) quitar de amigo a; **he has defriended her on Facebook** la ha quitado de amiga en Facebook

defrost [diːˈfrɒst] VT (frozen food, fridge) descongelar

defroster [diːˈfrɒstəʳ] N (US) eliminador m de vaho

deft [dɛft] ADJ diestro, hábil

defunct [dɪˈfʌŋkt] ADJ difunto; (organization etc) ya desaparecido

defuse [diːˈfjuːz] VT desarmar; (situation) calmar, apaciguar

defy [dɪˈfaɪ] VT (resist) oponerse a; (challenge) desafiar; (order) contravenir; **it defies description** resulta imposible describirlo

degenerate VI [dɪˈdʒɛnəreɪt] degenerar ▸ ADJ [dɪˈdʒɛnərɪt] degenerado

degradation [dɛgrəˈdeɪʃən] N degradación f

degrade [dɪˈgreɪd] VT degradar

degrading [dɪˈgreɪdɪŋ] ADJ degradante

★**degree** [dɪˈgriː] N grado; (Scol) título; **10 degrees below freezing** 10 grados bajo cero; **to have a ~ in maths** ser licenciado(-a) en matemáticas; **by degrees** (gradually) poco a poco, por etapas; **to some ~, to a certain ~** hasta cierto punto; **a considerable ~ of risk** un gran índice de riesgo

dehydrated [diːhaɪˈdreɪtɪd] ADJ deshidratado; (milk) en polvo

dehydration [diːhaɪˈdreɪʃən] N deshidratación f

de-ice [diːˈaɪs] VT (windscreen) deshelar

de-icer [diːˈaɪsəʳ] N descongelador m

deign [deɪn] VI: **to ~ to do** dignarse hacer

deity [ˈdiːɪtɪ] N deidad f, divinidad f

déjà vu [deɪʒɑːˈvuː] N: **I had a sense of ~** sentía como si ya lo hubiera vivido

dejected [dɪˈdʒɛktɪd] ADJ abatido, desanimado

dejection [dɪˈdʒɛkʃən] N abatimiento

Del. ABBR (US) = **Delaware**

★**delay** [dɪˈleɪ] VT demorar, aplazar; (person) entretener; (train) retrasar; (payment) aplazar ▸ VI tardar ▸ N demora, retraso; **without ~** en seguida, sin tardar

delayed-action [dɪleɪdˈækʃən] ADJ (bomb etc) de acción retardada

delectable [dɪˈlɛktəbl] ADJ (person) encantador(-a); (food) delicioso

delegate N [ˈdɛlɪgɪt] delegado(-a) ▸ VT [ˈdɛlɪgeɪt] (person) delegar en; (task) delegar; **to ~ sth to sb/sb to do sth** delegar algo en algn/en algn para hacer algo

delegation [dɛlɪˈgeɪʃən] N (of work etc) delegación f

delete [dɪˈliːt] VT suprimir, tachar; (Comput) suprimir, borrar

Delhi [ˈdɛlɪ] N Delhi m

deli [ˈdɛlɪ] N = **delicatessen**

deliberate ADJ [dɪˈlɪbərɪt] (intentional) intencionado; (slow) pausado, lento ▸ VI [dɪˈlɪbəreɪt] deliberar

deliberately [dɪˈlɪbərɪtlɪ] ADV (on purpose) a propósito; (slowly) pausadamente

deliberation [dɪlɪbəˈreɪʃən] N (consideration) reflexión f; (discussion) deliberación f, discusión f

delicacy [ˈdɛlɪkəsɪ] N delicadeza; (choice food) manjar m

delicate ['dɛlɪkɪt] ADJ (gen) delicado; (fragile) frágil

delicately ['dɛlɪkɪtlɪ] ADV con delicadeza, delicadamente; (act, express) con discreción

delicatessen [dɛlɪkə'tɛsn] N tienda especializada en alimentos de calidad

delicious [dɪ'lɪʃəs] ADJ delicioso, rico

delight [dɪ'laɪt] N (feeling) placer m, deleite m; (object) encanto, delicia; **to take ~ in** deleitarse en ▶ VT encantar, deleitar

★**delighted** [dɪ'laɪtɪd] ADJ: **~ (at or with/to do)** encantado (con/de hacer); **to be ~ that** estar encantado de que; **I'd be ~** con mucho or todo gusto

delightful [dɪ'laɪtful] ADJ encantador(a), delicioso

delimit [di:'lɪmɪt] VT delimitar

delineate [dɪ'lɪnɪeɪt] VT delinear

delinquency [dɪ'lɪŋkwənsɪ] N delincuencia

delinquent [dɪ'lɪŋkwənt] ADJ, N delincuente mf

delirious [dɪ'lɪrɪəs] ADJ (Med, fig) delirante; **to be ~** delirar, desvariar

delirium [dɪ'lɪrɪəm] N delirio

★**deliver** [dɪ'lɪvər] VT (distribute) repartir; (hand over) entregar; (message) comunicar; (speech) pronunciar; (blow) lanzar, dar; (Med) asistir al parto de

deliverance [dɪ'lɪvrəns] N liberación f

delivery [dɪ'lɪvərɪ] N reparto; entrega; (of speaker) modo de expresarse; (Med) parto, alumbramiento; **to take ~ of** recibir

delivery note N nota de entrega

delivery van N furgoneta de reparto

delta ['dɛltə] N delta m

delude [dɪ'lu:d] VT engañar

deluge ['dɛlju:dʒ] N diluvio ▶ VT (fig): **to ~ (with)** inundar (de)

delusion [dɪ'lu:ʒən] N ilusión f, engaño

de luxe [də'lʌks] ADJ de lujo

delve [dɛlv] VI: **to ~ into** hurgar en

Dem. ABBR (US Pol) = **democrat; democratic**

★**demand** [dɪ'mɑ:nd] VT (gen) exigir; (rights) reclamar; (need) requerir; **to ~ sth (from or of sb)** exigir algo (a algn) ▶ N (gen) exigencia; (claim) reclamación f; (Econ) demanda; **to be in ~** ser muy solicitado; **on ~** a solicitud

demanding [dɪ'mɑ:ndɪŋ] ADJ (boss) exigente; (work) absorbente

demarcation [di:mɑ:'keɪʃən] N demarcación f

demarcation dispute N conflicto de definición or demarcación del trabajo

demean [dɪ'mi:n] VT: **to ~ o.s.** rebajarse

demeanour, (US) **demeanor** [dɪ'mi:nər] N porte m, conducta, comportamiento

demented [dɪ'mɛntɪd] ADJ demente

demi- ['dɛmɪ] PREF semi..., medio...

demilitarize [di:'mɪlɪtəraɪz] VT desmilitarizar; **demilitarized zone** zona desmilitarizada

demise [dɪ'maɪz] N (death) fallecimiento

demist [di:'mɪst] VT (Aut) eliminar el vaho de

demister [di:'mɪstər] N (Aut) eliminador m de vaho

demo ['dɛməu] N ABBR (inf: = demonstration) manifestación f

demobilization [di:'məubɪlaɪ'zeɪʃən] N desmovilización f

★**democracy** [dɪ'mɒkrəsɪ] N democracia

democrat ['dɛməkræt] N demócrata mf

★**democratic** [dɛmə'krætɪk] ADJ democrático; **the D~ Party** el partido demócrata (estadounidense)

demography [dɪ'mɒgrəfɪ] N demografía

demolish [dɪ'mɒlɪʃ] VT derribar, demoler; (fig: argument) destruir

demolition [dɛmə'lɪʃən] N derribo, demolición f

demon ['di:mən] N (evil spirit) demonio ▶ CPD temible

★**demonstrate** ['dɛmənstreɪt] VT demostrar ▶ VI manifestarse; **to ~ (for/against)** manifestarse (a favor de/en contra de)

★**demonstration** [dɛmən'streɪʃən] N (Pol) manifestación f; (proof) prueba, demostración f; **to hold a ~** (Pol) hacer una manifestación

demonstrative [dɪ'mɒnstrətɪv] ADJ (person) expresivo; (Ling) demostrativo

demonstrator ['dɛmənstreɪtər] N (Pol) manifestante mf

demoralize [dɪ'mɒrəlaɪz] VT desmoralizar

demote [dɪ'məut] VT degradar

demotion [dɪ'məuʃən] N degradación f; (Comm) descenso

demur [dɪ'mər] VI: **to ~ (at)** hacer objeciones (a), vacilar (ante) ▶ N: **without ~** sin objeción

demure [dɪ'mjuər] ADJ recatado

demurrage [dɪ'mʌrɪdʒ] N sobrestadía

den [dɛn] N (of animal) guarida; (study) estudio

denationalization [di:næʃnəlaɪ'zeɪʃən] N desnacionalización f

denationalize [di:'næʃnəlaɪz] VT desnacionalizar

denatured alcohol [di:'neɪtʃəd-] N (US) alcohol m desnaturalizado

denial [dɪ'naɪəl] N (refusal) denegación f; (of report etc) desmentido

denier ['dɛnɪər] N denier m

denim ['dɛnɪm] N tela vaquera; see also **denims**

denim jacket N chaqueta vaquera, saco vaquero (LAm)

denims ['dɛnɪms] NPL vaqueros mpl

denizen ['dɛnɪzn] N (inhabitant) habitante mf; (foreigner) residente mf extranjero(-a)

★**Denmark** ['dɛnmɑ:k] N Dinamarca

denomination [dɪnɒmɪ'neɪʃən] N valor m; (Rel) confesión f

denominator [dɪ'nɒmɪneɪtər] N denominador m

509

denote [dɪ'nəut] vт indicar, significar

denounce [dɪ'nauns] vт denunciar

dense [dɛns] ADJ (*thick*) espeso; (*foliage etc*) tupido; (*inf: stupid*) torpe

densely ['dɛnslɪ] ADV: **~ populated** con una alta densidad de población

density ['dɛnsɪtɪ] N densidad *f*

dent [dɛnt] N abolladura ▶ vт (*also:* **make a dent in**) abollar

dental ['dɛntl] ADJ dental

dental floss [-flɔs] N seda dental

dental surgeon N odontólogo(-a)

dental surgery N clínica dental, consultorio dental

dentifrice ['dɛntɪfrɪs] N dentífrico

★**dentist** ['dɛntɪst] ADV n dentista *mf*; **~'s surgery** (BRIT) clínica dental, consultorio dental

dentistry ['dɛntɪstrɪ] N odontología

dentures ['dɛntʃəz] NPL dentadura *sg* (postiza)

denude [dɪ'njuːd] vт: **to ~ of** despojar de

denunciation [dɪnʌnsɪ'eɪʃən] N denuncia, denunciación *f*

deny [dɪ'naɪ] vт negar; (*charge*) rechazar; (*report*) desmentir; **to ~ o.s.** privarse (de); **he denies having said it** niega haberlo dicho

deodorant [diː'əudərənt] N desodorante *m*

depart [dɪ'pɑːt] vι irse, marcharse; (*train*) salir; **to ~ from** (*fig: differ from*) apartarse de

departed [dɪ'pɑːtɪd] ADJ (*bygone: days, glory*) pasado; (*dead*) difunto ▶ N: **the (dear) ~** el difunto/la difunta/los difuntos/las difuntas

★**department** [dɪ'pɑːtmənt] N (*Comm*) sección *f*; (*Scol*) departamento; (*Pol*) ministerio; **that's not my ~** (*fig*) no tiene que ver conmigo; **D~ of State** (US) Ministerio de Asuntos Exteriores

departmental [diːpɑːt'mɛntl] ADJ (*dispute*) departamental; (*meeting*) departamental, de departamento; **~ manager** jefe(-a) *m/f* de sección *or* de departamento *or* de servicio

department store N grandes almacenes *mpl*

★**departure** [dɪ'pɑːtʃər] N partida, ida; (*of train*) salida; **a new ~** un nuevo rumbo

departure lounge N (*at airport*) sala de embarque

★**depend** [dɪ'pɛnd] vι: **to ~ (up)on** (*be dependent upon*) depender de; (*rely on*) contar con; **it depends** depende, según; **depending on the result** según el resultado

dependable [dɪ'pɛndəbl] ADJ (*person*) formal, serio

dependant [dɪ'pɛndənt] N dependiente *mf*

dependence [dɪ'pɛndəns] N dependencia

dependent [dɪ'pɛndənt] ADJ: **to be ~ (on)** depender (de) ▶ N = **dependant**

depict [dɪ'pɪkt] vт (*in picture*) pintar; (*describe*) representar

depilatory [dɪ'pɪlətrɪ] N (*also:* **depilatory cream**) depilatorio

depleted [dɪ'pliːtɪd] ADJ reducido

deplorable [dɪ'plɔːrəbl] ADJ deplorable

deplore [dɪ'plɔːr] vт deplorar

deploy [dɪ'plɔɪ] vт desplegar

depopulate [diː'pɔpjuleɪt] vт despoblar

depopulation ['diːpɔpju'leɪʃən] N despoblación *f*

deport [dɪ'pɔːt] vт deportar

deportation [diːpɔː'teɪʃən] N deportación *f*

deportation order N orden *f* de expulsión *or* deportación

deportee [diːpɔː'tiː] N deportado(-a)

deportment [dɪ'pɔːtmənt] N comportamiento

depose [dɪ'pəuz] vт deponer

★**deposit** [dɪ'pɔzɪt] N depósito; (*Chem*) sedimento; (*of ore, oil*) yacimiento; **to put down a ~ of £50** dejar un depósito de 50 libras ▶ vт (*gen*) depositar

deposit account N (BRIT) cuenta de ahorros

depositor [dɪ'pɔzɪtər] N depositante *mf*, cuentacorrentista *mf*

depository [dɪ'pɔzɪtərɪ] N almacén *m* depositario

depot ['dɛpəu] N (*storehouse*) depósito; (*for vehicles*) parque *m*

deprave [dɪ'preɪv] vт depravar

depraved [dɪ'preɪvd] ADJ depravado, vicioso

depravity [dɪ'prævɪtɪ] N depravación *f*, vicio

deprecate ['dɛprɪkeɪt] vт desaprobar, lamentar

deprecating ['dɛprɪkeɪtɪŋ] ADJ (*disapproving*) de desaprobación; (*apologetic*): **a ~ smile** una sonrisa de disculpa

depreciate [dɪ'priːʃeɪt] vι depreciarse, perder valor

depreciation [dɪpriːʃɪ'eɪʃən] N depreciación *f*

depress [dɪ'prɛs] vт deprimir; (*press down*) apretar

depressant [dɪ'prɛsnt] N (*Med*) calmante *m*, sedante *m*

depressed [dɪ'prɛst] ADJ deprimido; (*Comm: market, economy*) deprimido; (: *area*) deprimido (económicamente); **to get ~** deprimirse

depressing [dɪ'prɛsɪŋ] ADJ deprimente

depression [dɪ'prɛʃən] N depresión *f*; **the economy is in a state of ~** la economía está deprimida

deprivation [dɛprɪ'veɪʃən] N privación *f*; (*loss*) pérdida

deprive [dɪ'praɪv] vт: **to ~ sb of** privar a algn de

deprived [dɪ'praɪvd] ADJ necesitado

dept. ABBR (= *department*) dpto.

★**depth** [dɛpθ] N profundidad *f*; **at a ~ of three metres** a tres metros de profundidad; **to be out of one's ~** (*swimmer*) perder pie; (*fig*) sentirse perdido; **to study sth in ~** estudiar algo a fondo; **in the depths of** en lo más hondo de

depth charge N carga de profundidad

deputation [dɛpju'teɪʃən] N delegación f

deputize ['dɛpjutaɪz] VI: **to ~ for sb** sustituir a algn

deputy ['dɛpjutɪ] ADJ: **~ head** subdirector(a) m/f ▶ N sustituto(-a), suplente mf; (Pol) diputado(-a); (agent) representante mf

deputy leader N vicepresidente(-a) m/f

derail [dɪ'reɪl] VT: **to be derailed** descarrilarse

derailment [dɪ'reɪlmənt] N descarrilamiento

deranged [dɪ'reɪndʒd] ADJ trastornado

derby ['dɑ:bɪ] N (US) hongo

deregulate [di:'rɛgjuleɪt] VT desreglamentar

deregulation [di:rɛgju'leɪʃən] N desreglamentación f

derelict ['dɛrɪlɪkt] ADJ abandonado

deride [dɪ'raɪd] VT ridiculizar, mofarse de

derision [dɪ'rɪʒən] N irrisión f, mofas fpl

derisive [dɪ'raɪsɪv] ADJ burlón(-ona)

derisory [dɪ'raɪzərɪ] ADJ (sum) irrisorio; (laughter, person) burlón(-ona), irónico

derivation [dɛrɪ'veɪʃən] N derivación f

derivative [dɪ'rɪvətɪv] N derivado ▶ ADJ (work) poco original

derive [dɪ'raɪv] VT derivar; (benefit etc) obtener ▶ VI: **to ~ from** derivarse de

derived [dɪ'raɪvd] ADJ derivado

dermatitis [də:mə'taɪtɪs] N dermatitis f

dermatology [də:mə'tɔlədʒɪ] N dermatología

derogatory [dɪ'rɔgətərɪ] ADJ despectivo

derrick ['dɛrɪk] N torre f de perforación

derv [də:v] N (BRIT) gasoil m

descend [dɪ'sɛnd] VT, VI descender, bajar; **to ~ from** descender de; **in descending order of importance** de mayor a menor importancia ▶ **descend on** VT FUS (enemy, angry person) caer sobre; (misfortune) sobrevenir; (gloom, silence) invadir; **visitors descended on us** las visitas nos invadieron

descendant [dɪ'sɛndənt] N descendiente mf

descent [dɪ'sɛnt] N descenso; (Geo) pendiente f, declive m; (origin) descendencia

★**describe** [dɪs'kraɪb] VT describir

★**description** [dɪs'krɪpʃən] N descripción f; (sort) clase f, género; **of every ~** de toda clase

descriptive [dɪs'krɪptɪv] ADJ descriptivo

desecrate ['dɛsɪkreɪt] VT profanar

desegregation [di:sɛgrɪ'geɪʃən] N desegregación f

★**desert** N ['dɛzət] desierto ▶ VT [dɪ'zə:t] abandonar, desamparar ▶ VI [dɪ'zə:t] (Mil) desertar; see also **deserts**

deserted [dɪ'zə:tɪd] ADJ desierto

deserter [dɪ'zə:tə'] N desertor(-a) m/f

desertion [dɪ'zə:ʃən] N deserción f

desert island N isla desierta

deserts [dɪ'zə:ts] NPL: **to get one's just ~** llevarse su merecido

★**deserve** [dɪ'zə:v] VT merecer, ser digno de, ameritar (LAM)

deservedly [dɪ'zə:vɪdlɪ] ADV con razón

deserving [dɪ'zə:vɪŋ] ADJ (person) digno; (action, cause) meritorio

desiccated ['dɛsɪkeɪtɪd] ADJ desecado

★**design** [dɪ'zaɪn] N (sketch) bosquejo; (of dress, car) diseño; (pattern) dibujo; **industrial ~** diseño industrial; **to have designs on sb** tener la(s) mira(s) puesta(s) en algn ▶ VT (gen) diseñar; **to be designed for sb/sth** estar hecho para algn/ algo

design and technology N (BRIT Scol) diseño y tecnología

designate VT ['dɛzɪgneɪt] (appoint) nombrar; (destine) designar ▶ ADJ ['dɛzɪgnɪt] designado

designation [dɛzɪg'neɪʃən] N (appointment) nombramiento; (name) denominación f

★**designer** [dɪ'zaɪnə'] N diseñador(a) m/f

designer baby N bebé m de diseño

desirability [dɪzaɪərə'bɪlɪtɪ] N ventaja, atractivo

desirable [dɪ'zaɪərəbl] ADJ (proper) deseable; (attractive) atractivo; **it is ~ that** es conveniente que

desire [dɪ'zaɪə'] N deseo ▶ VT desear; **to ~ sth/to do sth/that** desear algo/hacer algo/que

desirous [dɪ'zaɪərəs] ADJ deseoso

desist [dɪ'zɪst] VI: **to ~ (from)** desistir (de)

★**desk** [dɛsk] N (in office) escritorio; (for pupil) pupitre m; (in hotel, at airport) recepción f; (BRIT: in shop, restaurant) caja

desktop ['dɛsktɔp] N (Comput) escritorio

desktop computer N ordenador m de sobremesa

desktop publishing N autoedición f

desolate ['dɛsəlɪt] ADJ (place) desierto; (person) afligido

desolation [dɛsə'leɪʃən] N (of place) desolación f; (of person) aflicción f

despair [dɪs'pɛə'] N desesperación f; **in ~** desesperado ▶ VI: **to ~ of** desesperar de

despatch [dɪs'pætʃ] N, VT = **dispatch**

★**desperate** ['dɛspərɪt] ADJ desesperado; (fugitive) peligroso; (measures) extremo; **we are getting ~** estamos al borde de desesperación; **to be ~ for sth/to do** necesitar urgentemente algo/hacer

desperately ['dɛspərɪtlɪ] ADV desesperadamente; (very) terriblemente, gravemente; **~ ill** gravemente enfermo

desperation [dɛspə'reɪʃən] N desesperación f; **in ~** desesperado

despicable [dɪs'pɪkəbl] ADJ vil, despreciable

despise [dɪs'paɪz] VT despreciar

despite [dɪs'paɪt] PREP a pesar de, pese a

despondent [dɪs'pɔndənt] ADJ deprimido, abatido

despot ['dɛspɔt] N déspota mf

dessert [dɪˈzɜːt] N postre m

dessertspoon [dɪˈzɜːtspuːn] N cuchara (de postre)

destabilize [diːˈsteɪbɪlaɪz] VT desestabilizar

destination [dɛstɪˈneɪʃən] N destino

destine [ˈdɛstɪn] VT destinar

destined [ˈdɛstɪnd] ADJ: **~ for London** con destino a Londres

destiny [ˈdɛstɪnɪ] N destino

destitute [ˈdɛstɪtjuːt] ADJ desamparado, indigente

destitution [dɛstɪˈtjuːʃən] N indigencia, miseria

★**destroy** [dɪsˈtrɔɪ] VT destruir; (finish) acabar con

destroyer [dɪsˈtrɔɪəʳ] N (Naut) destructor m

destruction [dɪsˈtrʌkʃən] N destrucción f; (fig) ruina

destructive [dɪsˈtrʌktɪv] ADJ destructivo, destructor(a)

desultory [ˈdɛsəltərɪ] ADJ (reading) poco metódico; (conversation) inconexo; (contact) intermitente

detach [dɪˈtætʃ] VT separar; (unstick) despegar

detachable [dɪˈtætʃəbl] ADJ separable; (Tech) desmontable

detached [dɪˈtætʃt] ADJ (attitude) objetivo, imparcial

detached house N chalé m, chalet m

detachment [dɪˈtætʃmənt] N separación f; (Mil) destacamento; (fig) objetividad f, imparcialidad f

★**detail** [ˈdiːteɪl] N detalle m; (Mil) destacamento; **in ~** detalladamente; **to go into ~(s)** entrar en detalles ▸ VT detallar; (Mil) destacar

detailed [ˈdiːteɪld] ADJ detallado

detain [dɪˈteɪn] VT retener; (in captivity) detener

detainee [diːteɪˈniː] N detenido(-a)

detect [dɪˈtɛkt] VT (discover) descubrir; (Med, Police) identificar; (Mil, Radar, Tech) detectar; (notice) percibir

detection [dɪˈtɛkʃən] N descubrimiento; identificación f; **crime ~** investigación f; **to escape ~** (criminal) escaparse sin ser descubierto; (mistake) pasar inadvertido

★**detective** [dɪˈtɛktɪv] N detective mf

detective story N novela policíaca

detector [dɪˈtɛktəʳ] N detector m

détente [deɪˈtɑːnt] N distensión f, detente f

★**detention** [dɪˈtɛnʃən] N detención f, arresto; (Scol) castigo

deter [dɪˈtɜːʳ] VT (dissuade) disuadir; (prevent) impedir; **to ~ sb from doing sth** disuadir a algn de que haga algo

detergent [dɪˈtɜːdʒənt] N detergente m

deteriorate [dɪˈtɪərɪəreɪt] VI deteriorarse

deterioration [dɪtɪərɪəˈreɪʃən] N deterioro

determination [dɪtɜːmɪˈneɪʃən] N resolución f

determine [dɪˈtɜːmɪn] VT determinar; **to ~ to do sth** decidir hacer algo

determined [dɪˈtɜːmɪnd] ADJ: **to be ~ to do sth** estar decidido or resuelto a hacer algo; **a ~ effort** un esfuerzo enérgico

deterrence [dɪˈtɛrns] N disuasión f

deterrent [dɪˈtɛrənt] N fuerza de disuasión; **to act as a ~** servir para prevenir

detest [dɪˈtɛst] VT aborrecer

detestable [dɪˈtɛstəbl] ADJ aborrecible

dethrone [diːˈθrəun] VT destronar

detonate [ˈdɛtəneɪt] VI estallar ▸ VT hacer detonar

detonator [ˈdɛtəneɪtəʳ] N detonador m, fulminante m

detour [ˈdiːtuəʳ] N (gen, US Aut: diversion) desvío; **to make a ~** dar un rodeo ▸ VT (US: traffic) desviar

detox [ˈdiːtɔks] (inf) VI desintoxicarse ▸ N desintoxicación f

detoxification [diːtɔksɪfɪˈkeɪʃən] N desintoxicación f

detoxify [diːˈtɔksɪfaɪ] VI desintoxicarse

detract [dɪˈtrækt] VI: **to ~ from** quitar mérito a, restar valor a

detractor [dɪˈtræktəʳ] N detractor(-a) m/f

detriment [ˈdɛtrɪmənt] N: **to the ~ of** en perjuicio de; **without ~ to** sin detrimento de, sin perjuicio para

detrimental [dɛtrɪˈmɛntl] ADJ: **~ (to)** perjudicial (a)

deuce [djuːs] N (Tennis) cuarenta iguales

devaluation [dɪvæljuˈeɪʃən] N devaluación f

devalue [dɪˈvæljuː] VT devaluar

devastate [ˈdɛvəsteɪt] VT devastar; **he was devastated by the news** las noticias le dejaron desolado

devastating [ˈdɛvəsteɪtɪŋ] ADJ devastador(-a); (fig) arrollador(-a)

devastation [dɛvəsˈteɪʃən] N devastación f, ruina

★**develop** [dɪˈvɛləp] VT desarrollar; (Phot) revelar; (disease) contraer; (habit) adquirir; **this land is to be developed** se va a construir en este terreno; **to ~ a taste for sth** tomar gusto a algo ▸ VI desarrollarse; (advance) progresar; **to ~ into** transformarse or convertirse en

developer [dɪˈvɛləpəʳ] N (property developer) promotor(-a) m/f

developing country N país m en (vías de) desarrollo

development [dɪˈvɛləpmənt] N desarrollo; (advance) progreso; (of affair, case) desenvolvimiento; (of land) urbanización f

development area N zona de fomento or desarrollo

deviant [ˈdiːvɪənt] ADJ anómalo, pervertido

deviate [ˈdiːvɪeɪt] VI: **to ~ (from)** desviarse (de)

deviation [diːvɪˈeɪʃən] N desviación f

device [dɪˈvaɪs] N (scheme) estratagema,

recurso; (*apparatus*) aparato, mecanismo; (*explosive device*) artefacto explosivo

devil ['dɛvl] N diablo, demonio

devilish ['dɛvlɪʃ] ADJ diabólico

devil-may-care ['dɛvlmeɪ'kɛəʳ] ADJ despreocupado

devil's advocate N: **to play (the) ~** hacer de abogado del diablo

devious ['di:vɪəs] ADJ intricado, enrevesado; (*person*) taimado

devise [dɪ'vaɪz] VT idear, inventar

devoid [dɪ'vɔɪd] ADJ: **~ of** desprovisto de

devolution [di:və'lu:ʃən] N (*Pol*) descentralización f

devolve [dɪ'vɔlv] VI: **to ~ (up)on** recaer sobre

devote [dɪ'vəut] VT: **to ~ sth to** dedicar algo a

devoted [dɪ'vəutɪd] ADJ (*loyal*) leal, fiel; **to be ~ to sb** querer con devoción a algn; **the book is ~ to politics** el libro trata de política

devotee [dɛvəu'ti:] N devoto(-a)

devotion [dɪ'vəuʃən] N dedicación f; (*Rel*) devoción f

devour [dɪ'vauəʳ] VT devorar

devout [dɪ'vaut] ADJ devoto

dew [dju:] N rocío

dexterity [dɛks'tɛrɪtɪ] N destreza

dexterous, dextrous ['dɛkstrəs] ADJ (*skilful*) diestro, hábil; (*movement*) ágil

DfE N ABBR (*Brit*) = **Department for Education**

dg ABBR (= *decigram*) dg

diabetes [daɪə'bi:ti:z] N diabetes f

diabetic [daɪə'bɛtɪk] N diabético(-a) ▸ ADJ diabético; (*chocolate, jam*) para diabéticos

diabolical [daɪə'bɔlɪkəl] ADJ diabólico; (*inf: dreadful*) horrendo, horroroso

diagnose ['daɪəgnəuz] VT diagnosticar

diagnosis [daɪəg'nəusɪs] (*pl* **diagnoses** [-si:z]) N diagnóstico

diagonal [daɪ'ægənl] ADJ diagonal ▸ N diagonal f

diagram ['daɪəgræm] N diagrama m, esquema m

dial ['daɪəl] N esfera; (*of radio*) dial m; (*tuner*) sintonizador m; (*of phone*) disco ▸ VT (*number*) marcar, discar (*Lam*); **to ~ a wrong number** equivocarse de número; **can I ~ London direct?** ¿puedo marcar un número de Londres directamente?

dial. ABBR = **dialect**

dial code N (*US*) prefijo

dialect ['daɪəlɛkt] N dialecto

dialling code ['daɪəlɪŋ-] N (*Brit*) prefijo

dialling tone N (*Brit*) señal f or tono de marcar

★**dialogue**, (*US*) **dialog** ['daɪəlɔg] N diálogo

dial tone N (*US*) señal f or tono de marcar

dialysis [daɪ'ælɪsɪs] N diálisis f

diameter [daɪ'æmɪtəʳ] N diámetro

diametrically [daɪə'mɛtrɪklɪ] ADV: **~ opposed (to)** diametralmente opuesto (a)

diamond ['daɪəmənd] N diamante m ■ **diamonds** NPL (*Cards*) diamantes mpl

diamond ring N anillo or sortija de diamantes

diaper ['daɪəpəʳ] N (*US*) pañal m

diaphragm ['daɪəfræm] N diafragma m

diarrhoea, (*US*) **diarrhea** [daɪə'ri:ə] N diarrea

★**diary** ['daɪərɪ] N (*daily account*) diario; (*book*) agenda; **to keep a ~** escribir un diario

diatribe ['daɪətraɪb] N: **~ (against)** diatriba (contra)

dice [daɪs] N (*pl* **~**) dado ▸ VT (*Culin*) cortar en cuadritos

dicey ['daɪsɪ] ADJ (*inf*): **it's a bit ~** (*risky*) es un poco arriesgado; (*doubtful*) es un poco dudoso

dichotomy [daɪ'kɔtəmɪ] N dicotomía

dickhead ['dɪkhɛd] N (*Brit inf!*) gilipollas m inv (*inf!*)

Dictaphone® ['dɪktəfəun] N dictáfono

dictate VT [dɪk'teɪt] dictar ▸ N ['dɪkteɪt] dictado ▸ **dictate to** VT FUS (*person*) dar órdenes a; **I won't be dictated to** no recibo órdenes de nadie

dictation [dɪk'teɪʃən] N (*to secretary etc*) dictado; **at ~ speed** para tomar al dictado

dictator [dɪk'teɪtəʳ] N dictador(a) m/f

dictatorship [dɪk'teɪtəʃɪp] N dictadura

diction ['dɪkʃən] N dicción f

★**dictionary** ['dɪkʃənrɪ] N diccionario

did [dɪd] PT of **do**

didactic [daɪ'dæktɪk] ADJ didáctico

diddle ['dɪdl] VT estafar, timar

didn't ['dɪdənt] = **did not**

★**die** [daɪ] VI morir; **to ~ (of or from)** morirse (de); **to be dying** morirse, estar muriéndose; **to be dying for sth/to do sth** morirse por algo/de ganas de hacer algo
▸ **die away** VI (*sound, light*) desvanecerse
▸ **die down** VI (*gen*) apagarse; (*wind*) amainar
▸ **die out** VI desaparecer, extinguirse

diehard ['daɪhɑ:d] N intransigente mf

diesel ['di:zl] N diesel m

diesel engine N motor m diesel

diesel fuel, diesel oil N gasoil m

★**diet** ['daɪət] N dieta; (*restricted food*) régimen m; **to live on a ~ of** alimentarse de ▸ VI (*also:* **be on a diet**) estar a dieta, hacer régimen

dietician [daɪə'tɪʃən] N dietista mf

differ ['dɪfəʳ] VI (*be different*) ser distinto, diferenciarse; (*disagree*) discrepar

★**difference** ['dɪfrəns] N diferencia; (*quarrel*) desacuerdo; **it makes no ~ to me** me da igual or lo mismo; **to settle one's differences** arreglarse

★**different** ['dɪfrənt] ADJ diferente, distinto

differential [dɪfə'rɛnʃəl] N diferencial f

differentiate [dɪfə'rɛnʃɪeɪt] VT distinguir ▸ VI diferenciarse; **to ~ between** distinguir entre

differently [ˈdɪfrəntlɪ] ADV de otro modo, en forma distinta

★**difficult** [ˈdɪfɪkəlt] ADJ difícil; **~ to understand** difícil de entender

★**difficulty** [ˈdɪfɪkəltɪ] N dificultad f; **to have difficulties with** (police, landlord etc) tener problemas con; **to be in ~** estar en apuros

diffidence [ˈdɪfɪdəns] N timidez f, falta de confianza en sí mismo

diffident [ˈdɪfɪdənt] ADJ tímido

diffuse ADJ [dɪˈfjuːs] difuso ▶ VT [dɪˈfjuːz] difundir

★**dig** [dɪg] (pt, pp **dug** [dʌg]) VT (hole) cavar; (ground) remover; (coal) extraer; (nails etc) clavar; **to ~ one's nails into** clavar las uñas en ▶ VI: **to ~ into** (savings) consumir; **to ~ into one's pockets for sth** hurgar en el bolsillo buscando algo ▶ N (prod) empujón m; (archaeological) excavación f; (remark) indirecta; see also **digs**
  ▶ **dig in** VI (also: **dig o.s. in**: Mil) atrincherarse; (inf: eat) hincar los dientes ▶ VT (compost) añadir al suelo; (knife, claw) clavar; **to ~ in one's heels** (fig) mantenerse en sus trece
  ▶ **dig out** VT (hole) excavar; (survivors, car from snow) sacar
  ▶ **dig up** VT desenterrar; (plant) desarraigar

digest VT [daɪˈdʒɛst] (food) digerir; (facts) asimilar ▶ N [ˈdaɪdʒɛst] resumen m

digestible [daɪˈdʒɛstəbl] ADJ digerible

digestion [dɪˈdʒɛstʃən] N digestión f

digestive [daɪˈdʒɛstɪv] ADJ (juices, system) digestivo

digit [ˈdɪdʒɪt] N (number) dígito; (finger) dedo

digital [ˈdɪdʒɪtl] ADJ digital

digital camera N cámara digital

digital compact cassette N cas(s)et(t)e m or f digital compacto

digital TV N televisión f digital

dignified [ˈdɪgnɪfaɪd] ADJ grave, solemne; (action) decoroso

dignify [ˈdɪgnɪfaɪ] VT dignificar

dignitary [ˈdɪgnɪtərɪ] N dignatario(-a)

dignity [ˈdɪgnɪtɪ] N dignidad f

digress [daɪˈgrɛs] VI: **to ~ from** apartarse de

digression [daɪˈgrɛʃən] N digresión f

digs [dɪgz] NPL (BRIT inf) pensión f, alojamiento

dike [daɪk] N = **dyke**

dilapidated [dɪˈlæpɪdeɪtɪd] ADJ desmoronado, ruinoso

dilate [daɪˈleɪt] VT dilatar ▶ VI dilatarse

dilatory [ˈdɪlətərɪ] ADJ (person) lento; (action) dilatorio

dilemma [daɪˈlɛmə] N dilema m; **to be in a ~** estar en un dilema

dilettante [dɪlɪˈtæntɪ] N diletante mf

diligence [ˈdɪlɪdʒəns] N diligencia

diligent [ˈdɪlɪdʒənt] ADJ diligente

dill [dɪl] N eneldo

dilly-dally [ˈdɪlɪˈdælɪ] VI (hesitate) vacilar; (dawdle) entretenerse

dilute [daɪˈluːt] VT diluir

dim [dɪm] ADJ (light) débil; (sight) turbio; (outline) borroso; (inf: stupid) lerdo; (room) oscuro; **to take a ~ view of sth** tener una pobre opinión de algo ▶ VT (light) bajar

dime [daɪm] N (US) moneda de diez centavos

dimension [dɪˈmɛnʃən] N dimensión f

-dimensional [dɪˈmɛnʃənl] ADJ SUFF: **two-dimensional** de dos dimensiones

dimensions [dɪˈmɛnʃənz] NPL dimensiones fpl

diminish [dɪˈmɪnɪʃ] VT, VI disminuir

diminished [dɪˈmɪnɪʃt] ADJ: **~ responsibility** (Law) responsabilidad f disminuida

diminutive [dɪˈmɪnjutɪv] ADJ diminuto ▶ N (Ling) diminutivo

dimly [ˈdɪmlɪ] ADV débilmente; (not clearly) vagamente

dimmer [ˈdɪməʳ] N (also: **dimmer switch**) regulador m (de intensidad); (US Aut) interruptor m

dimple [ˈdɪmpl] N hoyuelo

dim-witted [ˈdɪmˈwɪtɪd] ADJ (inf) lerdo, de pocas luces

din [dɪn] N estruendo, estrépito ▶ VT: **to ~ sth into sb** (inf) meter algo en la cabeza a algn

dine [daɪn] VI cenar

diner [ˈdaɪnəʳ] N (person: in restaurant) comensal mf; (US) restaurante económico; (BRIT Rail) = **dining car**

dinghy [ˈdɪŋgɪ] N bote m; (also: **rubber dinghy**) lancha (neumática)

dingy [ˈdɪndʒɪ] ADJ (room) sombrío; (dirty) sucio; (dull) deslucido

dining car [ˈdaɪnɪŋ-] N (BRIT) coche-restaurante m

dining room [ˈdaɪnɪŋ-] N comedor m

dining table N mesa f de comedor

dinkum [ˈdɪŋkəm] ADJ (AUSTRALIA, NEW ZEALAND inf: also: **fair dinkum**) de verdad, auténtico; **to be fair ~ about sth** (serious) tomarse algo en serio; **fair ~?** ¿de verdad?

★**dinner** [ˈdɪnəʳ] N (evening meal) cena, comida (LAM); (lunch) comida; (public) cena, banquete m; **~'s ready!** ¡la cena está servida!

dinner jacket N smoking m

dinner party N cena

dinner time N (evening) hora de cenar; (midday) hora de comer

dinosaur [ˈdaɪnəsɔːʳ] N dinosaurio

dint [dɪnt] N: **by ~ of (doing) sth** a fuerza de (hacer) algo

diocese [ˈdaɪəsɪs] N diócesis f

dioxide [daɪˈɒksaɪd] N bióxido; **carbon ~** bióxido de carbono

dip [dɪp] N (slope) pendiente f; (in sea) chapuzón m ▶ VT (in water) mojar; (ladle etc) meter; (BRIT Aut): **to ~ one's lights** poner la luz de cruce ▶ VI descender, bajar

Dip. ABBR (BRIT) = **diploma**

diphtheria [dɪfˈθɪərɪə] N difteria

diphthong [ˈdɪfθɒŋ] N diptongo

diploma [dɪˈpləʊmə] N diploma m

diplomacy [dɪˈpləʊməsɪ] N diplomacia

diplomat [ˈdɪpləmæt] N diplomático(-a)

diplomatic [dɪpləˈmætɪk] ADJ diplomático; **to break off ~ relations** romper las relaciones diplomáticas

diplomatic corps N cuerpo diplomático

diplomatic immunity N inmunidad f diplomática

dipstick [ˈdɪpstɪk] N (Aut) varilla de nivel (del aceite)

dipswitch [ˈdɪpswɪtʃ] N (BRIT Aut) interruptor m

dire [ˈdaɪəʳ] ADJ calamitoso

★**direct** [daɪˈrɛkt] ADJ (gen) directo; (manner, person) franco ▸ VT dirigir; **can you ~ me to …?** ¿puede indicarme dónde está …?; **to ~ sb to do sth** mandar a algn hacer algo

direct cost N costo directo

direct current N corriente f continua

direct debit N domiciliación f bancaria de recibos; **to pay by ~** domiciliar el pago

direct dialling N servicio automático de llamadas

★**direction** [dɪˈrɛkʃən] N dirección f; **sense of ~** sentido de la orientación; **in the ~ of** hacia, en dirección a ■ **directions** NPL (advice) órdenes fpl, instrucciones fpl; (to a place) señas fpl; **directions for use** modo de empleo; **to ask for directions** preguntar el camino

directional [dɪˈrɛkʃənl] ADJ direccional

directive [daɪˈrɛktɪv] N orden f, instrucción f; **a government ~** una orden del gobierno

direct labour N mano f de obra directa

directly [dɪˈrɛktlɪ] ADV (in straight line) directamente; (at once) en seguida

direct mail N correspondencia personalizada

direct mailshot N (BRIT) promoción f por correspondencia personalizada

directness [dɪˈrɛktnɪs] N (of person, speech) franqueza

★**director** [dɪˈrɛktəʳ] N director(a) m/f; **managing ~** director(a) m/f gerente

Director of Public Prosecutions N ≈ fiscal mf general del Estado

directory [dɪˈrɛktərɪ] N (Tel) guía (telefónica); (street directory) callejero; (trade directory) directorio de comercio; (Comput) directorio

directory enquiries, (US) **directory assistance** N (service) (servicio m de) información f

dirt [dəːt] N suciedad f

dirt-cheap [ˈdəːtˈtʃiːp] ADJ baratísimo

dirt road N (US) camino sin firme

★**dirty** [ˈdəːtɪ] ADJ sucio; (joke) verde, colorado (LAm) ▸ VT ensuciar; (stain) manchar

dirty trick N mala jugada, truco sucio

disability [dɪsəˈbɪlɪtɪ] N incapacidad f

disability allowance N pensión f de invalidez

disable [dɪsˈeɪbl] VT (illness, accident) dejar incapacitado or inválido; (tank, gun) inutilizar; (Law: disqualify) incapacitar

disabled [dɪsˈeɪbld] ADJ (physically) minusválido(-a); (mentally) deficiente mental

disabuse [dɪsəˈbjuːz] VT desengañar

disadvantage [dɪsədˈvɑːntɪdʒ] N desventaja, inconveniente m

disadvantaged [dɪsədˈvɑːntɪdʒd] ADJ (person) desventajado

disadvantageous [dɪsædvənˈteɪdʒəs] ADJ desventajoso

disaffected [dɪsəˈfɛktɪd] ADJ descontento; **to be ~ (to or towards)** estar descontento (de)

disaffection [dɪsəˈfɛkʃən] N desafecto, descontento

disagree [dɪsəˈgriː] VI (differ) discrepar; **to ~ (with)** no estar de acuerdo (con); **I ~ with you** no estoy de acuerdo contigo

disagreeable [dɪsəˈgrɪəbl] ADJ desagradable

disagreement [dɪsəˈgriːmənt] N (gen) desacuerdo; (quarrel) riña; **to have a ~ with sb** estar en desacuerdo con algn

disallow [ˈdɪsəˈlaʊ] VT (goal) anular; (claim) rechazar

★**disappear** [dɪsəˈpɪəʳ] VI desaparecer

disappearance [dɪsəˈpɪərəns] N desaparición f

disappoint [dɪsəˈpɔɪnt] VT decepcionar; (hopes) defraudar

★**disappointed** [dɪsəˈpɔɪntɪd] ADJ decepcionado

disappointing [dɪsəˈpɔɪntɪŋ] ADJ decepcionante

disappointment [dɪsəˈpɔɪntmənt] N decepción f

disapproval [dɪsəˈpruːvəl] N desaprobación f

disapprove [dɪsəˈpruːv] VI: **to ~ of** desaprobar

disapproving [dɪsəˈpruːvɪŋ] ADJ de desaprobación, desaprobador(a)

disarm [dɪsˈɑːm] VT desarmar

disarmament [dɪsˈɑːməmənt] N desarme m

disarmament talks NPL conversaciones fpl de or sobre desarme

disarming [dɪsˈɑːmɪŋ] ADJ (smile) que desarma, encantador(a)

disarray [dɪsəˈreɪ] N: **in ~** (troops) desorganizado; (thoughts) confuso; (hair, clothes) desarreglado; **to throw into ~** provocar el caos

★**disaster** [dɪˈzɑːstəʳ] N desastre m

disaster area N zona catastrófica

disastrous [dɪˈzɑːstrəs] ADJ desastroso

disband [dɪsˈbænd] VT disolver ▸ VI desbandarse

disbelief [dɪsbəˈliːf] N incredulidad f; **in ~** con incredulidad

disbelieve [ˈdɪsbəˈliːv] VT (person, story) poner en duda, no creer

disc [dɪsk] N disco; (Comput) = **disk**

discard [dɪsˈkɑːd] vt tirar; (fig) descartar

discern [dɪˈsɜːn] vt percibir, discernir; (understand) comprender

discernible [dɪˈsɜːnəbl] ADJ perceptible

discerning [dɪˈsɜːnɪŋ] ADJ perspicaz

discharge vt [dɪsˈtʃɑːdʒ] (task, duty) cumplir; (ship etc) descargar; (patient) dar de alta; (employee) despedir; (soldier) licenciar; (defendant) poner en libertad; (settle: debt) saldar; **discharged bankrupt** quebrado(-a) rehabilitado(-a) ▸ N [ˈdɪstʃɑːdʒ] (Elec) descarga; (vaginal discharge) emisión f vaginal; (dismissal) despedida; (of duty) desempeño; (of debt) pago, descargo; (of gas, chemicals) escape m

disciple [dɪˈsaɪpl] N discípulo(-a)

disciplinary [ˈdɪsɪplɪnərɪ] ADJ: **to take ~ action against sb** disciplinar a algn

★**discipline** [ˈdɪsɪplɪn] N disciplina ▸ vt disciplinar; **to ~ o.s. to do sth** obligarse a hacer algo

disc jockey N pinchadiscos mf

disclaim [dɪsˈkleɪm] vt negar tener

disclaimer [dɪsˈkleɪməʳ] N rectificación f; **to issue a ~** hacer una rectificación

disclose [dɪsˈkləuz] vt revelar

disclosure [dɪsˈkləuʒəʳ] N revelación f

Discman® [ˈdɪskmən] N Discman® m

disco [ˈdɪskəu] N ABBR = **discothèque**

discolouration, (US) **discoloration** [dɪskʌləˈreɪʃən] N descoloramiento, decoloración f

discoloured, (US) **discolored** [dɪsˈkʌləd] ADJ descolorido

discomfort [dɪsˈkʌmfət] N incomodidad f; (unease) inquietud f; (physical) malestar m

disconcert [dɪskənˈsɜːt] vt desconcertar

disconnect [dɪskəˈnekt] vt (gen) separar; (Elec etc) desconectar; (supply) cortar (el suministro) a

disconsolate [dɪsˈkɔnsəlɪt] ADJ desconsolado

discontent [dɪskənˈtent] N descontento

discontented [dɪskənˈtentɪd] ADJ descontento

discontinue [dɪskənˈtɪnjuː] vt interrumpir; (payments) suspender

discord [ˈdɪskɔːd] N discordia; (Mus) disonancia

discordant [dɪsˈkɔːdənt] ADJ disonante

discothèque [ˈdɪskəutek] N discoteca

★**discount** N [ˈdɪskaunt] descuento; **at a ~** con descuento; **~ for cash** descuento por pago en efectivo; **to give sb a ~ on sth** hacer un descuento a algn en algo ▸ vt [dɪsˈkaunt] descontar; (report etc) descartar

discount house N (Finance) banco de descuento; (Comm: also: **discount store**) = tienda de saldos

discount rate N (Comm) tipo de descuento

discount store N = tienda de saldos

discourage [dɪsˈkʌrɪdʒ] vt desalentar; (oppose) oponerse a; (dissuade, deter) desanimar, disuadir; **to ~ sb from doing** disuadir a algn de hacer

discouragement [dɪsˈkʌrɪdʒmənt] N (dissuasion) disuasión f; (depression) desánimo, desaliento; **to act as a ~ to** servir para disuadir

discouraging [dɪsˈkʌrɪdʒɪŋ] ADJ desalentador(a)

discourteous [dɪsˈkəːtɪəs] ADJ descortés

★**discover** [dɪsˈkʌvəʳ] vt descubrir

discovery [dɪsˈkʌvərɪ] N descubrimiento

discredit [dɪsˈkredɪt] vt desacreditar

discreet [dɪˈskriːt] ADJ (tactful) discreto; (careful) circunspecto, prudente

discreetly [dɪˈskriːtlɪ] ADV discretamente

discrepancy [dɪˈskrepənsɪ] N (difference) diferencia; (disagreement) discrepancia

discretion [dɪˈskreʃən] N (tact) discreción f; (care) prudencia, circunspección f; **use your own ~** haz lo que creas oportuno; **at the ~ of** a criterio de

discretionary [dɪˈskreʃənrɪ] ADJ (powers) discrecional

discriminate [dɪˈskrɪmɪneɪt] vi: **to ~ between** distinguir entre; **to ~ against** discriminar contra

discriminating [dɪˈskrɪmɪneɪtɪŋ] ADJ entendido

discrimination [dɪskrɪmɪˈneɪʃən] N (discernment) perspicacia; (bias) discriminación f; **racial/sexual ~** discriminación racial/sexual

discus [ˈdɪskəs] N disco

★**discuss** [dɪˈskʌs] vt (gen) discutir; (a theme) tratar

★**discussion** [dɪˈskʌʃən] N discusión f; **under ~** en discusión

disdain [dɪsˈdeɪn] N desdén m ▸ vt desdeñar

disease [dɪˈziːz] N enfermedad f

diseased [dɪˈziːzd] ADJ enfermo

disembark [dɪsɪmˈbɑːk] vt, vi desembarcar

disembarkation [dɪsembɑːˈkeɪʃən] N desembarque m

disenchanted [dɪsɪnˈtʃɑːntɪd] ADJ: **~ (with)** desilusionado (con)

disenfranchise [ˈdɪsɪnˈfræntʃaɪz] vt privar del derecho al voto; (Comm) privar de franquicias

disengage [dɪsɪnˈgeɪdʒ] vt soltar; **to ~ the clutch** (Aut) desembragar

disentangle [dɪsɪnˈtæŋgl] vt desenredar

disfavour, (US) **disfavor** [dɪsˈfeɪvəʳ] N desaprobación f

disfigure [dɪsˈfɪgəʳ] vt desfigurar

disgorge [dɪsˈgɔːdʒ] vt verter

disgrace [dɪsˈgreɪs] N ignominia; (downfall) caída; (shame) vergüenza, escándalo ▸ vt deshonrar

disgraceful [dɪsˈgreɪsful] ADJ vergonzoso; (behaviour) escandaloso

disgruntled [dɪsˈgrʌntld] ADJ disgustado, descontento

disguise [dɪsˈgaɪz] N disfraz m; **in ~** disfrazado

▶ vt disfrazar; (voice) disimular; (feelings etc) ocultar; **to ~ o.s. as** disfrazarse de; **there's no disguising the fact that ...** no puede ocultarse el hecho de que ...

disgust [dɪs'gʌst] N repugnancia ▶ vt repugnar, dar asco a

disgusted [dɪs'gʌstɪd] ADJ indignado

disgusting [dɪs'gʌstɪŋ] ADJ repugnante, asqueroso

★**dish** [dɪʃ] N (gen) plato; **to do** or **wash the dishes** fregar los platos
▶ **dish out** vt (money, exam papers) repartir; (food) servir; (advice) dar
▶ **dish up** vt servir

dishcloth ['dɪʃklɔθ] N (for washing) bayeta; (for drying) paño de cocina

dishearten [dɪs'hɑːtn] vt desalentar

dishevelled, (US) **disheveled** [dɪ'ʃevəld] ADJ (hair) despeinado; (clothes, appearance) desarreglado

dishonest [dɪs'ɔnɪst] ADJ (person) poco honrado, tramposo; (means) fraudulento

dishonesty [dɪs'ɔnɪstɪ] N falta de honradez

dishonour, (US) **dishonor** [dɪs'ɔnər] N deshonra

dishonourable, (US) **dishonorable** [dɪs'ɔnərəbl] ADJ deshonroso

dish soap N (US) lavavajillas m inv

dishtowel ['dɪʃtauəl] N (US) bayeta

dishwasher ['dɪʃwɔʃər] N lavaplatos m inv; (person) friegaplatos mf

dishy ['dɪʃɪ] ADJ (BRIT old) buenón(-ona)

disillusion [dɪsɪ'luːʒən] vt desilusionar; **to become disillusioned (with)** quedar desilusionado (con)

disillusionment [dɪsɪ'luːʒənmənt] N desilusión f

disincentive [dɪsɪn'sentɪv] N freno; **to act as a ~ (to)** actuar de freno (a); **to be a ~** ser un freno a

disinclined ['dɪsɪn'klaɪnd] ADJ: **to be ~ to do sth** estar poco dispuesto a hacer algo

disinfect [dɪsɪn'fekt] vt desinfectar

disinfectant [dɪsɪn'fektənt] N desinfectante m

disinflation [dɪsɪn'fleɪʃən] N desinflación f

disinformation [dɪsɪnfə'meɪʃən] N desinformación f

disingenuous [dɪsɪn'dʒenjuəs] ADJ poco sincero, falso

disinherit [dɪsɪn'herɪt] vt desheredar

disintegrate [dɪs'ɪntɪgreɪt] vi disgregarse, desintegrarse

disinterested [dɪs'ɪntrəstɪd] ADJ desinteresado

disjointed [dɪs'dʒɔɪntɪd] ADJ inconexo

disk [dɪsk] N (Comput) disco, disquete m; **single-/ double-sided ~** disco de una cara/dos caras

disk drive N unidad f (de disco)

diskette [dɪs'ket] N diskette m, disquete m, disco flexible

disk operating system N sistema m operativo de discos

dislike [dɪs'laɪk] N antipatía, aversión f; **to take a ~ to sb/sth** cogerle or (LAM) agarrarle antipatía a algn/algo ▶ vt tener antipatía a; **I ~ the idea** no me gusta la idea

dislocate ['dɪsləkeɪt] vt dislocar; **he dislocated his shoulder** se dislocó el hombro

dislodge [dɪs'lɔdʒ] vt sacar; (enemy) desalojar

disloyal [dɪs'lɔɪəl] ADJ desleal

dismal ['dɪzml] ADJ (dark) sombrío; (depressing) triste; (very bad) fatal

dismantle [dɪs'mæntl] vt desmontar, desarmar

dismay [dɪs'meɪ] N consternación f; **much to my ~** para gran consternación mía ▶ vt consternar

dismiss [dɪs'mɪs] vt (worker) despedir; (official) destituir; (idea) rechazar; (Law) rechazar; (possibility) descartar ▶ vi (Mil) romper filas

dismissal [dɪs'mɪsl] N despido; destitución f

dismount [dɪs'maunt] vi apearse; (rider) desmontar

disobedience [dɪsə'biːdɪəns] N desobediencia

disobedient [dɪsə'biːdɪənt] ADJ desobediente

disobey [dɪsə'beɪ] vt desobedecer; (rule) infringir

disorder [dɪs'ɔːdər] N desorden m; (rioting) disturbio; (Med) trastorno; (disease) enfermedad f; **civil ~** desorden m civil

disorderly [dɪs'ɔːdəlɪ] ADJ (untidy) desordenado; (meeting) alborotado; **~ conduct** (Law) conducta escandalosa

disorganized [dɪs'ɔːgənaɪzd] ADJ desorganizado

disorientated [dɪs'ɔːrɪenteɪtəd] ADJ desorientado

disown [dɪs'əun] vt renegar de

disparaging [dɪs'pærɪdʒɪŋ] ADJ despreciativo; **to be ~ about sth/sb** menospreciar algo/a algn

disparate ['dɪspərɪt] ADJ dispar

disparity [dɪs'pærɪtɪ] N disparidad f

dispassionate [dɪs'pæʃənɪt] ADJ (unbiased) imparcial; (unemotional) desapasionado

dispatch [dɪs'pætʃ] vt enviar; (kill) despachar; (deal with: business) despachar ▶ N (sending) envío; (speed) prontitud f; (Press) informe m; (Mil) parte m

dispatch department N (Comm) departamento de envíos

dispatch rider N (Mil) correo

dispel [dɪs'pel] vt disipar, dispersar

dispensary [dɪs'pensərɪ] N dispensario

dispensation [dɪspen'seɪʃən] N (Rel) dispensa

dispense [dɪs'pens] vt dispensar, repartir; (medicine) preparar
▶ **dispense with** vt FUS (make unnecessary) prescindir de

dispenser [dɪs'pensər] N (container) distribuidor m automático

dispensing chemist [dɪsˈpɛnsɪŋ-] N (BRIT) farmacia

dispersal [dɪsˈpəːsl] N dispersión f

disperse [dɪsˈpəːs] VT dispersar ▶ VI dispersarse

dispirited [dɪˈspɪrɪtɪd] ADJ desanimado, desalentado

displace [dɪsˈpleɪs] VT (person) desplazar; (replace) reemplazar

displaced person N (Pol) desplazado(-a)

displacement [dɪsˈpleɪsmənt] N cambio de sitio

display [dɪsˈpleɪ] N (in shop window) escaparate m; (exhibition) exposición f; (Comput) visualización f; (Mil) desfile m; (of feeling) manifestación f; (pej) aparato, pompa; **on ~** (exhibits) expuesto, exhibido; (goods) en el escaparate ▶ VT exponer; manifestar; (ostentatiously) lucir

display advertising N publicidad f gráfica

displease [dɪsˈpliːz] VT (offend) ofender; (annoy) fastidiar; **displeased with** disgustado con

displeasure [dɪsˈplɛʒəʳ] N disgusto

disposable [dɪsˈpəuzəbl] ADJ (not reusable) desechable; **~ personal income** ingresos mpl personales disponibles

disposable nappy N pañal m desechable

disposal [dɪsˈpəuzl] N (sale) venta; (of house) traspaso; (by giving away) donación f; (arrangement) colocación f; (of rubbish) destrucción f; **at one's ~** a la disposición de algn; **to put sth at sb's ~** poner algo a disposición de algn

dispose [dɪsˈpəuz] VI: **~ of** (time, money) disponer de; (unwanted goods) deshacerse de; (Comm: sell) traspasar, vender; (throw away) tirar

disposed [dɪsˈpəuzd] ADJ: **~ to do** dispuesto a hacer

disposition [dɪspəˈzɪʃən] N disposición f; (temperament) carácter m

dispossess [ˈdɪspəˈzɛs] VT: **to ~ sb (of)** desposeer a algn (de)

disproportion [dɪsprəˈpɔːʃən] N desproporción f

disproportionate [dɪsprəˈpɔːʃənət] ADJ desproporcionado

disprove [dɪsˈpruːv] VT refutar

dispute [dɪsˈpjuːt] N disputa; (verbal) discusión f; (also: **industrial dispute**) conflicto (laboral); **to be in** or **under ~** (matter) discutirse; (territory) estar en disputa; (Law) estar en litigio ▶ VT (argue) disputar; (question) cuestionar

disqualification [dɪskwɔlɪfɪˈkeɪʃən] N inhabilitación f; (Sport) descalificación f; (from driving) descalificación f

disqualify [dɪsˈkwɔlɪfaɪ] VT (Sport) desclasificar; **to ~ sb for sth/from doing sth** incapacitar a algn para algo/para hacer algo

disquiet [dɪsˈkwaɪət] N preocupación f, inquietud f

disquieting [dɪsˈkwaɪətɪŋ] ADJ inquietante

disregard [dɪsrɪˈɡɑːd] VT desatender; (ignore) no

hacer caso de ▶ N (indifference: to feelings, danger, money): **~ (for)** indiferencia (a); **~ (of)** (nonobservance: of law, rules) violación f (de)

disrepair [dɪsrɪˈpɛəʳ] N: **to fall into ~** (building) desmoronarse; (street) deteriorarse

disreputable [dɪsˈrɛpjutəbl] ADJ (person, area) de mala fama; (behaviour) vergonzoso

disrepute [ˈdɪsrɪˈpjuːt] N descrédito, ignominia; **to bring into ~** desacreditar

disrespectful [dɪsrɪˈspɛktful] ADJ irrespetuoso

disrupt [dɪsˈrʌpt] VT (plans) desbaratar, alternar, trastornar; (meeting, public transport, conversation) interrumpir

disruption [dɪsˈrʌpʃən] N desbaratamiento; trastorno; interrupción f

disruptive [dɪsˈrʌptɪv] ADJ (influence) disruptivo; (strike action) perjudicial

dissatisfaction [dɪssætɪsˈfækʃən] N disgusto, descontento

dissatisfied [dɪsˈsætɪsfaɪd] ADJ insatisfecho

dissect [dɪˈsɛkt] VT (also fig) disecar

disseminate [dɪˈsɛmɪneɪt] VT divulgar, difundir

dissent [dɪˈsɛnt] N disensión f

dissenter [dɪˈsɛntəʳ] N (Rel, Pol etc) disidente mf

dissertation [dɪsəˈteɪʃən] N (Univ) tesina; see also **master's degree**

disservice [dɪsˈsəːvɪs] N: **to do sb a ~** perjudicar a algn

dissident [ˈdɪsɪdnt] ADJ, N disidente mf

dissimilar [dɪˈsɪmɪləʳ] ADJ distinto

dissipate [ˈdɪsɪpeɪt] VT disipar; (waste) desperdiciar

dissipated [ˈdɪsɪpeɪtɪd] ADJ disoluto

dissipation [dɪsɪˈpeɪʃən] N disipación f (moral), libertinaje m, vicio; (waste) derroche m

dissociate [dɪˈsəuʃɪeɪt] VT disociar; **to ~ o.s. from** disociarse de

dissolute [ˈdɪsəluːt] ADJ disoluto

dissolution [dɪsəˈluːʃən] N disolución f

dissolve [dɪˈzɔlv] VT disolver ▶ VI disolverse

dissuade [dɪˈsweɪd] VT: **to ~ sb (from)** disuadir a algn (de)

distaff [ˈdɪstæf] N: **~ side** rama femenina

★**distance** [ˈdɪstns] N distancia; **in the ~** a lo lejos; **what ~ is it to London?** ¿qué distancia hay de aquí a Londres?; **it's within walking ~** se puede ir andando

distant [ˈdɪstnt] ADJ lejano; (manner) reservado, frío

distaste [dɪsˈteɪst] N repugnancia

distasteful [dɪsˈteɪstful] ADJ repugnante, desagradable

Dist. Atty. ABBR (US) = **district attorney**

distemper [dɪsˈtɛmpəʳ] N (of dogs) moquillo

distend [dɪsˈtɛnd] VT dilatar, hinchar ▶ VI dilatarse, hincharse

distended [dɪˈstɛndɪd] ADJ (stomach) hinchado

distil, (US) **distill** [dɪsˈtɪl] VT destilar

distillery [dɪsˈtɪlərɪ] N destilería

distinct [dɪsˈtɪŋkt] ADJ (*different*) distinto; (*clear*) claro; (*unmistakeable*) inequívoco; **as ~ from** a diferencia de

distinction [dɪsˈtɪŋkʃən] N distinción f; (*in exam*) sobresaliente m; **a writer of ~** un escritor destacado; **to draw a ~ between** hacer una distinción entre

distinctive [dɪsˈtɪŋktɪv] ADJ distintivo

distinctly [dɪsˈtɪŋktlɪ] ADV claramente

distinguish [dɪsˈtɪŋgwɪʃ] VT distinguir ▶ VI: **to ~ (between)** distinguir (entre)

distinguished [dɪsˈtɪŋgwɪʃt] ADJ (*eminent*) distinguido; (*career*) eminente; (*refined*) distinguido, de categoría

distinguishing [dɪsˈtɪŋgwɪʃɪŋ] ADJ (*feature*) distintivo

distort [dɪsˈtɔ:t] VT deformar; (*sound*) distorsionar; (*account, news*) tergiversar

distortion [dɪsˈtɔ:ʃən] N deformación f; (*of sound*) distorsión f; (*of truth etc*) tergiversación f; (*of facts*) falseamiento

distract [dɪsˈtrækt] VT distraer

distracted [dɪsˈtræktɪd] ADJ distraído

distracting [dɪsˈtræktɪŋ] ADJ que distrae la atención, molesto

distraction [dɪsˈtrækʃən] N distracción f; (*confusion*) aturdimiento; (*amusement*) diversión f; **to drive sb to ~** (*distress, anxiety*) volver loco a algn

distraught [dɪsˈtrɔ:t] ADJ turbado, enloquecido

distress [dɪsˈtres] N (*anguish*) angustia; (*want*) miseria; (*pain*) dolor m; (*danger*) peligro; **in ~** (*ship etc*) en peligro ▶ VT afligir; (*pain*) doler

distressing [dɪsˈtresɪŋ] ADJ angustioso; doloroso

distress signal N señal f de socorro

distribute [dɪsˈtrɪbju:t] VT (*gen*) distribuir; (*share out*) repartir

distribution [dɪstrɪˈbju:ʃən] N distribución f

distribution cost N gastos mpl de distribución

distributor [dɪsˈtrɪbjutəʳ] N (*Aut*) distribuidor m; (*Comm*) distribuidora

★**district** [ˈdɪstrɪkt] N (*of country*) zona, región f; (*of town*) barrio; (*Admin*) distrito

district attorney N (US) fiscal mf

district council N ≈ municipio

district manager N representante mf regional

district nurse N (BRIT) enfermera que atiende a pacientes a domicilio

distrust [dɪsˈtrʌst] N desconfianza ▶ VT desconfiar de

distrustful [dɪsˈtrʌstful] ADJ desconfiado

disturb [dɪsˈtə:b] VT (*person: bother, interrupt*) molestar; (*meeting*) interrumpir; (*disorganize*) desordenar; **sorry to ~ you** perdone la molestia

disturbance [dɪsˈtə:bəns] N (*political etc*) disturbio; (*violence*) alboroto; (*of mind*) trastorno; **to cause a ~** causar alboroto; **~ of the peace** alteración f del orden público

disturbed [dɪsˈtə:bd] ADJ (*worried, upset*) preocupado, angustiado; **to be emotionally/mentally ~** tener problemas emocionales/ser un trastornado mental

disturbing [dɪsˈtə:bɪŋ] ADJ inquietante, perturbador(a)

disuse [dɪsˈju:s] N: **to fall into ~** caer en desuso

disused [dɪsˈju:zd] ADJ abandonado

ditch [dɪtʃ] N zanja; (*irrigation ditch*) acequia ▶ VT (*inf: partner*) deshacerse de; (: *plan, car etc*) abandonar

dither [ˈdɪðəʳ] VI vacilar

ditto [ˈdɪtəu] ADV ídem, lo mismo

divan [dɪˈvæn] N diván m

divan bed N cama turca

dive [daɪv] N (*from board*) salto; (*underwater*) buceo; (*of submarine*) inmersión f; (*pej: café, bar etc*) garito m; (*Aviat*) picada ▶ VI (*swimmer: into water*) saltar; (: *under water*) zambullirse, bucear; (*fish, submarine*) sumergirse; (*bird*) lanzarse en picado; **to ~ into** (*bag etc*) meter la mano en; (*place*) meterse de prisa en

diver [ˈdaɪvəʳ] N (*Sport*) saltador(a) m/f; (*underwater*) buzo

diverge [daɪˈvə:dʒ] VI divergir

divergent [daɪˈvə:dʒənt] ADJ divergente

diverse [daɪˈvə:s] ADJ diversos(-as), varios(-as)

diversification [daɪvə:sɪfɪˈkeɪʃən] N diversificación f

diversify [daɪˈvə:sɪfaɪ] VT diversificar

diversion [daɪˈvə:ʃən] N (BRIT Aut) desviación f; (*distraction*) diversión f; (*Mil*) diversión f

diversionary tactics [daɪˈvə:ʃənrɪ-] NPL tácticas fpl de diversión

diversity [daɪˈvə:sɪtɪ] N diversidad f

divert [daɪˈvə:t] VT (BRIT: *train, plane, traffic*) desviar; (*amuse*) divertir

divest [daɪˈvest] VT: **to ~ sb of sth** despojar a algn de algo

★**divide** [dɪˈvaɪd] VT dividir; (*separate*) separar; **to ~ (between** or **among)** repartir or dividir (entre); **40 divided by 5** 40 dividido por 5 ▶ VI dividirse; (*road*) bifurcarse
▶ **divide out** VT: **to ~ out (between** or **among)** (*sweets, tasks etc*) repartir (entre)

divided [dɪˈvaɪdɪd] ADJ (*country, couple*) dividido; (*opinions*) en desacuerdo

divided highway N (US) carretera de doble calzada

dividend [ˈdɪvɪdɛnd] N dividendo; (*fig*) beneficio

dividend cover N cobertura de dividendo

dividers [dɪˈvaɪdəz] NPL compás msg de puntas

divine [dɪˈvaɪn] ADJ divino ▶ VT (*future*) vaticinar; (*truth*) alumbrar; (*water, metal*) descubrir, detectar

diving ['daɪvɪŋ] N (Sport) salto; (underwater) buceo

diving board N trampolín m

diving suit N escafandra

divinity [dɪ'vɪnɪtɪ] N divinidad f; (Scol) teología

divisible [dɪ'vɪzɪbl] ADJ divisible

division [dɪ'vɪʒən] N (also BRIT Football) división f; (sharing out) reparto; (disagreement) diferencias fpl; (Comm) sección f; (BRIT Pol) votación f; ~ of labour división f del trabajo

divisive [dɪ'vaɪsɪv] ADJ divisivo

divorce [dɪ'vɔːs] N divorcio ▶ VT divorciarse de

★**divorced** [dɪ'vɔːst] ADJ divorciado

divorcee [dɪvɔː'siː] N divorciado(-a)

divot ['dɪvət] N (Golf) chuleta

divulge [daɪ'vʌldʒ] VT divulgar, revelar

Diwali [dɪ'wɑːli], **Divali** [dɪ'vɑːli] N Diwali m

★**DIY** ADJ, N ABBR (BRIT) = **do-it-yourself**

dizziness ['dɪzɪnɪs] N vértigo

dizzy ['dɪzɪ] ADJ (person) mareado; (height) vertiginoso; **to feel ~** marearse; **I feel ~** estoy mareado

DJ N ABBR (= disc jokey) DJ mf; = **dinner jacket**

Djakarta [dʒə'kɑːtə] N Yakarta

DJIA N ABBR (US Stock Exchange) = **Dow-Jones Industrial Average**

Djibouti [dʒɪ'buːtɪ] N Yibuti m

dl ABBR (= decilitre(s)) dl

DLit, DLitt ABBR (= Doctor of Literature, Doctor of Letters) título universitario

dm ABBR (= decimetre(s)) dm

DMus ABBR (= Doctor of Music) título universitario

DMZ N ABBR (= demilitarized zone) zona desmilitarizada

DNA N ABBR (= deoxyribonucleic acid) ADN m

DNA test N prueba f del ADN

---

do [duː]

(pt **did** [dɪd], pp **done** [dʌn]) N 1 (inf: party etc): **we're having a little do on Saturday** damos una fiestecita el sábado; **it was rather a grand do** fue un acontecimiento a lo grande 2: **the dos and don'ts** lo que se debe y no se debe hacer

▶ AUX VB 1 (in negative constructions: not translated): **I don't understand** no entiendo

2 (to form questions: not translated): **do you speak English?** ¿habla (usted) inglés?; **didn't you know?** ¿no lo sabías?; **what do you think?** ¿qué opinas?

3 (for emphasis, in polite expressions): **people do make mistakes sometimes** a veces sí se cometen errores; **she does seem rather late** a mí también me parece que se ha retrasado; **do sit down/help yourself** siéntate/sírvete por favor; **do take care!** ¡ten cuidado! ¿eh?; **I DO wish I could …** ojalá (que) pudiera …; **but I DO like it** pero, sí (que) me gusta

4 (used to avoid repeating vb): **she sings better than I do** canta mejor que yo; **do you agree?** — **yes, I do/no, I don't** ¿estás de acuerdo? — sí (lo estoy)/no (lo estoy); **she lives in Glasgow — so do I** vive en Glasgow — yo también; **he didn't like it and neither did we** no le gustó y a nosotros tampoco; **who made this mess?** — **I did** ¿quién hizo esta chapuza? — yo; **he asked me to help him and I did** me pidió que le ayudara y lo hice

5 (in question tags): **you like him, don't you?** te gusta, ¿verdad? or ¿no?; **I don't know him, do I?** creo que no le conozco; **he laughed, didn't he?** se rio ¿no?

▶ VT 1 (gen): **what are you doing tonight?** ¿qué haces esta noche?; **what can I do for you?** (in shop) ¿en qué puedo servirle?; **what does he do for a living?** ¿a qué se dedica?; **I'll do all I can** haré todo lo que pueda; **what have you done with my slippers?** ¿qué has hecho con mis zapatillas?; **to do the washing-up/cooking** fregar los platos/cocinar; **to do one's teeth/hair/nails** lavarse los dientes/arreglarse el pelo/arreglarse las uñas

2 (Aut etc): **the car was doing 100** el coche iba a 100; **we've done 200 km already** ya hemos hecho 200 km; **he can do 100 in that car** puede ir a 100 en ese coche

3 (visit: city, museum) visitar, recorrer

4 (cook): **a steak — well done please** un filete bien hecho, por favor

▶ VI 1 (act, behave) hacer; **do as I do** haz como yo

2 (get on, fare): **he's doing well/badly at school** va bien/mal en la escuela; **the firm is doing well** la empresa anda or va bien; **how do you do?** mucho gusto; (less formal) ¿qué tal?

3 (suit): **will it do?** ¿sirve?, ¿está or va bien?; **it doesn't do to upset her** cuidado en ofenderla

4 (be sufficient) bastar; **will £10 do?** ¿será bastante con £10?; **that'll do** así está bien; **that'll do!** (in annoyance) ¡ya está bien!, ¡basta ya!; **to make do (with)** arreglárselas (con)

▶ **do away with** VT FUS (inf: kill) eliminar; (eradicate: disease) eliminar; (abolish: law etc) abolir; (withdraw) retirar

▶ **do out of** VT FUS: **to do sb out of sth** pisar algo a algn

▶ **do up** VT (laces) atar; (zip, dress, shirt) abrochar; (renovate: room, house) renovar

▶ **do with** VT FUS (need): **I could do with a drink/some help** no me vendría mal un trago/un poco de ayuda; (be connected with) tener que ver con; **what has it got to do with you?** ¿qué tiene que ver contigo?

▶ **do without** VI: **if you're late for dinner then you'll do without** si llegas tarde tendrás que quedarte sin cenar ▶ VT FUS pasar sin; **I can do without a car** puedo pasar sin coche

---

do. ABBR = **ditto**

DOA ABBR = **dead on arrival**

d.o.b. ABBR = **date of birth**

doc [dɔk] N (inf) médico(-a)

docile [ˈdəʊsaɪl] ADJ dócil

dock [dɔk] N (Naut: wharf) dársena, muelle m; (Law) banquillo (de los acusados) ▶ VI (enter dock) atracar (en el muelle) ▶ VT (pay etc) descontar ■ **docks** NPL muelles mpl, puerto sg

dock dues NPL derechos mpl de muelle

docker [ˈdɔkəʳ] N trabajador m portuario, estibador m

docket [ˈdɔkɪt] N (on parcel etc) etiqueta

dockyard [ˈdɔkjɑːd] N astillero

★**doctor** [ˈdɔktəʳ] N médico(-a); (PhD etc) doctor(a) m/f ▶ VT (fig) arreglar, falsificar; (drink etc) adulterar

doctorate [ˈdɔktərɪt] N doctorado

El grado más alto que conceden las universidades es el doctorado (**doctorate**), tras un período de estudio e investigación original no inferior a tres años que culmina con la presentación de una tesis (thesis) en la que se exponen los resultados. El título más frecuente es el de PhD (Doctor of Philosophy), que se obtiene en Letras, Ciencias e Ingeniería, aunque también existen otros doctorados específicos en Música, Derecho etc.

Doctor of Philosophy N Doctor m (en Filosofía y Letras)

doctrinaire [dɔktrɪˈnɛəʳ] ADJ doctrinario

doctrine [ˈdɔktrɪn] N doctrina

docudrama [dɔkjuˈdrɑːmə] N (TV) docudrama m

document [ˈdɔkjumənt] N documento ▶ VT documentar

documentary [dɔkjuˈmɛntərɪ] ADJ documental ▶ N documental m

documentation [dɔkjumɛnˈteɪʃən] N documentación f

DOD N ABBR (US: = Department of Defense) Ministerio de Defensa

doddering [ˈdɔdərɪŋ], **doddery** [ˈdɔdərɪ] ADJ vacilante

doddle [ˈdɔdl] N: **it's a ~** (BRIT inf) es pan comido

Dodecanese [dəʊdɪkəˈniːz], **Dodecanese Islands** NPL Dodecaneso sg

dodge [dɔdʒ] N (of body) regate m; (fig) truco ▶ VT (gen) evadir; (blow) esquivar ▶ VI escabullirse; (Sport) hacer una finta; **to ~ out of the way** echarse a un lado; **to ~ through the traffic** esquivar el tráfico

Dodgems® [ˈdɔdʒəmz] NPL (BRIT) autos or coches mpl de choque

dodgy [ˈdɔdʒɪ] ADJ (BRIT inf: uncertain) dudoso; (: shady) sospechoso; (: risky) arriesgado

DOE N ABBR (US) = **Department of Energy**

doe [dəʊ] N (deer) cierva, gama; (rabbit) coneja

does [dʌz] VB see **do**

★**doesn't** [ˈdʌznt] = **does not**

★**dog** [dɔg] N perro; **to go to the dogs** (person) echarse a perder; (nation etc) ir a la ruina ▶ VT seguir (de cerca); (fig: memory etc) perseguir

dog biscuit N galleta de perro

dog collar N collar m de perro; (fig) alzacuello(s) msg

dog-eared [ˈdɔgɪəd] ADJ sobado; (page) con la esquina doblada

dogfish [ˈdɔgfɪʃ] N cazón m, perro marino

dog food N comida para perros

dogged [ˈdɔgɪd] ADJ tenaz, obstinado

doggy [ˈdɔgɪ] N (inf) perrito

doggy bag N bolsa para llevarse las sobras de la comida

dogma [ˈdɔgmə] N dogma m

dogmatic [dɔgˈmætɪk] ADJ dogmático

do-gooder [duːˈgudəʳ] N (pej): **to be a ~** ser una persona bien intencionada or un filantropista

dogsbody [ˈdɔgzbɔdɪ] N (BRIT) burro de carga

doily [ˈdɔɪlɪ] N pañito de adorno

doing [ˈduːɪŋ] N: **this is your ~** esto es obra tuya ■ **doings** NPL (events) sucesos mpl; (acts) hechos mpl

do-it-yourself [duːɪtjɔːˈsɛlf] N bricolaje m

doldrums [ˈdɔldrəmz] NPL: **to be in the ~** (person) estar abatido; (business) estar estancado

dole [dəʊl] N (BRIT: payment) subsidio de paro; **on the ~** parado ▶ **dole out** VT repartir

doleful [ˈdəʊlful] ADJ triste, lúgubre

doll [dɔl] N muñeca ▶ **doll up** VT: **to ~ o.s. up** ataviarse

★**dollar** [ˈdɔləʳ] N dólar m

dollop [ˈdɔləp] N buena cucharada

dolphin [ˈdɔlfɪn] N delfín m

domain [dəˈmeɪn] N (fig) campo, competencia; (land) dominios mpl

dome [dəʊm] N (Arch) cúpula; (shape) bóveda

★**domestic** [dəˈmɛstɪk] ADJ (animal, duty) doméstico; (flight, news, policy) nacional

domestic appliance N aparato m doméstico, aparato m de uso doméstico

domesticated [dəˈmɛstɪkeɪtɪd] ADJ domesticado; (person: home-loving) casero, hogareño

domesticity [dəʊmɛsˈtɪsɪtɪ] N vida casera

domestic servant N sirviente(-a) m/f

domicile [ˈdɔmɪsaɪl] N domicilio

dominant [ˈdɔmɪnənt] ADJ dominante

dominate [ˈdɔmɪneɪt] VT dominar

domination [dɔmɪˈneɪʃən] N dominación f

domineering [dɔmɪˈnɪərɪŋ] ADJ dominante

Dominica [dɔmɪˈniːkə, dəˈmɪnɪkə] N Dominica

Dominican Republic [dəˈmɪnɪkən-] N República Dominicana

dominion [dəˈmɪnɪən] N dominio

domino [ˈdɔmɪnəʊ] (pl **dominoes**) N ficha de dominó

d

dominoes [ˈdɔmɪnəuz] N (*game*) dominó

don [dɔn] N (*Brit*) profesor(a) m/f de universidad

donate [dəˈneɪt] vt donar

donation [dəˈneɪʃən] N donativo

★**done** [dʌn] pp of **do**

dongle [ˈdɔŋgl] N (*Comput: for wireless connection*) adaptador m; (: *for protected software*) llave f de seguridad

donkey [ˈdɔŋkɪ] N burro

donkey-work [ˈdɔŋkɪwəːk] N (*Brit inf*) trabajo pesado

donor [ˈdəunəʳ] N donante mf

donor card N carnet m de donante de órganos

★**don't** [dəunt] = **do not**

donut [ˈdəunʌt] N (*US*) = **doughnut**

doodle [ˈduːdl] N garabato ▶ vi pintar dibujitos or garabatos

doom [duːm] N (*fate*) suerte f; (*death*) muerte f ▶ vt: **to be doomed to failure** estar condenado al fracaso

doomsday [ˈduːmzdeɪ] N día m del juicio final

★**door** [dɔːʳ] N puerta; (*of car*) portezuela; (*entry*) entrada; **from ~ to ~** de puerta en puerta

doorbell [ˈdɔːbɛl] N timbre m

door handle N tirador m; (*of car*) manija

doorknob N pomo m de la puerta, manilla f (*Lam*)

door knocker N aldaba

doorman [ˈdɔːmən] N (*irreg*) (*in hotel*) portero

doormat [ˈdɔːmæt] N felpudo, estera

doorstep [ˈdɔːstɛp] N peldaño; **on your ~** en la puerta de casa; (*fig*) al lado de casa

door-to-door [ˈdɔːtəˈdɔːʳ] ADJ: **~ selling** venta a domicilio

doorway [ˈdɔːweɪ] N entrada, puerta; **in the ~** en la puerta

dope [dəup] N (*inf: illegal drug*) droga; (: *person*) imbécil mf; (: *information*) información f, informes mpl ▶ vt (*horse etc*) drogar

dopey [ˈdəupɪ] ADJ (*inf*) atontado

dormant [ˈdɔːmənt] ADJ inactivo; (*latent*) latente

dormer [ˈdɔːməʳ] N (*also:* **dormer window**) buhardilla

dormitory [ˈdɔːmɪtrɪ] N (*Brit*) dormitorio; (*US: hall of residence*) residencia, colegio mayor

dormouse [ˈdɔːmaus] (*pl* **dormice** [-maɪs]) N lirón m

Dors ABBR (*Brit*) = **Dorset**

dosage [ˈdəusɪdʒ] N (*on medicine bottle*) dosis f inv, dosificación f

dose [dəus] N (*of medicine*) dosis f inv; **a ~ of flu** un ataque de gripe ▶ vt: **to ~ o.s. with** automedicarse con

dosser [ˈdɔsəʳ] N (*Brit pej*) mendigo(-a); (*lazy person*) vago(-a)

doss house [ˈdɔs-] N (*Brit*) pensión f de mala muerte

dossier [ˈdɔsɪeɪ] N: **~ (on)** expediente m (sobre)

DOT N ABBR (*US:* = *Department of Transportation*) ministerio de transporte

dot [dɔt] N punto; **on the ~** en punto ▶ vt: **dotted with** salpicado de

dotcom [ˈdɔtkɔm] N puntocom f inv

dot command N (*Comput*) instrucción f (precedida) de punto

dote [dəut]: **to ~ on** vt fus adorar, idolatrar

dotted line [ˈdɔtɪd-] N línea de puntos; **to sign on the ~** firmar

dotty [ˈdɔtɪ] ADJ (*inf*) disparatado, chiflado

★**double** [ˈdʌbl] ADJ doble; **~ five two six (5526)** (*Tel*) cinco cinco dos seis; **spelt with a ~ "s"** escrito con dos "eses" ▶ ADV (*twice*): **to cost ~** costar el doble ▶ N (*gen*) doble m; **on the ~**, (*Brit*) **at the ~** corriendo ▶ vt doblar; (*efforts*) redoblar ▶ vi doblarse; (*have two uses etc*): **to ~ as** hacer las veces de

▶ **double back** vi (*person*) volver sobre sus pasos

▶ **double up** vi (*bend over*) doblarse; (*share bedroom*) compartir

double bass N contrabajo

double bed N cama de matrimonio

double-breasted [ˈdʌblˈbrɛstɪd] ADJ cruzado

double-check [ˈdʌblˈtʃɛk] vt volver a revisar ▶ vi: **I'll ~** voy a revisarlo otra vez

double-click [ˈdʌblˈklɪk] (*Comput*) vi hacer doble clic

double cream N nata enriquecida

double-cross [ˈdʌblˈkrɔs] vt (*trick*) engañar; (*betray*) traicionar

doubledecker [ˈdʌblˈdɛkəʳ] N autobús m de dos pisos

double glazing N (*Brit*) doble acristalamiento

double indemnity N doble indemnización f

double-page [ˈdʌblpeɪdʒ] ADJ: **~ spread** doble página

double room N habitación f doble

doubles [ˈdʌblz] N (*Tennis*) juego de dobles

double time N tarifa doble

double whammy [-ˈwæmɪ] N (*inf*) palo doble

double yellow lines NPL (*Brit Aut*) línea doble amarilla de prohibido aparcar, ≈ línea sg amarilla continua

doubly [ˈdʌblɪ] ADV doblemente

★**doubt** [daut] N duda; **there is no ~ that** no cabe duda de que; **without (a) ~** sin duda (alguna); **beyond ~** fuera de duda ▶ vt dudar; (*suspect*) dudar de; **I ~ it very much** lo dudo mucho; **to ~ that** dudar que

doubtful [ˈdautful] ADJ dudoso; (*arousing suspicion: person*) sospechoso; (*unconvinced*): **to be ~ about sth** tener dudas sobre algo; **I'm a bit ~** no estoy convencido

doubtless [ˈdautlɪs] ADV sin duda

dough [dəu] N masa, pasta; (*inf: money*) pasta, lana (*Lam*)

doughnut [ˈdəunʌt] N dónut m

douse [daus] VT (*drench: with water*) mojar; (*extinguish: flames*) apagar

dove [dʌv] N paloma

Dover ['dəuvə'] N Dover

dovetail ['dʌvteɪl] VI (*fig*) encajar

dowager ['dauɪdʒə'] N: **~ duchess** duquesa viuda

dowdy ['daudɪ] ADJ desaliñado; (*inelegant*) poco elegante

Dow-Jones average ['daudʒəunz-] N índice *m* Dow-Jones

Dow-Jones index N índice *m* Dow-Jones

★**down** [daun] N (*fluff*) pelusa; (*feathers*) plumón *m*, flojel *m*; (*hill*) loma ▶ ADV (*also*: **downwards**) abajo, hacia abajo; (*on the ground*) por/en tierra; **~ with X!** ¡abajo X!; **~ there** allí abajo; **~ here** aquí abajo; **I'll be ~ in a minute** ahora bajo; **England is two goals ~** Inglaterra está perdiendo por dos tantos; **I've been ~ with flu** he estado con gripe; **the price of meat is ~** ha bajado el precio de la carne; **I've got it ~ in my diary** lo he apuntado en mi agenda; **to pay £2 ~** dejar 2 libras de depósito; **~ under** (*in Australia etc*) en Australia/Nueva Zelanda ▶ PREP abajo; **he went ~ the hill** fue cuesta abajo ▶ VT (*inf: drink*) beberse, tragar(se); **to ~ tools** (*fig*) declararse en huelga

down-and-out ['daunəndaut] N (*tramp*) vagabundo(-a)

down-at-heel ['daunət'hi:l] ADJ venido a menos; (*appearance*) desaliñado

downbeat ['daunbi:t] N (*Mus*) compás *m* ▶ ADJ (*gloomy*) pesimista

downcast ['daunkɑ:st] ADJ abatido

downer ['daunə'] N (*inf: drug*) tranquilizante; **to be on a ~** estar pasando un mal bache

downfall ['daunfɔ:l] N caída, ruina

downgrade [daun'greɪd] VT (*job*) degradar; (*hotel*) bajar de categoría

downhearted [daun'hɑ:tɪd] ADJ desanimado

downhill [daun'hɪl] ADV: **to go ~** ir cuesta abajo; (*business*) estar en declive

Downing Street ['daunɪŋ-] N (*BRIT*) Downing Street *f*

Downing Street es la calle de Londres en la que tienen su residencia oficial tanto el Primer Ministro (*Prime Minister*) como el Ministro de Economía (*Chancellor of the Exchequer*). El primero vive normalmente en el "number 10" y el segundo en el "number 11". Es una calle cerrada al público que se encuentra en el barrio de Westminster, en el centro de Londres. *Downing Street* se usa también en lenguaje periodístico para referirse al Primer Ministro o al Gobierno.

★**download** ['daunləud] VT (*Comput*) descargar, bajar

downloadable [daun'ləudəbl] ADJ (*Comput*) descargable

down-market ['daun'mɑ:kɪt] ADJ de escasa calidad

down payment N entrada, pago al contado

downplay ['daunpleɪ] VT (*US*) quitar importancia a

downpour ['daunpɔ:'] N aguacero

downright ['daunraɪt] ADJ (*nonsense, lie*) manifiesto; (*refusal*) terminante

downsize [daun'saɪz] VT reducir la plantilla de

Down's syndrome [daunz-] N síndrome *m* de Down

★**downstairs** [daun'stɛəz] ADV (*below*) (en el piso de) abajo; (*motion*) escaleras abajo; **to come/go ~** bajar la escalera

downstream [daun'stri:m] ADV aguas *or* río abajo

downtime ['dauntaɪm] N (*Comm*) tiempo inactivo

down-to-earth [dauntu'ə:θ] ADJ práctico

downtown [daun'taun] ADV en el centro de la ciudad

downtrodden ['dauntrɔdn] ADJ oprimido

down under ADV en Australia (*or* Nueva Zelanda)

downward ['daunwəd] ADV hacia abajo; **face ~** (*person*) boca abajo; (*object*) cara abajo ▶ ADJ: **a ~ trend** una tendencia descendente

downwards ['daunwədz] ADV hacia abajo; **face ~** (*person*) boca abajo; (*object*) cara abajo

dowry ['daurɪ] N dote *f*

doz. ABBR = **dozen**

doze [dəuz] VI dormitar
▶ **doze off** VI echar una cabezada

★**dozen** ['dʌzn] N docena; **a ~ books** una docena de libros; **dozens of** cantidad de; **dozens of times** cantidad de veces; **80p a ~** 80 peniques la docena

DPh, DPhil N ABBR (= *Doctor of Philosophy*) título universitario

DPP N ABBR (*BRIT*) = **Director of Public Prosecutions**

DPT N ABBR (*Med*: = *diphtheria, pertussis, tetanus*) vacuna trivalente

DPW N ABBR (*US*: = *Department of Public Works*) ministerio de obras públicas

Dr, Dr. ABBR (= *doctor*) Dr; (*in street names*) = **drive**

dr ABBR (*Comm*) = **debtor**

drab [dræb] ADJ gris, monótono

★**draft** [drɑ:ft] N (*first copy: of document, report*) borrador *m*; (*Comm*) giro; (*US: call-up*) quinta ▶ VT (*write roughly*) hacer un borrador de; *see also* **draught**

draftsman *etc* ['drɑ:ftsmən] (*US*) = **draughtsman** *etc*

drag [dræg] VT arrastrar; (*river*) dragar, rastrear; **to ~ and drop** (*Comput*) arrastrar y soltar ▶ VI arrastrarse por el suelo ▶ N (*Aviat: resistance*) resistencia aerodinámica; (*inf*) lata; (*women's clothing*): **in ~** vestido de mujer

▸ **drag away** VT: **to ~ away (from)** separar a rastras (de)

▸ **drag on** VI ser interminable

dragnet ['drægnɛt] N (*Naut*) rastra; (*fig*) emboscada

dragon ['drægən] N dragón *m*

dragonfly ['drægənflaɪ] N libélula

dragoon [drə'guːn] N (*cavalryman*) dragón *m* ▸ VT: **to ~ sb into doing sth** forzar a algn a hacer algo

★**drain** [dreɪn] N desaguadero; (*in street*) sumidero; (*drain cover*) rejilla del sumidero; **to be a ~ on** consumir, agotar ▸ VT (*land, marshes*) desecar; (*Med*) drenar; (*reservoir*) desecar; (*fig*) agotar; **to feel drained (of energy)** (*fig*) sentirse agotado ▸ VI escurrirse

drainage ['dreɪnɪdʒ] N (*act*) desagüe *m*; (*Med, Agr*) drenaje *m*; (*sewage*) alcantarillado

draining board ['dreɪnɪŋ-], (*US*) **drainboard** ['dreɪnbɔːd] N escurridero, escurridor *m*

drainpipe ['dreɪnpaɪp] N tubo de desagüe

drake [dreɪk] N pato (macho)

dram [dræm] N (*drink*) traguito, copita

★**drama** ['drɑːmə] N (*art*) teatro; (*play*) drama *m*

★**dramatic** [drə'mætɪk] ADJ dramático; (*sudden, marked*) espectacular

dramatist ['dræmətɪst] N dramaturgo(-a)

dramatize ['dræmətaɪz] VT (*events etc*) dramatizar; (*adapt: novel: for TV, cinema*) adaptar

drank [dræŋk] PT of **drink**

drape [dreɪp] VT (*cloth*) colocar; (*flag*) colgar

draper ['dreɪpəʳ] N (*BRIT*) pañero(-a)

drapes [dreɪps] NPL (*US*) cortinas *fpl*

drastic ['dræstɪk] ADJ (*measure, reduction*) severo; (*change*) radical

draught, (*US*) **draft** [drɑːft] N (*of air*) corriente *f* de aire; (*drink*) trago; (*Naut*) calado; **on ~** (*beer*) de barril

draught beer N cerveza de barril

draughtboard ['drɑːftbɔːd] (*BRIT*) N tablero de damas

draughts [drɑːfts] N (*BRIT*) juego de damas

draughtsman, (*US*) **draftsman** ['drɑːftsmən] N (*irreg*) proyectista *m*, delineante *m*

draughtsmanship, (*US*) **draftsmanship** ['drɑːftsmənʃɪp] N (*drawing*) dibujo lineal; (*skill*) habilidad *f* para el dibujo

★**draw** [drɔː] (*pt* **drew** [druː], *pp* **drawn** [drɔːn]) VT (*pull*) tirar; (*take out*) sacar; (*attract*) atraer; (*picture*) dibujar; (*money*) retirar; (*formulate: conclusion*): **to ~ (from)** sacar (de); (*comparison, distinction*): **to ~ (between)** hacer (entre) ▸ VI (*Sport*) empatar; **to ~ near** acercarse ▸ N (*Sport*) empate *m*; (*lottery*) sorteo; (*attraction*) atracción *f*

▸ **draw back** VI: **to ~ back (from)** echarse atrás (de)

▸ **draw in** VI (*car*) aparcar; (*train*) entrar en la estación

▸ **draw on** VT (*resources*) utilizar, servirse de; (*imagination, person*) recurrir a

▸ **draw out** VI (*lengthen*) alargarse

▸ **draw up** VI (*stop*) pararse ▸ VT (*document*) redactar; (*plan*) trazar

drawback ['drɔːbæk] N inconveniente *m*, desventaja

drawbridge ['drɔːbrɪdʒ] N puente *m* levadizo

drawee [drɔː'iː] N girado, librado

drawer [drɔːʳ] N cajón *m*; (*of cheque*) librador(a) *m/f*

★**drawing** ['drɔːɪŋ] N dibujo

drawing board N tablero (de dibujante)

drawing pin N (*BRIT*) chincheta *m*

drawing room N salón *m*

drawl [drɔːl] N habla lenta y cansina

drawn [drɔːn] PP of **draw** ▸ ADJ (*haggard: with tiredness*) ojeroso; (*: with pain*) macilento

drawstring ['drɔːstrɪŋ] N cordón *m*

DRC N ABBR (= *Democratic Republic of the Congo*) RDC *f*

dread [drɛd] N pavor *m*, terror *m* ▸ VT temer, tener miedo *or* pavor a

dreadful ['drɛdful] ADJ espantoso; **I feel ~!** (*ill*) ¡me siento fatal *or* malísimo!; (*ashamed*) ¡qué vergüenza!

★**dream** [driːm] N sueño; **to have a ~ about sb/ sth** soñar con algn/algo; **sweet dreams!** ¡que sueñes con los angelitos! ▸ VT, VI (*pt, pp* **dreamed** *or* **dreamt** [drɛmt]) soñar

▸ **dream up** VT (*reason, excuse*) inventar; (*plan, idea*) idear

dreamer ['driːməʳ] N soñador(a) *m/f*

dreamt [drɛmt] PT, PP of **dream**

dream world N mundo imaginario *or* de ensueño

dreamy ['driːmɪ] ADJ (*person*) soñador(a), distraído; (*music*) de sueño

dreary ['drɪərɪ] ADJ monótono, aburrido

dredge [drɛdʒ] VT dragar

▸ **dredge up** VT sacar con draga; (*fig: unpleasant facts*) pescar, sacar a luz

dredger ['drɛdʒəʳ] N (*ship, machine*) draga; (*Culin*) tamiz *m*

dregs [drɛgz] NPL heces *fpl*

drench [drɛntʃ] VT empapar; **drenched to the skin** calado hasta los huesos

★**dress** [drɛs] N vestido; (*clothing*) ropa ▸ VT vestir; (*wound*) vendar; (*Culin*) aliñar; (*shop window*) decorar, arreglar; **to ~ o.s., get dressed** vestirse ▸ VI vestirse; **she dresses very well** se viste muy bien

▸ **dress up** VI vestirse de etiqueta; (*in fancy dress*) disfrazarse

dress circle N (*BRIT*) principal *m*

dress designer N modisto(-a)

dresser ['drɛsəʳ] N (*furniture*) aparador *m*; (*: US*) tocador *m*; (*Theat*) camarero(-a)

dressing ['drɛsɪŋ] N (*Med*) vendaje *m*; (*Culin*) aliño

dressing gown N (*BRIT*) bata

dressing room N (*Theat*) camarín m; (*Sport*) vestuario

dressing table N tocador m

dressmaker ['drɛsmeɪkəʳ] N modista, costurera

dressmaking ['drɛsmeɪkɪŋ] N costura

dress rehearsal N ensayo general

dress shirt N camisa de frac

dressy ['drɛsɪ] ADJ (*inf*) elegante

drew [dru:] PT *of* **draw**

dribble ['drɪbl] VI gotear, caer gota a gota; (*baby*) babear ▶ VT (*ball*) driblar, regatear

dried [draɪd] ADJ (*gen*) seco; (*fruit*) paso; (*milk*) en polvo

drier ['draɪəʳ] N = **dryer**

drift [drɪft] N (*of current etc*) flujo; (*of sand*) montón m; (*of snow*) ventisquero; (*meaning*) significado; **to catch sb's ~** cogerle el hilo a algn ▶ VI (*boat*) ir a la deriva; (*sand, snow*) amontonarse; **to let things ~** dejar las cosas como están; **to ~ apart** (*friends*) seguir su camino; (*lovers*) disgustarse, romper

drifter ['drɪftəʳ] N vagabundo(-a)

driftwood ['drɪftwud] N madera flotante

drill [drɪl] N taladro; (*bit*) broca; (*of dentist*) fresa; (*for mining etc*) perforadora, barrena; (*Mil*) instrucción f ▶ VT perforar, taladrar; (*soldiers*) ejercitar; (*pupils: in grammar*) hacer ejercicios con ▶ VI (*for oil*) perforar

drilling ['drɪlɪŋ] N (*for oil*) perforación f

drilling rig N (*on land*) torre f de perforación; (*at sea*) plataforma de perforación

drily ['draɪlɪ] ADV secamente

★**drink** [drɪŋk] N bebida; **to have a ~** tomar algo; tomar una copa *or* un trago; **a ~ of water** un trago de agua; **to invite sb for drinks** invitar a algn a tomar unas copas; **there's food and ~ in the kitchen** hay de comer y de beber en la cocina ▶ VT, VI (*pt* **drank** [dræŋk], *pp* **drunk** [drʌŋk]) beber, tomar (LAm); **would you like something to ~?** ¿quieres beber *or* tomar algo?
▶ **drink in** VT (*person: fresh air*) respirar; (: *story, sight*) beberse

drinkable ['drɪŋkəbl] ADJ (*not poisonous*) potable; (*palatable*) aguantable

drink-driving [drɪŋk'draɪvɪŋ] N: **to be charged with ~** ser acusado de conducir borracho *or* en estado de embriaguez

drinker ['drɪŋkəʳ] N bebedor(a) m/f

drinking ['drɪŋkɪŋ] N (*drunkenness*) beber m

drinking fountain N fuente f de agua potable

drinking water N agua potable

drip [drɪp] N (*act*) goteo; (*one drip*) gota; (*Med*) gota a gota m; (*sound: of water etc*) goteo; (*inf: spineless person*) soso(-a) ▶ VI gotear, caer gota a gota

drip-dry ['drɪp'draɪ] ADJ (*shirt*) de lava y pon

dripping ['drɪpɪŋ] N (*animal fat*) pringue m ▶ ADJ: **~ wet** calado

★**drive** [draɪv] (*pt* **drove** [drəuv], *pp* **driven** ['drɪvn]) N paseo (en coche); (*journey*) viaje m (en coche); (*also:* **driveway**) entrada; (*street*) calle f; (*energy*) energía, vigor m; (*Psych*) impulso; (*Sport*) ataque m; (*Comput: also:* **disk drive**) unidad f (de disco); **to go for a ~** dar una vuelta en coche; **it's three hours' ~ from London** es un viaje de tres horas en coche desde Londres; **left-/right-hand ~** conducción f a la izquierda/derecha; **front-/rear-wheel ~** tracción f delantera/trasera; **sales ~** promoción f de ventas ▶ VT (*car*) conducir, manejar (LAm); (*nail*) clavar; (*push*) empujar; (*Tech: motor*) impulsar; **to ~ sb mad** volverle loco a algn; **to ~ sb to (do) sth** empujar a algn a (hacer) algo; **he drives a taxi** es taxista; **he drives a Mercedes** tiene un Mercedes ▶ VI (*Aut: at controls*) conducir, manejar (LAm); (: *travel*) pasearse en coche; **can you ~?** ¿sabes conducir *or* (LAm) manejar?; **to ~ at 50 km an hour** ir a 50km por hora
▶ **drive at** VT FUS (*fig: intend, mean*) querer decir, insinuar
▶ **drive on** VI no parar, seguir adelante ▶ VT (*incite, encourage*) empujar
▶ **drive out** VT (*force out*) expulsar, echar

drive-by ['draɪvbaɪ] N: **~ shooting** tiroteo desde el coche

drive-in ['draɪvɪn] ADJ (*esp US*): **~ cinema** autocine m

drivel ['drɪvl] N (*inf*) tonterías fpl

driven ['drɪvn] PP *of* **drive**

★**driver** ['draɪvəʳ] N conductor(a) m/f, chofer mf (LAm); (*of taxi*) taxista mf

driver's license N (*US*) carnet m *or* permiso de conducir

driveway ['draɪvweɪ] N camino de entrada

driving ['draɪvɪŋ] N conducir m, manejar m (LAm) ▶ ADJ (*force*) impulsor(a)

driving instructor N instructor(a) m/f de autoescuela

driving lesson N clase f de conducir

driving licence N (*Brit*) carnet m *or* permiso de conducir

driving school N autoescuela

driving test N examen m de conducir

drizzle ['drɪzl] N llovizna, garúa (LAm) ▶ VI lloviznar

droll [drəul] ADJ gracioso

dromedary ['drɔmɪdərɪ] N dromedario

drone [drəun] VI (*bee, aircraft, engine*) zumbar; (*also:* **drone on**) murmurar sin interrupción ▶ N zumbido; (*male bee*) zángano

drool [dru:l] VI babear; **to ~ over sb/sth** caérsele la baba por algn/algo

droop [dru:p] VI (*flower*) marchitarse; (*shoulders*) encorvarse; (*head*) inclinarse; (*fig: spirits*) decaer, desanimarse

★**drop** [drɔp] N (*of water*) gota; (*fall: in price*) bajada; (: *in salary*) disminución f; **cough drops** pastillas fpl para la tos; **a ~ of 10%** una bajada del 10 por ciento ▶ VT (*allow to fall*) dejar caer; (*voice, eyes, price*) bajar; (*set down from car*) dejar; **to ~ sb a line** mandar unas líneas a algn; **to ~ anchor** echar el ancla ▶ VI (*object*) caer; (*price, temperature*) bajar; (*wind*) calmarse, amainar; (*numbers, attendance*) disminuir ■ **drops** NPL (*Med*) gotas *fpl*

▶ **drop in** VI (*inf: visit*): **to ~ in (on)** pasar por casa (de)

▶ **drop off** VI (*sleep*) dormirse ▶ VT (*passenger*) bajar, dejar

▶ **drop out** VI (*withdraw*) retirarse

droplet [ˈdrɔplɪt] N gotita

dropout [ˈdrɔpaut] N (*from society*) marginado(-a); (*from university*) estudiante *mf* que ha abandonado los estudios

dropper [ˈdrɔpəʳ] N (*Med*) cuentagotas *m inv*

droppings [ˈdrɔpɪŋz] NPL excremento *sg*

dross [drɔs] N (*fig*) escoria

drought [draut] N sequía

drove [drəuv] PT of **drive**

drown [draun] VT (*also*: **drown out**: *sound*) ahogar ▶ VI ahogarse

drowse [drauz] VI estar medio dormido

drowsy [ˈdrauzɪ] ADJ soñoliento; **to be ~** tener sueño

drudge [drʌdʒ] N esclavo(-a) del trabajo

drudgery [ˈdrʌdʒərɪ] N trabajo pesado or monótono

★**drug** [drʌg] N (*Med*) medicamento, droga; (*narcotic*) droga; **to be on drugs** drogarse; **he's on drugs** se droga ▶ VT drogar

drug addict N drogadicto(-a)

drug dealer N traficante *mf* de drogas

drug-driving [drʌgˈdraivɪŋ] N conducción *f* bajo los efectos de las drogas

druggist [ˈdrʌgɪst] N (*US*) farmacéutico(-a)

drug peddler N traficante *mf* de drogas

drugstore [ˈdrʌgstɔːʳ] N (*US*) tienda (*de comestibles, periódicos y medicamentos*)

drug trafficker N narcotraficante *mf*

★**drum** [drʌm] N tambor *m*; (*large*) bombo; (*for oil, petrol*) bidón *m* ▶ VI tocar el tambor; (*with fingers*) tamborilear ▶ VT: **to ~ one's fingers on the table** tamborilear con los dedos sobre la mesa ■ **drums** NPL batería *sg*

▶ **drum up** VT (*enthusiasm, support*) movilizar, fomentar

drummer [ˈdrʌməʳ] N (*in military band*) tambor *mf*; (*in jazz/pop group*) batería *mf*

drumstick [ˈdrʌmstɪk] N (*Mus*) palillo, baqueta; (*chicken leg*) muslo (de pollo)

drunk [drʌŋk] PP of **drink** ▶ ADJ borracho; **to get ~** emborracharse ▶ N (*also*: **drunkard**) borracho(-a)

drunken [ˈdrʌŋkən] ADJ borracho

drunkenness [ˈdrʌŋkənnɪs] N embriaguez *f*

★**dry** [draɪ] ADJ seco; (*day*) sin lluvia; (*climate*) árido, seco; (*humour*) agudo; (*uninteresting*: lec-

ture) aburrido, pesado; **on ~ land** en tierra firme ▶ VT secar; (*tears*) enjugarse; **to ~ one's hands/hair/eyes** secarse las manos/el pelo/las lágrimas ▶ VI secarse

▶ **dry up** VI (*river*) secarse; (*supply, imagination etc*) agotarse; (*in speech*) atascarse

dry-clean [ˈdraɪˈkliːn] VT limpiar or lavar en seco; **"~ only"** (*on label*) "limpieza or lavado en seco"

dry-cleaner's [ˈdraɪˈkliːnəz] N tintorería

dry-cleaning [ˈdraɪˈkliːnɪŋ] N lavado en seco

dry dock N (*Naut*) dique *m* seco

dryer [ˈdraɪəʳ] N (*for hair*) secador *m*; (*for clothes*) secadora

dry goods NPL (*Comm*) mercería *sg*

dry goods store N (*US*) mercería

dry ice N nieve *f* carbónica, hielo seco

dryness [ˈdraɪnɪs] N sequedad *f*

dry rot N putrefacción *f*

dry run N (*fig*) ensayo

dry ski slope N pista artificial de esquí

DSc N ABBR (= *Doctor of Science*) título universitario

DST N ABBR (*US*: = *Daylight Saving Time*) hora de verano

DT N ABBR (*Comput*) = **data transmission**

DTP N ABBR = **desktop publishing**; (*Med: vaccination*) = **diphtheria, tetanus, pertussis**

DT's N ABBR (*inf*: = *delirium tremens*) delirium *m* tremens

dual [ˈdjuəl] ADJ doble

dual carriageway N (*BRIT*) ≈ autovía

dual-control [ˈdjuəlkənˈtrəul] ADJ de doble mando

dual nationality N doble nacionalidad *f*

dual-purpose [ˈdjuəlˈpəːpəs] ADJ de doble uso

dubbed [dʌbd] ADJ (*Cine*) doblado

dubious [ˈdjuːbɪəs] ADJ (*questionable*: *reputation*) dudoso; (: *character*) sospechoso; (*unsure*) indeciso; **I'm very ~ about it** tengo mis dudas sobre ello

Dublin [ˈdʌblɪn] N Dublín

Dubliner [ˈdʌblɪnəʳ] N dublinés(-esa) *m/f*

duchess [ˈdʌtʃɪs] N duquesa

★**duck** [dʌk] N pato ▶ VI agacharse ▶ VT (*plunge in water*) zambullir

duckling [ˈdʌklɪŋ] N patito

duct [dʌkt] N conducto, canal *m*

dud [dʌd] N (*shell*) obús *m* que no estalla; (*object, tool*): **it's a ~** es una filfa ▶ ADJ: **~ cheque** (*BRIT*) cheque *m* sin fondos

★**due** [djuː] ADJ (*proper*) debido; (*fitting*) conveniente, oportuno; **in ~ course** a su debido tiempo; **~ to** debido a; **to be ~ to** deberse a; **the train is ~ to arrive at 8.00** el tren tiene (prevista) la llegada a las ocho; **the rent's ~ on the 30th** hay que pagar el alquiler el día 30; **I am ~ six days' leave** me deben seis días de vacaciones; **she is ~ back tomorrow** ella debe volver mañana ▶ ADV: **~ north** derecho al norte ■ **dues** NPL (for club, union) cuota sg; (in harbour) derechos mpl

due date N fecha de vencimiento

duel ['djuəl] N duelo

duet [dju:'ɛt] N dúo

duff [dʌf] ADJ (BRIT inf) sin valor

duffel bag ['dʌfl-] N macuto

duffel coat ['dʌfl-] N trenca

dug [dʌg] PT, PP of **dig**

dugout ['dʌgaut] N (canoe) piragua (hecha de un solo tronco); (Sport) banquillo; (Mil) refugio subterráneo

duke [dju:k] N duque m

dull [dʌl] ADJ (light) apagado; (stupid) torpe; (boring) pesado; (sound, pain) sordo; (weather, day) gris ▶ VT (pain, grief) aliviar; (mind, senses) entorpecer

duly ['dju:lɪ] ADV debidamente; (on time) a su debido tiempo

dumb [dʌm] ADJ (!) mudo; (stupid) estúpido; **to be struck ~** (fig) quedar boquiabierto

dumbbell ['dʌmbɛl] N (Sport) pesa

dumbfounded [dʌm'faundɪd] ADJ pasmado

dummy ['dʌmɪ] N (tailor's model) maniquí m; (BRIT: for baby) chupete m ▶ ADJ falso, postizo; **~ run** ensayo

★**dump** [dʌmp] N (heap) montón m de basura; (place) basurero, vertedero; (: inf) tugurio; (Mil) depósito; (Comput) copia vaciada; **to be (down) in the dumps** (inf) tener murria, estar deprimido ▶ VT (put down) dejar; (get rid of) deshacerse de; (Comput) tirar (a la papelera); (Comm: goods) inundar el mercado de

dumping ['dʌmpɪŋ] N (Econ) dumping m; (of rubbish): **"no ~"** "prohibido verter basura"

dumpling ['dʌmplɪŋ] N bola de masa hervida

dumpy ['dʌmpɪ] ADJ regordete(-a)

dunce [dʌns] N zopenco(-a)

dune [dju:n] N duna

dung [dʌŋ] N estiércol m

dungarees [dʌŋgə'ri:z] NPL mono sg, overol msg (LAm)

dungeon ['dʌndʒən] N calabozo

dunk [dʌŋk] VT mojar

duo ['dju:əu] N (Mus) dúo

duodenal [dju:ə'di:nl] ADJ (ulcer) de duodeno

duodenum [dju:ə'di:nəm] N duodeno

dupe [dju:p] N (victim) víctima ▶ VT engañar

duplex ['dju:plɛks] N (US: also: **duplex apartment**) dúplex m

duplicate N ['dju:plɪkət] duplicado; (copy of letter etc) copia; **in ~** por duplicado ▶ ADJ (copy) duplicado ▶ VT ['dju:plɪkeɪt] duplicar; (photocopy) fotocopiar; (repeat) repetir

duplicate key N duplicado de una llave

duplicity [dju:'plɪsɪtɪ] N doblez f, duplicidad f

durability [djuərə'bɪlɪtɪ] N durabilidad f

durable ['djuərəbl] ADJ duradero

duration [djuə'reɪʃən] N duración f

duress [djuə'rɛs] N: **under ~** por coacción

Durex® ['djuərɛks] N (BRIT) preservativo

★**during** ['djuərɪŋ] PREP durante

dusk [dʌsk] N crepúsculo, anochecer m

dusky ['dʌskɪ] ADJ oscuro; (complexion) moreno

★**dust** [dʌst] N polvo ▶ VT (furniture) desempolvar; (cake etc): **to ~ with** espolvorear de
▶ **dust off** VT (also fig) desempolvar, quitar el polvo de

★**dustbin** ['dʌstbɪn] N (BRIT) cubo de la basura, balde m (LAM)

dustbin liner N bolsa de basura

duster ['dʌstər] N paño, trapo; (feather duster) plumero

dust jacket N sobrecubierta

dustman ['dʌstmən] N (irreg) (BRIT) basurero

dustpan ['dʌstpæn] N cogedor m

dust storm N vendaval m de polvo

dusty ['dʌstɪ] ADJ polvoriento

★**Dutch** [dʌtʃ] ADJ holandés(-esa) ▶ N (Ling) holandés m ▶ ADV: **to go ~** (inf) pagar a escote ■ **the Dutch** NPL los holandeses

Dutch auction N subasta a la rebaja

Dutchman ['dʌtʃmən], **Dutchwoman** ['dʌtʃwumən] N (irreg) holandés(-esa) m/f

dutiful ['dju:tɪful] ADJ (child) obediente; (husband) sumiso; (employee) cumplido

★**duty** ['dju:tɪ] N deber m; (tax) derechos mpl de aduana; (Med: in hospital) servicio, guardia; **on ~** de servicio; (at night etc) de guardia; **off ~** libre (de servicio); **to make it one's ~ to do sth** encargarse de hacer algo sin falta; **to pay ~ on sth** pagar los derechos sobre algo

duty-free [dju:tɪ'fri:] ADJ libre de impuestos; **~ shop** tienda libre de impuestos

duty officer N (Mil etc) oficial mf de guardia

★**duvet** ['du:veɪ] N (BRIT) edredón m (nórdico)

DV ABBR (= Deo volente) Dios mediante

★**DVD** N ABBR (= digital versatile or video disc) DVD m

DVD player N lector m de DVD

DVD writer N grabadora de DVD

DVLA N ABBR (BRIT: = Driver and Vehicle Licensing Agency) organismo encargado de la expedición de permisos de conducir y matriculación de vehículos

DVM N ABBR (US: = Doctor of Veterinary Medicine) título universitario

DVT N ABBR = **deep-vein thrombosis**

dwarf [dwɔ:f] (pl **dwarves** [dwɔ:vz]) N (!) enano(-a) ▶ VT empequeñecer

dwell [dwɛl] (pt, pp **dwelt** [dwɛlt]) VI morar
▶ **dwell on** VT FUS explayarse en

dweller ['dwɛlər] N habitante mf; **city ~** habitante mf de la ciudad

dwelling ['dwɛlɪŋ] N vivienda

dwelt [dwɛlt] PT, PP of **dwell**

dwindle ['dwɪndl] vi menguar, disminuir

dwindling ['dwɪndlɪŋ] ADJ (*strength, interest*) menguante; (*resources, supplies*) en disminución

DWP N ABBR (*BRIT*) = **Department for Work and Pensions**

dye [daɪ] N tinte *m*; **hair ~** tinte *m* para el pelo ▸ vt teñir

dying ['daɪɪŋ] ADJ moribundo, agonizante; (*moments*) final; (*words*) último

dyke [daɪk] N (*barrier*) dique *m*; (*channel*) arroyo, acequia; (*causeway*) calzada

dynamic [daɪ'næmɪk] ADJ dinámico

dynamics [daɪ'næmɪks] N, NPL dinámica *sg*

dynamite ['daɪnəmaɪt] N dinamita ▸ vt dinamitar

dynamo ['daɪnəməu] N dinamo *f*, dinamo *m* (*LAm*)

dynasty ['dɪnəstɪ] N dinastía

dysentery ['dɪsɪntrɪ] N disentería

dyslexia [dɪs'lɛksɪə] N dislexia

dyslexic [dɪs'lɛksɪk] ADJ disléxico

dyspepsia [dɪs'pɛpsɪə] N dispepsia

dyspraxia [dɪs'præksɪə] N dispraxia

dystrophy ['dɪstrəfɪ] N distrofia; **muscular ~** distrofia muscular

Ee

E, e [iː] N (*letter*) E, e *f*; (*Mus*): **E** mi *m*; **E for Edward**, (*US*) **E for Easy** E de Enrique

E ABBR (= *east*) E ▶ N ABBR (= *ecstasy*) éxtasis *m*

ea. ABBR = **each**

E.A. ABBR (*US*: = *educational age*) nivel escolar

★**each** [iːtʃ] ADJ cada *inv*; **~ day** cada día ▶ PRON cada uno; **~ other** el uno al otro; **they hate ~ other** se odian (entre ellos *or* mutuamente); **~ of us** cada uno de nosotros ▶ ADV cada uno; **they have two books ~** tienen dos libros cada uno; **they cost £5 ~** cuestan cinco libras cada uno

> Use a reflexive verb to translate *each other*: They don't know each other. **No se conocen**.

eager [ˈiːɡəʳ] ADJ (*gen*) impaciente; (*hopeful*) ilusionado; (*keen*) entusiasmado; (*pupil*) apasionado; **to be ~ to do sth** estar deseoso de hacer algo; **to be ~ for** tener muchas ganas de, ansiar

eagerly [ˈiːɡəlɪ] ADV con impaciencia; con ilusión; con entusiasmo

eagerness [ˈiːɡənɪs] N impaciencia; ilusión *f*; entusiasmo

eagle [ˈiːɡl] N águila

E & OE ABBR = **errors and omissions excepted**

★**ear** [ɪəʳ] N oreja; (*sense of hearing*) oído; (*of corn*) espiga; **up to the ears in debt** abrumado de deudas

earache [ˈɪəreɪk] N dolor *m* de oídos

eardrum [ˈɪədrʌm] N tímpano

earful [ˈɪəful] N: **to give sb an ~** (*inf*) echar una bronca a algn

earl [əːl] N conde *m*

★**earlier** [ˈəːlɪəʳ] ADJ anterior ▶ ADV antes

★**early** [ˈəːlɪ] ADV (*gen*) temprano; (*ahead of time*) con tiempo, con anticipación; **~ in the morning/afternoon** a primeras horas de la mañana/tarde; **I can't come any earlier** no puedo llegar antes ▶ ADJ (*gen*) temprano; (*reply*) pronto; (*man*) primitivo; (*first: Christians, settlers*) primero; **to have an ~ night** acostarse temprano; **in the ~** *or* **~ in the spring/19th century** a principios de primavera/del siglo diecinueve; **you're ~!** ¡has llegado temprano *or* pronto!; **she's in her ~ forties** tiene poco más de cuarenta años; **at your earliest convenience** (*Comm*) con la mayor brevedad posible

early retirement N jubilación *f* anticipada

early warning system N sistema *m* de alerta inmediata

earmark [ˈɪəmɑːk] VT: **to ~ for** reservar para, destinar a

★**earn** [əːn] VT (*gen*) ganar; (*salary*) percibir; (*interest*) devengar; (*praise*) ganarse; **to ~ one's living** ganarse la vida

earned income N renta del trabajo

earnest [ˈəːnɪst] ADJ (*wish*) fervoroso; (*person*) serio, formal ▶ N (*also:* **earnest money**) anticipo, señal *f*; **in ~** *adv* en serio

★**earnings** [ˈəːnɪŋz] NPL (*personal*) ingresos *mpl*; (*of company etc*) ganancias *fpl*

earphones [ˈɪəfəunz] NPL auriculares *mpl*

earplugs [ˈɪəplʌgz] NPL tapones *mpl* para los oídos

earring [ˈɪərɪŋ] N pendiente *m*, arete *m* (LAM)

earshot [ˈɪəʃɔt] N: **out of/within ~** fuera del/al alcance del oído

★**earth** [əːθ] N (*gen*) tierra; (BRIT *Elec*) toma de tierra ▶ VT (BRIT *Elec*) conectar a tierra

earthenware [ˈəːθnwɛəʳ] N loza (de barro)

earthly [ˈəːθlɪ] ADJ terrenal, mundano; **~ paradise** paraíso terrenal; **there is no ~ reason to think ...** no existe razón para pensar ...

earthquake [ˈəːθkweɪk] N terremoto

earth-shattering [ˈəːθʃætərɪŋ] ADJ trascendental

earthworm [ˈəːθwəːm] N lombriz *f*

earthy [ˈəːθɪ] ADJ (*fig: uncomplicated*) sencillo; (*coarse*) grosero

earwig [ˈɪəwɪg] N tijereta
ease [iːz] N facilidad f; (comfort) comodidad f; **with ~** con facilidad; **to feel at ~/ill at ~** sentirse a gusto/a disgusto; **at ~!** (Mil) ¡descansen!
▶ VT (task) facilitar; (problem) mitigar; (pain) aliviar; (loosen) soltar; (relieve: pressure, tension) aflojar; (weight) aligerar; (help pass): **to ~ sth in/out** meter/sacar algo con cuidado ▶ VI (situation) relajarse
▶ **ease off, ease up** VI (work, business) aflojar; (person) relajarse
easel [ˈiːzl] N caballete m
★**easily** [ˈiːzɪlɪ] ADV fácilmente
easiness [ˈiːzɪnɪs] N facilidad f; (of manners) soltura
★**east** [iːst] N este m, oriente m; **the E~** el Oriente; (Pol) el Este ▶ ADJ del este, oriental ▶ ADV al este, hacia el este
eastbound ADJ en dirección al este
Easter [ˈiːstəʳ] N Pascua (de Resurrección)
Easter egg N huevo de Pascua
Easter holidays NPL Semana Santa sg
Easter Island N Isla de Pascua
easterly [ˈiːstəlɪ] ADJ (to the east) al este; (from the east) del este
Easter Monday N lunes m de Pascua
★**eastern** [ˈiːstən] ADJ del este, oriental; **E~ Europe** Europa del Este; **the E~ bloc** (Pol) los países del Este
Easter Sunday N Domingo de Resurrección
East Germany N (formerly) Alemania Oriental or del Este
East Timor [ˈiːstˈiːmɔː] N Timor Este m
eastward [ˈiːstwəd], **eastwards** [ˈiːstwədz] ADV hacia el este
★**easy** [ˈiːzɪ] ADJ fácil; (life) holgado, cómodo; (relaxed) natural; **payment on ~ terms** (Comm) facilidades de pago; **I'm ~** (inf) me da igual, no me importa; **easier said than done** del dicho al hecho hay buen trecho ▶ ADV: **to take it** or **things ~** (not worry) no preocuparse; (go slowly) tomarlo con calma; (rest) descansar
easy chair N butaca
easy-going [ˈiːzɪˈgəʊɪŋ] ADJ acomodadizo
easy touch [iːzɪˈtʌtʃ] N: **he's an ~** (inf) es fácil de convencer
★**eat** [iːt] (pt ate [eɪt], pp eaten [ˈiːtn]) VT comer
▶ **eat away** VT (sea) desgastar; (acid) corroer
▶ **eat away at, eat into** VT FUS corroer
▶ **eat out** VI comer fuera
▶ **eat up** VT (meal etc) comerse; **it eats up electricity** devora la electricidad
eatable [ˈiːtəbl] ADJ comestible
eau de Cologne [əʊdəkəˈləʊn] N (agua de) colonia
eaves [iːvz] NPL alero sg
eavesdrop [ˈiːvzdrɔp] VI: **to ~ (on sb)** escuchar a escondidas or con disimulo (a algn)
ebb [ɛb] N reflujo; **~ and flow** el flujo y reflujo;

to be at a low ~ (fig: person) estar de capa caída
▶ VI bajar; (fig: also: **ebb away**) decaer
ebb tide N marea menguante
e-bike [ˈiːbaɪk] N bici f eléctrica
ebony [ˈɛbənɪ] N ébano
e-book [ˈiːbuk] N libro electrónico, e-book m
ebullient [ɪˈbʌlɪənt] ADJ entusiasta, animado
e-business [ˈiːbɪznɪs] N (commerce) comercio electrónico; (company) negocio electrónico
EC N ABBR (formerly: = European Community) CE f
e-card [ˈiːkɑːd] N tarjeta de felicitación electrónica, e-card f
ECB N ABBR (= European Central Bank) BCE m
eccentric [ɪkˈsɛntrɪk] ADJ, N excéntrico(-a) m/f
ecclesiastical [ɪkliːzɪˈæstɪkəl] ADJ eclesiástico
ECG N ABBR (= electrocardiogram) E.C.G. m
★**echo** [ˈɛkəʊ] (pl **echoes**) N eco m ▶ VT (sound) repetir ▶ VI resonar, hacer eco
e-cigarette [ˈiːsɪgərɛt] N cigarrillo electrónico
ECLA N ABBR (= Economic Commission for Latin America) CEPAL f
éclair [ˈeɪklɛəʳ] N petisú m
eclipse [ɪˈklɪps] N eclipse m ▶ VT eclipsar
ECM N ABBR (US: = European Common Market) MCE m
eco- [ˈiːkəʊ] PREF eco-
eco-friendly [ˈiːkəʊfrɛndlɪ] ADJ ecológico
ecological [iːkəˈlɔdʒɪkl] ADJ ecológico
ecologist [ɪˈkɔlədʒɪst] N ecologista mf; (scientist) ecólogo(-a)
ecology [ɪˈkɔlədʒɪ] N ecología
e-commerce [ˈiːkɔməːs] N comercio electrónico
★**economic** [iːkəˈnɔmɪk] ADJ (profitable: price) económico; (: business etc) rentable
economical [iːkəˈnɔmɪkl] ADJ económico
economically [iːkəˈnɔmɪklɪ] ADV económicamente
★**economics** [iːkəˈnɔmɪks] N (Scol) economía ▶ NPL (financial aspects) finanzas fpl
economic warfare N guerra económica
economist [ɪˈkɔnəmɪst] N economista mf
economize [ɪˈkɔnəmaɪz] VI economizar, ahorrar
★**economy** [ɪˈkɔnəmɪ] N economía; **economies of scale** economías fpl de escala
economy class N (Aviat etc) clase f turista
economy class syndrome N síndrome m de la clase turista
economy size N tamaño familiar
ecosystem [ˈiːkəʊsɪstəm] N ecosistema m
eco-tourism [iːkəʊˈtuərɪzm] N turismo verde or ecológico
ecstasy [ˈɛkstəsɪ] N éxtasis m inv; (drug) éxtasis m inv
ecstatic [ɛksˈtætɪk] ADJ extático, extasiado
ECT N ABBR = **electroconvulsive therapy**

Ecuador [ˈɛkwədɔːʳ] N Ecuador *m*

Ecuadoran [ɛkwəˈdɔːrən], **Ecuadorian** [ɛkwəˈdɔːrɪən] ADJ, N ecuatoriano(-a) *m/f*

ecumenical [iːkjuˈmɛnɪkl] ADJ ecuménico

eczema [ˈɛksɪmə] N eczema *m*

eddy [ˈɛdɪ] N remolino

★**edge** [ɛdʒ] N (of knife etc) filo; (of object) borde *m*; (of lake etc) orilla; **on ~** (fig) = **edgy** ▶ VT (Sewing) ribetear ▶ VI: **to ~ past** pasar con dificultad; **to ~ away from** alejarse poco a poco de; **to ~ forward** avanzar poco a poco; **to ~ up** subir lentamente

edgeways [ˈɛdʒweɪz] ADV: **he couldn't get a word in ~** no pudo meter baza

edging [ˈɛdʒɪŋ] N (Sewing) ribete *m*; (of path) borde *m*

edgy [ˈɛdʒɪ] ADJ nervioso, inquieto

edible [ˈɛdɪbl] ADJ comestible

edict [ˈiːdɪkt] N edicto

edifice [ˈɛdɪfɪs] N edificio

edifying [ˈɛdɪfaɪɪŋ] ADJ edificante

Edinburgh [ˈɛdɪnbərə] N Edimburgo

El **Edinburgh Festival** (Festival de Edimburgo) es uno de los grandes eventos culturales europeos. Se celebra todos los años durante tres semanas del mes de agosto. Es famoso tanto por su programación oficial como por su festival alternativo, The Fringe, que presenta teatro, música, comedia y danza de vanguardia. Sus estrenos de más éxito aparecerán en las carteleras de otras ciudades del país después del festival. Durante el festival también se celebra, en la explanada delante del Castillo de Edimburgo, un gran espectáculo de música militar, el Military Tattoo.

edit [ˈɛdɪt] VT (be editor of) dirigir; (re-write) redactar; (cut) cortar; (Comput) editar

edition [ɪˈdɪʃən] N (gen) edición *f*; (number printed) tirada

★**editor** [ˈɛdɪtəʳ] N (of newspaper) director(a) *m/f*; (of book) redactor(a) *m/f*; (also: **film editor**) montador(a) *m/f*

editorial [ɛdɪˈtɔːrɪəl] ADJ editorial; **~ staff** redacción *f* ▶ N editorial *m*

EDP N ABBR (= electronic data processing) PED *m*

EDT N ABBR (US: = Eastern Daylight Time) hora de verano de Nueva York

educate [ˈɛdjukeɪt] VT (gen) educar; (instruct) instruir

educated [ˈɛdjukeɪtɪd] ADJ culto

educated guess [ˈɛdjukeɪtɪd-] N hipótesis *f* sólida

★**education** [ɛdjuˈkeɪʃən] N educación *f*; (schooling) enseñanza; (Scol: subject etc) pedagogía; **primary/secondary ~** enseñanza primaria/ secundaria

★**educational** [ɛdjuˈkeɪʃənl] ADJ (policy etc) de educación, educativo; (teaching) docente;

(instructive) educativo; **~ technology** tecnología educacional

Edwardian [ɛdˈwɔːdɪən] ADJ eduardiano

EEG N ABBR = **electroencephalogram**

eel [iːl] N anguila

EENT N ABBR (US Med) = **eye, ear, nose and throat**

EEOC N ABBR (US: = Equal Employment Opportunity Commission) comisión que investiga discriminación racial o sexual en el empleo

eerie [ˈɪərɪ] ADJ (sound, experience) espeluznante

EET N ABBR (= Eastern European Time) hora de Europa oriental

efface [ɪˈfeɪs] VT borrar

★**effect** [ɪˈfɛkt] N efecto; **to take ~** (law) entrar en vigor or vigencia; (drug) surtir efecto; **in ~** en realidad; **to have an ~ on sb/sth** hacerle efecto a algn/afectar algo; **to put into ~** (plan) llevar a la práctica; **his letter is to the ~ that ...** su carta viene a decir que ... ▶ VT efectuar, llevar a cabo ■ **effects** NPL (property) efectos *mpl*

★**effective** [ɪˈfɛktɪv] ADJ (gen) eficaz; (striking: display, outfit) impresionante; (real) efectivo; **to become ~** (law) entrar en vigor; **~ date** fecha de vigencia

effectively [ɪˈfɛktɪvlɪ] ADV (efficiently) eficazmente; (strikingly) de manera impresionante; (in reality) de hecho

effectiveness [ɪˈfɛktɪvnɪs] N eficacia

effeminate [ɪˈfɛmɪnɪt] ADJ afeminado

effervescent [ɛfəˈvɛsnt] ADJ efervescente

efficacy [ˈɛfɪkəsɪ] N eficacia

efficiency [ɪˈfɪʃənsɪ] N (gen) eficiencia; (of machine) rendimiento

★**efficient** [ɪˈfɪʃənt] ADJ eficiente; (remedy, product, system) eficaz; (machine, car) de buen rendimiento

efficiently [ɪˈfɪʃəntlɪ] ADV eficientemente, de manera eficiente

effigy [ˈɛfɪdʒɪ] N efigie *f*

effluent [ˈɛfluənt] N vertidos *mpl*

★**effort** [ˈɛfət] N esfuerzo; **to make an ~ to do sth** hacer un esfuerzo or esforzarse para hacer algo

effortless [ˈɛfətlɪs] ADJ sin ningún esfuerzo

effrontery [ɪˈfrʌntərɪ] N descaro

effusive [ɪˈfjuːsɪv] ADJ efusivo

EFL N ABBR (Scol) = **English as a foreign language**

EFTA [ˈɛftə] N ABBR (= European Free Trade Association) EFTA *f*

e.g. ADV ABBR (= exempli gratia) p.ej.

★**egg** [ɛg] N huevo; **hard-boiled/soft-boiled/ poached ~** huevo duro or (LAM) a la copa or (LAM) tibio/pasado por agua/escalfado; **scrambled eggs** huevos revueltos
▶ **egg on** VT incitar

eggcup [ˈɛgkʌp] N huevera

eggnog [ɛgˈnɔg] N ponche *m* de huevo

eggplant [ˈɛgplɑːnt] N (esp US) berenjena

eggshell ['ɛgʃɛl] N cáscara de huevo

egg-timer ['ɛgtaɪməʳ] N reloj m de arena (para cocer huevos)

egg white N clara de huevo

egg yolk N yema de huevo

ego ['iːgəu] N ego

egotism ['ɛgəutɪzəm] N egoísmo

egotist ['ɛgəutɪst] N egoísta mf

ego trip N: **to be on an ~** creerse el centro del mundo

Egypt ['iːdʒɪpt] N Egipto

Egyptian [ɪ'dʒɪpʃən] ADJ, N egipcio(-a) m/f

eiderdown ['aɪdədaun] N edredón m

★**eight** [eɪt] NUM ocho

★**eighteen** [eɪ'tiːn] NUM dieciocho

★**eighteenth** ['eɪ'tiːnθ] ADJ decimoctavo; **the ~ floor** la planta dieciocho; **the ~ of August** el dieciocho de agosto

★**eighth** [eɪtθ] ADJ octavo

eightieth ['eɪtɪɪθ] ADJ octogésimo

★**eighty** ['eɪtɪ] NUM ochenta

★**Eire** ['ɛərə] N Eire m

EIS N ABBR (= Educational Institute of Scotland) sindicato de profesores escoceses

★**either** ['aɪðəʳ] ADJ cualquiera de los dos ...; (both, each) cada; **on ~ side** en ambos lados ▸ PRON: **~ (of them)** cualquiera (de los dos); **I don't like ~** no me gusta ninguno de los dos ▸ ADV tampoco; **no, I don't ~** no, yo tampoco ▸ CONJ: **~ yes or no** o sí o no

eject [ɪ'dʒɛkt] VT echar; (tenant) desahuciar ▸ VI eyectarse

ejector seat [ɪ'dʒɛktə-] N asiento proyectable

eke out [iːk-] VT FUS (money) hacer que llegue

EKG N ABBR (US) see **electrocardiogram**

el [ɛl] N ABBR (US inf) = **elevated railroad**

elaborate ADJ [ɪ'læbərɪt] (design, pattern) complejo ▸ VT [ɪ'læbəreɪt] elaborar; (expand) ampliar; (refine) refinar ▸ VI [ɪ'læbəreɪt] explicarse con muchos detalles

elaborately [ɪ'læbərɪtlɪ] ADV de manera complicada; (decorated) profusamente

elaboration [ɪlæbə'reɪʃən] N elaboración f

elapse [ɪ'læps] VI transcurrir

elastic [ɪ'læstɪk] ADJ, N elástico

elastic band N (BRIT) gomita

elated [ɪ'leɪtɪd] ADJ: **to be ~** estar eufórico

elation [ɪ'leɪʃən] N euforia

elbow ['ɛlbəu] N codo ▸ VT: **to ~ one's way through the crowd** abrirse paso a codazos por la muchedumbre

elbow grease N (inf): **to use some** or **a bit of ~** menearse

★**elder** ['ɛldəʳ] ADJ mayor ▸ N (tree) saúco; (person) mayor; (of tribe) anciano

★**elderly** ['ɛldəlɪ] ADJ de edad, mayor; **~ people** los mayores, los ancianos

elder statesman N (irreg) estadista m veterano; (fig) figura respetada

★**eldest** ['ɛldɪst] ADJ, N el/la mayor

elect [ɪ'lɛkt] VT elegir; (choose): **to ~ to do** optar por hacer ▸ ADJ: **the president ~** el presidente electo

★**election** [ɪ'lɛkʃən] N elección f; **to hold an ~** convocar elecciones

election campaign N campaña electoral

electioneering [ɪlɛkʃə'nɪərɪŋ] N campaña electoral

elector [ɪ'lɛktəʳ] N elector(a) m/f

electoral [ɪ'lɛktərəl] ADJ electoral

electoral college N colegio electoral

electoral roll N censo electoral

electorate [ɪ'lɛktərɪt] N electorado

★**electric** [ɪ'lɛktrɪk] ADJ eléctrico

electrical [ɪ'lɛktrɪkl] ADJ eléctrico

electrical engineer N ingeniero(-a) electricista

electrical failure N fallo eléctrico

electric blanket N manta eléctrica

electric chair N silla eléctrica

electric cooker N cocina eléctrica

electric current N corriente f eléctrica

electric fire N estufa eléctrica

electrician [ɪlɛk'trɪʃən] N electricista mf

★**electricity** [ɪlɛk'trɪsɪtɪ] N electricidad f; **to switch on/off the ~** conectar/desconectar la electricidad

electricity board N (BRIT) compañía eléctrica (estatal)

electric light N luz f eléctrica

electric shock N electrochoque m

electrification [ɪlɛktrɪfɪ'keɪʃən] N electrificación f

electrify [ɪ'lɛktrɪfaɪ] VT (Rail) electrificar; (fig: audience) electrizar

electro... [ɪ'lɛktrəu] PREF electro...

electrocardiogram [ɪ'lɛktrə'kɑːdɪəgræm] N electrocardiograma m

electrocardiograph [ɪ'lɛktrə'kɑːdɪəgræf] N electrocardiógrafo

electro-convulsive therapy [ɪ'lɛktrəkən'vʌlsɪv-] N electroterapia

electrocute [ɪ'lɛktrəkjuːt] VT electrocutar

electrode [ɪ'lɛktrəud] N electrodo

electroencephalogram [ɪ'lɛktrəuen-'sɛfələgræm] N electroencefalograma m

electrolysis [ɪlɛk'trɔlɪsɪs] N electrólisis f inv

electromagnetic [ɪ'lɛktrəmæg'nɛtɪk] ADJ electromagnético

electron [ɪ'lɛktrɔn] N electrón m

★**electronic** [ɪlɛk'trɔnɪk] ADJ electrónico

electronic data processing N tratamiento or proceso electrónico de datos

electronic mail N correo electrónico

electronics [ɪlɛk'trɔnɪks] N electrónica

electron microscope N microscopio electrónico

electroplated [ɪ'lɛktrə'pleɪtɪd] ADJ galvanizado

electrotherapy [ɪ'lɛktrə'θɛrəpɪ] N electroterapia

elegance ['ɛlɪgəns] N elegancia

★**elegant** ['ɛlɪgənt] ADJ elegante

elegy ['ɛlɪdʒɪ] N elegía

element ['ɛlɪmənt] N (gen) elemento; (of heater, kettle etc) resistencia

elementary [ɛlɪ'mɛntərɪ] ADJ elemental; (primitive) rudimentario; (school, education) primario

elementary school N (US) escuela de enseñanza primaria

> En Estados Unidos y Canadá se llama **elementary school** al centro estatal en el que los niños reciben los primeros seis u ocho años de su educación, también llamado *grade school* o *grammar school*.

★**elephant** ['ɛlɪfənt] N elefante m

elevate ['ɛlɪveɪt] VT (gen) elevar; (in rank) ascender

elevated railroad N (US) *ferrocarril urbano elevado*

elevation [ɛlɪ'veɪʃən] N elevación f; (rank) ascenso; (height) altitud f

elevator ['ɛlɪveɪtər] N (US) ascensor m, elevador m (LAM)

★**eleven** [ɪ'lɛvn] NUM once

elevenses [ɪ'lɛvnzɪz] NPL (BRIT) ≈ café m de media mañana

★**eleventh** [ɪ'lɛvnθ] ADJ undécimo; **at the ~ hour** (fig) a última hora

elf [ɛlf] (pl **elves** [ɛlvz]) N duende m

elicit [ɪ'lɪsɪt] VT: **to ~ sth (from sb)** obtener algo (de algn)

eligible ['ɛlɪdʒəbl] ADJ: **an ~ young man/ woman** un buen partido; **to be ~ for sth** llenar los requisitos para algo; **to be ~ for a pension** tener derecho a una pensión

eliminate [ɪ'lɪmɪneɪt] VT eliminar; (score out) suprimir; (a suspect, possibility) descartar

elimination [ɪlɪmɪ'neɪʃən] N eliminación f; supresión f; **by process of ~** por eliminación

elite [eɪ'liːt] N élite f

elitist [eɪ'liːtɪst] ADJ (pej) elitista

elixir [ɪ'lɪksɪər] N elixir m

Elizabethan [ɪlɪzə'biːθən] ADJ isabelino

elm [ɛlm] N olmo

elocution [ɛlə'kjuːʃən] N elocución f

elongated ['iːlɔŋɡeɪtɪd] ADJ alargado

elope [ɪ'ləup] VI fugarse

elopement [ɪ'ləupmənt] N fuga

eloquence ['ɛləkwəns] N elocuencia

eloquent ['ɛləkwənt] ADJ elocuente

El Salvador [ɛl'sælvədɔː] N El Salvador m

★**else** [ɛls] ADV: **or ~** si no; **something ~** otra cosa or algo más; **somewhere ~** en otra parte; **everywhere ~** en todas partes menos aquí; **everyone ~** todos los demás; **nothing ~** nada más; **is there anything ~ I can do?** ¿puedo hacer algo más?; **where ~?** ¿dónde más?, ¿en qué otra parte?; **there was little ~ to do** apenas quedaba otra cosa que hacer; **nobody ~** nadie más

elsewhere [ɛls'wɛər] ADV (be) en otra parte; (go) a otra parte

ELT N ABBR (Scol) = **English Language Teaching**

elucidate [ɪ'luːsɪdeɪt] VT esclarecer, elucidar

elude [ɪ'luːd] VT eludir; (blow, pursuer) esquivar

elusive [ɪ'luːsɪv] ADJ esquivo; (answer) difícil de encontrar; **he is very ~** no es fácil encontrarlo

elves [ɛlvz] NPL of **elf**

emaciated [ɪ'meɪsɪeɪtɪd] ADJ escuálido

★**email** ['iːmeɪl] N ABBR (= electronic mail) email m, correo electrónico ▶ VT: **to ~ sb** mandar un email or un correo electrónico a algn; **to ~ sb sth** mandar algo a algn por Internet, mandar algo a algn en un email or un correo electrónico

email account N cuenta de correo

★**email address** N dirección f electrónica, email m

emanate ['ɛməneɪt] VI emanar, provenir

emancipate [ɪ'mænsɪpeɪt] VT emancipar

emancipated [ɪ'mænsɪpeɪtɪd] ADJ liberado

emancipation [ɪmænsɪ'peɪʃən] N emancipación f, liberación f

emasculate [ɪ'mæskjuleɪt] VT castrar; (fig) debilitar

embalm [ɪm'bɑːm] VT embalsamar

embankment [ɪm'bæŋkmənt] N (of railway) terraplén m; (riverside) dique m

embargo [ɪm'bɑːɡəu] (pl **embargoes**) N prohibición f; (Comm, Naut) embargo; **to put an ~ on sth** poner un embargo en algo

embark [ɪm'bɑːk] VI embarcarse; **to ~ on** (journey) emprender, iniciar; (fig) emprender ▶ VT embarcar

embarkation [ɛmbɑː'keɪʃən] N (of people) embarco; (of goods) embarque m

embarrass [ɪm'bærəs] VT avergonzar, dar vergüenza a; (financially etc) poner en un aprieto

★**embarrassed** [ɪm'baerəst] ADJ azorado, violento; **to be ~** sentirse azorado or violento

embarrassing [ɪm'bærəsɪŋ] ADJ (situation) violento; (question) embarazoso

embarrassment [ɪm'bærəsmənt] N vergüenza, azoramiento; (financial) apuros mpl

★**embassy** ['ɛmbəsɪ] N embajada

embed [ɪm'bɛd] VT (jewel) empotrar; (teeth etc) clavar

embellish [ɪm'bɛlɪʃ] VT embellecer; (fig: story, truth) adornar

embers ['ɛmbəz] NPL rescoldo *sg*, ascuas

embezzle [ɪm'bɛzl] VT desfalcar, malversar

embezzlement [ɪm'bɛzlmənt] N desfalco, malversación *f*

embezzler [ɪm'bɛzlər] N malversador(a) *m/f*

embitter [ɪm'bɪtər] VT (*person*) amargar; (*relationship*) envenenar

embittered [ɪm'bɪtəd] ADJ resentido, amargado

emblem ['ɛmbləm] N emblema *m*

embody [ɪm'bɔdɪ] VT (*spirit*) encarnar; (*ideas*) expresar

embolden [ɪm'bəuldən] VT envalentonar

embolism ['ɛmbəlɪzəm] N embolia

emboss [ɪm'bɔs] VT estampar en relieve; (*metal, leather*) repujar

embossed [ɪm'bɔst] ADJ realzado; **~ with ...** con ... en relieve

embrace [ɪm'breɪs] VT abrazar, dar un abrazo a; (*include*) abarcar; (*adopt: idea*) adherirse a ▶ VI abrazarse ▶ N abrazo

embroider [ɪm'brɔɪdər] VT bordar; (*fig: story*) adornar, embellecer

embroidery [ɪm'brɔɪdərɪ] N bordado

embroil [ɪm'brɔɪl] VT: **to become embroiled (in sth)** enredarse (en algo)

embryo ['ɛmbrɪəu] N (*also fig*) embrión *m*

emcee [ɛm'siː] N ABBR (*US*: = *master of ceremonies*) presentador(a) *m/f*

emend [ɪ'mɛnd] VT (*text*) enmendar

emerald ['ɛmərəld] N esmeralda

emerge [ɪ'məːdʒ] VI (*gen*) salir; (*arise*) surgir; **it emerges that** resulta que

emergence [ɪ'məːdʒəns] N (*of nation*) surgimiento

★**emergency** [ɪ'məːdʒənsɪ] N (*event*) emergencia; (*crisis*) crisis *f inv*; **in an ~** en caso de urgencia; **(to declare a) state of ~** (declarar) estado de emergencia *or* de excepción

emergency brake N (*US*) freno de mano

emergency cord N (*US*) timbre *m* de alarma

emergency exit N salida de emergencia

emergency landing N aterrizaje *m* forzoso

emergency lane N (*US*) arcén *m*

emergency meeting N reunión *f* extraordinaria

emergency room (*US Med*) N sala *f* de urgencias

emergency service N servicio de urgencia

emergency stop N (*Aut*) parada en seco

emergent [ɪ'məːdʒənt] ADJ (*nation*) recientemente independizado

emery board ['ɛmərɪ-] N lima de uñas

emetic [ɪ'mɛtɪk] N vomitivo, emético

emigrant ['ɛmɪɡrənt] N emigrante *mf*

emigrate ['ɛmɪɡreɪt] VI emigrar

emigration [ɛmɪ'ɡreɪʃən] N emigración *f*

émigré ['ɛmɪɡreɪ] N emigrado(-a)

eminence ['ɛmɪnəns] N eminencia; **to gain** *or* **win ~** ganarse fama

eminent ['ɛmɪnənt] ADJ eminente

eminently ['ɛmɪnəntlɪ] ADV eminentemente

emirate ['ɛmɪrɪt] N emirato

emission [ɪ'mɪʃən] N emisión *f*

emit [ɪ'mɪt] VT emitir; (*smell, smoke*) despedir

emoji [ɪ'məudʒɪ] N emoji *m*

emolument [ɪ'mɔljumənt] N (*gen pl: formal*) honorario, emolumento

emoticon [ɪ'məutɪkɔn] N emoticón *m*

emotion [ɪ'məuʃən] N emoción *f*

★**emotional** [ɪ'məuʃənl] ADJ (*person*) sentimental; (*scene*) conmovedor(a), emocionante

emotionally [ɪ'məuʃnəlɪ] ADV (*behave, speak*) con emoción; (*be involved*) sentimentalmente

emotive [ɪ'məutɪv] ADJ emotivo

empathy ['ɛmpəθɪ] N empatía; **to feel ~ with sb** sentirse identificado con algn

emperor ['ɛmpərər] N emperador *m*

emphasis ['ɛmfəsɪs] (*pl* **emphases** [-siːz]) N énfasis *m inv*; **to lay** *or* **place ~ on sth** (*fig*) hacer hincapié en algo; **the ~ is on sport** se da mayor importancia al deporte

★**emphasize** ['ɛmfəsaɪz] VT (*word, point*) subrayar, recalcar; (*feature*) hacer resaltar

emphatic [ɛm'fætɪk] ADJ (*condemnation*) enérgico; (*denial*) rotundo

emphatically [ɛm'fætɪklɪ] ADV con énfasis

emphysema [ɛmfɪ'siːmə] N (*Med*) enfisema *m*

empire ['ɛmpaɪər] N imperio

empirical [ɛm'pɪrɪkl] ADJ empírico

★**employ** [ɪm'plɔɪ] VT (*give job to*) emplear; (*make use of: thing, method*) emplear, usar; **he's employed in a bank** está empleado en un banco

★**employee** [ɪmplɔɪ'iː] N empleado(-a)

★**employer** [ɪm'plɔɪər] N patrón(-ona) *m/f*; (*businessman*) empresario(-a)

★**employment** [ɪm'plɔɪmənt] N empleo; **full ~** pleno empleo; **without ~** sin empleo; **to find ~** encontrar trabajo; **place of ~** lugar *m* de trabajo

employment agency N agencia de colocaciones *or* empleo

employment exchange N bolsa de trabajo

empower [ɪm'pauər] VT: **to ~ sb to do sth** autorizar a algn para hacer algo

empress ['ɛmprɪs] N emperatriz *f*

emptiness ['ɛmptɪnɪs] N vacío

★**empty** ['ɛmptɪ] ADJ vacío; (*street, area*) desierto; (*threat*) vano ▶ N (*bottle*) envase *m* ▶ VT vaciar; (*place*) dejar vacío ▶ VI vaciarse; (*house*) quedar(se) vacío *or* desocupado; (*place*) quedar(se) desierto; **to ~ into** (*river*) desembocar en

empty-handed ['ɛmptɪ'hændɪd] ADJ con las manos vacías

empty-headed [ˈɛmptɪˈhɛdɪd] ADJ casquivano

EMT N ABBR (US) = **emergency medical technician**

EMU N ABBR (= *Ecomomic and Monetary Union*; *European Monetary Union*) UME f

emulate [ˈɛmjuleɪt] VT emular

emulsion [ɪˈmʌlʃən] N emulsión f

enable [ɪˈneɪbl] VT: **to ~ sb to do sth** (*allow*) permitir a algn hacer algo; (*prepare*) capacitar a algn para hacer algo

enact [ɪnˈækt] VT (*law*) promulgar; (*play, scene, role*) representar

enamel [ɪˈnæməl] N esmalte m

enamel paint N esmalte m

enamoured [ɪˈnæməd] ADJ: **to be ~ of** (*person*) estar enamorado de; (*activity etc*) tener gran afición a; (*idea*) aferrarse a

enc. ABBR (*on letters etc*: = *enclosed, enclosure*) adj

encampment [ɪnˈkæmpmənt] N campamento

encase [ɪnˈkeɪs] VT: **to ~ in** (*contain*) encajar; (*cover*) cubrir

encased [ɪnˈkeɪst] ADJ: **~ in** (*covered*) revestido de

enchant [ɪnˈtʃɑːnt] VT encantar

enchanting [ɪnˈtʃɑːntɪŋ] ADJ encantador(a)

encircle [ɪnˈsəːkl] VT (*gen*) rodear; (*waist*) ceñir

encl. ABBR (= *enclosed*) adj

enclave [ˈɛnkleɪv] N enclave m

enclose [ɪnˈkləʊz] VT (*land*) cercar; (*with letter etc*) adjuntar; (*in receptacle*): **to ~ (with)** encerrar (con); **please find enclosed** le mandamos adjunto

enclosure [ɪnˈkləʊʒəʳ] N cercado, recinto; (*Comm*) carta adjunta

encoder [ɪnˈkəʊdəʳ] N (*Comput*) codificador m

encompass [ɪnˈkʌmpəs] VT abarcar

encore [ɔŋˈkɔːʳ] EXCL ¡otra!, ¡bis! ▶ N bis m

encounter [ɪnˈkaʊntəʳ] N encuentro ▶ VT encontrar, encontrarse con; (*difficulty*) tropezar con

★**encourage** [ɪnˈkʌrɪdʒ] VT alentar, animar; (*growth*) estimular; **to ~ sb (to do sth)** animar a algn (a hacer algo)

encouragement [ɪnˈkʌrɪdʒmənt] N estímulo; (*of industry*) fomento

encouraging [ɪnˈkʌrɪdʒɪŋ] ADJ alentador(a)

encroach [ɪnˈkrəʊtʃ] VI: **to ~ (up)on** (*gen*) invadir; (*time*) adueñarse de

encrust [ɪnˈkrʌst] VT incrustar

encrusted [ɪnˈkrʌstəd] ADJ: **~ with** recubierto de

encrypt [ɪnˈkrɪpt] VT (*Comput, Tel*) encriptar

encumber [ɪnˈkʌmbəʳ] VT: **to be encumbered with** (*carry*) estar cargado de; (*debts*) estar gravado de

encyclopaedia, encyclopedia [ɛnsaɪkləʊˈpiːdɪə] N enciclopedia

★**end** [ɛnd] N fin m; (*of table*) extremo; (*of line, rope etc*) cabo; (*of pointed object*) punta; (*of town*) barrio; (*of street*) final m; (*Sport*) lado; **in the ~** al final; **to be at an ~** llegar a su fin; (*fig*) al fin y al cabo, a fin de cuentas; **to this ~, with this ~ in view** con este propósito; **from ~ to ~** de punta a punta; **on ~** (*object*) de punta, de cabeza; **to stand on ~** (*hair*) erizarse, ponerse de punta; **for hours on ~** hora tras hora ▶ VT terminar, acabar; (*also:* **bring to an end, put an end to**) acabar con ▶ VI terminar, acabar; **to ~ (with)** terminar (con)

▶ **end up** VI: **to ~ up in** terminar en; (*place*) ir a parar a

endanger [ɪnˈdeɪndʒəʳ] VT poner en peligro; **an endangered species** (*of animal*) una especie en peligro de extinción

endear [ɪnˈdɪəʳ] VT: **to ~ o.s. to sb** ganarse la simpatía de algn

endearing [ɪnˈdɪərɪŋ] ADJ entrañable

endearment [ɪnˈdɪəmənt] N cariño, palabra cariñosa; **to whisper endearments** decir unas palabras cariñosas al oído; **term of ~** nombre m cariñoso

endeavour, (US) **endeavor** [ɪnˈdɛvəʳ] N esfuerzo; (*attempt*) tentativa ▶ VI: **to ~ to do** esforzarse por hacer; (*try*) procurar hacer

endemic [ɛnˈdɛmɪk] ADJ (*poverty, disease*) endémico

ending [ˈɛndɪŋ] N fin m, final m; (*of book*) desenlace m; (*Ling*) terminación f

endive [ˈɛndaɪv] N (*curly*) escarola; (*smooth, flat*) endibia

endless [ˈɛndlɪs] ADJ interminable, inacabable; (*possibilities*) infinito

endorse [ɪnˈdɔːs] VT (*cheque*) endosar; (*approve*) aprobar

endorsee [ɪndɔːˈsiː] N endosatario(-a)

endorsement [ɪnˈdɔːsmənt] N (*approval*) aprobación f; (*signature*) endoso; (*Brit: on driving licence*) nota de sanción

endorser [ɪnˈdɔːsəʳ] N avalista mf

endow [ɪnˈdau] VT (*provide with money*) dotar; (*found*) fundar; **to be endowed with** (*fig*) estar dotado de

endowment [ɪnˈdaumənt] ADJ (*amount*) donación f

endowment mortgage N hipoteca dotal

endowment policy N póliza dotal

end product N (*Industry*) producto final; (*fig*) resultado

end result N resultado

endurable [ɪnˈdjuərəbl] ADJ soportable, tolerable

endurance [ɪnˈdjuərəns] N resistencia

endurance test N prueba de resistencia

endure [ɪnˈdjuəʳ] VT (*bear*) aguantar, soportar; (*resist*) resistir ▶ VI (*last*) perdurar; (*resist*) resistir

enduring [ɪnˈdjuərɪŋ] ADJ duradero

end user N (*Comput*) usuario final

enema [ˈɛnɪmə] N (*Med*) enema m

★enemy ['ɛnəmɪ] ADJ, N enemigo(-a) *m/f*; **to make an ~ of sb** enemistarse con algn

energetic [ɛnə'dʒɛtɪk] ADJ enérgico

★energy ['ɛnədʒɪ] N energía

energy crisis N crisis *f* energética

energy drink N bebida energética, bebida isotónica

energy-saving ['ɛnədʒɪseɪvɪŋ] ADJ (*policy*) para ahorrar energía; (*device*) que ahorra energía ▸ N ahorro de energía

enervating ['ɛnəveɪtɪŋ] ADJ deprimente

enforce [ɪn'fɔːs] VT (*law*) hacer cumplir

enforced [ɪn'fɔːst] ADJ forzoso, forzado

enfranchise [ɪn'fræntʃaɪz] VT (*give vote to*) conceder el derecho de voto a; (*set free*) emancipar

engage [ɪn'geɪdʒ] VT (*attention*) captar; (*in conversation*) abordar; (*worker, lawyer*) contratar; **to ~ sb in conversation** entablar conversación con algn; **to ~ the clutch** embragar ▸ VI (*Tech*) engranar; **to ~ in** dedicarse a, ocuparse en

★engaged [ɪn'geɪdʒd] ADJ (BRIT: *busy, in use*) ocupado; (*betrothed*) prometido; **to get ~** prometerse; **he is ~ in research** se dedica a la investigación

engaged tone N (BRIT Tel) señal *f* de comunicando

engagement [ɪn'geɪdʒmənt] N (*appointment*) compromiso, cita; (*battle*) combate *m*; (*to marry*) compromiso; (*period*) noviazgo; **I have a previous ~** ya tengo un compromiso

engagement ring N anillo de pedida

engaging [ɪn'geɪdʒɪŋ] ADJ atractivo, simpático

engender [ɪn'dʒɛndə^r] VT engendrar

★engine ['ɛndʒɪn] N (Aut) motor *m*; (Rail) locomotora

engine driver N (BRIT: *of train*) maquinista *mf*

★engineer [ɛndʒɪ'nɪə^r] N ingeniero(-a); (BRIT: *for repairs*) técnico(-a); (US Rail) maquinista *mf*; **civil/mechanical ~** ingeniero(-a) de caminos, canales y puertos/industrial

★engineering [ɛndʒɪ'nɪərɪŋ] N ingeniería ▸ CPD (*works, factory*) de componentes mecánicos

engine failure, engine trouble N avería del motor

★England ['ɪŋglənd] N Inglaterra

★English ['ɪŋglɪʃ] ADJ inglés(-esa) ▸ N (Ling) el inglés ∎ **the English** NPL los ingleses

English Channel N: **the ~** el Canal de la Mancha

★Englishman ['ɪŋglɪʃmən], **Englishwoman** ['ɪŋglɪʃwumən] (*irreg*) inglés(-esa) *m/f*

English-speaker ['ɪŋglɪʃspiːkə^r] N persona de habla inglesa

English-speaking ['ɪŋglɪʃspiːkɪŋ] ADJ de habla inglesa

engrave [ɪn'greɪv] VT grabar

engraving [ɪn'greɪvɪŋ] N grabado

engrossed [ɪn'grəʊst] ADJ: **~ in** absorto en

engulf [ɪn'gʌlf] VT sumergir, hundir; (*fire*) devorar

enhance [ɪn'hɑːns] VT (*gen*) aumentar; (*beauty*) realzar; (*position, reputation*) mejorar

enigma [ɪ'nɪgmə] N enigma *m*

enigmatic [ɛnɪg'mætɪk] ADJ enigmático

★enjoy [ɪn'dʒɔɪ] VT (*have: health, fortune*) disfrutar de, gozar de; (: *food*) comer con gusto; **I ~ doing ...** me gusta hacer ...; **to ~ o.s.** divertirse, pasarlo bien

enjoyable [ɪn'dʒɔɪəbl] ADJ (*pleasant*) agradable; (*amusing*) divertido

enjoyment [ɪn'dʒɔɪmənt] N (*use*) disfrute *m*; (*joy*) placer *m*

enlarge [ɪn'lɑːdʒ] VT aumentar; (*broaden*) extender; (Phot) ampliar ▸ VI: **to ~ on** (*subject*) tratar con más detalles

enlarged [ɪn'lɑːdʒd] ADJ (*edition*) aumentado; (Med: *organ, gland*) dilatado

enlargement [ɪn'lɑːdʒmənt] N (Phot) ampliación *f*

enlighten [ɪn'laɪtn] VT informar, instruir

enlightened [ɪn'laɪtnd] ADJ iluminado; (*tolerant*) comprensivo

enlightening [ɪn'laɪtnɪŋ] ADJ informativo, instructivo

Enlightenment [ɪn'laɪtnmənt] N (History): **the ~** la Ilustración, el Siglo de las Luces

enlist [ɪn'lɪst] VT alistar; (*support*) conseguir; **enlisted man** (US Mil) soldado raso ▸ VI alistarse

enliven [ɪn'laɪvn] VT (*people*) animar; (*events*) avivar, animar

enmity ['ɛnmɪtɪ] N enemistad *f*

ennoble [ɪ'nəʊbl] VT ennoblecer

enormity [ɪ'nɔːmɪtɪ] N enormidad *f*

★enormous [ɪ'nɔːməs] ADJ enorme

★enough [ɪ'nʌf] ADJ: **~ time/books** bastante tiempo/bastantes libros ▸ N: **have you got ~?** ¿tiene usted bastante?; **(that's) ~!** ¡basta ya!, ¡ya está bien!; **that's ~, thanks** con eso basta, gracias; **I've had ~** estoy harto ▸ ADV: **big ~** bastante grande; **he has not worked ~** no ha trabajado bastante; **will five be ~?** ¿bastará con cinco?; **he was kind ~ to lend me the money** tuvo la bondad *or* amabilidad de prestarme el dinero; **... which, funnily ~ ...** ... lo que, por extraño que parezca ...

enquire [ɪn'kwaɪə^r] VT, VI = **inquire**

enrage [ɪn'reɪdʒ] VT enfurecer

enrich [ɪn'rɪtʃ] VT enriquecer

enrol, (US) **enroll** [ɪn'rəʊl] VT (*member*) inscribir; (Scol) matricular ▸ VI inscribirse; (Scol) matricularse

enrolment, (US) **enrollment** [ɪn'rəʊlmənt] N inscripción *f*; matriculación *f*

en route [ɔn'ruːt] ADV durante el viaje; **~ for/ from/to** camino de/de/a

ensconce [ɪn'skɔns] VT: **to ~ o.s.** instalarse cómodamente, acomodarse

ensemble [ɔn'sɔmbl] N (Mus) conjunto

enshrine [ɪn'ʃraɪn] VT recoger

ensign ['ensaɪn] N (flag) bandera; (Naut) alférez m

enslave [ɪn'sleɪv] VT esclavizar

ensue [ɪn'sjuː] VI seguirse; (result) resultar

ensuing [ɪn'sjuːɪŋ] ADJ subsiguiente

en suite [ɔn'swiːt] ADJ: **with ~ bathroom** con baño

ensure [ɪn'ʃuər] VT asegurar

ENT N ABBR (Med: = ear, nose and throat) otorrinolaringología

entail [ɪn'teɪl] VT (imply) suponer; (result in) acarrear

entangle [ɪn'tæŋgl] VT (thread etc) enredar, enmarañar; **to become entangled in sth** (fig) enredarse en algo

entanglement [ɪn'tæŋglmənt] N enredo

★**enter** ['entər] VT (room, profession) entrar en; (club) hacerse socio de; (army) alistarse en; (sb for a competition) inscribir; (write down) anotar, apuntar; (Comput) introducir ▶ VI entrar
  ▶ **enter for** VT FUS presentarse a
  ▶ **enter into** VT FUS (relations) establecer; (plans) formar parte de; (debate) tomar parte en; (negotiations) entablar; (agreement) llegar a, firmar
  ▶ **enter (up)on** VT FUS (career) emprender

enteritis [entə'raɪtɪs] N enteritis f

enterprise ['entəpraɪz] N empresa; (spirit) iniciativa; **free ~** la libre empresa; **private ~** la iniciativa privada

enterprising ['entəpraɪzɪŋ] ADJ emprendedor(a)

★**entertain** [entə'teɪn] VT (amuse) divertir; (receive: guest) recibir (en casa); (idea) abrigar

entertainer [entə'teɪnər] N artista mf

entertaining [entə'teɪnɪŋ] ADJ divertido, entretenido ▶ N: **to do a lot of ~** dar muchas fiestas, tener muchos invitados

entertainment [entə'teɪnmənt] N (amusement) diversión f; (show) espectáculo; (party) fiesta

entertainment allowance N (Comm) gastos mpl de representación

enthral [ɪn'θrɔːl] VT embelesar, cautivar

enthralled [ɪn'θrɔːld] ADJ cautivado

enthralling [ɪn'θrɔːlɪŋ] ADJ cautivador(a)

enthuse [ɪn'θuːz] VI: **to ~ about** or **over** entusiasmarse por

★**enthusiasm** [ɪn'θuːzɪæzəm] N entusiasmo

enthusiast [ɪn'θuːzɪæst] N entusiasta mf

enthusiastic [ɪnθuːzɪ'æstɪk] ADJ entusiasta; **to be ~ about sb/sth** estar entusiasmado con algn/algo

entice [ɪn'taɪs] VT tentar; (seduce) seducir

entire [ɪn'taɪər] ADJ entero, todo

entirely [ɪn'taɪəlɪ] ADV totalmente

entirety [ɪn'taɪərətɪ] N: **in its ~** en su totalidad

entitle [ɪn'taɪtl] VT: **to ~ sb to sth** dar a algn derecho a algo

entitled [ɪn'taɪtld] ADJ (book) titulado; **to be ~ to sth/to do sth** tener derecho a algo/a hacer algo

entity ['entɪtɪ] N entidad f

entourage [ɔntu'rɑːʒ] N séquito

entrails ['entreɪlz] NPL entrañas fpl; (US: offal) asadura sg, menudos mpl

★**entrance** N ['entrəns] entrada; **to gain ~ to** (university etc) ingresar en ▶ VT [ɪn'trɑːns] encantar, hechizar

entrance examination N (to school) examen m de ingreso

entrance fee N (to a show) entrada; (to a club) cuota

entrance ramp N (US Aut) rampa de acceso

entrancing [ɪn'trɑːnsɪŋ] ADJ encantador(a)

entrant ['entrənt] N (in race, competition) participante mf; (in exam) candidato(-a)

entreat [en'triːt] VT rogar, suplicar

entrenched [en'trentʃd] ADJ: **~ interests** intereses mpl creados

entrepreneur [ɔntrəprə'nəːr] N empresario(-a), capitalista mf

entrepreneurial [ɔntrəprə'nəːrɪəl] ADJ empresarial

entrust [ɪn'trʌst] VT: **to ~ sth to sb** confiar algo a algn

★**entry** ['entrɪ] N entrada; (permission to enter) acceso; (in register, diary, ship's log) apunte m; (in account book, ledger, list) partida; **no ~** prohibido el paso; (Aut) dirección prohibida; **single/double ~ book-keeping** contabilidad f simple/por partida doble

entry form N boletín m de inscripción

entry phone N (BRIT) portero automático

E-number ['iːnʌmbər] N número E

enumerate [ɪ'njuːməreɪt] VT enumerar

enunciate [ɪ'nʌnsɪeɪt] VT pronunciar; (principle etc) enunciar

envelop [ɪn'veləp] VT envolver

envelope ['envələup] N sobre m

enviable ['envɪəbl] ADJ envidiable

envious ['envɪəs] ADJ envidioso; (look) de envidia

★**environment** [ɪn'vaɪrnmənt] N medio ambiente; (surroundings) entorno; **Department of the E~** ministerio del medio ambiente

★**environmental** [ɪnvaɪərn'mentl] ADJ (medio) ambiental; **~ studies** (in school etc) ecología sg

environmentalist [ɪnvaɪərn'mentlɪst] N ecologista mf

environmentally [ɪnvaɪərn'mentlɪ] ADV: **~ sound/friendly** ecológico

envisage [ɪn'vɪzɪdʒ] VT (foresee) prever; (imagine) concebir

envision [ɪn'vɪʒən] VT imaginar

envoy ['envɔɪ] N enviado(-a)

envy ['envɪ] N envidia ▶ VT tener envidia a; **to ~ sb sth** envidiar algo a algn

enzyme ['enzaɪm] N enzima m or f

EPA N ABBR (US: = Environmental Protection Agency) Agencia del Medio Ambiente

ephemeral [ɪˈfemərl] ADJ efímero

epic [ˈepɪk] N épica ▶ ADJ épico

epicentre, (US) **epicenter** [ˈepɪsentəʳ] N epicentro

epidemic [epɪˈdemɪk] N epidemia

epigram [ˈepɪgræm] N epigrama m

epilepsy [ˈepɪlepsɪ] N epilepsia

epileptic [epɪˈleptɪk] ADJ epiléptico

epileptic fit [epɪˈleptɪk-] N ataque m de epilepsia, acceso m epiléptico

epilogue [ˈepɪlɔg] N epílogo

episcopal [ɪˈpɪskəpl] ADJ episcopal

episode [ˈepɪsəud] N episodio

epistle [ɪˈpɪsl] N epístola

epitaph [ˈepɪtɑːf] N epitafio

epithet [ˈepɪθet] N epíteto

epitome [ɪˈpɪtəmɪ] N arquetipo

epitomize [ɪˈpɪtəmaɪz] VT representar

epoch [ˈiːpɔk] N época

eponymous [ɪˈpɔnɪməs] ADJ epónimo

equable [ˈekwəbl] ADJ (climate) estable; (character) ecuánime

★**equal** [ˈiːkwl] ADJ (gen) igual; (treatment) equitativo; **to be ~ to** (task) estar a la altura de; **the E~ Opportunities Commission** (BRIT) comisión para la igualdad de la mujer en el trabajo ▶ N igual mf ▶ VT ser igual a; (fig) igualar

equality [iːˈkwɔlɪtɪ] N igualdad f

equalize [ˈiːkwəlaɪz] VT, VI igualar; (Sport) empatar

equalizer [ˈiːkwəlaɪzəʳ] N igualada

equally [ˈiːkwəlɪ] ADV igualmente; (share etc) a partes iguales; **they are ~ clever** son tan listos uno como otro

equals sign N signo igual

equanimity [ekwəˈnɪmɪtɪ] N ecuanimidad f

equate [ɪˈkweɪt] VT: **to ~ sth with** equiparar algo con

equation [ɪˈkweɪʒən] N (Math) ecuación f

equator [ɪˈkweɪtəʳ] N ecuador m

equatorial [ekwəˈtɔːrɪəl] ADJ ecuatorial

Equatorial Guinea N Guinea Ecuatorial

equestrian [ɪˈkwestrɪən] ADJ ecuestre ▶ N jinete mf

equilibrium [iːkwɪˈlɪbrɪəm] N equilibrio

equinox [ˈiːkwɪnɔks] N equinoccio

equip [ɪˈkwɪp] VT (gen) equipar; (person) proveer; **equipped with** (machinery etc) provisto de; **to be well equipped** estar bien equipado; **he is well equipped for the job** está bien preparado para este puesto

★**equipment** [ɪˈkwɪpmənt] N equipo

equitable [ˈekwɪtəbl] ADJ equitativo

equities [ˈekwɪtɪz] NPL (BRIT Comm) acciones fpl ordinarias

equity [ˈekwɪtɪ] N (fairness) equidad f; (Econ: of debtor) valor m líquido

equity capital N capital m propio, patrimonio neto

★**equivalent** [ɪˈkwɪvələnt] ADJ, N equivalente m; **to be ~ to** equivaler a

equivocal [ɪˈkwɪvəkl] ADJ equívoco

equivocate [ɪˈkwɪvəkeɪt] VI andarse con ambigüedades

equivocation [ɪkwɪvəˈkeɪʃən] N ambigüedad f

ER ABBR (BRIT: = Elizabeth Regina) la reina Isabel; (US Med) = **emergency room**

er [əː] EXCL (inf: in hesitation) esto, este (LAm)

ERA N ABBR (US Pol: = Equal Rights Amendment) enmienda sobre la igualdad de derechos de la mujer

era [ˈɪərə] N era, época

eradicate [ɪˈrædɪkeɪt] VT erradicar, extirpar

erase [ɪˈreɪz] VT (Comput) borrar

eraser [ɪˈreɪzəʳ] N goma de borrar

e-reader, eReader [ˈiːriːdəʳ] N lector m de libros electrónicos

erect [ɪˈrekt] ADJ erguido ▶ VT erigir, levantar; (assemble) montar

erection [ɪˈrekʃən] N (of building) construcción f; (of machinery) montaje m; (structure) edificio; (Med) erección f

ergonomics [əːgəˈnɔmɪks] N ergonomía

ERISA N ABBR (US: = Employee Retirement Income Security Act) ley que regula las pensiones de jubilados

Eritrea [erɪˈtreɪə] N Eritrea

ERM N ABBR (= Exchange Rate Mechanism) (mecanismo de cambios del) SME m

ermine [ˈəːmɪn] N armiño

ERNIE [ˈəːnɪ] N ABBR (BRIT: = Electronic Random Number Indicator Equipment) ordenador que elige al azar los números ganadores de los bonos del Estado

erode [ɪˈrəud] VT (Geo) erosionar; (metal) corroer, desgastar

erogenous zone [ɪˈrɔdʒənəs-] N zona erógena

erosion [ɪˈrəuʒən] N erosión f; desgaste m

erotic [ɪˈrɔtɪk] ADJ erótico

eroticism [ɪˈrɔtɪsɪzm] N erotismo

err [əːʳ] VI errar; (Rel) pecar

errand [ˈernd] N recado, mandado (LAm); **to run errands** hacer recados; **~ of mercy** misión f de caridad

errand boy N recadero

erratic [ɪˈrætɪk] ADJ variable; (results etc) desigual, poco uniforme

erroneous [ɪˈrəunɪəs] ADJ erróneo

★**error** [ˈerəʳ] N error m, equivocación f; **typing/spelling ~** error de mecanografía/ortografía; **in ~** por equivocación; **errors and omissions excepted** salvo error u omisión

error message N (Comput) mensaje m de error

erstwhile [ˈəːstwaɪl] ADJ antiguo, previo

erudite [ˈerudaɪt] ADJ erudito

erudition [ɛruˈdɪʃən] N erudición f

erupt [ɪˈrʌpt] vɪ entrar en erupción; (Med) hacer erupción; (fig) estallar

eruption [ɪˈrʌpʃən] N erupción f; (fig: of anger, violence) explosión f, estallido

ESA N ABBR (= European Space Agency) Agencia Espacial Europea

escalate [ˈɛskəleɪt] vɪ extenderse, intensificarse; (costs) aumentar vertiginosamente

escalation clause [ɛskəˈleɪʃən-] N cláusula de reajuste de los precios

escalator [ˈɛskəleɪtəʳ] N escalera mecánica

escapade [ɛskəˈpeɪd] N aventura

★**escape** [ɪˈskeɪp] N (gen) fuga; (Tech) escape m; (from duties) escapatoria; (from chase) evasión f ▶ vɪ (gen) escaparse; (flee) huir, evadirse; **to ~ from** (place) escaparse de; (person) huir de; (clutches) librarse de; **to ~ to** (another place, freedom, safety) huir a ▶ vт evitar, eludir; (consequences) escapar a; **his name escapes me** no me sale su nombre; **to ~ notice** pasar desapercibido

escape artist N artista mf de la evasión

escape clause N (fig: in agreement) cláusula de excepción

escapee [ɪskeɪˈpiː] N fugado(-a)

escape hatch N (in submarine, space rocket) escotilla de salvamento

escape key N (Comput) tecla de escape

escape route N (from fire) vía de escape

escapism [ɪˈskeɪpɪzəm] N escapismo, evasión f

escapist [ɪˈskeɪpɪst] ADJ escapista, de evasión ▶ N escapista mf

escapologist [ɛskəˈpɔlədʒɪst] N (BRIT) = **escape artist**

escarpment [ɪˈskɑːpmənt] N escarpa

eschew [ɪsˈtʃuː] vт evitar, abstenerse de

escort N [ˈɛskɔːt] acompañante mf; (Mil) escolta; (Naut) convoy m ▶ vт [ɪˈskɔːt] acompañar; (Mil, Naut) escoltar

escort agency N agencia de acompañantes

Eskimo [ˈɛskɪməu] (often !) ADJ esquimal ▶ N esquimal mf; (Ling) esquimal m

ESL N ABBR (Scol) = **English as a Second Language**

esophagus [iːˈsɔfəgəs] N (US) = **oesophagus**

esoteric [ɛsəuˈtɛrɪk] ADJ esotérico

ESP N ABBR = **extrasensory perception**; (Scol: = English for Specific (or Special) Purposes) inglés especializado

esp. ABBR = **especially**

★**especially** [ɪˈspɛʃlɪ] ADV (gen) especialmente; (above all) sobre todo; (particularly) en especial

espionage [ˈɛspɪənɑːʒ] N espionaje m

esplanade [ɛspləˈneɪd] N (by sea) paseo marítimo

espouse [ɪˈspauz] vт adherirse a

Esq. ABBR (= Esquire) D.

Esquire [ɪˈskwaɪəʳ] N: **J. Brown, ~** Sr. D. J. Brown

essay [ˈɛseɪ] N (Scol) redacción f; (: longer) trabajo

essayist [ˈɛseɪɪst] N ensayista mf

essence [ˈɛsns] N esencia; **in ~** esencialmente; **speed is of the ~** es esencial hacerlo con la mayor prontitud

★**essential** [ɪˈsɛnʃl] ADJ (necessary) imprescindible; (basic) esencial; **it is ~ that** es imprescindible que ▶ N (gen pl) lo esencial

essentially [ɪˈsɛnʃlɪ] ADV esencialmente

EST N ABBR (US: = Eastern Standard Time) hora de invierno de Nueva York

est. ABBR (= established) fundado; (= estimated) aprox.

establish [ɪˈstæblɪʃ] vт establecer; (prove: fact) comprobar, demostrar; (identity) verificar; (relations) entablar

established [ɪˈstæblɪʃt] ADJ (business) de buena reputación; (staff) de plantilla

establishment [ɪˈstæblɪʃmənt] N establecimiento; **the E~** la clase dirigente; **a teaching ~** un centro de enseñanza

estate [ɪˈsteɪt] N (land) finca, hacienda; (property) propiedad f; (inheritance) herencia; (Pol) estado; **housing ~** (BRIT) urbanización f; **industrial ~** polígono industrial

estate agency N (BRIT) agencia inmobiliaria

estate agent N (BRIT) agente mf inmobiliario(-a)

estate agent's N agencia inmobiliaria

estate car N (BRIT) ranchera, coche m familiar

esteem [ɪˈstiːm] N: **to hold sb in high ~** estimar en mucho a algn ▶ vт estimar

esthetic [iːsˈθɛtɪk] ADJ (US) = **aesthetic**

★**estimate** N [ˈɛstɪmət] estimación f; (assessment) tasa, cálculo; (Comm) presupuesto; **to give sb an ~ of** presentar a algn un presupuesto de; **at a rough ~** haciendo un cálculo aproximado ▶ vт [ˈɛstɪmeɪt] estimar; tasar, calcular ▶ vɪ [ˈɛstɪmeɪt]: **to ~ for** (Comm) hacer un presupuesto de, presupuestar

estimation [ɛstɪˈmeɪʃən] N opinión f, juicio; (esteem) aprecio; **in my ~** a mi juicio

Estonia [ɛˈstəunɪə] N Estonia

Estonian [ɛˈstəunɪən] ADJ estonio ▶ N estonio(-a); (Ling) estonio

estranged [ɪˈstreɪndʒd] ADJ separado

estrangement [ɪˈstreɪndʒmənt] N alejamiento, distanciamiento

estrogen [ˈiːstrəudʒən] N (US) = **oestrogen**

estuary [ˈɛstjuərɪ] N estuario, ría

ET N ABBR (BRIT: = Employment Training) plan estatal de formación para los desempleados ▶ ABBR (US) = **Eastern Time**

ETA N ABBR = **estimated time of arrival**

e-tailing [ˈiːteɪlɪŋ] N venta en línea, venta vía or por Internet

et al. ABBR (= et alii) et al.

★etc ABBR (= *et cetera*) etc

etch [ɛtʃ] VT grabar al aguafuerte

etching [ˈɛtʃɪŋ] N aguafuerte *m or f*

ETD N ABBR = **estimated time of departure**

eternal [ɪˈtəːnl] ADJ eterno

eternity [ɪˈtəːnɪtɪ] N eternidad *f*

ether [ˈiːθəʳ] N éter *m*

ethereal [ɪˈθɪərɪəl] ADJ etéreo

ethical [ˈɛθɪkl] ADJ ético; (*honest*) honrado

ethics [ˈɛθɪks] N ética ▶ NPL moralidad *f*

Ethiopia [iːθɪˈəupɪə] N Etiopía

Ethiopian [iːθɪˈəupɪən] ADJ, N etíope *mf*

★ethnic [ˈɛθnɪk] ADJ étnico

ethnic cleansing [-klɛnzɪŋ] N limpieza étnica

ethnic minority N minoría étnica

ethos [ˈiːθɔs] N (*of culture, group*) sistema *m* de valores

e-ticket [ˈiːtɪkɪt] N billete electrónico, boleto electrónico (*LAM*)

etiquette [ˈɛtɪkɛt] N etiqueta

ETV N ABBR (*US:* = *Educational Television*) televisión escolar

etymology [ɛtɪˈmɔlədʒɪ] N etimología

EU N ABBR (= *European Union*) UE *f*

eucalyptus [juːkəˈlɪptəs] N eucalipto

Eucharist [ˈjuːkərɪst] N Eucaristía

eulogy [ˈjuːlədʒɪ] N elogio, encomio

eunuch [ˈjuːnək] N eunuco

euphemism [ˈjuːfəmɪzm] N eufemismo

euphemistic [juːfəˈmɪstɪk] ADJ eufemístico

euphoria [juːˈfɔːrɪə] N euforia

Eurasia [juəˈreɪʃə] N Eurasia

Eurasian [juəˈreɪʃən] ADJ, N eurasiático(-a) *m/f*

Euratom [juəˈrætəm] N ABBR (= *European Atomic Energy Commission*) Euratom *m*

★euro [ˈjuərəu] N (*currency*) euro

Euro- PREF euro-

Eurocheque [ˈjuərəutʃɛk] N Eurocheque *m*

Eurocrat [ˈjuərəukræt] N eurócrata *mf*

Eurodollar [ˈjuərəudɔləʳ] N eurodólar *m*

Euroland [ˈjuərəulænd] N Eurolandia

★Europe [ˈjuərəp] N Europa

★European [juərəˈpiːən] ADJ, N europeo(-a) *m/f*

European Community N Comunidad *f* Europea

European Court of Justice N Tribunal *m* de Justicia de las Comunidades Europeas

European Union N Unión *f* Europea

Euro-sceptic [juərəuˈskɛptɪk] N euroescéptico(-a)

Eurostar® [ˈjuərəustɑːʳ] N Eurostar® *m*

Eurozone [ˈjuərəuzəun] N eurozona, zona euro

euthanasia [juːθəˈneɪzɪə] N eutanasia

evacuate [ɪˈvækjueɪt] VT evacuar; (*place*) desocupar

evacuation [ɪvækjuˈeɪʃən] N evacuación *f*

evacuee [ɪvækjuˈiː] N evacuado(-a)

evade [ɪˈveɪd] VT evadir, eludir

evaluate [ɪˈvæljueɪt] VT evaluar; (*value*) tasar; (*evidence*) interpretar

evangelical [iːvænˈdʒɛlɪkəl] ADJ evangélico

evangelist [ɪˈvændʒəlɪst] N evangelista *m*; (*preacher*) evangelizador(a) *m/f*

evaporate [ɪˈvæpəreɪt] VI evaporarse; (*fig*) desvanecerse ▶ VT evaporar

evaporation [ɪvæpəˈreɪʃən] N evaporación *f*

evasion [ɪˈveɪʒən] N evasión *f*

evasive [ɪˈveɪsɪv] ADJ evasivo

eve [iːv] N: **on the ~ of** en vísperas de

★even [ˈiːvn] ADJ (*level*) llano; (*smooth*) liso; (*speed, temperature*) uniforme; (*number*) par; (*Sport*) igual(es); **to break ~** cubrir los gastos; **to get ~ with sb** ajustar cuentas con algn ▶ ADV hasta, incluso; **~ more** aun más; **~ so** aun así; **not ~** ni siquiera; **~ he was there** hasta él estaba allí; **~ on Sundays** incluso los domingos; **~ faster** aún más rápido; **~ if** aunque + *subjun*, así + *subjun* (*LAM*); **~ if you tried** aunque lo intentaras, así lo procuraras (*LAM*); **~ though** aunque; **~ though he knew** aunque lo sabía ▶ VI: **to ~ out** nivelarse

even-handed [iːvnˈhændɪd] ADJ imparcial

★evening [ˈiːvnɪŋ] N tarde *f*; (*dusk*) atardecer *m*; (*night*) noche *f*; **in the ~** por la tarde; **this ~** esta tarde *or* noche; **tomorrow/yesterday ~** mañana/ayer por la tarde *or* noche

evening class N clase *f* nocturna

evening dress N (*man's*) traje *m* de etiqueta; (*woman's*) traje *m* de noche

evenly [ˈiːvnlɪ] ADV (*distribute, space, spread*) de modo uniforme; (*divide*) equitativamente

evensong [ˈiːvnsɔŋ] N vísperas *fpl*

★event [ɪˈvɛnt] N suceso, acontecimiento; (*Sport*) prueba; **in the ~ of** en caso de; **in the ~** en realidad; **in the course of events** en el curso de los acontecimientos; **at all events, in any ~** en cualquier caso

eventful [ɪˈvɛntful] ADJ (*life*) azaroso; (*day*) ajetreado; (*game*) lleno de emoción; (*journey*) lleno de incidentes

eventing [ɪˈvɛntɪŋ] N (*Horseriding*) competición *f*

eventual [ɪˈvɛntʃuəl] ADJ final

eventuality [ɪvɛntʃuˈælɪtɪ] N eventualidad *f*

★eventually [ɪˈvɛntʃuəlɪ] ADV (*finally*) por fin; (*in time*) con el tiempo

★ever [ˈɛvəʳ] ADV nunca, jamás; (*at all times*) siempre; **for ~** (para) siempre; **the best ~** lo nunca visto; **did you ~ meet him?** ¿llegaste a conocerle?; **have you ~ been there?** ¿has estado allí alguna vez?; **have you ~ seen it?** ¿lo has visto alguna vez?; **better than ~** mejor que nunca; **thank you ~ so much** muchísimas gracias; **yours ~** (*in letters*) un abrazo de; **~ since** *adv* desde entonces; *conj* después de que

Everest ['ɛvərɪst] N (*also:* **Mount Everest**) el Everest *m*

evergreen ['ɛvəgri:n] N árbol *m* de hoja perenne

everlasting [ɛvə'lɑ:stɪŋ] ADJ eterno, perpetuo

---

every ['ɛvrɪ]

ADJ **1** (*each*) cada; **every one of them** (*persons*) todos ellos(-as); (*objects*) cada uno de ellos(-as); **every shop in the town was closed** todas las tiendas de la ciudad estaban cerradas

2 (*all possible*) todo(-a); **I gave you every assistance** te di toda la ayuda posible; **I have every confidence in him** tiene toda mi confianza; **we wish you every success** te deseamos toda suerte de éxitos

3 (*showing recurrence*) todo(-a); **every day/week** todos los días/todas las semanas; **every other car had been broken into** habían forzado uno de cada dos coches; **she visits me every other/third day** me visita cada dos/tres días; **every now and then** de vez en cuando

---

★**everybody** ['ɛvrɪbɒdɪ] PRON todos *pron pl*, todo el mundo; **~ knows about it** todo el mundo lo sabe; **~ else** todos los demás

everyday ['ɛvrɪdeɪ] ADJ (*daily: use, occurrence, experience*) diario, cotidiano; (*usual: expression*) corriente; (*common*) vulgar; (*routine*) rutinario

★**everyone** ['ɛvrɪwʌn] PRON = **everybody**

★**everything** ['ɛvrɪθɪŋ] PRON todo; **~ is ready** todo está dispuesto; **he did ~ possible** hizo todo lo posible

★**everywhere** ['ɛvrɪwɛəʳ] ADV (*be*) en todas partes; (*go*) a o por todas partes; **~ you go you meet …** en todas partes encuentras …

evict [ɪ'vɪkt] VT desahuciar

eviction [ɪ'vɪkʃən] N desahucio

eviction notice N orden *f* de desahucio *or* (*LAm*) desalojo

evidence ['ɛvɪdəns] N (*proof*) prueba; (*of witness*) testimonio; (*facts*) datos *mpl*, hechos *mpl*; **to give ~** prestar declaración, dar testimonio

evident ['ɛvɪdənt] ADJ evidente, manifiesto

evidently ['ɛvɪdəntlɪ] ADV (*obviously*) obviamente, evidentemente; (*apparently*) por lo visto

★**evil** ['i:vl] ADJ malo; (*influence*) funesto; (*smell*) horrible ▸ N mal *m*

evildoer ['i:vldu:əʳ] N malhechor(a) *m/f*

evince [ɪ'vɪns] VT mostrar, dar señales de

evocative [ɪ'vɒkətɪv] ADJ sugestivo, evocador(a)

evoke [ɪ'vəuk] VT evocar; (*admiration*) provocar

evolution [i:və'lu:ʃən] N evolución *f*, desarrollo

evolve [ɪ'vɒlv] VT desarrollar ▸ VI evolucionar, desarrollarse

ewe [ju:] N oveja

ex [ɛks] N (*inf*): **my ex** mi ex

ex- [ɛks] PREF (*former: husband, president etc*) ex-; (*out of*): **the price ex-works** precio de fábrica

exacerbate [ɛk'sæsəbeɪt] VT exacerbar

★**exact** [ɪg'zækt] ADJ exacto ▸ VT: **to ~ sth (from)** exigir algo (de)

exacting [ɪg'zæktɪŋ] ADJ exigente; (*conditions*) arduo

exactitude [ɪg'zæktɪtju:d] N exactitud *f*

★**exactly** [ɪg'zæktlɪ] ADV exactamente; (*time*) en punto; **~!** ¡exacto!

exactness [ɪg'zæktnɪs] N exactitud *f*

exaggerate [ɪg'zædʒəreɪt] VT, VI exagerar

exaggerated [ɪg'zædʒəreɪtɪd] ADJ exagerado

exaggeration [ɪgzædʒə'reɪʃən] N exageración *f*

exalt [ɪg'zɔ:lt] VT (*praise*) ensalzar; (*elevate*) elevar

exalted [ɪg'zɔ:ltɪd] ADJ (*position*) elevado; (*elated*) enardecido

★**exam** [ɪg'zæm] N ABBR (*Scol*) = **examination**

examination [ɪgzæmɪ'neɪʃən] N (*gen*) examen *m*; (*Law*) interrogación *f*; (*Med*) reconocimiento; (*inquiry*) investigación *f*; **to take** *or* **sit an ~** hacer un examen; **the matter is under ~** se está examinando el asunto

examine [ɪg'zæmɪn] VT (*gen*) examinar; (*inspect: machine, premises*) inspeccionar; (*Scol, Law: person*) interrogar; (*at customs: luggage, passport*) registrar; (*Med*) reconocer, examinar

examiner [ɪg'zæmɪnəʳ] N examinador(a) *m/f*

★**example** [ɪg'zɑ:mpl] N ejemplo; **for ~** por ejemplo; **to set a good/bad ~** dar buen/mal ejemplo

exasperate [ɪg'zɑ:spəreɪt] VT exasperar, irritar; **exasperated by** *or* **at** *or* **with** exasperado por *or* con

exasperating [ɪg'zɑ:spəreɪtɪŋ] ADJ irritante

exasperation [ɪgzɑ:spə'reɪʃən] N exasperación *f*, irritación *f*

excavate ['ɛkskəveɪt] VT excavar

excavation [ɛkskə'veɪʃən] N excavación *f*

excavator ['ɛkskəveɪtəʳ] N excavadora

exceed [ɪk'si:d] VT exceder; (*number*) pasar de; (*speed limit*) sobrepasar; (*limits*) rebasar; (*powers*) excederse en; (*hopes*) superar

exceedingly [ɪk'si:dɪŋlɪ] ADV sumamente, sobremanera

excel [ɪk'sɛl] VI sobresalir; **to ~ o.s.** lucirse

excellence ['ɛksələns] N excelencia

Excellency ['ɛksələnsɪ] N: **His ~** Su Excelencia

★**excellent** ['ɛksələnt] ADJ excelente

★**except** [ɪk'sɛpt] PREP (*also:* **except for, excepting**) excepto, salvo; **~ if/when** excepto si/cuando; **~ that** salvo que ▸ VT exceptuar, excluir

exception [ɪk'sɛpʃən] N excepción *f*; **to take ~ to** ofenderse por; **with the ~ of** a excepción de; **to make an ~** hacer una excepción

exceptional [ɪkˈsɛpʃənl] ADJ excepcional

exceptionally [ɪkˈsɛpʃənəlɪ] ADV excepcionalmente, extraordinariamente

excerpt [ˈɛksəːpt] N extracto

excess [ɪkˈsɛs] N exceso; **in ~ of** superior a ■ **excesses** NPL excesos mpl

excess baggage N exceso de equipaje

excess fare N suplemento

excessive [ɪkˈsɛsɪv] ADJ excesivo

excess supply N exceso de oferta

excess weight N exceso de peso

★exchange [ɪksˈtʃeɪndʒ] N cambio; (of prisoners) canje m; (of ideas) intercambio; (also: **telephone exchange**) central f (telefónica); **in ~ for** a cambio de; **foreign ~** (Comm) divisas fpl ▶ VT intercambiar; **to ~ (for)** cambiar (por)

exchange control N control m de divisas

★exchange rate N tipo de cambio

exchequer [ɪksˈtʃɛkəʳ] N: **the ~** (BRIT) Hacienda

excisable [ɛkˈsaɪzəbl] ADJ sujeto al pago de impuestos sobre el consumo

excise [ˈɛksaɪz] N impuestos sobre el consumo interior

excitable [ɪkˈsaɪtəbl] ADJ excitable

excite [ɪkˈsaɪt] VT (stimulate) estimular; (anger) suscitar, provocar; (move) emocionar; **to get excited** emocionarse

excitement [ɪkˈsaɪtmənt] N emoción f

★exciting [ɪkˈsaɪtɪŋ] ADJ emocionante

excl. ABBR = **excluding; exclusive (of)**

exclaim [ɪkˈskleɪm] VI exclamar

exclamation [ɛkskləˈmeɪʃən] N exclamación f

exclamation mark, (US) **exclamation point** N signo de admiración

exclude [ɪkˈskluːd] VT excluir; (except) exceptuar

excluding [ɪksˈkluːdɪŋ] PREP: **~ VAT** IVA no incluido

exclusion [ɪkˈskluːʒən] N exclusión f; **to the ~ of** con exclusión de

exclusion clause N cláusula de exclusión

exclusion zone N zona de exclusión

exclusive [ɪkˈskluːsɪv] ADJ exclusivo; (club, district) selecto; **~ of tax** excluyendo impuestos; **~ of postage/service** franqueo/servicio no incluido; **from 1st to 13th March** ~ del 1 al 13 de marzo exclusive

exclusively [ɪkˈskluːsɪvlɪ] ADV únicamente

excommunicate [ɛkskəˈmjuːnɪkeɪt] VT excomulgar

excrement [ˈɛkskrəmənt] N excremento

excrete [ɪkˈskriːt] VI excretar

excruciating [ɪkˈskruːʃɪeɪtɪŋ] ADJ (pain) agudísimo, atroz

excursion [ɪkˈskəːʃən] N excursión f

excursion ticket N billete m (especial) de excursión

excusable [ɪkˈskjuːsəbl] ADJ perdonable

★excuse N [ɪkˈskjuːs] disculpa, excusa; (evasion) pretexto; **to make excuses for sb** presentar disculpas por algn ▶ VT [ɪkˈskjuːz] disculpar, perdonar; (justify) justificar; **to ~ sb from doing sth** dispensar a algn de hacer algo; **to ~ o.s. (for (doing) sth)** pedir disculpas a algn (por (hacer) algo); **~ me!** ¡perdone!; (attracting attention) ¡oiga(, por favor)!; **if you will ~ me** con su permiso

ex-directory [ˈɛksdɪˈrɛktərɪ] ADJ (BRIT): **~ (phone) number** número que no figura en la guía (telefónica)

execrable [ˈɛksɪkrəbl] ADJ execrable, abominable; (manners) detestable

executable [ˈɛksɪkjuːtəbl] ADJ (Comput) ejecutable

execute [ˈɛksɪkjuːt] VT (plan) realizar; (order) cumplir; (person) ajusticiar, ejecutar

execution [ɛksɪˈkjuːʃən] N realización f; cumplimiento; ejecución f

executioner [ɛksɪˈkjuːʃənəʳ] N verdugo

executive [ɪgˈzɛkjutɪv] N (Comm) ejecutivo(-a); (Pol) poder m ejecutivo ▶ ADJ ejecutivo; (car, plane, position) de ejecutivo; (offices, suite) de la dirección; (secretary) de dirección

executive director N director(a) m/f ejecutivo(-a)

executor [ɪgˈzɛkjutəʳ] N albacea m, testamentario

exemplary [ɪgˈzɛmplərɪ] ADJ ejemplar

exemplify [ɪgˈzɛmplɪfaɪ] VT ejemplificar

exempt [ɪgˈzɛmpt] ADJ: **~ from** exento de ▶ VT: **to ~ sb from** eximir a algn de

exemption [ɪgˈzɛmpʃən] N exención f; (immunity) inmunidad f

★exercise [ˈɛksəsaɪz] N ejercicio ▶ VT ejercer; (patience etc) proceder con; (dog) sacar de paseo ▶ VI hacer ejercicio

exercise bike N bicicleta estática

exercise book N cuaderno de ejercicios

exert [ɪgˈzəːt] VT ejercer; (strength, force) emplear; **to ~ o.s.** esforzarse

exertion [ɪgˈzəːʃən] N esfuerzo

exfoliant [ɛksˈfəʊlɪənt] N exfoliante m

ex gratia [ˈɛksˈgreɪʃə] ADJ: **~ payment** pago a título voluntario

exhale [ɛksˈheɪl] VT despedir, exhalar ▶ VI espirar, exhalar

exhaust [ɪgˈzɔːst] N (pipe) (tubo de) escape m; (fumes) gases mpl de escape ▶ VT agotar; **to ~ o.s.** agotarse

★exhausted [ɪgˈzɔːstɪd] ADJ agotado

exhausting [ɪgˈzɔːstɪŋ] ADJ: **an ~ journey/day** un viaje/día agotador

exhaustion [ɪgˈzɔːstʃən] N agotamiento; **nervous ~** agotamiento nervioso

exhaustive [ɪgˈzɔːstɪv] ADJ exhaustivo

exhibit [ɪgˈzɪbɪt] N (Art) obra expuesta; (Law)

objeto expuesto ▶ VT (*show: emotions*) manifestar; (: *courage, skill*) demostrar; (*paintings*) exponer

★**exhibition** [ɛksɪˈbɪʃən] N exposición *f*

exhibitionist [ɛksɪˈbɪʃənɪst] N exhibicionista *mf*

exhibitor [ɪgˈzɪbɪtəʳ] N expositor(a) *m/f*

exhilarating [ɪgˈzɪləreɪtɪŋ] ADJ estimulante, tónico

exhilaration [ɪgzɪləˈreɪʃən] N júbilo

exhort [ɪgˈzɔːt] VT exhortar

exile [ˈɛksaɪl] N exilio; (*person*) exiliado(-a) ▶ VT desterrar, exiliar

exist [ɪgˈzɪst] VI existir

existence [ɪgˈzɪstəns] N existencia

existentialism [ɛgzɪsˈtɛnʃəlɪzəm] N existencialismo

existing [ɪgˈzɪstɪŋ] ADJ existente, actual

★**exit** [ˈɛksɪt] N salida ▶ VI (*Theat*) hacer mutis; (*Comput*) salir (del sistema)

exit no debe traducirse por *éxito*.

exit poll N encuesta a la salida de los colegios electorales

exit ramp N (*US Aut*) vía de acceso

exit visa N visado de salida

exodus [ˈɛksədəs] N éxodo

ex officio [ˈɛksəˈfɪʃɪəu] ADJ de pleno derecho ▶ ADV ex oficio

exonerate [ɪgˈzɒnəreɪt] VT: **to ~ from** exculpar de

exorbitant [ɪgˈzɔːbɪtənt] ADJ (*price, demands*) exorbitante, excesivo

exorcize [ˈɛksɔːsaɪz] VT exorcizar

exotic [ɪgˈzɒtɪk] ADJ exótico

expand [ɪkˈspænd] VT ampliar, extender; (*number*) aumentar ▶ VI (*trade etc*) ampliarse, expandirse; (*gas, metal*) dilatarse; **to ~ on** (*notes, story etc*) ampliar

expanse [ɪkˈspæns] N extensión *f*

expansion [ɪkˈspænʃən] N ampliación *f*; aumento; (*of trade*) expansión *f*

expansionism [ɪkˈspænʃənɪzəm] N expansionismo

expansionist [ɪkˈspænʃənɪst] ADJ expansionista

expatriate [ɛksˈpætrɪət] N expatriado(-a)

★**expect** [ɪkˈspɛkt] VT (*gen*) esperar; (*count on*) contar con; (*suppose*) suponer; **as expected** como era de esperar; **I ~ so** supongo que sí; **to ~ to do sth** esperar hacer algo ▶ VI: **to be expecting** estar encinta

expectancy [ɪkˈspɛktənsɪ] N (*anticipation*) expectación *f*; **life ~** esperanza de vida

expectantly [ɪkˈspɛktəntlɪ] ADV (*look, listen*) con expectación

expectant mother [ɪkˈspɛktənt-] N futura madre *f*

expectation [ɛkspɛkˈteɪʃən] N (*hope*) esperanza; (*belief*) expectativa; **in ~ of** esperando; **against** *or* **contrary to all ~(s)** en contra de todas las previsiones; **to come** *or* **live up to sb's expectations** resultar tan bueno como se esperaba; **to fall short of sb's expectations** no cumplir las esperanzas de algn, decepcionar a algn

expedience [ɪkˈspiːdɪəns], **expediency** [ɪkˈspiːdɪənsɪ] N conveniencia

expedient [ɪkˈspiːdɪənt] ADJ conveniente, oportuno ▶ N recurso, expediente *m*

expedite [ˈɛkspɪdaɪt] VT (*speed up*) acelerar; (: *progress*) facilitar

expedition [ɛkspəˈdɪʃən] N expedición *f*

expeditionary force [ɛkspəˈdɪʃnrɪ-] N cuerpo expedicionario

expel [ɪkˈspɛl] VT expulsar

expend [ɪkˈspɛnd] VT gastar; (*use up*) consumir

expendable [ɪkˈspɛndəbl] ADJ prescindible

expenditure [ɪkˈspɛndɪtʃəʳ] N gastos *mpl*, desembolso; (*of time, effort*) gasto

expense [ɪkˈspɛns] N gasto, gastos *mpl*; (*high cost*) coste *m*; **at the ~ of** a costa de; **to meet the ~ of** hacer frente a los gastos de ■ **expenses** NPL (*Comm*) gastos *mpl*

expense account N cuenta de gastos (de representación)

★**expensive** [ɪkˈspɛnsɪv] ADJ caro, costoso

★**experience** [ɪkˈspɪərɪəns] N experiencia; **to learn by ~** aprender con la experiencia ▶ VT experimentar; (*suffer*) sufrir

experienced [ɪkˈspɪərɪənst] ADJ experimentado

★**experiment** [ɪkˈspɛrɪmənt] N experimento; **to perform** *or* **carry out an ~** realizar un experimento; **as an ~** como experimento ▶ VI hacer experimentos, experimentar; **to ~ with a new vaccine** experimentar con una vacuna nueva

experimental [ɪkspɛrɪˈmɛntl] ADJ experimental; **the process is still at the ~ stage** el proceso está todavía en prueba

★**expert** [ˈɛkspəːt] ADJ experto, perito; **~ witness** (*Law*) testigo pericial ▶ N experto(-a), perito(-a); (*specialist*) especialista *mf*; **~ in** *or* **at doing sth** experto *or* perito en hacer algo; **an ~ on sth** un experto en algo

expertise [ɛkspəːˈtiːz] N pericia

expiration [ɛkspɪˈreɪʃən] N (*gen*) expiración *f*, vencimiento

expire [ɪkˈspaɪəʳ] VI (*gen*) caducar, vencerse

expiry [ɪkˈspaɪərɪ] N caducidad *f*, vencimiento

expiry date N (*of medicine, food item*) fecha de caducidad

★**explain** [ɪkˈspleɪn] VT explicar; (*mystery*) aclarar ▶ **explain away** VT justificar

★**explanation** [ɛkspləˈneɪʃən] N explicación *f*; aclaración *f*; **to find an ~ for sth** encontrarle una explicación a algo

explanatory [ɪk'splænətrɪ] ADJ explicativo; aclaratorio

expletive [ɪk'spliːtɪv] N imprecación f

explicable [ɪk'splɪkəbl] ADJ explicable

explicit [ɪk'splɪsɪt] ADJ explícito

explicitly [ɪk'splɪsɪtlɪ] ADV explícitamente

★**explode** [ɪk'spləud] VI estallar, explotar; (with anger) reventar ▸ VT hacer explotar; (fig: theory, myth) demoler

exploit N ['ɛksplɔɪt] hazaña ▸ VT [ɪk'splɔɪt] explotar

exploitation [ɛksplɔɪ'teɪʃən] N explotación f

exploration [ɛksplə'reɪʃən] N exploración f

exploratory [ɪk'splɔrətrɪ] ADJ (fig: talks) exploratorio, preliminar

explore [ɪk'splɔːᵊ] VT explorar; (fig) examinar, sondear

explorer [ɪk'splɔːrəᵊ] N explorador(a) m/f

★**explosion** [ɪk'spləuʒən] N explosión f

explosive [ɪk'spləusɪv] ADJ, N explosivo

exponent [ɪk'spəunənt] N partidario(-a); (of skill, activity) exponente mf

export VT [ɛk'spɔːt] exportar ▸ N ['ɛkspɔːt] exportación f ▸ CPD ['ɛkspɔːt] de exportación

exportation [ɛkspɔː'teɪʃən] N exportación f

export drive N campaña de exportación

exporter [ɛk'spɔːtəᵊ] N exportador(a) m/f

export licence N licencia de exportación

export manager N gerente mf de exportación

export trade N comercio exterior

expose [ɪk'spəuz] VT exponer; (unmask) desenmascarar

exposé [ɪk'spəuzeɪ] N revelación f

exposed [ɪk'spəuzd] ADJ expuesto; (land, house) desprotegido; (Elec: wire) al aire; (pipe, beam) al descubierto

exposition [ɛkspə'zɪʃən] N exposición f

exposure [ɪk'spəuʒəᵊ] N exposición f; (Phot: speed) (tiempo m de) exposición f; (: shot) fotografía; **to die from ~** (Med) morir de frío

exposure meter N fotómetro

expound [ɪk'spaund] VT exponer; (theory, text) comentar; (one's views) explicar

★**express** [ɪk'sprɛs] ADJ (definite) expreso, explícito; (BRIT: letter etc) urgente ▸ N (train) rápido ▸ ADV: **to send sth ~** enviar algo por correo urgente ▸ VT expresar; (squeeze) exprimir; **to ~ o.s.** expresarse

★**expression** [ɪk'sprɛʃən] N expresión f

expressionism [ɪk'sprɛʃənɪzm] N expresionismo

expressive [ɪk'sprɛsɪv] ADJ expresivo

expressly [ɪk'sprɛslɪ] ADV expresamente

expressway [ɪk'sprɛsweɪ] N (US: urban motorway) autopista

expropriate [ɛks'prəuprɪeɪt] VT expropiar

expulsion [ɪk'spʌlʃən] N expulsión f

expurgate ['ɛkspəgeɪt] VT expurgar

exquisite [ɛk'skwɪzɪt] ADJ exquisito

exquisitely [ɛk'skwɪzɪtlɪ] ADV exquisitamente

ex-serviceman ['ɛks'səːvɪsmən] N (irreg) excombatiente m

ext. ABBR (Tel) = **extension**

extemporize [ɪk'stɛmpəraɪz] VI improvisar

extend [ɪk'stɛnd] VT (visit, street) prolongar; (building) ampliar; (thanks, friendship etc) extender; (Comm: credit) conceder; (deadline) prorrogar; (invitation) ofrecer ▸ VI (land) extenderse; **the contract extends to/for ...** el contrato se prolonga hasta/por ...

extension [ɪk'stɛnʃən] N extensión f; (building) ampliación f; (Tel: line) extensión f; (: telephone) supletorio m; (of deadline) prórroga; **~ 3718** extensión 3718

extension cable N (Elec) alargador m

extensive [ɪk'stɛnsɪv] ADJ (gen) extenso; (damage) importante; (knowledge) amplio

extensively [ɪk'stɛnsɪvlɪ] ADV (altered, damaged etc) extensamente; **he's travelled ~** ha viajado por muchos países

★**extent** [ɪk'stɛnt] N (breadth) extensión f; (scope: of knowledge, activities) alcance m; (degree: of damage, loss) grado; **to some ~** hasta cierto punto; **to a certain ~** hasta cierto punto; **to a large ~** en gran parte; **to the ~ of ...** hasta el punto de ...; **to such an ~ that ...** hasta tal punto que ...; **to what ~?** ¿hasta qué punto?; **debts to the ~ of £5000** deudas por la cantidad de £5000

extenuating [ɪk'stɛnjueɪtɪŋ] ADJ: **~ circumstances** circunstancias fpl atenuantes

exterior [ɛk'stɪərɪəᵊ] ADJ exterior, externo ▸ N exterior m

exterminate [ɪk'stəːmɪneɪt] VT exterminar

extermination [ɪkstəːmɪ'neɪʃən] N exterminio

external [ɛk'stəːnl] ADJ externo, exterior; **~ affairs** asuntos mpl exteriores; **for ~ use only** (Med) para uso tópico ▸ N: **the externals** la apariencia exterior

externally [ɛk'stəːnəlɪ] ADV por fuera

extinct [ɪk'stɪŋkt] ADJ (volcano) extinguido, apagado; (race) extinguido

extinction [ɪk'stɪŋkʃən] N extinción f

extinguish [ɪk'stɪŋgwɪʃ] VT extinguir, apagar

extinguisher [ɪk'stɪŋgwɪʃəᵊ] N extintor m

extol, (US) **extoll** [ɪk'stəul] VT (merits, virtues) ensalzar, alabar; (person) alabar, elogiar

extort [ɪk'stɔːt] VT sacar a la fuerza; (confession) arrancar

extortion [ɪk'stɔːʃən] N extorsión f

extortionate [ɪk'stɔːʃnət] ADJ excesivo, exorbitante

★**extra** ['ɛkstrə] ADJ adicional ▸ ADV (in addition) más; **wine will cost ~** el vino se paga aparte; **~ large sizes** tallas extragrandes ▸ N (addition) extra m, suplemento; (Theat) extra mf, comparsa *mf*; *(newspaper)* edición *f* extraordinaria ▪ **extras** NPL *(additional expense)* extras *mpl*

extra… [ˈɛkstrə] PREF extra…

extract VT [ɪkˈstrækt] sacar; *(tooth)* extraer; *(confession)* arrancar ▶ N [ˈɛkstrækt] fragmento; *(Culin)* extracto

extraction [ɪkˈstrækʃən] N extracción *f*; *(origin)* origen *m*

extractor fan [ɪkˈstræktə-] N extractor *m* de humos

extracurricular [ɛkstrəkəˈrɪkjuləʳ] ADJ *(Scol)* extraescolar

extradite [ˈɛkstrədaɪt] VT extraditar

extradition [ɛkstrəˈdɪʃən] N extradición *f*

extramarital [ɛkstrəˈmærɪtl] ADJ extramatrimonial

extramural [ɛkstrəˈmjuərl] ADJ extraacadémico

extraneous [ɪkˈstreɪnɪəs] ADJ extraño, ajeno

★**extraordinary** [ɪkˈstrɔːdnrɪ] ADJ extraordinario; *(odd)* raro; **the ~ thing is that …** lo más extraordinario es que …

extraordinary general meeting N junta general extraordinaria

extrapolation [ɪkstræpəˈleɪʃən] N extrapolación *f*

extrasensory perception [ˈɛkstrəˈsɛnsərɪ-] N percepción *f* extrasensorial

extra time N *(Football)* prórroga

extravagance [ɪkˈstrævəgəns] N *(excessive spending)* derroche *m*; *(thing bought)* extravagancia

extravagant [ɪkˈstrævəgənt] ADJ *(wasteful)* derrochador(a); *(taste, gift)* excesivamente caro; *(price)* exorbitante; *(praise)* excesivo

★**extreme** [ɪkˈstriːm] ADJ extremo; *(poverty etc)* extremado; *(case)* excepcional; **the ~ left/right** *(Pol)* la extrema izquierda/derecha ▶ N extremo; **extremes of temperature** temperaturas extremas

★**extremely** [ɪkˈstriːmlɪ] ADV sumamente, extremadamente

extremist [ɪkˈstriːmɪst] ADJ, N extremista *mf*

extremity [ɪkˈstrɛmətɪ] N extremidad *f*, punta; *(need)* apuro, necesidad *f* ▪ **extremities** NPL *(hands and feet)* extremidades *fpl*

extricate [ˈɛkstrɪkeɪt] VT: **to ~ o.s. from** librarse de

extrovert [ˈɛkstrəvɜːt] N extrovertido(-a)

exuberance [ɪɡˈzjuːbərns] N exuberancia

exuberant [ɪɡˈzjuːbərnt] ADJ *(person)* eufórico; *(style)* exuberante

exude [ɪɡˈzjuːd] VT rezumar

exult [ɪɡˈzʌlt] VI regocijarse

exultant [ɪɡˈzʌltənt] ADJ *(person)* regocijado, jubiloso; *(shout, expression, smile)* de júbilo

exultation [ɛɡzʌlˈteɪʃən] N regocijo, júbilo

★**eye** [aɪ] N ojo; **to keep an ~ on** vigilar; **as far as the ~ can see** hasta donde alcanza la vista; **with an ~ to doing sth** con vistas *or* miras a hacer algo; **to have an ~ for sth** tener mucha vista *or* buen ojo para algo; **there's more to this than meets the ~** esto tiene su miga ▶ VT mirar

eyeball [ˈaɪbɔːl] N globo ocular

eyebath [ˈaɪbɑːθ] N baño ocular, lavaojos *m inv*

eyebrow [ˈaɪbrau] N ceja

eyebrow pencil N lápiz *m* de cejas

eye-catching [ˈaɪkætʃɪŋ] ADJ llamativo

eye cup N *(US)* = **eyebath**

eyedrops [ˈaɪdrɒps] NPL gotas *fpl* para los ojos

eyeful [ˈaɪful] N *(inf)*: **to get an ~ of sth** ver bien algo

eyelash [ˈaɪlæʃ] N pestaña

eyelet [ˈaɪlɪt] N ojete *m*

eye-level [ˈaɪlɛvl] ADJ a la altura de los ojos

eyelid [ˈaɪlɪd] N párpado

eyeliner [ˈaɪlaɪnəʳ] N lápiz *m* de ojos

eye-opener [ˈaɪəupnəʳ] N revelación *f*, gran sorpresa

eyeshadow [ˈaɪʃædəu] N sombra de ojos

eyesight [ˈaɪsaɪt] N vista

eyesore [ˈaɪsɔːʳ] N monstruosidad *f*

eyestrain [ˈaɪstreɪn] N: **to get ~** cansar la vista *or* los ojos

eyetooth [ˈaɪtuːθ] *(pl* **eyeteeth** *[-tiːθ])* N colmillo; **to give one's eyeteeth for sth/to do sth** *(fig: inf)* dar un ojo de la cara por algo/por hacer algo

eyewash [ˈaɪwɒʃ] N *(fig)* disparates *mpl*, tonterías *fpl*

eye witness N testigo *mf* ocular

eyrie [ˈɪərɪ] N aguilera

Ff

F, f [ɛf] N (*letter*) F, f *f*; (*Mus*): F fa *m*; **F for Frederick**, (*US*) **F for Fox** F de Francia

F. ABBR = **Fahrenheit**

FA N ABBR (*BRIT*: = *Football Association*) ≈ AFE *f* (*SP*)

FAA N ABBR (*US*) = **Federal Aviation Administration**

fable ['feɪbl] N fábula

fabric ['fæbrɪk] N tejido, tela

> **fabric** no debe traducirse por *fábrica*.

fabricate ['fæbrɪkeɪt] VT fabricar; (*fig*) inventar

fabrication [fæbrɪ'keɪʃən] N fabricación *f*; (*fig*) invención *f*

fabric ribbon N cinta de tela

fabulous ['fæbjʊləs] ADJ (*inf*) fabuloso

façade [fə'sɑːd] N fachada

★face [feɪs] N (*Anat*) cara, rostro; (*of clock*) esfera; (*side*) cara; (*surface*) superficie *f*; **~ down** (*person, card*) boca abajo; **to lose ~** desprestigiarse; **to save ~** salvar las apariencias; **to make** *or* **pull a ~** hacer muecas; **in the ~ of** (*difficulties etc*) en vista de, ante; **on the ~ of it** a primera vista; **~ to ~** cara a cara ▸ VT (*direction*) estar de cara a; (*situation*) hacer frente a; (*facts*) aceptar; **to ~ the fact that ...** reconocer que ...
> ▸ **face up to** VT FUS hacer frente a, enfrentarse a

Facebook® ['feɪsbʊk] N Facebook® *m*

facebook® ['feɪsbʊk] VT, VI enviar un mensaje por el Facebook®

face cloth N (*BRIT*) toallita

face cream N crema (de belleza)

faceless ['feɪslɪs] ADJ (*fig*) anónimo

face lift N lifting *m*, estirado facial

face pack N (*BRIT*) mascarilla

face powder N polvos *mpl* para la cara

face-saving ['feɪsseɪvɪŋ] ADJ para salvar las apariencias

facet ['fæsɪt] N faceta

facetious [fə'siːʃəs] ADJ chistoso

facetiously [fə'siːʃəslɪ] ADV chistosamente

face value N (*of stamp*) valor *m* nominal; **to take sth at ~** (*fig*) tomar algo en sentido literal, aceptar las apariencias de algo

facial ['feɪʃəl] ADJ de la cara ▸ N (*also:* **beauty facial**) tratamiento facial, limpieza

facile ['fæsaɪl] ADJ superficial

facilitate [fə'sɪlɪteɪt] VT facilitar

facility [fə'sɪlɪtɪ] N facilidad *f*; **credit ~** facilidades de crédito ▪ **facilities** NPL (*buildings*) instalaciones *fpl*

facing ['feɪsɪŋ] PREP frente a ▸ ADJ de enfrente

facsimile [fæk'sɪmɪlɪ] N facsímil(e) *m*

★fact [fækt] N hecho; **in ~** en realidad; **to know for a ~ that ...** saber a ciencia cierta que ...

fact-finding ['fæktfaɪndɪŋ] ADJ: **a ~ tour/mission** un viaje/una misión de reconocimiento

faction ['fækʃən] N facción *f*

factional ['fækʃənl] ADJ (*fighting*) entre distintas facciones

factor ['fæktəʳ] N factor *m*; (*Comm: person*) agente *mf* comisionado(-a); **safety ~** factor de seguridad ▸ VI (*Comm*) comprar deudas

★factory ['fæktərɪ] N fábrica

factory farming N cría industrial

factory floor N (*workers*) trabajadores *mpl*, mano *f* de obra directa; (*area*) talleres *mpl*

factory ship N buque *m* factoría

factual ['fæktjʊəl] ADJ basado en los hechos

faculty ['fækəltɪ] N facultad *f*; (*US: teaching staff*) personal *m* docente

fad [fæd] N novedad *f*, moda

fade [feɪd] VI descolorarse, desteñirse; (*sound, hope*) desvanecerse; (*light*) apagarse; (*flower*) marchitarse
> ▸ **fade away** VI (*sound*) apagarse
> ▸ **fade in** VT (*TV, Cine*) fundir; (*Radio: sound*) mezclar ▸ VI (*TV, Cine*) fundirse; (*Radio*) oírse por encima
> ▸ **fade out** VT (*TV, Cine*) fundir; (*Radio*) apagar,

disminuir el volumen de ▶ vɪ (*TV, Cine*) desvanecerse; (*Radio*) apagarse, dejarse de oír

faded [ˈfeɪdɪd] ADJ (*clothes, colour*) descolorido; (*flower*) marchito

faeces, (*US*) **feces** [ˈfiːsiːz] NPL excremento *sg*, heces *fpl*

fag [fæg] N (*BRIT inf: cigarette*) pitillo (*SP*), cigarro; (*US !: homosexual*) maricón *m* (!)

fag end N (*BRIT inf*) colilla

fagged [fægd] ADJ (*BRIT inf: exhausted*) rendido, agotado

Fahrenheit [ˈfɑːrənhaɪt] N Fahrenheit *m*

★**fail** [feɪl] VT suspender; (*memory etc*) fallar a; **to ~ to do sth** (*neglect*) dejar de hacer algo; (*be unable*) no poder hacer algo; **words ~ me!** ¡no sé qué decir! ▶ vɪ suspender; (*be unsuccessful*) fracasar; (*strength, brakes, engine*) fallar; **without ~** sin falta

failing [ˈfeɪlɪŋ] N falta, defecto ▶ PREP a falta de; **~ that** de no ser posible eso

failsafe [ˈfeɪlseɪf] ADJ (*device etc*) de seguridad

★**failure** [ˈfeɪljəʳ] N fracaso; (*person*) fracasado(-a); (*mechanical etc*) fallo; (*in exam*) suspenso; (*of crops*) pérdida, destrucción *f*; **it was a complete ~** fue un fracaso total

★**faint** [feɪnt] ADJ débil; (*smell, breeze, trace*) leve; (*recollection*) vago; (*mark*) apenas visible; **to feel ~** estar mareado, marearse ▶ N desmayo ▶ vɪ desmayarse

faintest [ˈfeɪntɪst] ADJ: **I haven't the ~ idea** no tengo la más remota idea

faint-hearted [ˈfeɪntˈhɑːtɪd] ADJ apocado

faintly [ˈfeɪntlɪ] ADV débilmente; (*vaguely*) vagamente

faintness [ˈfeɪntnɪs] N debilidad *f*; vaguedad *f*

★**fair** [fɛəʳ] ADJ justo; (*hair, person*) rubio; (*weather*) bueno; (*good enough*) suficiente; (*sizeable*) considerable; **it's not ~!** ¡no es justo!, ¡no hay derecho!; **~ copy** copia en limpio; **a ~ amount of** bastante; **~ play** juego limpio; **~ wear and tear** desgaste *m* natural ▶ ADV: **to play ~** jugar limpio ▶ N feria; (*BRIT: funfair*) parque *m* de atracciones; **trade ~** feria de muestras

fair game N: **to be ~** ser blanco legítimo

fairground [ˈfɛəgraund] N recinto ferial

fair-haired [fɛəˈhɛəd] ADJ (*person*) rubio

★**fairly** [ˈfɛəlɪ] ADV (*justly*) con justicia; (*equally*) equitativamente; (*quite*) bastante; **I'm ~ sure** estoy bastante seguro

fairness [ˈfɛənɪs] N justicia; (*impartiality*) imparcialidad *f*; **in all ~** a decir verdad

fair trade N comercio justo

fairway [ˈfɛəweɪ] N (*Golf*) calle *f*

fairy [ˈfɛərɪ] N hada

fairy godmother N hada madrina

fairyland [ˈfɛərɪlænd] N el país de ensueño

fairy lights NPL bombillas *fpl* de colores

fairy tale N cuento de hadas

★**faith** [feɪθ] N fe *f*; (*trust*) confianza; (*sect*) religión *f*; **to have ~ in sb/sth** confiar en algn/algo

faithful [ˈfeɪθful] ADJ (*loyal: troops etc*) leal; (*spouse*) fiel; (*account*) exacto

faithfully [ˈfeɪθfulɪ] ADV fielmente; **yours ~** (*BRIT: in letters*) le saluda atentamente

faith healer N curador(a) *m/f* por fe

fake [feɪk] N (*painting etc*) falsificación *f*; (*person*) impostor(a) *m/f* ▶ ADJ falso ▶ vɪ fingir; (*painting etc*) falsificar

falcon [ˈfɔːlkən] N halcón *m*

Falkland Islands [ˈfɔːlklənd-] NPL Islas *fpl* Malvinas

★**fall** [fɔːl] N caída; (*US: season*) fall otoño: fall; (*decrease*) disminución *f*; **a ~ of earth** un desprendimiento de tierra; **a ~ of snow** una nevada ▶ vɪ (*pt* **fell** [fɛl], *pp* **fallen** [ˈfɔːlən]) caer; (*accidentally*) caerse; (*price*) bajar; **to ~ flat** (*on one's face*) caerse de bruces; (*joke, story*) no hacer gracia; **to ~ in love (with sb/sth)** enamorarse (de algn/algo); **to ~ short of sb's expectations** decepcionar a algn ■ **falls** NPL (*waterfall*) cataratas *fpl*, salto *sg* de agua

▶ **fall apart** vɪ deshacerse

▶ **fall back** vɪ retroceder

▶ **fall back on** VT FUS (*remedy etc*) recurrir a; **to have sth to ~ back on** tener algo a que recurrir

▶ **fall behind** vɪ quedarse atrás; (*fig: with payments*) retrasarse

▶ **fall down** vɪ (*person*) caerse; (*building*) derrumbarse

▶ **fall for** VT FUS (*trick*) tragar; (*person*) enamorarse de

▶ **fall in** vɪ (*roof*) hundirse; (*Mil*) alinearse

▶ **fall in with** VT FUS: **to ~ in with sb's plans** acomodarse con los planes de algn

▶ **fall off** vɪ caerse; (*diminish*) disminuir

▶ **fall out** vɪ (*friends etc*) reñir; (*hair, teeth*) caerse; (*Mil*) romper filas

▶ **fall over** vɪ caer(se)

▶ **fall through** vɪ (*plan, project*) fracasar

fallacy [ˈfæləsɪ] N error *m*

fallback position [ˈfɔːlbæk-] N posición *f* de repliegue

fallen [ˈfɔːlən] PP *of* **fall**

fallible [ˈfæləbl] ADJ falible

falling [ˈfɔːlɪŋ] ADJ: **~ market** mercado en baja

falling-off [ˈfɔːlɪŋˈɔf] N (*reduction*) disminución *f*

Fallopian tube [fəˈləupɪən-] N (*Anat*) trompa de Falopio

fallout [ˈfɔːlaut] N lluvia radioactiva

fallout shelter N refugio antinuclear

fallow [ˈfæləu] ADJ (*land, field*) en barbecho

★**false** [fɔːls] ADJ (*gen*) falso; (*teeth etc*) postizo; (*disloyal*) desleal, traidor(a); **under ~ pretences** con engaños

false alarm N falsa alarma

falsehood [ˈfɔːlshud] N falsedad *f*

falsely [ˈfɔːlslɪ] ADV falsamente

false teeth NPL (*BRIT*) dentadura *sg* postiza

falsify [ˈfɔːlsɪfaɪ] VT falsificar

falter [ˈfɔːltəʳ] vɪ vacilar

fame [feɪm] N fama

★**familiar** [fəˈmɪlɪəʳ] ADJ familiar; (*well-known*) conocido; (*tone*) de confianza; **to be ~ with** (*subject*) conocer (bien); **to make o.s. ~ with** familiarizarse con; **to be on ~ terms with sb** tener confianza con algn

familiarity [fəmɪlɪˈærɪtɪ] N familiaridad f

familiarize [fəˈmɪlɪəraɪz] VT: **to ~ o.s. with** familiarizarse con

★**family** [ˈfæmɪlɪ] N familia

family business N negocio familiar

family credit N (*BRIT*) ≈ ayuda familiar

family doctor N médico(-a) de cabecera

family life N vida doméstica *or* familiar

family man N (*irreg*) (*home-loving*) hombre m casero; (*having family*) padre m de familia

family planning N planificación f familiar

family planning clinic N clínica de planificación familiar

family tree N árbol m genealógico

famine [ˈfæmɪn] N hambre f, hambruna

famished [ˈfæmɪʃt] ADJ hambriento; **I'm ~!** (*inf*) ¡estoy muerto de hambre!, ¡tengo un hambre canina!

★**famous** [ˈfeɪməs] ADJ famoso, célebre

famously [ˈfeɪməslɪ] ADV (*get on*) estupendamente

★**fan** [fæn] N abanico; (*Elec*) ventilador m; (*person*) aficionado(-a); (*Sport*) hincha mf; (*of pop star*) fan mf ▶ VT abanicar; (*fire, quarrel*) atizar
▶ **fan out** VI desplegarse

fanatic [fəˈnætɪk] N fanático(-a)

fanatical [fəˈnætɪkəl] ADJ fanático

fan belt N correa del ventilador

fancied [ˈfænsɪd] ADJ imaginario

fanciful [ˈfænsɪful] ADJ (*gen*) fantástico; (*imaginary*) fantasioso; (*design*) rebuscado

fan club N club m de fans

fancy [ˈfænsɪ] N (*whim*) capricho, antojo; (*imagination*) imaginación f; **to take a ~ to sb** tomar cariño a algn; **when the ~ takes him** cuando se le antoja; **it took** *or* **caught my ~** me cayó en gracia ▶ ADJ (*luxury*) de lujo; (*price*) desorbitado ▶ VT (*feel like, want*) tener ganas de; (*imagine*) imaginarse, figurarse; **to ~ that ...** imaginarse que ...; **he fancies her** le gusta (ella) mucho

fancy dress N disfraz m

fancy-dress ball [ˈfænsɪdrɛs-] N baile m de disfraces

fancy goods N artículos mpl de fantasía

fanfare [ˈfænfɛəʳ] N fanfarria (de trompeta)

fanfold paper [ˈfænfəuld-] N papel m plegado en abanico *or* en acordeón

fang [fæŋ] N colmillo

fan heater N calefactor m de aire

fanlight [ˈfænlaɪt] N (montante m en) abanico

fanny [ˈfænɪ] N (*BRIT inf!: genitals*) chocho (*inf!*); (*US inf: buttocks*) pompis m, culo (*inf!*)

fantasize [ˈfæntəsaɪz] VI fantasear, hacerse ilusiones

★**fantastic** [fænˈtæstɪk] ADJ fantástico

fantasy [ˈfæntəzɪ] N fantasía

fanzine [ˈfænziːn] N fanzine m

FAO N ABBR (= *Food and Agriculture Organization*) OAA f, FAO f

FAQ ABBR (= *free alongside quay*) franco sobre muelle

FAQs NPL ABBR (= *frequently asked questions*) preguntas fpl frecuentes

★**far** [fɑːʳ] ADJ (*distant*) lejano; **the ~ left/right** (*Pol*) la extrema izquierda/derecha ▶ ADV lejos; **~ away, ~ off** (a lo) lejos; **~ better** mucho mejor; **~ from** lejos de; **by ~** con mucho; **it's by ~ the best** es con mucho el mejor; **go as ~ as the farm** vaya hasta la granja; **is it ~ to London?** ¿estamos lejos de Londres?, ¿Londres queda lejos?; **it's not ~ (from here)** no está lejos (de aquí); **as ~ as I know** que yo sepa; **how ~?** ¿hasta dónde?; (*fig*) ¿hasta qué punto?; **how ~ have you got with your work?** ¿hasta dónde has llegado en tu trabajo?

faraway [ˈfɑːrəweɪ] ADJ remoto; (*look*) ausente, perdido

farce [fɑːs] N farsa

farcical [ˈfɑːsɪkəl] ADJ absurdo

★**fare** [fɛəʳ] N (*on trains, buses*) precio (del billete); (*in taxi: cost*) tarifa; (*: passenger*) pasajero; (*food*) comida; **half/full ~** medio billete m/billete m completo

Far East N: **the ~** el Extremo *or* Lejano Oriente

farewell [fɛəˈwɛl] EXCL, N adiós m

far-fetched [fɑːˈfɛtʃt] ADJ inverosímil

★**farm** [fɑːm] N granja, finca, estancia (*LAM*), chacra (*LAM*) ▶ VT cultivar
▶ **farm out** VT (*work*): **to ~ out (to sb)** mandar hacer fuera (a algn)

★**farmer** [ˈfɑːməʳ] N granjero(-a), estanciero(-a) (*LAM*)

farmhand [ˈfɑːmhænd] N peón m

farmhouse [ˈfɑːmhaus] N granja, casa de hacienda (*LAM*)

farming [ˈfɑːmɪŋ] N (*gen*) agricultura; (*tilling*) cultivo; **sheep ~** cría de ovejas

farm labourer N = **farmhand**

farmland [ˈfɑːmlænd] N tierra de cultivo

farm produce N productos mpl agrícolas

farm worker N = **farmhand**

farmyard [ˈfɑːmjɑːd] N corral m

Faroe Islands [ˈfɛərəu-], **Faroes** [ˈfɛərəuz] NPL: **the ~** las Islas Feroe

far-reaching [fɑːˈriːtʃɪŋ] ADJ (*reform, effect*) de gran alcance

far-sighted [fɑːˈsaɪtɪd] ADJ previsor(a)

fart [fɑːt] (*inf!*) N pedo (*inf!*) ▶ VI tirarse un pedo (*inf!*)

farther [ˈfɑːðəʳ] ADV más lejos, más allá ▶ ADJ más lejano

farthest [ˈfɑːðɪst] SUPERLATIVE of **far**

FAS ABBR (BRIT: = free alongside ship) franco al costado del buque

fascinate [ˈfæsɪneɪt] VT fascinar

fascinated [ˈfæsɪneɪtəd] ADJ fascinado

fascinating [ˈfæsɪneɪtɪŋ] ADJ fascinante

fascination [fæsɪˈneɪʃən] N fascinación f

fascinator [ˈfæsɪneɪtəʳ] N (hat) tocado (de plumas, flores o cintas)

fascism [ˈfæʃɪzəm] N fascismo

fascist [ˈfæʃɪst] ADJ, N fascista mf

★**fashion** [ˈfæʃən] N moda; (fashion industry) industria de la moda; (manner) manera; in ~ a la moda; **out of ~** pasado de moda; **in the Greek ~** a la griega, al estilo griego; **after a ~** (finish, manage etc) en cierto modo ▶ VT formar

fashionable [ˈfæʃnəbl] ADJ de moda; (writer) de moda, popular; **it is ~ to do ...** está de moda hacer ...

fashion designer N diseñador(a) m/f de modas, modisto(-a)

fashionista [fæʃəˈnɪstə] N fashionista mf

fashion show N desfile m de modelos

★**fast** [fɑːst] ADJ (also Phot: film) rápido; (dye, colour) sólido; (clock): **to be ~** estar adelantado; **my watch is five minutes ~** mi reloj está adelantado cinco minutos; **in the ~ lane** (Aut) en el carril de adelantamiento; **to make a boat ~** amarrar una barca ▶ ADV rápidamente, de prisa; (stuck, held) firmemente; **as ~ as I etc can** lo más rápido posible; **~ asleep** profundamente dormido ▶ N ayuno ▶ VI ayunar

fasten [ˈfɑːsn] VT asegurar, sujetar; (coat, belt) abrochar ▶ VI cerrarse
▶ **fasten (up)on** VT FUS (idea) aferrarse a

fastener [ˈfɑːsnəʳ] N cierre m; (of door etc) cerrojo; (BRIT: also: **zip fastener**) cremallera

fastening [ˈfɑːsnɪŋ] N = **fastener**

fast food N comida rápida, platos mpl preparados

fastidious [fæsˈtɪdɪəs] ADJ (fussy) delicado; (demanding) exigente

★**fat** [fæt] ADJ gordo; (meat) con mucha grasa; (greasy) grasiento; (book) grueso; (profit) grande, pingüe ▶ N grasa; (on person) carnes fpl; (lard) manteca; **to live off the ~ of the land** vivir a cuerpo de rey

fatal [ˈfeɪtl] ADJ (mistake) fatal; (injury) mortal; (consequence) funesto

fatalism [ˈfeɪtəlɪzəm] N fatalismo

fatality [fəˈtælɪtɪ] N (road death etc) víctima f mortal

fatally [ˈfeɪtəlɪ] ADV: **~ injured** herido de muerte

fate [feɪt] N destino, sino

fated [ˈfeɪtɪd] ADJ predestinado

fateful [ˈfeɪtful] ADJ fatídico

fat-free [ˈfætfriː] ADJ sin grasa

★**father** [ˈfɑːðəʳ] N padre m

Father Christmas N Papá m Noel

fatherhood [ˈfɑːðəhud] N paternidad f

father-in-law [ˈfɑːðərɪnlɔː] N suegro

fatherland [ˈfɑːðəlænd] N patria

fatherly [ˈfɑːðəlɪ] ADJ paternal

fathom [ˈfæðəm] N braza ▶ VT (unravel) desentrañar; (understand) explicarse

fatigue [fəˈtiːg] N fatiga, cansancio; **metal ~** fatiga del metal

fatness [ˈfætnɪs] N gordura

fatten [ˈfætn] VT, VI engordar; **chocolate is fattening** el chocolate engorda

fatty [ˈfætɪ] ADJ (food) graso ▶ N (pej) gordito(-a), gordinflón(-ona) m/f

fatuous [ˈfætjuəs] ADJ fatuo, necio

faucet [ˈfɔːsɪt] N (US) grifo, llave f, canilla (LAM)

★**fault** [fɔːlt] N (blame) culpa; (defect: in character) defecto; (: in manufacture) desperfecto; (Geo) falla; **it's my ~** es culpa mía; **to find ~ with** criticar, poner peros a; **at ~** culpable ▶ VT criticar

faultless [ˈfɔːltlɪs] ADJ (action) intachable; (person) sin defectos

faulty [ˈfɔːltɪ] ADJ defectuoso

fauna [ˈfɔːnə] N fauna

faux pas [ˈfəuˈpɑː] N desacierto

favour, (US) **favor** [ˈfeɪvəʳ] N favor m; (approval) aprobación f; **to ask a ~ of** pedir un favor a; **to do sb a ~** hacer un favor a algn; **to find ~ with sb** (person) caer en gracia a algn; (suggestion) tener buena acogida por parte de algn; **in ~ of** a favor de; **to be in ~ of sth/of doing sth** ser partidario or estar a favor de algo/de hacer algo ▶ VT (proposition) estar a favor de, aprobar; (person etc) preferir; (assist) favorecer

favourable, (US) **favorable** [ˈfeɪvərəbl] ADJ favorable

favourably, (US) **favorably** [ˈfeɪvərəblɪ] ADV favorablemente

favourite, (US) **favorite** [ˈfeɪvərɪt] ADJ, N favorito(-a) m/f, preferido(-a) m/f

favouritism, (US) **favoritism** [ˈfeɪvərɪtɪzəm] N favoritismo

fawn [fɔːn] N cervato ▶ ADJ (also: **fawn-coloured**) de color cervato, leonado ▶ VI: **to ~ (up)on** adular

fax [fæks] N fax m ▶ VT mandar or enviar por fax

FBI N ABBR (US: = Federal Bureau of Investigation) FBI m

FCC N ABBR (US) = **Federal Communications Commission**

FCO N ABBR (BRIT: = Foreign and Commonwealth Office) ≈ Min. de AA. EE.

FD N ABBR (US) = **fire department**

FDA N ABBR (US: = Food and Drug Administration) oficina que se ocupa del control de los productos alimenticios y farmacéuticos

FE N ABBR = **further education**

★**fear** [fɪəʳ] N miedo, temor m; **for ~ of** por temor

a; **~ of heights** vértigo ▶ VT temer; **to ~ for/ that** temer por/que

fearful ['fɪəful] ADJ temeroso; *(awful)* espantoso; **to be ~ of** *(frightened)* tener miedo de

fearfully ['fɪəfulɪ] ADV *(timidly)* con miedo; *(old: very)* terriblemente

fearless ['fɪəlɪs] ADJ *(gen)* sin miedo *or* temor; *(bold)* audaz

fearlessly ['fɪəlɪslɪ] ADV temerariamente

fearlessness ['fɪəlɪsnɪs] N temeridad *f*

fearsome ['fɪəsəm] ADJ *(opponent)* temible; *(sight)* espantoso

feasibility [fi:zə'bɪlɪtɪ] N factibilidad *f*, viabilidad *f*

feasibility study N estudio de viabilidad

feasible ['fi:zəbl] ADJ factible, viable

feast [fi:st] N banquete *m*; *(Rel: also:* **feast day***)* fiesta ▶ VI festejar

feat [fi:t] N hazaña

feather ['fɛðə^r] N pluma ▶ VT: **to ~ one's nest** *(fig)* hacer su agosto, sacar tajada ▶ CPD *(mattress, bed, pillow)* de plumas

feather-weight ['fɛðəweɪt] N *(Boxing)* peso pluma

★**feature** ['fi:tʃə^r] N *(gen)* característica; *(Anat)* rasgo; *(article)* reportaje *m*; **a (special) ~ on sth/ sb** un reportaje (especial) sobre algo/algn ▶ VT *(film)* presentar ▶ VI figurar; **it featured prominently in ...** tuvo un papel destacado en ... ■ **features** NPL *(of face)* facciones *fpl*

feature film N largometraje *m*

Feb. ABBR *(= February)* feb.

★**February** ['fɛbruərɪ] N febrero; *see also* **July**

feces ['fi:si:z] NPL *(US)* = **faeces**

feckless ['fɛklɪs] ADJ irresponsable, irreflexivo

Fed [fɛd] ABBR *(US)* = **federal; federation**

fed [fɛd] PT, PP of **feed**

Fed. [fɛd] N ABBR *(US inf)* = **Federal Reserve Board**

federal ['fɛdərəl] ADJ federal

Federal Republic of Germany N República Federal de Alemania

federation [fɛdə'reɪʃən] N federación *f*

fed up [fɛd'ʌp] ADJ: **to be ~ (with)** estar harto (de)

fee [fi:] N *(professional)* honorarios *mpl*; *(for examination)* derechos *mpl*; *(of school)* matrícula; *(also:* **membership fee***)* cuota; *(also:* **entrance fee***)* entrada; **for a small ~** por poco dinero

feeble ['fi:bl] ADJ débil

feeble-minded [fi:bl'maɪndɪd] ADJ imbécil

★**feed** [fi:d] N *(gen)* comida; *(of animal)* pienso; *(on printer)* dispositivo de alimentación ▶ VT *(pt, pp* **fed** [fɛd]*)* *(gen)* alimentar; *(Brit: breastfeed)* dar el pecho a; *(animal, baby)* dar de comer a ▶ VI *(baby, animal)* comer

▶ **feed back** VT *(results)* pasar

▶ **feed in** VT *(Comput)* introducir

▶ **feed into** VT *(data, information)* suministrar a;

to ~ sth into a machine introducir algo en una máquina

▶ **feed on** VT FUS alimentarse de

feedback ['fi:dbæk] N *(from person)* reacción *f*; *(Tech)* realimentación *f*, feedback *m*

feeder ['fi:də^r] N *(bib)* babero

feeding bottle ['fi:dɪŋ-] N *(Brit)* biberón *m*

★**feel** [fi:l] N *(sensation)* sensación *f*; *(sense of touch)* tacto; **to get the ~ of sth** *(fig)* acostumbrarse a algo ▶ VI sentirse; **to ~ lonely/ better** sentirse solo/mejor; **I don't ~ well** no me siento bien; **to ~ hungry/cold** tener hambre/frío; **it feels soft** es suave al tacto; **it feels colder out here** se siente más frío aquí fuera; **to ~ like** *(want)* tener ganas de ▶ VT tocar; *(cold, pain etc)* sentir; *(think, believe)* creer; **I'm still feeling my way** *(fig)* todavía me estoy orientando; **I ~ that you ought to do it** creo que debes hacerlo

▶ **feel about, feel around** VI tantear

feeler ['fi:lə^r] N *(of insect)* antena; **to put out feelers** *(fig)* tantear el terreno

★**feeling** ['fi:lɪŋ] N *(physical)* sensación *f*; *(foreboding)* presentimiento; *(impression)* impresión *f*; *(emotion)* sentimiento; **what are your feelings about the matter?** ¿qué opinas tú del asunto?; **to hurt sb's feelings** herir los sentimientos de algn; **feelings ran high about it** causó mucha controversia; **I got the ~ that ...** me dio la impresión de que ...; **there was a general ~ that ...** la opinión general fue que ...

fee-paying school ['fi:peɪɪŋ-] N colegio de pago

feet [fi:t] NPL of **foot**

feign [feɪn] VT fingir

feigned [feɪnd] ADJ fingido

feline ['fi:laɪn] ADJ felino

fell [fɛl] PT of **fall** ▶ VT *(tree)* talar ▶ ADJ: **with one ~ blow** con un golpe feroz; **at one ~ swoop** de un solo golpe ▶ N *(Brit: mountain)* montaña; *(moorland)*: **the fells** los páramos

fellow ['fɛləu] N tipo, tío *(Sp)*; *(of learned society)* socio(-a); *(Univ)* miembro de la junta de gobierno de un colegio ▶ CPD: **~ students** compañeros(-as) *mpl/fpl* de curso

fellow citizen N conciudadano(-a)

fellow countryman N *(irreg)* compatriota *m*

fellow feeling N compañerismo

fellow men NPL semejantes *mpl*

fellowship ['fɛləuʃɪp] N compañerismo; *(grant)* beca

fellow traveller N compañero(-a) de viaje; *(Pol: with communists)* simpatizante *mf*

fellow worker N colega *mf*

felon ['fɛlən] N criminal *mf*

felony ['fɛlənɪ] N crimen *m*, delito mayor

felt [fɛlt] PT, PP of **feel** ▶ N fieltro

felt-tip pen ['fɛlttɪp-] N rotulador *m*

★**female** ['fi:meɪl] N *(pej: woman)* mujer *f*; *(Zool)* hembra ▶ ADJ femenino

feminine [ˈfɛmɪnɪn] ADJ femenino

femininity [fɛmɪˈnɪnɪtɪ] N feminidad f

feminism [ˈfɛmɪnɪzəm] N feminismo

feminist [ˈfɛmɪnɪst] N feminista mf

★**fence** [fɛns] N valla, cerca; (Racing) valla; **to sit on the ~** (fig) nadar entre dos aguas ▶ VT (also: **fence in**) cercar ▶ VI hacer esgrima
  ▶ **fence in** VT cercar
  ▶ **fence off** VT separar con cerca

fencing [ˈfɛnsɪŋ] N esgrima

fend [fɛnd] VI: **to ~ for o.s.** valerse por sí mismo
  ▶ **fend off** VT (attack, attacker) rechazar, repeler; (blow) desviar; (awkward question) esquivar

fender [ˈfɛndər] N pantalla; (US Aut) parachoques m inv; (Rail) trompa

fennel [ˈfɛnl] N hinojo

Fens [fɛnz] NPL (BRIT): **the ~** las tierras bajas de Norfolk (antiguamente zona de marismas)

ferment VI [fəˈmɛnt] fermentar ▶ N [ˈfəːmɛnt] (fig) agitación f

fermentation [fəːmɛnˈteɪʃən] N fermentación f

fern [fəːn] N helecho

ferocious [fəˈrəʊʃəs] ADJ feroz

ferociously [fəˈrəʊʃəslɪ] ADV ferozmente, con ferocidad

ferocity [fəˈrɒsɪtɪ] N ferocidad f

ferret [ˈfɛrɪt] N hurón m
  ▶ **ferret about, ferret around** VI rebuscar
  ▶ **ferret out** VT (secret, truth) desentrañar

ferry [ˈfɛrɪ] N (small) barca de pasaje, balsa; (large: also: **ferryboat**) transbordador m, ferry m
  ▶ VT transportar; **to ~ sth/sb across** or **over** transportar algo/a algn a la otra orilla; **to ~ sb to and fro** llevar a algn de un lado para otro

ferryman [ˈfɛrɪmən] N (irreg) barquero

fertile [ˈfəːtaɪl] ADJ fértil; (Biol) fecundo

fertility [fəˈtɪlɪtɪ] N fertilidad f; fecundidad f

fertility drug N medicamento contra la infertilidad

fertilization [fəːtɪlaɪˈzeɪʃən] N fertilización f; (Biol) fecundación f

fertilize [ˈfəːtɪlaɪz] VT fertilizar; (Biol) fecundar; (Agr) abonar

fertilizer [ˈfəːtɪlaɪzər] N abono, fertilizante m

fervent [ˈfəːvənt] ADJ ferviente

fervour, (US) **fervor** [ˈfəːvər] N fervor m, ardor m

fester [ˈfɛstər] VI supurar

★**festival** [ˈfɛstɪvəl] N (Rel) fiesta; (Art, Mus) festival m

festive [ˈfɛstɪv] ADJ festivo; **the ~ season** (BRIT: Christmas) las Navidades

festivities [fɛsˈtɪvɪtɪz] NPL festejos mpl

festoon [fɛsˈtuːn] VT: **to ~ with** festonear or engalanar con

fetch [fɛtʃ] VT ir a buscar; (BRIT: sell for) venderse por; **how much did it ~?** ¿por cuánto se vendió?
  ▶ **fetch up** VI ir a parar

fetching [ˈfɛtʃɪŋ] ADJ atractivo

fête [feɪt] N fiesta

fetid [ˈfɛtɪd] ADJ fétido

fetish [ˈfɛtɪʃ] N fetiche m

fetter [ˈfɛtər] VT (person) encadenar, poner grillos a; (horse) trabar; (fig) poner trabas a

fetters [ˈfɛtəz] NPL grillos mpl

fettle [ˈfɛtl] N: **in fine ~** en buenas condiciones

fetus [ˈfiːtəs] N (US) = **foetus**

feud [fjuːd] N (hostility) enemistad f; (quarrel) disputa; **a family ~** una pelea familiar

feudal [ˈfjuːdl] ADJ feudal

feudalism [ˈfjuːdəlɪzəm] N feudalismo

fever [ˈfiːvər] N fiebre f; **he has a ~** tiene fiebre

feverish [ˈfiːvərɪʃ] ADJ febril

feverishly [ˈfiːvərɪʃlɪ] ADV febrilmente

★**few** [fjuː] ADJ (not many) pocos; (some) algunos, unos; **~ people** poca gente; **in** or **over the next ~ days** en los próximos días; **every ~ weeks** cada dos o tres semanas; **a ~ more days** unos días más ▶ PRON algunos; **a ~** unos pocos; **a good ~, quite a ~** bastantes

fewer [ˈfjuːər] ADJ menos

fewest [ˈfjuːɪst] ADJ los/las menos

FFA N ABBR = **Future Farmers of America**

FH ABBR (BRIT) = **fire hydrant**

FHA N ABBR (US: = Federal Housing Administration) oficina federal de la vivienda

fiancé [fɪˈɑːŋseɪ] N novio, prometido

fiancée [fɪˈɑːŋseɪ] N novia, prometida

fiasco [fɪˈæskəʊ] N fiasco

fib [fɪb] N mentirijilla ▶ VI decir mentirijillas

fibre, (US) **fiber** [ˈfaɪbər] N fibra

fibreboard, (US) **fiberboard** [ˈfaɪbəbɔːd] N fibra vulcanizada

fibreglass, (US) **fiberglass** [ˈfaɪbəɡlɑːs] N fibra de vidrio

fibrositis [faɪbrəˈsaɪtɪs] N fibrositis f inv

FICA N ABBR (US) = **Federal Insurance Contributions Act**

fickle [ˈfɪkl] ADJ inconstante

fiction [ˈfɪkʃən] N (gen) ficción f

fictional [ˈfɪkʃənl] ADJ novelesco

fictionalize [ˈfɪkʃənəlaɪz] VT novelar

fictitious [fɪkˈtɪʃəs] ADJ ficticio

fiddle [ˈfɪdl] N (Mus) violín m; (cheating) trampa; **tax ~** evasión f fiscal; **to work a ~** hacer trampa ▶ VT (BRIT: accounts) falsificar
  ▶ **fiddle with** VT FUS juguetear con

fiddler [ˈfɪdlər] N violinista mf

fiddly [ˈfɪdlɪ] ADJ (task) delicado, mañoso; (object) enrevesado

fidelity [fɪˈdɛlɪtɪ] N fidelidad f

fidget [ˈfɪdʒɪt] VI moverse (nerviosamente)

fidgety [ˈfɪdʒɪtɪ] ADJ nervioso

fiduciary [fɪˈduːʃɪərɪ] N fiduciario(-a)

f

★**field** [fiːld] N (gen) campo; (Comput) campo; (fig) campo, esfera; (Sport) campo, cancha (LAm); (competitors) competidores mpl; **to lead the ~** (Sport, Comm) llevar la delantera; **to give sth a year's trial in the ~** (fig) sacar algo al mercado a prueba por un año; **my particular ~** mi especialidad ▶ CPD: **to have a ~ day** (fig) ponerse las botas

field glasses NPL gemelos mpl

field hospital N hospital m de campaña

field marshal N mariscal m

fieldwork [ˈfiːldwəːk] N (Archeol, Geo) trabajo de campo

fiend [fiːnd] N demonio

fiendish [ˈfiːndɪʃ] ADJ diabólico

★**fierce** [fɪəs] ADJ feroz; (wind, attack) violento; (heat) intenso; (fighting, enemy) encarnizado

fiercely [ˈfɪəslɪ] ADV con ferocidad; violentamente; intensamente; encarnizadamente

fierceness [ˈfɪəsnɪs] N ferocidad f; violencia; intensidad f; encarnizamiento

fiery [ˈfaɪərɪ] ADJ (burning) ardiente; (temperament) apasionado

FIFA [ˈfiːfə] N ABBR (= Fédération Internationale de Football Association) FIFA f

★**fifteen** [fɪfˈtiːn] NUM quince

★**fifteenth** [fɪfˈtiːnθ] ADJ decimoquinto; **the ~ floor** la planta quince; **the ~ of August** el quince de agosto

★**fifth** [fɪfθ] ADJ quinto

fiftieth [ˈfɪftɪɪθ] ADJ quincuagésimo

★**fifty** [ˈfɪftɪ] NUM cincuenta; **the fifties** los años cincuenta; **to be in one's fifties** andar por los cincuenta

fifty-fifty [ˈfɪftɪˈfɪftɪ] ADJ (deal, split) a medias; **we have a ~ chance of success** tenemos un cincuenta por ciento de posibilidades de tener éxito ▶ ADV: **to go ~ with sb** ir a medias con algn

fig [fɪg] N higo

★**fight** [faɪt] (pt, pp fought [fɔːt]) N (gen) pelea; (Mil) combate m; (struggle) lucha ▶ VT luchar contra; (cancer, alcoholism) combatir; (Law): **to ~ a case** defenderse ▶ VI pelear, luchar; (quarrel): **to ~ (with sb)** pelear (con algn); (fig): **to ~ (for/against)** luchar (por/contra)
▶ **fight back** VI defenderse; (after illness) recuperarse ▶ VT (tears) contener
▶ **fight down** VT (anger, anxiety, urge) reprimir
▶ **fight off** VT (attack, attacker) rechazar; (disease, sleep, urge) luchar contra
▶ **fight out** VT: **to ~ it out** decidirlo en una pelea

fighter [ˈfaɪtə] N combatiente mf; (fig) luchador(a) m/f; (plane) caza m

fighter-bomber [ˈfaɪtəbɔmə] N cazabombardero

fighter pilot N piloto de caza

fighting [ˈfaɪtɪŋ] N (gen) luchas fpl; (battle) combate m, pelea; (in streets) disturbios mpl

figment [ˈfɪgmənt] N: **a ~ of the imagination** un producto de la imaginación

figurative [ˈfɪgjurətɪv] ADJ (meaning) figurado; (Art) figurativo

★**figure** [ˈfɪgə] N (Drawing, Geom) figura, dibujo; (number, cipher) cifra; (person, outline) figura; (body shape) línea; (: attractive) tipo; **~ of speech** (Ling) figura retórica; **public ~** personaje m ▶ VT (esp US: think, calculate) calcular, imaginarse ▶ VI (appear) figurar; (esp US: make sense) ser lógico
▶ **figure on** VT FUS (US) contar con
▶ **figure out** VT (work out) resolver; (understand) comprender

figurehead [ˈfɪgəhed] N (fig) figura decorativa

figure skating N patinaje m artístico

Fiji [ˈfiːdʒiː], **Fiji Islands** NPL (Islas fpl) Fiji

filament [ˈfɪləmənt] N (Elec) filamento

filch [fɪltʃ] VT (inf: steal) birlar

★**file** [faɪl] N (tool) lima; (for nails) lima de uñas; (dossier) expediente m; (folder) carpeta; (in cabinet) archivo; (Comput) fichero; (row) fila; **to open/close a ~** (Comput) abrir/cerrar un fichero ▶ VT limar; (papers) clasificar; (Law: claim) presentar; (store) archivar; **to ~ a suit against sb** entablar pleito contra algn ▶ VI: **to ~ in/out** entrar/salir en fila; **to ~ past** desfilar ante

file name N (Comput) nombre m de fichero

file sharing [-ʃɛərɪŋ] N (Comput) uso m compartido de archivos

filibuster [ˈfɪlɪbʌstə] (esp US Pol) N obstruccionista mf, filibustero(-a) ▶ VI usar maniobras obstruccionistas

filing [ˈfaɪlɪŋ] N: **to do the ~** llevar los archivos

filing cabinet N archivo

filing clerk N oficinista mf

Filipino [fɪlɪˈpiːnəu] ADJ filipino ▶ N (person) filipino(-a); (Ling) tagalo

★**fill** [fɪl] VT llenar; (tooth) empastar; (vacancy) cubrir; **we've already filled that vacancy** ya hemos cubierto esa vacante; **filled with admiration (for)** lleno de admiración (por) ▶ N: **to eat one's ~** comer hasta hartarse
▶ **fill in** VT rellenar; (details, report) completar; **to ~ sb in on sth** (inf) poner a algn al corriente or al día sobre algo
▶ **fill out** VT (form, receipt) rellenar
▶ **fill up** VT llenar (hasta el borde) ▶ VI (Aut) echar gasolina

fillet [ˈfɪlɪt] N filete m

fillet steak N filete m de ternera

filling [ˈfɪlɪŋ] N (Culin) relleno; (for tooth) empaste m

filling station N estación f de servicio

fillip [ˈfɪlɪp] N estímulo

filly [ˈfɪlɪ] N potra

★**film** [fɪlm] N película ▶ VT (scene) filmar ▶ VI rodar

film script N guión m

film star N estrella de cine

filmstrip [ˈfɪlmstrɪp] N tira de diapositivas

film studio N estudio de cine

Filofax® [ˈfaɪləufæks] N agenda (profesional)
filter [ˈfɪltəʳ] N filtro ▸ vт filtrar
  ▸ **filter in, filter through** vi filtrarse
filter coffee N café m (molido) para filtrar
filter lane N (BRIT) carril m de selección
filter-tipped [ˈfɪltətɪpt] ADJ con filtro
filth [fɪlθ] N suciedad f
filthy [ˈfɪlθɪ] ADJ sucio; (language) obsceno
fin [fɪn] N (gen) aleta
★**final** [ˈfaɪnl] ADJ (last) final, último; (definitive)
  definitivo ▸ N (Sport) final f ■ **finals** NPL (Scol)
  exámenes mpl finales
final demand N (on invoice etc) último aviso
final dividend N dividendo final
finale [fɪˈnɑːlɪ] N final m
finalist [ˈfaɪnəlɪst] N (Sport) finalista mf
finality [faɪˈnælɪtɪ] N finalidad f; **with an air of**
  ~ en tono resuelto, de modo terminante
finalize [ˈfaɪnəlaɪz] vт ultimar
★**finally** [ˈfaɪnəlɪ] ADV (lastly) por último, finalmente; (eventually) por fin; (irrevocably) de modo
  definitivo; (once and for all) definitivamente
finance [faɪˈnæns] N (money, funds) fondos mpl
  ▸ vт financiar ■ **finances** NPL finanzas fpl
financial [faɪˈnænʃəl] ADJ financiero
financially [faɪˈnænʃəlɪ] ADV económicamente
financial management N gestión f financiera
financial statement N estado financiero
financial year N ejercicio (financiero)
financier [faɪˈnænsɪəʳ] N financiero(-a)
★**find** [faɪnd] vт (pt, pp found [faund]) (gen) encontrar, hallar; (come upon) descubrir; **to ~ sb guilty**
  (Law) declarar culpable a algn; **I ~ it easy** me
  resulta fácil ▸ N hallazgo; descubrimiento
  ▸ **find out** vт averiguar; (truth, secret) descubrir
  ▸ vi: **to ~ out about** enterarse de
findings [ˈfaɪndɪŋz] NPL (Law) veredicto sg, fallo
  sg; (of report) recomendaciones fpl
★**fine** [faɪn] ADJ (delicate) fino; (beautiful) hermoso;
  the weather is ~ hace buen tiempo; **he's ~** está
  muy bien ▸ ADV (well) bien; **you're doing ~** lo
  estás haciendo muy bien; **to cut it ~** (of time,
  money) calcular muy justo ▸ N (Law) multa; **to**
  get a ~ for (doing) sth recibir una multa por
  (hacer) algo ▸ vт (Law) multar
fine arts NPL bellas artes fpl
finely [ˈfaɪnlɪ] ADV (splendidly) con elegancia; (chop)
  en trozos pequeños, fino; (adjust) con precisión
fineness [ˈfaɪnnɪs] N (of cloth) finura
fine print N: **the ~** la letra pequeña or menuda
finery [ˈfaɪnərɪ] N galas fpl
finesse [fɪˈnɛs] N sutileza
fine-tooth comb [ˈfaɪntuːθ-] N: **to go through**
  sth with a ~ revisar algo a fondo
★**finger** [ˈfɪŋɡəʳ] N dedo; **little/index ~** (dedo)
  meñique m/índice m ▸ vт (touch) manosear;
  (Mus) puntear
fingernail [ˈfɪŋɡəneɪl] N uña

fingerprint [ˈfɪŋɡəprɪnt] N huella dactilar
fingertip [ˈfɪŋɡətɪp] N yema del dedo; **to have**
  sth at one's fingertips saberse algo al dedillo
finicky [ˈfɪnɪkɪ] ADJ (fussy) delicado
★**finish** [ˈfɪnɪʃ] N (end) fin m; (Sport) meta; (polish
  etc) acabado ▸ vт acabar, terminar; **to ~ doing**
  sth acabar de hacer algo ▸ vi acabar, terminar;
  to ~ first/second/third (Sport) llegar el pri-
  mero/segundo/tercero; **I've finished with the**
  paper he terminado con el periódico; **she's fin-**
  ished with him ha roto or acabado con él
  ▸ **finish off** vт acabar, terminar; (kill) rematar
  ▸ **finish up** vт acabar, terminar ▸ vi ir a parar,
  terminar
finished [ˈfɪnɪʃt] ADJ (product) acabado; (performance) pulido; (inf: tired) rendido, hecho polvo
finishing [ˈfɪnɪʃɪŋ] ADJ: **~ touches** toque m final
finishing line N línea de llegada or meta
finishing school N colegio para la educación social
  de señoritas
finite [ˈfaɪnaɪt] ADJ finito
★**Finland** [ˈfɪnlənd] N Finlandia
Finn [fɪn] N finlandés(-esa) m/f
★**Finnish** [ˈfɪnɪʃ] ADJ finlandés(-esa) ▸ N (Ling)
  finlandés m
fiord [fjɔːd] N fiordo
fir [fəːʳ] N abeto
★**fire** [ˈfaɪəʳ] N fuego; (accidental, damaging) incendio; (heater) estufa; **electric/gas ~** estufa eléc-
  trica/de gas; **on ~** ardiendo, en llamas; **to be**
  on ~ estar ardiendo; **to catch ~** prenderse
  fuego; **to set ~ to sth, set sth on ~** prender
  fuego a algo; **insured against ~** asegurado
  contra incendios; **to be/come under ~** estar/
  caer bajo el fuego enemigo ▸ vт (gun) disparar;
  (set fire to) incendiar; (excite) exaltar; (interest)
  despertar; (dismiss) despedir ▸ vi encenderse;
  (Aut: engine) encender
fire alarm N alarma de incendios
firearm [ˈfaɪərɑːm] N arma de fuego
fire brigade, (US) **fire department** N (cuerpo
  de) bomberos mpl
fire door N puerta contra incendios
fire drill N (ejercicio de) simulacro de incendio
fire engine N coche m de bomberos
fire escape N escalera de incendios
fire exit N salida de incendios
fire extinguisher N extintor m
fireguard [ˈfaɪəɡɑːd] N pantalla (guardallama)
fire hazard N = **fire risk**
fire hydrant N boca de incendios
fire insurance N seguro contra incendios
fireman [ˈfaɪəmən] N (irreg) bombero
fireplace [ˈfaɪəpleɪs] N chimenea
fireplug [ˈfaɪəplʌɡ] N (US) boca de incendios
fire practice N = **fire drill**
fireproof [ˈfaɪəpruːf] ADJ a prueba de fuego;
  (material) incombustible

fire regulations NPL reglamentos *mpl* contra incendios

fire risk N peligro de incendio

firescreen [ˈfaɪəskriːn] N pantalla refractaria

fireside [ˈfaɪəsaɪd] N: **by the ~** al lado de la chimenea

fire station N parque *m* de bomberos

firetruck N (US) = **fire engine**

firewall [ˈfaɪəwɔːl] N (Internet) firewall *m*

firewood [ˈfaɪəwʊd] N leña

fireworks [ˈfaɪəwəːks] NPL fuegos *mpl* artificiales

firing [ˈfaɪərɪŋ] N (Mil) disparos *mpl*, tiroteo

firing line N línea de fuego; **to be in the ~** (fig: liable to be criticised) estar en la línea de fuego

firing squad N pelotón *m* de ejecución

★**firm** [fəːm] ADJ firme; (offer, decision) en firme; **to be a ~ believer in sth** ser un partidario convencido de algo; **to take a ~ stand** or **stand ~ stand on sth** (fig) mantenerse firme ante algo ▶ N empresa

firmly [ˈfəːmlɪ] ADV firmemente

firmness [ˈfəːmnɪs] N firmeza

★**first** [fəːst] ADJ primero; **in the ~ instance** en primer lugar; **I'll do it ~ thing tomorrow** lo haré mañana a primera hora; **for the ~ time** por primera vez ▶ ADV (before others) primero; (when listing reasons etc) en primer lugar, primeramente; **at ~** al principio; **~ of all** ante todo; **head ~** de cabeza ▶ N (person: in race) primero(-a); (Aut: also: **first gear**) primera; **the ~ of January** el uno or primero de enero; **from the (very) ~** desde el principio

first aid N primeros auxilios *mpl*

first aid kit N botiquín *m*

first aid post, (US) **first aid station** N puesto de auxilio

first-class [ˈfəːstklɑːs] ADJ de primera clase; **~ ticket** (Rail etc) billete *m* or (LAM) boleto de primera clase; **~ mail** correo de primera clase

first-hand [fəːstˈhænd] ADJ de primera mano

first lady N (esp US) primera dama

firstly [ˈfəːstlɪ] ADV en primer lugar

first name N nombre *m* de pila

first night N estreno

first-rate [fəːstˈreɪt] ADJ de primera (clase)

first-time buyer [fəːsttaɪm-] N persona que compra su primera vivienda

fir tree N abeto

fiscal [ˈfɪskəl] ADJ fiscal; **~ year** año fiscal, ejercicio

★**fish** [fɪʃ] N pl inv pez *m*; (food) pescado; **~ and chips** pescado frito con patatas fritas ▶ VT pescar en ▶ VI pescar; **to go fishing** ir de pesca ▶ **fish out** VT (from water, box etc) sacar

There are two different words for *fish* in Spanish. **Pez** is used to refer to the animal and **pescado** is used to talk about the food.

fish-and-chip shop N = **chip shop**

fishbone [ˈfɪʃbəʊn] N espina

fisherman [ˈfɪʃəmən] N (irreg) pescador *m*

fishery [ˈfɪʃərɪ] N pesquería

fish factory N fábrica de elaboración de pescado

fish farm N piscifactoría

fish fingers NPL (BRIT) palitos *mpl* de pescado (empanado)

fishing boat [ˈfɪʃɪŋ-] N barca de pesca

fishing industry [ˈfɪʃɪŋ-] N industria pesquera

fishing line [ˈfɪʃɪŋ-] N sedal *m*

fishing net [ˈfɪʃɪŋ-] N red *f* de pesca

fishing rod [ˈfɪʃɪŋ-] N caña (de pescar)

fishing tackle [ˈfɪʃɪŋ-] N aparejo (de pescar)

fish market N mercado de pescado

fishmonger [ˈfɪʃmʌŋgəʳ] N (BRIT) pescadero(-a)

fishmonger's, fishmonger's shop N (BRIT) pescadería

fishseller [ˈfɪʃsɛləʳ] N (US) = **fishmonger**

fish slice N paleta para pescado

fish sticks NPL (US) = **fish fingers**

fishstore [ˈfɪʃstɔːʳ] N (US) = **fishmonger's**

fishy [ˈfɪʃɪ] ADJ (fig) sospechoso

fission [ˈfɪʃən] N fisión *f*; **atomic/nuclear ~** fisión *f* atómica/nuclear

fissure [ˈfɪʃəʳ] N fisura

fist [fɪst] N puño

fistfight [ˈfɪstfaɪt] N lucha a puñetazos

★**fit** [fɪt] ADJ (Med, Sport) en (buena) forma; (proper) adecuado, apropiado; **~ for** apropiado para; **~ to** apto para; **to keep ~** mantenerse en forma; **to be ~ for work** (after illness) estar en condiciones para trabajar; **do as you think** or **see ~** haz lo que te parezca mejor ▶ VT (clothes) quedar bien a; (try on: clothes) probar; (install) poner; (equip) proveer; (match: facts) cuadrar or corresponder or coincidir con; (: description) estar de acuerdo con; (accommodate) ajustar, adaptar ▶ VI (clothes) quedar bien; (in space, gap) caber; (facts) coincidir ▶ N (Med) ataque *m*; (outburst) arranque *m*; **~ of coughing** acceso de tos; **a ~ of anger/enthusiasm** un arranque de cólera/entusiasmo; **to have** or **suffer a ~** tener un ataque or acceso; **this dress is a good ~** este vestido me queda bien; **by fits and starts** a rachas ▶ **fit in** VI encajar; **to ~ in with sb's plans** acomodarse a los planes de algn ▶ VT (object) acomodar; (fig: appointment, visitor) encontrar un hueco para

▶ **fit out**, (BRIT) **fit up** VT equipar

fitful [ˈfɪtful] ADJ espasmódico, intermitente

fitfully [ˈfɪtfəlɪ] ADV irregularmente; **to sleep ~** dormir a rachas

fitment [ˈfɪtmənt] N mueble *m*

fitness [ˈfɪtnɪs] N (Med) forma física; (of remark) conveniencia

fitness instructor N instructor(a) *m/f* de fitness

fitted ['fɪtɪd] ADJ (*jacket, shirt*) entallado; (*sheet*) de cuatro picos

fitted carpet N moqueta

fitted cupboards NPL armarios *mpl* empotrados

fitted kitchen N cocina amueblada

fitter ['fɪtə'] N ajustador(a) *m/f*

fitting ['fɪtɪŋ] ADJ apropiado ▶ N (*of dress*) prueba; *see also* **fittings**

fitting room N (*in shop*) probador *m*

fittings ['fɪtɪŋz] NPL instalaciones *fpl*

★**five** [faɪv] NUM cinco; **she is ~ (years old)** tiene cinco años (de edad); **it costs ~ pounds** cuesta cinco libras; **it's ~ (o'clock)** son las cinco

five-day week ['faɪvdeɪ] N semana inglesa

fiver ['faɪvə'] N (*inf*: BRIT) billete *m* de cinco libras; (: US) billete *m* de cinco dólares

★**fix** [fɪks] VT (*secure*) fijar, asegurar; (*mend*) arreglar; (*make ready: meal, drink*) preparar; **to ~ sth in one's mind** fijar algo en la memoria ▶ N: **to be in a ~** estar en un aprieto; **the fight was a ~** (*inf*) la pelea estaba amañada
   ▶ **fix on** VT (*decide on*) fijar
   ▶ **fix up** VT (*arrange: date, meeting*) arreglar; **to ~ sb up with sth** conseguir algo a algn

fixation [fɪk'seɪʃən] N (*Psych*) fijación *f*

fixative ['fɪksətɪv] N fijador *m*

★**fixed** [fɪkst] ADJ (*prices etc*) fijo; **how are you ~ for money?** (*inf*) ¿qué tal andas de dinero?

fixed assets NPL activo *sg* fijo

fixed charge N gasto fijo

fixture ['fɪkstʃə'] N (*Sport*) encuentro ▪ **fixtures** NPL (*equipment*) instalaciones *fpl* fijas

fizz [fɪz] VI burbujear

fizzle out ['fɪzl-] VI apagarse; (*enthusiasm, interest*) decaer; (*plan*) quedar en agua de borrajas

fizzy ['fɪzɪ] ADJ (*drink*) gaseoso

fjord [fjɔːd] N = **fiord**

FL, Fla. ABBR (*US*) = **Florida**

flabbergasted ['flæbəgɑːstɪd] ADJ pasmado

flabby ['flæbɪ] ADJ flojo (de carnes); (*skin*) fofo

★**flag** [flæg] N bandera; (*stone*) losa; **~ of convenience** pabellón *m* de conveniencia ▶ VI decaer
   ▶ **flag down** VT: **to ~ sb down** hacer señas a algn para que se pare
   ▶ **flag up** VT recalcar

flagpole ['flægpəul] N asta de bandera

flagrant ['fleɪgrənt] ADJ flagrante

flagship ['flægʃɪp] N buque *m* insignia *or* almirante

flagstone ['flægstəun] N losa

flag stop N (*US*) parada discrecional

flair [fleə'] N aptitud *f* especial

flak [flæk] N (*Mil*) fuego antiaéreo; (*inf: criticism*) lluvia de críticas

flake [fleɪk] N (*of rust, paint*) desconchón *m*; (*of snow*) copo; (*of soap powder*) escama ▶ VI (*also:* **flake off**: *paint*) desconcharse; (*skin*) descamarse

flaky ['fleɪkɪ] ADJ (*paintwork*) desconchado; (*skin*) escamoso

flaky pastry N (*Culin*) hojaldre *m*

flamboyant [flæm'bɔɪənt] ADJ (*dress*) vistoso; (*person*) extravagante

flame [fleɪm] N llama; **to burst into flames** incendiarse; **old ~** (*inf*) antiguo amor *mf*

flamingo [flə'mɪŋgəu] N flamenco

flammable ['flæməbl] ADJ inflamable

flan [flæn] N (*BRIT*) tarta

flank [flæŋk] N flanco; (*of person*) costado ▶ VT flanquear

flannel ['flænl] N (*BRIT: also:* **face flannel**) toallita; (*fabric*) franela ▪ **flannels** NPL (*trousers*) pantalones *mpl* de franela

flannelette [flænə'let] N franela de algodón

flap [flæp] N (*of pocket, envelope*) solapa; (*of table*) hoja (plegadiza); (*wing movement*) aletazo; (*Aviat*) flap *m* ▶ VT (*wings*) batir ▶ VI (*sail, flag*) ondear; (*inf: also:* **be in a flap**) ponerse nervioso

flapjack ['flæpdʒæk] N (*US: pancake*) torta, panqueque *m* (*LAM*)

flare [fleə'] N llamarada; (*Mil*) bengala; (*in skirt etc*) vuelo ▪ **flares** NPL (*trousers*) pantalones *mpl* de campana
   ▶ **flare up** VI encenderse; (*fig: person*) encolerizarse; (: *revolt*) estallar

★**flash** [flæʃ] N relámpago; (*also:* **news flash**) noticias *fpl* de última hora; (*Phot*) flash *m*; (*US: torch*) linterna; **in a ~** en un instante; **~ of inspiration** ráfaga de inspiración ▶ VT (*light, headlights*) lanzar destellos con; (*torch*) encender; **to ~ sth about** (*fig: inf: flaunt*) ostentar algo, presumir con algo ▶ VI brillar; (*hazard light etc*) lanzar destellos; **he flashed by** *or* **past** pasó como un rayo

flashback ['flæʃbæk] N flashback *m*, escena retrospectiva

flashbulb ['flæʃbʌlb] N bombilla de flash

flash card N (*Scol*) tarjeta

flash drive N (*Comput*) memoria flash, flash drive *m*

flasher ['flæʃə'] N exhibicionista *m*

flashlight ['flæʃlaɪt] N (*US: torch*) linterna

flashpoint ['flæʃpɔɪnt] N punto de inflamación; (*fig*) punto de explosión

flashy ['flæʃɪ] ADJ (*pej*) ostentoso

flask [flɑːsk] N petaca; (*also:* **vacuum flask**) termo

★**flat** [flæt] ADJ llano; (*smooth*) liso; (*tyre*) desinflado; (*battery*) descargado; (*beer*) sin gas; (*Mus: instrument*) desafinado; **~ rate of pay** sueldo fijo ▶ N (*BRIT: apartment*) piso (*SP*), departamento (*LAM*), apartamento; (*Aut*) pinchazo; (*Mus*) bemol *m* ▶ ADV: **(to work) ~ out** (trabajar) a tope

flatfooted [flæt'futɪd] ADJ de pies planos

flatly ['flætlɪ] ADV rotundamente, de plano

flatmate ['flætmeɪt] N compañero(-a) de piso

flatness ['flætnɪs] N (of land) llanura, lo llano

flat pack N: **it comes in a ~** viene en un paquete plano para su automontaje

flat-pack ['flætpæk] ADJ: **~ furniture** muebles mpl automontables (embalados en paquetes planos)

flatscreen ['flætskriːn] ADJ pantalla plana

flatten ['flætn] VT (also: **flatten out**) allanar; (: smooth out) alisar; (house, city) arrasar

flatter ['flætər] VT adular, halagar; (show to advantage) favorecer

flatterer ['flætərər] N adulador(a) m/f

flattering ['flætərɪŋ] ADJ halagador(a); (clothes etc) que favorece, favorecedor(a)

flattery ['flætərɪ] N adulación f

flatulence ['flætjuləns] N flatulencia

flaunt [flɔːnt] VT ostentar, lucir

flavour, (US) **flavor** ['fleɪvər] N sabor m, gusto ▸ VT sazonar, condimentar; **strawberry flavoured** con sabor a fresa

flavouring, (US) **flavoring** ['fleɪvərɪŋ] N (in product) aromatizante m

flaw [flɔː] N defecto

flawless ['flɔːlɪs] ADJ impecable

flax [flæks] N lino

flaxen ['flæksən] ADJ muy rubio

flea [fliː] N pulga

flea market N rastro, mercadillo

fleck [flɛk] N mota ▸ VT (with blood, mud etc) salpicar; **brown flecked with white** marrón con motas blancas

fledgeling, fledgling ['flɛdʒlɪŋ] N (fig) novato(-a), principiante mf

flee [fliː] (pt, pp **fled** [flɛd]) VT huir de, abandonar ▸ VI huir

fleece [fliːs] N (of sheep) vellón m; (wool) lana; (top) forro polar ▸ VT (inf) desplumar

fleecy ['fliːsɪ] ADJ (blanket) lanoso, lanudo; (cloud) aborregado

fleet [fliːt] N flota; (of cars, lorries etc) parque m

fleeting ['fliːtɪŋ] ADJ fugaz

Flemish ['flɛmɪʃ] ADJ flamenco ▸ N (Ling) flamenco; **the ~** los flamencos

flesh [flɛʃ] N carne f; (skin) piel f; (of fruit) pulpa; **of ~ and blood** de carne y hueso

flesh wound N herida superficial

flew [fluː] PT of **fly**

flex [flɛks] N cable m ▸ VT (muscles) tensar

flexibility [flɛksɪ'bɪlɪtɪ] N flexibilidad f

★**flexible** ['flɛksəbl] ADJ flexible; **~ working hours** horario sg flexible

flexitarian [flɛksɪ'tɛərɪən] ADJ, N semivegetariano(-a) m/f, vegetariano(-a) m/f flexible

flexitime ['flɛksɪtaɪm] N horario flexible

flick [flɪk] N golpecito; (with finger) capirotazo; (BRIT inf: film) película ▸ VT dar un golpecito a ▸ **flick off** VT quitar con el dedo ▸ **flick through** VT FUS hojear

flicker ['flɪkər] VI (light) parpadear; (flame) vacilar ▸ N parpadeo

flick knife N navaja de muelle

flier ['flaɪər] N aviador(a) m/f

flies [flaɪz] NPL of **fly**

★**flight** [flaɪt] N vuelo; (escape) huida, fuga; (also: **flight of steps**) tramo (de escaleras); **to take ~** huir, darse a la fuga; **to put to ~** ahuyentar; **how long does the ~ take?** ¿cuánto dura el vuelo?

flight attendant N (US) auxiliar mf de vuelo

flight deck N (Aviat) cabina de mandos

flight path N trayectoria de vuelo

flight recorder N registrador m de vuelo

flighty ['flaɪtɪ] ADJ caprichoso

flimsy ['flɪmzɪ] ADJ (thin) muy ligero; (excuse) flojo

flinch [flɪntʃ] VI encogerse; **to ~ from** retroceder ante

fling [flɪŋ] VT (pt, pp **flung** [flʌŋ]) arrojar ▸ N (love affair) aventura amorosa

flint [flɪnt] N pedernal m; (in lighter) piedra

flip [flɪp] VT: **to ~ a coin** echar a cara o cruz ▸ **flip over** VT dar la vuelta a ▸ **flip through** VT FUS (book) hojear; (records) ver de pasada

flip-flops ['flɪpflɒps] NPL (esp BRIT) chancletas fpl

flippancy ['flɪpənsɪ] N ligereza

flippant ['flɪpənt] ADJ poco serio

flipper ['flɪpər] N aleta

flip side N (of record) cara B

flirt [fləːt] VI coquetear, flirtear ▸ N coqueta f

flirtation [fləː'teɪʃən] N coqueteo, flirteo

flit [flɪt] VI revolotear

★**float** [fləʊt] N flotador m; (in procession) carroza; (sum of money) reserva ▸ VI (Comm: currency) flotar; (swimmer) hacer la plancha ▸ VT (gen) hacer flotar; (company) lanzar; **to ~ an idea** plantear una idea

floating ['fləʊtɪŋ] ADJ: **~ vote** voto indeciso; **~ voter** votante mf indeciso(-a)

flock [flɒk] N (of sheep) rebaño; (of birds) bandada; (of people) multitud f ▸ VI: **to ~ to** acudir en tropel a

floe [fləʊ] N: **ice ~** témpano de hielo

flog [flɒg] VT azotar; (inf) vender

★**flood** [flʌd] N inundación f; (of words, tears etc) torrente m; (of letters, imports etc) avalancha ▸ VT (Aut: carburettor) inundar; **to ~ the market** (Comm) inundar el mercado ▸ VI (place) inundarse; (people): **to ~ into** inundar

flooding ['flʌdɪŋ] N inundaciones fpl

floodlight ['flʌdlaɪt] N foco ▸ VT (irreg: like **light**) iluminar con focos

floodlit ['flʌdlɪt] PT, PP of **floodlight** ▸ ADJ iluminado

flood tide N pleamar f

floodwater ['flʌdwɔːtəʳ] N aguas fpl (de la inundación)

★**floor** [flɔːʳ] N suelo, piso (LAM); (storey) piso; (of sea, valley) fondo; (dance floor) pista; **ground ~**, (US) **first ~** planta baja; **first ~**, (US) **second ~** primer piso; **top ~** último piso; **to have the ~** (speaker) tener la palabra ▶ VT (with blow) derribar; (fig: baffle) dejar anonadado

floorboard ['flɔːbɔːd] N tabla

flooring ['flɔːrɪŋ] N suelo; (material) solería

floor lamp N (US) lámpara de pie

floor show N cabaret m

floorwalker ['flɔːwɔːkəʳ] N (US Comm) supervisor(a) m/f

flop [flɔp] N fracaso ▶ VI (fail) fracasar

floppy ['flɔpɪ] ADJ flojo ▶ N (Comput: also: **floppy disk**) floppy m

flora ['flɔːrə] N flora

floral ['flɔːrl] ADJ floral; (pattern) floreado; (dress, wallpaper) de flores

Florence ['flɔrəns] N Florencia

Florentine ['flɔrəntaɪn] ADJ, N florentino(-a) m/f

florid ['flɔrɪd] ADJ (style) florido

florist ['flɔrɪst] N florista mf; **~'s (shop)** n floristería

flotation [fləu'teɪʃən] N (of shares) emisión f; (of company) lanzamiento

flounce [flauns] N volante m
  ▶ **flounce in** VI entrar con gesto exagerado
  ▶ **flounce out** VI salir con gesto airado

flounder ['flaundəʳ] VI tropezar ▶ N (Zool) platija

flour ['flauəʳ] N harina

flourish ['flʌrɪʃ] VI florecer ▶ N ademán m, movimiento (ostentoso)

flourishing ['flʌrɪʃɪŋ] ADJ floreciente

flout [flaut] VT burlarse de; (order) no hacer caso de, hacer caso omiso de

★**flow** [fləu] N (movement) flujo; (of traffic) circulación f; (direction) curso; (Elec) corriente f ▶ VI (river, blood) fluir; (traffic) circular

flow chart N organigrama m

flow diagram N organigrama m

★**flower** ['flauəʳ] N flor f; **in ~** en flor ▶ VI florecer

flower bed N macizo

flowerpot ['flauəpɔt] N tiesto

flowery ['flauərɪ] ADJ florido; (perfume, pattern) de flores

flowing ['fləuɪŋ] ADJ (hair, clothes) suelto; (style) fluido

flown [fləun] PP of **fly**

fl. oz. ABBR = **fluid ounce**

flu [fluː] N gripe f; **to have ~** tener la gripe

fluctuate ['flʌktjueɪt] VI fluctuar

fluctuation [flʌktju'eɪʃən] N fluctuación f

flue [fluː] N cañón m

fluency ['fluːənsɪ] N fluidez f, soltura

fluent ['fluːənt] ADJ (speech) elocuente; **he speaks ~ French**, **he's ~ in French** domina el francés

fluently ['fluːəntlɪ] ADV con soltura

fluff [flʌf] N pelusa

fluffy ['flʌfɪ] ADJ de pelo suave

fluid ['fluːɪd] ADJ (movement) fluido, líquido; (situation) inestable ▶ N fluido, líquido; (in diet) líquido

fluid ounce N onza f líquida

fluke [fluːk] N (inf) chiripa

flummox ['flʌməks] VT desconcertar

flung [flʌŋ] PT, PP of **fling**

flunky ['flʌŋkɪ] N lacayo

fluorescent [fluə'rɛsnt] ADJ fluorescente

fluoride ['fluəraɪd] N fluoruro

fluoride toothpaste N pasta de dientes con flúor

flurry ['flʌrɪ] N (of snow) ventisca; (haste) agitación f; **~ of activity** frenesí m de actividad

flush [flʌʃ] N (on face) rubor m; (fig: of youth, beauty) resplandor m; **hot flushes** (Med) sofocos mpl ▶ VT limpiar con agua; (also: **flush out**: game, birds) levantar; (: fig: criminal) poner al descubierto; **to ~ the toilet** tirar de la cadena (del wáter) ▶ VI ruborizarse ▶ ADJ: **~ with** a ras de

flushed [flʌʃt] ADJ ruborizado

fluster ['flʌstəʳ] N aturdimiento ▶ VT aturdir

flustered ['flʌstəd] ADJ aturdido

flute [fluːt] N flauta travesera

flutter ['flʌtəʳ] N (of wings) revoloteo, aleteo; (inf: bet) apuesta; **to be in a ~** estar nervioso ▶ VI revolotear

flux [flʌks] N flujo; **in a state of ~** cambiando continuamente

★**fly** [flaɪ] (pt **flew** [fluː], pp **flown** [fləun]) N (insect) mosca; (on trousers: also: **flies**) bragueta ▶ VT (plane) pilotar; (cargo) transportar (en avión); (distance) recorrer (en avión) ▶ VI volar; (passenger) ir en avión; (escape) evadirse; (flag) ondear
  ▶ **fly away** VI (bird, insect) irse volando
  ▶ **fly in** VI (person) llegar en avión; (plane) aterrizar; **he flew in from Bilbao** llegó en avión desde Bilbao
  ▶ **fly off** VI irse volando
  ▶ **fly out** VI irse en avión

fly-drive N: **~ holiday** vacaciones que incluyen vuelo y alquiler de coche

fly-fishing ['flaɪfɪʃɪŋ] N pesca con mosca

flying ['flaɪɪŋ] N (activity) (el) volar ▶ ADJ: **~ visit** visita relámpago; **with ~ colours** con lucimiento

flying buttress N arbotante m

flying picket N piquete m volante

flying saucer N platillo volante

flying squad N (Police) brigada móvil

flying start N: **to get off to a ~** empezar con buen pie

557

flyleaf [ˈflaɪliːf] (pl **flyleaves** [-liːvz]) N (hoja de) guarda

flyover [ˈflaɪəʊvəʳ] N (BRIT: *bridge*) paso elevado *or* (LAM) a desnivel

flypast [ˈflaɪpɑːst] N desfile *m* aéreo

flysheet [ˈflaɪʃiːt] N (*for tent*) doble techo

flyswatter [ˈflaɪswɔtəʳ] N matamoscas *m inv*

flyweight [ˈflaɪweɪt] ADJ de peso mosca ▶ N peso mosca

flywheel [ˈflaɪwiːl] N volante *m* (de motor)

FM ABBR (*Radio*: = *frequency modulation*) FM; (BRIT *Mil*) = **field marshal**

FMB N ABBR (*US*) = **Federal Maritime Board**

FMCS N ABBR (*US*: = *Federal Mediation and Conciliation Services*) organismo de conciliación en conflictos laborales

FO N ABBR (BRIT: = *Foreign Office*) ≈ Min. de AA. EE. (= *Ministerio de Asuntos Exteriores*)

foal [fəʊl] N potro

foam [fəʊm] N espuma ▶ VI hacer espuma

foam rubber N goma espuma

FOB ABBR (= *free on board*) f.a.b.

fob [fɔb] N (*also*: **watch fob**) leontina ▶ VT: **to ~ sb off with sth** deshacerse de algn con algo

focal [ˈfəʊkəl] ADJ focal; **~ point** punto focal; (*fig*) centro de atención

★**focus** [ˈfəʊkəs] (pl **focuses**) N foco; (*centre*) centro; **in/out of ~** enfocado/desenfocado ▶ VT (*field glasses etc*) enfocar ▶ VI: **to ~ (on)** enfocar (a); (*issue etc*) centrarse en

fodder [ˈfɔdəʳ] N pienso

FOE N ABBR (= *Friends of the Earth*) Amigos *mpl* de la Tierra; (*US*: = *Fraternal Order of Eagles*) organización benéfica

foe [fəʊ] N enemigo(-a)

foetus, (*US*) **fetus** [ˈfiːtəs] N feto

★**fog** [fɔg] N niebla

fogbound [ˈfɔgbaʊnd] ADJ inmovilizado por la niebla

★**foggy** [ˈfɔgɪ] ADJ: **it's ~** hay niebla

fog lamp, (*US*) **fog light** N (*Aut*) faro antiniebla

foible [ˈfɔɪbl] N manía

foil [fɔɪl] VT frustrar ▶ N hoja; (*also*: **kitchen foil**) papel *m* (de) aluminio; (*Fencing*) florete *m*

foist [fɔɪst] VT: **to ~ sth on sb** endilgarle algo a algn

★**fold** [fəʊld] N (*bend, crease*) pliegue *m*; (*Agr*) redil *m* ▶ VT doblar; **to ~ one's arms** cruzarse de brazos ▶ **fold up** VI plegarse, doblarse; (*business*) quebrar ▶ VT (*map etc*) plegar

folder [ˈfəʊldəʳ] N (*for papers*) carpeta; (*binder*) carpeta de anillas; (*brochure*) folleto; (*Comput*) directorio

folding [ˈfəʊldɪŋ] ADJ (*chair, bed*) plegable

foliage [ˈfəʊlɪɪdʒ] N follaje *m*

folio [ˈfəʊlɪəʊ] N folio

folk [fəʊk] NPL gente *f* ▶ ADJ popular, folklórico ■ **folks** NPL (*family*) familia, parientes *mpl*

folklore [ˈfəʊklɔːʳ] N folklore *m*

folk music N música folk

folk singer N cantante *mf* de música folk

folk song N canción *f* popular *or* folk

★**follow** [ˈfɔləʊ] VT (*also on Twitter*) seguir; **to ~ sb's advice** seguir el consejo de algn; **I don't quite ~ you** no te comprendo muy bien; **he followed suit** hizo lo mismo ▶ VI seguir; (*result*) resultar; **to ~ in sb's footsteps** seguir los pasos de algn; **it doesn't ~ that ...** no se deduce que .... ▶ **follow on** VI seguir; (*continue*): **to ~ on from** ser la consecuencia lógica de ▶ **follow out** VT (*implement: idea, plan*) realizar, llevar a cabo ▶ **follow through** VT llevar hasta el fin ▶ VI (*Sport*) dar el remate ▶ **follow up** VT (*letter, offer*) responder a; (*case*) investigar

follower [ˈfɔləʊəʳ] N seguidor(a) *m/f*; (*Pol*) partidario(-a)

★**following** [ˈfɔləʊɪŋ] ADJ siguiente ▶ N seguidores *mpl*, afición *f*

follow-up [ˈfɔləʊʌp] N continuación *f*

follow-up letter N carta recordatoria

folly [ˈfɔlɪ] N locura

fond [fɔnd] ADJ (*loving*) cariñoso; **to be ~ of sb** tener cariño a algn; **she's ~ of swimming** tiene afición a la natación, le gusta nadar

fondle [ˈfɔndl] VT acariciar

fondly [ˈfɔndlɪ] ADV (*lovingly*) con cariño; **he ~ believed that ...** creía ingenuamente que ...

fondness [ˈfɔndnɪs] N (*for things*) afición *f*; (*for people*) cariño

font [fɔnt] N pila bautismal

★**food** [fuːd] N comida

food chain N cadena alimenticia

food mixer N batidora

food poisoning N intoxicación *f* alimentaria

food processor N robot *m* de cocina

food stamp N (*US*) vale *m* para comida

foodstuffs [ˈfuːdstʌfs] NPL comestibles *mpl*

★**fool** [fuːl] N tonto(-a); (*Culin*) puré *m* de frutas con nata; **to make a ~ of o.s.** ponerse en ridículo ▶ VT engañar; **you can't ~ me** a mí no me engañas; *see also* **April Fools' Day** ▶ **fool about, fool around** VI hacer el tonto

foolhardy [ˈfuːlhɑːdɪ] ADJ temerario

foolish [ˈfuːlɪʃ] ADJ tonto; (*careless*) imprudente

foolishly [ˈfuːlɪʃlɪ] ADV tontamente, neciamente

foolproof [ˈfuːlpruːf] ADJ (*plan etc*) infalible

foolscap [ˈfuːlskæp] N ≈ papel *m* tamaño folio

★**foot** [fut] (pl **feet**) N (*Anat*) pie *m*; (*of page, stairs, mountain*) pie *m*; (*measure*) pie *m* (= 304 *mm*); (*of animal, table*) pata; **on ~** a pie; **to find one's feet** acostumbrarse; **to put one's ~ down** (*say no*) plantarse; (*Aut*) pisar el acelerador ▶ VT (*bill*) pagar

footage [ˈfutɪdʒ] N (*Cine*) imágenes *fpl*

foot-and-mouth [futənd'mauθ], **foot-and-mouth disease** N fiebre f aftosa

★**football** ['futbɔːl] N balón m; (game: BRIT) fútbol m; (: US) fútbol m americano

★**footballer** ['futbɔːləʳ] N (BRIT) = **football player**

football match N partido de fútbol

football player N futbolista mf, jugador(a) m/f de fútbol

footbrake ['futbreɪk] N freno de pie

footbridge ['futbrɪdʒ] N pasarela, puente m para peatones

footfall ['futfɔːl] N (footstep) paso, pisada; (Comm) afluencia

foothills ['futhɪlz] NPL estribaciones fpl

foothold ['futhəuld] N pie m firme

footing ['futɪŋ] N (fig) nivel m; **to lose one's ~** perder pie; **on an equal ~** en pie de igualdad

footlights ['futlaɪts] NPL candilejas fpl

footman ['futmən] N (irreg) lacayo

footnote ['futnəut] N nota (de pie de página)

footpath ['futpɑːθ] N sendero

footprint ['futprɪnt] N huella, pisada

footrest ['futrest] N apoyapiés m inv

footsie ['futsɪ] N: **to play ~ with sb** (inf) juguetear con los pies de algn

footsore ['futsɔːʳ] ADJ con los pies doloridos

footstep ['futstep] N paso

footwear ['futweəʳ] N calzado

FOR ABBR (= free on rail) franco (puesto sobre) vagón

---

for [fɔː]

PREP **1** (indicating destination, intention) para; **the train for London** el tren para Londres; (in announcements) el tren con destino a Londres; **he left for Rome** marchó para Roma; **he went for the paper** fue por el periódico; **is this for me?** ¿es esto para mí?; **it's time for lunch** es la hora de comer

2 (indicating purpose) para; **what('s it) for?** ¿para qué (es)?; **what's this button for?** ¿para qué sirve este botón?; **to pray for peace** rezar por la paz

3 (on behalf of, representing): **the MP for Hove** el diputado por Hove; **he works for the government/a local firm** trabaja para el gobierno/en una empresa local; **I'll ask him for you** se lo pediré por ti; **G for George** G de Gerona

4 (because of) por esta razón; **for fear of being criticized** por temor a ser criticado

5 (with regard to) para; **it's cold for July** hace frío para julio; **he has a gift for languages** tiene don de lenguas

6 (in exchange for) por; **I sold it for £5** lo vendí por £5; **to pay 50 pence for a ticket** pagar 50 peniques por un billete

7 (in favour of): **are you for or against us?** ¿estás con nosotros o contra nosotros?; **I'm all for it** estoy totalmente a favor; **vote for X** vote (a) X

8 (referring to distance): **there are roadworks for 5 km** hay obras en 5 km; **we walked for miles** caminamos kilómetros y kilómetros

9 (referring to time): **he was away for two years** estuvo fuera (durante) dos años; **it hasn't rained for three weeks** no ha llovido durante or en tres semanas; **I have known her for years** la conozco desde hace años; **can you do it for tomorrow?** ¿lo podrás hacer para mañana?

10 (with infinitive clauses): **it is not for me to decide** la decisión no es cosa mía; **it would be best for you to leave** sería mejor que te fueras; **there is still time for you to do it** todavía te queda tiempo para hacerlo; **for this to be possible ...** para que esto sea posible ...

11 (in spite of) a pesar de; **for all his complaints** a pesar de sus quejas

▶ CONJ (since, as: formal) puesto que

---

for can be translated by **para** or **por**. Use **para** to indicate intention or purpose:
a present for me **un regalo para mí**
What's this for? **¿Para qué es esto?**
Use **por** to indicate reason or cause: *Oxford is famous for its university.* **Oxford es famoso por su universidad**.

---

forage ['fɔrɪdʒ] N forraje m

foray ['fɔreɪ] N incursión f

forbid [fə'bɪd] (pt **forbad(e)** [fə'bæd], pp **forbidden** [fə'bɪdn]) VT prohibir; **to ~ sb to do sth** prohibir a algn hacer algo

forbidden [fə'bɪdn] PT of **forbid** ▶ ADJ (food, area) prohibido; (word, subject) tabú

forbidding [fə'bɪdɪŋ] ADJ (landscape) inhóspito; (severe) severo

★**force** [fɔːs] N fuerza; **the Forces** npl (BRIT) las Fuerzas Armadas; **sales ~** (Comm) personal m de ventas; **a ~ 5 wind** un viento fuerza 5; **to join forces** unir fuerzas; **in ~** (law etc) en vigor ▶ VT obligar, forzar; **to ~ o.s. to do** hacer un esfuerzo por hacer; **to ~ sb to do sth** obligar a algn a hacer algo

▶ **force back** VT (crowd, enemy) hacer retroceder; (tears) reprimir

▶ **force down** VT (food) tragar con esfuerzo

forced [fɔːst] ADJ (smile) forzado; (landing) forzoso

force-feed ['fɔːsfiːd] VT (animal, prisoner) alimentar a la fuerza

forceful ['fɔːsful] ADJ enérgico

forcemeat ['fɔːsmiːt] N (Culin) relleno

forceps ['fɔːseps] NPL fórceps m inv

forcible ['fɔːsəbl] ADJ (violent) a la fuerza; (telling) convincente

forcibly ['fɔːsəblɪ] ADV a la fuerza

ford [fɔːd] N vado ▶ VT vadear

fore [fɔːʳ] N: **to bring to the ~** sacar a la luz pública; **to come to the ~** empezar a destacar

forearm ['fɔ:rɑ:m] N antebrazo
forebear ['fɔ:bɛəʳ] N antepasado(-a)
foreboding [fɔ:'bəudɪŋ] N presentimiento
★forecast ['fɔ:kɑ:st] N pronóstico; **weather ~** previsión f meteorológica ▸ VT (irreg: like **cast**) pronosticar
foreclose [fɔ:'kləuz] VT (Law: also: **foreclose on**) extinguir el derecho de redimir
foreclosure [fɔ:'kləuʒəʳ] N apertura de un juicio hipotecario
forecourt ['fɔ:kɔ:t] N patio; (of garage) área de entrada
forefathers ['fɔ:fɑ:ðəz] NPL antepasados mpl
forefinger ['fɔ:fɪŋgəʳ] N (dedo) índice m
forefront ['fɔ:frʌnt] N: **in the ~ of** en la vanguardia de
forego [fɔ:'gəu] VT (irreg: like **go**) = **forgo**
foregoing ['fɔ:gəuɪŋ] ADJ anterior, precedente
foregone ['fɔ:gɔn] PP of **forego** ▸ ADJ: **it's a ~ conclusion** es una conclusión inevitable
foreground ['fɔ:graund] N (also Comput) primer plano m
forehand ['fɔ:hænd] N (Tennis) derechazo directo
forehead ['fɔrɪd] N frente f
★foreign ['fɔrɪn] ADJ extranjero; (trade) exterior
foreign currency N divisas fpl
★foreigner ['fɔrɪnəʳ] N extranjero(-a)
foreign exchange N (system) cambio de divisas; (money) divisas fpl, moneda extranjera
foreign investment N inversión f en el extranjero; (money, stock) inversiones fpl extranjeras
Foreign Minister N Ministro(-a) de Asuntos Exteriores, Canciller m (LAm)
Foreign Office N (BRIT) Ministerio de Asuntos Exteriores
Foreign Secretary N (BRIT) Ministro(-a) de Asuntos Exteriores, Canciller m (LAm)
foreleg ['fɔ:lɛg] N pata delantera
foreman ['fɔ:mən] N (irreg) capataz m; (Law: of jury) presidente mf
foremost ['fɔ:məust] ADJ principal ▸ ADV: **first and ~** ante todo, antes que nada
forename ['fɔ:neɪm] N nombre m (de pila)
forensic [fə'rɛnsɪk] ADJ forense; **~ scientist** forense mf
foreplay ['fɔ:pleɪ] N preámbulos mpl (de estimulación sexual)
forerunner ['fɔ:rʌnəʳ] N precursor(a) m/f
foresee [fɔ:'si:] VT (irreg: like **see**) prever
foreseeable [fɔ:'si:əbl] ADJ previsible
foreshadow [fɔ:'ʃædəu] VT prefigurar, anunciar
foreshore ['fɔ:ʃɔːʳ] N playa
foreshorten [fɔ:'ʃɔ:tn] VT (figure, scene) escorzar
foresight ['fɔ:saɪt] N previsión f

foreskin ['fɔ:skɪn] N (Anat) prepucio
★forest ['fɔrɪst] N bosque m
forestall [fɔ:'stɔ:l] VT anticiparse a
forestry ['fɔrɪstrɪ] N silvicultura
foretaste ['fɔ:teɪst] N anticipo
foretell [fɔ:'tɛl] VT (irreg: like **tell**) predecir, pronosticar
forethought ['fɔ:θɔ:t] N previsión f
forever [fə'rɛvəʳ] ADV siempre; (for good) para siempre; (endlessly) constantemente
forewarn [fɔ:'wɔ:n] VT avisar, advertir
forewent [fɔ:'wɛnt] PT of **forego**
foreword ['fɔ:wə:d] N prefacio
forfeit ['fɔ:fɪt] N (in game) prenda ▸ VT perder (derecho a)
forgave [fə'geɪv] PT of **forgive**
forge [fɔ:dʒ] N fragua; (smithy) herrería ▸ VT (BRIT: money, signature) falsificar; (metal) forjar ▸ **forge ahead** VI avanzar mucho
forger ['fɔ:dʒəʳ] N falsificador(a) m/f
forgery ['fɔ:dʒərɪ] N falsificación f
★forget [fə'gɛt] (pt **forgot** [fə'gɔt], pp **forgotten** [fə'gɔtn]) VT olvidar, olvidarse de ▸ VI olvidarse
forgetful [fə'gɛtful] ADJ olvidadizo, despistado
forget-me-not [fə'gɛtmɪnɔt] N nomeolvides f inv
★forgive [fə'gɪv] VT (irreg: like **give**) perdonar; **to ~ sb for sth/for doing sth** perdonar algo a algn/a algn por haber hecho algo
forgiveness [fə'gɪvnɪs] N perdón m
forgiving [fə'gɪvɪŋ] ADJ compasivo
forgo [fɔ:'gəu] VT (irreg: like **go**) (give up) renunciar a; (go without) privarse de
forgot [fə'gɔt] PT of **forget**
forgotten [fə'gɔtn] PP of **forget**
fork [fɔ:k] N (for eating) tenedor m; (for gardening) horca; (of roads) bifurcación f; (in tree) horcadura ▸ VI (road) bifurcarse ▸ **fork out** VT (inf: pay) soltar
forked [fɔ:kt] ADJ (lightning) en zigzag
fork-lift truck ['fɔ:klɪft-] N máquina elevadora
forlorn [fə'lɔ:n] ADJ (person) triste, melancólico; (deserted: cottage) abandonado; (desperate: attempt) desesperado
★form [fɔ:m] N forma; (BRIT Scol) curso; (document) formulario, planilla (LAm); **in the ~ of** en forma de; **in top ~** en plena forma; **to be in good ~** (Sport: fig) estar en plena forma ▸ VT formar; **to ~ part of sth** formar parte de algo; **to ~ a circle/a queue** hacer una curva/una cola
★formal ['fɔ:məl] ADJ (offer, receipt) por escrito; (person etc) correcto; (occasion, dinner) ceremonioso; **~ dress** traje m de vestir; (evening dress) traje m de etiqueta
formalities [fɔ:'mælɪtɪz] NPL formalidades fpl
formality [fɔ:'mælɪtɪ] N ceremonia
formalize ['fɔ:məlaɪz] VT formalizar
formally ['fɔ:məlɪ] ADV oficialmente

format [ˈfɔːmæt] N formato ▸ VT (*Comput*) formatear

formation [fɔːˈmeɪʃən] N formación f

formative [ˈfɔːmətɪv] ADJ (*years*) de formación

formatting [ˈfɔːmætɪŋ] N (*Comput*) formateado, formateo

★**former** [ˈfɔːməʳ] ADJ anterior; (*earlier*) antiguo; (*ex*) ex; **the ~ ... the latter ...** aquel ... este ...; **the ~ president** el antiguo *or* ex presidente; **the ~ Yugoslavia/Soviet Union** la antigua *or* ex Yugoslavia/Unión Soviética

formerly [ˈfɔːməlɪ] ADV antes

form feed N (*on printer*) salto de página

Formica® [fɔːˈmaɪkə] N formica®

formidable [ˈfɔːmɪdəbl] ADJ formidable

formula [ˈfɔːmjulə] N fórmula; **F~ One** (*Aut*) Fórmula Uno

formulate [ˈfɔːmjuleɪt] VT formular

fornicate [ˈfɔːnɪkeɪt] VI fornicar

forsake [fəˈseɪk] (*pt* **forsook** [fəˈsuk], *pp* **forsaken** [fəˈseɪkən]) VT (*gen*) abandonar; (*plan*) renunciar a

fort [fɔːt] N fuerte *m*; **to hold the ~** (*fig*) quedarse a cargo

forte [ˈfɔːtɪ] N fuerte *m*

★**forth** [fɔːθ] ADV: **back and ~** de acá para allá; **and so ~** y así sucesivamente

forthcoming [fɔːθˈkʌmɪŋ] ADJ próximo, venidero; (*character*) comunicativo

forthright [ˈfɔːθraɪt] ADJ franco

forthwith [ˈfɔːθˈwɪθ] ADV en el acto, acto seguido

fortieth [ˈfɔːtɪɪθ] ADJ cuadragésimo

fortification [fɔːtɪfɪˈkeɪʃən] N fortificación f

fortified wine [ˈfɔːtɪfaɪd-] N vino encabezado

fortify [ˈfɔːtɪfaɪ] VT fortalecer

fortitude [ˈfɔːtɪtjuːd] N (*city*) fortificar; (*person*) fortalecer

fortnight [ˈfɔːtnaɪt] N (*BRIT*) quincena; **it's a ~ since ...** hace quince días que ...

fortnightly [ˈfɔːtnaɪtlɪ] ADJ quincenal ▸ ADV quincenalmente

FORTRAN [ˈfɔːtræn] N FORTRAN *m*

fortress [ˈfɔːtrɪs] N fortaleza

fortuitous [fɔːˈtjuːɪtəs] ADJ fortuito

fortunate [ˈfɔːtʃənɪt] ADJ: **it is ~ that ...** (es una) suerte que ...

fortunately [ˈfɔːtʃənɪtlɪ] ADV afortunadamente

★**fortune** [ˈfɔːtʃən] N suerte f; (*wealth*) fortuna; **to make a ~** hacer un dineral

fortune-teller [ˈfɔːtʃəntɛləʳ] N adivino(-a)

★**forty** [ˈfɔːtɪ] NUM cuarenta

forum [ˈfɔːrəm] N (*also fig*) foro

★**forward** [ˈfɔːwəd] ADJ (*position*) avanzado; (*movement*) hacia delante; (*front*) delantero; (*not shy*) atrevido ▸ N (*Sport*) delantero ▸ VT (*letter*) remitir; (*career*) promocionar; **"please ~"** "remítase al destinatario" ▸ ADV: **to move ~** avanzar

forward contract N contrato a término

forward exchange N cambio a término

forwarding address N destinatario

forward planning N planificación f por anticipado

forward rate N tipo a término

forwards [ˈfɔːwədz] ADV (hacia) adelante

forward sales NPL ventas fpl a término

forward slash N barra diagonal

forwent [fɔːˈwɛnt] PT of **forgo**

fossick [ˈfɔsɪk] VI (*AUSTRALIA, NEW ZEALAND inf*) buscar; **to ~ for sth** buscar algo

fossil [ˈfɔsl] N fósil *m*

fossil fuel N combustible *m* fósil

foster [ˈfɔstəʳ] VT (*child*) acoger en familia; (*idea*) fomentar

foster brother N hermano de leche

foster child N (*irreg*) hijo(-a) adoptivo(-a)

foster mother N madre f adoptiva

foster sister N hermana de leche

fought [fɔːt] PT, PP of **fight**

foul [faul] ADJ (*gen*) sucio, puerco; (*weather, smell etc*) asqueroso; (*language*) grosero; (*temper*) malísimo ▸ N (*Football*) falta ▸ VT (*dirty*) ensuciar; (*block*) atascar; (*entangle: anchor, propeller*) atascar, enredarse en; (*football player*) cometer una falta contra

foul play N (*Sport*) mala jugada; (*Law*) muerte f violenta

★**found** [faund] PT, PP of **find** ▸ VT (*establish*) fundar

foundation [faunˈdeɪʃən] N (*act*) fundación f; (*basis*) base f; (*also:* **foundation cream**) crema de base ▪ **foundations** NPL (*of building*) cimientos *mpl*; **to lay the foundations** poner los cimientos

foundation stone N: **to lay the ~** poner la primera piedra

founder [ˈfaundəʳ] N fundador(a) *m/f* ▸ VI irse a pique

founding [ˈfaundɪŋ] ADJ: **~ fathers** (*esp US*) fundadores *mpl*, próceres *mpl*; **~ member** miembro fundador

foundry [ˈfaundrɪ] N fundición f

★**fountain** [ˈfauntɪn] N fuente f

fountain pen N (pluma) estilográfica, plumafuente f (*LAM*)

★**four** [fɔːʳ] NUM cuatro; **on all fours** a gatas

four-by-four [ˈfɔːbaɪˈfɔːʳ] N todoterreno, 4x4 *m* (*cuatro por cuatro*)

four-footed [fɔːˈfutɪd] ADJ cuadrúpedo

four-letter word [ˈfɔːlɛtə-] N taco

four-poster [ˈfɔːˈpəustəʳ] N (*also:* **four-poster bed**) cama de columnas

foursome [ˈfɔːsəm] N grupo de cuatro personas

★**fourteen** [ˈfɔːˈtiːn] NUM catorce

★**fourteenth** [fɔːˈtiːnθ] ADJ decimocuarto

★**fourth** [fɔ:θ] ADJ cuarto ▶ N (*Aut: also:* **fourth gear**) cuarta (velocidad)

four-wheel drive [ˈfɔ:wi:l-] N tracción f a las cuatro ruedas

fowl [faul] N ave f (de corral)

★**fox** [fɔks] N zorro ▶ VT confundir

fox fur N piel f de zorro

foxglove [ˈfɔksglʌv] N (*Bot*) dedalera

fox-hunting [ˈfɔkshʌntɪŋ] N caza de zorros

foxtrot [ˈfɔkstrɔt] N fox(trot) m

foyer [ˈfɔɪeɪ] N vestíbulo

FPA N ABBR (*Brit:* = *Family Planning Association*) asociación de planificación familiar

Fr. ABBR (*Rel:* = *father*) P.; (*:* = *friar*) Fr.

fracas [ˈfrækɑ:] N gresca, refriega

fracking [ˈfrækɪŋ] N fracturación f *or* fractura hidráulica, fracking m

fraction [ˈfrækʃən] N fracción f

fractionally [ˈfrækʃnəlɪ] ADV ligeramente

fractious [ˈfrækʃəs] ADJ (*person, mood*) irascible

fracture [ˈfræktʃəʳ] N fractura ▶ VT fracturar

fragile [ˈfrædʒaɪl] ADJ frágil

fragment [ˈfrægmənt] N fragmento

fragmentary [frægˈmɛntərɪ] ADJ fragmentario

fragrance [ˈfreɪgrəns] N fragancia

fragrant [ˈfreɪgrənt] ADJ fragante, oloroso

frail [freɪl] ADJ (*fragile*) frágil, quebradizo; (*weak*) delicado

★**frame** [freɪm] N (*Tech*) armazón f; (*of picture, door etc*) marco; (*of spectacles: also:* **frames**) montura ▶ VT encuadrar; (*picture*) enmarcar; (*reply*) formular; **to ~ sb** (*inf*) inculpar por engaños a algn

frame of mind N estado de ánimo

framework [ˈfreɪmwɜ:k] N marco

★**France** [frɑ:ns] N Francia

franchise [ˈfræntʃaɪz] N (*Pol*) derecho al voto, sufragio; (*Comm*) licencia, concesión f

franchisee [fræntʃaɪˈzi:] N concesionario(-a)

franchiser [ˈfræntʃaɪzəʳ] N compañía concesionaria

frank [fræŋk] ADJ franco ▶ VT (*Brit: letter*) franquear

frankfurter [ˈfræŋkfɜ:təʳ] N salchicha de Frankfurt

frankincense [ˈfræŋkɪnsɛns] N incienso

franking machine [ˈfræŋkɪŋ-] N máquina de franqueo

frankly [ˈfræŋklɪ] ADV francamente

frankness [ˈfræŋknɪs] N franqueza

frantic [ˈfræntɪk] ADJ (*desperate: need, desire*) desesperado; (*: search*) frenético; (*: person*) desquiciado

fraternal [frəˈtɜ:nl] ADJ fraterno

fraternity [frəˈtɜ:nɪtɪ] N (*club*) fraternidad f; (*US*) club m de estudiantes; (*guild*) gremio

fraternization [frætənaɪˈzeɪʃən] N fraternización f

fraternize [ˈfrætənaɪz] VI confraternizar

fraud [frɔ:d] N fraude m; (*person*) impostor(a) m/f

fraudulent [ˈfrɔ:djulənt] ADJ fraudulento

fraught [frɔ:t] ADJ (*tense*) tenso; **~ with** cargado de

fray [freɪ] N combate m, lucha, refriega ▶ VI deshilacharse; **tempers frayed** el ambiente se ponía tenso

FRB N ABBR (*US*) = **Federal Reserve Board**

FRCM N ABBR (*Brit*) = **Fellow of the Royal College of Music**

FRCO N ABBR (*Brit*) = **Fellow of the Royal College of Organists**

FRCP N ABBR (*Brit*) = **Fellow of the Royal College of Physicians**

FRCS N ABBR (*Brit*) = **Fellow of the Royal College of Surgeons**

freak [fri:k] N (*person*) fenómeno; (*event*) suceso anormal; (*pej: enthusiast*) adicto(-a); **health ~** (*pej*) maniático(-a) en cuestión de salud ▶ ADJ (*storm, conditions*) anormal
  ▶ **freak out** VI (*inf: on drugs*) flipar

freakish [ˈfri:kɪʃ] ADJ (*result*) inesperado; (*appearance*) estrambótico; (*weather*) cambiadizo

freckle [ˈfrɛkl] N peca

freckled [ˈfrɛkld] ADJ pecoso, lleno de pecas

★**free** [fri:] ADJ (*person: at liberty*) libre; (*not fixed*) suelto; (*gratis*) gratuito; (*unoccupied*) desocupado; (*liberal*) generoso; **~ and easy** despreocupado; **to give sb a ~ hand** dar carta blanca a algn; **is this seat ~?** ¿está libre este asiento?; **~ of tax** libre de impuestos; **~ of charge** gratis; **admission ~** entrada libre ▶ VT (*prisoner etc*) poner en libertad; (*jammed object*) soltar; **for ~** *adv* gratis

freebie [ˈfri:bɪ] N (*inf*): **it's a ~** es gratis

★**freedom** [ˈfri:dəm] N libertad f; **~ of association** libertad de asociación

freedom fighter N luchador(a) m/f por la libertad

free enterprise N libre empresa

Freefone® [ˈfri:fəun] N (*Brit*) número gratuito

free-for-all [ˈfri:fərɔ:l] N riña general

free gift N regalo

freehold [ˈfri:həuld] N propiedad f absoluta

free kick N tiro libre

freelance [ˈfri:lɑ:ns] ADJ independiente; **to do ~ work** trabajar por su cuenta ▶ ADV por cuenta propia

freeloader [ˈfri:ləudəʳ] N (*pej*) gorrón(-ona) (*inf*)

freely [ˈfri:lɪ] ADV libremente; (*liberally*) generosamente

free-market economy [ˈfri:ˈmɑ:kɪt-] N economía de libre mercado

freemason [ˈfri:meɪsn] N francmasón m

freemasonry [ˈfri:meɪsnrɪ] N (*franc*)masonería

Freepost® [ˈfri:pəust] N porte m pagado

free-range ['fri:'reɪndʒ] ADJ (hen, egg) de granja

free sample N muestra gratuita

freesia ['fri:ʒə] N fresia

free speech N libertad f de expresión

free trade N libre comercio

Freeview® ['fri:vju:] N (BRIT) servicio británico de televisión digital abierta

freeway ['fri:weɪ] N (US) autopista

freewheel [fri:'wi:l] VI ir en punto muerto

freewheeling [fri:'wi:lɪŋ] ADJ libre, espontáneo; (careless) irresponsable

free will N libre albedrío; **of one's own ~** por su propia voluntad

★**freeze** [fri:z] (pt **froze** [frəuz], pp **frozen** ['frəuzn]) VI helarse, congelarse ▶ VT helar; (prices, food, salaries) congelar ▶ N helada; (on arms, wages) congelación f
  ▶ **freeze over** VI (lake, river) helarse, congelarse; (window, windscreen) cubrirse de escarcha
  ▶ **freeze up** VI helarse, congelarse

freeze-dried ['fri:zdraɪd] ADJ liofilizado

★**freezer** ['fri:zə'] N congelador m, congeladora

★**freezing** ['fri:zɪŋ] ADJ helado

freezing point N punto de congelación; **3 degrees below ~** tres grados bajo cero

freight [freɪt] N (goods) carga; (money charged) flete m

freight car N vagón m de mercancías

freighter ['freɪtə'] N buque m de carga; (Aviat) avión m de transporte de mercancías

freight forward N contra reembolso del flete, flete por pagar

freight forwarder [-'fɔ:wədə'] N agente m expedidor

freight inward N flete sobre compras

freight train N (US) tren m de mercancías

★**French** [frɛntʃ] ADJ francés(-esa) ▶ N (Ling) francés m ■ **the French** NPL (people) los franceses

French bean N judía verde

French bread N pan m francés

French Canadian ADJ, N francocanadiense mf

French dressing N (Culin) vinagreta

French fried potatoes, (US) **French fries** NPL patatas fpl or (LAM) papas fpl fritas

French Guiana [-gaɪ'ænə] N la Guayana Francesa

French loaf N barra de pan

★**Frenchman** ['frɛntʃmən] N (irreg) francés m

French Riviera N: **the ~** la Riviera, la Costa Azul

French stick N barra de pan

French window N puerta ventana

★**Frenchwoman** ['frɛntʃwumən] N (irreg) francesa

frenetic [frə'nɛtɪk] ADJ frenético

frenzy ['frɛnzɪ] N frenesí m

frequency ['fri:kwənsɪ] N frecuencia

frequency modulation N frecuencia modulada

★**frequent** ADJ ['fri:kwənt] frecuente ▶ VT [frɪ'kwɛnt] frecuentar

frequently ['fri:kwəntlɪ] ADV frecuentemente, a menudo

fresco ['frɛskəu] N fresco

★**fresh** [frɛʃ] ADJ (gen) fresco; (bread) tierno; (new) nuevo; (water) dulce; **to make a ~ start** empezar de nuevo

freshen ['frɛʃən] VI (wind) arreciar; (air) refrescar
  ▶ **freshen up** VI (person) arreglarse

freshener ['frɛʃnə'] N: **air ~** ambientador m; **skin ~** tónico

fresher ['frɛʃə'] N (BRIT Scol: inf) estudiante mf de primer año

freshly ['frɛʃlɪ] ADV: **~ painted/arrived** recién pintado/llegado

freshman ['frɛʃmən] N (irreg) (US Scol) = **fresher**

freshness ['frɛʃnɪs] N frescura

freshwater ['frɛʃwɔ:tə'] ADJ (fish) de agua dulce

fret [frɛt] VI inquietarse

fretful ['frɛtful] ADJ (child) quejumbroso

Freudian ['frɔɪdɪən] ADJ freudiano; **~ slip** lapsus m (freudiano)

FRG N ABBR (= Federal Republic of Germany) RFA f

Fri. ABBR (= Friday) vier.

friar ['fraɪə'] N fraile m; (before name) fray

friction ['frɪkʃən] N fricción f

friction feed N (on printer) avance m por fricción

★**Friday** ['fraɪdɪ] N viernes m inv; see also **Tuesday**

★**fridge** [frɪdʒ] N (BRIT) nevera, frigo, refrigeradora (LAM), heladera (LAM)

fridge-freezer ['frɪdʒ'fri:zə'] N frigorífico-congelador m, combi m

fried [fraɪd] PT, PP of **fry** ▶ ADJ: **~ egg** huevo frito, huevo estrellado

★**friend** [frɛnd] N amigo(-a) ▶ VT (Internet) añadir como amigo a

friendliness ['frɛndlɪnɪs] N simpatía

★**friendly** ['frɛndlɪ] ADJ simpático; (government) amigo; (place) acogedor(a); (match) amistoso

friendly fire N fuego amigo, disparos mpl del propio bando

friendly society N mutualidad f, montepío

★**friendship** ['frɛndʃɪp] N amistad f

fries [fraɪz] NPL (esp US) = **French fried potatoes**

frieze [fri:z] N friso

frigate ['frɪgɪt] N fragata

fright [fraɪt] N susto; **to take ~** asustarse

frighten ['fraɪtn] VT asustar
  ▶ **frighten away, frighten off** VT (birds, children etc) espantar, ahuyentar

★**frightened** ['fraɪtnd] ADJ asustado

frightening ['fraɪtnɪŋ] ADJ: **it's ~** da miedo

frightful ['fraɪtful] ADJ espantoso, horrible

563

frightfully ['fraɪtfulɪ] ADV terriblemente; **I'm ~ sorry** lo siento muchísimo

frigid ['frɪdʒɪd] ADJ (Med) frígido

frigidity [frɪ'dʒɪdɪtɪ] N (Med) frigidez f

frill [frɪl] N volante m; **without frills** (fig) sin adornos

frilly ['frɪlɪ] ADJ con volantes

fringe [frɪndʒ] N (BRIT: of hair) flequillo; (edge: of forest etc) borde m, margen m

fringe benefits NPL ventajas fpl complementarias

fringe theatre N teatro experimental

Frisbee® ['frɪzbɪ] N frisbee® m

frisk [frɪsk] VT cachear, registrar

frisky ['frɪskɪ] ADJ juguetón(-ona)

fritter ['frɪtər] N buñuelo
▶ **fritter away** VT desperdiciar

frivolity [frɪ'vɔlɪtɪ] N frivolidad f

frivolous ['frɪvələs] ADJ frívolo

frizzy ['frɪzɪ] ADJ crespo

fro [frəu] see **to**

frock [frɔk] N vestido

★**frog** [frɔg] N rana; **to have a ~ in one's throat** tener carraspera

frogman ['frɔgmən] N (irreg) hombre-rana m

frogmarch ['frɔgmɑːtʃ] VT: **to ~ sb in/out** meter/sacar a algn a rastras

frolic ['frɔlɪk] VI juguetear

---

from [frɔm]

PREP **1** (indicating starting place) de, desde; **where do you come from?, where are you from?** ¿de dónde eres?; **where has he come from?** ¿de dónde ha venido?; **from London to Glasgow** de Londres a Glasgow; **to escape from sth/sb** escaparse de algo/algn

2 (indicating origin etc) de; **a letter/telephone call from my sister** una carta/llamada de mi hermana; **tell him from me that ...** dígale de mi parte que ...

3 (indicating time): **from one o'clock to** or **until** or **till nine** de la una a las nueve, desde la una hasta las nueve; **from January (on)** a partir de enero; **(as) from Friday** a partir del viernes

4 (indicating distance) de; **the hotel is 1 km from the beach** el hotel está a 1 km de la playa

5 (indicating price, number etc) de; **prices range from £10 to £50** los precios van desde £10 a or hasta £50; **the interest rate was increased from 9% to 10%** el tipo de interés fue incrementado de un 9% a un 10%

6 (indicating difference) de; **he can't tell red from green** no sabe distinguir el rojo del verde; **to be different from sb/sth** ser diferente a algn/algo

7 (because of, on the basis of): **from what he says** por lo que dice; **weak from hunger** debilitado por el hambre

---

frond [frɔnd] N fronda

★**front** [frʌnt] N (foremost part) parte f delantera; (of house) fachada; (promenade: also: **sea front**) paseo marítimo; (Mil, Pol, Meteorology) frente m; (fig: appearances) apariencia; **in ~ (of)** delante (de) ▶ ADJ (wheel, leg) delantero; (row, line) primero ▶ VI: **to ~ onto sth** dar a algo

frontage ['frʌntɪdʒ] N (of building) fachada

frontal ['frʌntl] ADJ frontal

front bench N (BRIT Pol) ver nota

El término genérico **front bench** se usa para referirse a los escaños situados en primera fila a ambos lados del Presidente (Speaker) de la Cámara de los Comunes (House of Commons) del Parlamento británico. Dichos escaños son ocupados por los miembros del gobierno a un lado y los del gobierno en la oposición (shadow cabinet) al otro. Por esta razón a todos ellos se les denomina frontbenchers.

frontbencher ['frʌnt'bentʃər] N (BRIT) see **front bench**

front desk N (US) recepción f

front door N puerta principal

frontier ['frʌntɪər] N frontera

frontispiece ['frʌntɪspiːs] N frontispicio

front page N primera plana

front room N (BRIT) salón m, sala

front runner N favorito(-a)

front-wheel drive ['frʌntwiːl-] N tracción f delantera

★**frost** [frɔst] N (gen) helada; (also: **hoarfrost**) escarcha ▶ VT (US Culin) escarchar

frostbite ['frɔstbaɪt] N congelación f

frosted ['frɔstɪd] ADJ (glass) esmerilado; (esp US: cake) glaseado

frosting ['frɔstɪŋ] N (esp US: icing) glaseado

★**frosty** ['frɔstɪ] ADJ (weather) de helada; (surface) cubierto de escarcha; (welcome etc) glacial

froth [frɔθ] N espuma

frothy ['frɔθɪ] ADJ espumoso

frown [fraun] VI fruncir el ceño ▶ N: **with a ~** frunciendo el entrecejo
▶ **frown on** VT FUS desaprobar

froze [frəuz] PT of **freeze**

★**frozen** ['frəuzn] PP of **freeze** ▶ ADJ (food) congelado; (Comm): **~ assets** activos mpl congelados or bloqueados

FRS N ABBR (BRIT: = Fellow of the Royal Society) miembro de la principal asociación de investigación científica; (US: = Federal Reserve System) banco central de los EE. UU.

frugal ['fruːgəl] ADJ (person) frugal

★**fruit** [fruːt] N pl inv fruta

fruiterer ['fruːtərər] N frutero(-a); **~'s (shop)** frutería

fruit fly N mosca de la fruta

fruitful ['fruːtful] ADJ provechoso

fruition [fruːˈɪʃən] N: **to come to ~** realizarse

fruit juice N jugo or (SP) zumo de fruta

fruitless [ˈfruːtlɪs] ADJ (fig) infructuoso, inútil

fruit machine N (BRIT) máquina tragaperras

fruit salad N macedonia or (LAM) ensalada de frutas

frump [frʌmp] N espantajo, adefesio

frustrate [frʌsˈtreɪt] VT frustrar

frustrated [frʌsˈtreɪtɪd] ADJ frustrado

frustrating [frʌsˈtreɪtɪŋ] ADJ (job, day) frustrante

frustration [frʌsˈtreɪʃən] N frustración f

★**fry** [fraɪ] (pt, pp **fried** [fraɪd]) VT freír ▶ N: **small ~** gente f menuda

frying pan [ˈfraɪɪŋ-] N sartén f, sartén m (LAM)

FT N ABBR (BRIT: = Financial Times) periódico financiero; (= the FT index) el índice de valores del Financial Times

ft. ABBR = **foot**; **feet**

FTC N ABBR (US) = **Federal Trade Commission**

fuchsia [ˈfjuːʃə] N fucsia

fuck [fʌk] (inf!) VT joder (SP inf!), coger (LAM inf!) ▶ VI joder (SP inf!), coger (LAM inf!); **~ off!** ¡vete a tomar por culo! (inf!)

fuddled [ˈfʌdld] ADJ (muddled) confuso, aturdido; (inf: tipsy) borracho

fuddy-duddy [ˈfʌdɪdʌdɪ] (pej) N carcamal m, carroza mf ▶ ADJ chapado a la antigua

fudge [fʌdʒ] N (Culin) caramelo blando ▶ VT (issue, problem) rehuir, esquivar

★**fuel** [ˈfjuəl] N (for heating) combustible m; (coal) carbón m; (wood) leña; (for engine) carburante m ▶ VT (furnace etc) alimentar; (aircraft, ship etc) aprovisionar de combustible

fuel oil N fueloil m

fuel poverty N pobreza energética

fuel pump N (Aut) surtidor m de gasolina

fuel tank N depósito de combustible

fug [fʌɡ] N aire m viciado

fugitive [ˈfjuːdʒɪtɪv] N (from prison) fugitivo(-a)

fulfil, (US) **fulfill** [fulˈfɪl] VT (function) desempeñar; (condition) cumplir; (wish, desire) realizar

fulfilled [fulˈfɪld] ADJ (person) realizado

fulfilment, (US) **fulfillment** [fulˈfɪlmənt] N realización f; (of promise) cumplimiento

★**full** [ful] ADJ lleno; (fig) pleno; (complete) completo; (maximum) máximo; (information) detallado; (price) íntegro, sin descuento; **I'm ~ (up)** estoy lleno; **we're ~ up for July** estamos completos para julio; **~ employment** pleno empleo; **~ name** nombre m completo; **a ~ two hours** dos horas enteras; **at ~ speed** a toda velocidad ▶ ADV: **~ well** perfectamente; **in ~** (reproduce, quote) íntegramente; **to write sth in ~** escribir algo por extenso; **to pay in ~** pagar la deuda entera

fullback [ˈfulbæk] N (Football) defensa m; (Rugby) zaguero

full-blooded [ˈfulˈblʌdɪd] ADJ (vigorous: attack) vigoroso; (pure) puro

full-cream [ˈfulˈkriːm] ADJ: **~ milk** leche f entera

full driving licence N (BRIT Aut) carnet m de conducir (definitivo); see also **L-plates**

full-fledged [ˈfulfledʒd] ADJ (US) = **fully-fledged**

full-grown [ˈfulˈɡrəun] ADJ maduro

full-length [ˈfulˈleŋθ] ADJ (portrait) de cuerpo entero; (film) de largometraje

full moon N luna llena, plenilunio

fullness [ˈfulnɪs] N plenitud f, amplitud f

full-scale [ˈfulskeɪl] ADJ (attack, war, search, retreat) en gran escala; (plan, model) de tamaño natural

full stop N punto

full-time [ˈfulˈtaɪm] ADJ (work) de tiempo completo ▶ ADV: **to work ~** trabajar a tiempo completo

fully [ˈfulɪ] ADV completamente; (at least) al menos

fully-fledged [ˈfulɪˈfledʒd], (US) **full-fledged** ADJ (teacher, barrister) diplomado; (bird) con todas sus plumas, capaz de volar; (fig) de pleno derecho

fully-paid [ˈfulɪpeɪd] ADJ: **~ share** acción f liberada

fulsome [ˈfulsəm] ADJ (pej: praise, gratitude) excesivo, exagerado; (: manner) obsequioso

fumble [ˈfʌmbl] VI: **to ~ with** manejar torpemente, manosear

fume [fjuːm] VI estar furioso, echar humo

fumes [fjuːmz] NPL humo sg, gases mpl

fumigate [ˈfjuːmɪɡeɪt] VT fumigar

★**fun** [fʌn] N (amusement) diversión f; (joy) alegría; **to have ~** divertirse; **for ~** por gusto; **to make ~ of** reírse de

function [ˈfʌŋkʃən] N función f ▶ VI funcionar; **to ~ as** hacer (las veces) de, fungir de (LAM)

functional [ˈfʌŋkʃənl] ADJ funcional

function key N (Comput) tecla de función

fund [fʌnd] N fondo; (reserve) reserva ∎ **funds** NPL (money) fondos mpl

fundamental [fʌndəˈmentl] ADJ fundamental ∎ **fundamentals** NPL fundamentos mpl

fundamentalism [fʌndəˈmentəlɪzəm] N fundamentalismo, integrismo

fundamentalist [fʌndəˈmentəlɪst] N fundamentalista mf, integrista mf

fundamentally [fʌndəˈmentəlɪ] ADV fundamentalmente

funding [ˈfʌndɪŋ] N financiación f

fund-raising [ˈfʌndreɪzɪŋ] N recaudación f de fondos

funeral [ˈfjuːnərəl] N (burial) entierro; (ceremony) funerales mpl

funeral director N director(a) m/f de pompas fúnebres

funeral parlour N (BRIT) funeraria

funeral service N misa de cuerpo presente

funereal [fjuːˈnɪərɪəl] ADJ fúnebre

funfair [ˈfʌnfɛəʳ] N (BRIT) parque m de atracciones; (travelling) feria

fungus [ˈfʌŋgəs] (pl **fungi** [-gaɪ]) N hongo; (mould) moho

funicular [fjuːˈnɪkjuləʳ] N (also: **funicular railway**) funicular m

funky [ˈfʌŋkɪ] ADJ (music) funky; (inf: good) guay

funnel [ˈfʌnl] N embudo; (of ship) chimenea

funnily [ˈfʌnɪlɪ] ADV de modo divertido, graciosamente; (oddly) de una manera rara; **~ enough** aunque parezca extraño

★**funny** [ˈfʌnɪ] ADJ gracioso, divertido; (strange) curioso, raro

funny bone N hueso de la alegría

fun run N maratón m popular

fur [fəːʳ] N piel f; (BRIT: on tongue etc) sarro

fur coat N abrigo de pieles

furious [ˈfjuərɪəs] ADJ furioso; (effort, argument) violento; **to be ~ with sb** estar furioso con algn

furiously [ˈfjuərɪəslɪ] ADV con furia

furl [fəːl] VT (sail) recoger

furlong [ˈfəːlɔŋ] N octava parte de una milla

furlough [ˈfəːləu] N (US Mil) permiso

furnace [ˈfəːnɪs] N horno

furnish [ˈfəːnɪʃ] VT amueblar; (supply) proporcionar; (information) facilitar

furnished [ˈfəːnɪʃt] ADJ: **~ flat** or (US) **apartment** piso amueblado

furnishings [ˈfəːnɪʃɪŋz] NPL mobiliario sg

★**furniture** [ˈfəːnɪtʃəʳ] N muebles mpl; **piece of ~** mueble m

furniture polish N cera para muebles

furore [fjuəˈrɔːrɪ] N (protests) escándalo

furrier [ˈfʌrɪəʳ] N peletero(-a)

furrow [ˈfʌrəu] N surco ▶ VT (forehead) arrugar

furry [ˈfəːrɪ] ADJ peludo; (toy) de peluche

★**further** [ˈfəːðəʳ] ADJ (new) nuevo; (place) más lejano ▶ ADV más lejos; (more) más; (moreover) además; **how much ~ is it?** ¿a qué distancia queda?; **~ to your letter of ...** (Comm) con referencia a su carta de ... ▶ VT hacer avanzar; **to**

~ one's interests fomentar sus intereses

further education N educación f postescolar

furthermore [fəːðəˈmɔːʳ] ADV además

furthermost [ˈfəːðəməust] ADJ más lejano

furthest [ˈfəːðɪst] SUPERLATIVE of **far**

furtive [ˈfəːtɪv] ADJ furtivo

furtively [ˈfəːtɪvlɪ] ADV furtivamente, a escondidas

fury [ˈfjuərɪ] N furia

fuse, (US) **fuze** [fjuːz] N fusible m; (for bomb etc) mecha; **a ~ has blown** se ha fundido un fusible ▶ VT (metal) fundir; (fig) fusionar ▶ VI fundirse; fusionarse; (BRIT Elec): **to ~ the lights** fundir los plomos

fuse box N caja de fusibles

fuselage [ˈfjuːzəlɑːʒ] N fuselaje m

fuse wire N hilo fusible

fusillade [fjuːzɪˈleɪd] N descarga cerrada; (fig) lluvia

fusion [ˈfjuːʒən] N fusión f

fuss [fʌs] N (excitement) conmoción f; (complaint) alboroto, protesta; (noise) bulla; (dispute) lío, jaleo; **to make a ~** armar jaleo ▶ VI preocuparse (por pequeñeces) ▶ VT (person) molestar
▶ **fuss over** VT FUS (person) contemplar, mimar

fusspot [ˈfʌspɔt] N (inf) quisquilloso(-a)

fussy [ˈfʌsɪ] ADJ (person) quisquilloso; **I'm not ~** (inf) me da igual

fusty [ˈfʌstɪ] ADJ (pej) rancio; **to smell ~** oler a cerrado

futile [ˈfjuːtaɪl] ADJ vano

futility [fjuːˈtɪlɪtɪ] N inutilidad f

futon [ˈfuːtɔn] N futón m

★**future** [ˈfjuːtʃəʳ] ADJ (gen) futuro; (coming) venidero ▶ N futuro, porvenir; **in ~** de ahora en adelante ■ **futures** NPL (Comm) operaciones fpl a término, futuros mpl

futuristic [fjuːtʃəˈrɪstɪk] ADJ futurista

fuze [fjuːz] N, VB (US) = **fuse**

fuzzy [ˈfʌzɪ] ADJ (Phot) borroso; (hair) muy rizado

fwd. ABBR = **forward**

FY ABBR = **fiscal year**

FYI ABBR = **for your information**

Gg

G, g [dʒiː] N (letter) G, g f; (Mus): **G** sol m; **G for George** G de Gerona

G N ABBR (BRIT Scol: mark: = good) N; (US Cine: = general audience) todos los públicos

g. ABBR (= gram(s), gravity) g

G8 N ABBR (Pol: = Group of Eight) G8 m

G20 N ABBR (Pol: = Group of Twenty) G20 m

GA ABBR (US Post) = **Georgia**

gab [gæb] N: **to have the gift of the ~** (inf) tener mucha labia

gabble [ˈgæbl] VI hablar atropelladamente; (gossip) cotorrear

gaberdine [gæbəˈdiːn] N gabardina

gable [ˈgeɪbl] N aguilón m

Gabon [gəˈbɔn] N Gabón m

gad about [gæd-] VI (inf) moverse mucho

gadget [ˈgædʒɪt] N aparato

gadgetry [ˈgædʒɪtrɪ] N chismes mpl

Gaelic [ˈgeɪlɪk] ADJ, N (Ling) gaélico

gaffe [gæf] N plancha, patinazo, metedura de pata

gaffer [ˈgæfəʳ] N (BRIT inf: boss) jefe m; (: (old) man) vejete m

gag [gæg] N (on mouth) mordaza; (joke) chiste m ▶ VT (prisoner etc) amordazar ▶ VI (choke) tener arcadas

gaga [ˈgɑːgɑː] ADJ: **to go ~** (senile) chochear; (ecstatic) caérsele a algn la baba

gage [geɪdʒ] N, VT (US) = **gauge**

gaiety [ˈgeɪtɪ] N alegría

gaily [ˈgeɪlɪ] ADV alegremente

gain [geɪn] N ganancia ▶ VT ganar; **to ~ by sth** ganar con algo; **to ~ ground** ganar terreno; **to ~ 3 lbs (in weight)** engordar 3 libras ▶ VI (watch) adelantarse
▶ **gain (up)on** VT FUS alcanzar

gainful [ˈgeɪnful] ADJ (employment) remunerado

gainfully [ˈgeɪnfulɪ] ADV: **to be ~ employed** tener un trabajo remunerado

gait [geɪt] N forma de andar, andares mpl

gal., gall. ABBR = **gallon**

gala [ˈgɑːlə] N gala; **swimming ~** certamen m de natación

Galapagos Islands [gəˈlæpəgəs-] NPL: **the ~** las Islas Galápagos

galaxy [ˈgæləksɪ] N galaxia

gale [geɪl] N (wind) vendaval m; **~ force 10** vendaval de fuerza 10

gall [gɔːl] N (Anat) bilis f, hiel f; (fig: impudence) descaro, caradura ▶ VT molestar

gallant [ˈgælənt] ADJ valeroso; (towards ladies) galante

gallantry [ˈgæləntrɪ] N valentía; (courtesy) galantería

gall bladder N vesícula biliar

galleon [ˈgælɪən] N galeón m

gallery [ˈgælərɪ] N (Theat) galería; (for spectators) tribuna; (also: **art gallery**: state-owned) pinacoteca or museo de arte; (: private) galería de arte

galley [ˈgælɪ] N (ship's kitchen) cocina; (ship) galera

galley proof N (Typ) prueba de galera, galerada

Gallic [ˈgælɪk] ADJ galo

gallon [ˈgæln] N galón m (= 8 pintas; Brit = 4,546 litros; US = 3,785 litros)

gallop [ˈgæləp] N galope m ▶ VI galopar; **galloping inflation** inflación f galopante

gallows [ˈgæləuz] N horca

gallstone [ˈgɔːlstəun] N cálculo biliar

Gallup poll [ˈgæləp-] N sondeo de opinión

galore [gəˈlɔːʳ] ADV en cantidad, en abundancia

galvanize [ˈgælvənaɪz] VT (metal) galvanizar; (fig): **to ~ sb into action** mover or impulsar a algn a actuar

Gambia [ˈgæmbɪə] N Gambia

gambit [ˈgæmbɪt] N (fig): **opening ~** táctica inicial

gamble [ˈgæmbl] N (risk) jugada arriesgada;

(*bet*) apuesta ▶ vt jugar, apostar ▶ vi jugar; (*take a risk*) jugárselas; (*Comm*) especular; **to ~ on** apostar a; (*fig*) contar con, confiar en que; **to ~ on the Stock Exchange** jugar a la bolsa

gambler ['gæmblə^r] N jugador(a) *m/f*

gambling ['gæmblɪŋ] N juego

gambol ['gæmbl] vi brincar, juguetear

★**game** [geɪm] N (*gen*) juego; (*match*) partido; (*of cards*) partida; (*Hunting*) caza; **big ~** caza mayor ▶ ADJ valiente; (*ready*): **to be ~ for anything** estar dispuesto a todo ■ **games** NPL (*Scol*) deportes *mpl*

game bird N ave *f* de caza

gamekeeper ['geɪmki:pə^r] N guardabosque *mf*

gamely ['geɪmlɪ] ADV con decisión

game plan N (*for game*) plan *m* de juego; (*gen*) táctica

gamer ['geɪmə^r] N jugador(a) *m/f* de videojuegos, videojugador(a) *m/f*

game reserve N coto de caza

games console [geɪmz-] N consola de juegos

game show N programa *m* concurso *inv*, concurso

gamesmanship ['geɪmzmənʃɪp] N (uso de) artimañas *fpl* para ganar

gaming ['geɪmɪŋ] N (*gambling*) juego; (*with video games*) juegos *mpl* de ordenador *or* computadora

gammon ['gæmən] N (*bacon*) tocino ahumado; (*ham*) jamón *m* ahumado

gamut ['gæmət] N (*Mus*) gama; **to run the (whole) ~ of emotions** (*fig*) recorrer toda la gama de emociones

gander ['gændə^r] N ganso

★**gang** [gæŋ] N (*of criminals etc*) banda; (*of kids*) pandilla; (*of colleagues*) peña; (*of workmen*) brigada ▶ vi: **to ~ up on sb** conchabarse contra algn

Ganges ['gændʒi:z] N: **the ~** el Ganges

gangland ['gæŋglænd] ADJ: **~ bosses** cabecillas mafiosos; **~ killings** asesinatos entre bandas

gangling ['gæŋglɪŋ] ADJ larguirucho

gangly ['gæŋglɪ] ADJ desgarbado

gangplank ['gæŋplæŋk] N pasarela, plancha

gangrene ['gæŋgri:n] N gangrena

gangster ['gæŋstə^r] N gángster *m*

gang warfare N guerra entre bandas

gangway ['gæŋweɪ] N (*Brit: in theatre, bus etc*) pasillo; (*on ship*) pasarela

gantry ['gæntrɪ] N (*for crane, railway signal*) pórtico; (*for rocket*) torre *f* de lanzamiento

GAO N ABBR (*US: = General Accounting Office*) tribunal de cuentas

gaol [dʒeɪl] N, vt (*Brit*) = **jail**

gap [gæp] N hueco; (*in trees, traffic*) claro; (*in market, records*) laguna; (*in time*) intervalo

gape [geɪp] vi mirar boquiabierto

gaping ['geɪpɪŋ] ADJ (*hole*) muy abierto

gap year N año sabático (*antes de empezar a estudiar en la universidad*)

garage ['gærɑ:ʒ] N garaje *m*; (*for repairs*) taller *m*

garage sale N venta de objetos usados (*en el jardín de una casa particular*)

garb [gɑ:b] N atuendo

garbage ['gɑ:bɪdʒ] N (*US*) basura; (*nonsense*) bobadas *fpl*; (*inf: film, book etc*) basura

garbage can N (*US*) cubo *or* (*LAm*) balde *m or* (*LAm*) bote *m* de la basura

garbage collector N (*US*) basurero(-a)

garbage disposal unit N triturador *m* (de basura)

garbage man N (*irreg*) basurero

garbage truck N (*US*) camión *m* de la basura

garbled ['gɑ:bld] ADJ (*account, explanation*) confuso

★**garden** ['gɑ:dn] N jardín *m* ■ **gardens** NPL (*public*) parque *m*, jardines *mpl*; (*private*) huertos *mpl*

garden centre N (*Brit*) centro de jardinería

garden city N (*Brit*) ciudad *f* jardín

gardener ['gɑ:dnə^r] N jardinero(-a)

gardening ['gɑ:dnɪŋ] N jardinería

garden party N recepción *f* al aire libre

gargle ['gɑ:gl] vi hacer gárgaras, gargarear (*LAm*)

gargoyle ['gɑ:gɔɪl] N gárgola

garish ['gɛərɪʃ] ADJ chillón(-ona)

garland ['gɑ:lənd] N guirnalda

garlic ['gɑ:lɪk] N ajo

garment ['gɑ:mənt] N prenda (de vestir)

garner ['gɑ:nə^r] vt hacer acopio de

garnish ['gɑ:nɪʃ] vt adornar; (*Culin*) aderezar

garret ['gærɪt] N desván *m*, buhardilla

garrison ['gærɪsn] N guarnición *f* ▶ vt guarnecer

garrulous ['gærjuləs] ADJ charlatán(-ana)

garter ['gɑ:tə^r] N (*US*) liga

garter belt N (*US*) liguero, portaligas *m inv*

★**gas** [gæs] N gas *m*; (*US: gasoline*) gasolina; **Calor ~®** (*gas m*) butano ▶ vt asfixiar con gas

gas chamber N cámara de gas

Gascony ['gæskənɪ] N Gascuña

gas cooker N (*Brit*) cocina de gas

gas cylinder N bombona de gas

gaseous ['gæsɪəs] ADJ gaseoso

gas fire N estufa de gas

gas-fired ['gæsfaɪəd] ADJ de gas

gash [gæʃ] N brecha, raja; (*from knife*) cuchillada ▶ vt rajar; (*with knife*) acuchillar

gasket ['gæskɪt] N (*Aut*) junta

gas mask N careta antigás

gas meter N contador *m* de gas

gasoline ['gæsəli:n] N (*US*) gasolina

gasp [gɑ:sp] N grito sofocado ▶ vi (*pant*) jadear ▶ **gasp out** vt (*say*) decir jadeando

gas pedal N (*esp US*) acelerador *m*

gas ring N hornillo de gas

gas station N (US) gasolinera

gas stove N cocina de gas

gassy ['gæsɪ] ADJ con mucho gas

gas tank N (US Aut) depósito (de gasolina)

gas tap N llave f del gas

gastric ['gæstrɪk] ADJ gástrico

gastric band N banda gástrica

gastric ulcer N úlcera gástrica

gastroenteritis ['gæstrəʊɛntə'raɪtɪs] N gastroenteritis f

gasworks ['gæswɜːks] NSG, NPL fábrica de gas

★**gate** [geɪt] N (also at airport) puerta; (Rail: at level crossing) barrera; (metal) verja

gâteau ['gætəʊ] (pl **gâteaux** ['gætəʊz]) N tarta

gatecrash ['geɪtkræʃ] VT colarse en

gatecrasher ['geɪtkræʃə^r] N intruso(-a)

gated community ['geɪtɪd-] N urbanización f cerrada

gatehouse ['geɪthaʊs] N casa del guarda

gateway ['geɪtweɪ] N puerta

gather ['gæðə^r] VT (flowers, fruit) coger (SP), recoger (LAM); (assemble) reunir; (pick up) recoger; (Sewing) fruncir; (understand) sacar en consecuencia; **to ~ speed** ganar velocidad; **to ~ (from/that)** deducir (por/que) ▶ VI (assemble) reunirse; (dust) acumularse; (clouds) cerrarse; **as far as I can ~** por lo que tengo entendido

gathering ['gæðərɪŋ] N reunión f, asamblea

gauche [gəʊʃ] ADJ torpe

gaudy ['gɔːdɪ] ADJ chillón(-ona)

gauge, (US) **gage** [geɪdʒ] N calibre m; (Rail) ancho de vía, entrevía; (instrument) indicador m; **petrol ~** indicador m (del nivel) de gasolina ▶ VT medir; (fig: sb's capabilities, character) juzgar, calibrar; **to ~ the right moment** elegir el momento (oportuno)

gaunt [gɔːnt] ADJ descarnado; (fig) adusto

gauntlet ['gɔːntlɪt] N (fig): **to run the ~ of sth** exponerse a algo; **to throw down the ~** arrojar el guante

gauze [gɔːz] N gasa

gave [geɪv] PT of **give**

gawk [gɔːk] VI mirar pasmado

gawky ['gɔːkɪ] ADJ desgarbado

gay [geɪ] ADJ gay; (old: colour, person) alegre

gaze [geɪz] N mirada fija ▶ VI: **to ~ at sth** mirar algo fijamente

gazelle [gə'zɛl] N gacela

gazette [gə'zɛt] N (newspaper) gaceta; (official publication) boletín m oficial

gazetteer [gæzə'tɪə^r] N índice geográfico

gazump [gə'zʌmp] VT, VI (BRIT inf) echarse atrás en la venta ya acordada de una casa por haber una oferta más alta

GB ABBR (= Great Britain) GB

GBH N ABBR (BRIT Law: inf) = **grievous bodily harm**

GC N ABBR (BRIT: = George Cross) distinción honorífica

GCE N ABBR (BRIT: = General Certificate of Education) ≈ certificado de bachillerato

GCHQ N ABBR (BRIT: = Government Communications Headquarters) centro de intercepción de las telecomunicaciones internacionales

★**GCSE** N ABBR (BRIT: = General Certificate of Secondary Education) certificado del último ciclo de la enseñanza secundaria obligatoria

Los **GCSE** (General Certificate of Secondary Education) son exámenes realizados por estudiantes de 16 años de edad en Inglaterra, Gales e Irlanda del Norte. Es imprescindible aprobarlos para poder continuar con los estudios y realizar los A Levels de las asignaturas correspondientes (ver A Level). Los resultados de los GSCE también son importantes para los que concluyen el ciclo de educación secundaria obligatoria y se ponen a buscar trabajo. El número de asignaturas que se suelen estudiar varía entre 8 y 12. Algunas, como el inglés, las matemáticas y las ciencias, son obligatorias para todos los estudiantes.

Gdns. ABBR (= gardens) jdns

GDP N ABBR (= gross domestic product) PIB m

GDR N ABBR (History: = German Democratic Republic) RDA f

gear [gɪə^r] N equipo; (Tech) engranaje m; (Aut) velocidad f, marcha; **top** or (US) **high/low ~** quinta (or sexta)/primera; **in ~** con la marcha metida ▶ VT (fig: adapt): **to ~ sth to** adaptar or ajustar algo a; **our service is geared to meet the needs of disabled people** nuestro servicio va enfocado a responder a las necesidades de los discapacitados

▶ **gear up** VI prepararse

gear box N caja de cambios

gear lever, (US) **gear shift** N palanca de cambio

gear stick N (BRIT) = **gear lever**

gear wheel N rueda dentada

GED N ABBR (US Scol) = **general educational development**

geese [giːs] NPL of **goose**

geezer ['giːzə^r] N (BRIT inf) tipo, maromo (SP)

Geiger counter ['gaɪgə-] N contador m Geiger

gel [dʒɛl] N gel m

gelatin, gelatine ['dʒɛlətiːn] N gelatina

gelignite ['dʒɛlɪgnaɪt] N gelignita

gem [dʒɛm] N gema, piedra preciosa; (fig) joya

Gemini ['dʒɛmɪnaɪ] N Géminis m

gen [dʒɛn] N (BRIT inf): **to give sb the ~ on sth** poner a algn al tanto de algo

Gen. ABBR (Mil: = General) Gen., Gral.

gen. ABBR (= general) grl.; = **generally**

gender ['dʒɛndə^r] N género

gene [dʒiːn] N gen(e) m

genealogy [dʒiːnɪˈælədʒɪ] N genealogía

★**general** [ˈdʒɛnərl] N general *m*; **in ~** en general ▸ ADJ general; **~ audit** auditoría general; **the ~ public** el gran público

general anaesthetic, (US) **general anesthetic** N anestesia general

general delivery N (US) lista de correos

general election N elecciones *fpl* generales

generalization [dʒɛnrəlaɪˈzeɪʃən] N generalización *f*

generalize [ˈdʒɛnrəlaɪz] VI generalizar

★**generally** [ˈdʒɛnrəlɪ] ADV generalmente, en general

general manager N director(a) *m/f* general

general practitioner N médico(-a) de medicina general

general store N tienda (*que vende de todo*)

general strike N huelga general

generate [ˈdʒɛnəreɪt] VT generar

★**generation** [dʒɛnəˈreɪʃən] N generación *f*

generator [ˈdʒɛnəreɪtə'] N generador *m*

generic [dʒɪˈnɛrɪk] ADJ genérico

generosity [dʒɛnəˈrɔsɪtɪ] N generosidad *f*

★**generous** [ˈdʒɛnərəs] ADJ generoso; (*copious*) abundante

generously [ˈdʒɛnərəslɪ] ADV generosamente; abundantemente

genesis [ˈdʒɛnɪsɪs] N génesis *f*

genetic [dʒɪˈnɛtɪk] ADJ genético; **~ engineering** ingeniería genética; **~ fingerprinting** identificación *f* genética

genetically modified organism [dʒɪˈnɛtɪkəlɪ-] N organismo genéticamente modificado, organismo transgénico

genetic engineering N ingeniería genética

genetic fingerprinting [-ˈfɪŋgəprɪntɪŋ] N identificación *f* genética

genetics [dʒɪˈnɛtɪks] N genética

Geneva [dʒɪˈniːvə] N Ginebra

genial [ˈdʒiːnɪəl] ADJ afable

genitals [ˈdʒɛnɪtlz] NPL (órganos *mpl*) genitales *mpl*

genitive [ˈdʒɛnɪtɪv] N genitivo

genius [ˈdʒiːnɪəs] N genio

Genoa [ˈdʒɛnəuə] N Génova

genocide [ˈdʒɛnəusaɪd] N genocidio

genome [ˈgiːnəum] N genoma *m*

gent [dʒɛnt] N ABBR (BRIT *inf*) = **gentleman**

genteel [dʒɛnˈtiːl] ADJ fino, distinguido

★**gentle** [ˈdʒɛntl] ADJ (*sweet*) dulce; (*touch etc*) ligero, suave

★**gentleman** [ˈdʒɛntlmən] N (*irreg*) señor *m*; (*well-bred man*) caballero; **~'s agreement** acuerdo entre caballeros

gentlemanly [ˈdʒɛntlmənlɪ] ADJ caballeroso

gentleness [ˈdʒɛntlnɪs] N dulzura; (*of touch*) suavidad *f*

gently [ˈdʒɛntlɪ] ADV suavemente

gentrification [dʒɛntrɪfɪˈkeɪʃən] N aburguesamiento

gentry [ˈdʒɛntrɪ] NPL pequeña nobleza *sg*

gents [dʒɛnts] N (BRIT *inf*) servicios *mpl* (de caballeros)

★**genuine** [ˈdʒɛnjuɪn] ADJ auténtico; (*person*) sincero

genuinely [ˈdʒɛnjuɪnlɪ] ADV sinceramente

geographer [dʒɪˈɔgrəfə'] N geógrafo(-a)

geographic [dʒɪəˈgræfɪk], **geographical** [dʒɪəˈgræfɪkl] ADJ geográfico

geography [dʒɪˈɔgrəfɪ] N geografía

geolocate [dʒiːələuˈkeɪt] VT geolocalizar

geological [dʒɪəˈlɔdʒɪkl] ADJ geológico

geologist [dʒɪˈɔlədʒɪst] N geólogo(-a)

geology [dʒɪˈɔlədʒɪ] N geología

geometric [dʒɪəˈmɛtrɪk], **geometrical** [dʒɪəˈmɛtrɪkl] ADJ geométrico

geometry [dʒɪˈɔmətrɪ] N geometría

Geordie [ˈdʒɔːdɪ] N (*inf*) habitante *mf* de Tyneside

Georgia [ˈdʒɔːdʒə] N Georgia

Georgian [ˈdʒɔːdʒən] ADJ georgiano ▸ N georgiano(-a); (*Ling*) georgiano

geranium [dʒɪˈreɪnjəm] N geranio

gerbil [ˈdʒɛrbl] N gerbo

geriatric [dʒɛrɪˈætrɪk] ADJ geriátrico

germ [dʒɜːm] N (*microbe*) microbio, bacteria; (*seed*) germen *m*

★**German** [ˈdʒɜːmən] ADJ alemán(-ana) ▸ N alemán(-ana) *m/f*; (*Ling*) alemán *m*

German Democratic Republic N (*History*) República Democrática Alemana

germane [dʒɜːˈmeɪn] ADJ: **~ (to)** pertinente (a)

German measles N rubeola, rubéola

German shepherd N (*dog*) pastor *m* alemán

★**Germany** [ˈdʒɜːmənɪ] N Alemania; **East/West ~** (*History*) Alemania Oriental *or* Democrática/Occidental *or* Federal

germination [dʒɜːmɪˈneɪʃən] N germinación *f*

germ warfare N guerra bacteriológica

gesticulate [dʒɛsˈtɪkjuleɪt] VI gesticular

gesticulation [dʒɛstɪkjuˈleɪʃən] N gesticulación *f*

gesture [ˈdʒɛstjə'] N gesto; **as a ~ of friendship** en señal de amistad

---

get [gɛt]

(*pt*, *pp* **got** [gɔt], US *pp* **gotten** [ˈgɔtn]) VI
1 (*become, be*) ponerse, volverse; **to get old/tired** envejecer/cansarse; **to get drunk** emborracharse; **to get dirty** ensuciarse; **to get ready/washed** prepararse/lavarse; **to get married** casarse; **when do I get paid?** ¿cuándo me pagan *or* se me paga?; **it's getting late** se está haciendo tarde

2 (*go*): **to get to/from** llegar a/de; **to get home** llegar a casa; **he got under the fence** pasó por debajo de la barrera

3 (*begin*) empezar a; **to get to know sb** (llegar a) conocer a algn; **I'm getting to like him** me está empezando a gustar; **let's get going** or **started** ¡vamos (a empezar)!

4 (*modal aux vb*): **you've got to do it** tienes que hacerlo

▶ VT **1**: **to get sth done** (*finish*) hacer algo; (*have done*) mandar hacer algo; **to get one's hair cut** cortarse el pelo; **to get the car going** or **to go** arrancar el coche; **to get sb to do sth** conseguir or hacer que algn haga algo; **to get sth/sb ready** preparar algo/a algn

2 (*obtain: money, permission, results*) conseguir; (*find: job, flat*) encontrar; (*fetch: person, doctor*) buscar; (: *object*) ir a buscar, traer; **to get sth for sb** conseguir algo para algn; **get me Mr Jones, please** (*Tel*) póngame or (*LAM*) comuníqueme con el Sr. Jones, por favor; **can I get you a drink?** ¿quieres algo de beber?

3 (*receive: present, letter*) recibir; (*acquire: reputation*) alcanzar; (: *prize*) ganar; **what did you get for your birthday?** ¿qué te regalaron por tu cumpleaños?; **how much did you get for the painting?** ¿cuánto sacaste por el cuadro?

4 (*catch*) coger (*SP*), agarrar (*LAM*); (*hit: target etc*) dar en; **to get sb by the arm/throat** coger or agarrar a algn por el brazo/cuello; **get him!** ¡cógelo! (*SP*), ¡atrápalo! (*LAM*); **the bullet got him in the leg** la bala le dio en la pierna

5 (*take, move*) llevar; **to get sth to sb** hacer llegar algo a algn; **do you think we'll get it through the door?** ¿crees que lo podremos meter por la puerta?

6 (*catch, take: plane, bus etc*) coger (*SP*), tomar (*LAM*); **where do I get the train for Birmingham?** ¿dónde se coge or se toma el tren para Birmingham?

7 (*understand*) entender; (*hear*) oír; **I've got it!** ¡ya lo tengo!, ¡eureka!; **I don't get your meaning** no te entiendo; **I'm sorry, I didn't get your name** lo siento, no me he enterado de su nombre

8 (*have, possess*): **to have got** tener

9 (*inf: annoy*) molestar; (: *thrill*) chiflar

▶ **get about** VI salir mucho; (*news*) divulgarse

▶ **get across** VT (*message, meaning*) lograr comunicar ▶ VI: **to get across to sb** hacer que algn comprenda

▶ **get along** VI (*agree*) llevarse bien; (*depart*) marcharse; (*manage*) = **get by**

▶ **get at** VT FUS (*attack*) meterse con; (*reach*) alcanzar; (*the truth*) descubrir; **what are you getting at?** ¿qué insinúas?

▶ **get away** VI marcharse; (*escape*) escaparse

▶ **get away with** VT FUS hacer impunemente

▶ **get back** VI (*return*) volver ▶ VT recobrar

▶ **get back at** VT FUS (*inf*): **to get back at sb (for sth)** vengarse de algn (por algo)

▶ **get by** VI (*pass*) (lograr) pasar; (*manage*) arreglárselas; **I can get by in Dutch** me defiendo en holandés

▶ **get down** VI bajar(se) ▶ VT FUS bajar ▶ VT bajar; (*depress*) deprimir

▶ **get down to** VT FUS (*work*) ponerse a

▶ **get in** VI entrar; (*train*) llegar; (*arrive home*) volver a casa, regresar; (*political party*) salir ▶ VT (*bring in: harvest*) recoger; (: *coal, shopping, supplies*) comprar, traer; (*insert*) meter

▶ **get into** VT FUS entrar en; (*vehicle*) subir a; **to get into a rage** enfadarse

▶ **get off** VI (*from train etc*) bajar(se); (*depart: person, car*) marcharse ▶ VT (*remove*) quitar; (*send off*) mandar; (*have as leave: day, time*) tener libre ▶ VT FUS (*train, bus*) bajar(se) de; **to get off to a good start** (*fig*) empezar muy bien or con buen pie

▶ **get on** VI (*at exam etc*): **how are you getting on?** ¿cómo te va?; **to get on (with)** (*agree*) llevarse bien (con) ▶ VT FUS (*train, bus*) subir(se) a

▶ **get on to** VT FUS (*deal with*) ocuparse de; (*inf: contact on phone etc*) hablar con

▶ **get out** VI salir; (*of vehicle*) bajar(se); (*news*) saberse ▶ VT sacar

▶ **get out of** VT FUS salir de; (*duty etc*) escaparse de; (*gain from: pleasure, benefit*) sacar de

▶ **get over** VT FUS (*illness*) recobrarse de

▶ **get round** VT FUS rodear; (*fig: person*) engatusar a ▶ VI: **to get round to doing sth** encontrar tiempo para hacer algo

▶ **get through** VT FUS (*finish*) acabar ▶ VI (*Tel*) (lograr) comunicar

▶ **get through to** VT FUS (*Tel*) comunicar con

▶ **get together** VI reunirse ▶ VT reunir, juntar

▶ **get up** VI (*rise*) levantarse ▶ VT FUS subir; **to get up enthusiasm for sth** cobrar entusiasmo por algo

▶ **get up to** VT FUS (*reach*) llegar a; (*prank*) hacer

getaway [ˈɡɛtəweɪ] N fuga

getaway car N: **the thieves' ~** el coche en que huyeron los ladrones

get-together [ˈɡɛtəɡɛðəʳ] N reunión f; (*party*) fiesta

get-up [ˈɡɛtʌp] N (*BRIT inf: outfit*) atavío, atuendo

get-well card [ɡɛtˈwɛl-] N tarjeta en la que se desea a un enfermo que se mejore

geyser [ˈɡiːzəʳ] N (*water heater*) calentador m de agua; (*Geo*) géiser m

Ghana [ˈɡɑːnə] N Ghana

Ghanaian [ɡɑːˈneɪən] ADJ, N ghanés(-esa) m/f

ghastly [ˈɡɑːstlɪ] ADJ horrible; (*pale*) pálido

gherkin [ˈɡəːkɪn] N pepinillo

ghetto [ˈɡɛtəu] N gueto

ghetto blaster [-ˈblɑːstəʳ] N radiocas(s)et(t)e m portátil (*de gran tamaño*)

ghost [ɡəust] N fantasma m ▶ VT (*book*) escribir por otro

ghostly [ˈɡəustlɪ] ADJ fantasmal

ghost story N cuento de fantasmas

ghostwriter [ˈɡəustraɪtəʳ] N negro(-a)

ghoul [ɡuːl] N espíritu m necrófago

GHQ N ABBR (*Mil*: = *general headquarters*) cuartel *m* general

GI N ABBR (*US inf*: = *government issue*) soldado del ejército norteamericano

★**giant** ['dʒaɪənt] N gigante *mf* ▶ ADJ gigantesco, gigante; **~ (size) packet** paquete *m* (de tamaño) gigante *or* familiar

giant killer N (*Sport*) matagigantes *m inv*

gibber ['dʒɪbə'] VI farfullar

gibberish ['dʒɪbərɪʃ] N galimatías *m*

gibe [dʒaɪb] N pulla

giblets ['dʒɪblɪts] NPL menudillos *mpl*

Gibraltar [dʒɪ'brɔːltə'] N Gibraltar *m*

giddiness ['gɪdɪnɪs] N mareo

giddy ['gɪdɪ] ADJ (*dizzy*) mareado; (*height, speed*) vertiginoso; **it makes me ~** me marea; **I feel ~** me siento mareado

★**gift** [gɪft] N (*gen*) regalo; (*Comm*: *also*: **free gift**) obsequio; (*ability*) don *m*; **to have a ~ for sth** tener dotes para algo

gifted ['gɪftɪd] ADJ dotado

gift shop, (*US*) **gift store** N tienda de regalos

gift token, gift voucher N vale-regalo *m*

gig¹ [gɪg] N (*inf*: *concert*) actuación *f*

gig² [gɪg] N ABBR (*inf*: = *gigabyte*) giga *m*

gigabyte ['gɪgəbaɪt] N gigabyte *m*

gigantic [dʒaɪ'gæntɪk] ADJ gigantesco

giggle ['gɪgl] VI reírse tontamente ▶ N risilla

GIGO ['gaɪgəu] ABBR (*Comput*: *inf*) = **garbage in, garbage out**

gill [dʒɪl] N (*measure*) 0.25 *pintas* (Brit = 0,148 *litros*; US = 0,118 *litros*)

gills [gɪlz] NPL (*of fish*) branquias *fpl*, agallas *fpl*

gilt [gɪlt] ADJ, N dorado

gilt-edged ['gɪltedʒd] ADJ (*Comm*: *stocks, securities*) de máxima garantía

gimlet ['gɪmlɪt] N barrena de mano

gimmick ['gɪmɪk] N reclamo; **sales ~** reclamo promocional

gimmicky ['gɪmɪkɪ] ADJ de reclamo

gin [dʒɪn] N (*liquor*) ginebra

ginger ['dʒɪndʒə'] N jengibre *m*

ginger ale N ginger ale *m*

ginger beer N refresco *m* de jengibre

gingerbread ['dʒɪndʒəbred] N pan *m* de jengibre

ginger-haired [dʒɪndʒə'heəd] ADJ pelirrojo

gingerly ['dʒɪndʒəlɪ] ADV con pies de plomo

ginseng ['dʒɪnsen] N ginseng *m*

gipsy ['dʒɪpsɪ] N gitano(-a)

★**giraffe** [dʒɪ'rɑːf] N jirafa

girder ['gə:də'] N viga

girdle ['gə:dl] N (*corset*) faja ▶ VT ceñir

★**girl** [gə:l] N (*small*) niña; (*young woman*) chica, joven *f*, muchacha; **an English ~** una (chica) inglesa

girl band N girl band *m* (*grupo musical de chicas*)

★**girlfriend** ['gə:lfrend] N (*female friend*) amiga; (*romantic partner*) novia

Girl Guide N exploradora

girlish ['gə:lɪʃ] ADJ de niña

Girl Scout N (*US*) = **Girl Guide**

giro ['dʒaɪrəu] N (*BRIT*: *bank giro*) giro bancario; (: *post office giro*) giro postal

girth [gə:θ] N circunferencia; (*of saddle*) cincha

gist [dʒɪst] N lo esencial

★**give** [gɪv] (*pt* **gave** [geɪv], *pp* **given** ['gɪvn]) VT dar; (*deliver*) entregar; (*as gift*) regalar; **to ~ sb sth, ~ sth to sb** dar algo a algn; **how much did you ~ for it?** ¿cuánto pagaste por él?; **12 o'clock, ~ or take a few minutes** más o menos las doce; **~ them my regards** dales recuerdos de mi parte; **I can ~ you 10 minutes** le puedo conceder 10 minutos ▶ VI (*break*) romperse; (*stretch*: *fabric*) dar de sí; **to ~ way** (*BRIT Aut*) ceder el paso; **to ~ way to despair** ceder a la desesperación

▶ **give away** VT (*give free*) regalar; (*betray*) traicionar; (*disclose*) revelar

▶ **give back** VT devolver

▶ **give in** VI ceder ▶ VT entregar

▶ **give off** VT despedir

▶ **give out** VT distribuir ▶ VI (*be exhausted*: *supplies*) agotarse; (*fail*: *engine*) averiarse; (: *strength*) fallar

▶ **give up** VI rendirse, darse por vencido ▶ VT renunciar a; **to ~ up smoking** dejar de fumar; **to ~ o.s. up** entregarse

give-and-take ['gɪvənd'teɪk] N (*inf*) toma y daca *m*

giveaway ['gɪvəweɪ] N (*inf*): **her expression was a ~** su expresión la delataba; **the exam was a ~!** ¡el examen estaba tirado! ▶ CPD: **~ prices** precios *mpl* de regalo

given ['gɪvn] PP *of* **give** ▶ ADJ (*fixed*: *time, amount*) determinado ▶ CONJ: **~ (that) ...** dado (que) ...; **~ the circumstances ...** dadas las circunstancias ...

glacial ['gleɪsɪəl] ADJ glacial

glacier ['glæsɪə'] N glaciar *m*

★**glad** [glæd] ADJ contento; **to be ~ about sth/that** alegrarse de algo/de que; **I was ~ of his help** agradecí su ayuda

gladden ['glædn] VT alegrar

glade [gleɪd] N claro

gladiator ['glædɪeɪtə'] N gladiador *m*

gladioli [glædɪ'əulaɪ] NPL gladiolos *mpl*

gladly ['glædlɪ] ADV con mucho gusto

glamorous ['glæmərəs] ADJ con glamour, glam(o)uroso

glamour, (*US*) **glamor** ['glæmə'] N encanto, atractivo

glance [glɑːns] N ojeada, mirada ▶ VI: **to ~ at** echar una ojeada a

▶ **glance off** VT FUS (*bullet*) rebotar en

glancing ['glɑːnsɪŋ] ADJ (*blow*) oblicuo

gland [glænd] N glándula

glandular [ˈglændjuləʳ] ADJ: **~ fever** mononucleosis f infecciosa

glare [glɛəʳ] N deslumbramiento, brillo ▸ VI deslumbrar; **to ~ at** mirar con odio

glaring [ˈglɛərɪŋ] ADJ (*mistake*) manifiesto

★glass [glɑːs] N vidrio, cristal m; (*for drinking*) vaso; (*with stem*) copa; (*also:* **looking glass**) espejo

glass-blowing [ˈglɑːsbləʊɪŋ] N soplado de vidrio

glass ceiling N (*fig*) techo *or* barrera invisible (*que impide ascender profesionalmente a las mujeres o miembros de minorías étnicas*)

glasses [ˈglɑːsəz] NPL gafas *fpl*, anteojos *mpl* (LAM)

glass fibre, (US) **glass fiber** N fibra de vidrio

glasshouse [ˈglɑːshaʊs] N invernadero

glassware [ˈglɑːswɛəʳ] N cristalería

glassy [ˈglɑːsɪ] ADJ (*eyes*) vidrioso

Glaswegian [glæsˈwiːdʒən] ADJ de Glasgow ▸ N nativo(-a) *or* habitante *m/f* de Glasgow

glaze [gleɪz] VT (*window*) acristalar; (*pottery*) vidriar; (*Culin*) glasear ▸ N barniz *m*; (*Culin*) glaseado

glazed [gleɪzd] ADJ (*eye*) vidrioso; (*pottery*) vidriado

glazier [ˈgleɪzɪəʳ] N vidriero(-a)

gleam [gliːm] N destello; **a ~ of hope** un rayo de esperanza ▸ VI relucir

gleaming [ˈgliːmɪŋ] ADJ reluciente

glean [gliːn] VT (*gather: information*) recoger

glee [gliː] N alegría, regocijo

gleeful [ˈgliːful] ADJ alegre

glen [glɛn] N cañada

glib [glɪb] ADJ (*person*) de mucha labia; (*comment*) fácil

glibly [ˈglɪblɪ] ADV (*explain*) con mucha labia

glide [glaɪd] VI deslizarse; (*Aviat, bird*) planear

glider [ˈglaɪdəʳ] N (*Aviat*) planeador *m*

gliding [ˈglaɪdɪŋ] N (*Aviat*) vuelo sin motor

glimmer [ˈglɪməʳ] N luz *f* tenue; (*of hope*) rayo

glimpse [glɪmps] N vislumbre *m*; **to catch a ~ of** vislumbrar ▸ VT vislumbrar, entrever

glint [glɪnt] N destello; (*in the eye*) chispa ▸ VI centellear

glisten [ˈglɪsn] VI relucir, brillar

glitter [ˈglɪtəʳ] VI relucir, brillar ▸ N brillo

glittering [ˈglɪtərɪŋ] ADJ reluciente, brillante

glitz [glɪts] N (*inf*) vistosidad *f*

gloat [gləʊt] VI: **to ~ over** regodearse con

★global [ˈgləʊbl] ADJ (*world-wide*) mundial; (*comprehensive*) global

globalization [gləʊbəlaɪzeɪʃən] N globalización *f*, mundialización *f*

global warming [-ˈwɔːmɪŋ] N (re)calentamiento global *or* de la tierra

globe [gləʊb] N globo, esfera; (*model*) bola del mundo; globo terráqueo

globetrotter [ˈgləʊbtrɔtəʳ] N trotamundos *mf*

globule [ˈglɔbjuːl] N glóbulo

gloom [gluːm] N penumbra; (*sadness*) desaliento, melancolía

gloomily [ˈgluːmɪlɪ] ADV tristemente; de modo pesimista

gloomy [ˈgluːmɪ] ADJ (*dark*) oscuro; (*sad*) triste; (*pessimistic*) pesimista; **to feel ~** sentirse pesimista

glorification [glɔːrɪfɪˈkeɪʃən] N glorificación *f*

glorify [ˈglɔːrɪfaɪ] VT glorificar

glorious [ˈglɔːrɪəs] ADJ glorioso; (*weather, sunshine*) espléndido

glory [ˈglɔːrɪ] N gloria

gloss [glɔs] N (*shine*) brillo; (*also:* **gloss paint**) (pintura) esmalte *m*
▸ **gloss over** VT FUS restar importancia a; (*omit*) pasar por alto

glossary [ˈglɔsərɪ] N glosario

glossy [ˈglɔsɪ] ADJ lustroso; (*hair*) brillante; (*photograph*) con brillo; (*magazine*) de papel satinado *or* cuché

glove [glʌv] N guante *m*

glove compartment N (*Aut*) guantera

glow [gləʊ] VI (*shine*) brillar ▸ N brillo

glower [ˈglaʊəʳ] VI: **to ~ at** mirar con ceño

glowing [ˈgləʊɪŋ] ADJ (*fire*) vivo; (*complexion*) encendido; (*fig: report, description*) entusiasta

glow-worm [ˈgləʊwəːm] N luciérnaga

glucose [ˈgluːkəʊs] N glucosa

glue [gluː] N pegamento, cemento (LAM) ▸ VT pegar

glue-sniffing [ˈgluːsnɪfɪŋ] N inhalación *f* de pegamento *or* (LAM) cemento

glum [glʌm] ADJ (*mood*) abatido; (*person, tone*) melancólico

glut [glʌt] N superabundancia

glute [gluːt] N (*inf*) glúteo

glutinous [ˈgluːtɪnəs] ADJ glutinoso, pegajoso

glutton [ˈglʌtn] N glotón(-ona) *m/f*; **~ for punishment** masoquista *mf*

gluttony [ˈglʌtənɪ] N gula, glotonería

glycerin, glycerine [ˈglɪsəriːn] N glicerina

GM ADJ ABBR (= *genetically-modified*) transgénico

gm ABBR (= *gram*) g

GMAT N ABBR (*US*: = *Graduate Management Admissions Test*) examen de admisión al segundo ciclo de la enseñanza superior

GMB N ABBR (*BRIT*) = **General, Municipal, Boilermakers and Allied Trade Union**

GM crop N cultivo transgénico

GM foods N alimentos *mpl* transgénicos

GMO N ABBR (= *genetically modified organism*) organismo transgénico, OGM *m*

GMT ABBR (= *Greenwich Mean Time*) GMT

gnarled [nɑːld] ADJ nudoso

gnash [næʃ] VT: **to ~ one's teeth** hacer rechinar los dientes

gnat [næt] N mosquito

gnaw [nɔː] VT roer

gnome [nəum] N gnomo

GNP N ABBR (= *gross national product*) PNB m

GNVQ N ABBR (BRIT: = *general national vocational qualification*) título general de formación profesional

★**go** [gəu] (*pt* **went** [wɛnt], *pp* **gone** [gɔn]) VI ir; (*travel*) viajar; (*depart*) irse, marcharse; (*work*) funcionar, marchar; (*be sold*) venderse; (*time*) pasar; (*become*) ponerse; (*break etc*) estropearse, romperse; **to go by car/on foot** ir en coche/a pie; **he's going to do it** va a hacerlo; **to go for a walk** ir a dar un paseo; **to go dancing** ir a bailar; **to go looking for sth/sb** ir a buscar algo/a algn; **to make sth go, get sth going** poner algo en marcha; **my voice has gone** he perdido la voz; **the cake is all gone** se acabó la tarta; **the money will go towards our holiday** el dinero es para (ayuda de) nuestras vacaciones; **how did it go?** ¿qué tal salió *or* resultó?, ¿cómo ha ido?; **the meeting went well** la reunión salió bien; **to go and see sb** ir a ver a algn; **to go to sleep** dormirse; **I'll take whatever is going** acepto lo que haya; **... to go** (US: *food*) ... para llevar ▸ N (*pl* **goes**): **to have a go (at)** probar suerte (con); **to be on the go** no parar; **whose go is it?** ¿a quién le toca?
▸ **go about** VI (*rumour*) propagarse; (*also:* **go round**: *wander*) andar (de un sitio para otro) ▸ VT FUS: **how do I go about this?** ¿cómo me las arreglo para hacer esto?; **to go about one's business** ocuparse de sus asuntos
▸ **go after** VT FUS (*pursue*) perseguir; (*job, record etc*) andar tras
▸ **go against** VT FUS (*be unfavourable to*: *results*) ir en contra de; (*be contrary to*: *principles*) ser contrario a
▸ **go ahead** VI seguir adelante
▸ **go along** VI ir ▸ VT FUS bordear; **as you go along** sobre la marcha
▸ **go along with** VT FUS (*accompany*) acompañar; (*agree with*: *idea*) estar de acuerdo con
▸ **go around** VI = **go round**
▸ **go away** VI irse, marcharse
▸ **go back** VI volver
▸ **go back on** VT FUS (*promise*) faltar a
▸ **go by** VI (*years, time*) pasar ▸ VT FUS guiarse por
▸ **go down** VI bajar; (*ship*) hundirse; (*sun*) ponerse; **that should go down well with him** eso le va a gustar; **he's gone down with flu** ha cogido la gripe ▸ VT FUS bajar por
▸ **go for** VT FUS (*fetch*) ir por; (*like*) gustar; (*attack*) atacar
▸ **go in** VI entrar
▸ **go in for** VT FUS (*competition*) presentarse a
▸ **go into** VT FUS entrar en; (*investigate*) investigar; (*embark on*) dedicarse a
▸ **go off** VI irse, marcharse; (*food*) pasarse; (*lights etc*) apagarse; (*explode*) estallar; (*event*) realizarse; **the party went off well** la fiesta salió bien ▸ VT FUS perder el interés por; **I'm going off him/the idea** ya no me gusta tanto él/la idea
▸ **go on** VI (*continue*) seguir, continuar; (*lights*)

encenderse; (*happen*) pasar, ocurrir; (*be guided by*: *evidence etc*) partir de; **to go on doing sth** seguir haciendo algo; **what's going on here?** ¿qué pasa aquí?
▸ **go on at** VT FUS (*nag*) soltarle el rollo a
▸ **go out** VI salir; (*fire, light*) apagarse; (*ebb*: *tide*) bajar, menguar; **to go out with sb** salir con algn
▸ **go over** VI (*ship*) zozobrar ▸ VT FUS (*check*) revisar; **to go over sth in one's mind** repasar algo mentalmente
▸ **go past** VI, VT FUS pasar
▸ **go round** VI (*circulate*: *news, rumour*) correr; (*suffice*) alcanzar, bastar; (*revolve*) girar, dar vueltas; (*make a detour*): **to go round (by)** dar la vuelta (por); (*visit*): **to go round (to sb's)** pasar a ver (a algn) ▸ VT FUS: **to go round the back** pasar por detrás
▸ **go through** VT FUS (*town etc*) atravesar; (*search through*) revisar; (*perform*: *ceremony*) realizar; (*examine*: *list, book*) repasar
▸ **go through with** VT FUS (*plan, crime*) llevar a cabo; **I couldn't go through with it** no pude llevarlo a cabo
▸ **go together** VI entenderse
▸ **go under** VI (*sink*: *ship, person*) hundirse; (*fig*: *business, firm*) quebrar
▸ **go up** VI subir; **to go up in flames** estallar en llamas
▸ **go with** VT FUS (*accompany*) ir con; (*fit, suit*) hacer juego con, acompañar a
▸ **go without** VT FUS pasarse sin

goad [gəud] VT aguijonear

go-ahead ['gəuəhɛd] ADJ emprendedor(a) ▸ N luz f verde; **to give sth/sb the ~** dar luz verde a algo/algn

★**goal** [gəul] N meta, arco (LAm); (*score*) gol m

goal difference N diferencia por goles

goalie ['gəulɪ] N (*inf*) = **goalkeeper**

goalkeeper ['gəulkiːpəʳ] N portero, guardameta mf, arquero (LAm)

goal post N poste m (de la portería)

goat [gəut] N cabra

gobble ['gɔbl] VT (*also:* **gobble down**, **gobble up**) engullir

go-between ['gəubɪtwiːn] N intermediario(-a)

Gobi Desert ['gəubɪ-] N Desierto de Gobi

goblet ['gɔblɪt] N copa

goblin ['gɔblɪn] N duende m

go-cart ['gəukɑːt] N = **go-kart**

god [gɔd] N dios m; **G~** Dios m

god-awful [gɔd'ɔːfəl] ADJ (*inf*) de puta pena

godchild ['gɔdtʃaɪld] N (*irreg*) ahijado(-a)

goddamn ['gɔddæm] ADJ (*inf*: *also*: **goddamned**) maldito, puñetero ▸ EXCL: **~!** ¡cagüen diez!

goddaughter ['gɔddɔːtəʳ] N ahijada

goddess ['gɔdɪs] N diosa

godfather ['gɔdfɑːðəʳ] N padrino

god-fearing ['gɔdfɪərɪŋ] ADJ temeroso de Dios

god-forsaken ['gɔdfəseɪkən] ADJ dejado de la mano de Dios

godmother [ˈgɔdmʌðəʳ] N madrina

godparents [ˈgɔdpɛərənts] NPL: **the ~** los padrinos

godsend [ˈgɔdsɛnd] N: **to be a ~** venir como llovido del cielo

godson [ˈgɔdsʌn] N ahijado

goes [gəuz] VB see **go**

gofer [ˈgəufəʳ] N (inf) chico(-a) para todo

go-getter [ˈgəugɛtəʳ] N ambicioso(-a)

goggle [ˈgɔgl] VI: **to ~ (at)** mirar con ojos desorbitados

goggles [ˈgɔglz] NPL (Aut) gafas fpl, anteojos mpl (LAm); (diver's) gafas fpl submarinas

going [ˈgəuɪŋ] N (conditions) cosas fpl; **it was slow ~** las cosas iban lentas ▶ ADJ: **the ~ rate** la tarifa corriente or en vigor

going-over [ˈgəuɪŋˈəuvəʳ] N (inf) revisión f; (beating) paliza

goings-on [ˈgəuɪŋzˈɔn] NPL (inf) tejemanejes mpl

go-kart [ˈgəukɑːt] N kart m

★**gold** [gəuld] N oro ▶ ADJ (reserves) de oro

golden [ˈgəuldn] ADJ (made of gold) de oro; (colour) dorado

Golden Age N Siglo de Oro

golden handshake N cuantiosa gratificación por los servicios prestados

golden rule N regla de oro

goldfish [ˈgəuldfɪʃ] N pez m de colores

gold leaf N pan m de oro

gold medal N (Sport) medalla de oro

goldmine [ˈgəuldmaɪn] N mina de oro

gold-plated [ˈgəuldˈpleɪtɪd] ADJ chapado en oro

goldsmith [ˈgəuldsmɪθ] N orfebre mf

gold standard N patrón m oro

★**golf** [gɔlf] N golf m

golf ball N (for game) pelota de golf

golf club N club m de golf; (stick) palo (de golf)

golf course N campo de golf

golfer [ˈgɔlfəʳ] N jugador(a) m/f de golf, golfista mf

golfing [ˈgɔlfɪŋ] N: **to go ~** jugar al golf

gondola [ˈgɔndələ] N góndola

gondolier [gɔndəˈlɪəʳ] N gondolero

★**gone** [gɔn] PP of **go**

goner [ˈgɔnəʳ] N (inf): **to be a ~** estar en las últimas

gong [gɔŋ] N gong m

gonorrhea [gɔnəˈrɪə] N gonorrea

★**good** [gud] ADJ bueno; (before nmsg) buen; (well-behaved) educado; **he's ~ at it** se le da bien; **to be ~ for** servir para; **it's ~ for you** te hace bien; **would you be ~ enough to …?** ¿podría hacerme el favor de …?, ¿sería tan amable de …?; **that's very ~ of you** es usted muy amable; **to feel ~** sentirse bien; **it's ~ to see you** me alegro de

verte; **a ~ deal (of)** mucho; **a ~ many** muchos; **is this any ~?** (will it do?) ¿sirve esto?; (what's it like?) ¿qué tal es esto?; **it's a ~ thing you were there** menos mal que estabas allí; **to make ~** reparar; **~!** ¡qué bien!; **~ morning/afternoon** ¡buenos días/buenas tardes!; **~ evening!** ¡buenas noches!; **~ night!** ¡buenas noches! ▶ N bien m; **for ~** (for ever) para siempre, definitivamente; **it's no ~ complaining** no sirve de nada quejarse; **he's up to no ~** está tramando algo; **for the common ~** para el bien común; see also **goods**

goodbye [gudˈbaɪ] EXCL ¡adiós!; **to say ~ (to)** (person) despedirse (de)

good faith N buena fe f

good-for-nothing [ˈgudfənʌθɪŋ] N inútil mf

Good Friday N Viernes m Santo

good-humoured [ˈgudˈhjuːməd] ADJ (person) afable, de buen humor; (remark, joke) bien intencionado

good-looking [ˈgudˈlukɪŋ] ADJ guapo

good-natured [ˈgudˈneɪtʃəd] ADJ (person) de buen carácter; (discussion) cordial

goodness [ˈgudnɪs] N (of person) bondad f; **for ~ sake!** ¡por Dios!; **~ gracious!** ¡madre mía!

★**goods** [gudz] NPL bienes mpl; (Comm etc) géneros mpl, mercancías fpl, artículos mpl; **all his ~ and chattels** todos sus bienes

goods train N (BRIT) tren m de mercancías

goodwill [gudˈwɪl] N buena voluntad f; (Comm) fondo de comercio; (customer connections) clientela

goody-goody [ˈgudɪgudɪ] N (pej) santurrón(-ona) m/f

gooey [ˈguːɪ] ADJ (inf) pegajoso; (cake, behaviour) empalagoso

Google® [ˈguːgl] N Google® m ▶ VT buscar en Google®

goose [guːs] (pl **geese** [giːs]) N ganso, oca

gooseberry [ˈguzbərɪ] N grosella espinosa or silvestre; **to play ~** hacer de carabina

gooseflesh [ˈguːsflɛʃ] N, **goosepimples** [ˈguːspɪmplz] NPL carne f de gallina

goose step N (Mil) paso de la oca

GOP N ABBR (US Pol: inf: = Grand Old Party) Partido Republicano

gopher [ˈgəufəʳ] N = **gofer**

gore [gɔːʳ] VT dar una cornada a, cornear ▶ N sangre f

gorge [gɔːdʒ] N garganta ▶ VR: **to ~ o.s. (on)** atracarse (de)

gorgeous [ˈgɔːdʒəs] ADJ precioso; (weather) estupendo; (person) guapísimo

gorilla [gəˈrɪlə] N gorila m

gormless [ˈgɔːmlɪs] ADJ (inf) ceporro, zoquete

gorse [gɔːs] N tojo

gory [ˈgɔːrɪ] ADJ sangriento

gosh [gɔʃ] (inf) EXCL ¡cielos!

go-slow [ˈgəuˈsləu] N (BRIT) huelga de celo

575

gospel ['gɔspl] N evangelio

gossamer ['gɔsəmə'] N gasa

gossip ['gɔsɪp] N cotilleo; (*person*) cotilla *mf*; **a piece of ~** un cotilleo ▶ vɪ cotillear, comadrear (*LAм*)

gossip column N ecos *mpl* de sociedad

★**got** [gɔt] PT, PP *of* **get**

Gothic ['gɔθɪk] ADJ gótico

gotten ['gɔtn] (*US*) PP *of* **get**

gouge [gaudʒ] vᴛ (*also:* **gouge out:** *hole etc*) excavar; (*initials*) grabar; **to ~ sb's eyes out** sacar los ojos a algn

goulash ['guːlæʃ] N g(o)ulash *m*

gourd [guəd] N calabaza

gourmet ['guəmeɪ] N gastrónomo(-a) ▶ ADJ gourmet *inv*

gout [gaut] N gota

govern ['gʌvən] vᴛ (*gen*) gobernar; (*event, conduct*) regir

governess ['gʌvənɪs] N institutriz *f*

governing ['gʌvənɪŋ] ADJ (*Pol*) de gobierno, gubernamental; **~ body** organismo de gobierno

★**government** ['gʌvnmənt] N gobierno; **local ~** administración *f* municipal

governmental [gʌvn'mentl] ADJ gubernamental

government stock N papel *m* del Estado

governor ['gʌvənə'] N gobernador(a) *m/f*; (*of school etc*) miembro del consejo; (*of jail*) director(a) *m/f*

Govt ABBR (= *Government*) gobno.

gown [gaun] N vestido; (*of teacher, judge*) toga

★**GP** N ABBR (*Med*) = **general practitioner**

GPO N ABBR (*BRIT old*) = **General Post Office**; (*US*) = **Government Printing Office**

GPS N ABBR (= *global positioning system*) GPS *m*

gr. ABBR (*Comm*: = *gross*) bto.

★**grab** [græb] vᴛ agarrar, coger (*SP*); **to ~ at** intentar agarrar

grace [greɪs] N (*Rel*) gracia; (*gracefulness*) elegancia, gracia; (*graciousness*) cortesía, gracia; **5 days' ~** un plazo de 5 días; **to say ~** bendecir la mesa; **his sense of humour is his saving ~** lo que le salva es su sentido del humor ▶ vᴛ (*favour*) honrar; (*adorn*) adornar

graceful ['greɪsful] ADJ grácil, ágil; (*style, shape*) elegante, gracioso

gracious ['greɪʃəs] ADJ amable ▶ EXCL: **good ~!** ¡Dios mío!

★**grade** [greɪd] N (*quality*) clase *f*, calidad *f*; (*in hierarchy*) grado; (*Scol: mark*) nota; (*US: Scol*) curso; (: *gradient*) pendiente *f*, cuesta; **to make the ~** (*fig*) dar el nivel ▶ vᴛ clasificar; *see also* **high school**

grade crossing N (*US*) paso a nivel

grade school N (*US*) escuela primaria; *see also* **elementary school**

gradient ['greɪdɪənt] N pendiente *f*

gradual ['grædjuəl] ADJ gradual

★**gradually** ['grædjuəlɪ] ADV gradualmente

★**graduate** N ['grædjuɪt] licenciado(-a), graduado(-a), egresado(-a) (*LAм*); (*US Scol*) bachiller *mf* ▶ vɪ ['grædjueɪt] licenciarse, graduarse, recibirse (*LAм*); (*US*) obtener el título de bachillerato

graduated pension ['grædjueɪtɪd-] N pensión *f* escalonada

graduation [grædju'eɪʃən] N graduación *f*; (*US Scol*) entrega de los títulos de bachillerato

graffiti [grə'fiːtɪ] NPL pintadas *fpl*

graft [grɑːft] N (*Agr, Med*) injerto; (*bribery*) corrupción *f*; **hard ~** (*inf*) trabajo duro ▶ vᴛ injertar

grain [greɪn] N (*single particle*) grano; (*no pl: cereals*) cereales *mpl*; (*US: corn*) trigo; (*in wood*) veta

gram [græm] N gramo

grammar ['græmə'] N gramática

grammar school N (*BRIT*) ≈ instituto (de segunda enseñanza); (*US*) escuela primaria; *see also* **comprehensive (school)**

grammatical [grə'mætɪkl] ADJ gramatical

gramme [græm] N = **gram**

gramophone ['græməfəun] N (*BRIT*) gramófono

gran [græn] (*inf*) N (*BRIT*) abuelita

granary ['grænərɪ] N granero

grand [grænd] ADJ magnífico, imponente; (*wonderful*) estupendo; (*gesture etc*) grandioso ▶ N (*US inf*) mil dólares *mpl*

grandad ['grændæd] (*inf*) N = **granddad**

grandchild ['græntʃaɪld] N (*irreg*) nieto(-a)

granddad ['grændæd] N (*inf*) yayo, abuelito

★**granddaughter** ['grændɔːtə'] N nieta

grandeur ['grændjə'] N grandiosidad *f*

★**grandfather** ['grænfɑːðə'] N abuelo

grandiose ['grændɪəuz] ADJ grandioso; (*pej*) pomposo

grand jury N (*US*) jurado de acusación

grandma ['grænmɑː] N (*inf*) yaya, abuelita

★**grandmother** ['grænmʌðə'] N abuela

grandpa ['grænpɑː] N (*inf*) = **granddad**

★**grandparents** ['grændpɛərənts] NPL abuelos *mpl*

grand piano N piano de cola

Grand Prix ['grɑ̃ː'priː] N (*Aut*) gran premio, Grand Prix *m*

★**grandson** ['grænsʌn] N nieto

grandstand ['grændstænd] N (*Sport*) tribuna

grand total N suma total, total *m*

granite ['grænɪt] N granito

granny ['grænɪ] N (*inf*) abuelita, yaya

grant [grɑːnt] vᴛ (*concede*) conceder; (*admit*): **to ~ (that)** reconocer (que); **to take sth for granted** dar algo por sentado ▶ N (*Scol*) beca

granular ['grænjulə'] ADJ granular; (detailed) detallado

granulated sugar ['grænjuleitid-] N (BRIT) azúcar m granulado

granule ['grænju:l] N gránulo

★**grape** [greip] N uva; **a bunch of grapes** un racimo de uvas; **sour grapes** (fig) envidia sg

grapefruit ['greipfru:t] N pomelo, toronja (LAM)

grape juice N jugo or (SP) zumo de uva

grapevine ['greipvain] N vid f, parra; **I heard it on the ~** (fig) me enteré, me lo contaron

graph [grɑ:f] N gráfica

graphic ['græfik] ADJ gráfico

graphic designer N diseñador(a) m/f gráfico(-a)

graphic equalizer N ecualizador m gráfico

graphics ['græfiks] N (art, process) artes fpl gráficas ▶ NPL (drawings, Comput) gráficos mpl

graphite ['græfait] N grafito

graph paper N papel m cuadriculado

grapple ['græpl] VI: **to ~ with a problem** enfrentarse a un problema

grappling iron ['græpliŋ-] N (Naut) rezón m

grasp [grɑ:sp] VT agarrar, asir; (understand) comprender ▶ N (grip) asimiento; (reach) alcance m; (understanding) comprensión f; **to have a good ~ of** (subject) dominar
▶ **grasp at** VT FUS (rope etc) tratar de agarrar; (fig: opportunity) aprovechar

grasping ['grɑ:spiŋ] ADJ avaro

★**grass** [grɑ:s] N hierba; (lawn) césped m; (pasture) pasto; (inf: informer) soplón(-ona) m/f

grasshopper ['grɑ:shɔpə'] N saltamontes m inv

grassland ['grɑ:slænd] N pradera, pampa (LAM)

grass roots ADJ de base ▶ NPL (Pol) bases fpl

grass snake N culebra

grassy ['grɑ:si] ADJ cubierto de hierba

grate [greit] N parrilla ▶ VI chirriar, rechinar ▶ VT (Culin) rallar

grateful ['greitful] ADJ agradecido

gratefully ['greitfəli] ADV con agradecimiento

grater ['greitə'] N rallador m

gratification [grætifi'keiʃən] N satisfacción f

gratify ['grætifai] VT complacer; (whim) satisfacer

gratifying ['grætifaiŋ] ADJ gratificante

grating ['greitiŋ] N (iron bars) rejilla ▶ ADJ (noise) chirriante

gratitude ['grætitju:d] N agradecimiento

gratuitous [grə'tju:itəs] ADJ gratuito

gratuity [grə'tju:iti] N gratificación f

grave [greiv] N tumba ▶ ADJ serio, grave

gravedigger ['greivdigə'] N sepulturero(-a)

gravel ['grævl] N grava

gravely ['greivli] ADV seriamente; **~ ill** muy grave

gravestone ['greivstəun] N lápida

graveyard ['greivja:d] N cementerio, camposanto

gravitate ['græviteit] VI gravitar

gravitation [grævi'teiʃən] N gravitación f

gravity ['græviti] N gravedad f; (seriousness) seriedad f

gravy ['greivi] N salsa de carne

gravy boat N salsera

gravy train N (inf): **to get on the ~** coger un chollo

gray [grei] ADJ (US) = **grey**

graze [greiz] VI pacer ▶ VT (touch lightly, scrape) rozar ▶ N (Med) rozadura

grazing ['greiziŋ] N (for livestock) pastoreo

grease [gri:s] N (fat) grasa; (lubricant) lubricante m ▶ VT engrasar; **to ~ the skids** (US fig) engrasar el mecanismo

grease gun N pistola engrasadora

greasepaint ['gri:speint] N maquillaje m

greaseproof ['gri:spru:f] ADJ a prueba de grasa; (BRIT: paper) de grasa

greasy ['gri:si] ADJ (hands, clothes) grasiento; (road, surface) resbaladizo

★**great** [greit] ADJ grande; (before n sing) gran; (inf) estupendo, macanudo (LAM), regio (LAM); (pain, heat) intenso; **we had a ~ time** nos lo pasamos muy bien; **they're ~ friends** son íntimos or muy amigos; **the ~ thing is that ...** lo bueno es que ...; **it was ~!** ¡fue estupendo!

Great Barrier Reef N Gran Barrera de Coral

★**Great Britain** N Gran Bretaña

> Aunque con frecuencia se usan los términos **Great Britain** (Gran Bretaña) y United Kindgom (Reino Unido) como si fueran sinónimos, no describen la misma realidad. Gran Bretaña comprende la unión de Inglaterra, Gales y Escocia, nacida en 1707. El Reino Unido, por otra parte, comprende Gran Bretaña y también Irlanda del Norte.

greater ['greitə'] ADJ mayor; **G~ London** el área metropolitana de Londres

greatest ['greitist] ADJ (el/la) mayor

great-grandchild [greit'grændtʃaild] N (irreg) bisnieto(-a)

great-grandfather [greit'grændfɑ:ðə'] N bisabuelo

great-grandmother [greit'grændmʌðə'] N bisabuela

Great Lakes NPL: **the ~** los Grandes Lagos

greatly ['greitli] ADV muy; (with verb) mucho

greatness ['greitnis] N grandeza

★**Greece** [gri:s] N Grecia

greed [gri:d] N (also: **greediness**) codicia; (for food) gula; (for power etc) avidez f

greedily ['gri:dili] ADV con avidez

greedy ['gri:di] ADJ codicioso; (for food) glotón(-ona)

577

Greek [griːk] ADJ griego ▸ N griego(-a); (*Ling*) griego; **ancient/modern ~** griego antiguo/moderno

★**green** [griːn] ADJ verde; (*inexperienced*) novato; **the G~ party** (*Pol*) el partido verde; **to have ~ fingers** (*fig*) tener buena mano para las plantas ▸ N verde *m*; (*stretch of grass*) césped *m*; (*of golf course*) campo, green *m* ■ **greens** NPL verduras *fpl*

green belt N cinturón *m* verde

green card N (*Aut*) carta verde; (*US: work permit*) *permiso de trabajo para los extranjeros en EE. UU.*

greenery [ˈgriːnərɪ] N vegetación *f*

greenfly [ˈgriːnflaɪ] N pulgón *m*

greengage [ˈgriːngeɪdʒ] N (ciruela) claudia

greengrocer [ˈgriːngrəʊsəʳ] N (*Brit*) frutero(-a), verdulero(-a)

greenhouse [ˈgriːnhaʊs] N invernadero

greenhouse effect N efecto invernadero

greenhouse gas N gas *m* que produce el efecto invernadero

greenish [ˈgriːnɪʃ] ADJ verdoso

Greenland [ˈgriːnlənd] N Groenlandia

Greenlander [ˈgriːnləndəʳ] N groenlandés(-esa) *m/f*

green light N luz *f* verde

green pepper N pimiento verde

green salad N ensalada *f* (*de lechuga, pepino, pimiento verde etc*)

green tax N ecotasa, impuesto ecológico; impuesto ambiental

greet [griːt] VT saludar; (*news*) recibir

greeting [ˈgriːtɪŋ] N (*gen*) saludo; (*welcome*) bienvenida; **greetings** saludos *mpl*; **season's greetings** Felices Pascuas

greetings card N tarjeta de felicitación

gregarious [grəˈgɛərɪəs] ADJ gregario

Grenada [grɛˈneɪdə] N Granada

grenade [grəˈneɪd] N (*also*: **hand grenade**) granada

grew [gruː] PT *of* **grow**

★**grey** [greɪ] ADJ gris; **to go ~** salirle canas

grey-haired [greɪˈhɛəd] ADJ canoso

greyhound [ˈgreɪhaʊnd] N galgo

grey vote N voto de la tercera edad

grid [grɪd] N rejilla; (*Elec*) red *f*; **off-grid** sin conexión a la red

griddle [ˈgrɪdl] N (*esp US*) plancha

gridiron [ˈgrɪdaɪən] N (*Culin*) parrilla

gridlock [ˈgrɪdlɔk] N (*esp US*) retención *f*

grief [griːf] N dolor *m*, pena; **to come to ~** (*plan*) fracasar, ir al traste; (*person*) acabar mal, desgraciarse

grievance [ˈgriːvəns] N (*cause for complaint*) motivo de queja, agravio

grieve [griːv] VI afligirse, acongojarse; **to ~ for** llorar por; **to ~ for sb** (*dead person*) llorar la pérdida de algn ▸ VT afligir, apenar

grievous [ˈgriːvəs] ADJ grave; (*loss*) cruel; **~ bodily harm** (*Law*) daños *mpl* corporales graves

grill [grɪl] N (*on cooker*) parrilla ▸ VT (*Brit*) asar a la parrilla; (*inf: question*) interrogar; **grilled meat** (*Brit*) carne *f* (asada) a la parrilla *or* plancha

grille [grɪl] N rejilla

grim [grɪm] ADJ (*place*) lúgubre; (*person*) adusto

grimace [grɪˈmeɪs] N mueca ▸ VI hacer muecas

grime [graɪm] N mugre *f*

grimly [ˈgrɪmlɪ] ADV (*say*) sombríamente

grimy [ˈgraɪmɪ] ADJ mugriento

grin [grɪn] N sonrisa abierta ▸ VI: **to ~ (at)** sonreír abiertamente (a)

grind [graɪnd] (*pt, pp* **ground** [graʊnd]) VT (*coffee, pepper etc*) moler; (*US: meat*) picar; (*make sharp*) afilar; (*polish: gem, lens*) esmerilar; **to ~ one's teeth** hacer rechinar los dientes ▸ VI (*car gears*) rechinar; **to ~ to a halt** (*vehicle*) pararse con gran estruendo de frenos; (*fig: talks, scheme*) interrumpirse; (*work, production*) paralizarse ▸ N: **the daily ~** (*inf*) la rutina diaria

grinder [ˈgraɪndəʳ] N (*machine: for coffee*) molinillo

grindstone [ˈgraɪndstəʊn] N: **to keep one's nose to the ~** trabajar sin descanso

grip [grɪp] N (*hold*) asimiento; (*of hands*) apretón *m*; (*handle*) asidero; (*of racquet etc*) mango; (*understanding*) comprensión *f*; **to get to grips with** enfrentarse con; **to lose one's ~** (*fig*) perder el control; **he lost his ~ of the situation** la situación se le fue de las manos ▸ VT agarrar

gripe [graɪp] N (*inf: complaint*) queja ▸ VI (*inf: complain*): **to ~ (about)** quejarse (de) ■ **gripes** NPL (*pain*) retortijones *mpl*

gripping [ˈgrɪpɪŋ] ADJ absorbente

grisly [ˈgrɪzlɪ] ADJ horripilante, horrible

gristle [ˈgrɪsl] N cartílago

grit [grɪt] N gravilla; (*courage*) valor *m*; **I've got a piece of ~ in my eye** tengo una arenilla en el ojo ▸ VT (*road*) poner gravilla en; **to ~ one's teeth** apretar los dientes

grits [grɪts] NPL (*US*) maíz *msg* a medio moler

grizzle [ˈgrɪzl] VI (*cry*) lloriquear

grizzly [ˈgrɪzlɪ] N (*also*: **grizzly bear**) oso pardo

groan [grəʊn] N gemido, quejido ▸ VI gemir, quejarse

grocer [ˈgrəʊsəʳ] N tendero (de ultramarinos); **~'s (shop)** *n* tienda de ultramarinos *or* (*LAm*) de abarrotes

groceries [ˈgrəʊsərɪz] NPL comestibles *mpl*

grocery [ˈgrəʊsərɪ] N (*shop*) tienda de ultramarinos

grog [grɔg] N (*Brit*) grog *m*

groggy [ˈgrɔgɪ] ADJ atontado

groin [grɔɪn] N ingle *f*

groom [gruːm] N mozo(-a) de cuadra; (also: **bridegroom**) novio ▶ VT (horse) almohazar; (fig): **to ~ sb for** preparar a algn para; **well-groomed** acicalado

groove [gruːv] N ranura; (of record) surco

grope [grəup] VI ir a tientas; **to ~ for** buscar a tientas

gross [grəus] ADJ (neglect, injustice) grave; (vulgar: behaviour) grosero; (: appearance) de mal gusto; (Comm) bruto ▶ VT (Comm) recaudar en bruto

gross domestic product N producto interior bruto

gross income N ingresos mpl brutos

grossly ['grəuslɪ] ADV (greatly) enormemente

gross national product N producto nacional bruto

gross profit N beneficios mpl brutos

gross sales NPL ventas fpl brutas

grotesque [grə'tɛsk] ADJ grotesco

grotto ['grɒtəu] N gruta

grotty ['grɒtɪ] ADJ (inf) asqueroso

grouch [grautʃ] VI (inf) refunfuñar ▶ N (inf: person) refunfuñón(-ona) m/f

★**ground** [graund] PT, PP of **grind** ▶ N suelo, tierra; (Sport) campo, terreno; (reason: gen pl) motivo, razón f; (US: also: **ground wire**) tierra; **on the ~** en el suelo; **common ~** terreno común; **to gain/lose ~** ganar/perder terreno; **to the ~** al suelo; **below ~** bajo tierra; **he covered a lot of ~ in his lecture** abarcó mucho en la clase ▶ VT (plane) mantener en tierra; (US Elec) conectar con tierra ▶ VI (ship) varar, encallar ▶ ADJ (coffee etc) molido ■ **grounds** NPL (of coffee etc) poso sg; (gardens etc) jardines mpl, parque m

ground cloth N (US) = **groundsheet**

ground control N control m desde tierra

ground floor N (BRIT) planta baja

grounding ['graundɪŋ] N (in education) conocimientos mpl básicos

groundkeeper ['graundkiːpər] N = **groundsman**

groundless ['graundlɪs] ADJ infundado, sin fundamento

groundnut ['graundnʌt] N cacahuete m

ground rent N alquiler m del terreno

ground rules NPL normas básicas

groundsheet ['graundʃiːt] N (BRIT) tela impermeable

groundsman ['graundzmən] (irreg), (US) **groundskeeper** ['graundzkiːpər] N (Sport) encargado de pista de deportes

ground staff N personal m de tierra

ground swell N mar m or f de fondo; (fig) ola

ground-to-air ['grauntə'ɛər] ADJ tierra-aire

ground-to-ground ['grauntə'graund] ADJ tierra-tierra

groundwork ['graundwəːk] N trabajo preliminar

Ground Zero N zona cero

★**group** [gruːp] N grupo; (Mus: pop group) conjunto, grupo ▶ VT (also: **group together**) agrupar ▶ VI agruparse

groupie ['gruːpɪ] N groupie f

group therapy N terapia de grupo

grouse [graus] N pl inv (bird) urogallo ▶ VI (complain) quejarse

grove [grəuv] N arboleda

grovel ['grɒvl] VI (fig) arrastrarse

★**grow** [grəu] (pt **grew** [gruː], pp **grown** [grəun]) VI crecer; (increase) aumentar; (expand) desarrollarse; (become) volverse; **to ~ tired of waiting** cansarse de esperar; **to ~ rich/weak** enriquecerse/debilitarse ▶ VT cultivar; (hair, beard) dejar crecer

▶ **grow apart** VI (fig) alejarse uno del otro
▶ **grow away from** VT FUS (fig) alejarse de
▶ **grow on** VT FUS: **that painting is growing on me** ese cuadro me gusta cada vez más
▶ **grow out of** VT FUS (habit) perder; (clothes): **I've grown out of this shirt** esta camisa se me ha quedado pequeña
▶ **grow up** VI crecer, hacerse hombre/mujer

grower ['grəuər] N (Agr) cultivador(a) m/f, productor(a) m/f

growing ['grəuɪŋ] ADJ creciente; **~ pains** (also fig) problemas mpl de crecimiento

growl [graul] VI gruñir

grown [grəun] PP of **grow**

grown-up [grəun'ʌp] N adulto(-a), mayor mf

growth [grəuθ] N crecimiento, desarrollo; (what has grown) brote m; (Med) tumor m

growth rate N tasa de crecimiento

grub [grʌb] N gusano; (inf: food) comida

grubby ['grʌbɪ] ADJ sucio, mugriento, mugroso (LAM)

grudge [grʌdʒ] N rencor; **to bear sb a ~** guardar rencor a algn ▶ VT: **to ~ sb sth** dar algo a algn de mala gana; **he grudges (giving) the money** da el dinero de mala gana

grudgingly ['grʌdʒɪŋlɪ] ADV de mala gana

gruelling, (US) **grueling** ['gruəlɪŋ] ADJ agotador

gruesome ['gruːsəm] ADJ horrible

gruff [grʌf] ADJ (voice) ronco; (manner) brusco

grumble ['grʌmbl] VI refunfuñar, quejarse

grumpy ['grʌmpɪ] ADJ gruñón(-ona)

grunge [grʌndʒ] N (Mus: fashion) grunge m

grunt [grʌnt] VI gruñir ▶ N gruñido

G-string ['dʒiːstrɪŋ] N tanga m

GSUSA N ABBR = **Girl Scouts of the United States of America**

GT ABBR (Aut: = gran turismo) GT

★**guarantee** [gærən'tiː] N garantía ▶ VT garantizar; **he can't ~ (that) he'll come** no está seguro de poder venir

guarantor [gærən'tɔːʳ] N garante *mf*, fiador(a) *m/f*

★**guard** [gɑːd] N guardia; (*person*) guarda *mf*; (BRIT Rail) jefe *m* de tren; (*safety device: on machine*) cubierta de protección; (*protection*) protección *f*; (*fireguard*) pantalla; (*mudguard*) guardabarros *m inv*; **to be on one's ~** (*fig*) estar en guardia ▶ VT guardar
▶ **guard against** VI: **to ~ against doing sth** guardarse de hacer algo; **to ~ against** *or* **from** proteger (de)

guard dog N perro guardián

guarded ['gɑːdɪd] ADJ (*fig*) cauteloso

guardian ['gɑːdɪən] N guardián(-ana) *m/f*; (*of minor*) tutor(a) *m/f*

guardrail ['gɑːdreɪl] N pretil *m*

guard's van N (BRIT Rail) furgón *m* del jefe de tren

Guatemala [gwɑːtə'mɑːlə] N Guatemala

Guatemalan [gwɑːtə'mɑːlən] ADJ, N guatemalteco(-a) *m/f*

Guernsey ['gəːnzɪ] N Guernsey *m*

guerrilla [gə'rɪlə] N guerrillero(-a)

guerrilla warfare N guerra de guerrillas

★**guess** [gɛs] VI, VT (*gen*) adivinar; (*suppose*) suponer; **I ~ you're right** (*esp US*) supongo que tienes razón; **to keep sb guessing** mantener a algn a la expectativa ▶ N suposición *f*, conjetura; **to take** *or* **have a ~** tratar de adivinar; **my ~ is that ...** yo creo que ...

guesstimate ['gɛstɪmɪt] N (*inf*) cálculo aproximado

guesswork ['gɛswəːk] N conjeturas *fpl*; **I got the answer by ~** acerté a ojo de buen cubero

★**guest** [gɛst] N invitado(-a); (*in hotel*) huésped(a) *m/f*; **be my ~** (*inf*) estás en tu casa

guest-house ['gɛsthaus] N casa de huéspedes, pensión *f*

guest room N cuarto de huéspedes

guff [gʌf] N (*inf*) bobadas *fpl*

guffaw [gʌ'fɔː] N carcajada ▶ VI reírse a carcajadas

guidance ['gaɪdəns] N (*gen*) dirección *f*; (*advice*) consejos *mpl*; **marriage/vocational ~** orientación *f* matrimonial/profesional

★**guide** [gaɪd] N (*person*) guía *mf*; (*book, fig*) guía *f*; (*also*: **girl guide**) exploradora ▶ VT guiar; **to be guided by sb/sth** dejarse guiar por algn/ algo

guidebook ['gaɪdbuk] N guía

guided missile ['gaɪdɪd-] N misil *m* teledirigido

guide dog N perro guía

guided tour N visita *f* con guía

guidelines ['gaɪdlaɪnz] NPL (*fig*) directrices *fpl*

guild [gɪld] N gremio

guildhall ['gɪldhɔːl] N (BRIT: *town hall*) ayuntamiento

guile [gaɪl] N astucia

guileless ['gaɪllɪs] ADJ cándido

guillotine ['gɪlətiːn] N guillotina

guilt [gɪlt] N culpabilidad *f*

★**guilty** ['gɪltɪ] ADJ culpable; **to feel ~ (about)** sentirse culpable (de); **to plead ~/not ~** declararse culpable/inocente

Guinea ['gɪnɪ] N: **Republic of ~** República de Guinea

guinea ['gɪnɪ] N (BRIT old) guinea (*21 chelines: en la actualidad ya no se usa esta moneda*)

Guinea-Bissau ['gɪnɪbɪ'sau] N Guinea-Bissau *f*

★**guinea pig** N cobaya; (*fig*) conejillo de Indias

guise [gaɪz] N: **in** *or* **under the ~ of** bajo la apariencia de

★**guitar** [gɪ'tɑːʳ] N guitarra

guitarist [gɪ'tɑːrɪst] N guitarrista *mf*

gulch [gʌltʃ] N (US) barranco

gulf [gʌlf] N golfo; (*abyss*) abismo; **the G~** el Golfo (Pérsico)

Gulf States NPL: **the ~** los países del Golfo

Gulf Stream N: **the ~** la Corriente del Golfo

gull [gʌl] N gaviota

gullet ['gʌlɪt] N esófago

gullibility [gʌlɪ'bɪlɪtɪ] N credulidad *f*

gullible ['gʌlɪbl] ADJ crédulo

gully ['gʌlɪ] N barranco

gulp [gʌlp] VI tragar saliva ▶ VT (*also*: **gulp down**) tragarse ▶ N (*of liquid*) trago; (*of food*) bocado; **in** *or* **at one ~** de un trago

gum [gʌm] N (Anat) encía; (*glue*) goma, cemento (LAM); (*sweet*) gominola; (*also*: **chewing-gum**) chicle *m* ▶ VT pegar con goma
▶ **gum up** VT: **to ~ up the works** (*inf*) entorpecerlo todo

gumboots ['gʌmbuːts] NPL (BRIT) botas *fpl* de goma

gumption ['gʌmpʃən] N (*inf*) iniciativa

gum tree N árbol *m* gomero

★**gun** [gʌn] N (*small*) pistola; (*shotgun*) escopeta; (*rifle*) fusil *m*; (*cannon*) cañón *m*; **to stick to one's guns** (*fig*) mantenerse firme en sus trece ▶ VT (*also*: **gun down**) abatir a tiros

gunboat ['gʌnbəut] N cañonero

gun dog N perro de caza

gunfire ['gʌnfaɪəʳ] N disparos *mpl*

gung-ho [gʌŋ'həu] ADJ (*inf*) patriotero

gunk [gʌŋk] N (*inf*) masa viscosa

gunman ['gʌnmən] N (*irreg*) pistolero

gunner ['gʌnəʳ] N artillero

gunpoint ['gʌnpɔɪnt] N: **at ~** a mano armada

gunpowder ['gʌnpaudəʳ] N pólvora

gunrunner ['gʌnrʌnəʳ] N traficante *mf* de armas

gunrunning ['gʌnrʌnɪŋ] N tráfico de armas

gunshot ['gʌnʃɔt] N disparo

gunsmith ['gʌnsmɪθ] N armero

gurgle ['gəːgl] VI gorgotear

guru [ˈguːruː] N gurú m
gush [gʌʃ] VI chorrear, salir a raudales; (fig) deshacerse en efusiones
gushing [ˈgʌʃɪŋ] ADJ efusivo
gusset [ˈgʌsɪt] N (in tights, pants) escudete m
gust [gʌst] N (of wind) ráfaga
gusto [ˈgʌstəu] N entusiasmo
gusty [ˈgʌstɪ] ADJ racheado
gut [gʌt] N intestino; (Mus etc) cuerda de tripa
▶ VT (poultry, fish) destripar; (building): **the blaze gutted the entire building** el fuego destruyó el edificio entero
gut reaction N reacción f instintiva
guts [gʌts] NPL (courage) agallas fpl, valor m; (inf: innards: of people, animals) tripas fpl; **to hate sb's** ~ odiar a algn (a muerte)
gutsy [ˈgʌtsɪ] ADJ: **to be** ~ (inf) tener agallas
gutted [ˈgʌtɪd] ADJ (inf: disappointed): **I was** ~ me quedé hecho polvo
gutter [ˈgʌtəʳ] N (of roof) canalón m; (in street) cuneta; **the** ~ (fig) el arroyo
gutter press N (inf): **the** ~ la prensa sensacionalista or amarilla; see also **tabloid press**
guttural [ˈgʌtərl] ADJ gutural
★**guy** [gaɪ] N (also: **guyrope**) viento, cuerda; (inf: man) tío (SP), tipo
Guyana [gaɪˈænə] N Guayana
Guy Fawkes Night [gaɪˈfɔːks-] N ver nota

La noche del cinco de noviembre, **Guy Fawkes Night**, se celebra el fracaso de la conspiración de la pólvora (Gunpowder Plot), el intento fallido de volar el parlamento de Jaime 1 en 1605. Esa noche se lanzan fuegos artificiales y se encienden hogueras en los jardines privados o en plan más oficial en parques públicos. La antigua tradición de quemar muñecos de trapo representando al cabecilla del intento Guy Fawkes ya ha caído en desuso.

guzzle [ˈgʌzl] VI tragar ▶ VT engullir
★**gym** [dʒɪm] N (also: **gymnasium**) gimnasio; (also: **gymnastics**) gimnasia
gymkhana [dʒɪmˈkɑːnə] N gincana
gymnasium [dʒɪmˈneɪzɪəm] N gimnasio
gymnast [ˈdʒɪmnæst] N gimnasta mf
gymnastics [dʒɪmˈnæstɪks] N gimnasia
gym shoes NPL zapatillas fpl de gimnasia
gym slip N (BRIT) pichi m
gynaecologist, (US) **gynecologist** [gaɪnɪˈkɔlədʒɪst] N ginecólogo(-a)
gynaecology, (US) **gynecology** [gaɪnɪˈkɔlədʒɪ] N ginecología
gypsy [ˈdʒɪpsɪ] N = **gipsy**
gyrate [dʒaɪˈreɪt] VI girar
gyroscope [ˈdʒaɪrəskəup] N giroscopio

g

Hh

H, h [eɪtʃ] N (*letter*) H, h *f*; **H for Harry,** (*US*) **H for How** H de Historia

habeas corpus [ˈheɪbɪəsˈkɔːpəs] N (*Law*) hábeas corpus *m*

haberdashery [ˈhæbəˈdæʃərɪ] N (*BRIT*) mercería; (*US: men's clothing*) prendas *fpl* de caballero

★**habit** [ˈhæbɪt] N hábito, costumbre *f*; (*drug habit*) adicción *f*; **to get out of/into the ~ of doing sth** perder la costumbre de/acostumbrarse a hacer algo

habitable [ˈhæbɪtəbl] ADJ habitable

habitat [ˈhæbɪtæt] N hábitat *m*

habitation [hæbɪˈteɪʃən] N habitación *f*

habitual [həˈbɪtjuəl] ADJ acostumbrado, habitual; (*drinker, liar*) empedernido

habitually [həˈbɪtjuəlɪ] ADV por costumbre

hack [hæk] VT (*cut*) cortar; (*slice*) tajar ▶ N corte *m*; (*axe blow*) hachazo; (*pej: writer*) escritor(a) *m/f* a sueldo; (*old horse*) jamelgo

hacker [ˈhækəʳ] N (*Comput*) pirata *m* informático

hackles [ˈhæklz] NPL: **to make sb's ~ rise** (*fig*) poner furioso a algn

hackney cab [ˈhæknɪ-] N coche *m* de alquiler

hackneyed [ˈhæknɪd] ADJ trillado, gastado

hacksaw [ˈhæksɔː] N sierra para metales

had [hæd] PT, PP *of* **have**

haddock [ˈhædək] (*pl* ~ *or* **haddocks**) N *especie de merluza*

hadn't [ˈhædnt] = **had not**

haematology, (*US*) **hematology** [ˈhiːməˈtɔlədʒɪ] N hematología

haemoglobin, (*US*) **hemoglobin** [ˈhiːməˈɡləubɪn] N hemoglobina

haemophilia, (*US*) **hemophilia** [ˈhiːməˈfɪlɪə] N hemofilia

haemorrhage, (*US*) **hemorrhage** [ˈhɛmərɪdʒ] N hemorragia

haemorrhoids, (*US*) **hemorrhoids** [ˈhɛmərɔɪdz] NPL hemorroides *fpl*, almorranas *fpl*

hag [hæg] N (*ugly*) vieja fea, tarasca; (*nasty*) bruja; (*witch*) hechicera

haggard [ˈhæɡəd] ADJ ojeroso

haggis [ˈhæɡɪs] N (*SCOTTISH*) *asadura de cordero cocida; see also* **Burns Night**

haggle [ˈhæɡl] VI (*argue*) discutir; (*bargain*) regatear

haggling [ˈhæɡlɪŋ] N regateo

Hague [heɪɡ] N: **The ~** La Haya

hail [heɪl] N (*weather*) granizo ▶ VT saludar; (*call*) llamar a; **to ~ (as)** aclamar (como), celebrar (como) ▶ VI granizar; **he hails from Scotland** es natural de Escocia

hailstone [ˈheɪlstəun] N (piedra de) granizo

hailstorm [ˈheɪlstɔːm] N granizada

★**hair** [hɛəʳ] N (*gen*) pelo, cabellos *mpl*; (*one hair*) pelo, cabello; (*head of hair*) pelo, cabellera; (*on legs etc*) vello; **to do one's ~** arreglarse el pelo; **grey ~** canas *fpl*

hairband [ˈhɛəbænd] N cinta

hairbrush [ˈhɛəbrʌʃ] N cepillo (para el pelo)

haircut [ˈhɛəkʌt] N corte *m* de pelo

hairdo [ˈhɛəduː] N peinado

★**hairdresser** [ˈhɛədrɛsəʳ] N peluquero(-a); **~'s** peluquería

hairdryer [ˈhɛədraɪəʳ] N secador *m* (de pelo)

-haired [hɛəd] ADJ SUFF: **fair/long-haired** (de pelo) rubio *or* (*LAM*) güero/de pelo largo

hair gel N fijador *m*

hairgrip [ˈhɛəɡrɪp] N horquilla

hairline [ˈhɛəlaɪn] N nacimiento del pelo

hairline fracture N fractura muy fina

hairnet [ˈhɛənɛt] N redecilla

hair oil N brillantina

hairpiece [ˈhɛəpiːs] N trenza postiza

hairpin [ˈhɛəpɪn] N horquilla

hairpin bend, (US) **hairpin curve** N curva muy cerrada

hair-raising ['hεəreızıŋ] ADJ espeluznante

hair remover N depilatorio

hair's breadth N: **by a ~** por un pelo

hair spray N laca

hairstyle ['hεəstaıl] N peinado

hairy ['hεərı] ADJ peludo, velludo; (inf: frightening) espeluznante

Haiti ['heıtı] N Haití m

haka ['hɑːkə] N (NEW ZEALAND) haka m or f

hake [heık] N merluza

halcyon ['hælsıən] ADJ feliz

hale [heıl] ADJ: **~ and hearty** sano y fuerte

half [hɑːf] (pl **halves** [hɑːvz]) N mitad f; (Sport: of match) tiempo, parte f; (: of ground) campo; (of beer) ≈ caña (SP), media pinta; (Rail) billete m de niño; **half-an-hour** media hora; **two and a ~** dos y media; **~ a dozen** media docena; **~ a pound** media libra, ≈ 250 gr; **to cut sth in ~** cortar algo por la mitad; **to go halves (with sb)** ir a medias (con algn) ► ADJ medio ► ADV medio, a medias; **~ asleep** medio dormido; **~ empty/closed** medio vacío/entreabierto; **~ past 3** las 3 y media

half-back ['hɑːfbæk] N (Sport) medio mf

half-baked ['hɑːf'beıkt] ADJ (inf: idea, scheme) mal concebido or pensado

half board N (BRIT: in hotel) media pensión

half-breed ['hɑːfbriːd] N (!) = **half-caste**

half-brother ['hɑːfbrʌðəʳ] N hermanastro

half-caste ['hɑːfkɑːst] N (!) mestizo(-a)

half day N medio día m, media jornada

half fare N medio pasaje m

half-hearted ['hɑːf'hɑːtıd] ADJ indiferente, poco entusiasta

half-hour [hɑːf'auəʳ] N media hora

half-mast ['hɑːf'mɑːst] N: **at ~** (flag) a media asta

halfpenny ['heıpnı] N medio penique m

half-price ['hɑːf'praıs] ADJ a mitad de precio

half term N (BRIT Scol) vacaciones de mediados del trimestre

half-time [hɑːf'taım] N descanso

halfway ['hɑːf'weı] ADV a medio camino; **to meet sb ~** (fig) llegar a un acuerdo con algn

halfway house N centro de readaptación de antiguos presos; (fig) solución f intermedia

half-wit ['hɑːfwıt] N (!) zoquete m

half-yearly [hɑːf'jıəlı] ADV semestralmente ► ADJ semestral

halibut ['hælıbət] N pl inv halibut m

halitosis [hælı'təusıs] N halitosis f

hall [hɔːl] N (for concerts) sala; (entrance way) entrada, vestíbulo

hallmark ['hɔːlmɑːk] N (mark) rasgo distintivo; (seal) sello

hallo [hə'ləu] EXCL = **hello**

hall of residence N (BRIT) colegio mayor, residencia universitaria

Hallowe'en [hæləu'iːn] N víspera de Todos los Santos

> **Hallowe'en** es una tradición que se celebra en los Estados Unidos, y cada vez más en el Reino Unido, el 31 de octubre, víspera de Todos los Santos. Es una ocasión festiva en la que se decoran las entradas de las casas con linternas hechas de calabazas esculpidas y los niños se disfrazan y van de puerta en puerta gritando "trick or treat" para indicar que gastarán una broma a quien no les dé un pequeño regalo (como golosinas o dinero).

hallucination [həluːsı'neıʃən] N alucinación f

hallucinogenic [həluːsınəu'dʒɛnık] ADJ alucinógeno

hallway ['hɔːlweı] N vestíbulo

halo ['heıləu] N (of saint) aureola, halo

halt [hɔːlt] N (stop) alto, parada; (Rail) apeadero; **to call a ~ (to sth)** (fig) poner fin (a algo) ► VT parar ► VI pararse; (process) interrumpirse

halter ['hɔːltəʳ] N (for horse) cabestro

halterneck ['hɔːltənɛk] ADJ de espalda escotada

halve [hɑːv] VT partir por la mitad

halves [hɑːvz] PL of **half**

★**ham** [hæm] N jamón m (cocido); (inf: also: **radio ham**) radioaficionado(-a); (also: **ham actor**) comicastro(-a)

★**hamburger** ['hæmbəːgəʳ] N hamburguesa

ham-fisted ['hæm'fıstıd] ADJ torpe, desmañado

hamlet ['hæmlıt] N aldea

hammer ['hæməʳ] N martillo ► VT (nail) clavar; **to ~ a point home to sb** remacharle un punto a algn
> **hammer out** VT (metal) forjar a martillo; (fig: solution, agreement) elaborar (trabajosamente)

hammock ['hæmək] N hamaca

hamper ['hæmpəʳ] VT estorbar ► N cesto

★**hamster** ['hæmstəʳ] N hámster m

hamstring ['hæmstrıŋ] N (Anat) tendón m de la corva

★**hand** [hænd] N mano f; (of clock) aguja, manecilla; (writing) letra; (worker) obrero; (measurement: of horse) palmo; **to give sb a ~** echar una mano a algn, ayudar a algn; **to force sb's ~** forzarle la mano a algn; **at ~** a mano; **in ~** entre manos; **we have the matter in ~** tenemos el asunto entre manos; **to have in one's ~** (knife, victory) tener en la mano; **to have a free ~** tener carta blanca; **on ~** (person, services) a mano, al alcance; **to ~** (information etc) a mano; **on the one ~ ..., on the other ~ ...** por una parte ... por

h

otra (parte) ... ▸ VT (*give*) dar, pasar; (*deliver*) entregar

▸ **hand down** VT pasar, bajar; (*tradition*) transmitir; (*heirloom*) dejar en herencia; (US: *sentence, verdict*) imponer

▸ **hand in** VT entregar

▸ **hand out** VT (*leaflets, advice*) repartir, distribuir

▸ **hand over** VT (*deliver*) entregar; (*surrender*) ceder

▸ **hand round** VT (BRIT: *information, papers*) pasar (de mano en mano); (: *chocolates etc*) ofrecer

★**handbag** ['hændbæg] N bolso, cartera (LAM)

hand baggage N = **hand luggage**

handball ['hændbɔːl] N balonmano

handbasin ['hændbeɪsn] N lavabo

handbook ['hændbuk] N manual *m*

handbrake ['hændbreɪk] N freno de mano

h & c (BRIT) ABBR = **hot and cold (water)**

hand cream N crema para las manos

handcuffs ['hændkʌfs] NPL esposas *fpl*

handful ['hændful] N puñado

hand-held ['hænd'held] ADJ de mano

handicap ['hændɪkæp] N desventaja; (*Sport*) hándicap *m* ▸ VT estorbar

handicraft ['hændɪkrɑːft] N artesanía

handiwork ['hændɪwəːk] N manualidad(es) *f(pl)*; (*fig*) obra; **this looks like his ~** (*pej*) es obra de él, parece

★**handkerchief** ['hæŋkətʃɪf] N pañuelo

★**handle** ['hændl] N (*of door etc*) pomo, tirador *m*; (*of cup etc*) asa; (*of knife etc*) mango; (*for winding*) manivela; **to fly off the ~** perder los estribos ▸ VT (*touch*) tocar; (*deal with*) encargarse de; (*treat: people*) manejar; **"~ with care"** "(manéjese) con cuidado"

handlebar ['hændlbɑː] N, **handlebars** ['hændlbɑːz] NPL manillar *msg*

handling ['hændlɪŋ] N (*Aut*) conducción *f*; **his ~ of the matter** su forma de llevar el asunto

handling charges NPL gastos *mpl* de tramitación

hand luggage N equipaje *m* de mano

handmade ['hændmeɪd] ADJ hecho a mano

handout ['hændaut] N (*distribution*) repartición *f*; (*charity*) limosna; (*leaflet*) folleto, octavilla; (*press handout*) nota

hand-picked ['hænd'pɪkt] ADJ (*produce*) escogido a mano; (*staff etc*) seleccionado cuidadosamente

handrail ['hændreɪl] N (*on staircase etc*) pasamanos *m inv*, barandilla

handset ['hændset] N (*Tel*) auricular *m*

hands-free ['hændzfriː] ADJ (*Tel: telephone*) manos libres; **~ kit** manos libres *m inv*

handshake ['hændʃeɪk] N apretón *m* de manos; (*Comput*) coloquio

★**handsome** ['hænsəm] ADJ guapo

hands-on ['hændz'ɔn] ADJ práctico; **she has a very ~ approach** le gusta tomar parte activa; **~ experience** (*Comput*) experiencia práctica

handstand ['hændstænd] N voltereta, salto mortal

hand-to-mouth ['hændtə'mauθ] ADJ (*existence*) precario

handwriting ['hændraɪtɪŋ] N letra

handwritten ['hændrɪtn] ADJ escrito a mano, manuscrito

handy ['hændɪ] ADJ (*close at hand*) a mano; (*useful: machine, tool etc*) práctico; (*skilful*) hábil, diestro; **to come in ~** venir bien

handyman ['hændɪmæn] N (*irreg*) manitas *m inv*

★**hang** [hæŋ] (*pt, pp* **hung** [hʌŋ]) VT colgar; (*head*) bajar; (*pt, pp* **hanged**: *criminal*) ahorcar

▸ N: **to get the ~ of sth** (*inf*) coger el tranquillo a algo

▸ **hang about, hang around** VI haraganear

▸ **hang back** VI (*hesitate*): **to ~ back (from doing)** vacilar (en hacer)

▸ **hang down** VI colgar, pender

▸ **hang on** VI (*wait*) esperar ▸ VT FUS (*depend on: decision etc*) depender de; **to ~ on to** (*keep*) guardar, quedarse con

▸ **hang out** VT (*washing*) tender, colgar ▸ VI (*inf: live*) vivir; (: *often be found*) moverse; **to ~ out of sth** colgar fuera de algo

▸ **hang round** VI = **hang about**

▸ **hang together** VI (*cohere: argument etc*) sostenerse

▸ **hang up** VT (*coat*) colgar ▸ VI (*Tel*) colgar; **to ~ up on sb** colgarle a algn

hangar ['hæŋə] N hangar *m*

hangdog ['hæŋdɔg] ADJ (*guilty: look, expression*) avergonzado

hanger ['hæŋə] N percha

hanger-on [hæŋər'ɔn] N parásito

hang-glider ['hæŋglaɪdə] N ala delta

hang-gliding ['hæŋglaɪdɪŋ] N vuelo con ala delta

hanging ['hæŋɪŋ] N (*execution*) ejecución *f* (en la horca)

hangman ['hæŋmən] N (*irreg*) verdugo

hangover ['hæŋəuvə] N (*after drinking*) resaca

hang-up ['hæŋʌp] N complejo

hanker ['hæŋkə] VI: **to ~ after** (*miss*) echar de menos; (*long for*) añorar

hankie, hanky ['hæŋkɪ] N ABBR = **handkerchief**

Hansard ['hænsɑːd] N actas oficiales de las sesiones del parlamento británico

haphazard [hæp'hæzəd] ADJ fortuito

hapless ['hæplɪs] ADJ desventurado

happen ['hæpən] VI suceder, ocurrir; (*take place*) tener lugar, realizarse; (*chance*): **he happened to hear/see** dio la casualidad de que oyó/vio; **as it happens** da la casualidad de que; **what's happening?** ¿qué pasa?

▶ **happen (up)on** VT FUS tropezar *or* dar con

happening [ˈhæpnɪŋ] N suceso, acontecimiento

happily [ˈhæpɪlɪ] ADV (*luckily*) afortunadamente; (*cheerfully*) alegremente

happiness [ˈhæpɪnɪs] N (*contentment*) felicidad f; (*joy*) alegría

★**happy** [ˈhæpɪ] ADJ feliz; (*cheerful*) alegre; **to be ~ (with)** estar contento (con); **yes, I'd be ~ to** sí, con mucho gusto; **H~ Christmas!** ¡Feliz Navidad!; **H~ New Year!** ¡Feliz Año Nuevo!; **~ birthday!** ¡feliz cumpleaños!

happy-go-lucky [ˈhæpɪgəʊˈlʌkɪ] ADJ despreocupado

happy hour N horas en las que la bebida es más barata en un bar

harangue [həˈræŋ] VT arengar

harass [ˈhærəs] VT acosar, hostigar

harassed [ˈhærəst] ADJ agobiado, presionado

harassment [ˈhærəsmənt] N persecución f, acoso; (*worry*) preocupación f

harbour, (*US*) **harbor** [ˈhɑːbəʳ] N puerto ▶ VT (*fugitive*) dar abrigo a; (*hope etc*) abrigar; (*hide*) dar abrigo a; (*retain: grudge etc*) guardar

harbour dues, (*US*) **harbor dues** NPL derechos *mpl* portuarios

★**hard** [hɑːd] ADJ duro; (*difficult*) difícil; (*work*) arduo; (*person*) severo; **no ~ feelings!** ¡sin rencor(es)!; **to be ~ of hearing** ser duro de oído; **I find it ~ to believe that ...** me cuesta trabajo creer que ... ▶ ADV (*work*) mucho, duro; (*think*) profundamente; **to look ~ at sb/sth** clavar los ojos en algn/algo; **to try ~** esforzarse; **to be ~ done by** ser tratado injustamente

hard-and-fast [ˈhɑːdənˈfɑːst] ADJ rígido, definitivo

hardback [ˈhɑːdbæk] N libro de tapa dura

hardboard [ˈhɑːdbɔːd] N aglomerado *m* (*de madera*)

hard cash N dinero en efectivo

hard copy N (*Comput*) copia impresa

hard-core [ˈhɑːdˈkɔːʳ] ADJ (*pornography*) duro; (*supporters*) incondicional

hard court N (*Tennis*) pista *or* cancha (de tenis) de cemento

hard disk N (*Comput*) disco duro

hard drive N (*Comput*) unidad f de disco duro

harden [ˈhɑːdn] VT endurecer; (*steel*) templar; (*fig*) curtir; (*: determination*) fortalecer ▶ VI (*substance*) endurecerse; (*fig*) curtirse

hardened [ˈhɑːdnd] ADJ (*criminal*) habitual; **to be ~ to sth** estar acostumbrado a algo

hard-headed [ˈhɑːdˈhɛdɪd] ADJ poco sentimental, realista

hard-hearted [ˈhɑːdˈhɑːtɪd] ADJ insensible

hard-hitting [ˈhɑːdˈhɪtɪŋ] ADJ (*speech, article*) contundente

hard labour N trabajos *mpl* forzados

hardliner [hɑːdˈlaɪnəʳ] N partidario(-a) de la línea dura

hard-luck story [ˈhɑːdlʌk-] N dramón *m*

★**hardly** [ˈhɑːdlɪ] ADV (*scarcely*) apenas; **that can ~ be true** eso difícilmente puede ser cierto; **~ ever** casi nunca; **I can ~ believe it** apenas me lo puedo creer

hardness [ˈhɑːdnɪs] N dureza

hard-nosed [ˈhɑːdˈnəʊzd] ADJ duro, sin contemplaciones

hard-pressed [ˈhɑːdˈprɛst] ADJ en apuros

hard sell N publicidad f agresiva; **~ techniques** técnicas *fpl* agresivas de venta

hardship [ˈhɑːdʃɪp] N (*troubles*) penas *fpl*; (*financial*) apuro

hard shoulder N (*Aut*) arcén *m*

hard-up [hɑːdˈʌp] ADJ (*inf*) sin un duro (*SP*), sin plata (*LAM*)

hardware [ˈhɑːdwɛəʳ] N ferretería; (*Comput*) hardware *m*

hardware shop, (*US*) **hardware store** N ferretería

hard-wearing [hɑːdˈwɛərɪŋ] ADJ resistente, duradero; (*shoes*) resistente

hard-won [ˈhɑːdˈwʌn] ADJ ganado con esfuerzo

hard-working [hɑːdˈwəːkɪŋ] ADJ trabajador(a)

hardy [ˈhɑːdɪ] ADJ fuerte; (*plant*) resistente

hare [hɛəʳ] N liebre f

hare-brained [ˈhɛəbreɪnd] ADJ atolondrado

harelip [ˈhɛəlɪp] N labio leporino

harem [hɑːˈriːm] N harén *m*

haricot [ˈhærɪkəʊ], **haricot bean** N alubia

hark back [hɑːk-] VI: **to ~ to** (*former days, earlier occasion*) recordar

★**harm** [hɑːm] N daño, mal *m*; **out of ~'s way** a salvo; **there's no ~ in trying** no se pierde nada con intentar ▶ VT (*person*) hacer daño a; (*health, interests*) perjudicar; (*thing*) dañar

harmful [ˈhɑːmful] ADJ (*gen*) dañino; (*reputation*) perjudicial

harmless [ˈhɑːmlɪs] ADJ (*person*) inofensivo; (*drug*) inocuo; (*joke etc*) inocente

harmonica [hɑːˈmɔnɪkə] N armónica

harmonious [hɑːˈməʊnɪəs] ADJ armonioso

harmonize [ˈhɑːmənaɪz] VT, VI armonizar

harmony [ˈhɑːmənɪ] N armonía

harness [ˈhɑːnɪs] N arreos *mpl* ▶ VT (*horse*) enjaezar; (*resources*) aprovechar

harp [hɑːp] N arpa ▶ VI: **to ~ on (about)** machacar (con)

harpoon [hɑːˈpuːn] N arpón *m*

harrow [ˈhærəʊ] N grada ▶ VT gradar

harrowing [ˈhærəʊɪŋ] ADJ angustioso

harry [ˈhærɪ] VT (*Mil*) acosar; (*person*) hostigar

harsh [hɑːʃ] ADJ (*cruel*) duro, cruel; (*severe*) severo; (*words*) hosco; (*colour*) chillón(-ona); (*contrast*) violento

h

harshly ['hɑːʃlɪ] ADV (say) con aspereza; (treat) con mucha dureza

harshness ['hɑːʃnɪs] N dureza

harvest ['hɑːvɪst] N (harvest time) siega; (of cereals etc) cosecha; (of grapes) vendimia ▶ VT, VI cosechar

harvester ['hɑːvɪstər] N (machine) cosechadora; (person) segador(a) m/f; **combine ~** segadora trilladora

has [hæz] VB see **have**

has-been ['hæzbiːn] N (inf: person) persona acabada; (: thing) vieja gloria

hash [hæʃ] N (Culin) picadillo; (inf: mess) lío; (symbol) almohadilla

hashish ['hæʃɪʃ] N hachís m

hashtag ['hæʃtæg] N (on Twitter) hashtag m, etiqueta

hasn't ['hæznt] = **has not**

hassle ['hæsl] N (inf) lío, rollo ▶ VT incordiar

haste [heɪst] N prisa

hasten ['heɪsn] VT acelerar ▶ VI darse prisa; **I ~ to add that ...** me apresuro a añadir que ...

hastily ['heɪstɪlɪ] ADV de prisa

hasty ['heɪstɪ] ADJ apresurado

★**hat** [hæt] N sombrero

hatbox ['hætbɒks] N sombrerera

hatch [hætʃ] N (Naut: also: **hatchway**) escotilla ▶ VI salir del cascarón; **5 eggs have hatched** han salido 5 pollos ▶ VT incubar; (fig: scheme, plot) idear, tramar

hatchback ['hætʃbæk] N (Aut) tres or cinco puertas m

hatchet ['hætʃɪt] N hacha

hatchet job N (inf) varapalo

hatchet man N (irreg) (inf) ejecutor de faenas desagradables por cuenta de otro

★**hate** [heɪt] VT odiar, aborrecer; **I ~ to trouble you, but ...** siento or lamento molestarle, pero ... ▶ N odio

hateful ['heɪtful] ADJ odioso

hater ['heɪtər] N: **cop-hater** persona que siente aversión a la policía; **woman-hater** misógino

hatred ['heɪtrɪd] N odio

hat trick N: **to score a ~** (BRIT Sport) marcar tres tantos (or triunfos) seguidos

haughtily ['hɔːtɪlɪ] ADV con arrogancia

haughty ['hɔːtɪ] ADJ altanero, arrogante

haul [hɔːl] VT tirar, jalar (LAm); (by lorry) transportar ▶ N (of fish) redada; (of stolen goods etc) botín m

haulage ['hɔːlɪdʒ] N (BRIT) transporte m; (costs) gastos mpl de transporte

haulage contractor N (firm) empresa de transportes; (person) transportista mf

haulier ['hɔːlɪər], (US) **hauler** ['hɔːlər] N transportista mf

haunch [hɔːntʃ] N anca; (of meat) pierna

haunt [hɔːnt] VT (ghost) aparecer en; (frequent) frecuentar; (obsess) obsesionar ▶ N guarida

haunted ['hɔːntɪd] ADJ (castle etc) embrujado; (look) de angustia

haunting ['hɔːntɪŋ] ADJ (sight, music) evocativo

Havana [həˈvɑːnə] N La Habana

---

have [hæv]

(pt, pp **had** [hæd]) AUX VB **1** (gen) haber; **to have arrived/eaten** haber llegado/comido; **having finished** or **when he had finished, he left** cuando hubo acabado, se fue

2 (in tag questions): **you've done it, haven't you?** lo has hecho, ¿verdad? or ¿no?

3 (in short answers and questions): **I haven't** no; **so I have** pues, es verdad; **we haven't paid — yes we have!** no hemos pagado — ¡sí que hemos pagado!; **I've been there before, have you?** he estado allí antes, ¿y tú?

▶ MODAL AUX VB (be obliged): **to have (got) to do sth** tener que hacer algo; **you haven't to tell her** no hay que or no debes decírselo

▶ VT **1** (possess) tener; **he has (got) blue eyes/dark hair** tiene los ojos azules/el pelo negro

2 (referring to meals etc): **to have breakfast/lunch/dinner** desayunar/comer/cenar; **to have a drink/a cigarette** tomar algo/fumar un cigarrillo

3 (receive) recibir; (obtain) obtener; **may I have your address?** ¿puedes darme tu dirección?; **you can have it for £5** te lo puedes quedar por £5; **I must have it by tomorrow** lo necesito para mañana; **to have a baby** tener un niño or bebé

4 (maintain, allow): **I won't have it!** ¡no lo permitiré!; **I won't have this nonsense!** ¡no permitiré estas tonterías!; **we can't have that** no podemos permitir eso

5: **to have sth done** hacer or mandar hacer algo; **to have one's hair cut** cortarse el pelo; **to have sb do sth** hacer que algn haga algo

6 (experience, suffer): **to have a cold/flu** tener un resfriado/la gripe; **she had her bag stolen/her arm broken** le robaron el bolso/se rompió un brazo; **to have an operation** operarse

7 (+ noun): **to have a swim/walk/bath/rest** nadar/dar un paseo/darse un baño/descansar; **let's have a look** vamos a ver; **to have a meeting/party** celebrar una reunión/una fiesta; **let me have a try** déjame intentarlo

▶ **have in** VT: **to have it in for sb** (inf) tenerla tomada con algn

▶ **have on** VT: **have you anything on tomorrow?** ¿vas a hacer algo mañana?; **I don't have any money on me** no llevo dinero (encima); **to have sb on** (BRIT inf) tomarle el pelo a algn

▶ **have out** VT: **to have it out with sb** (settle a problem etc) dejar las cosas en claro con algn

Use the verb **haber** to form the perfect tenses: *I've already seen that film.* **Ya he visto esa película.**
If you are using have in question tags to confirm a statement, use **¿no?** or **¿verdad?**: *You've done it, haven't you?* **Lo has hecho, ¿verdad?**
have is not usually translated when giving simple negative or positive answers to questions: *Have you read that book? — Yes, I have.* **¿Has leído el libro? — Sí.**

haven ['heɪvn] N puerto; *(fig)* refugio

haven't ['hævnt] = **have not**

haversack ['hævəsæk] N macuto

haves [hævz] NPL *(inf)*: **the ~ and the have-nots** los ricos y los pobres

havoc ['hævək] N estragos *mpl*; **to play ~ with sth** hacer estragos en algo

Hawaii [hə'waɪiː] N (Islas *fpl*) Hawai *m*

Hawaiian [hə'waɪjən] ADJ, N hawaiano(-a) *m/f*

hawk [hɔːk] N halcón *m* ▸ VT *(goods for sale)* pregonar

hawkish ['hɔːkɪʃ] ADJ beligerante

hawthorn ['hɔːθɔːn] N espino

hay [heɪ] N heno

hay fever N fiebre *f* del heno

haystack ['heɪstæk] N almiar *m*

haywire ['heɪwaɪər] ADJ *(inf)*: **to go ~** *(person)* volverse loco; *(plan)* irse al garete

hazard ['hæzəd] N riesgo; *(danger)* peligro; **to be a health ~** ser un peligro para la salud ▸ VT *(remark)* aventurar; *(one's life)* arriesgar; **to ~ a guess** aventurar una respuesta *or* hipótesis

hazardous ['hæzədəs] ADJ *(dangerous)* peligroso; *(risky)* arriesgado

hazard warning lights NPL *(Aut)* señales *fpl* de emergencia

haze [heɪz] N neblina

hazel ['heɪzl] N *(tree)* avellano ▸ ADJ *(eyes)* color *m* de avellano

hazelnut ['heɪzlnʌt] N avellana

hazy ['heɪzɪ] ADJ brumoso; *(idea)* vago

H-bomb ['eɪtʃbɒm] N bomba H

HD ABBR (= high definition) HD *m*

HDTV ABBR (= high definition television) HDTV *f*

HE ABBR = **high explosive**; *(Rel, Diplomacy*: = His (or Her) Excellency) S. Exc^a

★**he** [hiː] PRON él; **he who ...** aquel que ..., quien ...

he is not usually translated unless it is emphatic: *He is very tall.* **Es muy alto.**
Use **él** for emphasis: *He went but she didn't.* **Él fue pero ella no.**

★**head** [hɛd] N cabeza; *(leader)* jefe(-a) *m/f*; **heads (or tails)** cara (o cruz); **~ first** de cabeza; **~ over heels** patas arriba; **~ over heels in love** perdidamente enamorado; **on your ~ be it!** ¡allá tú!; **they went over my ~ to the manager** fueron directamente al gerente sin hacerme caso; **it was above** *or* **over their heads** no alcanzaron a entenderlo; **to come to a ~** *(fig: situation etc)* llegar a un punto crítico; **to have a ~ for business** tener talento para los negocios; **to have no ~ for heights** no resistir las alturas; **to lose/keep one's ~** perder la cabeza/mantener la calma; **to sit at the ~ of the table** sentarse a la cabecera de la mesa ▸ VT *(list)* encabezar; *(group)* capitanear; **to ~ the ball** cabecear (el balón)
  ▸ **head for** VT FUS dirigirse a; *(disaster)* ir camino de
  ▸ **head off** VT *(threat, danger)* evitar

★**headache** ['hɛdeɪk] N dolor *m* de cabeza; **to have a ~** tener dolor de cabeza

headband ['hɛdbænd] N cinta (para la cabeza), vincha *(LAm)*

headboard ['hɛdbɔːd] N cabecera

headdress ['hɛddrɛs] N *(of bride, Indian)* tocado

headed notepaper ['hɛdɪd-] N papel *m* con membrete

header ['hɛdər] N *(Brit inf: Football)* cabezazo; *(: fall)* caída de cabeza

headfirst [hɛd'fəːst] ADV de cabeza

headhunt ['hɛdhʌnt] VT: **to be headhunted** ser seleccionado por un cazatalentos

headhunter ['hɛdhʌntər] N *(fig)* cazaejecutivos *mf*

heading ['hɛdɪŋ] N título

headlamp ['hɛdlæmp] N *(Brit)* = **headlight**

headland ['hɛdlənd] N promontorio

headlight ['hɛdlaɪt] N faro

★**headline** ['hɛdlaɪn] N titular *m*

headlong ['hɛdlɒŋ] ADV *(fall)* de cabeza; *(rush)* precipitadamente

headmaster [hɛd'mɑːstər] N director *m* (de escuela)

headmistress [hɛd'mɪstrɪs] N directora *f* (de escuela)

head office N oficina central, central *f*

head-on [hɛd'ɒn] ADJ *(collision)* de frente

headphones ['hɛdfəunz] NPL auriculares *mpl*

★**headquarters** ['hɛdkwɔːtəz] NPL sede *f* central; *(Mil)* cuartel *m* general

head-rest ['hɛdrɛst] N reposa-cabezas *m inv*

headroom ['hɛdrum] N *(in car)* altura interior; *(under bridge)* (límite *m* de) altura

headscarf ['hɛdskɑːf] N pañuelo

headset ['hɛdsɛt] N cascos *mpl*

headstone ['hɛdstəun] N lápida

headstrong ['hɛdstrɒŋ] ADJ testarudo

head teacher N director(a)

head waiter N maître *m*

headway ['hɛdweɪ] N: **to make ~** *(fig)* hacer progresos

headwind ['hɛdwɪnd] N viento contrario

heady ['hɛdɪ] ADJ *(experience, period)* apasionante; *(wine)* fuerte

★**heal** [hiːl] vt curar ▸ vi cicatrizar

★**health** [hɛlθ] n salud f

health care n asistencia sanitaria

health centre n ambulatorio, centro médico

health food n, **health foods** npl alimentos mpl orgánicos

health hazard n riesgo para la salud

Health Service n (Brit) Servicio Nacional de Salud

★**healthy** [ˈhɛlθɪ] adj (gen) sano; (economy, bank balance) saludable

heap [hiːp] n montón m; **heaps of** (inf: lots) montones de ▸ vt amontonar; (plate) colmar; **to ~ favours/praise/gifts** etc **on sb** colmar a algn de favores/elogios/regalos etc

★**hear** [hɪəʳ] (pt, pp **heard** [haːd]) vt oír; (news) saber; (perceive) sentir; (listen to) escuchar; (lecture) asistir a; (Law: case) ver ▸ vi oír; **to ~ about** oír hablar de; **to ~ from sb** tener noticias de algn; **I've never heard of that book** nunca he oído hablar de ese libro
▸ **hear out** vt: **to ~ sb out** dejar que algn termine de hablar

heard [haːd] pt, pp of **hear**

hearing [ˈhɪərɪŋ] n (sense) oído; (Law) vista; **to give sb a ~** dar a algn la oportunidad de hablar, escuchar a algn

hearing aid n audífono

hearsay [ˈhɪəseɪ] n rumores mpl, habladurías fpl

hearse [haːs] n coche m fúnebre

★**heart** [haːt] n corazón m; (fig) valor m; (of lettuce) cogollo; **at ~** en el fondo; **by ~** (learn, know) de memoria; **to have a weak ~** tener el corazón débil; **to set one's ~ on sth/on doing sth** anhelar algo/hacer algo; **I did not have the ~ to tell her** no tuve valor para decírselo; **to take ~** cobrar ánimos; **the ~ of the matter** lo esencial or el meollo del asunto ■ **hearts** npl (Cards) corazones mpl

heartache [ˈhaːteɪk] n angustia

heart attack n infarto (de miocardio)

heartbeat [ˈhaːtbiːt] n latido (del corazón)

heartbreak [ˈhaːtbreɪk] n angustia, congoja

heartbreaking [ˈhaːtbreɪkɪŋ] adj desgarrador(a)

heartbroken [ˈhaːtbrəukən] adj: **she was ~ about it** eso le partió el corazón

heartburn [ˈhaːtbaːn] n acedía

heart disease n enfermedad f cardíaca

-hearted [ˈhaːtɪd] adj suff: **a kind-hearted person** una persona bondadosa

heartening [ˈhaːtnɪŋ] adj alentador(a)

heart failure n (Med) paro cardíaco

heartfelt [ˈhaːtfɛlt] adj (cordial) cordial; (deeply felt) sincero

hearth [haːθ] n (gen) hogar m; (fireplace) chimenea

heartily [ˈhaːtɪlɪ] adv sinceramente, cordial-

mente; (laugh) a carcajadas; (eat) con buen apetito; **to be ~ sick of** estar completamente harto de

heartland [ˈhaːtlænd] n zona interior or central; (fig) corazón m

heartless [ˈhaːtlɪs] adj despiadado

heartstrings [ˈhaːtstrɪŋz] npl: **to tug (at) sb's ~** tocar la fibra sensible de algn

heart-throb [ˈhaːtθrɔb] n ídolo

heart-to-heart [ˈhaːttəˈhaːt] n (also: **heart-to-heart talk**) conversación f íntima

heart transplant n transplante m de corazón

hearty [ˈhaːtɪ] adj (person) campechano; (laugh) sano; (dislike, support) absoluto

★**heat** [hiːt] n (gen) calor m; (Sport: also: **qualifying heat**) prueba eliminatoria ▸ vt calentar
▸ **heat up** vi (gen) calentarse ▸ vt calentar

heated [ˈhiːtɪd] adj caliente; (fig) acalorado

heater [ˈhiːtəʳ] n calentador m, estufa

heath [hiːθ] n (Brit) brezal m

heathen [ˈhiːðn] adj, n pagano(-a) m/f

heather [ˈhɛðəʳ] n brezo

heating [ˈhiːtɪŋ] n calefacción f

heat-resistant [ˈhiːtrɪzɪstənt] adj refractario

heat-seeking [ˈhiːtsiːkɪŋ] adj guiado por infrarrojos, termoguiado

heatstroke [ˈhiːtstrəuk] n insolación f

heatwave [ˈhiːtweɪv] n ola de calor

heave [hiːv] vt (pull) tirar; (push) empujar con esfuerzo; (lift) levantar (con esfuerzo); **to ~ a sigh** dar or echar un suspiro, suspirar ▸ vi (water) subir y bajar ▸ n tirón m; empujón m; (effort) esfuerzo; (throw) echada
▸ **heave to** vi (Naut) ponerse al pairo

heaven [ˈhɛvn] n cielo; (Rel) paraíso; **thank ~!** ¡gracias a Dios!; **for ~'s sake!** (pleading) ¡por el amor de Dios!, ¡por lo que más quiera!; (protesting) ¡por Dios!

heavenly [ˈhɛvnlɪ] adj celestial; (Rel) divino

heavenly body n cuerpo celeste

heavily [ˈhɛvɪlɪ] adv pesadamente; (drink, smoke) en exceso; (sleep, sigh) profundamente

★**heavy** [ˈhɛvɪ] adj pesado; (work) duro; (sea, rain, meal) fuerte; (drinker, smoker) empedernido; (eater) comilón(-ona); (responsibility) grave; (schedule) ocupado; (weather) bochornoso

heavy-duty [ˈhɛvɪˈdjuːtɪ] adj resistente

heavy goods vehicle n (Brit) vehículo pesado

heavy-handed [ˈhɛvɪˈhændɪd] adj (clumsy, tactless) torpe

heavy industry n industria pesada

heavy metal n (Mus) heavy m (metal)

heavy-set [hɛvɪˈsɛt] adj (esp US) corpulento, fornido

heavy user n consumidor m intensivo

heavyweight [ˈhɛvɪweɪt] n (Sport) peso pesado

Hebrew [ˈhiːbruː] adj, n (Ling) hebreo

Hebrides ['hɛbrɪdiːz] NPL: **the ~** las Hébridas

heck [hɛk] N (inf): **why the ~ ...?** ¿por qué porras ...?; **a ~ of a lot of** cantidad de

heckle ['hɛkl] VT interrumpir

heckler ['hɛklə'] N el/la que interrumpe a un orador

hectare ['hɛktɑː'] N (BRIT) hectárea

hectic ['hɛktɪk] ADJ agitado; (busy) ocupado

hector ['hɛktə'] VT intimidar con bravatas

he'd [hiːd] = **he would; he had**

hedge [hɛdʒ] N seto; **as a ~ against inflation** como protección contra la inflación ▶ VT cercar (con un seto); **one's bets** (fig) cubrirse ▶ VI contestar con evasivas

hedgehog ['hɛdʒhɔg] N erizo

hedgerow ['hɛdʒrəu] N seto vivo

hedonism ['hiːdənɪzəm] N hedonismo

heed [hiːd] N (also: **take heed of**: pay attention) hacer caso de; (: bear in mind) tener en cuenta; **to pay (no) ~ to, take (no) ~ of** (no) hacer caso a, (no) tener en cuenta

heedless ['hiːdlɪs] ADJ desatento

heel [hiːl] N talón m; (of shoe) tacón m; **to take to one's heels** (inf) poner pies en polvorosa; **to bring to ~** meter en cintura ▶ VT (shoe) poner tacón a; see also **dig**

hefty ['hɛftɪ] ADJ (person) fornido; (piece) grande; (price) alto

heifer ['hɛfə'] N novilla, ternera

★**height** [haɪt] N (of person) talla, estatura; (of building) altura; (high ground) cerro; (altitude) altitud f; **what ~ are you?** ¿cuánto mides?; **of average ~** de estatura mediana; **to be afraid of heights** tener miedo a las alturas; **at the ~ of summer** en los días más calurosos del verano; **it's the ~ of fashion** es el último grito en moda

heighten ['haɪtn] VT elevar; (fig) aumentar

heinous ['heɪnəs] ADJ atroz, nefasto

heir [ɛə'] N heredero(-a)

heir apparent N presunto heredero

heiress ['ɛərɛs] N heredera

heirloom ['ɛəluːm] N reliquia de familia

heist [haɪst] N (inf: hold-up) atraco a mano armada

held [hɛld] PT, PP of **hold**

★**helicopter** ['hɛlɪkɔptə'] N helicóptero

heliport ['hɛlɪpɔːt] N (Aviat) helipuerto

helium ['hiːlɪəm] N helio

★**hell** [hɛl] N infierno; **oh ~!** (inf) ¡demonios!, ¡caramba!

he'll [hiːl] = **he will; he shall**

hellbent [hɛl'bɛnt] ADJ (inf): **he was ~ on going** se le metió entre ceja y ceja ir

hellish ['hɛlɪʃ] ADJ infernal; (inf) horrible

★**hello** [hə'ləu] EXCL ¡hola!; (to attract attention) ¡oiga!; (surprise) ¡caramba!; (Tel) ¡dígame! (esp SP), ¡aló! (LAM)

helm [hɛlm] N (Naut) timón m

helmet ['hɛlmɪt] N casco

helmsman ['hɛlmzmən] N (irreg) timonel m

★**help** [hɛlp] N ayuda; (cleaner etc) criada, asistenta; **with the ~ of** con la ayuda de; **to be of ~ to sb** servir a algn ▶ VT ayudar; **can I ~ you?** (in shop) ¿qué desea?; **to ~ sb (to) do sth** echarle una mano or ayudar a algn a hacer algo; **~ yourself** sírvete; **he can't ~ it** no lo puede evitar; **~!** ¡socorro!
▶ **help out** VI ayudar, echar una mano ▶ VT: **to ~ sb out** ayudar a algn, echar una mano a algn

help desk N (esp Comput) centro de asistencia

helper ['hɛlpə'] N ayudante mf

helpful ['hɛlpful] ADJ útil; (person) servicial

helping ['hɛlpɪŋ] N ración f

helping hand N: **to give sb a ~** echar una mano a algn

helpless ['hɛlplɪs] ADJ (incapable) incapaz; (defenceless) indefenso

helpline ['hɛlplaɪn] N teléfono de asistencia al público

Helsinki ['hɛlsɪŋkɪ] N Helsinki m

helter-skelter ['hɛltə'skɛltə'] N (in funfair) tobogán m

hem [hɛm] N dobladillo ▶ VT poner or coser el dobladillo a
▶ **hem in** VT cercar; **to feel hemmed in** (fig) sentirse acosado

he-man ['hiːmæn] N (irreg) macho

hematology [hiːmə'tɔlədʒɪ] N (US) = **haematology**

hemisphere ['hɛmɪsfɪə'] N hemisferio

hemline ['hɛmlaɪn] N bajo (del vestido)

hemlock ['hɛmlɔk] N cicuta

hemoglobin [hiːmə'gləubɪn] N (US) = **haemoglobin**

hemophilia [hiːmə'fɪlɪə] N (US) = **haemophilia**

hemorrhage ['hɛmərɪdʒ] N (US) = **haemorrhage**

hemorrhoids ['hɛmərɔɪdz] NPL (US) = **haemorrhoids**

hemp [hɛmp] N cáñamo

hen [hɛn] N gallina; (female bird) hembra

hence [hɛns] ADV (therefore) por lo tanto; **two years ~** de aquí a dos años

henceforth [hɛns'fɔːθ] ADV de hoy en adelante

henchman ['hɛntʃmən] N (irreg) (pej) secuaz m

henna ['hɛnə] N alheña

hen night N (inf) despedida de soltera

hen party N (inf) reunión f de mujeres

henpecked ['hɛnpɛkt] ADJ: **to be ~** ser un calzonazos

hepatitis [hɛpə'taɪtɪs] N hepatitis f inv

★**her** [hɜː'] PRON (direct) la; (indirect) le; (stressed, after prep) ella ▶ ADJ su; see also **me; my**

herald ['hɛrəld] N (forerunner) precursor(a) m/f ▶ VT anunciar

heraldic [hɛ'rældɪk] ADJ heráldico

heraldry ['hɛrəldrɪ] N heráldica

herb [həːb] N hierba

herbaceous [həːˈbeɪʃəs] ADJ herbáceo

herbal [ˈhəːbl] ADJ de hierbas

herbal tea N infusión f de hierbas

herbicide [ˈhəːbɪsaɪd] N herbicida m

herd [həːd] N rebaño; (of wild animals, swine) piara ▶ VT (drive, gather: animals) llevar en manada; (: people) reunir
   ▶ **herd together** VT agrupar, reunir ▶ VI apiñarse, agruparse

★**here** [hɪər] ADV aquí; **~!** (present) ¡presente!; **~ is/ are** aquí está/están; **~ she is** aquí está; **come ~!** ¡ven aquí or acá!; **~ and there** aquí y allá

hereabouts [ˈhɪərəˈbauts] ADV por aquí (cerca)

hereafter [hɪərˈɑːftər] ADV en el futuro ▶ N: **the ~** el más allá

hereby [hɪəˈbaɪ] ADV (in letter) por la presente

hereditary [hɪˈredɪtrɪ] ADJ hereditario

heredity [hɪˈredɪtɪ] N herencia

heresy [ˈherəsɪ] N herejía

heretic [ˈherətɪk] N hereje mf

heretical [hɪˈretɪkəl] ADJ herético

herewith [hɪəˈwɪθ] ADV: **I send you ~** ... le mando adjunto ...

heritage [ˈherɪtɪdʒ] N (gen) herencia; (fig) patrimonio; **our national ~** nuestro patrimonio nacional

hermetically [həːˈmetɪkəlɪ] ADV: **~ sealed** herméticamente cerrado

hermit [ˈhəːmɪt] N ermitaño(-a)

hernia [ˈhəːnɪə] N hernia

★**hero** [ˈhɪərəu] (pl **heroes**) N héroe m; (in book, film) protagonista m

heroic [hɪˈrəuɪk] ADJ heroico

heroin [ˈherəuɪn] N heroína

heroin addict N heroinómano(-a), adicto(-a) a la heroína

heroine [ˈherəuɪn] N heroína; (in book, film) protagonista

heroism [ˈherəuɪzm] N heroísmo

heron [ˈherən] N garza

hero worship N veneración f

herring [ˈherɪŋ] N pl inv arenque m

hers [həːz] PRON (el) suyo/(la) suya etc; **a friend of ~** un amigo suyo; **this is ~** esto es suyo or de ella; see also **mine¹**

★**herself** [həːˈself] PRON (reflexive) se; (emphatic) ella misma; (after prep) sí (misma); see also **oneself**

he's [hiːz] = **he is; he has**

hesitant [ˈhezɪtənt] ADJ indeciso; **to be ~ about doing sth** no decidirse a hacer algo

hesitate [ˈhezɪteɪt] VI dudar, vacilar; (in speech) titubear; (be unwilling) resistirse a; **don't ~ to ask (me)** no dudes en pedírmelo

hesitation [hezɪˈteɪʃən] N indecisión f; **I have no ~ in saying (that)** ... no tengo el menor reparo en afirmar que ...

hessian [ˈhesɪən] N arpillera

heterogeneous [hetərəˈdʒiːnɪəs] ADJ heterogéneo

heterosexual [hetərəuˈseksjuəl] ADJ, N heterosexual mf

het up [hetˈʌp] ADJ (inf) agitado, nervioso

hew [hjuː] VT cortar

hex [heks] (US) N maleficio, mal m de ojo ▶ VT embrujar

hexagon [ˈheksəgən] N hexágono

hexagonal [hekˈsægənl] ADJ hexagonal

hey [heɪ] EXCL ¡oye!, ¡oiga!

heyday [ˈheɪdeɪ] N: **the ~ of** el apogeo de

HF N ABBR = **high frequency**

HGV N ABBR = **heavy goods vehicle**

HI ABBR (US) = **Hawaii**

★**hi** [haɪ] EXCL ¡hola!

hiatus [haɪˈeɪtəs] N vacío, interrupción f; (Ling) hiato

hibernate [ˈhaɪbəneɪt] VI invernar

hibernation [haɪbəˈneɪʃən] N hibernación f

hiccough, hiccup [ˈhɪkʌp] VI hipar ■ **hiccoughs** NPL hipo sg

hick [hɪk] N (US pej) paleto(-a)

hid [hɪd] PT of **hide**

hidden [ˈhɪdn] PP of **hide** ▶ ADJ: **there are no ~ extras** no hay suplementos ocultos; **~ agenda** plan m encubierto

★**hide** [haɪd] (pt **hid** [hɪd], pp **hidden** [ˈhɪdn]) N (skin) piel f ▶ VT esconder, ocultar; (feelings, truth) encubrir, ocultar ▶ VI: **to ~ (from sb)** esconderse or ocultarse (de algn)

hide-and-seek [ˈhaɪdənˈsiːk] N escondite m

hideaway [ˈhaɪdəweɪ] N escondite m

hideous [ˈhɪdɪəs] ADJ horrible

hideously [ˈhɪdɪəslɪ] ADV horriblemente

hide-out [ˈhaɪdaut] N escondite m, refugio

hiding [ˈhaɪdɪŋ] N (beating) paliza; **to be in ~** (concealed) estar escondido

hiding place N escondrijo

hierarchy [ˈhaɪərɑːkɪ] N jerarquía

hieroglyphic [haɪərəˈglɪfɪk] ADJ jeroglífico ▶ N: **hieroglyphics** jeroglíficos mpl

hi-fi [ˈhaɪfaɪ] ABBR = **high fidelity** ▶ N estéreo, hifi m ▶ ADJ de alta fidelidad

higgledy-piggledy [ˈhɪgldɪˈpɪgldɪ] ADV en desorden, de cualquier modo

★**high** [haɪ] ADJ alto; (speed, number) grande, alto; (price) elevado; (wind) fuerte; (voice) agudo; (inf: on drugs) colocado; (: on drink) borracho; (Culin: meat, game) pasado; (: spoilt) estropeado; **it is 20 m ~** tiene 20 m de altura; **to pay a ~ price for sth** pagar algo muy caro; **~ in the air** en las alturas ▶ ADV alto, a gran altura ▶ N: **exports have reached a new ~** las exportaciones han alcanzado niveles inusitados

highball [ˈhaɪbɔːl] N (US: drink) whisky m soda, highball m (LAM), jaibol m (LAM)

highboy [ˈhaɪbɔɪ] N (US) cómoda alta
highbrow [ˈhaɪbrau] ADJ culto
highchair [ˈhaɪtʃɛəʳ] N silla alta (para niños)
high-class [ˈhaɪˈklɑːs] ADJ (neighbourhood) de alta sociedad; (hotel) de lujo; (person) distinguido, de categoría; (food) de alta categoría
High Court N (Law) tribunal m supremo

> En el sistema legal de Inglaterra y Gales **High Court** es la forma abreviada de High Court of Justice, tribunal superior que junto con el de apelación (Court of Appeal) forma el Tribunal Supremo (Supreme Court). En el sistema legal escocés es la forma abreviada de High Court of Justiciary, tribunal con jurado que juzga los delitos más serios, que pueden dar lugar a una pena de gran severidad.

higher [ˈhaɪəʳ] ADJ (form of life, study etc) superior ▶ ADV más alto ▶ N (Scottish Scol): **H~** cada una de las asignaturas que se estudian entre los 16 y los 17 años generalmente, así como el certificado de haberlas probado
★**higher education** N educación f or enseñanza superior
high explosive N explosivo de gran potencia
highfalutin [haɪfəˈluːtɪn] ADJ (inf) de altos vuelos, encopetado
high finance N altas finanzas fpl
high-flier, high-flyer [haɪˈflaɪəʳ] N ambicioso(-a)
high-handed [haɪˈhændɪd] ADJ despótico
high-heeled [haɪˈhiːld] ADJ de tacón alto
high heels NPL (heels) tacones mpl altos; (shoes) zapatos mpl de tacón
highjack [ˈhaɪdʒæk] VB, N = **hijack**
high jump N (Sport) salto de altura
highlands [ˈhaɪləndz] NPL tierras fpl altas; **the H~** (in Scotland) las Tierras Altas de Escocia
high-level [ˈhaɪlɛvl] ADJ (talks etc) de alto nivel
★**highlight** [ˈhaɪlaɪt] N (fig: of event) punto culminante ▶ VT subrayar ■ **highlights** NPL (in hair) reflejos mpl
highlighter N rotulador m
highly [ˈhaɪlɪ] ADV sumamente; **~ paid** muy bien pagado; **to speak ~ of** hablar muy bien de; **~ strung** muy excitable
High Mass N misa mayor
highness [ˈhaɪnɪs] N altura; **Her** or **His H~** Su Alteza
high-pitched [haɪˈpɪtʃt] ADJ agudo
high point N: **the ~** el punto culminante
high-powered [ˈhaɪˈpauəd] ADJ (engine) de gran potencia; (fig: person) importante
high-pressure [ˈhaɪprɛʃəʳ] ADJ de alta presión; (fig: salesman etc) enérgico
high-rise [ˈhaɪraɪz] N (also: **high-rise block**, **high-rise building**) torre f de pisos

high school N centro de enseñanza secundaria, ≈ Instituto Nacional de Bachillerato (SP), liceo (LAM)

> El término **high school** se aplica en Estados Unidos a dos tipos de centros de educación secundaria: Junior High Schools, en los que se imparten normalmente del 7° al 9° curso (llamado grade) y Senior High Schools, que abarcan los cursos 10°, 11° y 12° y en ocasiones el 9°. Aquí pueden estudiarse asignaturas tanto de contenido académico como profesional. En Gran Bretaña también se llaman high school algunos centros de enseñanza secundaria.

high season N (BRIT) temporada alta
high-speed [ˈhaɪspiːd] ADJ de alta velocidad
high-spirited [haɪˈspɪrɪtɪd] ADJ animado
high spirits NPL ánimos mpl
high street N (BRIT) calle f mayor
high-tech (inf) ADJ al-tec (inf), de alta tecnología
high tide N marea alta
highway [ˈhaɪweɪ] N carretera; (US) autopista
Highway Code N (BRIT) código de la circulación
highwayman [ˈhaɪweɪmən] N (irreg) salteador m de caminos
hijack [ˈhaɪdʒæk] VT secuestrar ▶ N (also: **hijacking**) secuestro
hijacker [ˈhaɪdʒækəʳ] N secuestrador(a) m/f
hike [haɪk] VI (go walking) ir de excursión (a pie); (tramp) caminar ▶ N caminata; (inf: in prices etc) aumento
▶ **hike up** VT (raise) aumentar
hiker [ˈhaɪkəʳ] N excursionista mf
hiking [ˈhaɪkɪŋ] N senderismo
hilarious [hɪˈlɛərɪəs] ADJ divertidísimo
hilarity [hɪˈlærɪtɪ] N (laughter) risas fpl, carcajadas fpl
★**hill** [hɪl] N colina; (high) montaña; (slope) cuesta
hillbilly [ˈhɪlbɪlɪ] N (US) rústico(-a) montañés(-esa); (pej) palurdo(-a)
hillock [ˈhɪlək] N montecillo, altozano
hillside [ˈhɪlsaɪd] N ladera
hilltop [ˈhɪltɒp] N cumbre f
hill walking N senderismo (de montaña)
hilly [ˈhɪlɪ] ADJ montañoso; (uneven) accidentado
hilt [hɪlt] N (of sword) empuñadura; **to the ~** (fig: support) incondicionalmente; **to be in debt up to the ~** estar hasta el cuello de deudas
★**him** [hɪm] PRON (direct) lo, le (SP); (indirect) le; (stressed, after prep) él; see also **me**
Himalayas [hɪməˈleɪəz] NPL: **the ~** el Himalaya
★**himself** [hɪmˈsɛlf] PRON (reflexive) se; (emphatic) él mismo; (after prep) sí (mismo); see also **oneself**
hind [haɪnd] ADJ posterior ▶ N cierva
hinder [ˈhɪndəʳ] VT estorbar, impedir
hindquarters [ˈhaɪndkwɔːtəz] NPL (Zool) cuartos mpl traseros

hindrance [ˈhɪndrəns] N estorbo, obstáculo

hindsight [ˈhaɪndsaɪt] N percepción *f* tardía *or* retrospectiva; **with ~** en retrospectiva; **with the benefit of ~** con la perspectiva del tiempo transcurrido

Hindu [ˈhɪnduː] N hindú *mf*

Hinduism [ˈhɪnduːɪzm] N (*Rel*) hinduismo

hinge [hɪndʒ] N bisagra, gozne *m* ▶ VI (*fig*): **to ~ on** depender de

★**hint** [hɪnt] N indirecta; (*advice*) consejo; **to drop a ~** soltar *or* tirar una indirecta; **give me a ~** dame una pista ▶ VT: **to ~ that** insinuar que ▶ VI: **to ~ at** aludir a

★**hip** [hɪp] N cadera; (*Bot*) escaramujo

hip flask N petaca

hip-hop [ˈhɪphɔp] N hip hop *m*

hippie [ˈhɪpɪ] N hippie *mf*, jipi *mf*

hippo [ˈhɪpəu] (*pl* **hippos**) N hipopótamo

hip pocket N bolsillo de atrás

hippopotamus [hɪpəˈpɔtəməs] (*pl* **hippopotamuses** *or* **hippopotami** [-ˈpɔtəmaɪ]) N hipopótamo

hippy [ˈhɪpɪ] N = **hippie**

hipster [ˈhɪpstər] N (*inf: fashionable person*) hipster *mf*

★**hire** [ˈhaɪər] VT (*Brit: car, equipment*) alquilar; (*worker*) contratar ▶ N alquiler *m*; **for ~** se alquila; (*taxi*) libre; **on ~** de alquiler ▶ **hire out** VT alquilar, arrendar

hire car, hired car N (*Brit*) coche *m* de alquiler

hire purchase N (*Brit*) compra a plazos; **to buy sth on ~** comprar algo a plazos

★**his** [hɪz] PRON (el) suyo/(la) suya *etc*; **this is ~** esto es suyo *or* de él ▶ ADJ su; *see also* **my; mine¹**

Hispanic [hɪsˈpænɪk] ADJ hispánico

hiss [hɪs] VI sisear; (*in protest*) silbar ▶ N siseo; silbido

histogram [ˈhɪstəgræm] N histograma *m*

historian [hɪˈstɔːrɪən] N historiador(a) *m/f*

historic [hɪˈstɔrɪk], **historical** [hɪˈstɔrɪkl] ADJ histórico

★**history** [ˈhɪstərɪ] N historia; **there's a long ~ of that illness in his family** esa enfermedad corre en su familia

histrionics [hɪstrɪˈɔnɪks] NPL histrionismo

★**hit** [hɪt] VT (*pt, pp* **~**) (*strike*) golpear, pegar; (*reach: target*) alcanzar; (*collide with: car*) chocar contra; (*fig: affect*) afectar; **to ~ the headlines** salir en primera plana; **to ~ the road** (*inf*) largarse; **to ~ it off with sb** llevarse bien con algn ▶ N golpe *m*; (*success*) éxito; (*on website*) visita; (*in web search*) correspondencia

▶ **hit back** VI defenderse; (*fig*) devolver golpe por golpe

▶ **hit out at** VT FUS asestar un golpe a; (*fig*) atacar

▶ **hit (up)on** VT FUS (*answer*) dar con; (*solution*) hallar, encontrar

hit and miss ADJ: **it's very ~**, **it's a ~ affair** es cuestión de suerte

hit-and-run driver [ˈhɪtənˈrʌn-] N conductor *que tras atropellar a algn se da a la fuga*

hitch [hɪtʃ] VT (*fasten*) atar, amarrar; (*also*: **hitch up**) arremangarse; **to ~ a lift** hacer autostop ▶ N (*difficulty*) problema, pega; **technical ~** problema *m* técnico

▶ **hitch up** VT (*horse, cart*) enganchar, uncir

hitch-hike [ˈhɪtʃhaɪk] VI hacer autostop

hitch-hiker [ˈhɪtʃhaɪkər] N autostopista *mf*

hitch-hiking [ˈhɪtʃhaɪkɪŋ] N autostop *m*

hi-tech [ˈhaɪˈtek] ADJ de alta tecnología

hitherto [ˈhɪðəˈtuː] ADV hasta ahora, hasta aquí

hit list N lista negra

hitman [ˈhɪtmæn] N (*irreg*) asesino a sueldo

hit or miss [ˈhɪtəˈmɪs] ADJ = **hit and miss**

hit parade N: **the ~** los cuarenta principales

HIV N ABBR (= *human immunodeficiency virus*) VIH *m*; **HIV-negative** VIH negativo; **HIV-positive** VIH positivo, seropositivo

hive [haɪv] N colmena; **the shop was a ~ of activity** (*fig*) la tienda era una colmena humana

▶ **hive off** VT (*inf: separate*) separar; (*: privatize*) privatizar

hl ABBR (= *hectolitre*) hl

HM ABBR (= *His* (*or Her*) *Majesty*) S.M.

HMG ABBR (*Brit*) = **Her/His Majesty's Government**

HMI N ABBR (*Brit Scol*) = **Her/His Majesty's Inspector**

HMO N ABBR (*US*: = *Health Maintenance Organization*) seguro médico global

HMS ABBR = **Her/His Majesty's Ship**

HMSO N ABBR (*Brit*: = *Her/His Majesty's Stationery Office*) distribuidor oficial de las publicaciones del gobierno del Reino Unido

HNC N ABBR (*Brit*: = *Higher National Certificate*) título académico

HND N ABBR (*Brit*: = *Higher National Diploma*) título académico

hoard [hɔːd] N (*treasure*) tesoro; (*stockpile*) provisión *f* ▶ VT acumular

hoarding [ˈhɔːdɪŋ] N (*for posters*) valla publicitaria

hoarfrost [ˈhɔːfrɔst] N escarcha

hoarse [hɔːs] ADJ ronco

hoax [həuks] N engaño

hob [hɔb] N quemador *m*

hobble [ˈhɔbl] VI cojear

hobby [ˈhɔbɪ] N pasatiempo, afición *f*

hobby-horse [ˈhɔbɪhɔːs] N (*fig*) tema preferido

hobnob [ˈhɔbnɔb] VI: **to ~ (with)** alternar (con)

hobo [ˈhəubəu] N (*US*) vagabundo

hock [hɔk] N corvejón *m*; (*inf*): **to be in ~** (*person*) estar empeñado *or* endeudado; (*object*) estar empeñado

hockey [ˈhɔkɪ] N hockey m
hockey stick N palo de hockey
hocus-pocus [həukəsˈpəukəs] N (trickery) engañifa; (words: of magician) abracadabra m
hod [hɔd] N capacho
hodge-podge [ˈhɔdʒpɔdʒ] N (US) = **hotchpotch**
hoe [həu] N azadón m ▶ VT azadonar
hog [hɔg] N cerdo, puerco; **to go the whole ~** echar el todo por el todo ▶ VT (fig) acaparar
Hogmanay [hɔgməˈneɪ] N (SCOTTISH) Nochevieja

> La Nochevieja o *New Year's Eve* se conoce como **Hogmanay** en Escocia, donde se festeja de forma especial. La familia y los amigos se suelen juntar para oír las campanadas del reloj y luego se hace el *first-footing*, costumbre que consiste en visitar a los amigos y vecinos llevando algo de beber (generalmente whisky) y un trozo de carbón que se supone que traerá buena suerte para el año entrante.

hoist [hɔɪst] N (crane) grúa ▶ VT levantar, alzar
hoity-toity [hɔɪtɪˈtɔɪtɪ] ADJ (inf): **to be ~** darse humos
hold [həuld] (pt, pp **held** [held]) VT sostener; (contain) contener; (have: power, qualification) tener; (keep back) retener; (believe) sostener; (take hold of) coger (SP), agarrar (LAM); (bear: weight) soportar; (: meeting) celebrar; **~ the line!** (Tel) ¡no cuelgue!; **to ~ one's own** (fig) defenderse; **to ~ office** (Pol) ocupar un cargo; **he holds the view that ...** opina or es su opinión que ...; **to ~ sb responsible for sth** culpar or echarle la culpa a algn de algo ▶ VI (withstand: pressure) resistir; (be valid) ser válido; (stick) pegarse; **to ~ firm** or **fast** mantenerse firme ▶ N (grasp) asimiento; (fig) dominio; (Wrestling) presa; (Naut) bodega; **where can I get ~ of ...?** ¿dónde puedo encontrar (a) ...?; **to catch** or **get (a) ~ of** agarrarse or asirse de
▶ **hold back** VT retener; (secret) ocultar; **to ~ sb back from doing sth** impedir a algn hacer algo, impedir que algn haga algo
▶ **hold down** VT (person) sujetar; (job) mantener
▶ **hold forth** VI perorar
▶ **hold off** VT (enemy) rechazar ▶ VI: **if the rain holds off** si no llueve
▶ **hold on** VI agarrarse bien; (wait) esperar; **~ on!** (Tel) ¡(espere) un momento!
▶ **hold on to** VT FUS agarrarse a; (keep) guardar
▶ **hold out** VT ofrecer ▶ VI (resist) resistir; **to ~ out (against)** resistir (a), sobrevivir
▶ **hold over** VT (meeting etc) aplazar
▶ **hold up** VT (raise) levantar; (support) apoyar; (delay) retrasar; (: traffic) demorar; (: rob: bank) asaltar, atracar
holdall [ˈhəuldɔːl] N (BRIT) bolsa
holder [ˈhəuldəʳ] N (of ticket, record) poseedor(a) m/f; (of passport, post, office, title etc) titular mf
holding [ˈhəuldɪŋ] N (share) participación f
holding company N holding m

holdup [ˈhəuldʌp] N (robbery) atraco; (delay) retraso; (BRIT: in traffic) embotellamiento
★**hole** [həul] N agujero; **~ in the heart** (Med) boquete m en el corazón; **to pick holes in** (fig) encontrar defectos en ▶ VT agujerear; **the ship was holed** se abrió una vía de agua en el barco
▶ **hole up** VI esconderse
★**holiday** [ˈhɔlɪdɪ] N vacaciones fpl; (day off) (día m de) fiesta, día m festivo or (LAM) feriado; **on ~** de vacaciones; **to be on ~** estar de vacaciones
holiday camp N (BRIT) colonia or centro vacacional; (for children) colonia veraniega infantil
holiday home N residencia vacacional
holiday job N (BRIT) trabajo para las vacaciones
holidaymaker [ˈhɔlɪdɪmeɪkəʳ] N (BRIT) turista mf
holiday pay N paga de las vacaciones
holiday resort N centro turístico
holiday season N temporada de vacaciones
holiness [ˈhəulɪnɪs] N santidad f
holistic [həuˈlɪstɪk] ADJ holístico
★**Holland** [ˈhɔlənd] N Holanda
holler [ˈhɔləʳ] VI (inf) gritar, vocear
hollow [ˈhɔləu] ADJ hueco; (fig) vacío; (eyes) hundido; (sound) sordo ▶ N (gen) hueco; (in ground) hoyo ▶ VT: **to ~ out** ahuecar
holly [ˈhɔlɪ] N acebo
hollyhock [ˈhɔlɪhɔk] N malva loca
Hollywood [ˈhɔlɪwud] N Hollywood m
holocaust [ˈhɔləkɔːst] N holocausto
hologram [ˈhɔləgræm] N holograma m
holster [ˈhəulstəʳ] N pistolera
★**holy** [ˈhəulɪ] ADJ (gen) santo, sagrado; (water) bendito; **the H~ Father** el Santo Padre
Holy Communion N Sagrada Comunión f
Holy Ghost, Holy Spirit N Espíritu m Santo
homage [ˈhɔmɪdʒ] N homenaje m; **to pay ~ to** rendir homenaje a
★**home** [həum] N casa; (country) patria; (institution) asilo; (Comput) punto inicial or de partida; **at ~** en casa; **to go/come ~** ir/volver a casa; **make yourself at ~** ¡estás en tu casa!; **it's near my ~** está cerca de mi casa ▶ ADJ (domestic) casero, de casa; (Econ, Pol) nacional; (Sport: team) de casa; (: match, win) en casa ▶ ADV (direction) a casa
▶ **home in on** VT FUS (missile) dirigirse hacia
home address N domicilio
home-brew [həumˈbruː] N cerveza etc casera
homecoming [ˈhəumkʌmɪŋ] N regreso (al hogar)
home computer N ordenador m doméstico
Home Counties NPL condados que rodean Londres
home economics N economía doméstica
home ground N: **to be on ~** estar en su etc terreno
home-grown [ˈhəumgrəun] ADJ de cosecha propia

h

home help N (BRIT) trabajador(a) *m/f* del servicio de atención domiciliaria

homeland ['həumlænd] N tierra natal

★**homeless** ['həumlɪs] ADJ sin hogar, sin casa
▶ NPL: **the ~** las personas sin hogar

home loan N préstamo para la vivienda

homely ['həumlɪ] ADJ (*domestic*) casero; (*simple*) sencillo

home-made [həum'meɪd] ADJ casero

home match N partido en casa

Home Office N (BRIT) Ministerio del Interior

homeopathy *etc* [həumɪ'ɔpəθɪ] (US) = **homoeopathy** *etc*

home owner N propietario(-a) de una casa

★**home page** N (*Comput*) página de inicio

home rule N autonomía

Home Secretary N (BRIT) Ministro del Interior

homesick ['həumsɪk] ADJ: **to be ~** tener morriña *or* nostalgia

homestead ['həumstɛd] N hacienda

home town N ciudad *f* natal

home truth N: **to tell sb a few ~s** decir cuatro verdades a algn

homeward ['həumwəd] ADJ (*journey*) de vuelta
▶ ADV hacia casa

homewards ['həumwədz] ADV hacia casa

★**homework** ['həumwə:k] N deberes *mpl*

homicidal [hɔmɪ'saɪdl] ADJ homicida

homicide ['hɔmɪsaɪd] N (US) homicidio

homily ['hɔmɪlɪ] N homilía

homing ['həumɪŋ] ADJ (*device, missile*) buscador(a); **~ pigeon** paloma mensajera

homoeopath, (US) **homeopath** ['həumɪəupæθ] N homeópata *mf*

homoeopathic, (US) **homeopathic** [həumɪəu'pæθɪk] ADJ homeopático

homoeopathy, (US) **homeopathy** [həumɪ'ɔpəθɪ] N homeopatía

homogeneous [hɔmə'dʒi:nɪəs] ADJ homogéneo

homogenize [hə'mɔdʒənaɪz] VT homogeneizar

homosexual [hɔməu'sɛksjuəl] ADJ, N homosexual *mf*

Hon. ABBR (= *honourable, honorary*) en títulos

Honduras [hɔn'djuərəs] N Honduras *fpl*

hone [həun] VT (*sharpen*) afilar; (*fig*) perfeccionar

★**honest** ['ɔnɪst] ADJ honrado; (*sincere*) franco, sincero; **to be quite ~ with you ...** para serte franco ...

honestly ['ɔnɪstlɪ] ADV honradamente; francamente, de verdad

honesty ['ɔnɪstɪ] N honradez *f*

honey ['hʌnɪ] N miel *f*; (US *inf*) cariño; (: *to strangers*) guapo, linda

honeycomb ['hʌnɪkəum] N panal *m*; (*fig*) laberinto

honeymoon ['hʌnɪmu:n] N luna de miel

honeysuckle ['hʌnɪsʌkl] N madreselva

Hong Kong ['hɔŋ'kɔŋ] N Hong-Kong *m*

honk [hɔŋk] VI (*Aut*) tocar la bocina

Honolulu [hɔnə'lu:lu:] N Honolulú *m*

honorary ['ɔnərərɪ] ADJ no remunerado; (*duty, title*) honorífico; **~ degree** doctorado honoris causa

honour, (US) **honor** ['ɔnə^r] VT honrar; (*commitment, promise*) cumplir con ▶ N honor *m*, honra; **in ~ of** en honor de; **it's a great ~** es un gran honor

honourable, (US) **honorable** ['ɔnərəbl] ADJ honrado, honorable

honour-bound, (US) **honor-bound** ['ɔnə-'baund] ADJ moralmente obligado

honours degree N (*Univ*) licenciatura superior

Tras un período de estudios de tres años normalmente (cuatro en Escocia), los universitarios obtienen una licenciatura llamada **honours degree**. La calificación global que se recibe, en una escala de mayor a menor es la siguiente: *first class* (I), *upper-second class* (II:1), *lower-second class* (II:2) y *third class* (III). El licenciado puede añadir las letras *Hons* al título obtenido tras su nombre y apellidos, por ejemplo *Peter Jones BA Hons*.

honours list N (BRIT) *lista de distinciones honoríficas que entrega la reina*

A la lista con los títulos honoríficos y condecoraciones que el monarca británico otorga en Año Nuevo y en el día de su cumpleaños se la conoce con el nombre de **honours list**. Las personas que reciben dichas distinciones suelen ser miembros destacados de la vida pública en el Reino Unido y la *Commonwealth* (ámbito empresarial, ejército, deportes, espectáculos), aunque últimamente también se reconoce con ellas el trabajo abnegado y anónimo de la gente de la calle.

Hons. [ɔnz] ABBR (*Univ*) = **honours degree**

hood [hud] N capucha; (BRIT *Aut*) capota; (US *Aut*) capó *m*; (US *inf*) matón *m*; (*of cooker*) campana de humos

hooded ['hudɪd] ADJ (*robber*) encapuchado

hoodie ['hudɪ] N (*pullover*) sudadera *f* con capucha; (*young person*) joven *mf* encapuchado(-a)

hoodlum ['hu:dləm] N matón *m*

hoodwink ['hudwɪŋk] VT (BRIT) timar, engañar

hoof [hu:f] (*pl* **hoofs** *or* **hooves** [hu:vz]) N pezuña

★**hook** [huk] N gancho; (*on dress*) corchete *m*, broche *m*; (*for fishing*) anzuelo; **hooks and eyes** corchetes *mpl*, macho y hembra *m*; **by ~ or by crook** por las buenas o por las malas, cueste lo que cueste ▶ VT enganchar; **to be hooked on** (*inf*) estar enganchado a
▶ **hook up** VT (*Radio, TV*) transmitir en cadena

hooligan ['hu:lɪgən] N gamberro

hooliganism [ˈhuːlɪɡənɪzəm] N gamberrismo

hoop [huːp] N aro

hooray [huːˈreɪ] EXCL = **hurrah**

hoot [huːt] VI (BRIT Aut) tocar la bocina; (siren) sonar; (owl) ulular; **to ~ with laughter** morirse de risa ▶ N bocinazo, toque m de sirena

hooter [ˈhuːtəʳ] N (BRIT Aut) bocina; (of ship, factory) sirena

hoover® [ˈhuːvəʳ] (BRIT) N aspiradora ▶ VT pasar la aspiradora por

hooves [huːvz] PL of **hoof**

hop [hɒp] VI saltar, brincar; (on one foot) saltar con un pie ▶ N salto, brinco; see also **hops**

hope [həʊp] VT, VI esperar; **I ~ so/not** espero que sí/no ▶ N esperanza

hopeful [ˈhəʊpful] ADJ (person) optimista; (situation) prometedor(a); **I'm ~ that she'll manage to come** confío en que podrá venir

hopefully [ˈhəʊpfulɪ] ADV con optimismo, con esperanza; **~ he will recover** esperamos que se recupere

hopeless [ˈhəʊplɪs] ADJ desesperado

hopelessly [ˈhəʊplɪslɪ] ADV (live etc) sin esperanzas; **I'm ~ confused/lost** estoy totalmente despistado/perdido

hopper [ˈhɒpəʳ] N (chute) tolva

hops [hɒps] NPL lúpulo sg

horde [hɔːd] N horda

horizon [həˈraɪzn] N horizonte m

horizontal [hɒrɪˈzɒntl] ADJ horizontal

hormone [ˈhɔːməʊn] N hormona

hormone replacement therapy N terapia hormonal sustitutiva

horn [hɔːn] N cuerno, cacho (LAM); (Mus: also: **French horn**) trompa; (Aut) bocina, claxon m

horned [hɔːnd] ADJ con cuernos

hornet [ˈhɔːnɪt] N avispón m

horny [ˈhɔːnɪ] ADJ (material) córneo; (hands) calloso; (US inf) cachondo

horoscope [ˈhɒrəskəʊp] N horóscopo

horrendous [hɒˈrendəs] ADJ horrendo

horrible [ˈhɒrɪbl] ADJ horrible

horribly [ˈhɒrɪblɪ] ADV horriblemente

horrid [ˈhɒrɪd] ADJ horrible, horroroso

horridly [ˈhɒrɪdlɪ] ADV (behave) tremendamente mal

horrific [hɒˈrɪfɪk] ADJ (accident) horroroso; (film) horripilante

horrify [ˈhɒrɪfaɪ] VT horrorizar

horrifying [ˈhɒrɪfaɪɪŋ] ADJ horroroso

horror [ˈhɒrəʳ] N horror m

horror film N película de terror or miedo

horror-struck [ˈhɒrəstrʌk], **horror-stricken** [ˈhɒrəstrɪkn] ADJ horrorizado

hors d'œuvre [ɔːˈdəːvrə] N entremeses mpl

horse [hɔːs] N caballo

horseback [ˈhɔːsbæk] N: **on ~** a caballo

horsebox [ˈhɔːsbɒks] N remolque m para transportar caballos

horse chestnut N (tree) castaño de Indias; (nut) castaña de Indias

horsedrawn [ˈhɔːsdrɔːn] ADJ de tracción animal

horsefly [ˈhɔːsflaɪ] N tábano

horseman [ˈhɔːsmən] N (irreg) jinete m

horsemanship [ˈhɔːsmənʃɪp] N equitación f, manejo del caballo

horseplay [ˈhɔːspleɪ] N pelea amistosa

horsepower [ˈhɔːspaʊəʳ] N caballo (de fuerza), potencia en caballos

horse-racing [ˈhɔːsreɪsɪŋ] N carreras fpl de caballos

horseradish [ˈhɔːsrædɪʃ] N rábano picante

horse riding N (BRIT) equitación f

horseshoe [ˈhɔːsʃuː] N herradura

horse show N concurso hípico

horse-trader [ˈhɔːstreɪdəʳ] N chalán(-ana) m/f

horse trials NPL = **horse show**

horsewhip [ˈhɔːswɪp] VT azotar

horsewoman [ˈhɔːswumən] N (irreg) amazona

horsey [ˈhɔːsɪ] ADJ (inf: person) aficionado a los caballos

horticulture [ˈhɔːtɪkʌltʃəʳ] N horticultura

hose [həʊz] N (also: **hosepipe**) manguera ▶ **hose down** VT limpiar con manguera

hosiery [ˈhəʊzɪərɪ] N calcetería

hospice [ˈhɒspɪs] N hospicio

hospitable [ˈhɒspɪtəbl] ADJ hospitalario

★**hospital** [ˈhɒspɪtl] N hospital m

hospitality [hɒspɪˈtælɪtɪ] N hospitalidad f

hospitalize [ˈhɒspɪtəlaɪz] VT hospitalizar

host [həʊst] N anfitrión m; (TV, Radio) presentador(a) m/f; (of inn etc) mesonero; (Rel) hostia; (large number): **a ~ of** multitud de

★**hostage** [ˈhɒstɪdʒ] N rehén m

hostel [ˈhɒstl] N hostal m; (for students, nurses etc) residencia; (for homeless people) albergue; **(youth) ~** albergue m juvenil

hostelling [ˈhɒstlɪŋ] N: **to go (youth) ~** hospedarse en albergues

hostess [ˈhəʊstɪs] N anfitriona; (BRIT: air hostess) azafata; (TV, Radio) presentadora; (in night-club) señorita de compañía

hostile [ˈhɒstaɪl] ADJ hostil

hostility [hɒˈstɪlɪtɪ] N hostilidad f

★**hot** [hɒt] ADJ caliente; (weather) caluroso, de calor; (as opposed to only warm) muy caliente; (spicy) picante; (fig) ardiente, acalorado; **to be ~** (person) tener calor; (object) estar caliente; (weather) hacer calor
▶ **hot up** VI (inf: situation) ponerse difícil or apurado; (: party) animarse ▶ VT (inf: pace) apretar; (: engine) aumentar la potencia de

hot air N (inf) palabras fpl huecas

hot-air balloon [hɔt'ɛə-] N (Aviat) globo aeroestático or de aire caliente

hotbed ['hɔtbɛd] N (fig) semillero

hot-blooded [hɔt'blʌdɪd] ADJ impetuoso

hotchpotch ['hɔtʃpɔtʃ] N mezcolanza, baturrillo

hot dog N perrito caliente

★**hotel** [həu'tɛl] N hotel m

hotelier [həu'tɛlɪə'] N hotelero(-a)

hotel industry N industria hotelera

hotel room N habitación f de hotel

hot flush N (BRIT) sofoco

hotfoot ['hɔtfut] ADV a toda prisa

hothead ['hɔthɛd] N (fig) exaltado(-a)

hot-headed [hɔt'hɛdɪd] ADJ exaltado

hothouse ['hɔthaus] N invernadero

hot line N (Pol) teléfono rojo, línea directa

hotly ['hɔtlɪ] ADV con pasión, apasionadamente

hotplate ['hɔtpleɪt] N (on cooker) hornillo

hotpot ['hɔtpɔt] N (BRIT Culin) estofado

hot potato N (BRIT inf) asunto espinoso; **to drop sth/sb like a ~** no querer saber ya nada de algo/algn

hot seat N primera fila

hotspot ['hɔt'spɔt] N (Comput: also: **wireless hotspot**) punto de acceso inalámbrico

hot spot N (trouble spot) punto caliente; (night club etc) lugar m popular

hot-tempered ['hɔt'tɛmpəd] ADJ de mal genio or carácter

hot-water bottle [hɔt'wɔːtə-] N bolsa de agua caliente

hot-wire ['hɔtwaɪə'] VT (inf: car) hacer el puente en

hound [haund] VT acosar ▶ N perro de caza

★**hour** ['auə'] N hora; **at 30 miles an ~** a 30 millas por hora; **lunch ~** la hora del almuerzo or de comer; **to pay sb by the ~** pagar a algn por horas

hourly ['auəlɪ] ADJ (de) cada hora; (rate) por hora ▶ ADV cada hora

★**house** N [haus] (pl **houses** ['hauzɪz]) casa; (Pol) cámara; (Theat) sala; **at/to my ~** en/a mi casa; **the H~ of Commons/Lords** (BRIT) la Cámara de los Comunes/Lores; **the H~ of Representatives** (US) la Cámara de Representantes; **it's on the ~** (fig) la casa invita ▶ VT [hauz] (person) alojar

El parlamento de Gran Bretaña está formado por dos cámaras. La **House of Commons** (Cámara de los Comunes) está presidida por el Speaker y formada por 650 MPs o Members of Parliament (diputados), elegidos por sufragio universal directo. La cámara se reúne 175 días por año. La **House of Lords** (Cámara de los Lores) está presidida por el **Lord Chancellor** y formada por lores, que reciben del monarca este título vitalicio. Puede debatir y modificar leyes aprobadas por la Cámara de los Comunes.

En Estados Unidos, el parlamento, llamado Congress (el Congreso), está formado por el Senate (Senado) y la **House of Representatives** (la Cámara de Representantes). Esta segunda está formada por 435 miembros, representando de forma proporcional a la población de cada estado que representan. Son elegidos por un mandato de dos años por sufragio universal directo, y se reúnen en el Capitolio, en Washington DC.

house arrest N arresto domiciliario

houseboat ['hausbəut] N casa flotante

housebound ['hausbaund] ADJ confinado en casa

housebreaking ['hausbreɪkɪŋ] N allanamiento de morada

house-broken ['hausbrəukən] ADJ (US) = **house-trained**

housecoat ['hauskəut] N bata

household ['haushəuld] N familia

householder ['haushəuldə'] N propietario(-a); (head of house) cabeza de familia

househunting ['haushʌntɪŋ] N: **to go ~** ir en busca de vivienda

housekeeper ['hauskiːpə'] N ama de llaves

housekeeping ['hauskiːpɪŋ] N (work) trabajos mpl domésticos; (Comput) gestión f interna; (also: **housekeeping money**) dinero para gastos domésticos

house-owner ['hausəunə'] N propietario(a) de una vivienda

house plant N planta de interior

house-proud ['hauspraud] ADJ preocupado por el embellecimiento de la casa

house-to-house ['haustə'haus] ADJ (search) casa por casa; (collection) de casa en casa

house-train ['haustreɪn] VT (pet) enseñar (a hacer sus necesidades en el sitio apropiado)

house-trained ['haustreɪnd] ADJ (BRIT: animal) enseñado

house-warming ['hauswɔːmɪŋ] N (also: **house-warming party**) fiesta de estreno de una casa

housewife ['hauswaɪf] N (irreg) ama de casa

house wine N vino m de la casa

housework ['hauswəːk] N faenas fpl (de la casa)

housing ['hauzɪŋ] N (act) alojamiento; (houses) viviendas fpl ▶ CPD (problem, shortage) de (la) vivienda

housing association N asociación f de la vivienda

housing benefit N (BRIT) subsidio por alojamiento

housing conditions NPL condiciones fpl de habitabilidad

housing development, (BRIT) **housing estate** N urbanización f

hovel [ˈhɔvl] N casucha

hover [ˈhɔvəʳ] VI flotar (en el aire); (*helicopter*) cernerse; **to ~ on the brink of disaster** estar al borde mismo del desastre

hovercraft [ˈhɔvəkrɑːft] N aerodeslizador m, hovercraft m

hoverport [ˈhɔvəpɔːt] N puerto de aerodeslizadores

★**how** [hau] ADV cómo; **~ are you?** ¿cómo estás?; (*formal*) ¿cómo está usted?; **~ do you do?** encantado, mucho gusto; **~ far is it to ...?** ¿qué distancia hay de aquí a ...?; **~ long have you been here?** ¿cuánto (tiempo) hace que estás aquí?, ¿cuánto (tiempo) llevas aquí?; **~ lovely!** ¡qué bonito!; **~ many/much?** ¿cuántos/cuánto?; **~ much does it cost?** ¿cuánto cuesta?; **~ old are you?** ¿cuántos años tienes?; **~ is school?** ¿qué tal la escuela?; **~ was the film?** ¿qué tal la película?; **~ about a drink?** ¿te gustaría algo de beber?, ¿qué te parece una copa?

★**however** [hauˈevəʳ] ADV de cualquier manera; (+ *adjective*) por muy ... que; (*in questions*) cómo; **~ cold it is** por mucho frío que haga; **~ did you do it?** ¿cómo lo hiciste? ► CONJ sin embargo, no obstante; **~ I do it** lo haga como lo haga

howitzer [ˈhauɪtsəʳ] N (*Mil*) obús m

howl [haul] N aullido ► VI aullar; (*person*) dar alaridos; (*wind*) ulular

howler [ˈhauləʳ] N plancha, falta garrafal

howling [ˈhaulɪŋ] ADJ (*wind*) huracanado

HP N ABBR (*Brit*) = **hire purchase**

hp ABBR (*Aut*) = **horsepower**

HQ N ABBR = **headquarters**

HR N ABBR = **human resources**; (*US*) = **House of Representatives**

hr, hrs ABBR (= *hour(s)*) h

HRH ABBR (= *His (or Her) Royal Highness*) S.A.R.

HRT N ABBR = **hormone replacement therapy**

HS ABBR (*US*) = **high school**

HST ABBR (*US*: = *Hawaiian Standard Time*) hora de Hawai

HT ABBR = **high tension**

HTML N ABBR (*Comput*: = *hypertext markup language*) HTML m

hub [hʌb] N (*of wheel*) cubo; (*fig*) centro

hubbub [ˈhʌbʌb] N barahúnda, barullo

hubcap [ˈhʌbkæp] N tapacubos m inv

HUD N ABBR (*US*: = *Department of Housing and Urban Development*) ministerio de la vivienda y urbanismo

huddle [ˈhʌdl] VI: **to ~ together** amontonarse

hue [hjuː] N color m, matiz m; **~ and cry** n protesta

huff [hʌf] N: **in a ~** enojado

huffy [ˈhʌfɪ] ADJ (*inf*) mosqueado

hug [hʌg] VT abrazar ► N abrazo

★**huge** [hjuːdʒ] ADJ enorme

hulk [hʌlk] N (*ship*) barco viejo; (*person, building etc*) mole f

hulking [ˈhʌlkɪŋ] ADJ pesado

hull [hʌl] N (*of ship*) casco

hullabaloo [ˌhʌləbəˈluː] N (*inf: noise*) algarabía, jaleo

hullo [həˈləu] EXCL = **hello**

hum [hʌm] VT tararear, canturrear ► VI tararear, canturrear; (*insect*) zumbar ► N (*Elec*) zumbido; (*of traffic, machines*) zumbido, ronroneo; (*of voices etc*) murmullo

★**human** [ˈhjuːmən] ADJ humano ► N (*also:* **human being**) ser m humano

humane [hjuːˈmeɪn] ADJ humano, humanitario

humanism [ˈhjuːmənɪzəm] N humanismo

humanitarian [hjuːmænɪˈtɛərɪən] ADJ humanitario

humanity [hjuːˈmænɪtɪ] N humanidad f

humanly [ˈhjuːmənlɪ] ADV humanamente

humanoid [ˈhjuːmənɔɪd] ADJ, N humanoide mf

human relations NPL relaciones fpl humanas

human rights NPL derechos mpl humanos

humble [ˈhʌmbl] ADJ humilde ► VT humillar

humbly [ˈhʌmblɪ] ADV humildemente

humbug [ˈhʌmbʌg] N patrañas fpl; (*Brit: sweet*) caramelo de menta

humdrum [ˈhʌmdrʌm] ADJ (*boring*) monótono, aburrido; (*routine*) rutinario

humid [ˈhjuːmɪd] ADJ húmedo

humidifier [hjuːˈmɪdɪfaɪəʳ] N humectador m

humidity [hjuːˈmɪdɪtɪ] N humedad f

humiliate [hjuːˈmɪlɪeɪt] VT humillar

humiliating [hjuːˈmɪlɪeɪtɪŋ] ADJ humillante, vergonzoso

humiliation [hjuːmɪlɪˈeɪʃən] N humillación f

humility [hjuːˈmɪlɪtɪ] N humildad f

hummus [ˈhuməs] N humus m

humorist [ˈhjuːmərɪst] N humorista mf

humorous [ˈhjuːmərəs] ADJ gracioso, divertido

humour, (*US*) **humor** [ˈhjuːməʳ] N humorismo, sentido del humor; (*mood*) humor m; **sense of ~** sentido del humor; **to be in a good/bad ~** estar de buen/mal humor ► VT (*person*) complacer

humourless, (*US*) **humorless** [ˈhjuːməlɪs] ADJ serio

hump [hʌmp] N (*in ground*) montículo; (*camel's*) giba

humus [ˈhjuːməs] N (*Biol*) humus m

hunch [hʌntʃ] N (*premonition*) presentimiento; **I have a ~ that** tengo la corazonada or el presentimiento de que

hunchback [ˈhʌntʃbæk] N jorobado(-a)

hunched [hʌntʃt] ADJ jorobado

★**hundred** [ˈhʌndrəd] NUM ciento; (*before n*) cien; **about a ~ people** unas cien personas, alrededor de cien personas; **hundreds of** centenares de; **hundreds of people** centenares de personas; **I'm a ~ per cent sure** estoy completamente seguro

hundredth [ˈhʌndrɪdθ] ADJ centésimo

hundredweight [ˈhʌndrədweɪt] N (*Brit*) = 50.8 kg; 112 lb; (*US*) = 45.3 kg; 100 lb

h

hung [hʌŋ] PT, PP of **hang**

Hungarian [hʌŋ'gɛərɪən] ADJ húngaro ▸ N húngaro(-a); (Ling) húngaro

Hungary ['hʌŋgərɪ] N Hungría

hunger ['hʌŋgə'] N hambre f ▸ VI: **to ~ for** (fig) tener hambre de, anhelar

hunger strike N huelga de hambre

hungover [hʌŋ'əuvə'] ADJ (inf): **to be ~** tener resaca

hungrily ['hʌŋgrəlɪ] ADV ávidamente, con ganas

hungry ['hʌŋgrɪ] ADJ hambriento; **to be ~** tener hambre; **~ for** (fig) sediento de

hung up ADJ (inf: obsessed): **to be ~ about sth** estar obsesionado por algo

hunk [hʌŋk] N (of bread etc) trozo, pedazo

hunt [hʌnt] VT (seek) buscar; (Sport) cazar ▸ VI (search): **to ~ (for)** buscar; (Sport) cazar ▸ N caza, cacería
  ▸ **hunt down** VT acorralar, seguir la pista a

hunter ['hʌntə'] N cazador(a) m/f; (horse) caballo de caza

hunting ['hʌntɪŋ] N caza

hurdle ['hə:dl] N (Sport) valla; (fig) obstáculo

hurl [hə:l] VT lanzar, arrojar

hurling ['hə:lɪŋ] N (Sport) juego irlandés semejante al hockey

hurly-burly ['hə:lɪ'bə:lɪ] N jaleo, follón m

hurrah [hu'rɑ:], **hurray** [hu'reɪ] N ¡viva!, ¡hurra!

hurricane ['hʌrɪkən] N huracán m

hurried ['hʌrɪd] ADJ (fast) apresurado; (rushed) hecho de prisa

hurriedly ['hʌrɪdlɪ] ADV con prisa, apresuradamente

hurry ['hʌrɪ] N prisa; **to be in a ~** tener prisa, tener apuro (LAM), estar apurado (LAM) ▸ VI apresurarse, darse prisa, apurarse (LAM); **to ~ back/home** darse prisa en volver/volver a casa ▸ VT (person) dar prisa a; (work) apresurar, hacer de prisa
  ▸ **hurry along** VI pasar de prisa
  ▸ **hurry away, hurry off** VI irse corriendo
  ▸ **hurry on** VI: **to ~ on to say** apresurarse a decir
  ▸ **hurry up** VI darse prisa, apurarse (LAM)

⋆**hurt** [hə:t] (pt, pp ~) VT hacer daño a; (business, interests etc) perjudicar; **I ~ my arm** me lastimé el brazo ▸ VI doler; **where does it ~?** ¿dónde te duele? ▸ ADJ lastimado

hurtful ['hə:tful] ADJ (remark etc) hiriente, dañino

hurtle ['hə:tl] VI: **to ~ past** pasar como un rayo

⋆**husband** ['hʌzbənd] N marido

hush [hʌʃ] N silencio ▸ VT hacer callar; (cover up) encubrir; **~!** ¡chitón!, ¡cállate!
  ▸ **hush up** VT (fact) encubrir, callar

hushed [hʌʃt] ADJ (voice) bajo

hush-hush [hʌʃ'hʌʃ] ADJ (inf) muy secreto

husk [hʌsk] N (of wheat) cáscara

husky ['hʌskɪ] ADJ ronco; (burly) fornido ▸ N perro esquimal

hustings ['hʌstɪŋz] NPL (Pol) mitin msg preelectoral

hustle ['hʌsl] VT (push) empujar; (hurry) dar prisa a ▸ N bullicio, actividad f febril; **~ and bustle** ajetreo

hut [hʌt] N cabaña; (shed) cobertizo

hutch [hʌtʃ] N conejera

hyacinth ['haɪəsɪnθ] N jacinto

hybrid ['haɪbrɪd] ADJ, N híbrido; **~ car** coche híbrido; **~ engine** motor híbrido

hydrangea [haɪ'dreɪnʒə] N hortensia

hydrant ['haɪdrənt] N (also: **fire hydrant**) boca de incendios

hydraulic [haɪ'drɔ:lɪk] ADJ hidráulico

hydraulics [haɪ'drɔ:lɪks] N hidráulica

hydrochloric ['haɪdrəu'klɔrɪk] ADJ: **~ acid** ácido clorhídrico

hydroelectric [haɪdrəuɪ'lɛktrɪk] ADJ hidroeléctrico

hydrofoil ['haɪdrəfɔɪl] N aerodeslizador m

hydrogen ['haɪdrədʒən] N hidrógeno

hydrogen bomb N bomba de hidrógeno

hydrophobia [haɪdrə'fəubɪə] N hidrofobia

hydroplane ['haɪdrəpleɪn] N hidroavión m, hidroavioneta

hyena [haɪ'i:nə] N hiena

hygiene ['haɪdʒi:n] N higiene f

hygienic [haɪ'dʒi:nɪk] ADJ higiénico

hymn [hɪm] N himno

hype [haɪp] N (inf) bombo

hyperactive [haɪpər'æktɪv] ADJ hiperactivo

hyperconnectivity ['haɪpəkənɛk'tɪvəti] N hiperconectividad f

hyperlink ['haɪpəlɪŋk] N hiperenlace m

hypermarket ['haɪpəmɑ:kɪt] N hipermercado

hypertension ['haɪpə'tɛnʃən] N hipertensión f

hypertext ['haɪpə'tɛkst] N (Comput) hipertexto m

hyperventilation [haɪpəvɛntɪ'leɪʃən] N hiperventilación f

hyphen ['haɪfn] N guión m

hypnosis [hɪp'nəusɪs] N hipnosis f

hypnotic [hɪp'nɔtɪk] ADJ hipnótico

hypnotism ['hɪpnətɪzəm] N hipnotismo

hypnotist ['hɪpnətɪst] N hipnotista mf

hypnotize ['hɪpnətaɪz] VT hipnotizar

hypoallergenic ['haɪpəuælə'dʒɛnɪk] ADJ hipoalergénico

hypochondriac [haɪpəu'kɔndriæk] N hipocondríaco(-a)

hypocrisy [hɪ'pɔkrɪsɪ] N hipocresía

hypocrite ['hɪpəkrɪt] N hipócrita mf

hypocritical [hɪpə'krɪtɪkl] ADJ hipócrita

hypodermic [haɪpə'də:mɪk] ADJ hipodérmico
  ▸ N (syringe) aguja hipodérmica

hypotenuse [haɪˈpɔtɪnjuːz] N hipotenusa

hypothermia [haɪpəuˈθəːmɪə] N hipotermia

hypothesis [haɪˈpɔθɪsɪs] (*pl* **hypotheses** [-siːz]) N hipótesis *f inv*

hypothetical [haɪpəˈθɛtɪkl] ADJ hipotético

hysterectomy [hɪstəˈrɛktəmɪ] N histerectomía

hysteria [hɪˈstɪərɪə] N histeria

hysterical [hɪˈstɛrɪkl] ADJ histérico

hysterics [hɪˈstɛrɪks] NPL histeria *sg*, histerismo *sg*; **to have ~** ponerse histérico; **to be in ~** (*fig*) morirse de risa

Hz ABBR (= *Hertz*) Hz

h

I i

I, i [aɪ] N (*letter*) I, i *f*; **I for Isaac,** (*US*) **I for Item** I de Inés, I de Israel

I [aɪ] PRON yo ▶ ABBR = **island; isle**

IA, Ia. ABBR (*US*) = **Iowa**

IAEA N ABBR = **International Atomic Energy Agency**

ib., ibid. ABBR (= *ibidem*) ibídem

Iberian [aɪˈbɪərɪən] ADJ ibero, ibérico

Iberian Peninsula N: **the ~** la Península Ibérica

IBEW N ABBR (*US*: = *International Brotherhood of Electrical Workers*) *sindicato internacional de electricistas*

i/c ABBR (*BRIT*) = **in charge**

ICBM N ABBR (= *intercontinental ballistic missile*) misil *m* balístico intercontinental

ICC N ABBR (*US*) = **Interstate Commerce Commission**

★**ice** [aɪs] N hielo; **to keep sth on ~** (*fig: plan, project*) tener algo en reserva ▶ VT (*cake*) alcorzar ▶ VI (*also*: **ice over, ice up**) helarse

ice age N período glaciar

ice axe N piqueta (de alpinista)

iceberg [ˈaɪsbə:g] N iceberg *m*; **the tip of the ~** la punta del iceberg

icebox [ˈaɪsbɔks] N (*BRIT*) congelador *m*; (*US*) nevera, refrigeradora (*LAM*)

icebreaker [ˈaɪsbreɪkəʳ] N rompehielos *m inv*

ice bucket N cubo para el hielo

icecap [ˈaɪskæp] N casquete *m* polar

ice-cold [aɪsˈkəʊld] ADJ helado

★**ice cream** N helado

ice-cream soda N soda mezclada con helado

ice cube N cubito de hielo

iced [aɪst] ADJ (*drink*) con hielo; (*cake*) escarchado

ice hockey N hockey *m* sobre hielo

Iceland [ˈaɪslənd] N Islandia

Icelander [ˈaɪsləndəʳ] N islandés(-esa) *m/f*

Icelandic [aɪsˈlændɪk] ADJ islandés(-esa) ▶ N (*Ling*) islandés *m*

ice lolly N (*BRIT*) polo

ice pick N piolet *m*

ice rink N pista de hielo

ice-skate [ˈaɪsskeɪt] N patín *m* de hielo ▶ VI patinar sobre hielo

ice-skating [ˈaɪsskeɪtɪŋ] N patinaje *m* sobre hielo

icicle [ˈaɪsɪkl] N carámbano

icing [ˈaɪsɪŋ] N (*Culin*) alcorza; (*Aviat etc*) formación *f* de hielo

icing sugar N (*BRIT*) azúcar *m* glas(eado)

ICJ N ABBR = **International Court of Justice**

icon [ˈaɪkɔn] N (*gen*) icono; (*Comput*) icono

ICR N ABBR (*US*) = **Institute for Cancer Research**

ICT N ABBR (= *Information and Communication(s) Technology*) TIC *f*, tecnología de la información; (*BRIT Scol*) informática

ICU N ABBR (= *intensive care unit*) UVI *f*

icy [ˈaɪsɪ] ADJ (*road*) helado; (*fig*) glacial

ID ABBR (*US Post*) = **Idaho**

I'd [aɪd] = **I would; I had**

ID card N (*identity card*) DNI *m*

IDD N ABBR (*BRIT Tel*: = *international direct dialling*) *servicio automático internacional*

★**idea** [aɪˈdɪə] N idea; **good ~!** ¡buena idea!; **to have an ~ that ...** tener la impresión de que ...; **I haven't the least ~** no tengo ni (la más remota) idea

★**ideal** [aɪˈdɪəl] N ideal *m* ▶ ADJ ideal

idealism [aɪˈdɪəlɪzəm] N idealismo

idealist [aɪˈdɪəlɪst] N idealista *mf*

ideally [aɪˈdɪəlɪ] ADV: **~, the book should have ...** lo ideal sería que el libro tuviera ...

identical [aɪˈdɛntɪkl] ADJ idéntico

identification [aɪdɛntɪfɪˈkeɪʃən] N identificación *f*; **means of ~** documentos *mpl* personales

★**identify** [aɪˈdɛntɪfaɪ] VT identificar ▶ VI: **to ~ with** identificarse con

Identikit® [aɪˈdɛntɪkɪt] N: **~ (picture)** retratorobot *m*

identity [aɪˈdɛntɪtɪ] N identidad f

identity card N carnet m de identidad, cédula (de identidad) (LAm)

identity papers NPL documentos mpl (de identidad), documentación fsg

identity parade N identificación f de acusados

identity theft N robo de identidad

ideological [aɪdɪəˈlɒdʒɪkəl] ADJ ideológico

ideology [aɪdɪˈɒlədʒɪ] N ideología

idiocy [ˈɪdɪəsɪ] N idiotez f; (stupid act) estupidez f

idiom [ˈɪdɪəm] N modismo; (style of speaking) lenguaje m

> **idiom** no debe traducirse por idioma.

idiomatic [ɪdɪəˈmætɪk] ADJ idiomático

idiosyncrasy [ɪdɪəuˈsɪŋkrəsɪ] N idiosincrasia

idiot [ˈɪdɪət] N (gen) idiota mf; (fool) tonto(-a)

idiotic [ɪdɪˈɒtɪk] ADJ idiota; tonto

idle [ˈaɪdl] ADJ (inactive) ocioso; (lazy) holgazán(-ana); (unemployed) parado, desocupado; (talk) frívolo; **~ capacity** (Comm) capacidad f sin utilizar; **~ money** (Comm) capital m improductivo; **~ time** (Comm) tiempo de paro ▶ VI (machine) funcionar or marchar en vacío
> **idle away** VT: **to ~ away one's time** malgastar or desperdiciar el tiempo

idleness [ˈaɪdlnɪs] N holgazanería; paro, desocupación f

idler [ˈaɪdlər] N holgazán(-ana) m/f, vago(-a)

idol [ˈaɪdl] N ídolo

idolize [ˈaɪdəlaɪz] VT idolatrar

idyllic [ɪˈdɪlɪk] ADJ idílico

i.e. ABBR (= id est) es decir

IED [aɪiːˈdiː] N (= Improvised Explosive Device) artefacto explosivo improvisado, bomba caminera

★**if** [ɪf] CONJ si; **(even) if** aunque, si bien; **I'd be pleased if you could do it** yo estaría contento si pudieras hacerlo; **if necessary** si resultase necesario; **if I were you** yo en tu lugar; **if only** si solamente; **as if** como si ▶ N: **there are a lot of ifs and buts** hay muchas dudas sin resolver

> Don't confuse **si** without an accent, which means if, with the accented **sí**, which means yes:
> If you go, I'll go with you. **Si vas, te acompaño**.
> He said yes. **Dijo que sí**.

iffy [ˈɪfɪ] ADJ (inf) dudoso

igloo [ˈɪgluː] N iglú m

ignite [ɪgˈnaɪt] VT (set fire to) encender ▶ VI encenderse

ignition [ɪgˈnɪʃən] N (Aut: process) ignición f; (: mechanism) encendido; **to switch on/off the ~** arrancar/apagar el motor

ignition key N (Aut) llave f de contacto

ignoble [ɪgˈnəubl] ADJ innoble, vil

ignominious [ɪgnəˈmɪnɪəs] ADJ ignominioso, vergonzoso

ignoramus [ɪgnəˈreɪməs] N ignorante mf, inculto(-a)

ignorance [ˈɪgnərəns] N ignorancia; **to keep sb in ~ of sth** ocultarle algo a algn

ignorant [ˈɪgnərənt] ADJ ignorante; **to be ~ of** (subject) desconocer; (events) ignorar

★**ignore** [ɪgˈnɔːr] VT (person) no hacer caso de; (fact) pasar por alto

ikon [ˈaɪkɒn] N = **icon**

IL ABBR (US Post) = **Illinois**

ILA N ABBR (US: = International Longshoremen's Association) sindicato internacional de trabajadores portuarios

★**ill** [ɪl] ADJ enfermo, malo; **to take** or **be taken ~** caer or ponerse enfermo; **to feel ~ (with)** encontrarse mal (de); **to speak/think ~ of sb** hablar/pensar mal de algn ▶ N mal m; (fig) infortunio ▶ ADV mal; see also **ills**

Ill. ABBR (US Post) = **Illinois**

I'll [aɪl] = **I will; I shall**

ill-advised [ɪləd'vaɪzd] ADJ poco recomendable; **he was ~ to go** se equivocaba al ir

ill-at-ease [ɪlət'iːz] ADJ incómodo

ill-considered [ɪlkən'sɪdəd] ADJ (plan) poco pensado

ill-disposed [ɪldɪs'pəuzd] ADJ: **to be ~ towards sb/sth** estar maldispuesto hacia algn/algo

★**illegal** [ɪˈliːgl] ADJ ilegal

illegible [ɪˈlɛdʒɪbl] ADJ ilegible

illegitimate [ɪlɪˈdʒɪtɪmət] ADJ ilegítimo

ill-fated [ɪlˈfeɪtɪd] ADJ malogrado

ill-favoured, (US) **ill-favored** [ɪlˈfeɪvəd] ADJ poco agraciado

ill feeling N rencor m

ill-gotten [ˈɪlgɒtn] ADJ (gains etc) mal adquirido

ill health N mala salud f; **to be in ~** estar mal de salud

illicit [ɪˈlɪsɪt] ADJ ilícito

ill-informed [ɪlɪn'fɔːmd] ADJ (judgement) erróneo; (person) mal informado

illiterate [ɪˈlɪtərət] ADJ analfabeto

ill-mannered [ɪlˈmænəd] ADJ mal educado

★**illness** [ˈɪlnɪs] N enfermedad f

illogical [ɪˈlɒdʒɪkl] ADJ ilógico

ills [ɪlz] NPL males mpl

ill-suited [ɪlˈsuːtɪd] ADJ (couple) incompatible; **he is ~ to the job** no es la persona indicada para el trabajo

ill-timed [ɪlˈtaɪmd] ADJ inoportuno

ill-treat [ɪlˈtriːt] VT maltratar

ill-treatment [ɪlˈtriːtmənt] N malos tratos mpl

illuminate [ɪˈluːmɪneɪt] VT (room, street) iluminar, alumbrar; (subject) aclarar; **illuminated sign** letrero luminoso

illuminating [ɪˈluːmɪneɪtɪŋ] ADJ revelador(a)

illumination [ɪluːmɪˈneɪʃən] N alumbrado
■ **illuminations** NPL luminarias fpl, luces fpl

illusion [ɪ'lu:ʒən] N ilusión f; **to be under the ~ that ...** estar convencido de que ...

illusive [ɪ'lu:sɪv], **illusory** [ɪ'lu:sərɪ] ADJ ilusorio

illustrate ['ɪləstreɪt] VT ilustrar

★**illustration** [ɪlə'streɪʃən] N (example) ejemplo, ilustración f; (in book) lámina, ilustración f

illustrator ['ɪləstreɪtə'] N ilustrador(a) m/f

illustrious [ɪ'lʌstrɪəs] ADJ ilustre

ill will N rencor m

ILO N ABBR (= International Labour Organization) OIT f

IM N ABBR (= instant messaging) IM f ▶ VT enviar un mensaje instantáneo

I'm [aɪm] = **I am**

★**image** ['ɪmɪdʒ] N imagen f

imagery ['ɪmɪdʒərɪ] N imágenes fpl

imaginable [ɪ'mædʒɪnəbl] ADJ imaginable

imaginary [ɪ'mædʒɪnərɪ] ADJ imaginario

★**imagination** [ɪmædʒɪ'neɪʃən] N imaginación f; (inventiveness) inventiva; (illusion) fantasía

imaginative [ɪ'mædʒɪnətɪv] ADJ imaginativo

★**imagine** [ɪ'mædʒɪn] VT imaginarse; (suppose) suponer

imam [ɪ'mɑ:m] N imán m

imbalance [ɪm'bæləns] N desequilibrio

imbecile ['ɪmbəsi:l] N imbécil mf

imbue [ɪm'bju:] VT: **to ~ sth with** imbuir algo de

IMF N ABBR (= International Monetary Fund) FMI m

imitate ['ɪmɪteɪt] VT imitar

imitation [ɪmɪ'teɪʃən] N imitación f; (copy) copia; (pej) remedo

imitator ['ɪmɪteɪtə'] N imitador(a) m/f

immaculate [ɪ'mækjulət] ADJ limpísimo, inmaculado; (Rel) inmaculado

immaterial [ɪmə'tɪərɪəl] ADJ incorpóreo; **it is ~ whether ...** no importa si ...

immature [ɪmə'tjuə'] ADJ (person) inmaduro; (of one's youth) joven

immaturity [ɪmə'tjuərɪtɪ] N inmadurez f

immeasurable [ɪ'mɛʒrəbl] ADJ inconmensurable

immediacy [ɪ'mi:dɪəsɪ] N urgencia, proximidad f

★**immediate** [ɪ'mi:dɪət] ADJ inmediato; (pressing) urgente, apremiante; (nearest: family) próximo; (: neighbourhood) inmediato; **in the ~ future** en un futuro próximo

★**immediately** [ɪ'mi:dɪətlɪ] ADV (at once) en seguida; (directly) inmediatamente; **~ next to** justo al lado de

immense [ɪ'mɛns] ADJ inmenso, enorme

immensely [ɪ'mɛnslɪ] ADV enormemente

immensity [ɪ'mɛnsɪtɪ] N (of size, difference) inmensidad f; (of problem) enormidad f

immerse [ɪ'mə:s] VT (submerge) sumergir; **to be immersed in** (fig) estar absorto en

immersion heater [ɪ'mə:ʃən-] N (BRIT) calentador m de inmersión

★**immigrant** ['ɪmɪgrənt] N inmigrante mf

immigrate ['ɪmɪgreɪt] VI inmigrar

immigration [ɪmɪ'greɪʃən] N inmigración f

immigration authorities NPL servicio sg de inmigración

immigration laws NPL leyes fpl de inmigración

imminent ['ɪmɪnənt] ADJ inminente

immobile [ɪ'məubaɪl] ADJ inmóvil

immobilize [ɪ'məubɪlaɪz] VT inmovilizar

immoderate [ɪ'mɔdərɪt] ADJ (person) desmesurado; (opinion, reaction, demand) excesivo

immodest [ɪ'mɔdɪst] ADJ (indecent) desvergonzado, impúdico; (boasting) jactancioso

immoral [ɪ'mɔrl] ADJ inmoral

immorality [ɪmə'rælɪtɪ] N inmoralidad f

immortal [ɪ'mɔ:tl] ADJ inmortal

immortality [ɪmɔ:'tælɪtɪ] N inmortalidad f

immortalize [ɪ'mɔ:tlaɪz] VT inmortalizar

immovable [ɪ'mu:vəbl] ADJ (object) imposible de mover; (person) inconmovible

immune [ɪ'mju:n] ADJ: **~ (to)** inmune (a)

immune system N sistema m inmunitario

immunity [ɪ'mju:nɪtɪ] N (Med: of diplomat) inmunidad f; (Comm) exención f

immunization [ɪmjunaɪ'zeɪʃən] N inmunización f

immunize ['ɪmjunaɪz] VT inmunizar

imp [ɪmp] N (small devil, child) diablillo

impact ['ɪmpækt] N (gen) impacto

impair [ɪm'pɛə'] VT perjudicar

-impaired [ɪm'pɛəd] SUFF: **visually-impaired** con defectos de visión

impale [ɪm'peɪl] VT (with sword) atravesar

impart [ɪm'pɑ:t] VT comunicar; (make known) participar; (bestow) otorgar

impartial [ɪm'pɑ:ʃl] ADJ imparcial

impartiality [ɪmpɑ:ʃɪ'ælɪtɪ] N imparcialidad f

impassable [ɪm'pɑ:səbl] ADJ (barrier) infranqueable; (road) intransitable

impasse [ɪm'pɑ:s] N callejón m sin salida; **to reach an ~** llegar a un punto muerto

impassioned [ɪm'pæʃənd] ADJ apasionado, exaltado

impassive [ɪm'pæsɪv] ADJ impasible

impatience [ɪm'peɪʃəns] N impaciencia

impatient [ɪm'peɪʃənt] ADJ impaciente; **to get or grow ~** impacientarse

impatiently [ɪm'peɪʃəntlɪ] ADV con impaciencia

impeachment [ɪm'pi:tʃmənt] N denuncia, acusación f

impeccable [ɪm'pɛkəbl] ADJ impecable

impecunious [ɪmpɪ'kju:nɪəs] ADJ sin dinero

impede [ɪm'pi:d] VT estorbar, dificultar

impediment [ɪm'pɛdɪmənt] N obstáculo, estorbo; (also: **speech impediment**) defecto (del habla)

impel [ɪm'pɛl] VT (force): **to ~ sb (to do sth)** obligar a algn (a hacer algo)

impending [ɪm'pɛndɪŋ] ADJ inminente

impenetrable [ɪm'pɛnɪtrəbl] ADJ (jungle, fortress) impenetrable; (unfathomable) insondable

imperative [ɪm'pɛrətɪv] ADJ (tone) imperioso; (necessary) imprescindible ▶ N (Ling) imperativo

imperceptible [ɪmpə'sɛptɪbl] ADJ imperceptible

imperfect [ɪm'pə:fɪkt] ADJ imperfecto; (goods etc) defectuoso ▶ N (Ling: also: **imperfect tense**) imperfecto

imperfection [ɪmpə'fɛkʃən] N (blemish) desperfecto; (fault, flaw) defecto

imperial [ɪm'pɪərɪəl] ADJ imperial

imperialism [ɪm'pɪərɪəlɪzəm] N imperialismo

imperil [ɪm'pɛrɪl] VT poner en peligro

imperious [ɪm'pɪərɪəs] ADJ señorial, apremiante

impersonal [ɪm'pə:sənl] ADJ impersonal

impersonate [ɪm'pə:səneɪt] VT hacerse pasar por

impersonation [ɪmpə:sə'neɪʃən] N imitación f

impersonator [ɪm'pə:səneɪtə'] N (Theat etc) imitador(a) m/f

impertinence [ɪm'pə:tɪnəns] N impertinencia, insolencia

impertinent [ɪm'pə:tɪnənt] ADJ impertinente, insolente

imperturbable [ɪmpə'tə:bəbl] ADJ imperturbable, impasible

impervious [ɪm'pə:vɪəs] ADJ impermeable; (fig): **~ to** insensible a

impetuous [ɪm'pɛtjuəs] ADJ impetuoso

impetus ['ɪmpətəs] N ímpetu m; (fig) impulso

impinge [ɪm'pɪndʒ]: **to ~ on** vt fus (affect) afectar a

impish ['ɪmpɪʃ] ADJ travieso

implacable [ɪm'plækəbl] ADJ implacable

implant [ɪm'plɑ:nt] VT (Med) injertar, implantar; (fig: idea, principle) inculcar

implausible [ɪm'plɔ:zɪbl] ADJ inverosímil

implement N ['ɪmplɪmənt] instrumento, herramienta ▶ VT ['ɪmplɪmɛnt] hacer efectivo; (carry out) realizar

implicate ['ɪmplɪkeɪt] VT (compromise) comprometer; (involve) enredar; **to ~ sb in sth** comprometer a algn en algo

implication [ɪmplɪ'keɪʃən] N consecuencia; **by ~** indirectamente

implicit [ɪm'plɪsɪt] ADJ (gen) implícito; (complete) absoluto

implicitly [ɪm'plɪsɪtlɪ] ADV implícitamente

implore [ɪm'plɔ:'] VT (person) suplicar

imploring [ɪm'plɔ:rɪŋ] ADJ de súplica

imply [ɪm'plaɪ] VT (involve) implicar, suponer; (hint) insinuar

impolite [ɪmpə'laɪt] ADJ mal educado

impolitic [ɪm'pɒlɪtɪk] ADJ poco diplomático

imponderable [ɪm'pɒndərəbl] ADJ imponderable

import VT [ɪm'pɔ:t] importar ▶ N ['ɪmpɔ:t] (Comm) importación f; (: article) producto importado; (meaning) significado, sentido ▶ CPD (duty, licence etc) de importación

★**importance** [ɪm'pɔ:təns] N importancia; **to be of great/little ~** tener mucha/poca importancia

★**important** [ɪm'pɔ:tənt] ADJ importante; **it's not ~** no importa, no tiene importancia; **it is ~ that** es importante que

importantly [ɪm'pɔ:təntlɪ] ADV (pej) dándose importancia; **but, more ~ ...** pero, lo que es aún más importante ...

import duty N derechos mpl de importación

imported [ɪm'pɔ:tɪd] ADJ importado

importer [ɪm'pɔ:tə'] N importador(a) m/f

import licence, (US) **import license** N licencia de importación

impose [ɪm'pəuz] VT imponer ▶ VI: **to ~ on sb** abusar de algn

imposing [ɪm'pəuzɪŋ] ADJ imponente, impresionante

imposition [ɪmpə'zɪʃn] N (of tax etc) imposición f; **to be an ~** (on person) molestar

impossibility [ɪmpɒsə'bɪlɪtɪ] N imposibilidad f

★**impossible** [ɪm'pɒsɪbl] ADJ imposible; (person) insoportable; **it is ~ for me to leave now** me es imposible salir ahora

impossibly [ɪm'pɒsɪblɪ] ADV imposiblemente

impostor [ɪm'pɒstə'] N impostor(a) m/f

impotence ['ɪmpətəns] N impotencia

impotent ['ɪmpətənt] ADJ impotente

impound [ɪm'paund] VT embargar

impoverished [ɪm'pɒvərɪʃt] ADJ necesitado; (land) agotado

impracticable [ɪm'præktɪkəbl] ADJ no factible, irrealizable

impractical [ɪm'præktɪkl] ADJ (person) poco práctico

imprecise [ɪmprɪ'saɪs] ADJ impreciso

impregnable [ɪm'prɛgnəbl] ADJ invulnerable; (castle) inexpugnable

impregnate ['ɪmprɛgneɪt] VT (gen) impregnar; (soak) empapar; (fertilize) fecundar

impresario [ɪmprɪ'sɑ:rɪəu] N empresario(-a)

impress [ɪm'prɛs] VT impresionar; (mark) estampar; **to ~ sth on sb** convencer a algn de la importancia de algo ▶ VI causar buena impresión

impression [ɪm'prɛʃən] N impresión f; (footprint etc) huella; (print run) edición f; **to be under the ~ that** tener la impresión de que; **to make a**

good/bad ~ on sb causar buena/mala impresión a algn

impressionable [ɪmˈprɛʃnəbl] ADJ impresionable

impressionist [ɪmˈprɛʃənɪst] N impresionista mf

impressive [ɪmˈprɛsɪv] ADJ impresionante

imprint [ˈɪmprɪnt] N (Publishing) pie m de imprenta; (fig) sello

imprison [ɪmˈprɪzn] VT encarcelar

imprisonment [ɪmˈprɪznmənt] N encarcelamiento; (term of imprisonment) cárcel f; **life ~** cadena perpetua

improbable [ɪmˈprɔbəbl] ADJ improbable, inverosímil

impromptu [ɪmˈprɔmptjuː] ADJ improvisado ▸ ADV de improviso

improper [ɪmˈprɔpəʳ] ADJ (incorrect) impropio; (unseemly) indecoroso; (indecent) indecente; (dishonest: activities) deshonesto

impropriety [ɪmprəˈpraɪətɪ] N falta de decoro; (indecency) indecencia; (of language) impropiedad f

★**improve** [ɪmˈpruːv] VT mejorar; (foreign language) perfeccionar ▸ VI mejorar
  ▸ **improve (up)on** VT FUS (offer) mejorar

★**improvement** [ɪmˈpruːvmənt] N mejora; perfeccionamiento; **to make improvements to** mejorar

improvise [ˈɪmprəvaɪz] VT, VI improvisar

imprudence [ɪmˈpruːdns] N imprudencia

imprudent [ɪmˈpruːdnt] ADJ imprudente

impudent [ˈɪmpjudnt] ADJ descarado, insolente

impugn [ɪmˈpjuːn] VT impugnar

impulse [ˈɪmpʌls] N impulso; **to act on ~** actuar sin reflexionar, dejarse llevar por el impulso

impulse buying N compra impulsiva

impulsive [ɪmˈpʌlsɪv] ADJ irreflexivo, impulsivo

impunity [ɪmˈpjuːnɪtɪ] N: **with ~** impunemente

impure [ɪmˈpjuəʳ] ADJ (adulterated) adulterado; (morally) impuro

impurity [ɪmˈpjuərɪtɪ] N impureza

IN ABBR (US Post) = **Indiana**

---

in [ɪn]

PREP **1** (indicating place, position, with place names) en; **in the house/garden** en (la) casa/el jardín; **in here/there** aquí/ahí or allí dentro; **in London/England** en Londres/Inglaterra; **in town** en el centro (de la ciudad)
2 (indicating time) en; **in spring** en (la) primavera; **in 1988/May** en 1988/mayo; **in the afternoon** por la tarde; **at four o'clock in the afternoon** a las cuatro de la tarde; **I did it in three hours/days** lo hice en tres horas/días; **I'll see you in two weeks** or **in two weeks'**

time te veré dentro de dos semanas; **once in a hundred years** una vez cada cien años
3 (indicating manner etc) en; **in a loud/soft voice** en voz alta/baja; **in pencil/ink** a lápiz/bolígrafo; **the boy in the blue shirt** el chico de la camisa azul; **in writing** por escrito; **to pay in dollars** pagar en dólares
4 (indicating circumstances): **in the sun/shade** al sol/a la sombra; **in the rain** bajo la lluvia; **a change in policy** un cambio de política; **a rise in prices** un aumento de precios
5 (indicating mood, state): **in tears** llorando; **in anger/despair** enfadado/desesperado; **to live in luxury** vivir lujosamente; **in that** conj ya que
6 (with ratios, numbers): **1 in 10 households, 1 household in 10** una de cada 10 familias; **20 pence in the pound** 20 peniques por libra; **they lined up in twos** se alinearon de dos en dos; **in hundreds** a or por centenares
7 (referring to people, works) en; entre; **the disease is common in children** la enfermedad es común entre los niños; **in (the works of) Dickens** en (las obras de) Dickens
8 (indicating profession etc): **to be in teaching** dedicarse a la enseñanza
9 (after superlative) de; **the best pupil in the class** el/la mejor alumno(-a) de la clase
10 (with present participle): **in saying this** al decir esto
  ▸ ADV: **to be in** (person: at home) estar en casa; (: at work) estar; (train, ship, plane) haber llegado; (in fashion) estar de moda; **she'll be in later today** llegará más tarde hoy; **to ask sb in** hacer pasar a algn; **to run/limp** etc **in** entrar corriendo/cojeando etc
  ▸ N: **the ins and outs** (of proposal, situation etc) los detalles

in., ins ABBR = **inch; inches**

inability [ɪnəˈbɪlɪtɪ] N: **~ (to do)** incapacidad f (de hacer); **~ to pay** insolvencia en el pago

inaccessible [ɪnækˈsesɪbl] ADJ inaccesible

inaccuracy [ɪnˈækjurəsɪ] N inexactitud f

inaccurate [ɪnˈækjurət] ADJ inexacto, incorrecto

inaction [ɪnˈækʃən] N inacción f

inactive [ɪnˈæktɪv] ADJ inactivo

inactivity [ɪnækˈtɪvɪtɪ] N inactividad f

inadequacy [ɪnˈædɪkwəsɪ] N insuficiencia; incapacidad f

inadequate [ɪnˈædɪkwət] ADJ (insufficient) insuficiente; (unsuitable) inadecuado; (person) incapaz

inadmissible [ɪnədˈmɪsəbl] ADJ improcedente, inadmisible

inadvertent [ɪnədˈvəːtənt] ADJ descuidado, involuntario

inadvertently [ɪnədˈvəːtntlɪ] ADV por descuido

inadvisable [ɪnədˈvaɪzəbl] ADJ poco aconsejable

inane [ɪˈneɪn] ADJ necio, fatuo

inanimate [ɪnˈænɪmət] ADJ inanimado

inapplicable [ɪnˈæplɪkəbl] ADJ inaplicable

inappropriate [ɪnəˈprəʊprɪət] ADJ inadecuado

inapt [ɪnˈæpt] ADJ impropio

inaptitude [ɪnˈæptɪtjuːd] N incapacidad f

inarticulate [ɪnɑːˈtɪkjulət] ADJ (person) incapaz de expresarse; (speech) mal pronunciado

inartistic [ɪnɑːˈtɪstɪk] ADJ antiestético

inasmuch as [ɪnəzˈmʌtʃ-] ADV en la medida en que

inattention [ɪnəˈtenʃən] N desatención f

inattentive [ɪnəˈtentɪv] ADJ distraído

inaudible [ɪnˈɔːdɪbl] ADJ inaudible

inaugural [ɪˈnɔːɡjʊrəl] ADJ inaugural; (speech) de apertura

inaugurate [ɪˈnɔːɡjʊreɪt] VT inaugurar; (president, official) investir

inauguration [ɪnɔːɡjʊˈreɪʃən] N inauguración f; (of official) investidura; (of event) ceremonia de apertura

inauspicious [ɪnɔːsˈpɪʃəs] ADJ poco propicio, inoportuno

in-between [ɪnbɪˈtwiːn] ADJ intermedio

inborn [ɪnˈbɔːn] ADJ (feeling) innato

inbox [ˈɪnbɒks] N (Comput) buzón m de entrada; (US: in-tray) bandeja de entrada

inbred [ɪnˈbred] ADJ innato; (family) consanguíneo

inbreeding [ɪnˈbriːdɪŋ] N endogamia

Inc. ABBR = **incorporated**

Inca [ˈɪŋkə] ADJ (also: **Incan**) inca, de los incas ▸ N inca m/f

incalculable [ɪnˈkælkjuləbl] ADJ incalculable

incapability [ɪnkeɪpəˈbɪlɪtɪ] N incapacidad f

incapable [ɪnˈkeɪpəbl] ADJ: **~ (of doing sth)** incapaz (de hacer algo)

incapacitate [ɪnkəˈpæsɪteɪt] VT: **to ~ sb** incapacitar a algn

incapacitated [ɪnkəˈpæsɪteɪtɪd] ADJ incapacitado

incapacity [ɪnkəˈpæsɪtɪ] N (inability) incapacidad f

incarcerate [ɪnˈkɑːsəreɪt] VT encarcelar

incarnate ADJ [ɪnˈkɑːnɪt] en persona ▸ VT [ˈɪnkɑːneɪt] encarnar

incarnation [ɪnkɑːˈneɪʃən] N encarnación f

incendiary [ɪnˈsendɪərɪ] ADJ incendiario ▸ N (bomb) bomba incendiaria

incense N [ˈɪnsens] incienso ▸ VT [ɪnˈsens] (anger) indignar, encolerizar

incentive [ɪnˈsentɪv] N incentivo, estímulo

incentive bonus N prima

incentive scheme N plan m de incentivos

inception [ɪnˈsepʃən] N comienzo, principio

incessant [ɪnˈsesnt] ADJ incesante, continuo

incessantly [ɪnˈsesntlɪ] ADV constantemente

incest [ˈɪnsest] N incesto

★**inch** [ɪntʃ] N pulgada; **a few inches** unas pulgadas; **to be within an ~ of** estar a dos dedos de; **he didn't give an ~** no hizo la más mínima concesión
▸ **inch forward** VI avanzar palmo a palmo

incidence [ˈɪnsɪdns] N (of crime, disease) incidencia

★**incident** [ˈɪnsɪdnt] N incidente m; (in book) episodio

incidental [ɪnsɪˈdentl] ADJ circunstancial, accesorio; (unplanned) fortuito; **~ to** relacionado con; **~ expenses** (gastos mpl) imprevistos mpl

incidentally [ɪnsɪˈdentəlɪ] ADV (by the way) por cierto

incidental music N música de fondo

incident room N (Police) centro de coordinación

incinerate [ɪnˈsɪnəreɪt] VT incinerar, quemar

incinerator [ɪnˈsɪnəreɪtər] N incinerador m, incineradora

incipient [ɪnˈsɪpɪənt] ADJ incipiente

incision [ɪnˈsɪʒən] N incisión f

incisive [ɪnˈsaɪsɪv] ADJ (mind) penetrante; (remark etc) incisivo

incisor [ɪnˈsaɪzər] N incisivo

incite [ɪnˈsaɪt] VT provocar, incitar

incl. ABBR = **including; inclusive (of)**

inclement [ɪnˈklemənt] ADJ inclemente

inclination [ɪnklɪˈneɪʃən] N (tendency) tendencia, inclinación f

incline [n ˈɪnklaɪn, vt, vi ɪnˈklaɪn] N pendiente f, cuesta ▸ VT (slope) inclinar; (head) poner de lado; **to be inclined to** (tend) ser propenso a; (be willing) estar dispuesto a ▸ VI inclinarse

★**include** [ɪnˈkluːd] VT incluir, comprender; (in letter) adjuntar; **the tip is/is not included** la propina está/no está incluida

★**including** [ɪnˈkluːdɪŋ] PREP incluso, inclusive; **~ tip** propina incluida

inclusion [ɪnˈkluːʒən] N inclusión f

inclusive [ɪnˈkluːsɪv] ADJ inclusivo; **~ of tax** incluidos los impuestos; **$50, ~ of all surcharges** 50 dólares, incluidos todos los recargos ▸ ADV inclusive

incognito [ɪnkɒɡˈniːtəʊ] ADV de incógnito

incoherent [ɪnkəʊˈhɪərənt] ADJ incoherente

income [ˈɪnkʌm] N (personal) ingresos mpl; (from property etc) renta; (profit) rédito; **gross/net ~** ingresos mpl brutos/netos; **~ and expenditure account** cuenta de gastos e ingresos

income bracket N categoría económica

income support N (Brit) ≈ ayuda familiar

income tax N impuesto sobre la renta

income tax inspector N inspector(a) m/f de Hacienda

income tax return N declaración f de ingresos

incoming [ˈɪnkʌmɪŋ] ADJ (passengers, flight) de llegada; (government) entrante; (tenant) nuevo

incommunicado [ˌɪnkəmjuːˈkɑːdəu] ADJ: **to hold sb ~** mantener incomunicado a algn

incomparable [ɪnˈkɒmpərəbl] ADJ incomparable, sin par

incompatible [ɪnkəmˈpætɪbl] ADJ incompatible

incompetence [ɪnˈkɒmpɪtəns] N incompetencia

incompetent [ɪnˈkɒmpɪtənt] ADJ incompetente

incomplete [ɪnkəmˈpliːt] ADJ incompleto; (*unfinished*) sin terminar

incomprehensible [ɪnkɒmprɪˈhɛnsɪbl] ADJ incomprensible

inconceivable [ɪnkənˈsiːvəbl] ADJ inconcebible

inconclusive [ɪnkənˈkluːsɪv] ADJ sin resultado (definitivo); (*argument*) poco convincente

incongruity [ɪnkɒŋˈgruːɪtɪ] N incongruencia

incongruous [ɪnˈkɒŋgruəs] ADJ discordante

inconsequential [ɪnkɒnsɪˈkwɛnʃl] ADJ intrascendente

inconsiderable [ɪnkənˈsɪdərəbl] ADJ insignificante

inconsiderate [ɪnkənˈsɪdərət] ADJ desconsiderado; **how ~ of him!** ¡qué falta de consideración (de su parte)!

inconsistency [ɪnkənˈsɪstənsɪ] N inconsecuencia; (*of actions etc*) falta de lógica; (*of work*) carácter *m* desigual, inconsistencia; (*of statement etc*) contradicción *f*

inconsistent [ɪnkənˈsɪstnt] ADJ inconsecuente; (*contradictory*) incongruente; **~ with** que no concuerda con

inconsolable [ɪnkənˈsəuləbl] ADJ inconsolable

inconspicuous [ɪnkənˈspɪkjuəs] ADJ (*discreet*) discreto; (*person*) que llama poco la atención

inconstancy [ɪnˈkɒnstənsɪ] N inconstancia

inconstant [ɪnˈkɒnstənt] ADJ inconstante

incontinence [ɪnˈkɒntɪnəns] N incontinencia

incontinent [ɪnˈkɒntɪnənt] ADJ incontinente

incontrovertible [ɪnkɒntrəˈvɜːtəbl] ADJ incontrovertible

inconvenience [ɪnkənˈviːnjəns] N (*gen*) inconvenientes mpl; (*trouble*) molestia; **to put sb to great ~** causar mucha molestia a algn ▶ VT incomodar; **don't ~ yourself** no se moleste

inconvenient [ɪnkənˈviːnjənt] ADJ incómodo, poco práctico; (*time, place*) inoportuno; **that time is very ~ for me** esa hora me es muy inconveniente

incorporate [ɪnˈkɔːpəreɪt] VT incorporar; (*contain*) comprender; (*add*) agregar

incorporated [ɪnˈkɔːpəreɪtɪd] ADJ: **~ company** (*US*) ≈ Sociedad *f* Anónima (S.A.)

incorrect [ɪnkəˈrɛkt] ADJ incorrecto

incorrigible [ɪnˈkɒrɪdʒəbl] ADJ incorregible

incorruptible [ɪnkəˈrʌptɪbl] ADJ incorruptible

★**increase** N [ˈɪnkriːs] aumento; **an ~ of 5%** un aumento de 5%; **to be on the ~** ir en aumento ▶ VI [ɪnˈkriːs] aumentar; (*grow*) crecer; (*price*) subir ▶ VT [ɪnˈkriːs] aumentar; (*price*) subir

increasing [ɪnˈkriːsɪŋ] ADJ (*number*) creciente, que va en aumento

increasingly [ɪnˈkriːsɪŋlɪ] ADV cada vez más

★**incredible** [ɪnˈkrɛdɪbl] ADJ increíble

incredibly [ɪnˈkrɛdɪblɪ] ADV increíblemente

incredulity [ɪnkrɪˈdjuːlɪtɪ] N incredulidad *f*

incredulous [ɪnˈkrɛdjuləs] ADJ incrédulo

increment [ˈɪnkrɪmənt] N aumento, incremento

incriminate [ɪnˈkrɪmɪneɪt] VT incriminar

incriminating [ɪnˈkrɪmɪneɪtɪŋ] ADJ incriminatorio

incrust [ɪnˈkrʌst] VT = **encrust**

incubate [ˈɪnkjubeɪt] VT (*egg*) incubar, empollar ▶ VI (*egg, disease*) incubar

incubation [ɪnkjuˈbeɪʃən] N incubación *f*

incubation period N período de incubación

incubator [ˈɪnkjubeɪtə'] N incubadora

inculcate [ˈɪnkʌlkeɪt] VT: **to ~ sth in sb** inculcar algo en algn

incumbent [ɪnˈkʌmbənt] N ocupante *mf* ▶ ADJ: **it is ~ on him to ...** le incumbe ...

incur [ɪnˈkɜː'] VT (*expenses*) incurrir en; (*loss*) sufrir; (*anger, disapproval*) provocar

incurable [ɪnˈkjuərəbl] ADJ incurable

incursion [ɪnˈkɜːʃən] N incursión *f*

Ind. ABBR (*US*) = **Indiana**

indebted [ɪnˈdɛtɪd] ADJ: **to be ~ to sb** estar agradecido a algn

indecency [ɪnˈdiːsnsɪ] N indecencia

indecent [ɪnˈdiːsnt] ADJ indecente

indecent assault N (*BRIT*) atentado contra el pudor

indecent exposure N exhibicionismo

indecipherable [ɪndɪˈsaɪfərəbl] ADJ indescifrable

indecision [ɪndɪˈsɪʒən] N indecisión *f*

indecisive [ɪndɪˈsaɪsɪv] ADJ indeciso; (*discussion*) no resuelto, inconcluyente

★**indeed** [ɪnˈdiːd] ADV efectivamente, en realidad; (*in fact*) en efecto; (*furthermore*) es más; **yes ~!** ¡claro que sí!

indefatigable [ɪndɪˈfætɪgəbl] ADJ incansable, infatigable

indefensible [ɪndɪˈfɛnsəbl] ADJ (*conduct*) injustificable

indefinable [ɪndɪˈfaɪnəbl] ADJ indefinible

indefinite [ɪnˈdɛfɪnɪt] ADJ indefinido; (*uncertain*) incierto

indefinitely [ɪnˈdɛfɪnɪtlɪ] ADV (*wait*) indefinidamente

indelible [ɪnˈdɛlɪbl] ADJ imborrable

indelicate [ɪnˈdɛlɪkɪt] ADJ (*tactless*) indiscreto, inoportuno; (*not polite*) poco delicado

indemnify [ɪnˈdɛmnɪfaɪ] VT indemnizar, resarcir

indemnity [ɪnˈdɛmnɪtɪ] N (*insurance*) indemnidad *f*; (*compensation*) indemnización *f*

indent [ɪnˈdɛnt] VT (*text*) sangrar

indentation [ɪndɛnˈteɪʃən] N mella; (*Typ*) sangría

indenture [ɪnˈdɛntʃəʳ] N escritura, instrumento

★**independence** [ɪndɪˈpɛndns] N independencia

Independence Day N Día *m* de la Independencia

El cuatro de julio es la fiesta nacional de los Estados Unidos, **Independence Day**, en conmemoración de la Declaración de Independencia escrita por Thomas Jefferson y adoptada en 1776. En ella se proclamaba la ruptura total con Gran Bretaña de las trece colonias americanas que fueron el origen de los Estados Unidos de América.

★**independent** [ɪndɪˈpɛndənt] ADJ independiente; **to become ~** independizarse

independent school N (*Brit*) escuela privada, colegio privado

in-depth [ˈɪndɛpθ] ADJ en profundidad, a fondo

indescribable [ɪndɪˈskraɪbəbl] ADJ indescriptible

indestructible [ɪndɪsˈtrʌktəbl] ADJ indestructible

indeterminate [ɪndɪˈtəːmɪnɪt] ADJ indeterminado

★**index** [ˈɪndɛks] N (*pl* **indexes**) (*in book*) índice *m*; (*in library etc*) catálogo; (*pl* **indices** [ˈɪndɪsiːz]) (*ratio, sign*) exponente *m*

index card N ficha

index finger N (dedo) índice *m*

index-linked [ˈɪndɛksˈlɪŋkt], (*US*) **indexed** [ˈɪndɛkst] ADJ indexado

★**India** [ˈɪndɪə] N la India

Indian [ˈɪndɪən] ADJ, N indio(-a) *m/f*; (*also:* **American Indian**) indio(-a) *m/f* de América, amerindio(-a) *m/f*

Indian Ocean N: **the ~** el océano Índico, el mar de las Indias

Indian summer N (*fig*) veranillo de San Martín

india rubber N caucho

indicate [ˈɪndɪkeɪt] VT indicar ▶ VI (*Brit Aut*): **to ~ left/right** indicar a la izquierda/a la derecha

indication [ɪndɪˈkeɪʃən] N indicio, señal *f*

indicative [ɪnˈdɪkətɪv] ADJ: **to be ~ of sth** indicar algo ▶ N (*Ling*) indicativo

indicator [ˈɪndɪkeɪtəʳ] N (*gen*) indicador *m*; (*Aut*) intermitente *m*, direccional *m* (*Lam*)

indices [ˈɪndɪsiːz] NPL *of* **index**

indict [ɪnˈdaɪt] VT acusar

indictable [ɪnˈdaɪtəbl] ADJ: **~ offence** delito procesable

indictment [ɪnˈdaɪtmənt] N acusación *f*

indifference [ɪnˈdɪfrəns] N indiferencia

indifferent [ɪnˈdɪfrənt] ADJ indiferente; (*poor*) regular

indigenous [ɪnˈdɪdʒɪnəs] ADJ indígena

indigestible [ɪndɪˈdʒɛstɪbl] ADJ indigesto

indigestion [ɪndɪˈdʒɛstʃən] N indigestión *f*

indignant [ɪnˈdɪgnənt] ADJ: **to be ~ about sth** indignarse por algo

indignation [ɪndɪgˈneɪʃən] N indignación *f*

indignity [ɪnˈdɪgnɪtɪ] N indignidad *f*

indigo [ˈɪndɪgəʊ] ADJ (*colour*) (de color) añil ▶ N añil *m*

indirect [ɪndɪˈrɛkt] ADJ indirecto

indirectly [ɪndɪˈrɛktlɪ] ADV indirectamente

indiscernible [ɪndɪˈsəːnəbl] ADJ imperceptible

indiscreet [ɪndɪˈskriːt] ADJ indiscreto, imprudente

indiscretion [ɪndɪˈskrɛʃən] N indiscreción *f*, imprudencia

indiscriminate [ɪndɪˈskrɪmɪnət] ADJ indiscriminado

indispensable [ɪndɪˈspɛnsəbl] ADJ indispensable, imprescindible

indisposed [ɪndɪˈspəʊzd] ADJ (*unwell*) indispuesto

indisposition [ɪndɪspəˈzɪʃən] N indisposición *f*

indisputable [ɪndɪˈspjuːtəbl] ADJ incontestable

indistinct [ɪndɪˈstɪŋkt] ADJ indistinto

indistinguishable [ɪndɪˈstɪŋgwɪʃəbl] ADJ indistinguible

★**individual** [ɪndɪˈvɪdjuəl] N individuo ▶ ADJ individual; (*personal*) personal; (*particular*) particular

individualist [ɪndɪˈvɪdjuəlɪst] N individualista *mf*

individuality [ɪndɪvɪdjuˈælɪtɪ] N individualidad *f*

individually [ɪndɪˈvɪdjuəlɪ] ADV individualmente; particularmente

indivisible [ɪndɪˈvɪzəbl] ADJ indivisible

Indo-China [ˈɪndəʊˈtʃaɪnə] N Indochina

indoctrinate [ɪnˈdɔktrɪneɪt] VT adoctrinar

indoctrination [ɪndɔktrɪˈneɪʃən] N adoctrinamiento

indolence [ˈɪndələns] N indolencia

indolent [ˈɪndələnt] ADJ indolente, perezoso

Indonesia [ɪndəˈniːzɪə] N Indonesia

Indonesian [ɪndəˈniːzɪən] ADJ, N indonesio(-a) *m/f*; (*Ling*) indonesio

indoor [ˈɪndɔːʳ] ADJ (*swimming pool*) cubierto; (*plant*) de interior; (*sport*) bajo cubierta

indoors [ɪnˈdɔːz] ADV dentro; (*at home*) en casa

indubitable [ɪnˈdjuːbɪtəbl] ADJ indudable

indubitably [ɪnˈdjuːbɪtəblɪ] ADV indudablemente

induce [ɪnˈdjuːs] VT inducir, persuadir; (*bring*

about) producir; **to ~ sb to do sth** persuadir a algn a que haga algo

inducement [ɪnˈdjuːsmənt] N (*incentive*) incentivo, aliciente *m*

induct [ɪnˈdʌkt] VT iniciar; (*in job, rank, position*) instalar

induction [ɪnˈdʌkʃən] N (*Med: of birth*) inducción *f*

induction course N (*BRIT*) cursillo introductorio or de iniciación

indulge [ɪnˈdʌldʒ] VT (*whim*) satisfacer; (*person*) complacer; (*child*) mimar ▶ VI: **to ~ in** darse el gusto de

indulgence [ɪnˈdʌldʒəns] N vicio

indulgent [ɪnˈdʌldʒənt] ADJ indulgente

industrial [ɪnˈdʌstrɪəl] ADJ industrial

industrial action N huelga

industrial estate N (*BRIT*) polígono or (*LAM*) zona industrial

industrial goods NPL bienes *mpl* de producción

industrialist [ɪnˈdʌstrɪəlɪst] N industrial *mf*

industrialize [ɪnˈdʌstrɪəlaɪz] VT industrializar

industrial park N (*US*) = **industrial estate**

industrial relations NPL relaciones *fpl* empresariales

industrial tribunal N magistratura de trabajo, tribunal *m* laboral

industrial unrest N (*BRIT*) agitación *f* obrera

industrious [ɪnˈdʌstrɪəs] ADJ (*gen*) trabajador(a); (*student*) aplicado

industry [ˈɪndəstrɪ] N industria; (*diligence*) aplicación *f*

inebriated [ɪˈniːbrɪeɪtɪd] ADJ borracho

inedible [ɪnˈɛdɪbl] ADJ incomible; (*plant etc*) no comestible

ineffective [ɪnɪˈfɛktɪv], **ineffectual** [ɪnɪˈfɛktʃuəl] ADJ ineficaz, inútil

inefficiency [ɪnɪˈfɪʃənsɪ] N ineficacia

inefficient [ɪnɪˈfɪʃənt] ADJ ineficaz, ineficiente

inelegant [ɪnˈɛlɪgənt] ADJ poco elegante

ineligible [ɪnˈɛlɪdʒɪbl] ADJ inelegible

inept [ɪˈnɛpt] ADJ incompetente, incapaz

ineptitude [ɪˈnɛptɪtjuːd] N incapacidad *f*, ineptitud *f*

inequality [ɪnɪˈkwɒlɪtɪ] N desigualdad *f*

inequitable [ɪnˈɛkwɪtəbl] ADJ injusto

ineradicable [ɪnɪˈrædɪkəbl] ADJ inextirpable

inert [ɪˈnɜːt] ADJ inerte, inactivo; (*immobile*) inmóvil

inertia [ɪˈnɜːʃə] N inercia; (*laziness*) pereza

inertia-reel seat-belt [ɪˈnɜːʃəˈriːl-] N cinturón *m* de seguridad retráctil

inescapable [ɪnɪˈskeɪpəbl] ADJ ineludible, inevitable

inessential [ɪnɪˈsɛnʃl] ADJ no esencial

inestimable [ɪnˈɛstɪməbl] ADJ inestimable

inevitability [ɪnɛvɪtəˈbɪlɪtɪ] N inevitabilidad *f*

inevitable [ɪnˈɛvɪtəbl] ADJ inevitable; (*necessary*) forzoso

inevitably [ɪnˈɛvɪtəblɪ] ADV inevitablemente; **as ~ happens ...** como siempre pasa ...

inexact [ɪnɪgˈzækt] ADJ inexacto

inexcusable [ɪnɪksˈkjuːzəbl] ADJ imperdonable

inexhaustible [ɪnɪgˈzɔːstɪbl] ADJ inagotable

inexorable [ɪnˈɛksərəbl] ADJ inexorable, implacable

inexpensive [ɪnɪkˈspɛnsɪv] ADJ económico

inexperience [ɪnɪkˈspɪərɪəns] N falta de experiencia

inexperienced [ɪnɪkˈspɪərɪənst] ADJ inexperto; **to be ~ in sth** no tener experiencia en algo

inexplicable [ɪnɪkˈsplɪkəbl] ADJ inexplicable

inexpressible [ɪnɪkˈsprɛsəbl] ADJ inexpresable

inextricable [ɪnɪksˈtrɪkəbl] ADJ inseparable

inextricably [ɪnɪksˈtrɪkəblɪ] ADV indisolublemente

infallibility [ɪnfæləˈbɪlɪtɪ] N infalibilidad *f*

infallible [ɪnˈfælɪbl] ADJ infalible

infamous [ˈɪnfəməs] ADJ infame

infamy [ˈɪnfəmɪ] N infamia

infancy [ˈɪnfənsɪ] N infancia

infant [ˈɪnfənt] N niño(-a); (*baby*) niño(-a) pequeño(-a), bebé *mf*

infantile [ˈɪnfəntaɪl] ADJ infantil; (*pej*) aniñado

infant mortality N mortalidad *f* infantil

infantry [ˈɪnfəntrɪ] N infantería

infantryman [ˈɪnfəntrɪmən] N (*irreg*) soldado de infantería

infant school N (*BRIT*) escuela infantil; *see also* **primary school**

infatuated [ɪnˈfætjueɪtɪd] ADJ: **~ with** (*in love*) loco por; **to become ~ (with sb)** enamoriscarse (de algn), encapricharse (con algn)

infatuation [ɪnfætjuˈeɪʃən] N enamoramiento

infect [ɪnˈfɛkt] VT (*wound*) infectar; (*food*) contaminar; (*person, animal*) contagiar; (*fig: pej*) corromper; **infected with** (*illness*) contagiado de; **to become infected** (*wound*) infectarse

★**infection** [ɪnˈfɛkʃən] N infección *f*; (*fig*) contagio

infectious [ɪnˈfɛkʃəs] ADJ contagioso; (*fig*) infeccioso

infer [ɪnˈfɜː] VT deducir, inferir; **to ~ (from)** inferir (de), deducir (de)

inference [ˈɪnfərəns] N deducción *f*, inferencia

inferior [ɪnˈfɪərɪə] ADJ, N inferior *mf*; **to feel ~** sentirse inferior

inferiority [ɪnfɪərɪˈɒrətɪ] N inferioridad *f*

inferiority complex N complejo de inferioridad

infernal [ɪnˈfɜːnl] ADJ infernal

inferno [ɪnˈfɜːnəʊ] N infierno; (*fig*) hoguera

infertile [ɪnˈfɜːtaɪl] ADJ estéril; (*person*) infecundo

infertility [ɪnfəˈtɪlɪtɪ] N esterilidad f; infecundidad f

infest [ɪnˈfɛst] VT infestar

infested [ɪnˈfɛstɪd] ADJ: **~ (with)** plagado (de)

infidel [ˈɪnfɪdəl] N infiel mf

infidelity [ɪnfɪˈdɛlɪtɪ] N infidelidad f

in-fighting [ˈɪnfaɪtɪŋ] N (fig) lucha(s) f (pl) interna(s)

infiltrate [ˈɪnfɪltreɪt] VT (troops etc) infiltrarse en ▶ VI infiltrarse

infinite [ˈɪnfɪnɪt] ADJ infinito; **an ~ amount of money/time** un sinfín de dinero/tiempo

infinitely [ˈɪnfɪnɪtlɪ] ADV infinitamente

infinitesimal [ɪnfɪnɪˈtɛsɪməl] ADJ infinitésimo

infinitive [ɪnˈfɪnɪtɪv] N infinitivo

infinity [ɪnˈfɪnɪtɪ] N (Math) infinito; **an ~** infinidad f

infirm [ɪnˈfəːm] ADJ enfermizo, débil

infirmary [ɪnˈfəːmərɪ] N hospital m

infirmity [ɪnˈfəːmɪtɪ] N debilidad f; (illness) enfermedad f, achaque m

inflame [ɪnˈfleɪm] VT inflamar

inflamed [ɪnˈfleɪmd] ADJ: **to become ~** inflamarse

inflammable [ɪnˈflæməbl] ADJ inflamable; (situation etc) explosivo

inflammation [ɪnfləˈmeɪʃən] N inflamación f

inflammatory [ɪnˈflæmətərɪ] ADJ (speech) incendiario

inflatable [ɪnˈfleɪtəbl] ADJ inflable

inflate [ɪnˈfleɪt] VT (tyre) inflar; (fig) hinchar

inflated [ɪnˈfleɪtɪd] ADJ (tyre etc) inflado; (price, self-esteem etc) exagerado

★**inflation** [ɪnˈfleɪʃən] N (Econ) inflación f

inflationary [ɪnˈfleɪʃnərɪ] ADJ inflacionario

inflationary spiral N espiral f inflacionista

inflexible [ɪnˈflɛksɪbl] ADJ inflexible

inflict [ɪnˈflɪkt] VT: **to ~ on** infligir en; (tax etc) imponer a

in-flight [ˈɪnflaɪt] ADJ durante el vuelo

inflow [ˈɪnfləʊ] N afluencia

★**influence** [ˈɪnfluəns] N influencia; **under the ~ of alcohol** en estado de embriaguez ▶ VT influir en, influenciar

influential [ɪnfluˈɛnʃl] ADJ influyente

influenza [ɪnfluˈɛnzə] N gripe f

influx [ˈɪnflʌks] N afluencia

info [ˈɪnfəʊ] N (inf) = **information**

★**inform** [ɪnˈfɔːm] VT: **to ~ sb of sth** informar a algn sobre or de algo; (warn) avisar a algn de algo; (communicate) comunicar algo a algn ▶ VI: **to ~ on sb** delatar a algn

informal [ɪnˈfɔːml] ADJ (manner, tone) desenfadado; (dress, occasion) informal; (visit, meeting) extraoficial

informality [ɪnfɔːˈmælɪtɪ] N falta de ceremonia; (intimacy) intimidad f; (familiarity) familiaridad f; (ease) afabilidad f

informally [ɪnˈfɔːməlɪ] ADV sin ceremonia; (invite) informalmente

informant [ɪnˈfɔːmənt] N informante mf

informatics [ɪnfɔːˈmætɪks] N informática

★**information** [ɪnfəˈmeɪʃən] N información f; (news) noticias fpl; (knowledge) conocimientos mpl; (Law) delación f; **a piece of ~** un dato; **for your ~** para su información; **~ and communication(s) technology** (gen) tecnología de la información y de las comunicaciones; (BRIT Scol) informática

information bureau N oficina de información

information office N información f

information processing N procesamiento de datos

information retrieval N recuperación f de información

information science N gestión f de la información

information technology N informática

informative [ɪnˈfɔːmətɪv] ADJ informativo

informed [ɪnˈfɔːmd] ADJ (observer) informado, al corriente; **an ~ guess** una opinión bien fundamentada

informer [ɪnˈfɔːməʳ] N delator(a) m/f; (also: **police informer**) soplón(-ona) m/f

infra dig [ˈɪnfrəˈdɪɡ] ADJ ABBR (inf: = infra dignitatem) denigrante

infra-red [ɪnfrəˈrɛd] ADJ infrarrojo

infrastructure [ˈɪnfrəstrʌktʃəʳ] N infraestructura

infrequent [ɪnˈfriːkwənt] ADJ infrecuente

infringe [ɪnˈfrɪndʒ] VT infringir, violar ▶ VI: **to ~ on** invadir

infringement [ɪnˈfrɪndʒmənt] N infracción f; (of rights) usurpación f; (Sport) falta

infuriate [ɪnˈfjʊərɪeɪt] VT: **to become infuriated** ponerse furioso

infuriating [ɪnˈfjʊərɪeɪtɪŋ] ADJ (habit, noise) enloquecedor(a); **I find it ~** me saca de quicio

infuse [ɪnˈfjuːz] VT (with courage, enthusiasm): **to ~ sb with sth** infundir algo a algn

infusion [ɪnˈfjuːʒən] N (tea etc) infusión f

ingenious [ɪnˈdʒiːnjəs] ADJ ingenioso

ingenuity [ɪndʒɪˈnjuːɪtɪ] N ingeniosidad f

ingenuous [ɪnˈdʒɛnjuəs] ADJ ingenuo

ingot [ˈɪŋɡət] N lingote m, barra

ingrained [ɪnˈɡreɪnd] ADJ arraigado

ingratiate [ɪnˈɡreɪʃɪeɪt] VT: **to ~ o.s. with** congraciarse con

ingratiating [ɪnˈɡreɪʃɪeɪtɪŋ] ADJ (smile, speech) insinuante; (person) zalamero, congraciador(a)

ingratitude [ɪnˈɡrætɪtjuːd] N ingratitud f

★**ingredient** [ɪnˈɡriːdɪənt] N ingrediente m

ingrowing [ˈɪnɡrəʊɪŋ] ADJ: **~ (toe)nail** uña encarnada

inhabit [ɪnˈhæbɪt] VT vivir en; (occupy) ocupar

inhabitable [ɪnˈhæbɪtəbl] ADJ habitable

inhabitant [ɪnˈhæbɪtənt] N habitante *mf*

inhale [ɪnˈheɪl] VT inhalar ▶ VI (*breathe in*) aspirar; (*in smoking*) tragar

inhaler [ɪnˈheɪləʳ] N inhalador *m*

inherent [ɪnˈhɪərənt] ADJ: ~ **in** *or* **to** inherente a

inherently [ɪnˈhɪərəntlɪ] ADV intrínsecamente

inherit [ɪnˈhɛrɪt] VT heredar

inheritance [ɪnˈhɛrɪtəns] N herencia; (*fig*) patrimonio

inhibit [ɪnˈhɪbɪt] VT inhibir, impedir; **to ~ sb from doing sth** impedir a algn hacer algo

inhibited [ɪnˈhɪbɪtɪd] ADJ (*person*) cohibido

inhibition [ɪnhɪˈbɪʃən] N cohibición *f*

inhospitable [ɪnhɔsˈpɪtəbl] ADJ (*person*) inhospitalario; (*place*) inhóspito

in-house [ˈɪnhaus] ADJ dentro de la empresa

inhuman [ɪnˈhjuːmən] ADJ inhumano

inhumane [ɪnhjuːˈmeɪn] ADJ inhumano

inimitable [ɪˈnɪmɪtəbl] ADJ inimitable

iniquity [ɪˈnɪkwɪtɪ] N iniquidad *f*; (*injustice*) injusticia

initial [ɪˈnɪʃl] ADJ inicial; (*first*) primero ▶ N inicial *f* ▶ VT firmar con las iniciales ■ **initials** NPL iniciales *fpl*; (*abbreviation*) siglas *fpl*

initialize [ɪˈnɪʃəlaɪz] VT (*Comput*) inicializar

initially [ɪˈnɪʃəlɪ] ADV en un principio

initiate [ɪˈnɪʃɪeɪt] VT (*start*) iniciar; **to ~ sb into a secret** iniciar a algn en un secreto; **to ~ proceedings against sb** (*Law*) poner una demanda contra algn

initiation [ɪnɪʃɪˈeɪʃən] N (*into secret etc*) iniciación *f*; (*beginning*) comienzo

initiative [ɪˈnɪʃətɪv] N iniciativa; **to take the ~** tomar la iniciativa

inject [ɪnˈdʒɛkt] VT inyectar; (*money, enthusiasm*) aportar

injection [ɪnˈdʒɛkʃən] N inyección *f*; **to have an ~** ponerse una inyección

injudicious [ɪndʒuˈdɪʃəs] ADJ imprudente, indiscreto

injunction [ɪnˈdʒʌŋkʃən] N entredicho, interdicto

injure [ˈɪndʒəʳ] VT herir; (*hurt*) lastimar; (*fig: reputation etc*) perjudicar; (*feelings*) herir; **to ~ o.s.** hacerse daño, lastimarse

★**injured** [ˈɪndʒəd] ADJ (*also fig*) herido; ~ **party** (*Law*) parte *f* perjudicada

injurious [ɪnˈdʒuərɪəs] ADJ: ~ **(to)** perjudicial (para)

★**injury** [ˈɪndʒərɪ] N herida, lesión *f*; (*wrong*) perjuicio, daño; **to escape without ~** salir ileso

injury time N (*Sport*) descuento

injustice [ɪnˈdʒʌstɪs] N injusticia; **you do me an ~** usted es injusto conmigo

ink [ɪŋk] N tinta

ink-jet printer [ˈɪŋkdʒɛt-] N impresora de chorro de tinta

inkling [ˈɪŋklɪŋ] N sospecha; (*idea*) idea

inkpad [ˈɪŋkpæd] N almohadilla

inlaid [ˈɪnleɪd] ADJ (*wood*) taraceado; (*tiles*) entarimado

inland ADJ [ˈɪnlənd] interior; (*town*) del interior ▶ ADV [ɪnˈlænd] tierra adentro

Inland Revenue N (*BRIT*) ≈ Hacienda, ≈ Agencia Tributaria

in-laws [ˈɪnlɔːz] NPL suegros *mpl*

inlet [ˈɪnlɛt] N (*Geo*) ensenada, cala; (*Tech*) admisión *f*, entrada

inmate [ˈɪnmeɪt] N (*in prison*) preso(-a), presidiario(-a); (*in asylum*) internado(-a)

inmost [ˈɪnməust] ADJ más íntimo, más secreto

inn [ɪn] N posada, mesón *m*

innards [ˈɪnədz] NPL (*inf*) tripas *fpl*

innate [ɪˈneɪt] ADJ innato

inner [ˈɪnəʳ] ADJ interior, interno; (*feelings*) íntimo

inner city N barrios deprimidos del centro de una ciudad

inner-city ADJ (*schools, problems*) de las zonas céntricas pobres, de los barrios céntricos pobres

innermost [ˈɪnəməust] ADJ más íntimo, más secreto

inner tube N (*of tyre*) cámara, llanta (*LAM*)

inning [ˈɪnɪŋ] N (*US Baseball*) inning *m*, entrada; **innings** (*Cricket*) entrada, turno

innocence [ˈɪnəsns] N inocencia

★**innocent** [ˈɪnəsnt] ADJ inocente

innocuous [ɪˈnɔkjuəs] ADJ inocuo

innovation [ɪnəuˈveɪʃən] N novedad *f*

innovative [ˈɪnəuvətɪv] ADJ innovador

innuendo [ɪnjuˈɛndəu] (*pl* **innuendoes** [-əuz]) N indirecta

innumerable [ɪˈnjuːmrəbl] ADJ innumerable

inoculate [ɪˈnɔkjuleɪt] VT: **to ~ sb with sth/ against sth** inocular *or* vacunar a algn con algo/contra algo

inoculation [ɪnɔkjuˈleɪʃən] N inoculación *f*

inoffensive [ɪnəˈfɛnsɪv] ADJ inofensivo

inopportune [ɪnˈɔpətjuːn] ADJ inoportuno

inordinate [ɪˈnɔːdɪnət] ADJ excesivo, desmesurado

inordinately [ɪˈnɔːdɪnətlɪ] ADV excesivamente, desmesuradamente

inorganic [ɪnɔːˈgaenɪk] ADJ inorgánico

in-patient [ˈɪnpeɪʃənt] N (paciente *mf*) interno(-a)

input [ˈɪnput] N (*Elec*) entrada; (*of resources*) inversión *f*; (*Comput*) entrada de datos ▶ VT (*Comput*) introducir, entrar

inquest [ˈɪnkwɛst] N (*coroner's*) investigación *f* post-mortem

inquire [ɪnˈkwaɪəʳ] VI preguntar; **to ~ about** (*person*) preguntar por; (*fact*) informarse de ▶ VT: **to ~ when/where/whether** preguntar cuándo/dónde/si

▶ **inquire into** VT FUS: **to ~ into sth** investigar or indagar algo

inquiring [ɪnˈkwaɪərɪŋ] ADJ (mind) inquieto; (look) interrogante

★**inquiry** [ɪnˈkwaɪərɪ] N pregunta; (Law) investigación f, pesquisa; (commission) comisión f investigadora; **to hold an ~ into sth** emprender una investigación sobre algo; **"Inquiries"** "Información"

inquiry desk N mesa de información

inquiry office N (BRIT) oficina de información

inquisition [ɪnkwɪˈzɪʃən] N inquisición f

inquisitive [ɪnˈkwɪzɪtɪv] ADJ (mind) inquisitivo; (person) fisgón(-ona)

inroad [ˈɪnrəud] N incursión f; (fig) invasión f; **to make inroads into** (time) ocupar parte de; (savings, supplies) agotar parte de

insane [ɪnˈseɪn] ADJ loco; (Med) demente

insanitary [ɪnˈsænɪtərɪ] ADJ insalubre

insanity [ɪnˈsænɪtɪ] N demencia, locura

insatiable [ɪnˈseɪʃəbl] ADJ insaciable

inscribe [ɪnˈskraɪb] VT inscribir; (book etc): **to ~ (to sb)** dedicar (a algn)

inscription [ɪnˈskrɪpʃən] N (gen) inscripción f; (in book) dedicatoria

inscrutable [ɪnˈskruːtəbl] ADJ inescrutable, insondable

inseam measurement [ˈɪnsiːm-] N (US) = **inside leg measurement**

insect [ˈɪnsɛkt] N insecto

insect bite N picadura

insecticide [ɪnˈsɛktɪsaɪd] N insecticida m

insect repellent N loción f contra los insectos

insecure [ɪnsɪˈkjuər] ADJ inseguro

insecurity [ɪnsɪˈkjuərɪtɪ] N inseguridad f

insemination [ɪnsɛmɪˈneɪʃn] N: **artificial ~** inseminación f artificial

insensible [ɪnˈsɛnsɪbl] ADJ inconsciente; (unconscious) sin conocimiento

insensitive [ɪnˈsɛnsɪtɪv] ADJ insensible

insensitivity [ɪnsɛnsɪˈtɪvɪtɪ] N insensibilidad f

inseparable [ɪnˈsɛprəbl] ADJ inseparable; **they were ~ friends** los unía una estrecha amistad

insert VT [ɪnˈsəːt] (into sth) introducir; (Comput) insertar ▶ N [ˈɪnsəːt] encarte m

insertion [ɪnˈsəːʃən] N inserción f

in-service [ɪnˈsəːvɪs] ADJ (training, course) en el trabajo, a cargo de la empresa

inshore [ɪnˈʃɔːr] ADJ: **~ fishing** pesca f costera ▶ ADV (fish) a lo largo de la costa; (move) hacia la orilla

★**inside** [ˈɪnˈsaɪd] N interior m; (lining) forro; (of road: BRIT) izquierdo; (: in US, Europe etc) derecho; **~ out** adv (turn) al revés; (know) a fondo ▶ ADJ interior, interno ▶ ADV (within) (por) dentro, adentro (esp LAM); (with movement) hacia dentro; (inf: in prison) en chirona ▶ PREP dentro de; (of time): **~ 10 minutes** en menos de 10 minutos ▦ **insides** NPL (inf) tripas fpl

inside forward N (Sport) interior m

inside information N información f confidencial

inside lane N (Aut: BRIT) carril m izquierdo; (: in US, Europe etc) carril m derecho

inside leg measurement N medida de pernera

insider [ɪnˈsaɪdər] N enterado(-a)

insider dealing, insider trading N (Stock Exchange) abuso de información privilegiada

inside story N historia íntima

insidious [ɪnˈsɪdɪəs] ADJ insidioso

insight [ˈɪnsaɪt] N perspicacia, percepción f; **to gain** or **get an ~ into sth** comprender algo mejor

insignia [ɪnˈsɪgnɪə] NPL insignias fpl

insignificant [ɪnsɪgˈnɪfɪknt] ADJ insignificante

insincere [ɪnsɪnˈsɪər] ADJ poco sincero

insincerity [ɪnsɪnˈsɛrɪtɪ] N falta de sinceridad, doblez f

insinuate [ɪnˈsɪnjueɪt] VT insinuar

insinuation [ɪnsɪnjuˈeɪʃən] N insinuación f

insipid [ɪnˈsɪpɪd] ADJ soso, insulso

★**insist** [ɪnˈsɪst] VI insistir; **to ~ on doing** empeñarse en hacer; **to ~ that** insistir en que; (claim) exigir que

insistence [ɪnˈsɪstəns] N insistencia; (stubbornness) empeño

insistent [ɪnˈsɪstənt] ADJ insistente; (noise, action) persistente

insofar as [ɪnsəuˈfɑː-] CONJ en la medida en que, en tanto que

insole [ˈɪnsəul] N plantilla

insolence [ˈɪnsələns] N insolencia, descaro

insolent [ˈɪnsələnt] ADJ insolente, descarado

insoluble [ɪnˈsɔljubl] ADJ insoluble

insolvency [ɪnˈsɔlvənsɪ] N insolvencia

insolvent [ɪnˈsɔlvənt] ADJ insolvente

insomnia [ɪnˈsɔmnɪə] N insomnio

insomniac [ɪnˈsɔmnɪæk] N insomne mf

inspect [ɪnˈspɛkt] VT inspeccionar, examinar; (troops) pasar revista a

inspection [ɪnˈspɛkʃən] N inspección f, examen m; (of troops) revista

★**inspector** [ɪnˈspɛktər] N inspector(a) m/f; (BRIT: on buses, trains) revisor(a) m/f

inspiration [ɪnspəˈreɪʃən] N inspiración f

inspire [ɪnˈspaɪər] VT inspirar; **to ~ sb (to do sth)** alentar a algn (a hacer algo)

inspired [ɪnˈspaɪəd] ADJ (writer, book etc) inspirado, genial, iluminado; **in an ~ moment** en un momento de inspiración

inspiring [ɪnˈspaɪərɪŋ] ADJ inspirador(a)

inst. [ɪnst] ABBR (BRIT Comm: = instant, of the present month) cte.

instability [ɪnstəˈbɪlɪtɪ] N inestabilidad f

install, (US) **instal** [ɪnˈstɔːl] VT instalar

installation [ɪnstəˈleɪʃən] N instalación f
installer [ɪnˈstɔːlə] N (*Comput*) instalador m
installment plan N (*US*) compra a plazos
instalment, (*US*) **installment** [ɪnˈstɔːlmənt]
N plazo; (*of story*) entrega; (*of TV serial etc*) capítulo; **in instalments** (*pay, receive*) a plazos; **to pay in instalments** pagar a plazos *or* por abonos
★**instance** [ˈɪnstəns] N ejemplo, caso; **for ~** por ejemplo; **in the first ~** en primer lugar; **in that ~** en ese caso
★**instant** [ˈɪnstənt] N instante m, momento ▸ ADJ inmediato; (*coffee*) instantáneo
instantaneous [ɪnstənˈteɪnɪəs] ADJ instantáneo
instantly [ˈɪnstəntlɪ] ADV en seguida, al instante
instant message N mensaje m instantáneo
instant messaging [-ˈmɛsədʒɪŋ] N mensajería instantánea
instant replay N (*US TV*) repetición f de la jugada
★**instead** [ɪnˈstɛd] ADV en cambio; **~ of** en lugar de, en vez de
instep [ˈɪnstɛp] N empeine m
instigate [ˈɪnstɪɡeɪt] VT (*rebellion, strike, crime*) instigar; (*new ideas etc*) fomentar
instigation [ɪnstɪˈɡeɪʃən] N instigación f; **at sb's ~** a instigación de algn
instil [ɪnˈstɪl] VT: **to ~ into** inculcar a
instinct [ˈɪnstɪŋkt] N instinto
instinctive [ɪnˈstɪŋktɪv] ADJ instintivo
instinctively [ɪnˈstɪŋktɪvlɪ] ADV por instinto
★**institute** [ˈɪnstɪtjuːt] N instituto; (*professional body*) colegio ▸ VT (*begin*) iniciar, empezar; (*proceedings*) entablar
★**institution** [ɪnstɪˈtjuːʃən] N institución f; (*beginning*) iniciación f; (*Med: home*) asilo; (: *asylum*) manicomio; (: *custom*) costumbre f arraigada
institutional [ɪnstɪˈtjuːʃənl] ADJ institucional
instruct [ɪnˈstrʌkt] VT: **to ~ sb in sth** instruir a algn en *or* sobre algo; **to ~ sb to do sth** dar instrucciones a algn de *or* mandar a algn hacer algo
instruction [ɪnˈstrʌkʃən] N (*teaching*) instrucción f; **instructions (for use)** modo *sg* de empleo ■ **instructions** NPL órdenes *fpl*
instruction book N manual m
instructive [ɪnˈstrʌktɪv] ADJ instructivo
instructor [ɪnˈstrʌktəʳ] N instructor(a) *m/f*
★**instrument** [ˈɪnstrəmənt] N instrumento
instrumental [ɪnstrəˈmɛntl] ADJ (*Mus*) instrumental; **to be ~ in** ser el artífice de; **to be ~ in sth/in doing sth** ser responsable de algo/de hacer algo
instrumentalist [ɪnstrəˈmɛntəlɪst] N instrumentista *mf*

instrument panel N tablero (de instrumentos)
insubordinate [ɪnsəˈbɔːdənɪt] ADJ insubordinado
insubordination [ɪnsəbɔːdəˈneɪʃən] N insubordinación f
insufferable [ɪnˈsʌfrəbl] ADJ insoportable
insufficient [ɪnsəˈfɪʃənt] ADJ insuficiente
insufficiently [ɪnsəˈfɪʃəntlɪ] ADV insuficientemente
insular [ˈɪnsjuləʳ] ADJ insular; (*outlook*) estrecho de miras
insularity [ɪnsjuˈlærɪtɪ] N insularidad f
insulate [ˈɪnsjuleɪt] VT aislar
insulating tape [ˈɪnsjuleɪtɪŋ-] N cinta aislante
insulation [ɪnsjuˈleɪʃən] N aislamiento
insulator [ˈɪnsjuleɪtəʳ] N aislante m
insulin [ˈɪnsjulɪn] N insulina
insult N [ˈɪnsʌlt] insulto; (*offence*) ofensa ▸ VT [ɪnˈsʌlt] insultar; ofender
insulting [ɪnˈsʌltɪŋ] ADJ insultante; ofensivo
insuperable [ɪnˈsjuːprəbl] ADJ insuperable
★**insurance** [ɪnˈʃuərəns] N seguro; **fire/life ~** seguro contra incendios/de vida; **to take out ~ (against)** hacerse un seguro (contra)
insurance agent N agente *mf* de seguros
insurance broker N corredor(a) *m/f or* agente *mf* de seguros
insurance company N compañía f de seguros
insurance policy N póliza (de seguros)
insurance premium N prima de seguros
insure [ɪnˈʃuəʳ] VT asegurar; **to ~ sb** *or* **sb's life** hacer un seguro de vida a algn; **to ~ (against)** asegurar (contra); **to be insured for £5000** tener un seguro de 5000 libras
insured [ɪnˈʃuəd] N: **the ~** el asegurado(-a)
insurer [ɪnˈʃuərəʳ] N asegurador(a)
insurgent [ɪnˈsɜːdʒənt] ADJ, N insurgente *mf*, insurrecto(-a) *m/f*
insurmountable [ɪnsəˈmauntəbl] ADJ insuperable
insurrection [ɪnsəˈrɛkʃən] N insurrección f
intact [ɪnˈtækt] ADJ íntegro; (*untouched*) intacto
intake [ˈɪnteɪk] N (*Tech*) entrada, toma; (: *pipe*) tubo de admisión; (*of food*) ingestión f; (*Brit Scol*): **an ~ of 200 a year** 200 matriculados al año
intangible [ɪnˈtændʒɪbl] ADJ intangible
integer [ˈɪntɪdʒəʳ] N (*número*) entero
integral [ˈɪntɪɡrəl] ADJ (*whole*) íntegro; (*part*) integrante
integrate [ˈɪntɪɡreɪt] VT integrar ▸ VI integrarse
integrated circuit [ˈɪntɪɡreɪtɪd-] N (*Comput*) circuito integrado
integration [ɪntɪˈɡreɪʃən] N integración f; **racial ~** integración de razas

integrity [ɪnˈtɛɡrɪtɪ] N honradez f, rectitud f; (*Comput*) integridad f

intellect [ˈɪntəlɛkt] N intelecto

intellectual [ɪntəˈlɛktjuəl] ADJ, N intelectual mf

intelligence [ɪnˈtɛlɪdʒəns] N inteligencia

intelligence quotient N coeficiente m intelectual

Intelligence Service N Servicio de Inteligencia

intelligence test N prueba de inteligencia

★**intelligent** [ɪnˈtɛlɪdʒənt] ADJ inteligente

intelligently [ɪnˈtɛlɪdʒəntlɪ] ADV inteligentemente

intelligentsia [ɪntɛlɪˈdʒɛntsɪə] N intelectualidad f

intelligible [ɪnˈtɛlɪdʒɪbl] ADJ inteligible, comprensible

intemperate [ɪnˈtɛmpərət] ADJ inmoderado

★**intend** [ɪnˈtɛnd] VT (*gift etc*): **to ~ sth for** destinar algo a; **to ~ to do sth** tener intención de or pensar hacer algo

intended [ɪnˈtɛndɪd] ADJ (*effect*) deseado

★**intense** [ɪnˈtɛns] ADJ intenso; **to be ~** (*person*) tomárselo todo muy en serio

intensely [ɪnˈtɛnslɪ] ADV intensamente; (*very*) sumamente

intensify [ɪnˈtɛnsɪfaɪ] VT intensificar; (*increase*) aumentar

intensity [ɪnˈtɛnsɪtɪ] N (*gen*) intensidad f

intensive [ɪnˈtɛnsɪv] ADJ intensivo

intensive care N: **to be in ~** estar bajo cuidados intensivos; **~ unit** unidad f de vigilancia intensiva

intensively [ɪnˈtɛnsɪvlɪ] ADV intensivamente

intent [ɪnˈtɛnt] N propósito; (*Law*) premeditación f; **to all intents and purposes** a efectos prácticos ▶ ADJ (*absorbed*) absorto; (*attentive*) atento; **to be ~ on doing sth** estar resuelto or decidido a hacer algo

★**intention** [ɪnˈtɛnʃən] N intención f, propósito

intentional [ɪnˈtɛnʃənl] ADJ deliberado

intentionally [ɪnˈtɛnʃnəlɪ] ADV a propósito

intently [ɪnˈtɛntlɪ] ADV atentamente, fijamente

inter [ɪnˈtəːʳ] VT enterrar, sepultar

inter- [ˈɪntəʳ] PREF inter-

interact [ɪntərˈækt] VI (*substances*) influirse mutuamente; (*people*) relacionarse

interaction [ɪntərˈækʃən] N interacción f, acción f recíproca

interactive [ɪntərˈæktɪv] ADJ (*Comput*) interactivo

intercede [ɪntəˈsiːd] VI interceder; **to ~ with sb/on behalf of sb** interceder con algn/en nombre de algn

intercept [ɪntəˈsɛpt] VT interceptar; (*stop*) detener

interception [ɪntəˈsɛpʃən] N interceptación f; detención f

interchange N [ˈɪntətʃeɪndʒ] intercambio; (*on motorway*) intersección f ▶ VT [ɪntəˈtʃeɪndʒ] intercambiar

interchangeable [ɪntəˈtʃeɪndʒəbl] ADJ intercambiable

intercity [ɪntəˈsɪtɪ] ADJ: **~ (train)** (tren m) intercity m

intercom [ˈɪntəkəm] N interfono

interconnect [ɪntəkəˈnɛkt] VI (*rooms*) comunicar(se)

intercontinental [ˈɪntəkɔntɪˈnɛntl] ADJ intercontinental

intercourse [ˈɪntəkɔːs] N (*also*: **sexual intercourse**) relaciones fpl sexuales, contacto sexual; (*social*) trato

interdependence [ɪntədɪˈpɛndəns] N interdependencia

interdependent [ɪntədɪˈpɛndənt] ADJ interdependiente

★**interest** [ˈɪntrɪst] N (*Comm*) interés m; **compound/simple ~** interés compuesto/simple; **business interests** negocios mpl; **British interests in the Middle East** los intereses británicos en el Medio Oriente ▶ VT interesar

interested [ˈɪntrɪstɪd] ADJ interesado; **to be ~ in** interesarse por

interest-free [ˈɪntrɪstˈfriː] ADJ libre de interés

★**interesting** [ˈɪntrɪstɪŋ] ADJ interesante

interest rate N tipo de interés

interface [ˈɪntəfeɪs] N (*Comput*) junción f, interface m

interfere [ɪntəˈfɪəʳ] VI: **to ~ in** (*quarrel, other people's business*) entrometerse en; **to ~ with** (*hinder*) estorbar; (*damage*) estropear; (*Radio*) interferir con

interference [ɪntəˈfɪərəns] N (*gen*) intromisión f; (*Radio, TV*) interferencia

interfering [ɪntəˈfɪərɪŋ] ADJ entrometido

interim [ˈɪntərɪm] ADJ provisional; **~ dividend** dividendo parcial ▶ N: **in the ~** en el ínterin

★**interior** [ɪnˈtɪərɪəʳ] N interior m ▶ ADJ interior

interior decorator, interior designer N interiorista mf, diseñador(a) m/f de interiores

interior design N interiorismo, decoración f de interiores

interjection [ɪntəˈdʒɛkʃən] N interrupción f

interlock [ɪntəˈlɔk] VI entrelazarse; (*wheels etc*) endentarse

interloper [ˈɪntələupəʳ] N intruso(-a)

interlude [ˈɪntəluːd] N intervalo; (*rest*) descanso; (*Theat*) intermedio

intermarriage [ɪntəˈmærɪdʒ] N endogamia

intermarry [ɪntəˈmærɪ] VI casarse (entre parientes)

intermediary [ɪntəˈmiːdɪərɪ] N intermediario(-a)

intermediate [ɪntəˈmiːdɪət] ADJ intermedio

interminable [ɪnˈtəːmɪnəbl] ADJ inacabable

intermission [ɪntəˈmɪʃən] N (Theat) descanso

intermittent [ɪntəˈmɪtnt] ADJ intermitente

intermittently [ɪntəˈmɪtntlɪ] ADV intermitentemente

intern VT [ɪnˈtəːn] internar; (enclose) encerrar ▶ N [ˈɪntəːn] (esp US: doctor) médico(-a) interno(-a); (: on work placement) becario(-a)

★**internal** [ɪnˈtəːnl] ADJ interno, interior; (injury, structure, memo) interno; **~ injuries** heridas fpl or lesiones fpl internas

internally [ɪnˈtəːnəlɪ] ADV interiormente; **"not to be taken ~"** "uso externo"

Internal Revenue Service N (US) ≈ Hacienda, ≈ Agencia Tributaria

★**international** [ɪntəˈnæʃənl] ADJ internacional; **~ (game)** partido internacional; **~ (player)** jugador(a) m/f internacional

International Atomic Energy Agency N Organismo Internacional de Energía Atómica

International Chamber of Commerce N Cámara de Comercio Internacional

International Court of Justice N Corte f Internacional de Justicia

international date line N línea de cambio de fecha

internationally [ɪntəˈnæʃnəlɪ] ADV internacionalmente

International Monetary Fund N Fondo Monetario Internacional

internecine [ɪntəˈniːsaɪn] ADJ de aniquilación mutua

internee [ɪntəːˈniː] N interno(-a), recluso(-a)

★**internet, Internet** [ˈɪntənet] N: **the ~** (el or la) Internet

internet café N cibercafé m

internet service provider N proveedor m de (acceso a) Internet

internet user N internauta mf

internment [ɪnˈtəːnmənt] N internamiento

interplanetary [ɪntəˈplænɪtərɪ] ADJ interplanetario

interplay [ˈɪntəpleɪ] N interacción f

Interpol [ˈɪntəpɔl] N Interpol f

interpret [ɪnˈtəːprɪt] VT interpretar; (translate) traducir; (understand) entender ▶ VI hacer de intérprete

interpretation [ɪntəːprɪˈteɪʃən] N interpretación f; traducción f

interpreter [ɪnˈtəːprɪtər] N intérprete mf

interrelated [ɪntərɪˈleɪtɪd] ADJ interrelacionado

interrogate [ɪnˈterəʊgeɪt] VT interrogar

interrogation [ɪnterəʊˈgeɪʃən] N interrogatorio

interrogative [ɪntəˈrɔgətɪv] ADJ interrogativo

interrupt [ɪntəˈrʌpt] VT, VI interrumpir

interruption [ɪntəˈrʌpʃən] N interrupción f

intersect [ɪntəˈsekt] VT cruzar ▶ VI (roads) cruzarse

intersection [ɪntəˈsekʃən] N intersección f; (of roads) cruce m

intersperse [ɪntəˈspəːs] VT: **to ~ with** salpicar de

interstate [ˈɪntəsteɪt] N (US) carretera interestatal

intertwine [ɪntəˈtwaɪn] VT entrelazar ▶ VI entrelazarse

interval [ˈɪntəvl] N intervalo; (BRIT Theat, Sport) descanso; (Scol) recreo; **at intervals** a ratos, de vez en cuando; **sunny intervals** (Meteorology) claros mpl

intervene [ɪntəˈviːn] VI intervenir; (take part) participar; (occur) sobrevenir

intervening [ɪntəˈviːnɪŋ] ADJ intermedio

intervention [ɪntəˈvenʃən] N intervención f

★**interview** [ˈɪntəvjuː] N (Radio, TV etc) entrevista ▶ VT entrevistar a

interviewee [ɪntəvjuːˈiː] N entrevistado(-a)

interviewer [ˈɪntəvjuːər] N entrevistador(a) m/f

intestate [ɪnˈtesteɪt] ADJ intestado

intestinal [ɪnˈtestɪnl] ADJ intestinal

intestine [ɪnˈtestɪn] N: **large/small ~** intestino grueso/delgado

intimacy [ˈɪntɪməsɪ] N intimidad f; (relations) relaciones fpl íntimas

intimate ADJ [ˈɪntɪmət] íntimo; (friendship) estrecho; (knowledge) profundo ▶ VT [ˈɪntɪmeɪt] (announce) dar a entender

intimately [ˈɪntɪmətlɪ] ADV íntimamente

intimidate [ɪnˈtɪmɪdeɪt] VT intimidar, amedrentar

intimidating [ɪnˈtɪmɪdeɪtɪŋ] ADJ amedrentador, intimidante

intimidation [ɪntɪmɪˈdeɪʃən] N intimidación f

★**into** [ˈɪntuː] PREP (gen) en; (towards) a; (inside) hacia el interior de; **~ three pieces/French** en tres pedazos/al francés; **to change pounds ~ euros** cambiar libras por euros

intolerable [ɪnˈtɔlərəbl] ADJ intolerable, insoportable

intolerance [ɪnˈtɔlərəns] N intolerancia

intolerant [ɪnˈtɔlərənt] ADJ: **~ (of)** intolerante (con)

intonation [ɪntəuˈneɪʃən] N entonación f

intoxicate [ɪnˈtɔksɪkeɪt] VT embriagar

intoxicated [ɪnˈtɔksɪkeɪtɪd] ADJ embriagado

intoxication [ɪntɔksɪˈkeɪʃən] N embriaguez f

intractable [ɪnˈtræktəbl] ADJ (person) intratable; (problem) irresoluble; (illness) incurable

intranet [ˈɪntrənet] N intranet f

intransigence [ɪnˈtrænsɪdʒəns] N intransigencia

intransigent [ɪnˈtrænsɪdʒənt] ADJ intransigente

intransitive [ɪnˈtrænsɪtɪv] ADJ intransitivo

intravenous [ɪntrəˈviːnəs] ADJ intravenoso

in-tray ['ɪntreɪ] N bandeja de entrada

intrepid [ɪn'trɛpɪd] ADJ intrépido

intricacy ['ɪntrɪkəsɪ] N complejidad f

intricate ['ɪntrɪkət] ADJ (design, pattern) intrincado; (plot, problem) complejo

intrigue [ɪn'triːg] N intriga ▶ VT fascinar ▶ VI andar en intrigas

intriguing [ɪn'triːgɪŋ] ADJ fascinante

intrinsic [ɪn'trɪnsɪk] ADJ intrínseco

★**introduce** [ɪntrə'djuːs] VT introducir, meter; (speaker, TV show etc) presentar; **to ~ sb (to sb)** presentar algn (a algn); **to ~ sb to** (pastime, technique) introducir a algn a; **may I ~ …?** permítame presentarle a …

introduction [ɪntrə'dʌkʃən] N introducción f; (of person) presentación f; **a letter of ~** una carta de recomendación

introductory [ɪntrə'dʌktərɪ] ADJ introductorio; **an ~ offer** una oferta introductoria; **~ remarks** comentarios mpl preliminares

introspection [ɪntrəu'spɛkʃən] N introspección f

introspective [ɪntrəu'spɛktɪv] ADJ introspectivo

introvert ['ɪntrəuvəːt] ADJ, N introvertido(-a) m/f

intrude [ɪn'truːd] VI (person) entrometerse; **to ~ on** estorbar

intruder [ɪn'truːdər] N intruso(-a)

intrusion [ɪn'truːʒən] N invasión f

intrusive [ɪn'truːsɪv] ADJ intruso

intuition [ɪntju:'ɪʃən] N intuición f

intuitive [ɪn'tjuːɪtɪv] ADJ intuitivo

intuitively [ɪn'tjuːɪtɪvlɪ] ADV por intuición, intuitivamente

inundate ['ɪnʌndeɪt] VT: **to ~ with** inundar de

inure [ɪn'juər] VT: **to ~ (to)** acostumbrar or habituar (a)

invade [ɪn'veɪd] VT invadir

invader [ɪn'veɪdər] N invasor(a) m/f

invalid N ['ɪnvəlɪd] minusválido(-a) ▶ ADJ [ɪn'vælɪd] (not valid) inválido, nulo

invalidate [ɪn'vælɪdeɪt] VT invalidar, anular

invalid chair N silla de ruedas

invaluable [ɪn'væljuəbl] ADJ inestimable

invariable [ɪn'vɛərɪəbl] ADJ invariable

invariably [ɪn'vɛərɪəblɪ] ADV sin excepción, siempre; **she is ~ late** siempre llega tarde

invasion [ɪn'veɪʒən] N invasión f

invective [ɪn'vɛktɪv] N invectiva

inveigle [ɪn'viːgl] VT: **to ~ sb into (doing) sth** embaucar or engatusar a algn para (que haga) algo

invent [ɪn'vɛnt] VT inventar

invention [ɪn'vɛnʃən] N invento; (inventiveness) inventiva; (lie) invención f

inventive [ɪn'vɛntɪv] ADJ inventivo

inventiveness [ɪn'vɛntɪvnɪs] N ingenio, inventiva

inventor [ɪn'vɛntər] N inventor(a) m/f

inventory ['ɪnvəntrɪ] N inventario

inventory control N control m de existencias

inverse [ɪn'vəːs] ADJ, N inverso; **in ~ proportion (to)** en proporción inversa (a)

inversely [ɪn'vəːslɪ] ADV a la inversa

invert [ɪn'vəːt] VT invertir

invertebrate [ɪn'vəːtɪbrət] N invertebrado

inverted commas [ɪn'vəːtɪd-] NPL (BRIT) comillas fpl

invest [ɪn'vɛst] VT invertir; (fig: time, effort) dedicar; **to ~ sb with sth** conferir algo a algn ▶ VI: **to ~ in** (company etc) invertir dinero en; (fig: sth useful) comprar

investigate [ɪn'vɛstɪgeɪt] VT investigar; (study) estudiar, examinar

investigation [ɪnvɛstɪ'geɪʃən] N investigación f, pesquisa; examen m

investigative journalism [ɪn'vɛstɪgətɪv-] N periodismo de investigación

investigator [ɪn'vɛstɪgeɪtər] N investigador(a) m/f; **private ~** investigador(a) m/f privado(-a)

investiture [ɪn'vɛstɪtʃər] N investidura

investment [ɪn'vɛstmənt] N inversión f

investment grant N subvención f para la inversión

investment income N ingresos mpl procedentes de inversiones

investment portfolio N cartera de inversiones

investment trust N compañía inversionista, sociedad f de cartera

investor [ɪn'vɛstər] N inversor(a) m/f

inveterate [ɪn'vɛtərət] ADJ empedernido

invidious [ɪn'vɪdɪəs] ADJ odioso

invigilate [ɪn'vɪdʒɪleɪt] VT, VI (in exam) vigilar

invigilator [ɪn'vɪdʒɪleɪtər] N celador(a) m/f

invigorating [ɪn'vɪgəreɪtɪŋ] ADJ vigorizante

invincible [ɪn'vɪnsɪbl] ADJ invencible

inviolate [ɪn'vaɪələt] ADJ inviolado

invisible [ɪn'vɪzɪbl] ADJ invisible

invisible assets NPL activo invisible

invisible ink N tinta simpática

invisible mending N puntada invisible

★**invitation** [ɪnvɪ'teɪʃən] N invitación f; **at sb's ~** a invitación de algn; **by ~ only** solamente por invitación

★**invite** [ɪn'vaɪt] VT invitar; (opinions etc) solicitar, pedir; (trouble) buscarse; **to ~ sb (to do)** invitar a algn (a hacer); **to ~ sb to dinner** invitar a algn a cenar

▶ **invite out** VT invitar a salir

▶ **invite over** VT invitar a casa

inviting [ɪn'vaɪtɪŋ] ADJ atractivo; (look) provocativo; (food) apetitoso

615

invoice [ˈɪnvɔɪs] N factura ▸ VT facturar; **to ~ sb for goods** facturar a algn las mercancías

invoicing [ˈɪnvɔɪsɪŋ] N facturación f

invoke [ɪnˈvəuk] VT invocar; *(aid)* pedir; *(law)* recurrir a

involuntary [ɪnˈvɔləntrɪ] ADJ involuntario

★**involve** [ɪnˈvɔlv] VT *(entail)* suponer, implicar, tener que ver con; *(concern, affect)* corresponder a; **to ~ sb (in sth)** involucrar a algn (en algo), comprometer a algn (con algo)

involved [ɪnˈvɔlvd] ADJ complicado; **to be ~ in sth** *(take part)* estar involucrado en algo; *(engrossed in)* estar muy metido

involvement [ɪnˈvɔlvmənt] N participación f, dedicación f; *(obligation)* compromiso; *(difficulty)* apuro

invulnerable [ɪnˈvʌlnərəbl] ADJ invulnerable

inward [ˈɪnwəd] ADJ *(movement)* interior, interno; *(thought, feeling)* íntimo ▸ ADV hacia dentro

inwardly [ˈɪnwədlɪ] ADV *(feel, think etc)* para sí, para dentro

inwards [ˈɪnwədz] ADV hacia dentro

I/O ABBR *(Comput: = input/output)* E/S; **I/O error** error m de E/S

IOC N ABBR *(= International Olympic Committee)* COI m

iodine [ˈaɪəudiːn] N yodo

IOM ABBR *(BRIT)* = **Isle of Man**

ion [ˈaɪən] N ion m

Ionian Sea [aɪˈəunɪən-] N: **the ~** el mar Jónico

ioniser [ˈaɪənaɪzəʳ] N ionizador m

iota [aɪˈəutə] N *(fig)* jota, ápice m

IOU N ABBR *(= I owe you)* pagaré m

IOW ABBR *(BRIT)* = **Isle of Wight**

IPA N ABBR *(= International Phonetic Alphabet)* AFI m

iPad® [ˈaɪpæd] N iPad® m, tableta (digital)

iPhone® [ˈaɪfəun] N iPhone® m, teléfono inteligente

iPlayer® [ˈaɪpleɪəʳ] N servicio de vídeo a la carta de la BBC

iPod® [ˈaɪpɔd] N iPod® m

IQ N ABBR *(= intelligence quotient)* C.I. m

IRA N ABBR *(= Irish Republican Army)* IRA m; *(US)* = **individual retirement account**

Iran [ɪˈrɑːn] N Irán m

Iranian [ɪˈreɪnɪən] ADJ, N iraní mf; *(Ling)* iraní m

Iraq [ɪˈrɑːk] N Irak m

Iraqi [ɪˈrɑːkɪ] ADJ, N irakí mf

irascible [ɪˈræsɪbl] ADJ irascible

irate [aɪˈreɪt] ADJ enojado, airado

★**Ireland** [ˈaɪələnd] N Irlanda; **Republic of ~** República de Irlanda

iris [ˈaɪrɪs] *(pl* **irises** [-ɪz]*)* N *(Anat)* iris m; *(Bot)* lirio

★**Irish** [ˈaɪrɪʃ] ADJ irlandés(-esa) ▸ N *(Ling)* irlandés m; **the ~** npl los irlandeses

★**Irishman** [ˈaɪrɪʃmən] N *(irreg)* irlandés m

Irish Sea N: **the ~** el mar de Irlanda

★**Irishwoman** [ˈaɪrɪʃwumən] N *(irreg)* irlandesa

irk [əːk] VT fastidiar

irksome [ˈəːksəm] ADJ fastidioso

IRN N ABBR *(= Independent Radio News)* servicio de noticias en las cadenas de radio privadas

IRO N ABBR *(US)* = **International Refugee Organization**

★**iron** [ˈaɪən] N hierro; *(for clothes)* plancha ▸ ADJ de hierro ▸ VT *(clothes)* planchar ■ **irons** NPL *(chains)* grilletes mpl
▸ **iron out** VT *(crease)* quitar; *(fig)* allanar, resolver

Iron Curtain N: **the ~** el Telón de Acero

iron foundry N fundición f, fundidora

ironic [aɪˈrɔnɪk], **ironical** [aɪˈrɔnɪkl] ADJ irónico

ironically [aɪˈrɔnɪklɪ] ADV irónicamente

ironing [ˈaɪənɪŋ] N *(act)* planchado; *(ironed clothes)* ropa planchada; *(clothes to be ironed)* ropa por planchar

ironing board N tabla de planchar

iron lung N *(Med)* pulmón m de acero

ironmonger [ˈaɪənmʌŋgəʳ] N *(BRIT)* ferretero(-a); **~'s (shop)** ferretería

iron ore N mineral m de hierro

ironworks [ˈaɪənwəːks] N fundición f

irony [ˈaɪrənɪ] N ironía; **the ~ of it is that ...** lo irónico del caso es que ...

irrational [ɪˈræʃənl] ADJ irracional

irreconcilable [ɪrɛkənˈsaɪləbl] ADJ inconciliable; *(enemies)* irreconciliable

irredeemable [ɪrɪˈdiːməbl] ADJ irredimible

irrefutable [ɪrɪˈfjuːtəbl] ADJ irrefutable

irregular [ɪˈrɛgjuləʳ] ADJ irregular; *(surface)* desigual; *(action, event)* anómalo; *(behaviour)* poco ortodoxo

irregularity [ɪrɛgjuˈlærɪtɪ] N irregularidad f; desigualdad f

irrelevance [ɪˈrɛləvəns] N irrelevancia

irrelevant [ɪˈrɛləvənt] ADJ irrelevante; **to be ~** estar fuera de lugar, no venir al caso

irreligious [ɪrɪˈlɪdʒəs] ADJ irreligioso

irreparable [ɪˈrɛprəbl] ADJ irreparable

irreplaceable [ɪrɪˈpleɪsəbl] ADJ irreemplazable

irrepressible [ɪrɪˈprɛsəbl] ADJ incontenible

irreproachable [ɪrɪˈprəutʃəbl] ADJ irreprochable

irresistible [ɪrɪˈzɪstɪbl] ADJ irresistible

irresolute [ɪˈrɛzəluːt] ADJ indeciso

irrespective [ɪrɪˈspɛktɪv]: **~ of** prep sin tener en cuenta, no importa

irresponsibility [ɪrɪspɔnsɪˈbɪlɪtɪ] N irresponsabilidad f

irresponsible [ɪrɪˈspɔnsɪbl] ADJ *(act)* irresponsable; *(person)* poco serio

irretrievable [ɪrɪ'triːvəbl] ADJ (*object*) irrecuperable; (*loss, damage*) irremediable, irreparable

irretrievably [ɪrɪ'triːvəblɪ] ADV irremisiblemente

irreverence [ɪ'revərns] N irreverencia

irreverent [ɪ'revərnt] ADJ irreverente, irrespetuoso

irrevocable [ɪ'revəkəbl] ADJ irrevocable

irrigate ['ɪrɪɡeɪt] VT regar

irrigation [ɪrɪ'ɡeɪʃən] N riego

irritability [ɪrɪtə'bɪlɪtɪ] N irritabilidad *f*

irritable ['ɪrɪtəbl] ADJ (*person: temperament*) irritable; (: *mood*) de mal humor

irritant ['ɪrɪtənt] N agente *m* irritante

irritate ['ɪrɪteɪt] VT fastidiar; (*Med*) picar

irritating ['ɪrɪteɪtɪŋ] ADJ fastidioso

irritation [ɪrɪ'teɪʃən] N fastidio; picazón *f*, picor *m*

IRS N ABBR (*US*) = **Internal Revenue Service**

is [ɪz] VB *see* **be**

ISA ['aɪsə] N ABBR (*BRIT*: = *individual savings account*) plan de ahorro personal para pequeños inversores con fiscalidad cero

ISBN N ABBR (= *International Standard Book Number*) ISBN *m*

ISDN N ABBR (= *Integrated Services Digital Network*) RDSI *f*

Islam ['ɪzlɑːm] N Islam *m*

Islamic [ɪz'læmɪk] ADJ islámico

★**island** ['aɪlənd] N isla; (*also*: **traffic island**) isleta

islander ['aɪləndər] N isleño(-a)

isle [aɪl] N isla

isn't ['ɪznt] = **is not**

isobar ['aɪsəʊbɑːr] N isobara

isolate ['aɪsəleɪt] VT aislar

isolated ['aɪsəleɪtɪd] ADJ aislado

isolation [aɪsə'leɪʃən] N aislamiento

isolationism [aɪsə'leɪʃənɪzəm] N aislacionismo

isolation ward N pabellón *m* de aislamiento

isotope ['aɪsəʊtəʊp] N isótopo

ISP N ABBR = **Internet Service Provider**

Israel ['ɪzreɪl] N Israel *m*

Israeli [ɪz'reɪlɪ] ADJ, N israelí *mf*

★**issue** ['ɪsjuː] N cuestión *f*, asunto; (*outcome*) resultado; (*of banknotes etc*) emisión *f*; (*of newspaper etc*) número; (*offspring*) sucesión *f*, descendencia; **at ~** en cuestión; **to take ~ with sb (over)** disentir con algn (en); **to avoid the ~** andarse con rodeos; **to confuse** *or* **obscure the ~** confundir las cosas; **to make an ~ of sth** dar a algo más importancia de lo necesario ▸ VT (*rations, equipment*) distribuir, repartir; (*orders*) dar; (*certificate, passport*) expedir; (*decree*) promulgar; (*magazine*) publicar; (*cheque*) extender; (*banknotes, stamp*) emitir; **to ~ sth to sb**, **to ~ sb with sth** entregar algo a algn ▸ VI: **to ~ (from)** derivar (de), brotar (de)

Istanbul [ɪstæn'buːl] N Estambul *m*

isthmus ['ɪsməs] N istmo

★**IT** N ABBR = **information technology**

---

it [ɪt]

PRON **1** (*specific subject: not generally translated*) él (ella); (*direct object*) lo (la); (*indirect object*) le; (*after prep*) él (ella); (*abstract concept*) ello; **it's on the table** está en la mesa; **I can't find it** no lo (*or* la) encuentro; **give it to me** dámelo (*or* dámela); **I spoke to him about it** le hablé del asunto; **what did you learn from it?** ¿qué aprendiste de él (*or* ella)?; **did you go to it?** (*party, concert etc*) ¿fuiste?

2 (*impersonal*): **it's raining** llueve, está lloviendo; **it's 6 o'clock/the 10th of August** son las 6/es el 10 de agosto; **how far is it? — it's 10 miles/2 hours on the train** ¿a qué distancia está? — a 10 millas/2 horas en tren; **who is it? — it's me** ¿quién es? — soy yo

---

it is not usually translated when it is the subject of a sentence: *Where's my book? — It's on the table.* **¿Dónde está mi libro? — Está sobre la mesa.**

When *it* is the direct object of the verb in a sentence, use **lo** if it stands for a masculine noun or **la** if it stands for a feminine noun: *There's a croissant left. Do you want it?* **Queda un croissant. ¿Lo quieres?**

ITA N ABBR (*BRIT*: = *initial teaching alphabet*) *alfabeto parcialmente fonético, ayuda para enseñar a leer*

Italian [ɪ'tæljən] ADJ italiano ▸ N italiano(-a); (*Ling*) italiano

italic [ɪ'tælɪk] ADJ cursivo ▪ **italics** NPL cursiva *sg*

★**Italy** ['ɪtəlɪ] N Italia

ITC N ABBR (*BRIT*) = **Independent Television Commission**

itch [ɪtʃ] N picazón *f*; (*fig*) prurito ▸ VI (*person*) sentir *or* tener comezón; (*part of body*) picar; **to be itching to do sth** rabiar por *or* morirse de ganas de hacer algo

itching ['ɪtʃɪŋ] N picazón *f*, comezón *f*

itchy ['ɪtʃɪ] ADJ: **to be ~** picar; **my hand is ~** me pica la mano

it'd [ɪtd] = **it would**; **it had**

★**item** ['aɪtəm] N artículo; (*on agenda*) asunto (a tratar); (*in programme*) número; (*also*: **news item**) noticia; **items of clothing** prendas *fpl* de vestir

itemize ['aɪtəmaɪz] VT detallar

itemized bill ['aɪtəmaɪzd-] N recibo detallado

itinerant [ɪ'tɪnərənt] ADJ ambulante

itinerary [aɪ'tɪnərərɪ] N itinerario

it'll ['ɪtl] = **it will**; **it shall**

ITN N ABBR (*BRIT*) = **Independent Television News**

★**its** [ɪts] ADJ su

it's [ɪts] = **it is**; **it has**

★**itself** [ɪtˈsɛlf] PRON (*reflexive*) sí mismo(-a); (*emphatic*) él mismo(-a)

ITV N ABBR (BRIT: = *Independent Television*) cadena de televisión comercial

IUD N ABBR (= *intra-uterine device*) DIU *m*

I've [aɪv] = **I have**

ivory [ˈaɪvərɪ] N marfil *m*

Ivory Coast N: **the ~** la Costa de Marfil

ivory tower N (*fig*) torre *f* de marfil

ivy [ˈaɪvɪ] N hiedra

Ivy League N (US) *ver nota*

Las ocho universidades más prestigiosas del nordeste de los Estados Unidos reciben el nombre colectivo de **Ivy League**, por sus muros cubiertos de hiedra. Son: Brown, Columbia, Cornell, Dartmouth College, Harvard, Princeton, la universidad de Pennsylvania y Yale. Tienen un proceso de selección muy estricto y una matrícula muy cara. Muchos de los conocidos personajes del mundo político y cultural americano estudiaron en una de estas universidades. Hoy en día el término *Ivy League* es sinónimo al mismo tiempo de excelencia y elitismo. También se llaman así las competiciones deportivas que celebran entre ellas.

J j

J, j [dʒeɪ] N (*letter*) J, j f; **J for Jack**, (*US*) **J for Jig** J de José

JA N ABBR = **judge advocate**

J/A ABBR = **joint account**

jab [dʒæb] N codazo; golpe m (rápido); (*Med: inf*) pinchazo ▶ VT (*elbow*) dar un codazo a; (*punch*) dar un golpe rápido a; **to ~ sth into sth** clavar algo en algo ▶ VI: **to ~ at** intentar golpear a

jabber ['dʒæbə'] VT, VI farfullar

jack [dʒæk] N (*Aut*) gato; (*Bowls*) boliche m; (*Cards*) sota
▶ **jack in** VT (*inf*) dejar
▶ **jack up** VT (*Aut*) levantar con el gato

jackal ['dʒækl] N (*Zool*) chacal m

jackass ['dʒækæs] N (*also fig*) asno, burro

jackdaw ['dʒækdɔ:] N grajo(-a), chova

★jacket ['dʒækɪt] N chaqueta, americana, saco (*LAM*); (*of boiler etc*) camisa; (*of book*) sobrecubierta

jacket potato N patata asada (con piel)

jack-in-the-box ['dʒækɪnðəbɔks] N caja sorpresa, caja de resorte

jack-knife ['dʒæknaɪf] VI colear

jack-of-all-trades ['dʒækəv'ɔ:ltreɪdz] N aprendiz m de todo

jack plug N (*Elec*) enchufe m de clavija

jackpot ['dʒækpɔt] N premio gordo

Jacuzzi® [dʒə'ku:zɪ] N jacuzzi® m

jade [dʒeɪd] N (*stone*) jade m

jaded ['dʒeɪdɪd] ADJ (*tired*) cansado; (*fed up*) hastiado

jagged ['dʒægɪd] ADJ dentado

jaguar ['dʒægjuə'] N jaguar m

★jail [dʒeɪl] N cárcel f ▶ VT encarcelar

jailbird ['dʒeɪlbə:d] N preso(-a) reincidente

jailbreak ['dʒeɪlbreɪk] N fuga or evasión f (de la cárcel)

jailer ['dʒeɪlə'] N carcelero(-a)

jail sentence N pena f de cárcel

jalopy [dʒə'lɔpɪ] N (*inf*) cacharro, armatoste m

jam [dʒæm] N mermelada; (*also*: **traffic jam**) atasco, embotellamiento; (*inf*: *difficulty*) apuro; **to get sb out of a ~** sacar a algn del paso *or* de un apuro ▶ VT (*passage etc*) obstruir; (*mechanism, drawer etc*) atascar; (*Radio*) interferir; **to ~ sth into sth** meter algo a la fuerza en algo; **the telephone lines are jammed** las líneas están saturadas ▶ VI atascarse, trabarse

Jamaica [dʒə'meɪkə] N Jamaica

Jamaican [dʒə'meɪkən] ADJ, N jamaicano(-a) m/f

jamb [dʒæm] N jamba

jamboree [dʒæmbə'ri:] N congreso de niños exploradores

jammed [dʒæmd] ADJ atascado

jam-packed [dʒæm'pækt] ADJ: **~ (with)** atestado (de)

jam session N concierto improvisado de jazz/rock etc

Jan. ABBR (= *January*) ene.

jangle ['dʒæŋgl] VI sonar (de manera) discordante

janitor ['dʒænɪtə'] N (*caretaker*) portero, conserje m

★January ['dʒænjuərɪ] N enero; *see also* **July**

★Japan [dʒə'pæn] N (el) Japón

Japanese [dʒæpə'ni:z] ADJ japonés(-esa) ▶ N pl inv japonés(-esa) m/f; (*Ling*) japonés m

jar [dʒɑ:'] N (*glass: large*) jarra; (: *small*) tarro ▶ VI (*sound*) chirriar; (*colours*) desentonar

jargon ['dʒɑ:gən] N jerga

jarring ['dʒɑ:rɪŋ] ADJ (*sound*) discordante, desafinado; (*colour*) chocante

Jas. ABBR = **James**

jasmine, jasmin ['dʒæzmɪn] N jazmín m

jaundice ['dʒɔ:ndɪs] N ictericia

jaundiced ['dʒɔ:ndɪst] ADJ (*fig: embittered*) amargado; (: *disillusioned*) desilusionado

jaunt [dʒɔ:nt] N excursión f
jaunty ['dʒɔ:ntɪ] ADJ alegre; (relaxed) desenvuelto
Java ['dʒɑ:və] N Java
javelin ['dʒævlɪn] N jabalina
jaw [dʒɔ:] N mandíbula ▪ **jaws** NPL (Tech: of vice etc) mordaza sg
jawbone ['dʒɔ:bəun] N mandíbula, quijada
jay [dʒeɪ] N (Zool) arrendajo
jaywalker ['dʒeɪwɔ:kəʳ] N peatón(-ona) m/f imprudente
★**jazz** [dʒæz] N jazz m
  ▸ **jazz up** VT (liven up) animar
jazz band N orquesta de jazz
jazzy ['dʒæzɪ] ADJ de colores llamativos
JCB® N ABBR excavadora
JCS N ABBR (US) = **Joint Chiefs of Staff**
JD N ABBR (US: = Doctor of Laws) título universitario; (= Justice Department) Ministerio de Justicia
★**jealous** ['dʒeləs] ADJ (gen) celoso; (envious) envidioso; **to be ~** tener celos
jealously ['dʒeləslɪ] ADV (enviously) envidiosamente; (watchfully) celosamente
jealousy ['dʒeləsɪ] N celos mpl; envidia
★**jeans** [dʒi:nz] NPL vaqueros mpl or tejanos mpl, bluejean m inv (LAM)
Jeep® [dʒi:p] N jeep m
jeer [dʒɪəʳ] VI: **to ~ (at)** (boo) abuchear; (mock) mofarse (de)
jeering ['dʒɪərɪŋ] ADJ (crowd) insolente, ofensivo
  ▸ N protestas fpl; (mockery) burlas fpl
jeggings ['dʒegɪŋz] NPL jeggings mpl
Jello® ['dʒeləu] N (US) gelatina
jelly ['dʒelɪ] N (jam) jalea; (dessert etc) gelatina
jellyfish ['dʒelɪfɪʃ] N medusa
jemmy ['dʒemɪ] N palanqueta
jeopardize ['dʒepədaɪz] VT arriesgar, poner en peligro
jeopardy ['dʒepədɪ] N: **to be in ~** estar en peligro
jerk [dʒə:k] N (jolt) sacudida; (wrench) tirón m; (US pej) imbécil mf ▸ VT dar una sacudida a; tirar bruscamente de ▸ VI (vehicle) dar una sacudida
jerkin ['dʒə:kɪn] N chaleco
jerky ['dʒə:kɪ] ADJ espasmódico
jerry-built ['dʒerɪbɪlt] ADJ mal construido
jerry can ['dʒerɪ-] N bidón m
Jersey ['dʒə:zɪ] N Jersey m
★**jersey** ['dʒə:zɪ] N jersey m; (fabric) tejido de punto
Jerusalem [dʒə'ru:sləm] N Jerusalén m
jest [dʒest] N broma
jester ['dʒestəʳ] N bufón m
Jesus ['dʒi:zəs] N Jesús m; **~ Christ** Jesucristo
jet [dʒet] N (of gas, liquid) chorro m; (Aviat) avión m a reacción
jet-black ['dʒet'blæk] ADJ negro como el azabache

jet engine N motor m a reacción
jet lag N desorientación f por desfase horario
jetsam ['dʒetsəm] N echazón f
jet-setter ['dʒetsetəʳ] N personaje m de la jet
jet-ski ['dʒetski:] VI practicar el motociclismo acuático
jettison ['dʒetɪsn] VT desechar
jetty ['dʒetɪ] N muelle m, embarcadero
Jew [dʒu:] N judío(-a)
jewel ['dʒu:əl] N joya; (in watch) rubí m
jeweller, (US) **jeweler** ['dʒu:ələʳ] N joyero(-a); **~'s (shop)** joyería
jewellery, (US) **jewelry** ['dʒu:əlrɪ] N joyas fpl, alhajas fpl
Jewess ['dʒu:ɪs] N (!) judía
Jewish ['dʒu:ɪʃ] ADJ judío
JFK N ABBR (US) = **John Fitzgerald Kennedy International Airport**
jib [dʒɪb] VI (horse) plantarse; **to ~ at doing sth** resistirse a hacer algo
jibe [dʒaɪb] N mofa
jiffy ['dʒɪfɪ] N (inf): **in a ~** en un santiamén
jig [dʒɪg] N (dance, tune) giga
jigsaw ['dʒɪgsɔ:] N (also: **jigsaw puzzle**) rompecabezas m inv, puzle m; (tool) sierra de vaivén
jilbab [dʒɪl'ba:b] N hiyab m
jilt [dʒɪlt] VT dejar plantado a
jingle ['dʒɪŋgl] N (advert) musiquilla ▸ VI tintinear
jingoism ['dʒɪŋgəuɪzəm] N patriotería, jingoísmo
jinx [dʒɪŋks] N (inf): **there's a ~ on it** está gafado
jitters ['dʒɪtəz] NPL (inf): **to get the ~** ponerse nervioso
jittery ['dʒɪtərɪ] ADJ (inf) agitado
jiujitsu [dʒu:'dʒɪtsu:] N jiujitsu m
★**job** [dʒɔb] N trabajo; (task) tarea; (duty) deber m; (post) empleo; (inf: difficulty) dificultad f; **it's a good ~ that ...** menos mal que ...; **just the ~!** ¡justo lo que necesito!; **a part-time/full-time ~** un trabajo a tiempo parcial/tiempo completo; **that's not my ~** eso no me incumbe or toca a mí; **he's only doing his ~** está cumpliendo nada más
job centre N (BRIT) oficina de empleo
job creation scheme N plan m de creación de puestos de trabajo
job description N descripción f del puesto de trabajo
jobless ['dʒɔblɪs] ADJ sin trabajo ▸ NPL: **the ~** los parados
job lot N lote m de mercancías, saldo
job satisfaction N satisfacción f en el trabajo
job security N garantía de trabajo
job specification N especificación f del trabajo, profesiograma m
Jock N (pej: Scotsman) escocés m

jockey ['dʒɔkɪ] N jockey *mf* ▶ VI: **to ~ for position** maniobrar para sacar delantera

jockey box N (*US Aut*) guantera

jockstrap ['dʒɔkstræp] N suspensorio

jocular ['dʒɔkjuləʳ] ADJ (*humorous*) gracioso; (*merry*) alegre

jodhpurs ['dʒɔdpəːz] NPL pantalón *msg* de montar

jog [dʒɔg] VT empujar (ligeramente); **to ~ sb's memory** refrescar la memoria a algn ▶ VI (*run*) hacer footing; **to ~ along** (*fig*) ir tirando

jogger ['dʒɔgəʳ] N corredor(a) *m/f*

jogging ['dʒɔgɪŋ] N footing *m*

john [dʒɔn] N (*US inf*) wáter *m*

★**join** [dʒɔɪn] VT (*things*) unir, juntar; (*become member of: club*) hacerse socio de; (*Pol: party*) afiliarse a; (*meet: people*) reunirse con; (*fig*) unirse a; **will you ~ us for dinner?** ¿quieres cenar con nosotros?; **I'll ~ you later** me reuniré contigo luego; **to ~ forces (with)** aliarse (con) ▶ VI (*roads*) empalmar; (*rivers*) confluir ▶ N juntura ▶ **join in** VI tomar parte, participar ▶ VT FUS tomar parte *or* participar en ▶ **join up** VI unirse; (*Mil*) alistarse

joiner ['dʒɔɪnəʳ] N carpintero(-a)

joinery ['dʒɔɪnərɪ] N carpintería

★**joint** [dʒɔɪnt] N (*Tech*) juntura, unión *f*; (*Anat*) articulación *f*; (*BRIT Culin*) pieza de carne (para asar); (*inf: place*) garito; (*of cannabis*) porro ▶ ADJ (*common*) común; (*combined*) conjunto; (*responsibility*) compartido; (*committee*) mixto

joint account N (*with bank etc*) cuenta común

jointly ['dʒɔɪntlɪ] ADV (*gen*) en común; (*together*) conjuntamente

joint owners NPL copropietarios *mpl*

joint ownership N copropiedad *f*, propiedad *f* común

joint-stock bank ['dʒɔɪntstɔk-] N banco por acciones

joint-stock company ['dʒɔɪntstɔk-] N sociedad *f* anónima

joint venture N empresa conjunta

joist [dʒɔɪst] N viga

★**joke** [dʒəuk] N chiste *m*; (*also:* **practical joke**) broma; **to play a ~ on** gastar una broma a ▶ VI bromear

joker ['dʒəukəʳ] N chistoso(-a), bromista *mf*; (*Cards*) comodín *m*

joking ['dʒəukɪŋ] N bromas *fpl*

jokingly ['dʒəukɪŋlɪ] ADV en broma

jollity ['dʒɔlɪtɪ] N alegría

jolly ['dʒɔlɪ] ADJ (*merry*) alegre; (*enjoyable*) divertido ▶ ADV (*inf*) muy, la mar de; **~ good!** ¡estupendo! ▶ VT: **to ~ sb along** animar *or* darle ánimos a algn

jolt [dʒəult] N (*shake*) sacudida; (*blow*) golpe *m*; (*shock*) susto ▶ VT (*physically*) sacudir; (*emotionally*) asustar

Jordan ['dʒɔːdən] N (*country*) Jordania; (*river*) Jordán *m*

joss stick [dʒɔs-] N barrita de incienso, pebete *m*

jostle ['dʒɔsl] VT dar empujones *or* empellones a

jot [dʒɔt] N: **not one ~** ni pizca, ni un ápice ▶ **jot down** VT apuntar

jotter ['dʒɔtəʳ] N (*BRIT*) bloc *m*

journal ['dʒəːnl] N (*paper*) periódico; (*magazine*) revista; (*diary*) diario

journalese [dʒəːnə'liːz] N (*pej*) lenguaje *m* periodístico

journalism ['dʒəːnəlɪzəm] N periodismo

★**journalist** ['dʒəːnəlɪst] N periodista *mf*

★**journey** ['dʒəːnɪ] N viaje *m*; (*distance covered*) trayecto; **return ~** viaje de regreso; **a five-hour ~** un viaje de cinco horas ▶ VI viajar

jovial ['dʒəuvɪəl] ADJ risueño, alegre

jowl [dʒaul] N quijada

★**joy** [dʒɔɪ] N alegría

joyful ['dʒɔɪful] ADJ alegre

joyfully ['dʒɔɪfulɪ] ADV alegremente

joyous ['dʒɔɪəs] ADJ alegre

joyride ['dʒɔɪraɪd] N: **to go for a ~** darse una vuelta en un coche robado

joyrider ['dʒɔɪraɪdəʳ] N persona que se da una vuelta en un coche robado

joystick ['dʒɔɪstɪk] N (*Aviat*) palanca de mando; (*Comput*) palanca de control

JP N ABBR = **Justice of the Peace**

Jr ABBR = **junior**

JTPA N ABBR (*US:* = *Job Training Partnership Act*) programa gubernamental de formación profesional

jubilant ['dʒuːbɪlnt] ADJ jubiloso

jubilation [dʒuːbɪ'leɪʃən] N júbilo

jubilee ['dʒuːbɪliː] N aniversario; **silver ~** vigésimo quinto aniversario

★**judge** [dʒʌdʒ] N juez(a) *m/f* ▶ VT juzgar; (*competition*) actuar de *or* ser juez en; (*estimate*) considerar; (: *weight, size etc*) calcular; **I judged it necessary to inform him** consideré necesario informarle ▶ VI: **judging** *or* **to ~ by his expression** a juzgar por su expresión; **as far as I can ~** por lo que puedo entender, a mi entender

judge advocate N (*Mil*) auditor *m* de guerra

judgment, judgement ['dʒʌdʒmənt] N juicio; (*punishment*) sentencia, fallo; **to pass ~ (on)** (*Law*) pronunciar *or* dictar sentencia (sobre); (*fig*) emitir un juicio crítico *or* dictaminar (sobre); **in my ~** a mi juicio

judicial [dʒuː'dɪʃl] ADJ judicial

judiciary [dʒuː'dɪʃɪərɪ] N poder *m* judicial, magistratura

judicious [dʒuː'dɪʃəs] ADJ juicioso

judo ['dʒuːdəu] N judo

jug [dʒʌg] N jarra

jugged hare [dʒʌgd-] N (*BRIT*) estofado de liebre

juggernaut ['dʒʌgənɔːt] N (*BRIT: huge truck*) camión *m* de carga pesada

juggle [ˈdʒʌgl] VI hacer juegos malabares

juggler [ˈdʒʌglə^r] N malabarista mf

Jugoslav etc [ˈjuːgəʊslɑːv] = **Yugoslav** etc

jugular [ˈdʒʌgjulə^r] ADJ: ~ **vein** (vena) yugular f

★**juice** [dʒuːs] N jugo, zumo (Sp); (of meat) jugo; (inf: petrol): **we've run out of** ~ se nos acabó la gasolina

juiciness [ˈdʒuːsɪnɪs] N jugosidad f

juicy [ˈdʒuːsɪ] ADJ jugoso

jujitsu [dʒuːˈdʒɪtsuː] N jujitsu m

jukebox [ˈdʒuːkbɔks] N máquina de discos

Jul. ABBR (= July) jul.

★**July** [dʒuːˈlaɪ] N julio; **the first of** ~ el uno or primero de julio; **during** ~ en el mes de julio; **in** ~ **of next year** en julio del año que viene

jumble [ˈdʒʌmbl] N revoltijo ▸ VT (also: **jumble together, jumble up**: mix up) revolver; (: disarrange) mezclar

jumble sale N (BRIT) mercadillo

jumbo [ˈdʒʌmbəʊ], **jumbo jet** N jumbo

★**jump** [dʒʌmp] VI saltar, dar saltos; (start) sobresaltarse; (increase) aumentar ▸ VT saltar; **to** ~ **the queue** (BRIT) colarse ▸ N salto; (fence) obstáculo; (increase) aumento
  ▸ **jump about** VI dar saltos, brincar
  ▸ **jump at** VT FUS (fig) apresurarse a aprovechar; **he jumped at the offer** se apresuró a aceptar la oferta
  ▸ **jump down** VI bajar de un salto, saltar a tierra
  ▸ **jump up** VI levantarse de un salto

jumped-up [ˈdʒʌmptʌp] ADJ (pej) engreído

jumper [ˈdʒʌmpə^r] N (BRIT: pullover) jersey m, suéter m; (US: dress) pichi m; (Sport) saltador(a) m/f

jump leads, (US) **jumper cables** NPL cables mpl puente de batería

jump-start [ˈdʒʌmpstɑːt] VT (car) arrancar con ayuda de otra batería or empujando; (fig: economy) reactivar

jump suit N mono

jumpy [ˈdʒʌmpɪ] ADJ nervioso

Jun. ABBR = **junior**; (= June) jun.

junction [ˈdʒʌŋkʃən] N (BRIT: of roads) cruce m; (: Rail) empalme m

juncture [ˈdʒʌŋktʃə^r] N: **at this** ~ en este momento, en esta coyuntura

★**June** [dʒuːn] N junio; see also **July**

jungle [ˈdʒʌŋgl] N selva, jungla

junior [ˈdʒuːnɪə^r] ADJ (in age) menor, más joven; (competition) juvenil; (position) subalterno; **he's** ~ **to me** es menor que yo ▸ N menor mf, joven mf

junior executive N ejecutivo(-a) subalterno(-a)

junior high school N (US) centro de educación secundaria; see also **high school**

junior school N (BRIT) escuela primaria; see also **primary school**

junk [dʒʌŋk] N (cheap goods) baratijas fpl; (lumber) trastos mpl viejos; (rubbish) basura; (ship) junco ▸ VT (esp US) deshacerse de

junk bond N (Comm) obligación f basura inv

junk dealer N vendedor(a) m/f de objetos usados

junket [ˈdʒʌŋkɪt] N (Culin) dulce de leche cuajada; (BRIT inf): **to go on a** ~, **go junketing** viajar a costa ajena or del erario público

junk food N comida basura or de plástico

junkie [ˈdʒʌŋkɪ] N (inf) yonqui mf, heroinómano(-a)

junk mail N propaganda (buzoneada), correo m basura inv

junk room N trastero

junk shop N tienda de objetos usados

junta [ˈdʒʌntə] N junta militar

Jupiter [ˈdʒuːpɪtə^r] N (Mythology, Astro) Júpiter m

jurisdiction [dʒuərɪsˈdɪkʃən] N jurisdicción f; **it falls** or **comes within/outside our** ~ es/no es de nuestra competencia

jurisprudence [dʒuərɪsˈpruːdəns] N jurisprudencia

juror [ˈdʒuərə^r] N jurado

★**jury** [ˈdʒuərɪ] N jurado

jury box N tribuna del jurado

juryman [ˈdʒuərɪmən] N (irreg) miembro del jurado

★**just** [dʒʌst] ADJ justo m/f ▸ ADV (exactly) exactamente; (only) solo, solamente, no más (LAm); **he's** ~ **done it/left** acaba de hacerlo/irse; **I've** ~ **seen him** acabo de verle; ~ **right** perfecto; ~ **two o'clock** las dos en punto; **she's** ~ **as clever as you** es tan lista como tú; ~ **as well that ...** menos mal que ...; **it's** ~ **as well you didn't go** menos mal que no fuiste; **it's** ~ **as good (as)** es igual (que), es tan bueno (como); ~ **as he was leaving** en el momento en que se marchaba; **we were** ~ **going** ya nos íbamos; **I was** ~ **about to phone** estaba a punto de llamar; ~ **before/enough** justo antes/lo suficiente; ~ **here** aquí mismo; **he** ~ **missed** falló por poco; ~ **listen to this** escucha esto un momento; ~ **ask someone the way** simplemente pregúntale a alguien por dónde se va; **not** ~ **now** ahora no

★**justice** [ˈdʒʌstɪs] N justicia; (US: judge) juez(a) m/f; **to do** ~ **to** (fig) hacer justicia a; **this photo doesn't do you** ~ esta foto no te favorece

Justice of the Peace N juez(a) m/f de paz; see also **crown court**

justifiable [dʒʌstɪˈfaɪəbl] ADJ justificable, justificado

justifiably [dʒʌstɪˈfaɪəblɪ] ADV justificadamente, con razón

justification [dʒʌstɪfɪˈkeɪʃən] N justificación f

★**justify** [ˈdʒʌstɪfaɪ] VT justificar; (text) alinear, justificar; **to be justified in doing sth** tener motivo para or razón al hacer algo

justly [ˈdʒʌstlɪ] ADV (gen) justamente; (with reason) con razón

justness [ˈdʒʌstnɪs] N justicia
jut [dʒʌt] VI (*also:* **jut out**) sobresalir
jute [dʒuːt] N yute *m*
juvenile [ˈdʒuːvənaɪl] ADJ juvenil; (*humour, mentality*) infantil; (*court*) de menores ▸ N joven *mf*, menor *mf* de edad

juvenile delinquency N delincuencia juvenil
juvenile delinquent N delincuente *mf* juvenil
juxtapose [ˈdʒʌkstəpəuz] VT yuxtaponer
juxtaposition [ˈdʒʌkstəpəˈzɪʃən] N yuxtaposición *f*

j

Kk

K, k [keɪ] N (*letter*) K, k f; **K for King** K de Kilo

K ABBR (= *one thousand*) mil; (BRIT: = *Knight*) título; (= *kilobyte*) K

kaftan [ˈkæftæn] N caftán m

Kalahari Desert [kæləˈhɑːrɪ-] N desierto de Kalahari

kale [keɪl] N col f rizada

kaleidoscope [kəˈlaɪdəskəup] N calidoscopio

kamikaze [kæmɪˈkɑːzɪ] ADJ kamikaze

Kampala [kæmˈpɑːlə] N Kampala

Kampuchea [kæmpuˈtʃɪə] N Kampuchea

kangaroo [kæŋgəˈruː] N canguro

Kans. ABBR (*US*) = **Kansas**

kaput [kəˈput] ADJ (*inf*) roto, estropeado

karaoke [kɑːrəˈəukɪ] N karaoke

karate [kəˈrɑːtɪ] N karate m

Kashmir [kæʃˈmɪər] N Cachemira

kayak [ˈkaɪæk] N kayak m

Kazakhstan [kæzəkˈstɑːn] N Kazajstán m

KC N ABBR (BRIT *Law*: = *King's Counsel*) título concedido a determinados abogados

kebab [kəˈbæb] N pincho moruno, brocheta

keel [kiːl] N quilla; **on an even ~** (*fig*) en equilibrio
▸ **keel over** VI (*Naut*) zozobrar, volcarse; (*person*) desplomarse

★**keen** [kiːn] ADJ (*interest, desire*) grande, vivo; (*eye, intelligence*) agudo; (*competition*) reñido; (*edge*) afilado; (BRIT: *eager*) entusiasta; **to be ~ to do** or **on doing sth** tener muchas ganas de hacer algo; **to be ~ on sth/sb** interesarse por algo/algn; **I'm not ~ on going** no tengo ganas de ir

keenly [ˈkiːnlɪ] ADV (*enthusiastically*) con entusiasmo; (*acutely*) vivamente; (*intensely*) intensamente

keenness [ˈkiːnnɪs] N (*eagerness*) entusiasmo, interés m

★**keep** [kiːp] (*pt, pp* **kept** [kept]) VT (*retain, preserve*) guardar; (*hold back*) quedarse con; (*shop*) ser propietario de; (*feed: family etc*) mantener; (*promise*) cumplir; (*chickens, bees etc*) criar; **to ~ sb from doing sth** impedir a algn hacer algo; **to ~ sth from happening** impedir que algo ocurra; **to ~ sb happy** tener a algn contento; **to ~ sb waiting** hacer esperar a algn; **to ~ a place tidy** mantener un lugar limpio; **to ~ sth to o.s.** no decirle algo a nadie; **to ~ time** (*clock*) mantener la hora exacta; **~ the change** quédese con la vuelta; **to ~ a record** or **note of sth** tomar nota de or apuntar algo ▸ VI (*food*) conservarse; (*remain*) seguir, continuar; **to ~ doing sth** seguir haciendo algo ▸ N (*of castle*) torreón m; (*food etc*) comida, sustento; *see also* **keeps**
▸ **keep away** VT: **to ~ sth/sb away from sb** mantener algo/a algn apartado de algn ▸ VI: **to ~ away (from)** mantenerse apartado (de)
▸ **keep back** VT (*crowd, tears*) contener; (*money*) quedarse con; (*conceal: information*): **to ~ sth back from sb** ocultar algo a algn ▸ VI hacerse a un lado
▸ **keep down** VT (*control: prices, spending*) controlar; (*retain: food*) retener ▸ VI seguir agachado, no levantar la cabeza
▸ **keep in** VT (*invalid, child*) impedir que salga, no dejar salir; (*Scol*) castigar (a quedarse en el colegio) ▸ VI (*inf*): **to ~ in with sb** mantener la relación con algn
▸ **keep off** VT (*dog, person*) mantener a distancia; **~ your hands off!** ¡no toques!; **"~ off the grass"** "prohibido pisar el césped" ▸ VI evitar
▸ **keep on** VI seguir, continuar; **to ~ on doing** seguir or continuar haciendo; **to ~ on (about sth)** no parar de hablar (de algo)
▸ **keep out** VI (*stay out*) permanecer fuera; **"~ out"** "prohibida la entrada"
▸ **keep up** VT mantener, conservar ▸ VI no rezagarse; (*fig: in comprehension*) seguir (el hilo); **to ~ up with** (*pace*) ir al paso de; (*level*) mantenerse a la altura de; **to ~ up with sb** seguir el ritmo a algn

keeper [ˈkiːpər] N guarda mf

keep-fit [kiːpˈfɪt] N gimnasia (de mantenimiento)

keeping [ˈkiːpɪŋ] N (*care*) cuidado; **in ~ with** de acuerdo con

keeps [kiːps] N: **for ~** (*inf*) para siempre

keepsake [ˈkiːpseɪk] N recuerdo

keg [kɛg] N barrilete *m*, barril *m*

Ken. ABBR (*US*) = **Kentucky**

kennel [ˈkɛnl] N perrera ∎ **kennels** NPL (*dogs' home*) residencia canina

Kenya [ˈkɛnjə] N Kenia

Kenyan [ˈkɛnjən] ADJ, N keniata *mf*, keniano(-a) *m/f*

kept [kɛpt] PT, PP of **keep**

kerb [kəːb] N (*BRIT*) bordillo

kerb crawler [-krɔːlər] N conductor en busca de prostitutas desde su coche

kerbside [ˈkəːbsaɪd] N borde *m* de la acera

kernel [ˈkəːnl] N (*nut*) fruta; (*fig*) meollo

kerosene [ˈkɛrəsiːn] N keroseno

kestrel [ˈkɛstrəl] N cernícalo

ketchup [ˈkɛtʃəp] N salsa de tomate, ketchup *m*

kettle [ˈkɛtl] N hervidor *m*

kettle drum N (*Mus*) timbal *m*

kettling [ˈkɛtəlɪŋ] N (*BRIT inf*) acorralamiento (mediante cordón) policial

★**key** [kiː] N (*gen*) llave *f*; (*Mus*) tono; (*of piano, typewriter*) tecla; (*on map*) clave *f* ▶ CPD (*vital: position, issue, industry etc*) clave ▶ VT (*also:* **key in**) teclear

keyboard [ˈkiːbɔːd] N teclado ▶ VT (*text*) teclear

keyboarder [ˈkiːbɔːdər] N teclista *mf*

keyed up [kiːd-] ADJ (*person*) nervioso; **to be (all) ~** estar nervioso or emocionado

keyhole [ˈkiːhəul] N ojo (de la cerradura)

keyhole surgery N cirugía cerrada or no invasiva

key man N (*irreg*) hombre *m* clave

keynote [ˈkiːnəut] N (*Mus*) tónica; (*fig*) idea fundamental

keynote speech N discurso de apertura

keypad [ˈkiːpæd] N teclado numérico

keyring [ˈkiːrɪŋ] N llavero

keystone [ˈkiːstəun] N piedra clave

keystroke [ˈkiːstrəuk] N pulsación *f* (de una tecla)

kg ABBR (= *kilogram*) kg

KGB N ABBR KGB *m*

khaki [ˈkɑːkɪ] N caqui

kibbutz [kɪˈbuts] (*pl* **kibbutzim** [-ɪm]) N kibutz *m*

★**kick** [kɪk] VT (*person*) dar una patada a; (*ball*) dar un puntapié a; (*inf: habit*) quitarse de ▶ VI (*horse*) dar coces ▶ N patada; puntapié *m*, tiro; (*of rifle*) culatazo; (*inf: thrill*): **he does it for kicks** lo hace por pura diversión
  ▶ **kick around** VT (*idea*) dar vueltas a; (*person*) tratar a patadas a
  ▶ **kick off** VI (*Sport*) hacer el saque inicial

kick-off [ˈkɪkɔf] N saque inicial; **the ~ is at 10 o'clock** el partido empieza a las diez

kick-start [ˈkɪkstɑːt] N (*also:* **kick-starter**) (pedal *m* de) arranque *m*

★**kid** [kɪd] N (*inf: child*) niño(-a), chiquillo(-a); (*animal*) cabrito; (*leather*) cabritilla ▶ VI (*inf*) bromear

kid gloves NPL: **to treat sb with ~** andarse con pies de plomo con algn

kidnap [ˈkɪdnæp] VT secuestrar

kidnapper [ˈkɪdnæpər] N secuestrador(a) *m/f*

kidnapping [ˈkɪdnæpɪŋ] N secuestro

kidney [ˈkɪdnɪ] N riñón *m*

kidney bean N judía, alubia

kidney machine N riñón *m* artificial

★**kill** [kɪl] VT matar; (*murder*) asesinar; (*fig: rumour, conversation*) acabar con; **to ~ time** matar el tiempo ▶ N matanza
  ▶ **kill off** VT exterminar, terminar con; (*fig*) echar por tierra

★**killer** [ˈkɪlər] N asesino(-a)

killer app N ABBR (*inf:* = *killer application*) aplicación *f* rompedora, aplicación *f* de excelente rendimiento

killer instinct N: **to have the ~** ir a por todas

killing [ˈkɪlɪŋ] N (*one*) asesinato; (*several*) matanza; **to make a ~** (*inf: Comm*) hacer su agosto

killjoy [ˈkɪldʒɔɪ] N (*BRIT*) aguafiestas *mf*

kiln [kɪln] N horno

★**kilo** [ˈkiːləu] N ABBR (= *kilogram(me)*) kilo

kilobyte [ˈkɪləubaɪt] N (*Comput*) kilobyte *m*

kilogram, kilogramme [ˈkɪləugræm] N kilogramo

kilometre, (*US*) **kilometer** [ˈkɪləmiːtər] N kilómetro

kilowatt [ˈkɪləuwɔt] N kilovatio

kilt [kɪlt] N falda escocesa

kilter [ˈkɪltər] N: **out of ~** desbaratado

kimono [kɪˈməunəu] N quimono

kin [kɪn] N parientes *mpl*

★**kind** [kaɪnd] ADJ (*treatment*) bueno, cariñoso; (*person, act, word*) amable, atento; **would you be ~ enough to …?, would you be so ~ as to …?** ¿me hace el favor de …?; **it's very ~ of you (to do)** le agradezco mucho (el que haya hecho) ▶ N clase *f*, especie *f*; (*species*) género; **in ~** (*Comm*) en especie; **a ~ of** una especie de; **to be two of a ~** ser tal para cual

kindergarten [ˈkɪndəgɑːtn] N jardín *m* de infancia

kind-hearted [kaɪndˈhɑːtɪd] ADJ bondadoso, de buen corazón

Kindle® [ˈkɪndl] N Kindle® *m*, libro electrónico

kindle [ˈkɪndl] VT encender

kindliness [ˈkaɪndlɪnəs] N bondad *f*, amabilidad *f*

kindling [ˈkɪndlɪŋ] N leña (menuda)

kindly [ˈkaɪndlɪ] ADJ bondadoso; (*gentle*) cariñoso ▶ ADV bondadosamente, amablemente; **will you ~ …** sería usted tan amable de …

k

kindness [ˈkaɪndnɪs] N bondad f, amabilidad f; (act) favor m

kindred [ˈkɪndrɪd] N familia, parientes mpl ▶ ADJ: ~ **spirits** almas fpl gemelas

kinetic [kɪˈnɛtɪk] ADJ cinético

★**king** [kɪŋ] N rey m

kingdom [ˈkɪŋdəm] N reino

kingfisher [ˈkɪŋfɪʃəʳ] N martín m pescador

kingpin [ˈkɪŋpɪn] N (Tech) perno real or pinzote; (fig) persona clave

king-size [ˈkɪŋsaɪz], **king-sized** [ˈkɪŋsaɪzd] ADJ de tamaño gigante; (cigarette) extra largo; ~ **bed** cama de matrimonio extragrande

kink [kɪŋk] N (in rope etc) enroscadura; (in hair) rizo; (fig: emotional, psychological) manía

kinky [ˈkɪŋkɪ] ADJ (pej) perverso

kinship [ˈkɪnʃɪp] N parentesco; (fig) afinidad f

kinsman [ˈkɪnzmən] N (irreg) pariente m

kinswoman [ˈkɪnzwumən] N (irreg) parienta

kiosk [ˈkiːɔsk] N quiosco; (BRIT Tel) cabina; **newspaper** ~ quiosco, kiosco

kipper [ˈkɪpəʳ] N arenque m ahumado

Kiribati [kɪrɪˈbætɪ] N Kiribati m

★**kiss** [kɪs] N beso; ~ **of life** (artificial respiration) respiración f boca a boca ▶ VT besar; **to** ~ **sb goodbye** dar un beso de despedida a algn; **to** ~ (each other) besarse

kissagram [ˈkɪsəgræm] N servicio de felicitaciones mediante el que se envía a una persona vestida de manera sugerente para besar a algn

kit [kɪt] N equipo; (set of tools etc) (caja de) herramientas fpl; (assembly kit) juego de armar; **tool** ~ juego or estuche m de herramientas ▶ **kit out** VT equipar

kitbag [ˈkɪtbæg] N (Mil) macuto

★**kitchen** [ˈkɪtʃɪn] N cocina

kitchen garden N huerto

kitchen sink N fregadero

kitchen unit N módulo de cocina

kitchenware [ˈkɪtʃɪnwɛəʳ] N batería de cocina

kite [kaɪt] N (toy) cometa

kith [kɪθ] N: ~ **and kin** parientes mpl y allegados

kitten [ˈkɪtn] N gatito(-a)

kitty [ˈkɪtɪ] N (pool of money) fondo común; (Cards) bote m

kiwi [ˈkiːwiː] N (also: **kiwi fruit**) kiwi m; **K~** (inf: New Zealander) neozelandés(-esa) m/f

KKK N ABBR (US) = **Ku Klux Klan**

kleptomaniac [klɛptəuˈmeɪniæk] N cleptómano(-a)

km ABBR (= kilometre) km

km/h ABBR (= kilometres per hour) km/h

knack [næk] N: **to have the** ~ **of doing sth** tener facilidad para hacer algo

knackered [ˈnækəd] ADJ (inf) hecho polvo

knapsack [ˈnæpsæk] N mochila

knead [niːd] VT amasar

★**knee** [niː] N rodilla

kneecap [ˈniːkæp] VT destrozar a tiros la rótula de ▶ N rótula

knee-deep [ˈniːˈdiːp] ADJ: **the water was** ~ el agua llegaba hasta la rodilla

kneel [niːl] (pt, pp **knelt** [nɛlt]) VI (also: **kneel down**) arrodillarse

kneepad [ˈniːpæd] N rodillera

knell [nɛl] N toque m de difuntos

knelt [nɛlt] PT, PP of **kneel**

knew [njuː] PT of **know**

★**knickers** [ˈnɪkəz] NPL (BRIT) bragas fpl, calzones mpl (LAM)

knick-knack [ˈnɪknæk] N chuchería, baratija

★**knife** [naɪf] (pl **knives**) N cuchillo; ~, **fork and spoon** cubiertos mpl ▶ VT acuchillar

knife edge N: **to be on a** ~ estar en la cuerda floja

knight [naɪt] N caballero; (Chess) caballo

knighthood [ˈnaɪthud] N (title): **to get a** ~ recibir el título de Sir

knit [nɪt] VT tejer, tricotar; (brows) fruncir; (fig): **to** ~ **together** unir, juntar ▶ VI hacer punto, tejer, tricotar; (bones) soldarse

knitted [ˈnɪtɪd] ADJ de punto

knitting [ˈnɪtɪŋ] N labor f de punto

knitting machine N máquina de tricotar

knitting needle N, (US) **knit pin** N aguja de hacer punto or tejer

knitting pattern N patrón m para tricotar

knitwear [ˈnɪtwɛəʳ] N prendas fpl de punto

knives [naɪvz] PL of **knife**

knob [nɔb] N (of door) pomo; (of stick) puño; (on radio, TV) botón m; (lump) bulto; (fig): **a** ~ **of butter** (BRIT) un pedazo de mantequilla

knobbly [ˈnɔblɪ], (US) **knobby** [ˈnɔbɪ] ADJ (wood, surface) nudoso; (knee) huesudo

★**knock** [nɔk] VT (strike) golpear; (bump into) chocar contra; (fig: inf) criticar ▶ VI (at door etc): **to** ~ **at/on** llamar a; **he knocked at the door** llamó a la puerta ▶ N golpe m; (on door) llamada
▶ **knock down** VT (pedestrian) atropellar; (price) rebajar
▶ **knock off** VI (inf: finish) salir del trabajo ▶ VT (inf: steal) birlar; (strike off) quitar; (fig: from price, record): **to** ~ **off £10** rebajar en £10
▶ **knock out** VT dejar sin sentido; (Boxing) poner fuera de combate, dejar K.O.; (in competition) eliminar; (stop) estropear, dejar fuera de servicio
▶ **knock over** VT (object) derribar, tirar; (pedestrian) atropellar

knockdown [ˈnɔkdaun] ADJ (price) de saldo

knocker [ˈnɔkəʳ] N (on door) aldaba

knocking [ˈnɔkɪŋ] N golpes mpl, golpeteo

knock-kneed [nɔkˈniːd] ADJ patizambo

knockout [ˈnɔkaut] N (Boxing) K.O. m, knockout m

knock-up [ˈnɔkʌp] N (Tennis) peloteo

knot [nɔt] N (gen) nudo; **to tie a ~** hacer un nudo
▶ VT anudar

knotted [ˈnɔtɪd] ADJ anudado

knotty [ˈnɔtɪ] ADJ (fig) complicado

★**know** [nəu] (pt **knew** [njuː], pp **known** [nəun])
VT (gen) saber; (person, author, place) conocer; (recognize) reconocer; **to ~ how to do** saber hacer;
to ~ how to swim saber nadar; **to get to ~ sth**
enterarse de algo; **I ~ nothing about it** no sé
nada de eso; **I don't ~ him** no lo or le conozco; **to
~ right from wrong** saber distinguir el bien del
mal ▶ VI: **as far as I ~ ...** que yo sepa ...; **yes, I ~**
sí, ya lo sé; **I don't ~** no lo sé; **to ~ about** or **of sb/
sth** saber de algn/algo

> Use **saber** when talking about facts, and
> **conocer** when talking about knowing people
> or places:
> *I didn't know that.* **No lo sabía.**
> *I know her.* **La conozco.**

know-all [ˈnəuɔːl] N (BRIT pej) sabelotodo mf,
sabihondo(-a)

know-how [ˈnəuhau] N conocimientos mpl

knowing [ˈnəuɪŋ] ADJ (look etc) de complicidad

knowingly [ˈnəuɪŋlɪ] ADV (purposely) a sabiendas; (smile, look) con complicidad

know-it-all [ˈnəuɪtɔːl] N (US) = **know-all**

★**knowledge** [ˈnɔlɪdʒ] N (gen) conocimiento;
(learning) saber m, conocimientos mpl; **to have
no ~ of** no saber nada de; **with my ~** con mis
conocimientos, sabiéndolo; **to (the best of)
my ~** a mi entender, que yo sepa; **not to my ~**
que yo sepa, no; **it is common ~ that ...** es del
dominio público que ...; **it has come to my
~ that ...** me he enterado de que ...; **to have a
working ~ of Spanish** defenderse con el español

knowledgeable [ˈnɔlɪdʒəbl] ADJ entendido,
erudito

known [nəun] PP of **know** ▶ ADJ (thief, facts) conocido; (expert) reconocido

knuckle [ˈnʌkl] N nudillo
▶ **knuckle down** VI (inf) ponerse a trabajar en
serio
▶ **knuckle under** VI someterse

knuckleduster [ˈnʌkldʌstər] N puño de hierro

KO ABBR (= knock out) K.O. m ▶ VT (knock out) dejar
K.O.

koala [kəuˈɑːlə] N (also: **koala bear**) koala m

kook [kuːk] N (US inf) chiflado(-a), majareta mf

Koran [kɔˈrɑːn] N Corán m

Korea [kəˈrɪə] N Corea; **North/South ~** Corea
del Norte/Sur

Korean [kəˈrɪən] ADJ, N coreano(-a) m/f

kosher [ˈkəuʃər] ADJ autorizado por la ley judía

Kosovar [ˈkɔsəvɑːr], **Kosovan** [ˈkɔsəvən] ADJ
kosovar

Kosovo [ˈkɔsəvəu] N Kosovo m

kowtow [ˈkauˈtau] VI: **to ~ to sb** humillarse
ante algn

Kremlin [ˈkremlɪn] N: **the ~** el Kremlin

KS ABBR (US) = **Kansas**

Kt ABBR (BRIT: = Knight) caballero de una orden

Kuala Lumpur [ˈkwɑːləˈlumpuər] N Kuala
Lumpur m

kudos [ˈkjuːdɔs] N gloria, prestigio

Kurd [kəːd] N kurdo(-a)

Kuwait [kuˈweɪt] N Kuwait m

Kuwaiti [kuˈweɪtɪ] ADJ, N Kuwaití mf

kW ABBR (= kilowatt) Kv

KY, Ky. ABBR (US) = **Kentucky**

Kyrgyzstan [ˈkɪəgɪzstɑːn] N Kirguistán m, Kirguizistán m

k

Ll

L, l [εl] N (*letter*) L, l *f*; **L for Lucy**, (*US*) **L for Love** L de Lorenzo

L ABBR (*on maps etc*) = **lake**; (*size*) = **large**; (= *left*) izq.; (*BRIT Aut*: = *learner*) L

l ABBR = **litre**

LA N ABBR (*US*) = **Los Angeles** ▸ ABBR (*US*) = **Louisiana**

La. ABBR (*US*) = **Louisiana**

lab [læb] N ABBR = **laboratory**

Lab. ABBR (*CANADA*) = **Labrador**

⋆**label** ['leɪbl] N etiqueta; (*brand: of record*) sello (discográfico) ▸ VT poner una etiqueta a, etiquetar

labor ['leɪbəʳ] N, VB (*US*) = **labour**

⋆**laboratory** [ləˈbɒrətərɪ] N laboratorio

Labor Day N (*US*) día *m* de los trabajadores (*primer lunes de septiembre*)

> En Estados Unidos y Canadá, **Labor Day**, el día de los trabajadores, se celebra el primer lunes de septiembre. La celebración fue instituida por el Congreso en 1894, respondiendo a doce años de demandas de los trabajadores. Ha perdido gran parte de su carácter reivindicativo para convertirse en un festivo normal y corriente, ofreciendo la oportunidad de hacer un puente antes de la vuelta al colegio.

laborious [ləˈbɔːrɪəs] ADJ penoso

laboriously [ləˈbɔːrɪəslɪ] ADV penosamente

labor union N (*US*) sindicato

labor unrest N (*US*) conflictividad *f* laboral

Labour ['leɪbəʳ] N (*BRIT Pol*: *also*: **the Labour Party**) el partido laborista, los laboristas

labour, (*US*) **labor** ['leɪbəʳ] N (*task*) trabajo; (*also*: **labour force**) mano *f* de obra; (*workers*) trabajadores *mpl*; (*Med*) (dolores *mpl* de) parto; **hard ~** trabajos *mpl* forzados; **to be in ~** (*Med*) estar de parto ▸ VI: **to ~ (at)** trabajar (en) ▸ VT: **to ~ a point** insistir en un punto

labour cost, (*US*) **labor cost** N costo de la mano de obra

labour dispute, (*US*) **labor dispute** N conflicto laboral

laboured, (*US*) **labored** ['leɪbəd] ADJ (*breathing*) fatigoso; (*style*) forzado, pesado

labourer, (*US*) **laborer** ['leɪbərəʳ] N peón *m*; (*on farm*) peón *m*, obrero(-a); (*day labourer*) jornalero(-a)

labour force, (*US*) **labor force** N mano *f* de obra

labour-intensive, (*US*) **labor-intensive** [leɪbərɪnˈtɛnsɪv] ADJ que necesita mucha mano de obra

labour relations, (*US*) **labor relations** NPL relaciones *fpl* laborales

labour-saving, (*US*) **labor-saving** ['leɪbəseɪvɪŋ] ADJ que ahorra trabajo

laburnum [ləˈbəːnəm] N codeso

labyrinth ['læbɪrɪnθ] N laberinto

lace [leɪs] N encaje *m*; (*of shoe etc*) cordón *m* ▸ VT (*shoes: also*: **lace up**) atarse; (*drink: fortify with spirits*) echar licor a

lacemaking ['leɪsmeɪkɪŋ] N obra de encaje

lacerate ['læsəreɪt] VT lacerar

laceration [læsəˈreɪʃən] N laceración *f*

lace-up ['leɪsʌp] ADJ (*shoes etc*) con cordones

⋆**lack** [læk] N (*absence*) falta, carencia; (*scarcity*) escasez *f*; **through** *or* **for ~ of** por falta de ▸ VT faltarle a algn, carecer de; **to be lacking** faltar, no haber; **to be lacking in sth** faltarle a algn algo

lackadaisical [lækəˈdeɪzɪkl] ADJ (*careless*) descuidado; (*indifferent*) indiferente

lackey ['lækɪ] N (*also fig*) lacayo

lacklustre, (*US*) **lackluster** ['læklʌstəʳ] ADJ (*surface*) deslustrado, deslucido; (*style*) inexpresivo; (*eyes*) apagado

laconic [ləˈkɒnɪk] ADJ lacónico

lacquer ['lækəʳ] N laca; **hair ~** laca para el pelo

lacrosse [ləˈkrɒs] N lacrosse *f*

lacy ['leɪsɪ] ADJ (*like lace*) como de encaje

lad [læd] N (*inf*) muchacho, chico; (*in stable etc*) mozo

ladder ['lædə'] N escalera (de mano); (*BRIT: in tights*) carrera ▸ VT (*BRIT: tights*) hacer una carrera en

laden ['leɪdn] ADJ: **~ (with)** cargado (de); **fully ~** (*truck, ship*) cargado hasta el tope

ladle ['leɪdl] N cucharón m

lady ['leɪdɪ] N señora; (*distinguished, noble*) dama; **young ~** señorita; **the ladies' (room)** los servicios de señoras; **"ladies and gentlemen ..."** "señoras y caballeros ..."

ladybird ['leɪdɪbəːd], (*US*) **ladybug** ['leɪdɪbʌg] N mariquita

lady doctor N médica, doctora

lady-in-waiting ['leɪdɪɪn'weɪtɪŋ] N dama de honor

ladykiller ['leɪdɪkɪlə'] N robacorazones m inv

ladylike ['leɪdɪlaɪk] ADJ fino

Ladyship ['leɪdɪʃɪp] N: **your ~** su Señoría

lag [læg] VI (*also:* **lag behind**) retrasarse, quedarse atrás ▸ VT (*pipes*) revestir

lager ['lɑːgə'] N cerveza (rubia)

lager lout N (*BRIT pej*) gamberro borracho

lagging ['lægɪŋ] N revestimiento

lagoon [lə'guːn] N laguna

Lagos ['leɪgɔs] N Lagos m

laid [leɪd] PT, PP *of* **lay**

laid-back [leɪd'bæk] ADJ (*inf*) tranquilo, relajado

laid up ADJ: **to be ~** (*person*) tener que guardar cama

lain [leɪn] PP *of* **lie**

lair [lɛə'] N guarida

laissez-faire [lɛseɪ'fɛə'] N laissez-faire m

laity ['leɪtɪ] N laicado

lake [leɪk] N lago

Lake District N (*BRIT*): **the ~** la Región de los Lagos

lamb [læm] N cordero; (*meat*) carne f de cordero

lamb chop N chuleta de cordero

lambswool ['læmzwul] N lana de cordero

lame [leɪm] ADJ cojo, rengo (*LAM*); (*weak*) débil; (*excuse*) poco convincente; **~ duck** (*fig: person*) inútil mf (*: firm*) empresa en quiebra

lamely ['leɪmlɪ] ADV (*fig*) sin convicción

lament [lə'ment] N lamento ▸ VT lamentarse de

lamentable ['læməntəbl] ADJ lamentable

lamentation [læmən'teɪʃən] N lamento

laminated ['læmɪneɪtɪd] ADJ laminado

lamp [læmp] N lámpara

lamplight ['læmplaɪt] N: **by ~** a la luz de la lámpara

lampoon [læm'puːn] VT satirizar

lamppost ['læmppəust] N (*BRIT*) farola

lampshade ['læmpʃeɪd] N pantalla

lance [lɑːns] N lanza ▸ VT (*Med*) abrir con lanceta

lance corporal N (*BRIT*) soldado de primera clase

lancet ['lɑːnsɪt] N (*Med*) lanceta

Lancs [læŋks] ABBR (*BRIT*) = **Lancashire**

★**land** [lænd] N tierra; (*country*) país m; (*piece of land*) terreno; (*estate*) tierras fpl, finca; (*Agr*) campo; **to go/travel by ~** ir/viajar por tierra; **to own ~** ser dueño de tierras ▸ VI (*from ship*) desembarcar; (*Aviat*) aterrizar; (*fig: fall*) caer; **to ~ on one's feet** caer de pie; (*fig: to be lucky*) salir bien parado ▸ VT (*obtain*) conseguir; (*passengers, goods*) desembarcar; **to ~ sb with sth** (*inf*) hacer cargar a algn con algo

▸ **land up** VI: **to ~ up in/at** ir a parar a/en

landed ['lændɪd] ADJ: **~ gentry** terratenientes mpl

landfill site ['lændfɪl-] N vertedero

landing ['lændɪŋ] N desembarco; aterrizaje m; (*of staircase*) rellano

landing card N tarjeta de desembarque

landing craft N lancha de desembarco

landing gear N (*Aviat*) tren m de aterrizaje

landing stage N (*BRIT*) desembarcadero

landing strip N pista de aterrizaje

landlady ['lændleɪdɪ] N (*owner*) dueña; (*of boarding house*) patrona

landline ['lændlaɪn] N (teléfono) fijo; **can I ring you on your ~?** ¿te puedo llamar al fijo?

landlocked ['lændlɔkt] ADJ cercado de tierra

landlord ['lændlɔːd] N propietario; (*of pub etc*) patrón m

landlubber ['lændlʌbə'] N marinero de agua dulce

landmark ['lændmɑːk] N lugar m conocido; **to be a ~** (*fig*) hacer época

landowner ['lændəunə'] N terrateniente mf

★**landscape** ['lænskeɪp] N paisaje m

landscape architecture N arquitectura paisajista

landscaped ['lænskeɪpt] ADJ reformado artísticamente

landscape gardener N diseñador(a) m/f de paisajes

landscape gardening N jardinería paisajista

landscape painting N (*Art*) paisaje m

landslide ['lændslaɪd] N (*Geo*) corrimiento de tierras; (*fig, Pol*) victoria arrolladora

★**lane** [leɪn] N (*in country*) camino; (*in town*) callejón m; (*Aut*) carril m; (*in race*) calle f; (*for air or sea traffic*) ruta; **shipping ~** ruta marina

★**language** ['læŋgwɪdʒ] N lenguaje m; (*national tongue*) idioma m, lengua; **bad ~** palabrotas fpl

language laboratory N laboratorio de idiomas

language school N academia de idiomas

language studies NPL estudios mpl filológicos

languid ['læŋgwɪd] ADJ lánguido

languish [ˈlæŋgwɪʃ] VI languidecer
languor [ˈlæŋgəʳ] N languidez f
languorous [ˈlæŋgərəs] ADJ lánguido
lank [læŋk] ADJ (hair) lacio
lanky [ˈlæŋkɪ] ADJ larguirucho
lanolin, lanoline [ˈlænəlɪn] N lanolina
lantern [ˈlæntn] N linterna, farol m
lanyard [ˈlænjed] N acollador m
Laos [laus] N Laos m
★**lap** [læp] N (of track) vuelta; (of body) regazo; **to sit on sb's ~** sentarse en las rodillas de algn ▶ VI (waves) chapotear
  ▶ **lap up** VT beber a lengüetadas or con la lengua; (fig: compliments, attention) disfrutar; (: lies etc) tragarse
La Paz [læˈpæz] N La Paz
lapdog [ˈlæpdɒg] N perro faldero
lapel [ləˈpɛl] N solapa
Lapland [ˈlæplænd] N Laponia
Laplander [ˈlæplændəʳ] N lapón(-ona) m/f
lapse [læps] N (fault) error m, fallo; (moral) desliz m; **~ of time** lapso, intervalo; **a ~ of memory** un lapsus de memoria ▶ VI (expire) caducar; (morally) cometer un desliz; (time) pasar, transcurrir; **to ~ into bad habits** volver a las andadas
★**laptop** [ˈlæptɒp] N (also: **laptop computer**) (ordenador m) portátil m
larceny [ˈlɑːsənɪ] N latrocinio
lard [lɑːd] N manteca (de cerdo)
larder [ˈlɑːdəʳ] N despensa
★**large** [lɑːdʒ] ADJ grande; **a ~ number of people** una gran cantidad de personas; **on a ~ scale** a gran escala; **to make ~(r)** hacer mayor or más extenso ▶ ADV: **by and ~** en general, en términos generales; **at ~** (free) en libertad; (generally) en general

---

large no debe traducirse por largo.

★**largely** [ˈlɑːdʒlɪ] ADV (mostly) en su mayor parte; (introducing reason) en gran parte
large-scale [ˈlɑːdʒˈskeɪl] ADJ (map, drawing) a gran escala; (reforms, business activities) importante
largesse [lɑːˈʒɛs] N generosidad f
lark [lɑːk] N (bird) alondra; (joke) broma
  ▶ **lark about** VI bromear, hacer el tonto
larrikin [ˈlærɪkɪn] N (AUSTRALIA, NEW ZEALAND inf) gamberro(-a)
larva [ˈlɑːvə] (pl **larvae** [-iː]) N larva
laryngitis [lærɪnˈdʒaɪtɪs] N laringitis f
larynx [ˈlærɪŋks] N laringe f
lasagne [ləˈzænjə] N lasaña
lascivious [ləˈsɪvɪəs] ADJ lascivo
laser [ˈleɪzəʳ] N láser m
laser beam N rayo láser
laser printer N impresora láser
lash [læʃ] N latigazo; (punishment) azote m; (also: **eyelash**) pestaña ▶ VT azotar; (tie) atar

  ▶ **lash down** VT sujetar con cuerdas ▶ VI (rain) caer a trombas
  ▶ **lash out** VI (inf: spend) gastar a la loca; **to ~ out (at sb)** (hit) arremeter (contra algn); **to ~ out against sb** lanzar invectivas contra algn
lashing [ˈlæʃɪŋ] N (beating) azotaina, flagelación f; **lashings of** (BRIT old) montones mpl de
lass [læs] N chica
lassitude [ˈlæsɪtjuːd] N lasitud f
lasso [læˈsuː] N lazo ▶ VT coger con lazo (SP), lazar (MEX)
★**last** [lɑːst] ADJ (gen) último; (final) último, final; **~ night** anoche; **~ week** la semana pasada; **~ but one** penúltimo; **~ time** la última vez ▶ ADV (finally) por último; **at ~** por fin ▶ VI (endure) durar; (continue) continuar, seguir; **it lasts (for) two hours** dura dos horas
last-ditch [ˈlɑːstˈdɪtʃ] ADJ (attempt) de último recurso, último, desesperado
lasting [ˈlɑːstɪŋ] ADJ duradero
lastly [ˈlɑːstlɪ] ADV por último, finalmente
last-minute [ˈlɑːstmɪnɪt] ADJ de última hora
latch [lætʃ] N picaporte m, pestillo
  ▶ **latch on to** VT FUS (cling to: person) pegarse a; (: idea) aferrarse a
latchkey [ˈlætʃkiː] N llavín m
latchkey child N (irreg) niño cuyos padres trabajan
★**late** [leɪt] ADJ (not on time) tarde, atrasado; (towards end of period, life) tardío; (hour) avanzado; (deceased) fallecido; **to be ~ with** estar atrasado con; **~ delivery** entrega tardía; **in ~ May** hacia fines de mayo; **the ~ Mr X** el difunto Sr. X ▶ ADV tarde; (behind time, schedule) con retraso; **to be (10 minutes) ~** llegar con (10 minutos de) retraso; **~ in life** a una edad avanzada; **of ~** últimamente; **~ at night** a última hora de la noche; **to work ~** trabajar hasta tarde
latecomer [ˈleɪtkʌməʳ] N recién llegado(-a)
lately [ˈleɪtlɪ] ADV últimamente
lateness [ˈleɪtnɪs] N (of person) demora; (of event) tardanza
latent [ˈleɪtnt] ADJ latente; **~ defect** defecto latente
★**later** [ˈleɪtəʳ] ADJ (date etc) posterior; (version etc) más reciente ▶ ADV más tarde, después; **~ on today** hoy más tarde
lateral [ˈlætərl] ADJ lateral
★**latest** [ˈleɪtɪst] ADJ último; **at the ~** a más tardar
latex [ˈleɪtɛks] N látex m
lathe [leɪð] N torno
lather [ˈlɑːðəʳ] N espuma (de jabón) ▶ VT enjabonar
★**Latin** [ˈlætɪn] N latín m ▶ ADJ latino
Latin America N América Latina, Latinoamérica
Latin American ADJ, N latinoamericano(-a) m/f
Latino [læˈtiːnəu] ADJ, N latino(-a) m/f

latitude ['lætɪtjuːd] N latitud f; (fig: freedom) libertad f

latrine [lə'triːn] N letrina

latter ['lætə'] ADJ último; (of two) segundo ▶ N: **the ~** el último, este

latter-day ['lætədeɪ] ADJ moderno

latterly ['lætəlɪ] ADV últimamente

lattice ['lætɪs] N enrejado

lattice window N ventana enrejada or de celosía

lattice work N enrejado

Latvia ['lætvɪə] N Letonia

Latvian ['lætvɪən] ADJ letón(-ona) ▶ N letón(-ona) m/f; (Ling) letón m

laudable ['lɔːdəbl] ADJ loable

★**laugh** [lɑːf] N risa; (loud) carcajada; **(to do sth) for a ~** (hacer algo) en broma ▶ VI reírse, reír; reírse a carcajadas
  ▶ **laugh at** VT FUS reírse de
  ▶ **laugh off** VT tomar a risa

laughable ['lɑːfəbl] ADJ ridículo

laughing ['lɑːfɪŋ] ADJ risueño ▶ N: **it's no ~ matter** no es cosa de risa

laughing gas N gas m hilarante

laughing stock N: **to be the ~ of the town** ser el hazmerreír de la ciudad

laughter ['lɑːftə'] N risa

launch [lɔːntʃ] N (boat) lancha; see also **launching** ▶ VT (ship) botar; (rocket, plan) lanzar; (fig) comenzar
  ▶ **launch forth** VI: **to ~ forth (into)** lanzarse a or en, emprender
  ▶ **launch into** VT FUS lanzarse a
  ▶ **launch out** VI = **launch forth**

launching ['lɔːntʃɪŋ] N (of rocket etc) lanzamiento; (inauguration) estreno

launching pad, launch pad N plataforma de lanzamiento

launder ['lɔːndə'] VT lavar

Launderette® [lɔːn'drɛt], (US) **Laundromat®** ['lɔːndrəmæt] N lavandería (automática)

laundry ['lɔːndrɪ] N lavandería; (clothes: dirty) ropa sucia; (: clean) colada; **to do the ~** hacer la colada

laureate ['lɔːrɪət] ADJ see **poet laureate**

laurel ['lɔrl] N laurel m; **to rest on one's laurels** dormirse en or sobre los laureles

lava ['lɑːvə] N lava

lavatory ['lævətərɪ] N wáter m ■ **lavatories** NPL servicios mpl, aseos mpl, sanitarios mpl (LAM)

lavatory paper N papel m higiénico

lavender ['lævəndə'] N lavanda

lavish ['lævɪʃ] ADJ abundante; (giving freely): **~ with** pródigo en ▶ VT: **to ~ sth on sb** colmar a algn de algo

lavishly ['lævɪʃlɪ] ADV (give, spend) generosamente; (furnished) lujosamente

★**law** [lɔː] N ley f; (study) derecho; (of game) regla; **against the ~** contra la ley; **to study ~** estudiar derecho; **to go to ~** recurrir a la justicia

law-abiding ['lɔːəbaɪdɪŋ] ADJ respetuoso con la ley

law and order N orden m público

lawbreaker ['lɔːbreɪkə'] N infractor(a) m/f de la ley

law court N tribunal m (de justicia)

lawful ['lɔːful] ADJ legítimo, lícito

lawfully ['lɔːfulɪ] ADV legalmente

lawless ['lɔːlɪs] ADJ (act) ilegal; (person) rebelde; (country) ingobernable

Law Lord N (BRIT) miembro de la Cámara de los Lores y del más alto tribunal de apelación

lawmaker ['lɔːmeɪkə'] N legislador(a) m/f

lawn [lɔːn] N césped m

lawnmower ['lɔːnməuə'] N cortacésped m

lawn tennis N tenis m sobre hierba

law school N (US) facultad f de derecho

law student N estudiante mf de derecho

lawsuit ['lɔːsuːt] N pleito; **to bring a ~ against** entablar un pleito contra

★**lawyer** ['lɔːjə'] N abogado(-a); (for sales, wills etc) notario(-a)

lax [læks] ADJ (discipline) relajado; (person) negligente

laxative ['læksətɪv] N laxante m

laxity ['læksɪtɪ] N flojedad f; (moral) relajamiento; (negligence) negligencia

★**lay** [leɪ] PT of **lie** ▶ ADJ laico; (not expert) lego ▶ VT (pt, pp **laid** [leɪd]) (place) colocar; (eggs, table) poner; (trap) tender; (carpet) extender; **to ~ the facts/one's proposals before sb** presentar los hechos/sus propuestas a algn
  ▶ **lay aside, lay by** VT dejar a un lado
  ▶ **lay down** VT (pen etc) dejar; (arms) rendir; (policy) trazar; (rules etc) establecer; **to ~ down the law** imponer las normas
  ▶ **lay in** VT abastecerse de
  ▶ **lay into** VT FUS (inf: attack, scold) arremeter contra
  ▶ **lay off** VT (workers) despedir
  ▶ **lay on** VT (water, gas) instalar; (meal, facilities) proveer
  ▶ **lay out** VT (plan) trazar; (display) exponer; (spend) gastar
  ▶ **lay up** VT (store) guardar; (ship) desarmar; (illness) obligar a guardar cama

layabout ['leɪəbaut] N vago(-a)

lay-by ['leɪbaɪ] N (BRIT Aut) área de descanso

lay days NPL días mpl de inactividad

★**layer** ['leɪə'] N capa

layette [leɪ'ɛt] N ajuar m (de niño)

layman ['leɪmən] N (irreg) lego

lay-off ['leɪɔf] N despido, paro forzoso

layout ['leɪaut] N (design) plan m, trazado; (disposition) disposición f; (Press) composición f

laze [leɪz] VI no hacer nada; (pej) holgazanear

lazily ['leɪzɪlɪ] ADV perezosamente
laziness ['leɪzɪnɪs] N pereza
★**lazy** ['leɪzɪ] ADJ perezoso, vago, flojo (LAM)
LB ABBR (CANADA) = **Labrador**
lb. ABBR (weight) = **pound**
lbw ABBR (Cricket) = **leg before wicket**
LC N ABBR (US) = **Library of Congress**
lc ABBR (Typ: = lower case) min.
L/C ABBR = **letter of credit**
LCD N ABBR = **liquid crystal display**
Ld ABBR (BRIT: = Lord) título de nobleza
LDS N ABBR (= Licentiate in Dental Surgery) diploma universitario; (= Latter-day Saints) Iglesia de Jesucristo de los Santos del último día
LEA N ABBR (BRIT: = local education authority) organismo local encargado de la enseñanza
★**lead¹** [li:d] (pt, pp **led** [lɛd]) N (front position) delantera; (distance, time ahead) ventaja; (clue) pista; (Elec) cable m; (for dog) correa; (Theat) papel m principal; **to be in the ~** (Sport) llevar la delantera; (fig) ir a la cabeza; **to take the ~** (Sport) tomar la delantera; (fig) tomar la iniciativa ▸ VT conducir; (life) llevar; (be leader of) dirigir; (Sport) ir en cabeza de; (orchestra: BRIT) ser el primer violín en; (: US) dirigir; **to ~ sb to believe that ...** hacer creer a algn que ...; **to ~ sb to do sth** llevar a algn a hacer algo ▸ VI ir primero
  ▸ **lead astray** VT llevar por mal camino
  ▸ **lead away** VT llevar
  ▸ **lead back** VT hacer volver
  ▸ **lead off** VT llevar ▸ VI (in game) abrir
  ▸ **lead on** VT (tease) engañar; **to ~ sb on to** (induce) incitar a algn a
  ▸ **lead to** VT FUS producir, provocar
  ▸ **lead up to** VT FUS (events) conducir a; (in conversation) preparar el terreno para
lead² [lɛd] N (metal) plomo; (in pencil) mina
leaded ['lɛdɪd] ADJ: **~ windows** ventanas fpl emplomadas
leaden ['lɛdn] ADJ (sky, sea) plomizo; (heavy: footsteps) pesado
★**leader** ['li:də'] N jefe(-a) m/f, líder m; (of union etc) dirigente mf; (guide) guía mf; (of newspaper) editorial m; **they are leaders in their field** (fig) llevan la delantera en su especialidad
leadership ['li:dəʃɪp] N dirección f; **qualities of ~** iniciativa sg; **under the ~ of ...** bajo la dirección de ..., al mando de ...
lead-free ['lɛdfri:] ADJ sin plomo
leading ['li:dɪŋ] ADJ (main) principal; (outstanding) destacado; (first) primero; (front) delantero; **a ~ question** una pregunta tendenciosa
leading lady N (Theat) primera actriz f
leading light N (fig: person) figura principal
leading man N (irreg) (Theat) primer actor m
leading role N papel m principal
lead pencil N lápiz m
lead poisoning N envenenamiento plúmbico

lead singer [li:d-] N cantante mf
lead time N (Comm) plazo de entrega
lead-up ['li:dʌp] N: **in the ~ to the election** cuando falta etc poco para las elecciones
lead weight N peso de plomo
★**leaf** [li:f] (pl **leaves** [li:vz]) N hoja; **to turn over a new ~** (fig) hacer borrón y cuenta nueva; **to take a ~ out of sb's book** (fig) seguir el ejemplo de algn
  ▸ **leaf through** VT FUS (book) hojear
leaflet ['li:flɪt] N folleto
leafleting ['li:flətɪŋ] N (for company, political party) reparto de folletos
leafy ['li:fɪ] ADJ frondoso
★**league** [li:g] N sociedad f; (Football) liga; **to be in ~ with** estar confabulado con
league table N clasificación f
★**leak** [li:k] N (of liquid, gas) escape m, fuga; (in pipe) agujero; (in roof) gotera; (fig: of information, in security) filtración f ▸ VI (ship) hacer agua; (shoes) tener un agujero; (pipe) tener un escape; (roof) tener goteras; (liquid, gas: also: **leak out**) escaparse, salirse; (fig: news) trascender, divulgarse ▸ VT (gen) dejar escapar; (fig: information) filtrar
leakage ['li:kɪdʒ] N (of water, gas etc) escape m, fuga
leaky ['li:kɪ] ADJ (roof) con goteras; (bucket, shoe) con agujeros; (pipe) con un escape; (boat) que hace agua
★**lean** [li:n] (pt, pp **leaned** or **leant** [lɛnt]) ADJ (thin) flaco; (meat) magro ▸ VT: **to ~ sth on sth** apoyar algo en algo ▸ VI (slope) inclinarse; (rest): **to ~ against** apoyarse contra; **to ~ on** apoyarse en
  ▸ **lean back** VI inclinarse hacia atrás
  ▸ **lean forward** VI inclinarse hacia adelante
  ▸ **lean out** VI: **to ~ out (of)** asomarse (a)
  ▸ **lean over** VI inclinarse
leaning ['li:nɪŋ] ADJ inclinado; **the L~ Tower of Pisa** la Torre Inclinada de Pisa ▸ N: **~ (towards)** inclinación f (hacia)
leant [lɛnt] PT, PP of **lean**
lean-to ['li:ntu:] N (roof) tejado de una sola agua; (building) cobertizo
★**leap** [li:p] N salto ▸ VI (pt, pp **leaped** or **leapt** [lɛpt]) saltar; **to ~ at an offer** apresurarse a aceptar una oferta
  ▸ **leap up** VI (person) saltar
leapfrog ['li:pfrɔg] N pídola ▸ VI: **to ~ over sb/sth** saltar por encima de algn/algo
leapt [lɛpt] PT, PP of **leap**
leap year N año bisiesto
★**learn** [lə:n] (pt, pp **learned**, **learnt** [lə:nt]) VT (gen) aprender; (come to know of) enterarse de; **to ~ how to do sth** aprender a hacer algo; **to ~ that ...** enterarse or informarse de que ...; **we were sorry to ~ that ...** nos dio tristeza saber que ... ▸ VI aprender; **to ~ about sth** (Scol) aprender algo; (hear) enterarse or informarse de algo
learned ['lə:nɪd] ADJ erudito

learner [ˈləːnəʳ] N principiante *mf*; (BRIT: *also:* **learner driver**) conductor(a) *m/f* en prácticas; *see also* **L-plates**

learning [ˈləːnɪŋ] N saber *m*, conocimientos *mpl*

learning difficulties, learning disabilities NPL dificultades *fpl* de aprendizaje

learnt [ləːnt] PP *of* **learn**

lease [liːs] N arriendo; **on ~** en arriendo ▸ VT arrendar
▸ **lease back** VT subarrendar

leaseback [ˈliːsbæk] N subarriendo

leasehold [ˈliːshəuld] N (*contract*) derechos *mpl* de arrendamiento ▸ ADJ arrendado

leash [liːʃ] N correa

★**least** [liːst] ADJ (*slightest*) menor, más pequeño; (*smallest amount of*) mínimo ▸ ADV menos; **the ~ expensive car** el coche menos caro ▸ N: **the ~** lo menos; **at ~** por lo menos, al menos; **you could at ~ have phoned** por lo menos podías haber llamado; **not in the ~** en absoluto

★**leather** [ˈlɛðəʳ] N cuero ▸ CPD: **~ goods** artículos *mpl* de cuero *or* piel

leathery [ˈlɛðərɪ] ADJ (*skin*) curtido

★**leave** [liːv] (*pt, pp* **left** [lɛft]) VT dejar, (*go away from*) abandonar; **to ~ school** dejar la escuela *or* el colegio; **~ it to me!** ¡yo me encargo!; **to be left** quedar, sobrar; **there's some milk left over** sobra *or* queda algo de leche ▸ VI irse; (*train*) salir; **he's already left for the airport** ya se ha marchado al aeropuerto ▸ N permiso; **on ~** de permiso; **to take one's ~ of** despedirse de
▸ **leave behind** VT (*on purpose*) dejar (atrás); (*accidentally*) olvidar
▸ **leave off** VT (*lid*) no poner; (*switch*) no encender; (*inf: stop*): **to ~ off doing sth** dejar de hacer algo
▸ **leave on** VT (*lid*) dejar puesto; (*light, fire, cooker*) dejar encendido
▸ **leave out** VT omitir
▸ **leave over** VT (*postpone*) dejar, aplazar

leave of absence N excedencia

leaver [ˈliːvəʳ] N (BRIT: *from EU*) partidario de la *salida de la Unión Europea*

leaves [liːvz] PL *of* **leaf**

leavetaking [ˈliːvteɪkɪŋ] N despedida

Lebanon [ˈlɛbənən] N: **the ~** el Líbano

lecherous [ˈlɛtʃərəs] ADJ lascivo

lectern [ˈlɛktəːn] N atril *m*

★**lecture** [ˈlɛktʃəʳ] N conferencia; (*Scol*) clase *f*; **to give a ~ on** dar una conferencia sobre ▸ VI dar clase(s) ▸ VT (*scold*) sermonear; (*reprove*) echar una reprimenda a

lecture hall N sala de conferencias; (*Univ*) aula

lecturer [ˈlɛktʃərəʳ] N conferenciante *mf*; (BRIT: *at university*) profesor(a) *m/f*

lecture theatre N = **lecture hall**

LED N ABBR (*Elec:* = *light-emitting diode*) LED *m*

led [lɛd] PT, PP *of* **lead¹**

ledge [lɛdʒ] N (*on wall*) repisa; (*of window*) alféizar *m*; (*of mountain*) saliente *m*

ledger [ˈlɛdʒəʳ] N libro mayor

lee [liː] N sotavento; **in the ~ of** al abrigo de

leech [liːtʃ] N sanguijuela

leek [liːk] N puerro

leer [lɪəʳ] VI: **to ~ at sb** mirar de manera lasciva a algn

leeway [ˈliːweɪ] N (*fig*): **to have some ~** tener cierta libertad de acción

★**left** [lɛft] PT, PP *of* **leave** ▸ ADJ izquierdo; (*remaining*): **there are two ~** quedan dos ▸ N izquierda; **on** *or* **to the ~** a la izquierda; **the L~** (*Pol*) la izquierda ▸ ADV a la izquierda

left-click [ˈlɛftklɪk] VI clicar con el botón izquierdo del ratón ▸ VT: **to ~ an icon** clicar en un icono con el botón izquierdo del ratón

left-hand [ˈlɛfthænd] ADJ: **the ~ side** la izquierda

left-hand drive N conducción *f* por la izquierda

left-handed [lɛftˈhændɪd] ADJ zurdo; **~ scissors** tijeras *fpl* zurdas *or* para zurdos

left-hand side [ˈlɛfthænd-] N izquierda

leftie [ˈlɛftɪ] N (*inf*) = **lefty**

leftist [ˈlɛftɪst] ADJ (*Pol*) izquierdista

left-luggage [lɛftˈlʌgɪdʒ], **left-luggage office** N (BRIT) consigna

left-luggage locker N (BRIT) consigna *f* automática

left-overs [ˈlɛftəuvəz] NPL sobras *fpl*

left-wing [lɛftˈwɪŋ] ADJ (*Pol*) de izquierda(s), izquierdista

left-winger [ˈlɛftˈwɪŋəʳ] N (*Pol*) izquierdista *mf*

lefty [ˈlɛftɪ] N (*inf: Pol*) rojillo(-a)

★**leg** [lɛg] N pierna; (*of animal, chair*) pata; (*Culin: of meat*) pierna; (: *of chicken*) pata; (*of journey*) etapa; **1st/2nd ~** (*Sport*) partido de ida/de vuelta; **to pull sb's ~** tomar el pelo a algn; **to stretch one's legs** dar una vuelta

legacy [ˈlɛgəsɪ] N herencia; (*fig*) herencia, legado

★**legal** [ˈliːgl] ADJ (*permitted by law*) lícito; (*of law*) legal; (*inquiry etc*) jurídico; **to take ~ action** *or* **proceedings against sb** entablar *or* levantar un pleito contra algn

legal adviser N asesor(a) *m/f* jurídico(-a)

legal holiday N (US) fiesta oficial

legality [lɪˈgælɪtɪ] N legalidad *f*

legalize [ˈliːgəlaɪz] VT legalizar

legally [ˈliːgəlɪ] ADV legalmente; **~ binding** con fuerza legal

legal tender N moneda de curso legal

legend [ˈlɛdʒənd] N leyenda

legendary [ˈlɛdʒəndərɪ] ADJ legendario

-legged [ˈlɛgɪd] SUFF: **two-legged** (*table etc*) de dos patas

leggings [ˈlɛgɪŋz] NPL mallas *fpl*, leggins *mpl*

leggy [ˈlɛgɪ] ADJ de piernas largas

legibility [lɛdʒɪˈbɪlɪtɪ] N legibilidad *f*

legible [ˈlɛdʒəbl] ADJ legible

legibly [ˈlɛdʒəblɪ] ADV legiblemente

legion [ˈliːdʒən] N legión f

legionnaire [liːdʒəˈnɛəʳ] N legionario

legionnaire's disease N enfermedad f del legionario

legislation [lɛdʒɪsˈleɪʃən] N legislación f; **a piece of ~** (bill) un proyecto de ley; (act) una ley

legislative [ˈlɛdʒɪslətɪv] ADJ legislativo

legislator [ˈlɛdʒɪsleɪtəʳ] N legislador(a) m/f

legislature [ˈlɛdʒɪslətʃəʳ] N cuerpo legislativo

legitimacy [lɪˈdʒɪtɪməsɪ] N legitimidad f

legitimate [lɪˈdʒɪtɪmət] ADJ legítimo

legitimize [lɪˈdʒɪtɪmaɪz] VT legitimar

legless [ˈlɛglɪs] ADJ (BRIT inf) mamado

leg-room [ˈlɛgruːm] N espacio para las piernas

leisure [ˈlɛʒəʳ] N ocio, tiempo libre; **at ~** con tranquilidad

leisure centre N polideportivo

leisurely [ˈlɛʒəlɪ] ADJ sin prisa; lento

leisure suit N conjunto tipo chandal

lemon [ˈlɛmən] N limón m

lemonade [lɛməˈneɪd] N (fruit juice) limonada; (fizzy) gaseosa

lemon cheese, lemon curd N queso de limón

lemon juice N zumo de limón

lemon tea N té m con limón

★ **lend** [lɛnd] (pt, pp **lent** [lɛnt]) VT: **to ~ sth to sb** prestar algo a algn

lender [ˈlɛndəʳ] N prestamista mf

lending library [ˈlɛndɪŋ-] N biblioteca de préstamo

★ **length** [lɛŋθ] N (size) largo, longitud f; (section: of road, pipe) tramo; (: of rope etc) largo; (of wood, string) trozo; (amount of time) duración f; **at ~** (at last) por fin, finalmente; (lengthily) largamente; **it is two metres in ~** tiene dos metros de largo; **what ~ is it?** ¿cuánto tiene de largo?; **to fall full ~** caer de bruces; **to go to any ~(s) to do sth** ser capaz de hacer cualquier cosa para hacer algo

lengthen [ˈlɛŋθn] VT alargar ▸ VI alargarse

lengthways [ˈlɛŋθweɪz] ADV a lo largo

lengthy [ˈlɛŋθɪ] ADJ largo, extenso; (meeting) prolongado

lenient [ˈliːnɪənt] ADJ indulgente

★ **lens** [lɛnz] N (of spectacles) lente f; (of camera) objetivo

Lent [lɛnt] N Cuaresma

lent [lɛnt] PT, PP of **lend**

lentil [ˈlɛntl] N lenteja

Leo [ˈliːəu] N Leo

leopard [ˈlɛpəd] N leopardo

leotard [ˈliːətɑːd] N malla

leper [ˈlɛpəʳ] N leproso(-a)

leper colony N colonia de leprosos

leprosy [ˈlɛprəsɪ] N lepra

lesbian [ˈlɛzbɪən] ADJ lesbiano ▸ N lesbiana

lesion [ˈliːʒən] N (Med) lesión f

Lesotho [lɪˈsuːtuː] N Lesotho

★ **less** [lɛs] ADJ (in size, degree etc) menor; (in quantity) menos ▸ PRON, ADV menos; **~ than half** menos de la mitad; **~ than £1/a kilo/3 metres** menos de una libra/un kilo/3 metros; **~ than ever** menos que nunca; **~ 5%** menos el cinco por ciento; **~ and ~** cada vez menos; **the ~ he works ...** cuanto menos trabaja ...

lessee [lɛˈsiː] N inquilino(-a), arrendatario(-a)

lessen [ˈlɛsn] VI disminuir, reducirse ▸ VT disminuir, reducir

lesser [ˈlɛsəʳ] ADJ menor; **to a ~ extent** or **degree** en menor grado

★ **lesson** [ˈlɛsn] N clase f; **a maths ~** una clase de matemáticas; **to give lessons in** dar clases de; **it taught him a ~** (fig) le sirvió de lección

lessor [ˈlɛsɔːʳ, lɛˈsɔːʳ] N arrendador(a) m/f

lest [lɛst] CONJ: **~ it happen** para que no pase

★ **let** [lɛt] (pt, pp **~**) VT (allow) dejar, permitir; (BRIT: lease) alquilar; **to ~ sb do sth** dejar que algn haga algo; **to ~ sb have sth** dar algo a algn; **to ~ sb know sth** comunicar algo a algn; **~'s go** ¡vamos!; **~ him come** que venga; **"to ~"** "se alquila"

▸ **let down** VT (lower) bajar; (dress) alargar; (tyre) desinflar; (hair) soltar; (disappoint) defraudar

▸ **let go** VI soltar; (fig) dejarse ir ▸ VT soltar

▸ **let in** VT dejar entrar; (visitor etc) hacer pasar; **what have you ~ yourself in for?** ¿en qué te has metido?

▸ **let off** VT dejar escapar; (firework etc) disparar; (bomb) accionar; (passenger) dejar, bajar; **to ~ off steam** (fig: inf) desahogarse, desfogarse

▸ **let on** VI: **to ~ on that ...** revelar que ...

▸ **let out** VT dejar salir; (dress) ensanchar; (rent out) alquilar

▸ **let up** VI disminuir; (rain etc) amainar

---

let is usually translated by **dejar** or **permitir**. Both verbs can be followed either by an infinitive or by **que** plus the subjunctive:
Let me do it. **Déjame hacerlo**. or **Déjame que lo haga**.
They didn't let us see it. **No nos permitieron verlo**. or **No permitieron que lo viéramos**.
When you use *let's* to suggest doing something, in Spanish use **vamos a** followed by the infinitive: *Let's go for a walk.* **Vamos a dar un paseo**.

---

let-down [ˈlɛtdaun] N (disappointment) decepción f

lethal [ˈliːθl] ADJ (weapon) mortífero; (poison, wound) mortal

lethargic [lɛˈθɑːdʒɪk] ADJ aletargado

lethargy [ˈlɛθədʒɪ] N letargo

★ **letter** [ˈlɛtəʳ] N (of alphabet) letra; (correspondence) carta; **small/capital ~** minúscula/mayúscula; **covering ~** carta adjunta ■ **letters** NPL (literature, learning) letras fpl

letter bomb N carta-bomba

letterbox [ˈlɛtəbɒks] N (BRIT) buzón m

letterhead [ˈlɛtəhɛd] N membrete m, encabezamiento

lettering [ˈlɛtərɪŋ] N letras fpl

letter of credit N carta de crédito; **documentary ~** carta de crédito documentaria; **irrevocable ~** carta de crédito irrevocable

letter-opener [ˈlɛtərəupnə^r] N abrecartas m inv

letterpress [ˈlɛtəprɛs] N (method) prensa de copiar; (printed page) impresión f tipográfica

letter quality N calidad f de correspondencia

letters patent NPL letra sg de patente

lettuce [ˈlɛtɪs] N lechuga

let-up [ˈlɛtʌp] N descanso, tregua

leukaemia, (US) **leukemia** [luːˈkiːmɪə] N leucemia

★**level** [ˈlɛvl] ADJ (flat) llano; (flattened) nivelado; (uniform) igual; **to be ~ with** estar a nivel de; **a ~ spoonful** (Culin) una cucharada rasa ▶ ADV a nivel; **to draw ~ with** (team) igualar; (runner, car) alcanzar a ▶ N nivel m; (height) altura; **A levels** (BRIT) ≈ exámenes mpl de bachillerato superior; **O levels** npl (BRIT: formerly) ≈ bachillerato sg elemental, octavo sg de Básica; **on the ~** (fig: honest) en serio; **talks at ministerial ~** charlas fpl a nivel ministerial ▶ VT nivelar, allanar; (destroy: building) derribar; (gun) apuntar; (accusation): **to ~ (against)** levantar (contra) ▶ VI (inf): **to ~ with sb** ser franco con algn ▶ **level off, level out** VI (prices etc) estabilizarse; (ground) nivelarse; (aircraft) ponerse en una trayectoria horizontal

level crossing N (BRIT) paso a nivel

level-headed [lɛvlˈhɛdɪd] ADJ sensato

levelling, (US) **leveling** [ˈlɛvlɪŋ] ADJ (process, effect) de nivelación ▶ N igualación f, allanamiento

level playing field N situación f de igualdad; **to compete on a ~** competir en igualdad de condiciones

lever [ˈliːvə^r] N palanca ▶ VT: **to ~ up** levantar con palanca

leverage [ˈliːvərɪdʒ] N (fig: influence) influencia

levity [ˈlɛvɪtɪ] N frivolidad f, informalidad f

levy [ˈlɛvɪ] N impuesto ▶ VT exigir, recaudar

lewd [luːd] ADJ lascivo, obsceno, colorado (LAM)

lexicographer [lɛksɪˈkɔgrəfə^r] N lexicógrafo(-a)

lexicography [lɛksɪˈkɔgrəfɪ] N lexicografía

LGBT ABBR (= lesbian, gay, bisexual and/or transgender) LGTB

LGV N ABBR (= Large Goods Vehicle) vehículo pesado

LI ABBR (US) = **Long Island**

liabilities [laɪəˈbɪlətɪz] NPL obligaciones fpl; pasivo sg

liability [laɪəˈbɪlətɪ] N (pej: person, thing) estorbo, lastre m; (Law: responsibility) responsabilidad f; (handicap) desventaja

liable [ˈlaɪəbl] ADJ (subject): **~ to** sujeto a; (responsible): **~ for** responsable de; (likely): **~ to do** propenso a hacer; **to be ~ to a fine** exponerse a una multa

liaise [liːˈeɪz] VI: **to ~ (with)** colaborar (con); **to ~ with sb** mantener informado a algn

liaison [liːˈeɪzɔn] N (coordination) enlace m; (affair) relación f

liar [ˈlaɪə^r] N mentiroso(-a)

libel [ˈlaɪbl] N calumnia ▶ VT calumniar

libellous [ˈlaɪbləs] ADJ difamatorio, calumnioso

★**liberal** [ˈlɪbərl] ADJ (gen) liberal; (generous): **~ with** generoso con ▶ N: **L~** (Pol) liberal mf

Liberal Democrat N (BRIT) demócrata mf liberal

liberality [lɪbəˈrælɪtɪ] N (generosity) liberalidad f, generosidad f

liberalize [ˈlɪbərəlaɪz] VT liberalizar

liberally [ˈlɪbərəlɪ] ADV liberalmente

liberal-minded [ˈlɪbərlˈmaɪndɪd] ADJ de miras anchas, liberal

liberate [ˈlɪbəreɪt] VT (people: from poverty etc) librar; (prisoner) libertar; (country) liberar

liberation [lɪbəˈreɪʃən] N liberación f

liberation theology N teología de la liberación

Liberia [laɪˈbɪərɪə] N Liberia

Liberian [laɪˈbɪərɪən] ADJ, N liberiano(-a) m/f

liberty [ˈlɪbətɪ] N libertad f; **to be at ~** (criminal) estar en libertad; **to be at ~ to do** estar libre para hacer; **to take the ~ of doing sth** tomarse la libertad de hacer algo

libido [lɪˈbiːdəu] N libido

Libra [ˈliːbrə] N Libra

librarian [laɪˈbrɛərɪən] N bibliotecario(-a)

★**library** [ˈlaɪbrərɪ] N biblioteca

> **library** no debe traducirse por librería.

library book N libro de la biblioteca

libretto [lɪˈbrɛtəu] N libreto

Libya [ˈlɪbɪə] N Libia

Libyan [ˈlɪbɪən] ADJ, N libio(-a) m/f

lice [laɪs] PL of **louse**

licence, (US) **license** [ˈlaɪsns] N licencia; (permit) permiso; (also: **driving licence**, US: **driver's license**) carnet m de conducir, permiso de manejar (LAM); (excessive freedom) libertad f; **import ~** licencia or permiso de importación; **produced under ~** elaborado bajo licencia

licence number N (número de) matrícula

licence plate N (placa de) matrícula

license [ˈlaɪsns] N (US) = **licence** ▶ VT autorizar, dar permiso a; (car) sacar la matrícula de or (LAM) la patente de

licensed [ˈlaɪsnst] ADJ (for alcohol) autorizado para vender bebidas alcohólicas

licensed trade N comercio or negocio autorizado

licensee [laɪsən'si:] N (*in a pub*) concesionario(-a), dueño(-a) de un bar

license plate N (*US*) placa (de matrícula)

licensing hours NPL (*BRIT*) *horas durante las cuales se permite la venta y consumo de alcohol* (*en un bar etc*)

licentious [laɪ'sɛnʃəs] ADJ licencioso

lichen ['laɪkən] N liquen *m*

lick [lɪk] VT lamer; (*inf: defeat*) dar una paliza a; **to ~ one's lips** relamerse ▸ N lamedura; **a ~ of paint** una mano de pintura

licorice ['lɪkərɪs] N = **liquorice**

lid [lɪd] N (*of box, case, pan*) tapa, tapadera; **to take the ~ off sth** (*fig*) exponer algo a la luz pública

lido ['laɪdəu] N (*BRIT*) piscina, alberca (*LAM*)

★**lie** [laɪ] N mentira; **to tell lies** mentir ▸ VI mentir; (*pt* **lay** [leɪ], *pp* **lain** [leɪn]) (*rest*) estar echado, estar acostado; (*be situated: object*) estar, encontrarse; **to ~ low** (*fig*) mantenerse a escondidas
▸ **lie about, lie around** VI (*things*) estar tirado; (*BRIT: people*) estar acostado *or* tumbado
▸ **lie back** VI recostarse
▸ **lie down** VI echarse, tumbarse
▸ **lie up** VI (*hide*) esconderse

Liechtenstein ['lɪktənstaɪn] N Liechtenstein *m*

lie detector N detector *m* de mentiras

lie-down ['laɪdaun] N (*BRIT*): **to have a ~** echarse (una siesta)

lie-in ['laɪɪn] N (*BRIT*): **to have a ~** quedarse en la cama

lieu [lu:] N: **in ~ of** *prep* en lugar de

Lieut. ABBR = **lieutenant**

lieutenant [lɛf'tɛnənt, (*US*) lu:'tɛnənt] N (*Mil*) teniente *mf*

lieutenant colonel N teniente *m* coronel

★**life** [laɪf] (*pl* **lives** [laɪvz]) N vida; (*of licence etc*) vigencia; **to be sent to prison for ~** ser condenado a cadena perpetua; **country/city ~** la vida en el campo/en la ciudad; **true to ~** fiel a la realidad; **to paint from ~** pintar del natural; **to put** *or* **breathe new ~ into** (*person*) reanimar; (*project, area etc*) infundir nueva vida a

life assurance N (*BRIT*) seguro de vida

lifebelt ['laɪfbɛlt] N (*BRIT*) cinturón *m* salvavidas

lifeblood ['laɪfblʌd] N (*fig*) alma, nervio

lifeboat ['laɪfbəut] N lancha de socorro

life-buoy ['laɪfbɔɪ] N boya *or* guindola salvavidas

life coach N *profesional encargado de mejorar la situación laboral y personal de sus clientes*

life expectancy N esperanza de vida

lifeguard ['laɪfgɑ:d] N vigilante *mf*, socorrista *mf*

life imprisonment N cadena perpetua

life insurance N = **life assurance**

life jacket N chaleco salvavidas

lifeless ['laɪflɪs] ADJ sin vida; (*dull*) soso

lifelike ['laɪflaɪk] ADJ natural

lifeline ['laɪflaɪn] N (*fig*) cordón *m* umbilical

lifelong ['laɪflɔŋ] ADJ de toda la vida

life preserver N (*US*) = **lifebelt**

lifer ['laɪfə] N (*inf*) condenado(-a) a cadena perpetua

life-saver ['laɪfseɪvə] N socorrista *mf*

life sentence N cadena perpetua

life-sized ['laɪfsaɪzd] ADJ de tamaño natural

life span N vida

lifestyle ['laɪfstaɪl] N estilo de vida

life support system N (*Med*) sistema *m* de respiración asistida

lifetime ['laɪftaɪm] N: **in his ~** durante su vida; **once in a ~** una vez en la vida; **the chance of a ~** una oportunidad única

★**lift** [lɪft] VT levantar; (*copy*) plagiar ▸ VI (*fog*) disiparse ▸ N (*BRIT: elevator*) ascensor *m*, elevador *m* (*LAM*); **to give sb a ~** (*BRIT*) llevar a algn en coche
▸ **lift off** VT levantar, quitar ▸ VI (*rocket, helicopter*) despegar
▸ **lift out** VT sacar; (*troops, evacuees etc*) evacuar
▸ **lift up** VT levantar

lift-off ['lɪftɔf] N despegue *m*

ligament ['lɪgəmənt] N ligamento

★**light** [laɪt] N luz *f*; (*flame*) lumbre *f*; (*lamp*) luz *f*, lámpara; (*daylight*) luz *f* del día; (*headlight*) faro; (*rear light*) luz *f* trasera; (*for cigarette etc*): **have you got a ~?** ¿tienes fuego?; **to turn the ~ on/off** encender/apagar la luz; **in the ~ of** a la luz de; **to come to ~** salir a la luz; **to cast** *or* **shed** *or* **throw ~ on** arrojar luz sobre ▸ VT (*pt, pp* **lighted** *or* **lit** [lɪt]) (*candle, cigarette, fire*) encender; (*room*) alumbrar ▸ ADJ (*colour*) claro; (*room*) con mucha luz; **to make ~ of sth** (*fig*) no dar importancia a algo ▸ ADV (*travel*) con poco equipaje ■ **lights** NPL (*traffic lights*) semáforo *msg*
▸ **light up** VI (*smoke*) encender un cigarrillo; (*face*) iluminarse ▸ VT (*illuminate*) iluminar, alumbrar; (*set fire to*) encender

light bulb N bombilla, bombillo (*LAM*), foco (*LAM*)

lighten ['laɪtn] VI (*grow light*) clarear ▸ VT (*give light to*) iluminar; (*make lighter*) aclarar; (*make less heavy*) aligerar

lighter ['laɪtə] N (*also*: **cigarette lighter**) encendedor *m* (*LAM*), mechero

light-fingered [laɪt'fɪŋgəd] ADJ de manos largas

light-headed [laɪt'hɛdɪd] ADJ (*dizzy*) mareado; (*excited*) exaltado; (*by nature*) atolondrado

light-hearted [laɪt'hɑ:tɪd] ADJ (*person*) alegre; (*remark etc*) divertido

lighthouse ['laɪthaus] N faro

lighting ['laɪtɪŋ] N (*act*) iluminación *f*; (*system*) alumbrado

lighting-up time [laɪtɪŋ'ʌp-] N (*BRIT*) hora de encendido del alumbrado

lightly ['laɪtlɪ] ADV ligeramente; (*not seriously*)

con poca seriedad; **to get off** ~ ser castigado con poca severidad

light meter N (*Phot*) fotómetro

lightness ['laɪtnɪs] N claridad *f*; (*in weight*) ligereza

★**lightning** ['laɪtnɪŋ] N relámpago, rayo

lightning conductor, (*US*) **lightning rod** N pararrayos *m inv*

lightning strike N huelga relámpago

lightweight ['laɪtweɪt] ADJ (*suit*) ligero ▸ N (*Boxing*) peso ligero

light year N año luz

★**like** [laɪk] VT (*person*): **I** ~ **him** me cae bien; (*thing*): **I** ~ **swimming/apples** me gusta nadar/me gustan las manzanas; **I would** ~, **I'd** ~ me gustaría; (*for purchase*) quisiera; **would you** ~ **a coffee?** ¿quieres un café?; **I** ~ **swimming** me gusta nadar ▸ VI querer; **if you** ~ si quieres ▸ PREP como; **that's just** ~ **him** es muy de él, es típico de él; **do it** ~ **this** hazlo así; **it is nothing** ~ ... no tiene parecido alguno con ...; **what's he** ~? ¿cómo es (él)?; **what's the weather** ~? ¿qué tiempo hace?; **to be or look** ~ **sb/sth** parecerse a algn/algo; **something** ~ **that** algo así o por el estilo; **I feel** ~ **a drink** me apetece algo de beber ▸ ADJ parecido, semejante ▸ N: **did you ever see the** ~ **(of it)?** ¿has visto cosa igual?; **his likes and dislikes** sus gustos y aversiones; **the likes of him** personas como él

> The most common translation for *to like* when talking about things and activities is **gustar**. The construction is the opposite of English, with the thing you like being the subject of the sentence:
> *I like apples.* **Me gustan las manzanas**.
> *Do you like swimming?* **¿Te gusta nadar?**
> To talk about liking someone, use the phrase **caer bien**: *I like your brother.* **Tu hermano me cae bien**.
> To ask someone if they would like something, or would like to do something, use **querer**:
> *Would you like some coffee?* **¿Quieres café?**

likeable ['laɪkəbl] ADJ simpático, agradable

likelihood ['laɪklɪhud] N probabilidad *f*; **in all** ~ según todas las probabilidades

★**likely** ['laɪklɪ] ADJ probable, capaz (*LAM*); **he's** ~ **to leave** es probable *or* (*LAM*) capaz que se vaya ▸ ADV: **not** ~! (*inf*) ¡ni hablar!

like-minded [laɪk'maɪndɪd] ADJ de la misma opinión

liken ['laɪkən] VT: **to** ~ **to** comparar con

likeness ['laɪknɪs] N (*similarity*) semejanza, parecido

likewise ['laɪkwaɪz] ADV igualmente; **to do** ~ hacer lo mismo

liking ['laɪkɪŋ] N: ~ **(for)** (*person*) cariño (a); (*thing*) afición (a); **to take a** ~ **to sb** tomar cariño a algn; **to be to sb's** ~ ser del gusto de algn

lilac ['laɪlək] N (*tree*) lilo; (*flower*) lila ▸ ADJ (*colour*) de color lila

Lilo® ['laɪləu] N colchoneta inflable

lilt [lɪlt] N deje *m*

lilting ['lɪltɪŋ] ADJ melodioso

lily ['lɪlɪ] N lirio, azucena

Lima ['liːmə] N Lima

limb [lɪm] N miembro; (*of tree*) rama; **to be out on a** ~ (*fig*) estar aislado

limber up ['lɪmbə⁻'] VI (*fig*) entrenarse; (*Sport*) hacer (ejercicios de) precalentamiento

limbo ['lɪmbəu] N: **to be in** ~ (*fig*) quedar a la expectativa

lime [laɪm] N (*tree*) limero; (*fruit*) lima; (*Geo*) cal *f*

lime juice N zumo (*SP*) *or* jugo de lima

limelight ['laɪmlaɪt] N: **to be in the** ~ (*fig*) ser el centro de atención

limerick ['lɪmərɪk] N quintilla humorística

limestone ['laɪmstəun] N piedra caliza

★**limit** ['lɪmɪt] N límite *m*; **weight/speed** ~ peso máximo/velocidad *f* máxima; **within limits** entre límites ▸ VT limitar

limitation [lɪmɪ'teɪʃən] N limitación *f*

limited ['lɪmɪtɪd] ADJ limitado; **to be** ~ **to** limitarse a; ~ **edition** edición limitada

limited company, limited liability company N (*BRIT*) sociedad *f* anónima

limitless ['lɪmɪtlɪs] ADJ sin límites

limousine ['lɪməziːn] N limusina

limp [lɪmp] N: **to have a** ~ tener cojera ▸ VI cojear, renguear (*LAM*) ▸ ADJ flojo

limpet ['lɪmpɪt] N lapa

limpid ['lɪmpɪd] ADJ (*poetic*) límpido, cristalino

limply ['lɪmplɪ] ADV desmayadamente; **to say** ~ decir débilmente

linchpin ['lɪntʃpɪn] N pezonera; (*fig*) eje *m*

★**line** [laɪn] N (*Comm*) línea; (*straight line*) raya; (*rope*) cuerda; (*for fishing*) sedal *m*; (*wire*) hilo; (*row, series*) fila, hilera; (*of writing*) renglón *m*; (*on face*) arruga; (*Rail*) vía; (*speciality*) rama; **in** ~ **with** de acuerdo con; **she's in** ~ **for promotion** (*fig*) tiene muchas posibilidades de que la asciendan; **to bring sth into** ~ **with sth** poner algo de acuerdo con algo; ~ **of research/business** campo de investigación/comercio; **to take the** ~ **that ...** ser de la opinión que ...; **hold the** ~ **please** (*Tel*) no cuelgue usted, por favor; **to draw the** ~ **at doing sth** negarse a hacer algo; no permitir que se haga algo; **on the right lines** por buen camino; **a new** ~ **in cosmetics** una nueva línea en cosméticos ▸ VT (*Sewing*): **to** ~ **(with)** forrar (de); **to** ~ **the streets** ocupar las aceras; *see also* **lines**

▸ **line up** VI hacer cola ▸ VT alinear, poner en fila; **to have sth lined up** tener algo arreglado

linear ['lɪnɪə⁻'] ADJ lineal

lined [laɪnd] ADJ (*face*) arrugado; (*paper*) rayado; (*clothes*) forrado

line editing N (*Comput*) corrección *f* por líneas

line feed N (*Comput*) avance *m* de línea

lineman ['laɪnmən] N (*irreg*) (*US*) técnico de las líneas; (*Football*) delantero

linen [ˈlɪnɪn] N ropa blanca; (*cloth*) lino

line printer N impresora de línea

liner [ˈlaɪnəʳ] N vapor *m* de línea transatlántico; **dustbin ~** bolsa de la basura

lines [laɪnz] NPL (*Rail*) vía *sg*, raíles *mpl*

linesman [ˈlaɪnzmən] N (*irreg*) (*Sport*) juez *m* de línea

line-up [ˈlaɪnʌp] N (*US: queue*) cola; (*Sport*) alineación *f*

linger [ˈlɪŋgəʳ] VI retrasarse, tardar en marcharse; (*smell, tradition*) persistir

lingerie [ˈlænʒəriː] N ropa interior (de mujer), lencería

lingering [ˈlɪŋgərɪŋ] ADJ persistente; (*death*) lento

lingo [ˈlɪŋgəu] (*pl* **lingoes** [-gəuz]) N (*pej*) jerga

linguist [ˈlɪŋgwɪst] N lingüista *mf*

linguistic [lɪŋˈgwɪstɪk] ADJ lingüístico

linguistics [lɪŋˈgwɪstɪks] N lingüística

liniment [ˈlɪnɪmənt] N linimento

lining [ˈlaɪnɪŋ] N forro; (*Tech*) revestimiento; (*of brake*) guarnición *f*

★**link** [lɪŋk] N (*of chain*) eslabón *m*; (*connection*) conexión *f*; (*relationship*) relación *f*; (*bond*) vínculo, lazo; (*Internet*) enlace *m*; **rail ~** línea de ferrocarril, servicio de trenes ▶ VT vincular, unir; (*associate*): **to ~ with** *or* **to** relacionar con ■ **links** NPL (*Golf*) campo *sg* de golf
▶ **link up** VT acoplar ▶ VI unirse

link-up [ˈlɪŋkʌp] N (*gen*) unión *f*; (*meeting*) encuentro, reunión *f*; (*of roads*) empalme *m*; (*of spaceships*) acoplamiento; (*Radio, TV*) enlace *m*

lino [ˈlaɪnəu], **linoleum** [lɪˈnəuliəm] N linóleo

linseed oil [ˈlɪnsiːd-] N aceite *m* de linaza

lint [lɪnt] N gasa

lintel [ˈlɪntl] N dintel *m*

★**lion** [ˈlaɪən] N león *m*

lioness [ˈlaɪənɪs] N leona

★**lip** [lɪp] N labio; (*of jug*) pico; (*of cup etc*) borde *m*

liposuction [ˈlɪpəusʌkʃən] N liposucción *f*

lip-read [ˈlɪpriːd] VI leer los labios

lip salve N crema protectora para labios

lip service N: **to pay ~ to sth** alabar algo pero sin hacer nada

lipstick [ˈlɪpstɪk] N lápiz *m or* barra de labios, carmín *m*

liquefy [ˈlɪkwɪfaɪ] VT licuar ▶ VI licuarse

liqueur [lɪˈkjuəʳ] N licor *m*

liquid [ˈlɪkwɪd] ADJ, N líquido

liquidate [ˈlɪkwɪdeɪt] VT liquidar

liquidation [lɪkwɪˈdeɪʃən] N liquidación *f*; **to go into ~** entrar en liquidación

liquid crystal display N pantalla de cristal líquido

liquidity [lɪˈkwɪdɪtɪ] N (*Comm*) liquidez *f*

liquidize [ˈlɪkwɪdaɪz] VT (*Culin*) licuar

liquidizer [ˈlɪkwɪdaɪzəʳ] N (*Culin*) licuadora

liquor [ˈlɪkəʳ] N licor *m*, bebidas *fpl* alcohólicas

liquorice [ˈlɪkərɪs] N regaliz *m*

liquor store N (*US*) bodega, *tienda de vinos y bebidas alcohólicas*

Lisbon [ˈlɪzbən] N Lisboa

lisp [lɪsp] N ceceo ▶ VI cecear

lissom [ˈlɪsəm] ADJ ágil

★**list** [lɪst] N lista; (*of ship*) inclinación *f*; **shopping ~** lista de las compras ▶ VT (*write down*) hacer una lista de; (*mention*) enumerar; (*Comput*) hacer un listado de ▶ VI (*ship*) inclinarse; *see also* **lists**

listed building [ˈlɪstɪd-] N (*Arch*) edificio de interés histórico-artístico

listed company [ˈlɪstɪd-] N compañía cotizable

★**listen** [ˈlɪsn] VI escuchar, oír; (*pay attention*) atender; **to ~ to sth/sb** escuchar algo/a algn

listener [ˈlɪsnəʳ] N oyente *mf*

listeria [lɪsˈtɪərɪə] N listeria

listing [ˈlɪstɪŋ] N (*Comput*) listado

listless [ˈlɪstlɪs] ADJ apático, indiferente

listlessly [ˈlɪstlɪslɪ] ADV con indiferencia

listlessness [ˈlɪstlɪsnɪs] N indiferencia, apatía

list price N precio de catálogo

lists [lɪsts] NPL (*History*) liza *sg*; **to enter the ~ (against sb/sth)** salir a la palestra (contra algn/algo)

lit [lɪt] PT, PP *of* **light**

litany [ˈlɪtənɪ] N letanía

liter [ˈliːtəʳ] N (*US*) = **litre**

literacy [ˈlɪtərəsɪ] N capacidad *f* de leer y escribir

literacy campaign N campaña de alfabetización

literal [ˈlɪtərl] ADJ literal

literally [ˈlɪtrəlɪ] ADV literalmente

literary [ˈlɪtərərɪ] ADJ literario

literate [ˈlɪtərət] ADJ que sabe leer y escribir; (*educated*) culto

★**literature** [ˈlɪtərɪtʃəʳ] N literatura; (*brochures etc*) folletos *mpl*

lithe [laɪð] ADJ ágil

lithography [lɪˈθɔgrəfɪ] N litografía

Lithuania [lɪθjuˈeɪnɪə] N Lituania

Lithuanian [lɪθjuˈeɪnɪən] ADJ lituano ▶ N lituano(-a); (*Ling*) lituano

litigate [ˈlɪtɪgeɪt] VI litigar

litigation [lɪtɪˈgeɪʃən] N litigio

litmus paper [ˈlɪtməs-] N papel *m* de tornasol

litre, (*US*) **liter** [ˈliːtəʳ] N litro

litter [ˈlɪtəʳ] N (*rubbish*) basura; (*paper*) papeles *mpl* (tirados); (*young animals*) camada, cría

litter bin N (*BRIT*) papelera

littered [ˈlɪtəd] ADJ: **~ with** lleno de

litter lout, (*US*) **litterbug** [ˈlɪtəbʌg] N *persona que tira papeles usados en la vía pública*

★**little** [ˈlɪtl] ADJ (*small*) pequeño, chico (*LAM*); (*not* *much*) poco; (*diminutive*): **~ house** casita; **a ~ bit** un poquito; **~ finger** (dedo) meñique *m*; **for a ~ while** (durante) un rato; **with ~ difficulty** sin problema *or* dificultad ▶ ADV poco; **a ~** un poco (de); **~ by ~** poco a poco; **as ~ as possible** lo menos posible

little-known [ˈlɪtlˈnəʊn] ADJ poco conocido

liturgy [ˈlɪtədʒɪ] N liturgia

★**live¹** [laɪv] ADJ (*animal*) vivo; (*wire*) conectado; (*broadcast*) en directo; (*issue*) de actualidad; (*unexploded*) sin explotar

★**live²** [lɪv] VI vivir; **to ~ in London** vivir en Londres; **to ~ together** vivir juntos ▶ VT (*a life*) llevar; (*experience*) vivir
▶ **live down** VT hacer olvidar
▶ **live off** VT FUS (*land, fish etc*) vivir de; (*pej: parents etc*) vivir a costa de
▶ **live on** VT FUS (*food*) vivir de, alimentarse de; **to ~ on £50 a week** vivir con 50 libras semanales *or* a la semana
▶ **live out** VI (*student*) ser externo ▶ VT: **to ~ out one's days** *or* **life** pasar el resto de la vida
▶ **live up** VT: **to ~ it up** (*inf*) tirarse la gran vida
▶ **live up to** VT FUS (*fulfil*) cumplir con; (*justify*) justificar

liveblog [ˈlaɪvblɒg] N blog *m* en directo ▶ VT, VI bloguear en directo

live-in [ˈlɪvɪn] ADJ: **~ partner** pareja, compañero(-a) sentimental; **~ maid** asistenta interna

livelihood [ˈlaɪvlɪhʊd] N sustento

liveliness [ˈlaɪvlɪnɪs] N viveza

lively [ˈlaɪvlɪ] ADJ (*gen*) vivo; (*interesting: place, book etc*) animado; (*pace*) rápido; (*party, tune*) alegre

liven up [ˈlaɪvn-] VT (*discussion, evening*) animar ▶ VI animarse

liver [ˈlɪvəʳ] N hígado

liverish [ˈlɪvərɪʃ] ADJ: **to feel ~** sentirse *or* encontrarse mal, no estar muy católico

Liverpudlian [lɪvəˈpʌdlɪən] ADJ de Liverpool ▶ N nativo(-a) *or* habitante *m/f* de Liverpool

livery [ˈlɪvərɪ] N librea

lives [laɪvz] NPL *of* **life**

livestock [ˈlaɪvstɒk] N ganado

livestream [ˈlaɪvstriːm] N transmisión *f* en directo ▶ VT transmitir en directo

live wire [laɪv-] N (*fig: inf*): **he's a real ~!** ¡tiene una marcha!

livid [ˈlɪvɪd] ADJ lívido; (*furious*) furioso

living [ˈlɪvɪŋ] ADJ (*alive*) vivo; **in ~ memory** que se recuerde *or* recuerda ▶ N: **to earn** *or* **make a ~** ganarse la vida; **cost of ~** coste *m* de la vida

living conditions NPL condiciones *fpl* de vida

living expenses NPL gastos *mpl* de mantenimiento

living room N sala (de estar), living *m* (LAM)

living standards NPL nivel *msg* de vida

living wage N sueldo suficiente para vivir

living will N testamento vital

lizard [ˈlɪzəd] N lagartija

llama [ˈlɑːmə] N llama

LLB N ABBR (= *Bachelor of Laws*) Ldo.(-a.) en Dcho.; *see also* **bachelor's degree**

LLD N ABBR (= *Doctor of Laws*) Dr(a). en Dcho.

LMT N ABBR (*US*: = *Local Mean Time*) hora local

★**load** [ləʊd] N (*gen*) carga; (*weight*) peso; **a ~ of, loads of** (*fig*) (gran) cantidad de, montones de ▶ VT (*also Comput*) cargar; **to ~ (up) with** cargar con *or* de

loaded [ˈləʊdɪd] ADJ (*dice*) cargado; (*question*) intencionado; (*inf: rich*) forrado (de dinero)

loading [ˈləʊdɪŋ] N (*Comm*) sobreprima

loading bay N área de carga y descarga

loaf [ləʊf] (*pl* **loaves** [ləʊvz]) N (barra de) pan *m* ▶ VI (*also*: **loaf about, loaf around**) holgazanear

loam [ləʊm] N marga

★**loan** [ləʊn] N préstamo; (*Comm*) empréstito; **on ~** (*book, painting*) prestado; **to raise a ~** (*money*) procurar un empréstito ▶ VT prestar

loan account N cuenta de crédito

loan capital N empréstito

loan shark N (*pej*) prestamista *mf* sin escrúpulos

loath [ləʊθ] ADJ: **to be ~ to do sth** ser reacio a hacer algo

loathe [ləʊð] VT aborrecer; (*person*) odiar

loathing [ˈləʊðɪŋ] N aversión *f*; odio

loathsome [ˈləʊðsəm] ADJ asqueroso, repugnante; (*person*) odioso

loaves [ləʊvz] PL *of* **loaf**

lob [lɒb] VT (*ball*) volear por alto

lobby [ˈlɒbɪ] N vestíbulo, sala de espera; (*Pol: pressure group*) grupo de presión ▶ VT presionar

lobbyist [ˈlɒbɪɪst] N cabildero(-a)

lobe [ləʊb] N lóbulo

lobster [ˈlɒbstəʳ] N langosta

lobster pot N nasa, langostera

★**local** [ˈləʊkl] ADJ local ▶ N (*pub*) bar *m* ■ **the locals** NPL los vecinos, los del lugar

local anaesthetic, (*US*) **local anesthetic** N (*Med*) anestesia local

local authority N municipio, ayuntamiento (*SP*)

local call N (*Tel*) llamada local

local government N gobierno municipal

locality [ləʊˈkælɪtɪ] N localidad *f*

localize [ˈləʊkəlaɪz] VT localizar

locally [ˈləʊkəlɪ] ADV en la vecindad

locate [ləʊˈkeɪt] VT (*find*) localizar; (*situate*): **to be located in** estar situado en

location [ləʊˈkeɪʃən] N situación *f*; **on ~** (*Cine*) en exteriores, fuera del estudio

loch [lɒx] N lago

★**lock** [lɒk] N (*of door, box*) cerradura, chapa (LAM); (*of canal*) esclusa; (*of hair*) mechón *m*; **~ stock and barrel** (*fig*) por completo *or* entero; **on full ~**

(*Aut*) con el volante girado al máximo ▸ VT (*with key*) cerrar con llave; (*immobilize*) inmovilizar ▸ VI (*door etc*) cerrarse con llave; (*wheels*) trabarse
▸ **lock away** VT (*valuables*) guardar bajo llave; (*criminal*) encerrar
▸ **lock in** VT encerrar
▸ **lock out** VT (*person*) cerrar la puerta a; **the workers were locked out** los trabajadores tuvieron que enfrentarse con un cierre patronal
▸ **lock up** VT (*criminal*) meter en la cárcel; (*psychiatric patient*) encerrar; (*house*) cerrar (con llave) ▸ VI echar la llave

lockdown [ˈlɔkdaun] N: **to be in** or **under ~** (*place*) estar cerrado por una emergencia; **to be on ~** (*prisoner*) estar aislado

locker [ˈlɔkəʳ] N casillero

locker-room [ˈlɔkərum] N (*US Sport*) vestuario

locket [ˈlɔkɪt] N medallón m

lockout [ˈlɔkaut] N (*Industry*) paro or cierre m patronal, lockout m

locksmith [ˈlɔksmɪθ] N cerrajero(-a)

lock-up [ˈlɔkʌp] N (*prison*) cárcel f; (*cell*) jaula; (*also*: **lock-up garage**) jaula, cochera

locomotive [ləukəˈməutɪv] N locomotora

locum [ˈləukəm] N (*Med*) (médico(-a)) suplente m/f

locust [ˈləukəst] N langosta

lodge [lɔdʒ] N casa del guarda; (*porter's*) portería; (*Freemasonry*) logia ▸ VI (*person*): **to ~ (with)** alojarse (en casa de) ▸ VT (*complaint*) presentar

lodger [ˈlɔdʒəʳ] N huésped mf

lodging [ˈlɔdʒɪŋ] N alojamiento, hospedaje m

lodging house [ˈlɔdʒɪŋ-] N pensión f, casa de huéspedes

lodgings [ˈlɔdʒɪŋz] NPL alojamiento sg; (*house*) casa sg de huéspedes

loft [lɔft] N desván m

lofty [ˈlɔftɪ] ADJ alto; (*haughty*) altivo, arrogante; (*sentiments, aims*) elevado, noble

★**log** [lɔg] N (*of wood*) leño, tronco; (*written account*) diario; (*book*) = **logbook** ▸ N ABBR (= *logarithm*) log ▸ VT anotar, registrar
▸ **log in, log on** VI (*Comput*) iniciar la sesión
▸ **log off, log out** VI (*Comput*) finalizar la sesión

logarithm [ˈlɔgərɪðəm] N logaritmo

logbook [ˈlɔgbuk] N (*Naut*) diario de a bordo; (*Aviat*) libro de vuelo; (*of car*) documentación f (del coche)

log cabin N cabaña de troncos

log fire N fuego de leña

logger [ˈlɔgəʳ] N leñador(a) m/f

loggerheads [ˈlɔgəhɛdz] NPL: **at ~ (with)** de pique (con)

logic [ˈlɔdʒɪk] N lógica

logical [ˈlɔdʒɪkl] ADJ lógico

logically [ˈlɔdʒɪkəlɪ] ADV lógicamente

login [ˈlɔgɪn] N (*Comput*) login m

logistics [lɔˈdʒɪstɪks] N logística

log jam N: **to break the ~** poner fin al estancamiento

logo [ˈləugəu] N logotipo

loin [lɔɪn] N (*Culin*) lomo, solomillo ■ **loins** NPL lomos mpl

loin cloth N taparrabos m inv

loiter [ˈlɔɪtəʳ] VI vagar; (*pej*) merodear

LOL ABBR (*inf*: = *laughing out loud*) LOL, qué risa

loll [lɔl] VI (*also*: **loll about**) repantigarse

lollipop [ˈlɔlɪpɔp] N piruleta f, pirulí m; (*iced*) polo

lollipop lady N (BRIT) ver nota

lollipop man N (*irreg*) (BRIT) persona encargada de ayudar a los niños a cruzar la calle

> Se llama **lollipop man** o **lollipop lady** a la persona encargada de parar el tráfico en las carreteras cercanas a los colegios británicos para que los niños las crucen sin peligro. Van vestidas con un abrigo de color luminoso y llevan una señal de stop en un poste portátil, la cual recuerda por su forma a una piruleta, de ahí su nombre.

lollop [ˈlɔləp] VI (BRIT) moverse desgarbadamente

lolly [ˈlɔlɪ] N (*inf*: *ice cream*) polo; (: *lollipop*) piruleta; (: *money*) guita

★**London** [ˈlʌndən] N Londres m

★**Londoner** [ˈlʌndənəʳ] N londinense mf

lone [ləun] ADJ solitario

loneliness [ˈləunlɪnɪs] N soledad f, aislamiento

lonely [ˈləunlɪ] ADJ (*situation*) solitario; (*person*) solo; (*place*) aislado

lonely hearts ADJ: **~ ad** anuncio de la sección de contactos; **~ column** sección f de contactos

lone parent family N familia monoparental

loner [ˈləunəʳ] N solitario(-a)

lonesome [ˈləunsəm] ADJ (*esp US*) = **lonely**

★**long** [lɔŋ] ADJ largo; **in the ~ run** a la larga; **how ~ is the street?** ¿cuánto tiene la calle de largo?; **how ~ is the lesson?** ¿cuánto dura la clase?; **six metres ~** que mide seis metros, de seis metros de largo; **at ~ last** al fin, por fin ▸ ADV mucho tiempo, largamente; **don't be ~!** ¡no tardes!, ¡vuelve pronto!; **I shan't be ~** termino pronto; **so** or **as ~ as** mientras, con tal de que; **six months ~** que dura seis meses, de seis meses de duración; **all night ~** toda la noche; **~ ago** hace mucho (tiempo); **he no longer comes** ya no viene; **~ before** mucho antes ▸ VI: **to ~ for sth** anhelar algo ▸ N: **the ~ and the short of it is that ...** (*fig*) en resumidas cuentas ...; **before ~** (+ *future*) dentro de poco; (+ *past*) poco tiempo después

long-distance [lɔŋˈdɪstəns] ADJ (*race*) de larga distancia; (*call*) interurbano

longevity [lɔnˈdʒɛvɪtɪ] N longevidad f

long-haired [ˈlɔŋˈhɛəd] ADJ de pelo largo

longhand [ˈlɔŋhænd] N escritura (corriente)

long-haul [ˈlɔŋhɔːl] ADJ (*flight*) de larga distancia

longing ['lɔŋɪŋ] N anhelo, ansia; (*nostalgia*) nostalgia ► ADJ anhelante

longingly ['lɔŋɪŋlɪ] ADV con ansia

longitude ['lɔŋɡɪtjuːd] N longitud *f*

long jump N salto de longitud

long-life ['lɔŋlaɪf] ADJ (*batteries*) de larga duración; (*milk*) uperizado

long-lost ['lɔŋlɔst] ADJ desaparecido hace mucho tiempo

long-playing record ['lɔŋpleɪɪŋ-] N elepé *m*, disco de larga duración

long-range ['lɔŋ'reɪndʒ] ADJ de gran alcance; (*weather forecast*) a largo plazo

longshoreman ['lɔŋʃɔːmən] N (*irreg*) (US) estibador *m*

long-sighted ['lɔŋ'saɪtɪd] ADJ (BRIT) présbita

long-standing ['lɔŋ'stændɪŋ] ADJ de mucho tiempo

long-suffering [lɔŋ'sʌfərɪŋ] ADJ sufrido

long-term ['lɔŋtəːm] ADJ a largo plazo

long wave N onda larga

long-winded [lɔŋ'wɪndɪd] ADJ prolijo

loo [luː] N (BRIT *inf*) wáter *m*

loofah ['luːfə] N esponja de lufa

★look [luk] VI mirar; (*seem*) parecer; (*building etc*): **to ~ south/on to the sea** dar al sur/al mar; **to ~ ahead** mirar hacia delante; **it looks about four metres long** yo calculo que tiene unos cuatro metros de largo; **it looks all right to me** a mí me parece que está bien; **~ (here)!** (*expressing annoyance etc*) ¡oye!; **~!** (*expressing surprise*) ¡mira! ► N mirada; (*glance*) vistazo; (*appearance*) aire *m*, aspecto; **to have a ~ at sth** echar un vistazo a algo; **to have a ~ for sth** buscar algo ▓ **looks** NPL físico *sg*, belleza *sg*
► **look after** VT FUS (*care for*) cuidar a; (*deal with*) encargarse de
► **look around** VI echar una mirada alrededor
► **look at** VT FUS mirar; (*consider*) considerar
► **look back** VI mirar hacia atrás; **to ~ back at sb/sth** mirar hacia atrás algo/a algn; **to ~ back on** (*event, period*) recordar
► **look down on** VT FUS (*fig*) despreciar, mirar con desprecio
► **look for** VT FUS buscar
► **look forward to** VT FUS esperar con ilusión; (*in letters*): **we ~ forward to hearing from you** quedamos a la espera de su respuesta *or* contestación; **I'm not looking forward to it** no tengo ganas de eso, no me hace ilusión
► **look in** VI: **to ~ in on sb** (*visit*) pasar por casa de algn
► **look into** VT FUS investigar
► **look on** VI mirar (como espectador)
► **look out** VI (*beware*): **to ~ out (for)** tener cuidado (de)
► **look out for** VT FUS (*seek*) buscar; (*await*) esperar
► **look over** VT (*essay*) revisar; (*town, building*) inspeccionar, registrar; (*person*) examinar
► **look round** VI (*turn*) volver la cabeza; **to ~ round for sth** buscar algo

► **look through** VT FUS (*papers, book*) hojear; (*briefly*) echar un vistazo a; (*telescope*) mirar por
► **look to** VT FUS ocuparse de; (*rely on*) contar con
► **look up** VI mirar hacia arriba; (*improve*) mejorar ► VT (*word*) buscar; (*friend*) visitar
► **look up to** VT FUS admirar

look-out ['lukaut] N (*tower etc*) puesto de observación; (*person*) vigía *mf*; **to be on the ~ for sth** estar al acecho de algo

look-up table ['lukʌp-] N (*Comput*) tabla de consulta

loom [luːm] N telar *m* ► VI: **~ (up)** (*threaten*) surgir, amenazar; (*event: approach*) aproximarse

loony ['luːnɪ] ADJ, N (!) loco(-a) *m/f*

loop [luːp] N lazo; (*bend*) vuelta, recodo; (*Comput*) bucle *m*

loophole ['luːphəul] N laguna

★loose [luːs] ADJ (*gen*) suelto; (*not tight*) flojo; (*wobbly etc*) movedizo; (*clothes*) ancho; (*morals, discipline*) relajado; **~ connection** (*Elec*) hilo desempalmado; **to be at a ~ end** *or* (US) **at ~ ends** no saber qué hacer; **to tie up ~ ends** (*fig*) no dejar ningún cabo suelto, atar cabos ► VT (*free*) soltar; (*slacken*) aflojar; (*also*: **loose off**: *arrow*) disparar, soltar

loose change N cambio

loose chippings [-'tʃɪpɪŋz] NPL (*on road*) gravilla *sg* suelta

loose-fitting ['luːsfɪtɪŋ] ADJ suelto

loose-leaf ['luːsliːf] ADJ: **~ binder** *or* **folder** carpeta de anillas

loose-limbed ['luːslɪmd] ADJ ágil, suelto

loosely ['luːslɪ] ADV libremente, aproximadamente

loosely-knit [-nɪt] ADJ de estructura abierta

loosen ['luːsn] VT (*free*) soltar; (*untie*) desatar; (*slacken*) aflojar
► **loosen up** VI (*before game*) hacer (ejercicios de) precalentamiento; (*inf*: *relax*) soltarse, relajarse

looseness ['luːsnɪs] N soltura; flojedad *f*

loot [luːt] N botín *m* ► VT saquear

looter ['luːtər] N saqueador(a) *m/f*

looting ['luːtɪŋ] N pillaje *m*

lop [lɔp] **: to ~ off** VT cortar; (*branches*) podar

lop-sided ['lɔp'saɪdɪd] ADJ torcido; (*fig*) desequilibrado

lord [lɔːd] N señor *m*; **L~ Smith** Lord Smith; **the L~** el Señor; **the (House of) Lords** (BRIT) la Cámara de los Lores

lordly ['lɔːdlɪ] ADJ señorial

Lordship ['lɔːdʃɪp] N: **your ~** su Señoría

lore [lɔːr] N saber *m* popular, tradiciones *fpl*

lorry ['lɔrɪ] N (BRIT) camión *m*

lorry driver N camionero(-a)

lorry load N carga

★lose [luːz] (*pt, pp* **lost** [lɔst]) VT perder; **to ~ (time)** (*clock*) atrasarse; **to ~ no time (in doing sth)** no tardar (en hacer algo); **to get lost**

(*object*) extraviarse; (*person*) perderse ▶ VI perder, ser vencido

▶ **lose out** VI salir perdiendo

loser ['luːzə^r] N perdedor(a) *m/f*; **to be a bad ~** no saber perder

losing ['luːzɪŋ] ADJ (*team etc*) vencido, perdedor(a)

★**loss** [lɒs] N pérdida; **heavy losses** (*Mil*) grandes pérdidas *fpl*; **to be at a ~** no saber qué hacer; **to be a dead ~** ser completamente inútil; **to make a ~** sufrir pérdidas; **to cut one's losses** reducir las pérdidas; **to sell sth at a ~** vender algo perdiendo dinero

loss adjuster N (*Insurance*) perito(-a) *or* tasador(a) *m/f* de pérdidas

loss leader N (*Comm*) artículo de promoción

★**lost** [lɒst] PT, PP *of* **lose** ▶ ADJ perdido; **~ in thought** absorto, ensimismado

lost and found N (*US*) objetos *mpl* perdidos

lost cause N causa perdida

lost property N (*BRIT*) objetos *mpl* perdidos

lost property office, lost property department N (*BRIT*) departamento de objetos perdidos

★**lot** [lɒt] N (*at auction*) lote *m*; (*destiny*) suerte *f*; **the ~** el todo, todos *mpl*, todas *fpl*; **a ~** mucho, bastante; **a ~ of, lots of** muchos(-as); (*with singular noun*) mucho(-a); **I read a ~** leo bastante; **to draw lots (for sth)** echar suertes (para decidir algo)

lotion ['ləʊʃən] N loción *f*

lottery ['lɒtəri] N lotería

★**loud** [laud] ADJ (*voice, sound*) fuerte; (*laugh, shout*) estrepitoso; (*gaudy*) chillón(-ona) ▶ ADV (*speak etc*) fuerte; **out ~** en voz alta

loudhailer [laud'heɪlə^r] N (*BRIT*) megáfono

loudly ['laudli] ADV (*noisily*) fuerte; (*aloud*) en alta voz

loudness ['laudnɪs] N (*of sound etc*) fuerza

loudspeaker [laud'spiːkə^r] N altavoz *m*

lounge [laundʒ] N salón *m*, sala de estar; (*of hotel*) salón *m*; (*of airport*) sala de embarque ▶ VI (*also:* **lounge about, lounge around**) holgazanear, no hacer nada; *see also* **pub**

lounge bar N salón *m*

lounge suit N (*BRIT*) traje *m* de calle

louse [laus] (*pl* **lice** [laɪs]) N piojo

▶ **louse up** VT (*inf*) echar a perder

lousy ['lauzi] ADJ (*inf*) vil, asqueroso; (*ill*) fatal

lout [laut] N gamberro(-a)

louvre, (*US*) **louver** ['luːvə^r] ADJ: **~ door** puerta de rejilla; **~ window** ventana de libro

lovable ['lʌvəbl] ADJ amable, simpático

★**love** [lʌv] N (*romantic, sexual*) amor *m*; (*kind, caring*) cariño; **to send one's ~ to sb** dar sus recuerdos a algn; **~ from Anne** (*in letter*) con cariño de Anne; **to be in ~ with** estar enamorado de; **to make ~** hacer el amor; **for the ~ of** por amor a; **"15 ~"** (*Tennis*) "15 a cero" ▶ VT amar, querer; **I**

~ to read me encanta leer; **I ~ you** te quiero; **I ~ paella** me encanta la paella; **I'd ~ to come** me gustaría muchísimo venir

love affair N aventura sentimental *or* amorosa

love child N (*irreg*) hijo(-a) natural

loved ones ['lʌvdwʌnz] NPL seres *mpl* queridos

love-hate relationship ['lʌvheɪt-] N relación *f* de amor y odio

love letter N carta de amor

love life N vida sentimental

★**lovely** ['lʌvli] ADJ (*delightful*) precioso, encantador(a), lindo (*esp LAM*); (*beautiful*) precioso, lindo (*esp LAM*); **we had a ~ time** lo pasamos estupendo

lovemaking ['lʌvmeɪkɪŋ] N relaciones *fpl* sexuales

lover ['lʌvə^r] N amante *mf*; (*amateur*): **a ~ of** un(a) aficionado(-a) *or* un(a) amante de

lovesick ['lʌvsɪk] ADJ enfermo de amor, amartelado

love song ['lʌvsɔŋ] N canción *f* de amor

loving ['lʌvɪŋ] ADJ amoroso, cariñoso

lovingly ['lʌvɪŋli] ADV amorosamente, cariñosamente

★**low** [ləʊ] ADJ, ADV bajo; **to feel ~** sentirse deprimido; **to turn (down) ~** bajar ▶ N (*Meteorology*) área de baja presión; **to reach a new** *or* **an all-time ~** llegar a su punto más bajo ▶ VI (*cow*) mugir

low-alcohol [ləʊ'ælkəhɒl] ADJ bajo en alcohol

lowbrow ['ləʊbrau] ADJ (*person*) de poca cultura

low-calorie ['ləʊ'kælərɪ] ADJ bajo en calorías

low-carb [ləʊ'kɑːb] ADJ (*inf*) bajo(-a) en carbohidratos

low-cut ['ləʊkʌt] ADJ (*dress*) escotado

low-down ['ləʊdaun] N (*inf*): **he gave me the ~ on it** me puso al corriente ▶ ADJ (*mean*) vil, bajo

★**lower** ['ləʊə^r] ADJ más bajo; (*less important*) menos importante ▶ VT bajar; (*reduce: price*) reducir, rebajar; (: *resistance*) debilitar; **to ~ o.s. to** (*fig*) rebajarse a ▶ VI ['lauə^r]: **to ~ (at sb)** fulminar (a algn) con la mirada

lower case N (*Typ*) minúscula

Lower House N (*Pol*): **the ~** la Cámara baja

lowering ['lauərɪŋ] ADJ (*sky*) amenazador(a)

low-fat ['ləʊ'fæt] ADJ (*milk, yoghurt*) desnatado; (*diet*) bajo en calorías

low-key ['ləʊ'kiː] ADJ de mínima intensidad; (*operation*) de poco perfil

lowland ['ləʊlənd] N tierra baja

low-level ['ləʊlɛvl] ADJ de bajo nivel; (*flying*) a poca altura

low-loader ['ləʊləʊdə^r] N camión *m* de caja a bajo nivel

lowly ['ləʊli] ADJ humilde

low-lying [ləʊ'laɪɪŋ] ADJ bajo

low-rise ['ləʊraɪz] ADJ bajo

low-tech ['ləutɛk] ADJ de baja tecnología, tradicional

loyal ['lɔɪəl] ADJ leal

loyalist ['lɔɪəlɪst] N legitimista *mf*

loyally ['lɔɪəlɪ] ADV lealmente

loyalty ['lɔɪəltɪ] N lealtad *f*

loyalty card N (*Brit*) tarjeta cliente

lozenge ['lɔzɪndʒ] N (*Med*) pastilla

LP N ABBR (= *long-playing record*) elepé *m*

LPG N ABBR (= *liquefied petroleum gas*) GLP *m* (= *Gas Licuado de Petróleo*)

L-plates ['ɛlpleɪts] NPL (*Brit*) (placas *fpl* de) la L

LPN N ABBR (*US*: = *Licensed Practical Nurse*) enfermero(-a) practicante

LRAM N ABBR (*Brit*) = **Licentiate of the Royal Academy of Music**

LSAT N ABBR (*US*) = **Law School Admissions Test**

LSD N ABBR (= *lysergic acid diethylamide*) LSD *m*; (*Brit*: = *pounds, shillings and pence*) sistema monetario usado en Gran Bretaña hasta 1971

LSE N ABBR = **London School of Economics**

LT ABBR (*Elec*) = **low tension**

Lt. ABBR (= *lieutenant*) Tte.

Ltd ABBR (*Comm*: = *limited company*) S.A.

lubricant ['lu:brɪkənt] N lubricante *m*

lubricate ['lu:brɪkeɪt] VT lubricar, engrasar

lubrication [lu:brɪ'keɪʃən] N lubricación *f*

lucid ['lu:sɪd] ADJ lúcido

lucidity [lu:'sɪdɪtɪ] N lucidez *f*

lucidly ['lu:sɪdlɪ] ADV lúcidamente

★**luck** [lʌk] N suerte *f*; **good/bad ~** buena/mala suerte; **good ~!** ¡(que tengas) suerte!; **to be in ~** estar de suerte; **to be out of ~** tener mala suerte; **bad** or **hard** or **tough ~!** ¡qué pena!

luckily ['lʌkɪlɪ] ADV afortunadamente

luckless ['lʌklɪs] ADJ desafortunado

★**lucky** ['lʌkɪ] ADJ afortunado; (*at cards etc*) con suerte; (*object*) que trae suerte

lucrative ['lu:krətɪv] ADJ lucrativo

ludicrous ['lu:dɪkrəs] ADJ absurdo

ludo ['lu:dəu] N parchís *m*

lug [lʌg] VT (*drag*) arrastrar

luggage ['lʌgɪdʒ] N equipaje *m*

luggage rack N (*in train*) rejilla, redecilla; (*on car*) baca, portaequipajes *m inv*

luggage van N furgón *m* or vagón *m* de equipaje

lugubrious [lu'gu:brɪəs] ADJ lúgubre

lukewarm ['lu:kwɔ:m] ADJ tibio, templado

lull [lʌl] N tregua ▶ VT (*child*) acunar; (*person, fear*) calmar; **to ~ sb to sleep** arrullar a algn; **to ~ sb into a false sense of security** dar a algn una falsa sensación de seguridad

lullaby ['lʌləbaɪ] N nana

lumbago [lʌm'beɪgəu] N lumbago

lumber ['lʌmbə'] N (*junk*) trastos *mpl* viejos; (*wood*) maderos *mpl* ▶ VT (*Brit inf*): **to ~ sb with sth/sb** hacer que algn cargue con algo/algn ▶ VI (*also:* **lumber about, lumber along**) moverse pesadamente

lumberjack ['lʌmbədʒæk] N maderero

lumber room N (*Brit*) cuarto trastero

lumber yard N (*US*) almacén *m* de madera

luminous ['lu:mɪnəs] ADJ luminoso

lump [lʌmp] N terrón *m*; (*fragment*) trozo; (*in sauce*) grumo; (*in throat*) nudo; (*swelling*) bulto ▶ VT (*also:* **lump together**) juntar; (: *persons*) poner juntos

lump sum N suma global

lumpy ['lʌmpɪ] ADJ (*sauce*) lleno de grumos

lunacy ['lu:nəsɪ] N locura

lunar ['lu:nə'] ADJ lunar

lunatic ['lu:nətɪk] ADJ, N (!) loco(-a) *m/f*

lunatic asylum N (!) manicomio

★**lunch** [lʌntʃ] N almuerzo, comida; **to invite sb to** or **for ~** invitar a algn a almorzar ▶ VI almorzar

lunch break, lunch hour N hora del almuerzo

luncheon ['lʌntʃən] N almuerzo

luncheon meat N *tipo de fiambre*

luncheon voucher N vale *m* de comida

lunchtime ['lʌntʃtaɪm] N hora del almuerzo or de comer

lung [lʌŋ] N pulmón *m*

lung cancer N cáncer *m* del pulmón

lunge [lʌndʒ] VI (*also:* **lunge forward**) abalanzarse; **to ~ at** arremeter contra

lupin ['lu:pɪn] N altramuz *m*

lurch [lə:tʃ] VI dar sacudidas ▶ N sacudida; **to leave sb in the ~** dejar a algn plantado

lure [luə'] N (*bait*) cebo; (*decoy*) señuelo; (*attraction*) atracción *f* ▶ VT convencer con engaños

lurid ['luərɪd] ADJ (*colour*) chillón(-ona); (*account*) sensacional; (*detail*) horripilante

lurk [lə:k] VI (*hide*) esconderse; (*wait*) estar al acecho; (*fig*) acechar

luscious ['lʌʃəs] ADJ delicioso

lush [lʌʃ] ADJ exuberante

lust [lʌst] N lujuria; (*greed*) codicia
▶ **lust after** VT FUS codiciar

lustful ['lʌstful] ADJ lascivo, lujurioso

lustre, (*US*) **luster** ['lʌstə'] N lustre *m*, brillo

lustrous ['lʌstrəs] ADJ brillante

lusty ['lʌstɪ] ADJ robusto, fuerte

lute [lu:t] N laúd *m*

★**Luxembourg** ['lʌksəmbə:g] N Luxemburgo

luxuriant [lʌg'zjuərɪənt] ADJ exuberante

luxurious [lʌg'zjuərɪəs] ADJ lujoso

★**luxury** ['lʌkʃərɪ] N lujo ▶ CPD de lujo

luxury tax N impuesto de lujo

LV N ABBR (*Brit*) = **luncheon voucher**

LW ABBR (*Radio*) = **long wave**

Lycra® ['laɪkrə] N licra®

lying [ˈlaɪɪŋ] N mentiras *fpl* ▶ ADJ (*statement, story*) falso; (*person*) mentiroso

lynch [lɪntʃ] VT linchar

lynx [lɪnks] N lince *m*

Lyons [ˈlaɪənz] N Lyón *m*

lyre [ˈlaɪə^r] N lira

lyric [ˈlɪrɪk] ADJ lírico ■ **lyrics** NPL (*of song*) letra *sg*

lyrical [ˈlɪrɪkl] ADJ lírico

Mm

M, m [ɛm] N (letter) M, m f; **M for Mary**, (US) **M for Mike** M de Madrid

M N ABBR (BRIT) = **motorway; the M8** ≈ la A8 ▶ ABBR (= medium) M

m ABBR (= metre) m.; = **mile; million**

MA N ABBR (Scol) = **Master of Arts**; (US) = **Military Academy** ▶ ABBR (US) = **Massachusetts**

ma [mɑ:] (inf) N mamá

mac [mæk] N (BRIT) impermeable m

macabre [məˈkɑ:brə] ADJ macabro

macaroni [mækəˈrəʊnɪ] N macarrones mpl

macaroon [mækəˈru:n] N macarrón m, mostachón m

mace [meɪs] N (weapon, ceremonial) maza; (spice) macis f

Macedonia [mæsɪˈdəʊnɪə] N Macedonia

Macedonian [mæsɪˈdəʊnɪən] ADJ macedonio ▶ N macedonio(-a); (Ling) macedonio

machinations [mæʃɪˈneɪʃənz] NPL intrigas fpl, maquinaciones fpl

★machine [məˈʃi:n] N máquina ▶ VT (dress etc) coser a máquina; (Tech) trabajar a máquina

machine code N (Comput) código máquina

machine gun N ametralladora

machine language N (Comput) lenguaje m máquina

machine readable ADJ (Comput) legible por máquina

machinery [məˈʃi:nərɪ] N maquinaria; (fig) mecanismo

machine shop N taller m de máquinas

machine tool N máquina herramienta

machine translation N traducción f automática

machine washable ADJ lavable a máquina

machinist [məˈʃi:nɪst] N operario(-a) (de máquina)

macho [ˈmætʃəʊ] ADJ macho

mackerel [ˈmækrl] N pl inv caballa

mackintosh [ˈmækɪntɔʃ] N (BRIT) impermeable m

macro... [mækrəʊ] PREF macro...

macro-economics [ˈmækrəʊi:kəˈnɔmɪks] N macroeconomía

★mad [mæd] ADJ loco; (idea) disparatado; (angry) furioso, enojado (LAM); **~ (at or with sb)** furioso (con algn); **to be ~ (keen) about** or **on sth** estar loco por algo; **to go ~** volverse loco, enloquecer(se)

madam [ˈmædəm] N señora; **can I help you, ~?** ¿le puedo ayudar, señora?; **M~ Chairman** Señora Presidenta

madcap [ˈmædkæp] ADJ (inf) alocado, disparatado

mad cow disease N encefalopatía espongiforme bovina

madden [ˈmædn] VT volver loco

maddening [ˈmædnɪŋ] ADJ enloquecedor(a)

made [meɪd] PT, PP of **make**

Madeira [məˈdɪərə] N (Geo) Madeira; (wine) madeira m

made-to-measure [ˈmeɪdtəmɛʒəʳ] ADJ (BRIT) hecho a la medida

made-up [ˈmeɪdʌp] ADJ (story) ficticio

madhouse [ˈmædhaʊs] N (also fig) manicomio

madly [ˈmædlɪ] ADV locamente

madman [ˈmædmən] N (irreg) loco

madness [ˈmædnɪs] N locura

Madonna [məˈdɔnə] N Virgen f

Madrid [məˈdrɪd] N Madrid m

madrigal [ˈmædrɪgəl] N madrigal m

Mafia [ˈmæfɪə] N Mafia

mag [mæg] N ABBR (BRIT inf) = **magazine**

★magazine [mægəˈzi:n] N revista; (Mil: store) almacén m; (of firearm) recámara

maggot [ˈmægət] N gusano

★magic [ˈmædʒɪk] N magia ▶ ADJ mágico

magical [ˈmædʒɪkəl] ADJ mágico

magician [mə'dʒɪʃən] N mago(-a)

magistrate ['mædʒɪstreɪt] N juez(a) m/f (municipal); **Magistrates' Court** (BRIT) see **crown court**

magnanimity [mægnə'nɪmɪtɪ] N magnanimidad f

magnanimous [mæg'nænɪməs] ADJ magnánimo

magnate ['mægneɪt] N magnate mf

magnesium [mæg'niːzɪəm] N magnesio

magnet ['mægnɪt] N imán m

magnetic [mæg'nɛtɪk] ADJ magnético

magnetic disk N (Comput) disco magnético

magnetic tape N cinta magnética

magnetism ['mægnɪtɪzəm] N magnetismo

magnification [mægnɪfɪ'keɪʃən] N aumento

magnificence [mæg'nɪfɪsns] N magnificencia

magnificent [mæg'nɪfɪsnt] ADJ magnífico

magnificently [mæg'nɪfɪsntlɪ] ADV magníficamente

magnify ['mægnɪfaɪ] VT (object) ampliar; (sound) aumentar; (fig) exagerar

magnifying glass ['mægnɪfaɪɪŋ-] N lupa

magnitude ['mægnɪtjuːd] N magnitud f

magnolia [mæg'nəʊlɪə] N magnolia

magpie ['mægpaɪ] N urraca

maharajah [mɑːhə'rɑːdʒə] N maharajá m

mahogany [mə'hɒgənɪ] N caoba ▸ CPD de caoba

maid [meɪd] N criada; **old ~** (pej) solterona

maiden ['meɪdn] N doncella ▸ ADJ (aunt etc) soltera; (speech, voyage) inaugural

maiden name N apellido de soltera

★**mail** [meɪl] N correo; (letters) cartas fpl; **by ~** por correo ▸ VT (post) echar al correo; (send) mandar por correo

mailbox ['meɪlbɒks] N (Comput, US: for letters etc) buzón m

mailing list ['meɪlɪŋ-] N lista de direcciones

mailman ['meɪlmæn] N (irreg) (US) cartero

mail-order ['meɪlɔːdəʳ] N pedido postal; (business) venta por correo ▸ ADJ: **~ firm** or **house** casa de venta por correo

mailshot ['meɪlʃɒt] N mailing m inv

mailtrain ['meɪltreɪn] N tren m correo

mail van, (US) **mail truck** N (Aut) camioneta de correos or de reparto

maim [meɪm] VT mutilar, lisiar

★**main** [meɪn] ADJ principal, mayor ▸ N (pipe) cañería principal or maestra; (US) red f eléctrica; **the mains** (BRIT Elec) la red eléctrica; **in the ~** en general

main course N (Culin) plato principal

mainframe ['meɪnfreɪm] N (also: **mainframe computer**) ordenador m or computadora central

mainland ['meɪnlənd] N continente m

main line N línea principal

★**mainly** ['meɪnlɪ] ADV principalmente, en su mayoría

main road N carretera principal

mainstay ['meɪnsteɪ] N (fig) pilar m

mainstream ['meɪnstriːm] N (fig) corriente f principal

main street N calle f mayor

★**maintain** [meɪn'teɪn] VT mantener; (affirm) sostener; **to ~ that ...** mantener or sostener que ...

maintenance ['meɪntənəns] N mantenimiento; (alimony) pensión f alimenticia

maintenance contract N contrato de mantenimiento

maintenance order N (Law) obligación f de pagar una pensión alimenticia al cónyuge

maisonette [meɪzə'nɛt] N dúplex m

maize [meɪz] N (BRIT) maíz m, choclo (LAM)

Maj. ABBR (Mil) = **major**

majestic [mə'dʒɛstɪk] ADJ majestuoso

majesty ['mædʒɪstɪ] N majestad f; **Your M~** Su Majestad

★**major** ['meɪdʒəʳ] N (Mil) comandante m; **a ~ operation** una operación or intervención de gran importancia ▸ ADJ principal; (Mus) mayor ▸ VI (US Univ): **to ~ in** especializarse en

Majorca [mə'jɔːkə] N Mallorca

major general N (Mil) general m de división

★**majority** [mə'dʒɔrɪtɪ] N mayoría ▸ CPD (verdict) mayoritario

majority holding N (Comm): **to have a ~** tener un interés mayoritario

★**make** [meɪk] (pt, pp **made** [meɪd]) VT hacer; (manufacture) hacer, fabricar; (mistake) cometer; (speech) pronunciar; (cause to be): **to ~ sb sad** poner triste or entristecer a algn; (force): **to ~ sb do sth** obligar a algn a hacer algo; (equal): **2 and 2 ~ 4** 2 y 2 son 4; **to ~ a fool of sb** poner a algn en ridículo; **to ~ a profit/loss** obtener ganancias/sufrir pérdidas; **to ~ a profit of £500** sacar una ganancia de 500 libras; **to ~ it** (arrive) llegar; (achieve sth) tener éxito; **what time do you ~ it?** ¿qué hora tienes?; **to ~ do with** contentarse con ▸ N marca
▸ **make for** VT FUS (place) dirigirse a
▸ **make off** VI largarse
▸ **make out** VT (decipher) descifrar; (understand) entender; (see) distinguir; (write: cheque) extender; **to ~ out (that)** (claim, imply) dar a entender (que); **to ~ out a case for sth** dar buenas razones en favor de algo
▸ **make over** VT (assign): **to ~ over (to)** ceder or traspasar (a)
▸ **make up** VT (invent) inventar; (parcel) hacer; **to be made up of** estar compuesto de ▸ VI reconciliarse; (with cosmetics) maquillarse
▸ **make up for** VT FUS compensar

make-believe ['meɪkbɪliːv] N ficción f, fantasía

makeover ['meɪkəʊvəʳ] N cambio de imagen; **to give sb a ~** hacerle a algn un cambio de imagen

★**maker** [ˈmeɪkəʳ] N fabricante *mf*; (*of film, programme*) autor(a) *m/f*

makeshift [ˈmeɪkʃɪft] ADJ improvisado

★**make-up** [ˈmeɪkʌp] N maquillaje *m*

make-up bag N bolsita del maquillaje *or* de los cosméticos

make-up remover N desmaquillador *m*

making [ˈmeɪkɪŋ] N (*fig*): **in the ~** en vías de formación; **to have the makings of** (*person*) tener madera de

maladjusted [mæləˈdʒʌstɪd] ADJ inadaptado

maladroit [maeləˈdrɔɪt] ADJ torpe

malaise [mæˈleɪz] N malestar *m*

malaria [məˈlɛərɪə] N malaria

Malawi [məˈlɑːwɪ] N Malawi *m*

Malay [məˈleɪ] ADJ malayo ▶ N malayo(-a); (*Ling*) malayo

Malaya [məˈleɪə] N Malaya, Malaca

Malayan [məˈleɪən] ADJ, N = **Malay**

Malaysia [məˈleɪzɪə] N Malaisia, Malaysia

Malaysian [məˈleɪzɪən] ADJ, N malaisio(-a) *m/f*, malasio(-a) *m/f*

Maldive Islands [ˈmɔːldɪv-], **Maldives** [ˈmɔːldɪvz] NPL: **the ~** las Maldivas

★**male** [meɪl] N (*Biol, Elec*) macho ▶ ADJ (*sex, attitude*) masculino; (*child etc*) varón

male chauvinist, male chauvinist pig N machista *m*

male nurse N enfermero

malevolence [məˈlɛvələns] N malevolencia

malevolent [məˈlɛvələnt] ADJ malévolo

malfunction [mælˈfʌŋkʃən] N mal funcionamiento

Mali [ˈmɑːlɪ] N Mali *m*, Malí *m*

malice [ˈmælɪs] N (*ill will*) malicia; (*rancour*) rencor *m*

malicious [məˈlɪʃəs] ADJ malicioso; rencoroso

maliciously [məˈlɪʃəslɪ] ADV con malevolencia, con malicia; rencorosamente

malign [məˈlaɪn] VT difamar, calumniar ▶ ADJ maligno

malignant [məˈlɪɡnənt] ADJ (*Med*) maligno

malinger [məˈlɪŋɡəʳ] VI fingirse enfermo

malingerer [məˈlɪŋɡərəʳ] N enfermo(-a) fingido(-a)

mall [mɔːl] N (*US: also:* **shopping mall**) centro comercial

malleable [ˈmælɪəbl] ADJ maleable

mallet [ˈmælɪt] N mazo

malnutrition [mælnjuːˈtrɪʃən] N desnutrición *f*

malpractice [mælˈpræktɪs] N negligencia profesional

malt [mɔːlt] N malta; (*whisky*) whisky *m* de malta

Malta [ˈmɔːltə] N Malta

Maltese [mɔːlˈtiːz] ADJ maltés(-esa) ▶ N *pl inv* maltés(-esa) *m/f*; (*Ling*) maltés *m*

maltreat [mælˈtriːt] VT maltratar

malware [ˈmælwɛəʳ] N (*Comput*) malware *m*, software *m* malicioso

mammal [ˈmæml] N mamífero

mammoth [ˈmæməθ] N mamut *m* ▶ ADJ gigantesco

★**man** [mæn] (*pl* **men** [mɛn]) N hombre *m*; (*mankind*) el hombre; (*Chess*) pieza; **an old ~** un viejo; **~ and wife** marido y mujer ▶ VT (*Naut*) tripular; (*Mil*) defender; (*operate: machine*) manejar

manacle [ˈmænəkl] N esposa, manilla ■ **manacles** NPL grillos *mpl*

★**manage** [ˈmænɪdʒ] VI arreglárselas; **to ~ without sth/sb** poder prescindir de algo/algn ▶ VT (*be in charge of*) dirigir; (*person etc*) manejar; **to ~ to do sth** conseguir hacer algo

manageable [ˈmænɪdʒəbl] ADJ manejable

★**management** [ˈmænɪdʒmənt] N dirección *f*, administración *f*; **"under new ~"** "bajo nueva dirección"

management accounting N contabilidad *f* de gestión

management buyout N adquisición *f* por parte de la dirección

management consultant N consultor(a) *m/f* en dirección de empresas

★**manager** [ˈmænɪdʒəʳ] N director(a) *m/f*; (*of pop star*) mánager *mf*; (*Sport*) entrenador(a) *m/f*; **sales ~** jefe(-a) *m/f* de ventas

manageress [ˈmænɪdʒərɛs] N directora; (*Sport*) entrenadora

managerial [mænəˈdʒɪərɪəl] ADJ directivo

managing director [ˈmænɪdʒɪŋ-] N director(a) *m/f* general

Mancunian [mæŋˈkjuːnɪən] ADJ de Manchester ▶ N nativo(-a) *or* habitante *m/f* de Manchester

mandarin [ˈmændərɪn] N (*also:* **mandarin orange**) mandarina; (*person*) mandarín *m*

mandate [ˈmændeɪt] N mandato

mandatory [ˈmændətərɪ] ADJ obligatorio

mandolin, mandoline [ˈmændəlɪn] N mandolina

mane [meɪn] N (*of horse*) crin *f*; (*of lion*) melena

maneuver [məˈnuːvəʳ] VB, N (*US*) = **manoeuvre**

manful [ˈmænful] ADJ resuelto

manfully [ˈmænfəlɪ] ADV resueltamente

mangetout [mɔnʒ̃ˈtuː] N tirabeque *m*

mangle [ˈmæŋɡl] VT mutilar, destrozar ▶ N escurridor *m*

mango [ˈmæŋɡəu] (*pl* **mangoes**) N mango

mangrove [ˈmæŋɡrəuv] N mangle *m*

mangy [ˈmeɪndʒɪ] ADJ roñoso; (*Med*) sarnoso

manhandle [ˈmænhændl] VT maltratar; (*move by hand: goods*) manipular

manhole [ˈmænhəul] N boca de alcantarilla

manhood [ˈmænhud] N edad *f* viril; (*manliness*) virilidad *f*

man-hour [ˈmænˈauəʳ] N hora-hombre f
manhunt [ˈmænhʌnt] N caza de hombre
mania [ˈmeɪnɪə] N manía
maniac [ˈmeɪnɪæk] N maníaco(-a); (fig) maniático(-a)
manic [ˈmænɪk] ADJ (behaviour, activity) frenético
manic-depressive [ˈmænɪkdɪˈprɛsɪv] ADJ, N maniacodepresivo(-a) m/f
manicure [ˈmænɪkjuəʳ] N manicura
manicure set N estuche m de manicura
manifest [ˈmænɪfɛst] VT manifestar, mostrar ▶ ADJ manifiesto ▶ N manifiesto
manifestation [mænɪfɛsˈteɪʃən] N manifestación f
manifestly [ˈmænɪfɛstlɪ] ADV evidentemente
manifesto [mænɪˈfɛstəu] N manifiesto
manifold [ˈmænɪfəuld] ADJ múltiples ▶ N (Aut etc): **exhaust ~** colector m de escape
Manila [məˈnɪlə] N Manila
manila, manilla [məˈnɪlə] N (paper, envelope) manila
manipulate [məˈnɪpjuleɪt] VT manipular
manipulation [mənɪpjuˈleɪʃən] N manipulación f, manejo
mankind [mænˈkaɪnd] N humanidad f, género humano
manliness [ˈmænlɪnɪs] N virilidad f, hombría
manly [ˈmænlɪ] ADJ varonil
man-made [ˈmænˈmeɪd] ADJ artificial
manna [ˈmænə] N maná m
mannequin [ˈmænɪkɪn] N (dummy) maniquí m; (fashion model) maniquí mf
★**manner** [ˈmænəʳ] N manera, modo; (behaviour) conducta, manera de ser; (type) clase f; **bad manners** falta sg de educación, malos modales mpl; **all ~ of** toda clase or suerte de ■ **manners** NPL modales mpl, educación fsg; **(good) manners** (buena) educación fsg, (buenos) modales mpl
mannerism [ˈmænərɪzəm] N gesto típico
mannerly [ˈmænəlɪ] ADJ bien educado, formal
manoeuvrable, (US) **maneuverable** [məˈnuːvrəbl] ADJ (car etc) manejable
manoeuvre, (US) **maneuver** [məˈnuːvəʳ] VT, VI maniobrar; **to ~ sb into doing sth** manipular a algn para que haga algo ▶ N maniobra
manor [ˈmænəʳ] N (also: **manor house**) casa solariega
manpower [ˈmænpauəʳ] N mano f de obra
manservant [ˈmænsəːvənt] N criado
mansion [ˈmænʃən] N mansión f
manslaughter [ˈmænslɔːtəʳ] N homicidio involuntario
mantelpiece [ˈmæntlpiːs] N repisa de la chimenea
mantle [ˈmæntl] N manto
man-to-man [ˈmæntəˈmæn] ADJ de hombre a hombre

manual [ˈmænjuəl] ADJ manual; **~ worker** obrero(-a), trabajador(a) m/f manual ▶ N manual m
★**manufacture** [mænjuˈfæktʃəʳ] VT fabricar ▶ N fabricación f
manufactured goods [mænjuˈfæktʃəd-] NPL manufacturas fpl, bienes mpl manufacturados
★**manufacturer** [mænjuˈfæktʃərəʳ] N fabricante mf
manufacturing industries [mænjuˈfæktʃrɪŋ-] NPL industrias fpl manufactureras
manure [məˈnjuəʳ] N estiércol m, abono
manuscript [ˈmænjuskrɪpt] N manuscrito
Manx [mæŋks] ADJ de la Isla de Man
★**many** [ˈmɛnɪ] ADJ muchos(-as); **~ a time** muchas veces; **too ~ difficulties** demasiadas dificultades ▶ PRON muchos(-as); **a great ~** muchísimos, un buen número de; **twice as ~** el doble; **how ~?** ¿cuántos?
Maori [ˈmauri] ADJ, N maorí mf
★**map** [mæp] N mapa m ▶ VT trazar el mapa de ▶ **map out** VT (fig: career, holiday, essay) proyectar, planear
maple [ˈmeɪpl] N arce m, maple m (LAm)
mar [mɑːʳ] VT estropear
Mar. ABBR (= March) mar.
marathon [ˈmærəθən] N maratón m ▶ ADJ: **a ~ session** una sesión maratoniana
marathon runner N corredor(a) m/f de maratones
marauder [məˈrɔːdəʳ] N merodeador(a) m/f
marble [ˈmɑːbl] N mármol m; (toy) canica
★**March** [mɑːtʃ] N marzo; see also **July**
★**march** [mɑːtʃ] VI (Mil) marchar; (demonstrators) manifestarse; (fig) caminar con resolución ▶ N marcha; (demonstration) manifestación f
marcher [ˈmɑːtʃəʳ] N manifestante mf
marching [ˈmɑːtʃɪŋ] N: **to give sb his ~ orders** (fig) mandar a paseo a algn; (employee) poner de patitas en la calle a algn
march-past [ˈmɑːtʃpɑːst] N desfile m
mare [mɛəʳ] N yegua
margarine [mɑːdʒəˈriːn] N margarina
marge, marg [mɑːdʒ] N ABBR (inf) = **margarine**
★**margin** [ˈmɑːdʒɪn] N margen m; (Comm: profit margin) margen m de beneficios
marginal [ˈmɑːdʒɪnl] ADJ marginal
marginally [ˈmɑːdʒɪnəlɪ] ADV ligeramente
marginal seat N (Pol) circunscripción f políticamente no definida
marigold [ˈmærɪgəuld] N caléndula
marijuana [mærɪˈwɑːnə] N marihuana
marina [məˈriːnə] N puerto deportivo
marinade [mærɪˈneɪd] N adobo
marinate [ˈmærɪneɪt] VT adobar
marine [məˈriːn] ADJ marino ▶ N soldado de infantería de marina

marine insurance N seguro marítimo

mariner ['mærɪnəʳ] N marinero, marino

marionette [mærɪə'nɛt] N marioneta, títere m

marital ['mærɪtl] ADJ matrimonial; **~ status** estado civil

maritime ['mærɪtaɪm] ADJ marítimo

marjoram ['mɑːdʒərəm] N mejorana

★**mark** [mɑːk] N marca, señal f; (*in snow, mud etc*) huella; (*stain*) mancha; (BRIT Scol) nota; (*currency*) marco; **punctuation marks** signos mpl de puntuación; **to be quick off the ~** (*fig*) ser listo; **up to the ~** (*in efficiency*) a la altura de las circunstancias ▶ VT (*Sport: player*) marcar; (*stain*) manchar; (BRIT Scol) calificar, corregir; **to ~ time** marcar el paso; (*fig*) marcar(se) un ritmo
  ▶ **mark down** VT (*reduce: prices, goods*) rebajar
  ▶ **mark off** VT (*tick*) indicar, señalar
  ▶ **mark out** VT trazar
  ▶ **mark up** VT (*price*) aumentar

marked [mɑːkt] ADJ marcado, acusado

markedly ['mɑːkɪdlɪ] ADV marcadamente, apreciablemente

marker ['mɑːkəʳ] N (*sign*) marcador m; (*bookmark*) registro

★**market** ['mɑːkɪt] N mercado; **open ~** mercado libre; **to be on the ~** estar en venta; **to play the ~** jugar a la bolsa ▶ VT (Comm) comercializar; (*promote*) publicitar

marketable ['mɑːkɪtəbl] ADJ comerciable

market analysis N análisis m del mercado

market day N día m de mercado

market demand N demanda de mercado

market economy N economía de mercado

market forces NPL tendencias fpl del mercado

market garden N (BRIT) huerto

★**marketing** ['mɑːkɪtɪŋ] N marketing m, mercadotecnia

marketing manager N director m de marketing

market leader N líder m de ventas

marketplace ['mɑːkɪtpleɪs] N mercado

market price N precio de mercado

market research N (Comm) estudios mpl de mercado

market value N valor m en el mercado

marking ['mɑːkɪŋ] N (*on animal*) pinta; (*on road*) señal f

marking ink N tinta indeleble or de marcar

marksman ['mɑːksmən] N (*irreg*) tirador m

marksmanship ['mɑːksmənʃɪp] N puntería

mark-up ['mɑːkʌp] N (Comm: *margin*) margen m de beneficio; (: *increase*) aumento

marmalade ['mɑːməleɪd] N mermelada de naranja

maroon [mə'ruːn] VT: **to be marooned** (*shipwrecked*) quedar aislado; (*fig*) quedar abandonado ▶ N (*colour*) granate m ▶ ADJ (*colour*) granate inv

marquee [mɑː'kiː] N carpa, entoldado

marquess, marquis ['mɑːkwɪs] N marqués m

Marrakech, Marrakesh [mærə'kɛʃ] N Marrakech m

★**marriage** ['mærɪdʒ] N (*state*) matrimonio; (*wedding*) boda; (*act*) casamiento

marriage bureau N agencia matrimonial

marriage certificate N partida de casamiento

marriage guidance, (US) **marriage counseling** N orientación f matrimonial

marriage of convenience N matrimonio de conveniencia

★**married** ['mærɪd] ADJ casado; (*life, love*) conyugal

marrow ['mærəu] N médula; (*vegetable*) calabacín m

★**marry** ['mærɪ] VT casarse con; (*father, priest etc*) casar ▶ VI (*also:* **get married**) casarse

Mars [mɑːz] N Marte m

Marseilles [mɑː'seɪ] N Marsella

marsh [mɑːʃ] N pantano; (*salt marsh*) marisma

marshal ['mɑːʃl] N (Mil) mariscal m; (*at sports meeting, demonstration etc*) oficial mf; (US: *of police, fire department*) jefe(-a) m/f ▶ VT (*facts*) ordenar; (*soldiers*) formar

marshalling yard ['mɑːʃəlɪŋ-] N (Rail) estación f clasificadora

Marshall Islands ['mɑːʃəl-] NPL Islas Marshall fpl

marshmallow ['mɑːʃmæləu] N (Bot) malvavisco; (*sweet*) nube f, dulce m de merengue blando

marshy ['mɑːʃɪ] ADJ pantanoso

marsupial [mɑː'suːpɪəl] ADJ, N marsupial m

martial ['mɑːʃl] ADJ marcial

martial arts NPL artes fpl marciales

martial law N ley f marcial

martin ['mɑːtɪn] N (*also:* **house martin**) avión m

martyr ['mɑːtəʳ] N mártir mf ▶ VT martirizar

martyrdom ['mɑːtədəm] N martirio

marvel ['mɑːvl] N maravilla, prodigio ▶ VI: **to ~ (at)** maravillarse (de)

marvellous, (US) **marvelous** ['mɑːvləs] ADJ maravilloso

marvellously, (US) **marvelously** ['mɑːvləslɪ] ADV maravillosamente

Marxism ['mɑːksɪzəm] N marxismo

Marxist ['mɑːksɪst] ADJ, N marxista mf

marzipan ['mɑːzɪpæn] N mazapán m

mascara [mæs'kɑːrə] N rímel m

mascot ['mæskət] N mascota

masculine ['mæskjuˌlɪn] ADJ masculino

masculinity [mæskju'lɪnɪtɪ] N masculinidad f

mash [mæʃ] VT machacar ▶ N (*mix*) mezcla; (Culin) puré m; (*pulp*) amasijo

mashed potatoes [mæʃt-] NPL puré m de patatas or (LAM) papas

★**mask** [mɑːsk] N máscara ▶ VT (hide: feelings) esconder; **to ~ one's face** (cover) ocultarse la cara

masochism ['mæsəkɪzəm] N masoquismo

masochist ['mæsəukɪst] N masoquista mf

mason ['meɪsn] N (also: **stonemason**) albañil m; (also: **freemason**) masón m

masonic [mə'sɔnɪk] ADJ masónico

masonry ['meɪsnrɪ] N masonería; (in building) mampostería

masquerade [mæskə'reɪd] N baile m de máscaras; (fig) mascarada ▶ VI: **to ~ as** disfrazarse de, hacerse pasar por

★**mass** [mæs] N (people) muchedumbre f; (Physics) masa; (Rel) misa; (great quantity) montón m; **the masses** las masas; **to go to ~** ir a or oír misa ▶ VI reunirse; (Mil) concentrarse

massacre ['mæsəkər] N masacre f ▶ VT masacrar

massage ['mæsɑːʒ] N masaje m ▶ VT dar masajes or un masaje a

masseur [mæ'səːr] N masajista m

masseuse [mæ'səːz] N masajista f

★**massive** ['mæsɪv] ADJ enorme; (support, intervention) masivo

mass media NPL medios mpl de comunicación de masas

mass meeting N (of everyone concerned) reunión f en masa; (huge) mitin m

mass-produce ['mæsprə'djuːs] VT fabricar en serie

mass-production ['mæsprə'dʌkʃən] N fabricación f or producción f en serie

mast [mɑːst] N (Naut) mástil m; (Radio etc) torre f, antena

mastectomy [mæs'tɛktəmɪ] N mastectomía

★**master** ['mɑːstər] N (of servant, animal) amo; (fig: of situation) dueño; (Art, Mus) maestro; (in secondary school) profesor m; (title for boys): **M~ X** Señorito X ▶ VT dominar

master disk N (Comput) disco maestro

masterful ['mɑːstəful] ADJ magistral, dominante

master key N llave f maestra

masterly ['mɑːstəlɪ] ADJ magistral

mastermind ['mɑːstəmaɪnd] N inteligencia superior ▶ VT dirigir, planear

Master of Arts N licenciatura superior en Letras; see also **master's degree**

Master of Ceremonies N encargado de protocolo

Master of Science N licenciatura superior en Ciencias; see also **master's degree**

masterpiece ['mɑːstəpiːs] N obra maestra

master plan N plan m rector

master's degree N máster m

Los estudios de postgrado británicos que llevan a la obtención de un **master's degree** consisten generalmente en una combinación de curso(s) académico(s) y tesina (dissertation) sobre un tema original, o bien únicamente la redacción de una tesina. El primer caso es el más frecuente para los títulos de MA (Master of Arts) y MSc (Master of Science), mientras que los de MLitt (Master of Letters) o MPhil (Master of Philosophy) se obtienen normalmente mediante tesina. En algunas universidades, como las escocesas, el título de master's degree no es de postgrado, sino que corresponde a la licenciatura.

master stroke N golpe m maestro

mastery ['mɑːstərɪ] N maestría

mastiff ['mæstɪf] N mastín m

masturbate ['mæstəbeɪt] VI masturbarse

masturbation [mæstə'beɪʃən] N masturbación f

MAT N ABBR (= machine-assisted translation) TAO

mat [mæt] N alfombrilla; (also: **doormat**) felpudo ▶ ADJ = **matt**

★**match** [mætʃ] N (for lighting) cerilla, fósforo; (game) partido; (fig) igual mf; **to be a good ~** hacer buena pareja ▶ VT emparejar; (go well with) hacer juego con; (equal) igualar; (correspond to) corresponderse con; (pair: also: **match up**) casar con ▶ VI hacer juego

matchbox ['mætʃbɔks] N caja de cerillas

matching ['mætʃɪŋ] ADJ que hace juego

matchless ['mætʃlɪs] ADJ sin par, incomparable

matchmaker ['mætʃmeɪkər] N casamentero

★**mate** [meɪt] N (workmate) compañero(-a), colega mf; (inf: friend) amigo(-a), compadre mf (LAM); (animal) macho (hembra); (in merchant navy) primer oficial m, segundo de a bordo ▶ VI acoplarse, aparearse ▶ VT acoplar, aparear

maté ['mɑːteɪ] N mate m (cocido), yerba mate

★**material** [mə'tɪərɪəl] N (substance) materia; (equipment) material m; (cloth) tela, tejido ▶ ADJ material; (important) esencial ■ **materials** NPL materiales mpl; (equipment etc) artículos mpl

materialistic [mətɪərɪə'lɪstɪk] ADJ materialista

materialize [mə'tɪərɪəlaɪz] VI materializarse

materially [mə'tɪərɪəlɪ] ADV materialmente

maternal [mə'təːnl] ADJ maternal; **~ grandmother** abuela materna

maternity [mə'təːnɪtɪ] N maternidad f

maternity benefit N subsidio por maternidad

maternity dress N vestido premamá

maternity hospital N hospital m de maternidad

maternity leave N baja por maternidad

math [mæθ] N ABBR (US: = mathematics) matemáticas fpl

mathematical [mæθə'mætɪkl] ADJ matemático

mathematically [mæθɪˈmætɪklɪ] ADV matemáticamente

mathematician [mæθəməˈtɪʃən] N matemático(-a)

mathematics [mæθəˈmætɪks] N matemáticas *fpl*

maths [mæθs] N ABBR (BRIT: = *mathematics*) matemáticas *fpl*

matinée [ˈmætɪneɪ] N sesión *f* de tarde, vermut *m* (LAM)

mating [ˈmeɪtɪŋ] N aparejamiento

mating call N llamada del macho

mating season N época de celo

matins [ˈmætɪnz] N maitines *mpl*

matriarchal [meɪtrɪˈɑːkl] ADJ matriarcal

matrices [ˈmeɪtrɪsiːz] PL *of* **matrix**

matriculation [mətrɪkjuˈleɪʃən] N matriculación *f*, matrícula

matrimonial [mætrɪˈməʊnɪəl] ADJ matrimonial

matrimony [ˈmætrɪmənɪ] N matrimonio

matrix [ˈmeɪtrɪks] (*pl* **matrices** [ˈmeɪtrɪsiːz]) N matriz *f*

matron [ˈmeɪtrən] N (*in hospital*) enfermera jefe; (*in school*) ama de llaves

matronly [ˈmeɪtrənlɪ] ADJ de matrona; (*fig: figure*) corpulento

matt [mæt] ADJ mate

matted [ˈmætɪd] ADJ enmarañado

★**matter** [ˈmætəʳ] N cuestión *f*, asunto; (*Physics*) sustancia, materia; (*content*) contenido; (*Med: pus*) pus *m*; **what's the ~?** ¿qué pasa?; **no ~ what** pase lo que pase; **as a ~ of course** por rutina; **as a ~ of fact** en realidad; **printed ~** impresos *mpl*; **reading ~** material *m* de lectura, lecturas *fpl* ▶ VI importar; **it doesn't ~** no importa

matter-of-fact [ˈmætərəvˈfækt] ADJ (*style*) prosaico; (*person*) práctico; (*voice*) neutro

mattress [ˈmætrɪs] N colchón *m*

mature [məˈtjuəʳ] ADJ maduro ▶ VI madurar

mature student N *estudiante de más de 21 años*

maturity [məˈtjuərɪtɪ] N madurez *f*

maudlin [ˈmɔːdlɪn] ADJ llorón(-ona)

maul [mɔːl] VT magullar

Mauritania [mɔːrɪˈteɪnɪə] N Mauritania

Mauritius [məˈrɪʃəs] N Mauricio

mausoleum [mɔːsəˈlɪəm] N mausoleo

mauve [məʊv] ADJ de color malva

maverick [ˈmævrɪk] N (*fig*) inconformista *mf*, persona independiente

mawkish [ˈmɔːkɪʃ] ADJ sensiblero, empalagoso

max ABBR = **maximum**

maxim [ˈmæksɪm] N máxima

maxima [ˈmæksɪmə] PL *of* **maximum**

maximize [ˈmæksɪmaɪz] VT (*profits etc*) llevar al máximo; (*chances*) maximizar

★**maximum** [ˈmæksɪməm] ADJ máximo ▶ N (*pl* **maxima** [ˈmæksɪmə]) máximo

★**May** [meɪ] N mayo; *see also* **July**

★**may** [meɪ] VI (*conditional* **might**) (*indicating possibility*): **he ~ come** puede que venga; (*be allowed to*): **~ I smoke?** ¿puedo fumar?; (*wishes*): **~ God bless you!** ¡que Dios le bendiga!; **~ I sit here?** ¿me puedo sentar aquí?

★**maybe** [ˈmeɪbiː] ADV quizá(s); **~ not** quizá(s) no

mayday [ˈmeɪdeɪ] N señal *f* de socorro

May Day N el primero de Mayo

mayhem [ˈmeɪhɛm] N caos *m* total

mayonnaise [meɪəˈneɪz] N mayonesa

★**mayor** [mɛəʳ] N alcalde *m*

mayoress [ˈmɛərɛs] N alcaldesa

maypole [ˈmeɪpəʊl] N mayo

maze [meɪz] N laberinto

MB ABBR (*Comput*) = **megabyte**; (CANADA) = **Manitoba**

MBA N ABBR (= *Master of Business Administration*) máster *m* en administración de empresas

MBBS, MBChB N ABBR (BRIT: = *Bachelor of Medicine and Surgery*) título universitario

MBE N ABBR (BRIT: = *Member of the Order of the British Empire*) título ceremonial

MBO N ABBR *see* **management buyout**

MC N ABBR (= *master of ceremonies*) e.p.; (US: = *Member of Congress*) diputado del Congreso de los Estados Unidos

MCAT N ABBR (US: = *Medical College Admissions Test*) examen de ingreso en los estudios superiores de Medicina

MD N ABBR (= *Doctor of Medicine*) título universitario; (*Comm*) = **managing director** ▶ ABBR (US) = **Maryland**

MD player N MiniDisc *m*, minidisc *m*

MDT N ABBR (US: = *Mountain Daylight Time*) hora de verano de las Montañas Rocosas

ME ABBR (*US Post*) = **Maine** ▶ N ABBR (*US Med*) = **medical examiner**; (*Med*: = *myalgic encephalomyelitis*) encefalomielitis *f* miálgica

★**me** [miː] PRON (*direct*) me; (*stressed, after pronoun*) mí; **can you hear me?** ¿me oyes?; **he heard ME!** me oyó a mí; **it's me** soy yo; **give them to me** dámelos; **with/without me** conmigo/sin mí; **it's for me** es para mí

meadow [ˈmɛdəʊ] N prado, pradera

meagre, (US) **meager** [ˈmiːgəʳ] ADJ escaso, pobre

★**meal** [miːl] N comida; (*flour*) harina; **to go out for a ~** salir a comer

meals on wheels NSG (BRIT) *servicio de alimentación a domicilio para necesitados y tercera edad*

mealtime [ˈmiːltaɪm] N hora de comer

mealy-mouthed [ˈmiːlɪmaʊðd] ADJ: **to be ~** no decir nunca las cosas claras

★**mean** [miːn] ADJ (*with money*) tacaño; (*unkind*) mezquino, malo; (*average*) medio; (US: *vicious: animal*)

m

resabiado; (: *person*) malicioso ▶ VT (*pt, pp* **meant** [mɛnt]) (*signify*) querer decir, significar; (*intend*): **to ~ to do sth** tener la intención de *or* pensar hacer algo; **do you ~ it?** ¿lo dices en serio?; **what do you ~?** ¿qué quieres decir?; **to be meant for sb/sth** ser para algn/algo ▶ N medio, término medio; *see also* **means**

meander [mɪˈændə^r] VI (*river*) serpentear; (*person*) vagar

★**meaning** [ˈmiːnɪŋ] N significado, sentido

meaningful [ˈmiːnɪŋful] ADJ significativo

meaningless [ˈmiːnɪŋlɪs] ADJ sin sentido

meanness [ˈmiːnnɪs] N (*with money*) tacañería; (*unkindness*) maldad *f*, mezquindad *f*

★**means** [miːnz] NPL medio *sg*, manera *sg*; (*resource*) recursos *mpl*, medios *mpl*; **by ~ of** mediante, por medio de; **by all ~!** ¡naturalmente!, ¡claro que sí!

means test N control *m* de los recursos económicos

meant [mɛnt] PT, PP *of* **mean**

meantime [ˈmiːntaɪm], **meanwhile** [ˈmiːnwaɪl] ADV (*also:* **in the meantime**) mientras tanto

measles [ˈmiːzlz] N sarampión *m*

measly [ˈmiːzlɪ] ADJ (*inf*) miserable

measurable [ˈmɛʒərəbl] ADJ mensurable, que se puede medir

★**measure** [ˈmɛʒə^r] VT medir; (*for clothes etc*) tomar las medidas a ▶ VI medir ▶ N medida; (*ruler*) cinta métrica, metro; **a litre ~** una medida de un litro; **some ~ of success** cierto éxito; **to take measures to do sth** tomar medidas para hacer algo

▶ **measure up** VI: **to ~ up (to)** estar a la altura (de)

measured [ˈmɛʒəd] ADJ moderado; (*tone*) mesurado

measurement [ˈmɛʒəmənt] N (*measure*) medida; (*act*) medición *f*; **to take sb's measurements** tomar las medidas a algn

★**meat** [miːt] N carne *f*; **cold meats** fiambres *mpl*; **crab ~** carne *f* de cangrejo

meatball [ˈmiːtbɔːl] N albóndiga

meat pie N pastel *m* de carne

meaty [ˈmiːtɪ] ADJ (*person*) fuerte, corpulento; (*role*) sustancioso; **a ~ meal** una comida con bastante carne

Mecca [ˈmɛkə] N (*city*) la Meca; (*fig*) meca

mechanic [mɪˈkænɪk] N mecánico(-a)

mechanical [mɪˈkænɪkl] ADJ mecánico

mechanical engineering N (*science*) ingeniería mecánica; (*industry*) construcción *f* mecánica

mechanics [məˈkænɪks] N mecánica ▶ NPL mecanismo *sg*

mechanism [ˈmɛkənɪzəm] N mecanismo

mechanization [mɛkənaɪˈzeɪʃən] N mecanización *f*

mechanize [ˈmɛkənaɪz] VT mecanizar; (*factory etc*) automatizar

MEd N ABBR (= *Master of Education*) título universitario

★**medal** [ˈmɛdl] N medalla

medallion [mɪˈdælɪən] N medallón *m*

medallist, (US) **medalist** [ˈmɛdlɪst] N (*Sport*) medallista *mf*

meddle [ˈmɛdl] VI: **to ~ in** entrometerse en; **to ~ with sth** manosear algo

meddlesome [ˈmɛdlsəm], **meddling** [ˈmɛdlɪŋ] ADJ (*interfering*) entrometido; (*touching things*) curioso

★**media** [ˈmiːdɪə] NPL medios *mpl* de comunicación

media circus N circo mediático

mediaeval [mɛdɪˈiːvl] ADJ = **medieval**

median [ˈmiːdɪən] N (US: *also:* **median strip**) mediana

media research N estudio de los medios de publicidad

mediate [ˈmiːdɪeɪt] VI mediar

mediation [miːdɪˈeɪʃən] N mediación *f*

mediator [ˈmiːdɪeɪtə^r] N mediador(a) *m/f*

Medicaid [ˈmɛdɪkeɪd] N (US) *programa de ayuda médica*

★**medical** [ˈmɛdɪkl] ADJ médico ▶ N (*also:* **medical examination**) reconocimiento médico

medical certificate N certificado médico

medicalize [ˈmɛdɪkəlaɪz] VT medicalizar

Medicare [ˈmɛdɪkɛə^r] N (US) *seguro médico del Estado*

medicated [ˈmɛdɪkeɪtɪd] ADJ medicinal

medication [mɛdɪˈkeɪʃən] N (*drugs etc*) medicación *f*

medicinal [mɛˈdɪsɪnl] ADJ medicinal

★**medicine** [ˈmɛdsɪn] N medicina; (*drug*) medicamento

medicine chest N botiquín *m*

medicine man N (*irreg*) hechicero

medieval, mediaeval [mɛdɪˈiːvl] ADJ medieval

mediocre [miːdɪˈəukə^r] ADJ mediocre

mediocrity [miːdɪˈɔkrɪtɪ] N mediocridad *f*

meditate [ˈmɛdɪteɪt] VI meditar

meditation [mɛdɪˈteɪʃən] N meditación *f*

Mediterranean [mɛdɪtəˈreɪnɪən] ADJ mediterráneo; **the ~ (Sea)** el (mar) Mediterráneo

★**medium** [ˈmiːdɪəm] ADJ mediano; (*level, height*) medio ▶ N (*pl* **media**) (*means*) medio; (*pl* **mediums**) (*person*) médium *mf*; **happy ~** punto justo

medium-dry [ˈmiːdɪəmˈdraɪ] ADJ semiseco

medium-sized [ˈmiːdɪəmˈsaɪzd] ADJ de tamaño mediano; (*clothes*) de (la) talla mediana

medium wave N onda media

medley [ˈmɛdlɪ] N mezcla; (*Mus*) popurrí *m*

meek [miːk] ADJ manso, sumiso

meekly ['mi:klɪ] ADV mansamente, dócilmente

★**meet** [mi:t] (*pt, pp* **met** [mɛt]) VT encontrar; (*accidentally*) encontrarse con; (*by arrangement*) reunirse con; (*for the first time*) conocer; (*go and fetch*) ir a buscar; (*opponent*) enfrentarse con; (*obligations*) cumplir; (*bill, expenses*) pagar, costear; **pleased to ~ you!** ¡encantado (de conocerle)!, ¡mucho gusto! ▶ VI encontrarse; (*in session*) reunirse; (*join: objects*) unirse; (*get to know*) conocerse ▶ N (BRIT *Hunting*) cacería; (*US Sport*) encuentro
▶ **meet up** VI: **to ~ up with sb** reunirse con algn
▶ **meet with** VT FUS reunirse con; (*difficulty*) tropezar con

★**meeting** ['mi:tɪŋ] N (*also Sport: rally*) encuentro; (*arranged*) cita, compromiso (LAM); (*formal session, business meeting*) reunión *f*; (*Pol*) mitin *m*; **to call a ~** convocar una reunión

meeting place N lugar *m* de reunión *or* encuentro

meg [mɛg] N ABBR (*inf*: = *megabyte*) megabyte *m*

megabit ['mɛgəbɪt] N (*Comput*) megabit *m*

megabyte ['mɛgə'baɪt] N (*Comput*) megabyte *m*, megaocteto

megalomaniac [mɛgələʊ'meɪnɪæk] ADJ, N megalómano(-a) *m/f*

megaphone ['mɛgəfəʊn] N megáfono

megapixel ['mɛgəpɪksl] N megapíxel *m*

megastore ['mɛgəstɔːʳ] N macrotienda

megawatt ['mɛgəwɔt] N megavatio

meh [mɛ] EXCL ¡bah!

melancholy ['mɛlənkəlɪ] N melancolía ▶ ADJ melancólico

melee ['mɛleɪ] N refriega

mellow ['mɛləʊ] ADJ (*wine*) añejo; (*sound, colour*) suave; (*fruit*) maduro ▶ VI (*person*) madurar

melodious [mɪ'ləʊdɪəs] ADJ melodioso

melodrama ['mɛləʊdrɑːmə] N melodrama *m*

melodramatic [mɛləʊdrə'mætɪk] ADJ melodramático

melody ['mɛlədɪ] N melodía

melon ['mɛlən] N melón *m*

melt [mɛlt] VI (*metal*) fundirse; (*snow*) derretirse; (*fig*) ablandarse ▶ VT (*also*: **melt down**) fundir; **melted butter** mantequilla derretida
▶ **melt away** VI desvanecerse

meltdown ['mɛltdaʊn] N (*in nuclear reactor*) fusión *f* (de un reactor nuclear)

melting point ['mɛltɪŋ-] N punto de fusión

melting pot ['mɛltɪŋ-] N (*fig*) crisol *m*; **to be in the ~** estar sobre el tapete

★**member** ['mɛmbəʳ] N (*of political party*) miembro; (*of club*) socio(-a); **M~ of Parliament** (BRIT) diputado(-a); **M~ of the European Parliament** (BRIT) eurodiputado(-a); **M~ of Congress** (US) miembro del Congreso; **M~ of the House of Representatives** (US) miembro *mf* de la Cámara de Representantes; **M~ of the Scottish Parliament** (BRIT) diputado(-a) del Parlamento escocés

★**membership** ['mɛmbəʃɪp] N (*members*) miembros *mpl*; socios *mpl*; (*numbers*) número de miembros *or* socios; **to seek ~ of** pedir el ingreso a

membership card N carnet *m* de socio

membrane ['mɛmbreɪn] N membrana

meme [mi:m] N (*Internet*) meme *m*

memento [mə'mɛntəʊ] N recuerdo

memo ['mɛməʊ] N apunte *m*, nota

memoirs ['mɛmwɑːz] NPL memorias *fpl*

memo pad N bloc *m* de notas

memorable ['mɛmərəbl] ADJ memorable

memorandum [mɛmə'rændəm] (*pl* **memoranda** [-də]) N nota (de servicio); (*Pol*) memorándum *m*

memorial [mɪ'mɔːrɪəl] N monumento conmemorativo ▶ ADJ conmemorativo

Memorial Day N (US) *día de conmemoración de los caídos en la guerra*

memorize ['mɛməraɪz] VT aprender de memoria

★**memory** ['mɛmərɪ] N memoria; (*recollection*) recuerdo; (*Comput*) memoria; **to have a good/bad ~** tener buena/mala memoria; **loss of ~** pérdida de memoria

memory card N tarjeta de memoria

memory stick N (*Comput*) llave *f* de memoria

men [mɛn] PL *of* **man**

menace ['mɛnəs] N amenaza; (*inf: nuisance*) lata; **a public ~** un peligro público ▶ VT amenazar

menacing ['mɛnɪsɪŋ] ADJ amenazador(-a)

menacingly ['mɛnɪsɪŋlɪ] ADV amenazadoramente

menagerie [mɪ'nædʒərɪ] N casa de fieras

mend [mɛnd] VT reparar, arreglar; (*darn*) zurcir; **to ~ one's ways** enmendarse ▶ VI reponerse ▶ N (*gen*) remiendo; (*darn*) zurcido; **to be on the ~** ir mejorando

mending ['mɛndɪŋ] N arreglo, reparación *f*; (*clothes*) ropa por remendar

menial ['mi:nɪəl] ADJ (*pej*) bajo, servil

meningitis [mɛnɪn'dʒaɪtɪs] N meningitis *f*

menopause ['mɛnəʊpɔːz] N menopausia

men's room N (US): **the ~** el servicio de caballeros

menstrual ['mɛnstruəl] ADJ menstrual

menstruate ['mɛnstrueɪt] VI menstruar

menstruation [mɛnstru'eɪʃən] N menstruación *f*

menswear ['mɛnzwɛəʳ] N confección *f* de caballero

★**mental** ['mɛntl] ADJ mental; **~ illness** enfermedad *f* mental

mentality [mɛn'tælɪtɪ] N mentalidad *f*

mentally ['mɛntlɪ] ADV: **to be ~ ill** tener una enfermedad mental

menthol ['mɛnθɒl] N mentol *m*

★**mention** ['mɛnʃən] N mención *f* ▶ VT mencionar; (*speak of*) hablar de; **not to ~, without mentioning** sin contar; **I need hardly ~ that ...** huelga decir que ...; **don't ~ it!** ¡de nada!

mentor [ˈmɛntɔːʳ] N mentor *m*

menu [ˈmɛnjuː] N (*set menu*) menú *m*; (*printed*) carta; (*Comput*) menú *m*

menu-driven [ˈmɛnjuːdrɪvn] ADJ (*Comput*) guiado por menú

MEP N ABBR = **Member of the European Parliament**

mercantile [ˈmɜːkəntaɪl] ADJ mercantil

mercenary [ˈmɜːsɪnərɪ] ADJ, N mercenario(-a) *m/f*

merchandise [ˈmɜːtʃəndaɪz] N mercancías *fpl*

merchandiser [ˈmɜːtʃəndaɪzəʳ] N comerciante *mf*, tratante *m*

★**merchant** [ˈmɜːtʃənt] N comerciante *mf*

merchant bank N (*BRIT*) banco comercial

merchantman [ˈmɜːtʃəntmən] N (*irreg*) buque *m* mercante

merchant navy, (*US*) **merchant marine** N marina mercante

merciful [ˈmɜːsɪful] ADJ compasivo

mercifully [ˈmɜːsɪfulɪ] ADV con compasión; (*fortunately*) afortunadamente

merciless [ˈmɜːsɪlɪs] ADJ despiadado

mercilessly [ˈmɜːsɪlɪslɪ] ADV despiadadamente, sin piedad

mercurial [mɜːˈkjuərɪəl] ADJ veleidoso, voluble

mercury [ˈmɜːkjurɪ] N mercurio

mercy [ˈmɜːsɪ] N compasión *f*; (*Rel*) misericordia; **at the ~ of** a la merced de

mercy killing N eutanasia

mere [mɪəʳ] ADJ simple, mero

merely [ˈmɪəlɪ] ADV simplemente, solo

merge [mɜːdʒ] VT (*join*) unir; (*mix*) mezclar; (*fuse*) fundir; (*Comput: files, text*) fusionar ▶ VI unirse; (*Comm*) fusionarse

merger [ˈmɜːdʒəʳ] N (*Comm*) fusión *f*

meridian [məˈrɪdɪən] N meridiano

meringue [məˈræŋ] N merengue *m*

merit [ˈmɛrɪt] N mérito ▶ VT merecer

meritocracy [mɛrɪˈtɔkrəsɪ] N meritocracia

mermaid [ˈmɜːmeɪd] N sirena

merrily [ˈmɛrɪlɪ] ADV alegremente

merriment [ˈmɛrɪmənt] N alegría

merry [ˈmɛrɪ] ADJ alegre; **M~ Christmas!** ¡Felices Pascuas!

merry-go-round [ˈmɛrɪɡəuraund] N tiovivo

mesh [mɛʃ] N malla; (*Tech*) engranaje *m*; **wire ~** tela metálica ▶ VI (*gears*) engranar

mesmerize [ˈmɛzməraɪz] VT hipnotizar

★**mess** [mɛs] N confusión *f*; (*of objects*) revoltijo; (*dirt*) porquería; (*tangle*) lío; (*Mil*) comedor *m*; **to be (in) a ~** (*room*) estar revuelto; **to be/get o.s. in a ~** estar/meterse en un lío
   ▶ **mess about, mess around** VI (*inf*) perder el tiempo; (: *pass the time*) pasar el rato

▶ **mess about with, mess around with** VT FUS (*inf: play with*) divertirse con; (: *handle*) manosear

▶ **mess up** VT (*inf: disarrange*) desordenar; (: *spoil*) estropear; (: *dirty*) ensuciar

▶ **mess with** VT FUS (*inf: challenge, confront*) meterse con (*inf*); (: *interfere with*) interferir con

★**message** [ˈmɛsɪdʒ] N mensaje *m*, recado; **to get the ~** (*fig: inf*) enterarse ▶ VT (*inf: person*) mandar un mensaje a; (: *comment*) comentar

message board N (*Internet*) foro de debate

message switching N (*Comput*) conmutación *f* de mensajes

messenger [ˈmɛsɪndʒəʳ] N mensajero(-a)

Messiah [mɪˈsaɪə] N Mesías *m*

Messrs, Messrs. ABBR (*on letters: = Messieurs*) Sres.

messy [ˈmɛsɪ] ADJ (*dirty*) sucio; (*untidy*) desordenado; (*confused: situation etc*) confuso

Met [mɛt] N ABBR (*US*) = **Metropolitan Opera**

met [mɛt] PT, PP *of* **meet** ▶ ADJ ABBR = **meteorological**

metabolism [mɛˈtæbəlɪzəm] N metabolismo

★**metal** [ˈmɛtl] N metal *m*

metallic [mɛˈtælɪk] ADJ metálico

metallurgy [mɛˈtælədʒɪ] N metalurgia

metalwork [ˈmɛtlwəːk] N (*craft*) metalistería

metamorphosis [mɛtəˈmɔːfəsɪs] (*pl* **metamorphoses** [-siːz]) N metamorfosis *f inv*

metaphor [ˈmɛtəfəʳ] N metáfora

metaphorical [mɛtəˈfɔrɪkl] ADJ metafórico

metaphysics [mɛtəˈfɪzɪks] N metafísica

mete [miːt]: **to ~ out** VT (*punishment*) imponer

meteor [ˈmiːtɪəʳ] N meteoro

meteoric [miːtɪˈɔrɪk] ADJ (*fig*) meteórico

meteorite [ˈmiːtɪəraɪt] N meteorito

meteorological [miːtɪərəˈlɔdʒɪkl] ADJ meteorológico

meteorology [miːtɪəˈrɔlədʒɪ] N meteorología

meter [ˈmiːtəʳ] N (*instrument*) contador *m*; (*US: unit*) = **metre**; **parking ~** parquímetro ▶ VT (*US Post*) franquear

methane [ˈmiːθeɪn] N metano

★**method** [ˈmɛθəd] N método; **~ of payment** método de pago

methodical [mɪˈθɔdɪkl] ADJ metódico

Methodist [ˈmɛθədɪst] ADJ, N metodista *mf*

methodology [mɛθəˈdɔlədʒɪ] N metodología

meths [mɛθs] N (*BRIT*) = **methylated spirit**

methylated spirit [ˈmɛθɪleɪtɪd-] N (*BRIT*) alcohol *m* metilado *or* desnaturalizado

meticulous [mɛˈtɪkjuləs] ADJ meticuloso

★**metre**, (*US*) **meter** [ˈmiːtəʳ] N metro

metric [ˈmɛtrɪk] ADJ métrico; **to go ~** pasar al sistema métrico

metrication [mɛtrɪˈkeɪʃən] N conversión *f* al sistema métrico

metric system N sistema *m* métrico

metric ton N tonelada métrica

metronome ['mɛtrənəum] N metrónomo

metropolis [mɪ'trɔpəlɪs] N metrópoli(s) f

metropolitan [mɛtrə'pɔlɪtən] ADJ metropolitano

Metropolitan Police N (BRIT): **the ~** la policía londinense

mettle ['mɛtl] N valor m, ánimo

mew [mjuː] VI (cat) maullar

mews [mjuːz] (BRIT) N: **~ cottage** casa acondicionada en antiguos establos o cocheras; **~ flat** piso en antiguos establos o cocheras

Mexican ['mɛksɪkən] ADJ, N mexicano(-a) m/f, mejicano(-a) m/f

★**Mexico** ['mɛksɪkəu] N México, Méjico

Mexico City N Ciudad f de México or Méjico

mezzanine ['mɛtsəniːn] N entresuelo

MFA N ABBR (US: = Master of Fine Arts) título universitario

mfr ABBR (= manufacturer) fab.; = **manufacture**

mg ABBR (= milligram) mg

Mgr ABBR (= Monseigneur, Monsignor) Mons; (Comm) = **manager**

mgr ABBR = **manager**

MHR N ABBR (US) = **Member of the House of Representatives**

MHz ABBR (= megahertz) MHz

MI ABBR (US) = **Michigan**

MI5 N ABBR (BRIT: = Military Intelligence, section five) servicio de contraespionaje del gobierno británico

MI6 N ABBR (BRIT: = Military Intelligence, section six) servicio de inteligencia del gobierno británico

MIA ABBR (Mil: = missing in action) desaparecido

miaow [miː'au] VI maullar

mice [maɪs] PL of **mouse**

mickey ['mɪkɪ] N: **to take the ~ out of sb** tomar el pelo a algn

micro ['maɪkrəu] N = **microcomputer**

micro... [maɪkrəu] PREF micro...

microbe ['maɪkrəub] N microbio

microbiology [maɪkrəubaɪ'ɔlədʒɪ] N microbiología

microblog ['maɪkrəublɔg] N microblog m

microchip ['maɪkrəutʃɪp] N microchip m, microplaqueta

microcomputer ['maɪkrəukəm'pjuːtə'] N microordenador m, microcomputador m (LAM)

microcosm ['maɪkrəukɔzəm] N microcosmo

microeconomics ['maɪkrəui:kə'nɔmɪks] N microeconomía

microfiche ['maɪkrəufiːʃ] N microficha

microfilm ['maɪkrəufɪlm] N microfilm m

microlight ['maɪkrəulaɪt] N ultraligero

micrometer [maɪ'krɔmɪtə'] N micrómetro

microphone ['maɪkrəfəun] N micrófono

microprocessor ['maɪkrəu'prəusɛsə'] N microprocesador m

microscope ['maɪkrəskəup] N microscopio; **under the ~** al microscopio

microscopic [maɪkrə'skɔpɪk] ADJ microscópico

microwave ['maɪkrəuweɪv] N (also: **microwave oven**) horno microondas

mid [mɪd] ADJ: **in ~ May** a mediados de mayo; **~ afternoon** a media tarde; **in ~ air** en el aire; **he's in his ~ thirties** tiene unos treinta y cinco años

midday [mɪd'deɪ] N mediodía m

★**middle** ['mɪdl] N centro; (half-way point) medio; (waist) cintura; **in the ~ of the night** en plena noche; **I'm in the ~ of reading it** lo estoy leyendo ahora mismo ▶ ADJ de en medio

middle-aged [mɪdl'eɪdʒd] ADJ de mediana edad

Middle Ages NPL: **the ~** la Edad Media

middle class N: **the ~(es)** la clase media ▶ ADJ: **middle-class** de clase media

Middle East N Oriente m Medio

middleman ['mɪdlmæn] N (irreg) intermediario

middle management N dirección f de nivel medio

middle name N segundo nombre m

middle-of-the-road ['mɪdləvðə'rəud] ADJ moderado

middle school N (US) colegio para niños de doce a catorce años; (BRIT) colegio para niños de ocho o nueve a doce o trece años

middleweight ['mɪdlweɪt] N (Boxing) peso medio

middling ['mɪdlɪŋ] ADJ mediano

Middx ABBR (BRIT) = **Middlesex**

midge [mɪdʒ] N mosquito

midget ['mɪdʒɪt] N (!) enano(-a)

midi system N minicadena

Midlands ['mɪdləndz] NPL región central de Inglaterra

★**midnight** ['mɪdnaɪt] N medianoche f; **at ~** a medianoche

midriff ['mɪdrɪf] N diafragma m

midst [mɪdst] N: **in the ~ of** entre, en medio de; (situation, action) en mitad de

midsummer [mɪd'sʌmə'] N: **a ~ day** un día de pleno verano

Midsummer's Day N Día m de San Juan

midway [mɪd'weɪ] ADJ, ADV: **~ (between)** a medio camino (entre); **~ through** a la mitad (de)

midweek [mɪd'wiːk] ADV entre semana

midwife ['mɪdwaɪf] (pl **midwives** [-waɪvz]) N matrona, comadrona

midwifery ['mɪdwɪfərɪ] N tocología

midwinter [mɪd'wɪntə'] N: **in ~** en pleno invierno

miffed [mɪft] ADJ (inf) mosqueado

★**might** [maɪt] AUX VB: **you ~ like to try** podría intentar; **he ~ be there** puede que esté allí, a lo mejor está allí; **I ~ as well go** más vale que vaya; see also **may** ▶ N fuerza, poder m

m

mightily [ˈmaɪtɪlɪ] ADV fuertemente, poderosamente; **I was ~ surprised** me sorprendí enormemente

mightn't [ˈmaɪtnt] = **might not**

mighty [ˈmaɪtɪ] ADJ fuerte, poderoso

migraine [ˈmiːɡreɪn] N jaqueca

migrant [ˈmaɪɡrənt] ADJ migratorio; (worker) emigrante ▸ N (bird) ave f migratoria; (worker) emigrante mf

migrate [maɪˈɡreɪt] VI emigrar

migration [maɪˈɡreɪʃən] N emigración f

mike [maɪk] N ABBR (= microphone) micro

Milan [mɪˈlæn] N Milán m

★**mild** [maɪld] ADJ (person) apacible; (climate) templado; (slight) ligero; (taste) suave; (illness) leve

mildew [ˈmɪldjuː] N moho

mildly [ˈmaɪldlɪ] ADV ligeramente; suavemente; **to put it ~** por no decir algo peor

mildness [ˈmaɪldnɪs] N suavidad f; (of illness) levedad f

★**mile** [maɪl] N milla; **to do 20 miles per gallon** hacer 20 millas por galón

mileage [ˈmaɪlɪdʒ] N número de millas; (Aut) kilometraje m

mileage allowance N ≈ asignación f por kilometraje

mileometer [maɪˈlɒmɪtər] N (BRIT) = **milometer**

milestone [ˈmaɪlstəʊn] N mojón m; (fig) hito

milieu [ˈmiːljəː] N (medio) ambiente m, entorno

militant [ˈmɪlɪtnt] ADJ, N militante mf

militarism [ˈmɪlɪtərɪzəm] N militarismo

militaristic [mɪlɪtəˈrɪstɪk] ADJ militarista

★**military** [ˈmɪlɪtərɪ] ADJ militar

military service N servicio militar

militate [ˈmɪlɪteɪt] VI: **to ~ against** militar en contra de

militia [mɪˈlɪʃə] N milicia

★**milk** [mɪlk] N leche f ▸ VT (cow) ordeñar; (fig) chupar

milk chocolate N chocolate m con leche

milk float N (BRIT) furgoneta de la leche

milking [ˈmɪlkɪŋ] N ordeño

milkman [ˈmɪlkmən] N (irreg) lechero, repartidor m de la leche

milk shake N batido, malteada (LAM)

milk tooth N diente m de leche

milk truck N (US) = **milk float**

milky [ˈmɪlkɪ] ADJ lechoso

Milky Way N Vía Láctea

mill [mɪl] N (windmill etc) molino; (coffee mill) molinillo; (factory) fábrica; (spinning mill) hilandería ▸ VT moler ▸ VI (also: **mill about**) arremolinarse

milled [mɪld] ADJ (grain) molido; (coin, edge) acordonado

millennium [mɪˈlɛnɪəm] (pl **millenniums** or **millennia** [-ˈlɛnɪə]) N milenio

millennium bug N (Comput): **the ~** el (problema del) efecto 2000

miller [ˈmɪlər] N molinero

millet [ˈmɪlɪt] N mijo

milli... [mɪlɪ] PREF mili...

milligram, milligramme [ˈmɪlɪɡræm] N miligramo

millilitre, (US) **milliliter** [ˈmɪlɪliːtər] N mililitro

millimetre, (US) **millimeter** [ˈmɪlɪmiːtər] N milímetro

milliner [ˈmɪlɪnər] N sombrerero(-a)

millinery [ˈmɪlɪnərɪ] N sombrerería

★**million** [ˈmɪljən] N millón m; **a ~ times** un millón de veces

millionaire [mɪljəˈnɛər] N millonario(-a)

millionth [ˈmɪljənθ] ADJ millonésimo

millipede [ˈmɪlɪpiːd] N milpiés m inv

millstone [ˈmɪlstəʊn] N piedra de molino

millwheel [ˈmɪlwiːl] N rueda de molino

milometer [maɪˈlɒmɪtər] N (BRIT) cuentakilómetros m inv

mime [maɪm] N mímica; (actor) mimo(-a) ▸ VT remedar ▸ VI actuar de mimo

mimic [ˈmɪmɪk] N imitador(a) m/f ▸ ADJ mímico ▸ VT remedar, imitar

mimicry [ˈmɪmɪkrɪ] N imitación f

Min ABBR (BRIT Pol: = Ministry) Min

min. ABBR (= minute(s)) m.; = **minimum**

minaret [mɪnəˈrɛt] N alminar m, minarete m

mince [mɪns] VT picar ▸ VI (in walking) andar con pasos menudos ▸ N (BRIT Culin) carne f picada, picadillo

mincemeat [ˈmɪnsmiːt] N conserva de fruta picada; (US: meat) carne f picada

mince pie N pastelillo relleno de fruta picada

mincer [ˈmɪnsər] N picadora de carne

mincing [ˈmɪnsɪŋ] ADJ afectado

★**mind** [maɪnd] N (gen) mente f; (contrasted with matter) espíritu m; **it is on my ~** me preocupa; **to my ~** a mi parecer or juicio; **to change one's ~** cambiar de idea or de parecer; **to bring** or **call sth to ~** recordar algo; **to have sth/sb in ~** tener algo/a algn en mente; **to be out of one's ~** haber perdido el juicio; **to bear sth in ~** tomar or tener algo en cuenta; **to make up one's ~** decidirse; **it went right out of my ~** se me fue por completo (de la cabeza); **to be in two minds about sth** estar indeciso or dudar ante algo ▸ VT (attend to, look after) ocuparse de, cuidar; (be careful of) tener cuidado con; (object to): **I don't ~ the noise** no me molesta el ruido; **~ you, ...** te advierto que ...; **"~ the step"** "cuidado con el escalón" ▸ VI: **I don't ~** me es igual; **never ~!** ¡es igual!, ¡no importa!; (don't worry) ¡no te preocupes!

mind-boggling [ˈmaɪndbɒɡlɪŋ] ADJ (inf) alucinante, increíble

-minded [-maɪndɪd] ADJ: **fair-minded** imparcial; **an industrially-minded nation** una nación orientada a la industria

minder ['maɪndə^r] N guardaespaldas *m inv*

mindful ['maɪndful] ADJ: **~ of** consciente de

mindfulness ['maɪndfulnəs] N atención *f* plena, conciencia plena

mindless ['maɪndlɪs] ADJ (*violence, crime*) sin sentido; (*work*) de autómata

★**mine¹** [maɪn] PRON (el) mío/(la) mía *etc* ▶ ADJ: **this book is ~** este libro es mío

mine² [maɪn] N mina ▶ VT (*coal*) extraer; (*ship, beach*) minar

mine detector N detector *m* de minas

minefield ['maɪnfi:ld] N campo de minas

miner ['maɪnə^r] N minero(-a)

mineral ['mɪnərəl] ADJ mineral ▶ N mineral *m* ■ **minerals** NPL (*BRIT: soft drinks*) refrescos *mpl* con gas

mineral water N agua mineral

minesweeper ['maɪnswi:pə^r] N dragaminas *m inv*

mingle ['mɪŋgl] VI: **to ~ with** mezclarse con

mingy ['mɪndʒɪ] ADJ (*inf*) tacaño

mini... [mɪnɪ] PREF mini..., micro...

miniature ['mɪnətʃə^r] ADJ (en) miniatura ▶ N miniatura

minibar ['mɪnɪbɑ:^r] N minibar *m*

minibus ['mɪnɪbʌs] N microbús *m*

minicab ['mɪnɪkæb] N taxi *m* (*que solo puede pedirse por teléfono*)

minicomputer ['mɪnɪkəm'pju:tə^r] N miniordenador *m*, minicomputador *m* (*LAm*)

MiniDisc® ['mɪnɪdɪsk] N MiniDisc® *m*

minim ['mɪnɪm] N (*BRIT Mus*) blanca

minimal ['mɪnɪml] ADJ mínimo

minimalist ['mɪnɪməlɪst] ADJ, N minimalista *mf*

minimize ['mɪnɪmaɪz] VT minimizar; (*play down*) empequeñecer

★**minimum** ['mɪnɪməm] N (*pl* **minima** ['mɪnɪmə]) mínimo; **to reduce to a ~** reducir algo al mínimo ▶ ADJ mínimo; **~ wage** salario mínimo

minimum lending rate N tipo de interés mínimo

mining ['maɪnɪŋ] N minería ▶ ADJ minero

minion ['mɪnjən] N (*pej*) secuaz *m*

mini-series ['mɪnɪsɪərɪz] N miniserie *f*

miniskirt ['mɪnɪskə:t] N minifalda

★**minister** ['mɪnɪstə^r] N (*BRIT Pol*) ministro(-a); (: *junior*) secretario(-a) de Estado; (*Rel*) pastor *m* ▶ VI: **to ~** atender a

ministerial [mɪnɪs'tɪərɪəl] ADJ (*BRIT Pol*) ministerial

ministry ['mɪnɪstrɪ] N (*BRIT Pol*) ministerio; (*Rel*) sacerdocio; **M~ of Defence** Ministerio de Defensa

mink [mɪŋk] N visón *m*

mink coat N abrigo de visón

minnow ['mɪnəu] N pececillo (de agua dulce)

★**minor** ['maɪnə^r] ADJ (*repairs, injuries*) leve; (*poet, planet*) menor; (*unimportant*) secundario; (*Mus*) menor ▶ N (*Law*) menor *mf* de edad

Minorca [mɪ'nɔ:kə] N Menorca

minority [maɪ'nɔrɪtɪ] N minoría; **to be in a ~** estar en *or* ser minoría

minority interest N participación *f* minoritaria

minster ['mɪnstə^r] N catedral *f*

minstrel ['mɪnstrəl] N juglar *m*

mint [mɪnt] N (*plant*) menta, hierbabuena; (*sweet*) caramelo de menta; **the (Royal) M~**, (*US*) **the (US) M~** la Casa de la Moneda ▶ VT (*coins*) acuñar; **in ~ condition** en perfecto estado

mint sauce N salsa de menta

minuet [mɪnju'et] N minué *m*

minus ['maɪnəs] N (*also:* **minus sign**) signo menos ▶ PREP menos; **12 ~ 6 equals 6** 12 menos 6 son 6 ▶ ADJ: **~ 24°C** 24°C bajo cero

minuscule ['mɪnəskju:l] ADJ minúsculo

★**minute¹** ['mɪnɪt] N minuto; (*fig*) momento; **it is 5 minutes past 3** son las 3 y 5 (minutos); **at the last ~** a última hora; **wait a ~!** ¡espera un momento!; **up to the ~** de última hora ■ **minutes** NPL (*of meeting*) actas *fpl*

minute² [maɪ'nju:t] ADJ diminuto; (*search*) minucioso; **in ~ detail** con todo detalle

minute book N libro de actas

minute hand N minutero

minutely [maɪ'nju:tlɪ] ADV (*by a small amount*) por muy poco; (*in detail*) detalladamente, minuciosamente

minutiae [mɪ'nju:ʃɪi:] NPL minucias *fpl*

miracle ['mɪrəkl] N milagro

miracle play N auto, milagro

miraculous [mɪ'rækjuləs] ADJ milagroso

miraculously [mɪ'rækjuəslɪ] ADV milagrosamente

mirage ['mɪrɑ:ʒ] N espejismo

mire ['maɪə^r] N fango, lodo

★**mirror** ['mɪrə^r] N espejo; (*in car*) retrovisor *m* ▶ VT reflejar

mirror image N reflejo inverso

mirth [mə:θ] N alegría; (*laughter*) risa, risas *fpl*

misadventure [mɪsəd'ventʃə^r] N desventura; **death by ~** muerte *f* accidental

misanthropist [mɪ'zænθrəpɪst] N misántropo(-a)

misapply [mɪsə'plaɪ] VT emplear mal

misapprehension ['mɪsæprɪ'henʃən] N equivocación *f*

misappropriate [mɪsə'prəuprɪeɪt] VT (*funds*) malversar

misappropriation ['mɪsəprəuprɪ'eɪʃən] N malversación *f*, desfalco

misbehave [mɪsbɪ'heɪv] VI portarse mal

misbehaviour, (*US*) **misbehavior** [mɪsbɪ'heɪvjə^r] N mala conducta

m

misc. ABBR = **miscellaneous**

miscalculate [mɪsˈkælkjuleɪt] VT calcular mal

miscalculation [mɪskælkjuˈleɪʃən] N error *m* (de cálculo)

miscarriage [ˈmɪskærɪdʒ] N (*Med*) aborto (no provocado); **~ of justice** error *m* judicial

miscarry [mɪsˈkærɪ] VI (*Med*) abortar (de forma natural); (*fail: plans*) fracasar, malograrse

miscellaneous [mɪsɪˈleɪnɪəs] ADJ varios(-as), diversos(-as); **~ expenses** gastos diversos

miscellany [mɪˈsɛlənɪ] N miscelánea

mischance [mɪsˈtʃɑːns] N desgracia, mala suerte *f*; **by (some) ~** por (alguna) desgracia

mischief [ˈmɪstʃɪf] N (*naughtiness*) travesura; (*harm*) mal *m*, daño; (*maliciousness*) malicia

mischievous [ˈmɪstʃɪvəs] ADJ travieso; dañino; (*playful*) malicioso

mischievously [ˈmɪstʃɪvəslɪ] ADV por travesura; maliciosamente

misconception [ˈmɪskənˈsɛpʃən] N idea equivocada; equivocación *f*

misconduct [mɪsˈkɒndʌkt] N mala conducta; **professional ~** falta profesional

misconstrue [mɪskənˈstruː] VT interpretar mal

miscount [mɪsˈkaunt] VT, VI contar mal

misdeed [mɪsˈdiːd] N (*old*) fechoría, delito

misdemeanour, (US) **misdemeanor** [mɪsdɪˈmiːnəʳ] N delito, ofensa

misdirect [mɪsdɪˈrɛkt] VT (*person*) informar mal; (*letter*) poner señas incorrectas en

miser [ˈmaɪzəʳ] N avaro(-a)

miserable [ˈmɪzərəbl] ADJ (*unhappy*) triste, desgraciado; (*wretched*) miserable; **to feel ~** sentirse triste

miserably [ˈmɪzərəblɪ] ADV (*smile, answer*) tristemente; (*fail*) rotundamente; **to pay ~** pagar una miseria

miserly [ˈmaɪzəlɪ] ADJ avariento, tacaño

misery [ˈmɪzərɪ] N (*unhappiness*) tristeza; (*wretchedness*) miseria, desdicha

misfire [mɪsˈfaɪəʳ] VI fallar

misfit [ˈmɪsfɪt] N (*person*) inadaptado(-a)

misfortune [mɪsˈfɔːtʃən] N desgracia

misgiving [mɪsˈgɪvɪŋ] N, **misgivings** [mɪsˈgɪvɪŋz] NPL (*mistrust*) recelo; (*apprehension*) presentimiento; **to have misgivings about sth** tener dudas sobre algo

misguided [mɪsˈgaɪdɪd] ADJ equivocado

mishandle [mɪsˈhændl] VT (*treat roughly*) maltratar; (*mismanage*) manejar mal

mishap [ˈmɪshæp] N desgracia, contratiempo

mishear [mɪsˈhɪəʳ] VT, VI (*irreg: like* **hear**) oír mal

mishmash [ˈmɪʃmæʃ] N (*inf*) revoltijo

misinform [mɪsɪnˈfɔːm] VT informar mal

misinterpret [mɪsɪnˈtəːprɪt] VT interpretar mal

misinterpretation [ˈmɪsɪntəːprɪˈteɪʃən] N mala interpretación *f*

misjudge [mɪsˈdʒʌdʒ] VT juzgar mal

mislay [mɪsˈleɪ] VT (*irreg: like* **lay**) extraviar, perder

mislead [mɪsˈliːd] VT (*irreg: like* **lead**¹) llevar a conclusiones erróneas; (*deliberately*) engañar

misleading [mɪsˈliːdɪŋ] ADJ engañoso

misled [mɪsˈlɛd] PT, PP *of* **mislead**

mismanage [mɪsˈmænɪdʒ] VT administrar mal

mismanagement [mɪsˈmænɪdʒmənt] N mala administración *f*

misnomer [mɪsˈnəuməʳ] N término inapropiado *or* equivocado

misogynist [mɪˈsɒdʒɪnɪst] N misógino(-a)

misplace [mɪsˈpleɪs] VT (*lose*) extraviar; **misplaced** (*trust etc*) inmerecido

misprint [ˈmɪsprɪnt] N errata, error *m* de imprenta

mispronounce [mɪsprəˈnauns] VT pronunciar mal

misquote [ˈmɪsˈkwəut] VT citar incorrectamente

misread [mɪsˈriːd] VT (*irreg: like* **read**) leer mal

misrepresent [mɪsreprɪˈzɛnt] VT falsificar

misrepresentation [mɪsreprɪzɛnˈteɪʃən] N (*Law*) falsa declaración *f*

★**Miss** [mɪs] N Señorita; **Dear ~ Smith** Estimada Señorita Smith

★**miss** [mɪs] VT (*train etc*) perder; (*target*) errar; (*appointment, class*) faltar a; (*escape, avoid*) evitar; (*notice loss of: money etc*) notar la falta de, echar en falta; (*regret the absence of*): **I ~ him** le echo de menos; **the bus just missed the wall** faltó poco para que se estrella contra el muro; **you're missing the point** no has entendido la idea ▶ VI fallar ▶ N (*shot*) tiro fallido
▶ **miss out** VT (*BRIT*) omitir
▶ **miss out on** VT FUS (*fun, party, opportunity*) perderse

missal [ˈmɪsl] N misal *m*

misshapen [mɪsˈʃeɪpən] ADJ deforme

missile [ˈmɪsaɪl] N (*Aviat*) misil *m*; (*object thrown*) proyectil *m*

missile base N base *f* de misiles

missile launcher N lanzamisiles *m inv*

★**missing** [ˈmɪsɪŋ] ADJ (*pupil*) ausente, que falta; (*thing*) perdido; **to be ~** faltar; **~ person** desaparecido(-a); **~ in action** desaparecido en combate

mission [ˈmɪʃən] N misión *f*; **on a ~ for sb** en una misión para algn

missionary [ˈmɪʃənrɪ] N misionero(-a)

misspell [mɪsˈspɛl] VT (*irreg: like* **spell**) escribir mal

misspent [ˈmɪsˈspɛnt] ADJ: **his ~ youth** su juventud disipada

mist [mɪst] N (*light*) neblina; (*heavy*) niebla; (*at sea*) bruma ▶ VI (*also:* **mist over**, **mist up**: *weather*) nublarse; (: *BRIT: windows*) empañarse

★**mistake** [mɪsˈteɪk] N error *m*; **by ~** por equivocación; **to make a ~** (*about sb/sth*) equivocarse; (*in writing, calculating etc*) cometer un error ▶ VT (*irreg: like* **take**) entender mal; **to ~ A for B** confundir A con B

mistaken [mɪsˈteɪkən] PP *of* **mistake** ▶ ADJ (*idea etc*) equivocado; **~ identity** identificación *f* errónea; **to be ~** equivocarse, engañarse

mistakenly [mɪsˈteɪkənlɪ] ADV erróneamente

mister [ˈmɪstəʳ] N (*inf*) señor *m*; *see also* **Mr**

mistletoe [ˈmɪsltəu] N muérdago

mistook [mɪsˈtuk] PT *of* **mistake**

mistranslation [mɪstrænsˈleɪʃən] N mala traducción *f*

mistreat [mɪsˈtriːt] VT maltratar, tratar mal

mistress [ˈmɪstrɪs] N (*lover*) amante *f*; (*of house*) señora (de la casa); (*BRIT: in primary school*) maestra; (: *in secondary school*) profesora; *see also* **Mrs**

mistrust [mɪsˈtrʌst] VT desconfiar de ▶ N: **~ (of)** desconfianza (de)

mistrustful [mɪsˈtrʌstful] ADJ: **~ (of)** desconfiado (de), receloso (de)

misty [ˈmɪstɪ] ADJ nebuloso, brumoso; (*day*) de niebla; (*glasses*) empañado

misty-eyed [ˈmɪstɪˈaɪd] ADJ sentimental

misunderstand [mɪsʌndəˈstænd] VT, VI (*irreg: like* **stand**) entender mal

misunderstanding [mɪsʌndəˈstændɪŋ] N malentendido

misunderstood [mɪsʌndəˈstud] PT, PP *of* **misunderstand** ▶ ADJ (*person*) incomprendido

misuse N [mɪsˈjuːs] mal uso; (*of power*) abuso; (*of funds*) malversación *f* ▶ VT [mɪsˈjuːz] abusar de; (*funds*) malversar

MIT N ABBR (*US*) = **Massachusetts Institute of Technology**

mite [maɪt] N (*small quantity*) pizca; **poor ~!** ¡pobrecito!

mitigate [ˈmɪtɪgeɪt] VT mitigar; **mitigating circumstances** circunstancias *fpl* atenuantes

mitigation [mɪtɪˈgeɪʃən] N mitigación *f*, alivio

mitre, (*US*) **miter** [ˈmaɪtəʳ] N mitra

mitt [mɪt], **mitten** [ˈmɪtn] N manopla

★**mix** [mɪks] VT (*gen*) mezclar; (*combine*) unir; **to ~ sth with sth** mezclar algo con algo; **to ~ business with pleasure** combinar los negocios con el placer ▶ VI mezclarse; (*people*) llevarse bien ▶ N mezcla; **cake ~** preparado para pastel ▶ **mix in** VT (*eggs etc*) añadir ▶ **mix up** VT mezclar; (*confuse*) confundir; **to be mixed up in sth** estar metido en algo

★**mixed** [mɪkst] ADJ (*assorted*) variado, surtido; (*school, marriage etc*) mixto; (*feelings etc*) encontrado

mixed-ability [ˈmɪkstəˈbɪlɪtɪ] ADJ (*class etc*) de alumnos de distintas capacidades

mixed blessing N: **it's a ~** tiene su lado bueno y su lado malo

mixed doubles N (*Sport*) dobles *mpl* mixtos

mixed economy N economía mixta

mixed grill N (*BRIT*) parrillada mixta

mixed salad N ensalada mixta

mixed-up [mɪkstˈʌp] ADJ (*confused*) confuso, revuelto

mixer [ˈmɪksəʳ] N (*for food*) batidora; (*person*): **he's a good ~** tiene don de gentes

mixer tap N (grifo) monomando

★**mixture** [ˈmɪkstʃəʳ] N mezcla

mix-up [ˈmɪksʌp] N confusión *f*

Mk ABBR (*BRIT Tech*: = *mark*) Mk

mkt ABBR = **market**

ml ABBR (= *millilitre(s)*) ml

MLA N ABBR (*BRIT Pol: Northern Ireland*: = *Member of the Legislative Assembly*) miembro de la asamblea legislativa

MLitt N ABBR = **Master of Literature**; (= *Master of Letters*) título universitario de postgrado; *see also* **master's degree**

MLR N ABBR (*BRIT*) = **minimum lending rate**

mm ABBR (= *millimetre*) mm

MMR vaccine N (*against measles, mumps, rubella*) vacuna triple vírica

MMS N ABBR (= *multimedia messaging service*) MMS *m*

MN ABBR (*BRIT*) = **Merchant Navy**; (*US*) = **Minnesota**

MO N ABBR (*Med*) = **medical officer**; (*US inf*) = **modus operandi** ▶ ABBR (*US*) = **Missouri**

m.o. ABBR (= *money order*) g/

moan [məun] N gemido ▶ VI gemir; (*inf: complain*): **to ~ (about)** quejarse (de)

moaning [ˈməunɪŋ] N gemidos *mpl*; quejas *fpl*

moat [məut] N foso

mob [mɔb] N multitud *f*; (*pej*): **the ~** el populacho ▶ VT acosar

mobbing [ˈmɔbɪŋ] N acoso

★**mobile** [ˈməubaɪl] ADJ móvil ▶ N móvil *m*

mobile home N caravana

★**mobile phone** N (*BRIT*) teléfono móvil

mobile phone mast N (*BRIT Tel*) torre *f* de telefonía móvil, antena de telefonía móvil

mobility [məuˈbɪlɪtɪ] N movilidad *f*; **~ of labour** *or* (*US*) **labor** movilidad *f* de la mano de obra

mobilize [ˈməubɪlaɪz] VT movilizar

moccasin [ˈmɔkəsɪn] N mocasín *m*

mock [mɔk] VT (*make ridiculous*) ridiculizar; (*laugh at*) burlarse de ▶ ADJ fingido; **~ exams** (*BRIT Scol*) exámenes *mpl* de prueba

mockery [ˈmɔkərɪ] N burla; **to make a ~ of** desprestigiar

mocking [ˈmɔkɪŋ] ADJ (*tone*) burlón(-ona)

mockingbird [ˈmɔkɪŋbəːd] N sinsonte *m* (*LAm*), zenzontle *m* (*LAm*)

mock-up [ˈmɔkʌp] N maqueta

MOD N ABBR (*BRIT*) = **Ministry of Defence**; *see* **defence**

mod cons [ˈmɔdˈkɔnz] NPL ABBR (= *modern conveniences*) *see* **convenience**

mode [məud] N modo; (*of transport*) medio; (*Comput*) modo, modalidad *f*

★**model** ['mɔdl] N (*gen*) modelo; (*Arch*) maqueta; (*person: for fashion, art*) modelo *mf* ▶ ADJ modelo *inv*; **~ railway** ferrocarril *m* de juguete ▶ VT modelar; **to ~ o.s. on** tomar como modelo a; **to ~ clothes** pasar modelos, ser modelo; **to ~ on** crear a imitación de ▶ VI ser modelo

modelling, (*US*) **modeling** ['mɔdlɪŋ] N (*model-making*) modelado

modem ['məudəm] N módem *m*

★**moderate** ADJ, N ['mɔdərət] moderado(-a) *m/f* ▶ VI ['mɔdəreɪt] moderarse, calmarse ▶ VT ['mɔdəreɪt] moderar

moderately ['mɔdərətlɪ] ADV (*act*) con moderación; (*expensive, difficult*) medianamente; (*pleased, happy*) bastante

moderation [mɔdə'reɪʃən] N moderación *f*; **in ~** con moderación

moderator ['mɔdəreɪtər] N (*mediator*) moderador(a) *m/f*

★**modern** ['mɔdən] ADJ moderno; **~ languages** lenguas *fpl* modernas

modernity [mə'dɔːnɪtɪ] N modernidad *f*

modernization [mɔdənaɪ'zeɪʃən] N modernización *f*

modernize ['mɔdənaɪz] VT modernizar

★**modest** ['mɔdɪst] ADJ modesto; (*small*) módico

modestly ['mɔdɪstlɪ] ADV modestamente

modesty ['mɔdɪstɪ] N modestia

modicum ['mɔdɪkəm] N: **a ~ of** un mínimo de

modification [mɔdɪfɪ'keɪʃən] N modificación *f*; **to make modifications** hacer cambios *or* modificaciones

modify ['mɔdɪfaɪ] VT modificar

modish ['məudɪʃ] ADJ de moda

Mods [mɔdz] N ABBR (*BRIT*: = (*Honour*) *Moderations*) *examen de licenciatura de la universidad de Oxford*

modular ['mɔdjulər] ADJ (*filing, unit*) modular

modulate ['mɔdjuleɪt] VT modular

modulation [mɔdju'leɪʃən] N modulación *f*

module ['mɔdjuːl] N módulo

modus operandi ['məudəsɔpə'rændiː] N manera de actuar

Mogadishu [mɔgə'diːʃuː] N Mogadiscio

mogul ['məugəl] N (*fig*) magnate *m*

MOH N ABBR (*BRIT*) = **Medical Officer of Health**

mohair ['məuhɛər] N mohair *m*

Mohammed [mə'hæmɛd] N Mahoma *m*

moist [mɔɪst] ADJ húmedo

moisten ['mɔɪsn] VT humedecer

moisture ['mɔɪstʃər] N humedad *f*

moisturize ['mɔɪstʃəraɪz] VT (*skin*) hidratar

moisturizer ['mɔɪstʃəraɪzər] N crema hidratante

mojo ['məudʒəu] N (*US inf*) magnetismo personal

molar ['məulər] N muela

molasses [məu'læsɪz] N melaza

mold [məuld] N, VT (*US*) = **mould**

Moldavia [mɔl'deɪvɪə], **Moldova** [mɔl'dəuvə] N Moldavia, Moldova

Moldavian [mɔl'deɪvɪən], **Moldovan** [mɔl'dəuvən] ADJ, N moldavo(-a) *m/f*

mole [məul] N (*animal*) topo; (*spot*) lunar *m*

molecular [mə'lɛkjulər] ADJ molecular

molecule ['mɔlɪkjuːl] N molécula

molest [məu'lɛst] VT importunar; (*sexually*) abusar sexualmente de

moll [mɔl] N (*inf*) amiga

mollusc, (*US*) **mollusk** ['mɔləsk] N molusco

mollycoddle ['mɔlɪkɔdl] VT mimar

Molotov cocktail ['mɔlətɔf-] N cóctel *m* Molotov

molt [məult] VI (*US*) = **moult**

molten ['məultən] ADJ fundido; (*lava*) líquido

mom [mɔm] N (*US*) = **mum**

★**moment** ['məumənt] N momento; **at** *or* **for the ~** de momento, por el momento, por ahora; **in a ~** dentro de un momento

momentarily ['məuməntrɪlɪ] ADV momentáneamente; (*US: very soon*) de un momento a otro

momentary ['məuməntərɪ] ADJ momentáneo

momentous [məu'mɛntəs] ADJ trascendental, importante

momentum [məu'mɛntəm] N momento; (*fig*) ímpetu *m*; **to gather ~** cobrar velocidad; (*fig*) cobrar fuerza

mommy ['mɔmɪ] N (*US*) = **mummy**

Mon. ABBR (= *Monday*) lun.

Monaco ['mɔnəkəu] N Mónaco

monarch ['mɔnək] N monarca *mf*

monarchist ['mɔnəkɪst] N monárquico(-a)

monarchy ['mɔnəkɪ] N monarquía

monastery ['mɔnəstərɪ] N monasterio

monastic [mə'næstɪk] ADJ monástico

★**Monday** ['mʌndɪ] N lunes *m inv*; *see also* **Tuesday**

Monegasque [mɔnɪ'gæsk] ADJ, N monegasco(-a) *m/f*

monetarist ['mʌnɪtərɪst] N monetarista *mf*

monetary ['mʌnɪtərɪ] ADJ monetario

monetary policy N política monetaria

monetization [mʌnɪtaɪ'zeɪʃən] N monetización *f*

monetize ['mʌnɪtaɪz] VT monetizar

★**money** ['mʌnɪ] N dinero, plata (*LAm*); **to make ~** ganar dinero; **I've got no ~ left** no me queda dinero

money belt N riñonera

moneyed ['mʌnɪd] ADJ adinerado

moneylender ['mʌnɪlɛndər] N prestamista *mf*

moneymaker ['mʌnɪmeɪkər] N (*BRIT inf: business*) filón *m*

moneymaking [ˈmʌnɪmeɪkɪŋ] ADJ rentable

money market N mercado monetario

money order N giro

money-spinner [ˈmʌnɪspɪnəʳ] N (inf: person, idea, business) filón m

money supply N oferta monetaria, medio circulante, volumen m monetario

Mongol [ˈmɔŋgəl] N mongol(a) m/f; (Ling) mongol m

Mongolia [mɔŋˈgəulɪə] N Mongolia

Mongolian [mɔŋˈgəulɪən] ADJ mongol(a) ▶ N mongol(a) m/f; (Ling) mongol m

mongoose [ˈmɔŋguːs] N mangosta

mongrel [ˈmʌŋgrəl] N (dog) perro cruzado

★**monitor** [ˈmɔnɪtəʳ] N (Scol) monitor m; (also: **television monitor**) receptor m de control; (of computer) monitor m ▶ VT controlar; (foreign station) escuchar

monk [mʌŋk] N monje m

★**monkey** [ˈmʌŋkɪ] N mono

monkey business N, **monkey tricks** NPL tejemanejes mpl

monkey nut N (BRIT) cacahuete m, maní m (LAM)

monkey wrench N llave f inglesa

mono [ˈmɔnəu] ADJ (broadcast etc) mono inv

mono... [mɔnəu] PREF mono...

monochrome [ˈmɔnəukrəum] ADJ monocromo

monocle [ˈmɔnəkl] N monóculo

monogamous [məˈnɔgəməs] ADJ monógamo

monogram [ˈmɔnəgræm] N monograma m

monolith [ˈmɔnəlɪθ] N monolito

monolithic [mɔnəˈlɪθɪk] ADJ monolítico

monologue [ˈmɔnəlɔg] N monólogo

monoplane [ˈmɔnəpleɪn] N monoplano

monopolist [məˈnɔpəlɪst] N monopolista mf

monopolize [məˈnɔpəlaɪz] VT monopolizar

monopoly [məˈnɔpəlɪ] N monopolio; **Monopolies and Mergers Commission** (BRIT) comisión reguladora de monopolios y fusiones

monorail [ˈmɔnəureɪl] N monocarril m, monorraíl m

monosodium glutamate [mɔnəˈsəudɪəmˈgluːtəmeɪt] N glutamato monosódico

monosyllabic [mɔnɔsɪˈlæbɪk] ADJ monosílabo

monosyllable [ˈmɔnəsɪləbl] N monosílabo

monotone [ˈmɔnətəun] N voz f (or tono) monocorde

monotonous [məˈnɔtənəs] ADJ monótono

monotony [məˈnɔtənɪ] N monotonía

monoxide [məˈnɔksaɪd] N: **carbon ~** monóxido de carbono

monseigneur [mɔnsɛnˈjəːʳ], **monsignor** [mɔnˈsiːnjəʳ] N monseñor m

monsoon [mɔnˈsuːn] N monzón m

monster [ˈmɔnstəʳ] N monstruo

monstrosity [mɔnsˈtrɔsɪtɪ] N monstruosidad f

monstrous [ˈmɔnstrəs] ADJ (huge) enorme; (atrocious) monstruoso

montage [mɔnˈtɑːʒ] N montaje m

Mont Blanc [mɔ̃ˈblɑ̃] N Mont Blanc m

Montenegro [mɔntɪˈniːgrəu] N Montenegro

★**month** [mʌnθ] N mes m; **300 dollars a ~** 300 dólares al mes; **every ~** cada mes

★**monthly** [ˈmʌnθlɪ] ADJ mensual; **~ instalment** mensualidad f ▶ ADV mensualmente; **twice ~** dos veces al mes ▶ N (magazine) revista mensual

monument [ˈmɔnjumənt] N monumento

monumental [mɔnjuˈmɛntl] ADJ monumental

moo [muː] VI mugir

★**mood** [muːd] N humor m; **to be in a good/bad ~** estar de buen/mal humor

moodily [ˈmuːdɪlɪ] ADV malhumoradamente

moodiness [ˈmuːdɪnɪs] N humor m cambiante; (bad mood) mal humor m

moody [ˈmuːdɪ] ADJ (changeable) de humor variable; (sullen) malhumorado

★**moon** [muːn] N luna

moonbeam [ˈmuːnbiːm] N rayo de luna

moon landing N alunizaje m

moonless [ˈmuːnlɪs] ADJ sin luna

moonlight [ˈmuːnlaɪt] N luz f de la luna ▶ VI hacer pluriempleo

moonlighting [ˈmuːnlaɪtɪŋ] N pluriempleo

moonlit [ˈmuːnlɪt] ADJ: **a ~ night** una noche de luna

moonshot [ˈmuːnʃɔt] N lanzamiento de una astronave a la luna

moonstruck [ˈmuːnstrʌk] ADJ chiflado

moony [ˈmuːnɪ] ADJ: **to have ~ eyes** estar soñando despierto, estar pensando en las musarañas

Moor [muəʳ] N moro(-a)

moor [muəʳ] N páramo ▶ VT (ship) amarrar ▶ VI echar las amarras

moorings [ˈmuərɪŋz] NPL (chains) amarras fpl; (place) amarradero sg

Moorish [ˈmuərɪʃ] ADJ moro; (architecture) árabe

moorland [ˈmuələnd] N páramo, brezal m

moose [muːs] N pl inv alce m

moot [muːt] VT proponer para la discusión, sugerir ▶ ADJ: **~ point** punto discutible

mop [mɔp] N fregona; (of hair) melena ▶ VT fregar

▶ **mop up** VT limpiar

mope [məup] VI estar deprimido

▶ **mope about, mope around** VI andar abatido

moped [ˈməupɛd] N ciclomotor m

moquette [mɔˈkɛt] N moqueta

MOR ADJ ABBR (Mus: = middle-of-the-road) para el gran público

m

★**moral** [ˈmɔrl] ADJ moral ▶ N moraleja ■ **morals** NPL moralidad f, moral f

morale [mɔˈrɑːl] N moral f

morality [məˈrælɪtɪ] N moralidad f

moralize [ˈmɔrəlaɪz] VI: **to ~ (about)** moralizar (sobre)

morally [ˈmɔrəlɪ] ADV moralmente

moral victory N victoria moral

morass [məˈræs] N pantano

moratorium [mɔrəˈtɔːrɪəm] N moratoria

morbid [ˈmɔːbɪd] ADJ (interest) morboso; (Med) mórbido

---

more [mɔːʳ]

ADJ **1** (greater in number etc) más; **more people/ work than before** más gente/trabajo que antes

2 (additional) más; **do you want (some) more tea?** ¿quieres más té?; **is there any more wine?** ¿queda vino?; **it'll take a few more weeks** tardará unas semanas más; **it's 2 kms more to the house** faltan 2 km para la casa; **more time/letters than we expected** más tiempo del que/más cartas de las que esperábamos; **I have no more money, I don't have any more money** (ya) no tengo más dinero

▶ PRON (greater amount, additional amount) más; **more than 10** más de 10; **it cost more than the other one/than we expected** costó más que el otro/más de lo que esperábamos; **is there any more?** ¿hay más?; **I want more** quiero más; **and what's more …** y además …; **many/much more** muchos(-as) más, mucho(-a) más

▶ ADV más; **more dangerous/easily (than)** más peligroso/fácilmente (que); **more and more expensive** cada vez más caro; **more or less** más o menos; **more than ever** más que nunca; **she doesn't live here any more** ya no vive aquí

---

moreover [mɔːˈrəuvəʳ] ADV además, por otra parte

morgue [mɔːg] N depósito de cadáveres

MORI [ˈmɔːrɪ] N ABBR (BRIT) = **Market and Opinion Research Institute**

moribund [ˈmɔrɪbʌnd] ADJ moribundo

Mormon [ˈmɔːmən] N mormón(-ona) m/f

★**morning** [ˈmɔːnɪŋ] N (gen) mañana; (early morning) madrugada; **in the ~** por la mañana; **7 o'clock in the ~** las 7 de la mañana; **this ~** esta mañana

morning-after pill [ˈmɔːnɪŋˈɑːftə-] N píldora del día después

morning sickness N (Med) náuseas fpl del embarazo

Moroccan [məˈrɔkən] ADJ, N marroquí mf

Morocco [məˈrɔkəu] N Marruecos m

moron [ˈmɔːrɔn] N (!) imbécil mf

morose [məˈrəus] ADJ hosco, malhumorado

morphine [ˈmɔːfiːn] N morfina

morris dancing [ˈmɔrɪs] N (BRIT) baile tradicional inglés en el que se llevan cascabeles en la ropa

Morse [mɔːs] N (also: **Morse code**) (código) morse m

morsel [ˈmɔːsl] N (of food) bocado

mortal [ˈmɔːtl] ADJ, N mortal m

mortality [mɔːˈtælɪtɪ] N mortalidad f

mortality rate N tasa de mortalidad

mortally [ˈmɔːtəlɪ] ADV mortalmente

mortar [ˈmɔːtəʳ] N argamasa; (implement) mortero

★**mortgage** [ˈmɔːgɪdʒ] N hipoteca; **to take out a ~** sacar una hipoteca ▶ VT hipotecar

mortgage company N (US) ≈ banco hipotecario

mortgagee [mɔːgəˈdʒiː] N acreedor(a) m/f hipotecario(-a)

mortgager [ˈmɔːgədʒəʳ] N deudor(a) m/f hipotecario(-a)

mortice [ˈmɔːtɪs] N = **mortise**

mortician [mɔːˈtɪʃən] N (US) director(a) m/f de pompas fúnebres

mortification [ˈmɔːtɪfɪˈkeɪʃən] N mortificación f, humillación f

mortified [ˈmɔːtɪfaɪd] ADJ: **I was ~** me dio muchísima vergüenza

mortise [ˈmɔːtɪs], **mortise lock** N cerradura de muesca

mortuary [ˈmɔːtjuərɪ] N depósito de cadáveres

mosaic [məuˈzeɪɪk] N mosaico

Moscow [ˈmɔskəu] N Moscú m

Moslem [ˈmɔzləm] ADJ, N = **Muslim**

mosque [mɔsk] N mezquita

mosquito [mɔsˈkiːtəu] (pl **mosquitoes**) N mosquito, zancudo (LAM)

moss [mɔs] N musgo

mossy [ˈmɔsɪ] ADJ musgoso, cubierto de musgo

★**most** [məust] ADJ la mayor parte de, la mayoría de; **I saw the ~** yo fui el que más vi ▶ PRON la mayor parte, la mayoría; **~ of them** la mayor parte de ellos; **the ~** (also: + adjective) el más; **at the (very) ~** a lo sumo, todo lo más; **to make the ~ of** aprovechar (al máximo) ▶ ADV el más; (very) muy; **a ~ interesting book** un libro interesantísimo

★**mostly** [ˈməustlɪ] ADV en su mayor parte, principalmente

MOT N ABBR (BRIT) = **Ministry of Transport**; **the ~ (test)** ≈ la ITV

motel [məuˈtel] N motel m

moth [mɔθ] N mariposa nocturna; (clothes moth) polilla

mothball [ˈmɔθbɔːl] N bola de naftalina

moth-eaten [ˈmɔθiːtn] ADJ apolillado

★**mother** [ˈmʌðəʳ] N madre f ▶ ADJ materno ▶ VT (care for) cuidar (como una madre)

mother board N (*Comput*) placa madre

motherhood ['mʌðəhud] N maternidad f

mother-in-law ['mʌðərɪnlɔ:] N suegra

motherly ['mʌðəlɪ] ADJ maternal

mother-of-pearl ['mʌðərəv'pə:l] N nácar m

Mother's Day N Día m de la Madre

mother's help N niñera

mother-to-be ['mʌðətə'bi:] N futura madre

mother tongue N lengua materna

mothproof ['mɔθpru:f] ADJ a prueba de polillas

motif [məu'ti:f] N motivo; (*theme*) tema m

motion ['məuʃən] N movimiento; (*gesture*) ademán m, señal f; (*at meeting*) moción f; (*BRIT: also*: **bowel motion**) evacuación f intestinal; **to be in ~** (*vehicle*) estar en movimiento; **to set in ~** poner en marcha; **to go through the motions of doing sth** (*fig*) hacer algo mecánicamente *or* sin convicción ▶ VT, VI: **to ~ (to) sb to do sth** hacer señas a algn para que haga algo

motionless ['məuʃənlɪs] ADJ inmóvil

motion picture N película

motivate ['məutɪveɪt] VT motivar

motivated ['məutɪveɪtɪd] ADJ motivado

motivation [məutɪ'veɪʃən] N motivación f

motivational research [məutɪ'veɪʃənl-] N estudios mpl de motivación

motive ['məutɪv] N motivo; **from the best motives** con las mejores intenciones

motley ['mɔtlɪ] ADJ variopinto

★**motor** ['məutə'] N motor m; (*BRIT inf: vehicle*) coche m, carro (*LAM*), automóvil m, auto m (*LAM*) ▶ ADJ motor(a), motriz

motorbike ['məutəbaɪk] N moto f

motorboat ['məutəbəut] N lancha motora

motorcade ['məutəkeɪd] N desfile m de automóviles

motorcar ['məutəka:'] N (*BRIT*) coche m, carro (*LAM*), automóvil m, auto m (*LAM*)

motorcoach ['məutəkəutʃ] N autocar m, autobús m, camión m (*LAM*)

motorcycle ['məutəsaɪkl] N motocicleta

motorcycle racing N motociclismo

motorcyclist ['məutəsaɪklɪst] N motociclista mf

motoring ['məutərɪŋ] N (*BRIT*) automovilismo ▶ ADJ (*accident, offence*) de tráfico *or* tránsito

motorist ['məutərɪst] N conductor(a) m/f, automovilista mf

motorize ['məutəraɪz] VT motorizar

motor oil N aceite m para motores

motor racing N (*BRIT*) carreras fpl de coches, automovilismo

motor scooter N vespa®, motoneta (*LAM*)

motor vehicle N automóvil m

motorway ['məutəweɪ] N (*BRIT*) autopista

mottled ['mɔtld] ADJ moteado

motto ['mɔtəu] (*pl* **mottoes**) N lema m; (*watchword*) consigna

mould, (*US*) **mold** [məuld] N molde m; (*mildew*) moho ▶ VT moldear; (*fig*) formar

moulder, (*US*) **molder** ['məuldə'] VI (*decay*) decaer

moulding, (*US*) **molding** ['məuldɪŋ] N (*Arch*) moldura

mouldy, (*US*) **moldy** ['məuldɪ] ADJ enmohecido

moult, (*US*) **molt** [məult] VI mudar la piel; (*bird*) mudar las plumas

mound [maund] N montón m, montículo

mount [maunt] N monte m; (*horse*) montura; (*for jewel etc*) engarce m; (*for picture*) marco ▶ VT montar en, subir a; (*stairs*) subir; (*exhibition*) montar; (*attack*) lanzar; (*stamp*) pegar, fijar; (*picture*) enmarcar ▶ VI (*also*: **mount up**: *increase*) aumentar; (*on horse*) montar

★**mountain** ['mauntɪn] N montaña; **to make a ~ out of a molehill** hacer una montaña de un grano de arena ▶ CPD de montaña

mountain bike N bicicleta de montaña

mountaineer [mauntɪ'nɪə'] N montañero(-a), alpinista mf, andinista mf (*LAM*)

mountaineering [mauntɪ'nɪərɪŋ] N montañismo, alpinismo, andinismo (*LAM*)

mountainous ['mauntɪnəs] ADJ montañoso

mountain range N sierra

mountain rescue team N equipo de rescate de montaña

mountainside ['mauntɪnsaɪd] N ladera de la montaña

mounted ['mauntɪd] ADJ montado

Mount Everest N Monte m Everest

mourn [mɔ:n] VT llorar, lamentar ▶ VI: **to ~ for** llorar la muerte de, lamentarse por

mourner ['mɔ:nə'] N doliente mf

mournful ['mɔ:nful] ADJ triste, lúgubre

mourning ['mɔ:nɪŋ] N luto; **in ~** de luto ▶ CPD (*dress*) de luto

★**mouse** [maus] (*pl* **mice** [maɪs]) N (*also Comput*) ratón m

mouse mat, mouse pad N (*Comput*) alfombrilla, almohadilla

mousetrap ['maustræp] N ratonera

mousse [mu:s] N (*Culin*) mousse f; (*for hair*) espuma (moldeadora)

moustache [məs'ta:ʃ], (*US*) **mustache** ['mʌstæʃ] N bigote m

mousy ['mausɪ] ADJ (*person*) tímido; (*hair*) pardusco

★**mouth** [mauθ] (*pl* **mouths** [-ðz]) N boca; (*of river*) desembocadura

mouthful ['mauθful] N bocado

mouth organ N armónica

mouthpiece ['mauθpi:s] N (*of musical instru-*

ment) boquilla; (*Tel*) micrófono; (*spokesman*) portavoz *mf*

mouth-to-mouth ['mauθtə'mauθ] ADJ (*also:* **mouth-to-mouth resuscitation**) boca a boca *m*

mouthwash ['mauθwɔʃ] N enjuague *m* bucal

mouth-watering ['mauθwɔːtərɪŋ] ADJ apetitoso

movable ['muːvəbl] ADJ movible

★**move** [muːv] N (*movement*) movimiento; (*in game*) jugada; (: *turn to play*) turno; (*change of house*) mudanza; **to get a ~ on** darse prisa ▶ VT mover; (*emotionally*) conmover; (*Pol: resolution etc*) proponer; **to ~ sb to do sth** mover a algn a hacer algo; **to be moved** estar conmovido ▶ VI (*gen*) moverse; (*traffic*) circular; (*BRIT: also:* **move house**) trasladarse, mudarse
  ▶ **move about, move around** VI moverse; (*travel*) viajar
  ▶ **move along** VI (*stop loitering*) circular; (*along seat etc*) correrse
  ▶ **move away** VI (*leave*) marcharse
  ▶ **move back** VI (*return*) volver
  ▶ **move down** VT (*demote*) degradar
  ▶ **move forward** VI avanzar ▶ VT adelantar
  ▶ **move in** VI (*to a house*) instalarse
  ▶ **move off** VI ponerse en camino
  ▶ **move on** VI seguir viaje ▶ VT (*onlookers*) hacer circular
  ▶ **move out** VI (*of house*) mudarse
  ▶ **move over** VI hacerse a un lado, correrse
  ▶ **move up** VI subir; (*employee*) ascender

★**movement** ['muːvmənt] N movimiento; (*Tech*) mecanismo; **~ (of the bowels)** (*Med*) evacuación *f*

mover ['muːvəʳ] N proponente *mf*

★**movie** ['muːvɪ] N película; **to go to the movies** ir al cine

movie camera N cámara cinematográfica

moviegoer ['muːvɪɡəuəʳ] N (*US*) aficionado(-a) al cine

movie theater N (*US*) cine *m*

moving ['muːvɪŋ] ADJ (*emotional*) conmovedor(a); (*that moves*) móvil; (*instigating*) motor(a)

mow [məu] (*pt* **mowed**, *pp* **mowed** *or* **mown** [məun]) VT (*grass*) cortar; (*corn*) segar; (*also:* **mow down**: *shoot*) acribillar

mower ['məuəʳ] N (*also:* **lawnmower**) cortacésped *m*

Mozambique [məuzæm'biːk] N Mozambique *m*

★**MP** N ABBR (= *Military Police*) PM; (*BRIT*) = **Member of Parliament**; (*CANADA*) = **Mounted Police**

mpg N ABBR (= *miles per gallon*) *30 mpg = 9.4 l. per 100 km*

mph ABBR (= *miles per hour*) *60 mph = 96 km/h*

MPhil N ABBR (= *Master of Philosophy*) título universitario de postgrado; *see also* **master's degree**

MPS N ABBR (*BRIT*) = **Member of the Pharmaceutical Society**

MP3 ['ɛmpiː'θriː] N MP3 *m*

MP3 player N reproductor *m* MP3

★**Mr, Mr.** ['mɪstəʳ] N: **Mr Smith** (el) Sr. Smith

Use the article with **Sr./señor**, **Sra./señora**, **Srta./señorita** when you are talking about someone rather than to them: *Mr Smith is not at home*. **El señor Smith no está en casa**. Don't use the article before the title when addressing someone directly: *Dear Mrs Ramírez* **Estimada Sra. Ramírez**.

MRC N ABBR (*BRIT*: = *Medical Research Council*) departamento estatal que controla la investigación médica

MRCP N ABBR (*BRIT*) = **Member of the Royal College of Physicians**

MRCS N ABBR (*BRIT*) = **Member of the Royal College of Surgeons**

MRCVS N ABBR (*BRIT*) = **Member of the Royal College of Veterinary Surgeons**

★**Mrs, Mrs.** ['mɪsɪz] N: **~ Smith** (la) Sra. de Smith

MS N ABBR (= *manuscript*) MS; = **multiple sclerosis**; (*US*: = *Master of Science*) título universitario ▶ ABBR (*US*) = **Mississippi**

★**Ms, Ms.** [mɪz] N (*Miss or Mrs*) abreviatura con la que se evita hacer expreso el estado civil de una mujer; **Ms Smith** (la) Sra. Smith

MSA N ABBR (*US*: = *Master of Science in Agriculture*) título universitario

MSc ABBR *see* **Master of Science**

MSG N ABBR = **monosodium glutamate**

MSP N ABBR (*BRIT*) = **Member of the Scottish Parliament**

MST ABBR (*US*: = *Mountain Standard Time*) hora de invierno de las Montañas Rocosas

MSW N ABBR (*US*: = *Master of Social Work*) título universitario

MT ABBR (*US*) = **Montana** ▶ N ABBR = **machine translation**

Mt ABBR (*Geo*: = *mount*) m.

mth ABBR (= *month*) m

MTV N ABBR = **music television**

★**much** [mʌtʃ] ADJ mucho ▶ ADV, N, PRON mucho; (*before pp*) muy; **how ~ is it?** ¿cuánto es?, ¿cuánto cuesta?; **too ~** demasiado; **so ~** tanto; **it's not ~** no es mucho; **as ~ as** tanto como; **however ~ he tries** por mucho que se esfuerce; **I like it very/so ~** me gusta mucho/tanto; **thank you very ~** muchas gracias, muy agradecido

muck [mʌk] N (*dirt*) suciedad *f*; (*fig*) porquería
  ▶ **muck about, muck around** VI (*inf*) perder el tiempo; (: *enjoy o.s.*) entretenerse; (: *tinker*) manosear
  ▶ **muck in** VI (*inf*) arrimar el hombro
  ▶ **muck out** VT (*stable*) limpiar
  ▶ **muck up** VT (*inf*: *dirty*) ensuciar; (: *spoil*) echar a perder; (: *ruin*) estropear

muckraking ['mʌkreɪkɪŋ] (*fig*: *inf*) N amarillismo ▶ ADJ especializado en escándalos

mucky [ˈmʌkɪ] ADJ (*dirty*) sucio

mucus [ˈmjuːkəs] N mucosidad *f*, moco

mud [mʌd] N barro, lodo

muddle [ˈmʌdl] N desorden *m*, confusión *f*; (*mix-up*) embrollo, lío ▶ VT (*also:* **muddle up**) embrollar, confundir
▶ **muddle along, muddle on** VI arreglárselas de alguna manera
▶ **muddle through** VI salir del paso

muddle-headed [mʌdlˈhɛdɪd] ADJ (*person*) despistado, confuso

muddy [ˈmʌdɪ] ADJ fangoso, cubierto de lodo

mudguard [ˈmʌdgɑːd] N guardabarros *m inv*

mudpack [ˈmʌdpæk] N mascarilla

mudslide [ˈmʌdslaɪd] N desprendimiento de tierra

mud-slinging [ˈmʌdslɪŋɪŋ] N injurias *fpl*, difamación *f*

muesli [ˈmjuːzlɪ] N muesli *m*

muff [mʌf] N manguito ▶ VT (*chance*) desperdiciar; (*lines*) estropear; (*shot, catch etc*) fallar; **to ~ it** fracasar

muffin [ˈmʌfɪn] N bollo, ≈ magdalena

muffle [ˈmʌfl] VT (*sound*) amortiguar; (*against cold*) abrigar

muffled [ˈmʌfld] ADJ sordo, apagado; (*noise etc*) amortiguado

muffler [ˈmʌfləʳ] N (*scarf*) bufanda; (*US: Aut*) silenciador *m*; (: *on motorbike*) silenciador *m*, mofle *m*

mufti [ˈmʌftɪ] N: **in ~** (vestido) de paisano

mug [mʌg] N (*cup*) taza alta; (*for beer*) jarra; (*inf: face*) jeta; (: *fool*) bobo; **it's a ~'s game** es cosa de bobos ▶ VT (*assault*) atracar
▶ **mug up** VT (*inf: also:* **mug up on**) empollar

mugger [ˈmʌgəʳ] N atracador(a) *m/f*

mugging [ˈmʌgɪŋ] N atraco callejero

muggins [ˈmʌgɪnz] NSG (*inf*) tonto(-a) del bote

muggy [ˈmʌgɪ] ADJ bochornoso

mug shot N (*inf*) foto *f* (para la ficha policial)

mulatto [mjuːˈlætəu] (*pl* **mulattoes**) N (!) mulato(-a)

mulberry [ˈmʌlbrɪ] N (*fruit*) mora; (*tree*) morera, moral *m*

mule [mjuːl] N mula

mull [mʌl]: **to ~ over** VT meditar sobre

mulled [mʌld] ADJ: **~ wine** vino caliente (*con especias*)

mullioned [ˈmʌlɪənd] ADJ (*window*) dividido por parteluces

multi... [mʌltɪ] PREF multi...

multi-access [ˈmʌltɪˈækses] ADJ (*Comput*) multiacceso, de acceso múltiple

multicoloured, (*US*) **multicolored** [ˈmʌltɪkʌləd] ADJ multicolor

multifarious [mʌltɪˈfɛərɪəs] ADJ múltiple, vario

multigrain [ˈmʌltɪgreɪn] ADJ multigrano

multilateral [mʌltɪˈlætərl] ADJ (*Pol*) multilateral

multi-level [mʌltɪˈlɛvl] ADJ (*US*) = **multistorey**

multimedia [ˈmʌltɪˈmiːdɪə] ADJ multimedia *inv*

multimillionaire [mʌltɪmɪljəˈnɛəʳ] N multimillonario(-a)

multinational [mʌltɪˈnæʃənl] N multinacional *f* ▶ ADJ multinacional

multiple [ˈmʌltɪpl] ADJ múltiple ▶ N múltiplo; (*BRIT: also:* **multiple store**) (cadena de) grandes almacenes *mpl*

multiple choice N (*also:* **multiple choice test**) examen *m* de tipo test

multiple crash N colisión *f* en cadena

multiple sclerosis [-sklɪˈrəusɪs] N esclerosis *f* múltiple

multiplex [ˈmʌltɪplɛks] N (*also:* **multiplex cinema**) multicines *m inv*

multiplication [mʌltɪplɪˈkeɪʃən] N multiplicación *f*

multiplication table N tabla de multiplicar

multiplicity [mʌltɪˈplɪsɪtɪ] N multiplicidad *f*

multiply [ˈmʌltɪplaɪ] VT multiplicar ▶ VI multiplicarse

multiracial [mʌltɪˈreɪʃl] ADJ multirracial

multistorey [mʌltɪˈstɔːrɪ] ADJ (*BRIT: building, car park*) de muchos pisos

multitask [ˈmʌltɪtɑːsk] VI (*also Comput*) trabajar en multitarea

multitasking [ˈmʌltɪtɑːskɪŋ] N (*also Comput*) multitarea

multi-tasking [ˈmʌltɪtɑːskɪŋ] N (*Comput*) ejecución *f* de tareas múltiples, multitarea

multitude [ˈmʌltɪtjuːd] N multitud *f*

★**mum** [mʌm] N (*BRIT*) mamá *f* ▶ ADJ: **to keep ~ (about sth)** no decir ni mu (de algo)

mumble [ˈmʌmbl] VT decir entre dientes ▶ VI hablar entre dientes, musitar

mumbo jumbo [ˈmʌmbəu-] N (*inf*) galimatías *m inv*

mummify [ˈmʌmɪfaɪ] VT momificar

mummy [ˈmʌmɪ] N (*BRIT: mother*) mamá *f*; (*embalmed*) momia

mumps [mʌmps] N paperas *fpl*

munch [mʌntʃ] VT, VI mascar

mundane [mʌnˈdeɪn] ADJ mundano

municipal [mjuːˈnɪsɪpl] ADJ municipal

municipality [mjuːnɪsɪˈpælɪtɪ] N municipio

munificence [muːˈnɪfɪsns] N munificencia

munitions [mjuːˈnɪʃənz] NPL municiones *fpl*

mural [ˈmjuərl] N (pintura) mural *m*

★**murder** [ˈməːdəʳ] N asesinato; (*in law*) homicidio; **to commit ~** cometer un asesinato *or* homicidio ▶ VT asesinar, matar

murderer [ˈməːdərəʳ] N asesino(-a)

murderess [ˈməːdərɪs] N asesina

murderous [ˈməːdərəs] ADJ homicida

murk [məːk] N oscuridad f, tinieblas fpl

murky [ˈməːkɪ] ADJ (water, past) turbio; (room) sombrío

murmur [ˈməːməʳ] N murmullo; **heart ~** soplo cardíaco ▶ VT, VI murmurar

MusB, MusBac N ABBR (= Bachelor of Music) título universitario

★**muscle** [ˈmʌsl] N músculo; (fig: strength) garra, fuerza
▶ **muscle in** VI entrometerse

muscular [ˈmʌskjuləʳ] ADJ muscular; (person) musculoso

muscular dystrophy N distrofia muscular

MusD, MusDoc N ABBR (= Doctor of Music) título universitario

muse [mjuːz] VI meditar ▶ N musa

★**museum** [mjuːˈzɪəm] N museo

mush [mʌʃ] N gachas fpl

★**mushroom** [ˈmʌʃrum] N (gen) seta, hongo; (small) champiñón m ▶ VI (fig) crecer de la noche a la mañana

mushy [ˈmʌʃɪ] ADJ (vegetables) casi hecho puré; (story) sentimentaloide

★**music** [ˈmjuːzɪk] N música

★**musical** [ˈmjuːzɪkl] ADJ musical; (sound) melodioso; (person) con talento musical ▶ N (show) (comedia) musical m

musical box N = **music box**

musical chairs N juego de las sillas; (fig): **to play ~** cambiar de puesto continuamente

musical instrument N instrumento musical

musically [ˈmjuːzɪklɪ] ADV melodiosamente, armoniosamente

music box N caja de música

music centre N equipo de música

music hall N teatro de variedades

★**musician** [mjuːˈzɪʃən] N músico(-a)

music stand N atril m

musk [mʌsk] N (perfume m de) almizcle m

musket [ˈmʌskɪt] N mosquete m

musk rat N ratón m almizclero

musk rose N (Bot) rosa almizcleña

Muslim [ˈmʌzlɪm] ADJ, N musulmán(-ana) m/f

muslin [ˈmʌzlɪn] N muselina

musquash [ˈmʌskwɔʃ] N (fur) piel f del ratón almizclero

muss [mʌs] VT (inf: hair) despeinar; (: dress) arrugar

mussel [ˈmʌsl] N mejillón m

★**must** [mʌst] AUX VB (obligation): **I ~ do it** debo hacerlo, tengo que hacerlo; (probability): **he ~ be there by now** ya debe (de) estar allí ▶ N: **it's a ~** es imprescindible

mustache [ˈmʌstæʃ] N (US) = **moustache**

mustard [ˈmʌstəd] N mostaza

mustard gas N gas m mostaza

muster [ˈmʌstəʳ] VT juntar, reunir; (also: **muster up**) reunir; (: courage) armarse de

mustiness [ˈmʌstɪnɪs] N olor m a cerrado

mustn't [ˈmʌsnt] = **must not**

musty [ˈmʌstɪ] ADJ mohoso, que huele a humedad

mutant [ˈmjuːtənt] ADJ, N mutante m

mutate [mjuːˈteɪt] VI sufrir mutación, transformarse

mutation [mjuːˈteɪʃən] N mutación f

mute [mjuːt] ADJ mudo(-a)

muted [ˈmjuːtɪd] ADJ (noise) sordo; (criticism) callado

mutilate [ˈmjuːtɪleɪt] VT mutilar

mutilation [mjuːtɪˈleɪʃən] N mutilación f

mutinous [ˈmjuːtɪnəs] ADJ (troops) amotinado; (attitude) rebelde

mutiny [ˈmjuːtɪnɪ] N motín m ▶ VI amotinarse

mutter [ˈmʌtəʳ] VT, VI murmurar

mutton [ˈmʌtn] N (carne f de) cordero

mutual [ˈmjuːtʃuəl] ADJ mutuo; (friend) común

mutually [ˈmjuːtʃuəlɪ] ADV mutuamente

Muzak® [ˈmjuːzæk] N hilo musical

muzzle [ˈmʌzl] N hocico; (protective device) bozal m; (of gun) boca ▶ VT amordazar; (dog) poner un bozal a

MV ABBR = **motor vessel**

MVP N ABBR (US Sport) = **most valuable player**

MW ABBR (Radio: = medium wave) onda media

★**my** [maɪ] ADJ mi(s); **my house/brother** mi casa/hermano; **my sisters** mis hermanas; **I've washed my hair/cut my finger** me he lavado el pelo/cortado un dedo; **is this my pen or yours?** ¿este bolígrafo es mío o tuyo?

---

el/los or **la/las** are usually used to translate my when talking about possessions or referring to clothing or parts of the body:
They stole my car. **Me robaron el coche.**
I took off my coat. **Me quité el abrigo.**
I'm washing my hair. **Me estoy lavando la cabeza.**

Myanmar [ˈmaɪænmɑːʳ] N Myanmar m

myopic [maɪˈɔpɪk] ADJ miope

myriad [ˈmɪrɪəd] N (of people, things) miríada

myrrh [məːʳ] N mirra

★**myself** [maɪˈsɛlf] PRON (reflexive) me; (emphatic) yo mismo; (after prep) mí (mismo); see also **oneself**

mysterious [mɪsˈtɪərɪəs] ADJ misterioso

mysteriously [mɪsˈtɪərɪəslɪ] ADV misteriosamente

★**mystery** [ˈmɪstərɪ] N misterio

mystery play N auto, misterio

mystic [ˈmɪstɪk] ADJ, N místico(-a) m/f

mystical [ˈmɪstɪkl] ADJ místico

mysticism [ˈmɪstɪsɪzəm] N misticismo

mystification [ˌmɪstɪfɪˈkeɪʃən] N perplejidad f;
desconcierto
mystify [ˈmɪstɪfaɪ] VT (*perplex*) dejar perplejo;
(*disconcert*) desconcertar
mystique [mɪsˈtiːk] N misterio

myth [mɪθ] N mito
mythical [ˈmɪθɪkl] ADJ mítico
mythological [ˌmɪθəˈlɒdʒɪkl] ADJ mitológico
mythology [mɪˈθɒlədʒɪ] N mitología

Nn

N, n [ɛn] N (*letter*) N, n f; **N for Nellie**, (*US*) **N for Nan** N de Navarra

N ABBR (= *North*) N

NA N ABBR (*US*: = *Narcotics Anonymous*) organización de ayuda a los drogadictos; (*US*) = **National Academy**

n/a ABBR (= *not applicable*) no interesa; (*Comm etc*) = **no account**

NAACP N ABBR (*US*) = **National Association for the Advancement of Colored People**

NAAFI [ˈnæfɪ] N ABBR (*BRIT*: = *Navy, Army & Air Force Institutes*) servicio de cantinas etc para las fuerzas armadas

naan [nɑːn] N = **nan bread**

nab [næb] VT (*inf: grab*) coger (*SP*), agarrar (*LAM*); (: *catch out*) pillar

NACU N ABBR (*US*) = **National Association of Colleges and Universities**

nadir [ˈneɪdɪəʳ] N (*Astro*) nadir m; (*fig*) punto más bajo

NAFTA [ˈnæftə] N ABBR (= *North Atlantic Free Trade Agreement*) TLC m

nag [næg] N (*pej: horse*) rocín m ▶ VT (*scold*) regañar; (*annoy*) fastidiar

nagging [ˈnægɪŋ] ADJ (*doubt*) persistente; (*pain*) continuo ▶ N quejas *fpl*

nail [neɪl] N (*human*) uña; (*metal*) clavo; **to pay cash on the ~** pagar a tocateja ▶ VT clavar; (*fig: catch*) coger (*SP*), pillar; **to ~ sb down to a date/price** hacer que algn se comprometa a una fecha/un precio

nailbrush [ˈneɪlbrʌʃ] N cepillo para las uñas

nailfile [ˈneɪlfaɪl] N lima para las uñas

nail polish N esmalte m or laca para las uñas

nail polish remover N quitaesmalte m

nail scissors NPL tijeras *fpl* para las uñas

nail varnish N (*BRIT*) = **nail polish**

Nairobi [naɪˈrəʊbɪ] N Nairobi m

naïve [naɪˈiːv] ADJ ingenuo

naïvely [naɪˈiːvlɪ] ADV ingenuamente

naïveté [nɑːˈiːvteɪ], **naivety** [naɪˈiːvɪtɪ] N ingenuidad f, candidez f

naked [ˈneɪkɪd] ADJ (*nude*) desnudo; (*flame*) expuesto al aire; **with the ~ eye** a simple vista

NAM N ABBR (*US*) = **National Association of Manufacturers**

★**name** [neɪm] N (*gen*) nombre m; (*surname*) apellido; (*reputation*) fama, renombre m; **by ~** de nombre; **in the ~ of** en nombre de; **what's your ~?** ¿cómo se llama usted?; **my ~ is Peter** me llamo Peter; **to give one's ~ and address** dar sus señas; **to take sb's ~ and address** apuntar las señas de algn; **to make a ~ for o.s.** hacerse famoso; **to get (o.s.) a bad ~** forjarse una mala reputación ▶ VT (*child*) poner nombre a; (*criminal*) identificar; (*price, date etc*) fijar; (*appoint*) nombrar

name-drop [ˈneɪmdrɔp] VI: **he's always name-dropping** siempre está presumiendo de la gente que conoce

nameless [ˈneɪmlɪs] ADJ anónimo, sin nombre

namely [ˈneɪmlɪ] ADV a saber

nameplate [ˈneɪmpleɪt] N (*on door etc*) placa

namesake [ˈneɪmseɪk] N tocayo(-a)

Namibia [nɑːˈmɪbɪə] N Namibia

nan bread [nɑːn-] N pan indio sin apenas levadura

nanny [ˈnænɪ] N niñera

nanobot [ˈnænəʊbɔt] N (*Comput*) nanorobot m

nap [næp] N (*sleep*) sueñecito, siesta; **they were caught napping** les pilló desprevenidos

NAPA N ABBR (*US*: = *National Association of Performing Artists*) sindicato de trabajadores del espectáculo

napalm [ˈneɪpɑːm] N napalm m

nape [neɪp] N: **~ of the neck** nuca, cogote m

napkin [ˈnæpkɪn] N (*also*: **table napkin**) servilleta

Naples [ˈneɪplz] N Nápoles m

nappy [ˈnæpɪ] N (*BRIT*) pañal m

nappy liner N gasa

nappy rash N prurito

narcissism [nɑːˈsɪsɪzəm] N narcisismo

narcissus [nɑːˈsɪsəs] (pl **narcissi** [-saɪ]) N narciso

narcotic [nɑːˈkɔtɪk] ADJ, N narcótico ■ **narcotics** NPL estupefacientes mpl, narcóticos mpl

narrate [nəˈreɪt] VT narrar, contar

narration [nəˈreɪʃən] N narración f, relato

narrative [ˈnærətɪv] N narrativa ▶ ADJ narrativo

narrator [nəˈreɪtəʳ] N narrador(a) m/f

★**narrow** [ˈnærəʊ] ADJ estrecho; (resources, means) escaso; **to have a ~ escape** escaparse por los pelos ▶ VI estrecharse; (diminish) reducirse ▶ **narrow down** VT (search, investigation, possibilities) restringir, limitar; (list) reducir

narrow gauge ADJ (Rail) de vía estrecha

narrowly [ˈnærəlɪ] ADV (miss) por poco

narrow-minded [nærəʊˈmaɪndɪd] ADJ de miras estrechas

narrow-mindedness [ˈnærəʊˈmaɪndɪdnɪs] N estrechez f de miras

NAS N ABBR (US) = **National Academy of Sciences**

NASA [ˈnæsə] N ABBR (US: = National Aeronautics and Space Administration) NASA f

nasal [ˈneɪzl] ADJ nasal

Nassau [ˈnæsɔː] N (in Bahamas) Nassau m

nastily [ˈnɑːstɪlɪ] ADV (unpleasantly) de mala manera; (spitefully) con rencor

nastiness [ˈnɑːstɪnɪs] N (malice) malevolencia; (rudeness) grosería; (of person, remark) maldad f; (spitefulness) rencor m

nasturtium [nəsˈtəːʃəm] N capuchina

nasty [ˈnɑːstɪ] ADJ (remark) feo; (person) antipático; (revolting: taste, smell) asqueroso; (wound, disease etc) peligroso, grave; **to turn ~** (situation) ponerse feo; (weather) empeorar; (person) ponerse negro

NAS/UWT N ABBR (BRIT: = National Association of Schoolmasters/Union of Women Teachers) sindicato de profesores

★**nation** [ˈneɪʃən] N nación f

★**national** [ˈnæʃənl] ADJ nacional ▶ N súbdito(-a)

national anthem N himno nacional

National Curriculum N (BRIT) plan m general de estudios (en Inglaterra y Gales)

national debt N deuda pública

national dress N traje m típico del país

National Guard N (US) Guardia Nacional

National Health Service N (BRIT) Servicio Nacional de Salud

Desde su creación en 1948, el **National Health Service** (a menudo se le llama por sus siglas NHS) ha sido el responsable de ofrecer asistencia sanitaria a todos los residentes en el Reino Unido. Es el mayor sistema de salud público del mundo. Financiado por los contribuyentes, está basado en un principio: asistencia sanitaria gratuita para todos, independientemente de sus ingresos. Con algunas excepciones (la salud bucal y las medicinas en Inglaterra, Gales e Irlanda del Norte), todos los beneficios, incluyendo las consultas médicas y el tratamiento hospitalario, son gratuitas. Cada una de las cuatro naciones que forman el Reino Unido tiene su propio sistema, financiado y gestionado de forma independiente. El NHS recibe muchas críticas por las listas de espera quirúrgicas y por la falta de personal en los hospitales. Pasa por reformas continuas para mejorar el servicio que ofrece.

National Insurance N (BRIT) seguro social nacional, ≈ Seguridad f Social

El **National Insurance** es un sistema de contribuciones obligatorias pagadas por los trabajadores (a través de retenciones en sus nóminas), autónomos y los empresarios del Reino Unido, para financiar los gastos con diversos beneficios sociales como las pensiones, las bajas por maternidad, el seguro de desempleo y las ayudas por discapacidad. Introducido en 1911 como un sistema de seguro contra la enfermedad y el desempleo, fue ampliado considerablemente en 1948.

nationalism [ˈnæʃnəlɪzəm] N nacionalismo

nationalist [ˈnæʃnəlɪst] ADJ, N nacionalista mf

nationality [næʃəˈnælɪtɪ] N nacionalidad f

nationalization [næʃnəlaɪˈzeɪʃən] N nacionalización f

nationalize [ˈnæʃnəlaɪz] VT nacionalizar; **nationalized industry** industria nacionalizada

nationally [ˈnæʃnəlɪ] ADV (nationwide) a escala nacional; (as a nation) como nación

national press N prensa nacional

national service N (Mil) servicio militar

National Trust N (BRIT) organización encargada de preservar el patrimonio histórico británico

El **National Trust** es una organización independiente, sin ánimo de lucro, cuya misión es mantener y proteger los monumentos y lugares británicos de interés histórico o belleza natural. Su catálogo incluye un gran número de atracciones en todo el país, visitadas por turistas nacionales y extranjeros y con un variado programa de actividades.

nationwide [ˈneɪʃənwaɪd] ADJ a escala nacional

★**native** [ˈneɪtɪv] N (local inhabitant) natural mf; (!: in colonies) indígena mf, nativo(-a); **a ~ of Russia** un(a) natural de Rusia ▶ ADJ (indigenous) indígena; (country) natal; (innate) natural, innato; **~ language** lengua materna; **a ~ speaker of French** un hablante nativo de francés

Native American ADJ, N americano(-a) indígena *m/f*, amerindio(-a) *m/f*

native speaker N hablante *mf* nativo(-a)

Nativity [nə'tɪvɪtɪ] N: **the ~** Navidad *f*

nativity play N auto del nacimiento

NATO ['neɪtəʊ] N ABBR (= *North Atlantic Treaty Organization*) OTAN *f*

natter ['nætə'] VI (*BRIT*) charlar ▶ N: **to have a ~** charlar

★**natural** ['nætʃrəl] ADJ natural; **death from ~ causes** (*Law*) muerte *f* por causas naturales

natural childbirth N parto natural

natural gas N gas *m* natural

natural history N historia natural

naturalist ['nætʃrəlɪst] N naturalista *mf*

naturalization [nætʃrəlaɪ'zeɪʃən] N naturalización *f*

naturalize ['nætʃrəlaɪz] VT: **to become naturalized** (*person*) naturalizarse; (*plant*) aclimatarse

★**naturally** ['nætʃrəlɪ] ADV (*speak etc*) naturalmente; (*of course*) desde luego, por supuesto, ¡cómo no! (*LAM*); (*instinctively*) por naturaleza

naturalness ['nætʃrəlnɪs] N naturalidad *f*

natural resources NPL recursos *mpl* naturales

natural selection N selección *f* natural

natural wastage N (*Industry*) desgaste *m* natural

★**nature** ['neɪtʃə'] N naturaleza; (*group, sort*) género, clase *f*; (*character*) modo de ser, carácter *m*; **by ~** por naturaleza; **documents of a confidential ~** documentos *mpl* de tipo confidencial

-natured ['neɪtʃəd] SUFF: **ill-natured** malhumorado

nature reserve N reserva natural

nature trail N camino forestal educativo

naturist ['neɪtʃərɪst] N naturista *mf*

naught [nɔːt] N = **nought**

naughtily ['nɔːtɪlɪ] ADV (*behave*) mal; (*say*) con malicia

naughtiness ['nɔːtɪnɪs] N travesuras *fpl*

naughty ['nɔːtɪ] ADJ (*child*) travieso; (*story, film*) picante, escabroso, colorado (*LAM*)

Nauru [nɑː'uːruː] N Nauru *m*

nausea ['nɔːsɪə] N náusea

nauseate ['nɔːsɪeɪt] VT dar náuseas a; (*fig*) dar asco a

nauseating ['nɔːsɪeɪtɪŋ] ADJ nauseabundo; (*fig*) asqueroso, repugnante

nauseous ['nɔːsɪəs] ADJ nauseabundo; **to feel ~** sentir náuseas

nautical ['nɔːtɪkl] ADJ náutico, marítimo; **~ mile** milla marina

naval ['neɪvl] ADJ naval, de marina

naval officer N oficial *mf* de marina

nave [neɪv] N nave *f*

navel ['neɪvl] N ombligo

navigable ['nævɪgəbl] ADJ navegable

navigate ['nævɪgeɪt] VT (*ship*) gobernar; (*river etc*) navegar por ▶ VI navegar; (*Aut*) ir de copiloto

navigation [nævɪ'geɪʃən] N (*action*) navegación *f*; (*science*) náutica

navigator ['nævɪgeɪtə'] N navegante *mf*

navvy ['nævɪ] N (*BRIT*) peón *m* caminero

★**navy** ['neɪvɪ] N marina de guerra; (*ships*) armada, flota ▶ ADJ azul marino

navy-blue ['neɪvɪ'bluː] ADJ azul marino

Nazareth ['næzərɪθ] N Nazaret *m*

Nazi ['nɑːtsɪ] ADJ, N nazi *mf*

NB ABBR (= *nota bene*) nótese; (*CANADA*) = **New Brunswick**

NBA N ABBR (*US*) = **National Basketball Association; National Boxing Association**

NBC N ABBR (*US*: = *National Broadcasting Company*) cadena de televisión

NC ABBR (*US*) = **North Carolina**

NCC N ABBR (*US*) = **National Council of Churches**

NCCL N ABBR (*BRIT*: = *National Council for Civil Liberties*) asociación para la defensa de las libertades públicas

NCO N ABBR = **non-commissioned officer**

ND, N. Dak. ABBR (*US*) = **North Dakota**

NE ABBR (*US*) = **Nebraska; New England**

NEA N ABBR (*US*) = **National Education Association**

Neapolitan [nɪə'pɒlɪtən] ADJ, N napolitano(-a) *m/f*

neap tide [niːp-] N marea muerta

★**near** [nɪə'] ADJ (*place, relation*) cercano; (*time*) próximo; **£25,000 or nearest offer** 25,000 libras o precio a discutir; **in the ~ future** en fecha próxima ▶ ADV cerca; **he lives quite ~** vive bastante cerca ▶ PREP (*also:* **near to:** *space*) cerca de, junto a; (: *time*) cerca de; **~ here/there** cerca de aquí/de allí ▶ VT acercarse a, aproximarse a; **the building is nearing completion** el edificio está casi terminado

★**nearby** [nɪə'baɪ] ADJ cercano, próximo ▶ ADV cerca

★**nearly** ['nɪəlɪ] ADV casi, por poco; **I ~ fell** por poco me caigo; **not ~** ni mucho menos, ni con mucho

near miss N (*shot*) tiro casi en el blanco; (*Aviat*) accidente evitado por muy poco

nearness ['nɪənɪs] N cercanía, proximidad *f*

nearside ['nɪəsaɪd] N (*Aut: right-hand drive*) lado izquierdo; (: *left-hand drive*) lado derecho

near-sighted [nɪə'saɪtɪd] ADJ miope, corto de vista

★**neat** [niːt] ADJ (*place*) ordenado, bien cuidado; (*person*) pulcro; (*plan*) ingenioso; (*spirits*) solo

neatly ['niːtlɪ] ADV (*tidily*) con esmero; (*skilfully*) ingeniosamente

neatness ['niːtnɪs] N (*tidiness*) orden *m*; (*skilfulness*) destreza, habilidad *f*

nebulous ['nɛbjuləs] ADJ (*fig*) vago, confuso

★**necessarily** ['nɛsɪsrɪlɪ] ADV necesariamente; **not ~** no necesariamente

★**necessary** ['nɛsɪsrɪ] ADJ necesario, preciso; **he did all that was ~** hizo todo lo necesario; **if ~** si es necesario

necessitate [nɪ'sɛsɪteɪt] VT necesitar, precisar

necessity [nɪ'sɛsɪtɪ] N necesidad *f*; **in case of ~** en caso de urgencia ■ **necessities** NPL artículos *mpl* de primera necesidad

★**neck** [nɛk] N (*Anat*) cuello; (*of animal*) pescuezo; **~ and ~** parejos; **to stick one's ~ out** (*inf*) arriesgarse ▸ VI besuquearse

necklace ['nɛklɪs] N collar *m*

neckline ['nɛklaɪn] N escote *m*

necktie ['nɛktaɪ] N (*US*) corbata

nectar ['nɛktə^r] N néctar *m*

nectarine ['nɛktərɪn] N nectarina

née [neɪ] ADJ: **~ Scott** de soltera Scott

★**need** [niːd] N (*lack*) escasez *f*, falta; (*necessity*) necesidad *f*; **in case of ~** en caso de necesidad; **there's no ~ for ...** no hace(n) falta ...; **to be in ~ of, have ~ of** necesitar; **10 will meet my immediate needs** 10 satisfarán mis necesidades más apremiantes; **the needs of industry** las necesidades de la industria ▸ VT (*require*) necesitar; **I ~ it** lo necesito; **a signature is needed** se requiere una firma; **I ~ to do it** tengo que hacerlo; **you don't ~ to go** no hace falta que vayas

needle ['niːdl] N aguja ▸ VT (*fig: inf*) picar, fastidiar

needless ['niːdlɪs] ADJ innecesario, inútil; **~ to say** huelga decir que

needlessly ['niːdlɪslɪ] ADV innecesariamente, inútilmente

needlework ['niːdlwəːk] N (*activity*) costura, labor *f* de aguja

needn't ['niːdnt] = **need not**

needy ['niːdɪ] ADJ necesitado

negation [nɪ'geɪʃən] N negación *f*

★**negative** ['nɛgətɪv] N (*Phot*) negativo; (*answer*) negativa; (*Ling*) negación *f* ▸ ADJ negativo

negative cash flow N flujo negativo de efectivo

negative equity N *situación en la que el valor de la vivienda es menor que el que el de la hipoteca que pesa sobre ella*

neglect [nɪ'glɛkt] VT (*one's duty*) faltar a, no cumplir con; (*child*) descuidar, desatender; **to ~ to do sth** olvidarse de hacer algo ▸ N (*state*) abandono; (*personal*) dejadez *f*; (*of child*) desatención *f*; (*of duty*) incumplimiento

neglected [nɪ'glɛktɪd] ADJ abandonado

neglectful [nɪ'glɛktful] ADJ negligente; **to be ~ of sth/sb** desatender algo/a algn

negligee ['nɛglɪʒeɪ] N (*nightdress*) salto de cama

negligence ['nɛglɪdʒəns] N negligencia

negligent ['nɛglɪdʒənt] ADJ negligente; (*casual*) descuidado

negligently ['nɛglɪdʒəntlɪ] ADV negligentemente; (*casually*) con descuido

negligible ['nɛglɪdʒɪbl] ADJ insignificante, despreciable

negotiable [nɪ'gəuʃɪəbl] ADJ: **not ~** (*cheque*) no trasferible

★**negotiate** [nɪ'gəuʃɪeɪt] VT (*treaty, loan*) negociar; (*obstacle*) franquear; (*bend in road*) tomar ▸ VI: **to ~ (with)** negociar (con); **to ~ with sb for sth** tratar or negociar con algn por algo

negotiating table [nɪ'gəuʃɪeɪtɪŋ-] N mesa de negociaciones

negotiation [nɪgəuʃɪ'eɪʃən] N negociación *f*, gestión *f* ■ **negotiations** NPL negociaciones; **to enter into negotiations with sb** entrar en negociaciones con algn

negotiator [nɪ'gəuʃɪeɪtə^r] N negociador(a) *m/f*

neigh [neɪ] N relincho ▸ VI relinchar

neighbour, (*US*) **neighbor** ['neɪbə^r] N vecino(-a)

neighbourhood, (*US*) **neighborhood** ['neɪbəhud] N (*place*) vecindad *f*, barrio; (*people*) vecindario

neighbourhood watch N (BRIT: *also:* **neighbourhood watch scheme**) *vigilancia del barrio por los propios vecinos*

neighbouring, (*US*) **neighboring** ['neɪbərɪŋ] ADJ vecino

neighbourly, (*US*) **neighborly** ['neɪbəlɪ] ADJ amigable, sociable

★**neither** ['naɪðə^r] ADJ ni ▸ CONJ: **I didn't move and ~ did John** no me he movido, ni Juan tampoco ▸ PRON ninguno ▸ ADV: **~ good nor bad** ni bueno ni malo

neo... [niːəu] PREF neo...

Neolithic [niːəu'lɪθɪk] ADJ neolítico

neologism [nɪ'ɔlədʒɪzəm] N neologismo

neon ['niːɔn] N neón *m*

neon light N lámpara de neón

Nepal [nɪ'pɔːl] N Nepal *m*

★**nephew** ['nɛvjuː] N sobrino

nepotism ['nɛpətɪzəm] N nepotismo

nerd [nəːd] N (*pej*) primo(-a)

★**nerve** [nəːv] N (*Anat*) nervio; (*courage*) valor *m*; (*impudence*) descaro, frescura; **to lose one's ~** (*self-confidence*) perder el valor ■ **nerves** (*nervousness*) nerviosismo *msg*, nervios *mpl*; **a fit of nerves** un ataque de nervios

nerve centre N (*Anat*) centro nervioso; (*fig*) punto neurálgico

nerve gas N gas *m* nervioso

nerve-racking ['nəːvrækɪŋ] ADJ angustioso

★**nervous** ['nəːvəs] ADJ (*anxious*) nervioso; (*Anat*) nervioso; (*timid*) tímido, miedoso

nervous breakdown N crisis *f* nerviosa

nervously [ˈnəːvəslɪ] ADV nerviosamente; tímidamente

nervousness [ˈnəːvəsnɪs] N nerviosismo; timidez f

nervous wreck N (inf): **to be a ~** estar de los nervios

nervy [ˈnəːvɪ] ADJ: **to be ~** estar nervioso

nest [nɛst] N (of bird) nido ► VI anidar

nest egg N (fig) ahorros mpl

nestle [ˈnɛsl] VI: **to ~ down** acurrucarse

nestling [ˈnɛstlɪŋ] N pajarito

★**Net** [nɛt] N: **the ~** (Internet) la Red

★**net** [nɛt] N (gen) red f; (fabric) tul m ► ADJ (Comm) neto, líquido; (weight, price, salary) neto; **~ of tax** neto ► ADV: **he earns £10,000 ~ per year** gana 10,000 libras netas por año ► VT coger (SP) or agarrar (LAM) con red; (money: person) cobrar; (: deal, sale) conseguir; (Sport) marcar

netball [ˈnɛtbɔːl] N balonred m

net curtain N visillo

★**Netherlands** [ˈnɛðələndz] NPL: **the ~** los Países Bajos

net income N renta neta

netiquette [ˈnɛtɪkɛt] N netiqueta

net loss N pérdida neta

net profit N beneficio neto

nett [nɛt] ADJ = **net**

netting [ˈnɛtɪŋ] N red f, redes fpl

nettle [ˈnɛtl] N ortiga

★**network** [ˈnɛtwəːk] N red f; **local area ~** red local; **there's no ~ coverage here** (Tel) aquí no hay cobertura ► VT (Radio, TV) difundir por la red de emisores

neuralgia [njuəˈrældʒə] N neuralgia

neurological [njuərəˈlɒdʒɪkl] ADJ neurológico

neurosis [njuəˈrəusɪs] (pl **neuroses** [-siːz]) N neurosis f inv

neurotic [njuəˈrɒtɪk] ADJ, N neurótico(-a) m/f

neuter [ˈnjuːtəʳ] ADJ (Ling) neutro ► VT castrar, capar

neutral [ˈnjuːtrəl] ADJ (person) neutral; (colour etc) neutro; (Elec) neutro ► N (Aut) punto muerto

neutrality [njuːˈtrælɪtɪ] N neutralidad f

neutralize [ˈnjuːtrəlaɪz] VT neutralizar

neutron [ˈnjuːtrɒn] N neutrón m

neutron bomb N bomba de neutrones

★**never** [ˈnɛvəʳ] ADV nunca, jamás; **I ~ went** no fui nunca; **~ in my life** jamás en la vida; see also **mind**

never-ending [nɛvərˈɛndɪŋ] ADJ interminable, sin fin

nevertheless [nɛvəðəˈlɛs] ADV sin embargo, no obstante

★**new** [njuː] ADJ nuevo; (recent) reciente; **as good as ~** como nuevo

New Age N Nueva era

newbie [ˈnjuːbɪ] N recién llegado(-a) m/f

newborn [ˈnjuːbɔːn] ADJ recién nacido

newcomer [ˈnjuːkʌməʳ] N recién venido or llegado

new-fangled [ˈnjuːfæŋgld] ADJ (pej) modernísimo

new-found [ˈnjuːfaund] ADJ (friend) nuevo; (enthusiasm) recién adquirido

New Guinea N Nueva Guinea

newly [ˈnjuːlɪ] ADV recién

newly-weds [ˈnjuːlɪwɛdz] NPL recién casados

new moon N luna nueva

newness [ˈnjuːnɪs] N novedad f; (fig) inexperiencia

★**news** [njuːz] N noticias fpl; **a piece of ~** una noticia; **the ~** (Radio, TV) las noticias fpl, el telediario; **good/bad ~** buenas/malas noticias fpl; **financial ~** noticias fpl financieras

news agency N agencia de noticias

★**newsagent** [ˈnjuːzeɪdʒənt] N (BRIT: shop) tienda f or quiosco m de periódicos; (: shopkeeper) vendedor(a) m/f de periódicos

news bulletin N (Radio, TV) noticiario

newscaster [ˈnjuːzkɑːstəʳ] N presentador(a) m/f, locutor(a) m/f

news dealer N (US) = **newsagent**

news flash N noticia de última hora

newsletter [ˈnjuːzlɛtəʳ] N hoja informativa, boletín m

★**newspaper** [ˈnjuːzpeɪpəʳ] N periódico, diario; **daily ~** diario; **weekly ~** periódico semanal

newsprint [ˈnjuːzprɪnt] N papel m de periódico

newsreader [ˈnjuːzriːdəʳ] N = **newscaster**

newsreel [ˈnjuːzriːl] N noticiario

newsroom [ˈnjuːzruːm] N (Press, Radio, TV) sala de redacción

news stand N quiosco or puesto de periódicos

newsworthy [ˈnjuːzwəːðɪ] ADJ: **to be ~** ser de interés periodístico

newt [njuːt] N tritón m

new town N (BRIT) ciudad f nueva (construida con subsidios estatales)

★**New Year** N Año Nuevo; **Happy ~!** ¡Feliz Año Nuevo!; **to wish sb a happy ~** desear a algn un feliz Año Nuevo

New Year's Day N Día m de Año Nuevo

New Year's Eve N Nochevieja

New York [-ˈjɔːk] N Nueva York

New Zealand [-ˈziːlənd] N Nueva Zelanda (SP), Nueva Zelandia (LAM) ► ADJ neozelandés(-esa)

New Zealander [-ˈziːləndəʳ] N neozelandés(-esa) m/f

★**next** [nɛkst] ADJ (house, room) vecino, de al lado; (meeting) próximo; (page) siguiente; **the ~ day** el día siguiente; **~ time** la próxima vez; **~ year** el año próximo or que viene; **~ month** el mes que viene or entrante; **"turn to the ~ page"** "vuelva a la página siguiente"; **the week after ~** no la semana que viene sino la otra ► ADV después;

you're ~ le toca; **~ to** prep junto a, al lado de; **~ to nothing** casi nada

next door ADV en la casa de al lado ▶ ADJ vecino, de al lado

next-of-kin ['nɛkstəv'kɪn] N pariente(s) m(pl) más cercano(s)

NF N ABBR (BRIT Pol: = National Front) partido político de la extrema derecha ▶ ABBR (CANADA) = **Newfoundland**

NFL N ABBR (US) = **National Football League**

NG ABBR (US) = **National Guard**

NGO N ABBR (= non-governmental organization) ONG f

NH ABBR (US) = **New Hampshire**

NHL N ABBR (US) = **National Hockey League**

NHS N ABBR (BRIT) = **National Health Service**

NI ABBR = **Northern Ireland**; (BRIT) = **National Insurance**

nib [nɪb] N plumilla

nibble ['nɪbl] VT mordisquear

Nicaragua [nɪkə'rægjuə] N Nicaragua

Nicaraguan [nɪkə'rægjuən] ADJ, N nicaragüense mf

Nice [niːs] N Niza

★**nice** [naɪs] ADJ (likeable) simpático, majo; (kind) amable; (pleasant) agradable; (attractive) bonito, mono; (distinction) fino; (taste, smell, meal) rico

nice-looking ['naɪslukɪŋ] ADJ guapo

nicely ['naɪslɪ] ADV amablemente; (of health etc) bien; **that will do ~** perfecto

niceties ['naɪsɪtɪz] NPL detalles mpl

niche [niːʃ] N (Arch) nicho, hornacina

nick [nɪk] N (wound) rasguño; (cut, indentation) mella, muesca; **in the ~ of time** justo a tiempo; **in good ~** en buen estado ▶ VT (cut) cortar; (inf) birlar, mangar; (: arrest) pillar; **to ~ o.s.** cortarse

nickel ['nɪkl] N níquel m; (US) moneda de 5 centavos

nickname ['nɪkneɪm] N apodo, mote m ▶ VT apodar

Nicosia [nɪkə'siːə] N Nicosia

nicotine ['nɪkətiːn] N nicotina

nicotine patch N parche m de nicotina

★**niece** [niːs] N sobrina

nifty ['nɪftɪ] ADJ (inf: car, jacket) elegante, chulo; (: gadget, tool) ingenioso

Niger ['naɪdʒəʳ] N (country, river) Níger m

Nigeria [naɪ'dʒɪərɪə] N Nigeria

Nigerian [naɪ'dʒɪərɪən] ADJ, N nigeriano(-a) m/f

niggardly ['nɪɡədlɪ] ADJ (person) avaro, tacaño; (allowance, amount) miserable

niggle ['nɪɡl] VT preocupar ▶ VI (complain) quejarse; (fuss) preocuparse por minucias

niggling ['nɪɡlɪŋ] ADJ (detail: trifling) nimio, insignificante; (: annoying) molesto; (doubt, pain) constante

★**night** [naɪt] N (gen) noche f; (evening) tarde f; **last ~** anoche; **the ~ before last** anteanoche, antes de ayer por la noche; **at ~, by ~** de noche, por la

noche; **in the ~, during the ~** durante la noche, por la noche

night-bird ['naɪtbəːd] N (fig) trasnochador(a) m/f, madrugador(a) m/f (LAM)

nightcap ['naɪtkæp] N (drink) bebida que se toma antes de acostarse

night club N club nocturno, discoteca

nightdress ['naɪtdrɛs] N (BRIT) camisón m

nightfall ['naɪtfɔːl] N anochecer m

nightgown ['naɪtɡaun], (BRIT) **nightie** ['naɪtɪ] N = **nightdress**

nightingale ['naɪtɪŋɡeɪl] N ruiseñor m

night life N vida nocturna

nightly ['naɪtlɪ] ADJ de todas las noches ▶ ADV todas las noches, cada noche

★**nightmare** ['naɪtmɛəʳ] N pesadilla

night porter N guardián m nocturno

night safe N caja fuerte

night school N clase(s) f(pl) nocturna(s)

nightshade ['naɪtʃeɪd] N: **deadly ~** (Bot) belladona

night shift N turno nocturno or de noche

night-time ['naɪttaɪm] N noche f

night watchman N (irreg) vigilante m nocturno, sereno

nihilism ['naɪɪlɪzəm] N nihilismo

nil [nɪl] N (BRIT Sport) cero, nada

Nile [naɪl] N: **the ~** el Nilo

nimble ['nɪmbl] ADJ (agile) ágil, ligero; (skilful) diestro

nimbly ['nɪmblɪ] ADV ágilmente; con destreza

★**nine** [naɪn] NUM nueve

9-11, Nine-Eleven [naɪn'lɛvn] N 11-S m

★**nineteen** ['naɪn'tiːn] NUM diecinueve

★**nineteenth** [naɪn'tiːnθ] ADJ decimonoveno, decimonono

ninetieth ['naɪntɪɪθ] ADJ nonagésimo

★**ninety** ['naɪntɪ] NUM noventa

★**ninth** [naɪnθ] ADJ noveno

nip [nɪp] VT (pinch) pellizcar; (bite) morder ▶ VI (BRIT inf): **to ~ out/down/up** salir/bajar/subir un momento ▶ N (drink) trago

nipple ['nɪpl] N (Anat) pezón m; (of bottle) tetilla; (Tech) boquilla, manguito

nippy ['nɪpɪ] ADJ (BRIT: person) rápido; (US: taste) picante; **it's a very ~ car** es un coche muy potente para el tamaño que tiene

nit [nɪt] N (of louse) liendre f; (inf: idiot) imbécil mf

nit-pick ['nɪtpɪk] VI (inf) sacar punta a todo

nitrogen ['naɪtrədʒən] N nitrógeno

nitroglycerin, nitroglycerine ['naɪtrəu-'ɡlɪsəriːn] N nitroglicerina

nitty-gritty ['nɪtɪ'ɡrɪtɪ] N (inf): **to get down to the ~** ir al grano

nitwit ['nɪtwɪt] N (pej) cretino(-a)

NJ ABBR (US) = **New Jersey**

NLF N ABBR (= National Liberation Front) FLN m

n

NLRB N ABBR (US: = *National Labor Relations Board*) organismo de protección al trabajador

NM, N. Mex. ABBR (US) = **New Mexico**

no [nəu]

ADV (*opposite of "yes"*) no; **are you coming? — no (I'm not)** ¿vienes? — no; **would you like some more? — no thank you** ¿quieres más? — no gracias
▶ ADJ **1** (*not any*): **I have no money/time/books** no tengo dinero/tiempo/libros; **no other man would have done it** ningún otro lo hubiera hecho
2: "no entry" "prohibido el paso"; **"no smoking"** "prohibido fumar"
▶ N (*pl* **noes**) no *m*

no. ABBR (= *number*) n°, núm.

nobble ['nɔbl] VT (BRIT *inf: bribe*) sobornar; (: *catch*) pescar; (: *Racing*) drogar

Nobel prize [nəu'bɛl-] N premio Nobel

nobility [nəu'bɪlɪtɪ] N nobleza

noble ['nəubl] ADJ (*person*) noble; (*title*) de nobleza

nobleman ['nəublmən] N (*irreg*) noble *m*

nobly ['nəublɪ] ADV (*selflessly*) noblemente

★**nobody** ['nəubədɪ] PRON nadie

no-claims bonus ['nəukleɪmz-] N bonificación *f* por carencia de reclamaciones

nocturnal [nɔk'tə:nl] ADJ nocturno

★**nod** [nɔd] VI saludar con la cabeza; (*in agreement*) asentir con la cabeza ▶ VT: **to ~ one's head** inclinar la cabeza; **they nodded their agreement** asintieron con la cabeza ▶ N inclinación *f* de cabeza
▶ **nod off** VI cabecear

no-fly zone [nəu'flaɪ-] N zona de exclusión aérea

★**noise** [nɔɪz] N ruido; (*din*) escándalo, estrépito

noisily ['nɔɪzɪlɪ] ADV ruidosamente, estrepitosamente

noisy ['nɔɪzɪ] ADJ (*gen*) ruidoso; (*child*) escandaloso

nomad ['nəumæd] N nómada *mf*

nomadic [nəu'mædɪk] ADJ nómada

no man's land N tierra de nadie

nominal ['nɔmɪnl] ADJ nominal

nominate ['nɔmɪneɪt] VT (*propose*) proponer; (*appoint*) nombrar

nomination [nɔmɪ'neɪʃən] N propuesta; nombramiento

nominee [nɔmɪ'ni:] N candidato(-a)

non... [nɔn] PREF no, des..., in...

nonalcoholic [nɔnælkə'hɔlɪk] ADJ sin alcohol

nonaligned [nɔnə'laɪnd] ADJ no alineado

nonarrival [nɔnə'raɪvl] N falta de llegada

nonce word [nɔns-] N hápax *m*

nonchalant ['nɔnʃələnt] ADJ indiferente

noncommissioned [nɔnkə'mɪʃənd] ADJ: **~ officer** suboficial *mf*

noncommittal ['nɔnkə'mɪtl] ADJ (*reserved*) reservado; (*uncommitted*) evasivo

nonconformist [nɔnkən'fɔ:mɪst] ADJ inconformista ▶ N inconformista *mf*; (BRIT *Rel*) no conformista *mf*

noncontributory [nɔnkən'trɪbjutərɪ] ADJ: **~ pension scheme** *or* (US) **plan** fondo de pensiones no contributivo

noncooperation ['nɔnkəuɔpə'reɪʃən] N no cooperación *f*

nondescript ['nɔndɪskrɪpt] ADJ anodino, soso

★**none** [nʌn] PRON ninguno(-a); **I've ~ left** no me queda ninguno(-a); **~ of you** ninguno de vosotros; **I have ~** no tengo ninguno; **~ at all** (*not one*) ni uno ▶ ADV de ninguna manera; **he's ~ the worse for it** no le ha perjudicado

nonentity [nɔ'nɛntɪtɪ] N cero a la izquierda, nulidad *f*

nonessential [nɔnɪ'sɛnʃl] ADJ no esencial ▶ N: **nonessentials** cosas *fpl* secundarias *or* sin importancia

nonetheless [nʌnðə'lɛs] ADV sin embargo, no obstante, aún así

non-EU [nɔni:'ju:] ADJ (*citizen, passport*) no comunitario; (*imports*) de fuera de la Unión Europea

non-event [nɔnɪ'vɛnt] N acontecimiento sin importancia; **it was a ~** no pasó absolutamente nada

nonexecutive [nɔnɪg'zɛkjutɪv] ADJ: **~ director** director *m* no ejecutivo

nonexistent [nɔnɪg'zɪstənt] ADJ inexistente

non-fiction [nɔn'fɪkʃən] N no ficción *f*

nonintervention [nɔnɪntə'vɛnʃən] N no intervención *f*

no-no ['nəunəu] N (*inf*): **it's a ~** de eso ni hablar

non obst. ABBR (= *non obstante*) no obstante

no-nonsense [nəu'nɔnsəns] ADJ sensato

nonpayment [nɔn'peɪmənt] N falta de pago

nonplussed [nɔn'plʌst] ADJ perplejo

non-profit-making [nɔn'prɔfɪtmeɪkɪŋ] ADJ no lucrativo

nonsense ['nɔnsəns] N tonterías *fpl*, disparates *fpl*; **~!** ¡qué tonterías!; **it is ~ to say that ...** es absurdo decir que ...

nonsensical [nɔn'sɛnsɪkl] ADJ disparatado, absurdo

nonshrink [nɔn'ʃrɪŋk] ADJ que no encoge

nonskid [nɔn'skɪd] ADJ antideslizante

non-smoker ['nɔn'sməukə'] N no fumador(a) *m/f*

non-smoking ['nɔn'sməukɪŋ] ADJ (de) no fumador

nonstarter [nɔn'stɑ:tə'] N: **it's a ~** no tiene futuro

non-stick ['nɔn'stɪk] ADJ (*pan, surface*) antiadherente

nonstop ['nɔn'stɔp] ADJ continuo; (*Rail*) directo ▶ ADV sin parar

nontaxable [nɔn'tæksəbl] ADJ: ~ **income** renta no imponible

non-U ['nɔnjuː] ADJ ABBR (BRIT inf: = non-upper class) que no pertenece a la clase alta

nonvolatile [nɔn'vɔlətaɪl] ADJ: ~ **memory** (Comput) memoria permanente

nonvoting [nɔn'vəutɪŋ] ADJ: ~ **shares** acciones fpl sin derecho a voto

non-White ['nɔn'waɪt] (!) ADJ de color ▸ N (person) persona de color

noodles ['nuːdlz] NPL tallarines mpl

nook [nuk] N rincón m; **nooks and crannies** escondrijos mpl

noon [nuːn] N mediodía m

no-one ['nəuwʌn] PRON = **nobody**

noose [nuːs] N lazo corredizo

★**nor** [nɔːʳ] CONJ = **neither** ▸ ADV see **neither**

norm [nɔːm] N norma

★**normal** ['nɔːml] ADJ normal; **to return to** ~ volver a la normalidad

normality [nɔː'mælɪtɪ] N normalidad f

★**normally** ['nɔːməlɪ] ADV normalmente

Normandy ['nɔːməndɪ] N Normandía

★**north** [nɔːθ] N norte m ▸ ADJ (del) norte ▸ ADV al or hacia el norte

North Africa N África del Norte

North African ADJ, N norteafricano(-a) m/f

North America N América del Norte

North American ADJ, N norteamericano(-a) m/f

northbound ['nɔːθbaund] ADJ en dirección al norte

north-east [nɔːθ'iːst] N nor(d)este m

northeastern [nɔːθ'iːstən] ADJ nor(d)este, del nor(d)este

northerly ['nɔːðəlɪ] ADJ (point, direction) hacia el norte, septentrional; (wind) del norte

★**northern** ['nɔːðən] ADJ norteño, del norte

★**Northern Ireland** N Irlanda del Norte

> **Northern Ireland** (Irlanda del Norte) es una parte del Reino Unido formada por seis condados en el noreste de la isla de Irlanda. Nació en 1921 tras la división de la isla en Irlanda del Norte e Irlanda del Sur, que más tarde se convirtió en un estado independiente. Su población está compuesta mayoritariamente por unionistas protestantes, favorables a la permanencia dentro del Reino Unido, con una importante minoría de nacionalistas católicos, partidarios de una Irlanda unida e independiente. La existencia de Irlanda del Norte ha estado marcada por el enfrentamiento entre las dos comunidades. Desde finales de la década de 1960 hasta finales de la década de 1990, sufrió una fase de violencia, conocida como The Troubles, que causó miles de víctimas. El Good Friday Agreement (Acuerdo del Viernes Santo) marcó un paso muy importante hacia la paz, aunque el sectarismo y la división religiosa continúe planteando problemas.

North Korea N Corea del Norte

North Pole N: **the** ~ el Polo Norte

North Sea N: **the** ~ el mar del Norte

North Sea oil N petróleo del mar del Norte

northward ['nɔːθwəd], **northwards** ['nɔːθwədz] ADV hacia el norte

north-west [nɔːθ'wɛst] N noroeste m

northwestern ['nɔːθ'wɛstən] ADJ noroeste, del noroeste

★**Norway** ['nɔːweɪ] N Noruega

★**Norwegian** [nɔː'wiːdʒən] ADJ noruego(-a) ▸ N noruego(-a); (Ling) noruego

nos. ABBR (= numbers) núms.

★**nose** [nəuz] N (Anat) nariz f; (Zool) hocico; (sense of smell) olfato; **to pay through the ~ (for sth)** (inf) pagar un dineral (por algo) ▸ VI (also: **nose one's way**) avanzar con cautela
▸ **nose about, nose around** VI curiosear

nosebleed ['nəuzbliːd] N hemorragia nasal

nose-dive ['nəuzdaɪv] N picado vertical

nose drops NPL gotas fpl para la nariz

nosey ['nəuzɪ] ADJ curioso, fisgón(-ona)

nostalgia [nɔs'tældʒɪə] N nostalgia

nostalgic [nɔs'tældʒɪk] ADJ nostálgico

nostril ['nɔstrɪl] N ventana or orificio de la nariz

nosy ['nəuzɪ] ADJ = **nosey**

★**not** [nɔt] ADV no; ~ **at all** no ... en absoluto; ~ **that** ... no es que ...; **it's too late, isn't it?** es demasiado tarde, ¿verdad?; ~ **yet** todavía no; ~ **now** ahora no; **why** ~? ¿por qué no?; **I hope** ~ espero que no; ~ **at all** no ... nada; (after thanks) de nada

notable ['nəutəbl] ADJ notable

notably ['nəutəblɪ] ADV especialmente; (in particular) sobre todo

notary ['nəutərɪ] N (also: **notary public**) notario(-a)

notation [nəu'teɪʃən] N notación f

notch [nɔtʃ] N muesca, corte m
▸ **notch up** VT (score, victory) apuntarse

★**note** [nəut] N (Mus: record, letter) nota; (banknote) billete m; (tone) tono; **delivery** ~ nota de entrega; **to compare notes** (fig) cambiar impresiones; **of** ~ conocido, destacado; **to take** ~ prestar atención a; **just a quick** ~ **to let you know that ...** solo unas líneas para informarte que ... ▸ VT (observe) notar, observar; (write down) apuntar, anotar

notebook ['nəutbuk] N libreta, cuaderno; (for shorthand) libreta

notecase ['nəutkeɪs] N (BRIT) cartera, billetero

noted ['nəutɪd] ADJ célebre, conocido

notepad ['nəutpæd] N bloc m

notepaper ['nəutpeɪpə] N papel m para cartas

noteworthy ['nəutwəːðɪ] ADJ notable, digno de atención

★**nothing** ['nʌθɪŋ] N nada; (zero) cero; **he does** ~ no hace nada; ~ **new** nada nuevo; ~ **much** no mucho; **for ~** *(free)* gratis; *(in vain)* en balde; **~ at all** nada en absoluto

★**notice** ['nəʊtɪs] N *(announcement)* anuncio; *(warning)* aviso; *(dismissal)* despido; *(resignation)* dimisión f; *(review: of play etc)* reseña; **to bring sth to sb's ~** *(attention)* llamar la atención de algn sobre algo; **to take ~ of** hacer caso de, prestar atención a; **at short ~** con poca antelación; **without ~** sin previo aviso; **advance ~** previo aviso; **until further ~** hasta nuevo aviso; **to give sb ~ of sth** avisar a algn de algo; **to hand in one's ~, give ~** dimitir, renunciar; **it has come to my ~ that ...** he llegado a saber que ...; **to escape** *or* **avoid ~** pasar inadvertido ▸ VT *(observe)* notar, observar

noticeable ['nəʊtɪsəbl] ADJ evidente, obvio

notice board N *(BRIT)* tablón *m* de anuncios

notification [nəʊtɪfɪ'keɪʃən] N aviso; *(announcement)* anuncio

notify ['nəʊtɪfaɪ] VT: **to ~ sb (of sth)** comunicar (algo) a algn

notion ['nəʊʃən] N noción f, idea; *(opinion)* opinión f

notions ['nəʊʃənz] NPL *(US)* mercería

notoriety [nəʊtə'raɪətɪ] N notoriedad f, mala fama

notorious [nəʊ'tɔːrɪəs] ADJ notorio, tristemente célebre

notoriously [nəʊ'tɔːrɪəslɪ] ADV notoriamente

notwithstanding [nɒtwɪθ'stændɪŋ] ADV no obstante, sin embargo; **~ this** a pesar de esto

nougat ['nuːgɑː] N turrón *m*

nought [nɔːt] N cero

noun [naʊn] N nombre *m*, sustantivo

nourish ['nʌrɪʃ] VT nutrir; *(fig)* alimentar

nourishing ['nʌrɪʃɪŋ] ADJ nutritivo, rico

nourishment ['nʌrɪʃmənt] N alimento, sustento

Nov. ABBR (= *November*) nov.

★**novel** ['nɒvl] N novela ▸ ADJ *(new)* nuevo, original; *(unexpected)* insólito

novelist ['nɒvəlɪst] N novelista *mf*

novelty ['nɒvəltɪ] N novedad f

★**November** [nəʊ'vɛmbə'] N noviembre *m*; *see also* **July**

novice ['nɒvɪs] N principiante *mf*, novato(-a); *(Rel)* novicio(-a)

NOW [naʊ] N ABBR *(US)* = **National Organization for Women**

★**now** [naʊ] ADV *(at the present time)* ahora; *(these days)* actualmente, hoy día; **right ~** ahora mismo; **by ~** ya; **I'll do it just ~** ahora mismo lo hago; **~ and then, ~ and again** de vez en cuando; **from ~ on** de ahora en adelante; **between ~ and Monday** entre hoy y el lunes; **in 3 days from ~** de hoy en 3 días; **that's all for ~** eso es todo por ahora ▸ CONJ: **~ (that)** ya que, ahora que

nowadays ['naʊədeɪz] ADV hoy (en) día, actualmente

★**nowhere** ['nəʊwɛə'] ADV *(direction)* a ninguna parte; *(location)* en ninguna parte; **~ else** en *or* a ninguna otra parte

no-win situation [nəʊ'wɪn-] N: **I'm in a ~** haga lo que haga, llevo las de perder

noxious ['nɒkʃəs] ADJ nocivo

nozzle ['nɒzl] N boquilla

NP N ABBR = **notary public**

nr ABBR *(BRIT)* = **near**

NS ABBR *(CANADA)* = **Nova Scotia**

NSC N ABBR *(US)* = **National Security Council**

NSF N ABBR *(US)* = **National Science Foundation**

NSPCC N ABBR *(BRIT)* = **National Society for the Prevention of Cruelty to Children**

NSW ABBR *(AUSTRALIA)* = **New South Wales**

NT N ABBR = **New Testament** ▸ ABBR *(CANADA)* = **Northwest Territories**

nth [ɛnθ] ADJ: **for the ~ time** *(inf)* por enésima vez

nuance ['njuːɑːns] N matiz *m*

nubile ['njuːbaɪl] ADJ núbil

★**nuclear** ['njuːklɪə'] ADJ nuclear

nuclear disarmament N desarme *m* nuclear

nuclear family N familia nuclear

nuclear-free zone ['njuːklɪə'friː-] N zona desnuclearizada

nucleus ['njuːklɪəs] *(pl* **nuclei** ['njuːklɪaɪ]*)* N núcleo

nude [njuːd] ADJ, N desnudo *m*; **in the ~** desnudo

nudge [nʌdʒ] VT dar un codazo a

nudist ['njuːdɪst] N nudista *mf*

nudist colony N colonia nudista

nudity ['njuːdɪtɪ] N desnudez f

nugget ['nʌgɪt] N pepita

nuisance ['njuːsns] N molestia, fastidio; *(person)* pesado, latoso; **what a ~!** ¡qué lata!

NUJ N ABBR *(BRIT:* = *National Union of Journalists) sindicato de periodistas*

nuke [njuːk] *(inf)* N bomba atómica ▸ VT atacar con arma nuclear

null [nʌl] ADJ: **~ and void** nulo y sin efecto

nullify ['nʌlɪfaɪ] VT anular, invalidar

NUM N ABBR *(BRIT:* = *National Union of Mineworkers) sindicato de mineros*

numb [nʌm] ADJ entumecido; *(fig)* insensible; **to be ~ with cold** estar entumecido de frío; **~ with fear/grief** paralizado de miedo/dolor ▸ VT quitar la sensación a, entumecer, entorpecer

★**number** ['nʌmbə'] N número; *(numeral)* número, cifra; *(quantity)* cantidad f; **reference ~** número de referencia; **telephone ~** número de teléfono; **wrong ~** *(Tel)* número equivocado; **opposite ~** *(person)* homólogo(-a); **a ~ of** varios, algunos; **they were ten in ~** eran diez ▸ VT *(pages etc)* numerar, poner número a; *(amount to)* sumar, ascender a; **to be numbered among** figurar entre

number plate N (*Brit*) matrícula, placa

Number Ten N (*Brit*: 10 Downing Street) *residencia del primer ministro*

numbness ['nʌmnɪs] N insensibilidad f, parálisis f inv; (*due to cold*) entumecimiento

numbskull ['nʌmskʌl] N (*pej*) papanatas *mf*

numeral ['nju:mərəl] N número, cifra

numerate ['nju:mərɪt] ADJ competente en aritmética

numerical [nju:'mɛrɪkl] ADJ numérico

numerous ['nju:mərəs] ADJ numeroso, muchos

nun [nʌn] N monja, religiosa

nunnery ['nʌnərɪ] N convento de monjas

nuptial ['nʌpʃəl] ADJ nupcial

★**nurse** [nə:s] N enfermero(-a); (*nanny*) niñera; **male ~** enfermero ▶ VT (*patient*) cuidar, atender; (*baby*: *Brit*) mecer; (: *US*) criar, amamantar

nursery ['nə:sərɪ] N (*institution*) guardería infantil; (*room*) cuarto de los niños; (*for plants*) criadero, semillero

nursery rhyme N canción f infantil

nursery school N escuela infantil

nursery slope N (*Brit Ski*) cuesta para principiantes

nursing ['nə:sɪŋ] N (*profession*) profesión f de enfermera; (*care*) asistencia, cuidado ▶ ADJ (*mother*) lactante

nursing home N clínica de reposo

nurture ['nə:tʃə'] VT (*child, plant*) alimentar, nutrir

NUS N ABBR (*Brit*: = *National Union of Students*) *sindicato de estudiantes*

NUT N ABBR (*Brit*: = *National Union of Teachers*) *sindicato de profesores*

nut [nʌt] N (*Tech*) tuerca; (*Bot*) nuez f; **nuts** (*Culin*) frutos secos ▶ ADJ (*chocolate etc*) con nueces

nutcrackers ['nʌtkrækəz] NPL cascanueces *m inv*

nutmeg ['nʌtmɛg] N nuez f moscada

nutrient ['nju:trɪənt] ADJ nutritivo ▶ N elemento nutritivo

nutrition [nju:'trɪʃən] N nutrición f, alimentación f

nutritionist [nju:'trɪʃənɪst] N dietista *mf*

nutritious [nju:'trɪʃəs] ADJ nutritivo

nuts [nʌts] ADJ (*inf*) chiflado

nutshell ['nʌtʃɛl] N cáscara de nuez; **in a ~** en resumidas cuentas

nutty ['nʌtɪ] ADJ (*flavour*) a frutos secos; (*inf*: *foolish*) chalado

nuzzle ['nʌzl] VI: **to ~ up to** arrimarse a

NV ABBR (*US*) = **Nevada**

NVQ N ABBR (*Brit*: = *national vocational qualification*) *título de formación profesional*

NWT ABBR (*Canada*) = **Northwest Territories**

NY ABBR (*US*) = **New York**

NYC ABBR (*US*) = **New York City**

nylon ['naɪlɔn] N nilón *m* ▶ ADJ de nilón

nymph [nɪmf] N ninfa

nymphomaniac ['nɪmfəu'meɪnɪæk] ADJ, N ninfómana

NYSE N ABBR (*US*) = **New York Stock Exchange**

n

Oo

O, o [əu] N (letter) O, o f; **O for Oliver**, (US) **O for Oboe** O de Oviedo

oaf [əuf] N zoquete mf

oak [əuk] N roble m ▸ ADJ de roble

O & M N ABBR = **organization and method**

OAP N ABBR (BRIT) = **old-age pensioner**

oar [ɔːʳ] N remo; **to put** or **shove one's ~ in** (fig: inf) entrometerse

oarsman [ˈɔːzmən] N (irreg) remero

OAS N ABBR (= Organization of American States) OEA f

oasis [əuˈeɪsɪs] (pl **oases** [əuˈeɪsiːz]) N oasis m inv

oath [əuθ] N juramento; (swear word) palabrota; **on** (BRIT) or **under ~** bajo juramento

oatmeal [ˈəutmiːl] N harina de avena

oats [əuts] NPL avena

OAU N ABBR (= Organization of African Unity) OUA f

obdurate [ˈɔbdjurɪt] ADJ (stubborn) terco, obstinado; (sinner) empedernido; (unyielding) inflexible, firme

OBE N ABBR (BRIT: = Order of the British Empire) título ceremonial

obedience [əˈbiːdɪəns] N obediencia; **in ~ to** de acuerdo con

obedient [əˈbiːdɪənt] ADJ obediente

obelisk [ˈɔbɪlɪsk] N obelisco

obese [əuˈbiːs] ADJ obeso

obesity [əuˈbiːsɪtɪ] N obesidad f

obey [əˈbeɪ] VT obedecer; (instructions) cumplir

obituary [əˈbɪtjuərɪ] N necrología

★**object** N [ˈɔbdʒɪkt] (gen) objeto; (purpose) objeto, propósito; (Ling) objeto, complemento; **expense is no ~** no importa lo que cueste ▸ VI [əbˈdʒɛkt]: **to ~ to** (attitude) estar en contra de; (proposal) oponerse a; **I ~!** ¡protesto! ▸ VT objetar; **to ~ that** objetar que

objection [əbˈdʒɛkʃən] N objeción f; **I have no ~ to ...** no tengo inconveniente en que ...

objectionable [əbˈdʒɛkʃənəbl] ADJ (gen) desagradable; (conduct) censurable

★**objective** [əbˈdʒɛktɪv] ADJ, N objetivo

objectively [əbˈdʒɛktɪvlɪ] ADV objetivamente

objectivity [ɔbdʒɪkˈtɪvɪtɪ] N objetividad f

object lesson N (fig) (buen) ejemplo

objector [əbˈdʒɛktəʳ] N objetor(a) m/f

obligation [ɔblɪˈɡeɪʃən] N obligación f; (debt) deber m; **"without ~"** "sin compromiso"; **to be under an ~ to sb/to do sth** estar comprometido con algn/a hacer algo

obligatory [əˈblɪɡətərɪ] ADJ obligatorio

oblige [əˈblaɪdʒ] VT (do a favour for) complacer, hacer un favor a; **to ~ sb to do sth** obligar a algn a hacer algo; **to be obliged to sb for sth** estarle agradecido a algn por algo; **anything to ~!** (inf) todo sea por complacerte

obliging [əˈblaɪdʒɪŋ] ADJ servicial, atento

oblique [əˈbliːk] ADJ oblicuo; (allusion) indirecto ▸ N (Typ) barra

obliterate [əˈblɪtəreɪt] VT arrasar; (memory) borrar

oblivion [əˈblɪvɪən] N olvido

oblivious [əˈblɪvɪəs] ADJ: **~ of** inconsciente de

oblong [ˈɔblɔŋ] ADJ rectangular ▸ N rectángulo

obnoxious [əbˈnɔkʃəs] ADJ odioso, detestable; (smell) nauseabundo

o.b.o. ABBR (US: = or best offer) abierto a ofertas

oboe [ˈəubəu] N oboe m

obscene [əbˈsiːn] ADJ obsceno

obscenity [əbˈsɛnɪtɪ] N obscenidad f

obscure [əbˈskjuəʳ] ADJ oscuro ▸ VT oscurecer; (hide: sun) ocultar

obscurity [əbˈskjuərɪtɪ] N oscuridad f; (obscure point) punto oscuro; **to rise from ~** salir de la nada

obsequious [əbˈsiːkwɪəs] ADJ servil

observable [əbˈzəːvəbl] ADJ observable, perceptible

observance [əbˈzəːvns] N observancia, cumplimiento; (ritual) práctica; **religious observances** prácticas fpl religiosas

observant [əbˈzɜːvnt] ADJ observador(a)

observation [ɔbzəˈveɪʃən] N (Med) observación f; (by police etc) vigilancia

observation post N (Mil) puesto de observación

observatory [əbˈzɜːvətrɪ] N observatorio

observe [əbˈzɜːv] VT (gen) observar; (rule) cumplir

observer [əbˈzɜːvəʳ] N observador(a) m/f

obsess [əbˈsɛs] VT obsesionar; **to be obsessed by** or **with sb/sth** estar obsesionado con algn/algo

obsession [əbˈsɛʃən] N obsesión f

obsessive [əbˈsɛsɪv] ADJ obsesivo

obsolescence [ɔbsəˈlɛsns] N obsolescencia

obsolescent [ɔbsəˈlɛsnt] ADJ que está cayendo en desuso

obsolete [ˈɔbsəliːt] ADJ obsoleto

obstacle [ˈɔbstəkl] N obstáculo; (nuisance) estorbo

obstacle race N carrera de obstáculos

obstetrician [ɔbstəˈtrɪʃən] N obstetra mf

obstetrics [ɔbˈstɛtrɪks] N obstetricia

obstinacy [ˈɔbstɪnəsɪ] N terquedad f, obstinación f; (determination) tenacidad f

obstinate [ˈɔbstɪnɪt] ADJ terco, obstinado; (determined) tenaz

obstinately [ˈɔbstɪnɪtlɪ] ADV tercamente, obstinadamente

obstreperous [əbˈstrɛpərəs] ADJ ruidoso; (unruly) revoltoso

obstruct [əbˈstrʌkt] VT (block) obstruir; (hinder) estorbar, obstaculizar

obstruction [əbˈstrʌkʃən] N obstrucción f; (object) estorbo, obstáculo

obstructive [əbˈstrʌktɪv] ADJ obstruccionista; **stop being ~!** ¡deja de poner peros!

obtain [əbˈteɪn] VT (get) obtener; (achieve) conseguir; **to ~ sth (for o.s.)** conseguir or adquirir algo

obtainable [əbˈteɪnəbl] ADJ asequible

obtrusive [əbˈtruːsɪv] ADJ (person) importuno; (: interfering) entrometido; (building etc) demasiado visible

obtuse [əbˈtjuːs] ADJ obtuso

obverse [ˈɔbvəːs] N (of medal) anverso; (fig) complemento

obviate [ˈɔbvɪeɪt] VT obviar, evitar

★**obvious** [ˈɔbvɪəs] ADJ (clear) obvio, evidente; (unsubtle) poco sutil; **it's ~ that ...** está claro que ..., es evidente que ...

★**obviously** [ˈɔbvɪəslɪ] ADV obviamente, evidentemente; **~ not!** ¡por supuesto que no!; **he was ~ not drunk** era evidente que no estaba borracho; **he was not ~ drunk** no se le notaba que estaba borracho

OCAS N ABBR (= Organization of Central American States) ODECA f

★**occasion** [əˈkeɪʒən] N oportunidad f, ocasión f; (event) acontecimiento; **on that ~** esa vez, en aquella ocasión; **to rise to the ~** ponerse a la altura de las circunstancias ▶ VT ocasionar, causar

occasional [əˈkeɪʒənl] ADJ poco frecuente, ocasional

occasionally [əˈkeɪʒənlɪ] ADV de vez en cuando; **very ~** muy de tarde en tarde, en muy contadas ocasiones

occasional table N mesita

occult [ɔˈkʌlt] ADJ (gen) oculto

occupancy [ˈɔkjupənsɪ] N ocupación f

occupant [ˈɔkjupənt] N (of house) inquilino(-a); (of boat, car) ocupante mf

occupation [ɔkjuˈpeɪʃən] N (of house) tenencia; (job) trabajo; (pastime) ocupaciones fpl; (calling) oficio

occupational accident [ɔkjuˈpeɪʃənl-] N accidente m laboral

occupational guidance N orientación f profesional

occupational hazard N gajes mpl del oficio

occupational pension scheme N plan m profesional de jubilación

occupational therapy N terapia ocupacional

occupier [ˈɔkjupaɪəʳ] N inquilino(-a)

occupy [ˈɔkjupaɪ] VT (seat, post, time) ocupar; (house) habitar; **to ~ o.s. with** or **by doing** (as job) dedicarse a hacer; (to pass time) entretenerse haciendo; **to be occupied with sth/in doing sth** estar ocupado con algo/haciendo algo

occur [əˈkəːʳ] VI ocurrir, suceder; **to ~ to sb** ocurrírsele a algn

occurrence [əˈkʌrəns] N suceso

OCD N ABBR (= obsessive compulsive disorder) TOC m

★**ocean** [ˈəuʃən] N océano; **oceans of** (inf) la mar de

ocean bed N fondo del océano

ocean-going [ˈəuʃəngəuɪŋ] ADJ de alta mar

Oceania [əuʃɪˈɑːnɪə] N Oceanía

ocean liner N buque m transoceánico

ochre, (US) **ocher** [ˈəukəʳ] N ocre m

★**o'clock** [əˈklɔk] ADV: **it is five o'clock** son las cinco

OCR N ABBR = **optical character recognition/reader**

Oct. ABBR (= October) oct.

octagonal [ɔkˈtægənl] ADJ octagonal

octane [ˈɔkteɪn] N octano; **high ~ petrol** or (US) **gas** gasolina de alto octanaje

octave [ˈɔktɪv] N octava

★**October** [ɔkˈtəubəʳ] N octubre m; see also **July**

octogenarian [ˈɔktəudʒɪˈnɛərɪən] N octogenario(-a)

octopus [ˈɔktəpəs] N pulpo

oculist [ˈɔkjulɪst] N oculista *mf*

★**odd** [ɔd] ADJ (*strange*) extraño, raro; (*number*) impar; (*sock, shoe etc*) suelto; **60-odd** 60 y pico; **at ~ times** de vez en cuando; **to be the ~ one out** estar de más; **if you have the ~ minute** si tienes unos minutos libres; *see also* **odds**

oddball [ˈɔdbɔːl] N (*inf*) bicho raro

oddity [ˈɔdɪtɪ] N rareza; (*person*) excéntrico(-a)

odd-job man [ɔdˈdʒɔb-] N (*irreg*) hombre *m* que hace chapuzas

odd jobs NPL chapuzas *fpl*

oddly [ˈɔdlɪ] ADV extrañamente

oddments [ˈɔdmənts] NPL (*BRIT Comm*) restos *mpl*

odds [ɔdz] NPL (*in betting*) puntos *mpl* de ventaja; **it makes no ~** da lo mismo; **at ~** reñidos(-as); **to succeed against all the ~** tener éxito contra todo pronóstico; **~ and ends** cachivaches *mpl*

odds-on [ɔdzˈɔn] ADJ (*inf*): **the ~ favourite** el máximo favorito; **it's ~ he'll come** seguro que viene

ode [əud] N oda

odious [ˈəudɪəs] ADJ odioso

odometer [ɔˈdɔmɪtər] N (*US*) cuentakilómetros *m inv*

odour, (*US*) **odor** [ˈəudər] N olor *m*; (*unpleasant*) hedor *m*; (*perfume*) perfume *m*

odourless, (*US*) **odorless** [ˈəudəlɪs] ADJ sin olor

OECD N ABBR (= *Organization for Economic Cooperation and Development*) OCDE *f*

oesophagus, (*US*) **esophagus** [iːˈsɔfəgəs] N esófago

oestrogen, (*US*) **estrogen** [ˈiːstrədʒən] N estrógeno

of [ɔv, əv]

PREP **1** (*gen*) de; **a friend of ours** un amigo nuestro; **a boy of 10** un chico de 10 años; **that was kind of you** eso fue muy amable de tu parte

2 (*expressing quantity, amount, dates etc*) de; **a kilo of flour** un kilo de harina; **there were three of them** había tres; **three of us went** tres de nosotros fuimos; **the 5th of July** el 5 de julio; **a quarter of four** (*US*) las cuatro menos cuarto

3 (*from, out of*) de; **made of wood** (hecho) de madera

Ofcom [ˈɔfkɔm] N ABBR (*BRIT*) = **Office of Communications**

★**off** [ɔf] ADJ, ADV (*engine, light*) apagado; (*tap*) cerrado; (*BRIT: food: bad*) pasado, malo; (*: milk*) cortado; (*cancelled*) suspendido; (*removed*): **the lid was ~** no estaba puesta la tapadera; **he had his coat ~** se había quitado el abrigo; **to be ~** (*leave*) irse, marcharse; **to be ~ sick** estar enfermo *or* de baja; **a day ~** un día libre; **to have an ~ day** tener un mal día; **10% ~** (*Comm*) (con el) 10% de descuento; **it's a long way ~** está muy lejos; **on the ~ chance** por si acaso;

~ and on, on and ~ de vez en cuando; **I must be ~** tengo que irme; **to be well/badly ~** andar bien/mal de dinero; **I'm afraid the chicken is ~** (*in restaurant*) desgraciadamente ya no queda pollo; **that's a bit ~, isn't it?** (*fig: inf*) ¡eso no se hace! ▶ PREP de; **5 km ~ (the road)** a 5 km (de la carretera); **~ the coast** frente a la costa; **I'm ~ meat** (*no longer eat/like it*) paso de la carne

offal [ˈɔfl] N (*BRIT Culin*) menudillos *mpl*, asaduras *fpl*

off-centre, (*US*) **off-center** [ɔfˈsɛntər] ADJ descentrado, ladeado

off-colour [ˈɔfˈkʌlər] ADJ (*BRIT: ill*) indispuesto; **to feel ~** sentirse *or* estar mal

offence, (*US*) **offense** [əˈfɛns] N (*crime*) delito; (*insult*) ofensa; **to take ~ at** ofenderse por; **to commit an ~** cometer un delito

offend [əˈfɛnd] VT (*person*) ofender ▶ VI: **to ~ against** (*law, rule*) infringir

offender [əˈfɛndər] N delincuente *mf*; (*against regulations*) infractor(a) *m/f*

offending [əˈfɛndɪŋ] ADJ culpable; (*object*) molesto; (*word*) problemático

offense [əˈfɛns] N (*US*) = **offence**

offensive [əˈfɛnsɪv] ADJ ofensivo; (*smell etc*) repugnante ▶ N (*Mil*) ofensiva

★**offer** [ˈɔfər] N (*gen*) oferta, ofrecimiento; (*proposal*) propuesta; **"on ~"** (*Comm*) "en oferta"; **to make an ~ for sth** hacer una oferta por algo ▶ VT ofrecer; **to ~ sth to sb, ~ sb sth** ofrecer algo a algn; **to ~ to do sth** ofrecerse a hacer algo

offering [ˈɔfərɪŋ] N (*Rel*) ofrenda

offer price N precio de oferta

offertory [ˈɔfətrɪ] N (*Rel*) ofertorio

offhand [ɔfˈhænd] ADJ informal; (*brusque*) desconsiderado ▶ ADV de improviso, sin pensarlo; **I can't tell you ~** no te lo puedo decir así de improviso *or* (*LAM*) así nomás

★**office** [ˈɔfɪs] N (*place*) oficina; (*room*) despacho; (*position*) cargo, oficio; **doctor's ~** (*US*) consultorio; **to take ~** entrar en funciones; **through his good offices** gracias a sus buenos oficios

office automation N ofimática, buromática

office bearer N (*of club etc*) titular *mf* (de una cartera)

office block, (*US*) **office building** N bloque *m* de oficinas

office boy N ordenanza *m*

office hours NPL horas *fpl* de oficina; (*US Med*) horas *fpl* de consulta

office manager N jefe(-a) *m/f* de oficina

★**officer** [ˈɔfɪsər] N (*Mil etc*) oficial *mf*; (*of organization*) director(a) *m/f*; (*also*: **police officer**) agente *mf* de policía

office work N trabajo de oficina

office worker N oficinista *mf*

★**official** [əˈfɪʃl] ADJ (*authorized*) oficial, autorizado; (*strike*) oficial ▶ N funcionario(-a)

officialdom [əˈfɪʃldəm] N burocracia

officially [əˈfɪʃəlɪ] ADV oficialmente

official receiver N síndico

officiate [əˈfɪʃɪeɪt] VI (Rel) oficiar; **to ~ as Mayor** ejercer las funciones de alcalde; **to ~ at a marriage** celebrar una boda

officious [əˈfɪʃəs] ADJ oficioso

offing [ˈɔfɪŋ] N: **in the ~** (fig) en perspectiva

off-key [ɔfˈkiː] ADJ desafinado ▶ ADV desafinadamente

off-licence [ˈɔflaɪsns] N (BRIT: shop) tienda de bebidas alcohólicas

off-limits [ɔfˈlɪmɪts] ADJ (US Mil) prohibido al personal militar

off line ADJ, ADV (Comput) fuera de línea; (switched off) desconectado

off-load [ˈɔfləud] VT descargar, desembarcar

off-peak [ˈɔfˈpiːk] ADJ (holiday) de temporada baja; (electricity) de banda económica; (ticket) de precio reducido para viajar fuera de las horas punta

off-putting [ˈɔfputɪŋ] ADJ (BRIT: person) poco amable, difícil; (: behaviour) chocante; (: remark) desalentador(a)

off-season [ˈɔfˈsiːzn] ADJ, ADV fuera de temporada

offset [ˈɔfset] VT (irreg: like **set**) (counteract) contrarrestar, compensar ▶ N (also: **offset printing**) offset m

offshoot [ˈɔfʃuːt] N (Bot) vástago; (fig) ramificación f

offshore [ɔfˈʃɔːʳ] ADJ (breeze, island) costero; (fishing) de bajura; **~ oilfield** campo petrolífero submarino

offside [ˈɔfˈsaɪd] N (Aut: with right-hand drive) lado derecho; (: with left-hand drive) lado izquierdo ▶ ADJ (Sport) fuera de juego; (Aut: in UK) del lado derecho; (: in US, Europe etc) del lado izquierdo

offspring [ˈɔfsprɪŋ] N descendencia

offstage [ɔfˈsteɪdʒ] ADV entre bastidores

off-the-cuff [ɔfðəˈkʌf] ADJ espontáneo

off-the-job [ɔfðəˈdʒɔb] ADJ: **~ training** formación f fuera del trabajo

off-the-peg [ɔfðəˈpeg], (US) **off-the-rack** [ɔfðəˈræk] ADJ confeccionado

off-the-record [ˈɔfðəˈrekɔːd] ADJ extraoficial, confidencial ▶ ADV extraoficialmente, confidencialmente

off-white [ˈɔfwaɪt] ADJ blanco grisáceo

Ofgem [ˈɔfdʒem] N ABBR (BRIT: = Office of Gas and Electricity Markets) organismo regulador del sector energético en el Reino Unido

Oftel [ˈɔftel] N ABBR (BRIT: = Office of Telecommunications) organismo que controla las telecomunicaciones británicas

★**often** [ˈɔfn] ADV a menudo, con frecuencia, seguido (LAM); **how ~ do you go?** ¿cada cuánto vas?

Ofwat [ˈɔfwɔt] N ABBR (BRIT: = Office of Water Services) organismo que controla a las empresas suministradoras del agua en Inglaterra y Gales

ogle [ˈəugl] VT comerse con los ojos a

ogre [ˈəugəʳ] N ogro

OH ABBR (US) = **Ohio**

oh [əu] EXCL ¡ah!

OHMS ABBR (BRIT) = **On Her/His Majesty's Service**

★**oil** [ɔɪl] N aceite m; (petroleum) petróleo; **fried in ~** frito en aceite ▶ VT (machine) engrasar

oilcan [ˈɔɪlkæn] N lata de aceite

oilfield [ˈɔɪlfiːld] N campo petrolífero

oil filter N (Aut) filtro de aceite

oil-fired [ˈɔɪlfaɪəd] ADJ de fueloil

oil gauge N indicador m del aceite

oil industry N industria petrolífera

oil level N nivel m del aceite

oil painting N pintura al óleo

oil refinery N refinería de petróleo

oil rig N torre f de perforación

oilskins [ˈɔɪlskɪnz] NPL impermeable msg, chubasquero sg

oil slick N marea negra

oil tanker N petrolero; (truck) camión m cisterna

oil well N pozo (de petróleo)

oily [ˈɔɪlɪ] ADJ aceitoso; (food) grasiento

ointment [ˈɔɪntmənt] N ungüento

OK ABBR (US) = **Oklahoma**

O.K., okay [ˈəuˈkeɪ] EXCL O.K., ¡está bien!, ¡vale! ▶ ADJ bien; **it's ~ with** or **by me** estoy de acuerdo, me parece bien; **are you ~ for money?** ¿andas or vas bien de dinero? ▶ N: **to give sth one's ~** dar el visto bueno a or aprobar algo ▶ VT dar el visto bueno a

★**old** [əuld] ADJ viejo; (former) antiguo; **how ~ are you?** ¿cuántos años tienes?, ¿qué edad tienes?; **he's 10 years ~** tiene 10 años; **older brother** hermano mayor; **any ~ thing will do** sirve cualquier cosa

---

old can be translated by **viejo**, **antiguo**, or **anciano**. Use **viejo** when you are referring to old things or people in general: These shoes are really old. **Estos zapatos son muy viejos.**
When you mean former, you can use **viejo** or **antiguo** before the noun: I'm meeting an old friend tomorrow. **He quedado con un antiguo** or **viejo amigo mañana.**
However, when **antiguo** goes after the noun, it means ancient: **Visitamos un templo antiguo.** We went to see an ancient temple.
Anciano is used when referring to someone's age: I have a very old aunt. **Tengo una tía muy anciana.**

---

old age N vejez f

old-age pension [ˈəuldeɪdʒ-] N (BRIT) jubilación f, pensión f

old-age pensioner [ˈəuldeɪdʒ-] N (BRIT) jubilado(-a)

olden [ˈəʊldən] ADJ antiguo

old-fashioned [ˈəʊldˈfæʃənd] ADJ anticuado, pasado de moda

old maid N solterona

old people's home N (esp BRIT) residencia de ancianos

old-style [ˈəʊldstaɪl] ADJ tradicional, chapado a la antigua

old-time [ˈəʊldˈtaɪm] ADJ antiguo, de antaño

old-timer [əʊldˈtaɪməʳ] N veterano(-a); (old person) anciano(-a)

old wives' tale N cuento de viejas, patraña

oligarch [ˈɒlɪɡɑːk] N oligarca mf

olive [ˈɒlɪv] N (fruit) aceituna; (tree) olivo ▶ ADJ (also: **olive-green**) verde oliva inv

olive branch N (fig): **to offer an ~ to sb** ofrecer hacer las paces con algn

olive oil N aceite m de oliva

Olympic® [əʊˈlɪmpɪk] ADJ olímpico; **the ~ Games**®, **the Olympics**® npl los Juegos Olímpicos, las Olimpiadas

OM N ABBR (BRIT: = Order of Merit) título ceremonial

Oman [əʊˈmɑːn] N Omán m

OMB N ABBR (US: = Office of Management and Budget) servicio que asesora al presidente en materia presupuestaria

omelette, omelet [ˈɒmlɪt] N tortilla, tortilla de huevo (LAM)

omen [ˈəʊmən] N presagio

OMG ABBR (inf: = Oh my God!) Dios mío, cielos

ominous [ˈɒmɪnəs] ADJ de mal agüero, amenazador(a)

omission [əʊˈmɪʃən] N omisión f; (error) descuido

omit [əʊˈmɪt] VT omitir; (by mistake) olvidar, descuidar; **to ~ to do sth** olvidarse or dejar de hacer algo

omnivorous [ɒmˈnɪvərəs] ADJ omnívoro

ON ABBR (CANADA) = **Ontario**

---

on [ɒn]

PREP **1** (indicating position) en, sobre; **on the wall** en la pared; **it's on the table** está sobre or en la mesa; **on the left** a la izquierda; **I haven't got any money on me** no llevo dinero encima

2 (indicating means, method, condition etc): **on foot** a pie; **on the train/plane** (go) en tren/avión; (be) en el tren/el avión; **on the radio/television** por or en la radio/televisión; **on the telephone** al teléfono; **to be on drugs** drogarse; (Med) estar a tratamiento; **to be on holiday/business** estar de vacaciones/en viaje de negocios; **we're on irregular verbs** estamos con los verbos irregulares

3 (referring to time): **on Friday** el viernes; **on Fridays** los viernes; **on June 20th** el 20 de junio; **a week on Friday** del viernes en una semana; **on arrival** al llegar; **on seeing this** al ver esto

---

4 (about, concerning) sobre, acerca de; **a book on physics** un libro de or sobre física

5 (at the expense of): **this round's on me** esta ronda la pago yo, invito yo a esta ronda; (earning): **he's on sixteen thousand pounds a year** gana dieciséis mil libras al año

▶ ADV **1** (referring to dress): **to have one's coat on** tener or llevar el abrigo puesto; **she put her gloves on** se puso los guantes

2 (referring to covering): **"screw the lid on tightly"** "cerrar bien la tapa"

3 (further, continuously): **to walk/run** etc **on** seguir caminando/corriendo etc; **from that day on** desde aquel día; **it was well on in the evening** estaba ya entrada la tarde

4 (in phrases): **I'm on to sth** creo haber encontrado algo; **my father's always on at me to get a job** (inf) mi padre siempre me está dando la lata para que me ponga a trabajar

▶ ADJ **1** (functioning, in operation: machine, radio, TV, light) encendido (SP), prendido (LAM); (: tap) abierto; (: brakes) echado, puesto; **is the meeting still on?** (in progress) ¿todavía continúa la reunión?; (not cancelled) ¿va a haber reunión al fin?; **there's a good film on at the cinema** ponen una buena película en el cine

2: that's not on! (inf: not possible) ¡eso ni hablar!; (: not acceptable) ¡eso no se hace!

ONC N ABBR (BRIT: = Ordinary National Certificate) título escolar

★once [wʌns] ADV una vez; (formerly) antiguamente; **I knew him ~** le conocía hace tiempo; **at ~** en seguida, inmediatamente; (simultaneously) a la vez; **~ a week** una vez a la semana; **~ more** otra vez; **~ and for all** de una vez por todas; **~ upon a time** érase una vez ▶ CONJ una vez que; **~ he had left/it was done** una vez que se había marchado/se hizo

oncoming [ˈɒnkʌmɪŋ] ADJ (traffic) que viene de frente

OND N ABBR (BRIT: = Ordinary National Diploma) título escolar

---

one [wʌn]

NUM un/una; **one hundred and fifty** ciento cincuenta; **one by one** uno a uno; **it's one (o'clock)** es la una

▶ ADJ **1** (sole) único; **the one book which** el único libro que; **the one man who** el único que

2 (same) mismo(-a); **they came in the one car** vinieron en un solo coche

▶ PRON **1: this one** este, éste; **that one** ese, ése; (more remote) aquel, aquél; **I've already got (a red) one** ya tengo uno(-a) rojo(-a); **one by one** uno(-a) por uno(-a); **to be one up on sb** llevar ventaja a algn; **to be at one (with sb)** estar completamente de acuerdo (con algn)

2: one another (us) nos; (you) os (SP); (you: formal, them) se; **do you two ever see one another?** ¿os veis alguna vez? (SP), ¿se ven alguna vez?; **the two boys didn't dare look**

at one another los dos chicos no se atrevieron a mirarse (el uno al otro); **they all kissed one another** se besaron unos a otros
3 *impers*: **one never knows** nunca se sabe; **to cut one's finger** cortarse el dedo; **one needs to eat** hay que comer

one-armed bandit [ˈwʌnɑːmd-] N máquina tragaperras

one-day excursion [ˈwʌndeɪ-] N (US) billete m de ida y vuelta en un día

One-hundred share index [ˈwʌnhʌndrəd-] N índice m bursátil (*del Financial Times*)

one-man [ˈwʌnˈmæn] ADJ (*business*) individual

one-man band N hombre-orquesta m

one-off [wʌnˈɔf] N (BRIT *inf*: *object*) artículo único; (: *event*) caso especial

one-parent family [ˈwʌnpeərənt-] N familia monoparental

one-piece [ˈwʌnpiːs] ADJ (*bathing suit*) de una pieza

onerous [ˈɔnərəs] ADJ (*task, duty*) pesado; (*responsibility*) oneroso

oneself [wʌnˈsɛlf] PRON (*reflexive*) se; (*after prep*) sí; (*emphatic*) uno(-a) mismo(-a); **to hurt ~** hacerse daño; **to keep sth for ~** guardarse algo; **to talk to ~** hablar solo

one-shot [wʌnˈʃɔt] N (US) = **one-off**

one-sided [wʌnˈsaɪdɪd] ADJ (*argument*) parcial; (*decision, view*) unilateral; (*game, contest*) desigual

onesie [ˈwʌnzɪ] N pijama m de una pieza, pijama m entero

one-time [ˈwʌntaɪm] ADJ antiguo, ex-

one-to-one [ˈwʌntəwʌn] ADJ (*relationship*) individualizado

one-upmanship [wʌnˈʌpmənʃɪp] N: **the art of ~** el arte de quedar siempre por encima

one-way [ˈwʌnweɪ] ADJ (*street, traffic*) de dirección única; (*ticket*) sencillo

ongoing [ˈɔngəʊɪŋ] ADJ continuo

★**onion** [ˈʌnjən] N cebolla

★**online** [ɔnˈlaɪn] ADJ, ADV (*Comput*) en línea; (*switched on*) conectado

onlooker [ˈɔnlʊkəʳ] N espectador(a) m/f

★**only** [ˈəʊnlɪ] ADV solo, sólo (*to avoid confusion with adj*), solamente, nomás (LAM); **I'd be ~ too pleased to help** encantado de ayudarles; **I saw her ~ yesterday** le vi ayer mismo; **not ~ ... but also ...** no solo ... sino también ... ▶ ADJ único, solo; **an ~ child** un hijo único ▶ CONJ solamente que, pero; **I would come, ~ I'm very busy** iría, solo que estoy muy atareado

---

only is translated by **solo**, which can also mean *alone*. Previously, **solo** had an accent when it meant *only* but now the context is relied on to distinguish them. Where there is any confusion, **sólo** retains the accent to clarify the meaning: *He only stayed two days.* **Estuvo sólo dos días.** *He was alone for two days.* **Estuvo solo dos días.**

---

ono ABBR (= *or nearest offer*) abierto a ofertas

on-screen [ɔnˈskriːn] ADJ (*Comput etc*) en pantalla; (*romance, kiss*) cinematográfico

onset [ˈɔnsɛt] N comienzo

onshore [ˈɔnʃɔːʳ] ADJ (*wind*) que sopla del mar hacia la tierra

onslaught [ˈɔnslɔːt] N ataque m, embestida

on-the-job [ˈɔnðəˈdʒɔb] ADJ: **~ training** formación f en el trabajo or sobre la práctica

onto [ˈɔntu] PREP = **on to**

onus [ˈəʊnəs] N responsabilidad f; **the ~ is upon him to prove it** le incumbe a él demostrarlo

onward [ˈɔnwəd], **onwards** [ˈɔnwədz] ADV (*move*) (hacia) adelante; **from that time ~** desde entonces en adelante

onyx [ˈɔnɪks] N ónice m, ónix m

oops [ups] EXCL (*also*: **oops-a-daisy!**) ¡huy!

ooze [uːz] VI rezumar

opal [ˈəʊpl] N ópalo

opaque [əʊˈpeɪk] ADJ opaco

OPEC [ˈəʊpek] N ABBR (= *Organization of Petroleum-Exporting Countries*) OPEP f

★**open** [ˈəʊpn] ADJ abierto; (*car*) descubierto; (*road, view*) despejado; (*meeting*) público; (*admiration*) manifiesto; **in the ~ (air)** al aire libre; **~ verdict** veredicto inconcluso; **~ ticket** billete m abierto; **~ ground** (*among trees*) claro; (*waste ground*) solar m; **to have an ~ mind (on sth)** estar sin decidirse aún (sobre algo) ▶ VT abrir; **to ~ a bank account** abrir una cuenta en el banco ▶ VI (*flower, eyes, door, debate*) abrirse; (*book etc: commence*) comenzar
▶ **open on to** VT FUS (*room, door*) dar a
▶ **open out** VT abrir ▶ VI (*person*) abrirse
▶ **open up** VT abrir; (*blocked road*) despejar ▶ VI abrirse

open-and-shut [ˈəʊpənənˈʃʌt] ADJ: **~ case** caso claro or evidente

open day N (BRIT) jornada de puertas abiertas or acceso público

open-ended [əʊpnˈɛndɪd] ADJ (*fig*) indefinido, sin definir

opener [ˈəʊpnəʳ] N (*also*: **can opener, tin opener**) abrelatas m inv

open-heart surgery [əʊpnˈhɑːt-] N cirugía a corazón abierto

opening [ˈəʊpnɪŋ] N abertura; (*beginning*) comienzo; (*opportunity*) oportunidad f; (*job*) puesto vacante, vacante f

opening hours NPL horario de apertura

opening night N estreno

open learning N enseñanza flexible a tiempo parcial

openly [ˈəʊpnlɪ] ADV abiertamente

open-minded [əʊpnˈmaɪndɪd] ADJ de amplias miras, sin prejuicios

open-necked [ˈəʊpnnɛkt] ADJ sin corbata

openness [ˈəʊpnnɪs] N (*frankness*) franqueza

open-plan [ˈəʊpnˈplæn] ADJ diáfano, sin tabiques

o

open prison N centro penitenciario de régimen abierto

open return N vuelta con fecha abierta

open shop N *empresa que contrata a mano de obra no afiliada a ningún sindicato*

Open University N (BRIT) ≈ Universidad f Nacional de Educación a Distancia, ≈ UNED f

> La **Open University**, fundada en 1969, está especializada en impartir cursos a distancia y a tiempo parcial con sus propios materiales de apoyo diseñados para tal fin, entre ellos muchos recursos en línea y programas de radio y televisión emitidos por la BBC. Los trabajos se envían electrónicamente o por correo y se complementan con la asistencia obligatoria a cursos de verano. Para obtener la licenciatura es necesario estudiar un mínimo de módulos y alcanzar un determinado número de créditos. Con más de 250 000 inscritos, entre ellos muchos estudiantes del extranjero, la *Open University* es la organización educativa más grande del Reino Unido y una de las más grandes de todo el mundo. Cuenta con un nivel excelente en lo que respecta a los resultados como a la satisfacción de los estudiantes.

opera ['ɔpərə] N ópera

opera glasses NPL gemelos *mpl*

opera house N teatro de la ópera

opera singer N cantante *mf* de ópera

★**operate** ['ɔpəreɪt] VT (*machine*) hacer funcionar; (*company*) dirigir ▶ VI funcionar; (*drug*) hacer efecto; **to ~ on sb** (*Med*) operar a algn

operatic [ɔpə'rætɪk] ADJ de ópera

operating costs ['ɔpəreɪtɪŋ-] NPL gastos *mpl* operacionales

operating profit N beneficio de explotación

operating room N (*US*) quirófano, sala de operaciones

operating table N mesa de operaciones

operating theatre N quirófano, sala de operaciones

★**operation** [ɔpə'reɪʃən] N (*gen*) operación f; (*of machine*) funcionamiento; **to be in ~** estar funcionando *or* en funcionamiento; **to have an ~** (*Med*) ser operado; **to have an ~ for** operarse de; **the company's operations during the year** las actividades de la compañía durante el año

operational [ɔpə'reɪʃənl] ADJ operacional, en buen estado; (*Comm*) en condiciones de servicio; (*ready for use or action*) en condiciones de funcionar; **when the service is fully ~** cuando el servicio esté en pleno funcionamiento

operative ['ɔpərətɪv] ADJ (*measure*) en vigor; **the ~ word** la palabra clave

operator ['ɔpəreɪtə^r] N (*of machine*) operario(-a), maquinista *mf*; (*Tel*) operador(a) *m/f*, telefonista *mf*

operetta [ɔpə'retə] N opereta

ophthalmic [ɔf'θælmɪk] ADJ oftálmico

ophthalmologist [ɔfθæl'mɔlədʒɪst] N oftalmólogo(-a)

★**opinion** [ə'pɪnjən] N (*gen*) opinión f; **in my ~** en mi opinión, a mi juicio; **to seek a second ~** pedir una segunda opinión

opinionated [ə'pɪnjəneɪtɪd] ADJ testarudo

opinion poll N encuesta, sondeo

opium ['əupɪəm] N opio

★**opponent** [ə'pəunənt] N adversario(-a), contrincante *mf*

opportune ['ɔpətjuːn] ADJ oportuno

opportunism [ɔpə'tjuːnɪzm] N oportunismo

opportunist [ɔpə'tjuːnɪst] N oportunista *mf*

★**opportunity** [ɔpə'tjuːnɪtɪ] N oportunidad f, chance *m or f* (*LAM*); **to take the ~ to do** *or* **of doing** aprovechar la ocasión para hacer

oppose [ə'pəuz] VT oponerse a; **to be opposed to sth** oponerse a algo; **as opposed to** en vez de; (*unlike*) a diferencia de

opposing [ə'pəuzɪŋ] ADJ (*side*) opuesto, contrario

★**opposite** ['ɔpəzɪt] ADJ opuesto, contrario; (*house etc*) de enfrente; **the ~ sex** el otro sexo, el sexo opuesto ▶ ADV en frente ▶ PREP en frente de, frente a ▶ N lo contrario

opposite number N (*BRIT*) homólogo(-a)

★**opposition** [ɔpə'zɪʃən] N oposición f

oppress [ə'pres] VT oprimir

oppression [ə'preʃən] N opresión f

oppressive [ə'presɪv] ADJ opresivo

opprobrium [ə'prəubrɪəm] N (*formal*) oprobio

opt [ɔpt] VI: **to ~ for** optar por; **to ~ to do** optar por hacer

▶ **opt out** VI: **to ~ out of** optar por no hacer

optical ['ɔptɪkl] ADJ óptico

optical character reader N lector *m* óptico de caracteres

optical character recognition N reconocimiento *m* óptico de caracteres

optical fibre N fibra óptica

optician [ɔp'tɪʃən] N óptico(-a)

optics ['ɔptɪks] N óptica

optimism ['ɔptɪmɪzəm] N optimismo

optimist ['ɔptɪmɪst] N optimista *mf*

★**optimistic** [ɔptɪ'mɪstɪk] ADJ optimista

optimum ['ɔptɪməm] ADJ óptimo

★**option** ['ɔpʃən] N opción f; **to keep one's options open** (*fig*) mantener las opciones abiertas; **I have no ~** no tengo más *or* otro remedio

optional ['ɔpʃənl] ADJ opcional; (*course*) optativo; **~ extras** opciones *fpl* extras

opulence ['ɔpjuləns] N opulencia

opulent ['ɔpjulənt] ADJ opulento

OR ABBR (*US*) = **Oregon**

★**or** [ɔː^r] CONJ o; (*before o, ho*) u; (*with negative*): **he hasn't seen or heard anything** no ha visto ni oído nada; **or else** si no; **let me go or I'll scream!** ¡suélteme, o me pongo a gritar!

While *or* is usually translated by **o**, use **u** before words beginning with **o** and **ho** to avoid two 'o' sounds coming together: *two or three photos* **dos o tres fotos**; *for one reason or another* **por un motivo u otro**.
Write **ó** instead of **o** between numerals to prevent confusion with zero: 5 *or* 6 **5 ó 6**.

oracle [ˈɔrəkl] N oráculo

oral [ˈɔːrəl] ADJ oral ▶ N examen *m* oral

★**orange** [ˈɒrɪndʒ] N (*fruit*) naranja ▶ ADJ (de color) naranja *inv*

orangeade [ɒrɪndʒˈeɪd] N naranjada, refresco de naranja

orange juice N jugo *m* de naranja, zumo *m* de naranja (*Sp*)

orange squash N bebida de naranja

orang-outang, orang-utan [ɔˈræŋuːˈtæn] N orangután *m*

oration [ɔːˈreɪʃən] N discurso solemne; **funeral ~** oración *f* fúnebre

orator [ˈɔrətər] N orador(a) *m/f*

oratorio [ɒrəˈtɔːrɪəu] N oratorio

orbit [ˈɔːbɪt] N órbita; **to be in/go into ~ (round)** estar en/entrar en órbita (alrededor de) ▶ VT, VI orbitar

orbital [ˈɔːbɪtl] N (*also*: **orbital motorway**) autopista de circunvalación

orchard [ˈɔːtʃəd] N huerto; **apple ~** manzanar *m*, manzanal *m*

orchestra [ˈɔːkɪstrə] N orquesta; (*US*: *seating*) platea

orchestral [ɔːˈkestrəl] ADJ de orquesta

orchestrate [ˈɔːkɪstreɪt] VT orquestar

orchid [ˈɔːkɪd] N orquídea

ordain [ɔːˈdeɪn] VT (*Rel*) ordenar

ordeal [ɔːˈdiːl] N experiencia terrible

★**order** [ˈɔːdər] N orden *m*; (*command*) orden *f*; (*type, kind*) clase *f*; (*state*) estado; (*Comm*) pedido, encargo; **in ~** (*gen*) en orden; (*of document*) en regla; **in (working) ~** en funcionamiento; **a machine in working ~** una máquina en funcionamiento; **to be out of ~** estar desordenado; (*not working*) no funcionar; **in ~ to do** para hacer; **in ~ that** para que + *subjun*; **on ~** (*Comm*) pedido; **to be on ~** estar pedido; **we are under orders to do it** tenemos orden de hacerlo; **a point of ~** una cuestión de procedimiento; **to place an ~ for sth with sb** hacer un pedido de algo a algn; **made to ~** hecho a la medida; **his income is of the ~ of £24,000 per year** sus ingresos son del orden de 24 mil libras al año; **to the ~ of** (*Banking*) a la orden de ▶ VT (*also*: **put in order**) ordenar, poner en orden; (*Comm*) encargar, pedir; (*command*) mandar, ordenar; **to ~ sb to do sth** mandar a algn hacer algo

order book N cartera de pedidos

order form N hoja de pedido

orderly [ˈɔːdəlɪ] N (*Mil*) ordenanza *m*; (*Med*) auxiliar *mf* (de hospital) ▶ ADJ ordenado

orderly officer N (*Mil*) oficial *m* del día

order number N número de pedido

ordinal [ˈɔːdɪnl] ADJ ordinal

ordinarily [ˈɔːdnrɪlɪ] ADV por lo común

★**ordinary** [ˈɔːdnrɪ] ADJ corriente, normal; (*pej*) común y corriente; **out of the ~** fuera de lo común, extraordinario

ordinary degree N (*Brit*) diploma *m*

Después de tres años de estudios, algunos universitarios obtienen la titulación de **ordinary degree**. Esto ocurre en el caso poco frecuente de que no aprueben los exámenes que conducen al título de *honours degree* pero sus examinadores consideren que a lo largo de la carrera han logrado unos resultados mínimos satisfactorios. También es una opción que tienen los estudiantes de las universidades escocesas no interesados en estudiar en la universidad más de tres años.

ordinary seaman N (*irreg*) (*Brit*) marinero

ordinary shares NPL acciones *fpl* ordinarias

ordination [ɔːdɪˈneɪʃən] N ordenación *f*

ordnance [ˈɔːdnəns] N (*Mil*: *unit*) artillería

ordnance factory N fábrica de artillería

Ordnance Survey N (*Brit*) *servicio oficial de topografía y cartografía*

ore [ɔːr] N mineral *m*

oregano [ɒrɪˈgɑːnəu] N orégano

organ [ˈɔːgən] N órgano

organic [ɔːˈgænɪk] ADJ orgánico; (*vegetables, produce*) biológico

organism [ˈɔːgənɪzəm] N organismo

organist [ˈɔːgənɪst] N organista *mf*

★**organization** [ɔːgənaɪˈzeɪʃən] N organización *f*

organization chart N organigrama *m*

★**organize** [ˈɔːgənaɪz] VT organizar

organized [ˈɔːgənaɪzd] ADJ organizado; **to get ~** organizarse

organized crime N crimen *m* organizado

organizer [ˈɔːgənaɪzər] N organizador(a) *m/f*

orgasm [ˈɔːgæzəm] N orgasmo

orgy [ˈɔːdʒɪ] N orgía

Orient [ˈɔːrɪənt] N Oriente *m*

oriental [ɔːrɪˈentl] ADJ oriental

orientate [ˈɔːrɪənteɪt] VT orientar

orientation [ɔːrɪenˈteɪʃən] N orientación *f*

origin [ˈɒrɪdʒɪn] N origen *m*; (*point of departure*) procedencia

★**original** [əˈrɪdʒɪnl] ADJ original; (*first*) primero; (*earlier*) primitivo ▶ N original *m*

originality [ərɪdʒɪˈnælɪtɪ] N originalidad *f*

★**originally** [əˈrɪdʒɪnəlɪ] ADV (*at first*) al principio; (*with originality*) con originalidad

originate [əˈrɪdʒɪneɪt] VI: **to ~ from, to ~ in** surgir de, tener su origen en

originator [əˈrɪdʒɪneɪtər] N inventor(a) *m/f*, autor(a) *m/f*

Orkneys ['ɔːknɪz] NPL: **the ~** (*also:* **the Orkney Islands**) las Orcadas

ornament ['ɔːnəmənt] N adorno; (*trinket*) chuchería

ornamental [ɔːnə'mɛntl] ADJ decorativo, de adorno

ornamentation [ɔːnəmɛn'teɪʃən] N ornamentación f

ornate [ɔː'neɪt] ADJ recargado

ornithologist [ɔːnɪ'θɔlədʒɪst] N ornitólogo(-a)

ornithology [ɔːnɪ'θɔlədʒɪ] N ornitología

orphan ['ɔːfn] N huérfano(-a) ▶ VT: **to be orphaned** quedar huérfano(-a)

orphanage ['ɔːfənɪdʒ] N orfanato

orthodox ['ɔːθədɔks] ADJ ortodoxo

orthodoxy ['ɔːθədɔksɪ] N ortodoxia

orthopaedic, (*US*) **orthopedic** [ɔːθə'piːdɪk] ADJ ortopédico

orthopaedics, (*US*) **orthopedics** [ɔːθə'piːdɪks] N ortopedia

OS ABBR (*Brit*: = *Ordnance Survey*) *servicio oficial de topografía y cartografía*; (: *Naut*) = **ordinary seaman**; (: *Dress*) = **outsize**

O.S. ABBR = **out of stock**

Oscar ['ɔskəʳ] N óscar m

oscillate ['ɔsɪleɪt] VI oscilar; (*person*) vacilar

oscillation [ɔsɪ'leɪʃən] N oscilación f; (*of prices*) fluctuación f

OSHA N ABBR (*US*: = *Occupational Safety and Health Administration*) *oficina de la higiene y la seguridad en el trabajo*

Oslo ['ɔzləu] N Oslo

ostensible [ɔs'tɛnsɪbl] ADJ aparente

ostensibly [ɔs'tɛnsɪblɪ] ADV aparentemente

ostentatious [ɔstɛn'teɪʃəs] ADJ pretencioso, aparatoso; (*person*) ostentativo

osteopath ['ɔstɪəpæθ] N osteópata mf

ostracize ['ɔstrəsaɪz] VT hacer el vacío a

ostrich ['ɔstrɪtʃ] N avestruz m

OT N ABBR (= *Old Testament*) A.T.

OTB N ABBR (*US*: = *off-track betting*) *apuestas hechas fuera del hipódromo*

OTE ABBR (= *on-target earnings*) *beneficios según objetivos*

★**other** ['ʌðəʳ] ADJ otro; **the ~ day** el otro día; **some ~ people have still to arrive** quedan por llegar otros; **the ~ one** el (la) otro(-a) ▶ PRON: **others** (*other people*) otros; **~ than** (*apart from*) aparte de; **some actor or ~** un actor cualquiera; **somebody or ~** alguien, alguno; **it was no ~ than the bishop** no era otro que el obispo

★**otherwise** ['ʌðəwaɪz] ADV, CONJ de otra manera; (*if not*) si no; **an ~ good piece of work** un trabajo que, quitando eso, es bueno

OTT ABBR (*inf*) = **over the top**; *see* **top**

otter ['ɔtəʳ] N nutria

OU N ABBR (*Brit*) = **Open University**

ouch [autʃ] EXCL ¡ay!

★**ought** [ɔːt] AUX VB: **I ~ to do it** debería hacerlo; **this ~ to have been corrected** esto debiera de haberse corregido; **he ~ to win** (*probability*) debiera ganar; **you ~ to go and see it** vale la pena ir a verlo

ounce [auns] N onza (=*28.35g*: *16oz* = *1lb*)

★**our** ['auəʳ] ADJ nuestro; *see also* **my**

★**ours** ['auəz] PRON (el) nuestro/(la) nuestra *etc*; *see also* **mine**[1]

★**ourselves** [auə'sɛlvz] PRON PL (*reflexive, after prep*) nosotros(-as); (*emphatic*) nosotros(-as) mismos(-as); **we did it (all) by ~** lo hicimos nosotros solos; *see also* **oneself**

oust [aust] VT desalojar

★**out** [aut] ADV fuera, afuera; (*not at home*) fuera (de casa); (*light, fire*) apagado; (*on strike*) en huelga; **~ there** allí (fuera); **he's ~** (*absent*) no está, ha salido; **to be ~ in one's calculations** equivocarse (en sus cálculos); **to run ~** salir corriendo; **~ loud** en voz alta; **to be ~ and about again** estar repuesto y levantado; **the journey ~** el viaje de ida; **the boat was 10 km ~** el barco estaba a 10 kilómetros de la costa; **before the week was ~** antes del fin de la semana; **he's ~ for all he can get** busca sus propios fines, anda detrás de lo suyo; **~ of** *prep* (*outside*) fuera de; (*because of: anger etc*) por; **to look ~ of the window** mirar por la ventana; **to drink ~ of a cup** beber de una taza; **made ~ of wood** de madera; **~ of petrol** sin gasolina; **"~ of order"** "no funciona"; **it's ~ of stock** (*Comm*) está agotado ▶ VT: **to ~ sb** revelar públicamente la homosexualidad de algn

out-and-out ['autəndaut] ADJ (*liar, thief etc*) redomado, empedernido

outback ['autbæk] N interior m

outbid [aut'bɪd] VT pujar más alto que, sobrepujar

outboard ['autbɔːd] ADJ: **~ motor** (motor m) fuera borda m

outbound ['autbaund] ADJ (*flight*) de salida; (*flight: not return*) de ida; **~ from/for** con salida de/hacia

outbox ['autbɔks] N (*Comput*) buzón m de salida; (*US: out-tray*) bandeja de salida

outbreak ['autbreɪk] N (*of war*) comienzo; (*of disease*) epidemia; (*of violence etc*) ola

outbuilding ['autbɪldɪŋ] N dependencia; (*shed*) cobertizo

outburst ['autbəːst] N explosión f, arranque m

outcast ['autkɑːst] N paria mf

outclass [aut'klɑːs] VT aventajar, superar

★**outcome** ['autkʌm] N resultado

outcrop ['autkrɔp] N (*of rock*) afloramiento

outcry ['autkraɪ] N protestas fpl

outdated [aut'deɪtɪd] ADJ anticuado

outdistance [aut'dɪstəns] VT dejar atrás

outdo [aut'duː] VT (*irreg: like* **do**) superar

outdoor [aut'dɔːʳ] ADJ al aire libre; (*clothes*) de calle

outdoors [aut'dɔːz] ADV al aire libre

outer [ˈautəʳ] ADJ exterior, externo

outer space N espacio exterior

outfit [ˈautfɪt] N equipo; (*clothes*) traje *m*; (*inf: organization*) grupo, organización *f*

outfitter's [ˈautfɪtəz] N (BRIT) sastrería

outgoing [ˈautgəuɪŋ] ADJ (*president, tenant*) saliente; (*means of transport*) que sale; (*character*) extrovertido

outgoings [ˈautgəuɪŋz] NPL (BRIT) gastos *mpl*

outgrow [autˈgrəu] VT (*irreg: like* **grow**): **he has outgrown his clothes** su ropa le queda pequeña ya

outhouse [ˈauthaus] N dependencia

outing [ˈautɪŋ] N excursión *f*, paseo

outlandish [autˈlændɪʃ] ADJ estrafalario

outlast [autˈlɑːst] VT durar más tiempo que, sobrevivir a

outlaw [ˈautlɔː] N proscrito(-a) ▸ VT (*person*) declarar fuera de la ley; (*practice*) declarar ilegal

outlay [ˈautleɪ] N inversión *f*

outlet [ˈautlɛt] N salida; (*of pipe*) desagüe *m*; (*US Elec*) toma de corriente; (*for emotion*) desahogo; (*also:* **retail outlet**) punto de venta

★**outline** [ˈautlaɪn] N (*shape*) contorno, perfil *m*; (*sketch, plan*) esbozo; **in ~** (*fig*) a grandes rasgos ▸ VT (*plan etc*) esbozar

outlive [autˈlɪv] VT sobrevivir a

outlook [ˈautluk] N (*fig: prospects*) perspectivas *fpl*; (: *for weather*) pronóstico; (: *opinion*) punto de vista

outlying [ˈautlaɪɪŋ] ADJ remoto, aislado

outmanoeuvre, (US) **outmaneuver** [autməˈnuːvəʳ] VT (*Mil, fig*) superar en la estrategia

outmoded [autˈməudɪd] ADJ anticuado, pasado de moda

outnumber [autˈnʌmbəʳ] VT exceder *or* superar en número

out of bounds [autəvˈbaundz] ADJ: **it's ~** está prohibido el paso

out-of-court [autəvˈkɔːt] ADJ, ADV sin ir a juicio

out-of-date [autəvˈdeɪt] ADJ (*passport*) caducado, vencido; (*theory, idea*) anticuado; (*clothes, customs*) pasado de moda

out-of-doors [autəvˈdɔːz] ADV al aire libre

out-of-the-way [autəvðəˈweɪ] ADJ (*remote*) apartado; (*unusual*) poco común *or* corriente

out-of-touch [autəvˈtʌtʃ] ADJ: **to be ~** estar desconectado

out-of-town [autəvˈtaun] ADJ (*shopping centre etc*) en las afueras

outpatient [ˈautpeɪʃənt] N paciente *mf* externo(-a)

outpost [ˈautpəust] N puesto avanzado

outpouring [ˈautpɔːrɪŋ] N (*fig*) efusión *f*

output [ˈautput] N (volumen *m* de) producción *f*, rendimiento; (*Comput*) salida ▸ VT (*Comput*) imprimir

outrage [ˈautreɪdʒ] N (*scandal*) escándalo; (*atrocity*) atrocidad *f* ▸ VT ultrajar

outrageous [autˈreɪdʒəs] ADJ (*clothes*) extravagante; (*behaviour*) escandaloso

outright ADV [autˈraɪt] (*ask, deny*) francamente; (*refuse*) rotundamente; (*win*) de manera absoluta; (*be killed*) en el acto; (*completely*) completamente ▸ ADJ [ˈautraɪt] completo; (*winner*) absoluto; (*refusal*) rotundo

outrun [autˈrʌn] VT (*irreg: like* **run**) correr más que, dejar atrás

outset [ˈautsɛt] N principio

outshine [autˈʃaɪn] VT (*irreg: like* **shine**) (*fig*) eclipsar, brillar más que

★**outside** [autˈsaɪd] N exterior *m*; **at the ~** (*fig*) a lo sumo ▸ ADJ exterior, externo; **an ~ chance** una posibilidad remota; **~ left/right** (*esp Football*) extremo izquierdo/derecho ▸ ADV fuera, afuera (*LAm*) ▸ PREP fuera de; (*beyond*) más allá de

outside broadcast N (*Radio, TV*) emisión *f* exterior

outside contractor N contratista *mf* independiente

outside lane N (*Aut: in Britain*) carril *m* de la derecha; (: *in US, Europe etc*) carril *m* de la izquierda

outside line N (*Tel*) línea (exterior)

outsider [autˈsaɪdəʳ] N (*stranger*) forastero(-a)

outsize [ˈautsaɪz] ADJ (*clothes*) de talla grande

outskirts [ˈautskəːts] NPL alrededores *mpl*, afueras *fpl*

outsmart [autˈsmɑːt] VT ser más listo que

outsourcing [autˈsɔːsɪŋ] N contratación *f* externa, subcontratación *f*

outspoken [autˈspəukən] ADJ muy franco

outspread [autˈsprɛd] ADJ extendido; (*wings*) desplegado

★**outstanding** [autˈstændɪŋ] ADJ excepcional, destacado; (*unfinished*) pendiente

outstay [autˈsteɪ] VT: **to ~ one's welcome** quedarse más de lo conveniente

outstretched [autˈstrɛtʃt] ADJ (*arm*) extendido

outstrip [autˈstrɪp] VT (*competitors, demand, also fig*) dejar atrás, aventajar

out-tray [ˈauttreɪ] N bandeja de salida

outvote [autˈvəut] VT: **it was outvoted (by ...)** fue rechazado en el voto (por ...)

outward [ˈautwəd] ADJ (*sign, appearances*) externo; (*journey*) de ida ▸ ADV hacia afuera

outwardly [ˈautwədlɪ] ADV por fuera

outwards [ˈautwədz] ADV (*esp* BRIT) = **outward**

outweigh [autˈweɪ] VT pesar más que

outwit [autˈwɪt] VT ser más listo que

outworn [autˈwɔːn] ADJ (*expression*) cansado

oval [ˈəuvl] ADJ ovalado ▸ N óvalo

ovarian [əuˈvɛərɪən] ADJ ovárico; (*cancer*) de ovario

ovary [ˈəuvərɪ] N ovario

ovation [əʊˈveɪʃən] N ovación f

oven [ˈʌvn] N horno

oven glove N guante m para el horno, manopla para el horno

ovenproof [ˈʌvnpruːf] ADJ refractario, resistente al horno

oven-ready [ˈʌvnrɛdɪ] ADJ listo para el horno

ovenware [ˈʌvnwɛəʳ] N artículos mpl para el horno

★**over** [ˈəʊvəʳ] ADV encima, por encima; ~ here (por) aquí; ~ there (por) allí or allá; all ~ (everywhere) por todas partes; ~ and ~ (again) una y otra vez; to ask sb ~ invitar a algn a casa; to bend ~ inclinarse; now ~ to our Paris correspondent damos la palabra a nuestro corresponsal de París; the world ~ en todo el mundo, en el mundo entero; she's not ~ intelligent no es muy lista que digamos ▶ ADJ (finished) terminado; (surplus) de sobra; (excessively) demasiado ▶ PREP (por) encima de; (above) sobre; (on the other side of) al otro lado de; (more than) más de; (during) durante; (about, concerning): they fell out ~ money riñeron por una cuestión de dinero; ~ and above además de

over... [ˈəʊvəʳ] PREF sobre..., super...

overact [əʊvərˈækt] VI (Theat) exagerar el papel

★**overall** [ˈəʊvərɔːl] ADJ (length) total; (study) de conjunto ▶ ADV [əʊvərˈɔːl] en conjunto ▶ N (BRIT) guardapolvo ■ **overalls** NPL mono sg, overol msg (LAM)

overall majority N mayoría absoluta

overanxious [əʊvərˈæŋkʃəs] ADJ demasiado preocupado or ansioso

overawe [əʊvərˈɔː] VT intimidar

overbalance [əʊvəˈbæləns] VI perder el equilibrio

overbearing [əʊvəˈbɛərɪŋ] ADJ autoritario, imperioso

overboard [ˈəʊvəbɔːd] ADV (Naut) por la borda; to go ~ for sth (fig) enloquecer por algo

overbook [əʊvəˈbuk] VT sobrerreservar, reservar con exceso

overcame [əʊvəˈkeɪm] PT of overcome

overcapitalize [əʊvəˈkæpɪtəlaɪz] VI sobrecapitalizar

overcast [ˈəʊvəkɑːst] ADJ encapotado

overcharge [əʊvəˈtʃɑːdʒ] VT: to ~ sb cobrar un precio excesivo a algn

overcoat [ˈəʊvəkəʊt] N abrigo

overcome [əʊvəˈkʌm] VT (irreg: like come) (gen) vencer; (difficulty) superar; she was quite ~ by the occasion la ocasión le conmovió mucho

overconfident [əʊvəˈkɔnfɪdənt] ADJ demasiado confiado

overcrowded [əʊvəˈkraʊdɪd] ADJ atestado de gente; (city, country) superpoblado

overcrowding [əʊvəˈkraʊdɪŋ] N (in town, coun-

try) superpoblación f; (in bus etc) hacinamiento, apiñamiento

overdo [əʊvəˈduː] VT (irreg: like do) exagerar; (overcook) cocer demasiado; to ~ it (work etc) pasarse

overdone [əʊvəˈdʌn] ADJ (vegetables) recocido; (steak) demasiado hecho

overdose [ˈəʊvədəʊs] N sobredosis f inv

overdraft [ˈəʊvədrɑːft] N saldo deudor

overdrawn [əʊvəˈdrɔːn] ADJ (account) en descubierto

overdrive [ˈəʊvədraɪv] N (Aut) sobremarcha, superdirecta

overdue [əʊvəˈdjuː] ADJ retrasado; (recognition) tardío; (bill) vencido y no pagado; that change was long ~ ese cambio tenía que haberse hecho hace tiempo

overemphasis [əʊvərˈɛmfəsɪs] N: to put an ~ on poner énfasis excesivo en

overenthusiastic [ˈəʊvərənθuːzɪˈæstɪk] ADJ demasiado entusiasta

overestimate [əʊvərˈɛstɪmeɪt] VT sobreestimar

overexcited [əʊvərɪkˈsaɪtɪd] ADJ sobreexcitado

overexertion [əʊvərɪgˈzəːʃən] N agotamiento, fatiga

overexpose [əʊvərɪkˈspəʊz] VT (Phot) sobreexponer

overflow VI [əʊvəˈfləʊ] desbordarse ▶ N [ˈəʊvəfləʊ] (excess) exceso; (of river) desbordamiento; (also: overflow pipe) (cañería de) desagüe m

overfly [əʊvəˈflaɪ] VT (irreg: like fly) sobrevolar

overgenerous [əʊvəˈdʒɛnərəs] ADJ demasiado generoso

overgrown [əʊvəˈgrəʊn] ADJ (garden) cubierto de hierba; he's just an ~ schoolboy es un niño en grande

overhang [əʊvəˈhæŋ] VT (irreg: like hang) sobresalir por encima de ▶ VI sobresalir

overhaul VT [əʊvəˈhɔːl] revisar, repasar ▶ N [ˈəʊvəhɔːl] revisión f

overhead ADV [əʊvəˈhɛd] por arriba or encima ▶ ADJ [ˈəʊvəhɛd] (cable) aéreo; (railway) elevado, aéreo ▶ N [ˈəʊvəhɛd] (US) = overheads

overhead projector N retroproyector

overheads [ˈəʊvəhɛdz] NPL (BRIT) gastos mpl generales

overhear [əʊvəˈhɪəʳ] VT (irreg: like hear) oír por casualidad

overheat [əʊvəˈhiːt] VI (engine) recalentarse

overjoyed [əʊvəˈdʒɔɪd] ADJ encantado, lleno de alegría

overkill [ˈəʊvəkɪl] N (Mil) capacidad f excesiva de destrucción; (fig) exceso

overland [ˈəʊvəlænd] ADJ, ADV por tierra

overlap VI [əʊvəˈlæp] superponerse ▶ N [ˈəʊvələæp] superposición f

overleaf [əʊvəˈliːf] ADV al dorso

overload [əuvəˈləud] VT sobrecargar

overlook [əuvəˈluk] VT (have view of) dar a, tener vistas a; (miss) pasar por alto; (excuse) perdonar

overlord [ˈəuvəlɔːd] N señor m

overmanning [əuvəˈmænɪŋ] N exceso de mano de obra; (in organization) exceso de personal

overnight [əuvəˈnaɪt] ADV durante la noche; (fig) de la noche a la mañana; **to stay ~** pasar la noche ▸ ADJ de noche

overnight bag N neceser m de viaje

overnight stay N estancia de una noche

overpass [ˈəuvəpɑːs] N (US) paso elevado or a desnivel

overpay [əuvəˈpeɪ] VT: **to ~ sb by £50** pagar 50 libras de más a algn

overplay [əuvəˈpleɪ] VT exagerar; **to ~ one's hand** desmedirse

overpower [əuvəˈpauəʳ] VT dominar; (fig) embargar

overpowering [əuvəˈpauərɪŋ] ADJ (heat) agobiante; (smell) penetrante

overproduction [əuvəprəˈdʌkʃən] N superproducción f

overrate [əuvəˈreɪt] VT sobrevalorar

overreach [əuvəˈriːtʃ] VT: **to ~ o.s.** ir demasiado lejos, pasarse

overreact [əuvərɪˈækt] VI reaccionar de manera exagerada

override [əuvəˈraɪd] VT (irreg: like **ride**) (order, objection) no hacer caso de

overriding [əuvəˈraɪdɪŋ] ADJ predominante

overrule [əuvəˈruːl] VT (decision) anular; (claim) denegar

overrun [əuvəˈrʌn] VT (irreg: like **run**) (Mil: country) invadir; (time limit) rebasar, exceder; **the town is ~ with tourists** el pueblo está inundado de turistas ▸ VI rebasar el límite previsto

★**overseas** [əuvəˈsiːz] ADV en ultramar; (abroad) en el extranjero ▸ ADJ (trade) exterior; (visitor) extranjero

oversee [əuvəˈsiː] VT (irreg: like **see**) supervisar

overseer [ˈəuvəsɪəʳ] N (in factory) supervisor(a) m/f; (foreman) capataz m

overshadow [əuvəˈʃædəu] VT (fig) eclipsar; **to be overshadowed by** estar a la sombra de

overshoot [əuvəˈʃuːt] VT (irreg: like **shoot**) (turning) pasarse de; (runway) salirse de

oversight [ˈəuvəsaɪt] N descuido; **due to an ~** a causa de un descuido or una equivocación

oversimplify [əuvəˈsɪmplɪfaɪ] VT simplificar demasiado

oversleep [əuvəˈsliːp] VI (irreg: like **sleep**) dormir más de la cuenta, no despertarse a tiempo

overspend [əuvəˈspɛnd] VI (irreg: like **spend**) gastar más de la cuenta; **we have overspent by five dollars** hemos excedido el presupuesto en cinco dólares

overspill [ˈəuvəspɪl] N exceso de población

overstaffed [əuvəˈstɑːft] ADJ: **to be ~** tener exceso de plantilla

overstate [əuvəˈsteɪt] VT exagerar

overstatement [ˈəuvəsteɪtmənt] N exageración f

overstay [əuvəˈsteɪ] VT: **to ~ one's time** or **welcome** quedarse más de lo conveniente

overstep [əuvəˈstɛp] VT: **to ~ the mark** or **the limits** pasarse de la raya

overstock [əuvəˈstɔk] VT abarrotar

overstretched [əuvəˈstrɛtʃt] ADJ utilizado por encima de su capacidad

overstrike N [ˈəuvəstraɪk] (on printer) superposición f ▸ VT (irreg: like **strike**) superponer

oversubscribed [əuvəsəbˈskraɪbd] ADJ suscrito en exceso

overt [əuˈvəːt] ADJ abierto

overtake [əuvəˈteɪk] VT (irreg: like **take**) sobrepasar; (Brit Aut) adelantar

overtax [əuvəˈtæks] VT (Econ) exigir contribuciones fpl excesivas or impuestos mpl excesivos a; (fig: strength) poner a prueba; (: patience) agotar, abusar de; **to ~ o.s.** fatigarse demasiado

overthrow [əuvəˈθrəu] VT (irreg: like **throw**) (government) derrocar

overtime [ˈəuvətaɪm] N horas fpl extraordinarias; **to do** or **work ~** hacer or trabajar horas extraordinarias or extras

overtime ban N prohibición f de (hacer) horas extraordinarias

overtone [ˈəuvətəun] N (fig) tono

overtook [əuvəˈtuk] PT of **overtake**

overture [ˈəuvətʃuəʳ] N (Mus) obertura; (fig) propuesta

overturn [əuvəˈtəːn] VT volcar; (fig: plan) desbaratar; (: government) derrocar ▸ VI volcar

overview [ˈəuvəvjuː] N visión f de conjunto

overweight [əuvəˈweɪt] ADJ demasiado gordo or pesado

overwhelm [əuvəˈwɛlm] VT aplastar

overwhelming [əuvəˈwɛlmɪŋ] ADJ (victory, defeat) arrollador(a); (desire) irresistible; **one's ~ impression is of heat** lo que más impresiona es el calor

overwhelmingly [əuvəˈwɛlmɪŋlɪ] ADV abrumadoramente

overwork [əuvəˈwəːk] N trabajo excesivo ▸ VT hacer trabajar demasiado ▸ VI trabajar demasiado

overwrite [əuvəˈraɪt] VT (irreg: like **write**) (Comput: file, disk) sobre(e)scribir

overwrought [əuvəˈrɔːt] ADJ sobreexcitado

ovulation [ɔvjuˈleɪʃən] N ovulación f

★**owe** [əu] VT deber; **to ~ sb sth, to ~ sth to sb** deber algo a algn

owing to [ˈəuɪŋtuː] PREP debido a, por causa de

owl [aul] N (also: **long-eared owl**) búho; (also: **barn owl**) lechuza

★**own** [əun] VT tener, poseer ▶ VI: **to ~ to sth/to having done sth** confesar or reconocer algo/ haber hecho algo ▶ ADJ propio ▶ PRON: **a room of my ~** mi propia habitación; **to get one's ~ back** tomarse la revancha; **on one's ~** solo, a solas; **can I have it for my (very) ~?** ¿puedo quedarme con él?; **to come into one's ~** llegar a realizarse ▶ **own up** VI confesar

own brand N (*Comm*) marca propia

★**owner** [ˈəunəʳ] N dueño(-a)

owner-occupier [ˈəunərˈɔkjupaɪəʳ] N ocupante propietario(-a) *m/f*

ownership [ˈəunəʃɪp] N posesión *f*; **it's under new ~** está bajo nueva dirección

own goal N (*Sport*) autogol *m*; **to score an ~** marcar un gol en propia puerta, marcar un autogol

ox [ɔks] (*pl* **oxen** [ˈɔksn]) N buey *m*

Oxbridge [ˈɔksbrɪdʒ] N *universidades de Oxford y Cambridge*

El término **Oxbridge** es una fusión de Ox(ford) y (Cam)bridge, las dos universidades británicas más antiguas y con mayor prestigio académico y social. Muchos miembros destacados de la clase dirigente del país son antiguos alumnos de una de las dos. El mismo término suele aplicarse a todo lo que ambas representan en cuestión de prestigio y privilegios sociales.

oxen [ˈɔksən] NPL *of* **ox**

Oxfam [ˈɔksfæm] N ABBR (BRIT: = *Oxford Committee for Famine Relief*) OXFAM

oxide [ˈɔksaɪd] N óxido

oxtail [ˈɔksteɪl] N: **~ soup** sopa de rabo de buey

oxyacetylene [ˈɔksɪəˈsɛtɪliːn] ADJ oxiacetilénico; **~ burner, ~ torch** soplete *m* oxiacetilénico

oxygen [ˈɔksɪdʒən] N oxígeno

oxygen mask N máscara de oxígeno

oxygen tent N tienda de oxígeno

oyster [ˈɔɪstəʳ] N ostra

oz. ABBR = **ounce**

ozone [ˈəuzəun] N ozono

ozone-friendly ADJ que no daña la capa de ozono

ozone layer N capa de ozono

Pp

P, p [piː] N (*letter*) P, p *f*; **P for Peter** P de París

P ABBR = **president**; **prince**

p ABBR (= *page*) pág.; (*BRIT*) = **penny**; **pence**

PA N ABBR = **personal assistant**; **public address system** ▶ ABBR (*US*) = **Pennsylvania**

pa [paː] N (*inf*) papá *m*

p.a. ABBR = **per annum**

PAC N ABBR (*US*) = **political action committee**

pace [peɪs] N paso; (*rhythm*) ritmo; **to keep ~ with** llevar el mismo paso que; (*events*) mantenerse a la altura de *or* al corriente de; **to set the ~** (*running*) marcar el paso; (*fig*) marcar la pauta; **to put sb through his paces** (*fig*) poner a algn a prueba ▶ VI: **to ~ up and down** pasearse de un lado a otro

pacemaker ['peɪsmeɪkə^r] N (*Med*) marcapasos *m inv*; (*Sport: also:* **pacesetter**) liebre *f*

pacific [pə'sɪfɪk] ADJ pacífico ▶ N: **the P~ (Ocean)** el (océano) Pacífico

pacification [pæsɪfɪ'keɪʃən] N pacificación *f*

pacifier ['pæsɪfaɪə^r] N (*US: dummy*) chupete *m*

pacifism ['pæsɪfɪzəm] N pacifismo

pacifist ['pæsɪfɪst] N pacifista *mf*

pacify ['pæsɪfaɪ] VT (*soothe*) apaciguar; (*country*) pacificar

★pack [pæk] N (*packet*) paquete *m*; (*Comm*) embalaje *m*; (*of hounds*) jauría; (*of people*) manada; (*of thieves etc*) banda; (*of cards*) baraja; (*bundle*) fardo; (*US: of cigarettes*) paquete *m*, cajetilla ▶ VT (*wrap*) empaquetar; (*fill*) llenar; (*in suitcase etc*) meter, poner; (*cram*) llenar, atestar; (*fig: meeting etc*) llenar de partidarios; (*Comput*) comprimir; **to ~ one's bags** hacer las maletas; **to ~ sb off** (*inf*) despachar a algn ▶ VI hacer las maletas; **to send sb packing** (*inf*) echar a algn con cajas destempladas
▶ **pack in** (*inf*) VI (*break down*) estropearse ▶ VT dejar; **~ it in!** ¡para!, ¡basta ya!
▶ **pack up** VI (*inf: machine*) estropearse; (*person*) irse ▶ VT (*belongings, clothes*) recoger; (*goods, presents*) empaquetar, envolver

★package ['pækɪdʒ] N paquete *m*; (*bulky*) bulto; (*Comput*) paquete *m* (*de software*); (*also:* **package deal**) acuerdo global ▶ VT (*Comm: goods*) envasar, embalar

package holiday N viaje *m* organizado (con todo incluido)

package tour N viaje *m* organizado

packaging ['pækɪdʒɪŋ] N envase *m*

packed [pækt] ADJ abarrotado; **the place was ~** el local estaba abarrotado

packed lunch [pækt-] N almuerzo frío

packer ['pækə^r] N (*person*) empacador(a) *m/f*

packet ['pækɪt] N paquete *m*

packet switching [-'swɪtʃɪŋ] N (*Comput*) conmutación *f* por paquetes

packhorse ['pækhɔːs] N caballo de carga

pack ice N banco de hielo

packing ['pækɪŋ] N embalaje *m*

packing case N cajón *m* de embalaje

pact [pækt] N pacto

pad [pæd] N (*of paper*) bloc *m*; (*cushion*) cojinete *m*; (*launching pad*) plataforma (de lanzamiento); (*inf: flat*) casa ▶ VT rellenar

padded ['pædɪd] ADJ (*jacket*) acolchado; (*bra*) reforzado

padded cell N celda acolchada

padding ['pædɪŋ] N relleno; (*fig*) paja

paddle ['pædl] N (*oar*) canalete *m*, pala; (*US: for table tennis*) pala ▶ VT remar ▶ VI (*with feet*) chapotear

paddle steamer N vapor *m* de ruedas

paddling pool ['pædlɪŋ-] N (*BRIT*) piscina para niños

paddock ['pædək] N (*field*) potrero

paddy field ['pædɪ-] N arrozal *m*

padlock ['pædlɔk] N candado ▶ VT cerrar con candado

padre ['paːdrɪ] N capellán *m*

paediatrician, (*US*) **pediatrician** [piːdɪə'trɪʃən] N pediatra *mf*

paediatrics, (US) **pediatrics** [piːdɪˈætrɪks] N pediatría

paedophile, (US) **pedophile** [ˈpiːdəʊfaɪl] ADJ de pedófilos ▶ N pedófilo(-a)

pagan [ˈpeɪɡən] ADJ, N pagano(-a) m/f

★**page** [peɪdʒ] N página; (also: **page boy**) paje m ▶ VT (in hotel etc) llamar por altavoz a

pageant [ˈpædʒənt] N (procession) desfile m; (show) espectáculo

pageantry [ˈpædʒəntrɪ] N pompa

page break N límite m de la página

pager [ˈpeɪdʒəʳ] N busca m

paginate [ˈpædʒɪneɪt] VT paginar

pagination [pædʒɪˈneɪʃən] N paginación f

pagoda [pəˈɡəʊdə] N pagoda

paid [peɪd] PT, PP of **pay** ▶ ADJ (work) remunerado; (holiday) pagado; (official) a sueldo; **to put ~ to** (BRIT) acabar con

paid-up [ˈpeɪdʌp], (US) **paid-in** [ˈpeɪdɪn] ADJ (member) con sus cuotas pagadas or al día; (share) liberado; **~ capital** capital m desembolsado

pail [peɪl] N cubo, balde m

★**pain** [peɪn] N dolor m; **to be in ~** sufrir; **on ~ of death** so or bajo pena de muerte; see also **pains**

pained [peɪnd] ADJ (expression) afligido

★**painful** [ˈpeɪnful] ADJ doloroso; (difficult) penoso; (disagreeable) desagradable

painfully [ˈpeɪnfəlɪ] ADV (fig: very) terriblemente

painkiller [ˈpeɪnkɪləʳ] N analgésico

painless [ˈpeɪnlɪs] ADJ sin dolor; (method) fácil

pains [peɪnz] NPL (efforts) esfuerzos mpl; **to take ~ to do sth** tomarse el trabajo de hacer algo

painstaking [ˈpeɪnzteɪkɪŋ] ADJ (person) concienzudo, esmerado

★**paint** [peɪnt] N pintura; **a tin of ~** un bote de pintura ▶ VT pintar; **to ~ the door blue** pintar la puerta de azul

paintbox [ˈpeɪntbɒks] N caja de pinturas

paintbrush [ˈpeɪntbrʌʃ] N (artist's) pincel m; (decorator's) brocha

painter [ˈpeɪntəʳ] N pintor(a) m/f

★**painting** [ˈpeɪntɪŋ] N pintura

paintwork [ˈpeɪntwəːk] N pintura

★**pair** [pɛəʳ] N (of shoes, gloves etc) par m; (of people) pareja; **a ~ of scissors** unas tijeras; **a ~ of trousers** unos pantalones, un pantalón ▶ **pair off** VI: **to ~ off (with sb)** hacer pareja (con algn)

pajamas [pɪˈdʒɑːməz] NPL (US) pijama msg, piyama msg (LAM)

Pakistan [pɑːkɪˈstɑːn] N Paquistán m

Pakistani [pɑːkɪˈstɑːnɪ] ADJ, N paquistaní mf

PAL [pæl] N ABBR (TV) = **phase alternation line**

pal [pæl] N (inf) amiguete(-a) m/f, colega mf

★**palace** [ˈpæləs] N palacio

palatable [ˈpælɪtəbl] ADJ sabroso; (acceptable) aceptable

palate [ˈpælɪt] N paladar m

palatial [pəˈleɪʃəl] ADJ (surroundings, residence) suntuoso, espléndido

palaver [pəˈlɑːvəʳ] N (fuss) lío

★**pale** [peɪl] ADJ (gen) pálido; (colour) claro; **to grow** or **turn ~** palidecer ▶ N: **to be beyond the ~** pasarse de la raya ▶ VI palidecer; **to ~ into insignificance (beside)** no poderse comparar (con)

paleness [ˈpeɪlnɪs] N palidez f

Palestine [ˈpælɪstaɪn] N Palestina

Palestinian [pælɪsˈtɪnɪən] ADJ, N palestino(-a) m/f

palette [ˈpælɪt] N paleta

paling [ˈpeɪlɪŋ] N (stake) estaca; (fence) valla

palisade [pælɪˈseɪd] N palizada

pall [pɔːl] N (of smoke) cortina ▶ VI cansar

pallbearer [ˈpɔːlbɛərəʳ] N portador m del féretro

pallet [ˈpælɪt] N (for goods) pallet m

palletization [pælɪtaɪˈzeɪʃən] N paletización f

palliative [ˈpælɪətɪv] N paliativo

pallid [ˈpælɪd] ADJ pálido

pallor [ˈpæləʳ] N palidez f

pally [ˈpælɪ] ADJ (inf): **to be very ~ with sb** ser muy amiguete de algn

palm [pɑːm] N (Anat) palma; (also: **palm tree**) palmera, palma ▶ VT: **to ~ sth off on sb** (BRIT inf) endosarle algo a algn

palmist [ˈpɑːmɪst] N quiromántico(-a), palmista mf

Palm Sunday N Domingo de Ramos

palpable [ˈpælpəbl] ADJ palpable

palpably [ˈpælpəblɪ] ADV obviamente

palpitation [pælpɪˈteɪʃən] N palpitación f; **to have palpitations** tener palpitaciones

paltry [ˈpɔːltrɪ] ADJ (amount etc) miserable; (insignificant: person) insignificante

pamper [ˈpæmpəʳ] VT mimar

pamphlet [ˈpæmflət] N folleto; (political: handed out in street) panfleto

★**pan** [pæn] N (also: **saucepan**) cacerola, cazuela, olla; (also: **frying pan**) sartén f; (of lavatory) taza ▶ VI (Cine) tomar panorámicas; **to ~ for gold** cribar oro

pan- [pæn] PREF pan-

panacea [pænəˈsɪə] N panacea

panache [pəˈnæʃ] N gracia, garbo

Panama [ˈpænəmɑː] N Panamá m

Panama Canal N Canal m de Panamá

pancake [ˈpænkeɪk] N crepe f, panqueque m (LAM)

Pancake Day N martes m de carnaval

pancake roll N rollito de primavera

pancreas [ˈpæŋkrɪəs] N páncreas m

panda [ˈpændə] N panda m

panda car N (BRIT) coche m de la policía

pandemic [pæn'dɛmɪk] N pandemia; **flu ~** pandemia de gripe

pandemonium [pændɪ'məunɪəm] N (*mess*) caos *m*; (*noise*): **there was ~** se armó un tremendo jaleo

pander ['pændər] VI: **to ~ to** complacer a

p & h ABBR (*US*: = *postage and handling*) gastos *mpl* de envío

P & L ABBR = **profit and loss**

p & p ABBR (*BRIT*: = *postage and packing*) gastos *mpl* de envío

pane [peɪn] N cristal *m*

panel ['pænl] N (*of wood*) panel *m*; (*of cloth*) paño; (*Radio, TV*) panel *m* de invitados

panel game N (*TV*) programa *m* concurso para equipos

panelling, (*US*) **paneling** ['pænəlɪŋ] N paneles *mpl*

panellist, (*US*) **panelist** ['pænəlɪst] N miembro del jurado

pang [pæŋ] N: **pangs of conscience** remordimientos *mpl*; **pangs of hunger** dolores *mpl* del hambre

panhandler ['pænhændlər] N (*US pej*) mendigo(-a)

★**panic** ['pænɪk] N pánico ▸ VI dejarse llevar por el pánico

panic buying [-baɪɪŋ] N *compras masivas por miedo a futura escasez*

panicky ['pænɪkɪ] ADJ (*person*) asustadizo

panic-stricken ['pænɪkstrɪkən] ADJ preso del pánico

panini [pæ'ni:nɪ] N panini *m*

pannier ['pænɪər] N (*on bicycle*) cartera; (*on mule etc*) alforja

panorama [pænə'rɑ:mə] N panorama *m*

panoramic [pænə'ræmɪk] ADJ panorámico

pansy ['pænzɪ] N (*Bot*) pensamiento; (!) marica *m* (!)

pant [pænt] VI jadear

panther ['pænθər] N pantera

panties ['pæntɪz] NPL bragas *fpl*

pantihose ['pæntɪhəuz] N (*US*) medias *fpl*, pantis *mpl*

panto ['pæntəu] N (*BRIT inf*) = **pantomime**

pantomime ['pæntəmaɪm] N (*BRIT*) representación *f* musical navideña

En época navideña los teatros británicos ponen en escena representaciones llamadas **panto-mimes**, versiones libres de cuentos tradicionales como Aladino o El gato con botas. En ella nunca faltan personajes como la dama (*dame*), papel que siempre interpreta un actor, el protagonista joven (*principal boy*), normalmente interpretado por una actriz, y el malvado (*villain*). Es un espectáculo familiar dirigido a los niños pero con grandes dosis de humor para adultos en el que se alienta la participación del público.

pantry ['pæntrɪ] N despensa

pants [pænts] NPL (*BRIT*: *underwear*: *woman's*) bragas *fpl*; (: *man's*) calzoncillos *mpl*; (*US*: *trousers*) pantalones *mpl*

pantsuit ['pæntsju:t] N (*US*) traje *m* de chaqueta y pantalón

papal ['peɪpəl] ADJ papal

paparazzi [pæpə'rætsɪ] NPL paparazzi *mpl*

★**paper** ['peɪpər] N papel *m*; (*also*: **newspaper**) periódico, diario; (*study, article*) artículo; (*exam*) examen *m*; (**identity**) **papers** *npl* papeles *mpl*, documentos *mpl*; **a piece of ~** un papel; **to put sth down on ~** poner algo por escrito ▸ ADJ de papel ▸ VT empapelar

paper advance N (*on printer*) avance *m* de papel

paperback ['peɪpəbæk] N libro de bolsillo

paper bag N bolsa de papel

paperboy ['peɪpəbɔɪ] N (*selling*) vendedor *m* de periódicos; (*delivering*) repartidor *m* de periódicos

paper clip N clip *m*

paper hankie N pañuelo de papel

paper money N papel *m* moneda

paper profit N beneficio no realizado

paper shop N (*BRIT*) tienda de periódicos

paperweight ['peɪpəweɪt] N pisapapeles *m inv*

paperwork ['peɪpəwə:k] N trabajo administrativo; (*pej*) papeleo

papier-mâché ['pæpɪeɪ'mæʃeɪ] N cartón *m* piedra

paprika ['pæprɪkə] N pimentón *m*

Pap test ['pæp-] N (*Med*) frotis *m* (cervical)

Papua New Guinea ['pæpjuə-] N Papúa Nueva Guinea

papyrus [pə'paɪərəs] N papiro

par [pɑ:r] N par *f*; (*Golf*) par *m*; **to be on a ~ with** estar a la par con; **at ~** a la par; **to be above/below ~** estar sobre/bajo par; **to feel under ~** sentirse en baja forma ▸ ADJ a la par

parable ['pærəbl] N parábola

paracetamol [pærə'si:təmɔl] N (*BRIT*) paracetamol *m*

parachute ['pærəʃu:t] N paracaídas *m inv* ▸ VI lanzarse en paracaídas

parachutist ['pærəʃu:tɪst] N paracaidista *mf*

parade [pə'reɪd] N desfile *m*; **a fashion ~** un desfile de modelos ▸ VT (*gen*) recorrer, desfilar por; (*show off*) hacer alarde de ▸ VI desfilar; (*Mil*) pasar revista

parade ground N plaza de armas

paradise ['pærədaɪs] N paraíso

paradox ['pærədɔks] N paradoja

paradoxical [pærə'dɔksɪkl] ADJ paradójico

paradoxically [pærə'dɔksɪklɪ] ADV paradójicamente

paraffin ['pærəfɪn] N (*BRIT*): **~ (oil)** parafina

paraffin heater N estufa de parafina

paraffin lamp N quinqué *m*

paragon ['pærəgən] N modelo
paragraph ['pærəgrɑːf] N párrafo, acápite m (LAM); **new~** punto y aparte, punto acápite (LAM)
Paraguay ['pærəgwaɪ] N Paraguay m
Paraguayan [pærə'gwaɪən] ADJ, N paraguayo(-a) m/f, paraguayano(-a) m/f
parallel ['pærəlel] ADJ: **~ (with/to)** en paralelo (con/a); (fig) semejante (a) ▶ N (line) paralela; (fig) paralelo; (Geo) paralelo
paralysis [pə'ræləsɪs] N parálisis f inv
paralytic [pærə'lɪtɪk] ADJ paralítico
paralyze ['pærəlaɪz] VT paralizar; **paralyzed** paralizado
paramedic [pærə'medɪk] N auxiliar mf sanitario(-a)
parameter [pə'ræmɪtər] N parámetro
paramilitary [pærə'mɪlɪtərɪ] ADJ (organization, operations) paramilitar
paramount ['pærəmaunt] ADJ: **of ~ importance** de suma importancia
paranoia [pærə'nɔɪə] N paranoia
paranoid ['pærənɔɪd] ADJ (person, feeling) paranoico
paranormal [pærə'nɔːml] ADJ paranormal
parapet ['pærəpɪt] N parapeto
paraphernalia [pærəfə'neɪlɪə] N parafernalia
paraphrase ['pærəfreɪz] VT parafrasear
paraplegic [pærə'pliːdʒɪk] N parapléjico(-a)
parapsychology [pærəsaɪ'kɔlədʒɪ] N parapsicología
parasite ['pærəsaɪt] N parásito(-a)
parasol ['pærəsɔl] N sombrilla, quitasol m
paratrooper ['pærətruːpər] N paracaidista mf
parcel ['pɑːsl] N paquete m; **to be part and ~ of** ser parte integrante de ▶ VT (also: **parcel up**) empaquetar, embalar
▶ **parcel out** VT parcelar, repartir
parcel bomb N paquete m bomba
parcel post N servicio de paquetes postales
parch [pɑːtʃ] VT secar, resecar
parched [pɑːtʃt] ADJ (person) muerto de sed
parchment ['pɑːtʃmənt] N pergamino
pardon ['pɑːdn] N perdón m; (Law) indulto; **I beg your ~!** ¡perdone usted!; **(I beg your) ~?** ¿cómo (dice)? ▶ VT perdonar; indultar; **~ me!** ¡perdone usted!; (US) **~ me?** ¿cómo (dice)?
pare [peər] VT (nails) cortar; (fruit etc) pelar
parent ['peərənt] N (mother) madre f; (father) padre m ▷ **parents** NPL padres mpl

parent no debe traducirse por pariente.

parentage ['peərəntɪdʒ] N familia, linaje m; **of unknown ~** de padres desconocidos
parental [pə'rentl] ADJ paternal/maternal
parent company N casa matriz
parenthesis [pə'renθɪsɪs] (pl **parentheses** [-θɪsiːz]) N paréntesis m inv; **in parentheses** entre paréntesis

parenthood ['peərənthud] N el ser padres
parent ship N buque m nodriza
Paris ['pærɪs] N París m
parish ['pærɪʃ] N parroquia
parish council N consejo parroquial
parishioner [pə'rɪʃənər] N feligrés(-esa) m/f
Parisian [pə'rɪzɪən] ADJ, N parisino(-a) m/f, parisiense mf
parity ['pærɪtɪ] N paridad f, igualdad f
★**park** [pɑːk] N parque m, jardín m público ▶ VT, VI aparcar, estacionar
parka ['pɑːkə] N parka
park and ride N aparcamiento disuasorio
parking ['pɑːkɪŋ] N aparcamiento, estacionamiento; **"no ~"** "prohibido aparcar or estacionarse"
parking lights NPL luces fpl de estacionamiento
parking lot N (US) parking m, aparcamiento, playa f de estacionamiento (LAM)
parking meter N parquímetro
parking offence, (US) **parking violation** N ofensa por aparcamiento indebido
parking place N sitio para aparcar, aparcamiento
parking ticket N multa de aparcamiento
Parkinson's N (also: **Parkinson's disease**) (enfermedad f de) Parkinson m
parkour [pɑː'kuər] N parkour m
parkway ['pɑːkweɪ] N (US) alameda
parlance ['pɑːləns] N lenguaje m; **in common/modern ~** en lenguaje corriente/moderno
★**parliament** ['pɑːləmənt] N parlamento; (Spanish) las Cortes fpl

El Parlamento británico (**Parliament**) tiene como sede el palacio de Westminster, también llamado Houses of Parliament. Consta de dos cámaras; la Cámara de los Comunes (House of Commons) está formada por 650 diputados (Members of Parliament) que acceden a ella tras ser elegidos por sufragio universal en su respectiva área o circunscripción electoral (constituency). Se reúne 175 días al año y sus sesiones son presididas y moderadas por el Presidente de la Cámara (Speaker) y transmitidas por televisión. La cámara alta es la Cámara de los Lores (House of Lords) y sus miembros son nombrados por el monarca o bien han heredado su escaño. Su poder es limitado, aunque actúa como tribunal supremo de apelación, excepto en Escocia.

parliamentary [pɑːlə'mentərɪ] ADJ parlamentario
parlour, (US) **parlor** ['pɑːlər] N salón m, living m (LAM)
parlous ['pɑːləs] ADJ peligroso, alarmante
Parmesan [pɑːmɪ'zæn] N (also: **Parmesan cheese**) queso parmesano

parochial [pəˈrəukɪəl] ADJ parroquial; (pej) de miras estrechas

parody [ˈpærədɪ] N parodia ▶ VT parodiar

parole [pəˈrəul] N: **on ~** en libertad condicional

paroxysm [ˈpærəksɪzəm] N (Med) paroxismo, ataque m; (of anger, laughter, coughing) ataque m; (of grief) crisis f

parquet [ˈpɑːkeɪ] N: **~ floor(ing)** parquet m

parrot [ˈpærət] N loro, papagayo

parrot fashion ADV como un loro

parry [ˈpærɪ] VT parar

parsimonious [pɑːsɪˈməunɪəs] ADJ tacaño

parsley [ˈpɑːslɪ] N perejil m

parsnip [ˈpɑːsnɪp] N chirivía

parson [ˈpɑːsn] N cura m

★part [pɑːt] N (gen) parte f; (Mus) parte f; (bit) trozo; (of machine) pieza; (Theat etc) papel m; (of serial) entrega; (US: in hair) raya; **to take ~ in** participar or tomar parte en; **to take sb's ~** tomar partido por algn; **for my ~** por mi parte; **for the most ~** en su mayor parte; (people) en su mayoría; **for the better ~ of the day** durante la mayor parte del día; **~ of speech** (Ling) categoría gramatical, parte f de la oración; **to take sth in good/bad ~** aceptar algo bien/tomarse algo a mal ▶ ADV = **partly** ▶ VT separar; (break) partir ▶ VI (people) separarse; (roads) bifurcarse; (crowd) apartarse; (break) romperse
▶ **part with** VT FUS ceder, entregar; (money) pagar; (get rid of) deshacerse de

partake [pɑːˈteɪk] VI (irreg: like **take**) (formal): **to ~ of sth** (food) comer algo; (drink) tomar or beber algo

part exchange N (BRIT): **in ~** como parte del pago

partial [ˈpɑːʃl] ADJ parcial; **to be ~ to** (like) ser aficionado a

partially [ˈpɑːʃəlɪ] ADV en parte, parcialmente

participant [pɑːˈtɪsɪpənt] N (in competition) concursante mf

participate [pɑːˈtɪsɪpeɪt] VI: **to ~ in** participar en

participation [pɑːtɪsɪˈpeɪʃən] N participación f

participle [ˈpɑːtɪsɪpl] N participio

particle [ˈpɑːtɪkl] N partícula; (of dust) mota; (fig) pizca

particular [pəˈtɪkjulər] ADJ (special) particular; (concrete) concreto; (given) determinado; (detailed) detallado, minucioso; (fussy) quisquilloso; (demanding) exigente; **to be very ~ about** ser muy exigente en cuanto a; **I'm not ~** me es or da igual; **in ~** en particular ■ **particulars** NPL (information) datos mpl, detalles mpl; (details) pormenores mpl

particularly [pəˈtɪkjulələɪ] ADV (in particular) sobre todo; (difficult, good etc) especialmente

parting [ˈpɑːtɪŋ] N (act of) separación f; (farewell) despedida; (BRIT: in hair) raya ▶ ADJ de despedida; **~ shot** (fig) golpe m final

partisan [pɑːtɪˈzæn] ADJ partidista ▶ N partidario(-a); (fighter) partisano(-a)

partition [pɑːˈtɪʃən] N (Pol) división f; (wall) tabique m ▶ VT (country) dividir; (room, area) dividir con tabique

★partly [ˈpɑːtlɪ] ADV en parte

★partner [ˈpɑːtnər] N (Comm) socio(-a); (Sport) pareja; (at dance) pareja; (spouse) cónyuge mf; (friend etc) compañero(-a) ▶ VT acompañar

partnership [ˈpɑːtnəʃɪp] N (gen) asociación f; (Comm) sociedad f; **to go into ~ (with), form a ~ (with)** asociarse (con)

part payment N pago parcial

partridge [ˈpɑːtrɪdʒ] N perdiz f

part-time [ˈpɑːtˈtaɪm] ADJ, ADV a tiempo parcial

part-timer [pɑːtˈtaɪmər] N trabajador(a) m/f a tiempo parcial

★party [ˈpɑːtɪ] N (Pol) partido; (celebration) fiesta; (group) grupo; (Law) parte f (interesada); **to have** or **give** or **throw a ~** organizar una fiesta; **dinner ~** cena; **to be a ~ to a crime** ser cómplice mf de un crimen ▶ ADJ (Pol) de partido; (dress etc) de fiesta, de gala

party line N (Pol) línea política del partido; (Tel) línea compartida

party piece N: **to do one's ~** hacer su numerito (de fiesta)

party political broadcast N ≈ espacio electoral

★pass [pɑːs] VT (time, object) pasar; (place) pasar por; (exam, law) aprobar; (overtake, surpass) rebasar; (approve) aprobar; **to ~ sth through sth** pasar algo por algo; **to ~ the time of day with sb** pasar el rato con algn ▶ VI pasar; (Scol) aprobar ▶ N (permit) permiso, pase m; (membership card) carnet m; (in mountains) puerto; (Sport) pase m; (Scol: also: **pass mark**) aprobado; **things have come to a pretty ~!** ¡hasta dónde hemos llegado!; **to make a ~ at sb** (inf) insinuársele a algn
▶ **pass away** VI fallecer
▶ **pass by** VI pasar ▶ VT (ignore) pasar por alto
▶ **pass down** VT (customs, inheritance) pasar, transmitir
▶ **pass for** VT FUS pasar por; **she could ~ for 25** se podría creer que solo tiene 25 años
▶ **pass on** VI (die) fallecer, morir ▶ VT (hand on): **to ~ on (to)** transmitir (a); (cold, illness) pegar (a); (benefits) dar (a); (price rises) pasar (a)
▶ **pass out** VI desmayarse; (Mil) graduarse
▶ **pass over** VI (die) fallecer ▶ VT omitir, pasar por alto
▶ **pass up** VT (opportunity) dejar pasar, no aprovechar

passable [ˈpɑːsəbl] ADJ (road) transitable; (tolerable) pasable

passably [ˈpɑːsəblɪ] ADV pasablemente

passage [ˈpæsɪdʒ] N pasillo; (act of passing) tránsito; (fare, in book) pasaje m; (by boat) travesía

passageway [ˈpæsɪdʒweɪ] N (in house) pasillo, corredor m; (between buildings etc) pasaje m, pasadizo

★**passenger** ['pæsɪndʒəʳ] N pasajero(-a), viajero(-a)

passer-by [pɑːsə'baɪ] N transeúnte mf

passing ['pɑːsɪŋ] ADJ (fleeting) pasajero ▶ N: **in ~** de paso

passing place N (Aut) apartadero

passion ['pæʃən] N pasión f

passionate ['pæʃənɪt] ADJ apasionado

passionately ['pæʃənɪtlɪ] ADV apasionadamente, con pasión

passion fruit N fruta de la pasión, granadilla

passion play N drama m de la Pasión

passive ['pæsɪv] ADJ (also Ling) pasivo

passive smoking N efectos del tabaco en fumadores pasivos

passkey ['pɑːskiː] N llave f maestra

Passover ['pɑːsəuvəʳ] N Pascua (de los judíos)

passport ['pɑːspɔːt] N pasaporte m

passport control N control m de pasaporte

passport office N oficina de pasaportes

★**password** ['pɑːswəːd] N (also Comput) contraseña

★**past** [pɑːst] PREP (further than) más allá de; (later than) después de; **quarter/half ~ four** las cuatro y cuarto/media; **he's ~ forty** tiene más de cuarenta años; **I'm ~ caring** ya no me importa; **to be ~ it** (inf) (person) estar acabado ▶ ADJ pasado; (president etc) antiguo; **for the ~ few/three days** durante los últimos días/últimos tres días ▶ ADV: **to run ~** pasar corriendo ▶ N (time) pasado; (of person) antecedentes mpl; **in the ~** en el pasado, antes

★**pasta** ['pæstə] N pasta

paste [peɪst] N (gen) pasta; (glue) engrudo; **tomato ~** tomate m concentrado ▶ VT (stick) pegar; (glue) engomar

pastel ['pæstl] ADJ pastel; (painting) al pastel

pasteurized ['pæstəraɪzd] ADJ pasteurizado

pastille ['pæstl] N pastilla

pastime ['pɑːstaɪm] N pasatiempo

past master N: **to be a ~ at** ser un maestro en

pastor ['pɑːstəʳ] N pastor m

pastoral ['pɑːstərl] ADJ pastoral

past participle [-'pɑːtɪsɪpl] N (Ling) participio (de) pasado or (de) pretérito or pasivo

pastry ['peɪstrɪ] N (dough) pasta; (cake) pastel m

pasture ['pɑːstʃəʳ] N (grass) pasto

pasty N ['pæstɪ] empanada ▶ ADJ ['peɪstɪ] pastoso; (complexion) pálido

pat [pæt] VT dar una palmadita a; (dog etc) acariciar ▶ N (of butter) porción f; **to give sb/o.s. a ~ on the back** (fig) felicitar a algn/felicitarse ▶ ADV: **he knows it (off) ~** se lo sabe de memoria or al dedillo

patch [pætʃ] N (of material) parche m; (mended part) remiendo; (of land) terreno; (Comput) ajuste m; **(to go through) a bad ~** (pasar por) una mala racha ▶ VT (clothes) remendar

▶ **patch up** VT (mend temporarily) reparar; **to ~ up a quarrel** hacer las paces

patchwork ['pætʃwəːk] N labor f de retales

patchy ['pætʃɪ] ADJ desigual

pate [peɪt] N: **bald ~** calva

★**pâté** ['pæteɪ] N paté m

patent ['peɪtnt] N patente f ▶ VT patentar ▶ ADJ patente, evidente

patent leather N charol m

patently ['peɪtntlɪ] ADV evidentemente

patent medicine N específico

patent office N oficina de patentes y marcas

patent rights NPL derechos mpl de patente

paternal [pə'təːnl] ADJ paternal; (relation) paterno

paternalistic [pətəːnə'lɪstɪk] ADJ paternalista

paternity [pə'təːnɪtɪ] N paternidad f

paternity leave N permiso por paternidad, licencia por paternidad

paternity suit N (Law) caso de paternidad

★**path** [pɑːθ] N camino, sendero; (trail, track) pista; (of missile) trayectoria

pathetic [pə'θetɪk] ADJ (pitiful) penoso, patético; (very bad) malísimo; (moving) conmovedor(a)

pathetically [pə'θetɪklɪ] ADV penosamente, patéticamente; (very badly) malísimamente mal, de pena

pathname ['pɑːθneɪm] N (Comput) nombre m del directorio

pathological [pæθə'lɔdʒɪkəl] ADJ patológico

pathologist [pə'θɔlədʒɪst] N patólogo(-a)

pathology [pə'θɔlədʒɪ] N patología

pathos ['peɪθɔs] N patetismo

pathway ['pɑːθweɪ] N sendero, vereda

patience ['peɪʃns] N paciencia; (BRIT Cards) solitario; **to lose one's ~** perder la paciencia

★**patient** ['peɪʃnt] N paciente mf ▶ ADJ paciente, sufrido; **to be ~ with sb** tener paciencia con algn

patiently ['peɪʃəntlɪ] ADV pacientemente, con paciencia

patio ['pætɪəu] N patio

patriot ['peɪtrɪət] N patriota mf

patriotic [pætrɪ'ɔtɪk] ADJ patriótico

patriotism ['pætrɪətɪzəm] N patriotismo

patrol [pə'trəul] N patrulla; **to be on ~** patrullar, estar de patrulla ▶ VT patrullar por

patrol boat N patrullero, patrullera

patrol car N coche m patrulla

patrolman [pə'trəulmən] N (irreg) (US) policía m

patron ['peɪtrən] N (in shop) cliente mf; (of charity) patrocinador(a) m/f; **~ of the arts** mecenas mf

patronage ['pætrənɪdʒ] N patrocinio, protección f

patronize ['pætrənaɪz] VT (shop) ser cliente de; (look down on) tratar con condescendencia a

patronizing ['pætrənaɪzɪŋ] ADJ condescendiente

patron saint N santo(-a) patrón(-ona)

patter ['pætə'] N golpeteo; (*sales talk*) labia ▶ VI (*rain*) tamborilear

★**pattern** ['pætən] N (*Sewing*) patrón *m*; (*design*) dibujo; (*behaviour, events*) esquema *m*; **~ of events** curso de los hechos; **behaviour patterns** modelos *mpl* de comportamiento

patterned ['pætənd] ADJ (*material*) estampado

paucity ['pɔːsɪtɪ] N escasez *f*

paunch [pɔːntʃ] N panza, barriga

pauper ['pɔːpə'] N pobre *mf*

★**pause** [pɔːz] N pausa; (*interval*) intervalo ▶ VI hacer una pausa; **to ~ for breath** detenerse para tomar aliento

pave [peɪv] VT pavimentar; **to ~ the way for** preparar el terreno para

pavement ['peɪvmənt] N (*BRIT*) acera, vereda (*LAM*), andén *m* (*LAM*), banqueta (*LAM*); (*US*) calzada, pavimento

pavilion [pə'vɪlɪən] N pabellón *m*; (*Sport*) vestuarios *mpl*

paving ['peɪvɪŋ] N pavimento, enlosado

paving stone N losa

paw [pɔː] N pata; (*claw*) garra ▶ VT (*animal*) tocar con la pata; (*pej: touch*) tocar, manosear

pawn [pɔːn] N (*Chess*) peón *m*; (*fig*) instrumento ▶ VT empeñar

pawnbroker ['pɔːnbrəukə'] N prestamista *mf*

pawnshop ['pɔːnʃɔp] N casa de empeños

★**pay** [peɪ] (*pt, pp* **paid** [peɪd]) N paga; (*wage etc*) sueldo, salario; **to be in sb's ~** estar al servicio de algn ▶ VT pagar; (*visit*) hacer; (*respect*) ofrecer; **to ~ attention (to)** prestar atención (a); **how much did you ~ for it?** ¿cuánto pagaste por él?; **I paid £5 for that record** pagué 5 libras por ese disco; **to ~ one's way** (*contribute one's share*) pagar su parte; (*remain solvent: company*) ser solvente; **to ~ dividends** (*Comm*) pagar dividendos; (*fig*) compensar; **it won't ~ you to do that** no te merece la pena hacer eso; **to put paid to** (*plan, person*) acabar con ▶ VI pagar; (*be profitable*) rendir, compensar, ser rentable
  ▶ **pay back** VT (*money*) devolver, reembolsar; (*person*) pagar
  ▶ **pay for** VT FUS pagar
  ▶ **pay in** VT ingresar
  ▶ **pay off** VT liquidar; (*person*) pagar; (*debts*) liquidar, saldar; (*workers*) despedir; (*mortgage*) cancelar, redimir; **to ~ sth off in instalments** pagar algo a plazos ▶ VI (*scheme, decision*) dar resultado
  ▶ **pay out** VT (*rope*) ir dando; (*money*) gastar, desembolsar
  ▶ **pay up** VT, VI pagar

payable ['peɪəbl] ADJ pagadero; **to make a cheque ~ to sb** extender un cheque a favor de algn

pay-as-you-go [peɪəzjə'gəu] ADJ (*mobile phone*) (de) prepago

pay award N aumento de sueldo

payday ['peɪdeɪ] N día *m* de paga; **~ loan** (*BRIT Finance*) préstamo del día de pago

pay day N día *m* de paga

PAYE N ABBR (*BRIT*: = *pay as you earn*) sistema de retención fiscal en la fuente de ingresos

payee [peɪ'iː] N portador(a) *m/f*

pay envelope N (*US*) = **pay packet**

paying ['peɪɪŋ] ADJ: **~ guest** huésped(a) *m/f* de pago

payload ['peɪləud] N carga útil

★**payment** ['peɪmənt] N pago; **advance ~** (*part sum*) anticipo, adelanto; (*total sum*) saldo; **monthly ~** mensualidad *f*; **deferred ~, ~ by instalments** pago a plazos *or* diferido; **on ~ of £5** mediante pago de *or* pagando 5 libras; **in ~ for** en pago de

payout ['peɪjaut] N pago; (*in competition*) premio en metálico

pay packet N (*BRIT*) sobre *m* (de la paga)

pay-phone ['peɪfəun] N teléfono público

payroll ['peɪrəul] N plantilla, nómina; **to be on a firm's ~** estar en la plantilla *or* nómina de una empresa

pay slip N nómina, hoja del sueldo

pay station N (*US*) teléfono público

pay television N televisión *f* de pago

paywall ['peɪwɔːl] N (*Comput*) barrera de pago

PBS N ABBR (*US*: = *Public Broadcasting Service*) agrupación de ayuda a la realización de emisiones para la TV pública

PBX ABBR (*Tel*) = **private branch exchange**

★**PC** N ABBR (= *personal computer*) PC *m*; (*BRIT*) = **police constable** ▶ ABBR (*BRIT*) = **Privy Councillor** ▶ ADJ ABBR = **politically correct**

pc ABBR = **per cent; postcard**

p/c ABBR = **petty cash**

PCB N ABBR (= *printed circuit board*) TCI *f*

pcm ABBR = **per calendar month**

PD N ABBR (*US*) = **police department**

pd ABBR = **paid**

PDA N ABBR (= *personal digital assistant*) agenda electrónica

PDSA N ABBR (*BRIT*) = **People's Dispensary for Sick Animals**

PDT N ABBR (*US*: = *Pacific Daylight Time*) hora de verano del Pacífico

PE N ABBR (= *physical education*) ed. física ▶ ABBR (*CANADA*) = **Prince Edward Island**

★**pea** [piː] N guisante *m*, chícharo (*LAM*), arveja (*LAM*)

★**peace** [piːs] N paz *f*; (*calm*) paz *f*, tranquilidad *f*; **to be at ~ with sb/sth** estar en paz con algn/algo; **to keep the ~** (*policeman*) mantener el orden; (*citizen*) guardar el orden

peaceable ['piːsəbl] ADJ pacífico

peaceably ['piːsəblɪ] ADV pacíficamente

★**peaceful** ['piːsful] ADJ (*gentle*) pacífico; (*calm*) tranquilo, sosegado

peacekeeping [ˈpiːskiːpɪŋ] ADJ de pacificación ▶ N pacificación f

peacekeeping force N fuerza de pacificación

peace offering N (fig) prenda de paz

peacetime [ˈpiːstaɪm] N: **in ~** en tiempo de paz

★**peach** [piːtʃ] N melocotón m, durazno (LAM)

peacock [ˈpiːkɔk] N pavo real

peak [piːk] N (of mountain: top) cumbre f, cima; (: point) pico; (of cap) visera; (fig) cumbre f

peak-hour [ˈpiːkauəʳ] ADJ (traffic etc) de horas punta

peak hours NPL, **peak period** N horas fpl punta

peak rate N tarifa máxima

peaky [ˈpiːkɪ] ADJ (BRIT inf) pálido, paliducho; **I'm feeling a bit ~** estoy malucho, no me encuentro bien

peal [piːl] N (of bells) repique m; **~ of laughter** carcajada

★**peanut** [ˈpiːnʌt] N cacahuete m, maní m (LAM)

peanut butter N mantequilla de cacahuete

★**pear** [pɛəʳ] N pera

pearl [pɜːl] N perla

peasant [ˈpɛznt] N campesino(-a)

peat [piːt] N turba

pebble [ˈpɛbl] N guijarro

peck [pɛk] VT (also: **peck at**) picotear; (: food) comer sin ganas ▶ N picotazo; (kiss) besito

pecking order [ˈpɛkɪŋ-] N orden m de jerarquía

peckish [ˈpɛkɪʃ] ADJ (BRIT inf): **I feel ~** tengo ganas de picar algo

peculiar [pɪˈkjuːlɪəʳ] ADJ (odd) extraño, raro; (typical) propio, característico; (particular: importance, qualities) particular; **~ to** propio de

peculiarity [pɪkjuːlɪˈærɪtɪ] N peculiaridad f, característica

peculiarly [pɪˈkjuːlɪəlɪ] ADV (oddly) extrañamente; (particularly) particularmente

pedal [ˈpɛdl] N pedal m ▶ VI pedalear

pedal bin N cubo de la basura con pedal

pedalo [ˈpɛdələu] N patín m a pedal

pedant [ˈpɛdənt] N pedante mf

pedantic [pɪˈdæntɪk] ADJ pedante

pedantry [ˈpɛdəntrɪ] N pedantería

peddle [ˈpɛdl] VT (goods) ir vendiendo or vender de puerta en puerta; (drugs) traficar con; (gossip) divulgar

peddler [ˈpɛdləʳ] N vendedor(a) m/f ambulante

pedestal [ˈpɛdəstl] N pedestal m

pedestrian [pɪˈdɛstrɪən] N peatón m ▶ ADJ pedestre

pedestrian crossing N (BRIT) paso de peatones

pedestrianized ADJ: **a ~ street** una calle peatonal

pedestrian precinct, (US) **pedestrian zone** N zona peatonal

pediatrics [piːdɪˈætrɪks] N (US) = **paediatrics**

pedigree [ˈpɛdɪgriː] N genealogía; (of animal) pedigrí m ▶ CPD (animal) de raza, de casta

pedlar [ˈpɛdləʳ] N (BRIT) = **peddler**

pedophile [ˈpiːdəufaɪl] N (US) = **paedophile**

pee [piː] VI (inf) mear

peek [piːk] VI mirar a hurtadillas; (Comput) inspeccionar

peel [piːl] N piel f; (of orange, lemon) cáscara; (: removed) peladuras fpl ▶ VT pelar ▶ VI (paint etc) desconcharse; (wallpaper) despegarse, desprenderse; (skin) pelar
▶ **peel back** VT pelar

peeler [ˈpiːləʳ] N: **potato ~** mondador m or pelador m de patatas, pelapatatas m inv

peep [piːp] N (look) mirada furtiva; (sound) pío ▶ VI (look) mirar furtivamente
▶ **peep out** VI asomar la cabeza

peephole [ˈpiːphəul] N mirilla

peer [pɪəʳ] VI: **to ~ at** escudriñar ▶ N (noble) par m; (equal) igual m; (contemporary) contemporáneo(-a)

peerage [ˈpɪərɪdʒ] N nobleza

peerless [ˈpɪəlɪs] ADJ sin par, incomparable, sin igual

peeved [piːvd] ADJ enojado

peevish [ˈpiːvɪʃ] ADJ malhumorado

peevishness [ˈpiːvɪʃnɪs] N mal humor m

★**peg** [pɛg] N clavija; (for coat etc) gancho, colgador m; (BRIT: also: **clothes peg**) pinza; (also: **tent peg**) estaca ▶ VT (clothes) tender; (groundsheet) fijar con estacas; (fig: wages, prices) fijar

pejorative [pɪˈdʒɔrətɪv] ADJ peyorativo

Pekin [piːˈkɪn], **Peking** [piːˈkɪŋ] N Pekín m

pekinese [piːkɪˈniːz] N pequinés(-esa) m/f

pelican [ˈpɛlɪkən] N pelícano

pelican crossing N (BRIT Aut) paso de peatones señalizado

pellet [ˈpɛlɪt] N bolita; (bullet) perdigón m

pell-mell [ˈpɛlˈmɛl] ADV en tropel

pelmet [ˈpɛlmɪt] N galería

pelt [pɛlt] VT: **to ~ sb with sth** arrojarle algo a algn ▶ VI (rain: also: **pelt down**) llover a cántaros; (inf: run) correr ▶ N pellejo

pelvis [ˈpɛlvɪs] N pelvis f

★**pen** [pɛn] N (also: **ballpoint pen**) bolígrafo; (also: **fountain pen**) pluma; (for sheep) redil m; (US inf: prison) cárcel f, chirona; **to put ~ to paper** tomar la pluma

penal [ˈpiːnl] ADJ penal; **~ servitude** trabajos mpl forzados

penalize [ˈpiːnəlaɪz] VT (punish) castigar; (Sport) sancionar, penalizar

★**penalty** [ˈpɛnltɪ] N (gen) pena; (fine) multa; (Sport) sanción f; (also: **penalty kick**: Football) penalty m

penalty area N (BRIT Sport) área de castigo

penalty clause N cláusula de penalización

penalty shoot-out [-'ʃuːtaut] N (*Football*) tanda de penaltis

penance ['pɛnəns] N penitencia

pence [pɛns] PL *of* **penny**

penchant ['pɛnʃənt] N predilección *f*, inclinación *f*

★**pencil** ['pɛnsl] N lápiz *m*, lapicero (*LAM*) ▶ VT (*also*: **pencil in**) escribir con lápiz; (: *fig*) apuntar con carácter provisional

pencil case N estuche *m*

pencil sharpener N sacapuntas *m inv*

pendant ['pɛndnt] N pendiente *m*

pending ['pɛndɪŋ] PREP antes de; **~ the arrival of ...** hasta que llegue ..., hasta llegar ... ▶ ADJ pendiente

pendulum ['pɛndjuləm] N péndulo

penetrate ['pɛnɪtreɪt] VT penetrar

penetrating ['pɛnɪtreɪtɪŋ] ADJ penetrante

penetration [pɛnɪ'treɪʃən] N penetración *f*

penfriend ['pɛnfrɛnd] N (*BRIT*) amigo(-a) por correspondencia

penguin ['pɛŋgwɪn] N pingüino

penicillin [pɛnɪ'sɪlɪn] N penicilina

peninsula [pə'nɪnsjulə] N península

penis ['piːnɪs] N pene *m*

penitence ['pɛnɪtns] N penitencia

penitent ['pɛnɪtnt] ADJ arrepentido; (*Rel*) penitente

penitentiary [pɛnɪ'tɛnʃərɪ] N (*US*) cárcel *f*, presidio

penknife ['pɛnnaɪf] N navaja

pen name N seudónimo

pennant ['pɛnənt] N banderín *m*

penniless ['pɛnɪlɪs] ADJ sin dinero

Pennines ['pɛnaɪnz] NPL (Montes *mpl*) Peninos *mpl*

★**penny** ['pɛnɪ] (*pl* **pennies** ['pɛnɪz] *or BRIT* **pence** [pɛns]) N (*BRIT*) penique *m*; (*US*) centavo

penpal ['pɛnpæl] N amigo(-a) por correspondencia

penpusher ['pɛnpuʃər] N (*pej*) chupatintas *mf*

★**pension** ['pɛnʃən] N (*allowance, state payment*) pensión *f*; (*old-age*) jubilación *f* ▶ **pension off** VT jubilar

pensioner ['pɛnʃənər] N (*BRIT*) jubilado(-a)

pension fund N fondo de pensiones

pensive ['pɛnsɪv] ADJ pensativo; (*withdrawn*) preocupado

pentagon ['pɛntəgən] N pentágono; **the P~** (*US Pol*) el Pentágono

Pentecost ['pɛntɪkɔst] N Pentecostés *m*

penthouse ['pɛnthaus] N ático (de lujo)

pent-up ['pɛntʌp] ADJ (*feelings*) reprimido

penultimate [pɛ'nʌltɪmət] ADJ penúltimo

penury ['pɛnjurɪ] N miseria, pobreza

★**people** ['piːpl] NPL gente *f*; (*citizens*) pueblo *sg*, ciudadanos *mpl*; (*Pol*): **the ~** el pueblo; **several ~ came** vinieron varias personas; **~ say that ...** dice la gente que ...; **old/young ~** los ancianos/jóvenes; **~ at large** la gente en general; **a man of the ~** un hombre del pueblo ▶ N (*nation, race*) pueblo, nación *f* ▶ VT poblar

pep [pɛp] N (*inf*) energía ▶ **pep up** VT animar

★**pepper** ['pɛpər] N (*spice*) pimienta; (*vegetable*) pimiento, ají *m* (*LAM*), chile *m* (*LAM*) ▶ VT: **to ~ with** (*fig*) salpicar de

> Don't confuse **el pimiento**, the vegetable, with **la pimienta**, which is the spice.

peppermint ['pɛpəmɪnt] N menta; (*sweet*) pastilla de menta

pepperoni [pɛpə'rəunɪ] N ≈ salchichón *m* picante

pepper pot ['pɛpəpɔt] N pimentero

pep talk ['pɛptɔːk] N (*inf*): **to give sb a ~** darle a algn una inyección de ánimo

★**per** [pɜːr] PREP por; **~ day/person** por día/persona; **~ annum** al año; **as ~ your instructions** de acuerdo con sus instrucciones

per capita ADJ, ADV per cápita

perceive [pə'siːv] VT percibir; (*realize*) darse cuenta de

★**per cent**, (*US*) **percent** [pə'sɛnt] N por ciento; **a 20 ~ discount** un descuento del 20 por ciento

★**percentage** [pə'sɛntɪdʒ] N porcentaje *m*; **to get a ~ on all sales** percibir un tanto por ciento sobre todas las ventas; **on a ~ basis** a porcentaje

percentage point N punto (porcentual)

perceptible [pə'sɛptəbl] ADJ perceptible; (*notable*) sensible

perception [pə'sɛpʃən] N percepción *f*; (*insight*) perspicacia

perceptive [pə'sɛptɪv] ADJ perspicaz

perch [pɜːtʃ] N (*fish*) perca; (*for bird*) percha ▶ VI: **to ~ (on)** (*bird*) posarse (en); (*person*) encaramarse (en)

percolate ['pɜːkəleɪt] VT (*coffee*) filtrar ▶ VI (*coffee*) filtrarse; (*fig*) filtrarse

percolator ['pɜːkəleɪtər] N cafetera de filtro

percussion [pə'kʌʃən] N percusión *f*

percussionist [pə'kʌʃənɪst] N percusionista *mf*

peremptory [pə'rɛmptərɪ] ADJ perentorio

perennial [pə'rɛnɪəl] ADJ perenne

★**perfect** ADJ ['pɜːfɪkt] perfecto; **he's a ~ stranger to me** no le conozco de nada, me es completamente desconocido ▶ N ['pɜːfɪkt] (*also*: **perfect tense**) perfecto ▶ VT [pə'fɛkt] perfeccionar

perfection [pə'fɛkʃən] N perfección *f*

perfectionist [pə'fɛkʃənɪst] N perfeccionista *mf*

★**perfectly** ['pɜːfɪktlɪ] ADV perfectamente; **I'm ~ happy with the situation** estoy muy contento con la situación; **you know ~ well** lo sabes muy bien *or* perfectamente

perforate [ˈpəːfəreɪt] VT perforar
perforated ulcer N úlcera perforada
perforation [pəːfəˈreɪʃən] N perforación f
★**perform** [pəˈfɔːm] VT (carry out) realizar, llevar a cabo; (Theat) representar; (piece of music) interpretar ▸ VI (Theat) actuar; (Tech) funcionar
★**performance** [pəˈfɔːməns] N (of task) realización f; (of a play) representación f; (of player etc) actuación f; (of engine) rendimiento; (of car) prestaciones fpl; (of function) desempeño; **the team put up a good ~** el equipo se defendió bien
performer [pəˈfɔːməʳ] N (actor) actor m, actriz f; (Mus) intérprete mf
performing [pəˈfɔːmɪŋ] ADJ (animal) amaestrado
performing arts NPL: **the ~** las artes teatrales
perfume [ˈpəːfjuːm] N perfume m
perfunctory [pəˈfʌŋktərɪ] ADJ superficial
★**perhaps** [pəˈhæps] ADV quizá(s), tal vez; **~ so/not** puede que sí/no
peril [ˈpɛrɪl] N peligro, riesgo
perilous [ˈpɛrɪləs] ADJ peligroso
perilously [ˈpɛrɪləslɪ] ADV: **they came ~ close to being caught** por poco les cogen or agarran
perimeter [pəˈrɪmɪtəʳ] N perímetro
★**period** [ˈpɪərɪəd] N período, periodo; (History) época; (Scol) clase f; (full stop) punto; (Med) regla, periodo; (US Sport) tiempo; **for a ~ of three weeks** durante (un período de) tres semanas; **the holiday ~** el período de vacaciones ▸ ADJ (costume, furniture) de época
periodic [pɪərɪˈɔdɪk] ADJ periódico
periodical [pɪərɪˈɔdɪkl] ADJ periódico ▸ N revista, publicación f periódica
periodically [pɪərɪˈɔdɪklɪ] ADV de vez en cuando, cada cierto tiempo
period pains NPL dolores mpl de la regla or de la menstruación
peripatetic [pɛrɪpəˈtɛtɪk] ADJ (salesman) ambulante; (teacher) con trabajo en varios colegios
peripheral [pəˈrɪfərəl] ADJ periférico ▸ N (Comput) periférico, unidad f periférica
periphery [pəˈrɪfərɪ] N periferia
periscope [ˈpɛrɪskəup] N periscopio
perish [ˈpɛrɪʃ] VI perecer; (decay) echarse a perder
perishable [ˈpɛrɪʃəbl] ADJ perecedero
perishables [ˈpɛrɪʃəblz] NPL productos mpl perecederos
peritonitis [pɛrɪtəˈnaɪtɪs] N peritonitis f
perjure [ˈpəːdʒəʳ] VT: **to ~ o.s.** perjurar
perjury [ˈpəːdʒərɪ] N (Law) perjurio
perk [pəːk] N beneficio, extra m
  ▸ **perk up** VI (cheer up) animarse
perky [ˈpəːkɪ] ADJ alegre, animado
perm [pəːm] N permanente f ▸ VT: **to have one's hair permed** hacerse una permanente

permanence [ˈpəːmənəns] N permanencia
★**permanent** [ˈpəːmənənt] ADJ permanente; (job, position) fijo; (dye, ink) indeleble; **~ address** domicilio permanente; **I'm not ~ here** no estoy fijo aquí
permanently [ˈpəːmənəntlɪ] ADV (lastingly) para siempre, de modo definitivo; (all the time) permanentemente
permeate [ˈpəːmɪeɪt] VI penetrar, trascender ▸ VT penetrar, trascender a
permissible [pəˈmɪsɪbl] ADJ permisible, lícito
★**permission** [pəˈmɪʃən] N permiso; **to give sb ~ to do sth** autorizar a algn para que haga algo; **with your ~** con su permiso
permissive [pəˈmɪsɪv] ADJ permisivo
★**permit** N [ˈpəːmɪt] permiso, licencia; (entrance pass) pase m; **fishing ~** permiso de pesca; **building/export ~** licencia or permiso de construcción/exportación ▸ VT [pəˈmɪt] permitir; (accept) tolerar ▸ VI (pəˈmɪt]: **weather permitting** si el tiempo lo permite
permutation [pəːmjuˈteɪʃən] N permutación f
pernicious [pəːˈnɪʃəs] ADJ nocivo; (Med) pernicioso
pernickety [pəˈnɪkɪtɪ] ADJ (inf: person) quisquilloso; (: task) delicado
perpendicular [pəːpənˈdɪkjuləʳ] ADJ perpendicular
perpetrate [ˈpəːpɪtreɪt] VT cometer
perpetual [pəˈpɛtjuəl] ADJ perpetuo
perpetually [pəˈpɛtjuəlɪ] ADV (eternally) perpetuamente; (continuously) constantemente, continuamente
perpetuate [pəˈpɛtjueɪt] VT perpetuar
perpetuity [pəːpɪˈtjuɪt] N: **in ~** a perpetuidad
perplex [pəˈplɛks] VT dejar perplejo
perplexed [pəˈplɛkst] ADJ perplejo, confuso
perplexing [pəˈplɛksɪŋ] ADJ que causa perplejidad
perplexity [pəˈplɛksɪtɪ] N perplejidad f, confusión f
perquisites [ˈpəːkwɪzɪts] NPL (also: **perks**) beneficios mpl
persecute [ˈpəːsɪkjuːt] VT (pursue) perseguir; (harass) acosar
persecution [pəːsɪˈkjuːʃən] N persecución f
perseverance [pəːsɪˈvɪərəns] N perseverancia
persevere [pəːsɪˈvɪəʳ] VI perseverar
Persia [ˈpəːʃə] N Persia
Persian [ˈpəːʃən] ADJ, N persa mf; **the ~ Gulf** el Golfo Pérsico ▸ N (Ling) persa m
Persian cat N gato persa
persist [pəˈsɪst] VI persistir; **to ~ in doing sth** empeñarse en hacer algo
persistence [pəˈsɪstəns] N empeño
persistent [pəˈsɪstənt] ADJ (lateness, rain) persistente; (determined) porfiado; (continuing) constante; **~ offender** (Law) multirreincidente mf

persistently [pəˈsɪstntlɪ] ADV persistente-mente; (*continually*) constantemente

persnickety [pəˈsnɪkətɪ] ADJ (*US inf*) = **pernickety**

★**person** [ˈpəːsn] N persona; **in ~** en persona; **on** or **about one's ~** encima; **a ~ to ~ call** una llamada (de) persona a persona

personable [ˈpəːsnəbl] ADJ atractivo

★**personal** [ˈpəːsnl] ADJ personal, individual; (*visit*) en persona; (BRIT *Tel*) (de) persona a persona

personal allowance N desgravación f personal

personal assistant N ayudante *mf* personal

personal belongings NPL efectos *mpl* personales

personal column N anuncios *mpl* personales

personal computer N ordenador *m* personal

personal effects NPL efectos *mpl* personales

personal identification number N número personal de identificación

★**personality** [pəːsəˈnælɪtɪ] N personalidad f

★**personally** [ˈpəːsnəlɪ] ADV personalmente; (*in person*) en persona; **to take sth ~** tomarse algo a mal

personal organizer N agenda; (*electronic*) agenda electrónica

personal property N bienes *mpl* muebles

personal, social and health education N (BRIT *Scol*) *formación social y sanitaria para la vida adulta*

personal stereo N walkman® *m*

personification [pəːsɔnɪfɪˈkeɪʃən] N personificación f

personify [pəːˈsɔnɪfaɪ] VT encarnar, personificar

personnel [pəːsəˈnɛl] N personal *m*

personnel department N departamento de personal

personnel management N gestión f de personal

personnel manager N jefe *m* de personal

perspective [pəˈspɛktɪv] N perspectiva; **to get sth into ~** ver algo en perspectiva or como es

Perspex® [ˈpəːspɛks] N (BRIT) vidrio acrílico, plexiglás® *m*

perspiration [pəːspɪˈreɪʃən] N transpiración f, sudor *m*

perspire [pəˈspaɪəʳ] VI transpirar, sudar

★**persuade** [pəˈsweɪd] VT: **to ~ sb to do sth** persuadir a algn para que haga algo; **to ~ sb of sth/that** persuadir or convencer a algn de algo/de que; **I am persuaded that ...** estoy convencido de que ...

persuasion [pəˈsweɪʒən] N persuasión f; (*persuasiveness*) persuasiva; (*creed*) creencia

persuasive [pəˈsweɪsɪv] ADJ persuasivo

persuasively [pəˈsweɪsɪvlɪ] ADV de modo persuasivo

pert [pəːt] ADJ impertinente, fresco, atrevido

pertaining [pəːˈteɪnɪŋ]: **~ to** prep relacionado con

pertinent [ˈpəːtɪnənt] ADJ pertinente, a propósito

perturb [pəˈtəːb] VT perturbar

perturbing [pəˈtəːbɪŋ] ADJ inquietante, perturbador(a)

★**Peru** [pəˈruː] N el Perú

perusal [pəˈruːzəl] N (*quick*) lectura somera; (*careful*) examen *m*

peruse [pəˈruːz] VT (*examine*) leer con detención, examinar; (*glance at*) mirar por encima

Peruvian [pəˈruːvɪən] ADJ, N peruano(-a) *m/f*

pervade [pəˈveɪd] VT impregnar; (*influence, ideas*) extenderse por

pervasive [pəˈveɪsɪv] ADJ (*smell*) penetrante; (*influence*) muy extendido; (*gloom, feelings, ideas*) reinante

perverse [pəˈvəːs] ADJ perverso; (*stubborn*) terco; (*wayward*) travieso

perversely [pəˈvəːslɪ] ADV perversamente; tercamente; traviesamente

perverseness [pəˈvəːsnɪs] N perversidad f; terquedad f; travesura

perversion [pəˈvəːʃən] N perversión f

pervert N [ˈpəːvəːt] pervertido(-a) ▶ VT [pəˈvəːt] pervertir

pessary [ˈpɛsərɪ] N pesario

pessimism [ˈpɛsɪmɪzəm] N pesimismo

pessimist [ˈpɛsɪmɪst] N pesimista *mf*

pessimistic [pɛsɪˈmɪstɪk] ADJ pesimista

pest [pɛst] N (*insect*) insecto nocivo; (*fig*) lata, molestia ∎ **pests** NPL plaga

pest control N control *m* de plagas

pester [ˈpɛstəʳ] VT molestar, acosar

pesticide [ˈpɛstɪsaɪd] N pesticida *m*

pestilence [ˈpɛstɪləns] N pestilencia

pestle [ˈpɛsl] N mano f de mortero or de almirez

★**pet** [pɛt] N animal *m* doméstico, mascota f; (*favourite*) favorito(-a) ▶ VT acariciar ▶ VI (*inf*) besuquearse ▶ CPD: **teacher's ~** favorito(-a) (del profesor); **~ hate** manía

petal [ˈpɛtl] N pétalo

peter [ˈpiːtəʳ]: **to ~ out** vi agotarse, acabarse

petite [pəˈtiːt] ADJ menuda, chiquita

petition [pəˈtɪʃən] N petición f ▶ VT presentar una petición a ▶ VI: **to ~ for divorce** pedir el divorcio

pet name N nombre *m* cariñoso, apodo

petrified [ˈpɛtrɪfaɪd] ADJ (*fig*) pasmado, horrorizado

petrochemical [pɛtrəˈkɛmɪkl] ADJ petroquímico

petrodollars [ˈpɛtrəudɔləz] NPL petrodólares *mpl*

★**petrol** [ˈpɛtrəl] N (BRIT) gasolina; (*for lighter*) bencina

P

petrol bomb N cóctel *m* Molotov

petrol can N bidón *m* de gasolina

petrol engine N (BRIT) motor *m* de gasolina

petroleum [pəˈtrəuliəm] N petróleo

petroleum jelly N vaselina

petrolhead [ˈpetrəlhed] N (*inf*) fanático(-a) del automovilismo

petrol pump N (BRIT: *in car*) bomba de gasolina; (: *in garage*) surtidor *m* de gasolina

petrol station N (BRIT) gasolinera

petrol tank N (BRIT) depósito (de gasolina)

petticoat [ˈpetɪkəut] N combinación *f*, enagua(s) *f(pl)* (LAM)

pettifogging [ˈpetɪfɔgɪŋ] ADJ quisquilloso

pettiness [ˈpetɪnɪs] N mezquindad *f*

petty [ˈpetɪ] ADJ (*mean*) mezquino; (*unimportant*) insignificante

petty cash N dinero para gastos menores

petty cash book N libro de caja auxiliar

petty officer N contramaestre *m*

petulant [ˈpetjulənt] ADJ malhumorado

pew [pjuː] N banco

pewter [ˈpjuːtəʳ] N peltre *m*

Pfc ABBR (*US Mil*) = **private first class**

PG N ABBR (*Cine*) = **parental guidance**

PG 13 ABBR (*US Cine*: = *Parental Guidance 13*) no apto para menores de 13 años

PGA N ABBR = **Professional Golfers' Association**

PH N ABBR (*US Mil*: = *Purple Heart*) decoración otorgada a los heridos de guerra

pH N ABBR (= *pH value*) pH

PHA N ABBR (*US*) = **Public Housing Administration**

phallic [ˈfælɪk] ADJ fálico

phantom [ˈfæntəm] N fantasma *m*

Pharaoh [ˈfɛərəu] N faraón *m*

pharmaceutical [fɑːməˈsjuːtɪkl] ADJ farmacéutico

pharmacist [ˈfɑːməsɪst] N farmacéutico(-a)

pharmacy [ˈfɑːməsɪ] N (*US*) farmacia

phase [feɪz] N fase *f* ▶ VT: **phased withdrawal** retirada progresiva
  ▶ **phase in** VT introducir progresivamente
  ▶ **phase out** VT (*machinery, product*) retirar progresivamente; (*job, subsidy*) eliminar por etapas

PhD ABBR = **Doctor of Philosophy**

pheasant [ˈfeznt] N faisán *m*

phenomena [fəˈnɔmɪnə] NPL *of* **phenomenon**

phenomenal [frˈnɔmɪnl] ADJ fenomenal, extraordinario

phenomenally [frˈnɔmɪnlɪ] ADV extraordinariamente

phenomenon [fəˈnɔmɪnən] (*pl* **phenomena** [-nə]) N fenómeno

phial [ˈfaɪəl] N ampolla

philanderer [frˈlændərəʳ] N donjuán *m*, don Juan *m*

philanthropic [filənˈθrɔpɪk] ADJ filantrópico

philanthropist [frˈlænθrəpɪst] N filántropo(-a)

philatelist [frˈlætəlɪst] N filatelista *mf*

philately [frˈlætəlɪ] N filatelia

Philippines [ˈfɪlɪpiːnz] NPL: **the ~** (las Islas) Filipinas

philosopher [frˈlɔsəfəʳ] N filósofo(-a)

philosophical [filəˈsɔfɪkl] ADJ filosófico

★**philosophy** [frˈlɔsəfɪ] N filosofía

phishing [ˈfɪʃɪŋ] N phishing *m*, *método de estafa a través de Internet*

phlegm [flɛm] N flema

phlegmatic [flɛɡˈmætɪk] ADJ flemático

phobia [ˈfəubjə] N fobia

★**phone** [fəun] N teléfono; **to be on the ~** tener teléfono; (*be calling*) estar hablando por teléfono ▶ VT telefonear, llamar por teléfono
  ▶ **phone back** VT, VI volver a llamar
  ▶ **phone up** VT, VI llamar por teléfono

phone book N guía telefónica

★**phone box, phone booth** N cabina telefónica

★**phone call** N llamada (telefónica)

phonecard [ˈfəunkɑːd] N tarjeta telefónica

phone-in [ˈfəunɪn] N (BRIT *Radio, TV*) *programa de radio o televisión con las líneas abiertas al público*

★**phone number** N número de teléfono

phone tapping [-tæpɪŋ] N escuchas telefónicas

phonetics [fəˈnɛtɪks] N fonética

phoney [ˈfəunɪ] ADJ = **phony**

phonograph [ˈfəunəɡræf] N (*US*) fonógrafo, tocadiscos *m inv*

phonology [fəuˈnɔlədʒɪ] N fonología

phony [ˈfəunɪ] ADJ falso ▶ N (*person*) farsante *mf*

phosphate [ˈfɔsfeɪt] N fosfato

phosphorus [ˈfɔsfərəs] N fósforo

★**photo** [ˈfəutəu] N foto *f*

photo... [ˈfəutəu] PREF foto...

photo album N álbum *m* de fotos

photobomb [ˈfəutəubɔm] VT (*inf*) colarse en la foto de

photocall [ˈfəutəukɔːl] N sesión *f* fotográfica para la prensa

photocopier [ˈfəutəukɔpɪəʳ] N fotocopiadora

photocopy [ˈfəutəukɔpɪ] N fotocopia ▶ VT fotocopiar

photoelectric [fəutəurˈlɛktrɪk] ADJ: **~ cell** célula fotoeléctrica

photo finish N resultado comprobado por fotocontrol

Photofit® [ˈfəutəufɪt] N (*also*: **Photofit picture**) retrato robot

photogenic [fəutəuˈdʒɛnɪk] ADJ fotogénico

★**photograph** [ˈfəutəɡræf] N fotografía; **to take a ~ of** sb sacar una foto de algn ▶ VT fotografiar

★**photographer** [fəˈtɔɡrəfəʳ] N fotógrafo(-a)

photographic [fəutə'græfik] ADJ fotográfico
photography [fə'tɒgrəfɪ] N fotografía
photo opportunity N *oportunidad de salir en la foto*
Photoshop® ['fəutəuʃɒp] N Photoshop® *m* ▶ VT editar en Photoshop
Photostat® ['fəutəustæt] N fotostato
photosynthesis [fəutəu'sɪnθəsɪs] N fotosíntesis *f*
★**phrase** [freɪz] N frase *f* ▶ VT (*letter*) expresar, redactar
phrase book N libro de frases
★**physical** ['fɪzɪkl] ADJ físico; **~ examination** reconocimiento médico; **~ exercises** ejercicios *mpl* físicos
physical education N educación *f* física
physically ['fɪsɪklɪ] ADV físicamente
physical training N gimnasia
physician [fɪ'zɪʃən] N médico(-a)
physicist ['fɪzɪsɪst] N físico(-a)
★**physics** ['fɪzɪks] N física
physiological [fɪzɪə'lɒdʒɪkl] ADJ fisiológico
physiology [fɪzɪ'ɒlədʒɪ] N fisiología
physiotherapist [fɪzɪəu'θerəpɪst] N fisioterapeuta *mf*
physiotherapy [fɪzɪəu'θerəpɪ] N fisioterapia
physique [fɪ'ziːk] N físico
pianist ['pɪənɪst] N pianista *mf*
★**piano** [pɪ'ænəu] N piano
piano accordion N (BRIT) acordeón-piano *m*
piccolo ['pɪkələu] N (Mus) flautín *m*
★**pick** [pɪk] N (*tool: also:* **pickaxe**) pico, piqueta; **take your ~** escoja lo que quiera; **the ~ of** lo mejor de ▶ VT (*select*) elegir, escoger; (*gather*) coger (SP), recoger (LAM); (*lock*) abrir con ganzúa; (*scab, spot*) rascar; **to ~ one's nose/ teeth** hurgarse la nariz/escarbarse los dientes; **to ~ pockets** ratear, ser carterista; **to ~ one's way through** andar a tientas, abrirse camino; **to ~ a fight/quarrel with sb** buscar pelea/ camorra con algn; **to ~ sb's brains** aprovecharse de los conocimientos de algn ▶ VI: **to ~ and choose** ser muy exigente
▶ **pick at** VT FUS: **to ~ at one's food** comer con poco apetito
▶ **pick off** VT (*kill*) matar de un tiro
▶ **pick on** VT FUS (*person*) meterse con
▶ **pick out** VT escoger; (*distinguish*) identificar
▶ **pick up** VI (*improve: sales*) ir mejor; (*: patient*) reponerse; (*: Finance*) recobrarse; **to ~ up where one left off** volver a empezar algo donde lo había dejado ▶ VT (*from floor*) recoger; (*buy*) comprar; (*find*) encontrar; (*learn*) aprender; (*Police: arrest*) detener; (*Radio, TV, Tel*) captar; **to ~ up speed** acelerarse; **to ~ o.s. up** levantarse
pickaxe, (US) **pickax** ['pɪkæks] N pico, zapapico
picket ['pɪkɪt] N (*in strike*) piquete *m*; **to be on ~ duty** estar de piquete ▶ VT hacer un piquete en, piquetear

picketing ['pɪkɪtɪŋ] N organización *f* de piquetes
picket line N piquete *m*
pickings ['pɪkɪŋz] NPL (*pilferings*): **there are good ~ to be had here** se pueden sacar buenas ganancias de aquí
pickle ['pɪkl] N (*also:* **pickles**: *as condiment*) escabeche *m*; (*fig: mess*) apuro; **in a ~** en un lío, en apuros ▶ VT conservar en escabeche; (*in vinegar*) conservar en vinagre
pick-me-up ['pɪkmɪʌp] N reconstituyente *m*
pickpocket ['pɪkpɒkɪt] N carterista *mf*
pickup ['pɪkʌp] N (*also:* **pickup truck, pickup van**) furgoneta, camioneta
★**picnic** ['pɪknɪk] N picnic *m*, merienda ▶ VI hacer un picnic
picnic area N zona de picnic; (Aut) área de descanso
pictorial [pɪk'tɔːrɪəl] ADJ pictórico; (*magazine etc*) ilustrado
★**picture** ['pɪktʃər] N cuadro; (*painting*) pintura; (*photograph*) fotografía; (*film*) película; (*TV*) imagen *f*; (*fig: description*) descripción *f*; (*: situation*) situación *f*; **the pictures** (BRIT) el cine; **we get a good ~ here** captamos bien la imagen aquí; **to take a ~ of sb/sth** hacer *or* sacar una foto a algn/de algo; **the garden is a ~ in June** el jardín es una preciosidad en junio; **the overall ~** la impresión general; **to put sb in the ~** poner a algn al corriente *or* al tanto ▶ VT pintar; (*imagine*) imaginar
picture book N libro de dibujos
picture frame N marco
picture message N mensaje *m* con foto
picture messaging N (envío de) mensajes *mpl* con imágenes
picturesque [pɪktʃə'resk] ADJ pintoresco
piddling ['pɪdlɪŋ] ADJ (*inf*) insignificante
pidgin ['pɪdʒɪn] ADJ: **~ English** lengua franca basada en el inglés
★**pie** [paɪ] N (*of meat etc: large*) pastel *m*; (*: small*) empanada; (*sweet*) tarta
piebald ['paɪbɔːld] ADJ pío
★**piece** [piːs] N pedazo, trozo; (*of cake*) trozo; (*Draughts etc*) ficha; (*Chess*) pieza; (*part of a set*) pieza; (*item*): **a ~ of furniture/advice** un mueble/ un consejo; **to take to pieces** desmontar; **a ~ of news** una noticia; **a 10p ~** una moneda de 10 peniques; **a six-piece band** un conjunto de seis (músicos); **in one ~** (*object*) de una sola pieza; **~ by ~** pieza por *or* a pieza; **to say one's ~** decir su parecer ▶ VT: **to ~ together** juntar; (*Tech*) armar
piecemeal ['piːsmiːl] ADV poco a poco
piece rate N tarifa a destajo
piecework ['piːswəːk] N trabajo a destajo
pie chart N gráfico de sectores *or* de tarta
pier [pɪər] N muelle *m*, embarcadero
pierce [pɪəs] VT penetrar en, perforar; **to have one's ears pierced** hacerse los agujeros de las orejas

p

piercing ['pɪəsɪŋ] ADJ (*cry*) penetrante ▸ N (*body art*) piercing *m*

piety ['paɪətɪ] N piedad *f*

★**pig** [pɪg] N cerdo, puerco, chancho (*LAm*); (*person: greedy*) tragón(-ona) *m/f*, comilón(-ona) *m/f*; (*: nasty*) cerdo(-a)

pigeon ['pɪdʒən] N paloma; (*as food*) pichón *m*

pigeonhole ['pɪdʒənhəul] N casilla

piggy bank ['pɪgɪ'bæŋk] N hucha (*en forma de cerdito*)

pigheaded ['pɪg'hɛdɪd] ADJ terco, testarudo

piglet ['pɪglɪt] N cerdito, cochinillo

pigment ['pɪgmənt] N pigmento

pigmentation [pɪgmən'teɪʃən] N pigmentación *f*

pigmy ['pɪgmɪ] N = **pygmy**

pigskin ['pɪgskɪn] N piel *f* de cerdo

pigsty ['pɪgstaɪ] N pocilga

pigtail ['pɪgteɪl] N (*girl's*) trenza; (*Chinese*) coleta; (*Taur*) coleta

pike [paɪk] N (*spear*) pica; (*fish*) lucio

pilchard ['pɪltʃəd] N sardina

★**pile** [paɪl] N (*heap*) montón *m*; (*of carpet*) pelo; **in a ~** en un montón ▸ VI: **to ~ into** (*car*) meterse en
▸ **pile on** VT: **to ~ it on** (*inf*) exagerar
▸ **pile up** VI (*accumulate: work*) amontonarse, acumularse ▸ VT (*put in a heap: books, clothes*) apilar, amontonar; (*accumulate*) acumular

piles [paɪlz] NPL (*Med*) almorranas *fpl*, hemorroides *mpl*

pile-up ['paɪlʌp] N (*Aut*) accidente *m* múltiple

pilfer ['pɪlfə'] VT, VI ratear, robar, sisar

pilfering ['pɪlfərɪŋ] N ratería

pilgrim ['pɪlgrɪm] N peregrino(-a); **the P~ Fathers** or **Pilgrims** *los primeros colonos norteamericanos; see also* **Thanksgiving**

Los **Pilgrim Fathers** fueron un grupo de puritanos que partieron de Inglaterra en 1620 huyendo de la persecución religiosa. Después de atravesar el Atlántico a bordo del Mayflower, fundaron New Plymouth en Nueva Inglaterra, en lo que hoy es Massachusetts. Se considera a los *Pilgrim Fathers* como los fundadores de los Estados Unidos. Una vez al año, en *Thanksgiving* (el Día de Acción de Gracias), el cuarto jueves de noviembre, se celebra el éxito de su primera cosecha.

pilgrimage ['pɪlgrɪmɪdʒ] N peregrinación *f*, romería

★**pill** [pɪl] N píldora; **the ~** la píldora; **to be on the ~** tomar la píldora (anticonceptiva)

pillage ['pɪlɪdʒ] VT pillar, saquear

pillar ['pɪlə'] N pilar *m*, columna

pillar box N (*BRIT*) buzón *m*

pillion ['pɪljən] N (*of motorcycle*) asiento trasero; **to ride ~** ir en el asiento trasero

pillion passenger N pasajero que va detrás

pillory ['pɪlərɪ] VT poner en ridículo

pillow ['pɪləu] N almohada

pillowcase ['pɪləukeɪs], **pillowslip** ['pɪləuslɪp] N funda (de almohada)

★**pilot** ['paɪlət] N piloto *mf* ▸ ADJ (*scheme etc*) piloto *inv* ▸ VT pilotar; (*fig*) guiar, conducir

pilot light N piloto

pimento [pɪ'mɛntəu] N pimiento morrón

pimp [pɪmp] N chulo, cafiche *m* (*LAM*)

pimple ['pɪmpl] N grano

pimply ['pɪmplɪ] ADJ lleno de granos

PIN N ABBR (= *personal identification number*) PIN *m*

★**pin** [pɪn] N alfiler *m*; (*Elec: of plug*) clavija; (*Tech*) perno; (*: wooden*) clavija; (*drawing pin*) chincheta; (*in grenade*) percutor *m*; **pins and needles** hormigueo *sg* ▸ VT prender con (alfiler); sujetar con perno; **to ~ sth on sb** (*fig*) cargar a algn con la culpa de algo
▸ **pin down** VT (*fig*): **there's something strange here, but I can't quite ~ it down** aquí hay algo raro pero no puedo precisar qué es; **to ~ sb down** hacer que algn concrete

pinafore ['pɪnəfɔ:'] N delantal *m*

pinafore dress N (*BRIT*) pichi *m*

pinball ['pɪnbɔ:l] N (*also:* **pinball machine**) millón *m*, flipper *m*

pincers ['pɪnsəz] NPL pinzas *fpl*, tenazas *fpl*

pinch [pɪntʃ] N pellizco; (*of salt etc*) pizca; **at a ~** en caso de apuro; **to feel the ~** (*fig*) pasar apuros or estrecheces ▸ VT pellizcar; (*inf: steal*) birlar ▸ VI (*shoe*) apretar

pinched [pɪntʃt] ADJ (*drawn*) cansado; **~ with cold** transido de frío; **~ for money/space** mal or falto de dinero/espacio or sitio

pincushion ['pɪnkuʃən] N acerico

pine [paɪn] N (*also:* **pine tree**) pino ▸ VI: **to ~ for** suspirar por
▸ **pine away** VI morirse de pena

★**pineapple** ['paɪnæpl] N piña, ananá(s) *m* (*LAm*)

pine cone N piña

pine needle N aguja de pino

ping [pɪŋ] N (*noise*) sonido agudo

Ping-Pong® ['pɪŋpɔŋ] N ping-pong *m*

★**pink** [pɪŋk] ADJ (de color) rosa *inv* ▸ N (*colour*) rosa *m*; (*Bot*) clavel *m*

pinking shears ['pɪŋkɪŋ-] NPL tijeras *fpl* dentadas

pin money N dinero para gastos extra

pinnacle ['pɪnəkl] N cumbre *f*

pinpoint ['pɪnpɔɪnt] VT precisar

pinstripe ['pɪnstraɪp] ADJ: **~ suit** traje *m* a rayas

pint [paɪnt] N pinta (*Brit* = 0,57 l, *US* = 0,47 l); (*BRIT inf: of beer*) pinta de cerveza, ≈ jarra (*SP*)

pin-up ['pɪnʌp] N (*picture*) fotografía de mujer u hombre medio desnudos; **~ (girl)** ≈ chica de calendario

pioneer [paɪə'nɪə'] N pionero(-a) ▸ VT promover

pious ['paɪəs] ADJ piadoso, devoto

pip [pɪp] N (*seed*) pepita; **the pips** (*Brit Tel*) la señal

★**pipe** [paɪp] N tubería, cañería; (*for smoking*) pipa, cachimba (*Lam*), cachimbo (*Lam*); **(bag)pipes** *npl* gaita *sg* ▶ VT conducir en cañerías
▶ **pipe down** VI (*inf*) callarse

pipe cleaner N limpiapipas *m inv*

piped music [paɪpt-] N música ambiental

pipe dream N sueño imposible

pipeline [ˈpaɪplaɪn] N tubería, cañería; (*for oil*) oleoducto; (*for natural gas*) gasoducto; **it is in the ~** (*fig*) está en trámite

piper [ˈpaɪpəʳ] N (*gen*) flautista *mf*; (*with bagpipes*) gaitero(-a)

pipe tobacco N tabaco de pipa

piping [ˈpaɪpɪŋ] ADV: **to be ~ hot** estar calentito

piquant [ˈpiːkənt] ADJ picante

pique [piːk] N pique *m*, resentimiento

pirate [ˈpaɪərət] N pirata *mf* ▶ VT (*record, video, book*) hacer una copia pirata de, piratear

pirated [ˈpaɪərətɪd] ADJ (*book, record etc*) pirata *inv*

pirate radio N (*Brit*) emisora pirata

pirouette [pɪruˈɛt] N pirueta ▶ VI piruetear

Pisces [ˈpaɪsiːz] N Piscis *m*

piss [pɪs] VI (*inf*) mear

pissed [pɪst] ADJ (*inf!: drunk*) mamado, pedo

pistol [ˈpɪstl] N pistola

piston [ˈpɪstən] N pistón *m*, émbolo

pit [pɪt] N hoyo; (*also:* **coal pit**) mina; (*in garage*) foso de inspección; (*also:* **orchestra pit**) foso de la orquesta; (*quarry*) cantera ▶ VT (*chickenpox*) picar; (*rust*) comer; **to ~ A against B** oponer A a B; **to ~ one's wits against sb** medir fuerzas con algn; **pitted with** (*chickenpox*) picado de ■ **pits** NPL (*Aut*) box *msg*

pitapat [ˈpɪtəˈpæt] ADV: **to go ~** (*heart*) latir rápidamente; (*rain*) golpetear

★**pitch** [pɪtʃ] N (*throw*) lanzamiento; (*Mus*) tono; (*Brit Sport*) campo, terreno; (*tar*) brea; (*in market etc*) puesto; (*fig: degree*) nivel *m*, grado; **I can't keep working at this ~** no puedo seguir trabajando a este ritmo; **at its (highest) ~** en su punto máximo; **his anger reached such a ~ that ...** su ira *or* cólera llegó a tal extremo que ... ▶ VT (*throw*) arrojar, lanzar; **to ~ a tent** montar una tienda (de campaña); **to ~ one's aspirations too high** tener ambiciones desmesuradas ▶ VI (*fall*) caer(se); (*Naut*) cabecear

pitch-black [ˈpɪtʃˈblæk] ADJ negro como boca de lobo

pitched battle [pɪtʃt-] N batalla campal

pitcher [ˈpɪtʃəʳ] N cántaro, jarro

pitchfork [ˈpɪtʃfɔːk] N horca

piteous [ˈpɪtiəs] ADJ lastimoso

pitfall [ˈpɪtfɔːl] N riesgo

pith [pɪθ] N (*of orange*) piel *f* blanca; (*fig*) meollo

pithead [ˈpɪthɛd] N (*Brit*) bocamina

pithy [ˈpɪθɪ] ADJ jugoso

pitiful [ˈpɪtɪful] ADJ (*touching*) lastimoso, conmovedor(a); (*contemptible*) lamentable

pitifully [ˈpɪtɪfəlɪ] ADV: **it's ~ obvious** es tan evidente que da pena

pitiless [ˈpɪtɪlɪs] ADJ despiadado, implacable

pitilessly [ˈpɪtɪlɪslɪ] ADV despiadadamente, implacablemente

pittance [ˈpɪtns] N miseria

pity [ˈpɪtɪ] N (*compassion*) compasión *f*, piedad *f*; (*shame*) lástima; **to have** *or* **take ~ on sb** compadecerse de algn; **what a ~!** ¡qué pena!; **it is a ~ that you can't come** ¡qué pena que no puedas venir! ▶ VT compadecer(se de)

pitying [ˈpɪtɪɪŋ] ADJ compasivo, de lástima

pivot [ˈpɪvət] N eje *m* ▶ VI: **to ~ on** girar sobre; (*fig*) depender de

pixel [ˈpɪksl] N (*Comput*) píxel *m*

pixie [ˈpɪksɪ] N duendecillo

★**pizza** [ˈpiːtsə] N pizza

placard [ˈplækɑːd] N (*in march etc*) pancarta

placate [pləˈkeɪt] VT apaciguar

★**place** [pleɪs] N lugar *m*, sitio; (*rank*) rango; (*seat*) plaza, asiento; (*post*) puesto; (*in street names*) plaza; (*home*): **at/to his ~** en/a su casa; **to take ~** tener lugar; **out of ~** (*not suitable*) fuera de lugar; **in the first ~** (*first of all*) en primer lugar; **to change places with sb** cambiarse de sitio con algn; **~ of birth** lugar *m* de nacimiento; **from ~ to ~** de un sitio a *or* para otro; **all over the ~** por todas partes; **he's going places** (*fig: inf*) llegará lejos; **I feel rather out of ~ here** me encuentro algo desplazado; **to put sb in his ~** (*fig*) poner a algn en su lugar; **it is not my ~ to do it** no me incumbe a mí hacerlo ▶ VT (*object*) poner, colocar; (*identify*) reconocer; (*find a post for*) dar un puesto a, colocar; (*goods*) vender; **to be placed** (*in race, exam*) colocarse; **to ~ an order with sb (for)** hacer un pedido a algn (de); **we are better placed than a month ago** estamos en mejor posición que hace un mes

placebo [pləˈsiːbəu] N placebo

place mat N (*wooden etc*) salvamanteles *m inv*; (*in linen etc*) mantel *m* individual

placement [ˈpleɪsmənt] N colocación *f*; (*at work*) emplazamiento

place name N topónimo

placid [ˈplæsɪd] ADJ apacible, plácido

placidity [plæˈsɪdɪtɪ] N placidez *f*

plagiarism [ˈpleɪdʒjərɪzm] N plagio

plagiarist [ˈpleɪdʒjərɪst] N plagiario(-a)

plagiarize [ˈpleɪdʒjəraɪz] VT plagiar

plague [pleɪg] N plaga; (*Med*) peste *f* ▶ VT (*fig*) acosar, atormentar; **to ~ sb with questions** acribillar a algn a preguntas

plaice [pleɪs] N *pl inv* platija

plaid [plæd] N (*material*) tela de cuadros

★**plain** [pleɪn] ADJ (*clear*) claro, evidente; (*simple*) sencillo; (*frank*) franco, abierto; (*not handsome*) poco atractivo; (*pure*) natural, puro; **in ~ clothes** (*police*) vestido de paisano; **to make sth ~ to sb** dejar algo en claro a algn ▶ ADV claramente ▶ N llano, llanura

plain chocolate N chocolate *m* oscuro *or* amargo

plainly [ˈpleɪnlɪ] ADV claramente, evidentemente; (*frankly*) francamente

plainness [ˈpleɪnnɪs] N (*clarity*) claridad *f*; (*simplicity*) sencillez *f*; (*of face*) falta de atractivo

plain speaking N: **there has been some ~** se ha hablado claro

plaintiff [ˈpleɪntɪf] N demandante *mf*

plaintive [ˈpleɪntɪv] ADJ (*cry, voice*) lastimero, quejumbroso; (*look*) que da lástima

plait [plæt] N trenza ▶ VT trenzar

★**plan** [plæn] N (*drawing*) plano; (*scheme*) plan *m*, proyecto; **have you any plans for today?** ¿piensas hacer algo hoy? ▶ VT (*think*) pensar; (*prepare*) proyectar, planear; (*intend*) pensar, tener la intención de; **to ~ to do** pensar hacer; **how long do you ~ to stay?** ¿cuánto tiempo piensas quedarte? ▶ VI hacer proyectos; **to ~ for** planear, proyectar
▶ **plan out** VT planear detalladamente

★**plane** [pleɪn] N (*Aviat*) avión *m*; (*tree*) plátano; (*tool*) cepillo; (*Math*) plano

★**planet** [ˈplænɪt] N planeta *m*

planetarium [plænɪˈtɛərɪəm] N planetario

planetary [ˈplænɪtərɪ] ADJ planetario

plank [plæŋk] N tabla

plankton [ˈplæŋktən] N plancton *m*

planned economy [plænd-] N economía planificada

planner [ˈplænəʳ] N planificador(-a) *m/f*; (*chart*) diagrama *m* de planificación; **town ~** urbanista *mf*

★**planning** [ˈplænɪŋ] N (*Pol, Econ*) planificación *f*; **family ~** planificación familiar

planning committee N (*in local government*) comité *m* de planificación

planning permission N licencia de obras

★**plant** [plɑːnt] N planta; (*machinery*) maquinaria; (*factory*) fábrica ▶ VT plantar; (*field*) sembrar; (*bomb*) colocar

plantain [ˈplænteɪn] N llantén *m*

plantation [plænˈteɪʃən] N plantación *f*; (*estate*) hacienda

planter [ˈplɑːntəʳ] N hacendado

plant pot N maceta, tiesto

plaque [plæk] N placa

plasma [ˈplæzmə] N plasma *m*

plasma screen N pantalla de plasma

plaster [ˈplɑːstəʳ] N (*for walls*) yeso; (*also:* **plaster of Paris**) yeso mate; (*Med: for broken leg etc*) escayola; (*BRIT: also:* **sticking plaster**) tirita, esparadrapo ▶ VT enyesar; (*cover*): **to ~ with** llenar *or* cubrir de; **to be plastered with mud** estar cubierto de barro

plasterboard [ˈplɑːstəbɔːd] N cartón *m* yeso

plaster cast N (*Med*) escayola; (*model, statue*) vaciado de yeso

plastered [ˈplɑːstəd] ADJ (*inf*) borracho

plasterer [ˈplɑːstərəʳ] N yesero

★**plastic** [ˈplæstɪk] N plástico ▶ ADJ de plástico

plastic bag N bolsa de plástico

plastic bullet N bala de goma

plastic explosive N explosivo plástico

plasticine® [ˈplæstɪsiːn] N (*BRIT*) plastilina®

plastic surgery N cirugía plástica

plastinate [ˈplæstɪneɪt] VT plastinar

★**plate** [pleɪt] N (*dish*) plato; (*metal, in book*) lámina; (*Phot*) placa; (*on door*) placa; (*Aut: also:* **number plate**) matrícula; (*dental plate*) placa de dentadura postiza

plateau (*pl* **plateaus** *or* **plateaux** [ˈplætəuz]) N meseta, altiplanicie *f*

plateful [ˈpleɪtful] N plato

plate glass N vidrio *or* cristal *m* cilindrado

platen [ˈplætən] N (*on typewriter, printer*) rodillo

plate rack N escurreplatos *m inv*

★**platform** [ˈplætfɔːm] N (*Rail*) andén *m*; (*stage*) plataforma; (*at meeting*) tribuna; (*Pol*) programa *m* (electoral); **the train leaves from ~ seven** el tren sale del andén número siete

platform ticket N (*BRIT*) billete *m* de andén

platinum [ˈplætɪnəm] N platino

platitude [ˈplætɪtjuːd] N tópico, lugar *m* común

platonic [pləˈtɒnɪk] ADJ platónico

platoon [pləˈtuːn] N pelotón *m*

platter [ˈplætəʳ] N fuente *f*

plaudits [ˈplɔːdɪts] NPL aplausos *mpl*

plausibility [plɔːzɪˈbɪlɪtɪ] N verosimilitud *f*, credibilidad *f*

plausible [ˈplɔːzɪbl] ADJ verosímil; (*person*) convincente

★**play** [pleɪ] N (*gen*) juego; (*Theat*) obra; **to bring** *or* **call into ~** poner en juego ▶ VT (*game*) jugar; (*football, tennis, cards*) jugar a; (*compete against*) jugar contra; (*instrument*) tocar; (*Theat: part*) hacer el papel de; representar; (*fig*) desempeñar; **to ~ a trick on sb** gastar una broma a algn ▶ VI jugar; (*band*) tocar; (*tape, record*) sonar; (*frolic*) juguetear; **to ~ safe** ir a lo seguro; **to ~ into sb's hands** (*fig*) hacerle el juego a algn; **they're playing at soldiers** están jugando a (los) soldados; **to ~ for time** (*fig*) tratar de ganar tiempo; **a smile played on his lips** una sonrisa le bailaba en los labios
▶ **play about, play around** VI (*person*) hacer el tonto; **to ~ about** *or* **around with** (*fiddle with*) juguetear con; (*idea*) darle vueltas a
▶ **play along** VI: **to ~ along with** seguirle el juego a ▶ VT: **to ~ sb along** (*fig*) jugar con algn
▶ **play back** VT (*tape*) poner
▶ **play down** VT quitar importancia a
▶ **play on** VT FUS (*sb's feelings, credulity*) aprovecharse de; **to ~ on sb's nerves** atacarle los nervios a algn
▶ **play up** VI (*cause trouble*) dar guerra

playact ['pleɪækt] VI (*fig*) hacer comedia *or* teatro

play-acting ['pleɪæktɪŋ] N teatro

playboy ['pleɪbɔɪ] N playboy *m*

★**player** ['pleɪə^r] N jugador(a) *m/f*; (*Theat*) actor *m*, actriz *f*; (*Mus*) músico(-a)

playful ['pleɪful] ADJ juguetón(-ona)

★**playground** ['pleɪgraund] N (*in school*) patio de recreo; (*in park*) parque *m* infantil

playgroup ['pleɪgru:p] N jardín *m* de infancia

playing card ['pleɪɪŋ-] N naipe *m*, carta

playing field N campo de deportes

playmaker ['pleɪmeɪkə^r] N (*Sport*) creador(a) *m/f* de juego

playmate ['pleɪmeɪt] N compañero(-a) de juego

play-off ['pleɪɔf] N (*Sport*) (partido de) desempate *m*

playpen ['pleɪpɛn] N corral *m*

playroom ['pleɪru:m] N cuarto de juego

playschool ['pleɪsku:l] N = **playgroup**

plaything ['pleɪθɪŋ] N juguete *m*

★**playtime** ['pleɪtaɪm] N (*Scol*) (hora de) recreo

playwright ['pleɪraɪt] N dramaturgo(-a)

plc ABBR (*Brit*: = *public limited company*) S.A.

plea [pli:] N (*request*) súplica, petición *f*; (*excuse*) pretexto, disculpa; (*Law*) alegato, defensa

plea bargaining N (*Law*) *acuerdo entre fiscal y defensor para agilizar los trámites judiciales*

plead [pli:d] VT (*give as excuse*) poner como pretexto; (*Law*): **to ~ sb's case** defender a algn ▶ VI (*Law*) declararse; (*beg*): **to ~ with sb** suplicar *or* rogar a algn; **to ~ guilty/not guilty** (*defendant*) declararse culpable/inocente; **to ~ for sth** (*beg for*) suplicar algo

★**pleasant** ['plɛznt] ADJ agradable

pleasantly ['plɛzntlɪ] ADV agradablemente

pleasantries ['plɛzntrɪz] NPL (*polite remarks*) cortesías *fpl*; **to exchange ~** conversar amablemente

★**please** [pli:z] EXCL ¡por favor!; **~ don't cry!** ¡no llores! te lo ruego ▶ VT (*give pleasure to*) dar gusto a, agradar; **to ~ o.s.** hacer lo que le parezca; **~ yourself!** ¡haz lo que quieras!, ¡como quieras! ▶ VI (*think fit*): **do as you ~** haz lo que quieras *or* lo que te dé la gana

★**pleased** [pli:zd] ADJ (*happy*) alegre, contento; (*satisfied*): **~ (with)** satisfecho (de); **~ to meet you** ¡encantado!, ¡tanto *or* mucho gusto!; **to be ~ (about sth)** alegrarse (de algo); **we are ~ to inform you that ...** tenemos el gusto de comunicarle que ...

pleasing ['pli:zɪŋ] ADJ agradable, grato

pleasurable ['plɛʒərəbl] ADJ agradable, grato

pleasurably ['plɛʒərəblɪ] ADV agradablemente, gratamente

★**pleasure** ['plɛʒə^r] N placer *m*, gusto; (*will*) voluntad *f*; **"it's a ~"** "el gusto es mío"; **it's a ~ to see him** da gusto verle; **I have much ~ in informing you that ...** tengo el gran placer de comunicarles que ...; **with ~** con mucho *or* todo gusto; **is this trip for business or ~?** ¿este viaje es de negocios o de placer? ▶ CPD de recreo

pleasure cruise N crucero de placer

pleasure ground N parque *m* de atracciones

pleasure-seeking ['plɛʒəsi:kɪŋ] ADJ hedonista

pleat [pli:t] N pliegue *m*

pleb [plɛb] N: **the plebs** la gente baja, la plebe

plebeian [plɪ'bi:ən] N plebeyo(-a) ▶ ADJ plebeyo; (*pej*) ordinario

plebiscite ['plɛbɪsɪt] N plebiscito

plectrum ['plɛktrəm] N plectro

pledge [plɛdʒ] N (*object*) prenda; (*promise*) promesa, voto ▶ VT (*pawn*) empeñar; (*promise*) prometer; **to ~ support for sb** prometer su apoyo a algn; **to ~ sb to secrecy** hacer jurar a algn que guardará el secreto

plenary ['pli:nərɪ] ADJ: **in ~ session** en sesión plenaria

plentiful ['plɛntɪful] ADJ copioso, abundante

★**plenty** ['plɛntɪ] N abundancia; **~ of** mucho(s) (-a(s)); **we've got ~ of time to get there** tenemos tiempo de sobra para llegar

plethora ['plɛθərə] N plétora

pleurisy ['pluərɪsɪ] N pleuresía

pliability [plaɪə'bɪlɪtɪ] N flexibilidad *f*

pliable ['plaɪəbl] ADJ flexible

pliers ['plaɪəz] NPL alicates *mpl*, tenazas *fpl*

plight [plaɪt] N condición *f* or situación *f* difícil

plimsolls ['plɪmsɔlz] NPL (*Brit*) zapatillas *fpl* de tenis

plinth [plɪnθ] N plinto

PLO N ABBR (= *Palestine Liberation Organization*) OLP *f*

plod [plɔd] VI caminar con paso pesado; (*fig*) trabajar laboriosamente

plodder ['plɔdə^r] N *trabajador(a) diligente pero lento/a*

plodding ['plɔdɪŋ] ADJ (*student*) empollón(-ona); (*worker*) más aplicado que brillante

plonk [plɔŋk] (*inf*) N (*Brit*: *wine*) vino peleón ▶ VT: **to ~ sth down** dejar caer algo

★**plot** [plɔt] N (*scheme*) complot *m*, conjura; (*of story, play*) argumento; (*of land*) terreno, parcela; **a vegetable ~** un cuadro de hortalizas ▶ VT (*mark out*) trazar; (*conspire*) tramar, urdir ▶ VI conspirar

plotter ['plɔtə^r] N (*instrument*) trazador *m* (de gráficos)

plotting ['plɔtɪŋ] N conspiración *f*, intrigas *fpl*

plough, (*US*) **plow** [plau] N arado ▶ VT (*earth*) arar

▶ **plough back** VT (*Comm*) reinvertir

▶ **plough through** VT FUS (*crowd*) abrirse paso a la fuerza por

ploughing ['plauɪŋ] N labranza

707

ploughman [ˈplaumən] N (irreg): **~'s lunch** pan m con queso y cebolla

plow [plau] N, VB (US) = **plough**

ploy [plɔɪ] N truco, estratagema

pluck [plʌk] VT (fruit) coger (SP), recoger (LAM); (musical instrument) puntear; (bird) desplumar; **to ~ one's eyebrows** depilarse las cejas ▶ N valor m, ánimo; **to ~ up courage** hacer de tripas corazón

plucky [ˈplʌkɪ] ADJ valiente

plug [plʌg] N tapón m; (Elec) enchufe m, clavija; (Aut: also: **spark(ing) plug**) bujía; **to give sb/sth a ~** dar publicidad a algn/algo ▶ VT (hole) tapar; (inf: advertise) dar publicidad a; **to ~ a lead into a socket** enchufar un hilo en una toma
▶ **plug in** VT, VI (Elec) enchufar

plughole [ˈplʌghəul] N desagüe m

plug-in [ˈplʌgɪn] N (Comput) plug-in m

plum [plʌm] N (fruit) ciruela; (inf: also: **plum job**) chollo

plumage [ˈpluːmɪdʒ] N plumaje m

plumb [plʌm] ADJ vertical ▶ N plomo ▶ ADV (exactly) exactamente, en punto ▶ VT sondar; (fig) sondear
▶ **plumb in** VT (washing machine) conectar

plumber [ˈplʌmər] N fontanero(-a), plomero(-a) (LAM)

plumbing [ˈplʌmɪŋ] N (trade) fontanería, plomería (LAM); (piping) cañerías fpl

plume [pluːm] N (gen) pluma; (on helmet) penacho

plummet [ˈplʌmɪt] VI: **to ~ (down)** caer a plomo

plump [plʌmp] ADJ rechoncho, rollizo ▶ VT: **to ~ sth (down) on** dejar caer algo en
▶ **plump for** VT FUS (inf: choose) optar por
▶ **plump up** VT ahuecar

plumpness [ˈplʌmpnɪs] N gordura

plunder [ˈplʌndər] N pillaje m; (loot) botín m ▶ VT saquear, pillar

plunge [plʌndʒ] N zambullida; **to take the ~** lanzarse ▶ VT sumergir, hundir; **to ~ a room into darkness** sumir una habitación en la oscuridad ▶ VI (fall) caer; (dive) saltar; (person) arrojarse; (sink) hundirse

plunger [ˈplʌndʒər] N émbolo; (for drain) desatascador m

plunging [ˈplʌndʒɪŋ] ADJ (neckline) escotado

pluperfect [pluːˈpəːfɪkt] N pluscuamperfecto

plural [ˈpluərl] ADJ plural ▶ N plural m

★**plus** [plʌs] N (also: **plus sign**) signo más; (fig) punto a favor ▶ ADJ: **a ~ factor** (fig) un factor m a favor; **ten/twenty ~** más de diez/veinte ▶ PREP más, y, además de

plush [plʌʃ] ADJ de felpa

plus-one [ˈplʌsˈwʌn] N (inf) acompañante mf

plutonium [pluːˈtəunɪəm] N plutonio

ply [plaɪ] VT (a trade) ejercer; **to ~ sb with drink** no dejar de ofrecer copas a algn ▶ VI (ship) ir y venir; (for hire) ofrecerse (para alquilar) ▶ ADJ: **three ~** (wool) de tres cabos

plywood [ˈplaɪwud] N madera contrachapada

PM N ABBR (BRIT) = **Prime Minister**

p.m. ADV ABBR (= post meridiem) de la tarde or noche

PMS N ABBR (= premenstrual syndrome) SPM m

PMT N ABBR (= premenstrual tension) SPM m

pneumatic [njuːˈmætɪk] ADJ neumático

pneumatic drill N taladradora neumática

pneumonia [njuːˈməunɪə] N pulmonía, neumonía

PO N ABBR (= Post Office) Correos mpl; (Naut) = **petty officer**

po ABBR = **postal order**

POA N ABBR (BRIT) = **Prison Officers' Association**

poach [pəutʃ] VT (cook) escalfar; (steal) cazar/pescar en vedado ▶ VI cazar/pescar en vedado

poached [pəutʃt] ADJ (egg) escalfado

poacher [ˈpəutʃər] N cazador(a) m/f furtivo(-a)

poaching [ˈpəutʃɪŋ] N caza/pesca furtiva

PO Box N ABBR (= Post Office Box) apdo., aptdo.

★**pocket** [ˈpɔkɪt] N bolsillo; (of air, Geo, fig) bolsa; (Billiards) tronera; **breast ~** bolsillo de pecho; **~ of resistance** foco de resistencia; **~ of warm air** bolsa de aire caliente; **to be out of ~** salir perdiendo; **to be £5 in/out of ~** salir ganando/perdiendo 5 libras ▶ VT meter en el bolsillo; (steal) embolsarse; (Billiards) entronerar

pocketbook [ˈpɔkɪtbuk] N (US: wallet) cartera; (: handbag) bolso

pocketful [ˈpɔkɪtful] N bolsillo lleno

pocket knife N navaja

★**pocket money** N asignación f

pockmarked [ˈpɔkmɑːkt] ADJ (face) picado de viruelas

pod [pɔd] N vaina

podcast [ˈpɔdkɑːst] N podcast m ▶ VI podcastear

podcasting [ˈpɔdkɑːstɪŋ] N podcasting m

podgy [ˈpɔdʒɪ] ADJ gordinflón(-ona)

podiatrist [pɔˈdiːətrɪst] N (US) podólogo(-a)

podiatry [pɔˈdiːətrɪ] N (US) podología

podium [ˈpəudɪəm] N podio

POE N ABBR = **port of embarkation; port of entry**

★**poem** [ˈpəuɪm] N poema m

★**poet** [ˈpəuɪt] N poeta mf

poetic [pəuˈɛtɪk] ADJ poético

poet laureate [-ˈlɔːrɪɪt] N poeta(-isa) m/f laureado(-a)

El poeta (o la poetisa) de la corte, denominado **poet laureate**, ocupa como tal un puesto vitalicio al servicio de la Casa Real británica. Era tradición que escribiera poemas conmemorativos para ocasiones oficiales, aunque hoy día esto es poco frecuente. El primer poeta así distinguido fue John Dryden en 1668, aunque ya en 1616 Ben Jonson tuvo un papel parecido.

★**poetry** [ˈpəʊɪtrɪ] N poesía

poignant [ˈpɔɪnjənt] ADJ conmovedor(a)

poignantly [ˈpɔɪnjəntlɪ] ADV de modo conmovedor

★**point** [pɔɪnt] N punto; (*tip*) punta; (*purpose*) fin m, propósito; (BRIT Elec: also: **power point**) toma de corriente, enchufe m; (*use*) utilidad f; (*significant part*) lo esencial; (*place*) punto, lugar m; (*also:* **decimal point**): **2 ~ 3 (2.3)** dos coma tres (2,3); **to be on the ~ of doing sth** estar a punto de hacer algo; **to make a ~ of doing sth** poner empeño en hacer algo; **to get the ~** comprender; **to come to the ~** ir al meollo; **there's no ~ (in doing)** no tiene sentido (hacer); **~ of departure** (*also fig*) punto de partida; **~ of order** cuestión f de procedimiento; **~ of sale** (*Comm*) punto de venta; **point-of-sale advertising** publicidad f en el punto de venta; **the train stops at Carlisle and all points south** el tren para en Carlisle, y en todas las estaciones al sur; **when it comes to the ~** a la hora de la verdad; **in ~ of fact** en realidad; **that's the whole ~!** ¡de eso se trata!; **to be beside the ~** no venir al caso; **you've got a ~ there!** ¡tienes razón! ▶ VT (*gun etc*): **to ~ sth at sb** apuntar con algo a algn ▶ VI: **to ~ at** señalar ■ **points** NPL (*Aut*) contactos mpl; (*Rail*) agujas fpl

▶ **point out** VT señalar

▶ **point to** VT FUS indicar con el dedo; (*fig*) indicar, señalar

> Don't confuse **el punto**, which refers to a specific detail or something that someone says or believes, with **la punta**, which is the end or tip of something.

point-blank [ˈpɔɪntˈblæŋk] ADV (*say, refuse*) sin más hablar; (*also:* **at point-blank range**) a quemarropa

point duty N (BRIT) control m de circulación

pointed [ˈpɔɪntɪd] ADJ (*shape*) puntiagudo, afilado; (*remark*) intencionado

pointedly [ˈpɔɪntɪdlɪ] ADV intencionadamente

pointer [ˈpɔɪntəʳ] N (*stick*) puntero; (*needle*) aguja, indicador m; (*clue*) indicación f, pista; (*advice*) consejo

pointless [ˈpɔɪntlɪs] ADJ sin sentido

pointlessly [ˈpɔɪntlɪslɪ] ADV inútilmente, sin motivo

point of view N punto de vista

poise [pɔɪz] N (*of head, body*) porte m; (*calmness*) aplomo

poised [pɔɪzd] ADJ (*in temperament*) sereno

poison [ˈpɔɪzn] N veneno ▶ VT envenenar

poisoning [ˈpɔɪznɪŋ] N envenenamiento

poisonous [ˈpɔɪznəs] ADJ venenoso; (*fumes etc*) tóxico; (*fig: ideas, literature*) pernicioso; (: *rumours, individual*) nefasto

poke [pəʊk] VT (*fire*) hurgar, atizar; (*jab with finger, stick etc*) empujar; (*Comput*) almacenar; (*put*): **to ~ sth in(to)** introducir algo en; **to**

~ one's head out of the window asomar la cabeza por la ventana; **to ~ fun at sb** ridiculizar a algn ▶ N (*jab*) empujoncito; (*with elbow*) codazo; **to give the fire a ~** atizar el fuego

▶ **poke about** VI fisgonear

▶ **poke out** VI (*stick out*) salir

poker [ˈpəʊkəʳ] N atizador m; (*Cards*) póker m

poker-faced [ˈpəʊkəˈfeɪst] ADJ con cara de póker

poky [ˈpəʊkɪ] ADJ estrecho

★**Poland** [ˈpəʊlənd] N Polonia

polar [ˈpəʊləʳ] ADJ polar

polar bear N oso polar

polarization [pəʊləraɪˈzeɪʃən] N polarización f

polarize [ˈpəʊləraɪz] VT polarizar

Pole [pəʊl] N polaco(-a)

pole [pəʊl] N palo; (*Geo*) polo; (*Tel*) poste m; (*flagpole*) asta; (*tent pole*) mástil m

poleaxe [ˈpəʊlæks] VT (*fig*) desnucar

pole bean N (*US*) judía trepadora

polecat [ˈpəʊlkæt] N (*BRIT*) turón m; (*US*) mofeta

Pol. Econ. [ˈpɔlɪkɔn] N ABBR = **political economy**

polemic [pɔˈlɛmɪk] N polémica

polemicist [pɔˈlɛmɪsɪst] N polemista mf

pole star N estrella polar

pole vault N salto con pértiga

★**police** [pəˈliːs] N policía ▶ VT (*streets, city, frontier*) vigilar

police car N coche-patrulla m

police constable N (BRIT) guardia mf, policía mf

police department N (US) policía

police force N cuerpo de policía

★**policeman** [pəˈliːsmən] N (*irreg*) guardia m, policía m, agente m (LAM)

police officer N guardia mf, policía mf

police record N: **to have a ~** tener antecedentes penales

police state N estado policial

police station N comisaría

★**policewoman** [pəˈliːswʊmən] N (*irreg*) (*mujer f*) policía

policy [ˈpɔlɪsɪ] N política; (*also:* **insurance policy**) póliza; (*of newspaper, company*) política; **it is our ~ to do that** tenemos por norma hacer eso; **to take out a ~** sacar una póliza, hacerse un seguro

policy holder N asegurado(-a)

policy-making [ˈpɔlɪsɪmeɪkɪŋ] N elaboración f de directrices generales

policy-making body N *organismo encargado de elaborar las directrices generales*

polio [ˈpəʊlɪəʊ] N polio f

★**Polish** [ˈpəʊlɪʃ] ADJ polaco ▶ N (*Ling*) polaco

★**polish** [ˈpɔlɪʃ] N (*for shoes*) betún m; (*for floor*) cera (de lustrar); (*for nails*) esmalte m; (*shine*) brillo,

lustre *m*; (*fig: refinement*) refinamiento ▶ VT (*shoes*) limpiar; (*make shiny*) pulir, sacar brillo a; (*fig: improve*) perfeccionar, refinar
▶ **polish off** VT (*work*) terminar; (*food*) despachar
▶ **polish up** VT (*shoes, furniture etc*) limpiar, sacar brillo a; (*fig: language*) perfeccionar

polished [ˈpɔlɪʃt] ADJ (*fig: person*) refinado

★**polite** [pəˈlaɪt] ADJ cortés, atento; (*formal*) correcto; **it's not ~ to do that** es de mala educación hacer eso

politely [pəˈlaɪtlɪ] ADV cortésmente

politeness [pəˈlaɪtnɪs] N cortesía

politic [ˈpɔlɪtɪk] ADJ prudente

★**political** [pəˈlɪtɪkl] ADJ político

political asylum N asilo político

politically [pəˈlɪtɪkəlɪ] ADV políticamente

politically correct ADJ políticamente correcto

★**politician** [pɔlɪˈtɪʃən] N político(-a)

★**politics** [ˈpɔlɪtɪks] N política

polka [ˈpɔlkə] N polca

polka dot N lunar *m*

poll [pəul] N (*votes*) votación *f*, votos *mpl*; (*also:* **opinion poll**) sondeo, encuesta; **to go to the polls** (*voters*) votar; (*government*) acudir a las urnas
▶ VT (*votes*) obtener; (*in opinion poll*) encuestar

pollen [ˈpɔlən] N polen *m*

pollen count N índice *m* de polen

pollination [pɔlɪˈneɪʃən] N polinización *f*

polling [ˈpəulɪŋ] N (*Pol*) votación *f*; (*Tel*) interrogación *f*

polling booth N cabina de votar

polling day N día *m* de elecciones

polling station N centro electoral

pollster [ˈpəulstər] N (*person*) encuestador(a) *m/f*; (*organization*) empresa de encuestas *or* sondeos

poll tax N (*BRIT: formerly*) contribución *f* municipal (*no progresiva*)

pollutant [pəˈluːtənt] N (agente *m*) contaminante *m*

pollute [pəˈluːt] VT contaminar

★**pollution** [pəˈluːʃən] N contaminación *f*

polo [ˈpəuləu] N (*sport*) polo

polo-neck [ˈpəuləunɛk] ADJ de cuello vuelto
▶ N (*sweater*) suéter *m* de cuello vuelto

polo shirt N polo, niqui *m*

poly [ˈpɔlɪ] N ABBR (*BRIT*) = **polytechnic**

poly... [ˈpɔlɪ] PREF poli...

poly bag N (*BRIT inf*) bolsa de plástico

polyester [pɔlɪˈɛstər] N poliéster *m*

polyethylene [pɔlɪˈɛθiliːn] N (*US*) polietileno

polygamy [pəˈlɪɡəmɪ] N poligamia

polygraph [ˈpɔlɪɡrɑːf] N polígrafo

Polynesia [pɔlɪˈniːzɪə] N Polinesia

Polynesian [pɔlɪˈniːzɪən] ADJ, N polinesio(-a) *m/f*

polyp [ˈpɔlɪp] N (*Med*) pólipo

polystyrene [pɔlɪˈstaɪriːn] N poliestireno

polytechnic [pɔlɪˈtɛknɪk] N escuela politécnica

polythene [ˈpɔlɪθiːn] N (*BRIT*) polietileno

polythene bag N (*BRIT*) bolsa de plástico

polyurethane [pɔlɪˈjuərɪθeɪn] N poliuretano

pomegranate [ˈpɔmɪɡrænɪt] N granada

pommel [ˈpɔml] N pomo ▶ VT = **pummel**

pomp [pɔmp] N pompa

pompom [ˈpɔmpɔm] N borla

pompous [ˈpɔmpəs] ADJ pomposo; (*person*) presumido

pond [pɔnd] N (*natural*) charca; (*artificial*) estanque *m*

ponder [ˈpɔndər] VT, VI meditar

ponderous [ˈpɔndərəs] ADJ pesado

pong [pɔŋ] (*BRIT inf*) N peste *f* ▶ VI apestar

pontiff [ˈpɔntɪf] N pontífice *m*

pontificate [pɔnˈtɪfɪkeɪt] VI (*fig*): **to ~ (about)** pontificar (sobre)

pontoon [pɔnˈtuːn] N pontón *m*; (*BRIT: card game*) veintiuna

pony [ˈpəunɪ] N poney *m*, potro

ponytail [ˈpəunɪteɪl] N coleta, cola de caballo

pony trekking N (*BRIT*) excursión *f* a caballo

poodle [ˈpuːdl] N caniche *m*

★**pool** [puːl] N (*natural*) charca; (*pond*) estanque *m*; (*also:* **swimming pool**) piscina, alberca (*LAm*); (*billiards*) billar *m* americano; (*Comm: consortium*) consorcio; (*US: monopoly trust*) trust *m*; **typing ~** servicio de mecanografía; **(football) pools** *npl* quinielas *fpl* ▶ VT juntar

★**poor** [puər] ADJ pobre; (*bad*) malo ▶ NPL: **the ~** los pobres

> You generally put **pobre** after the noun when you mean *poor* in the sense of 'not rich' and before the noun in the sense of 'unfortunate':
> *It's a poor area.* **Es una región pobre.**
> *The poor boy was trembling.* **El pobre chico temblaba.**

poorly [ˈpuəlɪ] ADJ mal, enfermo ▶ ADV mal

★**pop** [pɔp] N ¡pum!; (*sound*) ruido seco; (*Mus*) (música) pop *m*; (*US inf: father*) papá *m*; (*inf: drink*) gaseosa ▶ VT (*burst*) hacer reventar; **she popped her head out (of the window)** sacó de repente la cabeza (por la ventana) ▶ VI reventar; (*cork*) saltar
▶ **pop in** VI entrar un momento
▶ **pop out** VI salir un momento
▶ **pop up** VI aparecer inesperadamente

pop concert N concierto pop

popcorn [ˈpɔpkɔːn] N palomitas *fpl* (de maíz)

pope [pəup] N papa *m*

poplar [ˈpɔplər] N álamo

poplin [ˈpɔplɪn] N popelina

popper [ˈpɒpəʳ] N corchete m, botón m automático

poppy [ˈpɒpɪ] N amapola; *see also* **Remembrance Day**

poppycock [ˈpɒpɪkɒk] N (*inf*) tonterías *fpl*

Popsicle® [ˈpɒpsɪkl] N (*US*) polo

pop star N estrella del pop

populace [ˈpɒpjuləs] N pueblo

★**popular** [ˈpɒpjuləʳ] ADJ popular; **a ~ song** una canción popular; **to be ~ (with)** (*person*) caer bien (a); (*decision*) ser popular (entre)

popularity [pɒpjuˈlærɪtɪ] N popularidad *f*

popularize [ˈpɒpjuləraɪz] VT popularizar; (*disseminate*) vulgarizar

populate [ˈpɒpjuleɪt] VT poblar

★**population** [pɒpjuˈleɪʃən] N población *f*

population explosion N explosión *f* demográfica

populous [ˈpɒpjuləs] ADJ populoso

pop-up [ˈpɒpʌp] ADJ desplegable, pop-up *inv* ▶ N desplegable *m*

pop-up book N libro desplegable

pop-up menu N (*Comput*) menú *m* desplegable

porcelain [ˈpɔːslɪn] N porcelana

porch [pɔːtʃ] N pórtico, entrada; (*US*) veranda

porcupine [ˈpɔːkjupaɪn] N puerco m espín

pore [pɔːʳ] N poro ▶ VI: **to ~ over** enfrascarse en

pork [pɔːk] N (carne *f* de) cerdo *or* (*LAm*) chancho

pork chop N chuleta de cerdo

pork pie N (*Brit Culin*) empanada de carne de cerdo

porn [pɔːn] ADJ (*inf*) porno *inv* ▶ N porno

pornographic [pɔːnəˈgræfɪk] ADJ pornográfico

pornography [pɔːˈnɒgrəfɪ] N pornografía

porous [ˈpɔːrəs] ADJ poroso

porpoise [ˈpɔːpəs] N marsopa

porridge [ˈpɒrɪdʒ] N gachas *fpl* de avena

★**port** [pɔːt] N (*harbour*) puerto; (*Naut: left side*) babor *m*; (*wine*) oporto; (*Comput*) puerta, puerto, port *m*; **~ of call** puerto de escala

portable [ˈpɔːtəbl] ADJ portátil

portal [ˈpɔːtl] N puerta (grande), portalón *m*

port authorities NPL autoridades *fpl* portuarias

portcullis [pɔːtˈkʌlɪs] N rastrillo

portend [pɔːˈtɛnd] VT presagiar, anunciar

portent [ˈpɔːtɛnt] N presagio, augurio

porter [ˈpɔːtəʳ] N (*for luggage*) maletero; (*doorkeeper*) portero(-a), conserje *mf*; (*US Rail*) mozo de los coches-cama

portfolio [pɔːtˈfəuliəu] N (*case, of artist*) cartera, carpeta; (*Pol, Finance*) cartera

porthole [ˈpɔːthəul] N portilla

portico [ˈpɔːtɪkəu] N pórtico

portion [ˈpɔːʃən] N porción *f*; (*helping*) ración *f*

portly [ˈpɔːtlɪ] ADJ corpulento

portrait [ˈpɔːtreɪt] N retrato

portray [pɔːˈtreɪ] VT retratar; (*in writing*) representar

portrayal [pɔːˈtreɪəl] N representación *f*

★**Portugal** [ˈpɔːtjugl] N Portugal *m*

★**Portuguese** [pɔːtjuˈgiːz] ADJ portugués(-esa) ▶ N *pl inv* portugués(-esa) *m/f*; (*Ling*) portugués *m*

Portuguese man-of-war [-mænəuˈwɔːʳ] N (*jellyfish*) especie de medusa

pose [pəuz] N postura, actitud *f*; (*pej*) afectación *f*, pose *f*; **to strike a ~** tomar *or* adoptar una pose *or* actitud ▶ VI posar; (*pretend*): **to ~ as** hacerse pasar por; **to ~ for** posar para ▶ VT (*question*) plantear

poser [ˈpəuzəʳ] N problema *m*/pregunta difícil; (*person*) = **poseur**

poseur [pəuˈzəːʳ] N (*inf*) presumido(-a), persona afectada

posh [pɒʃ] ADJ (*inf*) elegante, de lujo ▶ ADV (*inf*): **to talk ~** hablar con acento afectado

★**position** [pəˈzɪʃən] N posición *f*; (*job*) puesto; **to be in a ~ to do sth** estar en condiciones de hacer algo ▶ VT colocar

★**positive** [ˈpɒzɪtɪv] ADJ positivo; (*certain*) seguro; (*definite*) definitivo; **we look forward to a ~ reply** (*Comm*) esperamos que pueda darnos una respuesta en firme; **he's a ~ nuisance** es un auténtico pelmazo; **~ cash flow** (*Comm*) flujo positivo de efectivo

positively [ˈpɒzɪtɪvlɪ] ADV (*affirmatively, enthusiastically*) de forma positiva; (*inf: really*) absolutamente

posse [ˈpɒsɪ] N (*US*) pelotón *m*

possess [pəˈzɛs] VT poseer; **like one possessed** como un poseído; **whatever can have possessed you?** ¿cómo se te ocurrió?

possessed [pəˈzɛst] ADJ poseso, poseído

possession [pəˈzɛʃən] N posesión *f*; **to take ~ of sth** tomar posesión de algo ■ **possessions** NPL (*belongings*) pertenencias *fpl*

possessive [pəˈzɛsɪv] ADJ posesivo

possessiveness [pəˈzɛsɪvnɪs] N posesividad *f*

possessor [pəˈzɛsəʳ] N poseedor(a) *m/f*, dueño(-a)

★**possibility** [pɒsɪˈbɪlɪtɪ] N posibilidad *f*; **he's a ~ for the part** es uno de los posibles para el papel

★**possible** [ˈpɒsɪbl] ADJ posible; **as big as ~** lo más grande posible; **it is ~ to do it** es posible hacerlo; **as far as ~** en la medida de lo posible; **a ~ candidate** un(a) posible candidato(-a)

★**possibly** [ˈpɒsɪblɪ] ADV (*perhaps*) posiblemente, tal vez; **I cannot ~ come** me es imposible venir; **could you ~ ...?** ¿podrías ...?

★**post** [pəust] N (*Brit: system*) correos *mpl*; (*: letters, delivery*) correo; (*job, situation*) puesto; (*trading post*) factoría; (*pole*) poste *m*; (*on blog, social network*) post *m*; **by ~** por correo; **by return of ~** a vuelta de correo ▶ VT (*Brit: send by post*) mandar por correo; (*: put in mailbox*) echar al correo; (*on*

711

blog, social network) publicar; (Mil) apostar; (bills) fijar, pegar; (Brit: appoint): **to ~ to** destinar a; **to keep sb posted** tener a algn al corriente

post... [pəust] PREF post..., pos...; **post 1950** pos(t) 1950

postage ['pəustɪdʒ] N porte m, franqueo

postage stamp N sello (de correo)

postal ['pəustl] ADJ postal, de correos

postal order N giro postal

postbag ['pəustbæg] N (Brit) correspondencia, cartas fpl

postbox ['pəustbɔks] N (Brit) buzón m

★**postcard** ['pəustkɑ:d] N (tarjeta) postal f

postcode ['pəustkəud] N (Brit) código postal

postdate [pəust'deɪt] VT (cheque) poner fecha adelantada a

★**poster** ['pəustə^r] N cartel m, afiche m (LAm)

poste restante [pəust'rɛstɔ̃nt] N (Brit) lista de correos

posterior [pɔs'tɪərɪə^r] N (inf) trasero

posterity [pɔs'tɛrɪtɪ] N posteridad f

poster paint N pintura al agua

post-free [pəust'fri:] ADJ (con) porte pagado

postgraduate ['pəust'grædjuɪt] N posgraduado(-a)

posthumous ['pɔstjuməs] ADJ póstumo

posthumously ['pɔstjuməslɪ] ADV póstumamente, con carácter póstumo

posting ['pəustɪŋ] N destino

★**postman** ['pəustmən] N (irreg) (Brit) cartero

postmark ['pəustmɑ:k] N matasellos m inv

postmaster ['pəustmɑ:stə^r] N administrador m de correos

postmistress ['pəustmɪstrɪs] N administradora de correos

post-mortem [pəust'mɔ:təm] N autopsia

postnatal ['pəust'neɪtl] ADJ postnatal, posparto

★**post office** N (building) (oficina de) correos m; (organization): **the Post Office** Dirección f General de Correos

Post Office Box N apartado postal, casilla de correos (LAm)

post-paid ['pəust'peɪd] ADJ, ADV porte pagado

postpone [pəs'pəun] VT aplazar, postergar (LAm)

postponement [pəs'pəunmənt] N aplazamiento

postscript ['pəustskrɪpt] N posdata

postulate ['pɔstjuleɪt] VT postular

posture ['pɔstʃə^r] N postura, actitud f

post-war [pəust'wɔ:^r] ADJ de la posguerra

★**postwoman** ['pəustwumən] N (irreg) (Brit) cartera

posy ['pəuzɪ] N ramillete m (de flores)

★**pot** [pɔt] N (for cooking) olla; (teapot) tetera; (coffeepot) cafetera; (for flowers) maceta; (for jam) tarro,

pote m (LAm); (piece of pottery) cacharro; (inf: marijuana) costo, chocolate m; **pots of** (inf) montones de; **to go to ~** (inf: work, performance) irse al traste ▶ VT (plant) poner en tiesto; (conserve) conservar (en tarros)

potash ['pɔtæʃ] N potasa

potassium [pə'tæsɪəm] N potasio

★**potato** [pə'teɪtəu] (pl **potatoes**) N patata, papa (LAm)

potato crisps, (US) **potato chips** NPL patatas fpl fritas, papas fpl fritas (LAm)

potato peeler N pelapatatas m inv

potbellied ['pɔtbelɪd] ADJ (from overeating) barrigón(-ona); (from malnutrition) con el vientre hinchado

potency ['pəutnsɪ] N potencia

potent ['pəutnt] ADJ potente, poderoso; (drink) fuerte

potentate ['pəutnteɪt] N potentado

★**potential** [pə'tenʃl] ADJ potencial, posible ▶ N potencial m; **to have ~** prometer

potentially [pə'tenʃəlɪ] ADV en potencia

pothole ['pɔthəul] N (in road) bache m; (Brit: underground) gruta

potholer ['pɔthəulə^r] N (Brit) espeleólogo(-a)

potholing ['pɔthəulɪŋ] N (Brit): **to go ~** dedicarse a la espeleología

potion ['pəuʃən] N poción f, pócima

potluck [pɔt'lʌk] N: **to take ~** conformarse con lo que haya

pot plant N planta de interior

pot roast N carne f asada

potshot ['pɔtʃɔt] N: **to take a ~ at sth** tirar a algo sin apuntar

potted ['pɔtɪd] ADJ (food) en conserva; (plant) en tiesto or maceta; (fig: shortened) resumido

potter ['pɔtə^r] N alfarero(-a); **~'s wheel** torno de alfarero ▶ VI: **to ~ around, ~ about** entretenerse haciendo cosillas; **to ~ round the house** estar en casa haciendo cosillas

pottery ['pɔtərɪ] N cerámica; (factory) alfarería; **a piece of ~** un objeto de cerámica

potty ['pɔtɪ] ADJ (inf: mad) chiflado ▶ N orinal m de niño

potty-trained ['pɔtɪtreɪnd] ADJ que ya no necesita pañales

pouch [pautʃ] N (Zool) bolsa; (for tobacco) petaca

pouf, pouffe [pu:f] N (stool) puf m

poultry ['pəultrɪ] N aves fpl de corral; (meat) pollo

poultry farm N granja avícola

poultry farmer N avicultor(-a) m/f

pounce [pauns] VI: **to ~ on** precipitarse sobre ▶ N salto, ataque m

★**pound** [paund] N libra; (for dogs) perrera; (for cars) depósito; **half a ~** media libra; **a five ~ note** un billete de cinco libras ▶ VT (beat) golpear; (crush) machacar ▶ VI (beat) dar golpes

pounding ['paundɪŋ] N: **to take a ~** (team) recibir una paliza

pound sterling N libra esterlina

★**pour** [pɔːʳ] VT echar; (tea) servir; **to ~ sb a drink** servirle a algn una copa ▶ VI correr, fluir; (rain) llover a cántaros
▶ **pour away, pour off** VT vaciar, verter
▶ **pour in** VI (people) entrar en tropel; **to come pouring in** (water) entrar a raudales; (letters) llegar a montones; (cars, people) llegar en tropel
▶ **pour out** VI (people) salir en tropel ▶ VT (drink) echar, servir; (fig): **to ~ out one's feelings** desahogarse

pouring ['pɔːrɪŋ] ADJ: **~ rain** lluvia torrencial

pout [paut] VI hacer pucheros

★**poverty** ['pɔvətɪ] N pobreza, miseria; (fig) falta, escasez f

poverty line N: **below the ~** por debajo del umbral de pobreza

poverty-stricken ['pɔvətɪstrɪkn] ADJ necesitado

poverty trap N trampa de la pobreza

POW N ABBR = **prisoner of war**

powder ['paudəʳ] N polvo; (also: **face powder**) polvos mpl; (also: **gun powder**) pólvora ▶ VT empolvar; **to ~ one's face** empolvarse la cara; **to ~ one's nose** empolvarse la nariz, ponerse polvos; (euphemism) ir al baño

powder compact N polvera

powdered milk ['paudəd-] N leche f en polvo

powder keg N (fig) polvorín m

powder puff N borla (para empolvarse)

powder room N aseos mpl

powdery ['paudərɪ] ADJ polvoriento

★**power** ['pauəʳ] N poder m; (strength) fuerza; (nation) potencia; (drive) empuje m; (Tech) potencia; (Elec) energía; **to be in ~** (Pol) estar en el poder; **to do all in one's ~ to help sb** hacer todo lo posible por ayudar a algn; **the world powers** las potencias mundiales ▶ VT impulsar

powerboat ['pauəbəut] N lancha a motor

power cut N (BRIT) apagón m

powered ['pauəd] ADJ: **~ by** impulsado por; **nuclear-powered submarine** submarino nuclear

power failure N = **power cut**

★**powerful** ['pauəful] ADJ poderoso; (engine) potente; (strong) fuerte; (play, speech) convincente

powerhouse ['pauəhaus] N (fig: person) fuerza motriz; **a ~ of ideas** una cantera de ideas

powerless ['pauəlɪs] ADJ impotente

power line N línea de conducción eléctrica

power of attorney N poder m, procuración f

power point N (BRIT) enchufe m

power station N central f eléctrica

power steering N (Aut) dirección f asistida

powwow ['pauwau] N conferencia ▶ VI conferenciar

pp ABBR (= per procurationem) p.p.; = **pages**

PPE N ABBR (BRIT Scol) = **philosophy, politics and economics**

PPS N ABBR (= post postscriptum) posdata adicional; (BRIT: = Parliamentary Private Secretary) ayudante de un ministro

PQ ABBR (CANADA) = **Province of Quebec**

PR N ABBR see **proportional representation**; (= public relations) relaciones fpl públicas ▶ ABBR (US) = **Puerto Rico**

Pr. ABBR (= prince) P

practicability [præktɪkə'bɪlɪtɪ] N factibilidad f

practicable ['præktɪkəbl] ADJ (scheme) factible

★**practical** ['præktɪkl] ADJ práctico

practicality [præktɪ'kælɪtɪ] N (of situation etc) aspecto práctico

practical joke N broma pesada

practically ['præktɪklɪ] ADV (almost) casi, prácticamente

★**practice** ['præktɪs] N (habit) costumbre f; (exercise) práctica; (training) adiestramiento; (Med: of profession) práctica, ejercicio; (Med, Law: business) consulta; **in ~** (in reality) en la práctica; **out of ~** desentrenado; **to put sth into ~** poner algo en práctica; **it's common ~** es bastante corriente; **target ~** práctica de tiro; **he has a small ~** (doctor) tiene pocos pacientes; **to set up in ~ as** establecerse como ▶ VT, VI (US) = **practise**

practise, (US) **practice** ['præktɪs] VT (carry out) practicar; (profession) ejercer; (train at) practicar ▶ VI ejercer; (train) practicar

practised, (US) **practiced** ['præktɪst] ADJ (person) experto; (performance) experto; (liar) consumado; **with a ~ eye** con ojo experto

practising, (US) **practicing** ['præktɪsɪŋ] ADJ (Christian etc) practicante; (lawyer) en ejercicio; (homosexual) activo

practitioner [præk'tɪʃənəʳ] N practicante mf; (Med) médico(-a)

pragmatic [præg'mætɪk] ADJ pragmático

pragmatism ['prægmətɪzəm] N pragmatismo

pragmatist ['prægmətɪst] N pragmatista mf

Prague [prɑːg] N Praga

prairie ['prɛərɪ] N (US) pradera

★**praise** [preɪz] N alabanza(s) f(pl), elogio(s) m(pl) ▶ VT alabar, elogiar

praiseworthy ['preɪswəːðɪ] ADJ loable

pram [præm] N (BRIT) cochecito de niño

prance [prɑːns] VI (horse) hacer cabriolas

prank [præŋk] N travesura

prat [præt] N (BRIT pej) imbécil mf

prattle ['prætl] VI parlotear; (child) balbucear

prawn [prɔːn] N gamba

prawn cocktail N cóctel m de gambas

pray [preɪ] VI rezar; **to ~ for forgiveness** pedir perdón

prayer [prɛəʳ] N oración f, rezo; (entreaty) ruego, súplica

P

prayer book N devocionario, misal *m*

pre- ['pri:] PREF pre..., ante-; **pre-1970** pre 1970

preach [pri:tʃ] VI predicar

preacher ['pri:tʃə'] N predicador(a) *m/f*; (*US: minister*) pastor(a) *m/f*

preamble [prɪ'æmbl] N preámbulo

prearrange [pri:ə'reɪndʒ] VT organizar *or* acordar de antemano

prearrangement [pri:ə'reɪndʒmənt] N: **by ~** por previo acuerdo

precarious [prɪ'kɛərɪəs] ADJ precario

precariously [prɪ'kɛərɪəslɪ] ADV precariamente

precaution [prɪ'kɔ:ʃən] N precaución *f*

precautionary [prɪ'kɔ:ʃənrɪ] ADJ (*measure*) de precaución

precede [prɪ'si:d] VT, VI preceder

precedence ['prɛsɪdəns] N precedencia; (*priority*) preferencia

precedent ['prɛsɪdənt] N precedente *m*; **to establish** *or* **set a ~** sentar un precedente

preceding [prɪ'si:dɪŋ] ADJ precedente

precept ['pri:sɛpt] N precepto

precinct ['pri:sɪŋkt] N recinto; (*US: district*) distrito, barrio; **pedestrian ~** (*BRIT*) zona peatonal; **shopping ~** (*BRIT*) zona comercial ■ **precincts** NPL recinto

precious ['prɛʃəs] ADJ precioso; (*treasured*) querido; (*stylized*) afectado; **your ~ dog** (*ironic*) tu querido perro ▶ ADV (*inf*): **~ little/few** muy poco/pocos

precipice ['prɛsɪpɪs] N precipicio

precipitate ADJ [prɪ'sɪpɪtɪt] (*hasty*) precipitado ▶ VT [prɪ'sɪpɪteɪt] precipitar

precipitation [prɪsɪpɪ'teɪʃən] N precipitación *f*

precipitous [prɪ'sɪpɪtəs] ADJ (*steep*) escarpado; (*hasty*) precipitado

précis ['preɪsi:] N resumen *m*

precise [prɪ'saɪs] ADJ preciso, exacto; (*person*) escrupuloso

★**precisely** [prɪ'saɪslɪ] ADV exactamente, precisamente

precision [prɪ'sɪʒən] N precisión *f*

preclude [prɪ'klu:d] VT excluir

precocious [prɪ'kəʊʃəs] ADJ precoz

preconceived [pri:kən'si:vd] ADJ (*idea*) preconcebido

preconception [pri:kən'sɛpʃən] N (*idea*) idea preconcebida

precondition [pri:kən'dɪʃən] N condición *f* previa

precursor [pri:'kə:sə'] N precursor(a) *m/f*

predate ['pri:'deɪt] VT (*precede*) preceder

predator ['prɛdətə'] N depredador *m*

predatory ['prɛdətərɪ] ADJ depredador(a)

predecessor ['pri:dɪsɛsə'] N antecesor(a) *m/f*

predestination [pri:dɛstɪ'neɪʃən] N predestinación *f*

predestine [pri:'dɛstɪn] VT predestinar

predetermine [pri:dɪ'tə:mɪn] VT predeterminar

predicament [prɪ'dɪkəmənt] N apuro

predicate ['prɛdɪkɪt] N predicado

predict [prɪ'dɪkt] VT predecir, pronosticar

predictable [prɪ'dɪktəbl] ADJ previsible

predictably [prɪ'dɪktəblɪ] ADV (*behave, react*) de forma previsible; **~ she didn't arrive** como era de prever, no llegó

prediction [prɪ'dɪkʃən] N pronóstico, predicción *f*

predispose [pri:dɪs'pəuz] VT predisponer

predominance [prɪ'dɒmɪnəns] N predominio

predominant [prɪ'dɒmɪnənt] ADJ predominante

predominantly [prɪ'dɒmɪnəntlɪ] ADV en su mayoría

predominate [prɪ'dɒmɪneɪt] VI predominar

pre-eminent [pri:'ɛmɪnənt] ADJ preeminente

pre-empt [pri:'ɛmt] VT (*BRIT*) adelantarse a

pre-emptive [pri:'ɛmtɪv] ADJ: **~ strike** ataque *m* preventivo

preen [pri:n] VT: **to ~ itself** (*bird*) limpiarse las plumas; **to ~ o.s.** pavonearse

prefab ['pri:fæb] N casa prefabricada

prefabricated [pri:'fæbrɪkeɪtɪd] ADJ prefabricado

preface ['prɛfəs] N prefacio

prefect ['pri:fɛkt] N (*BRIT: in school*) monitor(a) *m/f*

★**prefer** [prɪ'fə:'] VT preferir; (*Law: charges, complaint*) presentar; (: *action*) entablar; **to ~ coffee to tea** preferir el café al té

preferable ['prɛfrəbl] ADJ preferible

preferably ['prɛfrəblɪ] ADV preferentemente, más bien

preference ['prɛfrəns] N preferencia; (*priority*) prioridad *f*; **in ~ to sth** antes que algo

preference shares NPL acciones *fpl* privilegiadas

preferential [prɛfə'rɛnʃəl] ADJ preferente

prefix ['pri:fɪks] N prefijo

pregnancy ['prɛgnənsɪ] N (*of woman*) embarazo; (*of animal*) preñez *f*

pregnancy test N prueba del embarazo

★**pregnant** ['prɛgnənt] ADJ (*woman*) embarazada; (*animal*) preñada; **3 months ~** embarazada de tres meses; **~ with meaning** cargado de significado

prehistoric ['pri:hɪs'tɔrɪk] ADJ prehistórico

prehistory [pri:'hɪstərɪ] N prehistoria

prejudge [pri:'dʒʌdʒ] VT prejuzgar

prejudice ['prɛdʒudɪs] N (*bias*) prejuicio; (*harm*) perjuicio ▶ VT (*bias*) predisponer; (*harm*) perjudicar; **to ~ sb in favour of/against** (*bias*) predisponer a algn a favor de/en contra de

prejudiced ['prɛdʒudɪst] ADJ (*person*) predispuesto; (*view*) parcial, interesado; **to be ~ against sb/sth** estar predispuesto en contra de algn/algo

prelate ['prɛlət] N prelado

preliminaries [prɪ'lɪmɪnərɪz] NPL preliminares *mpl*, preparativos *mpl*

preliminary [prɪ'lɪmɪnərɪ] ADJ preliminar

prelude ['prɛlju:d] N preludio

premarital ['pri:'mærɪtl] ADJ prematrimonial, premarital

premature ['prɛmətʃuə'] ADJ (*arrival etc*) prematuro; **you are being a little ~** te has adelantado

prematurely [prɛmə'tʃuəlɪ] ADV prematuramente, antes de tiempo

premeditate [pri:'mɛdɪteɪt] VT premeditar

premeditated [pri:'mɛdɪteɪtɪd] ADJ premeditado

premeditation [pri:mɛdɪ'teɪʃən] N premeditación *f*

premenstrual [pri:'mɛnstruəl] ADJ premenstrual

premenstrual tension N (*Med*) tensión *f* premenstrual

premier ['prɛmɪə'] ADJ primero, principal ▶ N (*Pol*) primer(a) ministro(-a)

première ['prɛmɪɛə'] N estreno

Premier League N primera división

premise ['prɛmɪs] N premisa

premises ['prɛmɪsɪs] NPL local *msg*; **on the ~** en el lugar mismo; **business ~** locales *mpl* comerciales

premium ['pri:mɪəm] N premio; (*insurance*) prima; **to be at a ~** estar muy solicitado; **to sell at a ~** (*shares*) vender caro

premium bond N (BRIT) bono del estado que participa en una lotería nacional

premium deal N (*Comm*) oferta extraordinaria

premium gasoline N (US) (gasolina) súper *m*

premonition [prɛmə'nɪʃən] N presentimiento

preoccupation [pri:ɔkju'peɪʃən] N preocupación *f*

preoccupied [pri:'ɔkjupaɪd] ADJ (*worried*) preocupado; (*absorbed*) ensimismado

pre-owned [pri:'əund] ADJ usado, de segunda mano

prep [prɛp] N ABBR (*Scol*: = *preparation*) deberes *mpl*

prepaid [pri:'peɪd] ADJ porte pagado; **~ envelope** sobre *m* de porte pagado

preparation [prɛpə'reɪʃən] N preparación *f*; **in ~ for sth** en preparación para algo ▪ **preparations** NPL preparativos *mpl*

preparatory [prɪ'pærətərɪ] ADJ preparatorio, preliminar; **~ to sth/to doing sth** como preparación para algo/para hacer algo

preparatory school N (BRIT) *colegio privado de enseñanza primaria*; (US) *colegio privado de enseñanza secundaria*; *see also* **public school**

★**prepare** [prɪ'pɛə'] VT preparar, disponer; (*Culin*) preparar ▶ VI: **to ~ for** (*action*) prepararse para; (*event*) hacer preparativos para

★**prepared** [prɪ'pɛəd] ADJ (*willing*): **to be ~ to help sb** estar dispuesto a ayudar a algn; **~ for** listo para

preponderance [prɪ'pɔndərns] N preponderancia, predominio

preposition [prɛpə'zɪʃən] N preposición *f*

prepossessing [pri:pə'zɛsɪŋ] ADJ agradable, atractivo

preposterous [prɪ'pɔstərəs] ADJ absurdo, ridículo

prep school [prɛp-] N = **preparatory school**

prerecorded ['pri:rɪ'kɔ:dɪd] ADJ: **~ broadcast** programa *m* grabado de antemano

prerequisite [pri:'rɛkwɪzɪt] N requisito previo

prerogative [prɪ'rɔgətɪv] N prerrogativa

Presbyterian [prɛzbɪ'tɪərɪən] ADJ, N presbiteriano(-a) *m/f*

presbytery ['prɛzbɪtərɪ] N casa parroquial

preschool ['pri:'sku:l] ADJ (*child, age*) preescolar

prescribe [prɪ'skraɪb] VT prescribir; (*Med*) recetar; **prescribed books** (BRIT *Scol*) libros *mpl* del curso

prescription [prɪ'skrɪpʃən] N (*Med*) receta; **to make up a ~**, (US) **fill a ~** preparar una receta; **only available on ~** se vende solamente con receta (médica)

prescription charges NPL (BRIT) precio *sg* de las recetas

prescriptive [prɪ'skrɪptɪv] ADJ normativo

presence ['prɛzns] N presencia; (*attendance*) asistencia; **in sb's ~** en presencia de algn; **~ of mind** aplomo

★**present** ADJ ['prɛznt] (*in attendance*) presente; (*current*) actual; **to be ~ at** asistir a, estar presente en; **those ~** los presentes ▶ N ['prɛznt] (*gift*) regalo; (*actuality*): **the ~** la actualidad, el presente; **to give sb a ~, make sb a ~ of sth** regalar algo a algn; **at ~** actualmente ▶ VT [prɪ'zɛnt] (*introduce*) presentar; (*expound*) exponer; (*give*) presentar, dar, ofrecer; (*Theat*) representar; **may I ~ Miss Clark** permítame presentarle *or* le presento a la Srta Clark; **to ~ o.s. for an interview** presentarse a una entrevista

presentable [prɪ'zɛntəbl] ADJ: **to make o.s. ~** arreglarse

presentation [prɛzn'teɪʃən] N presentación *f*; (*gift*) obsequio; (*of case*) exposición *f*; (*Theat*) representación *f*; **on ~ of the voucher** al presentar el vale

present-day ['prɛzntdeɪ] ADJ actual

presenter [prɪ'zɛntə'] N (*Radio, TV*) locutor(a) *m/f*

presently ['prɛzntlɪ] ADV (*soon*) dentro de poco; (US: *now*) ahora

present participle N participio (de) presente

present tense N (tiempo) presente m

preservation [prezə'veɪʃən] N conservación f

preservative [prɪ'zə:vətɪv] N conservante m

preserve [prɪ'zə:v] VT (keep safe) preservar, proteger; (maintain) mantener; (food) conservar; (in salt) salar ▸ N (for game) coto, vedado; (often pl: jam) confitura

preshrunk [pri:'ʃrʌŋk] ADJ inencogible

preside [prɪ'zaɪd] VI presidir

presidency ['prezɪdənsɪ] N presidencia

★**president** ['prezɪdənt] N presidente(-a) m/f; (US: of company) director(a) m/f

presidential [prezɪ'denʃl] ADJ presidencial

★**press** [pres] N (tool, machine, newspapers) prensa; (printer's) imprenta; (of hand) apretón m; **to go to ~** (newspaper) entrar en prensa; **to be in the ~** (being printed) estar en prensa; (in the newspapers) aparecer en la prensa ▸ VT (push) empujar; (: button) apretar; (grapes) pisar; (iron: clothes) planchar; (pressure) presionar; (doorbell) apretar, pulsar, tocar; (insist): **to ~ sth on sb** insistir en que algn acepte algo; **we are pressed for time** tenemos poco tiempo; **to ~ sb to do** or **into doing sth** (urge, entreat) presionar a algn para que haga algo; **to ~ sb for an answer** insistir a algn para que conteste; **to ~ charges against sb** (Law) demandar a algn ▸ VI (squeeze) apretar; (pressurize) ejercer presión
  ▸ **press ahead** VI seguir adelante
  ▸ **press on** VI avanzar; (hurry) apretar el paso

press agency N agencia de prensa

press clipping N = **press cutting**

press conference N rueda de prensa

press cutting N recorte m (de periódico)

pressing ['presɪŋ] ADJ apremiante

pressman ['presmæn] N (irreg) periodista m

press officer N jefe(-a) m/f de prensa

press release N comunicado de prensa

press stud N (BRIT) botón m de presión

press-up ['presʌp] N (BRIT) flexión f

★**pressure** ['preʃəʳ] N presión f; (urgency) apremio, urgencia; (influence) influencia; **high/low ~** alta/baja presión; **to put ~ on sb** presionar a algn, hacer presión sobre algn

pressure cooker N olla a presión

pressure gauge N manómetro

pressure group N grupo de presión

pressurize ['preʃəraɪz] VT presurizar; **to ~ sb (into doing sth)** presionar a algn (para que haga algo)

pressurized ['preʃəraɪzd] ADJ (container) a presión

prestige [pres'ti:ʒ] N prestigio

prestigious [pres'tɪdʒəs] ADJ prestigioso

★**presumably** [prɪ'zju:məblɪ] ADV es de suponer que, cabe presumir que; **~ he did it** es de suponer que lo hizo él

presume [prɪ'zju:m] VT: **to ~ (that)** presumir (que), suponer (que); **to ~ to do** (dare) atreverse a hacer

presumption [prɪ'zʌmpʃən] N suposición f; (pretension) presunción f

presumptuous [prɪ'zʌmptjuəs] ADJ presumido

presuppose [pri:sə'pəuz] VT presuponer

presupposition [pri:sʌpə'zɪʃən] N presuposición f

pre-tax [pri:'tæks] ADJ anterior al impuesto

pretence, (US) **pretense** [prɪ'tens] N (claim) pretensión f; (pretext) pretexto; (make-believe) fingimiento; **on** or **under the ~ of doing sth** bajo or con el pretexto de hacer algo; **she is devoid of all ~** no es pretenciosa; **under false pretences** con engaños

★**pretend** [prɪ'tend] VT (feign) fingir ▸ VI (feign) fingir; (claim): **to ~ to sth** pretender a algo

pretense [prɪ'tens] N (US) = **pretence**

pretension [prɪ'tenʃən] N (claim) pretensión f; **to have no pretensions to sth/to being sth** no engañarse en cuanto a algo/a ser algo

pretentious [prɪ'tenʃəs] ADJ pretencioso; (ostentatious) ostentoso, aparatoso

pretext ['pri:tekst] N pretexto; **on** or **under the ~ of doing sth** con el pretexto de hacer algo

prettily ['prɪtɪlɪ] ADV encantadoramente, con gracia

★**pretty** ['prɪtɪ] ADJ (gen) bonito, lindo (LAM) ▸ ADV bastante

prevail [prɪ'veɪl] VI (gain mastery) prevalecer; (be current) predominar; (persuade): **to ~ (up)on sb to do sth** persuadir a algn para que haga algo

prevailing [prɪ'veɪlɪŋ] ADJ (dominant) predominante

prevalent ['prevələnt] ADJ (dominant) dominante; (widespread) extendido; (fashionable) de moda

prevarication [prɪværɪ'keɪʃən] N evasivas fpl

★**prevent** [prɪ'vent] VT: **to ~ (sb) from doing sth** impedir (a algn) hacer algo; **to ~ sth from happening** evitar que ocurra algo

preventable [prɪ'ventəbl] ADJ evitable

preventative [prɪ'ventətɪv] ADJ preventivo

prevention [prɪ'venʃən] N prevención f

preventive [prɪ'ventɪv] ADJ preventivo

preview ['pri:vju:] N (of film) preestreno

★**previous** ['pri:vɪəs] ADJ previo, anterior; **he has no ~ experience in that field** no tiene experiencia previa en ese campo; **I have a ~ engagement** tengo un compromiso anterior

previously ['pri:vɪəslɪ] ADV antes

prewar [pri:'wɔ:ʳ] ADJ antes de la guerra

prey [preɪ] N presa ▸ VI: **to ~ on** vivir a costa de; (feed on) alimentarse de; **it was preying on his mind** le obsesionaba

★**price** [praɪs] N precio; (Betting: odds) puntos mpl de ventaja; **to go up** or **rise in ~** subir de precio; **what is the ~ of ...?** ¿qué precio tiene ...?; **to put a ~ on sth** poner precio a algo; **what ~ his promises now?** ¿para qué sirven ahora sus promesas?; **he regained his freedom, but at a ~**

recobró su libertad, pero le había costado caro
▶ VT (*goods*) fijar el precio de; **to be priced out of the market** (*article*) no encontrar comprador por ese precio; (*nation*) no ser competitivo

price control N control m de precios

price-cutting ['praɪskʌtɪŋ] N reducción f de precios

priceless ['praɪslɪs] ADJ que no tiene precio; (*inf: amusing*) divertidísimo

price list N tarifa

price range N gama de precios; **it's within my ~** está al alcance de mi bolsillo

price tag N etiqueta

price war N guerra de precios

pricey ['praɪsɪ] ADJ (BRIT *inf*) caro

prick [prɪk] N pinchazo; (*with pin*) alfilerazo; (*sting*) picadura ▶ VT pinchar; (*hurt*) picar; **to ~ up one's ears** aguzar el oído

prickle ['prɪkl] N (*sensation*) picor m; (*Bot*) espina; (*Zool*) púa

prickly ['prɪklɪ] ADJ espinoso; (*fig: person*) enojadizo

prickly heat N sarpullido causado por exceso de calor

prickly pear N higo chumbo

★**pride** [praɪd] N orgullo; (*pej*) soberbia; **to take (a) ~ in** enorgullecerse de; **her ~ and joy** su orgullo; **to have ~ of place** tener prioridad ▶ VT: **to ~ o.s. on** enorgullecerse de

★**priest** [priːst] N sacerdote m

★**priestess** ['priːstɪs] N sacerdotisa

priesthood ['priːsthud] N (*practice*) sacerdocio; (*priests*) clero

prig [prɪg] N gazmoño(-a)

prim [prɪm] ADJ (*demure*) remilgado; (*prudish*) gazmoño

primacy ['praɪməsɪ] N primacía

prima donna ['priːmə'dɔnə] N primadonna, diva

prima facie ['praɪmə'feɪʃɪ] ADJ: **to have a ~ case** (*Law*) tener razón a primera vista

primal ['praɪməl] ADJ original; (*important*) principal

primarily ['praɪmərɪlɪ] ADV (*above all*) ante todo, primordialmente

primary ['praɪmərɪ] ADJ primario; (*first in importance*) principal ▶ N (US: *also:* **primary election**) (elección f) primaria

primary colour, (US) **primary color** N color m primario

primary education N enseñanza primaria

primary school N (BRIT) escuela primaria

En el Reino Unido la escuela a la que van los niños entre cinco y once años se llama **primary school**, a menudo dividida en *infant school* (entre cinco y siete años de edad) y *junior school* (entre siete y once).

primate N ['praɪmɪt] (*Rel*) primado ▶ N ['praɪmeɪt] (*Zool*) primate m

prime [praɪm] ADJ primero, principal; (*basic*) fundamental; (*excellent*) selecto, de primera clase; **~ example** ejemplo típico ▶ N: **in the ~ of life** en la flor de la vida ▶ VT (*gun, pump*) cebar; (*wood, also fig*) preparar

Prime Minister N primer(a) ministro(-a); *see also* **Downing Street**

primer ['praɪmə*] N (*book*) texto elemental; (*paint*) capa preparatoria

prime time N (*Radio, TV*) horas fpl de mayor audiencia

primeval [praɪ'miːvəl] ADJ primitivo

primitive ['prɪmɪtɪv] ADJ primitivo; (*crude*) rudimentario; (*uncivilized*) inculto

primly ['prɪmlɪ] ADV remilgadamente; con gazmoñería

primrose ['prɪmrəuz] N primavera, prímula

primus® ['praɪməs], **primus stove** N (BRIT) hornillo de camping

★**prince** [prɪns] N príncipe m

prince charming N príncipe m azul

★**princess** [prɪn'ses] N princesa

★**principal** ['prɪnsɪpl] ADJ principal ▶ N director(a) m/f; (*in play*) protagonista mf principal; (*Comm*) capital m, principal m; *see also* **pantomime**

principality [prɪnsɪ'pælɪtɪ] N principado

principally ['prɪnsɪplɪ] ADV principalmente

principle ['prɪnsɪpl] N principio; **in ~** en principio; **on ~** por principio

★**print** [prɪnt] N (*impression*) marca, impresión f; (*footprint*) huella; (*fingerprint*) huella dactilar; (*letters*) letra de molde; (*fabric*) estampado; (*Art*) grabado; (*Phot*) impresión f; **out of ~** agotado ▶ VT (*gen*) imprimir; (*on mind*) grabar; (*write in capitals*) escribir en letras de molde
▶ **print out** VT (*Comput*) imprimir

printed circuit ['prɪntɪd-] N circuito impreso

printed circuit board N tarjeta de circuito impreso

printed matter N impresos mpl

printer ['prɪntə*] N (*person*) impresor(a) m/f; (*machine*) impresora

printhead ['prɪnthɛd] N cabeza impresora

printing ['prɪntɪŋ] N (*art*) imprenta; (*act*) impresión f; (*quantity*) tirada

printing press N prensa

printout ['prɪntaut] N (*Comput*) copia impresa

print wheel N rueda impresora

prior ['praɪə*] ADJ anterior, previo; (*more important*) más importante; **~ to doing** antes de or hasta hacer; **without ~ notice** sin previo aviso; **to have a ~ claim to sth** tener prioridad en algo ▶ N prior m

prioress [praɪə'res] N priora

★**priority** [praɪ'ɔrɪtɪ] N prioridad f; **to have** or **take ~ over sth** tener prioridad sobre algo

priory ['praɪərɪ] N priorato

prise, (US) **prize** [praɪz] VT: **to ~ open** abrir con palanca

prism ['prɪzəm] N prisma m

★**prison** ['prɪzn] N cárcel f, prisión f ▶ CPD carcelario

prison camp N campo de prisioneros

★**prisoner** ['prɪznəʳ] N (in prison) preso(-a); (captured person) prisionero(-a); (under arrest) detenido(-a); (in dock) acusado(-a); **the ~ at the bar** el acusado(-a); **to take sb ~** hacer or tomar prisionero a algn

prisoner of war N prisionero(-a) or preso(-a) de guerra

prissy ['prɪsɪ] ADJ remilgado

pristine ['prɪstiːn] ADJ prístino

privacy ['prɪvəsɪ] N (seclusion) soledad f; (intimacy) intimidad f; **in the strictest ~** con el mayor secreto

★**private** ['praɪvɪt] ADJ (personal) particular; (confidential) secreto, confidencial; (property, industry, discussion etc) privado; (person) reservado; (place) tranquilo; (sitting etc) a puerta cerrada; "**~**" (on envelope) "confidencial"; (on door) "privado"; **in (his) ~ life** en su vida privada; **to be in ~ practice** tener consulta particular ▶ N soldado raso; **in ~** en privado

private enterprise N la empresa privada

private eye N detective mf privado(-a)

private hearing N (Law) vista a puerta cerrada

private limited company N (BRIT) sociedad f de responsabilidad limitada

privately ['praɪvɪtlɪ] ADV en privado; (in o.s.) en secreto

private parts NPL partes fpl pudendas

private property N propiedad f privada

private school N colegio privado

privation [praɪ'veɪʃən] N (state) privación f; (hardship) privaciones fpl, estrecheces fpl

★**privatize** ['praɪvɪtaɪz] VT privatizar

privet ['prɪvɪt] N alheña

privilege ['prɪvɪlɪdʒ] N privilegio; (prerogative) prerrogativa

privileged ['prɪvɪlɪdʒd] ADJ privilegiado; **to be ~ to do sth** gozar del privilegio de hacer algo

privy ['prɪvɪ] ADJ: **to be ~ to** estar enterado de

Privy Council N consejo privado (de la Corona)

El consejo de asesores de la Corona conocido como **Privy Council** tuvo su origen en la época de los normandos, y fue adquiriendo mayor importancia hasta ser substituido en 1688 por el actual Consejo de Ministros (*Cabinet*). Hoy día sigue existiendo con un carácter fundamentalmente honorífico y los ministros del gobierno y otras personalidades políticas, eclesiásticas y jurídicas adquieren el rango de *Privy Councillors* de manera automática.

★**prize** [praɪz] N premio ▶ ADJ (first class) de primera clase ▶ VT apreciar, estimar; (US) = **prise**

prize fighter N boxeador m profesional

prize fighting N boxeo m profesional

prize-giving ['praɪzgɪvɪŋ] N distribución f de premios

prize money N (Sport) bolsa

prizewinner ['praɪzwɪnəʳ] N premiado(-a)

prizewinning ['praɪzwɪnɪŋ] ADJ (novel, essay) premiado

PRO N ABBR = **public relations officer**

pro [prəu] N (Sport) profesional mf; **the pros and cons** los pros y los contras

pro- [prəu] PREF (in favour of) pro, en pro de; **pro-Soviet** pro-soviético

proactive [prəu'æktɪv] ADJ: **to be ~** impulsar la actividad

probability [prɔbə'bɪlɪtɪ] N probabilidad f; **in all ~** lo más probable

probable ['prɔbəbl] ADJ probable; **it is ~/hardly ~ that** es probable/poco probable que

★**probably** ['prɔbəblɪ] ADV probablemente

probate ['prəubeɪt] N (Law) legalización f de un testamento

probation [prə'beɪʃən] N: **on ~** (employee) a prueba; (Law) en libertad condicional

probationary [prə'beɪʃnrɪ] ADJ: **~ period** período de prueba

probationer [prə'beɪʃənəʳ] N (Law) persona en libertad condicional; (nurse) ≈ enfermero(-a) en prácticas

probation officer N persona a cargo de los presos en libertad condicional

probe [prəub] N (Med, Space) sonda; (enquiry) investigación f ▶ VT sondar; (investigate) investigar

probity ['prəubɪtɪ] N probidad f

★**problem** ['prɔbləm] N problema m; **what's the ~?** ¿cuál es el problema?, ¿qué pasa?; **no ~!** ¡por supuesto!; **to have problems with the car** tener problemas con el coche

problematic [prɔblə'mætɪk], **problematical** [prɔblə'mætɪkl] ADJ problemático

problem-solving ['prɔbləmsɒlvɪŋ] N resolución f de problemas; **~ skills** técnicas de resolución de problemas

procedural [prəu'siːdʒərəl] ADJ de procedimiento; (Law) procesal

procedure [prə'siːdʒəʳ] N procedimiento; (bureaucratic) trámites mpl; **cashing a cheque is a simple ~** cobrar un cheque es un trámite sencillo

proceed [prə'siːd] VI proceder; (continue): **to ~ (with)** continuar (con); **to ~ against sb** (Law) proceder contra algn; **I am not sure how to ~** no sé cómo proceder; *see also* **proceeds**

proceedings [prə'siːdɪŋz] NPL acto(s) m(pl); (Law) proceso sg; (meeting) función fsg; (records) actas fpl

proceeds [ˈprəʊsiːdz] NPL ganancias *fpl*, ingresos *mpl*

★**process** N [ˈprəʊsɛs] proceso; (*method*) método, sistema *m*; (*proceeding*) procedimiento; **in ~** en curso; **we are in the ~ of moving to ...** estamos en vías de mudarnos a ... ▸ VT [ˈprəʊsɛs] tratar, elaborar ▸ VI [prəˈsɛs] (BRIT formal: *go in procession*) desfilar

processed cheese [ˈprəʊsɛst-], (US) **process cheese** N queso fundido

processing [ˈprəʊsɛsɪŋ] N elaboración *f*

procession [prəˈsɛʃən] N desfile *m*; **funeral ~** cortejo fúnebre

pro-choice [prəʊˈtʃɔɪs] ADJ en favor del derecho de elegir de la madre

proclaim [prəˈkleɪm] VT proclamar; (*announce*) anunciar

proclamation [prɒkləˈmeɪʃən] N proclamación *f*; (*written*) proclama

proclivity [prəˈklɪvɪtɪ] N propensión *f*, inclinación *f*

procrastinate [prəʊˈkræstɪneɪt] VI demorarse

procrastination [prəʊkræstɪˈneɪʃən] N dilación *f*

procreation [prəʊkrɪˈeɪʃən] N procreación *f*

Procurator Fiscal [ˈprɒkjʊreɪtə-] N (SCOTTISH) fiscal *mf*

procure [prəˈkjʊə] VT conseguir, obtener

procurement [prəˈkjʊəmənt] N obtención *f*

prod [prɒd] VT (*push*) empujar; (*with elbow*) dar un codazo a ▸ N empujoncito; codazo

prodigal [ˈprɒdɪɡl] ADJ pródigo

prodigious [prəˈdɪdʒəs] ADJ prodigioso

prodigy [ˈprɒdɪdʒɪ] N prodigio

★**produce** N [ˈprɒdjuːs] (*Agr*) productos *mpl* agrícolas ▸ VT [prəˈdjuːs] producir; (*yield*) rendir; (*bring*) sacar; (*show*) presentar, mostrar; (*proof of identity*) enseñar, presentar; (*Theat*) presentar, poner en escena; (*offspring*) dar a luz

produce dealer N (US) verdulero(-a)

★**producer** [prəˈdjuːsə] N (*Theat*) director(a) *m/f*; (*Agr, Cine*) productor(a) *m/f*

★**product** [ˈprɒdʌkt] N producto

★**production** [prəˈdʌkʃən] N (*act*) producción *f*; (*Theat*) representación *f*, montaje *m*; **to put into ~** lanzar a la producción

production agreement N (US) acuerdo de productividad

production line N línea de producción

production manager N jefe(-a) *m/f* de producción

productive [prəˈdʌktɪv] ADJ productivo

productivity [prɒdʌkˈtɪvɪtɪ] N productividad *f*

productivity agreement N (BRIT) acuerdo de productividad

productivity bonus N bono de productividad

Prof. [prɒf] ABBR (= *professor*) Prof

profane [prəˈfeɪn] ADJ profano

profess [prəˈfɛs] VT profesar; **I do not ~ to be an expert** no pretendo ser experto

professed [prəˈfɛst] ADJ (*self-declared*) declarado

★**profession** [prəˈfɛʃən] N profesión *f*

★**professional** [prəˈfɛʃnl] N profesional *mf*; (*skilled person*) perito ▸ ADJ profesional; (*by profession*) de profesión; **to take ~ advice** buscar un consejo profesional

professionalism [prəˈfɛʃnəlɪzm] N profesionalismo

professionally [prəˈfɛʃnəlɪ] ADV: **I only know him ~** solo le conozco por nuestra relación de trabajo

★**professor** [prəˈfɛsə] N (BRIT) catedrático(-a); (US: *teacher*) profesor(a) *m/f*

professorship [prəˈfɛsəʃɪp] N cátedra

proffer [ˈprɒfə] VT ofrecer

proficiency [prəˈfɪʃənsɪ] N capacidad *f*, habilidad *f*

proficiency test N prueba de capacitación

proficient [prəˈfɪʃənt] ADJ experto, hábil

profile [ˈprəʊfaɪl] N perfil *m*; **to keep a high/low ~** tratar de llamar la atención/pasar inadvertido

★**profit** [ˈprɒfɪt] N (*Comm*) ganancia; (*fig*) provecho; **~ and loss account** cuenta de ganancias y pérdidas; **with profits endowment assurance** seguro dotal con beneficios; **to sell sth at a ~** vender algo con ganancia ▸ VI: **to ~ by** or **from** aprovechar or sacar provecho de

profitability [prɒfɪtəˈbɪlɪtɪ] N rentabilidad *f*

profitable [ˈprɒfɪtəbl] ADJ (*Econ*) rentable; (*beneficial*) provechoso, útil

profitably [ˈprɒfɪtəblɪ] ADV rentablemente; provechosamente

profit centre, (US) **profit center** N centro de beneficios

profiteering [prɒfɪˈtɪərɪŋ] N (*pej*) explotación *f*

profit-making [ˈprɒfɪtmeɪkɪŋ] ADJ rentable

profit margin N margen *m* de ganancia

profit-sharing [ˈprɒfɪtʃɛərɪŋ] N participación *f* de empleados en los beneficios

profits tax N impuesto sobre los beneficios

profligate [ˈprɒflɪɡɪt] ADJ (*dissolute: behaviour, act*) disoluto; (: *person*) libertino; (*extravagant*): **he's very ~ with his money** es muy derrochador

pro forma [ˈprəʊˈfɔːmə] ADJ: **~ invoice** factura pro-forma

profound [prəˈfaʊnd] ADJ profundo

profoundly [prəˈfaʊndlɪ] ADV profundamente

profusely [prəˈfjuːslɪ] ADV profusamente

profusion [prəˈfjuːʒən] N profusión *f*, abundancia

progeny [ˈprɒdʒɪnɪ] N progenie *f*

★**programme**, (US, Comput) **program** [ˈprəʊɡræm] N programa *m* ▸ VT programar

programmer, (US) **programer** [ˈprəʊɡræmə] N programador(a) *m/f*

programming, (US) **programing** [ˈprəʊgræmɪŋ] N programación f

programming language, (US) **programing language** N lenguaje m de programación

★**progress** N [ˈprəʊgrɛs] progreso; (development) desarrollo; **in ~** (meeting, work etc) en curso ▶ VI [prəˈgrɛs] progresar, avanzar; desarrollarse; **as the match progressed** a medida que avanzaba el partido

progression [prəˈgrɛʃən] N progresión f

progressive [prəˈgrɛsɪv] ADJ progresivo; (person) progresista

progressively [prəˈgrɛsɪvlɪ] ADV progresivamente, poco a poco

progress report N (Med) informe m sobre el estado del paciente; (Admin) informe m sobre la marcha del trabajo

prohibit [prəˈhɪbɪt] VT prohibir; **to ~ sb from doing sth** prohibir a algn hacer algo; **"smoking prohibited"** "prohibido fumar"

prohibition [prəʊɪˈbɪʃən] N (US) prohibicionismo

prohibitive [prəˈhɪbɪtɪv] ADJ (price etc) prohibitivo

★**project** N [ˈprɔdʒɛkt] proyecto; (Scol, Univ: research) trabajo, proyecto ▶ VT [prəˈdʒɛkt] proyectar ▶ VI [prəˈdʒɛkt] (stick out) salir, sobresalir

projectile [prəˈdʒɛktaɪl] N proyectil m

projection [prəˈdʒɛkʃən] N proyección f; (overhang) saliente m

projectionist [prəˈdʒɛkʃənɪst] N (Cine) operador(a) m/f de cine

projection room N (Cine) cabina de proyección

projector [prəˈdʒɛktəʳ] N proyector m

proletarian [prəʊlɪˈtɛərɪən] ADJ proletario

proletariat [prəʊlɪˈtɛərɪət] N proletariado

pro-life [prəʊˈlaɪf] ADJ pro-vida

proliferate [prəˈlɪfəreɪt] VI proliferar, multiplicarse

proliferation [prəlɪfəˈreɪʃən] N proliferación f

prolific [prəˈlɪfɪk] ADJ prolífico

prologue, (US) **prolog** [ˈprəʊlɔg] N prólogo

prolong [prəˈlɔŋ] VT prolongar, extender

prom [prɔm] N ABBR (BRIT) = **promenade**; **promenade concert**; (ball) baile m de gala

Los conciertos de música clásica más conocidos en Inglaterra son los llamados *Proms* (o *promenade concerts*), que tienen lugar en el *Royal Albert Hall* de Londres, aunque también se llama así a cualquier concierto de esas características. Su nombre se debe al hecho de que en un principio el público paseaba durante las actuaciones; en la actualidad parte de la gente que acude a ellos permanece de pie. En Estados Unidos se llama **prom** a un baile de gala en un colegio o universidad, otra costumbre americana cada vez más popular en el Reino Unido.

promenade [prɔməˈnɑːd] N (by sea) paseo marítimo ▶ VI (stroll) pasearse

promenade concert N concierto (en que parte del público permanece de pie)

promenade deck N cubierta de paseo

prominence [ˈprɔmɪnəns] N (fig) importancia

prominent [ˈprɔmɪnənt] ADJ (standing out) saliente; (important) eminente, importante; **he is ~ in the field of …** destaca en el campo de …

prominently [ˈprɔmɪnəntlɪ] ADV (display, set) muy a la vista; **he figured ~ in the case** desempeñó un papel destacado en el juicio

promiscuity [prɔmɪsˈkjuːɪtɪ] N promiscuidad f

promiscuous [prəˈmɪskjuəs] ADJ (sexually) promiscuo

★**promise** [ˈprɔmɪs] N promesa; **to make sb a ~** prometer algo a algn; **a young man of ~** un joven con futuro ▶ VT, VI prometer; **to ~ (sb) to do sth** prometer (a algn) hacer algo; **to ~ well** ser muy prometedor

promising [ˈprɔmɪsɪŋ] ADJ prometedor(a)

promissory note [ˈprɔmɪsərɪ-] N pagaré m

promontory [ˈprɔməntrɪ] N promontorio

★**promote** [prəˈməʊt] VT promover; (new product) dar publicidad a, lanzar; (Mil) ascender; (employee) ascender; (ideas) fomentar; **the team was promoted to the second division** (BRIT Football) el equipo ascendió a la segunda división

promoter [prəˈməʊtəʳ] N (of sporting event) promotor(a) m/f; (of company, business) patrocinador(a) m/f

★**promotion** [prəˈməʊʃən] N (gen) promoción f; (Mil, of employee) ascenso

★**prompt** [prɔmpt] ADJ pronto; **to be ~ to do sth** no tardar en hacer algo; **they're very ~** (punctual) son muy puntuales ▶ ADV: **at six o'clock ~** a las seis en punto ▶ N (Comput) aviso, guía ▶ VT (urge) mover, incitar; (when talking) instar; (Theat) apuntar; **to ~ sb to do sth** instar a algn a hacer algo

prompter [ˈprɔmptəʳ] N (Theat) apuntador(a) m/f

promptly [ˈprɔmptlɪ] ADV (punctually) puntualmente; (rapidly) rápidamente

promptness [ˈprɔmptnɪs] N puntualidad f; rapidez f

promulgate [ˈprɔməlgeɪt] VT promulgar

prone [prəʊn] ADJ (lying) postrado; **~ to** propenso a

prong [prɔŋ] N diente m, punta

pronoun [ˈprəʊnaʊn] N pronombre m

pronounce [prəˈnaʊns] VT pronunciar; (declare) declarar; **they pronounced him unfit to plead** le declararon incapaz de defenderse ▶ VI: **to ~ (up)on** pronunciarse sobre

pronounced [prəˈnaʊnst] ADJ (marked) marcado

pronouncement [prəˈnaʊnsmənt] N declaración f

pronunciation [prənʌnsɪˈeɪʃən] N pronunciación f

★**proof** [pru:f] N prueba; **70°** ~ graduación f del 70 por 100 ▶ ADJ: ~ **against** a prueba de ▶ VT (tent, anorak) impermeabilizar

proofreader [ˈpru:fri:dəʳ] N corrector(a) m/f de pruebas

prop [prɔp] N apoyo; (fig) sostén m ▶ VT (lean): **to ~ sth against** apoyar algo contra ■ **props** NPL accesorios mpl, at(t)rezzo msg
▶ **prop up** VT (roof, structure) apuntalar; (economy) respaldar

Prop. ABBR (Comm) = **proprietor**

propaganda [prɔpəˈɡændə] N propaganda

propagate [ˈprɔpəɡeɪt] VT propagar

propagation [prɔpəˈɡeɪʃən] N propagación f

propel [prəˈpɛl] VT impulsar, propulsar

propeller [prəˈpɛləʳ] N hélice f

propelling pencil [prəˈpɛlɪŋ-] N (BRIT) portaminas m inv

propensity [prəˈpɛnsɪtɪ] N propensión f

★**proper** [ˈprɔpəʳ] ADJ (suited, right) propio; (exact) justo; (apt) apropiado, conveniente; (timely) oportuno; (seemly) correcto, decente; (authentic) verdadero; (inf: real) auténtico; **to go through the ~ channels** (Admin) ir por la vía oficial

★**properly** [ˈprɔpəlɪ] ADV (adequately) correctamente; (decently) decentemente

proper noun N nombre m propio

★**property** [ˈprɔpətɪ] N propiedad f; (estate) finca; **lost ~** objetos mpl perdidos; **personal ~** bienes mpl muebles ■ **properties** NPL (Theat) accesorios mpl, at(t)rezzo msg

property developer N promotor(a) m/f de construcciones

property owner N dueño(-a) de propiedades

property tax N impuesto sobre la propiedad

prophecy [ˈprɔfɪsɪ] N profecía

prophesy [ˈprɔfɪsaɪ] VT profetizar; (fig) predecir

prophet [ˈprɔfɪt] N profeta mf

prophetic [prəˈfɛtɪk] ADJ profético

proportion [prəˈpɔːʃən] N proporción f; (share) parte f; **to be in/out of ~ to** or **with sth** estar en/no guardar proporción con algo; **to see sth in ~** (fig) ver algo en su justa medida ■ **proportions** NPL (size) dimensiones fpl

proportional [prəˈpɔːʃənl] ADJ proporcional; ~ **(to)** en proporción (con)

proportionally [prəˈpɔːʃnəlɪ] ADV proporcionalmente, en proporción

proportional representation N (Pol) representación f proporcional

proportional spacing N (on printer) espaciado proporcional

proportionate [prəˈpɔːʃənɪt] ADJ proporcionado

proportionately [prəˈpɔːʃnɪtlɪ] ADV proporcionadamente, en proporción

proportioned [prəˈpɔːʃənd] ADJ proporcionado

★**proposal** [prəˈpəuzl] N propuesta; (offer of marriage) oferta de matrimonio; (plan) proyecto; (suggestion) sugerencia

★**propose** [prəˈpəuz] VT proponer; (have in mind): **to ~ sth/to do** or **doing sth** proponer algo/proponerse hacer algo; **to ~ to do** tener intención de hacer ▶ VI declararse

proposer [prəˈpəuzəʳ] N (of motion) proponente mf

proposition [prɔpəˈzɪʃən] N propuesta, proposición f; **to make sb a ~** proponer algo a algn

propound [prəˈpaund] VT (theory) exponer

proprietary [prəˈpraɪətərɪ] ADJ (Comm): ~ **article** artículo de marca; ~ **brand** marca comercial

proprietor [prəˈpraɪətəʳ] N propietario(-a), dueño(-a)

propriety [prəˈpraɪətɪ] N decoro

propulsion [prəˈpʌlʃən] N propulsión f

pro rata [prəuˈrɑːtə] ADV a prorrata

prosaic [prəuˈzeɪɪk] ADJ prosaico

Pros. Atty. ABBR (US) = **prosecuting attorney**

proscribe [prəˈskraɪb] VT proscribir

prose [prəuz] N prosa; (Scol) traducción f inversa

prosecute [ˈprɔsɪkju:t] VT (Law) procesar; **"trespassers will be prosecuted"** "se procesará a los intrusos"

prosecution [prɔsɪˈkju:ʃən] N proceso, causa; (accusing side) acusación f

prosecutor [ˈprɔsɪkju:təʳ] N acusador(a) m/f; (also: **public prosecutor**) fiscal mf

prospect N [ˈprɔspɛkt] (chance) posibilidad f; (outlook) perspectiva; (hope) esperanza; **to be faced with the ~ of** tener que enfrentarse a la posibilidad de que; **we were faced with the ~ of leaving early** se nos planteó la posibilidad de marcharnos pronto; **there is every ~ of an early victory** hay buenas perspectivas de una pronta victoria ▶ VT [prəˈspɛkt] explorar ▶ VI [prəˈspɛkt] buscar ■ **prospects** NPL (for work etc) perspectivas fpl

prospecting [prəˈspɛktɪŋ] N prospección f

prospective [prəˈspɛktɪv] ADJ (possible) probable, eventual; (certain) futuro; (buyer) presunto; (legislation, son-in-law) futuro

prospector [prəˈspɛktəʳ] N explorador(a) m/f; **gold ~** buscador m de oro

prospectus [prəˈspɛktəs] N prospecto

prosper [ˈprɔspəʳ] VI prosperar

prosperity [prɔˈspɛrɪtɪ] N prosperidad f

prosperous [ˈprɔspərəs] ADJ próspero

prostate [ˈprɔsteɪt] N (also: **prostate gland**) próstata

prostitute [ˈprɔstɪtju:t] N prostituta; **male ~** prostituto

prostitution [prɔstɪˈtju:ʃən] N prostitución f

prostrate [ˈprɔstreɪt] ADJ postrado; (fig) abatido ▶ VT: **to ~ o.s.** postrarse

protagonist [prə'tægənɪst] N protagonista *mf*

★**protect** [prə'tɛkt] VT proteger

protection [prə'tɛkʃən] N protección *f*; **to be under sb's ~** estar amparado por algn

protectionism [prə'tɛkʃənɪzəm] N proteccionismo

protection racket N chantaje *m*

protective [prə'tɛktɪv] ADJ protector(a); **~ custody** (*Law*) detención *f* preventiva

protector [prə'tɛktə'] N protector(a) *m/f*

protégé ['prəutɛʒeɪ] N protegido(-a)

protein ['prəuti:n] N proteína

pro tem [prəu'tɛm] ADV ABBR (= *pro tempore*) provisionalmente

★**protest** N ['prəutɛst] protesta; **to do sth under ~** hacer algo bajo protesta ▶ VI [prə'tɛst]: **to ~ about** *or* **at/against** protestar de/contra ▶ VT [prə'tɛst] (*affirm*) afirmar, declarar; (*insist*): **to ~ (that)** insistir en (que)

Protestant ['prɒtɪstənt] ADJ, N protestante *mf*

protester, protestor [prə'tɛstə'] N (*in demonstration*) manifestante *mf*

protest march N manifestación *f or* marcha (de protesta)

protocol ['prəutəkɒl] N protocolo

prototype ['prəutətaɪp] N prototipo

protracted [prə'træktɪd] ADJ prolongado

protractor [prə'træktə'] N (*Geom*) transportador *m*

protrude [prə'tru:d] VI salir, sobresalir

protuberance [prə'tju:bərəns] N protuberancia

★**proud** [praud] ADJ orgulloso; (*pej*) soberbio, altanero; **to be ~ to do sth** estar orgulloso de hacer algo ▶ ADV: **to do sb ~** tratar a algn a cuerpo de rey; **to do o.s. ~** lucirse

proudly ['praudlɪ] ADV orgullosamente, con orgullo; (*pej*) con soberbia, con altanería

★**prove** [pru:v] VT probar; (*verify*) comprobar; (*show*) demostrar; **to ~ o.s.** demostrar lo que uno vale; **he was proved right in the end** al final se vio que tenía razón ▶ VI: **to ~ correct** resultar correcto

proverb ['prɒvə:b] N refrán *m*

proverbial [prə'və:bɪəl] ADJ proverbial

proverbially [prə'və:bɪəlɪ] ADV proverbialmente

★**provide** [prə'vaɪd] VT proporcionar, dar; **to ~ sb with sth** proveer a algn de algo; **to be provided with** ser provisto de
  ▶ **provide for** VT FUS (*person*) mantener a; (*problem etc*) tener en cuenta

provided [prə'vaɪdɪd] CONJ: **~ (that)** con tal de que, a condición de que

Providence ['prɒvɪdəns] N Divina Providencia

providing [prə'vaɪdɪŋ] CONJ: **~ (that)** a condición de que, con tal de que

province ['prɒvɪns] N provincia; (*fig*) esfera

provincial [prə'vɪnʃəl] ADJ provincial; (*pej*) provinciano

provision [prə'vɪʒən] N provisión *f*; (*supply*) suministro, abastecimiento; **to make ~ for** (*one's family, future*) atender las necesidades de ■ **provisions** NPL provisiones *fpl*, víveres *mpl*

provisional [prə'vɪʒənl] ADJ provisional, provisorio (*LAm*); (*temporary*) interino ▶ N: **P~** (*IRELAND Pol*) Provisional *m* (*miembro de la tendencia activista del IRA*)

provisional driving licence N (*BRIT Aut*) carnet *m* de conducir provisional; *see also* **L-plates**

proviso [prə'vaɪzəu] N condición *f*, estipulación *f*; **with the ~ that** a condición de que

Provo ['prɒvəu] N ABBR (*inf*) = **Provisional**

provocation [prɒvə'keɪʃən] N provocación *f*

provocative [prə'vɒkətɪv] ADJ provocativo

provoke [prə'vəuk] VT (*arouse*) provocar, incitar; (*cause*) causar, producir; (*anger*) enojar; **to ~ sb to sth/to do** *or* **into doing sth** provocar a algn a algo/a hacer algo

provoking [prə'vəukɪŋ] ADJ provocador(a)

provost ['prɒvəst] N (*BRIT: of university*) rector(a) *m/f*; (*SCOTTISH*) alcalde(-esa) *m/f*

prow [prau] N proa

prowess ['prauɪs] N (*skill*) destreza, habilidad *f*; (*courage*) valor *m*; **his ~ as a footballer** (*skill*) su habilidad como futbolista

prowl [praul] VI (*also*: **prowl about, prowl around**) merodear ▶ N: **on the ~** de merodeo, merodeando

prowler ['praulə'] N merodeador(a) *m/f*

proximity [prɒk'sɪmɪtɪ] N proximidad *f*

proxy ['prɒksɪ] N poder *m*; (*person*) apoderado(-a); **by ~** por poderes

PRP N ABBR (= *performance related pay*) retribución en función del rendimiento en el trabajo

prude [pru:d] N gazmoño(-a), mojigato(-a)

prudence ['pru:dns] N prudencia

prudent ['pru:dnt] ADJ prudente

prudently ['pru:dntlɪ] ADV prudentemente, con prudencia

prudish ['pru:dɪʃ] ADJ gazmoño

prudishness ['pru:dɪʃnɪs] N gazmoñería

prune [pru:n] N ciruela pasa ▶ VT podar

pry [praɪ] VI: **to ~ into** entrometerse en

PS ABBR (= *postscript*) P.D.

psalm [sɑ:m] N salmo

PSAT N ABBR (*US*) = **Preliminary Scholastic Aptitude Test**

PSBR N ABBR (*BRIT*: = *public sector borrowing requirement*) necesidades de endeudamiento del sector público

pseud [sju:d] N (*BRIT inf: intellectually*) farsante *mf*; (*: socially*) pretencioso(-a)

pseudo... [sju:dəu] PREF seudo...

pseudonym ['sju:dənɪm] N seudónimo

PSHE N ABBR (BRIT Scol: = personal, social and health education) formación social y sanitaria para la vida adulta

PST N ABBR (US: = Pacific Standard Time) hora de invierno del Pacífico

PSV N ABBR (BRIT) = **public service vehicle**

psyche [ˈsaɪkɪ] N psique f

psychiatric [saɪkɪˈætrɪk] ADJ psiquiátrico

psychiatrist [saɪˈkaɪətrɪst] N psiquiatra mf

psychiatry [saɪˈkaɪətrɪ] N psiquiatría

psychic [ˈsaɪkɪk] ADJ (also: **psychical**) psíquico

psycho [ˈsaɪkəʊ] N (pej) psicópata mf, pirado(-a)

psychoanalyse, psychoanalyze [saɪkəʊˈænəlaɪz] VT psicoanalizar

psychoanalysis [saɪkəʊəˈnælɪsɪs] (pl **psychoanalyses** [-siːz]) N psicoanálisis m inv

psychoanalyst [saɪkəʊˈænəlɪst] N psicoanalista mf

★**psychological** [saɪkəˈlɒdʒɪkl] ADJ psicológico

psychologically [saɪkəˈlɒdʒɪklɪ] ADV psicológicamente

psychologist [saɪˈkɒlədʒɪst] N psicólogo(-a)

psychology [saɪˈkɒlədʒɪ] N psicología

psychopath [ˈsaɪkəʊpæθ] N psicópata mf

psychosis [saɪˈkəʊsɪs] (pl **psychoses** [-siːz]) N psicosis f inv

psychosomatic [ˈsaɪkəʊsəˈmætɪk] ADJ psicosomático

psychotherapy [saɪkəʊˈθerəpɪ] N psicoterapia

psychotic [saɪˈkɒtɪk] ADJ, N psicótico(-a) m/f

PT N ABBR (BRIT: = physical training) Ed. Fís.

pt ABBR = **pint; point**

Pt. ABBR (Geo: in place names: = Point) Pta

PTA N ABBR (BRIT: = Parent-Teacher Association) ≈ Asociación f de Padres de Alumnos

Pte. ABBR (BRIT Mil) = **private**

PTO ABBR (= please turn over) sigue

PTV N ABBR (US) = **pay television; public television**

★**pub** [pʌb] N ABBR (= public house) pub m, bar m

pub crawl N (inf): **to go on a ~** ir a recorrer bares

puberty [ˈpjuːbətɪ] N pubertad f

pubic [ˈpjuːbɪk] ADJ púbico

★**public** [ˈpʌblɪk] ADJ público; **to make sth ~** revelar or hacer público algo; **to go ~** (Comm) proceder a la venta pública de acciones; **to be ~ knowledge** ser del dominio público ▶ N: **the ~** el público; **in ~** en público

public address system N megafonía, sistema m de altavoces

publican [ˈpʌblɪkən] N dueño(-a) or encargado(-a) de un bar

publication [pʌblɪˈkeɪʃən] N publicación f

public company N sociedad f anónima

public convenience N (BRIT) aseos mpl públicos, sanitarios mpl (LAM)

public holiday N día m de fiesta, (día m) feriado (LAM)

public house N (BRIT) pub m, bar m

★**publicity** [pʌbˈlɪsɪtɪ] N publicidad f

publicize [ˈpʌblɪsaɪz] VT publicitar; (advertise) hacer propaganda para

public limited company N sociedad f anónima

publicly [ˈpʌblɪklɪ] ADV públicamente, en público

public opinion N opinión f pública

public ownership N propiedad f pública; **to be taken into ~** ser nacionalizado

Public Prosecutor N Fiscal mf del Estado

public relations N relaciones fpl públicas

public relations officer N encargado(-a) de relaciones públicas

public school N (BRIT) colegio privado; (US) instituto

En Inglaterra el término **public school** se usa para referirse a un colegio privado de pago, generalmente de alto prestigio social y en régimen de internado. Algunos de los más conocidos son Eton o Harrow. Muchos de sus alumnos estudian previamente hasta los 13 años en un centro privado de pago llamado prep(aratory) school y al terminar el bachiller pasan a estudiar en las universidades de Oxford y Cambridge. En otros lugares como Estados Unidos el mismo término se refiere a una escuela pública de enseñanza gratuita administrada por el Estado.

public sector N sector m público

public service vehicle N vehículo de servicio público

public-spirited [pʌblɪkˈspɪrɪtɪd] ADJ cívico

public transport, (US) public transportation N transporte m público

public utility N servicio público

public works NPL obras fpl públicas

★**publish** [ˈpʌblɪʃ] VT publicar

★**publisher** [ˈpʌblɪʃəʳ] N (person) editor(a) m/f; (firm) editorial f

publishing [ˈpʌblɪʃɪŋ] N (industry) industria del libro

publishing company N (casa) editorial f

pub lunch N almuerzo que se sirve en un pub; **to go for a ~** almorzar o comer en un pub

puce [pjuːs] ADJ de color pardo rojizo

puck [pʌk] N (Ice Hockey) puck m

pucker [ˈpʌkəʳ] VT (pleat) arrugar; (brow etc) fruncir

pudding [ˈpʊdɪŋ] N pudín m; (BRIT: sweet) postre m; **black ~** morcilla; **rice ~** arroz m con leche

puddle [ˈpʌdl] N charco

puerile [ˈpjʊəraɪl] ADJ pueril

Puerto Rican [ˈpwɜːtəʊˈriːkən] ADJ, N puertorriqueño(-a) m/f

Puerto Rico [-ˈriːkəʊ] N Puerto Rico

hacer circular; (*tongue etc*) sacar; (*inconvenience: person*) molestar, fastidiar; (*dislocate: shoulder, vertebra, knee*) dislocar(se) ▶ VI (*Naut*): **to ~ out to sea** hacerse a la mar; **to ~ out from Plymouth** salir de Plymouth

▶ **put through** VT (*call*) poner; (*plan etc*) hacer aprobar; **~ me through to Mr Low** póngame *or* (*LAM*) comuníqueme con el Señor Low

▶ **put together** VT unir, reunir; (*assemble: furniture*) armar, montar; (*meal*) preparar

▶ **put up** VT (*raise*) levantar, alzar; (*hang*) colgar; (*build*) construir; (*increase*) aumentar; (*accommodate*) alojar; (*incite*): **to ~ sb up to doing sth** instar *or* incitar a algn a hacer algo; **to ~ sth up for sale** poner algo a la venta

▶ **put upon** VT FUS: **to be ~ upon** (*imposed upon*) dejarse explotar

▶ **put up with** VT FUS aguantar

putrid ['pjuːtrɪd] ADJ podrido

putsch [pʊtʃ] N golpe *m* de estado

putt [pʌt] VT hacer un putt ▶ N putt *m*

putter ['pʌtəʳ] N putter *m*

putting green ['pʌtɪŋ-] N green *m*, minigolf *m*

putty ['pʌtɪ] N masilla

put-up ['pʊtʌp] ADJ: **~ job** (*BRIT*) estafa

puzzle ['pʌzl] N (*riddle*) acertijo; (*jigsaw*) rompecabezas *m inv*; (*also*: **crossword puzzle**) crucigrama *m*; (*mystery*) misterio ▶ VT dejar perplejo, confundir; **to be puzzled about sth** no llegar a entender algo ▶ VI: **to ~ about** quebrar la cabeza por; **to ~ over** (*sb's actions*) quebrarse la cabeza por; (*mystery, problem*) devanarse los sesos sobre

puzzling ['pʌzlɪŋ] ADJ (*question*) misterioso, extraño; (*attitude, instructions*) extraño

PVC N ABBR (= *polyvinyl chloride*) P.V.C. *m*

Pvt. ABBR (*US Mil*) = **private**

PW N ABBR (*US*) = **prisoner of war**

pw ABBR (= *per week*) por semana

PX N ABBR (*US Mil*: = *post exchange*) economato militar

pygmy ['pɪgmɪ] N pigmeo(-a)

pyjamas, (*US*) **pajamas** [pɪ'dʒɑːməz] NPL pijama *msg*, piyama *msg* (*LAM*); **a pair of ~** un pijama

pylon ['paɪlən] N torre *f* de conducción eléctrica

pyramid ['pɪrəmɪd] N pirámide *f*

Pyrenean [pɪrə'niːən] ADJ pirenaico

Pyrenees [pɪrə'niːz] NPL: **the ~** los Pirineos

Pyrex® ['paɪreks] N pírex *m* ▶ CPD: **~ casserole** cazuela de pírex

python ['paɪθən] N pitón *m*

Qq

Q, q [kjuː] N (*letter*) Q, q f; **Q for Queen** Q de Quebec

Qatar [kæˈtɑː] N Qatar m

QC N ABBR (BRIT: = *Queen's Counsel*) *título concedido a determinados abogados*

QCA N ABBR (BRIT: = *Qualifications and Curriculum Authority*) *organismo que se encarga del currículum educativo en Inglaterra*

QED ABBR (= *quod erat demonstrandum*) Q.E.D.

QM N ABBR *see* **quartermaster**

q.t. N ABBR (*inf*) = **quiet**; **on the ~** a hurtadillas

qty ABBR (= *quantity*) cantidad f

quack [kwæk] N (*of duck*) graznido; (*pej: doctor*) curandero(-a), matasanos m inv ▸ VI graznar

quad [kwɒd] ABBR = **quadrangle**; **quadruple**; **quadruplet**

quadrangle [ˈkwɒdræŋgl] N (BRIT: *courtyard: abbr: quad*) patio

quadruple [kwɒˈdruːpl] VT, VI cuadruplicar

quadruplet [kwɒˈdruːplɪt] N cuatrillizo

quagmire [ˈkwægmaɪəʳ] N lodazal m, cenagal m

quail [kweɪl] N (*bird*) codorniz f ▸ VI amedrentarse

quaint [kweɪnt] ADJ extraño; (*picturesque*) pintoresco

quaintly [ˈkweɪntlɪ] ADV extrañamente; pintorescamente

quaintness [ˈkweɪntnɪs] N lo pintoresco, tipismo

quake [kweɪk] VI temblar ▸ N ABBR = **earthquake**

Quaker [ˈkweɪkəʳ] N cuáquero(-a)

qualification [kwɒlɪfɪˈkeɪʃən] N (*ability*) capacidad f; (*often pl: diploma etc*) título; (*reservation*) salvedad f; (*modification*) modificación f; (*act*) calificación f; **what are your qualifications?** ¿qué títulos tienes?

★qualified [ˈkwɒlɪfaɪd] ADJ (*trained*) cualificado; (*fit*) capacitado; (*limited*) limitado; (*professionally*) titulado; **~ for/to do sth** capacitado para/para hacer algo; **he's not ~ for the job** no está capacitado para ese trabajo; **it was a ~ success** fue un éxito relativo

★qualify [ˈkwɒlɪfaɪ] VT (*Ling*) calificar a; (*capacitate*) capacitar; (*modify*) matizar; (*limit*) moderar ▸ VI: **to ~ (for)** (*in competition*) calificarse (para); (*be eligible*) reunir los requisitos (para); **to ~ (as)** (*pass examination*) calificarse (de), graduarse (en), recibirse (de) (LAM); **to ~ as an engineer** sacar el título de ingeniero

qualifying [ˈkwɒlɪfaɪɪŋ] ADJ (*exam, round*) eliminatorio

qualitative [ˈkwɒlɪtətɪv] ADJ cualitativo

★quality [ˈkwɒlɪtɪ] N calidad f; (*moral*) cualidad f; **of good/poor ~** de buena or alta/poca calidad

quality control N control m de calidad

quality of life N calidad f de vida

quality press N prensa seria

qualm [kwɑːm] N escrúpulo; **to have qualms about sth** sentir escrúpulos por algo

quandary [ˈkwɒndrɪ] N: **to be in a ~** verse en un dilema

quango [ˈkwæŋgəu] N ABBR (BRIT: = *quasi-autonomous non-governmental organization*) *organismo semiautónomo de subvención estatal*

quantifiable [kwɒntɪˈfaɪəbl] ADJ cuantificable

quantify [ˈkwɒntɪfaɪ] VT cuantificar

quantitative [ˈkwɒntɪtətɪv] ADJ cuantitativo

★quantity [ˈkwɒntɪtɪ] N cantidad f; **in ~** en grandes cantidades

quantity surveyor N aparejador(a) m/f

quantum leap [ˈkwɒntəm-] N (*fig*) avance m espectacular

quarantine [ˈkwɒrəntiːn] N cuarentena

quark [kwɑːk] N cuark m

quarrel [ˈkwɒrl] N riña, pelea; **to have a ~ with sb** reñir or pelearse con algn ▸ VI reñir, pelearse; **I can't ~ with that** no le veo pegas

quarrelsome [ˈkwɒrəlsəm] ADJ pendenciero

q

quarry [ˈkwɒrɪ] N (for stone) cantera; (animal) presa

quart [kwɔːt] N cuarto de galón (1.136 l)

★**quarter** [ˈkwɔːtəʳ] N cuarto, cuarta parte f; (US: coin) moneda de 25 centavos; (of year) trimestre m; (district) barrio; **a ~ of an hour** un cuarto de hora; **to pay by the ~** pagar trimestralmente or cada tres meses; **it's a ~ to** or (US) **of three** son las tres menos cuarto; **it's a ~ past** or (US) **after three** son las tres y cuarto; **from all quarters** de todas partes; **at close quarters** de cerca ▸ VT dividir en cuartos; (Mil: lodge) alojar ■ **quarters** NPL (barracks) cuartel msg; (living quarters) alojamiento sg

quarterback [ˈkwɔːtəbæk] N (US: football) mariscal m de campo

quarter-deck [ˈkwɔːtədɛk] N (Naut) alcázar m

quarter final N cuarto de final

quarterly [ˈkwɔːtəlɪ] ADJ trimestral ▸ ADV cada tres meses, trimestralmente

quartermaster [ˈkwɔːtəmɑːstəʳ] N (Mil) comisario, intendente m militar

quartet, quartette [kwɔːˈtɛt] N cuarteto

quarto [ˈkwɔːtəu] N tamaño holandés ▸ ADJ de tamaño holandés

quartz [kwɔːts] N cuarzo

quash [kwɒʃ] VT (verdict) anular, invalidar

quasi- [ˈkweɪzaɪ] PREF cuasi

quaver [ˈkweɪvəʳ] N (BRIT Mus) corchea ▸ VI temblar

quay [kiː] N (also: **quayside**) muelle m

queasiness [ˈkwiːzɪnɪs] N malestar m, náuseas fpl

queasy [ˈkwiːzɪ] ADJ: **to feel ~** tener náuseas

Quebec [kwɪˈbɛk] N Quebec m

★**queen** [kwiːn] N reina; (Cards etc) dama

queen mother N reina madre

Queen's Speech [kwiːnz-] N ver nota

Se llama **Queen's Speech** (o King's Speech) al discurso que pronuncia el monarca durante la sesión de apertura del Parlamento británico, en el que se expresan las líneas generales de la política del gobierno para la nueva legislatura. El Primer Ministro se encarga de redactarlo con la ayuda del Consejo de Ministros y es leído en la Cámara de los Lores (House of Lords) ante los miembros de ambas cámaras.

queer [kwɪəʳ] ADJ (odd) raro, extraño ▸ N (!) maricón m (!)

quell [kwɛl] VT calmar; (put down) sofocar

quench [kwɛntʃ] VT (flames) apagar; **to ~ one's thirst** apagar la sed

querulous [ˈkwɛruləs] ADJ (person, voice) quejumbroso

query [ˈkwɪərɪ] N (question) pregunta; (doubt) duda ▸ VT preguntar; (disagree with, dispute) no estar conforme con, dudar de

quest [kwɛst] N busca, búsqueda

★**question** [ˈkwɛstʃən] N pregunta; (matter) asunto, cuestión f; **to ask sb a ~, put a ~ to sb** hacerle una pregunta a algn; **the ~ is ...** el asunto es ...; **to bring** or **call sth into ~** poner algo en (tela de) duda; **beyond ~** fuera de toda duda; **out of the ~** imposible, ni hablar ▸ VT (doubt) dudar de; (interrogate) interrogar, hacer preguntas a

questionable [ˈkwɛstʃənəbl] ADJ discutible; (doubtful) dudoso

questioner [ˈkwɛstʃənəʳ] N interrogador(a) m/f

questioning [ˈkwɛstʃənɪŋ] ADJ inquisitivo ▸ N preguntas fpl; (by police etc) interrogatorio

question mark N punto de interrogación

questionnaire [kwɛstʃəˈnɛəʳ] N cuestionario

queue [kjuː] (BRIT) N cola; **to jump the ~** colarse ▸ VI hacer cola

quibble [ˈkwɪbl] VI andarse con sutilezas

quiche [kiːʃ] N quiche m

★**quick** [kwɪk] ADJ rápido; (temper) vivo; (agile) ágil; (mind) listo; (eye) agudo; (ear) fino; **be ~!** ¡date prisa!; **to be ~ to act** obrar con prontitud; **she was ~ to see that** se dio cuenta de eso en seguida ▸ N: **cut to the ~** (fig) herido en lo más vivo

quicken [ˈkwɪkən] VT apresurar ▸ VI acelerarse

quick-fire [ˈkwɪkfaɪəʳ] ADJ (questions etc) rápido, (hecho) a quemarropa

quick fix N (pej) parche m

★**quickly** [ˈkwɪklɪ] ADV rápidamente, de prisa; **we must act ~** tenemos que actuar cuanto antes

quickness [ˈkwɪknɪs] N rapidez f; (of temper) viveza; (agility) agilidad f; (of mind, eye etc) agudeza

quicksand [ˈkwɪksænd] N arenas fpl movedizas

quickstep [ˈkwɪkstɛp] N baile de ritmo rápido

quick-tempered [kwɪkˈtɛmpəd] ADJ de genio vivo

quick-witted [kwɪkˈwɪtɪd] ADJ listo, despabilado

quid [kwɪd] N pl inv (BRIT inf) libra

quid pro quo [ˈkwɪdprəuˈkwəu] N quid pro quo m, compensación f

★**quiet** [ˈkwaɪət] ADJ (voice, music etc) bajo; (person, place) tranquilo; (silent) callado; (reserved) reservado; (discreet) discreto; (not noisy: engine) silencioso; **keep ~!** ¡cállate!, ¡silencio!; **business is ~ at this time of year** hay poco movimiento en esta época ▸ N silencio; (calm) tranquilidad f ▸ VT, VI (US) = **quieten**

  quiet no debe traducirse por quieto.

quieten [ˈkwaɪətn], **quieten down** VI (grow calm) calmarse; (grow silent) callarse ▸ VT calmar; hacer callar

★**quietly** [ˈkwaɪətlɪ] ADV tranquilamente; (silently) silenciosamente

quietness [ˈkwaɪətnɪs] N (silence) silencio; (calm) tranquilidad f

quill [kwɪl] N (of porcupine) púa; (pen) pluma

quilt [kwɪlt] N (BRIT) edredón m

quin [kwɪn] N ABBR = **quintuplet**

quince [kwɪns] N membrillo

quinine [kwɪˈniːn] N quinina

quintet, quintette [kwɪnˈtɛt] N quinteto

quintuplet [kwɪnˈtjuːplɪt] N quintillizo

quip [kwɪp] N ocurrencia ▶ vi decir con ironía

quire [ˈkwaɪəʳ] N mano f de papel

quirk [kwəːk] N peculiaridad f; **by some ~ of fate** por algún capricho del destino

quirky [ˈkwəːkɪ] ADJ raro, estrafalario

★**quit** [kwɪt] (pt ~, pp ~ or **quitted**) vt dejar, abandonar; (premises) desocupar; (Comput) abandonar ▶ vi (give up) renunciar; (go away) irse; (resign) dimitir; ~ **stalling!** (US inf) ¡déjate de evasivas!

★**quite** [kwaɪt] ADV (rather) bastante; (entirely) completamente; ~ **a few of them** un buen número de ellos; ~ **(so)!** ¡así es!, ¡exactamente!; ~ **new** bastante nuevo; **that's not ~ right** eso no está del todo bien; **not ~ as many as last time** no tantos como la última vez; **she's ~ pretty** es bastante guapa

Quito [ˈkiːtəu] N Quito

quits [kwɪts] ADJ: ~ **(with)** en paz (con); **let's call it ~** quedamos en paz

quiver [ˈkwɪvəʳ] vi estremecerse ▶ N (for arrows) carcaj m

quiz [kwɪz] N (game) concurso; (: TV, Radio) programa-concurso; (questioning) interrogatorio ▶ vt interrogar

quizzical [ˈkwɪzɪkl] ADJ burlón(-ona)

quoits [kwɔɪts] NPL juego de aros

quorum [ˈkwɔːrəm] N quórum m

quota [ˈkwəutə] N cuota

quotation [kwəuˈteɪʃən] N cita; (estimate) presupuesto

quotation marks NPL comillas fpl

★**quote** [kwəut] N cita ▶ vt (sentence) citar; (Comm: sum, figure) cotizar; **the figure quoted for the repairs** el presupuesto dado para las reparaciones ▶ vi: **to ~ from** citar de; ~ **... unquote** (in dictation) comillas iniciales ... finales ▪ **quotes** NPL (inverted commas) comillas fpl; **in quotes** entre comillas

quotient [ˈkwəuʃənt] N cociente m

qv N ABBR (= quod vide) q.v.

qwerty keyboard [ˈkwəːtɪ-] N teclado QWERTY

q

Rr

R, r [ɑːʳ] N (letter) R, r f; **R for Robert**, (US) **R for Roger** R de Ramón

R ABBR (= right) dcha.; (US Cine: = restricted) solo mayores; (US Pol) = **republican**; (BRIT: = Rex, Regina) R.; (= river) R.; (= Réaumur (scale)) R

RA ABBR = **rear admiral** ▶ N ABBR (BRIT) = **Royal Academy**; **Royal Academician**

RAAF N ABBR = **Royal Australian Air Force**

Rabat [rə'bɑːt] N Rabat m

rabbi ['ræbaɪ] N rabino

★**rabbit** ['ræbɪt] N conejo ▶ VI: **to ~ (on)** (BRIT inf) hablar sin ton ni son

rabbit hutch N conejera

rabble ['ræbl] N (pej) chusma, populacho

rabies ['reɪbiːz] N rabia

RAC N ABBR (BRIT: = Royal Automobile Club) ≈ RACE m (SP)

raccoon, racoon [rə'kuːn] N mapache m

★**race** [reɪs] N carrera; (species) raza; **the arms ~** la carrera armamentista; **the human ~** el género humano ▶ VT (horse) hacer correr; (person) competir contra; (engine) acelerar ▶ VI (compete) competir; (run) correr; (pulse) latir a ritmo acelerado; **he raced across the road** cruzó corriendo la carretera; **to ~ in/out** entrar/salir corriendo

race car N (US) = **racing car**

race car driver N (US) = **racing driver**

racecourse ['reɪskɔːs] N hipódromo

racehorse ['reɪshɔːs] N caballo de carreras

race meeting N concurso hípico

race relations NPL relaciones fpl raciales

racetrack ['reɪstræk] N hipódromo; (for cars) circuito de carreras

racial ['reɪʃl] ADJ racial

racial discrimination N discriminación f racial

racial integration N integración f racial

racialism ['reɪʃəlɪzəm] N racismo

racialist ['reɪʃəlɪst] ADJ, N racista mf

racing ['reɪsɪŋ] N carreras fpl

racing car N (BRIT) coche m de carreras

racing driver N (BRIT) piloto mf de carreras

racism ['reɪsɪzəm] N racismo

racist ['reɪsɪst] ADJ, N racista mf

rack [ræk] N (also: **luggage rack**) rejilla (portaequipajes); (shelf) estante m; (also: **roof rack**) baca; (also: **clothes rack**) perchero; **to go to ~ and ruin** venirse abajo ▶ VT (cause pain to) atormentar; **to ~ one's brains** devanarse los sesos ▶ **rack up** VT conseguir, ganar

racket ['rækɪt] N (for tennis) raqueta; (inf: noise) ruido, estrépito; (: swindle) estafa, timo

racketeer [rækɪ'tɪəʳ] N (esp US) estafador(a) m/f

racquet ['rækɪt] N raqueta

racy ['reɪsɪ] ADJ picante, subido

RADA ['rɑːdə] N ABBR (BRIT) = **Royal Academy of Dramatic Art**

radar ['reɪdɑːʳ] N radar m

radar trap N trampa radar

radial ['reɪdɪəl] ADJ (tyre: also: **radial-ply**) radial

radiance ['reɪdɪəns] N brillantez f, resplandor m

radiant ['reɪdɪənt] ADJ brillante, resplandeciente

radiate ['reɪdɪeɪt] VT (heat) radiar, irradiar ▶ VI (lines) extenderse

radiation [reɪdɪ'eɪʃən] N radiación f

radiation sickness N enfermedad f de radiación

radiator ['reɪdɪeɪtəʳ] N (Aut) radiador m

radiator cap N tapón m del radiador

radiator grill N (Aut) rejilla del radiador

radical ['rædɪkl] ADJ radical

radically ['rædɪkəlɪ] ADV radicalmente

radii ['reɪdɪaɪ] NPL of **radius**

★**radio** ['reɪdɪəu] N radio f; **on the ~** en or por la radio ▶ VI: **to ~ to sb** mandar un mensaje por radio a algn ▶ VT (information) radiar, transmitir por radio; (*one's position*) indicar por radio; (*person*) llamar por radio

radioactive [reɪdɪəuˈæktɪv] ADJ radi(o)activo

radioactivity [reɪdɪəuækˈtɪvɪtɪ] N radi(o)actividad *f*

radio announcer N locutor(a) *m/f* de radio

radio-controlled [reɪdɪəukənˈtrəuld] ADJ teledirigido

radiographer [reɪdɪˈɔgrəfəʳ] N radiógrafo(-a)

radiography [reɪdɪˈɔgrəfɪ] N radiografía

radiology [reɪdɪˈɔlədʒɪ] N radiología

radio station N emisora

radio taxi N radio taxi *m*

radiotelephone [reɪdɪəuˈtɛlɪfəun] N radioteléfono

radio telescope [reɪdɪəuˈtɛlɪskəup] N radiotelescopio

radiotherapist [reɪdɪəuˈθɛrəpɪst] N radioterapeuta *mf*

radiotherapy [ˈreɪdɪəuθɛrəpɪ] N radioterapia

radish [ˈrædɪʃ] N rábano

radium [ˈreɪdɪəm] N radio

radius [ˈreɪdɪəs] (*pl* **radii** [-ɪaɪ]) N radio; **within a ~ of 50 miles** en un radio de 50 millas

RAF N ABBR (*BRIT*) = **Royal Air Force**

raffia [ˈræfɪə] N rafia

raffle [ˈræfl] N rifa, sorteo ▶ VT (*object*) rifar

raft [rɑ:ft] N (*craft*) balsa; (*also:* **life raft**) balsa salvavidas

rafter [ˈrɑ:ftəʳ] N viga

rag [ræg] N (*piece of cloth*) trapo; (*torn cloth*) harapo; (*pej: newspaper*) periodicucho; (*for charity*) actividades estudiantiles benéficas ▶ VT (*BRIT*) tomar el pelo a ∎ **rags** NPL harapos *mpl*; **in rags** en harapos, hecho jirones

rag-and-bone man [rægənˈbəunmæn] N (*irreg*) (*BRIT*) trapero

rag doll N muñeca de trapo

★**rage** [reɪdʒ] N (*fury*) rabia, furor *m*; **to fly into a ~** montar en cólera; **it's all the ~** es lo último; (*very fashionable*) está muy de moda ▶ VI (*person*) rabiar, estar furioso; (*storm*) bramar

ragged [ˈrægɪd] ADJ (*edge*) desigual, mellado; (*cuff*) roto; (*appearance*) andrajoso, harapiento; **~ left/right** (*text*) margen *m* izquierdo/derecho irregular

raging [ˈreɪdʒɪŋ] ADJ furioso; **in a ~ temper** de un humor de mil demonios

rag trade N: **the ~** (*inf*) el ramo de la confección

raid [reɪd] N (*Mil*) incursión *f*; (*criminal*) asalto; (*by police*) redada, allanamiento (*LAM*) ▶ VT invadir, atacar; asaltar

raider [ˈreɪdəʳ] N invasor(a) *m/f*

★**rail** [reɪl] N (*on stair*) barandilla, pasamanos *m inv*; (*on bridge*) pretil *m*; (*of balcony, ship*) barandilla; (*for train*) riel *m*, carril *m*; **by ~** por ferrocarril, en tren ∎ **rails** NPL vía *sg*

railcard [ˈreɪlkɑ:d] N (*BRIT*) tarjeta para obtener descuentos en el tren; **Young Person's R~** ≈ Tarjeta joven (*SP*)

railing [ˈreɪlɪŋ] N, **railings** [ˈreɪlɪŋz] NPL verja *sg*

★**railway** [ˈreɪlweɪ], (*US*) **railroad** [ˈreɪlrəud] N ferrocarril *m*, vía férrea

railway engine N (máquina) locomotora

railway line N (*BRIT*) línea (de ferrocarril)

railwayman [ˈreɪlweɪmən] N (*irreg*) (*BRIT*) ferroviario

railway station N (*BRIT*) estación *f* de ferrocarril

★**rain** [reɪn] N lluvia; **in the ~** bajo la lluvia ▶ VI llover; **it's raining** llueve, está lloviendo; **it's raining cats and dogs** está lloviendo a cántaros *or* a mares

rainbow [ˈreɪnbəu] N arco iris

raincoat [ˈreɪnkəut] N impermeable *m*

raindrop [ˈreɪndrɔp] N gota de lluvia

rainfall [ˈreɪnfɔ:l] N lluvia

rainforest [ˈreɪnfɔrɪst] N selva tropical

rainproof [ˈreɪnpru:f] ADJ impermeable, a prueba de lluvia

rainstorm [ˈreɪnstɔ:m] N temporal *m* (de lluvia)

rainwater [ˈreɪnwɔ:təʳ] N agua de lluvia

★**rainy** [ˈreɪnɪ] ADJ lluvioso

★**raise** [reɪz] N aumento ▶ VT (*lift*) levantar; (*build*) erigir, edificar; (*increase*) aumentar; (*improve: morale*) subir; (*: standards*) mejorar; (*doubts*) suscitar; (*a question*) plantear; (*cattle, family*) criar; (*crop*) cultivar; (*army*) reclutar; (*funds*) reunir; (*loan*) obtener; (*end: embargo*) levantar; **to ~ one's voice** alzar la voz; **to ~ one's glass to sb/sth** brindar por algn/algo; **to ~ a laugh/a smile** provocar risa/una sonrisa; **to ~ sb's hopes** dar esperanzas a algn

raisin [ˈreɪzn] N pasa de Corinto

rake [reɪk] N (*tool*) rastrillo; (*person*) libertino ▶ VT (*garden*) rastrillar; (*fire*) hurgar; (*with machine gun*) barrer
 ▶ **rake in, rake together** VT sacar

rake-off [ˈreɪkɔf] N (*inf*) comisión *f*, tajada

rakish [ˈreɪkɪʃ] ADJ (*dissolute*) libertino; **at a ~ angle** (*hat*) echado a un lado, de lado

rally [ˈrælɪ] N reunión *f*; (*Pol*) mitin *m*; (*Aut*) rally *m*; (*Tennis*) peloteo ▶ VT reunir ▶ VI reunirse; (*sick person*) recuperarse; (*Stock Exchange*) recuperarse
 ▶ **rally round** VT FUS (*fig*) dar apoyo a

rallying point [ˈrælɪŋ-] N (*Pol, Mil*) punto de reunión

RAM [ræm] N ABBR (*Comput: = random access memory*) RAM *f*

ram [ræm] N carnero; (*Tech*) pisón *m*; (*also:* **battering ram**) ariete *m* ▶ VT (*crash into*) dar contra, chocar con; (*push: fist etc*) empujar con fuerza; (*tread down*) apisonar

Ramadan [ˈræmədæn] N Ramadán *m*

ramble [ˈræmbl] N caminata, excursión *f* en el campo ▶ VI (*pej: also:* **ramble on**) divagar

r

rambler ['ræmblə'] N excursionista *mf*; (*Bot*) trepadora

rambling ['ræmblɪŋ] ADJ (*speech*) inconexo; (*Bot*) trepador(a); (*house*) laberíntico

rambunctious [ræm'bʌŋkʃəs] ADJ (*US*) = **rumbustious**

RAMC N ABBR (*BRIT*) = **Royal Army Medical Corps**

ramification [ræmɪfɪ'keɪʃən] N ramificación *f*

ramp [ræmp] N rampa; **on/off ~** *n* (*US Aut*) vía de acceso/salida; "**~**" (*Aut*) "rampa"

rampage [ræm'peɪdʒ] N: **to be on the ~** desmandarse ▶ VI: **they went rampaging through the town** recorrieron la ciudad armando alboroto

rampant ['ræmpənt] ADJ (*disease etc*): **to be ~** estar muy extendido

rampart ['ræmpɑ:t] N terraplén *m*; (*wall*) muralla

ram raid VT atracar (*rompiendo el escaparate con un coche*)

ramshackle ['ræmʃækl] ADJ destartalado

RAN N ABBR = **Royal Australian Navy**

ran [ræn] PT *of* **run**

ranch [rɑ:ntʃ] N (*US*) hacienda, estancia

rancher ['rɑ:ntʃə'] N ganadero

rancid ['rænsɪd] ADJ rancio

rancour, (*US*) **rancor** ['ræŋkə'] N rencor *m*

R & B N ABBR = **rhythm and blues**

R & D N ABBR (= *research and development*) I + D

random ['rændəm] ADJ fortuito, sin orden; (*Comput, Math*) aleatorio ▶ N: **at ~** al azar

random access N (*Comput*) acceso aleatorio

R & R N ABBR (*also US Mil*) = **rest and recreation**

randy ['rændɪ] ADJ (*BRIT inf*) cachondo, caliente

rang [ræŋ] PT *of* **ring**

★**range** [reɪndʒ] N (*of mountains*) cadena de montañas, cordillera; (*of missile*) alcance *m*; (*of voice*) registro; (*series*) serie *f*; (*of products*) surtido; (*Mil: also*: **shooting range**) campo de tiro; (*also*: **kitchen range**) fogón *m*; **within (firing) ~** a tiro; **do you have anything else in this price ~?** ¿tiene algo más de esta gama de precios? ▶ VT (*place*) colocar; (*arrange*) arreglar; **ranged left/ right** (*text*) alineado a la izquierda/derecha ▶ VI: **to ~ over** (*wander*) recorrer; (*extend*) extenderse por; **to ~ from ... to ...** oscilar entre ... y ...; **intermediate-/short-range missile** proyectil *m* de medio/corto alcance

ranger ['reɪndʒə'] N guardabosques *mf*

Rangoon [ræŋ'gu:n] N Rangún *m*

rangy ['reɪndʒɪ] ADJ alto y delgado

rank [ræŋk] N (*row*) fila; (*Mil*) rango; (*status*) categoría; (*BRIT: also*: **taxi rank**) parada; **the ~ and file** (*fig*) las bases; **to close ranks** (*Mil*) cerrar filas; (*fig*) hacer un frente común ▶ VT clasificar; **I ~ him sixth** yo le pongo en sexto lugar ▶ VI: **to ~ among** figurar entre ▶ ADJ (*stinking*) fétido, rancio; (*hypocrisy, injustice etc*) manifiesto;

~ outsider participante *mf* sin probabilidades de ganar

rankle ['ræŋkl] VI (*insult*) doler

ransack ['rænsæk] VT (*search*) registrar; (*plunder*) saquear

ransom ['rænsəm] N rescate *m*; **to hold sb to ~** (*fig*) poner a algn entre la espada y la pared

rant [rænt] VI despotricar

ranting ['ræntɪŋ] N desvaríos *mpl*

rap [ræp] VT golpear, dar un golpecito en ▶ N (*music*) rap *m*

rape [reɪp] N violación *f*; (*Bot*) colza ▶ VT violar

rape oil, rapeseed oil ['reɪpsi:d-] N aceite *m* de colza

rapid ['ræpɪd] ADJ rápido

rapidity [rə'pɪdɪtɪ] N rapidez *f*

rapidly ['ræpɪdlɪ] ADV rápidamente

rapids ['ræpɪdz] NPL (*Geo*) rápidos *mpl*

rapier ['reɪpɪə'] N estoque *m*

rapist ['reɪpɪst] N violador *m*

rapport [ræ'pɔ:] N entendimiento

rapprochement [ræ'prɔʃmɑ̃:ŋ] N acercamiento

rapt [ræpt] ADJ (*attention*) profundo; **to be ~ in contemplation** estar ensimismado

rapture ['ræptʃə'] N éxtasis *m*

rapturous ['ræptʃərəs] ADJ extático; (*applause*) entusiasta

★**rare** [reə'] ADJ raro, poco común; (*Culin: steak*) poco hecho; **it is ~ to find that ...** es raro descubrir que ...

rarefied ['reərɪfaɪd] ADJ (*air, atmosphere*) enrarecido

rarely ['reəlɪ] ADV rara vez, pocas veces

raring ['reərɪŋ] ADJ: **to be ~ to go** (*inf*) tener muchas ganas de empezar

rarity ['reərɪtɪ] N rareza

rascal ['rɑ:skl] N pillo(-a), pícaro(-a)

rash [ræʃ] ADJ imprudente, precipitado ▶ N (*Med*) sarpullido, erupción *f* (cutánea); **to come out in a ~** salirle a algn sarpullidos

rasher ['ræʃə'] N loncha

rashly ['ræʃlɪ] ADV imprudentemente, precipitadamente

rashness ['ræʃnɪs] N imprudencia, precipitación *f*

rasp [rɑ:sp] N (*tool*) escofina ▶ VT (*speak: also*: **rasp out**) decir con voz áspera

★**raspberry** ['rɑ:zbərɪ] N frambuesa

rasping ['rɑ:spɪŋ] ADJ: **a ~ noise** un ruido áspero

Rastafarian [ræstə'feərɪən] ADJ, N rastafari *mf*

rat [ræt] N rata

ratchet ['rætʃɪt] N (*Tech*) trinquete *m*

★**rate** [reɪt] N (*ratio*) razón *f*; (*percentage*) tanto por ciento; (*price*) precio; (: *of hotel*) tarifa; (*of interest*) tipo; (*speed*) velocidad *f*; **failure ~** porcentaje *m* de fallos; **pulse ~** pulsaciones *fpl* por minuto; **~ of pay** tipos *mpl* de sueldo; **at a ~ of 60 kph** a una velocidad de 60 kph; **~ of growth** ritmo de crecimiento; **~ of return** (*Comm*) tasa de rendimiento; **bank ~** tipo *or* tasa de interés bancario; **at any ~** en todo caso ▶ vt (*value*) tasar; (*estimate*) estimar; **to ~ as** ser considerado como; **to ~ sb/sth highly** tener a algn/algo en alta estima; **the property is rated at £840 per annum** (*Brit*) la propiedad está tasada en 840 libras al año ■ **rates** NPL (*Brit*) impuesto *sg* municipal; (*fees*) tarifa *sg*

rateable value ['reɪtəbl-] N (*Brit*) valor *m* impuesto

rate-capping ['reɪtkæpɪŋ] N (*Brit*) fijación *f* de las contribuciones

ratepayer ['reɪtpeɪər] N (*Brit*) contribuyente *mf*

★**rather** ['rɑːðər] ADV antes, más bien; (*somewhat*) algo, un poco; (*quite*) bastante; **it's ~ expensive** es algo caro; (*too much*) es demasiado caro; **there's ~ a lot** hay bastante; **I would** *or* **I'd ~ go** preferiría ir; **I'd ~ not** prefiero que no; **I ~ think he won't come** me inclino a creer que no vendrá; **or ~** (*more accurately*) o mejor dicho

ratification [rætɪfɪ'keɪʃən] N ratificación *f*

ratify ['rætɪfaɪ] vt ratificar

rating ['reɪtɪŋ] N (*valuation*) tasación *f*; (*standing*) posición *f*; (*Brit Naut: sailor*) marinero ■ **ratings** NPL (*Radio, TV*) niveles *mpl* de audiencia

ratio ['reɪʃɪəu] N razón *f*; **in the ~ of 100 to 1** razón *de or* en la proporción de 100 a 1

ration ['ræʃən] N ración *f* ▶ vt racionar ■ **rations** NPL víveres *mpl*

rational ['ræʃənl] ADJ racional; (*solution, reasoning*) lógico, razonable; (*person*) cuerdo, sensato

rationale [ræʃə'nɑːl] N razón *f* fundamental

rationalism ['ræʃnəlɪzəm] N racionalismo

rationalization [ræʃnəlaɪ'zeɪʃən] N racionalización *f*

rationalize ['ræʃnəlaɪz] vt (*reorganize: industry*) racionalizar

rationally ['ræʃnəlɪ] ADV racionalmente; (*logically*) lógicamente

rationing ['ræʃnɪŋ] N racionamiento

ratpack ['rætpæk] N (*Brit pej*) periodistas que persiguen a los famosos

rat race N lucha incesante por la supervivencia

rattan [ræ'tæn] N rota, caña de Indias

rattle ['rætl] N golpeteo; (*of train etc*) traqueteo; (*object: of baby*) sonaja, sonajero; (*: of sports fan*) matraca ▶ vi (*small objects*) castañetear; (*car, bus*): **to ~ along** traquetear ▶ vt hacer sonar agitando; (*inf: disconcert*) poner nervioso a

rattlesnake ['rætlsneɪk] N serpiente *f* de cascabel

ratty ['rætɪ] ADJ (*inf*) mosqueado; **to get ~** mosquearse

raucous ['rɔːkəs] ADJ estridente, ronco

raucously ['rɔːkəslɪ] ADV de modo estridente, roncamente

raunchy ['rɔːntʃɪ] ADJ (*inf*) lascivo

ravage ['rævɪdʒ] vt hacer estragos en, destrozar ■ **ravages** NPL estragos *mpl*

rave [reɪv] vi (*in anger*) encolerizarse; (*with enthusiasm*) entusiasmarse; (*Med*) delirar, desvariar ▶ cpd: **~ review** reseña entusiasta; **a ~ (party)** una (fiesta) rave; **~ music** música máquina ▶ N (*inf: party*) rave *m or f*

raven ['reɪvən] N cuervo

ravenous ['rævənəs] ADJ: **to be ~** tener un hambre canina

ravine [rə'viːn] N barranco

raving ['reɪvɪŋ] ADJ: **~ lunatic** (!) loco de atar

ravings ['reɪvɪŋz] NPL desvaríos *mpl*

ravioli [rævɪ'əulɪ] N ravioles *mpl*, ravioli *mpl*

ravish ['rævɪʃ] vt (*charm*) encantar, embelesar; (*rape*) violar

ravishing ['rævɪʃɪŋ] ADJ encantador(a)

★**raw** [rɔː] ADJ (*uncooked*) crudo; (*not processed*) bruto; (*sore*) vivo; (*inexperienced*) novato, inexperto; **~ materials** materias *fpl* primas

Rawalpindi [rɔːl'pɪndɪ] N Rawalpindi *m*

raw data N (*Comput*) datos *mpl* en bruto

raw deal N (*inf: bad deal*) mala pasada *or* jugada; (*: harsh treatment*) injusticia

raw material N materia prima

ray [reɪ] N rayo; **~ of hope** (rayo de) esperanza

rayon ['reɪɔn] N rayón *m*

raze [reɪz] vt (*also:* **raze to the ground**) arrasar, asolar

razor ['reɪzər] N (*open*) navaja; (*safety razor*) máquina de afeitar; (*electric razor*) máquina (eléctrica) de afeitar

razor blade N hoja de afeitar

razzle ['ræzl], **razzle-dazzle** ['ræzl'dæzl] N (*Brit inf*): **to be/go on the ~(-dazzle)** estar/irse de juerga

razzmatazz ['ræzmə'tæz] N (*inf*) animación *f*, bullicio

RC ABBR = **Roman Catholic**

RCAF N ABBR = **Royal Canadian Air Force**

RCMP N ABBR = **Royal Canadian Mounted Police**

RCN N ABBR = **Royal Canadian Navy**

RD ABBR (*US Post*) = **rural delivery**

Rd ABBR = **road**

RE N ABBR (*Brit Scol*) = **religious education**; (*Brit Mil*) = **Royal Engineers**

re [riː] PREP con referencia a

re... [riː] PREF re...

★**reach** [riːtʃ] N alcance *m*; (*Boxing*) envergadura; (*of river etc*) extensión *f* entre dos recodos; **within ~** al alcance (de la mano); **out of ~** fuera del alcance ▶ vt alcanzar, llegar a; (*achieve*) lograr; **to ~ sb by phone** comunicarse con algn por teléfono; **can I ~ you at your hotel?** ¿puedo localizarte en tu hotel? ▶ vi extenderse; (*stretch out hand: also:* **reach down, reach over, reach across** *etc*) tender la mano

r

733

▶ **reach out** VT (*hand*) tender ▶ VI: **to ~ out for sth** alargar *or* tender la mano para tomar algo

★**react** [ri:'ækt] VI reaccionar

★**reaction** [ri:'ækʃən] N reacción *f*

reactionary [ri:'ækʃənrɪ] ADJ, N reaccionario(-a) *m/f*

reactor [ri:'æktə^r] N (*also:* **nuclear reactor**) reactor *m* (nuclear)

★**read** [ri:d] (*pt, pp* ~ [rɛd]) VI leer; **to ~ between the lines** leer entre líneas ▶ VT leer; (*understand*) entender; (*study*) estudiar; **to take sth as ~** (*fig*) dar algo por sentado; **do you ~ me?** (*Tel*) ¿me escucha?

▶ **read out** VT leer en voz alta

▶ **read over** VT repasar

▶ **read through** VT (*quickly*) leer rápidamente, echar un vistazo a; (*thoroughly*) leer con cuidado *or* detenidamente

▶ **read up, read up on** VT FUS documentarse sobre

readable ['ri:dəbl] ADJ (*writing*) legible; (*book*) que merece la pena leer

★**reader** ['ri:də^r] N lector(a) *m/f*; (*book*) libro de lecturas; (*BRIT: at university*) profesor(a) *m/f*

readership ['ri:dəʃɪp] N (*of paper etc*) número de lectores

readily ['rɛdɪlɪ] ADV (*willingly*) de buena gana; (*easily*) fácilmente; (*quickly*) en seguida

readiness ['rɛdɪnɪs] N buena voluntad; (*preparedness*) preparación *f*; **in ~** (*prepared*) listo, preparado

★**reading** ['ri:dɪŋ] N lectura; (*understanding*) comprensión *f*; (*on instrument*) indicación *f*

reading lamp N lámpara portátil

reading matter N lectura

reading room N sala de lectura

readjust [ri:ə'dʒʌst] VT reajustar ▶ VI (*person*): **to ~ to** reajustarse a

readjustment [ri:ə'dʒʌstmənt] N reajuste *m*

★**ready** ['rɛdɪ] ADJ listo, preparado; (*willing*) dispuesto; (*available*) disponible; **to be ~ to do sth** estar listo para hacer algo; **~ for use** listo para usar; **to get ~** prepararse ▶ ADV: **ready-cooked** listo para comer ▶ N: **at the ~** (*Mil*) listo para tirar ▶ VT preparar

ready cash N efectivo

ready-made ['rɛdɪ'meɪd] ADJ confeccionado

ready money N dinero contante

ready reckoner N tabla de cálculos hechos

ready-to-wear ['rɛdɪtə'wɛə^r] ADJ confeccionado

reaffirm [ri:ə'fə:m] VT reafirmar

reagent [ri:'eɪdʒənt] N reactivo

★**real** [rɪəl] ADJ verdadero, auténtico; **in ~ terms** en términos reales; **in ~ life** en la vida real, en la realidad

real ale N cerveza elaborada tradicionalmente

real estate N bienes *mpl* raíces

real estate agency N = **estate agency**

realism ['rɪəlɪzəm] N (*also Art*) realismo

realist ['rɪəlɪst] N realista *mf*

realistic [rɪə'lɪstɪk] ADJ realista

realistically [rɪə'lɪstɪklɪ] ADV de modo realista

★**reality** [ri:'ælɪtɪ] N realidad *f*; **in ~** en realidad

reality TV N telerrealidad *f*

realization [rɪəlaɪ'zeɪʃən] N comprensión *f*; (*of a project*) realización *f*; (*Comm: of assets*) realización *f*

★**realize** ['rɪəlaɪz] VT (*understand*) darse cuenta de; (*a project*) realizar; (*Comm: asset*) realizar; **I ~ that …** comprendo *or* entiendo que …

★**really** ['rɪəlɪ] ADV realmente; (*for emphasis*) verdaderamente; **what ~ happened** (*actually*) lo que pasó en realidad; **~?** ¿de veras?; **~!** (*annoyance*) ¡vamos!, ¡por favor!

realm [rɛlm] N reino; (*fig*) esfera

real time N (*also Comput*) tiempo real

realtor ['rɪəltɔ:^r] N (*US*) corredor(a) *m/f* de bienes raíces

ream [ri:m] N resma; **reams** (*fig: inf*) montones *mpl*

reap [ri:p] VT segar; (*fig*) cosechar, recoger

reaper ['ri:pə^r] N segador(a) *m/f*

reappear [ri:ə'pɪə^r] VI reaparecer

reappearance [ri:ə'pɪərəns] N reaparición *f*

reapply [ri:ə'plaɪ] VI volver a presentarse, hacer *or* presentar una nueva solicitud

reappoint [ri:ə'pɔɪnt] VT volver a nombrar

reappraisal [ri:ə'preɪzl] N revaluación *f*

rear [rɪə^r] ADJ trasero ▶ N parte *f* trasera ▶ VT (*cattle, family*) criar ▶ VI (*also:* **rear up**: *animal*) encabritarse

rear-engined ['rɪər'ɛndʒɪnd] ADJ (*Aut*) con motor trasero

rearguard ['rɪəgɑ:d] N retaguardia

rearm [ri:'ɑ:m] VT rearmar ▶ VI rearmarse

rearmament [ri:'ɑ:məmənt] N rearme *m*

rearrange [ri:ə'reɪndʒ] VT ordenar *or* arreglar de nuevo

rear-view mirror ['rɪəvju:] N (*Aut*) espejo retrovisor

rear-wheel drive N tracción *f* trasera

★**reason** ['ri:zn] N razón *f*; **it stands to ~ that …** es lógico que …; **the ~ for/why** la causa de/la razón por la cual; **she claims with good ~ that she's underpaid** dice con razón que está mal pagada; **all the more ~ why you should not sell it** razón de más para que no lo vendas ▶ VI: **to ~ with sb** tratar de que algn entre en razón

★**reasonable** ['ri:znəbl] ADJ razonable; (*sensible*) sensato

reasonably ['ri:znəblɪ] ADV razonablemente; **a ~ accurate report** un informe bastante exacto

reasoned ['ri:znd] ADJ (*argument*) razonado

reasoning ['ri:znɪŋ] N razonamiento, argumentos *mpl*

reassemble [ri:ə'sɛmbl] VT volver a reunir;

(*machine*) montar de nuevo ▶ vi volver a reunirse

reassert [riːəˈsɜːt] vt reafirmar, reiterar

reassurance [riːəˈʃuərəns] N consuelo

reassure [riːəˈʃuəʳ] vt tranquilizar; **to ~ sb that** tranquilizar a algn asegurándole que

reassuring [riːəˈʃuərɪŋ] ADJ tranquilizador(a)

reawakening [riːəˈweɪknɪŋ] N despertar *m*

rebate [ˈriːbeɪt] N (*on product*) rebaja; (*on tax etc*) desgravación *f*; (*repayment*) reembolso

rebel N [ˈrɛbl] rebelde *mf* ▶ vi [rɪˈbɛl] rebelarse, sublevarse

rebellion [rɪˈbɛljən] N rebelión *f*, sublevación *f*

rebellious [rɪˈbɛljəs] ADJ rebelde; (*child*) revoltoso

rebirth [riːˈbɜːθ] N renacimiento

rebound vi [rɪˈbaund] (*ball*) rebotar ▶ N [ˈriːbaund] rebote *m*

rebrand [riːˈbrænd] vt relanzar

rebuff [rɪˈbʌf] N desaire *m*, rechazo ▶ vt rechazar

rebuild [riːˈbɪld] vt (*irreg: like* build) reconstruir

rebuilding [riːˈbɪldɪŋ] N reconstrucción *f*

rebuke [rɪˈbjuːk] N reprimenda ▶ vt reprender

rebut [rɪˈbʌt] vt rebatir

recalcitrant [rɪˈkælsɪtrənt] ADJ reacio

recall [rɪˈkɔːl] vt (*remember*) recordar; (*ambassador etc*) retirar; (*Comput*) volver a llamar ▶ N recuerdo

recant [rɪˈkænt] vi retractarse

recap [ˈriːkæp] vt, vi recapitular

recapitulate [riːkəˈpɪtjuleɪt] vt, vi = recap

recapture [riːˈkæptʃəʳ] vt (*town*) reconquistar; (*atmosphere*) hacer revivir

recd., rec'd ABBR (= *received*) recibido

recede [rɪˈsiːd] vi retroceder

receding [rɪˈsiːdɪŋ] ADJ (*forehead, chin*) hundido; **~ hairline** entradas *fpl*

★**receipt** [rɪˈsiːt] N (*document*) recibo; (*act of receiving*) recepción *f*; **to acknowledge ~ of** acusar recibo de; **we are in ~ of ...** obra en nuestro poder ... ∎ **receipts** NPL (*Comm*) ingresos *mpl*

receivable [rɪˈsiːvəbl] ADJ (*Comm*) a cobrar

★**receive** [rɪˈsiːv] vt recibir; (*guest*) acoger; (*wound*) sufrir; **"received with thanks"** "recibí"

Received Pronunciation [rɪˈsiːvd-] N *see* **RP**

receiver [rɪˈsiːvəʳ] N (*Tel*) auricular *m*; (*Radio*) receptor *m*; (*of stolen goods*) perista *mf*; (*Law*) administrador *m* jurídico

receivership [rɪˈsiːvəʃɪp] N: **to go into ~** entrar en liquidación

★**recent** [ˈriːsnt] ADJ reciente; **in ~ years** en los últimos años

★**recently** [ˈriːsntlɪ] ADV recientemente, recién (*LAm*); **~ arrived** recién llegado; **until ~** hasta hace poco

receptacle [rɪˈsɛptɪkl] N receptáculo

reception [rɪˈsɛpʃən] N (*in building, office etc*) recepción *f*; (*welcome*) acogida

reception centre N (*BRIT*) centro de recepción

reception desk N recepción *f*

receptionist [rɪˈsɛpʃənɪst] N recepcionista *mf*

receptive [rɪˈsɛptɪv] ADJ receptivo

recess [rɪˈsɛs] N (*in room*) hueco; (*for bed*) nicho; (*secret place*) escondrijo; (*Pol etc: holiday*) período vacacional; (*US Law: short break*) descanso; (*Scol: esp US*) recreo

★**recession** [rɪˈsɛʃən] N recesión *f*, depresión *f*

recessionista [rɪsɛʃəˈnɪstə] N recesionista *mf*

recharge [riːˈtʃɑːdʒ] vt (*battery*) recargar

rechargeable [riːˈtʃɑːdʒəbl] ADJ recargable

★**recipe** [ˈrɛsɪpɪ] N receta; (*for disaster, success*) fórmula

recipient [rɪˈsɪpɪənt] N recibidor(a) *m/f*; (*of letter*) destinatario(-a)

reciprocal [rɪˈsɪprəkl] ADJ recíproco

reciprocate [rɪˈsɪprəkeɪt] vt devolver, corresponder a ▶ vi corresponder

recital [rɪˈsaɪtl] N (*Mus*) recital *m*

recitation [rɛsɪˈteɪʃən] N (*of poetry*) recitado; (*of complaints etc*) enumeración *f*, relación *f*

recite [rɪˈsaɪt] vt (*poem*) recitar; (*complaints etc*) enumerar

reckless [ˈrɛkləs] ADJ temerario, imprudente; (*speed*) peligroso

recklessly [ˈrɛkləslɪ] ADV imprudentemente; de modo peligroso

recklessness [ˈrɛkləsnɪs] N temeridad *f*, imprudencia

★**reckon** [ˈrɛkən] vt (*calculate*) calcular; (*consider*) considerar; **I ~ that ...** me parece que ..., creo que ...; **he is somebody to be reckoned with** no se le puede descartar ▶ vi: **to ~ without sb/sth** dejar de contar con algn/algo
▶ **reckon on** vt fus contar con

reckoning [ˈrɛkənɪŋ] N (*calculation*) cálculo

reclaim [rɪˈkleɪm] vt (*land*) recuperar; (: *from sea*) rescatar; (*demand back*) reclamar

reclamation [rɛkləˈmeɪʃən] N recuperación *f*; rescate *m*

recline [rɪˈklaɪn] vi reclinarse

reclining [rɪˈklaɪnɪŋ] ADJ (*seat*) reclinable

recluse [rɪˈkluːs] N recluso(-a)

recognition [rɛkəɡˈnɪʃən] N reconocimiento; **transformed beyond ~** irreconocible; **in ~ of** en reconocimiento de

recognizable [ˈrɛkəɡnaɪzəbl] ADJ: **~ (by)** reconocible (por)

★**recognize** [ˈrɛkəɡnaɪz] vt reconocer, conocer; **to ~ (by/as)** reconocer (por/como)

recoil [rɪˈkɔɪl] vi (*person*): **to ~ from doing sth** retraerse de hacer algo ▶ N (*of gun*) retroceso

recollect [rɛkəˈlɛkt] vt recordar, acordarse de

recollection [rɛkəˈlɛkʃən] N recuerdo; **to the best of my ~** que yo recuerde

r

735

★**recommend** [rɛkə'mɛnd] vt recomendar; **she has a lot to ~ her** tiene mucho a su favor

recommendation [rɛkəmen'deɪʃən] n recomendación f

recommended retail price n (Brit) precio (recomendado) de venta al público

recompense ['rɛkəmpɛns] vt recompensar ▸ n recompensa

reconcilable ['rɛkənsaɪləbl] adj (re)conciliable

reconcile ['rɛkənsaɪl] vt (two people) reconciliar; (two facts) conciliar; **to ~ o.s. to sth** resignarse or conformarse a algo

reconciliation [rɛkənsɪlɪ'eɪʃən] n reconciliación f

recondite [rɪ'kɔndaɪt] adj recóndito

recondition [riːkən'dɪʃən] vt (machine) reparar, reponer

reconditioned [riːkən'dɪʃənd] adj renovado, reparado

reconfigure [riːkən'fɪgəʳ] vt reconfigurar

reconnaissance [rɪ'kɔnɪsns] n (Mil) reconocimiento

reconnoitre, (US) **reconnoiter** [rɛkə'nɔɪtəʳ] vt, vi (Mil) reconocer

reconsider [riːkən'sɪdəʳ] vt repensar

reconstitute [riː'kɔnstɪtjuːt] vt reconstituir

reconstruct [riːkən'strʌkt] vt reconstruir

reconstruction [riːkən'strʌkʃən] n reconstrucción f

reconvene [riːkən'viːn] vt volver a convocar ▸ vi volver a reunirse

★**record** n ['rɛkɔːd] (Mus) disco; (of meeting etc) acta; (register) registro, partida; (file) archivo; (also: **police** or **criminal record**) antecedentes mpl penales; (written) expediente m; (Sport) récord m; (Comput) registro; **public records** archivos mpl nacionales; **he is on ~ as saying that ...** hay pruebas de que ha dicho públicamente que ...; **Spain's excellent ~** el excelente historial de España; **off the ~** adj no oficial; adv confidencialmente ▸ adj ['rɛkɔːd] récord; **in ~ time** en un tiempo récord ▸ vt [rɪ'kɔːd] (set down) registrar; (Comput) registrar; (relate) hacer constar; (Mus: song etc) grabar

record card n (in file) ficha

recorded delivery [rɪ'kɔːdɪd-] n (Brit Post) entrega con acuse de recibo

recorded music n música grabada

recorder [rɪ'kɔːdəʳ] n (Mus) flauta de pico; (Tech) contador m

record holder n (Sport) actual poseedor(a) m/f del récord

★**recording** [rɪ'kɔːdɪŋ] n (Mus) grabación f

recording studio n estudio de grabación

record library n discoteca

record player n tocadiscos m inv

recount [rɪ'kaunt] vt contar

re-count n ['riːkaunt] (Pol: of votes) segundo escrutinio, recuento ▸ vt [riː'kaunt] volver a contar

recoup [rɪ'kuːp] vt: **to ~ one's losses** recuperar las pérdidas

recourse [rɪ'kɔːs] n recurso; **to have ~ to** recurrir a

★**recover** [rɪ'kʌvəʳ] vt recuperar; (rescue) rescatar ▸ vi recuperarse

★**recovery** [rɪ'kʌvərɪ] n recuperación f; rescate m; (Med): **to make a ~** restablecerse

recreate [riːkrɪ'eɪt] vt recrear

recreation [rɛkrɪ'eɪʃən] n recreación f; (amusement) recreo

recreational [rɛkrɪ'eɪʃənl] adj recreativo

recreational drug n droga recreativa

recreational vehicle n (US) caravana or roulotte f pequeña

recrimination [rɪkrɪmɪ'neɪʃən] n recriminación f

recruit [rɪ'kruːt] n recluta mf ▸ vt reclutar; (staff) contratar

recruiting office [rɪ'kruːtɪŋ-] n caja de reclutas

recruitment [rɪ'kruːtmənt] n reclutamiento

rectangle ['rɛktæŋgl] n rectángulo

rectangular [rɛk'tæŋgjuləʳ] adj rectangular

rectify ['rɛktɪfaɪ] vt rectificar

rector ['rɛktəʳ] n (Rel) párroco; (Scol) rector(a) m/f

rectory ['rɛktərɪ] n casa del párroco

rectum ['rɛktəm] n (Anat) recto

recuperate [rɪ'kuːpəreɪt] vi reponerse, restablecerse

recur [rɪ'kəːʳ] vi repetirse; (pain, illness) producirse de nuevo

recurrence [rɪ'kəːrns] n repetición f

recurrent [rɪ'kəːrnt] adj repetido

recurring [rɪ'kəːrɪŋ] adj (problem) repetido, constante

recyclable [riː'saɪkləbl] adj reciclable

recycle [riː'saɪkl] vt reciclar

recycled [riː'saɪkld] adj reciclado; **~ paper** papel m reciclado

recycling [riː'saɪklɪŋ] n reciclaje m

★**red** [rɛd] n rojo; **to be in the ~** (account) estar en números rojos; (business) tener un saldo negativo ▸ adj rojo; (hair) pelirrojo; (wine) tinto; **to give sb the ~ carpet treatment** recibir a algn con todos los honores

red alert n alerta roja

red-blooded ['rɛd'blʌdɪd] adj (inf) viril

redbrick university ['rɛdbrɪk-] n ver nota

El término **redbrick university** se aplica a las universidades construidas en los grandes centros urbanos industriales como Birmingham, Liverpool o Manchester a finales del siglo XIX o principios del XX. Deben su nombre a que sus edificios son normalmente de ladrillo, a diferencia de las universidades tradicionales como las de Oxford y Cambridge, cuyos edificios suelen ser de piedra y de interés histórico.

Red Cross N Cruz f Roja

redcurrant [ˈrɛdkʌrənt] N grosella roja

redden [ˈrɛdn] VT enrojecer ▸ VI enrojecerse

reddish [ˈrɛdɪʃ] ADJ (hair) rojizo

redecorate [riːˈdɛkəreɪt] VT volver a decorar; (with paint) pintar de nuevo

redecoration [riːdɛkəˈreɪʃən] N renovación f

redeem [rɪˈdiːm] VT redimir; (promises) cumplir; (sth in pawn) desempeñar; (Rel, fig) rescatar

redeemable [rɪˈdiːməbl] ADJ canjeable

redeeming [rɪˈdiːmɪŋ] ADJ: ~ feature punto bueno or favorable

redefine [riːdɪˈfaɪn] VT redefinir

redemption [rɪˈdɛmpʃən] N (Rel) redención f; to be past or beyond ~ no tener remedio

redeploy [riːdɪˈplɔɪ] VT disponer de nuevo

redeployment [riːdɪˈplɔɪmənt] N redistribución f

redevelop [riːdɪˈvɛləp] VT reorganizar

redevelopment [riːdɪˈvɛləpmənt] N reorganización f

red-handed [rɛdˈhændɪd] ADJ: he was caught ~ le pillaron con las manos en la masa

redhead [ˈrɛdhɛd] N pelirrojo(-a)

red herring N (fig) pista falsa

red-hot [rɛdˈhɔt] ADJ candente

redirect [riːdaɪˈrɛkt] VT (mail) reexpedir

rediscover [riːdɪsˈkʌvəʳ] VT redescubrir

rediscovery [riːdɪsˈkʌvərɪ] N redescubrimiento

redistribute [riːdɪsˈtrɪbjuːt] VT redistribuir, hacer una nueva distribución de

red-letter day [rɛdˈlɛtə-] N día m señalado, día m especial

red light N: to go through or jump a ~ (Aut) saltarse un semáforo

red-light district N barrio chino, zona de tolerancia

red meat N carne f roja

redness [ˈrɛdnɪs] N rojez f

redo [riːˈduː] VT (irreg: like do) rehacer

redolent [ˈrɛdələnt] ADJ: ~ of (smell) con fragancia a; to be ~ of (fig) evocar

redouble [riːˈdʌbl] VT: to ~ one's efforts redoblar los esfuerzos

redraft [riːˈdrɑːft] VT volver a redactar

redress [rɪˈdrɛs] N reparación f ▸ VT reparar, corregir; to ~ the balance restablecer el equilibrio

Red Sea N: the ~ el mar Rojo

red tape N (fig) trámites mpl, papeleo (inf)

★**reduce** [rɪˈdjuːs] VT reducir; (lower) rebajar; to ~ sth by/to reducir algo en/a; to ~ sb to silence/despair/tears hacer callar/desesperarse/llorar a algn; "~ speed now" (Aut) "reduzca la velocidad"

reduced [rɪˈdjuːst] ADJ (decreased) reducido,

rebajado; at a ~ price con rebaja or descuento; "greatly ~ prices" "grandes rebajas"

★**reduction** [rɪˈdʌkʃən] N reducción f; (of price) rebaja; (discount) descuento

redundancy [rɪˈdʌndənsɪ] N despido; (unemployment) desempleo; voluntary ~ baja voluntaria

redundancy payment N indemnización f por desempleo

redundant [rɪˈdʌndənt] ADJ (Brit: worker) parado, sin trabajo; (detail, object) superfluo; to be made ~ (Brit) quedar(se) sin trabajo, perder el empleo

reed [riːd] N (Bot) junco, caña; (Mus: of clarinet etc) lengüeta

re-educate [riːˈɛdjukeɪt] VT reeducar

reedy [ˈriːdɪ] ADJ (voice, instrument) aflautado

reef [riːf] N (at sea) arrecife m

reek [riːk] VI: to ~ (of) oler or apestar (a)

reel [riːl] N carrete m, bobina; (of film) rollo ▸ VT (Tech) devanar; (also: reel in) sacar ▸ VI (sway) tambalear(se); my head is reeling me da vueltas la cabeza

▸ **reel off** VT recitar de memoria

re-election [riːɪˈlɛkʃən] N reelección f

re-engage [riːɪnˈɡeɪdʒ] VT contratar de nuevo

re-enter [riːˈɛntəʳ] VT reingresar en, volver a entrar en

re-entry [riːˈɛntrɪ] N reingreso, reentrada

re-examine [riːɪɡˈzæmɪn] VT reexaminar

re-export VT [ˈriːˈɛksˈpɔːt] reexportar ▸ N [riːˈɛkspɔːt] reexportación f

ref [rɛf] N ABBR (inf) = referee

ref. ABBR (Comm: = with reference to) Ref

refectory [rɪˈfɛktərɪ] N comedor m

★**refer** [rɪˈfɜːʳ] VT (send: patient) referir; (: matter) remitir; (ascribe) referir a, relacionar con; he referred me to the manager me envió al gerente ▸ VI: to ~ to (allude to) referirse a, aludir a; (apply to) relacionarse con; (consult) remitirse a

referee [rɛfəˈriː] N árbitro(-a); (Brit: for job application): to be a ~ for sb proporcionar referencias a algn ▸ VT (match) arbitrar en

★**reference** [ˈrɛfrəns] N (mention: in book) referencia; (sending) remisión f; (relevance) relación f; (for job application: letter) carta de recomendación; with ~ to con referencia a; (Comm: in letter) me remito a

reference book N libro de consulta

reference library N biblioteca de consulta

reference number N número de referencia

referendum [rɛfəˈrɛndəm] (pl **referenda** [-də]) N referéndum m

referral [rɪˈfɜːrəl] N remisión f

refill VT [riːˈfɪl] rellenar ▸ N [ˈriːfɪl] repuesto, recambio

refine [rɪˈfaɪn] VT (sugar, oil) refinar

refined [rɪˈfaɪnd] ADJ *(person, taste)* refinado, fino

refinement [rɪˈfaɪnmənt] N *(of person)* cultura, educación f

refinery [rɪˈfaɪnərɪ] N refinería

refit *(also Naut)* N [ˈriːfɪt] reparación f ▸ VT [riːˈfɪt] reparar

reflate [riːˈfleɪt] VT *(economy)* reflacionar

reflation [riːˈfleɪʃən] N reflación f

reflationary [riːˈfleɪʃənrɪ] ADJ reflacionario

reflect [rɪˈflɛkt] VT *(light, image)* reflejar ▸ VI *(think)* reflexionar, pensar; **it reflects badly/well on him** le perjudica/le hace honor

reflection [rɪˈflɛkʃən] N *(act)* reflexión f; *(image)* reflejo; *(discredit)* crítica; **on ~** pensándolo bien

reflector [rɪˈflɛktəʳ] N *(Aut)* catafaros m inv; *(telescope)* reflector m

reflex [ˈriːflɛks] ADJ, N reflejo

reflexive [rɪˈflɛksɪv] ADJ *(Ling)* reflexivo

reform [rɪˈfɔːm] N reforma ▸ VT reformar

reformat [riːˈfɔːmæt] VT *(Comput)* volver a formatear

Reformation [rɛfəˈmeɪʃən] N: **the ~** la Reforma

reformatory [rɪˈfɔːmətərɪ] N *(US)* reformatorio

reformer [rɪˈfɔːməʳ] N reformador(a) m/f

refrain [rɪˈfreɪn] VI: **to ~ from doing** abstenerse de hacer ▸ N *(Mus etc)* estribillo

refresh [rɪˈfrɛʃ] VT refrescar

refresher course [rɪˈfrɛʃə-] N *(Brit)* curso de repaso

refreshing [rɪˈfrɛʃɪŋ] ADJ *(drink)* refrescante; *(sleep)* reparador; *(change etc)* estimulante; *(idea, point of view)* estimulante, interesante

refreshments [rɪˈfrɛʃmənts] NPL *(drinks)* refrescos mpl

refrigeration [rɪfrɪdʒəˈreɪʃən] N refrigeración f

refrigerator [rɪˈfrɪdʒəreɪtəʳ] N frigorífico, refrigeradora *(Lam)*, heladera *(Lam)*

refuel [riːˈfjuəl] VI repostar (combustible)

refuelling, *(US)* **refueling** [riːˈfjuəlɪŋ] N reabastecimiento de combustible

refuge [ˈrɛfjuːdʒ] N refugio, asilo; **to take ~ in** refugiarse en

★**refugee** [rɛfjuˈdʒiː] N refugiado(-a)

refugee camp N campamento para refugiados

refund N [ˈriːfʌnd] reembolso ▸ VT [rɪˈfʌnd] devolver, reembolsar

refurbish [riːˈfəːbɪʃ] VT restaurar, renovar

refurnish [riːˈfəːnɪʃ] VT amueblar de nuevo

refusal [rɪˈfjuːzəl] N negativa; **first ~** primera opción; **to have first ~ on sth** tener la primera opción a algo

refuse¹ [ˈrɛfjuːs] N basura

★**refuse²** [rɪˈfjuːz] VT *(reject)* rechazar; *(invitation)* declinar; *(permission)* denegar; *(say no to)* negarse a; **to ~ to do sth** negarse a *or* rehusar hacer algo ▸ VI negarse; *(horse)* rehusar

refuse bin N cubo *or* *(Lam)* bote m *or* *(Lam)* balde m de la basura

refuse collection N recogida de basuras

refuse disposal N eliminación f de basuras

refusenik [rɪˈfjuːznɪk] N *judío/a que tenía prohibido emigrar de la ex Unión Soviética*

refuse tip N vertedero

refute [rɪˈfjuːt] VT refutar, rebatir

regain [rɪˈɡeɪn] VT recobrar, recuperar

regal [ˈriːɡl] ADJ regio, real

regale [rɪˈɡeɪl] VT agasajar, entretener

regalia [rɪˈɡeɪlɪə] N galas fpl

regard [rɪˈɡɑːd] N *(gaze)* mirada; *(aspect)* respecto; *(esteem)* respeto; *(attention)* consideración f; **to give one's regards to** saludar de su parte a; **"(kind) regards"** "muy atentamente"; **"with kindest regards"** "con muchos recuerdos"; **regards to María, please give my regards to María** recuerdos a María, dele recuerdos a María de mi parte; **as regards, with ~ to** con respecto a, en cuanto a ▸ VT *(consider)* considerar; *(look at)* mirar

regarding [rɪˈɡɑːdɪŋ] PREP con respecto a, en cuanto a

regardless [rɪˈɡɑːdlɪs] ADV a pesar de todo; **~ of** sin reparar en

regatta [rɪˈɡætə] N regata

regency [ˈriːdʒənsɪ] N regencia

regenerate [rɪˈdʒɛnəreɪt] VT regenerar

regent [ˈriːdʒənt] N regente mf

reggae [ˈrɛɡeɪ] N reggae m

régime [reɪˈʒiːm] N régimen m

regiment N [ˈrɛdʒɪmənt] regimiento ▸ VT [ˈrɛdʒɪmɛnt] reglamentar

regimental [rɛdʒɪˈmɛntl] ADJ militar

regimentation [rɛdʒɪmɛnˈteɪʃən] N regimentación f

★**region** [ˈriːdʒən] N región f; **in the ~ of** *(fig)* alrededor de

regional [ˈriːdʒənl] ADJ regional

regional development N desarrollo regional

★**register** [ˈrɛdʒɪstəʳ] N registro ▸ VT registrar; *(birth)* declarar; *(car)* matricular; *(letter)* certificar; *(instrument)* marcar, indicar; **to ~ a protest** presentar una queja ▸ VI *(at hotel)* registrarse; *(as student)* matricularse; *(sign on)* inscribirse; *(make impression)* producir impresión; **to ~ for a course** matricularse *or* inscribirse en un curso

registered [ˈrɛdʒɪstəd] ADJ *(design)* registrado; *(Brit: letter)* certificado; *(student)* matriculado; *(voter)* registrado

registered company N sociedad f legalmente constituida

registered nurse N *(US)* enfermero(-a) titulado(-a)

registered office N domicilio social

registered trademark N marca registrada

registrar [ˈrɛdʒɪstrɑːʳ] N secretario(-a) (del registro civil)

registration [rɛdʒɪsˈtreɪʃən] N (act) declaración f; (Aut: also: **registration number**) matrícula

registry [ˈrɛdʒɪstrɪ] N registro

registry office N (BRIT) registro civil; **to get married in a ~** casarse por lo civil

★**regret** [rɪˈgrɛt] N sentimiento, pesar m; (remorse) remordimiento ▶ VT sentir, lamentar; (repent of) arrepentirse de; **we ~ to inform you that ...** sentimos informarle que ...

regretful [rɪˈgrɛtful] ADJ pesaroso, arrepentido

regretfully [rɪˈgrɛtfəlɪ] ADV con pesar, sentidamente

regrettable [rɪˈgrɛtəbl] ADJ lamentable; (loss) sensible

regrettably [rɪˈgrɛtəblɪ] ADV desgraciadamente

regroup [riːˈgruːp] VT reagrupar ▶ VI reagruparse

regt ABBR = **regiment**

★**regular** [ˈrɛgjuləʳ] ADJ regular; (soldier) profesional; (inf: intensive) verdadero; (listener, reader) asiduo; (usual) habitual ▶ N (client etc) cliente(-a) m/f habitual

regularity [rɛgjuˈlærɪtɪ] N regularidad f

regularly [ˈrɛgjuləlɪ] ADV con regularidad

regulate [ˈrɛgjuleɪt] VT (gen) controlar; (Tech) regular, ajustar

regulation [rɛgjuˈleɪʃən] N (rule) regla, reglamento; (adjustment) regulación f

rehabilitate [riːəˈbɪlɪteɪt] VT rehabilitar

rehabilitation [ˈriːəbɪlɪˈteɪʃən] N rehabilitación f

rehash [riːˈhæʃ] VT (inf) hacer un refrito de

rehearsal [rɪˈhəːsəl] N ensayo; **dress ~** ensayo general or final

rehearse [rɪˈhəːs] VT, VI ensayar

rehouse [riːˈhauz] VT dar nueva vivienda a

reign [reɪn] N reinado; (fig) predominio ▶ VI reinar; (fig) imperar

reigning [ˈreɪnɪŋ] ADJ (monarch) reinante, actual; (predominant) imperante

reiki [ˈreɪkɪ] N reiki m

reimburse [riːɪmˈbəːs] VT reembolsar

rein [reɪn] N (for horse) rienda; **to give sb free ~** dar rienda suelta a algn

reincarnation [riːɪnkɑːˈneɪʃən] N reencarnación f

★**reindeer** [ˈreɪndɪəʳ] N pl inv reno

reinforce [riːɪnˈfɔːs] VT reforzar

reinforced concrete [riːɪnˈfɔːst-] N hormigón m armado

reinforcement [riːɪnˈfɔːsmənt] N (action) refuerzo ■ **reinforcements** NPL (Mil) refuerzos mpl

reinstate [riːɪnˈsteɪt] VT (worker) reintegrar (a su puesto); (tax, law) reinstaurar

reinstatement [riːɪnˈsteɪtmənt] N reintegración f

reissue [riːˈɪʃuː] VT (record, book) reeditar

reiterate [riːˈɪtəreɪt] VT reiterar, repetir

reject N [ˈriːdʒɛkt] (thing) desecho ▶ VT [rɪˈdʒɛkt] rechazar; (proposition, offer etc) descartar

rejection [rɪˈdʒɛkʃən] N rechazo

rejoice [rɪˈdʒɔɪs] VI: **to ~ at** or **over** regocijarse or alegrarse de

rejoinder [rɪˈdʒɔɪndəʳ] N (retort) réplica

rejuvenate [rɪˈdʒuːvəneɪt] VT rejuvenecer

rekindle [riːˈkɪndl] VT volver a encender; (fig) despertar

relapse [rɪˈlæps] N (Med) recaída; (into crime) reincidencia

relate [rɪˈleɪt] VT (tell) contar, relatar; (connect) relacionar ▶ VI relacionarse; **to ~ to** (connect) relacionarse or tener que ver con

★**related** [rɪˈleɪtɪd] ADJ afín; (person) emparentado; **to be ~ to** (connected) guardar relación con; (by family) ser pariente de

relating [rɪˈleɪtɪŋ]: **~ to** prep referente a

★**relation** [rɪˈleɪʃən] N (person) pariente mf; (link) relación f; **in ~ to** en relación con, en lo que se refiere a; **to bear a ~** to guardar relación con; **diplomatic relations** relaciones fpl diplomáticas ■ **relations** NPL (relatives) familiares mpl

★**relationship** [rɪˈleɪʃənʃɪp] N relación f; (personal) relaciones fpl; (also: **family relationship**) parentesco

★**relative** [ˈrɛlətɪv] N pariente mf, familiar mf ▶ ADJ relativo

★**relatively** [ˈrɛlətɪvlɪ] ADV (fairly, rather) relativamente

relative pronoun N pronombre m relativo

★**relax** [rɪˈlæks] VI descansar; (quieten down) relajarse; **~!** (calm down) ¡tranquilo! ▶ VT relajar; (grip) aflojar

relaxation [riːlækˈseɪʃən] N (rest) descanso; (easing) relajación f, relajamiento; (amusement) recreo; (entertainment) diversión f

relaxed [rɪˈlækst] ADJ relajado; (tranquil) tranquilo

relaxing [rɪˈlæksɪŋ] ADJ relajante

relay N [ˈriːleɪ] (race) carrera de relevos ▶ VT [rɪˈleɪ] (Radio, TV) retransmitir; (pass on) retransmitir

★**release** [rɪˈliːs] N (liberation) liberación f; (discharge) puesta en libertad; (of gas etc) escape m; (of film etc) estreno; (of record) lanzamiento ▶ VT (prisoner) poner en libertad; (film) estrenar; (book) publicar; (piece of news) difundir; (gas etc) despedir, arrojar; (free: from wreckage etc) liberar; (Tech: catch, spring etc) desenganchar; (let go) soltar, aflojar

relegate [ˈrɛləgeɪt] VT relegar; (Sport): **to be relegated to** bajar a

relent [rɪˈlɛnt] VI ceder, ablandarse; (let up) descansar

relentless [rɪˈlɛntlɪs] ADJ implacable

relentlessly [rɪˈlɛntlɪslɪ] ADV implacablemente

relevance [ˈrɛləvəns] N relación f

relevant [ˈrɛləvənt] ADJ (fact) pertinente; ~ **to** relacionado con

reliability [rɪlaɪəˈbɪlɪtɪ] N (of method, source) fiabilidad f; (of machine, vehicle) seguridad f; (of facts) veracidad f

★**reliable** [rɪˈlaɪəbl] ADJ (person, firm) de confianza, de fiar; (method, machine) seguro; (source) fidedigno

reliably [rɪˈlaɪəblɪ] ADV: **to be ~ informed that ...** saber de fuente fidedigna que ...

reliance [rɪˈlaɪəns] N: ~ **(on)** dependencia (de)

reliant [rɪˈlaɪənt] ADJ: **to be ~ on sth/sb** depender de algo/algn

relic [ˈrɛlɪk] N (Rel) reliquia; (of the past) vestigio

★**relief** [rɪˈliːf] N (from pain, anxiety) alivio, desahogo; (help, supplies) socorro, ayuda; (Art, Geo) relieve m; **by way of light ~** a modo de diversión

relief road N carretera de descongestionamiento

relieve [rɪˈliːv] VT (pain, patient) aliviar; (bring help to) ayudar, socorrer; (burden) aligerar; (take over from: gen) sustituir a; (: guard) relevar; **to ~ sb of sth** quitar algo a algn; **to ~ sb of his command** (Mil) relevar a algn de su mando; **to ~ o.s.** hacer sus necesidades

relieved [rɪˈliːvd] ADJ: **to be ~** sentir un gran alivio

★**religion** [rɪˈlɪdʒən] N religión f

★**religious** [rɪˈlɪdʒəs] ADJ religioso

religious education N educación f religiosa

religiously [rɪˈlɪdʒəslɪ] ADV religiosamente

relinquish [rɪˈlɪŋkwɪʃ] VT abandonar; (plan, habit) renunciar a

relish [ˈrɛlɪʃ] N (Culin) salsa; (enjoyment) entusiasmo; (flavour) sabor m, gusto ▶ VT (food, challenge etc) saborear; **to ~ doing** gozar haciendo

relive [riːˈlɪv] VT vivir de nuevo, volver a vivir

relocate [riːləuˈkeɪt] VT trasladar ▶ VI trasladarse

reluctance [rɪˈlʌktəns] N desgana, renuencia

★**reluctant** [rɪˈlʌktənt] ADJ reacio; **to be ~ to do sth** resistirse a hacer algo

reluctantly [rɪˈlʌktəntlɪ] ADV de mala gana

rely [rɪˈlaɪ]: **to ~ on** VT fus confiar en, fiarse de; (: be dependent on) depender de; **you can ~ on my discretion** puedes contar con mi discreción

★**remain** [rɪˈmeɪn] VI (survive) quedar; (be left) sobrar; (continue) quedar(se), permanecer; **to ~ silent** permanecer callado; **I ~, yours faithfully** (in letters) le saluda atentamente

remainder [rɪˈmeɪndəʳ] N resto

remainer [rɪˈmeɪnəʳ] N (BRIT: in EU) partidario de permanecer en la Unión Europea

★**remaining** [rɪˈmeɪnɪŋ] ADJ restante, que queda(n)

remains [rɪˈmeɪnz] NPL restos mpl

remand [rɪˈmɑːnd] N: **on ~** detenido (bajo custodia) ▶ VT: **to ~ in custody** mantener bajo custodia

remand home N (BRIT) reformatorio

★**remark** [rɪˈmɑːk] N comentario ▶ VT comentar ▶ VI: **to ~ on sth** hacer observaciones sobre algo

★**remarkable** [rɪˈmɑːkəbl] ADJ notable; (outstanding) extraordinario

remarkably [rɪˈmɑːkəblɪ] ADV extraordinariamente

remarry [riːˈmærɪ] VI casarse por segunda vez, volver a casarse

remedial [rɪˈmiːdɪəl] ADJ: ~ **education** educación f de los niños atrasados

remedy [ˈrɛmədɪ] N remedio ▶ VT remediar, curar

★**remember** [rɪˈmɛmbəʳ] VT recordar, acordarse de; (bear in mind) tener presente; **I ~ seeing it, I ~ having seen it** recuerdo haberlo visto; **she remembered doing it** se acordó de hacerlo; ~ **me to your wife and children!** ¡dele recuerdos a su familia!

> Both **acordarse de** and **recordar** can be used in general contexts to translate to remember: Do you remember where he lives? **¿Te acuerdas de dónde vive?** or **¿Recuerdas dónde vive?** You can only use **acordarse de** to translate to remember to do something: Did you remember to close the door? **¿Te acordaste de cerrar la puerta?**
> **Recordar** is also used to translate remind: I must remind Richard to pay the rent. **Tengo que recordarle a Richard que pague el alquiler.**

remembrance [rɪˈmɛmbrəns] N (memory, souvenir) recuerdo; **in ~ of** en conmemoración de

Remembrance Day, Remembrance Sunday N (BRIT) ver nota

> En el Reino Unido el domingo más cercano al 11 de noviembre es **Remembrance Day** o **Remembrance Sunday**, aniversario de la firma del armisticio de 1918 que puso fin a la Primera Guerra Mundial. Tal día se recuerda a todos aquellos que murieron en las dos guerras mundiales con dos minutos de silencio a las once de la mañana (hora en que se firmó el armisticio), durante los actos de conmemoración celebrados en los monumentos a los caídos. Allí se colocan coronas de amapolas, flor que también se suele llevar prendida en el pecho tras pagar un donativo para los inválidos de guerra.

★**remind** [rɪˈmaɪnd] VT: **to ~ sb to do sth** recordar a algn que haga algo; **to ~ sb of sth** recordar algo a algn; **she reminds me of her mother** me recuerda a su madre; **that reminds me!** ¡a propósito!

reminder [rɪˈmaɪndəʳ] N notificación f; (memento) recuerdo

reminisce [rɛmɪ'nɪs] VI recordar (viejas historias)

reminiscences [rɛmɪ'nɪsnsɪz] NPL reminiscencias *fpl*, recuerdos *mpl*

reminiscent [rɛmɪ'nɪsnt] ADJ: **to be ~ of sth** recordar algo

remiss [rɪ'mɪs] ADJ descuidado; **it was ~ of me** fue un descuido de mi parte

remission [rɪ'mɪʃən] N remisión *f*; (*of sentence*) reducción *f* de la pena

remit [rɪ'mɪt] VT (*send: money*) remitir, enviar

remittance [rɪ'mɪtns] N remesa, envío

remnant ['rɛmnənt] N resto; (*of cloth*) retal *m*, retazo ■ **remnants** NPL (*Comm*) restos de serie

remonstrate ['rɛmənstreɪt] VI protestar

remorse [rɪ'mɔːs] N remordimientos *mpl*

remorseful [rɪ'mɔːsful] ADJ arrepentido

remorseless [rɪ'mɔːslɪs] ADJ (*fig*) implacable, inexorable

remorselessly [rɪ'mɔːslɪslɪ] ADV implacablemente, inexorablemente

remortgage [riː'mɔːgɪdʒ] VT: **to ~ one's house/home** volver a hipotecar la casa

★**remote** [rɪ'məut] ADJ remoto; (*distant*) lejano; (*person*) distante; **there is a ~ possibility that ...** hay una posibilidad remota de que ...

remote control N mando a distancia

remote-controlled [rɪ'məutkən'trəuld] ADJ teledirigido, con mando a distancia

remotely [rɪ'məutlɪ] ADV remotamente; (*slightly*) levemente

remoteness [rɪ'məutnɪs] N alejamiento; distancia

remould ['riː'məuld] N (*BRIT: tyre*) neumático *or* (*LAM*) llanta recauchutado(-a)

removable [rɪ'muː'vəbl] ADJ (*detachable*) separable

removal [rɪ'muː'vəl] N (*taking away*) (el) quitar; (*BRIT: from house*) mudanza; (*from office: dismissal*) destitución *f*; (*Med*) extirpación *f*

removal man N (*irreg*) (*BRIT*) mozo de mudanzas

removal van N (*BRIT*) camión *m* de mudanzas

★**remove** [rɪ'muːv] VT quitar; (*employee*) destituir; (*name: from list*) tachar, borrar; (*doubt*) disipar; (*Tech*) retirar, separar; (*Med*) extirpar; **first cousin once removed** (*parent's cousin*) tío(-a) segundo(-a); (*cousin's child*) sobrino(-a) segundo(-a)

remover [rɪ'muː'vəʳ] N: **make-up ~** desmaquilladora

remunerate [rɪ'mjuː'nəreɪt] VT remunerar

remuneration [rɪmjuː'nə'reɪʃən] N remuneración *f*

Renaissance [rɪ'neɪsɔ̃s] N: **the ~** el Renacimiento

rename [riː'neɪm] VT poner nuevo nombre a

render ['rɛndəʳ] VT (*thanks*) dar; (*aid*) proporcionar; (*honour*) dar, conceder; (*assistance*) dar, prestar; **to ~ sth + adj** volver algo + *adj*; **to ~ sth useless** hacer algo inútil

rendering ['rɛndərɪŋ] N (*Mus etc*) interpretación *f*

rendez-vous ['rɔndɪvuː] N cita ▶ VI reunirse, encontrarse; (*spaceship*) efectuar una reunión espacial

rendition [rɛn'dɪʃən] N (*Mus*) interpretación *f*

renegade ['rɛnɪgeɪd] N renegado(-a)

★**renew** [rɪ'njuː] VT renovar; (*resume*) reanudar; (*extend date*) prorrogar; (*negotiations*) volver a

renewable [rɪ'njuː'əbl] ADJ renovable; **~ energy**, **renewables** energías *fpl* renovables

renewal [rɪ'njuː'əl] N renovación *f*; reanudación *f*; prórroga

renounce [rɪ'nauns] VT renunciar a; (*right, inheritance*) renunciar

renovate ['rɛnəveɪt] VT renovar

renovation [rɛnə'veɪʃən] N renovación *f*

renown [rɪ'naun] N renombre *m*

renowned [rɪ'naund] ADJ renombrado

★**rent** [rɛnt] N alquiler *m*; (*for house*) arriendo, renta ▶ VT (*also: rent out*) alquilar

rental ['rɛntl] N (*for television, car*) alquiler *m*

rent boy N (*BRIT inf*) chapero

renunciation [rɪnʌnsɪ'eɪʃən] N renuncia

reoffend [riːə'fɛnd] VI reincidir

reopen [riː'əupən] VT volver a abrir, reabrir

reorder [riː'ɔːdəʳ] VT volver a pedir, repetir el pedido de; (*rearrange*) volver a ordenar *or* arreglar

reorganization [riːɔːgənaɪ'zeɪʃən] N reorganización *f*

reorganize [riː'ɔːgənaɪz] VT reorganizar

Rep ABBR (*US Pol*) = **representative**; **republican**

rep [rɛp] N ABBR (*Comm*) = **representative**; (*Theat*) = **repertory**

★**repair** [rɪ'pɛəʳ] N reparación *f*, arreglo; (*patch*) remiendo; **in good/bad ~** en buen/mal estado; **under ~** en obras ▶ VT reparar, arreglar

repair kit N caja de herramientas

repair man N (*irreg*) mecánico

repair shop N taller *m* de reparaciones

repartee [rɛpɑː'tiː] N réplicas *fpl* agudas

repast [rɪ'pɑːst] N (*formal*) comida

repatriate [riː'pætrɪeɪt] VT repatriar

repay [riː'peɪ] VT (*irreg: like* **pay**) (*money*) devolver, reembolsar; (*person*) pagar; (*debt*) liquidar; (*sb's efforts*) devolver, corresponder a

repayment [riː'peɪmənt] N reembolso, devolución *f*; (*sum of money*) recompensa

repeal [rɪ'piːl] N revocación *f* ▶ VT revocar

★**repeat** [rɪ'piːt] N (*Radio, TV*) reposición *f* ▶ VT repetir ▶ VI repetirse

repeatedly [rɪ'piːtɪdlɪ] ADV repetidas veces

repeat order N (*Comm*): **to place a ~ for** renovar un pedido de

741

repeat prescription N (BRIT) receta renovada

repel [rɪˈpɛl] VT repugnar

repellent [rɪˈpɛlənt] ADJ repugnante ▶ N: **insect ~** crema/loción f anti-insectos

repent [rɪˈpɛnt] VI: **to ~ (of)** arrepentirse (de)

repentance [rɪˈpɛntəns] N arrepentimiento

repercussion [riːpəˈkʌʃən] N (consequence) repercusión f; **to have repercussions** repercutir

repertoire [ˈrɛpətwɑːˈ] N repertorio

repertory [ˈrɛpətərɪ] N (also: **repertory theatre**) teatro de repertorio

repertory company N compañía de repertorio

repetition [rɛpɪˈtɪʃən] N repetición f

repetitious [rɛpɪˈtɪʃəs] ADJ repetidor(a), que se repite

repetitive [rɪˈpɛtɪtɪv] ADJ (movement, work) repetitivo, reiterativo; (speech) lleno de repeticiones

rephrase [riːˈfreɪz] VT decir or formular de otro modo

★**replace** [rɪˈpleɪs] VT (put back) devolver a su sitio; (take the place of) reemplazar, sustituir

replacement [rɪˈpleɪsmənt] N reemplazo; (act) reposición f; (thing) recambio; (person) suplente mf

replacement cost N costo de sustitución

replacement part N repuesto

replacement value N valor m de sustitución

replay [ˈriːpleɪ] N (Sport) partido de desempate; (TV: playback) repetición f

replenish [rɪˈplɛnɪʃ] VT (tank etc) rellenar; (stock etc) reponer; (with fuel) repostar

replete [rɪˈpliːt] ADJ repleto, lleno

replica [ˈrɛplɪkə] N réplica, reproducción f

★**reply** [rɪˈplaɪ] N respuesta, contestación f; **in ~** en respuesta; **there's no ~** (Tel) no contestan ▶ VI contestar, responder

reply coupon N cupón-respuesta m

reply-paid [rɪˈplaɪˈpeɪd] ADJ: **~ postcard** tarjeta postal con respuesta pagada

★**report** [rɪˈpɔːt] N informe m; (Press etc) reportaje m; (BRIT: also: **school report**) informe m escolar; (of gun) detonación f; **annual ~** (Comm) informe m anual ▶ VT informar sobre; (Press etc) hacer un reportaje sobre; (notify: accident, culprit) denunciar; **it is reported from Berlin that ...** se informa desde Berlín que ... ▶ VI (make a report) presentar un informe; (present o.s.): **to ~ (to sb)** presentarse (ante algn); **to ~ (on)** hacer un informe (sobre)

report card N (US, SCOTTISH) cartilla escolar

reportedly [rɪˈpɔːtɪdlɪ] ADV según se dice, según se informa

★**reporter** [rɪˈpɔːtəʳ] N (Press) periodista mf, reportero(-a); (Radio, TV) locutor(a) m/f

repose [rɪˈpəuz] N: **in ~** (face, mouth) en reposo

repossess [riːpəˈzɛs] VT recuperar

repossession order [riːpəˈzɛʃən-] N orden de devolución de la vivienda por el impago de la hipoteca

reprehensible [rɛprɪˈhɛnsɪbl] ADJ reprensible, censurable

★**represent** [rɛprɪˈzɛnt] VT representar; (Comm) ser agente de

representation [rɛprɪzɛnˈteɪʃən] N representación f; (petition) petición f ■ **representations** NPL (protest) quejas fpl

★**representative** [rɛprɪˈzɛntətɪv] N (US Pol) representante mf, diputado(-a); (Comm) representante mf ▶ ADJ: **~ (of)** representativo (de)

repress [rɪˈprɛs] VT reprimir

repression [rɪˈprɛʃən] N represión f

repressive [rɪˈprɛsɪv] ADJ represivo

reprieve [rɪˈpriːv] N (Law) indulto; (fig) alivio ▶ VT indultar; (fig) salvar

reprimand [ˈrɛprɪmɑːnd] N reprimenda ▶ VT reprender

reprint N [ˈriːprɪnt] reimpresión f ▶ VT [riːˈprɪnt] reimprimir

reprisal [rɪˈpraɪzl] N represalia; **to take reprisals** tomar represalias

reproach [rɪˈprəutʃ] N reproche m; **beyond ~** intachable ▶ VT: **to ~ sb with sth** reprochar algo a algn

reproachful [rɪˈprəutʃful] ADJ de reproche, de acusación

reproduce [riːprəˈdjuːs] VT reproducir ▶ VI reproducirse

reproduction [riːprəˈdʌkʃən] N reproducción f

reproductive [riːprəˈdʌktɪv] ADJ reproductor(a)

reproof [rɪˈpruːf] N reproche m

reprove [rɪˈpruːv] VT: **to ~ sb for sth** reprochar algo a algn

reptile [ˈrɛptaɪl] N reptil m

Repub. ABBR (US Pol) = **republican**

★**republic** [rɪˈpʌblɪk] N república

republican [rɪˈpʌblɪkən] ADJ, N republicano(-a) m/f

repudiate [rɪˈpjuːdɪeɪt] VT (charge) rechazar; (debt) negarse a reconocer

repudiation [rɪpjuːdɪˈeɪʃən] N (of charge) rechazo; (of debt) negativa a reconocer

repugnance [rɪˈpʌgnəns] N repugnancia

repugnant [rɪˈpʌgnənt] ADJ repugnante

repulse [rɪˈpʌls] VT rechazar

repulsion [rɪˈpʌlʃən] N repulsión f, repugnancia

repulsive [rɪˈpʌlsɪv] ADJ repulsivo

repurchase [riːˈpəːtʃəs] VT volver a comprar, readquirir

reputable [ˈrɛpjutəbl] ADJ (make etc) de renombre

★**reputation** [rɛpjuˈteɪʃən] N reputación f; **he has a ~ for being awkward** tiene fama de difícil

repute [rɪ'pjuːt] N reputación f, fama

reputed [rɪ'pjuːtɪd] ADJ supuesto; **to be ~ to be rich/intelligent** etc tener fama de rico/inteligente etc

reputedly [rɪ'pjuːtɪdlɪ] ADV según dicen or se dice

★**request** [rɪ'kwɛst] N solicitud f, petición f; **at the ~ of** a petición de ▶ VT: **to ~ sth of** or **from sb** solicitar algo a algn; **"you are requested not to smoke"** "se ruega no fumar"

request stop N (BRIT) parada discrecional

requiem ['rɛkwɪəm] N réquiem m

★**require** [rɪ'kwaɪəʳ] VT (need: person) necesitar, tener necesidad de; (: thing, situation) exigir, requerir; (want) pedir; (demand): **to ~ sb to do sth/sth of sb** exigir que algn haga algo; **what qualifications are required?** ¿qué títulos se requieren?; **required by law** requerido por la ley

★**requirement** [rɪ'kwaɪəmənt] N requisito; (need) necesidad f

requisite ['rɛkwɪzɪt] N requisito ▶ ADJ necesario, requerido

requisition [rɛkwɪ'zɪʃən] N solicitud f; (Mil) requisa ▶ VT (Mil) requisar

reroute [riː'ruːt] VT desviar

resale ['riːseɪl] N reventa

resale price maintenance N mantenimiento del precio de venta

resat [riː'sæt] PT, PP of **resit**

rescind [rɪ'sɪnd] VT (Law) abrogar; (contract) rescindir; (order etc) anular

★**rescue** ['rɛskjuː] N rescate m; **to come/go to sb's ~** ir en auxilio de algn, socorrer a algn ▶ VT rescatar; **to ~ from** librar de

rescue party N equipo de salvamento

rescuer ['rɛskjuəʳ] N salvador(a) m/f

★**research** [rɪ'səːtʃ] N investigaciones fpl; **a piece of ~** un trabajo de investigación ▶ VT investigar ▶ VI hacer investigaciones; **to ~ (into sth)** investigar (algo)

research and development N investigación f y desarrollo

researcher [rɪ'səːtʃəʳ] N investigador(a) m/f

research work N investigación f

resell [riː'sɛl] (pt, pp **resold** [-'səuld]) VT revender

resemblance [rɪ'zɛmbləns] N parecido; **to bear a strong ~ to** parecerse mucho a

resemble [rɪ'zɛmbl] VT parecerse a

resent [rɪ'zɛnt] VT resentirse por, ofenderse por; **he resents my being here** le molesta que esté aquí

resentful [rɪ'zɛntful] ADJ resentido

resentment [rɪ'zɛntmənt] N resentimiento

reservation [rɛzə'veɪʃən] N reserva; (BRIT: also: **central reservation**) mediana; **with reservations** con reservas

reservation desk N (US: in hotel) recepción f

★**reserve** [rɪ'zəːv] N reserva; (Sport) suplente mf; **in ~** en reserva ▶ VT (seats etc) reservar ▪ **reserves** NPL (Mil) reserva sg

reserve currency N divisa de reserva

reserved [rɪ'zəːvd] ADJ reservado

reserve price N (BRIT) precio mínimo

reserve team N (Sport) equipo reserva

reservist [rɪ'zəːvɪst] N (Mil) reservista m

reservoir ['rɛzəvwɑːʳ] N (artificial lake) embalse m, represa; (tank) depósito

reset [riː'sɛt] (pt, pp ~) VT (Comput) reinicializar

reshape [riː'ʃeɪp] VT (policy) reformar, rehacer

reshuffle [riː'ʃʌfl] N: **Cabinet ~** (Pol) remodelación f del gabinete

reside [rɪ'zaɪd] VI residir

residence ['rɛzɪdəns] N residencia; (formal: home) domicilio; (length of stay) permanencia; **in ~** (doctor) residente; **to take up ~** instalarse

residence permit N (BRIT) permiso de residencia

★**resident** ['rɛzɪdənt] N vecino(-a); (in hotel) huésped(a) m/f ▶ ADJ residente; (population) permanente

residential [rɛzɪ'dɛnʃəl] ADJ residencial

residue ['rɛzɪdjuː] N resto, residuo

★**resign** [rɪ'zaɪn] VT (gen) renunciar a; **to ~ o.s. to** (endure) resignarse a ▶ VI: **to ~ (from)** dimitir (de), renunciar (a)

resignation [rɛzɪg'neɪʃən] N dimisión f; (state of mind) resignación f; **to tender one's ~** presentar la dimisión

resigned [rɪ'zaɪnd] ADJ resignado

resilience [rɪ'zɪlɪəns] N (of material) elasticidad f; (of person) resistencia

resilient [rɪ'zɪlɪənt] ADJ (person) resistente

resin ['rɛzɪn] N resina

resist [rɪ'zɪst] VT resistirse a; (temptation, damage) resistir

resistance [rɪ'zɪstəns] N resistencia

resistant [rɪ'zɪstənt] ADJ: **~ (to)** resistente (a)

resit [riː'sɪt] (pt, pp **resat** [-'sæt]) VT (BRIT: exam) volver a presentarse a; (: subject) recuperar, volver a examinarse de (SP)

resolute ['rɛzəluːt] ADJ resuelto

resolutely ['rɛzəluːtlɪ] ADV resueltamente

★**resolution** [rɛzə'luːʃən] N (gen: Comput) resolución f; (purpose) propósito; **to make a ~** tomar una resolución

resolve [rɪ'zɔlv] N (determination) resolución f; (purpose) propósito ▶ VT resolver; **to ~ to do** resolver hacer ▶ VI resolverse

resolved [rɪ'zɔlvd] ADJ resuelto

resonance ['rɛzənəns] N resonancia

resonant ['rɛzənənt] ADJ resonante

★**resort** [rɪ'zɔːt] N (town) centro turístico; (recourse) recurso; **in the last ~** como último recurso; **seaside ~** playa, estación f balnearia;

r

winter sports ~ centro de deportes de invierno
▶ VI: **to ~ to** recurrir a

resound [rɪ'zaund] VI: **to ~ (with)** resonar (con)

resounding [rɪ'zaundɪŋ] ADJ sonoro; (fig) clamoroso

★**resource** [rɪ'sɔːs] N recurso; **natural resources** recursos mpl naturales; **to leave sb to his/her own resources** (fig) abandonar a algn/a sus propios recursos ■ **resources** NPL recursos mpl

resourceful [rɪ'sɔːsful] ADJ ingenioso

resourcefulness [rɪ'sɔːsfulnɪs] N inventiva, iniciativa

★**respect** [rɪs'pɛkt] N (consideration) respeto; (relation) respecto; **with ~ to** con respecto a; **in this ~** en cuanto a eso; **to have** or **show ~ for** tener or mostrar respeto a; **out of ~ for** por respeto a; **in some respects** en algunos aspectos; **with due ~, I still think you're wrong** con el respeto debido, sigo creyendo que está equivocado ▶ VT respetar ■ **respects** NPL recuerdos mpl, saludos mpl

> Don't confuse **respeto**, which refers to the esteem in which someone or something is held, with **respecto**, which means regard:
> They always treat me with respect. **Siempre me tratan con respeto.**
> With regard to the financial situation, ... **Respecto a la situación económica, ...**

respectability [rɪspɛktə'bɪlɪtɪ] N respetabilidad f

respectable [rɪs'pɛktəbl] ADJ respetable; (quite big: amount etc) apreciable; (passable) tolerable; (quite good: player, result etc) bastante bueno

respected [rɪs'pɛktɪd] ADJ respetado, estimado

respectful [rɪs'pɛktful] ADJ respetuoso

respectfully [rɪs'pɛktfulɪ] ADV respetuosamente; **Yours ~** Le saluda atentamente

respecting [rɪs'pɛktɪŋ] PREP (con) respecto a, en cuanto a

respective [rɪs'pɛktɪv] ADJ respectivo

respectively [rɪs'pɛktɪvlɪ] ADV respectivamente

respiration [rɛspɪ'reɪʃən] N respiración f

respiratory [rɛs'pɪrətərɪ] ADJ respiratorio

respite ['rɛspaɪt] N respiro; (Law) prórroga

resplendent [rɪs'plɛndənt] ADJ resplandeciente

respond [rɪs'pɔnd] VI responder; (react) reaccionar

respondent [rɪs'pɔndənt] N (Law) demandado(-a)

response [rɪs'pɔns] N respuesta; (reaction) reacción f; **in ~ to** como respuesta a

★**responsibility** [rɪspɔnsɪ'bɪlɪtɪ] N responsabilidad f; **to take ~ for sth/sb** admitir responsabilidad por algo/algn

★**responsible** [rɪs'pɔnsɪbl] ADJ (liable): **~ (for)** responsable (de); (character) serio, formal; (job) de responsabilidad; **to be ~ to sb (for sth)** ser responsable ante algn (de algo)

responsibly [rɪs'pɔnsɪblɪ] ADV con seriedad

responsive [rɪs'pɔnsɪv] ADJ sensible

★**rest** [rɛst] N descanso, reposo; (Mus) pausa, silencio; (support) apoyo; (remainder) resto; **the ~ of them** (people, objects) los demás; **to set sb's mind at ~** tranquilizar a algn ▶ VI descansar; (be supported): **to ~ on** apoyarse en; **it rests with him** depende de él; **~ assured that ...** tenga por seguro que ... ▶ VT (lean): **to ~ sth on/against** apoyar algo en or sobre/contra; **to ~ one's eyes** or **gaze on** fijar la mirada en

★**restaurant** ['rɛstərɔŋ] N restaurante m

restaurant car N (BRIT) coche-comedor m

restaurant owner N dueño(-a) or propietario(-a) de un restaurante

rest cure N cura de reposo

restful ['rɛstful] ADJ descansado, tranquilo

rest home N residencia de ancianos

restitution [rɛstɪ'tjuːʃən] N: **to make ~ to sb for sth** restituir algo a algn; (paying) indemnizar a algn por algo

restive ['rɛstɪv] ADJ inquieto; (horse) rebelón(-ona)

restless ['rɛstlɪs] ADJ inquieto; **to get ~** impacientarse

restlessly ['rɛstlɪslɪ] ADV inquietamente, con inquietud f

restlessness ['rɛstlɪsnɪs] N inquietud f

restock [riː'stɔk] VT reaprovisionar

restoration [rɛstə'reɪʃən] N restauración f; (giving back) devolución f, restitución f

restorative [rɪ'stɔːrətɪv] ADJ reconstituyente, fortalecedor(a) ▶ N reconstituyente m

restore [rɪ'stɔː] VT (building) restaurar; (sth stolen) devolver, restituir; (health) restablecer

restorer [rɪ'stɔːrə] N (Art etc) restaurador(a) m/f

restrain [rɪs'treɪn] VT (feeling) contener, refrenar; (person): **to ~ (from doing)** disuadir (de hacer)

restrained [rɪs'treɪnd] ADJ (style) reservado

restraint [rɪs'treɪnt] N (restriction) freno, control m; (moderation) moderación f; (of style) reserva; **wage ~** control m de los salarios

restrict [rɪs'trɪkt] VT restringir, limitar

restricted [rɪs'trɪktɪd] ADJ restringido, limitado

restriction [rɪs'trɪkʃən] N restricción f, limitación f

restrictive [rɪs'trɪktɪv] ADJ restrictivo

restrictive practices NPL (Industry) prácticas fpl restrictivas

rest room N (US) aseos mpl

restructure [riː'strʌktʃə] VT reestructurar

★**result** [rɪ'zʌlt] N resultado; **as a ~ of** a or como consecuencia de ▶ VI: **to ~ in** terminar en, tener por resultado; **to ~ (from)** resultar (de)

resultant [rɪ'zʌltənt] ADJ resultante

resume [rɪ'zju:m] VT (work, journey) reanudar; (sum up) resumir ▸ VI (meeting) continuar

résumé ['reɪzju:meɪ] N resumen m

resumption [rɪ'zʌmpʃən] N reanudación f

resurgence [rɪ'sə:dʒəns] N resurgimiento

resurrection [rɛzə'rɛkʃən] N resurrección f

resuscitate [rɪ'sʌsɪteɪt] VT (Med) resucitar

resuscitation [rɪsʌsɪ'teɪʃn] N resucitación f

retail ['ri:teɪl] N venta al por menor ▸ CPD al por menor ▸ VT vender al por menor or al detalle ▸ VI: **to ~ at** (Comm) tener precio de venta al público de

retailer ['ri:teɪlər] N minorista mf, detallista mf

retail outlet N punto de venta

retail price N precio de venta al público, precio al detalle or al por menor

retail price index N índice m de precios al por menor

retain [rɪ'teɪn] VT (keep) retener, conservar; (employ) contratar

retainer [rɪ'teɪnər] N (servant) criado(-a); (fee) anticipo

retaliate [rɪ'tælɪeɪt] VI: **to ~ (against)** tomar represalias (contra)

retaliation [rɪtælɪ'eɪʃən] N represalias fpl; **in ~ for** como represalia por

retaliatory [rɪ'tælɪətərɪ] ADJ de represalia

retarded [rɪ'tɑ:dɪd] ADJ (!) retrasado (mental) (!)

retch [rɛtʃ] VI darle a algn arcadas

retentive [rɪ'tɛntɪv] ADJ (memory) retentivo

rethink [ri:'θɪŋk] VT repensar

reticence ['rɛtɪsns] N reticencia, reserva

reticent ['rɛtɪsnt] ADJ reticente, reservado

retina ['rɛtɪnə] N retina

retinue ['rɛtɪnju:] N séquito, comitiva

★**retire** [rɪ'taɪər] VI (give up work) jubilarse; (withdraw) retirarse; (go to bed) acostarse

retired [rɪ'taɪəd] ADJ (person) jubilado

★**retirement** [rɪ'taɪəmənt] N jubilación f; **early ~** jubilación f anticipada

retiring [rɪ'taɪərɪŋ] ADJ (departing: chairman) saliente; (shy) retraído

retort [rɪ'tɔ:t] N (reply) réplica ▸ VI replicar

retrace [ri:'treɪs] VT: **to ~ one's steps** volver sobre sus pasos, desandar lo andado

retract [rɪ'trækt] VT (statement) retirar; (claws) retraer; (undercarriage, aerial) replegar ▸ VI retractarse

retractable [rɪ'træktəbl] ADJ replegable

retrain [ri:'treɪn] VT reciclar

retraining [ri:'treɪnɪŋ] N reciclaje m, readaptación f profesional

retread ['ri:trɛd] N neumático or (LAm) llanta recauchutado(-a)

retreat [rɪ'tri:t] N (place) retiro; (Mil) retirada;

to beat a hasty ~ (fig) retirarse en desbandada ▸ VI retirarse; (flood) bajar

retrial ['ri:traɪəl] N nuevo proceso

retribution [rɛtrɪ'bju:ʃən] N desquite m

retrieval [rɪ'tri:vəl] N recuperación f; **information ~** recuperación f de datos

retrieve [rɪ'tri:v] VT recobrar; (situation, honour) salvar; (Comput) recuperar; (error) reparar

retriever [rɪ'tri:vər] N perro cobrador

retroactive [rɛtrəu'æktɪv] ADJ retroactivo

retrograde ['rɛtrəgreɪd] ADJ retrógrado

retrospect ['rɛtrəspɛkt] N: **in ~** retrospectivamente

retrospective [rɛtrə'spɛktɪv] ADJ retrospectivo; (law) retroactivo ▸ N exposición f retrospectiva

★**return** [rɪ'tə:n] N (going or coming back) vuelta, regreso; (of sth stolen etc) devolución f; (recompense) recompensa; (Finance: from land, shares) ganancia, ingresos mpl; (Comm: of merchandise) devolución f; **tax ~** declaración f de la renta; **in ~ (for)** a cambio (de); **by ~ of post** a vuelta de correo; **many happy returns (of the day)!** ¡feliz cumpleaños! ▸ CPD (journey) de regreso; (Brit: ticket) de ida y vuelta; (match) de vuelta ▸ VI (person etc: come or go back) volver, regresar; (symptoms etc) reaparecer ▸ VT devolver; (favour, love etc) corresponder a; (verdict) pronunciar; (Pol: candidate) elegir ■ **returns** NPL (Comm) ingresos mpl

returnable [rɪ'tə:nəbl] ADJ: **~ bottle** envase m retornable

returner [rɪ'tə:nər] N mujer que vuelve a trabajar tras un tiempo dedicada a la familia

returning officer [rɪ'tə:nɪŋ-] N (Brit Pol) escrutador(a) m/f

return key N (Comput) tecla de retorno

return ticket N (esp Brit) billete m (Sp) or boleto m (LAm) de ida y vuelta, billete m redondo (Mex)

retweet [ri:'twi:t] VT (on Twitter) retuitear ▸ N retuit m

reunion [ri:'ju:nɪən] N (of family) reunión f; (of two people, school) reencuentro

reunite [ri:ju:'naɪt] VT reunir; (reconcile) reconciliar

rev [rɛv] N ABBR (Aut: = revolution) revolución f ▸ VT (also: **rev up**) acelerar

Rev., Revd. ABBR (= reverend) R., Rvdo.

revaluation [ri:vælju:'eɪʃən] N revalorización f

revamp [ri:'væmp] VT renovar

reveal [rɪ'vi:l] VT (make known) revelar

revealing [rɪ'vi:lɪŋ] ADJ revelador(a)

reveille [rɪ'vælɪ] N (Mil) diana

revel ['rɛvl] VI: **to ~ in sth/in doing sth** gozar de algo/haciendo algo

revelation [rɛvə'leɪʃən] N revelación f

reveller, (US) **reveler** ['rɛvlər] N jaranero(-a), juerguista mf

revelry ['rɛvlrɪ] N jarana, juerga

r

745

revenge [rɪˈvɛndʒ] N venganza; (*in sport*) revancha; **to take ~ on** vengarse de; **to get one's ~ (for sth)** vengarse (de algo)

revengeful [rɪˈvɛndʒful] ADJ vengativo

revenue [ˈrɛvənjuː] N ingresos *mpl*, rentas *fpl*

revenue account N cuenta de ingresos presupuestarios

revenue expenditure N gasto corriente

reverberate [rɪˈvəːbəreɪt] VI (*sound*) resonar, retumbar

reverberation [rɪvəːbəˈreɪʃən] N resonancia

revere [rɪˈvɪər] VT reverenciar, venerar

reverence [ˈrɛvərəns] N reverencia

Reverend [ˈrɛvərənd] ADJ (*in titles*): **the ~ John Smith** (*Anglican*) el Reverendo John Smith; (*Catholic*) el Padre John Smith; (*Protestant*) el Pastor John Smith

reverent [ˈrɛvərənt] ADJ reverente

reverie [ˈrɛvərɪ] N ensueño

reversal [rɪˈvəːsl] N (*of order*) inversión *f*; (*of policy*) cambio de rumbo; (*of decision*) revocación *f*

★**reverse** [rɪˈvəːs] N (*opposite*) contrario; (*back: of cloth*) revés *m*; (: *of coin*) reverso; (: *of paper*) dorso; (*Aut: also:* **reverse gear**) marcha atrás; **the ~** lo contrario; **to go into ~** dar marcha atrás ▶ ADJ (*order*) inverso; (*direction*) contrario; **in ~ order** en orden inverso ▶ VT (*decision*) dar marcha atrás a; (*Aut*) dar marcha atrás a; (*position, function*) invertir ▶ VI (*Brit Aut*) dar marcha atrás

reverse-charge call [rɪˈvəːstʃɑːdʒ-] N (*Brit*) llamada a cobro revertido

reverse video N vídeo inverso

reversible [rɪˈvəːsəbl] ADJ (*garment, procedure*) reversible

reversing lights [rɪˈvəːsɪŋ-] NPL (*Brit Aut*) luces *fpl* de marcha atrás

revert [rɪˈvəːt] VI: **to ~ to** volver *or* revertir a

★**review** [rɪˈvjuː] N (*magazine, also Mil*) revista; (*of book, film*) reseña; (*US: examination*) repaso, examen *m*; **to come under ~** ser examinado ▶ VT repasar, examinar; (*Mil*) pasar revista a; (*book, film*) reseñar

reviewer [rɪˈvjuːər] N crítico(-a)

revile [rɪˈvaɪl] VT injuriar, vilipendiar

revise [rɪˈvaɪz] VT (*manuscript*) corregir; (*opinion*) modificar; (*price, procedure*) revisar; (*Brit: study: subject*) repasar; (*look over*) revisar; **revised edition** edición *f* corregida

revision [rɪˈvɪʒən] N corrección *f*; modificación *f*; (*of subject*) repaso; (*revised version*) revisión *f*

revisit [riːˈvɪzɪt] VT volver a visitar

revitalize [riːˈvaɪtəlaɪz] VT revivificar

revival [rɪˈvaɪvəl] N (*recovery*) reanimación *f*; (*Pol*) resurgimiento; (*of interest*) renacimiento; (*Theat*) reestreno; (*of faith*) despertar *m*

revive [rɪˈvaɪv] VT resucitar; (*custom*) restablecer; (*hope, courage*) reanimar; (*play*) reestrenar ▶ VI (*person*) volver en sí; (*from tiredness*) reponerse; (*business*) reactivarse

revoke [rɪˈvəuk] VT revocar

revolt [rɪˈvəult] N rebelión *f* ▶ VI rebelarse, sublevarse; **to ~ (against sb/sth)** rebelarse (contra algn/algo) ▶ VT dar asco a, repugnar

revolting [rɪˈvəultɪŋ] ADJ asqueroso, repugnante

★**revolution** [rɛvəˈluːʃən] N revolución *f*

revolutionary [rɛvəˈluːʃənrɪ] ADJ, N revolucionario(-a) *m/f*

revolutionize [rɛvəˈluːʃənaɪz] VT revolucionar

revolve [rɪˈvɒlv] VI dar vueltas, girar; **to ~ (a) round** girar en torno a

revolver [rɪˈvɒlvər] N revólver *m*

revolving [rɪˈvɒlvɪŋ] ADJ (*chair, door etc*) giratorio

revue [rɪˈvjuː] N (*Theat*) revista

revulsion [rɪˈvʌlʃən] N asco, repugnancia

★**reward** [rɪˈwɔːd] N premio, recompensa ▶ VT: **to ~ (for)** recompensar *or* premiar (por)

rewarding [rɪˈwɔːdɪŋ] ADJ (*fig*) gratificante; **financially ~** económicamente provechoso

rewind [riːˈwaɪnd] (*pt, pp* **rewound** [-ˈwaund]) VT (*tape*) rebobinar; (*watch*) dar cuerda a; (*wool etc*) devanar

rewire [riːˈwaɪər] VT (*house*) renovar la instalación eléctrica de

reword [riːˈwəːd] VT expresar en otras palabras

rewritable [riːˈraɪtəbl] ADJ reescribible

rewrite [riːˈraɪt] VT (*irreg: like* **write**) reescribir

Reykjavik [ˈreɪkjəviːk] N Reykjavik *m*

RGN N ABBR (*Brit*) = **Registered General Nurse**

Rh ABBR (= *rhesus*) Rh *m*

rhapsody [ˈræpsədɪ] N (*Mus*) rapsodia; (*fig*): **to go into rhapsodies over** extasiarse por

rhesus negative [ˈriːsəs-] ADJ (*Med*) Rh negativo

rhesus positive ADJ (*Med*) Rh positivo

rhetoric [ˈrɛtərɪk] N retórica

rhetorical [rɪˈtɒrɪkl] ADJ retórico

rheumatic [ruːˈmætɪk] ADJ reumático

rheumatism [ˈruːmətɪzəm] N reumatismo, reúma *m or f*

rheumatoid arthritis [ˈruːmətɔɪd-] N reúma *m or f* articular

Rhine [raɪn] N: **the ~** el (río) Rin

rhinestone [ˈraɪnstəun] N diamante *m* de imitación

rhinoceros [raɪˈnɒsərəs] N rinoceronte *m*

Rhodes [rəudz] N Rodas *f*

rhododendron [rəudəˈdɛndrn] N rododendro

Rhone [rəun] N: **the ~** el Ródano

rhubarb [ˈruːbɑːb] N ruibarbo

rhyme [raɪm] N rima; (*verse*) poesía; **without ~ or reason** sin ton ni son ▶ VI: **to ~ (with)** rimar (con)

★**rhythm** [rɪðm] N ritmo

rhythmic [ˈrɪðmɪk], **rhythmical** [ˈrɪðmɪkl] ADJ rítmico

rhythmically [ˈrɪðmɪklɪ] ADV rítmicamente

rhythm method N método (de) Ogino

RI N ABBR (BRIT: = *religious instruction*) ed. religiosa
▶ ABBR (*US Post*) = **Rhode Island**

rib [rɪb] N (*Anat*) costilla ▶ VT (*mock*) tomar el pelo a

ribald [ˈrɪbəld] ADJ escabroso

ribbon [ˈrɪbən] N cinta; **in ribbons** (*torn*) hecho trizas

★**rice** [raɪs] N arroz *m*

ricefield [ˈraɪsfiːld] N arrozal *m*

rice pudding N arroz *m* con leche

★**rich** [rɪtʃ] ADJ rico; (*soil*) fértil; (*food*) pesado; (: *sweet*) empalagoso; **to be ~ in sth** abundar en algo ▶ NPL: **the ~** los ricos ▇ **riches** NPL riqueza *sg*

richly [ˈrɪtʃlɪ] ADV ricamente

richness [ˈrɪtʃnɪs] N riqueza; (*of soil*) fertilidad *f*

rickets [ˈrɪkɪts] N raquitismo

rickety [ˈrɪkɪtɪ] ADJ (*old*) desvencijado; (*shaky*) tambaleante

rickshaw [ˈrɪkʃɔː] N carro de culí

ricochet [ˈrɪkəʃeɪ] N rebote *m* ▶ VI rebotar

★**rid** [rɪd] (*pt, pp* **~**) VT: **to ~ sb of sth** librar a algn de algo; **to get ~ of** deshacerse *or* desembarazarse de

riddance [ˈrɪdns] N: **good ~!** ¡y adiós muy buenas!

ridden [ˈrɪdn] PP *of* **ride**

-ridden [ˈrɪdn] SUFF: **disease-ridden** plagado de enfermedades; **inflation-ridden** minado por la inflación

riddle [ˈrɪdl] N (*conundrum*) acertijo; (*mystery*) enigma *m*, misterio ▶ VT: **to be riddled with** ser lleno *or* plagado de

★**ride** [raɪd] (*pt* **rode** [rəʊd], *pp* **ridden** [ˈrɪdn]) N paseo; (*distance covered*) viaje *m*, recorrido; **to go for a ~** dar un paseo; **to take sb for a ~** (*fig*) tomar el pelo a algn ▶ VI (*on horse: as sport*) montar; (*go somewhere: on horse, bicycle*) dar un paseo, pasearse; (*journey: on bicycle, motor cycle, bus*) viajar; **to ~ at anchor** (*Naut*) estar fondeado ▶ VT (*a horse*) montar a; (*distance*) recorrer; **to ~ a bicycle** andar en bicicleta; **can you ~ a bike?** ¿sabes montar en bici(cleta)?
▶ **ride out** VT: **to ~ out the storm** (*fig*) capear el temporal

★**rider** [ˈraɪdəʳ] N (*on horse*) jinete *m*; (*on bicycle*) ciclista *mf*; (*on motorcycle*) motociclista *mf*

ridge [rɪdʒ] N (*of hill*) cresta; (*of roof*) caballete *m*; (*wrinkle*) arruga

ridicule [ˈrɪdɪkjuːl] N irrisión *f*, burla; **to hold sth/sb up to ~** poner algo/a algn en ridículo ▶ VT poner en ridículo a, burlarse de

ridiculous [rɪˈdɪkjʊləs] ADJ ridículo

ridiculously [rɪˈdɪkjʊləslɪ] ADV ridículamente, de modo ridículo

riding [ˈraɪdɪŋ] N equitación *f*; **I like ~** me gusta montar a caballo

riding habit N traje *m* de montar

riding school N escuela de equitación

rife [raɪf] ADJ: **to be ~** ser muy común; **to be ~ with** abundar en

riffraff [ˈrɪfræf] N chusma, gentuza

rifle [ˈraɪfl] N rifle *m*, fusil *m* ▶ VT saquear
▶ **rifle through** VT FUS saquear

rifle range N campo de tiro; (*at fair*) tiro al blanco

rift [rɪft] N (*fig: between friends*) desavenencia; (: *in party*) escisión *f*

rig [rɪg] N (*also:* **oil rig**: *on land*) torre *f* de perforación; (: *at sea*) plataforma petrolera ▶ VT (*election etc*) amañar los resultados de
▶ **rig out** VT (BRIT) ataviar
▶ **rig up** VT improvisar

rigging [ˈrɪgɪŋ] N (*Naut*) aparejo

★**right** [raɪt] ADJ (*true, correct*) correcto, exacto; (*suitable*) indicado, debido; (*proper*) apropiado, propio; (*just*) justo; (*morally good*) bueno; (*not left*) derecho; **to be ~** (*person*) tener razón; (*answer*) ser correcto; **to get sth ~** acertar en algo; **you did the ~ thing** hiciste bien; **let's get it ~ this time!** ¡a ver si esta vez nos sale bien!; **the ~ time** la hora exacta; (*fig*) el momento oportuno ▶ N (*title, claim*) derecho; (*not left*) derecha; **by rights** en justicia; **~ and wrong** el bien y el mal; **film rights** derechos *mpl* de la película; **on the ~** a la derecha; **to be in the ~** tener razón ▶ ADV (*correctly*) bien, correctamente; (*straight*) derecho, directamente; (*not on the left*) a la derecha; (*to the right*) hacia la derecha; **to put a mistake ~** corregir un error; **~ now** ahora mismo; **~ away** en seguida; **~ before/after** inmediatamente antes/después; **~ in the middle** exactamente en el centro; **to go ~ to the end of sth** llegar hasta el final de algo; **~, who's next?** bueno, ¿quién sigue? ▶ VT (*put straight*) enderezar; (*correct*) corregir ▶ EXCL ¡bueno!, ¡está bien!; **all ~!** ¡vale!

> Don't confuse the feminine noun **derecha**, which means *right* in the sense of position or direction, with the masculine noun **derecho**, which means someone's entitlement or law: *The park is on the right*. **El parque está a la derecha**.
> *human rights* **derechos humanos**.

right angle N ángulo recto

right-click [ˈraɪtklɪk] VI clicar con el botón derecho del ratón ▶ VT: **to ~ an icon** clicar en un icono con el botón derecho del ratón

righteous [ˈraɪtʃəs] ADJ justo, honrado; (*anger*) justificado

righteousness [ˈraɪtʃəsnɪs] N justicia

rightful [ˈraɪtful] ADJ (*heir*) legítimo

right-hand [ˈraɪthænd] ADJ: **~ drive** conducción *f* por la derecha; **the ~ side** la derecha

right-handed [raɪtˈhændɪd] ADJ (*person*) que usa la mano derecha, diestro

r

right-hand man N (*irreg*) brazo derecho

right-hand side N derecha

rightly ['raɪtlɪ] ADV correctamente, debidamente; (*with reason*) con razón; **if I remember ~** si recuerdo bien

right-minded ['raɪt'maɪndɪd] ADJ (*sensible*) sensato; (*decent*) honrado

right of way N (*on path etc*) derecho de paso; (*Aut*) prioridad *f* de paso

right-wing [raɪt'wɪŋ] ADJ (*Pol*) de derechas, derechista

right-winger [raɪt'wɪŋə^r] N (*Pol*) persona de derechas, derechista *mf*; (*Sport*) extremo derecha

rigid ['rɪdʒɪd] ADJ rígido; (*person, ideas*) inflexible

rigidity [rɪ'dʒɪdɪtɪ] N rigidez *f*; inflexibilidad *f*

rigidly ['rɪdʒɪdlɪ] ADV rígidamente; (*inflexibly*) inflexiblemente

rigmarole ['rɪgmərəul] N galimatías *m inv*

rigor mortis ['rɪgə'mɔ:tɪs] N rigidez *f* cadavérica

rigorous ['rɪgərəs] ADJ riguroso

rigorously ['rɪgərəslɪ] ADV rigurosamente

rigour, (*US*) **rigor** ['rɪgə^r] N rigor *m*, severidad *f*

rile [raɪl] VT irritar

rim [rɪm] N borde *m*; (*of spectacles*) montura, aro; (*of wheel*) llanta

rimless ['rɪmlɪs] ADJ (*spectacles*) sin aros

rimmed [rɪmd] ADJ: **~ with** con un borde de, bordeado de

rind [raɪnd] N (*of bacon, cheese*) corteza; (*of lemon etc*) cáscara

★**ring** [rɪŋ] (*pt* **rang** [ræŋ], *pp* **rung** [rʌŋ]) N (*of metal*) aro; (*on finger*) anillo; (*of people*) corro; (*of objects*) círculo; (*gang*) banda; (*for boxing*) cuadrilátero; (*of circus*) pista; (*bull ring*) ruedo, plaza; (*sound of bell*) toque *m*; (*telephone call*) llamada; **that has the ~ of truth about it** eso suena a verdad; **to give sb a ~** (*Brit Tel*) llamar a algn, dar un telefonazo a algn ▸ VI (*Brit: on telephone*) llamar por teléfono; (*large bell*) repicar; (*doorbell, phone*) sonar; (*also:* **ring out**: *voice, words*) sonar; (*ears*) zumbar ▸ VT (*Brit Tel: also:* **ring up**) llamar; (*bell etc*) hacer sonar; (*doorbell*) tocar; **the name doesn't ~ a bell (with me)** el nombre no me suena; **to ~ sb (up)** llamar a algn

▸ **ring back** VT, VI (*Brit Tel*) devolver la llamada

▸ **ring off** VI (*Brit Tel*) colgar, cortar la comunicación

▸ **ring up** VT (*Brit Tel*) llamar, telefonear

ring binder N carpeta de anillas

ring-fence ['rɪŋ'fɛns] VT proteger, blindar

ring finger N (*dedo*) anular *m*

ringing ['rɪŋɪŋ] N (*of bell*) toque *m*, tañido; (*of large bell*) repique *m*; (*in ears*) zumbido

ringing tone N (*Tel*) tono de llamada

ringleader ['rɪŋli:də^r] N cabecilla *mf*

ringlets ['rɪŋlɪts] NPL tirabuzones *mpl*, bucles *mpl*

ring road N (*Brit*) carretera periférica *or* de circunvalación

★**ringtone** ['rɪŋtəun] N tono de llamada

rink [rɪŋk] N (*also:* **ice rink**) pista de hielo; (*for roller-skating*) pista de patinaje

rinse [rɪns] N (*of dishes*) enjuague *m*; (*of clothes*) aclarado; (*hair colouring*) reflejo ▸ VT enjuagar, aclarar; (*hair*) dar reflejos a

Rio ['ri:əu], **Rio de Janeiro** ['ri:əudədʒə'nɪərəu] N Río de Janeiro

★**riot** ['raɪət] N motín *m*, disturbio; **to run ~** desmandarse ▸ VI amotinarse

rioter ['raɪətə^r] N amotinado(-a)

riot gear N uniforme *m* antidisturbios *inv*

riotous ['raɪətəs] ADJ alborotado; (*party*) bullicioso; (*uncontrolled*) desenfrenado

riotously ['raɪətəslɪ] ADV bulliciosamente

riot police N policía antidisturbios

RIP ABBR (= *requiescat or requiescant in pace*) q.e.p.d.

rip [rɪp] N rasgón *m*, desgarrón *m* ▸ VT rasgar, desgarrar ▸ VI rasgarse

▸ **rip off** VT (*inf: cheat*) estafar

▸ **rip up** VT hacer pedazos

ripcord ['rɪpkɔ:d] N cabo de desgarre

ripe [raɪp] ADJ (*fruit*) maduro

ripen ['raɪpən] VT, VI madurar

ripeness ['raɪpnɪs] N madurez *f*

rip-off ['rɪpɔf] N (*inf*): **it's a ~!** ¡es una estafa!, ¡es un timo!

riposte [rɪ'pɔst] N respuesta aguda, réplica

ripple ['rɪpl] N onda, rizo; (*sound*) murmullo ▸ VI rizarse ▸ VT rizar

★**rise** [raɪz] (*pt* **rose** [rəuz], *pp* **risen** ['rɪzn]) N (*slope*) cuesta, pendiente *f*; (*hill*) altura; (*increase: in wages: Brit*) aumento; (: *in prices, temperature*) subida, alza; (*fig: to power etc*) ascenso; (: *ascendancy*) auge *m*; **~ to power** ascenso al poder; **to give ~ to** dar lugar or origen a ▸ VI (*gen*) elevarse; (*prices*) subir; (*waters*) crecer; (*river*) nacer; (*sun*) salir; (*person: from bed etc*) levantarse; (*also:* **rise up**: *rebel*) sublevarse; (*in rank*) ascender; **to ~ to the occasion** ponerse a la altura de las circunstancias

risen ['rɪzn] PP *of* **rise**

rising ['raɪzɪŋ] ADJ (*increasing: number*) creciente; (: *prices*) en aumento or alza; (*tide*) creciente; (*sun, moon*) naciente ▸ N (*uprising*) sublevación *f*

rising damp N humedad *f* de paredes

rising star N (*fig*) figura en alza

★**risk** [rɪsk] N riesgo, peligro; **to take** *or* **run the ~ of doing** correr el riesgo de hacer; **at ~** en peligro; **at one's own ~** bajo su propia responsabilidad; **fire/health/security ~** peligro de incendio/para la salud/para la seguridad ▸ VT (*gen*) arriesgar; (*dare*) atreverse a

risk capital N capital *m* de riesgo

risky ['rɪskɪ] ADJ arriesgado, peligroso

risqué ['ri:skeɪ] ADJ (*joke*) subido de color

rissole ['rɪsəul] N croqueta

rite [raɪt] N rito; **last rites** últimos sacramentos *mpl*

ritual [ˈrɪtjuəl] ADJ ritual ▶ N ritual *m*, rito

★**rival** [ˈraɪvl] N rival *mf*; (*in business*) competidor(a) *m/f* ▶ ADJ rival, opuesto ▶ VT competir con

rivalry [ˈraɪvlrɪ] N rivalidad *f*, competencia

★**river** [ˈrɪvəʳ] N río; **up/down ~** río arriba/abajo ▶ CPD (*port, traffic*) de río, del río

riverbank [ˈrɪvəbæŋk] N orilla (del río)

riverbed [ˈrɪvəbɛd] N lecho, cauce *m*

rivet [ˈrɪvɪt] N roblón *m*, remache *m* ▶ VT remachar; (*fig*) fascinar

riveting [ˈrɪvɪtɪŋ] ADJ (*fig*) fascinante

Riviera [rɪvɪˈɛərə] N: **the (French) ~** la Costa Azul, la Riviera (francesa); **the Italian ~** la Riviera italiana

Riyadh [rɪˈjɑːd] N Riyadh *m*

RMT N ABBR (*BRIT: = National Union of Rail, Maritime and Transport Workers*) sindicato de transportes

RN N ABBR (*BRIT*) = **Royal Navy**; (*US*) = **registered nurse**

RNA N ABBR (= *ribonucleic acid*) ARN *m*, RNA *m*

RNLI N ABBR (*BRIT: = Royal National Lifeboat Institution*) organización benéfica que proporciona un servicio de lanchas de socorro

RNZAF N ABBR = **Royal New Zealand Air Force**

RNZN N ABBR = **Royal New Zealand Navy**

★**road** [rəud] N (*gen*) camino; (*motorway etc*) carretera; (*in town*) calle *f*; **major/minor ~** carretera general/secundaria; **main ~** carretera; **it takes four hours by ~** se tarda cuatro horas por carretera; **on the ~ to success** camino del éxito

roadblock [ˈrəudblɔk] N barricada, control *m*, retén *m* (LAM)

road haulage N transporte *m* por carretera

road hog [ˈrəudhɔg] N loco(-a) del volante

road map N mapa *m* de carreteras

road rage N *conducta agresiva de los conductores*

road safety N seguridad *f* vial

roadside [ˈrəudsaɪd] N borde *m* (del camino); **by the ~** al borde del camino ▶ CPD al lado de la carretera

roadsign [ˈrəudsaɪn] N señal *f* de tráfico

roadsweeper [ˈrəudswiːpəʳ] N (*BRIT: person*) barrendero(-a)

road tax N (*BRIT*) impuesto de rodaje

road user N usuario(-a) de la vía pública

roadway [ˈrəudweɪ] N calzada

roadworks [ˈrəudwəːks] NPL obras *fpl*

roadworthy [ˈrəudwəːðɪ] ADJ (*car*) en buen estado para circular

roam [rəum] VI vagar ▶ VT vagar por

roar [rɔːʳ] N (*of animal*) rugido, bramido; (*of crowd*) clamor *m*, rugido; (*of vehicle, storm*) estruendo; (*of laughter*) carcajada ▶ VI rugir, bramar; hacer estruendo; **to ~ with laughter** reírse a carcajadas

roaring [ˈrɔːrɪŋ] ADJ: **a ~ success** un tremendo éxito; **to do a ~ trade** hacer buen negocio

roast [rəust] N carne *f* asada, asado ▶ VT (*meat*) asar; (*coffee*) tostar

roast beef N rosbif *m*

roasting [ˈrəustɪŋ] N: **to give sb a ~** (*inf*) echar una buena bronca a algn

rob [rɔb] VT robar; **to ~ sb of sth** robar algo a algn; (*fig: deprive*) quitar algo a algn

robber [ˈrɔbəʳ] N ladrón(-ona) *m/f*

robbery [ˈrɔbərɪ] N robo

robe [rəub] N (*for ceremony etc*) toga; (*also:* **bath robe**) bata, albornoz *m*

robin [ˈrɔbɪn] N petirrojo

robot [ˈrəubɔt] N robot *m*

robotics [rəuˈbɔtɪks] N robótica

robust [rəuˈbʌst] ADJ robusto, fuerte

★**rock** [rɔk] N (*gen*) roca; (*boulder*) peña, peñasco; (*BRIT: sweet*) ≈ pirulí *m*; **on the rocks** (*drink*) con hielo; **their marriage is on the rocks** su matrimonio se está yendo a pique ▶ VT (*swing gently*) mecer; (*shake*) sacudir; **to ~ the boat** (*fig*) crear problemas ▶ VI mecerse, balancearse; sacudirse

rock and roll N rock and roll *m*, rocanrol *m*

rock-bottom [ˈrɔkˈbɔtəm] N (*fig*): **at ~** por los suelos; **to reach** *or* **touch ~** (*price*) estar por los suelos; (*person*) tocar fondo

rock cake N (*BRIT*) *bollito de pasas con superficie rugosa*

rock climber N escalador(a) *m/f*

rock climbing N (*Sport*) escalada

rockery [ˈrɔkərɪ] N cuadro alpino

★**rocket** [ˈrɔkɪt] N cohete *m* ▶ VI (*prices*) dispararse, ponerse por las nubes

rocket launcher N lanzacohetes *m inv*

rock face N pared *f* de roca

rocking chair [ˈrɔkɪŋ-] N mecedora

rocking horse N caballo de balancín

rocky [ˈrɔkɪ] ADJ (*gen*) rocoso; (*unsteady: table*) inestable

Rocky Mountains NPL: **the ~** las Montañas Rocosas

rococo [rəˈkəukəu] ADJ rococó *inv* ▶ N rococó

rod [rɔd] N vara, varilla; (*Tech*) barra; (*also:* **fishing rod**) caña

rode [rəud] PT *of* **ride**

rodent [ˈrəudnt] N roedor *m*

rodeo [ˈrəudɪəu] N rodeo

roe [rəu] N (*species: also:* **roe deer**) corzo; (*of fish*): **hard/soft ~** hueva/lecha

rogue [rəug] N pícaro, pillo

roguish [ˈrəugɪʃ] ADJ (*child*) travieso; (*smile etc*) pícaro

★**role** [rəul] N papel *m*, rol *m*

role-model [ˈrəulmɔdl] N modelo a imitar

role play N (*also:* **role playing**) juego de papeles *or* roles

r

★**roll** [rəul] N rollo; (*of bank notes*) fajo; (*also:* **bread roll**) panecillo; (*register*) lista, nómina; (*sound: of drums etc*) redoble m; (*movement: of ship*) balanceo; **cheese ~** panecillo de queso ▸ VT hacer rodar; (*also:* **roll up**: *string*) enrollar; (: *sleeves*) arremangar; (*cigarettes*) liar; (*also:* **roll out**: *pastry*) aplanar ▸ VI (*gen*) rodar; (*drum*) redoblar; (*in walking*) bambolearse; (*ship*) balancearse
  ▸ **roll about, roll around** VI (*person*) revolcarse
  ▸ **roll by** VI (*time*) pasar
  ▸ **roll in** VI (*mail, cash*) entrar a raudales
  ▸ **roll over** VI dar una vuelta
  ▸ **roll up** VI (*inf: arrive*) presentarse, aparecer
  ▸ VT (*carpet, cloth, map*) arrollar; (*sleeves*) arremangar; **to ~ o.s. up into a ball** acurrucarse, hacerse un ovillo

roll call N: **to take a ~** pasar lista

rolled [rəuld] ADJ (*umbrella*) plegado

roller ['rəulə^r] N rodillo; (*wheel*) rueda; (*for road*) apisonadora; (*for hair*) rulo

Rollerblades® ['rəuləbleidz] NPL patines mpl en línea

roller blind N (BRIT) persiana (enrollable)

roller coaster N montaña rusa

roller skates NPL patines mpl de rueda

roller-skating ['rəuləskeitiŋ] N patinaje m sobre ruedas; **to go ~** ir a patinar (*sobre ruedas*)

rollicking ['rɒlikiŋ] ADJ: **we had a ~ time** nos divertimos una barbaridad

rolling ['rəuliŋ] ADJ (*landscape*) ondulado

rolling mill N taller m de laminación

rolling pin N rodillo (de cocina)

rolling stock N (*Rail*) material m rodante

ROM [rɒm] N ABBR (*Comput*: = *read-only memory*) (memoria) ROM f

Roman ['rəumən] ADJ, N romano(-a) m/f

Roman Catholic ADJ, N católico(-a) m/f (romano(-a))

romance [rə'mæns] N (*love affair*) amor m, idilio; (*charm*) lo romántico; (*novel*) novela de amor

Romanesque [rəumə'nɛsk] ADJ románico

Romania [ru:'meiniə] N = **Rumania**

Romanian [ru:'meiniən] ADJ, N = **Rumanian**

Roman numeral N número romano

★**romantic** [rə'mæntik] ADJ romántico

romanticism [rə'mæntisizəm] N romanticismo

Romany ['rəuməni] ADJ gitano ▸ N (*person*) gitano(-a); (*Ling*) lengua gitana, caló (SP)

Rome [rəum] N Roma

romp [rɒmp] N retozo, jugueteo ▸ VI (*also:* **romp about**) juguetear; **to ~ home** (*horse*) ganar fácilmente

rompers ['rɒmpəz] NPL pelele m

★**roof** [ru:f] N (*gen*) techo; (*of house*) tejado; **~ of the mouth** paladar m ▸ VT techar, poner techo a

roofing ['ru:fiŋ] N techumbre f

roof rack N (*Aut*) baca, portaequipajes msg

rook [ruk] N (*bird*) graja; (*Chess*) torre f

rookie ['ruki] N (*inf*) novato(-a); (*Mil*) chivo

★**room** [ru:m] N (*in house*) cuarto, habitación f, pieza (*esp* LAm); (*also:* **bedroom**) dormitorio; (*in school etc*) sala; (*space*) sitio; **"rooms to let"**, (US) **"rooms for rent"** "se alquilan pisos *or* cuartos"; **single/double ~** habitación individual/doble *or* para dos personas; **is there ~ for this?** ¿cabe esto?; **to make ~ for sb** hacer sitio para algn; **there is ~ for improvement** podría mejorarse ■ **rooms** NPL (*lodging*) alojamiento sg

roominess ['ru:minis] N amplitud f, espaciosidad f

rooming house ['ru:miŋ-] N (US) pensión f

roommate ['ru:mmeit] N compañero(-a) de cuarto

room service N servicio de habitaciones

room temperature N temperatura ambiente

roomy ['ru:mi] ADJ espacioso

roost [ru:st] N percha ▸ VI pasar la noche

rooster ['ru:stə^r] N gallo

★**root** [ru:t] N (*Bot, Math*) raíz f; **to take ~** (*plant*) echar raíces; (*idea*) arraigar(se); **the ~ of the problem is that ...** la raíz del problema es que ... ▸ VI (*plant, belief*) arraigar(se)
  ▸ **root about** VI (*fig*) rebuscar
  ▸ **root for** VT FUS apoyar a
  ▸ **root out** VT desarraigar

root beer N (US) *refresco sin alcohol de extractos de hierbas*

rooted ['ru:tid] ADJ enraizado; (*opinions etc*) arraigado

rope [rəup] N cuerda; (*Naut*) cable m; **to know the ropes** (*fig*) conocer los trucos (del oficio) ▸ VT (*box*) atar *or* amarrar con (una) cuerda; (*climbers: also:* **rope together**) encordar; (*an area: also:* **rope off**) acordonar; **to ~ sb in** (*fig*) persuadir a algn a tomar parte

rope ladder N escala de cuerda

ropey ['rəupi] ADJ (*inf*) chungo

rort [rɔ:t] N (AUSTRALIA, NEW ZEALAND *inf*) N estafa ▸ VT estafar

rosary ['rəuzəri] N rosario

★**rose** [rəuz] PT *of* **rise** ▸ N rosa; (*also:* **rosebush**) rosal m; (*on watering can*) roseta ▸ ADJ color de rosa

rosé ['rəuzei] N vino rosado, clarete m

rosebed ['rəuzbɛd] N rosaleda

rosebud ['rəuzbʌd] N capullo de rosa

rosebush ['rəuzbuʃ] N rosal m

rosemary ['rəuzməri] N romero

rosette [rəu'zɛt] N rosetón m

ROSPA ['rɔspə] N ABBR (BRIT) = **Royal Society for the Prevention of Accidents**

roster ['rɒstə^r] N: **duty ~** lista de tareas

rostrum ['rɒstrəm] N tribuna

rosy ['rəuzi] ADJ rosado, sonrosado; **the future looks ~** el futuro parece prometedor

rot [rɒt] N (*decay*) putrefacción f, podredumbre f;

(fig: pej) tonterías *fpl*; **to stop the ~** *(fig)* poner fin a las pérdidas ▸ vt pudrir, corromper ▸ vi pudrirse, corromperse; **it has rotted** está podrido

rota ['rəutə] N lista (de tareas)

rotary ['rəutərɪ] ADJ rotativo

rotate [rəu'teɪt] VT *(revolve)* hacer girar, dar vueltas a; *(change round: crops)* cultivar en rotación; *(: jobs)* alternar ▸ vi *(revolve)* girar, dar vueltas

rotating [rəu'teɪtɪŋ] ADJ *(movement)* rotativo

rotation [rəu'teɪʃən] N rotación *f*; **in ~** por turno

rote [rəut] N: **by ~** de memoria

rotor ['rəutə'] N rotor *m*

rotten ['rɔtn] ADJ *(decayed)* podrido; *(: wood)* carcomido; *(fig)* corrompido; *(inf: bad)* pésimo; **to feel ~** *(ill)* sentirse fatal; **~ to the core** completamente podrido

rotund [rəu'tʌnd] ADJ rotundo

rouble, *(US)* **ruble** ['ru:bl] N rublo

rouge [ru:ʒ] N colorete *m*

★**rough** [rʌf] ADJ *(skin, surface)* áspero; *(terrain)* accidentado; *(road)* desigual; *(voice)* bronco; *(person, manner: coarse)* tosco, grosero; *(weather)* borrascoso; *(treatment)* brutal; *(sea)* embravecido; *(town, area)* peligroso; *(cloth)* basto; *(plan)* preliminar; *(guess)* aproximado; *(violent)* violento; **the sea is ~ today** el mar está agitado hoy; **to have a ~ time (of it)** pasar una mala racha; **~ estimate** cálculo aproximado ▸ ADV: **to sleep ~** *(BRIT)* pasar la noche al raso ▸ N *(Golf)*: **in the ~** en las hierbas altas ▸ vt: **to ~ it** vivir sin comodidades

roughage ['rʌfɪdʒ] N fibra(s) *f(pl)*, forraje *m*

rough-and-ready ['rʌfən'redɪ] ADJ improvisado, tosco

rough-and-tumble ['rʌfən'tʌmbl] N pelea

roughcast ['rʌfkɑ:st] N mezcla gruesa

rough copy, rough draft N borrador *m*

roughen ['rʌfn] VT *(a surface)* poner áspero

roughly ['rʌflɪ] ADV *(handle)* torpemente; *(make)* toscamente; *(approximately)* aproximadamente; **~ speaking** más o menos

roughness ['rʌfnɪs] N *(of surface)* aspereza; *(crudeness)* tosquedad *f*; *(violence)* brutalidad *f*

roughshod ['rʌfʃɔd] ADV: **to ride ~ over** *(person)* pisotear a; *(objections)* hacer caso omiso de

rough work N *(Scol etc)* borrador *m*

roulette [ru:'lɛt] N ruleta

Roumania [ru:'meɪnɪə] N = **Rumania**

★**round** [raund] ADJ redondo; **in ~ figures** en números redondos ▸ N círculo; *(of police officer)* ronda; *(of milkman)* recorrido; *(of doctor)* visitas *fpl*; *(game: in competition, cards)* partida; *(of ammunition)* cartucho; *(Boxing)* asalto; *(of talks)* ronda; **to go the rounds** *(story)* divulgarse; **a ~ of applause** una salva de aplausos; **a ~ of drinks/sandwiches** una ronda de bebidas/bocadillos; **a ~ of toast** *(BRIT)*

una tostada; **the daily ~** la rutina cotidiana ▸ vt *(corner)* doblar ▸ PREP alrededor de; *(surrounding)*: **~ his neck/the table** en su cuello/alrededor de la mesa; *(in a circular movement)*: **to move ~ the room/sail ~ the world** dar una vuelta a la habitación/circunnavegar el mundo; *(in various directions)*: **to move ~ the room/house** moverse por toda la habitación/casa; **it's just ~ the corner** *(fig)* está a la vuelta de la esquina; **she arrived ~ (about) noon** llegó alrededor del mediodía; **~ the clock** *adv* las 24 horas; **to go ~ the back** pasar por atrás ▸ ADV: **all ~** por todos lados; **all the year ~** durante todo el año; **the long way ~** por el camino menos directo; **to ask sb ~** invitar a algn a casa; **I'll be ~ at six o'clock** llegaré a eso de las seis; **to go ~ to sb's (house)** ir a casa de algn; **enough to go ~** bastante (para todos)

▸ **round off** VT *(speech etc)* acabar, poner término a

▸ **round up** VT *(cattle)* acorralar; *(people)* reunir; *(prices)* redondear

roundabout ['raundəbaut] N *(BRIT: Aut)* glorieta, rotonda; *(: at fair)* tiovivo ▸ ADJ *(route, means)* indirecto

rounded ['raundɪd] ADJ redondeado, redondo

rounders ['raundəz] N *(BRIT: game)* juego similar al béisbol

roundly ['raundlɪ] ADV *(fig)* rotundamente

round-robin ['raund'rɔbɪn] N *(Sport: also:* **round-robin tournament**) liguilla

round-shouldered ['raund'ʃəuldəd] ADJ cargado de espaldas

round trip N viaje *m* de ida y vuelta

roundup ['raundʌp] N rodeo; *(of criminals)* redada; **a ~ of the latest news** un resumen de las últimas noticias

rouse [rauz] VT *(wake up)* despertar; *(stir up)* suscitar

rousing ['rauzɪŋ] ADJ *(applause)* caluroso; *(speech)* conmovedor(a)

rout [raut] N *(Mil)* derrota; *(flight)* desbandada ▸ vt derrotar

★**route** [ru:t] N ruta, camino; *(of bus)* recorrido; *(of shipping)* rumbo, derrota; **the best ~ to London** el mejor camino *or* la mejor ruta para ir a Londres; **en ~ from ... to** en el viaje de ... a; **en ~ for** rumbo a, con destino en

route map N *(BRIT: for journey)* mapa *m* de carreteras

router ['ru:tə'] N *(Comput)* router *m*

★**routine** [ru:'ti:n] ADJ *(work)* rutinario; **~ procedure** trámite *m* rutinario ▸ N rutina; *(Theat)* número; *(Comput)* rutina

rover ['rəuvə'] N vagabundo(-a)

roving ['rəuvɪŋ] ADJ *(wandering)* errante; *(salesman)* ambulante; *(reporter)* volante

★**row**[1] [rau] N *(line)* fila, hilera; *(Knitting)* vuelta; **four days in a ~** cuatro días seguidos ▸ vi *(in boat)* remar ▸ vt *(boat)* conducir remando

★**row**[2] [rau] N *(noise)* escándalo; *(dispute)* bronca, pelea; *(fuss)* jaleo; *(scolding)* reprimenda; **to**

r

make a ~ armar un lío; **to have a ~** pelearse, reñir ▶ VI reñir(se)

rowboat [ˈrəʊbəʊt] N (US) bote m de remos

rowdy [ˈraʊdɪ] ADJ (person: noisy) ruidoso; (: quarrelsome) pendenciero; (occasion) alborotado ▶ N pendenciero(-a)

rowdyism [ˈraʊdɪɪzəm] N gamberrismo

row houses NPL (US) casas fpl adosadas

rowing [ˈrəʊɪŋ] N remo

rowing boat N (BRIT) bote m or barco de remos

rowlock [ˈrɒlək] N (BRIT) chumacera

★**royal** [ˈrɔɪəl] ADJ real

Royal Academy, Royal Academy of Arts N (BRIT) la Real Academia (de Bellas Artes)

La **Royal Academy (of Arts)**, fundada en 1768 durante el reinado de Jorge III, es una institución dedicada al fomento de la pintura, escultura y arquitectura en el Reino Unido. Además de dar cursos de arte, presenta una exposición anual de artistas contemporáneos en su sede de Burlington House, en el centro de Londres. Todos los veranos celebra una exposición importante de artistas contemporáneos. No existe una institución equivalente a la Real Academia de la Lengua.

Royal Air Force N (BRIT) Fuerzas fpl Aéreas Británicas

royal blue N azul m marino

royalist [ˈrɔɪəlɪst] ADJ, N monárquico(-a) m/f

Royal Navy N (BRIT) Marina Británica

royalty [ˈrɔɪəltɪ] N (royal persons) (miembros mpl de la) familia real; (payment to author) derechos mpl de autor

RP N ABBR (BRIT) = **Received Pronunciation**

rpm ABBR (= revolutions per minute) r.p.m.

RR ABBR (US) = **railway**

RRP N ABBR (BRIT: = recommended retail price) PVP m

RSA N ABBR (BRIT) = **Royal Society of Arts; Royal Scottish Academy**

RSI N ABBR (Med: = repetitive strain injury) lesión f por esfuerzo repetitivo

RSPB N ABBR (BRIT) = **Royal Society for the Protection of Birds**

RSPCA N ABBR (BRIT) = **Royal Society for the Prevention of Cruelty to Animals**

RSVP ABBR (= répondez s'il vous plaît) SRC

RTA N ABBR (= road traffic accident) accidente m de carretera

Rt. Hon. ABBR (BRIT: = Right Honourable) tratamiento honorífico de diputado

Rt. Rev. ABBR (= Right Reverend) Rvdo.

rub [rʌb] VT (gen) frotar; (hard) restregar; **to ~ sb up** or (US) **~ sb the wrong way** sacar de quicio a algn ▶ N (gen) frotamiento; (touch) roce m; **to give sth a ~** frotar algo
▶ **rub down** VT (body) secar frotando; (horse) almohazar

▶ **rub in** VT (ointment) frotar

▶ **rub off** VT borrar ▶ VI quitarse (frotando); **to ~ off on sb** influir en algn, pegársele a algn

▶ **rub out** VT borrar ▶ VI borrarse

rubber [ˈrʌbəʳ] N caucho, goma; (BRIT: eraser) goma de borrar

rubber band N goma, gomita

rubber bullet N bala de goma

rubber gloves NPL guantes mpl de goma

rubber plant N ficus m

rubber ring N (for swimming) flotador m

rubber stamp N sello (de caucho) ▶ VT: **rubber-stamp** (fig) aprobar maquinalmente

rubbery [ˈrʌbərɪ] ADJ (como) de goma

★**rubbish** [ˈrʌbɪʃ] (BRIT) N (from household) basura; (waste) desperdicios mpl; (fig: pej) tonterías fpl; (trash) basura, porquería; **what you've just said is ~** lo que acabas de decir es una tontería ▶ VT (inf) poner por los suelos

rubbish bin N (BRIT) cubo or bote m (LAM) de la basura

rubbish dump N (BRIT: in town) vertedero, basurero

rubbishy [ˈrʌbɪʃɪ] ADJ (inf) de mala calidad, de pacotilla

rubble [ˈrʌbl] N escombros mpl

ruby [ˈruːbɪ] N rubí m

RUC N ABBR (= Royal Ulster Constabulary) fuerza de policía en Irlanda del Norte

★**rucksack** [ˈrʌksæk] N mochila

ructions [ˈrʌkʃənz] NPL: **there will be ~** se va a armar la gorda

rudder [ˈrʌdəʳ] N timón m

ruddy [ˈrʌdɪ] ADJ (face) rubicundo; (inf: damned) condenado

rude [ruːd] ADJ (impolite: person) grosero, maleducado; (: word, manners) rudo, grosero; (indecent) indecente; **to be ~ to sb** ser grosero con algn

rudeness [ˈruːdnɪs] N grosería, tosquedad f

rudiment [ˈruːdɪmənt] N rudimento

rudimentary [ruːdɪˈmentərɪ] ADJ rudimentario

rue [ruː] VT arrepentirse de

rueful [ˈruːful] ADJ arrepentido

ruffian [ˈrʌfɪən] N matón m, criminal m

ruffle [ˈrʌfl] VT (hair) despeinar; (clothes) arrugar; (fig: person) agitar

rug [rʌg] N alfombra; (BRIT: for knees) manta

★**rugby** [ˈrʌgbɪ] N (also: **rugby football**) rugby m

rugged [ˈrʌgɪd] ADJ (landscape) accidentado; (features) robusto

rugger [ˈrʌgəʳ] N (BRIT inf) rugby m

★**ruin** [ˈruːɪn] N ruina; **in ruins** en ruinas ▶ VT arruinar; (spoil) estropear ■ **ruins** NPL ruinas fpl, restos mpl

ruinous [ˈruːɪnəs] ADJ ruinoso

★**rule** [ruːl] N (norm) norma, costumbre f; (regulation, ruler) regla; (government) dominio; (dominion

etc): **under British ~** bajo el dominio británico; **it's against the rules** está prohibido; **as a ~** por regla general, generalmente; **by ~ of thumb** por experiencia; **majority ~** (*Pol*) gobierno mayoritario ▶ VT (*country, person*) gobernar; (*decide*) disponer; (*draw: lines*) trazar; **to ~ that ...** (*umpire, judge*) fallar que ... ▶ VI gobernar; (*Law*) fallar; **to ~ against/in favour of/on** fallar en contra de/a favor de/sobre
▶ **rule out** VT excluir

ruled [ru:ld] ADJ (*paper*) rayado

ruler ['ru:lə'] N (*sovereign*) soberano(-a); (*for measuring*) regla

ruling ['ru:lɪŋ] ADJ (*party*) gobernante; (*class*) dirigente ▶ N (*Law*) fallo, decisión *f*

rum [rʌm] N ron *m*

Rumania [ru:'meɪnɪə] N Rumanía

Rumanian [ru:'meɪnɪən] ADJ, N rumano(-a) *m/f*

rumble ['rʌmbl] N ruido sordo; (*of thunder*) redoble *m* ▶ VI retumbar, hacer un ruido sordo; (*stomach, pipe*) sonar

rumbustious [rʌm'bʌstʃəs] ADJ (*person*) bullicioso

rummage ['rʌmɪdʒ] VI revolverlo todo

rumour, (*US*) **rumor** ['ru:mə'] N rumor *m*; **~ has it that ...** corre la voz de que ... ▶ VT: **it is rumoured that ...** se rumorea que ...

rump [rʌmp] N (*of animal*) ancas *fpl*, grupa

rumple ['rʌmpl] VT (*clothes*) arrugar; (*hair*) despeinar

rump steak N filete *m* de lomo

rumpus ['rʌmpəs] N (*inf*) lío, jaleo; (*quarrel*) pelea, riña; **to kick up a ~** armar un follón *or* armar bronca

★**run** [rʌn] (*pt* **ran** [ræn], *pp* **~**) N (*Sport*) carrera; (*outing*) paseo, excursión *f*; (*distance travelled*) trayecto; (*series*) serie *f*; (*Theat*) temporada; (*Ski*) pista; (*in tights, stockings*) carrera; **to go for a ~** ir a correr; **to make a ~ for it** echar(se) a correr, escapar(se), huir; **to have the ~ of sb's house** tener el libre uso de la casa de algn; **a ~ of luck** una racha de suerte; **there was a ~ on** (*meat, tickets*) hubo mucha demanda de; **in the long ~** a la larga; **on the ~** en fuga ▶ VT (*operate: business*) dirigir; (: *competition, course*) organizar; (: *hotel, house*) administrar, llevar; (*Comput: program*) ejecutar; (*to pass: hand*) pasar; (*Press: feature*) publicar; **I'll ~ you to the station** te llevaré a la estación en coche; **to ~ a risk** correr un riesgo; **to ~ a bath** llenar la bañera; **to ~ errands** hacer recados; **it's very cheap to ~** es muy económico ▶ VI (*gen*) correr; (*work: machine*) funcionar, marchar; (*bus, train: operate*) circular, ir; (: *travel*) ir; (*continue: play*) seguir en cartel; (: *contract*) ser válido; (*flow: river, bath*) fluir; (*colours, washing*) desteñirse; (*in election*) ser candidato; **to ~ for the bus** correr tras el autobús; **we shall have to ~ for it** tendremos que escapar; **the train runs between Gatwick and Victoria** el tren circula entre Gatwick y Victoria; **the bus runs every 20 minutes** el autobús pasa cada 20 minutos; **to**

~ on petrol/on diesel/off batteries funcionar con gasolina/gasoil/baterías; **my salary won't ~ to a car** mi sueldo no me da para comprarme un coche; **the car ran into the lamppost** el coche chocó contra el farol
▶ **run about, run around** VI (*children*) correr por todos lados
▶ **run across** VT FUS (*find*) dar *or* topar con
▶ **run after** VT FUS (*to catch up*) correr tras; (*chase*) perseguir
▶ **run away** VI huir
▶ **run down** VI (*clock*) pararse ▶ VT (*reduce: production*) ir reduciendo; (*factory*) restringir la producción de; (*Aut*) atropellar; (*criticize*) criticar; **to be ~ down** (*person: tired*) encontrarse agotado
▶ **run in** VT (*BRIT: car*) rodar
▶ **run into** VT FUS (*meet: person, trouble*) tropezar con; (*collide with*) chocar con; **to ~ into debt** contraer deudas, endeudarse
▶ **run off** VT (*water*) dejar correr; **to be ~ off one's feet** estar ocupadísimo ▶ VI huir corriendo
▶ **run out** VI (*person*) salir corriendo; (*liquid*) irse; (*lease*) caducar, vencer; (*money*) acabarse
▶ **run out of** VT FUS quedar sin; **I've ~ out of petrol** se me acabó la gasolina
▶ **run over** VT (*Aut*) atropellar ▶ VT FUS (*revise*) repasar
▶ **run through** VT FUS (*instructions*) repasar
▶ **run up** VT (*debt*) incurrir en ▶ VI: **to ~ up against** (*difficulties*) tropezar con

run-around ['rʌnəraund] N: **to give sb the ~** traer a algn al retortero

runaway ['rʌnəweɪ] ADJ (*horse*) desbocado; (*truck*) sin frenos; (*person*) fugitivo

rundown ['rʌndaun] N (*BRIT: of industry etc*) cierre *m* gradual

rung [rʌŋ] PP *of* **ring** ▶ N (*of ladder*) escalón *m*, peldaño

run-in ['rʌnɪn] N (*inf*) altercado

★**runner** ['rʌnə'] N (*in race: person*) corredor(a) *m/f*; (: *horse*) caballo; (*on sledge*) patín *m*; (*wheel*) ruedecilla

runner bean N (*BRIT*) judía verde

runner-up [rʌnər'ʌp] N subcampeón(-ona) *m/f*

★**running** ['rʌnɪŋ] N (*sport*) atletismo; (*race*) carrera; **to be in/out of the ~ for sth** tener/no tener posibilidades de ganar algo ▶ ADJ (*costs, water*) corriente; (*commentary*) en directo ▶ ADV: **6 days ~** 6 días seguidos

running costs NPL (*of business*) gastos *mpl* corrientes; (*of car*) gastos *mpl* de mantenimiento

running head N (*Typ*) encabezamiento normal

running mate N (*US Pol*) candidato(-a) a la vicepresidencia

runny ['rʌnɪ] ADJ líquido; (*eyes*) lloroso; **to have a ~ nose** tener mocos

run-off ['rʌnɔf] N (*in contest, election*) desempate *m*; (*extra race*) carrera de desempate

run-of-the-mill ['rʌnəvðə'mɪl] ADJ común y corriente

r

runt [rʌnt] N (*also pej*) enano

run-up [ˈrʌnʌp] N: ~ **to** (*election etc*) período previo a

runway [ˈrʌnweɪ] N (*Aviat*) pista (de aterrizaje)

rupee [ruːˈpiː] N rupia

rupture [ˈrʌptʃəʳ] N (*Med*) hernia ▶ VT: **to ~ o.s.** causarse una hernia

★**rural** [ˈrʊərl] ADJ rural

ruse [ruːz] N ardid *m*

★**rush** [rʌʃ] N ímpetu *m*; (*hurry*) prisa, apuro (*LAM*); (*Comm*) demanda repentina; (*Bot*) junco; (*current*) corriente *f* fuerte, ráfaga; (*of feeling*) torrente *m*; **gold ~** fiebre *f* del oro; **we've had a ~ of orders** ha habido una gran demanda; **I'm in a ~ (to do)** tengo prisa *or* (*LAM*) apuro (por hacer); **is there any ~ for this?** ¿te corre prisa esto? ▶ VT apresurar; (*work*) hacer de prisa; (*attack: town etc*) asaltar; **to ~ sth off** hacer algo de prisa y corriendo ▶ VI correr, precipitarse ▶ **rush through** VT (*meal*) comer de prisa; (*book*) leer de prisa; (*work*) hacer de prisa; (*town*) atravesar a toda velocidad ▶ VT SEP (*Comm: order*) despachar rápidamente

rush hour N hora *f* punta

rush job N (*urgent*) trabajo urgente

rusk [rʌsk] N bizcocho tostado

★**Russia** [ˈrʌʃə] N Rusia

Russian [ˈrʌʃən] ADJ ruso ▶ N ruso(-a); (*Ling*) ruso

rust [rʌst] N herrumbre *f*, moho ▶ VI oxidarse

rustic [ˈrʌstɪk] ADJ rústico

rustle [ˈrʌsl] VI susurrar ▶ VT (*paper*) hacer crujir; (*US: cattle*) hurtar, robar

rustproof [ˈrʌstpruːf] ADJ inoxidable

rusty [ˈrʌstɪ] ADJ oxidado

rut [rʌt] N surco; (*Zool*) celo; **to be in a ~** ser esclavo de la rutina

ruthless [ˈruːθlɪs] ADJ despiadado

RV ABBR (= *revised version*) traducción inglesa de la *Biblia de 1855* ▶ N ABBR (*US*) = **recreational vehicle**

Rwanda [ruˈændə] N Ruanda

rye [raɪ] N centeno

rye bread N pan de centeno

Ss

S, s [ɛs] N (*letter*) S, s *f*; **S for Sugar** S de sábado

S ABBR (= *Saint*) Sto.(-a.); (*US Scol: mark: = satisfactory*) suficiente; (*on clothes*) = **small**; (= *south*) S

SA N ABBR = **South Africa; South America**

Sabbath ['sæbəθ] N domingo; (*Jewish*) sábado

sabbatical [sə'bætɪkl] ADJ: **~ year** año sabático

sabotage ['sæbətɑːʒ] N sabotaje *m* ▸ VT sabotear

sabre, (US) **saber** ['seɪbəʳ] N sable *m*

saccharin, saccharine ['sækərɪn] N sacarina

sachet ['sæʃeɪ] N sobrecito

★sack [sæk] N (*bag*) saco, costal *m*; **to get the ~** ser despedido; **to give sb the ~** despedir *or* echar a algn ▸ VT (*dismiss*) despedir, echar; (*plunder*) saquear

sackful ['sækful] N saco

sacking ['sækɪŋ] N (*material*) arpillera

sacrament ['sækrəmənt] N sacramento

sacred ['seɪkrɪd] ADJ sagrado, santo

sacred cow N (*fig*) vaca sagrada

★sacrifice ['sækrɪfaɪs] N sacrificio; **to make sacrifices (for sb)** sacrificarse (por algn) ▸ VT sacrificar

sacrilege ['sækrɪlɪdʒ] N sacrilegio

sacrosanct ['sækrəusæŋkt] ADJ sacrosanto

★sad [sæd] ADJ (*unhappy*) triste; (*deplorable*) lamentable

sadden ['sædn] VT entristecer

saddle ['sædl] N silla (de montar); (*of cycle*) sillín *m* ▸ VT (*horse*) ensillar; **to ~ sb with sth** (*inf: task, bill, name*) cargar a algn con algo; **to be saddled with sth** (*inf*) tener que cargar con algo

saddlebag ['sædlbæg] N alforja

sadism ['seɪdɪzm] N sadismo

sadist ['seɪdɪst] N sádico(-a)

sadistic [sə'dɪstɪk] ADJ sádico

sadly ['sædlɪ] ADV tristemente; (*regrettably*) desgraciadamente; **~ lacking (in)** muy deficiente (en)

sadness ['sædnɪs] N tristeza

sado-masochism [seɪdəu'mæsəkɪzɪm] N sado-masoquismo

sae ABBR (BRIT: = *stamped addressed envelope*) sobre franqueado con la dirección propia

safari [sə'fɑːrɪ] N safari *m*

safari park N safari *m*

★safe [seɪf] ADJ (*out of danger*) fuera de peligro; (*not dangerous, sure*) seguro; (*unharmed*) ileso; (*trustworthy*) digno de confianza; **it is ~ to say that ...** se puede decir con confianza que ...; **(just) to be on the ~ side** para mayor seguridad; **~ and sound** sano y salvo; **~ journey!** ¡buen viaje! ▸ N caja de caudales, caja fuerte

safe bet N apuesta segura; **it's a ~ she'll turn up** seguro que viene

safe-breaker ['seɪfbreɪkəʳ] N (BRIT) ladrón(-ona) *m/f* de cajas fuertes

safe-conduct [seɪf'kɔndakt] N salvoconducto

safe-cracker ['seɪfkrækəʳ] N (US) = **safe-breaker**

safe-deposit ['seɪfdɪpɔzɪt] N (*vault*) cámara acorazada; (*box*) caja de seguridad *or* de caudales

safeguard ['seɪfgɑːd] N protección *f*, garantía ▸ VT proteger, defender

safe haven N refugio

safekeeping ['seɪf'kiːpɪŋ] N custodia

safely ['seɪflɪ] ADV seguramente, con seguridad; (*without mishap*) sin peligro; **I can ~ say** puedo decir *or* afirmar con toda seguridad; **to arrive ~** llegar bien

safeness ['seɪfnɪs] N seguridad *f*

safe passage N garantías *fpl* para marcharse en libertad

safe sex N sexo seguro *or* sin riesgo

★safety ['seɪftɪ] N seguridad *f*; **road ~** seguridad *f* en carretera; **~ first!** ¡precaución! ▸ CPD de seguridad

safety belt N cinturón *m* (de seguridad)

safety catch N seguro

safety net N red *f* (de seguridad)

safety pin N imperdible *m*, seguro (*LAM*)

safety valve N válvula de seguridad *or* de escape

saffron ['sæfrən] N azafrán *m*

sag [sæg] VI aflojarse

saga ['sɑːɡə] N (*History*) saga; (*fig*) epopeya

sage [seɪdʒ] N (*herb*) salvia; (*man*) sabio

Sagittarius [sædʒɪ'tɛərɪəs] N Sagitario

sago ['seɪɡəu] N sagú *m*

Sahara [sə'hɑːrə] N: **the ~ (Desert)** el (desierto del) Sáhara

Sahel [sæ'hɛl] N Sahel *m*

said [sɛd] PT, PP *of* **say**

Saigon [saɪ'ɡɔn] N Saigón *m*

★**sail** [seɪl] N (*on boat*) vela; **to go for a ~** dar un paseo en barco ▶ VT (*boat*) gobernar ▶ VI (*travel: ship*) navegar; (: *passenger*) pasear en barco; (*Sport*) hacer vela; (*set off: also:* **to set sail**) zarpar; **they sailed into Copenhagen** arribaron a Copenhague
 ▶ **sail through** VT FUS (*exam*) aprobar fácilmente

sailboat ['seɪlbəut] N (*US*) velero, barco de vela

sailing ['seɪlɪŋ] N (*Sport*) vela; **to go ~** hacer vela

sailing boat N velero, barco de vela

sailing ship N barco de vela

sailor ['seɪləʳ] N marinero, marino

★**saint** [seɪnt] N santo(-a); **S~ John** San Juan

saintliness ['seɪntlɪnɪs] N santidad *f*

saintly ['seɪntlɪ] ADJ santo

★**sake** [seɪk] N: **for the ~ of** por; **for the ~ of argument** digamos, es un decir; **art for art's ~** el arte por el arte

salad ['sæləd] N ensalada; **tomato ~** ensalada de tomate

salad bowl N ensaladera

salad cream N (*BRIT*) mayonesa

salad dressing N aliño

salad oil N aceite *m* para ensalada

salami [sə'lɑːmɪ] N salami *m*, salchichón *m*

salaried ['sælərɪd] ADJ asalariado

★**salary** ['sælərɪ] N sueldo

salary earner N asalariado(-a)

salary scale N escala salarial

★**sale** [seɪl] N venta; (*at reduced prices*) liquidación *f*, saldo; (*auction*) subasta; **closing-down** *or* (*US*) **liquidation ~** liquidación *f*; **on ~ or return** (*goods*) venta por reposición; **on ~** en venta; **"for ~"** "se vende"; **~ and lease back** venta y arrendamiento al vendedor ■ **sales** NPL (*total amount sold*) ventas *fpl*, facturación *f*

saleroom ['seɪlruːm] N sala de subastas

sales assistant N (*BRIT*) dependiente(-a) *m/f*

sales campaign N campaña de venta

sales clerk N (*US*) dependiente(-a) *m/f*

sales conference N conferencia de ventas

sales drive N promoción *f* de ventas

sales figures NPL cifras *fpl* de ventas

sales force N personal *m* de ventas

salesman ['seɪlzmən] N (*irreg*) vendedor *m*; (*in shop*) dependiente *m*; (*representative*) viajante *m*

sales manager N gerente *mf* de ventas

salesmanship ['seɪlzmənʃɪp] N arte *m* de vender

sales meeting N reunión *f* de ventas

salesperson ['seɪlzpəːsən] N vendedor(a) *m/f*, dependiente(-a) *m/f*

sales rep N representante *mf*, agente *mf* comercial

sales tax N (*US*) = **purchase tax**

saleswoman ['seɪlzwumən] N (*irreg*) vendedora; (*in shop*) dependienta; (*representative*) viajante *f*

salient ['seɪlɪənt] ADJ (*features, points*) sobresaliente

saline ['seɪlaɪn] ADJ salino

saliva [sə'laɪvə] N saliva

sallow ['sæləu] ADJ cetrino

sally forth, sally out ['sælɪ-] VI salir, ponerse en marcha

salmon ['sæmən] N *pl inv* salmón *m*

salon ['sælɔn] N (*hairdressing salon, beauty salon*) salón *m*

saloon [sə'luːn] N (*US*) bar *m*, taberna; (*BRIT Aut*) (coche *m* de) turismo; (*ship's lounge*) cámara, salón *m*

SALT [sɔːlt] N ABBR (= *Strategic Arms Limitation Talks/Treaty*) tratado SALT

★**salt** [sɔːlt] N sal *f*; **an old ~** un lobo de mar ▶ VT salar; (*put salt on*) poner sal en
 ▶ **salt away** VT (*inf: money*) ahorrar

salt cellar N salero

salt mine N mina de sal

saltwater ['sɔːltwɔːtəʳ] ADJ (*fish etc*) de agua salada, de mar

salty ['sɔːltɪ] ADJ salado

salubrious [sə'luːbrɪəs] ADJ sano; (*fig: district etc*) atractivo

salutary ['sæljutərɪ] ADJ saludable

salute [sə'luːt] N saludo; (*of guns*) salva ▶ VT saludar

salvage ['sælvɪdʒ] N (*saving*) salvamento, recuperación *f*; (*things saved*) objetos *mpl* salvados ▶ VT salvar

salvage vessel N buque *m* de salvamento

salvation [sæl'veɪʃən] N salvación *f*

Salvation Army N Ejército de Salvación

salve [sælv] N (*cream etc*) ungüento, bálsamo

salvo ['sælvəu] N (*Mil*) salva

Samaritan [sə'mærɪtən] N: **to call the Samaritans** llamar al teléfono de la esperanza

★**same** [seɪm] ADJ mismo; **at the ~ time** (*at the same moment*) al mismo tiempo; (*yet*) sin embargo; **the ~ book as** el mismo libro que; **on the ~ day** el mismo día ▸ PRON: **the ~** el mismo (la misma); **all** *or* **just the ~** sin embargo, aun así; **they're one and the ~** (*person*) son la misma persona; (*thing*) son iguales; **to do the ~ (as sb)** hacer lo mismo (que algn); **and the ~ to you!** ¡igualmente!; **~ here!** ¡yo también!; **the ~ again** (*in bar etc*) otro igual

same-sex marriage ['seɪmseks-] N matrimonio gay

same-sex relationship ['seɪmseks-] N relación *f* entre personas del mismo sexo

Samoa [sə'məuə] N Samoa

sampan ['sæmpæn] N sampán *m*

★**sample** ['sɑːmpl] N muestra; **to take a ~** tomar una muestra; **free ~** muestra gratuita ▸ VT (*food, wine*) probar

sanatorium [sænə'tɔːrɪəm] (*pl* **sanatoria** [-rɪə]) N (*BRIT*) sanatorio

sanctify ['sæŋktɪfaɪ] VT santificar

sanctimonious [sæŋktɪ'məunɪəs] ADJ santurrón(-ona)

sanction ['sæŋkʃən] N sanción *f* ▸ VT sancionar ■ **sanctions** NPL (*Pol*) sanciones *fpl*; **to impose economic sanctions on** *or* **against** imponer sanciones económicas a *or* contra

sanctity ['sæŋktɪtɪ] N (*gen*) santidad *f*; (*inviolability*) inviolabilidad *f*

sanctuary ['sæŋktjuərɪ] N (*gen*) santuario; (*refuge*) asilo, refugio; (*for wildlife*) reserva

★**sand** [sænd] N arena; (*beach*) playa ■ **sands** NPL playa *sg* de arena ▸ VT (*also:* **sand down**: *wood etc*) lijar

sandal ['sændl] N sandalia

sandalwood ['sændlwud] N sándalo

sandbag ['sændbæg] N saco de arena

sandblast ['sændblɑːst] VT limpiar con chorro de arena

sandbox ['sændbɔks] N (*US*) = **sandpit**

sandcastle ['sændkɑːsl] N castillo de arena

sand dune N duna

sander ['sændər] N pulidora

sandpaper ['sændpeɪpər] N papel *m* de lija

sandpit ['sændpɪt] N (*BRIT: for children*) cajón *m* de arena

sandstone ['sændstəun] N piedra arenisca

sandstorm ['sændstɔːm] N tormenta de arena

★**sandwich** ['sændwɪtʃ] N bocadillo (SP), sandwich *m* (LAM); **cheese/ham ~** sandwich de queso/jamón ▸ VT (*also:* **sandwich in**) intercalar; **to be sandwiched between** estar apretujado entre

sandwich board N cartelón *m*

sandwich course N (*BRIT*) programa que intercala períodos de estudio con prácticas profesionales

sandy ['sændɪ] ADJ arenoso; (*colour*) rojizo

sane [seɪn] ADJ cuerdo, sensato

sang [sæŋ] PT *of* **sing**

sanitarium [sænɪ'tɛərɪəm] N (*US*) = **sanatorium**

sanitary ['sænɪtərɪ] ADJ (*system, arrangements*) sanitario; (*clean*) higiénico

sanitary towel, (*US*) **sanitary napkin** N paño higiénico, compresa

sanitation [sænɪ'teɪʃən] N (*in house*) servicios *mpl* higiénicos; (*in town*) servicio de desinfección

sanitation department N (*US*) departamento de limpieza y recogida de basuras

sanity ['sænɪtɪ] N cordura; (*of judgment*) sensatez *f*

sank [sæŋk] PT *of* **sink**

San Marino ['sænmə'riːnəu] N San Marino

Santa Claus [sæntə'klɔːz] N San Nicolás *m*, Papá Noel *m*

Santiago [sæntɪ'ɑːgəu] N (*also:* **Santiago de Chile**) Santiago (de Chile)

sap [sæp] N (*of plants*) savia ▸ VT (*strength*) minar, agotar

sapling ['sæplɪŋ] N árbol nuevo *or* joven

sapphire ['sæfaɪər] N zafiro

Saragossa [særə'gɔsə] N Zaragoza

sarcasm ['sɑːkæzm] N sarcasmo

sarcastic [sɑː'kæstɪk] ADJ sarcástico; **to be ~** ser sarcástico

sarcophagus [sɑː'kɔfəgəs] (*pl* **sarcophagi** [-gaɪ]) N sarcófago

sardine [sɑː'diːn] N sardina

Sardinia [sɑː'dɪnɪə] N Cerdeña

Sardinian [sɑː'dɪnɪən] ADJ, N sardo(-a) *m/f*

sardonic [sɑː'dɔnɪk] ADJ sardónico

sari ['sɑːrɪ] N sari *m*

SARS [sɑːz] N ABBR (= *severe acute respiratory syndrome*) neumonía asiática, SARS *m*

SAS N ABBR (*BRIT Mil*: = *Special Air Service*) cuerpo del ejército británico encargado de misiones clandestinas

SASE N ABBR (*US*: = *self-addressed stamped envelope*) sobre franqueado con la dirección propia

sash [sæʃ] N faja

Sask. ABBR (*CANADA*) = **Saskatchewan**

SAT N ABBR (*US*) = **Scholastic Aptitude Test**

En Estados Unidos, los estudiantes de secundaria que quieren ir a la universidad tienen que realizar un examen: el **SAT** o el *ACT*. El SAT, introducido en 1926, incluye tres pruebas: matemáticas, comprensión lectora y redacción. El *ACT* (*American College Test*) fue creado en 1959 e incluye cuatro pruebas: inglés, matemáticas, lectura y razonamiento científico, además de una prueba optativa de redacción. En Inglaterra, los niños realizan una serie de pruebas llamadas *SATs* (*Standard Assessment Test*), a los 7 y a los 11 años, para que los colegios puedan evaluar el progreso de cada niño.

sat [sæt] PT, PP of **sit**

Sat. ABBR (= *Saturday*) sáb.

Satan ['seɪtn] N Satanás *m*

satanic [sə'tænɪk] ADJ satánico

satchel ['sætʃl] N bolsa; (*child's*) cartera, mochila (*LAM*)

sated ['seɪtɪd] ADJ (*appetite, person*) saciado

★**satellite** ['sætəlaɪt] N satélite *m*

satellite dish N (antena) parabólica

satellite navigation system N sistema *m* de navegación por satélite

satellite television N televisión *f* por satélite

satiate ['seɪʃɪeɪt] VT saciar, hartar

satin ['sætɪn] N raso ▶ ADJ de raso; **with a ~ finish** satinado

satire ['sætaɪə^r] N sátira

satirical [sə'tɪrɪkl] ADJ satírico

satirist ['sætɪrɪst] N (*writer etc*) escritor(a) *m/f* satírico(-a); (*cartoonist*) caricaturista *mf*

satirize ['sætɪraɪz] VT satirizar

satisfaction [sætɪs'fækʃən] N satisfacción *f*; **it gives me great ~** es para mí una gran satisfacción; **has it been done to your ~?** ¿se ha hecho a su satisfacción?

satisfactorily [sætɪs'fæktərɪlɪ] ADV satisfactoriamente, de modo satisfactorio

satisfactory [sætɪs'fæktərɪ] ADJ satisfactorio

satisfied ['sætɪsfaɪd] ADJ satisfecho; **to be ~ (with sth)** estar satisfecho (de algo)

satisfy ['sætɪsfaɪ] VT satisfacer; (*pay*) liquidar; (*convince*) convencer; **to ~ the requirements** llenar los requisitos; **to ~ sb that** convencer a algn de que; **to ~ o.s. of sth** convencerse de algo

satisfying ['sætɪsfaɪɪŋ] ADJ satisfactorio

satnav ['sætnæv] N ABBR (= *satellite navigation*) navegador *m* (GPS)

satsuma [sæt'su:mə] N satsuma

saturate ['sætʃəreɪt] VT: **to ~ (with)** empapar *or* saturar (de)

saturated fat [sætʃəreɪtɪd-] N grasa saturada

saturation [sætʃə'reɪʃən] N saturación *f*

★**Saturday** ['sætədɪ] N sábado; *see also* **Tuesday**

★**sauce** [sɔːs] N salsa; (*sweet*) crema; (*fig: cheek*) frescura

saucepan ['sɔːspən] N cacerola, olla

saucer ['sɔːsə^r] N platillo

saucily ['sɔːsɪlɪ] ADV con frescura, descaradamente

sauciness ['sɔːsɪnɪs] N frescura, descaro

saucy ['sɔːsɪ] ADJ fresco, descarado

Saudi, Saudi Arabian ['saudɪ-] ADJ, N saudí *mf*, saudita *mf*

Saudi Arabia N Arabia Saudí *or* Saudita

sauna ['sɔːnə] N sauna

saunter ['sɔːntə^r] VI deambular

★**sausage** ['sɔsɪdʒ] N salchicha; (*salami etc*) salchichón *m*

sausage roll N empanadilla de salchicha

sauté ['səuteɪ] ADJ (*Culin: potatoes*) salteado; (*: onions*) dorado, rehogado ▶ VT saltear; dorar

sautéed ['səuteɪd] ADJ salteado

savage ['sævɪdʒ] ADJ (*cruel, fierce*) feroz, furioso; (*primitive*) salvaje ▶ N salvaje *mf* ▶ VT (*attack*) embestir

savagely ['sævɪdʒlɪ] ADV con ferocidad, furiosamente; de modo salvaje

savagery ['sævɪdʒrɪ] N ferocidad *f*; salvajismo

★**save** [seɪv] VT (*rescue*) salvar, rescatar; (*money, time*) ahorrar; (*put by*) guardar; (*Comput*) salvar, guardar; (*avoid: trouble*) evitar; (*Sport*) parar; **to ~ face** salvar las apariencias; **it will ~ me an hour** con ello ganaré una hora; **I saved you a piece of cake** te he guardado un trozo de tarta; **God ~ the Queen!** ¡Dios guarde a la Reina!, ¡Viva la Reina! ▶ VI (*also:* **save up**) ahorrar ▶ N (*Sport*) parada ▶ PREP salvo, excepto

saving ['seɪvɪŋ] N (*on price etc*) economía ▶ ADJ: **the ~ grace of** el único mérito de ■ **savings** NPL ahorros *mpl*; **to make savings** economizar

savings account N cuenta de ahorros

savings and loan association N (*US*) sociedad *f* de ahorro y préstamo

savings bank N caja de ahorros

saviour, (*US*) **savior** ['seɪvjə^r] N salvador(a) *m/f*

savoir-faire ['sævwɑː'fɛə^r] N don *m* de gentes

savour, (*US*) **savor** ['seɪvə^r] N sabor *m*, gusto ▶ VT saborear

savoury, (*US*) **savory** ['seɪvərɪ] ADJ sabroso; (*dish: not sweet*) salado

savvy ['sævɪ] N (*inf*) conocimiento, experiencia

saw [sɔː] PT of **see** ▶ N (*tool*) sierra ▶ VT (*pt sawed, pp sawed* [sɔːd] *or sawn* [sɔːn]) serrar; **to ~ sth up** (a)serrar algo

sawdust ['sɔːdʌst] N (a)serrín *m*

sawmill ['sɔːmɪl] N aserradero

sawn [sɔːn] PP of **saw**

sawn-off ['sɔːnɔf], (*US*) **sawed-off** ['sɔːdɔf] ADJ: **~ shotgun** escopeta de cañones recortados

saxophone ['sæksəfəun] N saxófono

★**say** [seɪ] (*pt, pp said* [sɛd]) N: **to have one's ~** expresar su opinión; **to have a** *or* **some ~ in sth** tener voz y voto en algo ▶ VT, VI decir; **to ~ yes/ no** decir que sí/no; **my watch says 3 o'clock** mi reloj marca las tres; **that is to ~** es decir; **that goes without saying** ni que decir tiene; **when all is said and done** al fin y al cabo, a fin de cuentas; **there is something** *or* **a lot to be said for it** hay algo *or* mucho que decir a su favor; **I should ~ it's worth about £100** yo diría que vale unas 100 libras; **she said (that) I was to give you this** me pidió que te diera esto; **~ after me** repite lo que yo diga; **shall we ~ Tuesday?** ¿quedamos, por ejemplo, el martes?; **that doesn't ~ much for him** eso no dice nada a su favor

saying ['seɪɪŋ] N dicho, refrán m

say-so ['seɪsəu] N (inf) autorización f

SBA N ABBR (US) = **Small Business Administration**

SC N ABBR (US) = **Supreme Court** ▶ ABBR (US) = **South Carolina**

s/c ABBR = **self-contained**

scab [skæb] N costra; (pej) esquirol(a) m/f

scaffold ['skæfəld] N (for execution) cadalso

scaffolding ['skæfəldɪŋ] N andamio, andamiaje m

scald [skɔ:ld] N escaldadura ▶ VT escaldar

scalding ['skɔ:ldɪŋ] ADJ (also: **scalding hot**) hirviendo, que arde

★**scale** [skeɪl] N (gen) escala; (Mus) escala; (of fish) escama; (of salaries, fees etc) escalafón m; **pay ~** escala salarial; **~ of charges** tarifa, lista de precios; **on a large ~** a gran escala; **to draw sth to ~** dibujar algo a escala ▶ VT (mountain) escalar; (tree) trepar ■ **scales** NPL (small) balanza sg; (large) báscula sg
▶ **scale down** VT reducir

scaled-down [skeɪld'daun] ADJ reducido proporcionalmente

scale model N modelo a escala

scallion ['skæljən] N (US) cebolleta

scallop ['skɔləp] N (Zool) venera; (Sewing) festón m

scalp [skælp] N cabellera ▶ VT escalpar

scalpel ['skælpl] N bisturí m

scam [skæm] N (inf) estafa, timo

scamper ['skæmpəʳ] VI: **to ~ away, ~ off** escabullirse

scampi ['skæmpɪ] NPL gambas fpl

scan [skæn] VT (examine) escudriñar; (glance at quickly) dar un vistazo a; (TV, Radar) explorar, registrar; (Comput) escanear ▶ N (Med) examen m ultrasónico; **to have a ~** pasar por el escáner

★**scandal** ['skændl] N escándalo; (gossip) chismes mpl

scandalize ['skændəlaɪz] VT escandalizar

scandalous ['skændələs] ADJ escandaloso

Scandinavia [skændɪ'neɪvɪə] N Escandinavia

Scandinavian [skændɪ'neɪvɪən] ADJ, N escandinavo(-a) m/f

scanner ['skænəʳ] N (Radar, Med, Comput) escáner m

scant [skænt] ADJ escaso

scantily ['skæntɪlɪ] ADV: **~ clad** or **dressed** ligero de ropa

scantiness ['skæntɪnɪs] N escasez f, insuficiencia

scanty ['skæntɪ] ADJ (meal) insuficiente; (clothes) ligero

scapegoat ['skeɪpgəut] N cabeza de turco, chivo expiatorio

scar [skɑ:] N cicatriz f ▶ VT marcar con una cicatriz ▶ VI cicatrizarse

scarce [skɛəs] ADJ escaso; **to make o.s. ~** (inf) esfumarse

scarcely ['skɛəslɪ] ADV apenas; **~ anybody** casi nadie; **I can ~ believe it** casi no puedo creerlo

scarceness ['skɛəsnɪs], **scarcity** ['skɛəsɪtɪ] N escasez f

scarcity value N valor m de escasez

scare [skɛəʳ] N susto, sobresalto; (panic) pánico; **bomb ~** amenaza de bomba ▶ VT asustar, espantar; **to ~ sb stiff** dar a algn un susto de muerte
▶ **scare away, scare off** VT espantar, ahuyentar

scarecrow ['skɛəkrəu] N espantapájaros m inv

scared [skɛəd] ADJ: **to be ~** asustarse, estar asustado

scaremonger ['skɛəmʌŋgəʳ] N alarmista mf

scarf [skɑ:f] (pl **scarves** [skɑ:vz]) N (long) bufanda; (square) pañuelo

scarlet ['skɑ:lɪt] ADJ escarlata

scarlet fever N escarlatina

scarper ['skɑ:pəʳ] VI (BRIT inf) largarse

scarred [skɑ:d] ADJ lleno de cicatrices

scarves [skɑ:vz] NPL of **scarf**

scary ['skɛərɪ] ADJ (inf) de miedo; **it's ~** da miedo

scathing ['skeɪðɪŋ] ADJ mordaz; **to be ~ about sth** criticar algo duramente

scatter ['skætəʳ] VT (spread) esparcir, desparramar; (put to flight) dispersar ▶ VI desparramarse; dispersarse

scatterbrained ['skætəbreɪnd] ADJ ligero de cascos

scavenge ['skævɪndʒ] VI: **to ~ (for)** (person) revolver entre la basura (para encontrar); **to ~ for food** (hyenas etc) nutrirse de carroña

scavenger ['skævɪndʒəʳ] N (person) mendigo/a que rebusca en la basura; (Zool: animal) animal m de carroña; (: bird) ave f de carroña

scenario [sɪ'nɑ:rɪəu] N (Theat) argumento; (Cine) guión m; (fig) escenario

★**scene** [si:n] N (Theat) escena; (of crime, accident) escenario; (sight, view) vista, panorama; (fuss) escándalo; **the political ~ in Spain** el panorama político español; **behind the scenes** (also fig) entre bastidores; **to appear** or **come on the ~** (also fig) aparecer, presentarse; **to make a ~** (inf: fuss) armar un escándalo

scenery ['si:nərɪ] N (Theat) decorado; (landscape) paisaje m

scenic ['si:nɪk] ADJ (picturesque) pintoresco

scent [sɛnt] N perfume m, olor m; (fig: track) rastro, pista; (sense of smell) olfato; **to put** or **throw sb off the ~** (fig) despistar a algn ▶ VT perfumar; (suspect) presentir

sceptic, (US) **skeptic** ['skɛptɪk] N escéptico(-a)

sceptical, (US) **skeptical** ['skɛptɪkl] ADJ escéptico

S

scepticism, (US) **skepticism** ['skɛptɪsɪzm] N escepticismo

sceptre, (US) **scepter** ['sɛptə'] N cetro

★**schedule** ['ʃɛdjuːl, (US) 'skɛdjuːl] N (of trains) horario; (of events) programa m; (list) lista; **we are working to a very tight ~** tenemos un programa de trabajo muy apretado; **to be ahead of/behind ~** ir adelantado/retrasado; **on ~** a la hora, sin retraso; **everything went according to ~** todo salió según lo previsto ► VT (timetable) establecer el horario de; (list) catalogar; (visit) fijar la hora de; **the meeting is scheduled for seven** or **to begin at seven** la reunión está fijada para las siete

scheduled ['ʃɛdjuːld, (US) 'skɛdjuːld] ADJ (date, time) fijado; (visit, event, bus, train) programado; (stop) previsto; **~ flight** vuelo regular

schematic [skɪ'mætɪk] ADJ (diagram etc) esquemático

scheme [skiːm] N (plan) plan m, proyecto; (method) esquema m; (plot) intriga; (trick) ardid m; (arrangement) disposición f; (pension scheme etc) sistema m; **colour ~** combinación f de colores ► VT proyectar ► VI (plan) hacer proyectos; (intrigue) intrigar

scheming ['skiːmɪŋ] ADJ intrigante

schism ['skɪzəm] N cisma m

schizophrenia [skɪtsə'friːnɪə] N esquizofrenia

schizophrenic [skɪtsə'frɛnɪk] ADJ esquizofrénico

scholar ['skɔlə'] N (pupil) alumno(-a), estudiante mf; (learned person) sabio(-a), erudito(-a)

scholarly ['skɔləlɪ] ADJ erudito

scholarship ['skɔləʃɪp] N erudición f; (grant) beca

★**school** [skuːl] N (gen) escuela, colegio; (in university) facultad f; (of fish) banco; **to be at** or **go to ~** ir al colegio or a la escuela ► VT (animal) amaestrar

school age N edad f escolar

schoolbook ['skuːlbuk] N libro de texto

★**schoolboy** ['skuːlbɔɪ] N alumno

schoolchild ['skuːltʃaɪld] N (irreg) alumno(-a)

schooldays ['skuːldeɪz] NPL años mpl del colegio

★**schoolgirl** ['skuːlgəːl] N alumna

schooling ['skuːlɪŋ] N enseñanza

school-leaver ['skuːlliːvə'] N (BRIT) joven que ha terminado la educación secundaria

schoolmaster ['skuːlmɑːstə'] N (primary) maestro; (secondary) profesor m

schoolmistress ['skuːlmɪstrɪs] N (primary) maestra; (secondary) profesora

schoolroom ['skuːlrum] N clase f

schoolteacher ['skuːltiːtʃə'] N (primary) maestro(-a); (secondary) profesor(a) m/f

schoolyard ['skuːljɑːd] N (US) patio del colegio

schooner ['skuːnə'] N (ship) goleta

sciatica [saɪ'ætɪkə] N ciática

★**science** ['saɪəns] N ciencia; **the sciences** las ciencias

science fiction N ciencia-ficción f

scientific [saɪən'tɪfɪk] ADJ científico

★**scientist** ['saɪəntɪst] N científico(-a)

sci-fi ['saɪfaɪ] N ABBR (inf) = **science fiction**

Scilly Isles ['sɪlɪ-], **Scillies** ['sɪlɪz] NPL: **the ~** las Islas Sorlingas

scintillating ['sɪntɪleɪtɪŋ] ADJ (wit, conversation, company) brillante, chispeante, ingenioso

★**scissors** ['sɪzəz] NPL tijeras fpl; **a pair of ~** unas tijeras

scoff [skɔf] VT (BRIT inf: eat) engullir ► VI: **to ~ (at)** (mock) mofarse (de)

scold [skəuld] VT regañar

scolding ['skəuldɪŋ] N riña, reprimenda

scone [skɔn] N pastel de pan

scoop [skuːp] N cucharón m; (for flour etc) pala; (Press) exclusiva ► VT (Comm: market) adelantarse a; (: profit) sacar; (Comm, Press: competitors) adelantarse a
► **scoop out** VT excavar
► **scoop up** VT recoger

scooter ['skuːtə'] N (motor cycle) Vespa®; (toy) patinete m

scope [skəup] N (of plan, undertaking) ámbito; (reach) alcance m; (of person) competencia; (opportunity) libertad f (de acción); **there is plenty of ~ for improvement** hay bastante campo para efectuar mejoras

scorch [skɔːtʃ] VT (clothes) chamuscar; (earth, grass) quemar, secar

scorcher ['skɔːtʃə'] N (inf: hot day) día m abrasador

scorching ['skɔːtʃɪŋ] ADJ abrasador(a)

★**score** [skɔː'] N (points etc) puntuación f; (Mus) partitura; (reckoning) cuenta; (twenty) veintena; **on that ~** en lo que se refiere a eso; **to have an old ~ to settle with sb** (fig) tener cuentas pendientes con algn; **to keep (the) ~** llevar la cuenta; **scores of people** (fig) muchísima gente, cantidad de gente ► VT (goal, point) ganar; (mark, cut) rayar; **to ~ 6 out of 10** obtener una puntuación de 6 sobre 10 ► VI marcar un tanto; (Football) marcar un gol; (keep score) llevar el tanteo
► **score out** VT tachar

scoreboard ['skɔːbɔːd] N marcador m

scoreline ['skɔːlaɪn] N (Sport) resultado final

scorer ['skɔːrə'] N marcador(a) m/f; (keeping score) encargado(-a) del marcador

scorn [skɔːn] N desprecio ► VT despreciar

scornful ['skɔːnful] ADJ desdeñoso, despreciativo

scornfully ['skɔːnfulɪ] ADV desdeñosamente, con desprecio

Scorpio ['skɔːpɪəu] N Escorpión m

scorpion ['skɔːpɪən] N alacrán m, escorpión m

Scot [skɔt] N escocés(-esa) m/f

Scotch [skɔtʃ] N whisky *m* escocés

scotch [skɔtʃ] VT (*rumour*) desmentir; (*plan*) frustrar

Scotch tape® N (*US*) cinta adhesiva, celo, scotch® *m*

scot-free [skɔt'friː] ADV: **to get off ~** (*unpunished*) salir impune; (*unhurt*) salir ileso

★**Scotland** ['skɔtlənd] N Escocia

Scots [skɔts] ADJ escocés(-esa)

★**Scotsman** ['skɔtsmən] N (*irreg*) escocés *m*

★**Scotswoman** ['skɔtswumən] N (*irreg*) escocesa

★**Scottish** ['skɔtɪʃ] ADJ escocés(-esa); **the ~ National Party** *partido político independista escocés*; **the ~ Parliament** el Parlamento escocés

En 1997, después de casi trescientos años de unión política entre Inglaterra y Escocia, esta segunda aprobó en referéndum establecer un parlamento autónomo en Edimburgo. En 1999, 129 parlamentarios fueron elegidos, con competencias en áreas como la educación, el medio ambiente, la salud, la justicia, los impuestos y el gobierno local. El *First Minister* (Primer Ministro) es jefe del gobierno escocés, pero la soberana británica sigue siendo la jefa del Estado. En septiembre de 2014, en un nuevo referéndum, la mayoría de los escoceses rechazó la independencia plena del Reino Unido.

scoundrel ['skaundrəl] N canalla *mf*, sinvergüenza *mf*

scour ['skauə'] VT (*clean*) fregar, estregar; (*search*) recorrer, registrar

scourer ['skauərə'] N (*pad*) estropajo; (*powder*) limpiador *m*

scourge [skəːdʒ] N azote *m*

scout [skaut] N explorador *m*; **girl ~** (*US*) niña exploradora
  ▶ **scout around** VI reconocer el terreno

scowl [skaul] VI fruncir el ceño; **to ~ at sb** mirar con ceño a algn

scrabble ['skræbl] VI (*claw*): **to ~ (at)** arañar; **to ~ around for sth** revolver todo buscando algo ▶ N: **S~®** Scrabble® *m*, Intelect® *m*

scraggy ['skrægɪ] ADJ flaco, delgaducho

scram [skræm] VI (*inf*) largarse

scramble ['skræmbl] N (*climb*) subida (difícil); (*struggle*) pelea ▶ VI: **to ~ out/through** salir/abrirse paso con dificultad; **to ~ for** pelear por; **to go scrambling** (*Sport*) hacer motocross

scrambled eggs ['skræmbld-] NPL huevos *mpl* revueltos

scrap [skræp] N (*bit*) pedacito; (*fig*) pizca; (*fight*) riña, bronca; (*also*: **scrap iron**) chatarra, hierro viejo; **to sell sth for ~** vender algo como chatarra ▶ VT (*discard*) desechar, descartar ▶ VI reñir, armar (una) bronca ■ **scraps** NPL (*waste*) sobras *fpl*, desperdicios *mpl*

scrapbook ['skræpbuk] N álbum *m* de recortes

scrap dealer N chatarrero(-a)

scrape [skreɪp] N (*fig*) lío, apuro; **to get into a ~** meterse en un lío ▶ VT raspar; (*skin etc*) rasguñar; (*also*: **scrape against**) rozar
  ▶ **scrape through** VI (*succeed*) salvarse por los pelos; (*in exam*) aprobar por los pelos

scraper ['skreɪpə'] N raspador *m*

scrap heap N (*fig*): **on the ~** desperdiciado; **to throw sth on the ~** desechar *or* descartar algo

scrap iron N chatarra

scrap merchant N (*BRIT*) chatarrero(-a)

scrap metal N chatarra, desecho de metal

scrap paper N pedazos *mpl* de papel

scrappy ['skræpɪ] ADJ (*essay etc*) deshilvanado; (*education*) incompleto

scrap yard N depósito de chatarra; (*for cars*) cementerio de coches

scratch [skrætʃ] N rasguño; (*from claw*) arañazo; **to start from ~** partir de cero; **to be up to ~** cumplir con los requisitos ▶ ADJ: **~ team** equipo improvisado ▶ VT (*paint, car*) rayar; (*with claw, nail*) rasguñar, arañar; (*Comput*) borrar ▶ VI rascarse

scratch card N (*BRIT*) tarjeta *f* de "rasque y gane"

scratchpad ['skrætʃpæd] N (*US*) bloc *m* de notas

scrawl [skrɔːl] N garabatos *mpl* ▶ VI hacer garabatos

scrawny ['skrɔːnɪ] ADJ (*person, neck*) flaco

★**scream** [skriːm] N chillido; **it was a ~** (*fig: inf*) fue para morirse de risa *or* muy divertido; **he's a ~** (*fig: inf*) es muy divertido *or* de lo más gracioso ▶ VI chillar; **to ~ at sb (to do sth)** gritarle a algn (para que haga algo)

scree [skriː] N cono de desmoronamiento

screech [skriːtʃ] VI chirriar

★**screen** [skriːn] N (*Cine, TV*) pantalla; (*movable*) biombo; (*wall*) tabique *m*; (*also*: **windscreen**) parabrisas *m inv* ▶ VT (*conceal*) tapar; (*from the wind etc*) proteger; (*film*) proyectar; (*fig: person: for security*) investigar; (: *for illness*) hacer una exploración a

screen editing N (*Comput*) corrección *f* en pantalla

screenful ['skriːnful] N pantalla

screening ['skriːnɪŋ] N (*of film*) proyección *f*; (*for security*) investigación *f*; (*Med*) exploración *f*

screen memory N (*Comput*) memoria de la pantalla

screenplay ['skriːnpleɪ] N guión *m*

screen saver [-seɪvə'] N (*Comput*) salvapantallas *m inv*

screenshot ['skriːnʃɔt] N (*Comput*) pantallazo, captura de pantalla

screen test N prueba de pantalla

screw [skruː] N tornillo; (*propeller*) hélice *f* ▶ VT atornillar; **to ~ sth to the wall** fijar algo a la pared con tornillos
  ▶ **screw up** VT (*paper, material etc*) arrugar; (*inf: ruin*) fastidiar; **to ~ up one's eyes** arrugar

S

el entrecejo; **to ~ up one's face** torcer or arrugar la cara

screwdriver ['skru:draɪvə^r] N destornillador m

screwed-up ['skru:d'ʌp] ADJ (inf): **she's totally ~** está trastornada

screwy ['skru:ɪ] ADJ (inf) chiflado

scribble ['skrɪbl] N garabatos mpl ▶ vɪ garabatear ▶ vт escribir con prisa; **to ~ sth down** garabatear algo

script [skrɪpt] N (Cine etc) guión m; (writing) escritura, letra

scripted ['skrɪptɪd] ADJ (Radio, TV) escrito

Scripture ['skrɪptʃə^r] N Sagrada Escritura

scriptwriter ['skrɪptraɪtə^r] N guionista mf

scroll [skrəʊl] N rollo ▶ vт (Comput) desplazar

scrotum ['skrəʊtəm] N escroto

scrounge [skraʊndʒ] (inf) vт: **to ~ sth off** or **from sb** gorronear algo a algn ▶ vɪ: **to ~ on sb** vivir a costa de algn

scrounger ['skraʊndʒə^r] N gorrón(-ona) m/f

scrub [skrʌb] N (clean) fregado; (land) maleza ▶ vт fregar, restregar; (reject) cancelar, anular

scrubbing brush ['skrʌbɪŋ-] N cepillo de fregar

scruff [skrʌf] N: **by the ~ of the neck** por el pescuezo

scruffy ['skrʌfɪ] ADJ desaliñado, desaseado

scrum [skrʌm], **scrummage** ['skrʌmɪdʒ] N (Rugby) melé f

scruple ['skru:pl] N escrúpulo; **to have no scruples about doing sth** no tener reparos en or escrúpulos para hacer algo

scrupulous ['skru:pjuləs] ADJ escrupuloso

scrupulously ['skru:pjuləslɪ] ADV escrupulosamente; **to be ~ fair/honest** ser sumamente justo/honesto

scrutinize ['skru:tɪnaɪz] vт escudriñar; (votes) escrutar

scrutiny ['skru:tɪnɪ] N escrutinio, examen m; **under the ~ of sb** bajo la mirada or el escrutinio de algn

scuba ['sku:bə] N escafandra autónoma

scuba diving ['sku:bə'daɪvɪŋ] N submarinismo

scuff [skʌf] vт (shoes, floor) rayar

scuffle ['skʌfl] N refriega

scullery ['skʌlərɪ] N trascocina

sculptor ['skʌlptə^r] N escultor(a) m/f

sculpture ['skʌlptʃə^r] N escultura

scum [skʌm] N (on liquid) espuma; (pej: people) escoria

scupper ['skʌpə^r] vт (boat) hundir; (BRIT fig: plans etc) acabar con

scurrilous ['skʌrɪləs] ADJ difamatorio, calumnioso

scurry ['skʌrɪ] vɪ: **to ~ off** escabullirse

scurvy ['skə:vɪ] N escorbuto

scuttle ['skʌtl] N (also: **coal scuttle**) cubo, carbonera ▶ vт (ship) barrenar ▶ vɪ (scamper): **to ~ away**, **~ off** escabullirse

scythe [saɪð] N guadaña

SD, S. Dak. ABBR (US) = **South Dakota**

SDLP N ABBR (BRIT Pol) = **Social Democratic and Labour Party**

★**sea** [si:] N mar m or f; **by ~** (travel) en barco; **on the ~** (boat) en el mar; (town) junto al mar; **to be all at ~** (fig) estar despistado; **out to** or **at ~** en alta mar; **to go by ~** ir en barco; **heavy** or **rough seas** marejada; **by** or **beside the ~** (holiday) en la playa; (village) a orillas del mar; **a ~ of faces** una multitud de caras

sea bed N fondo del mar

sea bird N ave f marina

seaboard ['si:bɔ:d] N litoral m

sea breeze N brisa de mar

seadog ['si:dɔg] N lobo de mar

seafarer ['si:fɛərə^r] N marinero

seafaring ['si:fɛərɪŋ] ADJ (community) marinero; (life) de marinero

★**seafood** ['si:fu:d] N mariscos mpl

sea front N (beach) playa; (prom) paseo marítimo

seagoing ['si:gəʊɪŋ] ADJ (ship) de alta mar

seagull ['si:gʌl] N gaviota

seal [si:l] N (animal) foca; (stamp) sello; **~ of approval** sello de aprobación ▶ vт (close) cerrar; (: with seal) sellar; (decide: sb's fate) decidir; (: bargain) cerrar
▶ **seal off** vт obturar

seal cull N matanza de crías de foca

sea level N nivel m del mar

sealing wax ['si:lɪŋ-] N lacre m

sea lion N león m marino

sealskin ['si:lskɪn] N piel f de foca

seam [si:m] N costura; (of metal) juntura; (of coal) veta, filón m; **the hall was bursting at the seams** la sala rebosaba de gente

seaman ['si:mən] N (irreg) marinero

seamanship ['si:mənʃɪp] N náutica

seamy ['si:mɪ] ADJ sórdido

seance ['seɪɔns] N sesión f de espiritismo

seaplane ['si:pleɪn] N hidroavión m

seaport ['si:pɔ:t] N puerto de mar

★**search** [sə:tʃ] N (for person, thing) busca, búsqueda; (of drawer, pockets) registro; (inspection) reconocimiento; **in ~ of** en busca de ▶ vт (look in) buscar en; (examine) examinar; (person, place) registrar; (Comput) buscar ▶ vɪ: **to ~ for** buscar; **"~ and replace"** (Comput) "buscar y reemplazar"
▶ **search through** vт FUS registrar

search engine N (Internet) buscador m

searcher ['sə:tʃə^r] N buscador(a) m/f

searching ['sə:tʃɪŋ] ADJ (question) penetrante

searchlight ['sə:tʃlaɪt] N reflector m

search party N equipo de salvamento

search warrant N mandamiento judicial

searing ['sɪərɪŋ] ADJ (*heat*) abrasador(a); (*pain*) agudo

seashore ['siːʃɔː] N playa, orilla del mar; **on the ~** a la orilla del mar

seasick ['siːsɪk] ADJ mareado; **to be ~** marearse

★**seaside** ['siːsaɪd] N playa, orilla del mar; **to go to the ~** ir a la playa

seaside resort N centro turístico costero

★**season** ['siːzn] N (*of year*) estación *f*; (*sporting etc*) temporada; (*gen*) época, período; **the busy ~** (*for shops, hotels etc*) la temporada alta; **to be in/out of ~** estar en sazón/fuera de temporada; **the open ~** (*Hunting*) la temporada de caza *or* de pesca ▶ VT (*food*) sazonar

seasonal ['siːznl] ADJ estacional

seasoned ['siːznd] ADJ (*wood*) curado; (*fig: worker, actor*) experimentado; (*troops*) curtido; **~ campaigner** veterano(-a)

seasoning ['siːznɪŋ] N condimento

season ticket N abono

★**seat** [siːt] N (*in bus, train: place*) asiento; (*chair*) silla; (*Parliament*) escaño; (*buttocks*) trasero; (*centre: of government etc*) sede *f*; **are there any seats left?** ¿quedan plazas?; **to take one's ~** sentarse, tomar asiento ▶ VT sentar; (*have room for*) tener cabida para; **to be seated** estar sentado, sentarse

seat belt N cinturón *m* de seguridad

seating ['siːtɪŋ] N asientos *mpl*

seating arrangements NPL distribución *fsg* de los asientos

seating capacity N número de asientos, aforo

SEATO ['siːtəu] N ABBR (= *Southeast Asia Treaty Organization*) OTASE *f*

sea water N agua del mar

seaweed ['siːwiːd] N alga marina

seaworthy ['siːwəːðɪ] ADJ en condiciones de navegar

SEC N ABBR (*US: = Securities and Exchange Commission*) comisión *de operaciones bursátiles*

sec. ABBR = **second¹**

secateurs [sɛkəˈtəːz] NPL podadera *sg*

secede [sɪˈsiːd] VI: **to ~ (from)** separarse (de)

secluded [sɪˈkluːdɪd] ADJ retirado

seclusion [sɪˈkluːʒən] N retiro

★**second¹** ['sɛkənd] ADJ segundo; **to have ~ thoughts** cambiar de opinión; **on ~ thoughts** *or* (*US*) **thought** pensándolo bien; **to ask for a ~ opinion** (*Med*) pedir una segunda opinión; **~ floor** (*BRIT*) segundo piso; (*US*) primer piso; **~ mortgage** segunda hipoteca; **Charles the S~** Carlos Segundo ▶ ADV (*in race etc*) en segundo lugar ▶ N (*gen*) segundo; (*Aut: also:* **second gear**) segunda; (*Comm*) artículo con algún desperfecto; (*BRIT Scol: degree*) título universitario de segunda clase; **just a ~!** ¡un momento! ▶ VT (*motion*) apoyar

second² [sɪˈkɔnd] VT (*employee*) trasladar temporalmente

secondary ['sɛkəndərɪ] ADJ secundario

secondary education N enseñanza secundaria

★**secondary school** N escuela secundaria

second-best [sɛkəndˈbɛst] N segundo

second-class ['sɛkəndˈklɑːs] ADJ de segunda clase; **~ citizen** ciudadano(-a) de segunda (clase) ▶ ADV: **to send sth ~** enviar algo por correo de segunda clase; **to travel ~** viajar en segunda

second cousin N primo(-a) segundo(-a)

seconder ['sɛkəndə'] N el (la) que apoya una moción

second-guess ['sɛkəndˈgɛs] VT (*evaluate*) juzgar (a posteriori); (*anticipate*): **to ~ sth/sb** (intentar) adivinar algo/lo que va a hacer algn

secondhand ['sɛkəndˈhænd] ADJ de segunda mano, usado ▶ ADV: **to buy sth ~** comprar algo de segunda mano; **to hear sth ~** oír algo indirectamente

second hand N (*on clock*) segundero

second-in-command ['sɛkəndɪnkəˈmɑːnd] N (*Mil*) segundo en el mando; (*Admin*) segundo(-a), ayudante *mf*

secondly ['sɛkəndlɪ] ADV en segundo lugar

secondment [sɪˈkɔndmənt] N (*BRIT*) traslado temporal

second-rate ['sɛkəndˈreɪt] ADJ de segunda categoría

secrecy ['siːkrəsɪ] N secreto

★**secret** ['siːkrɪt] ADJ, N secreto; **in ~** *adv* en secreto; **to keep sth ~ (from sb)** ocultarle algo (a algn); **to make no ~ of sth** no ocultar algo

secret agent N agente *mf* secreto(-a), espía *mf*

secretarial [sɛkrɪˈtɛərɪəl] ADJ (*course*) de secretariado; (*staff*) de secretaría; (*work, duties*) de secretaria

secretariat [sɛkrɪˈtɛərɪət] N secretaría

★**secretary** ['sɛkrətərɪ] N secretario(-a); **S~ of State** (*BRIT Pol*) Ministro (con cartera)

secretary-general ['sɛkrətərɪˈdʒɛnərl] N secretario(-a) general

secretary pool N (*US*) = **typing pool**

secrete [sɪˈkriːt] VT (*Med, Anat, Biol*) secretar; (*hide*) ocultar, esconder

secretion [sɪˈkriːʃən] N secreción *f*

secretive ['siːkrətɪv] ADJ reservado, sigiloso

secretly ['siːkrɪtlɪ] ADV en secreto

secret police N policía secreta

secret service N servicio secreto

sect [sɛkt] N secta

sectarian [sɛkˈtɛərɪən] ADJ sectario

★**section** ['sɛkʃən] N sección *f*; (*part*) parte *f*; (*of document*) artículo; (*of opinion*) sector *m*; **business ~** (*Press*) sección *f* de economía

S

763

sectional [ˈsɛkʃənl] ADJ (*regional*) regional, local

sector [ˈsɛktər] N sector *m*

secular [ˈsɛkjulər] ADJ secular, seglar

secure [sɪˈkjuər] ADJ (*free from anxiety*) seguro; (*firmly fixed*) firme, fijo; **to make sth ~** afianzar algo ▸ VT (*fix*) asegurar, afianzar; (*get*) conseguir; (*Comm: loan*) garantizar; **to ~ sth for sb** conseguir algo para algn

secured creditor [sɪˈkjuər-] N acreedor(a) *m/f* con garantía

securely [sɪˈkjuəlɪ] ADV firmemente; **it is ~ fastened** está bien sujeto

★**security** [sɪˈkjuərɪtɪ] N seguridad *f*; (*for loan*) fianza; (: *object*) prenda; **to increase/tighten ~** aumentar/estrechar las medidas de seguridad; **~ of tenure** tenencia asegurada; **job ~** seguridad *f* en el empleo ■ **securities** NPL (*Comm*) valores *mpl*, títulos *mpl*

Security Council N: **the ~** el Consejo de Seguridad

security forces NPL fuerzas *fpl* de seguridad

security guard N guardia *mf* de seguridad

security risk N riesgo para la seguridad

secy. ABBR (= *secretary*) Sec.

sedan [sɪˈdæn] N (*US Aut*) sedán *m*

sedate [sɪˈdeɪt] ADJ tranquilo ▸ VT administrar sedantes a, sedar

sedation [sɪˈdeɪʃən] N (*Med*) sedación *f*; **to be under ~** estar bajo sedación

sedative [ˈsɛdɪtɪv] N sedante *m*, calmante *m*

sedentary [ˈsɛdntrɪ] ADJ sedentario

sediment [ˈsɛdɪmənt] N sedimento

sedimentary [sɛdɪˈmɛntərɪ] ADJ (*Geo*) sedimentario

sedition [sɪˈdɪʃən] N sedición *f*

seduce [sɪˈdjuːs] VT (*gen*) seducir

seduction [sɪˈdʌkʃən] N seducción *f*

seductive [sɪˈdʌktɪv] ADJ seductor(-a)

★**see** [siː] (*pt* **saw** [sɔː], *pp* **seen** [siːn]) VT (*gen*) ver; (*understand*) ver, comprender; (*look at*) mirar; **to go and ~ sb** ir a ver a algn; **there was nobody to be seen** no se veía a nadie; **as far as I can ~** por lo visto *or* por lo que veo; **~ you soon/later/tomorrow!** ¡hasta pronto/luego/mañana!; **to ~ that** (*ensure*) asegurarse de que; **to ~ sb to the door** acompañar a algn a la puerta; **I don't know what she sees in him** no sé qué le encuentra ▸ VI ver; **let me ~** (*show me*) a ver; (*let me think*) vamos a ver; **~ for yourself** compruébalo tú mismo ▸ N sede *f*
▸ **see about** VT FUS atender a, encargarse de
▸ **see off** VT despedir
▸ **see out** VT (*take to the door*) acompañar hasta la puerta
▸ **see through** VT FUS (*person, behaviour*) calar
▸ VT llevar a cabo
▸ **see to** VT FUS atender a, encargarse de

★**seed** [siːd] N semilla; (*in fruit*) pepita; (*fig*) germen *m*; (*Tennis*) preseleccionado(-a); **to go to ~** (*plant*) granar; (*fig*) descuidarse

seedless [ˈsiːdlɪs] ADJ sin semillas *or* pepitas

seedling [ˈsiːdlɪŋ] N planta de semillero

seedy [ˈsiːdɪ] ADJ (*person*) desaseado; (*place*) sórdido

seeing [ˈsiːɪŋ] CONJ: **~ (that)** visto que, en vista de que

seek [siːk] (*pt, pp* **sought** [sɔːt]) VT (*gen*) buscar; (*post*) solicitar; **to ~ advice/help from sb** pedir consejos/solicitar ayuda a algn
▸ **seek out** VT (*person*) buscar

★**seem** [siːm] VI parecer; **there seems to be ...** parece que hay ...; **it seems (that) ...** parece que ...; **what seems to be the trouble?** ¿qué pasa?; **I did what seemed best** hice lo que parecía mejor

seemingly [ˈsiːmɪŋlɪ] ADV aparentemente, según parece

seen [siːn] PP *of* **see**

seep [siːp] VI filtrarse

seer [sɪər] N vidente *mf*, profeta *mf*

seersucker [ˈsɪəsʌkər] N sirsaca

seesaw [ˈsiːsɔː] N balancín *m*, subibaja *m*

seethe [siːð] VI hervir; **to ~ with anger** enfurecerse

see-through [ˈsiːθruː] ADJ transparente

segment [ˈsɛgmənt] N segmento; (*of citrus fruit*) gajo

segregate [ˈsɛgrɪgeɪt] VT segregar

segregation [sɛgrɪˈgeɪʃən] N segregación *f*

Seine [seɪn] N Sena *m*

seismic [ˈsaɪzmɪk] ADJ sísmico

seize [siːz] VT (*grasp*) agarrar, asir; (*take possession of*) secuestrar; (: *territory*) apoderarse de; (*opportunity*) aprovecharse de
▸ **seize up** VI (*Tech*) agarrotarse
▸ **seize (up)on** VT FUS valerse de

seizure [ˈsiːʒər] N (*Med*) ataque *m*; (*Law*) incautación *f*

seldom [ˈsɛldəm] ADV rara vez

★**select** [sɪˈlɛkt] ADJ selecto, escogido; (*hotel, restaurant, clubs*) exclusivo; **a ~ few** una minoría selecta ▸ VT escoger, elegir; (*Sport*) seleccionar

★**selection** [sɪˈlɛkʃən] N selección *f*, elección *f*; (*Comm*) surtido

selection committee N comisión *f* de nombramiento

selective [sɪˈlɛktɪv] ADJ selectivo

self [sɛlf] N (*pl* **selves** [sɛlvz]) uno mismo; **the ~** el yo ▸ PREF auto...

self-addressed [ˈsɛlfəˈdrɛst] ADJ: **~ envelope** sobre *m* con la dirección propia

self-adhesive [sɛlfədˈhiːzɪv] ADJ autoadhesivo, autoadherente

self-appointed [sɛlfəˈpɔɪntɪd] ADJ autonombrado

self-assurance [sɛlfəˈʃuərəns] N confianza en sí mismo

self-assured [sɛlfəˈʃuəd] ADJ seguro de sí mismo

self-catering [sɛlf'keɪtərɪŋ] ADJ (BRIT) sin pensión or servicio de comida; **~ apartment** apartamento con cocina propia

self-centred, (US) **self-centered** [sɛlf'sɛntəd] ADJ egocéntrico

self-cleaning [sɛlf'kliːnɪŋ] ADJ autolimpiador

self-confessed [sɛlfkən'fɛst] ADJ (alcoholic etc) confeso

self-confidence [sɛlf'kɒnfɪdns] N confianza en sí mismo

self-confident [sɛlf'kɒnfɪdnt] ADJ seguro de sí (mismo), lleno de confianza en sí mismo

self-conscious [sɛlf'kɒnʃəs] ADJ cohibido

self-contained [sɛlfkən'teɪnd] ADJ (gen) independiente; (BRIT: flat) con entrada particular

self-control [sɛlfkən'trəʊl] N autodominio

self-defeating [sɛlfdɪ'fiːtɪŋ] ADJ contraproducente

self-defence, (US) **self-defense** [sɛlfdɪ'fɛns] N defensa propia

self-discipline [sɛlf'dɪsɪplɪn] N autodisciplina

self-employed [sɛlfɪm'plɔɪd] ADJ que trabaja por cuenta propia, autónomo

self-esteem [sɛlfɪ'stiːm] N amor m propio

self-evident [sɛlf'ɛvɪdnt] ADJ patente

self-explanatory [sɛlfɪks'plænətərɪ] ADJ que no necesita explicación

self-financing [sɛlffaɪ'nænsɪŋ] ADJ autofinanciado

self-governing [sɛlf'ɡʌvənɪŋ] ADJ autónomo

self-harm [sɛlf'hɑːm] VI autolesionarse ▶ N autolesión f

self-help [ˈsɛlf'hɛlp] N autosuficiencia, ayuda propia

selfie [ˈsɛlfɪ] N selfie m, autofoto f

self-importance [sɛlfɪm'pɔːtns] N presunción f, vanidad f

self-important [sɛlfɪm'pɔːtnt] ADJ vanidoso

self-indulgent [sɛlfɪn'dʌldʒənt] ADJ indulgente consigo mismo

self-inflicted [sɛlfɪn'flɪktɪd] ADJ infligido a sí mismo

self-interest [sɛlf'ɪntrɪst] N egoísmo

selfish [ˈsɛlfɪʃ] ADJ egoísta

selfishly [ˈsɛlfɪʃlɪ] ADV con egoísmo, de modo egoísta

selfishness [ˈsɛlfɪʃnɪs] N egoísmo

selfless [ˈsɛlflɪs] ADJ desinteresado

selflessly [ˈsɛlflɪslɪ] ADV desinteresadamente

self-made man [ˈsɛlfmeɪd-] N (irreg) hombre m hecho a sí mismo

self-pity [sɛlf'pɪtɪ] N lástima de sí mismo

self-portrait [sɛlf'pɔːtreɪt] N autorretrato

self-possessed [sɛlfpə'zɛst] ADJ sereno, dueño de sí mismo

self-preservation [ˈsɛlfprɛzə'veɪʃən] N propia conservación f

self-propelled [sɛlfprə'pɛld] ADJ autopropulsado, automotor(-triz)

self-raising [sɛlf'reɪzɪŋ], (US) **self-rising** [sɛlf'raɪzɪŋ] ADJ: **~ flour** harina con levadura

self-reliant [sɛlfrɪ'laɪənt] ADJ independiente, autosuficiente

self-respect [sɛlfrɪ'spɛkt] N amor m propio

self-respecting [sɛlfrɪ'spɛktɪŋ] ADJ que tiene amor propio

self-righteous [sɛlf'raɪtʃəs] ADJ santurrón(-ona)

self-rising [sɛlf'raɪzɪŋ] ADJ (US) = **self-raising**

self-sacrifice [sɛlf'sækrɪfaɪs] N abnegación f

self-same [ˈsɛlfseɪm] ADJ mismo, mismísimo

self-satisfied [sɛlf'sætɪsfaɪd] ADJ satisfecho de sí mismo

self-service [sɛlf'sə:vɪs] ADJ de autoservicio

self-styled [ˈsɛlfstaɪld] ADJ supuesto, sediciente

self-sufficient [sɛlfsə'fɪʃənt] ADJ autosuficiente

self-supporting [sɛlfsə'pɔːtɪŋ] ADJ económicamente independiente

self-tanning [sɛlf'tænɪŋ] ADJ autobronceador

self-taught [sɛlf'tɔːt] ADJ autodidacta

self-test [ˈsɛlftɛst] N (Comput) autocomprobación f

★**sell** [sɛl] (pt, pp **sold** [səʊld]) VT vender; **to ~ sb an idea** (fig) convencer a algn de una idea ▶ VI venderse; **to ~ at** or **for £10** venderse a 10 libras
  ▶ **sell off** VT liquidar
  ▶ **sell out** VI transigir, transar (LAM); **to ~ out (to sb/sth)** (Comm) vender su negocio (a algn/algo) ▶ VT agotar las existencias de, venderlo todo; **the tickets are all sold out** las entradas están agotadas
  ▶ **sell up** VI (Comm) liquidarse

sell-by date [ˈsɛlbaɪ-] N fecha de caducidad

seller [ˈsɛləʳ] N vendedor(a) m/f; **~'s market** mercado de demanda

selling price [ˈsɛlɪŋ-] N precio de venta

Sellotape® [ˈsɛləʊteɪp] N (BRIT) cinta adhesiva, celo, scotch® m

sellout [ˈsɛlaʊt] N traición f; **it was a ~** (Theat etc) fue un éxito de taquilla

selves [sɛlvz] NPL of **self**

semantic [sɪ'mæntɪk] ADJ semántico

semaphore [ˈsɛməfɔːʳ] N semáforo

semblance [ˈsɛmbləns] N apariencia

semen [ˈsiːmən] N semen m

semester [sɪ'mɛstəʳ] N (US) semestre m

semi [ˈsɛmɪ] N = **semidetached**

semi... [sɛmɪ] PREF semi..., medio...

semicircle [ˈsɛmɪsəːkl] N semicírculo

semicircular [ˈsɛmɪ'səːkjuləʳ] ADJ semicircular

semicolon [sɛmɪ'kəʊlən] N punto y coma

semiconductor [sɛmɪkən'dʌktəʳ] N semiconductor m

S

765

semiconscious [sɛmɪˈkɔnʃəs] ADJ semiconsciente

semidetached [sɛmɪdɪˈtætʃt], **semidetached house** N casa adosada

semi-final [sɛmɪˈfaɪnl] N semifinal f

seminar [ˈsɛmɪnɑː ʳ] N seminario

seminary [ˈsɛmɪnərɪ] N (Rel) seminario

semiprecious stone [sɛmɪˈprɛʃəs-] N piedra semipreciosa

semiquaver [ˈsɛmɪkweɪvə ʳ] N (BRIT) semicorchea

semiskilled [ˈsɛmɪskɪld] ADJ (work, worker) semicualificado

semi-skimmed [ˈsɛmɪˈskɪmd] ADJ semidesnatado

semi-skimmed (milk) N leche semidesnatada

semitone [ˈsɛmɪtəun] N semitono

semolina [sɛməˈliːnə] N sémola

Sen., sen. ABBR = **senator; senior**

senate [ˈsɛnɪt] N senado; see also **Congress**

El **Senate** (Senado) es la cámara alta del Congress, el parlamento de los Estados Unidos. Está compuesto por cien senadores, dos por cada estado de la Unión, elegidos cada seis años por sufragio universal directo. Cada dos años se procede a la renovación de un tercio del Senado.

senator [ˈsɛnɪtə ʳ] N senador(a) m/f

★**send** [sɛnd] (pt, pp **sent** [sɛnt]) VT mandar, enviar; **to ~ by post** mandar por correo; **to ~ sb for sth** mandar a algn a buscar algo; **to ~ word that ...** avisar or mandar aviso de que ...; **she sends (you) her love** te manda or envía cariñosos recuerdos; **to ~ sb to sleep/into fits of laughter** dormir/hacer reír a algn; **to ~ sb flying** echar a algn; **to ~ sth flying** tirar algo
▶ **send away** VT (letter, goods) despachar
▶ **send away for** VT FUS pedir
▶ **send back** VT devolver
▶ **send for** VT FUS mandar traer; (by post) escribir pidiendo
▶ **send in** VT (report, application, resignation) mandar
▶ **send off** VT (goods) despachar; (BRIT Sport: player) expulsar
▶ **send on** VT (letter, luggage) remitir
▶ **send out** VT (invitation) mandar; (emit: light, heat) emitir, difundir; (: signal) emitir
▶ **send round** VT (letter, document etc) hacer circular
▶ **send up** VT (person, price) hacer subir; (BRIT: parody) parodiar

sender [ˈsɛndə ʳ] N remitente mf

send-off [ˈsɛndɔf] N: **a good ~** una buena despedida

send-up [ˈsɛndʌp] N (inf) parodia, sátira

Senegal [sɛnɪˈgɔːl] N Senegal m

Senegalese [sɛnɪgəˈliːz] ADJ, N senegalés(-esa) m/f

senile [ˈsiːnaɪl] ADJ senil

senility [sɪˈnɪlɪtɪ] N senilidad f

★**senior** [ˈsiːnɪə ʳ] ADJ (older) mayor, más viejo; (on staff) de más antigüedad; (of higher rank) superior; **P. Jones ~** P. Jones padre ▶ N mayor m

senior citizen N persona de la tercera edad

senior high school N (US) = instituto de enseñanza media; see also **high school**

seniority [siːnɪˈɔrɪtɪ] N antigüedad f; (in rank) rango superior

sensation [sɛnˈseɪʃən] N (physical feeling, impression) sensación f

sensational [sɛnˈseɪʃənl] ADJ sensacional

★**sense** [sɛns] N (faculty, meaning) sentido; (feeling) sensación f; (good sense) sentido común, juicio; **~ of humour** or (US) **humor** sentido del humor; **it makes ~** tiene sentido; **there is no ~ in (doing) that** no tiene sentido (hacer) eso; **to come to one's senses** (regain consciousness) volver en sí, recobrar el sentido; **to take leave of one's senses** perder el juicio ▶ VT sentir, percibir

senseless [ˈsɛnslɪs] ADJ estúpido, insensato; (unconscious) sin conocimiento

senselessly [ˈsɛnslɪslɪ] ADV estúpidamente, insensatamente

sensibility [sɛnsɪˈbɪlɪtɪ] N sensibilidad f ■ **sensibilities** NPL delicadeza sg

★**sensible** [ˈsɛnsɪbl] ADJ sensato; (reasonable) razonable, lógico

La palabra inglesa **sensible** no debe traducirse por sensible.

sensibly [ˈsɛnsɪblɪ] ADV sensatamente; razonablemente, de modo lógico

★**sensitive** [ˈsɛnsɪtɪv] ADJ sensible; (touchy) susceptible; **he is very ~ about it** es muy susceptible acerca de eso

sensitivity [sɛnsɪˈtɪvɪtɪ] N sensibilidad f; susceptibilidad f

sensual [ˈsɛnsjuəl] ADJ sensual

sensuous [ˈsɛnsjuəs] ADJ sensual

sent [sɛnt] PT, PP of **send**

★**sentence** [ˈsɛntəns] N (Ling) frase f, oración f; (Law) sentencia, fallo; **to pass ~ on sb** (also fig) sentenciar or condenar a algn ▶ VT: **to ~ sb to death/to five years** condenar a algn a muerte/a cinco años de cárcel

sentiment [ˈsɛntɪmənt] N sentimiento; (opinion) opinión f

sentimental [sɛntɪˈmɛntl] ADJ sentimental

sentimentality [sɛntɪmɛnˈtælɪtɪ] N sentimentalismo, sensiblería

sentinel [ˈsɛntɪnl] N centinela m

sentry [ˈsɛntrɪ] N centinela m

sentry duty N: **to be on ~** estar de guardia, hacer guardia

Seoul [səul] N Seúl m

Sep. ABBR (= September) sep., set.

separable [ˈsɛpərəbl] ADJ separable

★separate ADJ ['sɛprɪt] separado; (*distinct*) distinto; **~ from** separado *or* distinto de; **under ~ cover** (*Comm*) por separado ■ **separates** NPL (*clothes*) coordinados *mpl* ▶ VT ['sɛpəreɪt] separar; (*part*) dividir; **to ~ into** dividir *or* separar en; **he is separated from his wife, but not divorced** está separado de su mujer, pero no (está) divorciado ▶ VI ['sɛpəreɪt] separarse

separately ['sɛprɪtlɪ] ADV por separado

separation [sɛpə'reɪʃən] N separación *f*

sepia ['si:pɪə] ADJ color sepia *inv*

Sept. ABBR (= *September*) sep.

★September [sɛp'tɛmbəʳ] N se(p)tiembre *m*; *see also* **July**

septic ['sɛptɪk] ADJ séptico; **to go ~** ponerse séptico

septicaemia, (US) **septicemia** [sɛptɪ'si:mɪə] N septicemia

septic tank N fosa séptica

sequel ['si:kwl] N consecuencia, resultado; (*of story*) continuación *f*

sequence ['si:kwəns] N sucesión *f*, serie *f*; (*Cine*) secuencia; **in ~** en orden *or* serie

sequencing ['si:kwənsɪŋ] N secuenciado

sequential [sɪ'kwɛnʃəl] ADJ: **~ access** (*Comput*) acceso en serie

sequin ['si:kwɪn] N lentejuela

Serb [sə:b] ADJ, N = **Serbian**

Serbia ['sə:bɪə] N Serbia

Serbian ['sə:bɪən] ADJ serbio ▶ N serbio(-a); (*Ling*) serbio

Serbo-Croat ['sə:bəu'krəuæt] N (*Ling*) serbo-croata *m*

serenade [sɛrə'neɪd] N serenata ▶ VT dar serenata a

serene [sɪ'ri:n] ADJ sereno, tranquilo

serenely [sɪ'ri:nlɪ] ADV serenamente, tranquilamente

serenity [sə'rɛnɪtɪ] N serenidad *f*, tranquilidad *f*

sergeant ['sɑ:dʒənt] N sargento *mf*

sergeant major N sargento mayor

serial ['sɪərɪəl] N novela por entregas; (*TV*) serie *f*

serial access N (*Comput*) acceso en serie

serial interface N (*Comput*) interface *m* en serie

serialize ['sɪərɪəlaɪz] VT publicar/televisar por entregas

serial killer N asesino(-a) en serie

serial number N número de serie

★series ['sɪəri:z] N *pl inv* serie *f*

★serious ['sɪərɪəs] ADJ serio; (*grave*) grave; **are you ~ (about it)?** ¿lo dices en serio?

★seriously ['sɪərɪəslɪ] ADV en serio; (*ill, wounded etc*) gravemente; (*inf: extremely*) de verdad; **to take sth/sb ~** tomar algo/a algn en serio; **he's ~ rich** es una pasada de rico

seriousness ['sɪərɪəsnɪs] N seriedad *f*; gravedad *f*

sermon ['sə:mən] N sermón *m*

serpent ['sə:pənt] N serpiente *f*

serrated [sɪ'reɪtɪd] ADJ serrado, dentellado

serum ['sɪərəm] N suero

servant ['sə:vənt] N (*gen*) servidor(a) *m/f*; (*also:* **house servant**) criado(-a)

★serve [sə:v] VT servir; (*customer*) atender; (*train*) tener parada en; (*apprenticeship*) hacer; (*prison term*) cumplir; **it serves him right** se lo merece, se lo tiene merecido; **to ~ a summons on sb** entregar una citación a algn; **it serves my purpose** me sirve para lo que quiero; **are you being served?** ¿le atienden?; **the power station serves the entire region** la central eléctrica abastece a toda la región; **to ~ to do** servir para hacer ▶ VI (*servant, soldier etc*) servir; (*Tennis*) sacar; **to ~ as/for** servir de/para; **to ~ on a committee/a jury** ser miembro de una comisión/un jurado ▶ N (*Tennis*) saque *m*
▶ **serve out**, **serve up** VT (*food*) servir

server N (*Comput*) servidor *m*

★service ['sə:vɪs] N (*gen*) servicio; (*Rel: Catholic*) misa; (*: other*) oficio (religioso); (*Aut*) mantenimiento; (*of dishes*) juego; **funeral ~** exequias *fpl*; **to hold a ~** celebrar un oficio religioso; **the train ~ to London** los trenes a Londres; **~ included/not included** servicio incluido/no incluido; **to be of ~ to sb** ser útil a algn ▶ VT (*car, washing machine*) revisar; (*: repair*) reparar ■ **services** NPL (*Econ: tertiary sector*) sector *m* terciario *or* (de) servicios; (*BRIT: on motorway*) área de servicio; **the Services** las fuerzas armadas; **the essential services** los servicios esenciales; **medical/social services** servicios *mpl* médicos/sociales

serviceable ['sə:vɪsəbl] ADJ servible, utilizable

service area N (*on motorway*) área de servicio

service charge N (*BRIT*) servicio

service industries NPL industrias *fpl* de servicios

serviceman ['sə:vɪsmən] N (*irreg*) militar *m*

service station N estación *f* de servicio

servicing ['sə:vɪsɪŋ] N (*of car*) revisión *f*; (*of washing machine etc*) servicio de reparaciones

serviette [sə:vɪ'ɛt] N (*BRIT*) servilleta

servile ['sə:vaɪl] ADJ servil

session ['sɛʃən] N (*sitting*) sesión *f*; **to be in ~** estar en sesión

session musician N músico *mf* de estudio

★set [sɛt] (*pt, pp* **~**) N juego; (*Radio*) aparato; (*TV*) televisor *m*; (*of utensils*) batería; (*of cutlery*) cubierto; (*of books*) colección *f*; (*Tennis*) set *m*; (*group of people*) grupo; (*Cine*) plató *m*; (*Theat*) decorado; (*Hairdressing*) marcado; **a ~ of false teeth** una dentadura postiza; **a ~ of dining-room furniture** muebles *mpl* de comedor ▶ ADJ (*fixed*) fijo; (*ready*) listo; (*resolved*) resuelto, decidido; **a ~ phrase** una frase hecha; **~ in one's ways** con costumbres arraigadas; **to be all ~ to do sth** estar listo para hacer algo; **to be ~ on doing sth** estar empeñado en hacer algo; **a novel ~ in Valencia** una novela ambientada en Valencia ▸ VT (*place*) poner, colocar; (*fix*) fijar; (*adjust*) ajustar, arreglar; (*decide: rules etc*) establecer, decidir; (*assign: task*) asignar; (: *homework*) poner; **to ~ to music** poner música a; **to ~ on fire** incendiar, prender fuego a; **to ~ free** poner en libertad; **to ~ sth going** poner algo en marcha; **to ~ sail** zarpar, hacerse a la mar ▸ VI (*sun*) ponerse; (*jam, jelly*) cuajarse; (*concrete*) fraguar

▸ **set about** VT FUS: **to ~ about doing sth** ponerse a hacer algo

▸ **set aside** VT poner aparte, dejar de lado

▸ **set back** VT (*progress*): **to ~ back (by)** retrasar (por); **a house ~ back from the road** una casa apartada de la carretera

▸ **set down** VT (*bus, train*) dejar; (*record*) poner por escrito

▸ **set in** VI (*infection*) declararse; (*complications*) comenzar; **the rain has ~ in for the day** parece que va a llover todo el día

▸ **set off** VI partir ▸ VT (*bomb*) hacer estallar; (*cause to start*) poner en marcha; (*show up well*) hacer resaltar

▸ **set out** VI partir; **to ~ out (from)** salir (de); **to ~ out to do sth** proponerse hacer algo ▸ VT (*arrange*) disponer; (*state*) exponer

▸ **set up** VT (*organization*) establecer

setback ['sɛtbæk] N (*hitch*) revés *m*, contratiempo; (*in health*) recaída

set menu N menú *m*

set phrase N frase *f* hecha

set square N cartabón *m*

settee [sɛ'tiː] N sofá *m*

setting ['sɛtɪŋ] N (*scenery*) marco; (*of jewel*) engaste *m*, montadura

setting lotion N fijador *m* (para el pelo)

★**settle** ['sɛtl] VT (*argument, matter*) resolver; (*pay: bill, accounts*) pagar, liquidar; (*colonize: land*) colonizar; (*Med: calm*) calmar, sosegar; **to ~ one's stomach** asentar el estómago; **that's settled then** bueno, está arreglado ▸ VI (*dust etc*) depositarse; (*weather*) estabilizarse; **to ~ for sth** convenir en aceptar algo; **to ~ on sth** decidirse por algo

▸ **settle down** VI (*get comfortable*) ponerse cómodo, acomodarse; (*calm down*) calmarse, tranquilizarse; (*live quietly*) echar raíces

▸ **settle in** VI instalarse

▸ **settle up** VI: **to ~ up with sb** ajustar cuentas con algn

settlement ['sɛtlmənt] N (*payment*) liquidación *f*; (*agreement*) acuerdo, convenio; (*village etc*) poblado; **in ~ of our account** (*Comm*) en pago or liquidación de nuestra cuenta

settler ['sɛtlər] N colono(-a), colonizador(a) *m/f*

setup ['sɛtʌp] N sistema *m*

★**seven** ['sɛvn] NUM siete

★**seventeen** [sɛvn'tiːn] NUM diecisiete

★**seventeenth** [sɛvn'tiːnθ] ADJ decimoséptimo

★**seventh** ['sɛvnθ] ADJ séptimo

seventieth ['sɛvntɪθ] ADJ septuagésimo

★**seventy** ['sɛvntɪ] NUM setenta

sever ['sɛvər] VT cortar; (*relations*) romper

★**several** ['sɛvərl] ADJ, PRON varios(-as) *m/fpl*, algunos(-as) *m/fpl*; **~ of us** varios de nosotros; **~ times** varias veces

severance ['sɛvərəns] N (*of relations*) ruptura

severance pay N indemnización *f* por despido

severe [sɪ'vɪər] ADJ severo; (*serious*) grave; (*hard*) duro; (*pain*) intenso

severely [sɪ'vɪəlɪ] ADV severamente; (*wounded, ill*) de gravedad, gravemente

severity [sɪ'vɛrɪtɪ] N severidad *f*; gravedad *f*; intensidad *f*

Seville [sə'vɪl] N Sevilla

sew [səu] (*pt* **sewed** [səud], *pp* **sewn** [səun]) VT, VI coser

▸ **sew up** VT coser

sewage ['suːɪdʒ] N (*effluence*) aguas *fpl* residuales; (*system*) alcantarillado

sewage works N estación *f* depuradora (de aguas residuales)

sewer ['suːər] N alcantarilla, cloaca

sewing ['səuɪŋ] N costura

sewing machine N máquina de coser

sewn [səun] PP *of* **sew**

sex [sɛks] N sexo; **the opposite ~** el sexo opuesto; **to have ~** hacer el amor

sex act N acto sexual, coito

sex appeal N sex-appeal *m*, gancho

sex education N educación *f* sexual

sexism ['sɛksɪzəm] N sexismo

sexist ['sɛksɪst] ADJ, N sexista *mf*

sex life N vida sexual

sex object N objeto sexual

sextant ['sɛkstənt] N sextante *m*

sextet [sɛks'tɛt] N sexteto

sexting ['sɛkstɪŋ] N (*inf*) sexteo

sexual ['sɛksjuəl] ADJ sexual; **~ assault** atentado contra el pudor; **~ harassment** acoso sexual; **~ intercourse** relaciones *fpl* sexuales

sexuality [sɛksju'ælɪtɪ] N sexualidad *f*

sexually ['sɛksjuəlɪ] ADV sexualmente

sexy ['sɛksɪ] ADJ sexy

Seychelles [seɪ'ʃɛlz] NPL: **the ~** las Seychelles

SF N ABBR = **science fiction**

SG N ABBR (*US*: = *Surgeon General*) jefe del servicio federal de sanidad

Sgt. ABBR (= *sergeant*) Sgto.

shabbily ['ʃæbɪlɪ] ADV (*treat*) injustamente; (*dressed*) pobremente

shabbiness ['ʃæbɪnɪs] N (*of dress, person*) aspecto desharrapado; (*of building*) mal estado

shabby [ˈʃæbɪ] ADJ (*person*) desharrapado; (*clothes*) raído, gastado

shack [ʃæk] N choza, chabola

shackle [ˈʃækl] VT encadenar; (*fig*): **to be shackled by sth** verse obstaculizado por algo

shackles [ˈʃæklz] NPL grillos *mpl*, grilletes *mpl*

★**shade** [ʃeɪd] N sombra; (*for lamp*) pantalla; (*for eyes*) visera; (*of colour*) tono *m*, tonalidad *f*; (*US: window shade*) persiana; **in the ~** a la sombra; **a ~ more** (*small quantity*) un poquito más; **a ~ smaller** un poquito más pequeño ▶ VT dar sombra a ■ **shades** NPL (*US: sunglasses*) gafas *fpl* de sol

★**shadow** [ˈʃædəʊ] N sombra; **without** or **beyond a ~ of doubt** sin lugar a dudas ▶ VT (*follow*) seguir y vigilar

shadow cabinet N (BRIT Pol) gobierno en la oposición

shadowy [ˈʃædəʊɪ] ADJ oscuro; (*dim*) indistinto

shady [ˈʃeɪdɪ] ADJ sombreado; (*fig: dishonest*) sospechoso; (*deal*) turbio

shaft [ʃɑːft] N (*of arrow, spear*) astil *m*; (*Aut, Tech*) eje *m*, árbol *m*; (*of mine*) pozo; (*of lift*) hueco, caja; (*of light*) rayo; **ventilator ~** chimenea de ventilación

shaggy [ˈʃægɪ] ADJ peludo

★**shake** [ʃeɪk] (*pt* **shook** [ʃʊk], *pp* **shaken** [ˈʃeɪkn]) VT sacudir; (*building*) hacer temblar; (*perturb*) inquietar, perturbar, (*weaken*) debilitar; (*alarm*) trastornar; **to ~ one's head** (*in refusal*) negar con la cabeza; (*in dismay*) mover or menear la cabeza, incrédulo; **to ~ hands with sb** estrechar la mano a algn ▶ VI estremecerse; (*tremble*) temblar; **to ~ in one's shoes** (*fig*) temblar de miedo ▶ N (*movement*) sacudida
▶ **shake off** VT sacudirse; (*fig*) deshacerse de
▶ **shake up** VT agitar

shake-up [ˈʃeɪkʌp] N reorganización *f*

shakily [ˈʃeɪkɪlɪ] ADV (*reply*) con voz temblorosa or trémula; (*walk*) con paso vacilante; (*write*) con mano temblorosa

shaky [ˈʃeɪkɪ] ADJ (*unstable*) inestable, poco firme; (*trembling*) tembloroso; (*health*) delicado; (*memory*) defectuoso; (*person: from illness*) temblando; (*premise etc*) incierto

shale [ʃeɪl] N esquisto

★**shall** [ʃæl] AUX VB: **I ~ go** iré; **~ I help you?** ¿quieres que te ayude?; **I'll buy three, ~ I?** compro tres, ¿no te parece?

shallot [ʃəˈlɔt] N (BRIT) cebollita, chalote *m*

shallow [ˈʃæləʊ] ADJ poco profundo; (*fig*) superficial

shallows [ˈʃæləʊz] NPL bajío *sg*, bajos *mpl*

sham [ʃæm] N fraude *m*, engaño ▶ ADJ falso, fingido ▶ VT fingir, simular

shambles [ˈʃæmblz] N desorden *m*, confusión *f*; **the economy is (in) a complete ~** la economía está en un estado desastroso

shambolic [ʃæmˈbɔlɪk] ADJ (*inf*) caótico

★**shame** [ʃeɪm] N vergüenza; (*pity*) lástima, pena; **it is a ~ that/to do** es una lástima or pena que/ hacer; **what a ~!** ¡qué lástima or pena!; **to put sth/sb to ~** (*fig*) ridiculizar algo/a algn ▶ VT avergonzar

shamefaced [ˈʃeɪmfeɪst] ADJ avergonzado

shameful [ˈʃeɪmful] ADJ vergonzoso

shamefully [ˈʃeɪmfulɪ] ADV vergonzosamente

shameless [ˈʃeɪmlɪs] ADJ descarado

★**shampoo** [ʃæmˈpuː] N champú *m* ▶ VT lavar con champú

shampoo and set N lavado y marcado

shamrock [ˈʃæmrɔk] N trébol *m*

shandy [ˈʃændɪ], (US) **shandygaff** [ˈʃændɪgæf] N clara, cerveza con gaseosa

shan't [ʃɑːnt] = **shall not**

shanty town [ˈʃæntɪ-] N barrio de chabolas

SHAPE [ʃeɪp] N ABBR (= *Supreme Headquarters Allied Powers, Europe*) cuartel general de las fuerzas aliadas en Europa

★**shape** [ʃeɪp] N forma; **to take ~** tomar forma; **to get o.s. into ~** ponerse en forma or en condiciones; **in the ~ of a heart** en forma de corazón; **I can't bear gardening in any ~ or form** no aguanto la jardinería de ningún modo ▶ VT formar, dar forma a; (*clay*) modelar; (*stone*) labrar; (*sb's ideas*) formar; (*sb's life*) determinar ▶ VI (*also:* **shape up**: *events*) desarrollarse; (*person*) formarse

-shaped SUFF: **heart-shaped** en forma de corazón

shapeless [ˈʃeɪplɪs] ADJ informe, sin forma definida

shapely [ˈʃeɪplɪ] ADJ bien formado or proporcionado

★**share** [ʃɛəʳ] N (*part*) parte *f*, porción *f*; (*contribution*) cuota; (*Comm*) acción *f*; **to have a ~ in the profits** tener una proporción de las ganancias; **he has a 50% ~ in a new business venture** tiene una participación del 50% en un nuevo negocio ▶ VT dividir; (*fig: have in common*) compartir; **to ~ out (among** or **between)** repartir (entre) ▶ VI: **to ~ in** participar en

share capital N (*Comm*) capital *m* social en acciones

share certificate N certificado or título de una acción

shareholder [ˈʃɛəhəʊldəʳ] N (BRIT) accionista *mf*

share index N (*Comm*) índice *m* de la bolsa

share issue N emisión *f* de acciones

share price N (*Comm*) cotización *f*

shark [ʃɑːk] N tiburón *m*

★**sharp** [ʃɑːp] ADJ (*razor, knife*) afilado; (*point*) puntiagudo; (*outline*) definido; (*pain*) intenso; (*Mus*) desafinado; (*contrast*) marcado; (*voice*) agudo; (*curve, bend*) cerrado; (*person: quick-witted*) avispado; (*: dishonest*) poco escrupuloso; **to be ~ with sb** hablar a algn de forma brusca y tajante ▶ N (*Mus*) sostenido ▶ ADV: **at two**

S

o'clock ~ a las dos en punto; **turn ~ left** tuerce del todo a la izquierda

sharpen ['ʃɑːpn] VT afilar; (pencil) sacar punta a; (fig) agudizar

sharpener ['ʃɑːpnər] N (gen) afilador m; (also: **pencil sharpener**) sacapuntas m inv

sharp-eyed [ʃɑːp'aɪd] ADJ de vista aguda

sharpish ['ʃɑːpɪʃ] ADV (BRIT inf: quickly) prontito, bien pronto

sharply ['ʃɑːplɪ] ADV (abruptly) bruscamente; (clearly) claramente; (harshly) severamente

sharp-tempered [ʃɑːp'tɛmpəd] ADJ de genio arisco

sharp-witted [ʃɑːp'wɪtɪd] ADJ listo, despabilado

shatter ['ʃætər] VT hacer añicos or pedazos; (fig: ruin) destruir, acabar con ▸ VI hacerse añicos

shattered ['ʃætəd] ADJ (grief-stricken) destrozado, deshecho; (exhausted) agotado, hecho polvo

shattering ['ʃætərɪŋ] ADJ (experience) devastador(a), anonadante

shatterproof ['ʃætəpruːf] ADJ inastillable

shave [ʃeɪv] VT afeitar, rasurar ▸ VI afeitarse ▸ N: **to have a ~** afeitarse

shaven ['ʃeɪvn] ADJ (head) rapado

shaver ['ʃeɪvər] N (also: **electric shaver**) máquina de afeitar (eléctrica)

shaving ['ʃeɪvɪŋ] N (action) afeitado ∎ **shavings** NPL (of wood etc) virutas fpl

shaving brush N brocha (de afeitar)

shaving cream N crema (de afeitar)

shaving foam N espuma de afeitar

shaving point N enchufe m para máquinas de afeitar

shaving soap N jabón m de afeitar

shawl [ʃɔːl] N chal m

★**she** [ʃiː] PRON ella; **there ~ is** allí está; **she-cat** gata

> she is not usually translated unless it is emphatic: She's very nice. **Es muy maja**. Use **ella** for emphasis: She did it but he didn't. **Ella lo hizo, pero él no**.

sheaf [ʃiːf] (pl **sheaves** [ʃiːvz]) N (of corn) gavilla; (of arrows) haz m; (of papers) fajo

shear [ʃɪər] VT (pt **sheared**, pp **sheared** or **shorn** [ʃɔːn]) (sheep) esquilar, trasquilar
▸ **shear off** VI romperse

shears ['ʃɪəz] NPL (for hedge) tijeras fpl de jardín

sheath [ʃiːθ] N vaina; (contraceptive) preservativo

sheath knife N cuchillo de monte

sheaves [ʃiːvz] NPL of **sheaf**

★**shed** (pt, pp ~) [ʃɛd] N cobertizo; (Industry, Rail) nave f ▸ VT (skin) mudar; (tears) derramar; (workers) despedir; **to ~ light on** (problem, mystery) aclarar, arrojar luz sobre

she'd [ʃiːd] = **she had; she would**

sheen [ʃiːn] N brillo, lustre m

★**sheep** [ʃiːp] N pl inv oveja

sheepdog ['ʃiːpdɔg] N perro pastor

sheep farmer N ganadero (de ovejas)

sheepish ['ʃiːpɪʃ] ADJ tímido, vergonzoso

sheepskin ['ʃiːpskɪn] N piel f de carnero

sheepskin jacket N zamarra

sheer [ʃɪər] ADJ (utter) puro, completo; (steep) escarpado; (material) diáfano; **by ~ chance** de pura casualidad ▸ ADV verticalmente

★**sheet** [ʃiːt] N (on bed) sábana; (of paper) hoja; (of glass, metal) lámina

sheet feed N (on printer) alimentador m de papel

sheet lightning N relámpago (difuso)

sheet metal N metal m en lámina

sheet music N hojas fpl de partitura

sheik, sheikh [ʃeɪk] N jeque m

shelf [ʃɛlf] (pl **shelves** [ʃɛlvz]) N estante m

shelf life N (Comm) período de conservación antes de la venta

★**shell** [ʃɛl] N (on beach) concha, caracol m (LAM); (of egg, nut etc) cáscara; (explosive) proyectil m, obús m; (of building) armazón m ▸ VT (peas) desenvainar; (Mil) bombardear
▸ **shell out** VI (inf): **to ~ out (for)** soltar el dinero (para), desembolsar (para)

she'll [ʃiːl] = **she will; she shall**

shellfish ['ʃɛlfɪʃ] N pl inv crustáceo; (pl: as food) mariscos mpl

shellsuit ['ʃɛlsuːt] N chándal m (de Tactel®)

★**shelter** ['ʃɛltər] N abrigo, refugio; **to take ~ (from)** refugiarse or asilarse (de); **bus ~** marquesina ▸ VT (aid) amparar, proteger; (give lodging to) abrigar; (hide) esconder ▸ VI abrigarse, refugiarse

sheltered ['ʃɛltəd] ADJ (life) protegido; (spot) abrigado

shelve [ʃɛlv] VT (fig) dar carpetazo a

shelves [ʃɛlvz] NPL of **shelf**

shelving ['ʃɛlvɪŋ] N estantería

shepherd ['ʃɛpəd] N pastor m ▸ VT (guide) guiar, conducir

shepherdess ['ʃɛpədɪs] N pastora

shepherd's pie N pastel de carne y puré de patatas

sherbet ['ʃəːbət] N (BRIT: powder) polvos mpl azucarados; (US: water ice) sorbete m

sheriff ['ʃɛrɪf] N (US) sheriff m

sherry ['ʃɛrɪ] N jerez m

she's [ʃiːz] = **she is; she has**

Shetland ['ʃɛtlənd] N (also: **the Shetlands, the Shetland Isles**) las Islas fpl Shetland

Shetland pony N pony m de Shetland

shield [ʃiːld] N escudo; (Tech) blindaje m ▸ VT: **to ~ (from)** proteger (de)

shift [ʃɪft] N (change) cambio; (at work) turno; **a ~ in demand** (Comm) un desplazamiento de la demanda ▸ vt trasladar; (*remove*) quitar ▸ vi moverse; (*change place*) cambiar de sitio; **the wind has shifted to the south** el viento ha virado al sur

shift key N (*on keyboard*) tecla de mayúsculas

shiftless ['ʃɪftlɪs] ADJ (*person*) vago

shift work N (*BRIT*) trabajo por turnos; **to do ~** trabajar por turnos

shifty ['ʃɪftɪ] ADJ tramposo; (*eyes*) furtivo

Shiite ['ʃiːaɪt] ADJ, N chiita *mf*

shilling ['ʃɪlɪŋ] N (*BRIT: formerly*) chelín *m* (= 12 peniques antiguos; una libra tenía 20 chelines)

shilly-shally ['ʃɪlɪʃælɪ] vi titubear, vacilar

shimmer ['ʃɪmər] N reflejo trémulo ▸ vi relucir

shimmering ['ʃɪmərɪŋ] ADJ reluciente; (*haze*) trémulo; (*satin etc*) lustroso

shin [ʃɪn] N espinilla ▸ vi: **to ~ down/up a tree** bajar de/trepar un árbol

shindig ['ʃɪndɪg] N (*inf*) fiesta, juerga

shine [ʃaɪn] (*pt, pp shone* [ʃɒn]) N brillo, lustre *m* ▸ vi brillar, relucir ▸ vt (*shoes*) lustrar, sacar brillo a; **to ~ a torch on sth** dirigir una linterna hacia algo

shingle ['ʃɪŋgl] N (*on beach*) guijarras *fpl*

shingles ['ʃɪŋglz] N (*Med*) herpes *msg*

shining ['ʃaɪnɪŋ] ADJ (*surface, hair*) lustroso; (*light*) brillante

shiny ['ʃaɪnɪ] ADJ brillante, lustroso

★**ship** [ʃɪp] N buque *m*, barco; **~'s manifest** manifiesto del buque; **on board ~** a bordo ▸ vt (*goods*) embarcar; (*oars*) desarmar; (*send*) transportar or enviar por vía marítima

shipbuilder ['ʃɪpbɪldər] N constructor(a) *m/f* naval

shipbuilding ['ʃɪpbɪldɪŋ] N construcción *f* naval

ship canal N canal *m* de navegación

ship chandler [-'tʃɑːndlər] N proveedor *m* de efectos navales

shipment ['ʃɪpmənt] N (*act*) embarque *m*; (*goods*) envío

shipowner ['ʃɪpəunər] N naviero, armador *m*

shipper ['ʃɪpər] N compañía naviera

shipping ['ʃɪpɪŋ] N (*act*) embarque *m*; (*traffic*) buques *mpl*

shipping agent N agente *mf* marítimo(-a)

shipping company N compañía naviera

shipping lane N ruta de navegación

shipping line N = **shipping company**

shipshape ['ʃɪpʃeɪp] ADJ en buen orden

shipwreck ['ʃɪprɛk] N naufragio ▸ vt: **to be shipwrecked** naufragar

shipyard ['ʃɪpjɑːd] N astillero

shire ['ʃaɪər] N (*BRIT*) condado

shirk [ʃəːk] vt eludir, esquivar; (*obligations*) faltar a

★**shirt** [ʃəːt] N camisa; **in ~ sleeves** en mangas de camisa

shirty ['ʃəːtɪ] ADJ (*BRIT inf*): **to be ~** estar de malas pulgas

shit [ʃɪt] (*inf!*) N mierda (*inf!*); (*nonsense*) chorradas *fpl* ▸ EXCL ¡mierda! (*inf!*); **tough ~!** ¡te jodes! (*inf!*)

shiver ['ʃɪvər] N escalofrío ▸ vi temblar, estremecerse; (*with cold*) tiritar

shoal [ʃəul] N (*of fish*) banco

★**shock** [ʃɒk] N (*impact*) choque *m*; (*Elec*) descarga (eléctrica); (*emotional*) conmoción f; (*start*) sobresalto, susto; (*Med*) postración f nerviosa; **to get a ~** (*Elec*) sentir una sacudida eléctrica; **to give sb a ~** dar un susto a algn; **to be suffering from ~** padecer una postración nerviosa; **it came as a ~ to hear that ...** me *etc* asombró descubrir que ... ▸ vt dar un susto a; (*offend*) escandalizar

shock absorber [-əbsɔːbər] N amortiguador *m*

shocker ['ʃɒkər] N (*inf*): **it was a real ~** fue muy fuerte

shocking ['ʃɒkɪŋ] ADJ (*awful: weather, handwriting*) espantoso, horrible; (*improper*) escandaloso; (*result*) inesperado

shock therapy, shock treatment N (*Med*) terapia de choque

shock wave N onda expansiva or de choque

shod [ʃɒd] PT, PP of **shoe** ▸ ADJ calzado

shoddiness ['ʃɒdɪnɪs] N baja calidad f

shoddy ['ʃɒdɪ] ADJ de pacotilla

★**shoe** [ʃuː] (*pt, pp shod* [ʃɒd]) N zapato; (*for horse*) herradura; (*brake shoe*) zapata ▸ vt (*horse*) herrar

shoebrush ['ʃuːbrʌʃ] N cepillo para zapatos

shoehorn ['ʃuːhɔːn] N calzador *m*

shoelace ['ʃuːleɪs] N cordón *m*

shoemaker ['ʃuːmeɪkər] N zapatero(-a)

shoe polish N betún *m*

shoeshop ['ʃuːʃɒp] N zapatería

shoestring ['ʃuːstrɪŋ] N (*shoelace*) cordón *m*; (*fig*): **on a ~** con muy poco dinero, a lo barato

shone [ʃɒn] PT, PP of **shine**

shonky ['ʃɒŋkɪ] ADJ (*AUSTRALIA, NEW ZEALAND inf*) chapucero

shoo [ʃuː] EXCL ¡fuera!; (*to animals*) ¡zape! ▸ vt (*also*: **shoo away, shoo off**) ahuyentar

shook [ʃuk] PT of **shake**

★**shoot** [ʃuːt] (*pt, pp shot* [ʃɒt]) N (*on branch, seedling*) retoño, vástago; (*shooting party*) cacería; (*competition*) concurso de tiro; (*preserve*) coto de caza ▸ vt disparar; (*kill*) matar a tiros; (*execute*) fusilar; (*Cine: film, scene*) rodar, filmar ▸ vi (*Football*) chutar; **to ~ (at)** tirar (a); **to ~ past** pasar como un rayo; **to ~ in/out** entrar corriendo/salir disparado
   ▸ **shoot down** vt (*plane*) derribar
   ▸ **shoot up** vi (*prices*) dispararse

shooting ['ʃuːtɪŋ] N (*shots*) tiros *mpl*, tiroteo; (*Hunting*) caza con escopeta; (*act, murder*) asesinato (a tiros); (*Cine*) rodaje *m*

shooting star N estrella fugaz

★**shop** [ʃɔp] N tienda; (*workshop*) taller *m*; **to talk ~** (*fig*) hablar del trabajo; **repair ~** taller *m* de reparaciones ▶ VI (*also:* **go shopping**) ir de compras
▶ **shop around** VI comparar precios

shopaholic [ˈʃɔpəˈhɔlɪk] N (*inf*) adicto(-a) a las compras

★**shop assistant** N (BRIT) dependiente(-a) *m/f*

shop floor N (BRIT *fig*) taller *m*, fábrica

★**shopkeeper** [ˈʃɔpkiːpəʳ] N (BRIT) tendero(-a)

shoplift [ˈʃɔplɪft] VI robar en las tiendas

shoplifter [ˈʃɔplɪftəʳ] N ratero(-a)

shoplifting [ˈʃɔplɪftɪŋ] N ratería, robo (en las tiendas)

shopper [ˈʃɔpəʳ] N comprador(a) *m/f*

★**shopping** [ˈʃɔpɪŋ] N (*goods*) compras *fpl*

shopping bag N bolsa (de compras)

shopping cart N (US also *Comput*) carrito de la compra

shopping centre, (US) **shopping center** N centro comercial

shopping mall N centro comercial

shopping trolley N (BRIT) carrito de la compra

shop-soiled [ˈʃɔpsɔɪld] ADJ (BRIT) usado

shop steward N (BRIT *Industry*) enlace *mf* sindical

shop window N escaparate *m*, vidriera (LAM)

shopworn [ˈʃɔpwɔːn] ADJ (US) usado

shore [ʃɔːʳ] N (*of sea, lake*) orilla; **on ~** en tierra
▶ VT: **to ~ (up)** reforzar

shore leave N (*Naut*) permiso para bajar a tierra

shorn [ʃɔːn] PP *of* **shear**

★**short** [ʃɔːt] ADJ (*not long*) corto; (*in time*) breve, de corta duración; (*person*) bajo; (*curt*) brusco, seco; **to be ~ of sth** estar falto de algo; **a ~ time ago** hace poco (tiempo); **in the ~ term** a corto plazo; **to be in ~ supply** escasear, haber escasez de; **I'm ~ of time** me falta tiempo; **it is ~ for** es la forma abreviada de ▶ ADV (*suddenly*) inesperadamente; **to fall ~ of** no alcanzar; **to run ~ of sth** acabársele algo; **everything ~ of ...** todo menos ...; **~ of doing ...** a menos que hagamos *etc* ...; **to stop ~** parar en seco; **to stop ~ of** detenerse antes de; **in ~** en pocas palabras; **to cut ~** (*speech, visit*) interrumpir, terminar inesperadamente ▶ N (*also:* **short film**) cortometraje *m* ▪ **shorts** NPL pantalones *mpl* cortos; **a pair of shorts** unos pantalones cortos ▶ VI (*Elec*) ponerse en cortocircuito

shortage [ˈʃɔːtɪdʒ] N escasez *f*, falta

shortbread [ˈʃɔːtbred] N *galleta de mantequilla, especie de mantecada*

short-change [ʃɔːtˈtʃeɪndʒ] VT: **to ~ sb** no dar el cambio completo a algn

short-circuit [ʃɔːtˈsəːkɪt] VT poner en cortocircuito ▶ VI ponerse en cortocircuito

shortcoming [ˈʃɔːtkʌmɪŋ] N defecto, deficiencia

shortcrust pastry [ˈʃɔːtkrʌst-], **short pastry** N (BRIT) pasta quebradiza

shortcut [ˈʃɔːtkʌt] N atajo

shorten [ˈʃɔːtn] VT acortar; (*visit*) interrumpir

shortfall [ˈʃɔːtfɔːl] N déficit *m*, deficiencia

shorthand [ˈʃɔːthænd] N (BRIT) taquigrafía; **to take sth down in ~** taquigrafiar algo

shorthand notebook N cuaderno de taquigrafía

shorthand typist N (BRIT) taquimecanógrafo(-a)

short list N (BRIT: *for job*) lista de candidatos pre-seleccionados

short-lived [ˈʃɔːtˈlɪvd] ADJ efímero

★**shortly** [ˈʃɔːtlɪ] ADV en breve, dentro de poco

shortness [ˈʃɔːtnɪs] N (*of distance*) cortedad *f*; (*of time*) brevedad *f*; (*manner*) brusquedad *f*

short-sighted [ʃɔːtˈsaɪtɪd] ADJ (BRIT) miope, corto de vista; (*fig*) imprudente

short-sightedness [ʃɔːtˈsaɪtɪdnɪs] N (BRIT) miopía; (*fig*) falta de previsión, imprudencia

short-sleeved ADJ de manga corta

short-staffed [ʃɔːtˈstɑːft] ADJ falto de personal

short story N cuento

short-tempered [ʃɔːtˈtempəd] ADJ enojadizo

short-term [ˈʃɔːttəːm] ADJ (*effect*) a corto plazo

short time N: **to work ~, be on ~** (*Industry*) trabajar con sistema de horario reducido

short-time working [ˈʃɔːttaɪm-] N trabajo de horario reducido

short wave N (*Radio*) onda corta

★**shot** [ʃɔt] PT, PP *of* **shoot** ▶ N (*sound*) tiro, disparo; (*person*) tirador(a) *m/f*; (*try*) tentativa; (*injection*) inyección *f*; (*Phot*) toma, fotografía; (*shotgun pellets*) perdigones *mpl*; **to fire a ~ at sb/sth** tirar or disparar contra algn/algo; **to have a ~ at (doing) sth** probar suerte con algo; **like a ~** (*without any delay*) como un rayo; **a big ~** (*inf*) un pez gordo ▶ ADJ (*inf*): **to get ~ of sth/sb** deshacerse de algo/algn, quitarse algo/a algn de encima

shotgun [ˈʃɔtɡʌn] N escopeta

★**should** [ʃud] AUX VB: **I ~ go now** debo irme ahora; **he ~ be there now** debe de haber llegado (ya); **I ~ go if I were you** yo en tu lugar me iría; **I ~ like to** me gustaría; **~ he phone ...** si llamara ..., en caso de que llamase ...

When *should* means *ought to*, use the conditional of **deber**: *You should take more exercise*. **Deberías hacer más ejercicio.**
tener que is also a very common way to translate *should*: *I should have told you before*. **Tendría que habértelo dicho antes.**
When *should* means *would*, use the conditional: *I should go if I were you*. **Yo que tú, iría.**

★**shoulder** [ˈʃəʊldəʳ] N hombro; (BRIT: *of road*): **hard ~** arcén *m*; **to look over one's ~** mirar hacia atrás; **to rub shoulders with sb** (*fig*) codearse con algn; **to give sb the cold ~** (*fig*) dar de lado a algn ▶ VT (*fig*) cargar con

shoulder bag N bolso de bandolera

shoulder blade N omóplato

shoulder strap N tirante *m*

shouldn't [ˈʃʊdnt] = **should not**

★**shout** [ʃaʊt] N grito ▶ VT gritar ▶ VI gritar, dar voces
▶ **shout down** VT hundir a gritos

shouting [ˈʃaʊtɪŋ] N griterío

shouting match N (*inf*) discusión *f* a voz en grito

shove [ʃʌv] N empujón *m* ▶ VT empujar; (*inf: put*): **to ~ sth in** meter algo a empellones; **he shoved me out of the way** me quitó de en medio de un empujón
▶ **shove off** VI (*Naut*) alejarse del muelle; (*fig: inf*) largarse

shovel [ˈʃʌvl] N pala; (*mechanical*) excavadora ▶ VT mover con pala

★**show** [ʃəʊ] (*pt* **showed** [ʃəʊd], *pp* **shown** [ʃəʊn]) N (*of emotion*) demostración *f*; (*semblance*) apariencia; (*Comm, Tech: exhibition*) exhibición *f*, exposición *f*; (*Theat*) función *f*, espectáculo; (*organization*) negocio, empresa; **on ~** (*exhibits etc*) expuesto; **to be on ~** estar expuesto; **it's just for ~** es solo para impresionar; **to ask for a ~ of hands** pedir una votación a mano alzada; **who's running the ~ here?** ¿quién manda aquí? ▶ VT mostrar, enseñar; (*courage etc*) mostrar, manifestar; (*exhibit*) exponer; (*film*) proyectar; **to ~ a profit/loss** (*Comm*) arrojar un saldo positivo/negativo; **I have nothing to ~ for it** no saqué ningún provecho (de ello); **to ~ sb to her seat/to the door** acompañar a algn a su asiento/a la puerta; **as shown in the illustration** como se ve en el grabado; **it just goes to ~ that ...** queda demostrado que ... ▶ VI mostrarse; (*appear*) aparecer; **it doesn't ~** no se ve *or* nota
▶ **show in** VT (*person*) hacer pasar
▶ **show off** VI (*pej*) presumir ▶ VT (*display*) lucir; (*pej*) hacer alarde de
▶ **show out** VT: **to ~ sb out** acompañar a algn a la puerta
▶ **show up** VI (*stand out*) destacar; (*inf: turn up*) presentarse ▶ VT (*defect*) poner de manifiesto; (*unmask*) desenmascarar

showbiz [ˈʃəʊbɪz] N (*inf*) = **show business**

show business N el mundo del espectáculo

showcase [ˈʃəʊkeɪs] N vitrina; (*fig*) escaparate *m*

showdown [ˈʃəʊdaʊn] N crisis *f*, momento decisivo

★**shower** [ˈʃaʊəʳ] N (*rain*) chaparrón *m*, chubasco; (*of stones etc*) lluvia; (*also:* **shower bath**) ducha; **to have** *or* **take a ~** ducharse ▶ VI llover ▶ VT: **to ~ sb with sth** colmar a algn de algo

shower cap N gorro de baño

shower gel N gel de ducha

showerproof [ˈʃaʊəpruːf] ADJ impermeable

showery [ˈʃaʊərɪ] ADJ (*weather*) lluvioso

showground [ˈʃəʊgraʊnd] N ferial *m*, real *m* (de la feria)

showing [ˈʃəʊɪŋ] N (*of film*) proyección *f*

show jumping N hípica

showman [ˈʃəʊmən] N (*irreg*) (*at fair, circus*) empresario (de espectáculos); (*fig*) actor *m* consumado

showmanship [ˈʃəʊmənʃɪp] N dotes *fpl* teatrales

shown [ʃəʊn] PP *of* **show**

show-off [ˈʃəʊɔf] N (*inf: person*) fanfarrón(-ona) *m/f*

showpiece [ˈʃəʊpiːs] N (*of exhibition etc*) objeto más valioso, joya; **that hospital is a ~** ese hospital es un modelo del género

showroom [ˈʃəʊruːm] N sala de muestras

show trial N juicio propagandístico

showy [ˈʃəʊɪ] ADJ ostentoso

shrank [ʃræŋk] PT *of* **shrink**

shrapnel [ˈʃræpnl] N metralla

shred [ʃred] N (*gen pl*) triza, jirón *m*; (*fig: of truth, evidence*) pizca, chispa ▶ VT hacer trizas; (*documents*) triturar; (*Culin*) desmenuzar

shredder [ˈʃredəʳ] N (*vegetable shredder*) picadora; (*document shredder*) trituradora (de papel)

shrewd [ʃruːd] ADJ astuto

shrewdly [ˈʃruːdlɪ] ADV astutamente

shrewdness [ˈʃruːdnɪs] N astucia

shriek [ʃriːk] N chillido ▶ VT, VI chillar

shrill [ʃrɪl] ADJ agudo, estridente

shrimp [ʃrɪmp] N camarón *m*

shrine [ʃraɪn] N santuario, sepulcro

shrink [ʃrɪŋk] (*pt* **shrank** [ʃræŋk], *pp* **shrunk** [ʃrʌŋk]) VI encogerse; (*be reduced*) reducirse; **to ~ from (doing) sth** no atreverse a hacer algo ▶ VT encoger ▶ N (*inf, pej*) loquero(-a)
▶ **shrink away** VI retroceder, retirarse

shrinkage [ˈʃrɪŋkɪdʒ] N encogimiento; reducción *f*; (*Comm: in shops*) pérdidas *fpl*

shrink-wrap [ˈʃrɪŋkræp] VT empaquetar en envase termoretráctil

shrivel [ˈʃrɪvl], **shrivel up** VT (*dry*) secar; (*crease*) arrugar ▶ VI secarse; arrugarse

shroud [ʃraʊd] N sudario ▶ VT: **shrouded in mystery** envuelto en el misterio

Shrove Tuesday [ˈʃrəʊv-] N martes *m* de carnaval

shrub [ʃrʌb] N arbusto

shrubbery [ˈʃrʌbərɪ] N arbustos *mpl*

shrug [ʃrʌg] N encogimiento de hombros ▶ VT, VI: **to ~ (one's shoulders)** encogerse de hombros
▶ **shrug off** VT negar importancia a; (*cold, illness*) deshacerse de

shrunk [ʃrʌŋk] PP *of* **shrink**

shrunken [ˈʃrʌŋkn] ADJ encogido

shudder [ˈʃʌdəʳ] N estremecimiento, escalofrío ▸ VI estremecerse

shuffle [ˈʃʌfl] VT (*cards*) barajar; **to ~ (one's feet)** arrastrar los pies

shun [ʃʌn] VT rehuir, esquivar

shunt [ʃʌnt] VT (*Rail*) maniobrar

shunting yard [ˈʃʌntɪŋ-] N estación *f* de maniobras

★**shut** [ʃʌt] (*pt, pp* **~**) VT cerrar ▸ VI cerrarse
  ▸ **shut down** VT, VI cerrar; (*machine*) parar
  ▸ **shut off** VT (*stop: power, water supply etc*) interrumpir, cortar; (: *engine*) parar
  ▸ **shut out** VT (*person*) excluir, dejar fuera; (*noise, cold*) no dejar entrar; (*block: view*) tapar; (: *memory*) tratar de olvidar
  ▸ **shut up** VI (*inf: keep quiet*) callarse ▸ VT (*close*) cerrar; (*silence*) callar

shutdown [ˈʃʌtdaʊn] N cierre *m*

shutter [ˈʃʌtəʳ] N contraventana; (*Phot*) obturador *m*

shuttle [ˈʃʌtl] N lanzadera; (*also:* **shuttle service:** *Aviat*) puente *m* aéreo ▸ VI (*vehicle, person*) ir y venir ▸ VT (*passengers*) transportar, trasladar

shuttlecock [ˈʃʌtlkɔk] N volante *m*

shuttle diplomacy N viajes *mpl* diplomáticos

shy [ʃaɪ] ADJ tímido; **to be ~ of doing sth** esquivar hacer algo ▸ VI: **to ~ away from doing sth** (*fig*) rehusar hacer algo

shyly [ˈʃaɪlɪ] ADV tímidamente

shyness [ˈʃaɪnɪs] N timidez *f*

Siam [saɪˈæm] N Siam *m*

Siamese [saɪəˈmiːz] ADJ siamés(-esa); **~ cat** gato siamés; **~ twins** gemelos(-as) *mpl/fpl* siameses(-as) ▸ N (*person*) siamés(-esa) *m/f*; (*Ling*) siamés *m*

Siberia [saɪˈbɪərɪə] N Siberia

sibling [ˈsɪblɪŋ] N (*formal*) hermano(-a)

Sicilian [sɪˈsɪlɪən] ADJ, N siciliano(-a) *m/f*

Sicily [ˈsɪsɪlɪ] N Sicilia

★**sick** [sɪk] ADJ (*ill*) enfermo; (*nauseated*) mareado; (*humour*) morboso; **to be ~** (*BRIT*) vomitar; **to feel ~** tener náuseas; **to be ~ of** (*fig*) estar harto de; **a ~ person** un(a) enfermo(-a); **to be (off) ~** estar ausente por enfermedad; **to fall** *or* **take ~** ponerse enfermo

sickbag [ˈsɪkbæg] N bolsa para el mareo

sick bay N enfermería

sickbed [ˈsɪkbɛd] N lecho de enfermo

sick building syndrome N enfermedad causada por falta de ventilación y luz natural en un edificio

sicken [ˈsɪkn] VT dar asco a ▸ VI enfermar; **to be sickening for** (*cold, flu etc*) mostrar síntomas de

sickening [ˈsɪknɪŋ] ADJ (*fig*) asqueroso

sickle [ˈsɪkl] N hoz *f*

sick leave N baja por enfermedad

sickle-cell anaemia [ˈsɪklsɛl-] N anemia de células falciformes, drepanocitosis *f*

sick list N: **to be on the ~** estar de baja

sickly [ˈsɪklɪ] ADJ enfermizo; (*taste*) empalagoso

sickness [ˈsɪknɪs] N enfermedad *f*, mal *m*; (*vomiting*) náuseas *fpl*

sickness benefit N subsidio de enfermedad

sick pay N prestación por enfermedad pagada por la empresa

sickroom [ˈsɪkruːm] N cuarto del enfermo

★**side** [saɪd] N (*gen*) lado; (*face, surface*) cara; (*of paper*) cara; (*slice of bread*) rebanada; (*of body*) costado; (*of animal*) ijar *m*, ijada; (*of lake*) orilla; (*part*) lado; (*aspect*) aspecto; (*team: Sport*) equipo; (: *Pol etc*) partido; (*of hill*) ladera; **by the ~ of** al lado de; **~ by ~** juntos(-as); **from all sides** de todos lados; **the right/wrong ~** el derecho/revés; **to take sides (with)** tomar partido (por); **~ of beef** flanco de vaca; **from ~ to ~** de un lado a otro ▸ ADJ (*door, entrance*) lateral ▸ VI: **to ~ with sb** tomar partido por algn

sidebar [ˈsaɪdbɑːʳ] N (*on web page*) barra lateral

sideboard [ˈsaɪdbɔːd] N aparador *m*

sideboards [ˈsaɪdbɔːdz] (*BRIT*), **sideburns** [ˈsaɪdbəːnz] NPL patillas *fpl*

sidecar [ˈsaɪdkɑːʳ] N sidecar *m*

side dish N entremés *m*

side drum N (*Mus*) tamboril *m*

side effect N efecto secundario

sidekick [ˈsaɪdkɪk] N compinche *m*

sidelight [ˈsaɪdlaɪt] N (*Aut*) luz *f* lateral

sideline [ˈsaɪdlaɪn] N (*Sport*) línea de banda; (*fig*) empleo suplementario

sidelong [ˈsaɪdlɔŋ] ADJ de soslayo; **to give a ~ glance at sth** mirar algo de reojo

side plate N platito

side road N (*BRIT*) calle *f* lateral

side-saddle [ˈsaɪdsædl] ADV a la amazona

side show N (*stall*) caseta; (*fig*) atracción *f* secundaria

sidestep [ˈsaɪdstɛp] VT (*question*) eludir; (*problem*) esquivar ▸ VI (*Boxing etc*) dar un quiebro

side street N calle *f* lateral

sidetrack [ˈsaɪdtræk] VT (*fig*) desviar (de su propósito)

sidewalk [ˈsaɪdwɔːk] N (*US*) acera, vereda (*LAM*), andén *m* (*LAM*), banqueta (*LAM*)

sideways [ˈsaɪdweɪz] ADV de lado

siding [ˈsaɪdɪŋ] N (*Rail*) apartadero, vía muerta

sidle [ˈsaɪdl] VI: **to ~ up (to)** acercarse furtivamente (a)

SIDS [sɪdz] N ABBR (= *sudden infant death syndrome*) (síndrome *m* de la) muerte *f* súbita

siege [siːdʒ] N cerco, sitio; **to lay ~ to** cercar, sitiar

siege economy N economía de sitio or de asedio

Sierra Leone [sɪˈɛrəlɪˈəun] N Sierra Leona

siesta [sɪˈɛstə] N siesta

sieve [sɪv] N colador m ▶ VT cribar

sift [sɪft] VT cribar ▶ VI: **to ~ through** (information) examinar cuidadosamente

sigh [saɪ] N suspiro ▶ VI suspirar

★**sight** [saɪt] N (faculty) vista; (spectacle) espectáculo; (on gun) mira, alza; **in ~** a la vista; **out of ~** fuera de (la) vista; **at ~** a la vista; **at first ~** a primera vista; **to lose ~ of sth/sb** perder algo/a algn de vista; **to catch ~ of sth/sb** divisar algo/a algn; **I know her by ~** la conozco de vista; **to set one's sights on (doing) sth** aspirar a or ambicionar (hacer) algo ▶ VT ver, divisar

sighted [ˈsaɪtɪd] ADJ vidente, de vista normal; **partially ~** de vista limitada

★**sightseeing** [ˈsaɪtsiːɪŋ] N turismo; **to go ~** hacer turismo

sightseer [ˈsaɪtsiːəʳ] N turista mf

★**sign** [saɪn] N (with hand) señal f, seña; (trace) huella, rastro; (notice) letrero; (written) signo; (also: **road sign**) indicador m; (: with instructions) señal f de tráfico; **as a ~ of** en señal de; **it's a good/bad ~** es buena/mala señal; **plus/minus ~** signo de más/de menos ▶ VT firmar; (Sport) fichar; **to ~ one's name** firmar
  ▶ **sign away** VT (rights etc) ceder
  ▶ **sign in** VI firmar el registro (al entrar)
  ▶ **sign off** VI (Radio, TV) cerrar el programa
  ▶ **sign on** VI (Mil) alistarse; (as unemployed) apuntarse al paro; (employee) firmar un contrato ▶ VT (Mil) alistar; (employee) contratar
  ▶ **sign out** VI firmar el registro (al salir)
  ▶ **sign over** VT: **to ~ sth over to sb** traspasar algo a algn
  ▶ **sign up** VI (Mil) alistarse; (for course) inscribirse ▶ VT (player) fichar; (contract) contratar

★**signal** [ˈsɪgnl] N señal f; **the engaged ~** (Tel) la señal de comunicando; **the ~ is very weak** (TV) no captamos bien el canal ▶ VI (Aut) señalizar; **to ~ to sb (to do sth)** hacer señas a algn (para que haga algo) ▶ VT (person) hacer señas a; (message) transmitir; **to ~ a left/right turn** (Aut) indicar que se va a doblar a la izquierda/derecha

signal box N (Rail) garita de señales

signalman [ˈsɪgnlmən] N (irreg) (Rail) guardavía m

signatory [ˈsɪgnətərɪ] N firmante mf

signature [ˈsɪgnətʃəʳ] N firma

signature tune N sintonía

signet ring [ˈsɪgnət-] N (anillo de) sello

significance [sɪgˈnɪfɪkəns] N significado; (importance) trascendencia; **that is of no ~** eso no tiene importancia

★**significant** [sɪgˈnɪfɪkənt] ADJ significativo; (important) trascendente; **it is ~ that ...** es significativo que ...

significantly [sɪgˈnɪfɪkəntlɪ] ADV (smile) expresivamente; (improve, increase) sensiblemente; **and, ~ ...** y debe notarse que ...

signify [ˈsɪgnɪfaɪ] VT significar

sign language N mímica, lenguaje m por or de señas

signpost [ˈsaɪnpəust] N indicador m

Sikh [siːk] ADJ, N sij mf

silage [ˈsaɪlɪdʒ] N ensilaje m

★**silence** [ˈsaɪlns] N silencio ▶ VT hacer callar, acallar; (guns) reducir al silencio

silencer [ˈsaɪlnsəʳ] N silenciador m

★**silent** [ˈsaɪlnt] ADJ (gen) silencioso; (not speaking) callado; (film) mudo; **to keep or remain ~** guardar silencio

silently [ˈsaɪlntlɪ] ADV silenciosamente, en silencio

silent partner N (Comm) socio(-a) comanditario(-a)

silhouette [sɪluːˈɛt] N silueta; **silhouetted against** destacado sobre or contra

silicon [ˈsɪlɪkən] N silicio

silicon chip N chip m, plaqueta de silicio

silicone [ˈsɪlɪkəun] N silicona

silk [sɪlk] N seda ▶ CPD de seda

silky [ˈsɪlkɪ] ADJ sedoso

sill [sɪl] N (also: **windowsill**) alféizar m; (Aut) umbral m

silliness [ˈsɪlɪnɪs] N (of person) necedad f; (of idea) lo absurdo

★**silly** [ˈsɪlɪ] ADJ (person) tonto; (idea) absurdo; **to do sth ~** hacer una tontería

silo [ˈsaɪləu] N silo

silt [sɪlt] N sedimento

★**silver** [ˈsɪlvəʳ] N plata; (money) moneda suelta ▶ ADJ de plata

silver foil, (BRIT) **silver paper** N papel m de plata

silver plate N vajilla de plata

silver-plated [sɪlvəˈpleɪtɪd] ADJ plateado

silversmith [ˈsɪlvəsmɪθ] N platero(-a)

silverware [ˈsɪlvəwɛəʳ] N plata

silver wedding, silver wedding anniversary N (BRIT) bodas fpl de plata

silvery [ˈsɪlvrɪ] ADJ plateado

SIM card [ˈsɪm-] N (Tel) SIM card m or f, tarjeta SIM

★**similar** [ˈsɪmɪləʳ] ADJ: **~ to** parecido or semejante a

similarity [sɪmɪˈlærɪtɪ] N parecido, semejanza

similarly [ˈsɪmɪləlɪ] ADV del mismo modo; (in a similar way) de manera parecida; (equally) igualmente

simile [ˈsɪmɪlɪ] N símil m

simmer [ˈsɪməʳ] VI hervir a fuego lento
  ▶ **simmer down** VI (fig: inf) calmarse, tranquilizarse

simpering [ˈsɪmpərɪŋ] ADJ afectado; (*foolish*) bobo

★**simple** [ˈsɪmpl] ADJ (*easy*) sencillo; (*foolish*) simple; (*Comm*) simple; **the ~ truth** la pura verdad

simple interest N (*Comm*) interés *m* simple

simple-minded [sɪmplˈmaɪndɪd] ADJ simple, ingenuo

simpleton [ˈsɪmpltən] N inocentón(-ona) *m/f*

simplicity [sɪmˈplɪsɪtɪ] N sencillez *f*; (*foolishness*) ingenuidad *f*

simplification [sɪmplɪfɪˈkeɪʃən] N simplificación *f*

simplify [ˈsɪmplɪfaɪ] VT simplificar

★**simply** [ˈsɪmplɪ] ADV (*in a simple way: live, talk*) sencillamente; (*just, merely*) solo

simulate [ˈsɪmjuleɪt] VT simular

simulation [sɪmjuˈleɪʃən] N simulación *f*

simultaneous [sɪməlˈteɪnɪəs] ADJ simultáneo

simultaneously [sɪməlˈteɪnɪəslɪ] ADV simultáneamente, a la vez

sin [sɪn] N pecado ▶ VI pecar

★**since** [sɪns] ADV desde entonces ▶ PREP desde; **~ then**, **ever ~** desde entonces; **~ Monday** desde el lunes ▶ CONJ (*time*) desde que; (*because*) ya que, puesto que; **(ever) ~ I arrived** desde que llegué

sincere [sɪnˈsɪər] ADJ sincero

sincerely [sɪnˈsɪəlɪ] ADV sinceramente; **yours ~** (*in letters*) le saluda (afectuosamente); **~ yours** (*US*) (*in letters*) le saluda atentamente

sincerity [sɪnˈsɛrɪtɪ] N sinceridad *f*

sinecure [ˈsaɪnɪkjuər] N chollo

sinew [ˈsɪnjuː] N tendón *m*

sinful [ˈsɪnful] ADJ (*thought*) pecaminoso; (*person*) pecador(a)

★**sing** [sɪŋ] (*pt* **sang** [sæŋ], *pp* **sung** [sʌŋ]) VT cantar ▶ VI (*gen*) cantar; (*bird*) trinar; (*ears*) zumbar

Singapore [sɪŋəˈpɔːr] N Singapur *m*

singe [sɪndʒ] VT chamuscar

★**singer** [ˈsɪŋər] N cantante *mf*

Singhalese [sɪŋəˈliːz] ADJ = **Sinhalese**

singing [ˈsɪŋɪŋ] N (*of person, bird*) canto; (*songs*) canciones *fpl*; (*in the ears*) zumbido; (*of kettle*) silbido

★**single** [ˈsɪŋgl] ADJ único, solo; (*unmarried*) soltero; (*not double*) individual, sencillo; **not a ~ one was left** no quedaba ni uno; **every ~ day** todos los días (sin excepción) ▶ N (*BRIT: also:* **single ticket**) billete *m* sencillo; (*record*) sencillo, single *m* ■ **singles** NPL (*Tennis*) individuales *mpl*
▶ **single out** VT (*choose*) escoger; (*point out*) singularizar

single bed N cama individual

single-breasted [sɪŋglˈbrɛstɪd] ADJ (*jacket, suit*) recto, sin cruzar

single-entry book-keeping [ˈsɪŋglɛntrɪ-] N contabilidad *f* por partida simple

Single European Market N: **the ~** el Mercado Único Europeo

single file N: **in ~** en fila de uno

single-handed [sɪŋglˈhændɪd] ADV sin ayuda

single-minded [sɪŋglˈmaɪndɪd] ADJ resuelto, firme

single parent N (*mother*) madre *f* soltera; (*father*) padre *m* soltero

single-parent family [ˈsɪŋglpɛərənt-] N familia monoparental

single room N habitación *f* individual

singles bar N (*esp US*) bar *m* para solteros

single-sex school [ˈsɪŋglsɛks-] N escuela no mixta

single-sided [sɪŋglˈsaɪdɪd] ADJ (*Comput: disk*) de una cara

single spacing N (*Typ*): **in ~** a un espacio

singlet [ˈsɪŋglɪt] N camiseta

singly [ˈsɪŋglɪ] ADV uno por uno

singsong [ˈsɪŋsɔŋ] ADJ (*tone*) cantarín(-ina) ▶ N (*songs*): **to have a ~** tener un concierto improvisado

singular [ˈsɪŋgjulər] ADJ singular, extraordinario, raro, extraño; (*outstanding*) excepcional; (*Ling*) singular ▶ N (*Ling*) singular *m*; **in the feminine ~** en femenino singular

singularly [ˈsɪŋgjuləlɪ] ADV singularmente, extraordinariamente

Sinhalese [sɪnhəˈliːz] ADJ cingalés(-esa)

sinister [ˈsɪnɪstər] ADJ siniestro

★**sink** [sɪŋk] (*pt* **sank** [sæŋk], *pp* **sunk** [sʌŋk]) N fregadero ▶ VT (*ship*) hundir, echar a pique; (*foundations*) excavar; (*piles etc*): **to ~ sth into** hundir algo en ▶ VI (*gen*) hundirse; **he sank into a chair/the mud** se dejó caer en una silla/se hundió en el barro; **the shares** *or* **share prices have sunk to three dollars** las acciones han bajado a tres dólares
▶ **sink in** VI (*fig*) penetrar, calar; **the news took a long time to ~ in** la noticia tardó mucho en hacer mella en él (*or* mí *etc*)

sinking [ˈsɪŋkɪŋ] ADJ: **that ~ feeling** la sensación esa de desmoralización

sinking fund N fondo de amortización

sink unit N fregadero

sinner [ˈsɪnər] N pecador(a) *m/f*

Sinn Féin [ʃɪnˈfeɪn] N partido político republicano de Irlanda del Norte

sinuous [ˈsɪnjuəs] ADJ sinuoso

sinus [ˈsaɪnəs] N (*Anat*) seno

sip [sɪp] N sorbo ▶ VT sorber, beber a sorbitos

siphon [ˈsaɪfən] N sifón *m* ▶ VT (*also:* **siphon off**: *funds*) desviar

★**sir** [sɜːr] N señor *m*; **S~ John Smith** Sir John Smith; **yes, ~** sí, señor; **Dear S~** (*in letter*) Muy señor mío, Estimado Señor; **Dear Sirs** Muy señores nuestros, Estimados Señores

siren [ˈsaɪərn] N sirena

sirloin [ˈsɜːlɔɪn] N solomillo

sirloin steak N filete m de solomillo

sisal ['saɪsəl] N pita, henequén m (LAm)

sissy ['sɪsɪ] N (!) marica m (!)

★**sister** ['sɪstə^r] N hermana; (BRIT: nurse) enfermera jefe

sister-in-law ['sɪstərɪnlɔ:] N cuñada

sister organization N organización f hermana

sister ship N barco gemelo

★**sit** [sɪt] (pt, pp **sat** [sæt]) VI sentarse; (be sitting) estar sentado; (assembly) reunirse; (dress etc) caer, sentar; (for painter) posar; **that jacket sits well** esa chaqueta sienta bien ▸ VT (BRIT: exam) presentarse a
  ▸ **sit about, sit around** VI holgazanear
  ▸ **sit back** VI (in seat) recostarse
  ▸ **sit down** VI sentarse; **to be sitting down** estar sentado
  ▸ **sit in on** VT FUS: **to ~ in on a discussion** asistir a una discusión
  ▸ **sit on** VT FUS (jury, committee) ser miembro de, formar parte de; **to ~ on a committee** ser miembro de una comisión or un comité
  ▸ **sit up** VI incorporarse; (not go to bed) no acostarse

sitcom ['sɪtkɔm] N ABBR (TV: = situation comedy) comedia de situación, telecomedia

sit-down ['sɪtdaun] ADJ: **~ strike** huelga de brazos caídos; **a ~ meal** una comida sentada

site [saɪt] N sitio; (also: **building site**) solar m ▸ VT situar

sit-in ['sɪtɪn] N (demonstration) sentada f

siting ['saɪtɪŋ] N (location) situación f, emplazamiento

sitter ['sɪtə^r] N (Art) modelo mf; (babysitter) canguro mf

sitting ['sɪtɪŋ] N (of assembly etc) sesión f; (in canteen) turno

sitting member N (Pol) titular mf de un escaño

sitting room N sala de estar

sitting tenant N inquilino con derechos de estancia en una vivienda

situate ['sɪtjueɪt] VT situar, ubicar (LAm)

situated ['sɪtjueɪtɪd] ADJ situado, ubicado (LAm)

★**situation** [sɪtju'eɪʃən] N situación f; **"situations vacant"** (BRIT) "ofertas de trabajo"

situation comedy N (TV, Radio) comedia de situación, telecomedia

★**six** [sɪks] NUM seis

six-pack ['sɪkspæk] N (esp US) paquete m de seis cervezas

★**sixteen** [sɪks'ti:n] NUM dieciséis

★**sixteenth** [sɪks'ti:nθ] ADJ decimosexto

★**sixth** [sɪksθ] ADJ sexto; **the upper/lower ~** (Scol) el séptimo/sexto año

sixth form N (BRIT) clase f de alumnos del sexto año (de 16 a 18 años de edad)

sixth-form college N instituto m para alumnos de 16 a 18 años

sixtieth ['sɪkstɪɪθ] ADJ sexagésimo

★**sixty** ['sɪkstɪ] NUM sesenta

★**size** [saɪz] N (gen) tamaño; (extent) extensión f; (of clothing) talla; (of shoes) número; **I take ~ 5 shoes** ≈ calzo el número treinta y ocho; **I take ~ 14** ≈ mi talla es la 42; **I'd like the small/large ~** (of soap powder etc) quisiera el tamaño pequeño/grande
  ▸ **size up** VT formarse una idea de

sizeable ['saɪzəbl] ADJ importante, considerable

sizzle ['sɪzl] VI crepitar

SK ABBR (CANADA) = **Saskatchewan**

skate [skeɪt] N patín m; (fish: pl inv) raya ▸ VI patinar
  ▸ **skate over, skate round** VT FUS (problem, issue) pasar por alto

skateboard ['skeɪtbɔ:d] N monopatín m

skateboarding N monopatín m

skatepark ['skeɪtpɑ:k] N pista de skate

skater ['skeɪtə^r] N patinador(a) m/f

skating ['skeɪtɪŋ] N patinaje m; **figure ~** patinaje m artístico

skating rink N pista de patinaje

skeleton ['skɛlɪtn] N esqueleto; (Tech) armazón m; (outline) esquema m

skeleton key N llave f maestra

skeleton staff N personal m reducido

skeptic etc ['skɛptɪk] (US) = **sceptic** etc

sketch [skɛtʃ] N (drawing) dibujo; (outline) esbozo, bosquejo; (Theat) pieza corta, sketch m ▸ VT dibujar; (plan etc: also: **sketch out**) esbozar

sketch book N bloc m de dibujo

sketching ['skɛtʃɪŋ] N dibujo

sketch pad N bloc m de dibujo

sketchy ['skɛtʃɪ] ADJ incompleto

skewer ['skju:ə^r] N brocheta

★**ski** [ski:] N esquí m ▸ VI esquiar

ski boot N bota de esquí

skid [skɪd] N patinazo; **to go into a ~** comenzar a patinar ▸ VI patinar

skid mark N señal f de patinazo

skier ['ski:ə^r] N esquiador(a) m/f

★**skiing** ['ski:ɪŋ] N esquí m; **to go ~** practicar el esquí, (ir a) esquiar

ski instructor N instructor(a) m/f de esquí

ski jump N (course) pista para salto de esquí

skilful, (US) **skillful** ['skɪlful] ADJ diestro, experto

skilfully, (US) **skillfully** ['skɪlfulɪ] ADV hábilmente, con destreza

ski lift N telesilla m, telesquí m

★**skill** [skɪl] N destreza, pericia; (technique) arte m, técnica; **there's a certain ~ to doing it** se necesita cierta habilidad para hacerlo

777

skilled [skɪld] ADJ hábil, diestro; (*worker*) cualificado

skillet ['skɪlɪt] N sartén *f* pequeña

skillful ['skɪlful] (*US*) = **skilful**

skim [skɪm] VT (*milk*) desnatar; (*glide over*) rozar, rasar ▸ VI: **to ~ through** (*book*) hojear

skimmed milk [skɪmd-] N leche *f* desnatada *or* descremada

skimp [skɪmp] VT (*work*) chapucear; (*cloth etc*) escatimar; **to ~ on** (*material etc*) economizar; (*work*) escatimar

skimpy ['skɪmpɪ] ADJ (*meagre*) escaso; (*skirt*) muy corto

★**skin** [skɪn] N (*gen*) piel *f*; (*complexion*) cutis *m*; (*of fruit, vegetable*) piel *f*, cáscara; (*crust: on pudding, paint*) nata; **wet** *or* **soaked to the ~** calado hasta los huesos ▸ VT (*fruit etc*) pelar; (*animal*) despellejar

skin cancer N cáncer *m* de piel

skin-deep ['skɪn'diːp] ADJ superficial

skin diver N buceador(a) *m/f*

skin diving N buceo

skinflint ['skɪnflɪnt] N tacaño(-a), roñoso(-a)

skinhead ['skɪnhɛd] N cabeza *mf* rapada, skin(head) *mf*

skinny ['skɪnɪ] ADJ flaco, magro

skintight ['skɪntaɪt] ADJ (*dress etc*) muy ajustado

skip [skɪp] N brinco, salto; (*container*) contenedor *m* ▸ VI brincar; (*with rope*) saltar a la comba ▸ VT (*pass over*) omitir, saltarse

ski pants NPL pantalones *mpl* de esquí

ski pass N forfait *m* (de esquí)

ski pole N bastón *m* de esquiar

skipper ['skɪpə^r] N (*Naut, Sport*) capitán(-ana)

skipping rope ['skɪpɪŋ-] N (*BRIT*) comba, cuerda (de saltar)

ski resort N estación *f* de esquí

skirmish ['skəːmɪʃ] N escaramuza

★**skirt** [skəːt] N falda, pollera (*LAM*) ▸ VT (*surround*) ceñir, rodear; (*go round*) ladear

skirting board ['skəːtɪŋ-] N (*BRIT*) rodapié *m*

ski run N pista de esquí

ski slope N pista de esquí

ski suit N traje *m* de esquiar

skit [skɪt] N sátira, parodia

ski tow N arrastre *m* (de esquí)

skittle ['skɪtl] N bolo; **skittles** (*game*) boliche *m*

skive [skaɪv] VI (*BRIT inf*) gandulear

skulk [skʌlk] VI esconderse

skull [skʌl] N calavera; (*Anat*) cráneo

skullcap ['skʌlkæp] N (*worn by Jews*) casquete *m*; (*worn by Pope*) solideo

skunk [skʌŋk] N mofeta

★**sky** [skaɪ] N cielo; **to praise sb to the skies** poner a algn por las nubes

sky-blue [skaɪ'bluː] ADJ (azul) celeste

skydiving ['skaɪdaɪvɪŋ] N paracaidismo acrobático

sky-high ['skaɪ'haɪ] ADJ (*inf*) por las nubes ▸ ADV (*throw*) muy alto; **prices have gone ~** (*inf*) los precios están por las nubes

skylark ['skaɪlɑːk] N (*bird*) alondra

skylight ['skaɪlaɪt] N tragaluz *m*, claraboya

skyline ['skaɪlaɪn] N (*horizon*) horizonte *m*; (*of city*) perfil *m*

Skype® [skaɪp] (*Internet, Tel*) N Skype® *m* ▸ VT hablar con algn a través de Skype

skyscraper ['skaɪskreɪpə^r] N rascacielos *m inv*

slab [slæb] N (*stone*) bloque *m*; (*of wood*) tabla, plancha; (*flat*) losa; (*of cake*) trozo; (*of meat, cheese*) tajada, trozo

slack [slæk] ADJ (*loose*) flojo; (*slow*) de poca actividad; (*careless*) descuidado; (*Comm: market*) poco activo; (*: demand*) débil; (*period*) bajo; **business is ~** hay poco movimiento en el negocio

slacken ['slækn] VI (*also:* **slacken off**) aflojarse ▸ VT aflojar; (*speed*) disminuir

slackness ['slæknɪs] N flojedad *f*; (*carelessness*) negligencia

slacks [slæks] NPL pantalones *mpl*

slag [slæg] N escoria, escombros *mpl*

slag heap N escorial *m*, escombrera

slain [sleɪn] PP of **slay**

slake [sleɪk] VT (*one's thirst*) apagar

slalom ['slɑːləm] N eslálom *m*

slam [slæm] VT (*door*) cerrar de golpe; (*throw*) arrojar (violentamente); (*criticize*) vapulear, vituperar; **to ~ the door** dar un portazo ▸ VI cerrarse de golpe

slammer ['slæmə^r] N (*inf*): **the ~** la trena, el talego

slander ['slɑːndə^r] N calumnia, difamación *f* ▸ VT calumniar, difamar

slanderous ['slɑːndərəs] ADJ calumnioso, difamatorio

slang [slæŋ] N argot *m*; (*jargon*) jerga

slanging match ['slæŋɪŋ-] N (*BRIT inf*) bronca gorda

slant [slɑːnt] N sesgo, inclinación *f*; (*fig*) punto de vista, interpretación *f*; **to get a new ~ on sth** obtener un nuevo punto de vista sobre algo

slanted ['slɑːntɪd], **slanting** ['slɑːntɪŋ] ADJ inclinado

slap [slæp] N palmada; (*in face*) bofetada ▸ VT dar una palmada/bofetada a; (*paint etc*): **to ~ sth on sth** embadurnar algo con algo ▸ ADV (*directly*) de lleno

slapdash ['slæpdæʃ] ADJ chapucero

slaphead ['slæphɛd] N (*BRIT inf*) colgado(-a)

slapstick ['slæpstɪk] N: **~ comedy** comedia de payasadas

slap-up ['slæpʌp] ADJ: **a ~ meal** (*BRIT*) un banquetazo, una comilona

slash [slæʃ] VT acuchillar; (*fig: prices*) fulminar

slat [slæt] N (*of wood, plastic*) tablilla, listón *m*

slate [sleɪt] N pizarra ▶ VT (BRIT *fig: criticize*) vapulear

slaughter [ˈslɔːtəʳ] N (*of animals*) matanza; (*of people*) carnicería ▶ VT matar

slaughterhouse [ˈslɔːtəhaus] N matadero

Slav [slɑːv] ADJ eslavo

slave [sleɪv] N esclavo(-a) ▶ VI (*also:* **slave away**) trabajar como un negro; **to ~ (away) at sth** trabajar como un negro en algo

slave driver N (*inf, pej*) tirano(-a)

slave labour, (US) **slave labor** N trabajo de esclavos

slaver [ˈslævəʳ] VI (*dribble*) babear

slavery [ˈsleɪvərɪ] N esclavitud *f*

slavish [ˈsleɪvɪʃ] ADJ (*devotion*) de esclavo; (*imitation*) servil

slay [sleɪ] (*pt* **slew** [sluː], *pp* **slain** [sleɪn]) VT (*literary*) matar

sleazy [ˈsliːzɪ] ADJ (*fig: place*) sórdido

sledge [slɛdʒ], (US) **sled** [slɛd] N trineo

sledgehammer [ˈslɛdʒhæməʳ] N mazo

sleek [sliːk] ADJ (*shiny*) lustroso

★**sleep** [sliːp] (*pt, pp* **slept** [slɛpt]) N sueño; **to go to ~** dormirse; **to have a good night's ~** dormir toda la noche; **to put to ~** (*patient*) dormir; (*animal: euphemism: kill*) sacrificar ▶ VI dormir; **to ~ lightly** tener el sueño ligero; **to ~ with sb** (*euphemism*) acostarse con algn ▶ VT: **we can ~ 4** podemos alojar a 4, tenemos cabida para 4 ▶ **sleep in** VI (*oversleep*) quedarse dormido

sleeper [ˈsliːpəʳ] N (*person*) durmiente *mf*; (BRIT *Rail: on track*) traviesa; (: *train*) coche-cama *m*

sleepiness [ˈsliːpɪnɪs] N somnolencia

★**sleeping bag** [ˈsliːpɪŋ-] N saco de dormir

sleeping car N coche-cama *m*

sleeping partner N (*Comm*) socio(-a) comanditario(-a)

sleeping pill N somnífero

sleeping sickness N enfermedad *f* del sueño

sleepless [ˈsliːplɪs] ADJ: **a ~ night** una noche en blanco

sleeplessness [ˈsliːplɪsnɪs] N insomnio

sleepover [ˈsliːpəuvəʳ] N: **we're having a ~ at Fiona's** nos quedamos a dormir en casa de Fiona

sleepwalk [ˈsliːpwɔːk] VI caminar dormido; (*habitually*) ser sonámbulo

sleepwalker [ˈsliːpwɔːkəʳ] N sonámbulo(-a)

sleepy [ˈsliːpɪ] ADJ soñoliento; (*place*) soporífero; **to be** *or* **feel ~** tener sueño

sleet [sliːt] N aguanieve *f*

sleeve [sliːv] N manga; (*Tech*) manguito; (*of record*) funda

sleeveless [ˈsliːvlɪs] ADJ (*garment*) sin mangas

sleigh [sleɪ] N trineo

sleight [slaɪt] N: **~ of hand** prestidigitación *f*

slender [ˈslɛndəʳ] ADJ delgado; (*means*) escaso

slept [slɛpt] PT, PP *of* **sleep**

sleuth [sluːθ] N (*inf*) detective *mf*

slew [sluː] VI (*veer*) torcerse ▶ PT *of* **slay**

★**slice** [slaɪs] N (*of meat*) tajada; (*of bread*) rebanada; (*of lemon*) rodaja; (*utensil*) paleta ▶ VT cortar, tajar; rebanar; **sliced bread** pan *m* de molde

slick [slɪk] ADJ (*skilful*) hábil, diestro; (*clever*) astuto ▶ N (*also:* **oil slick**) marea negra

slid [slɪd] PT, PP *of* **slide**

★**slide** [slaɪd] (*pt, pp* **slid** [slɪd]) N (*in playground*) tobogán *m*; (*Phot*) diapositiva; (*microscope slide*) portaobjetos *m inv*, plaquilla de vidrio; (BRIT: *also:* **hair slide**) pasador *m* ▶ VT correr, deslizar ▶ VI (*slip*) resbalarse; (*glide*) deslizarse; **to let things ~** (*fig*) dejar que ruede la bola

slide projector N (*Phot*) proyector *m* de diapositivas

slide rule N regla de cálculo

slide show N (*Comput*) pase *m* de diapositivas

sliding [ˈslaɪdɪŋ] ADJ (*door*) corredizo; **~ roof** (*Aut*) techo de corredera

sliding scale N escala móvil

★**slight** [slaɪt] ADJ (*slim*) delgado; (*frail*) delicado; (*pain etc*) leve; (*trifling*) insignificante; (*small*) pequeño; **a ~ improvement** una ligera mejora; **not in the slightest** en absoluto; **there's not the slightest possibility** no hay la menor *or* más mínima posibilidad ▶ N desaire *m* ▶ VT (*offend*) ofender, desairar

★**slightly** [ˈslaɪtlɪ] ADV ligeramente, un poco; **~ built** delgado

★**slim** [slɪm] ADJ delgado, esbelto ▶ VI adelgazar

slime [slaɪm] N limo, cieno

slimming [ˈslɪmɪŋ] N adelgazamiento ▶ ADJ (*diet, pills*) adelgazante

slimness [ˈslɪmnɪs] N delgadez *f*

slimy [ˈslaɪmɪ] ADJ cenagoso; (*covered with mud*) fangoso; (*also fig: person*) adulón, zalamero

sling [slɪŋ] (*pt, pp* **slung** [slʌŋ]) N (*Med*) cabestrillo; (*weapon*) honda; **to have one's arm in a ~** llevar el brazo en cabestrillo ▶ VT tirar, arrojar

slink [slɪŋk] (*pt, pp* **slunk** [slʌŋk]) VI: **to ~ away, ~ off** escabullirse

slinky [ˈslɪŋkɪ] ADJ (*clothing*) pegado al cuerpo, superajustado

★**slip** [slɪp] N (*slide*) resbalón *m*; (*mistake*) descuido; (*underskirt*) combinación *f*; (*of paper*) papelito; **to give sb the ~** dar esquinazo a algn; **a ~ of the tongue** un lapsus; **wages ~** (BRIT) hoja del sueldo ▶ VT (*slide*) deslizar; **to ~ sth on/off** ponerse/quitarse algo; **to ~ on a jumper** ponerse un jersey *or* un suéter ▶ VI (*slide*) deslizarse; (*stumble*) resbalar(se); (*decline*) decaer; (*move smoothly*): **to ~ into/out of** (*room etc*) colarse en/salirse de; **to let a chance ~ by** dejar escapar una oportunidad; **it slipped from her hand** se la cayó de la mano ▶ **slip away** VI escabullirse

socialist [ˈsəuʃəlɪst] ADJ, N socialista *mf*

socialite [ˈsəuʃəlaɪt] N *persona que alterna con la buena sociedad*

socialize [ˈsəuʃəlaɪz] VI hacer vida social; **to ~ with** *(colleagues)* salir con

social life N vida social

socially [ˈsəuʃəlɪ] ADV socialmente

social media NPL medios sociales

social networking [-ˈnetwɔːkɪŋ] N interacción *f* social a través de la red

social networking site N red *f* social

social science N, **social sciences** NPL ciencias *fpl* sociales

social security N seguridad *f* social

social services NPL servicios *mpl* sociales

social welfare N asistencia social

social work N asistencia social

social worker N asistente(-a) *m/f* social

society [səˈsaɪətɪ] N sociedad *f; (club)* asociación *f; (also:* **high society)** alta sociedad ▶ CPD *(party, column)* social, de sociedad

socio-economic [ˈsəusɪəuɪːkəˈnɒmɪk] ADJ socioeconómico

sociological [səusɪəˈlɒdʒɪkəl] ADJ sociológico

sociologist [səusɪˈɒlədʒɪst] N sociólogo(-a)

sociology [səusɪˈɒlədʒɪ] N sociología

sock [sɒk] N calcetín *m*, media *(LAM);* **to pull one's socks up** *(fig)* hacer esfuerzos, despabilarse

socket [ˈsɒkɪt] N *(Elec)* enchufe *m*

sod [sɒd] N *(of earth)* césped *m; (pej)* cabrón(-ona) *m/f (inf!)* ▶ EXCL: **~ off!** *(inf!)* ¡vete a la porra!

soda [ˈsəudə] N *(Chem)* sosa; *(also:* **soda water)** soda; *(US: also:* **soda pop)** gaseosa

sodden [ˈsɒdn] ADJ empapado

sodium [ˈsəudɪəm] N sodio

sodium chloride N cloruro sódico *or* de sodio

sofa [ˈsəufə] N sofá *m*

sofa bed N sofá-cama *m*

Sofia [ˈsəufɪə] N Sofía

★**soft** [sɒft] ADJ *(teacher, parent)* blando; *(gentle, not loud)* suave; *(stupid)* bobo; **~ currency** divisa blanda *or* débil

soft-boiled [ˈsɒftbɔɪld] ADJ *(egg)* pasado por agua

soft copy N *(Comput)* copia transitoria

soft drink N bebida no alcohólica

soft drugs NPL drogas *fpl* blandas

soften [ˈsɒfn] VT *(butter, ground, leather)* ablandar; *(skin, fabric, outline)* suavizar ▶ VI ablandarse; suavizarse

softener [ˈsɒfnəʳ] N suavizante *m*

soft fruit N bayas *fpl*

soft furnishings NPL tejidos *mpl* para el hogar

soft-hearted [sɒftˈhɑːtɪd] ADJ bondadoso

softly [ˈsɒftlɪ] ADV suavemente; *(gently)* delicadamente, con delicadeza

softness [ˈsɒftnɪs] N blandura; suavidad *f*

soft option N alternativa fácil

soft sell N venta persuasiva

soft target N blanco *or* objetivo fácil

soft toy N juguete *m* de peluche

★**software** [ˈsɒftwɛəʳ] N *(Comput)* software *m*

soft water N agua blanda

soggy [ˈsɒgɪ] ADJ empapado

★**soil** [sɔɪl] N *(earth)* tierra, suelo ▶ VT ensuciar

soiled [sɔɪld] ADJ sucio, manchado

sojourn [ˈsɒdʒəːn] N *(formal)* estancia

solace [ˈsɒlɪs] N consuelo

solar [ˈsəuləʳ] ADJ solar

solarium [səˈlɛərɪəm] *(pl* **solaria** [-rɪə]*)* N solario

solar panel N panel *m* solar

solar plexus [-ˈplɛksəs] N *(Anat)* plexo solar

solar power N energía solar

solar system N sistema *m* solar

sold [səuld] PT, PP *of* **sell**

solder [ˈsəuldəʳ] VT soldar ▶ N soldadura

★**soldier** [ˈsəuldʒəʳ] N *(gen)* soldado *mf; (army man)* militar *m;* **toy ~** soldadito de plomo ▶ VI: **to ~ on** seguir adelante

sold out ADJ *(Comm)* agotado

sole [səul] N *(of foot)* planta; *(of shoe)* suela; *(fish: pl inv)* lenguado ▶ ADJ único; **the ~ reason** la única razón

solely [ˈsəullɪ] ADV únicamente, solo, solamente; **I will hold you ~ responsible** le consideraré el único responsable

solemn [ˈsɒləm] ADJ solemne

sole trader N *(Comm)* comerciante *mf* exclusivo(-a)

solicit [səˈlɪsɪt] VT *(request)* solicitar ▶ VI *(prostitute)* abordar clientes

★**solicitor** [səˈlɪsɪtəʳ] N *(BRIT: for wills etc)* ≈ notario(-a); *(: in court)* ≈ abogado(-a); *see also* **barrister**

solid [ˈsɒlɪd] ADJ sólido; *(gold etc)* macizo; *(line)* continuo; *(vote)* unánime; **we waited two ~ hours** esperamos dos horas enteras; **to be on ~ ground** estar en tierra firme; *(fig)* estar seguro ▶ N sólido

solidarity [sɒlɪˈdærɪtɪ] N solidaridad *f*

solid fuel N combustible *m* sólido

solidify [səˈlɪdɪfaɪ] VI solidificarse

solidity [səˈlɪdɪtɪ] N solidez *f*

solidly [ˈsɒlɪdlɪ] ADV sólidamente; *(fig)* unánimemente

solid-state [ˈsɒlɪdsteɪt] ADJ *(Elec)* estado sólido

soliloquy [səˈlɪləkwɪ] N soliloquio

solitaire [sɒlɪˈtɛəʳ] N *(game, gem)* solitario

solitary [ˈsɒlɪtərɪ] ADJ solitario, solo; *(isolated)* apartado, aislado; *(only)* único

solitary confinement N incomunicación *f;* **to be in ~** estar incomunicado

solitude [ˈsɒlɪtjuːd] N soledad *f*

solo [ˈsəuləu] N solo ▶ ADV *(fly)* en solitario

soloist [ˈsəʊləʊɪst] N solista mf

Solomon Islands [ˈsɒləmən-] NPL: **the ~** las Islas Salomón

solstice [ˈsɒlstɪs] N solsticio

soluble [ˈsɒljʊbl] ADJ soluble

★**solution** [səˈluːʃən] N solución f

★**solve** [sɒlv] VT resolver, solucionar

solvency [ˈsɒlvənsɪ] N (Comm) solvencia

solvent [ˈsɒlvənt] ADJ (Comm) solvente ▶ N (Chem) solvente m

solvent abuse N uso indebido de disolventes

Somali [səˈmɑːlɪ] ADJ, N somalí mf

Somalia [səˈmɑːlɪə] N Somalia

sombre, (US) **somber** [ˈsɒmbəʳ] ADJ sombrío

---

some [sʌm]

ADJ **1** (a certain amount or number of): **some tea/water/biscuits** té/agua/(unas) galletas; **have some tea** tómese un té; **there's some milk in the fridge** hay leche en el frigo; **there were some people outside** había algunas personas fuera; **I've got some money, but not much** tengo algo de dinero, pero no mucho

2 (certain: in contrasts) algunos(-as); **some people say that …** hay quien dice que …; **some films were excellent, but most were mediocre** hubo películas excelentes, pero la mayoría fueron mediocres

3 (unspecified): **some woman was asking for you** una mujer estuvo preguntando por ti; **some day** algún día; **some day next week** un día de la semana que viene; **he was asking for some book (or other)** pedía no sé qué libro; **in some way or other** de alguna que otra manera

4 (considerable amount of) bastante; **some days ago** hace unos cuantos días; **after some time** pasado algún tiempo; **at some length** con mucho detalle

5 (inf: intensive): **that was some party!** ¡menuda fiesta!

▶ PRON **1** (a certain number): **I've got some** (books etc) tengo algunos(-as)

2 (a certain amount) algo; **I've got some** (money, milk) tengo algo; **would you like some?** (coffee etc) ¿quiere un poco?; (books etc) ¿quiere alguno?; **could I have some of that cheese?** ¿me puede dar un poco de ese queso?; **I've read some of the book** he leído parte del libro

▶ ADV: **some 10 people** unas 10 personas, una decena de personas

---

★**somebody** [ˈsʌmbədɪ] PRON alguien; **~ or other** alguien

someday [ˈsʌmdeɪ] ADV algún día

★**somehow** [ˈsʌmhaʊ] ADV de alguna manera; (for some reason) por una u otra razón

★**someone** [ˈsʌmwʌn] PRON = **somebody**

someplace [ˈsʌmpleɪs] ADV (US) = **somewhere**

somersault [ˈsʌməsɔːlt] N (deliberate) salto mortal; (accidental) vuelco ▶ VI dar un salto mortal; dar vuelcos

★**something** [ˈsʌmθɪŋ] PRON algo; **~ to do** algo que hacer; **it's ~ of a problem** es bastante problemático; **would you like ~ to eat/drink?** ¿te gustaría cenar/tomar algo? ▶ ADV: **he's ~ like me** es un poco como yo

sometime [ˈsʌmtaɪm] ADV (in future) algún día, en algún momento; **~ last month** durante el mes pasado; **I'll finish it ~** lo terminaré un día de estos

★**sometimes** [ˈsʌmtaɪmz] ADV a veces

somewhat [ˈsʌmwɒt] ADV algo

★**somewhere** [ˈsʌmwɛəʳ] ADV (be) en alguna parte; (go) a alguna parte; **~ else** (be) en otra parte; (go) a otra parte

★**son** [sʌn] N hijo

sonar [ˈsəʊnɑːʳ] N sonar m

sonata [səˈnɑːtə] N sonata

★**song** [sɒŋ] N canción f

songwriter [ˈsɒŋraɪtəʳ] N compositor(a) m/f de canciones

sonic [ˈsɒnɪk] ADJ (boom) sónico

son-in-law [ˈsʌnɪnlɔː] N yerno

sonnet [ˈsɒnɪt] N soneto

sonny [ˈsʌnɪ] N (inf) hijo

★**soon** [suːn] ADV pronto, dentro de poco; **~ afterwards** poco después; **very/quite ~** muy/bastante pronto; **how ~ can you be ready?** ¿cuánto tardas en prepararte?; **it's too ~ to tell** es demasiado pronto para saber; **see you ~!** ¡hasta pronto!; see also **as**

sooner [ˈsuːnəʳ] ADV (time) antes, más temprano; **I would ~ do that** preferiría hacer eso; **~ or later** tarde o temprano; **no ~ said than done** dicho y hecho; **the ~ the better** cuanto antes mejor; **no ~ had we left than …** apenas nos habíamos marchado cuando …

soot [sʊt] N hollín m

soothe [suːð] VT tranquilizar; (pain) aliviar

soothing [ˈsuːðɪŋ] ADJ (ointment etc) sedante; (tone, words etc) calmante, tranquilizante

SOP N ABBR = **standard operating procedure**

sophisticated [səˈfɪstɪkeɪtɪd] ADJ sofisticado

sophistication [səfɪstɪˈkeɪʃən] N sofisticación f

sophomore [ˈsɒfəmɔːʳ] N (US) estudiante mf de segundo año

soporific [sɒpəˈrɪfɪk] ADJ soporífero

sopping [ˈsɒpɪŋ] ADJ: **~ (wet)** empapado

soppy [ˈsɒpɪ] ADJ (inf) bobo, tonto

soprano [səˈprɑːnəʊ] N soprano f

sorbet [ˈsɔːbeɪ] N sorbete m

sorcerer [ˈsɔːsərəʳ] N hechicero

sordid [ˈsɔːdɪd] ADJ (place etc) sórdido; (motive etc) mezquino

sore [sɔːʳ] ADJ (painful) doloroso, que duele;

S

(*offended*) resentido; **~ throat** dolor *m* de garganta; **my eyes are ~, I have ~ eyes** me duelen los ojos; **it's a ~ point** es un asunto delicado *or* espinoso ▶ N llaga

sorely ADV: **I am ~ tempted to (do it)** estoy muy tentado a (hacerlo)

soreness ['sɔːnɪs] N dolor *m*

sorrel ['sɔrəl] N (*Bot*) acedera

sorrow ['sɔrəu] N pena, dolor *m*

sorrowful ['sɔrəuful] ADJ afligido, triste

sorrowfully ['sɔrəufulɪ] ADV tristemente

★**sorry** ['sɔrɪ] ADJ (*regretful*) arrepentido; (*condition, excuse*) lastimoso; (*sight, failure*) triste; **~!** ¡perdón!, ¡perdone!; **~?** ¿cómo?; **I am ~** lo siento; **I feel ~ for him** me da lástima *or* pena; **I'm ~ to hear that ...** siento saber que ...; **to be ~ about sth** lamentar algo

★**sort** [sɔːt] N clase *f*, género, tipo; (*make: of coffee, car etc*) marca; **what ~ do you want?** (*make*) ¿qué marca quieres?; **what ~ of car?** ¿qué tipo de coche?; **I shall do nothing of the ~** no pienso hacer nada parecido ▶ VT (*also:* **sort out:** *papers*) clasificar; (: *organize*) ordenar, organizar; (: *resolve: problem, situation etc*) arreglar, solucionar; (: *Comput*) clasificar; **it's ~ of awkward** (*inf*) es bastante difícil

sortie ['sɔːtɪ] N salida

sorting office ['sɔːtɪŋ-] N oficina de clasificación del correo

SOS N SOS *m*

so-so ['səusəu] ADV regular, así así

soufflé ['suːfleɪ] N suflé *m*

sought [sɔːt] PT, PP *of* **seek**

sought-after ['sɔːtɑːftə'] ADJ solicitado, codiciado

soul [səul] N alma *f*; **God rest his ~** Dios le reciba en su seno *or* en su gloria; **I didn't see a ~** no vi a nadie; **the poor ~ had nowhere to sleep** el pobre no tenía dónde dormir

soul-destroying ['səuldɪstrɔɪɪŋ] ADJ (*work*) deprimente

soulful ['səulful] ADJ lleno de sentimiento

soulmate ['səulmeɪt] N compañero(-a) del alma

soul-searching ['səulsəːtʃɪŋ] N: **after much ~** después de pensarlo mucho, después de darle muchas vueltas

★**sound** [saund] ADJ (*healthy*) sano; (*safe, not damaged*) en buen estado; (*valid: argument, policy, claim*) válido; (: *move*) acertado; (*dependable: person*) de fiar; (*sensible*) sensato, razonable; **to be of ~ mind** estar en su sano juicio ▶ ADV: **~ asleep** profundamente dormido ▶ N (*noise*) sonido, ruido; (*volume: on TV etc*) volumen *m*; (*Geo*) estrecho; **I don't like the ~ of it** no me gusta nada ▶ VT (*alarm*) sonar; (*also:* **sound out:** *opinions*) consultar, sondear ▶ VI sonar, resonar; (*fig: seem*) parecer; **to ~ like** sonar a; **it sounds as if ...** parece que ...
▶ **sound off** VI (*inf*): **to ~ off (about)** (*give one's opinions*) despotricar (contra)

sound barrier N barrera del sonido

sound bite N cita jugosa

sound effects NPL efectos *mpl* sonoros

sound engineer N ingeniero(-a) de sonido

sounding ['saundɪŋ] N (*Naut etc*) sondeo

sounding board N caja de resonancia

soundly ['saundlɪ] ADV (*sleep*) profundamente; (*beat*) completamente

soundproof ['saundpruːf] ADJ insonorizado

sound system N equipo de sonido

soundtrack ['saundtræk] N (*of film*) banda sonora

sound wave N (*Physics*) onda sonora

★**soup** [suːp] N (*thick*) sopa; (*thin*) caldo; **in the ~** (*fig*) en apuros

soup kitchen N comedor *m* de beneficencia

soup plate N plato sopero

soupspoon ['suːpspuːn] N cuchara sopera

sour ['sauə'] ADJ agrio; (*milk*) cortado; **it's just ~ grapes!** (*fig*) ¡pura envidia!, ¡están verdes!; **to go** *or* **turn ~** (*milk*) cortarse; (*wine*) agriarse; (*fig: relationship*) agriarse; (: *plans*) irse a pique

source [sɔːs] N fuente *f*; **I have it from a reliable ~ that ...** sé de fuente fidedigna que ...

source language N (*Comput*) lenguaje *m* fuente *or* de origen

★**south** [sauθ] N sur *m*; **the S~ of France** el Sur de Francia ▶ ADJ del sur ▶ ADV al sur, hacia el sur; **(to the) ~ of** al sur de; **to travel ~** viajar hacia el sur

South Africa N Sudáfrica

South African ADJ, N sudafricano(-a) *m/f*

★**South America** N América del Sur, Sudamérica

★**South American** ADJ, N sudamericano(-a) *m/f*

southbound ['sauθbaund] ADJ en dirección al sur

south-east [sauθ'iːst] N sudeste *m*, sureste *m* ▶ ADJ (*counties etc*) (del) sudeste, (del) sureste

Southeast Asia N Sudeste *m* asiático

southeastern [sauθ'iːstən] ADJ (del) sudeste, (del) sureste

southerly ['sʌðəlɪ] ADJ sur; (*from the south*) del sur

★**southern** ['sʌðən] ADJ del sur, meridional; **the ~ hemisphere** el hemisferio sur

South Korea N Corea del Sur

South Pole N Polo Sur

South Sea Islands NPL: **the ~** Oceanía

South Seas NPL: **the ~** los Mares del Sur

South Sudan N Sudán *m* del Sur

South Vietnam N Vietnam *m* del Sur

southward ['sauθwəd], **southwards** ['sauθwədz] ADV hacia el sur

south-west [sauθ'wɛst] N suroeste *m*

southwestern [sauθ'wɛstən] ADJ suroeste

souvenir [suːvə'nɪə'] N recuerdo

sovereign ['sɔvrɪn] ADJ, N soberano(-a) *m/f*

sovereignty ['sɔvrɪntɪ] N soberanía

soviet ['səuvɪət] ADJ soviético

Soviet Union N: **the ~** la Unión Soviética

sow¹ [sau] N cerda, puerca

sow² [səu] (*pt* **sowed** [səud], *pp* **sown** [səun]) VT sembrar

soya ['sɔɪə], (US) **soy** [sɔɪ] N soja

soya bean, (US) **soy bean** N semilla de soja

soya sauce, (US) **soy sauce** N salsa de soja

sozzled ['sɔzld] ADJ (BRIT *inf*) mamado

spa [spɑː] N balneario

★**space** [speɪs] N espacio; (*room*) sitio; **(with)in the ~ of an hour/three generations** en el espacio de una hora/tres generaciones; **in a short ~ of time** en poco *or* un corto espacio de tiempo; **in a confined ~** en un espacio restringido; **to clear a ~ for sth** hacer sitio para algo ▶ VT (*also:* **space out**) espaciar

space bar N (*on keyboard*) barra espaciadora

spacecraft ['speɪskrɑːft] N nave *f* espacial, astronave *f*

spaceman ['speɪsmæn] N (*irreg*) astronauta *m*, cosmonauta *m*

spaceship ['speɪsʃɪp] N = **spacecraft**

space shuttle N transportador *m* espacial

spacesuit ['speɪssuːt] N traje *m* espacial

spacewoman ['speɪswumən] N (*irreg*) astronauta, cosmonauta

spacing ['speɪsɪŋ] N espacio

spacious ['speɪʃəs] ADJ amplio

spade [speɪd] N (*tool*) pala ■ **spades** NPL (*Cards: British*) picas *fpl*; (: *Spanish*) espadas *fpl*

spadework ['speɪdwəːk] N (*fig*) trabajo preliminar

spaghetti [spə'ɡɛtɪ] N espaguetis *mpl*

★**Spain** [speɪn] N España

spam [spæm] N (*junk email*) correo basura

spamming ['spæmɪŋ] N (*Comput*) spamming *m*

span [spæn] N (*of bird, plane*) envergadura; (*of hand*) palmo; (*of arch*) luz *f*; (*in time*) lapso ▶ VT extenderse sobre, cruzar; (*fig*) abarcar

★**Spaniard** ['spænjəd] N español(a) *m/f*

spaniel ['spænjəl] N perro de aguas

★**Spanish** ['spænɪʃ] ADJ español(a); **~ omelette** tortilla española *or* de patata ▶ N (*Ling*) español *m*, castellano ■ **the Spanish** NPL (*people*) los españoles

spank [spæŋk] VT zurrar, dar unos azotes a

spanner ['spænər] N (BRIT) llave *f* inglesa

spar [spɑːr] N palo, verga ▶ VI (*Boxing*) entrenarse (en el boxeo)

★**spare** [spɛər] ADJ de reserva; (*surplus*) sobrante, de más; **there are two going ~** sobran *or* quedan dos ▶ N (*part*) pieza de repuesto ▶ VT (*do without*) pasarse sin; (*afford to give*) tener de sobra; (*refrain from hurting*) perdonar; (*details etc*) ahorrar; **to ~** (*surplus*) sobrante, de sobra; **to ~ no expense** no escatimar gastos; **can you ~ (me) £10?** ¿puedes prestarme *or* darme 10 libras?; **can you ~ the**

time? ¿tienes tiempo?; **I've a few minutes to ~** tengo unos minutos libres; **there is no time to ~** no hay tiempo que perder

spare part N pieza de repuesto

spare room N cuarto de los invitados

spare time N ratos *mpl* de ocio, tiempo libre

spare tyre, (US) **spare tire** N (*Aut*) neumático *or* (*LAM*) llanta de recambio

spare wheel N (*Aut*) rueda de recambio

sparing ['spɛərɪŋ] ADJ: **to be ~ with** ser parco en

sparingly ['spɛərɪŋlɪ] ADV escasamente

spark [spɑːk] N chispa; (*fig*) chispazo

sparking plug N = **spark plug**

sparkle ['spɑːkl] N centelleo, destello ▶ VI centellear; (*shine*) relucir, brillar

sparkler ['spɑːklər] N bengala

sparkling ['spɑːklɪŋ] ADJ centelleante; (*wine*) espumoso

spark plug N bujía

sparring partner ['spɑːrɪŋ-] N spárring *m*; (*fig*) contrincante *mf*

sparrow ['spærəu] N gorrión *m*

sparse [spɑːs] ADJ esparcido, escaso

sparsely ['spɑːslɪ] ADV escasamente; **a ~ furnished room** un cuarto con pocos muebles

spartan ['spɑːtən] ADJ (*fig*) espartano

spasm ['spæzəm] N (*Med*) espasmo; (*fig*) arranque *m*, ataque *m*

spasmodic [spæz'mɔdɪk] ADJ espasmódico

spastic ['spæstɪk] ADJ espástico

spat [spæt] PT, PP *of* **spit** ▶ N (US) riña

spate [speɪt] N (*fig*): **~ of** torrente *m* de; **in ~** (*river*) crecido

spatial ['speɪʃl] ADJ espacial

spatter ['spætər] VT: **to ~ with** salpicar de

spatula ['spætjulə] N espátula

spawn [spɔːn] VT (*pej*) engendrar ▶ VI desovar, frezar ▶ N huevas *fpl*

SPCA N ABBR (US) = **Society for the Prevention of Cruelty to Animals**

SPCC N ABBR (US) = **Society for the Prevention of Cruelty to Children**

★**speak** [spiːk] (*pt* **spoke** [spəuk], *pp* **spoken** ['spəukn]) VT (*language*) hablar; (*truth*) decir; **to ~ one's mind** hablar claro *or* con franqueza ▶ VI hablar; (*make a speech*) intervenir; **to ~ to sb/of or about sth** hablar con algn/de *or* sobre algo; **to ~ at a conference/in a debate** hablar en un congreso/un debate; **he has no money to ~ of** no tiene mucho dinero que digamos; **speaking!** ¡al habla!; **~ up!** ¡habla más alto!
  ▶ **speak for** VT FUS: **to ~ for sb** hablar por *or* en nombre de algn; **that picture is already spoken for** (*in shop*) ese cuadro está reservado

★**speaker** ['spiːkər] N (*in public*) orador(a) *m/f*; (*also:* **loudspeaker**) altavoz *m*; (: *for stereo etc*) bafle *m*; **the S~** (*Pol: BRIT*) el Presidente de la

S

Cámara de los Comunes; (: US) el Presidente del Congreso; **are you a Welsh ~?** ¿habla Vd galés?

speaking ['spi:kɪŋ] ADJ hablante

-speaking ['spi:kɪŋ] SUFF -hablante; **Spanish-speaking people** los hispanohablantes

spear [spɪə'] N lanza; (for fishing) arpón m ▶ VT alancear; arponear

spearhead ['spɪəhɛd] VT (attack etc) encabezar ▶ N punta de lanza, vanguardia

spearmint ['spɪəmɪnt] N menta verde

spec [spɛk] N (inf): **on ~** por si acaso; **to buy on ~** arriesgarse a comprar

★**special** ['spɛʃl] ADJ especial; (edition etc) extraordinario; (delivery) urgente; **nothing ~** nada de particular, nada extraordinario ▶ N (train) tren m especial

special agent N agente mf especial

special correspondent N corresponsal mf especial

special delivery N (Post): **by ~** por entrega urgente

special effects NPL (Cine) efectos mpl especiales

★**specialist** ['spɛʃəlɪst] N especialista mf; **a heart ~** (Med) un(-a) especialista del corazón

speciality [spɛʃɪ'ælɪtɪ], (US) **specialty** ['spɛʃəltɪ] N especialidad f

★**specialize** ['spɛʃəlaɪz] VI: **to ~ (in)** especializarse (en)

specially ['spɛʃlɪ] ADV especialmente

special offer N (Comm) oferta especial

special school N (BRIT) colegio m de educación especial

special train N tren m especial

specialty ['spɛʃəltɪ] N (US) = **speciality**

★**species** ['spi:ʃi:z] N especie f

★**specific** [spə'sɪfɪk] ADJ específico

★**specifically** [spə'sɪfɪklɪ] ADV (explicitly: state, warn) específicamente, expresamente; (especially: design, intend) especialmente

specification [spɛsɪfɪ'keɪʃən] N especificación f ■ **specifications** NPL (plan) presupuesto sg; (of car, machine) descripción f técnica; (for building) plan msg detallado

specify ['spɛsɪfaɪ] VT, VI especificar, precisar; **unless otherwise specified** salvo indicaciones contrarias

specimen ['spɛsɪmən] N ejemplar m; (Med: of urine) espécimen m; (: of blood) muestra

specimen copy N ejemplar m de muestra

specimen signature N muestra de firma

speck [spɛk] N grano, mota

speckled ['spɛkld] ADJ moteado

specs [spɛks] NPL (inf) gafas fpl (SP), anteojos mpl

spectacle ['spɛktəkl] N espectáculo ■ **spectacles** NPL (BRIT: glasses) gafas fpl (SP), anteojos mpl

spectacle case N estuche m or funda (de gafas)

★**spectacular** [spɛk'tækjulə'] ADJ espectacular; (success) impresionante

spectator [spɛk'teɪtə'] N espectador(a) m/f

spectator sport N deporte m espectáculo

spectra ['spɛktrə] NPL of **spectrum**

spectre, (US) **specter** ['spɛktə'] N espectro, fantasma m

spectrum ['spɛktrəm] (pl **spectra** [-trə]) N espectro

speculate ['spɛkjuleɪt] VI especular; (try to guess): **to ~ about** especular sobre

speculation [spɛkju'leɪʃən] N especulación f

speculative ['spɛkjulətɪv] ADJ especulativo

speculator ['spɛkjuleɪtə'] N especulador(a) m/f

sped [spɛd] PT, PP of **speed**

★**speech** [spi:tʃ] N (faculty) habla; (formal talk) discurso; (words) palabras fpl; (manner of speaking) forma de hablar; (language) idioma m, lenguaje m

speech day N (BRIT Scol) ≈ día de reparto de premios

speech impediment N defecto del habla

speechless ['spi:tʃlɪs] ADJ mudo, estupefacto

speech therapy N logopedia

★**speed** [spi:d] (pt, pp **sped** [spɛd] or esp Aut **speeded**) N (also Aut, Tech: gear) velocidad f; (haste) prisa; (promptness) rapidez f; **at full** or **top ~** a máxima velocidad; **at a ~ of 70 km/h** a una velocidad de 70 km por hora; **at ~** a gran velocidad; **a five-speed gearbox** una caja de cambios de cinco velocidades; **shorthand/typing ~** rapidez f en taquigrafía/mecanografía ▶ VI (Aut: exceed speed limit) conducir con exceso de velocidad; **the years sped by** los años pasaron volando ▶ **speed up** VI acelerarse ▶ VT acelerar

speedboat ['spi:dbəut] N lancha motora

speed camera N cámara de control de velocidad

speedily ['spi:dɪlɪ] ADV rápido, rápidamente

speeding ['spi:dɪŋ] N (Aut) exceso de velocidad

speed limit N límite m de velocidad, velocidad f máxima

speedometer [spɪ'dɔmɪtə'] N velocímetro

speed trap N (Aut) control m de velocidad

speedway ['spi:dweɪ] N (Sport) pista de carrera

speedy ['spi:dɪ] ADJ (fast) veloz, rápido; (prompt) pronto

★**spell** [spɛl] N (also: **magic spell**) encanto, hechizo; (period of time) rato, período; (turn) turno; **to cast a ~ on sb** hechizar a algn ▶ VT (pt, pp **spelt** [spɛlt] or **spelled** [spɛld]) deletrear; (fig) anunciar, presagiar; **can you ~ it for me?** ¿cómo se deletrea or se escribe?; **how do you ~ your name?** ¿cómo se escribe tu nombre? ▶ VI: **he can't ~** no sabe escribir bien, comete faltas de ortografía

▶ **spell out** vt (*explain*):**to ~ sth out for sb** explicar algo a algn en detalle

spellbound ['spɛlbaund] ADJ embelesado, hechizado

spellchecker N (*Comput*) corrector m (ortográfico)

spelling ['spɛlɪŋ] N ortografía

spelling mistake N falta de ortografía

spelt [spɛlt] PT, PP *of* **spell**

★**spend** [spɛnd] (*pt, pp* **spent** [spɛnt]) vt (*money*) gastar; (*time*) pasar; (*life*) dedicar; **to ~ time/ money/effort on sth** gastar tiempo/dinero/ energías en algo

spending ['spɛndɪŋ] N: **government ~** gastos *mpl* del gobierno

spending money N dinero para gastos

spending power N poder m adquisitivo

spendthrift ['spɛndθrɪft] N derrochador(a) *m/f*, manirroto(-a)

spent [spɛnt] PT, PP *of* **spend** ▶ ADJ (*cartridge, bullets, match*) usado

sperm [spəːm] N esperma

sperm bank N banco de esperma

sperm whale N cachalote m

spew [spjuː] vt vomitar, arrojar

sphere [sfɪəʳ] N esfera

spherical ['sfɛrɪkl] ADJ esférico

sphinx [sfɪŋks] N esfinge f

spice [spaɪs] N especia ▶ vt especiar

spiciness ['spaɪsɪnɪs] N lo picante

spick-and-span ['spɪkən'spæn] ADJ impecable

spicy ['spaɪsɪ] ADJ picante

★**spider** ['spaɪdəʳ] N araña

spider's web N telaraña

spiel [ʃpiːl] N (*inf*) rollo

spike [spaɪk] N (*point*) punta; (*Zool*) pincho, púa; (*Bot*) espiga; (*Elec*) pico parásito ▶ vt: **to ~ a quote** cancelar una cita ■ **spikes** NPL (*Sport*) zapatillas *fpl* con clavos

spiky ['spaɪkɪ] ADJ (*bush, branch*) cubierto de púas; (*animal*) erizado

spill [spɪl] (*pt, pp* **spilt** [spɪlt] *or* **spilled** [spɪld]) vt derramar, verter; (*blood*) derramar; **to ~ the beans** (*inf*) descubrir el pastel ▶ vi derramarse

▶ **spill out** vi derramarse, desparramarse

▶ **spill over** vi desbordarse

spillage ['spɪlɪdʒ] N (*event*) derrame m; (*substance*) vertidos *mpl*

spin [spɪn] (*pt, pp* **spun** [spʌn]) N (*revolution of wheel*) vuelta, revolución f; (*Aviat*) barrena; (*trip in car*) paseo (en coche) ▶ vt (*wool etc*) hilar; (*wheel*) girar ▶ vi girar, dar vueltas; **the car spun out of control** el coche se descontroló y empezó a dar vueltas

▶ **spin out** vt alargar, prolongar

spina bifida ['spaɪnə'bɪfɪdə] N espina bífida

spinach ['spɪnɪtʃ] N espinacas *fpl*

spinal ['spaɪnl] ADJ espinal

spinal column N columna vertebral

spinal cord N médula espinal

spin class N (*Sport*) clase f de spinning

spindly ['spɪndlɪ] ADJ (*leg*) zanquivano

spin doctor N (*inf*) informador(a) parcial al servicio de un partido político

spin-dry ['spɪn'draɪ] vt centrifugar

spin-dryer [spɪn'draɪəʳ] N (*Brit*) secadora centrífuga

spine [spaɪn] N espinazo, columna vertebral; (*thorn*) espina

spine-chilling ['spaɪntʃɪlɪŋ] ADJ terrorífico

spineless ['spaɪnlɪs] ADJ (*fig*) débil, flojo

spinet [spɪ'nɛt] N espineta

spinning ['spɪnɪŋ] N (*of thread*) hilado; (*art*) hilandería; (*Sport*) spinning m

spinning top N peonza

spinning wheel N rueca, torno de hilar

spin-off ['spɪnɔf] N derivado, producto secundario

spinster ['spɪnstəʳ] N soltera; (*pej*) solterona

spiral ['spaɪərl] N espiral f; **the inflationary ~** la espiral inflacionista ▶ ADJ en espiral ▶ vi (*prices*) dispararse

spiral staircase N escalera de caracol

spire ['spaɪəʳ] N aguja, chapitel m

★**spirit** ['spɪrɪt] N (*soul*) alma f; (*ghost*) fantasma m; (*attitude*) espíritu m; (*courage*) valor m, ánimo; **in good spirits** alegre, de buen ánimo; **community ~**, **public ~** civismo; **Holy S~** Espíritu m Santo ■ **spirits** NPL (*drink*) alcohol *msg*, bebidas *fpl* alcohólicas

spirited ['spɪrɪtɪd] ADJ enérgico, vigoroso

spirit level N nivel m de aire

★**spiritual** ['spɪrɪtjuəl] ADJ espiritual ▶ N (*also:* **Negro spiritual**) canción f religiosa, espiritual m

spiritualism ['spɪrɪtjuəlɪzəm] N espiritualismo

spit [spɪt] (*pt, pp* **spat** [spæt]) N (*for roasting*) asador m, espetón m; (*spittle*) esputo, escupitajo; (*saliva*) saliva ▶ vi escupir; (*sound*) chisporrotear

★**spite** [spaɪt] N rencor m, ojeriza; **in ~ of** a pesar de, pese a ▶ vt fastidiar

spiteful ['spaɪtful] ADJ rencoroso, malévolo

spitting ['spɪtɪŋ] N: **"~ prohibited"** "se prohíbe escupir" ▶ ADJ: **to be the ~ image of sb** ser la viva imagen de algn

spittle ['spɪtl] N saliva, baba

splash [splæʃ] N (*sound*) chapoteo; (*of colour*) mancha ▶ vt salpicar; **to ~ paint on the floor** manchar el suelo de pintura ▶ vi (*also:* **splash about**) chapotear

▶ **splash out** vi (*Brit inf*) derrochar dinero

splashdown ['splæʃdaun] N amaraje m, amerizaje m

spleen [spliːn] N (*Anat*) bazo

S

789

splendid ['splɛndɪd] ADJ espléndido

splendidly ['splɛndɪdlɪ] ADV espléndidamente; **everything went ~** todo fue a las mil maravillas

splendour, (US) **splendor** ['splɛndəʳ] N esplendor m; (fig) brillo, gloria

splice [splaɪs] VT empalmar

splint [splɪnt] N tablilla

splinter ['splɪntəʳ] N astilla; (in finger) espigón m ▶ VI astillarse, hacer astillas

splinter group N grupo disidente, facción f

★**split** [splɪt] (pt, pp ~) N hendedura, raja; (fig) división f; (Pol) escisión f; **to do the splits** hacer el spagat ▶ VT partir, rajar; (party) dividir; (work, profits) repartir; **to ~ the difference** partir la diferencia; **to ~ sth down the middle** (also fig) dividir algo en dos ▶ VI (divide) dividirse, escindirse ▶ **split up** VI (couple) separarse, romper; (meeting) acabarse

split-level ['splɪtlɛvl] ADJ (house) dúplex

split peas NPL guisantes mpl secos

split personality N doble personalidad f

split second N fracción f de segundo

splitting ['splɪtɪŋ] ADJ (headache) horrible

splutter ['splʌtəʳ] VI chisporrotear; (person) balbucear

spoil [spɔɪl] (pt, pp spoilt [spɔɪlt] or spoiled [spɔɪld]) VT (damage) dañar; (ruin) estropear, echar a perder; (child) mimar, consentir; (ballot paper) invalidar ▶ VI: **to be spoiling for a fight** estar con ganas de lucha, andar con ganas de pelea

spoiled [spɔɪld] ADJ (US: food: bad) pasado, malo; (: milk) cortado

spoils [spɔɪlz] NPL despojo sg, botín msg

spoilsport ['spɔɪlspɔːt] N aguafiestas mf

spoilt [spɔɪlt] PT, PP of **spoil** ▶ ADJ (child) mimado, consentido; (ballot paper) invalidado

spoke [spəuk] PT of **speak** ▶ N rayo, radio

spoken ['spəukn] PP of **speak**

★**spokesman** ['spəuksmən] N (irreg) portavoz m, vocero (LAM)

spokesperson ['spəukspəːsn] N portavoz mf, vocero(-a) (LAM)

★**spokeswoman** ['spəukswumən] N (irreg) portavoz f, vocera (LAM)

sponge [spʌndʒ] N esponja; (Culin: also: **sponge cake**) bizcocho ▶ VT (wash) lavar con esponja ▶ VI: **to ~ on** or (US) **off sb** vivir a costa de algn

sponge bag N (BRIT) neceser m

sponge cake N bizcocho, pastel m

sponger ['spʌndʒəʳ] N (pej) gorrón(-ona) m/f

spongy ['spʌndʒɪ] ADJ esponjoso

★**sponsor** ['spɒnsəʳ] N (Radio, TV) patrocinador(a) m/f; (for membership) padrino (madrina); (Comm) fiador(a) m/f, avalador(a) m/f ▶ VT patrocinar; apadrinar; (parliamentary bill) apoyar, respaldar; (idea etc) presentar, promover; **I sponsored him**

at 3p a mile (in fund-raising race) me apunté para darle 3 peniques la milla

sponsorship ['spɒnsəʃɪp] N patrocinio

spontaneity [spɒntə'neɪɪtɪ] N espontaneidad f

spontaneous [spɒn'teɪnɪəs] ADJ espontáneo

spontaneously [spɒn'teɪnɪəslɪ] ADV espontáneamente

spooky ['spuːkɪ] ADJ (inf: place, atmosphere) espeluznante, horripilante

spool [spuːl] N carrete m; (of sewing machine) canilla

★**spoon** [spuːn] N cuchara

spoon-feed ['spuːnfiːd] VT dar de comer con cuchara a; (fig) dárselo todo mascado a

spoonful ['spuːnful] N cucharada

sporadic [spə'rædɪk] ADJ esporádico

★**sport** [spɔːt] N deporte m; (amusement) juego, diversión f; **to be a good ~** (person) ser muy majo; **indoor/outdoor sports** deportes mpl en pista cubierta/al aire libre; **to say sth in ~** decir algo en broma

sport coat N (US) = **sports jacket**

sporting ['spɔːtɪŋ] ADJ deportivo; **to give sb a ~ chance** darle a algn su oportunidad

sport jacket N (US) = **sports jacket**

sports car N coche m sport

sports centre N (BRIT) polideportivo

sports coat N (US) = **sports jacket**

sports drink N bebida energética, bebida isotónica

sports ground N campo de deportes, centro deportivo

sports jacket, (US) **sport jacket** N chaqueta deportiva

sportsman ['spɔːtsmən] N (irreg) deportista m

sportsmanship ['spɔːtsmənʃɪp] N deportividad f

sports pages NPL páginas fpl deportivas

sports utility vehicle N SUV m, todoterreno m inv

sportswear ['spɔːtswɛəʳ] N ropa de deporte

sportswoman ['spɔːtswumən] N (irreg) deportista

sporty ['spɔːtɪ] ADJ deportivo

★**spot** [spɒt] N sitio, lugar m; (dot: on pattern) punto, mancha; (pimple) grano; (also: **advertising spot**) spot m; **on the ~** en el acto; (in difficulty) en un aprieto; **to do sth on the ~** hacer algo en el acto; **to put sb on the ~** poner a algn en un apuro ▶ VT (notice) notar, observar ▶ ADJ (Comm) inmediatamente efectivo

spot check N reconocimiento rápido

spotless ['spɒtlɪs] ADJ (clean) inmaculado; (reputation) intachable

spotlessly ['spɒtlɪslɪ] ADV: **~ clean** limpísimo

spotlight ['spɒtlaɪt] N foco, reflector m; (Aut) faro auxiliar

spot-on [spɔt'ɔn] ADJ (BRIT inf) exacto

spot price N precio de entrega inmediata

spotted ['spɔtɪd] ADJ (pattern) de puntos

spotty ['spɔtɪ] ADJ (face) con granos

spouse [spauz] N cónyuge mf

spout [spaut] N (of jug) pico; (pipe) caño ▶ VI chorrear

sprain [spreɪn] N torcedura, esguince m ▶ VT: **to ~ one's ankle** torcerse el tobillo

sprang [spræŋ] PT of **spring**

sprawl [sprɔːl] VI tumbarse; **to send sb sprawling** tirar a algn al suelo ▶ N: **urban ~** crecimiento urbano descontrolado

sprawling ['sprɔːlɪŋ] ADJ (town) desparramado

★**spray** [spreɪ] N rociada; (of sea) espuma; (container) atomizador m; (of paint) pistola rociadora; (of flowers) ramita ▶ VT rociar; (crops) regar ▶ CPD (deodorant) en atomizador

★**spread** [spred] (pt, pp ~) N extensión f; (of idea) diseminación f; (inf: food) comilona; (Press, Typ: two pages) plana; **middle-age ~** gordura de la mediana edad ▶ VT extender; diseminar; (butter) untar; (wings, sails) desplegar; (scatter) esparcir; **repayments will be ~ over 18 months** los pagos se harán a lo largo de 18 meses ▶ VI (also: **spread out**: stain) extenderse; (news) diseminarse

▶ **spread out** VI (move apart) separarse

spread-eagled ['spredi:gld] ADJ: **to be ~** estar despatarrado

spreadsheet ['spredʃi:t] N (Comput) hoja de cálculo

spree [spri:] N: **to go on a ~** ir de juerga or (LAM) farra

sprightly ['spraɪtlɪ] ADJ vivo, enérgico

★**spring** [sprɪŋ] (pt **sprang** [spræŋ], pp **sprung** [sprʌŋ]) N (season) primavera; (leap) salto, brinco; (coiled metal) resorte m; (of water) fuente f, manantial m; (bounciness) elasticidad f; **in (the) ~** en (la) primavera; **to walk with a ~ in one's step** andar dando saltos or brincos ▶ VI (arise) brotar, nacer; (leap) saltar, brincar; **to ~ into action** lanzarse a la acción ▶ VT: **to ~ a leak** (pipe etc) empezar a hacer agua; **he sprang the news on me** de repente me soltó la noticia

▶ **spring up** VI (thing: appear) aparecer; (problem) surgir

springboard ['sprɪŋbɔːd] N trampolín m

spring-clean [sprɪŋ'kliːn] N (also: **spring-cleaning**) limpieza general

spring onion N cebolleta

spring roll N rollito de primavera

springtime ['sprɪŋtaɪm] N primavera

springy ['sprɪŋɪ] ADJ elástico; (grass) mullido

sprinkle ['sprɪŋkl] VT (pour: liquid) rociar; (: salt, sugar) espolvorear; **to ~ water** etc **on**, **~ with water** etc rociar or salpicar de agua etc

sprinkler ['sprɪŋklə'] N (for lawn) aspersor m; (to put out fire) aparato de rociadura automática

sprinkling ['sprɪŋklɪŋ] N (of water) rociada; **a ~ of salt/sugar** un poco de sal/azúcar

sprint [sprɪnt] N (e)sprint m; **the 200 metres ~** los 200 metros lisos ▶ VI (gen) correr a toda velocidad; (Sport) esprintar

sprinter ['sprɪntə'] N velocista mf

spritzer ['sprɪtsə'] N vino blanco con soda

sprocket ['sprɔkɪt] N (on printer etc) rueda dentada

sprocket feed N avance m por rueda dentada

sprout [spraut] VI brotar, retoñar ▶ N: **(Brussels) sprouts** npl coles fpl de Bruselas

spruce [spru:s] N (Bot) pícea ▶ ADJ aseado, pulcro

▶ **spruce up** VT (tidy) arreglar, acicalar; (smarten up: room etc) ordenar; **to ~ o.s. up** arreglarse

sprung [sprʌŋ] PP of **spring**

spry [spraɪ] ADJ ágil, activo

SPUC N ABBR (= Society for the Protection of Unborn Children) ≈ Federación f Española de Asociaciones Provida

spun [spʌn] PT, PP of **spin**

spur [spə:'] N espuela; (fig) estímulo, aguijón m; **on the ~ of the moment** de improviso ▶ VT (also: **spur on**) estimular, incitar

spurious ['spjuərɪəs] ADJ falso

spurn [spə:n] VT desdeñar, rechazar

spurt [spə:t] N chorro; (of energy) arrebato; **to put in** or **on a ~** (runner) acelerar; (fig: in work etc) hacer un gran esfuerzo ▶ VI chorrear

sputter ['spʌtə'] VI = **splutter**

spy [spaɪ] N espía mf ▶ VI: **to ~ on** espiar a ▶ VT (see) divisar, lograr ver ▶ CPD (film, story) de espionaje

spycam ['spaɪkæm] N cámara f oculta

spying ['spaɪɪŋ] N espionaje m

spyware ['spaɪwɛə'] N (Comput) spyware m

Sq. ABBR (in address: = Square) Pl.

sq. ABBR (Math etc) = **square**

squabble ['skwɔbl] N riña, pelea ▶ VI reñir, pelear

squad [skwɔd] N (Mil) pelotón m; (Police) brigada; (Sport) equipo; **flying ~** (Police) brigada móvil

squad car N (Police) coche-patrulla m

squaddie ['skwɔdɪ] N (Mil: inf) chivo

squadron ['skwɔdrn] N (Mil) escuadrón m; (Aviat, Naut) escuadra

squalid ['skwɔlɪd] ADJ miserable

squall [skwɔːl] N (storm) chubasco; (wind) ráfaga

squalor ['skwɔlə'] N miseria

squander ['skwɔndə'] VT (money) derrochar, despilfarrar; (chances) desperdiciar

★**square** [skwɛə'] N cuadro; (in town) plaza; (US: block of houses) manzana, cuadra (LAM); (inf: person) carca mf; **we're back to ~ one** (fig) hemos vuelto al punto de partida ▶ ADJ cua-

S

drado; (inf: *ideas, tastes*) trasnochado; **all ~** igual(es); **a ~ meal** una comida decente; **two metres ~** dos metros por dos; **one ~ metre** un metro cuadrado; **to get one's accounts ~** dejar las cuentas claras ▶ VT (*arrange*) arreglar; (*Math*) cuadrar; (*reconcile*) compaginar; **I'll ~ it with him** (inf) yo lo arreglo con él; **can you ~ it with your conscience?** ¿cómo se justifica ante sí mismo? ▶ VI cuadrar, conformarse

▶ **square up** VI (*settle*): **to ~ up (with sb)** ajustar cuentas (con algn)

square bracket N (*Typ*) corchete *m*

squarely [ˈskwɛəlɪ] ADV (*fully*) de lleno; (*honestly, fairly*) honradamente, justamente

square root N raíz *f* cuadrada

squash [skwɔʃ] N (*vegetable*) calabaza; (*Sport*) squash *m*; (BRIT: *drink*): **lemon/orange ~** zumo (SP) *or* jugo (LAM) de limón/naranja ▶ VT aplastar

squat [skwɔt] ADJ achaparrado ▶ VI agacharse, sentarse en cuclillas; **to ~ in/on** (*property*) ocupar (ilegalmente)

squatter [ˈskwɔtəʳ] N ocupante *mf* ilegal, okupa *mf*

squawk [skwɔːk] VI graznar

squeak [skwiːk] VI (*hinge, wheel*) chirriar, rechinar; (*shoe, wood*) crujir; (*mouse*) chillar ▶ N (*of hinge, wheel etc*) chirrido, rechinamiento; (*of shoes*) crujir *m*; (*of mouse etc*) chillido

squeaky [ˈskwiːkɪ] ADJ que cruje; **to be ~ clean** (*fig*) ser superhonrado

squeal [skwiːl] VI chillar, dar gritos agudos

squeamish [ˈskwiːmɪʃ] ADJ delicado, remilgado

★**squeeze** [skwiːz] N presión *f*; (*of hand*) apretón *m*; (*Comm: credit squeeze*) restricción *f*; **a ~ of lemon** unas gotas de limón ▶ VT (*lemon etc*) exprimir; (*hand, arm*) apretar ▶ VI: **to ~ past/under sth** colarse al lado de/por debajo de algo
▶ **squeeze out** VT exprimir; (*fig*) excluir
▶ **squeeze through** VI abrirse paso con esfuerzos

squelch [skwɛltʃ] VI chapotear

squid [skwɪd] N *pl inv* calamar *m*

squiggle [ˈskwɪɡl] N garabato

squint [skwɪnt] VI bizquear, ser bizco; **to ~ at sth** mirar algo entornando los ojos ▶ N (*Med*) estrabismo

squire [ˈskwaɪəʳ] N (BRIT) terrateniente *m*

squirm [skwəːm] VI retorcerse, revolverse

★**squirrel** [ˈskwɪrəl] N ardilla

squirt [skwəːt] VI salir a chorros ▶ VT chiscar

Sr ABBR = **senior**; (*Rel*) = **sister**

SRC N ABBR (BRIT: = *Students' Representative Council*) *consejo de estudiantes*

Sri Lanka [srɪˈlæŋkə] N Sri Lanka *m*

SRO ABBR (US) = **standing room only**

SS ABBR (= *steamship*) M.V.

SSA N ABBR (US: = *Social Security Administration*) = Seguro Social

SST N ABBR (US) = **supersonic transport**

ST ABBR (US: = *Standard Time*) hora oficial

St ABBR (= *saint*) Sto.(-a.); (= *street*) c/

stab [stæb] N (*with knife etc*) puñalada; (*of pain*) pinchazo; **to have a ~ at (doing) sth** (inf) probar (a hacer) algo ▶ VT apuñalar; **to ~ sb to death** matar a algn a puñaladas

stabbing [ˈstæbɪŋ] N: **there's been a ~** han apuñalado a alguien ▶ ADJ (*pain*) punzante

stability [stəˈbɪlɪtɪ] N estabilidad *f*

stabilization [steɪbəlaɪˈzeɪʃən] N estabilización *f*

stabilize [ˈsteɪbəlaɪz] VT estabilizar ▶ VI estabilizarse

stabilizer [ˈsteɪbəlaɪzəʳ] N (*Aviat, Naut*) estabilizador *m*

★**stable** [ˈsteɪbl] ADJ estable ▶ N cuadra, caballeriza; **riding stables** escuela hípica

staccato [stəˈkɑːtəu] ADJ, ADV staccato

stack [stæk] N montón *m*, pila; (inf) mar *f*; **there's stacks of time to finish it** hay cantidad de tiempo para acabarlo ▶ VT amontonar, apilar

stacker [ˈstækəʳ] N (*for printer*) apiladora

★**stadium** [ˈsteɪdɪəm] N estadio

★**staff** [stɑːf] N (*work force*) personal *m*, plantilla; (BRIT Scol: *also*: **teaching staff**) cuerpo docente; (*stick*) bastón *m* ▶ VT proveer de personal; **to be staffed by Asians/women** tener una plantilla asiática/femenina

staffroom [ˈstɑːfruːm] N sala de profesores

stag [stæg] N ciervo, venado; (BRIT Stock Exchange) especulador *m* con nuevas emisiones

★**stage** [steɪdʒ] N escena; (*point*) etapa; (*platform*) plataforma; **the ~** el escenario, el teatro; **in stages** por etapas; **in the early/final stages** en las primeras/últimas etapas; **to go through a difficult ~** pasar una fase *or* etapa mala ▶ VT (*play*) poner en escena, representar; (*organize*) montar, organizar; (*fig: perform: recovery etc*) efectuar

stagecoach [ˈsteɪdʒkəutʃ] N diligencia

stage door N entrada de artistas

stagehand [ˈsteɪdʒhænd] N tramoyista *mf*

stage-manage [ˈsteɪdʒmænɪdʒ] VT (*fig*) manipular

stage manager N director(a) *m/f* de escena

stagger [ˈstæɡəʳ] VI tambalear ▶ VT (*amaze*) asombrar; (*hours, holidays*) escalonar

staggering [ˈstæɡərɪŋ] ADJ (*amazing*) asombroso, pasmoso

staging post [ˈsteɪdʒɪŋ-] N escala

stagnant [ˈstæɡnənt] ADJ estancado

stagnate [stæɡˈneɪt] VI estancarse; (*fig: economy, mind*) quedarse estancado

stagnation [stæɡˈneɪʃən] N estancamiento

stag night, stag party N despedida de soltero

staid [steɪd] ADJ (clothes) serio, formal

stain [steɪn] N mancha; (colouring) tintura ▶ VT manchar; (wood) teñir

stained glass N vidrio m de color

stained glass window [steɪnd-] N vidriera de colores

stainless ['steɪnlɪs] ADJ (steel) inoxidable

stainless steel N acero inoxidable

stain remover N quitamanchas m inv

stair [steə'] N (step) peldaño, escalón m ■ **stairs** NPL escaleras fpl

staircase ['steəkeɪs], **stairway** ['steəweɪ] N escalera

stairwell ['steəwel] N hueco or caja de la escalera

stake [steɪk] N estaca, poste m; (Comm) interés m; (Betting) apuesta; **to be at ~** estar en juego; **to have a ~ in sth** tener interés en algo ▶ VT (bet) apostar; (also: **stake out**: area) cercar con estacas; **to ~ a claim to (sth)** presentar reclamación por or reclamar (algo)

stake-out ['steɪkaut] N vigilancia; **to be on a ~** estar de vigilancia

stalactite ['stæləktaɪt] N estalactita

stalagmite ['stæləgmaɪt] N estalagmita

stale [steɪl] ADJ (bread) duro; (food) pasado; (smell) rancio; (beer) agrio

stalemate ['steɪlmeɪt] N tablas fpl; **to reach ~** (fig) estancarse, alcanzar un punto muerto

stalk [stɔːk] N tallo, caña ▶ VT acechar, cazar al acecho ▶ VI: **to ~ off** irse airado

stall [stɔːl] N (in market) puesto; (in stable) casilla (de establo); **a newspaper ~** un quiosco (de periódicos); **a flower ~** un puesto de flores ■ **stalls** NPL (BRIT) (in cinema, theatre) butacas fpl ▶ VT (Aut) parar, calar; (fig) dar largas a ▶ VI (Aut) pararse, calarse; (fig) buscar evasivas

stallholder ['stɔːlhəuldə'] N dueño(-a) de un puesto

stallion ['stæliən] N semental m, garañón m

stalwart ['stɔːlwət] N partidario(-a) incondicional

stamen ['steɪmən] N estambre m

stamina ['stæmɪnə] N resistencia

stammer ['stæmə'] N tartamudeo, balbuceo ▶ VI tartamudear, balbucir

★**stamp** [stæmp] N sello, estampilla (LAm); (mark) marca, huella; (on document) timbre m ▶ VI (also: **stamp one's foot**) patear ▶ VT patear, golpear con el pie; (letter) poner sellos en, franquear; (with rubber stamp) marcar con sello; **stamped addressed envelope (sae)** sobre m franqueado con la dirección propia

▶ **stamp out** VT (fire) apagar con el pie; (crime, opposition) acabar con

stamp album N álbum m para sellos

stamp collecting N filatelia

stamp duty N (BRIT) derecho de timbre

stampede [stæm'piːd] N (of cattle) estampida

stamp machine N máquina (expendedora) de sellos

stance [stæns] N postura

★**stand** [stænd] (pt, pp **stood** [stud]) N (attitude) posición f, postura; (for taxis) parada; (also: **music stand**) atril m; (Sport) tribuna; (at exhibition) stand m; **to make a ~** (fig) resistir, mantener una postura firme; **to take a ~ on an issue** adoptar una actitud hacia una cuestión ▶ VI (be) estar, encontrarse; (be on foot) estar de pie; (rise) levantarse; (remain) quedar en pie; **to ~ for parliament** (BRIT) presentarse (como candidato) a las elecciones; **nothing stands in our way** nada nos lo impide; **to ~ still** quedarse inmóvil; **to let sth ~ as it is** dejar algo como está; **as things ~** tal como están las cosas; **to ~ guard** or **watch** (Mil) hacer guardia ▶ VT (place) poner, colocar; (tolerate, withstand) aguantar, soportar; **to ~ sb a drink/meal** invitar a algn a una copa/a comer; **the company will have to ~ the loss** la empresa tendrá que hacer frente a las pérdidas; **I can't ~ him** no le aguanto, no le puedo ver

▶ **stand aside** VI apartarse, mantenerse aparte

▶ **stand back** VI retirarse

▶ **stand by** VI (be ready) estar listo ▶ VT FUS (opinion) mantener

▶ **stand down** VI (withdraw) ceder el puesto; (Mil, Law) retirarse

▶ **stand for** VT FUS (signify) significar; (tolerate) aguantar, permitir

▶ **stand in for** VT FUS suplir a

▶ **stand out** VI (be prominent) destacarse

▶ **stand up** VI (rise) levantarse, ponerse de pie

▶ **stand up for** VT FUS defender

▶ **stand up to** VT FUS hacer frente a

stand-alone ['stændələun] ADJ (Comput) autónomo

★**standard** ['stændəd] N patrón m, norma; (flag) estandarte m; **the gold ~** (Comm) el patrón oro; **high/low ~** alto/bajo nivel; **below** or **not up to ~** (work) de calidad inferior; **to apply a double ~** aplicar un doble criterio ▶ ADJ (size etc) normal, corriente, estándar ■ **standards** NPL (morals) valores mpl morales

Standard Grade N (SCOTTISH Scol) certificado del último ciclo de la enseñanza secundaria obligatoria

standardization [stændədaɪ'zeɪʃən] N normalización f

standardize ['stændədaɪz] VT estandarizar

standard lamp N (BRIT) lámpara de pie

standard model N modelo estándar

standard of living N nivel m de vida

standard practice N norma, práctica común

standard rate N tasa de imposición

standard time N hora oficial

stand-by ['stændbaɪ] N (alert) alerta, aviso; (also: **stand-by ticket**: Theat) entrada reducida de última hora; (: Aviat) billete m standby; **to be on ~** estar preparado; (doctor) estar listo para acudir; (Aviat) estar en la lista de espera

S

793

stand-by generator N generador *m* de reserva

stand-by passenger N (*Aviat*) pasajero(-a) en lista de espera

stand-by ticket N (*Aviat*) (billete *m*) standby *m*

stand-in ['stændɪn] N suplente *mf*; (*Cine*) doble *mf*

standing ['stændɪŋ] ADJ (*upright*) derecho; (*on foot*) de pie, en pie; (*permanent: committee*) permanente; (*: rule*) fijo; (*: army*) permanente, regular; (*grievance*) constante, viejo; **he was given a ~ ovation** le dieron una calurosa ovación de pie; **~ joke** motivo constante de broma ▶ N reputación *f*; (*duration*): **of six months' ~** que lleva seis meses; **of many years' ~** que lleva muchos años; **a man of some ~** un hombre de cierta posición *or* categoría

standing order N (*BRIT: at bank*) giro bancario; **~s** *npl* (*Mil*) reglamento *sg* general

standing room N sitio para estar de pie

stand-off ['stændɔf] N punto muerto

stand-offish [stænd'ɔfɪʃ] ADJ distante

standpipe ['stændpaɪp] N tubo vertical

standpoint ['stændpɔɪnt] N punto de vista

standstill ['stændstɪl] N: **at a ~** (*industry, traffic*) paralizado, en un punto muerto; **to come to a ~** pararse, quedar paralizado

stank [stæŋk] PT of **stink**

staple ['steɪpl] N (*for papers*) grapa; (*product*) producto *or* artículo de primera necesidad ▶ ADJ (*crop, industry, food etc*) básico ▶ VT grapar

stapler ['steɪpləʳ] N grapadora

★**star** [stɑːʳ] N estrella; (*celebrity*) estrella, astro; **4-star petrol** gasolina súper; **four-star hotel** hotel *m* de cuatro estrellas ▶ VI: **to ~ in** ser la estrella de ▶ VT (*Theat, Cine*) tener como protagonista ■ **the stars** NPL (*Astrology*) el horóscopo

star attraction N atracción *f* principal

starboard ['stɑːbəd] N estribor *m*

starch [stɑːtʃ] N almidón *m*

starchy ['stɑːtʃɪ] ADJ (*food*) feculento

stardom ['stɑːdəm] N estrellato

★**stare** [stɛəʳ] N mirada fija ▶ VI: **to ~ at** mirar fijo

starfish ['stɑːfɪʃ] N estrella de mar

stark [stɑːk] ADJ (*bleak*) severo, escueto; (*simplicity, colour*) austero; (*reality, truth*) puro; (*poverty*) absoluto ▶ ADV: **~ naked** en cueros

starkers ['stɑːkəz] ADJ (*BRIT inf*): **to be ~** estar en cueros

starlet ['stɑːlɪt] N (*Cine*) actriz *f* principiante

starling ['stɑːlɪŋ] N estornino

starry ['stɑːrɪ] ADJ estrellado

starry-eyed [stɑːrɪ'aɪd] ADJ (*gullible, innocent*) inocentón(-ona), ingenuo; (*idealistic*) idealista; (*from wonder*) asombrado; (*from love*) enamoradísimo

Stars and Stripes NPL: **the ~** las barras y las estrellas, la bandera de EE.UU.

star sign N signo del zodíaco

star-studded ['stɑːstʌdɪd] ADJ: **a ~ cast** un elenco estelar

★**start** [stɑːt] N (*beginning*) principio, comienzo; (*departure*) salida; (*sudden movement*) sobresalto; (*advantage*) ventaja; **to give sb a ~** dar un susto a algn; **at the ~** al principio; **for a ~** en primer lugar; **to make an early ~** ponerse en camino temprano; **the thieves had three hours' ~** los ladrones llevaban tres horas de ventaja ▶ VT empezar, comenzar; (*cause*) causar; (*found: business, newspaper*) establecer, fundar; (*engine*) poner en marcha; **to ~ a fire** provocar un incendio; **to ~ doing** *or* **to do sth** empezar a hacer algo ▶ VI (*begin*) comenzar, empezar; (*with fright*) asustarse, sobresaltarse; (*train etc*) salir; **to ~ (off) with ...** (*firstly*) para empezar ...; (*at the beginning*) al principio

▶ **start off** VI empezar, comenzar; (*leave*) salir, ponerse en camino

▶ **start out** VI (*begin*) empezar; (*set out*) partir, salir

▶ **start over** VI (*US*) volver a empezar

▶ **start up** VI comenzar; (*car*) ponerse en marcha ▶ VT comenzar; (*car*) poner en marcha

starter ['stɑːtəʳ] N (*Aut*) botón *m* de arranque; (*BRIT Culin*) entrada, entrante *m*; (*Sport: official*) juez(a) *m/f* de salida; (*: runner*) corredor(a) *m/f*

starting point ['stɑːtɪŋ-] N punto de partida

starting price N (*Comm*) precio inicial

startle ['stɑːtl] VT sobresaltar

startling ['stɑːtlɪŋ] ADJ alarmante

star turn N (*BRIT*) atracción *f* principal

starvation [stɑː'veɪʃən] N hambre *f*, hambruna (*LAM*); (*Med*) inanición *f*

starvation wages NPL sueldo *sg* de hambre

starve [stɑːv] VI pasar hambre; (*to death*) morir de hambre; **I'm starving** estoy muerto de hambre ▶ VT hacer pasar hambre; (*fig*) privar

stash [stæʃ] VT: **to ~ sth away** (*inf*) poner algo a buen recaudo

★**state** [steɪt] N estado; (*pomp*): **in ~** con mucha ceremonia; **~ of emergency** estado de excepción *or* emergencia; **~ of mind** estado de ánimo; **to lie in ~** (*corpse*) estar de cuerpo presente; **to be in a ~** estar agitado; **the States** los Estados Unidos ▶ VT (*say, declare*) afirmar; (*a case*) presentar, exponer

State Department N (*US*) Ministerio de Asuntos Exteriores

state education N (*BRIT*) enseñanza pública

stateless ['steɪtlɪs] ADJ desnacionalizado

stately ['steɪtlɪ] ADJ majestuoso, imponente

★**statement** ['steɪtmənt] N afirmación *f*; (*Law*) declaración *f*; (*Comm*) estado; **official ~** informe *m* oficial; **~ of account, bank ~** estado de cuenta

state-of-the-art ['steɪtəvðɪ'ɑːt] ADJ (*technology etc*) puntero

state-owned ['steɪtəund] ADJ estatal, del estado

state school N escuela or colegio estatal

statesman ['steɪtsmən] N (irreg) estadista m

statesmanship ['steɪtsmənʃɪp] N habilidad f política, arte m de gobernar

static ['stætɪk] N (Radio) parásitos mpl ▶ ADJ estático

static electricity N electricidad f estática

★**station** ['steɪʃən] N (gen) estación f; (place) puesto, sitio; (Radio) emisora; (rank) posición f social; **action stations!** ¡a los puestos de combate! ▶ VT colocar, situar; (Mil) apostar; **to be stationed in** (Mil) estar estacionado en

stationary ['steɪʃnərɪ] ADJ estacionario, fijo

stationer ['steɪʃənər] N papelero(-a)

stationer's, stationer's shop N (BRIT) papelería

stationery ['steɪʃənərɪ] N (writing paper) papel m de escribir; (writing materials) artículos mpl de escritorio

station master N (Rail) jefe m de estación

station wagon N (US) ranchera

statistic [stə'tɪstɪk] N estadística

statistical [stə'tɪstɪkl] ADJ estadístico

statistics [stə'tɪstɪks] N (science) estadística

statue ['stætju:] N estatua

statuette [stætju'et] N figurilla

stature ['stætʃər] N estatura; (fig) talla

status ['steɪtəs] N condición f, estado; (reputation) reputación f, estatus m

status line N (Comput) línea de situación or de estado

status quo N (e)statu quo m

status symbol N símbolo de prestigio

statute ['stætju:t] N estatuto, ley f

statute book N código de leyes

statutory ['stætjutrɪ] ADJ estatutario; **~ meeting** junta ordinaria

staunch [stɔ:ntʃ] ADJ leal, incondicional ▶ VT (flow, blood) restañar

stave [steɪv] VT: **to ~ off** (attack) rechazar; (threat) evitar

★**stay** [steɪ] N (period of time) estancia; (Law): **~ of execution** aplazamiento de una sentencia ▶ VI (remain) quedar(se); (as guest) hospedarse; **to ~ put** seguir en el mismo sitio ▶ VT (spend) pasar; **to ~ the night/5 days** pasar la noche/ estar or quedarse 5 días
  ▶ **stay away** VI (from person, building) no acercarse; (from event) no acudir
  ▶ **stay behind** VI quedar atrás
  ▶ **stay in** VI (at home) quedarse en casa
  ▶ **stay on** VI quedarse
  ▶ **stay out** VI (of house) no volver a casa; (strikers) no volver al trabajo
  ▶ **stay up** VI (at night) velar, no acostarse

staycation [steɪ'keɪʃən] N (inf) vacaciones fpl en casa

staying power ['steɪɪŋ-] N resistencia, aguante m

STD N ABBR (= sexually transmitted disease) ETS f; (BRIT: = subscriber trunk dialling) servicio de conferencias automáticas

stead [sted] N: **in sb's ~** en lugar de algn; **to stand sb in good ~** ser muy útil a algn

steadfast ['stedfɑ:st] ADJ firme, resuelto

steadily ['stedɪlɪ] ADV (firmly) firmemente; (unceasingly) sin parar; (fixedly) fijamente; (drive) a velocidad constante

★**steady** ['stedɪ] ADJ (fixed) firme, fijo; (regular) regular; (boyfriend etc) formal, fijo; (person, character) sensato, juicioso ▶ VT (hold) mantener firme; (stabilize) estabilizar; (nerves) calmar; **to ~ o.s. on** or **against sth** afirmarse en algo

steak [steɪk] N (gen) filete m; (beef) bistec m

★**steal** [sti:l] (pt stole [stəul], pp stolen ['stəuln]) VT, VI robar
  ▶ **steal away, steal off** VI marcharse furtivamente, escabullirse

stealth [stelθ] N: **by ~** a escondidas, sigilosamente

stealthy ['stelθɪ] ADJ cauteloso, sigiloso

★**steam** [sti:m] N vapor m; (mist) vaho, humo; **under one's own ~** (fig) por sus propios medios or propias fuerzas; **to run out of ~** (fig: person) quedar(se) agotado, quemarse; **to let off ~** (fig) desahogarse ▶ VT (Culin) cocer al vapor ▶ VI echar vapor; (ship): **to ~ along** avanzar, ir avanzando
  ▶ **steam up** VT empañar; **to get steamed up about sth** (fig) ponerse negro por algo ▶ VI (window) empañarse

steam engine N máquina de vapor

steamer ['sti:mər] N (buque m de) vapor m; (Culin) recipiente para cocinar al vapor

steam iron N plancha de vapor

steamroller ['sti:mrəulər] N apisonadora

steamship ['sti:mʃɪp] N = **steamer**

steamy ['sti:mɪ] ADJ (room) lleno de vapor; (window) empañado; (heat, atmosphere) bochornoso

★**steel** [sti:l] N acero ▶ ADJ de acero

steel band N banda de percusión del Caribe

steel industry N industria siderúrgica

steel mill N fábrica de acero

steelworks ['sti:lwə:ks] N acería, fundición f de acero

steely ['sti:lɪ] ADJ (determination) inflexible; (gaze) duro; (eyes) penetrante; **~ grey** gris m metálico

steelyard ['sti:ljɑ:d] N romana

steep [sti:p] ADJ escarpado, abrupto; (stair) empinado; (price) exorbitante, excesivo ▶ VT empapar, remojar

steeple ['sti:pl] N aguja, campanario

steeplechase ['sti:pltʃeɪs] N carrera de obstáculos

steeplejack ['sti:pldʒæk] N reparador(a) m/f de chimeneas or de campanarios

S

steer [stɪə^r] VT (car) conducir (SP), manejar (LAM); (person) dirigir, guiar ▶ VI conducir (SP), manejar (LAM); **to ~ clear of sb/sth** (fig) esquivar a algn/evadir algo

steering ['stɪərɪŋ] N (Aut) dirección f

steering committee N comisión f directiva

steering wheel N volante m

stellar ['stɛlə^r] ADJ estelar

stem [stɛm] N (of plant) tallo; (of glass) pie m; (of pipe) cañón m ▶ VT detener; (blood) restañar
  ▶ **stem from** VT FUS ser consecuencia de

stem cell N célula madre

stench [stɛntʃ] N hedor m

stencil ['stɛnsl] N (typed) cliché m, clisé m; (lettering) plantilla ▶ VT hacer un cliché de

stenographer [stɛ'nɔgrəfə^r] N (US) taquígrafo(-a)

★**step** [stɛp] N paso; (sound) paso, pisada; (stair) peldaño, escalón m; **~ by ~** paso a paso; (fig) poco a poco; **to keep in ~ (with)** llevar el paso de; (fig) llevar el paso de, estar de acuerdo con; **to be in/out of ~ with** estar acorde con/estar en disonancia con; **to take steps to solve a problem** tomar medidas para resolver un problema ▶ VI: **to ~ forward** dar un paso adelante ■ **steps** NPL (BRIT) = **stepladder**
  ▶ **step down** VI (fig) retirarse
  ▶ **step in** VI entrar; (fig) intervenir
  ▶ **step off** VT FUS bajar de
  ▶ **step on** VT FUS pisar
  ▶ **step over** VT FUS pasar por encima de
  ▶ **step up** VT (increase) aumentar

step aerobics NPL step m

★**stepbrother** ['stɛpbrʌðə^r] N hermanastro

stepchild ['stɛptʃaɪld] N (irreg) hijastro(-a)

stepdad ['stɛpdæd] N padrastro

★**stepdaughter** ['stɛpdɔːtə^r] N hijastra

★**stepfather** ['stɛpfɑːðə^r] N padrastro

stepladder ['stɛplædə^r] N escalera doble or de tijera

★**stepmother** ['stɛpmʌðə^r] N madrastra

stepmum ['stɛpmʌm] N madrastra

stepping stone ['stɛpɪŋ-] N pasadera

step Reebok® [-'riːbɔk] N step m

★**stepsister** ['stɛpsɪstə^r] N hermanastra

★**stepson** ['stɛpsʌn] N hijastro

stereo ['stɛrɪəu] N estéreo; **in ~** en estéreo ▶ ADJ (also: **stereophonic**) estéreo, estereofónico

stereotype ['stɪərɪətaɪp] N estereotipo ▶ VT estereotipar

sterile ['stɛraɪl] ADJ estéril

sterilization [stɛrɪlaɪ'zeɪʃən] N esterilización f

sterilize ['stɛrɪlaɪz] VT esterilizar

sterling ['stəːlɪŋ] ADJ (silver) de ley; **a pound ~** una libra esterlina; **he is of ~ character** tiene un carácter excelente ▶ N (Econ) libras fpl esterlinas

stern [stəːn] ADJ severo, austero ▶ N (Naut) popa

sternum ['stəːnəm] N esternón m

steroid ['stɪərɔɪd] N esteroide m

stethoscope ['stɛθəskəup] N estetoscopio

stevedore ['stiːvədɔː^r] N estibador m

stew [stjuː] N cocido, estofado, guisado (LAM) ▶ VT, VI estofar, guisar; (fruit) cocer; **stewed fruit** compota de fruta

★**steward** ['stjuːəd] N (gen) camarero; (shop steward) enlace mf sindical

★**stewardess** ['stjuːədəs] N azafata

stewardship ['stjuːədʃɪp] N tutela

stewing steak ['stjuːɪŋ-], (US) **stew meat** N carne f de vaca

St. Ex. ABBR = **stock exchange**

★**stick** [stɪk] (pt, pp **stuck** [stʌk]) N palo; (as weapon) porra; (also: **walking stick**) bastón m; **to get hold of the wrong end of the ~** entender al revés ▶ VT (glue) pegar; (inf: put) meter; (: tolerate) aguantar, soportar; **to ~ sth into** clavar or hincar algo en ▶ VI pegarse; (come to a stop) quedarse parado; (get jammed: door, lift) atascarse; **to ~ to** (word, principles) atenerse a, ser fiel a; (promise) cumplir; **it stuck in my mind** se me quedó grabado
  ▶ **stick around** VI (inf) quedarse
  ▶ **stick out** VI sobresalir ▶ VT: **to ~ it out** (inf) aguantar
  ▶ **stick up** VI sobresalir
  ▶ **stick up for** VT FUS defender

sticker ['stɪkə^r] N (label) etiqueta adhesiva; (with slogan) pegatina

sticking plaster ['stɪkɪŋ-] N (BRIT) esparadrapo

sticking point N (fig) punto de fricción

stick insect N insecto palo

stickler ['stɪklə^r] N: **to be a ~ for** insistir mucho en

stick shift N (US Aut) palanca de cambios

stick-up ['stɪkʌp] N (inf) asalto, atraco

sticky ['stɪkɪ] ADJ pegajoso; (label) adhesivo; (fig) difícil

stiff [stɪf] ADJ rígido, tieso; (hard) duro; (difficult) difícil; (person) inflexible; (price) exorbitante; **to have a ~ neck/back** tener tortícolis/dolor de espalda; **the door's ~** la puerta está atrancada ▶ ADV: **scared/bored ~** muerto de miedo/aburrimiento

stiffen ['stɪfn] VT hacer más rígido; (limb) entumecer ▶ VI endurecerse; (grow stronger) fortalecerse

stiffness ['stɪfnɪs] N rigidez f

stifle ['staɪfl] VT ahogar, sofocar

stifling ['staɪflɪŋ] ADJ (heat) sofocante, bochornoso

stigma ['stɪgmə] N (pl Bot, Med, Rel **stigmata** [stɪg'mɑːtə], fig **stigmas**) estigma m

stile [staɪl] N escalera (para pasar una cerca)

stiletto [stɪˈlɛtəu] N (BRIT: *also*: **stiletto heel**) tacón *m* de aguja

★**still** [stɪl] ADJ inmóvil, quieto; *(orange juice etc)* sin gas; **keep ~!** ¡estate quieto!, ¡no te muevas! ▶ ADV *(up to this time)* todavía; *(even)* aún; *(nonetheless)* sin embargo, aun así; **he ~ hasn't arrived** todavía no ha llegado ▶ N *(Cine)* foto *f* fija

stillborn [ˈstɪlbɔːn] ADJ nacido muerto

still life N naturaleza muerta

stilt [stɪlt] N zanco; *(pile)* pilar *m*, soporte *m*

stilted [ˈstɪltɪd] ADJ afectado, artificial

stimulant [ˈstɪmjulənt] N estimulante *m*

stimulate [ˈstɪmjuleɪt] VT estimular

stimulating [ˈstɪmjuleɪtɪŋ] ADJ estimulante

stimulation [stɪmjuˈleɪʃən] N estímulo

stimulus [ˈstɪmjuləs] *(pl* **stimuli** [-laɪ]*)* N estímulo, incentivo

sting [stɪŋ] *(pt, pp* **stung** [stʌŋ]*)* N *(wound)* picadura; *(pain)* escozor *m*, picazón *m*; *(organ)* aguijón *m*; *(inf: confidence trick)* timo ▶ VT picar ▶ VI picar, escocer; **my eyes are stinging** me pican *or* escuecen los ojos

stingy [ˈstɪndʒɪ] ADJ tacaño

stink [stɪŋk] *(pt* **stank** [stæŋk], *pp* **stunk** [stʌŋk]*)* N hedor *m*, tufo ▶ VI heder, apestar

stinking [ˈstɪŋkɪŋ] ADJ hediondo, fétido; *(fig: inf)* horrible

stint [stɪnt] N tarea, destajo; **to do one's ~ (at sth)** hacer su parte (de algo), hacer lo que corresponde (de algo) ▶ VI: **to ~ on** escatimar

stipend [ˈstaɪpɛnd] N salario, remuneración *f*

stipendiary [staɪˈpɛndɪərɪ] ADJ: **~ magistrate** magistrado(-a) estipendiario(-a)

stipulate [ˈstɪpjuleɪt] VT estipular

stipulation [stɪpjuˈleɪʃən] N estipulación *f*

★**stir** [stəːʳ] N *(fig: agitation)* conmoción *f*; **to give sth a ~** remover algo; **to cause a ~** causar conmoción *or* sensación ▶ VT *(tea etc)* remover; *(fire)* atizar; *(move)* agitar; *(fig: emotions)* provocar ▶ VI moverse
▶ **stir up** VT excitar; *(trouble)* fomentar

stir-fry [ˈstəːfraɪ] VT sofreír removiendo ▶ N plato preparado sofriendo y removiendo los ingredientes

stirrup [ˈstɪrəp] N estribo

stitch [stɪtʃ] N *(Sewing)* puntada; *(Knitting)* punto; *(Med)* punto (de sutura); *(pain)* punzada ▶ VT coser; *(Med)* suturar

St Kitts and Nevis [seɪnt kɪtsændˈniːvɪs] N San Cristóbal y Nieves *m*

St Lucia [seɪntˈluːʃə] N Santa Lucía

stoat [stəut] N armiño

★**stock** [stɔk] N *(Comm: reserves)* existencias *fpl*, stock *m*; *(: selection)* surtido; *(Agr)* ganado, ganadería; *(Culin)* caldo; *(fig: lineage)* estirpe *f*, cepa; *(Finance)* capital *m*; *(: shares)* acciones *fpl*; *(Rail: rolling stock)* material *m* rodante; **in ~** en existencia *or* almacén; **out of ~** agotado; **to have sth in ~** tener existencias de algo; **to**

take ~ of *(fig)* considerar, examinar; **government ~** papel *m* del Estado; **stocks and shares** acciones y valores ▶ ADJ *(Comm: goods, size)* normal, de serie; *(fig: reply etc)* clásico, trillado; *(: greeting)* acostumbrado ▶ VT *(have in stock)* tener existencias de; *(: supply)* proveer, abastecer ■ **stocks** NPL *(History: punishment)* cepo *sg*
▶ **stock up with** VT FUS abastecerse de

stockbroker [ˈstɔkbrəukəʳ] N agente *mf or* corredor(a) *m/f* de bolsa

stock control N *(Comm)* control *m* de existencias

stock cube N pastilla *or* cubito de caldo

stock exchange N bolsa

stockholder [ˈstɔkhəuldəʳ] N *(US)* accionista *mf*

Stockholm [ˈstɔkhəum] N Estocolmo

stocking [ˈstɔkɪŋ] N media

stock-in-trade [ˈstɔkɪnˈtreɪd] N *(tools etc)* herramientas *fpl*; *(stock)* existencia de mercancías; *(fig)*: **it's his ~** es su especialidad

stockist [ˈstɔkɪst] N *(BRIT)* distribuidor(a) *m/f*

stock market N bolsa (de valores)

stock phrase N vieja frase *f*

stockpile [ˈstɔkpaɪl] N reserva ▶ VT acumular, almacenar

stockroom [ˈstɔkruːm] N almacén *m*, depósito

stocktaking [ˈstɔkteɪkɪŋ] N *(BRIT Comm)* inventario, balance *m*

stocky [ˈstɔkɪ] ADJ *(strong)* robusto; *(short)* achaparrado

stodgy [ˈstɔdʒɪ] ADJ indigesto, pesado

stoical [ˈstəuɪkəl] ADJ estoico

stoke [stəuk] VT atizar

stole [stəul] PT *of* **steal** ▶ N estola

stolen [ˈstəuln] PP *of* **steal**

stolid [ˈstɔlɪd] ADJ *(person)* imperturbable, impasible

★**stomach** [ˈstʌmək] N *(Anat)* estómago; *(belly)* vientre *m* ▶ VT tragar, aguantar

stomachache N dolor *m* de estómago

stomach pump N bomba gástrica

stomach ulcer N úlcera de estómago

stomp [stɔmp] VI: **to ~ in/out** entrar/salir con pasos ruidosos

★**stone** [stəun] N piedra; *(in fruit)* hueso; *(BRIT: weight)* = 6.348 *kg*; 14*lb*; **within a ~'s throw of the station** a tiro de piedra *or* a dos pasos de la estación ▶ ADJ de piedra ▶ VT apedrear; *(fruit)* deshuesar

Stone Age N: **the ~** la Edad de Piedra

stone-cold [ˈstəunˈkəuld] ADJ helado

stoned [stəund] ADJ *(inf: drunk)* trompa, borracho, colocado

stone-deaf [ˈstəunˈdɛf] ADJ sordo como una tapia

stonemason [ˈstəunmeɪsən] N albañil *m*

797

stonewall [stəun'wɔːl] vi alargar la cosa innecesariamente ▸ vт dar largas a

stonework ['stəunwɜːk] N (art) cantería

stonking ['stɔŋkɪŋ] (BRIT inf) ADJ, ADV cojonudo, de puta madre; **a ~ prize** un premio cojonudo; **a ~ good idea** una idea de puta madre

stony ['stəunɪ] ADJ pedregoso; (glance) glacial

stood [stud] PT, PP of **stand**

stooge [stuːdʒ] N (pej) hombre m de paja

stool [stuːl] N taburete m

stoop [stuːp] vi (also: **stoop down**) doblarse, agacharse; (also: **have a stoop**) ser cargado de espaldas; (bend) inclinarse, encorvarse; **to ~ to (doing) sth** rebajarse a (hacer) algo

★**stop** [stɔp] N parada, alto; (in punctuation) punto ▸ vт parar, detener; (break off) suspender; (block: pay) suspender; (: cheque) invalidar; (prevent) impedir; (also: **put a stop to**) poner término a; **to ~ doing sth** dejar de hacer algo; **to ~ sb (from) doing sth** impedir a algn hacer algo; **~ it!** ¡basta ya!, ¡párate! ▸ vi pararse, detenerse; (end) acabarse; **to ~ dead** pararse en seco
  ▸ **stop by** vi pasar por
  ▸ **stop off** vi interrumpir el viaje
  ▸ **stop up** vт (hole) tapar

stopcock ['stɔpkɔk] N llave f de paso

stopgap ['stɔpgæp] N interino; (person) sustituto(-a); (measure) medida provisional ▸ CPD (situation) provisional

stoplights ['stɔplaɪts] NPL (Aut) luces fpl de detención

stopover ['stɔpəuvə'] N parada intermedia; (Aviat) escala

stoppage ['stɔpɪdʒ] N (strike) paro; (temporary stop) interrupción f; (of pay) suspensión f; (blockage) obstrucción f

stopper ['stɔpə'] N tapón m

stop press N noticias fpl de última hora

stopwatch ['stɔpwɔtʃ] N cronómetro

storage ['stɔːrɪdʒ] N almacenaje m; (Comput) almacenamiento

storage capacity N capacidad f de almacenaje

storage heater N acumulador m de calor

★**store** [stɔː'] N (stock) provisión f; (depot) almacén m; (BRIT: large shop) almacén m; (US) tienda; (reserve) reserva, repuesto; **who knows what is in ~ for us** quién sabe lo que nos espera; **to set great/little ~ by sth** dar mucha/poca importancia a algo, valorar mucho/poco algo ▸ vт (gen) almacenar; (Comput) almacenar; (keep) guardar; (in filing system) archivar ▪ **stores** NPL víveres mpl
  ▸ **store up** vт acumular

storehouse ['stɔːhaus] N almacén m, depósito

storekeeper ['stɔːkiːpə'] N (US) tendero(-a)

storeroom ['stɔːruːm] N despensa

storey, (US) **story** ['stɔːrɪ] N piso

stork [stɔːk] N cigüeña

★**storm** [stɔːm] N tormenta; (wind) vendaval m; (fig: of applause) salva; (: of criticism) nube f; **to take a town by ~** (Mil) tomar una ciudad por asalto ▸ vi (fig) rabiar ▸ vт tomar por asalto, asaltar

storm cloud N nubarrón m

storm door N contrapuerta

stormy ['stɔːmɪ] ADJ tempestuoso

★**story** ['stɔːrɪ] N historia; (Press) artículo; (joke) cuento, chiste m; (plot) argumento; (lie) cuento; (US) = **storey**

storybook ['stɔːrɪbuk] N libro de cuentos

storyteller ['stɔːrɪtelə'] N cuentista mf

stout [staut] ADJ (strong) sólido; (fat) gordo, corpulento ▸ N cerveza negra

stove [stəuv] N (for cooking) cocina; (for heating) estufa; **gas/electric ~** cocina de gas/eléctrica

stow [stəu] vт meter, poner; (Naut) estibar

stowaway ['stəuəweɪ] N polizón(-ona) m/f

straddle ['strædl] vт montar a horcajadas

straggle ['strægl] vi (wander) vagar en desorden; (lag behind) rezagarse

straggler ['stræglə'] N rezagado(-a)

straggling ['stræglɪŋ], **straggly** ['stræglɪ] ADJ (hair) desordenado

★**straight** [streɪt] ADJ (direct) recto, derecho; (plain, uncomplicated) sencillo; (frank) franco, directo; (in order) en orden; (continuous) continuo; (Theat: part, play) serio; (person: conventional) recto, convencional; (: heterosexual) heterosexual; **10 ~ wins** 10 victorias seguidas; **to be (all) ~** (tidy) estar en orden; (clarified) estar claro; **to put or get sth ~** dejar algo en claro ▸ ADV derecho, directamente; (drink) solo; **I went ~ home** (me) fui directamente a casa; **~ away, ~ off** (at once) en seguida

straighten ['streɪtn] vт (also: **straighten out**) enderezar, poner derecho; **to ~ things out** poner las cosas en orden ▸ vi (also: **straighten up**) enderezarse, ponerse derecho

straighteners ['streɪtnəz] NPL (for hair) plancha de pelo

straight-faced [streɪt'feɪst] ADJ serio ▸ ADV sin mostrar emoción, impávido

straightforward [streɪt'fɔːwəd] ADJ (simple) sencillo; (honest) sincero

strain [streɪn] N (gen) tensión f; (Tech) presión f; (Med) distensión f, torcedura; (breed) raza; (lineage) linaje m; (of virus) variedad f; **she's under a lot of ~** está bajo mucha tensión ▸ vт (back etc) distender, torcerse; (resources) agotar; (tire) cansar; (stretch) estirar; (filter) filtrar; (meaning) tergiversar ▸ vi esforzarse ▪ **strains** NPL (Mus) son msg

strained [streɪnd] ADJ (muscle) torcido; (laugh) forzado; (relations) tenso

strainer ['streɪnə'] N colador m

strait [streɪt] N (Geo) estrecho; **to be in dire straits** (fig) estar en un gran aprieto

straitjacket ['streɪtdʒækɪt] N camisa de fuerza

strait-laced [streɪtˈleɪst] ADJ mojigato, gazmoño

strand [strænd] N (of thread) hebra; (of rope) ramal m; **a ~ of hair** un pelo

stranded [ˈstrændɪd] ADJ (person: without money) desamparado; (: without transport) colgado

★**strange** [streɪndʒ] ADJ (not known) desconocido; (odd) extraño, raro

strangely ADV de un modo raro; see also **enough**

stranger [ˈstreɪndʒəʳ] N desconocido(-a); (from another area) forastero(-a); **I'm a ~ here** no soy de aquí

strangle [ˈstræŋgl] VT estrangular

stranglehold [ˈstræŋglhəʊld] N (fig) dominio completo

strangulation [stræŋgjuˈleɪʃən] N estrangulación f

strap [stræp] N correa; (of slip, dress) tirante m ▶ VT atar con correa

straphanging [ˈstræphæŋɪŋ] N viajar m de pie or (LAM) parado

strapless [ˈstræplɪs] ADJ (bra, dress) sin tirantes

strapped [stræpt] ADJ: **to be ~ for cash** (inf) andar mal de dinero

strapping [ˈstræpɪŋ] ADJ robusto, fornido

Strasbourg [ˈstræzbɜːg] N Estrasburgo

strata [ˈstrɑːtə] NPL of **stratum**

stratagem [ˈstrætɪdʒəm] N estratagema

strategic [strəˈtiːdʒɪk] ADJ estratégico

strategy [ˈstrætɪdʒɪ] N estrategia

stratum [ˈstrɑːtəm] (pl **strata** [ˈstrɑːtə]) N estrato

straw [strɔː] N paja; (also: **drinking straw**) caña, pajita; **that's the last ~!** ¡eso es el colmo!

★**strawberry** [ˈstrɔːbərɪ] N fresa, frutilla (LAM)

stray [streɪ] ADJ (animal) extraviado; (bullet) perdido; (scattered) disperso ▶ VI extraviarse, perderse; (wander: walker) vagar, ir sin rumbo fijo; (: speaker) desvariar

streak [striːk] N raya; (fig: of madness etc) vena; **to have streaks in one's hair** tener vetas en el pelo; **a winning/losing ~** una racha de buena/mala suerte ▶ VT rayar ▶ VI: **to ~ past** pasar como un rayo

streaker [ˈstriːkəʳ] N corredor(a) m/f desnudo(-a)

streaky [ˈstriːkɪ] ADJ rayado

★**stream** [striːm] N riachuelo, arroyo; (jet) chorro; (flow) corriente f; (of people) oleada; **against the ~** a contracorriente; **on ~** (new power plant etc) en funcionamiento ▶ VT (Scol) dividir en grupos por habilidad ▶ VI correr, fluir; **to ~ in/out** (people) entrar/salir en tropel

streamer [ˈstriːməʳ] N serpentina

stream feed N (on photocopier etc) alimentación f continua

streamline [ˈstriːmlaɪn] VT aerodinamizar; (fig) racionalizar

streamlined [ˈstriːmlaɪnd] ADJ aerodinámico

★**street** [striːt] N calle f; **to be on the streets** (homeless) estar sin vivienda; (as prostitute) hacer la calle; **the back streets** las callejuelas ▶ ADJ callejero

streetcar [ˈstriːtkɑː] N (US) tranvía m

street cred [-krɛd] N (inf) imagen de estar en la onda

street lamp N farol m (LAM), farola (SP)

street light N farol m (LAM), farola (SP)

street lighting N alumbrado público

street map N plano (de la ciudad)

street market N mercado callejero

street plan N plano callejero

streetwise [ˈstriːtwaɪz] ADJ (inf) pícaro

★**strength** [strɛŋθ] N fuerza; (of girder, knot etc) resistencia; (of chemical solution) potencia; (of wine) graduación f de alcohol; (fig: power) poder m; **on the ~ of** a base de, en base a; **to be at full/below ~** tener/no tener completo el cupo

strengthen [ˈstrɛŋθn] VT fortalecer, reforzar

strenuous [ˈstrɛnjuəs] ADJ (tough) arduo; (energetic) enérgico; (opposition) firme, tenaz; (efforts) intensivo

★**stress** [strɛs] N (force, pressure) presión f; (mental strain) estrés m, tensión f; (accent, emphasis) énfasis m, acento; (Ling, Poetry) acento; (Tech) tensión f, carga; **to be under ~** estar estresado; **to lay great ~ on sth** hacer hincapié en algo ▶ VT subrayar, recalcar

stressed [strɛst] ADJ (tense) estresado, agobiado; (syllable) acentuado

stressful [ˈstrɛsful] ADJ (job) estresante

★**stretch** [strɛtʃ] N (of sand etc) trecho; (of road) tramo; (of time) período, tiempo ▶ VI estirarse; (extend): **to ~ to** or **as far as** extenderse hasta; (be enough: money, food): **to ~ to** alcanzar para, dar de sí para ▶ VT extender, estirar; (make demands of) exigir el máximo esfuerzo a; **to ~ one's legs** estirar las piernas

▶ **stretch out** VI tenderse ▶ VT (arm etc) extender; (spread) estirar

stretcher [ˈstrɛtʃəʳ] N camilla

stretcher-bearer [ˈstrɛtʃəbɛərəʳ] N camillero(-a)

stretch marks NPL estrías fpl

strewn [struːn] ADJ: **~ with** cubierto or sembrado de

stricken [ˈstrɪkən] ADJ (person) herido; (city, industry etc) condenado; **~ with** (arthritis, disease) afligido por; **grief-stricken** destrozado por el dolor

★**strict** [strɪkt] ADJ (order, rule etc) estricto; (discipline, ban) severo; **in ~ confidence** en la más absoluta confianza

strictly [ˈstrɪktlɪ] ADV estrictamente; (totally) terminantemente; **~ confidential** estrictamente confidencial; **~ speaking** en (el) sentido estricto (de la palabra); **~ between ourselves …** entre nosotros …

stridden [ˈstrɪdn] PP of **stride**

S

stride [straɪd] (*pt* **strode** [strəud], *pp* **stridden** ['strɪdn]) N zancada, tranco; **to take in one's ~** (*fig: changes etc*) tomar con calma ▶ vɪ dar zancadas, andar a trancos

strident ['straɪdnt] ADJ estridente; (*colour*) chillón(-ona)

strife [straɪf] N lucha

★**strike** [straɪk] (*pt, pp* **struck** [strʌk]) N huelga; (*of oil etc*) descubrimiento; (*attack*) ataque *m*; (*Sport*) golpe *m*; **on ~** (*workers*) en huelga; **to call a ~** declarar una huelga; **to go on** *or* **come out on ~** ponerse *or* declararse en huelga ▶ vT golpear, pegar; (*oil etc*) descubrir; (*obstacle*) topar con; (*produce: coin, medal*) acuñar; (: *agreement, deal*) alcanzar; **to ~ a balance** (*fig*) encontrar un equilibrio; **to ~ a match** encender una cerilla; **to ~ a bargain** cerrar un trato; **the clock struck nine o'clock** el reloj dio las nueve ▶ vɪ declarar la huelga; (*attack: Mil etc*) atacar; (*clock*) dar la hora
  ▶ **strike back** vɪ (*Mil*) contraatacar; (*fig*) devolver el golpe
  ▶ **strike down** vT derribar
  ▶ **strike off** vT (*from list*) tachar; (*doctor etc*) suspender
  ▶ **strike out** vT borrar, tachar
  ▶ **strike up** vT (*Mus*) empezar a tocar; (*conversation*) entablar; (*friendship*) trabar

strikebreaker ['straɪkbreɪkər] N rompehuelgas *mf*, esquirol *mf*

striker ['straɪkər] N huelguista *mf*; (*Sport*) delantero

striking ['straɪkɪŋ] ADJ (*colour*) llamativo; (*obvious*) notorio

Strimmer® ['strɪmər] N cortacéspedes *m inv* (*especial para los bordes*)

★**string** [strɪŋ] (*pt, pp* **strung** [strʌŋ]) N (*gen*) cuerda; (*row*) hilera; (*Comput*) cadena; **to pull strings** (*fig*) mover palancas; **to get a job by pulling strings** conseguir un trabajo por enchufe; **with no strings attached** (*fig*) sin compromiso ▶ vT: **to ~ together** ensartar; **to be strung out** extenderse ■ **the strings** NPL (*Mus*) los instrumentos de cuerda

string bean N judía verde, habichuela

stringed instrument [strɪŋd-], **string instrument** N (*Mus*) instrumento de cuerda

stringent ['strɪndʒənt] ADJ riguroso, severo

string quartet N cuarteto de cuerdas

strip [strɪp] N tira; (*of land*) franja; (*of metal*) cinta, lámina ▶ vT desnudar; (*also:* **strip down**: *machine*) desmontar ▶ vɪ desnudarse
  ▶ **strip off** vT (*paint etc*) quitar ▶ vɪ (*person*) desnudarse

strip cartoon N tira cómica, historieta (*LAm*)

stripe [straɪp] N raya; (*Mil*) galón *m*; **white with green stripes** blanco con rayas verdes

striped [straɪpt] ADJ a rayas, rayado

strip lighting N alumbrado fluorescente

stripper ['strɪpər] N artista *mf* de striptease

strip-search ['strɪpsəːtʃ] vT: **to ~ sb** desnudar y registrar a algn

striptease ['strɪptiːz] N striptease *m*

strive [straɪv] (*pt* **strove** [strəuv], *pp* **striven** ['strɪvn]) vɪ: **to ~ to do sth** esforzarse *or* luchar por hacer algo

strobe [strəub] N (*also:* **strobe light**) luz *f* estroboscópica

strode [strəud] PT *of* **stride**

stroke [strəuk] N (*blow*) golpe *m*; (*Swimming*) brazada; (*Med*) apoplejía; (*caress*) caricia; (*of pen*) trazo; (*Swimming: style*) estilo; (*of piston*) carrera; **at a ~** de golpe; **a ~ of luck** un golpe de suerte; **two-stroke engine** motor *m* de dos tiempos ▶ vT acariciar

stroll [strəul] N paseo, vuelta; **to go for a ~**, **have** *or* **take a ~** dar un paseo ▶ vɪ dar un paseo *or* una vuelta

stroller ['strəulər] N (*US: pushchair*) cochecito

★**strong** [strɔŋ] ADJ fuerte; (*bleach, acid*) concentrado; **they are 50 ~** son 50 ▶ ADV: **to be going ~** (*company*) marchar bien; (*person*) conservarse bien

strong-arm ['strɔŋɑːm] ADJ (*tactics, methods*) represivo

strongbox ['strɔŋbɔks] N caja fuerte

strong drink N bebida cargada *or* fuerte

stronghold ['strɔŋhəuld] N fortaleza; (*fig*) baluarte *m*

strong language N lenguaje *m* fuerte

strongly ['strɔŋlɪ] ADV fuertemente, con fuerza; (*believe*) firmemente; **to feel ~ about sth** tener una opinión firme sobre algo

strongman ['strɔŋmæn] N (*irreg*) forzudo; (*fig*) hombre *m* robusto

strongroom ['strɔŋruːm] N cámara acorazada

stroppy ['strɔpɪ] ADJ (*Brit inf*) borde; **to get ~** ponerse borde

strove [strəuv] PT *of* **strive**

struck [strʌk] PT, PP *of* **strike**

structural ['strʌktʃərəl] ADJ estructural

structure ['strʌktʃər] N estructura; (*building*) construcción *f*

struggle ['strʌgl] N lucha; **to have a ~ to do sth** esforzarse por hacer algo ▶ vɪ luchar

strum [strʌm] vT (*guitar*) rasguear

strung [strʌŋ] PT, PP *of* **string**

strut [strʌt] N puntal *m* ▶ vɪ pavonearse

strychnine ['strɪkniːn] N estricnina

stub [stʌb] N (*of ticket etc*) matriz *f*; (*of cigarette*) colilla ▶ vT: **to ~ one's toe on sth** dar con el dedo del pie contra algo
  ▶ **stub out** vT (*cigarette*) apagar

stubble ['stʌbl] N rastrojo; (*on chin*) barba (incipiente)

stubborn ['stʌbən] ADJ terco, testarudo

stucco ['stʌkəu] N estuco

stuck [stʌk] PT, PP *of* **stick** ▶ ADJ (*jammed*) atascado

stuck-up [stʌk'ʌp] ADJ engreído, presumido

stud [stʌd] N (*shirt stud*) corchete *m*; (*of boot*) taco; (*earring*) pendiente *m* (de bolita); (*also:* **stud farm**) caballeriza; (*also:* **stud horse**) caballo semental ▶ VT (*fig*): **studded with** salpicado de

★**student** ['stjuːdənt] N estudiante *mf*; **a law/medical ~** un(a) estudiante de derecho/medicina ▶ ADJ estudiantil

student driver N (*US Aut*) aprendiz(a) *m/f* de conductor

students' union N (*BRIT: association*) sindicato de estudiantes; (*: building*) centro de estudiantes

studio ['stjuːdɪəu] N estudio; (*artist's*) taller *m*

studio flat, (*US*) **studio apartment** N estudio

studious ['stjuːdɪəs] ADJ estudioso; (*studied*) calculado

studiously ['stjuːdɪəslɪ] ADV (*carefully*) con esmero

★**study** ['stʌdɪ] N estudio; **to make a ~ of sth** realizar una investigación de algo ▶ VT estudiar; (*examine*) examinar, investigar ▶ VI estudiar; **to ~ for an exam** preparar un examen

★**stuff** [stʌf] N materia; (*cloth*) tela; (*substance*) material *m*, sustancia; (*things, belongings*) cosas *fpl* ▶ VT llenar; (*Culin*) rellenar; (*animal: for exhibition*) disecar; **my nose is stuffed up** tengo la nariz tapada; **stuffed toy** juguete *m* or muñeco de trapo

stuffing ['stʌfɪŋ] N relleno

stuffy ['stʌfɪ] ADJ (*room*) mal ventilado; (*person*) de miras estrechas

stumble ['stʌmbl] VI tropezar, dar un traspié ▶ **stumble across** VT FUS (*fig*) tropezar con

stumbling block ['stʌmblɪŋ-] N tropiezo, obstáculo

stump [stʌmp] N (*of tree*) tocón *m*; (*of limb*) muñón *m* ▶ VT: **to be stumped** quedarse perplejo; **to be stumped for an answer** quedarse sin saber qué contestar

stun [stʌn] VT aturdir

stung [stʌŋ] PT, PP *of* **sting**

stunk [stʌŋk] PP *of* **stink**

stunned [stʌnd] ADJ (*dazed*) aturdido, atontado; (*amazed*) pasmado; (*shocked*) anonadado

stunning ['stʌnɪŋ] ADJ (*fig: news*) pasmoso; (*: outfit etc*) sensacional

stunt [stʌnt] N (*Aviat*) vuelo acrobático; (*in film*) escena peligrosa; (*also:* **publicity stunt**) truco publicitario

stunted ['stʌntɪd] ADJ enano, achaparrado

stuntman ['stʌntmæn] N (*irreg*) especialista *m*

stupefaction [stjuːpɪ'fækʃən] N estupefacción *f*

stupefy ['stjuːpɪfaɪ] VT dejar estupefacto

stupendous [stjuː'pendəs] ADJ estupendo, asombroso

★**stupid** ['stjuːpɪd] ADJ estúpido, tonto

stupidity [stjuː'pɪdɪtɪ] N estupidez *f*

stupor ['stjuːpər] N estupor *m*

sturdy ['stɜːdɪ] ADJ robusto, fuerte

stutter ['stʌtər] N tartamudeo ▶ VI tartamudear

St Vincent and the Grenadines [seɪnt'vɪnsəntændðə'grenədiːnz] N San Vicente y las Granadinas *m*

sty [staɪ] N (*for pigs*) pocilga

stye [staɪ] N (*Med*) orzuelo

★**style** [staɪl] N estilo; (*fashion*) moda; (*of dress etc*) hechura; (*hair style*) corte *m*; **in the latest ~** en el último modelo

stylish ['staɪlɪʃ] ADJ elegante, a la moda

stylist ['staɪlɪst] N (*hair stylist*) peluquero(-a)

stylus ['staɪləs] (*pl* **styli** [-laɪ] *or* **styluses**) N (*of record player*) aguja

Styrofoam® ['staɪrəfəum] N (*US*) poliestireno ▶ ADJ (*cup*) de poliestireno

suave [swɑːv] ADJ cortés, fino

sub [sʌb] N ABBR = **submarine**; **subscription**

sub... [sʌb] PREF sub...

subcommittee ['sʌbkəmɪtɪ] N subcomisión *f*

subconscious [sʌb'kɔnʃəs] ADJ subconsciente ▶ N subconsciente *m*

subcontinent [sʌb'kɔntɪnənt] N: **the Indian ~** el subcontinente de la India

subcontract N ['sʌb'kɔntrækt] subcontrato ▶ VT ['sʌbkən'trækt] subcontratar

subcontractor ['sʌbkən'træktər] N subcontratista *mf*

subdivide [sʌbdɪ'vaɪd] VT subdividir

subdue [səb'djuː] VT sojuzgar; (*passions*) dominar

subdued [səb'djuːd] ADJ (*light*) tenue; (*person*) sumiso, manso

sub-editor ['sʌb'edɪtər] N (*BRIT*) redactor(a) *m/f*

★**subject** N ['sʌbdʒɪkt] súbdito; (*Scol*) tema *m*, materia; (*Grammar*) sujeto; **to change the ~** cambiar de tema ▶ VT [səb'dʒɛkt]: **to ~ sb to sth** someter a algn a algo ▶ ADJ ['sʌbdʒɪkt]: **to be ~ to** (*law*) estar sujeto a; (*person*) ser propenso a; **~ to confirmation in writing** sujeto a confirmación por escrito

subjective [səb'dʒɛktɪv] ADJ subjetivo

subject matter N materia; (*content*) contenido

sub judice [sʌb'djuːdɪsɪ] ADJ (*Law*) pendiente de resolución

subjugate ['sʌbdʒugeɪt] VT subyugar, sojuzgar

subjunctive [səb'dʒʌŋktɪv] ADJ, N subjuntivo

sublet [sʌb'let] VT, VI subarrendar, realquilar

sublime [sə'blaɪm] ADJ sublime

subliminal [sʌb'lɪmɪnl] ADJ subliminal

submachine gun ['sʌbmə'ʃiːn-] N metralleta

submarine [sʌbmə'riːn] N submarino

submerge [səb'mɜːdʒ] VT sumergir; (*flood*) inundar ▶ VI sumergirse

submersion [səbˈməːʃən] N sumersión f

submission [səbˈmɪʃən] N sumisión f; (to committee etc) ponencia

submissive [səbˈmɪsɪv] ADJ sumiso

submit [səbˈmɪt] VT someter; (proposal, claim) presentar; **I ~ that ...** me permito sugerir que ... ▶ VI someterse

subnormal [sʌbˈnɔːməl] ADJ subnormal

subordinate [səˈbɔːdɪnət] ADJ, N subordinado(-a) m/f

subpoena [səbˈpiːnə] (Law) N citación f ▶ VT citar

subprime [ˈsʌbpraɪm] ADJ de alto riesgo; **~ mortgage** (Finance) hipoteca de alto riesgo

subroutine [sʌbruːˈtiːn] N (Comput) subrutina

subscribe [səbˈskraɪb] VI suscribir; **to ~ to** (fund, opinion) suscribir, aprobar; (opinion) estar de acuerdo con; (newspaper) suscribirse a

subscribed capital [səbˈskraɪbd-] N capital m suscrito

subscriber [səbˈskraɪbəʳ] N (to periodical) suscriptor(a) m/f; (to telephone) abonado(-a)

subscript [ˈsʌbskrɪpt] N (Typ) subíndice m

subscription [səbˈskrɪpʃən] N (to club) abono; (to magazine) suscripción f; **to take out a ~ to** suscribirse a

subsequent [ˈsʌbsɪkwənt] ADJ subsiguiente, posterior; **~ to** posterior a

subsequently [ˈsʌbsɪkwəntlɪ] ADV posteriormente, más tarde

subservient [səbˈsəːvɪənt] ADJ: **~ (to)** servil (a)

subside [səbˈsaɪd] VI hundirse; (flood) bajar; (wind) amainar

subsidence [səbˈsaɪdns] N hundimiento; (in road) socavón m

subsidiarity [səbsɪdɪˈærɪtɪ] N (Pol) subsidiariedad f

subsidiary [səbˈsɪdɪərɪ] N sucursal f, filial f ▶ ADJ (Univ: subject) secundario

subsidize [ˈsʌbsɪdaɪz] VT subvencionar

subsidy [ˈsʌbsɪdɪ] N subvención f

subsist [səbˈsɪst] VI: **to ~ on sth** subsistir a base de algo, sustentarse con algo

subsistence [səbˈsɪstəns] N subsistencia

subsistence allowance N dietas fpl

subsistence level N nivel m de subsistencia

subsistence wage N sueldo de subsistencia

★**substance** [ˈsʌbstəns] N sustancia; (fig) esencia; **to lack ~** (argument) ser poco convincente; (accusation) no tener fundamento; (film, book) tener poca profundidad

substance abuse N uso indebido de sustancias tóxicas

substandard [sʌbˈstændəd] ADJ (goods) inferior; (housing) deficiente

substantial [səbˈstænʃl] ADJ sustancial, sustancioso; (fig) importante

substantially [səbˈstænʃəlɪ] ADV sustancialmente; **~ bigger** bastante más grande

substantiate [səbˈstænʃɪeɪt] VT comprobar

★**substitute** [ˈsʌbstɪtjuːt] N (person) suplente mf; (thing) sustituto ▶ VT: **to ~ A for B** sustituir B por A, reemplazar A por B

substitution [sʌbstɪˈtjuːʃən] N sustitución f

subterfuge [ˈsʌbtəfjuːdʒ] N subterfugio

subterranean [sʌbtəˈreɪnɪən] ADJ subterráneo

subtitle [ˈsʌbtaɪtl] N subtítulo

subtle [ˈsʌtl] ADJ sutil

subtlety [ˈsʌtltɪ] N sutileza

subtly [ˈsʌtlɪ] ADV sutilmente

subtotal [sʌbˈtəutl] N subtotal m

subtract [səbˈtrækt] VT restar; (fig) sustraer

subtraction [səbˈtrækʃən] N resta; (fig) sustracción f

suburb [ˈsʌbəːb] N barrio residencial; **the suburbs** las afueras (de la ciudad)

suburban [səˈbəːbən] ADJ suburbano; (train etc) de cercanías

suburbia [səˈbəːbɪə] N barrios mpl residenciales

subversion [səbˈvəːʃən] N subversión f

subversive [səbˈvəːsɪv] ADJ subversivo

subway [ˈsʌbweɪ] N (Brit) paso subterráneo or inferior; (US) metro

sub-zero [sʌbˈzɪərəu] ADJ: **~ temperatures** temperaturas fpl bajo cero

★**succeed** [səkˈsiːd] VI (person) tener éxito; (plan) salir bien; **to ~ in doing** lograr hacer ▶ VT suceder a

succeeding [səkˈsiːdɪŋ] ADJ (following) sucesivo; **~ generations** generaciones fpl futuras

★**success** [səkˈses] N éxito; (gain) triunfo

★**successful** [səkˈsesful] ADJ (venture) de éxito, exitoso (esp LAm); **to be ~ (in doing)** lograr (hacer)

successfully [səkˈsesfulɪ] ADV con éxito

succession [səkˈseʃən] N (series) sucesión f, serie f; (descendants) descendencia; **in ~** sucesivamente

successive [səkˈsesɪv] ADJ sucesivo, consecutivo; **on three ~ days** tres días seguidos

successor [səkˈsesəʳ] N sucesor(a) m/f

succinct [səkˈsɪŋkt] ADJ sucinto

succulent [ˈsʌkjulənt] ADJ suculento ■ **succulents** NPL (Bot) plantas fpl carnosas

succumb [səˈkʌm] VI sucumbir

★**such** [sʌtʃ] ADJ (so much): **~ courage** tanto valor; tal, semejante; (of that kind): **~ a book** tal libro; **~ books** tales libros; **~ books as I have** cuantos libros tengo; **I said no ~ thing** no dije tal cosa ▶ ADV tan; **~ a long trip** un viaje tan largo; **~ a lot of** tanto; **~ as** (like) tal como; **a noise ~ as to** un ruido tal que; **it's ~ a long time since we saw each other** hace tanto tiempo que no nos vemos; **~ a long time ago** hace tantísimo tiempo; **as ~** como tal

such-and-such ['sʌtʃənsʌtʃ] ADJ tal o cual

suchlike ['sʌtʃlaɪk] PRON (inf): **and ~** y cosas por el estilo

suck [sʌk] VT chupar; (bottle) sorber; (breast) mamar; (pump, machine) aspirar

sucker ['sʌkəʳ] N (Bot) serpollo; (Zool) ventosa; (pej) bobo(-a), primo(-a)

sucrose ['su:krəuz] N sacarosa

suction ['sʌkʃən] N succión f

suction pump N bomba aspirante or de succión

Sudan [su'dæn] N Sudán m

Sudanese [su:də'ni:z] ADJ, N sudanés(-esa) m/f

★**sudden** ['sʌdn] ADJ (rapid) repentino, súbito; (unexpected) imprevisto; **all of a ~** de repente

sudden-death [sʌdn'dɛθ] N (also: **sudden-death play off**) muerte f súbita

★**suddenly** ['sʌdnlɪ] ADV de repente

sudoku [su'dəuku:] N sudoku m

suds [sʌdz] NPL espuma sg de jabón

sue [su:] VT demandar; **to ~ (for)** demandar (por); **to ~ for divorce** solicitar or pedir el divorcio; **to ~ for damages** demandar por daños y perjuicios

suede [sweɪd] N ante m, gamuza (LAM)

suet ['suɪt] N sebo

Suez Canal ['su:ɪz-] N Canal m de Suez

★**suffer** ['sʌfəʳ] VT sufrir, padecer; (tolerate) aguantar, soportar; (undergo: loss, setback) experimentar ► VI sufrir, padecer; **to ~ from** padecer, sufrir; **to ~ from the effects of alcohol/a fall** sufrir los efectos del alcohol/resentirse de una caída

sufferance ['sʌfərns] N: **he was only there on ~** estuvo allí solo porque se lo toleraron

sufferer ['sʌfərəʳ] N víctima f; (Med): **~ from** enfermo(-a) de

suffering ['sʌfərɪŋ] N (hardship, deprivation) sufrimiento; (pain) dolor m

suffice [sə'faɪs] VI bastar, ser suficiente

sufficient [sə'fɪʃənt] ADJ suficiente, bastante

sufficiently [sə'fɪʃəntlɪ] ADV suficientemente, bastante

suffix ['sʌfɪks] N sufijo

suffocate ['sʌfəkeɪt] VI ahogarse, asfixiarse

suffocation [sʌfə'keɪʃən] N sofocación f, asfixia

suffrage ['sʌfrɪdʒ] N sufragio

suffuse [sə'fju:z] VT: **to ~ (with)** (colour) bañar (de); **her face was suffused with joy** su cara estaba llena de alegría

★**sugar** ['ʃugəʳ] N azúcar m ► VT echar azúcar a, azucarar

sugar basin N (BRIT) = **sugar bowl**

sugar beet N remolacha

sugar bowl N azucarero

sugar cane N caña de azúcar

sugar-coated [ʃugə'kəutɪd] ADJ azucarado

sugar lump N terrón m de azúcar

sugar refinery N refinería de azúcar

sugary ['ʃugərɪ] ADJ azucarado

★**suggest** [sə'dʒest] VT sugerir; (recommend) aconsejar; **what do you ~ I do?** ¿qué sugieres que haga?; **this suggests that ...** esto hace pensar que ...

★**suggestion** [sə'dʒestʃən] N sugerencia; **there's no ~ of ...** no hay indicación or evidencia de ...

suggestive [sə'dʒestɪv] ADJ sugestivo; (pej: indecent) indecente

suicidal ['suɪsaɪdl] ADJ suicida

★**suicide** ['suɪsaɪd] N suicidio; (person) suicida mf; **to commit ~** suicidarse

suicide attack N atentado suicida

suicide attempt, suicide bid N intento de suicidio

suicide bomber N terrorista mf suicida

suicide bombing N atentado m suicida

★**suit** [su:t] N traje m; (Law) pleito; (Cards) palo; **to bring a ~ against sb** entablar demanda contra algn; **to follow ~** (Cards) seguir el palo; (fig) seguir el ejemplo (de algn) ► VT convenir; (clothes) sentar bien a, ir bien a; (adapt): **to ~ sth to** adaptar or ajustar algo a; **to be suited to sth** (suitable for) ser apto para algo; **well suited** (couple) hechos el uno para el otro; **that suits me** me va bien

★**suitable** ['su:təbl] ADJ conveniente; (apt) indicado

suitably ['su:təblɪ] ADV convenientemente; (appropriately) en forma debida

suitcase ['su:tkeɪs] N maleta, valija (LAM)

suite [swi:t] N (of rooms) suite f; (Mus) suite f; (furniture): **bedroom/dining room ~** (juego de) dormitorio/comedor m; **a three-piece ~** un tresillo

suitor ['su:təʳ] N pretendiente m

sulfate ['sʌlfeɪt] N (US) = **sulphate**

sulfur ['sʌlfəʳ] N (US) = **sulphur**

sulk [sʌlk] VI estar de mal humor

sulky ['sʌlkɪ] ADJ malhumorado

sullen ['sʌlən] ADJ hosco, malhumorado

sulphate, (US) **sulfate** ['sʌlfeɪt] N sulfato; **copper ~** sulfato de cobre

sulphur, (US) **sulfur** ['sʌlfəʳ] N azufre m

sulphur dioxide N dióxido de azufre

sultan ['sʌltən] N sultán m

sultana [sʌl'tɑ:nə] N (fruit) pasa de Esmirna

sultry ['sʌltrɪ] ADJ (weather) bochornoso; (seductive) seductor(a)

★**sum** [sʌm] N suma; (total) total m
► **sum up** VT resumir; (evaluate rapidly) evaluar ► VI hacer un resumen

Sumatra [su'mɑ:trə] N Sumatra

summarize ['sʌməraɪz] VT resumir

summary ['sʌmərɪ] N resumen m ► ADJ (justice) sumario

S

★**summer** ['sʌməʳ] N verano; **in (the) ~** en (el) verano ▸ ADJ de verano

summer holidays NPL vacaciones *fpl* de verano

summerhouse ['sʌməhaus] N (*in garden*) cenador *m*, glorieta

summertime ['sʌmətaɪm] N (*season*) verano

summer time N (*by clock*) hora de verano

summery ['sʌmərɪ] ADJ veraniego

summing-up [sʌmɪŋ'ʌp] N (*Law*) resumen *m*

★**summit** ['sʌmɪt] N cima, cumbre *f*; (*also:* **summit conference**) (conferencia) cumbre *f*

summit conference N (conferencia) cumbre *f*

summon ['sʌmən] VT (*person*) llamar; (*meeting*) convocar; **to ~ a witness** citar a un testigo ▸ **summon up** VT (*courage*) armarse de

summons ['sʌmənz] N llamamiento, llamada; **to serve a ~ on sb** citar a algn ante el juicio ▸ VT citar, emplazar

sumo ['suːməu] N (*also:* **sumo wrestling**) sumo

sump [sʌmp] N (*Brit Aut*) cárter *m*

sumptuous ['sʌmptjuəs] ADJ suntuoso

★**sun** [sʌn] N sol *m*; **they have everything under the ~** no les falta nada, tienen de todo.

Sun. ABBR (= *Sunday*) dom.

sunbathe ['sʌnbeɪð] VI tomar el sol

sunbeam ['sʌnbiːm] N rayo de sol

sunbed ['sʌnbed] N cama solar

sunblock ['sʌnblɔk] N filtro solar

sunburn ['sʌnbəːn] N (*painful*) quemadura del sol; (*tan*) bronceado

sunburnt ['sʌnbəːnt], **sunburned** ['sʌnbəːnd] ADJ (*tanned*) bronceado; (*painfully*) quemado por el sol

sundae ['sʌndeɪ] N *helado con frutas y nueces*

★**Sunday** ['sʌndɪ] N domingo; *see also* **Tuesday**

Sunday paper N (periódico) dominical *m*

Los **Sunday papers** (dominicales) son una verdadera institución tanto en Gran Bretaña como en los Estados Unidos. La mayoría de los periódicos tiene una edición dominical, que se publica tanto en papel como en internet, con una redacción diferente de la que elabora el diario durante la semana. El dominical suele venir acompañado de suplementos sobre negocios, deporte, viajes, literatura, etc., así como un suplemento en color.

Sunday school N catequesis *f*

sundial ['sʌndaɪəl] N reloj *m* de sol

sundown ['sʌndaun] N anochecer *m*, puesta de sol

sundries ['sʌndrɪz] NPL géneros *mpl* diversos

sundry ['sʌndrɪ] ADJ varios, diversos; **all and ~** todos sin excepción

sunflower ['sʌnflauəʳ] N girasol *m*

sung [sʌŋ] PP *of* **sing**

sunglasses ['sʌnglɑːsɪz] NPL gafas *fpl* de sol

sunk [sʌŋk] PP *of* **sink**

sunken ['sʌŋkn] ADJ (*bath*) hundido

sunlamp ['sʌnlæmp] N lámpara solar ultravioleta

sunlight ['sʌnlaɪt] N luz *f* del sol

sunlit ['sʌnlɪt] ADJ iluminado por el sol

sun lounger N tumbona, perezosa (*LAM*)

sunny ['sʌnɪ] ADJ soleado; (*day*) de sol; (*fig*) alegre; **it is ~** hace sol

sunrise ['sʌnraɪz] N salida del sol

sun roof N (*Aut*) techo corredizo *or* solar; (*on building*) azotea, terraza

sunscreen ['sʌnskriːn] N filtro solar

sunset ['sʌnset] N puesta del sol

sunshade ['sʌnʃeɪd] N (*over table*) sombrilla

sunshine ['sʌnʃaɪn] N sol *m*

sunstroke ['sʌnstrəuk] N insolación *f*

suntan ['sʌntæn] N bronceado

suntan lotion N bronceador *m*

suntanned ['sʌntænd] ADJ bronceado

suntan oil N aceite *m* bronceador

★**super** ['suːpəʳ] ADJ (*inf*) genial

superannuation [suːpərænjuˈeɪʃən] N jubilación *f*, pensión *f*

★**superb** [suːˈpəːb] ADJ magnífico, espléndido

Super Bowl N (*US Sport*) super copa de fútbol americano

La **Super Bowl** es la final de la *NFL* (*National Football League*), la máxima competición del fútbol americano profesional. 40 años después de su primera celebración, en 1967, el domingo de la *Super Bowl* se ha convertido en una tradición, famoso por la cantidad de comida que devoran los millones de fans que se juntan para ver la final y por los comentarios televisivos postpartido. La *Super Bowl* es la retransmisión televisiva de los Estados Unidos con mayor audiencia. Eso hace que en el *Halftime Show*, la actuación durante el descanso de la final, aparezcan los mayores artistas del momento.

supercilious [suːpəˈsɪlɪəs] ADJ (*disdainful*) desdeñoso; (*haughty*) altanero

superconductor [suːpəkənˈdʌktəʳ] N superconductor *m*

superficial [suːpəˈfɪʃəl] ADJ superficial

superfluous [suːˈpəːfluəs] ADJ superfluo, de sobra

superfood ['suːpəfuːd] N superalimento

superglue ['suːpəgluː] N cola de contacto, supercola

superhighway ['suːpəhaɪweɪ] N (*US*) superautopista; **the information ~** la superautopista de la información

superhuman [suːpəˈhjuːmən] ADJ sobrehumano

superimpose ['suːpərɪmˈpəuz] VT sobreponer

superintend [su:pərɪn'tɛnd] VT supervisar

superintendent [su:pərɪn'tɛndənt] N director(a) *m/f*; (*also:* **police superintendent**) subjefe(-a) *m/f*

superior [su'pɪərɪə'] ADJ superior; (*smug: person*) altivo, desdeñoso; (: *smile, air*) de suficiencia; (: *remark*) desdeñoso; **Mother S~** (*Rel*) madre *f* superiora ▶ N superior *m*

superiority [supɪərɪ'ɔrɪtɪ] N superioridad *f*; desdén *m*

superlative [su'pə:lətɪv] ADJ, N superlativo

superman ['su:pəmæn] N (*irreg*) superhombre *m*

★**supermarket** ['su:pəmɑ:kɪt] N supermercado

supermodel ['su:pəmɔdl] N top model *f*, supermodelo *f*

supernatural [su:pə'nætʃərəl] ADJ sobrenatural ▶ N: **the ~** lo sobrenatural

supernova [su:pə'nəuvə] N supernova

superpower ['su:pəpauə'] N (*Pol*) superpotencia

supersede [su:pə'si:d] VT suplantar

supersonic ['su:pə'sɔnɪk] ADJ supersónico

superstar ['su:pəstɑ:'] N superestrella ▶ ADJ de superestrella

superstition [su:pə'stɪʃən] N superstición *f*

superstitious [su:pə'stɪʃəs] ADJ supersticioso

superstore ['su:pəstɔ:'] N (*BRIT*) hipermercado

supertanker ['su:pətæŋkə'] N superpetrolero

supertax ['su:pətæks] N sobretasa, sobreimpuesto

supervise ['su:pəvaɪz] VT supervisar

supervision [su:pə'vɪʒən] N supervisión *f*

supervisor ['su:pəvaɪzə'] N supervisor(a) *m/f*

supervisory ['su:pəvaɪzərɪ] ADJ de supervisión

supper ['sʌpə'] N cena; **to have ~** cenar

supplant [sə'plɑ:nt] VT suplantar, reemplazar

supple ['sʌpl] ADJ flexible

supplement N ['sʌplɪmənt] suplemento ▶ VT [sʌplɪ'mɛnt] suplir

supplementary [sʌplɪ'mɛntərɪ] ADJ suplementario

supplier [sə'plaɪə'] N suministrador(a) *m/f*; (*Comm*) distribuidor(a) *m/f*

★**supply** [sə'plaɪ] VT (*provide*) suministrar; (*information*) facilitar; (*fill: need, want*) suplir, satisfacer; (*equip*): **to ~ (with)** proveer (de) ▶ N provisión *f*; (*of gas, water etc*) suministro; **to be in short ~** escasear, haber escasez de; **the electricity/water/gas ~** el suministro de electricidad/agua/gas; **~ and demand** la oferta y la demanda ▶ ADJ (*BRIT: teacher etc*) suplente ■ **supplies** NPL (*food*) víveres *mpl*; (*Mil*) pertrechos *mpl*; **office supplies** materiales *mpl* de oficina

★**support** [sə'pɔ:t] N (*moral, financial etc*) apoyo; (*Tech*) soporte *m*; **they stopped work in ~ (of)** pararon de trabajar en apoyo (de) ▶ VT apoyar; (*financially*) mantener; (*uphold*) sostener; (*Sport: team*) seguir, ser hincha de; **to ~ o.s.** (*financially*) ganarse la vida

support buying [-'baɪɪŋ] N compra proteccionista

★**supporter** [sə'pɔ:tə'] N (*Pol etc*) partidario(-a); (*Sport*) aficionado(-a); (*Football*) hincha *mf*

supporting [sə'pɔ:tɪŋ] ADJ (*wall*) de apoyo; **~ role** papel *m* secundario; **~ actor/actress** actor/actriz *m/f* secundario(-a)

supportive [sə'pɔ:tɪv] ADJ de apoyo; **I have a ~ family/wife** mi familia/mujer me apoya

★**suppose** [sə'pəuz] VT, VI suponer; (*imagine*) imaginarse; **to be supposed to do sth** deber hacer algo; **I don't ~ she'll come** no creo que venga; **he's supposed to be an expert** se le supone un experto

supposedly [sə'pəuzɪdlɪ] ADV según cabe suponer

supposing [sə'pəuzɪŋ] CONJ en caso de que; **always ~ (that) he comes** suponiendo que venga

supposition [sʌpə'zɪʃən] N suposición *f*

suppository [sə'pɔzɪtrɪ] N supositorio

suppress [sə'prɛs] VT suprimir; (*yawn*) ahogar

suppression [sə'prɛʃən] N represión *f*

supremacy [su'prɛməsɪ] N supremacía

supreme [su'pri:m] ADJ supremo

Supreme Court N (*US*) Tribunal *m* Supremo, Corte *f* Suprema

La **Supreme Court** (Tribunal Supremo) de Estados Unidos, establecida en 1789, es la más alta instancia de la justicia en el país. Está compuesta por un *Chief Justice* (presidente) y ocho *Associate Justices* (jueces) nombrados por el presidente de los Estados Unidos y confirmados por el Senado. El cargo de los jueces es vitalicio, a no ser que dimitan, sean cesados o que el Congreso les obligue a retirarse. Cada estado cuenta también con un tribunal supremo propio, responsable por los asuntos legales y jurídicos en el estado en cuestión.

supremo [su'pri:məu] N autoridad *f* máxima

Supt. ABBR (*Police*) = **superintendent**

surcharge ['sə:tʃɑ:dʒ] N sobretasa, recargo

★**sure** [ʃuə'] ADJ seguro; (*definite, convinced*) cierto; (*aim*) certero; **to be ~ of sth** estar seguro de algo; **to be ~ of o.s.** estar seguro de sí mismo; **to make ~ of sth/that** asegurarse de algo/asegurar que; **I'm not ~ how/why/when** no estoy seguro de cómo/por qué/cuándo ▶ ADV (*inf*): **that ~ is pretty, that's ~ pretty** (*US*) ¡qué bonito es!; **~!** (*of course*) ¡claro!, ¡por supuesto!; **~ enough** efectivamente

sure-fire ['ʃuəfaɪə'] ADJ (*inf*) infalible

sure-footed [ʃuə'futɪd] ADJ de pie firme

★**surely** ['ʃuəlɪ] ADV (*certainly*) seguramente; **~ you don't mean that!** ¡no lo dices en serio!

surety ['ʃuərətɪ] N fianza; (*person*) fiador(a) *m/f*; **to go** or **stand - for sb** ser fiador de algn, salir garante por algn

surf [səːf] N olas *fpl* ▶ VI hacer surf ▶ VT (*Internet*): **to - the Net** navegar por Internet

★**surface** ['səːfɪs] N superficie *f*; **on the - it seems that ...** (*fig*) a primera vista parece que ... ▶ VT (*road*) revestir ▶ VI salir a la superficie ▶ CPD (*Mil, Naut*) de (la) superficie

surface area N área de la superficie

surface mail N vía terrestre

surface-to-air ['səːfɪstə'ɛəʳ] ADJ (*Mil*) tierra-aire

surface-to-surface ['səːfɪstə'səːfɪs] ADJ (*Mil*) tierra-tierra

surfboard ['səːfbɔːd] N tabla (de surf)

surfeit ['səːfɪt] N: **a - of** un exceso de

surfer ['səːfəʳ] N surfista *mf*; **web** or **net -** internauta *mf*

surfing ['səːfɪŋ] N surf *m*

surge [səːdʒ] N oleada, oleaje *m*; (*Elec*) sobretensión *f* transitoria ▶ VI (*wave*) romper; (*people*) avanzar a tropel; **to - forward** avanzar rápidamente

surgeon ['səːdʒən] N cirujano(-a)

★**surgery** ['səːdʒərɪ] N cirugía; (*BRIT: room*) consultorio; (: *Pol*) horas en las que los electores pueden reunirse personalmente con su diputado; **to undergo - operarse**; *see also* **constituency**

surgery hours NPL (*BRIT*) horas *fpl* de consulta

surgical ['səːdʒɪkl] ADJ quirúrgico

surgical spirit N (*BRIT*) alcohol *m*

Suriname [suərɪ'næm] N Surinam *m*

surly ['səːlɪ] ADJ hosco, malhumorado

surmount [səː'maunt] VT superar, vencer

surname ['səːneɪm] N apellido

surpass [səː'pɑːs] VT superar, exceder

surplus ['səːpləs] N excedente *m*; (*Comm*) superávit *m*; **to have a - of sth** tener un excedente de algo ▶ ADJ (*Comm*) excedente, sobrante; **it is - to our requirements** nos sobra; **- stock** saldos *mpl*

★**surprise** [sə'praɪz] N sorpresa; **to take by -** (*person*) coger desprevenido or por sorpresa a, sorprender a; (*Mil: town, fort*) atacar por sorpresa ▶ VT sorprender

★**surprised** [sə'praɪzd] ADJ (*look, smile*) de sorpresa; **to be - sorprenderse**

★**surprising** [sə'praɪzɪŋ] ADJ sorprendente

surprisingly [sə'praɪzɪŋlɪ] ADV (*easy, helpful*) de modo sorprendente; **(somewhat) -, he agreed** para sorpresa de todos, aceptó

surrealism [sə'rɪəlɪzəm] N surrealismo

★**surrender** [sə'rɛndəʳ] N rendición *f*, entrega ▶ VI rendirse, entregarse ▶ VT renunciar

surrender value N valor *m* de rescate

surreptitious [sʌrəp'tɪʃəs] ADJ subrepticio

surrogate ['sʌrəgɪt] N (*BRIT*) sustituto(-a)

surrogate mother N madre *f* de alquiler

★**surround** [sə'raund] VT rodear, circundar; (*Mil etc*) cercar

surrounding [sə'raundɪŋ] ADJ circundante

surroundings [sə'raundɪŋz] NPL alrededores *mpl*, cercanías *fpl*

surtax ['səːtæks] N sobretasa, sobreimpuesto

surveillance [səː'veɪləns] N vigilancia

★**survey** N ['səːveɪ] inspección *f*, reconocimiento; (*inquiry*) encuesta; (*comprehensive view: of situation etc*) vista de conjunto; **to carry out a - of** inspeccionar, examinar ▶ VT [səː'veɪ] examinar, inspeccionar; (*Surveying: building*) inspeccionar; (: *land*) hacer un reconocimiento de, reconocer; (*look at*) mirar, contemplar; (*make inquiries about*) hacer una encuesta de

surveyor [səː'veɪəʳ] N (*BRIT: of building*) perito *mf*; (*of land*) agrimensor(a) *m/f*

survival [sə'vaɪvl] N supervivencia

survival course N curso de supervivencia

survival kit N equipo de emergencia

survive [sə'vaɪv] VI sobrevivir; (*custom etc*) perdurar ▶ VT sobrevivir a

survivor [sə'vaɪvəʳ] N superviviente *mf*

susceptibility [səsɛptə'bɪlɪtɪ] N (*to illness*) propensión *f*

susceptible [sə'sɛptəbl] ADJ (*easily influenced*) influenciable; (*to disease, illness*): **- to** propenso a

sushi ['suːʃɪ] N sushi *m*

★**suspect** ADJ, N ['sʌspɛkt] sospechoso(-a) *m/f* ▶ VT [səs'pɛkt] sospechar

suspected [səs'pɛktɪd] ADJ presunto; **to have a - fracture** tener una posible fractura

★**suspend** [səs'pɛnd] VT suspender

suspended animation [səs'pɛndəd-] N: **in a state of -** en (estado de) hibernación

suspended sentence N (*Law*) libertad *f* condicional

suspender belt [səs'pɛndəʳ-] N (*BRIT*) liguero, portaligas *m inv* (*LAM*)

suspenders [səs'pɛndəz] NPL (*BRIT*) ligas *fpl*; (*US*) tirantes *mpl*

suspense [səs'pɛns] N incertidumbre *f*, duda; (*in film etc*) suspense *m*; **to keep sb in -** mantener a algn en suspense

suspension [səs'pɛnʃən] N (*gen*) suspensión *f*; (*of driving licence*) privación *f*

suspension bridge N puente *m* colgante

suspension file N archivador *m* colgante

suspicion [səs'pɪʃən] N sospecha; (*distrust*) recelo; (*trace*) traza; **to be under -** estar bajo sospecha; **arrested on - of murder** detenido bajo sospecha de asesinato

suspicious [səs'pɪʃəs] ADJ (*suspecting*) receloso; (*causing suspicion*) sospechoso; **to be - of** or **about sb/sth** tener sospechas de algn/algo

suss out [sʌs-] VT (*BRIT inf*) calar

sustain [səs'teɪn] VT sostener, apoyar; (*suffer*) sufrir, padecer

sustainable [səs'teɪnəbl] ADJ sostenible; **~ development** desarrollo sostenible

sustained [səs'teɪnd] ADJ (*effort*) sostenido

sustenance ['sʌstɪnəns] N sustento

suture ['suːtʃə^r] N sutura

SUV ['es'juː'viː] N ABBR (= *sports utility vehicle*) SUV *m*, todoterreno *m inv*

SVQ N ABBR (= *Scottish Vocational Qualification*) *titulación de formación profesional en Escocia*

SW ABBR = **short wave**

swab [swɔb] N (*Med*) algodón *m*, frotis *m inv* ▸ VT (*Naut: also:* **swab down**) limpiar, fregar

swagger ['swægə^r] VI pavonearse

swallow ['swɔləu] N (*bird*) golondrina; (*of food*) bocado; (*of drink*) trago ▸ VT tragar
▸ **swallow up** (*savings etc*) consumir

swam [swæm] PT *of* **swim**

swamp [swɔmp] N pantano, ciénaga ▸ VT abrumar, agobiar

swampy ['swɔmpɪ] ADJ pantanoso

swan [swɔn] N cisne *m*

swank [swæŋk] (*inf*) N (*vanity, boastfulness*) fanfarronada ▸ VI fanfarronear, presumir

swan song N (*fig*) canto del cisne

swap [swɔp] N canje *m*, trueque *m* ▸ VT: **to ~ (for)** canjear (por), cambiar (por)

SWAPO ['swɑːpəu] N ABBR (= *South-West Africa People's Organization*) SWAPO *f*

swarm [swɔːm] N (*of bees*) enjambre *m*; (*fig*) multitud *f* ▸ VI (*bees*) formar un enjambre; (*fig*) hormiguear, pulular

swarthy ['swɔːðɪ] ADJ moreno

swashbuckling ['swɔʃbʌklɪŋ] ADJ (*person*) aventurero; (*film*) de capa y espada

swastika ['swɔstɪkə] N esvástica, cruz *f* gamada

SWAT [swɔt] N ABBR (*US:* = *Special Weapons and Tactics*) *unidad especial de la policía*

swat [swɔt] VT aplastar ▸ N (*also:* **fly swat**) matamoscas *m inv*

swathe [sweɪð] VT: **to ~ in** (*blankets*) envolver en; (*bandages*) vendar en

sway [sweɪ] VI mecerse, balancearse ▸ VT (*influence*) mover, influir en ▸ N (*rule, power*): **~ (over)** dominio (sobre); **to hold ~ over sb** dominar a algn, mantener el dominio sobre algn

Swaziland ['swɑːzɪlænd] N Swazilandia

swear [swɛə^r] (*pt* **swore** [swɔː^r], *pp* **sworn** [swɔːn]) VI jurar; (*with swearwords*) decir tacos; **to ~ to sth** declarar algo bajo juramento ▸ VT: **to ~ an oath** prestar juramento, jurar
▸ **swear in** VT tomar juramento (a); **to be sworn in** prestar juramento

swearword ['swɛəwəːd] N taco, palabrota

sweat [swɛt] N sudor *m* ▸ VI sudar

sweatband ['swɛtbænd] N (*Sport: on head*) banda; (*: on wrist*) muñequera

sweater ['swɛtə^r] N suéter *m*

sweatshirt ['swɛtʃəːt] N sudadera

sweatshop ['swɛtʃɔp] N fábrica donde se explota al obrero

sweaty ['swɛtɪ] ADJ sudoroso

★**Swede** [swiːd] N sueco(-a)

swede [swiːd] N (*Brit*) nabo

★**Sweden** ['swiːdn] N Suecia

★**Swedish** ['swiːdɪʃ] ADJ, N (*Ling*) sueco

★**sweep** [swiːp] (*pt, pp* **swept** [swɛpt]) N (*act*) barrida; (*of arm*) manotazo *m*; (*curve*) curva, alcance *m*; (*also:* **chimney sweep**) deshollinador(a) *m/f* ▸ VT barrer; (*with arm*) empujar; (*current*) arrastrar; (*disease, fashion*) recorrer ▸ VI barrer
▸ **sweep away** VT barrer; (*rub out*) borrar
▸ **sweep past** VI pasar rápidamente; (*brush by*) rozar
▸ **sweep up** VI barrer

sweeper ['swiːpə^r] N (*person*) barrendero(-a); (*machine*) barredora; (*Football*) líbero, libre *m*

sweeping ['swiːpɪŋ] ADJ (*gesture*) dramático; (*generalized*) generalizado; (*changes, reforms*) radical

sweepstake ['swiːpsteɪk] N lotería

★**sweet** [swiːt] N (*Brit*: *candy*) dulce *m*, caramelo; (*: pudding*) postre *m* ▸ ADJ dulce; (*sugary*) azucarado; (*charming: person*) encantador(a); (*: smile, character*) dulce, amable, agradable; **to smell/ taste ~** oler/saber dulce

sweet and sour ADJ agridulce

sweetcorn ['swiːtkɔːn] N maíz *m* (dulce)

sweeten ['swiːtn] VT (*person*) endulzar; (*add sugar to*) poner azúcar a

sweetener ['swiːtnə^r] N (*Culin*) edulcorante *m*

sweetheart ['swiːthɑːt] N amor *m*, novio(-a); (*in speech*) amor, cariño

sweetness ['swiːtnɪs] N (*gen*) dulzura

sweet pea N guisante *m* de olor

sweet potato N batata, camote *m* (*LAM*)

sweetshop ['swiːtʃɔp] N (*Brit*) confitería, bombonería

swell [swel] (*pt* **swelled** [sweld], *pp* **swollen** ['swəulən] *or* **swelled**) N (*of sea*) marejada, oleaje *m* ▸ ADJ (*US inf: excellent*) estupendo, fenomenal ▸ VT hinchar, inflar ▸ VI (*also:* **swell up**) hincharse; (*numbers*) aumentar; (*sound, feeling*) ir aumentando

swelling ['swelɪŋ] N (*Med*) hinchazón *f*

sweltering ['sweltərɪŋ] ADJ sofocante, de mucho calor

swept [swept] PT, PP *of* **sweep**

swerve [swəːv] N regate *m*; (*in car*) desvío brusco ▸ VI desviarse bruscamente

swift [swɪft] N (*bird*) vencejo ▸ ADJ rápido, veloz

swiftly ['swɪftlɪ] ADV rápidamente

swiftness ['swɪftnɪs] N rapidez *f*, velocidad *f*

swig [swɪg] N (*inf: drink*) trago

swill [swɪl] N bazofia ▸ VT (*also*: **swill out, swill down**) lavar, limpiar con agua

★**swim** [swɪm] (*pt* **swam** [swæm], *pp* **swum** [swʌm]) N: **to go for a ~** ir a nadar *or* a bañarse ▸ VI nadar; (*head, room*) dar vueltas; **to go swimming** ir a nadar ▸ VT pasar a nado; **to ~ a length** nadar *or* hacer un largo

swimmer ['swɪmə^r] N nadador(a) *m/f*

★**swimming** ['swɪmɪŋ] N natación *f*

swimming cap N gorro de baño

swimming costume N bañador *m*, traje *m* de baño

swimmingly ['swɪmɪŋlɪ] ADV: **to go ~** (*wonderfully*) ir como una seda *or* sobre ruedas

swimming pool N piscina, alberca (*LAM*)

swimming trunks NPL bañador *msg*

★**swimsuit** ['swɪmsuːt] N = **swimming costume**

swindle ['swɪndl] N estafa ▸ VT estafar

swine [swaɪn] N *pl inv* cerdo, puerco; (*pej*) canalla *m*

swine flu ['swaɪn-] N gripe *f* porcina

★**swing** [swɪŋ] (*pt, pp* **swung** [swʌŋ]) N (*in playground*) columpio; (*movement*) balanceo, vaivén *m*; (*change of direction*) viraje *m*; (*rhythm*) ritmo; (*Pol: in votes etc*): **there has been a ~ towards/away from Labour** ha habido un viraje en favor/en contra del Partido Laborista; **a ~ to the left** un movimiento hacia la izquierda; **to be in full ~** estar en plena marcha; **to get into the ~ of things** meterse en situación ▸ VT balancear; (*on a swing*) columpiar; (*also*: **swing round**) voltear, girar ▸ VI balancearse, columpiarse; (*also*: **swing round**) dar media vuelta; **the road swings south** la carretera gira hacia el sur

swing bridge N puente *m* giratorio

swing door, (*US*) **swinging door** ['swɪŋɪŋ-] N puerta giratoria

swingeing ['swɪndʒɪŋ] ADJ (*BRIT*) abrumador(a)

swipe [swaɪp] N golpe *m* fuerte ▸ VT (*hit*) golpear fuerte; (*inf: steal*) guindar; (*credit card etc*) pasar

swipe card [swaɪp-] N tarjeta magnética deslizante, tarjeta swipe

swirl [swəːl] VI arremolinarse

swish [swɪʃ] N (*sound: of whip*) chasquido; (: *of skirts*) frufrú *m*; (: *of grass*) crujido ▸ ADJ (*old: smart*) elegante ▸ VI chasquear

★**Swiss** [swɪs] ADJ, N *pl inv* suizo(-a) *m/f*

★**switch** [swɪtʃ] N (*for light, radio etc*) interruptor *m*; (*change*) cambio ▸ VT (*change*) cambiar de; (*invert: also*: **switch round, switch over**) intercambiar
  ▸ **switch off** VT apagar; (*engine*) parar
  ▸ **switch on** VT (*Aut: ignition*) encender, prender (*LAM*); (*engine, machine*) arrancar; (*water supply*) conectar

switchboard ['swɪtʃbɔːd] N (*Tel*) centralita (de teléfonos), conmutador *m* (*LAM*)

★**Switzerland** ['swɪtsələnd] N Suiza

swivel ['swɪvl] VI (*also*: **swivel round**) girar

swollen ['swəulən] PP *of* **swell**

swoon [swuːn] VI desmayarse

swoop [swuːp] N (*by police etc*) redada; (*of bird etc*) descenso en picado, calada ▸ VI (*also*: **swoop down**) caer en picado

swop [swɔp] N, VB = **swap**

sword [sɔːd] N espada

swordfish ['sɔːdfɪʃ] N pez *m* espada

swore [swɔː^r] PT *of* **swear**

sworn [swɔːn] PP *of* **swear** ▸ ADJ (*statement*) bajo juramento; (*enemy*) implacable

swot [swɔt] (*BRIT*) VT, VI empollar ▸ N empollón(-ona) *m/f*

swum [swʌm] PP *of* **swim**

swung [swʌŋ] PT, PP *of* **swing**

sycamore ['sɪkəmɔː^r] N sicomoro

sycophant ['sɪkəfænt] N adulador(a) *m/f*, pelotillero(-a)

Sydney ['sɪdnɪ] N Sídney *m*

syllable ['sɪləbl] N sílaba

syllabus ['sɪləbəs] N programa *m* de estudios; **on the ~** en el programa de estudios

★**symbol** ['sɪmbl] N símbolo

symbolic [sɪm'bɔlɪk], **symbolical** [sɪm'bɔlɪkl] ADJ simbólico; **to be ~ of sth** simbolizar algo

symbolism ['sɪmbəlɪzəm] N simbolismo

symbolize ['sɪmbəlaɪz] VT simbolizar

symmetrical [sɪ'metrɪkl] ADJ simétrico

symmetry ['sɪmɪtrɪ] N simetría

sympathetic [sɪmpə'θetɪk] ADJ compasivo; (*understanding*) comprensivo; **to be ~ to a cause** (*well-disposed*) apoyar una causa; **to be ~ towards** (*person*) ser comprensivo con

> **sympathetic** no debe traducirse por *simpático*.

sympathize ['sɪmpəθaɪz] VI: **to ~ with** (*person*) compadecerse de; (*feelings*) comprender; (*cause*) apoyar

sympathizer ['sɪmpəθaɪzə^r] N (*Pol*) simpatizante *mf*

★**sympathy** ['sɪmpəθɪ] N (*pity*) compasión *f*; (*understanding*) comprensión *f*; **a letter of ~** un pésame; **with our deepest ~** nuestro más sentido pésame

symphony ['sɪmfənɪ] N sinfonía

symposium [sɪm'pəuzɪəm] N simposio

★**symptom** ['sɪmptəm] N síntoma *m*, indicio

symptomatic [sɪmptə'mætɪk] ADJ: **~ (of)** sintomático (de)

synagogue ['sɪnəgɔg] N sinagoga

sync [sɪŋk] N (*inf*): **to be in/out of ~ (with)** ir/no ir al mismo ritmo (que); (*fig: people*) conectar/no conectar (con)

synchromesh ['sɪŋkrəumeʃ] N cambio sincronizado de velocidades

synchronize [ˈsɪŋkrənaɪz] VT sincronizar ▸ VI: **to ~ with** sincronizarse con

synchronized swimming [ˈsɪŋkrənaɪzd-] N natación f sincronizada

syncopated [ˈsɪŋkəpeɪtɪd] ADJ sincopado

syndicate [ˈsɪndɪkɪt] N (gen) sindicato; (Press) agencia (de noticias)

syndrome [ˈsɪndrəum] N síndrome m

synonym [ˈsɪnənɪm] N sinónimo

synonymous [sɪˈnɒnɪməs] ADJ: **~ (with)** sinónimo (de)

synopsis [sɪˈnɒpsɪs] (pl **synopses** [-siːz]) N sinopsis f inv

syntax [ˈsɪntæks] N sintaxis f

syntax error N (Comput) error m sintáctico

synthesis [ˈsɪnθəsɪs] (pl **syntheses** [-siːz]) N síntesis f inv

synthesizer [ˈsɪnθəsaɪzəʳ] N sintetizador m

synthetic [sɪnˈθɛtɪk] ADJ sintético ▸ N sintético

syphilis [ˈsɪfɪlɪs] N sífilis f

syphon [ˈsaɪfən] N, VB = **siphon**

Syria [ˈsɪrɪə] N Siria

Syrian [ˈsɪrɪən] ADJ, N sirio(-a) m/f

syringe [sɪˈrɪndʒ] N jeringa

syrup [ˈsɪrəp] N jarabe m, almíbar m

★**system** [ˈsɪstəm] N sistema m; (Anat) organismo; **it was quite a shock to his ~** fue un golpe para él

systematic [sɪstəˈmætɪk] ADJ sistemático, metódico

system disk N (Comput) disco del sistema

systems analyst N analista mf de sistemas

Tt

T, t [ti:] N (*letter*) T, t *f*; **T for Tommy** T de Tarragona

TA N ABBR (*BRIT*) = **Territorial Army**

ta [tɑ:] EXCL (*BRIT inf*) ¡gracias!

tab [tæb] N ABBR = **tabulator** ▶ N lengüeta; (*label*) etiqueta; **to keep tabs on** (*fig*) vigilar

tabby ['tæbɪ] N (*also:* **tabby cat**) gato atigrado

tabernacle ['tæbənækl] N tabernáculo

★table ['teɪbl] N mesa; (*chart: of statistics etc*) cuadro, tabla; **to lay** *or* **set the ~** poner la mesa; **to clear the ~** quitar *or* levantar la mesa; **league ~** (*Football, Rugby*) clasificación *f* del campeonato; **~ of contents** índice *m* de materias ▶ VT (*BRIT: motion etc*) presentar

tablecloth ['teɪblklɔθ] N mantel *m*

table d'hôte [tɑ:bl'dəut] N menú *m*

table lamp N lámpara de mesa

tablemat ['teɪblmæt] N (*for plate*) posaplatos *m inv*; (*for hot dish*) salvamanteles *m inv*

tablespoon ['teɪblspu:n] N cuchara grande; (*also:* **tablespoonful:** *as measurement*) cucharada grande

tablet ['tæblɪt] N (*Med*) pastilla, comprimido; (*for writing*) bloc *m*; (*of stone*) lápida; (*Comput*) tableta, tablet *f*; **~ of soap** pastilla de jabón

table talk N conversación *f* de sobremesa

table tennis N ping-pong *m*, tenis *m* de mesa

table wine N vino de mesa

tabloid ['tæblɔɪd] N (*newspaper*) periódico popular sensacionalista

tabloid press N ver nota

El término **tabloid press** o *tabloids* se usa para referirse a los periódicos populares británicos. Aunque el nombre viene de su tamaño reducido se sigue usando de forma genérica para las versiones publicadas en línea. A diferencia de la llamada *quality press*, estos periódicos se caracterizan por su lenguaje sencillo, presentación llamativa y contenido a menudo sensacionalista, con gran énfasis en noticias sobre escándalos financieros y sexuales de los famosos, por lo que también reciben el nombre peyorativo de *gutter press*.

taboo [tə'bu:] ADJ, N tabú *m*

tabulate ['tæbjuleɪt] VT disponer en tablas

tabulator ['tæbjuleɪtəʳ] N tabulador *m*

tachograph ['tækəgrɑ:f] N tacógrafo

tachometer [tæ'kɔmɪtəʳ] N taquímetro

tacit ['tæsɪt] ADJ tácito

tacitly ['tæsɪtlɪ] ADV tácitamente

taciturn ['tæsɪtə:n] ADJ taciturno

tack [tæk] N (*nail*) tachuela; (*stitch*) hilván *m*; (*Naut*) bordada ▶ VT (*nail*) clavar con tachuelas; (*stitch*) hilvanar; **to ~ sth on to (the end of) sth** (*of letter, book*) añadir algo a(l final de) algo ▶ VI virar

★tackle ['tækl] N (*gear*) equipo; (*fishing tackle, for lifting*) aparejo; (*Football*) entrada, tackle *m*; (*Rugby*) placaje *m* ▶ VT (*difficulty*) enfrentarse a, abordar; (*challenge: person*) hacer frente a; (*grapple with*) agarrar; (*Football*) entrar a; (*Rugby*) placar

tacky ['tækɪ] ADJ pegajoso; (*inf*) hortera *inv*, de mal gusto

tact [tækt] N tacto, discreción *f*

tactful ['tæktful] ADJ discreto, diplomático; **to be ~** tener tacto, actuar discretamente

tactfully ['tæktfulɪ] ADV diplomáticamente, con tacto

tactical ['tæktɪkl] ADJ táctico

tactical voting N voto útil

tactician [tæk'tɪʃən] N táctico(-a)

tactics ['tæktɪks] NPL táctica *sg*

tactless ['tæktlɪs] ADJ indiscreto

tactlessly ['tæktlɪslɪ] ADV indiscretamente, sin tacto

tadpole ['tædpəul] N renacuajo

taffy ['tæfɪ] N (*US*) melcocha

tag [tæg] N (*label*) etiqueta; **price/name ~** etiqueta del precio/con el nombre
▶ **tag along** VI: **to ~ along with sb** engancharse a algn

tag question N pregunta coletilla

Tahiti [tɑːˈhiːtɪ] N Tahití *m*

★**tail** [teɪl] N cola; (*Zool*) rabo; (*of shirt, coat*) faldón *m*; **heads or tails** cara o cruz; **to turn ~** volver la espalda ▶ VT (*follow*) vigilar a ■ **tails** NPL (*formal suit*) levita
  ▶ **tail away, tail off** VI (*in size, quality etc*) ir disminuyendo

tailback [ˈteɪlbæk] N (*Brit Aut*) cola

tail coat N frac *m*

tail end N cola, parte *f* final

tailgate [ˈteɪlɡeɪt] N (*Aut*) puerta trasera

tail light N (*Aut*) luz *f* trasera

tailor [ˈteɪlə^r] N sastre *m*; **~'s (shop)** sastrería
  ▶ VT: **to ~ sth (to)** confeccionar algo a medida (para)

tailoring [ˈteɪlərɪŋ] N (*cut*) corte *m*; (*craft*) sastrería

tailor-made [ˈteɪləˈmeɪd] ADJ (*also fig*) hecho a (la) medida

tailwind [ˈteɪlwɪnd] N viento de cola

taint [teɪnt] VT (*meat, food*) contaminar; (*fig: reputation*) manchar, tachar (*LAm*)

tainted [ˈteɪntɪd] ADJ (*water, air*) contaminado; (*fig*) manchado

Taiwan [taɪˈwɑːn] N Taiwán *m*

Taiwanese [taɪwəˈniːz] ADJ, N taiwanés(-esa) *m/f*

Tajikistan [tɑːdʒɪkɪˈstɑːn] N Tayikistán *m*

★**take** [teɪk] (*pt* **took** [tuk], *pp* **taken** [ˈteɪkən]) VT tomar; (*grab*) coger (*Sp*), agarrar (*LAm*); (*gain: prize*) ganar; (*require: effort, courage*) exigir; (*support weight of*) aguantar; (*hold: passengers etc*) tener cabida para; (*accompany, bring, carry*) llevar; (*exam*) presentarse a; (*conduct: meeting*) presidir; **to ~ sth from** (*drawer etc*) sacar algo de; (*person*) quitar algo a, coger algo a (*Sp*); **to ~ notes** tomar apuntes; **to ~ sb's hand** tomar de la mano a algn; **to be taken ill** ponerse enfermo; **~ the first on the left** toma la primera a la izquierda; **I only took Russian for one year** solo estudié ruso un año; **I took him for a doctor** le tenía por médico; **it won't ~ long** durará poco; **it will ~ at least five litres** tiene cabida por lo menos para cinco litros; **to be taken with sb/sth** (*attracted*) tomarle cariño a algn/tomarle gusto a algo; **I ~ it that ...** supongo que ... ▶ VI (*fire*) prender; (*dye*) coger (*Sp*), agarrar, tomar ▶ N (*Cine*) toma
  ▶ **take after** VT FUS parecerse a
  ▶ **take apart** VT desmontar
  ▶ **take away** VT (*remove*) quitar; (*carry off*) llevar
  ▶ VI: **to ~ away from** quitar mérito a
  ▶ **take back** VT (*return*) devolver; (*one's words*) retractar
  ▶ **take down** VT (*building*) derribar; (*dismantle: scaffolding*) desmantelar; (*message etc*) apuntar, tomar nota de
  ▶ **take in** VT (*deceive*) engañar; (*understand*) entender; (*include*) abarcar; (*lodger*) acoger, recibir; (*orphan, stray dog*) recoger; (*Sewing*) achicar

  ▶ **take off** VI (*Aviat*) despegar, decolar (*LAM*) ▶ VT (*remove*) quitar; (*imitate*) imitar, remedar
  ▶ **take on** VT (*work*) emprender; (*employee*) contratar; (*opponent*) desafiar
  ▶ **take out** VT sacar; (*remove*) quitar; **don't ~ it out on me!** ¡no te desquites conmigo!
  ▶ **take over** VT (*business*) tomar posesión de
  ▶ VI: **to ~ over from sb** reemplazar a algn
  ▶ **take to** VT FUS (*person*) coger cariño a (*Sp*), encariñarse con (*LAm*); (*activity*) aficionarse a; **to ~ to doing sth** aficionarse a (hacer) algo
  ▶ **take up** VT (*a dress*) acortar; (*occupy: time, space*) ocupar; (*engage in: hobby etc*) dedicarse a; (*absorb: liquids*) absorber; (*accept: offer, challenge*) aceptar; **to ~ sb up on sth** aceptar algo de algn
  ▶ VI: **to ~ up with sb** hacerse amigo de algn
  ▶ **take upon** VT: **to ~ it upon o.s. to do sth** encargarse de hacer algo

takeaway [ˈteɪkəweɪ] ADJ (*Brit: food*) para llevar
  ▶ N tienda *or* restaurante *m* de comida para llevar

take-home pay [ˈteɪkhəum-] N salario neto

taken [ˈteɪkən] PP *of* **take**

takeoff [ˈteɪkɔf] N (*Aviat*) despegue *m*, decolaje *m* (*LAm*)

takeover [ˈteɪkəuvə^r] N (*Comm*) absorción *f*

takeover bid N oferta pública de adquisición

takings [ˈteɪkɪŋz] NPL (*Comm*) ingresos *mpl*

talc [tælk] N (*also*: **talcum powder**) talco

★**tale** [teɪl] N (*story*) cuento; (*account*) relación *f*; **to tell tales** (*fig*) contar chismes

★**talent** [ˈtælnt] N talento

talented [ˈtæləntɪd] ADJ talentoso, de talento

talisman [ˈtælɪzmən] N talismán *m*

★**talk** [tɔːk] N charla; (*gossip*) habladurías *fpl*, chismes *mpl*; (*conversation*) conversación *f*; **to give a ~** dar una charla *or* conferencia ▶ VI (*speak*) hablar; (*chatter*) charlar; **to ~ about** hablar de; **talking of films, have you seen ...?** hablando de películas, ¿has visto ...? ▶ VT hablar; **to ~ shop** hablar del trabajo; **to ~ sb into doing sth** convencer a algn para que haga algo; **to ~ sb out of doing sth** disuadir a algn de que haga algo ■ **talks** NPL (*Pol etc*) conversaciones *fpl*
  ▶ **talk over** VT discutir

talkative [ˈtɔːkətɪv] ADJ hablador(a)

talker [ˈtɔːkə^r] N hablador(a) *m/f*

talking point [ˈtɔːkɪŋ-] N tema *m* de conversación

talking-to [ˈtɔːkɪŋtuː] N: **to give sb a good ~** echar una buena bronca a algn

talk show N programa *m* magazine

★**tall** [tɔːl] ADJ alto; (*tree*) grande; **to be 6 feet ~** ≈ medir 1 metro 80, tener 1 metro 80 de alto; **how ~ are you?** ¿cuánto mides?

tallboy [ˈtɔːlbɔɪ] N (*Brit*) cómoda alta

tallness [ˈtɔːlnɪs] N altura

tall story N cuento chino

tally [ˈtælɪ] N cuenta; **to keep a ~ of sth** llevar la cuenta de algo ▶ VI: **to ~ (with)** concordar (con), cuadrar (con)

talon ['tælən] N garra

tambourine [tæmbə'ri:n] N pandereta

tame [teɪm] ADJ (*mild*) manso; (*tamed*) domesticado; (*fig: story, style, person*) soso, anodino

tameness ['teɪmnɪs] N mansedumbre f

Tamil ['tæmɪl] ADJ tamil ▶ N tamil mf; (*Ling*) tamil m

tamper ['tæmpəʳ] VI: **to ~ with** (*lock etc*) intentar forzar; (*papers*) falsificar

tampon ['tæmpɒn] N tampón m

tan [tæn] N (*also:* **suntan**) bronceado; **to get a ~** broncearse, ponerse moreno ▶ VT broncear ▶ VI ponerse moreno ▶ ADJ (*colour*) marrón

tandem ['tændəm] N tándem m

tandoori [tæn'duərɪ] ADJ, N tandoori m (*asado a la manera hindú, en horno de barro*)

tang [tæŋ] N sabor m fuerte

tangent ['tændʒənt] N (*Math*) tangente f; **to go off at a ~** (*fig*) salirse por la tangente

tangerine [tændʒə'ri:n] N mandarina

tangible ['tændʒəbl] ADJ tangible; **~ assets** bienes mpl tangibles

Tangier [tæn'dʒɪəʳ] N Tánger m

tangle ['tæŋgl] N enredo; **to get in(to) a ~** enredarse

tango ['tæŋgəu] N tango

tank [tæŋk] N (*also:* **water tank**) depósito, tanque m; (*for fish*) acuario; (*Mil*) tanque m

tankard ['tæŋkəd] N bock m

tanker ['tæŋkəʳ] N (*ship*) petrolero; (*truck*) camión m cisterna

tankful ['tæŋkful] N: **to get a ~ of petrol** llenar el depósito de gasolina

tankini [taŋ'ki:nɪ] N tankini m

tanned [tænd] ADJ (*skin*) moreno, bronceado

tannin ['tænɪn] N tanino

tanning ['tænɪŋ] N (*of leather*) curtido

tannoy® ['tænɔɪ] N: **over the ~** por el altavoz

tantalizing ['tæntəlaɪzɪŋ] ADJ tentador(a)

tantamount ['tæntəmaunt] ADJ: **~ to** equivalente a

tantrum ['tæntrəm] N rabieta; **to throw a ~** coger una rabieta

Tanzania [tænzə'nɪə] N Tanzania

Tanzanian [tænzə'nɪən] ADJ, N tanzano(-a) m/f

★**tap** [tæp] N (*BRIT: on sink etc*) grifo, canilla (*LAM*); (*gentle blow*) golpecito; (*gas tap*) llave f; **on ~** (*fig: resources*) a mano; **beer on ~** cerveza de barril ▶ VT (*table etc*) tamborilear; (*shoulder etc*) dar palmaditas en; (*resources*) utilizar, explotar; (*telephone conversation*) intervenir, pinchar

tap dancing ['tæpdɑ:nsɪŋ] N claqué m

★**tape** [teɪp] N cinta; (*also:* **magnetic tape**) cinta magnética; (*sticky tape*) cinta adhesiva; **on ~** (*song etc*) grabado (en cinta) ▶ VT (*record*) grabar (en cinta)

tape deck N pletina

tape measure N cinta métrica, metro

taper ['teɪpəʳ] N cirio ▶ VI afilarse

tape-record ['teɪprɪkɔ:d] VT grabar (en cinta)

tape recorder N grabadora

tape recording N grabación f

tapered ['teɪpəd], **tapering** ['teɪpərɪŋ] ADJ terminado en punta

tapestry ['tæpɪstrɪ] N (*object*) tapiz m; (*art*) tapicería

tape-worm ['teɪpwə:m] N solitaria, tenia

tapioca [tæpɪ'əukə] N tapioca

tappet ['tæpɪt] N excéntrica

tar [tɑ:ʳ] N alquitrán m, brea; **low/middle ~ cigarettes** cigarrillos mpl con contenido bajo/medio de alquitrán

tarantula [tə'ræntjulə] N tarántula

tardy ['tɑ:dɪ] ADJ (*late*) tardío; (*slow*) lento

tare [tɛəʳ] N (*Comm*) tara

★**target** ['tɑ:gɪt] N (*gen*) blanco; **to be on ~** (*project*) seguir el curso previsto

target audience N público al que va destinado un programa etc

target market N (*Comm*) mercado al que va destinado un producto etc

target practice N tiro al blanco

tariff ['tærɪf] N (*on goods*) arancel m; (*BRIT: in hotels etc*) tarifa

tariff barrier N (*Comm*) barrera arancelaria

tarmac ['tɑ:mæk] N (*BRIT: on road*) asfalto; (*Aviat*) pista (de aterrizaje)

tarn [tɑ:n] N lago pequeño de montaña

tarnish ['tɑ:nɪʃ] VT deslustrar

tarot ['tærəu] N tarot m

tarpaulin [tɑ:'pɔ:lɪn] N lona (impermeabilizada)

tarragon ['tærəgən] N estragón m

tarry ['tærɪ] VI entretenerse, quedarse atrás

tart [tɑ:t] N (*Culin*) tarta; (*BRIT inf, pej: woman*) fulana ▶ ADJ (*flavour*) agrio, ácido
▶ **tart up** VT (*room, building*) dar tono a

tartan ['tɑ:tn] N tartán m, tela escocesa ▶ ADJ de tartán

tartar ['tɑ:təʳ] N (*on teeth*) sarro

tartar sauce, **tartare sauce** N salsa tártara

tartly ['tɑ:tlɪ] ADV (*answer*) ásperamente

★**task** [tɑ:sk] N tarea; **to take to ~** reprender

task force N (*Mil, Police*) grupo de operaciones

taskmaster ['tɑ:skmɑ:stəʳ] N: **he's a hard ~** es muy exigente

tassel ['tæsl] N borla

★**taste** [teɪst] N sabor m, gusto; (*also:* **aftertaste**) dejo; (*sip*) sorbo; (*fig: glimpse, idea*) muestra, idea; **can I have a ~ of this wine?** ¿puedo probar este vino?; **to have a ~ for sth** ser aficionado a algo; **in good/bad ~** de buen/mal gusto; **to be in bad** or **poor ~** ser de mal gusto ▶ VT probar; **you can**

~ the garlic (in it) se nota el sabor a ajo ▶ VI: **to ~ of** or **like** (*fish etc*) saber a

taste bud N papila gustativa or del gusto

tasteful [ˈteɪstful] ADJ de buen gusto

tastefully [ˈteɪstfulɪ] ADV elegantemente, con buen gusto

tasteless [ˈteɪstlɪs] ADJ (*food*) soso; (*remark*) de mal gusto

tastelessly [ˈteɪstlɪslɪ] ADV con mal gusto

tastily [ˈteɪstɪlɪ] ADV sabrosamente

tastiness [ˈteɪstɪnɪs] N (buen) sabor *m*, lo sabroso

tasty [ˈteɪstɪ] ADJ sabroso, rico

ta-ta [ˈtæˈtɑː] EXCL (*BRIT inf*) hasta luego, adiós

tatters [ˈtætəz] NPL: **in ~** (*also:* **tattered**) hecho jirones

tattoo [təˈtuː] N tatuaje *m*; (*spectacle*) espectáculo militar ▶ VT tatuar

tatty [ˈtætɪ] ADJ (*BRIT inf*) cochambroso

taught [tɔːt] PT, PP of **teach**

taunt [tɔːnt] N pulla ▶ VT lanzar pullas a

Taurus [ˈtɔːrəs] N Tauro

taut [tɔːt] ADJ tirante, tenso

tavern [ˈtævən] N (*old*) posada, fonda

tawdry [ˈtɔːdrɪ] ADJ de mal gusto

tawny [ˈtɔːnɪ] ADJ leonado

★**tax** [tæks] N impuesto; **before/after ~** impuestos excluidos/incluidos; **free of ~** libre de impuestos ▶ VT gravar (con un impuesto); (*fig: test*) poner a prueba; (: *patience*) agotar

taxable [ˈtæksəbl] ADJ (*income*) imponible, sujeto a impuestos

tax allowance N desgravación *f* fiscal

taxation [tækˈseɪʃən] N impuestos *mpl*; **system of ~** sistema *m* tributario

tax avoidance N evasión *f* de impuestos

tax collector N recaudador(a) *m/f*

tax disc N (*BRIT Aut*) pegatina del impuesto de circulación

tax evasion N evasión *f* fiscal

tax exemption N exención *f* de impuestos

tax-free [ˈtæksfriː] ADJ libre de impuestos

tax haven N paraíso fiscal

taxi [ˈtæksɪ] N taxi *m* ▶ VI (*Aviat*) rodar por la pista

taxidermist [ˈtæksɪdəːmɪst] N taxidermista *mf*

taxi driver N taxista *mf*

tax inspector N inspector(a) *m/f* de Hacienda

taxi rank, (*US*) **taxi stand** N parada de taxis

tax payer N contribuyente *mf*

tax rebate N devolución *f* de impuestos, reembolso fiscal

tax relief N desgravación *f* fiscal

tax return N declaración *f* de la renta

tax shelter N protección *f* fiscal

tax year N año fiscal

TB N ABBR = **tuberculosis**

tbc ABBR (= *to be confirmed*) por confirmar

TD N ABBR (*US*) = **Treasury Department**; (*Football*) = **touchdown**

★**tea** [tiː] N té *m*; (*BRIT: snack*) ≈ merienda; **high ~** (*BRIT*) ≈ merienda-cena

tea bag N bolsita de té

tea break N (*BRIT*) descanso para el té

teacake [ˈtiːkeɪk] N bollito, queque *m* (*LAM*)

★**teach** [tiːtʃ] (*pt, pp* **taught** [tɔːt]) VT: **to ~ sb sth, ~ sth to sb** enseñar algo a algn; **it taught him a lesson** (eso) le sirvió de escarmiento ▶ VI enseñar; (*be a teacher*) ser profesor(a)

★**teacher** [ˈtiːtʃəʳ] N (*in secondary school*) profesor(a) *m/f*; (*in primary school*) maestro(-a); **Spanish ~** profesor(a) *m/f* de español

teacher training college N (*for primary schools*) escuela normal; (*for secondary schools*) centro de formación del profesorado

teach-in [ˈtiːtʃɪn] N seminario

teaching [ˈtiːtʃɪŋ] N enseñanza

teaching aids NPL materiales *mpl* pedagógicos

teaching hospital N hospital universitario

tea cloth N (*BRIT*) paño de cocina, trapo de cocina (*LAM*)

tea cosy N cubretetera *m*

teacup [ˈtiːkʌp] N taza de té

teak [tiːk] N (madera de) teca

tea leaves NPL hojas *fpl* de té

★**team** [tiːm] N equipo; (*of animals*) pareja ▶ **team up** VI asociarse

team spirit N espíritu *m* de equipo

teamwork [ˈtiːmwəːk] N trabajo en equipo

tea party N té *m*

teapot [ˈtiːpɔt] N tetera

★**tear**[1] [tɪəʳ] N lágrima; **in tears** llorando; **to burst into tears** deshacerse en lágrimas

★**tear**[2] [tɛəʳ] (*pt* **tore** [tɔːʳ], *pp* **torn** [tɔːn]) N rasgón *m*, desgarrón *m* ▶ VT romper, rasgar; **to ~ to pieces** or **to bits** or **to shreds** (*also fig*) hacer pedazos, destrozar ▶ VI rasgarse
▶ **tear along** VI (*rush*) precipitarse
▶ **tear apart** VT (*also fig*) hacer pedazos
▶ **tear away** VT: **to ~ o.s. away (from sth)** alejarse de algo)
▶ **tear down** VT (*building, statue*) derribar; (*poster, flag*) arrancar
▶ **tear off** VT (*sheet of paper etc*) arrancar; (*one's clothes*) quitarse a tirones
▶ **tear out** VT (*sheet of paper, cheque*) arrancar
▶ **tear up** VT (*sheet of paper etc*) romper

tearaway [ˈtɛərəweɪ] N (*inf*) gamberro(-a)

teardrop [ˈtɪədrɔp] N lágrima

tearful [ˈtɪəful] ADJ lloroso

tear gas N gas *m* lacrimógeno

tearing [ˈtɛərɪŋ] ADJ: **to be in a ~ hurry** tener muchísima prisa

tearoom [ˈtiːruːm] N salón *m* de té

t

tease [tiːz] N bromista *mf* ▶ VT tomar el pelo a

tea set N servicio de té

teashop ['tiːʃɔp] N café *m*, cafetería

Teasmaid® ['tiːzmeɪd] N tetera automática

teaspoon ['tiːspuːn] N cucharita; (*also:* **tea-spoonful**: *as measurement*) cucharadita

tea strainer N colador *m* de té

teat [tiːt] N (*of bottle*) boquilla, tetilla

teatime ['tiːtaɪm] N hora del té

tea towel N (*BRIT*) paño de cocina

tea urn N tetera grande

tech [tɛk] N ABBR (*inf*) = **technology**; **technical college**

★**technical** ['tɛknɪkl] ADJ técnico

technical college N centro de formación profesional

technicality [tɛknɪ'kælɪtɪ] N detalle *m* técnico; **on a legal ~** por una cuestión formal

technically ['tɛknɪklɪ] ADV técnicamente

technician [tɛk'nɪʃn] N técnico(-a)

★**technique** [tɛk'niːk] N técnica

techno ['tɛknəʊ] N (*Mus*) (música) tecno

technocrat ['tɛknəkræt] N tecnócrata *mf*

technological [tɛknə'lɔdʒɪkl] ADJ tecnológico

technologist [tɛk'nɔlədʒɪst] N tecnólogo(-a)

★**technology** [tɛk'nɔlədʒɪ] N tecnología

teddy ['tɛdɪ], **teddy bear** N osito de peluche

tedious ['tiːdɪəs] ADJ pesado, aburrido

tedium ['tiːdɪəm] N tedio

tee [tiː] N (*Golf*) tee *m*

teem [tiːm] VI: **to ~ with** rebosar de; **it is teeming (with rain)** llueve a mares

teen [tiːn] ADJ = **teenage** ▶ N (*US*) = **teenager**

teenage ['tiːneɪdʒ] ADJ (*fashions etc*) juvenil

★**teenager** ['tiːneɪdʒə^r] N adolescente *mf*, quinceañero(-a)

teens [tiːnz] NPL: **to be in one's ~** ser adolescente

tee-shirt ['tiːʃəːt] N = **T-shirt**

teeter ['tiːtə^r] VI balancearse

teeth [tiːθ] NPL *of* **tooth**

teethe [tiːð] VI echar los dientes

teething ring ['tiːðɪŋ-] N mordedor *m*

teething troubles ['tiːðɪŋ-] NPL (*fig*) dificultades *fpl* iniciales

teetotal ['tiː'təʊtl] ADJ (*person*) abstemio

teetotaller, (*US*) **teetotaler** ['tiː'təʊtlə^r] N (*person*) abstemio(-a)

TEFL ['tɛfl] N ABBR = **Teaching of English as a Foreign Language**; **~ qualification** título para la enseñanza del inglés como lengua extranjera

Teflon® ['tɛflɔn] N teflón® *m*

Teheran [tɛə'rɑːn] N Teherán *m*

tel. ABBR (= *telephone*) tel.

Tel Aviv ['tɛlə'viːv] N Tel Aviv *m*

telecast ['tɛlɪkɑːst] VT, VI transmitir por televisión

telecommunications ['tɛlɪkəmjuːnɪ'keɪʃənz] N telecomunicaciones *fpl*

teleconferencing ['tɛlɪkɔnfərənsɪŋ] N teleconferencias *fpl*

telefax ['tɛlɪfæks] N telefax *m*

telegram ['tɛlɪgræm] N telegrama *m*

telegraph ['tɛlɪgrɑːf] N telégrafo

telegraphic [tɛlɪ'græfɪk] ADJ telegráfico

telegraph pole N poste *m* telegráfico

telegraph wire N hilo telegráfico

telepathic [tɛlɪ'pæθɪk] ADJ telepático

telepathy [tə'lɛpəθɪ] N telepatía

★**telephone** ['tɛlɪfəʊn] N teléfono; **to be on the ~** (*subscriber*) tener teléfono; (*be speaking*) estar hablando por teléfono ▶ VT llamar por teléfono, telefonear

telephone book N guía *f* telefónica

telephone booth, (*BRIT*) **telephone box** N cabina telefónica

telephone call N llamada telefónica

telephone directory N guía telefónica

telephone exchange N central *f* telefónica

telephone number N número de teléfono

telephonist [tə'lɛfənɪst] N (*BRIT*) telefonista *mf*

telephoto ['tɛlɪ'fəʊtəʊ] ADJ: **~ lens** teleobjetivo

teleprinter ['tɛlɪprɪntə^r] N teletipo, teleimpresora

teleprompter® ['tɛlɪprɔmptə^r] N teleapuntador *m*

telesales ['tɛlɪseɪlz] NPL televentas *fpl*

telescope ['tɛlɪskəʊp] N telescopio

telescopic [tɛlɪ'skɔpɪk] ADJ telescópico; (*umbrella*) plegable

Teletext® ['tɛlɪtɛkst] N teletexto *m*

telethon ['tɛlɪθɔn] N telemaratón *m*, maratón *m* televisivo (*con fines benéficos*)

televise ['tɛlɪvaɪz] VT televisar

★**television** ['tɛlɪvɪʒən] N televisión *f*; **to watch ~** mirar *or* ver la televisión

television licence N (*BRIT*) licencia que se paga por el uso del televisor, destinada a financiar la BBC

television programme N programa *m* de televisión

television set N televisor *m*

teleworking ['tɛlɪwəːkɪŋ] N teletrabajo

telex ['tɛlɛks] N télex *m* ▶ VT (*message*) enviar por télex; (*person*) enviar un télex a ▶ VI enviar un télex

★**tell** [tɛl] (*pt, pp* **told** [təʊld]) VT decir; (*relate: story*) contar; (*distinguish*): **to ~ sth from** distinguir algo de; **to ~ sb to do sth** decir a algn que haga algo; **to ~ sb about sth** contar algo a algn; **to ~ the time** dar *or* decir la hora; **can you ~ me the time?** ¿me puedes decir la hora?; **(I) ~ you what ...** fíjate ...; **I couldn't ~ them apart** no podía distinguirlos ▶ VI (*talk*): **to ~ (of)** contar; (*have effect*) tener efecto

▶ **tell off** VT: **to ~ sb off** regañar a algn

▶ **tell on** VT FUS: **to ~ on sb** chivarse de algn

teller ['tɛləᵊ] N (*in bank*) cajero(-a)

telling ['tɛlɪŋ] ADJ (*remark, detail*) revelador(a)

telltale ['tɛlteɪl] ADJ (*sign*) indicador(a)

telly ['tɛlɪ] N (BRIT *inf*) tele f

temerity [tə'mɛrɪtɪ] N temeridad f

temp [tɛmp] N ABBR (BRIT: = *temporary office worker*) empleado(-a) eventual ▶ VI trabajar como empleado(-a) eventual

temper ['tɛmpəᵊ] N (*mood*) humor m; (*bad temper*) (mal) genio; (*fit of anger*) ira; (*of child*) rabieta; **to be in a ~** estar furioso; **to lose one's ~** enfadarse, enojarse (LAM); **to keep one's ~** contenerse, no alterarse ▶ VT (*moderate*) moderar

temperament ['tɛmprəmənt] N (*nature*) temperamento

temperamental [tɛmprə'mɛntl] ADJ temperamental

temperance ['tɛmpərns] N moderación f; (*in drinking*) sobriedad f

temperate ['tɛmprət] ADJ moderado; (*climate*) templado

★**temperature** ['tɛmprətʃəᵊ] N temperatura; **to have** *or* **run a ~** tener fiebre

tempered ['tɛmpəd] ADJ (*steel*) templado

tempest ['tɛmpɪst] N tempestad f

tempestuous [tɛm'pɛstjuəs] ADJ (*relationship, meeting*) tempestuoso

tempi ['tɛmpiː] NPL *of* **tempo**

template ['tɛmplɪt] N plantilla

★**temple** ['tɛmpl] N (*building*) templo; (*Anat*) sien f

templet ['tɛmplɪt] N = **template**

tempo ['tɛmpəu] (*pl* **tempos** *or* **tempi** ['tɛmpiː]) N tempo; (*fig: of life etc*) ritmo

temporal ['tɛmpərl] ADJ temporal

temporarily ['tɛmpərərɪlɪ] ADV temporalmente

temporary ['tɛmpərərɪ] ADJ provisional, temporal; (*passing*) transitorio; (*worker*) eventual; (*job*) temporal; **~ teacher** maestro(-a) interino(-a)

tempt [tɛmpt] VT tentar; **to ~ sb into doing sth** tentar *or* inducir a algn a hacer algo; **to be tempted to do sth** (*person*) sentirse tentado de hacer algo

temptation [tɛmp'teɪʃən] N tentación f

tempting ['tɛmptɪŋ] ADJ tentador(a); (*food*) apetitoso

★**ten** [tɛn] NUM diez; **tens of thousands** decenas fpl de miles

tenable ['tɛnəbl] ADJ sostenible

tenacious [tə'neɪʃəs] ADJ tenaz

tenaciously [tə'neɪʃəslɪ] ADV tenazmente

tenacity [tə'næsɪtɪ] N tenacidad f

tenancy ['tɛnənsɪ] N alquiler m

tenant ['tɛnənt] N (*rent-payer*) inquilino(-a); (*occupant*) habitante mf

tend [tɛnd] VT (*sick etc*) cuidar, atender; (*cattle,*

machine) vigilar, cuidar ▶ VI: **to ~ to do sth** tener tendencia a hacer algo

tendency ['tɛndənsɪ] N tendencia

tender ['tɛndəᵊ] ADJ tierno, blando; (*delicate*) delicado; (*meat*) tierno; (*sore*) sensible; (*affectionate*) tierno, cariñoso ▶ N (Comm: *offer*) oferta; (*money*): **legal ~** moneda de curso legal; **to put in a ~ (for)** hacer una oferta (para); **to put work out to ~** sacar un trabajo a concurso ▶ VT ofrecer; **to ~ one's resignation** presentar la dimisión

tenderize ['tɛndəraɪz] VT (Culin) ablandar

tenderly ['tɛndəlɪ] ADV tiernamente

tenderness ['tɛndənɪs] N ternura; (*of meat*) blandura

tendinitis [tɛndə'naɪtɪs] N tendinitis f

tendon ['tɛndən] N tendón m

tendril ['tɛndrɪl] N zarcillo

tenement ['tɛnəmənt] N casa *or* bloque m de pisos *or* (LAM) vecinos

Tenerife [tɛnə'riːf] N Tenerife m

tenet ['tɛnət] N principio

tenner ['tɛnəᵊ] N (*inf*) (billete m de) diez libras fpl

★**tennis** ['tɛnɪs] N tenis m

tennis ball N pelota de tenis

tennis club N club m de tenis

tennis court N cancha de tenis

tennis elbow N (Med) codo de tenista, sinovitis f del codo

tennis match N partido de tenis

tennis player N tenista mf

tennis racket N raqueta de tenis

tennis shoes NPL zapatillas fpl de tenis

tenor ['tɛnəᵊ] N (Mus) tenor m

tenpin bowling ['tɛnpɪn-] N bolos mpl

tense [tɛns] ADJ tenso; (*stretched*) tirante; (*stiff*) rígido, tieso; (*person*) nervioso ▶ N (Ling) tiempo ▶ VT (*tighten: muscles*) tensar

tensely ['tɛnslɪ] ADV: **they waited ~** esperaban tensos

tenseness ['tɛnsnɪs] N tirantez f, tensión f

tension ['tɛnʃən] N tensión f

tent [tɛnt] N tienda (de campaña), carpa (LAM)

tentacle ['tɛntəkl] N tentáculo

tentative ['tɛntətɪv] ADJ (*person*) indeciso; (*provisional*) provisional

tentatively ['tɛntətɪvlɪ] ADV con indecisión; (*provisionally*) provisionalmente

tenterhooks ['tɛntəhuks] NPL: **on ~** sobre ascuas

★**tenth** [tɛnθ] ADJ décimo

tent peg N clavija, estaca

tent pole N mástil m

tenuous ['tɛnjuəs] ADJ tenue

tenure ['tɛnjuəᵊ] N posesión f, tenencia; **to have ~** tener posesión *or* título de propiedad

tepid ['tɛpɪd] ADJ tibio

Ter. ABBR = **terrace**

t

★term [təːm] N (*limit*) límite *m*; (*Comm*) plazo; (*word*) término; (*period*) período; (*Scol*) trimestre *m*; **in the short/long ~** a corto/largo plazo; **during his ~ of office** bajo su mandato; **to be on good terms with sb** llevarse bien con algn; **to come to terms with** (*problem*) aceptar; **in terms of …** en cuanto a …, en términos de … ▶ VT llamar, calificar de ■ **terms** NPL (*conditions*) condiciones *fpl*; (*Comm*) precio, tarifa

terminal [ˈtəːmɪnl] ADJ (*disease*) mortal; (*patient*) terminal ▶ N (*Elec*) borne *m*; (*Comput*) terminal *m*; (*also*: **air terminal**) terminal *f*; (*Brit*: *also*: **coach terminal**) (estación *f*) terminal *f*

terminate [ˈtəːmɪneɪt] VT poner término a; (*pregnancy*) interrumpir ▶ VI: **to ~ in** acabar en

termination [təːmɪˈneɪʃən] N fin *m*; (*of contract*) terminación *f*; **~ of pregnancy** interrupción *f* del embarazo

termini [ˈtəːmɪnaɪ] NPL *of* **terminus**

terminology [təːmɪˈnɔlədʒɪ] N terminología

terminus [ˈtəːmɪnəs] (*pl* **termini** [ˈtəːmɪnaɪ]) N término, (estación *f*) terminal *f*

termite [ˈtəːmaɪt] N termita, comején *m*

term paper N (*US Univ*) trabajo escrito trimestral *or* semestral

Terr. ABBR = **terrace**

terrace [ˈtɛrəs] N terraza; (*Brit*: *row of houses*) hilera de casas adosadas; **the terraces** (*Brit Sport*) las gradas *fpl*

terraced [ˈtɛrəst] ADJ (*garden*) escalonado; (*house*) adosado

terracotta [ˈtɛrəˈkɔtə] N terracota

terrain [tɛˈreɪn] N terreno

terrestrial [tɪˈrestrɪəl] ADJ (*life*) terrestre; (*Brit*: *channel*) de transmisión (por) vía terrestre

★terrible [ˈtɛrɪbl] ADJ terrible, horrible; (*inf*) malísimo

terribly [ˈtɛrɪblɪ] ADV terriblemente; (*very badly*) malísimamente

terrier [ˈtɛrɪəʳ] N terrier *m*

terrific [təˈrɪfɪk] ADJ fantástico, fenomenal, macanudo (*Lam*); (*wonderful*) maravilloso

terrify [ˈtɛrɪfaɪ] VT aterrorizar; **to be terrified** estar aterrado *or* aterrorizado

terrifying [ˈtɛrɪfaɪɪŋ] ADJ aterrador(a)

territorial [tɛrɪˈtɔːrɪəl] ADJ territorial

territorial waters NPL aguas *fpl* jurisdiccionales

territory [ˈtɛrɪtərɪ] N territorio

terror [ˈtɛrəʳ] N terror *m*

terror attack N atentado (terrorista)

terrorism [ˈtɛrərɪzəm] N terrorismo

★terrorist [ˈtɛrərɪst] N terrorista *mf*

terrorist attack N atentado (terrorista)

terrorize [ˈtɛrəraɪz] VT aterrorizar

terse [təːs] ADJ (*style*) conciso; (*reply*) brusco

tertiary [ˈtəːʃərɪ] ADJ terciario; **~ education** enseñanza superior

Terylene® [ˈtɛrəliːn] N (*Brit*) terylene® *m*

TESL [ˈtɛsl] N ABBR = **Teaching of English as a Second Language**

★test [tɛst] N (*trial, check*) prueba, ensayo; (: *of goods in factory*) control *m*; (*of courage etc*) prueba; (*Chem, Med*) prueba; (*of blood, urine*) análisis *m inv*; (*exam*) examen *m*, test *m*; (*also*: **driving test**) examen *m* de conducir; **to put sth to the ~** someter algo a prueba ▶ VT probar, poner a prueba; (*Med*) examinar; (: *blood*) analizar; **to ~ sth for sth** analizar algo en busca de algo

testament [ˈtɛstəmənt] N testamento; **the Old/New T~** el Antiguo/Nuevo Testamento

test ban N (*also*: **nuclear test ban**) suspensión *f* de pruebas nucleares

test card N (*TV*) carta de ajuste

test case N juicio que sienta precedente

testes [ˈtɛstiːz] NPL testes *mpl*

test flight N vuelo de ensayo

testicle [ˈtɛstɪkl] N testículo

testify [ˈtɛstɪfaɪ] VI (*Law*) prestar declaración; **to ~ to sth** atestiguar algo

testimonial [tɛstɪˈməʊnɪəl] N (*of character*) (carta de) recomendación *f*

testimony [ˈtɛstɪmənɪ] N (*Law*) testimonio, declaración *f*

testing [ˈtɛstɪŋ] ADJ (*difficult: time*) duro

test match N partido internacional

testosterone [tɛsˈtɒstərəʊn] N testosterona

test paper N examen *m*, test *m*

test pilot N piloto *mf* de pruebas

test tube N probeta

test-tube baby N bebé *m* probeta *inv*

testy [ˈtɛstɪ] ADJ irritable

tetanus [ˈtɛtənəs] N tétano

tetchy [ˈtɛtʃɪ] ADJ irritable

tether [ˈtɛðəʳ] VT atar ▶ N: **to be at the end of one's ~** no aguantar más

★text [tɛkst] N texto; (*on mobile*) mensaje *m* de texto ▶ VT: **to ~ sb** enviar un mensaje (de texto) a algn

textbook [ˈtɛkstbuk] N libro de texto

textiles [ˈtɛkstaɪlz] NPL tejidos *mpl*

★text message N mensaje *m* de texto

text messaging [-ˈmɛsɪdʒɪŋ] N (envío de) mensajes *mpl* de texto

textual [ˈtɛkstjuəl] ADJ del texto, textual

texture [ˈtɛkstʃəʳ] N textura

TGIF ABBR (*inf*) = **thank God it's Friday**

Thai [taɪ] ADJ, N tailandés(-esa) *m/f*

Thailand [ˈtaɪlænd] N Tailandia

thalidomide® [θəˈlɪdəmaɪd] N talidomida®

Thames [tɛmz] N: **the ~** el Támesis

★than [ðæn, ðən] CONJ que; (*with numerals*): **more ~ 10/once** más de 10/una vez; **I have more/less ~ you** tengo más/menos que tú; **it is better to phone ~ to write** es mejor llamar por teléfono que escribir; **no sooner did he leave ~ the phone rang** en cuanto se marchó, sonó el teléfono

★**thank** [θæŋk] vt dar las gracias a, agradecer; **~ you (very much)** (muchas) gracias; **~ heavens, ~ God!** ¡gracias a Dios!, ¡menos mal!; *see also* **thanks**

thankful ['θæŋkful] ADJ: **~ for** agradecido (por)

thankfully ['θæŋkfəlɪ] ADV (*gratefully*) con agradecimiento; (*with relief*) por suerte; **~ there were few victims** afortunadamente hubo pocas víctimas

thankless ['θæŋklɪs] ADJ ingrato

thanks [θæŋks] NPL gracias *fpl*; **~ to** prep gracias a ▶ EXCL ¡gracias!; **many ~, ~ a lot** ¡muchas gracias!

Thanksgiving (Day) ['θæŋksgɪvɪŋ-] N día *m* de Acción de Gracias

En Estados Unidos el cuarto jueves de noviembre es **Thanksgiving Day**, fiesta oficial en la que se conmemora la celebración que tuvieron los primeros colonos norteamericanos (*Pilgrims* o *Pilgrim Fathers*) tras la estupenda cosecha de 1621, por la que se dan gracias a Dios. Se acostumbra hacer una gran comida en familia consistiendo en pavo con salsa de arándanos, batatas y, de postre, tarta de calabaza. También se celebran importantes eventos deportivos que las familias y amigos suelen ver juntos. En Canadá se celebra una fiesta semejante el segundo lunes de octubre, aunque no está relacionada con dicha fecha histórica.

that [ðæt]

(*pl* **those**) ADJ (*demonstrative*) ese(-a) (*to avoid confusion with adj*); (*: more remote*) aquel (aquella); **leave that book on the table** deja ese libro sobre la mesa; **that one** ese (esa), ése (ésa); (*more remote*) aquel (aquella), aquél (aquélla) (*to avoid confusion with adj*); **that one over there** ese (esa) de ahí, ése (ésa) de ahí; aquel (aquella) de allí, aquél (aquélla) de allí; *see also* **those**

▶ PRON **1** (*demonstrative*) ese(-a), ése(-a) (*to avoid confusion with adj*), eso (*neuter*); (*: more remote*) aquel (aquella), aquél (aquélla) (*to avoid confusion with adj*), aquello (*neuter*); **what's that?** ¿qué es eso (or aquello)?; **who's that?** ¿quién es?; (*pointing etc*) ¿quién es ese/a?; **is that you?** ¿eres tú?; **will you eat all that?** ¿vas a comer todo eso?; **that's my house** esa es mi casa; **that's what he said** eso es lo que dijo; **that is (to say)** es decir; **at** or **with that she ...** en eso, ella ...; **do it like that** hazlo así; *see also* **those 2** (*relative: subject, object*) que; (*: with preposition*) (el (la)) que, el (la) cual; **the book (that) I read** el libro que leí; **the books that are in the library** los libros que están en la biblioteca; **all (that) I have** todo lo que tengo; **the box (that) I put it in** la caja en la que or donde lo puse; **the people (that) I spoke to** la gente

con la que hablé; **not that I know of** que yo sepa, no

3 (*relative: of time*) que; **the day (that) he came** el día (en) que vino

▶ CONJ que; **he thought that I was ill** creyó que yo estaba enfermo

▶ ADV (*demonstrative*): **I can't work that much** no puedo trabajar tanto; **I didn't realize it was that bad** no creí que fuera tan malo; **that high** así de alto

thatched [θætʃt] ADJ (*roof*) de paja; **~ cottage** casita con tejado de paja

Thatcherism ['θætʃərɪzəm] N thatcherismo

thaw [θɔː] N deshielo ▶ VI (*ice*) derretirse; (*food*) descongelarse ▶ VT descongelar

the [ðiː, ðə]

DEF ART **1** (*gen*) el *m*, la *f*, los *mpl*, las *fpl* (NB = **el** *immediately before feminine noun beginning with stressed* (**h**)**a**; **a + el = al**; **de + el = del**): **the boy/ girl** el chico/la chica; **the books/flowers** los libros/las flores; **to the postman** al cartero; **from the drawer** del cajón; **I haven't the time/money** no tengo tiempo/dinero; **1.10 euros to the dollar** 1,10 euros por dólar; **paid by the hour** pagado por hora

2 (**+** *adj to form noun*) los *pl*; lo *sg*; **the rich and the poor** los ricos y los pobres; **to attempt the impossible** intentar lo imposible

3 (*in titles, surnames*): **Elizabeth the First** Isabel Primera; **Peter the Great** Pedro el Grande; **do you know the Smiths?** ¿conoce a los Smith?

4 (*in comparisons*): **the more he works the more he earns** cuanto más trabaja más gana

theatre, (US) **theater** ['θɪətə'] N teatro; (*also:* **lecture theatre**) aula; (*BRIT Med: also:* **operating theatre**) quirófano

theatre-goer, (US) **theater-goer** ['θɪətəgəuə'] N aficionado(-a) al teatro

theatrical [θɪ'ætrɪkl] ADJ teatral

theft [θeft] N robo

★**their** [ðeə'] ADJ su

theirs [ðeəz] PRON (el) suyo/(la) suya *etc*; *see also* **my; mine**¹

★**them** [ðem, ðəm] PRON (*direct*) los (las); (*indirect*) les; (*stressed, after prep*) ellos (ellas); **I see ~** los veo; **both of ~** ambos(-as), los (las) dos; **give me a few of ~** dame algunos(-as); *see also* **me**

★**theme** [θiːm] N tema *m*

theme park N parque *m* temático

theme song N tema *m* (musical)

★**themselves** [ðəm'selvz] PRON PL (*subject*) ellos mismos (ellas mismas); (*complement*) se; (*after prep*) sí (mismos(-as)); *see also* **oneself**

★**then** [ðen] ADV (*at that time*) entonces; (*next*) pues; (*later*) luego, después; (*and also*) además; **from ~ on** desde entonces; **until ~** hasta entonces; **and ~ what?** y luego, ¿qué?; **what do you**

t

want me to do, ~? ¿entonces, qué quiere que haga? ▶ CONJ (*therefore*) en ese caso, entonces ▶ ADJ: **the ~ president** el entonces presidente

theologian [θɪəˈləudʒən] N teólogo(-a)

theological [θɪəˈlɔdʒɪkl] ADJ teológico

theology [θɪˈɔlədʒɪ] N teología

theorem [ˈθɪərəm] N teorema *m*

theoretical [θɪəˈrɛtɪkl] ADJ teórico

theoretically [θɪəˈrɛtɪklɪ] ADV teóricamente, en teoría

theorize [ˈθɪəraɪz] VI teorizar

theory [ˈθɪərɪ] N teoría

therapeutic [θɛrəˈpjuːtɪk], **therapeutical** [θɛrəˈpjuːtɪkl] ADJ terapéutico

therapist [ˈθɛrəpɪst] N terapeuta *mf*

★**therapy** [ˈθɛrəpɪ] N terapia

---

there [ðɛəʳ]

ADV **1: there is, there are** hay; **there is no-one here** no hay nadie aquí; **there is no bread left** no queda pan; **there has been an accident** ha habido un accidente

2 (*referring to place*) ahí; (: *distant*) allí; **it's there** está ahí; **put it in/on/up/down there** ponlo ahí dentro/encima/arriba/abajo; **I want that book there** quiero ese libro de ahí; **there he is!** ¡ahí está!; **there's the bus** ahí or ya viene el autobús; **back/down there** allí atrás/abajo; **over there, through there** por allí

3: there, there (*esp to child*) venga, venga, bueno

Whereas *there is* and *there are* agree with the number of things they refer to, **hay**, **hubo**, **había**, etc do not change:
There was a murder. **Hubo un asesinato.**
There were two kidnappings. **Hubo dos secuestros.**
To talk about the number of people there are, use **ser**, which does change to reflect whether you are talking about singular or plural: *There are four of us.* **Somos cuatro.**

---

thereabouts [ˈðɛərəˈbauts] ADV por ahí

thereafter [ðɛərˈɑːftəʳ] ADV después

thereby [ˈðɛəbaɪ] ADV así, de ese modo

★**therefore** [ˈðɛəfɔːʳ] ADV por lo tanto

there's [ðɛəz] = **there is; there has**

thereupon [ðɛərəˈpɔn] ADV (*at that point*) en eso, en seguida

thermal [ˈθəːml] ADJ termal; (*paper*) térmico

thermal printer N termoimpresora

thermodynamics [ˈθəːmədaɪnæmɪks] N termodinámica

thermometer [θəˈmɔmɪtəʳ] N termómetro

thermonuclear [ˈθəːməuˈnjuːklɪəʳ] ADJ termonuclear

Thermos® [ˈθəːməs] N (*also*: **Thermos flask**) termo

thermostat [ˈθəːməustæt] N termostato

thesaurus [θɪˈsɔːrəs] N tesoro, diccionario de sinónimos

★**these** [ðiːz] ADJ PL estos(-as); **~ children/flowers** estos chicos/estas flores ▶ PRON PL estos(-as), éstos(-as) (*to avoid confusion with adj*); *see also* **this**

thesis [ˈθiːsɪs] (*pl* **theses** [-siːz]) N tesis *f inv*; *see also* **doctorate**

★**they** [ðeɪ] PRON PL ellos (ellas); **~ say that ...** (*it is said that*) se dice que ...

they'd [ðeɪd] = **they had; they would**

they'll [ðeɪl] = **they will; they shall**

they're [ðɛəʳ] = **they are**

they've [ðeɪv] = **they have**

★**thick** [θɪk] ADJ (*wall, slice*) grueso; (*dense: liquid, smoke etc*) espeso; (: *vegetation, beard*) tupido; (*stupid*) torpe; **it's 20 cm ~** tiene 20 cm de espesor ▶ N: **in the ~ of the battle** en lo más reñido de la batalla

thicken [ˈθɪkn] VI espesarse ▶ VT (*sauce etc*) espesar

thicket [ˈθɪkɪt] N espesura

thickly [ˈθɪklɪ] ADV (*spread*) en capa espesa; (*cut*) en lonchas/rebanadas gruesas; (*populated*) densamente

thickness [ˈθɪknɪs] N espesor *m*, grosor *m*

thickset [θɪkˈsɛt] ADJ fornido

thick-skinned [θɪkˈskɪnd] ADJ (*fig*) insensible

★**thief** [θiːf] (*pl* **thieves** [θiːvz]) N ladrón(-ona) *m/f*

thieving [ˈθiːvɪŋ] N robo, hurto ▶ ADJ ladrón(-ona)

thigh [θaɪ] N muslo

thighbone [ˈθaɪbəun] N fémur *m*

thimble [ˈθɪmbl] N dedal *m*

★**thin** [θɪn] ADJ delgado; (*wall, layer*) fino; (*watery*) aguado; (*light*) tenue; (*hair*) escaso; (*fog*) ligero; (*crowd*) disperso ▶ VT: **to ~ (down)** (*sauce, paint*) diluir ▶ VI (*fog*) aclararse; (*also*: **thin out**: *crowd*) dispersarse; **his hair is thinning** se está quedando calvo

★**thing** [θɪŋ] N cosa; (*object*) objeto, artículo; (*contraption*) chisme *m*; (*mania*) manía; **the best ~ would be to ...** lo mejor sería ...; **the main ~ is ...** lo principal es ...; **first ~ (in the morning)** a primera hora (de la mañana); **last ~ (at night)** a última hora (de la noche); **the ~ is ...** lo que pasa es que ...; **how are things?** ¿qué tal van las cosas?; **she's got a ~ about mice** le dan no sé qué los ratones; **poor ~!** ¡pobre! *mf*, ¡pobrecito(-a)! ■ **things** NPL (*belongings*) cosas *fpl*

★**think** [θɪŋk] (*pl* **thought** [θɔːt]) VI pensar; **what did you ~ of it?** ¿qué te pareció?; **what did you ~ of them?** ¿qué te parecieron?; **to ~ about sth/sb** pensar en algo/algn; **I'll ~ about it** lo pensaré; **to ~ of doing sth** pensar en hacer algo; **~ again!** ¡piénsalo bien!; **to ~ aloud** pensar en voz alta; **to ~ well of sb** tener buen concepto de algn ▶ VT pensar, creer; (*imagine*) imaginar; **I ~ so/not** creo que sí/no

▶ **think out** VT (*plan*) elaborar, tramar; (*solution*) encontrar

▶ **think over** VT reflexionar sobre, meditar; **I'd like to ~ things over** me gustaría pensármelo

▶ **think through** VT pensar bien

▶ **think up** VT imaginar

thinking ['θɪŋkɪŋ] N: **to my (way of) ~** a mi parecer

think tank N grupo de expertos

thinly ['θɪnlɪ] ADV (*cut*) en lonchas/rebanadas finas; (*spread*) en una capa fina

thinness ['θɪnnɪs] N delgadez *f*

★**third** [θəːd] ADJ (*before n*) tercer(a); (*following n*) tercero(-a) ▶ N tercero(-a); (*fraction*) tercio; (BRIT: *degree*) título universitario de tercera clase

third degree ADJ (*burns*) de tercer grado

thirdly ['θəːdlɪ] ADV en tercer lugar

third party insurance N (BRIT) seguro a terceros

third-rate ['θəːd'reɪt] ADJ de poca calidad

★**Third World** N: **the ~** el Tercer Mundo ▶ CPD tercermundista

thirst [θəːst] N sed *f*

★**thirsty** ['θəːstɪ] ADJ (*person*) sediento; **to be ~** tener sed

★**thirteen** [θəːˈtiːn] NUM trece

★**thirteenth** [θəːˈtiːnθ] ADJ decimotercero ▶ N (*in series*) decimotercero(-a); (*fraction*) decimotercio

thirtieth ['θəːtɪəθ] ADJ trigésimo ▶ N (*in series*) trigésimo(-a); (*fraction*) treintavo

★**thirty** ['θəːtɪ] NUM treinta

---

this [ðɪs]

(*pl* **these**) ADJ (*demonstrative*) este(-a); **this man/woman** este hombre/esta mujer; **this way** por aquí; **this time last year** hoy hace un año; **this one (here)** este(-a), éste(-a), esto (de aquí); *see also* **these**

▶ PRON (*demonstrative*) este(-a), éste(-a) (*to avoid confusion with adj*), esto *neuter*; **who is this?** ¿quién es este (esta)?; **what is this?** ¿qué es esto?; **this is where I live** aquí vivo; **this is what he said** esto es lo que dijo; **this is Mr Brown** (*in introductions*) le presento al Sr. Brown; (*photo*) este es el Sr. Brown; (*on telephone*) habla el Sr. Brown; **they were talking of this and that** hablaban de esto y lo otro; *see also* **these**

▶ ADV (*demonstrative*): **this high/long** así de alto/largo; **this far** hasta aquí

---

thistle ['θɪsl] N cardo

thong [θɒŋ] N correa

thorn [θɔːn] N espina

thorny ['θɔːnɪ] ADJ espinoso

★**thorough** ['θʌrə] ADJ (*search*) minucioso; (*knowledge*) profundo; (*research*) a fondo

thoroughbred ['θʌrəbrɛd] ADJ (*horse*) de pura sangre

thoroughfare ['θʌrəfɛəʳ] N calle *f*; **"no ~"** "prohibido el paso"

thoroughgoing ['θʌrəgəʊɪŋ] ADJ a fondo

thoroughly ['θʌrəlɪ] ADV (*search*) minuciosamente; (*study*) profundamente; (*wash*) a fondo; (*utterly: bad, wet etc*) completamente, totalmente

thoroughness ['θʌrənɪs] N minuciosidad *f*

★**those** [ðəʊz] ADJ PL esos (esas); (*more remote*) aquellos(-as); **leave ~ books on the table** deja esos libros sobre la mesa ▶ PRON PL esos (esas), ésos (ésas) (*to avoid confusion with adj*); (*more remote*) aquellos(-as), aquéllos(-as) (*to avoid confusion with adj*)

---

esos or **esas** is used to translate *those*, but to refer to something more distant, use **aquellos** or **aquellas**:
I want those! ¡Quiero esos!
Which ones? Those over there? ¿Cuáles? ¿Aquellos?

★**though** [ðəʊ] CONJ aunque; **even ~** aunque ▶ ADV sin embargo, aún así; **it's not so easy, ~** sin embargo no es tan fácil

★**thought** [θɔːt] PT, PP *of* **think** ▶ N pensamiento; (*opinion*) opinión *f*; (*intention*) intención *f*; **to give sth some ~** pensar algo detenidamente; **after much ~** después de pensarlo bien; **I've just had a ~** se me acaba de ocurrir una idea

thoughtful ['θɔːtful] ADJ pensativo; (*considerate*) atento

thoughtfully ['θɔːtfəlɪ] ADV pensativamente; atentamente

thoughtless ['θɔːtlɪs] ADJ desconsiderado

thoughtlessly ['θɔːtlɪslɪ] ADV insensatamente

thought-provoking ['θɔːtprəvəʊkɪŋ] ADJ estimulante

★**thousand** ['θaʊzənd] NUM mil; **two ~** dos mil; **thousands of** miles de

thousandth ['θaʊzəntθ] NUM milésimo

thrash [θræʃ] VT dar una paliza a

▶ **thrash about** VI revolverse

▶ **thrash out** VT discutir a fondo

thrashing ['θræʃɪŋ] N: **to give sb a ~** dar una paliza a algn

thread [θrɛd] N hilo; (*of screw*) rosca ▶ VT (*needle*) enhebrar

threadbare ['θrɛdbɛəʳ] ADJ raído

★**threat** [θrɛt] N amenaza; **to be under ~ of** estar amenazado de

★**threaten** ['θrɛtn] VI amenazar ▶ VT: **to ~ sb with sth/to do** amenazar a algn con algo/con hacer

threatening ['θrɛtnɪŋ] ADJ amenazador(a), amenazante

★**three** [θriː] NUM tres

three-dimensional [θriːdɪˈmɛnʃənl] ADJ tridimensional

threefold ['θriːfəʊld] ADV: **to increase ~** triplicar

three-piece ['θriːpiːs] CPD: **~ suit** traje *m* de tres piezas; **~ suite** tresillo

three-ply [ˈθriːplaɪ] ADJ (*wood*) de tres capas; (*wool*) triple

three-quarter [θriːˈkwɔːtəʳ] ADJ: **~ length sleeves** mangas *fpl* tres cuartos

three-quarters [θriːˈkwɔːtəz] NPL tres cuartas partes; **~ full** tres cuartas partes lleno

three-wheeler [θriːˈwiːləʳ] N (*car*) coche *m* cabina

thresh [θrɛʃ] VT (*Agr*) trillar

threshing machine [ˈθrɛʃɪŋ-] N trilladora

threshold [ˈθrɛʃhəʊld] N umbral *m*; **to be on the ~ of** (*fig*) estar al borde de

threshold agreement N convenio de nivel crítico

threw [θruː] PT *of* **throw**

thrift [θrɪft] N economía

thrifty [ˈθrɪftɪ] ADJ económico

thrill [θrɪl] N (*excitement*) emoción *f* ▸ VT emocionar; **to be thrilled** (*with gift etc*) estar encantado

thriller [ˈθrɪləʳ] N película/novela de suspense

thrilling [ˈθrɪlɪŋ] ADJ emocionante

thrive [θraɪv] (*pt* **thrived** *or* **throve** [θrəʊv], *pp* **thrived** *or* **thriven** [ˈθrɪvn]) VI (*grow*) crecer; (*do well*) prosperar

thriving [ˈθraɪvɪŋ] ADJ próspero

★**throat** [θrəʊt] N garganta; **I have a sore ~** me duele la garganta

throb [θrɒb] N (*of heart*) latido; (*of engine*) vibración *f* ▸ VI latir; vibrar; (*with pain*) dar punzadas; **my head is throbbing** la cabeza me da punzadas

throes [θrəʊz] NPL: **in the ~ of** en medio de

thrombosis [θrɒmˈbəʊsɪs] (*pl* **thromboses** [-siːz]) N trombosis *f*

throne [θrəʊn] N trono

throng [θrɒŋ] N multitud *f*, muchedumbre *f* ▸ VT, VI apiñarse, agolparse

throttle [ˈθrɒtl] N (*Aut*) acelerador *m* ▸ VT estrangular

★**through** [θruː] PREP por, a través de; (*time*) durante; (*by means of*) por medio de, mediante; (*owing to*) gracias a; **(from) Monday ~ Friday** (*US*) de lunes a viernes; **to go ~ sb's papers** mirar entre los papeles de algn; **I am halfway ~ the book** voy por la mitad del libro ▸ ADJ (*ticket, train*) directo; **"no ~ road"** (*BRIT*) "calle sin salida" ▸ ADV completamente, de parte a parte; **the soldiers didn't let us ~** los soldados no nos dejaron pasar; **to put sb ~ to sb** (*Tel*) poner *or* pasar a algn con algn; **to be ~** (*Tel*) tener comunicación; (*have finished*) haber terminado

★**throughout** [θruːˈaʊt] PREP (*place*) por todas partes de, por todo; (*time*) durante todo ▸ ADV por *or* en todas partes

throughput [ˈθruːpʊt] N (*of goods, materials*) producción *f*; (*Comput*) capacidad *f* de procesamiento

throve [θrəʊv] PT *of* **thrive**

★**throw** [θrəʊ] (*pt* **threw** [θruː], *pp* **thrown** [θrəʊn]) N tiro; (*Sport*) lanzamiento ▸ VT tirar, echar, botar (*LAM*); (*Sport*) lanzar; (*rider*) derribar; (*fig*) desconcertar; **to ~ a party** dar una fiesta

▸ **throw about, throw around** VT (*litter etc*) tirar, esparcir

▸ **throw away** VT tirar, botar (*LAM*)

▸ **throw in** VT (*Sport: ball*) sacar; (*include*) incluir

▸ **throw off** VT deshacerse de

▸ **throw open** VT (*doors, windows*) abrir de par en par; (*house, gardens etc*) abrir al público; (*competition, race*) abrir a todos

▸ **throw out** VT tirar, botar (*LAM*)

▸ **throw together** VT (*clothes*) amontonar; (*meal*) preparar a la carrera; (*essay*) hacer sin cuidado

▸ **throw up** VI vomitar, devolver

throwaway [ˈθrəʊəweɪ] ADJ para tirar, desechable

throwback [ˈθrəʊbæk] N: **it's a ~ to** (*fig*) eso nos lleva de nuevo a

throw-in [ˈθrəʊɪn] N (*Sport*) saque *m* de banda

thrown [θrəʊn] PP *of* **throw**

thru [θruː] PREP, ADJ, ADV (*US*) = **through**

thrush [θrʌʃ] N zorzal *m*, tordo; (*Med*) candidiasis *f*

thrust [θrʌst] (*pt, pp* **~**) N (*Tech*) empuje *m* ▸ VT empujar; (*push in*) introducir

thrusting [ˈθrʌstɪŋ] ADJ (*person*) dinámico, con empuje

thud [θʌd] N golpe *m* sordo

thug [θʌg] N gamberro(-a)

thumb [θʌm] N (*Anat*) pulgar *m*; **to give sth/sb the thumbs up/down** aprobar/desaprobar algo/a algn ▸ VT: **to ~ a lift** hacer dedo

▸ **thumb through** VT FUS (*book*) hojear

thumb index N uñero, índice *m* recortado

thumbnail [ˈθʌmneɪl] N uña del pulgar

thumbnail sketch N esbozo

thumbtack [ˈθʌmtæk] N (*US*) chincheta, chinche *f* (*LAM*)

thump [θʌmp] N golpe *m*; (*sound*) ruido seco *or* sordo ▸ VT, VI golpear

thumping [ˈθʌmpɪŋ] ADJ (*inf: huge*) descomunal

thunder [ˈθʌndəʳ] N trueno; (*of applause etc*) estruendo ▸ VI tronar; (*train etc*): **to ~ past** pasar como un trueno

thunderbolt [ˈθʌndəbəʊlt] N rayo

thunderclap [ˈθʌndəklæp] N trueno

thunderous [ˈθʌndərəs] ADJ ensordecedor(a), estruendoso

thunderstorm [ˈθʌndəstɔːm] N tormenta

thunderstruck [ˈθʌndəstrʌk] ADJ pasmado

thundery [ˈθʌndərɪ] ADJ tormentoso

Thur., Thurs. ABBR (= *Thursday*) juev.

★**Thursday** [ˈθəːzdɪ] N jueves *m inv*; *see also* **Tuesday**

thus [ðʌs] ADV así, de este modo

thwart [θwɔːt] vt frustrar

thyme [taɪm] n tomillo

thyroid ['θaɪrɔɪd] n tiroides m inv

tiara [tɪ'ɑːrə] n tiara, diadema

Tiber ['taɪbəʳ] n Tíber m

Tibet [tɪ'bɛt] n el Tibet

Tibetan [tɪ'bɛtən] adj tibetano ▶ n tibetano(-a); (Ling) tibetano

tibia ['tɪbɪə] n tibia

tic [tɪk] n tic m

tick [tɪk] n (sound: of clock) tictac m; (mark) señal f (de visto bueno), palomita (Lam); (Zool) garrapata; (Brit inf): **in a ~** en un instante; (Brit inf: credit): **to buy sth on ~** comprar algo a crédito; **to put a ~ against sth** poner una señal a algo ▶ vi hacer tictac ▶ vt marcar, señalar
  ▶ **tick off** vt marcar; (person) reñir
  ▶ **tick over** vi (Brit: engine) girar en marcha lenta; (: fig) ir tirando

ticker tape ['tɪkə-] n cinta perforada

★**ticket** ['tɪkɪt] n billete m, tique m, boleto (Lam); (for cinema etc) entrada, boleto (Lam); (in shop: on goods) etiqueta; (for library) tarjeta; (US Pol) lista (de candidatos); **to get a parking ~** (Aut) ser multado por estacionamiento ilegal

ticket agency n (Theat) agencia de venta de entradas

ticket barrier n (Brit Rail) barrera más allá de la cual se necesita billete/boleto

ticket collector n revisor(a) m/f

ticket holder n poseedor(a) m/f de billete or entrada

ticket inspector n revisor(a) m/f, inspector(a) m/f de boletos (Lam)

ticket machine n máquina de billetes (Sp) or boletos (Lam)

ticket office n (Theat) taquilla, boletería (Lam); (Rail) despacho de billetes or (Lam) boletos

ticking-off ['tɪkɪŋ'ɔf] n (inf): **to give sb a ~** echarle una bronca a algn

tickle ['tɪkl] n: **to give sb a ~** hacer cosquillas a algn ▶ vt hacer cosquillas a ▶ vi hacer cosquillas; (material) picar

ticklish ['tɪklɪʃ] adj (which tickles: blanket) que pica; (: cough) irritante; (fig: problem) delicado; **to be ~** tener cosquillas

tidal ['taɪdl] adj de marea

tidal wave n maremoto

tidbit ['tɪdbɪt] n (US) = **titbit**

tiddlywinks ['tɪdlɪwɪŋks] n juego de la pulga

★**tide** [taɪd] n marea; (fig: of events) curso, marcha; **high/low ~** marea alta/baja; **the ~ of public opinion** la tendencia de la opinión pública ▶ vt: **to ~ sb over** or **through (until)** sacar a algn del apuro (hasta)

tidily ['taɪdɪlɪ] adv bien, ordenadamente; **to arrange ~** ordenar; **to dress ~** vestir bien

tidiness ['taɪdɪnɪs] n (order) orden m; (cleanliness) aseo

★**tidy** ['taɪdɪ] adj (room) ordenado; (drawing, work) limpio; (person) (bien) arreglado; (: in character) metódico; (mind) claro, metódico ▶ vt (also: **tidy up**) ordenar, poner en orden

★**tie** [taɪ] n (string etc) atadura; (Brit: necktie) corbata; (fig: link) vínculo, lazo; (Sport: draw) empate m; **family ties** obligaciones fpl familiares; **cup ~** (Sport: match) partido de copa ▶ vt atar; **to ~ in a bow** hacer un lazo con; **to ~ a knot in sth** hacer un nudo en algo ▶ vi (Sport) empatar
  ▶ **tie down** vt atar; (fig): **to ~ sb down to** obligar a algn a
  ▶ **tie in** vi: **to ~ in (with)** (correspond) concordar (con)
  ▶ **tie on** vt (Brit: label etc) atar
  ▶ **tie up** vt (parcel) envolver; (dog) atar; (boat) amarrar; (arrangements) concluir; **to be tied up** (busy) estar ocupado

tie-break ['taɪbreɪk], **tie-breaker** ['taɪbreɪkəʳ] n (Tennis) tiebreak m, muerte f súbita; (in quiz) punto decisivo

tie-on ['taɪɔn] adj (Brit: label) para atar

tie-pin ['taɪpɪn] n (Brit) alfiler m de corbata

tier [tɪəʳ] n grada; (of cake) piso

tie tack n (US) alfiler m de corbata

tiff [tɪf] n (inf) pelea, riña

tiger ['taɪgəʳ] n tigre m

★**tight** [taɪt] adj (rope) tirante; (money) escaso; (clothes, budget) ajustado; (programme) apretado; (budget) ajustado; (security) estricto; (inf: drunk) borracho ▶ adv (squeeze) muy fuerte; (shut) herméticamente; **to be packed ~** (suitcase) estar completamente lleno; (people) estar apretados; **everybody hold ~!** ¡agárrense bien!

tighten ['taɪtn] vt (rope) tensar, estirar; (screw) apretar ▶ vi estirarse; apretarse

tight-fisted [taɪt'fɪstɪd] adj tacaño

tight-lipped ['taɪt'lɪpt] adj: **to be ~** (silent) rehusar hablar; (angry) apretar los labios

tightly ['taɪtlɪ] adv (grasp) muy fuerte

tightness ['taɪtnɪs] n (of rope) tirantez f; (of clothes) estrechez f; (of budget) lo ajustado

tightrope ['taɪtrəʊp] n cuerda floja

tightrope walker n equilibrista mf, funambulista mf

tights [taɪts] npl (Brit) medias fpl, pantis mpl

tigress ['taɪgrɪs] n tigresa

tilde ['tɪldə] n tilde f

tile [taɪl] n (on roof) teja; (on floor) baldosa; (on wall) azulejo ▶ vt (floor) poner baldosas en; (wall) alicatar

tiled [taɪld] adj (floor) embaldosado; (wall, bathroom) alicatado; (roof) con tejas

★**till** [tɪl] n caja (registradora) ▶ vt (land) cultivar ▶ prep, conj = **until**

tiller ['tɪləʳ] n (Naut) caña del timón

tilt [tɪlt] vt inclinar ▶ vi inclinarse ▶ n (slope) inclinación f; **to wear one's hat at a ~** llevar el sombrero echado a un lado or terciado; **(at) full ~** a toda velocidad or carrera

timber ['tɪmbə^r] N (*material*) madera; (*trees*) árboles *mpl*

★**time** [taɪm] N tiempo; (*epoch: often pl*) época; (*by clock*) hora; (*moment*) momento; (*occasion*) vez *f*; (*Mus*) compás *m*; **a long ~** mucho tiempo; **four at a ~** cuatro a la vez; **for the ~ being** de momento, por ahora; **at times** a veces, a ratos; **~ after ~, ~ and again** repetidas veces, una y otra vez; **from ~ to ~** de vez en cuando; **in ~** (*soon enough*) a tiempo; (*after some time*) con el tiempo; (*Mus*) al compás; **in a week's ~** dentro de una semana; **in no ~** en un abrir y cerrar de ojos; **any ~** cuando sea; **on ~** a la hora; **to be 30 minutes behind/ahead of ~** llevar media hora de retraso/adelanto; **to take one's ~** tomárselo con calma; **he'll do it in his own ~** (*without being hurried*) lo hará sin prisa; (*out of working hours*) lo hará en su tiempo libre; **by the ~ he arrived** cuando llegó; **5 times 5** 5 por 5; **what ~ is it?** ¿qué hora es?; **what ~ do you make it?** ¿qué hora es *or* tiene?; **to be behind the times** estar atrasado; **to carry three boxes at a ~** llevar tres cajas a la vez; **to keep ~** llevar el ritmo *or* el compás; **to have a good ~** pasarlo bien, divertirse ▶ VT calcular *or* medir el tiempo de; (*race*) cronometrar; (*remark etc*) elegir el momento para; **to ~ sth well/badly** elegir un buen/mal momento para algo; **the bomb was timed to explode five minutes later** la bomba estaba programada para explotar cinco minutos más tarde

time-and-motion expert ['taɪmənd'məʊʃən-] N experto(-a) en la ciencia de la producción

time-and-motion study ['taɪmənd'məʊʃən-] N estudio de desplazamientos y tiempos

time bomb N bomba de relojería

time card N tarjeta de registro horario

time clock N reloj *m* registrador

time-consuming ['taɪmkənsju:mɪŋ] ADJ que requiere mucho tiempo

time frame N plazo

time-honoured, (*US*) **time-honored** ['taɪmɔnəd] ADJ consagrado

timekeeper ['taɪmki:pə^r] N (*Sport*) cronómetro

time lag N desfase *m*

time-lapse (photography) ['taɪmlæps-] N fotografía secuencial

timeless ['taɪmlɪs] ADJ eterno

time limit N (*gen*) límite *m* de tiempo; (*Comm*) plazo

timeline ['taɪmlaɪn] N línea de tiempo

timely ['taɪmlɪ] ADJ oportuno

time off N tiempo libre

timer ['taɪmə^r] N (*also:* **timer switch**) interruptor *m*; (*in kitchen*) temporizador *m*; (*Tech*) temporizador *m*

time-saving ['taɪmseɪvɪŋ] ADJ que ahorra tiempo

time scale N escala de tiempo

time sharing N (*Comput*) tiempo compartido

time sheet N = **time card**

time signal N señal *f* horaria

time switch N (*Brit*) interruptor *m* (horario)

★**timetable** ['taɪmteɪbl] N horario; (*programme of events etc*) programa *m*

time zone N huso horario

timid ['tɪmɪd] ADJ tímido

timidity [tɪ'mɪdɪtɪ] N timidez *f*

timidly ['tɪmɪdlɪ] ADV tímidamente

timing ['taɪmɪŋ] N (*Sport*) cronometraje *m*; **the ~ of his resignation** el momento que eligió para dimitir

timpani ['tɪmpənɪ] NPL tímpanos *mpl*

★**tin** [tɪn] N estaño; (*also:* **tin plate**) hojalata; (*Brit: can*) lata

tinfoil ['tɪnfɔɪl] N papel *m* de estaño

tinge [tɪndʒ] N matiz *m* ▶ VT: **tinged with** teñido de

tingle ['tɪŋgl] N hormigueo ▶ VI (*cheeks, skin: from cold*) sentir comezón; (*: from bad circulation*) sentir hormigueo; **to ~ with** estremecerse de

tinker ['tɪŋkə^r] N calderero(-a); (*gipsy*) gitano(-a) ▶ **tinker with** VT FUS jugar con, tocar

tinkle ['tɪŋkl] VI tintinear

tin mine N mina de estaño

tinned [tɪnd] ADJ (*Brit: food*) en lata, en conserva

tinnitus ['tɪnɪtəs] N (*Med*) acúfeno

tinny ['tɪnɪ] ADJ (*sound, taste*) metálico; (*pej: car*) poco sólido, de pacotilla

tin opener [-əupnə^r] N (*Brit*) abrelatas *m inv*

tinsel ['tɪnsl] N oropel *m*

tint [tɪnt] N matiz *m*; (*for hair*) tinte *m* ▶ VT (*hair*) teñir

tinted ['tɪntɪd] ADJ (*hair*) teñido; (*glass, spectacles*) ahumado

★**tiny** ['taɪnɪ] ADJ minúsculo, pequeñito

★**tip** [tɪp] N (*end*) punta; (*gratuity*) propina; (*Brit: for rubbish*) vertedero; (*advice*) consejo ▶ VT (*waiter*) dar una propina a; (*tilt*) inclinar; (*empty: also:* **tip out**) vaciar, echar; (*predict: winner*) pronosticar; (*: horse*) recomendar; **he tipped out the contents of the box** volcó el contenido de la caja ▶ **tip off** VT avisar, poner sobre aviso a ▶ **tip over** VT volcar ▶ VI volcarse

tip-off ['tɪpɔf] N (*hint*) advertencia

tipped [tɪpt] ADJ (*Brit: cigarette*) con filtro

Tipp-Ex® ['tɪpeks] N Tipp-Ex® *m*

tipple ['tɪpl] N (*Brit*): **his ~ is Cointreau** bebe Cointreau

tipster ['tɪpstə^r] N (*Racing*) pronosticador(a) *m/f*

tipsy ['tɪpsɪ] ADJ alegre, achispado

tiptoe ['tɪptəu] N (*Brit*): **on ~** de puntillas

tiptop ['tɪptɔp] ADJ: **in ~ condition** en perfectas condiciones

tirade [taɪ'reɪd] N diatriba

tire ['taɪə^r] N (*US*) = **tyre** ▶ VT cansar ▶ VI (*gen*) cansarse; (*become bored*) aburrirse ▶ **tire out** VT agotar, rendir

★**tired** [ˈtaɪəd] ADJ cansado; **to be ~ of sth** estar harto de algo; **to be/feel/look ~** estar/sentirse/parecer cansado

tiredness [ˈtaɪədnɪs] N cansancio

tireless [ˈtaɪəlɪs] ADJ incansable

tirelessly [ˈtaɪəlɪslɪ] ADV incansablemente

tire pressure N (US) = **tyre pressure**

tiresome [ˈtaɪəsəm] ADJ aburrido

tiring [ˈtaɪrɪŋ] ADJ cansado

★**tissue** [ˈtɪʃuː] N tejido; (paper handkerchief) pañuelo de papel, kleenex® m

tissue paper N papel m de seda

tit [tɪt] N (bird) herrerillo común; **to give ~ for tat** dar ojo por ojo

titbit [ˈtɪtbɪt], (US) **tidbit** [ˈtɪdbɪt] N (food) golosina; (news) pedazo

titillate [ˈtɪtɪleɪt] VT estimular, excitar

titillation [tɪtɪˈleɪʃən] N estimulación f, excitación f

titivate [ˈtɪtɪveɪt] VT emperejilar

★**title** [ˈtaɪtl] N título; (Law: right): **~ (to)** derecho (a)

title deed N (Law) título de propiedad

title page N portada

title role N papel m principal

titter [ˈtɪtə'] VI reírse entre dientes

tittle-tattle [ˈtɪtltætl] N chismes mpl

titular [ˈtɪtjʊlə'] ADJ (in name only) nominal

T-junction [ˈtiːdʒʌŋkʃən] N cruce m en T

TM ABBR (= trademark) marca de fábrica; = **transcendental meditation**

TN ABBR (US) = **Tennessee**

TNT N ABBR (= trinitrotoluene) TNT m

---

to [tuː, tə]

PREP **1** (direction) a; **to go to France/London/school/the station** ir a Francia/Londres/al colegio/a la estación; **to go to Claude's/the doctor's** ir a casa de Claude/al médico; **the road to Edinburgh** la carretera de Edimburgo; **to the left/right** a la izquierda/derecha

2 (as far as) hasta, a; **from here to London** de aquí a or hasta Londres; **to count to 10** contar hasta 10; **from 40 to 50 people** entre 40 y 50 personas

3 (with expressions of time): **a quarter/twenty to five** las cinco menos cuarto/veinte

4 (for, of): **the key to the front door** la llave de la puerta principal; **she is secretary to the director** es la secretaria del director; **a letter to his wife** una carta a or para su mujer

5 (expressing indirect object) a; **to give sth to sb** darle algo a algn; **give it to me** dámelo; **to talk to sb** hablar con algn; **to be a danger to sb** ser un peligro para algn; **to carry out repairs to sth** hacer reparaciones en algo

6 (in relation to): **3 goals to 2** 3 goles a 2; **30 miles to the gallon** ≈ 9,4 litros a los cien (kilómetros); **8 apples to the kilo** 8 manzanas por kilo

7 (purpose, result): **to come to sb's aid** venir en auxilio or ayuda de algn; **to sentence sb to death** condenar a algn a muerte; **to my great surprise** con gran sorpresa mía

▶ INFIN PARTICLE **1** (simple infin): **to go/eat** ir/comer

2 (following another vb; see also relevant vb): **to want/try/start to do** querer/intentar/empezar a hacer

3 (with vb omitted): **I don't want to** no quiero

4 (purpose, result) para; **I did it to help you** lo hice para ayudarte; **he came to see you** vino a verte

5 (equivalent to relative clause): **I have things to do** tengo cosas que hacer; **the main thing is to try** lo principal es intentar

6 (after adj etc): **ready to go** listo para irse; **too old to ...** demasiado viejo (como) para ...

▶ ADV: **pull/push the door to** tirar de/empujar la puerta; **to go to and fro** ir y venir

---

toad [təud] N sapo

toadstool [ˈtəudstuːl] N seta venenosa

toady [ˈtəudɪ] N pelota mf ▶ VI: **to ~ to sb** hacer la pelota or dar coba a algn

★**toast** [təust] N (Culin: also: **piece of toast**) tostada; (drink, speech) brindis m inv ▶ VT (Culin) tostar; (drink to) brindar por

toaster [ˈtəustə'] N tostador m

toastmaster [ˈtəustmɑːstə'] N persona que propone brindis y anuncia a los oradores en un banquete

toast rack N rejilla para tostadas

tobacco [təˈbækəu] N tabaco; **pipe ~** tabaco de pipa

tobacconist [təˈbækənɪst] N estanquero(-a), tabaquero(-a) (LAM); **~'s (shop)** (BRIT) estanco, tabaquería (LAM)

tobacco plantation N plantación f de tabaco, tabacal m

Tobago [təˈbeɪɡəu] N see **Trinidad and Tobago**

toboggan [təˈbɔɡən] N tobogán m

★**today** [təˈdeɪ] ADV, N (also fig) hoy m; **what day is it ~?** ¿qué día es hoy?; **what date is it ~?** ¿a qué fecha estamos hoy?; **~ is the 4th of March** hoy es el 4 de marzo; **~'s paper** el periódico de hoy; **a fortnight ~** de hoy en 15 días, dentro de 15 días

toddle [ˈtɔdl] VI empezar a andar, dar los primeros pasos

toddler [ˈtɔdlə'] N niño(-a) (que empieza a andar)

toddy [ˈtɔdɪ] N ponche m

to-do [təˈduː] N (fuss) lío

★**toe** [təu] N dedo (del pie); (of shoe) punta; **big/little ~** dedo gordo/pequeño del pie ▶ VT: **to ~ the line** (fig) acatar las normas

TOEFL [ˈtəufl] N ABBR = **Test(ing) of English as a Foreign Language**

toehold [ˈtəuhəuld] N punto de apoyo (para el pie)

823

toenail [ˈtəʊneɪl] N uña del pie
toffee [ˈtɒfɪ] N caramelo
toffee apple N (BRIT) manzana de caramelo
tofu [ˈtəʊfuː] N tofu m
toga [ˈtəʊɡə] N toga
★**together** [təˈɡɛðəʳ] ADV juntos; (at same time) al mismo tiempo, a la vez; ~ **with** junto con
togetherness [təˈɡɛðənɪs] N compañerismo
toggle switch [ˈtɒɡl-] N (Comput) conmutador m de palanca
Togo [ˈtəʊɡəʊ] N Togo
togs [tɒɡz] NPL (inf: clothes) atuendo, ropa
toil [tɔɪl] N trabajo duro, labor f ▶ VI esforzarse
★**toilet** [ˈtɔɪlət] N (BRIT: lavatory) servicios mpl, baño; **to go to the** ~ ir al baño ▶ CPD (bag, soap etc) de aseo; see also **toilets**
toilet bag N neceser m, bolsa de aseo
toilet bowl N taza (de retrete)
toilet paper N papel m higiénico
toiletries [ˈtɔɪlətrɪz] NPL artículos mpl de aseo; (make-up etc) artículos mpl de tocador
toilet roll N rollo de papel higiénico
toilets [ˈtɔɪləts] NPL (BRIT) servicios mpl, baño
toilet soap N jabón m de tocador
toilet water N (agua de) colonia
to-ing and fro-ing [ˈtuːɪŋənˈfrəʊɪŋ] N vaivén m
token [ˈtəʊkən] N (sign) señal f, muestra; (souvenir) recuerdo; (voucher) vale m; (disc) ficha; **book/record** ~ (BRIT) vale m para comprar libros/discos; **by the same** ~ (fig) por la misma razón ▶ CPD (fee, strike) nominal, simbólico
tokenism [ˈtəʊkənɪzəm] N (Pol) política simbólica or de fachada
Tokyo [ˈtəʊkjəʊ] N Tokio
told [təʊld] PT, PP of **tell**
tolerable [ˈtɒlərəbl] ADJ (bearable) soportable; (fairly good) pasable
tolerably [ˈtɒlərəblɪ] ADV (good, comfortable) medianamente
tolerance [ˈtɒlərns] N (also Tech) tolerancia
tolerant [ˈtɒlərnt] ADJ: ~ **of** tolerante con
tolerantly [ˈtɒlərntlɪ] ADV con tolerancia
tolerate [ˈtɒləreɪt] VT tolerar
toleration [tɒləˈreɪʃən] N tolerancia
toll [təʊl] N (of casualties) número de víctimas; (tax, charge) peaje m ▶ VI (bell) doblar
toll bridge N puente m de peaje
toll call N (US Tel) conferencia, llamada interurbana
toll-free [ˈtɒlˈfriː] ADJ, ADV (US) gratis
toll road N carretera de peaje
★**tomato** [təˈmɑːtəʊ] (pl **tomatoes**) N tomate m
tomato puree N puré m de tomate
tomato sauce N salsa de tomate
tomb [tuːm] N tumba
tombola [tɒmˈbəʊlə] N tómbola

tomboy [ˈtɒmbɔɪ] N marimacho
tombstone [ˈtuːmstəʊn] N lápida
tombstoning [ˈtuːmstəʊnɪŋ] N (BRIT) tirarse de pie al mar desde gran altura
tomcat [ˈtɒmkæt] N gato
★**tomorrow** [təˈmɔrəu] ADV, N (also fig) mañana; **the day after** ~ pasado mañana; ~ **morning** mañana por la mañana; **a week** ~ de mañana en ocho (días)
★**ton** [tʌn] N tonelada; **tons of** (inf) montones de
tonal [ˈtəʊnl] ADJ tonal
tone [təʊn] N tono; **dialling** ~ (Tel) señal f para marcar ▶ VI armonizar
▶ **tone down** VT (criticism) suavizar; (colour) atenuar
▶ **tone up** VT (muscles) tonificar
tone-deaf [təʊnˈdɛf] ADJ sin oído musical
toner [ˈtəʊnəʳ] N (for photocopier) virador m
Tonga [ˈtɒŋə] N Islas fpl Tonga
tongs [tɒŋz] NPL (for coal) tenazas fpl; (for hair) tenacillas fpl
★**tongue** [tʌŋ] N lengua; ~ **in cheek** en broma
tongue-tied [ˈtʌŋtaɪd] ADJ (fig) mudo
tongue-twister [ˈtʌŋtwɪstəʳ] N trabalenguas m inv
tonic [ˈtɒnɪk] N (Med) tónico; (Mus) tónica; (also: **tonic water**) (agua) tónica
★**tonight** [təˈnaɪt] ADV, N esta noche; **I'll see you** ~ nos vemos esta noche
tonnage [ˈtʌnɪdʒ] N (Naut) tonelaje m
tonsil [ˈtɒnsl] N amígdala; **to have one's tonsils out** sacarse las amígdalas or anginas
tonsillitis [tɒnsɪˈlaɪtɪs] N amigdalitis f
★**too** [tuː] ADV, ADJ (excessively) demasiado; (very) muy; (also) también; **it's** ~ **sweet** está demasiado dulce; **I'm not** ~ **sure about that** no estoy muy seguro de eso; **I went** ~ yo también fui; ~ **much** adv, adj demasiado; ~ **many** adj demasiados(-as); ~ **bad!** ¡mala suerte!
took [tuk] PT of **take**
★**tool** [tuːl] N herramienta; (fig: person) instrumento
toolbar [ˈtuːlbɑːʳ] N barra de herramientas
tool box N caja de herramientas
tool kit N juego de herramientas
tool shed N cobertizo (para herramientas)
toot [tuːt] N (of horn) bocinazo; (of whistle) silbido ▶ VI (with car horn) tocar la bocina
★**tooth** [tuːθ] (pl **teeth** [tiːθ]) N (Anat, Tech) diente m; (molar) muela; **to clean one's teeth** lavarse los dientes; **to have a** ~ **out** sacarse una muela; **by the skin of one's teeth** por un pelo
★**toothache** [ˈtuːθeɪk] N dolor m de muelas
★**toothbrush** [ˈtuːθbrʌʃ] N cepillo de dientes
★**toothpaste** [ˈtuːθpeɪst] N pasta de dientes
toothpick [ˈtuːθpɪk] N palillo
tooth powder N polvos mpl dentífricos
★**top** [tɒp] N (of mountain) cumbre f, cima; (of head)

coronilla; (of ladder) (lo) alto; (of cupboard, table) superficie f; (lid: of box, jar) tapa; (: of bottle) tapón m; (of list, table, queue, page) cabeza; (toy) peonza; (Dress: blouse) blusa; (: T-shirt) camiseta; (: of pyjamas) chaqueta; **on ~ of** sobre, encima de; **from ~ to bottom** de pies a cabeza; **the ~ of the milk** la nata; **at the ~ of the stairs** en lo alto de la escalera; **at the ~ of the street** al final de la calle; **at the ~ of one's voice** (fig) a voz en grito; **over the ~** (inf) excesivo, desmesurado; **to go over the ~** pasarse ▶ ADJ de arriba; (in rank) principal, primero; (best) mejor; **at ~ speed** a máxima velocidad; **a ~ surgeon** un cirujano eminente ▶ VT (exceed) exceder; (be first in) encabezar

▶ **top off** (US) VT volver a llenar

▶ **top up** VT volver a llenar; (mobile phone) recargar el saldo de

topaz ['təupæz] N topacio

top-class ['tɔp'klɑːs] ADJ de primera clase

topcoat ['tɔpkəut] N sobretodo, abrigo

topflight ['tɔpflaɪt] ADJ de primera (categoría or clase)

top floor N último piso

top hat N sombrero de copa

top-heavy [tɔp'hɛvɪ] ADJ (object) con más peso en la parte superior

topic ['tɔpɪk] N tema m

topical ['tɔpɪkl] ADJ actual

topless ['tɔplɪs] ADJ (bather etc) topless inv

top-level ['tɔplɛvl] ADJ (talks) al más alto nivel

topmost ['tɔpməust] ADJ más alto

top-notch ['tɔp'nɔtʃ] ADJ (inf) de primerísima categoría

topography [tə'pɔgrəfɪ] N topografía

topping ['tɔpɪŋ] N (Culin): **with a ~ of cream** con nata por encima

topple ['tɔpl] VT volcar, derribar ▶ VI caerse

top-ranking ['tɔpræŋkɪŋ] ADJ de alto rango

top-secret [tɔp'siːkrɪt] ADJ de alto secreto

top-security ['tɔpsɪ'kjuərɪtɪ] ADJ (BRIT) de máxima seguridad

topsy-turvy ['tɔpsɪ'təːvɪ] ADJ, ADV patas arriba

top-up ['tɔpʌp] N: **would you like a ~?** ¿quiere que se lo vuelva a llenar?

top-up card N (for mobile phone) tarjeta prepago

top-up loan N (BRIT) préstamo complementario

torch [tɔːtʃ] N antorcha; (BRIT: electric) linterna

tore [tɔːr] PT of **tear¹**

torment N ['tɔːmɛnt] tormento ▶ VT [tɔː'mɛnt] atormentar; (fig: annoy) fastidiar

torn [tɔːn] PP of **tear¹**

tornado [tɔː'neɪdəu] (pl **tornadoes**) N tornado

torpedo [tɔː'piːdəu] (pl **torpedoes**) N torpedo

torpedo boat N torpedero, lancha torpedera

torpor ['tɔːpər] N letargo

torrent ['tɔrnt] N torrente m

torrential [tɔ'rɛnʃl] ADJ torrencial

torrid ['tɔrɪd] ADJ tórrido; (fig) apasionado

torso ['tɔːsəu] N torso

tortoise ['tɔːtəs] N tortuga

tortoiseshell ['tɔːtəʃɛl] ADJ de carey

tortuous ['tɔːtjuəs] ADJ tortuoso

★**torture** ['tɔːtʃər] N tortura ▶ VT torturar; (fig) atormentar

torturer ['tɔːtʃərər] N torturador(a) m/f

Tory ['tɔːrɪ] ADJ, N (BRIT Pol) conservador(a) m/f

toss [tɔs] VT tirar, echar; (head) sacudir; **to ~ a coin** echar a cara o cruz ▶ VI: **to ~ up for sth** jugar algo a cara o cruz; **to ~ and turn** (in bed) dar vueltas (en la cama) ▶ N (movement: of head etc) sacudida; (: of coin) tirada, echada (LAM); **to win/lose the ~** (also Sport) ganar/perder (a cara o cruz)

tot [tɔt] N (BRIT: drink) copita; (child) nene(-a) m/f

▶ **tot up** VT sumar

★**total** ['təutl] ADJ total, entero; (emphatic: failure etc) completo, total ▶ N total m, suma; **grand ~** cantidad f total; (cost) importe m total; **in ~** en total, en suma ▶ VT (add up) sumar; (amount to) ascender a

totalitarian [təutælɪ'tɛərɪən] ADJ totalitario

totality [təu'tælɪtɪ] N totalidad f

total loss N siniestro total

totally ['təutəlɪ] ADV totalmente

tote [təut] VT (inf) acarrear, cargar con

tote bag N bolsa

totem pole ['təutəm-] N poste m totémico

totter ['tɔtər] VI tambalearse

★**touch** [tʌtʃ] N (sense) tacto; (contact) contacto; (Football) lateral m; **a ~ of** (fig) una pizca o un poquito de; **to get in ~ with sb** ponerse en contacto con algn; **I'll be in ~** le llamaré/escribiré; **to lose ~** (friends) perder contacto; **to be out of ~ with events** no estar al corriente de (los acontecimientos); **the personal ~** el toque personal; **to put the finishing touches to sth** dar el último toque a algo ▶ VT tocar; (emotionally) conmover; **no artist in the country can ~ him** no hay artista en todo el país que le iguale

▶ **touch down** VI (on land) aterrizar

▶ **touch on** VT FUS (topic) aludir (brevemente) a

▶ **touch up** VT (paint) retocar

touch-and-go ['tʌtʃən'gəu] ADJ arriesgado

touchdown ['tʌtʃdaun] N aterrizaje m; (US Football) ensayo

touched [tʌtʃt] ADJ conmovido; (inf) chiflado

touchiness ['tʌtʃɪnɪs] N susceptibilidad f

touching ['tʌtʃɪŋ] ADJ conmovedor(a)

touchline ['tʌtʃlaɪn] N (Sport) línea de banda

touch screen N (Tech) pantalla táctil; **~ mobile** móvil m con pantalla táctil; **~ technology** tecnología táctil

touch-sensitive ['tʌtʃ'sɛnsɪtɪv] ADJ táctil, sensible al tacto

touch-type ['tʌtʃtaɪp] VI mecanografiar al tacto

t

touchy ['tʌtʃɪ] ADJ (*person*) quisquilloso

★tough [tʌf] ADJ (*meat*) duro; (*journey*) penoso; (*task, problem, situation*) difícil; (*resistant*) resistente; (*person*) fuerte; (: *pej*) bruto; **they got ~ with the workers** se pusieron muy duros con los trabajadores ▶ N (*gangster etc*) gorila *m*

toughen ['tʌfn] VT endurecer

toughness ['tʌfnɪs] N dureza; (*resistance*) resistencia; (*strictness*) inflexibilidad *f*

toupée ['tu:peɪ] N peluquín *m*

★tour ['tuə^r] N viaje *m*; (*also:* **package tour**) viaje *m* con todo incluido; (*of town, museum*) visita; **to go on a ~ of** (*region, country*) ir de viaje por; (*museum, castle*) visitar; **to go on ~** partir *or* ir de gira ▶ VT viajar por

tour guide N guía *mf* turístico(-a)

touring ['tuərɪŋ] N viajes *mpl* turísticos, turismo

tourism ['tuərɪzm] N turismo

★tourist ['tuərɪst] N turista *mf* ▶ CPD turístico; **the ~ trade** el turismo

tourist class N (*Aviat*) clase *f* turista

tourist office N oficina de turismo

★tournament ['tuənəmənt] N torneo

tourniquet ['tuənɪkeɪ] N (*Med*) torniquete *m*

tour operator N touroperador(a) *m/f*, operador(a) *m/f* turístico(-a)

tousled ['tauzld] ADJ (*hair*) despeinado

tout [taut] VI: **to ~ for business** solicitar clientes ▶ N: **ticket ~** revendedor(a) *m/f*

tow [təu] (*Aut*) N: **to give sb a ~** remolcar a algn; **"on** *or* (*US*) **in ~"** "a remolque" ▶ VT remolcar ▶ **tow away** VT llevarse a remolque

toward [tə'wɔːd], **towards** [tə'wɔːdz] PREP hacia; (*of attitude*) respecto a, con; (*of purpose*) para; **~(s) noon** alrededor de mediodía; **~(s) the end of the year** hacia finales de año; **to feel friendly ~(s) sb** sentir amistad hacia algn

★towel ['tauəl] N toalla; **to throw in the ~** (*fig*) darse por vencido, renunciar

towelling, (*US*) **toweling** ['tauəlɪŋ] N (*fabric*) felpa

towel rail, (*US*) **towel rack** N toallero

★tower ['tauə^r] N torre *f* ▶ VI (*building, mountain*) elevarse; **to ~ above** *or* **over sth/sb** dominar algo/destacarse sobre algn

tower block N (*BRIT*) bloque *m* de pisos

towering ['tauərɪŋ] ADJ muy alto, imponente

★town [taun] N ciudad *f*; **to go to ~** ir a la ciudad; (*fig*) tirar la casa por la ventana; **in the ~** en la ciudad; **to be out of ~** estar fuera de la ciudad

town centre N centro de la ciudad

town clerk N secretario(-a) del Ayuntamiento

town council N Ayuntamiento, consejo municipal

town crier [-kraɪə^r] N (*BRIT*) pregonero

town hall N ayuntamiento

townie ['taunɪ] N (*BRIT inf*) urbanita *mf*, persona de la ciudad

town plan N plano de la ciudad

town planner N urbanista *mf*

town planning N urbanismo

township ['taunʃɪp] N asentamiento urbano creado en tiempos del apartheid para gente de raza negra en Sudáfrica

townspeople ['taunzpi:pl] NPL gente *f* de ciudad

towpath ['təupɑ:θ] N camino de sirga

towrope ['təurəup] N cable *m* de remolque

tow truck N (*US*) camión *m* grúa

toxic ['tɔksɪk] ADJ tóxico

toxic asset N (*Econ*) activo tóxico

toxic bank N (*Econ*) banco malo

toxin ['tɔksɪn] N toxina

★toy [tɔɪ] N juguete *m* ▶ **toy with** VT FUS jugar con; (*idea*) acariciar

toyshop ['tɔɪʃɔp] N juguetería

toy train N tren *m* de juguete

trace [treɪs] N rastro; **there was no ~ of it** no había ningún indicio de ello ▶ VT (*draw*) trazar, delinear; (*locate*) encontrar

traceability [treɪsə'bɪlɪtɪ] N rastreabilidad *f*

trace element N oligoelemento

trachea [trə'kɪə] N (*Anat*) tráquea

tracing paper ['treɪsɪŋ-] N papel *m* de calco

track [træk] N (*mark*) huella, pista; (*path: gen*) camino, senda; (: *of bullet etc*) trayectoria; (: *of suspect, animal*) pista, rastro; (*Rail*) vía; (*Comput, Sport*) pista; (*on album*) canción *f*; **to keep ~ of** mantenerse al tanto de, seguir; **a four-track tape** una cinta de cuatro pistas; **the first ~ on the record/tape** la primera canción en el disco/la cinta; **to be on the right ~** (*fig*) ir por buen camino ▶ VT seguir la pista de ▶ **track down** VT (*person*) localizar; (*sth lost*) encontrar

tracker dog ['trækə^r-] N (*BRIT*) perro rastreador

track events NPL (*Sport*) pruebas *fpl* en pista

tracking station ['trækɪŋ-] N (*Space*) estación *f* de seguimiento

track meet N (*US*) concurso de carreras y saltos

track record N: **to have a good ~** (*fig*) tener un buen historial

★tracksuit ['træksu:t] N chandal *m*

tract [trækt] N (*Geo*) región *f*; (*pamphlet*) folleto

traction ['trækʃən] N (*Aut: power*) tracción *f*; **in ~** (*Med*) en tracción

traction engine N locomotora de tracción

tractor ['træktə^r] N tractor *m*

trade [treɪd] N comercio, negocio; (*skill, job*) oficio, empleo; (*industry*) industria; **foreign ~** comercio exterior ▶ VI negociar, comerciar ▶ VT (*exchange*): **to ~ sth (for sth)** cambiar algo (por algo) ▶ **trade in** VT (*old car etc*) ofrecer como parte del pago

trade barrier N barrera comercial

trade deficit N déficit m comercial

Trade Descriptions Act N (BRIT) ley sobre descripciones comerciales

trade discount N descuento comercial

trade fair N feria de muestras

trade-in ['treɪdɪn] ADJ: **~ price/value** precio/valor de un artículo usado que se descuenta del precio de otro nuevo

trademark ['treɪdmɑ:k] N marca de fábrica

trade mission N misión f comercial

trade name N marca registrada

trade-off ['treɪdɔf] N: **a ~ (between)** un equilibrio (entre)

trade price N precio al detallista

trader ['treɪdəʳ] N comerciante mf

trade reference N referencia comercial

trade secret N secreto profesional

tradesman ['treɪdzmən] N (irreg) (shopkeeper) comerciante mf

trade union N sindicato

trade unionist [-'juːnjənɪst] N sindicalista mf

trade wind N viento alisio

trading ['treɪdɪŋ] N comercio

trading account N cuenta de compraventa

trading estate N (BRIT) polígono industrial

trading stamp N cupón m, sello de prima

★**tradition** [trə'dɪʃən] N tradición f

★**traditional** [trə'dɪʃənl] ADJ tradicional

traditionally [trə'dɪʃənlɪ] ADV tradicionalmente

★**traffic** ['træfɪk] N tráfico, circulación f, tránsito; **air ~** tráfico aéreo ▶ VI: **to ~ in** (pej: liquor, drugs) traficar en

traffic calming [-'kɑːmɪŋ] N reducción f de la velocidad de la circulación

traffic circle N (US) rotonda, glorieta

traffic island N refugio, isleta

traffic jam N embotellamiento, atasco

trafficker ['træfɪkəʳ] N traficante mf

★**traffic lights** NPL semáforo sg

traffic offence, (US) **traffic violation** N infracción f de tráfico

traffic warden N guardia mf de tráfico

tragedy ['trædʒədɪ] N tragedia

tragic ['trædʒɪk] ADJ trágico

tragically ['trædʒɪkəlɪ] ADV trágicamente

trail [treɪl] N (tracks) rastro, pista; (path) camino, sendero; (dust, smoke) estela; **to be on sb's ~** seguir la pista de algn ▶ VT (drag) arrastrar; (follow) seguir la pista de; (follow closely) vigilar ▶ VI arrastrarse; (in contest etc) ir perdiendo
▶ **trail away, trail off** VI (sound) desvanecerse; (interest, voice) desaparecer
▶ **trail behind** VI quedar a la zaga

trailer ['treɪləʳ] N (Aut) remolque m; (caravan) caravana; (Cine) trailer m, avance m

trailer truck N (US) camión articulado

★**train** [treɪn] N tren m; (of dress) cola; (series): **~ of events** curso de los acontecimientos; **to go by ~** ir en tren; **one's ~ of thought** el razonamiento de uno ▶ VT (educate) formar; (teach skills to) adiestrar; (sportsperson) entrenar; (dog) adiestrar, amaestrar; (point: gun etc): **to ~ on** apuntar a; **to ~ sb to do sth** enseñar a algn a hacer algo ▶ VI (Sport) entrenarse; (be educated, learn a skill) formarse; **to ~ as a teacher** etc estudiar para profesor etc

train attendant N (US Rail) empleado(-a) de coches-cama

trained [treɪnd] ADJ (worker) cualificado; (animal) amaestrado

trainee [treɪ'niː] N trabajador(a) m/f en prácticas ▶ CPD: **he's a ~ teacher** (primary) es estudiante de magisterio; (secondary) está haciendo las prácticas del I.C.E.

trainer ['treɪnəʳ] N (Sport) entrenador(a) m/f; (of animals) domador(a) m/f ■ **trainers** NPL (shoes) zapatillas fpl (de deporte)

★**training** ['treɪnɪŋ] N formación f; (Sport) entrenamiento; **to be in ~** (Sport) estar entrenando

training college N (gen) colegio de formación profesional; (for teachers) escuela normal

training course N curso de formación

training shoes NPL zapatillas fpl (de deporte)

train wreck N (fig) destrozo; **he's a complete ~** está completamente destrozado

traipse [treɪps] VI andar penosamente

trait [treɪt] N rasgo

traitor ['treɪtəʳ] N traidor(a) m/f

trajectory [trə'dʒɛktərɪ] N trayectoria, curso

tram [træm] N (BRIT: also: **tramcar**) tranvía m

tramline ['træmlaɪn] N carril m de tranvía

tramp [træmp] N (pej) (person) vagabundo(-a); (woman) puta ▶ VI andar con pasos pesados

trample ['træmpl] VT: **to ~ (underfoot)** pisotear

trampoline ['træmpəliːn] N trampolín m

trance [trɑːns] N trance m; **to go into a ~** entrar en trance

tranquil ['træŋkwɪl] ADJ tranquilo

tranquillity, (US) **tranquility** [træŋ'kwɪlɪtɪ] N tranquilidad f

tranquillizer, (US) **tranquilizer** ['træŋkwɪlaɪzəʳ] N (Med) tranquilizante m

trans- [trænz] PREF trans-, tras-

transact [træn'zækt] VT (business) tramitar

transaction [træn'zækʃən] N transacción f, operación f; **cash transactions** transacciones fpl al contado

transatlantic ['trænzət'læntɪk] ADJ transatlántico

transcend [træn'sɛnd] VT rebasar

transcendent [træn'sɛndənt] ADJ trascendente

transcendental [trænsɛn'dɛntl] ADJ: **~ meditation** meditación f transcendental

transcribe [trænˈskraɪb] VT transcribir, copiar

transcript [ˈtrænskrɪpt] N copia

transcription [trænˈskrɪpʃən] N transcripción f

transept [ˈtrænsɛpt] N crucero

transfer N [ˈtrænsfəʳ] transferencia; (*Sport*) traspaso; (*picture, design*) calcomanía; **by bank ~** por transferencia bancaria *or* giro bancario ▶ VT [trænsˈfəːʳ] trasladar, pasar; **to ~ the charges** (*Brit Tel*) llamar a cobro revertido; **to ~ money from one account to another** transferir dinero de una cuenta a otra; **to ~ sth to sb's name** transferir algo al nombre de algn

transferable [trænsˈfəːrəbl] ADJ: **not ~** intransferible

transfix [trænsˈfɪks] VT traspasar; (*fig*): **transfixed with fear** paralizado por el miedo

transform [trænsˈfɔːm] VT transformar

transformation [trænsfəˈmeɪʃən] N transformación f

transformer [trænsˈfɔːməʳ] N (*Elec*) transformador m

transfusion [trænsˈfjuːʒən] N transfusión f

transgress [trænsˈgrɛs] VT (*go beyond*) traspasar; (*violate*) violar, infringir

tranship [trænˈʃɪp] VT trasbordar

transient [ˈtrænzɪənt] ADJ transitorio

transistor [trænˈzɪstəʳ] N (*Elec*) transistor m

transistorized [trænˈzɪstəraɪzd] ADJ (*circuit*) transistorizado

transistor radio N transistor m

transit [ˈtrænzɪt] N: **in ~** en tránsito

transit camp N campamento de tránsito

transition [trænˈzɪʃən] N transición f

transitional [trænˈzɪʃənl] ADJ transitorio

transition period N período de transición

transitive [ˈtrænzɪtɪv] ADJ (*Ling*) transitivo

transitively [ˈtrænzɪtɪvlɪ] ADV transitivamente

transitory [ˈtrænzɪtərɪ] ADJ transitorio

transit visa N visado de tránsito

translate [trænzˈleɪt] VT: **to ~ (from/into)** traducir (de/a)

translation [trænzˈleɪʃən] N traducción f

translator [trænzˈleɪtəʳ] N traductor(a) m/f

translucent [trænzˈluːsnt] ADJ traslúcido

transmission [trænzˈmɪʃən] N transmisión f

transmit [trænzˈmɪt] VT transmitir

transmitter [trænzˈmɪtəʳ] N transmisor m; (*station*) emisora

transparency [trænsˈpɛərnsɪ] N (*Brit Phot*) diapositiva

transparent [trænsˈpærnt] ADJ transparente

transpire [trænsˈpaɪəʳ] VI (*turn out*) resultar (ser); (*happen*) ocurrir, suceder; (*become known*): **it finally transpired that …** por fin se supo que …

transplant VT [trænsˈplɑːnt] transplantar ▶ N [ˈtrænsplɑːnt] (*Med*) transplante m; **to have a heart ~** hacerse un transplante de corazón

★**transport** N [ˈtrænspɔːt] transporte m; **public ~** transporte m público ▶ VT [trænsˈpɔːt] transportar

transportable [trænsˈpɔːtəbl] ADJ transportable

transportation [trænspɔːˈteɪʃən] N transporte m; (*of prisoners*) deportación f

transport café N (*Brit*) bar-restaurante m de carretera

transpose [trænsˈpəuz] VT transponer

transsexual [trænzˈsɛksjuəl] ADJ, N transexual mf

transverse [ˈtrænzvəːs] ADJ transverso, transversal

transvestite [trænzˈvɛstaɪt] N travesti mf

trap [træp] N (*snare, trick*) trampa; (*carriage*) cabriolé m; **to set** *or* **lay a ~ (for sb)** poner(le) una trampa (a algn) ▶ VT coger (*Sp*) *or* agarrar (*Lam*) en una trampa; (*trick*) engañar; (*confine*) atrapar; (*immobilize*) bloquear; (*jam*) atascar; **to ~ one's finger in the door** pillarse el dedo en la puerta

trap door N escotilla

trapeze [trəˈpiːz] N trapecio

trapper [ˈtræpəʳ] N trampero, cazador m

trappings [ˈtræpɪŋz] NPL adornos mpl

trash [træʃ] N basura; (*inf: nonsense*) tonterías fpl; **the book/film is ~** el libro/la película no vale nada

trash can N (*US*) cubo *or* balde m (*Lam*) *or* bote m (*Lam*) de la basura

trash can liner N (*US*) bolsa de basura

trashy [ˈtræʃɪ] ADJ (*inf*) chungo

trauma [ˈtrɔːmə] N trauma m

traumatic [trɔːˈmætɪk] ADJ traumático

★**travel** [ˈtrævl] N los viajes, el viajar ▶ VI viajar; **this wine doesn't ~ well** este vino pierde con los viajes ▶ VT (*distance*) recorrer

travel agency N agencia de viajes

travel agent N (*agency*) agencia de viajes; (*person*) agente mf de viajes

travel brochure N folleto turístico

travel insurance N seguro de viaje

traveller, (*US*) **traveler** [ˈtrævləʳ] N viajero(-a); (*Comm*) viajante mf

traveller's cheque, (*US*) **traveler's check** N cheque m de viaje

travelling, (*US*) **traveling** [ˈtrævlɪŋ] N los viajes, el viajar ▶ ADJ (*circus, exhibition*) ambulante ▶ CPD (*bag, clock*) de viaje

travelling expenses, (*US*) **traveling expenses** NPL dietas fpl

travelling salesman, (*US*) **traveling salesman** N (*irreg*) viajante m

travelogue [ˈtrævəlɔg] N (*book*) relación f de viajes; (*film*) documental m de viajes; (*talk*) recuento de viajes

travel-sick [ˈtrævəlsɪk] ADJ: **to get ~** marearse al viajar

travel sickness N mareo

traverse ['trævəs] VT atravesar

travesty ['trævəstɪ] N parodia

trawler ['trɔːlə'] N pesquero de arrastre

tray [treɪ] N (for carrying) bandeja; (on desk) cajón m

treacherous ['trɛtʃərəs] ADJ traidor(a); **road conditions are ~** el estado de las carreteras es peligroso

treachery ['trɛtʃərɪ] N traición f

treacle ['triːkl] N (BRIT) melaza

tread [trɛd] (pt **trod** [trɔd], pp **trodden** ['trɔdn]) N paso, pisada; (of tyre) banda de rodadura ▶ VI pisar
  ▶ **tread on** VT FUS pisar

treas. ABBR = **treasurer**

treason ['triːzn] N traición f

treasure ['trɛʒə'] N tesoro ▶ VT (value) apreciar, valorar

treasure hunt N caza del tesoro

treasurer ['trɛʒərə'] N tesorero(-a)

treasury ['trɛʒərɪ] N: **the T~**, (US) **the T~ Department** = el Ministerio de Economía y Hacienda

treasury bill N bono del Tesoro

★**treat** [triːt] N (present) regalo; (pleasure) placer m; **to give sb a ~** hacer un regalo a algn ▶ VT tratar; (consider) considerar; **to ~ sb to sth** invitar a algn a algo; **to ~ sth as a joke** tomar algo a broma

treatise ['triːtɪz] N tratado

★**treatment** ['triːtmənt] N tratamiento; **to have ~ for sth** recibir tratamiento por algo

treaty ['triːtɪ] N tratado

treble ['trɛbl] ADJ triple ▶ VT triplicar ▶ VI triplicarse

treble clef N (Mus) clave f de sol

★**tree** [triː] N árbol m

tree-lined ['triːlaɪnd] ADJ bordeado de árboles

tree trunk N tronco de árbol

trek [trɛk] N (long journey) expedición f; (tiring walk) caminata

trellis ['trɛlɪs] N enrejado

tremble ['trɛmbl] VI temblar

trembling ['trɛmblɪŋ] N temblor m ▶ ADJ tembloroso

tremendous [trɪ'mɛndəs] ADJ tremendo; (enormous) enorme; (excellent) estupendo

tremendously [trɪ'mɛndəslɪ] ADV enormemente, sobremanera; **he enjoyed it ~** lo disfrutó de lo lindo

tremor ['trɛmə'] N temblor m; (also: **earth tremor**) temblor m de tierra

trench [trɛntʃ] N zanja; (Mil) trinchera

trench coat N trinchera

trench warfare N guerra de trincheras

★**trend** [trɛnd] N (tendency) tendencia; (of events) curso; (fashion) moda; **~ towards/away from sth** tendencia hacia/en contra de algo; **to set the ~** marcar la pauta

trendy ['trɛndɪ] ADJ de moda

trepidation [trɛpɪ'deɪʃən] N inquietud f

trespass ['trɛspəs] VI: **to ~ on** entrar sin permiso en; **"no trespassing"** "prohibido el paso"

trespasser ['trɛspəsə'] N intruso(-a); **"trespassers will be prosecuted"** "se procesará a los intrusos"

tress [trɛs] N guedeja

trestle ['trɛsl] N caballete m

trestle table N mesa de caballete

tri- [traɪ] PREF tri-

★**trial** ['traɪəl] N (Law) juicio, proceso; (test: of machine etc) prueba; (hardship) desgracia; **to bring sb to ~ (for a crime)** llevar a algn a juicio (por un delito); **~ by jury** juicio ante jurado; **to be sent for ~** ser remitido al tribunal; **by ~ and error** a fuerza de probar ■ **trials** NPL (Athletics) pruebas fpl; (of horses) pruebas fpl

trial balance N balance m de comprobación

trial basis N: **on a ~** a modo de prueba

trial offer N oferta de prueba

trial period N período de prueba

trial run N prueba

triangle ['traɪæŋgl] N (Math, Mus) triángulo

triangular [traɪ'æŋgjulə'] ADJ triangular

triathlon [traɪ'æθlən] N triatlón m

tribal ['traɪbəl] ADJ tribal

tribe [traɪb] N tribu f

tribesman ['traɪbzmən] N (irreg) miembro de una tribu

tribulation [trɪbju'leɪʃən] N tribulación f

tribunal [traɪ'bjuːnl] N tribunal m

tributary ['trɪbjutərɪ] N (river) afluente m

tribute ['trɪbjuːt] N homenaje m, tributo; **to pay ~ to** rendir homenaje a

trice [traɪs] N: **in a ~** en un santiamén

★**trick** [trɪk] N trampa; (conjuring trick, deceit) truco; (joke) broma; (Cards) baza; **it's a ~ of the light** es una ilusión óptica; **to play a ~ on sb** gastar una broma a algn; **that should do the ~** eso servirá ▶ VT engañar; **to ~ sb out of sth** quitarle algo a algn con engaños; **to ~ sb into doing sth** hacer que algn haga algo con engaños

trickery ['trɪkərɪ] N engaño

trickle ['trɪkl] N (of water etc) hilo ▶ VI gotear

trick question N pregunta capciosa

trickster ['trɪkstə'] N estafador(a) m/f

tricky ['trɪkɪ] ADJ difícil; (problem) delicado

tricycle ['traɪsɪkl] N triciclo

tried [traɪd] ADJ probado

trifle ['traɪfl] N bagatela; (Culin) dulce de bizcocho, gelatina, fruta y natillas ▶ ADV: **a ~ long** un pelín largo ▶ VI: **to ~ with** jugar con

trifling ['traɪflɪŋ] ADJ insignificante

trigger ['trɪgə'] N (of gun) gatillo
  ▶ **trigger off** VT desencadenar

trigonometry [trɪgə'nɔmətrɪ] N trigonometría

t

trilby [ˈtrɪlbɪ] N (also: **trilby hat**) sombrero flexible or tirolés

trill [trɪl] N (of bird) gorjeo; (Mus) trino

trilogy [ˈtrɪlədʒɪ] N trilogía

trim [trɪm] ADJ (elegant) aseado; (house, garden) en buen estado; (figure): **to be ~** tener buen talle ▶ N (haircut etc) recorte m; **to keep in (good) ~** mantener en buen estado ▶ VT (neaten) arreglar; (cut) recortar; (decorate) adornar; (Naut: a sail) orientar

trimmings [ˈtrɪmɪŋz] NPL (extras) accesorios mpl; (cuttings) recortes mpl

Trinidad and Tobago [ˈtrɪnɪdæd-] N Trinidad f y Tobago

Trinity [ˈtrɪnɪtɪ] N: **the ~** la Trinidad

trinket [ˈtrɪŋkɪt] N chuchería, baratija

trio [ˈtriːəu] N trío

★**trip** [trɪp] N viaje m; (excursion) excursión f; (stumble) traspié m; **on a ~** de viaje ▶ VI (stumble) tropezar; (go lightly) andar a paso ligero
▶ **trip over** VT FUS tropezar con
▶ **trip up** VI tropezar, caerse ▶VT hacer tropezar or caer

tripartite [traɪˈpɑːtaɪt] ADJ (agreement, talks) tripartita

tripe [traɪp] N (Culin) callos mpl; (pej: rubbish) bobadas fpl

triple [ˈtrɪpl] ADJ triple ▶ ADV: **~ the distance/ the speed** tres veces la distancia/la velocidad

triple jump N triple salto

triplets [ˈtrɪplɪts] NPL trillizos(-as) m/fpl

triplicate [ˈtrɪplɪkət] N: **in ~** por triplicado

tripod [ˈtraɪpɒd] N trípode m

Tripoli [ˈtrɪpəlɪ] N Trípoli m

tripper [ˈtrɪpəʳ] N turista mf, excursionista mf

tripwire [ˈtrɪpwaɪəʳ] N cable m de trampa

trite [traɪt] ADJ trillado

triumph [ˈtraɪʌmf] N triunfo ▶ VI: **to ~ (over)** vencer

triumphal [traɪˈʌmfl] ADJ triunfal

triumphant [traɪˈʌmfənt] ADJ triunfante

triumphantly [traɪˈʌmfəntlɪ] ADV triunfalmente, en tono triunfal

trivia [ˈtrɪvɪə] NPL trivialidades fpl

trivial [ˈtrɪvɪəl] ADJ insignificante, trivial

triviality [trɪvɪˈælɪtɪ] N insignificancia, trivialidad f

trivialize [ˈtrɪvɪəlaɪz] VT trivializar

trod [trɒd] PT of **tread**

trodden [ˈtrɒdn] PP of **tread**

troll [trɒl] N (Comput) troll m

trolley [ˈtrɒlɪ] N carrito; (in hospital) camilla

trolley bus N trolebús m

trolling [ˈtrəulɪŋ] N (Internet) troleo

trombone [trɒmˈbəun] N trombón m

troop [truːp] N grupo, banda ■ **troops** NPL (Mil) tropas fpl

▶ **troop in** VI entrar en tropel
▶ **troop out** VI salir en tropel

troop carrier N (plane) transporte m (militar); (Naut) (buque m de) transporte m

trooper [ˈtruːpəʳ] N (Mil) soldado (de caballería); (US: police officer) policía mf montado(-a)

trooping the colour [ˈtruːpɪŋ-] N (ceremony) presentación f de la bandera

troopship [ˈtruːpʃɪp] N (buque m de) transporte m

trophy [ˈtrəufɪ] N trofeo

tropic [ˈtrɒpɪk] N trópico; **the tropics** los trópicos, la zona tropical; **T~ of Cancer/Capricorn** trópico de Cáncer/Capricornio

tropical [ˈtrɒpɪkl] ADJ tropical

trot [trɒt] N trote m; **on the ~** (BRIT fig) seguidos(-as) ▶ VI trotar
▶ **trot out** VT (excuse, reason) volver a usar; (names, facts) sacar a relucir

★**trouble** [ˈtrʌbl] N problema m, dificultad f; (worry) preocupación f; (bother, effort) molestia, esfuerzo; (unrest) inquietud f; (with machine etc) fallo, avería; (Med): **stomach ~** problemas mpl gástricos; **to be in ~** estar en un apuro; (for doing wrong) tener problemas; **to have ~ doing sth** tener dificultad en or para hacer algo; **to go to the ~ of doing sth** tomarse la molestia de hacer algo; **it's no ~!** ¡no es molestia (ninguna)!; **what's the ~?** ¿qué pasa?; **the ~ is ...** el problema es ..., lo que pasa es ... ▶ VT molestar; **please don't ~ yourself** por favor no se moleste; (worry) preocupar, inquietar ▶ VI: **to ~ to do sth** molestarse en hacer algo ■ **troubles** NPL (Pol etc) conflictos mpl

troubled [ˈtrʌbld] ADJ (person) preocupado; (epoch, life) agitado

trouble-free [ˈtrʌblfriː] ADJ sin problemas or dificultades

troublemaker [ˈtrʌblmeɪkəʳ] N agitador(a) m/f

troubleshooter [ˈtrʌblʃuːtəʳ] N (in conflict) mediador(a) m/f

troublesome [ˈtrʌblsəm] ADJ molesto, inoportuno

trouble spot N centro de fricción, punto caliente

troubling [ˈtrʌblɪŋ] ADJ (thought) preocupante; **these are ~ times** son malos tiempos

trough [trɒf] N (also: **drinking trough**) abrevadero; (also: **feeding trough**) comedero; (channel) canal m

trounce [trauns] VT dar una paliza a

troupe [truːp] N grupo

trouser press N prensa para pantalones

★**trousers** [ˈtrauzəz] NPL pantalones mpl; **short ~** pantalones mpl cortos

trouser suit N traje m de chaqueta y pantalón

trousseau [ˈtruːsəu] (pl **trousseaux** or **trousseaus** [-z]) N ajuar m

trout [traut] N pl inv trucha

trowel [ˈtrauəl] N paleta

truant ['truənt] N: **to play ~** (BRIT) hacer novillos

truce [truːs] N tregua

★**truck** [trʌk] N (US) camión m; (Rail) vagón m

truck driver N camionero(-a)

trucker ['trʌkəʳ] N (esp US) camionero(-a)

truck farm N (US) huerto de hortalizas

trucking ['trʌkɪŋ] N (esp US) transporte m en camión

trucking company N (US) compañía de transporte por carretera

truckload ['trʌkləud] N camión m lleno

truculent ['trʌkjulənt] ADJ agresivo

trudge [trʌdʒ] VI caminar penosamente

★**true** [truː] ADJ verdadero; (accurate) exacto; (genuine) auténtico; (faithful) fiel; (wheel) centrado; (wall) a plomo; (beam) alineado; **~ to life** verídico; **to come ~** realizarse, cumplirse

truffle ['trʌfl] N trufa

truly ['truːlɪ] ADV realmente; (faithfully) fielmente; **yours ~** (in letter-writing) atentamente

trump [trʌmp] N (Cards) triunfo; **to turn up trumps** (fig) salir or resultar bien

trump card N triunfo; (fig) baza

trumped-up ['trʌmptʌp] ADJ inventado

trumpet ['trʌmpɪt] N trompeta

truncated [trʌŋ'keɪtɪd] ADJ truncado

truncheon ['trʌntʃən] N (BRIT) porra

trundle ['trʌndl] VT, VI: **to ~ along** rodar haciendo ruido

trunk [trʌŋk] N (of tree, person) tronco; (of elephant) trompa; (case) baúl m; (US Aut) maletero, baúl m (LAM)

trunk call N (BRIT Tel) llamada interurbana

trunk road N carretera principal

trunks [trʌŋks] NPL (also: **swimming trunks**) bañador m

truss [trʌs] N (Med) braguero ▶ VT: **to ~ (up)** atar

★**trust** [trʌst] N confianza; (Comm) trust m; (Law) fideicomiso; **in ~** en fideicomiso; **you'll have to take it on ~** tienes que aceptarlo a ojos cerrados ▶ VT (rely on) tener confianza en; **to ~ sth to sb** (entrust) confiar algo a algn; **to ~ (that)** (hope) esperar (que)

trust company N banco fideicomisario

trusted ['trʌstɪd] ADJ de confianza, fiable, de fiar

trustee [trʌs'tiː] N (Law) fideicomisario

trustful ['trʌstful] ADJ confiado

trust fund N fondo fiduciario or de fideicomiso

trusting ['trʌstɪŋ] ADJ confiado

trustworthy ['trʌstwəː ðɪ] ADJ digno de confianza, fiable, de fiar

trusty ['trʌstɪ] ADJ fiel

★**truth** [truːθ] (pl **truths** [truːðz]) N verdad f

truthful ['truːθful] ADJ (person) sincero; (account) fidedigno

truthfully ['truːθfulɪ] ADV (answer) con sinceridad

truthfulness ['truːθfulnɪs] N (of account) verdad f; (of person) sinceridad f

★**try** [traɪ] N tentativa, intento; (Rugby) ensayo; **to give sth a ~** intentar hacer algo ▶ VT (Law) juzgar, procesar; (test: sth new) probar, someter a prueba; (attempt) intentar; (strain: patience) hacer perder; **to ~ to do sth** intentar hacer algo; **to ~ one's (very) best** or **hardest** poner todo su empeño, esmerarse ▶ VI probar; **~ again!** ¡vuelve a probar!; **~ harder!** ¡esfuérzate más!; **well, I tried** al menos lo intenté
▶ **try on** VT (clothes) probarse
▶ **try out** VT probar, poner a prueba

trying ['traɪɪŋ] ADJ cansado; (person) pesado

tsar [zɑːʳ] N zar m

T-shirt ['tiːʃəːt] N camiseta

TSO N ABBR (BRIT) = **The Stationery Office**

T-square ['tiːskwɛəʳ] N regla en T

tsunami [tsuˈnɑːmɪ] N tsunami m

TT ADJ ABBR (BRIT inf) = **teetotal** ▶ ABBR (US) = **Trust Territory**

tub [tʌb] N cubo (SP), balde m (LAM); (bath) bañera, tina (LAM)

tuba ['tjuːbə] N tuba

tubby ['tʌbɪ] ADJ regordete

★**tube** [tjuːb] N tubo; (BRIT: underground) metro; (US inf: television) tele f

tubeless ['tjuːblɪs] ADJ (tyre) sin cámara

tuber ['tjuːbəʳ] N (Bot) tubérculo

tuberculosis [tjubəːkjuˈləusɪs] N tuberculosis f inv

tube station N (BRIT) estación f de metro

tubing ['tjuːbɪŋ] N tubería (SP), cañería; **a piece of ~** un trozo de tubo

tubular ['tjuːbjuləʳ] ADJ tubular

TUC N ABBR (BRIT: = Trades Union Congress) federación nacional de sindicatos

tuck [tʌk] N (Sewing) pliegue m ▶ VT (put) poner
▶ **tuck away** VT esconder
▶ **tuck in** VT meter; (child) arropar ▶ VI (eat) comer con apetito
▶ **tuck up** VT (child) arropar

tucker ['tʌkəʳ] N (AUSTRALIA, NEW ZEALAND inf) papeo

tuck shop N (Scol) tienda de golosinas

Tue., Tues. ABBR (= Tuesday) mart.

★**Tuesday** ['tjuːzdɪ] N martes m inv; **on ~** el martes; **on Tuesdays** los martes; **every ~** todos los martes; **every other ~** cada dos martes, un martes sí y otro no; **last/next ~** el martes pasado/próximo; **a week/fortnight on ~**, **~ week/fortnight** del martes en 8/15 días, del martes en una semana/dos semanas

tuft [tʌft] N mechón m; (of grass etc) manojo

tug [tʌg] N (ship) remolcador m ▶ VT remolcar

tug-of-love [tʌgəvˈlʌv] N: **~ children** hijos envueltos en el litigio de los padres por su custodia

tug-of-war [tʌgəv'wɔːʳ] N juego de la cuerda

tuition [tjuː'ɪʃən] N (*Brit*) enseñanza; (: *private tuition*) clases *fpl* particulares; (*US*: *school fees*) matrícula

tulip ['tjuːlɪp] N tulipán *m*

tumble ['tʌmbl] N (*fall*) caída ▸ vi caerse, tropezar; **to ~ to sth** (*inf*) caer en la cuenta de algo

tumbledown ['tʌmbldaun] ADJ ruinoso

tumble dryer N (*Brit*) secadora

tumbler ['tʌmbləʳ] N vaso

tummy ['tʌmɪ] N (*inf*) barriga, vientre *m*

tumour, (*US*) **tumor** ['tjuːməʳ] N tumor *m*

tumult ['tjuːmʌlt] N tumulto

tumultuous [tjuː'mʌltjuəs] ADJ tumultuoso

tuna ['tjuːnə] N *pl inv* (*also*: **tuna fish**) atún *m*

tundra ['tʌndrə] N tundra

⋆**tune** [tjuːn] N (*melody*) melodía; **to be in/out of ~** (*instrument*) estar afinado/desafinado; (*singer*) afinar/desafinar; **to be in/out of ~ with** (*fig*) armonizar/desentonar con; **to the ~ of** (*fig*: *amount*) por (la) cantidad de ▸ vt (*Mus*) afinar; (*Radio, TV, Aut*) sintonizar
▸ **tune in** vi (*Radio, TV*): **to ~ in (to)** sintonizar (con)
▸ **tune up** vi (*musician*) afinar (su instrumento)

tuneful ['tjuːnful] ADJ melodioso

tuner ['tjuːnəʳ] N (*radio set*) sintonizador *m*; **piano ~** afinador(a) *m/f* de pianos

tungsten ['tʌŋstn] N tungsteno

tunic ['tjuːnɪk] N túnica

tuning ['tjuːnɪŋ] N sintonización *f*; (*Mus*) afinación *f*

tuning fork N diapasón *m*

Tunis ['tjuːnɪs] N Túnez *m*

Tunisia [tjuː'nɪzɪə] N Túnez *m*

Tunisian [tjuː'nɪzɪən] ADJ, N tunecino(-a) *m/f*

⋆**tunnel** ['tʌnl] N túnel *m*; (*in mine*) galería ▸ vi construir un túnel/una galería

tunnel vision N (*Med*) visión *f* periférica restringida; (*fig*) estrechez *f* de miras

tunny ['tʌnɪ] N atún *m*

turban ['təːbən] N turbante *m*

turbid ['təːbɪd] ADJ turbio

turbine ['təːbaɪn] N turbina

turbo ['təːbəu] N turbo

turboprop ['təːbəuprɔp] N turbohélice *m*

turbot ['təːbət] N *pl inv* rodaballo

turbulence ['təːbjuləns] N (*Aviat*) turbulencia

turbulent ['təːbjulənt] ADJ turbulento

tureen [təˈriːn] N sopera

turf [təːf] N césped *m*; (*clod*) tepe *m* ▸ vt cubrir con césped
▸ **turf out** vt (*inf*) echar a la calle

turf accountant N corredor(a) *m/f* de apuestas

turgid ['təːdʒɪd] ADJ (*prose*) pesado

Turin [tjuəˈrɪn] N Turín *m*

Turk [təːk] N turco(-a)

Turkey ['təːkɪ] N Turquía

turkey ['təːkɪ] N pavo

Turkish ['təːkɪʃ] ADJ turco ▸ N (*Ling*) turco

Turkish bath N baño turco

Turkmenistan [təːkmɛnɪˈstɑːn] N Turkmenistán *m*

turmeric ['təːmərɪk] N cúrcuma

turmoil ['təːmɔɪl] N desorden *m*, alboroto; **in ~** revuelto

⋆**turn** [təːn] N turno; (*in road*) curva; (*Theat*) número; (*Med*) ataque *m*; **a good ~** un favor; **it gave me quite a ~** me dio un susto; **"no left ~"** (*Aut*) "prohibido girar a la izquierda"; **it's your ~** te toca a ti; **in ~** por turnos; **to take turns** turnarse; **at the ~ of the year/century** a fin de año/a finales de siglo; **to take a ~ for the worse** (*situation, patient*) empeorar ▸ vt girar, volver, voltear (*Lam*); (*collar, steak*) dar la vuelta a; (*shape: wood, metal*) tornear; (*change*): **to ~ sth into** convertir algo en; **they turned him against us** le pusieron en contra nuestra; **the car turned the corner** el coche dobló la esquina ▸ vi volver, voltearse (*Lam*); (*person: look back*) volverse; (*reverse direction*) dar la vuelta, voltearse (*Lam*); (*milk*) cortarse; (*change*) cambiar; (*become*): **to ~ into sth** convertirse *or* transformarse en algo; **to ~ left** (*Aut*) torcer *or* girar a la izquierda; **she has no-one to ~ to** no tiene a quién recurrir
▸ **turn around** vi (*person*) volverse, darse la vuelta ▸ vt (*object*) dar la vuelta a, voltear (*Lam*)
▸ **turn away** vi apartar la vista ▸ vt (*reject: person, business*) rechazar
▸ **turn back** vi volverse atrás ▸ vt hacer retroceder; (*clock*) retrasar
▸ **turn down** vt (*refuse*) rechazar; (*reduce*) bajar; (*fold*) doblar
▸ **turn in** vi (*inf: go to bed*) acostarse ▸ vt (*fold*) doblar hacia dentro
▸ **turn off** vi (*from road*) desviarse ▸ vt (*light, radio etc*) apagar; (*engine*) parar
▸ **turn on** vt (*light, radio etc*) encender, prender (*Lam*); (*engine*) poner en marcha
▸ **turn out** vt (*light, gas*) apagar; (*produce: goods, novel etc*) producir ▸ vi (*attend: troops*) presentarse; (: *doctor*) atender; **to ~ out to be ...** resultar ser ...
▸ **turn over** vi (*person*) volverse ▸ vt (*mattress, card*) dar la vuelta a; (*page*) volver
▸ **turn round** vi volverse; (*rotate*) girar
▸ **turn to** vt fus: **to ~ to sb** acudir a algn
▸ **turn up** vi (*person*) llegar, presentarse; (*lost object*) aparecer ▸ vt (*radio*) subir, poner más alto; (*heat, gas*) poner más fuerte

turnabout ['təːnəbaut], **turnaround** ['təːnəraund] N (*fig*) giro total

turncoat ['təːnkəut] N renegado(-a)

turned-up ['təːndʌp] ADJ (*nose*) respingón(-ona)

turning ['təːnɪŋ] N (*side road*) bocacalle *f*; (*bend*) curva; **the first ~ on the right** la primera bocacalle a la derecha

turning point N (*fig*) momento decisivo

turnip ['tə:nɪp] N nabo

turnkey system ['tə:nki:-] N (*Comput*) sistema *m* de seguridad

turnout ['tə:naut] N (*attendance*) asistencia; (*number of people attending*) número de asistentes; (*spectators*) público

turnover ['tə:nəuvə'] N (*Comm: amount of money*) facturación *f*; (*of goods*) movimiento; **there is a rapid ~ in staff** hay mucho movimiento de personal

turnpike ['tə:npaɪk] N (*US*) autopista de peaje

turnstile ['tə:nstaɪl] N torniquete *m*

turntable ['tə:nteɪbl] N plato

turn-up ['tə:nʌp] N (*BRIT: on trousers*) vuelta

turpentine ['tə:pəntaɪn] N (*also:* **turps**) trementina

turquoise ['tə:kwɔɪz] N (*stone*) turquesa ▶ ADJ color turquesa *inv*

turret ['tʌrɪt] N torreón *m*

turtle ['tə:tl] N tortuga (marina)

turtleneck ['tə:tlnɛk], **turtleneck sweater** N (jersey *m* de) cuello cisne

Tuscany ['tʌskənɪ] N Toscana

tusk [tʌsk] N colmillo

tussle ['tʌsl] N lucha, pelea

tutor ['tju:tə'] N profesor(a) *m/f*

tutorial [tju:'tɔ:rɪəl] N (*Scol*) seminario

Tuvalu [tu:'və'lu:] N Tuvalu *m*

tuxedo [tʌk'si:dəu] N (*US*) smoking *m*, esmoquin *m*

★**TV** [ti:'vi:] N ABBR (= *television*) televisión *f*

TV dinner N cena precocinada

TV licence N (*BRIT*) *licencia que se paga por el uso del televisor, destinada a financiar la BBC*

twaddle ['twɔdl] N (*inf*) tonterías *fpl*

twang [twæŋ] N (*of instrument*) tañido; (*of voice*) timbre *m* nasal

tweak [twi:k] VT (*nose, ear*) pellizcar; (*hair*) tirar

tweed [twi:d] N tweed *m*

tweet [twi:t] N (*on Twitter*) tweet *m*, tuit *m* ▶ VT, VI (*on Twitter*) tuitear

tweetable ['twi:təbl] ADJ (*on Twitter*) tuitable

tweezers ['twi:zəz] NPL pinzas *fpl* (de depilar)

★**twelfth** [twɛlfθ] NUM duodécimo

Twelfth Night N (Día *m* de) Reyes *mpl*

★**twelve** [twɛlv] NUM doce; **at ~ o'clock** (*midday*) a mediodía; (*midnight*) a medianoche

★**twentieth** ['twɛntɪɪθ] NUM vigésimo

★**twenty** ['twɛntɪ] NUM veinte; **in ~ fourteen** en dos mil catorce

twerking ['twə:kɪŋ] N perreo

twerp [twə:p] N (*pej*) idiota *mf*

★**twice** [twaɪs] ADV dos veces; **~ as much** dos veces más, el doble; **she is ~ your age** ella te dobla en edad; **~ a week** dos veces a la *or* por semana

twiddle ['twɪdl] VT, VI: **to ~ (with) sth** dar vuel-

tas a algo; **to ~ one's thumbs** (*fig*) estar de brazos cruzados

twig [twɪg] N ramita ▶ VI (*inf*) caer en la cuenta

twilight ['twaɪlaɪt] N crepúsculo; (*morning*) madrugada; **in the ~** en la media luz

twill [twɪl] N sarga, estameña

★**twin** [twɪn] ADJ, N gemelo(-a) *m/f* ▶ VT hermanar

twin-bedded room ['twɪn'bɛdɪd-] N = **twin room**

twin beds NPL camas *fpl* gemelas

twin-carburettor ['twɪnkɑ:bju'rɛtə'] ADJ de dos carburadores

twine [twaɪn] N bramante *m* ▶ VI (*plant*) enroscarse

twin-engined [twɪn'ɛndʒɪnd] ADJ bimotor; **~ aircraft** avión *m* bimotor

twinge [twɪndʒ] N (*of pain*) punzada; (*of conscience*) remordimiento

twinkle ['twɪŋkl] N centelleo ▶ VI centellear; (*eyes*) parpadear

twin room N habitación *f* con dos camas

twin town N ciudad *f* hermanada *or* gemela

twirl [twə:l] N giro ▶ VT dar vueltas a ▶ VI piruetear

★**twist** [twɪst] N (*action*) torsión *f*; (*in road, coil*) vuelta; (*in wire, flex*) doblez *f*; (*in story*) giro ▶ VT torcer, retorcer; (*roll around*) enrollar; (*fig*) deformar; **to ~ one's ankle/wrist** (*Med*) torcerse el tobillo/la muñeca ▶ VI serpentear

twisted ['twɪstɪd] ADJ (*wire, rope*) trenzado, enroscado; (*ankle, wrist*) torcido; (*fig: logic, mind*) retorcido

twit [twɪt] N (*inf*) tonto(-a)

twitch [twɪtʃ] N sacudida; (*nervous*) tic *m* nervioso ▶ VI moverse nerviosamente

Twitter® ['twɪtə'] N Twitter® *m* ▶ VI conectarse a Twitter

Twitterati [twɪtə'rɑ:tɪ] NPL (*inf*) tuiteros

Twittersphere ['twɪtəsfɪə'] N (*inf*): **the ~** el universo Twitter

★**two** [tu:] NUM dos; **~ by ~**, **in twos** de dos en dos; **to put ~ and ~ together** (*fig*) atar cabos

two-bit ['tu:'bɪt] ADJ (*esp US inf, pej*) de poca monta, de tres al cuarto

two-door ['tu:'dɔ:'] ADJ (*Aut*) de dos puertas

two-faced ['tu:'feɪst] ADJ (*pej: person*) falso, hipócrita

twofold ['tu:'fəuld] ADV: **to increase ~** duplicarse ▶ ADJ (*increase*) doble; (*reply*) en dos partes

two-piece ['tu:'pi:s] N (*also:* **two-piece suit**) traje *m* de dos piezas; (*also:* **two-piece swimsuit**) dos piezas *m inv*, bikini *m*

two-seater ['tu:'si:tə'] N (*plane, car*) avión *m*/coche *m* de dos plazas, biplaza *m*

twosome ['tu:səm] N (*people*) pareja

two-stroke ['tu:strəuk] N (*also:* **two-stroke engine**) motor *m* de dos tiempos ▶ ADJ de dos tiempos

t

two-tone [ˈtuːtəun] ADJ (*colour*) bicolor, de dos tonos

two-way [ˈtuːweɪ] ADJ: **~ traffic** circulación *f* de dos sentidos; **~ radio** radio *f* emisora y receptora

TX ABBR (*US*) = **Texas**

tycoon [taɪˈkuːn] N: **(business) ~** magnate *mf*

★**type** [taɪp] N (*category*) tipo, género; (*model*) modelo; (*Typ*) tipo, letra; **what ~ do you want?** ¿qué tipo quieres?; **in bold/italic ~** en negrita/cursiva ▸ VT (*letter etc*) escribir a máquina

type-cast [ˈtaɪpkɑːst] ADJ (*actor*) encasillado

typeface [ˈtaɪpfeɪs] N tipo de letra

typescript [ˈtaɪpskrɪpt] N texto mecanografiado

typeset [ˈtaɪpsɛt] VT (*irreg: like* **set**) componer

typesetter [ˈtaɪpsɛtəʳ] N cajista *mf*

typewriter [ˈtaɪpraɪtəʳ] N máquina de escribir

typewritten [ˈtaɪprɪtn] ADJ mecanografiado

typhoid [ˈtaɪfɔɪd] N (fiebre *f*) tifoidea

typhoon [taɪˈfuːn] N tifón *m*

typhus [ˈtaɪfəs] N tifus *m*

★**typical** [ˈtɪpɪkl] ADJ típico

typically [ˈtɪpɪklɪ] ADV típicamente

typify [ˈtɪpɪfaɪ] VT tipificar

typing [ˈtaɪpɪŋ] N mecanografía

typing pool N (*BRIT*) servicio de mecanógrafos

typist [ˈtaɪpɪst] N mecanógrafo(-a)

typo [ˈtaɪpəu] N ABBR (*inf*: = *typographical error*) errata

typography [taɪˈpɒɡrəfɪ] N tipografía

tyranny [ˈtɪrənɪ] N tiranía

tyrant [ˈtaɪərənt] N tirano(-a)

tyre, (*US*) **tire** [ˈtaɪəʳ] N neumático, llanta (*LAm*)

tyre pressure N presión *f* de los neumáticos

Tyrol [tɪˈrəul] N Tirol *m*

Tyrolean [tɪrəˈlɪən], **Tyrolese** [tɪrəˈliːz] ADJ tirolés(-esa)

Tyrrhenian Sea [tɪˈriːnɪən-] N mar *m* Tirreno

tzar [zɑːʳ] N = **tsar**

Uu

U, u [ju:] N (*letter*) U, u f; **U for Uncle** U de Uruguay

U N ABBR (*BRIT Cine:* = *universal*) todos los públicos

UAW N ABBR (*US*) = **United Automobile Workers**

U-bend ['ju:bɛnd] N recodo

ubiquitous [ju:'bɪkwɪtəs] ADJ omnipresente, ubicuo

UCAS ['ju:kæs] N ABBR (*BRIT*) = **Universities and Colleges Admissions Service**

UDA N ABBR (*BRIT:* = *Ulster Defence Association*) *organización paramilitar protestante de Irlanda del Norte*

udder ['ʌdəʳ] N ubre f

UDR N ABBR (*BRIT:* = *Ulster Defence Regiment*) *fuerza de seguridad de Irlanda del Norte*

UEFA [ju:'eɪfə] N ABBR (= *Union of European Football Associations*) UEFA f

UFO ['ju:fəu] N ABBR (= *unidentified flying object*) OVNI m

Uganda [ju:'gændə] N Uganda

Ugandan [ju:'gændən] ADJ, N ugandés(-esa) m/f

ugh [ə:h] EXCL ¡uf!

ugliness ['ʌglɪnɪs] N fealdad f

★**ugly** ['ʌglɪ] ADJ feo; (*dangerous*) peligroso

UHF ABBR (= *ultra-high frequency*) UHF f

UHT ADJ ABBR = **ultra heat treated**; **~ milk** leche f uperizada

★**UK** N ABBR (= *United Kingdom*) Reino Unido, R.U.

Ukraine [ju:'kreɪn] N Ucrania

Ukrainian [ju:'kreɪnɪən] ADJ ucraniano ▸ N ucraniano(-a); (*Ling*) ucraniano

ulcer ['ʌlsəʳ] N úlcera; **mouth ~** llaga bucal

Ulster ['ʌlstəʳ] N Ulster m

ulterior [ʌl'tɪərɪəʳ] ADJ ulterior; **~ motive** segundas intenciones fpl

ultimate ['ʌltɪmət] ADJ último, final; (*greatest*) mayor ▸ N: **the ~ in luxury** el colmo del lujo

ultimately ['ʌltɪmətlɪ] ADV (*in the end*) por

último, al final; (*fundamentally*) a fin de cuentas

ultimatum [ʌltɪ'meɪtəm] (*pl* **ultimatums** *or* **ultimata** [-tə]) N ultimátum m

ultra- ['ʌltrə] PREF ultra-

ultrasonic [ʌltrə'sɔnɪk] ADJ ultrasónico

ultrasound ['ʌltrəsaund] N (*Med*) ultrasonido

ultraviolet ['ʌltrə'vaɪəlɪt] ADJ ultravioleta

um [ʌm] EXCL (*inf: in hesitation*) esto, este (*LAm*)

umbilical cord [ʌmbɪ'laɪkl-] N cordón m umbilical

umbrage ['ʌmbrɪdʒ] N: **to take ~ (at)** ofenderse (por)

★**umbrella** [ʌm'brɛlə] N paraguas m inv; **under the ~ of** (*fig*) bajo la protección de

umlaut ['umlaut] N diéresis f inv

umpire ['ʌmpaɪəʳ] N árbitro ▸ VT arbitrar

umpteen [ʌmp'ti:n] NUM enésimos(-as); **for the umpteenth time** por enésima vez

UMW N ABBR (*US:* = *United Mineworkers of America*) *sindicato de mineros*

UN N ABBR (= *United Nations*) ONU f

un- [ʌn] PREF in-; des-; no ...; poco ...; nada ...

unabashed [ʌnə'bæʃt] ADJ nada avergonzado

unabated [ʌnə'beɪtɪd] ADJ: **to continue ~** seguir con la misma intensidad

★**unable** [ʌn'eɪbl] ADJ: **to be ~ to do sth** no poder hacer algo; (*not know how to*) ser incapaz de hacer algo, no saber hacer algo

unabridged [ʌnə'brɪdʒd] ADJ íntegro

unacceptable [ʌnək'sɛptəbl] ADJ (*proposal, behaviour, price*) inaceptable; **it's ~ that** no se puede aceptar que

unaccompanied [ʌnə'kʌmpənɪd] ADJ no acompañado; (*singing, song*) sin acompañamiento

unaccountably [ʌnə'kauntəblɪ] ADV inexplicablemente

unaccounted [ʌnə'kauntɪd] ADJ: **two passengers are ~ for** faltan dos pasajeros

u

unaccustomed [ʌnə'kʌstəmd] ADJ: **to be ~ to** no estar acostumbrado a

unacquainted [ʌnə'kweɪntɪd] ADJ: **to be ~ with** *(facts)* desconocer, ignorar

unadulterated [ʌnə'dʌltəreɪtɪd] ADJ *(gen)* puro; *(wine)* sin mezcla

unaffected [ʌnə'fɛktɪd] ADJ *(person, behaviour)* sin afectación, sencillo; *(emotionally):* **to be ~ by** no estar afectado por

unafraid [ʌnə'freɪd] ADJ: **to be ~** no tener miedo

unaided [ʌn'eɪdɪd] ADJ sin ayuda, por sí solo

unanimity [ju:nə'nɪmɪtɪ] N unanimidad *f*

unanimous [ju:'nænɪməs] ADJ unánime

unanimously [ju:'nænɪməslɪ] ADV unánimemente

unanswered [ʌn'ɑ:nsəd] ADJ *(question, letter)* sin contestar; *(criticism)* incontestado

unappetizing [ʌn'æpɪtaɪzɪŋ] ADJ poco apetitoso

unappreciative [ʌnə'pri:ʃɪətɪv] ADJ desagradecido

unarmed [ʌn'ɑ:md] ADJ *(person)* desarmado; *(combat)* sin armas

unashamed [ʌnə'ʃeɪmd] ADJ desvergonzado

unassisted [ʌnə'sɪstɪd] ADJ, ADV sin ayuda

unassuming [ʌnə'sju:mɪŋ] ADJ modesto, sin pretensiones

unattached [ʌnə'tætʃt] ADJ *(person)* soltero; *(part etc)* suelto

unattended [ʌnə'tɛndɪd] ADJ *(car, luggage)* desatendido

unattractive [ʌnə'træktɪv] ADJ poco atractivo

unauthorized [ʌn'ɔ:θəraɪzd] ADJ no autorizado

unavailable [ʌnə'veɪləbl] ADJ *(article, room, book)* no disponible; *(person)* ocupado

unavoidable [ʌnə'vɔɪdəbl] ADJ inevitable

unavoidably [ʌnə'vɔɪdəblɪ] ADV *(detained)* por causas ajenas a su voluntad

unaware [ʌnə'wɛəʳ] ADJ: **to be ~ of** ignorar

unawares [ʌnə'wɛəz] ADV: **to catch sb ~** pillar a algn desprevenido

unbalanced [ʌn'bælənst] ADJ desequilibrado; *(mentally)* trastornado

unbearable [ʌn'bɛərəbl] ADJ insoportable

unbeatable [ʌn'bi:təbl] ADJ *(gen)* invencible; *(price)* inmejorable

unbeaten [ʌn'bi:tn] ADJ *(team)* imbatido; *(army)* invicto; *(record)* no batido

unbecoming [ʌnbɪ'kʌmɪŋ] ADJ *(unseemly: language, behaviour)* indecoroso, impropio; *(unflattering: garment)* poco favorecedor(a)

unbeknown [ʌnbɪ'nəun], **unbeknownst** [ʌnbɪ'nəunst] ADV: **~(st) to me** sin saberlo yo

unbelief [ʌnbɪ'li:f] N incredulidad *f*

unbelievable [ʌnbɪ'li:vəbl] ADJ increíble

unbelievingly [ʌnbɪ'li:vɪŋlɪ] ADV sin creer

unbend [ʌn'bɛnd] VI *(irreg: like* **bend***)* *(fig: person)* relajarse ▶ VT *(wire)* enderezar

unbending [ʌn'bɛndɪŋ] ADJ *(fig)* inflexible

unbiased, unbiassed [ʌn'baɪəst] ADJ imparcial

unblemished [ʌn'blɛmɪʃt] ADJ sin mancha

unblock [ʌn'blɔk] VT *(pipe)* desatascar; *(road)* despejar

unborn [ʌn'bɔ:n] ADJ que va a nacer

unbounded [ʌn'baundɪd] ADJ ilimitado, sin límite

unbreakable [ʌn'breɪkəbl] ADJ irrompible

unbridled [ʌn'braɪdld] ADJ *(fig)* desenfrenado

unbroken [ʌn'brəukən] ADJ *(seal)* intacto; *(series)* continuo, ininterrumpido; *(record)* no batido; *(spirit)* indómito

unbuckle [ʌn'bʌkl] VT desabrochar

unburden [ʌn'bə:dn] VT: **to ~ o.s.** desahogarse

unbusinesslike [ʌn'bɪznɪslaɪk] ADJ *(trader)* poco profesional; *(transaction)* incorrecto; *(fig: person)* poco práctico; *(: without method)* desorganizado

unbutton [ʌn'bʌtn] VT desabrochar

uncalled-for [ʌn'kɔ:ldfɔ:ʳ] ADJ gratuito, inmerecido

uncanny [ʌn'kænɪ] ADJ extraño, extraordinario

unceasing [ʌn'si:sɪŋ] ADJ incesante

unceremonious ['ʌnserɪ'məunɪəs] ADJ *(abrupt, rude)* brusco, hosco

uncertain [ʌn'sə:tn] ADJ incierto; *(indecisive)* indeciso; **it's ~ whether** no se sabe si; **in no ~ terms** sin dejar lugar a dudas

uncertainty [ʌn'sə:tntɪ] N incertidumbre *f*

unchallenged [ʌn'tʃælɪndʒd] ADJ *(Law etc)* incontestado; **to go ~** no encontrar respuesta

unchanged [ʌn'tʃeɪndʒd] ADJ sin cambiar *or* alterar

uncharitable [ʌn'tʃærɪtəbl] ADJ *(remark, behaviour)* demasiado duro

uncharted [ʌn'tʃɑ:tɪd] ADJ inexplorado

unchecked [ʌn'tʃɛkt] ADJ desenfrenado

uncivil [ʌn'sɪvɪl] ADJ descortés, grosero

uncivilized [ʌn'sɪvɪlaɪzd] ADJ *(gen)* inculto, poco civilizado; *(fig: behaviour etc)* bárbaro

★**uncle** ['ʌŋkl] N tío

unclear [ʌn'klɪəʳ] ADJ poco claro; **I'm still ~ about what I'm supposed to do** todavía no tengo muy claro lo que tengo que hacer

uncoil [ʌn'kɔɪl] VT desenrollar ▶ VI desenrollarse

★**uncomfortable** [ʌn'kʌmfətəbl] ADJ incómodo; *(uneasy)* inquieto

uncomfortably [ʌn'kʌmfətəblɪ] ADV *(uneasily: say)* con inquietud; *(: think)* con remordimiento *or* nerviosismo

uncommitted [ʌnkə'mɪtɪd] ADJ *(attitude, country)* no comprometido; **to remain ~ to** *(policy, party)* no comprometerse a

uncommon [ʌn'kɔmən] ADJ poco común, raro

uncommunicative [ʌnkə'mju:nɪkətɪv] ADJ poco comunicativo, reservado

uncomplicated [ʌnˈkɔmplɪkeɪtɪd] ADJ sin complicaciones

uncompromising [ʌnˈkɔmprəmaɪzɪŋ] ADJ intransigente

unconcerned [ʌnkənˈsəːnd] ADJ indiferente; **to be ~ about** ser indiferente a, no preocuparse de

unconditional [ʌnkənˈdɪʃənl] ADJ incondicional

uncongenial [ʌnkənˈdʒiːnɪəl] ADJ desagradable

unconnected [ʌnkəˈnɛktɪd] ADJ (*unrelated*): **to be ~ with** no estar relacionado con

unconscious [ʌnˈkɔnʃəs] ADJ sin sentido; (*unaware*) inconsciente; **to knock sb ~** dejar a algn sin sentido ▶ N: **the ~** el inconsciente

unconsciously [ʌnˈkɔnʃəslɪ] ADV inconscientemente

unconsciousness [ʌnˈkɔnʃəsnɪs] N inconsciencia

unconstitutional [ʌnkɔnstɪˈtjuːʃənl] ADJ anticonstitucional

uncontested [ʌnkənˈtɛstɪd] ADJ (*champion*) incontestado; (*Parliament: seat*) ganado sin oposición

uncontrollable [ʌnkənˈtrəuləbl] ADJ (*temper*) indomable; (*laughter*) incontenible

uncontrolled [ʌnkənˈtrəuld] ADJ (*child, dog, emotion*) incontrolado; (*inflation, price rises*) desenfrenado

unconventional [ʌnkənˈvɛnʃənl] ADJ poco convencial

unconvinced [ʌnkənˈvɪnst] ADJ: **to be** or **remain ~** seguir sin convencerse

unconvincing [ʌnkənˈvɪnsɪŋ] ADJ poco convincente

uncork [ʌnˈkɔːk] VT descorchar

uncorroborated [ʌnkəˈrɔbəreɪtɪd] ADJ no confirmado

uncouth [ʌnˈkuːθ] ADJ grosero, inculto

uncover [ʌnˈkʌvəʳ] VT (*gen*) descubrir; (*take lid off*) destapar

undamaged [ʌnˈdæmɪdʒd] ADJ (*goods*) en buen estado; (*fig: reputation*) intacto

undaunted [ʌnˈdɔːntɪd] ADJ: **~ by** sin dejarse desanimar por

undecided [ʌndɪˈsaɪdɪd] ADJ (*person*) indeciso; (*question*) no resuelto, pendiente

undelivered [ʌndɪˈlɪvəd] ADJ no entregado al destinatario; **if ~ return to sender** en caso de no llegar a su destino devolver al remitente

undeniable [ʌndɪˈnaɪəbl] ADJ innegable

undeniably [ʌndɪˈnaɪəblɪ] ADV innegablemente

★**under** [ˈʌndəʳ] PREP debajo de; (*less than*) menos de; (*according to*) según, de acuerdo con; **~ there** ahí debajo; **~ construction** en construcción, en obras; **~ the circumstances** dadas las circunstancias; **in ~ two hours** en menos de dos

horas; **~ anaesthetic** bajo los efectos de la anestesia; **~ discussion** en discusión, sobre el tapete ▶ ADV debajo, abajo

under... [ˈʌndəʳ] PREF sub...

under-age [ˈʌndərˈeɪdʒ] ADJ menor de edad

underarm [ˈʌndərɑːm] N axila, sobaco ▶ CPD: **~ deodorant** desodorante *m* corporal

undercapitalised [ʌndəˈkæpɪtəlaɪzd] ADJ descapitalizado

undercarriage [ˈʌndəkærɪdʒ] N (*BRIT Aviat*) tren *m* de aterrizaje

undercharge [ʌndəˈtʃɑːdʒ] VT cobrar de menos

underclass [ˈʌndəklɑːs] N clase *f* marginada

underclothes [ˈʌndəkləuðz] NPL ropa *sg* interior or (*LAM*) íntima

undercoat [ˈʌndəkəut] N (*paint*) primera mano

undercover [ʌndəˈkʌvəʳ] ADJ clandestino

undercurrent [ˈʌndəkʌrnt] N corriente *f* submarina; (*fig*) tendencia oculta

undercut [ˈʌndəkʌt] VT (*irreg: like* **cut**) vender más barato que

underdeveloped [ʌndədɪˈvɛləpt] ADJ subdesarrollado

underdog [ˈʌndədɔg] N desvalido(-a)

underdone [ʌndəˈdʌn] ADJ (*Culin*) poco hecho

underemployment [ʌndərɪmˈplɔɪmənt] N subempleo

underestimate [ʌndərˈɛstɪmeɪt] VT subestimar

underexposed [ʌndərɪksˈpəuzd] ADJ (*Phot*) subexpuesto

underfed [ʌndəˈfɛd] ADJ subalimentado

underfoot [ʌndəˈfut] ADV: **it's wet ~** el suelo está mojado

underfunded [ʌndəˈfʌndɪd] ADJ infradotado (económicamente)

undergo [ʌndəˈgəu] VT (*irreg: like* **go**) sufrir; (*treatment*) recibir, someterse a; **the car is undergoing repairs** están reparando el coche

undergraduate [ˈʌndəˈgrædjuət] N estudiante *mf* ▶ CPD: **~ courses** cursos *mpl* de licenciatura

★**underground** [ˈʌndəgraund] N (*BRIT: railway*) metro; (*Pol*) movimiento clandestino ▶ ADJ subterráneo ▶ ADV (*work*) en la clandestinidad

undergrowth [ˈʌndəgrəuθ] N maleza

underhand [ʌndəˈhænd], **underhanded** [ʌndəˈhændɪd] ADJ (*fig*) poco limpio

underinsured [ʌndərɪnˈʃuəd] ADJ insuficientemente asegurado

underlie [ʌndəˈlaɪ] VT (*irreg: like* **lie**) (*fig*) ser la razón fundamental de; **the underlying cause** la causa fundamental

underline [ʌndəˈlaɪn] VT subrayar

underling [ˈʌndəlɪŋ] N (*pej*) subalterno(-a)

undermanning [ʌndəˈmænɪŋ] N falta de personal

undermentioned [ʌndəˈmɛnʃənd] ADJ abajo citado

u

837

undermine [ˌʌndəˈmaɪn] vt socavar, minar

underneath [ˌʌndəˈniːθ] ADV debajo ▸ PREP debajo de, bajo

undernourished [ˌʌndəˈnʌrɪʃt] ADJ desnutrido

underpaid [ˌʌndəˈpeɪd] ADJ mal pagado

underpants [ˈʌndəpænts] NPL calzoncillos mpl

underpass [ˈʌndəpɑːs] N (BRIT) paso subterráneo

underpin [ˌʌndəˈpɪn] vt (argument, case) secundar, sostener

underplay [ˌʌndəˈpleɪ] vt (BRIT) minimizar

underpopulated [ˌʌndəˈpɔpjuleɪtɪd] ADJ poco poblado

underprice [ˌʌndəˈpraɪs] vt vender demasiado barato

underpriced [ˌʌndəˈpraɪst] ADJ con precio demasiado bajo

underprivileged [ˌʌndəˈprɪvɪlɪdʒd] ADJ desposeído

underrate [ˌʌndəˈreɪt] vt infravalorar, subestimar

underscore [ˈʌndəskɔːʳ] vt subrayar, sostener

underseal [ˌʌndəˈsiːl] vt (Aut) proteger contra la corrosión

undersecretary [ˌʌndəˈsɛkrətrɪ] N subsecretario(-a)

undersell [ˌʌndəˈsel] (pt, pp **undersold** [-ˈsəuld]) vt (competitors) vender más barato que

undershirt [ˈʌndəʃəːt] N (US) camiseta

undershorts [ˈʌndəʃɔːts] NPL (US) calzoncillos mpl

underside [ˈʌndəsaɪd] N parte f inferior, revés m

undersigned [ˈʌndəsaɪnd] ADJ, N: **the ~** el/la etc abajo firmante

underskirt [ˈʌndəskəːt] N (BRIT) enaguas fpl

understaffed [ˌʌndəˈstɑːft] ADJ falto de personal

understaffing [ˌʌndəˈstɑːfɪŋ] N falta de personal

★**understand** [ˌʌndəˈstænd] vt, vi (irreg: like **stand**) entender, comprender; (assume) tener entendido; **to make o.s. understood** hacerse entender; **I ~ you have been absent** tengo entendido que (usted) ha estado ausente

understandable [ˌʌndəˈstændəbl] ADJ comprensible

★**understanding** [ˌʌndəˈstændɪŋ] ADJ comprensivo ▸ N comprensión f, entendimiento; (agreement) acuerdo; **to come to an ~ with sb** llegar a un acuerdo con algn; **on the ~ that** a condición de que + subjun

understate [ˌʌndəˈsteɪt] vt minimizar

understatement [ˌʌndəˈsteɪtmənt] N subestimación f; (modesty) modestia (excesiva); **to say it was good is quite an ~** decir que estuvo bien es quedarse corto

understood [ˌʌndəˈstud] PT, PP of **understand** ▸ ADJ entendido; (implied): **it is ~ that** se sobreentiende que

understudy [ˈʌndəstʌdɪ] N suplente mf

undertake [ˌʌndəˈteɪk] vt (irreg: like **take**) emprender; **to ~ to do sth** comprometerse a hacer algo

undertaker [ˈʌndəteɪkəʳ] N director(a) m/f de pompas fúnebres

undertaking [ˈʌndəteɪkɪŋ] N empresa; (promise) promesa

undertone [ˈʌndətəun] N (of criticism) connotación f; (low voice): **in an ~** en voz baja

undervalue [ˌʌndəˈvæl]uː] vt (fig) subestimar, infravalorar; (Comm etc) valorizar por debajo de su precio

underwater [ˌʌndəˈwɔːtəʳ] ADV bajo el agua ▸ ADJ submarino

underway [ˌʌndəˈweɪ] ADJ: **to be ~** (meeting) estar en marcha; (investigation) estar llevándose a cabo

★**underwear** [ˈʌndəwɛəʳ] N ropa interior or (LAM) íntima

underweight [ˌʌndəˈweɪt] ADJ de peso insuficiente; (person) demasiado delgado

underwent [ˌʌndəˈwɛnt] vB see **undergo**

underworld [ˈʌndəwəːld] N (of crime) hampa, inframundo

underwrite [ˌʌndəˈraɪt] vt (irreg: like **write**) (Comm) suscribir; (Insurance) asegurar (contra riesgos)

underwriter [ˈʌndəraɪtəʳ] N (Insurance) asegurador(a) m/f

undeserving [ˌʌndɪˈzəːvɪŋ] ADJ: **to be ~ of** no ser digno de

undesirable [ˌʌndɪˈzaɪərəbl] ADJ indeseable

undeveloped [ˌʌndɪˈveləpt] ADJ (land, resources) sin explotar

undies [ˈʌndɪz] NPL (inf) paños mpl menores

undiluted [ˌʌndaɪˈluːtɪd] ADJ (concentrate) concentrado

undiplomatic [ˌʌndɪpləˈmætɪk] ADJ poco diplomático

undischarged [ˌʌndɪsˈtʃɑːdʒd] ADJ: **~ bankrupt** quebrado(-a) no rehabilitado(-a)

undisciplined [ʌnˈdɪsɪplɪnd] ADJ indisciplinado

undiscovered [ˌʌndɪsˈkʌvəd] ADJ no descubierto; (unknown) desconocido

undisguised [ˌʌndɪsˈɡaɪzd] ADJ franco, abierto

undisputed [ˌʌndɪˈspjuːtɪd] ADJ incontestable

undistinguished [ˌʌndɪsˈtɪŋɡwɪʃt] ADJ mediocre

undisturbed [ˌʌndɪsˈtəːbd] ADJ (sleep) ininterrumpido; **to leave sth ~** dejar algo tranquilo or como está

undivided [ˌʌndɪˈvaɪdɪd] ADJ: **I want your ~ attention** quiero su completa atención

undo [ʌnˈduː] vt (irreg: like **do**) (laces) desatar; (button etc) desabrochar; (spoil) deshacer

undoing [ʌnˈduːɪŋ] N ruina, perdición f

undone [ʌn'dʌn] PP of **undo** ▶ ADJ: **to come ~** (*clothes*) desabrocharse; (*parcel*) desatarse

undoubted [ʌn'dautɪd] ADJ indubable

undoubtedly [ʌn'dautɪdlɪ] ADV indubablemente, sin duda

undress [ʌn'drɛs] VI desnudarse, desvestirse (*esp LAm*)

undrinkable [ʌn'drɪŋkəbl] ADJ (*unpalatable*) imbebible; (*poisonous*) no potable

undue [ʌn'djuː] ADJ indebido, excesivo

undulating ['ʌndjuleɪtɪŋ] ADJ ondulante

unduly [ʌn'djuːlɪ] ADV excesivamente, demasiado

undying [ʌn'daɪɪŋ] ADJ eterno

unearned [ʌn'əːnd] ADJ (*praise, respect*) inmerecido; **~ income** ingresos mpl no ganados, renta no ganada or salarial

unearth [ʌn'əːθ] VT desenterrar

unearthly [ʌn'əːθlɪ] ADJ: **~ hour** (*inf*) hora intempestiva

unease [ʌn'iːz] N malestar *m*

uneasy [ʌn'iːzɪ] ADJ intranquilo; (*worried*) preocupado; **to feel ~ about doing sth** sentirse incómodo con la idea de hacer algo

uneconomic ['ʌniːkə'nɔmɪk], **uneconomical** ['ʌniːkə'nɔmɪkl] ADJ no económico

uneducated [ʌn'ɛdjukeɪtɪd] ADJ ignorante, inculto

★**unemployed** [ʌnɪm'plɔɪd] ADJ parado, sin trabajo ▶ N: **the ~** los parados

★**unemployment** [ʌnɪm'plɔɪmənt] N paro, desempleo, cesantía (*LAm*)

unemployment benefit N (*BRIT*) subsidio de desempleo or paro

unending [ʌn'ɛndɪŋ] ADJ interminable

unenviable [ʌn'ɛnvɪəbl] ADJ poco envidiable

unequal [ʌn'iːkwəl] ADJ (*length, objects etc*) desigual; (*amounts*) distinto; (*division of labour*) poco justo

unequalled, (*US*) **unequaled** [ʌn'iːkwəld] ADJ inigualado, sin par

unequivocal [ʌnɪ'kwɪvəkəl] ADJ (*answer*) inequívoco, claro; (*person*) claro

unerring [ʌn'əːrɪŋ] ADJ infalible

UNESCO [juː'nɛskəu] N ABBR (= *United Nations Educational, Scientific and Cultural Organization*) UNESCO f

unethical [ʌn'ɛθɪkəl] ADJ (*methods*) inmoral; (*doctor's behaviour*) que infringe la ética profesional

uneven [ʌn'iːvn] ADJ desigual; (*road etc*) con baches

uneventful [ʌnɪ'vɛntful] ADJ sin incidentes

unexceptional [ʌnɪk'sɛpʃənl] ADJ sin nada de extraordinario, corriente

unexciting [ʌnɪk'saɪtɪŋ] ADJ (*news*) sin interés; (*film, evening*) aburrido

★**unexpected** [ʌnɪk'spɛktɪd] ADJ inesperado

unexpectedly [ʌnɪk'spɛktɪdlɪ] ADV inesperadamente

unexplained [ʌnɪks'pleɪnd] ADJ inexplicado

unexploded [ʌnɪks'pləudɪd] ADJ sin explotar

unfailing [ʌn'feɪlɪŋ] ADJ (*support*) indefectible; (*energy*) inagotable

★**unfair** [ʌn'fɛəʳ] ADJ: **~ (to sb)** injusto (con algn); **it's ~ that ...** es injusto que ..., no es justo que ...

unfair dismissal N despido improcedente

unfairly [ʌn'fɛəlɪ] ADV injustamente

unfaithful [ʌn'feɪθful] ADJ infiel

unfamiliar [ʌnfə'mɪlɪəʳ] ADJ extraño, desconocido; **to be ~ with sth** desconocer or ignorar algo

unfashionable [ʌn'fæʃnəbl] ADJ (*clothes*) pasado or fuera de moda; (*district*) poco elegante

unfasten [ʌn'fɑːsn] VT desatar

unfathomable [ʌn'fæðəməbl] ADJ insondable

unfavourable, (*US*) **unfavorable** [ʌn'feɪvərəbl] ADJ desfavorable

unfavourably, (*US*) **unfavorably** [ʌn'feɪvrəblɪ] ADV: **to look ~ upon** ser adverso a

unfeeling [ʌn'fiːlɪŋ] ADJ insensible

unfinished [ʌn'fɪnɪʃt] ADJ inacabado, sin terminar

unfit [ʌn'fɪt] ADJ en baja forma; (*incompetent*) incapaz; **~ for work** incapacitado para trabajar

unflagging [ʌn'flægɪŋ] ADJ incansable

unflappable [ʌn'flæpəbl] ADJ imperturbable

unflattering [ʌn'flætərɪŋ] ADJ (*dress, hairstyle*) poco favorecedor

unflinching [ʌn'flɪntʃɪŋ] ADJ impávido

unfold [ʌn'fəuld] VT desdoblar; (*fig*) revelar ▶ VI abrirse; revelarse

unforeseeable [ʌnfɔː'siːəbl] ADJ imprevisible

unforeseen ['ʌnfɔː'siːn] ADJ imprevisto

unforgettable [ʌnfə'gɛtəbl] ADJ inolvidable

unforgivable [ʌnfə'gɪvəbl] ADJ imperdonable

unformatted [ʌn'fɔːmætɪd] ADJ (*disk, text*) sin formatear

unfortunate [ʌn'fɔːtʃnət] ADJ desgraciado; (*event, remark*) inoportuno

★**unfortunately** [ʌn'fɔːtʃnətlɪ] ADV desgraciadamente, por desgracia

unfounded [ʌn'faundɪd] ADJ infundado

unfriend [ʌn'frɛnd] VT (*Internet*) quitar de amigo a; **he has unfriended her on Facebook** la ha quitado de amiga en Facebook

unfriendly [ʌn'frɛndlɪ] ADJ antipático; (*behaviour, remark*) hostil, poco amigable

unfulfilled [ʌnful'fɪld] ADJ (*ambition*) sin realizar; (*prophecy, promise, terms of contract*) incumplido; (*desire, person*) insatisfecho

unfurl [ʌn'fəːl] VT desplegar

unfurnished [ʌn'fəːnɪʃt] ADJ sin amueblar

ungainly [ʌn'geɪnlɪ] ADJ (*walk*) desgarbado

ungodly [ʌn'gɔdlɪ] ADJ: **at an ~ hour** a una hora intempestiva

u

ungrateful [ʌnˈɡreɪtful] ADJ ingrato

unguarded [ʌnˈɡɑːdɪd] ADJ (*moment*) de descuido

unhappily [ʌnˈhæpɪlɪ] ADV (*unfortunately*) desgraciadamente

unhappiness [ʌnˈhæpɪnɪs] N tristeza

★**unhappy** [ʌnˈhaepɪ] ADJ (*sad*) triste; (*unfortunate*) desgraciado; (*childhood*) infeliz; **~ with** (*arrangements etc*) poco contento con, descontento de

unharmed [ʌnˈhɑːmd] ADJ (*person*) ileso

UNHCR N ABBR (= *United Nations High Commission for Refugees*) ACNUR *m*

unhealthy [ʌnˈhelθɪ] ADJ (*gen*) malsano, insalubre; (*person*) enfermizo; (*interest*) morboso

unheard-of [ʌnˈhɜːdɒv] ADJ inaudito, sin precedente

unhelpful [ʌnˈhelpful] ADJ (*person*) poco servicial; (*advice*) inútil

unhesitating [ʌnˈhezɪteɪtɪŋ] ADJ (*loyalty*) automático; (*reply, offer*) inmediato; (*person*) resuelto

unholy [ʌnˈhəʊlɪ] ADJ: **an ~ alliance** una alianza nefasta; **he returned at an ~ hour** volvió a una hora intempestiva

unhook [ʌnˈhuk] VT desenganchar; (*from wall*) descolgar; (*undo*) desabrochar

unhurt [ʌnˈhɜːt] ADJ ileso

unhygienic [ʌnhaɪˈdʒiːnɪk] ADJ antihigiénico

UNICEF [ˈjuːnɪsef] N ABBR (= *United Nations International Children's Emergency Fund*) UNICEF *f*

unidentified [ʌnaɪˈdentɪfaɪd] ADJ no identificado; **~ flying object** objeto volante no identificado

unification [juːnɪfɪˈkeɪʃən] N unificación *f*

★**uniform** [ˈjuːnɪfɔːm] N uniforme *m* ▶ ADJ uniforme

uniformity [juːnɪˈfɔːmɪtɪ] N uniformidad *f*

unify [ˈjuːnɪfaɪ] VT unificar, unir

unilateral [juːnɪˈlætərəl] ADJ unilateral

unimaginable [ʌnɪˈmædʒɪnəbl] ADJ inconcebible, inimaginable

unimaginative [ʌnɪˈmædʒɪnətɪv] ADJ falto de imaginación

unimpaired [ʌnɪmˈpeəd] ADJ (*unharmed*) intacto; (*not lessened*) no disminuido; (*unaltered*) inalterado

unimportant [ʌnɪmˈpɔːtənt] ADJ sin importancia

unimpressed [ʌnɪmˈprest] ADJ poco impresionado

uninhabited [ʌnɪnˈhæbɪtɪd] ADJ desierto; (*country*) despoblado; (*house*) deshabitado, desocupado

uninhibited [ʌnɪnˈhɪbɪtɪd] ADJ nada cohibido, desinhibido

uninjured [ʌnˈɪndʒəd] ADJ (*person*) ileso

uninspiring [ʌnɪnˈspaɪərɪŋ] ADJ anodino

uninstall [ˈʌnɪnstɔːl] VT (*Comput*) desinstalar

unintelligent [ʌnɪnˈtelɪdʒənt] ADJ poco inteligente

unintentional [ʌnɪnˈtenʃənəl] ADJ involuntario

unintentionally [ʌnɪnˈtenʃnəlɪ] ADV sin querer

uninvited [ʌnɪnˈvaɪtɪd] ADJ (*guest*) sin invitación

uninviting [ʌnɪnˈvaɪtɪŋ] ADJ (*place, offer*) poco atractivo; (*food*) poco apetecible

union [ˈjuːnjən] N unión *f*; (*also*: **trade union**) sindicato; **the U~** (*US*) la Unión ▶ CPD sindical

union card N carnet *m* de sindicato

unionize [ˈjuːnjənaɪz] VT sindicalizar

Union Jack N bandera del Reino Unido

union shop N (*US*) empresa de afiliación sindical obligatoria

unique [juːˈniːk] ADJ único

unisex [ˈjuːnɪseks] ADJ unisex

Unison [ˈjuːnɪsn] N (*BRIT*: *trade union*) gran sindicato del sector público

unison [ˈjuːnɪsn] N: **in ~** en armonía

unissued capital [ʌnˈɪʃuːd-] N capital *m* no emitido

unit [ˈjuːnɪt] N unidad *f*; (*team, squad*) grupo; **kitchen ~** módulo de cocina; **production ~** taller *m* de fabricación; **sink ~** fregadero

unit cost N costo unitario

unite [juːˈnaɪt] VT unir ▶ VI unirse

united [juːˈnaɪtɪd] ADJ unido

United Arab Emirates NPL Emiratos *mpl* Árabes Unidos

★**United Kingdom** N Reino Unido

United Nations, United Nations Organization N Naciones Unidas *fpl*

★**United States, United States of America** N Estados Unidos *mpl* (de América)

unit price N precio unitario

unit trust N (*BRIT*) bono fiduciario

unity [ˈjuːnɪtɪ] N unidad *f*

Univ. ABBR = **university**

universal [juːnɪˈvɜːsl] ADJ universal

universally [juːnɪˈvɜːsəlɪ] ADV universalmente

★**universe** [ˈjuːnɪvɜːs] N universo

★**university** [juːnɪˈvɜːsɪtɪ] N universidad *f*; **to be at/go to ~** estudiar en/ir a la universidad ▶ CPD (*student, professor, education, degree*) universitario; (*year*) académico

unjust [ʌnˈdʒʌst] ADJ injusto

unjustifiable [ʌndʒʌstɪˈfaɪəbl] ADJ injustificable

unjustified [ʌnˈdʒʌstɪfaɪd] ADJ (*text*) no alineado *or* justificado

unkempt [ʌnˈkempt] ADJ descuidado; (*hair*) despeinado

unkind [ʌnˈkaɪnd] ADJ poco amable; (*comment etc*) cruel

unkindly [ʌnˈkaɪndlɪ] ADV (*speak*) severamente; (*treat*) cruelmente, mal

unknown [ʌnˈnəʊn] ADJ desconocido; **~ quantity** incógnita ▶ ADV: **~ to me** sin saberlo yo

unladen [ʌnˈleɪdən] ADJ (*weight*) vacío, sin cargamento

unlawful [ʌnˈlɔːful] ADJ ilegal, ilícito

unleaded [ʌnˈlɛdɪd] N (*also:* **unleaded petrol**) gasolina sin plomo

unleash [ʌnˈliːʃ] VT desatar

unleavened [ʌnˈlɛvənd] ADJ ácimo, sin levadura

★**unless** [ʌnˈlɛs] CONJ a menos que; **~ he comes** a menos que venga; **~ otherwise stated** salvo indicación contraria; **~ I am mistaken** si no mi equivoco

unlicensed [ʌnˈlaɪsənst] ADJ (BRIT: *to sell alcohol*) no autorizado

unlike [ʌnˈlaɪk] ADJ distinto ▸ PREP a diferencia de

unlikelihood [ʌnˈlaɪklɪhud] N improbabilidad f

★**unlikely** [ʌnˈlaɪklɪ] ADJ improbable

unlimited [ʌnˈlɪmɪtɪd] ADJ ilimitado; **~ liability** responsabilidad f ilimitada

unlisted [ʌnˈlɪstɪd] ADJ (US Tel) que no figura en la guía; **~ company** empresa sin cotización en bolsa

unlit [ʌnˈlɪt] ADJ (*room*) oscuro, sin luz

unload [ʌnˈləud] VT descargar

unlock [ʌnˈlɔk] VT abrir (con llave)

★**unlucky** [ʌnˈlʌkɪ] ADJ desgraciado; (*object, number*) que trae mala suerte; **to be ~** (*person*) tener mala suerte

unmanageable [ʌnˈmænɪdʒəbl] ADJ (*unwieldy: tool, vehicle*) difícil de manejar; (: *situation*) incontrolable

unmanned [ʌnˈmænd] ADJ (*spacecraft*) sin tripulación

unmannerly [ʌnˈmænəlɪ] ADJ mal educado, descortés

unmarked [ʌnˈmɑːkt] ADJ (*unstained*) sin mancha; **~ police car** vehículo policial camuflado

unmarried [ʌnˈmærɪd] ADJ soltero

unmask [ʌnˈmɑːsk] VT desenmascarar

unmatched [ʌnˈmætʃt] ADJ incomparable

unmentionable [ʌnˈmɛnʃnəbl] ADJ (*topic, vice*) indecible; (*word*) que no se debe decir

unmerciful [ʌnˈməːsɪful] ADJ despiadado

unmistakable [ʌnmɪsˈteɪkəbl] ADJ inconfundible

unmistakably [ʌnmɪsˈteɪkəblɪ] ADV de modo inconfundible

unmitigated [ʌnˈmɪtɪgeɪtɪd] ADJ rematado, absoluto

unnamed [ʌnˈneɪmd] ADJ (*nameless*) sin nombre; (*anonymous*) anónimo

unnatural [ʌnˈnætʃrəl] ADJ (*gen*) antinatural; (*manner*) afectado; (*habit*) perverso

unnecessary [ʌnˈnɛsəsərɪ] ADJ innecesario, inútil

unnerve [ʌnˈnəːv] VT (*accident*) poner nervioso; (*hostile attitude*) acobardar; (*long wait, interview*) intimidar

unnoticed [ʌnˈnəutɪst] ADJ: **to go** *or* **pass ~** pasar desapercibido

UNO [ˈjuːnəu] N ABBR (= *United Nations Organization*) ONU f

unobservant [ʌnəbˈzəːvnt] ADJ: **to be ~** ser poco observador, ser distraído

unobtainable [ʌnəbˈteɪnəbl] ADJ inasequible; (Tel) inexistente

unobtrusive [ʌnəbˈtruːsɪv] ADJ discreto

unoccupied [ʌnˈɔkjupaɪd] ADJ (*house etc*) libre, desocupado

unofficial [ʌnəˈfɪʃl] ADJ no oficial; **~ strike** huelga no oficial

unopened [ʌnˈəupənd] ADJ (*letter, present*) sin abrir

unopposed [ʌnəˈpəuzd] ADV (*enter, be elected*) sin oposición

unorthodox [ʌnˈɔːθədɔks] ADJ poco ortodoxo

unpack [ʌnˈpæk] VI deshacer las maletas, desempacar (LAM) ▸ VT deshacer

unpaid [ʌnˈpeɪd] ADJ (*bill, debt*) sin pagar, impagado; (*Comm*) pendiente; (*holiday*) sin sueldo; (*work*) no remunerado

unpalatable [ʌnˈpælətəbl] ADJ (*truth*) desagradable

unparalleled [ʌnˈpærəlɛld] ADJ (*unequalled*) sin par; (*unique*) sin precedentes

unpatriotic [ʌnpætrɪˈɔtɪk] ADJ (*person*) poco patriota; (*speech, attitude*) antipatriótico

unplanned [ʌnˈplænd] ADJ (*visit*) imprevisto; (*baby*) no planeado

unpleasant [ʌnˈplɛznt] ADJ (*disagreeable*) desagradable; (*person, manner*) antipático

unplug [ʌnˈplʌg] VT desenchufar, desconectar

unpolluted [ʌnpəˈluːtɪd] ADJ impoluto, no contaminado

unpopular [ʌnˈpɔpjuləʳ] ADJ poco popular; **to be ~ with sb** (*person, law*) no ser popular con algn; **to make o.s. ~ (with)** hacerse impopular (con)

unprecedented [ʌnˈprɛsɪdəntɪd] ADJ sin precedentes

unpredictable [ʌnprɪˈdɪktəbl] ADJ imprevisible

unprejudiced [ʌnˈprɛdʒudɪst] ADJ (*not biased*) imparcial; (*having no prejudices*) sin prejuicio

unprepared [ʌnprɪˈpɛəd] ADJ (*person*) desprevenido; (*speech*) improvisado

unprepossessing [ʌnpriːpəˈzɛsɪŋ] ADJ poco atractivo

unprincipled [ʌnˈprɪnsɪpld] ADJ sin escrúpulos

unproductive [ʌnprəˈdʌktɪv] ADJ improductivo; (*discussion*) infructuoso

unprofessional [ʌnprəˈfɛʃənl] ADJ poco profesional; **~ conduct** negligencia

unprofitable [ʌnˈprɔfɪtəbl] ADJ poco provechoso, no rentable

u

841

unprotected [ˌʌnprəˈtɛktɪd] ADJ (sex) sin protección

unprovoked [ˌʌnprəˈvəukt] ADJ no provocado

unpunished [ʌnˈpʌnɪʃt] ADJ: **to go ~** quedar sin castigo, salir impune

unqualified [ʌnˈkwɒlɪfaɪd] ADJ sin título, no cualificado; (success) total, incondicional

unquestionably [ʌnˈkwɛstʃənəblɪ] ADV indiscutiblemente

unquestioning [ʌnˈkwɛstʃənɪŋ] ADJ (obedience, acceptance) incondicional

unravel [ʌnˈrævl] VT desenmarañar

unreal [ʌnˈrɪəl] ADJ irreal

unrealistic [ˌʌnrɪəˈlɪstɪk] ADJ poco realista

unreasonable [ʌnˈriːznəbl] ADJ irrazonable; **to make ~ demands on sb** hacer demandas excesivas a algn

unrecognizable [ʌnˈrɛkəgnaɪzəbl] ADJ irreconocible

unrecognized [ʌnˈrɛkəgnaɪzd] ADJ (talent, genius) ignorado; (Pol: regime) no reconocido

unrecorded [ˌʌnrɪˈkɔːdɪd] ADJ no registrado

unrefined [ˌʌnrɪˈfaɪnd] ADJ (sugar, petroleum) sin refinar

unrehearsed [ˌʌnrɪˈhəːst] ADJ (Theat etc) improvisado; (spontaneous) espontáneo

unrelated [ˌʌnrɪˈleɪtɪd] ADJ sin relación; (family) no emparentado

unrelenting [ˌʌnrɪˈlɛntɪŋ] ADJ implacable

unreliable [ˌʌnrɪˈlaɪəbl] ADJ (person) informal; (machine) poco fiable

unrelieved [ˌʌnrɪˈliːvd] ADJ (monotony) constante

unremitting [ˌʌnrɪˈmɪtɪŋ] ADJ incesante

unrepeatable [ˌʌnrɪˈpiːtəbl] ADJ irrepetible

unrepentant [ˌʌnrɪˈpɛntənt] ADJ (smoker, sinner) impenitente; **to be ~ about sth** no arrepentirse de algo

unrepresentative [ˌʌnrɛprɪˈzɛntətɪv] ADJ (untypical) poco representativo

unreserved [ˌʌnrɪˈzəːvd] ADJ (seat) no reservado; (approval, admiration) total

unreservedly [ˌʌnrɪˈzəːvɪdlɪ] ADV sin reserva

unresponsive [ˌʌnrɪˈspɒnsɪv] ADJ insensible

unrest [ʌnˈrɛst] N inquietud f, malestar m; (Pol) disturbios mpl

unrestricted [ˌʌnrɪˈstrɪktɪd] ADJ (power, time) sin restricción; (access) libre

unrewarded [ˌʌnrɪˈwɔːdɪd] ADJ sin recompensa

unripe [ʌnˈraɪp] ADJ verde, inmaduro

unrivalled, (US) **unrivaled** [ʌnˈraɪvəld] ADJ incomparable, sin par

unroll [ʌnˈrəul] VT desenrollar

unruffled [ʌnˈrʌfld] ADJ (person) imperturbable; (hair) liso

unruly [ʌnˈruːlɪ] ADJ indisciplinado

unsafe [ʌnˈseɪf] ADJ (journey) peligroso; (car etc)

inseguro; (method) arriesgado; **~ to drink/eat** no apto para el consumo humano

unsaid [ʌnˈsɛd] ADJ: **to leave sth ~** dejar algo sin decir

unsaleable, (US) **unsalable** [ʌnˈseɪləbl] ADJ invendible

unsatisfactory [ˈʌnsætɪsˈfæktərɪ] ADJ poco satisfactorio

unsatisfied [ʌnˈsætɪsfaɪd] ADJ (desire, need etc) insatisfecho

unsavoury, (US) **unsavory** [ʌnˈseɪvərɪ] ADJ (fig) repugnante

unscathed [ʌnˈskeɪðd] ADJ ileso

unscientific [ˌʌnsaɪənˈtɪfɪk] ADJ poco científico

unscrew [ʌnˈskruː] VT destornillar

unscrupulous [ʌnˈskruːpjuləs] ADJ sin escrúpulos

unseat [ʌnˈsiːt] VT (rider) hacer caerse de la silla a; (fig: official) hacer perder su escaño a

unsecured [ˌʌnsɪˈkjuəd] ADJ: **~ creditor** acreedor(a) m/f común

unseeded [ʌnˈsiːdɪd] ADJ (Sport) no preseleccionado

unseen [ʌnˈsiːn] ADJ (person, danger) oculto

unselfish [ʌnˈsɛlfɪʃ] ADJ generoso, poco egoísta; (act) desinteresado

unsettled [ʌnˈsɛtld] ADJ inquieto; (situation) inestable; (weather) variable

unsettling [ʌnˈsɛtlɪŋ] ADJ perturbador(a), inquietante

unshakable, unshakeable [ʌnˈʃeɪkəbl] ADJ inquebrantable

unshaven [ʌnˈʃeɪvn] ADJ sin afeitar

unsightly [ʌnˈsaɪtlɪ] ADJ desagradable

unskilled [ʌnˈskɪld] ADJ: **~ workers** mano f de obra no cualificada

unsociable [ʌnˈsəuʃəbl] ADJ insociable

unsocial [ʌnˈsəuʃl] ADJ: **~ hours** horario nocturno

unsold [ʌnˈsəuld] ADJ sin vender

unsolicited [ˌʌnsəˈlɪsɪtɪd] ADJ no solicitado

unsophisticated [ˌʌnsəˈfɪstɪkeɪtɪd] ADJ (person) sencillo, ingenuo; (method) poco sofisticado

unsound [ʌnˈsaund] ADJ (health) malo; (in construction: floor, foundations) defectuoso; (: policy, advice, judgment) erróneo; (: investment) poco seguro

unspeakable [ʌnˈspiːkəbl] ADJ indecible; (awful) incalificable

unspoiled [ˈʌnspɔɪld], **unspoilt** [ˈʌnspɔɪlt] ADJ (place) que no ha perdido su belleza natural

unspoken [ʌnˈspəukn] ADJ (words) sobreentendido; (agreement, approval) tácito

unstable [ʌnˈsteɪbl] ADJ inestable

unsteady [ʌnˈstɛdɪ] ADJ inestable

unstinting [ʌnˈstɪntɪŋ] ADJ (support etc) pródigo

unstuck [ʌnˈstʌk] ADJ: **to come ~** despegarse; (fig) fracasar

unsubscribe [ʌnsəb'skraɪb] vɪ (*Internet*) borrarse

unsubstantiated [ʌnsəb'stænʃɪeɪtɪd] ADJ (*rumour, accusation*) no comprobado

unsuccessful [ʌnsək'sɛsful] ADJ (*attempt*) infructuoso; (*writer, proposal*) sin éxito; **to be ~** (*in attempting sth*) no tener éxito, fracasar

unsuccessfully [ʌnsək'sɛsfulɪ] ADV en vano, sin éxito

unsuitable [ʌn'suːtəbl] ADJ inconveniente, inapropiado; (*time*) inoportuno

unsuited [ʌn'suːtɪd] ADJ: **to be ~ for** *or* **to** (*clothes, tools etc*) no ser apropiado para

unsung [ˈʌnsʌŋ] ADJ: **an ~ hero** un héroe desconocido

unsupported [ʌnsə'pɔːtɪd] ADJ (*claim*) sin fundamento; (*theory*) sin base firme

unsure [ʌn'ʃuəʳ] ADJ inseguro, poco seguro; **to be ~ of o.s.** estar poco seguro de sí mismo

unsuspecting [ʌnsə'spɛktɪŋ] ADJ confiado

unsweetened [ʌn'swiːtnd] ADJ sin azúcar

unsympathetic [ʌnsɪmpə'θɛtɪk] ADJ (*attitude*) poco comprensivo; (*person*) sin compasión; **~ (to)** indiferente (a)

untangle [ʌn'tæŋgl] vᴛ desenredar

untapped [ʌn'tæpt] ADJ (*resources*) sin explotar

untaxed [ʌn'tækst] ADJ (*goods*) libre de impuestos; (*income*) antes de impuestos

unthinkable [ʌn'θɪŋkəbl] ADJ inconcebible, impensable

unthinkingly [ʌn'θɪŋkɪŋlɪ] ADV irreflexivamente

untidy [ʌn'taɪdɪ] ADJ (*room*) desordenado, en desorden; (*appearance*) desaliñado

untie [ʌn'taɪ] vᴛ desatar

★**until** [ən'tɪl] PREP hasta; **~ now** hasta ahora; **~ then** hasta entonces; **from morning ~ night** de la mañana a la noche ▶ CONJ hasta que; **~ he comes** hasta que venga

untimely [ʌn'taɪmlɪ] ADJ inoportuno; (*death*) prematuro

untold [ʌn'təuld] ADJ (*story*) nunca contado; (*suffering*) indecible; (*wealth*) incalculable

untouched [ʌn'tʌtʃt] ADJ (*not used etc*) intacto, sin tocar; (*safe: person*) indemne, ileso; (*unaffected*): **~ by** insensible a

untoward [ʌntə'wɔːd] ADJ (*behaviour*) impropio; (*event*) adverso

untrained [ʌn'treɪnd] ADJ (*worker*) sin formación; (*troops*) no entrenado; **to the ~ eye** para los no entendidos

untrammelled, (US) **untrammeled** [ʌn'træməld] ADJ ilimitado

untranslatable [ʌntrænz'leɪtəbl] ADJ intraducible

untried [ʌn'traɪd] ADJ (*plan*) no probado

untrue [ʌn'truː] ADJ (*statement*) falso

untrustworthy [ʌn'trʌstwəːðɪ] ADJ (*person*) poco fiable

unusable [ʌn'juːzəbl] ADJ inservible

unused¹ [ʌn'juːzd] ADJ sin usar, nuevo

unused² [ʌn'juːst] ADJ: **to be ~ to (doing) sth** no estar acostumbrado a (hacer) algo

★**unusual** [ʌn'juːʒuəl] ADJ insólito, poco común

unusually [ʌn'juːʒuəlɪ] ADV: **he arrived ~ early** llegó más temprano que de costumbre

unveil [ʌn'veɪl] vᴛ (*statue*) descubrir

unwanted [ʌn'wɒntɪd] ADJ (*person, effect*) no deseado

unwarranted [ʌn'wɒrəntɪd] ADJ injustificado

unwary [ʌn'wɛərɪ] ADJ imprudente, incauto

unwavering [ʌn'weɪvərɪŋ] ADJ inquebrantable

unwelcome [ʌn'wɛlkəm] ADJ (*at a bad time*) inoportuno, molesto; **I felt ~** sentí que allí sobraba

unwell [ʌn'wɛl] ADJ: **to feel ~** estar indispuesto, sentirse mal

unwieldy [ʌn'wiːldɪ] ADJ difícil de manejar

unwilling [ʌn'wɪlɪŋ] ADJ: **to be ~ to do sth** estar poco dispuesto a hacer algo

unwillingly [ʌn'wɪlɪŋlɪ] ADV de mala gana

unwind [ʌn'waɪnd] vᴛ (*irreg: like* **wind²**) desenvolver ▶ vɪ (*relax*) relajarse

unwise [ʌn'waɪz] ADJ imprudente

unwitting [ʌn'wɪtɪŋ] ADJ inconsciente

unwittingly [ʌn'wɪtɪŋlɪ] ADV inconscientemente, sin darse cuenta

unworkable [ʌn'wəːkəbl] ADJ (*plan*) impracticable

unworthy [ʌn'wəːðɪ] ADJ indigno; **to be ~ of sth/to do sth** ser indigno de algo/de hacer algo

unwrap [ʌn'ræp] vᴛ desenvolver

unwritten [ʌn'rɪtn] ADJ (*agreement*) tácito; (*rules, law*) no escrito

unzip [ʌn'zɪp] vᴛ abrir la cremallera de; (*Comput*) descomprimir

---

up [ʌp]

PREP: **to go/be up sth** subir/estar subido en algo; **he went up the stairs/the hill** subió las escaleras/la colina; **we walked/climbed up the hill** subimos la colina; **they live further up the street** viven más arriba en la calle; **go up that road and turn left** sigue por esa calle y gira a la izquierda

▶ ADV **1** (*upwards, higher*) más arriba; **up in the mountains** en lo alto (de la montaña); **put it a bit higher up** ponlo un poco más arriba *or* alto; **to stop halfway up** pararse a la mitad del camino *or* de la subida; **up there** ahí *or* allí arriba; **up above** en lo alto, por encima, arriba; **"this side up"** "este lado hacia arriba"; **to live/go up North** vivir en el norte/ ir al norte

2: to be up (*out of bed*) estar levantado; (*prices, level*) haber subido; (*building*) estar construido; (*tent*) estar montado; (*curtains, paper etc*) estar puesto; **time's up** se acabó el tiempo; **when**

u

the year was up al terminarse el año; **he's well up in** or **on politics** (Brit: *knowledgeable*) está muy al día en política; **what's up?** (*wrong*) ¿qué pasa?; **what's up with him?** ¿qué le pasa?; **prices are up on last year** los precios han subido desde el año pasado

3: **up to** (*as far as*) hasta; **up to now** hasta ahora or la fecha

4: **to be up to** (*depending on*): **it's up to you** depende de ti; **he's not up to it** (*job, task etc*) no es capaz de hacerlo; **I don't feel up to it** no me encuentro con ánimos para ello; **his work is not up to the required standard** su trabajo no da la talla; **what is he up to?** (*inf: doing*) ¿qué estará tramando?

▶ vi (*inf*): **she upped and left** se levantó y se marchó

▶ vt (*inf: price*) subir

▶ n: **ups and downs** altibajos *mpl*

up-and-coming [ˌʌpəndˈkʌmɪŋ] ADJ prometedor(a)

upbeat [ˈʌpbiːt] N (*Mus*) tiempo no acentuado; (*in economy, prosperity*) aumento ▶ ADJ (*inf*) optimista, animado

upbraid [ʌpˈbreɪd] vt censurar, reprender

upbringing [ˈʌpbrɪŋɪŋ] N educación *f*

upcoming [ˈʌpkʌmɪŋ] ADJ próximo

upcycle [ˈʌpsaɪkl] vt reciclar creativamente

update [ʌpˈdeɪt] vt poner al día

upend [ʌpˈend] vt poner vertical

upfront [ʌpˈfrʌnt] ADJ claro, directo; **to be ~ about sth** admitir algo claramente ▶ ADV a las claras; (*pay*) por adelantado

upgrade [ʌpˈgreɪd] vt ascender; (*Comput*) actualizar

upheaval [ʌpˈhiːvl] N trastornos *mpl*; (*Pol*) agitación *f*

uphill [ʌpˈhɪl] ADJ en cuesta; (*fig: task*) penoso, difícil ▶ ADV: **to go ~** ir cuesta arriba

uphold [ʌpˈhəʊld] vt (*irreg: like* **hold**) sostener

upholstery [ʌpˈhəʊlstərɪ] N tapicería

upkeep [ˈʌpkiːp] N mantenimiento

upload [ʌpˈləʊd] vt (*Comput*) subir

upmarket [ʌpˈmɑːkɪt] ADJ (*product*) de categoría

upon [əˈpɒn] PREP sobre

upper [ˈʌpəʳ] ADJ superior, de arriba ▶ N (*of shoe: also:* **uppers**) pala

upper case N (*Typ*) mayúsculas *fpl*

upper-class [ˈʌpəˈklɑːs] ADJ (*district, people, accent*) de clase alta; (*attitude*) altivo

uppercut [ˈʌpəkʌt] N uppercut *m*, gancho a la cara

upper hand N: **to have the ~** tener la sartén por el mango

Upper House N (*Pol*): **the ~** la Cámara alta

uppermost [ˈʌpəməʊst] ADJ el más alto; **what was ~ in my mind** lo que más me preocupaba

Upper Volta [-ˈvɒltə] N Alto Volta *m*

upright [ˈʌpraɪt] ADJ vertical; (*fig*) honrado

uprising [ˈʌpraɪzɪŋ] N sublevación *f*

uproar [ˈʌprɔːʳ] N tumulto, escándalo

uproarious [ʌpˈrɔːrɪəs] ADJ escandaloso; (*hilarious*) graciosísimo

uproot [ʌpˈruːt] vt desarraigar

★**upset** N [ˈʌpsɛt] (*to plan etc*) revés *m*, contratiempo; (*Med*) trastorno; **to have a stomach ~** (*Brit*) tener el estómago revuelto ▶ vt [ʌpˈsɛt] (*irreg: like* **set**) (*glass etc*) volcar; (*spill*) derramar; (*plan*) alterar; (*person*) molestar, perturbar ▶ ADJ [ʌpˈsɛt] preocupado, perturbado; (*stomach*) revuelto; **to get ~** molestarse, llevarse un disgusto

upset price N (*US, Scottish*) precio mínimo or de reserva

upsetting [ʌpˈsɛtɪŋ] ADJ (*worrying*) inquietante; (*offending*) ofensivo; (*annoying*) molesto

upshot [ˈʌpʃɒt] N resultado

upside-down [ˈʌpsaɪdˈdaʊn] ADV al revés; **to turn a place ~** (*fig*) revolverlo todo

upstage [ˈʌpˈsteɪdʒ] vt robar protagonismo a

upstairs [ˈʌpˈstɛəz] ADV arriba ▶ ADJ (*room*) de arriba ▶ N el piso superior

upstart [ˈʌpstɑːt] N advenedizo(-a)

upstream [ʌpˈstriːm] ADV río arriba

upsurge [ˈʌpsəːdʒ] N (*of enthusiasm etc*) arrebato

uptake [ˈʌpteɪk] N: **he is quick/slow on the ~** es muy listo/torpe

uptight [ʌpˈtaɪt] ADJ (*inf*) tenso, nervioso

★**up-to-date** [ˈʌptəˈdeɪt] ADJ actual, moderno; **to bring sb ~ (on sth)** poner a algn al corriente/tanto (de algo)

uptown [ˈʌptaʊn] ADV (*US*) hacia las afueras ▶ ADJ exterior, de las afueras

upturn [ˈʌptəːn] N (*in luck*) mejora; (*Comm: in market*) resurgimiento económico; (: *in value of currency*) aumento

upturned [ˈʌptəːnd] ADJ: **~ nose** nariz *f* respingona

upward [ˈʌpwəd], **upwards** [ˈʌpwədz] ADV hacia arriba; (*more than*): **~(s) of** más de

upwardly-mobile [ˈʌpwədlɪˈməʊbaɪl] ADJ: **to be ~** mejorar socialmente

Ural Mountains [ˈjuərəl-] NPL: **the ~** (*also:* **the Urals**) los Montes Urales

uranium [juəˈreɪnɪəm] N uranio

Uranus [juəˈreɪnəs] N (*Astro*) Urano

urban [ˈəːbən] ADJ urbano

urbane [əːˈbeɪn] ADJ cortés, urbano

urbanization [ˈəːbənaɪˈzeɪʃən] N urbanización *f*

urchin [ˈəːtʃɪn] N pilluelo, golfillo

Urdu [ˈuəduː] N urdu *m*

urge [əːdʒ] N (*force*) impulso; (*desire*) deseo ▶ vt: **to ~ sb to do sth** animar a algn a hacer algo

▶ **urge on** vt animar

urgency [ˈəːdʒənsɪ] N urgencia

★**urgent** [ˈəːdʒənt] ADJ (earnest, persistent: plea) insistente; (: tone) urgente

urgently [ˈəːdʒəntlɪ] ADV con urgencia, urgentemente

urinal [ˈjuərɪnl] N (building) urinario; (vessel) orinal m

urinate [ˈjuərɪneɪt] VI orinar

urine [ˈjuərɪn] N orina

URL N ABBR (= uniform resource locator) URL m

urn [əːn] N urna; (also: **tea urn**) tetera (grande)

Uruguay [ˈjuərəgwaɪ] N el Uruguay

Uruguayan [juərəˈgwaɪən] ADJ, N uruguayo(-a) m/f

★**US** N ABBR (= United States) EE.UU.

★**us** [ʌs] PRON nos; (after prep) nosotros(-as); (inf: me): **give us a kiss** dame un beso; see also **me**

★**USA** N ABBR = **United States of America**; (Mil) = **United States Army**

usable [ˈjuːzəbl] ADJ utilizable

USAF N ABBR = **United States Air Force**

usage [ˈjuːzɪdʒ] N (Ling) uso; (utilization) utilización f

USB ABBR (= universal serial bus) USB m

USB key N llave f USB, memoria USB

USB stick N memoria USB, llave f de memoria

USCG N ABBR = **United States Coast Guard**

USDA N ABBR = **United States Department of Agriculture**

USDAW [ˈʌzdɔː] N ABBR (BRIT: = Union of Shop, Distributive, and Allied Workers) sindicato de empleados de comercio

USDI N ABBR = **United States Department of the Interior**

★**use** N [juːs] uso, empleo; (usefulness) utilidad f; **in ~** en uso; **out of ~** en desuso; **to be of ~** servir; **ready for ~** listo (para usar); **to make ~ of sth** aprovechar or servirse de algo; **it's no ~** (pointless) es inútil; (not useful) no sirve ▸ VT [juːz] usar, emplear; **what's this used for?** ¿para qué sirve esto?

▸ **use up** VT (food) consumir; (money) gastar

used[1] [juːzd] ADJ (car) usado

used[2] [juːst] ADJ: **to be ~ to** estar acostumbrado(-a) a (SP), acostumbrar; **to get ~ to** acostumbrarse a ▸ AUX VB: **she ~ to do it** (ella) solía or acostumbraba hacerlo

> To describe what someone *used to do* or what *used to happen*, you should generally just use the imperfect tense of the main verb: We used to buy our food at the corner shop. **Comprábamos la comida en la tienda de la esquina**.
> Alternatively, to describe someone's habits, you can use **solía** or **acostumbraba (a)** plus the infinitive: He used to go for a walk every day. **Solía** or **Acostumbraba (a) dar un paseo todos los días**.

★**useful** [ˈjuːsful] ADJ útil; **to come in ~** ser útil

usefulness [ˈjuːsfəlnɪs] N utilidad f

★**useless** [ˈjuːslɪs] ADJ inútil; (unusable: object) inservible

uselessly [ˈjuːslɪslɪ] ADV inútilmente, en vano

uselessness [ˈjuːslɪsnɪs] N inutilidad f

★**user** [ˈjuːzəʳ] N usuario(-a); (of petrol, gas etc) consumidor(a) m/f

user-friendly [ˈjuːzəˈfrɛndlɪ] ADJ (Comput) fácil de utilizar

username [ˈjuːzəneɪm] N (Comput) nombre m de usuario

USES N ABBR = **United States Employment Service**

usher [ˈʌʃəʳ] N (at wedding) ujier mf; (in cinema etc) acomodador(a) m/f ▸ VT: **to ~ sb in** (into room) hacer pasar a algn; **it ushered in a new era** (fig) inició una nueva era

usherette [ʌʃəˈrɛt] N (in cinema) acomodadora

USM N ABBR = **United States Mail; United States Mint**

USN N ABBR = **United States Navy**

USP N ABBR = **unique selling point; unique selling proposition**

USPHS N ABBR = **United States Public Health Service**

USPO N ABBR = **United States Post Office**

USS ABBR = **United States Ship; United States Steamer**

USSR N ABBR (History) = **Union of Soviet Socialist Republics; the (former) ~** la (antigua) U.R.S.S. (= Unión de Repúblicas Socialistas Soviéticas)

usu. ABBR = **usually**

★**usual** [ˈjuːʒuəl] ADJ normal, corriente; **as ~** como de costumbre, como siempre

★**usually** [ˈjuːʒuəlɪ] ADV normalmente

usurer [ˈjuːʒərəʳ] N usurero(-a)

usurp [juːˈzəːp] VT usurpar

usury [ˈjuːʒərɪ] N usura

UT ABBR (US) = **Utah**

ute [juːt] N ABBR (AUSTRALIA, NEW ZEALAND: inf: = utility truck) camioneta

utensil [juːˈtɛnsl] N utensilio; **kitchen utensils** batería de cocina

uterus [ˈjuːtərəs] N útero

utilitarian [juːtɪlɪˈtɛərɪən] ADJ utilitario

utility [juːˈtɪlɪtɪ] N utilidad f; (public utility) (empresa de) servicio público

utility room N trascocina

utilization [juːtɪlaɪˈzeɪʃən] N utilización f

utilize [ˈjuːtɪlaɪz] VT utilizar

utmost [ˈʌtməust] ADJ mayor; **it is of the ~ importance that …** es de la mayor importancia que … ▸ N: **to do one's ~** hacer todo lo posible

utter [ˈʌtəʳ] ADJ total, completo ▸ VT pronunciar, proferir

u

utterance [ˈʌtərns] N palabras *fpl*, declaración *f*

utterly [ˈʌtəlɪ] ADV completamente, totalmente

U-turn [ˈjuːˈtəːn] N cambio de sentido; (*fig*) giro de 180 grados

Uzbekistan [ʌzbɛkɪˈstɑːn] N Uzbekistán *m*

Vv

V, v [viː] N *(letter)* V, v f; **V for Victor** V de Valencia

v. ABBR (= *verse*) vers.°; (= *see*) V, vid., vide; (= *versus*) vs.; = **volt**

VA, Va. ABBR *(US)* = **Virginia**

vac [væk] N ABBR *(BRIT inf)* = **vacation**

vacancy ['veɪkənsɪ] N *(job)* vacante f; *(room)* cuarto libre; **have you any vacancies?** ¿tiene or hay alguna habitación or algún cuarto libre?; **"no vacancies"** "completo"

vacant ['veɪkənt] ADJ desocupado, libre; *(expression)* distraído

vacant lot N *(US)* solar m

vacate [və'keɪt] VT *(house)* desocupar; *(job)* dejar (vacante)

vacation [və'keɪʃən] N vacaciones fpl; **on ~** de vacaciones; **to take a ~** *(esp US)* tomarse unas vacaciones

vacation course N curso de vacaciones

vacationer [və'keɪʃənəʳ], **vacationist** [və'keɪʃənɪst] N *(US)* turista mf

vaccinate ['væksɪneɪt] VT vacunar

vaccination [væksɪ'neɪʃən] N vacunación f

vaccine ['væksiːn] N vacuna

vacuum ['vækjum] N vacío

vacuum bottle N *(US)* = **vacuum flask**

vacuum cleaner N aspiradora

vacuum flask N *(BRIT)* termo

vacuum-packed ['vækjum'pækt] ADJ envasado al vacío

vagabond ['vægəbɒnd] N vagabundo(-a)

vagary ['veɪgərɪ] N capricho

vagina [və'dʒaɪnə] N vagina

vagrancy ['veɪgrənsɪ] N vagabundeo

vagrant ['veɪgrənt] N vagabundo(-a)

vague [veɪg] ADJ vago; *(blurred: memory)* borroso; *(uncertain)* incierto; *(ambiguous)* impreciso; *(person: absent-minded)* distraído; (: *evasive*): **to be ~** no decir las cosas clara-

mente; **I haven't the vaguest idea** no tengo la más remota idea

vaguely ['veɪglɪ] ADV vagamente

vagueness ['veɪgnɪs] N vaguedad f, imprecisión f; *(absent-mindedness)* despiste m

vain [veɪn] ADJ *(conceited)* presumido; *(useless)* vano, inútil; **in ~** en vano

vainly ['veɪnlɪ] ADV *(to no effect)* en vano; *(conceitedly)* vanidosamente

valance ['væləns] N *(for bed)* volante alrededor de la colcha o sábana que cuelga hasta el suelo

valedictory [vælɪ'dɪktərɪ] ADJ de despedida

valentine ['væləntaɪn] N *(also: **valentine card**)* tarjeta del Día de los Enamorados

Valentine's Day N día m de los enamorados *(el 14 de febrero, día de San Valentín)*

valet ['væleɪ] N ayuda m de cámara

valet service N *(for clothes)* planchado

valiant ['væljənt] ADJ valiente

valiantly ['væljəntlɪ] ADV valientemente, con valor

valid ['vælɪd] ADJ válido; *(ticket)* valedero; *(law)* vigente

validate ['vælɪdeɪt] VT *(contract, document)* convalidar; *(argument, claim)* dar validez a

validity [və'lɪdɪtɪ] N validez f; vigencia

valise [və'liːz] N maletín m

★**valley** ['vælɪ] N valle m

valour, *(US)* **valor** ['væləʳ] N valor m, valentía

★**valuable** ['væljuəbl] ADJ *(jewel)* de valor; *(time)* valioso ■ **valuables** NPL objetos mpl de valor

valuation [vælju'eɪʃən] N tasación f, valuación f

★**value** ['væljuː] N valor m; *(importance)* importancia; **to lose (in) ~** *(currency)* bajar; *(property)* desvalorizarse; **to gain (in) ~** *(currency)* subir; *(property)* revalorizarse; **you get good ~ (for money) in that shop** la relación calidad-precio es muy buena en esa tienda; **to be of great ~ to**

sb ser de gran valor para algn ▶ VT (*fix price of*) tasar, valorar; (*esteem*) apreciar; **it is valued at £8** está valorado en ocho libras ■ **values** NPL (*moral*) valores *mpl* morales

value added tax N (BRIT) impuesto sobre el valor añadido *or* (LAM) agregado

valued ['væljuːd] ADJ (*appreciated*) apreciado

valueless ['væljuːlɪs] ADJ sin valor

valuer ['væljuːəʳ] N tasador(a) *m/f*

valve [vælv] N (*Anat*, *Tech*) válvula

vampire ['væmpaɪəʳ] N vampiro

★**van** [væn] N (*Aut*) furgoneta, camioneta (LAM); (BRIT *Rail*) furgón *m* (de equipajes)

V and A N ABBR (BRIT) = **Victoria and Albert Museum**

vandal ['vændl] N vándalo(-a)

vandalism ['vændəlɪzəm] N vandalismo

vandalize ['vændəlaɪz] VT dañar, destruir, destrozar

vanguard ['vænɡɑːd] N vanguardia

vanilla [və'nɪlə] N vainilla

vanish ['vænɪʃ] VI desaparecer, esfumarse

vanity ['vænɪtɪ] N vanidad *f*

vanity case N neceser *m*

vantage point ['vɑːntɪdʒ-] N posición *f* ventajosa

Vanuatu ['vænuːætuː] N Vanuatu *m*

vape [veɪp] VT, VI vapear

vaper ['veɪpəʳ] N fumador(a) *m/f* de cigarrillos electrónicos

vaping ['veɪpɪŋ] N cigarrillos *mpl* electrónicos

vaporize ['veɪpəraɪz] VT vaporizar ▶ VI vaporizarse

vapour, (US) **vapor** ['veɪpəʳ] N vapor *m*; (*on breath, window*) vaho

vapour trail, (US) **vapor trail** N (*Aviat*) estela

variable ['vɛərɪəbl] ADJ variable ▶ N variable *f*

variance ['vɛərɪəns] N: **to be at ~ (with)** estar en desacuerdo (con), no cuadrar (con)

variant ['vɛərɪənt] N variante *f*

variation [vɛərɪ'eɪʃən] N variación *f*

varicose ['værɪkəus] ADJ: **~ veins** varices *fpl*

varied ['vɛərɪd] ADJ variado

★**variety** [və'raɪətɪ] N variedad *f*, diversidad *f*; (*quantity*) surtido; **for a ~ of reasons** por varias *or* diversas razones

variety show N espectáculo de variedades

★**various** ['vɛərɪəs] ADJ varios(-as), diversos(-as); **at ~ times** (*different*) en distintos momentos; (*several*) varias veces

varnish ['vɑːnɪʃ] N (*gen*) barniz *m*; (*also*: **nail varnish**) esmalte *m* ▶ VT (*gen*) barnizar; (*nails*) pintar (con esmalte)

vary ['vɛərɪ] VT variar; (*change*) cambiar ▶ VI variar; (*disagree*) discrepar; **to ~ with** *or* **according to** variar según *or* de acuerdo con

varying ['vɛərɪŋ] ADJ diversos(-as)

vase [vɑːz] N florero, jarrón *m*

vasectomy [və'sɛktəmɪ] N vasectomía

Vaseline® ['væsɪliːn] N vaselina®

vast [vɑːst] ADJ (*quantity, organization*) enorme; (*area, knowledge*) vasto

vastly ['vɑːstlɪ] ADV enormemente

vastness ['vɑːstnɪs] N inmensidad *f*

VAT [væt] N ABBR (BRIT: = *value added tax*) IVA *m*

vat [væt] N tina, tinaja

Vatican ['vætɪkən] N: **the ~** el Vaticano

vatman ['vætmæn] N (*irreg*) (BRIT *inf*) inspector *m or* recaudador *m* del IVA; **"how to avoid the ~"** "cómo evitar pagar el IVA"

vaudeville ['vɔːdəvɪl] N (US) vodevil *m*

vault [vɔːlt] N (*of roof*) bóveda; (*tomb*) panteón *m*; (*in bank*) cámara acorazada ▶ VT (*also*: **vault over**) saltar (por encima de)

vaunted ['vɔːntɪd] ADJ: **much ~** cacareado

VC N ABBR = **vice-chairman**; **vice-chancellor**; (BRIT: = *Victoria Cross*) *condecoración militar*

VCR N ABBR = **video cassette recorder**

VD N ABBR = **venereal disease**

VDU N ABBR (= *visual display unit*) UPV *f*

veal [viːl] N ternera

veer [vɪəʳ] VI (*vehicle*) virar; (*wind*) girar

veg. [vɛdʒ] N ABBR (BRIT *inf*) = **vegetable(s)**

vegan ['viːɡən] N vegano(-a)

vegeburger, veggieburger ['vɛdʒɪbəːɡəʳ] N hamburguesa vegetal

★**vegetable** ['vɛdʒtəbl] N (*Bot*) vegetal *m*; (*edible plant*) legumbre *f*, hortaliza ▶ ADJ vegetal ■ **vegetables** NPL (*cooked*) verduras *fpl*

vegetable garden N huerta, huerto

★**vegetarian** [vɛdʒɪ'tɛərɪən] ADJ, N vegetariano(-a) *m/f*

vegetate ['vɛdʒɪteɪt] VI vegetar

vegetation [vɛdʒɪ'teɪʃən] N vegetación *f*

vegetative ['vɛdʒɪtətɪv] ADJ vegetativo; (*Bot*) vegetal

vehemence ['viːɪməns] N vehemencia; violencia

vehement ['viːɪmənt] ADJ vehemente, apasionado; (*dislike, hatred*) violento

★**vehicle** ['viːɪkl] N vehículo; (*fig*) vehículo, medio

vehicular [vɪ'hɪkjuləʳ] ADJ: **~ traffic** circulación *f* rodada

veil [veɪl] N velo; **under a ~ of secrecy** (*fig*) en el mayor secreto ▶ VT velar

veiled [veɪld] ADJ (*also fig*) disimulado, velado

vein [veɪn] N vena; (*of ore etc*) veta

Velcro® ['vɛlkrəu] N velcro® *m*

vellum ['vɛləm] N (*writing paper*) papel *m* vitela

velocity [vɪ'lɔsɪtɪ] N velocidad *f*

velour [və'luəʳ] N terciopelo

velvet [ˈvɛlvɪt] N terciopelo ▸ ADJ aterciopelado

vendetta [vɛnˈdɛtə] N vendetta

vending machine [ˈvɛndɪŋ-] N máquina expendedora, expendedor m

vendor [ˈvɛndəʳ] N vendedor(a) m/f; **street ~** vendedor(a) m/f callejero(-a)

veneer [vəˈnɪəʳ] N chapa, enchapado; (fig) barniz m

venereal [vɪˈnɪərɪəl] ADJ: **~ disease** enfermedad f venérea

Venetian blind [vɪˈniːʃən-] N persiana

Venezuela [vɛnəˈzweɪlə] N Venezuela

Venezuelan [vɛnəˈzweɪlən] ADJ, N venezolano(-a) m/f

vengeance [ˈvɛndʒəns] N venganza; **with a ~** (fig) con creces

vengeful [ˈvɛndʒful] ADJ vengativo

Venice [ˈvɛnɪs] N Venecia

venison [ˈvɛnɪsn] N carne f de venado

venom [ˈvɛnəm] N veneno

venomous [ˈvɛnəməs] ADJ venenoso

venomously [ˈvɛnəməslɪ] ADV con odio

vent [vɛnt] N (opening) abertura; (air-hole) respiradero; (in wall) rejilla (de ventilación) ▸ VT (fig: feelings) desahogar

ventilate [ˈvɛntɪleɪt] VT ventilar

ventilation [vɛntɪˈleɪʃən] N ventilación f

ventilation shaft N pozo de ventilación

ventilator [ˈvɛntɪleɪtəʳ] N ventilador m

ventriloquist [vɛnˈtrɪləkwɪst] N ventrílocuo(-a)

venture [ˈvɛntʃəʳ] N empresa; **a business ~** una empresa comercial ▸ VT arriesgar; (opinion) ofrecer; **to ~ to do sth** aventurarse a hacer algo ▸ VI arriesgarse, lanzarse

venture capital N capital m de riesgo

venue [ˈvɛnjuː] N (meeting place) lugar m de reunión; (for concert) local m

Venus [ˈviːnəs] N (Astro) Venus m

veracity [vəˈræsɪtɪ] N veracidad f

veranda, verandah [vəˈrændə] N terraza; (with glass) galería

verb [vəːb] N verbo

verbal [ˈvəːbl] ADJ verbal

verbally [ˈvəːbəlɪ] ADV verbalmente, de palabra

verbatim [vəːˈbeɪtɪm] ADJ, ADV al pie de la letra, palabra por palabra

verbose [vəːˈbəus] ADJ prolijo

★**verdict** [ˈvəːdɪkt] N veredicto, fallo; (fig: opinion) opinión f, juicio; **~ of guilty/not guilty** veredicto de culpabilidad/inocencia

verge [vəːdʒ] N (BRIT) borde m; **to be on the ~ of doing sth** estar a punto de hacer algo ▸ **verge on** VT FUS rayar en

verger [ˈvəːdʒəʳ] N sacristán m

verification [vɛrɪfɪˈkeɪʃən] N comprobación f, verificación f

verify [ˈvɛrɪfaɪ] VT comprobar, verificar; (prove the truth of) confirmar

veritable [ˈvɛrɪtəbl] ADJ verdadero, auténtico

vermin [ˈvəːmɪn] NPL (animals) bichos mpl; (insects) sabandijas fpl; (fig) sabandijas fpl

vermouth [ˈvəːməθ] N vermut m

vernacular [vəˈnækjuləʳ] N lengua vernácula

versatile [ˈvəːsətaɪl] ADJ (person) polifacético; (machine, tool etc) versátil

versatility [vəːsəˈtɪlɪtɪ] N versatilidad f

verse [vəːs] N versos mpl, poesía; (stanza) estrofa; (in bible) versículo; **in ~** en verso

versed [vəːst] ADJ: **(well-)versed in** versado en

version [ˈvəːʃən] N versión f

versus [ˈvəːsəs] PREP contra

vertebra [ˈvəːtɪbrə] (pl **vertebrae** [briː]) N vértebra

vertebrate [ˈvəːtɪbrɪt] N vertebrado

vertical [ˈvəːtɪkl] ADJ vertical

vertically [ˈvəːtɪkəlɪ] ADV verticalmente

vertigo [ˈvəːtɪgəu] N vértigo; **to suffer from ~** tener vértigo

verve [vəːv] N brío

★**very** [ˈvɛrɪ] ADV muy; **the ~ last** el último (de todos); **at the ~ least** al menos; **~ much** muchísimo; **~ well/little** muy bien/poco; **~ high frequency** (Radio) frecuencia muy alta; **it's ~ cold** hace mucho frío ▸ ADJ: **the ~ book which** el mismo libro que; **the ~ thought (of it) alarms me** con solo pensarlo me entra miedo

vespers [ˈvɛspəz] NPL vísperas fpl

vessel [ˈvɛsl] N (Anat) vaso; (ship) barco; (container) vasija

vest [vɛst] N (BRIT) camiseta; (US: waistcoat) chaleco

vested interests [ˈvɛstɪd-] NPL (Comm) intereses mpl creados

vestibule [ˈvɛstɪbjuːl] N vestíbulo

vestige [ˈvɛstɪdʒ] N vestigio, rastro

vestry [ˈvɛstrɪ] N sacristía

Vesuvius [vɪˈsuːvɪəs] N Vesubio

vet [vɛt] N ABBR = **veterinary surgeon**; (US inf) = **veteran** ▸ VT revisar; **to ~ sb for a job** someter a investigación a algn para un trabajo

veteran [ˈvɛtərn] N veterano(-a) ▸ ADJ: **she is a ~ campaigner for ...** es una veterana de la campaña de ...

veteran car N coche m antiguo

veterinarian [vɛtrɪˈnɛərɪən] N (US) = **veterinary surgeon**

veterinary [ˈvɛtrɪnərɪ] ADJ veterinario

veterinary surgeon N (BRIT) veterinario(-a)

veto [ˈviːtəu] N (pl **vetoes**) veto; **to put a ~ on** vetar ▸ VT prohibir, vedar

vetting [ˈvɛtɪŋ] N: **positive ~** investigación guber-

V

849

namental de los futuros altos cargos de la Administración

vex [vɛks] VT (irritate) fastidiar; (make impatient) impacientar

vexed [vɛkst] ADJ (question) controvertido

vexing ['vɛksɪŋ] ADJ molesto, engorroso

VFD N ABBR (US) = **voluntary fire department**

VG N ABBR (BRIT Scol etc: = very good) S (= sobresaliente)

VHF ABBR (= very high frequency) VHF f

VI ABBR (US) = **Virgin Islands**

★**via** ['vaɪə] PREP por, por vía de

viability [vaɪə'bɪlɪtɪ] N viabilidad f

viable ['vaɪəbl] ADJ viable

viaduct ['vaɪədʌkt] N viaducto

vial ['vaɪəl] N frasco pequeño

vibes [vaɪbz] NPL (inf): **I got good/bad ~** me dio buen/mal rollo

vibrant ['vaɪbrənt] ADJ (lively, bright) vivo; (full of emotion: voice) vibrante; (: colour) fuerte

vibraphone ['vaɪbrəfəun] N vibráfono

vibrate [vaɪ'breɪt] VI vibrar

vibration [vaɪ'breɪʃən] N vibración f

vibrator [vaɪ'breɪtəʳ] N vibrador m

vicar ['vɪkəʳ] N párroco

vicarage ['vɪkərɪdʒ] N parroquia

vicarious [vɪ'kɛərɪəs] ADJ indirecto; (responsibility) delegado

★**vice** [vaɪs] N (evil) vicio; (Tech) torno de banco

vice- [vaɪs] PREF vice...

vice-chairman ['vaɪs'tʃɛəmən] N (irreg) presidente(-a) m/f

vice-chancellor [vaɪs'tʃɑːnsələʳ] N (BRIT Univ) rector(a) m/f

vice-president [vaɪs'prɛzɪdənt] N vicepresidente(-a) m/f

viceroy ['vaɪsrɔɪ] N virrey m

vice versa ['vaɪsɪ'vəːsə] ADV viceversa

vicinity [vɪ'sɪnɪtɪ] N (area) vecindad f; (nearness) proximidad f; **in the ~ (of)** cercano (a)

vicious ['vɪʃəs] ADJ (remark) malicioso; (blow) brutal; (dog, horse) resabido; **a ~ circle** un círculo vicioso

viciousness ['vɪʃəsnɪs] N brutalidad f

vicissitudes [vɪ'sɪsɪtjuːdz] NPL vicisitudes fpl, peripecias fpl

★**victim** ['vɪktɪm] N víctima; **to be the ~ of** ser víctima de

victimization [vɪktɪmaɪ'zeɪʃən] N persecución f; (of striker etc) represalias fpl

victimize ['vɪktɪmaɪz] VT (strikers etc) tomar represalias contra

victor ['vɪktəʳ] N vencedor(a) m/f

Victorian [vɪk'tɔːrɪən] ADJ victoriano

victorious [vɪk'tɔːrɪəs] ADJ vencedor(a)

★**victory** ['vɪktərɪ] N victoria; **to win a ~ over sb** obtener una victoria sobre algn

★**video** ['vɪdɪəu] CPD de vídeo ▶ N vídeo ▶ VT grabar (en vídeo)

video call N videollamada

videocam ['vɪdɪəukæm] N videocámara

video camera N videocámara, cámara de vídeo

videodisk ['vɪdɪəudɪsk] N videodisco

video game N videojuego

video nasty N vídeo de violencia y/o porno duro

videophone ['vɪdɪəufəun] N videoteléfono, videófono

video recorder N vídeo, videocassette f

video recording N videograbación f

video tape N cinta de vídeo

vie [vaɪ] VI: **to ~ with** competir con

Vienna [vɪ'ɛnə] N Viena

Viennese [vɪə'niːz] ADJ, N vienés(-esa) m/f

Vietnam, Viet Nam [vjɛt'næm] N Vietnam m

Vietnamese [vjɛtnə'miːz] ADJ vietnamita ▶ N pl inv vietnamita mf; (Ling) vietnamita m

★**view** [vjuː] N vista; (landscape) paisaje m; (opinion) opinión f, criterio; **on ~** (in museum etc) expuesto; **in full ~ of sb** a la vista de algn; **to be within ~ (of sth)** estar a la vista (de algo); **an overall ~ of the situation** una visión de conjunto de la situación; **in ~ of the fact that** en vista de que; **to take or hold the ~ that ...** opinar or pensar que ...; **with a ~ to doing sth** con miras or vistas a hacer algo ▶ VT (look at) mirar; (examine) examinar

viewdata ['vjuːdeɪtə] N videodatos mpl

★**viewer** ['vjuːəʳ] N (small projector) visionadora; (TV) televidente mf, telespectador(a) m/f

viewfinder ['vjuːfaɪndəʳ] N visor m de imagen

viewpoint ['vjuːpɔɪnt] N punto de vista

vigil ['vɪdʒɪl] N vigilia; **to keep ~** velar

vigilance ['vɪdʒɪləns] N vigilancia

vigilance committee N (US) comité m de autodefensa

vigilant ['vɪdʒɪlənt] ADJ vigilante

vigilante [vɪdʒɪ'læntɪ] N vecino/a que se toma la justicia por su mano

vigorous ['vɪɡərəs] ADJ enérgico, vigoroso

vigorously ['vɪɡərəslɪ] ADV enérgicamente, vigorosamente

vigour, (US) **vigor** ['vɪɡəʳ] N energía, vigor m

vile [vaɪl] ADJ (action) vil, infame; (smell) repugnante; (temper) endemoniado

vilify ['vɪlɪfaɪ] VT denigrar, vilipendiar

villa ['vɪlə] N (country house) casa de campo; (suburban house) chalet m

★**village** ['vɪlɪdʒ] N aldea

villager ['vɪlɪdʒəʳ] N aldeano(-a)

villain ['vɪlən] N (scoundrel) malvado(-a); (criminal) maleante mf; see also **pantomime**

VIN N ABBR (US) = **vehicle identification number**

vinaigrette [vɪneɪˈgret] N vinagreta

vindicate [ˈvɪndɪkeɪt] VT vindicar, justificar

vindication [vɪndɪˈkeɪʃən] N: **in ~ of** en justificación de

vindictive [vɪnˈdɪktɪv] ADJ vengativo

vine [vaɪn] N vid f

★**vinegar** [ˈvɪnɪgəʳ] N vinagre m

vine-growing [ˈvaɪngrəʊɪŋ] ADJ (region) viticultor(a)

vineyard [ˈvɪnjɑːd] N viña, viñedo

vintage [ˈvɪntɪdʒ] N (year) vendimia, cosecha; **the 1970 ~** la cosecha de 1970

vintage car N coche m antiguo or de época

vintage wine N vino añejo

vintage year N: **it's been a ~ for plays** ha sido un año destacado en lo que a teatro se refiere

vinyl [ˈvaɪnl] N vinilo

viola [vɪˈəʊlə] N (Mus) viola

violate [ˈvaɪəleɪt] VT violar

violation [vaɪəˈleɪʃən] N violación f; **in ~ of sth** en violación de algo

★**violence** [ˈvaɪələns] N violencia; **acts of ~** actos mpl de violencia

★**violent** [ˈvaɪələnt] ADJ (gen) violento; (pain) intenso; **a ~ dislike of sb/sth** una profunda antipatía or manía a algn/algo

violently [ˈvaɪələntlɪ] ADV (severely: ill, angry) muy

violet [ˈvaɪələt] ADJ violado, violeta inv ▶ N (plant) violeta

★**violin** [vaɪəˈlɪn] N violín m

violinist [vaɪəˈlɪnɪst] N violinista mf

VIP N ABBR (= very important person) VIP mf

viper [ˈvaɪpəʳ] N víbora

viral [ˈvaɪərəl] ADJ (Med) vírico; (Comput) viral; **~ marketing** márketing m viral; **to go ~** difundirse de forma viral

virgin [ˈvəːdʒɪn] N virgen mf; **the Blessed V~** la Santísima Virgen ▶ ADJ virgen

virginity [vəːˈdʒɪnɪtɪ] N virginidad f

Virgo [ˈvəːgəʊ] N Virgo

virile [ˈvɪraɪl] ADJ viril

virility [vɪˈrɪlɪtɪ] N virilidad f

virtual [ˈvəːtjuəl] ADJ (also Comput, Physics) virtual

virtually [ˈvəːtjuəlɪ] ADV (almost) prácticamente, virtualmente; **it is ~ impossible** es prácticamente imposible

virtual reality N (Comput) realidad f virtual

virtue [ˈvəːtjuː] N virtud f; **by ~ of** en virtud de

virtuosity [vəːtjuˈɔsɪtɪ] N virtuosismo

virtuoso [vəːtjuˈəʊsəʊ] N virtuoso

virtuous [ˈvəːtjuəs] ADJ virtuoso

virulence [ˈvɪrʊləns] N virulencia

virulent [ˈvɪrʊlənt] ADJ virulento, violento

★**virus** [ˈvaɪərəs] N virus m inv

visa [ˈviːzə] N visado, visa (LAM)

vis-à-vis [viːzəˈviː] PREP con respecto a

viscount [ˈvaɪkaunt] N vizconde m

viscous [ˈvɪskəs] ADJ viscoso

vise [vaɪs] N (US Tech) = **vice**

visibility [vɪzɪˈbɪlɪtɪ] N visibilidad f

visible [ˈvɪzəbl] ADJ visible; **~ exports/imports** exportaciones fpl/importaciones fpl visibles

visibly [ˈvɪzɪblɪ] ADV visiblemente

vision [ˈvɪʒən] N (sight) vista; (foresight, in dream) visión f

visionary [ˈvɪʒənrɪ] N visionario(-a)

★**visit** [ˈvɪzɪt] N visita; **to pay a ~ to** (person) visitar a; **on a private/official ~** en visita privada/oficial ▶ VT (person) visitar, hacer una visita a; (place) ir a, (ir a) conocer

visiting [ˈvɪzɪtɪŋ] ADJ (speaker, professor) invitado; (team) visitante

visiting card N tarjeta de visita

visiting hours NPL (in hospital etc) horas fpl de visita

★**visitor** [ˈvɪzɪtəʳ] N (gen) visitante mf; (to one's house) visita; (tourist) turista mf; (tripper) excursionista mf; **to have visitors** (at home) tener visita

visitor centre, (US) **visitor center** N centro m de información

visitors' book N libro de visitas

visor [ˈvaɪzəʳ] N visera

vista [ˈvɪstə] N vista, panorama

visual [ˈvɪzjuəl] ADJ visual

visual aid N medio visual

visual arts NPL artes fpl plásticas

visual display unit N unidad f de despliegue visual, monitor m

visualize [ˈvɪzjuəlaɪz] VT imaginarse; (foresee) prever

visually [ˈvɪzjuəlɪ] ADV: **~ handicapped** (!) con visión deficiente

★**vital** [ˈvaɪtl] ADJ (essential) esencial, imprescindible; (crucial) crítico; (person) enérgico, vivo; (organ) vital; **of ~ importance (to sb/sth)** de suma importancia (para algn/algo)

vitality [vaɪˈtælɪtɪ] N energía, vitalidad f

vitally [ˈvaɪtəlɪ] ADV: **~ important** de suma importancia

vital statistics NPL (of population) estadísticas fpl demográficas; (inf: of woman) medidas fpl (corporales)

★**vitamin** [ˈvɪtəmɪn] N vitamina

vitamin pill N pastilla de vitaminas

vitreous [ˈvɪtrɪəs] ADJ (china, enamel) vítreo

vitriolic [vɪtrɪˈɔlɪk] ADJ mordaz

viva [ˈvaɪvə] N (also: **viva voce**) examen m oral

V

851

vivacious [vɪˈveɪʃəs] ADJ vivaz, alegre
vivacity [vɪˈvæsɪtɪ] N vivacidad f
vivid [ˈvɪvɪd] ADJ (account) gráfico; (light) intenso; (imagination) vivo
vividly [ˈvɪvɪdlɪ] ADV (describe) gráficamente; (remember) como si fuera hoy
vivisection [vɪvɪˈsɛkʃən] N vivisección f
vixen [ˈvɪksn] N (Zool) zorra, raposa; (pej: woman) arpía, bruja
viz ABBR (= videlicet) v. gr.
VLF ABBR = **very low frequency**
vlog [vlɔg] N videoblog m, vlog m
vlogger [ˈvlɔgəʳ] N videobloguero(-a)
vlogging [ˈvlɔgɪŋ] N los videoblogs
V-neck [ˈviːnɛk] N cuello de pico
VOA N ABBR (= Voice of America) Voz f de América
vocabulary [vəuˈkæbjulərɪ] N vocabulario
vocal [ˈvəukl] ADJ vocal; (articulate) elocuente
vocal cords NPL cuerdas fpl vocales
vocalist [ˈvəukəlɪst] N cantante mf
vocation [vəuˈkeɪʃən] N vocación f
vocational [vəuˈkeɪʃənl] ADJ profesional; **~ guidance** orientación f profesional; **~ training** formación f profesional
vociferous [vəˈsɪfərəs] ADJ vociferante
vociferously [vəˈsɪfərəslɪ] ADV a gritos
vodka [ˈvɔdkə] N vodka m
vogue [vəug] N boga, moda; **to be in ~**, **be the ~** estar de moda or en boga
★**voice** [vɔɪs] N voz f; **in a loud/soft ~** en voz alta/baja; **to give ~ to** expresar ▸ VT (opinion) expresar
voice mail N (Tel) correo de voz, buzón m de voz
voice-over [ˈvɔɪsəuvəʳ] N voz f en off
void [vɔɪd] N vacío m; (hole) hueco ▸ ADJ (invalid) nulo, inválido; (empty): **~ of** carente or desprovisto de
voile [vɔɪl] N gasa
vol. ABBR (= volume) t
volatile [ˈvɔlətaɪl] ADJ (situation) inestable; (person) voluble; (liquid) volátil; (Comput: memory) no permanente
volcanic [vɔlˈkænɪk] ADJ volcánico
volcano [vɔlˈkeɪnəu] (pl **volcanoes**) N volcán m
volition [vəˈlɪʃən] N: **of one's own ~** por su propia voluntad
volley [ˈvɔlɪ] N (of gunfire) descarga; (of stones etc) lluvia; (Tennis etc) volea
volleyball [ˈvɔlɪbɔːl] N voleibol m, balonvolea m
volt [vəult] N voltio
voltage [ˈvəultɪdʒ] N voltaje m; **high/low ~** alto/bajo voltaje, alta/baja tensión
volte-face [ˈvɔltˈfɑːs] N viraje m
voluble [ˈvɔljubl] ADJ locuaz, hablador(a)

volume [ˈvɔljuːm] N (of tank) volumen m; (book) tomo; **~ one/two** (of book) tomo primero/segundo ■ **volumes** NPL (great quantities) cantidad fsg; **his expression spoke volumes** su expresión (lo) decía todo
volume control N (Radio, TV) (botón m del) volumen m
volume discount N (Comm) descuento por volumen de compras
voluminous [vəˈluːmɪnəs] ADJ (large) voluminoso; (prolific) prolífico
voluntarily [ˈvɔləntrɪlɪ] ADV libremente, voluntariamente
★**voluntary** [ˈvɔləntərɪ] ADJ voluntario, espontáneo
voluntary liquidation N (Comm) liquidación f voluntaria
voluntary redundancy N (BRIT) despido voluntario
★**volunteer** [vɔlənˈtɪəʳ] N voluntario(-a) ▸ VT (information) ofrecer; **to ~ to do** ofrecerse a hacer ▸ VI ofrecerse (de voluntario)
voluptuous [vəˈlʌptjuəs] ADJ voluptuoso
vomit [ˈvɔmɪt] N vómito ▸ VT, VI vomitar
voracious [vəˈreɪʃəs] ADJ voraz; (reader) ávido
★**vote** [vəut] N voto; (votes cast) votación f; (right to vote) derecho a votar; (franchise) sufragio; **~ of thanks** voto de gracias; **to put sth to the ~**, **to take a ~ on sth** someter algo a votación; **to pass a ~ of confidence/no confidence** aprobar un voto de confianza/de censura ▸ VT (chairman) elegir; **to ~ to do sth** votar por hacer algo; **he was voted secretary** fue elegido secretario por votación ▸ VI votar, ir a votar; **~ for** or **in favour of/against** voto a favor de/en contra de
voter [ˈvəutəʳ] N votante mf
voting [ˈvəutɪŋ] N votación f
voting paper N (BRIT) papeleta de votación
voting right N derecho a voto
vouch [vautʃ] N: **to ~ for** vt fus garantizar, responder de
voucher [ˈvautʃəʳ] N (for meal, petrol) vale m; **luncheon/travel ~** vale m de comida/de viaje
vow [vau] N voto; **to take** or **make a ~ to do sth** jurar hacer algo, comprometerse a hacer algo ▸ VI hacer voto ▸ VT: **to ~ to do/that** jurar hacer/que
vowel [ˈvauəl] N vocal f
voyage [ˈvɔɪɪdʒ] N (journey) viaje m; (crossing) travesía
voyeur [vwaːˈjəːʳ] N voyeur mf, mirón(-ona) m/f
VP N ABBR (= vice-president) V.P.
vs ABBR (= versus) vs.
VSO N ABBR (BRIT: = Voluntary Service Overseas) organización que envía jóvenes voluntarios a trabajar y enseñar en los países del Tercer Mundo

VT, Vt. ABBR (*US*) = **Vermont**

vulgar ['vʌlgəʳ] ADJ (*rude*) ordinario, grosero; (*in bad taste*) de mal gusto

vulgarity [vʌl'gærɪtɪ] N grosería; mal gusto

vulnerability [vʌlnərə'bɪlɪtɪ] N vulnerabilidad *f*

vulnerable ['vʌlnərəbl] ADJ vulnerable

vulture ['vʌltʃəʳ] N buitre *m*, gallinazo (*LAM*)

V

W, w [ˈdʌblju:] N (*letter*) W, w f; **W for William** W de Washington

W ABBR (= *west*) O; (*Elec*: = *watt*) v

WA ABBR (*US*) = **Washington**

wad [wɔd] N (*of cotton wool, paper*) bolita; (*of banknotes etc*) fajo

wadding [ˈwɔdɪŋ] N relleno

waddle [ˈwɔdl] VI andar como un pato

wade [weɪd] VI: **to ~ through** (*fig: a book*) leer con dificultad; **to ~ through the water** caminar por el agua

wading pool [ˈweɪdɪŋ-] N (*US*) piscina para niños

wafer [ˈweɪfəʳ] N (*biscuit*) barquillo; (*Rel*) oblea; (: *consecrated*) hostia; (*Comput*) oblea, microplaqueta

wafer-thin [ˈweɪfəˈθɪn] ADJ finísimo

waffle [ˈwɔfl] N (*Culin*) gofre m ▸ VI meter el rollo

waffle iron N molde m para hacer gofres

waft [wɔft] VT llevar por el aire ▸ VI flotar

wag [wæg] VT menear, agitar; **the dog wagged its tail** el perro meneó la cola ▸ VI moverse, menearse

★**wage** [weɪdʒ] N (*also*: **wages**) sueldo, salario; **a day's ~** el sueldo de un día ▸ VT: **to ~ war** hacer la guerra

wage claim N reivindicación f salarial

wage differential N diferencia salarial

wage earner N asalariado(-a)

wage freeze N congelación f de salarios

wage packet N sobre m de la paga

wager [ˈweɪdʒəʳ] N apuesta ▸ VT apostar

waggle [ˈwægl] VT menear, mover

wagon, waggon [ˈwægən] N (*horse-drawn*) carro; (*BRIT Rail*) vagón m

wail [weɪl] N gemido ▸ VI gemir

waist [weɪst] N cintura, talle m

waistcoat [ˈweɪstkəut] N (*BRIT*) chaleco

waistline [ˈweɪstlaɪn] N talle m

★**wait** [weɪt] N espera; (*interval*) pausa; **to lie in ~ for** acechar a ▸ VI esperar; **I can't ~ to** (*fig*) estoy deseando; **to ~ for** esperar (a); **to keep sb waiting** hacer esperar a algn; **~ a moment!** ¡un momento!, ¡un momentito!; **"repairs while you ~"** "reparaciones en el acto"
▸ **wait behind** VI quedarse
▸ **wait on** VT FUS servir a
▸ **wait up** VI esperar levantado

★**waiter** [ˈweɪtəʳ] N camarero

waiting [ˈweɪtɪŋ] N: **"no ~"** (*BRIT Aut*) "prohibido estacionar"

waiting list N lista de espera

waiting room N sala de espera

★**waitress** [ˈweɪtrɪs] N camarera

waive [weɪv] VT suspender

waiver [ˈweɪvəʳ] N renuncia

wake [weɪk] (*pt* **woke** [wəuk] *or* **waked**, *pp* **woken** [ˈwəukn] *or* **waked**) VT (*also*: **wake up**) despertar ▸ VI (*also*: **wake up**) despertarse; **to ~ up to sth** (*fig*) darse cuenta de algo ▸ N (*for dead person*) velatorio; (*Naut*) estela; **in the ~ of** tras, después de; **to follow in sb's ~** (*fig*) seguir las huellas de algn

wakeboard [ˈweɪkbɔ:d] N wakeboard m ▸ VI practicar wakeboard

waken [ˈweɪkn] VT, VI = **wake**

★**Wales** [weɪlz] N País m de Gales

La **National Assembly for Wales** (Asamblea Nacional de Gales) fue creada en 1998, cuando la mayoría del electorado galés eligió dotarse de un gobierno autónomo en un referéndum celebrado un año antes. Se diferencia del Parlamento Escocés en que mientras este tiene considerables poderes legislativos sobre los asuntos de su competencia, y también en materia fiscal, la Asamblea Nacional de Gales tiene competencias más limitadas y no puede recaudar impuestos. La Asamblea está compuesta por 60 diputados, los AMs (*Assembly Members*), que son elegidos para un mandato de cuatro años y que están bajo la autoridad del *First Minister* (Primer Ministro).

★**walk** [wɔːk] N (*stroll*) paseo; (*hike*) excursión f a pie, caminata; (*gait*) paso, andar m; (*in park etc*) paseo; **to go for a ~** ir a dar un paseo; **10 minutes' ~ from here** a 10 minutos de aquí andando; **people from all walks of life** gente de todas las esferas ▶ VI andar, caminar; (*for pleasure, exercise*) pasearse; **to ~ in one's sleep** ser sonámbulo(-a) ▶ VT (*distance*) recorrer a pie, andar; (*dog*) (sacar a) pasear; **I'll ~ you home** te acompañaré a casa
▶ **walk out** VI (*go out*) salir; (*as protest*) marcharse, salirse; (*strike*) declararse en huelga; **to ~ out on sb** abandonar a algn

walkabout [ˈwɔːkəbaut] N: **to go (on a) ~** darse un baño de multitudes

walker [ˈwɔːkəʳ] N (*person*) paseante mf, caminante mf

walkie-talkie [ˈwɔːkɪˈtɔːkɪ] N walkie-talkie m

walking [ˈwɔːkɪŋ] N (el) andar; **it's within ~ distance** se puede ir andando or a pie

walking shoes NPL zapatos mpl para andar

walking stick N bastón m

walk-on [ˈwɔːkɔn] ADJ (*Theat: part*) de comparsa

walkout [ˈwɔːkaut] N (*of workers*) huelga

walkover [ˈwɔːkəuvəʳ] N (*inf*) pan m comido

walkway [ˈwɔːkweɪ] N paseo

★**wall** [wɔːl] N pared f; (*exterior*) muro; (*city wall etc*) muralla; **to go to the ~** (*fig: firm etc*) quebrar, ir a la bancarrota
▶ **wall in** VT (*garden etc*) cercar con una tapia

walled [wɔːld] ADJ (*city*) amurallado; (*garden*) con tapia

wallet [ˈwɔlɪt] N cartera, billetera (*esp LAM*)

wallflower [ˈwɔːlflauəʳ] N alhelí m; **to be a ~** (*fig*) comer pavo

wall hanging N tapiz m

wallop [ˈwɔləp] VT (*inf*) zurrar

wallow [ˈwɔləu] VI revolcarse; **to ~ in one's grief** sumirse en su pena

wallpaper [ˈwɔːlpeɪpəʳ] N (*for walls*) papel m pintado; (*Comput*) fondo de escritorio ▶ VT empapelar

wall-to-wall [ˈwɔːltəˈwɔːl] ADJ: **~ carpeting** moqueta

wally [ˈwɔlɪ] N (*inf*) majadero(-a)

walnut [ˈwɔːlnʌt] N nuez f; (*tree*) nogal m

walrus [ˈwɔːlrəs] (*pl ~ or* **walruses**) N morsa

waltz [wɔːlts] N vals m ▶ VI bailar el vals

wan [wɔn] ADJ pálido

wand [wɔnd] N (*also:* **magic wand**) varita (mágica)

wander [ˈwɔndəʳ] VI (*person*) vagar; deambular; (*thoughts*) divagar; (*get lost*) extraviarse ▶ VT recorrer, vagar por

wanderer [ˈwɔndərəʳ] N vagabundo(-a)

wandering [ˈwɔndərɪŋ] ADJ (*tribe*) nómada; (*minstrel, actor*) ambulante; (*path, river*) sinuoso; (*glance, mind*) distraído

wane [weɪn] VI menguar

wangle [ˈwæŋgl] (*BRIT inf*) VT: **to ~ sth** agenciarse or conseguir algo ▶ N chanchullo

wanker [ˈwæŋkəʳ] N (*inf!*) pajero(-a); (*: as insult*) mamón(-ona) m/f

★**want** [wɔnt] VT (*wish for*) querer, desear; (*need*) necesitar; (*lack*) carecer de; **to ~ to do** querer hacer; **to ~ sb to do sth** querer que algn haga algo; **you're wanted on the phone** te llaman al teléfono ▶ N (*poverty*) pobreza; **for ~ of** por falta de; **to be in ~** estar necesitado ■ **wants** NPL (*needs*) necesidades fpl

want ads NPL (*US*) anuncios mpl por palabras

wanted [ˈwɔntɪd] ADJ (*criminal*) buscado; **"~"** (*in advertisements*) "se busca"

wanting [ˈwɔntɪŋ] ADJ: **to be ~ (in)** estar falto (de); **to be found ~** no estar a la altura de las circunstancias

wanton [ˈwɔntn] ADJ (*licentious*) lascivo

WAP [wæp] N ABBR (= *wireless application protocol*) WAP m

WAP phone N teléfono WAP

★**war** [wɔːʳ] N guerra; **to make ~** hacer la guerra; **the First/Second World W~** la Primera/Segunda Guerra Mundial

warble [ˈwɔːbl] N (*of bird*) trino, gorjeo ▶ VI (*bird*) trinar

war cry N grito de guerra

ward [wɔːd] N (*in hospital*) sala; (*Pol*) distrito electoral; (*Law: child: also:* **ward of court**) pupilo(-a) ▶ **ward off** VT desviar, parar; (*attack*) rechazar

warden [ˈwɔːdn] N (*BRIT: of institution*) director(a) m/f; (*of park, game reserve*) guardián(-ana) m/f; (*BRIT: also:* **traffic warden**) guardia mf

warder [ˈwɔːdəʳ] N (*BRIT*) guardián(-ana) m/f, carcelero(-a)

wardrobe [ˈwɔːdrəub] N armario, guardarropa, ropero, clóset/closet m (*LAM*)

warehouse [ˈwɛəhaus] N almacén m, depósito

wares [wɛəz] NPL mercancías fpl

warfare [ˈwɔːfɛəʳ] N guerra

war game N juego de estrategia militar

warhead [ˈwɔːhɛd] N cabeza armada; **nuclear warheads** cabezas fpl nucleares

warily [ˈwɛərɪlɪ] ADV con cautela, cautelosamente

warlike [ˈwɔːlaɪk] ADJ guerrero

★**warm** [wɔːm] ADJ caliente; (*person, greeting, heart*) afectuoso, cariñoso; (*supporter*) entusiasta; (*thanks, congratulations, apologies*) efusivo; (*clothes etc*) que abriga; (*welcome, day*) caluroso; **it's ~** hace calor; **I'm ~** tengo calor; **to keep sth ~** mantener algo caliente
▶ **warm up** VI (*room*) calentarse; (*person*) entrar en calor; (*athlete*) hacer ejercicios de calentamiento; (*discussion*) acalorarse ▶ VT calentar

warm-blooded [ˈwɔːmˈblʌdɪd] ADJ de sangre caliente

war memorial N monumento a los caídos

warm-hearted [wɔːmˈhɑːtɪd] ADJ afectuoso

W

warmly ['wɔ:mlɪ] ADV afectuosamente
warmonger ['wɔ:mʌŋɡə'] N belicista *mf*
warmongering ['wɔ:mʌŋɡrɪŋ] N belicismo
warmth [wɔ:mθ] N calor *m*
warm-up ['wɔ:mʌp] N (*Sport*) ejercicios *mpl* de calentamiento
★**warn** [wɔ:n] VT avisar, advertir; **to ~ sb not to do sth** or **against doing sth** aconsejar a algn que no haga algo
★**warning** ['wɔ:nɪŋ] N aviso, advertencia; **gale ~** (*Meteorology*) aviso de vendaval; **without (any) ~** sin aviso or avisar
warning light N luz *f* de advertencia
warning triangle N (*Aut*) triángulo señalizador
warp [wɔ:p] VI (*wood*) combarse
warpath ['wɔ:pɑ:θ] N: **to be on the ~** (*fig*) estar en pie de guerra
warped [wɔ:pt] ADJ (*wood*) alabeado; (*fig: character, sense of humour etc*) pervertido
warrant ['wɔrnt] N (*Law: to arrest*) orden *f* de detención; (*: to search*) mandamiento de registro ▸ VT (*justify, merit*) merecer
warrant officer N (*Mil*) brigada *m*; (*Naut*) contramaestre *m*
warranty ['wɔrəntɪ] N garantía; **under ~** (*Comm*) bajo garantía
warren ['wɔrən] N (*of rabbits*) madriguera; (*fig*) laberinto
warring ['wɔ:rɪŋ] ADJ (*interests etc*) opuesto; (*nations*) en guerra
warrior ['wɔrɪə'] N guerrero(-a)
Warsaw ['wɔ:sɔ:] N Varsovia
warship ['wɔ:ʃɪp] N buque *m* or barco de guerra
wart [wɔ:t] N verruga
wartime ['wɔ:taɪm] N: **in ~** en tiempos de guerra, en la guerra
wary ['wɛərɪ] ADJ cauteloso; **to be ~ about** or **of doing sth** tener cuidado con hacer algo
was [wɔz] PT of **be**
★**wash** [wɔʃ] VT lavar; (*sweep, carry: sea etc*) llevar; **he was washed overboard** fue arrastrado del barco por las olas ▸ VI lavarse ▸ N (*clothes etc*) lavado; (*bath*) baño; (*of ship*) estela; **to have a ~** lavarse
  ▸ **wash away** VT (*stain*) quitar lavando; (*river etc*) llevarse; (*fig*) limpiar
  ▸ **wash down** VT lavar
  ▸ **wash off** VT quitar lavando
  ▸ **wash up** VI (*Brit*) fregar los platos; (*US: have a wash*) lavarse
washable ['wɔʃəbl] ADJ lavable
washbasin ['wɔʃbeɪsn], (*US*) **washbowl** ['wɔʃbəul] N lavabo
washcloth ['wɔʃklɔθ] N (*US*) manopla
washer ['wɔʃə'] N (*Tech*) arandela
washing ['wɔʃɪŋ] N (*dirty*) ropa sucia; (*clean*) colada
washing line N cuerda de (colgar) la ropa

washing machine N lavadora
washing powder N (*Brit*) detergente *m* (en polvo)
Washington ['wɔʃɪŋtən] N (*city, state*) Washington *m*
★**washing-up** [wɔʃɪŋ'ʌp] N (*Brit*) fregado; (*: dishes*) platos *mpl* (para fregar); **to do the ~** fregar los platos
washing-up liquid N (*Brit*) lavavajillas *m inv*
wash leather N gamuza
wash-out ['wɔʃaut] N (*inf*) fracaso
washroom ['wɔʃrum] N servicios *mpl*
wasn't ['wɔznt] = **was not**
WASP, Wasp [wɔsp] N ABBR (*US inf*: = *White Anglo-Saxon Protestant*) sobrenombre, en general peyorativo, que se da a los americanos de origen anglosajón, acomodados y de tendencia conservadora
wasp [wɔsp] N avispa
waspish ['wɔspɪʃ] ADJ (*character*) irascible; (*comment*) mordaz, punzante
wastage ['weɪstɪdʒ] N desgaste *m*; (*loss*) pérdida; **natural ~** desgaste natural
★**waste** [weɪst] N derroche *m*, despilfarro; (*misuse*) desgaste *m*; (*of time*) pérdida; (*food*) sobras *fpl*; (*rubbish*) basura, desperdicios *mpl*; **to lay ~** devastar, arrasar; **it's a ~ of money** es tirar el dinero; **to go to ~** desperdiciarse ▸ ADJ (*material*) de desecho; (*left over*) sobrante; (*energy, heat*) desperdiciado; (*land, ground: in city*) sin construir; (*: in country*) baldío ▸ VT (*squander*) malgastar, derrochar; (*time*) perder; (*opportunity*) desperdiciar
  ■ **wastes** NPL (*area of land*) tierras *fpl* baldías
  ▸ **waste away** VI consumirse
wastebasket ['weɪstbɑ:skɪt] N (*esp US*) = **wastepaper basket**
waste disposal, waste disposal unit N (*Brit*) triturador *m* de basura
wasteful ['weɪstful] ADJ derrochador(a); (*process*) antieconómico
wastefully ['weɪstfulɪ] ADV: **to spend money ~** derrochar dinero
waste ground N (*Brit*) terreno baldío
wasteland ['weɪstlənd] N (*urban*) descampados *mpl*
wastepaper basket ['weɪstpeɪpə-] N papelera; (*Comput*) papelera de reciclaje
waste pipe N tubo de desagüe
waste products NPL (*Industry*) residuos *mpl*
waster ['weɪstə'] N (*pej*) gandul *mf*
★**watch** [wɔtʃ] N reloj *m*; (*vigil*) vigilia; (*vigilance*) vigilancia; (*Mil: guard*) centinela *m*; (*Naut: spell of duty*) guardia; **to keep a close ~ on sth/sb** vigilar algo/a algn de cerca ▸ VT (*look at*) mirar, observar; (*: match, programme*) ver; (*spy on, guard*) vigilar; (*be careful of*) cuidar, tener cuidado de; **~ how you drive/what you're doing** ten cuidado al conducir/con lo que haces ▸ VI ver, mirar; (*keep guard*) montar guardia
  ▸ **watch out** VI cuidarse, tener cuidado

watch band N (US) pulsera (de reloj)

watchdog ['wɔtʃdɔg] N perro guardián; (fig) organismo de control

watchful ['wɔtʃful] ADJ vigilante, sobre aviso

watchfully ['wɔtʃfulɪ] ADV: **to stand ~** permanecer vigilante

watchmaker ['wɔtʃmeɪkəʳ] N relojero(-a)

watchman ['wɔtʃmən] N (irreg) guardián m; (also: **night watchman**) sereno, vigilante m; (: in factory) vigilante m nocturno

watch stem N (US) cuerda

watch strap N pulsera (de reloj)

watchword ['wɔtʃwəːd] N consigna, contraseña

★**water** ['wɔːtəʳ] N agua; **I'd like a drink of ~** quisiera un vaso de agua; **in British waters** en aguas británicas; **to pass ~** orinar ▶ VT (plant) regar ▶ VI (eyes) llorar; **his mouth watered** se le hizo la boca agua
▶ **water down** VT (milk etc) aguar; (fig: story) dulcificar, diluir

waterboarding ['wɔːtəbɔːdɪŋ] N submarino

water closet N wáter m

watercolour, (US) **watercolor** ['wɔːtəkʌləʳ] N acuarela

water-cooled ['wɔːtəkuːld] ADJ refrigerado (por agua)

watercress ['wɔːtəkrɛs] N berro

waterfall ['wɔːtəfɔːl] N cascada, salto de agua

waterfront ['wɔːtəfrʌnt] N (seafront) parte f que da al mar; (at docks) muelles mpl

water heater N calentador m de agua

water hole N abrevadero

watering can ['wɔːtərɪŋ-] N regadera

water level N nivel m del agua

water lily N nenúfar m

waterline ['wɔːtəlaɪn] N (Naut) línea de flotación

waterlogged ['wɔːtəlɔgd] ADJ (boat) anegado; (ground) inundado

water main N cañería del agua

watermark ['wɔːtəmɑːk] N (on paper) filigrana

watermelon ['wɔːtəmɛlən] N sandía

water polo N waterpolo, polo acuático

waterproof ['wɔːtəpruːf] ADJ impermeable

water-repellent ['wɔːtərɪ'pɛlənt] ADJ hidrófugo

watershed ['wɔːtəʃɛd] N (Geo) cuenca; (fig) momento crítico

water-skiing ['wɔːtəskiːɪŋ] N esquí m acuático

water softener N ablandador m de agua

water tank N depósito de agua

watertight ['wɔːtətaɪt] ADJ hermético

water vapour, (US) **water vapor** N vapor m de agua

waterway ['wɔːtəweɪ] N vía fluvial or navegable

waterworks ['wɔːtəwəːks] NPL central fsg depuradora

watery ['wɔːtərɪ] ADJ (colour) desvaído; (coffee) aguado; (eyes) lloroso

watt [wɔt] N vatio

wattage ['wɔtɪdʒ] N potencia en vatios

wattle ['wɔtl] N zarzo

★**wave** [weɪv] N ola; (of hand) señal f con la mano; (Radio) onda; (in hair) onda; (fig: of enthusiasm, strikes) oleada; **short/medium/long ~** (Radio) onda corta/media/larga; **the new ~** (Cine, Mus) la nueva ola ▶ VI agitar la mano; (flag) ondear ▶ VT (handkerchief, gun) agitar; **to ~ goodbye to sb** decir adiós a algn con la mano; **he waved us over to his table** nos hizo señas (con la mano) para que nos acercásemos a su mesa
▶ **wave aside**, **wave away** VT (person): **to ~ sb aside** apartar a algn con la mano; (fig: suggestion, objection) rechazar; (doubts) desechar

waveband ['weɪvbænd] N banda de ondas

wavelength ['weɪvlɛŋθ] N longitud f de onda

waver ['weɪvəʳ] VI oscilar; (confidence) disminuir; (faith) flaquear

wavy ['weɪvɪ] ADJ ondulado

wax [wæks] N cera ▶ VT encerar ▶ VI (moon) crecer

waxen ['wæksn] ADJ (fig: pale) blanco como la cera

waxworks ['wækswəːks] NPL museo sg de cera

★**way** [weɪ] N camino; (distance) trayecto, recorrido; (direction) dirección f, sentido; (manner) modo, manera; (habit) costumbre f; **which ~? — this ~** ¿por dónde? or ¿en qué dirección? — por aquí; **on the ~** (en route) en (el) camino; (expected) en camino; **to be on one's ~** estar en camino; **you pass it on your ~ home** está de camino a tu casa; **to be in the ~** bloquear el camino; (fig) estorbar; **to keep out of sb's ~** esquivar a algn; **to make ~ (for sb/sth)** dejar paso (a algn/algo); (fig) abrir camino (a algn/algo); **to go out of one's ~ to do sth** desvivirse por hacer algo; **to lose one's ~** perderse, extraviarse; **to be the wrong ~ round** estar del or al revés; **in a ~** en cierto modo or sentido; **by the ~** a propósito; **by ~ of** (via) pasando por; (as a sort of) como, a modo de; **"~ in"** (BRIT) "entrada"; **"~ out"** (BRIT) "salida"; **the ~ back** el camino de vuelta; **the village is rather out of the ~** el pueblo está un poco apartado or retirado; **it's a long ~ away** está muy lejos; **to get one's own ~** salirse con la suya; **"give ~"** (BRIT Aut) "ceda el paso"; **no ~!** (inf) ¡ni pensarlo!; **put it the right ~ up** ponlo boca arriba; **he's in a bad ~** está grave; **to be under ~** (work, project) estar en marcha

waybill ['weɪbɪl] N (Comm) hoja de ruta, carta de porte

waylay [weɪ'leɪ] VT (irreg: like **lay**) atacar

wayside ['weɪsaɪd] N borde m del camino; **to fall by the ~** (fig) fracasar

way station N (US Rail) apeadero

W

wayward ['weɪwəd] ADJ díscolo, caprichoso

WC ['dʌblju'si:] N ABBR (BRIT: = water closet) wáter m

WCC N ABBR = **World Council of Churches**

★**we** [wi:] PRON PL nosotros(-as); **we understand** (nosotros) entendemos; **here we are** aquí estamos

★**weak** [wi:k] ADJ débil, flojo; (tea, coffee) flojo, aguado; **to grow ~(er)** debilitarse

weaken ['wi:kən] VI debilitarse; (give way) ceder ▶ VT debilitar

weak-kneed [wi:k'ni:d] ADJ (fig) sin voluntad or carácter

weakling ['wi:klɪŋ] N debilucho(-a)

weakly ['wi:klɪ] ADJ enfermizo, débil ▶ ADV débilmente

weakness ['wi:knɪs] N debilidad f; (fault) punto débil; **to have a ~ for** tener debilidad por

wealth [wɛlθ] N (money, resources) riqueza; (of details) abundancia

wealth tax N impuesto sobre el patrimonio

wealthy ['wɛlθɪ] ADJ rico

wean [wi:n] VT destetar

★**weapon** ['wɛpən] N arma; **weapons of mass destruction** armas de destrucción masiva

★**wear** [wɛəʳ] (pt **wore** [wɔːʳ], pp **worn** [wɔːn]) N (use) uso; (deterioration through use) desgaste m; (clothing): **casual ~** ropa de sport; **evening ~** (man's) traje m de etiqueta; (woman's) traje m de noche ▶ VT (clothes, beard) llevar; (shoes) calzar; (look, smile) tener; (damage: through use) gastar, usar; **to ~ a hole in sth** hacer un agujero en algo ▶ VI (last) durar; (rub through etc) desgastarse
 ▶ **wear away** VT gastar ▶ VI desgastarse
 ▶ **wear down** VT gastar; (strength) agotar
 ▶ **wear off** VI (pain, excitement etc) pasar, desaparecer
 ▶ **wear out** VT desgastar; (person, strength) agotar

wearable ['wɛərəbl] ADJ que se puede llevar, ponible

wear and tear N desgaste m

wearer ['wɛərəʳ] N: **the ~ of this jacket** el/la que lleva puesta esta chaqueta

wearily ['wɪərɪlɪ] ADV con cansancio

weariness ['wɪərɪnɪs] N cansancio; abatimiento

wearisome ['wɪərɪsəm] ADJ (tiring) cansado, pesado; (boring) aburrido

weary ['wɪərɪ] ADJ (tired) cansado; (dispirited) abatido ▶ VT cansar ▶ VI: **to ~ of** cansarse de, aburrirse de

weasel ['wi:zl] N (Zool) comadreja

★**weather** ['wɛðəʳ] N tiempo; **under the ~** (fig: ill) mal, pachucho; **what's the ~ like?** ¿qué tiempo hace?, ¿cómo hace? ▶ VT (storm, crisis) hacer frente a

weather-beaten ['wɛðəbi:tn] ADJ curtido

weathercock ['wɛðəkɔk] N veleta

★**weather forecast** N boletín m meteorológico

weatherman ['wɛðəmæn] N (irreg) hombre m del tiempo

weatherproof ['wɛðəpru:f] ADJ (garment) impermeable

weather report N parte m meteorológico

weather vane N = **weathercock**

weave [wi:v] (pt **wove** [wəuv], pp **woven** ['wəuvn]) VT (cloth) tejer; (fig) entretejer ▶ VI (pt, pp **weaved**) (fig: move in and out) zigzaguear

weaver ['wi:vəʳ] N tejedor(a) m/f

weaving ['wi:vɪŋ] N tejeduría

web [wɛb] N (of spider) telaraña; (on foot) membrana; (Comput: network) red f; **the W~** la Red

web address N dirección f de página web

webbed [wɛbd] ADJ (foot) palmeado

webbing ['wɛbɪŋ] N (on chair) cinchas fpl

★**webcam** ['wɛbkæm] N webcam f

webinar ['wɛbmɑːʳ] N (Comput) seminario web, webinar m

weblog ['wɛblɔg] N weblog m

webmail ['wɛbmeɪl] N (Comput) correo web, webmail m

web page N página web

★**website** ['wɛbsaɪt] N sitio web

wed [wɛd] (pt, pp **wedded** ['wɛdɪd]) VT casar ▶ VI casarse ▶ N: **the newly-weds** los recién casados

Wed. ABBR (= Wednesday) miérc.

we'd [wi:d] = **we had**; **we would**

wedded ['wɛdɪd] PT, PP of **wed**

★**wedding** ['wɛdɪŋ] N boda, casamiento

wedding anniversary N aniversario de boda; **silver/golden ~** bodas fpl de plata/de oro

wedding day N día m de la boda

wedding dress N traje m de novia

wedding present N regalo de boda

wedding ring N alianza

wedge [wɛdʒ] N (of wood etc) cuña; (of cake) trozo ▶ VT acuñar; (push) apretar

wedge-heeled ['wɛdʒ'hi:ld] ADJ con suela de cuña

wedlock ['wɛdlɔk] N matrimonio

★**Wednesday** ['wɛdnzdɪ] N miércoles m inv; see also **Tuesday**

wee [wi:] ADJ (SCOTTISH) pequeñito

weed [wi:d] N mala hierba, maleza ▶ VT escardar, desherbar
 ▶ **weed out** VT eliminar

weedkiller ['wi:dkɪləʳ] N herbicida m

weedy ['wi:dɪ] ADJ (person) debilucho

★**week** [wi:k] N semana; **a ~ today** de hoy en ocho días; **Tuesday ~, a ~ on Tuesday** del martes en una semana; **once/twice a ~** una vez/dos veces a la semana; **this ~** esta semana; **in two weeks' time** dentro de dos semanas; **every other ~** cada dos semanas

weekday ['wi:kdeɪ] N día m laborable; **on weekdays** entre semana, en días laborables

★**weekend** [wi:k'ɛnd] N fin m de semana

weekend case N neceser m

weekly ['wi:klɪ] ADV semanalmente, cada semana ▶ ADJ semanal; **~ newspaper** semanario ▶ N semanario

weep [wi:p] (pt, pp **wept** [wɛpt]) VI, VT llorar; (Med: wound etc) supurar

weeping willow ['wi:pɪŋ-] N sauce m llorón

weepy ['wi:pɪ] N (inf: film) película lacrimógena; (: story) historia lacrimógena

weft [wɛft] N (Textiles) trama

★**weigh** [weɪ] VT, VI pesar; **to ~ anchor** levar anclas; **to ~ the pros and cons** pesar los pros y los contras
▶ **weigh down** VT sobrecargar; (fig: with worry) agobiar
▶ **weigh out** VT (goods) pesar
▶ **weigh up** VT sopesar

weighbridge ['weɪbrɪdʒ] N báscula para camiones

weighing machine ['weɪɪŋ-] N báscula, peso

★**weight** [weɪt] N peso; (on scale) pesa; **to lose/ put on ~** adelgazar/engordar; **weights and measures** pesas fpl y medidas

weighting ['weɪtɪŋ] N (allowance): **(London) ~** dietas (por residir en Londres)

weightlessness ['weɪtlɪsnɪs] N ingravidez f

weight lifter N levantador(a) m/f de pesas

weightlifting ['weɪtlɪftɪŋ] N levantamiento de pesas

weight limit N límite m de peso

weight training N musculación f (con pesas)

weighty ['weɪtɪ] ADJ pesado

weir [wɪər] N presa

weird [wɪəd] ADJ raro, extraño

weirdo ['wɪədəu] N (inf) tío(-a) raro(-a)

★**welcome** ['wɛlkəm] ADJ bienvenido; **to make sb ~** recibir or acoger bien a algn; **thank you — you're ~** gracias — de nada; **you're ~ to try** puede intentar cuando quiera ▶ N bienvenida ▶ VT dar la bienvenida a; (be glad of) alegrarse de; **we ~ this step** celebramos esta medida

weld [wɛld] N soldadura ▶ VT soldar

welding ['wɛldɪŋ] N soldadura

welfare ['wɛlfɛər] N bienestar m; (social aid) asistencia social; **W~** (US) subsidio de paro; **to look after sb's ~** cuidar del bienestar de algn

welfare state N estado del bienestar

welfare work N asistencia social

★**well** [wɛl] N pozo ▶ ADV bien; **as ~** (in addition) además, también; **as ~ as** además de; **you might as ~ tell me** más vale que me lo digas; **it would be as ~ to ask** más valdría preguntar; **~ done!** ¡bien hecho!; **to do ~** (business) ir bien; **I did ~ in my exams** me han salido bien los exámenes; **they are doing ~ now** les va bien ahora; **to think ~ of sb** pensar bien de algn; **I don't feel ~** no me encuentro or siento bien

▶ ADJ: **to be ~** estar bien (de salud); **get ~ soon!** ¡que te mejores pronto! ▶ EXCL ¡vaya!, ¡bueno!; **~, as I was saying ...** bueno, como decía ...
▶ **well up** VI brotar

we'll [wi:l] = **we will; we shall**

well-behaved ['wɛlbɪ'heɪvd] ADJ: **to be ~** portarse bien

well-being ['wɛl'bi:ɪŋ] N bienestar m

well-bred ['wɛl'brɛd] ADJ bien educado

well-built ['wɛl'bɪlt] ADJ (person) fornido

well-chosen ['wɛl'tʃəuzn] ADJ (remarks, words) acertado

well-deserved ['wɛldɪ'zə:vd] ADJ merecido

well-developed ['wɛldɪ'vɛləpt] ADJ (arm, muscle etc) bien desarrollado; (sense) agudo, fino

well-disposed ['wɛldɪs'pəuzd] ADJ: **~ to(wards)** bien dispuesto a

well-dressed ['wɛl'drɛst] ADJ bien vestido

well-earned ['wɛl'ə:nd] ADJ (rest) merecido

well-groomed ['wɛl'gru:md] ADJ de apariencia cuidada

well-heeled ['wɛl'hi:ld] ADJ (inf: wealthy) rico

wellies ['wɛlɪz] NPL (BRIT inf) botas de goma

well-informed ['wɛlɪn'fɔ:md] ADJ (having knowledge of sth) enterado, al corriente

Wellington ['wɛlɪŋtən] N Wellington m

wellingtons ['wɛlɪŋtənz] NPL (also: **Wellington boots**) botas fpl de goma

well-kept ['wɛl'kɛpt] ADJ (secret) bien guardado; (hair, hands, house, grounds) bien cuidado

★**well-known** ['wɛl'nəun] ADJ (person) conocido

well-mannered ['wɛl'mænəd] ADJ educado

well-meaning ['wɛl'mi:nɪŋ] ADJ bienintencionado

well-nigh ['wɛl'naɪ] ADV: **~ impossible** casi imposible

well-off ['wɛl'ɔf] ADJ acomodado

well-paid [wɛl'peɪd] ADJ bien pagado, bien retribuido

well-read ['wɛl'rɛd] ADJ culto

well-spoken ['wɛl'spəukən] ADJ bienhablado

well-stocked ['wɛl'stɔkt] ADJ (shop, larder) bien surtido

well-timed ['wɛl'taɪmd] ADJ oportuno

well-to-do ['wɛltə'du:] ADJ acomodado

well-wisher ['wɛlwɪʃər] N admirador(a) m/f

well-woman clinic ['wɛlwumən-] N centro de prevención médica para mujeres

★**Welsh** [wɛlʃ] ADJ galés(-esa); **the ~ Assembly** el Parlamento galés ▶ N (Ling) galés m ■ **the Welsh** NPL los galeses

★**Welshman** ['wɛlʃmən] N (irreg) galés m

Welsh rarebit [-'rɛəbɪt] N pan m con queso tostado

★**Welshwoman** ['wɛlʃwumən] N (irreg) galesa

welter ['wɛltər] N mescolanza, revoltijo

went [wɛnt] PT of **go**

W

wept [wɛpt] PT, PP of **weep**

were [wəːʳ] PT of **be**

we're [wɪəʳ] = **we are**

weren't [wəːnt] = **were not**

werewolf ['wɪəwulf] (pl **werewolves** [-wulvz]) N hombre m lobo

★**west** [wɛst] N oeste m; **the W~** Occidente m ▶ ADJ occidental, del oeste ▶ ADV al or hacia el oeste

westbound ['wɛstbaund] ADJ (traffic, carriageway) en dirección al oeste

West Country N: **the ~** el suroeste de Inglaterra

westerly ['wɛstəlɪ] ADJ (wind) del oeste

★**western** ['wɛstən] ADJ occidental ▶ N (Cine) película del oeste

westerner ['wɛstənəʳ] N (Pol) occidental mf

westernized ['wɛstənaɪzd] ADJ occidentalizado

West German (formerly) ADJ de Alemania Occidental ▶ N alemán(-ana) m/f (de Alemania Occidental)

West Germany N (formerly) Alemania Occidental

West Indian ADJ, N antillano(-a) m/f

West Indies [-ˈɪndɪz] NPL: **the ~** las Antillas

Westminster ['wɛstmɪnstəʳ] N el parlamento británico, Westminster m

westward ['wɛstwəd], **westwards** ['wɛstwədz] ADV hacia el oeste

★**wet** [wɛt] ADJ (damp) húmedo; (wet through) mojado; (rainy) lluvioso; **to get ~** mojarse; **"~ paint"** "recién pintado" ▶ VT: **to ~ one's pants** or **o.s.** mearse

wet blanket N: **to be a ~** (fig) ser un (una) aguafiestas

wetness ['wɛtnɪs] N humedad f

wet rot N putrefacción f por humedad

wetsuit ['wɛtsuːt] N traje m de buzo

we've [wiːv] = **we have**

whack [wæk] VT dar un buen golpe a

whale [weɪl] N (Zool) ballena

whaler ['weɪləʳ] N (ship) ballenero

whaling ['weɪlɪŋ] N pesca de ballenas

wharf [wɔːf] (pl **wharves** [wɔːvz]) N muelle m

---

what [wɔt]

ADJ **1** (in direct/indirect questions) qué; **what size is he?** ¿qué talla usa?; **what colour/shape is it?** ¿de qué color/forma es?; **what books do you need?** ¿qué libros necesitas?

2 (in exclamations): **what a mess!** ¡qué desastre!; **what a fool I am!** ¡qué tonto soy!

▶ PRON **1** (interrogative) qué; **what are you doing?** ¿qué haces or estás haciendo?; **what is happening?** ¿qué pasa or está pasando?; **what is it called?** ¿cómo se llama?; **what about me?** ¿y yo qué?; **what about doing …?** ¿qué tal si hacemos …?; **what is his address?**

¿cuáles son sus señas?; **what will it cost?** ¿cuánto costará?

2 (relative) lo que; **I saw what you did/was on the table** vi lo que hiciste/había en la mesa; **what I want is a cup of tea** lo que quiero es una taza de té; **I don't know what to do** no sé qué hacer; **tell me what you're thinking about** dime en qué estás pensando

3 (reported questions): **she asked me what I wanted** me preguntó qué quería

▶ EXCL (disbelieving) ¡cómo!; **what, no coffee!** ¡que no hay café!

whatever [wɔtˈɛvəʳ] ADJ: **~ book you choose** cualquier libro que elijas ▶ PRON: **do ~ is necessary** haga lo que sea necesario; **~ it costs** cueste lo que cueste ▶ ADV: **no reason ~** ninguna razón en absoluto; **nothing ~** nada en absoluto

whatsoever [wɔtsəuˈɛvəʳ] ADJ see **whatever**

wheat [wiːt] N trigo

wheatgerm ['wiːtdʒəːm] N germen m de trigo

wheatmeal ['wiːtmiːl] N harina de trigo

wheedle ['wiːdl] VT: **to ~ sb into doing sth** engatusar a algn para que haga algo; **to ~ sth out of sb** sonsacar algo a algn

★**wheel** [wiːl] N rueda; (Aut: also: **steering wheel**) volante m; (Naut) timón m ▶ VT (pram etc) empujar ▶ VI (also: **wheel round**) dar la vuelta, girar

wheelbarrow ['wiːlbærəu] N carretilla

wheelbase ['wiːlbeɪs] N batalla

wheelchair ['wiːltʃɛəʳ] N silla de ruedas

wheel clamp N (Aut) cepo

wheeler-dealer ['wiːləˈdiːləʳ] N chanchullero(-a)

wheelie-bin ['wiːlɪbɪn] N (BRIT) contenedor m de basura

wheeling ['wiːlɪŋ] N: **~ and dealing** (pej) chanchullos mpl

wheeze [wiːz] VI resollar

wheezy ['wiːzɪ] ADJ silbante

---

when [wɛn]

ADV cuándo; **when did it happen?** ¿cuándo ocurrió?; **I know when it happened** sé cuándo ocurrió

▶ CONJ **1** (at, during, after the time that) cuando; **be careful when you cross the road** ten cuidado al cruzar la calle; **that was when I needed you** entonces era cuando te necesitaba; **I'll buy you a car when you're 18** te compraré un coche cuando cumplas 18 años

2 (on, at which): **on the day when I met him** el día en que le conocí

3 (whereas) cuando; **you said I was wrong when in fact I was right** dijiste que no tenía razón, cuando en realidad sí la tenía

---

whenever [wɛnˈɛvəʳ] CONJ cuando; (every time) cada vez que; **I go ~ I can** voy siempre or todas las veces que puedo

★**where** [wɛə^r] ADV dónde; **this is ~** aquí es donde; **~ are you from?** ¿de dónde es usted? ▶ CONJ donde; **~ possible** donde sea posible

---

where can be translated by **dónde** or **donde**. Use **dónde** to ask about the location of something or someone: *Where's your mum?* **¿Dónde está tu madre?**
Use **donde** to refer to where something or someone is: *The keys are where you left them.* **Las llaves están donde las dejaste**.

---

whereabouts ['wɛərəbauts] ADV dónde ▶ N: **nobody knows his ~** nadie conoce su paradero

whereas [wɛər'æz] CONJ mientras

whereby [wɛə'baɪ] ADV mediante el (la) cual *etc*, por lo (la) cual *etc*

whereupon [wɛərə'pɒn] CONJ con lo cual, después de lo cual

wherever [wɛər'ɛvə^r] ADV dondequiera que; (*interrogative*) dónde; **sit ~ you like** siéntese donde quiera

wherewithal ['wɛəwɪðɔːl] N recursos *mpl*; **the ~ (to do sth)** los medios económicos (para hacer algo)

whet [wɛt] VT estimular; (*appetite*) abrir

★**whether** ['wɛðə^r] CONJ si; **I don't know ~ to accept or not** no sé si aceptar o no; **~ you go or not** vayas o no vayas

whey [weɪ] N suero

---

which [wɪtʃ]

ADJ **1** (*interrogative: direct, indirect*) qué; **which picture(s) do you want?** ¿qué cuadro(s) quieres?; **which one?** ¿cuál?; **which one of you?** ¿cuál de vosotros?; **tell me which one you want** dime cuál (es el que) quieres

2: **in which case** en cuyo caso; **we got there at eight pm, by which time the cinema was full** llegamos allí a las ocho, cuando el cine estaba lleno

▶ PRON **1** (*interrogative*) cuál; **I don't mind which** el (la) que sea; **which do you want?** ¿cuál quieres?

2 (*relative: replacing noun*) que; (: *replacing clause*) lo que; (: *after preposition*) (el (la)) que, el (la) cual; **the apple which you ate/which is on the table** la manzana que comiste/que está en la mesa; **the chair on which you are sitting** la silla en la que estás sentado; **he didn't believe it, which upset me** no se lo creyó, lo cual *or* lo que me disgustó; **after which** después de lo cual

---

whichever [wɪtʃ'ɛvə^r] ADJ: **take ~ book you prefer** coja el libro que prefiera; **~ book you take** cualquier libro que coja

whiff [wɪf] N bocanada; **to catch a ~ of sth** oler algo

★**while** [waɪl] N rato, momento; **for a ~** durante algún tiempo; **in a ~** dentro de poco; **all the ~** todo el tiempo; **we'll make it worth your ~** te compensaremos generosamente ▶ CONJ

durante; (*whereas*) mientras; (*although*) aunque ▶ VT: **to ~ away the time** pasar el rato

whilst [waɪlst] CONJ = **while**

whim [wɪm] N capricho

whimper ['wɪmpə^r] N (*weeping*) lloriqueo; (*moan*) quejido ▶ VI lloriquear; quejarse

whimsical ['wɪmzɪkl] ADJ (*person*) caprichoso

whine [waɪn] N (*of pain*) gemido; (*of engine*) zumbido ▶ VI gemir; zumbar; (*fig: complain*) gimotear

★**whip** [wɪp] N látigo; (*BRIT Pol*) diputado encargado de la disciplina del partido en el parlamento ▶ VT azotar; (*snatch*) arrebatar; (*US Culin*) batir ▶ **whip up** VT (*cream etc*) batir (rápidamente); (*inf: meal*) preparar rápidamente; (: *stir up: support, feeling*) avivar

whiplash ['wɪplæʃ] N (*Med: also:* **whiplash injury**) latigazo

whipped cream [wɪpt-] N nata montada

whipping boy ['wɪpɪŋ-] N (*fig*) cabeza de turco

whip-round ['wɪpraund] N (*BRIT*) colecta

whirl [wəːl] N remolino ▶ VT hacer girar, dar vueltas a ▶ VI (*dancers*) girar, dar vueltas; (*leaves, dust, water etc*) arremolinarse

whirlpool ['wəːlpuːl] N remolino

whirlwind ['wəːlwɪnd] N torbellino

whirr [wəː^r] VI zumbar

whisk [wɪsk] N (*BRIT Culin*) batidor *m* ▶ VT (*BRIT Culin*) batir; **to ~ sb away** *or* **off** llevarse volando a algn

whiskers ['wɪskəz] NPL (*of animal*) bigotes *mpl*; (*of man*) patillas *fpl*

whisky, (*US, IRELAND*) **whiskey** ['wɪskɪ] N whisky *m*

★**whisper** ['wɪspə^r] N cuchicheo; (*rumour*) rumor *m*; (*fig*) susurro, murmullo ▶ VI cuchichear, hablar bajo; (*fig*) susurrar ▶ VT susurrar; **to ~ sth to sb** decirle algo al oído a algn

whispering ['wɪspərɪŋ] N cuchicheo

whist [wɪst] N (*BRIT*) whist *m*

whistle ['wɪsl] N (*sound*) silbido; (*object*) silbato ▶ VT, VI silbar; **to ~ (a tune)** silbar (una melodía)

whistleblower ['wɪslbləuə^r] N denunciante *mf*

whistleblowing ['wɪslbləuɪŋ] N denuncias *fpl*

whistle-stop ['wɪslstɒp] ADJ: **~ tour** (*US Pol*) gira electoral rápida; (*fig*) recorrido rápido

Whit [wɪt] N Pentecostés *m*

★**white** [waɪt] ADJ blanco; (*pale*) pálido; **to turn** *or* **go ~** (*person*) palidecer, ponerse blanco; (*hair*) encanecer ▶ N blanco; (*of egg*) clara; **the whites** (*washing*) la ropa blanca; **tennis whites** ropa *f* de tenis

whitebait ['waɪtbeɪt] N chanquetes *mpl*

whiteboard ['waɪtbɔːd] N pizarra blanca; **interactive ~** pizarra interactiva

white coffee N (*BRIT*) café *m* con leche

W

white-collar worker [ˈwaɪtkɔlə-] N oficinista *mf*

white elephant N (*fig*) maula

white goods NPL (*appliances*) electrodomésticos *mpl* de línea blanca; (*linen etc*) ropa blanca

white-hot [waɪtˈhɔt] ADJ (*metal*) candente, calentado al (rojo) blanco

White House N (*US*) Casa Blanca

white lie N mentirijilla

whiteness [ˈwaɪtnɪs] N blancura

white noise N sonido blanco

whiteout [ˈwaɪtaut] N resplandor *m* sin sombras; (*fig*) masa confusa

white paper N (*Pol*) libro blanco

whitewash [ˈwaɪtwɔʃ] N (*paint*) cal *f*, jalbegue *m* ▶ VT encalar, blanquear; (*fig*) encubrir

whiting [ˈwaɪtɪŋ] N *pl inv* (*fish*) pescadilla

Whit Monday N lunes *m* de Pentecostés

Whitsun [ˈwɪtsn] N (*BRIT*) Pentecostés *m*

whittle [ˈwɪtl] VT: **to ~ away**, **~ down** ir reduciendo

whizz [wɪz] VI: **to ~ past** *or* **by** pasar a toda velocidad

whizz kid N (*inf*) prodigio(-a)

WHO N ABBR (= *World Health Organization*) OMS *f*

---

who [huː]

PRON **1** (*interrogative*) quién; **who is it?**, **who's there?** ¿quién es?; **who are you looking for?** ¿a quién buscas?; **I told her who I was** le dije quién era yo

2 (*relative*) que; **the man/woman who spoke to me** el hombre/la mujer que habló conmigo; **those who can swim** los que saben *or* sepan nadar

---

whodunit, whodunnit [huːˈdʌnɪt] N (*inf*) novela policíaca

whoever [huːˈɛvəʳ] PRON: **~ finds it** cualquiera *or* quienquiera que lo encuentre; **ask ~ you like** pregunta a quien quieras; **~ he marries** se case con quien se case

★**whole** [həul] ADJ (*complete*) todo, entero; (*not broken*) intacto; **~ villages were destroyed** pueblos enteros fueron destruidos ▶ N (*total*) total *m*; (*sum*) conjunto; **the ~ of the town** toda la ciudad, la ciudad entera; **on the ~**, **as a ~** en general

wholefood [ˈhəulfuːd] N, **wholefoods** [ˈhəulfuːdz] NPL alimento(s) *m(pl)* integral(es)

wholehearted [həulˈhɑːtɪd] ADJ (*support, approval*) total; (*sympathy*) todo

wholeheartedly [həulˈhɑːtɪdlɪ] ADV con entusiasmo

wholemeal [ˈhəulmiːl] ADJ (*BRIT: flour, bread*) integral

wholesale [ˈhəulseɪl] N venta al por mayor ▶ ADJ al por mayor; (*destruction*) sistemático

wholesaler [ˈhəulseɪləʳ] N mayorista *mf*

wholesome [ˈhəulsəm] ADJ sano

wholewheat [ˈhəulwiːt] ADJ = **wholemeal**

wholly [ˈhəulɪ] ADV totalmente, enteramente

---

whom [huːm]

PRON **1** (*interrogative*): **whom did you see?** ¿a quién viste?; **to whom did you give it?** ¿a quién se lo diste?; **tell me from whom you received it** dígame de quién lo recibió

2 (*relative*) que; **to whom** a quien(es); **of whom** de quien(es), del/de la que; **the man whom I saw** el hombre que vi; **the man to whom I wrote** el hombre a quien escribí; **the lady about whom I was talking** la señora de (la) que hablaba; **the lady with whom I was talking** la señora con quien *or* (la) que hablaba

---

whooping cough [ˈhuːpɪŋ-] N tos *f* ferina

whoops [wuːps] EXCL (*also:* **whoops-a-daisy!**) ¡huy!

whoosh [wuʃ] N: **it came out with a ~** (*sauce etc*) salió todo de repente; (*air*) salió con mucho ruido

whopper [ˈwɔpəʳ] N (*inf: lie*) embuste *m*; (*large thing*): **a ~** uno(-a) enorme

whopping [ˈwɔpɪŋ] ADJ (*inf*) enorme

whore [hɔːʳ] N (*!*) puta (*!*)

---

whose [huːz]

ADJ **1** (*possessive: interrogative*) de quién; **whose book is this?**, **whose is this book?** ¿de quién es este libro?; **whose pencil have you taken?** ¿de quién es el lápiz que has cogido?; **whose daughter are you?** ¿de quién eres hija?

2 (*possessive: relative*) cuyo(-a) *m/f*, cuyos(-as) *mpl/fpl*; **the man whose son they rescued** el hombre cuyo hijo rescataron; **the girl whose sister he was speaking to** la chica con cuya hermana estaba hablando; **those whose passports I have** aquellas personas cuyos pasaportes tengo; **the woman whose car was stolen** la mujer a quien le robaron el coche

▶ PRON de quién; **whose is this?** ¿de quién es esto?; **I know whose it is** sé de quién es

---

why [waɪ]

ADV por qué; **why not?** ¿por qué no?; **why not do it now?** ¿por qué no lo haces (*or* hacemos) ahora?

▶ CONJ: **I wonder why he said that** me pregunto por qué dijo eso; **that's not why I'm here** no es por eso (por lo) que estoy aquí; **the reason why** la razón por la que

▶ EXCL (*expressing surprise, shock, annoyance*) ¡hombre!, ¡vaya!; (*explaining*): **why, it's you!** ¡hombre, eres tú!; **why, that's impossible** ¡pero si eso es imposible!

When *why* is used in questions it is translated by **por qué**: *Why didn't you come to the party?* **¿Por qué no viniste a la fiesta?**
When **porque** is written as one word and with no accent, it means *because: I didn't go because I wasn't feeling well.* **No fui porque no me sentía bien**.

whyever [waɪˈɛvəʳ] ADV por qué

WI N ABBR (*BRIT*: = *Women's Institute*) *asociación de amas de casa* ▸ ABBR (*Geo*) = **West Indies**; (*US*) = **Wisconsin**

wick [wɪk] N mecha

★**wicked** [ˈwɪkɪd] ADJ malvado, cruel

wickedness [ˈwɪkɪdnɪs] N maldad *f*, crueldad *f*

wicker [ˈwɪkəʳ] N mimbre *m*

wickerwork [ˈwɪkəwəːk] N artículos *mpl* de mimbre

wicket [ˈwɪkɪt] N (*Cricket*) palos *mpl*

wicket keeper N guardameta *m*

★**wide** [waɪd] ADJ ancho; (*area, knowledge*) vasto, grande; (*choice*) amplio; **it is three metres ~** tiene tres metros de ancho; **to open ~** abrir de par en par; **to shoot ~** errar el tiro

wide-angle lens [ˈwaɪdæŋgl-] N (objetivo) gran angular *m*

wide-awake [waɪdəˈweɪk] ADJ bien despierto

wide-eyed [waɪdˈaɪd] ADJ con los ojos muy abiertos; (*fig*) ingenuo

widely [ˈwaɪdlɪ] ADV (*differing*) muy; **it is ~ believed that ...** existe la creencia generalizada de que ...; **to be ~ read** (*author*) ser muy leído; (*reader*) haber leído mucho

widen [ˈwaɪdn] VT ensanchar; (*experience*) ampliar ▸ VI ensancharse

wideness [ˈwaɪdnɪs] N anchura; amplitud *f*

wide open ADJ abierto de par en par

wide-ranging [waɪdˈreɪndʒɪŋ] ADJ (*survey, report*) de gran alcance; (*interests*) muy diversos

widespread [ˈwaɪdsprɛd] ADJ (*belief etc*) extendido, general

widget [ˈwɪdʒɪt] N (*Comput*) mini aplicación *f*, widget *m*

widow [ˈwɪdəu] N viuda

widowed [ˈwɪdəud] ADJ viudo

widower [ˈwɪdəuəʳ] N viudo

width [wɪdθ] N anchura; (*of cloth*) ancho; **it's seven metres in ~** tiene siete metros de ancho

widthways [ˈwɪdθweɪz] ADV a lo ancho

wield [wiːld] VT (*sword*) blandir; (*power*) ejercer

★**wife** [waɪf] (*pl* **wives** [waɪvz]) N mujer *f*, esposa

Wi-Fi [ˈwaɪfaɪ] N ABBR (= *wireless fidelity*) wi-fi *m* ▸ ADJ (*hot spot, network etc*) wi-fi

wig [wɪg] N peluca

wigging [ˈwɪgɪŋ] N (*BRIT inf*) rapapolvo, bronca

wiggle [ˈwɪgl] VT menear ▸ VI menearse

wiggly [ˈwɪglɪ] ADJ (*line*) ondulado

wigwam [ˈwɪgwæm] N tipi *m*, tienda india

wiki [ˈwɪkiː] N (*Comput*) wiki *f*

★**wild** [waɪld] ADJ (*animal*) salvaje; (*plant*) silvestre; (*idea*) descabellado; (*rough: sea*) bravo; (: *land*) agreste; (: *weather*) muy revuelto; (*inf: angry*) furioso; **to be ~ about** (*enthusiastic*) estar *or* andar loco por; **in its ~ state** en estado salvaje ▸ N: **the ~** la naturaleza ■ **wilds** NPL regiones *fpl* salvajes, tierras *fpl* vírgenes

wild card N (*Comput*) comodín *m*

wildcat [ˈwaɪldkæt] N gato montés

wildcat strike N huelga salvaje

wilderness [ˈwɪldənɪs] N desierto; (*jungle*) jungla

wildfire [ˈwaɪldfaɪəʳ] N: **to spread like ~** correr como un reguero de pólvora

wild-goose chase [waɪldˈguːs-] N (*fig*) búsqueda inútil

wildlife [ˈwaɪldlaɪf] N fauna

wildly [ˈwaɪldlɪ] ADV (*roughly*) violentamente; (*foolishly*) locamente; (*rashly*) descabelladamente; (*lash out*) a diestro y siniestro; (*guess*) a lo loco; (*happy*) a más no poder

wiles [waɪlz] NPL artimañas *fpl*, ardides *mpl*

wilful, (*US*) **willful** [ˈwɪlful] ADJ (*action*) deliberado; (*obstinate*) testarudo

---

will [wɪl]

AUX VB **1** (*forming future tense*): **I will finish it tomorrow** lo terminaré *or* voy a terminar mañana; **I will have finished it by tomorrow** lo habré terminado para mañana; **will you do it? — yes I will/no I won't** ¿lo harás? — sí/no; **you won't lose it, will you?** no lo vayas a perder *or* no lo perderás ¿verdad?

2 (*in conjectures: predictions*): **he will** *or* **he'll be there by now** ya habrá llegado, ya debe (de) haber llegado; **that will be the postman** será el cartero, debe ser el cartero

3 (*in commands, requests, offers*): **will you be quiet!** ¿quieres callarte?; **will you help me?** ¿quieres ayudarme?; **will you have a cup of tea?** ¿te apetece un té?; **I won't put up with it!** ¡no lo soporto!

4 (*habits, persistence*): **the car won't start** el coche no arranca; **accidents will happen** son cosas que pasan

▸ VT (*pt, pp willed*): **to will sb to do sth** desear que algn haga algo; **he willed himself to go on** con gran fuerza de voluntad, continuó

▸ N **1** (*desire*) voluntad *f*; **against sb's will** contra la voluntad de algn; **he did it of his own free will** lo hizo por su propia voluntad

2 (*Law*) testamento; **to make a** *or* **one's will** hacer su testamento

W

will is often translated by the present tense: Will you help me? **¿Me ayudas?**
Use **voy a, va a**, etc followed by the infinitive to talk about plans and intentions: We'll be having lunch late. **Vamos a comer tarde**.
Use the future tense when talking about what will happen: How long will it take? **¿Cúanto tiempo llevará?**

willful ['wɪfʊl] ADJ (US) = **wilful**

★**willing** ['wɪlɪŋ] ADJ (with goodwill) de buena voluntad; (enthusiastic) entusiasta; **he's ~ to do it** está dispuesto a hacerlo; **to show ~** mostrarse dispuesto

willingly ['wɪlɪŋlɪ] ADV con mucho gusto

willingness ['wɪlɪŋnɪs] N buena voluntad

will-o'-the-wisp ['wɪləðə'wɪsp] N fuego fatuo; (fig) quimera

willow ['wɪləu] N sauce m

willpower ['wɪlpauə'] N fuerza de voluntad

willy-nilly [wɪlɪ'nɪlɪ] ADV quiérase o no

wilt [wɪlt] VI marchitarse

wily ['waɪlɪ] ADJ astuto

wimp [wɪmp] N (inf) enclenque mf; (character) calzonazos m inv

★**win** [wɪn] (pt, pp **won** [wʌn]) N (in sports etc) victoria, triunfo ▶ VT ganar; (obtain: contract etc) conseguir, lograr ▶ VI ganar
▶ **win over**, (BRIT) **win round** VT convencer a

wince [wɪns] VI encogerse

winch [wɪntʃ] N torno

Winchester disk® ['wɪntʃɪstə-] N (Comput) disco Winchester®

★**wind**¹ [wɪnd] N viento; (Med) gases mpl; (breath) aliento; **into** or **against the ~** contra el viento; **to get ~ of sth** enterarse de algo; **to break ~** ventosear ▶ VT (take breath away from) dejar sin aliento a

wind² [waɪnd] (pt, pp **wound** [waund]) VT enrollar; (wrap) envolver; (clock, toy) dar cuerda a ▶ VI (road, river) serpentear
▶ **wind down** VT (car window) bajar; (fig: production, business) disminuir
▶ **wind up** VT (clock) dar cuerda a; (debate) concluir, terminar

windbreak ['wɪndbreɪk] N barrera contra el viento

windcheater ['wɪndtʃiːtə'], (US) **windbreaker** ['wɪndbreɪkə'] N cazadora

winder ['waɪndə'] N (on watch) cuerda

wind erosion N erosión f del viento

windfall ['wɪndfɔːl] N golpe m de suerte

wind farm N parque m eólico

winding ['waɪndɪŋ] ADJ (road) tortuoso

wind instrument N (Mus) instrumento de viento

windmill ['wɪndmɪl] N molino de viento

★**window** ['wɪndəu] N ventana; (in car, train) ventana; (in shop etc) escaparate m, vitrina (LAM), vidriera (LAM); (Comput) ventana

window box N jardinera (de ventana)

window cleaner N (person) limpiacristales m inv

window dressing N decoración f de escaparates

window envelope N sobre m de ventanilla

window frame N marco de ventana

window ledge N alféizar m, repisa

window pane N cristal m

window seat N asiento junto a la ventana

window-shopping ['wɪndəuʃɔpɪŋ] N: **to go ~** ir a ver o mirar escaparates

windowsill ['wɪndəusɪl] N alféizar m, repisa

windpipe ['wɪndpaɪp] N tráquea

wind power N energía eólica

windscreen ['wɪndskriːn], (US) **windshield** ['wɪndʃiːld] N parabrisas m inv

windscreen washer, (US) **windshield washer** N lavaparabrisas m inv

windscreen wiper, (US) **windshield wiper** N limpiaparabrisas m inv

windsurfing ['wɪndsəːfɪŋ] N windsurf m

windswept ['wɪndswept] ADJ azotado por el viento

wind tunnel N túnel m aerodinámico

wind turbine ['wɪndtəːbaɪn] N aerogenerador m

windy ['wɪndɪ] ADJ de mucho viento; **it's ~** hace viento

★**wine** [waɪn] N vino ▶ VT: **to ~ and dine sb** agasajar or festejar a algn

wine bar N bar especializado en vinos

wine cellar N bodega

wine glass N copa (de or para vino)

wine-growing ['waɪngrəuɪŋ] ADJ viticultor(a)

wine list N lista de vinos

wine merchant N vinatero

wine tasting N degustación f de vinos

wine waiter N escanciador m

★**wing** [wɪŋ] N ala; (BRIT Aut) aleta ■ **wings** NPL (Theat) bastidores mpl

winger ['wɪŋə'] N (Sport) extremo mf

wing mirror N (espejo) retrovisor m

wing nut N tuerca (de) mariposa

wingspan ['wɪŋspæn], **wingspread** ['wɪŋspred] N envergadura

wink [wɪŋk] N guiño; (blink) pestañeo ▶ VI guiñar; (blink) pestañear; (light etc) parpadear

winkle ['wɪŋkl] N bígaro, bigarro

★**winner** ['wɪnə'] N ganador(a) m/f

★**winning** ['wɪnɪŋ] ADJ (team) ganador(a); (goal) decisivo; (charming) encantador(a)

winning post N meta

winnings ['wɪnɪŋz] NPL ganancias fpl

★**winter** ['wɪntə'] N invierno ▶ VI invernar

winter sports NPL deportes mpl de invierno

wintertime [ˈwɪntətaɪm] N invierno

wintry [ˈwɪntrɪ] ADJ invernal

★**wipe** [waɪp] N: **to give sth a ~** pasar un trapo sobre algo ▶ VT limpiar; (*tape*) borrar; **to ~ one's nose** limpiarse la nariz
▶ **wipe off** VT limpiar con un trapo
▶ **wipe out** VT (*debt*) liquidar; (*memory*) borrar; (*destroy*) destruir
▶ **wipe up** VT limpiar

★**wire** [ˈwaɪəʳ] N alambre *m*; (*Elec*) cable *m* (eléctrico); (*Tel*) telegrama *m* ▶ VT (*house*) poner la instalación eléctrica en; (*also*: **wire up**) conectar

wire cutters NPL cortaalambres *msg inv*

wireless [ˈwaɪəlɪs] N (*BRIT*) radio *f* ▶ ADJ inalámbrico

wireless technology N tecnología inalámbrica

wire mesh, wire netting N tela metálica

wire service N (*US*) agencia de noticias

wire-tapping [ˈwaɪəˈtæpɪŋ] N intervención *f* telefónica

wiring [ˈwaɪərɪŋ] N instalación *f* eléctrica

wiry [ˈwaɪərɪ] ADJ enjuto y fuerte

wisdom [ˈwɪzdəm] N sabiduría, saber *m*; (*good sense*) cordura

wisdom tooth N muela del juicio

★**wise** [waɪz] ADJ sabio; (*sensible*) juicioso; **I'm none the wiser** sigo sin entender
▶ **wise up** VI (*inf*): **to ~ up (to sth)** enterarse (de algo)

...wise [waɪz] SUFF: **timewise** en cuanto a *or* respecto al tiempo

wisecrack [ˈwaɪzkræk] N broma

★**wish** [wɪʃ] N (*desire*) deseo; **best wishes** (*on birthday etc*) felicidades *fpl*; **with best wishes** (*in letter*) saludos *mpl*, recuerdos *mpl* ▶ VT desear; (*want*) querer; **he wished me well** me deseó mucha suerte; **to ~ sth on sb** imponer algo a algn; **to ~ to do/sb to do sth** querer hacer/que algn haga algo ▶ VI desear; **to ~ for** desear

wishbone [ˈwɪʃbəun] N espoleta (*de la que tiran dos personas; quien se quede con el hueso más largo pide un deseo*)

wishful [ˈwɪʃful] ADJ: **it's ~ thinking** eso es hacerse ilusiones

wishy-washy [ˈwɪʃɪwɔʃɪ] ADJ (*inf: colour*) desvaído; (: *ideas, thinking*) flojo

wisp [wɪsp] N mechón *m*; (*of smoke*) voluta

wistful [ˈwɪstful] ADJ pensativo; (*nostalgic*) nostálgico

wit [wɪt] N (*wittiness*) ingenio, gracia; (*intelligence: also*: **wits**) inteligencia; (: *person*) chistoso(-a); **to have** *or* **keep one's wits about one** no perder la cabeza

witch [wɪtʃ] N bruja

witchcraft [ˈwɪtʃkrɑːft] N brujería

witch doctor N hechicero

witch-hunt [ˈwɪtʃhʌnt] N (*Pol*) caza de brujas

---

with [wɪð, wɪθ]

PREP **1** (*accompanying, in the company of*) con (*con + mí, ti, sí = conmigo, contigo, consigo*); **I was with him** estaba con él; **we stayed with friends** nos quedamos en casa de unos amigos
2 (*descriptive, indicating manner etc*) con, de; **a room with a view** una habitación con vistas; **the man with the grey hat/blue eyes** el hombre del sombrero gris/de los ojos azules; **red with anger** rojo de ira; **to shake with fear** temblar de miedo; **to fill sth with water** llenar algo de agua
3: **I'm with you/I'm not with you** (*understand*) ya te entiendo/no te entiendo; **to be with it** (*inf: person: up-to-date*) estar al tanto; (: *alert*) ser despabilado; **I'm not really with it today** no doy pie con bola hoy

withdraw [wɪθˈdrɔː] VT (*irreg: like draw*) retirar; **to ~ money (from the bank)** retirar fondos (del banco) ▶ VI retirarse; (*go back on promise*) retractarse; **to ~ into o.s.** ensimismarse

withdrawal [wɪθˈdrɔːəl] N retirada; (*of money*) reintegro

withdrawal symptoms NPL síndrome *m* de abstinencia

withdrawn [wɪθˈdrɔːn] ADJ (*person*) reservado, introvertido ▶ PP of **withdraw**

withdrew [wɪθˈdruː] PT of **withdraw**

wither [ˈwɪðəʳ] VI marchitarse

withered [ˈwɪðəd] ADJ marchito, seco

withhold [wɪθˈhəuld] VT (*irreg: like hold*) (*money*) retener; (*decision*) aplazar; (*permission*) negar; (*information*) ocultar

★**within** [wɪðˈɪn] PREP dentro de; **~ reach** al alcance de la mano; **~ sight of** a la vista de; **~ the week** antes de que acabe la semana; **to be ~ the law** atenerse a la legalidad; **~ an hour from now** dentro de una hora; **~ a mile (of)** a menos de una milla (de) ▶ ADV dentro

★**without** [wɪðˈaut] PREP sin; **to go** *or* **do ~ sth** prescindir de algo; **~ anybody knowing** sin saberlo nadie

withstand [wɪθˈstænd] VT (*irreg: like stand*) resistir a

★**witness** [ˈwɪtnɪs] N (*person*) testigo *mf*; (*evidence*) testimonio; **~ for the prosecution/defence** testigo de cargo/descargo; **to bear ~ to** (*fig*) ser testimonio de ▶ VT (*event*) presenciar, ser testigo de; (*document*) atestiguar la veracidad de ▶ VI: **to ~ to (having seen) sth** dar testimonio de (haber visto) algo

witness box, (US) witness stand N tribuna de los testigos

witticism [ˈwɪtɪsɪzm] N dicho ingenioso

wittily [ˈwɪtɪlɪ] ADV ingeniosamente

witty [ˈwɪtɪ] ADJ ingenioso

wives [waɪvz] NPL of **wife**

wizard [ˈwɪzəd] N hechicero

W

865

wizened [ˈwɪznd] ADJ arrugado, marchito

wk ABBR = **week**

WMD N ABBR *see* **weapons of mass destruction**

WO N ABBR = **warrant officer**

wobble [ˈwɔbl] VI tambalearse

wobbly [ˈwɔblɪ] ADJ (*hand, voice*) tembloroso; (*table, chair*) tambaleante, cojo

woe [wəu] N desgracia

woeful [ˈwəuful] ADJ (*bad*) lamentable; (*sad*) apesadumbrado

wok [wɔk] N wok *m*

woke [wəuk] PT *of* **wake**

woken [ˈwəukn] PP *of* **wake**

wolf [wulf] (*pl* **wolves** [wulvz]) N lobo

★**woman** [ˈwumən] (*pl* **women** [ˈwɪmɪn]) N mujer *f*; **young ~** (mujer *f*) joven *f*; **women's page** (*Press*) sección *f* de la mujer

woman doctor N doctora

woman friend N amiga

womanize [ˈwumənaɪz] VI ser un mujeriego

womanly [ˈwumənlɪ] ADJ femenino

womb [wuːm] N (*Anat*) matriz *f*, útero

women [ˈwɪmɪn] NPL *of* **woman**

Women's Liberation Movement, Women's Movement N (*also*: **women's lib**) Movimiento de liberación de la mujer

won [wʌn] PT, PP *of* **win**

★**wonder** [ˈwʌndəʳ] N maravilla, prodigio; (*feeling*) asombro; **it's no ~ that** no es de extrañar que ▶ VI: **to ~ whether** preguntarse si; **to ~ at** asombrarse de; **to ~ about** pensar sobre *or* en

★**wonderful** [ˈwʌndəful] ADJ maravilloso

wonderfully [ˈwʌndəfəlɪ] ADV maravillosamente, estupendamente

wonky [ˈwɔŋkɪ] ADJ (BRIT: *inf*: *unsteady*) poco seguro, cojo; (: *broken down*) estropeado

wont [wɔnt] N: **as is his/her ~** como tiene por costumbre

won't [wəunt] = **will not**

woo [wuː] VT (*woman*) cortejar

★**wood** [wud] N (*timber*) madera; (*forest*) bosque *m* ▶ CPD de madera

wood alcohol N (US) alcohol *m* desnaturalizado

wood carving N tallado en madera

wooded [ˈwudɪd] ADJ arbolado

★**wooden** [ˈwudn] ADJ de madera; (*fig*) inexpresivo

woodland [ˈwudlənd] N bosque *m*

woodpecker [ˈwudpɛkəʳ] N pájaro carpintero

wood pigeon N paloma torcaz

woodwind [ˈwudwɪnd] N (*Mus*) instrumentos *mpl* de viento de madera

woodwork [ˈwudwəːk] N carpintería

woodworm [ˈwudwəːm] N carcoma

woof [wuf] N (*of dog*) ladrido ▶ VI ladrar ▶ EXCL: **~, ~!** ¡guau, guau!

wool [wul] N lana; **knitting ~** lana (de hacer punto); **to pull the ~ over sb's eyes** (*fig*) dar a algn gato por liebre

woollen, (US) **woolen** [ˈwulən] ADJ de lana ▶ N: **woollens** géneros *mpl* de lana

woolly, (US) **wooly** [ˈwulɪ] ADJ de lana; (*fig: ideas*) confuso

woozy [ˈwuːzɪ] ADJ (*inf*) mareado

★**word** [wəːd] N palabra; (*news*) noticia; (*promise*) palabra (de honor); **~ for ~** palabra por palabra; **what's the ~ for "pen" in Spanish?** ¿cómo se dice "pen" en español?; **to put sth into words** expresar algo en palabras; **to have a ~ with sb** hablar (dos palabras) con algn; **in other words** en otras palabras; **to break/keep one's ~** faltar a la palabra/cumplir la promesa; **to leave ~ (with/for sb) that ...** dejar recado (con/para algn) de que ...; **to have words with sb** (*quarrel with*) discutir *or* reñir con algn ▶ VT redactar

wording [ˈwəːdɪŋ] N redacción *f*

word-of-mouth [wəːdəvˈmauθ] N: **by** *or* **through ~** de palabra, por el boca a boca

word-perfect [wəːdˈpəːfɪkt] ADJ (*speech etc*) sin faltas de expresión

word processing N procesamiento *or* tratamiento de textos

word processor [-ˈprəusɛsəʳ] N procesador *m* de textos

word wrap [ˈwəːdræp] N (*Comput*) salto de línea automático

wordy [ˈwəːdɪ] ADJ verboso, prolijo

wore [wɔːʳ] PT *of* **wear**

★**work** [wəːk] N trabajo; (*job*) empleo, trabajo; (*Art, Lit*) obra; **to go to ~** ir a trabajar *or* al trabajo; **to be at ~ (on sth)** estar trabajando (en algo); **to set to ~, start ~** ponerse a trabajar; **to be out of ~** estar parado, no tener trabajo; **his life's ~** el trabajo de su vida ▶ VI trabajar; (*mechanism*) funcionar, marchar; (*medicine*) ser eficaz, surtir efecto; **to ~ hard** trabajar mucho *or* duro; **to ~ to rule** (*Industry*) hacer una huelga de celo; **to ~ loose** (*part*) desprenderse; (*knot*) aflojarse ▶ VT (*shape*) trabajar; (*stone etc*) tallar; (*mine etc*) explotar; (*machine*) manejar, hacer funcionar; (*cause*) producir; *see also* **works**

▶ **work off** VT: **to ~ off one's feelings** desahogarse

▶ **work on** VT FUS trabajar en, dedicarse a; (*principle*) basarse en; **he's working on the car** está reparando el coche

▶ **work out** VI (*plans etc*) salir bien, funcionar; (*Sport*) hacer ejercicios; **it works out at £100** asciende a 100 libras ▶ VT (*problem*) resolver; (*plan*) elaborar

▶ **work up** VT: **he worked his way up in the company** ascendió en la compañía mediante sus propios esfuerzos

workable [ˈwəːkəbl] ADJ (*solution*) práctico, factible

workaholic [wəːkəˈhɔlɪk] N adicto(-a) al trabajo

workbench ['wə:kbɛntʃ] N banco or mesa de trabajo

worked up [wə:kt-] ADJ: **to get ~** excitarse

★**worker** ['wə:kər] N trabajador(a) m/f, obrero(-a); **office ~** oficinista mf

work experience N: **I'm going to do my ~ in a factory** voy a hacer las prácticas en una fábrica

workforce ['wə:kfɔ:s] N mano f de obra

work-in ['wə:kɪn] N (BRIT) ocupación f (de la empresa sin interrupción del trabajo)

working ['wə:kɪŋ] ADJ (day, week) laborable; (tools, conditions, clothes) de trabajo; (wife) que trabaja; (partner) activo

working capital N (Comm) capital m circulante

working class N clase f obrera ▶ ADJ: **working-class** obrero

working knowledge N conocimientos mpl básicos

working man N (irreg) obrero

working order N: **in ~** en funcionamiento

working party N comisión f de investigación, grupo de trabajo

working week N semana laboral

work-in-progress ['wə:kɪn'prəugrɛs] N (Comm) trabajo en curso

workload ['wə:kləud] N cantidad f de trabajo

workman ['wə:kmən] N (irreg) obrero

workmanship ['wə:kmənʃɪp] N (art) hechura; (skill) habilidad f

workmate ['wə:kmeɪt] N compañero(-a) de trabajo

work of art N obra de arte

workout ['wə:kaut] N (Sport) sesión f de ejercicios

work permit N permiso de trabajo

workplace ['wə:kpleɪs] N lugar m de trabajo

works [wə:ks] NSG (BRIT: factory) fábrica ▶ NPL (of clock, machine) mecanismo

works council N comité m de empresa

worksheet ['wə:kʃi:t] N (Comput) hoja de trabajo; (Scol) hoja de ejercicios

workshop ['wə:kʃɔp] N taller m

work station N estación f de trabajo

work study N estudio del trabajo

work surface N encimera

worktop ['wə:ktɔp] N encimera

work-to-rule ['wə:ktə'ru:l] N (BRIT) huelga de celo

★**world** [wə:ld] N mundo; **all over the ~** por todo el mundo, en el mundo entero; **the business ~** el mundo de los negocios; **what in the ~ is he doing?** ¿qué diablos está haciendo?; **to think the ~ of sb** (fig) tener un concepto muy alto de algn; **to do sb a ~ of good** sentar muy bien a algn ▶ CPD (champion) del mundo; (power, war) mundial; **W~ War**

One/Two la Primera/Segunda Guerra Mundial

World Cup N (Football): **the ~** el Mundial, los Mundiales

world-famous [wə:ld'feɪməs] ADJ de fama mundial, mundialmente famoso

worldly ['wə:ldlɪ] ADJ mundano

world music N música étnica

World Series N: **the ~** (US Baseball) el campeonato nacional de béisbol de EE.UU.

World Service N see BBC

world-wide ['wə:ldwaɪd] ADJ mundial, universal

World-Wide Web N: **the ~** la World Wide Web

worm [wə:m] N gusano; (earthworm) lombriz f

worn [wɔ:n] PP of **wear** ▶ ADJ usado

worn-out ['wɔ:naut] ADJ (object) gastado; (person) rendido, agotado

★**worried** ['wʌrɪd] ADJ preocupado; **to be ~ about sth** estar preocupado por algo

worrisome ['wʌrɪsəm] ADJ preocupante, inquietante

★**worry** ['wʌrɪ] N preocupación f ▶ VT preocupar, inquietar ▶ VI preocuparse; **to ~ about or over sth/sb** preocuparse por algo/algn

worrying ['wʌrɪɪŋ] ADJ inquietante

★**worse** [wə:s] ADJ, ADV peor; **to get ~, to grow ~** empeorar; **he is none the ~ for it** se ha quedado tan fresco or tan tranquilo; **so much the ~ for you** tanto peor para ti ▶ N el peor, lo peor; **a change for the ~** un empeoramiento

worsen ['wə:sn] VT, VI empeorar

worse off ADJ (financially): **to be ~** tener menos dinero; (fig): **you'll be ~ this way** de esta forma estarás peor que antes

worship ['wə:ʃɪp] N (organized worship) culto; (act) adoración f; **Your W~** (BRIT: to mayor) su Ilustrísima; (: to judge) su señoría ▶ VT adorar

worshipper, (US) **worshiper** ['wə:ʃɪpər] N devoto(-a)

★**worst** [wə:st] ADJ, ADV (el/la) peor; **at ~** en el peor de los casos; **to come off ~** llevar la peor parte ▶ N lo peor; **if the ~ comes to the ~** en el peor de los casos

worst-case ['wə:stkeɪs] ADJ: **the ~ scenario** el peor de los casos

worsted ['wustɪd] N: (wool) **~** estambre m

★**worth** [wə:θ] N valor m ▶ ADJ: **to be ~** valer; **how much is it ~?** ¿cuánto vale?; **it's ~ it** vale or merece la pena; **to be ~ one's while (to do)** merecer la pena (hacer); **it's not ~ the trouble** no vale or merece la pena

worthless ['wə:θlɪs] ADJ sin valor; (useless) inútil

worthwhile ['wə:θwaɪl] ADJ (activity) que merece la pena; (cause) loable

worthy ['wə:ðɪ] ADJ (person) respetable; (motive) honesto; **~ of** digno de

W

---

would [wud]

AUX VB **1** (*conditional tense*): **if you asked him he would do it** si se lo pidieras, lo haría; **if you had asked him he would have done it** si se lo hubieras pedido, lo habría *or* hubiera hecho
2 (*in offers, invitations, requests*): **would you like a biscuit?** ¿quieres una galleta?; (*formal*) ¿querría una galleta?; **would you ask him to come in?** ¿quiere hacerle pasar?; **would you open the window please?** ¿quiere *or* podría abrir la ventana, por favor?
3 (*in indirect speech*): **I said I would do it** dije que lo haría
4 (*emphatic*): **it WOULD have to snow today!** ¡tenía que nevar precisamente hoy!
5 (*insistence*): **she wouldn't behave** no quiso comportarse bien
6 (*conjecture*): **it would have been midnight** sería medianoche; **it would seem so** parece ser que sí
7 (*indicating habit*): **he would go there on Mondays** iba allí los lunes

---

The conditional is often used to translate *would* when it is followed by a verb: *I said I would do it*. **Dije que lo haría**.
When *would* is used to make requests, translate it using **poder** in the present: *Would you close the door, please?* **¿Puedes cerrar la puerta, por favor?**
To translate *I'd like* ... when talking about aspirations, use **Me gustaría ...**: *I'd like to go to China*. **Me gustaría ir a China**.
To ask if someone would like something, use **querer**: *Would you like a biscuit?* **¿Quieres una galleta?**

---

would-be ['wudbi:] ADJ (*pej*) presunto
wouldn't ['wudnt] = **would not**
★**wound¹** [wu:nd] N herida ▸ VT herir
wound² [waund] PT, PP *of* **wind²**
wove [wəuv] PT *of* **weave**
woven ['wəuvən] PP *of* **weave**
WP N ABBR = **word processing; word processor**
▸ ABBR (*BRIT inf*: = *weather permitting*) si lo permite el tiempo
wpm ABBR (= *words per minute*) p.p.m.
wrangle ['ræŋgl] N riña ▸ VI reñir
★**wrap** [ræp] N (*stole*) chal *m*; **under wraps** (*fig*: *plan, scheme*) oculto, tapado ▸ VT (*also*: **wrap up**) envolver, abrigar; (: *gift*) envolver
▸ **wrap up** VI (*dress warmly*) abrigarse
wrapper ['ræpə^r] N (*BRIT*: *of book*) sobrecubierta; (*on chocolate etc*) envoltura
wrapping paper ['ræpɪŋ-] N papel *m* de envolver
wrath [rɔθ] N cólera
wreak [ri:k] VT (*destruction*) causar; **to ~ havoc (on)** hacer *or* causar estragos (en); **to ~ vengeance (on)** vengarse (en)

wreath [ri:θ] (*pl* **wreaths** [ri:ðz]) N (*also*: **funeral wreath**) corona; (*of flowers*) guirnalda
wreck [rek] N (*ship*: *destruction*) naufragio; (: *remains*) restos *mpl* del barco; (*pej*: *person*) ruina ▸ VT destrozar; (*chances*) arruinar; **to be wrecked** (*Naut*) naufragar
wreckage ['rekɪdʒ] N (*remains*) restos *mpl*; (*of building*) escombros *mpl*
wrecker ['rekə^r] N (*US*: *breakdown van*) camión-grúa *m*
wren [ren] N (*Zool*) reyezuelo
wrench [rentʃ] N (*Tech*) llave *f* inglesa; (*tug*) tirón *m* ▸ VT arrancar; **to ~ sth from sb** arrebatar algo violentamente a algn
wrest [rest] VT: **to ~ sth from sb** arrebatar *or* arrancar algo a algn
wrestle ['resl] VI: **to ~ (with sb)** luchar (con *or* contra algn)
wrestler ['reslə^r] N luchador(a) *m/f* (de lucha libre)
wrestling ['reslɪŋ] N lucha libre
wrestling match N combate *m* de lucha libre
wretch [retʃ] N desgraciado(-a), miserable *mf*; **little ~!** (*often hum*) ¡granuja!
wretched ['retʃɪd] ADJ (*inf*) miserable
wriggle ['rɪgl] VI serpentear; (*also*: **wriggle about**) menearse, retorcerse
wring [rɪŋ] (*pt, pp* **wrung** [rʌŋ]) VT torcer, retorcer; (*wet clothes*) escurrir; (*fig*): **to ~ sth out of sb** sacar algo por la fuerza a algn
wringer ['rɪŋə^r] N escurridor *m*
wringing ['rɪŋɪŋ] ADJ (*also*: **wringing wet**) empapado
wrinkle ['rɪŋkl] N arruga ▸ VT arrugar ▸ VI arrugarse
wrinkled ['rɪŋkld], **wrinkly** ['rɪŋklɪ] ADJ (*fabric, paper etc*) arrugado
wrist [rɪst] N muñeca
wristband ['rɪstbænd] N (*BRIT*: *of shirt*) puño; (: *of watch*) correa
wrist watch N reloj *m* de pulsera
writ [rɪt] N mandato judicial; **to serve a ~ on sb** notificar un mandato judicial a algn
writable ['raɪtəbl] ADJ (*CD, DVD*) escribible
★**write** [raɪt] (*pt* **wrote** [rəut], *pp* **written** ['rɪtn]) VT escribir; (*cheque*) extender; **to ~ sb a letter** escribir una carta a algn ▸ VI escribir
▸ **write away** VI: **to ~ away for** (*information, goods*) pedir por escrito *or* carta
▸ **write down** VT escribir; (*note*) apuntar
▸ **write off** VT (*debt*) borrar (como incobrable); (*fig*) desechar por inútil; (*smash up*: *car*) destrozar
▸ **write out** VT escribir
▸ **write up** VT redactar
write-off ['raɪtɔf] N siniestro total; **the car is a ~** el coche es pura chatarra
write-protect ['raɪtprə'tekt] VT (*Comput*) proteger contra escritura
★**writer** ['raɪtə^r] N escritor(a) *m/f*

write-up ['raɪtʌp] N (*review*) crítica, reseña

writhe [raɪð] VI retorcerse

★**writing** ['raɪtɪŋ] N escritura; (*handwriting*) letra; (*of author*) obras *fpl*; **in ~** por escrito; **to put sth in ~** poner algo por escrito; **in my own ~** escrito por mí; *see also* **writings**

writing case N estuche *m* de papel de escribir

writing desk N escritorio

writing paper N papel *m* de escribir

writings ['raɪtɪŋz] NPL obras *fpl*

★**written** ['rɪtn] PP *of* **write**

★**wrong** [rɔŋ] ADJ (*wicked*) malo; (*unfair*) injusto; (*incorrect*) equivocado, incorrecto; (*not suitable*) inoportuno, inconveniente; **to be ~** (*answer*) estar equivocado; (*in doing, saying*) equivocarse; **it's ~ to steal, stealing is ~** robar está mal; **you are ~ to do it** haces mal en hacerlo; **you are ~ about that, you've got it ~** en eso estás equivocado; **what's ~?** ¿qué pasa?; **what's ~ with the car?** ¿qué le pasa al coche?; **there's nothing ~** no pasa nada; **you have the ~ number** (*Tel*) se ha equivocado de número ▶ ADV mal; **to go ~** (*person*) equivocarse; (*plan*) salir mal; (*machine*) estropearse ▶ N mal *m*; (*injustice*) injusticia; **to be in the ~** no tener razón; (*guilty*) tener la culpa ▶ VT ser injusto con; (*hurt*) agraviar

wrongdoer ['rɔŋduəʳ] N malhechor(a) *m/f*

wrong-foot [rɔŋ'fut] VT (*Sport*) hacer perder el equilibrio a; (*fig*) poner en un aprieto a

wrongful ['rɔŋful] ADJ injusto; **~ dismissal** (*Industry*) despido improcedente

wrongly ['rɔŋlɪ] ADV (*answer, do, count*) incorrectamente; (*treat*) injustamente

wrong number N (*Tel*): **you've got the ~** se ha equivocado de número

wrote [rəut] PT *of* **write**

wrought [rɔːt] ADJ: **~ iron** hierro forjado

wrung [rʌŋ] PT, PP *of* **wring**

wry [raɪ] ADJ irónico

wt. ABBR = **weight**

WTO N ABBR (= *World Trade Organisation*) OMC *f* (= *Organización mundial del comercio*)

WV, W.Va. ABBR (*US*) = **West Virginia**

WWW N ABBR (= *World Wide Web*) WWW *f*

WY, Wyo. ABBR (*US*) = **Wyoming**

WYSIWYG ['wɪzɪwɪg] ABBR (*Comput*: = *what you see is what you get*) tipo de presentación en un procesador de textos

W

X, x [eks] N (*letter*) X, x *f*; (BRIT *Cine: formerly*) no apto para menores de 18 años; **X for Xmas** X de Xiquena; **if you earn X dollars a year** si ganas X dólares al año

X-certificate [ˈɛkssəˈtɪfɪkɪt] ADJ (BRIT *Cine: formerly*) no apto para menores de 18 años

Xerox® [ˈzɪərɒks] N (*also:* **Xerox machine**) fotocopiadora; (*photocopy*) fotocopia ▶ VT fotocopiar

XL ABBR = **extra large**

Xmas [ˈɛksməs] N ABBR = **Christmas**

X-rated [ˈeksˈreɪtɪd] ADJ (*US Cine*) no apto para menores de 18 años

X-ray [ˈɛksreɪ] N radiografía ▶ VT radiografiar ■ **X-rays** NPL rayos *mpl* X

xylophone [ˈzaɪləfəʊn] N xilófono

Yy

Y, y [waɪ] N (letter) Y, y f; **Y for Yellow**, (US) **Y for Yoke** Y de Yegua

Y2K [waɪtu:'keɪ] ABBR = **Year 2000**; **the ~ problem** (Comput) el efecto 2000

★**yacht** [jɔt] N yate m

yachting ['jɔtɪŋ] N (sport) balandrismo

yachtsman ['jɔtsmən] N (irreg) balandrista m

yachtswoman ['jɔtswumən] N (irreg) balandrista

yakka ['jækə] N (AUSTRALIA, NEW ZEALAND inf) curro

yam [jæm] N ñame m; (sweet potato) batata, camote m (LAM)

Yank [jæŋk], **Yankee** ['jæŋkɪ] N (pej) yanqui mf

yank [jæŋk] VT tirar de, jalar de (LAM) ▶ N tirón m

yap [jæp] VI (dog) aullar

★**yard** [jɑːd] N patio; (US: garden) jardín m; (measure) yarda; **builder's ~** almacén m

yard sale N (US) venta de objetos usados (en el jardín de una casa particular)

yardstick ['jɑːdstɪk] N (fig) criterio, norma

yarn [jɑːn] N hilo; (tale) cuento (chino), historia

yawn [jɔːn] N bostezo ▶ VI bostezar

yawning ['jɔːnɪŋ] ADJ (gap) muy abierto

yd. ABBR (= yard) yda

yeah [jɛə] ADV (inf) sí

★**year** [jɪər] N año; (Scol, Univ) curso; **this ~** este año; **~ in, ~ out** año tras año; **a** or **per ~** al año; **to be eight years old** tener ocho años; **she's three years old** tiene tres años; **an eight-year-old child** un niño de ocho años (de edad)

yearbook ['jɪəbuk] N anuario

yearling ['jɪəlɪŋ] N (racehorse) potro de un año

yearly ['jɪəlɪ] ADJ anual ▶ ADV anualmente, cada año; **twice ~** dos veces al año

yearn [jəːn] VI: **to ~ for sth** añorar algo, suspirar por algo

yearning ['jəːnɪŋ] N ansia; (longing) añoranza

yeast [jiːst] N levadura

yell [jɛl] N grito, alarido ▶ VI gritar

★**yellow** ['jɛləu] ADJ, N amarillo

yellow fever N fiebre f amarilla

yellowish ['jɛləuɪʃ] ADJ amarillento

Yellow Pages® NPL páginas fpl amarillas

Yellow Sea N: **the ~** el mar Amarillo

yelp [jɛlp] N aullido ▶ VI aullar

Yemen ['jɛmən] N Yemen m

Yemeni ['jɛmənɪ] ADJ, N yemení mf, yemenita mf

yen [jɛn] N (currency) yen m

yeoman ['jəumən] N (irreg): **Y~ of the Guard** alabardero de la Casa Real

★**yes** [jɛs] ADV, N sí m; **to say/answer ~** decir/contestar que sí; **to say ~ (to)** decir que sí (a), conformarse (con)

yes man N (irreg) pelotillero

★**yesterday** ['jɛstədɪ] ADV, N ayer m; **~ morning/evening** ayer por la mañana/tarde; **all day ~** todo el día de ayer; **the day before ~** antes de ayer, anteayer

★**yet** [jɛt] ADV todavía; **it is not finished ~** todavía no está acabado; **the best ~** el/la mejor hasta ahora; **as ~** hasta ahora, todavía; **~ again** de nuevo ▶ CONJ sin embargo, a pesar de todo

yew [juː] N tejo

Y-fronts® ['waɪfrʌnts] NPL (BRIT) calzoncillos mpl, eslip msg tradicional

YHA N ABBR (BRIT: = Youth Hostel Association) ≈ Red f Española de Albergues Juveniles

Yiddish ['jɪdɪʃ] N yídish m, judeoalemán m

yield [jiːld] N producción f; (Agr) cosecha; (Comm) rendimiento; **a ~ of 5%** un rédito del 5 por ciento ▶ VT producir, dar; (profit) rendir ▶ VI rendirse, ceder; (US Aut) ceder el paso

yikes [jaɪks] EXCL (inf: esp hum) ostras

YMCA N ABBR (= Young Men's Christian Association) Asociación f de Jóvenes Cristianos

yob [jɔb], **yobbo** ['jɔbbəu] N (BRIT pej) gamberro

y

yodel [ˈjəudl] vi cantar a la tirolesa

yoga [ˈjəugə] N yoga m

★**yoghurt, yogurt** [ˈjəugət] N yogur m

yoke [jəuk] N (of oxen) yunta; (on shoulders) balancín m; (fig) yugo ▸ vt (also: **yoke together**: oxen) uncir

yolk [jəuk] N yema (de huevo)

yonder [ˈjɔndər] ADV allá (a lo lejos)

yonks [jɔŋks] NPL (inf): **I haven't seen him for ~** hace siglos que no lo veo

---

you [juː]

PRON **1** (subject: familiar, singular) tú; (: plural) vosotros(-as) (SP), ustedes (LAM); (: polite) usted sg, ustedes pl; **you are very kind** eres/es etc muy amable; **you French enjoy your food** a vosotros (or ustedes) los franceses os (or les) gusta la comida; **you and I will go** iremos tú y yo
2 (object: direct: familiar: singular) te; (: plural) os (SP), les (LAM); (: polite: singular masc) lo or le; (: plural masc) los or les; (: singular fem) la; (: plural fem) las; **I know you** te/le etc conozco
3 (object: indirect: familiar: singular) te; (: plural) os (SP), les (LAM); (: polite) le sg, les pl; **I gave the letter to you yesterday** te/os etc di la carta ayer
4 (stressed): **I told YOU to do it** te dije a ti que lo hicieras, es a ti a quien dije que lo hicieras
5 (after prep: NB: con + ti = contigo: familiar: singular) ti; (: plural) vosotros(-as) (SP), ustedes (LAM); (: polite) usted, ustedes pl; **it's for you** es para ti/vosotros etc
6 (comparisons: familiar: singular) tú; (: plural) vosotros(-as) (SP), ustedes (LAM); (: polite) usted sg, ustedes pl; **she's younger than you** es más joven que tú/vosotros etc
7 (impersonal: one): **fresh air does you good** el aire puro (te) hace bien; **you never know** nunca se sabe; **you can't do that!** ¡eso no se hace!

There are different ways of saying you in Spanish. If you are talking to people your own age or that you know well, use the familiar **tú/vosotros** or the corresponding form of the verb. Otherwise, use the formal option **usted**. In Argentina and certain Central American countries, **vos** is used instead of **tú**. Note that subject pronouns are usually omitted in Spanish:

You don't understand me. **No me entiendes**.
How are you? **¿Cómo estáis?**

In Latin America, **ustedes** is used instead of **vosotros**: How are you? **¿Cómo están?** When you means one or people in general, the impersonal **se** is often used: I doubt it, but you never know. **Lo dudo, pero nunca se sabe**.

you'd [juːd] = **you had; you would**

you'll [juːl] = **you will; you shall**

★**young** [jʌŋ] ADJ joven; **a ~ man/lady** un(a) joven; **my younger brother** mi hermano menor or pequeño; **the younger generation** la nueva generación ▸ NPL (of animal) cría; (people): **the ~** los jóvenes, la juventud

youngster [ˈjʌŋstər] N joven mf

★**your** [jɔːr] ADJ tu, vuestro pl; (formal) su; **~ house** tu etc casa; see also **my**

you're [juər] = **you are**

★**yours** [jɔːz] PRON tuyo, vuestro pl; (formal) suyo; **a friend of ~** un amigo tuyo etc; see also **faithfully; mine**[1]; **sincerely**

★**yourself** [jɔːˈself] PRON (reflexive) tú mismo; (complement) te; (after prep) ti (mismo); (formal) usted mismo; (: complement) se; (: after prep) sí (mismo); **you ~ told me** me lo dijiste tú mismo; **(all) by ~** sin ayuda de nadie, solo; see also **oneself**

yourselves [jɔːˈselvz] PRON PL vosotros mismos, ustedes mismos (LAM); (after prep) vosotros (mismos), ustedes (mismos) (LAM); (formal) ustedes (mismos); (: complement) se; (: after prep) sí mismos

youth [juːθ] N juventud f; (pl **youths** [juːðz]) (young man) joven m; **in my ~** en mi juventud

youth club N club m juvenil

youthful [ˈjuːθful] ADJ juvenil

youthfulness [ˈjuːθfəlnɪs] N juventud f

youth hostel N albergue m juvenil

youth movement N movimiento juvenil

you've [juːv] = **you have**

yowl [jaul] N (of animal, person) aullido ▸ vi aullar

yr ABBR (= year) a

YT ABBR (CANADA) = **Yukon Territory**

Yugoslav [ˈjuːgəuslɑːv] ADJ, N (formerly) yugoslavo(-a) m/f

Yugoslavia [juːgəuˈslɑːvɪə] N (History) Yugoslavia

Yugoslavian [juːgəuˈslɑːvɪən] ADJ (History) yugoslavo(-a)

yuppie [ˈjʌpɪ] (inf) ADJ, N yuppie mf

YWCA N ABBR (= Young Women's Christian Association) Asociación f de Jóvenes Cristianas

Zz

Z, z [zɛd, (US) ziː] N (*letter*) Z, z *f*; **Z for Zebra** Z de Zaragoza

Zaire [zɑːˈiːəʳ] N Zaire *m*

Zambia [ˈzæmbɪə] N Zambia

Zambian [ˈzæmbɪən] ADJ, N zambiano(-a) *m/f*

zany [ˈzeɪnɪ] ADJ estrafalario

zap [zæp] VT (*Comput*) borrar

zeal [ziːl] N celo, entusiasmo

zealot [ˈzɛlət] N fanático(-a)

zealous [ˈzɛləs] ADJ celoso, entusiasta

zebra [ˈziːbrə] N cebra

zebra crossing N (*BRIT*) paso de peatones

zenith [ˈzɛnɪθ] N (*Astro*) cénit *m*; (*fig*) apogeo

★**zero** [ˈzɪərəu] N cero; **5 degrees below ~** 5 grados bajo cero

zero hour N hora cero

zero option N (*Pol*) opción *f* cero

zero-rated [ˈzɪərəureɪtɪd] ADJ (*BRIT*) de tasa cero

zest [zɛst] N ánimo, vivacidad *f*; (*of orange*) piel *f*; **~ for living** brío

zigzag [ˈzɪgzæg] N zigzag *m* ▶ VI zigzaguear

Zimbabwe [zɪmˈbɑːbwɪ] N Zimbabwe *m*

Zimbabwean [zɪmˈbɑːbwɪən] ADJ, N zimbabuense *mf*

Zimmer® [ˈzɪməʳ] N (*also:* **Zimmer frame**) andador *m*, andaderas *fpl*

zinc [zɪŋk] N cinc *m*, zinc *m*

Zionism [ˈzaɪənɪzm] N sionismo

Zionist [ˈzaɪənɪst] ADJ, N sionista *mf*

zip [zɪp] N (*also:* **zip fastener**, *US:* **zipper**) cremallera, cierre *m* relámpago (*LAM*); (*energy*) energía, vigor *m* ▶ VT (*Comput*) comprimir; (*also:* **zip up**) cerrar la cremallera de ▶ VI: **to ~ along to the shops** ir de compras volando

zip code N (*US*) código postal

zip file N (*Comput*) archivo *m* comprimido

zipper [ˈzɪpəʳ] N (*US*) cremallera

zit [zɪt] N grano

zither [ˈzɪðəʳ] N cítara

zodiac [ˈzəudɪæk] N zodíaco

zombie [ˈzɔmbɪ] N zombi *m*

★**zone** [zəun] N zona

zonked [zɔŋkt] ADJ (*inf*) hecho polvo

★**zoo** [zuː] N zoo, (parque *m*) zoológico

zoological [zuːəˈlɔdʒɪkəl] ADJ zoológico

zoologist [zuˈɔlədʒɪst] N zoólogo(-a)

zoology [zuːˈɔlədʒɪ] N zoología

zoom [zuːm] VI: **to ~ past** pasar zumbando; **to ~ in (on sth/sb)** (*Phot, Cine*) enfocar (algo/a algn) con el zoom

zoom lens N zoom *m*

zucchini [zuːˈkiːnɪ] (*pl ~ or* **zucchinis**) N (*US*) calabacín *m*, calabacita (*LAM*)

Zumba® [ˈzumbə] N zumba *f*

Grammar
Gramática

Using the grammar

The Grammar section deals systematically and comprehensively with all the information you will need in order to communicate accurately in Spanish. The user-friendly layout explains the grammar point on a left-hand page, leaving the facing page free for illustrative examples. The circled numbers, → ❶ etc, direct you to the relevant example in every case. Another strong point of the Grammar section is its comprehensive treatment of verbs. Regular verbs are fully explained, and 80 major irregular verbs are conjugated in their simple tenses. The irregular verbs are given in alphabetical order and laid out in tables, making them easy and efficient to consult. In addition, a verb index lists every Spanish verb in this dictionary, each cross-referred to the appropriate conjugation model.

The Grammar section also provides invaluable guidance on the danger of translating English structures by identical structures in Spanish. Use of numbers and punctuation are important areas covered towards the end of the section. Finally, the index lists the main words and grammatical terms in both English and Spanish.

Abbreviations

cond.	conditional
fem.	feminine
masc.	masculine
plur.	plural
sing.	singular
subj	subjunctive
algn	**alguien**
sb	somebody
sth	something

Contents

Verbs

Simple Tenses: Formation

In Spanish the simple tenses are:

      Present → **①**

      Imperfect → **②**

      Future → **③**

      Conditional → **④**

      Preterite → **⑤**

      Present Subjunctive → **⑥**

      Imperfect Subjunctive → **⑦**

They are formed by adding endings to a verb stem. The endings show the number and person of the subject of the verb → **⑧**

The stem and endings of regular verbs are totally predictable. The following sections show all the patterns for regular verbs. For irregular verbs, see page 80 onwards.

Regular Verbs

There are three regular verb patterns (called conjugations), each identifiable by the ending of the infinitive:

First conjugation verbs end in **-ar** e.g. **hablar** to speak.

Second conjugation verbs end in **-er** e.g. **comer** to eat.

Third conjugation verbs end in **-ir** e.g. **vivir** to live.

These three conjugations are treated in order on the following pages. The subject pronouns will appear in brackets because they are not always necessary in Spanish (see page 230).

Examples

❶ (yo) hablo

I speak
I am speaking
I do speak

❷ (yo) hablaba

I spoke
I was speaking
I used to speak

❸ (yo) hablaré

I shall speak
I shall be speaking

❹ (yo) hablaría

I should/would speak
I should/would be speaking

❺ (yo) hablé

I spoke

❻ (que) (yo) hable

(that) I speak

❼ (que) (yo) hablara *or* **hablase**

(that) I spoke

❽ (yo) hablo
(nosotros) hablamos
(yo) hablaría
(nosotros) hablaríamos

I speak
we speak
I would speak
we would speak

Verbs

Simple Tenses: First Conjugation

The stem is formed as follows:

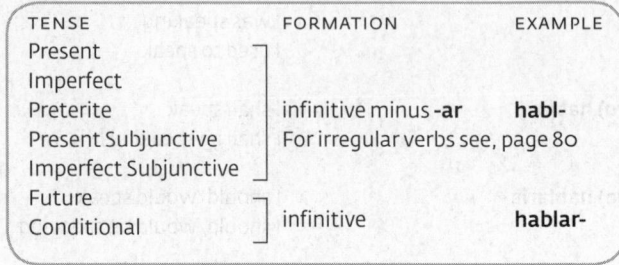

TENSE	FORMATION	EXAMPLE
Present		
Imperfect		
Preterite	infinitive minus **-ar**	**habl-**
Present Subjunctive	For irregular verbs see, page 80	
Imperfect Subjunctive		
Future	infinitive	**hablar-**
Conditional		

To the appropriate stem add the following endings:

		❶ PRESENT	**❷ IMPERFECT**	**❸ PRETERITE**
sing.	1st person	**-o**	**-aba**	**-é**
	2nd person	**-as**	**-abas**	**-aste**
	3rd person	**-a**	**-aba**	**-ó**
plur.	1st person	**-amos**	**-ábamos**	**-amos**
	2nd person	**-áis**	**-abais**	**-asteis**
	3rd person	**-an**	**-aban**	**-aron**

		❹ PRESENT SUBJUNCTIVE	**❺ IMPERFECT SUBJUNCTIVE**
sing.	1st person	**-e**	**-ara** or **-ase**
	2nd person	**-es**	**-aras** or **-ases**
	3rd person	**-e**	**-ara** or **-ase**
plur.	1st person	**-emos**	**-áramos** or **-ásemos**
	2nd person	**-éis**	**-arais** or **-aseis**
	3rd person	**-en**	**-aran** or **-asen**

		❻ FUTURE	**❼ CONDITIONAL**
sing.	1st person	**-é**	**-ía**
	2nd person	**-ás**	**-ías**
	3rd person	**-á**	**-ía**
plur.	1st person	**-emos**	**-íamos**
	2nd person	**-éis**	**-íais**
	3rd person	**-án**	**-ían**

Examples

1 PRESENT

(yo)	hablo
(tú)	hablas
(él/ella/Vd)	habla
(nosotros/as)	hablamos
(vosotros/as)	habláis
(ellos/as/Vds)	hablan

2 IMPERFECT

hablaba
hablabas
hablaba
hablábamos
hablabais
hablaban

3 PRETERITE

hablé
hablaste
habló
hablamos
hablasteis
hablaron

4 PRESENT SUBJUNCTIVE

(yo)	hable
(tú)	hables
(él/ella/Vd)	hable
(nosotros/as)	hablemos
(vosotros/as)	habléis
(ellos/as/Vds)	hablen

5 IMPERFECT SUBJUNCTIVE

hablara *or* hablase
hablaras *or* hablases
hablara *or* hablase
habláramos *or* hablásemos
hablarais *or* hablaseis
hablaran *or* hablasen

6 FUTURE

(yo)	hablaré
(tú)	hablarás
(él/ella/Vd)	hablará
(nosotros/as)	hablaremos
(vosotros/as)	hablaréis
(ellos/as/Vds)	hablarán

7 CONDITIONAL

hablaría
hablarías
hablaría
hablaríamos
hablaríais
hablarían

Verbs

Simple Tenses: Second Conjugation

The stem is formed as follows:

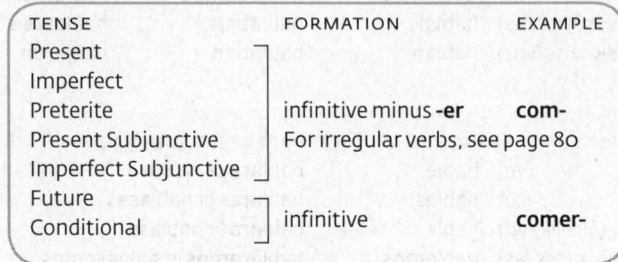

TENSE	FORMATION	EXAMPLE
Present Imperfect Preterite Present Subjunctive Imperfect Subjunctive	infinitive minus **-er** For irregular verbs, see page 80	**com-**
Future Conditional	infinitive	**comer-**

To the appropriate stem add the following endings:

		1 PRESENT	**2** IMPERFECT	**3** PRETERITE
	1st person	**-o**	**-ía**	**-í**
sing.	2nd person	**-es**	**-ías**	**-iste**
	3rd person	**-e**	**-ía**	**-ió**
	1st person	**-emos**	**-íamos**	**-imos**
plur.	2nd person	**-éis**	**-íais**	**-isteis**
	3rd person	**-en**	**-ían**	**-ieron**

		4 PRESENT SUBJUNCTIVE	**5** IMPERFECT SUBJUNCTIVE
	1st person	**-a**	**-iera** or **-iese**
sing.	2nd person	**-as**	**-ieras** or **-ieses**
	3rd person	**-a**	**-iera** or **-iese**
	1st person	**-amos**	**-iéramos** or **-iésemos**
plur.	2nd person	**-áis**	**-ierais** or **-ieseis**
	3rd person	**-an**	**-ieran** or **-iesen**

		6 FUTURE	**7** CONDITIONAL
	1st person	**-é**	**-ía**
sing.	2nd person	**-ás**	**-ías**
	3rd person	**-á**	**-ía**
	1st person	**-emos**	**-íamos**
plur.	2nd person	**-éis**	**-íais**
	3rd person	**-án**	**-ían**

Examples

1 PRESENT

(yo)	com**o**
(tú)	com**es**
(él/ella/Vd)	com**e**
(nosotros/as)	com**emos**
(vosotros/as)	com**éis**
(ellos/as/Vds)	com**en**

2 IMPERFECT

com**ía**
com**ías**
com**ía**
com**íamos**
com**íais**
com**ían**

3 PRETERITE

com**í**
com**iste**
com**ió**
com**imos**
com**isteis**
com**ieron**

4 PRESENT SUBJUNCTIVE

(yo)	com**a**
(tú)	com**as**
(él/ella/Vd)	com**a**
(nosotros/as)	com**amos**
(vosotros/as)	com**áis**
(ellos/as/Vds)	com**an**

5 IMPERFECT SUBJUNCTIVE

com**iera** or com**iese**
com**ieras** or com**ieses**
com**iera** or com**iese**
com**iéramos** or com**iésemos**
com**ierais** or com**ieseis**
com**ieran** or com**iesen**

6 FUTURE

(yo)	comer**é**
(tú)	comer**ás**
(él/ella/Vd)	comer**á**
(nosotros/as)	comer**emos**
(vosotros/as)	comer**éis**
(ellos/as/Vds)	comer**án**

7 CONDITIONAL

comer**ía**
comer**ías**
comer**ía**
comer**íamos**
comer**íais**
comer**ían**

11

Verbs

Simple Tenses: Third Conjugation

The stem is formed as follows:

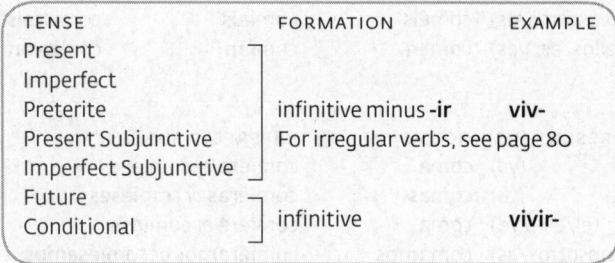

TENSE	FORMATION	EXAMPLE
Present		
Imperfect		
Preterite	infinitive minus **-ir**	**viv-**
Present Subjunctive	For irregular verbs, see page 80	
Imperfect Subjunctive		
Future	infinitive	**vivir-**
Conditional		

To the appropriate stem add the following endings:

		① PRESENT	**②** IMPERFECT	**③** PRETERITE
	1st person	**-o**	**-ía**	**-í**
sing.	2nd person	**-es**	**-ías**	**-iste**
	3rd person	**-e**	**-ía**	**-ió**
	1st person	**-imos**	**-íamos**	**-imos**
plur.	2nd person	**-ís**	**-íais**	**-isteis**
	3rd person	**-en**	**-ían**	**-ieron**

		④ PRESENT SUBJUNCTIVE	**⑤** IMPERFECT SUBJUNCTIVE
	1st person	**-a**	**-iera** or **-iese**
sing.	2nd person	**-as**	**-ieras** or **-ieses**
	3rd person	**-a**	**-iera** or **-iese**
	1st person	**-amos**	**-iéramos** or **-iésemos**
plur.	2nd person	**-áis**	**-ierais** or **-ieseis**
	3rd person	**-an**	**-ieran** or **-iesen**

		⑥ FUTURE	**⑦** CONDITIONAL
	1st person	**-é**	**-ía**
sing.	2nd person	**-ás**	**-ías**
	3rd person	**-á**	**-ía**
	1st person	**-emos**	**-íamos**
plur.	2nd person	**-éis**	**-íais**
	3rd person	**-án**	**-ían**

Examples

❶ PRESENT

(yo)	viv**o**
(tú)	viv**es**
(él/ella/Vd)	viv**e**
(nosotros/as)	viv**imos**
(vosotros/as)	viv**ís**
(ellos/as/Vds)	viv**en**

❷ IMPERFECT

viv**ía**
viv**ías**
viv**ía**
viv**íamos**
viv**íais**
viv**ían**

❸ PRETERITE

viv**í**
viv**iste**
viv**ió**
viv**imos**
viv**isteis**
viv**ieron**

❹ PRESENT SUBJUNCTIVE

(yo)	viv**a**
(tú)	viv**as**
(él/ella/Vd)	viv**a**
(nosotros/as)	viv**amos**
(vosotros/as)	viv**áis**
(ellos/as/Vds)	viv**an**

❺ IMPERFECT SUBJUNCTIVE

viv**iera** *or* viv**iese**
viv**ieras** *or* viv**ieses**
viv**iera** *or* viv**iese**
viv**iéramos** *or* viv**iésemos**
viv**ierais** *or* viv**ieseis**
viv**ieran** *or* viv**iesen**

❻ FUTURE

(yo)	vivir**é**
(tú)	vivir**ás**
(él/ella/Vd)	vivir**á**
(nosotros/as)	vivir**emos**
(vosotros/as)	vivir**éis**
(ellos/as/Vds)	vivir**án**

❼ CONDITIONAL

vivir**ía**
vivir**ías**
vivir**ía**
vivir**íamos**
vivir**íais**
vivir**ían**

Verbs

The Imperative

The imperative is the form of the verb used to give commands or orders. It can be used politely, as in English 'Shut the door, please'.

In *positive* commands, the imperative forms for **Vd**, **Vds** and **nosotros** are the same as the subjunctive. The other forms are as follows:

> **tú** (same as 3rd person singular present indicative)
> **vosotros** (final **-r** of infinitive changes to **-d**) → ❶

(tú)	**habla** speak	**come** eat	**vive** live
(Vd)	**hable** speak	**coma** eat	**viva** live
(nosotros)	**hablemos** let's speak	**comamos** let's eat	**vivamos** let's live
(vosotros)	**hablad** speak	**comed** eat	**vivid** live
(Vds)	**hablen** speak	**coman** eat	**vivan** live

In *negative* commands, all the imperative forms are exactly the same as the present subjunctive.

The imperative of irregular verbs is given in the verb tables, pages 82 to 160.

Position of object pronouns with the imperative:
- in *positive* commands: they follow the verb and are attached to it. An accent may be needed to show the correct position for stress (see page 296). The **nosotros** form drops the final **-s** before the pronoun **se** → ❷
- in *negative* commands: they precede the verb and are not attached to it → ❸

For the order of object pronouns, see page 236.

Examples

① **cantar** — to sing
cantad — sing

② **Perdóneme** — Excuse me
Enviémoselos — Let's send them to him/her/them

Elíjanos — Choose us
Explíquemelo — Explain it to me

Esperémosla — Let's wait for her/it
Devuélvaselo — Give it back to him/her/them

③ **No me molestes** — Don't disturb me
No se la devolvamos — Let's not give it back to him/her/them

No les castiguemos — Let's not punish them
No me lo mandes — Don't send it to me
No las conteste — Don't answer them
No nos lo hagan — Don't do it to us

Verbs

The Imperative *continued*

For reflexive verbs – e.g. **levantarse** to get up – the object pronoun is the reflexive pronoun. It should be noted that the imperative forms need an accent to show the correct position for stress (see page 296). The forms **nosotros** and **vosotros** also drop the final **-s** and **-d** respectively before the pronouns **nos** and **os** → ❶

> BUT: **idos (vosotros)** go

ⓘ Note: For general instructions, the infinitive is used instead of the imperative → ❷, but when it is preceded by **vamos a**, the construction is often translated as *let's* ... → ❸

Examples

❶ Levántate — Get up
No te levantes — Don't get up
Levántese (Vd) — Get up
No se levante (Vd) — Don't get up
Levantémonos — Let's get up
No nos levantemos — Let's not get up
Levantaos — Get up
No os levantéis — Don't get up
Levántense (Vds) — Get up
No se levanten (Vds) — Don't get up

❷ Ver pág ... — See page ...
No pasar — Do not pass

❸ Vamos a ver — Let's see
Vamos a empezar — Let's start

Verbs

Compound Tenses: formation

In Spanish the compound tenses are:

      Perfect → ❶
      Pluperfect → ❷
      Future Perfect → ❸
      Conditional Perfect → ❹
      Past Anterior → ❺
      Perfect Subjunctive → ❻
      Pluperfect Subjunctive → ❼

They consist of the past participle of the verb together with the auxiliary verb **haber**.

Compound tenses are formed in exactly the same way for both regular and irregular verbs, the only difference being that irregular verbs may have an irregular past participle.

The Past Participle

For all compound tenses you need to know how to form the past participle of the verb. For regular verbs this is as follows:

    First conjugation: replace the **-ar** of the infinitive by **-ado** → ❽

    Second conjugation: replace the **-er** of the infinitive by **-ido** → ❾

    Third conjugation: replace the **-ir** of the infinitive by **-ido** → ❿

Examples

① (yo) he hablado — I have spoken

② (yo) había hablado — I had spoken

③ (yo) habré hablado — I shall have spoken

④ (yo) habría hablado — I should/would have spoken

⑤ (yo) hube hablado — I had spoken

⑥ (que) (yo) haya hablado — (that) I spoke, have spoken

⑦ (que) (yo) hubiera/hubiese hablado — (that) I had spoken

⑧ **cantar** to sing → **cantado** sung

⑨ **comer** to eat → **comido** eaten

⑩ **vivir** to live → **vivido** lived

Verbs

Compound Tenses: formation *continued*

PERFECT TENSE
The present tense of **haber** plus the past participle → ❶

PLUPERFECT TENSE
The imperfect tense of **haber** plus the past participle → ❷

FUTURE PERFECT
The future tense of **haber** plus the past participle → ❸

CONDITIONAL PERFECT
The conditional of **haber** plus the past participle → ❹

Examples

❶ PERFECT

(yo)	**he** hablado
(tú)	**has** hablado
(él/ella/Vd)	**ha** hablado
(nosotros/as)	**hemos** hablado
(vosotros/as)	**habéis** hablado
(ellos/as/Vds)	**han** hablado

❷ PLUPERFECT

(yo)	**había** hablado
(tú)	**habías** hablado
(él/ella/Vd)	**había** hablado
(nosotros/as)	**habíamos** hablado
(vosotros/as)	**habíais** hablado
(ellos/as/Vds)	**habían** hablado

❸ FUTURE PERFECT

(yo)	**habré** hablado
(tú)	**habrás** hablado
(él/ella/Vd)	**habrá** hablado
(nosotros/as)	**habremos** hablado
(vosotros/as)	**habréis** hablado
(ellos/as/Vds)	**habrán** hablado

❹ CONDITIONAL PERFECT

(yo)	**habría** hablado
(tú)	**habrías** hablado
(él/ella/Vd)	**habría** hablado
(nosotros/as)	**habríamos** hablado
(vosotros/as)	**habríais** hablado
(ellos/as/Vds)	**habrían** hablado

Verbs

Compound Tenses: Formation *continued*

PAST ANTERIOR
The preterite of **haber** plus the past participle → **1**

PERFECT SUBJUNCTIVE
The present subjunctive of **haber** plus the past participle → **2**

PLUPERFECT SUBJUNCTIVE
The imperfect subjunctive of **haber** plus the past participle → **3**

For how to form the past participle of regular verbs, see page 18.
The past participle of irregular verbs is given for each verb in the verb
tables, pages 82 to 160.

Examples

1 PAST ANTERIOR

(yo)	**hube** habl**ado**
(tú)	**hubiste** habl**ado**
(él/ella/Vd)	**hubo** habl**ado**
(nosotros/as)	**hubimos** habl**ado**
(vosotros/as)	**hubisteis** habl**ado**
(ellos/as/Vds)	**hubieron** habl**ado**

2 PERFECT SUBJUNCTIVE

(yo)	**haya** habl**ado**
(tú)	**hayas** habl**ado**
(él/ella/Vd)	**haya** habl**ado**
(nosotros/as)	**hayamos** habl**ado**
(vosotros/as)	**hayáis** habl**ado**
(ellos/as/Vds)	**hayan** habl**ado**

3 PLUPERFECT SUBJUNCTIVE

(yo)	**hubiera** or **hubiese** habl**ado**
(tú)	**hubieras** or **hubieses** habl**ado**
(él/ella/Vd)	**hubiera** or **hubiese** habl**ado**
(nosotros/as)	**hubiéramos** or **hubiésemos** habl**ado**
(vosotros/as)	**hubierais** or **hubieseis** habl**ado**
(ellos/as/Vds)	**hubieran** or **hubiesen** habl**ado**

Verbs

Reflexive Verbs

A reflexive verb is one accompanied by a reflexive pronoun. The infinitive of a reflexive verb ends with the pronoun **se**, which is added to the verb form e.g. **levantarse** *to get up*; **lavarse** *to wash (oneself)*.
The reflexive pronouns are:

	SINGULAR	PLURAL
1st person	**me**	**nos**
2nd person	**te**	**os**
3rd person	**se**	**se**

The reflexive pronoun 'reflects back' to the subject, but it is not always translated in English → **①**

> The plural pronouns are sometimes translated as 'one another', 'each other' (the *reciprocal* meaning) → **②**

> The reciprocal meaning may be emphasized by **el uno al otro/ la una a la otra (los unos a los otros/las unas a las otras)** → **③**

Both simple and compound tenses of reflexive verbs are conjugated in exactly the same way as those of non-reflexive verbs, except that the reflexive pronoun is always used.

The only irregularity is in the 1st and 2nd person plural of the affirmative imperative (see page 16). A sample reflexive verb is conjugated in full on pages 28 to 31.

Position of reflexive pronouns

Except with the infinitive, gerund and positive commands, the pronoun comes before the verb → **④**

In the infinitive, gerund and positive commands, the pronoun follows the verb and is attached to it (but see also page 232) → **⑤**

Examples

❶ Me visto   I'm dressing (myself)
Nos lavamos   We're washing (ourselves)
Se levanta   He gets up

❷ Nos queremos   We love each other
Se parecen   They resemble one another

❸ Se miraban el uno al otro   They were looking at each other

❹ Me acuesto temprano   I go to bed early
¿Cómo se llama Vd?   What is your name?
No se ha despertado   He hasn't woken up
No te levantes   Don't get up

❺ Quiero irme   I want to go away
Estoy levantándome   I am getting up
Siéntense   Sit down
Vámonos   Let's go

Verbs

Reflexive Verbs *continued*

Some verbs have both a reflexive and non-reflexive form. When used reflexively, they have a different but closely related meaning, as shown in the following examples.

NON-REFLEXIVE	REFLEXIVE
acostar to put to bed	**acostarse** to go to bed
casar to marry (off)	**casarse** to get married
detener to stop	**detenerse** to come to a halt
dormir to sleep	**dormirse** to go to sleep
enfadar to annoy	**enfadarse** to get annoyed
hacer to make	**hacerse** to become
ir to go	**irse** to leave, go away
lavar to wash	**lavarse** to get washed
levantar to raise	**levantarse** to get up
llamar to call	**llamarse** to be called
poner to put	**ponerse** to put on (clothing), to become
sentir to feel (something)	**sentirse** to feel (sick, tired, *etc*)
vestir to dress (someone)	**vestirse** to get dressed
volver to return	**volverse** to turn round

Some other verbs exist only in the reflexive:

arrepentirse to repent	**jactarse** to boast
atreverse to dare	**quejarse** to complain

Some verbs acquire a different nuance when used reflexively:

caer to fall → ❶	**caerse** to fall down (by accident) → ❷
morir to die, be killed (by accident or on purpose) → ❸	**morirse** to die (from natural causes) → ❹

Often a reflexive verb can be used:
- to avoid the passive (see page 32) → ❺
- in impersonal expressions (see page 40) → ❻

Examples

1 El agua caía desde las rocas — Water fell from the rocks

2 Me caí y me rompí el brazo — I fell and broke my arm

3 Tres personas han muerto en un accidente/atentado terrorista — Three people were killed in an accident/a terrorist attack

4 Mi abuelo se murió a los ochenta años — My grandfather died at the age of eighty

5 Se perdió la batalla — The battle was lost
No se veían las casas — The houses could not be seen

6 Se dice que ... — (It is said that) People say that ...
No se puede entrar — You/One can't go in
No se permite — It is not allowed

Verbs

Reflexive Verbs *continued*

Conjugation of **lavarse** to wash (oneself)

1 SIMPLE TENSES

PRESENT

(yo)	**me** lav**o**
(tú)	**te** lav**as**
(él/ella/Vd)	**se** lav**a**
(nosotros/as)	**nos** lav**amos**
(vosotros/as)	**os** lav**áis**
(ellos/as/Vds)	**se** lav**an**

IMPERFECT

(yo)	**me** lav**aba**
(tú)	**te** lav**abas**
(él/ella/Vd)	**se** lav**aba**
(nosotros/as)	**nos** lav**ábamos**
(vosotros/as)	**os** lav**abais**
(ellos/as/Vds)	**se** lav**aban**

FUTURE

(yo)	**me** lav**aré**
(tú)	**te** lav**arás**
(él/ella/Vd)	**se** lav**ará**
(nosotros/as)	**nos** lav**aremos**
(vosotros/as)	**os** lav**aréis**
(ellos/as/Vds)	**se** lav**arán**

CONDITIONAL

(yo)	**me** lav**aría**
(tú)	**te** lav**arías**
(él/ella/Vd)	**se** lav**aría**
(nosotros/as)	**nos** lav**aríamos**
(vosotros/as)	**os** lav**aríais**
(ellos/as/Vds)	**se** lav**arían**

Examples

ReflexiveVerbs *continued*

Conjugation of **lavarse** to wash (oneself)

PRETERITE
(yo)	**me** lav**é**
(tú)	**te** lav**aste**
(él/ella/Vd)	**se** lav**ó**
(nosotros/as)	**nos** lav**amos**
(vosotros/as)	**os** lav**asteis**
(ellos/as/Vds)	**se** lav**aron**

PRESENT SUBJUNCTIVE
(yo)	**me** lav**e**
(tú)	**te** lav**es**
(él/ella/Vd)	**se** lav**e**
(nosotros/as)	**nos** lav**emos**
(vosotros/as)	**os** lav**éis**
(ellos/as/Vds)	**se** lav**en**

IMPERFECT SUBJUNCTIVE
(yo)	**me** lav**ara** *or* lav**ase**
(tú)	**te** lav**aras** *or* lav**ases**
(él/ella/Vd)	**se** lav**ara** *or* lav**ase**
(nosotros/as)	**nos** lav**áramos** *or* lav**ásemos**
(vosotros/as)	**os** lav**arais** *or* lav**aseis**
(ellos/as/Vds)	**se** lav**aran** *or* lav**asen**

Verbs

Reflexive Verbs *continued*

Conjugation of **lavarse** to wash (oneself)

PERFECT

(yo)	**me he** lav**ado**
(tú)	**te has** lav**ado**
(él/ella/Vd)	**se ha** lav**ado**
(nosotros/as)	**nos hemos** lav**ado**
(vosotros/as)	**os habéis** lav**ado**
(ellos/as/Vds)	**se han** lav**ado**

PLUPERFECT

(yo)	**me había** lav**ado**
(tú)	**te habías** lav**ado**
(él/ella/Vd)	**se había** lav**ado**
(nosotros/as)	**nos habíamos** lav**ado**
(vosotros/as)	**os habíais** lav**ado**
(ellos/as/Vds)	**se habían** lav**ado**

FUTURE PERFECT

(yo)	**me habré** lav**ado**
(tú)	**te habrás** lav**ado**
(él/ella/Vd)	**se habrá** lav**ado**
(nosotros/as)	**nos habremos** lav**ado**
(vosotros/as)	**os habréis** lav**ado**
(ellos/as/Vds)	**se habrán** lav**ado**

Examples

Reflexive Verbs *continued*

Conjugation of **lavarse** to wash (oneself)

PAST ANTERIOR
(yo)	**me hube** lavado
(tú)	**te hubiste** lavado
(él/ella/Vd)	**se hubo** lavado
(nosotros/as)	**nos hubimos** lavado
(vosotros/as)	**os hubisteis** lavado
(ellos/as/Vds)	**se hubieron** lavado

PERFECT SUBJUNCTIVE
(yo)	**me haya** lavado
(tú)	**te hayas** lavado
(él/ella/Vd)	**se haya** lavado
(nosotros/as)	**nos hayamos** lavado
(vosotros/as)	**os hayáis** lavado
(ellos/as/Vds)	**se hayan** lavado

PLUPERFECT SUBJUNCTIVE
(yo)	**me hubiera** *or* **hubiese** lavado
(tú)	**te hubieras** *or* **hubieses** lavado
(él/ella/Vd)	**se hubiera** *or* **hubiese** lavado
(nosotros/as)	**nos hubiéramos** *or* **hubiésemos** lavado
(vosotros/as)	**os hubierais** *or* **hubieseis** lavado
(ellos/as/Vds)	**se hubieran** *or* **hubiesen** lavado

Verbs

The Passive

In active sentences, the subject of a verb carries out the action of that verb, but in passive sentences the subject receives the action. Compare the following:

> The car hit Jane (*subject*: the car)
> Jane was hit by the car (*subject*: Jane)

English uses the verb 'to be' with the past participle to form passive sentences. Spanish forms them in the same way, i.e.:
a tense of **ser** + *past participle*.

The past participle agrees in number and gender with the subject → ❶

A sample verb is conjugated in the passive voice on pages 36 to 39.

In English, the word 'by' usually introduces the agent through which the action of a passive sentence is performed. In Spanish this agent is preceded by **por** → ❷

The passive voice is used much less frequently in Spanish than English. It is, however, often used in expressions where the identity of the agent is unknown or unimportant → ❸

Examples

❶ Pablo ha sido despedido — Paul has been sacked
Su madre era muy admirada — His mother was greatly admired
El palacio será vendido — The palace will be sold
Las puertas habían sido cerradas — The doors had been closed

❷ La casa fue diseñada por mi hermano — The house was designed by my brother

❸ La ciudad fue conquistada tras un largo asedio — The city was conquered after a long siege
Ha sido declarado el estado de excepción — A state of emergency has been declared

33

Verbs

The Passive *continued*

In English the indirect object in an active sentence can become the subject of the related passive sentence, e.g.

> 'His mother gave him the book' (*indirect object*: him)
> He was given the book by his mother

This is not possible in Spanish. The indirect object remains as such, while the object of the active sentence becomes the subject of the passive sentence → **❶**

Other ways to express a passive meaning

Since modern Spanish tends to avoid the passive, it uses various other constructions to replace it:

If the agent (person or object performing the action) is known, the active is often preferred where English might prefer the passive → **❷**

The 3rd person plural of the active voice can be used. The meaning is equivalent to 'they' + *verb* → **❸**

When the action of the sentence is performed on a person, the reflexive form of the verb can be used in the 3rd person singular, and the person becomes the object → **❹**

When the action is performed on a thing, this becomes the subject of the sentence and the verb is made reflexive, agreeing in number with the subject → **❺**

Examples

❶ Su madre le regaló el libro
His mother gave him the book
BECOMES:
El libro le fue regalado por su madre
The book was given to him by his mother

❷ La policía interrogó al sospechoso
The police questioned the suspect
RATHER THAN:
El sospechoso fue interrogado por la policía

❸ Usan demasiada publicidad en la televisión
Too much advertising is used on television

❹ Últimamente no se lo/los ha visto mucho en público
He has/They have not been seen much in public recently

❺ Esta palabra ya no se usa
This word is no longer used
Todos los libros se han vendido
All the books have been sold

Verbs

The Passive *continued*

Conjugation of **ser amado** to be loved

PRESENT

(yo)	**soy** am**ado/a**
(tú)	**eres** am**ado/a**
(él/ella/Vd)	**es** am**ado/a**
(nosotros/as)	**somos** am**ados/as**
(vosotros/as)	**sois** am**ados/as**
(ellos/as/Vds)	**son** am**ados/as**

IMPERFECT

(yo)	**era** am**ado/a**
(tú)	**eras** am**ado/a**
(él/ella/Vd)	**era** am**ado/a**
(nosotros/as)	**éramos** am**ados/as**
(vosotros/as)	**erais** am**ados/as**
(ellos/as/Vds)	**eran** am**ados/as**

FUTURE

(yo)	**seré** am**ado/a**
(tú)	**serás** am**ado/a**
(él/ella/Vd)	**será** am**ado/a**
(nosotros/as)	**seremos** am**ados/as**
(vosotros/as)	**seréis** am**ados/as**
(ellos/as/Vds)	**serán** am**ados/as**

CONDITIONAL

(yo)	**sería** am**ado/a**
(tú)	**serías** am**ado/a**
(él/ella/Vd)	**sería** am**ado/a**
(nosotros/as)	**seríamos** am**ados/as**
(vosotros/as)	**seríais** am**ados/as**
(ellos/as/Vds)	**serían** am**ados/as**

Examples

The Passive *continued*

Conjugation of **ser amado** to be loved

PRETERITE

(yo)	**fui** am**ado/a**
(tú)	**fuiste** am**ado/a**
(él/ella/Vd)	**fue** am**ado/a**
(nosotros/as)	**fuimos** am**ados/as**
(vosotros/as)	**fuisteis** am**ados/as**
(ellos/as/Vds)	**fueron** am**ados/as**

PRESENT SUBJUNCTIVE

(yo)	**sea** am**ado/a**
(tú)	**seas** am**ado/a**
(él/ella/Vd)	**sea** am**ado/a**
(nosotros/as)	**seamos** am**ados/as**
(vosotros/as)	**seáis** am**ados/as**
(ellos/as/Vds)	**sean** am**ados/as**

IMPERFECT SUBJUNCTIVE

(yo)	**fuera** *or* **fuese** am**ado/a**
(tú)	**fueras** *or* **fueses** am**ado/a**
(él/ella/Vd)	**fuera** *or* **fuese** am**ado/a**
(nosotros/as)	**fuéramos** *or* **fuésemos** am**ados/as**
(vosotros/as)	**fuerais** *or* **fueseis** am**ados/as**
(ellos/as/Vds)	**fueran** *or* **fuesen** am**ados/as**

Verbs

The Passive *continued*

Conjugation of **ser amado** to be loved

PERFECT

(yo)	**he sido** amado/a
(tú)	**has sido** amado/a
(él/ella/Vd)	**ha sido** amado/a
(nosotros/as)	**hemos sido** amados/as
(vosotros/as)	**habéis sido** amados/as
(ellos/as/Vds)	**han sido** amados/as

PLUPERFECT

(yo)	**había sido** amado/a
(tú)	**habías sido** amado/a
(él/ella/Vd)	**había sido** amado/a
(nosotros/as)	**habíamos sido** amados/as
(vosotros/as)	**habíais sido** amados/as
(ellos/as/Vds)	**habían sido** amados/as

FUTURE PERFECT

(yo)	**habré sido** amado/a
(tú)	**habrás sido** amado/a
(él/ella/Vd)	**habrá sido** amado/a
(nosotros/as)	**habremos sido** amados/as
(vosotros/as)	**habréis sido** amados/as
(ellos/as/Vds)	**habrán sido** amados/as

CONDITIONAL PERFECT

(yo)	**habría sido** amado/a
(tú)	**habrías sido** amado/a
(él/ella/Vd)	**habría sido** amado/a
(nosotros/as)	**habríamos sido** amados/as
(vosotros/as)	**habríais sido** amados/as
(ellos/as/Vds)	**habrían sido** amados/as

Examples

The Passive *continued*

Conjugation of **ser amado** to be loved

PAST ANTERIOR

(yo)	**hube sido** amado/a
(tú)	**hubiste sido** amado/a
(él/ella/Vd)	**hubo sido** amado/a
(nosotros/as)	**hubimos sido** amados/as
(vosotros/as)	**hubisteis sido** amados/as
(ellos/as/Vds)	**hubieron sido** amados/as

PERFECT SUBJUNCTIVE

(yo)	**haya sido** amado/a
(tú)	**hayas sido** amado/a
(él/ella/Vd)	**haya sido** amado/a
(nosotros/as)	**hayamos sido** amados/as
(vosotros/as)	**hayáis sido** amados/as
(ellos/as/Vds)	**hayan sido** amados/as

PLUPERFECT SUBJUNCTIVE

(yo)	**hubiera/-se sido** amado/a
(tú)	**hubieras/-ses sido** amado/a
(él/ella/Vd)	**hubiera/-se sido** amado/a
(nosotros/as)	**hubiéramos/-semos sido** amados/as
(vosotros/as)	**hubierais/-seis sido** amados/as
(ellos/as/Vds)	**hubieran/-sen sido** amados/as

Verbs

Impersonal Verbs

Impersonal verbs are used only in the infinitive, the gerund, and in the 3rd person (usually singular); unlike English, Spanish does not use the subject pronoun with impersonal verbs, e.g.

> **llueve** it's raining
> **es fácil decir que ...** it's easy to say that ...

The most common impersonal verbs are:

INFINITIVE	CONSTRUCTION
amanecer	**amanece/está amaneciendo** it's daybreak
anochecer	**anochece/está anocheciendo** it's getting dark
granizar	**graniza/está granizando** it's hailing
llover	**llueve/está lloviendo** it's raining → ❶
lloviznar	**llovizna/está lloviznando** it's drizzling
nevar	**nieva/está nevando** it's snowing → ❶
tronar	**truena/está tronando** it's thundering

Some reflexive verbs are also used impersonally:

INFINITIVE	CONSTRUCTION
creerse	**se cree que*** + *indicative* → ❷ it is thought that; people think that
decirse	**se dice que*** + *indicative* → ❸ it is said that; people say that

* This impersonal construction conveys the same meaning as the 3rd person plural of these verbs: **creen que**, **dicen que**

Examples

❶ Llovía a cántaros   It was raining cats and dogs
   Estaba nevando cuando salieron   It was snowing when they left

❷ Se cree que llegarán mañana   It is thought they will arrive
                          tomorrow

❸ Se dice que ha sido el peor   People say it's been the worst
   invierno en 50 años   winter in 50 years

Verbs

Impersonal Verbs *continued*

INFINITIVE	CONSTRUCTION
poderse	**se puede** + *infinitive* → ❶
	one/people can, it is possible to
tratarse de	**se trata de** + *noun* → ❷
	it's a question/matter of something
	it's about something
	se trata de + *infinitive* → ❸
	it's a question/matter of doing; somebody must do
venderse	**se vende*** + *noun* → ❹
	to be sold; for sale

*This impersonal construction conveys the same meaning as the 3rd person plural of this verb: **venden**

The following verbs are also commonly used in impersonal constructions:

INFINITIVE	CONSTRUCTION
bastar	**basta con** + *infinitive* → ❺
	it is enough to do
	basta con + *noun* → ❻
	something is enough, it only takes something
faltar	**falta** + *infinitive* → ❼
	we still have to/one still has to
haber	**hay** + *noun* → ❽
	there is/are
	hay que + *infinitive* → ❾
	one has to/we have to
hacer	**hace** + *noun/adjective depicting weather/dark/light etc* → ❿
	it is
	hace + *time expression* + **que** + *indicative* → ⓫
	somebody has done *or* been doing something since ...
	hace + *time expression* + **que** + *negative indicative* → ⓬
	it is ... since

Examples

① Aquí se puede aparcar One can park here

② No se trata de dinero It isn't a question/matter of money

③ Se trata de poner fin al asunto We must put an end to the matter

④ Se vende coche Car for sale

⑤ Basta con telefonear para reservar un asiento You just need to phone to reserve a seat

⑥ Basta con un error para que todo se estropee One single error is enough to ruin everything

⑦ Aún falta cerrar las maletas We/One still have/has to close the suitcases

⑧ Hay una habitación libre There is one room free
No había cartas esta mañana There were no letters this morning

⑨ Hay que cerrar las puertas We have/One has to shut the doors

⑩ Hace calor/viento/sol It is hot/windy/sunny
Mañana hará bueno It'll be nice (weather) tomorrow

⑪ Hace seis meses que vivo/ vivimos aquí I/We have lived or been living here for six months

⑫ Hace tres años que no le veo It is three years since I last saw him

Verbs

Impersonal Verbs *continued*

INFINITIVE	CONSTRUCTION
hacer falta	**hace falta** + *noun object* (+ *indirect object*) → ❶
	(somebody) needs something; something is
	necessary (to somebody)
	hace falta + *infinitive* (+ *indirect object*) → ❷
	it is necessary to do
	hace falta que + *subjunctive* → ❸
	it is necessary to do, somebody must do
parecer	**parece que** (+ *indirect object*) + *indicative* → ❹
	it seems/appears that
ser	**es/son** + *time expression* → ❺
	it is
	es + **de día/noche** → ❻
	it is
	es + *adjective* + *infinitive* → ❼
	it is
ser mejor	**es mejor** + *infinitive* → ❽
	it's better to do
	es mejor que + *subjunctive* → ❾
	it's better if/that
valer más	**más vale** + *infinitive* → ❿
	it's better to do
	más vale que + *subjunctive* → ⓫
	it's better to do/that somebody does

Examples

1 **Hace falta valor para hacer eso**

One needs courage to do that/
Courage is needed to do that

Me hace falta otro vaso más

I need an extra glass

2 **Hace falta volver**

It is necessary to return/
We/I/You must return*

Me hacía falta volver

I had to return

3 **Hace falta que Vd se vaya**

You have to/must leave

4 **(Me) parece que estás equivocado**

It seems (to me) you are wrong

5 **Son las tres y media**

It is half past three

Ya es primavera

It is spring now

6 **Era de noche cuando llegamos**

It was night when we arrived

7 **Era inútil protestar**

It was useless to complain

8 **Es mejor no decir nada**

It's better to keep quiet

9 **Es mejor que lo pongas aquí**

It would be better if/that you
put it here

10 **Más vale prevenir que curar**

Prevention is better than cure

11 **Más valdría que no fuéramos**

It would be better if we didn't go/
We'd better not go

*The translation here obviously depends on context

Verbs

The Infinitive

The infinitive is the form of the verb found in dictionary entries meaning 'to ...', e.g. **hablar** *to speak*, **vivir** *to live*.

The infinitive is used in the following ways:

After a preposition → **①**

As a verbal noun → **②**
In this use the article may precede the infinitive, especially when the infinitive is the subject and begins the sentence → **③**

As a dependent infinitive, in the following verbal constructions:
- with no linking preposition → **④**
- with the linking preposition **a** → **⑤**
  (see also page 66)
- with the linking preposition **de** → **⑥**
  (see also page 66)
- with the linking preposition **en** → **⑦**
  (see also page 66)
- with the linking preposition **con** → **⑧**
  (see also page 66)
- with the linking preposition **por** → **⑨**
  (see also page 66)

The following construction should also be noted:
   indefinite pronoun + **que** + *infinitive* → **⑩**

The object pronouns generally follow the infinitive and are attached to it. For exceptions, see page 232.

Examples

1 **Después de acabar el desayuno, salió de casa**
After finishing her breakfast she went out

Al enterarse de lo ocurrido se puso furiosa
When she found out what had happened she was furious

Me hizo daño sin saberlo
She hurt me without realizing

2 **Su deporte preferido es montar a caballo**
His favourite sport is horse riding

Ver es creer
Seeing is believing

3 **El viajar tanto me resulta cansado**
I find all this travelling tiring

4 **¿Quiere Vd esperar?**
Would you like to wait?

5 **Aprenderán pronto a nadar**
They will soon learn to swim

6 **Pronto dejará de llover**
It'll stop raining soon

7 **La comida tarda en hacerse**
The meal takes a long time to cook

8 **Amenazó con denunciarlos**
He threatened to report them (to the police)

9 **Comience Vd por decirme su nombre**
Please start by giving me your name

10 **Tengo algo que decirte**
I have something to tell you

Verbs

The Infinitive *continued*

The verbs set out below are followed by the infinitive with no linking preposition.

deber, **poder**, **saber**, **querer** and **tener que** (**hay que** in impersonal constructions) → **1**

valer más, **hacer falta**: see Impersonal Verbs, page 44.

verbs of seeing or hearing, e.g. **ver** *to see*, **oír** *to hear* → **2**

hacer → **3**

dejar to let, allow → **3**

The following common verbs:

aconsejar to advise → **4**　　　　**necesitar** to need → **11**
conseguir to manage to → **5**　　　**odiar** to hate
decidir to decide　　　　　　　　　**olvidar** to forget → **12**
desear to wish, want → **6**　　　　**pensar** to think → **13**
esperar to hope → **7**　　　　　　**preferir** to prefer → **14**
evitar to avoid → **8**　　　　　　**procurar** to try → **10**
impedir to prevent → **9**　　　　　**prohibir** to forbid → **15**
intentar to try → **10**　　　　　　**prometer** to promise → **16**
lograr to manage to → **5**　　　　　**proponer** to propose → **17**

Examples

1 **¿Quiere Vd esperar?**
    No puede venir

Would you like to wait?
She can't come

2 **Nos ha visto llegar**
    Se los oye cantar

She saw us arriving
You can hear them singing

3 **No me hagas reír**
    Déjeme pasar

Don't make me laugh
Let me past

4 **Le aconsejamos dejarlo para
    mañana**

We'd advise you to leave it until
tomorrow

5 **Aún no he conseguido/logrado
    entenderlo**

I still haven't managed to work
it out

6 **No desea tener más hijos**

She doesn't want to have any
more children

7 **Esperamos ir de vacaciones
    este verano**

We are hoping to go on holiday
this summer

8 **Evite beber cuando conduzca**

Avoid drinking and driving

9 **No pudo impedirle hablar**

He couldn't prevent him from
speaking

10 **Intentamos/Procuramos pasar
    desapercibidos**

We tried not to be noticed

11 **Necesitaba salir a la calle**

I/He/She needed to go out

12 **Olvidó dejar su dirección**

He/She forgot to leave his/
her address

13 **¿Piensan venir por Navidad?**

Are you thinking of coming for
Christmas?

14 **Preferiría elegirlo yo mismo**

I'd rather choose it myself

15 **Prohibió fumar a los alumnos**

He forbade the pupils to smoke

16 **Prometieron volver pronto**

They promised to come back soon

17 **Propongo salir cuanto antes**

I propose to leave as soon as
possible

Verbs

The Infinitive: Set Expressions

The following are set expressions in Spanish:

> **dejar caer** to drop → ❶
> **hacer entrar** to show in → ❷
> **hacer saber** to let know, make known → ❸
> **hacer salir** to let out → ❹
> **hacer venir** to send for → ❺
> **ir(se) a buscar** to go for, go and get → ❻
> **mandar hacer** to order → ❼
> **mandar llamar** to send for → ❽
> **oír decir que** to hear it said that → ❾
> **oír hablar de** to hear of/about → ❿
> **querer decir** to mean → ⓫

The Perfect Infinitive

The perfect infinitive is formed using the auxiliary verb **haber** with the past participle of the verb → ⓬

The perfect infinitive is found:
- following certain prepositions, especially **después de** *after* → ⓭
- following certain verbal constructions → ⓮

Examples

1 Al verla, dejó caer lo que llevaba en las manos

When he saw her he dropped what he was carrying

2 Haz entrar a nuestros invitados

Show our guests in

3 Quiero hacerles saber que no serán bien recibidos

I want to let them know that they won't be welcome

4 Hágale salir, por favor

Please let him out

5 Le he hecho venir a Vd porque ...

I sent for you because ...

6 Vete a buscar los guantes

Go and get your gloves

7 Me he mandado hacer un traje

I have ordered a suit

8 Mandaron llamar al médico

They sent for the doctor

9 He oído decir que está enfermo

I've heard it said that he's ill

10 No he oído hablar más de él

I haven't heard anything more (said) of him

11 ¿Qué quiere decir eso?

What does that mean?

12 haber terminado
haberse vestido

to have finished
to have got dressed

13 Después de haber comprado el regalo, volvió a casa
Después de haber madrugado tanto, el taxi se retrasó

After buying/having bought the present, he went back home
After she got up so early, the taxi arrived late

14 perdonar a alguien por haber hecho
dar las gracias a alguien por haber hecho
pedir perdón por haber hecho

to forgive somebody for doing/having done
to thank somebody for doing/having done
to be sorry for doing/having done

Verbs

The Gerund

Formation

First conjugation:
- replace the **-ar** of the infinitive by **-ando** → ❶

Second conjugation:
- replace the **-er** of the infinitive by **-iendo** → ❷

Third conjugation:
- replace the **-ir** of the infinitive by **-iendo** → ❸

For irregular gerunds, see irregular verbs, page 80 onwards.

Uses

After the verb **estar**, to form the continuous tenses → ❹

After the verbs **seguir** and **continuar** *to continue*, and **ir** when meaning to *happen gradually* → ❺

In time constructions, after **llevar** → ❻

When the action in the main clause needs to be complemented by another action → ❼

The position of object pronouns is the same as for the infinitive (see page 46).

The gerund is invariable and strictly verbal in sense.

The Present Participle

It is formed by replacing the **-ar** of the infinitive of 1st conjugation verbs by **-ante**, and the **-er** and **-ir** of the 2nd and 3rd conjugations by **-iente** → ❽

A very limited number of verbs have a present participle used either as an adjective or a noun → ❾/❿

Examples

1 **cantar** to sing → **cantando** singing

2 **temer** to fear → **temiendo** fearing

3 **partir** to leave → **partiendo** leaving

4 **Estoy escribiendo una carta** I am writing a letter
   Estaban esperándonos They were waiting for us

5 **Sigue viniendo todos los días** He/She is still coming every day
   Continuarán subiendo los precios Prices will continue to go up
   El ejército iba avanzando poco The army was gradually
   a poco advancing

6 **Lleva dos años estudiando inglés** He/She has been studying
   English for two years

7 **Pasamos el día tomando el sol** We spent the day sunbathing
   en la playa on the beach
   Iba cojeando He/She/I was limping
   Salieron corriendo They ran out

8 **cantar** to sing → **cantante** singing/singer
   pender to hang → **pendiente** hanging
   seguir to follow → **siguiente** following

9 **agua corriente** running water

10 **un estudiante** a student

Verbs

Use of Tenses

The Present

Unlike English, the Spanish simple present can be used to talk both about what is true at present and what is happening right now → **①**

Normally, however, the continuous present is used to describe actions that are going on at this very moment:

estar haciendo to be doing → **②**

Spanish uses the present tense where English uses the perfect in the following cases:

- with certain prepositions of time – notably **desde** *for/since* – when an action begun in the past is continued in the present → **③**
  - ⓘ Note: The perfect can be used as in English when the verb is negative → **④**
- in the construction **acabar de hacer** *to have just done* → **⑤**

Like English, Spanish often uses the present where a future action is implied → **⑥**

The Future

The future is generally used as in English → **⑦**, but note the following:

Immediate future time is often expressed by means of the present tense of **ir** + **a** + infinitive → **⑧**

When 'will' or 'shall' mean 'wish to', 'are willing to', **querer** is used → **⑨**

The Future Perfect

Used as in English shall/will have done → **⑩**

It can also express conjecture, usually about things in the recent past → **⑪**

Examples

1 **Fumo**
Lee
Vivimos

I smoke *or* I am smoking
He reads *or* He is reading
We live *or* We are living

2 **Está fumando**

He is smoking

3 **Linda estudia español desde hace seis meses**
Estoy de pie desde las siete
¿Hace mucho que esperan?
Ya hace dos semanas que estamos aquí

Linda's been learning Spanish for six months (and still is)
I've been up since seven
Have you been waiting long?
We've been here for two weeks now

4 **No se han visto desde hace meses**

They haven't seen each other for months

5 **Isabel acaba de salir**

Isabel has just left

6 **Mañana voy a Madrid**
Voy de vacaciones en agosto
Te llamo el viernes

I am going to Madrid tomorrow
I am going on holiday in August
I'll call you on Friday

7 **Lo haré mañana**

I'll do it tomorrow

8 **Te vas a caer si no tienes cuidado**
Va a perder el tren
Va a llevar una media hora

You'll fall if you're not careful
He's going to miss the train
It'll take about half an hour

9 **¿Me quieres esperar un momento, por favor?**

Will you wait for me a second, please?

10 **Lo habré acabado para mañana**

I will have finished it for tomorrow

11 **Ya habrán llegado a casa**

They must have arrived home by now

Verbs

Use of Tenses *continued*

The Imperfect

The imperfect describes:
- an action or state in the past without definite limits in time → **❶**
- habitual action(s) in the past (often expressed in English by means of *would* or *used to*) → **❷**

Spanish uses the imperfect tense where English uses the pluperfect in the following cases:
- with certain prepositions of time – notably **desde** *for/since* – when an action begun in the remoter past was continued in the more recent past → **❸**
  - ⓘ Note: The pluperfect is used as in English when the verb is negative or the action has been completed → **❹**
- in the construction **acabar de hacer** *to have just done* → **❺**

Both the continuous and simple forms in English can be translated by the Spanish simple imperfect, but the continuous imperfect is used when the emphasis is on the fact that an action was going on at a precise moment in the past → **❻**

The Perfect

The perfect is generally used as in English → **❼**

The Preterite

The preterite generally corresponds to the English simple past in both written and spoken Spanish → **❽**

However, while English can use the simple past to describe habitual actions or settings, Spanish uses the imperfect (see above) → **❾**

The Past Anterior

This tense is only ever used in written, literary Spanish, to replace the pluperfect in time clauses where the verb in the main clause is in the preterite → **❿**

Examples

1 **Todos mirábamos en silencio**
We were all watching in silence

Nuestras habitaciones daban a la playa
Our rooms overlooked the beach

2 **En su juventud se levantaba de madrugada**
In his youth he used to get up really early

Hablábamos sin parar durante horas
We would talk non-stop for hours on end

Mi hermano siempre me tomaba el pelo
My brother was always teasing me

3 **Hacía dos años que vivíamos en Irlanda**
We had been living in Ireland for two years

Estaba enfermo desde 2012
He had been ill since 2012

Hacía mucho tiempo que salían juntos
They had been going out together for a long time

4 **Hacía un año que no le había visto**
I hadn't seen him for a year

Hacía una hora que había llegado
She had arrived an hour before

5 **Acababa de encontrármelos**
I had just met them

6 **Cuando llegué, todos estaban fumando**
When I arrived, they were all smoking

7 **Todavía no han salido**
They haven't come out yet

8 **Me desperté y salté de la cama**
I woke up and jumped out of bed

9 **Siempre iban en coche al trabajo**
They always travelled to work by car

10 **Apenas hubo acabado, se oyeron unos golpes en la puerta**
She had scarcely finished when there was a knock at the door

Verbs

The Subjunctive: when to use it

For how to form the subjunctive, see page 6 onwards.

After verbs of:

- 'wishing'

  querer que ⎤
  desear que ⎦ to wish that, want → ❶

- 'emotion' (e.g. regret, surprise, shame, pleasure, etc)

  sentir que   to be sorry that → ❷
  sorprender que   to be surprised that → ❸
  alegrarse de que to be pleased that → ❹

- 'asking' and 'advising'

  pedir que   to ask that → ❺
  aconsejar que   to advise that → ❻

In all the above constructions, when the subject of the verbs in the main and subordinate clause is the same, the infinitive is used, and the conjunction **que** omitted → ❼

- 'ordering', 'forbidding', 'allowing'

  mandar que* ⎤
  ordenar que ⎦ to order that → ❽

  permitir que* ⎤
  dejar que* ⎦ to allow that → ❾

  prohibir que*   to forbid that → ❿
  impedir que*   to prevent that → ⓫

  * With these verbs either the subjunctive or the infinitive is used when the object of the main verb is the subject of the subordinate verb → ⓬

Always after verbs expressing doubt or uncertainty, and verbs of opinion used negatively.

  dudar que   to doubt that → ⓭

  no creer que ⎤
  no pensar que ⎦ not to think that → ⓮

Examples

① **Queremos que esté contenta**

We want her to be happy
(*literally*: We want that she is happy)

¿Desea Vd que lo haga yo?

Do you want me to do it?

② **Sentí mucho que no vinieran**

I was very sorry that they didn't come

③ **Nos sorprendió que no les vieran Vds**

We were surprised you didn't see them

④ **Me alegro de que te gusten**

I'm pleased that you like them

⑤ **Solo les pedimos que tengan cuidado**

We're only asking you to take care

⑥ **Le aconsejé que no llegara tarde**

I advised him not to be late

⑦ **Quiero que lo termines pronto**
BUT:
Quiero terminarlo pronto

I want you to finish it soon

I want to finish it soon

⑧ **Ha mandado que vuelvan**
Ordenó que fueran castigados

He has ordered them to come back
He ordered them to be punished

⑨ **No permitas que te tomen el pelo**
No me dejó que la llevara a casa

Don't let them pull your leg
She wouldn't let me take her home

⑩ **Te prohíbo que digas eso**

I forbid you to say that

⑪ **No les impido que vengan**

I am not preventing them from coming

⑫ **Les ordenó que salieran**
or **Les ordenó salir**

She ordered them to go out

⑬ **Dudo que lo sepan hacer**

I doubt they can do it

⑭ **No creo que sean tan listos**

I don't think they are as clever as that

Verbs

The Subjunctive: when to use it *continued*

In impersonal constructions which express necessity, possibility, etc:

hace falta que ⎤	it is necessary that → ❶
es necesario que ⎦	
es posible que	it is possible that → ❷
más vale que	it is better that → ❸
es una lástima que	it is a pity that → ❹

ⓘ Note: In impersonal constructions which state a fact or express certainty the indicative is used when the impersonal verb is affirmative. When it is negative, the subjunctive is used → ❺

After certain conjunctions:

para que ⎤	so that → ❻
a fin de que* ⎦	
como si	as if → ❼
sin que*	without → ❽
a condición de que* ⎤	provided that,
con tal (de) que* ⎥	on condition that → ❾
siempre que ⎦	
a menos que ⎤	unless → ❿
a no ser que ⎦	
antes (de) que*	before → ⓫
no sea que	lest/in case → ⓬
mientras (que) ⎤	as long as → ⓭
siempre que ⎦	
(el) que	the fact that → ⓮

* When the subject of both verbs is the same, the infinitive is used, and the final **que** is omitted → ❽

Examples

1 **¿Hace falta que vaya Jaime?**   Does Jaime have to go?

2 **Es posible que tengan razón**   It's possible that they are right

3 **Más vale que se quede Vd en su casa**   You'd be better to stay at home

4 **Es una lástima que haya perdido su perrito**   It's a shame/pity that she has lost her puppy

5 **Es verdad que va a venir**   It's true that he's coming
   BUT:
   No es verdad que vayan a hacerlo   It's not true that they are going to do it

6 **Átalas bien para que no se caigan**   Tie them on securely so that they won't fall off

7 **Hablaba como si no creyera en sus propias palabras**   He spoke as if he didn't believe his own words

8 **Salimos sin que nos vieran**   We left without them seeing us
   BUT:
   Me fui sin esperarla   I left without waiting for her

9 **Lo haré con tal de que me cuentes todo lo que pasó**   I'll do it provided you tell me exactly what happened

10 **Saldremos de paseo a menos que esté lloviendo**   We'll go for a walk unless it's raining

11 **Avísale antes de que sea demasiado tarde**   Tell him before it's too late

12 **Habla en voz baja, no sea que alguien nos oiga**   Speak softly in case anyone hears us

13 **Eso no pasará mientras yo sea el jefe aquí**   That won't happen as long as I am the boss here

14 **El que no me escribiera no me importaba demasiado**   The fact that he didn't write didn't bother me too much

Verbs

The Subjunctive: when to use it *continued*

After the conjunctions:
> **de modo que**
> **de forma que**   so that (*indicating a purpose*) → **❶**
> **de manera que**

> ⓘ Note: When these conjunctions introduce a result and not a
> purpose the subjunctive is not used → **❷**

In relative clauses with an antecedent which is:
- negative → **❸**
- indefinite → **❹**
- non-specific → **❺**

In main clauses, to express a wish or exhortation. The verb may be
preceded by expressions like **ojalá** or **que** → **❻**

In the **si** clause of conditions where the English sentence contains a
conditional tense → **❼**

In set expressions → **❽**

In the following constructions which translate however:
- **por** + *adjective* + *subjunctive* → **❾**
- **por** + *adverb* + *subjunctive* → **❿**
- **por** + **mucho** + *subjunctive* → **⓫**

Examples

1 Vuélvanse de manera que los vea bien

Turn round so that I can see you properly

2 No quieren hacerlo, de manera que tendré que hacerlo yo

They won't do it, so I'll have to do it myself

3 No he encontrado a nadie que la conociera

I haven't met anyone who knows her

No dijo nada que no supiéramos ya

He/She didn't say anything we didn't already know

4 Necesito alguien que sepa conducir

I need someone who can drive

Busco algo que me distraiga

I'm looking for something to take my mind off it

5 Busca una casa que tenga calefacción central

He's/She's looking for a house which has central heating
(*subjunctive used since such a house may or may not exist*)

El que lo haya visto tiene que decírmelo

Anyone who has seen it must tell me
(*subjunctive used since it is not known who has seen it*)

6 ¡Ojalá haga buen tiempo!

Let's hope the weather will be good!

¡Que te diviertas!

Have a good time!

7 Si fuéramos en coche llegaríamos a tiempo

If we went by car we'd be there on time

8 Diga lo que diga ...

Whatever he may say ...

Sea lo que sea ...

Be that as it may ...

Pase lo que pase ...

Come what may ...

Sea como sea ...

One way or another ...

9 Por cansado que esté, seguirá trabajando

No matter how/However tired he may be, he'll go on working

10 Por lejos que viva, iremos a buscarlo

No matter how/However far away he lives, we'll go and pick him up

11 Por mucho que lo intente, nunca lo conseguirá

No matter how/However hard he tries, he'll never succeed

63

Verbs

The Subjunctive: when to use it *continued*

Clauses taking either a subjunctive or an indicative

In certain constructions, a subjunctive is needed when the action refers to future events or hypothetical situations, whereas an indicative is used when stating a fact or experience → ❶

The commonest of these are:

The conjunctions:

cuando	when → ❶
en cuanto	as soon as → ❷
tan pronto como	
después (de) que*	after → ❸
hasta que	until → ❹
mientras	while → ❺
siempre que	whenever → ❻
aunque	even if/though → ❼

All conjunctions and pronouns ending in **-quiera** (*-ever*) → ❽

* ⓘ Note: If the subject of both verbs is the same, the subjunctive introduced by **después (de) que** may be replaced by **después de** + *infinitive* → ❾

Sequence of tenses in Subordinate Clauses

If the verb in the main clause is in the present, future or imperative, the verb in the dependent clause will be in the present or perfect subjunctive → ❿

If the verb in the main clause is in the conditional or any past tense, the verb in the dependent clause will be in the imperfect or pluperfect subjunctive → ⓫

Examples

1 **Le aconsejé que oyera música**
   cuando estuviera nervioso

I advised him to listen to music
when he felt nervous

Me gusta nadar cuando hace
calor

I like to swim when it is warm

2 **Te devolveré el libro tan pronto**
   como lo haya leído

I'll give you back the book as
soon as I have read it

3 **Te lo diré después de que te**
   hayas sentado

I'll tell you after you've sat down

4 **Quédate aquí hasta que**
   volvamos

Stay here until we come back

5 **No hablen en voz alta mientras**
   estén ellos aquí

Don't speak loudly while they
are here

6 **Vuelvan por aquí siempre que**
   quieran

Come back whenever you wish to

7 **No le creeré aunque diga la**
   verdad

I won't believe him even if he
tells the truth

8 **La encontraré dondequiera**
   que esté

I will find her wherever she
might be

9 **Después de cenar me acosté**

After dinner I went to bed

10 **Quiero que lo hagas**
   (*pres + pres subj*)

I want you to do it

Temo que no haya venido
(*pres + perf subj*)

I fear he hasn't come (might not
have come)

Iremos por aquí para que no
nos vean (*future + pres subj*)

We'll go this way so that they
won't see us

11 **Me gustaría que llegaras**
   temprano (*cond + imperf subj*)

I'd like you to arrive early

Les pedí que me esperaran
(*preterite + imperf subj*)

I asked them to wait for me

Sentiría mucho que hubiese
muerto (*cond + pluperf subj*)

I would be very sorry if he were
dead

65

Verbs

Verbs governing *a*, *de*, *con*, *en*, *por* and *para*

The following lists (pages 66 to 73) contain common verbal constructions using the prepositions **a**, **de**, **con**, **en**, **por** and **para**.

Note the following abbreviations:

infin.	*infinitive*
perf. infin.	*perfect infinitive**
algn	**alguien**
sb	somebody
sth	something

* For information see page 50.

aburrirse de + *infin.*	to get bored with doing → **1**
acabar con algo/algn	to put an end to sth/finish with sb → **2**
acabar de* + *infin.*	to have just done → **3**
acabar por + *infin.*	to end up doing → **4**
acercarse a algo/algn	to approach sth/sb
acordarse de algo/algn/de + *infin.*	to remember sth/sb/doing → **5**
acostumbrarse a algo/algn/a + *infin.*	to get used to sth/sb/to doing → **6**
acusar a algn de algo/de + *perf. infin.*	to accuse sb of sth/of doing *or* having done → **7**
advertir a algn de algo	to notify *or* warn sb about sth → **8**
aficionarse a algo/a + *infin.*	to grow fond of sth/of doing → **9**
alegrarse de algo/de + *perf. infin.*	to be glad about sth/of doing *or* having done → **10**
alejarse de algn/algo	to move away from sb/sth
amenazar a algn con algo/con + *infin.*	to threaten sb with sth/to do → **11**
animar a algn a + *infin.*	to encourage sb to do
apresurarse a + *infin.*	to hurry to do → **12**

* See also Use of Tenses, pages 54 and 56

Examples

① **Me aburría de no poder salir de casa**
I used to get bored with not being able to leave the house

② **Quiso acabar con su vida**
He wanted to put an end to his life

③ **Acababan de llegar cuando ...**
They had just arrived when ...

④ **El acusado acabó por confesarlo todo**
The accused ended up by confessing everything

⑤ **Nos acordamos muy bien de aquellas vacaciones**
We remember that holiday very well

⑥ **Me he acostumbrado a levantarme temprano**
I've got used to getting up early

⑦ **Lo acusó de haber mentido**
She accused him of lying

⑧ **Advertí a mi amigo del peligro que corría**
I warned my friend about the danger he was in

⑨ **Nos hemos aficionado a la música clásica**
We've become interested in classical music

⑩ **Me alegro de haberlo conocido**
I'm glad I met him

⑪ **Amenazó con denunciarlos**
He threatened to report them

⑫ **Se apresuraron a coger sitio**
They hurried to find a seat

Verbs

Verbs governing *a*, *de*, *con*, *en*, *por* and *para* continued

aprender a + *infin.*	to learn to do → **1**
aprovecharse de algo/algn	to take advantage of sth/sb
aproximarse a algn/algo	to approach sb/sth
asistir a algo	to attend sth, be at sth
asomarse a/por	to lean out of → **2**
asombrarse de + *infin.*	to be surprised at doing → **3**
atreverse a + *infin.*	to dare to do
avergonzarse de algo/algn/de + *perf. infin.*	to be ashamed of sth/sb/of doing *or* having done → **4**
ayudar a algn a + *infin.*	to help sb to do → **5**
bajarse de (+ *place/vehicle*)	to get off/out of → **6**
burlarse de algn	to make fun of sb
cansarse de algo/algn/de + *infin.*	to tire of sth/sb/of doing
carecer de algo	to lack sth → **7**
cargar de algo	to load with sth → **8**
casarse con algn	to get married to sb → **9**
cesar de + *infin.*	to stop doing
chocar con algo	to crash/bump into sth → **10**
comenzar a + *infin.*	to begin to do
comparar con algn/algo	to compare with sb/sth
consentir en + *infin.*	to agree to do
consistir en + *infin.*	to consist of doing → **11**
constar de algo	to consist of sth → **12**
contar con algn/algo	to rely on sb/sth → **13**
convenir en + *infin.*	to agree to do → **14**
darse cuenta de algo	to realize sth
dejar de + *infin.*	to stop doing → **15**
depender de algo/algn	to depend on sth/sb → **16**
despedirse de algn	to say goodbye to sb
dirigirse a algn/+ place	to address sb/head for
disponerse a + *infin.*	to get ready to do
empezar a + *infin.*	to begin to do
empezar por + *infin.*	to begin by doing → **17**

Examples

1. **Me gustaría aprender a nadar** — I'd like to learn to swim

2. **No te asomes a la ventana** — Don't lean out of the window

3. **Nos asombramos mucho de verlos ahí** — We were very surprised at seeing them there

4. **No me avergüenzo de haberlo hecho** — I'm not ashamed of having done it

5. **Ayúdeme a llevar estas maletas** — Help me to carry these cases

6. **Se bajó del coche** — He got out of the car

7. **La casa carecía de jardín** — The house lacked (did not have) a garden

8. **El carro iba cargado de paja** — The cart was loaded with straw

9. **Se casó con Andrés** — She married Andrés

10. **Enciende la luz, o chocarás con la puerta** — Turn the light on, or you'll bump into the door

11. **Mi plan consistía en vigilarlos de cerca** — My plan consisted of keeping a close eye on them

12. **El examen consta de tres partes** — The exam consists of three parts

13. **Cuento contigo para que me ayudes a hacerlo** — I'm relying on you to help me do it

14. **Convinieron en reunirse al día siguiente** — They agreed to meet the following day

15. **¿Quieres dejar de hablar?** — Will you stop talking?

16. **No depende de mí** — It's not up to me

17. **Empieza por enterarte de lo que se trata** — Begin by finding out what it is about

69

Verbs

Verbs governing *a*, *de*, *con*, *en*, *por* and *para* *continued*

encontrarse con algn	to meet sb (by chance) → ❶
enfadarse con algn	to get annoyed with sb
enseñar a algn a + *infin.*	to teach sb to → ❷
enterarse de algo	to find out about sth → ❸
entrar en (+ *place*)	to enter, go into
esperar a + *infin.*	to wait until → ❹
estar de acuerdo con algn/algo	to agree with sb/sth
fiarse de algn/algo	to trust sb/sth
fijarse en algo/algn	to notice sth/sb → ❺
hablar con algn	to talk to sb → ❻
hacer caso a algn	to pay attention to sb
hartarse de algo/algn/de + *infin.*	to get fed up with sth/sb/with doing → ❼
interesarse por algo/algn	to be interested in sth/sb → ❽
invitar a algn a + *infin.*	to invite sb to do
jugar a (+ sports, games)	to play
luchar por algo/por + *infin.*	to fight *or* strive for/to do → ❾
llegar a + *infin./*(place)	to manage to do/to reach → ❿
llenar de algo	to fill with sth
negarse a + *infin.*	to refuse to do → ⓫
obligar a algn a + *infin.*	to make sb do → ⓬
ocuparse de algn/algo	to take care of sb/attend to sth
oler a algo	to smell of sth → ⓭
olvidarse de algo/algn/de + *infin.*	to forget sth/sb/to do → ⓮
oponerse a algo/a + *infin.*	to be opposed to sth/to doing
parecerse a algn/algo	to resemble sb/sth
pensar en algo/algn/en + *infin.*	to think about sth/sb/about doing → ⓯
preguntar por algn	to ask for/about sb
preocuparse de *or* **por algo/algn**	to worry about sth/sb → ⓰

Examples

1 **Me encontré con ella al entrar en el banco**

I met her as I was going into the bank

2 **Le estoy enseñando a nadar**

I am teaching him to swim

3 **¿Te has enterado del sitio adonde hay que ir?**

Have you found out where we have to go?

4 **Espera a saber lo que quiere antes de comprar el regalo**

Wait until you know what he wants before buying the present

5 **Me fijé en él cuando subía a su coche**

I noticed him when he was getting into his car

6 **¿Puedo hablar con Vd un momento?**

May I talk to you for a moment?

7 **Me he hartado de escribirle**

I've got fed up with writing to him

8 **Me interesaba mucho por la arqueología**

I was very interested in archaeology

9 **Hay que luchar por mantener la paz**

We need to strive to preserve peace

10 **Lo intenté sin llegar a conseguirlo**

I tried but didn't manage to do it

11 **Se negó a hacerlo**

He refused to do it

12 **Lo obligó a sentarse**

He made him sit down

13 **Este perfume huele a jazmín**

This perfume smells of jasmine

14 **Siempre me olvido de cerrar la puerta**

I always forget to shut the door

15 **No quiero pensar en eso**

I don't want to think about that

16 **Se preocupa mucho de/por su apariencia**

He worries a lot about his appearance

71

Verbs

Verbs governing *a*, *de*, *con*, *en*, *por* and *para* *continued*

prepararse a + *infin.*	to prepare to do
probar a + *infin.*	to try to do
quedar en + *infin.*	to agree to do → ❶
quedar por + *infin.*	to remain to be done → ❷
quejarse de algo	to complain of sth
referirse a algo	to refer to sth
reírse de algo/algn	to laugh at sth/sb
rodear de	to surround with → ❸
romper a + *infin.*	to (suddenly) start to do → ❹
salir de (+ *place*)	to leave
sentarse a (+ *table etc*)	to sit down at
subir(se) a (+ *vehicle/place*)	to get on *or* into/to climb → ❺
servir de algo a algn	to be useful to/serve sb as sth → ❻
servir para algo/para + *infin.*	to be good as sth/for doing → ❼
servirse de algo	to use sth → ❽
soñar con algn/algo/con + *infin.*	to dream about/of sb/sth/of doing
sorprenderse de algo	to be surprised at sth
tardar en + *infin.*	to take time to do → ❾
tener ganas de algo/de + *infin.*	to want sth/to do → ❿
tener miedo de algo	to be afraid of sth → ⓫
tener miedo a algn	to be afraid of sb → ⓬
terminar por + *infin.*	to end by doing
tirar de algo/algn	to pull sth/sb
trabajar de (+ *occupation*)	to work as → ⓭
trabajar en (+ *place of work*)	to work at/in → ⓮
traducir a (+ *language*)	to translate into
tratar de + *infin.*	to try to do → ⓯
tratarse de algo/algn/de + *infin.*	to be a question of sth/about sb/ about doing → ⓰
vacilar en + *infin.*	to hesitate to do → ⓱
volver a + *infin.*	to do again → ⓲

Examples

1 Habíamos quedado en encontrarnos a las 8

We had agreed to meet at 8

2 Queda por averiguar dónde se ocultan

It remains to be discovered where they are hiding

3 Habían rodeado el jardín de un seto de cipreses

They had surrounded the garden with a hedge of cypress trees

4 Al apagarse la luz, el niño rompió a llorar

When the lights went out, the little boy suddenly started to cry

5 ¡De prisa, sube al coche!

Get into the car, quick!

6 Esto me servirá de bastón

This will serve me as a walking stick

7 No sirvo para (ser) jardinero

I'm no good as a gardener

8 Se sirvió de un destornillador para abrirlo

She used a screwdriver to open it

9 Tardaron mucho en salir

They took a long time to come out

10 Tengo ganas de volver a España

I want to go back to Spain

11 Mi hija tiene miedo de la oscuridad

My daughter is afraid of the dark

12 Nunca tuvieron miedo a su padre

They were never afraid of their father

13 Pedro trabaja de camarero en Londres

Pedro works as a waiter in London

14 Trabajaba en una oficina

I used to work in an office

15 No trates de engañarme

Don't try to deceive me

16 Se trata de nuestro nuevo vecino

It's about our new neighbour

17 Nunca vacilaban en pedir dinero

They never hesitated to ask for money

18 No vuelvas a hacerlo nunca más

Don't ever do it again

73

Verbs

Ser and *Estar*

Spanish has two verbs – **ser** and **estar** – for 'to be'.

They are not interchangeable and each one is used in defined contexts.

ser is used:
- with an adjective, to express a permanent or inherent quality → ❶
- to express occupation or nationality → ❷
- to express possession → ❸
- to express origin or the material from which something is made → ❹
- with a noun, pronoun or infinitive following the verb → ❺
- to express the time and date → ❻
- to form the passive, with the past participle (see page 32).

ⓘ Note: This use emphasizes the action of the verb. If, however, the resultant state or condition needs to be emphasized, **estar** is used. The past participle then functions as an adjective (see page 208) and has to agree in gender and in number with the noun → ❼

estar is used:
- to indicate place or location of a person, animal or thing* → ❽
- with an adjective or adjectival phrase, to express a quality or state seen by the speaker as subject to change or different from expected → ❾
- when speaking of a person's state of health → ❿
- to form the continuous tenses, used with the gerund (see page 52) → ⓫
- with **de** + *noun*, to indicate a temporary occupation → ⓬

*To talk about where an event is taking place, use **ser** → ⓭

Examples

1 Mi hermano es alto — My brother is tall
María es inteligente — María is clever

2 Javier es aviador — Javier is a pilot
Sus padres son italianos — His parents are Italian

3 La casa es de Miguel — The house belongs to Miguel

4 Mi mujer es de Granada — My wife is from Granada
Las paredes son de ladrillo — The walls are made of brick

5 Andrés es un niño travieso — Andrés is a naughty boy
Soy yo, Enrique — It's me, Enrique
Todo es proponérselo — It's all a question of putting your mind to it

6 Son las tres y media — It's half past three
Mañana es sábado — Tomorrow is Saturday

7 Las puertas eran cerradas sigilosamente — The doors were being silently closed
Las puertas estaban cerradas — The doors were closed (resultant action)

8 La comida está en la mesa — The meal is on the table

9 Su amigo está enfermo — Her friend is ill
El lavabo está ocupado — The toilet is engaged
Hoy estoy de mal humor — I'm in a bad mood today
El café estaba frío — The coffee was cold

10 ¿Cómo están Vds? — How are you?
Estamos todos bien — We are all well

11 Estamos aprendiendo mucho — We are learning a great deal

12 Mi primo está de camarero en un bar — My cousin is working as a waiter in a bar

13 La boda será en Madrid — The wedding will be in Madrid

Verbs

Ser and *Estar* continued

With certain adjectives, both **ser** and **estar** can be used, although they are not interchangeable when used in this way:

- **ser** will express a permanent or inherent quality → **1**
- **estar** will express a temporary state or quality → **2**

Both **ser** and **estar** may also be used in set expressions.

The commonest of these are:

With **ser**

Sea como sea	Be that as it may
Es igual/Es lo mismo	It's all the same
llegar a ser	to become
¿Cómo fue eso?	How did that happen?
¿Qué ha sido de él?	What has become of him?
ser para (*with the idea of purpose*)	to be for → **3**

With **estar**

estar de pie/de rodillas	to be standing/kneeling
estar de viaje	to be travelling
estar de vacaciones	to be on holiday
estar de vuelta	to be back
estar de moda	to be in fashion
Está bien	It's all right
estar para	to be about to do sth/to be in a mood for → **4**
estar por	to be inclined to/to be (all) for → **5**
estar a punto de	to be just about to do sth → **6**

Examples

❶ Su tía es muy joven/vieja
His aunt is very young/old
Son muy ricos/pobres
They are very rich/poor
Mi hijo es bueno/malo
My son is good/naughty
Viajar es cansado
Travelling is tiring

❷ Está muy joven/vieja con ese vestido
She looks very young/old in that dress
Ahora están muy ricos/pobres
They're very well/badly off at the moment

Estaba enfermo
He was ill
Está borracho
He is drunk
El café está bueno/malo
The coffee tastes good/bad
Hoy estoy cansada
I am tired today

❸ Este paquete es para Vd
This parcel is for you
Esta caja es para guardar semillas
This box is for keeping seeds in

❹ Están para llegar
They're about to arrive

❺ Estoy por irme a vivir a España
I'm inclined to go and live in Spain

❻ Las rosas están a punto de salir
The roses are about to come out

Verbs

Verbal Idioms

Special Intransitive Verbs

With the following verbs the Spanish construction is the opposite of the English. The subject in English becomes the indirect object of the Spanish verb, while the object in English becomes the subject of the Spanish verb. Compare the following:

> I like that house (subject: I, object: that house)
> **Esa casa me gusta** (subject: **esa casa**, indirect object: **me**)

The commonest of these verbs are:

gustar	to like → ❶
gustar más	to prefer → ❷
encantar	(colloquial) to love → ❸
faltar	to need/to be short of/to have missing → ❹
quedar	to be/have left → ❺
doler	to have a pain in/to hurt, ache → ❻
interesar	to be interested in → ❼
importar	to mind → ❽

Examples

1 **Me gusta este vestido** I like this dress (This dress pleases me)

2 **Me gustan más estas** I prefer these

3 **Nos encanta hacer deporte** We love doing sport

4 **Me faltaban 100 euros** I needed 100 euros
   Solo le falta el toque final It just needs the finishing touch
   Le faltaban tres dientes He/She had three teeth missing

5 **Solo nos quedan dos kilómetros** We only have two kilometres (left) to go

6 **Me duele la cabeza** I have a headache

7 **Nos interesa mucho la política** We are very interested in politics

8 **No me importa la lluvia** I don't mind rain

Irregular Verbs

Irregular Verbs

The verbs listed opposite and conjugated on pages 82 to 160 provide the main patterns for irregular verbs and verbs that change their stems (radical-changing verbs). The verbs are grouped opposite according to their infinitive ending and are shown in the following tables in alphabetical order.

In the tables, the most important irregular verbs are given in their most common simple tenses, together with the imperative and the gerund.

The past participle is also shown for each verb, to enable you to form all the compound tenses, as on pages 18 to 23.

The pronouns **ella** and **Vd** take the same verb endings as **él**, while **ellas** and **Vds** take the same endings as **ellos**.

> All the verbs included in the tables differ from the three conjugations set out on pages 8 to 13. Many – e.g. **contar** – serve as models for groups of verbs, while others – e.g. **ir** – are unique. On pages 161–190 you will find every verb in this dictionary listed alphabetically and cross-referred either to the relevant basic conjugation or to the appropriate model in the verb tables.

Imperfect Subjunctive of Irregular Verbs

For verbs with an irregular stem in the preterite tense – e.g. **andar** → **anduvieron** – the imperfect subjunctive is formed by using the root form of the 3rd person plural of the preterite tense, and adding the imperfect subjunctive endings **-iera/-iese** etc where the verb has an 'i' in the preterite ending – e.g. anduv**ieron** → anduv**iera/iese**. Where the verb has no 'i' in the preterite ending, add **-era/-ese** etc – e.g. produj**eron** → produj**era/ese**.

Irregular Verbs

'-ar':
- actuar
- almorzar
- andar
- aullar
- avergonzar
- averiguar
- contar
- cruzar
- dar
- empezar
- enviar
- errar
- estar
- jugar
- negar
- pagar
- pensar
- rehusar
- rogar
- sacar
- volcar

'-er':
- caber
- caer
- cocer
- coger
- crecer
- entender
- haber
- hacer
- hay
- leer
- llover
- mover
- nacer
- oler
- poder
- poner
- querer
- resolver
- romper

- saber
- satisfacer
- ser
- tener
- torcer
- traer
- valer
- vencer
- ver
- volver

'-ir':
- abolir
- abrir
- adquirir
- bendecir
- conducir
- construir
- decir
- dirigir
- distinguir
- dormir
- elegir
- erguir
- escribir
- freír
- gruñir
- ir
- lucir
- morir
- oír
- pedir
- prohibir
- reír
- reñir
- reunir
- salir
- seguir
- sentir
- venir
- zurcir

abolir (to abolish)

	PRESENT		IMPERFECT
yo	abolo	yo	abolía
tú	aboles	tú	abolías
él	abole	él	abolía
nosotros	abolimos	nosotros	abolíamos
vosotros	abolís	vosotros	abolíais
ellos	abolen	ellos	abolían

	FUTURE		CONDITIONAL
yo	aboliré	yo	aboliría
tú	abolirás	tú	abolirías
él	abolirá	él	aboliría
nosotros	aboliremos	nosotros	aboliríamos
vosotros	aboliréis	vosotros	aboliríais
ellos	abolirán	ellos	abolirían

	PRESENT SUBJUNCTIVE		PRETERITE
yo	abola	yo	abolí
tú	abolas	tú	aboliste
él	abola	él	abolío
nosotros	abolamos	nosotros	abolimos
vosotros	aboláis	vosotros	abolisteis
ellos	abolan	ellos	abolieron

PAST PARTICIPLE	IMPERATIVE
abolido	abole
	abolid

GERUND
aboliendo

Irregular Verbs

abrir (to open)

	PRESENT		IMPERFECT
yo	abro	yo	abría
tú	abres	tú	abrías
él	abre	él	abría
nosotros	abrimos	nosotros	abríamos
vosotros	abrís	vosotros	abríais
ellos	abren	ellos	abrían

	FUTURE		CONDITIONAL
yo	abriré	yo	abriría
tú	abrirás	tú	abrirías
él	abrirá	él	abriría
nosotros	abriremos	nosotros	abriríamos
vosotros	abriréis	vosotros	abriríais
ellos	abrirán	ellos	abrirían

	PRESENT SUBJUNCTIVE		PRETERITE
yo	abra	yo	abrí
tú	abras	tú	abriste
él	abra	él	abrió
nosotros	abramos	nosotros	abrimos
vosotros	abráis	vosotros	abristeis
ellos	abran	ellos	abrieron

PAST PARTICIPLE	IMPERATIVE
abierto	abre
	abrid

GERUND
abriendo

actuar (to act)

	PRESENT		IMPERFECT
yo	**actúo**	yo	actuaba
tú	**actúas**	tú	actuabas
él	**actúa**	él	actuaba
nosotros	actuamos	nosotros	actuábamos
vosotros	actuáis	vosotros	actuabais
ellos	**actúan**	ellos	actuaban

	FUTURE		CONDITIONAL
yo	actuaré	yo	actuaría
tú	actuarás	tú	actuarías
él	actuará	él	actuaría
nosotros	actuaremos	nosotros	actuaríamos
vosotros	actuaréis	vosotros	actuaríais
ellos	actuarán	ellos	actuarían

	PRESENT SUBJUNCTIVE		PRETERITE
yo	**actúe**	yo	actué
tú	**actúes**	tú	actuaste
él	**actúe**	él	actuó
nosotros	actuemos	nosotros	actuamos
vosotros	actuéis	vosotros	actuasteis
ellos	**actúen**	ellos	actuaron

PAST PARTICIPLE	IMPERATIVE
actuado	**actúa**
	actuad

GERUND
actuando

Irregular Verbs

adquirir (to acquire)

	PRESENT		IMPERFECT
yo	**adquiero**	yo	adquir**ía**
tú	**adquieres**	tú	adquir**ías**
él	**adquiere**	él	adquir**ía**
nosotros	adquir**imos**	nosotros	adquir**íamos**
vosotros	adquir**ís**	vosotros	adquir**íais**
ellos	**adquieren**	ellos	adquir**ían**

	FUTURE		CONDITIONAL
yo	adquirir**é**	yo	adquirir**ía**
tú	adquirir**ás**	tú	adquirir**ías**
él	adquirir**á**	él	adquirir**ía**
nosotros	adquirir**emos**	nosotros	adquirir**íamos**
vosotros	adquirir**éis**	vosotros	adquirir**íais**
ellos	adquirir**án**	ellos	adquirir**ían**

	PRESENT SUBJUNCTIVE		PRETERITE
yo	**adquiera**	yo	adquir**í**
tú	**adquieras**	tú	adquir**iste**
él	**adquiera**	él	adquir**ió**
nosotros	adquir**amos**	nosotros	adquir**imos**
vosotros	adquir**áis**	vosotros	adquir**isteis**
ellos	**adquieran**	ellos	adquir**ieron**

PAST PARTICIPLE	IMPERATIVE
adquir**ido**	**adquiere**
	adquir**id**

GERUND
adquir**iendo**

Irregular Verbs

almorzar (to have lunch)

	PRESENT		IMPERFECT
yo	**almuerzo**	yo	almorz**aba**
tú	**almuerzas**	tú	almorz**abas**
él	**almuerza**	él	almorz**aba**
nosotros	almorz**amos**	nosotros	almorz**ábamos**
vosotros	almorz**áis**	vosotros	almorz**abais**
ellos	**almuerzan**	ellos	almorz**aban**

	FUTURE		CONDITIONAL
yo	almorzar**é**	yo	almorzar**ía**
tú	almorzar**ás**	tú	almorzar**ías**
él	almorzar**á**	él	almorzar**ía**
nosotros	almorzar**emos**	nosotros	almorzar**íamos**
vosotros	almorzar**éis**	vosotros	almorzar**íais**
ellos	almorzar**án**	ellos	almorzar**ían**

	PRESENT SUBJUNCTIVE		PRETERITE
yo	**almuerce**	yo	**almorcé**
tú	**almuerces**	tú	almorz**aste**
él	**almuerce**	él	almorz**ó**
nosotros	**almorcemos**	nosotros	almorz**amos**
vosotros	**almorcéis**	vosotros	almorz**asteis**
ellos	**almuercen**	ellos	almorz**aron**

PAST PARTICIPLE	IMPERATIVE
almorz**ado**	**almuerza**
	almorz**ad**

GERUND
almorz**ando**

Irregular Verbs

andar (to walk)

	PRESENT		IMPERFECT
yo	ando	yo	andaba
tú	andas	tú	andabas
él	anda	él	andaba
nosotros	andamos	nosotros	andábamos
vosotros	andáis	vosotros	andabais
ellos	andan	ellos	andaban

	FUTURE		CONDITIONAL
yo	andaré	yo	andaría
tú	andarás	tú	andarías
él	andará	él	andaría
nosotros	andaremos	nosotros	andaríamos
vosotros	andaréis	vosotros	andaríais
ellos	andarán	ellos	andarían

	PRESENT SUBJUNCTIVE		PRETERITE
yo	ande	yo	anduve
tú	andes	tú	anduviste
él	ande	él	anduvo
nosotros	andemos	nosotros	anduvimos
vosotros	andéis	vosotros	anduvisteis
ellos	anden	ellos	anduvieron

PAST PARTICIPLE	IMPERATIVE
andado	anda
	andad

GERUND
andando

aullar (to howl)

	PRESENT		IMPERFECT
yo	aúllo	yo	aullaba
tú	aúllas	tú	aullabas
él	aúlla	él	aullaba
nosotros	aullamos	nosotros	aullábamos
vosotros	aulláis	vosotros	aullabais
ellos	aúllan	ellos	aullaban

	FUTURE		CONDITIONAL
yo	aullaré	yo	aullaría
tú	aullarás	tú	aullarías
él	aullará	él	aullaría
nosotros	aullaremos	nosotros	aullaríamos
vosotros	aullaréis	vosotros	aullaríais
ellos	aullarán	ellos	aullarían

	PRESENT SUBJUNCTIVE		PRETERITE
yo	aúlle	yo	aullé
tú	aúlles	tú	aullaste
él	aúlle	él	aulló
nosotros	aullemos	nosotros	aullamos
vosotros	aulléis	vosotros	aullasteis
ellos	aúllen	ellos	aullaron

PAST PARTICIPLE	IMPERATIVE
aullado	aúlla
	aullad

GERUND
aullando

Irregular Verbs

avergonzar (to shame)

	PRESENT		IMPERFECT
yo	avergüenzo	yo	avergonzaba
tú	avergüenzas	tú	avergonzabas
él	avergüenza	él	avergonzaba
nosotros	avergonzamos	nosotros	avergonzábamos
vosotros	avergonzáis	vosotros	avergonzabais
ellos	avergüenzan	ellos	avergonzaban

	FUTURE		CONDITIONAL
yo	avergonzaré	yo	avergonzaría
tú	avergonzarás	tú	avergonzarías
él	avergonzará	él	avergonzaría
nosotros	avergonzaremos	nosotros	avergonzaríamos
vosotros	avergonzaréis	vosotros	avergonzaríais
ellos	avergonzarán	ellos	avergonzarían

	PRESENT SUBJUNCTIVE		PRETERITE
yo	avergüence	yo	avergoncé
tú	avergüences	tú	avergonzaste
él	avergüence	él	avergonzó
nosotros	avergoncemos	nosotros	avergonzamos
vosotros	avergoncéis	vosotros	avergonzasteis
ellos	avergüencen	ellos	avergonzaron

PAST PARTICIPLE	IMPERATIVE
avergonzado	avergüenza
	avergonzad

GERUND
avergonzando

averiguar (to find out)

	PRESENT		IMPERFECT
yo	averiguo	yo	averiguaba
tú	averiguas	tú	averiguabas
él	averigua	él	averiguaba
nosotros	averiguamos	nosotros	averiguábamos
vosotros	averiguáis	vosotros	averiguabais
ellos	averiguan	ellos	averiguaban

	FUTURE		CONDITIONAL
yo	averiguaré	yo	averiguaría
tú	averiguarás	tú	averiguarías
él	averiguará	él	averiguaría
nosotros	averiguaremos	nosotros	averiguaríamos
vosotros	averiguaréis	vosotros	averiguaríais
ellos	averiguarán	ellos	averiguarían

	PRESENT SUBJUNCTIVE		PRETERITE
yo	averigüe	yo	averigüé
tú	averigües	tú	averiguaste
él	averigüe	él	averiguó
nosotros	averigüemos	nosotros	averiguamos
vosotros	averigüéis	vosotros	averiguasteis
ellos	averigüen	ellos	averiguaron

PAST PARTICIPLE	IMPERATIVE
averiguado	averigua
	averiguad

GERUND
averiguando

Irregular Verbs

bendecir (to bless)

	PRESENT		IMPERFECT
yo	bendigo	yo	bendecía
tú	bendices	tú	bendecías
él	bendice	él	bendecía
nosotros	bendecimos	nosotros	bendecíamos
vosotros	bendecís	vosotros	bendecíais
ellos	bendicen	ellos	bendecían

	FUTURE		CONDITIONAL
yo	bendeciré	yo	bendeciría
tú	bendecirás	tú	bendecirías
él	bendecirá	él	bendeciría
nosotros	bendeciremos	nosotros	bendeciríamos
vosotros	bendeciréis	vosotros	bendeciríais
ellos	bendecirán	ellos	bendecirían

	PRESENT SUBJUNCTIVE		PRETERITE
yo	bendiga	yo	bendije
tú	bendigas	tú	bendijiste
él	bendiga	él	bendijo
nosotros	bendigamos	nosotros	bendijimos
vosotros	bendigáis	vosotros	bendijisteis
ellos	bendigan	ellos	bendijeron

PAST PARTICIPLE	IMPERATIVE
bendecido	bendice
	bendecid

GERUND
bendiciendo

Irregular Verbs

caber (to fit)

	PRESENT		IMPERFECT
yo	quepo	yo	cabía
tú	cabes	tú	cabías
él	cabe	él	cabía
nosotros	cabemos	nosotros	cabíamos
vosotros	cabéis	vosotros	cabíais
ellos	caben	ellos	cabían

	FUTURE		CONDITIONAL
yo	cabré	yo	cabría
tú	cabrás	tú	cabrías
él	cabrá	él	cabría
nosotros	cabremos	nosotros	cabríamos
vosotros	cabréis	vosotros	cabríais
ellos	cabrán	ellos	cabrían

	PRESENT SUBJUNCTIVE		PRETERITE
yo	quepa	yo	cupe
tú	quepas	tú	cupiste
él	quepa	él	cupo
nosotros	quepamos	nosotros	cupimos
vosotros	quepáis	vosotros	cupisteis
ellos	quepan	ellos	cupieron

PAST PARTICIPLE	IMPERATIVE
cabido	cabe
	cabed

GERUND
cabiendo

Irregular Verbs

caer (to fall)

	PRESENT		IMPERFECT
yo	caigo	yo	caía
tú	caes	tú	caías
él	cae	él	caía
nosotros	caemos	nosotros	caíamos
vosotros	caéis	vosotros	caíais
ellos	caen	ellos	caían

	FUTURE		CONDITIONAL
yo	caeré	yo	caería
tú	caerás	tú	caerías
él	caerá	él	caería
nosotros	caeremos	nosotros	caeríamos
vosotros	caeréis	vosotros	caeríais
ellos	caerán	ellos	caerían

	PRESENT SUBJUNCTIVE		PRETERITE
yo	caiga	yo	caí
tú	caigas	tú	caíste
él	caiga	él	cayó
nosotros	caigamos	nosotros	caímos
vosotros	caigáis	vosotros	caísteis
ellos	caigan	ellos	cayeron

PAST PARTICIPLE	IMPERATIVE
caído	cae
	caed

GERUND
cayendo

cocer (to boil)

	PRESENT		IMPERFECT
yo	**cuezo**	yo	coc**ía**
tú	**cueces**	tú	coc**ías**
él	**cuece**	él	coc**ía**
nosotros	coc**emos**	nosotros	coc**íamos**
vosotros	coc**éis**	vosotros	coc**íais**
ellos	**cuecen**	ellos	coc**ían**

	FUTURE		CONDITIONAL
yo	cocer**é**	yo	cocer**ía**
tú	cocer**ás**	tú	cocer**ías**
él	cocer**á**	él	cocer**ía**
nosotros	cocer**emos**	nosotros	cocer**íamos**
vosotros	cocer**éis**	vosotros	cocer**íais**
ellos	cocer**án**	ellos	cocer**ían**

	PRESENT SUBJUNCTIVE		PRETERITE
yo	**cueza**	yo	coc**í**
tú	**cuezas**	tú	coc**iste**
él	**cueza**	él	coc**ió**
nosotros	**cozamos**	nosotros	coc**imos**
vosotros	**cozáis**	vosotros	coc**isteis**
ellos	**cuezan**	ellos	coc**ieron**

PAST PARTICIPLE	IMPERATIVE
coc**ido**	**cuece**
	coc**ed**

GERUND
coc**iendo**

Irregular Verbs

coger (to take)

	PRESENT		IMPERFECT
yo	cojo	yo	cogía
tú	coges	tú	cogías
él	coge	él	cogía
nosotros	cogemos	nosotros	cogíamos
vosotros	cogéis	vosotros	cogíais
ellos	cogen	ellos	cogían

	FUTURE		CONDITIONAL
yo	cogeré	yo	cogería
tú	cogerás	tú	cogerías
él	cogerá	él	cogería
nosotros	cogeremos	nosotros	cogeríamos
vosotros	cogeréis	vosotros	cogeríais
ellos	cogerán	ellos	cogerían

	PRESENT SUBJUNCTIVE		PRETERITE
yo	coja	yo	cogí
tú	cojas	tú	cogiste
él	coja	él	cogió
nosotros	cojamos	nosotros	cogimos
vosotros	cojáis	vosotros	cogisteis
ellos	cojan	ellos	cogieron

PAST PARTICIPLE	IMPERATIVE
cogido	coge
	coged

GERUND
cogiendo

Irregular Verbs

conducir (to drive, to lead)

	PRESENT		IMPERFECT
yo	**conduzco**	yo	conduc**ía**
tú	conduc**es**	tú	conduc**ías**
él	conduc**e**	él	conduc**ía**
nosotros	conduc**imos**	nosotros	conduc**íamos**
vosotros	conduc**ís**	vosotros	conduc**íais**
ellos	conduc**en**	ellos	conduc**ían**

	FUTURE		CONDITIONAL
yo	conducir**é**	yo	conducir**ía**
tú	conducir**ás**	tú	conducir**ías**
él	conducir**á**	él	conducir**ía**
nosotros	conducir**emos**	nosotros	conducir**íamos**
vosotros	conducir**éis**	vosotros	conducir**íais**
ellos	conducir**án**	ellos	conducir**ían**

	PRESENT SUBJUNCTIVE		PRETERITE
yo	**conduzca**	yo	**conduje**
tú	**conduzcas**	tú	**condujiste**
él	**conduzca**	él	**condujo**
nosotros	**conduzcamos**	nosotros	**condujimos**
vosotros	**conduzcáis**	vosotros	**condujisteis**
ellos	**conduzcan**	ellos	**condujeron**

PAST PARTICIPLE	IMPERATIVE
conduc**ido**	conduc**e**
	conduc**id**

GERUND
conduc**iendo**

Irregular Verbs

construir (to build)

	PRESENT		IMPERFECT
yo	**construyo**	yo	construía
tú	**construyes**	tú	construías
él	**construye**	él	construía
nosotros	construimos	nosotros	construíamos
vosotros	construís	vosotros	construíais
ellos	**construyen**	ellos	construían

	FUTURE		CONDITIONAL
yo	construiré	yo	construiría
tú	construirás	tú	construirías
él	construirá	él	construiría
nosotros	construiremos	nosotros	construiríamos
vosotros	construiréis	vosotros	construiríais
ellos	construirán	ellos	construirían

	PRESENT SUBJUNCTIVE		PRETERITE
yo	**construya**	yo	construí
tú	**construyas**	tú	construiste
él	**construya**	él	**construyó**
nosotros	**construyamos**	nosotros	construimos
vosotros	**construyáis**	vosotros	construisteis
ellos	**construyan**	ellos	**construyeron**

PAST PARTICIPLE	IMPERATIVE
construido	**construye**
	construid

GERUND
construyendo

Irregular Verbs

contar (to tell, to count)

	PRESENT		IMPERFECT
yo	**cuento**	yo	cont**aba**
tú	**cuentas**	tú	cont**abas**
él	**cuenta**	él	cont**aba**
nosotros	cont**amos**	nosotros	cont**ábamos**
vosotros	cont**áis**	vosotros	cont**abais**
ellos	**cuentan**	ellos	cont**aban**

	FUTURE		CONDITIONAL
yo	contar**é**	yo	contar**ía**
tú	contar**ás**	tú	contar**ías**
él	contar**á**	él	contar**ía**
nosotros	contar**emos**	nosotros	contar**íamos**
vosotros	contar**éis**	vosotros	contar**íais**
ellos	contar**án**	ellos	contar**ían**

	PRESENT SUBJUNCTIVE		PRETERITE
yo	**cuente**	yo	cont**é**
tú	**cuentes**	tú	cont**aste**
él	**cuente**	él	cont**ó**
nosotros	cont**emos**	nosotros	cont**amos**
vosotros	cont**éis**	vosotros	cont**asteis**
ellos	**cuenten**	ellos	cont**aron**

PAST PARTICIPLE	IMPERATIVE
cont**ado**	**cuenta**
	contad

GERUND
cont**ando**

Irregular Verbs

crecer (to grow)

	PRESENT		IMPERFECT
yo	crezco	yo	crecía
tú	creces	tú	crecías
él	crece	él	crecía
nosotros	crecemos	nosotros	crecíamos
vosotros	crecéis	vosotros	crecíais
ellos	crecen	ellos	crecían

	FUTURE		CONDITIONAL
yo	creceré	yo	crecería
tú	crecerás	tú	crecerías
él	crecerá	él	crecería
nosotros	creceremos	nosotros	creceríamos
vosotros	creceréis	vosotros	creceríais
ellos	crecerán	ellos	crecerían

	PRESENT SUBJUNCTIVE		PRETERITE
yo	crezca	yo	crecí
tú	crezcas	tú	creciste
él	crezca	él	creció
nosotros	crezcamos	nosotros	crecimos
vosotros	crezcáis	vosotros	crecisteis
ellos	crezcan	ellos	crecieron

PAST PARTICIPLE	IMPERATIVE
crecido	crece
	creced

GERUND
creciendo

Irregular Verbs

cruzar (to cross)

	PRESENT		IMPERFECT
yo	cruz**o**	yo	cruz**aba**
tú	cruz**as**	tú	cruz**abas**
él	cruz**a**	él	cruz**aba**
nosotros	cruz**amos**	nosotros	cruz**ábamos**
vosotros	cruz**áis**	vosotros	cruz**abais**
ellos	cruz**an**	ellos	cruz**aban**

	FUTURE		CONDITIONAL
yo	cruzar**é**	yo	cruzar**ía**
tú	cruzar**ás**	tú	cruzar**ías**
él	cruzar**á**	él	cruzar**ía**
nosotros	cruzar**emos**	nosotros	cruzar**íamos**
vosotros	cruzar**éis**	vosotros	cruzar**íais**
ellos	cruzar**án**	ellos	cruzar**ían**

	PRESENT SUBJUNCTIVE		PRETERITE
yo	**cruce**	yo	**crucé**
tú	**cruces**	tú	cruz**aste**
él	**cruce**	él	cruz**ó**
nosotros	**crucemos**	nosotros	cruz**amos**
vosotros	**crucéis**	vosotros	cruz**asteis**
ellos	**crucen**	ellos	cruz**aron**

PAST PARTICIPLE	IMPERATIVE
cruz**ado**	cruz**a**
	cruz**ad**

GERUND
cruz**ando**

Irregular Verbs

dar (to give)

	PRESENT		IMPERFECT
yo	doy	yo	daba
tú	das	tú	dabas
él	da	él	daba
nosotros	damos	nosotros	dábamos
vosotros	dais	vosotros	dabais
ellos	dan	ellos	daban

	FUTURE		CONDITIONAL
yo	daré	yo	daría
tú	darás	tú	darías
él	dará	él	daría
nosotros	daremos	nosotros	daríamos
vosotros	daréis	vosotros	daríais
ellos	darán	ellos	darían

	PRESENT SUBJUNCTIVE		PRETERITE
yo	dé	yo	di
tú	des	tú	diste
él	dé	él	dio
nosotros	demos	nosotros	dimos
vosotros	deis	vosotros	disteis
ellos	den	ellos	dieron

PAST PARTICIPLE	IMPERATIVE
dado	da
	dad

GERUND
dando

Irregular Verbs

decir (to say, to tell)

	PRESENT		IMPERFECT
yo	digo	yo	decía
tú	dices	tú	decías
él	dice	él	decía
nosotros	decimos	nosotros	decíamos
vosotros	decís	vosotros	decíais
ellos	dicen	ellos	decían

	FUTURE		CONDITIONAL
yo	diré	yo	diría
tú	dirás	tú	dirías
él	dirá	él	diría
nosotros	diremos	nosotros	diríamos
vosotros	diréis	vosotros	diríais
ellos	dirán	ellos	dirían

	PRESENT SUBJUNCTIVE		PRETERITE
yo	diga	yo	dije
tú	digas	tú	dijiste
él	diga	él	dijo
nosotros	digamos	nosotros	dijimos
vosotros	digáis	vosotros	dijisteis
ellos	digan	ellos	dijeron

PAST PARTICIPLE	IMPERATIVE
dicho	di
	decid

GERUND
diciendo

Irregular Verbs

dirigir (to direct)

	PRESENT		IMPERFECT
yo	dirijo	yo	dirigía
tú	diriges	tú	dirigías
él	dirige	él	dirigía
nosotros	dirigimos	nosotros	dirigíamos
vosotros	dirigís	vosotros	dirigíais
ellos	dirigen	ellos	dirigían

	FUTURE		CONDITIONAL
yo	dirigiré	yo	dirigiría
tú	dirigirás	tú	dirigirías
él	dirigirá	él	dirigiría
nosotros	dirigiremos	nosotros	dirigiríamos
vosotros	dirigiréis	vosotros	dirigiríais
ellos	dirigirán	ellos	dirigirían

	PRESENT SUBJUNCTIVE		PRETERITE
yo	dirija	yo	dirigí
tú	dirijas	tú	dirigiste
él	dirija	él	dirigió
nosotros	dirijamos	nosotros	dirigimos
vosotros	dirijáis	vosotros	dirigisteis
ellos	dirijan	ellos	dirigieron

PAST PARTICIPLE	IMPERATIVE
dirigido	dirige
	dirigid

GERUND
dirigiendo

Irregular Verbs

distinguir (to distinguish)

	PRESENT		IMPERFECT
yo	**distingo**	yo	distinguía
tú	distingues	tú	distinguías
él	distingue	él	distinguía
nosotros	distinguimos	nosotros	distinguíamos
vosotros	distinguís	vosotros	distinguíais
ellos	distinguen	ellos	distinguían

	FUTURE		CONDITIONAL
yo	distinguiré	yo	distinguiría
tú	distinguirás	tú	distinguirías
él	distinguirá	él	distinguiría
nosotros	distinguiremos	nosotros	distinguiríamos
vosotros	distinguiréis	vosotros	distinguiríais
ellos	distinguirán	ellos	distinguirían

	PRESENT SUBJUNCTIVE		PRETERITE
yo	**distinga**	yo	distinguí
tú	**distingas**	tú	distinguiste
él	**distinga**	él	distinguió
nosotros	**distingamos**	nosotros	distinguimos
vosotros	**distingáis**	vosotros	distinguisteis
ellos	**distingan**	ellos	distinguieron

PAST PARTICIPLE	IMPERATIVE
distinguido	distingue
	distinguid

GERUND
distinguiendo

Irregular Verbs

dormir (to sleep)

	PRESENT		IMPERFECT
yo	**duermo**	yo	dormía
tú	**duermes**	tú	dormías
él	**duerme**	él	dormía
nosotros	dorm**imos**	nosotros	dorm**íamos**
vosotros	dorm**ís**	vosotros	dorm**íais**
ellos	**duermen**	ellos	dorm**ían**

	FUTURE		CONDITIONAL
yo	dormir**é**	yo	dormir**ía**
tú	dormir**ás**	tú	dormir**ías**
él	dormir**á**	él	dormir**ía**
nosotros	dormir**emos**	nosotros	dormir**íamos**
vosotros	dormir**éis**	vosotros	dormir**íais**
ellos	dormir**án**	ellos	dormir**ían**

	PRESENT SUBJUNCTIVE		PRETERITE
yo	**duerma**	yo	dorm**í**
tú	**duermas**	tú	dorm**iste**
él	**duerma**	él	**durmió**
nosotros	**durmamos**	nosotros	dorm**imos**
vosotros	**durmáis**	vosotros	dorm**isteis**
ellos	**duerman**	ellos	**durmieron**

PAST PARTICIPLE	IMPERATIVE
dorm**ido**	**duerme**
	dorm**id**

GERUND
durmiendo

Irregular Verbs

elegir (to choose)

	PRESENT		IMPERFECT
yo	elijo	yo	elegía
tú	eliges	tú	elegías
él	elige	él	elegía
nosotros	elegimos	nosotros	elegíamos
vosotros	elegís	vosotros	elegíais
ellos	eligen	ellos	elegían

	FUTURE		CONDITIONAL
yo	elegiré	yo	elegiría
tú	elegirás	tú	elegirías
él	elegirá	él	elegiría
nosotros	elegiremos	nosotros	elegiríamos
vosotros	elegiréis	vosotros	elegiríais
ellos	elegirán	ellos	elegirían

	PRESENT SUBJUNCTIVE		PRETERITE
yo	elija	yo	elegí
tú	elijas	tú	elegiste
él	elija	él	eligió
nosotros	elijamos	nosotros	elegimos
vosotros	elijáis	vosotros	elegisteis
ellos	elijan	ellos	eligieron

PAST PARTICIPLE	IMPERATIVE
elegido	elige
	elegid

GERUND
eligiendo

Irregular Verbs

empezar (to begin)

	PRESENT		IMPERFECT
yo	empiezo	yo	empezaba
tú	empiezas	tú	empezabas
él	empieza	él	empezaba
nosotros	empezamos	nosotros	empezábamos
vosotros	empezáis	vosotros	empezabais
ellos	empiezan	ellos	empezaban

	FUTURE		CONDITIONAL
yo	empezaré	yo	empezaría
tú	empezarás	tú	empezarías
él	empezará	él	empezaría
nosotros	empezaremos	nosotros	empezaríamos
vosotros	empezaréis	vosotros	empezaríais
ellos	empezarán	ellos	empezarían

	PRESENT SUBJUNCTIVE		PRETERITE
yo	empiece	yo	empecé
tú	empieces	tú	empezaste
él	empiece	él	empezó
nosotros	empecemos	nosotros	empezamos
vosotros	empecéis	vosotros	empezasteis
ellos	empiecen	ellos	empezaron

PAST PARTICIPLE	IMPERATIVE
empezado	empieza
	empezad

GERUND
empezando

Irregular Verbs

entender (to understand)

	PRESENT		IMPERFECT
yo	**entiendo**	yo	entend**ía**
tú	**entiendes**	tú	entend**ías**
él	**entiende**	él	entend**ía**
nosotros	entend**emos**	nosotros	entend**íamos**
vosotros	entend**éis**	vosotros	entend**íais**
ellos	**entienden**	ellos	entend**ían**

	FUTURE		CONDITIONAL
yo	entender**é**	yo	entender**ía**
tú	entender**ás**	tú	entender**ías**
él	entender**á**	él	entender**ía**
nosotros	entender**emos**	nosotros	entender**íamos**
vosotros	entender**éis**	vosotros	entender**íais**
ellos	entender**án**	ellos	entender**ían**

	PRESENT SUBJUNCTIVE		PRETERITE
yo	**entienda**	yo	entend**í**
tú	**entiendas**	tú	entend**iste**
él	**entienda**	él	entend**ió**
nosotros	entend**amos**	nosotros	entend**imos**
vosotros	entend**áis**	vosotros	entend**isteis**
ellos	**entiendan**	ellos	entend**ieron**

PAST PARTICIPLE	IMPERATIVE
entend**ido**	**entiende**
	entend**ed**

GERUND
entend**iendo**

Irregular Verbs

enviar (to send)

	PRESENT		IMPERFECT
yo	envío	yo	enviaba
tú	envías	tú	enviabas
él	envía	él	enviaba
nosotros	enviamos	nosotros	enviábamos
vosotros	enviáis	vosotros	enviabais
ellos	envían	ellos	enviaban

	FUTURE		CONDITIONAL
yo	enviaré	yo	enviaría
tú	enviarás	tú	enviarías
él	enviará	él	enviaría
nosotros	enviaremos	nosotros	enviaríamos
vosotros	enviaréis	vosotros	enviaríais
ellos	enviarán	ellos	enviarían

	PRESENT SUBJUNCTIVE		PRETERITE
yo	envíe	yo	envié
tú	envíes	tú	enviaste
él	envíe	él	envió
nosotros	enviemos	nosotros	enviamos
vosotros	enviéis	vosotros	enviasteis
ellos	envíen	ellos	enviaron

PAST PARTICIPLE	IMPERATIVE
enviado	envía
	enviad

GERUND
enviando

Irregular Verbs

erguir (to erect)

	PRESENT		IMPERFECT
yo	**yergo**	yo	ergu**ía**
tú	**yergues**	tú	ergu**ías**
él	**yergue**	él	ergu**ía**
nosotros	ergu**imos**	nosotros	ergu**íamos**
vosotros	ergu**ís**	vosotros	ergu**íais**
ellos	**yerguen**	ellos	ergu**ían**

	FUTURE		CONDITIONAL
yo	erguir**é**	yo	erguir**ía**
tú	erguir**ás**	tú	erguir**ías**
él	erguir**á**	él	erguir**ía**
nosotros	erguir**emos**	nosotros	erguir**íamos**
vosotros	erguir**éis**	vosotros	erguir**íais**
ellos	erguir**án**	ellos	erguir**ían**

	PRESENT SUBJUNCTIVE		PRETERITE
yo	**yerga**	yo	ergu**í**
tú	**yergas**	tú	ergu**iste**
él	**yerga**	él	**irguió**
nosotros	**irgamos**	nosotros	ergu**imos**
vosotros	**irgáis**	vosotros	ergu**isteis**
ellos	**yergan**	ellos	**irguieron**

PAST PARTICIPLE	IMPERATIVE
ergu**ido**	**yergue**
	ergu**id**

GERUND
irguiendo

Irregular Verbs

errar (to err)

	PRESENT		IMPERFECT
yo	yerro	yo	erraba
tú	yerras	tú	errabas
él	yerra	él	erraba
nosotros	erramos	nosotros	errábamos
vosotros	erráis	vosotros	errabais
ellos	yerran	ellos	erraban

	FUTURE		CONDITIONAL
yo	erraré	yo	erraría
tú	errarás	tú	errarías
él	errará	él	erraría
nosotros	erraremos	nosotros	erraríamos
vosotros	erraréis	vosotros	erraríais
ellos	errarán	ellos	errarían

	PRESENT SUBJUNCTIVE		PRETERITE
yo	yerre	yo	erré
tú	yerres	tú	erraste
él	yerre	él	erró
nosotros	erremos	nosotros	erramos
vosotros	erréis	vosotros	errasteis
ellos	yerren	ellos	erraron

PAST PARTICIPLE	IMPERATIVE
errado	yerra
	errad

GERUND
errando

Irregular Verbs

escribir (to write)

	PRESENT		IMPERFECT
yo	escribo	yo	escribía
tú	escribes	tú	escribías
él	escribe	él	escribía
nosotros	escribimos	nosotros	escribíamos
vosotros	escribís	vosotros	escribíais
ellos	escriben	ellos	escribían

	FUTURE		CONDITIONAL
yo	escribiré	yo	escribiría
tú	escribirás	tú	escribirías
él	escribirá	él	escribiría
nosotros	escribiremos	nosotros	escribiríamos
vosotros	escribiréis	vosotros	escribiríais
ellos	escribirán	ellos	escribirían

	PRESENT SUBJUNCTIVE		PRETERITE
yo	escriba	yo	escribí
tú	escribas	tú	escribiste
él	escriba	él	escribió
nosotros	escribamos	nosotros	escribimos
vosotros	escribáis	vosotros	escribisteis
ellos	escriban	ellos	escribieron

PAST PARTICIPLE	IMPERATIVE
escrito	escribe
	escribid

GERUND
escribiendo

Irregular Verbs

estar (to be)

	PRESENT		IMPERFECT
yo	estoy	yo	estaba
tú	estás	tú	estabas
él	está	él	estaba
nosotros	estamos	nosotros	estábamos
vosotros	estáis	vosotros	estabais
ellos	están	ellos	estaban

	FUTURE		CONDITIONAL
yo	estaré	yo	estaría
tú	estarás	tú	estarías
él	estará	él	estaría
nosotros	estaremos	nosotros	estaríamos
vosotros	estaréis	vosotros	estaríais
ellos	estarán	ellos	estarían

	PRESENT SUBJUNCTIVE		PRETERITE
yo	esté	yo	estuve
tú	estés	tú	estuviste
él	esté	él	estuvo
nosotros	estemos	nosotros	estuvimos
vosotros	estéis	vosotros	estuvisteis
ellos	estén	ellos	estuvieron

PAST PARTICIPLE	IMPERATIVE
estado	está
	estad

GERUND
estando

Irregular Verbs

freír (to fry)

	PRESENT			IMPERFECT
yo	**frío**		yo	freía
tú	**fríes**		tú	freías
él	**fríe**		él	freía
nosotros	freímos		nosotros	freíamos
vosotros	freís		vosotros	freíais
ellos	**fríen**		ellos	freían

	FUTURE			CONDITIONAL
yo	freiré		yo	freiría
tú	freirás		tú	freirías
él	freirá		él	freiría
nosotros	freiremos		nosotros	freiríamos
vosotros	freiréis		vosotros	freiríais
ellos	freirán		ellos	freirían

	PRESENT SUBJUNCTIVE			PRETERITE
yo	**fría**		yo	freí
tú	**frías**		tú	freíste
él	**fría**		él	**frio**
nosotros	**friamos**		nosotros	freímos
vosotros	**friais**		vosotros	freísteis
ellos	**frían**		ellos	**frieron**

PAST PARTICIPLE	IMPERATIVE
frito	**fríe**
	freíd

GERUND
friendo

Irregular Verbs

gruñir (to grunt)

	PRESENT			IMPERFECT
yo	gruño		yo	gruñía
tú	gruñes		tú	gruñías
él	gruñe		él	gruñía
nosotros	gruñimos		nosotros	gruñíamos
vosotros	gruñís		vosotros	gruñíais
ellos	gruñen		ellos	gruñían

	FUTURE			CONDITIONAL
yo	gruñiré		yo	gruñiría
tú	gruñirás		tú	gruñirías
él	gruñirá		él	gruñiría
nosotros	gruñiremos		nosotros	gruñiríamos
vosotros	gruñiréis		vosotros	gruñiríais
ellos	gruñirán		ellos	gruñirían

	PRESENT SUBJUNCTIVE			PRETERITE
yo	gruña		yo	gruñí
tú	gruñas		tú	gruñiste
él	gruña		él	gruñó
nosotros	gruñamos		nosotros	gruñimos
vosotros	gruñáis		vosotros	gruñisteis
ellos	gruñan		ellos	gruñeron

PAST PARTICIPLE	IMPERATIVE
gruñido	gruñe
	gruñid

GERUND
gruñendo

Irregular Verbs

haber (to have, *auxiliary*)

	PRESENT		IMPERFECT
yo	he	yo	había
tú	has	tú	habías
él	ha	él	había
nosotros	hemos	nosotros	habíamos
vosotros	habéis	vosotros	habíais
ellos	han	ellos	habían

	FUTURE		CONDITIONAL
yo	habré	yo	habría
tú	habrás	tú	habrías
él	habrá	él	habría
nosotros	habremos	nosotros	habríamos
vosotros	habréis	vosotros	habríais
ellos	habrán	ellos	habrían

	PRESENT SUBJUNCTIVE		PRETERITE
yo	haya	yo	hube
tú	hayas	tú	hubiste
él	haya	él	hubo
nosotros	hayamos	nosotros	hubimos
vosotros	hayáis	vosotros	hubisteis
ellos	hayan	ellos	hubieron

PAST PARTICIPLE	IMPERATIVE
habido	he
	habed

GERUND
habiendo

Irregular Verbs

hacer (to do, to make)

	PRESENT		IMPERFECT
yo	hago	yo	hacía
tú	haces	tú	hacías
él	hace	él	hacía
nosotros	hacemos	nosotros	hacíamos
vosotros	hacéis	vosotros	hacíais
ellos	hacen	ellos	hacían

	FUTURE		CONDITIONAL
yo	haré	yo	haría
tú	harás	tú	harías
él	hará	él	haría
nosotros	haremos	nosotros	haríamos
vosotros	haréis	vosotros	haríais
ellos	harán	ellos	harían

	PRESENT SUBJUNCTIVE		PRETERITE
yo	haga	yo	hice
tú	hagas	tú	hiciste
él	haga	él	hizo
nosotros	hagamos	nosotros	hicimos
vosotros	hagáis	vosotros	hicisteis
ellos	hagan	ellos	hicieron

PAST PARTICIPLE	IMPERATIVE
hecho	haz
	haced

GERUND
haciendo

Irregular Verbs

hay (there is, there are)

PRESENT
hay

IMPERFECT
había

FUTURE
habrá

CONDITIONAL
habría

PRESENT SUBJUNCTIVE
haya

PRETERITE
hubo

PAST PARTICIPLE
habido

IMPERATIVE
not used

GERUND
habiendo

Irregular Verbs

ir (to go)

	PRESENT		IMPERFECT
yo	voy	yo	iba
tú	vas	tú	ibas
él	va	él	iba
nosotros	vamos	nosotros	íbamos
vosotros	vais	vosotros	ibais
ellos	van	ellos	iban

	FUTURE		CONDITIONAL
yo	iré	yo	iría
tú	irás	tú	irías
él	irá	él	iría
nosotros	iremos	nosotros	iríamos
vosotros	iréis	vosotros	iríais
ellos	irán	ellos	irían

	PRESENT SUBJUNCTIVE		PRETERITE
yo	vaya	yo	fui
tú	vayas	tú	fuiste
él	vaya	él	fue
nosotros	vayamos	nosotros	fuimos
vosotros	vayáis	vosotros	fuisteis
ellos	vayan	ellos	fueron

PAST PARTICIPLE	IMPERATIVE
ido	ve
	id

GERUND
yendo

Irregular Verbs

jugar (to play)

	PRESENT		IMPERFECT
yo	**juego**	yo	jug**aba**
tú	**juegas**	tú	jug**abas**
él	**juega**	él	jug**aba**
nosotros	jug**amos**	nosotros	jug**ábamos**
vosotros	jug**áis**	vosotros	jug**abais**
ellos	**juegan**	ellos	jug**aban**

	FUTURE		CONDITIONAL
yo	jugar**é**	yo	jugar**ía**
tú	jugar**ás**	tú	jugar**ías**
él	jugar**á**	él	jugar**ía**
nosotros	jugar**emos**	nosotros	jugar**íamos**
vosotros	jugar**éis**	vosotros	jugar**íais**
ellos	jugar**án**	ellos	jugar**ían**

	PRESENT SUBJUNCTIVE		PRETERITE
yo	**juegue**	yo	**jugué**
tú	**juegues**	tú	jug**aste**
él	**juegue**	él	jug**ó**
nosotros	**juguemos**	nosotros	jug**amos**
vosotros	**juguéis**	vosotros	jug**asteis**
ellos	**jueguen**	ellos	jug**aron**

PAST PARTICIPLE	IMPERATIVE
jug**ado**	**juega**
	jug**ad**

GERUND
jug**ando**

Irregular Verbs

leer (to read)

	PRESENT		IMPERFECT
yo	leo	yo	leía
tú	lees	tú	leías
él	lee	él	leía
nosotros	leemos	nosotros	leíamos
vosotros	leéis	vosotros	leíais
ellos	leen	ellos	leían

	FUTURE		CONDITIONAL
yo	leeré	yo	leería
tú	leerás	tú	leerías
él	leerá	él	leería
nosotros	leeremos	nosotros	leeríamos
vosotros	leeréis	vosotros	leeríais
ellos	leerán	ellos	leerían

	PRESENT SUBJUNCTIVE		PRETERITE
yo	lea	yo	leí
tú	leas	tú	leíste
él	lea	él	leyó
nosotros	leamos	nosotros	leímos
vosotros	leáis	vosotros	leísteis
ellos	lean	ellos	leyeron

PAST PARTICIPLE	IMPERATIVE
leído	lee
	leed

GERUND
leyendo

Irregular Verbs

lucir (to shine)

	PRESENT		IMPERFECT
yo	**luzco**	yo	lucía
tú	luces	tú	lucías
él	luce	él	lucía
nosotros	lucimos	nosotros	lucíamos
vosotros	lucís	vosotros	lucíais
ellos	lucen	ellos	lucían

	FUTURE		CONDITIONAL
yo	luciré	yo	luciría
tú	lucirás	tú	lucirías
él	lucirá	él	luciría
nosotros	luciremos	nosotros	luciríamos
vosotros	luciréis	vosotros	luciríais
ellos	lucirán	ellos	lucirían

	PRESENT SUBJUNCTIVE		PRETERITE
yo	**luzca**	yo	lucí
tú	**luzcas**	tú	luciste
él	**luzca**	él	lució
nosotros	**luzcamos**	nosotros	lucimos
vosotros	**luzcáis**	vosotros	lucisteis
ellos	**luzcan**	ellos	lucieron

PAST PARTICIPLE	IMPERATIVE
lucido	luce
	lucid

GERUND
luciendo

Irregular Verbs

llover (to rain)

PRESENT	**IMPERFECT**
llueve	llovía
FUTURE	**CONDITIONAL**
lloverá	llovería
PRESENT SUBJUNCTIVE	**PRETERITE**
llueva	llovió

PAST PARTICIPLE	**IMPERATIVE**
llovido	*not used*
GERUND	
lloviendo	

morir (to die)

	PRESENT		IMPERFECT
yo	muero	yo	moría
tú	mueres	tú	morías
él	muere	él	moría
nosotros	morimos	nosotros	moríamos
vosotros	morís	vosotros	moríais
ellos	mueren	ellos	morían

	FUTURE		CONDITIONAL
yo	moriré	yo	moriría
tú	morirás	tú	morirías
él	morirá	él	moriría
nosotros	moriremos	nosotros	moriríamos
vosotros	moriréis	vosotros	moriríais
ellos	morirán	ellos	morirían

	PRESENT SUBJUNCTIVE		PRETERITE
yo	muera	yo	morí
tú	mueras	tú	moriste
él	muera	él	murió
nosotros	muramos	nosotros	morimos
vosotros	muráis	vosotros	moristeis
ellos	mueran	ellos	murieron

PAST PARTICIPLE	IMPERATIVE
muerto	muere
	morid

GERUND
muriendo

Irregular Verbs

mover (to move)

	PRESENT		IMPERFECT
yo	muevo	yo	movía
tú	mueves	tú	movías
él	mueve	él	movía
nosotros	movemos	nosotros	movíamos
vosotros	movéis	vosotros	movíais
ellos	mueven	ellos	movían

	FUTURE		CONDITIONAL
yo	moveré	yo	movería
tú	moverás	tú	moverías
él	moverá	él	movería
nosotros	moveremos	nosotros	moveríamos
vosotros	moveréis	vosotros	moveríais
ellos	moverán	ellos	moverían

	PRESENT SUBJUNCTIVE		PRETERITE
yo	mueva	yo	moví
tú	muevas	tú	moviste
él	mueva	él	movió
nosotros	movamos	nosotros	movimos
vosotros	mováis	vosotros	movisteis
ellos	muevan	ellos	movieron

PAST PARTICIPLE	IMPERATIVE
movido	mueve
	moved

GERUND
moviendo

Irregular Verbs

nacer (to be born)

	PRESENT		IMPERFECT
yo	nazco	yo	nacía
tú	naces	tú	nacías
él	nace	él	nacía
nosotros	nacemos	nosotros	nacíamos
vosotros	nacéis	vosotros	nacíais
ellos	nacen	ellos	nacían

	FUTURE		CONDITIONAL
yo	naceré	yo	nacería
tú	nacerás	tú	nacerías
él	nacerá	él	nacería
nosotros	naceremos	nosotros	naceríamos
vosotros	naceréis	vosotros	naceríais
ellos	nacerán	ellos	nacerían

	PRESENT SUBJUNCTIVE		PRETERITE
yo	nazca	yo	nací
tú	nazcas	tú	naciste
él	nazca	él	nació
nosotros	nazcamos	nosotros	nacimos
vosotros	nazcáis	vosotros	nacisteis
ellos	nazcan	ellos	nacieron

PAST PARTICIPLE	IMPERATIVE
nacido	nace
	naced

GERUND
naciendo

Irregular Verbs

negar (to deny)

	PRESENT		IMPERFECT
yo	niego	yo	negaba
tú	niegas	tú	negabas
él	niega	él	negaba
nosotros	negamos	nosotros	negábamos
vosotros	negáis	vosotros	negabais
ellos	niegan	ellos	negaban

	FUTURE		CONDITIONAL
yo	negaré	yo	negaría
tú	negarás	tú	negarías
él	negará	él	negaría
nosotros	negaremos	nosotros	negaríamos
vosotros	negaréis	vosotros	negaríais
ellos	negarán	ellos	negarían

	PRESENT SUBJUNCTIVE		PRETERITE
yo	niegue	yo	negué
tú	niegues	tú	negaste
él	niegue	él	negó
nosotros	neguemos	nosotros	negamos
vosotros	neguéis	vosotros	negasteis
ellos	nieguen	ellos	negaron

PAST PARTICIPLE	IMPERATIVE
negado	niega
	negad

GERUND
negando

Irregular Verbs

oír (to hear)

	PRESENT		IMPERFECT
yo	oigo	yo	oía
tú	oyes	tú	oías
él	oye	él	oía
nosotros	oímos	nosotros	oíamos
vosotros	oís	vosotros	oíais
ellos	oyen	ellos	oían

	FUTURE		CONDITIONAL
yo	oiré	yo	oiría
tú	oirás	tú	oirías
él	oirá	él	oiría
nosotros	oiremos	nosotros	oiríamos
vosotros	oiréis	vosotros	oiríais
ellos	oirán	ellos	oirían

	PRESENT SUBJUNCTIVE		PRETERITE
yo	oiga	yo	oí
tú	oigas	tú	oíste
él	oiga	él	oyó
nosotros	oigamos	nosotros	oímos
vosotros	oigáis	vosotros	oísteis
ellos	oigan	ellos	oyeron

PAST PARTICIPLE	IMPERATIVE
oído	oye
	oíd

GERUND
oyendo

Irregular Verbs

oler (to smell)

	PRESENT		IMPERFECT
yo	huelo	yo	olía
tú	hueles	tú	olías
él	huele	él	olía
nosotros	olemos	nosotros	olíamos
vosotros	oléis	vosotros	olíais
ellos	huelen	ellos	olían

	FUTURE		CONDITIONAL
yo	oleré	yo	olería
tú	olerás	tú	olerías
él	olerá	él	olería
nosotros	oleremos	nosotros	oleríamos
vosotros	oleréis	vosotros	oleríais
ellos	olerán	ellos	olerían

	PRESENT SUBJUNCTIVE		PRETERITE
yo	huela	yo	olí
tú	huelas	tú	oliste
él	huela	él	olió
nosotros	olamos	nosotros	olimos
vosotros	oláis	vosotros	olisteis
ellos	huelan	ellos	olieron

PAST PARTICIPLE	IMPERATIVE
olido	huele
	oled

GERUND
oliendo

Irregular Verbs

pagar (to pay)

	PRESENT		IMPERFECT
yo	pago	yo	pagaba
tú	pagas	tú	pagabas
él	paga	él	pagaba
nosotros	pagamos	nosotros	pagábamos
vosotros	pagáis	vosotros	pagabais
ellos	pagan	ellos	pagaban

	FUTURE		CONDITIONAL
yo	pagaré	yo	pagaría
tú	pagarás	tú	pagarías
él	pagará	él	pagaría
nosotros	pagaremos	nosotros	pagaríamos
vosotros	pagaréis	vosotros	pagaríais
ellos	pagarán	ellos	pagarían

	PRESENT SUBJUNCTIVE		PRETERITE
yo	pague	yo	pagué
tú	pagues	tú	pagaste
él	pague	él	pagó
nosotros	paguemos	nosotros	pagamos
vosotros	paguéis	vosotros	pagasteis
ellos	paguen	ellos	pagaron

PAST PARTICIPLE	IMPERATIVE
pagado	paga
	pagad

GERUND
pagando

Irregular Verbs

pedir (to ask for)

	PRESENT		IMPERFECT
yo	pido	yo	pedía
tú	pides	tú	pedías
él	pide	él	pedía
nosotros	pedimos	nosotros	pedíamos
vosotros	pedís	vosotros	pedíais
ellos	piden	ellos	pedían

	FUTURE		CONDITIONAL
yo	pediré	yo	pediría
tú	pedirás	tú	pedirías
él	pedirá	él	pediría
nosotros	pediremos	nosotros	pediríamos
vosotros	pediréis	vosotros	pediríais
ellos	pedirán	ellos	pedirían

	PRESENT SUBJUNCTIVE		PRETERITE
yo	pida	yo	pedí
tú	pidas	tú	pediste
él	pida	él	pidió
nosotros	pidamos	nosotros	pedimos
vosotros	pidáis	vosotros	pedisteis
ellos	pidan	ellos	pidieron

PAST PARTICIPLE	IMPERATIVE
pedido	pide
	pedid

GERUND
pidiendo

Irregular Verbs

pensar (to think)

	PRESENT		IMPERFECT
yo	**pienso**	yo	pens**aba**
tú	**piensas**	tú	pens**abas**
él	**piensa**	él	pens**aba**
nosotros	pens**amos**	nosotros	pens**ábamos**
vosotros	pens**áis**	vosotros	pens**abais**
ellos	**piensan**	ellos	pens**aban**

	FUTURE		CONDITIONAL
yo	pensar**é**	yo	pensar**ía**
tú	pensar**ás**	tú	pensar**ías**
él	pensar**á**	él	pensar**ía**
nosotros	pensar**emos**	nosotros	pensar**íamos**
vosotros	pensar**éis**	vosotros	pensar**íais**
ellos	pensar**án**	ellos	pensar**ían**

	PRESENT SUBJUNCTIVE		PRETERITE
yo	**piense**	yo	pens**é**
tú	**pienses**	tú	pens**aste**
él	**piense**	él	pens**ó**
nosotros	pens**emos**	nosotros	pens**amos**
vosotros	pens**éis**	vosotros	pens**asteis**
ellos	**piensen**	ellos	pens**aron**

PAST PARTICIPLE	IMPERATIVE
pens**ado**	**piensa**
	pensa**d**

GERUND
pens**ando**

Irregular Verbs

poder (to be able)

	PRESENT		IMPERFECT
yo	puedo	yo	podía
tú	puedes	tú	podías
él	puede	él	podía
nosotros	podemos	nosotros	podíamos
vosotros	podéis	vosotros	podíais
ellos	pueden	ellos	podían

	FUTURE		CONDITIONAL
yo	podré	yo	podría
tú	podrás	tú	podrías
él	podrá	él	podría
nosotros	podremos	nosotros	podríamos
vosotros	podréis	vosotros	podríais
ellos	podrán	ellos	podrían

	PRESENT SUBJUNCTIVE		PRETERITE
yo	pueda	yo	pude
tú	puedas	tú	pudiste
él	pueda	él	pudo
nosotros	podamos	nosotros	pudimos
vosotros	podáis	vosotros	pudisteis
ellos	puedan	ellos	pudieron

PAST PARTICIPLE	IMPERATIVE
podido	puede
	poded

GERUND
pudiendo

Irregular Verbs

poner (to put)

	PRESENT		IMPERFECT
yo	**pongo**	yo	pon**ía**
tú	pon**es**	tú	pon**ías**
él	pon**e**	él	pon**ía**
nosotros	pon**emos**	nosotros	pon**íamos**
vosotros	pon**éis**	vosotros	pon**íais**
ellos	pon**en**	ellos	pon**ían**

	FUTURE		CONDITIONAL
yo	**pondré**	yo	**pondría**
tú	**pondrás**	tú	**pondrías**
él	**pondrá**	él	**pondría**
nosotros	**pondremos**	nosotros	**pondríamos**
vosotros	**pondréis**	vosotros	**pondríais**
ellos	**pondrán**	ellos	**pondrían**

	PRESENT SUBJUNCTIVE		PRETERITE
yo	**ponga**	yo	**puse**
tú	**pongas**	tú	**pusiste**
él	**ponga**	él	**puso**
nosotros	**pongamos**	nosotros	**pusimos**
vosotros	**pongáis**	vosotros	**pusisteis**
ellos	**pongan**	ellos	**pusieron**

PAST PARTICIPLE	IMPERATIVE
puesto	**pon**
	pon**ed**

GERUND
pon**iendo**

Irregular Verbs

prohibir (to forbid)

	PRESENT		IMPERFECT
yo	**prohíbo**	yo	prohib**ía**
tú	**prohíbes**	tú	prohib**ías**
él	**prohíbe**	él	prohib**ía**
nosotros	prohib**imos**	nosotros	prohib**íamos**
vosotros	prohib**ís**	vosotros	prohib**íais**
ellos	**prohíben**	ellos	prohib**ían**

	FUTURE		CONDITIONAL
yo	prohibir**é**	yo	prohibir**ía**
tú	prohibir**ás**	tú	prohibir**ías**
él	prohibir**á**	él	prohibir**ía**
nosotros	prohibir**emos**	nosotros	prohibir**íamos**
vosotros	prohibir**éis**	vosotros	prohibir**íais**
ellos	prohibir**án**	ellos	prohibir**ían**

	PRESENT SUBJUNCTIVE		PRETERITE
yo	**prohíba**	yo	prohib**í**
tú	**prohíbas**	tú	prohib**iste**
él	**prohíba**	él	prohib**ió**
nosotros	prohib**amos**	nosotros	prohib**imos**
vosotros	prohib**áis**	vosotros	prohib**isteis**
ellos	**prohíban**	ellos	prohib**ieron**

PAST PARTICIPLE	IMPERATIVE
prohib**ido**	**prohíbe**
	prohib**id**

GERUND
prohib**iendo**

Irregular Verbs

querer (to want)

	PRESENT		IMPERFECT
yo	quiero	yo	quería
tú	quieres	tú	querías
él	quiere	él	quería
nosotros	queremos	nosotros	queríamos
vosotros	queréis	vosotros	queríais
ellos	quieren	ellos	querían

	FUTURE		CONDITIONAL
yo	querré	yo	querría
tú	querrás	tú	querrías
él	querrá	él	querría
nosotros	querremos	nosotros	querríamos
vosotros	querréis	vosotros	querríais
ellos	querrán	ellos	querrían

	PRESENT SUBJUNCTIVE		PRETERITE
yo	quiera	yo	quise
tú	quieras	tú	quisiste
él	quiera	él	quiso
nosotros	queramos	nosotros	quisimos
vosotros	queráis	vosotros	quisisteis
ellos	quieran	ellos	quisieron

PAST PARTICIPLE	IMPERATIVE
querido	quiere
	quered

GERUND
queriendo

Irregular Verbs

rehusar (to refuse)

	PRESENT		IMPERFECT
yo	rehúso	yo	rehusaba
tú	rehúsas	tú	rehusabas
él	rehúsa	él	rehusaba
nosotros	rehusamos	nosotros	rehusábamos
vosotros	rehusáis	vosotros	rehusabais
ellos	rehúsan	ellos	rehusaban

	FUTURE		CONDITIONAL
yo	rehusaré	yo	rehusaría
tú	rehusarás	tú	rehusarías
él	rehusará	él	rehusaría
nosotros	rehusaremos	nosotros	rehusaríamos
vosotros	rehusaréis	vosotros	rehusaríais
ellos	rehusarán	ellos	rehusarían

	PRESENT SUBJUNCTIVE		PRETERITE
yo	rehúse	yo	rehusé
tú	rehúses	tú	rehusaste
él	rehúse	él	rehusó
nosotros	rehusemos	nosotros	rehusamos
vosotros	rehuséis	vosotros	rehusasteis
ellos	rehúsen	ellos	rehusaron

PAST PARTICIPLE	IMPERATIVE
rehusado	rehúsa
	rehusad

GERUND
rehusando

Irregular Verbs

reír (to laugh)

	PRESENT		IMPERFECT
yo	río	yo	reía
tú	ríes	tú	reías
él	ríe	él	reía
nosotros	reímos	nosotros	reíamos
vosotros	reís	vosotros	reíais
ellos	ríen	ellos	reían

	FUTURE		CONDITIONAL
yo	reiré	yo	reiría
tú	reirás	tú	reirías
él	reirá	él	reiría
nosotros	reiremos	nosotros	reiríamos
vosotros	reiréis	vosotros	reiríais
ellos	reirán	ellos	reirían

	PRESENT SUBJUNCTIVE		PRETERITE
yo	ría	yo	reí
tú	rías	tú	reíste
él	ría	él	rio
nosotros	riamos	nosotros	reímos
vosotros	riais	vosotros	reísteis
ellos	rían	ellos	rieron

PAST PARTICIPLE	IMPERATIVE
reído	ríe
	reíd

GERUND
riendo

Irregular Verbs

reñir (to scold)

	PRESENT		IMPERFECT
yo	riño	yo	reñía
tú	riñes	tú	reñías
él	riñe	él	reñía
nosotros	reñimos	nosotros	reñíamos
vosotros	reñís	vosotros	reñíais
ellos	riñen	ellos	reñían

	FUTURE		CONDITIONAL
yo	reñiré	yo	reñiría
tú	reñirás	tú	reñirías
él	reñirá	él	reñiría
nosotros	reñiremos	nosotros	reñiríamos
vosotros	reñiréis	vosotros	reñiríais
ellos	reñirán	ellos	reñirían

	PRESENT SUBJUNCTIVE		PRETERITE
yo	riña	yo	reñí
tú	riñas	tú	reñiste
él	riña	él	riñó
nosotros	riñamos	nosotros	reñimos
vosotros	riñáis	vosotros	reñisteis
ellos	riñan	ellos	riñeron

PAST PARTICIPLE	IMPERATIVE
reñido	riñe
	reñid

GERUND
riñendo

Irregular Verbs

resolver (to solve)

	PRESENT		IMPERFECT
yo	**resuelvo**	yo	resolv**ía**
tú	**resuelves**	tú	resolv**ías**
él	**resuelve**	él	resolv**ía**
nosotros	resolv**emos**	nosotros	resolv**íamos**
vosotros	resolv**éis**	vosotros	resolv**íais**
ellos	**resuelven**	ellos	resolv**ían**

	FUTURE		CONDITIONAL
yo	resolver**é**	yo	resolver**ía**
tú	resolver**ás**	tú	resolver**ías**
él	resolver**á**	él	resolver**ía**
nosotros	resolver**emos**	nosotros	resolver**íamos**
vosotros	resolver**éis**	vosotros	resolver**íais**
ellos	resolver**án**	ellos	resolver**ían**

	PRESENT SUBJUNCTIVE		PRETERITE
yo	**resuelva**	yo	resolv**í**
tú	**resuelvas**	tú	resolv**iste**
él	**resuelva**	él	resolv**ió**
nosotros	resolv**amos**	nosotros	resolv**imos**
vosotros	resolv**áis**	vosotros	resolv**isteis**
ellos	**resuelvan**	ellos	resolv**ieron**

PAST PARTICIPLE	IMPERATIVE
resuelto	**resuelve**
	resolv**ed**

GERUND
resolv**iendo**

Irregular Verbs

reunir (to put together, to gather)

	PRESENT		IMPERFECT
yo	reúno	yo	reunía
tú	reúnes	tú	reunías
él	reúne	él	reunía
nosotros	reunimos	nosotros	reuníamos
vosotros	reunís	vosotros	reuníais
ellos	reúnen	ellos	reunían

	FUTURE		CONDITIONAL
yo	reuniré	yo	reuniría
tú	reunirás	tú	reunirías
él	reunirá	él	reuniría
nosotros	reuniremos	nosotros	reuniríamos
vosotros	reuniréis	vosotros	reuniríais
ellos	reunirán	ellos	reunirían

	PRESENT SUBJUNCTIVE		PRETERITE
yo	reúna	yo	reuní
tú	reúnas	tú	reuniste
él	reúna	él	reunió
nosotros	reunamos	nosotros	reunimos
vosotros	reunáis	vosotros	reunisteis
ellos	reúnan	ellos	reunieron

PAST PARTICIPLE	IMPERATIVE
reunido	reúne
	reunid

GERUND
reuniendo

Irregular Verbs

rogar (to beg)

	PRESENT		IMPERFECT
yo	ruego	yo	rogaba
tú	ruegas	tú	rogabas
él	ruega	él	rogaba
nosotros	rogamos	nosotros	rogábamos
vosotros	rogáis	vosotros	rogabais
ellos	ruegan	ellos	rogaban

	FUTURE		CONDITIONAL
yo	rogaré	yo	rogaría
tú	rogarás	tú	rogarías
él	rogará	él	rogaría
nosotros	rogaremos	nosotros	rogaríamos
vosotros	rogaréis	vosotros	rogaríais
ellos	rogarán	ellos	rogarían

	PRESENT SUBJUNCTIVE		PRETERITE
yo	ruegue	yo	rogué
tú	ruegues	tú	rogaste
él	ruegue	él	rogó
nosotros	roguemos	nosotros	rogamos
vosotros	roguéis	vosotros	rogasteis
ellos	rueguen	ellos	rogaron

PAST PARTICIPLE	IMPERATIVE
rogado	ruega
	rogad

GERUND
rogando

Irregular Verbs

romper (to break)

	PRESENT		IMPERFECT
yo	rompo	yo	rompía
tú	rompes	tú	rompías
él	rompe	él	rompía
nosotros	rompemos	nosotros	rompíamos
vosotros	rompéis	vosotros	rompíais
ellos	rompen	ellos	rompían

	FUTURE		CONDITIONAL
yo	romperé	yo	rompería
tú	romperás	tú	romperías
él	romperá	él	rompería
nosotros	romperemos	nosotros	romperíamos
vosotros	romperéis	vosotros	romperíais
ellos	romperán	ellos	romperían

	PRESENT SUBJUNCTIVE		PRETERITE
yo	rompa	yo	rompí
tú	rompas	tú	rompiste
él	rompa	él	rompió
nosotros	rompamos	nosotros	rompimos
vosotros	rompáis	vosotros	rompisteis
ellos	rompan	ellos	rompieron

PAST PARTICIPLE	IMPERATIVE
roto	rompe
	romped

GERUND
rompiendo

Irregular Verbs

saber (to know)

	PRESENT		IMPERFECT
yo	**sé**	yo	sab**ía**
tú	sab**es**	tú	sab**ías**
él	sab**e**	él	sab**ía**
nosotros	sab**emos**	nosotros	sab**íamos**
vosotros	sab**éis**	vosotros	sab**íais**
ellos	sab**en**	ellos	sab**ían**

	FUTURE		CONDITIONAL
yo	**sabré**	yo	**sabría**
tú	**sabrás**	tú	**sabrías**
él	**sabrá**	él	**sabría**
nosotros	**sabremos**	nosotros	**sabríamos**
vosotros	**sabréis**	vosotros	**sabríais**
ellos	**sabrán**	ellos	**sabrían**

	PRESENT SUBJUNCTIVE		PRETERITE
yo	**sepa**	yo	**supe**
tú	**sepas**	tú	**supiste**
él	**sepa**	él	**supo**
nosotros	**sepamos**	nosotros	**supimos**
vosotros	**sepáis**	vosotros	**supisteis**
ellos	**sepan**	ellos	**supieron**

PAST PARTICIPLE	IMPERATIVE
sab**ido**	sab**e**
	sab**ed**

GERUND
sab**iendo**

Irregular Verbs

sacar (to take out)

	PRESENT		IMPERFECT
yo	saco	yo	sacaba
tú	sacas	tú	sacabas
él	saca	él	sacaba
nosotros	sacamos	nosotros	sacábamos
vosotros	sacáis	vosotros	sacabais
ellos	sacan	ellos	sacaban

	FUTURE		CONDITIONAL
yo	sacaré	yo	sacaría
tú	sacarás	tú	sacarías
él	sacará	él	sacaría
nosotros	sacaremos	nosotros	sacaríamos
vosotros	sacaréis	vosotros	sacaríais
ellos	sacarán	ellos	sacarían

	PRESENT SUBJUNCTIVE		PRETERITE
yo	saque	yo	saqué
tú	saques	tú	sacaste
él	saque	él	sacó
nosotros	saquemos	nosotros	sacamos
vosotros	saquéis	vosotros	sacasteis
ellos	saquen	ellos	sacaron

PAST PARTICIPLE	IMPERATIVE
sacado	saca
	sacad

GERUND
sacando

Irregular Verbs

salir (to go out)

	PRESENT		IMPERFECT
yo	salgo	yo	salía
tú	sales	tú	salías
él	sale	él	salía
nosotros	salimos	nosotros	salíamos
vosotros	salís	vosotros	salíais
ellos	salen	ellos	salían

	FUTURE		CONDITIONAL
yo	saldré	yo	saldría
tú	saldrás	tú	saldrías
él	saldrá	él	saldría
nosotros	saldremos	nosotros	saldríamos
vosotros	saldréis	vosotros	saldríais
ellos	saldrán	ellos	saldrían

	PRESENT SUBJUNCTIVE		PRETERITE
yo	salga	yo	salí
tú	salgas	tú	saliste
él	salga	él	salió
nosotros	salgamos	nosotros	salimos
vosotros	salgáis	vosotros	salisteis
ellos	salgan	ellos	salieron

PAST PARTICIPLE	IMPERATIVE
salido	sal
	salid

GERUND
saliendo

Irregular Verbs

satisfacer (to satisfy)

	PRESENT		IMPERFECT
yo	satisfago	yo	satisfacía
tú	satisfaces	tú	satisfacías
él	satisface	él	satisfacía
nosotros	satisfacemos	nosotros	satisfacíamos
vosotros	satisfacéis	vosotros	satisfacíais
ellos	satisfacen	ellos	satisfacían

	FUTURE		CONDITIONAL
yo	satisfaré	yo	satisfaría
tú	satisfarás	tú	satisfarías
él	satisfará	él	satisfaría
nosotros	satisfaremos	nosotros	satisfaríamos
vosotros	satisfaréis	vosotros	satisfaríais
ellos	satisfarán	ellos	satisfarían

	PRESENT SUBJUNCTIVE		PRETERITE
yo	satisfaga	yo	satisfice
tú	satisfagas	tú	satisficiste
él	satisfaga	él	satisfizo
nosotros	satisfagamos	nosotros	satisficimos
vosotros	satisfagáis	vosotros	satisficisteis
ellos	satisfagan	ellos	satisficieron

PAST PARTICIPLE	IMPERATIVE
satisfecho	satisfaz/satisface
	satisfaced

GERUND
satisfaciendo

Irregular Verbs

seguir (to follow)

	PRESENT		IMPERFECT
yo	**sigo**	yo	seguí**a**
tú	**sigues**	tú	seguí**as**
él	**sigue**	él	seguí**a**
nosotros	segu**imos**	nosotros	seguí**amos**
vosotros	segu**ís**	vosotros	seguí**ais**
ellos	**siguen**	ellos	seguí**an**

	FUTURE		CONDITIONAL
yo	seguir**é**	yo	seguir**ía**
tú	seguir**ás**	tú	seguir**ías**
él	seguir**á**	él	seguir**ía**
nosotros	seguir**emos**	nosotros	seguir**íamos**
vosotros	seguir**éis**	vosotros	seguir**íais**
ellos	seguir**án**	ellos	seguir**ían**

	PRESENT SUBJUNCTIVE		PRETERITE
yo	**siga**	yo	segu**í**
tú	**sigas**	tú	segu**iste**
él	**siga**	él	**siguió**
nosotros	**sigamos**	nosotros	segu**imos**
vosotros	**sigáis**	vosotros	segu**isteis**
ellos	**sigan**	ellos	**siguieron**

PAST PARTICIPLE	IMPERATIVE
segu**ido**	**sigue**
	segu**id**

GERUND
siguiendo

Irregular Verbs

sentir (to feel)

	PRESENT		IMPERFECT
yo	siento	yo	sentía
tú	sientes	tú	sentías
él	siente	él	sentía
nosotros	sentimos	nosotros	sentíamos
vosotros	sentís	vosotros	sentíais
ellos	sienten	ellos	sentían

	FUTURE		CONDITIONAL
yo	sentiré	yo	sentiría
tú	sentirás	tú	sentirías
él	sentirá	él	sentiría
nosotros	sentiremos	nosotros	sentiríamos
vosotros	sentiréis	vosotros	sentiríais
ellos	sentirán	ellos	sentirían

	PRESENT SUBJUNCTIVE		PRETERITE
yo	sienta	yo	sentí
tú	sientas	tú	sentiste
él	sienta	él	sintió
nosotros	sintamos	nosotros	sentimos
vosotros	sintáis	vosotros	sentisteis
ellos	sientan	ellos	sintieron

PAST PARTICIPLE	IMPERATIVE
sentido	siente
	sentid

GERUND
sintiendo

Irregular Verbs

ser (to be)

	PRESENT		IMPERFECT
yo	**soy**	yo	**era**
tú	**eres**	tú	**eras**
él	**es**	él	**era**
nosotros	**somos**	nosotros	**éramos**
vosotros	**sois**	vosotros	**erais**
ellos	**son**	ellos	**eran**

	FUTURE		CONDITIONAL
yo	ser**é**	yo	ser**ía**
tú	ser**ás**	tú	ser**ías**
él	ser**á**	él	ser**ía**
nosotros	ser**emos**	nosotros	ser**íamos**
vosotros	ser**éis**	vosotros	ser**íais**
ellos	ser**án**	ellos	ser**ían**

	PRESENT SUBJUNCTIVE		PRETERITE
yo	**sea**	yo	**fui**
tú	**seas**	tú	**fuiste**
él	**sea**	él	**fue**
nosotros	**seamos**	nosotros	**fuimos**
vosotros	**seáis**	vosotros	**fuisteis**
ellos	**sean**	ellos	**fueron**

PAST PARTICIPLE	IMPERATIVE
sido	**sé**
	se**d**

GERUND
siendo

Irregular Verbs

tener (to have)

	PRESENT		IMPERFECT
yo	tengo	yo	tenía
tú	tienes	tú	tenías
él	tiene	él	tenía
nosotros	tenemos	nosotros	teníamos
vosotros	tenéis	vosotros	teníais
ellos	tienen	ellos	tenían

	FUTURE		CONDITIONAL
yo	tendré	yo	tendría
tú	tendrás	tú	tendrías
él	tendrá	él	tendría
nosotros	tendremos	nosotros	tendríamos
vosotros	tendréis	vosotros	tendríais
ellos	tendrán	ellos	tendrían

	PRESENT SUBJUNCTIVE		PRETERITE
yo	tenga	yo	tuve
tú	tengas	tú	tuviste
él	tenga	él	tuvo
nosotros	tengamos	nosotros	tuvimos
vosotros	tengáis	vosotros	tuvisteis
ellos	tengan	ellos	tuvieron

PAST PARTICIPLE	IMPERATIVE
tenido	ten
	tened

GERUND
teniendo

torcer (to twist)

	PRESENT		IMPERFECT
yo	tuerzo	yo	torcía
tú	tuerces	tú	torcías
él	tuerce	él	torcía
nosotros	torcemos	nosotros	torcíamos
vosotros	torcéis	vosotros	torcíais
ellos	tuercen	ellos	torcían

	FUTURE		CONDITIONAL
yo	torceré	yo	torcería
tú	torcerás	tú	torcerías
él	torcerá	él	torcería
nosotros	torceremos	nosotros	torceríamos
vosotros	torceréis	vosotros	torceríais
ellos	torcerán	ellos	torcerían

	PRESENT SUBJUNCTIVE		PRETERITE
yo	tuerza	yo	torcí
tú	tuerzas	tú	torciste
él	tuerza	él	torció
nosotros	torzamos	nosotros	torcimos
vosotros	torzáis	vosotros	torcisteis
ellos	tuerzan	ellos	torcieron

PAST PARTICIPLE	IMPERATIVE
torcido	tuerce
	torced

GERUND
torciendo

Irregular Verbs

traer (to bring)

	PRESENT		IMPERFECT
yo	**traigo**	yo	traía
tú	traes	tú	traías
él	trae	él	traía
nosotros	traemos	nosotros	traíamos
vosotros	traéis	vosotros	traíais
ellos	traen	ellos	traían

	FUTURE		CONDITIONAL
yo	traeré	yo	traería
tú	traerás	tú	traerías
él	traerá	él	traería
nosotros	traeremos	nosotros	traeríamos
vosotros	traeréis	vosotros	traeríais
ellos	traerán	ellos	traerían

	PRESENT SUBJUNCTIVE		PRETERITE
yo	**traiga**	yo	**traje**
tú	**traigas**	tú	**trajiste**
él	**traiga**	él	**trajo**
nosotros	**traigamos**	nosotros	**trajimos**
vosotros	**traigáis**	vosotros	**trajisteis**
ellos	**traigan**	ellos	**trajeron**

PAST PARTICIPLE	IMPERATIVE
traído	trae
	traed

GERUND
trayendo

Irregular Verbs

valer (to be worth)

	PRESENT		IMPERFECT
yo	**valgo**	yo	valía
tú	val**es**	tú	valías
él	val**e**	él	valía
nosotros	val**emos**	nosotros	valíamos
vosotros	val**éis**	vosotros	valíais
ellos	val**en**	ellos	valían

	FUTURE		CONDITIONAL
yo	**valdré**	yo	**valdría**
tú	**valdrás**	tú	**valdrías**
él	**valdrá**	él	**valdría**
nosotros	**valdremos**	nosotros	**valdríamos**
vosotros	**valdréis**	vosotros	**valdríais**
ellos	**valdrán**	ellos	**valdrían**

	PRESENT SUBJUNCTIVE		PRETERITE
yo	**valga**	yo	valí
tú	**valgas**	tú	val**iste**
él	**valga**	él	val**ió**
nosotros	**valgamos**	nosotros	val**imos**
vosotros	**valgáis**	vosotros	val**isteis**
ellos	**valgan**	ellos	val**ieron**

PAST PARTICIPLE	IMPERATIVE
val**ido**	val**e**
	val**ed**

GERUND
val**iendo**

Irregular Verbs

vencer (to win)

	PRESENT		IMPERFECT
yo	venzo	yo	vencía
tú	vences	tú	vencías
él	vence	él	vencía
nosotros	vencemos	nosotros	vencíamos
vosotros	vencéis	vosotros	vencíais
ellos	vencen	ellos	vencían

	FUTURE		CONDITIONAL
yo	venceré	yo	vencería
tú	vencerás	tú	vencerías
él	vencerá	él	vencería
nosotros	venceremos	nosotros	venceríamos
vosotros	venceréis	vosotros	venceríais
ellos	vencerán	ellos	vencerían

	PRESENT SUBJUNCTIVE		PRETERITE
yo	venza	yo	vencí
tú	venzas	tú	venciste
él	venza	él	venció
nosotros	venzamos	nosotros	vencimos
vosotros	venzáis	vosotros	vencisteis
ellos	venzan	ellos	vencieron

PAST PARTICIPLE	IMPERATIVE
vencido	vence
	venced

GERUND

venciendo

venir (to come)

	PRESENT		IMPERFECT
yo	**vengo**	yo	venía
tú	**vienes**	tú	venías
él	**viene**	él	venía
nosotros	ven**imos**	nosotros	veníamos
vosotros	ven**ís**	vosotros	veníais
ellos	**vienen**	ellos	venían

	FUTURE		CONDITIONAL
yo	**vendré**	yo	**vendría**
tú	**vendrás**	tú	**vendrías**
él	**vendrá**	él	**vendría**
nosotros	**vendremos**	nosotros	**vendríamos**
vosotros	**vendréis**	vosotros	**vendríais**
ellos	**vendrán**	ellos	**vendrían**

	PRESENT SUBJUNCTIVE		PRETERITE
yo	**venga**	yo	**vine**
tú	**vengas**	tú	**viniste**
él	**venga**	él	**vino**
nosotros	**vengamos**	nosotros	**vinimos**
vosotros	**vengáis**	vosotros	**vinisteis**
ellos	**vengan**	ellos	**vinieron**

PAST PARTICIPLE	IMPERATIVE
ven**ido**	**ven**
	veni**d**

GERUND
viniendo

Irregular Verbs

ver (to see)

	PRESENT		IMPERFECT
yo	veo	yo	veía
tú	ves	tú	veías
él	ve	él	veía
nosotros	vemos	nosotros	veíamos
vosotros	veis	vosotros	veíais
ellos	ven	ellos	veían

	FUTURE		CONDITIONAL
yo	veré	yo	vería
tú	verás	tú	verías
él	verá	él	vería
nosotros	veremos	nosotros	veríamos
vosotros	veréis	vosotros	veríais
ellos	verán	ellos	verían

	PRESENT SUBJUNCTIVE		PRETERITE
yo	vea	yo	vi
tú	veas	tú	viste
él	vea	él	vio
nosotros	veamos	nosotros	vimos
vosotros	veáis	vosotros	visteis
ellos	vean	ellos	vieron

PAST PARTICIPLE
visto

IMPERATIVE
ve
ved

GERUND
viendo

Irregular Verbs

volcar (to overturn)

	PRESENT		IMPERFECT
yo	**vuelco**	yo	volc**aba**
tú	**vuelcas**	tú	volc**abas**
él	**vuelca**	él	volc**aba**
nosotros	volc**amos**	nosotros	volc**ábamos**
vosotros	volc**áis**	vosotros	volc**abais**
ellos	**vuelcan**	ellos	volc**aban**

	FUTURE		CONDITIONAL
yo	volcar**é**	yo	volcar**ía**
tú	volcar**ás**	tú	volcar**ías**
él	volcar**á**	él	volcar**ía**
nosotros	volcar**emos**	nosotros	volcar**íamos**
vosotros	volcar**éis**	vosotros	volcar**íais**
ellos	volcar**án**	ellos	volcar**ían**

	PRESENT SUBJUNCTIVE		PRETERITE
yo	**vuelque**	yo	**volqué**
tú	**vuelques**	tú	volc**aste**
él	**vuelque**	él	volc**ó**
nosotros	**volquemos**	nosotros	volc**amos**
vosotros	**volquéis**	vosotros	volc**asteis**
ellos	**vuelquen**	ellos	volc**aron**

PAST PARTICIPLE	IMPERATIVE
volc**ado**	**vuelca**
	volca**d**

GERUND
volc**ando**

Irregular Verbs

volver (to return)

	PRESENT		IMPERFECT
yo	**vuelvo**	yo	volv**ía**
tú	**vuelves**	tú	volv**ías**
él	**vuelve**	él	volv**ía**
nosotros	volv**emos**	nosotros	volv**íamos**
vosotros	volv**éis**	vosotros	volv**íais**
ellos	**vuelven**	ellos	volv**ían**

	FUTURE		CONDITIONAL
yo	volver**é**	yo	volver**ía**
tú	volver**ás**	tú	volver**ías**
él	volver**á**	él	volver**ía**
nosotros	volver**emos**	nosotros	volver**íamos**
vosotros	volver**éis**	vosotros	volver**íais**
ellos	volver**án**	ellos	volver**ían**

	PRESENT SUBJUNCTIVE		PRETERITE
yo	**vuelva**	yo	volv**í**
tú	**vuelvas**	tú	volv**iste**
él	**vuelva**	él	volv**ió**
nosotros	volv**amos**	nosotros	volv**imos**
vosotros	volv**áis**	vosotros	volv**isteis**
ellos	**vuelvan**	ellos	volv**ieron**

PAST PARTICIPLE	IMPERATIVE
vuelto	**vuelve**
	volv**ed**

GERUND

volv**iendo**

Irregular Verbs

zurcir (to darn)

	PRESENT		IMPERFECT
yo	**zurzo**	yo	zurcía
tú	zurces	tú	zurcías
él	zurce	él	zurcía
nosotros	zurcimos	nosotros	zurcíamos
vosotros	zurcís	vosotros	zurcíais
ellos	zurcen	ellos	zurcían

	FUTURE		CONDITIONAL
yo	zurciré	yo	zurciría
tú	zurcirás	tú	zurcirías
él	zurcirá	él	zurciría
nosotros	zurciremos	nosotros	zurciríamos
vosotros	zurciréis	vosotros	zurciríais
ellos	zurcirán	ellos	zurcirían

	PRESENT SUBJUNCTIVE		PRETERITE
yo	**zurza**	yo	zurcí
tú	**zurzas**	tú	zurciste
él	**zurza**	él	zurció
nosotros	**zurzamos**	nosotros	zurcimos
vosotros	**zurzáis**	vosotros	zurcisteis
ellos	**zurzan**	ellos	zurcieron

PAST PARTICIPLE	IMPERATIVE
zurcido	zurce
	zurcid

GERUND
zurciendo

Verb Index

The following pages, 162 to 190, contain an index of all the Spanish verbs in this dictionary cross-referred to the appropriate conjugation model:

- Regular verbs belonging to the first, second and third conjugation are numbered 1, 2 and 3 respectively. For the regular conjugations, see pages 6 to 13.

- Irregular verbs are numerically cross-referred to the appropriate model as conjugated on pages 82 to 160. Thus, **alzar** is cross-referred to page 100, where **cruzar**, the model for this verb group, is conjugated.

- Verbs which are most commonly used in the reflexive form – e.g. **amodorrarse** – have been cross-referred to the appropriate non-reflexive model. For the full conjugation of a reflexive verb, see pages 28 to 31.

- Verbs printed in **bold** – e.g. **abrir** – are themselves models.

- Superscript numbers refer you to notes on page 191 which indicate how the verb differs from its model.

Verb Index

Verb Index

Verb Index

Verb Index

Verb Index

Verb Index

Verb Index

Verb Index

Verb Index

Verb Index

Verb Index

Verb Index

Verb Index

Verb Index

Verb Index

Verb Index

Verb Index

Verb Index

Verb Index

Verb Index

Verb Index

Verb Index

Verb Index

Verb Index

Verb Index

Verb Index

Verb Index

Verb Index

Verb Index

Verb Index

Notes

The notes below indicate special peculiarities of individual verbs.
When only some forms of a given tense are affected, all these are shown.
When all forms of the tense are affected, only the 1st and 2nd persons are shown, followed by *etc*.

1 Gerund 2 Past Participle 3 Present 4 Preterite 5 Present Subjunctive
6 Imperfect Subjunctive

1 **acaecer, acontecer, amanecer, anochecer, competer, deshelar, escampar, granizar, helar, nevar, nublar, relampaguear, tronar, verdear**: used almost exclusively in infinitive and 3rd person singular
2 **asir** 3 asgo 5 asga, asgar *etc*
3 **atañer, -tañer** 1 atañendo 4 atañó: see also 1 above
4 **balbucir** 3 balbuceo 5 balbucee, balbucees *etc*
5 **concernir** 3 concierne, conciernen 5 concierna, conciernan: only used in 3rd person
6 **degollar** 3 degüello, degüellas, degüella, degüellan 5 degüelle, degüelles, degüellen
7 **delinquir** 3 delinco 5 delinca, delincas *etc*
8 **desasir** 3 desasgo 5 desasga, desasgas *etc*
9 **discernir** 3 discierno, disciernes, discierne, disciernen 5 discierna, disciernas, disciernan
10 **enraizar** 3 enraízo, enraízas, enraíza, enraízan 5 enraíce, enraíces, enraícen
11 **pudrir** 2 podrido
12 **rehuir** 3 rehúyo, rehúyes, rehúye, rehúyen 5 rehúya, rehúyas, rehúyan
13 **roer** 4 royó, royeron 6 royera, royeras *etc*
14 **soler**: used only in present and imperfect indicative
15 **yacer** 3 yazgo *or* yazco *or* yago 5 yazga *etc or* yazca *etc or* yaga *etc*

Nouns

The Gender of Nouns

In Spanish, all nouns are either masculine or feminine, whether denoting people, animals or things. Gender is largely unpredictable and has to be learnt for each noun. However, the following guidelines will help you determine the gender for certain types of nouns:

Nouns denoting male people and animals are usually – but not always – masculine, e.g.

un hombre a man
un toro a bull
un enfermero a (*male*) nurse
un semental a stallion

Nouns denoting female people and animals are usually – but not always – feminine, e.g.

una niña a girl
una vaca a cow
una enfermera a nurse
una yegua a mare

Some nouns are masculine *or* feminine depending on the sex of the person to whom they refer, e.g.

un camarada a (*male*) comrade
una camarada a (*female*) comrade
un belga a Belgian (*man*)
una belga a Belgian (*woman*)
un marroquí a Moroccan (*man*)
una marroquí a Moroccan (*woman*)

Other nouns referring to either men *or* women have only one gender which applies to both, e.g.

una persona a person
una visita a visitor
una víctima a victim
una estrella a star

Often the ending of a noun indicates its gender. Shown opposite are some of the most important to guide you.

Nouns

Masculine endings

-o	un **clavo** a nail, **un plátano** a banana
	EXCEPTIONS: **mano** hand, **foto** photograph, **moto(cicleta)** motorbike
-l	un **tonel** a barrel, **un hotel** a hotel
	EXCEPTIONS: **cal** lime, **cárcel** prison, **catedral** cathedral, **col** cabbage, **miel** honey, **piel** skin, **sal** salt, **señal** sign
-r	un **tractor** a tractor, **el altar** the altar
	EXCEPTIONS: **coliflor** cauliflower, **flor** flower, **labor** task
-y	**el rey** the king, **un buey** an ox
	EXCEPTION: **ley** law

Feminine endings

-a	una **casa** a house, **la cara** the face
	EXCEPTIONS: **día** day, **mapa** map, **planeta** planet, **tranvía** tram, and most words ending in -ma (**tema** subject, **problema** problem, *etc*)
-ión	una **canción** a song, **una procesión** a procession
	EXCEPTIONS: most nouns not ending in -ción or -sión, e.g. **avión** aeroplane, **camión** lorry, **gorrión** sparrow
-dad, -tad, -tud	una **ciudad** a town, **la libertad** freedom
	una **multitud** a crowd
-ed	una **pared** a wall, **la sed** thirst
	EXCEPTION: **césped** lawn
-itis	una **faringitis** pharyngitis, **la celulitis** cellulitis
-iz	una **perdiz** a partridge, **una matriz** a matrix
	EXCEPTIONS: **lápiz** pencil, **maíz** corn, **tapiz** tapestry
-sis	una **tesis** a thesis, **una dosis** a dose
	EXCEPTIONS: **análisis** analysis, **énfasis** emphasis, **paréntesis** parenthesis
-umbre	la **podredumbre** rot, **la muchedumbre** crowd

Nouns

The Gender of Nouns *continued*

Some nouns change meaning according to gender. The most common are set out below:

	MASCULINE	FEMININE
capital	capital (*money*)	capital (*city*) → ❶
clave	harpsichord	clue
cólera	cholera	anger → ❷
cometa	comet	kite
corriente	current month	current
corte	cut	court (*royal*) → ❸
coma	coma	comma → ❹
cura	priest	cure → ❺
frente	front (*in war*)	forehead → ❻
guardia	policeman	guard, policewoman → ❼
guía	guide (*man*)	guide (*woman, book*) → ❽
moral	mulberry tree	morals
orden	order (*arrangement*)	order (*command*) → ❾
ordenanza	office boy	ordinance
papa	Pope	potato
parte	dispatch	part → ❿
pendiente	earring	slope
pez	fish	pitch
policía	policeman	police, policewoman
radio	radius, radium	radio

Examples

1. **Invirtieron mucho capital** — They invested a lot of capital
   La capital es muy fea — The capital city is very ugly

2. **Es difícil luchar contra el cólera** — Cholera is difficult to combat
   Montó en cólera — He got angry

3. **Me encanta tu corte de pelo** — I love your haircut
   Se trasladó la corte a Madrid — The court was moved to Madrid

4. **Entró en un coma profundo** — He went into a deep coma
   Aquí hace falta una coma — You need to put a comma here

5. **¿Quién es? – El cura** — Who is it? – The priest
   No tiene cura — It's hopeless

6. **Han mandado a su hijo al frente** — Her son has been sent to the front
   Tiene la frente muy ancha — She has a very broad forehead

7. **Vino un guardia de tráfico** — A traffic policeman came
   Están relevando la guardia ahora — They're changing the guard now

8. **Nuestro guía nos hizo reír a carcajadas** — Our guide had us falling about laughing
   Busco una guía turística — I'm looking for a guidebook

9. **Están en orden alfabético** — They're in alphabetical order
   No hemos recibido la orden de pago — We haven't had the payment order

10. **Le mandó un parte al general** — He sent a dispatch to the general
    En alguna parte debe estar — It must be somewhere or other

Nouns

Gender: the Formation of Feminines

As in English, male and female are sometimes differentiated by the use of two quite separate words, e.g.

> **mi marido** my husband
> **mi mujer** my wife
> **un toro** a bull
> **una vaca** a cow

There are, however, some words in Spanish which show this distinction by the form of their ending:

Nouns ending in **-o** change to **-a** to form the feminine → ❶

If the masculine singular form already ends in **-a**, no further **-a** is added to the feminine → ❷

If the last letter of the masculine singular form is a consonant, an **-a** is normally added in the feminine* → ❸

* If the last syllable has an accent, it disappears in the feminine (see page 296) → ❹

Feminine forms to note

MASCULINE	FEMININE	
el abad	la abadesa	abbot/abbess
un actor	una actriz	actor/actress
el alcalde	la alcaldesa	mayor/mayoress
el conde	la condesa	count/countess
el duque	la duquesa	duke/duchess
el emperador	la emperatriz	emperor/empress
un poeta	una poetisa	poet/poetess
el príncipe	la princesa	prince/princess
el rey	la reina	king/queen
un sacerdote	una sacerdotisa	priest/priestess
un tigre	una tigresa	tiger/tigress
el zar	la zarina	tzar/tzarina

Examples

1 **un amigo** a (*male*) friend
un empleado a (*male*) employee
un gato a cat

una amiga a (*female*) friend
una empleada a (*female*) employee
una gata a (*female*) cat

2 **un deportista** a sportsman
un colega a (*male*) colleague
un camarada a (*male*) comrade

una deportista a sportswoman
una colega a (*female*) colleague
una camarada a (*female*) comrade

3 **un español** a Spaniard,
a Spanish man
un vendedor a salesman
un jugador a (*male*) player

una española a Spanish woman

una vendedora a saleswoman
una jugadora a (*female*) player

4 **un lapón** a Laplander (*man*)
un león a lion
un neocelandés
a New Zealander (*man*)

una lapona a Laplander (*woman*)
una leona a lioness
una neocelandesa
a New Zealander (*woman*)

Nouns

The Formation of Plurals

Nouns ending in an unstressed vowel add **-s** to the singular form → **1**

Nouns ending in a consonant or a stressed vowel add **-es** to the singular form → **2**

   (i) BUT: **café** coffee shop (*plural:* **cafés**)
            mamá mummy (*plural:* **mamás**)
            papá daddy (*plural:* **papás**)
            pie foot (*plural:* **pies**)
            sofá sofa (*plural:* **sofás**)
            té tea (*plural:* **tes**)

and words of foreign origin ending in a consonant, e.g.:

            coñac brandy (*plural:* **coñacs**)
            ballet ballet (*plural:* **ballets**)

   (i) Note:

- nouns ending in **-n** or **-s** with an accent on the last syllable drop this accent in the plural (see page 296) → **3**
- nouns ending in **-n** with the stress on the last syllable but one in the singular add an accent to that syllable in the plural in order to show the correct position for stress (see page 296) → **4**
- nouns ending in **-z** change this to **c** in the plural → **5**

Nouns with an unstressed final syllable ending in **-s** do not change in the plural → **6**

Examples

1 **la casa** the house **las casas** the houses
   el libro the book **los libros** the books

2 **un rumor** a rumour **unos rumores** (some) rumours
   un jabalí a boar **unos jabalíes** (some) boars

3 **la canción** the song **las canciones** the songs
   el autobús the bus **los autobuses** the buses

4 **un examen** an exam **unos exámenes** (some) exams
   un crimen a crime **unos crímenes** (some) crimes

5 **la luz** the light **las luces** the lights

6 **un paraguas** an umbrella **unos paraguas** (some) umbrellas
   la dosis the dose **las dosis** the doses
   el lunes Monday **los lunes** Mondays

Articles

The Definite Article

	WITH MASC. NOUN	WITH FEM. NOUN	
SING.	**el**	**la**	the
PLUR.	**los**	**las**	the

The article used depends on both the gender of the noun and whether it is singular or plural → **❶**

ⓘ Note: use **el** not **la** immediately before a feminine singular noun starting with a stressed **a-** or **ha-** → **❷**

For uses of the definite article, see page 203.

a + **el** becomes **al** → **❸**

de + **el** becomes **del** → **❹**

Examples

❶ el tren the train   **la estación** the station
  el actor the actor   **la actriz** the actress
  los hoteles the hotels   **las escuelas** the schools
  los profesores the teachers   **las mujeres** the women

❷ el agua pura   the pure water
  BUT:
  la misma agua   the same water

  el hacha   the axe
  BUT:
  la mejor hacha   the best axe

❸ al cine   to the cinema
  al empleado   to the employee
  al hospital   to the hospital

❹ del departamento   from/of the department
  del autor   from/of the author
  del presidente   from/of the president

Articles

Uses of the Definite Article

While the Spanish definite article usually translates as 'the', it is often used where English has no article or uses another construction:

with abstract nouns, except when following certain prepositions → ❶

in generalizations, especially with plural or uncountable* nouns → ❷

with parts of the body → ❸
'Ownership' is often indicated by an indirect object pronoun or a reflexive pronoun → ❹

with titles/ranks/professions followed by a proper name → ❺
EXCEPTIONS: with **Don/Doña**, **San/Santo/Santa** → ❻

before nouns of official, academic and religious buildings, and names of meals and games → ❼

The definite article is *not* used with nouns in apposition unless those nouns are qualified → ❽

* An uncountable noun is one which cannot be used in the plural or with an indefinite article, e.g. **el acero** *steel*; **la leche** *milk*.

Examples

1 **El tiempo es oro** Time is money
   BUT:
   con pasión with passion
   sin esperanza without hope

2 **No me gusta el café** I don't like coffee
   Los niños necesitan ser queridos Children need to be loved
   Los precios suben Prices are rising

3 **Vuelva la cabeza hacia la izquierda** Turn your head to the left
   No puedo mover las piernas I can't move my legs

4 **La cabeza me da vueltas** My head is spinning
   Lávate las manos Wash your hands

5 **El rey Jorge III** King George III
   el capitán Menéndez Captain Menéndez
   el doctor Ochoa Doctor Ochoa
   el señor Ramírez Mr Ramírez

6 **Don Arturo Ruiz** Mr Arturo Ruiz
   Santa Teresa Saint Teresa

7 **en la cárcel** in prison
   en la universidad at university
   en la iglesia at church
   la cena dinner
   el tenis tennis
   el ajedrez chess

8 **Madrid, capital de España,** Madrid, the capital of Spain,
   es la ciudad que ... is the city which ...
   BUT:
   Maria Callas, la famosa Maria Callas, the famous opera
   cantante de ópera ... singer ...

Articles

The Indefinite Article

	WITH MASC. NOUN	WITH FEM. NOUN	
SING.	un	una	a
PLUR.	unos	unas	some

The indefinite article is used in Spanish largely as it is in English.

BUT:

There is no article when a person's profession is being stated → ❶

The article is used, however, when the profession is qualified by an adjective → ❷

The article is not used with the following words:

otro	another	→ ❸
cierto	certain	→ ❹
semejante	such (a)	→ ❺
tal	such (a)	→ ❻
cien	a hundred	→ ❼
mil	a thousand	→ ❽
sin	without	→ ❾
qué	what a	→ ❿

There is no article with a noun in apposition → ⓫. When an abstract noun is qualified by an adjective, the indefinite article is used, but is not translated in English → ⓬

Examples

1 **Es profesor**
He's a teacher
Mi madre es enfermera
My mother is a nurse

2 **Es un buen médico**
He's a good doctor
Se hizo una escritora célebre
She became a famous writer

3 **otro libro**
another book

4 **cierta calle**
a certain street

5 **semejante ruido**
such a noise

6 **tal mentira**
such a lie

7 **cien soldados**
a hundred soldiers

8 **mil años**
a thousand years

9 **sin casa**
without a house

10 **¡Qué sorpresa!**
What a surprise!

11 **Baroja, gran escritor de la Generación del 98**
Baroja, a great writer of the 'Generación del 98'

12 **con una gran sabiduría/un valor admirable**
with great wisdom/admirable courage
Dieron pruebas de una sangre fría increíble
They showed incredible coolness
una película de un mal gusto espantoso
a film in appallingly bad taste

Articles

The Article '*lo*'

This is never used with a noun. Instead, it is used in the following ways:

As an intensifier before an adjective or adverb in the construction

lo + adjective/adverb + **que** → ❶

ⓘ Note: The adjective agrees with the noun it refers to → ❷

With an adjective or participle to form an abstract noun → ❸

In the phrase **lo de** to refer to a subject of which speaker and listener are already aware. It can often be translated as *the business/affair of/about* ... → ❹

In set expressions, the commonest of which are:

a lo mejor	maybe, perhaps	→ ❺
a lo lejos	in the distance	→ ❻
a lo largo de	along, through	→ ❼
por lo menos	at least	→ ❽
por lo tanto	therefore, so	→ ❾
por lo visto	apparently	→ ❿

Examples

① **No sabíamos lo pequeña que era la casa**
We didn't know how small the house was

Sé lo mucho que te gusta la música
I know how much you like music

② **No te imaginas lo simpáticos que son**
You can't imagine how nice they are

Ya sabes lo buenas que son estas manzanas
You already know how good these apples are

③ **Lo bueno de eso es que ...**
The good thing about it is that ...

Sentimos mucho lo ocurrido
We are very sorry about what happened

④ **Lo de ayer es mejor que lo olvides**
It's best you forget what happened yesterday

Lo de tu hermano me preocupa mucho
That business with your brother worries me a lot

⑤ **A lo mejor ha salido**
Perhaps he's gone out

⑥ **A lo lejos se veían unas casas**
Some houses could be seen in the distance

⑦ **a lo largo de su vida**
throughout his life

a lo largo de la carretera
along the road

⑧ **Hubo por lo menos cincuenta heridos**
At least fifty people were injured

⑨ **No hemos recibido ninguna instrucción al respecto, y por lo tanto no podemos ...**
We have not received any instructions about it, therefore we cannot ...

⑩ **Por lo visto, no viene**
Apparently or It seems he's not coming

Adjectives

Adjectives

Most adjectives agree in number and gender with the noun or pronoun.

(i) Note that:

- if the adjective refers to two or more singular nouns of the same gender, a plural ending of that gender is required → **1**
- if the adjective refers to two or more singular nouns of different genders, a masculine plural ending is required → **2**

The formation of feminines

Adjectives ending in **-o** change to **-a** → **3**

Some groups of adjectives add **-a**:
- adjectives of nationality or geographical origin → **4**
- adjectives ending in **-or** (except irregular comparatives: see page 214), **-án**, **-ón**, **-ín** → **5**

(i) Note: When there is an accent on the last syllable, it disappears in the feminine (see page 296).

Other adjectives do not change → **6**

The formation of plurals

Adjectives ending in an unstressed vowel add **-s** → **7**

Adjectives ending in a stressed vowel or a consonant add **-es** → **8**

(i) Note:

- if there is an accent on the last syllable of a word ending in a consonant, it will disappear in the plural (see page 296) → **9**
- if the last letter is a **z** it will become a **c** in the plural → **10**

Examples

① **la lengua y la literatura españolas**
(the) Spanish language and literature

② **Nunca había visto árboles y flores tan raros**
I had never seen such strange trees and flowers

③ **mi hermano pequeño**
my little brother
mi hermana pequeña
my little sister

④ **un chico español**
a Spanish boy
una chica española
a Spanish girl
el equipo barcelonés
the team from Barcelona
la vida barcelonesa
the Barcelona way of life

⑤ **un niño encantador**
a charming little boy
una niña encantadora
a charming little girl
un hombre holgazán
an idle man
una mujer holgazana
an idle woman
un gesto burlón
a mocking gesture
una sonrisa burlona
a mocking smile
un chico cantarín
a boy who's fond of singing
una chica cantarina
a girl who's fond of singing

⑥ **un final feliz**
a happy ending
una infancia feliz
a happy childhood
mi amigo belga
my Belgian (*male*) friend
mi amiga belga
my Belgian (*female*) friend
el vestido verde
the green dress
la blusa verde
the green blouse

⑦ **el último tren**
the last train
los últimos trenes
the last trains
una casa vieja
an old house
unas casas viejas
(some) old houses

⑧ **un médico iraní**
an Iranian doctor
unos médicos iraníes
(some) Iranian doctors
un examen fácil
an easy exam
unos exámenes fáciles
(some) easy exams

⑨ **un río francés**
a French river
unos ríos franceses
(some) French rivers

⑩ **un día feliz**
a happy day
unos días felices
(some) happy days

Adjectives

Invariable Adjectives

Some adjectives and other parts of speech used adjectivally do not change in the feminine or plural.

The commonest of these are:
- nouns used to denote colour → ❶
- compound adjectives → ❷
- nouns used as adjectives → ❸

Shortening of adjectives

The following drop the final **-o** before a masculine singular noun:

bueno good → ❹
malo bad
alguno* some → ❺
ninguno* no
uno one → ❻
primero first → ❼
tercero third
postrero last → ❽

> * ⓘ Note: An accent is required to show the correct position for stress.

Grande _big, great_ is shortened to **gran** before a masculine _or_ feminine singular noun → ❾

Santo _Saint_ changes to **San** except with saints' names beginning with **Do-** _or_ **To-** → ❿

Ciento _a hundred_ is shortened to **cien** before a masculine _or_ feminine plural noun → ⓫

Cualquiera drops the final **-a** before a masculine _or_ feminine singular noun → ⓬

Examples

❶	**los vestidos naranja**	the orange dresses
❷	**las chaquetas azul marino**	the navy blue jackets
❸	**bebés probeta**	test-tube babies
	mujeres soldado	women soldiers
❹	**un buen libro**	a good book
❺	**algún libro**	some book
❻	**cuarenta y un años**	forty-one years
❼	**el primer hijo**	the first child
❽	**un postrer deseo**	a last wish
❾	**un gran actor**	a great actor
	una gran decepción	a great disappointment
❿	**San Antonio**	Saint Anthony
	Santo Tomás	Saint Thomas
⓫	**cien años**	a hundred years
	cien millones	a hundred million
⓬	**cualquier día**	any day
	a cualquier hora	any time

Adjectives

Comparatives and Superlatives

Comparatives

These are formed using the following constructions:

 más ... (que) more ... (than) → ❶
 menos ... (que) less ... (than) → ❷
 tanto ... como as ... as → ❸
 tan ... como as ... as → ❹
 tan ... que so ... that → ❺
 demasiado ... ⎫ too ... ⎫
 bastante ... **para** ... enough to → ❻
 suficiente ... ⎭ ... enough ⎭

'Than' followed by a clause is translated by **de lo que** → ❼

Superlatives

These are formed using the following constructions:

 el/la/los/las más ... (que) the most ... (that) → ❽
 el/la/los/las menos ... (que) the least ... (that) → ❾

After a superlative the preposition **de** is often translated as 'in' → ❿

The absolute superlative (*very, most, extremely + adjective*) is expressed in Spanish by **muy** + adjective, or by adding **-ísimo/a/os/as** to the adjective when it ends in a consonant, or to its stem (adjective minus final vowel) when it ends in a vowel → ⓫

ⓘ Note: It is sometimes necessary to change the spelling of the adjective when **-ísimo** is added, in order to maintain the same sound (see page 300) → ⓬

Examples

1   **una razón más seria**   a more serious reason
       Es más alto que mi hermano   He's taller than my brother

2   **una película menos conocida**   a less well-known film
       Luis es menos tímido que tú   Luis is less shy than you

3   **Pablo tenía tanto miedo como yo**   Pablo was as frightened as I was

4   **No es tan grande como creía**   It isn't as big as I thought

5   **El examen era tan difícil que**   The exam was so difficult that
       nadie aprobó   nobody passed

6   **Eres (lo) bastante grande para**   You're old enough to do it by
       hacerlo solo   yourself

7   **Está más cansada de lo que**   She is more tired than she seems
       parece

8   **el caballo más veloz**   the fastest horse
       la casa más pequeña   the smallest house
       los días más lluviosos   the wettest days
       las manzanas más maduras   the ripest apples

9   **el hombre menos simpático**   the least likeable man
       la niña menos habladora   the least talkative girl
       los cuadros menos bonitos   the least attractive paintings
       las camisas menos viejas   the least old shirts

10 **la estación más ruidosa**   the noisiest station in London
       de Londres

11 **Este libro es muy interesante**   This book is very interesting

12 **Tienen un coche rapidísimo**   They have an extremely fast car
       Era facilísimo de hacer   It was very easy to make
       Mi tío era muy rico   My uncle was very rich
       Se hizo riquísimo   He became extremely rich
       un león muy feroz   a very ferocious lion
       un tigre ferocísimo   an extremely ferocious tiger

Adjectives

Comparatives and Superlatives *continued*

Adjectives with irregular comparatives/superlatives

ADJECTIVE	COMPARATIVE	SUPERLATIVE
bueno	**mejor**	**el/la mejor**
good	better	the best
malo	**peor**	**el/la peor**
bad	worse	the worst
grande	**mayor** or **más grande**	**el/la mayor** or **el/la más grande**
big	bigger; older	the biggest; the oldest
pequeño	**menor** or **más pequeño**	**el/la menor** or **el/la más pequeño/a**
small	smaller; younger; lesser	the smallest; the youngest; the least

The irregular comparative and superlative forms of **grande** and
pequeño are used mainly to express:
- age, in which case they come after the noun → ❶
- abstract size and degrees of importance, in which case they
  come before the noun → ❷

The regular forms are used mainly to express physical size → ❸

Irregular comparatives and superlatives have one form for both
masculine and feminine, but always agree in number with the
noun → ❶

Examples

1 **mis hermanos mayores**   my older brothers
    la hija menor   the youngest daughter

2 **el menor ruido**   the slightest sound
    las mayores dificultades   the biggest difficulties

3 **Este plato es más grande que**   This plate is bigger than that
    aquel   one
    Mi casa es más pequeña que   My house is smaller than yours
    la tuya

Adjectives

Demonstrative Adjectives

	MASCULINE	FEMININE	
SING.	**este**	**esta**	this
	ese	**esa**	that
	aquel	**aquella**	
PLUR.	**estos**	**estas**	these
	esos	**esas**	those
	aquellos	**aquellas**	

Demonstrative adjectives normally precede the noun and always agree in number and gender with it → ❶

The forms **ese/a/os/as** are used:
- to indicate distance from the speaker but proximity to the person addressed → ❷
- to indicate a not too remote distance → ❸

The forms **aquel/la/los/las** are used to indicate distance, in space or time → ❹

Examples

1 **Este bolígrafo no escribe** This pen is not working
Esa revista es muy mala That is a very bad magazine
Aquella montaña es muy alta That mountain (over there) is very high

¿Conoces a esos señores? Do you know those gentlemen?
Siga Vd hasta aquellos edificios Carry on until you come to those buildings

¿Ves a aquellas personas? Can you see those people (over there)?

2 **Ese papel en donde escribes ...** That paper you are writing on ...

3 **No me gustan esos cuadros** I don't like those pictures

4 **Aquella calle parece muy ancha** That street (over there) looks very wide

Aquellos años sí que fueron felices Those were really happy years

Adjectives

Interrogative Adjectives

		MASCULINE	FEMININE	
SING.		¿qué?	¿qué?	what?, which?
		¿cuánto?	¿cuánta?	how much?
PLUR.		¿qué?	¿qué?	what?, which?
		¿cuántos?	¿cuántas?	how many?

Interrogative adjectives, when not invariable, agree in number and gender with the noun → ❶

The forms shown above are also used in indirect questions → ❷

Exclamatory Adjectives

		MASCULINE	FEMININE	
SING.		¡qué!	¡qué!	what (a)
		¡cuánto!	¡cuánta!	what (a lot of)
PLUR.		¡qué!	¡qué!	what
		¡cuántos!	¡cuántas!	what (a lot of)

Exclamatory adjectives, when not invariable, agree in number and gender with the noun → ❸

Examples

❶ ¿Qué libro te gustó más?   Which book did you like most?
¿Qué clase de hombre es?   What type of man is he?
¿Qué instrumentos toca Vd?   What instruments do you play?
¿Qué ofertas ha recibido Vd?   What offers have you received?
¿Cuánto dinero te queda?   How much money have you got
     left?

¿Cuánta lluvia ha caído?   How much rain have we had?
¿Cuántos vestidos quieres   How many dresses do you want
comprar?   to buy?
¿Cuántas personas van a venir?   How many people are coming?

❷ No sé a qué hora llegó   I don't know at what time she
     arrived

Dígame cuántas postales quiere   Tell me how many postcards
     you'd like

❸ ¡Qué pena!   What a pity!
¡Qué tiempo tan/más malo!   What lousy weather!
¡Cuánto tiempo!   What a long time!
¡Cuánta pobreza!   What poverty!
¡Cuántos autobuses!   What a lot of buses!
¡Cuántas mentiras!   What a lot of lies!

Adjectives

Possessive Adjectives

Weak forms

WITH SING. NOUN		WITH PLUR. NOUN		
MASC.	FEM.	MASC.	FEM.	
mi	mi	mis	mis	my
tu	tu	tus	tus	your
su	su	sus	sus	his; her; its; your (of **Vd**)
nuestro	nuestra	nuestros	nuestras	our
vuestro	vuestra	vuestros	vuestras	your
su	su	sus	sus	their; your (of **Vds**)

All possessive adjectives agree in number and (when applicable) in gender with the noun, not with the owner → ❶
The weak forms always precede the noun → ❶

Since the form **su(s)** can mean his, her, your (of **Vd**, **Vds**) or their, clarification is often needed. This is done by adding **de él**, **de ella**, **de Vds** etc to the noun, and usually (but not always) changing the possessive to a definite article → ❷

Examples

1 **Pilar no ha traído nuestros libros**   Pilar hasn't brought our books
     Antonio irá a vuestra casa   Antonio will go to your house
     ¿Han vendido su coche tus   Have your neighbours sold their
       vecinos?   car?
     Mi hermano y tu primo no se   My brother and your cousin
       llevan bien   don't get on

2 **su casa → la casa de él**   his house
     sus amigos → los amigos de Vd   your friends
     sus coches → los coches de ellos   their cars
     su abrigo → el abrigo de ella   her coat

Adjectives

Possessive Adjectives *continued*

Strong forms

WITH SING. NOUN		WITH PLUR. NOUN		
MASC.	FEM.	MASC.	FEM.	
mío	mía	míos	mías	my
tuyo	tuya	tuyos	tuyas	your
suyo	suya	suyos	suyas	his; her; its; your (of **Vd**)
nuestro	nuestra	nuestros	nuestras	our
vuestro	vuestra	vuestros	vuestras	your
suyo	suya	suyos	suyas	their; your (of **Vds**)

The strong forms agree in the same way as the weak forms (see page 220)

The strong forms follow the noun, or the verb **ser**, and are used:
- to translate the English (*of*) *mine*, (*of*) *yours*, etc → **❶**
- to address people → **❷**

Examples

❶ Es un capricho suyo   It's a whim of hers
    un amigo nuestro   a friend of ours
    una revista tuya   a magazine of yours
    Este abrigo es mío.   This coat is mine.

❷ Muy señor mío (in letters)   Dear Sir
    hija mía   my daughter
    ¡Dios mío!   My God!
    Amor mío   Darling/My love

Adjectives

Indefinite Adjectives

alguno/a/os/as	some
ambos/as	both
cada	each; every
cierto/a/os/as	certain; definite
cualquiera, plural cualesquiera	some; any
los/las demás	the others; the remainder
mismo/a/os/as	same; -self
mucho/a/os/as	many; much
ningún, ninguna, plural ningunos, ningunas	any; no
otro/a/os/as	other; another
poco/a/os/as	few; little
tal(es)	such (a)
tanto/a/os/as	so much; so many
todo/a/os/as	all; every
varios/as	several; various

Unless invariable, all indefinite adjectives agree in number and gender with the noun → **1**

alguno
Before a masculine singular noun, this drops the final **-o** and adds an accent to show the correct position for stress → **2** (see also page 296)

ambos
This is usually only used in written Spanish. The spoken language prefers the form **los dos/las dos** → **3**

cierto and mismo
These change their meaning according to their position in relation to the noun (see also Position of Adjectives, page 228) → **4**

cualquiera
This drops the final **-a** before a masculine *or* feminine noun → **5**

Examples

❶ el mismo día — the same day
las mismas películas — the same films
mucha/poca gente — many/few people
mucho/poco dinero — much/little money

❷ algún día — some day
alguna razón — some reason

❸ Me gustan los dos cuadros — I like both pictures
¿Conoces a las dos enfermeras? — Do you know both nurses?

❹ cierto tiempo — a certain time
BUT:
éxito cierto — sure success
el mismo color — the same colour
BUT:
en la iglesia misma — in the church itself

❺ cualquier casa — any house
BUT:
una revista cualquiera — any magazine

225

Adjectives

Indefinite Adjectives *continued*

ningún is only used in negative sentences or phrases → **①**

otro is never preceded by an indefinite article → **②**

tal is never followed by an indefinite article → **③**

todo can be followed by a definite article, a demonstrative or possessive adjective or a place name → **④**

> EXCEPTIONS:
> - when **todo** in the singular means any, every, or each → **⑤**
> - in some set expressions → **⑥**

Examples

① No es ninguna tonta
¿No tienes parientes?
— No, ninguno

She's no fool
Haven't you any relatives?
— No, none

② ¿Me das otra manzana?
Prefiero estos otros zapatos

Will you give me another apple?
I prefer these other shoes

③ Nunca dije tal cosa

I never said such a thing

④ Estudian durante toda la noche
Ha llovido toda esta semana
Pondré en orden todos mis libros
Lo sabe todo Madrid

They study all night
It has rained all this week
I'll sort out all my books
All Madrid knows it

⑤ Podrá entrar toda persona que
lo desee
BUT:
Vienen todos los días

Any person who wishes to enter
may do so

They come every day

⑥ de todos modos
a toda velocidad
por todas partes
por todos lados
a/en todas partes
a/en todos lados

anyway
at full/top speed

everywhere

227

Adjectives

Position of Adjectives

Spanish adjectives usually follow the noun → ❶, ❷

Note that when used figuratively or to express a quality already inherent in the noun, adjectives can precede the noun → ❸

As in English, demonstrative, possessive (weak forms), numerical, interrogative and exclamatory adjectives precede the noun → ❹

Indefinite adjectives, such as **ambos** *both* and **cada** *each*, also usually precede the noun → ❺

ⓘ Note: **alguno** *some/any* in negative expressions follows the noun → ❻

Some adjectives can precede or follow the noun, but their meaning varies according to their position:

	BEFORE NOUN	AFTER NOUN
antiguo	former	old, ancient → ❼
diferente	various	different → ❽
grande	great	big → ❾
medio	half	average → ❿
mismo	same	-self, very/precisely → ⓫
nuevo	new, another, fresh	brand new → ⓬
pobre	poor (wretched)	poor (not rich) → ⓭
puro	sheer, mere	pure (clear) → ⓮
varios	several	assorted, different → ⓯
viejo	old (long known, etc)	old (aged) → ⓰

Adjectives following the noun are linked by **y** → ⓱

Examples

① **la página siguiente**   the following page
　 la hora exacta   the right time

② **una corbata azul**   a blue tie
　 una palabra española   a Spanish word

③ **un dulce sueño**   a sweet dream
　 un terrible desastre   a terrible disaster
　　 (all disasters are terrible)

④ **este sombrero**   this hat
　 mi padre   my father
　 ¿qué hombre?   what man?

⑤ **cada día**   every day
　 otra vez   another time
　 poco dinero   little money

⑥ **sin duda alguna**   without any doubt

⑦ **un antiguo colega**   a former colleague
　 la historia antigua   ancient history

⑧ **diferentes capítulos**   various chapters
　 personas diferentes   different people

⑨ **un gran pintor**   a great painter
　 una casa grande   a big house

⑩ **medio melón**   half a melon
　 velocidad media   average speed

⑪ **la misma respuesta**   the same answer
　 yo mismo   myself
　 eso mismo   precisely that

⑫ **mi nuevo coche**   my new car
　 unos zapatos nuevos   (some) brand new shoes

⑬ **esa pobre mujer**   that poor woman
　 un país pobre   a poor country

⑭ **la pura verdad**   the plain truth
　 aire puro   fresh air

⑮ **varios caminos**   several ways/paths
　 artículos varios   assorted items

⑯ **un viejo amigo**   an old friend
　 esas toallas viejas   those old towels

⑰ **una acción cobarde y falsa**   a cowardly, deceitful act

Pronouns

Personal Pronouns

	SUBJECT PRONOUNS		
	SINGULAR	PLURAL	
1st person	**yo** I	**nosotros** we	(masc./masc. + fem.)
		nosotras we	(all fem.)
2nd person	**tú** you	**vosotros** you	(masc./masc. + fem.)
		vosotras you	(all fem.)
3rd person	**él** he; it	**ellos** they	(masc./masc. + fem.)
	ella she; it	**ellas** they	(all fem.)
	usted (Vd) you	**ustedes (Vds)** you	

Subject pronouns have a limited usage in Spanish. Normally they are only used with verbs:

- for emphasis → ❶
- for clarity → ❷

BUT: **Vd** and **Vds** should always be used for politeness, whether they are otherwise needed or not → ❸

For subject pronouns used after certain prepositions as well as in comparative constructions, see page 238.

It as subject of a verb and *they* referring to things are never translated into Spanish → ❹

tú/usted

As a general rule, you should use **tú** (or **vosotros**, if plural) when addressing a friend, a child, a relative, someone you know well, or when invited to do so. In all other cases, use **usted** (or **ustedes**).

nosotros/as; vosotros/as; él/ella; ellos/ellas

All these forms reflect the number and gender of the noun(s) they replace. **Nosotros**, **vosotros** and **ellos** also replace a combination of masculine and feminine nouns.

Examples

1 **Ellos sí que llegaron tarde**
   They really did arrive late

   Tú no tienes por qué venir
   There is no reason for you to come

   Ella jamás creería eso
   She would never believe that

   Vosotros saldréis primero y nosotros os seguiremos
   You leave first and we will follow you

2 **Yo estudio español pero él estudia francés**
   I study Spanish but he studies French

   Ella era muy deportista pero él prefería jugar a las cartas
   She was a sporty type but he preferred to play cards

3 **Pase Vd por aquí**
   Please come this way

   ¿Habían estado Vds antes en esta ciudad?
   Had you been to this town before?

4 **¿Qué es? — Es una sorpresa**
   What is it? — It's a surprise

   ¿Qué son? — Son abrelatas
   What are they? — They are tin-openers

Pronouns

Personal Pronouns *continued*

	DIRECT OBJECT PRONOUNS	
	SINGULAR	PLURAL
1st person	**me** me	**nos** us
2nd person	**te** you	**os** you
3rd person (*masc.*)	**lo** him; it; you (of **Vd**)	**los** them; you (of **Vds**)
(*fem.*)	**la** her; it; you (of **Vd**)	**las** them; you (of **Vds**)

lo sometimes functions as a 'neuter' pronoun, referring to an idea or information contained in a previous statement or question. It is often not translated → ❶

Position of direct object pronouns

In constructions other than the affirmative imperative, the infinitive or the gerund, the pronoun always comes before the verb → ❷

> In the affirmative imperative, the infinitive and the gerund, the pronoun follows the verb and is attached to it. An accent is needed in certain cases to show the correct position for stress (see also page 296) → ❸

Where an infinitive or gerund depends on a previous verb, the pronoun may be used either after the infinitive or gerund, or before the main verb → ❹

ⓘ Note: see how this applies to reflexive verbs → ❹

For further information, see Order of Object Pronouns, page 236.

Reflexive Pronouns

These are dealt with under reflexive verbs, page 24.

Examples

1 **¿Va a venir Merche? — No lo sé** Is Merche coming? — I don't know
Hay que regar las plantas The plants need watering
  — Yo lo haré   — I'll do it
Habían comido ya pero no They had already eaten, but they
  nos lo dijeron   didn't tell us
Yo conduzco de prisa pero él I drive fast but he drives slowly
  lo hace despacio

2 **Te quiero** I love you
¿Las ve Vd? Can you see them?
¿No me oyen Vds? Can't you hear me?
Tu hija no nos conoce Your daughter doesn't know us
No los toques Don't touch them

3 **Ayúdame** Help me
Acompáñenos Come with us
Quiero decirte algo I want to tell you something
Estaban persiguiéndonos They were coming after us

4 **Lo está comiendo** or She is eating it
Está comiéndolo
Nos vienen a ver or They are coming to see us
Vienen a vernos
No quería levantarse or He didn't want to get up
No se quería levantar
Estoy afeitándome or I'm shaving
Me estoy afeitando

233

Pronouns

Personal Pronouns *continued*

	INDIRECT OBJECT PRONOUNS	
	SINGULAR	PLURAL
1st person	**me**	**nos**
2nd person	**te**	**os**
3rd person	**le**	**les**

The pronouns shown in the above table replace the preposition **a** + noun → ❶

Position of indirect object pronouns

In constructions other than the affirmative imperative, the infinitive and the gerund, the pronoun comes before the verb → ❷

> In the affirmative imperative, the infinitive and the gerund, the pronoun follows the verb and is attached to it. An accent is needed in certain cases to show the correct position for stress (see also page 296) → ❸

Where an infinitive or gerund depends on a previous verb, the pronoun may be used either after the infinitive or gerund, or before the main verb → ❹

For further information, see Order of Object Pronouns, page 236.

Reflexive Pronouns

These are dealt with under reflexive verbs, page 24.

Examples

❶ Estoy escribiendo a Teresa I am writing to Teresa
Le estoy escribiendo I am writing to her
Da de comer al gato Give the cat some food
Dale de comer Give it some food

❷ Sofía os ha escrito Sofía has written to you
¿Os ha escrito Sofía? Has Sofía written to you?
Carlos no nos habla Carlos doesn't speak to us
¿Qué te pedían? What were they asking you for?
No les haga caso Vd Don't take any notice of them

❸ Respóndame Vd Answer me
Díganos Vd la respuesta Tell us the answer
No quería darte la noticia todavía I didn't want to tell you the news yet
Llegaron diciéndome que ... When they arrived, they told me that ...

❹ Estoy escribiéndole or I am writing to him/her
Le estoy escribiendo
Les voy a hablar or I'm going to talk to them
Voy a hablarles

Pronouns

Personal Pronouns *continued*

Order of object pronouns

When two object pronouns of different persons are combined, the order is: indirect before direct, i.e.

me		lo
te	before	la
nos		los → ❶
os		las

ⓘ Note: When two 3rd person object pronouns are combined, the first (i.e. the indirect object pronoun) becomes **se** → ❷

Points to note on object pronouns

As **le/les** can refer to either gender, and **se** to either gender, singular or plural, sometimes clarification is needed. This is done by adding **a él** *to him*, **a ella** *to her*, **a Vd** *to you* etc to the phrase, usually after the verb → ❸

When a noun object precedes the verb, the corresponding object pronoun must be used too → ❹

Indirect object pronouns are often used instead of possessive adjectives with parts of the body or clothing to indicate 'ownership', and also in certain common constructions involving reflexive verbs (see also The Indefinite Article, page 202) → ❺

In some areas of Spain, **la** is sometimes used instead of **le** when referring to a feminine person or animal. While **leísmo** (the use of **le** and **les** instead of **lo** and **los**) is acceptable in most of Spain, **laísmo** (the use of **la** instead of **le**) is frowned upon in most Spanish-speaking regions → ❻

Examples

1 **Paloma os lo mandará mañana**　　Paloma is sending it to you tomorrow

　¿Te los ha enseñado mi hermana?　　Has my sister shown them to you?

　No me lo digas　　Don't tell me (that)

　Todos estaban pidiéndotelo　　They were all asking you for it

　No quiere prestárnosla　　He won't lend it to us

2 **Se lo di ayer**　　I gave it to him/her/them yesterday

3 **Le escriben mucho a ella**　　They write to her often

　Se lo van a mandar pronto a ellos　　They will be sending it to them soon

4 **A tu hermano lo conozco bien**　　I know your brother well

　A Elena la vemos algunas veces　　We sometimes see Elena

5 **La chaqueta le estaba ancha**　　His jacket was too loose

　Me duele el tobillo　　My ankle is aching

　Se me ha perdido el bolígrafo　　I have lost my pen

6 **Le/Lo encontraron en el cine**　　They met him at the cinema

　Les/Los oímos llegar　　We heard them coming

　Le/La* escribimos una carta　　We wrote a letter to her

* restricted usage. See note at point 6 on page 236.

Pronouns

Personal Pronouns *continued*

Pronouns after prepositions

These are the same as the subject pronouns, except for the forms **mí** *me*, **ti** *you (singular)*, and the reflexive **sí** *himself, herself, themselves, yourselves* → ❶

Con *with* combines with **mí**, **ti** and **sí** to form

conmigo	with me → ❷
contigo	with you
consigo	with him(self)/her(self) *etc*

The following prepositions always take a subject pronoun:

entre	between, among → ❸
hasta	
incluso	even, including → ❹
salvo	
menos	except → ❺
según	according to → ❻

ⓘ Note: Subject pronouns are also used in comparative constructions → ❼

Mí, **ti**, **él**, **ella**, **sí** and so on are used for emphasis, especially where contrast is involved → ❽

Ello *it, that* is used after a preposition when referring to an idea already mentioned, but never to a concrete noun → ❾

A él, **de él** never contract → ❿

Examples

① **Pienso en ti**   I think about you
  ¿Son para mí?   Are they for me?
  Es para ella   It's for her
  Iban hacia ellos   They were going towards them
  Volveréis sin nosotros You'll come back without us
  Volaban sobre vosotros They were flying over you
  Hablaba para sí   He was talking to himself

② **Venid conmigo**   Come with me
  Lo trajeron consigo   They brought it/him with them
  BUT:
  ¿Hablaron con vosotros? Did they talk to you?

③ **entre tú y ella**   between you and her

④ **Hasta yo puedo hacerlo** Even I can do it

⑤ **todos menos yo**   everybody except me

⑥ **según tú**   according to you

⑦ **Es más joven que yo**   He is younger than me
                        (*or* than I am)

⑧ **¿A ti no te escriben?**   Don't they write to you?
  Me lo manda a mí, no a ti She is sending it to me, not to you

⑨ **Nunca pensaba en ello** He never thought about it
  Por todo ello me parece que ... For all those reasons it seems to
                      me that ...

⑩ **A él no lo conozco**   I don't know him
  No he sabido nada de él I haven't heard from him

Pronouns

Indefinite Pronouns

algo	something, anything → ❶
alguien	somebody, anybody → ❷
alguno/a/os/as	some, a few → ❸
cada uno/a	each (one) → ❹
	everybody
cualquiera	anybody; any → ❺
los/las demás	the others
	the rest → ❻
mucho/a/os/as	many; much → ❼
nada	nothing → ❽
nadie	nobody → ❾
ninguno/a	none, not any → ❿
poco/a/os/as	few; little → ⓫
tanto/a/os/as	so much; so many → ⓬
todo/a/os/as	all; everything → ⓭
uno ... (el) otro ⎤	(the) one ... the other
una ... (la) otra ⎦	
unos ... (los) otros ⎤	→ ⓮
unas ... (las) otras ⎦	some ... (the) others
varios/as	several → ⓯

algo, alguien, alguno

These can never be used after a negative. The appropriate negative pronouns are used instead: **nada**, **nadie**, **ninguno** (see also negatives, page 276) → ⓰

Examples

① **Tengo algo para ti**
   ¿Viste algo?

I have something for you
Did you see anything?

② **Alguien me lo ha dicho**
   ¿Has visto a alguien?

Somebody told me
Have you seen anybody?

③ **Algunos de los niños ya sabían leer**

Some of the children could read already

④ **Le dio una manzana a cada uno**
   ¡Cada uno a su casa!

She gave each of them an apple
Everybody go home!

⑤ **Cualquiera puede hacerlo**
   Cualquiera de las explicaciones vale

Anybody can do it
Any of the explanations is a valid one

⑥ **Yo me fui, los demás se quedaron**

I went, the others stayed

⑦ **Muchas de las casas no tenían jardín**

Many of the houses didn't have a garden

⑧ **¿Qué tienes en la mano?**
   — Nada

What have you got in your hand?
— Nothing

⑨ **¿A quién ves? — A nadie**

Who can you see? — Nobody

⑩ **¿Cuántas tienes? — Ninguna**

How many have you got? — None

⑪ **Había muchos cuadros,**
   pero vi pocos que me gustaran

There were many pictures,
but I saw few that I liked

⑫ **¿Se oía mucho ruido? — No tanto**

Was there much noise? — Not all that much

⑬ **Lo ha estropeado todo**
   Todo va bien

He has spoiled everything
Everything is going well

⑭ **Unos cuestan 30 euros,**
   los otros 40 euros

Some cost 30 euros, the others 40 euros

⑮ **Varios de ellos me gustaron mucho**

I liked several of them very much

⑯ **Veo a alguien**
   No veo a nadie
   Tengo algo que hacer
   No tengo nada que hacer

I can see somebody
I can't see anybody
I have something to do
I don't have anything to do

Pronouns

Relative Pronouns

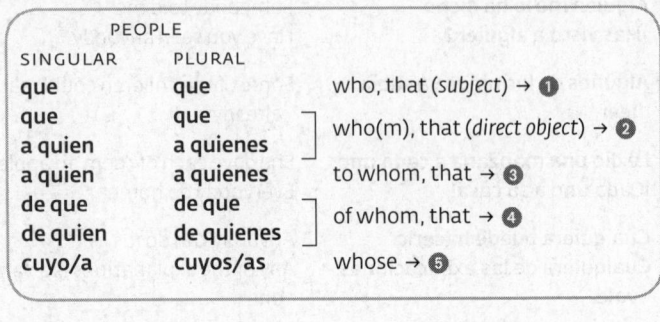

	PEOPLE	
SINGULAR	PLURAL	
que	que	who, that (*subject*) → ❶
que	que	who(m), that (*direct object*) → ❷
a quien	a quienes	
a quien	a quienes	to whom, that → ❸
de que	de que	of whom, that → ❹
de quien	de quienes	
cuyo/a	cuyos/as	whose → ❺

THINGS	
SINGULAR AND PLURAL	
que	which, that (*subject*) → ❻
que	which, that (*direct object*) → ❼
a que	to which, that → ❽
de que	of which, that → ❾
cuyo	whose → ❿

cuyo, which is in fact a relative adjective, agrees with the noun it accompanies → ❺/❿

You cannot omit the relative pronoun in Spanish as you can in English → ❷/❼

Examples

1 Mi hermano, que tiene veinte años, es el más joven

My brother, who is twenty, is the youngest

2 Los amigos que más quiero son ...
Pilar, a quien Daniel admira tanto, es ...

The friends (that) I like best are ...
Pilar, whom Daniel admires so much, is ...

3 Mis abogados, a quienes he escrito hace poco, están ...

My lawyers, to whom I wrote recently, are ...

4 La chica de que te hablé llega mañana
los niños de quienes se ocupa Vd

The girl (that) I told you about is coming tomorrow
the children (that) you look after

5 Vendrá la mujer cuyo hijo está enfermo

The woman whose son is ill will be coming

6 Hay una escalera que lleva a la buhardilla

There's a staircase which leads to the loft

7 La casa que hemos comprado tiene ...
Este es el regalo que me ha mandado mi amiga

The house (which) we've bought has ...
This is the present (that) my friend has sent to me

8 la tienda a que siempre va

the shop (which) she always goes to

9 las injusticias de que se quejan

the injustices (that) they're complaining about

10 la ventana cuyas cortinas están corridas

the window whose curtains are drawn

Pronouns

Relative Pronouns *continued*

el cual, el que

These are used when the relative is separated from the word it refers to, or when it would otherwise be unclear which word it refers to. The pronouns always agree in number and gender with the noun → **1**

> **El cual** may also be used when the verb in the relative clause is separated from the relative pronoun → **2**

lo que, lo cual

The neuter form **lo** is normally used when referring to an idea, statement or abstract noun. In certain expressions, the form **lo cual** may also be used as the subject of the relative clause → **3**

Relative pronouns after prepositions

Que or **el/la que** etc, when referring to things, and **quien(es)** and **el/la que** etc, when referring to people, are generally used after the prepositions:

a	to	→ **4**
con	with	→ **5**
de	from, about, of	→ **6**
en	in, on, into	→ **7**

It should be noted that **en que** can sometimes be translated by:
- *where*. In this case it can also be replaced by **en donde** or **donde** → **8**
- *when*. Sometimes here it can be replaced by **cuando** → **9**

El que or **el cual** are used after other prepositions, and they always agree → **10**

Examples

1 **El padre de Elena, el cual tiene mucho dinero, es ...**
Elena's father, who has a lot of money, is ...
(el cual is used here since que or quien might equally refer to Elena)

Su hermana, a la cual/la que hacía mucho que no veía, estaba también allí
His sister, whom I hadn't seen for a long time, was also there

2 **Vieron a su tío, el cual, después de levantarse, salió**
They saw their uncle, who, after having got up, went out

3 **No sabe lo que hace**
He doesn't know what he is doing

Lo que dijiste fue una tontería
What you said was foolish

Todo estaba en silencio, lo que (or lo cual) me pareció muy raro
All was silent, which I thought most odd

4 **las tiendas a (las) que íbamos**
the shops we used to go to

5 **la chica con quien (or la que) sale**
the girl he's going out with

6 **el libro de(l) que te hablé**
the book I told you about

7 **el lío en (el) que te has metido**
the trouble you've got yourself into

8 **el sitio en que (en donde/donde) se escondía**
the place where he/she was hiding

9 **el año en que naciste**
the year (when) you were born

10 **el puente debajo del que/del cual pasa el río**
the bridge under which the river flows

las obras por las cuales/ las que es famosa
the plays for which she is famous

245

Pronouns

Relative Pronouns *continued*

el que, **la que**; **los que**, **las que**
These mean *the one(s) who/which, those who* → ①

ⓘ Note: **quien(es)** can replace **el que** *etc* when used in a general
   sense → ②

todos los que, **todas las que**
These mean *all who, all those/the ones which* → ③

todo lo que
This translates *all that, everything that* → ④

el de, **la de**; **los de**, **las de**
These can mean:
  • *the one(s) of, that/those of* → ⑤
  • *the one(s) with* → ⑥

Examples

1 **Esa película es la que quiero ver**
That film is the one I want to see
¿Te acuerdas de ese amigo?
Do you remember that friend?
El que te presenté ayer
The one I introduced you to yesterday

Los que quieran entrar tendrán que pagar
Those who want to go in will have to pay

2 **Quien (*or* El que) llegue antes ganará el premio**
He who arrives first will win the prize

3 **Todos los que salían iban de negro**
All those who were coming out were dressed in black
¿Qué autobuses puedo tomar?
Which buses can I take?
– Todos los que pasen por aquí
– Any (All those) that come this way

4 **Quiero saber todo lo que ha pasado**
I want to know everything that has happened

5 **Trae la foto de tu novio y la de tu hermano**
Bring the photo of your boyfriend and the one of your brother
Viajamos en mi coche y en el de Alicia
We travelled in my car and Alicia's
Te doy estos libros y también los de mi hermana
I'll give you these books and my sister's too

6 **Tu amigo, el de las gafas, me lo contó**
Your friend, the one with glasses, told me

Pronouns

Interrogative Pronouns

> **¿qué?** what?; which?
> **¿cuál(es)?** which?; what?
> **¿quién(es)?** who?

qué

It translates *what* → ❶

ⓘ Note: **por** + **qué** is normally translated by *why* → ❷

cuál

It normally implies a choice, and translates *which* → ❸

ⓘ However, **cúal(es)** is also used in *what is/are* questions that require specific information rather than a definition as the answer → ❹

ⓘ Note: Whilst the pronoun **qué** can also work as an adjective, **cuál** only works as a pronoun → ❺

quién

SUBJECT *or* AFTER PREPOSITION	**quién(es)**	who → ❻
OBJECT	**a quién(es)**	whom → ❼
	de quién(es)	whose → ❽

All the forms shown above are also used in indirect questions → ❾

Examples

❶ **¿Qué están haciendo?**   What are they doing?
  ¿Qué dices?   What are you saying?
  ¿Qué es un tractor, papá?   What's a tractor, Daddy?
  ¿Qué son las alcaparras?   What are capers?
  ¿Para qué lo quieres?   What do you want it for?

❷ **¿Por qué no llegaron Vds antes?**   Why didn't you arrive earlier?

❸ **¿Cuál de estos vestidos te gusta más?**   Which of these dresses do you like best?
  ¿Cuáles viste?   Which ones did you see?

❹ **¿Cuál es la capital de España?**   What is the capital of Spain?
  ¿Cuál es tu consejo?   What is your advice?
  ¿Cuál es su fecha de nacimiento?   What is your date of birth?

❺ **¿Qué libro es más interesante?**   Which book is more interesting?
  ¿Cuál (de estos libros) es más interesante?   Which (of these books) is more interesting?

❻ **¿Quién ganó la carrera?**   Who won the race?
  ¿Con quiénes los viste?   Who did you see them with?

❼ **¿A quiénes ayudaste?**   Who(m) did you help?
  ¿A quién se lo diste?   Who did you give it to?

❽ **¿De quién es este libro?**   Whose is this book?

❾ **Le pregunté para qué lo quería**   I asked him/her what he/she wanted it for
  No me dijeron cuáles preferían   They didn't tell me which ones they preferred
  No sabía a quién acudir   I didn't know who to turn to

Pronouns

Possessive Pronouns

These are the same as the strong forms of the possessive adjectives, but they are always accompanied by the definite article.

Singular:

MASCULINE	FEMININE	
el mío	la mía	mine
el tuyo	la tuya	yours (of **tú**)
el suyo	la suya	his; hers; its; yours (of **Vd**)
el nuestro	la nuestra	ours
el vuestro	la vuestra	yours (of **vosotros**)
el suyo	la suya	theirs; yours (of **Vds**)

Plural:

MASCULINE	FEMININE	
los míos	las mías	mine
los tuyos	las tuyas	yours (of **tú**)
los suyos	las suyas	his; hers; its; yours (of **Vd**)
los nuestros	las nuestras	ours
los vuestros	las vuestras	yours (of **vosotros**)
los suyos	las suyas	theirs; yours (of **Vds**)

The pronoun agrees in number and gender with the noun it replaces, not with the owner, and can also be translated as 'my one(s)', 'your one(s)' etc → **1**

Alternative translations are 'my own', 'your own' (one(s)) etc → **2**

After the prepositions **a** and **de** the article **el** is contracted in the normal way (see page 200):

   a + el mío → al mío → **3**
   de + el mío → del mío → **4**

Examples

1 **Pregunta a Cristina si este bolígrafo es el suyo**

Ask Cristina if this pen is hers *or* her one

¿Qué equipo ha ganado, el suyo o el nuestro?

Which team won – theirs or ours?

Mi perro es más joven que el tuyo

My dog is younger than yours

Daniel pensó que esos libros eran los suyos

Daniel thought those books were his

Si no tienes lápices de color, te prestaré los míos

If you don't have any crayons, I'll lend you mine

Las habitaciones son menos amplias que las vuestras

The rooms are smaller than yours

2 **¿Es su familia tan grande como la tuya?**

Is his/her/their family as big as your own one?

Sus precios son más bajos que los nuestros

Their prices are lower than our own ones

3 **¿Por qué prefieres este sombrero al mío?**

Why do you prefer this hat to mine?

Su coche se parece al vuestro

His/Her/Their car looks like yours *or* your one

4 **Mi libro está encima del tuyo**

My book is on top of yours *or* your one

Su padre vive cerca del nuestro

His/Her/Their father lives near ours

Pronouns

Demonstrative Pronouns

	MASCULINE	FEMININE	NEUTER	
SING.	este	esta	esto	this
	ese	esa	eso	that
	aquel	aquella	aquello	
PLUR.	estos	estas		these
	esos	esas		those
	aquellos	aquellas		

The pronoun agrees in number and gender with the noun it replaces → **❶**

The difference in meaning between the forms **ese** and **aquel** is the same as between the corresponding adjectives (see page 216).

The masculine and feminine pronouns were always written with an accent in the past (**éste**, **ésta**, **éstos**, **éstas**; **ése**, **ésa**, **ésos**, **ésas**; **aquél**, **aquélla**, **aquéllos**, **aquéllas**) to distinguish them from demonstrative adjectives. Nowadays the accents are only considered essential where ambiguity is otherwise possible. The neuter forms are never written with an accent.

The neuter forms always refer to an idea or a statement or to an object when we want to identify it, etc, but never to specified nouns → **❷**

An additional meaning of **aquel** is *the former*, and of **este** *the latter* → **❸**

Examples

❶ **¿Qué abrigo te gusta más?**
   — **Este de aquí**

**Aquella casa era más grande
   que esta**

estos libros y aquellos

Quiero estas sandalias y esas

Which coat do you like best?
   — This one here

That house was bigger than
   this one

these books and those (over
   there)

I'd like these sandals and those
   ones

❷ **No puedo creer que esto me
   esté pasando a mí**

**Eso de madrugar es algo que
   no le gusta**

Aquello sí que me gustó

Esto es una bicicleta

I can't believe this is really
   happening to me

(This business of) getting up
   early is something she doesn't
   like

I really did like that

This is a bicycle

❸ **Hablaban Jaime y Andrés,
   este a voces y aquel casi
   en un susurro**

Jaime and Andrés were talking,
   the latter in a loud voice and
   the former almost in a whisper

253

Adverbs

Adverbs

Formation

Most adverbs are formed by adding **-mente** to the feminine form of the adjective. Accents on the adjective are not affected since the suffix **-mente** is stressed independently → **1**

> ⓘ Note: **-mente** is omitted:
> - in the first of two or more of these adverbs when joined by a conjunction → **2**
> - **recientemente** *recently* is replaced by **recién** immediately before a past participle → **3**

The following adverbs are formed in an irregular way:

bueno → **bien**	
good	well
malo → **mal**	
bad	badly

Adjectives used as adverbs

Certain adjectives are used adverbially. These include:
alto, **bajo**, **barato**, **caro**, **claro**, **derecho**, **fuerte** and **rápido** → **4**

> ⓘ Note: Other adjectives used where in English we would use an adverb agree with the subject, and can normally be replaced by an adverb ending in **-mente** or an adverbial phrase → **5**

Position of adverbs

When the adverb accompanies a verb, it may either immediately follow it or precede it for emphasis → **6**

> ⓘ Note: The adverb can never be placed between **haber** and the past participle in compound tenses → **7**

When the adverb accompanies an adjective or another adverb, it generally precedes the adjective or adverb → **8**

Examples

❶ FEM. ADJECTIVE   **ADVERB**

lenta slow	**lentamente** slowly
franca frank	**francamente** frankly
feliz happy	**felizmente** happily
fácil easy	**fácilmente** easily

❷ Lo hicieron lenta pero eficazmente   They did it slowly but efficiently

❸ El pan estaba recién hecho   The bread had just been baked

❹

hablar alto/bajo	to speak loudly/softly
cortar derecho	to cut (in a) straight (line)
costar barato/caro	to be cheap/expensive
Habla muy fuerte	He talks very loudly
ver claro	to see clearly
correr rápido	to run fast

❺ Esperaban impacientes (or **impacientemente/ con impaciencia**)   They were waiting impatiently

Vivieron muy felices (or **muy felizmente**)   They lived very happily

❻

No conocemos aún al nuevo médico	We still haven't met the new doctor
Aún estoy esperando	I'm still waiting
Han hablado muy bien	They spoke very well
Siempre le regalaban flores	They always gave her flowers

❼

Lo he hecho ya	I've already done it
No ha estado nunca en Italia	She's never been to Italy

❽

un sombrero muy bonito	a very nice hat
hablar demasiado alto	to talk too loud
mañana temprano	early tomorrow
hoy mismo	today

Adverbs

Comparatives and Superlatives

Comparatives

These are formed using the following constructions:

>**más ... (que)** more ... (than) → **❶**
>**menos ... (que)** less ... (than) → **❷**
>**tanto como** as much as → **❸**
>**tan ... como** as ... as → **❹**
>**tan ... que** so ... that → **❺**
>**demasiado ... para** too ... to → **❻**
>**(lo) bastante ...**
>**(lo) suficientemente ...** ⎤ **para** enough to → **❼**
>**cada vez más/menos** more and more/less and less → **❽**

ⓘ To translate *more than/fewer than* with a number, use **más de/menos de** (e.g. **más de 10** more than 10; **menos de 100** fewer than 100).

Superlatives

These are formed by placing **más/menos** *the most/the least* before the adverb → **❾**

lo is added before a superlative which is qualified → **❿**

The absolute superlative (*very, most, extremely* + adverb) is formed by placing **muy** before the adverb. The form **-ísimo** (see also page 296) is also occasionally found → **⓫**

Adverbs with irregular comparatives/superlatives

ADVERB	COMPARATIVE	SUPERLATIVE
bien well	**mejor*** better	**(lo) mejor** (the) best
mal badly	**peor** worse	**(lo) peor** (the) worst
mucho a lot	**más** more	**(lo) más** (the) most
poco little	**menos** less	**(lo) menos** (the) least

* **más bien** also exists, meaning *rather* → **⓬**

Examples

1 más deprisa — more quickly
más abiertamente — more openly
Mi hermana canta más fuerte que yo — My sister sings louder than me

2 menos fácilmente — less easily
menos a menudo — less often
Nos vemos menos frecuentemente que antes — We see each other less often than before

3 **Daniel no lee tanto como Andrés** — Daniel doesn't read as much as Andrés

4 **Hágalo tan rápido como le sea posible** — Do it as quickly as you can
Ganan tan poco como nosotros — They earn as little as we do

5 **Llegaron tan pronto que tuvieron que esperarnos** — They arrived so early that they had to wait for us

6 **Es demasiado tarde para ir al cine** — It's too late to go to the cinema

7 **Corrió lo suficientemente rápido para batir el récord** — She ran fast enough to break the record

8 **Me gusta el campo cada vez más** — I like the countryside more and more

9 **María es la que corre más rápido** — María is the one who runs fastest
El que llegó menos tarde fue Miguel — Miguel was the one who arrived the least late

10 **Lo hice lo más de prisa que pude** — I did it as quickly as I could

11 muy lentamente — very slowly
tempranísimo — extremely early
muchísimo — very much

12 **Era un hombre más bien bajito** — He was a rather short man
Estaba más bien inquieta que impaciente — I was restless rather than impatient

257

Adverbs

Common Adverbs and their Usage

Some common adverbs:

bastante	enough; quite → ❶
bien	well → ❷
cómo	how → ❸
cuánto	how much → ❹
demasiado	too much; too → ❺
más	more → ❻
menos	less → ❼
mucho	a lot; much → ❽
poco	little, not much; not very → ❾
siempre	always → ❿
también	also, too → ⓫
tan	as → ⓬
tanto	as much → ⓭
todavía/aún	still; yet; even → ⓮
ya	already → ⓯

bastante, **cuánto**, **demasiado**, **mucho**, **poco** and **tanto** are also used as adjectives that agree with the noun they qualify (see indefinite adjectives, page 224, and interrogative adjectives, page 218)

Examples

① **Es bastante tarde** — It's quite late

② **¡Bien hecho!** — Well done!

③ **¡Cómo me ha gustado!** — How I liked it!

④ **¿Cuánto cuesta este libro?** — How much is this book?

⑤ **He comido demasiado** — I've eaten too much
Es demasiado caro — It's too expensive

⑥ **Mi hermano trabaja más ahora** — My brother works more now
Es más tímida que Sofía — She is shyer than Sofía

⑦ **Se debe beber menos** — We should drink less
Estoy menos sorprendida que tú — I'm less surprised than you are

⑧ **¿Lees mucho?** — Do you read a lot?
¿Está mucho más lejos? — Is it much further?

⑨ **Comen poco** — They don't eat (very) much
Sofía es poco decidida — Sofía is not very decisive

⑩ **Siempre dicen lo mismo** — They always say the same (thing)

⑪ **A mí también me gusta** — I like it too

⑫ **Ana es tan alta como yo** — Ana is as tall as I am

⑬ **Nos aburrimos tanto como vosotros** — We got as bored as you did

⑭ **Todavía/Aún tengo dos** — I've still got two
Todavía/Aún no han llegado — They haven't arrived yet
Mejor aún/todavía — Even better

⑮ **Ya lo he hecho** — I've already done it

Prepositions

On the following pages you will find some of the most frequent uses of prepositions in Spanish. Particular attention is paid to cases where usage differs markedly from English. It is often difficult to give an English equivalent for Spanish prepositions, since usage *does* vary so much between the two languages. In the list below, the broad meaning of the preposition is given on the left, with examples of usage following. Prepositions are dealt with in alphabetical order, except **a**, **de**, **en** and **por** which are shown first.

a

at	**echar algo a algn**	to throw sth at sb
	a 50 euros el kilo	(at) 50 euros a kilo
	a 100 km por hora	at 100 km per hour
	sentarse a la mesa	to sit down at the table
in	**al sol**	in the sun
	a la sombra	in the shade
onto	**cayeron al suelo**	they fell onto the floor
	pegar una foto a la pared	to stick a photo onto the wall
to	**ir al cine**	to go to the cinema
	dar algo a algn	to give sth to sb
	venir a hacer	to come to do
from	**quitarle algo a algn**	to take sth from sb
	robarle algo a algn	to steal sth from sb
	arrebatarle algo a algn	to snatch sth from sb
	comprarle algo a algn	to buy sth from/for sb*
	esconderle algo a algn	to hide sth from sb
means	**a mano**	by hand
	a caballo	on horseback
	(*but note other forms of transport used with* **en** *and* **por**)	
	a pie	on foot

* The translation here obviously depends on the context.

Prepositions

manner	**a la inglesa** in the English manner
	a pasos lentos with slow steps
	poco a poco little by little
	a ciegas blindly
time, date:	**a medianoche** at midnight
at, on	**a las dos y cuarto** at quarter past two
	a tiempo on time
	a final/fines de mes at the end of the month
	a veces at times
distance	**a 8 km de aquí** (at a distance of) 8 kms from here
	a dos pasos de mi casa just a step from my house
	a lo lejos in the distance
with **el** + *infin.*	**al levantarse** on getting up
	al abrir la puerta on opening the door
after certain adjectives	**dispuesto a todo** ready for anything
	parecido a esto similar to this
	obligado a ello obliged to (do) that
after certain verbs	see page 66

Personal a

When the direct object of a verb is a person or pet animal, **a** must be
placed immediately before it.

EXAMPLES: **Querían mucho a sus hijos**
 They loved their children dearly
 El niño miraba a su perro con asombro
 The boy kept looking at his dog in astonishment

EXCEPTIONS: **tener**
 to have
 Tienen dos hijos
 They have two children

261

Prepositions

de

from	**venir de Londres** to come from London **un médico de Valencia** a doctor from Valencia **de la mañana a la noche** from morning till night **de 10 a 15** from 10 to 15
belonging to, of	**el sombrero de mi padre** my father's hat **las lluvias de abril** April showers
contents, composition, material	**una caja de cerillas** a box of matches **una taza de té** a cup of tea; a tea-cup **un vestido de seda** a silk dress
destined for	**una silla de cocina** a kitchen chair **un traje de noche** an evening dress
descriptive	**la mujer del sombrero verde** the woman with the green hat **el vecino de al lado** the next-door neighbour
manner	**de manera irregular** in an irregular way **de una puñalada** by stabbing
quality	**una mujer de edad** an elderly lady **objetos de valor** valuable items
comparative + a number	**Había más/menos de 100 personas** There were more/fewer than 100 people
in (*after superlatives*)	**la ciudad más/menos bonita del mundo** the most/least beautiful city in the world
after certain adjectives	**contento de ver** pleased to see **fácil/difícil de entender** easy/difficult to understand **capaz de hacer** capable of doing
after certain verbs	see page 66

Prepositions

en

in, at	**en el campo** in the country **en Londres** in London **en la cama** in bed **con un libro en la mano** with a book in his hand **en voz baja** in a low voice **en la escuela** in/at school
into	**Entra en la casa** Go into the house **Metió la mano en su bolso** She put her hand into her handbag
on	**un cuadro en la pared** a picture on the wall **sentado en una silla** sitting on a chair **en la planta baja** on the ground floor
time, dates, months: at, in	**en este momento** at this moment **en 2012** in 2012 **en enero** in January
transport: by	**en coche** by car **en avión** by plane **en tren** by train (but see also **por**)
language	**en español** in Spanish
duration	**Lo hice en una semana** I did it in a week

after certain adjectives	**Es muy buena/mala en geografía**
	  She is very good/bad at geography
	Fueron los primeros/últimos/únicos en + *infin.*
	  They were the first/last/only ones + *infin.*

after certain verbs	see page 66

Prepositions

por

motion: along, through, around	**Vaya por ese camino** Go along that path **por el túnel** through the tunnel **pasear por el campo** to walk around the countryside
vague location	**Tiene que estar por aquí** It's got to be somewhere around here **Lo busqué por todas partes** I looked for him everywhere
vague time	**por la tarde** in the afternoon **por aquellos días** in those days
rate	**90 km por hora** 90 km an hour **un cinco por ciento** five per cent **Ganaron por 3 a o** They won 3-o
by (*agent of passive*)	**descubierto por unos niños** discovered by some children **odiado por sus enemigos** hated by his enemies
by (*means of*)	**por barco** by boat **por tren** by train (freight) **por correo aéreo** by airmail **llamar por teléfono** to telephone
cause, reason: for, because	**¿por qué?** why?, for what reason? **por todo eso** because of all that **por lo que he oído** judging by what I've heard
+ *infinitive*: to	**libros por leer** books to be read **cuentas por pagar** bills to be paid
equivalence	**¿Me tienes por tonto?** Do you think I'm stupid?
+ *adjective*/+ *adverb* + **que**: however	**por buenos que sean** however good they are **por mucho que lo quieras** however much you want it

Prepositions

for	**¿Cuánto me darán por este libro?** How much will they give me for this book? **Te lo cambio por este** I'll swap you this one for it **No siento nada por ti** I feel nothing for you **si no fuera por ti** if it weren't for you **¡Por Dios!** For God's sake!
for the benefit of	**Lo hago por ellos** I'm doing it for their benefit
on behalf of	**Firma por mí** Sign on my behalf

por also combines with other prepositions to form double prepositions usually conveying the idea of movement. The commonest of these are:

over	**Saltó por encima de la mesa** She jumped over the table
under	**Nadamos por debajo del puente** We swam under the bridge
past	**Pasaron por delante de Correos** They went past the post office
behind	**por detrás de la puerta** behind the door
through	**La luz entraba por entre las cortinas** Light was coming in through the curtains
+ **donde**	**¿Por dónde has venido?** which way did you come?

ante

faced with, before	**Lo hicieron ante mis propios ojos** They did it before my very eyes **Ante eso no se puede hacer nada** There's nothing one can do when faced with that
preference	**la salud ante todo** health above everything else

antes de

before (*time*)	**antes de las 5** before 5 o'clock

Prepositions

bajo/debajo de

These are usually equivalent, although **bajo** is used more frequently in a figurative sense and with temperatures.

under	**bajo/debajo de la cama** under the bed
	bajo el dominio romano under Roman rule
below	**un grado bajo cero** one degree below zero

con

with	**Vino con su amigo** She came with her friend
after certain adjectives	**enfadado con ellos** angry with them
	magnánimo con sus súbditos
	magnanimous with his subjects

contra

against	**No tengo nada contra ti** I've nothing against you
	apoyado contra la pared leaning against the wall

delante de

in front of	**Iba delante de mí** She was walking in front of me

desde

from	**Desde aquí se puede ver** You can see it from here
	Llamaban desde España
	They were phoning from Spain
	desde otro punto de vista
	from a different point of view
	desde la 1 hasta las 6 from 1 till 6
	desde entonces from then onwards
since	**desde que volvieron** since they returned

Prepositions

for	**Viven en esa casa desde hace 3 años**
	They've been living in that house for 3 years
	(*note tense*)

detrás de

behind	**Están detrás de la puerta** They are behind the door

durante

during	**durante la guerra** during the war
for	**Anduvieron durante 3 días** They walked for 3 days

entre

between	**entre 8 y 10** between 8 and 10
among	**María y Elena, entre otras**
	María and Elena, among others
reciprocal	**ayudarse entre sí** to help each other

excepto

except (for)	**todos excepto tú** everybody except you

hacia

towards	**Van hacia ese edificio**
	They're going towards that building
around (*time*)	**hacia las 3** at around 3 (o'clock)
	hacia fines de enero around the end of January

Prepositions

Hacia can also combine with some adverbs to convey a sense of motion in a particular direction:

hacia arriba upwards
hacia abajo downwards
hacia adelante forwards
hacia atrás backwards
hacia adentro inwards
hacia afuera outwards

hasta

until	**hasta la noche** until night
as far as	**Viajaron hasta Sevilla** They travelled as far as Seville
up to	**Conté hasta 300 ovejas** I counted up to 300 lambs **Hasta ahora no los había visto** Up to now I hadn't seen them
even	**Hasta un tonto lo entendería** Even an imbecile would understand that

para

for	**Es para ti** It's for you **Es para mañana** It's for tomorrow **una habitación para dos noches** a room for two nights **Para ser un niño, lo hace muy bien** For a child he is very good at it **Salen para Cádiz** They are leaving for Cádiz **Se conserva muy bien para sus años** He keeps very well for his age
+ *infinitive*: (in order) to	**Es demasiado torpe para comprenderlo** He's too stupid to understand
+ **sí**: to oneself	**hablar para sí** to talk to oneself **reír para sí** to laugh to oneself
with time	**Todavía tengo para 1 hora** I'll be another hour (at it) yet

Prepositions

salvo

except (for)	**todos salvo él** everyone except him **salvo cuando llueve** except when it's raining
barring	**salvo imprevistos** barring the unexpected **salvo contraorden** unless you hear to the contrary

según

according to	**según su consejo** according to her advice **según lo que me dijiste** according to what you told me

sin

without	**sin agua/dinero** without water/money **sin mi marido** without my husband
+ *infinitive*	**sin contar a los otros** without counting the others

sobre

on	**sobre la cama** on the bed **sobre el armario** on (top of) the wardrobe
on (to)	**Póngalo sobre la mesa** Put it on the table
about, on	**un libro sobre Eva Perón** a book about Eva Perón
above, over	**Volábamos sobre el mar** We were flying over the sea **la nube sobre aquella montaña** the cloud above that mountain
approximately	**Vendré sobre las 4** I'll come about 4 o'clock
about	**Madrid tiene sobre 4 millones de habitantes** Madrid has about 4 million inhabitants

tras

behind	**Está tras el asiento** It's behind the seat
after	**uno tras otro** one after another **día tras día** day after day **Corrieron tras el ladrón** They ran after the thief

Conjunctions

Conjunctions

Some conjunctions introduce a main clause, such as **y** (*and*), **pero** (*but*), **si** (*if*), **o** (*or*) etc, and some introduce a subordinate clause, like **porque** (*because*), **mientras que** (*while*), **después de que** (*after*) etc. They are all used in much the same way as in English, but the following points are of note:

Some conjunctions in Spanish require a following subjunctive, see pages 60 to 63.

Some conjunctions are 'split' in Spanish like 'both ... and', 'either ... or' in English:

tanto ... como both ... and → ❶
ni ... ni neither ... nor → ❷
o (bien) ... o (bien) either ... or (else) → ❸
sea ... sea either ... or, whether ... or → ❹

y
- Before words beginning with **i-** or **hi-** + consonant it becomes **e** → ❺

o
- Before words beginning with **o-** or **ho-** it becomes **u** → ❻
- Between numerals it becomes **ó** → ❼

que
- meaning *that* → ❽
- in comparisons, meaning *than* → ❾
- followed by the subjunctive, see page 58.

porque (not to be confused with **por qué** *why*)
- como should be used instead at the beginning of a sentence → ❿

pero, sino
- pero normally translates *but* → ⓫
- sino is used when there is a direct contrast after a negative → ⓬

Examples

1 **Estas flores crecen tanto en verano como en invierno**
These flowers grow in both summer and winter

2 **Ni él ni ella vinieron**
Neither he nor she came
No tengo ni dinero ni comida
I have neither money nor food

3 **Debe de ser o ingenua o tonta**
She must be either naïve or stupid

O bien me huyen o bien no me reconocen
Either they're avoiding me or else they don't recognize me

4 **Sea en verano, sea en invierno, siempre me gusta andar**
I always like walking, whether in summer or in winter

5 **Diana e Isabel**
Diana and Isabel
madre e hija
mother and daughter
BUT:
árboles y hierba
trees and grass

6 **diez u once**
ten or eleven
minutos u horas
minutes or hours

7 **37 ó 38**
37 or 38

8 **Dicen que te han visto**
They say (that) they've seen you
¿Sabías que estábamos allí?
Did you know that we were there?

9 **Le gustan más que nunca**
He likes them more than ever
Miguel es menos guapo que su hermano
Miguel is less attractive than his brother

10 **Como estaba lloviendo no pudimos salir**
Because/As it was raining we couldn't go out
(*Compare with:* **No pudimos salir porque estaba lloviendo**)

11 **Me gustaría ir, pero estoy muy cansada**
I'd like to go, but I am very tired

12 **No es escocesa sino irlandesa**
She isn't Scottish but Irish

271

Suffixes

Augmentative, Diminutive and Pejorative Suffixes

These can be used after nouns, adjectives and some adverbs. They are attached to the end of the word after any final vowel has been removed:

e.g. **puerta → puertita**
 doctor → doctorcito

ⓘ Note: Further changes sometimes take place (see page 300).

Augmentatives

These are used mainly to imply largeness, but they can also suggest clumsiness, ugliness or grotesqueness. The commonest augmentatives are:
 ón/ona → ❶
 azo/a → ❷
 ote/a → ❸

Diminutives

These are used mainly to suggest smallness or to express a feeling of affection. Occasionally they can be used to express ridicule or contempt. The commonest diminutives are:
 ito/a → ❹
 (e)cito/a → ❺
 (ec)illo/a → ❻
 (z)uelo/a → ❼

Pejoratives

These are used to convey the idea that something is unpleasant or to express contempt. The commonest suffixes are:
 ucho/a → ❽
 acho/a → ❾
 uzo/a → ❿
 uco/a → ⓫
 astro/a → ⓬

Examples

1 **un hombre** a man

un hombrón a big man

2 **bueno** good
un perro a dog
gripe flu

buenazo (person) easily imposed on
un perrazo a really big dog
un gripazo a really bad bout of flu

3 **grande** big
palabra word
amigo friend

grandote huge
palabrota swear word
amigote old pal

4 **una casa** a house
un poco a little
un rato a while
mi hija my daughter
despacio slowly

una casita a cottage
un poquito a little bit
un ratito a little while
mi hijita my dear, sweet daughter
despacito nice and slowly

5 **un viejo** an old man
un pueblo a village
una voz a voice

un viejecito a little old man
un pueblecito a small village
una vocecita a sweet little voice

6 **una ventana** a window

una ventanilla a small window
(car, train etc)

un chico a boy
una campana a bell
un palo a stick
un médico a doctor

un chiquillo a small boy
una campanilla a small bell
un palillo a toothpick
un mediquillo a quack (doctor)

7 **los pollos** the chickens
hoyos hollows
un ladrón a thief
una mujer a woman

los polluelos the little chicks
hoyuelos dimples
un ladronzuelo a petty thief
una mujerzuela a whore

8 **un animal** an animal
un cuarto a room
una casa a house

un animalucho a wretched animal
un cuartucho a poky little room
una casucha a shack

9 **rico** rich

ricacho nouveau riche

10 **gente** people

gentuza scum

11 **una ventana** a window

un ventanuco a miserable little
window

12 **un político** a politician

un politicastro a third-rate
politician

273

Sentence structure

Word Order

Word order in Spanish is much more flexible than in English. You can often find the subject placed after the verb or the object before the verb, either for emphasis or for stylistic reasons → **1**

There are some cases, however, where the order is always different from English. Most of these have already been dealt with under the appropriate part of speech, but are summarized here along with other instances not covered elsewhere.

> Object pronouns nearly always come before the verb → **2**
> For details, see pages 232 to 235.
>
> Qualifying adjectives nearly always come after the noun → **3**
> For details, see page 228.
>
> Following direct speech the subject always follows the verb → **4**

For word order in negative sentences, see page 276.

For word order in interrogative sentences, see page 280 → **5**

Examples

1. **Ese libro te lo di yo**   I gave you that book
   No nos vio nadie   Nobody saw us

2. **Ya los veo**   I can see them now
   Me lo dieron ayer   They gave it to me yesterday

3. **una ciudad española**   a Spanish town
   vino tinto   red wine

4. **– Pienso que sí – dijo Ana**   'I think so,' said Ana
   – No importa – replicó Daniel   'It doesn't matter,' Daniel replied

Sentence structure

Negatives

A sentence is made negative by adding **no** between the subject (if stated explicitly) and the verb (and any preceding object pronouns) → **1**

There are, however, some points to note:
- in phrases like *not her, not now* etc, the Spanish **no** usually comes after the word it qualifies → **2**
- with verbs of saying, hoping, thinking etc, *not* is translated by **que no** → **3**

Double negatives

The following are the most common negative pairs:

> **no ... nada** nothing (*not ... anything*)
> **no ... nadie** nobody (*not ... anybody*)
> **no ... más** no longer (*not ... any more*)
> **no ... nunca** never (*not ... ever*)
> **no ... jamás** never (*not ... ever*)
> **no ... más que** only (*not ... more than*)
> **no ... ningún/ninguno/a** no (*not any*)
> **no ... tampoco** not ... either
> **no ... ni ... ni** neither ... nor
> **no ... ni siquiera** not even

Word order

No precedes the verb (and any object pronouns) in both simple and compound tenses, and the second element follows the verb → **4**

Sometimes the above negatives are placed before the verb (with the exception of **más** and **más que**), and **no** is then dropped → **5**

For use of **nada**, **nadie** and **ninguno** as pronouns, see page 240.

Examples

AFFIRMATIVE		NEGATIVE
① El coche es suyo	→	**El coche no es suyo**
The car is his		The car is not his
(Yo) me lo pondré	→	**(Yo) no me lo pondré**
I will put it on		I will not put it on

② ¿Quién lo ha hecho? — Ella no
Who did it? — Not her

¿Quieres un cigarrillo?
— Ahora no
Do you want a cigarette?
— Not now

Dame ese libro, el que está a tu lado no, el otro
Give me that book, not the one near you, the other one

③ Opino que no
I think not

Dijeron que no
They said not

④ No dicen nada
They don't say anything

No han visto a nadie
They haven't seen anybody

No me veréis más
You won't see me any more

No te olvidaré nunca/jamás
I'll never forget you

No habían recorrido más que 40 kms cuando ...
They hadn't travelled more than 40 kms when ...

No se me ha ocurrido ninguna idea
I haven't had any ideas

No les estaban esperando ni mi hijo ni mi hija
Neither my son nor my daughter was waiting for them

No ha venido ni siquiera Juan
Not even Juan has come

⑤ Nadie ha venido hoy
Nobody came today

Nunca me han gustado
I've never liked them

Ni mi hermano ni mi hermana fuman
Neither my brother nor my sister smokes

Sentence structure

Negatives *continued*

Negatives in short replies

No *no* is the usual negative response to a question → ❶

    ⓘ Note: It is often translated as 'not' → ❷
       (see also page 276)

Nearly all the other negatives listed on page 276 may be used without a verb in a short reply → ❸

Combination of negatives

These are the most common combinations of negative particles:

      no ... nunca más → ❹
      no ... nunca a nadie → ❺
      no ... nunca nada/nada nunca → ❻
      no ... nunca más que → ❼
      no ... ni ... nunca ... → ❽

Examples

1 **¿Quieres venir con nosotros?**
 — No

Do you want to come with us?
 — No

2 **¿Vienes o no?**

Are you coming or not?

3 **¿Ha venido alguien? — ¡Nadie!**
 ¿Has ido al Japón alguna vez?
 — Nunca

Has anyone come? — Nobody!
Have you ever been to Japan?
 — Never

4 **No lo haré nunca más**

I'll never do it again

5 **No se ve nunca a nadie por allí**

You never see anybody around
there

6 **No cambiaron nada nunca**

They never changed anything

7 **No he hablado nunca más que**
 con su mujer

I've only ever spoken to his wife

8 **No me ha escrito ni llamado**
 por teléfono nunca

He/She has never written to me
or phoned me

Sentence structure

Question Forms

Direct

There are two ways of forming direct questions in Spanish:

> by inverting the normal word order so that
> *subject + verb → verb + subject* → ❶

> by maintaining the word order *subject + verb*, but by using a rising
> intonation at the end of the sentence → ❷

> ⓘ Note: In compound tenses the auxiliary may never be
> separated from the past participle, as happens in English → ❸

Indirect

An indirect question is one that is 'reported', e.g. he asked me 'what the
time was', tell me 'which way to go'. Word order in indirect questions can
adopt one of the two following patterns:

> *interrogative word + subject + verb* → ❹

> *interrogative word + verb + subject* → ❺

¿verdad?, ¿no?

These are used wherever English would use 'isn't it?', 'don't they?', 'weren't
we?', 'is it?' etc tagged on to the end of a sentence → ❻

sí

Sí is the word for 'yes' in answer to a question put either in the affirmative
or in the negative → ❼

Examples

1 ¿Vendrá tu madre?　　　　　Will your mother come?
¿Lo trajo Vd?　　　　　　　Did you bring it?
¿Es posible eso?　　　　　　Is it possible?
¿Cuándo volverán Vds?　　　When will you come back?

2 El gato, ¿se bebió toda la leche?　Did the cat drink up all his milk?
Andrés, ¿va a venir?　　　　Is Andrés coming?

3 ¿Lo ha terminado Vd?　　　Have you finished it?
¿Había llegado tu amigo?　　Had your friend arrived?

4 Dime qué autobuses pasan por　Tell me which buses come this
aquí　　　　　　　　　　way
No sé cuántas personas vendrán　I don't know how many people
will turn up

5 Me preguntó dónde trabajaba　He asked me where my brother
mi hermano　　　　　　worked
No sabemos a qué hora　　We don't know what time the
empieza la película　　　　film starts

6 Hace calor, ¿verdad?　　　It's warm, isn't it?
No se olvidará Vd, ¿verdad?　You won't forget, will you?
Estaréis cansados, ¿no?　　You will be tired, won't you?
Te lo dijo Carmen, ¿no?　　Carmen told you, didn't she?

7 ¿Lo has hecho? — Sí　　　Have you done it? — Yes (I have)
¿No lo has hecho? — Sí　　Haven't you done it? — Yes
(I have)

Translation problems

Beware of translating word by word. While on occasions this is possible, quite often it is not. The need for caution is illustrated by the following:

> English phrasal verbs (i.e. verbs followed by a preposition), e.g. 'to run away', 'to fall down', are often translated by one word in Spanish → ❶

> English verbal constructions often contain a preposition where none exists in Spanish, and vice versa → ❷

> The Spanish preposition may not always be the one that the English sentence leads you to expect, and vice versa → ❸

> A word which is singular in English may be plural in Spanish, or vice versa → ❹

> Spanish has no equivalent of the possessive construction denoted by ...'s/...s' → ❺

Problems

-ing

This is translated in a variety of ways in Spanish:

> 'to be ... -ing' can sometimes be translated by a simple tense (see also pages 54 to 56) → ❻
> But, when a physical position is denoted, a past participle is used → ❼

in the construction 'to see/hear sb ... -ing', use an infinitive → ❽
'-ing' can also be translated by:
- an infinitive, see page 46 → ❾
- a perfect infinitive, see page 50 → ❿
- a gerund, see page 52 → ⓫
- a noun → ⓬

Examples

1
huir	to run away
caerse	to fall down
ceder	to give in

2
pagar	to pay for
mirar	to look at
escuchar	to listen to
encontrarse con	to meet
fijarse en	to notice
servirse de	to use

3
extrañarse de	to be surprised at
harto de	fed up with
soñar con	to dream of
contar con	to count on

4
| unas vacaciones | a holiday |
| la gente | people |

5
| el coche de mi hermano | my brother's car (*literally*: ... of my brother) |
| el cuarto de las niñas | the girls' bedroom (*literally*: ... of the girls) |

6
| Se va mañana | He/She is leaving tomorrow |
| ¿Qué haces? | What are you doing? |

7
| Está sentado ahí | He is sitting over there |
| Estaba tendida en el suelo | She was lying on the ground |

8
| Les veo venir | I can see them coming |
| La he oído cantar | I've heard her singing |

9
Me gusta ir al cine	I like going to the cinema
¡Deja de hablar!	Stop talking!
En vez de contestar	Instead of answering
Antes de salir	Before leaving

10
| Después de haber abierto la caja, María ... | After opening the box, María ... |

11
| Pasamos la tarde fumando y charlando | We spent the afternoon smoking and chatting |

12
| El esquí me mantiene en forma | Skiing keeps me fit |

283

Translation problems

to be (*see also Verbal Idioms, pages 74 to 76*)

In set expressions, describing physical and emotional conditions, **tener** is used:

> **tener calor/frío** to be warm/cold
> **tener hambre/sed** to be hungry/thirsty
> **tener miedo** to be afraid
> **tener razón** to be right

Describing the weather, e.g. 'what's the weather like?', 'it's windy/sunny', use **hacer** → ❶

For ages, e.g. 'he is 6', use **tener** (see also page 310) → ❷

there is/there are

Both are translated by **hay** → ❸

can, be able

Physical ability is expressed by **poder** → ❹

If the meaning is 'to know how to', use **saber** → ❺

'Can' + a 'verb of hearing or seeing etc' is not translated in Spanish → ❻

to

Generally translated by **a** → ❼

In time expressions, e.g. 10 to 6, use **menos** → ❽

When the meaning is 'in order to', use **para** → ❾

Following a verb, as in 'to try to do', 'to like to do', see pages 46 and 48.

'easy/difficult/impossible' etc 'to do' are translated by **fácil/difícil/ imposible** etc **de hacer** when the adjective describes something other than the infinitive → ❿

Examples

1 ¿Qué tiempo hace?
   Hace bueno/malo/viento

What's the weather like?
It's lovely/miserable/windy

2 ¿Cuántos años tienes?
   Tengo quince años

How old are you?
I'm fifteen

3 Hay un señor en la puerta
   Hay cinco libros en la mesa

There's a gentleman at the door
There are five books on the table

4 No puedo salir contigo

I can't go out with you

5 ¿Sabes nadar?

Can you swim?

6 No veo nada
   ¿Es que no me oyes?

I can't see anything
Can't you hear me?

7 Dale el libro a Isabel

Give the book to Isabel

8 las diez menos cinco
   a las siete menos cuarto

five to ten
at a quarter to seven

9 Lo hice para ayudaros
   Se inclinó para atarse el cordón
      de zapato

I did it to help you
He bent down to tie his
   shoelace

10 Este libro es fácil/difícil de leer
   BUT
   Es fácil confundirse

This book is easy/difficult to read

It's easy to get mixed up

Translation problems

must

When *must* expresses an assumption, **deber de** is often used → ❶

> ⓘ Note: This meaning is also often expressed by **deber** directly followed by the infinitive → ❷

When it expresses obligation, there are three possible translations:
- **tener que** → ❸
- **deber** → ❹
- **hay que** (impersonal) → ❺

may

If *may* expresses possibility, it can be translated by:
- **poder** → ❻
- **puede (ser) que** + *subjunctive*

To express permission, use **poder** → ❼

will

If *will* expresses willingness or desire rather than the future, the present tense of **querer** is used → ❽

would

If *would* expresses willingness, use the preterite or imperfect of **querer** → ❾

When a repeated or habitual action in the past is referred to, use
- the imperfect → ❿
- the imperfect of **soler** + *infinitive* → ⓫

Examples

❶ Ha debido de mentir He must have lied
Debe de gustarle She must like it

❷ Debe estar por aquí cerca It must be near here
Debo haberlo dejado en el tren I must have left it on the train

❸ Tenemos que salir temprano mañana We must leave early tomorrow
Tengo que irme I must go

❹ Debo visitarlos I must visit them
Debéis escuchar lo que se os dice You must listen to what is said to you

❺ Hay que entrar por ese lado One/We etc must go in that way

❻ Todavía puede cambiar de opinión He may still change his mind
Creo que puede llover esta tarde I think it may rain this afternoon
Puede (ser) que no lo sepa She may not know

❼ ¿Puedo irme? May I go?
Puede sentarse You may sit down

❽ ¿Quiere Vd esperar un momento, por favor? Will you wait a moment, please?
No quiere ayudarme He won't help me

❾ No quisieron venir They wouldn't come

❿ Las miraba hora tras hora She would watch them for hours on end

⓫ Últimamente solía comer muy poco Latterly he would eat very little

Pronunciation

Pronunciation of Vowels

Spanish vowels are always clearly pronounced and not relaxed in unstressed syllables as happens in English.

	EXAMPLES	HINTS ON PRONUNCIATION
[a]	casa	Between English *a* as in *hat* and *u* as in *hut*
[e]	pensar	Similar to English *e* in *pet*
[i]	filo	Between English *i* as in *pin* and *ee* as in *been*
[o]	loco	Similar to English *o* in *hot*
[u]	luna	Between English *ew* as in *few* and *u* as in *put*

Pronunciation of Diphthongs

All these diphthongs are shorter than similar English diphthongs.

[ai]	baile hay	Like *i* in *side*
[au]	causa	Like *ou* in *sound*
[ei]	peine rey	Like *ey* in *grey*
[eu]	deuda	Like the vowel sounds in English *may you*, but without the sound of the *y*
[oi]	boina voy	Like *oy* in *boy*

Semi-consonants

| [j] | hacia ya
tiene yeso
labio yo | *i* following a consonant and preceding a vowel, and **y** preceding a vowel are pronounced as *y* in English *yet* |
| [w] | agua bueno
arduo ruido | **u** following a consonant and preceding a vowel is pronounced as *w* in English *walk* |

EXCEPTIONS: **gue**, **gui** (see page 290)

Pronunciation

Pronunciation of Consonants

Some consonants are pronounced almost exactly as in English:
[l, m, n, f, k, and in some cases g].

Others, listed below, are similar to English, but differences should be noted.

	EXAMPLES	HINTS ON PRONUNCIATION
[p]	padre	They are not aspirated, unlike
[k]	coco	English pot, cook and ten.
[t]	tan	
[t]	todo tú	Pronounced with the tip of the
[d]	doy balde	tongue touching the upper front teeth and not the roof of the mouth as in English.

The following consonants are not heard in English:

[β]	labio	This is pronounced between upper and lower lips, which do not touch, unlike English b as in bend.
[ɣ]	haga	Similar to English g as in gate, but tongue does not touch the soft palate.
[ɲ]	año	Similar to ni in onion
[x]	jota	Like the guttural ch in loch
[r]	pera	A single trill with the tip of the tongue against the teeth ridge.
[rr]	rojo perro	A multiple trill with the tip of the tongue against the teeth ridge.

Pronunciation

From Spelling to Sounds

Note the pronunciation of the following (groups of) letters.

LETTER	PRONOUNCED	EXAMPLES
b,v	[b]	These letters have the same value. At the start of a breath group, and after written **m** and **n**, the sound is similar to English *boy* → ❶
	[β]	in all other positions, the sound is unknown in English (see page 289) → ❷
c	[k]	Before **a**, **o**, **u** or a consonant, like English *keep*, but not aspirated → ❸
	[θ/s]	Before **e**, **i** like English *thin*, or, in Latin America and parts of Spain, like English *same* → ❹
ch	[tʃ]	Like English *church* → ❺
d	[d]	At the start of the breath group and after **l** or **n**, it is pronounced similar to English *deep* (see page 289) → ❻
	[ð]	Between vowels and after consonants (except **l** or **n**), it is pronounced very like English *though* → ❼
	[(ð)]	At the end of words, and in the verb ending **-ado**, it is often not pronounced → ❽
g	[x]	Before **e**, **i**, pronounced gutturally, similar to English lo*ch* → ❾
	[g]	At the start of the breath group and after **n**, it is pronounced like English *get* → ❿
	[ɣ]	In other positions the sound is unknown in English → ⓫
gue	[ge/ɣe]	The **u** is silent → ⓬
gui	[gi/ɣi]	
güe	[gwe/ɣwe]	The **u** is pronounced like English
güi	[gwi/ɣwi]	*walk* → ⓭

Examples

1. **bomba** ['bomba]   **voy** [boi]   **vicio** ['biθjo]

2. **hubo** ['uβo]   **de veras** [de 'βeras]   **lavar** [la'βar]

3. **casa** ['kasa]   **coco** ['koko]   **cumbre** ['kumbre]

4. **cero** ['θero/'sero]   **cinco** ['θiŋko/'siŋko]

5. **mucho** ['mutʃo]   **chuchería** [tʃutʃe'ria]

6. **doy** [doi]   **balde** ['balde]   **bondad** [bon'dað]

7. **modo** ['moðo]   **ideal** [iðe'al]

8. **Madrid** [ma'ðri(ð)]   **comprado** [kom'pra(ð)o]

9. **gente** ['xente]   **giro** ['xiro]   **general** [xene'ral]

10. **ganar** [ga'nar]   **pongo** ['poŋgo]

11. **agua** ['aɣwa]   **agrícola** [a'ɣrikola]

12. **guija** ['gixa]   **guerra** ['gerra]   **pague** ['paɣe]

13. **agüero** [a 'ɣwero]   **argüir** [ar'ɣwir]

Pronunciation

From Spelling to Sounds *continued*

LETTER	PRONOUNCED	EXAMPLES
h	[-]	This is always silent → ❶
j	[x]	Like the guttural sound in English lo*ch*, but often aspirated at the end of a word → ❷
ll	[ʎ]	Similar to English -*y*- in *yes* → ❸
	[j/ʒ]	In some parts of Spain and in Latin America, like English *yet* or *pleasure* → ❹
-nv-	[mb]	This combination of letters is pronounced as in English i*mb*ibe → ❺
ñ	[ɲ]	As in English on*i*on → ❻
q	[k]	Always followed by silent letter **u**, and pronounced as in English *keep*, but not aspirated → ❼
s	[s]	Except where mentioned below, like English *sing* → ❽
	[z]	When followed by **b, d, g, l, m, n** like English *zoo* → ❾
w	[w]	Like English *v, w* → ❿
x	[ks]	Between vowels, often like English e*x*it → ⓫
	[s]	Before a consonant, and, increasingly, even between vowels, like English *send* → ⓬
y	[j]	Like English *yes* → ⓭
	[ʒ]	In some parts of Latin America, like English *leisure* → ⓮
z	[θ]	Like English *thin* → ⓯
	[s]	In some parts of Spain and in Latin America, like English *send* → ⓰

Examples

1. **hombre** ['ombre]   **hoja** ['oxa]   **ahorrar** [ao'rrar]

2. **jota** ['xota]   **tejer** [te'xer]   **reloj** [re'lo(h)]

3. **calle** ['kaʎe]   **llamar** [ʎa'mar]

4. **pillar** [pi'jar/pi'ʒar]   **olla** ['oja/'oʒa]

5. **enviar** [em'bjar]   **sin valor** ['sim ba'lor]

6. **uña** ['uɲa]   **bañar** [ba'ɲar]

7. **aquel** [a'kel]   **querer** [ke'rer]

8. **está** [es'ta]   **serio** ['serjo]

9. **desde** ['dezðe]   **mismo** ['mizmo]   **asno** ['azno]

10. **wáter** ['bater]   **web** [web]

11. **éxito** ['eksito]   **máximo** ['maksimo]

12. **extra** ['estra]   **sexto** ['sesto]

13. **yo** [jo]   **yedra** ['jeðra]

14. **yeso** ['ʒeso]   **yerno** ['ʒerno]

15. **zapato** [θa'pato]   **zona** ['θona]   **luz** [luθ]

16. **zaguán** [sa'ʎwan]   **zueco** ['sweko]   **pez** [pes]

Pronunciation

Normal Word Stress

There are simple rules to establish which syllable in a Spanish word is stressed. When an exception to these rules occurs an acute accent (stress mark) is needed (see page 296). These rules are as follows:

- words ending in a vowel or combination of vowels, or with the consonants **-s** or **-n** are stressed on the next to last syllable. The great majority of Spanish words fall into this category → **1**
- words ending in a consonant other than **-s** or **-n** bear the stress on the last syllable → **2**
- a minority of words bear the stress on the second to last syllable, and these always need an accent → **3**
- some nouns change their stress from singular to plural → **4**

Stress in Diphthongs

In the case of diphthongs there are rules to establish which of the vowels is stressed (see page 288 for pronunciation). These rules are as follows:

- diphthongs formed by the combination of a 'weak' vowel (**i**, **u**) and a 'strong' vowel (**a**, **e** or **o**) bear the stress on the strong vowel → **5**
- diphthongs formed by the combination of two 'weak' vowels bear the stress on the second vowel → **6**

ⓘ Note: Two 'strong' vowels don't form a diphthong but are pronounced as two separate vowels. In these cases stress follows the normal rules → **7**

Examples

1 **ca**sa house
corre he runs
pa**la**bra word
crisis crisis

casas houses
corren they run
pa**la**bras words
crisis crises

2 re**loj** watch
ver**dad** truth
bati**dor** beater

3 mur**cié**lago bat
pájaro bird

4 ca**rác**ter character
régimen regime

ca**rac**teres characters
re**gí**menes regimes

5 **bai**le dance
boina beret
peine comb
causa cause
reina queen

6 **fui** I went
vi**u**do widower

7 me ma**re**o I feel dizzy
ca**er** to fall
caos chaos
co**rrea** leash

Spelling

The Acute Accent (´)

This is used in writing to show that a word is stressed contrary to the normal rules for stress (see page 294) → **①**

The following points should be noted:

The same syllable is stressed in the plural form of adjectives and nouns as in the singular. To show this, it is necessary to
- add an accent in the case of unaccented nouns and adjectives ending in **-n** → **②**
- drop the accent from nouns and adjectives ending in **-n** or **-s** which have an accent on the last syllable → **③**

The feminine form of accented nouns or adjectives does not have an accent → **④**

When object pronouns are added to certain verb forms an accent is required to show that the syllable stressed in the verb form does not change. These verb forms are:
- the gerund → **⑤**
- the infinitive, when followed by two pronouns → **⑥**
- imperative forms, except for the 2nd person plural → **⑦**

The absolute superlative forms of adjectives are always accented → **⑧**

Accents on adjectives are not affected by the addition of the adverbial suffix **-mente** → **⑨**

Examples

① **autobús**
bus
relámpago
lightning

revolución
revolution
árboles
trees

② **orden** →
order
examen →
examination
joven →
young

órdenes
orders
exámenes
examinations
jóvenes
young

③ **revolución** →
revolution
autobús →
bus
parlanchín →
chatty

revoluciones
revolutions
autobuses
buses
parlanchines
chatty

④ **marqués** →
marquis
francés →
French (*masc.*)

marquesa
marchioness
francesa
French (*fem.*)

⑤ **comprando** →
buying

comprándo(se)lo
buying it (for him/her/them)

⑥ **vender** →
to sell

vendérselas
to sell them to him/her/them

⑦ **compra** →
buy
hagan →
do

cómpralo
buy it
háganselo
do it for him/her/them

⑧ **viejo** →
old
caro →
expensive

viejísimo
ancient
carísimo
very expensive

⑨ **fácil** →
easy

fácilmente
easily

Spelling

The Acute Accent *continued*

It is also used to distinguish between the written forms of words which are pronounced the same but have a different meaning or function. These are as follows:

Possessive adjectives/personal pronouns → **①**

Interrogative and exclamatory forms of adverbs, pronouns and adjectives → **②**

ⓘ Note: The accent is used in indirect as well as direct questions and exclamations → **③**

The pronoun **él** and the article **el** → **④**

A small group of words which could otherwise be confused. These are:

de	of, from	**dé**	give (*pres. subj.*)
mas	but	**más**	more
si	if	**sí**	yes; himself etc → **⑤**
te	you	**té**	tea

The Diaeresis (¨)

This is used only in the combinations **güi** or **güe** to show that the **u** is pronounced as a semi-consonant (see page 288) → **⑧**

Examples

1 **Han robado mi coche**
   A mí no me vio
   ¿Te gusta tu trabajo?
   Tú, ¿que opinas?

They've stolen my car
He didn't see me
Do you like your job?
What do you think?

2 **El chico con quien viajé**
   ¿Con quién viajaste?
   Donde quieras
   ¿Dónde encontraste eso?

The boy I travelled with
Who did you travel with?
Wherever you want
Where did you find that?

3 **¿Cómo se abre?**
   No sé cómo se abre

How does it open?
I don't know how it opens

4 **El puerto queda cerca**
   Él no quiso hacerlo

The harbour's nearby
He refused to do it

5 **si no viene**
   Sí que lo sabe

if he doesn't come
Yes he *does* know

6 **¡Qué vergüenza!**
   En seguida averigüé dónde
    estaba

How shocking!
I found out straight away where
  it was

Spelling

Regular Spelling Changes

The consonants **c**, **g** and **z** are modified by the addition of certain verb or plural endings and by some suffixes. Most of the cases where this occurs have already been dealt with under the appropriate part of speech, but are summarized here along with other instances not covered elsewhere.

Verbs

The changes set out below occur so that the consonant of the verb stem is always pronounced the same as in the infinitive. For verbs affected by these changes see the list of verbs on page 81.

INFINITIVE	CHANGE			TENSES AFFECTED
-car	c + e	→	-que	Present subj, pret → ❶
-cer, -cir	c + a, o	→	-za, -zo	Present, pres subj → ❷
-gar	g + e, i	→	-gue	Present subj, pret → ❸
-guar	gu + e	→	-güe	Present subj, pret → ❹
-ger, -gir	g + a, o	→	-ja, -jo	Present, pres subj → ❺
-guir	gu + a, o	→	-ga, -go	Present, pres subj → ❻
-zar	z + e	→	-ce	Present subj, pret → ❼

Noun and adjective plurals

SINGULAR		PLURAL
vowel + **z**	→	-ces → ❽

Nouns and adjectives + suffixes

ENDING	SUFFIX	NEW ENDING
vowel + **z** +	-cito	-cecito → ❾
-go, -ga +	-ito, -illo	-guito/a, -guillo/a → ❿
-co, -ca +	-ito, -illo	-quito/a, -quillo/a → ⓫

Adjective absolute superlatives

ENDING	SUPERLATVE
-co	-quísimo → ⓬
-go	-guísimo → ⓭
vowel + **z**	-císimo → ⓮

Examples

1 **Es inútil que lo busques aquí** — It's no good looking for it here
Saqué dos entradas — I got two tickets

2 **Hace falta que venzas tu miedo** — You must overcome your fear

3 **No creo que lleguemos antes** — I don't think we'll get there any sooner

Ya le pagué — I've already paid her

4 **Averigüé dónde estaba la casa** — I found out where the house was

5 **Cojo el autobús, es más barato** — I take the bus, it's cheaper

6 **¿Sigo?** — Shall I go on?

7 **No permiten que se cruce la frontera** — They don't allow people to cross the border
Nunca simpaticé mucho con él — I never got on very well with him

8
voz	→	**voces**	**luz**	→	**luces**
voice		voices	light		lights
veloz	→	**veloces**	**capaz**	→	**capaces**
quick			capable		

9 **luz** → **lucecita**
light — little light

10 **amigo** → **amiguito**
friend — chum

11 **chico** → **chiquillo**
boy — little boy

12 **rico** → **riquísimo**
rich — extremely rich

13 **largo** → **larguísimo**
long — very, very long

14 **feroz** → **ferocísimo**
fierce — extremely fierce

301

The alphabet

The Alphabet

A, a [a]	**J, j** ['xota]	**R, r** ['erre]
B, b [be]	**K, k** [ka]	**S, s** ['ese]
C, c [θe]	**L, l** ['ele]	**T, t** [te]
Ch, ch [tʃe]	**Ll, ll** ['eʎe]	**U, u** [u]
D, d [de]	**M, m** ['eme]	**V, v** ['uβe]
E, e [e]	**N, n** ['ene]	**W, w** ['uβe'doble]
F, f ['efe]	**Ñ, ñ** ['eɲe]	**X, x** ['ekis]
G, g [xe]	**O, o** [o]	**Y, y** [i'ɣrjeɣa]
H, h ['atʃe]	**P, p** [pe]	**Z, z** ['θeta]
I, i [i]	**Q, q** [ku]	

The letters are feminine and you therefore talk of **una a**, or **la a**.

Capital letters are used much as in English except for the following:

adjectives of nationality:
e.g. **una ciudad alemana** a German town
un autor español a Spanish author

languages:
e.g. **¿Habla Vd inglés?** Do you speak English?
Hablan español e italiano They speak Spanish and Italian

days of the week:
lunes Monday
martes Tuesday
miércoles Wednesday
jueves Thursday

viernes Friday
sábado Saturday
domingo Sunday

months of the year:
enero January
febrero February
marzo March
abril April
mayo May
junio June

julio July
agosto August
se(p)tiembre September
octubre October
noviembre November
diciembre December

Punctuation

Spanish punctuation differs from English in the following ways:

Question marks

There are inverted question marks and exclamation marks at the beginning of a question or exclamation, as well as upright ones at the end.

Indications of dialogue

Dashes are used to indicate dialogue, and are equivalent to the English inverted commas:

> **– ¿Vendrás conmigo? – le preguntó María**
> 'Will you come with me?' María asked him

ⓘ Note: When no expression of saying, replying etc follows, only one dash is used at the beginning:
– Sí. 'Yes.'

Letter headings

At the beginning of a letter, a colon is used instead of the English comma:
Querida Cristina: Dear Cristina, **Muy Sr. mío**: Dear Sir,

Punctuation terms in Spanish

.	**punto**	!	**se cierra admiración**
,	**coma**	" "	**comillas** (used as '…')
;	**punto y coma**	"	**se abren comillas**
:	**dos puntos**	"	**se cierran comillas**
…	**puntos suspensivos**	( )	**paréntesis**
¿?	**interrogación**	(	**se abre paréntesis**
¿	**se abre interrogación**	)	**se cierra paréntesis**
?	**se cierra interrogación**	–	**guión**
¡!	**admiración**		
¡	**se abre admiración** **punto y aparte**	new paragraph	
	punto final	last full stop	

Numbers

Cardinal (one, two, three *etc*)

cero	0	setenta	70
uno (un, una)	1	ochenta	80
dos	2	noventa	90
tres	3	cien (ciento)	100
cuatro	4	ciento uno (un, una)	101
cinco	5	ciento dos	102
seis	6	ciento diez	110
siete	7	ciento cuarenta y dos	142
ocho	8	doscientos/as	200
nueve	9	doscientos/as uno (un, una)	201
diez	10	doscientos/as dos	202
once	11	trescientos/as	300
doce	12	cuatrocientos/as	400
trece	13	quinientos/as	500
catorce	14	seiscientos/as	600
quince	15	setecientos/as	700
dieciséis	16	ochocientos/as	800
diecisiete	17	novecientos/as	900
dieciocho	18	mil	1.000
diecinueve	19	mil uno (un, una)	1.001
veinte	20	mil dos	1.002
veintiuno (veintiún, -una)	21	mil doscientos veinte	1.220
veintidós	22	dos mil	2.000
treinta	30	cien mil	100.000
treinta y uno (un, una)	31	doscientos/as mil	200.000
cuarenta	40	un millón	1.000.000
cincuenta	50	dos millones	2.000.000
sesenta	60	un billón	1.000.000.000.000

Fractions

un medio; medio/a	$\frac{1}{2}$
un tercio	$\frac{1}{3}$
dos tercios	$\frac{2}{3}$
un cuarto	$\frac{1}{4}$
tres cuartos	$\frac{3}{4}$
un quinto	$\frac{1}{5}$
cinco y tres cuartos	$5\frac{3}{4}$

Others

cero coma cinco	0,5
uno coma tres	1,3
(el, un) diez por ciento	10%
dos más/y dos	$2 + 2$
dos menos dos	$2 - 2$
dos por dos	2×2
dos dividido por dos	$2 \div 2$

Numbers

Points to note on cardinals

uno drops the **o** before masculine nouns, and the same applies when in compound numerals:
- **un libro** 1 book, **treinta y un niños** 31 children
- **un estudiante de veintiún años** a 21-year-old student

1, 21, 31 etc and 200, 300, 400 etc have feminine forms:
- **cuarenta y una euros** 41 euros, **quinientas libras** £500

ciento is used before numbers smaller than 100, otherwise **cien** is used:
- **ciento cuatro** 104 but **cien euros** 100 euros, **cien mil** 100,000 (see also page 210)

millón takes **de** before a noun:
- **un millón de personas** 1,000,000 people

mil is only found in the plural when meaning thousands of:
- **miles de solicitantes** thousands of applicants

cardinals normally precede ordinals:
- **los tres primeros pisos** the first three floors

ⓘ Note: The full stop is used with numbers over one thousand and the comma with decimals i.e. the opposite of English usage.

Numbers

Ordinal Numbers (first, second, third *etc*)

primero (primer, primera)	1º,1ª	**undécimo/a**	11º,11ª
segundo/a	2º,2ª	**duodécimo/a**	12º,12ª
tercero (tercer, tercera)	3º,3ª	**decimotercer(o/a)**	13º,13ª
cuarto/a	4º,4ª	**decimocuarto/a**	14º,14ª
quinto/a	5º,5ª	**decimoquinto/a**	15º,15ª
sexto/a	6º,6ª	**decimosexto/a**	16º,16ª
séptimo/a	7º,7ª	**decimoséptimo/a**	17º,17ª
octavo/a	8º,8ª	**decimoctavo/a**	18º,18ª
noveno/a	9º,9ª	**decimonoveno/a**	19º,19ª
décimo/a	10º,10ª	**vigésimo/a**	20º,20ª

Points to note on ordinals

They agree in gender and in number with the noun, which they normally precede, except with royal titles:

> **la primera vez** the first time
> **Felipe segundo** Philip II

primero and **tercero** drop the **o** before a masculine singular noun:

> **el primer premio** the first prize
> **el tercer día** the third day

Beyond **décimo** ordinal numbers are rarely used, and they are replaced by the cardinal number placed immediately after the noun:

> **el siglo diecisiete** the seventeenth century
> **Alfonso doce** Alfonso XII
> **en el piso trece** on the 13th floor

> BUT: **vigésimo/a** 20th
> (but not with royal titles or centuries)
> **centésimo/a** 100th
> **milésimo/a** 1,000th
> **millonésimo/a** 1,000,000th

Numbers

Other Uses

collective numbers:

un par	2, a couple
una decena (de personas)	about 10 (people)
una docena (de niños)	(about) a dozen (children)
una quincena (de hombres)	about fifteen (men)
una veintena* (de coches)	about twenty (cars)
un centenar, una centena (de casas)	about a hundred (houses)
cientos/centenares de personas	hundreds of people
un millar (de soldados)	about a thousand (soldiers)
miles/millares de moscas	thousands of flies

* 30, 40, 50 can also be converted in the same way.

measurements:

veinte metros cuadrados	20 square metres
veinte metros cúbicos	20 cubic metres
un puente de cuarenta metros de largo/longitud	a 40-metre-long bridge

distance:

De aquí a Madrid hay 400 km	Madrid is 400 km away
a 7 km de aquí	7 km from here

Telephone numbers

Póngame con Madrid, el cuatro, cincuenta y ocho, veintidós, noventa y tres I would like Madrid 458 22 93

Me da Valencia, el veinte, cincuenta y uno, setenta y tres Could you get me Valencia 20 51 73?

Extensión tres, tres, cinco/trescientos treinta y cinco Extension number 335

ⓘ Note: In Spanish telephone numbers may be read out individually, but more frequently they are broken down into groups of two. They are written in groups of two or three numbers (never four).

Time

The Time

¿Qué hora es? *What time is it?*
Es ... *(1 o'clock, midnight, noon)* ⎤ **It's ...**
Son las ... *(other times)* ⎦
Es la una y cuarto It's 1.15
Son las diez menos cinco It's 9.55

00.00	**medianoche**; **las doce (de la noche)**	midnight, twelve o'clock
00.10	**las doce y diez (de la noche)**	
00.15	**las doce y cuarto**	
00.30	**las doce y media**	
00.45	**la una menos cuarto**	
01.00	**la una (de la madrugada)**	one a.m., one o'clock in the morning
01.10	**la una y diez (de la madrugada)**	
02.45	**las tres menos cuarto**	
07.00	**las siete (de la mañana)**	
07.50	**las ocho menos diez**	
12.00	**mediodía**; **las doce (de la mañana)**	noon, twelve o'clock
13.00	**la una (de la tarde)**	one p.m., one o'clock in the afternoon
19.00	**las siete (de la tarde)**	seven p.m., seven o'clock in the evening
21.00	**las nueve (de la noche)**	nine p.m., nine o'clock at night

ⓘ Note: When referring to a timetable, the 24-hour clock is used:

las dieciséis cuarenta y cinco	16.45
las veintiuna quince	21.15

Examples

¿A qué hora vas a venir?	What time are you coming?
— A las siete	— At seven o'clock
Las oficinas cierran de dos a cuatro	The offices are closed from two until four
Vendré a eso de/hacia las siete y media	I'll come at around 7.30
a las seis y pico	just after 6 o'clock
a las cinco en punto	at 5 o'clock sharp
entre las ocho y las nueve	between 8 and 9 o'clock
Son más de las tres y media	It's after half past three
Hay que estar allí lo más tarde a las diez	You have to be there by ten o'clock at the latest
Tiene para media hora	He'll be half an hour (at it)
Estuvo sin conocimiento durante un cuarto de hora	She was unconscious for a quarter of an hour
Les estoy esperando desde hace una hora/desde las dos	I've been waiting for them for an hour/since two o'clock
Se fueron hace unos minutos	They left a few minutes ago
Lo hice en veinte minutos	I did it in twenty minutes
El tren llega dentro de una hora	The train arrives in an hour('s time)
¿Cuánto (tiempo) dura la película?	How long does the film last?
por la mañana/tarde/noche	in the morning/afternoon or evening/at night
mañana por la mañana	tomorrow morning
ayer por la tarde	yesterday afternoon or evening
anoche	last night
anteayer	the day before yesterday
pasado mañana	the day after tomorrow

Calendar

Dates

¿Qué día es hoy?	What day is it today?
¿A qué día (or fecha) estamos?	What's the date today?
Es (el) …	It's the …
Estamos a …	
uno/primero de mayo	1st of May
dos de mayo	2nd of May
veintiocho de mayo	28th of May
lunes tres de octubre	Monday the 3rd of October
Vienen el siete de marzo	They're coming on the 7th of March

ⓘ Note: Use cardinal numbers for dates. Only for the first of the month can the ordinal number sometimes be used.

Years

Nací en 2005	I was born in 2005
el veinte de enero de dos mil trece	(on) 20th January 2013

Other expressions

en los años cincuenta	during the fifties
en el siglo veintiuno	in the twenty-first century
en mayo	in May
lunes (quince)	Monday (the 15th)
el quince de marzo	on March the 15th
el/los lunes	on Monday/Mondays
dentro de diez días	in 10 days' time
hace diez días	10 days ago

Age

¿Qué edad tiene?	How old is he/she?
¿Cuántos años tiene?	
Tiene 23 años	He/She is 23
Tiene unos 40 años	He/She is around 40
A los 21 años	At the age of 21

Index

The following index lists comprehensively both grammatical terms and key words in English and Spanish.

Index

Index

Index

Index

Index

Index

Index

Index

Index